A Concordance to the Complete Writings of

GEORGE HERBERT

THE CORNELL CONCORDANCES

S. M. Parrish, *General Editor*

Supervisory Committee

M. H. Abrams
Donald D. Eddy
Ephim Fogel
Alain Seznec

POEMS OF MATTHEW ARNOLD, *edited by S. M. Parrish* (Out of Print)
POEMS OF W. B. YEATS, *edited by S. M. Parrish*
POEMS OF EMILY DICKINSON, *edited by S. P. Rosenbaum*
WRITINGS OF WILLIAM BLAKE, *edited by David V. Erdman*
BYRON'S *DON JUAN, edited by C. W. Hagelman, Jr., and R. J. Barnes*
THÉÂTRE ET POÉSIES DE JEAN RACINE, *edited by Bryant C. Freeman*
BEOWULF, edited by J. B. Bessinger, Jr.
PLAYS OF W. B. YEATS, *edited by Eric Domville*
POEMS OF JONATHAN SWIFT, *edited by Michael Shinagel*
PLAYS OF WILLIAM CONGREVE, *edited by David Mann*
POEMS OF SAMUEL JOHNSON, *edited by Helen Naugle*
FABLES AND TALES OF JEAN DE LA FONTAINE, *edited by J. Allen Tyler*
POEMS OF OSIP MANDELSTAM, *edited by Demetrius J. Koubourlis*
POEMS OF SIR PHILIP SIDNEY, *edited by Herbert S. Donow*
PLAYS AND POEMS OF FEDERICO GARCÍA LORCA, *edited by Alice M. Pollin*
PASCAL'S *PENSÉES, edited by Hugh M. Davidson and Pierre H. Dubé*
COMPLETE WRITINGS OF GEORGE HERBERT, *edited by Mario A. Di Cesare and Rigo Mignani*

A Concordance to the Complete Writings of

GEORGE HERBERT

Edited by

MARIO A. DI CESARE

and

RIGO MIGNANI

Cornell University Press

ITHACA AND LONDON

First published 1977 by Cornell University Press.
Published in the United Kingdom by Cornell University Press Ltd.,
2–4 Brook Street, London W1Y 1AA.

International Standard Book Number 0–8014–1106–8
Library of Congress Catalog Card Number 76–56642
Printed in the United States of America
Librarians: Library of Congress cataloging information appears on the last page of the book.

CONTENTS

PREFACE

Thy word is all, if we could spell.
—"The Flower"

Let not the winde
Scatter my words. . . .
—"Longing"

George Herbert's use of words in *The Temple*—simple, unassuming, and often elusive words—has aroused keen interest in recent years, and readers and critics have begun to think more vigorously about how his titles work hieroglyphically or how the disconnected images of "Prayer" joyously escape definition. Such interest stimulated us to attempt this concordance. Clichés and commonplaces fade and fail when one attempts to describe Herbert's language, so we have simply presented it, in as well-organized and useful a format as we could devise.

The concordance contains all of Herbert's available writings: English, Latin and Greek, poetry and prose. We have included the poems doubtfully attributed to him and the second part of *Outlandish Proverbs*, even though we share the reluctance of most scholars to consider these works authentic (reading the doubtful poems will not make anyone wish they were Herbert's). In any case, the user can easily disregard them if he wishes; all are clearly identified as of doubtful authorship.

The general principle of inclusiveness extends also to our procedures. Titles are concorded, and we have kept to a minimum the number of high-frequency words omitted. We have not concorded numerals, dates of letters (*Works*, pp. 363–381) and similar rubrics (pp. 53, 92–93, 169 of *The Temple*), or the long quotations from *Valdesso*. As to variants, we have been generally accommodating, excluding those which were modifications of spelling, but not excluding variations in verb form or in number.

By permission of the Oxford University Press, our copy text has been F. E. Hutchinson's magisterial Oxford English Texts edition (*The Works of George Herbert*, Oxford, 1941), supplemented by the texts of the 1613 Latin gratulatory poems recently edited by Leicester Bradner in *Renaissance News*, 15 (1962), 208–211. (A full edition of the MS used by Bradner has recently been prepared by P. C. Dust, *The Carmen Gratulans Adventu Serenissimi Principis Frederici Comitis Palantini ad Academiam Cantabrigiensem: An Edition with Introduction, Translation, and Commentary* . . . , Salzburg, 1975.) Our text for the variants has also been Hutchinson's, which was checked against the Williams manuscript (MS Jones B 62, Dr. Williams's Library, Gordon Square, London) and the Bodleian manuscript (MS Tanner 307, Bodleian Library, Oxford), and supplemented by G. M. Story's text of the "Inuenta Bellica," the variant version of "Triumphus Mortis," published in *Modern Philology*, 59 (1962), 271–272. In preparing the text of *The Temple*, however, we have regarded the 1633 edition (*The Temple* . . . , Cambridge, 1633) as authoritative in all matters of substance, though we have used Hutchinson for page citations and have kept a few of his modifications of spelling or punctuation. Most of the differences between the 1633 edition and Hutchinson's edition are minor; all are noted in his apparatus criticus.

Preparing the text has involved a number of editorial decisions; these were based less on a craving for consistency than on our intention to provide as direct and uncluttered access to the text as possible. We have made a very few specific changes. For typographical reasons, we have omitted the braces in two poems and juxtaposed the words with a slash between: *Mary / Army* (p. 77); *Life / Strife* and *Salvation / Damnation* (p. 170). We have silently adjusted the *v/u* and *i/j* exchanges in all lines from the Williams manuscript, the *Doubtful Poems*, and a few other places such as Herbert's *Will*—such adjustments were commonplace in seventeenth-century printing. In the printing of Latin works, however, the practice was not common; hence, we have made no adjustments in the Latin texts except to modify for the sake of consistency the initial letters of a few words in Bradner's transcription (e.g., *Juppiter* becomes *Iuppiter*). On the grounds that *&c* is a typographical device used in some poems to save space, we have expanded all refrains, specifically in "The Sacrifice," "Antiphon," and "Home." Finally, we have made these particular changes: in the poems from the Williams manuscript, we have changed initial *ff* to *F;* in *The Country Parson*, we have expanded the abbreviation of the biblical title from *King.* (p. 239) and *Kin.* (p. 285) to *Kings.*

NOTE TO USERS

Order

The book is separated into three parts—the English concordance, the Latin concordance, and the frequency lists. In both concordances, the poetry comes first, in the order of Hutchinson's edition; the three English translations of Latin poetry (pp. 438–439) are grouped with the English poetry before the prose. Lines are in text order; individual variants are grouped with the appropriate line. When an index word occurs two or more times in the line, the line is printed only once. Alphabetization throughout the list of entries ignores most apostrophes, both internal and external.

Format

Identifying information lists page number, title, and line number, and sometimes special information in the column after the title. The page citation is always to Hutchinson's edition, except for the Bradner text of the 1613 Latin poems (coded BR in the special information column) and the Story variants to

"Triumphus Mortis" (coded VS). The symbols used for the special information column and the abbreviated titles are explained in the section following this preface.

Context

For the poetry, the context is always the line, even though Herbert's lines are sometimes very short. For the prose, our program provides context based on logical rather than physical units; the context is controlled mainly by discrimination among various levels of punctuation (including certain specially inserted symbols which sometimes overrode the kind of nonpunctuation a computer could not detect, such as the period in a biblical verse reference or in an abbreviation, or which sometimes provided stops where they did not exist or where they might have been bypassed under our rules). Punctuation apart, context was determined on the principle that Herbert's prose style is generally periodic; so we have biased our context forward. We have also attempted to reduce clutter in these contexts by cutting off forward-pointing prepositions (for example, *by, of, to*) or conjunctions when one of these was the final word of the determined context.

The Entries

Hyphenated words. These are listed three (or more) times—under the full word and under each component. In first preparing the text, we attempted to discriminate between forms like *Christ-side-piercing* and *common-weal,* but by the time our editing was complete, it was clear that such distinctions were often tenuous, and we ended by considering all hyphenated words as compounds.

Possessives and contractions. Most of the texts, notably the 1633 edition of *The Temple,* do not use apostrophes for possessives. We have editorially discriminated all such possessives among the entries (but have, of course, made no change in the text itself). Contractions were a more complex matter. We have not tampered with contractions that involved unusual changes such as metathesis (like *o're*). When a contraction consisted of an apostrophe replacing a single, obvious letter, we separated the compound parts artificially for the entry list; the contraction *he's* remains in the text as *he's* but is entered under *he* and *'s,* sorted next to *is.*

Spelling. We have limited our normalizing to abbreviations of certain common names, especially the names of biblical books (see *Corinthians,* abbreviated to *1 Cor., 2 Cor.*). We have, however, provided cross references from the conventional modern spelling of a word to the seventeenth-century spellings which are not close by; in some cases, this meant inserting a modern spelling into the word list (see *ache,* with cross references to *ach, ake*). Cross references are provided usually for the singular noun or the infinitive of the verb, and usually only one cross reference is given; the user will always want to look over the entire neighborhood.

Homographs. Our criterion for homographs (the term is generally misused) is the standard one—the two words must be different in both etymology and meaning. We have attempted to be reasonably thorough, but we have not worried much about words which appear to be homographs because of stray variations in spelling, and we have no doubt overlooked some. Even C. T. Onions, whose authoritative *Oxford Dictionary of English Etymology* (Oxford, 1966) has been our guide, was sometimes uncertain of the exact boundaries around or between forms. "Will" is a good example of the problem. As Onions points out, one cannot distinguish with complete confidence among the various shades of intent or deliberation represented by the auxiliary verb; there are sharp differences between the two proverbs "What your glass telles you, will not be told by Councell" and "He that will not have peace, God gives him warre."

Variants. We have been accommodating toward variants to the text of *The Temple,* excluding variants in spelling but including practically everything else. Variants in the Williams manuscript are of three kinds—lines containing one or two words that differ from the final version; lines that are substantially or completely different from corresponding lines; lines (and whole poems) that do not exist in the final version. The latter two kinds present no problem. In the case of lines containing only one or two variant words, we originally planned to index only those words and to suppress the repetitive remainder. We have been persuaded, however, that there are uses for these duplicated lines. But while consenting to forgo both the elegant routines worked out by our programmer for suppression and our own scruples about the extra entries, we have not wished to clutter the text with numerous variant spellings. In these cases, therefore, we have retained the spelling used in the 1633 edition of *The Temple* for all words except the specifically variant words.

In the rest of Herbert's works, variants are less abundant (and generally less interesting). The very few verbal variants in *The Country Parson* have been inserted in brackets, to avoid extensive modification of the prose-context program. In *Valdesso,* the variants consisted almost entirely of substantial additions in the 1646 edition of the work (*Divine Considerations,* Cambridge, 1646). The main variants in the Latin were those in the manuscript published by Story. Some of these also exist in Pickering's text (*Works of George Herbert,* edited and published by William Pickering, vol. ii, 1835, vol. i, 1836), based on a manuscript in his possession; after comparing Pickering's text with Story's, we have given Story's priority and use Pickering only for variants not in the Story manuscript.

The Latin Concordance

Practically all of the remarks above also apply to the Latin text. A few particulars need to be added.

Given the highly inflected character of classical Latin and thus the variety of forms available to the writer, a huge proportion—over seventy-five percent—of the Latin entries are single-occurrence words. Hence, we omit this group from the frequency lists (see below).

The orthography of the Latin is regular; cross-referencing was not necessary. Herbert occasionally substitutes a *y* for an *i* (*hyemes, sydera*) or uses a Greek spelling (*charas*) or an archaic-looking form (*quum, sies*); his printers regularly use the older conventions of *v/u* and *i/j*. Homographs are rare and easily identified (*bellum* as adjective, *solum* as noun).

Since no system of transliteration of Greek is better than minimally adequate, we have used simple equivalents, generally those recommended by *Webster's New International Dictionary*. We use *o* and *e* for both long and short vowels; iota subscript we print as *i* following the appropriate letter.

We have provided separate entries for the enclitics *que, ue,* and *ne* and have listed both parts of each such word (but of course have made no change in the text itself). An interesting result is that *que* is the most frequent entry in the Latin section.

Frequency Lists

These are of two kinds—words listed by frequency and words listed alphabetically. The first is complete for the English, but the Latin frequency list omits single-frequency words. The alphabetical lists include all words of a frequency of 6 or higher for the English and of 3 or higher for the Latin; the aim is to provide the user in a few pages with a prospect of Herbert's vocabulary.

Omissions

Persuaded that concordances can be important tools for many kinds of linguistic study, we have omitted from the English concordance only a very few words, and those reluctantly. The specific words omitted and their frequencies are: *a,* 1,781; *and,* 3,568; *in,* 1,512; *it,* 923; *of,* 2,131; *that,* 1,575; *the,* 3,961. The word *to* is concorded only for the poetry but not for the prose (in which it occurs about 1,500 times); as Hutchinson points out, Herbert's use of the preposition in his poetry is often very interesting, as when he uses it to mean "in comparison to." No words were omitted from the Latin concordance.

The concordance was programmed on an IBM 360, in COBOL, at the Computer Center, State University of New York at Binghamton. A tape of the complete text of Herbert's works has been stored in the Rare Books Room of the University Library; copies are available at cost to interested users.

ACKNOWLEDGMENTS

This book could not have been completed without a great deal of cooperation, goodwill, and concrete help. Funds for keypunching were arranged by various officers of our university. We are particularly grateful to Assistant Vice-President Grace Dowling, Associate Dean Robert Melville, and Provost Arthur Smith. Amy Charles, biographer of Herbert, kindly answered numerous questions and gave us much useful information. Our collaborators in another concordance, Alfred G. Lynn, senior programmer at the SUNY Computer Center, and Lea Ann Boone, graduate student in English and programmer, gave us a lot of practical advice and assistance in particular chores. Stephen Parrish, the General Editor, has been patient, understanding, encouraging, and helpful in numerous ways.

Our main debt is to our programmer, Sergei Kucherov, whose work has been admirable on every count. His programming showed not only competence and clarity but also a high degree of imagination. He worked more hours than we could possibly recompense, and his care in keeping us from error has been exemplary.

MARIO A. DI CESARE
RIGO MIGNANI

State University of New York at Binghamton

ABBREVIATIONS

Symbols used in the special information column are listed below.

BR Bradner text of 1613 Latin gratulatory poems, published in *Renaissance News,* 15 (1962), 208–211.

D Doubtful work; specifically, the *Doubtful Poems* collected in Hutchinson, pp. 208–222, and the second part of the *Proverbs,* first published in 1651 (Hutchinson, pp. 356–362).

V Variant, except as noted below, mainly the variants to the 1633 text of *The Temple* from the Bodleian MS (also known as Tanner 307).

VS Variant from the manuscript of "Inuenta Bellica" (early version of "Triumphus Mortis") edited by G. M. Story, *Modern Philology,* 59 (1962), 271–272.

W Williams text. The Williams manuscript (in Dr. Williams's Library, London, also known as Jones B 62) contains the early text of part of *The Temple* and some Latin poems. Six poems in the Williams text were not included in the final version of *The Temple;* they are transcribed in Hutchinson, pp. 200–205.

WC In several cases, variants are the result of corrections made in Herbert's own hand in the Williams text itself; these are coded WC.

Title abbreviations are self-evident and are not elaborated here; those that may give trouble are listed below, with the page number in the Hutchinson edition on which the poem begins.

English Poems

Abbreviation	*Title*	*Page*
Bohemia	To the Queene of Bohemia.	211
Ch.–rents	Church–rents and schismes.	140
Charms & K	Charms and Knots.	96
Coloss.	Coloss. 3. 3. Our life is hid with Christ in God.	84
Ephes.	Ephes. 4. 30. Grieve not the Holy Spirit, &c.	135
H. Danvers	On Henry Danvers earl of Danby.	208
J. Danvers	On Sir John Danvers.	208
L. Bacon	To the Right Hon. the L. Chancellor (Bacon).	209
Walton 1	Sonnet, "My God, where is that ancient heat towards thee . . . "	206
Walton 2	Sonnet, "Sure, Lord, there is enough in thee . . . "	206
Walton 3, 4	To my Successor.	207
Walton 5, 6	Translations of "In Sacram Anchoram Piscatoris . . . "	439

English Prose

Abbreviation	*Title*	*Page*
Cornaro	A Treatise of Temperance and Sobrietie: Written by Lud. Cornarus; Translated into English by Mr. George Herbert.	291

Concordance to Writings in English

	PAGE	TITLE		LINE
A-DOING				
Nothing with labour, folly long a-doing.	14	Ch.-Porch		192
A-FOOT				
come a Horse-back, there is reason, that my desires should go a-foot;	363	Letters		23
AARON				
Aaron.	174	Aaron		T
Come people; Aaron's drest.	174	Aaron		25
AARON'S				
List, ye may heare great Aarons bell.	99	Decay		10
AARONS				
Thus are true Aarons drest.	174	Aaron		5
ABASH'D				
With that abash'd and struck with many a sting	142	Pilgrimage		25
ABATE (see also bate)				
Till your bright gift my darknesse did abate.	209	L. Bacon	D	8
ABHORR'D				
shall be abhorr'd by thee.	218	Psalm V	D	16
ABHORRES				
For above all things he abhorres deceit:	72	Constancie		18
ABHORRING				
in a true detestation of the soul, abhorring, and renouncing sin,	279	Priest 33		24
and abhorring from so sudden an end, and finding my self continually	292	Cornaro		18
ABIDE				
Because thou dost abide with me,	183	A Parodie		4
And are there any leaves, that still abide?	188	Heaven		7
And are there any leaves, which still abide?	188	Heaven	W	7
Shine on, Majestick soule, abide	213	L' Envoy	D	1
Things well fitted abide.	337	Proverbs		483
A scab'd horse cannot abide the comb.	359	Proverbs	D	1113
ABIDER				
Much spends the traveller, more then the abider.	330	Proverbs		276
ABIDETH				
because the anointing which we have received, and abideth in us,	314	Valdesso	V	6
ABIDING				
and finds no sure abiding place.	215	Psalm I	D	16
ABILITIES				
All my abilities, my designes confound,	164	The Crosse		11
my resolution to be, that my poor Abilities in Poetry, shall be all,	363	Letters		11
ABILITY				
herein is the greatest ability of a Parson to lead his people exactly	230	Priest 5		20
every gift or ability is a talent to be accounted for, and to be	274	Priest 32		24
ABJECTS				
Servants and abjects flout me; they are wittie:	31	Sacrifice		141
ABLE				
My soul hath felt, ev'n able to destroy,	172	The Glance		10
Able a heart of iron to appall,	187	Judgement		3
Sinne being not able to extirpate quite	194	Ch.-Milit.		161
Therefore he sent out able ministers,	195	Ch.-Milit.		199
able to stand the Judges doom:	215	Psalm I	D	18
is ever very well supplyed by some able man who treads in his steps,	232	Priest 7		26
which happily for his other children he is not able to do.	239	Priest 10		33
if poor, and he able, he easeth them therein.	244	Priest 12		25
working those that are able to the same charity, still pressing it in	245	Priest 12		12
he inlargeth himself, if he be able, to the neighbour-hood;	245	Priest 12		18
the person bee so poor, that he is not able to reward the Phisician:	262	Priest 23		14
which are two great lights able to dazle the eyes of the mis-led,	263	Priest 24		19
examined the nature of it, is able to explaine it after to others.	279	Priest 33		9
of perfection, and are able to make the man of God perfect, 2 Tim. 3.	306	Valdesso		19
The rage of a wild boar is able to spoil more then one wood.	360	Proverbs	D	1132
and yet I am scarce able with much ado to make one half years	365	Letters		10
that if all fail, yet I am able to stand on mine own legs.	370	Letters		10
ABLEST				
sends for three or four of the ablest of the Parish to hear the cause	260	Priest 23		9
ABODE				
He that loves Gods abode, and to combine	24	Ch.-Porch		437
Fain would I here have made abode,	142	Pilgrimage		9
Thy short abode and stay	154	Glimpse		11
Yea, in deaths shadie black abode	173	23 Psalme		13
Of thy abode,	183	A Parodie		8
and abode in those fenny places two whole moneths in the heat	302	Cornaro		18
ABOLISH				
To' abolish Sinn, not Wheat.	200	H. Commun.	W	21
ABOUND				
These are the scumme, with which course wits abound:	16	Ch.-Porch		237
The hills with health abound; the vales with store;	119	Providence		95
This is thy house, with these it doth abound:	137	Familie		21
What heats abound!	149	Longing		27
and make you abound in every good worke, to the joy of your ever	377	Letters		26
ABOUNDED				
so that then where sin abounded, not death, but grace superabounded;	288	Priest		24
no inconvenience thereby, because that humour abounded not in me.	294	Cornaro		22
ABOUT				
About thy neck do drown thee? raise thy head;	13	Ch.-Porch		170
Affect in things about thee cleanlinesse,	21	Ch.-Porch		367
Thy clothes being fast, but thy soul loose about thee.	23	Ch.-Porch		414
Canst thou finde hell about my lips? and misse	28	Sacrifice		42
Comes to about the many hundredth part.	38	The Sinner		11
Comes to about the many hundred part.	38	The Sinner	W	11
About some land, which he had dearly bought	40	Redemption		7
Each day doth round about us see.	48	Repentance		8
Going about the world, and giving light.	59	Whitsunday		16

ABOUT (cont'd)	PAGE	TITLE		LINE
Blows all the dust about the floore:	67	Ch.-floore		17
Gave them about to all.	70	Humilitie		8
When man was lost, thy pitie lookt about	107	Home		13
I blasted all the joyes about me:	108	Home		44
About her eares:	110	Brit. Ch.		21
Like moles within us, heave, and cast about:	126	Confession		14
A boyling caldron, round about whose verge	129	Love unkn.		27
Flowers look about, and die not in their prime.	154	Glimpse		10
Doe winde a rope about, and cut my heart:	165	The Crosse		33
Like leaves about me: or like summer friends,	169	The Answer		4
And wheel'd about again to spell Christ-Crosse.	191	Ch.-Milit.		54
Much about one and the same time and place,	192	Ch.-Milit.		101
Lyes round about us to helpe out the story,	212	Bohemia	D	26
About thy temples that the furious frowne	212	Bohemia	D	38
Nor all the people round about,	216	Psalm III	D	15
So shall the people round about	221	Psalm VII	D	25
as about prayers morning and evening on their knees, reading	248	Priest 14		32
carrying it about with him as fully, as if he had begot his whole	250	Priest 16		9
Correspondence with all the neighbouring Pastours round about him,	253	Priest 19		16
the Parson once demanded after other questions about mans misery;	257	Priest 21		2
because we are about a Calling, and a preparation thereunto.	276	Priest 32		36
hath considered how to carry himself at table about his appetite,	278	Priest 33		19
About foure yeares since, I was led by the advice of Physicians,	295	Cornaro		19
about mortification, and observation of Gods Kingdome within us,	305	Valdesso		9
These words about the H. Scripture suite with what he writes	306	Valdesso		15
to relieve my Neighbour, God hath already reveled his Will about it.	313	Valdesso		14
many places doe the Fathers bring about Untill against the Heretiques	318	Valdesso		10
The 98. Consid. about being justified by faith, or by good works,	319	Valdesso	V	16
Flies are busiest about leane horses.	323	Proverbs		73
yet that will be about 30 l. per an. but the commodiousness is beyond	369	Letters		32
from giving you cause, to apology, about your counselling me herein:	378	Letters		10
ABOVE				
Wine above all things doth Gods stamp deface.	8	Ch.-Porch		48
Which is above the heav'ns, whose spring and rent	44	H. Bapt.1		5
Which is above the heav'ns, whose spring and vent	44	H. Bapt.1	V	5
Waters above the Heavens. O sweet streams	44	H. Bapt.1	W	5
But above all, the heart	53	Antiphon 1		11
Sometimes I peere above them all;	55	Temper 1		6
Drop from above!	60	Grace		4
Drop from above!	60	Grace		8
Drop from above.	60	Grace		12
Drop from above.	60	Grace		16
Drop from above.	60	Grace		20
Drop from above.	61	Grace	W	20
Drop from above.	61	Grace		24
But much more blest be God above,	63	Even-song		4
But brings a favour from above;	64	Even-song		31
Leads to the Quire above,	67	Ch.-floore		8
For above all things he abhorres deceit:	72	Constancie		18
Below, our drink; above, our meat;	92	Man		40
And here above:	92	Antiphon 2		3
Entred for both, farre above their desert!	105	Obedience		45
Who above all things lov'd this life;	122	Time		8
Not that thou hast not still above	124	Gratefulnes		21
My sighs and tears as busie were above;	132	The Storm		3
Written above there? Yesterday	133	The Method		14
Thy hand above did burn and glow,	141	Justice 2		11
Yet can I mark how starres above	162	The Search		13
Before a court, ev'n that above so cleare,	167	Dotage		16
In heav'n above.	172	The Glance		24
As plainly as that above doth show;	175	The Foil		3
To thee, who art more farre above deceit,	185	A Wreath		7
Then deceit seems above simplicitie.	185	A Wreath		8
But above all, thy Church and Spouse doth prove	190	Ch.-Milit.		9
if God give any thing above those, and not spent in them,	240	Priest 10		11
his money for the poor, and his table for those that are above Alms.	243	Priest 11		9
or if he be of a condition above such gifts, he sends him a good	254	Priest 20		15
not hold in Christianity, because it contains things above nature:	256	Priest 21		24
which carries a reverence with it, even above contempt.	268	Priest 28		21
obligation to God, and their own soul, is above any temporall tye.	270	Priest 29		22
and above all things, they are to fréquent Sessions and Sizes;	276	Priest 32		37
Thou hast exalted thy mercy above all things;	288	Priest		23
Above all, taking care never to rise with a full stomack,	293	Cornaro		18
are verie beautifull and convenient above most in this age,	301	Cornaro		12
Truth and oyle are ever above.	328	Proverbs		234
To bee beloved is above all bargaines.	342	Proverbs		631
and sits above the Proctors, is Regent or Non-regent at his pleasure,	370	Letters		2
But perhaps being above the Common people, our Credit and estimation	373	Letters		25
And above all, If any care of future things molest you?	374	Letters		12
all these are over and above their wages, To Sara thirteene shillings	382	G.H.'s Will		26
ABRAHAM				
Advise with Abraham, when thy power could not	99	Decay		3
Where th' Ark did rest, there Abraham began	190	Ch.-Milit.		19
For first concerning Abraham and Sara, I ever tooke that	315	Valdesso		35
Neither doe I doubt but if Abraham had lived in our Kingdome under	316	Valdesso		23
ABRAHAM'S				
so need not Abraham's Equivocation, nor Paul's neither,	316	Valdesso		7
ABRIDGEMENTS				
and the Abridgements of the Statutes, as also by discourse with men	260	Priest 23		3

	PAGE	TITLE		LINE
ABROACH				
Did set again abroach; then let him say	37	The Agonie		15
ABROAD				
Gad not abroad at ev'ry quest and call	68	Content		5
But when I view abroad both Regiments;	71	Frailtie		9
Walkt by my self abroad, I saw a large	129	Love unkn.		25
I will abroad.	153	The Collar		2
I will abroad.	153	The Collar		28
And in my powers not stirre abroad,	183	A Parodie		9
services done by men-servants at home, and his linnen washed abroad.	237	Priest 9		10
And when they go abroad, his wife among her neighbours is	240	Priest 10		27
when his occasions carry him abroad, or bring strangers to him,	274	Priest 32		7
When none of these occasions call him abroad, every morning that hee	277	Priest 32		15
Dry bread at home is better then rost meate abroad.	344	Proverbs		681
ABSENCE				
For as thy absence doth excell	163	The Search		57
as knowing that absence breedes strangeness, but presence love.	284	Priest 35		15
my absence by how much it naturally augmenteth suspicion,	372	Letters		20
ABSENT				
The absent partie is still faultie.	332	Proverbs		318
The Mr. absent, and the house dead.	352	Proverbs		940
ABSOLUTE				
that he may be an absolute Master and commander of himself,	227	Priest 3		8
ABSOLUTELY				
pin unjustly from the richest, he absolutely restores it as a Judge;	260	Priest 23		15
For if he absolutely shut up mens mouths, and forbid all disclosing	286	Priest 37		33
to avoiding of costlier matters, if I should fall absolutely sick:	365	Letters		8
ABSTAIN				
Abstain wholly, or wed. Thy bounteous Lord	7	Ch.-Porch		13
there are some persons, who abstain not even from known sins;	264	Priest 26		10
I am more bound to abstain from those, which by mine own experience I	266	Priest 26		24
and I abstain from fruit, and fish, and the like, because they hurt	300	Cornaro		9
ABSTAINE				
Abstaine or wedd: if thou canst not abstaine	7	Ch.-Porch	W	13
ABSTINE				
Suffer and expect, sustine, abstine.	343	Proverbs	V	701
ABSTINENCE				
Besides the cleannesse of sweet abstinence,	86	Lent		19
very admirable) as at their daily temperance, abstinence, watchings,	237	Priest 9		31
which he celebrates not only with abstinence of diet, but also	241	Priest 10		38
either of Abstinence a morall vertue, or Mortification a divine.	267	Priest 26		16
ABSURD				
he goe into the world, esteeming it absurd, that he should exceed,	241	Priest 10		20
It's absurd to warme one in his armour.	347	Proverbs		775
ABUNDANCE				
But in th' abundance of thy Grace	218	Psalm V	D	17
ABUNDANTLY				
who have already abundantly discharg'd that part, having both ordered	373	Letters		11
ABUSE				
There they deride me, they abuse me all:	31	Sacrifice		154
Neither ought other mens abuse of Lent	86	Lent		28
A pair of Cheeks of them, is thy abuse.	206	Walton 2		7
I abuse the Creature, I am false to my reason which should guide me,	265	Priest 26		9
the Gallant, who is witty enough to abuse both others, and himself,	275	Priest 32		7
the one, the abuse of it, by taking petty Countrey bribes;	276	Priest 32		20
ABUS'D				
I have abus'd thy stock, destroy'd thy woods,	83	Sighs & Gr.		9
ABUSES				
Make not thy sport, abuses: for the fly	15	Ch.-Porch		233
ABUSIVENESSE				
Profanenesse, filthinesse, abusivenesse.	16	Ch.-Porch		236
ACADEMICALL				
yea, indeed of all, both Courtly, Militarie, Academicall.	441	Oration		28
ACADEMICK				
Thou often didst with Academick praise	47	Afflict.1		45
ACCENSIO				
distinction, for Fomes is not taken away, but Accensio Fomitis;	308	Valdesso		16
ACCEPT				
And must return. Accept of them and me,	5	Dedication		3
My God, accept of my confession.	49	Repentance		18
O accept	147	Offering		28
beseeching the Almighty to pardon and accept our poor services,	236	Priest 8		27
and, accept the good meaning of, Your most obedient Son,	374	Letters		31
ACCEPTABLE				
shewing them how acceptable such works are to God, and wishing them	247	Priest 14		18
comforts and condoles, doth perform an acceptable thing to thee;	298	Cornaro		7
ACCEPTANCE				
we for your gracious acceptance of these poore duties wish,	443	Oration		5
ACCEPTATION				
intent of the Gospell in the acceptation of Christs righteousnesse	304	Valdesso		22
ACCEPTING				
In Gods accepting you have done the good you intended, & whom serve	381	Woodnoth		17
ACCEPTS				
who more accepts a common course of devotion, then dislikes	273	Priest 31		8
ACCESSARY				
The Parsons Accessary Knowledges.	229	Priest 5		T
ACCESSE				
Whose sparkling light accesse denies:	82	Ungratef.		14
Of what an easie quick accesse,	103	Prayer 2		1
Which by the springs accesse grew much more great.	154	Glimpse		15
as his accesse to the poor is more comfortable, then to the rich;	249	Priest 14		8

ACCESSE (cont'd)	PAGE	TITLE	LINE
then the accesse of the Officers of the Catholike King?	442	Oration	9
ACCESSION			
The accession of which new title to your Excellencies, all the Muses	441	Oration	28
ACCIDENT			
or any other accident, he contrives how and in what manner to induce	236	Priest 8	1
ACCIDENTS			
and other accidents by his governing power, the fairest harvests come	271	Priest 30	17
ACCIPE			
Better is one Accipe, then twice to say, Dabo tibi.	358	Proverbs D	1079
ACCOMMODATE			
Patience, time and money accommodate all things.	338	Proverbs	498
ACCOMMODATION			
or place, under colour of accommodation, or necessary provision,	238	Priest 9	16
ACCOMPANIED			
the power and efficacie of that Temperance which ever accompanied me.	302	Cornaro	21
ACCOMPANYING			
and neighbourly accompanying one another, with reconciling	284	Priest 35	6
ACCOMPLISH			
so neither may thy word, but accomplish that for which it is given.	289	Priest	32
ACCOMPLISHED			
That when they have accomplished the round,	197	Ch.-Milit.	267
That when they have accomplished their round,	197	Ch.-Milit. W	267
ACCOMPT			
your care of Leighton, upon my accompt, & give you my self for it,	378	Letters	4
ACCORD			
That all together may accord in thee,	36	Thanksgvng	41
ACCORDING			
Number according to thy foes?	38	Good Fri.	6
If comforts fell according to desert,	138	The Size	39
According as the weather falls.	143	Complaining	10
According to my righteousness,	221	Psalm VII D	31
according to the grace that is given to us, whether prophecy,	226	Priest 2	4
prophecy, let us prophecy according to the proportion of faith;	226	Priest 2	5
according as his audience is, so he useth one, or other;	230	Priest 5	17
and sayings of others, according as his text invites him;	233	Priest 7	12
he thinks he hath in some measure, according to poor, and fraile man,	236	Priest 8	9
the seldomer, according as hee is satisfied of his Wifes discretion.	239	Priest 9	4
his servants between love, and fear, according as hee findes them;	241	Priest 10	8
and then he suits things faithfully according to that end.	253	Priest 19	5
giving age honour, according to the Apostles rule, 1 Tim. 5. 1.	255	Priest 21	25
according as I feele my self, either I take my wonted proportion,	267	Priest 26	8
But the Parson distinguisheth according to his double aime,	267	Priest 26	15
in his discourses occasionally, according to the pulse of the hearer.	268	Priest 27	7
according to the Apostles rule, he endeavours that none shall despise	268	Priest 28	16
but that God often changeth it according as he sees fit,	270	Priest 30	31
according to St. Pauls rule, Ephes. 4. 28. 1 Thes. 4. 11, 12.	275	Priest 32	2
and managing Commons, or Woods, according as the place suggests.	276	Priest 32	6
according as he discovers any of his Flock to be in one or the other	280	Priest 34	12
his preaching, The Lord (saith he) reward him according to his works.	285	Priest 36	34
a reverence, and makes him esteemed according to his Profession.	286	Priest 36	25
being so built by me according to the rules of Architecture,	301	Cornaro	13
invites us to all good, according to that singular place, Phil. 4. 8.	313	Valdesso	20
and they are to be judged according to the outward fact,	316	Valdesso	19
[according to the common and legal proceedings among men.]	316	Valdesso	28
God sends cold according to Cloathes.	322	Proverbs	33
Every one stretcheth his legges according to his coverlet.	325	Proverbs	147
of this parish to be devided according to my deare wives discretion.	382	G.H.'s Will	17
ACCORDINGLY			
Sought him accordingly in great resorts;	40	Redemption	10
And liv'd accordingly; my creditor	50	Faith	15
And livd accordingly with no new score,	50	Faith W	15
Accordingly his voyce is humble, his words treatable, and slow;	231	Priest 6	16
and accordingly either meets with their vices, or advanceth their	239	Priest 10	9
And accordingly, as he finds any defect in these, hee first considers	251	Priest 17	25
and accordingly by questions well ordered he found Philosophy in	256	Priest 21	22
and accordingly applies himselfe with Catechizings, and lively	258	Priest 22	25
Accordingly, for salves, his wife seeks not the city, but preferrs	262	Priest 23	3
accordingly, when we had sinned beyond any help in heaven or earth,	288	Priest	25
the next Friday it is tryed, and accordingly you shall hear.	371	Letters	17
and therefore entertaine it accordingly from Your very affectionate	379	Letters	26
ACCORDS			
Is, when the soul unto the lines accords.	168	a true Hymn	10
ACCOUNT			
In love or honour: take account of all;	20	Ch.-Porch	344
For what account can thy ill steward make?	83	Sighs & Gr.	8
demanding an account, but not by the way of an account.	239	Priest 9	2
demanding an account, but not by the way of an account.	239	Priest 9	3
and they all account, that to teach the ignorant is the greatest	240	Priest 10	22
or his Wife, takes account of Sermons, and how every one profits,	240	Priest 10	37
and which are such, as that men generally account me happie.	300	Cornaro	33
It takes much from the account, to which his sin doth amount.	327	Proverbs	192
Who must account for himselfe and others, must know both.	328	Proverbs	209
and I shou'd account my self most happy if I might change with you;	373	Letters	3
of monyes wherof he is to give as I know he will a Just account:	383	G.H.'s Will	26
ACCOUNTABLE			
his beck throughout the Kingdome, accountable for the publick good;	276	Priest 32	12
ACCOUNTED			
every gift or ability is a talent to be accounted for, and to be	274	Priest 32	25
why should I be accounted lesse happie, or lesse my self,	302	Cornaro	34

	PAGE	TITLE	LINE
ACCOUNTS			
Most surely judg'd, make thy accounts agree.	24	Ch.-Porch	456
That transferr'd th' accounts to me.	114	Dialogue	16
Traditions are accounts without our host.	194	Ch.-Milit. W	160
ACCRUE			
Where all my debts are payd, none can accrue	65	Ch.-mus. W	8
ACCRUES			
Because the benefit accrues to me.	117	Providence	28
ACCURATELY			
These and the like points hee hath accurately digested,	263	Priest 24	14
ACCURSED			
And on his own accursed pate	222	Psalm VII D	59
ACCURST			
Thy curse being laid on him, makes thee accurst.	169	Dial.-Anth	6
ACCUSE			
Then they accuse me of great blasphemie,	28	Sacrifice	61
The Jews accuse me with despitefulnesse;	29	Sacrifice	85
ACCUSTOME			
man should begin and by little and little accustome himself unto it.	299	Cornaro	9
ACCUSTOMED			
admits no vaine or idle names, but such as are usuall and accustomed.	258	Priest 22	4
ACH			
Musick helps not the tooth-ach.	339	Proverbs	532
The tooth-ach is more ease then to deale with ill people.	340	Proverbs	558
The Royall Crowne cures not the head-ach.	340	Proverbs	576
ACHE (see also ach,ake)			
ACHIEVE (see also atchieving)			
ACKNOWLEDG			
delights to have men feel, and acknowledg, and reverence his power,	271	Priest 30	19
ACKNOWLEDGE			
We all acknowledge both thy power and love	117	Providence	29
Lord, I acknowledge; take thy plagues away:	126	Confession	26
Much more do Common-weals acknowledge thee,	190	Ch.-Milit.	5
ACKNOWLEDGING			
of others by their sight, to the acknowledging of God, and his power,	282	Priest 34	15
ACQUAINT			
Now his desire is to acquaint you with those passages of newes which	368	Letters	1
These are the things I am to acquaint you with, of whose rude	369	Letters	1
ACQUAINTANCE			
Your first acquaintance might discredit all.	44	H. Bapt.1	14
May take acquaintance of this heap of dust;	64	Ch.-monum.	3
Finde their acquaintance there.	91	Man	24
And for their old acquaintance plead.	109	Home	70
he and I are ancient acquaintance, and I have a strong opinion	369	Letters	21
ACQUAINTED			
yet if my Sister were acquainted that they are ready, I dare say she	367	Letters	1
ACQUIT			
In brief, acquit thee bravely; play the man.	24	Ch.-Porch	457
ACQUITTS			
Acquitts yourselves and gives the sicke all greife.	209	Paradox D	6
ACT			
they come to pray, as a devout behaviour in the very act of praying.	231	Priest 6	16
esteeming that this private praying is a more voluntary act in them,	241	Priest 10	5
doing any thing of aversenesse, save in the very act of punishment:	263	Priest 25	28
One act in these things is bad, but it is the custome and habit that	266	Priest 26	17
an act against reason, because it is unnaturall to hurt ones self;	266	Priest 26	21
and be preserved in that act by his sustaining power, yet if he suite	271	Priest 30	15
that repentance is an act of the mind, not of the Body,	279	Priest 33	14
imprecation to Simon Magus, Act. 8. Thy mony perish with thee:	285	Priest 36	30
ACTED			
Sinnes are not knowne till they bee acted.	352	Proverbs	942
ACTING			
a tincture of private malice in the joy, and hast of acting his part;	287	Priest 37	27
ACTION			
Let me not think an action mine own way,	104	Obedience	18
When thou dost favour any action,	158	Praise 3	7
To runne into an action;	184	The Elixer	6
Makes that and th' action fine.	185	The Elixer	20
and this raiseth the action from the Shop, to the Church.	262	Priest 23	11
The Countrey Parson at spare times from action, standing on a hill,	264	Priest 26	3
to that which is presently unlawfull, even in one continued action.	264	Priest 26	22
not knowing the bounds of the action, nor when his eating begins	264	Priest 26	24
ACTIONS			
Thy mouth to it, thy actions to them both:	9	Ch.-Porch	74
To couzin thee. Look to thy actions well:	23	Ch.-Porch	425
They would not have their actions scann'd,	100	Miserie	21
Yet since thou canst not choose but see my actions;	104	Obedience	23
Thou mayst as well my actions guide, as see.	104	Obedience	25
And at my actions carp, or catch.	106	Conscience	18
These contrarieties crush me: these crosse actions	165	The Crosse	32
Lett in the Light to all their actions	185	The Elixer W	23
Both for their vertuous actions and their crimes.	197	Ch.-Milit.	262
but in all his words and actions slighting, and disesteeming it,	227	Priest 3	18
lust, and when not, and so in many circumstances of actions.	230	Priest 5	31
Parson hath throughly canvassed al the particulars of humane actions,	230	Priest 5	34
but in actions, in visiting other sick children, and tending their	239	Priest 10	25
with God, who weighs even childrens actions, 1 Kings 14. 12, 13.	239	Priest 10	29
of their generall Schoole rules ever to the smallest actions of Life;	266	Priest 26	1
that the world pierceth not godly mens actions no more then Gods,	315	Valdesso	30
us to judge of the doubtfull actions of Saints in the Scriptures;	316	Valdesso	12
Worldly learned men cannot judg spirituall mens actions,	317	Valdesso	6

	PAGE	TITLE		LINE
ACTIONS (cont'd)				
difficulty of applying their generall rules to particular actions,	319	Valdesso	V	32
Our owne actions are our security, not others judgements.	326	Proverbs		173
Our owne actions secure us not others judgements.	326	Proverbs	V	173
thy actions serve the turne.	347	Proverbs		771
Prayse not thyself, thy actions serve the Turne.	347	Proverbs	V	771
They favour learning whose actions are worthy of a learned pen.	357	Proverbs	D	1061
you bee like great Alexander, unlesse Historie delivered his actions?	443	Oration		3
ACTIVE				
Active and stirring spirits live alone.	20	Ch.-Porch		341
Yet active strength: whose long and bonie face	138	The Size		33
and his soul fervent, active, young, and lusty as an eagle.	237	Priest 9		27
Originall concupisence is such an active thing, by reason	238	Priest 9		12
ACTIVENESSE				
Embrace their activenesse, not vanities.	21	Ch.-Porch		363
ACTS				
with confession of sins, and all acts of Mortification.	242	Priest 10		1
and not break off their acts of dependance, how faire soever	271	Priest 30		26
Which acts of repentance are and must be found in all Gods servants:	279	Priest 33		25
but that, so the other acts be, that is not necessary:	279	Priest 33		28
who performes the other acts of repentance, when he cannot more,	279	Priest 33		30
or justify himselfe before God, by any acts or exercises of Religion;	312	Valdesso		16
There are two sorts of acts in religion;	312	Valdesso	V	23
acts of humiliation, and acts of confidence and joy;	312	Valdesso	V	23
acts of humiliation, and acts of confidence and joy;	312	Valdesso	V	24
ACTUALL				
that it is not to be understood of actuall sinnes, but habituall,	308	Valdesso		2
for I can no more free my selfe from actuall sinnes after Baptisme,	308	Valdesso		3
ACTUATES				
sustaining power he preserves and actuates every thing in his being;	271	Priest 30		3
AD				
for so he useth the same word in Consideration 68 ad finem.	317	Valdesso	V	8
ADAM				
Thus Adam my first breathing rendereth:	28	Sacrifice		71
For sure when Adam did not know	53	H.Commun.		33
What Adam had, and forfeited for all,	143	Holdfast		13
ADAM'S				
So sits the earths great curse in Adams fall	32	Sacrifice		165
From what life feeleth, Adams fall.	48	Repentance		12
And where sinne placeth me in Adams fall,	50	Faith		19
And where sinne places me in Adams fall,	50	Faith	W	19
ADAYES				
The world is now adayes, God save the Conquerour.	358	Proverbs	D	1075
ADD				
my poor labours, but add to those points, which I have observed,	224	Priest		15
he add a tincture of private malice in the joy, and hast of acting	287	Priest 37		27
ADDE				
This certain Anchor adde a Seal, and so	439	Walton 5		6
(Where nothing should be broke) to adde a Seal.	439	Walton 5		18
of my friends, to adde something to my usuall stint and measure.	295	Cornaro		20
ADDED				
To this may be added the consideration of any text with the coherence	229	Priest 4		9
To all this may be added, not for emboldening the unruly,	242	Priest 10		33
the Godly have ever added some houres of prayer, as at nine,	272	Priest 31		26
But here there are two Cautions to be added.	273	Priest 31		15
all other things shall be added, even it selfe is a Sermon.	278	Priest 33		14
To these might be added the Preaching of the Gospel in all Nations,	282	Priest 34		31
They added withall, that unlesse I speedily used that remedy,	292	Cornaro		13
like to that of the Jewes, which they added to their divine law.	320	Valdesso		4
ADDER'S				
valerian, mercury, adders tongue, yerrow, melilot, and Saint Johns	262	Priest 23		6
ADDES				
Feeds not, but addes to the desire of meat.	154	Glimpse		12
Addes to the union, as lights doe gather	212	Bohemia	D	36
and veal, if he addes any thing for a great day, or a stranger,	241	Priest 10		17
ADDEST				
Then all thou addest may be call'd his treasure.	11	Ch.-Porch		114
ADDICTED				
because Countrey people are much addicted to them, so that to favour	283	Priest 35		29
first caused me to leave Intemperance, to which I was much addicted:	291	Cornaro		20
I so addicted my self to this course of life, that I never went	292	Cornaro		33
ADDITION				
if there be any extraordinary addition to the customary exercises,	235	Priest 8		34
This addition after ten dayes wrought so much upon me, that	296	Cornaro		14
ADDITIONARY				
and that is, of what is Necessary, and what is Additionary.	272	Priest 31		21
But these prayers are not necessary, but additionary.	272	Priest 31		29
or by oversleeping himself at night, omits his additionary prayer.	272	Priest 31		31
Christian, that this prayer being additionary, not necessary;	273	Priest 31		5
in my heart) because this kinde of Prayer is additionary,	273	Priest 31		36
ADDRESSE				
I would addresse	78	Ang.&Sts.		8
ADDRESSES				
Particularly, I like all your Addresses, & for ought I see,	378	Letters		17
ADDS				
but adds to them, out of choyce and devotion, some other dayes	237	Priest 9		24
It adds to the glory both of soule and body.	327	Proverbs		193
ADJUDGE				
Lord, I adjudge my self to tears and grief,	136	Ephes.		25
ADMINISTER				
The Countrey Parson being to administer the Sacraments,	257	Priest 22		26

	PAGE	TITLE		LINE
ADVANTAGE				
Calmnesse is great advantage: he that lets	19	Ch.-Porch		313
Watch an advantage to appeare.	79	Employm.2		20
And with advantage mine the more.	157	Clasping		6
And with advantage mine the more, ...	157	Clasping		16
contrives how and in what manner to induce it to the best advantage.	236	Priest 8		2
is placed surer for his childrens advantage, then if it were given	240	Priest 10		9
which they can better employ to their own advantage, and sutably	243	Priest 11		16
by all means, that the delinquents returne is to his advantage.	264	Priest 25		2
to be accounted for, and to be improved to our Masters Advantage.	274	Priest 32		26
and ordering his land to the best advantage both of himself,	275	Priest 32		26
and it is a great advantage to know the practice of the Land;	277	Priest 32		4
as divers have done lately, to our Countrey's advantage. . . .	278	Priest 32		10
unlawful to open faults, no benefit or advantage can make it lawfull:	287	Priest 37		6
I can easily get on horseback without the advantage of the ground,	300	Cornaro		35
In spending lies the advantage.	323	Proverbs		85
consider what advantage you have over Youth and Health, . .	372	Letters		32
ADVANTAGES				
by which God turnes all outward blessings to inward advantages.	271	Priest 30		38
and utter this well, all his advantages are to his losse. . .	272	Priest 30		3
because there are contained therein 4 manifest advantages. . .	284	Priest 35		3
ADVENTURE				
He lies warm, and without adventure.	69	Content		20
But quickly seek some new adventure.	126	Confession		22
ADVERSARIES				
mine adversaries all.	217	Psalm III	D	20
and darkned by the Adversaries, and their great stumbling-block.	305	Valdesso		2
ADVERSITY				
fortitude in the cold midnight stormes of persecution and adversity.	237	Priest 9		38
ADVICE				
or else to examine with care, and advice, what they are fittest for,	275	Priest 32		16
I was led by the advice of Physicians, and the dayly importunitie	295	Cornaro		19
that my advice hath taken effect in the reducing of many rude	302	Cornaro		14
I refuse not advice from the meanest, that creeps upon Gods earth,	378	Letters		11
Gods earth, no not tho' the advice step so far, as to be reproof:	378	Letters		13
ADVISE				
I will no more advise:	95	Submission		18
Advise with Abraham, when thy power could not	99	Decay		3
Yet in their being joyn with one advise	121	Providence		146
Unto what you now advise:	177	The Rose		14
I advise, that in stead of a Physician a regular life is to be	298	Cornaro		11
Though old and wise, yet still advise.	325	Proverbs		134
Advise none to marry or to goe to warre.	329	Proverbs		236
Advise none to marry nor to goe to warre.	329	Proverbs	V	236
While the discreet advise, the foole doth his busines. . . .	330	Proverbs		273
ADVISETH				
he adviseth them so to labour for wealth and maintenance, . . .	248	Priest 14		5
He adviseth all to call to minde their Baptism often; . . .	258	Priest 22		14
the Parson adviseth them to read, or hear them read often, . .	270	Priest 29		13
he adviseth to insist and dwell chiefly on the two noble branches	277	Priest 32		36
he adviseth to be very vigilant, and not to let go the raines as soon	280	Priest 34		15
ADVIZE				
It is a different thing to advize you now, & before you took Sir	380	Woodnoth		7
AFARRE				
Better good afarre off, then evill at hand.	330	Proverbs		267
AFFAIRES				
reserving so much of the affaires, as serve for a diversion for him;	238	Priest 9		38
For there are two branches of his affaires;	275	Priest 32		22
but yet he will heare of no other affaires, untill they have	368	Letters		8
AFFAIRS				
most naturally as they are, wallowing in the midst of their affairs:	247	Priest 14		7
that they dive not too deep into worldly affairs, plunging themselves	247	Priest 14		24
wish them best, and that not a desire to meddle with others affairs,	251	Priest 17		31
and exposing to them the uncertainty of humane affairs, . . .	253	Priest 19		32
all the people so order their affairs as to receive just at those	259	Priest 22		26
of their health, nor of their affairs, (which being overburdened,	266	Priest 26		14
for every one to imploy himselfe to the advancement of his affairs,	275	Priest 32		29
to mark their Fathers discretion in ordering his House and Affairs;	276	Priest 32		29
thing to advize you now, & before you took Sir Johns affairs.	380	Woodnoth		8
AFFECT				
Affect in things about thee cleanlinesse, ...	21	Ch.-Porch		367
Did not affect thee much, was not thy aim;	106	Sion		8
And much affect thee, as tempestuous times	132	The Storm		5
I affect to own, ...	178	Discipline		10
hee may affect also his people, knowing that no Sermon moves them so	231	Priest 6		13
AFFECTED				
that being first affected himself, hee may affect also his people,	231	Priest 6		13
they do come, he be a little affected therewith, but not afflicted,	273	Priest 31		19
When therefore I was thus affected [afflicted] from the thirtie fifth	292	Cornaro		1
whom that matter ought to have affected most, received no . .	294	Cornaro		21
AFFECTING				
Many affecting wit beyond their power, ...	16	Ch.-Porch		245
truly affecting, and cordially expressing all that we say; . .	233	Priest 7		30
AFFECTION				
the same affection which made him not profit before, making him then	235	Priest 7		13
not his affection found out a fit wife for him, whose humble,	238	Priest 9		27
There is no heat of affection but is joyned	357	Proverbs	D	1050
AFFECTIONATE				
most heartily, affectionate Brother, and Servant, GEORGE HERBERT.	372	Letters		8
therefore entertaine it accordingly from Your very affectionate bro;	379	Letters		27

AFFECTIONATELY	PAGE	TITLE		LINE
that he ought to pray God affectionately and fervently to send him	312	Valdesso		17
AFFECTIONS				
With full crie of affections, quite astray;	80	Christmas		3
to get knowledg, but to subdue and mortifie all lusts and affections:	226	Priest 2		10
Mortification in regard of lusts and affections, and the stupifying	227	Priest 3		6
when the affections of the soul in desiring and procuring increase	230	Priest 5		26
how full of affections? he joyes, and he is sorry, he grieves,	234	Priest 7		19
and mastered all his lusts and affections within, and the whole Army	278	Priest 33		22
doubtlesse then also mens affections and words must turne,	288	Priest 37		4
AFFECTS				
Each little comforte much affects our hartes,	210	Paradox	D	33
yet your appearing in it, affects me strangely.	369	Letters		24
AFFLICT				
Afflict my houre,	144	Complaining		17
Can so afflict or so affright,	183	A Parodie		14
AFFLICTED				
of his cure is sick, or afflicted with losse of friend, or estate,	249	Priest 15		14
rather goes to them, then sends for the afflicted, though they can,	249	Priest 15		16
or otherwise afflicted, he followeth the Churches counsell,	249	Priest 15		28
some fitt day to carry it themselves, and cheere the Afflicted.	254	Priest 19		1
God dishonoured every day, and man afflicted.	267	Priest 27		32
he be a little affected therewith, but not afflicted, or troubled;	273	Priest 31		19
and find some poore afflicted soul, and there be bountifull,	281	Priest 34		3
therefore I was thus affected [afflicted] from the thirtie fifth	292	Cornaro		1
bodie and minde, wherewith infinite both young and old are afflicted.	302	Cornaro		26
AFFLICTING				
since fasting in Scripture language is an afflicting of our souls,	242	Priest 10		12
AFFLICTION				
Affliction shall advance the flight in me.	43	East.wings		20
Affliction.	46	Afflict.1		T
Affliction.	62	Afflict.2		T
Affliction.	73	Afflict.3		T
Affliction.	89	Afflict.4		T
Affliction.	97	Afflict.5		T
Affliction then is ours;	97	Afflict.5		19
A great affliction broke the little frame,	112	JESU		3
Doth give a hold and handle to affliction.	126	Confession		24
Was in great letters set AFFLICTION.	129	Love unkn.		28
Setting affliction to encounter pleasure;	194	Ch.-Milit.		148
from the Benefit of affliction, which softens, and works the stubborn	249	Priest 15		24
as they remember themselves were, when affliction did blow the Coals.	280	Priest 34		21
What hath Affliction grievous in it more then for a moment?	372	Letters		26
AFFLICTIONS				
Afflictions sorted, anguish of all sizes,	45	Sinne 1		6
As Gods afflictions into man,	126	Confession		9
Where of all plants afflictions soonest grow;	170	Water-crs.		3
Setting afflictions to encounter pleasure;	194	Ch.-Milit.	W	148
There is thy best Throne. For afflictions are	211	Bohemia	D	15
up that which is behinde of the afflictions of Christ in his flesh,	225	Priest 1		12
Patience in regard of afflictions, Mortification in regard of lusts	227	Priest 3		5
or why should our afflictions here, have so much power or boldness	372	Letters		27
And, for temporal Afflictions! I beseech you consider all that can	373	Letters		20
consider all that can happen to you are either afflictions of Estate,	373	Letters		21
And for afflictions of the Body, dear Madam, remember the holy	373	Letters		34
for those Afflictions of the Soul, consider that God intends that	374	Letters		9
of those that might say, What shall we rejoyce in afflictions?	374	Letters		23
AFFORD				
But gladly welcome what he doth afford;	7	Ch.-Porch		15
And make a suit unto him, to afford	40	Redemption		3
Yet in thy temple thou dost him afford	67	Windows		3
Till then, afford us so much wit;	92	Man		52
Cast down, yet help afford;	171	Bittersweet		3
do thou to us afford.	217	Psalm IV	D	24
fails not to afford his best comforts, and rather goes to them,	249	Priest 15		15
AFFORDS				
What fine varietie each tongue affords:	167	The Sonne		2
The finenesse which a hymne or psalme affords,	168	a true Hymn		9
to acquaint you with those passages of newes which this time affords;	368	Letters		2
AFFRAID				
neither is he affraid of praising, or praying to God at all times,	284	Priest 35		25
AFFRIGHT				
Affright both sinne and shame.	52	H.Commun.		18
Can so afflict or so affright,	183	A Parodie		14
AFFRIGHTED				
or if the poor Church-wardens be affrighted with their greatness,	232	Priest 6		14
and then when he hath affrighted them with this, exposing	253	Priest 19		34
AFFRIGHTS				
That as the first affrights,	82	Ungratef.		21
AFFRONT				
Affront those joyes, wherewith thou didst endow,	71	Frailtie		19
AFOOT				
To go where the King goes afoot (i.e. to the stool).	356	Proverbs	D	1034
AFORE				
Therefore he gives her respect both afore her servants,	238	Priest 9		36
Whitsuntide, afore and after Harvest, and the beginning of Lent.	259	Priest 22		22
AFOREHAND				
Brugensis uppon the Scripture and his halfe yeares wages aforehand,	382	G.H.'s Will		20
Bostocke St. Augustines workes and his halfe yeares wages aforehand,	382	G.H.'s Will		21
AFRAID				
he is not afraid of the pestilence that walketh in darkenesse,	238	Priest 9		6

AFRAID (cont'd)	PAGE	TITLE		LINE
and, though subject to death, yet continually afraid of it:	303	Cornaro		18
He that hath but one eye, must bee afraid to lose it.	358	Proverbs	D	1088
He that is afraid of leaves, goes not to the wood.	358	Proverbs	D	1092
AFRICK				
And ev'n all Africk; would at least I might	140	Ch.-rents		28
AFTER				
Nay, after death their spite shall further go;	34	Sacrifice		245
Nay, after death their spite shall farther go;	34	Sacrifice	W	245
And after death the fumes that spring	69	Content		22
After thy love.	74	The Starre		16
Oh glorious spirits, who after all your bands	77	Ang.&Sts.		1
All after pleasures as I rid one day,	80	Christmas		1
All after pleasures riding on a Day.	80	Christmas	W	1
After my sinnes! look not on my desert,	83	Sighs & Gr.		2
And after death for cures.	94	Life		15
After all this canst thou be strange?	108	Home		26
After, where ES, and next where U was graved.	112	JESU		6
Trees after bearing drop their leaves for soil:	119	Providence		70
But after death out of his grave	125	Peace		27
But you shall heare. After my heart was well,	129	Love unkn.		22
After the trimming, not the stuffe and ground.	131	Mans medly		18
He may attain to, after he is dead.	131	Mans medly		24
After so foul a journey death is fair,	142	Pilgrimage		35
Both then, and after, many a brunt	151	The Bag		21
But after thou hadst slipt a drop	158	Praise 3		31
And then when after much delay,	164	The Crosse		7
After so many deaths I live and write;	166	The Flower		37
After death can never die.	180	Invitation		30
After the losse of life and sense,	186	Death		7
Who after him should braver truths disclose.	194	Ch.-Milit.		138
How long will ye seek after lies,	217	Psalm IV	D	9
but after hee had fulfilled the work of Reconciliation,	225	Priest 1		7
which Christ did, and after his manner, both for Doctrine and Life.	225	Priest 1		19
but after a man is once Minister, he cannot agree to come into any	226	Priest 2		25
and what follows after, as also the scope of the Holy Ghost.	229	Priest 4		11
it is an honest joy ever after to looke upon his well spent houres.	230	Priest 5		6
but after divers gentle admonitions, if they persevere,	232	Priest 6		12
Chapt. 10. after he had complained of the desolation of Israel,	234	Priest 7		4
After religion, he teacheth them, that three things make a compleate	240	Priest 10		16
After the consideration of his own Parish, he inlargeth himself,	245	Priest 12		17
After these discourses, if they be poor and needy, whom he thus finds	248	Priest 14		8
so the hunger and thirst after it may come rather from themselves,	250	Priest 15		5
so also when after many admonitions, any continue to be refractory,	250	Priest 16		15
to the person, hungreth and thirsteth after righteous punishment	254	Priest 20		28
but after that the Catechisme is once learn'd, that which nature is	256	Priest 21		25
when the Parson once demanded after other questions about mans	257	Priest 21		2
Whitsuntide, afore and after Harvest, and the beginning of Lent.	259	Priest 22		22
or for quality is licorous after dainties, is a glutton;	266	Priest 26		8
So that if after dinner they are not fit (or un-weeldy) either	266	Priest 26		31
Not that all must presently work after dinner;	266	Priest 26		33
As when the people hungred and thirsted after our Saviours Doctrine,	267	Priest 26		22
but if after gentle, and neighbourly admonitions they still persist	270	Priest 29		19
As when a Merchant hath a ship come home after many a storme,	271	Priest 30		22
on God, not onely before the corne is inned, but after also;	271	Priest 30		35
But if after all this care well dispatched, the house-keepers Family	275	Priest 32		36
after he hath shew'd the unlawfulness of spending the day in	277	Priest 32		28
After the severall knowledg of these, he adviseth to insist and dwell	277	Priest 32		36
examined the nature of it, is able to explaine it after to others.	279	Priest 33		9
that there is none that can or will look after things, but all goes	281	Priest 34		8
A Prayer after Sermon.	290	Priest		T
then that after many troubles and griefs I should quickly come	291	Cornaro		25
But after I had resolved to follow Temperance and Reason,	292	Cornaro		31
I should be a conquerour, as also a little after it came to passe:	294	Cornaro		27
This addition after ten dayes wrought so much upon me, that	296	Cornaro		14
although after the fifteenth day it grew lesse and lesse.	296	Cornaro		20
but that he shall ever after live free from diseases, if he will keep	297	Cornaro		19
because that after one is once sixtie five yeares old, all the time	300	Cornaro		28
yeares old, all the time we live after, is rather death then life.	300	Cornaro		29
for I can no more free my selfe from actuall sinnes after Baptisme,	308	Valdesso		4
as if they were both but Alphabets and after a time to be left.	309	Valdesso		19
after the example of devout Cornelius.	312	Valdesso		21
After the house is finisht, leave it.	326	Proverbs		172
Step after step the ladder is ascended.	334	Proverbs		393
Hee that comes after must scrape.	335	Proverbs	V	415
Hee that workes after his owne manner,	335	Proverbs		421
He that lives not well one yeare, sorrowes seven after.	340	Proverbs		562
Hee hath not liv'd, that lives not after death.	350	Proverbs		873
One houres sleepe before midnight is worth three after.	350	Proverbs		882
the Germanes in the deede, the French after the deede.	352	Proverbs		947
feeles it all the winter after.	354	Proverbs		992
After Death the Doctor.	356	Proverbs	D	1037
No naked man is sought after to be rifled.	357	Proverbs	D	1063
The horse that drawes after him his halter,	359	Proverbs	D	1120
in some proportion, and after my manner, Your most obedient Servant,	364	Letters		3
after I enter'd into a Benefice, I should be most glad to entertain	367	Letters		9
and for ever after cease my clamorous and greedy bookish requests.	367	Letters		11
it is likely that the time after the Holydaye will bee fruitfuller	368	Letters		2
presently after Michaelmas, I am to make an Oration to the whole	369	Letters		12
is the encouragement of learning all the year after, except my cousin	375	Letters		29
done fairly, if they leave them a good portion after their decease.	376	Letters		16

AFTER (cont'd)	PAGE	TITLE		LINE
Doe this & be a man as David, after Gods hart.	381	Woodnoth		21
After many singular honors, remarkable commands, most noble . .	441	Oration		24
AFTERNOONE				
and catechized in the afternoone, he thinks he hath in some measure,	236	Priest 8		8
AFTERNOONS				
The Countrey Parson upon the afternoons in the weekdays, . .	247	Priest 14		3
AFTERWARD				
and then afterward they will attend it of themselves without his	318	Valdesso		21
AFTERWARDS				
who first shed teares over Jerusalem, and afterwards blood. . .	234	Priest 7		22
will lesse afterwards, the same affection which made him not profit	235	Priest 7		13
Afterwards when the hour calls, with his family attending him,	236	Priest 8		2
He afterwards turnes his care to fit all their dispositions with some	239	Priest 10		29
in eating, that he can eat more, then afterwards he finds true:)	267	Priest 26		4
his preaching, but afterwards also, as Mat. 22. 35. He was tempted:	280	Priest 34		9
but also afterwards I fell not into that yearely disease, . .	293	Cornaro		22
self to the reading of some learned book, and afterwards to writing;	301	Cornaro		7
forth her first borne Sonne, as if afterwards he had knowne her:	318	Valdesso		13
AGAIN (see also agen)				
Did set again abroach; then let him say	37	The Agonie		15
Reserving all for flesh again.	51	Faith		44
And there in hymnes send back thy fire again:	54	Love 2		8
Now come again, said I, and flout me.	108	Home		46
Thinks on it, and thinks again:	114	Businesse		35
Curl o're again.	115	Dulnesse		8
Wherefore I crie, and crie again;	124	Gratefulnes		25
Hath let thee out again:	128	Bunch Gr.		2
Then close again the seam, ...	138	The Size		42
And then again	145	Discharge		49
That your sweet sap might come again!	152	The Jews		12
So that again I now am mine, ...	157	Clasping		5
And now in age I bud again, ...	166	The Flower		36
A mirth but open'd and seal'd up again;	172	The Glance		18
By nailing Christ to fasten it again.	190	Ch.-Milit.		24
And wheel'd about again to spell Christ-Crosse.	191	Ch.-Milit.		54
Quitting his spear, lest it should pierce again	192	Ch.-Milit.		69
Though nail'd unto 't, but he ascends again, ...	439	Walton 5		2
When nail'd unto 't, but he ascends again	439	Walton 5	V	2
Unless the wicked turn again, ...	222	Psalm VII	D	41
He asked him again, what he would do, if he were in a ditch?	257	Priest 21		4
And again, of Hymeneus and Alexander, he saith, he had delivered them	285	Priest 36		34
Again notorious faults are either such as are made known by common	287	Priest 37		11
but they will object again, What becomes of your Annuity? . .	364	Letters		30
or rather increaseth, I wish earnestly that I were again with you:	372	Letters		18
Rejoyce in the Lord alwaies, and again I say rejoyce. . . .	374	Letters		21
yes, I say again rejoyce;	374	Letters		24
AGAINE				
Untill the graves againe restore	208	H. Danvers	D	3
to a reverence, which they forget againe, when they come to pray,	231	Priest 6		15
and reads it againe and againe, and the more the promise is delayed,	310	Valdesso		28
and reads it againe and againe, and the more the promise is delayed,	310	Valdesso		29
He thinkes not well, that thinkes not againe.	349	Proverbs		836
given her occasion to protest shee will never speake with him againe,	368	Letters		23
'GAINST				
'Gainst him, who seeks not life, but is the meek	28	Sacrifice		58
And taking councels 'gainst the Lord, ...	215	Psalm II	D	5
and 'gainst his Christ, presume to say, ...	215	Psalm II	D	6
His arrows are ordain'd 'gainst him	222	Psalm VII	D	47
AGAINST				
Against thee: for his light was onely lent.	9	Ch.-Porch		82
Against their Maker: they do wish me dead, ...	26	Sacrifice		6
They use that power against me, which I gave:	27	Sacrifice		11
Against thee, in thee I will overcome	37	Reprisall		15
The man, who once against thee fought.	37	Reprisall		16
Engine against th' Almightie, sinners towre, ...	51	Prayer 1		5
Engine against th' Almightie, sinners fort, ...	51	Prayer 1	W	5
Working against the states of death and hell.	58	H.Script.1		12
That thou mayst fit thy self against thy fall.	65	Ch.-monum.		24
Against the beasts: so joyntly bandying, ...	71	Humilitie		29
Against the beasts: so joyntly banding, ...	71	Humilitie	V	29
Cold fruits warm kernells help against the winde.	120	Providence		130
Against me there is none, but for me much.	141	Justice 2		24
Though my sinnes against me cried, ...	146	Praise 2		13
Against, but for me.	163	The Search		52
And tune mens hearts against the Gospel came:	192	Ch.-Milit.		76
And cleanse mens hearts against the Gospel came:	192	Ch.-Milit.	W	76
Against this meane & humble Blackamore.	209	L. Bacon	D	10
To second thee against there cunning hate.	211	Bohemia	D	22
Making a Head & spring against thy Reason.	213	Bohemia	D	59
Against me, saying, For my soul	216	Psalm III	D	3
that can against me rise.	216	Psalm III	D	16
Because against thy Majesty	219	Psalm V	D	33
against my foes disdain:	221	Psalm VII	D	22
or against some great Festivall, that he may the better celebrate it,	232	Priest 7		22
night and day against the proper and peculiar temptations of his	238	Priest 9		1
against these ghostly enemies he girdeth up his loynes, . .	238	Priest 9		3
is particular, and against mee, I am to follow our Saviours rule,	248	Priest 14		26
and against God, I am then to follow the Apostles rule, . .	248	Priest 14		28
and peace it administers against all temptations, even to death it	250	Priest 15		3
and yet hear Sermons against both, and himselfe condemn both in good	264	Priest 26		15

AGAINST (cont'd)	PAGE	TITLE		LINE
an act against reason, because it is unnaturall to hurt ones self;	266	Priest 26		21
touch him no more, then a stone thrown against heaven, where he is,	269	Priest 28		8
whereas there are usually three Objections made against the Place;	276	Priest 32		19
in all the fore-mentioned points against the time of their practice.	276	Priest 32		27
because infamy is a part of the sentence against malefactours,	287	Priest 37		18
of my kindred saw some great powerfull men pick quarrels against me,	294	Cornaro		17
But all these things could not defend me against their importunities.	296	Cornaro		5
the Fathers bring about Untill against the Heretiques who disputed	318	Valdesso		10
the Heretiques who disputed against the Virginity of the blessed	318	Valdesso		11
in a zeal against these, and in a strict performance of a few cheap	319	Valdesso	V	24
The best remedy against an ill man is much ground betweene both.	326	Proverbs		152
No lock will hold against the power of gold.	332	Proverbs		317
No Lockes can hold against gold.	332	Proverbs	V	317
Who spits against heaven, it falls in his face.	333	Proverbs		346
The Frier preached against stealing,	345	Proverbs		737
Set good against evill.	348	Proverbs		823
Craft against craft makes no living.	350	Proverbs		890
A wolfe will never make war against another wolfe.	359	Proverbs	D	1125
that are to come, you have strong preservatives against all disquiet.	373	Letters		19
AGE				
Ev'n with the yeare: but age, if it will hit,	13	Ch.-Porch		158
My tender age in sorrow did beginne:	43	East.wings		11
Not simpring all mine age,	47	Afflict.1		44
Not simpring all my age,	47	Afflict.1	W	44
Mans age is two houres work, or three:	48	Repentance		7
Prayer the Churches banquet, Angels age,	51	Prayer 1		1
And strengthen it in ev'ry age,	97	Afflict.5		5
When age grows low and weak,	98	Mortific.		25
Recover all thy sigh-blown age	153	The Collar		19
And now in age I bud again,	166	The Flower		36
these privately, giving age honour, according to the Apostles rule,	255	Priest 21		24
and the difference, hee ought to receive, of what age soever.	258	Priest 22		36
me contrariwise, at the age of eightie and one, strong and lustie;	291	Cornaro		10
[afflicted] from the thirtie fifth yeare of my age to the fortieth,	292	Cornaro		2
that old age could not be sustained with so little meat and drink;	295	Cornaro		22
For there is no malignitie of old age in the humours of my bodie,	296	Cornaro		36
of how great moment ten yeares are in mature age, wherein wisdome	298	Cornaro		29
which, but in that age, can hardly be perfected.	298	Cornaro		31
written by their Authors in that age, and those ten yeares,	298	Cornaro		34
and in our age, Paul the third, and Cardinal Bembo, who therefore	299	Cornaro		1
recounting the delights and pleasures in this age of eighty three,	300	Cornaro		31
are verie beautifull and convenient above most in this age,	301	Cornaro		12
and husbandrie, whereof in this age there is great plentie.	301	Cornaro		37
These are the delights and solaces of my old age, which is altogether	302	Cornaro		22
as a Tragedie with old Age, by reason of the sad events which it	302	Cornaro		32
of old was praised, that at the age of 73 yeares he writ a Tragedie;	302	Cornaro		33
Now lest there should be any delight wanting to my old age,	303	Cornaro		1
it is evident, That the life which I live at this age, is not a dead,	303	Cornaro		10
would I change age and constitution with them who follow their	303	Cornaro		12
I know how inconsiderate that age is, and, though subject to death,	303	Cornaro		17
When age is jocond it makes sport for death.	342	Proverbs		637
An Idle youth, a needy Age.	356	Proverbs	D	1042
therefore, if either Age or Sickness lead you to those Joyes?	372	Letters		31
and age, and knew none but one who could be no company to them.	375	Letters		14
Fame is sowne in this age, that it may be reaped in the following;	443	Oration		3
AGEN				
Mine own clothes on, they leade me out agen.	32	Sacrifice		190
Then flesh did lend thee, back agen.	202	love	W	18
AGENT				
that the patient might be proportionable to the agent, and especially	295	Cornaro		32
AGENTS				
certifies you that there are come agents hither from the low-Cuntries	368	Letters		4
demand of the Kings these Agents pretend they have no commission,	368	Letters		14
AGES				
that God in all ages hath had his servants, to whom he hath revealed	229	Priest 4		22
because all ages have thought that a competency, and he that profits	235	Priest 7		11
but with the Gospel it selfe be preached to all ages, Matth. 26. 13.	282	Priest 34		26
since the Saints of God in all ages have ever held in so pretious	317	Valdesso		33
of his praise, no, not, as in past ages, those Pillars of Hercules.	442	Oration		13
AGGRAVATED				
This also is aggravated, in that I apprehend what my Friends would	364	Letters		19
AGO				
Sev'n yeares ago: one vogue and vein,	128	Bunch Gr.		4
I writ thy purpose long ago.	155	Assurance		18
AGONIE				
The Agonie.	37	The Agonie		T
AGREE				
Most surely judg'd, make thy accounts agree.	24	Ch.-Porch		456
Sends me to Pilate. This makes them agree;	29	Sacrifice		74
They choose a murderer, and all agree	30	Sacrifice		113
Hath some good in him, all agree.	63	Sinne 2		3
In friendship, first I think, if that agree,	93	Unkindness		2
Do not so well agree.	95	Submission		16
To which I do agree,	104	Obedience		9
With his train-bands and mates agree	110	The Quip		2
To bear them out, and with my state agree.	164	Grief		8
For gold and grace did never yet agree:	197	Ch.-Milit.		251
he cannot agree to come into any house, where he shall not exercise	226	Priest 2		25
Fooles bite one another, but wise-men agree together.	336	Proverbs		452

AGREEABLE	PAGE	TITLE		LINE
to search out most diligently what meats were agreeable unto me,	293	Cornaro		5
and therefore it was agreeable to reason, that my yeares increasing,	295	Cornaro		28
is a naturall Physick most agreeable to us, and also doth preserve	298	Cornaro		14
but such meats as are agreeable to his disease, and that in much	299	Cornaro		31
especially since it is easie and most agreeable to the nature of Man.	300	Cornaro		5
any meat or drink (though most agreeable to them) then their stomack	300	Cornaro		13
AGREED				
To this agreed two Italian Proverbs, the one whereof was,	295	Cornaro		33
though in the point of Resurrection he agreed with them,	316	Valdesso		9
AGREEMENT				
An ill agreement is better then a good judgement.	329	Proverbs		264
Two sparrows on one Ear of Corn make an ill agreement.	358	Proverbs	D	1074
AGREES				
hidden properties it hath, what meat and drink agrees best with it:	297	Cornaro		28
AGUE				
Lord, how I am all ague, when I seek	38	The Sinner		1
One ague dwelleth in my bones,	165	The Crosse		13
Health without money is halfe an ague.	338	Proverbs		509
But I fear the heat of my late Ague hath dryed up those springs,	363	Letters		4
AGUES				
Consuming agues dwell in ev'ry vein,	47	Afflict.1		27
Autumnall Agues are long, or mortall.	326	Proverbs		148
AH				
Ah! how they scourge me! yet my tendernesse	30	Sacrifice		125
Ah! was it not enough that thou	37	Reprisall		9
Ah my deare God! though I am clean forgot,	48	Afflict.1		65
Ah my deare King! though I am clean forgot,	48	Afflict.1	W	65
Ah wretch! what verse	102	Miserie		65
Ah wretched man	102	Miserie	W	65
Ah! no more: thou break'st my heart.	115	Dialogue		32
Ah Loyterer! I'le no more, no more I'le bring:	121	Hope		7
Ah my deare Father, ease my smart!	165	The Crosse		31
Ah my deare angrie Lord,	171	Bittersweet		1
Ah Lord! do not withdraw,	183	A Parodie		16
I the unkinde, ungratefull? Ah my deare,	189	Love 3		9
Ah, what a thing is man devoid of grace,	193	Ch.-Milit.		111
AID				
Do I forbear to crave your speciall aid:	78	Ang.&Sts.		7
AIDED				
Aided by him, I will not fear	216	Psalm III	D	13
AIM				
Doth often aim at, never hit the sphere.	19	Ch.-Porch		318
Should aim and shoot at that which Is on high:	85	Coloss.		8
Did not affect thee much, was not thy aim;	106	Sion		8
What is thy aim? wouldst thou unlock the doore	155	Assurance		15
To have my aim, and yet to be	165	The Crosse		25
and Character of a true Pastour, that I may have a Mark to aim at:	224	Priest		7
whose aim and labour must be not only to get knowledg, but to subdue	226	Priest 2		8
an aim and mark of the whole discourse, whither to drive	256	Priest 21		30
making it my aim in all things, how I may help others to the furthest	301	Cornaro		7
much from Divinity, at which, not without cause, he thinks, I aim;	370	Letters		21
find out some thing not unworthy of those hands at which they aim.	377	Letters		1
AIME				
But the Parson having a double aime, and making a hook of his	244	Priest 12		31
But the Parson distinguisheth according to his double aime,	267	Priest 26		15
Now Love is his business, and aime;	284	Priest 35		16
AIMETH				
Sink not in spirit: who aimeth at the sky,	19	Ch.-Porch		333
AIMING				
A steadie aiming at a tombe.	48	Repentance		6
AIMS				
It moves, it creeps, it aims at thee:	149	Longing		38
shoots higher that threatens the Moon, then hee that aims at a Tree.	224	Priest		9
These are the Parsons generall aims in his Circuit;	249	Priest 14		10
AIR (see also ayre)				
also I ride to Newmarket, and there lie a day or two for fresh Air;	365	Letters		7
AIRE				
One aire of thoughts usurps my brain.	128	Bunch Gr.		5
They purge the aire without, within the breast.	132	The Storm		18
watching, ill aire, overmuch use of the benefit of marriage.	293	Cornaro		31
and the season of the yeare was winter and most cold aire.	296	Cornaro		28
But I drained the ground, and made the aire good:	301	Cornaro		28
It's an ill aire where wee gaine nothing.	350	Proverbs		872
AIRES				
But that these countrey-aires thy love	124	Gratefulnes		23
AKE				
Suckt all thy magazens: my head did ake,	83	Sighs & Gr.		10
His head to shoot and ake.	101	Miserie		48
but you married men laugh till your hearts ake.	361	Proverbs	D	1175
AKES				
The comforters head never akes.	334	Proverbs		392
his head akes not at the matter.	335	Proverbs		421
AL				
Parson hath throughly canvassed al the particulars of humane actions,	230	Priest 5		34
ALARMS				
Of alarms.	80	Deniall		10
ALAS				
Alas! what haste they make to be undone!	27	Sacrifice		34
Alas! I did so, when I left my crown	34	Sacrifice		222
Alas! I did so, when I lost my crown	34	Sacrifice	W	222

ALAS (cont'd)	PAGE	TITLE		LINE
Alas! what have I stollen from you? Death.	34	Sacrifice		231
Alas, my God, I know not what.	36	Thanksgvng		50
But now (alas!) I dare not; for our King,	78	Ang.&Sts.		16
But now alas I dare not; for my King,	78	Ang.&Sts.	W	16
Alas! our murmurings come not last.	128	Bunch Gr.		18
Brave rose, (alas!) where art thou? in the chair	140	Ch.-rents		1
Brave rose, (alas!) where art thou? in the place	140	Ch.-rents	V	1
I fell, and cry'd, Alas my King!	142	Pilgrimage		27
Oh that my prayers! mine, alas!	152	The Jews		7
Alas, my God!	164	Grief		19
Alas, poore Death, where is thy glorie?	169	Dial.-Anth		1
Alas poore mortall, void of storie,	169	Dial.-Anth		3
Dust, alas, no musick feels,	186	Dooms-day		9
in a doctrinall way, saying to the contemner, Alas, why do you thus?	269	Priest 28		12
alas Sir, what is that to those infinite Volumes of Divinity,	365	Letters		13
ALBION				
Not all the teams of Albion in a row	158	Praise 3		15
ALCHYMY				
No Alchymy to saving.	324	Proverbs		114
ALE				
or Ale-houses, to the dishonour of his person and office.	227	Priest 3		30
ALE-HOUSES				
or Ale-houses, to the dishonour of his person and office.	227	Priest 3		30
ALEXANDER				
Speaking of Alexander the Coppersmith, who had withstood his	285	Priest 36		32
And again, of Hymeneus and Alexander, he saith, he had delivered them	286	Priest 36		1
How could you bee like great Alexander, unlesse Historie delivered	443	Oration		2
ALEXANDER'S				
Who were cut short in Alexanders stemme.	192	Ch.-Milit.		74
ALIENATED				
and makes so much the more of him, as before he alienated himselfe;	263	Priest 25		34
ALIGHT				
Though he alight sometimes, still goeth on.	20	Ch.-Porch		340
ALIKE				
but a dictionary, and may be considered alike in all the Scripture.	235	Priest 7		10
yet the victory is alike in all, being by the self-same Spirit.	279	Priest 33		2
that it may be alike in all Gods children (which as concerning	279	Priest 33		21
ALIVE				
Were sinne alive, good cause there were	150	Longing		65
I am to grief alive, to them as dead.	165	The Crosse		24
ALL (see also al)				
Much lesse towards God, whose lust is all their book?	6	Ch.-Porch		12
If God had laid all common, certainly	7	Ch.-Porch		19
Is outlawd by himself: all kinde of ill	7	Ch.-Porch		33
Is outlawd by himself: all kinds of ill	7	Ch.-Porch	W	33
Hee that has all ill, & can have no good	7	Ch.-Porch	W	35
All worldly right, save what he hath by beast.	7	Ch.-Porch		36
Lose all mine own? God hath giv'n me a measure	8	Ch.-Porch		38
(All in a shipwrack shift their severall way)	8	Ch.-Porch		44
Wine above all things doth Gods stamp deface.	8	Ch.-Porch		48
If those bee all thy day, the sunne will crie	9	Ch.-Porch	W	81
Into a bed, to sleep out all ill weathers.	9	Ch.-Porch		84
Throughout the world. Fool not: for all may have,	10	Ch.-Porch		89
Thou hast run all thy race, ere thou beginn.	10	Ch.-Porch	W	90
O England, full of all sinn, most of sloth,	10	Ch.-Porch	W	91
Not that they all are so; but that the most	10	Ch.-Porch		95
Not that they are all so; but that the most	10	Ch.-Porch	W	95
All that they leave: this is flat povertie.	10	Ch.-Porch		106
All that is left: this is flat povertie.	10	Ch.-Porch	W	106
Then all thou addest may be call'd his treasure.	11	Ch.-Porch		114
Doe all things like a man, not sneakingly:	11	Ch.-Porch		121
Tast all, but feed not. if thy stomach call	11	Ch.-Porch	W	128
Who carves, is kind to two; who talks, to all.	11	Ch.-Porch		130
By all means use sometimes to be alone.	12	Ch.-Porch		145
Before thy journey fairly part with all.	13	Ch.-Porch		162
To all things els. Wealth is the conjurers devil;	13	Ch.-Porch		165
As all the day thou mayst hold out to go.	14	Ch.-Porch		186
That all the day thou mayst hold out to go.	14	Ch.-Porch	W	186
Be sweet to all. Is thy complexion sowre?	15	Ch.-Porch		211
Whom all his passions follow, as he goes.	15	Ch.-Porch		216
All things are bigge with jest: nothing that's plain,	16	Ch.-Porch		239
And the sad man is cock of all his jests.	16	Ch.-Porch		252
Thy drops of bloud must pay down all his fear:	17	Ch.-Porch		274
If thou be single, all thy goods and ground	17	Ch.-Porch		283
Submit to love; but yet not more then all.	17	Ch.-Porch		284
All such is courteous, usefull, new, or wittie.	18	Ch.-Porch		290
Entice all neatly to what they know best;	18	Ch.-Porch		295
If thou be Master-gunner, spend not all	18	Ch.-Porch		301
Will no more talk all, then eat all the feast.	18	Ch.-Porch		306
Mark all his wandrings, and enjoy his frets;	19	Ch.-Porch		315
Take all into thee; then with equall care	19	Ch.-Porch		321
And meet them there. All worldly joyes go lesse	19	Ch.-Porch		329
And meet them there. All wordly joyes go lesse	19	Ch.-Porch	W	329
In love or honour: take account of all;	20	Ch.-Porch		344
All forrain wisdome doth amount to this,	20	Ch.-Porch		355
To take all that is given; whether wealth,	20	Ch.-Porch		356
A good digestion turneth all to health:	20	Ch.-Porch		358
Strike off all scores; none are so cleare as they.	20	Ch.-Porch		360
Keep all thy native good, and naturalize	21	Ch.-Porch		361
All forrain of that name; but scorn their ill:	21	Ch.-Porch		362

ALL (cont'd)	PAGE	TITLE		LINE
Who follows all things, forfeiteth his will.	21	Ch.-Porch		364
In time they'l runne thee out of all thy wit.	21	Ch.-Porch		366
That all may gladly board thee, as a flowre.	21	Ch.-Porch		368
Give to all something; to a good poore man,	21	Ch.-Porch		377
For all the week thy food so oft he gave thee.	22	Ch.-Porch		392
We all are but cold suitours; let us move	22	Ch.-Porch		400
And make thy self all reverence and fear.	22	Ch.-Porch		406
All equall are within the churches gate.	22	Ch.-Porch		408
Those doores being shut, all by the eare comes in.	23	Ch.-Porch		418
Makes all their beautie his deformitie.	23	Ch.-Porch		420
Turns all their beauty to his uglines.	23	Ch.-Porch	W	420
All worldly thoughts are but theeves met together	23	Ch.-Porch		424
The worst speak something good: if all want sense,	23	Ch.-Porch		431
Oh all ye, who passe by, whose eyes and minde	26	Sacrifice		1
Though he had all I had, did not forbeare	27	Sacrifice		14
Curing all wounds, but mine; all, but my fears:	27	Sacrifice		27
All my Disciples flie; fear puts a barre	28	Sacrifice		49
The Priest and rulers all false witnesse seek	28	Sacrifice		57
The Priests and rulers all false witnesse seek	28	Sacrifice	W	57
Then they condemne me all with that same breath,	28	Sacrifice		69
Herod and all his bands do set me light,	29	Sacrifice		77
Who teach all hands to warre, fingers to fight,	29	Sacrifice		78
I him obey, who all things else command:	29	Sacrifice		83
They choose a murderer, and all agree	30	Sacrifice		113
All understanding, more then heav'n doth glasse:	30	Sacrifice		119
So they in me denie themselves all pitie:	31	Sacrifice		143
When all my tears were bloud, the while you slept:	31	Sacrifice		150
There they deride me, they abuse me all:	31	Sacrifice		154
For these are all the grapes Sion doth bear,	31	Sacrifice		162
Upon my head: so I remove it all	32	Sacrifice		166
They strike my head, the rock from whence all store	32	Sacrifice		170
And thorny all their crowns, bloudie their weeds;	32	Sacrifice		178
All Scepters, Reeds: Cloths, Scarlet: Crowns are Thorns:	32	Sacrifice	W	178
All spite in one, counting my life their losse,	33	Sacrifice		194
O all ye who passe by, behold and see;	33	Sacrifice		201
The tree of life to all, but onely me:	33	Sacrifice		203
Till all were melted, though he were all steel:	33	Sacrifice		211
All that salvation, which ye now resist;	34	Sacrifice		226
With Manna, Angels food, I fed them all:	34	Sacrifice		239
But now I die; now all is finished.	34	Sacrifice		249
King of all Grief (a title strange, yet true,	35	Thanksgvng	W	1
To thee of all kings onely due)	35	Thanksgvng		2
King of all wounds, how shall I grieve for thee,	35	Thanksgvng	W	3
Who in all grief preventest me?	35	Thanksgvng		4
That all thy body was one doore.	35	Thanksgvng		6
All back unto thee by the poore.	35	Thanksgvng		20
All back unto thee in the poore.	35	Thanksgvng	W	20
That all together may accord in thee,	36	Thanksgvng		41
But in all vict'ries overthrow me?	37	Reprisall		12
A man so wrung with pains, that all his hair,	37	The Agonie		9
Lord, how I am all ague, when I seek	38	The Sinner		1
Shall all thy death?	38	Good Fri.		8
That thy distresse through all may runne,	39	Good Fri.		15
All come to lodge there, sinne may say,	39	Good Fri.		27
All come to lodge there, he may say,	39	Good Fri.	W	27
For by the writings all may see	39	Good Fri.	W	31
And all the writings blot or burn.	39	Good Fri.		32
With all thy art.	41	Easter		8
The crosse taught all wood to resound his name,	41	Easter		9
His stretched sinews taught all strings, what key	41	Easter		11
Or since all musick is but three parts vied	42	Easter		15
And then beyond them all my Baptisme view	43	H. Bapt.1	W	2
In you Redemption measures all my time,	44	H. Bapt.1		10
Your first acquaintance might discredit all.	44	H. Bapt.1		14
Is all the passage, on my infancie	44	H. Bapt.2		3
My soul will bee all bubble straight,	45	Nature	W	9
Afflictions sorted, anguish of all sizes,	45	Sinne 1		6
Yet all these fences and their whole aray	46	Sinne 1		13
Yet all these fences with one bosome sinn	46	Sinne 1	W	13
Sorrow was all my soul; I scarce beleeved,	47	Afflict.1		29
Sorrow was all my soul; I did not know	47	Afflict.1	W	29
Not simpring all mine age,	47	Afflict.1		44
Not simpring all my age,	47	Afflict.1	W	44
Thus are we to delights: but we are all	48	Repentance		9
Looking on this side, & beyond us all:	48	Repentance	W	9
Bitternesse fills our bowels; all our hearts	49	Repentance		27
And bring by Faith all things to him?	49	Faith		4
Faith makes me any thing, or all	50	Faith		17
Where now by Faith all arms are of a length;	50	Faith		27
One size doth all conditions fit.	50	Faith		28
Reserving all for flesh again.	51	Faith		44
A kinde of tune, which all things heare and fear;	51	Prayer 1		8
And all our lump to leaven;	53	H.Commun.		30
Let all the world in ev'ry corner sing,	53	Antiphon 1		1
Let all the world in ev'ry corner sing,	53	Antiphon 1		7
But above all, the heart	53	Antiphon 1		11
Let all the world in ev'ry corner sing,	53	Antiphon 1		13
While mortall love doth all the title gain!	54	Love 1		5
While mortall love does all the title gain!	54	Love 1	W	5
Bear all the sway, possessing heart and brain,	54	Love 1		7

ALL (cont'd)

	PAGE	TITLE		LINE
All her invention on thine Altar lay,	54	Love 2		7
Thou shalt recover all thy goods in kinde,	54	Love 2		11
All knees shall bow to thee; all wits shall rise,	54	Love 2		13
Sometimes I peere above them all;	55	Temper 1		6
Which just now took up all my heart?	56	Temper 2		2
O fix thy chair of grace, that all my powers	56	Temper 2		9
Scatter, or binde them all to bend to thee:	56	Temper 2		13
Is all good structure in a winding stair?	56	Jordan 1		3
Must all be vail'd, while he that reades, divines,	56	Jordan 1		9
All things are busie; onely I	57	Employm. 1		17
But all my companie is a weed.	57	Employm. 1		22
To cleare the breast, to mollifie all pain.	58	H.Script.1		4
Thou art all health, health thriving, till it make	58	H.Script.1		5
Oh that I knew how all thy lights combine,	58	H.Script.2		1
But all the constellations of the storie.	58	H.Script.2		4
Feasting all comers by twelve chosen men.	59	Whitsunday		8
Melt into blessings all the sky,	59	Whitsunday	W	23
To write a verse or two is all the praise,	61	Praise 1		1
Man is all weaknesse; there is no such thing	61	Praise 1		9
O raise me then! poore bees, that work all day,	61	Praise 1		17
Spin all the day:	61	Praise 1	W	18
Is more then all my deaths can be,	62	Afflict.2		3
If all mens tears were let	62	Afflict.2		6
What were they all, compar'd to thine?	62	Afflict.2		8
All my delight, so all my smart:	62	Afflict.2		13
By way of imprest, all my future mone.	62	Afflict.2		15
Of all these things, or all of them in one?	62	Mattens		8
Powring upon it all thy art,	62	Mattens		11
Hath some good in him, all agree.	63	Sinne 2		3
I ranne; but all I brought, was fome.	64	Even-song		12
My God, thou art all love.	64	Even-song		29
Drives all at last. Therefore I gladly trust	64	Ch.-monum.		6
That measures all our time; which also shall	65	Ch.-monum.		21
Where all my debts are payd, none can accrue	65	Ch.-mus.	W	8
Is checker'd all along,	67	Ch.-floore		5
But all is cleansed when the marble weeps.	67	Ch.-floore		15
Blows all the dust about the floore:	67	Ch.-floore		17
Purge all my sinnes done heretofore:	68	Trin.Sun.		4
Complies and suits with all estates;	69	Content		14
Better by worms be all once spent,	69	Content		26
When all thy deeds, whose brunt thou feel'st alone,	69	Content		29
I am with thee, and Most take all.	70	Quidditie		12
Where all the beasts and fowls by their command	70	Humilitie		3
Where all the beasts and Foule by their command	70	Humilitie	W	3
Gave them about to all.	70	Humilitie		8
Spoil'd all the train: then saying, Here it is	71	Humilitie		27
Misuse them all the day:	71	Frailtie	W	6
In all, I think my foot doth ever tread	71	Frailtie		7
Unpinne, or wrench from giving all their due.	72	Constancie		5
All being brought into a summe,	72	Constancie		14
For above all things he abhorres deceit:	72	Constancie		18
All of a piece, and all are cleare and straight.	72	Constancie		20
Did th' earth and all things with it move.	76	Sunday		46
To all Angels and Saints.	77	Ang.&Sts.		T
Oh glorious spirits, who after all your bands	77	Ang.&Sts.		1
The great restorative for all decay	78	Ang.&Sts.		12
Whom we do all joyntly adore and praise,	78	Ang.&Sts.		17
All worship is prerogative, and a flower	78	Ang.&Sts.		21
And then not heare it crying! all day long	80	Deniall		18
All after pleasures as I rid one day,	80	Christmas		1
All after pleasures riding on a Day.	80	Christmas	W	1
To be all passengers most sweet relief?	81	Christmas		8
To Man of all beasts be not thou a stranger:	81	Christmas		12
Enriching all the place.	81	Christmas		20
Shepherd and flock shall sing, and all my powers	81	Christmas		21
Then we will sing, and shine all our own day,	81	Christmas		31
But all thy sweets are packt up in the other;	82	Ungratef.		19
For we have all of us just such another.	82	Ungratef.		24
Suckt all thy magazens: my head did ake,	83	Sighs & Gr.		10
Quickly reformed all with menaces.	84	Sighs & Gr.	W	10
Should thicken all my powers; because my lust	83	Sighs & Gr.		15
But Wisdome quickly swept them all away.	84	The World		5
Till she had weakned all by alteration:	84	The World		8
Reformed all at length with menaces.	84	The World		10
Quitting with daily labour all My pleasure,	85	Coloss.		9
We forfeit all our Creed.	86	Lent		30
As may all vice controll:	87	Lent	W	45
And all must die.	88	Vertue		12
All these stand open, or I have the keyes:	88	The Pearl		9
To all expressions both of hand and eye,	88	The Pearl		15
Where both their baskets are with all their store,	89	The Pearl	W	26
I know all these, and have them in my hand:	89	The Pearl		31
With all the circumstances that may move:	89	The Pearl		36
Broken in pieces all asunder,	89	Afflict.4		1
My thoughts are all a case of knives,	90	Afflict.4		7
All my attendants are at strife,	90	Afflict.4		13
All the rebellions of the night.	90	Afflict.4		24
All things are in decay.	90	Man		6
Man is all symmetrie,	91	Man		13
And all to all the world besides:	91	Man		15

ALL (cont'd)

	PAGE	TITLE		LINE
He is in little all the sphere.	91	Man		22
All things unto our flesh are kinde	91	Man		34
Then how are all things neat?	92	Man		42
The world thinks all things bigg and tall	97	Charms & K	W	17
And ruffle all their curious knots and store.	97	Afflict.5		22
All day exchanging mirth and breath	98	Mortific.		15
Till all do melt, and drown his breath	98	Mortific.		27
That all these dyings may be life in death.	99	Mortific.		36
And calling Justice, all things burn.	99	Decay		20
Folly and Sinne play all his game.	100	Miserie		3
Thou art all brightnesse, perfect puritie;	101	Miserie		32
As dirtie hands foul all they touch,	101	Miserie		37
And feed the swine, with all his mind & might:	101	Miserie	W	44
Give him his dirt to wallow in all night:	101	Miserie		46
They will be kind, and all his pains requite,	101	Miserie	W	46
The spring, whence all things flow:	101	Miserie		60
And all the bloud of God to run in vain.	102	Miserie		64
Whisper, How wide is all this long pretence!	103	Jordan 2		16
Whisper, How wide is all this preparation	103	Jordan 2	W	16
By it do all things live their measur'd houre:	103	Prayer 2		10
By it do all things live their silly houre:	103	Prayer 2	W	10
That were I to leave all but one,	103	Prayer 2		21
Wealth, fame, endowments, vertues, all should go;	103	Prayer 2		22
To passe it self and all it hath to thee.	104	Obedience		8
To passe it self and all it has to thee.	104	Obedience	W	8
All thy delight in me fulfill!	104	Obedience		17
Show'd a strange love to all our good:	104	Obedience		27
Wherefore I all forgo:	105	Obedience		31
Harmonious peace must rock them all the day:	105	Conscience		9
The wood was all embellished	106	Sion		4
All show'd the builders, crav'd the seers care.	106	Sion		6
Yet all this glorie, all this pomp and state	106	Sion		7
For all thy frame and fabrick is within.	106	Sion		12
All Solomons sea of brasse and world of stone	106	Sion		17
And all their motions upward be;	107	Sion		22
After all this canst thou be strange?	108	Home		26
This world of wo? hence all ye clouds, away,	108	Home		33
I blasted all the joyes about me:	108	Home		44
My thoughts and joyes are all packt up and gone,	109	Home		69
For all they either painted are,	109	Brit. Ch.		11
Allureth all in hope to be	110	Brit. Ch.		14
And all in sport to geere at me.	110	The Quip		4
Ev'n all to pieces: which I went to seek:	112	JESU		4
Tells to all he meets, his crosse:	114	Businesse		32
But when all my care and pains	114	Dialogue		5
That is all, if that I could	115	Dialogue		25
Left all joyes to feel all smart -	115	Dialogue		31
As if I were all earth?	115	Dulnesse		2
When all perfections as but one appeare,	115	Dulnesse		13
Of all the creatures both in sea and land	117	Providence		5
To thy renown: but all their hands and throats	117	Providence		11
The sacrifice for all; while they below	117	Providence		14
For me and all my fellows praise to thee:	117	Providence		26
We all acknowledge both thy power and love	117	Providence		29
While all things have their will, yet none but thine.	117	Providence		32
Lay hands on all: they are thy right and left.	117	Providence		34
Nothing escapes them both; all must appeare,	118	Providence		37
Who sweetly temper'st all. If we could heare	118	Providence		39
Thou art in all things one, in each thing many:	118	Providence		43
For thou art infinite in one and all.	118	Providence		44
Where all may reach: no beast but knows his feed.	118	Providence		50
As bouls go on, but turning all the way.	118	Providence		60
The common all men have; that which is rare,	119	Providence		98
All countreys have enough to serve their need:	120	Providence		105
Boat, cable, sail and needle, all in one.	120	Providence		128
Where all the guests sit close, and nothing wants.	121	Providence		134
All things that are, though they have sev'rall wayes,	121	Providence		145
In all my other hymnes, but in this twice.	121	Providence		148
Who above all things lov'd this life;	122	Time		8
All thou hast giv'n him heretofore	123	Gratefulnes		7
And didst allow us all our noise:	124	Gratefulnes		18
Through all the earth:	125	Peace		32
Yet grief knows all, and enters when he will.	126	Confession		6
Now all day spares.	127	Giddinesse		12
No sale or bargain passe: all would disperse,	127	Giddinesse		23
Of a great rock: I well remember all,	129	Love unkn.		15
But when I thought to sleep out all these faults	130	Love unkn.		49
But all my scores were by another paid,	130	Love unkn.		60
All did but strive to mend, what you had marr'd.	130	Love unkn.		67
All creatures have their joy: and man hath his.	131	Mans medly		3
And he of all things fears two deaths alone.	131	Mans medly		30
But all the doctrine, which he taught and gave,	135	Divinitie		13
Is all that saves, and not obscure.	135	Divinitie		24
Break all thy spheres, and save thy head.	135	Divinitie		26
All day complain.	136	Ephes.		21
For where thou dwellest all is neat.	136	Familie		8
First Peace and Silence all disputes controll,	137	Familie		9
And giving all things their set forms and houres,	137	Familie		11
Great joyes are all at once;	138	The Size		19
Grasp not at much, for fear thou losest all.	138	The Size		38

ALL (cont'd)

	PAGE	TITLE	LINE
The starres and all things are; If I refuse,	139	Artillerie	12
And those all bitten, in thy chair I see.	140	Ch.-rents	10
And those all sitten in thy chair I see.	140	Ch.-rents V	10
And ev'n all Africk; would at least I might	140	Ch.-rents	28
With these two poore ones lick up all the dew,	140	Ch.-rents	29
Here I was robb'd of all my gcld,	142	Pilgrimage	16
Was all I found.	142	Pilgrimage	24
And lives: If that be all, said I,	142	Pilgrimage	34
Of my deare God with all my power & might.	143	Holdfast	2
That all things were more ours by being his.	143	Holdfast	12
What Adam had, and forfeited for all,	143	Holdfast	13
Art thou all justice, Lord?	143	Complaining	11
More attributes? Am I all throat or eye,	143	Complaining	13
Hast thou not made thy counts, and summ'd up all?	144	Discharge	6
If it be his once, all is well.	144	Discharge	20
Grieve over freshly all thy pain?	145	Discharge	50
And the cream of all my heart	146	Praise 2	11
But all I fear is lest thy heart displease,	147	Offering	13
All sorts of wounds; of such strange force it is.	147	Offering	21
Seek out this All-heal, and seek no repose,	147	Offering	22
All were thine	148	Offering	34
From thee all pitie flows.	148	Longing	13
Hast thou left all things to their course,	149	Longing	44
Is all lockt? hath a sinners plea	149	Longing	47
Where all things have their leafe assign'd:	149	Longing	50
And all thy promises live and bide.	150	Longing	68
Lies all the yeare,	150	Longing	81
He did descend, undressing all the way.	151	The Bag	12
He, who came hither all alone,	151	The Bag	27
No flowers, no garlands gay? all blasted?	153	The Collar	15
All wasted?	153	The Collar	16
Recover all thy sigh-blown age	153	The Collar	19
That all was not so fair, as I conceiv'd,	155	Assurance	8
If all the hope and comfort that I gather,	155	Assurance	21
Yea, when both rocks and all things shall disband,	156	Assurance	34
Such a Truth, as ends all strife:	156	The Call	3
My busie heart shall spin it all my dayes:	157	Praise 3	3
All things concurre to give it a perfection.	158	Praise 3	9
Not all the teams of Albion in a row	158	Praise 3	15
In ruling all	158	Praise 3	20
Both all my praise, and more!	159	Praise 3	42
Who changeth all things, as him pleaseth best.	159	Jos.coat	4
Let us (said he) poure on him all we can:	159	The Pulley	3
When almost all was out, God made a stay,	160	The Pulley	8
Perceiving that alone of all his treasure	160	The Pulley	9
As serve him up, who all the world commands:	161	Priesthood	26
But all was one.	162	The Search	24
To it all strength, all subtilties	163	The Search	39
All distance known:	163	The Search	58
O who will give me tears? Come all ye springs,	164	Grief	1
My grief hath need of all the watry things,	164	Grief	3
Which want provision in the midst of all.	164	Grief	12
But all my wealth, and familie might combine	164	The Crosse	5
All my abilities, my designes confound,	164	The Crosse	11
I am in all a weak disabled thing,	165	The Crosse	17
Thou turnest th' edge of all things on me still,	165	The Crosse	21
Of all my woes another wo,	165	The Crosse	28
All the hard weather,	166	The Flower	13
Thy word is all, if we could spell.	166	The Flower	21
Where all things burn,	166	The Flower	33
On whom thy tempests fell all night.	166	The Flower	42
My heart was meaning all the day,	168	a true Hymn	2
He who craves all the minde,	168	a true Hymn	11
And all the soul, and strength, and time,	168	a true Hymn	12
I shake my head, and all the thoughts and ends,	169	The Answer	2
Flyes of estates and sunne-shine. But to all,	169	The Answer	5
In that dark state of tears: to all, that so	169	The Answer	12
Where of all plants afflictions soonest grow;	170	Water-crs.	3
And all my sowre-sweet dayes	171	Bittersweet	7
Passing all cordials made by any art,	171	The Glance	6
And all this not for my desert,	172	23 Psalme	11
Shall measure all my dayes;	173	23 Psalme	22
With these all day I do perfume my minde,	175	The Odour	6
Should all my life employ, and busie me.	175	The Odour	30
Ev'n all my heart, and what is lodged there:	176	Forerunners	8
My god must have my best, ev'n all I had.	176	Forerunners	18
For, Thou art still my God, is all that ye	177	Forerunners	32
So all within be livelier then before.	177	Forerunners	36
If then all that worldlings prize	178	The Rose	21
For they all produce repentance,	178	The Rose	27
Come ye hither all, whose taste	179	Invitation	1
God, in whom all dainties are.	179	Invitation	6
Come ye hither all, whom wine	180	Invitation	7
Come ye hither all, whom pain	180	Invitation	13
Bringing all your sinnes to sight:	180	Invitation	15
Come ye hither all, whom joy	180	Invitation	19
Come ye hither all, whose love	180	Invitation	25
Lord I have invited all,	180	Invitation	31
Where is all, there all shculd be.	180	Invitation	36
All their living,	181	Banquet	17

ALL (cont'd)	PAGE	TITLE		LINE
Of all thy mercies, is my posie still.	182	The Posie		4
Of all Gods mercies, is my posie still.	183	The Posie		12
In all things thee to see,	184	The Elixer		2
All things I doe to thee	184	The Elixer	W	2
All may of thee partake:	184	The Elixer		13
That turneth all to gold:	185	The Elixer		22
Lett in the Light to all their actions	185	The Elixer	W	23
I give to thee, who knowest all my wayes,	185	A Wreath		3
And all thy bones with beautie shall be clad.	186	Death		20
Summon all the dust to rise,	186	Dooms-day		3
Parcel'd out to all the world.	187	Dooms-day		28
Thou Echo, thou art mortall, all men know.	188	Heaven		3
Seest and rulest all things ev'n as one:	190	Ch.-Milit.		2
But above all, thy Church and Spouse doth prove	190	Ch.-Milit.		9
All, Emblems, which thy Darling doth improve.	190	Ch.-Milit.	W	16
But to the Gentiles he bore crosse and all,	190	Ch.-Milit.		25
Knocking at all doores, ever as she went.	190	Ch.-Milit.		30
Till all depart: so went the Church her way,	191	Ch.-Milit.		33
Till all be gone. so went the Church her way,	191	Ch.-Milit.	W	33
Gave her the highest place in all mens hearts.	191	Ch.-Milit.		50
Who, that they might subdue, made all their foes.	191	Ch.-Milit.		62
Who had subdued all the world for foes.	191	Ch.-Milit.	W	62
Then showres Religion, and makes all to bear.	192	Ch.-Milit.		88
To this great lotterie, and all would pull.	193	Ch.-Milit.		134
But all was glorious cheating, brave deceit,	193	Ch.-Milit.		135
Disparking oracles, and all their treasure,	194	Ch.-Milit.		147
And this is all the Rock, whereof they boast,	194	Ch.-Milit.		159
Yet that he might the better gain all nations,	195	Ch.-Milit.		183
From all these places, but at divers times,	195	Ch.-Milit.		185
And blending these he carri'd all mens eyes,	195	Ch.-Milit.		189
All poste to Rome: Princes submit their necks	195	Ch.-Milit.		195
And all her calender of sinnes fulfill;	197	Ch.-Milit.		244
The Church and Sunne with all their power and skill.	198	Ch.-Milit.		273
Make his sighs to use it all,	199	L'Envoy		14
Tak'st all the Lodging, leaving none	200	H. Commun.	W	5
But that both thou, and all thy traine	200	H. Commun.	W	10
That thou didst all those pains endure	200	H. Commun.	W	20
Sinn onely, which did all deface	200	H. Commun.	W	23
This gift of all gifts is the best,	201	H. Commun.	W	43
My God, give mee all Thee.	201	H. Commun.	W	48
Has all.	203	Trin.Sun.	W	19
Convert & colour all the other flood	204	The Knell	W	14
Let the world reel, we and all ours stand sure,	439	Walton 5		9
This holy Cable's of all storms secure.	439	Walton 5		10
This holy Cable's from all storms secure.	439	Walton 5	V	10
Meane while, if hee (which all thinges weares)	208	H. Danvers	D	5
Acquitts yourselves and gives the sicke all greife.	209	Paradox	D	6
When all things pull & hale, that they may bring	212	Bohemia	D	27
To serve it forth, & being stript of all	212	Bohemia	D	31
(Till now averse to all that's Good)	214	Convert	D	17
His leaf shall never fade, and all	214	Psalm I	D	11
Whose pow'r shall dash and break them all	216	Psalm II	D	23
are all that make the Son their stay.	216	Psalm II	D	32
Nor all the people round about,	216	Psalm III	D	15
mine adversaries all.	217	Psalm III	D	20
Then worldlings joy'd with all their store	218	Psalm IV	D	27
because of all my foes:	219	Psalm V	D	22
o Lord, reject them all,	219	Psalm V	D	32
But let all those that trust in thee	219	Psalm V	D	35
all night I make my Couch to swim;	220	Psalm VI	D	14
because of all mine Enemies;	220	Psalm VI	D	18
all ye that work Iniquities.	220	Psalm VI	D	20
And put them all to utter shame,	220	Psalm VI	D	27
From all that persecute my life,	220	Psalm VII	D	3
The Lord shall judge the people all:	221	Psalm VII	D	29
But I for all his righteousness	222	Psalm VII	D	61
if a man do not all which is here expressed, hee presently sinns,	224	Priest		10
to get knowledg, but to subdue and mortifie all lusts and affections:	226	Priest 2		10
and to preserve a boldness with them and all, even so farre	226	Priest 2		30
just, prudent, temperate, bold, grave in all his wayes.	227	Priest 3		2
the stupifying and deading of all the clamorous powers of the soul,	227	Priest 3		7
of himself, for all the purposes which God hath ordained him.	227	Priest 3		9
Countrey Parson is very circumspect in avoiding all coveteousnesse,	227	Priest 3		16
but in all his words and actions slighting, and disesteeming it,	227	Priest 3		18
the Parson is very carefull to avoid all the kinds thereof,	227	Priest 3		23
For sins make all equall, whom they finde together;	227	Priest 3		27
Countrey people (as indeed all honest men) do much esteem their	228	Priest 3		2
The Countrey Parson is full of all knowledg.	228	Priest 4		14
For all Truth being consonant to it self, and all being penn'd by one	229	Priest 4		5
and all being penn'd by one and the self-same Spirit, it cannot be,	229	Priest 4		6
that God in all ages hath had his servants, to whom he hath revealed	229	Priest 4		22
and that as one Countrey doth not bear all things, that there may be	229	Priest 4		24
or will open all to one, that there may be a traffick in knowledg	229	Priest 4		25
or a good proportion of all, out of all which he hath compiled	229	Priest 5		33
out of all which he hath compiled a book, and body of Divinity,	229	Priest 5		33
the storehouse of his Sermons, and which he preacheth all his Life;	230	Priest 5		2
the Church Catechisme, to which all divinity may easily be reduced.	230	Priest 5		8
at least all those which he observeth are most incident to his	230	Priest 5		34
read divine services, composeth himselfe to all possible reverence;	231	Priest 6		2
and using all other gestures which may expresse a hearty,	231	Priest 6		3

ALL (cont'd)	PAGE	TITLE	LINE
exacts of them all possible reverence, by no means enduring either	231	Priest 6	22
or kneel, to do all in a strait, and steady posture, as attending	231	Priest 6	26
and all other answers, which are on the Clerks and peoples part	231	Priest 6	28
he procures attention by all possible art, both by earnestnesse	232	Priest 7	31
and seasoning all our words and sentences in our hearts,	233	Priest 7	29
truly affecting, and cordially expressing all that we say;	233	Priest 7	31
for thou art Love, and when thou teachest, all are Scholers.	233	Priest 7	37
And herein St Paul excelled in all his Epistles.	234	Priest 7	11
How did he put the Romans in all his prayers? Rom. 1. 9.	234	Priest 7	12
Oh let us all take heed what we do, God sees us, he sees whether I	234	Priest 7	26
but a dictionary, and may be considered alike in all the Scripture.	235	Priest 7	10
because all ages have thought that a competency, and he that profits	235	Priest 7	11
himself, but that all may be done with reverence to his glory,	235	Priest 8	24
that the Lord would be pleased to sanctifie them all, that they may	235	Priest 8	29
and that the good God would pardon all those, who come with lesse	235	Priest 8	31
He is very circumspect in all companyes, both of his behaviour,	237	Priest 9	14
and out of liberality, make her fruitfull in all good works.	238	Priest 9	33
As hee is just in all things, so is he to his wife also,	238	Priest 9	34
with prayers, and catechizing, and all religious duties.	239	Priest 10	14
and healing of all wounds and sores with her owne hands;	239	Priest 10	15
Therefore having seasoned them with all Piety, not only of words in	239	Priest 10	23
afterwards turnes his care to fit all their dispositions with some	239	Priest 10	30
His servants are all religious, and were it not his duty to have them	240	Priest 10	13
for all in his house are either teachers or learners, or both,	240	Priest 10	20
and they all account, that to teach the ignorant is the greatest	240	Priest 10	22
in the house of those that are skill'd in Musick, all are Musicians;	240	Priest 10	30
so in the house of a Preacher, all are preachers.	240	Priest 10	31
to preserve a directnesse, and open plainnesse in all things;	240	Priest 10	34
so that all his house knowes, that there is no help for a fault done,	240	Priest 10	35
he straitly requires of all to pray by themselves before they sleep	241	Priest 10	1
but also of company, recreation, and all outward contentments;	241	Priest 10	39
with confession of sins, and all acts of Mortification.	242	Priest 10	1
To all this may be added, not for emboldening the unruly,	242	Priest 10	33
hee hath them all with him, because countrey people are very	243	Priest 11	19
Which perswasion the Parson by all means avoyds, knowing that where	243	Priest 11	22
For though he desire, that all should live well, and vertuously,	243	Priest 11	28
Wherefore all his works rellish of Charity.	244	Priest 12	15
but that all bee in a competent way of getting their living.	244	Priest 12	20
excellent statute, which bindes all Parishes to maintaine their own.	244	Priest 12	23
Yet in all his Charity, he distinguisheth, giving them most,	245	Priest 12	14
miseries have a naturall priviledge, and exemption from all law.	245	Priest 12	30
that all things there be decent, and befitting his Name by which it	246	Priest 13	2
Therefore first he takes order, that all things be in good repair;	246	Priest 13	3
where painted, and that all the painting be grave, and reverend,	246	Priest 13	12
That all the books appointed by Authority be there, and those	246	Priest 13	13
and all kept sweet and clean, in a strong and decent chest,	246	Priest 13	18
And all this he doth, not as out of necessity, or as putting	246	Priest 13	23
The first whereof is, Let all things be done decently, and in order:	246	Priest 13	27
The second, Let all things be done to edification, 1 Cor. 14.	246	Priest 13	28
To this end he hath throughly digested all the points of consolation,	249	Priest 15	18
from his promises, from the examples of all Saints, that ever were;	249	Priest 15	21
comfortable, and Soveraigne a Medicine it is to all sin-sick souls;	250	Priest 15	2
and peace it administers against all temptations, even to death it	250	Priest 15	3
his Parish being all his joy, and thought) leaveth not his Ministry	250	Priest 17	25
but the earnestnesse to do all the good he can, moves him to say thus	251	Priest 17	32
The Countrey Parson is sincere and upright in all his relations.	252	Priest 19	24
and true in all his wayes, as being the servant of him,	253	Priest 19	1
as to all the Fathers of the Church, so especially to his Diocesan,	253	Priest 19	6
keeps good Correspondence with all the neighbouring Pastours round	253	Priest 19	15
and debt of neighbourhood to all the Parishes which are neer him.	253	Priest 19	21
all together choosing some fitt day to carry it themselves,	253	Priest 19	37
paymaster, rewarding all good deeds to their full proportion.	254	Priest 20	21
He exacts of all the Doctrine of the Catechisme;	255	Priest 21	22
He requires all to be present at Catechizing:	255	Priest 21	25
When once all have learned the words of the Catechisme,	256	Priest 21	1
requiring answers to all these, and helping and cherishing	256	Priest 21	13
who held that the seeds of all truths lay in every body,	256	Priest 21	21
which the Parson so much commends to all his fellow-labourers;	257	Priest 21	17
he requires the presence of all, and Baptizeth not willingly,	258	Priest 22	2
He adviseth all to call to minde their Baptism often;	258	Priest 22	14
or Sundayes before the Communion, or on the Eves of all those dayes.	258	Priest 22	28
as the Parson useth all reverence himself, so he administers to none	259	Priest 22	11
who being to present all that receive not thrice a year;	259	Priest 22	25
neither can all the people so order their affairs as to receive just	259	Priest 22	26
The Countrey Parson desires to be all to his Parish, and not onely	259	Priest 23	29
but that they still fall from all compromises that have been made.	260	Priest 23	24
If all fail, then he keeps good correspondence with some neighbour	260	Priest 23	36
easie for the Parsons purse, and more familiar for all mens bodyes.	261	Priest 23	32
but preferrs her garden and fields before all outlandish gums.	262	Priest 23	4
But though the Parson sets forward all Charitable deeds,	262	Priest 23	12
useth all possible diligence to reduce them to the common Faith.	262	Priest 24	20
being unmoved in arguing, and voyd of all contentiousnesse:	263	Priest 24	18
and shewing by all means, that the delinquents returne is to his	264	Priest 25	1
hath exactly sifted the definitions of all vertues, and vices;	264	Priest 26	32
not because they are all that are of this dark, and creeping	265	Priest 26	2
either spends not at all, or not in some proportion to Gods blessing	265	Priest 26	6
if in all these, and those more which concerne me, I either do	265	Priest 26	16
and to give one instance for all, if God have given me servants,	265	Priest 26	20
throw into the fire, and so they pay them their wages, all is well.	265	Priest 26	27
of their health, and so they will stand to the pain, all is well.	266	Priest 26	20

ALL (cont'd)	PAGE	TITLE	LINE
Not that all must presently work after dinner;	266	Priest 26	32
wisheth all to incline rather to too much, then to too little;	267	Priest 26	12
not onely because all men shun the company of perpetuall severity,	268	Priest 27	2
that so the sentence lighting upon one, the example may reach to all.	269	Priest 28	2
he takes it either in an humble way, saying nothing at all;	269	Priest 28	6
people have to think that all things come by a kind of naturall	270	Priest 30	25
labours to reduce them to see Gods hand in all things,	270	Priest 30	29
So that if a farmer should depend upon God all the yeer,	271	Priest 30	28
hand to sickle, shall then secure himself, and think all cock-sure;	271	Priest 30	30
God further, even till he imbarn his corn, and then think all sure;	271	Priest 30	32
God sends a fire, and consumes all that he hath:	271	Priest 30	33
by which God turnes all outward blessings to inward advantages.	271	Priest 30	37
and utter this well, all his advantages are to his losse.	272	Priest 30	3
that all Christians should pray twice a day, every day of the week,	272	Priest 31	21
and when for all that they do come, he be a little affected	273	Priest 31	18
This distinction may runne through all Christian duties,	274	Priest 31	1
to whore, to scoffe, to revile, to all sorts of gamings.	274	Priest 32	12
the Common-wealth, that none should be idle, but all busied.	274	Priest 32	28
therfore all are to procure them honestly, and seasonably,	274	Priest 32	30
because when we have sold all, and given it to the poor,	274	Priest 32	33
All are either to have a Calling, or prepare for it:	275	Priest 32	11
Wherefore all are either presently to enter into a Calling,	275	Priest 32	14
they are fittest for, and to prepare for that with all diligence.	275	Priest 32	17
But if after all this care well dispatched, the house-keepers Family	275	Priest 32	36
and to restrain all those, who else might both trouble him	276	Priest 32	15
Wherefore it behoves all, who are come to the gravitie,	276	Priest 32	16
The Heirs are to prepare in all the fore-mentioned points against	276	Priest 32	26
and above all things, they are to frequent Sessions and Sizes;	276	Priest 32	37
he is to endeavour by all means to be a Knight or Burgess there;	277	Priest 32	9
For all Gentlemen, that are now weakned, and disarmed with sedentary	277	Priest 32	17
And the Parson is a lover of and exciter to justice in all things,	277	Priest 32	22
The one being usefull to all Ccuntreys, and the other especially	278	Priest 32	2
all other things shall be added, even it selfe is a Sermon.	278	Priest 33	13
and mastered all his lusts and affections within, and the whole Army	278	Priest 33	22
And if the same person had been sick of all diseases, and were	278	Priest 33	30
of all diseases, and were recovered of all by things that he knew;	278	Priest 33	31
yet the victory is alike in all, being by the self-same Spirit.	279	Priest 33	2
that it may be alike in all Gods children (which as concerning	279	Priest 33	21
Which acts of repentance are and must be found in all Gods servants:	279	Priest 33	26
And they must be likewise in all that are his.	280	Priest 34	11
not to eate of all those dishes at table, which even their present	280	Priest 34	22
nor to store their house with all those furnitures which even their	280	Priest 34	24
to extend themselves to all that mirth, which the present occasion	280	Priest 34	27
that can or will look after things, but all goes by chance, or wit:	281	Priest 34	9
though there be a great Governour of all things, yet to them he is	281	Priest 34	10
sea rage so much as it can, and all things do what they can, and all,	281	Priest 34	22
do what they can, and all, not only without dissolution of the whole,	281	Priest 34	22
if he had been at the Creation of all things, should lesse beleeve	281	Priest 34	29
should lesse beleeve it, seeing the Preservation of all things;	281	Priest 34	30
all the great wonders of old live in them, and then who can deny	282	Priest 34	5
And their very dispersion in all Lands, was intended not only	282	Priest 34	14
but with the Gospel it selfe be preached to all ages, Matth. 26. 13.	282	Priest 34	26
generation should not passe, till all were fulfilled, Luke 21. 32.	282	Priest 34	29
To these might be added the Preaching of the Gospel in all Nations,	282	Priest 34	32
And all may certainly conclude, that God loves them, till either they	283	Priest 34	22
Wherefore he exacts of all to bee present at the perambulation,	284	Priest 35	10
and goes with him to the other, and all dine or sup together.	284	Priest 35	21
or praying to God at all times, but is rather glad of catching	284	Priest 35	25
who was to shew all humility before his Passion, yet he allows in his	285	Priest 36	28
if all men are to blesse upon occasion, as appears Rom. 12. 14. how	286	Priest 36	26
and forbid all disclosing of faults, many an evill may not only be,	286	Priest 37	34
all are executioners, and the Law gives a malefactour to all to be	287	Priest 37	30
executioners, and the Law gives a malefactour to all to be defamed.	287	Priest 37	31
which before their offence and Judgment they had in all mens brests:	287	Priest 37	34
for all are honest, till the contrary be proved.	287	Priest 37	34
before thy face, who are contrary to thee, in all we call thee?	288	Priest	10
Thy hands both made us, and also made us Lords of all thy creatures;	288	Priest	13
Thou hast exalted thy mercy above all things;	288	Priest	23
awake all my powers to glorifie thee!	289	Priest	10
and inable all my powers, that in their full strength they may	289	Priest	27
and the Father of all mercy!	290	Priest	1
incomprehensible God, be ascribed all Honour, and Glory,	290	Priest	15
having tried all remedies fruitlesly, the Physicians told me that yet	292	Cornaro	2
I grew fully perswaded, that all my griefs arose out of Intemperance:	292	Cornaro	20
seem to some incredible) I was perfectly cured of all my infirmities.	292	Cornaro	38
and yet all these I found hurtfull.	293	Cornaro	14
I forsook all these kinde of meats and drinks, and chose that wine	293	Cornaro	15
Above all, taking care never to rise with a full stomack,	293	Cornaro	18
yeare I was not onely freed from all those evils which had so long	293	Cornaro	20
all superfluities passing away without difficultie, and no ill	293	Cornaro	28
Yet could I not so avoid all these, but that now and then I fell into	293	Cornaro	37
as all that know me, can testifie:	294	Cornaro	11
all these did hurt me little, whereas they hurt them very much who	294	Cornaro	14
But all these things could not defend me against their importunities.	296	Cornaro	5
so that all things were troublesome to me:	296	Cornaro	16
Besides all this, I could not sleep, no not a quarter of an houre:	296	Cornaro	21
whereupon all gave me for dead.	296	Cornaro	22
In all which time I felt no grief, save now and then a little	296	Cornaro	30
For the Temperance of so many yeares spent all ill humours,	296	Cornaro	32
because this will cut off all causes of diseases, so that he shall	297	Cornaro	21

ALL (cont'd)	PAGE	TITLE		LINE
then a Temperate Life, Temperance by all means is to be embraced.	298	Cornaro		2
wherein wisdome and all kinde of vertues is most vigorous;	298	Cornaro		30
are not almost all the learned books that we have, written by their	298	Cornaro		32
in all things wherein they deal, may be more lively and vigorous.	299	Cornaro		20
so decent, and so holy, it is worthy by all means to be embraced;	300	Cornaro		4
yet all must [needs] take heed, lest they take a greater quantitie	300	Cornaro		11
yeares old, all the time we live after, is rather death then life.	300	Cornaro		29
and well-contented, free from all troubles and troublesome thoughts;	300	Cornaro		37
making it my aim in all things, how I may help others to the furthest	301	Cornaro		7
All these things I do at my ease, and at fit seasons, and in mine own	301	Cornaro		9
are so ordered, that they all meet and end in a fair plot of ground;	301	Cornaro		21
which are all in their perfect vigour, but especially my Taste;	302	Cornaro		8
when I was given to disorder and all the delights that could be.	302	Cornaro		11
all the sonnes of one father and mother, all in perfect health;	303	Cornaro		3
all the sonnes of one father and mother, all in perfect health;	303	Cornaro		4
all, as farre as I can conjecture, very apt and well given both	303	Cornaro		4
For death to all young men is a terrible thing, as also to those that	303	Cornaro		18
by the regularitie of my life I have shut out death all other wayes.	303	Cornaro		28
but that I should wish all who have the care of themselves,	303	Cornaro		31
and to such, and all that is theirs, I owe diligence;	304	Valdesso		7
neverthelesse I wish you by all meanes to publish it, for these three	304	Valdesso		18
righteousnesse (as he sheweth through all his Considerations) a thing	305	Valdesso		1
And David (though David) studied all the day long in it:	306	Valdesso		20
All the Saints of God may be said in some sence to have put	306	Valdesso		28
that it makes him godly, righteous, and sober all his life long;	309	Valdesso		6
They shall be all taught of God, it being Scripture cannot be spoken	310	Valdesso		2
sence of that Text, wee shall overthrow all means, save catechizing,	310	Valdesso		12
amongst all divine and spirituall exercises and duties,	311	Valdesso	V	3
All the discourse from this line [place] till the end of this Chapter	311	Valdesso		20
or living, for all the point lies in believing or not believing.	311	Valdesso		29
for it invites us to all good, according to that singular place,	313	Valdesso		19
A man is to embrace all good, but because he cannot doe all,	313	Valdesso		21
but because he cannot doe all, God often chuseth which he shall doe,	313	Valdesso		21
such as are all vain conversations:	314	Valdesso		19
perhaps he meant all of this later not of the former.	317	Valdesso		4
since the Saints of God in all ages have ever held in so pretious	317	Valdesso		32
building it all upon the word untill the day starre arise,	318	Valdesso		8
All is well with him, who is beloved of his neighbours.	321	Proverbs		10
All is well to him, that is loved of his neighbours.	321	Proverbs	V	10
When all sinnes grow old, coveteousnesse is young.	321	Proverbs		18
When all sinnes grow old, coveteousnesse grows young.	321	Proverbs	V	18
One sound blow will serve to undo all.	322	Proverbs		34
Who gives to all, denies all.	322	Proverbs		38
All came from, and will goe to others.	322	Proverbs		41
In a good house all is quickly ready.	323	Proverbs		58
If all fooles had bables, wee should want fuell.	323	Proverbs		63
He that is warme, thinkes all so.	323	Proverbs		80
All truths are not to be told.	324	Proverbs		89
Good is the mora that makes all sure.	325	Proverbs		145
Of all smells, bread: of all tasts, salt.	326	Proverbs		166
In the house of a Fidler, all fiddle.	328	Proverbs		223
The wise hand doth not all that the foolish mouth speakes.	329	Proverbs		246
A journying woman speakes much of all, and all of her.	330	Proverbs		279
That is not good language which all understand not.	331	Proverbs		302
All is not gold that glisters.	331	Proverbs		306
Since you know all, and I nothing,	332	Proverbs		336
Hee that repaires not a part, builds all.	333	Proverbs		344
Hee that repaires not a part, at length must all.	333	Proverbs	V	344
He that beleeveth all, misseth;	333	Proverbs		364
All griefes with bread are lesse.	334	Proverbs		377
All griefes with bread are lesse, or Nor woe to want.	334	Proverbs	V	377
All things require skill, but an appetite.	334	Proverbs		378
All things have their place, knew wee how to place them.	334	Proverbs		379
To a crazy ship all winds are contrary.	334	Proverbs		395
Who hath bitter in his mouth, spits not all sweet.	335	Proverbs		422
He that hath children, all his morsels are not his owne.	335	Proverbs		423
He who hath children, all his morsels are not his owne.	335	Proverbs	V	423
All feete tread not in one shoe.	338	Proverbs		497
Patience, time and money accommodate all things.	338	Proverbs		498
If all fooles wore white Caps, wee should seeme a flock of geese.	338	Proverbs		513
All things in their beeing are good for something.	339	Proverbs		520
Love makes all hard hearts gentle.	339	Proverbs		542
When the tree is fallen, all goe with their hatchet.	340	Proverbs		566
To bee beloved is above all bargaines.	342	Proverbs		631
Pardon all but thy selfe.	344	Proverbs		677
If a good man thrive, all thrive with him.	344	Proverbs		695
If things were to be done twice, all would be wise.	344	Proverbs		700
If all things might be done twice, all would be wise.	343	Proverbs	V	700
you could not fill all to your mind.	343	Proverbs	V	700
you could not fit all to your mind.	344	Proverbs		701
All our pompe the earth covers.	345	Proverbs		716
All keyes hang not on one girdle.	345	Proverbs		719
All the Armes of England will not arme feare.	345	Proverbs		722
Let all live as they would die.	345	Proverbs		725
To a child all weather is cold.	345	Proverbs		732
Fooles give to please all but their owne.	345	Proverbs		735
The first dish pleaseth all.	346	Proverbs		744
All complaine.	346	Proverbs		750
Praise none too much, for all are fickle.	347	Proverbs		774
All are not merry that dance lightly.	348	Proverbs		808

ALL (cont'd)	PAGE	TITLE		LINE
He that gives all before hee dies provides to suffer.	349	Proverbs		855
He that gives all ere hee dies provides to suffer.	349	Proverbs	V	855
of a monke on all sides.	351	Proverbs		900
of a monke on all hands.	351	Proverbs	V	900
The Physitian owes all to the patient,	351	Proverbs		921
Wine makes all sorts of creatures at table.	352	Proverbs		931
All are presumed good, till they are found in a fault.	352	Proverbs		944
The great would have none great and the little all little.	352	Proverbs		946
To live peaceably with all breedes good blood.	353	Proverbs		963
When all men have what belongs to them, it cannot bee much.	353	Proverbs		979
When one is on horsebacke hee knowes all things.	353	Proverbs		982
feeles it all the winter after.	354	Proverbs		992
If you would bee at ease, all the world is not.	355	Proverbs		1019
all the world would turne Carpenters (to make them crutches).	355	Proverbs		1020
All that shakes falles not.	355	Proverbs		1022
All beasts of prey are strong or treacherous.	355	Proverbs		1023
All covet, all lose.	358	Proverbs	D	1078
All flesh is not venison.	358	Proverbs	D	1096
God strikes with his finger, and not with all his arme.	359	Proverbs	D	1114
all his life, could he find it.	360	Proverbs	D	1143
in Poetry, shall be all, and ever consecrated to Gods glory.	363	Letters		12
as that if all things proved not well, I had rather the fault should	364	Letters		28
all which tend to avoiding of costlier matters, if I should fall	365	Letters		7
of all good which you see in Frenchmen, whether it be in knowledge,	366	Letters		7
upon condition that I should surcease from all title to it,	367	Letters		9
I beseech you all, you and my dear Mother and Sister to pardon me,	369	Letters		17
for the Orator writes all the University Letters, makes all	369	Letters		33
all the University Letters, makes all the Orations, be it to King,	369	Letters		34
is at all their Assemblies and Meetings, and sits above the Proctors,	370	Letters		1
I hope I shall get this place without all your London helps,	370	Letters		8
that if all fail, yet I am able to stand on mine own legs.	370	Letters		10
the midst of much business, and all in a Fortnight, not long since.	371	Letters		4
Concerning the Orators place all goes well yet, the next Friday it is	371	Letters		16
I was in hope I should my self carry all sickness out of your family:	372	Letters		15
constant and the more earnest for you to the God of all Consolation.	372	Letters		23
and comfort your self in the God of all Comfort, who is not willing	372	Letters		25
that are to come, you have strong preservatives against all disquiet.	373	Letters		19
I beseech you consider all that can happen to you are either	373	Letters		20
And above all, If any care of future things molest you?	374	Letters		12
Casting all your Care on the Lord, for he careth for you. (1 Pet.	374	Letters		16
at all times rejoyce in the Lord, who taketh care for us:	374	Letters		25
Let your moderation appear to all men, the Lord is at hand:	374	Letters		27
trouble not your selves, God is at hand to deliver us from.all, or,	374	Letters		30
not your selves, God is at hand to deliver us from all, or, in all.	374	Letters		30
a good mind into the way of charity, and that was all I intended.	375	Letters		8
whom to receive were the greatest charitie of all, for she is	375	Letters		24
is the encouragement of learning all the year after, except my cousin	375	Letters		28
into your hart, and the LORD bless all your purposes to his glory.	375	Letters		34
I forgett all thinges, so I may doe them good who want it.	376	Letters		5
and all yours; and make your family, a housefull of GOD's servants.	376	Letters		19
of your Mother upon you, and cause all her wishes, diligence,	377	Letters		4
Particularly, I like all your Addresses, & for ought I see,	378	Letters		17
You write very lovingly that all your things are mine.	378	Letters		21
bless you more & more, & so turn you all, in your severall wayes,	378	Letters		25
be My God & Dear Master, the Spring & Fountain of all Goodness.	379	Letters		17
sent my Letters, to your Brother, investing him, in all that I have.	379	Letters		20
now Constancy is such & of great esteem with all.	380	Woodnoth		15
6. you doe not want all success.	381	Woodnoth		7
7. Though you want all success either in inclining or restraining,	381	Woodnoth		14
I give all my goods both within doores and without doores both	382	G.H.'s Will		3
all these are over and above their wages, To Sara thirteene shillings	382	G.H.'s Will		25
All those that are crost are discharged already the rest are to be	383	G.H.'s Will		3
yea, indeed of all, both Courtly, Militarie, Academicall.	441	Oration		27
title to your Excellencies, all the Muses and Graces congratulate;	442	Oration		1
for respect to you, embrace all that is cheerefull, joyous,	442	Oration		7
all we and our whole Kingdome exult with joy, to bee united with that	442	Oration		13
same order and habit, of which wee all in this Kingdome glorie to be.	442	Oration		21
neighboring Sea, wondrously sound through all our Coasts, and eares.	442	Oration		24
repose, peace with all but Booke-wormes, perpetuall povertie,	442	Oration		36
ALL-HEAL				
Seek out this All-heal, and seek no repose,	147	Offering		22
ALLAY				
Then keep such companie; make them thy allay:	15	Ch.-Porch		212
ALLEYS				
Parted with alleys or with grass	75	Sunday	W	27
ALLOW				
Couldst thou not griefs sad conquests me allow,	37	Reprisall		11
Impute a lustre, and allow them bright;	51	Faith		35
Impart a lustre, and allow them bright;	51	Faith	W	35
Give to thy Mother, what thou wouldst allow	86	Lent		5
And didst allow us all our noise:	124	Gratefulnes		18
Betwixt my God and me; that I allow	155	Assurance		9
We cannot allow this: or else if the thing will admit interpretation;	252	Priest 18		10
But some may say, though the Law allow this, the Gospel doth not,	287	Priest 37		22
our Colledge Customs allow not that, and I shou'd account my self	373	Letters		2
and will not allow any room there for such an in-mate as Grief;	374	Letters		10
or, allow that any sadness shall be his Competitor.	374	Letters		11
ALLOWABLE				
with his favours, can not but be not only allowable but commendable.	381	Woodnoth		26

ALLOWANCE	PAGE	TITLE		LINE
yet I am scarce able with much ado to make one half years allowance,	365	Letters		10
ALLOW'D				
He scarce allow'd me half an eie.	111	The Quip		15
Could be allcw'd for harmonie)	165	The Crosse		16
ALLOWED				
Those that can read, are allowed times for it, and those that cannot,	240	Priest 10		19
ALLOWES				
he himselfe allowes it for a holy conversation and refreshment.	311	Valdesso		2
ALLOWING				
allowing no Jurisdiction over the godly, this cannot stand,	316	Valdesso		15
ALLOWS				
Allows thee choise of paths: take no by-wayes;	7	Ch.-Porch		14
Allows for that, and keeps his constant way:	73	Constancie		28
Whose grief allows him musick and a ryme:	164	Grief		17
Listens behinde him, and allows some light,	191	Ch.-Milit.		32
yet considering that the Law allows these in case they be true,	245	Priest 12		24
but allows by no means to give without testimony, as he obeys	245	Priest 12		25
once satisfied, he allows his Charity some blindnesse in the other;	245	Priest 12		27
shew all humility before his Passion, yet he allows in his Apostles.	285	Priest 36		28
ALLSO				
But allso pleasing bee.	184	The Elixer	W	4
And travell'd Westward allso, coasting on,	193	Ch.-Milit.	W	104
That allso made thee dead.	201	H. Commun.	W	30
ALLURE				
This may allure us with delights;	82	Ungratef.		22
ALLURETH				
Allureth all in hope to be	110	Brit. Ch.		14
ALLWAYES				
You allwayes feare to feele those smarts	210	Paradox	D	31
ALMANACK				
The Court hath no Almanack.	350	Proverbs		894
ALMES				
In Almes regard thy means, and others merit.	21	Ch.-Porch		373
Let thy almes go before, and keep heav'ns gate	21	Ch.-Porch		383
they all account, that to teach the ignorant is the greatest almes.	240	Priest 10		23
and a Bason for Almes and offerings;	246	Priest 13		20
and syncere Religion, such as are Prayer, Fasting, Almes-deedes, &c.	312	Valdesso		21
Almes never make poore. Or thus,	327	Proverbs		189
Great almes-giving lessens no mans living.	327	Proverbs		190
To steale the Hog, and give the feet for almes.	329	Proverbs		237
He that preacheth giveth almes.	347	Proverbs		788
ALMES-DEEDES				
and syncere Religion, such as are Prayer, Fasting, Almes-deedes, &c.	312	Valdesso		21
ALMES-GIVING				
Great almes-giving lessens no mans living.	327	Proverbs		190
ALMIGHTIE				
Engine against th' Almightie, sinners towre,	51	Prayer 1		5
Engine against th' Almightie, sinners fort,	51	Prayer 1	W	5
Of what supreme almightie power	103	Prayer 2		7
Almightie God doth grieve, he puts on sense:	136	Ephes.		16
Be not Almightie, let me say,	163	The Search		51
Almightie Judge, how shall poore wretches brook	187	Judgement		1
Almightie Lord, who from thy glorious throne	190	Ch.-Milit.		1
commending my soule and body to Almightie God that made them doe thus	382	G.H.'s Will		2
ALMIGHTY				
Thwart not th' Almighty God: O be not crosse.	22	Ch.-Porch		395
Sinne is flat opposite to th' Almighty, seeing	63	Sinne 2		4
and presence of Almighty God, and blessing the people either openly,	236	Priest 8		5
humbly beseeching the Almighty to pardon and accept our poor	236	Priest 8		27
O almighty and ever-living Lord God!	288	Priest		7
God Almighty prosper the Work.	379	Letters		10
ALMOST				
And while it cometh, it is almost past.	145	Discharge		53
When almost all was out, God made a stay,	160	The Pulley		8
the beginning of the Gout, with almost a continuall fever and thirst.	291	Cornaro		23
evils which had so long beset me, and were almost become incurable;	293	Cornaro		21
are not almost all the learned books that we have, written by their	298	Cornaro		32
concluding every Consideration almost with his holy Name,	305	Valdesso		5
which depend almost wholly on their Canon law and Decretals,	319	Valdesso	V	29
ALMS (see also almes)				
his money for the poor, and his table for those that are above Alms.	243	Priest 11		9
ALONE				
By all means use sometimes to be alone.	12	Ch.-Porch		145
That thou hast gotten. Surely use alone	12	Ch.-Porch		155
Will canker both, yett thou alone shallt smart:	13	Ch.-Porch	W	166
As that thy self alone to hell shalt goe.	13	Ch.-Porch	W	168
Active and stirring spirits live alone.	20	Ch.-Porch		341
A HEART alone	26	The Altar		5
The sunne, which once did shine alone,	59	Whitsunday		13
Thou art my grief alone,	62	Afflict.2		11
Who gave me sight alone,	63	Even-song		5
A strong regard and aw: but speech alone	68	Windows		13
Content and warm t' it self alone:	68	Content		10
When all thy deeds, whose brunt thou feel'st alone,	69	Content		29
Since there is no place so alone,	75	Sunday		20
Praised be the God alone,	93	Antiphon 2		22
Thy words were then, Let me alone.	99	Decay		5
Beautie alone to me:	115	Dulnesse		10
And put the penne alone into his hand,	117	Providence		7
Doth not refrain unto himself alone,	117	Providence		18

ALONE (cont'd)	PAGE	TITLE		LINE
But Man alone, to show his heav'nly breed:	120	Providence		111
Sometimes unite. The Indian nut alone	120	Providence		126
Quitting the fruit, seiz'd on my heart alone,	129	Love unkn.		12
Man ties them both alone,	131	Mans medly		10
And he of all things fears two deaths alone.	131	Mans medly		30
To heav'n alone both go, and leade.	135	Divinitie		28
I sinne not to my grief alone,	136	Ephes.		17
Then will I trust, said I, in him alone.	143	Holdfast		5
Thy noon alone.	144	Discharge		14
And alone, when they replied,	146	Praise 2		15
Thy lusts have made, and not thy lusts alone;	147	Offering		15
Surely thine alone.	148	Offering		36
He, who came hither all alone,	151	The Bag		27
Thy praise alone.	157	Praise 3		2
Perceiving that alone of all his treasure	160	The Pulley		9
My alone onely heart and breast,	174	Aaron		17
For when My Master, which alone is sweet,	175	The Odour		21
And thy book alone.	178	Discipline		12
For with it alone I flie	182	Banquet		43
And I alone,	183	A Parodie		2
Thou and alone thou know'st.	183	A Parodie		25
Now with the crosse, as with a staffe, alone,	190	Ch.-Milit.		28
Europe alone and Rome do keep them free	194	Ch.-Milit.	W	157
Blessed be God alone,	199	L'Envoy		17
Or rather so, as thou alone	200	H. Commun.	W	4
Lett two of those alone	203	Trin.Sun.	W	15
And starres alone unto the pitch doe runne	211	Bohemia	D	4
and makes that law alone to be	214	Psalm I	D	6
For thy protection, Lord, alone	218	Psalm IV	D	31
yet not as himself alone, but as presenting with himself the whole	231	Priest 6		7
he never talkes with any woman alone, but in the audience of others,	237	Priest 9		11
from hot Countreys, where both flesh alone, and much more with wine,	242	Priest 10		17
thanking of him, he exacts of them to let him alone, and say rather,	245	Priest 12		32
whether he could get out of the ditch alone, or whether he needed	257	Priest 21		9
he never decides it alone, but sends for three or four of the ablest	260	Priest 23		8
Welcome evill, if thou commest alone.	325	Proverbs		140
Who eates his cock alone must saddle his horse alone.	333	Proverbs		348
Who eates his cake alone must saddle his horse alone.	333	Proverbs	V	348
Hast comes not alone.	348	Proverbs		826

ALONG				
And brought'st thy sweets along with thee.	42	Easter		22
Bringinge thy sweets along with thee.	42	Easter	W	22
And brought thy sweets along with thee.	42	Easter	WC	22
Is checker'd all along,	67	Ch.-floore		5

ALOOFE				
On painting and fighting looke aloofe.	329	Proverbs		247

ALOUD				
Heark how they crie aloud still, Crucifie:	29	Sacrifice		97
and child, answering aloud both Amen, and all other answers,	231	Priest 6		28

ALPHABETS				
as if they were both but Alphabets and after a time to be left.	309	Valdesso		19

ALREADIE				
which is alreadie burdened with a disease, would be wholly oppressed.	299	Cornaro		33

ALREADY				
But I am frailtie, and already dust;	83	Sighs & Gr.		17
Partakes already half of hell.	123	Time		24
but had already gone farre in me, first caused me to leave	291	Cornaro		18
to relieve my Neighbour, God hath already reveled his Will about it.	313	Valdesso		14
burden to you, since I can never answer what I have already received;	367	Letters		14
I have wrote to my dear sick Sister this week already, and therefore	367	Letters		21
who have already abundantly discharg'd that part, having both ordered	373	Letters		11
those that are crost are discharged already the rest are to be payd.	383	G.H.'s Will		3

ALSO (see also allso)				
Because to shun them also is so cheap:	9	Ch.-Porch		68
Servants and churches also play their part.	14	Ch.-Porch		196
To sell me also, and to put me there:	27	Sacrifice		15
The souldiers also spit upon that face,	32	Sacrifice		181
The souldiers also spit upon my Face,	32	Sacrifice	W	181
Was writ in stone; so thou, which also art	41	Sepulchre		18
My bodie also thither.	52	H.Commun.		26
May also fix their reverence:	56	Temper 2		10
That measures all our time; which also shall	65	Ch.-monum.		21
That he might save his life, and also hers,	85	Vanitie 1		12
And also thee,	90	Afflict.4		21
Just so the other heav'n they also serve,	134	Divinitie		5
But I have also starres and shooters too,	139	Artillerie		17
Nay, ev'n to trust in him, was also his:	143	Holdfast		6
Thy passions also have their set partitions.	147	Offering		16
But also mine; as when the league was made	156	Assurance		28
Bestow this jewell also on my creature,	160	The Pulley		12
Known also to each minute of an houre:	190	Ch.-Milit.		4
And travell'd westward also: journeying on	193	Ch.-Milit.		104
They have their period also and set times	197	Ch.-Milit.		261
Thus also Sinne and Darknesse follow still	198	Ch.-Milit.		272
Thus also sinn and darknes constantly	198	Ch.-Milit.	W	272
So also did the Church by going west	198	Ch.-Milit.		275
That thy death is also dead,	199	L'Envoy		7
Then of this also I am sure	200	H. Commun.	W	19
which also I will set as high as I can, since hee shoots higher that	224	Priest		8
and also therein setting aside the Reverend Prelates of the Church,	225	Priest 2		20

ALSO (cont'd)

	PAGE	TITLE	LINE
and apparell, the disorders thereof are also very manifest. . .	228	Priest 3	9
and what follows after, as also the scope of the Holy Ghost.	229	Priest 4	11
The Countrey Parson hath read the Fathers also, and the Schoolmen,	229	Priest 5	31
He greatly esteemes also of cases of conscience, wherein he is much	230	Priest 5	19
hee may affect also his people, knowing that no Sermon moves them so	231	Priest 6	13
which answers also are to be done not in a hudling, or slubbering	231	Priest 6	30
and of theirs also who gaze upon them when they come in, . .	232	Priest 6	10
whom also he intreats to press some point, that he himself hath often	232	Priest 7	27
Herein also he serves himselfe of the judgements of God, . .	233	Priest 7	6
for them also men heed, and remember better then exhortations;	233	Priest 7	13
and then also in a serious manner, never jestingly or sportfully.	237	Priest 9	12
so is he to his wife also, counting nothing so much his owne,	238	Priest 9	34
not only with abstinence of diet, but also of company, recreation,	241	Priest 10	38
which also in diseases of exinanition (as consumptions) must be	242	Priest 10	31
sicknesse breaks these obligations of fasting, but sicklinesse also.	242	Priest 10	36
Not but that the poor are welcome also to his table, whom he	243	Priest 11	10
for that also is some kind of obligation;	245	Priest 12	19
so doth he also to those at his door, whom God puts in his way,	245	Priest 12	20
For though these testimonies also may be falsifyed, yet considering	245	Priest 12	23
So doth hee also before giving make them say their Prayers first,	245	Priest 12	34
finds busie in the works of their calling, he commendeth them also:	247	Priest 14	21
encouraging also the servants to learn to read, and offering to have	248	Priest 14	36
For both God is there also, and those for whom God dyed: . .	249	Priest 14	6
he also urgeth them to do some pious charitable works, as a necessary	249	Priest 15	32
but also professeth himselfe throughly of the opinion, carrying it	250	Priest 16	8
so also when after many admonitions, any continue to be refractory,	250	Priest 16	15
things are otherwise equall, therefore he satisfies this duty also.	253	Priest 19	28
not the lesse, lest he cast their neighbours poverty on them also.	254	Priest 19	7
even containing in vertue the answer also, especially to the more	256	Priest 21	36
the safest course for Christians also to meditate on their Baptisme	258	Priest 22	18
but also for the discharge of the Church-wardens, who being . .	259	Priest 22	24
and not onely a Pastour, but a Lawyer also, and a Phisician.	259	Priest 23	30
as also by discourse with men of that profession, whom he hath ever	260	Priest 23	3
Now as the Parson is in Law, so is he in sicknesse also: . .	260	Priest 23	29
as also by way of illustration, even as our Saviour made plants	261	Priest 23	13
for as hee is Charitable, so he is just also.	262	Priest 23	15
be preferred, especially since in disobeying there is scandall also:	263	Priest 24	11
which is said of hurtfull meats, extends to hurtfull drinks also.	266	Priest 26	28
but also for that when they are in company, instructions seasoned	268	Priest 27	3
as also the visitation Articles, which are grounded upon the Canons,	270	Priest 29	14
on God, not onely before the corne is inned, but after also;	271	Priest 30	35
hath both a faire harvest, and that also well inned, and imbarned,	272	Priest 30	1
as that by this he may take into his Prayer humiliation also.	273	Priest 31	32
but a generall also of the diseases of the time, that so, . .	274	Priest 32	6
Yet is it also a debt to our Countrey to have a Calling, . .	274	Priest 32	26
and also an honourable Imployment of a Gentle, or Noble-man in	276	Priest 32	12
and also elsewhere, when they see any remarkable point of Education	276	Priest 32	29
he must not only be a morning man, but at Committees also; . .	277	Priest 32	12
but also as they may be handled, a religious imployment? . .	278	Priest 32	7
military state of a Christian life, but even in the peaceable also;	279	Priest 33	4
his preaching, but afterwards also, as Mat. 22. 35. He was tempted:	280	Priest 34	9
but also of any part, by taking away so much as the usuall seasons	281	Priest 34	23
wherewith also a carefull Joseph might meet.	281	Priest 34	26
their Countrey also is known, the places, and rivers travelled unto,	282	Priest 34	2
it not onely a grave, and reverend thing, but a beneficial also.	285	Priest 36	3
have the Ministers power of Blessing only, but also of cursing.	285	Priest 36	25
duty in Ministers themselves, hath made the people also neglect it;	286	Priest 36	12
The same is to be observed in writing Letters also. . . .	286	Priest 36	26
but also spread in his Parish, without any remedy (which cannot be	287	Priest 37	1
Of these also men may talk, and more, they may discover them to those	287	Priest 37	16
whom the Law would have defamed, except he also do it out of rancour.	287	Priest 37	29
doubtlesse then also mens affections and words must turne, . .	288	Priest 37	4
Thy hands both made us, and also made us Lords of all thy creatures;	288	Priest	13
a sober life, expressing also the means which I have used therein.	291	Cornaro	16
cool wines pleased my taste best, as also melons, and other fruit;	293	Cornaro	11
but also afterwards I fell not into that yearely disease, . .	293	Cornaro	22
Which benefits also still continue, because from the time that I was	293	Cornaro	24
Yet with this diet I avoided other hurtfull things also, . .	293	Cornaro	30
yet these forenamed things have also their force.	293	Cornaro	34
I preserved me also, asmuch as I could, from hatred and melancholie,	293	Cornaro	35
I should be a conquerour, as also a little after it came to passe:	294	Cornaro	27
whereupon also I joyed exceedingly;	294	Cornaro	29
was sore hurt, and also one of my arms and legges put out of joynt.	294	Cornaro	39
But my experience taught me another thing also, to wit, . .	295	Cornaro	16
but also to gather strength, which could not be but by meat & drink.	295	Cornaro	24
hath cured him, commends this also to him, if he will live in health.	297	Cornaro	18
and also doth preserve even ill tempers in good health, . .	298	Cornaro	14
so did Plato also, and Isocrates, and Tullie, and many others	298	Cornaro	39
not onely in the citie, but also in villages and hamlets. . .	299	Cornaro	4
as also that their minde, in all things wherein they deal, . .	299	Cornaro	20
I enjoy also my gardens, and those divers, parted with rills	301	Cornaro	15
where also I have fountains and gardens, and a very convenient house.	301	Cornaro	18
as also of excellent Artificers in Architecture, painting, . .	301	Cornaro	36
I am much pleased also in my travells, with the beauty of situation.	302	Cornaro	6
Moreover, by this also, in what estate I am, may be discovered,	302	Cornaro	27
with their musick and fashion, and I my self also sing often;	303	Cornaro	7
as daily experience sheweth, and I also, when I was a young man,	303	Cornaro	15
as also to those that live in sinne, and follow their appetites:	303	Cornaro	19
but also I hope, when I shall come to that point, I shall finde no	303	Cornaro	23
happily also with this (as his thoughts are fruitfull) intending	304	Valdesso	12

AM

	PAGE	TITLE		LINE
Who am the way of truth, the true relief;	27	Sacrifice		38
Who am the way & Truth, the true relief;	27	Sacrifice	W	38
And onely am the Lord of hosts and might:	29	Sacrifice		79
And now I am deliver'd unto death,	31	Sacrifice		145
I am the floore, the sink, where they it fling:	32	Sacrifice		175
I, who am Truth, turn into truth their deeds:	32	Sacrifice		179
I, who am Truth, turn into truth their scorns:	32	Sacrifice	W	179
Reproches, which are free, while I am bound.	33	Sacrifice		219
Yet by my subjects am condemn'd to die	34	Sacrifice		234
Onely let others say, when I am dead,	34	Sacrifice		251
Shall not perceive, that I am here.	36	Thanksgvng		38
For though I die for thee, I am behinde;	36	Reprisall		3
Lord, how I am all ague, when I seek	38	The Sinner		1
Now I am here, what thou wilt do with me	48	Afflict.1		55
Ah my deare God! though I am clean forgot,	48	Afflict.1		65
Ah my deare King! though I am clean forgot,	48	Afflict.1	W	65
Thy hands made both, and I am there:	55	Temper 1		26
I am no link of thy great chain,	57	Employm. 1		21
I am with thee, and Most take all.	70	Quidditie		12
But I am frailtie, and already dust;	83	Sighs & Gr.		17
I am a scandall to the Church, and not	86	Lent		11
Speak not at large, say, I am thine:	111	The Quip		23
But I am lost in flesh, whose sugred lyes	116	Dulnesse		21
Ask'd what it meant. I, (who am never loth	116	Love-joy		4
Sorrie I am, my God, sorrie I am,	122	Sinnes rd.		1
Sorrie I am, my God, sorrie I am.	122	Sinnes rd.		18
And now, me thinks, I am where I began	128	Bunch Gr.		3
I did toward Canaan draw; but now I am	128	Bunch Gr.		6
I did towards Canaan draw; but now I am	128	Bunch Gr.	V	6
Bid what he please; yet I am sure,	135	Divinitie		22
When I am sowre,	135	Ephes.		2
I am no Crystall, what shall I?	136	Ephes.		30
Not, but I am (I must say still)	139	Artillerie		21
Yet if thou shunnest, I am thine:	139	Artillerie		29
I must be so, if I am mine.	139	Artillerie		30
I am but finite, yet thine infinitely.	139	Artillerie		32
Because I am	143	Complaining		4
More attributes? Am I all throat or eye,	143	Complaining		13
In bitter grief: yet am I stil'd	150	Longing		59
Lord, thou art mine, and I am thine,	157	Clasping		1
If mine I am: and thine much more,	157	Clasping		2
So that again I now am mine,	157	Clasping		5
Lord, I am thine, and thou art mine:	157	Clasping		11
I am both foul and brittle; much unfit	160	Priesthood		11
I am in all a weak disabled thing,	165	The Crosse		17
I am to grief alive, to them as dead.	165	The Crosse		24
That I am he	166	The Flower		41
While he is mine, and I am his,	172	23 Psalme		3
Poore priest thus am I drest.	174	Aaron		10
In him I am well drest.	174	Aaron		15
First I am sure, whether bread stay	200	H. Commun.	W	7
Then of this also I am sure	200	H. Commun.	W	19
When winds and waves rise highest, I am sure,	439	walton 6		3
But I by God am seated King,	215	Psalm II	D	13
am nothing but Infirmitie.	219	Psalm VI	D	4
With groaning I am wearied,	220	Psalm VI	D	13
(thorow the Mercy of GOD) to please Him, for whom I am, and live,	224	Priest		2
to which I am inclined, as not to get out of that sicknesse,	242	Priest 10		37
as not to get out of that sicknesse, when I am in it, by any diet.	242	Priest 10		38
I am to follow our Saviours rule, and to take my brother aside,	248	Priest 14		26
I am then to follow the Apostles rule, 1 Timothy 5. 20. and to rebuke	248	Priest 14		29
I am false to my reason which should guide me, I offend the supreme	265	Priest 26		10
undecently to the station wherein God hath placed me, I am Covetous.	265	Priest 26		18
sometimes too salt, and so not competent nourishment, I am Covetous.	265	Priest 26		23
I am more bound to abstain from those, which by mine own experience I	266	Priest 26		23
and feeling when I go to meat in what disposition I am,	267	Priest 26		8
if I am to visit the sick in haste, and my neerest way ly through	273	Priest 31		33
And I am confident, that under God nothing holp me, but that exact	296	Cornaro		28
I am continually in health, and I am so nimble, that I can easily get	300	Cornaro		34
and I am so nimble, that I can easily get on horseback without	300	Cornaro		34
Then, I am ever cheerfull, merrie, and well-contented, free from all	300	Cornaro		37
I am not wearie of life, which I passe with great delight.	301	Cornaro		2
I am much pleased also in my travells, with the beauty of situation.	302	Cornaro		5
by this also, in what estate I am, may be discovered, because	302	Cornaro		27
I am delighted with their musick and fashion, and I my self also sing	303	Cornaro		6
Yet I am sure, that my end is farre from me:	303	Cornaro		24
Whether goest, griefe? where I am wont.	324	Proverbs		96
be silent, least while I think I am modest, I wrong both my self,	364	Letters		7
how I am now setting foot into Divinity, to lay the platform of my	364	Letters		11
it is true (God knows) I am weak, yet not so, but that every day,	364	Letters		26
neither am I yet recovered, so that I am fain ever and anon,	364	Letters		33
so that I am fain ever and anon, to buy somewhat tending towards my	364	Letters		33
Now this Lent I am forbid utterly to eat any Fish, so that I am fain	365	Letters		1
so that I am fain to dyet in my Chamber at mine own cost;	365	Letters		2
and yet I am scarce able with much ado to make one half years	365	Letters		9
for I am sure you love Your faithfullest Servant, GEORGE HERBERT.	365	Letters		25
The disease which I am troubled with now is the shortness of time,	365	Letters		30
But I am out of my time:	366	Letters		19
mee in your letters, for I am your ever loving brother, G. HERBERT.	366	Letters		21
for I am enjoined to write to you by Sir John Danvers, to which mine	367	Letters		27

AM (cont'd)	PAGE	TITLE	LINE
& therfore I am not over much beholding to those busnesses which	367	Letters	29
These are the things I am to acquaint you with, of whose rude	369	Letters	1
I am to make an Oration to the whole University of an hour long in	369	Letters	12
of which I am very proud, not but that I joy in your favours,	370	Letters	8
that if all fail, yet I am able to stand on mine own legs.	370	Letters	10
and paper enough, yet am I Your readiest Servant, GEORGE HERBERT.	370	Letters	32
and am glad that although you offer more, yet you will doe,	375	Letters	6
you take her not, I am thinking to do it, even beyond my strengthe;	375	Letters	35
I am glad I used you in it, and you have no cause to be sorry,	377	Letters	20
I humbly thank him, & am so far from giving you cause, to apology,	378	Letters	9
And as I am glad for the thing, so no less glad for the Heart,	379	Letters	14
other profitt, the work I may change, the profitt, I am master of.	381	Woodnoth	32
AMAZE			
Amaze poore mortals, and object their crimes.	132	The Storm	6
Little losses amaze, great tame.	354	Proverbs	1013
AMAZ'D			
That we have nought. I stood amaz'd at this,	143	Holdfast	10
AMAZED			
as being truly touched and amazed with the Majesty of God,	231	Priest 6	5
AMAZEMENT			
other Tortures, as the very mention of them might beget amazement;	374	Letters	1
AMBASSADOURS			
of Cambridge, when the Ambassadours were made Masters of Arts.	441	Oration	T
AMBASSAGES			
commands, most noble Ambassages, and other titles most pleasing,	441	Oration	25
AMBER			
As Amber-greese leaves a rich sent	174	The Odour	2
AMBER-GREESE			
As Amber-greese leaves a rich sent	174	The Odour	2
AMBITION			
or honour, be a sin of covetousnes or ambition, and when not;	230	Priest 5	28
Ambition, or untimely desire of promotion to an higher state,	238	Priest 9	14
AMBITIONS			
mens Covetousnesse, and Ambitions to the effecting of his word.	282	Priest 34	34
AMBUSH			
Who by an ambush lost his Paradise.	192	Ch.-Milit.	66
AMEN			
And Ergo was transform'd into Amen.	191	Ch.-Milit.	56
and child, answering aloud both Amen, and all other answers,	231	Priest 6	28
be ascribed all Honour, and Glory, and Praise, ever. Amen.	290	Priest	16
God Almighty prosper the Work. Amen.	379	Letters	10
Amen 1. Higher opportunities of doeing good are to be preferred	380	Woodnoth	2
AMENDED			
and the faults of Nature are often amended by Art, as barren grounds	292	Cornaro	11
AMENDMENT			
Put our amendment in our way,	64	Even-song	23
as a child, and forgives, so hee may have any signe of amendment;	250	Priest 16	15
AMERC'D			
And then amerc'd them, double gifts to bring	71	Humilitie	31
AMERICA			
Then shall Religion to America flee:	197	Ch.-Milit.	247
AMERICAN			
Readie to passe to the American strand.	196	Ch.-Milit.	236
AMIDST			
Slight those who say amidst their sickly healths,	12	Ch.-Porch	133
AMIENS			
Amiens was taken by the Fox, and retaken by the Lion.	356	Proverbs	D 1036
AMISS			
He that thinks amiss, concludes worse.	357	Proverbs	D 1046
AMISSE			
Or love, or language; nothing comes amisse:	20	Ch.-Porch	357
We say amisse,	166	The Flower	19
He that doth love, and love amisse	170	Self-cond.	7
Weep what ye have drunk amisse,	180	Invitation	10
We think we rob them, but we think amisse:	197	Ch.-Milit.	253
But it will not be amisse in this exceeding usefull point to descend	275	Priest 32	17
of Gods Worke in his heart through the Word, doth amisse;	309	Valdesso	31
when they doe amisse, and they are to be judged according	316	Valdesso	18
AMITIE			
For head with foot hath private amitie,	91	Man	17
AMONG			
Putting my life among their sinnes and fears,	30	Sacrifice	106
Among the beams, which crown the face	74	The Starre	22
That so among the rest I may	74	The Starre	25
And among those his soul.	87	Lent	48
Among thy trees, which in a ROW	132	Paradise	2
Among my many had his full career,	159	Jos.coat	6
Among the best in art.	168	a true Hymn	8
Wert thou not born among the trees and leaves?	188	Heaven	5
Wert thou not born among the woods and leaves?	188	Heaven W	5
Among the eastern nations for a time,	191	Ch.-Milit.	35
he is among us; for if we be here, hee must be here, since we are	234	Priest 7	29
and that among suspicious men, and other like circumstances	237	Priest 9	3
his wife among her neighbours is the beginner of good discourses,	240	Priest 10	27
his children among children, his servants among other servants;	240	Priest 10	29
parts his Living, and life among them, giving some corn outright,	245	Priest 12	10
propounds among his Brethren what were fitting to be done.	253	Priest 19	14
ever reputed, even among the Heathen, as an obligation to do good,	253	Priest 19	26
either blessing God, that he will be pleased to dwell among men;	273	Priest 31	25
nor when they are among them that are merry, to extend themselves	280	Priest 34	26

AMONG (cont'd)	PAGE	TITLE		LINE
and ranked backbiters among the generation of the wicked, . . .	287	Priest 37		23
and among our Dukes, Landus, and Donatus, and many others . .	299	Cornaro		2
in this land of light, and region of the Gospell, among his chosen.	304	Valdesso		15
Secondly, among Habits, some oppose Theologicall vertues, . .	308	Valdesso		6
[according to the common and legal proceedings among men.] . .	316	Valdesso		28
How the godly are exempt from Laws is a known point among Divines,	316	Valdesso		31
Let not him that feares feathers come among wild-foule. . .	322	Proverbs		48
fat Hogs among Jews, and Wine in a fishing net.	361	Proverbs	D	1163
AMONGST				
amongst all divine and spirituall exercises and duties, . .	311	Valdesso	V	3
Amongst good men two men suffice.	350	Proverbs		885
be amongst the chiefest also, so also have I required Mr W. for his	378	Letters		23
For amongst us what glorious shew is there, either of garments,	442	Oration		31
AMOUNT				
All forrain wisdome doth amount to this, ...	20	Ch.-Porch		355
Do amount to, onely he, ...	114	Dialogue		14
It takes much from the account, to which his sin doth amount.	327	Proverbs		192
It is the whole amount of this letter, and therefore entertaine it	379	Letters		25
AMOUNTS				
Amounts (and richly) to serve thee:	63	Mattens		14
AMPLIFY				
is but an occasion for you to amplify your favour to mee in pardoning	369	Letters		3
AMUSE				
Amuse poore mortals, and object their crimes.	132	The Storm	V	6
AMY				
To Amy Danvers thirty shillings, To Mrs Anne Danvers twenty . .	383	G.H.'s Will		9
AN				
It spoils an Angel: robs thee of thy God.	6	Ch.-Porch	W	10
Were I an Epicure, I could bate swearing.	8	Ch.-Porch		60
Wit's an unruly engine, wildly striking	16	Ch.-Porch		241
Have got to be a deare fool for an houre.	16	Ch.-Porch		246
To pick out treasures from an earthen pot.	23	Ch.-Porch		430
Make not an ell, by trifling in thy wo.	24	Ch.-Porch		460
Had to this day been an Egyptian slave.	27	Sacrifice		10
Thou hast an ancient claime to mee.	39	Good Fri.	W	32
With an exact and most particular trust, ...	51	Faith		43
The six-daies world transposing in an houre, ...	51	Prayer 1		7
The six-daies world-transposing in an houre, ...	51	Prayer 1	V	7
I goe to Church; make me an Angel, I	61	Praise 1	W	5
An herb destill'd, and drunk, may dwell next doore, . . .	61	Praise 1		13
Of an untrained hope or passion.	68	Content		6
Of an untrained hope & passion.	68	Content	V	6
Of an untrained hope and passion.	68	Content	W	6
In sev'rall ranks upon an azure throne, ...	70	Humilitie		2
How well her name an Army doth present, ...	77	Anagram		1
Watch an advantage to appeare.	79	Employm.2		20
Oh that I were an Orenge-tree, ...	79	Employm.2		21
I have deserv'd that an Egyptian night	83	Sighs & Gr.		14
To gain at harvest an eternall Treasure.	85	Coloss.		10
True Christians should be glad of an occasion	86	Lent		13
Of thy great love once spread, as in an urn	99	Decay		17
Of what an easie quick accesse, ...	103	Prayer 2		1
And quickly gain, for each inch lost, an ell.	103	Prayer 2		24
Let me not think an action mine own way, ...	104	Obedience		18
Where in the deed there was an intimation	105	Obedience		33
As an intangled, hamper'd thing.	109	Home		64
He scarce allow'd me half an eie.	111	The Quip		15
And, to be short, make an oration.	111	The Quip		19
Draws tears, or bloud, not want an handkerchief.	112	Dawning		16
Unto the service mutter an assent, ...	117	Providence		15
Is there an herb for that? O that thy care	119	Providence		75
And if an herb hath power, what have the starres?	119	Providence		77
An anchor gave to me.	121	Hope		2
Then an old prayer-book I did present:	121	Hope		3
And he an optick sent.	121	Hope		4
An executioner at best;	123	Time		15
An usher to convey our souls	123	Time		17
Onely an open breast	126	Confession		19
An answer get.	132	The Storm		16
An earthly globe, ...	138	The Size		45
And draw the bottome out an end.	145	Discharge		45
An Offering.	147	Offering		T
He did repair unto an inne.	151	The Bag		20
Wing'd like an arrow: but my scout	162	The Search		19
Thy will such an intrenching is, ...	163	The Search		37
And up to heaven in an houre;	166	The Flower		17
The world an ancient murderer is;	170	Self-cond.		10
An orientall fragrancie, My Master.	174	The Odour		5
To runne into an action;	184	The Elixer		6
Death, thou wast once an uncouth hideous thing, ...	185	Death		1
Unto an honest faithfull grave;	186	Death		23
Known also to each minute of an houre:	190	Ch.-Milit.		4
Which doth not meet with an eternall thought.	190	Ch.-Milit.		8
Which does not meet with an eternall thought.	190	Ch.-Milit.	W	8
Who by an ambush lost his Paradise.	192	Ch.-Milit.		66
Adoring garlick with an humble face, ...	193	Ch.-Milit.		112
His highest was an ox or crocodile, ...	193	Ch.-Milit.		122
He was a God, now he's an Emperour.	194	Ch.-Milit.		140
I could beleeve an Impanation	201	H. Commun.	W	25
At the rate of an Incarnation	201	H. Commun.	W	26

AN (cont'd)

	PAGE	TITLE		LINE
If thou dost find an house built to thy mind	207	Walton 4		1
When Love being weary made an end	439	Walton 5		11
The Convert. An Ode.	213	Convert	D	T
The Temple where an Idol stood,	214	Convert	D	18
he shall be like an happy tree,	214	Psalm I	D	8
and there an awful Scepter sway:	216	Psalm II	D	22
Their throat an open Sepulcher,	219	Psalm V	D	27
entertained to that end, either by an open, or implicite Covenant.	226	Priest 2		23
that he may be an absolute Master and commander of himself,	227	Priest 3		8
They say, it is an ill Mason that refuseth any stone:	228	Priest 4		15
but that an industrious, and judicious comparing of place with place	229	Priest 4		7
it is an honest joy ever after to looke upon his well spent houres.	230	Priest 5		6
What an admirable Epistle is the second to the Corinthians?	234	Priest 7		17
by an often urging of the presence, and majesty of God,	234	Priest 7		25
The Parson exceeds not an hour in preaching, because all ages have	235	Priest 7		11
and his soul fervent, active, young, and lusty as an eagle.	237	Priest 9		27
Originall concupisence is such an active thing, by reason	238	Priest 9		12
or untimely desire of promotion to an higher state, or place,	238	Priest 9		15
demanding an account, but not by the way of an account.	239	Priest 9		2
demanding an account, but not by the way of an account.	239	Priest 9		3
but an old good servant boards a child.	241	Priest 10		10
since fasting in Scripture language is an afflicting of our souls,	242	Priest 10		12
cold and flegmatick, the eating of flesh is an antidote to both.	242	Priest 10		21
One thing is evident, that an English body, and a Students body,	243	Priest 10		1
with an handsome, and seemly Carpet of good and costly Stuffe,	246	Priest 13		17
he hateth him not as an officer, but pityes him as a Father:	250	Priest 16		11
as when he is set at an armour, or horse, he borrowes them	252	Priest 19		26
as an obligation to do good, rather then to those that are further,	253	Priest 19		26
in Catechizing there is an humblenesse very sutable to Christian	255	Priest 21		10
may then by an honourable way take occasion to be better instructed.	255	Priest 21		31
And this is an admirable way of teaching, wherein the Catechized will	256	Priest 21		17
an aim and mark of the whole discourse, whither to drive	256	Priest 21		30
an illustrating the thing by something else, which he knows,	256	Priest 21		37
confesseth himself an unworthy one, and therefore differs from other	259	Priest 22		15
but hee that sits, or lies, puts up to an Apostle:	259	Priest 22		17
As in cases of an obscure and dark nature, not easily determinable	260	Priest 23		20
as they may be an help, and a recreation to more divine studies,	261	Priest 23		10
The Church needing both an evidence, and an exercise.	263	Priest 24		7
the other an humble, and ingenuous search of truth;	263	Priest 24		16
neither doth he esteem him for an enemy, but as a brother still,	263	Priest 25		29
but in brief, a poor man is an occasion, my countrey is an occasion,	265	Priest 26		13
is an occasion, my countrey is an occasion, my friend is an occasion,	265	Priest 26		14
is an occasion, my friend is an occasion, my Table is an occasion,	265	Priest 26		14
is an occasion, my Table is an occasion, my apparell is an occasion:	265	Priest 26		15
an act against reason, because it is unnaturall to hurt ones self;	266	Priest 26		21
live in health, not keep an uniform diet, but to feed variously,	267	Priest 26		10
he takes it either in an humble way, saying nothing at all;	269	Priest 28		6
that things are not set in such an inevitable order, but that God	270	Priest 30		30
that if anything could presume of an inevitable course,	271	Priest 30		8
who hath in his hand an apple, and a piece of Gold under it;	272	Priest 30		8
common course of devotion, then dislikes an occasionall interruption.	273	Priest 31		9
and it is an honest, and just care, so it exceed not bounds,	275	Priest 32		27
and also an honourable Imployment of a Gentle, or Noble-man in	276	Priest 32		12
for it is both an honor which they owe to the Reverend Judges	277	Priest 32		1
that repentance is an act of the mind, not of the Body,	279	Priest 33		14
but to them an unpenetrable rock, an unaccessible desert.	282	Priest 34		4
but for an exciting of others by their sight, to the acknowledging	282	Priest 34		15
and with an exceeding great victory, which in the Creation needed	283	Priest 34		15
many an evill may not only be, but also spread in his Parish,	287	Priest 37		1
and sold our God, our glorious, our gracious God for an apple.	288	Priest		18
for an apple once we lost our God, and still lose him for no more;	288	Priest		19
would have been an ornament to the world, and a comfort to their	291	Cornaro		4
that Intemperance was not such an evil, but it might easily be	291	Cornaro		6
that after many troubles and griefs I should quickly come to an end;	291	Cornaro		26
and abhorring from so sudden an end, and finding my self continually	292	Cornaro		18
and therefore out of an hope of avoiding death and pain,	292	Cornaro		21
considering what an orderly life I had led for many yeares together,	295	Cornaro		7
That an orderly and regular life can hardly be altered without	295	Cornaro		17
Besides all this, I could not sleep, no not a quarter of an houre:	296	Cornaro		22
That an orderly life is the most sure way & ground of health and long	297	Cornaro		11
comforts and condoles, doth perform an acceptable thing to thee;	298	Cornaro		7
that an orderly life is so hard a thing that it cannot be kept.	298	Cornaro		36
and divers labours, which suit not with an orderly life:	299	Cornaro		14
Wherefore since an orderly life is so profitable, so vertuous,	300	Cornaro		3
onely upon a hope of an happie issue, which yet befalls verie few.	300	Cornaro		24
An old man of an ill constitution, but living orderly, is more sure	300	Cornaro		24
An old man of an ill constitution, but living orderly, is more sure	300	Cornaro		25
that Temperance which I have found so good, I here make an end.	303	Cornaro		35
holy Scriptures have not only an Elementary use, but a use	306	Valdesso		18
H. Scriptures (as I wrote before) have not only an Elementary use,	309	Valdesso		21
the dayes of the Gospell will not give an outward Law of Ceremonies	310	Valdesso		5
reviling also of Ananias seemes, by his owne recalling, an oversight;	316	Valdesso		11
so it may be a fruit of it, and an exaltation. 1 John 5. 14.	319	Valdesso		13
but an analogat observation of Ecclesiasticall and Canonicall lawes,	320	Valdesso		1
A Cake and an ill custome must be broken.	322	Proverbs		27
A caske and an ill custome must both of them be broken.	322	Proverbs	V	27
The longest Day hath an Eveninge.	322	Proverbs	V	51
An old wise mans shaddow is better then a young buzzards sword.	324	Proverbs		90
Make hast to an ill way that you may get out of it.	325	Proverbs		124
Old wine, and an old friend, are good provisions.	325	Proverbs		136

AN (cont'd)	PAGE	TITLE		LINE
The best remedy against an ill man is much ground betweene both.	326	Proverbs		152
One stroke fells not an oke.	327	Proverbs		181
Send a wise man on an errand, and say nothing unto him.	328	Proverbs		217
The corne hides it self in the snow, as an old man in furrs.	329	Proverbs		241
An ill wound is cured, not an ill name.	329	Proverbs		245
I had rather ride on an asse that carries me,	329	Proverbs		258
An ill agreement is better then a good judgement.	329	Proverbs		264
Let an ill man lie in thy straw, and he lookes to be thy heire.	330	Proverbs		271
Chuse not an house neere an Inne (viz. for noise)	330	Proverbs		286
The best mirrour is an old friend.	331	Proverbs		296
Call me not an olive, till thou see me gathered.	331	Proverbs		301
Hee wrongs not an old man that steales his supper from him.	331	Proverbs		311
When you are an Anvill, hold you still;	332	Proverbs		338
All things require skill, but an appetite.	334	Proverbs		378
An old friend, a new house.	334	Proverbs		400
An old friend is a new house.	334	Proverbs	V	400
but an 100 sons are not enough to govern one Father.	335	Proverbs	V	404
An upbraided morsell never choaked any.	335	Proverbs		406
An ill labourer quarrells with his tooles.	335	Proverbs		408
Health without money is halfe an ague.	338	Proverbs		509
A flatterers throat is an open Sepulcher.	341	Proverbs		588
An examin'd enterprize goes on boldly.	342	Proverbs		618
Skill and confidence are an unconquered army.	342	Proverbs		626
An old Physitian, and a young Lawyer.	343	Proverbs		648
An idle head is a boxe for the winde.	343	Proverbs		651
but an ill man doubles his fault.	343	Proverbs		655
but an ill, it doubles his fault.	343	Proverbs	V	655
It's an ill councell that hath no escape.	345	Proverbs		715
A gentle heart is tyed with an easie thread.	345	Proverbs		726
A little lett lets an ill workeman.	346	Proverbs		755
You cannot hide an eele in a sacke.	346	Proverbs		762
To a crafty man, a crafty and an halfe.	347	Proverbs		796
An ill deede cannot bring honour.	348	Proverbs		806
an Usurers, a Taverne, a Spittle, and a Prison.	348	Proverbs		816
In an hundred elles of contention, there is not an inch of love.	348	Proverbs		817
He that passeth a winters day escapes an enemy.	349	Proverbs		864
It's an ill aire where wee gaine nothing.	350	Proverbs		872
Hee that would be a Gentleman, let him goe to an assault.	350	Proverbs		878
Take heede of an oxe before, of an horse behind,	351	Proverbs		900
The ignorant hath an Eagles wings, and an Owles eyes.	351	Proverbs		902
The way is an ill neighbour.	351	Proverbs		915
An old mans staffe is the rapper of deaths doore.	351	Proverbs		916
Wine is a turne-coate (first a friend, then an enemy).	351	Proverbs		929
An Oxe is taken by the horns, and a Man by the tongue.	353	Proverbs		967
Take an oxe by his hornes & a man by his tongue.	353	Proverbs	V	967
To speake of an Usurer at the table marres the wine.	353	Proverbs		974
An oath that is not to bee made is not to be kept.	354	Proverbs		1017
An old cat sports not with her prey.	355	Proverbs		1030
An Idle youth, a needy Age.	356	Proverbs	D	1042
an ill dyet was the mother.	357	Proverbs	D	1048
For the same man to be an heretick	357	Proverbs	D	1058
Two sparrows on one Ear of Corn make an ill agreement.	358	Proverbs	D	1074
An Asse endures his burden, but not more then his burden.	358	Proverbs	D	1080
He that steals an egge, will steal an oxe.	358	Proverbs	D	1090
An old dog barks not in vain.	358	Proverbs	D	1099
Such a Saint, such an offering.	359	Proverbs	D	1108
It is very hard to shave an egge.	359	Proverbs	D	1128
There is an hour wherein a man might be happy	360	Proverbs	D	1143
Stay a while, that we may make an end the sooner.	361	Proverbs	D	1161
To seek these things is lost labour; Geese in an oyle pot,	361	Proverbs	D	1163
Some men plant an opinion they seem to erradicate.	361	Proverbs	D	1164
so devout as to come to the Chappell an howre before prayers began,	368	Letters		17
my comfort is that this is but an occasion for you to amplify your	369	Letters		3
I am to make an Oration to the whole University of an hour long in	369	Letters		12
to make an Oration to the whole University of an hour long in Latin,	369	Letters		13
yet that will be about 30 l. per an. but the commodiousness is beyond	369	Letters		32
but, their Fiery-tryals have had an end:	374	Letters		1
and will not allow any room there for such an in-mate as Grief;	374	Letters		11
What an admirable thing is this, that God puts his shoulder to our	374	Letters		17
because they were to come into an unknown country, tender in	375	Letters		13
and it is an outlandish one, which I commend to you as being now	376	Letters		17
to an exceeding cheerfulness, in signing 100 lib. with her own hands	379	Letters		1
things inwardly good to have an eye to the world may be pharisaicall:	380	Woodnoth		16
having lately receaved an hundred and two pounds besides some	383	G.H.'s Will		23
ANAGRAM				
Anagram MARY / ARMY.	77	Anagram		T
ANALOGAT				
but an analogat observation of Ecclesiasticall and Canonicall lawes,	320	Valdesso		1
ANANIAS				
The reviling also of Ananias seemes, by his owne recalling,	316	Valdesso		10
ANATOMY				
This is done by seeing one Anatomy, reading one Book of Phisick,	261	Priest 23		4
ANCHOR				
And anchor thou art onely, to confirm	97	Afflict.5		4
An anchor gave to me.	121	Hope		2
But onely while thou speak'st; This Anchor will.	439	Walton 5		4
This certain Anchor adde a Seal, and so	439	Walton 5		6
This Anchor keeps my faith, that, me secure.	439	Walton 6		4
ANCHORISME				
From Egypt Anchorisme and retirednesse,	195	Ch.-Milit.		187

	PAGE	TITLE		LINE
ANCIENT (see also antient)				
Thou hast an ancient claime to mee.	39	Good Fri.	W	32
Unto his ancient and miraculous right.	60	Whitsunday		28
Wherefore thou quitt'st thy ancient claim:	106	Sion		10
Till they regain their ancient nest.	111	Vanitie 2		16
His ancient justice overflows our crimes.	128	Bunch Gr.		14
Where is thy famous force, thy ancient sting?	169	Dial.-Anth		2
The world an ancient murderer is;	170	Self-cond.		10
Then in memoriall of his ancient throne	195	Ch.-Milit.		181
Compare with ancient times and purer yeares;	196	Ch.-Milit.		227
To pay our debts, and leave our ancient place	197	Ch.-Milit.		256
To pay our debts, and leave her ancient place	197	Ch.-Milit.	W	256
And met in th' east their first and ancient sound,	197	Ch.-Milit.		268
Thy ancient baptism which when I was foule	202	love	W	11
My God, where is that ancient heat towards thee,	206	walton 1		1
Gentility is nothing but Ancient Riches.	356	Proverbs	D	1033
for your favours are so ancient, that they prevent my memory,	367	Letters		15
he and I are ancient acquaintance, and I have a strong opinion	369	Letters		21
ANCIENTS				
and Isocrates, and Tullie, and many others of the Ancients;	299	Cornaro		1
&				
Whose twigs are pleasures, & they whip thee bare,	6	Ch.-Porch	W	9
Yet wedding marrs thy fortune, fast & pray:	7	Ch.-Porch	W	14
If thou chuse bravely & rely on God	7	Ch.-Porch	W	17
And winne thy selfe: Compare the joyes & so	7	Ch.-Porch	W	23
Hee that has all ill, & can have no good	7	Ch.-Porch	W	35
Least gaining gaine on thee, & fill thy hart	13	Ch.-Porch	W	164
Need & bee glad, & wish thy presence still:	19	Ch.-Porch	W	326
First to bee Slovens, & forsake their nose.	21	Ch.-Porch	W	370
Let vain & busie thoughts have there no part:	23	Ch.-Porch	W	421
Who am the way & Truth, the true relief;	27	Sacrifice	W	38
What ever scoffes & scornfulnesse can bring,	32	Sacrifice	W	174
The Place, & keep possession still.	39	Good Fri.	W	30
In grottos, gardens, Palaces & Courts	40	Redemption	W	11
Who straight, Your suit is granted, said, & died.	40	Redemption		14
Though he give light, & th' East perfume;	42	Easter		24
Though hee bring light & th' other sents:	42	Easter	W	24
I pass the shades, & fixe upon the true	43	H. Bapt.1	W	4
You doe prevent most sins & for the rest	44	H. Bapt.1	W	6
And mend as rising starres & rivers doe.	44	H. Bapt.1	W	9
Looking on this side, & beyond us all:	48	Repentance	W	9
Melt & consume	49	Repentance	W	28
To smoke & fume	49	Repentance	W	29
Thus dost thou make proud knowledge bend & crouch	50	Faith		31
Thus dost thou make proud knowledge bow & crouch	50	Faith	W	31
Of strange delights, where we may wish & take.	58	H.Script.1		7
Thy words do finde me out, & parallels bring,	58	H.Script.2		11
Starres are poore books, & oftentimes do misse:	58	H.Script.2		13
Lord once more shake the Heaven & earth	59	Whitsunday	W	17
Armies of blessings would contend & vye	66	Ch.-lock	W	4
Mark you the floore? that square & speckled stone,	66	Ch.-floore		1
More rev'rend grows, & more doth win:	67	Windows		9
Which else shows watrish, bleak, & thin.	67	Windows		10
Of an untrained hope & passion.	68	Content	V	6
Make bracelets for the spouse & wife	76	Sunday	W	31
Money, thou bane of blisse, & sourse of wo,	77	Avarice		1
Both hart & knees, in crying night and day,	80	Deniall	W	13
Furnish & deck my soul, that thou mayst have	81	Christmas		13
But Love took Grace & Glory by the hand,	84	Sighs & Gr.	W	19
Whose leaves first sheltred man from drought & dew,	84	The World		12
My words & thoughts do both expresse this notion,	84	Coloss.		1
With showres and frosts, with love & aw,	85	Vanitie 1		25
Doubles the night, & trips by day.	96	Charms & K	W	8
In small draughts Heav'en does shine & dwell:	97	Charms & K	W	21
And feed the swine, with all his mind & might:	101	Miserie	W	44
Lovers are still pretending, & ev'n wrongs	116	Dulnesse		19
The South with marble; North with furres & woods.	119	Providence		96
Sponges, non-sense and sense; mines, th' earth & plants.	121	Providence		136
Then let me want thy hand & ART.	133	Paradise		9
Of my deare God with all my power & might.	143	Holdfast		2
Dwell in my head & eyes: come clouds, & rain:	164	Grief		2
And judge our selves. That light, which sin & passion	171	Self-cond.		20
That these two words might creep & grow	175	The Odour		14
But did bewitch both kings & many a nation	195	Ch.-Milit.	W	193
Who brought his doctrins & his deeds from Rome	195	Ch.-Milit.	W	201
The Church shall come, & Sinne the Church shall smother:	197	Ch.-Milit.		266
Judgement may meet them both & search them round.	197	Ch.-Milit.		269
Follow the Church & sunn where ere they fly.	198	Ch.-Milit.	W	273
Bee there, to thy truth, & my gaine	200	H. Commun.	W	11
Concerneth mee & Thee.	200	H. Commun.	W	12
In Bread & mee, the way thou takest	200	H. Commun.	W	17
Creatures are good, & have their place	200	H. Commun.	W	22
My flesh, & fleshly villany,	201	H. Commun.	W	29
Shall they be food & strength & might	201	H. Commun.	W	35
Bodyes & Minds are different Spheres	201	H. Commun.	W	40
Nor can they change their bounds & meres,	201	H. Commun.	W	41
When I contrive & plott to prove	201	love	W	4
Whereas if I orecome thee & thy Love	202	love	W	23
Hell, Death & Divel come short of mee.	202	love	W	24
Nature & Grace	202	Trin.Sun.	W	5
Steele & a flint strike fire,	202	Trin.Sun.	W	7

& (cont'd)

	PAGE	TITLE		LINE
Witt & desire	202	Trin.Sun.	W	8
Except life catch & hold those fast.	202	Trin.Sun.	W	10
Who God & Saints and Angels loose at last.	203	Trin.Sun.	W	17
The Day is spent, & hath his will on mee:	203	Even-song	W	1
Lord make my Losses up, & sett mee free:	203	Even-song	W	5
But thou art Light & darknes both togeather:	203	Even-song	W	13
Now the great combat of our flesh & reason	204	The Knell	W	8
Convert & colour all the other flood	204	The Knell	W	14
Julips & Cordials when wee call on thee	204	The Knell	W	17
Which warme these lines, & serve them up to thee	204	Persever.	W	2
(Whom Schollers Habitt & Obscurity	209	L. Bacon	D	6
Against this meane & humble Blackamore.	209	L. Bacon	D	10
But veywe yourselves, & inward turn your eyes;	210	Paradox	D	27
For though you vysit us, & wayle our case,	211	Paradox	D	39
Maintaine there Lustre still, & shining cleere	211	Bohemia	D	11
A foile to sett of worth, & make it rare.	211	Bohemia	D	16
Fairer & richer. Now wee know, what's thine,	211	Bohemia	D	18
Sorrowes & griefs, to fight with them a bout	211	Bohemia	D	20
Betwixt us & the people: when as glory	212	Bohemia	D	25
When all things pull & hale, that they may bring	212	Bohemia	D	27
To serve it forth, & being stript of all	212	Bohemia	D	31
To conquere new ones, & shall share the frame	212	Bohemia	D	43
Of th' universe, like as the windes, & name	212	Bohemia	D	44
There hands shall clipp the Eagles winges, & chase	212	Bohemia	D	47
Making a Head & spring against thy Reason.	213	Bohemia	D	59
That habitable sea, & brinish strand,	213	Bohemia	D	62
Of Divell, Jessuitt & Spaine,	213	L' Envoy	D	9
Secondly, by a courteous carriage, & winning behaviour:	268	Priest 28		22
as they think fit, & see cause, or rather as Gods spirit leads them.	272	Priest 31		27
both of Blessing, & cursing are expounded in the Common-Prayer-book:	286	Priest 36		3
and the discomfort, discredit, & hinderance of the Pastor.	287	Priest 37		4
passed judgment, & been corrected either by whipping, or imprisoning,	287	Priest 37		15
And as malefactors may lose & forfeit their goods, or life;	287	Priest 37		32
deliver thy message reverently, readily, faithfully, & fruitfully.	289	Priest		29
still striving & prospering so long within us, untill our obedience	290	Priest		10
(having a most cold & moist stomack) I fell into divers diseases,	291	Cornaro		21
whereinto I was wont, when I pleased my Sense & Appetite.	293	Cornaro		23
For having endured many heats & colds, and other like discommodities	294	Cornaro		12
but also to gather strength, which could not be but by meat & drink.	295	Cornaro		25
if our corporall life depend on the harmonie of humours & elements,	297	Cornaro		8
orderly life is the most sure way & ground of health and long dayes,	297	Cornaro		12
and greatly to be esteemed for the knowing & curing of diseases,	298	Cornaro		4
that I may enjoy the sight & communication of my friends,	301	Cornaro		35
that is in humano foro & secundum praesumptionem legalem,	316	Valdesso		28
Vertue now is in stones, herbs & words only.	337	Proverbs	V	478
Good & quickly seldome meete.	341	Proverbs		580
No prison is faire, & no love foule.	348	Proverbs	V	829
Take an oxe by his hornes & a man by his tongue.	353	Proverbs	V	967
& therfore I am not over much beholding to those busnesses which	367	Letters		29
& therfore deferr it untill they heare farther from the States.	368	Letters		15
Sir Charles Howard & his Lady are at much difference, & shee being	368	Letters		19
& shee being at London sent for him (as shee sayes) to make peace	368	Letters		20
& to threaten him that if he will not give her halfe her estate	368	Letters		23
spirituall livings into their owne hands, & taking it from the Popes:	368	Letters		28
this passeth in Spaine freely with consent of King & counsell.	368	Letters		29
who writt a poem heere in England & presented it to the King,	368	Letters		31
but not so great as he expected & therfore he grumblingly said that	368	Letters		32
upon this he was forbid Court & kingdome, yet was seene lately neere	368	Letters		35
denounced to him, told the King & so he is committed to prison.	368	Letters		37
upon my accompt, & give you my self for it, to be yours for ever.	378	Letters		4
& have endeavoured many wayes, to find out a man for it.	378	Letters		6
I humbly thank him, & am so far from giving you cause, to apology,	378	Letters		9
whome I esteem to be God's faithfull & diligent Servant,	378	Letters		15
all your Addresses, & for ought I see, they are ever to be liked.	378	Letters		17
Now God the Father of our Lord Jesus Christ bless you more & more,	378	Letters		25
bless you more & more, & so turn you all, in your severall wayes,	378	Letters		25
& the great Joy of Your Brother & Servant in Christ Jesus GEORGE	378	Letters		27
& the great Joy of Your Brother & Servant in Christ Jesus GEORGE	378	Letters		28
100 lib. with her own hands (& promising to get her Son to doe	379	Letters		2
liked our Book well, & has given order to the Tenants, at Leighton,	379	Letters		8
glad for the Heart, that God has given you & yours, to pious works.	379	Letters		15
Blessed be My God & Dear Master, the Spring & Fountain of all	379	Letters		16
be My God & Dear Master, the Spring & Fountain of all Goodness.	379	Letters		16
& for my power, I have sent my Letters, to your Brother,	379	Letters		18
7, 21. & in the whole chapter	380	Woodnoth		5
thing to advize you now, & before you took Sir Johns affairs.	380	Woodnoth		8
you have layed out thoughts & prayers you have sowed.	380	Woodnoth		10
3. To Change shewes not well & you are by the Apostles rule (Philip	380	Woodnoth		12
are lovely, & of good report if there be any vertue or any praise.	380	Woodnoth		14
now Constancy is such & of great esteem with all.	380	Woodnoth		15
so in things naturally visible & apparent, as the course of our life	380	Woodnoth		17
as the course of our life & the changes thereof, we are to regard	380	Woodnoth		18
& neither to scandalize them, nor wound our owne reputation.	380	Woodnoth		19
(whose the success of things is) & not into the hands of men or mens	380	Woodnoth		24
long God knocks at our harts, before he be heard, & yet desists not.	381	Woodnoth		2
that (which you are thinking to doe) to blessed Mary Magd. & Paul,	381	Woodnoth		5
& if upon your withdrawing it shold doe so, it would trouble your	381	Woodnoth		11
To desire good & endeavour it when we can doe no more, is to doe it.	381	Woodnoth		15
Gods accepting you have done the good you intended, & whom serve you?	381	Woodnoth		18
temple as much as Solomon because he desired it, & prepared for it.	381	Woodnoth		20

& (cont'd)	PAGE	TITLE		LINE
Doe this & be a man as David, after Gods hart.	381	Woodnoth		21
& to rise with his favours, can not but be not only allowable	381	Woodnoth		25
& therfore not relinquishable without their masters consent.	381	Woodnoth		29
ANEW				
The world anew: the sunne shall never rise	212	Bohemia	D	45
ANGEL				
It spoils an Angel: robs thee of thy God.	6	Ch.-Porch	W	10
I goe to Church; make me an Angel, I	61	Praise 1	W	5
What angel fit?	116	Dulnesse		28
Oh that some Angel might a trumpet sound;	152	The Jews		8
ANGEL'S				
so man did eat Angels food:	290	Priest		9
ANGELL				
Whether I Angell it, or fall to dust.	55	Temper 1	W	25
Save one good Angell, which a friend had ti'd	142	Pilgrimage		17
ANGELS				
Which Angels did desire to have the grace,	32	Sacrifice		182
Whom Angels did desire to have the grace,	32	Sacrifice	W	182
Angels and grace, eternall hopes and fears.	46	Sinne 1		12
Whether I flie with angels, fall with dust,	55	Temper 1		25
To all Angels and Saints.	77	Ang.&Sts.		T
Some Angels us'd the first; if our relief	97	Afflict.5		15
Lord, let the Angels praise thy name.	100	Miserie		1
In th' other Angels have a right by birth:	131	Mans medly		9
This spacious globe: Angels must have their joy,	158	Praise 3		21
Who God & Saints and Angels loose at last.	203	Trin.Sun.	W	17
and the Angels minister to us their owne food, even joy,	280	Priest 34		6
not to Thunder, or Angels, but to silly and sinfull men:	289	Priest		5
ANGELS'				
'Tis angels musick; therefore come not late.	22	Ch.-Porch		388
With Manna, Angels food, I fed them all:	34	Sacrifice		239
Prayer the Churches banquet, Angels age,	51	Prayer 1		1
ANGER				
In love I should: but anger is not love,	18	Ch.-Porch		311
Thy anger comes, and I decline:	166	The Flower		31
Wonders of anger once, but now of love.	191	Ch.-Milit.		38
and in sore anger vex their pride.	215	Psalm II	D	12
When once his anger burns, thrice blest	216	Psalm II	D	31
nor in thine anger chasten me:	219	Psalm VI	D	2
leaving anger, and retorting, and revenge to the children	269	Priest 28		20
When you enter into a house, leave the anger ever at the doore.	350	Proverbs		896
ANGRIE				
But as cold hands are angrie with the fire,	66	Ch.-lock		5
Yet as cold hands are angrie with the fire,	66	Ch.-lock	W	5
The angrie Lion did present his paw,	70	Humilitie		9
Sweet rose, whose hue angrie and brave	87	Vertue		5
Ah my deare angrie Lord,	171	Bittersweet		1
ANGRY				
He that is angry at a feast is rude.	340	Proverbs		564
ANGUISH				
Afflictions sorted, anguish of all sizes,	45	Sinne 1		6
But he hath spoil'd the race; and giv'n to anguish	159	Jos.coat		10
Anguish in grain, vexations ripe and blown,	167	Dotage		8
ANN				
besides that which is due to her, to Ann I leave thirty shillings:	382	G.H.'s Will		24
ANNE				
To the Right Honourable the Lady Anne, Countess of Pembr. and Montg.	376	Letters		T
To Mrs Anne Danvers twenty shillings, To Mrs Mary Danvers twenty	383	G.H.'s Will		10
Mary Gifford tenn shillings To Anne Hibbert tenn shillings To William	383	G.H.'s Will		16
ANNEAL				
But when thou dost anneal in glasse thy storie,	67	Windows		6
ANNEAL'D				
Anneal'd on every bunch. One standing by	116	Love-joy		3
ANNEXED				
payd out of it unto some whose names shal be annexed unto this bill.	382	G.H.'s Will		15
ANNUITY				
but they will object again, What becomes of your Annuity?	364	Letters		31
either by engaging my future Annuity, or any other way,	365	Letters		21
that if any course could be taken of doubling my Annuity now,	367	Letters		8
ANOINTED				
my arm and legge should be set, and my whole bodie anointed with oyl:	295	Cornaro		12
ANOINTING				
because the anointing which we have received, and abideth in us,	314	Valdesso	V	6
ANON				
As for thy passion - But of that anon,	35	Thanksgvng		29
so that I am fain ever and anon, to buy somewhat tending towards my	364	Letters		34
ANOTHER				
Why should I feel another mans mistakes	18	Ch.-Porch		309
Another chafe, may warm him at his fire,	19	Ch.-Porch		314
Mark what another sayes: for many are	19	Ch.-Porch		319
Then from one ruler to another bound	28	Sacrifice		53
Another lift like this will make	52	H.Commun.		27
As from one room t' another.	53	H.Commun.		36
And in another make me understood.	58	H.Script.2		12
And one another pay:	81	Christmas		32
For we have all of us just such another.	82	Ungratef.		24
Full of proportions, one limbe to another,	91	Man		14
Another to attend him.	92	Man		48
But all my scores were by another paid,	130	Love unkn.		60
I tun'd another (having store)	162	The Search		21

ANOTHER (cont'd)	PAGE	TITLE	LINE
I turn'd another (having store)	162	The Search V	21
Another in my soul (the memorie	165	The Crosse	14
Of all my woes another wo,	165	The Crosse	28
Onely another head	174	Aaron	11
I have, another heart and breast,	174	Aaron	12
Another musick, making live not dead,	174	Aaron	13
Light one another, and together runne.	198	Ch.-Milit.	271
Shal help another, but my judgment bee;	204	Persever. W	6
Poets to turn it to another use.	206	Walton 2	5
Another Monument for Thee.	209	H. Danvers D	10
how much more in things of another world, where the well is deep,	228	Priest 4	34
For the Law required one thing, and the Gospel another:	229	Priest 4	15
is another great stumbling block to the holinesse of Scholars.	238	Priest 9	19
for then commonly the stream of temptations is turned another way,	238	Priest 9	23
to visite in person, now one quarter of his Parish, now another.	247	Priest 14	5
in the person of another, making them to reprove themselves.	248	Priest 14	22
If he finde another giving a poor man a penny, he gives him a tester	254	Priest 20	13
This order being used to one, would be a little varyed to another.	256	Priest 21	16
therfore one anothers company, much lesse defaming one another.	260	Priest 23	28
being cunning to make use of another, and spare themselves:	265	Priest 26	34
he that throws a stone at another, hits himselfe;	269	Priest 28	14
overcome them, being told to another, whether in private conference,	278	Priest 33	16
at table about his appetite, if he tell this to another, preacheth;	278	Priest 33	19
and neighbourly accompanying one another, with reconciling	284	Priest 35	6
that his Parish at good times invite one another to their houses,	284	Priest 35	18
Another old Custome there is of saying, when light is brought in,	284	Priest 35	22
Now as the Apostle argues in another case;	285	Priest 36	18
and turne quite another man, doubtlesse then also mens affections	288	Priest 37	3
giving us one world in our selves, and another to serve us:	288	Priest	14
But my experience taught me another thing also, to wit,	295	Cornaro	16
For indeed no man can be a perfect Physician to another,	297	Cornaro	25
Wherefore one to another cannot be a perfect Physician.	297	Cornaro	36
if we make another sence of that Text, wee shall overthrow all means,	310	Valdesso	11
But it is one thing not to judge, another to defend them.	316	Valdesso	14
Three helping one another, beare the burthen of sixe.	325	Proverbs	135
Ever since we weare cloathes, we know not one another.	326	Proverbs	168
They that know one another salute a farre off.	327	Proverbs	185
Whose house is of glasse, must not throw stones at another.	327	Proverbs	196
The tree that growes slowly, keepes it selfe for another.	327	Proverbs	198
One hand washeth another, and both the face.	329	Proverbs	239
Hee is a foole that thinks not that another thinks.	330	Proverbs	287
must not say to another; Blow.	333	Proverbs	353
We are fooles one to another.	334	Proverbs	381
This world is nothing except it tend to another.	334	Proverbs	382
The horse thinkes one thing, and he that sadles him another.	334	Proverbs	387
He that hath one foot in the straw, hath another in the spittle.	336	Proverbs	438
Fooles bite one another, but wise-men agree together.	336	Proverbs	452
Disgraces are like cherries, one drawes another.	338	Proverbs	487
we ought not to trust another.	338	Proverbs	490
One slumber finds another.	339	Proverbs	528
A scepter is one thing, and a ladle another.	339	Proverbs	545
Wisedome hath one foot on Land, and another on Sea.	341	Proverbs	611
No barber shaves so close but another finds worke.	343	Proverbs	667
One sword keepes another in the sheath.	345	Proverbs	723
He that pitties another, remembers himselfe.	347	Proverbs	782
Hee that is a master must serve (another).	354	Proverbs	991
One month doth nothing without another.	355	Proverbs	1028
One mouth doth nothing without another.	355	Proverbs V	1028
What one day gives us, another takes away from us.	359	Proverbs D	1111
Fortune to one is Mother, to another is Step-mother.	359	Proverbs D	1118
A wolfe will never make war against another wolfe.	359	Proverbs D	1125
I have another judge, to whom I stand or fall.	376	Letters	8
The case of ministers and magistrates is another thing,	381	Woodnoth	28
ANOTHER'S			
Shall I, to please anothers wine-sprung minde,	8	Ch.-Porch	37
When thou dost tell anothers jest, therein	9	Ch.-Porch	61
Can on anothers hardly rest.	68	Content	4
Surely if each one saw anothers heart,	127	Giddinesse	21
when it is a fault to discover anothers fault, or when not;	230	Priest 5	25
of holinesse, then the procuring, and rejoycing in anothers good.	234	Priest 7	10
If he chance to finde any reading in anothers Bible, he provides him	254	Priest 20	12
neither avoyding therfore one anothers company, much lesse defaming	260	Priest 23	27
whom anothers ill mastereth, and leadeth captive without any	269	Priest 28	21
they may disclose anothers fault, finds it somwhat difficult how	286	Priest 37	32
Hee puls with a long rope, that waits for anothers death.	322	Proverbs	25
Hee puls with a long rope, who looks for anothers death.	322	Proverbs V	25
A foole knowes more in his house, then a wise man in anothers.	329	Proverbs	257
Anothers bread costs deare.	332	Proverbs	324
Thou hast death in thy house, and dost bewaile anothers.	334	Proverbs	376
Hee that's fed at anothers hand may stay long ere he be full.	336	Proverbs	439
Who is fed by anothers hand stays long ere he be full.	336	Proverbs V	439
He that tells a secret is anothers servant.	338	Proverbs	512
A good payer is master of anothers purse.	341	Proverbs	595
None knowes the weight of anothers burthen.	350	Proverbs	880
be fain alwayes to borrow Books, and build on anothers foundation?	364	Letters	14
it were in another's power to defeat my charity, and evill shold be	376	Letters	9
ANSWER			
Full of themselves, and answer their own notion.	19	Ch.-Porch	320
I answer nothing, but with patience prove	29	Sacrifice	89
But thou shalt answer, Lord, for me.	110	The Quip	8

ANSWER (cont'd)	PAGE	TITLE	LINE
But thou shalt answer, Lord, for me.	110	The Quip	12
But thou shalt answer, Lord, for me.	111	The Quip	16
But thou shalt answer, Lord, for me.	111	The Quip	20
To answer these fine things shall come;	111	The Quip	22
And then they have their answer home.	111	The Quip	24
A hollow winde did seem to answer, No:	124	Peace	5
An answer get.	132	The Storm	16
The Answer.	169	The Answer	T
And therein my answer lies.	177	The Rose	16
For my answer is a rose.	178	The Rose	32
other answers, which are on the Clerks and peoples part to answer;	231	Priest 6	29
or spitting even in the midst of their answer, but gently	231	Priest 6	32
so that while they answer, As it was in the beginning, &c.	231	Priest 6	33
even containing in vertue the answer also, especially to the more	256	Priest 21	35
This familiar illustration made the answer so plaine, that he was	257	Priest 21	5
because to answer in form may still admit ignorance:	259	Priest 22	7
To this I answer, that Galen kept it, and held it for the best	298	Cornaro	37
For I answer, That those inconveniences are of no great moment (as I	299	Cornaro	15
I answer first; Nature, which endeavours to preserve a man as much	299	Cornaro	25
Secondly, I answer better, That he which lives a temperate life,	299	Cornaro	35
The shortest answer is doing.	340	Proverbs	552
and hath nothing else to answer your infinite kindnesses,	363	Letters	19
burden to you, since I can never answer what I have already received;	367	Letters	14
therefore I desire him to send me a direct answer in his next Letter.	370	Letters	25
ANSWERABLE			
that there is nothing here answerable to the greatnesse of your	442	Oration	30
ANSWER'D			
A guest, I answer'd, worthy to be here:	189	Love 3	7
ANSWERED			
But this is easily answered:	287	Priest 37	25
how easily is that answered, when we consider that the Blessings in	373	Letters	28
ANSWERER			
and helping and cherishing the Answerer, by making the Question very	256	Priest 21	13
whither to drive the Answerer, which the Questionist must have in his	256	Priest 21	31
when the answerer sticks, an illustrating the thing by something	256	Priest 21	37
And the answerer could not tell;	257	Priest 21	3
loosely and wildely, and then the Answerer will discover what hee is.	259	Priest 22	9
ANSWERING			
and child, answering aloud both Amen, and all other answers,	231	Priest 6	28
now to the answering of this demand of the Kings these Agents pretend	368	Letters	13
ANSWERS			
and all other answers, which are on the Clerks and peoples part	231	Priest 6	28
which answers also are to be done not in a hudling, or slubbering	231	Priest 6	30
And the like in other answers.	232	Priest 6	2
and to satisfie the Congregation by their Catholick answers.	255	Priest 21	21
as they hear the answers prove, may when they come home,	255	Priest 21	28
requiring answers to all these, and helping and cherishing	256	Priest 21	12
ANT			
The smallest ant or atome knows thy power,	190	Ch.-Milit.	3
ANTEDATE			
Thou didst lay hold, and antedate	44	H. Bapt.2	4
ANTHEME			
A Dialogue-Antheme.	169	Dial.-Anth	T
ANTHONIE			
Holy Macarius and great Anthonie	191	Ch.-Milit.	41
ANTICHRIST			
So both together are one Antichrist,	196	Ch.-Milit.	206
ANTICIPATE			
Beforehand, and anticipate their last houre.	21	Ch.-Porch	370
ANTICIPATED			
shall he use in diseases, which being in health he hath anticipated?	299	Cornaro	24
ANTICKS			
and reverend, not with light colours, or foolish anticks.	246	Priest 13	13
ANTIDOTE			
cold and flegmatick, the eating of flesh is an antidote to both.	242	Priest 10	21
ANTIDOTES			
Since where are poysons, antidotes are most:	119	Providence	87
ANTIENT			
as of those of antient times, so especially of the late ones;	233	Priest 7	7
understand the great good use of this antient and pious ordinance,	249	Priest 15	31
ANTIPHON			
Antiphon.	53	Antiphon 1	T
Antiphon.	92	Antiphon 2	T
ANTIQUITIE			
I view their pieces, I compare them with those of Antiquitie;	302	Cornaro	2
ANTIQUITIES			
survey palaces, gardens, and antiquities, publick fabricks, temples,	302	Cornaro	3
ANVILE			
when there are many to strike on one Anvile.	340	Proverbs	551
ANVILL			
When you are an Anvill, hold you still;	332	Proverbs	338
ANXIOUSLY			
they so labour, as neither to labour anxiously, nor distrustfully,	247	Priest 14	26
Then they labour anxiously, when they overdo it, to the loss of their	247	Priest 14	27
ANY			
By any art, yet to be purchased.	13	Ch.-Porch	172
Much lesse make any one thine enemie.	20	Ch.-Porch	351
Much lesse make any one thy enemie.	20	Ch.-Porch W	351
Who never thought that any robberie:	28	Sacrifice	63
Can there be any day but this,	42	Easter	27

ANY (cont'd)	PAGE	TITLE		LINE
Faith makes me any thing, or all	50	Faith		17
Precious for any grief in any part;	58	H.Script.1		3
Mend my estate in any wayes,	61	Praise 1		3
To use in any thing a trick or sleight;	72	Constancie		17
Canst thou be any where	74	The Starre		3
If any one our Masters hand can show.	78	Ang.&Sts.		30
As good go any where, they say,	80	Deniall		11
If any touch my friend, or his good name,	93	Unkindness		6
Nor any sorrow tell them that they sinne,	100	Miserie		22
Convey a Lordship any way	104	Obedience		2
Convey a Lordship any waies.	104	Obedience	V	2
And hath any space of breath	114	Businesse		29
Any thought of waving.	114	Dialogue		4
Thou art in small things great, not small in any:	118	Providence		41
But who hath praise enough? nay who hath any?	121	Providence		141
Surpasse in brightnesse any flame.	135	Divinitie		16
Had I any,	148	Offering		32
If ye have any thing to send or write,	152	The Bag		31
Or if hereafter any of my friends	152	The Bag		37
Any thing to me. Heark despair, away.	152	The Bag		42
When thou dost favour any action,	158	Praise 3		7
O let not that of any thing;	163	The Search		33
Passing all cordials made by any art,	171	The Glance		6
And what I do in any thing,	184	The Elixer		3
And are there any leaves, that still abide?	188	Heaven		7
And are there any leaves, which still abide?	188	Heaven	W	7
If I lack'd any thing.	188	Love 3		6
What wretchednesse can give him any room,	193	Ch.-Milit.		117
As well as any she? Cannot thy Dove	206	Walton 1		8
Bright soule, of whome if any countrey knowne	211	Bohemia	D	1
and sin not any more.	217	Psalm IV	D	16
he cannot agree to come into any house, where he shall not exercise	226	Priest 2		26
They who for the hope of promotion neglect any necessary admonition,	226	Priest 2		37
are offended much with any, who by hard usage increase their travell,	227	Priest 3		14
nor nigardly to keep, nor troubled to lose any worldly wealth;	227	Priest 3		17
They say, it is an ill Mason that refuseth any stone:	228	Priest 4		15
that if any do Gods will, he shall know of the Doctrine,	228	Priest 4		28
be added the consideration of any text with the coherence thereof,	229	Priest 4		10
For it being indifferent in it selfe to choose any Method,	230	Priest 5		10
Neither let any think this a slight thing.	230	Priest 5		23
or any undutifull behaviour in them, but causing them,	231	Priest 6		24
If there be any of the gentry or nobility of the Parish,	232	Priest 6		7
that not any ill will draws him to it, but the debt and obligation	232	Priest 6		18
if he at any time intermit, it is either for want of health,	232	Priest 7		21
and if there be any extraordinary addition to the customary	235	Priest 8		33
or any other accident, he contrives how and in what manner to induce	236	Priest 8		1
he never talkes with any woman alone, but in the audience of others,	237	Priest 9		11
is a common temptation to men of any eminency, especially being	238	Priest 9		17
could out of humility, produce any speciall grace of faith, patience,	238	Priest 9		32
resolves with himself never to omit any present good deed of charity,	240	Priest 10		6
if God give any thing above those, and not spent in them,	240	Priest 10		11
He suffers not a ly or equivocation by any means in his house,	240	Priest 10		32
and veal, if he addes any thing for a great day, or a stranger,	241	Priest 10		17
he goes no further for any entertainment, lest he goe into the world,	241	Priest 10		19
For it is as unnatural to do any thing, that leads me to a sicknesse,	242	Priest 10		36
as not to get out of that sicknesse, when I am in it, by any diet.	242	Priest 10		38
and vertuously, not for any reward of his, but for vertues sake;	243	Priest 11		28
if not the best way, yet any way, make his Parish good.	244	Priest 11		5
But he gives no set pension to any;	244	Priest 12		26
not suffering any that day that hee receives, to want a good meal	245	Priest 12		7
When-ever hee gives any thing, and sees them labour in thanking	245	Priest 12		31
When he comes to any house, first he blesseth it, and then as hee	247	Priest 14		10
when any of his cure is sick, or afflicted with losse of friend,	249	Priest 15		13
or any ways distressed, fails not to afford his best comforts,	249	Priest 15		14
For by this means, when any sinns, he hateth him not as an officer,	250	Priest 16		11
as a child, and forgives, so hee may have any signe of amendment;	250	Priest 16		15
any continue to be refractory, yet hee gives him not over,	250	Priest 16		16
that if any be willing to partake, they may resort thither.	251	Priest 17		12
When he comes to any other house, where his kindred, or other	251	Priest 17		15
or other relations give him any authority over the Family,	251	Priest 17		16
as he finds any defect in these, hee first considers with himselfe,	251	Priest 17		25
if he perceive in company any discourse tending to ill,	252	Priest 18		16
Likewise in any other Countrey-duty, he considers what is the end	253	Priest 19		3
he considers what is the end of any Command, and then he suits things	253	Priest 19		4
and resorting unto him in any difficulty, either in his studies or in	253	Priest 19		8
about him, performing for them any Ministeriall office, which is	253	Priest 19		17
Likewise he welcomes to his house any Minister, how poor or mean	253	Priest 19		18
or of good report, if there be any vertue, or any praise;	253	Priest 19		25
if God have sent any calamity either by fire, or famine,	253	Priest 19		29
or famine, to any neighbouring Parish, then he expects no Briefe;	253	Priest 19		30
if any neighbouring village be overburdened with poore,	254	Priest 19		1
If he chance to finde any reading in anothers Bible, he provides him	254	Priest 20		11
Questionist must have in his mind before any question be propounded,	256	Priest 21		32
Neither findes he any issue in this, but to throw himself down	257	Priest 22		31
If there be any, who having not received yet, are to enter into this	258	Priest 22		29
When any one can distinguish the Sacramentall from common bread,	258	Priest 22		34
in a feast of Charity is more scandall then any posture.	259	Priest 22		18
Therefore hee endures not that any of his Flock should go to Law;	259	Priest 23		31
but in any Controversie, that they should resort to him as their	259	Priest 23		32
Yet when ever any controversie is brought to him, he never decides it	260	Priest 23		7

ANY (cont'd)	PAGE	TITLE	LINE
if there be any of his flock sick, hee is their Physician,	260	Priest 23	29
Yet is it easie for any Scholer to attaine to such a measure	261	Priest 23	2
In curing of any, the Parson and his Family use to premise prayers,	262	Priest 23	9
if there be any of his parish that hold strange Doctrins,	262	Priest 24	19
whether any rule in the world be obscure, and how then should	263	Priest 24	3
or punishing of any, as the vulgar ever consters for signes of ill	263	Priest 25	24
he forbears not in any wise to use the delinquent as before,	263	Priest 25	26
or doing any thing of aversenesse, save in the very act	263	Priest 25	28
When he deals with any that is heavy, and carnall;	267	Priest 26	17
or if he have any leisure to look off from thence, he meets	267	Priest 27	30
contempt shall proceed so far as to do any thing punishable by law,	268	Priest 28	31
then when any despises him, he takes it either in an humble way,	269	Priest 28	5
and leadeth captive without any resistance, even in resistance,	269	Priest 28	22
If himselfe reforme any thing, it is out of the overflowing of his	269	Priest 29	30
he wisheth them by no means to spare any, though never so great;	270	Priest 29	18
obligation to God, and their own soul, is above any temporall tye.	270	Priest 29	22
so that corne doth not grow by any other vertue, then by that which	271	Priest 30	4
So that if any scruple arise, I will throw it away, and be most	273	Priest 31	37
whereas now, of any place, they are least there.	275	Priest 32	36
These are so far from deterring any good man from the place,	276	Priest 32	23
when they see any remarkable point of Education or good husbandry,	276	Priest 32	29
according as he discovers any of his Flock to be in one or the other	280	Priest 34	13
but also of any part, by taking away so much as the usuall seasons	281	Priest 34	23
therefore this kind of Punishment was chosen rather then any other.	282	Priest 34	17
being no reason, why any should distrust Saint Luke, or Tertullian,	282	Priest 34	20
not any sin else, but is within his Love;	283	Priest 34	24
If there be any ill in the custome, that may be severed from	283	Priest 35	31
with reconciling of differences at that time, if there be any:	284	Priest 35	7
of Christs Cross, or for any shame to leave that which is good.	284	Priest 35	33
by speaking any good, this unusuall form begets a reverence,	286	Priest 36	23
without any remedy (which cannot be applyed without notice)	287	Priest 37	2
when we had sinned beyond any help in heaven or earth, then thou	288	Priest	26
and therefore never was sick by any of these inconveniences,	294	Cornaro	9
which excesse of joy neither could do me any hurt.	294	Cornaro	30
neither melancholie, nor any other passion can hurt a temperate life.	294	Cornaro	31
and suffered not any new of that kinde to arise, neither the good	296	Cornaro	33
or contract any ill qualitie, as usually happens in old mens bodies,	296	Cornaro	34
Neither can any man denie this, who will narrowly consider it.	297	Cornaro	14
take a greater quantitie of any meat or drink (though most agreeable	300	Cornaro	12
neither omit I any thing that may either teach, or delight me.	302	Cornaro	4
so that any simple fare is more savourie to me now, then heretofore,	302	Cornaro	9
I sleep well and quietly any where, and my dreams are fair	302	Cornaro	13
is very great) receiving not any hurt or inconvenience thereby:	302	Cornaro	19
Now lest there should be any delight wanting to my old age,	302	Cornaro	37
but lest in any thing I forsake that Temperance which I have found so	303	Cornaro	34
Hee that trusts in the Kings word for any thing trusts in the King.	307	Valdesso	4
and not any private Enthusiasmes, or Revelations:	308	Valdesso	33
and that no other sin or vertue hath any thing to doe with us;	311	Valdesso	24
or justify himselfe before God, by any acts or exercises of Religion;	312	Valdesso	15
For otherwise any Malefactor may pretend motions, which is	316	Valdesso	21
Prayers and provender never hinder any journey.	330	Proverbs	V 277
An upbraided morsell never choaked any.	335	Proverbs	406
Love makes one fitt for any work.	343	Proverbs	646
Good newes may bee told at any time, but ill in the morning.	350	Proverbs	877
neither do I make any question, but that you have performed your	363	Letters	24
if there be any truth in me, I find it little enough to keep me in	364	Letters	31
Now this Lent I am forbid utterly to eat any Fish, so that I am fain	365	Letters	2
there be any course, either by engaging my future Annuity,	365	Letters	20
either by engaging my future Annuity, or any other way, I desire you,	365	Letters	21
and if there be any such which you have found useful to yourself,	366	Letters	4
that if any course could be taken of doubling my Annuity now,	367	Letters	7
of all Comfort, who is not willing to behold any sorrow but for sin.	372	Letters	25
that if any of yours shou'd prove a Goliah-like trouble,	374	Letters	5
and will not allow any room there for such an in-mate as Grief;	374	Letters	11
or, allow that any sadness shall be his Competitor.	374	Letters	12
And above all, If any care of future things molest you?	374	Letters	12
Neither hath she any to repair unto at good times, as Christmas,	375	Letters	27
If there fall out yet any rubb, you shall heare of me;	377	Letters	22
not considering you any other wayes, as neyther I my self desire	378	Letters	15
are lovely, & of good report if there be any vertue or any praise.	380	Woodnoth	14
For any scruple of leaving your trade, throw it away.	381	Woodnoth	22
if there be any body els that owe me any thing else of old debt I	383	G.H.'s Will	26
be any body els that owe me any thing else of old debt I forgive	383	G.H.'s Will	26
glorious shew is there, either of garments, or of any thing else?	442	Oration	32
ANYTHING			
that if anything could presume of an inevitable course,	271	Priest 30	8
APACE			
Whereby he grew apace and scorn'd to use	195	Ch.-Milit.	191
APART			
Sinnes have their box apart,	82	Ungratef.	29
And live apart.	127	Giddinesse	24
since the words apart are not Scripture, but a dictionary,	235	Priest 7	9
APE			
The higher the Ape goes, the more he shewes his taile.	346	Proverbs	745
APOLOGY			
from giving you cause, to apology, about your counselling me herein:	378	Letters	10
doe as much) with some little Apology that she had done nothing in it	379	Letters	4
APOPLECTIQUE			
(as Hectique, Paralitique, Apoplectique. Lethargique).	357	Proverbs	D 1044

	PAGE	TITLE		LINE
APOSTLE				
Mine own Apostle, who the bag did beare,	27	Sacrifice		13
some live there in office, whose rule is that of the Apostle;	226	Priest 2		3
This is that which the Apostle cals a reasonable service,	232	Priest 6		2
but hee that sits, or lies, puts up to an Apostle:	259	Priest 22		17
Now as the Apostle argues in another case;	285	Priest 36		18
APOSTLE'S				
and as following the Apostles two great and admirable Rules in things	246	Priest 13		25
I am then to follow the Apostles rule, 1 Timothy 5. 20. and to rebuke	248	Priest 14		29
For the Apostles rule Philip. 4. being admirable, and large,	253	Priest 19		22
giving age honour, according to the Apostles rule, 1 Tim. 5. 1.	255	Priest 21		25
according to the Apostles rule, he endeavours that none shall despise	268	Priest 28		17
APOSTLES				
On thy Apostles? thou didst then	59	Whitsunday		6
When the Apostles would have called down fire from Heaven,	229	Priest 4		12
But that which the Apostles used so diligently in their writings,	285	Priest 36		9
or the Apostles only, no more then to be a spirituall Father was	285	Priest 36		12
shew all humility before his Passion, yet he allows in his Apostles.	285	Priest 36		29
APOSTLES'				
Whose streams we got by the Apostles sluce,	152	The Jews		3
by the Apostles rule. 1 Cor.	380	Woodnoth		5
not well & you are by the Apostles rule (Philip 4, 8.) not only	380	Woodnoth		12
APOSTROPHES				
by turning often, and making many Apostrophes to God, as,	233	Priest 7		33
APOTHECARIE'S				
The Apothecaries morter spoiles the Luters musick.	351	Proverbs		925
APOTHECARY				
So, where the Apothecary useth either for loosing, Rubarb,	261	Priest 23		33
APPALL				
Able a heart of iron to appall,	187	Judgement		3
APPARELL				
and apparell, the disorders thereof are also very manifest.	228	Priest 3		9
First, what disorders there are either in Apparell, or Diet,	251	Priest 17		19
is an occasion, my Table is an occasion, my apparell is an occasion:	265	Priest 26		15
APPARENT				
so in things naturally visible & apparent, as the course of our life	380	Woodnoth		17
APPARITIONS				
If apparitions make us sad,	63	Sinne 2		7
APPARRELL				
and his apparrell plaine, but reverend, and clean, without spots,	228	Priest 3		10
APPEAL				
Of his rich crown, from whom lyes no appeal	78	Ang.&Sts.		22
Of his great crown, from whom lyes no appeal	78	Ang.&Sts.	W	22
APPEAR				
which will make them appear exceeding reverend, and holy.	234	Priest 7		24
which will appear if the Pious soul foresee and prevent such	273	Priest 31		16
How shall we dare to appear before thy face, who are contrary	288	Priest		9
will better appear by his 98 Consideration of faith and good works.	312	Valdesso	V	4
Let your moderation appear to all men, the Lord is at hand:	374	Letters		27
APPEARE				
If thou shalt give me wit, it shall appeare,	36	Thanksgvng		43
That th' earth did like a heav'n appeare;	59	Whitsunday		10
But when it would appeare to others eye,	68	Content		11
Till thy release appeare.	75	Sunday		14
Watch an advantage to appeare.	79	Employm.2		20
They appeare trim and drest	85	Vanitie 1		20
So many yeares baptiz'd, and not appeare?	108	Home		27
When all perfections as but one appeare,	115	Dulnesse		13
Nothing escapes them both; all must appeare,	118	Providence		37
Flies have their table spread, ere they appeare.	118	Providence		54
And at your lodging with their thanks appeare.	120	Providence		120
What point so piercing can appeare	163	The Search		55
Make Sinne appeare;	183	A Parodie		18
To time and place, where judgement shall appeare.	198	Ch.-Milit.		277
unlesse he could have made it appeare, that it was done by Gods	316	Valdesso		26
in the choice of whom their judgement doth even now appeare.	442	Oration		27
perpetuall povertie, but when your Excellencies appeare.	442	Oration		38
APPEAR'D				
And then appear'd a glorious skie.	51	Faith		40
APPEARES				
At dinner my man appeares.	322	Proverbs		37
APPEARING				
yet your appearing in it, affects me strangely.	369	Letters		23
APPEARS				
as appears Rom. 12. 14. how much more those, who are spiritual	286	Priest 36		27
APPEASE				
Lord, how couldst thou so much appease	49	Faith		1
APPERTAINS				
To thee help appertains.	149	Longing		43
APPETITE				
The third is the observation with what appetite they sit down.	267	Priest 26		5
hath considered how to carry himself at table about his appetite,	278	Priest 33		19
followed my Appetite, and did eat meats pleasing to my taste;	292	Cornaro		27
whereinto I was wont, when I pleased my Sense & Appetite.	293	Cornaro		24
But sensuall men (as most are) desiring to satisfie their Appetite,	298	Cornaro		24
It is better to please the Appetite (though they live ten yeares	298	Cornaro		26
For suddenly it takes away our appetite, so that we can eat	299	Cornaro		27
But some, too much given to Appetite, object, That a long life is no	300	Cornaro		27
All things require skill, but an appetite.	334	Proverbs		378
APPETITES				
when the appetites of the body in eating, drinking, sleep,	230	Priest 5		28

ARCHITECTURE (cont'd)	PAGE	TITLE		LINE
being so built by me according to the rules of Architecture,	301	Cornaro		13
as also of excellent Artificers in Architecture, painting,	301	Cornaro		36
ARE				
Whose twigs are pleasures, & they whip thee bare,	6	Ch.-Porch	W	9
The cheapest sinnes most dearely punish are;	9	Ch.-Porch		67
If thou wilt die, the gates of hell are broad:	9	Ch.-Porch		71
Not that they all are so; but that the most	10	Ch.-Porch		95
Not that they are all so; but that the most	10	Ch.-Porch	W	95
Are gone to grasse, and in the pasture lost.	10	Ch.-Porch		96
A mast'ring minde; so both are lost thereby:	10	Ch.-Porch		104
Houses are built by rule, and common-wealths.	12	Ch.-Porch		135
And are like empty vessels under sail.	14	Ch.-Porch		184
Who strive to sit out losing hands, are lost.	14	Ch.-Porch		202
These are the scumme, with which course wits abound:	16	Ch.-Porch		237
All things are bigge with jest: nothing that's plain,	16	Ch.-Porch		239
When base men are exalted, do not bate	17	Ch.-Porch	W	265
And are her sureties, ere they are a friends.	17	Ch.-Porch		282
Mark what another sayes: for many are	19	Ch.-Porch		319
Kindnesse, good parts, great places are the way	19	Ch.-Porch		327
Strike off all scores; none are so cleare as they.	20	Ch.-Porch		360
We all are but cold suitours; let us move	22	Ch.-Porch		400
All equall are within the churches gate.	22	Ch.-Porch		408
All worldly thoughts are but theeves met together	23	Ch.-Porch		424
For churches are either our heav'n or hell.	23	Ch.-Porch		426
For churches either are our heav'n or hell.	23	Ch.-Porch	W	426
Whose parts are as thy hand did frame;	26	The Altar		3
To worldly things are sharp, but to me blinde;	26	Sacrifice		2
A Balsome are for both the Hemispheres:	27	Sacrifice		26
Most true to those, who are my greatest grief:	27	Sacrifice		39
Because the raging waters still are high:	29	Sacrifice		95
Used, and wished, are the whole worlds light:	30	Sacrifice		110
Servants and abjects flout me; they are wittie:	31	Sacrifice		141
For these are all the grapes Sion doth bear,	31	Sacrifice		162
Yet since mans scepters are as frail as reeds,	32	Sacrifice		177
All Scepters, Reeds: Cloths, Scarlet: Crowns are Thorns:	32	Sacrifice	W	178
Reproches, which are free, while I am bound.	33	Sacrifice		219
But there are two vast, spacious things,	37	The Agonie		4
Yet few there are that sound them; Sinne and Love.	37	The Agonie		6
Are blowne away, as if they nere had bin.	46	Sinne 1	W	14
Thus are we to delights: but we are all	48	Repentance		9
Wee are born old.	48	Repentance	W	10
Where now by Faith all arms are of a length;	50	Faith		27
The heav'ns are not too high,	53	Antiphon 1		3
Shepherds are honest people; let them sing:	57	Jordan 1		11
All things are busie; onely I	57	Employm. 1		17
Such are thy secrets, which my life makes good,	58	H.Script.2		9
Starres are poore books, & oftentimes do misse:	58	H.Script.2		13
But wee are falne from Heaven to Earth,	59	Whitsunday	W	13
So devils are our sinnes in perspective.	63	Sinne 2		10
How tame these ashes are, how free from lust,	65	Ch.-monum.		23
Where all my debts are payd, none can accrue	65	Ch.-mus.	W	8
But as cold hands are angrie with the fire,	66	Ch.-lock		5
Yet as cold hands are angrie with the fire,	66	Ch.-lock	W	5
The brags of life are but a nine dayes wonder;	69	Content		21
Are chaw'd by others pens and tongue;	69	Content		30
Are chaw'd by others pen and tongue;	69	Content	W	30
All of a piece, and all are cleare and straight.	72	Constancie		20
The worky-daies are the back-part;	75	Sunday		11
Sundaies the pillars are,	75	Sunday		22
They are the fruitfull beds and borders	75	Sunday		26
They are the rows of fruitfull trees	75	Sunday	W	26
Blessings are plentifull and rife,	76	Sunday		34
Since we are ever ready to disburse,	78	Ang.&Sts.		29
Since we are ever ready to discourse,	78	Ang.&Sts.	V	29
But we are still too young or old;	79	Employm.2		26
But we are ever young or old;	79	Employm.2	W	26
But all thy sweets are packt up in the other;	82	Ungratef.		19
Whereas in fulnesse there are sluttish fumes,	86	Lent		22
Yet are we bid, Be holy ev'n as he.	87	Lent		35
Where both their baskets are with all their store,	89	The Pearl	W	26
My thoughts are all a case of knives,	90	Afflict.4		7
All my attendants are at strife,	90	Afflict.4		13
The elements are let loose to fight,	90	Afflict.4		17
All things are in decay.	90	Man		6
Parrats may thank us, if they are not mute,	91	Man		11
All things unto our flesh are kinde	91	Man		34
Waters united are our navigation;	92	Man		38
Both are our cleanlinesse. Hath one such beautie?	92	Man		41
Both are our cleanlines: if one have beauty,	92	Man	W	41
Then how are all things neat?	92	Man		42
And both mine eyes are thine,	95	Submission		2
If either will convert us, we are thine:	97	Afflict.5		14
We are the trees, whom shaking fastens more,	97	Afflict.5		20
When clothes are taken from a chest of sweets	98	Mortific.		2
When cloths are taken from a chest of sweets	98	Mortific.	V	2
Those clouts are little winding sheets,	98	Mortific.		5
Convey them quickly, who are bound for death.	98	Mortific.		12
They are of cloth,	100	Miserie		17
And those things most, which are most pure and fine:	101	Miserie		38
Oh foolish man! where are thine eyes?	101	Miserie		49

ARE (cont'd)

	PAGE	TITLE	LINE
So great are thy perfections,	104	Obedience	24
And truly brasse and stones are heavie things,	107	Sion	19
But grones are quick, and full of wings,	107	Sion	21
We talk of harvests; there are no such things,	108	Home	55
My thoughts and joyes are all packt up and gone,	109	Home	69
For all they either painted are,	109	Brit. Ch.	11
Tell me, I pray, Whose hands are those?	110	The Quip	7
Where are my lines then? my approaches? views?	116	Dulnesse	17
Where are my window-songs?	116	Dulnesse	18
Lovers are still pretending, & ev'n wrongs	116	Dulnesse	19
Are brought to Man, while they are lame and mute.	117	Providence	12
Lay hands on all: they are thy right and left.	117	Providence	34
Tempests are calm to thee; they know thy hand,	118	Providence	45
When they are callow; but withdraw their food	118	Providence	63
When they are fledge, that need may teach them flying.	118	Providence	64
Are there much surer then our art is sure.	119	Providence	80
Since where are poysons, antidotes are most:	119	Providence	87
Are rul'd by him, and taught to serve his trade.	119	Providence	92
Hard things are glorious; easie things good cheap.	119	Providence	97
When they are ripe, their odour will ascend,	120	Providence	119
How harsh are thorns to pears! and yet they make	120	Providence	121
How smooth are silks compared with a stake,	120	Providence	123
Most herbs that grow in brooks, are hot and dry.	120	Providence	129
And none can know thy works, which are so many,	121	Providence	143
All things that are, though they have sev'rall wayes,	121	Providence	145
My thoughts are working like a busie flame,	122	Sinnes rd.	3
But words suffice not, where are lewd intentions:	122	Sinnes rd.	11
They are too subtill for the subt'llest hearts;	126	Confession	11
We are the earth; and they,	126	Confession	13
Closets are halls to them; and hearts, high-wayes.	126	Confession	18
Gods works are wide, and let in future times;	128	Bunch Gr.	13
But as his joyes are double;	131	Mans medly	25
Glorie and honour are set by till it	132	The Storm	15
Poets have wrong'd poore storms: such dayes are best;	132	The Storm	17
Ev'n fruitfull trees more fruitfull ARE.	133	Paradise	12
But, Lord, the house and familie are thine,	136	Familie	5
Joyes oft are there, and griefs as oft as joyes;	137	Familie	17
And where these are not found,	137	Familie	22
Are passing brave.	137	The Size	4
Great joyes are all at once;	138	The Size	19
Those are at home; these journey still,	138	The Size	23
These seas are tears, and heav'n the haven.	138	The Size	47
The starres and all things are; If I refuse,	139	Artillerie	12
Then we are shooters both, and thou dost deigne	139	Artillerie	25
Are the more foul, the more thou wert divine.	140	Ch.-rents	4
Are both thy due: but I a silly flie,	143	Complaining	8
Mothers are kinde, because thou art,	148	Longing	14
Storms are the triumph of his art:	151	The Bag	5
When he was come, as travellers are wont,	151	The Bag	19
My lines and life are free; free as the rode,	153	The Collar	4
Legs are but stumps, and Pharaohs wheels but logs,	158	Praise 3	17
And force of fire, what curious things are made	161	Priesthood	14
But th' holy men of God such vessels are,	161	Priesthood	25
My searches are my daily bread;	162	The Search	3
Are things of nought.	163	The Search	40
What are two shallow foords, two little spouts	164	Grief	9
Verses, ye are too fine a thing, too wise	164	Grief	13
Are properly a crosse felt by thy sonne,	165	The Crosse	35
Are thy returns! ev'n as the flowers in spring;	165	The Flower	2
These are thy wonders, Lord of power,	166	The Flower	15
These are thy wonders, Lord of love,	167	The Flower	43
To make us see we are but flowers that glide:	167	The Flower	44
These are the pleasures here.	167	Dotage	6
These are the sorrows here.	167	Dotage	12
Where are no sorrows, but delights more true,	167	Dotage	17
Then miseries are here!	167	Dotage	18
When once those snuffes are ta'ne away,	171	Self-cond.	22
In tears like seas, our sinnes are pil'd	173	Marie Magd	11
Thus are true Aarons drest.	174	Aaron	5
The harbingers are come. See, see their mark;	176	Forerunners	1
Colour'd griefs indeed there are,	177	The Rose	6
There are no such things to me,	177	The Rose	11
God, in whom all dainties are.	179	Invitation	6
Still are good,	181	Banquet	26
Yet being bruis'd are better sented:	181	Banquet	27
But these are high perfections:	185	The Elixer W	21
Happy are they that dare	185	The Elixer W	22
And show them as they are.	185	The Elixer W	24
There thou shalt finde my faults are thine.	188	Judgement	15
But are their cares and businesse with the pleasure?	188	Judgement V	17
And are there any leaves, that still abide?	188	Heaven	7
And are there any leaves, which still abide?	188	Heaven W	7
What leaves are they? impart the matter wholly.	188	Heaven	9
Are holy leaves the Echo then of blisse?	188	Heaven	11
But are there cares and businesse with the pleasure?	188	Heaven	17
How deare to me, O God, thy counsels are!	191	Ch.-Milit.	47
(As dying things are wont) untill it flew	192	Ch.-Milit.	80
How deare to me, O God, thy counsels are!	192	Ch.-Milit.	99
Are given over, for their curious arts,	194	Ch.-Milit.	152
How deare to me, O God, thy counsels are!	194	Ch.-Milit.	155

ARE (cont'd)

	PAGE	TITLE		LINE
Traditions are accounts without our host.	194	Ch.-Milit.	W	160
So both together are one Antichrist, ...	196	Ch.-Milit.		206
How deare to me, O God, thy counsels are!	196	Ch.-Milit.		209
Old and new Babylon are to hell and night, ...	196	Ch.-Milit.		215
They are hells land-marks, Satans double crest:	196	Ch.-Milit.		219
They are Sinnes nipples, feeding th' east and west.	196	Ch.-Milit.		220
We are more poore, and they more rich by this.	197	Ch.-Milit.		254
How deare to me, O God, thy counsels are!	198	Ch.-Milit.		278
Creatures are good, & have their place	200	H. Commun.	W	22
Bodyes & Minds are different Spheres	201	H. Commun.	W	40
Are so, as for the present, I did move	204	Persever.	W	3
Why are not Sonnets made of thee? and layes	206	Walton 1		5
Or, since thy wayes are deep, and still the same, ...	206	Walton 1		10
Are shed for him, dissolve thy frame, ...	209	H. Danvers	D	7
A Paradox. That the Sicke are in better State then the Whole.	209	Paradox	D	T
Are quit with them and more.	210	Paradox	D	10
The sicke are in themselves a State	210	Paradox	D	13
Your feares in number more, your joyes are lesse.	210	Paradox	D	36
Are thy dominion. Those that rule in clay	211	Bohemia	D	6
There is thy best Throne. For afflictions are	211	Bohemia	D	15
When scepters, state, Attendants are the screen	212	Bohemia	D	24
But joyes are stord for thee: thou shalt returne	212	Bohemia	D	55
And meet theire tast, who are thy bitter foes.	213	Bohemia	D	66
The wicked are not so, but they	215	Psalm I	D	13
are like the chaff, which from the face	215	Psalm I	D	14
Why are the Heathen swell'd with rage, ...	215	Psalm II	D	1
are all that make the Son their stay.	216	Psalm II	D	32
How are my foes increased, Lord?	216	Psalm III	D	1
many are they that rise	216	Psalm III	D	2
Many there are that say, O who	217	Psalm IV	D	21
For wickedness their insides are, ...	219	Psalm V	D	25
O heal me, for my bones are vex'd, ...	220	Psalm VI	D	5
the hearts and reins are try'd.	221	Psalm VII	D	36
those that in heart are right:	222	Psalm VII	D	38
His arrows are ordain'd 'gainst him	222	Psalm VII	D	47
he constituted Deputies in his place, and these are Priests.	225	Priest 1		9
Those that live in Noble Houses are called Chaplains, whose duty	226	Priest 2		15
Doubtlesse they are Parsons of the families they live in, . .	226	Priest 2		21
they live in, and are entertained to that end, either by an open,	226	Priest 2		22
Before they are in Orders, they may be received for Companions,	226	Priest 2		23
Wherfore they are not to be over-submissive, and base, but to keep up	226	Priest 2		27
wherein a Christian is most seen, are Patience, and Mortification;	227	Priest 3		4
most in those things which are most apt to scandalize his Parish.	227	Priest 3		11
are offended much with any, who by hard usage increase their travell,	227	Priest 3		14
and then they are worst, who ought to be best.	227	Priest 3		28
and apparell, the disorders thereof are also very manifest. . .	228	Priest 3		9
by what they understand, are best led to what they understand not.	228	Priest 4		20
the means he useth are first, a holy Life, remembring what his Master	228	Priest 4		27
and because they are not understood but with the same Spirit that	228	Priest 4		32
The fourth means are Commenters and fathers, who have handled	229	Priest 4		17
least all those which he observeth are most incident to his Parish.	230	Priest 5		35
other answers, which are on the Clerks and peoples part to answer;	231	Priest 6		29
which answers also are to be done not in a hudling, or slubbering	231	Priest 6		30
and those most, which are nearest to his Parish;	233	Priest 7		8
for people are very attentive at such discourses, and think it	233	Priest 7		9
which are thick, and heavy, and hard to raise to a poynt of Zeal,	233	Priest 7		15
that Sermons are dangerous things, that none goes out of Church as he	233	Priest 7		19
moving and ravishing texts, whereof the Scriptures are full.	233	Priest 7		28
for thou art Love, and when thou teachest, all are Scholers.	233	Priest 7		37
The Prophets are admirable in this.	234	Priest 7		2
since we are here by him, and without him could not be here.	234	Priest 7		29
There are but two devouring elements, fire, and water, he hath both	234	Priest 7		33
since the words apart are not Scripture, but a dictionary, . .	235	Priest 7		9
His thoughts are full of making the best of the day, and contriving	235	Priest 8		20
day he spends either in reconciling neighbours that are at variance,	236	Priest 8		11
he takes occasion to discourse of such things as are both profitable,	236	Priest 8		22
his state of Life, which are principally these two, Spirituall pride,	238	Priest 9		2
such as are tavernes for men, and lace-making for women; . .	240	Priest 10		2
and good breeding, are his two great stocks for his children;	240	Priest 10		10
His servants are all religious, and were it not his duty to have them	240	Priest 10		13
his profit, for none are so well served, as by religious servants,	240	Priest 10		14
Those that can read, are allowed times for it, and those that cannot,	240	Priest 10		19
are allowed times for it, and those that cannot, are taught;	240	Priest 10		20
for all in his house are either teachers or learners, or both,	240	Priest 10		20
Even the wals are not idle, but something is written, or painted	240	Priest 10		23
so that as in the house of those that are skill'd in Musick,	240	Priest 10		30
in the house of those that are skill'd in Musick, all are Musicians;	240	Priest 10		30
so in the house of a Preacher, all are preachers.	240	Priest 10		31
act in them, then when they are called to others prayers, and that,	241	Priest 10		5
for there being two things, which as they are, are unuseful to man,	241	Priest 10		27
which as they are, are unuseful to man, the one for smalnesse,	241	Priest 10		27
The two former obligations are much more essentiall to a true fast,	242	Priest 10		7
as most Students are, he cannot keep the last obligation, . .	242	Priest 10		29
nor suffer others in his house that are so, to keep it; . .	242	Priest 10		30
are two great obstructed vessels, and there is nothing that is food,	243	Priest 10		1
And obstructions are the cause of most diseases.	243	Priest 10		5
his money for the poor, and his table for those that are above Alms.	243	Priest 11		9
Not but that the poor are welcome also to his table, whom he	243	Priest 11		10
and their comfort, who are much cheered with such friendliness.	243	Priest 11		13
because countrey people are very observant of such things, . .	243	Priest 11		20

ARE (cont'd)

	PAGE	TITLE	LINE
and will not be perswaded, but being not invited, they are hated.	243	Priest 11	22
knowing that where there are such conceits, there is no room for his	243	Priest 11	23
For many and wonderfull things are spoken of thee, thou great Vertue.	244	Priest 12	8
working those that are able to the same charity, still pressing it in	245	Priest 12	12
who live best, and take most paines, and are most charged: . .	245	Priest 12	16
the two commands, we are more injoyned to be charitable, then wise.	245	Priest 12	28
may go the right way, and thither onely, where they are onely due.	245	Priest 12	34
For other givings are lay, and secular, but this is to give like	245	Priest 12	37
be as they ought, for those great duties that are performed in them.	246	Priest 13	7
For there he shall find his flock most naturally as they are,	247	Priest 14	6
shewing them how acceptable such works are to God, and wishing them	247	Priest 14	18
for they are not sensible of finenesse:	248	Priest 14	18
if they be of higher quality, they commonly are quick, and sensible,	248	Priest 14	19
These are the Parsons generall aims in his Circuit; . . .	249	Priest 14	9
such as are from Gods generall providence extended even to lillyes;	249	Priest 15	19
or otherwise are done to his owne person, hee considers the offender	250	Priest 16	13
that some are called at the eleventh houre, and therefore hee still	250	Priest 16	18
First, what disorders there are either in Apparell, or Diet,	251	Priest 17	19
other good books, how Sundayes, holy-days, and fasting days are kept.	251	Priest 17	24
baits which the enemy lays in company, are discovered and avoyded:	252	Priest 18	14
but such as are every way fitting to do his Countrey true . .	252	Priest 19	28
and debt of neighbourhood to all the Parishes which are neer him.	253	Priest 19	22
that we should do whatsoe̅ver things are honest, or just, . .	253	Priest 19	24
rather then to those that are further, where things are otherwise	253	Priest 19	27
where things are otherwise equall, therefore he satisfies this duty	253	Priest 19	27
knowing that Countrey people are drawne, or led by sense, . .	254	Priest 20	31
who like Christian Souldiers are to give the word, and to satisfie	255	Priest 21	20
who are not well grounded, may then by an honourable way take	255	Priest 21	30
that those who are well grown in the knowledg of Religion, . .	255	Priest 21	32
Then are there some things to be beleeved that are not seen?	256	Priest 21	8
Then are there some things to be beleeved that are not seen?	256	Priest 21	9
full of such things, as are not to be seen, but beleeved? . .	256	Priest 21	11
upon which and to which the questions are to be chained. . .	256	Priest 21	34
shewing that things of ordinary use are not only to serve in the way	257	Priest 21	14
admits no vaine or idle names, but such as are usuall and accustomed.	258	Priest 22	4
are to enter into this great work, he takes the more pains with them,	258	Priest 22	29
Children and youths are usually deferred too long, under pretence	258	Priest 22	37
of that, wherin they are most eminent, is the most gainfull way	260	Priest 23	6
when the persons in difference are of a contentious disposition,	260	Priest 23	23
For home-bred medicines are both more easie for the Parsons purse,	261	Priest 23	31
which are two great lights able to dazle the eyes of the mis-led,	263	Priest 24	18
There are some vices, whose natures are alwayes cleer, and evident,	264	Priest 26	5
There are some vices, whose natures are alwayes cleer, and evident,	264	Priest 26	6
There are other vices, whose natures, at least in the beginning,	264	Priest 26	7
whose natures, at least in the beginning, are dark and obscure:	264	Priest 26	8
So likewise there are some persons, who abstain not even from known	264	Priest 26	10
there are others, who when they know a sin evidently, they commit it	264	Priest 26	11
they are long a knowing it, being partiall to themselves, . .	264	Priest 26	12
or known commonly, the beginnings of them are not easily observable:	264	Priest 26	18
and the beginnings of them are not observed, because of the suddain	264	Priest 26	19
whose natures are most stealing, and beginnings uncertaine. . .	264	Priest 26	33
not because they are all that are of this dark, and creeping	265	Priest 26	2
for example sake, and because they are most common, he thus thinks:	265	Priest 26	3
that servants for their mony are as other things that they buy,	265	Priest 26	24
Country people are full of these petty injustices, being cunning	265	Priest 26	33
Many think they are at more liberty then they are, as if they were	266	Priest 26	18
Many think they are at more liberty then they are, as if they were	266	Priest 26	19
and this they are not masters of.	266	Priest 26	23
by a Common tradition, and vulgar knowledge are reputed to be so.	266	Priest 26	26
So that if after dinner they are not fit (or un-weeldy) either	266	Priest 26	31
not fit (or un-weeldy) either to pray, or work, they are gluttons.	266	Priest 26	32
and those that are weakly,) but that they must rise so, . .	266	Priest 26	34
To guide them in this, there are three rules:	266	Priest 26	37
because diseases of exinanition are more dangerous, then diseases	267	Priest 26	14
but also for that when they are in company, instructions seasoned	268	Priest 27	3
and which are described in this Book, he must be despised; . .	268	Priest 28	12
at least of those, who are apt to despise:	268	Priest 28	24
for this may produce hatred in those that are reproved, . .	268	Priest 28	29
to the examination, and punishment of those which are in Authority;	269	Priest 28	1
These are the five shields, wherewith the Godly receive the darts	269	Priest 28	18
of his Conscience, whereas they are to do it by Command, and by Oath.	269	Priest 29	31
by the Common Statute-Law they are taken for a kinde of Corporation,	269	Priest 29	33
and by the same Law they are to levy penalties for negligence in	270	Priest 29	4
which are grounded upon the Canons, that so they may know their duty,	270	Priest 29	15
that things are not set in such an inevitable order, but that God	270	Priest 30	30
he often overturnes things, when they are thought past danger;	271	Priest 30	21
and utter this well, all his advantages are to his losse. . . .	272	Priest 30	3
But these prayers are not necessary, but additionary. . . .	272	Priest 31	28
especially to pious minds, which are ever tender, and delicate.	273	Priest 31	14
But here there are two Cautions to be added.	273	Priest 31	14
riches are the blessing of God, and the great Instrument of doing	274	Priest 32	28
therfore all are to procure them honestly, and seasonably, . .	274	Priest 32	30
them honestly, and seasonably, when they are not better imployed.	274	Priest 32	31
establisheth it, since they that have nothing, are fittest to work.	275	Priest 32	5
All are either to have a Calling, or prepare for it: . . .	275	Priest 32	11
Wherefore all are either presently to enter into a Calling, . .	275	Priest 32	14
what they are fittest for, and to prepare for that with all . .	275	Priest 32	16
Men are either single, or marryed:	275	Priest 32	19
For there are two branches of his affaires;	275	Priest 32	21
whereas now, of any place, they are least there.	275	Priest 32	36

ARE (cont'd)	PAGE	TITLE		LINE
who are come to the gravitie, and ripenesse of judgement for so	276	Priest 32		16
And whereas there are usually three Objections made against . .	276	Priest 32		18
These are so far from deterring any good man from the place,	276	Priest 32		22
for single men, they are either Heirs, or younger Brothers: . .	276	Priest 32		25
The Heirs are to prepare in all the fore-mentioned points against	276	Priest 32		26
Therefore they are to mark their Fathers discretion in ordering his	276	Priest 32		27
Besides, they are to read Books of Law, and Justice; . . .	276	Priest 32		34
they are not in this Consideration, because we are about a Calling,	276	Priest 32		35
because we are about a Calling, and a preparation thereunto.	276	Priest 32		36
and above all things, they are to frequent Sessions and Sizes;	277	Priest 32		1
for there the particulars are exactly discussed, which are brought	277	Priest 32		13
which are brought from thence to the House but in generall. . .	277	Priest 32		13
that are now weakned, and disarmed with sedentary lives, . .	277	Priest 32		17
and disarmed with sedentary lives, are to know the use of their Arms:	277	Priest 32		18
which are not only a noble, but also as they may be handled,	278	Priest 32		6
whether in private conference, or in the Church, are a Sermon.	278	Priest 33		17
since we are not Masters of our bodies, this sufficeth. . .	279	Priest 33		19
Which acts of repentance are and must be found in all Gods servants:	279	Priest 33		26
when we are assaulted with temptations either from within or from	280	Priest 34		3
And they must be likewise in all that are his.	280	Priest 34		11
nor when they are among them that are merry, to extend themselves	280	Priest 34		26
Now in those that are tempted, whatsoever is unruly, falls upon two	281	Priest 34		6
The Jewes yet live, and are known:	281	Priest 34		35
they are Circumcised to this day, and expect the promises . .	281	Priest 34		36
There are two Prophesies in the Gospel, which evidently argue Christs	282	Priest 34		22
either he doth it as they are Creatures, dust and ashes; . .	283	Priest 34		10
or as they are sinfull.	283	Priest 34		11
because Countrey people are much addicted to them, so that to favour	283	Priest 35		29
because there are contained therein 4 manifest advantages. . .	284	Priest 35		2
As for those that are ashamed to use this forme, as being old,	284	Priest 35		29
both of Blessing, & cursing are expounded in the Common-Prayer-book:	286	Priest 36		3
so that they are so far from craving this benefit from their ghostly	286	Priest 36		12
and now we are fallen to the clean contrary, even from superstition	286	Priest 36		16
if all men are to blesse upon occasion, as appears Rom. 12. 14. how	286	Priest 36		27
appears Rom. 12. 14. how much more those, who are spiritual Fathers?	286	Priest 36		28
when they are at leasure, make others faults their entertainment	286	Priest 37		30
Faults are either notorious, or private.	287	Priest 37		11
Again notorious faults are either such as are made known by common	287	Priest 37		12
notorious faults are either such as are made known by common fame	287	Priest 37		12
by those, which are branded for rogues, that they may be known;	287	Priest 37		19
all are executioners, and the Law gives a malefactour to all to be	287	Priest 37		30
for all are honest, till the contrary be proved.	287	Priest 37		34
before thy face, who are contrary to thee, in all we call thee?	288	Priest		9
for we are darknesse, and weaknesse, and filthinesse, and shame.	288	Priest		10
therefore we sons of men are not consumed.	288	Priest		22
to convert those who are not yet thine, and to confirme those that	289	Priest		16
convert those who are not yet thine, and to confirme those that are:	289	Priest		17
and the faults of Nature are often amended by Art, as barren grounds	292	Cornaro		11
as barren grounds are made fruitfull by good husbandry. . .	292	Cornaro		12
can bring little grief or hurt to those that are temperate. . .	294	Cornaro		35
I denie not but that Physicians are necessarie, and greatly to be	298	Cornaro		3
But sensuall men (as most are) desiring to satisfie their Appetite,	298	Cornaro		23
of how great moment ten yeares are in mature age, wherein wisdome	298	Cornaro		29
are not almost all the learned books that we have, written by their	298	Cornaro		32
That they who are employed in the common wealth, cannot live	299	Cornaro		12
That those inconveniences are of no great moment (as I shewed before)	299	Cornaro		15
but such meats as are agreeable to his disease, and that in much	299	Cornaro		31
Let no man here object unto me, That there are many, who, . .	300	Cornaro		17
and which are such, as that men generally account me happie.	300	Cornaro		32
besides that they are in the fairest place of this learned Citie	301	Cornaro		10
are verie beautifull and convenient above most in this age, . .	301	Cornaro		11
of Architecture, that they are cool in summer, and warm in winter.	301	Cornaro		13
because many wayes thither are so ordered, that they all meet and end	301	Cornaro		21
on both sides whereof are great and fruitfull fields, well manured	301	Cornaro		24
which are all in their perfect vigour, but especially my Taste;	302	Cornaro		8
well and quietly any where, and my dreams are fair and pleasant.	302	Cornaro		13
These are the delights and solaces of my old age, which is altogether	302	Cornaro		22
bodie and minde, wherewith infinite both young and old are afflicted.	302	Cornaro		26
Because such are daily exposed to a thousand dangers and deaths,	303	Cornaro		14
also with this (as his thoughts are fruitfull) intending the honour	304	Valdesso		12
there are some things which I like not in him, as my fragments will	304	Valdesso		16
These three things are very eminent in the Author, and overweigh	305	Valdesso		12
of perfection, and are able to make the man of God perfect, 2 Tim. 3.	306	Valdesso		19
both are to be done, the Scriptures still used, and Gods worke within	309	Valdesso		31
In the Scripture are Doctrines, these ever teach more and more.	310	Valdesso		13
In the Scripture are Promises, these ever comfort more and more.	310	Valdesso		14
so are wee to doe with the Scriptures and this is the use . .	310	Valdesso		30
because even the godly are chastized but not punished) for evill	311	Valdesso		28
and syncere Religion, such as are Prayer, Fasting, Almes-deedes,	312	Valdesso		20
There are two sorts of acts in religion;	312	Valdesso	V	23
Of the first sort are repentance, prayers, fasting, Psalmes,	312	Valdesso	V	26
that restraining motions are much more frequent to the godly,	313	Valdesso		17
and not those which are in themselves occasions of sinne; . .	314	Valdesso		18
such as are all vain conversations:	314	Valdesso		19
is in some sort true because they are spiritually discerned,	315	Valdesso		31
So likewise are the godly in some sort exempt from Lawes, . .	315	Valdesso		32
Nay they are purposely recorded in holy Writ.	316	Valdesso		5
The godly are punishable as others, when they doe amisse, . .	316	Valdesso		17
and they are to be judged according to the outward fact, . .	316	Valdesso		18
How the godly are exempt from Laws is a known point among Divines,	316	Valdesso		30

ARE (cont'd)	PAGE	TITLE		LINE
but when he sayes they are equally exempt with God, that is dangerous	316	Valdesso		32
and the faith of miracles are divers guifts, and of a different	319	Valdesso		7
But there are other Cases of Conscience grounded on Piety	319	Valdesso	V	30
generall rules to particular actions, which are a most noble study.	319	Valdesso	V	32
For at least some of the Papists are come now, to what the Pharisees	320	Valdesso		6
Building and marrying of Children are great wasters.	321	Proverbs		11
Light burdens, long borne, are heavie.	321	Proverbs	V	15
Evening words are not like to morning.	323	Proverbs		65
When prayers are done, my Lady is ready.	323	Proverbs		71
Flies are busiest about leane horses.	323	Proverbs		73
They that are booted are not alwaies ready.	323	Proverbs		83
All truths are not to be told.	324	Proverbs		89
Vertue and a Trade are the best portion for Children.	324	Proverbs		107
saies they are not ripe.	325	Proverbs		130
Old wine, and an old friend, are good provisions.	325	Proverbs		136
The wrongs of a Husband or Master are not reproached.	325	Proverbs		139
Autumnall Agues are long, or mortall.	326	Proverbs		148
Good words are worth much, and cost little.	326	Proverbs		155
Debters are lyers.	326	Proverbs		165
In a great River great fish are found,	326	Proverbs		167
Our owne actions are our security, not others judgements.	326	Proverbs		173
The Smith and his penny both are black.	327	Proverbs		195
Diseases of the eye are to bee cured with the elbow.	327	Proverbs		203
Diseases of the eyes are to bee cured with the elbow.	326	Proverbs	V	203
In great pedigrees there are Governours and Chandlers.	328	Proverbs		222
Truth and oyle are ever above.	328	Proverbs		234
A woman and a glasse are ever in danger.	329	Proverbs		244
There are more men threatned then stricken.	329	Proverbs		256
By suppers more are killed then Galen ever cured.	330	Proverbs	V	272
A mountaine and a river are good neighbours.	330	Proverbs		274
Gossips are frogs, they drinke and talke.	330	Proverbs		275
When you are an Anvill, hold you still;	332	Proverbs		338
when you are a hammer, strike your fill.	332	Proverbs		338
Pardons and pleasantnesse are great revenges of slanders.	333	Proverbs		365
Pardons and pleasantnesse are great Revengers of slanders.	333	Proverbs	V	365
All griefes with bread are lesse.	334	Proverbs		377
All griefes with bread are lesse, or Nor woe to want.	334	Proverbs	V	377
We are fooles one to another.	334	Proverbs		381
There are three waies, the Universities, the Sea, the Court.	334	Proverbs		383
To a crazy ship all winds are contrary.	334	Proverbs		395
In sports and journeys men are knowne.	334	Proverbs		399
but an 100 sons are not enough to govern one Father.	335	Proverbs	V	404
The charges of building and making of gardens are unknowne.	335	Proverbs		412
He that hath children, all his morsels are not his owne.	335	Proverbs		423
He who hath children, all his morsels are not his owne.	335	Proverbs	V	423
Where your will is ready, your feete are light.	336	Proverbs		448
When your will is ready, the feete are swift.	336	Proverbs	V	448
Disgraces are like cherries, one drawes another.	338	Proverbs		487
All things in their beeing are good for something.	339	Proverbs		520
There are many waies to fame.	339	Proverbs		539
Great trees are good for nothing but shade.	339	Proverbs		546
when there are many to strike on one Anvile.	340	Proverbs		551
Happier are the hands compast with yron,	341	Proverbs		582
Willowes are weak, yet they bind other wood.	341	Proverbs		594
Skill and confidence are an unconquered army.	342	Proverbs		626
Feares are divided in the midst.	342	Proverbs		639
In a Leopard the spotts are not observed.	343	Proverbs		660
Divine ashes are better then earthly meale.	344	Proverbs		684
Comparisons are odious.	345	Proverbs		718
To him that will, waies are not wanting.	345	Proverbs		730
Good workemen are seldome rich.	346	Proverbs		756
Praise none too much, for all are fickle.	347	Proverbs		774
A shippe and a woman are ever repairing.	347	Proverbs		780
Good swimmers at length are drowned.	347	Proverbs		801
All are not merry that dance lightly.	348	Proverbs		808
Religion, Credit, and the Eye are not to be touched.	349	Proverbs		837
Words are women, deedes are men.	349	Proverbs		843
Goods are theirs that enjoy them.	349	Proverbs		850
In a retreat the lame are formost.	350	Proverbs		883
The ofspring of those that are very young, or very old, lasts not.	350	Proverbs		887
The Reverend are ever before.	350	Proverbs		891
There are more Physitians in health then drunkards.	351	Proverbs		903
Warre and Physicke are governed by the eye.	351	Proverbs		906
Conversation makes one what they are.	351	Proverbs	V	926
Castles are Forrests of stones.	352	Proverbs		936
The dainties of the great are the teares of the poore.	352	Proverbs		937
Parsons are soules waggoners.	352	Proverbs		938
Children when they are little make parents fooles,	352	Proverbs		939
when they are great they make them mad.	352	Proverbs		939
Children when they are little make their parents fooles,	352	Proverbs	V	939
Dogs are fine in the field.	352	Proverbs		941
Sinnes are not knowne till they bee acted.	352	Proverbs		942
All are presumed good, till they are found in a fault.	352	Proverbs		944
The Italians are wise before the deede,	352	Proverbs		947
Spectacles are deaths Harquebuze.	352	Proverbs		950
Lawyers houses are built on the heads of fooles.	352	Proverbs		951
The house is a fine house, when good folke are within.	352	Proverbs		952
The house is a fine house, when good folks are within.	352	Proverbs	V	952
The first and last frosts are the worst.	352	Proverbs		954
Manie things are lost for want of asking.	353	Proverbs		968

ARE (cont'd)	PAGE	TITLE		LINE
Citties are taken by the eares.	353	Proverbs		970
Health and sicknesse surely are mens double enemies.	354	Proverbs		1011
All beasts of prey are strong or treacherous.	355	Proverbs		1023
Benefits please like flowers while they are fresh.	356	Proverbs	D	40
Some evils are cured by contempt.	357	Proverbs	D	1052
Infants manners are moulded more by the example of Parents,	357	Proverbs	D	1060
They favour learning whose actions are worthy of a learned pen.	357	Proverbs	D	1061
Spies are the ears and eyes of Princes.	357	Proverbs	D	1067
(applyed to rich men that are unthankful to God).	359	Proverbs	D	1100
New things are fair.	359	Proverbs	D	1117
Princes are venison in Heaven.	360	Proverbs	D	1156
Criticks are like brushers of Noblemens cloaths.	360	Proverbs	D	1157
Souldiers in peace are like chimneys in summer.	361	Proverbs	D	1172
those many Love-poems, that are daily writ and consecrated to Venus;	363	Letters		7
nor to bewail that so few are writ, that look towards God and Heaven.	363	Letters		8
perhaps they will say, you are sickly, you must not study too hard;	364	Letters		25
for infirmities are both painful and costly.	365	Letters		1
hath bought a parcel of Books for me, and that they are coming over.	366	Letters		30
yet if my Sister were acquainted that they are ready, I dare say she	367	Letters		1
for your favours are so ancient, that they prevent my memory,	367	Letters		14
not but first certifies you that there are come agents hither from	368	Letters		4
certaine injuries which they are thought to have offerd to our	368	Letters		6
Sir Charles Howard & his Lady are at much difference, & shee being	368	Letters		19
These are the things I am to acquaint you with, of whose rude	369	Letters		1
for my Cambridge necessities are stronger to tye me here,	369	Letters		18
he and I are ancient acquaintance, and I have a strong opinion	369	Letters		21
of the heavens, so are earthly Troubles compar'd to heavenly Joyes;	372	Letters		30
have over Youth and Health, who are now so near those true Comforts.	372	Letters		33
but you are freed from that fear, who have already abundantly	373	Letters		10
or on the Joyes that are to come, you have strong preservatives	373	Letters		18
consider all that can happen to you are either afflictions of Estate,	373	Letters		21
since if we had Riches we are commanded to give them away:	373	Letters		23
in the holy Scripture, are never given to the rich, but to the poor.	373	Letters		29
and yours (which praised be God are less) are not like to continue	374	Letters		2
yours (which praised be God are less) are not like to continue long.	374	Letters		2
school-mistresse, and you know what those mercenary creatures are.	375	Letters		26
but difficulties are so farr from cooling christians, that they whett	376	Letters		10
all your Addresses, & for ought I see, they are ever to be liked.	378	Letters		17
You write very lovingly that all your things are mine.	378	Letters		22
Higher opportunities of doeing good are to be preferred before lower,	380	Woodnoth		3
2. yet are you now ingaged.	380	Woodnoth		7
To Change shewes not well & you are by the Apostles rule (Philip 4,	380	Woodnoth		12
but things that are lovely, & of good report if there be any vertue	380	Woodnoth		14
thereof, we are to regard others, & neither to scandalize them,	380	Woodnoth		18
if God had done that (which you are thinking to doe) to blessed Mary	381	Woodnoth		4
the one are Gods servants, the other the commonwealths,	381	Woodnoth		28
of my deceased Neece which are to be payd out of it unto some	382	G.H.'s Will		14
all these are over and above their wages, To Sara thirteene shillings	382	G.H.'s Will		26
On the other side are the names of those to whome my deceased Neece	383	G.H.'s Will		1
All those that are crost are discharged already the rest are to be	383	G.H.'s Will		3
those that are crost are discharged already the rest are to be payd.	383	G.H.'s Will		3
MS. that there are divers moneys of mine in Mr Stephens hands	383	G.H.'s Will		22
in that you are of the same order and habit, of which wee all in this	442	Oration		20
since you are so great both in your Princes, and your selves,	442	Oration		28
But yet the Arts in quietnes and silence here are reverenced,	442	Oration		35
ARGUE				
which evidently argue Christs Divinity by their success:	282	Priest 34		23
ARGU'D				
Thus argu'd into hopes, my thoughts reserved	46	Afflict.1		15
Thus argu'd into hopes, I was preserved	46	Afflict.1	W	15
ARGUED				
On the other side I argued, that Nature was contented with a little,	295	Cornaro		25
ARGUES				
for this argues a height and eminency of mind, which is not easily	268	Priest 28		25
Now as the Apostle argues in another case;	285	Priest 36		18
in their seasons argues a Deity.	347	Proverbs		773
ARGUING				
Be calm in arguing: for fiercenesse makes	18	Ch.-Porch		307
The Parson arguing.	262	Priest 24		T
being unmoved in arguing, and voyd of all contentiousnesse:	263	Priest 24		18
ARGUMENT				
Spoil the good use; lest by that argument	86	Lent		29
Spoil our good use; lest by that argument	86	Lent	W	29
since our Saviour hath made that the argument of a Pastour's love,	224	Priest		5
He hath one argument unanswerable.	283	Priest 34		9
ARGUMENTS				
for Atheisme) he scatters in his discourse three sorts of arguments;	281	Priest 34		16
ARIGHT				
See how spite cankers things. These words aright	30	Sacrifice		109
ARISE				
Arise, arise, they come. Look how they runne!	27	Sacrifice		33
Arise sad heart; if thou dost not withstand,	112	Dawning		9
Arise sad heart; if thou doe not withstand,	112	Dawning	V	9
Arise, arise;	112	Dawning		13
Early didst thou arise to plant this vine,	190	Ch.-Milit.		11
Arise, O Lord, and rescue me;	217	Psalm III	D	17
Arise in wrath, O Lord, advance	221	Psalm VII	D	21
So that if any scruple arise, I will throw it away, and be most	273	Priest 31		38
didst thou arise triumphant, and therein mad'st us victorious.	289	Priest		1
and suffered not any new of that kinde to arise, neither the good	296	Cornaro		33

ARISE (cont'd)	PAGE	TITLE		LINE
building it all upon the word untill the day starre arise, . . .	318	Valdesso		9
ARISETH				
to whom this discourse ariseth not) some live in the Universities,	225	Priest 2		22
ARISING				
The Sunne arising in the East, ...	42	Easter		23
With thy arising, they presume.	42	Easter		26
and arising from the improvement of things, which otherwise would be	241	Priest 10		23
ARISTIDES				
by the generall Providence of God, as Socrates and Aristides, &c.	308	Valdesso		13
ARISTOTLE				
Plato and Aristotle were at a losse, ...	191	Ch.-Milit.		53
ARK				
As was and is thy floting Ark; whose stay	97	Afflict.5		3
To hold the Ark, although it seem to shake	161	Priesthood		32
Where th' Ark did rest, there Abraham began	190	Ch.-Milit.		19
To bring the other Ark from Canaan.	190	Ch.-Milit.		20
To bring the other Ark to Canaan.	190	Ch.-Milit.	W	21
Onely whereas the Ark in glorie shone, ...	190	Ch.-Milit.		27
ARM				
His arm is short; yet with a sling	61	Praise 1		11
Is thy great arm which spans the east and west, ...	103	Prayer 2		8
While the inclosure is thine ARM?	133	Paradise		6
and onely commanded that my arm and legge should be set, . . .	295	Cornaro		11
ARME (martial)				
Cloath thee in war, arme thee in peace.	334	Proverbs		386
All the Armes of England will not arme feare.	345	Proverbs		722
ARME				
and then who can deny the stretched out arme of a mighty God?	282	Priest 34		6
The thrusting away of his arme makes us onely not embraced. . .	283	Priest 34		26
God strikes with his finger, and not with all his arme. . .	359	Proverbs	D	1114
ARMED				
bring strangers to him, he may be the better armed to encounter them.	274	Priest 32		8
ARMES				
All the Armes of England will not arme feare.	345	Proverbs		722
ARMIES				
Armies of blessings would contend & vye	66	Ch.-lock	W	4
and armies victorious, and retains and confirms kingdomes, . .	297	Cornaro		10
ARMOUR				
puts on the whole Armour of God, and by the vertue of the shield	238	Priest 9		5
as when he is set at an armour, or horse, he borrowes them . .	252	Priest 19		26
It's absurd to warme one in his armour.	347	Proverbs		775
Armour is light at table.	352	Proverbs		934
ARMS (martial)				
Bringing nor man, nor arms, nor fear, ...	151	The Bag		28
ARMS				
Where now by Faith all arms are of a length;	50	Faith		27
Wilt thou meet arms with man, that thou dost stretch . . .	55	Temper 1		13
These arms shall crush thee. Spare not, do thy worst. . . .	169	Dial.-Anth		8
and disarmed with sedentary lives, are to know the use of their Arms:	277	Priest 32		19
was sore hurt, and also one of my arms and legges put out of joynt.	295	Cornaro		1
all who have the care of themselves, to embrace it with open arms?	303	Cornaro		32
ARMY				
Anagram MARY / ARMY.	77	Anagram		T
How well her name an Army doth present, ...	77	Anagram		1
and the whole Army of Temptations without, hath ever so many sermons	278	Priest 33		23
Skill and confidence are an unconquered army.	342	Proverbs		626
AROSE				
I grew fully perswaded, that all my griefs arose out of Intemperance:	292	Cornaro		20
ARRAIGNE				
And missing this, most falsly did arraigne thee;	41	Sepulchre		14
Doth arraigne, ...	180	Invitation		14
ARRAS				
Not of rich arras, but mean tapestrie.	17	Ch.-Porch		270
Chases in Arras, guilded emptinesse, ...	167	Dotage		3
With canvas, not with arras clothe their shame:	177	Forerunners		26
ARRAY (see also aray)				
ARRIVAL				
by a due blessing of God for their safe arrival, and saying grace	251	Priest 17		9
ARRIVES				
and arrives not to the point it should, which if it did, . . .	319	Valdesso		11
ARROW				
Wing'd like an arrow: but my scout	162	The Search		19
ARROWS				
Shunne not my arrows, and behold my breast.	139	Artillerie		28
His arrows are ordain'd 'gainst him	222	Psalm VII	D	47
ART (noun)				
Studie this art, make it thy great designe;	10	Ch.-Porch		101
By any art, yet to be purchased.	13	Ch.-Porch		172
But love is lost, the art of friendship's gone, ...	17	Ch.-Porch	W	275
Thy art of love, which I'le turn back on thee:	36	Thanksgvng		47
And as of old, the law by heav'nly art	41	Sepulchre		17
With all thy art.	41	Easter		8
And make up our defects with his sweet art.	42	Easter		18
It is thy highest art	45	Nature		5
If blisse had lien in art or strength, ...	50	Faith		25
Meeting sinnes force and art.	52	H.Commun.		12
The grosser world stands to thy word and art;	56	Temper 2		5
Let suppling grace, to crosse his art, ...	60	Grace		19
O lett thy grace, to crosse his art, ...	60	Grace	W	19
Powring upon it all thy art, ...	62	Mattens		11

ART (cont'd)	PAGE	TITLE	LINE
Blest be the Architect, whcse art	67	Ch.-floore	19
It is no office, art, or news,	70	Quidditie	9
Do pinch and straiten thee, and use much art	99	Decay	14
Thy skill and art, what musick would it be!	118	Providence	40
Are there much surer then our art is sure.	119	Providence	80
Thy curious art in marshalling thy goods.	119	Providence	94
By art.	123	Gratefulnes	4
Hath found the art	132	Mans medly	35
Then let me want thy hand & ART.	133	Paradise	9
Wherefore with my utmost art	146	Praise 2	9
Storms are the triumph of his art:	151	The Bag	5
Among the best in art.	168	a true Hymn	8
Passing all cordials made by any art,	171	The Glance	6
Strength levels grounds, Art makes a garden there;	192	Ch.-Milit.	87
There is no dealing with thee in that Art:	201	love W	2
Here is copied out by art;	208	J. Danvers D	10
he procures attention by all possible art, both by earnestnesse	232	Priest 7	31
but counts it the art, and secret of governing to preserve	240	Priest 10	33
and the faults of Nature are often amended by Art, as barren grounds	292	Cornaro	11
In every Art it is good to have a master.	342	Proverbs	619
ART			
Then thou art modest, and the wine grows bold.	8	Ch.-Porch	42
Art thou a Magistrate? then be severe:	10	Ch.-Porch	85
If thou art nothing, think what thou wouldst bee	10	Ch.-Porch W	90
If cause require, thou art his sacrifice;	17	Ch.-Porch	273
God is more there, then thou: for thou art there	22	Ch.-Porch	404
The sonne, in whom thou art well pleas'd to be?	33	Sacrifice W	214
O blessed bodie! Whither art thou thrown?	40	Sepulchre	1
Was writ in stone; so thou, which also art	41	Sepulchre	18
Then of a sinner thou art rid,	55	Temper 1	19
And ev'ry day a new Creatour art.	56	Temper 2	8
Thou art all health, health thriving, till it make	58	H.Script.1	5
A full eternitie: thou art a masse	58	H.Script.1	6
Thy praise too much? thou art heav'ns Lidger here,	58	H.Script.1	11
Thy praise enough? thou art heav'ns Lidger here,	58	H.Script.1 W	11
Thou art joyes handsell: heav'n lies flat in thee,	58	H.Script.1	13
Lord, though we change, thou art the same;	60	Whitsunday	25
Thou art my grief alone,	62	Afflict.2	11
Thou Lord conceal it not: and as thou art	62	Afflict.2	12
But thou art ready there to catch	62	Mattens	2
My God, thou art all love.	64	Even-song	29
Thy life on earth was grief, and thou art still	73	Afflict.3	13
Make up one man; whose face thou art,	75	Sunday	9
Thou art a day of mirth:	76	Sunday	57
Whence com'st thou, that thou art so fresh and fine?	77	Avarice	2
Thou art the man, and man but drosse to thee.	77	Avarice	12
Thou art the holy mine, whence came the gold,	78	Ang.&Sts.	11
Thou art the sacred mine, whence came the gold,	78	Ang.&Sts. W	11
Thou art the cabinet where the jewell lay:	78	Ang.&Sts.	14
And not refuse me: for thou onely art	83	Sighs & Gr.	4
Thou art both Judge and Saviour, feast and rod,	83	Sighs & Gr.	27
Who art my life: dissolve the knot,	90	Afflict.4	22
But that thou art my wisdome, Lord,	95	Submission	1
And anchor thou art onely, to confirm	97	Afflict.5	4
Thou art all brightnesse, perfect puritie;	101	Miserie	32
My blessed Lord, art thou! how suddenly	103	Prayer 2	2
Art thou, my blessed King? how suddenly	103	Prayer 2 W	2
Art thou possest, who, when thou couldst not die,	103	Prayer 2	14
There thou art struggling with a peevish heart,	106	Sion	13
Thou art my lovelinesse, my life, my light,	115	Dulnesse	9
Thou art in small things great, not small in any:	118	Providence	41
Thou art in all things one, in each thing many:	118	Providence	43
For thou art infinite in one and all.	118	Providence	44
To show thou art not bound, as if thy lot	121	Providence	137
And in his blessing thou art blest:	123	Time	13
Thou art a gard'ner now, and more,	123	Time	16
And art thou grieved, sweet and sacred Dove,	135	Ephes.	1
And for the future time art heir	137	The Size	11
Brave rose, (alas!) where art thou? in the chair	140	Ch.-rents	1
Brave rose, (alas!) where art thou? in the place	140	Ch.-rents V	1
Because thou art	143	Complaining	2
Thou art the Lord of glorie;	143	Complaining	6
Art thou all justice, Lord?	143	Complaining	11
Mothers are kinde, because thou art,	148	Longing	14
That thou art grown	150	Longing	63
But thou art my desert:	156	Assurance	25
Thou art not onely to perform thy part,	156	Assurance	27
Lord, thou art mine, and I am thine,	157	Clasping	1
Lord, I am thine, and thou art mine:	157	Clasping	11
So mine thou art, that something more	157	Clasping	12
But thou art fire, sacred and hallow'd fire;	160	Priesthood	7
Whither, O, whither art thou fled,	162	The Search	1
That thou art there.	162	The Search	8
For thou art with me; and thy rod	173	23 Psalme	15
Yet have they left me, Thou art still my God.	176	Forerunners	6
So Thou art still my God, be out of fear.	176	Forerunners	10
For, Thou art still my God, is all that ye	177	Forerunners	32
Thou art God:	179	Discipline	31
Souls joy, when thou art gone,	183	A Parodie	1
Say, that thou art not here.	183	A Parodie	20

ART (cont'd)	PAGE	TITLE		LINE
That I may seek, but thou art lost;	183	A Parodie		24
To thee, who art more farre above deceit,	185	A Wreath		7
Thou art grown fair and full of grace,	186	Death		15
Thou Echo, thou art mortall, all men know.	188	Heaven		3
As thou art evry-where;	200	H. Commun.	W	3
Thou art too hard for me in Love:	201	love	W	1
But thou art Light & darknes both togeather:	203	Even-song	W	13
Yet Thou art not so dark, since I know this,	203	Even-song	W	17
Thou art my rock, thou art my rest.	205	Persever.	W	16
Thou art requited; for his Fame,	209	H. Danvers	D	8
He said to me, Thou art my Son,	216	Psalm II	D	17
But thou, O Lord, art still the shield	216	Psalm III	D	5
Thou art my glory, Lord, and he	216	Psalm III	D	7
Thou art a God whose puritie	218	Psalm V	D	9
Thou art that righteous God by whom	221	Psalm VII	D	35
for thou art Love, and when thou teachest, all are Scholers.	233	Priest 7		36
every one is more awaked, when we come, and say, Thou art the man.	236	Priest 8		15
for thou art not only the feast, but the way to it.	257	Priest 22		34
yet art thou our Creatour, and we thy work:	288	Priest		11
But thou Lord, art patience, and pity, and sweetnesse, and love;	288	Priest		21
My house, my house, though thou art small,	335	Proverbs		413
thou art to me the Escuriall.	335	Proverbs		413
ARTHUR				
Mr Herberts reasons for Arth. Woodenoths Living with Sir John	380	Woodnoth		T
ARTICLES				
as also the visitation Articles, which are grounded upon the Canons,	270	Priest 29		14
ARTICLING				
There is no articling with thee:	139	Artillerie		31
ARTIFICERS				
as also of excellent Artificers in Architecture, painting,	301	Cornaro		36
ARTIFICES				
and France, and observing the Artifices, and Manufactures there,	278	Priest 32		9
ARTILLERIE				
Artillerie.	139	Artillerie		T
ARTILLERIES				
Born where thy servants both artilleries use.	139	Artillerie		18
ARTIST				
for no perfect Artist ever yet hated his owne worke.	283	Priest 34		12
ARTISTS				
Of skilfull artists, for the boards of those	161	Priesthood		17
ARTS				
Religion thence fled into Greece, where arts	191	Ch.-Milit.		49
Thence into Greece she fled, where curious Arts	191	Ch.-Milit.	W	49
In both of these Prowesse and Arts did tame	192	Ch.-Milit.		75
That as before Empire and Arts made way,	192	Ch.-Milit.		83
Are given over, for their curious arts,	194	Ch.-Milit.		152
And where of old the Empire and the Arts	197	Ch.-Milit.		263
Spain hath done one; when Arts perform the other,	197	Ch.-Milit.		265
Order makes arts easie, and armies victorious, and retains	297	Cornaro		9
of Cambridge, when the Ambassadours were made Masters of Arts.	441	Oration		T
as to you deserving them, Wee at last salute you Masters of Arts;	441	Oration		27
But yet the Arts in quietnes and silence here are reverenced,	442	Oration		35
AS				
Mayst rule it, as thou list; and poure the shame,	7	Ch.-Porch		27
Lets his soul runne for nought, as little fearing.	8	Ch.-Porch		59
Thy Gentrie bleats, as if thy native cloth	10	Ch.-Porch		93
Is full as poore as he, that needs but five.	10	Ch.-Porch		108
As the day lessens, and his life with it.	13	Ch.-Porch		160
As that thy self alone to hell shalt goe.	13	Ch.-Porch	W	168
None is so wastefull as the scraping dame.	13	Ch.-Porch		173
As all the day thou mayst hold out to go.	14	Ch.-Porch		186
As empty boldnesse: therefore first assay	15	Ch.-Porch		207
Whom all his passions follow, as he goes.	15	Ch.-Porch		216
As hurts not others, but may make thee better,	16	Ch.-Porch		262
Give one estate, as one life. None is bound	17	Ch.-Porch		285
As if thou mad'st thy will. A civil guest	18	Ch.-Porch		305
As cunning fencers suffer heat to tire.	19	Ch.-Porch		316
As gunnes destroy, so may a little sling.	20	Ch.-Porch		352
As swords cause death, so may a little sting.	20	Ch.-Porch	W	352
And then as farre as fair behaviour may,	20	Ch.-Porch		359
Strike off all scores; none are so cleare as they.	20	Ch.-Porch		360
That all may gladly board thee, as a flowre.	21	Ch.-Porch		368
As if none could bee brave, but who profess	21	Ch.-Porch	W	369
As those, who mock at Gods way of salvation.	24	Ch.-Porch		446
Look not on pleasures as they come, but go.	24	Ch.-Porch		458
Whose parts are as thy hand did frame;	26	The Altar		3
As nothing but	26	The Altar		7
Not half so sweet as my sweet sacrifice:	27	Sacrifice		19
With clubs and staves they seek me, as a thief,	27	Sacrifice		37
In three dayes raz'd, and raised as before.	28	Sacrifice		66
But surely not their hearts, as I well trie:	30	Sacrifice		123
But surely not their hearts, as I will trie:	30	Sacrifice	V	123
But not their harts, as I by proofe doe try.	30	Sacrifice	W	123
They buffet me, and box me as they list,	30	Sacrifice		129
They buffet him, and box him as they list,	30	Sacrifice	W	129
As Moses face was vailed, so is mine,	31	Sacrifice		138
As Moses face was vailed, so was mine,	31	Sacrifice	W	138
Yet since mans scepters are as frail as reeds,	32	Sacrifice		177
With stronger blows strike mee as I come out:	32	Sacrifice	W	187
Such sorrow as, if sinfull man could feel,	33	Sacrifice		209

AS (cont'd)

	PAGE	TITLE		LINE
As he that for some robberie suffereth.	34	Sacrifice		230
That as sinne came, so Sacraments might flow:	34	Sacrifice		247
Was such a grief as cannot be.	35	Thanksgvng		10
As for thy passion - But of that anon,	35	Thanksgvng		29
As if I us'd them but for fashion.	36	Thanksgvng		36
Which my God feels as bloud; but I, as wine.	37	The Agonie		18
That as each beast his cure doth know,	39	Good Fri.		19
To write thy sorrows in, as blood	39	Good Fri.	W	22
And as of old, the law by heav'nly art	41	Sepulchre		17
Yet do we still persist as we began,	41	Sepulchre		21
That, as his death calcined thee to dust,	41	Easter		5
As thy discoverie presents.	42	Easter	W	26
As larks, harmoniously,	43	East.wings		8
As larks, doe by degree,	43	East.wings	W	8
As he that sees a dark and shadie grove,	43	H. Bapt.1		1
As he that Heaven beyond much thicket spyes	43	H. Bapt.1	W	3
Or else give tears to drown them, as they grow.	44	H. Bapt.1		9
And mend as rising starres & rivers doe.	44	H. Bapt.1	W	9
Are blowne away, as if they nere had bin.	46	Sinne 1	W	14
As we did rise, we die together.	49	Repentance		24
Thy wrath for sinne, as when mans sight was dimme,	49	Faith		2
I had it straight, and did as truly eat,	50	Faith		7
As ever did a welcome guest.	50	Faith		8
A peasant may beleeve as much	50	Faith		29
As a great Clerk, and reach the highest stature.	50	Faith		30
But as th' outworks, they may controll	52	H.Commun.		16
As from one room t' another.	53	H.Commun.		36
As may consume our lusts, and make thee way.	54	Love 2		5
If as a flowre doth spread and die,	57	Employm. 1		1
For as thou dost impart thy grace,	57	Employm. 1		9
A life as barren to thy praise,	57	Employm. 1		14
As is the dust, to which that life doth tend,	57	Employm. 1		15
Then as dispersed herbs do watch a potion,	58	H.Script.2		7
As Prince or King:	61	Praise 1		10
Who have a work, as well as they,	61	Praise 1		19
Thou Lord conceal it not: and as thou art	62	Afflict.2		12
As if that thou hadst nothing els to do?	62	Mattens		12
Yet as in sleep we see foul death, and live:	63	Sinne 2		9
But as cold hands are angrie with the fire,	66	Ch.-lock		5
Yet as cold hands are angrie with the fire,	66	Ch.-lock	W	5
From private bodies, make as big a thunder,	69	Content		23
As those which rise from a huge King.	69	Content		24
And as their wit is, their digestion,	69	Content		31
(For he would not) as they beheld the grace	70	Humilitie		18
And challenge it, as proper to his place,	70	Humilitie		20
And ever as I walk my foot doth tredd	71	Frailtie	W	7
So well as there?	74	The Starre		4
Glitter, and curle, and winde as they:	74	The Starre		26
That, as each beast his manger knows,	76	Sunday		38
As Sampson bore the doores away,	76	Sunday		47
Thy flight is higher, as thy birth.	76	Sunday		59
On men dropp blessings as I fly.	79	Employm.2	W	25
Then was my heart broken, as was my verse:	79	Deniall		3
As good go any where, they say,	80	Deniall		11
As to benumme	80	Deniall		12
All after pleasures as I rid one day,	80	Christmas		1
A willing shiner, that shall shine as gladly,	81	Christmas		29
As frost-nipt sunnes look sadly.	81	Christmas		30
That as the first affrights,	82	Ungratef.		21
But Grace shor'd these, and cut that as it grew.	84	The World		15
Surveys, as if he had design'd.	85	Vanitie 1		4
Yet are we bid, Be holy ev'n as he.	87	Lent		35
As may our faults controll:	87	Lent		45
As may all vice controll:	87	Lent	W	45
As watring pots give flowers their lives.	90	Afflict.4		10
As the sunne scatters by his light	90	Afflict.4		23
But Man hath caught and kept it, as his prey.	91	Man		20
But Man has caught and kept it, as his prey.	91	Man	W	20
As our delight, or as our treasure:	91	Man		28
That, as the world serves us, we may serve thee,	92	Man		53
That as the world to us is kind and free	92	Man	W	53
I would not use a friend, as I use Thee.	93	Unkindness		5
I could not use a friend, as I use Thee.	93	Unkindness		10
I cannot use a friend, as I use Thee.	93	Unkindness		15
Nor would I use a friend, as I use Thee.	94	Unkindness		20
Yet use I not my foes, as I use thee.	94	Unkindness		25
It be as short as yours.	94	Life		18
As was and is thy floting Ark; whose stay	97	Afflict.5		3
As we at first did board with thee,	97	Afflict.5		11
As yet to spare:	99	Mortific.		34
He is to Sinai gone, as we heard tell:	99	Decay		9
I see the world grows old, when as the heat	99	Decay		16
Of thy great love once spread, as in an urn	99	Decay		17
As he will swear,	100	Miserie		11
And make his own? as if none knew, but he.	100	Miserie		14
As dirtie hands foul all they touch,	101	Miserie		37
And yet as though he knew it not,	102	Miserie		61
Decking the sense, as if it were to sell.	102	Jordan 2		6
Praising the sense, as if it were to sell.	102	Jordan 2	W	6
As flames do work and winde, when they ascend,	103	Jordan 2		13

AS (cont'd)

	PAGE	TITLE	LINE
If this poore paper do as much as they.	104	Obedience	5
As many lines, as there doth need	104	Obedience	7
As many lines, as it does need	104	Obedience W	7
And here present it as my speciall deed.	104	Obedience	10
As if this passed with a reservation,	104	Obedience	13
But as thy love shall sway,	104	Obedience	19
Thou mayst as well my actions guide, as see.	104	Obedience	25
As I have mine, may set his hand	105	Obedience	37
Is not so deare to thee as one good grone.	106	Sion	18
And ever as they mount, like larks they sing;	107	Sion	23
As if thy love could fail or change.	108	Home	28
And scouling on them as they pin'd away,	108	Home	45
As an intangled, hamper'd thing.	109	Home	64
To whom the starres shine not so fair, as eyes;	111	Vanitie 2	3
Nor solid work, as false embroyderies;	111	Vanitie 2	4
Which as it riseth, raiseth thee:	112	Dawning	12
But as I can see no merit,	115	Dialogue	17
As the reason then is thine;	115	Dialogue	21
That as I did freely part	115	Dialogue	29
As if I were all earth?	115	Dulnesse	2
When all perfections as but one appeare,	115	Dulnesse	13
As on a window late I cast mine eye,	116	Love-joy	1
Such as springs use that fall, and windes that blow.	117	Providence	16
Is mine to write, as it is yours to raise.	117	Providence	24
And hold it fast, as children do their fathers,	118	Providence	46
Which as it lengthens windes, and windes us in,	118	Providence	59
As bouls go on, but turning all the way.	118	Providence	60
As fair as ever, and as fit to use;	118	Providence	67
He makes a grave; as if the thing had sense,	119	Providence	83
And as thy house is full, so I adore	119	Providence	93
To show thou art not bound, as if thy lot	121	Providence	137
As Babel grew, before there were dissensions.	122	Sinnes rd.	15
As if thy blessings had spare dayes:	124	Gratefulnes	30
As Gods afflictions into man,	126	Confession	9
One while he counts of heav'n, as of his treasure:	127	Giddinesse	5
As if a whirlwinde blew	127	Giddinesse	14
For as the Jews of old by Gods command	128	Bunch Gr.	8
Let me as well take up their joy, as sorrow.	128	Bunch Gr.	21
And clean and fair, as I one even-tide	129	Love unkn.	23
But as my heart did tender it, the man	129	Love unkn.	33
But as birds drink, and straight lift up their head,	131	Mans medly	21
But as his joyes are double;	131	Mans medly	25
If as the windes and waters here below	132	The Storm	1
My sighs and tears as busie were above;	132	The Storm	3
And much affect thee, as tempestuous times	132	The Storm	5
As well as we.	132	The Storm	8
As men, for fear the starres should sleep and nod,	134	Divinitie	1
As if a starre were duller then a clod,	134	Divinitie	3
Was cleare as heav'n, from whence it came.	135	Divinitie	14
Do as ye would be done unto.	135	Divinitie	18
O dark instructions; ev'n as dark as day!	135	Divinitie	19
For death is drie as dust. Yet if ye part,	135	Ephes.	10
End as the night, whose sable hue	135	Ephes.	11
As if they had a part?	136	Familie	2
As if there were no rule or eares?	136	Familie	4
Joyes oft are there, and griefs as oft as joyes;	137	Familie	17
What is so shrill as silent tears?	137	Familie	20
And in the flesh condemn'd it as unfit,	138	The Size	26
As I one ev'ning sat before my cell,	139	Artillerie	1
I rose, and shook my clothes, as knowing well,	139	Artillerie	3
Do as thou usest, disobey,	139	Artillerie	6
As many eyes as starres? since it is night,	140	Ch.-rents	26
Just as I went, None goes that way	142	Pilgrimage	33
According as the weather falls.	143	Complaining	10
Come, bring thy gift. If blessings were as slow	147	Offering	1
As mens returns, what would become of fools?	147	Offering	2
As neither good, nor one: so oft divisions	147	Offering	14
As thy due desert.	147	Offering	30
As theirs.	150	Longing	72
The God of power, as he did ride	151	The Bag	9
He smil'd and said as he did go,	151	The Bag	17
When he was come, as travellers are wont,	151	The Bag	19
But as he was returning, there came one	151	The Bag	25
My lines and life are free; free as the rode,	153	The Collar	4
Loose as the winde, as large as store.	153	The Collar	5
But as I rav'd and grew more fierce and wilde	153	The Collar	33
When as my fears foretold this, did replie,	154	Glimpse	19
That all was not so fair, as I conceiv'd,	155	Assurance	8
But also mine; as when the league was made	156	Assurance	28
Such a Way, as gives us breath:	156	The Call	2
Such a Truth, as ends all strife:	156	The Call	3
And such a Life, as killeth death.	156	The Call	4
Such a Light, as shows a feast:	156	The Call	6
Such a Feast, as mends in length:	156	The Call	7
Such a Strength, as makes his guest.	156	The Call	8
Such a Joy, as none can move:	156	The Call	10
Such a Love, as none can part:	156	The Call	11
Such a Heart, as joyes in love.	156	The Call	12
Yet then as mine didst me restore.	157	Clasping	18
(As we have boxes for the poore)	158	Praise 3	28

AS (cont'd)

	PAGE	TITLE		LINE
Who changeth all things, as him pleaseth best.	159	Jos.coat		4
As serve him up, who all the world commands:	161	Priesthood		26
As if to meet thee they did know,	162	The Search		11
As having keyes unto thy love,	162	The Search		15
As passeth thought:	163	The Search		38
As that to it	163	The Search		42
Since then my grief must be as large,	163	The Search		45
As is thy space,	163	The Search		46
For as thy absence doth excell	163	The Search		57
To set thy honour up, as our designe.	164	The Crosse		6
I am to grief alive, to them as dead.	165	The Crosse		24
Are thy returns! ev'n as the flowers in spring;	165	The Flower		2
As if there were no such cold thing.	165	The Flower		7
Quite under ground; as flowers depart	166	The Flower		10
Still upwards bent, as if heav'n were mine own,	166	The Flower		30
I like our language, as our men and coast:	167	The Sonne		3
As when th' heart sayes (sighing to be approved)	168	a true Hymn		19
As a young exhalation, newly waking,	169	The Answer		8
Who gives to man, as he sees fit Salvation. / Damnation.	170	Water-crs.		10
And as it never shall remove,	173	23 Psalme		23
As she had brought wherewith to stain,	173	Marie Magd		16
As Amber-greese leaves a rich sent	174	The Odour		2
As flesh may be;	175	The Odour		13
My servant, as thee not displeasing,	175	The Odour		24
(As sweet things traffick when they meet)	175	The Odour		27
As plainly as that above doth show;	175	The Foil		3
As if grief were not foul, nor vertue winning.	176	The Foil		8
Blushing woes, that look as cleare	177	The Rose		7
As if they could beautie spare.	177	The Rose		8
As a floud the lower grounds.	180	Invitation		24
Such as is, and makes divine!	181	Banquet		9
As we sugar melt in wine?	181	Banquet		12
But as Pomanders and wood	181	Banquet		25
Here, as broken, is presented:	181	Banquet		30
As thy eclipsed light.	183	A Parodie		15
To do it as for thee:	184	The Elixer		4
Not rudely, as a beast,	184	The Elixer		5
Who sweeps a room, as for thy laws,	185	The Elixer		19
And show them as they are.	185	The Elixer	W	24
Straight as a line, and ever tends to thee,	185	A Wreath		6
For we consider'd thee as at some six	186	Death		5
Much in request, much sought for, as a good.	186	Death		16
Much in request, much long'd for as a good.	186	Death	W	16
As at dooms-day;	186	Death		18
Therefore we can go die as sleep, and trust	186	Death		21
As peculiar notes and strains	186	Dooms-day		11
Seest and rulest all things ev'n as one:	190	Ch.-Milit.		2
Trimme as the light, sweet as the laden boughs	190	Ch.-Milit.		14
Of Noahs shadie vine, chaste as the dove;	190	Ch.-Milit.		15
As well our understanding as our sight.	190	Ch.-Milit.		18
Now with the crosse, as with a staffe, alone,	190	Ch.-Milit.		28
Knocking at all doores, ever as she went.	190	Ch.-Milit.		30
Yet as the sunne, though forward be his flight,	190	Ch.-Milit.		31
Though Greece took horse as soon as Egypt did,	191	Ch.-Milit.		57
And Rome as both; yet Egypt faster rid,	191	Ch.-Milit.		58
(As dying things are wont) untill it flew	192	Ch.-Milit.		80
That as before Empire and Arts made way,	192	Ch.-Milit.		83
As well what should befall, as what befell.	193	Ch.-Milit.		130
From Greece he went to Rome: and as before	194	Ch.-Milit.		139
So trimme, as Greece and Egypt? yet their hearts	194	Ch.-Milit.		151
So spruse, as Greece and Egypt? yet their hearts	194	Ch.-Milit.	W	151
As the old heathen would deem prodigies.	194	Ch.-Milit.		154
As Rome will one day finde unto her cost.	194	Ch.-Milit.		160
As Sinne in Greece a Prophet was before,	195	Ch.-Milit.		171
Such force as once did captivate the Jews;	195	Ch.-Milit.		192
As new and old Rome did one Empire twist;	196	Ch.-Milit.		205
Yet with two faces, as their Janus was;	196	Ch.-Milit.		207
Yet not as Sinne, but as Religion.	196	Ch.-Milit.		212
As is the moon and sunne to heav'n and light.	196	Ch.-Milit.		216
But as in vice the copie still exceeds	196	Ch.-Milit.		221
At Christs last coming, as his first did finde:	196	Ch.-Milit.		231
To these diminishings, as is between	196	Ch.-Milit.		233
They have their times of Gospel, ev'n as we.	197	Ch.-Milit.		248
They have their time of Gospel, ev'n as we.	197	Ch.-Milit.	W	248
Yet as the Church shall thither westward flie,	197	Ch.-Milit.		259
Thus do both lights, as well in Church as Sunne,	197	Ch.-Milit.		270
But as the Sunne still goes both west and east;	198	Ch.-Milit.		274
As thou art evry-where;	200	H. Commun.	W	3
Or rather so, as thou alone	200	H. Commun.	W	4
Sometimes, when as I wash, I say	202	love	W	7
And shrodely, as I think, Lord wash my soule	202	love	W	8
As if shades knew not Thee.	203	Even-song	W	12
Are so, as for the present, I did move	204	Persever.	W	3
Or rather as thou movedst mee.	204	Persever.	W	4
As a burst fouling-peece doth save the birds	204	Persever.	W	7
As well as any she? Cannot thy Dove	206	Walton 1		8
Oceans of Ink; for, as the Deluge did	206	Walton 2		2
As God gives thee store,	207	Walton 3		5
Gifts speake their Givers. For as those Refractions,	209	L. Bacon	D	3
As well show inward warblinge as decay.	210	Paradox	D	24

AS (cont'd)

	PAGE	TITLE		LINE
Betwixt us & the people: when as glory	212	Bohemia	D	25
Addes to the unicn, as lights doe gather	212	Bohemia	D	36
Of th' universe, like as the windes, & name	212	Bohemia	D	44
Then shall thy Glory, fresh as flowers	213	L' Envoy	D	7
which also I will set as high as I can, since hee shoots higher that	224	Priest		8
but that it is a good strife to go as farre as wee can in pleasing	224	Priest		12
it is a good strife to go as farre as wee can in pleasing of him,	224	Priest		12
that which Christ did, and by his auctority, and as his Vicegerent.	225	Priest 1		17
as a Parsons to his Parish, in describing the one (which is indeed	226	Priest 2		17
as many of them do, and because they have different Names,	226	Priest 2		20
even so farre as reproofe to their very face, when occasion cals,	226	Priest 2		30
and therefore as feeling their own sweat, and consequently knowing	227	Priest 3		13
as the Jewes and Judas did Christ, he may say as He did,	227	Priest 3		32
he may say as He did, I sate daily with you teaching in the Temple.	227	Priest 3		33
because Countrey people (as indeed all honest men) do much esteem	228	Priest 3		2
though it be to his own hinderance, as knowing, that if he be not so,	228	Priest 3		5
As for oaths, and apparell, the disorders thereof are also very	228	Priest 3		8
serves either positively as it is, or else to illustrate some other	228	Priest 4		17
of the Scripture with some short inward ejaculation, as, Lord,	229	Priest 4		2
and what follows after, as also the scope of the Holy Ghost.	229	Priest 4		11
they were reproved, as ignorant of what spirit they were.	229	Priest 4		13
yet as diverse, not as repugnant:	229	Priest 4		15
As he doth not so study others, as to neglect the grace of God in	229	Priest 4		19
as to neglect the grace of God in himself, and what the Holy Spirit	229	Priest 4		19
his servants, to whom he hath revealed his Truth, as well as to him;	229	Priest 4		23
and that as one Countrey doth not bear all things, that there may be	229	Priest 4		23
according as his audience is, so he useth one, or other;	230	Priest 5		17
as being truly touched and amazed with the Majesty of God,	231	Priest 6		5
yet not as himself alone, but as presenting with himself the whole	231	Priest 6		7
but as presenting with himself the whole Congregation, whose sins he	231	Priest 6		7
as this is the true reason of his inward feare, so he is content	231	Priest 6		10
they come to pray, as a devout behaviour in the very act of praying.	231	Priest 6		15
as to let the fervency of the supplicant hang and dy between	231	Priest 6		18
as attending to what is done in the Church, and every one,	231	Priest 6		26
so that while they answer, As it was in the beginning, &c.	231	Priest 6		33
they meditate as they speak, that God hath ever had his people,	231	Priest 6		34
that have glorified him as wel as now, and that he shall have so	231	Priest 6		35
service, Rom. 12. when we speak not as Parrats, without reason,	232	Priest 6		3
or offer up such sacrifices as they did of old, which was of beasts	232	Priest 6		4
as of those of antient times, so especially of the late ones;	233	Priest 7		7
and sayings of others, according as his text invites him;	233	Priest 7		12
that none goes out of Church as he came in, but either better,	233	Priest 7		20
and making many Apostrophes to God, as, Oh Lord blesse my people,	233	Priest 7		33
he sees whether I speak as I ought, or you hear as you ought,	234	Priest 7		27
whether I speak as I ought, or you hear as you ought, he sees hearts,	234	Priest 7		28
or you hear as you ought, he sees hearts, as we see faces:	234	Priest 7		28
and terrible, as great in mercy, so great in judgement:	234	Priest 7		32
His voyce is as the sound of many waters, Revelations 1.	234	Priest 7		34
as it lyes entire, and unbroken in the Scripture it self.	235	Priest 7		3
way of crumbling a text into small parts, as, the Person speaking,	235	Priest 7		6
as soon as he awakes on Sunday morning, presently falls to work,	235	Priest 8		16
and seems to himselfe so as a Market-man is, when the Market day	235	Priest 8		18
even as Princes have theirs, besides their publick disbursments.	236	Priest 8		17
he takes occasion to discourse of such things as are both profitable,	236	Priest 8		22
As he opened the day with prayer, so he closeth it, humbly beseeching	236	Priest 8		25
But yet as the temper of his body may be, or as the temper of his	237	Priest 9		1
or as the temper of his Parish may be, where he may have occasion	237	Priest 9		1
unto God, and as his grace shall direct him, so let him proceed.	237	Priest 9		6
and his soul fervent, active, young, and lusty as an eagle.	237	Priest 9		27
(though that indeed be very admirable) as at their daily temperance,	237	Priest 9		31
he findeth to be as necessary, and as difficult at least,	237	Priest 9		36
and as difficult at least, as to be cloathed with perfect patience,	237	Priest 9		36
as to be cloathed with perfect patience, and Christian fortitude in	237	Priest 9		36
means to continue so, he doth at least, as much as hath been said.	238	Priest 9		25
As hee is just in all things, so is he to his wife also,	238	Priest 9		34
counting nothing so much his owne, as that he may be unjust unto it.	238	Priest 9		35
reserving so much of the affaires, as serve for a diversion for him;	238	Priest 9		38
the seldomer, according as hee is satisfied of his Wifes discretion.	239	Priest 9		4
as that neither they want a competent sustentation, nor her husband	239	Priest 10		18
such as are tavernes for men, and lace-making for women;	240	Priest 10		2
not spent in them, he blesseth God, and lays it out as he sees cause.	240	Priest 10		12
so well served, as by religious servants, both because they do best,	240	Priest 10		15
which is expressed in a fayre table, as being the rule of a family.	240	Priest 10		26
so that as in the house of those that are skill'd in Musick,	240	Priest 10		30
his servants between love, and fear, according as hee findes them;	241	Priest 10		8
but clean, whole, and sweet, as sweet as his garden can make;	241	Priest 10		12
he refuseth not, as coming cheap, and easie, and arising from	241	Priest 10		22
for there being two things, which as they are, are unuseful to man,	241	Priest 10		27
the one for smalnesse, as crums, and scattered corn, and the like;	241	Priest 10		27
the other for the foulnesse, as wash, and durt, and things thereinto	241	Priest 10		29
do as it were dresse and prepare both for man in themselves,	241	Priest 10		33
as Sunday is his day of joy, so Friday his day of Humiliation,	241	Priest 10		36
or over-nourishing things, as the Israelites did eate sowre herbs:	242	Priest 10		4
as most Students are, he cannot keep the last obligation,	242	Priest 10		28
also in diseases of exinanition (as consumptions) must be broken:	242	Priest 10		31
For it is as unnatural to do any thing, that leads me to a sicknesse,	242	Priest 10		36
I am inclined, as not to get out of that sicknesse, when I am in it,	242	Priest 10		37
as being immoderately taken, it is exceeding obstructive.	243	Priest 10		4
and therefore as God, although we should love him onely for his own	243	Priest 11		30
sets up as many encouragements to goodnesse as he can, both in	244	Priest 11		3

AS (cont'd)

	PAGE	TITLE	LINE
for then they will reckon upon it, as on a debt;	244	Priest 12	28
and repine as much, as he that is disseized of his own inheritance.	244	Priest 12	29
and repine as much, as he that is disseized of his own inheritance.	244	Priest 12	30
paines in their vocation, as not knowing when they shal be relieved;	245	Priest 12	3
as at great Festivals, and Communicns;	245	Priest 12	7
as he obeys Authority in the one, so that being once satisfied,	245	Priest 12	25
Commandments, and as he finds them perfect, rewards them the more.	245	Priest 12	36
as walls plaistered, windows glazed, floore paved, seats whole,	246	Priest 13	4
and Font be as they ought, for those great duties that are performed	246	Priest 13	7
not as out of necessity, or as putting a holiness in the things,	246	Priest 13	23
or as putting a holiness in the things, but as desiring to keep	246	Priest 13	23
but as desiring to keep the middle way between superstition,	246	Priest 13	24
and as following the Apostles two great and admirable Rules in things	246	Priest 13	25
For there he shall find his flock most naturally as they are,	247	Priest 14	6
which they put on as their holy-day cloathes, and come to Church in	247	Priest 14	8
and then as hee finds the persons of the house imployed, . . .	247	Priest 14	11
as if hee findes them reading, hee furnisheth them with good books;	247	Priest 14	15
they so labour, as neither to labour anxiously, nor distrustfully,	247	Priest 14	26
as if it were in their own hands to thrive, or not to thrive.	247	Priest 14	30
as that they make not that the end of their labour, but that they may	248	Priest 14	6
and oftentimes, as Nathan did, in the person of another, . .	248	Priest 14	21
for as when the offence is particular, and against mee, . .	248	Priest 14	26
as about prayers morning and evening on their knees, reading	248	Priest 14	32
as his accesse to the poor is more comfortable, then to the rich;	249	Priest 14	7
as having continuall use of them, such as are from Gods generall	249	Priest 15	18
such as are from Gods generall providence extended even to lillyes;	249	Priest 15	19
as a necessary evidence and fruit of their faith, at that time	249	Priest 15	33
carrying it about with him as fully, as if he had begot his whole	250	Priest 16	9
it about with him as fully, as if he had begot his whole Parish.	250	Priest 16	9
he hateth him not as an officer, but pityes him as a Father:	250	Priest 16	11
he hateth him not as an officer, but pityes him as a Father:	250	Priest 16	12
his owne person, hee considers the offender as a child, and forgives,	250	Priest 16	14
which as hee cannot, touching the last day, so neither touching	250	Priest 16	21
good discourses, such as may edify, interposing sometimes some short,	251	Priest 17	4
as he finds any defect in these, hee first considers with himselfe,	251	Priest 17	25
This was not so well said, as it might have been forborn; . .	252	Priest 18	9
as when he is set at an armour, or horse, he borrowes them . .	252	Priest 19	25
but such as are every way fitting to do his Countrey true . .	252	Priest 19	27
as being the servant of him, in whom there was no guile. . .	253	Priest 19	2
as to all the Fathers of the Church, so especially to his Diocesan,	253	Priest 19	6
use of them, as of Clergy councels, for the benefit of the Diocese.	253	Priest 19	10
with as joyfull a countenance, as if he were to entertain some great	253	Priest 19	19
as joyfull a countenance, as if he were to entertain some great Lord.	253	Priest 19	19
as an obligation to do good, rather then to those that are further,	253	Priest 19	26
as concerning this life, who hath promised, that Godlinesse shall be	254	Priest 20	18
as the case requires, then by causing them to be presented, . .	254	Priest 20	24
And yet as the malice of the person, or hainousness of the crime may	254	Priest 20	25
which exceedingly delights him as by way of exercise upon himself,	255	Priest 21	11
as they hear the answers prove, may when they come home, . .	255	Priest 21	27
as parrats, without ever piercing into the sense of it. . .	256	Priest 21	4
as thus, in the Creed:	256	Priest 21	6
How came this world to be as it is?	256	Priest 21	7
full of such things, as are not to be seen, but beleeved? . .	256	Priest 21	10
As, when the Parson once demanded after other questions about mans	257	Priest 21	1
he could not but say, he would hast out of it as fast as he could.	257	Priest 21	7
as Sermons come short of questions in the one, so they farre exceed	257	Priest 21	22
in a great confusion, as being not only to receive God, but to break,	257	Priest 22	29
admits no vaine or idle names, but such as are usuall and accustomed.	258	Priest 22	4
as being done both in the presence of God, and his Saints, . .	258	Priest 22	12
ones first receiving is not so much by yeers, as by understanding:	258	Priest 22	33
as to a great purchase for their children, and servants; . .	259	Priest 22	3
as the Parson useth all reverence himself, so he administers to none	259	Priest 22	10
as, at Easter, Christmasse, Whitsuntide, afore and after Harvest,	259	Priest 22	21
the people so order their affairs as to receive just at those times,	259	Priest 22	27
in any Controversie, that they should resort to him as their Judge.	259	Priest 23	33
as also by discourse with men of that profession, whom he hath ever	260	Priest 23	3
pin unjustly from the richest, he absolutely restores it as a Judge;	260	Priest 23	16
As in cases of an obscure and dark nature, not easily determinable	260	Priest 23	20
or in cases of high consequence, as establishing of inheritances:	260	Priest 23	22
he shews them how to go to Law, even as Brethren, and not as enemies,	260	Priest 23	26
and not as enemies, neither avoyding therfore one anothers company,	260	Priest 23	26
Now as the Parson is in Law, so is he in sicknesse also: . .	260	Priest 23	28
as may be of much use to him both for himself, and others. . .	261	Priest 23	3
be diligently perused, as being the practicall part, and of most use.	261	Priest 23	8
as they may be an help, and a recreation to more divine studies,	261	Priest 23	10
as also by way of illustration, even as our Saviour made plants	261	Priest 23	13
even as our Saviour made plants and seeds to teach the people:	261	Priest 23	13
As for spices, he doth not onely prefer home-bred things before them,	261	Priest 23	36
for as hee is Charitable, so he is just also.	262	Priest 23	15
as in their tithes, or otherwise.	262	Priest 24	27
as if he be a Papist, the Church is the hinge he turnes on; . .	262	Priest 24	29
these two with himselfe, as what the Church is, how it began,	262	Priest 24	32
the Countrey Parson proceeds so farre as to call in Authority,	263	Priest 25	22
punishing of any, as the vulgar ever consters for signes of ill will;	263	Priest 25	24
he forbears not in any wise to use the delinquent as before,	263	Priest 25	26
but as a brother still, except some small and temporary estranging	263	Priest 25	30
and makes so much the more of him, as before he alienated himselfe;	263	Priest 25	34
natures are alwayes cleer, and evident, as Adultery, Murder, Hatred,	264	Priest 26	6
as Covetousnesse, and Gluttony. So likewise there are some persons,	264	Priest 26	9
that servants for their mony are as other things that they buy,	265	Priest 26	24

AS (cont'd)

	PAGE	TITLE	LINE
things that they buy, even as a piece of wood, which they may cut,	265	Priest 26	25
as he that eats more then his estate will bear, is a Prodigall;	266	Priest 26	8
as if they were Masters of their health, and so they will stand	266	Priest 26	19
As for the quantity, touching our imployments, none must eat so	266	Priest 26	28
none must eat so as to disable themselves from a fit discharging	266	Priest 26	29
as that it is not meate or drinke that hinders them from working.	266	Priest 26	35
according as I feele my self, either I take my wonted proportion,	267	Priest 26	8
As when the people hungred and thirsted after our Saviours Doctrine,	267	Priest 26	22
as knowing that nature will not bear everlasting droopings,	267	Priest 27	33
contempt shall proceed so far as to do any thing punishable by law,	268	Priest 28	31
punishable by law, as contempt is apt to do, if it be not thwarted,	268	Priest 28	32
and being in the world as he was, hath this undoubted pledge of his	269	Priest 28	17
as being persons enabled by that Name to take moveable goods,	270	Priest 29	1
or as David says, to be even a door-keeper in the house of God.	270	Priest 29	11
as also the visitation Articles, which are grounded upon the Canons,	270	Priest 29	14
but that God often changeth it according as he sees fit,	270	Priest 30	31
then by that which he continually supplyes, as the corn needs it;	271	Priest 30	6
instantly dry up, as a river would if the fountain were stopped.	271	Priest 30	7
if he suite not other things to the growth, as seasons, and weather,	271	Priest 30	16
As when a Merchant hath a ship come home after many a storme,	271	Priest 30	22
then God sends such weather, as lays the corn, and destroys it:	271	Priest 30	31
Just as a Father, who hath in his hand an apple, and a piece of Gold	272	Priest 30	7
As for example: It is necessary, that all Christians should pray	272	Priest 31	21
Godly have ever added some houres of prayer, as at nine, or at three,	272	Priest 31	26
or at midnight, cr as they think fit, & see cause, or rather as Gods	272	Priest 31	27
as they think fit, & see cause, or rather as Gods spirit leads them.	272	Priest 31	27
which none can perform so wel in trouble, as in calmness.	273	Priest 31	3
God knows the occasion as wel as he, and He is as a gracious Father,	273	Priest 31	7
God knows the occasion as wel as he, and He is as a gracious Father,	273	Priest 31	8
and He is as a gracious Father, who more accepts a common course	273	Priest 31	8
assure himself, as to admit no scruple, but to go on as cheerfully,	273	Priest 31	10
but to go on as cheerfully, as if he had not been interrupted.	273	Priest 31	11
As for example: A godly man, not out of superstition,	273	Priest 31	21
he may behave himself so as befits so great a presence;	273	Priest 31	27
as that by this he may take into his Prayer humiliation also.	273	Priest 31	32
as I passe, in my heart) because this kinde of Prayer is additionary,	273	Priest 31	35
in the soul, and a hand in the Body, as ingagements of working:	274	Priest 32	20
and take as much joy in a straight-growing childe, or servant,	275	Priest 32	33
childe, or servant, as a Gardiner doth in a choice tree.	275	Priest 32	33
and managing Commons, or Woods, according as the place suggests.	276	Priest 32	6
with the same care as others, when they meet with good fruit,	276	Priest 32	31
As for better Books of Divinity, they are not in this Consideration,	276	Priest 32	35
he may go to Court, as the eminent place both of good and ill.	277	Priest 32	5
and as the Husbandman labours for them, so must they fight for,	277	Priest 32	19
even as John the Baptist squared out to every one (even to Souldiers)	277	Priest 32	22
As for younger Brothers, those whom the Parson finds loose,	277	Priest 32	24
commends the study of the Civill Law, as a brave, and wise knowledg,	277	Priest 32	31
as the only wonder-working knowledg, and therefore requiring the best	277	Priest 32	34
but also as they may be handled, a religious imployment?	278	Priest 32	7
as divers have done lately, to our Countrey's advantage.	278	Priest 32	10
hath ever so many sermons ready penn'd, as he hath victories.	278	Priest 33	24
And it fares in this as it doth in Physick:	278	Priest 33	25
is a Physitian so far as he meetes with the same disease,	278	Priest 33	27
there were no such Physician as he, both for skill and tendernesse.	278	Priest 33	31
an act of the mind, not of the Body, even as the Originall signifies;	279	Priest 33	15
alike in all Gods children (which as concerning weeping it cannot be,	279	Priest 33	21
that so the body may joyn in the grief, as it did in the sin;	279	Priest 33	28
so that he as truly repents, who performes the other acts	279	Priest 33	29
when he cannot more, as he that weeps a floud of tears.	279	Priest 33	31
The like he doth in other Christian vertues, as of Faith, and Love,	279	Priest 33	34
wherein (as Saint Paul implyes that he ought, Romans 2.) hee first	279	Priest 33	35
as he did our Saviour, and the Angels minister to us their owne food,	280	Priest 34	5
his preaching, but afterwards also, as Mat. 22. 35. He was tempted:	280	Priest 34	9
according as he discovers any of his Flock to be in one or the other	280	Priest 34	12
and not to let go the raines as soon as the horse goes easie.	280	Priest 34	16
lest their quiet betray them (as it is apt to do) to a coldnesse,	280	Priest 34	18
but to labour still to be as fervent in Christian Duties,	280	Priest 34	19
as they remember themselves were, when affliction did blow the Coals.	280	Priest 34	20
he is lost, as if they said, God doth forsake and persecute them,	281	Priest 34	10
how the windes should blow so much as they can, and the sea rage so	281	Priest 34	21
and the sea rage so much as it can, and all things do what they can,	281	Priest 34	21
by taking away so much as the usuall seasons of summer and winter,	281	Priest 34	24
should be his proof, and witnesses, as he calls them, Isaiah 43. 12.	282	Priest 34	13
not so much doubting a God, as that he is theirs;	283	Priest 34	6
either he doth it as they are Creatures, dust and ashes;	283	Priest 34	10
or as they are sinfull.	283	Priest 34	11
As Creatures, he must needs love them;	283	Priest 34	11
As sinfull, he must much more love them;	283	Priest 34	13
and this as the more faulty in him, so the more glorious in God.	283	Priest 34	21
he mislikes, and reproves as uncharitable, and unneighbourly;	284	Priest 35	12
as knowing that absence breedes strangeness, but presence love.	284	Priest 35	15
is a great Blessing, and as great as food, for which we give thanks:	284	Priest 35	27
As for those that are ashamed to use this forme, as being old,	284	Priest 35	29
those that are ashamed to use this forme, as being old, and obsolete,	284	Priest 35	30
Now as the Apostle argues in another case;	285	Priest 36	17
which though our Saviour reproved as unfitting for his particular,	285	Priest 36	27
language, he shall be esteemed as ordinary complementers;	286	Priest 36	21
as appears Rom. 12. 14. how much more those, who are spiritual	286	Priest 36	27
notorious faults are either such as are made known by common fame	287	Priest 37	12
or else such as have passed judgment, & been corrected either	287	Priest 37	14

AS (cont'd)

	PAGE	TITLE		LINE
Law intends, as is evident by those, which are branded for rogues,	287	Priest 37		19
As the executioner is not uncharitable, that takes away the life	287	Priest 37		25
And as malefactors may lose & forfeit their goods, or life; . .	287	Priest 37		31
that as the rain returns not empty, so neither may thy word,	289	Priest		31
the measure of thy love, who hast done for us as much as may be.	290	Priest		12
whereas my life seemed as farre from it by Nature, as it was neare it	291	Cornaro		26
as farre from it by Nature, as it was neare it by Intemperance.	291	Cornaro		27
preserving of Health, as a disorderly life to the overthrowing of it;	292	Cornaro		6
as I too wel by experience found.	292	Cornaro		7
as barren grounds are made fruitfull by good husbandry. . .	292	Cornaro		11
was such as belonged to sickly constitutions, and that in a small	292	Cornaro		24
my Physicians nothing thereof, as is the custome of sick people.	292	Cornaro		30
If Temperance had so much power as to bring me health; . . .	293	Cornaro		3
cool wines pleased my taste best, as also melons, and other fruit;	293	Cornaro		11
fitted my stomack, and in such measure, as easily might be digested:	293	Cornaro		17
with a full stomack, but so as I might well both eat and drink more.	293	Cornaro		19
other hurtfull things also, as too much heat and cold, wearinesse,	293	Cornaro		30
I preserved me also, asmuch as I could, from hatred and melancholie,	293	Cornaro		35
as all that know me, can testifie:	294	Cornaro		11
I should be a conquerour, as also a little after it came to passe:	294	Cornaro		27
which seemed as a miracle to the Physicians.	295	Cornaro		13
as, that old age could not be sustained with so little meat . .	295	Cornaro		22
as usually happens in old mens bodies, which live without rule.	296	Cornaro		35
without such observation, as is not easily to be made upon others;	297	Cornaro		29
who not onely as a friend doth visit thee, but help thee! . .	298	Cornaro		9
as is manifest by experience, is a naturall Physick most agreeable	298	Cornaro		13
But sensuall men (as most are) desiring to satisfie their Appetite,	298	Cornaro		23
inconveniences are of no great moment (as I shewed before) if a man	299	Cornaro		16
as also that their minde, in all things wherein they deal, . .	299	Cornaro		20
which endeavours to preserve a man as much as she can, teacheth us	299	Cornaro		26
but such meats as are agreeable to his disease, and that in much	299	Cornaro		31
No man that followes it,.is bound to eat and drink so little as I:	300	Cornaro		7
as I will shew by my self, recounting the delights and pleasures in	300	Cornaro		30
and which are such, as that men generally account me happie.	300	Cornaro		32
as also of excellent Artificers in Architecture, painting, . .	301	Cornaro		35
as a Tragedie with old Age, by reason of the sad events which it	302	Cornaro		31
as farre as I can conjecture, very apt and well given both . .	303	Cornaro		4
thousand dangers and deaths, as daily experience sheweth, and I also,	303	Cornaro		15
as also to those that live in sinne, and follow their appetites:	303	Cornaro		19
hath put this into your hands (as he sent the fish with mony to S.	304	Valdesso		11
happily also with this (as his thoughts are fruitfull) intending	304	Valdesso		12
I like not in him, as my fragments will expresse, when you read them;	304	Valdesso		16
acceptation of Christs righteousnesse (as he sheweth through all his	304	Valdesso		22
and overweigh the defects (as I conceive) towards the publishing	305	Valdesso		13
but not as a naked Word severed from God, but as the Word of God:	306	Valdesso		29
but not as a naked Word severed from God, but as the Word of God:	307	Valdesso		1
together with many other, as namely Consid. 71. upon Our Father;	307	Valdesso		16
oppose Theologicall vertues, as Uncharitablenesse opposes Charity;	308	Valdesso		7
Habits oppose morall vertues, as Prodigality opposes Moderation;	308	Valdesso		10
by the generall Providence of God, as Socrates and Aristides, &c.	308	Valdesso		13
As if he should say:	308	Valdesso		33
as if they were both but Alphabets and after a time to be left.	309	Valdesso		19
The H. Scriptures (as I wrote before) have not only an Elementary	309	Valdesso		20
(as Pictures may be by a plenarie circumspection) but still even	309	Valdesso		22
as to neglect the Consideration of Gods Worke in his heart through	309	Valdesso		30
As for the Text, They shall be all taught of God, it being Scripture	310	Valdesso		2
of the Gospell will not give an cutward Law of Ceremonies as of old,	310	Valdesso		5
but such a one as shall still have the assistance of the holy spirit	310	Valdesso		6
ever outrunning the Teacher, as it did when Peter taught Cornelius:	310	Valdesso		8
For as the servant leaves not the letter when he hath read it,	310	Valdesso		27
us not with the same thing only when it is read as the promises doe,	310	Valdesso		34
Scriptures for the first and principall, as Consid. 47, and others;	311	Valdesso	V	5
which may be unto him as the sunne to a Travellour in his journey,	312	Valdesso		18
and syncere Religion, such as are Prayer, Fasting, Almes-deedes,	312	Valdesso		20
as to relieve my Neighbour, God hath already reveled his Will about	313	Valdesso		13
there be a restraining motion (as S. Paul had when hee would have	313	Valdesso		16
holy Scripture, he meaneth that we should not use it as the onely,	314	Valdesso	V	5
that we should not use it as the onely, or as the principall means;	314	Valdesso	V	5
such as are all vain conversations:	314	Valdesso		19
For as for these, pious persons ought alwaies to avoid them:	314	Valdesso		19
Gods Spirit will mortify and try them as gold in the fire. . .	314	Valdesso		21
or conditionally he prayed as man, though as God he knew the event.	315	Valdesso		11
Wherefore as David's Adultery cannot be excused, so need . .	316	Valdesso		6
The godly are punishable as others, when they doe amisse, . .	316	Valdesso		17
be evident to others, as well as to themselves, that God moved them.	316	Valdesso		20
for as a Magistrate judgeth in his tribunall, so a Scholar judgeth in	317	Valdesso		1
as if it were but childrens meat, whereas there is not onely milke	317	Valdesso		23
how this opinion could befall so good a man as it seems Valdesso was,	317	Valdesso		32
held in so pretious esteem the word of God, as their Joy, and Crowne,	317	Valdesso		34
it for a time onely, and then cast it away, as he sayes strangely.	318	Valdesso		3
As for the text of S. Pet. 2 Ep. 1. 19. which he makes the ground	318	Valdesso		6
forth her first borne Sonne, as if afterwards he had knowne her:	318	Valdesso		13
And miracle-working as it may be severed from justifying faith,	319	Valdesso		12
Who is so deafe, as he that will not heare?	323	Proverbs		79
Who is so deafe, as he who will not heare?	323	Proverbs	V	79
To a fair day open the window, but make you ready as to a foule.	325	Proverbs		119
A garden must be lookt unto and drest as the body. . . .	325	Proverbs		129
Water trotted is as good as oates.	325	Proverbs		131
Men speake of the faire, as things went with them there. . .	326	Proverbs		151
The corne hides it self in the snow, as an old man in furrs.	329	Proverbs		241

AS (cont'd)	PAGE	TITLE		LINE
The Lyon is not so fierce as they paint him.	330	Proverbs		289
As the yeere is, your pot must seeth.	332	Proverbs		335
The fault is as great as hee that is faulty.	333	Proverbs		369
If you could runne, as you drinke, you might catch a hare.	334	Proverbs		373
He that hath the spice, may season as he list.	335	Proverbs		424
He who hath the spice, may season as he pleaseth.	335	Proverbs	V	424
Labour as long liv'd, pray as ever dying.	337	Proverbs		480
Labour as long liv'd, pray as alwayes dying.	337	Proverbs	V	480
The Lame goes as farre as your staggerer.	339	Proverbs		517
He that looseth is Marchant as well as he that gaines.	339	Proverbs		518
A jade eates as much as a good horse.	339	Proverbs		519
Let all live as they would die.	345	Proverbs		725
The first blow is as much as two.	351	Proverbs		913
(as Hectique, Paralitique, Apoplectique. Lethargique).	357	Proverbs	D	1044
The War is not don so long as my Enemy lives.	357	Proverbs	D	1051
Favour will as surely perish as life.	357	Proverbs	D	1055
There's no such conquering weapon as the necessity of conquering.	357	Proverbs	D	1064
We must love, as looking one day to hate.	359	Proverbs	D	1126
as well as naturall bodies.	361	Proverbs	D	1166
as that if all things proved not well, I had rather the fault should	364	Letters		28
As I shal find occasion, as witty shal receive them by peeces;	366	Letters		3
as when you meet with a witty French speech, try to speak the like in	366	Letters		10
as of certaine injuries which they are thought to have offerd to our	368	Letters		5
as that either his subjects only should practise it, or at least that	368	Letters		11
on Christmas day to bee so devout as to come to the Chappell an howre	368	Letters		17
& shee being at London sent for him (as shee sayes) to make peace	368	Letters		20
but not so great as he expected & therfore he grumblingly said that	368	Letters		32
neither can I so much as go to Bugden, and deliver your Letter,	369	Letters		15
Sir send the Letter you receive from him to me as soon as you can,	370	Letters		6
brothers house of his own name (as I think) at the sign of the Pedler	370	Letters		27
Can I be so happy, as to hear of both these that they succeed well?	371	Letters		10
or, that my love is as dumb as my papers;	371	Letters		25
or, that my love is as dumb as my papers;	371	Letters		26
have so much power or boldness as to oppose the hope of our Joyes	372	Letters		28
As the Earth is but a point in respect of the heavens, so are earthly	372	Letters		29
most carry themselves so, as if they not only not desir'd, but,	373	Letters		33
other Tortures, as the very mention of them might beget amazement;	373	Letters		37
I beseech you let such thoughts as these, moderate your present fear	374	Letters		3
consider that God intends that to be as a sacred Temple for himself	374	Letters		10
and will not allow any room there for such an in-mate as Grief;	374	Letters		11
although you offer more, yet you will doe, as you write, that alsoe.	375	Letters		7
Neither hath she any to repair unto at good times, as Christmas, &c.	375	Letters		27
of taking her, as once you did, surely it were a great good deed,	375	Letters		31
these many years, as having spent two hundred pounds in building;	376	Letters		1
and not as many who think they have done fairly, if they leave them	376	Letters		14
which I commend to you as being now a father, "the best-bredd child	376	Letters		17
Gods earth, no not tho' the advice step so far, as to be reproof:	378	Letters		13
you any other wayes, as neyther I my self desire to be considered.	378	Letters		15
As I had written thus much, I received a Letter, from My Brother,	378	Letters		30
promising to get her Son to doe as much) with some little Apology	379	Letters		3
that she had done nothing in it (as my Brother writes) hitherto.	379	Letters		4
And as I am glad for the thing, so no less glad for the Heart,	379	Letters		14
As for my assistance, doubt not, through Gods blessing,	379	Letters		17
As in things inwardly good to have an eye to the world may be	380	Woodnoth		15
as the course of our life & the changes thereof, we are to regard	380	Woodnoth		17
the one for the nature thereof (as your trade) the other only	380	Woodnoth		22
trade) the other only for the success (as assistance of Sir John) doe	380	Woodnoth		22
only for the success (as assistance of Sir John) doe as David did:	380	Woodnoth		23
As God where he finds no roome for his Inclining grace,	381	Woodnoth		7
David built the temple as much as Solomon because he desired it,	381	Woodnoth		19
Doe this & be a man as David, after Gods hart.	381	Woodnoth		21
as God gives me higher thoughts, & to rise with his favours,	381	Woodnoth		25
of monyes wherof he is to give as I know he will a Just account:	383	G.H.'s Will		25
most pleasing, as well to us remembring, as to you deserving them,	441	Oration		26
as to you deserving them, Wee at last salute you Masters of Arts;	441	Oration		26
who tying, as with a knot, both Indias to his Spaine, knowes no	442	Oration		11
of his praise, no, not, as in past ages, those Pillars of Hercules.	442	Oration		12
we have, as much failed, as your Excellencies doe excel,	442	Oration		34
we have as much failed, as your Excellencies doe excel, in both.	442	Oration		34
ASCEND				
As flames do work and winde, when they ascend,	103	Jordan 2		13
When they are ripe, their odour will ascend,	120	Providence		119
And so my sinnes ascend three stories high,	122	Sinnes rd.		14
To thee my sighs, my tears ascend:	148	Longing		5
ASCENDED				
Step after step the ladder is ascended.	334	Proverbs		393
ASCENDS				
Though nail'd unto 't, but he ascends again,	439	Walton 5		2
When nail'd unto 't, but he ascends again	439	Walton 5	V	2
ASCENT				
In their ascent and cause.	91	Man		36
ASCRIBED				
incomprehensible God, be ascribed all Honour, and Glory,	290	Priest		15
ASHAMED				
If the Parson were ashamed of particularizing in these things,	248	Priest 14		38
made the answer so plaine, that he was even ashamed of his ignorance;	257	Priest 21		6
As for those that are ashamed to use this forme, as being old,	284	Priest 35		30
that at Baptisme they professed not to be ashamed of Christs Cross,	284	Priest 35		32
He that is ashamed in small things, will extend his pusillanimity	284	Priest 35		34
of whose rude delivery my hast makes mee ashamed, only my comfort is	369	Letters		2

ASHES	PAGE	TITLE		LINE
How tame these ashes are, how free from lust,	65	Ch.-monum.		23
Lets his own ashes choke his soul.	79	Employm.2		10
either he doth it as they are Creatures, dust and ashes;	283	Priest 34		10
The dog that licks ashes, trust not with meale.	334	Proverbs		389
Divine ashes are better then earthly meale.	344	Proverbs		684
ASIA				
And much of Asia and Europe fast asleep,	140	Ch.-rents		27
motion (as S. Paul had when hee would have preached in Asia),	313	Valdesso		17
ASIDE				
and also therein setting aside the Reverend Prelates of the Church,	225	Priest 2		21
setting aside his care of his Flock, were a madnesse to doubt of.	234	Priest 7		16
our Saviours rule, and to take my brother aside, and reprove him;	248	Priest 14		27
yet seasonably, and discreetly, by taking aside the Lord, or Lady;	251	Priest 17		28
I know that (setting casualties aside) I shall not die but by a pure	303	Cornaro		26
entreating that you would a while lay aside those warlike lookes,	442	Oration		2
ASK				
What to ask further. Doubts well rais'd do lock	18	Ch.-Porch		299
What to ask farther. Doubts well rais'd do lock	18	Ch.-Porch	W	299
We cannot ask the thing, which is not there,	103	Prayer 2		11
They ask enough; why shouldst thou further go?	145	Discharge		26
Then he proceeded to ask, whether he could get out of the ditch	257	Priest 21		8
whom he hath ever some cases to ask, when he meets with them;	260	Priest 23		4
and himself, and who is ready to ask, if he shall mend shoos,	275	Priest 32		7
He that serves well needes not ask his wages.	347	Proverbs		798
ASKE				
Ill natures, the more you aske them, the more they stick.	324	Proverbs		106
Better spare to have of thine own, then aske of other men.	330	Proverbs		266
I had rather aske of my sire browne bread,	330	Proverbs		269
Aske much to have a little.	332	Proverbs		322
ASK'D				
Ask'd what it meant. I, (who am never loth	116	Love-joy		4
And ask'd, if Peace were there.	124	Peace		4
And when they ask'd, what he would wear;	151	The Bag		16
ASKED				
He asked him again, what he would do, if he were in a ditch?	257	Priest 21		4
but when one is asked a question, he must discover what he is.	257	Priest 21		19
ASKES				
When a friend askes, there is no to morrow.	322	Proverbs		32
To a gratefull man give mony when he askes.	324	Proverbs		115
The foole askes much, but hee is more foole that grants it.	330	Proverbs		282
A great ship askes deepe waters.	336	Proverbs		449
Love askes faith, and faith firmenesse.	339	Proverbs		544
A pittifull looke askes enough.	347	Proverbs		790
ASKING				
Manie things are lost for want of asking.	353	Proverbs		968
ASKS				
but man's unpreparednesse asks kneeling.	259	Priest 22		13
he asks no other, but to have the skill of healing a wound,	260	Priest 23		31
for he asks counsell of the Dead (i.e. books).	361	Proverbs	D	1158
ASKT				
Yet still askt pardon, and was not deni'd.	129	Love unkn.		21
ASLEEP				
And much of Asia and Europe fast asleep,	140	Ch.-rents		27
ASMUCH				
I preserved me also, asmuch as I could, from hatred and melancholie,	293	Cornaro		35
ASPECT				
A fine aspect in fit aray,	109	Brit. Ch.		7
And one aspect of thine spend in delight	172	The Glance		22
His grave aspect had more of heav'n then hell:	194	Ch.-Milit.		168
His grave aspect was liker heav'n then hell:	194	Ch.-Milit.	W	168
ASPECTS				
Both their full-ey'd aspects, and secret glances.	85	Vanitie 1		7
to conquer your enemies, and assume more mild and gracious aspects;	442	Oration		4
ASPERSIONS				
Who by aspersions throw a stone	96	Charms & K		9
to redeem the Dignity either from true faults, or unjust aspersions.	276	Priest 32		24
ASPIRE				
I aspire	178	Discipline		7
Never to thee aspire,	202	Trin.Sun.	W	9
ASSAILE				
Assaile who will, the valiant attends.	324	Proverbs		95
ASSAILES				
The Divell never assailes a man, except he find him	361	Proverbs	D	1176
ASSAULT				
Dares to assault thee, and besiege thy doore.	132	The Storm		12
Though windes and waves assault my keel,	151	The Bag		2
Hee that would be a Gentleman, let him goe to an assault.	350	Proverbs		878
ASSAULTED				
when we are assaulted with temptations either from within or from	280	Priest 34		3
ASSAY				
As empty boldnesse: therefore first assay	15	Ch.-Porch		207
Who knows not Love, let him assay	37	The Agonie		13
ASSE				
I had rather ride on an asse that carries me,	329	Proverbs		258
An Asse endures his burden, but not more then his burden.	358	Proverbs	D	1080
It is good to hold the asse by the bridle.	360	Proverbs	D	1129
ASSEMBLED				
blesse this portion here assembled together, with thy unworthy	289	Priest		25
ASSEMBLIES				
he is so farre from condemning such assemblies, that he rather	284	Priest 35		14

ASSEMBLIES (cont'd)	PAGE	TITLE		LINE
is at all their Assemblies and Meetings, and sits above the Proctors,	370	Letters		2
ASSENT				
Unto the service mutter an assent, ...	117	Providence		15
or assent to the promises of the Gospell by heare-say, or relation	308	Valdesso		34
ASSERTION				
The reason of this assertion is taken from the nature of man,	274	Priest 32		18
But if it should be, the Assertion stands thus:	275	Priest 32		11
ASSIGN'D				
A daintie lodging me assign'd.	65	Ch.-mus.		4
Thou knowst my tallies; and when there's assign'd	73	Afflict.3		8
Where all things have their leafe assign'd:	149	Longing		50
Yet must there such proportions be assign'd	196	Ch.-Milit.		232
Yet must there such proportion be assign'd	196	Ch.-Milit.	W	232
ASSIGNS				
of the Pedler and the Pack on London-bridge, for there he assigns me.	370	Letters		28
ASSISTANCE				
a one as shall still have the assistance of the holy spirit applying	310	Valdesso		6
As for my assistance, doubt not, through Gods blessing, . .	379	Letters		17
other only for the success (as assistance of Sir John) doe as David	380	Woodnoth		23
ASSUME				
To assume thy flesh and bone;	113	Businesse		18
with himself, how or what behaviour to assume for so holy things.	257	Priest 22		28
to conquer your enemies, and assume more mild and gracious aspects;	442	Oration		4
ASSUMES				
Flesh assumes, ...	181	Banquet		23
he hath so done, then he assumes the Parson, and exhorts to Charity.	260	Priest 23		16
ASSURANCE				
Assurance.	155	Assurance		T
in assurance, because it is not performed by way of request,	286	Priest 36		6
ASSURANCES				
A good pay-master starts not at assurances.	324	Proverbs		113
ASSURE				
so doth he assure himself, that God in all ages hath had his	229	Priest 4		21
And of this he is so to assure himself, as to admit no scruple,	273	Priest 31		10
ASSURES				
but assures himselfe, that mony thus lent to God, is placed surer	240	Priest 10		7
ASSURING				
know of the Doctrine, John 7. and assuring himself, that wicked men,	228	Priest 4		29
ASSWAGED				
is not quite extinguished, but the heate of it asswaged. . .	308	Valdesso		17
ASTRAY				
With full crie of affections, quite astray;	80	Christmas		3
ASTROLOGERS				
Astrologie is true, but the Astrologers cannot finde it. . .	342	Proverbs		641
ASTROLOGIE				
Astrologie is true, but the Astrologers cannot finde it. . .	342	Proverbs		641
ASTRONOMER				
The fleet Astronomer can bore, ...	85	Vanitie 1		1
ASUNDER				
Did flie asunder:	80	Deniall		7
Broken in pieces all asunder, ...	89	Afflict.4		1
AT				
Stay at the third glasse: if thou lose thy hold, ...	8	Ch.-Porch		41
Stay at the third cup, or forgo the place.	8	Ch.-Porch		47
And rots to nothing at the next great thaw.	12	Ch.-Porch		140
Findes his crackt name at length in the church-glasse.	14	Ch.-Porch		198
If yet thou love game at so deere a rate, ...	14	Ch.-Porch		199
Catch not at quarrels. He that dares not speak	15	Ch.-Porch		217
Think not thy fame at ev'ry twitch will break:	15	Ch.-Porch		219
Lesse at thine own things laugh; lest in the jest	15	Ch.-Porch		231
Courtesie grows at Court; news in the citie.	18	Ch.-Porch	W	292
That thou canst speak, at once; but husband it, ...	18	Ch.-Porch		302
Another chafe, may warm him at his fire, ...	19	Ch.-Porch		314
Doth often aim at, never hit the sphere.	19	Ch.-Porch		318
Sink not in spirit: who aimeth at the sky, ...	19	Ch.-Porch		333
He that by being at church escapes the ditch, ...	24	Ch.-Porch		435
Jest not at preachers language, or expression:	24	Ch.-Porch		439
As those, who mock at Gods way of salvation.	24	Ch.-Porch		446
Summe up at night, what thou hast done by day;	24	Ch.-Porch		451
Summe up at night, what thou hast done that day;	24	Ch.-Porch	W	451
May at his perill further go.	25	Superlim		8
Who at three hundred did the ointment prize, ...	27	Sacrifice		18
Of life, just at the gates of life and blisse?	28	Sacrifice		43
Of faith, but furie: yet at their commands	28	Sacrifice		46
But who does hawk at eagles with a dove?	29	Sacrifice		91
God holds his peace at man, and man cries out:	32	Sacrifice		187
In heaven at his manour I him sought:	40	Redemption		5
At length I heard a ragged noise and mirth	40	Redemption		12
Therefore my sudden soul caught at the place, ...	46	Afflict.1		17
At first thou gav'st me milk and sweetnesses;	47	Afflict.1		19
To fruit or shade: at least some bird would trust	48	Afflict.1		59
A steadie aiming at a tombe.	48	Repentance		6
Sweeten at length this bitter bowl, ...	49	Repentance		19
While those to spirits refin'd, at doore attend	52	H.Commun.		23
Catching the sense at two removes?	56	Jordan 1		10
At thy great doom.	57	Employm. 1		8
And digs my grave at each remove:	60	Grace		14
Drives all at last. Therefore I gladly trust	64	Ch.-monum.		6
These laugh at Jeat and Marble put for signes, ...	65	Ch.-monum.		12
O make mee wholy guiltles, or at least	66	Ch.-lock	W	9

AT (cont'd)

	PAGE	TITLE	LINE
Sometimes Death, puffing at the doore,	67	Ch.-floore	16
Gad not abroad at ev'ry quest and call	68	Content	5
At length the Crow bringing the Peacocks plume,	70	Humilitie	17
Humilitie, who held the plume, at this	71	Humilitie	25
At the next Session-day.	71	Humilitie	32
At close tentations: when the day is done,	72	Constancie	22
Knocking at heaven with thy brow:	75	Sunday	10
With the same shake, which at his passion	76	Sunday	45
Having a new at his expence,	76	Sunday	53
O let me take thee at the bound,	76	Sunday	60
At the last houre:	78	Ang.&Sts.	23
For thou hast life and death at thy command;	83	Sighs & Gr.	26
Reformed all at length with menaces.	84	The World	10
Should aim and shoot at that which Is on high:	85	Coloss.	8
To gain at harvest an eternall Treasure.	85	Coloss.	10
To ordinarie suitours at the doore.	85	Vanitie 1	21
To finde out death, but missest life at hand.	86	Vanitie 1	28
Begins at home, and layes the burden there,	86	Lent	8
Quick thoughts and motions at a small expense,	86	Lent	20
That ev'ry man may revell at his doore,	87	Lent	46
And at what rate and price I have thy love;	89	The Pearl	35
All my attendants are at strife,	90	Afflict.4	13
That it may dwell with thee at last!	92	Man	51
And thou within them starve at doore.	93	Unkindness	14
At th' head of others, hit their own.	96	Charms & K	10
At th' hart of others, hit their own.	96	Charms & K W	10
At first we liv'd in pleasure;	97	Afflict.5	7
As we at first did board with thee,	97	Afflict.5	11
Which shall befriend him at the house of death.	98	Mortific.	18
Which shall befriend him at the houre of death.	98	Mortific. W	18
At some fair oak, or bush, or cave, or well:	99	Decay	7
For one poore minute, stumble at a pinne:	100	Miserie	20
Indeed at first Man was a treasure,	102	Miserie	67
My Saviours bloud: when ever at his board	106	Conscience	14
And at my actions carp, or catch.	106	Conscience	18
But there was none; at least no help without:	107	Home	15
Thraldome from those, who would not at a feast	107	Home	21
And all in sport to geere at me.	110	The Quip	4
Speak not at large, say, I am thine:	111	The Quip	23
For they can never be at rest,	111	Vanitie 2	15
But at his perill: when he digs the place,	119	Providence	82
And at your lodging with their thanks appeare.	120	Providence	120
If it at length deserve some blame:	122	Time	4
An executioner at best;	123	Time	15
But thou didst reckon, when at first	123	Gratefulnes	9
What it would come to at the worst	123	Gratefulnes	11
Perpetuall knockings at thy doore,	124	Gratefulnes	13
Peace at the root must dwell.	125	Peace	16
At length I met a rev'rend good old man,	125	Peace	19
At Salem dwelt, who liv'd with good increase	125	Peace	23
Which many wondring at, got some of those	125	Peace	29
He is some twentie sev'rall men at least	127	Giddinesse	3
Which at a board, while many drunk bare wine,	130	Love unkn.	42
To supple hardnesses. But at the length	130	Love unkn.	45
And trip at night, have spheres suppli'd;	134	Divinitie	2
At least those beams of truth, which onely save,	135	Divinitie	15
When sawcie mirth shall knock or call at doore,	136	Ephes.	13
Great joyes are all at once;	138	The Size	19
Those are at home; these journey still,	138	The Size	23
At least in lump: for such doth oft destroy;	138	The Size	27
Grasp not at much, for fear thou losest all.	138	The Size	38
And ev'n all Africk; would at least I might	140	Ch.-rents	28
At length I got unto the gladsome hill,	142	Pilgrimage	19
That we have nought. I stood amaz'd at this,	143	Holdfast	10
He is thy night at noon: he is at night	144	Discharge	13
It moves, it creeps, it aims at thee:	149	Longing	38
By these thy feet, at which my heart	150	Longing	80
At which the Church falling upon her face	152	The Jews	9
At every word,	153	The Collar	34
Thou didst at once thy self indite,	156	Assurance	29
And so take up at use good store:	159	Praise 3	40
When God at first made man,	159	The Pulley	1
Let him be rich and wearie, that at least,	160	The Pulley	18
So that at once both feeder, dish, and meat	161	Priesthood	21
I do not greatly wonder at the sight,	161	Priesthood	23
I throw me at his feet.	161	Priesthood	36
Offring at heav'n, growing and groning thither:	166	The Flower	25
Wine becomes a wing at last.	182	Banquet	42
For we consider'd thee as at some six	186	Death	5
As at dooms-day;	186	Death	18
Lest at length they plead possession:	187	Dooms-day	16
Knocking at all doores, ever as she went.	190	Ch.-Milit.	30
Plato and Aristotle were at a losse,	191	Ch.-Milit.	53
At length to Germanie, still westward bending,	192	Ch.-Milit.	81
At first he got to Egypt, and did sow	193	Ch.-Milit.	107
Fresh and fine deities. They were at great cost,	193	Ch.-Milit.	109
From all these places, but at divers times,	195	Ch.-Milit.	185
At Christs last coming, as his first did finde:	196	Ch.-Milit.	231
At the rate of an Incarnation	201	H. Commun. W	26
Who God & Saints and Angels loose at last.	203	Trin.Sun. W	17

AT (cont'd)

	PAGE	TITLE		LINE
At there owne weapons, without pomp or state	211	Bohemia	D	21
Those ravening Harpyes, which peck at thy face, ...	212	Bohemia	D	48
At once to Hell, without a baiting while	212	Bohemia	D	49
At Purgatory, there inchanted Ile, ...	212	Bohemia	D	50
that was at peace with me:	221	Psalm VII	D	12
and Character of a true Pastour, that I may have a Mark to aim at:	224	Priest		8
shoots higher that threatens the Moon, then hee that aims at a Tree.	224	Priest		9
Wherfore he hath one Comment at least upon every book of Scripture,	229	Priest 4		28
at least all those which he observeth are most incident to his	230	Priest 5		34
make it a piece of state not to come at the beginning of service	232	Priest 6		8
their poor neighbours, but at midprayers, both to their own loss,	232	Priest 6		9
if he at any time intermit, it is either for want of health,	232	Priest 7		21
of the hearers, that he may be heard at his returne more attentively.	232	Priest 7		24
for people are very attentive at such discourses, and think it	233	Priest 7		9
at his first entrance humbly adoring, and worshipping the invisible	236	Priest 8		4
day he spends either in reconciling neighbours that are at variance,	236	Priest 8		11
At night he thinks it a very fit time, both sutable to the joy	236	Priest 8		18
his meat dress'd and other services done by men-servants at home,	237	Priest 9		9
but only by those means, by which at first it was obtained. .	237	Priest 9		21
and wondreth not so much at their patient suffering, and cheerfull	237	Priest 9		29
(though that indeed be very admirable) as at their daily temperance,	237	Priest 9		31
and as difficult at least, as to be cloathed with perfect patience,	237	Priest 9		36
nor of the sicknesse that destroyeth at noone day, [Ghostly pride	238	Priest 9		8
means to continue so, he doth at least, as much as hath been said.	238	Priest 9		25
and halfe at least of the government of the house, reserving so much	238	Priest 9		37
requires of all to pray by themselves before they sleep at night,	241	Priest 10		2
if a peece of dry flesh at my table be more unpleasant to me,	242	Priest 10		13
and sutably to their needs, then so much given in meat at dinner.	243	Priest 11		17
men to Piety, and is content, if at least so, they will become good:	244	Priest 11		1
as at great Festivals, and Communions;	245	Priest 12		7
But specially, at hard times, and dearths, he even parts his Living,	245	Priest 12		9
giving some corn outright, and selling other at under rates;	245	Priest 12		11
so doth he also to those at his door, whom God puts in his way,	245	Priest 12		20
and at great festivalls strawed, and stuck with boughs, . .	246	Priest 13		9
ill imployed, he chides not at first, for that were neither civill,	248	Priest 14		14
catechizing, singing of Psalms at their work, and on holy days;	248	Priest 14		34
necessary evidence and fruit of their faith, at that time especially:	249	Priest 15		33
that some are called at the eleventh houre, and therefore hee still	250	Priest 16		19
and saying grace at meat, and at going to bed by giving the Host	251	Priest 17		9
and at going to bed by giving the Host notice, that he will have	251	Priest 17		10
as when he is set at an armour, or horse, he borrowes them . .	252	Priest 19		26
or at some other time of the day, propounds among his Brethren what	253	Priest 19		13
This I do, because at such, and such a time you were charitable.	254	Priest 20		17
He requires all to be present at Catechizing:	255	Priest 21		26
wherein the Catechized will at length finde delight, and by which	256	Priest 21		18
secret of whose good consists in this, that at Sermons, and Prayers,	257	Priest 21		18
is at a stand with himself, how or what behaviour to assume for so	257	Priest 22		27
Especially at Communion times he is in a great confusion, . .	257	Priest 22		28
but to throw himself down at the throne of grace, saying, . .	257	Priest 22		31
At Baptisme, being himselfe in white, he requires the presence	258	Priest 22		1
At the times of the Holy Communion, he first takes order . .	258	Priest 22		20
if not duly once a month, yet at least five or six times in the year;	259	Priest 22		20
as, at Easter, Christmasse, Whitsuntide, afore and after Harvest,	259	Priest 22		21
the people so order their affairs as to receive just at those times,	259	Priest 22		27
or at least his Wife, of whom in stead of the qualities of the world,	260	Priest 23		30
and the knowing of herbs may be done at such times, as they may be	261	Priest 23		9
at least in fundamentall things, the obscurity in some points being	263	Priest 24		4
The Countrey Parson at spare times from action, standing on a hill,	264	Priest 26		3
whose natures, at least in the beginning, are dark and obscure:	264	Priest 26		8
So a man dining, eats at first lawfully;	264	Priest 26		22
either spends not at all, or not in some proportion to Gods blessing	265	Priest 26		6
Many think they are at more liberty then they are, as if they were	266	Priest 26		18
and tarryed so long at it, that they would have fainted, . . .	267	Priest 26		23
at least of those, who are apt to despise:	268	Priest 28		24
he takes it either in an humble way, saying nothing at all; . .	269	Priest 28		6
or in a sad way, greived at his own, and others sins, which . .	269	Priest 28		9
he that throws a stone at another, hits himselfe;	269	Priest 28		14
and to be sued at the Law concerning such goods for the use . .	270	Priest 29		3
Man would sit down at this world, God bids him sell it, . .	272	Priest 30		6
Godly have ever added some houres of prayer, as at nine, or at three,	272	Priest 31		26
as at nine, or at three, or at midnight, or as they think fit,	272	Priest 31		26
or at three, or at midnight, or as they think fit, & see cause,	272	Priest 31		26
or by oversleeping himself at night, omits his additionary prayer.	272	Priest 31		31
hath so many dispersed Officers at his beck throughout the Kingdome,	276	Priest 32		11
especially, the Statutes at large.	276	Priest 32		35
Judges and Magistrates, to attend them, at least in their Shire;	277	Priest 32		3
At other times he is to travell over the King's Dominions, . .	277	Priest 32		6
he must not only be a morning man, but at Committees also; . .	277	Priest 32		12
every morning that hee is at home hee must either ride the Great	277	Priest 32		15
hath considered how to carry himself at table about his appetite,	278	Priest 33		18
or at least in that degree it ought to be, since he found himselfe	279	Priest 33		11
he came at length to this resolution, that repentance is an act	279	Priest 33		13
not to eate of all those dishes at table, which even their present	280	Priest 34		23
that at such, or such a time their peace and mirth have carryed them	280	Priest 34		32
if he had been at the Creation of all things, should lesse beleeve	281	Priest 34		28
at severall times and occasions, the Parson setleth wavering minds.	283	Priest 34		4
with reconciling of differences at that time, if there be any:	284	Priest 35		7
and largesse, which at that time is, or ought to be used. . .	284	Priest 35		9
Wherefore he exacts of all to bee present at the perambulation,	284	Priest 35		10
that his Parish at good times invite one another to their houses,	284	Priest 35		17

AT (cont'd)	PAGE	TITLE	LINE
or praying to God at all times, but is rather glad of catching	284	Priest 35	25
that at Baptisme they professed not to be ashamed of Christs Cross,	284	Priest 35	31
when they are at leasure, make others faults their entertainment	286	Priest 37	30
me contrariwise, at the age of eightie and one, strong and lustie;	291	Cornaro	10
That they who in these two things that enter in at the mouth,	294	Cornaro	4
and that at length I should be a conquerour, as also a little after	294	Cornaro	26
Neverthelesse at a venture two remedies might be used, letting	295	Cornaro	3
at length I yeelded, and permitted the quantitie of meat to be	296	Cornaro	7
and that at length they shut up their dayes like a Lamp, . .	298	Cornaro	16
those ten yeares, which they set at naught in regard of their belly?	298	Cornaro	34
Because since this is at the best but uncertain, dangerous, . .	300	Cornaro	19
All these things I do at my ease, and at fit seasons, and in mine own	301	Cornaro	9
things I do at my ease, and at fit seasons, and in mine own houses;	301	Cornaro	9
At other times, I repair to a village of mine, seated in the valley;	301	Cornaro	19
because at these yeares (viz. 83) I have made a most pleasant	302	Cornaro	28
of old was praised, that at the age of 73 yeares he writ a Tragedie;	302	Cornaro	33
it is evident, That the life which I live at this age, is not a dead,	303	Cornaro	9
For at least some of the Papists are come now, to what the Pharisees	320	Valdesso	6
The Devill is not alwaies at one doore.	322	Proverbs	31
At dinner my man appeares.	322	Proverbs	37
At Length the Fox turnes Monk.	323	Proverbs	72
At length the Fox is brought to the Furrier.	323	Proverbs	81
Praise day at night, and life at the end.	324	Proverbs	97
A good pay-master starts not at assurances.	324	Proverbs	113
Play with a foole at home, ...	325	Proverbs	146
Buy at a faire, but sell at home.	326	Proverbs	160
Whose house is of glasse, must not throw stones at another. . .	327	Proverbs	196
A gentlemans grayhound, and a salt-box; seeke them at the fire.	327	Proverbs	205
The Jewes spend at Easter, the Mores at marriages, ...	329	Proverbs	242
Better good afarre off, then evill at hand.	330	Proverbs	267
The groundsell speakes not save what it heard at the hinges.	331	Proverbs	295
Hee will spend a whole yeares rent at one meales meate. . .	331	Proverbs	305
The tongue talkes at the heads cost.	331	Proverbs	312
Although the sun shine, leave not thy cloake at home. . . .	332	Proverbs	326
at his time, and not till then.	332	Proverbs	333
Hee that repaires not a part, at length must all.	333	Proverbs	V 344
He that is not handsome at 20, nor strong at 30, nor rich at 40,	333	Proverbs	349
nor wise at 50, will never bee handsome, strong, rich, or wise.	333	Proverbs	349
He that owes nothing, if he makes not mouthes at us, is courteous.	333	Proverbs	362
his head akes not at the matter.	335	Proverbs	421
hath neede of a net at his girdle.	335	Proverbs	428
and his horse drinke at every water, ...	336	Proverbs	434
Hee that's fed at anothers hand may stay long ere he be full.	336	Proverbs	439
At the games end we shall see who gaines.	339	Proverbs	538
He that is angry at a feast is rude.	340	Proverbs	564
God is at the end, when we thinke he is furthest off it. . .	341	Proverbs	598
When my house burnes, it's not good playing at Chesse. . . .	343	Proverbs	666
Speake not of a dead man at the table.	343	Proverbs	672
Dry bread at home is better then rost meate abroad. . . .	344	Proverbs	681
At Court, every one for himselfe.	347	Proverbs	795
Good swimmers at length are drowned.	347	Proverbs	801
Good newes may bee told at any time, but ill in the morning.	350	Proverbs	877
When you enter into a house, leave the anger ever at the doore.	350	Proverbs	896
The Law is not the same at morning and at night.	351	Proverbs	905
Wine makes all sorts of creatures at table.	352	Proverbs	931
Armour is light at table.	352	Proverbs	934
The Citizen is at his businesse before he rise.	352	Proverbs	958
To speake of an Usurer at the table marres the wine. . . .	353	Proverbs	974
He that is at ease seekes dainties.	353	Proverbs	985
If the husband be not at home, there is nobodie.	354	Proverbs	1016
If you would bee at ease, all the world is not.	355	Proverbs	1019
Power seldome grows old at Court.	357	Proverbs	D 1053
then by stars at their nativities.	357	Proverbs	D 1060
To play at Chesse when the house is on fire.	360	Proverbs	D 1136
Take heed of winde that comes in at a hole, ...	360	Proverbs	D 1154
my case unto you, which I think deserves the reading at the least;	364	Letters	10
so that I am fain to dyet in my Chamber at mine own cost; . .	365	Letters	3
To my dear brother, Mr. Henry Herbert, at Paris.	366	Letters	27
To Sir Robert Harley, at Brampton.	367	Letters	T
to those busnesses which justly excuse him from writing at this time,	367	Letters	31
which they are thought to have offerd to our Merchants at the Indies,	368	Letters	7
or at least that the Hollanders should pay him tribute out of their	368	Letters	12
Sir Charles Howard & his Lady are at much difference, & shee being	368	Letters	19
& shee being at London sent for him (as shee sayes) to make peace	368	Letters	20
is at all their Assemblies and Meetings, and sits above the Proctors,	370	Letters	1
is Regent or Non-regent at his pleasure, and such like Gaynesses,	370	Letters	3
may divert me too much from Divinity, at which, not without cause,	370	Letters	20
brothers house of his own name (as I think) at the sign of the Pedler	370	Letters	27
At my last parting from you, I was the better content because I was	372	Letters	14
at all times rejoyce in the Lord, who taketh care for us: . .	374	Letters	25
Let your moderation appear to all men, the Lord is at hand: . .	374	Letters	28
trouble not your selves, God is at hand to deliver us from all, or,	374	Letters	29
when he urged one upon me, and but one, and that at my choice.	375	Letters	11
Neither hath she any to repair unto at good times, as Christmas,	375	Letters	27
take pitty of her, which yet at that distance is some difficulty.	375	Letters	30
especially at this time, being more beggarly now than I have been	375	Letters	36
To my very dear brother Sir Henry Herbert, at Court. . . .	376	Letters	25
Honourable the Lady Anne, Countess of Pembr. and Montg. at court.	376	Letters	T
if at length they may find out some thing not unworthy of those hands	376	Letters	29
find out some thing not unworthy of those hands at which they aim.	377	Letters	1

	PAGE	TITLE	LINE
AT (cont'd)			
To my deere brother, Sir Henry Herbert, at Court.	377	Letters	32
it also to My Brother, to name at first, what the summe should be,	379	Letters	6
& has given order to the Tenants, at Leighton, to make payment of it.	379	Letters	9
therfore your choice at first was good	380	Woodnoth	6
you have bin at charges:	380	Woodnoth	9
of want of success consider how long God knocks at our harts,	381	Woodnoth	2
due to Mrs Judeth Spenser is to be payd to Mrs Mary Lawly at Chelsey	383	G.H.'s Will	21
as to you deserving them, Wee at last salute you Masters of Arts;	441	Oration	27
ATCHIEVING			
hath guided me hitherto, and of atchieving my (I dare say) holy ends.	364	Letters	19
ATHEISM			
the clean contrary, even from superstition to coldnes, and Atheism.	286	Priest 36	18
ATHEISME			
disputation is no Cure for Atheisme) he scatters in his discourse	281	Priest 34	15
But if he sees them neerer desperation, then Atheisme; . . .	283	Priest 34	6
The Divell divides the world between Atheisme and Superstition	359	Proverbs	D 1107
ATHEIST			
that the Atheist, or Epicurian can have nothing to contradict.	281	Priest 34	34
ATHEISTS			
a million of Atheists, and 30000 Witches.	361	Proverbs	D 1174
ATOME			
The smallest ant or atome knows thy power, ...	190	Ch.-Milit.	3
ATTAIN			
He may attain to, after he is dead.	131	Mans medly	24
be no kind of excellency which it is possible for you to attain to,	366	Letters	14
ATTAIN'D			
up your Children that they have attain'd to the years of Discretion,	373	Letters	13
ATTAINE			
Which of them soonest should attaine my hart.	66	Ch.-lock W	4
With Glory may attaine thy Face.	202	Trin.Sun. W	6
is it easie for any Scholer to attaine to such a measure of Phisick,	261	Priest 23	2
ATTAINED			
first point, and but by Catechizing, the other cannot be attained.	255	Priest 21	8
ATTEMPTING			
that it is ever attempting, or doing one mischief or other. . .	238	Priest 9	14
ATTEMPTS			
And yet thy wounds still my attempts defie, ...	36	Reprisall	7
ATTEND			
While those to spirits refin'd, at doore attend	52	H.Commun.	23
Musick and light attend our head.	91	Man	33
Another to attend him.	92	Man	48
Thy scales like buckets, which attend	141	Justice 2	16
Judges and Magistrates, to attend them, at least in their Shire;	277	Priest 32	3
Indeed he that shall so attend to the bark of the letter, . .	309	Valdesso	29
bidding the dispersed Hebrews attend to the word till the day dawn,	318	Valdesso	18
but however he would have them attend to it till that time, . .	318	Valdesso	20
and then afterward they will attend it of themselves without his	318	Valdesso	21
If thou thy selfe canst doe it, attend no others helpe or hand.	348	Proverbs	813
ATTENDANTS			
All my attendants are at strife, ...	90	Afflict.4	13
When scepters, state, Attendants are the screen	212	Bohemia D	24
ATTENDED			
Keep open house, richly attended, ...	59	Whitsunday	7
Good is to bee sought out, and evill attended.	324	Proverbs	112
ATTENDING			
And there the Churches festivall attending:	192	Ch.-Milit.	82
as attending to what is done in the Church, and every one, . .	231	Priest 6	27
the hour calls, with his family attending him, he goes to Church,	236	Priest 8	3
ATTENDS			
Unto the coffin, that attends his death.	98	Mortific.	24
Assaile who will, the valiant attends.	324	Proverbs	95
ATTENTION			
he procures attention by all possible art, both by earnestnesse	232	Priest 7	30
By these and other means the Parson procures attention; . .	233	Priest 7	22
ATTENTIVE			
for people are very attentive at such discourses, and think it	233	Priest 7	9
ATTENTIVELY			
of the hearers, that he may be heard at his returne more attentively.	232	Priest 7	24
ATTIRE (see also tire)			
To wear thy habit, the severe attire	160	Priesthood	9
ATTIRES			
O what a sight were Man, if his attires	127	Giddinesse	17
ATTRACT			
Attract the lesser to it: let those fires, ...	54	Love 2	2
ATTRIBUTE			
Shall have his attribute to sing;	36	Thanksgvng	40
ATTRIBUTES			
More attributes? Am I all throat or eye, ...	143	Complaining	13
AUCTORITY			
and containes the direct steps of Pastorall Duty and Auctority.	225	Priest 1	4
that which Christ did, and by his auctority, and as his Vicegerent.	225	Priest 1	17
and the dayly prayers enjoyned him by auctority, which he observeth	237	Priest 9	23
AUDIBLY			
Therefore those he meets on the way he blesseth audibly, . . .	251	Priest 17	2
AUDIENCE			
according as his audience is, so he useth one, or other; . .	230	Priest 5	17
or somtimes both, if his audience be intermixed.	230	Priest 5	18
with any woman alone, but in the audience of others, and that seldom,	237	Priest 9	12
AUDITORS			
and busy cast of his eye on his auditors, with letting them know,	233	Priest 7	1

	PAGE	TITLE		LINE
AVOYDING (cont'd)				
not avoyding his company, or doing any thing of aversenesse,	263	Priest 25		27
AVOYDS				
Which perswasion the Parson by all means avoyds, knowing that where	243	Priest 11		23
AW				
A strong regard and aw: but speech alone	68	Windows		13
With showres and frosts, with love & aw,	85	Vanitie 1		25
Lest want of aw	183	A Parodie		17
AWAKE				
Awake, my lute, and struggle for thy part	41	Easter		7
Awake sad heart, whom sorrow ever drowns;	112	Dawning		1
Awake, awake;	112	Dawning		5
for particulars ever touch, and awake more then generalls.	233	Priest 7		6
Awake therefore, my Lute, and my Viol!	289	Priest		9
awake all my powers to glorifie thee!	289	Priest		10
AWAKED				
And every one is more awaked, when we come, and say, Thou art	236	Priest 8		14
AWAKES				
as soon as he awakes on Sunday morning, presently falls to work,	235	Priest 8		16
AWARE				
Man, ere he is aware,	99	Mortific.		31
but proceeding on, comes to do unlawfully, even before he is aware;	264	Priest 26		24
AWAY				
Play not away the vertue of that name,	9	Ch.-Porch		65
O crumble not away thy souls fair heap.	9	Ch.-Porch		70
Away thy blessings, and extreamly flout thee,	23	Ch.-Porch		413
Mine owne deare people, cry, away, away,	29	Sacrifice		102
No room for me, and flie away.	39	Good Fri.		28
One cunning bosome-sinne blows quite away.	46	Sinne 1		14
Are blowne away, as if they nere had bin.	46	Sinne 1	W	14
When I got health, thou took'st away my life,	47	Afflict.1		31
I could not go away, nor persevere.	47	Afflict.1		48
And drop away,	49	Repentance		29
And drope away,	49	Repentance	V	29
Vanisht away, when Faith did change the scene:	51	Faith		39
Till it get wing, and flie away with thee.	59	Whitsunday		4
Till I get wing to fly away with thee.	59	Whitsunday	W	4
They drive them soon away;	71	Humilitie		30
Can blow away, or glittering look it blinde:	72	Constancie		8
As Sampson bore the doores away,	76	Sunday		47
Wherefore that robe we cast away,	76	Sunday		52
But Wisdome quickly swept them all away.	84	The World		5
By noon most cunningly did steal away,	94	Life		5
This world of wo? hence all ye clouds, away,	108	Home		33
Away; I must get up and see.	108	Home		34
And scouling on them as they pin'd away,	108	Home		45
Lord, I acknowledge; take thy plagues away:	126	Confession		26
I passe away and leave it dead?	135	Ephes.		6
To wash away my stubborn thought:	139	Artillerie		15
My hill was further: so I flung away,	142	Pilgrimage		31
Away distrust:	145	Discharge		54
Thy beggars grow; rid them away	150	Longing		77
Away despair; my gracious Lord doth heare.	151	The Bag		1
Any thing to me. Heark despair, away.	152	The Bag		42
Away; take heed:	153	The Collar		27
Whither away delight?	154	Glimpse		1
O take these barres, these lengths away;	163	The Search		49
So much desir'd, is giv'n, to take away	164	The Crosse		9
Grief melts away	165	The Flower		5
My comforts drop and melt away like snow:	169	The Answer		1
When once those snuffes are ta'ne away,	171	Self-cond.		22
Who have pass'd my right away.	177	The Rose		12
Throw away thy rod,	178	Discipline		1
Throw away thy wrath:	178	Discipline		2
Throw away thy rod;	179	Discipline		29
Throw away thy wrath.	179	Discipline		32
Come away,	186	Dooms-day		1
Come away,	186	Dooms-day		7
Come away,	187	Dooms-day		13
Come away,	187	Dooms-day		19
Come away,	187	Dooms-day		25
He chid the Church away, where e're he came,	193	Ch.-Milit.		105
By carrying first their gold from them away:	197	Ch.-Milit.		250
Or whether Bread doe fly away	200	H. Commun.	W	8
And wash away my Shame.	214	Convert	D	10
Of earth is driven by winds away,	215	Psalm I	D	15
and from us cast their cords away.	215	Psalm II	D	8
But now from me depart away,	220	Psalm VI	D	19
and if it be taken away, though justly, they will murmur,	244	Priest 12		29
his Father bids him throw it away, and he will give him the gold	272	Priest 30		10
if any scruple arise, I will throw it away, and be most confident,	273	Priest 31		38
by taking away so much as the usuall seasons of summer and winter,	281	Priest 34		23
The thrusting away of his arme makes us onely not embraced.	283	Priest 34		25
that takes away the life of the condemned, except besides his office,	287	Priest 37		26
their parents and kindred snatcht away in the midst of their dayes,	291	Cornaro		9
all superfluities passing away without difficultie, and no ill	293	Cornaro		28
For suddenly it takes away our appetite, so that we can eat	299	Cornaro		27
because Temperance takes away the cause of diseases:	300	Cornaro		1
and the cause being taken away, there is no place for the effect.	300	Cornaro		2
distinction, for Fomes is not taken away, but Accensio Fomitis;	308	Valdesso		16
it for a time onely, and then cast it away, as he sayes strangely.	318	Valdesso		3

	PAGE	TITLE		LINE
AWAY (cont'd)				
I doe not then bid him goe away but rather stay longer, . . .	318	Valdesso		16
doth not bid them then cast away the word, or leave it off: . .	318	Valdesso		19
Take heede of still waters, the quick passe away.	326	Proverbs		171
Waight and measure take away strife.	328	Proverbs		213
Although it raine, throw not away thy watering pot. . . .	332	Proverbs		325
When God will punish, hee will first take away the understanding.	344	Proverbs		688
Three can hold their peace, if two be away.	345	Proverbs		714
Words and feathers the wind carries away.	359	Proverbs	D	1103
What one day gives us, another takes away from us. . . .	359	Proverbs	D	1111
since if we had Riches we are commanded to give them away: . .	373	Letters		24
He doubles it to take away the scruple of those that might say,	374	Letters		22
For any scruple of leaving your trade, throw it away. . . .	381	Woodnoth		22
AWE (see also aw)				
O learn to stand in awe of him, ...	217	Psalm IV	D	15
AWFUL				
and there an awful Scepter sway:	216	Psalm II	D	22
AWFULL				
and awfull mindes into the Congregation, and that the good God would	235	Priest 8		29
AYRE				
A feather in hand is better then a bird in the ayre.	340	Proverbs		578
AZURE				
In sev'rall ranks upon an azure throne, ...	70	Humilitie		2
The sky his azure mantle gain'd.	151	The Bag		15
BABEL				
It may a Babel prove	72	Frailtie		22
As Babel grew, before there were dissensions.	122	Sinnes rd.		15
BABLES				
If all fooles had bables, wee should want fuell.	323	Proverbs		63
BABYLON				
Sinne did set out of Eastern Babylon, ...	193	Ch.-Milit.		103
He did surname his palace, Babylon.	195	Ch.-Milit.		182
Thus Sinne triumphs in Western Babylon;	196	Ch.-Milit.		211
Old and new Babylon are to hell and night, ...	196	Ch.-Milit.		215
BACK				
And not the beast, that bears it on his back.	17	Ch.-Porch		268
My dove doth back into my bosome flie, ...	29	Sacrifice		94
All back unto thee by the poore.	35	Thanksgvng		20
All back unto thee in the poore.	35	Thanksgvng	W	20
Thy art of love, which I'le turn back on thee:	36	Thanksgvng		47
And there in hymnes send back thy fire again:	54	Love 2		8
The worky-daies are the back-part;	75	Sunday		11
Brought back to the Red Sea, the sea of shame.	128	Bunch Gr.		7
Look back upon thine own estate, ...	170	Self-cond.		4
Love bade me welcome: yet my soul drew back, ...	188	Love 3		1
Then flesh did lend thee, back agen.	202	love	W	18
exercise what he is, unlesse he forsake his plough, and look back.	226	Priest 2		27
his garden or orchard supplyes it, or his barne, and back-side:	241	Priest 10		19
The back-doore robs the house.	337	Proverbs		474
for, since your favours come a Horse-back, there is reason, . .	363	Letters		22
but, I have wrote him back, that this dignity, hath no such . .	370	Letters		21
BACK-DOORE				
The back-doore robs the house.	337	Proverbs		474
BACK-PART				
The worky-daies are the back-part;	75	Sunday		11
BACK-SIDE				
his garden or orchard supplyes it, or his barne, and back-side:	241	Priest 10		19
BACKBITERS				
and ranked backbiters among the generation of the wicked, . .	287	Priest 37		23
Were there no hearers, there would be no backbiters. . . .	323	Proverbs		69
BACKWARD				
When backward on my sins I turne mine eyes	43	H. Bapt.1	W	1
More backward still, and to that water flie, ...	43	H. Bapt.1		4
BACON				
To the Right Hon. the L. Chancellor (Bacon).	209	L. Bacon	D	T
Where you thinke there is bacon, there is no Chimney. . . .	324	Proverbs		99
BAD				
Take a bad lodging in my heart;	74	The Starre		6
Joy, I did lock thee up: but some bad man	128	Bunch Gr.		1
Playntes to bad fortunes dew:	211	Paradox	D	38
bad councels let them fall:	219	Psalm V	D	30
when his storing, which was even now good, passeth from good to bad.	264	Priest 26		30
One act in these things is bad, but it is the custome and habit that	266	Priest 26		17
A bad dog never sees the Wolfe.	323	Proverbs		59
In the mouth of a bad dog fals often a good bone.	358	Proverbs	D	1093
BADD				
Were there no fooles, badd ware would not passe.	323	Proverbs		66
BADE				
Love bade me welcome: yet my soul drew back, ...	188	Love 3		1
BAG				
What skills it, if a bag of stones or gold	13	Ch.-Porch		169
Mine own Apostle, who the bag did beare, ...	27	Sacrifice		13
The Bag.	151	The Bag		T
(I have no bag, but here is room):	152	The Bag		32
Covetousnesse breaks the bag.	358	Proverbs	D	1071
BAIT				
Ryme thee to good, and make a bait of pleasure.	6	Ch.-Porch		4
Where some poore truths were shuffled for a bait	193	Ch.-Milit.		136
The fish adores the bait.	341	Proverbs		607
The escaped mouse ever feeles the taste of the bait. . . .	344	Proverbs		679

	PAGE	TITLE		LINE
BAITING				
At once to Hell, without a baiting while	212	Bohemia	D	49
BAITS				
And sev'rall baits in either kinde	97	Afflict.5		17
when the baits which the enemy lays in company, are discovered	252	Priest 18		13
BAKER				
Bee not a Baker, if your head be of butter.	332	Proverbs		321
BALCONES				
Began to make Balcones, Terraces, ...	84	The World		7
BALL				
This oure great Sublunary Ball,°	213	L' Envoy	D	12
BALLANCE				
Ballance each dramme of reason, like a potion.	19	Ch.-Porch		322
What, (childe), is the ballance thine, ...	114	Dialogue		9
The dishes of thy ballance seem'd to gape, ...	141	Justice 2		7
The ballance distinguisheth not betweene gold and lead. . .	342	Proverbs		629
BALLS				
Do end in bubbles, balls of winde;	64	Even-song		14
But balls of wilde-fire to my troubled minde.	64	Even-song		16
BALM				
The couch of time; cares balm and bay:	75	Sunday		5
BALME				
The Couch of Time, the balme of tears, ...	75	Sunday	W	2
BALSAMES				
Whom oil and balsames kill, what salve can cure?	24	Ch.-Porch		447
BALSOME				
A Balsome are for both the Hemispheres:	27	Sacrifice		26
There is a balsome, or indeed a bloud, ...	147	Offering		19
BAND				
But the sweet cement, which in one sure band	67	Ch.-floore		10
Then Sinne combin'd with Death in a firm band	84	The World		16
My life within this band.	94	Life		3
BANDIE				
Which my fierce youth did bandie, fall and flow	169	The Answer		3
BANDING				
Against the beasts: so joyntly banding, ...	71	Humilitie	V	29
BANDS (group)				
Herod and all his bands do set me light, ...	29	Sacrifice		77
With his train-bands and mates agree	110	The Quip		2
BANDS				
I suffer binding, who have loos'd their bands:	28	Sacrifice		47
Oh glorious spirits, who after all your bands	77	Ang.&Sts.		1
Not the decrees of power, but bands of love.	190	Ch.-Milit.		10
BANDYING				
Against the beasts: so joyntly bandying, ...	71	Humilitie		29
BANE				
Money, thou bane of blisse, & sourse of wo, ...	77	Avarice		1
Hath some fond lover tic'd thee to thy bane?	176	Forerunners		21
(The marks of future bane) shall fill our cup	197	Ch.-Milit.		239
Now if a shepherd know not which grass will bane, or which not,	230	Priest 5		32
BANED				
which is unwholsome, being sometimes baned meat, sometimes too salt,	265	Priest 26		22
BANES				
May yet forbid the banes and bliss.	205	Persever.	W	12
BANQUET				
Prayer the Churches banquet, Angels age, ...	51	Prayer 1		1
No hawk, or banquet, or renown, ...	69	Quidditie		3
Nor hawke, nor banquet, nor renowne, ...	69	Quidditie	W	3
The Banquet.	181	Banquet		T
Ther's no great banquet but some fares ill.	343	Proverbs		668
BANQUETTING				
Not in his parlour; banquetting the poore, ...	87	Lent		47
BAPTISM				
Thy ancient baptism which when I was foule	202	love	W	11
He adviseth all to call to minde their Baptism often; . . .	258	Priest 22		15
BAPTISME				
Whom God in Baptisme washt with his own blood.	6	Ch.-Porch		8
H. Baptisme.	43	H. Bapt.1		T
And then beyond them all my Baptisme view	43	H. Bapt.1	W	2
H. Baptisme.	44	H. Bapt.2		T
And use in baptisme, while ye pine and die:	152	The Jews		4
Such power hath mightie Baptisme to produce	191	Ch.-Milit.		45
At Baptisme, being himselfe in white, he requires the presence	258	Priest 22		1
Baptisme being a blessing, that the word hath not the like. . .	258	Priest 22		6
also to meditate on their Baptisme often (being the first step	258	Priest 22		18
that at Baptisme they professed not to be ashamed of Christs Cross,	284	Priest 35		32
for I can no more free my selfe from actuall sinnes after Baptisme,	308	Valdesso		4
then I could of Originall before, and without Baptisme. . .	308	Valdesso		5
BAPTIST				
even as John the Baptist squared out to every one (even to Souldiers)	277	Priest 32		23
BAPTIZ'D				
So many yeares baptiz'd, and not appeare?	108	Home		27
BAPTIZED				
and upon what termes, and with what vowes they were Baptized.	258	Priest 22		20
BAPTIZETH				
the presence of all, and Baptizeth not willingly, but on Sundayes,	258	Priest 22		2
BAR (see also barre)				
BARABBAS				
For choosing Barabbas a murderer	170	Self-cond.		2
BARBER				
No barber shaves so close but another finds worke. . . .	343	Proverbs		667

	PAGE	TITLE		LINE
BARE				
Whose twigs are pleasures, & they whip thee bare,	6	Ch.-Porch	W	9
When once thy foot enters the church, be bare.	22	Ch.-Porch		403
In Gods rich garden: that is bare,	75	Sunday		27
Which at a board, while many drunk bare wine,	130	Love unkn.		42
Better a bare foote then none.	323	Proverbs		78
BAREFOOT				
Hee that goes barefoot, must not plant thornes.	323	Proverbs		82
BARELY				
one of our neeces into your hands but barely what I wrote I meant,	375	Letters		5
BARGAIN				
Think heav'n a better bargain, then to give	21	Ch.-Porch		374
The bargain made to serve thee: but thy love	100	Miserie		26
No sale or bargain passe: all would disperse,	127	Giddinesse		23
And then bargain with the winde	199	L'Envoy		15
BARGAINE				
A good bargaine is a pick-purse.	321	Proverbs		12
On a good bargaine thinke twice.	339	Proverbs		529
BARGAINES				
To bee beloved is above all bargaines.	342	Proverbs		631
BARK				
Indeed he that shall so attend to the bark of the letter,	309	Valdesso		29
BARKE				
If the old dog barke he gives counsell.	327	Proverbs		197
BARKS				
An old dog barks not in vain.	358	Proverbs	D	1099
BARNE				
his garden or orchard supplyes it, or his barne, and back-side:	241	Priest 10		18
BARRE				
All my Disciples flie; fear puts a barre	28	Sacrifice		49
BARRELL				
You cannot know wine by the barrell.	321	Proverbs		20
BARREN				
A life as barren to thy praise,	57	Employm. 1		14
as barren grounds are made fruitfull by good husbandry.	292	Cornaro		12
BARRES				
O take these barres, these lengths away;	163	The Search		49
BASE				
When base men are exalted, do not bate	17	Ch.-Porch	W	265
I know thy parentage is base and low:	77	Avarice		3
and base, but to keep up with the Lord and Lady of the house,	226	Priest 2		28
BASENESSE				
When basenesse is exalted, do not bate	17	Ch.-Porch		265
BASKETS				
Where both their baskets are with all their store,	89	The Pearl	W	26
BASON				
and a Bason for Almes and offerings;	246	Priest 13		20
BATCHELORS				
We Batchelors laugh and shew our teeth,	361	Proverbs	D	1175
BATE				
Were I an Epicure, I could bate swearing.	8	Ch.-Porch		60
When basenesse is exalted, do not bate	17	Ch.-Porch		265
When base men are exalted, do not bate	17	Ch.-Porch	W	265
Thy cheere is mended; bate not of the food,	22	Ch.-Porch		393
BATHE				
Hir waters alsoe and desired Bathe.	210	Paradox	D	18
The Bathe of the Blackamoor hath sworne not to whiten.	359	Proverbs	D	1105
BATH'D				
I bath'd it often, ev'n with holy bloud,	130	Love unkn.		41
BATHED				
and brings with his own to the heavenly altar to be bathed,	231	Priest 6		9
BATHS				
Clouds cool by heat, and baths by cooling boil.	119	Providence		72
BATS				
Frogs marry fish and flesh; bats, bird and beast;	121	Providence		135
BATTELL				
And bloudie battell which thou once didst trie)	158	Praise 3		35
BAY				
The couch of time; cares balm and bay:	75	Sunday		5
BAYES				
Have I no bayes to crown it?	153	The Collar		14
BE				
The holy lines cannot be understood.	6	Ch.-Porch		10
Sure to be crosse he would shift feet and face.	7	Ch.-Porch		24
Be not a beast in courtesie; but stay,	8	Ch.-Porch		46
Lie not; but let thy heart be true to God,	9	Ch.-Porch		73
Dare to be true. Nothing can need a ly:	9	Ch.-Porch		77
Art thou a Magistrate? then be severe:	10	Ch.-Porch		85
Then all thou addest may be call'd his treasure.	11	Ch.-Porch		114
Be sure to doe it, though it be but small:	11	Ch.-Porch		116
By all means use sometimes to be alone.	12	Ch.-Porch		145
Be thriftie, but not covetous: therefore give	12	Ch.-Porch		151
Take starres for money; starres not to be told	13	Ch.-Porch		171
By any art, yet to be purchased.	13	Ch.-Porch		172
But, This with my discretion will be brave.	14	Ch.-Porch		190
But know, that nothing can so foolish be,	15	Ch.-Porch		206
Be sweet to all. Is thy complexion sowre?	15	Ch.-Porch		211
And do them not: that shall thy wisdome be;	15	Ch.-Porch		221
If that thy fame with ev'ry toy be pos'd,	15	Ch.-Porch		223
But may be wittie, if thou hast the vein.	16	Ch.-Porch		240
Have got to be a deare fool for an houre.	16	Ch.-Porch		246

BE (cont'd)

	PAGE	TITLE		LINE
Be not thine own worm: yet such jealousie,	16	Ch.-Porch		261
I care not though the cloth of state should be	17	Ch.-Porch		269
Yet be not surety, if thou be a father.	17	Ch.-Porch		277
If thou be single, all thy goods and ground	17	Ch.-Porch		283
If thou be Master-gunner, spend not all	18	Ch.-Porch		301
Be calm in arguing: for fiercenesse makes	18	Ch.-Porch		307
If truth be with thy friend, be with them both:	19	Ch.-Porch		323
Be usefull where thou livest, that they may	19	Ch.-Porch		325
So shalt thou humble and magnanimous be:	19	Ch.-Porch		332
Let thy minde still be bent, still plotting where,	20	Ch.-Porch		337
And when, and how the businesse may be done.	20	Ch.-Porch		338
Slight not the smallest losse, whether it be	20	Ch.-Porch		343
Till thou change names, and be where he began.	21	Ch.-Porch		378
Write, So much giv'n to God; thou shalt be heard.	21	Ch.-Porch		382
Thwart not th' Almighty God: O be not crosse.	22	Ch.-Porch		395
Thwart not the mighty God: O be not crosse.	22	Ch.-Porch	W	395
Though private prayer be a brave designe,	22	Ch.-Porch		397
When once thy foot enters the church, be bare.	22	Ch.-Porch		403
Praying's the end of preaching. O be drest;	23	Ch.-Porch		410
God sent him, whatsoe're he be: O tarry,	24	Ch.-Porch		442
Though it be ill, makes him no ill Physician.	24	Ch.-Porch		444
Be down, then winde up both; since we shall be	24	Ch.-Porch		455
Or that which groneth to be so,	25	Superlim		7
O let thy blessed SACRIFICE be mine,	26	The Altar		15
O let thy onely SACRIFICE be mine,	26	The Altar	W	15
And sanctifie this ALTAR to be thine.	26	The Altar		16
O let this cup passe, if it be thy pleasure:	27	Sacrifice		23
Alas! what haste they make to be undone!	27	Sacrifice		34
My face they cover, though it be divine.	31	Sacrifice		137
Your tears for your own fortunes should be kept:	31	Sacrifice		151
Which shews my bloud to be the onely way,	31	Sacrifice		158
The sonne, in whom thou dost delight to be?	33	Sacrifice		214
The sonne, in whom thou art well pleas'd to be?	33	Sacrifice	W	214
Shall I be scourged, flouted, boxed, sold?	35	Thanksgvng		7
Was such a grief as cannot be.	35	Thanksgvng		10
Shall thy strokes be my stroking? thorns, my flower?	35	Thanksgvng		13
I will not marry; or, if she be mine,	35	Thanksgvng		23
She and her children shall be thine.	35	Thanksgvng		24
His skinne, his garments bloudie be.	37	The Agonie		10
Or cannot leaves, but fruit, be signe	38	Good Fri.		11
And be my sunne.	39	Good Fri.		16
Not thriving, I resolved to be bold,	40	Redemption		2
Though it be cold, hard, foul, from loving man	41	Sepulchre		23
Can there be any day but this,	42	Easter		27
Yet though my flours be lost, they say	42	Easter	W	27
Let me be soft and supple to thy will,	44	H. Bapt.2		8
Yet lest perchance I should too happie be	48	Afflict.1		49
Her houshold to me, and I should be just.	48	Afflict.1		60
Yet, though thou troublest me, I must be meek;	48	Afflict.1		61
In weaknesse must be stout.	48	Afflict.1		62
If life be told	48	Repentance		11
What can be lower then the common manger?	50	Faith		22
Them both to be together.	52	H.Commun.		28
It cannot be. Where is that mightie joy,	56	Temper 2		1
Must all be vail'd, while he that reades, divines,	56	Jordan 1		9
The greater shall our glorie be.	57	Employm. 1		10
Show that thy brests can not be dry,	59	Whitsunday	W	21
Is more then all my deaths can be,	62	Afflict.2		3
Yet studies them, not him by whom they be.	63	Mattens		16
Blest be the God of love,	63	Even-song		1
Both to be busie, and to play.	63	Even-song		3
But much more blest be God above,	63	Even-song		4
Be crumbled into dust. Mark here below	65	Ch.-monum.		22
Be broken into dust. Mark here below	65	Ch.-monum.	W	22
His blouds sweet current much more loud to be.	66	Ch.-lock		12
Blest be the Architect, whose art	67	Ch.-floore		19
To be a window, through thy grace.	67	Windows		5
Better by worms be all once spent,	69	Content		26
Who still is right, and prayes to be so still.	73	Constancie		35
Constant unto it, making it to be	73	Afflict.3		14
Canst thou be any where	74	The Starre		3
Ordain'd the highest to be best;	79	Employm.2		13
Then should I ever laden be,	79	Employm.2		23
To be all passengers most sweet relief?	81	Christmas		8
To Man of all beasts be not thou a stranger:	81	Christmas		12
Of better lodging thou maist be possest.	80	Christmas	W	14
The shepherds sing; and shall I silent be?	81	Christmas		15
Where now we shall be better Gods then he.	82	Ungratef.		6
True Christians should be glad of an occasion	86	Lent		13
Yet are we bid, Be holy ev'n as he.	87	Lent		35
Perhaps my God, though he be farre before,	87	Lent		40
How many drammes of spirit there must be	88	The Pearl		18
Or can be, then is Man? to whose creation	90	Man		5
A beast, yet is, or should be more:	91	Man		9
And both thy servants be.	92	Man		54
Praised be the God of love,	92	Antiphon 2		1
Lord, thy praises should be more.	93	Antiphon 2		19
Praised be the God alone,	93	Antiphon 2		22
Since if my sent be good, I care not, if	94	Life		17
It be as short as yours.	94	Life		18

BE (cont'd)

	PAGE	TITLE	LINE
My minde would be extreamly stirr'd	95	Submission	3
Shall ne're be troubled with ill eyes.	96	Charms & K	2
Shall ne're be troubled with scre eyes.	96	Charms & K W	2
That all these dyings may be life in death.	99	Mortific.	36
Not he: he knows, where he can better be,	100	Miserie	10
Though it be small,	100	Miserie	23
Who would, to be thy foes.	100	Miserie	30
They will be kind, and all his pains requite,	101	Miserie W	46
Of what we might not take, or be withstood.	104	Obedience	30
And the receit shall be	106	Conscience	13
And all their motions upward be;	107	Sion	22
After all this canst thou be strange?	108	Home	26
Allureth all in hope to be	110	Brit. Ch.	14
And long may be.	110	Brit. Ch.	27
Blessed be God, whose love it was	110	Brit. Ch.	28
And he would needs a comfort be,	111	The Quip	18
And, to be short, make an oration.	111	The Quip	19
If souls be made of earthly mold,	111	Vanitie 2	11
For they can never be at rest,	111	Vanitie 2	15
Christs resurrection thine may be:	112	Dawning	10
Canst be idle? canst thou play,	113	Businesse	1
Be the season cold, or hot:	113	Businesse	10
But if yet thou idle be,	113	Businesse	15
Two lives worse then ten deaths be.	113	Businesse	28
If I say, Thou shalt be mine;	114	Dialogue	11
Look onely; for to love thee, who can be,	116	Dulnesse	27
To be the bodie and the letters both	116	Love-joy	6
Trees would be tuning on their native lute	117	Providence	10
To be exact, transcendent, and divine;	117	Providence	30
And be dispos'd, and dress'd, and tun'd by thee,	118	Providence	38
Thy skill and art, what musick would it be!	118	Providence	40
Ev'n poysons praise thee. Should a thing be lost?	119	Providence	85
To be commerce and trade from sunne to sunne.	120	Providence	108
Of what strange length must that needs be,	123	Time	25
And sayes, If he in this be crost,	123	Gratefulnes	6
And in no quiet canst thou be,	124	Gratefulnes	26
But such a heart, whose pulse may be	124	Gratefulnes	31
They shall be thick and cloudie to my breast.	126	Confession	30
There would be no commerce,	127	Giddinesse	22
Blessed be God, who prosper'd Noahs vine,	128	Bunch Gr.	24
It must be he. Your heart was dull, I fear.	130	Love unkn.	56
Wherefore be cheer'd, and praise him to the full	130	Love unkn.	68
Who fain would have you be new, tender, quick.	131	Love unkn.	70
May be reliefs,	132	Mans medly	32
Be to me rather sharp and TART,	133	Paradise	8
To such indifferents chained be,	134	The Method	18
Which needs not man, be ty'd to those	134	The Method	26
Do as ye would be done unto.	135	Divinitie	18
There can no discord but in ceasing be.	136	Ephes.	22
But runnes, although I be not drie;	136	Ephes.	29
To be in both worlds full	138	The Size	13
I must be so, if I am mine.	139	Artillerie	30
Can both the way and end be tears?	142	Pilgrimage	28
And lives: If that be all, said I,	142	Pilgrimage	34
But I was told by one, it could not be;	143	Holdfast	3
Yet I might trust in God to be my light.	143	Holdfast	4
If it be his once, all is well.	144	Discharge	20
In Christ two natures met to be thy cure.	147	Offering	6
In publick judgements one may be a nation,	147	Offering	11
Then bring thy gift; and let thy hymne be this;	147	Offering	24
To be thy praise,	148	Offering	41
And be my salvation.	148	Offering	42
O be not now	149	Longing	33
Not to relieve? how can it be,	150	Longing	62
Shall still be open; what he sends	152	The Bag	39
Shall I be still in suit?	153	The Collar	6
And be thy law,	153	The Collar	25
Although thy heap be kept	154	Glimpse	23
The wheel shall go, so that thy stay be short.	155	Glimpse	27
Who by thy coming may be made a court!	155	Glimpse	30
No such rank poyson can there be.	155	Assurance	6
Then shalt thou be my rock and tower,	156	Assurance	35
Then I or ought, or can be mine.	157	Clasping	3
Yet to be thine, doth me restore;	157	Clasping	4
If I without thee would be mine,	157	Clasping	9
I neither should be mine nor thine.	157	Clasping	10
Not thee, but me, and to be mine:	157	Clasping	15
O be mine still! still make me thine!	157	Clasping	19
That to thy chests there might be coming in	159	Praise 3	41
That to thy chest there might be coming in	159	Praise 3 V	41
So both should losers be.	160	The Pulley	15
Let him be rich and wearie, that at least,	160	The Pulley	18
But since those great ones, be they ne're so great,	161	Priesthood	19
O what pure things, most pure must those things be,	161	Priesthood	29
Or steel, or mountains be thy ring,	163	The Search	35
Since then my grief must be as large,	163	The Search	45
Be not Almightie, let me say,	163	The Search	51
When thou dost turn, and wilt be neare;	163	The Search	53
For my rough sorrows: cease, be dumbe and mute,	164	Grief	14
Could be allow'd for harmonie)	165	The Crosse	16

BE (cont'd)

	PAGE	TITLE		LINE
So that, ev'n when my hopes seem to be sped,	165	The Crosse		23
To have my aim, and yet to be	165	The Crosse		25
And ev'n in Paradise to be a weed.	165	The Crosse		30
With but foure words, my words, Thy will be done.	165	The Crosse		36
It cannot be	166	The Flower		40
Who would be more,	167	The Flower		47
Whereas if th' heart be moved,	168	a true Hymn		16
Although the verse be somewhat scant,	168	a true Hymn		17
As when th' heart sayes (sighing to be approved)	168	a true Hymn		19
I shall be one day better then before:	169	Dial.-Anth		9
Thou so much worse, that thou shalt be no more.	169	Dial.-Anth		10
That choice may be thy storie.	170	Self-cond.		6
If thy first glance so powerfull be,	172	The Glance		17
Shewing his steps should be the street,	173	Marie Magd		4
To make him clean, who could not be defil'd?	173	Marie Magd		8
And be in him new drest.	174	Aaron		20
As flesh may be;	175	The Odour		13
Good men ye be, to leave me my best room,	176	Forerunners		7
So Thou art still my God, be out of fear.	176	Forerunners		10
He will be pleased with that dittie;	176	Forerunners		11
So all within be livelier then before.	177	Forerunners		36
Or if such deceits there be,-	177	The Rose		9
Be contracted to a rose;	178	The Rose		22
Worldly joyes to be a scourge:	178	The Rose		26
Where is all, there all should be.	180	Invitation		36
God took bloud, and needs would be	182	Banquet		34
Be my dittie,	182	Banquet		50
Which cannot be,	183	A Parodie		3
Nothing can be so mean,	184	The Elixer		14
Nothing can be so low,	184	The Elixer	W	14
Cannot for lesse be told.	185	The Elixer		24
And all thy bones with beautie shall be clad.	186	Death		20
And the musick shall be praise.	187	Dooms-day		30
Let that be scann'd.	188	Judgement		14
A guest, I answer'd, worthy to be here:	189	Love 3		7
Love said, you shall be he.	189	Love 3		8
Which might the more indeare it to be thine.	190	Ch.-Milit.		12
Yet as the sunne, though forward be his flight,	190	Ch.-Milit.		31
Till all be gone. so went the Church her way,	191	Ch.-Milit.	W	33
If God and man be sever'd infinitely!	193	Ch.-Milit.		116
None will beleeve this now, though money be	193	Ch.-Milit.		119
To be a Church-man too, and wear a Mitre:	194	Ch.-Milit.		163
Yet must there such proportions be assign'd	196	Ch.-Milit.		232
Yet must there such proportion be assign'd	196	Ch.-Milit.	W	232
The spacious world and Jurie to be seen.	196	Ch.-Milit.		234
But lends to us, shall be our desolation.	197	Ch.-Milit.		258
Lendeth to us, shall be our desolation.	197	Ch.-Milit.	W	258
Blessed be God alone,	199	L'Envoy		17
Shall they be food & strength & might	201	H. Commun.	W	35
Something that may be conquest on my part	201	love	W	5
Be good to the Poor,	207	Walton 3		4
Nor canst thou be content, unlesse thou to	439	Walton 5		5
(Where nothing should be broke) to adde a Seal.	439	Walton 5		18
Theire dead, and Time shal be no more:	208	H. Danvers	D	4
And be that Idol's URN.	214	Convert	D	20
and makes that law alone to be	214	Psalm I	D	6
he shall be like an happy tree,	214	Psalm I	D	8
Therefore shall not the wicked be	215	Psalm I	D	17
shall utterly be overthrown.	215	Psalm I	D	24
the Heathen shall thy portion be.	216	Psalm II	D	20
Now therefore, O ye Kings, be wise,	216	Psalm II	D	25
be learned, ye that judge the earth:	216	Psalm II	D	26
O kiss the Son, lest he be wrath,	216	Psalm II	D	29
upon thy people be.	217	Psalm III	D	24
of corn and wine can be.	218	Psalm IV	D	28
shall be abhorr'd by thee.	218	Psalm V	D	16
with perfect joy be fill'd.	219	Psalm V	D	36
if I so guilty be:	221	Psalm VII	D	10
in that prepared be:	222	Psalm VII	D	46
shall he himself be caught.	222	Psalm VII	D	56
shall be returned home:	222	Psalm VII	D	58
to be received up into heaven, he constituted Deputies in his place,	225	Priest 1		8
Chartre of the Priesthood may be plainly gathered both the Dignity	225	Priest 1		15
whose aim and labour must be not only to get knowledg, but to subdue	226	Priest 2		9
is indeed the bent of my Discourse) the other will be manifest.	226	Priest 2		19
are in Orders, they may be received for Companions, or discoursers;	226	Priest 2		24
Wherfore they are not to be over-submissive, and base, but to keep up	226	Priest 2		28
and shall be so farre from that which they seek with their	226	Priest 2		34
and cringings, that they shall ever be despised.	226	Priest 2		36
that he may be an absolute Master and commander of himself,	227	Priest 3		8
and then they are worst, who ought to be best.	227	Priest 3		29
in keeping his word, though it be to his own hinderance, as knowing,	228	Priest 3		5
as knowing, that if he be not so, he wil quickly be discovered,	228	Priest 3		6
that if he be not so, he wil quickly be discovered, and disregarded:	228	Priest 3		6
which if it be necessary even in temporall things, how much more in	228	Priest 4		33
one and the self-same Spirit, it cannot be, but that an industrious,	229	Priest 4		7
comparing of place with place must be a singular help for the right	229	Priest 4		8
To this may be added the consideration of any text with the coherence	229	Priest 4		9
therefore the spirit of both is to be considered, and weighed.	229	Priest 4		16
one Countrey doth not bear all things, that there may be a Commerce;	229	Priest 4		24

BE (cont'd)

	PAGE	TITLE	LINE
that there may be a traffick in knowledg between the servants of God,	229	Priest 4	25
this being to be done in his younger and preparatory times, . .	230	Priest 5	5
the Church Catechisme, to which all divinity may easily be reduced.	230	Priest 5	9
that is best to be chosen, of which there is likelyest to be most	230	Priest 5	10
is best to be chosen, of which there is likelyest to be most use.	230	Priest 5	11
expounding of our Catechisme must needs be the most usefull forme.	230	Priest 5	14
or somtimes both, if his audience be intermixed.	230	Priest 5	18
or honour, be a sin of covetousnes or ambition, and when not;	230	Priest 5	27
the pleasure that comes with sleep, be sins of gluttony, drunkenness,	230	Priest 5	29
which grass will bane, or which not, how is he fit to be a shepherd?	230	Priest 5	32
and brings with his own to the heavenly altar to be bathed, . .	231	Priest 6	9
which answers also are to be done not in a hudling, or slubbering	231	Priest 6	30
If there be any of the gentry or nobility of the Parish, . .	232	Priest 6	7
admonitions, if they persevere, he causes them to be presented:	232	Priest 6	13
or if the poor Church-wardens be affrighted with their greatness,	232	Priest 6	14
notwithstanding his instruction that they ought not to be so,	232	Priest 6	16
of the hearers, that he may be heard at his returne more attentively.	232	Priest 7	24
mouth of two or three witnesses the truth may be more established.	232	Priest 7	29
and think it behoves them to be so, when God is so neer them,	233	Priest 7	10
be with them, or Christ, verse 23. which, setting aside his care	234	Priest 7	16
Therefore this care may be learn'd there, and then woven into	234	Priest 7	23
for if we be here, hee must be here, since we are here by him,	234	Priest 7	29
since we are here by him, and without him could not be here.	234	Priest 7	30
but a dictionary, and may be considered alike in all the Scripture.	235	Priest 7	10
himself, but that all may be done with reverence to his glory,	235	Priest 8	24
that how or whenever he punish him, it be not in his Ministry:	235	Priest 8	27
that the Lord would be pleased to sanctifie them all, that they may	235	Priest 8	28
and if there be any extraordinary addition to the customary . .	235	Priest 8	33
or to be entertained of them, where he takes occasion to discourse	236	Priest 8	20
and that our feet may be like hindes feet ever climbing up higher,	236	Priest 8	29
But yet as the temper of his body may be, or as the temper of his	237	Priest 9	1
or as the temper of his Parish may be, where he may have occasion	237	Priest 9	2
If he be unmarried, and keepe house, he hath not a woman in his	237	Priest 9	7
If he be unmarryed, and sojourne, he never talkes with any woman	237	Priest 9	10
and very looks, knowing himself to be both suspected, and envyed.	237	Priest 9	15
knowing that it can no way be preserved, but only by those means,	237	Priest 9	20
(though that indeed be very admirable) as at their daily temperance,	237	Priest 9	31
he findeth to be as necessary, and as difficult at least, . .	237	Priest 9	36
as to be cloathed with perfect patience, and Christian fortitude in	237	Priest 9	37
If the Parson be unmarryed, and means to continue so, he doth	238	Priest 9	24
If he be marryed, the choyce of his wife was made rather by his eare,	238	Priest 9	26
counting nothing so much his owne, as that he may be unjust unto it.	238	Priest 9	35
want a competent sustentation, nor her husband be brought in debt.	239	Priest 10	19
from the improvement of things, which otherwise would be lost.	241	Priest 10	24
unpleasant, is the naturall rule of fasting, although it be flesh.	242	Priest 10	11
if a peece of dry flesh at my table be more unpleasant to me,	242	Priest 10	13
and where flesh may be much better spared, and with more safety then	242	Priest 10	18
the Parson, if he be in full health, keeps the three obligations,	242	Priest 10	26
If his body be weak and obstructed, as most Students are, . .	242	Priest 10	28
also in diseases of exinanition (as consumptions) must be broken:	242	Priest 10	32
To all this may be added, not for emboldening the unruly, . .	242	Priest 10	33
But since both is to be done, the better sort invited, and meaner	243	Priest 11	14
of such things, and will not be perswaded, but being not invited,	243	Priest 11	21
that so both they may be encouraged to persevere, and others spurred	243	Priest 11	26
yet that will not be so:	243	Priest 11	29
that there be not a begger, or idle person in his Parish, . .	244	Priest 12	19
If his Parish be rich, he exacts this of them;	244	Priest 12	24
and if it be taken away, though justly, they will murmur, . .	244	Priest 12	28
paines in their vocation, as not knowing when they shal be relieved;	245	Priest 12	4
he inlargeth himself, if he be able, to the neighbour-hood; . .	245	Priest 12	18
For though these testimonies also may be falsifyed, yet considering	245	Priest 12	23
yet considering that the Law allows these in case they be true,	245	Priest 12	24
the two commands, we are more injoyned to be charitable, then wise.	245	Priest 12	28
to let him alone, and say rather, God be praised, God be glorified;	245	Priest 12	32
to let him alone, and say rather, God be praised, God be glorified;	245	Priest 12	33
that all things there be decent, and befitting his Name by which it	246	Priest 13	2
Therefore first he takes order, that all things be in good repair;	246	Priest 13	4
and Font be as they ought, for those great duties that are performed	246	Priest 13	6
that the Church be swept, and kept cleane without dust, . .	246	Priest 13	8
That there be fit, and proper texts of Scripture every where painted,	246	Priest 13	11
where painted, and that all the painting be grave, and reverend,	246	Priest 13	12
That all the books appointed by Authority be there, and those	246	Priest 13	14
and that there be a fitting, and sightly Communion Cloth of fine	246	Priest 13	16
The first whereof is, Let all things be done decently, and in order:	246	Priest 13	27
The second, Let all things be done to edification, 1 Cor. 14.	246	Priest 13	28
even in externall and indifferent things, what course is to be taken;	247	Priest 13	1
and put them to great shame, who deny the Scripture to be perfect.	247	Priest 13	2
if they be poor and needy, whom he thus finds labouring, . .	248	Priest 14	9
in their vocation, and himself be ever the more welcome to them.	248	Priest 14	12
for if he be a plaine countryman, he reproves him plainly; . .	248	Priest 14	17
if they be of higher quality, they commonly are quick, and sensible,	248	Priest 14	18
that he may keep himself pure, and not be intangled in others sinnes.	248	Priest 14	24
Neither in this doth he forbear, though there be company by:	248	Priest 14	25
of particularizing in these things, hee were not fit to be a Parson:	249	Priest 14	1
any continue to be refractory, yet hee gives him not over, . .	250	Priest 16	16
that if any be willing to partake, they may resort thither. . .	251	Priest 17	12
if hee be to stay for a time, hee considers diligently the state	251	Priest 17	17
what means of Piety, whether daily prayers be used, Grace, . .	251	Priest 17	23
If it be well spoken, or done, he takes occasion to commend,	252	Priest 18	4
This is to be on Gods side, and be true to his party. . . .	252	Priest 18	15

BE (cont'd)	PAGE	TITLE	LINE
propounds among his Brethren what were fitting to be done.	253	Priest 19	14
or of good report, if there be any vertue, or any praise;	253	Priest 19	25
none knowing whose turne may be next, and then when he hath	253	Priest 19	33
making together a summe either to be sent, or, which were more	253	Priest 19	37
if any neighbouring village be overburdened with poore,	254	Priest 19	1
he gives him a tester for it, if the giver be fit to receive it;	254	Priest 20	14
or if he be of a condition above such gifts, he sends him a good	254	Priest 20	14
this life, who hath promised, that Godlinesse shall be gainfull:	254	Priest 20	20
then by causing them to be presented, or otherwise complained of.	254	Priest 20	24
or hainousness of the crime may be, he is carefull to see condign	254	Priest 20	26
the Parson endeavoureth to be in Gods stead, knowing that Countrey	254	Priest 20	30
first point, and but by Catechizing, the other cannot be attained.	255	Priest 21	8
that the same common truths may be every where professed,	255	Priest 21	18
He requires all to be present at Catechizing:	255	Priest 21	26
may then by an honourable way take occasion to be better instructed.	255	Priest 21	31
In this course the order of the Catechisme would be kept,	256	Priest 21	5
How came this world to be as it is?	256	Priest 21	7
Then are there some things to be beleeved that are not seen?	256	Priest 21	9
full of such things, as are not to be seen, but beleeved?	256	Priest 21	11
This order being used to one, would be a little varyed to another.	256	Priest 21	16
the singular dexterity of Socrates in this kind may be observed,	256	Priest 21	29
Questionist must have in his mind before any question be propounded,	256	Priest 21	33
upon which and to which the questions are to be chained.	256	Priest 21	34
since man is so miserable, what is to be done?	257	Priest 21	3
only to serve in the way of drudgery, but to be washed, and cleansed,	257	Priest 21	14
cannot inflame or ravish, that must be done by a set, and laboured,	257	Priest 21	25
knowest what thou didst, when thou appointedst it to be done thus;	257	Priest 22	33
the Church-Wardens, that the elements be of the best, not cheape,	258	Priest 22	22
If there be any, who having not received yet, are to enter into this	258	Priest 22	29
particularly, the rule may be this:	258	Priest 22	33
but the Questions must be propounded loosely and wildely,	259	Priest 22	8
if there be but three Communions, neither can all the people so order	259	Priest 22	25
The Countrey Parson desires to be all to his Parish, and not onely	259	Priest 23	29
of which he gathers, in case he be ignorant himself, what to hold;	260	Priest 23	11
and cannot be gained, but that they still fall from all compromises	260	Priest 23	24
if there be any of his flock sick, hee is their Physician,	260	Priest 23	29
as may be of much use to him both for himself, and others.	261	Priest 23	3
And let Fernelius be the Phisick Authour, for he writes briefly,	261	Priest 23	5
especially let his Method of Phisick be diligently perused,	261	Priest 23	7
and the knowing of herbs may be done at such times, as they may be	261	Priest 23	9
as they may be an help, and a recreation to more divine studies,	261	Priest 23	10
and so not be drowned altogether in the works of their vocation,	261	Priest 23	23
wherein the manifold wisedome of God is wonderfully to be seen,	261	Priest 23	28
God is wonderfully to be seen, one thing would be carefully observed;	261	Priest 23	28
to know what herbs may be used in stead of drugs of the same nature,	261	Priest 23	29
if there be any of his parish that hold strange Doctrins,	262	Priest 24	19
as if he be a Papist, the Church is the hinge he turnes on;	262	Priest 24	30
whether it be a rule to it selfe, whether it hath a rule,	263	Priest 24	1
whether having a rule, it ought not to be guided by it;	263	Priest 24	3
whether any rule in the world be obscure, and how then should	263	Priest 24	3
and how then should the best be so, at least in fundamentall things,	263	Priest 24	4
that ought not to be preferred, especially since in disobeying there	263	Priest 24	10
more then indifferent, it be in our power to omit or refuse them.	263	Priest 24	13
that God cannot be wanting to them in Doctrine, to whom he is so	263	Priest 24	20
A man may be both Covetous, and Intemperate, and yet hear Sermons	264	Priest 26	14
the bounds of the action, nor when his eating begins to be unlawfull.	264	Priest 26	25
The application of the ground would be infinite;	265	Priest 26	13
which yet ought to be done, since there is a Justice in the least	265	Priest 26	31
in the least things, and for the least there shall be a judgment.	265	Priest 26	33
And Scholers ought to be diligent in the observation of these,	265	Priest 26	35
by a Common tradition, and vulgar knowledge are reputed to be so.	266	Priest 26	26
and which are described in this Book, he must be despised;	268	Priest 28	13
this is foretold, that it shall be so still, until things be no more.	268	Priest 28	15
this is foretold, that it shall be so still, until things be no more.	268	Priest 28	16
he that wil be respected, must respect;	268	Priest 28	23
if it be not thwarted, the Parson having a due respect both	268	Priest 28	32
But if the Contempt be not punishable by Law, or being so,	269	Priest 28	3
and to be sued at the Law concerning such goods for the use	270	Priest 29	3
Wherefore the Parson suffers not the place to be vilified or debased,	270	Priest 29	7
or as David says, to be even a door-keeper in the house of God.	270	Priest 29	11
yea though they be tenants, or otherwise ingaged to the delinquent:	270	Priest 29	21
certainly it should be either the sun in heaven, or the fire	271	Priest 30	10
and be preserved in that act by his sustaining power, yet if he suite	271	Priest 30	15
or if the goods be housed, a fire hath broken forth, and suddenly	271	Priest 30	24
every day of the week, and four times on Sunday, if they be well.	272	Priest 31	23
Upon this his mind begins to be perplexed, and troubled,	272	Priest 31	32
But here there are two Cautions to be added.	273	Priest 31	15
they do come, he be a little affected therewith, but not afflicted,	273	Priest 31	19
either blessing God, that he will be pleased to dwell among men;	273	Priest 31	24
throw it away, and be most confident, that God is not displeased.	273	Priest 31	38
bring strangers to him, he may be the better armed to encounter them.	274	Priest 32	7
The great and nationall sin of this Land he esteems to be Idlenesse;	274	Priest 32	9
may be prevented, or diverted by reasonable imployment.	274	Priest 32	23
every gift or ability is a talent to be accounted for, and to be	274	Priest 32	25
to be accounted for, and to be improved to our Masters Advantage.	274	Priest 32	25
the Common-wealth, that none should be idle, but all busied.	274	Priest 32	28
given it to the poor, we must not be idle, but labour to get more,	275	Priest 32	1
But if it should be, the Assertion stands thus:	275	Priest 32	10
to enter into a Calling, if they be fit for it, and it for them;	275	Priest 32	15
But it will not be amisse in this exceeding usefull point to descend	275	Priest 32	17

BE (cont'd)	PAGE	TITLE	LINE
Could men finde out this delight, they would seldome be from home;	275	Priest 32	35
the house-keepers Family be so small, and his dexterity so great,	275	Priest 32	37
he is to endeavour by all means to be a Knight or Burgess there;	277	Priest 32	9
he must not only be a morning man, but at Committees also; . .	277	Priest 32	11
but also as they may be handled, a religious imployment? . .	278	Priest 32	7
that if the Kingdome of God be first sought, all other things shall	278	Priest 33	13
all other things shall be added, even it selfe is a Sermon. . .	278	Priest 33	14
for though the temptations may be diverse in divers Christians,	279	Priest 33	1
or at least in that degree it ought to be, since he found himselfe	279	Priest 33	11
that it may be alike in all Gods children (which as concerning	279	Priest 33	21
alike in all Gods children (which as concerning weeping it cannot be,	279	Priest 33	22
Which acts of repentance are and must be found in all Gods servants:	279	Priest 33	26
where it can be, that so the body may joyn in the grief, . .	279	Priest 33	27
but that, so the other acts be, that is not necessary: . . .	279	Priest 33	28
And they must be likewise in all that are his.	280	Priest 34	11
as he discovers any of his Flock to be in one or the other state,	280	Priest 34	13
he adviseth to be very vigilant, and not to let go the raines as soon	280	Priest 34	15
but to labour still to be as fervent in Christian Duties, . .	280	Priest 34	19
If we would judg ourselves, we should not be judged; . . .	280	Priest 34	31
and if we would bound our selves, we should not be bounded. . .	280	Priest 34	32
some poore afflicted soul, and there be bountifull, and liberall;	281	Priest 34	3
though there be a great Governour of all things, yet to them he is	281	Priest 34	9
he sees not how a house could be either built without a builder,	281	Priest 34	18
Let the weather be what it will, still we have bread, though	281	Priest 34	25
there may be so evident, though unused a proof of Divinity taken from	281	Priest 34	32
especially since it may be a just doubt, whether, considering	282	Priest 34	7
intended by God, that the Jewes should be his proof, and witnesses,	282	Priest 34	12
that it should never be forgotten, but with the Gospel it selfe be	282	Priest 34	25
but with the Gospel it selfe be preached to all ages, Matth. 26. 13.	282	Priest 34	26
To these might be added the Preaching of the Gospel in all Nations,	282	Priest 34	31
in the mouth of two or three witnesses every word may be established;	283	Priest 34	19
but the despising of Love must needs be without it. . . .	283	Priest 34	25
Parson is a Lover of old Customes, if they be good, and harmlesse;	283	Priest 35	28
If there be any ill in the custome, that may be severed from	283	Priest 35	31
the custome, that may be severed from the good, he pares the apple,	283	Priest 35	32
with reconciling of differences at that time, if there be any:	284	Priest 35	7
and largesse, which at that time is, or ought to be used. . .	284	Priest 35	9
that he rather procures them to be often, as knowing that absence	284	Priest 35	15
that at Baptisme they professed not to be ashamed of Christs Cross,	284	Priest 35	32
no more then to be a spirituall Father was appropriated to them.	285	Priest 36	13
language, he shall be esteemed as ordinary complementers; . .	286	Priest 36	21
The same is to be observed in writing Letters also. . . .	286	Priest 36	25
many an evill may not only be, but also spread in his Parish,	287	Priest 37	1
without any remedy (which cannot be applyed without notice) . .	287	Priest 37	2
if it be unlawful to open faults, no benefit or advantage can make it	287	Priest 37	5
by those, which are branded for rogues, that they may be known;	287	Priest 37	20
or put into the stocks, that they may be looked upon. . . .	287	Priest 37	21
executioners, and the Law gives a malefactour to all to be defamed.	287	Priest 37	31
for all are honest, till the contrary be proved.	287	Priest 37	35
that Rogues should be known, and Charity to the publick hath	287	Priest 37	36
if the punished delinquent shall be much troubled for his sins,	288	Priest 37	2
Blessed be the God of Heaven and Earth!	289	Priest	8
Blessed be God! and the Father of all mercy!	290	Priest	1
the measure of thy love, who hast done for us as much as may be.	290	Priest	12
incomprehensible God, be ascribed all Honour, and Glory, . .	290	Priest	15
Intemperance was not such an evil, but it might easily be remedied;	291	Cornaro	6
a great desire to know the way of my life, and how I came to be so.	291	Cornaro	12
From this ill temper there remained little else to be expected of me,	291	Cornaro	24
within a few moneths I should be driven to that exigent, . .	292	Cornaro	14
to that exigent, that there would be no help for me, but Death,	292	Cornaro	15
there would be no help for me, but Death, shortly to be expected.	292	Cornaro	15
That which savours, is good and nourisheth, be consonant to truth.	293	Cornaro	10
fitted my stomack, and in such measure, as easily might be digested:	293	Cornaro	17
fearing lest I should be overthrown, they were possessed with a deep	294	Cornaro	17
and that at length I should be a conquerour, as also a little after	294	Cornaro	26
Neverthelesse at a venture two remedies might be used, letting	295	Cornaro	4
and fever (which was certainly expected) might be hindred. . .	295	Cornaro	6
that they could not be much troubled, or make a great concourse,	295	Cornaro	9
and onely commanded that my arm and legge should be set, . .	295	Cornaro	11
and regular life can hardly be altered without exceeding great	295	Cornaro	17
that old age could not be sustained with so little meat and drink;	295	Cornaro	22
which yet needs not onely to be sustained, but also to gather	295	Cornaro	23
but also to gather strength, which could not be but by meat & drink.	295	Cornaro	24
my stint of meat and drink should be diminished, rather then	295	Cornaro	30
that the patient might be proportionable to the agent, and especially	295	Cornaro	31
and permitted the quantitie of meat to be increased, yet but two	296	Cornaro	8
neither the good humours to be corrupted, or contract any ill	296	Cornaro	34
By this it may clearely be perceived, how great is the power of order	297	Cornaro	3
Neither is it to be doubted, but that he shall ever after live free	297	Cornaro	18
For indeed no man can be a perfect Physician to another, . .	297	Cornaro	24
which things in others cannot be known without such observation,	297	Cornaro	29
without such observation, as is not easily to be made upon others;	297	Cornaro	30
Wherefore one to another cannot be a perfect Physician. . .	297	Cornaro	36
then a Temperate Life, Temperance by all means is to be embraced.	298	Cornaro	2
and greatly to be esteemed for the knowing & curing of diseases,	298	Cornaro	4
how much more dearely should a Physician be esteemed, who not onely	298	Cornaro	8
that in stead of a Physician a regular life is to be embraced,	298	Cornaro	12
Many have thought that this could be done by Aurum potabile,	298	Cornaro	19
But surely there is no such matter, if Temperance be wanting.	298	Cornaro	22
which, but in that age, can hardly be perfected.	298	Cornaro	31

BE (cont'd)

	PAGE	TITLE		LINE
that an orderly life is so hard a thing that it cannot be kept.	298	Cornaro		37
and later yeares, it is no such thing which may not be performed;	299	Cornaro		7
moment (as I shewed before) if a man be temperate in meat and drink;	299	Cornaro		16
in all things wherein they deal, may be more lively and vigorous.	299	Cornaro		21
which is alreadie burdened with a disease, would be wholly oppressed.	299	Cornaro		34
so decent, and so holy, it is worthy by all means to be embraced;	300	Cornaro		4
not the qualitie for his rule, which is very easie to be observed.	300	Cornaro		16
when I was given to disorder and all the delights that could be.	302	Cornaro		11
which is altogether to be preferred before others youth:	302	Cornaro		23
may be discovered, because at these yeares (viz. 83) I have made	302	Cornaro		27
which kinde of Poems useth to be the childe of Youth, which it most	302	Cornaro		30
why should I be accounted lesse happie, or lesse my self,	302	Cornaro		34
Now lest there should be any delight wanting to my old age,	302	Cornaro		37
their youthfull appetites, although they be of a most strong temper:	303	Cornaro		13
not onely a shamefull thing to fear that which cannot be avoided;	303	Cornaro		22
Many things more might be said in commendation hereof:	303	Cornaro		33
Print it, that with it the honour of my Lord might be published.	305	Valdesso		8
All the Saints of God may be said in some sence to have put	306	Valdesso		28
it were the Authors opinion, yet the truth of it would be examined.	307	Valdesso		22
The Doctrine of the last passage must be warily understood.	308	Valdesso		1
that it is not to be understood of actuall sinnes, but habituall,	308	Valdesso		2
so it be understood with the former distinction, for Fomes is	308	Valdesso		14
as if they were both but Alphabets and after a time to be left.	309	Valdesso		20
neither can they ever be exhausted, (as Pictures may be by a plenarie	309	Valdesso		22
(as Pictures may be by a plenarie circumspection) but still even	309	Valdesso		22
learned and perfect in them, there is somewhat to be learned more:	309	Valdesso		24
both are to be done, the Scriptures still used, and Gods worke within	309	Valdesso		31
They shall be all taught of God, it being Scripture cannot be spoken	310	Valdesso		2
it being Scripture cannot be spoken to the disparagement	310	Valdesso		3
yet Peter was to be sent for, and those that have inspirations must	310	Valdesso		9
Much more might be said, but this sufficeth, he himselfe allowes it	311	Valdesso		1
we shall not be punished (which word I like here better then	311	Valdesso		26
but the truth of the Doctrine would be examined, however it may passe	312	Valdesso		1
which may be unto him as the sunne to a Travellour in his journey,	312	Valdesso		18
the person here described to be in the dark, ought to use the first,	312	Valdesso	V	25
except there be a restraining motion (as S. Paul had when hee would	313	Valdesso		15
Wherefore as David's Adultery cannot be excused, so need	316	Valdesso		6
and they are to be judged according to the outward fact,	316	Valdesso		18
unlesse it be evident to others, as well as to themselves,	316	Valdesso		19
So may a warre be just on both sides, and was just in the Canaanites	316	Valdesso		29
There is no more to be said of this Chapter but that his opinion	318	Valdesso		5
And miracle-working as it may be severed from justifying faith,	319	Valdesso		12
so it may be a fruit of it, and an exaltation. 1 John 5. 14.	319	Valdesso		13
this were the Authors opinion, yet the truth of it would be examined.	319	Valdesso	V	16
A Cake and an ill custome must be broken.	322	Proverbs		27
A caske and an ill custome must both of them be broken.	322	Proverbs	V	27
Love and a Cough cannot be hid.	322	Proverbs		49
Were there no hearers, there would be no backbiters.	323	Proverbs		69
All truths are not to be told.	324	Proverbs		89
Keepe good men company, and you shall be of the number.	325	Proverbs		120
Better to be blinde, then to see ill.	325	Proverbs		126
A garden must be lookt unto and drest as the body.	325	Proverbs		129
Though the Mastiffe be gentle, yet bite him not by the lippe.	325	Proverbs		132
Though the Mastiffe be gentile, yet bite him not by the lippe.	325	Proverbs	V	132
Though a lie be well drest, it is ever overcome.	325	Proverbs		133
What your glasse telles you, will not be told by Councell.	329	Proverbs		255
Let an ill man lie in thy straw, and he lookes to be thy heire.	330	Proverbs		271
Say no ill of the yeere, till it be past.	331	Proverbs		297
Bee not a Baker, if your head be of butter.	332	Proverbs		321
how that which is to come will be drawne on.	332	Proverbs		329
He that will be served must bee patient.	333	Proverbs		354
Hee that demands misseth not, unlesse his demands be foolish.	333	Proverbs		359
Hee that's fed at anothers hand may stay long ere he be full.	336	Proverbs		439
Who is fed by anothers hand stays long ere he be full.	336	Proverbs	V	439
He that would be well, needs not goe from his owne house.	336	Proverbs		442
let him be wise in the punishment.	340	Proverbs		555
He that mockes a cripple, ought to be whole.	340	Proverbs		565
'Tis hard to be wretched, but worse to be knowne so.	340	Proverbs		577
It's better to be the head of a Lyzard, then the tayle of a Lyon.	340	Proverbs		579
It's better to be the head of a mouse, then the tayle of a Lyon.	340	Proverbs	V	579
If the staffe be crooked, the shadow cannot be straight.	341	Proverbs		583
Speake fitly, or be silent wisely.	342	Proverbs		625
He cannot be vertuous that is not rigorous.	343	Proverbs		664
That which will not be spun,	343	Proverbs		665
If things were to be done twice, all would be wise.	344	Proverbs		700
If all things might be done twice, all would be wise.	343	Proverbs	V	700
Three can hold their peace, if two be away.	345	Proverbs		714
Be what thou wouldst seeme to be.	345	Proverbs		724
To be too busie gets contempt.	346	Proverbs		738
take not to serve you, if you will be served neately.	347	Proverbs		794
God, and Parents, and our Master, can never be requited.	348	Proverbs		805
Religion, Credit, and the Eye are not to be touched.	349	Proverbs		837
It's good tying the sack before it be full.	349	Proverbs		842
Hee that would be a Gentleman, let him goe to an assault.	350	Proverbs		878
Wine that cost nothing is digested before it be drunke.	352	Proverbs		932
Better be a foole then a knave.	352	Proverbs		961
You may be on land, yet not in a garden.	353	Proverbs		964
If the husband be not at home, there is nobodie.	354	Proverbs		1016
An oath that is not to bee made is not to be kept.	354	Proverbs		1017
a space ought to be interposed.	356	Proverbs	D	40

BE (cont'd)

	PAGE	TITLE	LINE
Nothing is to be presumed on, or despaired of.	356	Proverbs	D 56
For the same man to be an heretick	357	Proverbs	D 1058
Heresie may be easier kept out, then shooke off.	357	Proverbs	D 1059
No naked man is sought after to be rifled.	357	Proverbs	D 1063
Not only ought fortune to be pictured on a wheel,	358	Proverbs	D 1077
He that will do thee a good turne, either he will be gon or dye.	358	Proverbs	D 1083
Hee that makes himself a sheep, shall be eat by the wolfe.	358	Proverbs	D 1089
He that will be surety, shall pay.	358	Proverbs	D 1091
We do it soon enough, if that we do be well.	359	Proverbs	D 1109
There is an hour wherein a man might be happy	360	Proverbs	D 1143
Wo be to him that reads but one book.	360	Proverbs	D 1146
Tithe, and be rich.	360	Proverbs	D 1147
A man is known to be mortal by two things, Sleep and Lust.	361	Proverbs	D 1159
Presents of love fear not to be ill taken of strangers.	361	Proverbs	D 1162
by the hand of man may be overturned.	362	Proverbs	D 1184
to declare my resolution to be, that my poor Abilities in Poetry,	363	Letters	11
in Poetry, shall be all, and ever consecrated to Gods glory.	363	Letters	12
And therefore let it be sufficient for me, that the same heart,	363	Letters	17
I dare no longer be silent, least while I think I am modest,	364	Letters	7
and shall I then be fain alwayes to borrow Books, and build	364	Letters	13
if there be any truth in me, I find it little enough to keep me in	364	Letters	31
there be any course, either by engaging my future Annuity,	365	Letters	20
I desire you, Sir, to be my Mediator to them in my behalf.	365	Letters	21
and if there be any such which you have found useful to yourself,	366	Letters	4
you see in Frenchmen, whether it be in knowledge, or in fashion,	366	Letters	8
Let there be no kind of excellency which it is possible for you	366	Letters	13
be proud, not with a foolish vanting of yourself when there is no	366	Letters	16
but upon the want of those Books which were not to be got in England;	367	Letters	5
that if any course could be taken of doubling my Annuity now,	367	Letters	7
into a Benefice, I should be most glad to entertain it, and both pay	367	Letters	10
It is high time now that I should be no more a burden to you,	367	Letters	13
Sister this week already, and therefore now I hope may be excused.	367	Letters	22
yet that will be about 30 l. per an. but the commodiousness is beyond	369	Letters	32
makes all the Orations, be it to King, Prince, or whatever comes	369	Letters	34
but that I have both time and work to be Your extreme Servant,	370	Letters	14
no such earthiness in it, but it may very well be joined with Heaven;	370	Letters	23
cause this inclosed to be carried to his brothers house of his own	370	Letters	26
whether my peace be yet made with her concerning my unkind departure.	371	Letters	8
Can I be so happy, as to hear of both these that they succeed well?	371	Letters	9
when I shall understand that a Letter will be seasonable,	371	Letters	15
I beseech you to be chearful, and comfort your self in the God of all	372	Letters	24
alwaies observ'd the thred of Life to be like other threds or skenes	373	Letters	4
Offices for which I came into the world, and must yet be kept in it;	373	Letters	10
So that now if they do not well the falt cannot be charg'd on you;	373	Letters	15
of what poor regard ought they to be, since if we had Riches we are	373	Letters	23
I never find Blessed be the Rich;	373	Letters	30
or, Blessed be the Noble;	373	Letters	30
but, Blessed be the Meek, and Blessed be the Poor, and,	373	Letters	31
Blessed be the Meek, and Blessed be the Poor, and, Blessed be	373	Letters	31
and, Blessed be the Mourners, for they shall be comforted.	373	Letters	32
as if they not only not desir'd, but, even fear'd to be blessed.	373	Letters	34
and yours (which praised be God are less) are not like to continue	374	Letters	2
consider that God intends that to be as a sacred Temple for himself	374	Letters	9
or, allow that any sadness shall be his Competitor.	374	Letters	12
be careful for nothing. What can be said more comfortably?	374	Letters	28
What can be said more comfortably?	374	Letters	28
and age, and knew none but one who could be no company to them.	375	Letters	15
power to defeat my charity, and evill shold be stronger then good:	376	Letters	10
and still they will be presenting or wishing to see, if at length	376	Letters	28
though it be none of the Court-stile, yet doubtless Madam,	377	Letters	2
and you have no cause to be sorry, since it is GOD's business.	377	Letters	21
upon my accompt, & give you my self for it, to be yours for ever.	378	Letters	5
Gods earth, no not tho' the advice step so far, as to be reproof:	378	Letters	13
whome I esteem to be God's faithfull & diligent Servant,	378	Letters	14
you any other wayes, as neyther I my self desire to be considered.	378	Letters	16
all your Addresses, & for ought I see, they are ever to be liked.	378	Letters	17
be amongst the chiefest also, so also have I required Mr W. for his	378	Letters	22
one to the other, that ye may be a heavenly comfort, to his prayse,	378	Letters	26
to name at first, what the summe should be, but he told her Grace,	379	Letters	6
that he would by no meanes do so, urging, that Charity must be free.	379	Letters	8
Blessed be My God & Dear Master, the Spring & Fountain of all	379	Letters	16
doubt not, through Gods blessing, but it shall be to the full;	379	Letters	18
Higher opportunities of doeing good are to be preferred before lower,	380	Woodnoth	3
are lovely, & of good report if there be any vertue or any praise.	380	Woodnoth	14
things inwardly good to have an eye to the world may be pharisaicall:	380	Woodnoth	16
long God knocks at our harts, before he be heard, & yet desists not.	381	Woodnoth	2
to be without dores with him, is no ill company.	381	Woodnoth	3
Doe this & be a man as David, after Gods hart.	381	Woodnoth	21
with his favours, can not but be not only allowable but commendable.	381	Woodnoth	26
bequeath unto my Neeces equally to be devided betweene them excepting	382	G.H.'s Will	13
of my deceased Neece which are to be payd out of it unto some whose	382	G.H.'s Will	14
payd out of it unto some whose names shal be annexed unto this bill.	382	G.H.'s Will	15
unto the poore of this parish to be devided according to my deare	382	G.H.'s Will	17
is that Mr Woodnoth should be mine Executor to whome I bequeath	382	G.H.'s Will	28
pound whereof fifteene pound shal be bestowed uppon Leighton Church,	382	G.H.'s Will	29
Sir John Danvers that he would be pleased to be Overseer of this	382	G.H.'s Will	32
John Danvers that he would be pleased to be Overseer of this Will.	382	G.H.'s Will	32
those that are crost are discharged already the rest are to be payd.	383	G.H.'s Will	4
due to Mrs Judeth Spenser is to be payd to Mrs Mary Lawly at Chelsey	383	G.H.'s Will	21
if there be any body els that owe me any thing else of old debt I	383	G.H.'s Will	26

BE (cont'd)	PAGE	TITLE		LINE
same order and habit, of which wee all in this Kingdome glorie to be.	442	Oration		22
Fame is sowne in this age, that it may be reaped in the following;	443	Oration		4
let the first be the care of your Excellencies;	443	Oration		4
BEACON				
Or a fir'd beacon frighteth from his ditties.	16	Ch.-Porch		250
BEADES				
The beades in the Hand,	358	Proverbs	D	1082
BEADS				
Drops bloud (the onely beads) my words to measure:	27	Sacrifice		22
BEAM				
Then by a sunne-beam I will climbe to thee.	63	Mattens		20
The beam and scape	141	Justice 2		9
BEAMES				
Which know not thee, suck in thy beames	203	Even-song	W	23
Yet thy brave beames excluded from their right	211	Bohemia	D	10
BEAMS				
You give us teares to wash them: lett those beams	44	H. Bapt.1	W	7
Where beams surround my Saviours face,	74	The Starre		2
Among the beams, which crown the face	74	The Starre		22
Unto that hive of beams	74	The Starre		31
His beams shall cheer my breast, and both so twine,	81	Christmas		33
Till ev'n his beams sing, and my musick shine.	81	Christmas		34
That thy bright beams may tame thy bow.	97	Afflict.5		24
At least those beams of truth, which onely save,	135	Divinitie		15
BEANE				
A beane in liberty is better then a comfit in prison.	343	Proverbs		653
BEAR (noun)				
That God who hath delivered me out of the paws of the Lyon and Bear,	374	Letters		7
BEAR				
In clothes, cheap handsomnesse doth bear the bell.	14	Ch.-Porch		187
For these are all the grapes Sion doth bear,	31	Sacrifice		162
From th' earth unto my brows, and bear the thrall:	32	Sacrifice		167
My crosse I bear my self, untill I faint:	33	Sacrifice		197
O let thy blessed Spirit bear a part,	42	Easter		17
Must bear the longest part.	53	Antiphon 1		12
Must bear the chiefest part.	53	Antiphon 1	V	12
Bear all the sway, possessing heart and brain,	54	Love 1		7
And bear the bundle, wheresoe're it goes:	88	The Pearl		17
Many a fault more then my lease will bear;	129	Love unkn.		20
To bear.	150	Longing		66
So doth thy nearenesse bear the bell,	163	The Search		59
To bear them out, and with my state agree.	164	Grief		8
To guide, thy staffe to bear.	173	23 Psalme		16
To bear her filth; and that her sinnes did dash	173	Marie Magd		14
Then showres Religion, and makes all to bear.	192	Ch.-Milit.		88
and that as one Countrey doth not bear all things, that there may be	229	Priest 4		24
shall much better brooke and bear a draught of beer, then if it had	242	Priest 10		23
for quantity eats more then his health or imployments will bear,	266	Priest 26		8
as he that eats more then his estate will bear, is a Prodigall;	266	Priest 26		9
as knowing that nature will not bear everlasting droopings,	267	Priest 27		34
to bud, blow and bear fruit in your Soul, to his glory,	377	Letters		6
BEARE				
Mine own Apostle, who the bag did beare,	27	Sacrifice		13
Three helping one another, beare the burthen of sixe.	325	Proverbs		135
The eye and Religion can beare no jesting.	326	Proverbs		158
Beare with evill, and expect good.	338	Proverbs		511
BEARER				
and sent, which to the bearer is but paper, but to the receiver,	282	Priest 34		37
BEARES				
Which now that moist land to thee beares.	213	L' Envoy	D	6
whose sins he then beares, and brings with his own to the heavenly	231	Priest 6		8
which he every where beares towards our deare [great] Master	305	Valdesso		4
BEARING				
Trees after bearing drop their leaves for soil:	119	Providence		70
they have their Law and Language bearing witnesse to them,	281	Priest 34		36
but the spirits bearing witnesse with our spirit, revealing	309	Valdesso		3
BEARS				
In conversation boldnesse now bears sway.	15	Ch.-Porch		205
And not the beast, that bears it on his back.	17	Ch.-Porch		268
Then Simon bears it for me by constraint,	33	Sacrifice		198
And more: He is a tree, yet bears no fruit;	91	Man		8
And more: He is a tree, yet bears more fruit;	91	Man	W	8
Will not a verse run smooth that bears thy name?	206	Walton 1		11
BEAST				
All worldly right, save what he hath by beast.	7	Ch.-Porch		36
Be not a beast in courtesie; but stay,	8	Ch.-Porch		46
And not the beast, that bears it on his back.	17	Ch.-Porch		268
That as each beast his cure doth know,	39	Good Fri.		19
That, as each beast his manger knows,	76	Sunday		38
A beast, yet is, or should be more:	91	Man		9
Where all may reach: no beast but knows his feed.	118	Providence		50
Frogs marry fish and flesh; bats, bird and beast;	121	Providence		135
Not rudely, as a beast,	184	The Elixer		5
The Wolfe knowes, what the ill beast thinkes.	321	Proverbs		16
The beast that goes alwaies never wants blowes.	329	Proverbs		260
Hee a beast doth die, that hath done no good to his country.	354	Proverbs		993
BEASTS				
Then may the beasts draw thee to happy light.	16	Ch.-Porch		264
Where all the beasts and fowls by their command	70	Humilitie		3
Where all the beasts and Foule by their command	70	Humilitie	W	3

BEASTS (cont'd)	PAGE	TITLE		LINE
When by the beasts the presents tendred were,	70	Humilitie		7
Till they fell out: which when the beasts espied,	70	Humilitie		21
Against the beasts: so joyntly bandying,	71	Humilitie		29
Against the beasts: so joyntly banding,	71	Humilitie	V	29
To Man of all beasts be not thou a stranger:	81	Christmas		12
Beasts fain would sing; birds dittie to their notes;	117	Providence		9
The beasts say, Eat me: but, if beasts must teach,	117	Providence		21
Preferring, like brute beasts, a lothsome den	167	Dotage		15
sacrifices as they did of old, which was of beasts devoyd of reason;	232	Priest 6		5
when they set themselves to work like brute beasts, never raising	248	Priest 14		1
the place was moorish and unhealthy, fitter for beasts then men.	301	Cornaro		27
All beasts of prey are strong or treacherous.	355	Proverbs		1023
BEAT				
No man shall beat into his head,	100	Miserie		15
If, though thou didst not beat thy future brow,	144	Discharge		23
BEATE				
Beate the dog before the Lyon.	348	Proverbs		825
BEATRICE				
George Herbert one hundred pound To Mrs Beatrice Herbert forty pound,	383	G.H.'s Will		7
BEAUTEOUS				
Their beauteous glories. Onely shreds of thee,	140	Ch.-rents		9
Beautie and beauteous words should go together.	177	Forerunners		30
BEAUTIE				
Makes all their beautie his deformitie.	23	Ch.-Porch		420
Sprung from that beautie which can never fade;	54	Love 1		2
Sprung from the beautie which can never fade;	54	Love 1	W	2
Wit fancies beautie, beautie raiseth wit:	54	Love 1		9
Become a verse? Is there in truth no beautie?	56	Jordan 1		2
Both are our cleanlinesse. Hath one such beautie?	92	Man		41
Beautie in thee takes up her place,	109	Brit. Ch.		4
Beautie in thee takes up the place,	109	Brit. Ch.	V	4
First, Beautie crept into a rose,	110	The Quip		5
Beautie alone to me:	115	Dulnesse		10
A rose, besides his beautie, is a cure.	119	Providence		78
Your health and beautie both began to break.	140	Ch.-rents		20
Then beautie flow'd, then wisdome, honour, pleasure:	160	The Pulley		7
True beautie dwells on high: ours is a flame	177	Forerunners		28
Beautie and beauteous words should go together.	177	Forerunners		30
As if they could beautie spare.	177	The Rose		8
And all thy bones with beautie shall be clad.	186	Death		20
BEAUTIES				
Makes beauties here;	115	Dulnesse		16
BEAUTIFULL				
are verie beautifull and convenient above most in this age,	301	Cornaro		11
BEAUTY				
Turns all their beauty to his uglines.	23	Ch.-Porch	W	420
Both are our cleanlines: if one have beauty,	92	Man	W	41
The beauty lies in the discovery.	206	Walton 2		14
Whose native beauty needs not dresse or lace	212	Bohemia	D	30
My beauty wears and doth decay	220	Psalm VI	D	17
and liberall disposition he preferred before beauty, riches,	238	Priest 9		29
I am much pleased also in my travells, with the beauty of situation.	302	Cornaro		6
A poore beauty finds more lovers then husbands.	337	Proverbs		481
Beauty drawes more then oxen.	344	Proverbs		685
BEAUTY'S				
Frail Beauty's Charms to Heav'n did raise,	214	Convert	D	13
BECAME				
Till he became	43	East.wings		4
That I became	43	East.wings		14
Till I became	43	East.wings	W	14
Who by not keeping once, became a debter;	152	The Jews		5
Nay, he became a poet, and would serve	193	Ch.-Milit.		131
A gown and pen became him wondrous well:	194	Ch.-Milit.		167
of a cheerfull and merrie man I became melancholie and cholerick;	296	Cornaro		15
BECAUSE				
Because no knowledg, is not earth but mudd.	7	Ch.-Porch	W	36
Because to shun them also is so cheap:	9	Ch.-Porch		68
Because 'tis better, and perhaps may save thee.	22	Ch.-Porch		394
Because the raging waters still are high:	29	Sacrifice		95
Because this box we know;	82	Ungratef.		23
Should thicken all my powers; because my lust	83	Sighs & Gr.		15
Herbs gladly cure our flesh; because that they	91	Man		23
Because the benefit accrues to me.	117	Providence		28
I blesse thee, Lord, because I GROW	132	Paradise		1
Then thou to grant mine: but because	139	Artillerie		23
Because thou art	143	Complaining		2
Because I am	143	Complaining		4
Mothers are kinde, because thou art,	148	Longing		14
Because the search was dumbe before:	162	The Search		23
Because thou dost abide with me,	183	A Parodie		4
Still eastward go; because it drew more neare	198	Ch.-Milit.		276
You whoe admire yourselves because	209	Paradox	D	1
because of all my foes:	219	Psalm V	D	22
Because against thy Majesty	219	Psalm V	D	33
because of all mine Enemies;	220	Psalm VI	D	18
Save me, my Lord, my God, because	220	Psalm VII	D	1
and because they have different Names, think their Office different.	226	Priest 2		20
And because the two highest points of Life, wherein a Christian is	227	Priest 3		3
because Countrey people live hardly, and therefore as feeling their	227	Priest 3		12
Secondly because Luxury is a very visible sinne, the Parson is very	227	Priest 3		21

BECAUSE (cont'd)	PAGE	TITLE	LINE
but especially that of drinking, because it is the most popular vice;	227	Priest 3	24
because Countrey people (as indeed all honest men) do much esteem	228	Priest 3	1
because people by what they understand, are best led to what they	228	Priest 4	19
because they feel them not, and because they are not understood	228	Priest 4	31
and because they are not understood but with the same Spirit that	228	Priest 4	31
because all ages have thought that a competency, and he that profits	235	Priest 7	11
because those trades, for the most part, serve but the vices	240	Priest 10	3
servants, both because they do best, and because what they do,	240	Priest 10	15
both because they do best, and because what they do, is blessed,	240	Priest 10	16
because countrey people are very observant of such things,	243	Priest 11	20
This I do, because at such, and such a time you were charitable.	254	Priest 20	17
not hold in Christianity, because it contains things above nature:	256	Priest 21	24
because to answer in form may still admit ignorance:	259	Priest 22	7
The Feast indeed requires sitting, because it is a Feast;	259	Priest 22	13
because the natures of these vices being not evidently discussed,	264	Priest 26	17
because of the suddain passing from that which was just now lawfull,	264	Priest 26	20
not because they are all that are of this dark, and creeping	265	Priest 26	2
for example sake, and because they are most common, he thus thinks:	265	Priest 26	3
because wealth is given to that end to supply our occasions.	265	Priest 26	8
because men usually think, that servants for their mony are as other	265	Priest 26	23
an act against reason, because it is unnaturall to hurt ones self;	266	Priest 26	22
of themselves in time of eating, which because it is deceitfull;	267	Priest 26	2
because diseases of exinanition are more dangerous, then diseases	267	Priest 26	13
because hee knows nothing but the Crosse of Christ, his minde being	267	Priest 27	27
not onely because all men shun the company of perpetuall severity,	268	Priest 27	2
because this hath been the portion of God his Master, and of Gods	268	Priest 28	13
in my heart) because this kinde of Prayer is additionary,	273	Priest 31	36
And because Idleness is twofold, the one in having no calling,	274	Priest 32	15
because when we have sold all, and given it to the poor,	274	Priest 32	32
Now because the onely opposer to this Doctrine is the Gallant,	275	Priest 32	5
because we are about a Calling, and a preparation thereunto.	276	Priest 32	36
because it is the key of Commerce, and discovers the Rules	277	Priest 32	32
because notwithstanding his infinite hate of sinne, his Love overcame	283	Priest 34	13
because Countrey people are much addicted to them, so that to favour	283	Priest 35	28
because there are contained therein 4 manifest advantages.	284	Priest 35	2
out of niceness, because they like the salutations, and complements,	285	Priest 36	4
Or else, because they think it empty and superfluous.	285	Priest 36	8
because it is not performed by way of request, but of confidence,	286	Priest 36	6
because infamy is a part of the sentence against malefactours,	287	Priest 37	18
Ride on Lord, because of the word of truth, and meeknesse,	289	Priest	22
because divers worthy young men have obliged me unto it.	291	Cornaro	7
because from the time that I was made whole, I never since departed	293	Cornaro	24
because in his meats and drinks he kept a due moderation;	294	Cornaro	8
no inconvenience thereby, because that humour abounded not in me.	294	Cornaro	22
because by eating little he prolongs his life.	295	Cornaro	35
because this will cut off all causes of diseases, so that he shall	297	Cornaro	20
because they say, It is better to please the Appetite (though they	298	Cornaro	26
live regularly, because they must often endure heats, and colds,	299	Cornaro	13
because Temperance takes away the cause of diseases:	300	Cornaro	1
For I eat little, because a little sufficeth my weak stomack:	300	Cornaro	8
I abstain from fruit, and fish, and the like, because they hurt me.	300	Cornaro	10
Because since this is at the best but uncertain, dangerous,	300	Cornaro	19
because that after one is once sixtie five yeares old, all the time	300	Cornaro	28
because many wayes thither are so ordered, that they all meet and end	301	Cornaro	20
because the place was moorish and unhealthy, fitter for beasts then	301	Cornaro	26
Because that by Temperance and the Grace of God I feel not those	302	Cornaro	23
because at these yeares (viz. 83) I have made a most pleasant	302	Cornaro	28
because I have now a clearer voice, then ever I had in my life.	303	Cornaro	7
Because such are daily exposed to a thousand dangers and deaths,	303	Cornaro	14
because that by the regularitie of my life I have shut out death all	303	Cornaro	27
because I would doe nothing negligently that you commit unto mee;	304	Valdesso	4
because even the godly are chastized but not punished) for evill	311	Valdesso	28
because the Scripture invites enough, for it invites us to all good,	313	Valdesso	18
but because he cannot doe all, God often chuseth which he shall doe,	313	Valdesso	21
because the anointing which we have received, and abideth in us,	314	Valdesso V	5
is in some sort true because they are spiritually discerned,	315	Valdesso	31
The dog gnawes the bone because he cannot swallow it.	337	Proverbs	457
Forbeare not sowing because of birds.	343	Proverbs	670
Now I write to you, Sir, because to you I have ever opened my heart;	365	Letters	23
Letter in yours, for it was because I know your Lodging, but not his.	367	Letters	24
because my recompenses of your favours consist in this only.	367	Letters	31
who because of his importunities gave him a reward, but not so great	368	Letters	31
I was the better content because I was in hope I should my self carry	372	Letters	15
because sickness hath made me unable to perform those Offices	373	Letters	8
because they were to come into an unknown country, tender in	375	Letters	13
David built the temple as much as Solomon because he desired it,	381	Woodnoth	20
BECK			
hath so many dispersed Officers at his beck throughout the Kingdome,	276	Priest 32	11
BECKEN			
When wanton pleasures becken us to thrall.	11	Ch.-Porch	118
From his Ecliptick line: becken the skie.	12	Ch.-Porch	137
But time did becken to the flowers, and they	94	Life	4
BECOME			
Become a verse? Is there in truth no beautie?	56	Jordan 1	2
As mens returns, what would become of fools?	147	Offering	2
When God vouchsafeth to become our fare,	161	Priesthood	27
I passe not, I, what of the rest become,	176	Forerunners	9
men to Piety, and is content, if at least so, they will become good:	244	Priest 11	1
evils which had so long beset me, and were almost become incurable;	293	Cornaro	21
I gave the mouse a hole, and she is become my heire.	324	Proverbs	94

BEE (cont'd)	PAGE	TITLE	LINE
nor wise at 50, will never bee handsome, strong, rich, or wise.	333	Proverbs	349
He that will be served must bee patient.	333	Proverbs	354
Hee that would bee well old, must bee old betimes. . . .	334	Proverbs	371
Hee that knowes what may bee gained in a day never steales. . .	336	Proverbs	445
To bee beloved is above all bargaines.	342	Proverbs	631
Good newes may bee told at any time, but ill in the morning.	350	Proverbs	877
The little cannot bee great, unlesse he devoure many. . . .	351	Proverbs	922
Sinnes are not knowne till they bee acted.	352	Proverbs	942
that a man would desire straight to bee buried there. . . .	353	Proverbs	969
When all men have what belongs to them, it cannot bee much. . .	353	Proverbs	979
An oath that is not to bee made is not to be kept. . . .	354	Proverbs	1017
If you would bee at ease, all the world is not.	355	Proverbs	1019
The life of spies is to know, not bee known.	357	Proverbs	D 1068
He that hath but one eye, must bee afraid to lose it. . . .	358	Proverbs	D 1088
Bee covetous, then, of all good which you see in Frenchmen, . .	366	Letters	7
that the time after the Holydaye will bee fruitfuller of novelties,	368	Letters	3
observed on Christmas day to bee so devout as to come to the Chappell	368	Letters	17
to bee united with that cloud, which useth to infuse so great	442	Oration	14
your Excellencies to bee more deare unto us, in that you are	442	Oration	20
How could you bee like great Alexander, unlesse Historie delivered	443	Oration	2
BEE'S			
Every bees hony is sweet.	341	Proverbs	609
BEEFE			
it consisteth most of mutton, beefe, and veal, if he addes any thing	241	Priest 10	17
BEEING			
All things in their beeing are good for something. . . .	339	Proverbs	520
BEEN (see also bin)			
Man would have been th' incloser: but since now	7	Ch.-Porch	20
Had to this day been an Egyptian slave.	27	Sacrifice	10
Having been tenant long to a rich Lord, ...	40	Redemption	1
For so thou should'st without me still have been, ...	52	H.Commun.	5
What house more stately hath there been, ...	90	Man	4
And two deaths had been thy fee.	113	Businesse	22
Full well I understood, who had been there:	130	Love unkn.	54
And jagg'd his seamlesse coat, had that been fine, ...	134	Divinitie	11
Which hath been broken now so long, ...	150	Longing	74
Know that much had been his worth;	208	J. Danvers	D 14
means to continue so, he doth at least, as much as hath been said.	238	Priest 9	25
This was not so well said, as it might have been forborn; . .	252	Priest 18	9
but that they still fall from all compromises that have been made.	260	Priest 23	25
because this hath been the portion of God his Master, and of Gods	268	Priest 28	14
but to go on as cheerfully, as if he had not been interrupted.	273	Priest 31	12
He that hath been sick of a Consumption, and knows what recovered	278	Priest 33	25
And if the same person had been sick of all diseases, and were	278	Priest 33	30
if he had been at the Creation of all things, should lesse beleeve	281	Priest 34	28
where he knowes there hath been or is a little difference, . .	284	Priest 35	19
passed judgment, & been corrected either by whipping, or imprisoning,	287	Priest 37	15
would have been an ornament to the world, and a comfort to their	291	Cornaro	4
the Authors sake, whom I conceive to have been a true servant of God;	304	Valdesso	6
but he might have been justly put to death for it by the Magistrate,	316	Valdesso	24
and yet he had been punished justly, that is in humano foro &	316	Valdesso	27
The wolfe eats oft of the sheep that have been warn'd. . . .	360	Proverbs	D 1134
in that I apprehend what my Friends would have been forward to say,	364	Letters	20
for it hath been my fortune of late to have such sudden warning,	365	Letters	31
knows also that my solliciting him has been much, and my tears many	372	Letters	3
how they have been burnt by thousands, and have endur'd such other	373	Letters	36
being more beggarly now than I have been these many years, . .	376	Letters	1
BEENE			
By suppers more have beene killed then Galen ever cured. . .	330	Proverbs	272
If the mother had not beene in the oven, ...	344	Proverbs	696
BEER			
shall much better brooke and bear a draught of beer, then if it had	242	Priest 10	23
BEES			
Neither bring hony with the bees, ...	57	Employm. 1	18
O raise me then! poore bees, that work all day, ...	61	Praise 1	17
Of laden Bees;	79	Employm.2	W 22
Bees work for man; and yet they never bruise	118	Providence	65
BEFALL			
As well what should befall, as what befell.	193	Ch.-Milit.	130
That nothing befall him unworthy of that Majesty before which he is	235	Priest 8	23
wonder how this opinion could befall so good a man as it seems	317	Valdesso	31
BEFALLS			
onely upon a hope of an happie issue, which yet befalls verie few.	300	Cornaro	24
BEFALS			
whatsoever befals us we must alwaies, at all times rejoyce in	374	Letters	25
BEFELL			
How shall I count what thee befell, ...	38	Good Fri.	3
And well it was for thee, when this befell, ...	144	Discharge	16
As well what should befall, as what befell.	193	Ch.-Milit.	130
BEFITS			
he may behave himself so as befits so great a presence; . .	273	Priest 31	27
BEFITTING			
things there be decent, and befitting his Name by which it is called.	246	Priest 13	2
BEFORE			
When once it is within thee; but before	7	Ch.-Porch	26
His minde with rest, before his trunk with riches:	11	Ch.-Porch	110
His minde with rest, before his trunks with riches:	11	Ch.-Porch	W 110
Before thy journey fairly part with all.	13	Ch.-Porch	162
Let thy almes go before, and keep heav'ns gate	21	Ch.-Porch	383
In three dayes raz'd, and raised as before.	28	Sacrifice	66

BEFORE (cont'd)

	PAGE	TITLE		LINE
That he before me well nigh suffereth:	31	Sacrifice		147
Then with the reed they gave to me before,	32	Sacrifice		169
But thou wast up before myne houre	42	Easter	W	21
Before that I could feare.	46	Afflict.1	W	16
Before I had the power to change my life.	47	Afflict.1		42
That which before was darkned clean	51	Faith		37
Before that sinne turn'd flesh to stone,	53	H.Commun.		29
Our eies shall see thee, which before saw dust;	54	Love 2		9
Before I were by frosts extremitie	57	Employm. 1		3
That which was dust before, doth quickly rise,	71	Frailtie		15
Before didst bow.	74	The Starre		20
Before we do our wares unfold:	79	Employm.2		28
And built a braver Palace then before.	84	The World		20
And knoweth long before,	85	Vanitie 1		6
Admitted to their bed-chamber, before	85	Vanitie 1		19
Perhaps my God, though he be farre before,	87	Lent		40
As Babel grew, before there were dissensions.	122	Sinnes rd.		15
For where thou onely wert before	123	Time		14
What do I here before his doore?	123	Time		29
As I one ev'ning sat before my cell,	139	Artillerie		1
And made you look much fresher then before.	140	Ch.-rents		15
For where before thou still didst call on me,	141	Justice 2		19
And having giv'n the rest before,	151	The Bag		23
Before my sighs did drie it: there was corn	153	The Collar		11
Before my tears did drown it.	153	The Collar		12
That which had but two legs before,	158	Praise 3		10
Because the search was dumbe before:	162	The Search		23
Before a court, ev'n that above so cleare,	167	Dotage		16
I shall be one day better then before:	169	Dial.-Anth		9
Before the Lord of glorie;	170	Self-cond.		3
This worlds delights before true Christian joy,	170	Self-cond.		8
False gain before the true,	171	Self-cond.		15
Did before dimme and choke,	171	Self-cond.		21
To look upon me, who before did lie	171	The Glance		3
(Whose precepts she had trampled on before)	173	Marie Magd		2
Then should the Pomander, which was before	175	The Odour		16
Would warm and work it sweeter then before.	175	The Odour		20
But will ye leave me thus? when ye before	176	Forerunners		14
So all within be livelier then before.	177	Forerunners		36
Which before ye drink is bloud.	180	Invitation		12
Then the ten bitter plagues had done before.	191	Ch.-Milit.		40
Before the other. Greece being past her prime,	191	Ch.-Milit.		60
Before the other two were in their prime.	191	Ch.-Milit.	W	60
That as before Empire and Arts made way,	192	Ch.-Milit.		83
From Greece he went to Rome: and as before	194	Ch.-Milit.		139
As Sinne in Greece a Prophet was before,	195	Ch.-Milit.		171
Give me not that I had before,	201	H. Commun.	W	46
Before they are in Orders, they may be received for Companions,	226	Priest 2		23
coherence thereof, touching what goes before, and what follows after,	229	Priest 4		11
amazed with the Majesty of God, before whom he then presents himself;	231	Priest 6		6
that none is careless before his Judg, and that the word of God shal	233	Priest 7		21
in our hearts, before they come into our mouths, truly affecting,	233	Priest 7		29
the same affection which made him not profit before, making him then	235	Priest 7		14
him unworthy of that Majesty before which he is to present himself,	235	Priest 8		23
and liberall disposition he preferred before beauty, riches,	238	Priest 9		29
requires of all to pray by themselves before they sleep at night,	241	Priest 10		1
draught of beer, then if it had taken before either fish, or rootes,	242	Priest 10		23
So doth hee also before giving make them say their Prayers first,	245	Priest 12		35
but always in the close, before he departs from them:	248	Priest 14		15
but is long before hee proceede to disinheriting, or perhaps never	250	Priest 16		17
spirits, and possesse them even before they themselves heed it.	252	Priest 18		7
And therefore before he comes, having observed some defects in	253	Priest 19		11
Questionist must have in his mind before any question be propounded,	256	Priest 21		32
or Sundayes before the Communion, or on the Eves of all those dayes.	258	Priest 22		28
he doth not onely prefer home-bred things before them, but condemns	261	Priest 23		37
but preferrs her garden and fields before all outlandish gums.	262	Priest 23		4
he forbears not in any wise to use the delinquent as before,	263	Priest 25		26
and makes so much the more of him, as before he alienated himselfe;	263	Priest 25		34
but proceeding on, comes to do unlawfully, even before he is aware;	264	Priest 26		24
on God, not onely before the corne is inned, but after also;	271	Priest 30		35
what he may, before they come, and when for all that they do come,	273	Priest 31		18
who was to shew all humility before his Passion, yet he allows in his	285	Priest 36		28
that they oftentimes goe out of church, before he hath blessed them.	286	Priest 36		14
which before their offence and Judgment they had in all mens brests:	287	Priest 37		33
The Authour's Prayer before Sermon.	288	Priest		T
How shall we dare to appear before thy face, who are contrary	288	Priest		9
This they had told me before:	292	Cornaro		26
For whereas before the measure of my whole dayes meat, viz.	296	Cornaro		9
of my drink, which before was foureteen ounces, I made now sixteen.	296	Cornaro		12
of no great moment (as I shewed before) if a man be temperate in meat	299	Cornaro		16
which is altogether to be preferred before others youth:	302	Cornaro		23
then I could of Originall before, and without Baptisme.	308	Valdesso		4
The H. Scriptures (as I wrote before) have not only an Elementary	309	Valdesso		20
or justify himselfe before God, by any acts or exercises of Religion;	312	Valdesso		15
place he preferres the Word before the sight of the Transfiguration	318	Valdesso		23
A child correct behind and not before.	324	Proverbs		118
A horse and a child correct behind and not before.	324	Proverbs	V	118
Hee that lookes not before, finds himselfe behind.	327	Proverbs		200
Fine dressing is a foule house swept before the doores.	329	Proverbs		243
Marry a widdow before she leave mourning.	329	Proverbs		252

BEFORE (cont'd)	PAGE	TITLE		LINE
In the kingdome of a cheater the wallet is carried before.	337	Proverbs		465
Before you make a friend, eate a bushell of salt with him.	342	Proverbs		624
It's not good fishing before the net.	343	Proverbs		663
Beate the dog before the Lyon.	348	Proverbs		825
It's good tying the sack before it be full.	349	Proverbs		842
He that gives all before hee dies provides to suffer.	349	Proverbs		855
One houres sleepe before midnight is worth three after.	350	Proverbs		882
The Reverend are ever before.	350	Proverbs		891
Take heede of an oxe before, of an horse behind,	351	Proverbs		900
Life is halfe spent before we know what it is.	351	Proverbs		917
Wine that cost nothing is digested before it be drunke.	352	Proverbs		932
The Italians are wise before the deede,	352	Proverbs		947
The Citizen is at his businesse before he rise.	352	Proverbs		958
He that followes the Lord hopes to goe before.	354	Proverbs		994
so devout as to come to the Chappell an howre before prayers began,	368	Letters		18
which if you can sent to Sir Francis before his departure,	369	Letters		26
Higher opportunities of doeing good are to be preferred before lower,	380	Woodnoth		4
thing to advize you now, & before you took Sir Johns affairs.	380	Woodnoth		8
long God knocks at our harts, before he be heard, & yet desists not.	381	Woodnoth		2
BEFOREHAND				
Beforehand, and anticipate their last houre.	21	Ch.-Porch		370
Blessings beforehand, tyes of gratefulnesse,	46	Sinne 1		9
BEFRIEND				
He treads down that which doth befriend him,	92	Man		45
Which shall befriend him at the house of death.	98	Mortific.		18
Which shall befriend him at the houre of death.	98	Mortific.	W	18
BEGAN				
Till thou change names, and be where he began.	21	Ch.-Porch		378
Yet do we still persist as we began,	41	Sepulchre		21
My flesh began unto my soul in pain,	47	Afflict.1		25
Of that brave gift, each one began to fume,	70	Humilitie		19
Began to make Balcones, Terraces,	84	The World		7
My thoughts began to burnish, sprout, and swell,	102	Jordan 2		4
My thoughts began to burnish, spredd, and swell,	102	Jordan 2	W	4
I did demand; he thus began:	125	Peace		21
And now, me thinks, I am where I began	128	Bunch Gr.		3
Began to spread and to expatiate there:	130	Love unkn.		39
But not of speech in starres, began to muse:	139	Artillerie		10
Your health and beautie both began to break.	140	Ch.-rents		20
What for it self love once began,	156	Assurance		41
For what Christ once in humblenesse began,	168	The Sonne		13
Where th' Ark did rest, there Abraham began	190	Ch.-Milit.		19
Both where and when the Church began her race,	192	Ch.-Milit.		102
as what the Church is, how it began, how it proceeded, whether it be	263	Priest 24		1
I began to consider the force of Temperance, and to think thus	293	Cornaro		1
Wherefore I began to search out most diligently what meats were	293	Cornaro		4
I began to perswade my self, that this suit and contention was raised	294	Cornaro		23
so devout as to come to the Chappell an howre before prayers began,	368	Letters		18
BEGET				
Which this dayes favour did beget?	64	Even-song		11
other Tortures, as the very mention of them might beget amazement;	374	Letters		1
BEGETS				
this unusuall form begets a reverence, and makes him esteemed	286	Priest 36		24
BEGGAR				
See how thy beggar works on thee	123	Gratefulnes		3
BEGGARLY				
being more beggarly now than I have been these many years,	375	Letters		36
BEGGARS				
Thy beggars grow; rid them away	150	Longing		77
BEGG'D				
Lime begg'd of old, (they say),	154	Glimpse		13
BEGGER				
that there be not a begger, or idle person in his Parish,	244	Priest 12		20
BEGGING				
Begging his food of that which he may eat,	193	Ch.-Milit.		113
incessantly begging some ease of your pains, with that earnestness,	371	Letters		29
BEGIN				
which did not onely begin, but had already gone farre in me,	291	Cornaro		18
but onely that a man should begin and by little and little accustome	299	Cornaro		9
BEGINN				
Thou hast run all thy race, ere thou beginn.	10	Ch.-Porch	W	90
BEGINNE				
My tender age in sorrow did beginne:	43	East.wings		11
BEGINNER				
his wife among her neighbours is the beginner of good discourses,	240	Priest 10		28
BEGINNING				
Have one beginning and one finall summe:	161	Priesthood		22
And therefore St. Paul in the beginning of his Epistles,	225	Priest 1		10
so that while they answer, As it was in the beginning, &c.	231	Priest 6		34
of state not to come at the beginning of service with their poor	232	Priest 6		9
Whitsuntide, afore and after Harvest, and the beginning of Lent.	259	Priest 22		22
whose natures, at least in the beginning, are dark and obscure:	264	Priest 26		8
not only in the beginning of his preaching, but afterwards also,	280	Priest 34		8
and the beginning of the Gout, with almost a continuall fever	291	Cornaro		22
BEGINNINGS				
And such beginnings touch their END.	133	Paradise		15
or known commonly, the beginnings of them are not easily observable:	264	Priest 26		18
and the beginnings of them are not observed, because of the suddain	264	Priest 26		19
whose natures are most stealing, and beginnings uncertaine.	264	Priest 26		33

BEING (cont'd)	PAGE	TITLE		LINE
Sinne being gone, oh fill the place, ...	39	Good Fri.		29
Sinn being gone o doe thou fill	39	Good Fri.	W	29
It wants the good of vertue, and of being.	63	Sinne 2		5
All being brought into a summe, ...	72	Constancie		14
Till that we both, being toss'd from earth, ...	77	Sunday		62
my soule to thee, that being drest	80	Christmas	W	13
Then he that curbs them, being but one to five:	89	The Pearl		29
In their descent and being; to our minde	91	Man		35
Yet in their being joyn with one advise	121	Providence		146
Ev'n God himself, being pressed for my sake.	128	Bunch Gr.		28
That all things were more ours by being his.	143	Holdfast		12
Since this being mine, brings with it thine, ...	157	Clasping		7
To fetch the bodie; both being due to grief.	159	Jos.coat		9
Thy curse being laid on him, makes thee accurst.	169	Dial.-Anth		6
She being stain'd her self, why did she strive	173	Marie Magd		7
Yet being bruis'd are better sented:	181	Banquet		27
But I still being low and short, ...	182	Banquet		40
Flesh being turn'd to dust, and bones to sticks.	186	Death		8
Before the other. Greece being past her prime, ...	191	Ch.-Milit.		60
And being craftier much then Goodnesse was, ...	193	Ch.-Milit.		124
Sinne being not able to extirpate quite	194	Ch.-Milit.		161
So now being Priest he plainly did professe	195	Ch.-Milit.		173
Being in this their old crackt looking-glasse.	196	Ch.-Milit.		208
When Love being weary made an end	439	Walton 5		11
How sweet a friend was he, who being griev'd	439	Walton 5		15
To serve it forth, & being stript of all	212	Bohemia	D	31
Being desirous (thorow the Mercy of GOD) to please Him, . . .	224	Priest		1
Christ being not to continue on earth, but after hee had fulfilled	225	Priest 1		6
whose duty and obligation being the same to the Houses they live in,	226	Priest 2		16
The Countrey Parson is exceeding exact in his Life, being holy, just,	227	Priest 3		2
coveteousnesse, neither being greedy to get, nor nigardly to keep,	227	Priest 3		16
do much esteem their word, it being the Life of buying, and selling,	228	Priest 3		3
For all Truth being consonant to it self, and all being penn'd by one	229	Priest 4		5
and all being penn'd by one and the self-same Spirit, it cannot be,	229	Priest 4		6
this being to be done in his younger and preparatory times, . .	230	Priest 5		5
For it being indifferent in it selfe to choose any Method, . .	230	Priest 5		9
Now Catechizing being a work of singular, and admirable benefit	230	Priest 5		11
as being truly touched and amazed with the Majesty of God, . .	231	Priest 6		5
that being first affected himself, hee may affect also his people,	231	Priest 6		12
and obligation of his calling, being to obey God rather then men.	232	Priest 6		19
it being naturall to men to think, that where is much earnestness,	232	Priest 7		32
for the humane soule being bounded, and kept in, in her sensitive	238	Priest 9		10
temptation to men of any eminency, especially being single men.	238	Priest 9		17
and that much more being single, then if he were marryed; . .	238	Priest 9		21
which is expressed in a fayre table, as being the rule of a family.	240	Priest 10		26
charity being his only perfume, which deserves cost when he can spare	241	Priest 10		14
for there being two things, which as they are, are unuseful to man,	241	Priest 10		26
where both the people and the drink being cold and flegmatick,	242	Priest 10		20
that a weak stomack being prepossessed with flesh, shall much better	242	Priest 10		22
as being immoderately taken, it is exceeding obstructive. . .	243	Priest 10		4
and will not be perswaded, but being not invited, they are hated.	243	Priest 11		21
so that being once satisfied, he allows his Charity some blindnesse	245	Priest 12		26
the first being for the honour of God;	246	Priest 13		30
his Parish being all his joy, and thought) leaveth not his Ministry	250	Priest 17		25
men being willing to sell the interest, and ingagement of their	252	Priest 18		20
as being the servant of him, in whom there was no guile. . .	253	Priest 19		2
He observes Visitations, and being there, makes due use of them,	253	Priest 19		10
For the Apostles rule Philip. 4. being admirable, and large,	253	Priest 19		22
and Neighbourhood being ever reputed, even among the Heathen,	253	Priest 19		25
for there being three points of his duty, the one, to infuse	255	Priest 21		2
This order being used to one, would be a little varyed to another.	256	Priest 21		16
but there being two things in Sermons, the one Informing, . .	257	Priest 21		21
The Countrey Parson being to administer the Sacraments, . .	257	Priest 22		26
in a great confusion, as being not only to receive God, but to break;	257	Priest 22		29
being himselfe in white, he requires the presence of all, . .	258	Priest 22		1
Baptisme being a blessing, that the word hath not the like. . .	258	Priest 22		7
as being done both in the presence of God, and his Saints, . .	258	Priest 22		12
meditate on their Baptisme often (being the first step into their	258	Priest 22		18
their understandings being ripe enough for ill things, and why	259	Priest 22		1
the other, in being worse served and obeyed.	259	Priest 22		5
who being to present all that receive not thrice a year; . .	259	Priest 22		24
be diligently perused, as being the practicall part, and of most use.	261	Priest 23		8
the obscurity in some points being the exercise of the Church,	263	Priest 24		5
exercise of the Church, the light in the foundations being the guide;	263	Priest 24		6
whether, there being two precepts, one of obeying Authority,	263	Priest 24		8
being made by the precept of Authority more then indifferent,	263	Priest 24		12
being unmoved in arguing, and voyd of all contentiousnesse: . .	263	Priest 24		17
being partiall to themselves, and witty to others who shall reprove	264	Priest 26		13
because the natures of these vices being not evidently discussed,	264	Priest 26		17
Wherefore the Parson being true to his businesse, hath exactly sifted	264	Priest 26		31
which is unwholsome, being sometimes baned meat, sometimes too salt,	265	Priest 26		21
being cunning to make use of another, and spare themselves: . .	265	Priest 26		34
but being seated in the Countrey, and doing their duty faithfully,	266	Priest 26		2
(which being overburdened, or studying dainties too much, . .	266	Priest 26		15
his minde being defixed on it with those nailes wherewith his Master	267	Priest 27		29
or being so, the Parson think it in his discretion either unfit,	269	Priest 28		3
in a Triumphant way, being glad, and joyfull, that hee is made	269	Priest 28		16
and being in the world as he was, hath this undoubted pledge of his	269	Priest 28		17
as being persons enabled by that Name to take moveable goods,	270	Priest 29		1
be vilified or debased, by being cast on the lower ranke of people;	270	Priest 29		7

BEING (cont'd)	PAGE	TITLE		LINE
it being the greatest honor of this world, to do God and his chosen	270	Priest 29		10
Now the Canons being the Church-wardens rule, the Parson adviseth	270	Priest 29		12
sustaining power he preserves and actuates every thing in his being;	271	Priest 30		4
and being ready to put hand to sickle, shall then secure himself,	271	Priest 30		29
Christian, that this prayer being additionary, not necessary;	273	Priest 31		5
The one being usefull to all Countreys, and the other especially	278	Priest 32		2
there being a promise, that if the Kingdome of God be first sought,	278	Priest 33		12
overcome them, being told to another, whether in private conference,	278	Priest 33		16
yet the victory is alike in all, being by the self-same Spirit.	279	Priest 33		2
some being of a more melting temper then others) consisteth in a true	279	Priest 33		22
(there being no reason, why any should distrust Saint Luke,	282	Priest 34		20
the one in his being, the other in his sinfull being:	283	Priest 34		20
those that are ashamed to use this forme, as being old, and obsolete,	284	Priest 35		30
So that it is so far from being a fault to discover such offenders,	287	Priest 37		38
being directed by them in the way I ought to hold, I understood,	292	Cornaro		23
Being now sound and well, I began to consider the force	293	Cornaro		1
without difficultie, and no ill humours being ingendred in the body.	293	Cornaro		29
Being carried home, when the Physicians saw in what case I was,	295	Cornaro		1
shall he use in diseases, which being in health he hath anticipated?	299	Cornaro		24
and the cause being taken away, there is no place for the effect.	300	Cornaro		2
being so built by me according to the rules of Architecture,	301	Cornaro		12
or lesse my self, who being ten yeares older have made a Comedie?	302	Cornaro		35
who being obscured in his own country he would have to flourish in	304	Valdesso		13
it being Scripture cannot be spoken to the disparagement	310	Valdesso		2
the Scriptures, or to themselves being still men, though godly men.	316	Valdesso		4
for the most of his Considerations being grounded upon some text	318	Valdesso		1
the one being gratia gratis data, the other gratia gratum faciens,	319	Valdesso		7
this being given only to the godly, and the other sometimes	319	Valdesso		8
The 98. Consid. about being justified by faith, or by good works,	319	Valdesso	V	16
This being well weighed, will make the Consideration easy,	320	Valdesso		4
nor being spoken to is silent.	330	Proverbs		278
Being on sea saile, being on land settle.	335	Proverbs		418
of your love, with being in some proportion, and after my manner,	364	Letters		3
& shee being at London sent for him (as shee sayes) to make peace	368	Letters		20
since this place being civil may divert me too much from Divinity,	370	Letters		19
does fix me here, it being now but a month to our Commencement:	372	Letters		19
But perhaps being above the Common people, our Credit and estimation	373	Letters		25
being more beggarly now than I have been these many years,	375	Letters		36
which I commend to you as being now a father, "the best-bredd child	376	Letters		17
BELEEFE				
That which beleefe	202	Trin.Sun.	W	11
BELEEV'D				
My Creditour beleev'd so too.	50	Faith	W	16
BELEEVE				
I did beleeve that I did nothing owe,	50	Faith		14
That I beleeve is in the sacred storie:	50	Faith		18
A peasant may beleeve as much	50	Faith		29
(Beleeve me), it shall safely come.	152	The Bag		34
I half beleeve,	184	A Parodie		28
None will beleeve this now, though money be	193	Ch.-Milit.		119
I could beleeve an Impanation	201	H. Commun.	W	25
neither will they beleeve him in the pulpit, whom they cannot trust	228	Priest 3		7
and to beleeve, that things are not set in such an inevitable order,	270	Priest 30		29
how he that would beleeve a Divinity, if he had been at the Creation	281	Priest 34		28
should lesse beleeve it, seeing the Preservation of all things;	281	Priest 34		29
Who would beleeve that old wine should hurt my stomack,	297	Cornaro		32
BELEEVED				
Would have their tale beleeved for their oathes,	14	Ch.-Porch		183
Sorrow was all my soul; I scarce beleeved,	47	Afflict.1		29
Then are there some things to be beleeved that are not seen?	256	Priest 21		9
full of such things, as are not to be seen, but beleeved?	256	Priest 21		11
BELEEVERS				
Quick beleevers neede broad shoulders.	322	Proverbs		39
BELEEVES				
Beleeves so too, and lets me go.	50	Faith		16
BELEEVETH				
He that beleeveth all, misseth;	333	Proverbs		364
hee that beleeveth nothing, hitts not.	333	Proverbs		364
BELEEVING				
He often useth this manner of speech Beleeving by Revelation,	308	Valdesso		29
this I call beleeving by Revelation, and not by Relation.	309	Valdesso		7
BELIEFE				
Your stronge beliefe	209	Paradox	D	5
Is this the nature of beliefe?	256	Priest 21		10
BELIEV'D				
His letters were broke rudely up, believ'd	439	Walton 5		16
BELIEVE				
if we believe, no sinne shall hurt us;	311	Valdesso		25
if we believe not, no vertue shall helpe us.	311	Valdesso		25
BELIEVING				
is not that which filleth the heart with joy and peace in believing;	309	Valdesso		3
or living, for all the point lies in believing or not believing.	311	Valdesso		30
BELL (see also bels)				
In clothes, cheap handsomnesse doth bear the bell.	14	Ch.-Porch		187
List, ye may heare great Aarons bell.	99	Decay		10
So doth thy nearenesse bear the bell,	163	The Search		59
Making a chiming of a passing-bell.	166	The Flower		18
The Bell doth tolle	204	The Knell	W	1
God comes to see without a bell.	334	Proverbs		384
To the counsell of fooles a woodden bell.	339	Proverbs		535

	PAGE	TITLE	LINE
BENEFITT			
lying upon you either for the execution or benefitt of a trade,	380	Woodnoth	26
BENJAMIN			
yet find leisure to write to my Lord, or Sir Benjamin Ruddyard;	370	Letters	30
BENT			
Let thy minde still be bent, still plotting where,	20	Ch.-Porch	337
My bent thoughts, like a brittle bow,	80	Deniall	6
Farther from it then when I bent my bow;	165	The Crosse	26
Further from it then when I bent my bow;	165	The Crosse V	26
Still upwards bent, as if heav'n were mine own,	166	The Flower	30
Unto thine is bent:	178	Discipline	6
Religion, like a pilgrime, westward bent,	190	Ch.-Milit.	29
His bow is bent, his quiver is	222	Psalm VII D	43
the one (which is indeed the bent of my Discourse) the other will	226	Priest 2	18
BENUMME			
As to benumme	80	Deniall	12
BEQUEATH			
sum of five hundred pounds I bequeath unto my Neeces equally to be	382	G.H.'s Will	12
Then I bequeath twenty pounds unto the poore of this parish to be	382	G.H.'s Will	16
Then I bequeath to Mr Hays the Comment of Lucas Brugensis uppon	382	G.H.'s Will	18
then I bequeath to Mr Bostocke St. Augustines workes and his halfe	382	G.H.'s Will	20
be mine Executor to whome I bequeath twenty pound whereof fifteene	382	G.H.'s Will	29
BERRY			
It is a sheep of Berry, it is marked on the nose	356	Proverbs D	1040
BESECH			
Lastlie I besech Sir John Danvers that he would be pleased to be	382	G.H.'s Will	31
BESEECH			
I beseech you all, you and my dear Mother and Sister to pardon me,	369	Letters	17
I beseech you to be chearful, and comfort your self in the God of all	372	Letters	24
I beseech you consider all that can happen to you are either	373	Letters	20
I beseech you let such thoughts as these, moderate your present fear	374	Letters	3
BESEECHING			
humbly beseeching his Master, that how or whenever he punish him,	235	Priest 8	26
humbly beseeching the Almighty to pardon and accept our poor	236	Priest 8	27
beseeching the Father of lights to open their eyes, and to give him	262	Priest 24	22
or beseeching him, that whenever he repaires to his house,	273	Priest 31	25
beseeching thee to blesse thy word, wher-ever spoken this day	289	Priest	14
BESET			
For the temptations with which a good man is beset, and the ways	278	Priest 33	15
was not onely freed from all those evils which had so long beset me,	293	Cornaro	21
BESIDE			
Like David's tree, planted beside	213	L' Envoy D	2
BESIDES			
Besides what I might have	46	Afflict.1	4
Besides the cleannesse of sweet abstinence,	86	Lent	19
And all to all the world besides:	91	Man	15
Besides, thy death and bloud	104	Obedience	26
Besides my physick, know there's some for thee:	106	Conscience	20
A rose, besides his beautie, is a cure.	119	Providence	78
Besides, things sort not to my will,	165	The Crosse	19
To which, besides their own demean,	165	The Flower	3
Besides their other flames? Doth Poetry	206	Walton 1	3
Besides, this being to be done in his younger and preparatory times,	230	Priest 5	5
besides this laborious work, a slighter forme of Catechizing,	230	Priest 5	15
Besides his example, he having often instructed his people how	231	Priest 6	20
besides his ordinary prayers, he makes a peculiar one for a blessing	235	Priest 8	21
even as Princes have theirs, besides their publick disbursments.	236	Priest 8	17
and besides the common prayers of the family, he straitly requires	240	Priest 10	38
and besides, with confession of sins, and all acts of Mortification.	241	Priest 10	39
Besides this generall provision, he hath other times of opening his	245	Priest 12	5
besides which, he hath a Poor-mans Box conveniently seated,	246	Priest 13	20
Besides these occasionall discourses, the Parson questions what order	248	Priest 14	30
Besides this, in his visiting the sick, or otherwise afflicted,	249	Priest 15	27
Besides, if he perceive in company any discourse tending to ill,	252	Priest 18	15
Besides, whereas in Sermons there is a kinde of state, in Catechizing	255	Priest 21	9
having ever besides two great helps and powerfull perswaders on his	263	Priest 24	15
comprehends, besides the hurt, an act against reason, because it is	266	Priest 26	21
Besides this, the Godly have ever added some houres of prayer,	272	Priest 31	25
Besides, every gift or ability is a talent to be accounted for,	274	Priest 32	24
Besides, they are to read Books of Law, and Justice;	276	Priest 32	33
for besides the blessing that that brings upon it, there being	278	Priest 33	12
Besides the continuall succession (since the Gospell) of holy men,	282	Priest 34	18
Besides, the Priests of the Old Testament were commanded to Blesse	285	Priest 36	15
except besides his office, he add a tincture of private malice in	287	Priest 37	26
Besides, it concerns the Common-Wealth, that Rogues should be known,	287	Priest 37	35
Besides all this, I could not sleep, no not a quarter of an houre:	296	Cornaro	21
Besides, these Belly-gods say, that an orderly life is so hard	298	Cornaro	36
besides that they are in the fairest place of this learned Citie	301	Cornaro	10
Besides he opposeth the teaching of the spirit to the teaching	317	Valdesso	26
three pound more besides that which is due to her, to Ann I leave	382	G.H.'s Will	23
an hundred and two pounds besides some Remainders of monyes wherof	383	G.H.'s Will	24
BESIEGE			
Dares to assault thee, and besiege thy doore.	132	The Storm	12
BESPOKE			
So I bespoke me much insinuation:	103	Jordan 2 W	14
BEST			
And make us strive, who shall sing best thy name.	5	Dedication	4
If it concurr with vertue: doe thy best	7	Ch.-Porch W	21
Which is thy best stake, when griefs make thee tame.	9	Ch.-Porch	66
A toy shunn'd cleanly passeth with the best.	15	Ch.-Porch	228
That suites him best, of whom thy speech is heard.	18	Ch.-Porch	294

BEST (cont'd)	PAGE	TITLE		LINE
Entice all neatly to what they know best;	18	Ch.-Porch		295
Is best to celebrate this most high day.	41	Easter		12
Exalted Manna, gladnesse of the best,	51	Prayer 1		10
Yet take thy way; for sure thy way is best:	55	Temper 1		21
Which dissolution sure doth best discern,	65	Ch.-monum.		10
Ordain'd the highest to be best;	79	Employm.2		13
In both let's do our best.	87	Lent		36
The best of men, turn but thy hand	100	Miserie		19
Shows who is best.	109	Brit. Ch.		9
An executioner at best;	123	Time		15
The clearest diamond: let them do their best,	126	Confession		29
Poets have wrong'd poore storms: such dayes are best;	132	The Storm		17
Who changeth all things, as him pleaseth best.	159	Jos.coat		4
Among the best in art.	168	a true Hymn		8
In both I have the best.	172	23 Psalme		8
Good men ye be, to leave me my best room,	176	Forerunners		7
My god must have my best, ev'n all I had.	176	Forerunners		18
Of his two thrones he made the latter best,	196	Ch.-Milit.		213
This gift of all gifts is the best,	201	H. Commun.	W	43
In the best face but filth, when, Lord, in thee	206	Walton 2		13
There is thy best Throne. For afflictions are	211	Bohemia	D	15
and then they are worst, who ought to be best.	227	Priest 3		29
by what they understand, are best led to what they understand not.	228	Priest 4		20
that is best to be chosen, of which there is likelyest to be most	230	Priest 5		10
His thoughts are full of making the best of the day, and contriving	235	Priest 8		20
of making the best of the day, and contriving it to his best gaines.	235	Priest 8		21
contrives how and in what manner to induce it to the best advantage.	236	Priest 8		2
and that the Ministry requires the best and highest things,	236	Priest 9		33
servants, both because they do best, and because what they do,	240	Priest 10		15
whom hee sees take best courses, that so both they may be encouraged	243	Priest 11		25
that he may, if not the best way, yet any way, make his Parish good.	244	Priest 11		4
giving them most, who live best, and take most paines, and are most	245	Priest 12		16
fails not to afford his best comforts, and rather goes to them,	249	Priest 15		15
what kind of remedy fits the temper of the house best, and then hee	251	Priest 17		27
who wish them best, and that not a desire to meddle with others	251	Priest 17		30
wise men have thought it the best way of preserving a state to reduce	258	Priest 22		15
the Church-Wardens, that the elements be of the best, not cheape,	258	Priest 22		22
and how then should the best be so, at least in fundamentall things,	263	Priest 24		4
even of the best in the Parish, when occasion requires:	268	Priest 28		28
but invites and urges the best unto it, shewing that they do	270	Priest 29		9
and ordering his land to the best advantage both of himself,	275	Priest 32		25
But his family is his best care, to labour Christian soules,	275	Priest 32		31
wonder-working knowledg, and therefore requiring the best spirits.	277	Priest 32		35
for strong and very cool wines pleased my taste best, as also melons,	293	Cornaro		11
hidden properties it hath, what meat and drink agrees best with it:	297	Cornaro		28
this I answer, that Galen kept it, and held it for the best Physick:	298	Cornaro		38
Because since this is at the best but uncertain, dangerous,	300	Cornaro		19
And that the best of Gods Servants should have weaknesses is no way	316	Valdesso		2
The best salve for the whole Chapter, is to distinguish Judgment:	316	Valdesso		34
Yet doubtlesse the best faith in us is defective, and arrives	319	Valdesso		10
Vertue and a Trade are the best portion for Children.	324	Proverbs		107
The best remedy against an ill man is much ground betweene both.	326	Proverbs		152
Sometimes the best gaine is to lose.	328	Proverbs		224
The best mirrour is an old friend.	331	Proverbs		296
Living well is the best revenge.	339	Proverbs		524
The best smell is bread, the best savour, salt,	346	Proverbs		741
the best love that of children.	346	Proverbs		741
That's the best gowne that goes up and downe the house.	346	Proverbs		742
The market is the best garden.	346	Proverbs		743
The best of the sport is to doe the deede, and say nothing.	348	Proverbs		812
The best bred have the best portion.	352	Proverbs		953
The best bred have the best portions.	352	Proverbs	V	953
Danger it selfe the best remedy for danger.	357	Proverbs	D	1054
Though I had the best wit in the World, yet it would easily tyre me,	363	Letters		14
so that the best use of them is, having, not to have them.	373	Letters		24
as being now a father, "the best-bredd child hath the best portion".	376	Letters		18
BEST-BREDD				
as being now a father, "the best-bredd child hath the best portion".	376	Letters		18
BESTOW				
Such glorious gifts thou didst bestow,	59	Whitsunday		9
Were it not better to bestow	95	Submission		5
Yet one pure heart is nothing to bestow:	147	Offering		5
Bestow this jewell also on my creature,	160	The Pulley		12
To praise, and on thee, Lord, some Ink bestow.	206	Walton 2		11
BESTOW'D				
On Justice was bestow'd the Foxes brain,	70	Humilitie		15
BESTOWED				
pound whereof fifteene pound shal be bestowed uppon Leighton Church,	382	G.H.'s Will		29
BETAKES				
refreshment, gladly betakes it selfe, even to the losse of honour.	252	Priest 18		22
BETHINKETH				
he bethinketh himselfe what good deeds he can do that day,	244	Priest 12		16
BETIMES				
Here I intombe my flesh, that it betimes	64	Ch.-monum.		2
O heare betimes, lest thy relenting	111	Vanitie 2		7
He that riseth betimes hath some thing in his head.	329	Proverbs		235
Hee that will deceive the fox, must rise betimes.	333	Proverbs		351
Hee that would deceive the fox, must rise betimes.	333	Proverbs	V	351
Hee that would bee well old, must bee old betimes.	334	Proverbs		371
Marry your daughters betimes, lest they marry themselves.	361	Proverbs	D	1171

	PAGE	TITLE		LINE
BETRAY				
Judas, dost thou betray me with a kisse?	28	Sacrifice		41
Thou didst betray me to a lingring book,	47	Afflict.1		39
lest their quiet betray them (as it is apt to do) to a coldnesse,	280	Priest 34		18
BETROTH				
And made them jewels to betroth	82	Ungratef.		10
BETT				
except my cousin Bett take pitty of her, which yet at that distance	375	Letters		29
BETTER				
As hurts not others, but may make thee better,	16	Ch.-Porch		262
Think heav'n a better bargain, then to give	21	Ch.-Porch		374
Because 'tis better, and perhaps may save thee.	22	Ch.-Porch		394
To make the musick better.	55	Temper 1		24
Better by worms be all once spent,	69	Content		26
And make it better.	74	The Starre		8
A better lodging then a rack or grave.	81	Christmas		14
Of better lodging thou maist be possest.	80	Christmas	W	14
Where now we shall be better Gods then he.	82	Ungratef.		6
Is better then to rest:	87	Lent		33
Were it not better to bestow	95	Submission		5
Not he: he knows, where he can better be,	100	Miserie		10
A better hedge, and need lesse reparation.	120	Providence		122
Since by thy cutting he grows better.	122	Time		12
Much better tunes, then grones can make;	124	Gratefulnes		22
Better then you know me, or (which is one)	129	Love unkn.		10
Better then you knew me, or (which is one)	129	Love unkn.	V	10
Of better drink	131	Mans medly		23
More skill in musick, and keep better time.	154	Glimpse		7
I shall be one day better then before:	169	Dial.-Anth		9
This were the better skie, the brighter place.	175	The Foil		4
Yet being bruis'd are better sented:	181	Banquet		27
Yet that he might the better gain all nations,	195	Ch.-Milit.		183
So though Sinne made his latter seat the better,	196	Ch.-Milit.		223
So though Sinne made his later seat the better,	196	Ch.-Milit.	W	223
A Paradox. That the Sicke are in better State then the Whole.	209	Paradox	D	T
And not from better fate,	210	Paradox	D	16
This is thy empire yet: till better season	213	Bohemia	D	60
that he may the better celebrate it, or for the variety	232	Priest 7		23
for them also men heed, and remember better then exhortations;	233	Priest 7		13
none goes out of Church as he came in, but either better, or worse;	233	Priest 7		20
and where flesh may be much better spared, and with more safety then	242	Priest 10		18
shall much better brooke and bear a draught of beer, then if it had	242	Priest 10		22
both is to be done, the better sort invited, and meaner relieved,	243	Priest 11		14
which they can better employ to their own advantage, and sutably	243	Priest 11		15
but that they may have wherewithall to serve God the better,	248	Priest 14		8
may then by an honourable way take occasion to be better instructed.	255	Priest 21		31
being ripe enough for ill things, and why not then for better?	259	Priest 22		2
but sometimes lift up their minds to better things, even in the midst	261	Priest 23		25
knot-grasse for the other, and that with better successe.	261	Priest 23		36
estranging may corroborate the punishment to a better subduing,	263	Priest 25		31
that so they may know their duty, and keep their oath the better;	270	Priest 29		16
Better were his corne burnt, then not spiritually improved.	272	Priest 30		3
sit down at this world, God bids him sell it, and purchase a better:	272	Priest 30		7
bring strangers to him, he may be the better armed to encounter them.	274	Priest 32		8
them honestly, and seasonably, when they are not better imployed.	274	Priest 32		31
in the world hath a braver [better] Institution then that of Justices	276	Priest 32		9
As for better Books of Divinity, they are not in this Consideration,	276	Priest 32		35
where can he busie himself better, then in those new Plantations,	278	Priest 32		5
and can much better, and particularly do it, then he that is	278	Priest 33		28
and complements, and formes of worldly language better;	285	Priest 36		6
Thou hast given us the blessings of this life, and of a better.	290	Priest		6
since none can have a better Physician then himself, nor better	298	Cornaro		1
nor better Physick then a Temperate Life, Temperance by all means is	298	Cornaro		1
It is better to please the Appetite (though they live ten yeares	298	Cornaro		26
Secondly, I answer better, That he which lives a temperate life,	299	Cornaro		35
not be punished (which word I like here better then chastizement,	311	Valdesso		27
will better appear by his 98 Consideration of faith and good works.	312	Valdesso	V	4
A handfull of good life is better then a bushell of learning.	321	Proverbs		3
Better the feet slip then the tongue.	322	Proverbs		53
Better thy foote slip then thy tongue.	322	Proverbs	V	53
Better a bare foote then none.	323	Proverbs		78
Better bend then break.	323	Proverbs	V	85
An old wise mans shaddow is better then a young buzzards sword.	324	Proverbs		90
Better to be blinde, then to see ill.	325	Proverbs		126
A naughty child is better sick then whole.	328	Proverbs		233
Providence is better then a rent.	329	Proverbs		254
An ill agreement is better then a good judgement.	329	Proverbs		264
Better spare to have of thine own, then aske of other men.	330	Proverbs		266
Better good afarre off, then evill at hand.	330	Proverbs		267
Feare keepes the garden better then the gardiner.	330	Proverbs		268
Your pot broken seemes better then my whole one.	330	Proverbs		270
Good is good, but better carries it.	337	Proverbs		454
A feather in hand is better then a bird in the ayre.	340	Proverbs		578
It's better to be the head of a Lyzard, then the tayle of a Lyon.	340	Proverbs		579
It's better to be the head of a mouse, then the tayle of a Lyon.	340	Proverbs	V	579
A beane in liberty is better then a comfit in prison.	343	Proverbs		653
Dry bread at home is better then rost meate abroad.	344	Proverbs		681
Divine ashes are better then earthly meale.	344	Proverbs		684
Better speake truth rudely, then lye covertly.	346	Proverbs		767
One foote is better then two crutches.	346	Proverbs		769
Better suffer ill, then doe ill.	346	Proverbs		770

BETTER (cont'd)	PAGE	TITLE		LINE
Better a snotty child, then his nose wip'd off.	348	Proverbs		828
It is better to have wings then hornes.	352	Proverbs		960
Better be a foole then a knave.	352	Proverbs		961
A trade is better then service.	354	Proverbs		1005
Better is one Accipe, then twice to say, Dabo tibi.	358	Proverbs	D	1079
He that hath time and looks for better time,	359	Proverbs	D	1102
We must recoile a little, to the end we may leap the better.	359	Proverbs	D	1121
yet my heart, a much better member, is alwayes with you:	371	Letters		27
I was the better content because I was in hope I should my self carry	372	Letters		14
Although you have a much better Paymaster then my self,	378	Letters		2
worse by your withdrawing which grow not better by your presence.	381	Woodnoth		11
BETTERS				
Chuse none for thy servant who have served thy betters.	354	Proverbs		1014
BETWEEN				
To come between?	163	The Search		56
Embroider'd lyes, nothing between two dishes;	167	Dotage		5
Between his soul and gold, and hath preferr'd	171	Self-cond.		14
To these diminishings, as is between	196	Ch.-Milit.		233
that there may be a traffick in knowledg between the servants of God,	229	Priest 4		26
to let the fervency of the supplicant hang and dy between speaking,	231	Priest 6		18
a grave livelinesse, between fear and zeal, pausing yet pressing,	231	Priest 6		19
He keeps his servants between love, and fear, according as hee findes	241	Priest 10		7
but as desiring to keep the middle way between superstition,	246	Priest 13		24
and so between gentle reasoning, and pitying, he overcomes the evill:	269	Priest 28		14
Between the businesse of life and the day of death,	356	Proverbs	D	40
The Divell divides the world between Atheisme and Superstition	359	Proverbs	D	1107
BETWEENE				
The best remedy against an ill man is much ground betweene both.	326	Proverbs		152
The ballance distinguisheth not betweene gold and lead.	342	Proverbs		629
let it not come betweene the spindle and the distaffe.	343	Proverbs		665
Reason lies betweene the spurre and the bridle.	345	Proverbs		711
my Neeces equally to be devided betweene them excepting some legacies	382	G.H.'s Will		13
'TWIXT				
'Twixt his sinnes and Saviours death?	114	Businesse		30
BETWIXT				
Betwixt my friends and me. They leave the starre,	28	Sacrifice		50
Betwixt my friends and me. They leave that starre,	28	Sacrifice	W	50
Betwixt two theeves I spend my utmost breath,	34	Sacrifice		229
Betwixt this world and that of grace.	90	Afflict.4		6
Betwixt my God and me; that I allow	155	Assurance		9
Betwixt us & the people: when as glory	212	Bohemia	D	25
BEWAIL				
I will bewail, approve:	171	Bittersweet		6
nor to bewail that so few are writ, that look towards God and Heaven.	363	Letters		8
BEWAILE				
In life you lov'd me not, in death you bewaile me.	328	Proverbs		218
Thou hast death in thy house, and dost bewaile anothers.	334	Proverbs		376
BEWAILES				
Hee that bewailes himselfe hath the cure in his hands.	336	Proverbs		441
The crow bewailes the sheepe, and then eates it.	337	Proverbs		458
BEWARE				
Beware of lust: it doth pollute and foul	6	Ch.-Porch		7
Beware of lust (startle not) o beware	6	Ch.-Porch	W	7
Onely by his permission. Then beware,	22	Ch.-Porch		405
Heark and beware, lest what you now do measure	111	Vanitie 2		5
When the Foxe preacheth, beware your geese.	332	Proverbs		337
BEWITCH				
Thy glorious houshold-stuffe did me bewitch	46	Afflict.1	W	9
But did bewitch, and finely work each nation	195	Ch.-Milit.		193
But did bewitch both kings & many a nation	195	Ch.-Milit.	W	193
BEYOND				
Many affecting wit beyond their power,	16	Ch.-Porch		245
Stayes not, but looks beyond it on the skie;	43	H. Bapt.1		2
And then beyond them all my Baptisme view	43	H. Bapt.1	W	2
As he that Heaven beyond much thicket spyes	43	H. Bapt.1	W	3
Looking on this side, & beyond us all:	48	Repentance	W	9
Church-bels beyond the starres heard, the souls bloud,	51	Prayer 1		13
May guard it safe beyond the highest starr.	66	Ch.-lock	W	12
Is beyond my savour.	115	Dialogue		20
Beyond the utmost starres and poles.	123	Time		18
yet he looks not in this point of Curing beyond his own Parish,	262	Priest 23		13
when we had sinned beyond any help in heaven or earth, then thou	288	Priest		26
Without danger we cannot get beyond danger.	354	Proverbs		1010
be about 30 l. per an. but the commodiousness is beyond the Revenue;	369	Letters		33
you take her not, I am thinking to do it, even beyond my strengthe;	375	Letters		35
BIAS				
Thus doth thy power crosse-bias me, not making	48	Afflict.1		53
When the wide world runnes bias, from his will	73	Constancie		32
BIBLE				
How dare those eyes upon a Bible look,	6	Ch.-Porch		11
If he chance to finde any reading in anothers Bible, he provides him	254	Priest 20		12
BIBLES				
Bibles laid open, millions of surprises,	45	Sinne 1		8
BID				
My soul bid nothing, but preserve her wealth:	44	H. Bapt.2		13
My soul bid nothing, but keep hir first wealth:	44	H. Bapt.2	W	13
The Scriptures bid us fast; the Church sayes, now:	86	Lent		4
Yet are we bid, Be holy ev'n as he.	87	Lent		35
Bid him but temper his excesse;	100	Miserie		9
But he doth bid us take his bloud for wine.	135	Divinitie		21

BID (cont'd)	PAGE	TITLE		LINE
Bid what he please; yet I am sure, ...	135	Divinitie		22
Yet Phisicians bid those that would live in health, not keep	267	Priest 26		10
if I bid a man stay in a place untill I come, I doe not then bid him	318	Valdesso		14
I doe not then bid him goe away but rather stay longer, . .	318	Valdesso		15
doth not bid them then cast away the word, or leave it off: . .	318	Valdesso		19
BIDDING				
pardoning my sins, and bidding me go feed the people of thy love.	289	Priest		6
So S. Peter bidding the dispersed Hebrews attend to the word till	318	Valdesso		17
BIDE				
And all thy promises live and bide.	150	Longing		68
Thou hast a garden for us, where to bide.	167	The Flower		46
Echo. Bide.	188	Heaven		8
BIDS				
Bids no such thing:	78	Ang.&Sts.		18
Bids the rash gazer wipe his eye:	87	Vertue		6
sit down at this world, God bids him sell it, and purchase a better:	272	Priest 30		7
his Father bids him throw it away, and he will give him the gold	272	Priest 30		10
BIERE				
A chair or litter shows the biere, ...	98	Mortific.		29
And both would runne untill they found a biere	159	Jos.coat		8
BIG				
A grave too big for me.	55	Temper 1		12
From private bodies, make as big a thunder, ...	69	Content		23
BIGG				
The world thinks all things bigg and tall	97	Charms & K	W	17
BIGGE				
Bigge with his sister: he hath lost the reins, ...	7	Ch.-Porch		32
Bigge with his sister: he hath lost his reins, ...	7	Ch.-Porch	W	32
All things are bigge with jest: nothing that's plain, ...	16	Ch.-Porch		239
BIGGER				
The eye is bigger then the belly.	355	Proverbs		1018
Volumes of Divinity, which yet every day swell, and grow bigger.	365	Letters		15
BILL				
Some wood and nails to make a staffe or bill	106	Conscience		21
payd out of it unto some whose names shal be annexed unto this bill.	382	G.H.'s Will		16
BIN				
Are blowne away, as if they nere had bin.	46	Sinne 1	W	14
Worthy had bin, thou hadst not lost thine owne:	211	Bohemia	D	2
you have bin at charges:	380	Woodnoth		8
BIND				
Willowes are weak, yet they bind other wood.	341	Proverbs		594
BINDE				
They binde, and leade me unto Herod: he	29	Sacrifice		73
Scatter, or binde them all to bend to thee:	56	Temper 2		13
The whey of milk doth loose, the milk doth binde.	120	Providence		132
BINDES				
And bindes thy hands, ...	66	Ch.-lock		2
Sleep bindes them fast; onely their breath	98	Mortific.		9
excellent statute, which bindes all Parishes to maintaine their own.	244	Priest 12		23
BINDING				
I suffer binding, who have loos'd their bands:	28	Sacrifice		47
Yet in binding them prentices (in case he think fit to do so) he	239	Priest 10		33
Rubarb, or for binding, Bolearmena, the Parson useth damask or white	261	Priest 23		33
BIRD				
To fruit or shade: at least some bird would trust	48	Afflict.1		59
The milkie way, the bird of Paradise, ...	51	Prayer 1		12
The bird that sees a daintie bowre	101	Miserie		55
Frogs marry fish and flesh; bats, bird and beast;	121	Providence		135
He that will take the bird, must not skare it.	322	Proverbs		42
The bird loves her nest.	323	Proverbs		75
Faire shooting never kild bird.	335	Proverbs		405
Farre shooting never kild bird.	335	Proverbs	V	405
A feather in hand is better then a bird in the ayre.	340	Proverbs		578
BIRDS				
Beasts fain would sing; birds dittie to their notes;	117	Providence		9
Birds teach us hawking; fishes have their net:	118	Providence		51
Heark, how the birds do sing, ...	131	Mans medly		1
But as birds drink, and straight lift up their head, ...	131	Mans medly		21
Go birds of spring: let winter have his fee, ...	177	Forerunners		34
As a burst fouling-peece doth save the birds	204	Persever.	W	7
Forbeare not sowing because of birds.	343	Proverbs		670
One faire day in winter makes not birds merrie.	353	Proverbs		977
BIRTH				
I straight return'd, and knowing his great birth, ...	40	Redemption		9
Whereas my birth and spirit rather took	47	Afflict.1		37
Gods breath in man returning to his birth, ...	51	Prayer 1		2
He that first fell from his great birth	59	Whitsunday	W	15
To spell his elements, and finde his birth	65	Ch.-monum.		8
Thy flight is higher, as thy birth.	76	Sunday		59
The other winds towards Him, whose happie birth	84	Coloss.		6
In th' other Angels have a right by birth:	131	Mans medly		9
When I had forgot my birth, ...	182	Banquet		31
BIT				
Look on meat, think it dirt, then eat a bit;	11	Ch.-Porch		131
Whereas a bit	138	The Size		28
otherwise they should do) then alwayes to live under bit and bridle.	298	Cornaro		28
The bit that one eates, no friend makes.	325	Proverbs		142
BITE				
And bite his lip;	131	Mans medly		29
This, this hath done it, this did bite the root	140	Ch.-rents		5

BITE (cont'd)	PAGE	TITLE		LINE
Though the Mastiffe be gentle, yet bite him not by the lippe.	325	Proverbs		132
Though the Mastiffe be gentile, yet bite him not by the lippe.	325	Proverbs	V	132
Fooles bite one another, but wise-men agree together.	336	Proverbs		452
In every country dogges bite.	342	Proverbs		620
BITES				
Fly the pleasure that bites to morrow.	336	Proverbs		444
BITETH				
But it biteth in the close.	178	The Rose		24
BITTEN				
And those all bitten, in thy chair I see.	140	Ch.-rents		10
BITTER				
None shall in hell such bitter pangs endure, ...	24	Ch.-Porch		445
They carrie me to my most bitter crosse:	33	Sacrifice		195
Sweeten at length this bitter bowl, ...	49	Repentance		19
With the turn'd viall of thy bitter wrath!	83	Sighs & Gr.		20
Into the bitter box; but O my God, ...	83	Sighs & Gr.		29
In bitter grief: yet am I stil'd	150	Longing		59
O spitefull bitter thought!	155	Assurance		1
Bitter-sweet.	171	Bittersweet		T
Since that time many a bitter storm	172	The Glance		9
Then the ten bitter plagues had done before.	191	Ch.-Milit.		40
And meet theire tast, who are thy bitter foes.	213	Bohemia	D	66
Who hath bitter in his mouth, spits not all sweet.	335	Proverbs		422
BITTER-SWEET				
Bitter-sweet.	171	Bittersweet		T
BITTERLY				
Bitterly spitefull thought! Couldst thou invent	155	Assurance		2
BITTERNESSE				
Doubles each lash: and yet their bitternesse	30	Sacrifice		126
Bitternesse fills our bowels; all our hearts	49	Repentance		27
BLACK				
And th' other black and grave, wherewith each one	67	Ch.-floore		4
Yea, in deaths shadie black abode	173	23 Psalme		13
Hath soild with Black) the colour of my state, ...	209	L. Bacon	D	7
Through that black tiffany thy vertues shine	211	Bohemia	D	17
The Smith and his penny both are black.	327	Proverbs		195
BLACKAMOOR				
The Bathe of the Blackamoor hath sworne not to whiten. . . .	359	Proverbs	D	1105
BLACKAMOORES				
So Blackamoores repute us fowle, and wee	210	Paradox	D	9
BLACKAMORE				
And I to you a Blackamore present.	209	L. Bacon	D	2
Against this meane & humble Blackamore.	209	L. Bacon	D	10
BLACKNESSE				
Into a blacknesse and distaste?	108	Home		40
BLAME				
From the least spot or thought of blame.	93	Unkindness		9
If it at length deserve some blame:	122	Time		4
And know you not, sayes Love, who bore the blame?	189	Love 3		15
And now my foes the Lord will blame	220	Psalm VI	D	25
Who praiseth Saint Peter, doth not blame Saint Paul.	349	Proverbs		859
BLAMES				
He that blames would buy.	335	Proverbs		410
BLAMING				
Blaming the shallownesse of our request.	103	Prayer 2		12
BLASPHEME				
My bosome friend, if he blaspheme thy name, ...	35	Thanksgvng		25
had delivered them to Satan, that they might learn not to Blaspheme.	286	Priest 36		2
BLASPHEMIE				
Then they accuse me of great blasphemie, ...	28	Sacrifice		61
BLAST				
To which the blast of deaths incessant motion, ...	64	Ch.-monum.		4
Can blast my fruit, or bring me HARM, ...	133	Paradise		5
BLASTED				
His blasted fame	93	Unkindness		8
I blasted all the joyes about me:	108	Home		44
No flowers, no garlands gay? all blasted?	153	The Collar		15
BLEAK				
Which else shows watrish, bleak, & thin.	67	Windows		10
Turned your ruddie into pale and bleak:	140	Ch.-rents		19
Let a bleak palenesse chalk the doore, ...	177	Forerunners		35
BLEATS				
Thy Gentrie bleats, as if thy native cloth	10	Ch.-Porch		93
BLEED				
On it my heart doth bleed	104	Obedience		6
Stonie hearts will bleed.	179	Discipline		20
BLEEDING				
Thought to let out, the bleeding did you good, ...	140	Ch.-rents		14
And lay my threatnings bleeding on the ground.	164	The Crosse		12
BLENDING				
And blending these he carri'd all mens eyes, ...	195	Ch.-Milit.		189
BLESS				
and them for ever bless.	219	Psalm V	D	42
if the Ministration of condemnation did bless, how shall . .	285	Priest 36		19
into your hart, and the LORD bless all your purposes to his glory.	375	Letters		34
the good GOD bless you more and more;	376	Letters		19
The LORD bless you, and make you abound in every good worke,	377	Letters		26
Now God the Father of our Lord Jesus Christ bless you more & more,	378	Letters		25
BLESSE				
I blesse thee, Lord, because I GROW	132	Paradise		1

BLESSE (cont'd)	PAGE	TITLE		LINE
When thou dost blesse, hath twelve: one wheel doth rise . .	158	Praise 3		11
With the other blesse thy sheep, ...	199	L'Envoy		3
as, Oh Lord blesse my people, and teach them this point; . .	233	Priest 7		34
And if temporall Fathers blesse their children, how much more may,	285	Priest 36		14
the Priests of the Old Testament were commanded to Blesse the people,	285	Priest 36		16
so that even ill Priests may blesse.	285	Priest 36		24
if all men are to blesse upon occasion, as appears Rom. 12. 14. how	286	Priest 36		27
we blesse thee! we magnifie thee for ever!	289	Priest		11
beseeching thee to blesse thy word, wher-ever spoken this day	289	Priest		14
blesse it in this thy own Kingdom, which thou hast made a Land	289	Priest		17
blesse this portion here assembled together, with thy unworthy	289	Priest		24
O Lord, blesse it: O Lord, make it health and strength unto us;	290	Priest		9
BLESSED				
O let thy blessed SACRIFICE be mine, ...	26	The Altar		15
O blessed bodie! Whither art thou thrown?	40	Sepulchre		1
O let thy blessed Spirit bear a part, ...	42	Easter		17
O blessed streams! either ye do prevent	44	H. Bapt.1		7
Come blessed Dove charm'd with my song, ...	59	Whitsunday	W	1
My vows to thee most gladly, blessed Maid, ...	78	Ang.&Sts.		9
My blessed Lord, art thou! how suddenly	103	Prayer 2		2
Art thou, my blessed King? how suddenly	103	Prayer 2	W	2
Blessed be God, whose love it was	110	Brit. Ch.		28
Blessed be God, who prosper'd Noahs vine, ...	128	Bunch Gr.		24
When blessed Marie wip'd her Saviours feet, ...	173	Marie Magd		1
Blessed be God alone, ...	199	L'Envoy		17
Thrice blessed Three in One.	199	L'Envoy		18
they do best, and because what they do, is blessed, and prospers.	240	Priest 10		16
for it was not the person, but Priesthood, that blessed; . .	285	Priest 36		23
effectually applying Gods favour to the blessed, by the interesting	286	Priest 36		8
that they oftentimes goe out of church, before he hath blessed them.	286	Priest 36		14
Blessed Saviour! many waters could not quench thy love! . .	288	Priest		30
Blessed be the God of Heaven and Earth!	289	Priest		8
and do so for thy blessed Son's sake, in whose sweet and pleasing	289	Priest		34
Blessed be God! and the Father of all mercy!	290	Priest		1
against the Virginity of the blessed Virgin out of that text Mat. 1.	318	Valdesso		11
I never find Blessed be the Rich;	373	Letters		30
or, Blessed be the Noble;	373	Letters		30
but, Blessed be the Meek, and Blessed be the Poor, and, . .	373	Letters		31
Blessed be the Meek, and Blessed be the Poor, and, Blessed be	373	Letters		31
and, Blessed be the Mourners, for they shall be comforted. . .	373	Letters		31
as if they not only not desir'd, but, even fear'd to be blessed.	373	Letters		34
Sir Henry H: of the blessed Success, that God had given us, . .	378	Letters		31
Blessed be My God & Dear Master, the Spring & Fountain of all	379	Letters		16
that (which you are thinking to doe) to blessed Mary Magd. & Paul,	381	Woodnoth		4
BLESSETH				
and blesseth God for the gift of continency, knowing that it can no	237	Priest 9		19
not spent in them, he blesseth God, and lays it out as he sees cause.	240	Priest 10		12
first he blesseth it, and then as hee finds the persons of the house	247	Priest 14		11
and blesseth them, encouraging also the servants to learn to read,	248	Priest 14		36
Therefore those he meets on the way he blesseth audibly, . .	251	Priest 17		2
BLESSING				
Hee'le make thy wife a blessing not a rodd.	7	Ch.-Porch	W	18
He that gets patience, and the blessing which	24	Ch.-Porch		433
And in his blessing thou art blest:	123	Time		13
Belongs, O Lord, thy blessing shall	217	Psalm III	D	23
he makes a peculiar one for a blessing on the exercises of the day,	235	Priest 8		22
Almighty God, and blessing the people either openly, or to himselfe.	236	Priest 8		5
raise up their mindes to apprehend Gods good blessing to our Church,	236	Priest 8		23
by a due blessing of God for their safe arrival, and saying grace	251	Priest 17		9
that the Blessing of God to them ought to make them the more	254	Priest 19		5
Baptisme being a blessing, that the word hath not the like. . .	258	Priest 22		7
or not in some proportion to Gods blessing upon him, is covetous.	265	Priest 26		6
either blessing God, that he will be pleased to dwell among men;	273	Priest 31		24
riches are the blessing of God, and the great Instrument of doing	274	Priest 32		28
for besides the blessing that that brings upon it, there being	278	Priest 33		12
First, a blessing of God for the fruits of the field: . . .	284	Priest 35		3
Light is a great Blessing, and as great as food, for which we give	284	Priest 35		27
The Parson Blessing.	285	Priest 36		T
that Blessing the people is in so little use with his brethren:	285	Priest 36		1
how shall not the ministration of the spirit exceed in blessing?	285	Priest 36		20
The fruit of this blessing good Hannah found, and received with great	285	Priest 36		20
Neither have the Ministers power of Blessing only, but also . .	285	Priest 36		25
The formes both of Blessing, & cursing are expounded in . .	286	Priest 36		2
Now blessing differs from prayer, in assurance, because it is	286	Priest 36		6
and ingaging of Gods own power and institution for a blessing.	286	Priest 36		11
but if he often interpose a Blessing, when the other gives him just	286	Priest 36		22
In the mean time a Priests blessing, though it be none . . .	377	Letters		2
Wherefore the Lord make good the blessing of your Mother upon you,	377	Letters		4
doubt not, through Gods blessing, but it shall be to the full;	379	Letters		18
BLESSINGS				
God then deals blessings: If a king did so, ...	22	Ch.-Porch		389
Away thy blessings, and extreamly flout thee, ...	23	Ch.-Porch		413
Our blessings from us, and extreamly flout thee, ...	23	Ch.-Porch	W	413
Of heav'nly blessings issue evermore:	32	Sacrifice		171
Of heav'nly blessings issue to the poore:	32	Sacrifice	W	171
Blessings beforehand, tyes of gratefulnesse, ...	46	Sinne 1		9
Melt into blessings all the sky, ...	59	Whitsunday	W	23
Armies of blessings would contend & vye	66	Ch.-lock	W	4
Blessings are plentifull and rife, ...	76	Sunday		34
On men dropp blessings as I fly.	79	Employm.2	W	25

	PAGE	TITLE	LINE
BLESSINGS (cont'd)			
As if thy blessings had spare dayes:	124	Gratefulnes	30
Come, bring thy gift. If blessings were as slow	147	Offering	1
Having a glasse of blessings standing by;	159	The Pulley	2
The blessings of this life, Proverbs 22. 9. Psalm 41. 2.	244	Priest 12	11
pains with them, that hee may lay the foundation of future Blessings.	258	Priest 22	31
by which God turnes all outward blessings to inward advantages.	271	Priest 30	37
Thou hast given us the blessings of this life, and of a better.	290	Priest	5
thy blessings hang in clusters, they come trooping upon us!	290	Priest	6
when we consider that the Blessings in the holy Scripture,	373	Letters	28
BLEST			
Blest be the God of love,	63	Even-song	1
But much more blest be God above,	63	Even-song	4
Blest be the Architect, whose art	67	Ch.-floore	19
And in his blessing thou art blest:	123	Time	13
Blest Order, which in power dost so excell,	160	Priesthood	1
Blest Order, which in power doth so excell,	160	Priesthood V	1
Blest is the man that never would	214	Psalm I D	1
When once his anger burns, thrice blest	216	Psalm II D	31
BLEW			
As if a whirlwinde blew	127	Giddinesse	14
Did once perceive, it blew them under foot,	140	Ch.-rents	7
Did once perceive, it blew thee under foot,	140	Ch.-rents V	7
BLIND			
Hee that saw Christ open a blind mans eyes, saw not more Divinity,	283	Priest 34	1
In the kingdome of blind men the one ey'd is king.	337	Proverbs	469
The blind eate many a flie.	340	Proverbs	556
BLINDE			
To worldly things are sharp, but to me blinde;	26	Sacrifice	2
Who by my spittle gave the blinde man eies,	31	Sacrifice	134
Who by my spittle gave that blinde man eies,	31	Sacrifice W	134
Dust blown by wit, till that they both were blinde:	54	Love 2	10
Can blow away, or glittering look it blinde:	72	Constancie	8
O do not blinde me!	83	Sighs & Gr.	13
Better to be blinde, then to see ill.	325	Proverbs	126
BLINDNESSE			
Leaving his blindnesse to mine enemies:	31	Sacrifice	135
Leaving his blindnesse to my enemies:	31	Sacrifice W	135
once satisfied, he allows his Charity some blindnesse in the other;	245	Priest 12	27
BLISS			
May yet forbid the banes and bliss.	205	Persever. W	12
BLISSE			
Of life, just at the gates of life and blisse?	28	Sacrifice	43
If blisse had lien in art or strength,	50	Faith	25
Softnesse, and peace, and joy, and love, and blisse,	51	Prayer 1	9
This book of starres lights to eternall blisse.	58	H.Script.2	14
This book of starres can spell eternall blisse.	58	H.Script.2 W	14
A gale to bring me sooner to my blisse.	73	Afflict.3	12
Money, thou bane of blisse, & sourse of wo,	77	Avarice	1
To raise him to the glimpse of blisse:	102	Miserie	75
Are holy leaves the Echo then of blisse?	188	Heaven	11
Wounds willingly endur'd to work his blisse,	192	Ch.-Milit.	65
BLISTER			
The growth of flesh is but a blister;	44	H. Bapt.2	14
BLOCK			
is another great stumbling block to the holinesse of Scholars.	238	Priest 9	19
and darkned by the Adversaries, and their great stumbling-block.	305	Valdesso	3
BLOOD (see also bloud)			
Whom God in Baptisme washt with his own blood.	6	Ch.-Porch	8
To write thy sorrows in, as blood	39	Good Fri. W	22
Lord make thy Blood	204	The Knell W	13
altar to be bathed, and washed in the sacred Laver of Christs blood.	231	Priest 6	10
who first shed teares over Jerusalem, and afterwards blood.	234	Priest 7	22
and squeeze blood undecently to the station wherein God hath placed	265	Priest 26	17
It is a great victory that comes without blood.	328	Proverbs	227
To live peaceably with all breedes good blood.	353	Proverbs	963
BLOODY			
The bloody man, the false one too,	218	Psalm V D	15
BLOOM			
With thy quick flow'r, thy momentarie bloom;	48	Repentance	3
BLOSSOME			
Like a nipt blossome, hung	80	Deniall	24
BLOT			
And all the writings blot or burn.	39	Good Fri.	32
They make his life a constant blot,	102	Miserie	63
BLOTS			
It blots thy lesson written in thy soul;	6	Ch.-Porch	9
BLOTT			
It makes thy soule a blott: it is a rodd	6	Ch.-Porch W	8
BLOTTED			
I often blotted what I had begunne;	102	Jordan 2	9
BLOUD			
Thy drops of bloud must pay down all his fear:	17	Ch.-Porch	274
Drops bloud (the onely beads) my words to measure:	27	Sacrifice	22
And therefore wish my bloud on them and theirs:	30	Sacrifice	107
When all my tears were bloud, the while you slept:	31	Sacrifice	150
Which shews my bloud to be the onely way,	31	Sacrifice	158
Shall I weep bloud? why, thou hast wept such store	35	Thanksgvng	5
Which my God feels as bloud; but I, as wine.	37	The Agonie	18
How shall I measure out thy bloud?	38	Good Fri.	2
Since bloud is fittest, Lord, to write	39	Good Fri.	21

	PAGE	TITLE	LINE
BLOUD (cont'd)			
Church-bels beyond the starres heard, the souls bloud,	51	Prayer 1	13
By this thy heav'nly bloud;	53	H.Commun.	38
And hast redeem'd me through thy bloud,	68	Trin.Sun.	2
Writ by a friend, and with his bloud;	75	Sunday	4
Whose drops of bloud paid the full price,	76	Sunday	54
For thou hast other vessels full of bloud,	83	Sighs & Gr.	21
The propositions of hot bloud and brains;	89	The Pearl	23
His bloud did spill	94	Unkindness	23
And all the bloud of God to run in vain.	102	Miserie	64
Besides, thy death and bloud	104	Obedience	26
My Saviours bloud: when ever at his board	106	Conscience	14
The bloud did make, which thou didst waste?	107	Home	8
Draws tears, or bloud, not want an handkerchief.	112	Dawning	16
A stream of bloud, which issu'd from the side	129	Love unkn.	14
I bath'd it often, ev'n with holy bloud,	130	Love unkn.	41
But he doth bid us take his bloud for wine.	135	Divinitie	21
My want of tears with store of bloud.	136	Ephes.	36
Then I refuse not ev'n with bloud	139	Artillerie	14
And shows it so? Indeed Christs precious bloud	140	Ch.-rents	12
There is a balsome, or indeed a bloud,	147	Offering	19
To let me bloud, and not restore	153	The Collar	8
Which before ye drink is bloud.	180	Invitation	12
God took bloud, and needs would be	182	Banquet	34
But since our Saviours death did put some bloud	186	Death	13
Bragging that thy bloud is cold,	199	L'Envoy	6
But though the streams of thy bloud were currant through darknesse,	288	Priest	32
a venture two remedies might be used, letting of bloud, and purging,	295	Cornaro	4
to bee united with that bloud, which useth to infuse so great	442	Oration	15
BLOUD'S			
Yet heare, O God, onely for his blouds sake	66	Ch.-lock	9
His blouds sweet current much more loud to be.	66	Ch.-lock	12
BLOUDIE			
And thorny all their crowns, bloudie their weeds;	32	Sacrifice	178
Copie thy fair, though bloudie hand?	35	Thanksgvng	16
His skinne, his garments bloudie be.	37	The Agonie	10
Thy sorrows in, and bloudie fight;	39	Good Fri.	22
The bloudie crosse of my deare Lord	106	Conscience	23
And bloudie battell which thou once didst trie)	158	Praise 3	35
BLOUDY			
They would discolour thy most bloudy sweat.	62	Afflict.2	10
Thy bloudy death and undeserv'd, makes thee	115	Dulnesse	11
BLOW (bloom)			
to bud, blow and bear fruit in your Soul, to his glory,	377	Letters	5
BLOW (hit)			
Receiv'd the blow upon his side,	151	The Bag	29
One sound blow will serve to undo all.	322	Proverbs	34
The first blow is as much as two.	351	Proverbs	913
(applyed to those that have a blow).	356	Proverbs D	1040
BLOW			
Can blow away, or glittering look it blinde:	72	Constancie	8
This fully to us, till death blow	82	Ungratef.	16
This to us fully, till death blow	82	Ungratef. W	16
For us the windes do blow,	91	Man	25
Such as springs use that fall, and windes that blow.	117	Providence	16
But when thou dost on businesse blow,	158	Praise 3	13
as they remember themselves were, when affliction did blow the Coals.	280	Priest 34	21
how the windes should blow so much as they can, and the sea rage so	281	Priest 34	20
must not say to another; Blow.	333	Proverbs	353
BLOWES (hit)			
The beast that goes alwaies never wants blowes.	329	Proverbs	260
BLOWES			
Hee that blowes in the dust fills his eyes with it.	340	Proverbs	570
BLOWING			
Blowing up houses with their whole increase.	14	Ch.-Porch	204
BLOWN			
I was blown through with ev'ry storm and winde.	47	Afflict.1	36
A fervent sigh might well have blown	53	H.Commun.	31
Dust blown by wit, till that they both were blinde:	54	Love 2	10
Recover all thy sigh-blown age	153	The Collar	19
To see their mother-root, when they have blown;	166	The Flower	11
Anguish in grain, vexations ripe and blown,	167	Dotage	8
Which soon was blown to such a mightie flame,	194	Ch.-Milit.	145
BLOWNE			
Are blowne away, as if they nere had bin.	46	Sinne 1 W	14
BLOWS			
With stronger blows strike mee as I come out:	32	Sacrifice W	187
One cunning bosome-sinne blows quite away.	46	Sinne 1	14
Blows all the dust about the floore:	67	Ch.-floore	17
Who blows it not, nor doth controll	79	Employm.2	8
blows the fire, endeavouring to disorder the Christian,	272	Priest 31	33
BLUNTED			
My mirth and edge was lost; a blunted knife	47	Afflict.1	33
BLURR'D			
If studious, copie fair, what time hath blurr'd;	10	Ch.-Porch	86
BLUSH			
Why doth my Mother blush? is she the rose,	140	Ch.-rents	11
A wise man needes not blush for changing his purpose.	342	Proverbs	613
and it is the part of a poor spirit to undervalue himself and blush.	366	Letters	19
BLUSHING			
Blushing woes, that look as cleare	177	The Rose	7

	PAGE	TITLE	LINE
BLUSTERING			
A blustering night, a faire day.	331	Proverbs	307
BLUSTRING			
While blustring windes destroy the wanton bowres,	97	Afflict.5	21
BOAR			
The rage of a wild boar is able to spoil more then one wood.	360	Proverbs	D 1132
BOARD			
That all may gladly board thee, as a flowre.	21	Ch.-Porch	368
As we at first did board with thee,	97	Afflict.5	11
My Saviours bloud: when ever at his board	106	Conscience	14
Which at a board, while many drunk bare wine,	130	Love unkn.	42
Thy board is full, yet humble guests	149	Longing	53
I struck the board, and cry'd, No more.	153	The Collar	1
BOARDS			
Of skilfull artists, for the boards of those	161	Priesthood	17
but an old good servant boards a child.	241	Priest 10	11
BOAST			
Boast not thereof; nor make thy shame thy glorie.	8	Ch.-Porch	50
Let forrain nations of their language boast,	167	The Sonne	1
And falsly boast,	183	A Parodie	23
And this is all the Rock, whereof they boast,	194	Ch.-Milit.	159
BOASTS			
But he that boasts, shuts that out of his storie.	8	Ch.-Porch	52
BOAT			
Boat, cable, sail and needle, all in one.	120	Providence	128
Ev'n when the boat seems most to reel.	151	The Bag	4
BODIE			
Short of his canne and bodie; must I finde	8	Ch.-Porch	39
Shame tears my soul, my bodie many a wound;	33	Sacrifice	217
O blessed bodie! Whither art thou thrown?	40	Sepulchre	1
What though my bodie runne to dust?	51	Faith	41
My bodie also thither.	52	H.Commun.	26
My bodie to this school, that it may learn	65	Ch.-monum.	7
Did through my bodie wound my minde,	65	Ch.-mus.	2
Now I in you without a bodie move,	65	Ch.-mus.	5
My horse and I, both tir'd, bodie and minde,	80	Christmas	2
To be the bodie and the letters both	116	Love-joy	6
To fetch the bodie; both being due to grief.	159	Jos.coat	9
Some to windes their bodie lend,	187	Dooms-day	21
In a fayre bodie	208	J. Danvers D	7
gives true strength to the bodie, all superfluities passing away	293	Cornaro	28
and other like discommodities of the bodie, and troubles	294	Cornaro	13
whereby my head and whole bodie was sore hurt, and also one of my	294	Cornaro	39
which must needs so temper the humours of the bodie, that they could	295	Cornaro	9
my arm and legge should be set, and my whole bodie anointed with oyl:	295	Cornaro	12
and my bodie spent with extream leannesse, and the season	296	Cornaro	26
For there is no malignitie of old age in the humours of my bodie,	296	Cornaro	37
the Grace of God I feel not those perturbations of bodie and minde,	302	Cornaro	25
BODIE'S			
of Christ in his flesh, for his Bodie's sake, which is the Church.	225	Priest 1	12
BODIES			
From private bodies, make as big a thunder,	69	Content	23
Some to windes their bodies lend,	187	Dooms-day W	21
If glorious bodies pass the sight	201	H. Commun. W	34
since we are not Masters of our bodies, this sufficeth.	279	Priest 33	19
that they had no great power to hurt those bodies, which were kept in	294	Cornaro	2
power a sober and temperate life hath over our bodies and mindes,	294	Cornaro	26
as usually happens in old mens bodies, which live without rule.	296	Cornaro	35
Unsound minds like unsound Bodies, if you feed, you poyson.	358	Proverbs	D 1076
as well as naturall bodies.	361	Proverbs	D 1166
BODY			
Upon thy body, clothes, and habitation.	21	Ch.-Porch	372
That all thy body was one doore.	35	Thanksgvng	6
mind breaking out, and dilating it selfe even to his body, cloaths,	228	Priest 3	13
and body of Divinity, which is the storehouse of his Sermons,	230	Priest 5	1
This Body he made by way of expounding the Church Catechisme,	230	Priest 5	7
when the appetites of the body in eating, drinking, sleep,	230	Priest 5	28
But yet as the temper of his body may be, or as the temper of his	237	Priest 9	1
and by these hee keeps his body tame, serviceable, and healthfull;	237	Priest 9	26
If his body be weak and obstructed, as most Students are,	242	Priest 10	28
One thing is evident, that an English body, and a Students body,	243	Priest 10	1
English body, and a Students body, are two great obstructed vessels,	243	Priest 10	1
In brief, it is the body of Religion, John 13. 35.	244	Priest 12	13
who held that the seeds of all truths lay in every body,	256	Priest 21	22
and knowledg of their own body, and what it can well disgest:	267	Priest 26	1
he first represents to every body the necessity of a vocation.	274	Priest 32	17
in the soul, and a hand in the Body, as ingagements of working:	274	Priest 32	20
an act of the mind, not of the Body, even as the Originall signifies;	279	Priest 33	15
that so the body may joyn in the grief, as it did in the sin;	279	Priest 33	27
without difficultie, and no ill humours being ingendred in the body.	293	Cornaro	29
A garden must be lookt unto and drest as the body.	325	Proverbs	129
It adds to the glory both of soule and body.	327	Proverbs	193
The soule needs few things, the body many.	342	Proverbs	640
The soule needs some things, the body many.	342	Proverbs V	640
The body is more drest then the soule.	351	Proverbs	919
The body is sooner drest then the soule.	351	Proverbs	920
A piece of a Churchyard fitts every body.	355	Proverbs	1027
There is no body will go to hell for company.	361	Proverbs	D 1177
can happen to you are either afflictions of Estate, or Body, or Mind.	373	Letters	22
And for afflictions of the Body, dear Madam, remember the holy	373	Letters	35
Herbert commending my soule and body to Almightie God that made them	382	G.H.'s Will	2

	PAGE	TITLE		LINE
BODY (cont'd)				
if there be any body els that owe me any thing else of old debt I	383	G.H.'s Will		26
BODYES				
Bodyes & Minds are different Spheres	201	H. Commun.	W	40
easie for the Parsons purse, and more familiar for all mens bodyes.	261	Priest 23		32
BOHEMIA				
To the Queene of Bohemia.	211	Bohemia	D	T
BOIL (see also boyle)				
Clouds cool by heat, and baths by cooling boil.	119	Providence		72
BOLD				
Then thou art modest, and the wine grows bold.	8	Ch.-Porch		42
Not thriving, I resolved to be bold,	40	Redemption		2
Still mock me, and grow bold:	116	Dulnesse		22
He that did but look up, was proud and bold.	141	Justice 2		6
And surging griefs, when they grew bold, controll,	172	The Glance		15
just, prudent, temperate, bold, grave in all his wayes.	227	Priest 3		2
by a bold and impartial reproof, even of the best in the Parish,	268	Priest 28		27
It's a bold mouse that nestles in the catts eare.	344	Proverbs		693
BOLDLY				
of the house best, and then hee faithfully, and boldly applyeth it;	251	Priest 17		27
An examin'd enterprize goes on boldly.	342	Proverbs		618
BOLDNESS				
and to preserve a boldness with them and all, even so farre	226	Priest 2		29
Pardon my boldness Sir, it is a most serious Case, nor can I write	364	Letters		15
pardon my boldness, and consider but these three things.	365	Letters		15
pardon my boldness of inclosing my Brothers Letter in yours,	367	Letters		23
have so much power or boldness as to oppose the hope of our Joyes	372	Letters		28
Dear Madam, pardon my boldness, and, accept the good meaning of,	374	Letters		31
BOLDNESSE				
In conversation boldnesse now bears sway.	15	Ch.-Porch		205
As empty boldnesse: therefore first assay	15	Ch.-Porch		207
Boldnesse guilds finely, and will set it forth.	15	Ch.-Porch		210
Towards great persons use respective boldnesse:	16	Ch.-Porch		253
Towards great persons use respectfull boldnesse:	16	Ch.-Porch	W	253
BOLEARMENA				
Bolearmena, the Parson useth damask or white Roses for the one,	261	Priest 23		34
BOND				
Who breaks his own bond, forfeiteth himself:	11	Ch.-Porch		119
BONDAGE				
Of a new Prince, new bondage.	359	Proverbs	D	1116
BONDS				
Fathers first enter bonds to natures ends;	17	Ch.-Porch		281
Let us in sunder break their bonds,	215	Psalm II	D	7
BONE				
In his poore cabinet of bone	82	Ungratef.		28
To assume thy flesh and bone;	113	Businesse		18
To hide thy shame: for thou hast cast a bone	156	Assurance		39
Fetching their proofs ev'n from the very bone;	167	Dotage		11
For thou upon the cheek-bone smit'st	217	Psalm III	D	19
Hee that gives thee a bone, would not have thee die.	333	Proverbs		355
The dog gnawes the bone because he cannot swallow it.	337	Proverbs		457
Were it not for the bone in the legge,	355	Proverbs		1020
In the mouth of a bad dog fals often a good bone.	358	Proverbs	D	1093
BONES				
Constancie knits the bones, and makes us stowre,	11	Ch.-Porch		117
Constancie knits the bones, and makes us sowre,	11	Ch.-Porch	W	117
Sicknesses cleave my bones;	47	Afflict.1		26
That so the broken bones may joy,	49	Repentance		32
My flesh and bones and joynts do pray:	109	Home		74
Would thou hadst no flesh and bones!	113	Businesse		13
With doubling knees and weary bones,	148	Longing		2
One ague dwelleth in my bones,	165	The Crosse		13
Nothing but bones,	185	Death		2
Flesh being turn'd to dust, and bones to sticks.	186	Death		8
And all thy bones with beautie shall be clad.	186	Death		20
Open the bones, and you shall nothing find	206	Walton 2		12
O heal me, for my bones are vex'd,	220	Psalm VI	D	5
BONIE				
Yet active strength: whose long and bonie face	138	The Size		33
BOOK				
Much lesse towards God, whose lust is all their book?	6	Ch.-Porch		12
Nay, I will reade thy book, and never move	36	Thanksgvng		45
Nay, I will reade thy book, and never linn	36	Thanksgvng	W	45
You taught the book of life my name, that so	44	H. Bapt.1		12
Thou didst betray me to a lingring book,	47	Afflict.1		39
If I go lower in the book,	50	Faith		21
Oh Book! infinite sweetnesse! let my heart	58	H.Script.1		1
This book of starres lights to eternall blisse.	58	H.Script.2		14
This book of starres can spell eternall blisse.	58	H.Script.2	W	14
Then an old prayer-book I did present:	121	Hope		3
Tumble thy breast, and turn thy book.	133	The Method		10
Indeed the world's thy book,	149	Longing		49
But by book,	178	Discipline		11
And thy book alone.	178	Discipline		12
This by my picture, in my book I write:	183	The Posie		6
For ev'ry mans peculiar book?	187	Judgement		5
which I have observed, untill the Book grow to a compleat Pastorall.	224	Priest		15
But the chief and top of his knowledge consists in the book of books,	228	Priest 4		22
Wherfore he hath one Comment at least upon every book of Scripture,	229	Priest 4		28
out of all which he hath compiled a book, and body of Divinity,	229	Priest 5		33
such gifts, he sends him a good book, or easeth him in his Tithes,	254	Priest 20		15

	PAGE	TITLE		LINE
BOSOM				
He that hath hornes in his boscm,	340	Proverbs		567
BOSOME				
Thy friend put in thy bosome: wear his eies	17	Ch.-Porch		271
My dove doth back into my bosome flie,	29	Sacrifice		94
My bosome friend, if he blaspheme thy name,	35	Thanksgvng		25
Yet all these fences with one bosome sinn	46	Sinne 1	W	13
One cunning bosome-sinne blows quite away.	46	Sinne 1		14
The help did in thy boscme lie.	107	Home		16
And in thy bosome poure my tears,	150	Longing		71
love for love, even the son of his love out of his bosome of love.	283	Priest 34		17
The ill that comes out of our mouth falles into our bosome.	328	Proverbs		221
BOSOME-SINNE				
One cunning bosome-sinne blows quite away.	46	Sinne 1		14
BOSTOCKE				
then I bequeath to Mr Bostocke St. Augustines workes and his halfe	382	G.H.'s Will		20
George Herbert (testes Nathaniell Bostocke, Elizabeth Burden)	382	G.H.'s Will		34
To Mr Bostocke forty shillings To Elizabeth Burthen thirty shillings	383	G.H.'s Will		15
BOTH				
Continence hath his joy: weigh both; and so	7	Ch.-Porch		17
Thy mouth to it, thy actions to them both:	9	Ch.-Porch		74
A mast'ring minde; so both are lost thereby:	10	Ch.-Porch		104
Will canker both, yett thou alone shallt smart:	13	Ch.-Porch	W	166
One common waight will press downe both, yet so	13	Ch.-Porch	W	167
Both friends should die, then hinder them to live.	17	Ch.-Porch		280
If truth be with thy friend, be with them both:	19	Ch.-Porch		323
Both want, and wish thy pleasing presence still.	19	Ch.-Porch		326
Cures both a fever and lethargicknesse.	19	Ch.-Porch		336
Cures both a fever and a drowsines.	19	Ch.-Porch	W	336
Christs stamp to boot: both images regard.	21	Ch.-Porch		380
Open for thee; or both may come too late.	21	Ch.-Porch		384
In time of service seal up both thine eies,	23	Ch.-Porch		415
Be down, then winde up both; since we shall be	24	Ch.-Porch		455
A Balsome are for both the Hemispheres:	27	Sacrifice		26
Weep not, deare friends, since I for both have wept	31	Sacrifice		149
One box doth lie both ink and sinne:	39	Good Fri.		24
Consort both heart and lute, and twist a song	42	Easter		13
Such starres I counted mine: both heav'n and earth	46	Afflict.1		11
Affright both sinne and shame.	52	H.Commun.		18
Them both to be together.	52	H.Commun.		28
Dust blown by wit, till that they both were blinde:	54	Love 2		10
Thy hands made both, and I am there:	55	Temper 1		26
Save that, and me; or sin for both destroy.	56	Temper 2		4
This verse marks that, and both do make a motion	58	H.Script.2		5
May both the work and workman show:	63	Mattens		19
Both to be busie, and to play.	63	Even-song		3
We both together sweetly live and love,	65	Ch.-mus.		7
But when I view abroad both Regiments;	71	Frailtie		9
But since thy breath gave me both life and shape,	73	Afflict.3		7
Till that we both, being toss'd from earth,	77	Sunday		62
Both knees and heart, in crying night and day,	80	Deniall		13
Both hart & knees, in crying night and day,	80	Deniall	W	13
My horse and I, both tir'd, bodie and minde,	80	Christmas		2
His beams shall cheer my breast, and both so twine,	81	Christmas		33
Thou hast unlockt them both,	82	Ungratef.		9
Thou hast layd open both,	82	Ungratef.	W	9
Thou art both Judge and Saviour, feast and rod,	83	Sighs & Gr.		27
My words & thoughts do both expresse this notion,	84	Coloss.		1
Both their full-ey'd aspects, and secret glances.	85	Vanitie 1		7
In both let's do our best.	87	Lent		36
I know the wayes of Learning; both the head	88	The Pearl		1
Both th' old discoveries, and the new-found seas,	88	The Pearl		7
To all expressions both of hand and eye,	88	The Pearl		15
Where both their baskets are with all their store,	89	The Pearl	W	26
What both the stops and pegs of pleasure bee:	89	The Pearl	W	28
Both the main sale, and the commodities;	89	The Pearl		34
Did both conduct and teach me, how by it	89	The Pearl		39
And both with moons and tides.	91	Man		18
Both are our cleanlinesse. Hath one such beautie?	92	Man		41
Both are our cleanlines: if one have beauty,	92	Man	W	41
And both thy servants be.	92	Man		54
That both grace and glorie tend	92	Antiphon 2		7
And both mine eyes are thine,	95	Submission		2
Since thou hast both mine eyes.	95	Submission		20
Is both a weapon and a guide.	96	Charms & K		4
Where yet both Sinne and Satan, thy old foes,	99	Decay		13
To both our goods, if he to it will stand.	105	Obedience		40
Entred for both, farre above their desert!	105	Obedience		45
I have both lost mine eyes and eares.	105	Conscience		6
Is both my physick and my sword.	106	Conscience		24
Both sweet and bright.	109	Brit. Ch.		3
To be the bodie and the letters both	116	Love-joy		6
Of all the creatures both in sea and land	117	Providence		5
We all acknowledge both thy power and love	117	Providence		29
Nothing escapes them both; all must appeare,	118	Providence		37
So both the flower doth stay, and hony run.	118	Providence		68
And curious vertues both of herbs and stones?	119	Providence		74
I hold for two lives, and both lives in me.	129	Love unkn.		5
Man ties them both alone,	131	Mans medly		10
Both frosts and thoughts dc nip,	131	Mans medly		28
To thee both fruit and order OW.	132	Paradise		3

BOTH (cont'd)

	PAGE	TITLE		LINE
To heav'n alone both go, and leade.	135	Divinitie		28
To be in both worlds full	138	The Size		13
Wouldst thou both eat thy cake, and have it?	138	The Size		18
Born where thy servants both artilleries use.	139	Artillerie		18
Then we are shooters both, and thou dost deigne	139	Artillerie		25
Your health and beautie both began to break.	140	Ch.-rents		20
Can both the way and end be tears?	142	Pilgrimage		28
Are both thy due: but I a silly flie, ...	143	Complaining		8
Dropping from heav'n, which doth both cleanse and close . . .	147	Offering		20
But now both sinne is dead, ...	150	Longing		67
Both then, and after, many a brunt	151	The Bag		21
Yea, when both rocks and all things shall disband, ...	156	Assurance		34
Both all my praise, and more!	159	Praise 3		42
And both would runne untill they found a biere	159	Jos.coat		8
To fetch the bodie; both being due to grief.	159	Jos.coat		9
So both should losers be.	160	The Pulley		15
I am both foul and brittle; much unfit	160	Priesthood		11
So that at once both feeder, dish, and meat	161	Priesthood		21
And centre both to me denie	162	The Search		7
For mine excludes both measure, tune, and time.	164	Grief		18
Where I both feed and rest;	172	23 Psalme		6
In both I have the best.	172	23 Psalme		8
And yet in washing one, she washed both.	173	Marie Magd		18
My minde ev'n thrust into them both:	175	The Odour		7
Till both removed to the western clime.	191	Ch.-Milit.		36
And Rome as both; yet Egypt faster rid, ...	191	Ch.-Milit.		58
In both of these Prowesse and Arts did tame	192	Ch.-Milit.		75
Thus both the Church and Sunne together ran	192	Ch.-Milit.		97
Both where and when the Church began her race, ...	192	Ch.-Milit.		102
The world came both with hands and purses full	193	Ch.-Milit.		133
United now in one both time and sphere.	195	Ch.-Milit.		176
But did bewitch both kings & many a nation	195	Ch.-Milit.	W	193
So both together are one Antichrist, ...	196	Ch.-Milit.		206
By letting in them both, pollutes her streams:	197	Ch.-Milit.		242
By letting in them both pollute her streams:	197	Ch.-Milit.	W	242
Shall both in France and England domineer:	197	Ch.-Milit.		246
Both for their vertuous actions and their crimes.	197	Ch.-Milit.		262
Judgement may meet them both & search them round.	197	Ch.-Milit.		269
Thus do both lights, as well in Church as Sunne, ...	197	Ch.-Milit.		270
But as the Sunne still goes both west and east;	198	Ch.-Milit.		274
But that both thou, and all thy traine	200	H. Commun.	W	10
But thou art Light & darknes both togeather:	203	Even-song	W	13
The Water, and the Earth both unto thee	439	Walton 5		7
He judgeth both the good, and those	222	Psalm VII	D	39
of the Priesthood may be plainly gathered both the Dignity thereof,	225	Priest 1		15
which Christ did, and after his manner, both for Doctrine and Life.	225	Priest 1		19
into which if he come, he prostitutes himself both to shame, and sin,	227	Priest 3		25
therefore the spirit of both is to be considered, and weighed.	229	Priest 4		16
the servants of God, for the planting both of love, and humility.	229	Priest 4		27
or somtimes both, if his audience be intermixed.	230	Priest 5		18
and child, answering aloud both Amen, and all other answers,	231	Priest 6		28
both to their own loss, and of theirs also who gaze upon them when	232	Priest 6		10
both by earnestnesse of speech, it being naturall to men to think,	232	Priest 7		31
are but two devouring elements, fire, and water, he hath both in him;	234	Priest 7		34
both sutable to the joy of the day, and without hinderance to publick	236	Priest 8		18
he takes occasion to discourse of such things as are both profitable,	236	Priest 8		22
is very circumspect in all companyes, both of his behaviour, speech,	237	Priest 9		14
and very looks, knowing himself to be both suspected, and envyed.	237	Priest 9		15
in high places doth the Parson fear, or experiment, or both;	238	Priest 9		21
Therefore he gives her respect both afore her servants, . . .	238	Priest 9		36
to his earthly, having no title to either, except he do good to both.	239	Priest 10		23
servants, both because they do best, and because what they do,	240	Priest 10		15
or learners, or both, so that his family is a Schoole of Religion,	240	Priest 10		21
God hath provided Creatures for both;	241	Priest 10		30
by taking both sorts of food into them, do as it were dresse	241	Priest 10		33
do as it were dresse and prepare both for man in themselves,	241	Priest 10		34
from hot Countreys, where both flesh alone, and much more with wine,	242	Priest 10		16
where both the people and the drink being cold and flegmatick,	242	Priest 10		19
cold and flegmatick, the eating of flesh is an antidote to both.	242	Priest 10		21
and carving for them, both for his own humility, and their comfort,	243	Priest 11		12
But since both is to be done, the better sort invited, and meaner	243	Priest 11		13
that so both they may be encouraged to persevere, and others spurred	243	Priest 11		25
encouragements to goodnesse as he can, both in honour, and profit,	244	Priest 11		3
and come to Church in frame, but commonly the next day put off both.	247	Priest 14		10
hee both commends them much, and furthers them when hee is gone,	247	Priest 14		13
For both God is there also, and those for whom God dyed: . .	249	Priest 14		6
from the certainty both of deliverance, and reward, if we faint not;	249	Priest 15		25
to his Diocesan, honouring him both in word, and behaviour, . .	253	Priest 19		7
Thus both in rewarding vertue, and in punishing vice, the Parson	254	Priest 20		29
their vowes, and by occasion of both, inlarge their meditations.	255	Priest 21		34
as being done both in the presence of God, and his Saints, . .	258	Priest 22		12
which while they deferr, both sides suffer;	259	Priest 22		4
as may be of much use to him both for himself, and others. . .	261	Priest 23		3
Now both the reading of him, and the knowing of herbs may be done	261	Priest 23		8
Nature serving Grace both in comfort of diversion, and the benefit	261	Priest 23		11
For home-bred medicines are both more easie for the Parsons purse,	261	Priest 23		31
sweet usage of them, both in going to, and sending for them often,	262	Priest 24		26
The Church needing both an evidence, and an exercise. . . .	263	Priest 24		7
A man may be both Covetous, and Intemperate, and yet hear Sermons	264	Priest 26		14
and yet hear Sermons against both, and himselfe condemn both in good	264	Priest 26		15

BOTH (cont'd)	PAGE	TITLE		LINE
hear Sermons against both, and himselfe condemn both in good earnest:	264	Priest 26		16
both in present for his family, and in future for his children,	264	Priest 26		26
in perverting that order which he hath set both to things, . .	265	Priest 26		12
seasoned with pleasantnesse, both enter sooner, and roote deeper.	268	Priest 27		4
he condescends to humane frailties both in himselfe and others;	268	Priest 27		6
knows well, that both for the generall ignominy which is cast upon	268	Priest 28		9
the Parson having a due respect both to the person, and to the cause,	268	Priest 28		33
both publickly, and privately instruct his Church-Wardens, . .	269	Priest 29		26
So that if a Farmer hath both a faire harvest, and that also well	271	Priest 30		38
the Gallant, who is witty enough to abuse both others, and himself,	275	Priest 32		7
and ordering his land to the best advantage both of himself,	275	Priest 32		26
For it is both a security to the King, who hath so many dispersed	276	Priest 32		10
all those, who else might both trouble him and the whole State.	276	Priest 32		15
for it is both an honor which they owe to the Reverend Judges	277	Priest 32		1
he may go to Court, as the eminent place both of good and ill.	277	Priest 32		6
and a shamefull wrong both to the Common-wealth, and their own House:	277	Priest 32		27
there were no such Physician as he, both for skill and tendernesse.	278	Priest 33		32
The formes both of Blessing, & cursing are expounded in . .	286	Priest 36		2
Thy hands both made us, and also made us Lords of all thy creatures;	288	Priest		12
with a full stomack, but so as I might well both eat and drink more.	293	Cornaro		19
refused both remedies, and onely commanded that my arm and legge	295	Cornaro		10
both of old times and later yeares, it is no such thing which may	299	Cornaro		5
which is both easie for common-weals-men, and very convenient,	299	Cornaro		17
both that they may preserve themselves from diseases, which hinder	299	Cornaro		18
on both sides whereof are great and fruitfull fields, well manured	301	Cornaro		24
That I have both given God a Temple, and men to worship him in it:	301	Cornaro		31
bodie and minde, wherewith infinite both young and old are afflicted.	302	Cornaro		25
very apt and well given both for learning and behaviour. . .	303	Cornaro		5
The exemption from both, is by the Grace of God.	308	Valdesso		5
as if they were both but Alphabets and after a time to be left.	309	Valdesso		19
both are to be done, the Scriptures still used, and Gods worke within	309	Valdesso		31
So may a warre be just on both sides, and was just in the Canaanites	316	Valdesso		29
on both sides, and was just in the Canaanites and Israelites both.	316	Valdesso		30
indeed sometime doubly teaching both in penning and in applying.	317	Valdesso		30
both of them having forms or vizars of godlinesse, but denying	319	Valdesso	V	26
A caske and an ill custome must both of them be broken. . .	322	Proverbs	V	27
The best remedy against an ill man is much ground betweene both.	326	Proverbs		152
It adds to the glory both of soule and body.	327	Proverbs		193
The Smith and his penny both are black.	327	Proverbs		195
Who must account for himselfe and others, must know both. . .	328	Proverbs		209
One hand washeth another, and both the face.	329	Proverbs		239
God strikes not with both hands, ...	331	Proverbs		315
both would last long.	344	Proverbs		697
It is good to have some friends both in heaven and hell. . .	359	Proverbs	D	1127
then either of them both.	361	Proverbs	D	1173
I wrong both my self, and also the confidence my Friends have in me;	364	Letters		8
for infirmities are both painful and costly.	365	Letters		1
and both pay for the surplusage of these Books, and for ever after	367	Letters		10
but that I have both time and work to be Your extreme Servant,	370	Letters		14
Can I be so happy, as to hear of both these that they succeed well?	371	Letters		10
having both ordered your Family, and so brought up your Children that	373	Letters		12
Care of them will justifie you both to the world and your own	373	Letters		16
I wrote to him that I would have both or neither;	375	Letters		12
to let them know your love, for which both they shall, and I doe,	375	Letters		22
But though I both consider this, and your observation, also,	376	Letters		3
a much better Paymaster then my self, even him, whome we both serve:	378	Letters		3
I heard from you, that I long to heare both how you and your's doe:	379	Letters		24
I give all my goods both within doores and without doores both	382	G.H.'s Will		3
doores and without doores both monneys and bookes and howshould	382	G.H.'s Will		4
yea, indeed of all, both Courtly, Militarie, Academicall. . .	441	Oration		27
both Indias to his Spaine, knowes no limits of his praise, . .	442	Oration		11
both the Spanish and Brittish Nation serve and worship James.	442	Oration		17
James is the protecting Saint unto us both;	442	Oration		19
since you are so great both in your Princes, and your selves,	442	Oration		28
we have as much failed, as your Excellencies doe excel, in both.	442	Oration		35
BOTTELL				
The wine in the bottell doth not quench thirst.	342	Proverbs		616
BOTTLE				
Did weep to heav'n, they found a bottle there	158	Praise 3		27
A drunkards purse is a bottle.	325	Proverbs		143
BOTTOM				
whose bottom is wound up and laid ready for work in the New . .	373	Letters		6
BOTTOME				
And bottome of the leaves: which when the winde	140	Ch.-rents		6
And draw the bottome out an end.	145	Discharge		45
Rest in the bottome lay.	160	The Pulley		10
In the world who knowes not to swimme, goes to the bottome. . .	330	Proverbs		285
In the world who can not swimme, goe to the bottome. . . .	330	Proverbs	V	285
BOUGHS				
I got me boughs off many a tree:	42	Easter		20
Trimme as the light, sweet as the laden boughs	190	Ch.-Milit.		14
festivalls strawed, and stuck with boughs, and perfumed with incense.	246	Priest 13		10
Short boughs, long vintage.	338	Proverbs		508
BOUGHT				
About some land, which he had dearly bought	40	Redemption		7
So high a torture? Is such poyson bought?	155	Assurance		3
that he hath bought a parcel of Books for me, and that they are	366	Letters		30
BOULS				
As bouls go on, but turning all the way.	118	Providence		60

BRAVE (cont'd)	PAGE	TITLE		LINE
And thought his god most brave;	82	Ungratef.		5
Sweet rose, whose hue angrie and brave	87	Vertue		5
So brave a Palace built; O dwell in it,	92	Man		50
Then came brave Glorie puffing by	111	The Quip		13
Are passing brave.	137	The Size		4
Brave rose, (alas!) where art thou? in the chair	140	Ch.-rents		1
Brave rose, (alas!) where art thou? in the place	140	Ch.-rents	V	1
But all was glorious cheating, brave deceit,	193	Ch.-Milit.		135
I thought it brave to praise thee then,	202	love	W	15
Yet thy brave beames excluded from their right	211	Bohemia	D	10
commends the study of the Civill Law, as a brave, and wise knowledg,	277	Priest 32		31
You live in a brave nation, where, except you wink, you cannot	366	Letters		5
except you wink, you cannot but see many brave examples.	366	Letters		7
BRAVELY				
If thou chuse bravely & rely on God	7	Ch.-Porch	W	17
In brief, acquit thee bravely; play the man.	24	Ch.-Porch		457
Nero and others lodg'd him bravely there,	194	Ch.-Milit.		141
The Churches here, bravely resolv'd one night	194	Ch.-Milit.		162
BRAVER				
Brave language, braver deeds:	71	Frailtie		14
And built a braver Palace then before.	84	The World		20
Who after him should braver truths disclose.	194	Ch.-Milit.		138
Each breast does feel, no braver fuel choose	206	walton 1		13
Common-wealth in the world hath a braver [better] Institution then	276	Priest 32		9
BRAVERIE				
To stuffe thy minde with solid braverie;	15	Ch.-Porch		208
And change thy temperance into braverie.	15	Ch.-Porch		222
BRAVES				
And if the braves of conqu'ring sinne	60	Whitsunday		23
BRAVEST				
Who make the bravest shows.	161	Priesthood		18
BRAWLING				
Brawling Curres never want sore eares.	322	Proverbs	V	52
BREAD				
Who cannot wish, except I give them bread:	26	Sacrifice		7
Make bread of it: and that repose	125	Peace		39
Now eat his bread in peace,	127	Giddinesse		10
My searches are my daily bread;	162	The Search		3
Or hath sweetnesse in the bread	181	Banquet		13
First I am sure, whether bread stay	200	H. Commun.	W	7
Or whether Bread doe fly away	200	H. Commun.	W	8
Concerneth bread not mee.	200	H. Commun.	W	9
In Bread & mee, the way thou takest	200	H. Commun.	W	17
If thou hadst dyde for Bread.	201	H. Commun.	W	27
and bread of Charity to some equality, representing to his people,	254	Priest 19		3
When any one can distinguish the Sacramentall from common bread,	258	Priest 22		35
weather be what it will, still we have bread, though sometimes more,	281	Priest 34		25
And now Lord, thou hast fed us with the bread of life:	290	Priest		9
of my bread, and egges, and flesh, and broth, was twelve ounces	296	Cornaro		10
Every day brings his bread with it.	321	Proverbs		5
Who hath no more bread then neede, must not keepe a dog.	325	Proverbs		128
Of all smells, bread: of all tasts, salt.	326	Proverbs		166
Estate in two parishes is bread in two wallets.	328	Proverbs		231
I had rather aske of my sire browne bread,	330	Proverbs		269
Anothers bread costs deare.	332	Proverbs		324
All griefes with bread are lesse.	334	Proverbs		377
All griefes with bread are lesse, or Nor woe to want.	334	Proverbs	V	377
Who likes not the drinke, God deprives him of bread.	334	Proverbs		394
Hope is the poore mans bread.	337	Proverbs		477
Under water, famine; under snow, bread.	339	Proverbs		516
Dry bread at home is better then rost meate abroad.	344	Proverbs		681
The best smell is bread, the best savour, salt,	346	Proverbs		741
Threatned men eat bread, says the Spaniard.	358	Proverbs	D	1081
BREAK				
Think not thy fame at ev'ry twitch will break:	15	Ch.-Porch		219
But thou wast up by break of day,	42	Easter		21
Do not by hanging down break from the hand,	112	Dawning		11
Did break and scatter.	124	Peace		12
I would say thorns. Deare, could my heart not break,	130	Love unkn.		52
Break all thy spheres, and save thy head.	135	Divinitie		26
Your health and beautie both began to break.	140	Ch.-rents		20
May oft break forth, and never break the lock.	154	Glimpse		25
Let us in sunder break their bonds,	215	Psalm II	D	7
Whose pow'r shall dash and break them all	216	Psalm II	D	23
as being not only to receive God, but to break, and administer him.	257	Priest 22		30
and not break off their acts of dependance, how faire soever	271	Priest 30		26
For that he ought not to break off, but to continue his dependance	271	Priest 30		34
either for fear or shame, break his custome, he shall do passing ill:	273	Priest 31		30
and find sparkes of such thoughts now and then to break forth,	281	Priest 34		13
they break forth like mighty waters on every side.	290	Priest		7
Better bend then break.	323	Proverbs	V	85
BREAK'ST				
Ah! no more: thou break'st my heart.	115	Dialogue		32
BREAKE				
See, they breake in	204	The Knell	W	10
which continually breake Gods Laws, and dishonour him with those	269	Priest 28		10
BREAKES				
Hee that makes a thing too fine, breakes it.	336	Proverbs		440
Councell breakes not the head.	336	Proverbs		443
The thread breakes, where it is weakest.	341	Proverbs		596

	PAGE	TITLE		LINE
BRIM-FULL				
Praise thee brim-full!	115	Dulnesse		4
BRIMME				
Unto the brimme, and make our measure up;	197	Ch.-Milit.		240
BRIMSTONE				
To deale with brimstone, that untamed stench	212	Bohemia	D	53
BRINE				
Into one common sewer, sea, and brine;	62	Afflict.2		7
BRING				
Bring not thy plough, thy plots, thy pleasures thither.	23	Ch.-Porch		422
What ever scoffes or scornfulnesse can bring,	32	Sacrifice		174
What ever scoffes & scornfulnesse can bring,	32	Sacrifice	W	174
Thus trimmed forth they bring me to the rout,	32	Sacrifice		185
Though hee bring light & th' other sents:	42	Easter	W	24
And bring by Faith all things to him?	49	Faith		4
Neither bring hony with the bees,	57	Employm. 1		18
Thy words do finde me out, & parallels bring,	58	H.Script.2		11
When they combine and mingle, bring	68	Windows		12
And then amerc'd them, double gifts to bring	71	Humilitie		31
A gale to bring me sooner to my blisse.	73	Afflict.3		12
Reason and speech we onely bring.	91	Man		10
Ah Loyterer! I'le no more, no more I'le bring:	121	Hope		7
Untill their cockatrice they hatch and bring:	122	Sinnes rd.		4
And made it bring forth grapes good store.	128	Bunch Gr.		25
Can blast my fruit, or bring me HARM,	133	Paradise		5
I will bring thee.	146	Praise 2		12
Come, bring thy gift. If blessings were as slow	147	Offering		1
Then bring thy gift; and let thy hymne be this;	147	Offering		24
I live to shew his power, who once did bring	159	Jos.coat		13
Who bring my God to me!	161	Priesthood		30
The late-past frosts tributes of pleasure bring.	165	The Flower		4
The late-past frosts tributes of pleasures bring.	165	The Flower	V	4
And bring my minde in frame:	172	23 Psalme		10
So to bring in wherewith to wash:	173	Marie Magd		17
To bring the other Ark from Canaan.	190	Ch.-Milit.		20
To bring the other Ark to Canaan.	190	Ch.-Milit.	W	21
When all things full & hale, that they may bring	212	Bohemia	D	27
Shall flow no more - until they bring	214	Convert	D	8
but shall bring forth a lye.	222	Psalm VII	D	52
that (the good instrument of God to bring women to heaven) a wise	238	Priest 9		30
except the evidence of the misery bring testimony with it.	245	Priest 12		22
I bring this example, because men usually think, that servants	265	Priest 26		23
few bring covetousness thus low, or consider it so narrowly,	265	Priest 26		30
or bring strangers to him, he may be the better armed to encounter	274	Priest 32		7
If Temperance had so much power as to bring me health;	293	Cornaro		3
can bring little grief or hurt to those that are temperate.	294	Cornaro		34
many places doe the Fathers bring about Untill against the Heretiques	318	Valdesso		10
Dry feet, warme head, bring safe to bed.	335	Proverbs		402
Little journeys and good cost bring safe home.	338	Proverbs		502
You may bring a horse to the river,	342	Proverbs		623
An ill deede cannot bring honour.	348	Proverbs		806
BRINGETH				
householder, who bringeth out of his treasure things new and old;	261	Priest 23		15
BRINGING				
At length the Crow bringing the Peacocks plume,	70	Humilitie		17
A secret vertue bringing peace and mirth	125	Peace		35
Bringing nor man, nor arms, nor fear,	151	The Bag		28
Killing and quickning, bringing down to hell	166	The Flower		16
Bringing all your sinnes to sight:	180	Invitation		15
by bringing them up in the fear and nurture of the Lord;	275	Priest 32		22
BRINGINGE				
Bringinge thy sweets along with thee.	42	Easter	W	22
BRINGS				
If this seeme Monkish; think which brings most paine	7	Ch.-Porch	W	15
But brings a favour from above;	64	Even-song		31
There is no fruitfull yeare, but that which brings	108	Home		57
Brings thy Saviours death no gain?	114	Businesse		36
Since this being mine, brings with it thine,	157	Clasping		7
and brings with his own to the heavenly altar to be bathed,	231	Priest 6		8
for besides the blessing that that brings upon it, there being	278	Priest 33		12
a fair and desirable death, which Nature brings by way of resolution.	303	Cornaro		29
Every day brings his bread with it.	321	Proverbs		5
When God will, no winde but brings raine.	332	Proverbs		332
Every sin brings its punishment with it.	346	Proverbs		760
Hee that brings good newes knockes hard.	348	Proverbs		824
Great Fortune brings with it Great misfortune.	360	Proverbs	D	1144
BRINISH				
That habitable sea, & brinish strand,	213	Bohemia	D	62
BRITAIN'S				
Remote from ours, then Spaine from Britains shoare.	438	Lat.Trans.		4
BRITISH				
The British Church.	109	Brit. Ch.		T
Constantines British line meant this of old,	192	Ch.-Milit.		93
BRITTISH				
both the Spanish and Brittish Nation serve and worship James.	442	Oration		18
BRITTLE				
He is a brittle crazie glasse:	67	Windows		2
My bent thoughts, like a brittle bow,	80	Deniall		6
I am both foul and brittle; much unfit	160	Priesthood		11
like vessels made of brittle clay.	216	Psalm II	D	24

	PAGE	TITLE		LINE
BROACH				
When that lay gather'd, thou didst broach the mountains: . . .	120	Providence		114
BROACHT				
Could not that wisdome, which first broacht the wine, ...	134	Divinitie		9
BROAD				
If thou wilt die, the gates of hell are broad:	9	Ch.-Porch		71
Quick beleevers neede broad shoulders.	322	Proverbs		39
BROIDER'D				
Fie, thou wilt soil thy broider'd coat, ...	176	Forerunners		23
BROK				
And thou hast brok th' ungodly's teeth:	217	Psalm III	D	21
BROKE				
Sure the unruly sigh had broke my heart.	73	Afflict.3		6
A great afflicticn broke the little frame, ...	112	JESU		3
Either the league was broke, or neare it;	155	Assurance		11
His letters were broke rudely up, believ'd	439	Walton 5		16
(Where nothing should be broke) to adde a Seal.	439	Walton 5		18
BROKEN				
A broken ALTAR, Lord, thy servant reares, ...	26	The Altar		1
That so the broken bones may joy, ...	49	Repentance		32
Though I in broken pay	62	Afflict.2		4
Be broken into dust. Mark here below	65	Ch.-monum.	W	22
Then was my heart broken, as was my verse:	79	Deniall		3
Broken in pieces all asunder, ...	89	Afflict.4		1
That to my broken heart he was I ease you, ...	112	JESU		9
Which hath been broken now so long, ...	150	Longing		74
Here, as broken, is presented.	181	Banquet		30
Lord, thy broken consort raise, ...	187	Dooms-day		29
also in diseases of exinanition (as consumptions) must be broken:	242	Priest 10		32
be housed, a fire hath broken forth, and suddenly consumed them.	271	Priest 30		25
A Cake and an ill custome must be broken.	322	Proverbs		27
A caske and an ill custome must both of them be broken. . . .	322	Proverbs	V	27
Your pot broken seemes better then my whole one.	330	Proverbs		270
BROOK				
O brook not this, lest if what even now	71	Frailtie		17
O brook not this, lest if that, which just now	71	Frailtie	W	17
How canst thou brook his foolishnesse?	100	Miserie		7
Almightie Judge, how shall poore wretches brook	187	Judgement		1
BROOKE				
shall much better brooke and bear a draught of beer, then if it had	242	Priest 10		23
BROOKS				
Most herbs that grow in brooks, are hot and dry.	120	Providence		129
BROOM				
Whose house is foul, while he adores his broom?	193	Ch.-Milit.		118
BROTH				
What cordials make this curious broth, ...	175	The Odour		9
This broth of smells, that feeds and fats my minde.	175	The Odour		10
and flesh, and broth, was twelve ounces exactly weighed; . . .	296	Cornaro		10
BROTHELS				
Of stews and brothels onely knew the doores, ...	176	Forerunners		15
BROTHER				
Each part may call the farthest, brother:	91	Man		16
Each part may call the furthest, brother:	91	Man	V	16
Each one whispring, Live ye brother?	186	Dooms-day		6
our Saviours rule, and to take my brother aside, and reprove him;	248	Priest 14		27
but as a brother still, except some small and temporary estranging	263	Priest 25		30
For when my brother and others of my kindred saw some great powerfull	294	Cornaro		15
My deare and deserving Brother, your Valdesso I now returne with many	304	Valdesso		1
mee in your letters, for I am your ever loving brother, G. HERBERT.	366	Letters		22
P.S. My brother is somewhat of the same temper, and perhaps a little	366	Letters		24
To my dear brother, Mr. Henry Herbert, at Paris.	366	Letters		26
I understand by a Letter from my Brother Henry, that he hath bought	366	Letters		29
most heartily, affectionate Brother, and Servant, GEORGE HERBERT.	372	Letters		8
but advance them, was lovingly done, and like a good brother.	375	Letters		3
I will tell you what I wrote to our eldest brother, when he urged one	375	Letters		10
So prayes Your ever loving brother, G. HERBERT.	376	Letters		21
To my very dear brother Sir Henry Herbert, at Court.	376	Letters		24
every good worke, to the joy of your ever loving brother, G. HERBERT.	377	Letters		28
To my deere brother, Sir Henry Herbert, at Court.	377	Letters		31
& the great Joy of Your Brother & Servant in Christ Jesus GEORGE	378	Letters		28
a Letter, from My Brother, Sir Henry H: of the blessed Success,	378	Letters		31
that she had done nothing in it (as my Brother writes) hitherto.	379	Letters		4
She referred it also to My Brother, to name at first, what the summe	379	Letters		5
I have sent my Letters, to your Brother, investing him, . . .	379	Letters		19
therefore entertaine it accordingly from Your very affectionate bro;	379	Letters		27
BROTHER'S				
pardon my boldness of inclosing my Brothers Letter in yours,	367	Letters		23
BROTHERS				
for single men, they are either Heirs, or younger Brothers: . . .	276	Priest 32		26
As for younger Brothers, those whom the Parson finds loose, . . .	277	Priest 32		24
inclosed to be carried to his brothers house of his own name (as I	370	Letters		27
BROUGHT				
To work for two, who brought himself to thrall.	17	Ch.-Porch		286
To work for two, that brought himself to thrall.	17	Ch.-Porch	W	286
That brought the wise men of the East from farre.	28	Sacrifice		51
And brought thy sweets along with thee.	42	Easter	WC	22
But since those pipes of gold, which brought	59	Whitsunday		17
What have I brought thee home	64	Even-song		9
I ranne; but all I brought, was fome.	64	Even-song		12
The jealous Turkie brought his corall-chain;	70	Humilitie		13
All being brought into a summe, ...	72	Constancie		14

BROUGHT (cont'd)	PAGE	TITLE	LINE
Of pleasures brought me to him, readie there	81	Christmas	7
Are brought to Man, while they are lame and mute.	117	Providence	12
Brought back to the Red Sea, the sea of shame.	128	Bunch Gr.	7
To him I brought a dish of fruit one day,	129	Love unkn.	6
My heart, that brought it (do you understand?)	130	Love unkn.	36
As she had brought wherewith to stain,	173	Marie Magd	16
Brought you to Church well drest and clad:	176	Forerunners	17
Brought thee low,	179	Discipline	27
Nilus for monsters brought forth Israelites.	191	Ch.-Milit.	44
Who brought his doctrins & his deeds from Rome	195	Ch.-Milit. W	201
Had he only brought them forth,	208	J. Danvers D	13
which skill either she brought with her, or he takes care she shall	239	Priest 10	16
want a competent sustentation, nor her husband be brought in debt.	239	Priest 10	19
Yet when ever any controversie is brought to him, he never decides it	260	Priest 23	8
which are brought from thence to the House but in generall.	277	Priest 32	13
when light is brought in, God send us the light of heaven;	284	Priest 35	23
those that pleased my taste brought me commoditie or discommoditie;	293	Cornaro	7
increased so much in them, that it brought them to a sudden end.	294	Cornaro	20
Divers reasons they brought, as, that old age could not be sustained	295	Cornaro	22
untill shee had brought forth her first borne Sonne, as if afterwards	318	Valdesso	13
At length the Fox is brought to the Furrier.	323	Proverbs	81
Drought never brought dearth.	346	Proverbs	749
and so brought up your Children that they have attain'd to the years	373	Letters	12
What a trouble hath your Goodness brought on you, by admitting our	376	Letters	26
BROUGHT'ST			
And brought'st thy sweets along with thee.	42	Easter	22
BROW			
Knocking at heaven with thy brow:	75	Sunday	10
When I had gain'd the brow and top,	142	Pilgrimage	22
If, though thou didst not beat thy future brow,	144	Discharge	23
BROWNE			
I had rather aske of my sire browne bread,	330	Proverbs	269
BROWS			
From th' earth unto my brows, and bear the thrall:	32	Sacrifice	167
BROWSE			
The goate must browse where she is tyed.	323	Proverbs	56
BRUGENSIS			
Mr Hays the Comment of Lucas Brugensis uppon the Scripture and his	382	G.H.'s Will	19
BRUISE			
O do not bruise me!	83	Sighs & Gr.	6
Bees work for man; and yet they never bruise	118	Providence	65
Who remove stones, bruise their fingers.	322	Proverbs	40
BRUIS'D			
Yet being bruis'd are better sented:	181	Banquet	27
BRUISES			
Moreover I say, that even bruises and squats, and falls,	294	Cornaro	33
BRUNT			
When all thy deeds, whose brunt thou feel'st alone,	69	Content	29
Both then, and after, many a brunt	151	The Bag	21
BRUSHERS			
Criticks are like brushers of Noblemens cloaths.	360	Proverbs D	1157
BRUTE			
Preferring, like brute beasts, a lothsome den	167	Dotage	15
when they set themselves to work like brute beasts, never raising	247	Priest 14	32
BRUTISH			
Since my dark soul and brutish is thy right,	81	Christmas	11
BUBBLE			
My soul will bee all bubble straight,	45	Nature W	9
Is but a bubble, and makes thee a boy.	111	Vanitie 2	18
BUBBLES			
My soul will turn to bubbles straight,	45	Nature	9
Do end in bubbles, balls of winde;	64	Even-song	14
BUCKET			
Good words quench more then a bucket of water.	329	Proverbs	263
BUCKETS			
Thy scales like buckets, which attend	141	Justice 2	16
BUCKINGHAM			
My Lord of Buckingham was observed on Christmas day to bee so devout	368	Letters	16
BUD			
Nipt in the bud;	57	Employm. 1	4
The fruit of this, the next worlds bud,	75	Sunday	2
And now in age I bud again,	166	The Flower	36
prayers and tears, to bud, blow and bear fruit in your Soul,	377	Letters	5
BUFFET			
They buffet me, and box me as they list,	30	Sacrifice	129
They buffet him, and box him as they list,	30	Sacrifice W	129
BUGDEN			
neither can I so much as go to Bugden, and deliver your Letter,	369	Letters	15
BUILD			
I'le build a spittle, or mend common wayes,	36	Thanksgvng	33
Could build so strong in a weak heart.	67	Ch.-floore	20
That none doth build a stately habitation,	90	Man	2
to multiply, and build up this knowledge to a spirituall Temple;	255	Priest 21	4
'Tis easier to build two chimneys, then to maintaine one.	350	Proverbs	893
To build castles in Spain.	356	Proverbs D	1041
be fain alwayes to borrow Books, and build on anothers foundation?	364	Letters	13
BUILDER			
he sees not how a house could be either built without a builder,	281	Priest 34	19
BUILDER'S			
All show'd the builders, crav'd the seers care.	106	Sion	6

	PAGE	TITLE		LINE
BUILDING				
To raze the building to the very floore:	84	The World		17
With care and courage building me,	90	Afflict.4		29
And crusht the building: and it's partly true,	127	Giddinesse		15
building it all upon the word untill the day starre arise,	318	Valdesso		8
Building and marrying of Children are great wasters.	321	Proverbs		11
The charges of building and making of gardens are unknowne.	335	Proverbs		412
Building is a sweet impoverishing.	337	Proverbs		459
these many years, as having spent two hundred pounds in building;	376	Letters		2
your relation of my Lady Duchess's forwardnes in our church building.	377	Letters		20
BUILDS				
That no man builds a stately habitation,	90	Man	W	2
He builds a house, which quickly down must go,	127	Giddinesse		13
Hee that repaires not a part, builds all.	333	Proverbs		344
but the Devill builds a Chappell hard by.	343	Proverbs		674
BUILT				
Houses are built by rule, and common-wealths.	12	Ch.-Porch		135
Why, he that built the world can do much more:	28	Sacrifice		67
Love built a stately house; where Fortune came,	84	The World		1
And built a braver Palace then before.	84	The World		20
So brave a Palace built; O dwell in it,	92	Man		50
And built without thy Cost:	207	Walton 3		3
If thou dost find an house built to thy mind	207	Walton 4		1
who treads in his steps, and will not throw down what he hath built;	232	Priest 7		27
he sees not how a house could be either built without a builder,	281	Priest 34		18
being so built by me according to the rules of Architecture,	301	Cornaro		12
Whereupon men flockt thither, and built houses with happy successe.	301	Cornaro		29
No sooner is a Temple built to God	343	Proverbs		674
Lawyers houses are built on the heads of fooles.	352	Proverbs		951
David built the temple as much as Solomon because he desired it,	381	Woodnoth		19
BULK				
First, the Bulk of Divinity.	365	Letters		16
BUNCH				
Anneal'd on every bunch. One standing by	116	Love-joy		3
The bunch of grapes.	128	Bunch Gr.		T
BUNDLE				
And bear the bundle, wheresoe're it goes:	88	The Pearl		17
BUNDLES				
Hee that hath charge of soules transports them not in bundles.	353	Proverbs		986
BURDEN (see also burthen)				
The decreed burden of each mortall Saint:	33	Sacrifice		199
The gladsome burden of a mortall saint.	33	Sacrifice	W	199
The burden of the week lies there,	75	Sunday		12
Begins at home, and layes the burden there,	86	Lent		8
and no less burden, as being done both in the presence of God,	258	Priest 22		12
An Asse endures his burden, but not more then his burden.	358	Proverbs	D	1080
It is high time now that I should be no more a burden to you,	367	Letters		13
George Herbert (testes Nathaniell Bostocke, Elizabeth Burden)	382	G.H.'s Will		34
BURDENED				
which is alreadie burdened with a disease, would be wholly oppressed.	299	Cornaro		34
BURDENS				
Light burdens, long borne, are heavie.	321	Proverbs	V	15
BURGESS				
he is to endeavour by all means to be a Knight or Burgess there;	277	Priest 32		10
BURIALL				
And with his buriall-linen drie thine eyes:	112	Dawning		14
BURIALL-LINEN				
And with his buriall-linen drie thine eyes:	112	Dawning		14
BURIED				
he sheweth through all his Considerations) a thing strangely buried,	305	Valdesso		2
that a man would desire straight to bee buried there.	353	Proverbs		969
BURN				
And all the writings blot or burn.	39	Good Fri.		32
First with thy fire-work burn to dust	74	The Starre		9
And calling Justice, all things burn.	99	Decay		20
Come Lord, my head doth burn, my heart is sick,	107	Home		1
Then burn thy Epicycles, foolish man;	135	Divinitie		25
Thy hand above did burn and glow,	141	Justice 2		11
Where all things burn,	166	The Flower		33
Wherewith whole showls of Martyrs once did burn,	206	Walton 1		2
Henceforth in Sacred Flames shall Burn,	214	Convert	D	19
BURNE				
He will burne his house, to warme his hands.	331	Proverbs		304
BURNED				
yet when God pleased, the sun stood stil, the fire burned not.	271	Priest 30		12
BURNES				
Well may hee smell fire, whose gowne burnes.	325	Proverbs		138
Hee that burnes his house warmes himselfe for once.	331	Proverbs		303
He that burnes most shines most.	340	Proverbs		568
When my house burnes, it's not good playing at Chesse.	343	Proverbs		666
He warmes too neere that burnes.	348	Proverbs		815
BURNISH				
My thoughts began to burnish, sprout, and swell,	102	Jordan 2		4
My thoughts began to burnish, spredd, and swell,	102	Jordan 2	W	4
BURNS				
His house still burns, and yet he still doth sing,	100	Miserie		4
Such poor invention burns in their low mind	206	Walton 2		9
When once his anger burns, thrice blest	216	Psalm II	D	31
BURNT				
Upon thine Altar burnt? Cannot thy love	206	Walton 1		6
Better were his corne burnt, then not spiritually improved.	272	Priest 30		4

BURNT (cont'd)	PAGE	TITLE		LINE
Wood halfe burnt is easily kindled.	341	Proverbs		606
how they have been burnt by thousands, and have endur'd such other	373	Letters		36
BURST				
As a burst fouling-peece doth save the birds	204	Persever.	W	7
BURTHEN				
The gladsome burthen of a mortall saint.	33	Sacrifice	WC	199
Three helping one another, beare the burthen of sixe.	325	Proverbs		135
Knowledge is no burthen.	344	Proverbs		692
None knowes the weight of anothers burthen.	350	Proverbs		880
admirable thing is this, that God puts his shoulder to our burthen;	374	Letters		18
forty shillings To Elizabeth Burthen thirty shillings To Mary Gifford	383	G.H.'s Will		15
BURTHENS				
Light burthens, long borne, growe heavie.	321	Proverbs		15
BUSH				
At some fair oak, or bush, or cave, or well:	99	Decay		7
Nothing but drought and dearth, but bush and brake, ...	108	Home		49
BUSHELL				
a hatchet, a bushell, leaven, boyes piping and dancing; . . .	257	Priest 21		12
A handfull of good life is better then a bushell of learning.	321	Proverbs		3
Before you make a friend, eate a bushell of salt with him. . .	342	Proverbs		624
BUSHIE				
With bushie groves, pricking the lookers eie, ...	51	Faith		38
BUSIE				
Let vain or busie thoughts have there no part:	23	Ch.-Porch		421
Let vain & busie thoughts have there no part:	23	Ch.-Porch	W	421
All things are busie; onely I	57	Employm. 1		17
Both to be busie, and to play.	63	Even-song		3
Nor the Exchange, or busie Hall;	70	Quidditie		10
That busie plant!	79	Employm.2		22
My thoughts are working like a busie flame, ...	122	Sinnes rd.		3
My sighs and tears as busie were above;	132	The Storm		3
Busie enquiring heart, what wouldst thou know?	144	Discharge		1
My busie heart shall spin it all my dayes:	157	Praise 3		3
Call home thine eye (that busie wanderer)	170	Self-cond.		5
Should all my life employ, and busie me.	175	The Odour		30
Busie in controversies sprung of late.	194	Ch.-Milit.		166
Those that he finds busie in the works of their calling, . . .	247	Priest 14		20
where can he busie himself better, then in those new Plantations,	278	Priest 32		5
To be too busie gets contempt.	346	Proverbs		738
BUSIED				
the Common-wealth, that none should be idle, but all busied.	274	Priest 32		28
BUSIEST				
Flies are busiest about leane horses.	323	Proverbs		73
BUSINES				
it is a good and just thing for every one to do their own busines.	247	Priest 14		23
While the discreet advise, the foole doth his busines.	330	Proverbs		273
BUSINESS				
Now Love is his business, and aime;	284	Priest 35		16
I knew not, in the midst of much business, and all in a Fortnight,	371	Letters		3
and you have no cause to be sorry, since it is GOD's business.	377	Letters		21
BUSINESSE				
And when, and how the businesse may be done.	20	Ch.-Porch		338
Life is a businesse, not good cheer;	79	Employm.2		16
Businesse.	113	Businesse		T
Thy businesse his, and in thy life partake:	144	Discharge		18
But when thou dost on businesse blow, ...	158	Praise 3		13
But are their cares and businesse with the pleasure?	188	Judgement	V	17
But are there cares and businesse with the pleasure?	188	Heaven		17
Wherefore the Parson being true to his businesse, hath exactly sifted	264	Priest 26		31
The Italian says, None fouls his hands in his own businesse:	275	Priest 32		27
He that staies does the businesse.	327	Proverbs		188
Who doth his owne businesse, foules not his hands.	335	Proverbs		419
Love and businesse teach eloquence.	345	Proverbs		704
Hee that hath a wife and children wants not businesse.	347	Proverbs		778
The Citizen is at his businesse before he rise.	352	Proverbs		958
Who hath no hast in his businesse, ...	354	Proverbs		997
Without businesse debauchery.	354	Proverbs		1009
Between the businesse of life and the day of death, ...	356	Proverbs	D	40
BUSINESSES				
Great businesses turne on a little pinne.	345	Proverbs		720
I have forty businesses in my hands, your Courtesie will pardon	371	Letters		18
though businesses may stop my hand, yet my heart, a much better	371	Letters		26
BUSNESSES				
over much beholding to those busnesses which justly excuse him from	367	Letters		30
BUSTIED				
But while I bustled, I might heare a friend	103	Jordan 2		15
BUSY (see also busie)				
and busy cast of his eye on his auditors, with letting them know,	233	Priest 7		1
BUT				
But gladly welcome what he doth afford;	7	Ch.-Porch		15
Man would have been th' incloser: but since now	7	Ch.-Porch		20
When once it is within thee; but before	7	Ch.-Porch		26
Because no knowledg, is not earth but mudd.	7	Ch.-Porch	W	36
Be not a beast in courtesie; but stay, ...	8	Ch.-Porch		46
But he that boasts, shuts that out of his storie.	8	Ch.-Porch		52
But the cheap swearer through his open sluce	8	Ch.-Porch		58
Pick out of tales the mirth, but not the sinne.	9	Ch.-Porch		63
Lie not; but let thy heart be true to God, ...	9	Ch.-Porch		73
But if thou coole, then take some shame to thee	10	Ch.-Porch	W	90
O England! full of sinne, but most of sloth;	10	Ch.-Porch		91

BUT (cont'd)

	PAGE	TITLE		LINE
Not that they all are so; but that the most	10	Ch.-Porch		95
Not that they are all so; but that the most	10	Ch.-Porch	W	95
Some till their ground, but let weeds choke their sonne:	10	Ch.-Porch		98
Some great estates provide, but doe not breed	10	Ch.-Porch		103
Is full as poore as he, that needs but five.	10	Ch.-Porch		108
But if thy sonne can make ten pound his measure,	11	Ch.-Porch		113
Be sure to doe it, though it be but small:	11	Ch.-Porch		116
Simpring is but a lay-hypocrisie:	11	Ch.-Porch		123
Tast all, but feed not. if thy stomach call	11	Ch.-Porch	W	128
But say withall, Earth to earth I commit.	11	Ch.-Porch	W	132
Thou liv'st by rule. What doth not so, but man?	12	Ch.-Porch		134
Thou liv'st by rule. What does not so, but man?	12	Ch.-Porch	W	134
Be thriftie, but not covetous: therefore give	12	Ch.-Porch		151
Ev'n with the yeare: but age, if it will hit,	13	Ch.-Porch		158
Gold thou mayst safely touch; but if it stick	13	Ch.-Porch		167
And spares himself, but would his taylor chide.	13	Ch.-Porch		180
But, This with my discretion will be brave.	14	Ch.-Porch		190
Play not for gain, but sport. Who playes for more	14	Ch.-Porch		193
But know, that nothing can so foolish be,	15	Ch.-Porch		206
But the great souldiers honour was compos'd	15	Ch.-Porch		225
But may be wittie, if thou hast the vein.	16	Ch.-Porch		240
But if thou want it, buy it not too deere.	16	Ch.-Porch		244
As hurts not others, but may make thee better,	16	Ch.-Porch		262
Not of rich arras, but mean tapestrie.	17	Ch.-Porch		270
But love is lost, the way of friendship's gone,	17	Ch.-Porch		275
But love is lost, the art of friendship's gone,	17	Ch.-Porch	W	275
Submit to love; but yet not more then all.	17	Ch.-Porch		284
(But a proud ignorance will lose his rest,	18	Ch.-Porch		297
That thou canst speak, at once; but husband it,	18	Ch.-Porch		302
In love I should: but anger is not love,	18	Ch.-Porch		311
Slacknesse breeds worms; but the sure traveller,	20	Ch.-Porch		339
All forrain of that name; but scorn their ill:	21	Ch.-Porch		362
As if none could bee brave, but who profess	21	Ch.-Porch	W	369
Man is Gods image; but a poore man is	21	Ch.-Porch		379
Fast when thou wilt; but then 'tis gain, not losse.	22	Ch.-Porch		396
We all are but cold suitours; let us move	22	Ch.-Porch		400
Resort to sermons, but to prayers most:	23	Ch.-Porch		409
Thy clothes being fast, but thy soul loose about thee.	23	Ch.-Porch		414
All worldly thoughts are but theeves met together	23	Ch.-Porch		424
How know'st thou, but thy sinnes made him miscarrie?	24	Ch.-Porch		440
Look not on pleasures as they come, but go.	24	Ch.-Porch		458
Nothing but holy, pure, and cleare,	25	Superlim		6
As nothing but	26	The Altar		7
To worldly things are sharp, but to me blinde;	26	Sacrifice		2
Curing all wounds, but mine; all, but my fears:	27	Sacrifice		27
One houre of watching; but their drowsie brain	27	Sacrifice		30
Of faith, but furie: yet at their commands	28	Sacrifice		46
'Gainst him, who seeks not life, but is the meek	28	Sacrifice		58
But yet their friendship is my enmitie:	29	Sacrifice		75
To whose powre Thunder is but weake and slight:	29	Sacrifice	W	79
I answer nothing, but with patience prove	29	Sacrifice		89
But who does hawk at eagles with a dove?	29	Sacrifice		91
Pilate a stranger holdeth off; but they,	29	Sacrifice		101
But hony is their gall, brightnesse their night:	30	Sacrifice		111
But I the Prince of peace; peace that doth passe	30	Sacrifice		118
But surely not their hearts, as I well trie:	30	Sacrifice		123
But surely not their hearts, as I will trie:	30	Sacrifice	V	123
But not their harts, as I by proofe doe try.	30	Sacrifice	W	123
And Prophets once to see, but found no place:	32	Sacrifice		183
Man stole the fruit, but I must climbe the tree;	33	Sacrifice		202
The tree of life to all, but onely me:	33	Sacrifice		203
Bywords, but this by sorrow I must win:	33	Sacrifice		207
But, O my God, my God! why leav'st thou me,	33	Sacrifice		213
Sharp nails pierce this, but sharper that confound;	33	Sacrifice		218
But more with malice: yet, when they did call,	34	Sacrifice		238
But now I die; now all is finished.	34	Sacrifice		249
'Tis but to tell the tale is told.	35	Thanksgvng		8
But how then shall I imitate thee, and	35	Thanksgvng		15
As for thy passion - But of that anon,	35	Thanksgvng		29
But mend mine own without delayes.	36	Thanksgvng		34
But mend my own without delayes.	36	Thanksgvng	W	34
As if I us'd them but for fashion.	36	Thanksgvng		36
But in all vict'ries overthrow me?	37	Reprisall		12
But there are two vast, spacious things,	37	The Agonie		4
Which my God feels as bloud; but I, as wine.	37	The Agonie		18
But shreds of holinesse, that dare not venture	38	The Sinner		6
Or cannot leaves, but fruit, be signe	38	Good Fri.		11
No lodging for thee, but a cold hard stone?	40	Sepulchre		2
But that which shews them large, shews them unfit.	41	Sepulchre		9
And so should perish, but that nothing can,	41	Sepulchre		22
Or since all musick is but three parts vied	42	Easter		15
But thou wast up by break of day,	42	Easter		21
But thou wast up before myne houre	42	Easter	W	21
Can there be any day but this,	42	Easter		27
We count three hundred, but we misse:	42	Easter		29
There is but one, and that one ever.	42	Easter		30
Stayes not, but looks beyond it on the skie;	43	H. Bapt.1		2
My soul bid nothing, but preserve her wealth:	44	H. Bapt.2		13
My soul bid nothing, but keep hir first wealth:	44	H. Bapt.2	W	13
The growth of flesh is but a blister;	44	H. Bapt.2		14

BUT (cont'd)

	PAGE	TITLE		LINE
There was no moneth but May.	47	Afflict.1		22
But with my yeares sorrow did twist and grow,	47	Afflict.1		23
But with my yeares sorrows did twist and grow,	47	Afflict.1	W	23
That I did live, but by a pang of woe.	47	Afflict.1	W	30
Thus are we to delights: but we are all	48	Repentance		9
But thou wilt sinne and grief destroy;	49	Repentance		31
None but the wise or strong had gained it:	50	Faith		26
But by the way of nourishment and strength	52	H.Commun.		7
But as th' outworks, they may controll	52	H.Commun.		16
But wee strangers grown, o Lord,	53	H.Commun.	W	37
But above all, the heart	53	Antiphon 1		11
This is but tuning of my breast,	55	Temper 1		23
But thy diviner world of grace	56	Temper 2		6
But keep a standing Majestie in me.	56	Temper 2		16
Not to a true, but painted chair?	56	Jordan 1		5
But the extension and the room,	57	Employm. 1		6
But with delaies.	57	Employm. 1		16
But all my companie is a weed.	57	Employm. 1		22
But all the constellations of the storie.	58	H.Script.2		4
But wee are falne from Heaven to Earth,	59	Whitsunday	W	13
But since those pipes of gold, which brought	59	Whitsunday		17
But that from them joyes purle for ever	59	Whitsunday	W	22
Thy house would but a dungeon prove,	60	Grace		6
Not flyes, but I shall bee his prey	61	Praise 1	W	19
But thou art ready there to catch	62	Mattens		2
But God more care of us hath had:	63	Sinne 2		6
But much more blest be God above,	63	Even-song		4
But I have got his sonne, and he hath none.	63	Even-song		8
I ranne; but all I brought, was fome.	64	Even-song		12
But balls of wilde-fire to my troubled minde.	64	Even-song		16
But brings a favour from above;	64	Even-song		31
That flesh is but the glasse, which holds the dust	65	Ch.-monum.		20
But if I travell in your companie,	66	Ch.-mus.		11
But as cold hands are angrie with the fire,	66	Ch.-lock		5
Not on my sinnes, or coldnesse, but thy will.	66	Ch.-lock		8
But the sweet cement, which in one sure band	67	Ch.-floore		10
But all is cleansed when the marble weeps.	67	Ch.-floore		15
But while he thinks to spoil the room, he sweeps.	67	Ch.-floore		18
But when thou dost anneal in glasse thy storie,	67	Windows		6
A strong regard and aw: but speech alone	68	Windows		13
But when it would appeare to others eye,	68	Content		11
The brags of life are but a nine dayes wonder;	69	Content		21
But it is that which while I use	70	Quidditie		11
But is fair dust!	71	Frailtie		4
But when I view abroad both Regiments;	71	Frailtie		9
Nor seeks, nor shunnes them; but doth calmly stay,	72	Constancie		12
His goodnesse sets not, but in dark can runne:	72	Constancie		23
But though men fail him, yet his part doth play.	73	Constancie		30
But since thy breath gave me both life and shape,	73	Afflict.3		7
The week were dark, but for thy light:	75	Sunday		6
The week were dark, but that thy light	75	Sunday	W	6
To endlesse death: but thou dost pull	75	Sunday		16
We could not choose but look on still;	75	Sunday		19
Thou art the man, and man but drosse to thee.	77	Avarice		12
But now (alas!) I dare not; for our King,	78	Ang.&Sts.		16
But now alas I dare not; for my King,	78	Ang.&Sts.	W	16
Man is no starre, but a quick coal	79	Employm.2		6
But we are still too young or old;	79	Employm.2		26
But we are ever young or old;	79	Employm.2	W	26
But no hearing.	80	Deniall		15
But no hearing.	80	Deniall		20
There when I came, whom found I but my deare,	81	Christmas		5
Thou hast but two rare cabinets full of treasure,	82	Ungratef.		7
Thou hadst but two rich cabinets of treasure,	82	Ungratef.	W	7
But all thy sweets are packt up in the other;	82	Ungratef.		19
But man is close, reserv'd, and dark to thee:	82	Ungratef.		25
When thou demandest but a heart,	82	Ungratef.		26
But on thy glorie! then thou wilt reform	83	Sighs & Gr.		3
The mightie God, but I a sillie worm;	83	Sighs & Gr.		5
But I am frailtie, and already dust;	83	Sighs & Gr.		17
But Love took Grace & Glory by the hand,	84	Sighs & Gr.	W	19
But O reprieve me!	83	Sighs & Gr.		25
Into the bitter box; but O my God,	83	Sighs & Gr.		29
But Wisdome quickly swept them all away.	84	The World		5
But rev'rend laws, and many a proclamation	84	The World		9
But Grace shor'd these, and cut that as it grew.	84	The World		15
But Love and Grace took Glorie by the hand,	84	The World		19
But his deare God? who yet his glorious law	85	Vanitie 1		23
To finde out death, but missest life at hand.	86	Vanitie 1		28
But is compos'd of passion.	86	Lent		3
But is a child of passion.	86	Lent	W	3
But though the whole world turn to coal,	88	Vertue		15
Then he that curbs them, being but one to five:	89	The Pearl		29
Therefore not sealed, but with open eyes	89	The Pearl		32
Therefore not seeled, but with open eyes	89	The Pearl	W	32
But thy silk twist let down from heav'n to me,	89	The Pearl		38
But he that means to dwell therein.	90	Man		3
But Man hath caught and kept it, as his prey.	91	Man		20
But Man has caught and kept it, as his prey.	91	Man	W	20
Nothing we see, but means our good,	91	Man		27

BUT (cont'd)

	PAGE	TITLE	LINE
But let the poore,	93	Unkindness	13
But when thy grace	94	Unkindness	18
But time did becken to the flowers, and they	94	Life	4
But that thou art my wisdome, Lord,	95	Submission	1
But when I thus dispute and grieve,	95	Submission	9
But when I mark my life and praise,	96	Justice 1	6
But who drinks on, to hell may go.	97	Charms & K	18
There is but joy and grief;	97	Afflict.5	13
But now thou dost thy self immure and close	99	Decay	11
Man is but grasse,	100	Miserie	5
Bid him but temper his excesse;	100	Miserie	9
And make his own? as if none knew, but he.	100	Miserie	14
The best of men, turn but thy hand	100	Miserie	19
The bargain made to serve thee: but thy love	100	Miserie	26
Wonders and sings, but not his power	101	Miserie	57
But Man doth know	101	Miserie	59
But sinne hath fool'd him. Now he is	102	Miserie	73
But while I bustled, I might heare a friend	103	Jordan 2	15
If I but lift mine eyes, my suit is made:	103	Prayer 2	5
That were I to leave all but one,	103	Prayer 2	21
But as thy love shall sway,	104	Obedience	19
Yet since thou canst not choose but see my actions;	104	Obedience	23
Not a fair look, but thou dost call it foul:	105	Conscience	2
Not a sweet dish, but thou dost call it sowre:	105	Conscience	3
My thoughts must work, but like a noiselesse sphere;	105	Conscience	8
I do but taste it, straight it cleanseth me,	106	Conscience	15
But grones are quick, and full of wings,	107	Sion	21
But there was none; at least no help without:	107	Home	15
Nothing but drought and dearth, but bush and brake,	108	Home	49
Some may dream merrily, but when they wake,	108	Home	51
But when we leave our corn and hay:	108	Home	56
There is no fruitfull yeare, but that which brings	108	Home	57
But dearest Mother, (what those misse),	110	Brit. Ch.	25
And none but thee.	110	Brit. Ch.	30
But thou shalt answer, Lord, for me.	110	The Quip	8
But thou shalt answer, Lord, for me.	110	The Quip	12
In silks that whistled, who but he?	111	The Quip	14
But thou shalt answer, Lord, for me.	111	The Quip	16
But thou shalt answer, Lord, for me.	111	The Quip	20
Is but a bubble, and makes thee a boy.	111	Vanitie 2	18
But thou dost still lament, and pine, and crie;	112	Dawning	7
And feel his death, but not his victorie.	112	Dawning	8
Is deeply carved there: but th' other week	112	JESU	2
But if yet thou idle be,	113	Businesse	15
Were but worth the having,	114	Dialogue	2
But when all my care and pains	114	Dialogue	5
But as I can see no merit,	115	Dialogue	17
When all perfections as but one appeare,	115	Dulnesse	13
But I am lost in flesh, whose sugred lyes	116	Dulnesse	21
I may but look towards thee:	116	Dulnesse	26
To thy renown: but all their hands and throats	117	Providence	11
But robs a thousand who would praise thee fain,	117	Providence	19
The beasts say, Eat me: but, if beasts must teach,	117	Providence	21
The tongue is yours to eat, but mine to praise.	117	Providence	22
The trees say, Pull me: but the hand you stretch,	117	Providence	23
While all things have their will, yet none but thine.	117	Providence	32
Where all may reach: no beast but knows his feed.	118	Providence	50
As bouls go on, but turning all the way.	118	Providence	60
When they are callow; but withdraw their food	118	Providence	63
Their masters flower, but leave it, having done,	118	Providence	66
But at his perill: when he digs the place,	119	Providence	82
Nothing wears clothes, but Man; nothing doth need	120	Providence	109
But he to wear them. Nothing useth fire,	120	Providence	110
But Man alone, to show his heav'nly breed:	120	Providence	111
Rain, do not hurt my flowers; but gently spend	120	Providence	117
Thy creatures leap not, but expresse a feast,	121	Providence	133
But who hath praise enough? nay who hath any?	121	Providence	141
None can expresse thy works, but he that knows them:	121	Providence	142
And so complete, but onely he that owes them.	121	Providence	144
In all my other hymnes, but in this twice.	121	Providence	148
I gave to Hope a watch of mine: but he	121	Hope	1
But he a few green eares:	121	Hope	6
But words suffice not, where are lewd intentions:	122	Sinnes rd.	11
But where one man would have me grinde it,	122	Time	5
Which now is but a pruning-knife.	122	Time	10
He doth not crave lesse time, but more.	123	Time	30
But thou didst reckon, when at first	123	Gratefulnes	9
But that these countrey-aires thy love	124	Gratefulnes	23
But such a heart, whose pulse may be	124	Gratefulnes	31
But while I lookt, the clouds immediately	124	Peace	11
But when I digg'd, I saw a worm devoure	125	Peace	17
But after death out of his grave	125	Peace	27
No smith can make such locks, but they have keyes:	126	Confession	17
But quickly seek some new adventure.	126	Confession	22
Smooth open hearts no fastning have; but fiction	126	Confession	23
But then a thought creeps in,	127	Giddinesse	6
Joy, I did lock thee up: but some bad man	128	Bunch Gr.	1
I did toward Canaan draw; but now I am	128	Bunch Gr.	6
I did towards Canaan draw; but now I am	128	Bunch Gr. V	6
But where's the cluster? where's the taste	128	Bunch Gr.	19

BUT (cont'd)

	PAGE	TITLE		LINE
But can he want the grape, who hath the wine?	128	Bunch Gr.		22
But can he want the grape, who hath the vine?	128	Bunch Gr.	V	22
But much more him I must adore,	128	Bunch Gr.		26
And in the middle plac'd my heart. But he	129	Love unkn.		7
But you shall heare. After my heart was well,	129	Love unkn.		22
But as my heart did tender it, the man	129	Love unkn.		33
But with a richer drug, then scalding water,	130	Love unkn.		40
To supple hardnesses. But at the length	130	Love unkn.		45
But when I thought to sleep out all these faults	130	Love unkn.		49
For I had giv'n the key to none, but one:	130	Love unkn.		55
But all my scores were by another paid,	130	Love unkn.		60
All did but strive to mend, what you had marr'd.	130	Love unkn.		67
But trimm'd with curious lace,	131	Mans medly		16
But as birds drink, and straight lift up their head,	131	Mans medly		21
But as his joyes are double;	131	Mans medly		25
He hath two winters, other things but one:	131	Mans medly		27
Could he but take them right, and in their wayes.	132	Mans medly		33
And with thy knife but prune and PARE,	133	Paradise		11
But stay! what's there?	134	The Method		21
Who heare not him, but quickly heare	134	The Method		27
But all the doctrine, which he taught and gave,	135	Divinitie		13
But he doth bid us take his bloud for wine.	135	Divinitie		21
Faith needs no staffe of flesh, but stoutly can	135	Divinitie		27
But to my Gods too; he doth grone.	136	Ephes.		18
There can no discord but in ceasing be.	136	Ephes.		22
But runnes, although I be not drie;	136	Ephes.		29
But, Lord, the house and familie are thine,	136	Familie		5
But griefs without a noise:	137	Familie		18
But not to make a constant stay.	137	Familie		24
But little do reserve themselves for more:	138	The Size		20
Is not a corpulent, but a thinne and spare,	138	The Size		32
Which have the face of fire, but end in rest.	139	Artillerie		8
But not of speech in starres, began to muse:	139	Artillerie		10
But turning to my God, whose ministers	139	Artillerie		11
But I have also starres and shooters too,	139	Artillerie		17
Not, but I am (I must say still)	139	Artillerie		21
Then thou to grant mine: but because	139	Artillerie		23
With thine own clay. But I would parley fain:	139	Artillerie		27
I am but finite, yet thine infinitely.	139	Artillerie		32
But when debates and fretting jealousies	140	Ch.-rents		16
He that did but look up, was proud and bold.	141	Justice 2		6
But now that Christs pure vail presents the sight,	141	Justice 2		13
Against me there is none, but for me much.	141	Justice 2		24
But I was quicken'd by my houre.	142	Pilgrimage		10
A wasted place, but sometimes rich.	142	Pilgrimage		15
And but a chair.	142	Pilgrimage		36
But I was told by one, it could not be;	143	Holdfast		3
But to have nought is ours, not to confesse	143	Holdfast		9
Are both thy due: but I a silly flie,	143	Complaining		8
Have I no parts but those of grief?	143	Complaining		15
Of future depths, but drink the cleare and good.	145	Discharge		28
But through a Church-yard which them bounds.	145	Discharge		40
Things present shrink and die: but they that spend	145	Discharge		41
But it extend,	145	Discharge		44
What hast thou there? a heart? but is it pure?	147	Offering		3
But all I fear is lest thy heart displease,	147	Offering		13
But now both sinne is dead,	150	Longing		67
Well may he close his eyes, but not his heart.	151	The Bag		6
But as he was returning, there came one	151	The Bag		25
(I have no bag, but here is room):	152	The Bag		32
Have I no harvest but a thorn	153	The Collar		7
Not so, my heart: but there is fruit,	153	The Collar		17
But as I rav'd and grew more fierce and wilde	153	The Collar		33
Thou cam'st but now; wilt thou so soon depart,	154	Glimpse		2
But one half houre of comfort for my heart?	154	Glimpse		5
But one half houre of comfort to my heart?	154	Glimpse	V	5
Feeds not, but addes to the desire of meat.	154	Glimpse		12
But constant to his part	154	Glimpse		18
Doubtlesse, but in the way of punishment,	155	Assurance		4
Thou said'st but even now,	155	Assurance		7
And coin large hopes; but, that I was deceiv'd:	155	Assurance		10
But I will to my Father,	155	Assurance		19
But thou art my desert:	156	Assurance		25
But also mine; as when the league was made	156	Assurance		28
Then can thy truth and I: but while rocks stand,	156	Assurance		32
Not thee, but me, and to be mine:	157	Clasping		15
That which had but two legs before,	158	Praise 3		10
But when thou dost on businesse blow,	158	Praise 3		13
Legs are but stumps, and Pharaohs wheels but logs,	158	Praise 3		17
But when mine eyes	158	Praise 3		26
But after thou hadst slipt a drop	158	Praise 3		31
For well he knows, if but one grief and smart	159	Jos.coat		5
But he hath spoil'd the race; and giv'n to anguish	159	Jos.coat		10
But keep them with repining restlesnesse:	160	The Pulley		17
But thou art fire, sacred and hallow'd fire;	160	Priesthood		7
And I but earth and clay: should I presume	160	Priesthood		8
But since those great ones, be they ne're so great,	161	Priesthood		19
But th' holy men of God such vessels are,	161	Priesthood		25
Wing'd like an arrow: but my scout	162	The Search		19
But all was one.	162	The Search		24

BUT (cont'd)

	PAGE	TITLE		LINE
Against, but for me.	163	The Search		52
Of a lesse world? the greater is but small,	164	Grief		10
But all my wealth, and familie might combine	164	The Crosse		5
With but foure words, my words, Thy will be done.	165	The Crosse		36
But while I grow in a straight line,	166	The Flower		29
To make us see we are but flowers that glide:	167	The Flower		44
But oh the folly of distracted men,	167	Dotage		13
Where are no sorrows, but delights more true,	167	Dotage		17
Flyes of estates and sunne-shine. But to all,	169	The Answer		5
But in my prosecutions slack and small;	169	The Answer		7
But cooling by the way, grows pursie and slow,	169	The Answer		10
But rather turn the pipe, and waters course	170	Water-crs.		6
But still thy sweet originall joy	172	The Glance		13
A mirth but open'd and seal'd up again;	172	The Glance		18
But for his holy name.	172	23 Psalme		12
But lives in me while I do rest)	174	Aaron		24
That call is but the breathing of the sweet.	175	The Odour		25
But must they have my brain? must they dispark	176	Forerunners		3
But will ye leave me thus? when ye before	176	Forerunners		14
But borrow'd thence to light us thither.	177	Forerunners		29
But I will not much oppose	177	The Rose		13
But it biteth in the close.	178	The Rose		24
But I health, not physick choose:	178	The Rose		29
But by book,	178	Discipline		11
For it seems but just and right	180	Invitation		34
But as Pomanders and wood	181	Banquet		25
But I still being low and short,	182	Banquet		40
But leave me to my load:	183	A Parodie		10
And when thou dost but shine lesse cleare,	183	A Parodie		19
That I may seek, but thou art lost;	183	A Parodie		24
That Sinne sayes true: but while I grieve,	184	A Parodie		29
But allso pleasing bee.	184	The Elixer	W	4
But still to make thee prepossest,	184	The Elixer		7
But these are high perfections:	185	The Elixer	W	21
Nothing but bones,	185	Death		2
Thy mouth was open, but thou couldst not sing.	185	Death		4
Dry dust, which sheds no tears, but may extort.	186	Death		12
But since our Saviours death did put some bloud	186	Death		13
But thy trumpet: then it kneels,	186	Dooms-day		10
But I resolve, when thou shalt call for mine,	188	Judgement		11
But are their cares and businesse with the pleasure?	188	Judgement	V	17
But are there cares and businesse with the pleasure?	188	Heaven		17
Light, joy, and leisure; but shall they persever?	188	Heaven		19
But quick-ey'd Love, observing me grow slack	188	Love 3		3
Who made the eyes but I?	189	Love 3		12
Truth Lord, but I have marr'd them: let my shame	189	Love 3		13
But above all, thy Church and Spouse doth prove	190	Ch.-Milit.		9
Not the decrees of power, but bands of love.	190	Ch.-Milit.		10
Moses pursu'd this: but King Solomon	190	Ch.-Milit.		21
But to the Gentiles he bore crosse and all,	190	Ch.-Milit.		25
Wonders of anger once, but now of love.	191	Ch.-Milit.		38
But seems to yeeld Christ hath the greater wounds,	191	Ch.-Milit.		64
But seems to yeeld Christ had the greater wounds,	191	Ch.-Milit.	W	64
But th' Empire dwelt in Greece, to comfort them	192	Ch.-Milit.		73
But England in the higher victorie:	192	Ch.-Milit.		90
But all was glorious cheating, brave deceit,	193	Ch.-Milit.		135
From all these places, but at divers times,	195	Ch.-Milit.		185
But did bewitch, and finely work each nation	195	Ch.-Milit.		193
But did bewitch both kings & many a nation	195	Ch.-Milit.	W	193
But when they were unto the Sorbon come,	196	Ch.-Milit.	W	202
That the whole world did seem but the Popes mule.	196	Ch.-Milit.		204
Yet not as Sinne, but as Religion.	196	Ch.-Milit.		212
But as in vice the copie still exceeds	196	Ch.-Milit.		221
The pattern, but not so in vertuous deeds;	196	Ch.-Milit.		222
But in the Jews and us deserveth tears.	196	Ch.-Milit.		228
We think we rob them, but we think amisse:	197	Ch.-Milit.		253
But lends to us, shall be our desolation.	197	Ch.-Milit.		258
But as the Sunne still goes both west and east;	198	Ch.-Milit.		274
But reserve his breath in store,	199	L'Envoy		12
But that both thou, and all thy traine	200	H. Commun.	W	10
Is more, but for mee still.	200	H. Commun.	W	18
But that which made my soule to dye	201	H. Commun.	W	28
And what shold flesh but flesh discry,	201	H. Commun.	W	32
But keep a constant Pole.	201	H. Commun.	W	42
But then there comes into my way	202	love	W	10
Let mee but once the conquest have	202	love	W	19
But thou art Light & darknes both togeather:	203	Even-song	W	13
But that my darknes may touch thine:	203	Even-song	W	18
But what shall issue, whither these my words	204	Persever.	W	5
Shal help another, but my judgment bee;	204	Persever.	W	6
But kill the man, is seald with thee.	204	Persever.	W	8
In the best face but filth, when, Lord, in thee	206	Walton 2		13
Though nail'd unto 't, but he ascends again,	439	Walton 5		2
When nail'd unto 't, but he ascends again	439	Walton 5	V	2
But onely while thou speak'st; This Anchor will.	439	Walton 5		4
But his heavenly and divine,	208	J. Danvers	D	11
But that my Inke was factious for this side.	209	L. Bacon	D	12
And judge of things but Mediocritie.	210	Paradox	D	12
But veywe yourselves, & inward turn your eyes;	210	Paradox	D	27
Which wee but somtymes prove:	210	Paradox	D	32

BUT (cont'd)

	PAGE	TITLE		LINE
None but gross joyes you move:	210	Paradox	D	34
Stick fast therein, but thy transcendent soule	211	Bohemia	D	7
When sense is made by Comments. But that face	212	Bohemia	D	29
Which misery cannot untwist but rather	212	Bohemia	D	35
But it shall spy some of there victories.	212	Bohemia	D	46
But joyes are stcrd for thee: thou shalt returne	212	Bohemia	D	55
Will pour full joyes to thee, but dregs to those,	213	Bohemia	D	65
But in God's Law sets his delight,	214	Psalm I	D	5
The wicked are nct so, but they	215	Psalm I	D	13
But He, that sits in Heaven, shall laugh,	215	Psalm II	D	9
But I by God am seated King,	215	Psalm II	D	13
but tremble in ycur highest mirth.	216	Psalm II	D	28
But thou, C Lord, art still the shield	216	Psalm III	D	5
But know the Lord himself doth chuse	217	Psalm IV	D	11
will shew us good? But, Lord,	217	Psalm IV	D	22
But in th' abundance of thy Grace	218	Psalm V	D	17
But let all those that trust in thee	219	Psalm V	D	35
am nothing but Infirmitie.	219	Psalm VI	D	4
But, Lord, hcw long so much perplex'd	220	Psalm VI	D	7
But now from me depart away,	220	Psalm VI	D	19
but just men ever guide:	221	Psalm VII	D	34
but shall bring forth a lye.	222	Psalm VII	D	52
But in the pit which he hath made	222	Psalm VII	D	55
But I for all his righteousness	222	Psalm VII	D	61
but that it is a good strife to go as farre as wee can in pleasing	224	Priest		11
my poor labours, but add tc those points, which I have observed,	224	Priest		14
but after hee had fulfilled the work of Reconciliation,	225	Priest 1		7
to get knowledg, but to subdue and mortifie all lusts and affections:	226	Priest 2		9
but after a man is once Minister, he cannot agree to come into any	226	Priest 2		24
but to keep up with the Lord and Lady of the house, and to preserve	226	Priest 2		28
their very face, when occasion cals, but seasonably and discreetly.	226	Priest 2		31
but in all his words and actions slighting, and disesteeming it,	227	Priest 3		18
but especially that of drinking, because it is the most popular vice;	227	Priest 3		23
but orders his Life in such a fashion, that when death takes him,	227	Priest 3		31
and his apparrell plaine, but reverend, and clean, without spots,	228	Priest 3		11
and there is no knowledg, but, in a skilfull hand, serves either	228	Priest 4		16
But the chief and top of his knowledge consists in the book of books,	228	Priest 4		21
But for the understanding of these;	228	Priest 4		26
because they are not understood but with the same Spirit that writ	228	Priest 4		32
but that an industrious, and judicious comparing of place with place	229	Priest 4		7
but diversly clothed, illustrated, and inlarged.	230	Priest 5		2
but as presenting with himself the whole Congregation, whose sins he	231	Priest 6		7
speaking, but with a grave livelinesse, between fear and zeal,	231	Priest 6		19
or any undutifull behaviour in them, but causing them, when they sit,	231	Priest 6		25
of their answer, but gently and pausably, thinking what they say;	231	Priest 6		32
but when we use our reason, and apply our powers to the service	232	Priest 6		5
their poor neighbours, but at midprayers, both to their own loss,	232	Priest 6		9
but after divers gentle admonitions, if they persevere,	232	Priest 6		12
but even to let the world sinke, so they do their duty;	232	Priest 6		16
but the debt and obligation of his calling, being to obey God rather	232	Priest 6		18
but stories and sayings they will well remember.	233	Priest 7		17
none goes out of Church as he came in, but either better, or worse;	233	Priest 7		20
but the character of his Sermon is Holiness;	233	Priest 7		23
he is not witty, or learned, or eloquent, but Holy.	233	Priest 7		24
But it is gained first, by choosing texts of Devotion,	233	Priest 7		26
There are but two devouring elements, fire, and water, he hath both	234	Priest 7		33
but a dictionary, and may be considered alike in all the Scripture.	235	Priest 7		9
himself, but that all may be done with reverence to his glory,	235	Priest 8		24
But yet as the temper of his body may be, or as the temper of his	237	Priest 9		1
but findes opportunities of having his meat dress'd and other	237	Priest 9		8
with any woman alone, but in the audience of others, and that seldom,	237	Priest 9		11
but hath power over his own will, and hath so decreed in his heart,	237	Priest 9		16
but only by those means, by which at first it was obtained.	237	Priest 9		20
but adds to them, out of choyce and devotion, some other dayes	237	Priest 9		24
but that he sometimes looks how things go, demanding an account,	239	Priest 9		1
demanding an account, but not by the way of an account.	239	Priest 9		2
but in actions, in visiting other sick children, and tending their	239	Priest 10		24
but giving him the prerogative of his Fathers profession,	239	Priest 10		31
serve but the vices and vanities of the world, which he is to deny,	240	Priest 10		3
but assures himselfe, that mony thus lent to God, is placed surer	240	Priest 10		7
the wals are not idle, but something is written, or painted there,	240	Priest 10		24
but counts it the art, and secret of governing to preserve	240	Priest 10		33
that there is no help for a fault done, but confession.	240	Priest 10		36
but generally he distributes it thus, To his Children he shewes more	241	Priest 10		8
but an old good servant boards a child.	241	Priest 10		10
The furniture of his house is very plain, but clean, whole,	241	Priest 10		12
fare is plain, and common, but wholsome, what hee hath, is little,	241	Priest 10		15
and common, but wholsome, what hee hath, is little, but very good;	241	Priest 10		16
But those which his home produceth, he refuseth not, as coming cheap,	241	Priest 10		21
not only with abstinence of diet, but also of company, recreation,	241	Priest 10		38
which is but the determination of the second rule by Authority	242	Priest 10		5
but only the two former, which also in diseases of exinanition	242	Priest 10		30
but for the comfort of the weak, that not onely sicknesse breaks	242	Priest 10		34
sicknesse breaks these obligations of fasting, but sicklinesse also.	242	Priest 10		35
Not but that the poor are welcome also to his table, whom he	243	Priest 11		9
But since both is to be done, the better sort invited, and meaner	243	Priest 11		13
and will not be perswaded, but being not invited, they are hated.	243	Priest 11		21
and vertuously, not for any reward of his, but for vertues sake;	243	Priest 11		29
but that all bee in a competent way of getting their living.	244	Priest 12		20
But he gives no set pension to any;	244	Priest 12		25

BUT (cont'd)

	PAGE	TITLE	LINE
But the Parson having a double aime, and making a hook of his	244	Priest 12	30
but resolved to himself, hee wins them to praise God more, . .	245	Priest 12	1
But specially, at hard times, and dearths, he even parts his Living,	245	Priest 12	9
But these he helps not without some testimony, except the evidence	245	Priest 12	21
but allows by no means to give without testimony, as he obeys	245	Priest 12	25
But evident miseries have a naturall priviledge, and exemption from	245	Priest 12	29
givings are lay, and secular, but this is to give like a Priest.	245	Priest 12	38
and those not torne, or fouled, but whole and clean, and well bound;	246	Priest 13	15
but as desiring to keep the middle way between superstition,	246	Priest 13	24
and come to Church in frame, but commonly the next day put off both.	247	Priest 14	9
But then he admonisheth them of two things;	247	Priest 14	23
but that they so labour, as neither to labour anxiously, . .	247	Priest 14	26
but that they may have wherewithall to serve God the better,	248	Priest 14	7
but his purse to their relief, that so they go on more cheerfully in	248	Priest 14	11
but always in the close, before he departs from them: . . .	248	Priest 14	15
but he holds the Rule, that Nothing is little in Gods service:	249	Priest 14	1
but with these he mingles other discourses for conversation sake,	249	Priest 14	10
but also professeth himselfe throughly of the opinion, carrying it	250	Priest 16	8
he hateth him not as an officer, but pityes him as a Father:	250	Priest 16	11
but is long before hee proceede to disinheriting, or perhaps never	250	Priest 16	17
but is himselfe where ever he is.	251	Priest 17	1
or breeding up children to no Calling, but in idleness, or the like.	251	Priest 17	21
but the earnestnesse to do all the good he can, moves him to say thus	251	Priest 17	31
in the Company where he is, but comes under his Test and censure:	252	Priest 18	3
But this he doth discretely, with mollifying, and suppling words;	252	Priest 18	7
Your meaning is not thus, but thus;	252	Priest 18	11
but this will not stand.	252	Priest 18	12
but such as are every way fitting to do his Countrey true . .	252	Priest 19	27
but taking his Parish together the next Sunday, or holy-day,	253	Priest 19	30
but in the other God is his own immediate paymaster, rewarding all	254	Priest 20	20
first point, and but by Catechizing, the other cannot be attained.	255	Priest 21	8
not himself, but is first a Sermon to himself, and then to others;	255	Priest 21	14
way that a Pastor can take, to go over the same, but in other words:	256	Priest 21	3
the order of the Catechisme would be kept, but the rest varyed:	256	Priest 21	6
full of such things, as are not to be seen, but beleeved? . .	256	Priest 21	11
but after that the Catechisme is once learn'd, that which nature is	256	Priest 21	25
Yet the skill consists but in these three points:	256	Priest 21	30
for he could not but say, he would hast out of it as fast as he	257	Priest 21	7
only to serve in the way of drudgery, but to be washed, and cleansed,	257	Priest 21	14
but when one is asked a question, he must discover what he is.	257	Priest 21	19
but there being two things in Sermons, the one Informing, . .	257	Priest 21	21
as being not only to receive God, but to break, and administer him.	257	Priest 22	30
but to throw himself down at the throne of grace, saying, . .	257	Priest 22	31
for thou art not only the feast, but the way to it. . . .	258	Priest 22	1
and Baptizeth not willingly, but on Sundayes, or great dayes.	258	Priest 22	3
admits no vaine or idle names, but such as are usuall and accustomed.	258	Priest 22	4
and thinketh the Ceremony not onely innocent, but reverend. . .	258	Priest 22	9
thing to sustain that place, but a great honour, and no less burden,	258	Priest 22	11
of the Communion only (for then it is too late) but the Sunday,	258	Priest 22	27
of devotion to the Sacrament, but it is for want of Instruction;	258	Priest 22	38
But Parents, and Masters should make hast in this, as to a great	259	Priest 22	2
The saying of the Catechism is necessary, but not enough; . .	259	Priest 22	7
but the Questions must be propounded loosely and wildely, . .	259	Priest 22	8
all reverence himself, so he administers to none but to the reverent.	259	Priest 22	12
but man's unpreparednesse asks kneeling.	259	Priest 22	13
but hee that sits, or lies, puts up to an Apostle: . . .	259	Priest 22	16
but also for the discharge of the Church-wardens, who being . .	259	Priest 22	23
if there be but three Communions, neither can all the people so order	259	Priest 22	25
and not onely a Pastour, but a Lawyer also, and a Phisician.	259	Priest 23	30
but in any Controversie, that they should resort to him as their	259	Priest 23	32
but sends for three or four of the ablest of the Parish to hear	260	Priest 23	8
poorest man of the Parish detain but a pin unjustly from the richest,	260	Priest 23	15
but when he hath so done, then he assumes the Parson, and exhorts	260	Priest 23	16
but that they still fall from all compromises that have been made.	260	Priest 23	24
But then he shews them how to go to Law, even as Brethren, . .	260	Priest 23	25
but to have the skill of healing a wound, or helping the sick.	260	Priest 23	31
But if neither himselfe, nor his wife have the skil, and his means	260	Priest 23	32
not to exceed his bounds, but in tickle cases to call in help.	260	Priest 23	36
but sometimes lift up their minds to better things, even in the midst	261	Priest 23	24
but condemns them for vanities, and so shuts them out of his family,	261	Priest 23	37
but preferrs her garden and fields before all outlandish gums.	262	Priest 23	4
But though the Parson sets forward all Charitable deeds, . .	262	Priest 23	11
not to incroach on others Professions, but to live on his own.	262	Priest 23	17
but as a brother still, except some small and temporary estranging	263	Priest 25	29
but proceeding on, comes to do unlawfully, even before he is aware;	264	Priest 26	23
but for example sake, and because they are most common, . .	265	Priest 26	3
but in brief, a poor man is an occasion, my countrey is an occasion,	265	Priest 26	13
but being seated in the Countrey, and doing their duty faithfully,	266	Priest 26	2
things is bad, but it is the custome and habit that names a glutton.	266	Priest 26	17
But to eat to ones hurt, comprehends, besides the hurt, . .	266	Priest 26	20
but that they must rise so, as that it is not meate or drinke that	266	Priest 26	34
not keep an uniform diet, but to feed variously, now more, . .	267	Priest 26	11
But the Parson distinguisheth according to his double aime, . .	267	Priest 26	15
but when he meets with a refined, and heavenly disposition, . .	267	Priest 26	18
but rather made food miraculously, then suffered so good desires	267	Priest 26	24
because hee knows nothing but the Crosse of Christ, his minde being	267	Priest 27	28
but also for that when they are in company, instructions seasoned	268	Priest 27	3
doing kindnesses, but receiving none;	268	Priest 28	24
that are reproved, but never contempt either in them, or others.	268	Priest 28	29
But if the Contempt be not punishable by Law, or being so, . .	269	Priest 28	3

BUT (cont'd)

	PAGE	TITLE	LINE
but invites and urges the best unto it, shewing that they do	270	Priest 29	8
shewing that they do not loose, or go lesse, but gaine by it;	270	Priest 29	9
but if after gentle, and neighbourly admonitions they still persist	270	Priest 29	19
but that God often changeth it according as he sees fit, . .	270	Priest 30	30
but to continue his dependance on God, not onely before the corne is	271	Priest 30	34
on God, not onely before the corne is inned, but after also;	271	Priest 30	35
But these prayers are not necessary, but additionary. . . .	272	Priest 31	28
but to go on as cheerfully, as if he had not been interrupted.	273	Priest 31	11
But here there are two Cautions to be added.	273	Priest 31	14
he be a little affected therewith, but not afflicted, or troubled;	273	Priest 31	19
if he resent it to a mislike, but not a griefe.	273	Priest 31	20
but of reverence to Gods house, resolves whenever he enters into	273	Priest 31	22
But it happens, that neer the place where he is to pray, . .	273	Priest 31	27
I will not doubt to go without staying to pray there (but onely,	273	Priest 31	35
but a generall also of the diseases of the time, that so, . .	274	Priest 32	5
the Common-wealth, that none should be idle, but all busied.	274	Priest 32	28
we must not be idle, but labour to get more, that we may give more,	275	Priest 32	1
But if it should be, the Assertion stands thus:	275	Priest 32	10
But it will not be amisse in this exceeding usefull point to descend	275	Priest 32	17
But his family is his best care, to labour Christian soules,	275	Priest 32	30
But if after all this care well dispatched, the house-keepers Family	275	Priest 32	36
But if hee may bee of the Commission of Peace, there is nothing	276	Priest 32	7
for so excellent a Place, not to refuse, but rather to procure it.	276	Priest 32	18
But chiefly, and above all things, they are to frequent Sessions	276	Priest 32	37
he must not only be a morning man, but at Committees also; . .	277	Priest 32	12
which are brought from thence to the House but in generall. . .	277	Priest 32	14
But if the young Gallant think these Courses dull, and phlegmatick,	278	Priest 32	3
but also as they may be handled, a religious imployment? . .	278	Priest 32	6
military state of a Christian life, but even in the peaceable also;	279	Priest 33	3
but that, so the other acts be, that is not necessary: . . .	279	Priest 33	28
his preaching, but afterwards also, as Mat. 22. 35. He was tempted:	280	Priest 34	9
but to labour still to be as fervent in Christian Duties, . .	280	Priest 34	19
but to put bounds, and hoopes to their joyes:	280	Priest 34	28
But if they shall fear, that at such, or such a time their peace	280	Priest 34	32
that can or will look after things, but all goes by chance, or wit:	281	Priest 34	8
but also of any part, by taking away so much as the usuall seasons	281	Priest 34	23
but to them an unpenetrable rock, an unaccessible desert. . .	282	Priest 34	3
but for an exciting of others by their sight, to the acknowledging	282	Priest 34	14
but with the Gospel it selfe be preached to all ages, Matth. 26. 13.	282	Priest 34	26
and sent, which to the bearer is but paper, but to the receiver,	282	Priest 34	37
which to the bearer is but paper, but to the receiver, and opener,	282	Priest 34	37
But if he sees them neerer desperation, then Atheisme; . . .	283	Priest 34	5
not any sin else, but is within his Love;	283	Priest 34	24
but the despising of Love must needs be without it. . . .	283	Priest 34	24
as knowing that absence breedes strangeness, but presence love.	284	Priest 35	16
but is rather glad of catching opportunities to do them. . .	284	Priest 35	25
it not onely a grave, and reverend thing, but a beneficial also.	285	Priest 36	3
But that which the Apostles used so diligently in their writings,	285	Priest 36	9
But this was not proper to Christ, or the Apostles only, . .	285	Priest 36	11
for it was not the person, but Priesthood, that blessed; . .	285	Priest 36	23
have the Ministers power of Blessing only, but also of cursing.	285	Priest 36	25
it is not performed by way of request, but of confidence, and power,	286	Priest 36	7
But the Parson first values the gift in himself, and then teacheth	286	Priest 36	18
but if he often interpose a Blessing, when the other gives him just	286	Priest 36	22
but also spread in his Parish, without any remedy (which cannot be	287	Priest 37	1
may talk, so they do it not with sport, but commiseration;) . .	287	Priest 37	14
But some may say, though the Law allow this, the Gospel doth not,	287	Priest 37	21
But this is easily answered:	287	Priest 37	24
But thou Lord, art patience, and pity, and sweetnesse, and love;	288	Priest	20
so that then where sin abounded, not death, but grace superabounded;	288	Priest	25
But though the streams of thy bloud were currant through darknesse,	288	Priest	32
not to Thunder, or Angels, but to silly and sinfull men: . .	289	Priest	5
but pardon our sins, and perfect what thou hast begun. . . .	289	Priest	21
so neither may thy word, but accomplish that for which it is given.	289	Priest	32
three Persons, but one most glorious, incomprehensible God, . .	290	Priest	14
Intemperance was not such an evil, but it might easily be remedied;	291	Cornaro	6
but had already gone farre in me, first caused me to leave . .	291	Cornaro	18
But Intemperance destroyes most healthy and flourishing . .	292	Cornaro	9
there would be no help for me, but Death, shortly to be expected.	292	Cornaro	15
But I, then not liking that kinde of Diet, followed my Appetite,	292	Cornaro	26
But after I had resolved to follow Temperance and Reason, . .	292	Cornaro	31
saw that it was no hard thing to do so, but the proper duty of man;	292	Cornaro	32
with a full stomack, but so as I might well both eat and drink more.	293	Cornaro	18
but also afterwards I fell not into that yearely disease, . .	293	Cornaro	22
I not so avoid all these, but that now and then I fell into them;	293	Cornaro	38
But mine own experience confirmeth this more;	294	Cornaro	10
But I, whom that matter ought to have affected most, received no	294	Cornaro	20
But I, considering what an orderly life I had led for many yeares	295	Cornaro	7
But my experience taught me another thing also, to wit, . .	295	Cornaro	16
but also to gather strength, which could not be but by meat & drink.	295	Cornaro	24
But all these things could not defend me against their importunities.	296	Cornaro	5
the quantitie of meat to be increased, yet but two ounces onely.	296	Cornaro	8
nothing holp me, but that exact rule which I had so long continued.	296	Cornaro	29
though it was but a little excesse, in a few dayes had so soon	297	Cornaro	5
but that he shall ever after live free from diseases, if he will keep	297	Cornaro	19
no man can be a perfect Physician to another, but to himself onely.	297	Cornaro	25
I denie not but that Physicians are necessarie, and greatly to be	298	Cornaro	3
who not onely as a friend doth visit thee, but help thee! . .	298	Cornaro	9
But that a man may preserve himself in health, I advise, . .	298	Cornaro	11
But surely there is no such matter, if Temperance be wanting.	298	Cornaro	21

BUT (cont'd)

	PAGE	TITLE		LINE
But sensuall men (as most are) desiring to satisfie their Appetite,	298	Cornaro		23
But they consider not, of how great moment ten yeares are in mature	298	Cornaro		28
which, but in that age, can hardly be perfected.	298	Cornaro		31
not onely in the citie, but also in villages and hamlets.	299	Cornaro		4
but onely that a man should begin and by little and little accustome	299	Cornaro		8
But some may say, He which lives a regular life, eating alwayes light	299	Cornaro		22
so that we can eat but a very little, wherewith she is very well	299	Cornaro		28
but such meats as are agreeable to his disease, and that in much	299	Cornaro		30
cannot fall into diseases, and but very seldome into indispositions;	299	Cornaro		36
But they who finde benefit in these meats, may, yea ought to use	300	Cornaro		10
Because since this is at the best but uncertain, dangerous,	300	Cornaro		19
man of an ill constitution, but living orderly, is more sure of life,	300	Cornaro		25
But some, too much given to Appetite, object, That a long life is no	300	Cornaro		27
But these erre greatly, as I will shew by my self, recounting	300	Cornaro		30
But I drained the ground, and made the aire good:	301	Cornaro		27
which are all in their perfect vigour, but especially my Taste;	302	Cornaro		9
But this chiefly delights me, that my advice hath taken effect in	302	Cornaro		14
but cheerfull, lively, and pleasant.	303	Cornaro		10
but also I hope, when I shall come to that point, I shall finde no	303	Cornaro		22
(setting casualties aside) I shall not die but by a pure resolution:	303	Cornaro		26
but that I should wish all who have the care of themselves,	303	Cornaro		31
but lest in any thing I forsake that Temperance which I have found so	303	Cornaro		34
But I like none of it, for it slights the Scripture too much:	306	Valdesso		16
but a use of perfection, and are able to make the man of God perfect,	306	Valdesso		18
but not as a naked Word severed from God, but as the Word of God:	306	Valdesso		29
but not as a naked Word severed from God, but as the Word of God:	307	Valdesso		1
But by trusting in the word of God they trust in God.	307	Valdesso		2
but habituall, for I can no more free my selfe from actuall sinnes	308	Valdesso		3
none can free themselves of themselves, but only by the Grace of God:	308	Valdesso		9
distinction, for Fomes is not taken away, but Accensio Fomitis;	308	Valdesso		16
is not quite extinguished, but the heate of it asswaged.	308	Valdesso		17
but the spirits bearing witnesse with our spirit, revealing	309	Valdesso		3
as if they were both but Alphabets and after a time to be left.	309	Valdesso		19
but a use of perfection, neither can they ever be exhausted,	309	Valdesso		21
be by a plenarie circumspection) but still even to the most learned	309	Valdesso		23
but the meaning is this, That God in the dayes of the Gospell will	310	Valdesso		4
but such a one as shall still have the assistance of the holy spirit	310	Valdesso		6
hath read it, but keepes it by him, and reads it againe and againe,	310	Valdesso		28
But the use of the Doctrinall part is more, in regard it presents us	310	Valdesso		32
but enlightens us with new Considerations the more we read it.	310	Valdesso		34
but this sufficeth, he himselfe allowes it for a holy conversation	311	Valdesso		1
but it is sutable to what the Author holds elsewhere, for he	311	Valdesso		21
even the godly are chastized but not punished) for evill doing	311	Valdesso		28
but the truth of the Doctrine would be examined, however it may passe	311	Valdesso		31
in the Church of God there is one fundamentall, but else variety.	312	Valdesso		3
but that he ought to pray God affectionately and fervently to send	312	Valdesso		16
but in things good, as to relieve my Neighbour, God hath already	313	Valdesso		13
but because he cannot doe all, God often chuseth which he shall doe,	313	Valdesso		21
but in those other occasions, Gods Spirit will mortify and try them	314	Valdesso		20
But with condition, or conditionally he prayed as man, though as God	315	Valdesso		10
Feare is given to Christ, but not doubt, and upon good ground.	315	Valdesso		12
But when he enlargeth he goes too farre.	315	Valdesso		34
But it is one thing not to judge, another to defend them.	316	Valdesso		13
Neither doe I doubt but if Abraham had lived in our Kingdome under	316	Valdesso		22
but he might have been justly put to death for it by the Magistrate,	316	Valdesso		24
but when he sayes they are equally exempt with God, that is dangerous	316	Valdesso		31
men cannot judg spirituall mens actions, but the Magistrate may.	317	Valdesso		6
as if it were but childrens meat, whereas there is not onely milke	317	Valdesso		23
whereas there is not onely milke there, but strong meat also.	317	Valdesso		24
more to be said of this Chapter but that his opinion of the scripture	318	Valdesso		5
I doe not then bid him goe away but rather stay longer,	318	Valdesso		16
but however he would have them attend to it till that time,	318	Valdesso		20
having forms or vizars of godlinesse, but denying the power thereof.	319	Valdesso	V	27
But there are other Cases of Conscience grounded on Piety	319	Valdesso	V	30
but an analogat observation of Ecclesiasticall and Canonicall lawes,	320	Valdesso		1
Not a long day, but a good heart rids worke.	321	Proverbs		24
The Chicken is the Countries, but the Citie eates it.	324	Proverbs		108
To a fair day open the window, but make you ready as to a foule.	325	Proverbs		119
Love your neighbour, but pull not downe your hedge.	325	Proverbs	V	141
Buy at a faire, but sell at home.	326	Proverbs		160
but take heede, lest you bee drowned.	326	Proverbs		167
Thinke of ease, but worke on.	327	Proverbs		178
you can have but water of it.	327	Proverbs		180
God complaines not, but doth what is fitting.	327	Proverbs		182
but the liberall makes of a farthing sixe pence.	328	Proverbs	V	211
The honey is sweet, but the Bee stings.	328	Proverbs		212
One graine fills not a sacke, but helpes his fellowes.	328	Proverbs		226
Punishment is lame, but it comes.	329	Proverbs		249
The Fox knowes much, but more he that catcheth him.	330	Proverbs		280
The foole askes much, but hee is more foole that grants it.	330	Proverbs		282
Feare nothing but sinne.	331	Proverbs		299
The child saies nothing, but what it heard by the fire.	331	Proverbs		300
He is not poore that hath little, but he that desireth much.	331	Proverbs		309
When God will, no winde but brings raine.	332	Proverbs		332
All things require skill, but an appetite.	334	Proverbs		378
but not a hundred sons one father.	335	Proverbs		404
but an 100 sons are not enough to govern one Father.	335	Proverbs	V	404
Hee who hath but one sonne makes him fat,	336	Proverbs	V	433
Fooles bite one another, but wise-men agree together.	336	Proverbs		452
Good is good, but better carries it.	337	Proverbs		454

BUT (cont'd)

	PAGE	TITLE		LINE
The good mother sayes not, Will you? but gives.	337	Proverbs		467
Praise a hill, but keepe below.	338	Proverbs		488
Praise the Sea, but keepe on land.	338	Proverbs		489
Faire is not faire, but that which pleaseth.	338	Proverbs		492
There is no jollitie but hath a smack of folly.	338	Proverbs		493
Great trees are good for nothing but shade.	339	Proverbs		546
Bells call others, but themselves enter not into the Church.	340	Proverbs		571
'Tis hard to be wretched, but worse to be knowne so.	340	Proverbs		577
The March sunne raises but dissolves not.	342	Proverbs		614
but he will drinke when and what he pleaseth.	342	Proverbs		623
Astrologie is true, but the Astrologers cannot finde it.	342	Proverbs		641
but an ill man doubles his fault.	343	Proverbs		655
but an ill, it doubles his fault.	343	Proverbs	V	655
None is offended but by himselfe.	343	Proverbs		656
Nothing lasts but the Church.	343	Proverbs		661
No barber shaves so close but another finds worke.	343	Proverbs		667
Ther's no great banquet but some fares ill.	343	Proverbs		668
but the Devill builds a Chappell hard by.	343	Proverbs		674
Pardon all but thy selfe.	344	Proverbs		677
None is so wise, but the foole overtakes him.	345	Proverbs		734
None is so wise, but that the foole overtakes him.	345	Proverbs	V	734
Fooles give to please all but their owne.	345	Proverbs		735
Gods Mill grinds slow, but sure.	346	Proverbs		747
There comes nought out of the sacke but what was there.	348	Proverbs		833
There come nought out of the sacke but what was there.	348	Proverbs	V	833
Good newes may bee told at any time, but ill in the morning.	350	Proverbs		877
The yeare doth nothing else but open and shut.	351	Proverbs		901
but the patient owes nothing to him but a little mony.	351	Proverbs		921
Trees eate but once.	352	Proverbs		933
Knowledge makes one laugh, but wealth makes one dance.	352	Proverbs		957
You cannot make the fire so low but it will get out.	353	Proverbs		965
With customes wee live well, but Lawes undoe us.	353	Proverbs		973
Hee that tells his wife newes is but newly married.	353	Proverbs		987
knowes nothing sure but what hee hath laid out.	354	Proverbs		1001
Gentility is nothing but Ancient Riches.	356	Proverbs	D	1033
but he would chuse to dy in Spain (where they say	357	Proverbs	D	1047
There is no heat of affection but is joyned	357	Proverbs	D	1050
but every thing else in this world.	358	Proverbs	D	1077
An Asse endures his burden, but not more then his burden.	358	Proverbs	D	1080
He that hath but one eye, must bee afraid to lose it.	358	Proverbs	D	1088
To seek in a Sheep five feet when there is but four.	359	Proverbs	D	1112
but sometimes he can hurt.	359	Proverbs	D	1119
No day so clear but hath dark clouds.	359	Proverbs	D	1123
No hair so small but hath his shadow.	359	Proverbs	D	1124
The mouse that hath but one hole is quickly taken.	360	Proverbs	D	1135
Wo be to him that reads but one book.	360	Proverbs	D	1146
but my next neighbour doth me more harm	361	Proverbs	D	1173
but you married men laugh till your hearts ake.	361	Proverbs	D	1175
But I fear the heat of my late Ague hath dryed up those springs,	363	Letters		4
but, I profess it not:	363	Letters		16
to answer your infinite kindnesses, but a constancy of obedience;	363	Letters		19
but that you have performed your kindness to the full, and that	363	Letters		24
But perhaps they will say, you are sickly, you must not study too	364	Letters		25
but that every day, I may step one step towards my journies end;	364	Letters		27
but they will object again, What becomes of your Annuity?	364	Letters		30
in our publick Halls, you know, is nothing but Fish and Whit-meats:	365	Letters		4
But, alas Sir, what is that to those infinite Volumes of Divinity,	365	Letters		13
pardon my boldness, and consider but these three things.	365	Letters		16
except you wink, you cannot but see many brave examples.	366	Letters		6
when there is no caus, but by setting a just price of your qualities:	366	Letters		17
But I am out of my time:	366	Letters		19
and perhaps a little more mild, but you will hardly perceive it.	366	Letters		25
but upon the want of those Books which were not to be got in England;	367	Letters		4
Letter in yours, for it was because I know your Lodging, but not his.	367	Letters		25
yet his love expects them not but first certifies you that there are	368	Letters		4
but yet he will heare of no other affaires, untill they have	368	Letters		8
but not so great as he expected & therfore he grumblingly said that	368	Letters		32
only my comfort is that this is but an occasion for you to amplify	369	Letters		3
I could have come in person to thank you, but it is not possible;	369	Letters		11
yet that will be about 30 l. per an. but the commodiousness is beyond	369	Letters		32
not but that I joy in your favours, but that you may see,	370	Letters		9
that I joy in your favours, but that you may see, that if all fail,	370	Letters		9
but that I have both time and work to be Your extreme Servant,	370	Letters		13
but, I have wrote him back, that this dignity, hath no such	370	Letters		21
no such earthiness in it, but it may very well be joined with Heaven;	370	Letters		22
but I hope I shall shortly, though for the reckoning of your favours,	370	Letters		30
but, since I know I did not, and that your share continues,	372	Letters		16
would quickly make good my wish but that my employment does fix me	372	Letters		19
does fix me here, it being now but a month to our Commencement:	372	Letters		20
of all Comfort, who is not willing to behold any sorrow but for sin.	372	Letters		26
As the Earth is but a point in respect of the heavens, so are earthly	372	Letters		29
but, wou'd you divide and choose too?	373	Letters		1
but you are freed from that fear, who have already abundantly	373	Letters		10
But perhaps being above the Common people, our Credit and estimation	373	Letters		25
but, Oh God! how easily is that answered, when we consider that	373	Letters		27
in the holy Scripture, are never given to the rich, but to the poor.	373	Letters		29
but, Blessed be the Meek, and Blessed be the Poor, and,	373	Letters		31
as if they not only not desir'd, but, even fear'd to be blessed.	373	Letters		34
but, their Fiery-tryals have had an end:	374	Letters		1
but, whatsoever befals us we must alwaies, at all times rejoyce in	374	Letters		25

	PAGE	TITLE		LINE
BUT (cont'd)				
not only entertain my proposals, but advance them, was lovingly done,	375	Letters		2
one of our neeces into your hands but barely what I wrote I meant,	375	Letters		5
when he urged one upon me, and but one, and that at my choice.	375	Letters		11
and age, and knew none but one who could be no company to them.	375	Letters		15
having none to doe it but her school-mistresse, and you know what	375	Letters		25
But I judge you not:	375	Letters		32
But though I both consider this, and your observation, also,	376	Letters		3
but difficulties are so farr from cooling christians, that they whett	376	Letters		10
But take this rule, and it is an outlandish one, which I commend	376	Letters		16
but you joyed me exceedingly with your relation of my Lady Duchess's	377	Letters		18
but he told her Grace, that he would by no meanes do so,	379	Letters		6
doubt not, through Gods blessing, but it shall be to the full;	379	Letters		18
but things that are lovely, & of good report if there be any vertue	380	Woodnoth		13
but to chuse a higher work, as God gives me higher thoughts,	381	Woodnoth		24
with his favours, can not but be not only allowable but commendable.	381	Woodnoth		26
with his favours, can not but be not only allowable but commendable.	381	Woodnoth		27
but a Trade having two things, the one imployment, the other profitt,	381	Woodnoth		30
But yet the Arts in quietnes and silence here are reverenced,	442	Oration		35
repose, peace with all but Booke-wormes, perpetuall povertie,	442	Oration		36
perpetuall povertie, but when your Excellencies appeare.	442	Oration		37
BUTTER				
Bee not a Baker, if your head be of butter.	332	Proverbs		321
BUTTERY				
or Diet, or too open a Buttery, or reading vain books, or swearing,	251	Priest 17		20
BUY				
But if thou want it, buy it not too deere.	16	Ch.-Porch		244
that servants for their mony are as other things that they buy,	265	Priest 26		25
if a man hath wherewithall to buy a spade, and yet hee chuseth rather	265	Priest 26		28
To buy deare is not bounty.	326	Proverbs		156
Buy at a faire, but sell at home.	326	Proverbs		160
He that blames would buy.	335	Proverbs		410
I am fain ever and anon, to buy somewhat tending towards my health;	364	Letters		34
or five Shillings come in my way, I buy it, though I fast for it;	365	Letters		12
BUYER				
Whither the buyer and the seller please;	104	Obedience		3
The buyer needes a hundred eyes, the seller not one.	334	Proverbs		390
BUYING				
do much esteem their word, it being the Life of buying, and selling,	228	Priest 3		3
In chusing a wife, and buying a sword,	338	Proverbs		490
BUZZARD'S				
An old wise mans shaddow is better then a young buzzards sword.	324	Proverbs		90
BY				
Allows thee choise of paths: take no by-wayes;	7	Ch.-Porch		14
Is outlawd by himself: all kinde of ill	7	Ch.-Porch		33
Is outlawd by himself: all kinds of ill	7	Ch.-Porch	W	33
All worldly right, save what he hath by beast.	7	Ch.-Porch		36
Frailtie gets pardon by submissivenesse;	8	Ch.-Porch		51
By dressing, mistressing, and complement.	9	Ch.-Porch		80
Thou liv'st by rule. What doth not so, but man?	12	Ch.-Porch		134
Thou liv'st by rule. What does not so, but man?	12	Ch.-Porch	W	134
Houses are built by rule, and common-wealths.	12	Ch.-Porch		135
Who lives by rule then, keeps good companie.	12	Ch.-Porch		138
By all means use sometimes to be alone.	12	Ch.-Porch		145
By any art, yet to be purchased.	13	Ch.-Porch		172
By no means runne in debt: take thine own measure.	13	Ch.-Porch		175
Spend not on hopes. They that by pleading clothes	14	Ch.-Porch		181
By great deeds shew, that thou canst little do;	15	Ch.-Porch		220
Usefulnesse comes by labour, wit by ease;	18	Ch.-Porch		291
By lavishnesse thine own, and others wit,	18	Ch.-Porch		304
Onely by his permission. Then beware,	22	Ch.-Porch		405
They may weep out the stains by them did rise:	23	Ch.-Porch		417
Those doores being shut, all by the eare comes in.	23	Ch.-Porch		418
He that by being at church escapes the ditch,	24	Ch.-Porch		435
Which he might fall in by companions, gains.	24	Ch.-Porch		436
Summe up at night, what thou hast done by day;	24	Ch.-Porch		451
Make not an ell, by trifling in thy wo.	24	Ch.-Porch		460
Oh all ye, who passe by, whose eyes and minde	26	Sacrifice		1
But not their harts, as I by proofe doe try.	30	Sacrifice	W	123
Who by my spittle gave the blinde man eies,	31	Sacrifice		134
Who by my spittle gave that blinde man eies,	31	Sacrifice	W	134
Then Simon bears it for me by constraint,	33	Sacrifice		198
O all ye who passe by, behold and see;	33	Sacrifice		201
Bywords, but this by sorrow I must win:	33	Sacrifice		207
Yet by my subjects am condemn'd to die	34	Sacrifice		234
They part my garments, and by lot dispose	34	Sacrifice		241
All back unto thee by the poore.	35	Thanksgvng		20
For by thy death I die for thee.	36	Reprisall		8
By thy eternall glorie didst outgo me?	37	Reprisall		10
Yet by confession will I come	37	Reprisall		13
Each seventh note by right is due to thee.	38	The Sinner		4
For by the writings all may see	39	Good Fri.	W	31
For they can lodge transgressions by the score:	40	Sepulchre		6
And as of old, the law by heav'nly art	41	Sepulchre		17
Who takes thee by the hand, that thou likewise	41	Easter		3
But thou wast up by break of day,	42	Easter		21
As larks, doe by degree,	43	East.wings	W	8
Although by stealth	44	H. Bapt.2		11
Though that by stealth	44	H. Bapt.2	W	11
And thence by kinde	45	Nature		10
That I did live, but by a pang of woe.	47	Afflict.1	W	30

BY (cont'd)

	PAGE	TITLE		LINE
And bring by Faith all things to him?	49	Faith		4
Where now by Faith all arms are of a length;	50	Faith		27
But by the way of nourishment and strength	52	H.Commun.		7
By this thy heav'nly bloud;	53	H.Commun.		38
Since thou hast taught us by thy word,	53	H.Commun.	W	39
That wee may gaine by crosses.	53	H.Commun.	W	40
Thou standing by: and though thy glorious name	54	Love 1		11
Dust blown by wit, till that they both were blinde:	54	Love 2		10
Who wert disseized by usurping lust:	54	Love 2		12
Before I were by frosts extremitie	57	Employm. 1		3
Feasting all comers by twelve chosen men.	59	Whitsunday		8
Were cut and martyr'd by the fault	59	Whitsunday		19
By way of imprest, all my future mone.	62	Afflict.2		15
Yet studies them, not him by whom they be.	63	Mattens		16
Then by a sunne-beam I will climbe to thee.	63	Mattens		20
By sight of sinne we should grow mad.	63	Sinne 2		8
Better by worms be all once spent,	69	Content		26
Are chaw'd by others pens and tongue;	69	Content		30
Are chaw'd by others pen and tongue;	69	Content	W	30
He that by seeking hath himself once found,	69	Content		35
Where all the beasts and fowls by their command	70	Humilitie		3
Where all the beasts and Foule by their command	70	Humilitie	W	3
When by the beasts the presents tendred were,	70	Humilitie		7
Which by consent was giv'n to Mansuetude.	70	Humilitie		10
The fearfull Hare her eares, which by their law	70	Humilitie		11
The fearfull Hare her eares, which by the law	70	Humilitie	W	11
Kill'd in the way by chance.	70	Humilitie		16
While the world now rides by, now lags behinde.	72	Constancie		10
By that I knew that thou wast in the grief,	73	Afflict.3		2
Sure thou wilt joy, by gaining me	74	The Starre		29
Writ by a friend, and with his bloud;	75	Sunday		4
We sullied by our foul offence:	76	Sunday		51
Then forcing thee, by fire he made thee bright:	77	Avarice		9
And by the others is opprest.	79	Employm.2		15
And by degrees	79	Employm.2	W	24
For by that powder thou wilt make us see.	82	Ungratef.		18
For by this powder thou wilt make us see.	82	Ungratef.	W	18
But Love took Grace & Glory by the hand,	84	Sighs & Gr.	W	19
Whereas they were supported by the same:	84	The World		4
Till she had weakned all by alteration:	84	The World		8
But Love and Grace took Glorie by the hand,	84	The World		19
Spoil the good use; lest by that argument	86	Lent		29
Spoil our good use; lest by that argument	86	Lent	W	29
That travelleth by-wayes:	87	Lent		39
May turn, and take me by the hand, and more	87	Lent		41
By starving sinne and taking such repast,	87	Lent		44
What willing nature speaks, what forc'd by fire;	88	The Pearl		6
Did both conduct and teach me, how by it	89	The Pearl		39
As the sunne scatters by his light	90	Afflict.4		23
And day by day	90	Afflict.4		27
I made a posie, while the day ran by:	94	Life		1
By noon most cunningly did steal away,	94	Life		5
Lord, thou relievest, yet I die by thee:	95	Justice 1		4
Doubles the night, & trips by day.	96	Charms & K	W	8
Who by aspersions throw a stone	96	Charms & K		9
By it do all things live their measur'd houre:	103	Prayer 2		10
By it do all things live their silly houre:	103	Prayer 2	W	10
That by destroying that which ty'd thy purse,	103	Prayer 2		17
Lord, let it now by way of purchase go.	105	Obedience		35
They were by winged souls	105	Obedience		44
By listning to thy chatting fears	105	Conscience		5
That chains us by the teeth so fast?	108	Home		38
And ev'n my verse, when by the ryme and reason	109	Home		75
By her preferr'd,	110	Brit. Ch.		15
That ev'n her face by kissing shines,	110	Brit. Ch.		17
Then came brave Glorie puffing by	111	The Quip		13
Do not by hanging down break from the hand,	112	Dawning		11
Anneal'd on every bunch. One standing by	116	Love-joy		3
And be dispos'd, and dress'd, and tun'd by thee,	118	Providence		38
Springs vent their streams, and by expense get store:	119	Providence		71
Clouds cool by heat, and baths by cooling boil.	119	Providence		72
Is by a ship the speedier passage made.	119	Providence		90
Are rul'd by him, and taught to serve his trade.	119	Providence		92
And by their breathing ventilate the ill.	122	Sinnes rd.		10
Since by thy cutting he grows better.	122	Time		12
By art.	123	Gratefulnes		4
By flight of sinne.	125	Peace		36
For as the Jews of old by Gods command	128	Bunch Gr.		8
Walkt by my self abroad, I saw a large	129	Love unkn.		25
But all my scores were by another paid,	130	Love unkn.		60
In th' other Angels have a right by birth:	131	Mans medly		9
A throbbing conscience spurred by remorse	132	The Storm		9
Glorie and honour are set by till it	132	The Storm		15
Reason triumphs, and faith lies by.	134	Divinitie		8
Which falls by night, and poure it out for you!	140	Ch.-rents		30
But I was quicken'd by my houre.	142	Pilgrimage		10
But I was told by one, it could not be;	143	Holdfast		3
That all things were more ours by being his.	143	Holdfast		12
And single things grow fruitfull by deserts.	147	Offering		10
By these thy feet, at which my heart	150	Longing		80

BY (cont'd)

	PAGE	TITLE		LINE
Whose streams we got by the Apostles sluce,	152	The Jews		3
Who by not keeping once, became a debter;	152	The Jews		5
And now by keeping lose the letter:	152	The Jews		6
And by that crie of her deare Lord obtain,	152	The Jews		11
Which by the springs accesse grew much more great.	154	Glimpse		15
Who by thy coming may be made a court!	155	Glimpse		30
What is objected by my foes.	155	Assurance		24
Having a glasse of blessings standing by;	159	The Pulley		2
Yet have I often seen, by cunning hand	161	Priesthood		13
That earth is fitted by the fire and trade	161	Priesthood		16
In praising might, the poore do by submission	161	Priesthood		41
What pride by opposition.	161	Priesthood		42
Are properly a crosse felt by thy sonne,	165	The Crosse		35
Forfeit their Paradise by their pride.	167	The Flower		49
But cooling by the way, grows pursie and slow,	169	The Answer		10
Passing all cordials made by any art,	171	The Glance		6
My doctrine tun'd by Christ, (who is not dead,	174	Aaron		23
A speaking sweet, mend by reflection,	175	The Odour		17
This breathing would with gains by sweetning me	175	The Odour		26
But by book,	178	Discipline		11
This by my picture, in my book I write:	183	The Posie		6
By nailing Christ to fasten it again.	190	Ch.-Milit.		24
Who by an ambush lost his Paradise.	192	Ch.-Milit.		66
Onely there was a handsome picture by,	194	Ch.-Milit.		169
By free dispensings of the Churches treasure.	195	Ch.-Milit.		180
By dispensations of the Churches treasure.	195	Ch.-Milit.	W	180
And make that name good by their transmigrations;	195	Ch.-Milit.		184
While Truth sat by, counting his victories:	195	Ch.-Milit.		190
By letting in them both, pollutes her streams:	197	Ch.-Milit.		242
By letting in them both pollute her streams:	197	Ch.-Milit.	W	242
By carrying first their gold from them away:	197	Ch.-Milit.		250
We are more poore, and they more rich by this.	197	Ch.-Milit.		254
So also did the Church by going west	198	Ch.-Milit.		275
That I who cannot now by day	203	Even-song	W	6
Why doth that fire, which by thy power and might	206	Walton 1		12
Passe not by,	208	J. Danvers	D	1
Here is copied out by art;	208	J. Danvers	D	10
So by the Other, you may read in mee	209	L. Bacon	D	5
By outward forme and showe,	210	Paradox	D	26
When sense is made by Comments. But that face	212	Bohemia	D	29
Which, planted by the waters, shall	214	Psalm I	D	9
Of earth is driven by winds away,	215	Psalm I	D	15
But I by God am seated King,	215	Psalm II	D	13
Aided by him, I will not fear	216	Psalm III	D	13
shall be abhorr'd by thee.	218	Psalm V	D	16
Destroy them, Lord, and by their own	219	Psalm V	D	29
protected still by thee:	219	Psalm V	D	38
Thou art that righteous God by whom	221	Psalm VII	D	35
For first, Man fell from God by disobedience.	225	Priest 1		4
that which Christ did, and by his auctority, and as his Vicegerent.	225	Priest 1		17
entertained to that end, either by an open, or implicite Covenant.	226	Priest 2		23
who by hard usage increase their travell, the Countrey Parson is very	227	Priest 3		14
and by having fellowship, with the unfruitfull works of darknesse,	227	Priest 3		25
because people by what they understand, are best led to what they	228	Priest 4		19
and all being penn'd by one and the self-same Spirit, it cannot be,	229	Priest 4		6
the places controverted, which the Parson by no means refuseth.	229	Priest 4		19
This Body he made by way of expounding the Church Catechisme,	230	Priest 5		7
possible reverence, by no means enduring either talking, or sleeping,	231	Priest 6		23
he by no means suffers it, but after divers gentle admonitions,	232	Priest 6		12
he is ever very well supplyed by some able man who treads in his	232	Priest 7		25
he procures attention by all possible art, both by earnestnesse	232	Priest 7		31
both by earnestnesse of speech, it being naturall to men to think,	232	Priest 7		31
and by a diligent, and busy cast of his eye on his auditors,	232	Priest 7		33
By these and other means the Parson procures attention;	233	Priest 7		22
it is gained first, by choosing texts of Devotion, not Controversie,	233	Priest 7		26
by dipping, and seasoning all our words and sentences in our hearts,	233	Priest 7		28
Thirdly, by turning often, and making many Apostrophes to God,	233	Priest 7		32
by frequent wishes of the peoples good, and joying therein,	234	Priest 7		6
by an often urging of the presence, and majesty of God,	234	Priest 7		25
of the presence, and majesty of God, by these, or such like speeches.	234	Priest 7		25
since we are here by him, and without him could not be here.	234	Priest 7		30
or from the State, or from God by a child born, or dead,	235	Priest 8		35
or in exhortations to some of his flock by themselves, whom his	236	Priest 8		13
Let him communicate the thing often by prayer unto God,	237	Priest 9		5
his meat dress'd and other services done by men-servants at home,	237	Priest 9		9
but only by those means, by which at first it was obtained.	237	Priest 9		20
and the dayly prayers enjoyned him by auctority, which he observeth	237	Priest 9		23
and by these hee keeps his body tame, serviceable, and healthfull;	237	Priest 9		26
and by the vertue of the shield of faith, he is not afraid	238	Priest 9		5
by reason of continuall inward, or outward temptations,	238	Priest 9		12
the choyce of his wife was made rather by his eare, then by his eye;	238	Priest 9		26
the choyce of his wife was made rather by his eare, then by his eye;	238	Priest 9		27
demanding an account, but not by the way of an account.	239	Priest 9		3
and sending his charity by them to the poor, and somtimes giving them	239	Priest 10		26
so well served, as by religious servants, both because they do best,	240	Priest 10		15
He suffers not a ly or equivocation by any means in his house,	240	Priest 10		32
he straitly requires of all to pray by themselves before they sleep	241	Priest 10		1
and till they have learned them, makes them kneel by him;	241	Priest 10		4
by taking both sorts of food into them, do as it were dresse	241	Priest 10		33
both for man in themselves, by growing them selves fit for his table.	241	Priest 10		34

BY (cont'd)

	PAGE	TITLE	LINE
the determination of the second rule by Authority to this particular.	242	Priest 10	6
and fasting dayes were fully performed by keeping of the two former,	242	Priest 10	9
which will discover it selfe by spitting, and rheume, or flegme.	242	Priest 10	25
as not to get out of that sicknesse, when I am in it, by any diet.	242	Priest 10	38
takes home with him, setting them close by him, and carving for them,	243	Priest 11	11
Which perswasion the Parson by all means avoyds, knowing that where	243	Priest 11	22
This he effects either by bounty, or perswasion, or by authority,	244	Priest 12	22
or perswasion, or by authority, making use of that excellent statute,	244	Priest 12	22
and so by continuall, and fresh bounties, unexpected to them,	244	Priest 12	32
but allows by no means to give without testimony, as he obeys	245	Priest 12	25
things there be decent, and befitting his Name by which it is called.	246	Priest 13	3
That all the books appointed by Authority be there, and those	246	Priest 13	14
Neither in this doth he forbear, though there be company by:	248	Priest 14	25
and offering to have them taught on holy-dayes by his servants.	248	Priest 14	37
perfecting our Redemption no other way, then by sorrow; . .	249	Priest 15	23
For by this means, when any sinns, he hateth him not as an officer,	250	Priest 16	10
by a due blessing of God for their safe arrival, and saying grace	251	Priest 17	8
and at going to bed by giving the Host notice, that he will have	251	Priest 17	10
yet seasonably, and discreetly, by taking aside the Lord, or Lady;	251	Priest 17	28
either by the wickedness or quarrelsomnesse thereof, he either	252	Priest 18	16
it judiciously, or breaks it off seasonably by some diversion.	252	Priest 18	18
if God have sent any calamity either by fire, or famine, . .	253	Priest 19	29
is rather by withdrawing his bounty and courtesie from the parties	254	Priest 20	22
from the parties offending, or by private, or publick reproof,	254	Priest 20	23
then by causing them to be presented, or otherwise complained of.	254	Priest 20	24
that Countrey people are drawne, or led by sense, more then by faith,	254	Priest 20	31
or led by sense, more then by faith, by present rewards, . .	254	Priest 20	32
more then by faith, by present rewards, or punishments, . .	254	Priest 20	32
by present rewards, or punishments, more then by future. . .	254	Priest 20	32
turning it to reformation of life, by pithy and lively exhortations;	255	Priest 21	7
first point, and but by Catechizing, the other cannot be attained.	255	Priest 21	8
which exceedingly delights him as by way of exercise upon himself,	255	Priest 21	11
and by way of preaching to himself, for the advancing of his own	255	Priest 21	12
and to satisfie the Congregation by their Catholick answers.	255	Priest 21	21
may then by an honourable way take occasion to be better instructed.	255	Priest 21	30
their vowes, and by occasion of both, inlarge their meditations.	255	Priest 21	34
for many say the Catechisme by rote, as parrats, without ever	256	Priest 21	3
Was it made, or came it by chance?	256	Priest 21	7
by making the Question very plaine with comparisons, and making much	256	Priest 21	13
and by which the Catechizer, if he once get the skill of it,	256	Priest 21	18
and accordingly by questions well ordered he found Philosophy in	256	Priest 21	22
an illustrating the thing by something else, which he knows,	256	Priest 21	37
cannot inflame or ravish, that must be done by a set, and laboured,	257	Priest 21	25
and his Saints, and by way of undertaking for a Christian soul.	258	Priest 22	13
a state to reduce it to its principles by which it grew great;	258	Priest 22	16
The time of every ones first receiving is not so much by yeers,	258	Priest 22	32
ones first receiving is not so much by yeers, as by understanding:	258	Priest 22	33
by experience, and by reading some initiatory treatises in the Law,	260	Priest 23	1
and by reading some initiatory treatises in the Law, with Daltons	260	Priest 23	1
as also by discourse with men of that profession, whom he hath ever	260	Priest 23	3
and dark nature, not easily determinable by Lawyers themselves;	260	Priest 23	21
This is done by seeing one Anatomy, reading one Book of Phisick,	261	Priest 23	4
reading one Book of Phisick, having one Herball by him. . .	261	Priest 23	5
as also by way of illustration, even as our Saviour made plants	261	Priest 23	13
that by familiar things hee might make his Doctrine slip the more	261	Priest 23	18
whether having a rule, it ought not to be guided by it; . .	263	Priest 24	3
being made by the precept of Authority more then indifferent,	263	Priest 24	12
and shewing by all means, that the delinquents returne is to his	264	Priest 25	1
which by mine own experience I have found hurtfull, then from those	266	Priest 26	24
then from those which by a Common tradition, and vulgar knowledge are	266	Priest 26	26
This he procures, first by his holy and unblameable life; . .	268	Priest 28	20
Secondly, by a courteous carriage, & winning behaviour: . .	268	Priest 28	22
by a bold and impartial reproof, even of the best in the Parish,	268	Priest 28	27
contempt shall proceed so far as to do any thing punishable by law,	268	Priest 28	32
But if the Contempt be not punishable by Law, or being so, . .	269	Priest 28	3
of his Conscience, whereas they are to do it by Command, and by Oath.	269	Priest 29	31
since even by the Common Statute-Law they are taken for a kinde	269	Priest 29	33
as being persons enabled by that Name to take moveable goods,	270	Priest 29	2
and by the same Law they are to levy penalties for negligence in	270	Priest 29	4
be vilified or debased, by being cast on the lower ranke of people;	270	Priest 29	7
shewing that they do not loose, or go lesse, but gaine by it;	270	Priest 29	10
he wisheth them by no means to spare any, though never so great;	270	Priest 29	18
have to think that all things come by a kind of naturall course;	270	Priest 30	25
By his sustaining power he preserves and actuates every thing in his	271	Priest 30	3
so that corne doth not grow by any other vertue, then by that which	271	Priest 30	4
then by that which he continually supplyes, as the corn needs it;	271	Priest 30	5
or the fire on earth, by reason of their fierce, strong, . .	271	Priest 30	11
By Gods governing power he preserves and orders the references	271	Priest 30	13
and be preserved in that act by his sustaining power, yet if he suite	271	Priest 30	15
and other accidents by his governing power, the fairest harvests come	271	Priest 30	17
by which God turnes all outward blessings to inward advantages.	271	Priest 30	37
This Liberty he compasseth by one distinction, and that is, . .	272	Priest 31	19
or by oversleeping himself at night, omits his additionary prayer.	272	Priest 31	30
omission thereof upon just occasion ought by no means to trouble him.	273	Priest 31	7
By this it is evident, that the distinction is of singular use	273	Priest 31	12
as that by this he may take into his Prayer humiliation also.	273	Priest 31	32
may be prevented, or diverted by reasonable imployment. . .	274	Priest 32	24
by bringing them up in the fear and nurture of the Lord; . .	275	Priest 32	22
the improvement of his grounds, by drowning, or draining, . .	275	Priest 32	24
the one, the abuse of it, by taking petty Countrey bribes; . .	276	Priest 32	20

BY (cont'd)

	PAGE	TITLE		LINE
he is to endeavour by all means to be a Knight or Burgess there;	277	Priest 32		9
and not ingaged into some Profession by their Parents, whose neglect	277	Priest 32		25
the Professours whereof were much imployed by Queen Elizabeth,	277	Priest 32		32
of all diseases, and were recovered of all by things that he knew;	278	Priest 33		31
yet the victory is alike in all, being by the self-same Spirit.	279	Priest 33		2
that can or will look after things, but all goes by chance, or wit:	281	Priest 34		9
by taking away so much as the usuall seasons of summer and winter,	281	Priest 34		23
and frequented by others, but to them an unpenetrable rock, . .	282	Priest 34		3
that this very thing was intended by God, that the Jews should be	282	Priest 34		12
but for an exciting of others by their sight, to the acknowledging	282	Priest 34		15
which evidently argue Christs Divinity by their success: . .	282	Priest 34		23
Mercy in releeving the poor by a liberall distribution and largesse,	284	Priest 35		8
1 Sam. 1. 18. though it came from a man disallowed by God: . .	285	Priest 36		22
because it is not performed by way of request, but of confidence,	286	Priest 36		7
by the interesting of that dignity wherewith God hath invested	286	Priest 36		8
by speaking any good, this unusuall form begets a reverence,	286	Priest 36		23
are either such as are made known by common fame (and of these,	287	Priest 37		12
passed judgment, & been corrected either by whipping, or imprisoning,	287	Priest 37		15
Law intends, as is evident by those, which are branded for rogues,	287	Priest 37		19
yet by these thy conflicts, and seemingly hazards, didst thou arise	288	Priest		33
Written by Lud. Cornarus, Translated into English by Mr. George	291	Cornaro		T
by Lud. Cornarus, Translated into English by Mr. George Herbert.	291	Cornaro		T
wit and noble disposition, overthrown and undone by Intemperance;	291	Cornaro		3
For by it, and my ill constitution, (having a most cold & moist	291	Cornaro		20
whereas my life seemed as farre from it by Nature, as it was neare it	291	Cornaro		27
as farre from it by Nature, as it was neare it by Intemperance.	291	Cornaro		27
as I too wel by experience found.	292	Cornaro		7
and the faults of Nature are often amended by Art, as barren grounds	292	Cornaro		11
as barren grounds are made fruitfull by good husbandry. . .	292	Cornaro		12
being directed by them in the way I ought to hold, I understood,	292	Cornaro		23
and by continuance thereof, within lesse then one yeare (although it	292	Cornaro		35
By this means, within lesse then a yeare I was not onely freed from	293	Cornaro		19
hurt those bodies, which were kept in good order by a moderate Diet:	294	Cornaro		3
and therefore never was sick by any of these inconveniences,	294	Cornaro		9
that this suit and contention was raised by the Divine Providence,	294	Cornaro		24
By which it is manifest, That neither melancholie, nor any other	294	Cornaro		30
This I found by experience, when I was seventie yeares old: . .	294	Cornaro		35
and then was dragged for a good space by the furie of the horses,	294	Cornaro		38
I was led by the advice of Physicians, and the dayly importunitie	295	Cornaro		19
but also to gather strength, which could not be but by meat & drink.	295	Cornaro		25
because by eating little he prolongs his life.	295	Cornaro		35
By which is intimated, that the hurt of too much meat is greater,	296	Cornaro		2
I by the grace of God cured my self, onely with returning to my	296	Cornaro		24
which I contracted by breaking my diet, although it was a sore evil,	297	Cornaro		1
By this it may clearely be perceived, how great is the power of order	297	Cornaro		3
Every one by long experience may know the qualities of his own	297	Cornaro		26
qualities to me, if I had not found them out by long experience?	297	Cornaro		35
then a Temperate Life, Temperance by all means is to be embraced.	298	Cornaro		2
as is manifest by experience, is a naturall Physick most agreeable	298	Cornaro		13
onely by a pure consumption of the radicall moisture, without grief	298	Cornaro		17
Many have thought that this could be done by Aurum potabile,	298	Cornaro		19
although they see themselves ill handled by their intemperance,	298	Cornaro		25
written by their Authors in that age, and those ten yeares, . .	298	Cornaro		33
onely that a man should begin and by little and little accustome	299	Cornaro		9
so decent, and so holy, it is worthy by all means to be embraced;	300	Cornaro		4
as I will shew by my self, recounting the delights and pleasures in	300	Cornaro		30
being so built by me according to the rules of Architecture,	301	Cornaro		12
By this means the place is come to that perfection we now see it is:	301	Cornaro		30
is this my pleasure made lesse by the decaying dulnesse of my senses,	302	Cornaro		7
Because that by Temperance and the Grace of God I feel not those	302	Cornaro		24
Moreover, by this also, in what estate I am, may be discovered,	302	Cornaro		27
Tragedie with old Age, by reason of the sad events which it contains.	302	Cornaro		32
By which it is evident, That the life which I live at this age,	303	Cornaro		9
whereas I by the experience of so many yeares have learned to give	303	Cornaro		20
(setting casualties aside) I shall not die but by a pure resolution:	303	Cornaro		26
because that by the regularitie of my life I have shut out death all	303	Cornaro		27
a fair and desirable death, which Nature brings by way of resolution.	303	Cornaro		29
A Copy of a letter written by MR. GEORGE HERBERT to his friend	304	Valdesso		T
Churches sake, to whom by Printing it I would have you consecrate it.	304	Valdesso		9
neverthelesse I wish you by all meanes to publish it, for these three	304	Valdesso		18
and darkned by the Adversaries, and their great stumbling-block.	305	Valdesso		2
But by trusting in the word of God they trust in God. . . .	307	Valdesso		2
The exemption from both, is by the Grace of God.	308	Valdesso		5
none can free themselves of themselves, but only by the Grace of God:	308	Valdesso		9
only by the generall Providence of God, as Socrates and Aristides,	308	Valdesso		12
He often useth this manner of speech Beleeving by Revelation,	308	Valdesso		29
not by relation, whereby I understand he meaneth only the effectuall	308	Valdesso		30
or assent to the promises of the Gospell by heare-say, or relation	309	Valdesso		1
this I call beleeving by Revelation, and not by Relation. . .	309	Valdesso		7
(as Pictures may be by a plenarie circumspection) but still even	309	Valdesso		22
Although by other words of the same Psalme it is evident, . .	309	Valdesso		27
observed, who workes by his Word, and ever in the reading of it.	310	Valdesso		1
hath read it, but keepes it by him, and reads it againe and againe,	310	Valdesso		28
will better appear by his 98 Consideration of faith and good works.	312	Valdesso	V	5
or justify himselfe before God, by any acts or exercises of Religion;	312	Valdesso		15
and that by restraining him from what he would not have him doe.	313	Valdesso		22
By renouncing the help of humane learning in the studying . .	314	Valdesso	V	3
By occasions (I suppose) hee meaneth the ordinary, or necessary	314	Valdesso		16
reviling also of Ananias seemes, by his owne recalling, an oversight;	316	Valdesso		11
but he might have been justly put to death for it by the Magistrate,	316	Valdesso		25

BY (cont'd)

	PAGE	TITLE		LINE
have made it appeare, that it was done by Gods immediate precept.	316	Valdesso		26
and surely this the Author meant by the word Jurisdiction,	317	Valdesso	V	7
The 98. Consid. about being justified by faith, or by good works,	319	Valdesso	V	17
justified by faith, or by good works, or condemned for unbelief,	319	Valdesso	V	17
By the Saints of the world he every where understands the cunning	319	Valdesso	V	19
understands the cunning hypocrite who by the world is counted a very	319	Valdesso	V	20
By Hebrew piety, he meaneth not the very Ceremonies of the Jewes,	319	Valdesso		34
OUTLANDISH PROVERBS SELECTED By Mr. G. H.	319	Proverbs		T
You cannot know wine by the barrell.	321	Proverbs		20
The Mill gets by going.	325	Proverbs		122
Though the Mastiffe be gentle, yet bite him not by the lippe.	325	Proverbs		132
Though the Mastiffe be gentile, yet bite him not by the lippe.	325	Proverbs	V	132
Ill comes in by ells, and goes out by inches.	327	Proverbs		194
What your glasse telles you, will not be told by Councell.	329	Proverbs		255
By suppers more have beene killed then Galen ever cured.	330	Proverbs		272
By suppers more are killed then Galen ever cured.	330	Proverbs	V	272
The child saies nothing, but what it heard by the fire.	331	Proverbs		300
By the needle you shall draw the thread,	332	Proverbs		329
and by that which is past, see	332	Proverbs		329
Who is fed by anothers hand stays long ere he be full.	336	Proverbs	V	439
He that trusts in a lie, shall perish by the truth.	340	Proverbs	V	569
I was taken by a morsell, saies the fish.	342	Proverbs		627
Foolish tongues talke by the dozen.	343	Proverbs		645
None is offended but by himselfe.	343	Proverbs		656
but the Devill builds a Chappell hard by.	343	Proverbs		674
He is onely bright that shines by himselfe.	345	Proverbs		707
By doing nothing we learne to do ill.	346	Proverbs		757
To a close shorne sheepe, God gives wind by measure.	349	Proverbs		867
Warre and Physicke are governed by the eye.	351	Proverbs		906
An Oxe is taken by the horns, and a Man by the tongue.	353	Proverbs		967
Take an oxe by his hornes & a man by his tongue.	353	Proverbs	V	967
Citties are taken by the eares.	353	Proverbs		970
Selected By Mr George Herbert, Late Orator	356	Proverbs	D	T
Slander is a shipwrack by a dry Tempest.	356	Proverbs	D	135
Amiens was taken by the Fox, and retaken by the Lion.	356	Proverbs	D	1036
Some evils are cured by contempt.	357	Proverbs	D	1052
Infants manners are moulded more by the example of Parents,	357	Proverbs	D	1060
then by stars at their nativities.	357	Proverbs	D	1060
Hee that makes himself a sheep, shall be eat by the wolfe.	358	Proverbs	D	1089
God gives his wrath by weight, and without weight his mercy.	359	Proverbs	D	1115
It is good to hold the asse by the bridle.	360	Proverbs	D	1129
A man is known to be mortal by two things, Sleep and Lust.	361	Proverbs	D	1159
Whatever is made by the hand of man,	362	Proverbs	D	1184
by the hand of man may be overturned.	362	Proverbs	D	1184
by which Scholars say, the Muses use to take up their habitations.	363	Letters		5
either by engaging my future Annuity, or any other way,	365	Letters		20
by the Patents of your perpetual favour to do so still,	365	Letters		24
As I shal find occasion, you shal receive them by peeces;	366	Letters		3
by transporting French commodities to your own country.	366	Letters		12
when there is no caus, but by setting a just price of your qualities:	366	Letters		17
I understand by a Letter from my Brother Henry, that he hath bought	366	Letters		29
for I am enjoined to write to you by Sir John Danvers, to which mine	367	Letters		28
her halfe her estate to live on by her selfe (for shee desires no	368	Letters		24
yet have I sent it thither by a faithful Messenger this day:	369	Letters		16
I understand by Sir Francis Nethersols Letter, that he fears I have	370	Letters		18
judge me then by those waters, and not by my ink, and then you shall	372	Letters		4
and not by my ink, and then you shall justly value Your most truly,	372	Letters		4
my absence by how much it naturally augmenteth suspicion,	372	Letters		21
by so much shall it make my prayers the more constant and the more	372	Letters		21
how they have been burnt by thousands, and have endur'd such other	373	Letters		36
hath your Goodness brought on you, by admitting our poor services?	376	Letters		26
by moving the Duches's heart, to an exceeding cheerfulness,	379	Letters		1
but he told her Grace, that he would by no meanes do so, urging,	379	Letters		7
by the Apostles rule. 1 Cor.	380	Woodnoth		5
Change shewes not well & you are by the Apostles rule (Philip 4, 8.)	380	Woodnoth		12
by the way of supporting either it (in regard of the citty) or your	380	Woodnoth		27
things may grow worse by your withdrawing which grow not better	381	Woodnoth		10
worse by your withdrawing which grow not better by your presence.	381	Woodnoth		11
Merchant of London which fell to me by the death of my deare Neece	382	G.H.'s Will		9
by which we well know how to convince the sterne, and more austere	442	Oration		5
wee might the more by love grow on, both the Spanish and Brittish	442	Oration		17

BY-WAYES

Allows thee choise of paths: take no by-wayes;	7	Ch.-Porch		14
That travelleth by-wayes:	87	Lent		39

BYWORDS

Bywords, but this by sorrow I must win:	33	Sacrifice		207

C

I saw a vine drop grapes with J and C	116	Love-joy		2

CABINET

Thou art the cabinet where the jewell lay:	78	Ang.&Sts.		14
The statelier cabinet is the Trinitie,	82	Ungratef.		13
In his poore cabinet of bone	82	Ungratef.		28
Or cabinet of pleasure.	91	Man		30

CABINETS

Thou hast but two rare cabinets full of treasure,	82	Ungratef.		7
Thou hadst but two rich cabinets of treasure,	82	Ungratef.	W	7

CABLE

Boat, cable, sail and needle, all in one.	120	Providence		128
Good cable, to enforce and draw,	153	The Collar		24
This holy Cable's of all storms secure.	439	Walton 5		10

	PAGE	TITLE		LINE
CABLE (cont'd)				
This holy Cable's from all storms secure.	439	Walton 5	V	10
CAESAR				
Why, Caesar is their onely King, not I:	30	Sacrifice		121
CAGE				
Of what is fit, and not. Forsake thy cage,	153	The Collar		21
CAKE				
Wouldst thou both eat thy cake, and have it?	138	The Size		18
pork, sausages, pulse, and cake, and py-crust, and the like:	293	Cornaro		13
A Cake and an ill custome must be broken.	322	Proverbs		27
Who eates his cake alone must saddle his horse alone.	333	Proverbs	V	348
CALAMITIES				
Your colour faded, and calamities	140	Ch.-rents		18
Your colour vaded, and calamities	140	Ch.-rents	V	18
Sure-footed griefs, solid calamities,	167	Dotage		9
CALAMITY				
if God have sent any calamity either by fire, or famine,	253	Priest 19		29
CALAMITYES				
Cease then to judge calamityes	210	Paradox	D	25
CALCINED				
That, as his death calcined thee to dust,	41	Easter		5
CALDRON				
A boyling caldron, round about whose verge	129	Love unkn.		27
Out of the caldron getting, soon I fled	130	Love unkn.		46
The Caldron suppled, what was grown too hard:	130	Love unkn.		65
CALENDER				
And all her calender of sinnes fulfill;	197	Ch.-Milit.		244
Death keepes no Calender.	351	Proverbs		908
CALL (see also cals)				
Thou hast two sconses, if thy stomack call;	11	Ch.-Porch		128
Tast all, but feed not. if thy stomach call	11	Ch.-Porch	W	128
Thy children, kindred, friends upon thee call;	13	Ch.-Porch		161
Yet for twelve heav'nly legions I could call:	31	Sacrifice		155
But more with malice: yet, when they did call,	34	Sacrifice		238
Yet Lord restore thine image, heare my call:	38	The Sinner		12
The dew, for which grasse cannot call,	60	Grace		11
Gad not abroad at ev'ry quest and call	68	Content		5
To execute their call,	70	Humilitie		6
Each part may call the farthest, brother:	91	Man		16
Each part may call the furthest, brother:	91	Man	V	16
Not a fair look, but thou dost call it foul:	105	Conscience		2
Not a sweet dish, but thou dost call it sowre:	105	Conscience		3
When sawcie mirth shall knock or call at doore,	136	Ephes.		13
In hope of great things. Call to minde thy dream,	138	The Size		44
For where before thou still didst call on me,	141	Justice 2		19
Some call the wold;	142	Pilgrimage		14
Some call the world;	142	Pilgrimage	V	14
Some call the would;	142	Pilgrimage	V	14
Yet call.	148	Longing		12
Call in thy deaths head there: tie up thy fears.	153	The Collar		29
The Call.	156	The Call		T
The windes their stint: and yet when I did call,	158	Praise 3		23
Thou heardst my call, and more.	158	Praise 3		24
We him in glorie call, The Sonne of Man.	168	The Sonne		14
Call home thine eye (that busie wanderer)	170	Self-cond.		5
Shall call and meet,	175	The Odour		23
That call is but the breathing of the sweet.	175	The Odour		25
Still invite, still call to thee:	180	Invitation		33
When thou shalt call	187	Judgement		4
But I resolve, when thou shalt call for mine,	188	Judgement		11
Julips & Cordials when wee call on thee	204	The Knell	W	17
Call thee from out of that surrounded land,	213	Bohemia	D	61
Lord hear me when I call on Thee,	217	Psalm IV	D	1
He adviseth all to call to minde their Baptism often;	258	Priest 22		14
not to exceed his bounds, but in tickle cases to call in help.	260	Priest 23		36
the Countrey Parson proceeds so farre as to call in Authority,	263	Priest 25		23
When none of these occasions call him abroad, every morning that hee	277	Priest 32		15
before thy face, who are contrary to thee, in all we call thee?	288	Priest		10
this I call beleeving by Revelation, and not by Relation.	309	Valdesso		6
Call me not an olive, till thou see me gathered.	331	Proverbs		301
Bells call others, but themselves enter not into the Church.	340	Proverbs		571
CALL'D				
Then all thou addest may be call'd his treasure.	11	Ch.-Porch		114
And when Justice call'd for fears,	146	Praise 2		23
CALLED				
Those that live in Noble Houses are called Chaplains, whose duty	226	Priest 2		15
When the Apostles would have called down fire from Heaven,	229	Priest 4		13
act in them, then when they are called to others prayers, and that,	241	Priest 10		5
things there be decent, and befitting his Name by which it is called.	246	Priest 13		3
that some are called at the eleventh houre, and therefore hee still	250	Priest 16		19
This is called keeping Gods watch, when the baits which the enemy	252	Priest 18		13
Thou hast elected us, thou hast called us, thou hast justified us,	290	Priest		3
CALLETH				
God calleth preaching folly. Do not grudge	23	Ch.-Porch		429
Man calleth thee his wealth, who made thee rich;	77	Avarice		13
when a just occasion calleth him out of his Parish (which he	250	Priest 17		23
CALLING				
And calling Justice, all things burn.	99	Decay		20
Me thoughts I heard one calling, childe:	154	The Collar		35
but the debt and obligation of his calling, being to obey God rather	232	Priest 6		19
turnes his care to fit all their dispositions with some calling,	239	Priest 10		31

	PAGE	TITLE	LINE
CALLING (cont'd)			
and unbefitting the reverence of their Fathers calling,	240	Priest 10	2
Those that he finds busie in the works of their calling,	247	Priest 14	21
or breeding up children to no Calling, but in idleness,	251	Priest 17	21
where God is thanked for calling us to the knowledg of his grace,	258	Priest 22	6
step into their great and glorious calling) and upon what termes,	258	Priest 22	19
fit discharging either of Divine duties, or duties of their calling.	266	Priest 26	30
the one in having no calling, the other in walking carelesly in our	274	Priest 32	16
the other in walking carelesly in our calling, he first represents	274	Priest 32	17
So that even in Paradise man had a calling, and how much more out	274	Priest 32	22
Yet is it also a debt to our Countrey to have a Calling,	274	Priest 32	27
All are either to have a Calling, or prepare for it:	275	Priest 32	11
Wherefore all are either presently to enter into a Calling,	275	Priest 32	15
because we are about a Calling, and a preparation thereunto.	276	Priest 32	36
necessary duties, and occasions of our calling and condition of life;	314	Valdesso	17
CALLOUS			
Indeed 'tis true. I found a callous matter	130	Love unkn.	38
Indeed it's true. I found a callous matter	130	Love unkn. V	38
CALLOW			
The callow principles within their nest:	85	Vanitie 1	17
When they are callow; but withdraw their food	118	Providence	63
CALLS			
Which each one calls for so with utmost breath,	31	Sacrifice	146
What place or person calls for, he doth pay.	72	Constancie	15
And calls for musick, while his veins do swell,	98	Mortific.	14
And calls him coward, who for fear of sinne	127	Giddinesse	7
Thy clay that weeps, thy dust that calls.	143	Complaining	5
Afterwards when the hour calls, with his family attending him,	236	Priest 8	3
so must they fight for, and defend them, when occasion calls.	277	Priest 32	20
should be his proof, and witnesses, as he calls them, Isaiah 43. 12.	282	Priest 34	13
The hole calls the thiefe.	327	Proverbs	204
our Credit and estimation calls on us to live in a more splendid	373	Letters	26
CALM			
Be calm in arguing: for fiercenesse makes	18	Ch.-Porch	307
O day most calm, most bright,	75	Sunday	1
O day so calm, sc bright:	75	Sunday W	1
Sweet day, so cool, so calm, so bright,	87	Vertue	1
Tempests are calm to thee; they know thy hand,	118	Providence	45
CALMLY			
Nor seeks, nor shunnes them; but doth calmly stay,	72	Constancie	12
CALMNESS			
which none can perform so wel in trouble, as in calmness.	273	Priest 31	3
CALMNESSE			
Calmnesse is great advantage: he that lets	19	Ch.-Porch	313
CALS			
their very face, when occasion cals, but seasonably and discreetly.	226	Priest 2	31
This is that which the Apostle cals a reasonable service,	232	Priest 6	2
and these exhortations he cals his privy purse, even as Princes have	236	Priest 8	16
Whosoever when a just occasion cals, either spends not at all,	265	Priest 26	5
CALVES			
keep and fodder well their cattel, they must have milk, and Calves;	270	Priest 30	28
CAM'ST			
Thou cam'st but now; wilt thou so soon depart,	154	Glimpse	2
CAMBRIDGE			
While Prince to Spaine, and King to Cambridge goes,	438	Lat.Trans.	1
of the Universitie of Cambridg.	356	Proverbs D	T
for my Cambridge necessities are stronger to tye me here,	369	Letters	18
I was glad of your Cambridge newes, but you joyed me exceedingly	377	Letters	18
Orator of the Universitie of Cambridge, when the Ambassadours were	441	Oration	T
CAME			
Yet not mine neither: for from thee they came,	5	Dedication	2
The greater world o' th' two; for that came in	33	Sacrifice	206
That as sinne came, so Sacraments might flow:	34	Sacrifice	247
I took thy sweetned pill, till I came neare;	47	Afflict.1	47
I took thy sweetned pill, till I came where	47	Afflict.1 W	47
My heart did heave, and there came forth, O God!	73	Afflict.3	1
Thou art the holy mine, whence came the gold,	78	Ang.&Sts.	11
Thou art the sacred mine, whence came the gold,	78	Ang.&Sts. W	11
There when I came, whom found I but my deare,	81	Christmas	5
Love built a stately house; where Fortune came,	84	The World	1
Then Pleasure came, who liking not the fashion,	84	The World	6
Where never yet came moth.	100	Miserie	18
He did, he came: O my Redeemer deare,	108	Home	25
Then Money came, and chinking still,	110	The Quip	9
Then came brave Glorie puffing by	111	The Quip	13
Then came quick Wit and Conversation,	111	The Quip	17
Was cleare as heav'n, from whence it came.	135	Divinitie	14
And so I came to phansies medow strow'd	142	Pilgrimage	7
And so I came to Fancies medow strow'd	142	Pilgrimage V	7
So to cares cops I came, and there got through	142	Pilgrimage	11
But as he was returning, there came one	151	The Bag	25
He, who came hither all alone,	151	The Bag	27
To Egypt first she came, where they did prove	191	Ch.-Milit.	37
And tune mens hearts against the Gospel came:	192	Ch.-Milit.	76
And cleanse mens hearts against the Gospel came:	192	Ch.-Milit. W	76
He chid the Church away, where e're he came,	193	Ch.-Milit.	105
The world came both with hands and purses full	193	Ch.-Milit.	133
The world came in with hands and purses full	193	Ch.-Milit. W	133
that none goes out of Church as he came in, but either better,	233	Priest 7	20
that the prohibiting of flesh came from hot Countreys, where both	242	Priest 10	16
How came this world to be as it is?	256	Priest 21	6

CAME (cont'd)	PAGE	TITLE		LINE
Was it made, or came it by chance?	256	Priest 21		7
he came at length to this resolution, that repentance is an act	279	Priest 33		13
1 Sam. 1. 18. though it came from a man disallowed by God:	285	Priest 36		22
a great desire to know the way of my life, and how I came to be so.	291	Cornaro		12
I should be a conquerour, as also a little after it came to passe:	294	Cornaro		27
Upon the neck of it came a terrible fever, which continued thirtie	296	Cornaro		19
All came from, and will goe to others.	322	Proverbs		41
me unable to perform those Offices for which I came into the world,	373	Letters		10
Therefore I considered that if one only came, the comfort intended	375	Letters		16
CAMELS				
Old Camels carry young Camels skins to the Market.	359	Proverbs	D	1101
CAMELS'				
Old Camels carry young Camels skins to the Market.	359	Proverbs	D	1101
CAMOMILL				
And Elder, camomill, mallowes, comphrey and smallage made into	262	Priest 23		7
CAN (see also canne,kan)				
Hee that has all ill, & can have no good	7	Ch.-Porch	W	35
Dare to be true. Nothing can need a ly:	9	Ch.-Porch		77
But if thy sonne can make ten pound his measure,	11	Ch.-Porch		113
Entice the trusty sunne, if that you can,	12	Ch.-Porch		136
Entice the trusty sunne, if that thou can,	12	Ch.-Porch	W	136
Then he can lose with pleasure, stakes his heart;	14	Ch.-Porch		194
But know, that nothing can so foolish be,	15	Ch.-Porch		206
Whom oil and balsames kill, what salve can cure?	24	Ch.-Porch		447
Whom oil and mercies kill, what salve can cure?	24	Ch.-Porch	W	447
Why, he that built the world can do much more:	28	Sacrifice		67
What ever scoffes or scornfulnesse can bring,	32	Sacrifice		174
What ever scoffes & scornfulnesse can bring,	32	Sacrifice	W	174
Into the conquest. Though I can do nought	37	Reprisall		14
Into thy conquest, though I can do nought	37	Reprisall	W	14
And though my hard heart scarce to thee can grone,	38	The Sinner		13
Since nothing Lord can bee so good	39	Good Fri.	W	21
For they can lodge transgressions by the score:	40	Sepulchre		6
And so should perish, but that nothing can,	41	Sepulchre		22
Can not make up so brave a feast	42	Easter	W	25
Can there be any day but this,	42	Easter		27
A hart can never come too late.	42	Easter	W	28
That I can walk to heav'n well neare.	50	Faith		12
What can be lower then the common manger?	50	Faith		22
Yet can these not get over to my soul,	52	H.Commun.		13
Which I can go to, when I please,	53	H.Commun.		39
No doore can keep them out:	53	Antiphon 1		10
Sprung from that beautie which can never fade;	54	Love 1		2
Sprung from the beautie which can never fade;	54	Love 1	W	2
That washes what it shows. Who can indeare	58	H.Script.1		10
This book of starres can spell eternall blisse.	58	H.Script.2	W	14
And if wee can stay there, it's well.	59	Whitsunday	W	14
Show that thy brests can not be dry,	59	Whitsunday	W	21
That I can raise:	61	Praise 1		2
They can do more.	61	Praise 1		16
Is more then all my deaths can be,	62	Afflict.2		3
Where all my debts are payd, none can accrue	65	Ch.-mus.	W	8
Lord, how can man preach thy eternall word?	67	Windows		1
Can on anothers hardly rest.	68	Content		4
Which can let loose to a crown, and yet with pleasure	69	Content		15
Nor can it entertain the day	70	Quidditie		7
Whom neither force nor fawning can	72	Constancie		4
Can blow away, or glittering look it blinde:	72	Constancie		8
Whom none can work or wooe	72	Constancie		16
His goodnesse sets not, but in dark can runne:	72	Constancie		23
Whom nothing can procure,	73	Constancie		31
If any one our Masters hand can show.	78	Ang.&Sts.		30
For what account can thy ill steward make?	83	Sighs & Gr.		8
The fleet Astronomer can bore,	85	Vanitie 1		1
The subtil Chymick can devest	85	Vanitie 1		15
Nothing their furie can controll,	90	Afflict.4		11
Or can be, then is Man? to whose creation	90	Man		5
Yet can a friend what thou hast done fulfill?	94	Unkindness		21
Not he: he knows, where he can better be,	100	Miserie		10
Can thy strange wayes rehearse?	102	Miserie		66
What is this woman-kinde, which I can wink	108	Home		39
For they can never be at rest,	111	Vanitie 2		15
Who for man was sold, can see;	114	Dialogue		15
But as I can see no merit,	115	Dialogue		17
Can praise his fairest fair;	115	Dulnesse		6
Look onely; for to love thee, who can be,	116	Dulnesse		27
Thy even praise can neither rise, nor fall.	118	Providence		42
Is clothing, meat and trencher, drink and Can,	120	Providence	V	127
None can expresse thy works, but he that knows them:	121	Providence		142
And none can know thy works, which are so many,	121	Providence		143
Much better tunes, then grones can make;	124	Gratefulnes		22
No scrue, no piercer can	126	Confession		7
No smith can make such locks, but they have keyes:	126	Confession		17
But can he want the grape, who hath the wine?	128	Bunch Gr.		22
But can he want the grape, who hath the vine?	128	Bunch Gr.	V	22
Can blast my fruit, or bring me HARM,	133	Paradise		5
Who can these Gordian knots undo?	135	Divinitie		20
Faith needs no staffe of flesh, but stoutly can	135	Divinitie		27
There can no discord but in ceasing be.	136	Ephes.		22
Marbles can weep; and surely strings	136	Ephes.		23

CAN (cont'd)

	PAGE	TITLE		LINE
Can both the way and end be tears?	142	Pilgrimage		28
That which is past who can recall?	144	Discharge		10
I can raise thee.	146	Praise 2		20
Not to relieve? how can it be,	150	Longing		62
No such rank poyson can there be.	155	Assurance		6
Then can thy truth and I: but while rocks stand,	156	Assurance		32
Such a Joy, as none can move:	156	The Call		10
Such a Love, as none can part:	156	The Call		11
Then I or ought, or can be mine.	157	Clasping		3
Can hale or draw it out of doore.	158	Praise 3		16
Let us (said he) poure on him all we can:	159	The Pulley		3
Yet can I mark how herbs below	162	The Search		9
Yet can I mark how starres above	162	The Search		13
What point so piercing can appeare	163	The Search		55
Fast in thy Paradise, where no flower can wither!	166	The Flower		23
Which when we once can finde and prove,	167	The Flower		45
For who can look for lesse, that loveth Life. / Strife.	170	Water-crs.		5
What can I want or need?	172	23 Psalme		4
Perhaps with more embellishment can say,	177	Forerunners		33
And can shoot,	179	Discipline		23
And can hit from farre.	179	Discipline		24
Who can scape his bow?	179	Discipline		25
After death can never die.	180	Invitation		30
Can so afflict or so affright,	183	A Parodie		14
Nothing can be so mean,	184	The Elixer		14
Nothing can be so low,	184	The Elixer	W	14
Therefore we can go die as sleep, and trust	186	Death		21
What wretchednesse can give him any room,	193	Ch.-Milit.		117
Nor can they change their bounds & meres,	201	H. Commun.	W	41
More spotted then my flesh can bee.	202	love	W	9
His fall can tell,	202	Trin.Sun.	W	13
If that bee dark we can not see:	203	Even-song	W	14
For who can tell, though thou hast dyde to winn	205	Persever.	W	9
Nothinge can see	210	Paradox	D	11
No Earth can bee thy Jointure. For the sunne	211	Bohemia	D	3
Whose fier, like there malice, nought can quench.	212	Bohemia	D	54
nor can I hide his sacred will.	215	Psalm II	D	16
that can against me rise.	216	Psalm III	D	16
of corn and wine can be.	218	Psalm IV	D	28
which also I will set as high as I can, since hee shoots higher that	224	Priest		8
it is a good strife to go as farre as wee can in pleasing of him,	224	Priest		12
knowing that it can no way be preserved, but only by those means,	237	Priest 9		20
Those that can read, are allowed times for it, and those that cannot,	240	Priest 10		19
but clean, whole, and sweet, as sweet as his garden can make;	241	Priest 10		13
being his only perfume, which deserves cost when he can spare it.	241	Priest 10		15
which they can better employ to their own advantage, and sutably	243	Priest 11		15
sets up as many encouragements to goodnesse as he can, both in	244	Priest 11		3
he bethinketh himselfe what good deeds he can do that day,	244	Priest 12		17
who can read, who not;	248	Priest 14		34
the afflicted, though they can, and otherwise ought to come to him.	249	Priest 15		16
but the earnestnesse to do all the good he can, moves him to say thus	251	Priest 17		32
stead to his Parish, and dischargeth God what he can of his promises.	254	Priest 20		9
he thinks it the most usefull way that a Pastor can take,	256	Priest 21		2
When any one can distinguish the Sacramentall from common bread,	258	Priest 22		34
neither can all the people so order their affairs as to receive just	259	Priest 22		26
and knowledg of their own body, and what it can well disgest:	267	Priest 26		1
in eating, that he can eat more, then afterwards he finds true:)	267	Priest 26		3
For knowing what one usually can well disgest, and feeling when I go	267	Priest 26		6
which none can perform so wel in trouble, as in calmness.	273	Priest 31		2
He that hath or can have yet no imployment, if he truly,	275	Priest 32		12
where can he busie himself better, then in those new Plantations,	278	Priest 32		5
and can much better, and particularly do it, then he that is	278	Priest 33		28
where it can be, that so the body may joyn in the grief,	279	Priest 33		27
that there is none that can or will look after things, but all goes	281	Priest 34		8
how the windes should blow so much as they can, and the sea rage so	281	Priest 34		21
and the sea rage so much as it can, and all things do what they can,	281	Priest 34		21
sea rage so much as it can, and all things do what they can, and all,	281	Priest 34		22
that the Atheist, or Epicurian can have nothing to contradict.	281	Priest 34		34
and then who can deny the stretched out arme of a mighty God?	282	Priest 34		6
unlawful to open faults, no benefit or advantage can make it lawfull:	287	Priest 37		6
So that I can truly say, That they who in these two things that enter	294	Cornaro		3
as all that know me, can testifie:	294	Cornaro		11
neither melancholie, nor any other passion can hurt a temperate life.	294	Cornaro		31
can bring little grief or hurt to those that are temperate.	294	Cornaro		34
a temperate life, can receive little hurt from other inconveniences.	295	Cornaro		15
an orderly and regular life can hardly be altered without exceeding	295	Cornaro		17
Neither can any man denie this, who will narrowly consider it.	297	Cornaro		14
For indeed no man can be a perfect Physician to another,	297	Cornaro		24
since none can have a better Physician then himself, nor better	297	Cornaro		37
which, but in that age, can hardly be perfected.	298	Cornaro		31
which endeavours to preserve a man as much as she can, teacheth us	299	Cornaro		26
so that we can eat but a very little, wherewith she is very well	299	Cornaro		28
(though most agreeable to them) then their stomack can easily digest:	300	Cornaro		13
that I can easily get on horseback without the advantage	300	Cornaro		34
So that I can truly say, That I have both given God a Temple,	301	Cornaro		31
as farre as I can conjecture, very apt and well given both	303	Cornaro		4
for I can no more free my selfe from actuall sinnes after Baptisme,	308	Valdesso		3
Of these none can free themselves of themselves, but only	308	Valdesso		8
neither can they ever be exhausted, (as Pictures may be by a plenarie	309	Valdesso		21
Saviour prayed with doubtfulnesse, is more then I can or dare say;	315	Valdesso		10

	PAGE	TITLE		LINE
CAN (cont'd)				
Marry your sonne when you will; your daughter when you can.	326	Proverbs		149
The eye and Religion can beare no jesting.	326	Proverbs		158
you can have but water of it.	327	Proverbs		180
Evils have their comfort, good none can support	328	Proverbs		208
In the world who can not swimme, goe to the bottome.	330	Proverbs	V	285
No Lockes can hold against gold.	332	Proverbs	V	317
Sit in your place and none can make you rise.	334	Proverbs		372
He that can make a fire well, can end a quarrell.	340	Proverbs		557
Three can hold their peace, if two be away.	345	Proverbs		714
God, and Parents, and our Master, can never be requited.	348	Proverbs		805
Doe what thou oughtest, and come what come can.	348	Proverbs		818
Women laugh when they can, and weepe when they will.	348	Proverbs		821
He can give little to his servant, that lickes his knife.	349	Proverbs		846
He that can stay obtaines.	349	Proverbs		852
No tye can oblige the perfidious.	357	Proverbs	D	1066
Of a pigs taile you can never make a good shaft.	359	Proverbs	D	1104
but sometimes he can hurt.	359	Proverbs	D	1119
The healthfull man can give counsell to the sick.	360	Proverbs	D	1130
nor can I write coldly in that, wherein consisteth the making good	364	Letters		16
burden to you, since I can never answer what I have already received;	367	Letters		13
neither can I so much as go to Bugden, and deliver your Letter,	369	Letters		15
opinion of him, that if he can do me a courtesie, he will of himself;	369	Letters		22
which if you can sent to Sir Francis before his departure,	369	Letters		25
Sir send the Letter you receive from him to me as soon as you can,	370	Letters		6
Can I be so happy, as to hear of both these that they succeed well?	371	Letters		9
beseech you consider all that can happen to you are either	373	Letters		21
What can be said more comfortably?	374	Letters		28
I doe my part to them, lett them think of me what they will or can.	376	Letters		7
be none of the Court-stile, yet doubtless Madam, can do you no hurt:	377	Letters		3
much less can I disesteem it from you, whome I esteem to be God's	378	Letters		13
To desire good & endeavour it when we can doe no more, is to doe it.	381	Woodnoth		15
with his favours, can not but be not only allowable but commendable.	381	Woodnoth		26
CANAAN				
I did toward Canaan draw; but now I am	128	Bunch Gr.		6
I did towards Canaan draw; but now I am	128	Bunch Gr.	V	6
To bring the other Ark from Canaan.	190	Ch.-Milit.		20
To bring the other Ark to Canaan.	190	Ch.-Milit.	W	21
CANAANITES				
on both sides, and was just in the Canaanites and Israelites both.	316	Valdesso		30
CANCELL				
A new small-rented lease, and cancell th' old.	40	Redemption		4
He did endure to cancell sinne:	151	The Bag		22
CANDLE				
Himself the candle hold.	81	Christmas		26
It's a poore sport that's not worth the candle.	346	Proverbs		752
CANE				
Lovely enchanting language, sugar-cane,	176	Forerunners		19
CANKER				
Will canker both, yett thou alone shallt smart:	13	Ch.-Porch	W	166
CANKERS				
A tithe purloin'd cankers the whole estate.	22	Ch.-Porch		386
See how spite cankers things. These words aright	30	Sacrifice		109
CANNE				
Short of his canne and bodie; must I finde	8	Ch.-Porch		39
CANNOT				
The holy lines cannot be understood.	6	Ch.-Porch		10
Omit the oathes, which true wit cannot need:	9	Ch.-Porch		62
Who cannot rest till hee good-fellows finde,	12	Ch.-Porch		149
Who cannot live on twentie pound a yeare,	13	Ch.-Porch		176
Cannot on fourtie: he's a man of pleasure,	13	Ch.-Porch		177
Love is a personall debt. I cannot give	17	Ch.-Porch		278
Who cannot wish, except I give them bread:	26	Sacrifice		7
Yet my Disciples sleep: I cannot gain	27	Sacrifice		29
Who cannot live lesse then eternally:	29	Sacrifice		99
Was such a grief as cannot be.	35	Thanksgvng		10
Or cannot leaves, but fruit, be signe	38	Good Fri.		11
It cannot be. Where is that mightie joy,	56	Temper 2		1
The dew, for which grasse cannot call,	60	Grace		11
I cannot ope mine eyes,	62	Mattens		1
Who cannot on his own bed sweetly sleep,	68	Content		3
It cannot vault, or dance, or play;	70	Quidditie		5
It's true, we cannot reach Christs forti'th day;	87	Lent		31
We cannot reach our Saviours puritie;	87	Lent		34
I cannot use a friend, as I use Thee.	93	Unkindness		15
I cannot skill of these thy wayes.	95	Justice 1		1
I cannot skill of these my wayes.	96	Justice 1		12
My God, Man cannot praise thy name:	101	Miserie		31
Man cannot serve thee; let him go,	101	Miserie		43
We cannot ask the thing, which is not there,	103	Prayer 2		11
Cannot give the name of gains	114	Dialogue		6
Doth shut them out, so that they cannot enter;	126	Confession		20
Or, if they enter, cannot rest,	126	Confession		21
Christ keepeth now, who cannot fail or fall.	143	Holdfast		14
And care for future chances, cannot go	145	Discharge		38
It cannot be	166	The Flower		40
Who cannot dresse it well, want wit, not words.	167	The Sonne		4
Which cannot be,	183	A Parodie		3
Cannot for lesse be told.	185	The Elixer		24
I cannot look on thee.	189	Love 3		10
Into my soule this cannot pass	201	H. Commun.	W	37

CANNOT (cont'd)	PAGE	TITLE		LINE
And cannot turn to soule.	201	H. Commun.	W	39
That I who cannot now by day	203	Even-song	W	6
Upon thine Altar burnt? Cannot thy love	206	Walton 1		6
As well as any she? Cannot thy Dove	206	Walton 1		8
Which misery cannot untwist but rather	212	Bohemia	D	35
Of opposition cannot place thee, where	212	Bohemia	D	39
cannot in sins delight:	218	Psalm V	D	10
he cannot agree to come into any house, where he shall not exercise	226	Priest 2		25
him in the pulpit, whom they cannot trust in his Conversation.	228	Priest 3		8
one and the self-same Spirit, it cannot be, but that an industrious,	229	Priest 4		7
his flock by themselves, whom his Sermons cannot, or doe not reach.	236	Priest 8		13
are allowed times for it, and those that cannot, are taught;	240	Priest 10		20
he cannot keep the last obligation, nor suffer others in his house	242	Priest 10		29
which as hee cannot, touching the last day, so neither touching	250	Priest 16		21
We cannot allow this: or else if the thing will admit interpretation;	252	Priest 18		9
first point, and but by Catechizing, the other cannot be attained.	255	Priest 21		8
For questions cannot inflame or ravish, that must be done by a set,	257	Priest 21		24
and cannot be gained, but that they still fall from all compromises	260	Priest 23		24
that God cannot be wanting to them in Doctrine, to whom he is so	263	Priest 24		20
they cannot wel dispatch) nor of their estate, nor of their brethren.	266	Priest 26		16
that he cannot without this maintain himself in a Christian state.	272	Priest 31		24
to weep, and cannot, since we are not Masters of our bodies,	279	Priest 33		18
alike in all Gods children (which as concerning weeping it cannot be,	279	Priest 33		22
when he cannot more, as he that weeps a floud of tears.	279	Priest 33		30
Saviour himselfe used, Marke 10. 16, cannot bee vain and superfluous.	285	Priest 36		11
without any remedy (which cannot be applyed without notice)	287	Priest 37		2
which things in others cannot be known without such observation,	297	Cornaro		29
Wherefore one to another cannot be a perfect Physician.	297	Cornaro		36
that an orderly life is so hard a thing that it cannot be kept.	298	Cornaro		37
cannot live regularly, because they must often endure heats,	299	Cornaro		12
cannot fall into diseases, and but very seldome into indispositions;	299	Cornaro		35
When I cannot have their companie, I give my self to the reading	301	Cornaro		5
not onely a shamefull thing to fear that which cannot be avoided;	303	Cornaro		22
it being Scripture cannot be spoken to the disparagement	310	Valdesso		3
but because he cannot doe all, God often chuseth which he shall doe,	313	Valdesso		21
Wherefore as David's Adultery cannot be excused, so need	316	Valdesso		6
this cannot stand, and it is ill Doctrine in a common-wealth.	316	Valdesso		16
Worldly learned men cannot judg spirituall mens actions,	317	Valdesso		5
You cannot know wine by the barrell.	321	Proverbs		20
Love and a Cough cannot be hid.	322	Proverbs		49
The Fox, when hee cannot reach the grapes,	325	Proverbs		130
The mill cannot grind with the water that's past.	326	Proverbs		153
If you loose your time, you cannot get mony nor gaine.	332	Proverbs		320
The dog gnawes the bone because he cannot swallow it.	337	Proverbs		457
which a hundred wise men cannot pull out.	339	Proverbs		527
We cannot come to honour under a Coverlet.	339	Proverbs		533
It's a poore stake that cannot stand one yeare in the ground.	340	Proverbs		553
If the staffe be crooked, the shadow cannot be straight.	341	Proverbs		583
Astrologie is true, but the Astrologers cannot finde it.	342	Proverbs		641
A wise man cares not for what he cannot have.	343	Proverbs		662
He cannot be vertuous that is not rigorous.	343	Proverbs		664
You cannot make a wind-mill goe with a paire of bellowes.	344	Proverbs		676
He that is fallen cannot helpe him that is downe.	346	Proverbs		753
You cannot hide an eele in a sacke.	346	Proverbs		762
You cannot hide a needle in a sacke.	346	Proverbs	V	762
You cannot flea a stone.	346	Proverbs		764
A good heart cannot lye.	347	Proverbs		800
An ill deede cannot bring honour.	348	Proverbs		806
The little cannot bee great, unlesse he devoure many.	351	Proverbs		922
You cannot make the fire so low but it will get out.	353	Proverbs		965
When all men have what belongs to them, it cannot bee much.	353	Proverbs		979
Without danger we cannot get beyond danger.	354	Proverbs		1010
A scab'd horse cannot abide the comb.	359	Proverbs	D	1113
except you wink, you cannot but see many brave examples.	366	Letters		6
yet if you cannot send it with much convenience, it is no matter,	369	Letters		27
I cannot yet find leisure to write to my Lord, or Sir Benjamin	370	Letters		29
who cannot think me lazy, since I rode 200 mile to see a Sister,	371	Letters		2
So that now if they do not well the falt cannot be charg'd on you;	373	Letters		15
CANON				
which depend almost wholly on their Canon law and Decretals,	319	Valdesso	V	29
CANONICALL				
and a thing required under Canonicall obedience, the expounding	230	Priest 5		13
but an analogat observation of Ecclesiasticall and Canonicall lawes,	320	Valdesso		2
CANONS				
Now the Canons being the Church-wardens rule, the Parson adviseth	270	Priest 29		12
which are grounded upon the Canons, that so they may know their duty,	270	Priest 29		15
CANST				
Abstaine or wedd: if thou canst not abstaine	7	Ch.-Porch	W	13
Drink not the third glasse, which thou canst not tame,	7	Ch.-Porch		25
Flie idlenesse, which yet thou canst not flie	9	Ch.-Porch		79
By great deeds shew, that thou canst little do;	15	Ch.-Porch		220
That thou canst speak, at once; but husband it,	18	Ch.-Porch		302
Canst thou finde hell about my lips? and misse	28	Sacrifice		42
Canst thou be any where	74	The Starre		3
For thou canst make a debter,	74	The Starre		7
How canst thou brook his foolishnesse?	100	Miserie		7
That thou within his curtains drawn canst see:	100	Miserie		16
Thou canst no more not heare, then thou canst die.	103	Prayer 2		6
Yet since thou canst not choose but see my actions;	104	Obedience		23
How canst thou stay, considering the pace	107	Home		7

CANST (cont'd)	PAGE	TITLE	LINE
After all this canst thou be strange?	108	Home	26
Canst be idle? canst thou play,	113	Businesse	1
And in no quiet canst thou be,	124	Gratefulnes	26
For thou canst tell,	144	Discharge	19
Wherefore if thou canst fail,	156	Assurance	31
And rivers stirre, thou canst not shrink or quail:	156	Assurance	33
Nor canst thou be content, unlesse thou to	439	Walton 5	5
If thou thy selfe canst doe it, attend no others helpe or hand.	348	Proverbs	813
CANVAS			
With canvas, not with arras clothe their shame:	177	Forerunners	26
CANVASING			
especially canvasing those, whose natures are most stealing,	264	Priest 26	32
CANVASSED			
the Parson hath throughly canvassed al the particulars of humane	230	Priest 5	33
CAPE			
and the Divell in Capuch (or cape of the cloak).	358	Proverbs	D 1082
CAPON			
He that gives thee a Capon, give him the leg and the wing.	324	Proverbs	109
CAPS			
If all fooles wore white Caps, wee should seeme a flock of geese.	338	Proverbs	513
CAPTIVATE			
To captivate strong holds to thee.	45	Nature	6
Such force as once did captivate the Jews;	195	Ch.-Milit.	192
CAPTIVE			
Give me my captive soul, or take	52	H.Commun.	25
and leadeth captive without any resistance, even in resistance,	269	Priest 28	22
CAPTIVES			
Thy works nights captives: O let grace	60	Grace	7
CAPUCH			
and the Divell in Capuch (or cape of the cloak).	358	Proverbs	D 1082
CARD			
Get a good stock of these, then draw the card	18	Ch.-Porch	293
CARDINAL			
Paul the third, and Cardinal Bembo, who therefore lived so long;	299	Cornaro	1
CARDS			
Rather then shew his cards.) Steal from his treasure	18	Ch.-Porch	298
CARE			
Nothing from thine: in service, care, or coldnesse	16	Ch.-Porch	255
I care not though the cloth of state should be	17	Ch.-Porch	269
Take all into thee; then with equall care	19	Ch.-Porch	321
Who say, I care not, those I give for lost;	20	Ch.-Porch	347
Who say, I care not, I give those for gone;	20	Ch.-Porch	W 347
Lord, with what care hast thou begirt us round!	45	Sinne 1	1
But God more care of us hath had:	63	Sinne 2	6
Thy diet, care, and cost	64	Even-song	13
With care and courage building me,	90	Afflict.4	29
Since if my sent be good, I care not, if	94	Life	17
All show'd the builders, crav'd the seers care.	106	Sion	6
But when all my care and pains	114	Dialogue	5
Is there an herb for that? O that thy care	119	Providence	75
Men therefore seek to have, and care to keep.	119	Providence	99
Content and care	138	The Size	34
This houre is mine: if for the next I care,	145	Discharge	33
And care for future chances, carnot go	145	Discharge	38
setting aside his care of his Flock, were a madnesse to doubt of.	234	Priest 7	17
never was there such care of a flock expressed, save in the great	234	Priest 7	20
Therefore this care may be learn'd there, and then woven into	234	Priest 7	22
or he takes care she shall learn it of some religious neighbour.	239	Priest 10	16
He afterwards turnes his care to fit all their dispositions with some	239	Priest 10	30
think fit to do so) he takes care not to put them into vain trades,	239	Priest 10	34
considers his own Parish, and takes care, that there be not a begger,	244	Priest 12	19
The Countrey Parson hath a speciall care of his Church,	246	Priest 13	1
or else to examine with care, and advice, what they are fittest for,	275	Priest 32	16
and it is an honest, and just care, so it exceed not bounds,	275	Priest 32	28
But his family is his best care, to labour Christian soules,	275	Priest 32	31
But if after all this care well dispatched, the house-keepers Family	275	Priest 32	36
with the same care as others, when they meet with good fruit,	276	Priest 32	31
taking care never to rise with a full stomack, but so as I might well	293	Cornaro	18
but that I should wish all who have the care of themselves,	303	Cornaro	32
in which perhaps you will discover some care, which I forbare not in	304	Valdesso	3
Cover your selfe with your shield, and care not for cryes.	326	Proverbs	161
Little wealth, little care.	338	Proverbs	501
If great men would have care of little ones,	344	Proverbs	697
Paines to get, care to keep, feare to lose.	353	Proverbs	975
whose Example and Care of them will justifie you both to the world	373	Letters	16
And above all, If any care of future things molest you?	374	Letters	13
Cast thy Care on the Lord and he shall nourish thee. (Psal. 55.)	374	Letters	14
Casting all your Care on the Lord, for he careth for you. (1 Pet.	374	Letters	16
entertains our Care for us that we may the more quietly intend his	374	Letters	18
at all times rejoyce in the Lord, who taketh care for us:	374	Letters	26
of kindred bredd up, (which generally is very true,) yet I care not;	376	Letters	5
yet I shall ever put your care of Leighton, upon my accompt,	378	Letters	4
let this of Leighton Church the care, be amongst the chiefest also,	378	Letters	22
I thanke you heartily for Leighton, your care, your Counsell,	379	Letters	13
let the first be the care of your Excellencies;	443	Oration	4
CARE'S			
The couch of time; cares balm and bay:	75	Sunday	5
So to cares cops I came, and there got through	142	Pilgrimage	11
CAREER			
Among my many had his full career,	159	Jos.coat	6

CAREER (cont'd)	PAGE	TITLE		LINE
Shadows well mounted, dreams in a career,	167	Dotage		4
CAREFUL				
be careful for nothing. What can be said more comfortably?	374	Letters		28
CAREFULL				
the Parson is very carefull to avoid all the kinds thereof,	227	Priest 3		22
he is carefull to see condign punishment inflicted, and with truly	254	Priest 20		26
wherewith also a carefull Joseph might meet.	281	Priest 34		27
CAREFULLY				
God is wonderfully to be seen, one thing would be carefully cbserved;	261	Priest 23		28
CARELESLY				
I did behave me carelesly,	133	The Method		15
the other in walking carelesly in our calling, he first represents	274	Priest 32		16
CARELESNESS				
or carelesness of his flock, and accordingly applies himselfe	258	Priest 22		24
CARELESNESSE				
and carelesnesse in their devotions, but to labour still to be	280	Priest 34		18
CARELESS				
that none is careless before his Judg, and that the word of God shal	233	Priest 7		21
CARES				
How hast thou lost them in a croud of cares?	101	Miserie		50
But are their cares and businesse with the pleasure?	188	Judgement	V	17
But are there cares and businesse with the pleasure?	188	Heaven		17
The resolved minde hath no cares.	337	Proverbs	V	464
A wise man cares not for what he cannot have.	343	Proverbs		662
CARETH				
all your Care on the Lord, for he careth for you. (1 Pet. 5.7.)	374	Letters		16
CARING				
plunging themselves over head and eares into carking, and caring;	247	Priest 14		25
CARKING				
plunging themselves over head and eares into carking, and caring;	247	Priest 14		25
CARNALL				
Yet did a rogue with hope of carnall joy	194	Ch.-Milit.		149
[carnall impurity,] nor of the sicknesse that destroyeth at noone	238	Priest 9		7
When he deals with any that is heavy, and carnall;	267	Priest 26		17
So is the carnall and wilfull man with the worm of the grave in this	272	Priest 30		12
CARP				
And at my actions carp, or catch.	106	Conscience		18
CARPENTERS				
all the world would turne Carpenters (to make them crutches).	355	Proverbs		1020
CARPET				
an handsome, and seemly Carpet of good and costly Stuffe, or Cloth,	246	Priest 13		17
CARRIAGE				
in his behaviour and carriage towards him, not avoyding his company,	263	Priest 25		27
Secondly, by a courteous carriage, & winning behaviour:	268	Priest 28		22
to church, or for disorderly carriage in time of divine service.	270	Priest 29		6
CARRIE				
They carrie me to my most bitter crosse:	33	Sacrifice		195
And carrie with them th' other parts.	49	Repentance		30
Sure it would carrie with it ev'n my heart,	159	Jos.coat		7
CARRI'D				
Chasing the fathers dimnesse, carri'd farre	168	The Sonne		8
And blending these he carri'd all mens eyes,	195	Ch.-Milit.		189
CARRIED				
Being carried home, when the Physicians saw in what case I was,	295	Cornaro		1
In the kingdome of a cheater the wallet is carried before.	337	Proverbs		465
cause this inclosed to be carried to his brothers house of his own	370	Letters		26
CARRIES				
which carries a reverence with it, even above contempt.	268	Priest 28		21
I had rather ride on an asse that carries me,	329	Proverbs		258
He carries well, to whom it waighes not.	334	Proverbs		391
Good is good, but better carries it.	337	Proverbs		454
Words and feathers the wind carries away.	359	Proverbs	D	1103
CARROWAY				
and for seeds, to Fennell, and Carroway seeds.	262	Priest 23		3
CARRY				
instructed his people how to carry themselves in divine service,	231	Priest 6		22
scatteringly in the Sermon, carry great holiness in them.	234	Priest 7		1
which when they leave the family, they carry with them.	241	Priest 10		7
all together choosing some fitt day to carry it themselves,	253	Priest 19		38
especially if they carry their eyes ever open, and fix them on their	266	Priest 26		4
when his occasions carry him abroad, or bring strangers to him,	274	Priest 32		7
that hath considered how to carry himself at table about his	278	Priest 33		18
It's a proud horse that will not carry his owne provender.	345	Proverbs		712
Old Camels carry young Camels skins to the Market.	359	Proverbs	D	1101
I was in hope I should my self carry all sickness out of your family:	372	Letters		15
most carry themselves so, as if they not only not desir'd,	373	Letters		33
CARRYED				
their peace and mirth have carryed them further then this moderation,	280	Priest 34		33
CARRYES				
he carryes himself very respectively, as to all the Fathers	253	Priest 19		5
he carryes them higher, even somtimes to a forgetting of themselves,	267	Priest 26		19
CARRYING				
My rebel-flesh, and carrying thy name,	52	H.Commun.		17
By carrying first their gold from them away:	197	Ch.-Milit.		250
carrying it about with him as fully, as if he had begot his whole	250	Priest 16		9
CARVE				
Carve, or discourse; do not a famine fear.	11	Ch.-Porch		129
Which with the edge of wit they cut and carve.	134	Divinitie		7
CARVED				
Is deeply carved there: but th' other week	112	JESU		2

	PAGE	TITLE		LINE
CARVES				
Who carves, is kind to two; who talks, to all.	11	Ch.-Porch		130
CARVING				
them close by him, and carving for them, both for his own humility,	243	Priest 11		11
CARVINGS				
With flowers and carvings, mysticall and rare:	106	Sion		5
CASE (receptacle)				
My thoughts are all a case of knives, ...	90	Afflict.4		7
CASE				
For it was their own case who killed me:	30	Sacrifice	W	115
('Tis your own case) ye never move a wing.	78	Ang.&Sts.		20
'tis your own case, ye never move your wing.	78	Ang.&Sts.	W	20
A Christians state and case	138	The Size		31
Lord, see my case.	163	The Search		48
For though you vysit us, & wayle our case, ...	211	Paradox	D	39
in binding them prentices (in case he think fit to do so) he takes	239	Priest 10		34
yet considering that the Law allows these in case they be true,	245	Priest 12		24
as the case requires, then by causing them to be presented, . .	254	Priest 20		24
of which he gathers, in case he be ignorant himself, what to hold;	260	Priest 23		11
Wherefore in case a Christian endeavour to weep, and cannot,	279	Priest 33		18
Now as the Apostle argues in another case;	285	Priest 36		18
when the Physicians saw in what case I was, they concluded that I	295	Cornaro		2
there the case is plaine, Cornelius had revelation, yet Peter was	310	Valdesso		8
wherefore I will open my case unto you, which I think deserves	364	Letters		9
it is a most serious Case, nor can I write coldly in that, . .	364	Letters		16
The case of ministers and magistrates is another thing, . .	381	Woodnoth		27
CASES				
He greatly esteemes also of cases of conscience, wherein he is much	230	Priest 5		19
except in the cases of extreme poverty, and in the seasons . .	248	Priest 14		4
antient and pious ordinance, and how necessary it is in some cases:	249	Priest 15		32
whom he hath ever some cases to ask, when he meets with them;	260	Priest 23		4
there may happen somtimes some cases, wherein he chooseth to permit	260	Priest 23		18
As in cases of an obscure and dark nature, not easily determinable	260	Priest 23		20
or in cases of high consequence, as establishing of inheritances:	260	Priest 23		21
not to exceed his bounds, but in tickle cases to call in help.	260	Priest 23		36
and the Cases of Conscience belonging thereto, wherein (as Saint Paul	279	Priest 33		34
These in diverse cases ought, and were of old forborn for a time.	312	Valdesso	V	27
This is true onley of the Popish Cases of Conscience, which depend	319	Valdesso	V	28
But there are other Cases of Conscience grounded on Piety . .	319	Valdesso	V	30
CASKE				
A caske and an ill custome must both of them be broken. . .	322	Proverbs	V	27
CASKS				
False glozing pleasures, casks of happinesse, ...	167	Dotage		1
CAST				
Wherefore that robe we cast away, ...	76	Sunday		52
As on a window late I cast mine eye, ...	116	Love-joy		1
Like moles within us, heave, and cast about:	126	Confession		14
They rushed in, and cast them in the dirt	140	Ch.-rents		23
To hide thy shame: for thou hast cast a bone	156	Assurance		39
Cast down, yet help afford;	171	Bittersweet		3
And on sinne doth cast the fright.	180	Invitation		18
Where first the Church should raise her down-cast face. . .	192	Ch.-Milit.		86
and from us cast their cords away.	215	Psalm II	D	8
and busy cast of his eye on his auditors, with letting them know,	233	Priest 7		1
not the lesse, lest he cast their neighbours poverty on them also.	254	Priest 19		6
both for the generall ignominy which is cast upon the profession,	268	Priest 28		10
be vilified or debased, by being cast on the lower ranke of people;	270	Priest 29		8
it for a time onely, and then cast it away, as he sayes strangely.	318	Valdesso		3
doth not bid them then cast away the word, or leave it off: . .	318	Valdesso		19
Cast thy Care on the Lord and he shall nourish thee. (Psal. 55.)	374	Letters		14
CASTING				
the casting of it on mean persons, especially in some Shires:	276	Priest 32		21
Casting all your Care on the Lord, for he careth for you. (1 Pet.	374	Letters		16
CASTLE				
A faire wife and a frontire Castle breede quarrels. . . .	324	Proverbs		103
CASTLES				
Castles are Forrests of stones.	352	Proverbs		936
To build castles in Spain.	356	Proverbs	D	1041
CASUALTIES				
Fine nets and casualties to catch us in, ...	45	Sinne 1	W	7
for I know that (setting casualties aside) I shall not die . .	303	Cornaro		26
CAT				
An old cat sports not with her prey.	355	Proverbs		1030
CATCH				
Catch not at quarrels. He that dares not speak	15	Ch.-Porch		217
Fine nets and stratagems to catch us in, ...	45	Sinne 1		7
Fine nets and casualties to catch us in, ...	45	Sinne 1	W	7
But thou art ready there to catch	62	Mattens		2
And at my actions carp, or catch.	106	Conscience		18
Except life catch & hold those fast.	202	Trin.Sun.	W	10
If you could runne, as you drinke, you might catch a hare. . .	334	Proverbs		373
You must loose a flie to catch a trout.	348	Proverbs		827
CATCHETH				
The Fox knowes much, but more he that catcheth him. . . .	330	Proverbs		280
Still fisheth he that catcheth one.	358	Proverbs	D	1095
CATCHING				
Catching the sense at two removes?	56	Jordan 1		10
but is rather glad of catching opportunities to do them. . .	284	Priest 35		26
CATECHISM				
and preferreth the ordinary Church-Catechism, partly for obedience	255	Priest 21		17
nature is towards Philosophy, the Catechism is towards Divinity.	256	Priest 21		26

CATECHISM (cont'd)	PAGE	TITLE		LINE
The saying of the Catechism is necessary, but not enough;	259	Priest 22		6
CATECHISME				
This Body he made by way of expounding the Church Catechisme,	230	Priest 5		8
the expounding of our Catechisme must needs be the most usefull	230	Priest 5		14
He exacts of all the Doctrine of the Catechisme;	255	Priest 21		22
When once all have learned the words of the Catechisme,	256	Priest 21		1
for many say the Catechisme by rote, as parrats, without ever	256	Priest 21		3
In this course the order of the Catechisme would be kept,	256	Priest 21		5
but after that the Catechisme is once learn'd, that which nature is	256	Priest 21		25
CATECHIZED				
and catechized in the afternoone, he thinks he hath in some measure,	236	Priest 8		8
wherein the Catechized will at length finde delight, and by which	256	Priest 21		17
CATECHIZER				
and by which the Catechizer, if he once get the skill of it,	256	Priest 21		18
CATECHIZETH				
Those he Catechizeth publickly, these privately, giving age honour,	255	Priest 21		24
CATECHIZING				
Now Catechizing being a work of singular, and admirable benefit	230	Priest 5		11
a slighter forme of Catechizing, fitter for country people;	230	Priest 5		16
with prayers, and catechizing, and all religious duties.	239	Priest 10		13
reading of Scripture, catechizing, singing of Psalms at their work,	248	Priest 14		33
The Parson Catechizing.	255	Priest 21		T
The Countrey Parson values Catechizing highly:	255	Priest 21		1
Catechizing is the first point, and but by Catechizing,	255	Priest 21		7
first point, and but by Catechizing, the other cannot be attained.	255	Priest 21		8
in Catechizing there is an humblenesse very sutable to Christian	255	Priest 21		10
He requires all to be present at Catechizing:	255	Priest 21		26
shall overthrow all means, save catechizing, and set up Enthusiasmes.	310	Valdesso		12
CATECHIZINGS				
and accordingly applies himselfe with Catechizings, and lively	258	Priest 22		25
CATHARINE				
To Mrs Catharine Vaughan One hundred pound, To Mr George Herbert one	383	G.H.'s Will		6
CATHOLICK				
and to satisfie the Congregation by their Catholick answers.	255	Priest 21		21
the Catholick Religion is professed with greatest strictness).	357	Proverbs	D	1047
CATHOLIKE				
then the accesse of the Officers of the Catholike King?	442	Oration		9
CATT				
The Catt sees not the mouse ever.	341	Proverbs		592
Send not a Catt for Lard.	342	Proverbs		644
CATT'S				
It's a bold mouse that nestles in the catts eare.	344	Proverbs		693
CATTEL				
if they keep and fodder well their cattel, they must have milk,	270	Priest 30		28
CAUGHT				
Therefore my sudden soul caught at the place,	46	Afflict.1		17
But Man hath caught and kept it, as his prey.	91	Man		20
But Man has caught and kept it, as his prey.	91	Man	W	20
shall he himself be caught.	222	Psalm VII	D	56
CAUS				
not with a foolish vanting of yourself when there is no caus,	366	Letters		17
CAUSE				
If cause require, thou art his sacrifice;	17	Ch.-Porch		273
As swords cause death, so may a little sting.	20	Ch.-Porch	W	352
For it was their own cause who killed me:	30	Sacrifice		115
The stock and surplus, cause and historie:	88	The Pearl		8
In their ascent and cause.	91	Man		36
And have good cause: there it was dipt and di'd,	129	Love unkn.		16
Were sinne alive, good cause there were	150	Longing		65
And, that I had great cause to fear it.	155	Assurance		12
not spent in them, he blesseth God, and lays it out as he sees cause.	240	Priest 10		13
And obstructions are the cause of most diseases.	243	Priest 10		5
thinking that their own labour is the cause of their thriving,	247	Priest 14		30
three or four of the ablest of the Parish to hear the cause with him,	260	Priest 23		10
is the main foundation, and pillar of their cause, whereon they rely;	262	Priest 24		29
and to the cause, referreth the whole matter to the examination,	268	Priest 28		34
as they think fit, & see cause, or rather as Gods spirit leads them.	272	Priest 31		27
because Temperance takes away the cause of diseases:	300	Cornaro		1
and the cause being taken away, there is no place for the effect.	300	Cornaro		2
much from Divinity, at which, not without cause, he thinks, I aim;	370	Letters		21
cause this inclosed to be carried to his brothers house of his own	370	Letters		26
of your Mother upon you, and cause all her wishes, diligence,	377	Letters		4
and you have no cause to be sorry, since it is GOD's business.	377	Letters		21
I humbly thank him, & am so far from giving you cause, to apology,	378	Letters		10
CAUSED				
first caused me to leave Intemperance, to which I was much addicted:	291	Cornaro		19
CAUSELESS				
that was my causeless foe:	221	Psalm VII	D	14
CAUSES				
admonitions, if they persevere, he causes them to be presented:	232	Priest 6		13
I will declare the causes which moved me to forsake Intemperance,	291	Cornaro		15
For contrarie causes have contrarie effects, and the faults of Nature	292	Cornaro		10
because this will cut off all causes of diseases, so that he shall	297	Cornaro		21
CAUSETH				
making a hook of his Charity, causeth them still to depend on him;	244	Priest 12		32
whose admirable power causeth that the meat and drink that is taken	293	Cornaro		26
CAUSING				
or any undutifull behaviour in them, but causing them, when they sit,	231	Priest 6		25
then by causing them to be presented, or otherwise complained of.	254	Priest 20		24

CAUTIONS	PAGE	TITLE		LINE
But here there are two Cautions to be added.	273	Priest 31		15
CAVE				
To digge thee out of thy dark cave and grot:	77	Avarice		8
At some fair oak, or bush, or cave, or well:	99	Decay		7
I sought thee in a secret cave, ...	124	Peace		3
The gloomy cave of Desperation	141	Pilgrimage		4
CAVILL				
Cavill, and claim her part and measure, ...	104	Obedience		12
CAVILS				
He cavils instantly.	82	Ungratef.		27
CEASE				
These stones to praise thee may not cease.	26	The Altar		14
Or feel his part, he would not cease to kneel, ...	33	Sacrifice		210
Or feel his share, he would not cease to kneel, ...	33	Sacrifice	W	210
So wee may cease to suck: to praise thee, never.	59	Whitsunday	W	24
O let thy graces without cease	60	Grace		3
Then cease discoursing soul, till thine own ground, ...	69	Content		33
And that love may never cease, ...	146	Praise 2		3
For my rough sorrows: cease, be dumbe and mute, ...	164	Grief		14
With the one make warre to cease;	199	L'Envoy		2
With the one make warrs to cease;	199	L'Envoy	W	2
Clinging and crying, crying without cease, ...	205	Persever.	W	15
Cease then to judge calamityes	210	Paradox	D	25
and for ever after cease my clamorous and greedy bookish requests.	367	Letters		11
CEASED				
And ceased not to give thanks for the Ephesians, Eph. 1. 16.	234	Priest 7		12
CEASING				
There can no discord but in ceasing be.	136	Ephes.		22
CELEBRATE				
Is best to celebrate this most high day.	41	Easter		12
that he may the better celebrate it, or for the variety . .	232	Priest 7		23
CELEBRATES				
which he celebrates not only with abstinence of diet, but also	241	Priest 10		37
of the Communion, the Parson celebrates it, if not duly once a month,	259	Priest 22		20
CELESTIALL				
Touch it with thy celestiall quicknesse, ...	74	The Starre		14
CELL				
As I one ev'ning sat before my cell, ...	139	Artillerie		1
CEMENT				
But the sweet cement, which in one sure band	67	Ch.-floore		10
CEMENTED				
Made of a heart, and cemented with teares:	26	The Altar		2
CENSORIOUS				
Examines me with a censorious hand:	29	Sacrifice		82
CENSURE				
When written Truths shall censure mans devise.	194	Ch.-Milit.	W	160
in the Company where he is, but comes under his Test and censure:	252	Priest 18		3
Every man's censure is first moulded in his own nature. . .	362	Proverbs	D	1181
CENSURES				
In thy just censures; fain would I draw nigh, ...	160	Priesthood		4
CENSURETH				
so a Scholar judgeth in his study, and censureth this or that;	317	Valdesso		3
CENTER				
and a point, or center, when his storing, which was even now good,	264	Priest 26		29
CENTRE				
There the circumference earth is, heav'n the centre. . . .	38	The Sinner		8
From either pole unto the centre:	69	Content		18
And tacks the centre to the sphere!	103	Prayer 2		9
And centre both to me denie	162	The Search		7
CENTURE				
There the circumference earth is, heav'n the centure. . . .	38	The Sinner	W	8
From either pole unto the centure:	69	Content	W	18
CEREMONIES				
of the Gospell will not give an outward Law of Ceremonies as of old,	310	Valdesso		5
he meaneth not the very Ceremonies of the Jewes, which no Christian	319	Valdesso		34
CEREMONIOUS				
consists in a few ceremonious and superstitious observations;	319	Valdesso	V	23
CEREMONY				
and thinketh the Ceremony not onely innocent, but reverend. . .	258	Priest 22		9
CERTAIN				
This certain Anchor adde a Seal, and so	439	Walton 5		6
CERTAINE				
For it is certaine, that a weak stomack being prepossessed . .	242	Priest 10		21
as of certaine injuries which they are thought to have offerd to our	368	Letters		6
CERTAINLY				
If God had laid all common, certainly	7	Ch.-Porch		19
then some fish there, certainly to eat the flesh, and not the fish,	242	Priest 10		14
certainly, it is the safest course for Christians also to meditate	258	Priest 22		17
certainly it should be either the sun in heaven, or the fire	271	Priest 30		9
And all may certainly conclude, that God loves them, till either they	283	Priest 34		22
and fever (which was certainly expected) might be hindred. . .	295	Cornaro		6
CERTAINTY				
Doe owe the symbole of their certainty.	439	Walton 5		8
from the certainty both of deliverance, and reward, if we faint not;	249	Priest 15		25
CERTIFIES				
expects them not but first certifies you that there are come agents	368	Letters		4
CHAFE				
Another chafe, may warm him at his fire, ...	19	Ch.-Porch		314
CHAFF				
are like the chaff, which from the face	215	Psalm I	D	14

	PAGE	TITLE	LINE
CHAFING			
Then chafing said, This man deludes:	123	Time	28
CHAIN			
I am no link of thy great chain,	57	Employm. 1	21
The jealous Turkie brought his corall-chain;	70	Humilitie	13
God chains the dog till night: wilt loose the chain,	145	Discharge	46
CHAINE			
Hee is not free that drawes his chaine.	348	Proverbs	830
CHAINED			
To such indifferents chained be,	134	The Method	18
upon which and to which the questions are to be chained.	256	Priest 21	34
CHAINS			
That chains us by the teeth so fast?	108	Home	38
God chains the dog till night: wilt loose the chain,	145	Discharge	46
CHAIR			
O fix thy chair of grace, that all my powers	56	Temper 2	9
Not to a true, but painted chair?	56	Jordan 1	5
A chair or litter shows the biere,	98	Mortific.	29
Brave rose, (alas!) where art thou? in the chair	140	Ch.-rents	1
And those all bitten, in thy chair I see.	140	Ch.-rents	10
And those all sitten in thy chair I see.	140	Ch.-rents V	10
And but a chair.	142	Pilgrimage	36
nor sitten in the scorners chair.	214	Psalm I D	4
CHALICE			
in a strong and decent chest, with a Chalice, and Cover,	246	Priest 13	19
CHALK			
Let a bleak palenesse chalk the doore,	177	Forerunners	35
CHALLENGE			
And challenge it, as proper to his place,	70	Humilitie	20
I challenge here the brightest day,	126	Confession	28
Since many gifts do challenge many hearts!	147	Offering	8
CHAMBER			
Admitted to their bed-chamber, before	85	Vanitie 1	19
Who sweeps a chamber, for thy laws,	185	The Elixer W	19
Within your chamber try your hearts,	217	Psalm IV D	17
childrens advantage, then if it were given to the Chamber of London.	240	Priest 10	9
so that I am fain to dyet in my Chamber at mine own cost;	365	Letters	3
CHAMBERS			
Empty Chambers make foolish maides.	322	Proverbs	29
CHANCE			
Hearken unto a Verser, who may chance	6	Ch.-Porch	3
The meanest tool, that he may chance to use.	20	Ch.-Porch	354
That if I chance to hold my peace,	26	The Altar	13
Kill'd in the way by chance.	70	Humilitie	16
Than that, which one day Worms may chance refuse?	206	Walton 1	14
If thou chance for to find	207	Walton 3	1
If he chance to finde any reading in anothers Bible, he provides him	254	Priest 20	11
Was it made, or came it by chance?	256	Priest 21	7
that can or will look after things, but all goes by chance, or wit:	281	Priest 34	9
CHANCELLOR			
To the Right Hon. the L. Chancellor (Bacon).	209	L. Bacon D	T
CHANCES			
And care for future chances, cannot go	145	Discharge	38
CHANDLERS			
In great pedigrees there are Governours and Chandlers.	328	Proverbs	222
CHANGE			
And change thy temperance into braverie.	15	Ch.-Porch	222
Till thou change names, and be where he began.	21	Ch.-Porch	378
Before I had the power to change my life.	47	Afflict.1	42
Well, I will change the service, and go seek	48	Afflict.1	63
Vanisht away, when Faith did change the scene:	51	Faith	39
Though elements change, and heaven move,	56	Temper 2	14
Lord, though we change, thou art the same;	60	Whitsunday	25
As if thy love could fail or change.	108	Home	28
Nor can they change their bounds & meres,	201	H. Commun. W	41
To change my bed, troubles me not;	302	Cornaro	12
would I change age and constitution with them who follow their	303	Cornaro	12
Cities seldome change Religion only.	356	Proverbs D	71
and I shou'd account my self most happy if I might change with you;	373	Letters	3
3. To Change shewes not well & you are by the Apostles rule (Philip	380	Woodnoth	12
the other profitt, the work I may change, the profitt, I am master	381	Woodnoth	31
CHANG'D			
Sorrow hath chang'd its note: such is his will,	159	Jos.coat	3
CHANGES			
as the course of our life & the changes thereof, we are to regard	380	Woodnoth	18
CHANGETH			
Who changeth all things, as him pleaseth best.	159	Jos.coat	4
but that God often changeth it according as he sees fit,	270	Priest 30	31
CHANGING			
O that I once past changing were,	166	The Flower	22
Made Pharaoh Moses, changing th' historie.	191	Ch.-Milit.	42
A wise man needes not blush for changing his purpose.	342	Proverbs	613
CHAP			
And for the Corinthians, chap. 1. 4.	234	Priest 7	14
CHAPLAINS			
Those that live in Noble Houses are called Chaplains, whose duty	226	Priest 2	16
Let not Chaplains think themselves so free, as many of them do,	226	Priest 2	19
CHAPPELL			
Unto some Chappell, die or live.	35	Thanksgvng	28
but the Devill builds a Chappell hard by.	343	Proverbs	674
so devout as to come to the Chappell an howre before prayers began,	368	Letters	17

	PAGE	TITLE	LINE
CHAPTER			
Who reade a chapter when they rise,	96	Charms & K	1
Chapt. 10. after he had complained of the desolation of Israel,	234	Priest 7	4
And for the Philippians made request with joy, ch. 1. 4.	234	Priest 7	15
this line [place] till the end of this Chapter may seeme strange,	311	Valdesso	20
And with this exposition the Chapter is cleare enough, but the truth	311	Valdesso	31
This Chapter is considerable. The intent of it, that the world	315	Valdesso	29
The best salve for the whole Chapter, is to distinguish Judgment:	316	Valdesso	34
There is no more to be said of this Chapter but that his opinion	318	Valdesso	5
7, 21. & in the whole chapter	380	Woodnoth	5
CHARACTER			
The Countrey PARSON HIS CHARACTER, AND Rule of Holy Life.	223	Priest	T
I have resolved to set down the Form and Character of a true Pastour,	224	Priest	7
but the character of his Sermon is Holiness;	233	Priest 7	23
A Character, that Hermogenes never dream'd of, and therefore he could	233	Priest 7	24
CHARGE			
Thy distance from me; see my charge,	163	The Search	47
and fix them on their charge, and not on their preferment.	266	Priest 26	5
what a great Charge lyes upon them, and that indeed the whole order	269	Priest 29	28
Hee that hath charge of soules transports them not in bundles.	353	Proverbs	986
Now though they have hitherto travelled upon your charge,	367	Letters	1
loved her even in my departure, in looking to her Son, and my charge.	371	Letters	13
CHARG'D			
Lo, here I hang, charg'd with a world of sinne,	33	Sacrifice	205
So that now if they do not well the falt cannot be charg'd on you;	373	Letters	15
CHARGED			
who live best, and take most paines, and are most charged:	245	Priest 12	16
and his owne lesse charged, hee findes some way of releeving it,	254	Priest 19	2
CHARGES			
The charges of building and making of gardens are unknowne.	335	Proverbs	412
you have bin at charges:	380	Woodnoth	9
CHARING			
pardoning Your most indebted kinsman GEORGE HERBERT. Charing Cross.	369	Letters	7
CHARITABLE			
the two commands, we are more injoyned to be charitable, then wise.	245	Priest 12	29
he also urgeth them to do some pious charitable works, as a necessary	249	Priest 15	32
the Blessing of God to them ought to make them the more charitable,	254	Priest 19	6
This I do, because at such, and such a time you were charitable.	254	Priest 20	18
But though the Parson sets forward all Charitable deeds,	262	Priest 23	12
for as hee is Charitable, so he is just also.	262	Priest 23	15
CHARITIE			
And Charitie.	67	Ch.-floore	12
With faith, with hope, with charitie;	68	Trin.Sun.	8
Of Joy and Charitie. Sir, you have not miss'd,	116	Love-joy	7
whom to receive were the greatest charitie of all, for she is	375	Letters	24
CHARITY			
and sending his charity by them to the poor, and somtimes giving them	239	Priest 10	26
resolves with himself never to omit any present good deed of charity,	240	Priest 10	6
charity being his only perfume, which deserves cost when he can spare	241	Priest 10	14
The Countrey Parson owing a debt of Charity to the poor,	243	Priest 11	6
The Parson's Charity.	244	Priest 12	T
The Countrey Parson is full of Charity;	244	Priest 12	6
To Charity is given the covering of sins, 1 Pet. 4. 8.	244	Priest 12	8
Wherefore all his works rellish of Charity.	244	Priest 12	15
counting that day lost, wherein he hath not exercised his Charity.	244	Priest 12	18
time will lose the name and effect of Charity with the poor people,	244	Priest 12	27
and making a hook of his Charity, causeth them still to depend	244	Priest 12	31
working those that are able to the same charity, still pressing it in	245	Priest 12	13
Yet in all his Charity, he distinguisheth, giving them most,	245	Priest 12	15
So is his charity in effect a Sermon.	245	Priest 12	17
once satisfied, he allows his Charity some blindnesse in the other;	245	Priest 12	27
to receive the charity of well minded people, and to lay up treasure	246	Priest 13	21
exposing the obligation of Charity, and Neighbour-hood,	253	Priest 19	34
and bread of Charity to some equality, representing to his people,	254	Priest 19	4
Contentiousnesse in a feast of Charity is more scandall then any	259	Priest 22	18
he hath so done, then he assumes the Parson, and exhorts to Charity.	260	Priest 23	17
And justice is the ground of Charity.	262	Priest 23	18
Charity in loving walking, and neighbourly accompanying one another,	284	Priest 35	5
which hath so much advanced Charity, and ranked backbiters among	287	Priest 37	23
and Charity to the publick hath the precedence of private charity.	287	Priest 37	36
and Charity to the publick hath the precedence of private charity.	287	Priest 37	37
oppose Theologicall vertues, as Uncharitablenesse opposes Charity;	308	Valdesso	7
I was desirous to putt a good mind into the way of charity,	375	Letters	8
it were in another's power to defeat my charity, and evill shold be	376	Letters	9
that he would by no meanes do so, urging, that Charity must be free.	379	Letters	8
CHARLES			
Sir Charles Howard & his Lady are at much difference, & shee being	368	Letters	19
CHARM			
What open force, or hidden CHARM	133	Paradise	4
CHARM'D			
Come blessed Dove charm'd with my song,	59	Whitsunday W	1
CHARMS			
Charms and Knots.	96	Charms & K	T
Frail Beauty's Charms to Heav'n did raise,	214	Convert D	13
CHARTRE			
Out of this Chartre of the Priesthood may be plainly gathered both	225	Priest 1	14
CHASE			
Chase brave employments with a naked sword	10	Ch.-Porch	88
Chase brave employment with a naked sword	10	Ch.-Porch W	88
There hands shall clipp the Eagles winges, & chase	212	Bohemia D	47

	PAGE	TITLE		LINE
CHAS'D				
Prayers chas'd syllogismes into their den,	191	Ch.-Milit.		55
CHASES				
Chases in Arras, guilded emptinesse,	167	Dotage		3
CHASING				
Chasing the fathers dimnesse, carri'd farre	168	The Sonne		8
CHASTE				
Of Noahs shadie vine, chaste as the dove;	190	Ch.-Milit.		15
CHASTEN				
nor in thine anger chasten me:	219	Psalm VI	D	2
CHASTENS				
Happie is hee that chastens himselfe.	325	Proverbs		137
He that chastens one, chastens 20.	333	Proverbs		356
CHASTIZED				
because even the godly are chastized but not punished) for evill	311	Valdesso		28
CHASTIZEMENT				
not be punished (which word I like here better then chastizement,	311	Valdesso		27
CHASTNINGS				
Corne is cleaned with winde, and the soule with chastnings.	326	Proverbs		154
CHATTELS				
enabled by that Name to take moveable goods, or chattels, and to sue,	270	Priest 29		2
CHATTING				
By listning to thy chatting fears	105	Conscience		5
CHAW'D				
Are chaw'd by others pens and tongue;	69	Content		30
Are chaw'd by others pen and tongue;	69	Content	W	30
CHAWES				
Redeem truth from his chawes: if souldier,	10	Ch.-Porch	W	87
CHEAP				
But the cheap swearer through his open sluce	8	Ch.-Porch		58
Because to shun them also is so cheap:	9	Ch.-Porch		68
In clothes, cheap handsomnesse doth bear the bell.	14	Ch.-Porch		187
Hard things are glorious; easie things good cheap.	119	Providence		97
he refuseth not, as coming cheap, and easie, and arising from	241	Priest 10		22
in a strict performance of a few cheap and easie duties of religion,	319	Valdesso	V	25
CHEAPE				
that the elements be of the best, not cheape, or course,	258	Priest 22		22
A Lyons skin is never cheape.	323	Proverbs		55
Ill ware is never cheape.	323	Proverbs		61
Good cheape is deare.	329	Proverbs		261
CHEAPEST				
The cheapest sinnes most dearely punisht are;	9	Ch.-Porch		67
CHEARFUL				
I beseech you to be chearful, and comfort your self in the God of all	372	Letters		24
CHEAT				
Cheat the most subtill nations. Who so coy,	194	Ch.-Milit.		150
CHEATER				
In the kingdome of a cheater the wallet is carried before.	337	Proverbs		465
CHEATING				
Lust and wine plead a pleasure, cheating gain:	8	Ch.-Porch	W	57
But all was glorious cheating, brave deceit,	193	Ch.-Milit.		135
CHECK				
Check the proud sea, ev'n when it swells and gathers.	118	Providence		48
CHECKER'D				
Is checker'd all along,	67	Ch.-floore		5
And make a twist checker'd with night and day!	118	Providence		58
CHEEK				
For thou upon the cheek-bone smit'st	217	Psalm III	D	19
CHEEK-BONE				
For thou upon the cheek-bone smit'st	217	Psalm III	D	19
CHEEKE				
Hee that wipes the childs nose, kisseth the mothers cheeke.	355	Proverbs		1032
CHEEKS				
A pair of Cheeks of them, is thy abuse.	206	Walton 2		7
CHEER				
Life is a businesse, not good cheer;	79	Employm.2		16
O cheer and tune my heartlesse breast,	80	Deniall		26
His beams shall cheer my breast, and both so twine,	81	Christmas		33
Others do sleep, and envie not their cheer.	118	Providence		56
Taste of the cheer,	131	Mans medly		20
Enact good cheer?	138	The Size		16
Exact good cheer?	138	The Size	V	16
In this cheer,	180	Invitation		17
Welcome sweet and scared cheer,	181	Banquet		1
CHEERE				
Thy cheere is mended; bate not of the food,	22	Ch.-Porch		393
some fitt day to carry it themselves, and cheere the Afflicted.	253	Priest 19		38
CHEER'D				
Wherefore be cheer'd, and praise him to the full	130	Love unkn.		68
CHEERED				
and their comfort, who are much cheered with such friendliness.	243	Priest 11		13
CHEEREFULL				
for respect to you, embrace all that is cheerefull, joyous,	442	Oration		7
CHEERFULL				
and cheerfull dying under persecuting Emperours, (though that indeed	237	Priest 9		30
that of a cheerfull and merrie man I became melancholie	296	Cornaro		15
Then, I am ever cheerfull, merrie, and well-contented, free from all	300	Cornaro		37
but cheerfull, lively, and pleasant.	303	Cornaro		10
CHEERFULLY				
that so they go on more cheerfully in their vocation, and himself be	248	Priest 14		12
He willingly and cheerfully crosseth the child, and thinketh	258	Priest 22		8

CHILD (cont'd)	PAGE	TITLE		LINE
Truly it grieves me to think of the child, how destitute she is,	376	Letters		12
as being now a father, "the best-bredd child hath the best portion".	376	Letters		18
CHILD'S				
A childs service is little, ...	327	Proverbs		206
Hee that wipes the childs nose, kisseth the mothers cheeke. . .	355	Proverbs		1032
CHILDE				
Write thee great God, and me a childe:	44	H. Bapt.2		7
What, (childe), is the ballance thine, ...	114	Dialogue		9
Thy childe.	150	Longing		60
Me thoughts I heard one calling, childe:	154	The Collar		35
and take as much joy in a straight-growing childe, or servant,	275	Priest 32		33
which kinde of Poems useth to be the childe of Youth, which it most	302	Cornaro		30
CHILDE'S				
Some mark a partridge, never their childes fashion:	10	Ch.-Porch		99
CHILDHOOD				
Childhood is health.	44	H. Bapt.2		15
CHILDREN				
Thy children, kindred, friends upon thee call;	13	Ch.-Porch		161
She and her children shall be thine.	35	Thanksgvng		24
And hold it fast, as children do their fathers, ...	118	Providence		46
Children for kingdomes to thee; they shall live	212	Bohemia	D	42
a trayning up of her children and mayds in the fear of God, . .	239	Priest 10		12
His children he first makes Christians, and then Commonwealths-men;	239	Priest 10		20
in visiting other sick children, and tending their wounds, . .	239	Priest 10		25
which happily for his other children he is not able to do. . .	239	Priest 10		32
in consideration of providing a stock for his children; . .	240	Priest 10		7
and good breeding, are his two great stocks for his children;	240	Priest 10		11
his children among children, his servants among other servants;	240	Priest 10		28
his children among children, his servants among other servants;	240	Priest 10		29
To his Children he shewes more love then terrour, to his servants	241	Priest 10		9
and sometimes he hears the children read himselfe, and blesseth them,	248	Priest 14		35
or breeding up children to no Calling, but in idleness, . .	251	Priest 17		21
Children and youths are usually deferred too long, under pretence	258	Priest 22		36
as to a great purchase for their children, and servants; . .	259	Priest 22		3
and in future for his children, hardly perceives when his storing	264	Priest 26		27
and revenge to the children of the world, whom anothers ill . .	269	Priest 28		21
it may be alike in all Gods children (which as concerning weeping	279	Priest 33		21
who sacrificed lest his Children should have transgressed in their	281	Priest 34		1
And if temporall Fathers blesse their children, how much more may,	285	Priest 36		14
So in the Old Testament Elisha cursed the children, 2 Kings 2. 24.	285	Priest 36		26
I finde eleven grand-children of mine, all the sonnes of one father	303	Cornaro		3
Building and marrying of Children are great wasters. . . .	321	Proverbs		11
Vertue and a Trade are the best portion for Children. . . .	324	Proverbs		107
Shee spins well that breedes her children.	325	Proverbs		144
He that hath children, all his morsels are not his owne. . .	335	Proverbs		423
He who hath children, all his morsels are not his owne. . .	335	Proverbs	V	423
When children stand quiet, they have done some ill. . . .	338	Proverbs		504
the best love that of children.	346	Proverbs		741
Hee that hath a wife and children wants not businesse. . . .	347	Proverbs		778
Children when they are little make parents fooles, . . .	352	Proverbs		939
Children when they are little make their parents fooles, . .	352	Proverbs	V	939
and so brought up your Children that they have attain'd to the years	373	Letters		13
For the time of breeding is the time of doing children good;	376	Letters		14
CHILDREN'S				
My childrens right, nor ought he take it: rather	17	Ch.-Porch		279
Foolish night-fires, womens and childrens wishes, ...	167	Dotage		2
with God, who weighs even childrens actions, 1 Kings 14. 12, 13.	239	Priest 10		29
is placed surer for his childrens advantage, then if it were given	240	Priest 10		8
as if it were but childrens meat, whereas there is not onely milke	317	Valdesso		23
CHILNESSE				
Or else the chilnesse of my faint demands.	66	Ch.-lock		4
CHIME				
Sundaies observe: think when the bells do chime, ...	22	Ch.-Porch		387
They and my minde may chime, ...	80	Deniall		29
They and my hart may chime, ...	80	Deniall	W	29
They and my soule may chime, ...	80	Deniall	WC	29
CHIMING				
Making a chiming of a passing-bell.	166	The Flower		18
CHIMNEY				
Where you thinke there is bacon, there is no Chimney. . . .	324	Proverbs		99
Silkes and Satins put out the fire in the chimney. . . .	351	Proverbs		912
Silkes and Satins put out the fire of the chimney. . . .	351	Proverbs	V	912
CHIMNEYS				
'Tis easier to build two chimneys, then to maintaine one. . .	350	Proverbs		893
Souldiers in peace are like chimneys in summer.	361	Proverbs	D	1172
CHINK				
Scarce a good joy creeps through the chink:	60	Whitsunday		22
CHINKING				
Then Money came, and chinking still, ...	110	The Quip		9
CHOAKED				
An upbraided morsell never choaked any.	335	Proverbs		406
CHOAKES				
Who hastens a glutton choakes him.	349	Proverbs		858
CHOICE (see also choyce)				
That choice may be thy storie.	170	Self-cond.		6
Hath made a Jewish choice:	170	Self-cond.		9
childe, or servant, as a Gardiner doth in a choice tree. . .	275	Priest 32		34
when he urged one upon me, and but one, and that at my choice.	375	Letters		11
therfore your choice at first was good	380	Woodnoth		6
in the choice of whom their judgement doth even now appeare.	442	Oration		26

	PAGE	TITLE		LINE
CHOISE				
Allows thee choise of paths: take no by-wayes;	7	Ch.-Porch		14
CHOKE				
Some till their ground, but let weeds choke their sonne:	10	Ch.-Porch		98
Lets his own ashes choke his soul.	79	Employm.2		10
Did before dimme and choke,	171	Self-cond.		21
Choke him, let him say no more,	199	L'Envoy		11
Choke him, let him speak no more,	199	L'Envoy	W	11
CHOLERICK				
of a cheerfull and merrie man I became melancholie and cholerick;	296	Cornaro		16
The cholerick man never wants woe.	339	Proverbs		536
A man well mounted is ever Cholerick.	355	Proverbs		1025
CHOLLERICK				
From a chollerick man withdraw a little;	326	Proverbs		164
The Chollerick drinkes, the Melancholick eates,	351	Proverbs		924
CHOOSE (see also chuse)				
They choose a murderer, and all agree	30	Sacrifice		113
We could not choose but look on still;	75	Sunday		19
Yet since thou canst not choose but see my actions;	104	Obedience		23
But I health, not physick choose:	178	The Rose		29
Each breast does feel, no braver fuel choose	206	Walton 1		13
For it being indifferent in it selfe to choose any Method,	230	Priest 5		10
but, wou'd you divide and choose too?	373	Letters		1
CHOOSETH				
he chooseth rather to give the poor money, which they can better	243	Priest 11		15
wherein he chooseth to permit his Parishioners rather to make use	260	Priest 23		18
CHOOSING				
For choosing Barabbas a murderer	170	Self-cond.		2
it is gained first, by choosing texts of Devotion, not Controversie,	233	Priest 7		26
all together choosing some fitt day to carry it themselves,	253	Priest 19		38
CHOSE				
and chose that wine that fitted my stomack, and in such measure,	293	Cornaro		16
CHOSEN				
Feasting all comers by twelve chosen men.	59	Whitsunday		8
that is best to be chosen, of which there is likelyest to be most	230	Priest 5		10
the greatest honor of this world, to do God and his chosen service;	270	Priest 29		11
therefore this kind of Punishment was chosen rather then any other.	282	Priest 34		17
in this land of light, and region of the Gospell, among his chosen.	304	Valdesso		15
CHOYCE				
some choyce Observations drawn out of the whole text, as it lyes	235	Priest 7		3
out of choyce and devotion, some other dayes for fasting,	237	Priest 9		24
the choyce of his wife was made rather by his eare, then by his eye;	238	Priest 9		26
CHOYSEST				
which out of his choysest judgment hee hath resolved to observe,	268	Priest 28		11
CHRIST				
Though David had his Jonathan, Christ his John.	17	Ch.-Porch		276
Christ purg'd his temple; so must thou thy heart.	23	Ch.-Porch		423
And in this shew, what Christ hath done.	51	Faith		36
This shadowes out what Christ hath done.	51	Faith	W	36
Reversed thunder, Christ-side-piercing spear,	51	Prayer 1		6
Christ hath took in this piece of ground,	76	Sunday		40
Coloss. 3. 3. Our life is hid with Christ in God.	84	Coloss.		T
Who goeth in the way which Christ hath gone,	87	Lent		37
Who goeth in that way which Christ hath gone,	87	Lent	V	37
Who goeth in the way that Christ hath gone,	87	Lent	W	37
Christ left his grave-clothes, that we might, when grief	112	Dawning		15
Christ left his grave-cloths, that we might, when grief	112	Dawning	V	15
The man reply'd; It figures JESUS CHRIST.	116	Love-joy		8
Christ keepeth now, who cannot fail or fall.	143	Holdfast		14
In Christ two natures met to be thy cure.	147	Offering		6
For what Christ once in humblenesse began,	168	The Sonne		13
Christ is my onely head,	174	Aaron		16
My doctrine tun'd by Christ, (who is not dead,	174	Aaron		23
By nailing Christ to fasten it again.	190	Ch.-Milit.		24
And wheel'd about again to spell Christ-Crosse.	191	Ch.-Milit.		54
But seems to yeeld Christ hath the greater wounds,	191	Ch.-Milit.		64
But seems to yeeld Christ had the greater wounds,	191	Ch.-Milit.	W	64
Although the Crosse could not Christ here detain,	439	Walton 5		1
and 'gainst his Christ, presume to say,	215	Psalm II	D	6
A Pastor is the Deputy of Christ for the reducing of Man	225	Priest 1		1
Christ is the glorious instrument of God for the revoking of Man.	225	Priest 1		5
Christ being not to continue on earth, but after hee had fulfilled	225	Priest 1		6
up that which is behinde of the afflictions of Christ in his flesh,	225	Priest 1		12
in that a Priest may do that which Christ did, and by his auctority,	225	Priest 1		17
in that a Priest is to do that which Christ did, and after his	225	Priest 1		18
Neither is it for the servant of Christ to haunt Innes,	227	Priest 3		29
as the Jewes and Judas did Christ, he may say as He did,	227	Priest 3		33
be with them, or Christ, verse 23. which, setting aside his care	234	Priest 7		16
from Christ himself, perfecting our Redemption no other way,	249	Priest 15		22
because hee knows nothing but the Crosse of Christ, his minde being	267	Priest 27		28
God) stands fast in the Liberty wherewith Christ hath made us free.	272	Priest 31		18
Hee that saw Christ open a blind mans eyes, saw not more Divinity,	282	Priest 34		38
But this was not proper to Christ, or the Apostles only,	285	Priest 36		12
the one in, The Grace of our Lord Jesus Christ, &c.	286	Priest 36		4
I shall finde no little comfort in the favour of Jesus Christ.	303	Cornaro		24
Feare is given to Christ, but not doubt, and upon good ground.	315	Valdesso		12
preferres the Word before the sight of the Transfiguration of Christ.	318	Valdesso		24
Your most faithful Servant in Christ Jesu, GEORGE HERBERT.	377	Letters		10
Now God the Father of our Lord Jesus Christ bless you more & more,	378	Letters		24
great Joy of Your Brother & Servant in Christ Jesus GEORGE HERBERT.	378	Letters		28

	PAGE	TITLE		LINE
CHRIST-CROSSE				
And wheel'd about again to spell Christ-Crosse.	191	Ch.-Milit.		54
CHRIST-SIDE-PIERCING				
Reversed thunder, Christ-side-piercing spear,	51	Prayer 1		6
CHRIST'S				
Christs stamp to boot: both images regard.	21	Ch.-Porch		380
Christs hands, though nail'd, wrought our salvation,	76	Sunday		48
It's true, we cannot reach Christs forti'th day;	87	Lent		31
Christs resurrection thine may be:	112	Dawning		10
Christs coming hath made man thy debter,	122	Time		11
And shows it so? Indeed Christs precious bloud	140	Ch.-rents		12
But now that Christs pure vail presents the sight,	141	Justice 2		13
To make a jest of Christs three offices:	195	Ch.-Milit.		174
At Christs last coming, as his first did finde:	196	Ch.-Milit.		231
altar to be bathed, and washed in the sacred Laver of Christs blood.	231	Priest 6		10
which evidently argue Christs Divinity by their success:	282	Priest 34		23
that at Baptisme they professed not to be ashamed of Christs Cross,	284	Priest 35		32
Gospell in the acceptation of Christs righteousnesse (as he sheweth	304	Valdesso		22
CHRISTIAN				
The Christian plummet sounding heav'n and earth;	51	Prayer 1		4
The Christian Temper.	55	Temper 1	W	T
The Christian Temper.	56	Temper 2	W	T
So now each Christian hath his journeys spann'd:	128	Bunch Gr.		10
This worlds delights before true Christian joy,	170	Self-cond.		8
points of Life, wherein a Christian is most seen, are Patience,	227	Priest 3		4
and Christian fortitude in the cold midnight stormes of persecution	237	Priest 9		37
And the top of Christian vertues, 1 Corin. 13.	244	Priest 12		14
there is an humblenesse very sutable to Christian regeneration,	255	Priest 21		10
who like Christian Souldiers are to give the word, and to satisfie	255	Priest 21		20
and his Saints, and by way of undertaking for a Christian soul.	258	Priest 22		14
and essentiall to a Christian, that he cannot without this maintain	272	Priest 31		24
that he cannot without this maintain himself in a Christian state.	272	Priest 31		25
endeavouring to disorder the Christian, and put him out of his	272	Priest 31		34
and shews the perplexed Christian, that this prayer being	273	Priest 31		4
This distinction may runne through all Christian duties,	274	Priest 31		2
to labour Christian soules, and raise them to their height,	275	Priest 32		31
Neither is this true onely in the military state of a Christian life,	279	Priest 33		3
Wherefore in case a Christian endeavour to weep, and cannot,	279	Priest 33		18
The like he doth in other Christian vertues, as of Faith,	279	Priest 33		33
that there is a double state of a Christian even in this Life,	280	Priest 34		2
but to labour still to be as fervent in Christian Duties,	280	Priest 34		20
Rather should a Christian Souldier take such occasions to harden	284	Priest 35		35
the very Ceremonies of the Jewes, which no Christian observes now;	320	Valdesso		1
CHRISTIAN'S				
These three make up some Christians destinie:	58	H.Script.2		8
A Christians state and case	138	The Size		31
CHRISTIANITY				
Is not Christianity full of such things, as are not to be seen,	256	Priest 21		10
That position will not hold in Christianity, because it contains	256	Priest 21		24
CHRISTIANS				
True Christians should be glad of an occasion	86	Lent		13
His children he first makes Christians, and then Commonwealths-men;	239	Priest 10		20
it is the safest course for Christians also to meditate on their	258	Priest 22		17
that all Christians should pray twice a day, every day of the week,	272	Priest 31		21
for though the temptations may be diverse in divers Christians,	279	Priest 33		1
the Christians in sutes.	329	Proverbs		242
but difficulties are so farr from cooling christians, that they whett	376	Letters		11
CHRISTMAS				
Christmas.	80	Christmas		T
Christmas-Day.	80	Christmas	W	T
They talke of Christmas so long, that it comes.	349	Proverbs		840
Buckingham was observed on Christmas day to bee so devout as to come	368	Letters		16
Neither hath she any to repair unto at good times, as Christmas, &c.	375	Letters		27
CHRISTMAS-DAY				
Christmas-Day.	80	Christmas	W	T
CHRISTMASSE				
at Easter, Christmasse, Whitsuntide, afore and after Harvest,	259	Priest 22		21
CHRONICLE				
Onely thy Chronicle is lost; and yet	69	Content		25
From times great Chronicle, and hither sent.	192	Ch.-Milit.		96
CHRYSOSTOME				
or Tertullian, or Chrysostome, more then Tully, Virgill,	282	Priest 34		21
CHRYSTAL				
Why should I Womens eyes for Chrystal take?	206	Walton 2		8
CHRYSTALLINE				
Turne watrish Holland to a chrystalline sphere.	211	Bohemia	D	12
CHURCH				
The Church-porch. Perirrhanterium.	6	Ch.-Porch		T
Findes his crackt name at length in the church-glasse.	14	Ch.-Porch		198
When once thy foot enters the church, be bare.	22	Ch.-Porch		403
Who marks in church-time others symmetrie,	23	Ch.-Porch		419
Who marks in church-time others comlines,	23	Ch.-Porch	W	419
He that by being at church escapes the ditch,	24	Ch.-Porch		435
Thy self in church; approach, and taste	25	Superlim		3
The Church.	26	The Church		T
Church-bels beyond the starres heard, the souls bloud,	51	Prayer 1		13
The church with psalms must shout,	53	Antiphon 1		9
I go to Church; help me to wings, and I	61	Praise 1		5
I goe to Church; make me an Angel, I	61	Praise 1	W	5
Church-monuments.	64	Ch.-monum.		T
Church-musick.	65	Ch.-mus.		T

	PAGE	TITLE		LINE
CHURCH-MUSICK				
Church-musick.	65	Ch.-mus.		T
CHURCH-PORCH				
The Church-porch. Perirrhanterium.	6	Ch.-Porch		T
CHURCH-RENTS				
Church-rents and schismes.	140	Ch.-rents		T
CHURCH-TIME				
Who marks in church-time others symmetrie,	23	Ch.-Porch		419
Whc marks in church-time others comlines,	23	Ch.-Porch	W	419
CHURCH-WARDENS				
or if the poor Church-wardens be affrighted with their greatness,	232	Priest 6		14
he first takes order with the Church-Wardens, that the elements be	258	Priest 22		21
but also for the discharge of the Church-wardens, who being	259	Priest 22		24
nor the Church-Wardens so well take notice who receive thrice,	259	Priest 22		27
The Parson with his Church-Wardens.	269	Priest 29		T
and privately instruct his Church-Wardens, what a great Charge lyes	269	Priest 29		27
CHURCH-WARDENS'				
Now the Canons being the Church-wardens rule, the Parson adviseth	270	Priest 29		13
CHURCH-YARD				
But through a Church-yard which them bounds.	145	Discharge		40
No Church-yard is so handsom,	353	Proverbs		969
CHURCHE'S				
All equall are within the churches gate.	22	Ch.-Porch		408
The churches mysticall repast.	25	Superlim		4
Prayer the Churches banquet, Angels age,	51	Prayer 1		1
And there the Churches festivall attending:	192	Ch.-Milit.		82
By free dispensings of the Churches treasure.	195	Ch.-Milit.		180
By dispensations of the Churches treasure.	195	Ch.-Milit.	W	180
or otherwise afflicted, he followeth the Churches counsell, namely,	249	Priest 15		29
CHURCHES				
Servants and churches also play their part.	14	Ch.-Porch		196
For churches are either our heav'n or hell.	23	Ch.-Porch		426
For churches either are our heav'n or hell.	23	Ch.-Porch	W	426
The Churches here, bravely resolv'd one night	194	Ch.-Milit.		162
Thirdly for the Churches sake, to whom by Printing it I would have	304	Valdesso		8
CHURCHYARD				
A piece of a Churchyard fitts every body.	355	Proverbs		1027
CHUSE				
If thou chuse bravely & rely on God	7	Ch.-Porch	W	17
But know the Lord himself doth chuse	217	Psalm IV	D	11
Chuse not an house neere an Inne (viz. for noise)	330	Proverbs		286
Chuse a horse made, and a wife to make.	350	Proverbs		871
Chuse none for thy servant who have served thy betters.	354	Proverbs		1014
but he would chuse to dy in Spain (where they say	357	Proverbs	D	1047
but to chuse a higher work, as God gives me higher thoughts,	381	Woodnoth		25
CHUSETH				
and yet hee chuseth rather to use his neighbours, and wear out that,	265	Priest 26		29
God often chuseth which he shall doe, and that by restraining him	313	Valdesso		22
CHUSING				
In chusing a wife, and buying a sword,	338	Proverbs		490
CHYMICK				
The subtil Chymick can devest	85	Vanitie 1		15
CICERO (see also tully)				
CINAMON				
Of cloves and nutmegs, and in cinamon sail;	137	The Size		8
CINNAMON				
or that cinnamon should heat me more then pepper?	297	Cornaro		33
CIRCLE				
Within the circle of his breath,	98	Mortific.		21
CIRCLING				
That zele and purenes circling my request	66	Ch.-lock	W	11
CIRCUIT				
The Parson in Circuit.	247	Priest 14		T
These are the Parsons generall aims in his Circuit;	249	Priest 14		10
CIRCUMCISED				
they are Circumcised to this day, and expect the promises	282	Priest 34		1
CIRCUMFERENCE				
There the circumference earth is, heav'n the centre.	38	The Sinner		8
There the circumference earth is, heav'n the centure.	38	The Sinner	W	8
CIRCUMSPECT				
Countrey Parson is very circumspect in avoiding all coveteousnesse,	227	Priest 3		16
He is very circumspect in all companyes, both of his behaviour,	237	Priest 9		14
CIRCUMSPECTION				
(as Pictures may be by a plenarie circumspection) but still even	309	Valdesso		23
CIRCUMSTANCE				
I fear only that I have omitted some fitting circumstance,	370	Letters		12
CIRCUMSTANCES				
With all the circumstances that may move:	89	The Pearl		36
lust, and when not, and so in many circumstances of actions.	230	Priest 5		31
and other like circumstances considered, he is rather married then	237	Priest 9		4
CITIE				
Courtesie grows in court; news in the citie.	18	Ch.-Porch		292
Courtesie grows at Court; news in the citie.	18	Ch.-Porch	W	292
not onely in the citie, but also in villages and hamlets.	299	Cornaro		4
that they are in the fairest place of this learned Citie of Padua,	301	Cornaro		11
The Chicken is the Countries, but the Citie eates it.	324	Proverbs		108
CITIES				
That leads the van, and swallows up the cities.	16	Ch.-Porch		248
In cities, theatres, gardens, parks, and courts:	40	Redemption		11
and retains and confirms kingdcmes, cities, and families in peace.	297	Cornaro		11
Sometimes I ride to some of the neighbour-cities, that I may enjoy	301	Cornaro		34

	PAGE	TITLE		LINE
CLEANSETH				
I do but taste it, straight it cleanseth me,	106	Conscience		15
CLEAR				
No day so clear but hath dark clouds.	359	Proverbs	D	1123
CLEARE				
Strike off all scores; none are so cleare as they.	20	Ch.-Porch		360
Nothing but holy, pure, and cleare,	25	Superlim		6
To cleare the breast, to mollifie all pain.	58	H.Script.1		4
To cleare the breast, to suple outward pain.	58	H.Script.1	W	4
All of a piece, and all are cleare and straight.	72	Constancie		20
Lord, cleare thy gift, that with a constant wit	116	Dulnesse		25
Was cleare as heav'n, from whence it came.	135	Divinitie		14
If a cleare spring for me no time forbears,	136	Ephes.		28
Of future depths, but drink the cleare and good.	145	Discharge		28
Thou didst cleare me;	146	Praise 2		14
Plain demonstrations, evident and cleare,	167	Dotage		10
Before a court, ev'n that above so cleare,	167	Dotage		16
Shines bright and cleare, ev'n unto condemnation,	171	Self-cond.		23
Blushing woes, that look as cleare	177	The Rose		7
And when thou dost but shine lesse cleare,	183	A Parodie		19
And with this exposition the Chapter is cleare enough, but the truth	311	Valdesso		31
CLEARELY				
Who for a God clearely a sallet lost.	193	Ch.-Milit.		110
By this it may clearely be perceived, how great is the power of order	297	Cornaro		3
one to understand and expresse so clearely and excellently the intent	304	Valdesso		21
CLEARER				
because I have now a clearer voice, then ever I had in my life.	303	Cornaro		7
CLEAREST				
The clearest diamond: let them do their best,	126	Confession		29
CLEARETH				
Doctrine of this Consideration cleareth that of the precedent	310	Valdesso		26
CLEAVE (see also clave)				
Which if it cleave to coine, one common rust	13	Ch.-Porch	W	165
Sicknesses cleave my bones;	47	Afflict.1		26
CLEAVES				
Faith cleaves unto it, counting evr'y grain	51	Faith		42
CLEER				
There are some vices, whose natures are alwayes cleer, and evident,	264	Priest 26		6
CLEERE				
Maintaine there Lustre still, & shining cleere	211	Bohemia	D	11
CLEERLY				
of the house, and shewing them cleerly, that they respect them most,	251	Priest 17		30
CLEFT				
The inward walls and Sommers cleft and tore:	84	The World		14
CLEMENCIE				
Lord, with what bountie and rare clemencie	82	Ungratef.		1
CLENSETH				
A holy habit clenseth not a foule soule.	343	Proverbs		669
CLERGY				
use of them, as of Clergy councels, for the benefit of the Diocese.	253	Priest 19		10
CLERK				
As a great Clerk, and reach the highest stature.	50	Faith		30
CLERK'S				
other answers, which are on the Clerks and peoples part to answer;	231	Priest 6		29
CLIMBE				
Man stole the fruit, but I must climbe the tree;	33	Sacrifice		202
Then by a sunne-beam I will climbe to thee.	63	Mattens		20
To climbe to thee.	89	The Pearl		40
That I may climbe and finde relief.	144	Complaining		20
CLIMBES				
For wealth without contentment, climbes a hill	11	Ch.-Porch		111
CLIMBING				
Where lay my heart; and climbing still,	142	Pilgrimage		21
and that our feet may be like hindes feet ever climbing up higher,	236	Priest 8		29
CLIME				
Till both removed to the western clime.	191	Ch.-Milit.		36
CLINGING				
With face and hands clinging unto thy brest,	205	Persever.	W	14
Clinging and crying, crying without cease,	205	Persever.	W	15
CLIPP				
There hands shall clipp the Eagles winges, & chase	212	Bohemia	D	47
CLOAK				
and the Divell in Capuch (or cape of the cloak).	358	Proverbs	D	1082
CLOAKE				
Although the sun shine, leave not thy cloake at home.	332	Proverbs		326
CLOATH				
Cloath thee in war, arme thee in peace.	334	Proverbs		386
CLOATHED				
as to be cloathed with perfect patience, and Christian fortitude in	237	Priest 9		37
CLOATHES				
which they put on as their holy-day cloathes, and come to Church in	247	Priest 14		9
God sends cold according to Cloathes.	322	Proverbs		33
Mend your cloathes, and you may hold out this yeare.	324	Proverbs		100
Ever since we weare cloathes, we know not one another.	326	Proverbs		168
CLOATHS				
and dilating it selfe even to his body, cloaths, and habitation.	228	Priest 3		13
Criticks are like brushers of Noblemens cloaths.	360	Proverbs	D	1157
CLOCKS				
And give new wheels to our disorder'd clocks.	64	Even-song		24
CLOD				
With his poore clod of earth the spacious sky.	8	Ch.-Porch		54

	PAGE	TITLE		LINE
CLOD (cont'd)				
As if a starre were duller then a clod,	134	Divinitie		3
Must dulnesse turn me to a clod?	176	Forerunners		5
CLODS				
Doth for two clods of earth ten spheres controule,	211	Bohemia	D	8
CLOGS				
It hangs, it clogs:	158	Praise 3		14
CLOISTER'S				
Take up within a cloisters gates.	69	Content		16
CLOISTERERS				
Statesmen within, without doores cloisterers:	195	Ch.-Milit.		200
CLOKE				
Without excuse or cloke.	171	Self-cond.		24
CLOSE				
At close tentations: when the day is done,	72	Constancie		22
But man is close, reserv'd, and dark to thee:	82	Ungratef.		25
But now thou dost thy self immure and close	99	Decay		11
The help stands close, and keeps the fear in view.	119	Providence		88
Where all the guests sit close, and nothing wants.	121	Providence		134
Then close again the seam,	138	The Size		42
Close to my side.	142	Pilgrimage		18
Dropping from heav'n, which doth both cleanse and close	147	Offering		20
Well may he close his eyes, but not his heart.	151	The Bag		6
But it biteth in the close.	178	The Rose		24
Splendour from darknes. So close sits the crowne	212	Bohemia	D	37
takes home with him, setting them close by him, and carving for them,	243	Priest 11		11
but always in the close, before he departs from them:	248	Priest 14		15
No barber shaves so close but another finds worke.	343	Proverbs		667
To a close shorne sheepe, God gives wind by measure.	349	Proverbs		867
Your thoughts close, and your countenance loose.	362	Proverbs	D	1183
CLOSENESSE				
Is wooll and furres: cool without closenesse, shade:	120	Providence		102
Is wooll and furre: cool without closenesse, shade:	120	Providence	V	102
CLOSES				
My musick shows ye have your closes,	88	Vertue		11
CLOSEST				
And now with darknesse closest wearie eyes,	64	Even-song		18
CLOSET				
Doth closet up it self, and still retreat,	99	Decay		18
CLOSETH				
so he closeth it, humbly beseeching the Almighty to pardon and accept	236	Priest 8		26
CLOSETS				
Closets; and in them many a chest;	126	Confession		3
Closets are halls to them; and hearts, high-wayes.	126	Confession		18
CLOTH				
Thy Gentrie bleats, as if thy native cloth	10	Ch.-Porch		93
The curious unthrift makes his cloth too wide,	13	Ch.-Porch		179
I care not though the cloth of state should be	17	Ch.-Porch		269
They are of cloth,	100	Miserie		17
and sightly Communion Cloth of fine linnen, with an handsome,	246	Priest 13		16
of good and costly Stuffe, or Cloth, and all kept sweet and clean,	246	Priest 13		18
Hee that dines and leaves, layes the cloth twice.	333	Proverbs		347
CLOTHE (see also cloath)				
Nothing could seem too rich to clothe the sunne,	102	Jordan 2		11
With canvas, not with arras clothe their shame:	177	Forerunners		26
CLOTHED				
but diversly clothed, illustrated, and inlarged.	230	Priest 5		2
CLOTHES (see also cloathes)				
Spend not on hopes. They that by pleading clothes	14	Ch.-Porch		181
In clothes, cheap handsomnesse doth bear the bell.	14	Ch.-Porch		187
Upon thy body, clothes, and habitation.	21	Ch.-Porch		372
Thy clothes being fast, but thy soul loose about thee.	23	Ch.-Porch		414
Mine own clothes on, they leade me out agen.	32	Sacrifice		190
When clothes are taken from a chest of sweets	98	Mortific.		2
Christ left his grave-clothes, that we might, when grief	112	Dawning		15
Nothing wears clothes, but Man; nothing doth need	120	Providence		109
And like a Dolphins skinne, his clothes combin'd	127	Giddinesse		19
I rose, and shook my clothes, as knowing well,	139	Artillerie		3
He had new clothes a making here below.	151	The Bag		18
CLOTHING				
Is clothing, meat and trencher, drink and kan,	120	Providence		127
Is clothing, meat and trencher, drink and Can,	120	Providence	V	127
CLOTHS				
All Scepters, Reeds: Cloths, Scarlet: Crowns are Thorns:	32	Sacrifice	W	178
When cloths are taken from a chest of sweets	98	Mortific.	V	2
Christ left his grave-cloths, that we might, when grief	112	Dawning	V	15
CLOUD				
The cloud his bow, the fire his spear,	151	The Bag		14
And setling to a cloud, doth live and die	169	The Answer		11
Each Cloud distills thy praise, and doth forbid	206	Walton 2		4
CLOUDIE				
They shall be thick and cloudie to my breast.	126	Confession		30
CLOUDS				
Truth dwels not in the clouds: the bow that's there	19	Ch.-Porch		317
Truth dwels not in the clouds: that Bow doth hit	19	Ch.-Porch	W	317
This world of wo? hence all ye clouds, away,	108	Home		33
Clouds cool by heat, and baths by cooling boil.	119	Providence		72
The windes grew gard'ners, and the clouds good fountains.	120	Providence		116
But while I lookt, the clouds immediately	124	Peace		11
Then have we too our guardian fires and clouds;	128	Bunch Gr.		15
Dwell in my head & eyes: come clouds, & rain:	164	Grief		2

	PAGE	TITLE	LINE
CLOUDS (cont'd)			
No day so clear but hath dark clouds.	359	Proverbs	D 1123
CLOUTS			
Those clouts are little winding sheets,	98	Mortific.	5
CLOVES			
Of cloves and nutmegs, and in cinamon sail;	137	The Size	8
CLOWNE			
Give a clowne your finger, and he will take your hand.	324	Proverbs	111
CLUBS			
With clubs and staves they seek me, as a thief,	27	Sacrifice	37
CLUE			
Give it a corner, and the clue undoes.	11	Ch.-Porch	124
CLUSTER			
But where's the cluster? where's the taste	128	Bunch Gr.	19
CLUSTERS			
thy blessings hang in clusters, they come trooping upon us!	290	Priest	6
CLUTCH			
And till they foot and clutch their prey,	126	Confession	15
COACH			
for riding in a coach in great haste, it happened that the coach was	294	Cornaro	36
it happened that the coach was overturned, and then was dragged	294	Cornaro	37
COAL			
Man is no starre, but a quick coal	79	Employm.2	6
But though the whole world turn to coal,	88	Vertue	15
COALS			
as they remember themselves were, when affliction did blow the Coals.	280	Priest 34	21
COARSE (see also course)			
COAST			
I like our language, as our men and coast:	167	The Sonne	3
COASTING			
And travell'd Westward allso, coasting on,	193	Ch.-Milit. W	104
COASTS			
also concerning the fishing which the Hollanders use in our coasts,	368	Letters	10
neighboring Sea, wondrously sound through all our Coasts, and eares.	442	Oration	24
COAT			
My coat, the type of love, which once cur'd those	34	Sacrifice	242
This is the lace of Peaces coat:	124	Peace	9
And jagg'd his seamlesse coat, had that been fine,	134	Divinitie	11
Spin out thy thread, and make thereof a coat	156	Assurance	38
Josephs coat.	159	Jos.coat	T
Fie, thou wilt soil thy broider'd coat,	176	Forerunners	23
COATE			
Wine is a turne-coate (first a friend, then an enemy).	351	Proverbs	929
COATS			
One of Joyes coats, ticing it with relief	159	Jos.coat	11
COBWEBS			
That her fine cobwebs did support the frame,	84	The World	3
cleane without dust, or Cobwebs, and at great festivalls strawed,	246	Priest 13	9
COCK			
And the sad man is cock of all his jests.	16	Ch.-Porch	252
hand to sickle, shall then secure himself, and think all cock-sure;	271	Priest 30	30
Who eates his cock alone must saddle his horse alone.	333	Proverbs	348
COCK-SURE			
hand to sickle, shall then secure himself, and think all cock-sure;	271	Priest 30	30
COCKATRICE			
Untill their cockatrice they hatch and bring:	122	Sinnes rd.	4
COCKERS			
He that cockers his child, provides for his enemie.	347	Proverbs	789
COFFERS			
Neither eyes on letters, nor hands in coffers.	330	Proverbs	288
COFFIN			
Unto the coffin, that attends his death.	98	Mortific.	24
COHERENCE			
be added the consideration of any text with the coherence thereof,	229	Priest 4	10
COIN			
And coin large hopes; but, that I was deceiv'd:	155	Assurance	10
COINE			
Which if it cleave to coine, one common rust	13	Ch.-Porch W	165
COLD			
We all are but cold suitours; let us move	22	Ch.-Porch	400
No lodging for thee, but a cold hard stone?	40	Sepulchre	2
Though it be cold, hard, foul, from loving man	41	Sepulchre	23
But as cold hands are angrie with the fire,	66	Ch.-lock	5
Yet as cold hands are angrie with the fire,	66	Ch.-lock W	5
To cold complexions needing it.	78	Employm.2	5
Untill the grave increase our cold.	79	Employm.2	30
Cold sinne still forcing it, till it return,	99	Decay	19
Be the season cold, or hot:	113	Businesse	10
Cold fruits warm kernells help against the winde.	120	Providence	130
To warm his love, which I did fear grew cold.	129	Love unkn.	32
On double pleasures: leave thy cold dispute	153	The Collar	20
To cold despairs, and gnawing pensivenesse?	155	Assurance	16
As if there were no such cold thing.	165	The Flower	7
O what a deadly cold	184	A Parodie	26
Pleasure succeeded straight, when that grew cold.	194	Ch.-Milit.	144
Bragging that thy bloud is cold,	199	L'Envoy	6
and Christian fortitude in the cold midnight stormes of persecution	237	Priest 9	38
is apt to nourish more then in cold regions, and where flesh may be	242	Priest 10	18
where both the people and the drink being cold and flegmatick,	242	Priest 10	20
(having a most cold & moist stomack) I fell into divers diseases,	291	Cornaro	21
other hurtfull things also, as too much heat and cold, wearinesse,	293	Cornaro	31

COME (cont'd)

	PAGE	TITLE		LINE
Come blessed Dove charm'd with my song,	59	Whitsunday	W	1
O come! for thou dost know the way.	61	Grace		21
Who, when great trials come,	72	Constancie		11
Come, come, my God, O come,	80	Deniall		14
Come Lord, my head doth burn, my heart is sick,	107	Home		1
Now come again, said I, and flout me.	108	Home		46
They dresse themselves and come to thee.	108	Home		52
Come dearest Lord, passe not this holy season,	109	Home		73
The word is, Stay, sayes ever, Come.	109	Home		76
To answer these fine things shall come;	111	The Quip		22
May come too late!	111	Vanitie 2		8
What it would come to at the worst	123	Gratefulnes		11
Alas! our murmurings come not last.	128	Bunch Gr.		18
Thy life is Gods, thy time to come is gone,	144	Discharge		11
In times to come; for it will grow.	145	Discharge		30
Either grief will not come: or if it must,	145	Discharge		51
Come, bring thy gift. If blessings were as slow	147	Offering		1
Sayes, Come?	149	Longing		42
When he was come, as travellers are wont,	151	The Bag		19
(Beleeve me), it shall safely come.	152	The Bag		34
That your sweet sap might come again!	152	The Jews		12
They quickly go and come with lesser crime:	154	Glimpse		9
Come, my Way, my Truth, my Life:	156	The Call		1
Come, my Light, my Feast, my Strength:	156	The Call		5
Come, my Joy, my Love, my Heart:	156	The Call		9
Come from the earth, from whence those vessels come;	161	Priesthood		20
Doth flatter power. Lest good come short of ill	161	Priesthood		40
To come between?	163	The Search		56
O who will give me tears? Come all ye springs,	164	Grief		1
Dwell in my head & eyes: come clouds, & rain:	164	Grief		2
Come people; Aaron's drest.	174	Aaron		25
The harbingers are come. See, see their mark;	176	Forerunners		1
Come ye hither all, whose taste	179	Invitation		1
Come ye hither all, whom wine	180	Invitation		7
Come ye hither all, whom pain	180	Invitation		13
Come ye hither all, whom joy	180	Invitation		19
Come ye hither all, whose love	180	Invitation		25
Come away,	186	Dooms-day		1
Come away,	186	Dooms-day		7
Come away,	187	Dooms-day		13
Come away,	187	Dooms-day		19
Come away,	187	Dooms-day		25
Spices come from the East; so did thy Spouse,	190	Ch.-Milit.		13
But when they were unto the Sorbon come,	196	Ch.-Milit.	W	202
The Church shall come, & Sinne the Church shall smother:	197	Ch.-Milit.		266
Thou dost come first to them, that showes	200	H. Commun.	W	14
Hell, Death & Divel come short of mee.	202	love	W	24
Come to our bed	211	Paradox	D	41
of good men shall the wicked come.	215	Psalm I	D	20
his cruelty shall come.	222	Psalm VII	D	60
he cannot agree to come into any house, where he shall not exercise	226	Priest 2		25
into which if he come, he prostitutes himself both to shame,	227	Priest 3		24
when they come to pray, as a devout behaviour in the very act	231	Priest 6		15
make it a piece of state not to come at the beginning of service	232	Priest 6		8
and of theirs also who gaze upon them when they come in,	232	Priest 6		11
in our hearts, before they come into our mouths, truly affecting,	233	Priest 7		30
Oh my Master, on whose errand I come, let me hold my peace,	233	Priest 7		35
that thou would'st rent the Heavens, that thou wouldst come down, &c.	234	Priest 7		3
the Market day comes, or a shopkeeper, when customers use to come in.	235	Priest 8		19
that they may come with holy hearts, and awfull mindes into	235	Priest 8		29
all those, who come with lesse prepared hearts then they ought.	235	Priest 8		31
And every one is more awaked, when we come, and say, Thou art	236	Priest 8		14
and come to Church in frame, but commonly the next day put off both.	247	Priest 14		9
the afflicted, though they can, and otherwise ought to come to him.	249	Priest 15		17
so the hunger and thirst after it may come rather from themselves,	250	Priest 15		6
answers prove, may when they come home, either commend or reprove,	255	Priest 21		28
as Sermons come short of questions in the one, so they farre exceed	257	Priest 21		22
have to think that all things come by a kind of naturall course;	270	Priest 30		25
by his governing power, the fairest harvests come to nothing.	271	Priest 30		18
As when a Merchant hath a ship come home after many a storme,	271	Priest 30		22
what he may, before they come, and when for all that they do come,	273	Priest 31		18
and when for all that they do come, he be a little affected	273	Priest 31		18
Come, say they, we have nothing to do, lets go to the Tavern,	274	Priest 32		12
who are come to the gravitie, and ripenesse of judgement for so	276	Priest 32		16
for we must not do evill, that good may come of it.	287	Priest 37		7
beyond any help in heaven or earth, then thou saidest, Lo, I come!	288	Priest		27
thy blessings hang in clusters, they come trooping upon us!	290	Priest		7
that after many troubles and griefs I should quickly come to an end;	291	Cornaro		26
By this means the place is come to that perfection we now see it is:	301	Cornaro		30
For when I come home, I finde eleven grand-children of mine,	303	Cornaro		2
when I shall come to that point, I shall finde no little comfort in	303	Cornaro		23
whence come so many Books of severall mens opinions:	317	Valdesso		3
if I bid a man stay in a place untill I come, I doe not then bid him	318	Valdesso		15
that I may speak with him or doe some thing else when I doe come.	318	Valdesso		17
For at least some of the Papists are come now, to what the Pharisees	320	Valdesso		6
are come now, to what the Pharisees were come in our Saviours time.	320	Valdesso		7
Let not him that feares feathers come among wild-foule.	322	Proverbs		48
To a boyling pot flies come not.	325	Proverbs		123
how that which is to come will be drawne on.	332	Proverbs		329
Stay till the lame messenger come,	332	Proverbs		331

COME (cont'd)	PAGE	TITLE		LINE
Dearths foreseene come not.	335	Proverbs		407
Deaths foreseene come not.	335	Proverbs	V	407
We cannot come to honour under a Coverlet.	339	Proverbs		533
Thursday come, and the week's gone.	341	Proverbs		587
let it not come betweene the spindle and the distaffe. . . .	343	Proverbs		665
Doe what thou oughtest, and come what come can.	348	Proverbs		818
There come nought out of the sacke but what was there. . . .	348	Proverbs	V	833
Modesty sets off one newly come to honour.	357	Proverbs	D	1062
The death of a young wolfe doth never come too soon. . . .	360	Proverbs	D	1131
for, since your favours come a Horse-back, there is reason, . .	363	Letters		22
And yet if a Book of four or five Shillings come in my way, . .	365	Letters		12
certifies you that there are come agents hither from the low-Cuntries	368	Letters		4
day to bee so devout as to come to the Chappell an howre before	368	Letters		17
I wish I could have come in person to thank you, but it is . .	369	Letters		11
If I could possibly have come, none should have done my message	369	Letters		20
or on the Joyes that are to come, you have strong preservatives	373	Letters		19
because they were to come into an unknown country, tender in	375	Letters		13
COMEDIE				
at these yeares (viz. 83) I have made a most pleasant comedie,	302	Cornaro		29
or lesse my self, who being ten yeares older have made a Comedie?	302	Cornaro		36
COMERS				
Feasting all comers by twelve chosen men.	59	Whitsunday		8
COMES				
Usefulnesse comes by labour, wit by ease;	18	Ch.-Porch		291
Or love, or language; nothing comes amisse:	20	Ch.-Porch		357
Those doores being shut, all by the eare comes in.	23	Ch.-Porch		418
The greater world o' th' two; for that comes in	33	Sacrifice	W	206
Comes to about the many hundredth part.	38	The Sinner		11
Comes to about the many hundred part.	38	The Sinner	W	11
Onely thy grace, which with these elements comes, ...	52	H.Commun.		19
Thy Saviour comes, and with him mirth:	112	Dawning		4
And comes.	124	Gratefulnes		16
That from small fires comes oft no small mishap.	139	Artillerie		4
Thy anger comes, and I decline:	166	The Flower		31
But then there comes into my way	202	love	W	10
and the pleasure that comes with sleep, be sins of gluttony,	230	Priest 5		29
so as a Market-man is, when the Market day comes, or a shopkeeper,	235	Priest 8		18
When he comes to any house, first he blesseth it, and then as hee	247	Priest 14		10
that he comes to the point very leasurely, and oftentimes, . .	248	Priest 14		20
And when he comes to his Inn, he refuseth not to joyne, . .	251	Priest 17		7
When he comes to any other house, where his kindred, or other	251	Priest 17		15
in the Company where he is, but comes under his Test and censure:	252	Priest 18		3
And therefore before he comes, having observed some defects in	253	Priest 19		11
Hee that comes to the Sacrament, hath the confidence of a Guest,	259	Priest 22		14
he then comes on the faster, and makes so much the more of him,	263	Priest 25		33
but proceeding on, comes to do unlawfully, even before he is aware;	264	Priest 26		23
the Child comes, and with pulling, gets the apple out of his Fathers	272	Priest 30		9
Hence it comes, that a Physician, when he cometh to visit his	297	Cornaro		15
Ill comes in by ells, and goes out by inches.	327	Proverbs		194
The ill that comes out of our mouth falles into our bosome. . .	328	Proverbs		221
It is a great victory that comes without blood.	328	Proverbs		227
The thorne comes forth with his point forwards.	329	Proverbs		238
Punishment is lame, but it comes.	329	Proverbs		249
Though you rise early, yet the day comes	332	Proverbs		333
the time comes that hee will repay thee.	333	Proverbs		368
God comes to see without a bell.	334	Proverbs		384
In time comes he whom God sends.	334	Proverbs		397
Hee that comes of a hen must scrape.	335	Proverbs		415
Hee that comes after must scrape.	335	Proverbs	V	415
Hast comes not alone.	348	Proverbs		826
There comes nought out of the sacke but what was there. . .	348	Proverbs		833
They talke of Christmas so long, that it comes.	349	Proverbs		840
When a Lackey comes to hells doore, the devills locke the gates.	353	Proverbs		984
Old men go to Death, Death comes to Young men.	356	Proverbs	D	1
time comes that he repents himself of time.	359	Proverbs	D	1102
Take heed of winde that comes in at a hole, ...	360	Proverbs	D	1154
be it to King, Prince, or whatever comes to the University; . .	369	Letters		35
COMETH				
And while it cometh, it is almost past.	145	Discharge		53
when he cometh to visit his patient, prescribes this Physick first,	297	Cornaro		15
COMFIT				
A beane in liberty is better then a comfit in prison.	343	Proverbs		653
COMFORT				
Comfort, I'le die; for if you poste from me, ...	66	Ch.-mus.		9
Comfort, I'le die; for if you part from me, ...	66	Ch.-mus.	W	9
And he would needs a comfort be, ...	111	The Quip		18
But one half houre of comfort for my heart?	154	Glimpse		5
But one half houre of comfort to my heart?	154	Glimpse	V	5
If all the hope and comfort that I gather, ...	155	Assurance		21
But th' Empire dwelt in Greece, to comfort them	192	Ch.-Milit.		73
which in the day of wrath hath not one dramme of comfort for us.	227	Priest 3		21
the storehouse and magazene of life and comfort, the holy Scriptures.	228	Priest 4		23
for knowledge, Examples for illustration, and Promises for comfort:	228	Priest 4		26
but for the comfort of the weak, that not onely sicknesse breaks	242	Priest 10		34
and their comfort, who are much cheered with such friendliness.	243	Priest 11		12
Nature serving Grace both in comfort of diversion, and the benefit	261	Priest 23		11
that the distinction is of singular use and comfort, especially	273	Priest 31		13
This Instruction and comfort the Parson getting for himself,	279	Priest 33		32
and comfort in the holy Ghost.	280	Priest 34		7
have been an ornament to the world, and a comfort to their friends:	291	Cornaro		4

COMMON (cont'd)	PAGE	TITLE	LINE
are either such as are made known by common fame (and of these,	287	Priest 37	12
it concerns the Common-Wealth, that Rogues should be known, . .	287	Priest 37	36
That they who are employed in the common wealth, cannot live	299	Cornaro	12
which is both easie for common-weals-men, and very convenient,	299	Cornaro	17
this cannot stand, and it is ill Doctrine in a common-wealth.	316	Valdesso	17
may pretend motions, which is unsufferable in a Common-wealth.	316	Valdesso	22
[according to the common and legal proceedings among men.] . .	316	Valdesso	28
and indeed in common sence, if I bid a man stay in a place untill I	318	Valdesso	14
But perhaps being above the Common people, our Credit and estimation	373	Letters	25
COMMON-PRAYER-BOOK			
both of Blessing, & cursing are expounded in the Common-Prayer-book:	286	Priest 36	3
COMMON-WEAL			
'Twas more secure in great Loves Common-weal	439	Walton 5	17
COMMON-WEALS			
Much more do Common-weals acknowledge thee, ...	190	Ch.-Milit.	5
COMMON-WEALS-MEN			
which is both easie for common-weals-men, and very convenient,	299	Cornaro	17
COMMON-WEALTH			
Now it is a justice and debt to the Common-wealth he lives in,	262	Priest 23	16
and it concernes the Common-wealth, that none should be idle,	274	Priest 32	27
No Common-wealth in the world hath a braver [better] Institution then	276	Priest 32	8
and a shamefull wrong both to the Common-wealth, and their own House:	277	Priest 32	27
it concerns the Common-Wealth, that Rogues should be known, . . .	287	Priest 37	36
this cannot stand, and it is ill Doctrine in a common-wealth.	316	Valdesso	17
may pretend motions, which is unsufferable in a Common-wealth.	316	Valdesso	22
COMMON-WEALTHS			
Houses are built by rule, and common-wealths.	12	Ch.-Porch	135
COMMONLY			
for then commonly the stream of temptations is turned another way,	238	Priest 9	22
and come to Church in frame, but commonly the next day put off both.	247	Priest 14	10
if they be of higher quality, they commonly are quick, and sensible,	248	Priest 14	19
or known commonly, the beginnings of them are not easily observable:	264	Priest 26	18
of old age in the humours of my bodie, which commonly kills men.	296	Cornaro	37
COMMONS			
of advancing the publick Stock, and managing Commons, or Woods,	276	Priest 32	6
COMMONWEALTH'S			
the other the commonwealths, & therfore not relinquishable without	381	Woodnoth	29
COMMONWEALTHS			
His children he first makes Christians, and then Commonwealths-men;	239	Priest 10	21
COMMONWEALTHS-MEN			
His children he first makes Christians, and then Commonwealths-men;	239	Priest 10	21
COMMUNICATE			
Let him communicate the thing often by prayer unto God, . . .	237	Priest 9	5
such which you have found useful to yourself, communicate them to me.	366	Letters	5
COMMUNICATION			
that I may enjoy the sight & communication of my friends, . .	301	Cornaro	35
COMMUNION			
The H. Communion.	52	H.Commun.	T
The H. Communion.	200	H. Commun. W	T
and Desk, and Communion Table, and Font be as they ought, . .	246	Priest 13	6
and sightly Communion Cloth of fine linnen, with an handsome,	246	Priest 13	16
Especially at Communion times he is in a great confusion, . .	257	Priest 22	28
At the times of the Holy Communion, he first takes order . .	258	Priest 22	21
not on the Sunday of the Communion only (for then it is too late)	258	Priest 22	27
or Sundayes before the Communion, or on the Eves of all those dayes.	258	Priest 22	28
touching the frequency of the Communion, the Parson celebrates it,	259	Priest 22	19
COMMUNIONS			
as at great Festivals, and Communions;	245	Priest 12	7
if there be but three Communions, neither can all the people so order	259	Priest 22	26
COMPACTED			
A box where sweets compacted lie;	88	Vertue	10
COMPANIE			
Who lives by rule then, keeps good companie.	12	Ch.-Porch	138
Then keep such companie; make them thy allay:	15	Ch.-Porch	212
A servile death in servile companie:	34	Sacrifice	235
But all my companie is a weed.	57	Employm. 1	22
But if I travell in your companie, ...	66	Ch.-mus.	11
In companie;	98	Mortific.	16
Of that good companie.	101	Miserie W	48
When I cannot have their companie, I give my self to the reading	301	Cornaro	6
COMPANIONS			
Which he might fall in by companions, gains.	24	Ch.-Porch	436
are in Orders, they may be received for Companions, or discoursers;	226	Priest 2	24
COMPANY			
The joyes of Company or Contemplation	89	The Pearl W	29
not only with abstinence of diet, but also of company, recreation,	241	Priest 10	38
Neither in this doth he forbear, though there be company by:	248	Priest 14	25
that he may enlarge the glory of God to the company he is in,	251	Priest 17	8
or done in the Company where he is, but comes under his Test	252	Priest 18	3
when the baits which the enemy lays in company, are discovered	252	Priest 18	14
if he perceive in company any discourse tending to ill, . . .	252	Priest 18	16
neither avoyding therfore one anothers company, much lesse defaming	260	Priest 23	27
not avoyding his company, or doing any thing of aversenesse,	263	Priest 25	27
and hee that eats offensively to the Company, either in his order,	266	Priest 26	10
not onely because all men shun the company of perpetuall severity, .	268	Priest 27	2
but also for that when they are in company, instructions seasoned	268	Priest 27	3
which the present occasion of wit and company otherwise admits;	280	Priest 34	28
Keepe good men company, and you shall be of the number. . .	325	Proverbs	120
Keep not ill men company, lest you increase the number. . .	331	Proverbs	314
He that dies without the company of good men	354	Proverbs	995

	PAGE	TITLE	LINE
COMPLEATE			
he teacheth them, that three things make a compleate servant, Truth,	240	Priest 10	18
COMPLEATNESS			
and I will strive to imitate the compleatness of your love,	364	Letters	2
COMPLEMENT			
By dressing, mistressing, and complement.	9	Ch.-Porch	80
COMPLEMENTALL			
that it is no complementall or light thing to sustain that place,	258	Priest 22	11
COMPLEMENTERS			
language, he shall be esteemed as ordinary complementers;	286	Priest 36	22
COMPLEMENTING			
of spending the day in dressing, Complementing, visiting,	277	Priest 32	29
with a great man in the ordinary course of complementing language,	286	Priest 36	21
COMPLEMENTS			
and complements, and formes of worldly language better;	285	Priest 36	5
COMPLETE (see also compleat)			
And so complete, but onely he that owes them.	121	Providence	144
Wherein is contained the complete definition of a Minister.	225	Priest 1	13
COMPLETENESSE			
The Parson's Completenesse.	259	Priest 23	T
COMPLEXION			
Be sweet to all. Is thy complexion sowre?	15	Ch.-Porch	211
A sad wise valour is the brave complexion,	16	Ch.-Porch	247
COMPLEXIONS			
To cold complexions needing it.	78	Employm.2	5
COMPLIE			
Will more complie, then help. A Lord I had,	129	Love unkn.	3
COMPLIES			
Complies and suits with all estates;	69	Content	14
COMPLYING			
Complying with thy counsels, doing nought	190	Ch.-Milit.	7
COMPOSE			
on Sundays it is easie for them to compose themselves to order,	247	Priest 14	8
COMPOS'D			
But the great souldiers honour was compos'd	15	Ch.-Porch	225
But is compos'd of passion.	86	Lent	3
The humble soul compos'd of love and fear	86	Lent	7
COMPOSETH			
read divine services, composeth himselfe to all possible reverence;	231	Priest 6	2
COMPOSITIONS			
My slender compositions might consume.	160	Priesthood	10
COMPOSURES			
For though the world is full of such composures, yet every mans own	230	Priest 5	4
COMPREHEND			
These three rules generally comprehend the faults of eating,	266	Priest 26	12
COMPREHENDS			
But to eat to ones hurt, comprehends, besides the hurt,	266	Priest 26	21
COMPRIZE			
For these two rules comprize and include the double object of our	246	Priest 13	29
COMPROMISES			
but that they still fall from all compromises that have been made.	260	Priest 23	25
CONCEAL			
Thou Lord conceal it not: and as thou art	62	Afflict.2	12
He took fine vizards to conceal his crimes:	195	Ch.-Milit.	186
CONCEALES			
A woman conceales what shee knowes not.	355	Proverbs	1031
CONCEALS			
Conceals thee still?	163	The Search	30
CONCEIT			
Thy person share, and the conceit advance.	15	Ch.-Porch	232
I did conceit a most delicious feast;	50	Faith	6
and have a good conceit of your wit, mark what I say, have a good	366	Letters	15
of your wit, mark what I say, have a good conceit of your wit;	366	Letters	16
CONCEITE			
that destroyeth at noone day, [Ghostly pride and self-conceite.]	238	Priest 9	8
CONCEITS			
knowing that where there are such conceits, there is no room for his	243	Priest 11	23
CONCEIV'ST			
If thou mislike him, thou conceiv'st him not.	23	Ch.-Porch	428
CONCEIVE			
And I conceive, our Saviour did this for three reasons:	261	Priest 23	17
the Authors sake, whom I conceive to have been a true servant of God;	304	Valdesso	6
overweigh the defects (as I conceive) towards the publishing thereof,	305	Valdesso	13
and I conceive that restraining motions are much more frequent	313	Valdesso	17
that you may well conceive, your Excellencies to bee more deare unto	442	Oration	19
CONCEIV'D			
That all was not so fair, as I conceiv'd,	155	Assurance	8
CONCEIVES			
Exploits of mischief he conceives,	222	Psalm VII D	51
He conceives not possibly, how the windes should blow so much as they	281	Priest 34	20
He conceives not possibly, how he that would beleeve a Divinity,	281	Priest 34	27
A good Judge conceives quickly, judges slowly.	341	Proverbs	599
CONCERNE			
in all these, and those more which concerne me, I either do nothing,	265	Priest 26	16
CONCERNES			
and exerciseth a threefold power in every thing which concernes man.	271	Priest 30	1
and it concernes the Common-wealth, that none should be idle,	274	Priest 32	27
CONCERNETH			
Concerneth bread not mee.	200	H. Commun. W	9
Concerneth mee & Thee.	200	H. Commun. W	12

	PAGE	TITLE		LINE
CONFERENCE				
told to another, whether in private conference, or in the Church,	278	Priest 33		17
CONFERRE				
I conferre often with worthie men, excelling in wit, learning,	301	Cornaro		4
CONFESS				
Did not confess in the first Theefe	202	Trin.Sun.	W	12
CONFESSE				
Share in the conquest, and confesse a troth.	19	Ch.-Porch		324
Lord, I confesse my sinne is great;	48	Repentance		1
I do confesse	49	Repentance		16
For I confesse my heavie score, ...	68	Trin.Sun.		5
We must confesse that nothing is our own.	143	Holdfast		7
Then I confesse, that he my succour is:	143	Holdfast		8
But to have nought is ours, not to confesse	143	Holdfast		9
Why then confesse	210	Paradox	D	35
CONFESSETH				
confesseth himself an unworthy one, and therefore differs from other	259	Priest 22		15
CONFESSION				
Then turn thy faults and his into confession:	24	Ch.-Porch		441
Then turn thy fault and his into confession:	24	Ch.-Porch	W	441
Yet by confession will I come	37	Reprisall		13
My God, accept of my confession.	49	Repentance		18
Confession.	126	Confession		T
For since confession pardon winnes, ...	126	Confession		27
Let the graves make their confession, ...	187	Dooms-day		15
that there is no help for a fault done, but confession. . .	240	Priest 10		36
with confession of sins, and all acts of Mortification. . .	242	Priest 10		1
in perswading them to particular confession, labouring to make them	249	Priest 15		30
CONFESSOR				
Deceive not thy Physitian, Confessor, nor Lawyer.	324	Proverbs		105
CONFIDENCE				
Is Confidence:	67	Ch.-floore		9
the Sacrament, hath the confidence of a Guest, and hee that kneels,	259	Priest 22		14
it is not performed by way of request, but of confidence, and power,	286	Priest 36		7
of God may be said in some sence to have put confidence in Scripture,	306	Valdesso		29
acts of humiliation, and acts of confidence and joy;	312	Valdesso	V	24
Skill and confidence are an unconquered army.	342	Proverbs		626
I wrong both my self, and also the confidence my Friends have in me;	364	Letters		8
CONFIDENT				
throw it away, and be most confident, that God is not displeased.	273	Priest 31		38
And I am confident, that under God nothing holp me, but that exact	296	Cornaro		28
CONFIGURATIONS				
And the configurations of their glorie!	58	H.Script.2		2
CONFIRM				
And anchor thou art onely, to confirm	97	Afflict.5		4
Wake and confirm that judgment now, ...	221	Psalm VII	D	23
CONFIRME				
convert those who are not yet thine, and to confirme those that are:	289	Priest		17
CONFIRMED				
and the event confirmed it.	285	Priest 36		31
CONFIRMETH				
Which Josephus's History confirmeth, and the continuance of which	282	Priest 34		30
But mine own experience confirmeth this more;	294	Cornaro		11
CONFIRMS				
This Galen confirms, when he sayes, that immoderate heats and colds,	294	Cornaro		6
and armies victorious, and retains and confirms kingdomes, cities,	297	Cornaro		10
CONFLICTS				
yet by these thy conflicts, and seemingly hazards, didst thou arise	288	Priest		33
CONFORMABLE				
and joyfull, that hee is made conformable to his Master; . .	269	Priest 28		17
CONFORMITY				
which he observeth out of humble conformity, and obedience; . .	237	Priest 9		24
which conformity and fashionableness is so exceeding unbefitting	285	Priest 36		6
CONFOUND				
What I taught: Comments would the text confound.	28	Sacrifice		55
Sharp nails pierce this, but sharper that confound;	33	Sacrifice		218
All my abilities, my designes confound, ...	164	The Crosse		11
The wicked's målice, Lord, confound, ...	221	Psalm VII	D	33
CONFRONTING				
Confronting equally the law and grace.	196	Ch.-Milit.		218
CONFUSED				
With noises confused frighting the day:	29	Sacrifice		103
CONFUSION				
and to confusion suddainly.	220	Psalm VI	D	28
Especially at Communion times he is in a great confusion, . .	257	Priest 22		29
CONFUTE				
Yet his owne practice seemes to confute his opinion, for the most	317	Valdesso		35
CONGRATULATE				
title to your Excellencies, all the Muses and Graces congratulate;	442	Oration		2
CONGREGATION				
but as presenting with himself the whole Congregation, whose sins he	231	Priest 6		8
and awfull mindes into the Congregation, and that the good God would	235	Priest 8		30
and fraile man, discharged the publick duties of the Congregation.	236	Priest 8		10
and to satisfie the Congregation by their Catholick answers.	255	Priest 21		21
CONJECTURE				
as farre as I can conjecture, very apt and well given both . .	303	Cornaro		4
CONJURER'S				
To all things els. Wealth is the conjurers devil;	13	Ch.-Porch		165
CONQUER				
Commodious to conquer heav'n and thee	72	Frailtie		23
Thou shalt not bee a Queene and conquer there.	212	Bohemia	D	40

	PAGE	TITLE		LINE
CONQUER (cont'd)				
with which you use to conquer your enemies, and assume more mild	442	Oration		3
CONQUERE				
To conquere new ones, & shall share the frame	212	Bohemia	D	43
CONQUER'D				
And having conquer'd, did so strangely rule,	196	Ch.-Milit.		203
CONQU'RING				
And if the braves of conqu'ring sinne	60	Whitsunday		23
CONQUERING				
There's no such conquering weapon as the necessity of conquering.	357	Proverbs	D	1064
CONQUEROUR				
and that at length I should be a conquerour, as also a little after	294	Cornaro		27
The world is now adayes, God save the Conquerour.	358	Proverbs	D	1075
CONQUEST				
Share in the conquest, and confesse a troth.	19	Ch.-Porch		324
Into the conquest. Though I can do nought	37	Reprisall		14
Into thy conquest, though I can do nought	37	Reprisall	W	14
Till thy conquest and his fall	199	L'Envoy	V	13
Something that may be conquest on my part	201	love	W	5
Let mee but once the conquest have	202	love	W	19
Upon the matter 'twill thy conquest prove:	202	love	W	20
CONQUESTS				
Couldst thou not griefs sad conquests me allow,	37	Reprisall		11
While his conquests dayly spread;	199	L'Envoy		8
Till thy conquests and his fall	199	L'Envoy		13
CONSCIENCE				
And in the eare, not conscience ring.	68	Windows		15
Conscience.	105	Conscience		T
A throbbing conscience spurred by remorse	132	The Storm		9
He greatly esteemes also of cases of conscience, wherein he is much	230	Priest 5		19
it is out of the overflowing of his Conscience, whereas they are	269	Priest 29		31
of the grave in this world, and the worm of Conscience in the next.	272	Priest 30		14
and the Cases of Conscience belonging thereto, wherein (as Saint Paul	279	Priest 33		34
This is true onley of the Popish Cases of Conscience, which depend	319	Valdesso	V	28
there are other Cases of Conscience grounded on Piety and Morality,	319	Valdesso	V	30
Some make a conscience of spitting in the Church,	343	Proverbs		650
Once a yeare a man may say: On his conscience.	353	Proverbs		971
of them will justifie you both to the world and your own Conscience:	373	Letters		17
your withdrawing it shold doe so, it would trouble your conscience.	381	Woodnoth		13
CONSCIENCES				
Without, our shame; within, our consciences;	46	Sinne 1		11
CONSECRATE				
Churches sake, to whom by Printing it I would have you consecrate it.	304	Valdesso		9
CONSECRATED				
those many Love-poems, that are daily writ and consecrated to Venus;	363	Letters		8
in Poetry, shall be all, and ever consecrated to Gods glory.	363	Letters		12
CONSENT				
Which by consent was giv'n to Mansuetude.	70	Humilitie		10
To a full consent.	178	Discipline		8
this passeth in Spaine freely with consent of King & counsell.	368	Letters		29
& therfore not relinquishable without their masters consent.	381	Woodnoth		30
CONSEQUENCE				
or in cases of high consequence, as establishing of inheritances:	260	Priest 23		22
considering the great Consequence of their place, and more of their	270	Priest 29		17
great in it selfe, and great in Consequence:	274	Priest 32		10
CONSEQUENTLY				
and consequently knowing the price of mony, are offended much	227	Priest 3		13
And consequently he found, that the essence of repentance,	279	Priest 33		20
CONSERVE				
His pills of sublimate in that conserve.	193	Ch.-Milit.		132
CONSIDER				
Consider, Lord; Lord, bow thine eare,	149	Longing		29
O God consider me	221	Psalm VII	D	30
while they consider, that God cannot be wanting to them in Doctrine,	263	Priest 24		20
or consider it so narrowly, which yet ought to be done,	265	Priest 26		31
I began to consider the force of Temperance, and to think thus	293	Cornaro		1
Neither can any man denie this, who will narrowly consider it.	297	Cornaro		15
But they consider not, of how great moment ten yeares are in mature	298	Cornaro		29
Of him that speakes ill, consider the life more then the words.	346	Proverbs		761
Of him that speakes ill, consider the life more then the word.	346	Proverbs	V	761
pardon my boldness, and consider but these three things.	365	Letters		16
consider what advantage you have over Youth and Health,	372	Letters		32
I beseech you consider all that can happen to you are either	373	Letters		20
when we consider that the Blessings in the holy Scripture,	373	Letters		28
consider that God intends that to be as a sacred Temple for himself	374	Letters		9
But though I both consider this, and your observation, also,	376	Letters		3
complaine of want of success consider how long God knocks at our	381	Woodnoth		1
CONSIDERABLE				
This Chapter is considerable. The intent of it, that the world	315	Valdesso		29
CONSIDERATION				
To this may be added the consideration of any text with the coherence	229	Priest 4		10
he sets himself to the Consideration of the duties of the day,	235	Priest 8		32
in consideration of providing a stock for his children;	240	Priest 10		6
After the consideration of his own Parish, he inlargeth himself,	245	Priest 12		17
The Parson's Consideration of Providence.	270	Priest 30		T
they are not in this Consideration, because we are about a Calling,	276	Priest 32		36
who will take this into consideration, I will declare the causes	291	Cornaro		14
concluding every Consideration almost with his holy Name,	305	Valdesso		5
Scripture suite with what he writes elsewhere, especially Consid. 32.	306	Valdesso		16
together with many other, as namely Consid. 71. upon Our Father;	307	Valdesso		16
and Consid. 94. upon these words:	307	Valdesso		17

CONSIDERATION (cont'd)	PAGE	TITLE		LINE
See the note upon Consid. 36.	307	Valdesso		23
as to neglect the Consideration of Gods Worke in his heart through	309	Valdesso		30
The Doctrine of this Consideration cleareth that of the precedent	310	Valdesso		26
Scriptures for the first and principall, as Consid. 47, and others;	311	Valdesso	V	5
will better appear by his 98 Consideration of faith and good works.	312	Valdesso	V	5
for so he useth the same word in Consideration 68 ad finem. . .	317	Valdesso	V	8
Things needing great Consideration. Mat. 24. 15.	317	Valdesso		26
2 Ep. 1. 19. which he makes the ground of his [this] Consideration,	318	Valdesso		8
The 98. Consid. about being justified by faith, or by good works,	319	Valdesso	V	16
will make the Consideration easy, and very observeable: . .	320	Valdesso		5
CONSIDERATIONS				
Briefe Notes on Valdesso's Considerations A Copy of a letter written	304	Valdesso		T
he sheweth through all his Considerations) a thing strangely buried,	305	Valdesso		1
to the dubious and offensive places in the following CONSIDERATIONS.	306	Valdesso		T
but enlightens us with new Considerations the more we read it.	310	Valdesso		35
for the most of his Considerations being grounded upon some text	318	Valdesso		1
CONSIDER'D				
I have consider'd it, and finde	36	Reprisall		1
For we consider'd thee as at some six	186	Death		5
CONSIDERED				
therefore the spirit of both is to be considered, and weighed.	229	Priest 4		16
but a dictionary, and may be considered alike in all the Scripture.	235	Priest 7		10
and other like circumstances considered, he is rather married then	237	Priest 9		4
people (whom he chiefly considered) might have every where monuments	261	Priest 23		21
Hee that hath considered how to carry himself at table about his	278	Priest 33		18
Therefore I considered that if one only came, the comfort intended	375	Letters		16
you any other wayes, as neyther I my self desire to be considered.	378	Letters		16
CONSIDERING				
How canst thou stay, considering the pace	107	Home		7
and considering with my self, That the way to please him, . .	224	Priest		3
The Country Parson considering that virginity is a higher state then	236	Priest 9		31
yet considering that the Law allows these in case they be true,	245	Priest 12		24
and considering his Flock, discovers two sorts of vices, . .	264	Priest 26		4
considering the great Consequence of their place, and more of their	270	Priest 29		17
The Countrey Parson considering the great aptnesse Countrey people	270	Priest 30		24
Thus the Parson considering that repentance is the great vertue	279	Priest 33		6
considering the stubbornnesse of the Nation, their living then in	282	Priest 34		7
considering what an orderly life I had led for many yeares together,	295	Cornaro		7
especially considering the time and place where he lived. . .	311	Valdesso	V	7
not considering you any other wayes, as neyther I my self desire	378	Letters		15
CONSIDERS				
He first considers his own Parish, and takes care, that there be	244	Priest 12		19
his owne person, hee considers the offender as a child, and forgives,	250	Priest 16		14
hee considers diligently the state thereof to Godward, and that in	251	Priest 17		17
hee first considers with himselfe, what kind of remedy fits . .	251	Priest 17		25
he considers what is the end of any Command, and then he suits things	253	Priest 19		3
hee considers and looks into the ignorance, or carelesness of his	258	Priest 22		24
Hee considers every one there, and either helps them in particular,	276	Priest 32		3
CONSIGNE				
Which do consigne and send them unto death.	98	Mortific.		6
CONSIST				
In healing not my self, there doth consist	34	Sacrifice		225
If the world consist of order, if our corporall life depend . .	297	Cornaro		7
because my recompenses of your favours consist in this only.	367	Letters		32
CONSISTETH				
it consisteth most of mutton, beefe, and veal, if he addes any thing	241	Priest 10		16
a more melting temper then others) consisteth in a true detestation	279	Priest 33		23
wherein consisteth the making good of my former education, . .	364	Letters		17
CONSISTS				
But the chief and top of his knowledge consists in the book of books,	228	Priest 4		21
The Parsons Method in handling of a text consists of two parts;	235	Priest 7		1
Yet the skill consists but in these three points:	256	Priest 21		30
the secret of whose good consists in this, that at Sermons, . .	257	Priest 21		18
although the power of health consists most in the proportion of meat	293	Cornaro		33
whose holinesse consists in a few ceremonious and superstitious	319	Valdesso	V	22
CONSOLATION				
To this end he hath throughly digested all the points of consolation,	249	Priest 15		18
constant and the more earnest for you to the God of all Consolation.	372	Letters		23
CONSONANT				
For all Truth being consonant to it self, and all being penn'd by one	229	Priest 4		5
That which savours, is good and nourisheth, be consonant to truth.	293	Cornaro		10
CONSORT				
Consort both heart and lute, and twist a song	42	Easter		13
Lord place me in thy consort; give one strain	57	Employm. 1		23
Lord, thy broken consort raise, ...	187	Dooms-day		29
CONSPIRE				
In laws and policie; what the starres conspire, ...	88	The Pearl		5
CONSTANCIE				
Constancie knits the bones, and makes us stowre, ...	11	Ch.-Porch		117
Constancie knits the bones, and makes us sowre, ...	11	Ch.-Porch	W	117
Constancie.	72	Constancie		T
CONSTANCY				
and constancy in its operations, certainly it should be either	271	Priest 30		9
The constancy of the benefits of the yeere	347	Proverbs		773
to answer your infinite kindnesses, but a constancy of obedience;	363	Letters		19
now Constancy is such & of great esteem with all.	380	Woodnoth		15
CONSTANT				
Allows for that, and keeps his constant way:	73	Constancie		28
Constant unto it, making it to be	73	Afflict.3		14
They make his life a constant blot, ...	102	Miserie		63

CONTEND (cont'd)	PAGE	TITLE	LINE
either unfit, or bootelesse to contend, then when any despises him,	269	Priest 28	5
CONTENT			
Content.	68	Content	T
Content and warm t' it self alone:	68	Content	10
This soul doth span the world, and hang content	69	Content	17
Content thee, greedie heart.	137	The Size	1
Content and care	138	The Size	34
So do these words a sweet content,	174	The Odour	4
Nor canst thou be content, unlesse thou to	439	Walton 5	5
so he is content to expresse this outwardly to the utmost of his	231	Priest 6	11
for a reward to draw men to Piety, and is content, if at least so,	243	Priest 11	32
He that studies his content, wants it.	321	Proverbs	4
I was the better content because I was in hope I should my self carry	372	Letters	14
CONTENTED			
that Nature was contented with a little, and that I had for many	295	Cornaro	26
we can eat but a very little, wherewith she is very well contented:	299	Cornaro	29
and well-contented, free from all troubles and troublesome thoughts;	300	Cornaro	37
(to wit - with a moderate and contented heart).	328	Proverbs	208
CONTENTION			
And is in contention for them whither to live, or dy;	234	Priest 7	15
that this suit and contention was raised by the Divine Providence,	294	Cornaro	24
In an hundred elles of contention, there is not an inch of love.	348	Proverbs	817
CONTENTIOUS			
when the persons in difference are of a contentious disposition,	260	Priest 23	23
CONTENTIOUSNESSE			
Contentiousnesse in a feast of Charity is more scandall then any	259	Priest 22	17
being unmoved in arguing, and voyd of all contentiousnesse:	263	Priest 24	18
CONTENTMENT			
For wealth without contentment, climbes a hill	11	Ch.-Porch	111
CONTENTMENTS			
but also of company, recreation, and all outward contentments;	241	Priest 10	39
CONTEST			
If they should offer to contest	42	Easter	25
When th' elements did for place contest	79	Employm.2	11
To enter combate with us, and contest	139	Artillerie	26
Let wits contest,	182	The Posie	1
CONTINENCE			
Continence hath his joy: weigh both; and so	7	Ch.-Porch	17
CONTINENCY			
and blesseth God for the gift of continency, knowing that it can no	237	Priest 9	19
CONTINUALL			
by reason of continuall inward, or outward temptations,	238	Priest 9	13
and so by continuall, and fresh bounties, unexpected to them,	244	Priest 12	32
as having continuall use of them, such as are from Gods generall	249	Priest 15	19
Besides the continuall succession (since the Gospell) of holy men,	282	Priest 34	18
the beginning of the Gout, with almost a continuall fever and thirst.	291	Cornaro	23
CONTINUALLY			
he meets continually with two most sad spectacles, Sin,	267	Priest 27	31
which continually breake Gods Laws, and dishonour him with those	269	Priest 28	10
him with those mouths, which he continually fils, and feeds:	269	Priest 28	11
then by that which he continually supplyes, as the corn needs it;	271	Priest 30	5
and indeed, to depend, and fear continually.	271	Priest 30	36
and finding my self continually oppressed with pain and sicknesse,	292	Cornaro	19
I am continually in health, and I am so nimble, that I can easily get	300	Cornaro	34
and, though subject to death, yet continually afraid of it:	303	Cornaro	17
shewes that he was continually conversant in it, and not used it	318	Valdesso	2
CONTINUANCE			
confirmeth, and the continuance of which verdict is yet evident.	282	Priest 34	30
and unworthy hearts rob us of the continuance of this thy sweet love:	289	Priest	20
and by continuance thereof, within lesse then one yeare (although it	292	Cornaro	36
CONTINUE			
Christ being not to continue on earth, but after hee had fulfilled	225	Priest 1	6
the Parson be unmarryed, and means to continue so, he doth at least,	238	Priest 9	25
any continue to be refractory, yet hee gives him not over,	250	Priest 16	16
but to continue his dependance on God, not onely before the corne is	271	Priest 30	34
Which benefits also still continue, because from the time that I was	293	Cornaro	24
they live disorderly, yet continue in health to their lives end:	300	Cornaro	18
Though you see a Church-man ill, yet continue in the Church still.	344	Proverbs	698
yours (which praised be God are less) are not like to continue long.	374	Letters	3
before lower, even where to continue in the lower is no sinn.	380	Woodnoth	4
When we exhort people to continue in their vocation, it is in	381	Woodnoth	23
CONTINUED			
that must be done by a set, and laboured, and continued speech.	257	Priest 21	25
to that which is presently unlawfull, even in one continued action.	264	Priest 26	22
it is a continued Creation, and a creation every moment.	281	Priest 34	31
and that I had for many yeares continued in good health,	295	Cornaro	27
came a terrible fever, which continued thirtie five dayes and nights;	296	Cornaro	20
nothing holp me, but that exact rule which I had so long continued.	296	Cornaro	30
CONTINUES			
know I did not, and that your share continues, or rather increaseth,	372	Letters	17
CONTINUETH			
who continueth to pour his benefits upon us.	290	Priest	2
CONTINUING			
and that also well inned, and imbarned, and continuing safe there;	272	Priest 30	2
CONTRACT			
Stretch or contract me thy poore debter:	55	Temper 1	22
Contract my houre,	144	Complaining	19
Contract into a span.	159	The Pulley	5
or contract any ill qualitie, as usually happens in old mens bodies,	296	Cornaro	34

CONVERT (cont'd)	PAGE	TITLE		LINE
Convert & colour all the other flood	204	The Knell	W	14
The Convert. An Ode.	213	Convert	D	T
How long will ye, vain men, convert	217	Psalm IV	D	7
that it may effectually pierce their hearts, and convert them.	262	Priest 24		24
to convert those who are not yet thine, and to confirme those that	289	Priest		16
CONVEY				
To me dost now thy self convey;	52	H.Commun.		4
Who did so sweetly deaths sad taste convey, ...	94	Life		10
Convey them quickly, who are bound for death.	98	Mortific.		12
Which shall convey him to the house of death.	98	Mortific.		30
Which shall convey him to the place of death.	98	Mortific.	W	30
Convey a Lordship any way	104	Obedience		2
Convey a Lordship any waies.	104	Obedience	V	2
An usher to convey our souls	123	Time		17
Not to his hurt. Sighs will convey	152	The Bag		41
Their hands convey him, who conveys their hands.	161	Priesthood		28
CONVEYED				
it were a great good deed, and I would have her conveyed to you.	375	Letters		32
CONVEYS				
Their hands convey him, who conveys their hands.	161	Priesthood		28
CONVINCE				
by which we well know how to convince the sterne, and more austere	442	Oration		6
COOL				
Sweet day, so cool, so calm, so bright, ...	87	Vertue		1
Clouds cool by heat, and baths by cooling boil.	119	Providence		72
Is wooll and furres: cool without closenesse, shade:	120	Providence		102
Is wooll and furre: cool without closenesse, shade:	120	Providence	V	102
They never cool, much lesse give out.	126	Confession		16
A neighbour spring to cool his inward heat;	154	Glimpse		14
for strong and very cool wines pleased my taste best, as also melons,	293	Cornaro		11
of Architecture, that they are cool in summer, and warm in winter.	301	Cornaro		13
COOLE				
But if thou coole, then take some shame to thee	10	Ch.-Porch	W	90
A coole mouth, and warme feet, live long.	321	Proverbs		21
COOLING				
Clouds cool by heat, and baths by cooling boil.	119	Providence		72
But cooling by the way, grows pursie and slow, ...	169	The Answer		10
but difficulties are so farr from cooling christians, that they whett	376	Letters		11
COOLS				
Which cools his will.	133	The Method		4
COPIE				
If studious, copie fair, what time hath blurr'd;	10	Ch.-Porch		86
Copie thy fair, though bloudie hand?	35	Thanksgvng		16
Copie out onely that, and save expense.	103	Jordan 2		18
But as in vice the copie still exceeds	196	Ch.-Milit.		221
COPIED				
Here is copied out by art;	208	J. Danvers	D	10
COPPERSMITH				
Speaking of Alexander the Coppersmith, who had withstood his	285	Priest 36		32
COPPY				
Coppy out that: there needs no alteration.	103	Jordan 2	W	18
COPS				
So to cares cops I came, and there got through	142	Pilgrimage		11
COPY				
governing of his house, making it a copy and modell for his Parish.	239	Priest 10		7
Thirdly, that he might set a Copy for Parsons.	261	Priest 23		26
on Valdesso's Considerations A Copy of a letter written by MR. GEORGE	304	Valdesso		T
CORALL				
The jealous Turkie brought his corall-chain;	70	Humilitie		13
CORALL-CHAIN				
The jealous Turkie brought his corall-chain;	70	Humilitie		13
CORDIALL				
And cordiall left to repair mans decay:	31	Sacrifice		159
That cordiall water to our ground, ...	59	Whitsunday		18
Cordiall and Corrosive: put not thy hand	83	Sighs & Gr.		28
What I have lost with cordiall fruit?	153	The Collar		9
CORDIALLY				
truly affecting, and cordially expressing all that we say; . . .	233	Priest 7		30
CORDIALS				
Passing all cordials made by any art, ...	171	The Glance		6
What cordials make this curious broth, ...	175	The Odour		9
Julips & Cordials when wee call on thee	204	The Knell	W	17
CORDS				
and from us cast their cords away.	215	Psalm II	D	8
CORINTHIANS				
The Odour. 2. Cor. 2.	174	The Odour		T
And for the Corinthians, chap. 1. 4.	234	Priest 7		13
What an admirable Epistle is the second to the Corinthians? . .	234	Priest 7		18
And the top of Christian vertues, 1 Corin. 13.	244	Priest 12		14
The second, Let all things be done to edification, 1 Cor. 14.	246	Priest 13		28
some sort true because they are spiritually discerned, 1 Cor. 2. 14.	315	Valdesso		32
by the Apostles rule. 1 Cor.	380	Woodnoth		5
CORN				
But when we leave our corn and hay:	108	Home		56
Before my sighs did drie it: there was corn	153	The Collar		11
of corn and wine can be.	218	Psalm IV	D	28
the one for smalnesse, as crums, and scattered corn, and the like;	241	Priest 10		28
giving some corn outright, and selling other at under rates;	245	Priest 12		11
in the field, his seed-corn, and tares;	261	Priest 23		23
and that if they sow and soyle their grounds, they must have corn;	270	Priest 30		27

COULD (cont'd)	PAGE	TITLE		LINE
What pleasures could I want, whose King I served,	46	Afflict.1		13
Before that I could feare.	46	Afflict.1	W	16
I could not go away, nor persevere.	47	Afflict.1		48
And could see little, to regard his ease,	49	Faith		3
Which when I could not get, I thought it here:	50	Faith		10
O that I could a sinne once see!	63	Sinne 2		1
Could build so strong in a weak heart.	67	Ch.-floore		20
We could not choose but look on still;	75	Sunday		19
When my devotions could not pierce	79	Deniall		1
I took up in the next inne I could finde.	80	Christmas		4
Which they effected, none could them withstand.	84	The World		18
I could not use a friend, as I use Thee.	93	Unkindness		10
Advise with Abraham, when thy power could not	99	Decay		3
Nothing could seem too rich to clothe the sunne,	102	Jordan 2		11
As if thy love could fail or change.	108	Home		28
That is all, if that I could	115	Dialogue		25
Sure thou didst put a minde there, if I could	116	Dulnesse		23
Who sweetly temper'st all. If we could heare	118	Providence		39
When yet some places could no moisture get,	120	Providence		115
I would say thorns. Deare, could my heart not break,	130	Love unkn.		52
Could he but take them right, and in their wayes.	132	Mans medly		33
Thy Father could	133	The Method		5
Could not that wisdome, which first broacht the wine,	134	Divinitie		9
But I was told by one, it could not be;	143	Holdfast		3
Could poyson, if it had a tongue, expresse?	155	Assurance		14
Could be allow'd for harmonie)	165	The Crosse		16
Could have recover'd greennesse? It was gone	166	The Flower		9
Thy word is all, if we could spell.	166	The Flower		21
O, could I love! and stops: God writeth, Loved,	168	a true Hymn		20
To make him clean, who could not be defil'd?	173	Marie Magd		8
And not his feet? Though we could dive	173	Marie Magd		10
Without whom I could have no rest:	174	Aaron		14
If we could see below	175	The Foil		1
As if they could beautie spare.	177	The Rose		8
Could improve,	181	Banquet		29
The second Temple could not reach the first:	196	Ch.-Milit.		225
I could beleeve an Impanation	201	H. Commun.	W	25
Although the Crosse could not Christ here detain,	439	Walton 5		1
He writ; when 's hand could write no more,	439	Walton 5		13
When my dear Friend, could write no more,	439	Walton 6		1
never dream'd of, and therefore he could give no precepts thereof.	233	Priest 7		25
since we are here by him, and without him could not be here.	234	Priest 7		30
women to heaven) a wise and loving husband could out of humility,	238	Priest 9		31
and doing that which either he could not do, or was not fit for him	241	Priest 10		32
And the answerer could not tell;	257	Priest 21		4
for he could not but say, he would hast out of it as fast as he	257	Priest 21		7
he could not but say, he would hast out of it as fast as he could.	257	Priest 21		7
whether he could get out of the ditch alone, or whether he needed	257	Priest 21		8
that if anything could presume of an inevitable course,	271	Priest 30		8
Could men finde out this delight, they would seldome be from home;	275	Priest 32		34
he sees not how a house could be either built without a builder,	281	Priest 34		18
many waters could not quench thy love!	288	Priest		31
there was one help for me, if I could constantly pursue it, to wit,	292	Cornaro		4
I preserved me also, asmuch as I could, from hatred and melancholie,	293	Cornaro		35
Yet could I not so avoid all these, but that now and then I fell into	293	Cornaro		37
which excesse of joy neither could do me any hurt.	294	Cornaro		30
that they could not be much troubled, or make a great concourse,	295	Cornaro		9
that old age could not be sustained with so little meat and drink;	295	Cornaro		22
but also to gather strength, which could not be but by meat & drink.	295	Cornaro		24
But all these things could not defend me against their importunities.	296	Cornaro		5
Besides all this, I could not sleep, no not a quarter of an houre:	296	Cornaro		21
What Physician could have discovered these hidden qualities to me,	297	Cornaro		34
Many have thought that this could be done by Aurum potabile,	298	Cornaro		19
when I was given to disorder and all the delights that could be.	302	Cornaro		11
then I could of Originall before, and without Baptisme.	308	Valdesso		4
unlesse he could have made it appeare, that it was done by Gods	316	Valdesso		25
I wonder how this opinion could befall so good a man as it seems	317	Valdesso		31
If you could runne, as you drinke, you might catch a hare.	334	Proverbs		373
you could not fill all to your mind.	343	Proverbs	V	700
you could not fit all to your mind.	344	Proverbs		701
There is a remedy for every thing, could men find it.	360	Proverbs	D	1142
all his life, could he find it.	360	Proverbs	D	1143
that if any course could be taken of doubling my Annuity now,	367	Letters		7
I wish I could have come in person to thank you, but it is	369	Letters		11
If I could possibly have come, none should have done my message	369	Letters		19
and age, and knew none but one who could be no company to them.	375	Letters		15
If you could think of taking her, as once you did, surely it were	375	Letters		30
what could have happened more pleasing to us, then the accesse	442	Oration		8
How could you bee like great Alexander, unlesse Historie delivered	443	Oration		2
COULDST				
Couldst thou not griefs sad conquests me allow,	37	Reprisall		11
Lord, how couldst thou so much appease	49	Faith		1
Art thou possest, who, when thou couldst not die,	103	Prayer 2		14
Thou couldst well see	144	Discharge		24
Bitterly spitefull thought! Couldst thou invent	155	Assurance		2
Thy mouth was open, but thou couldst not sing.	185	Death		4
COUNCELL				
What your glasse telles you, will not be told by Councell.	329	Proverbs		255
Councell breakes not the head.	336	Proverbs		443
It's an ill councell that hath no escape.	345	Proverbs		715

COUNTREY (cont'd)	PAGE	TITLE	LINE
Whensoever the Ccuntrey Parson proceeds so farre as to call in	263	Priest 25	22
The Countrey Parson at spare times from action, standing on a hill,	264	Priest 26	3
is an occasion, my countrey is an occasion, my friend is an occasion,	265	Priest 26	14
but being seated in the Countrey, and doing their duty faithfully,	266	Priest 26	3
The Countrey Parson is generally sad, because hee knows nothing	267	Priest 27	27
The Countrey Parson knows well, that both for the generall ignominy	268	Priest 28	9
The Countrey Parson doth often, both publickly, and privately	269	Priest 29	26
The Countrey Parson considering the great aptnesse Countrey people	270	Priest 30	24
considering the great aptnesse Countrey people have to think that all	270	Priest 30	25
The Countrey Parson observing the manifold wiles of Satan (who playes	272	Priest 31	15
The Countrey Parson hath not onely taken a particular Survey	274	Priest 32	4
Yet is it also a debt to our Countrey to have a Calling, . . .	274	Priest 32	26
the one, the abuse of it, by taking petty Countrey bribes; . .	276	Priest 32	20
The Countrey Parson's Library is a holy Life:	278	Priest 33	11
The Countrey Parson knows, that there is a double state . .	280	Priest 34	1
their Countrey also is known, the places, and rivers travelled unto,	282	Priest 34	2
their living then in their Countrey under so many miracles were	282	Priest 34	9
then their present exile, and disability to live in their Countrey.	282	Priest 34	10
The Countrey Parson is a Lover of old Customes, if they be good,	283	Priest 35	27
because Countrey people are much addicted to them, so that to favour	283	Priest 35	29
The Countrey Parson wonders, that Blessing the people is in so little	285	Priest 36	1
The Countrey Parson perceiving, that most, when they are at leasure,	286	Priest 37	29
in the reducing of many rude and untoiled places in my countrey,	302	Cornaro	16
In every countrey the sun rises in the morning.	342	Proverbs	621
Much money makes a Countrey poor, ...	361	Proverbs	D 1178
COUNTREY-AIRES			
But that these countrey-aires thy love	124	Gratefulnes	23
COUNTREY-DUTY			
Likewise in any other Countrey-duty, he considers what is the end	253	Priest 19	3
COUNTREY'S			
as divers have done lately, to our Countrey's advantage. . .	278	Priest 32	10
COUNTREYS			
All countreys have enough to serve their need:	120	Providence	105
that the prohibiting of flesh came from hot Countreys, where both	242	Priest 10	16
The one being usefull to all Ccuntreys, and the other especially	278	Priest 32	3
COUNTRIE'S			
The Chicken is the Countries, but the Citie eates it.	324	Proverbs	108
COUNTRY (see also cuntry)			
a slighter forme of Catechizing, fitter for country people; . .	230	Priest 5	16
The Country Parson, as soon as he awakes on Sunday morning, . .	235	Priest 8	16
The Country Parson considering that virginity is a higher state then	236	Priest 9	31
Country people are full of these petty injustices, being cunning	265	Priest 26	33
or Noble-man in the Country he lives in, inabling him with power	276	Priest 32	13
who being obscured in his own country he would have to flourish in	304	Valdesso	14
In every country dogges bite.	342	Proverbs	620
Hee a beast doth die, that hath done no good to his country.	354	Proverbs	993
by transporting French commodities to your own country. . .	366	Letters	13
because they were to come into an unknown country, tender in	375	Letters	14
COUNTRYMAN			
for if he be a plaine countryman, he reproves him plainly; . .	248	Priest 14	17
COUNTS			
God reckons for him, counts the favour his:	21	Ch.-Porch	381
One while he counts of heav'n, as of his treasure: . . .	127	Giddinesse	5
Hast thou not made thy counts, and summ'd up all?	144	Discharge	6
but counts it the art, and secret of governing to preserve . .	240	Priest 10	33
COURAGE			
Lest sinne take courage and return, ...	39	Good Fri.	31
With care and courage building me, ...	90	Afflict.4	29
COURSE (coarse)			
These are the scumme, with which course wits abound:	16	Ch.-Porch	237
And sudden arbours shadow course-spunne lines?	56	Jordan 1	7
He wears a stuffe whose thread is course and round, ...	131	Mans medly	15
not cheape, or course, much lesse ill-tasted, or unwholsome.	258	Priest 22	23
COURSE			
That my offences course it in a ring.	122	Sinnes rd.	2
Hast thou left all things to their course, ...	149	Longing	44
The Water-course.	170	Water-crs.	T
But rather turn the pipe, and waters course	170	Water-crs.	6
The course was westward, that the sunne might light	190	Ch.-Milit.	17
even in externall and indifferent things, what course is to be taken;	247	Priest 13	1
In this course the order of the Catechisme wculd be kept, . .	256	Priest 21	5
it is the safest course for Christians also to meditate on their	258	Priest 22	17
have to think that all things come by a kind of naturall course;	270	Priest 30	26
that if anything could presume of an inevitable course, . .	271	Priest 30	9
who more accepts a common course of devotion, then dislikes . .	273	Priest 31	9
then to take Jobs admirable Course, who sacrificed lest his Children	281	Priest 34	1
with a great man in the ordinary course of complementing language,	286	Priest 36	21
I so addicted my self to this course of life, that I never went	292	Cornaro	33
I never since departed from my setled course of Sobrietie, . .	293	Cornaro	26
onely with returning to my former course of Diet, although I was now	296	Cornaro	25
after live free from diseases, if he will keep such a course of life;	297	Cornaro	20
there be any course, either by engaging my future Annuity, . .	365	Letters	20
that if any course could be taken of doubling my Annuity now,	367	Letters	7
as the course of our life & the changes thereof, we are to regard	380	Woodnoth	18
COURSE-SPUNNE			
And sudden arbours shadow course-spunne lines?	56	Jordan 1	7
COURSES			
whom hee sees take best courses, that so both they may be encouraged	243	Priest 11	25
But if the young Gallant think these Courses dull, and phlegmatick,	278	Priest 32	4
been forward to say, if I had taken ill courses, Follow your Book,	364	Letters	21

	PAGE	TITLE		LINE
COURT				
Courtesie grows in court; news in the citie.	18	Ch.-Porch		292
Courtesie grows at Court; news in the citie.	18	Ch.-Porch	W	292
Let not thy higher Court remove,	56	Temper 2		15
To court each place or fortune that doth fall,	68	Content		7
To court each place or fortune that does fall,	68	Content	W	7
Although then others court you, if ye know	78	Ang.&Sts.		26
Into these lines; till in heav'ns court of rolls	105	Obedience		43
Who by thy coming may be made a court!	155	Glimpse		30
Before a court, ev'n that above so cleare,	167	Dotage		16
Farre from court,	182	Banquet		41
Sometimes he may go to Court, as the eminent place both of good	277	Priest 32		5
There are three waies, the Universities, the Sea, the Court.	334	Proverbs		383
At Court, every one for himselfe.	347	Proverbs		795
So many men in Court and so many strangers.	350	Proverbs		874
The Court hath no Almanack.	350	Proverbs		894
Power seldome grows old at Court.	357	Proverbs	D	1053
upon this he was forbid Court & kingdome, yet was seene lately neere	368	Letters		35
To my very dear brother Sir Henry Herbert, at Court.	376	Letters		25
Honourable the Lady Anne, Countess of Pembr. and Montg. at court.	376	Letters		T
though it be none of the Court-stile, yet doubtless Madam,	377	Letters		2
To my deere brother, Sir Henry Herbert, at Court.	377	Letters		32
COURT-STILE				
though it be none of the Court-stile, yet doubtless Madam,	377	Letters		2
COURTEOUS				
All such is courteous, usefull, new, or wittie.	18	Ch.-Porch		290
Secondly, by a courteous carriage, & winning behaviour:	268	Priest 28		22
He that owes nothing, if he makes not mouthes at us, is courteous.	333	Proverbs		362
COURTESIE				
Be not a beast in courtesie; but stay,	8	Ch.-Porch		46
Courtesie grows in court; news in the citie.	18	Ch.-Porch		292
Courtesie grows at Court; news in the citie.	18	Ch.-Porch	W	292
In him to do themselves a courtesie:	30	Sacrifice		114
The quick returns of courtesie and wit:	88	The Pearl		12
The Parson's Courtesie.	243	Priest 11		T
and of Courtesie to his other parishioners, he so distinguisheth,	243	Priest 11		7
others spurred to do well, that they may enjoy the like courtesie.	243	Priest 11		27
by withdrawing his bounty and courtesie from the parties offending,	254	Priest 20		23
opinion of him, that if he can do me a courtesie, he will of himself;	369	Letters		23
your Courtesie will pardon the haste of Your humblest Servant,	371	Letters		18
COURTESIES				
And trade in courtesies and wit,	78	Employm.2		3
for them often, and in finding out Courtesies to place on them;	262	Priest 24		27
COURTIER				
The Courtier getts it, that has grace.	97	Charms & K	W	20
COURTIERS				
Old courtiers know this; therefore set out so,	14	Ch.-Porch		185
COURTLY				
yea, indeed of all, both Courtly, Militarie, Academicall.	441	Oration		28
COURTS				
In cities, theatres, gardens, parks, and courts:	40	Redemption		11
In grottos, gardens, Palaces & Courts	40	Redemption	W	11
COUSIN				
except my cousin Bett take pitty of her, which yet at that distance	375	Letters		29
COUZIN				
To couzin thee. Look to thy actions well:	23	Ch.-Porch		425
COVENANT				
preach my Laws, and takest my Covenant in thy mouth? Psal. 50. 16.	226	Priest 2		14
entertained to that end, either by an open, or implicite Covenant.	226	Priest 2		23
COVER				
My face they cover, though it be divine.	31	Sacrifice		137
Holds them unto it, and doth cover	100	Miserie		27
Cover the Earth, so doth thy Majesty:	206	Walton 2		3
and decent chest, with a Chalice, and Cover, and a Stoop, or Flagon;	246	Priest 13		19
Cover your selfe with your shield, and care not for cryes.	326	Proverbs		161
COVERING				
To Charity is given the covering of sins, 1 Pet. 4. 8.	244	Priest 12		9
COVERLET				
Every one stretcheth his legges according to his coverlet.	325	Proverbs		147
We cannot come to honour under a Coverlet.	339	Proverbs		533
COVERS				
All our pompe the earth covers.	345	Proverbs		716
COVERT				
What covert dare eclipse thy face?	163	The Search		31
COVERTLY				
Better speake truth rudely, then lye covertly.	346	Proverbs		767
COVET				
All covet, all lose.	358	Proverbs	D	1078
COVETEOUS				
Poore and liberall, rich and coveteous.	332	Proverbs		339
The coveteous spends more then the liberall.	344	Proverbs		683
COVETEOUSNESSE				
Countrey Parson is very circumspect in avoiding all coveteousnesse,	227	Priest 3		16
When all sinnes grow old, coveteousnesse is young.	321	Proverbs		18
When all sinnes grow old, coveteousnesse grows young.	321	Proverbs	V	18
COVETOUS				
Be thriftie, but not covetous: therefore give	12	Ch.-Porch		151
A man may be both Covetous, and Intemperate, and yet hear Sermons	264	Priest 26		14
or not in some proportion to Gods blessing upon him, is covetous.	265	Priest 26		7
undecently to the station wherein God hath placed me, I am Covetous.	265	Priest 26		19
sometimes too salt, and so not competent nourishment, I am Covetous.	265	Priest 26		23

COVETOUS (cont'd)	PAGE	TITLE	LINE
rather to use his neighbours, and wear out that, he is covetous.	265	Priest 26	30
Bee covetous, then, of all good which you see in Frenchmen, . . .	366	Letters	7
COVETOUSNES			
or honour, be a sin of covetousnes or ambition, and when not;	230	Priest 5	27
first, for covetousnes, he lays this ground:	265	Priest 26	4
COVETOUSNESS			
few bring covetousness thus low, or consider it so narrowly,	265	Priest 26	30
COVETOUSNESSE			
is turned another way, into Covetousnesse, Love of pleasure,	238	Priest 9	23
as Covetousnesse, and Gluttony. So likewise there are some persons,	264	Priest 26	9
God turning mens Covetousnesse, and Ambitions to the effecting of his	282	Priest 34	34
Covetousnesse breaks the bag.	358	Proverbs	D 1071
COW			
A curst Cow hath short hornes.	339	Proverbs	531
Who will sell the Cow, must say the word.	347	Proverbs	791
A poore mans Cow dies, a rich mans child.	350	Proverbs	869
The Cow knowes not what her taile is worth, till she have lost it.	350	Proverbs	870
COWARD			
Plainly and home, is coward of the two.	15	Ch.-Porch	218
And calls him coward, who for fear of sinne	127	Giddinesse	7
The vertue of a coward is suspition.	362	Proverbs	D 1179
COWARD'S			
A valiant mans looke is more then a cowards sword.	345	Proverbs	708
COWARDS			
Cowards tell lies, and those that fear the rod;	9	Ch.-Porch	75
COY			
Lord, make me coy and tender to offend:	93	Unkindness	1
Cheat the most subtill nations. Who so coy, ...	194	Ch.-Milit.	150
COZEN (see also couzin)			
CRACKT			
Findes his crackt name at length in the church-glasse.	14	Ch.-Porch	198
Being in this their old crackt looking-glasse.	196	Ch.-Milit.	208
CRAFT			
He that hath not the craft, let him shut up shop.	349	Proverbs	860
Craft against craft makes no living.	350	Proverbs	890
CRAFTIER			
And being craftier much then Goodnesse was, ...	193	Ch.-Milit.	124
CRAFTY			
To a crafty man, a crafty and an halfe.	347	Proverbs	796
CRAVE			
Do I forbear to crave your speciall aid:	78	Ang.&Sts.	7
He doth not crave lesse time, but more.	123	Time	30
Thy word our hearts and hands did crave, ...	123	Gratefulnes	10
Sweet Peace, where dost thou dwell? I humbly crave, ...	124	Peace	1
CRAV'D			
All show'd the builders, crav'd the seers care.	106	Sion	6
CRAVES			
He who craves all the minde, ...	168	a true Hymn	11
CRAVING			
so that they are so far from craving this benefit from their ghostly	286	Priest 36	13
CRAVINGS			
And wanton in thy cravings, thou mayst know, ...	65	Ch.-monum.	19
CRAZIE			
He is a brittle crazie glasse:	67	Windows	2
CRAZY			
To a crazy ship all winds are contrary.	334	Proverbs	395
CREAM			
And the cream of all my heart	146	Praise 2	11
CREATE			
He did not heav'n and earth create, ...	63	Mattens	15
CREATEDST			
Lord, who createdst man in wealth and store, ...	43	East.wings	1
CREATION			
Then I will use the works of thy creation, ...	36	Thanksgvng	35
Then will I use the works of thy creation, ...	36	Thanksgvng W	35
The rest of our Creation	76	Sunday	43
The work of thy creation	82	Ungratef.	11
Or can be, then is Man? to whose creation	90	Man	5
Lord, mend or rather make us: one creation	127	Giddinesse	25
if he had been at the Creation of all things, should lesse beleeve	281	Priest 34	28
For Preservation is a Creation;	281	Priest 34	30
it is a continued Creation, and a creation every moment. . .	281	Priest 34	31
which in the Creation needed not, gave them love for love, . .	283	Priest 34	16
CREATOUR			
And ev'ry day a new Creatour art.	56	Temper 2	8
yet art thou our Creatour, and we thy work:	288	Priest	12
CREATURE			
And strip the creature naked, till he finde	85	Vanitie 1	16
Once a poore creature, now a wonder, ...	89	Afflict.4	4
And my clay my creature would	115	Dialogue	27
Each creature hath a wisdome for his good.	118	Providence	61
Bestow this jewell also on my creature, ...	160	The Pulley	12
For thy poore creature there	200	H. Commun. W	6
I abuse the Creature, I am false to my reason which should guide me,	265	Priest 26	9
CREATURES			
When creatures had no reall light	51	Faith	33
Of all the creatures both in sea and land	117	Providence	5
Some creatures have in winter what to eat;	118	Providence	55
Should creatures want for want of heed their due?	119	Providence	86
Thy creatures leap not, but expresse a feast, ...	121	Providence	133

	PAGE	TITLE		LINE
CREATURES (cont'd)				
All creatures have their joy: and man hath his.	131	Mans medly		3
Creatures are good, & have their place	200	H. Commun.	W	22
God hath provided Creatures for both;	241	Priest 10		30
either he doth it as they are Creatures, dust and ashes;	283	Priest 34		10
As Creatures, he must needs love them;	283	Priest 34		11
Thy hands both made us, and also made us Lords of all thy creatures;	288	Priest		13
Wine makes all sorts of creatures at table.	352	Proverbs		931
school-mistresse, and you know what those mercenary creatures are.	375	Letters		26
CREDIT				
Whether thy stock of credit swell, or fall.	20	Ch.-Porch		346
To credit him, and to discredit those	193	Ch.-Milit.		137
To credit him, and so discredit those	193	Ch.-Milit.	W	137
He that hath lost his credit is dead to the world.	333	Proverbs		357
Religion, Credit, and the Eye are not to be touched.	349	Proverbs		837
Take heed of credit decaid, and people that have nothing.	360	Proverbs	D	1150
our Credit and estimation calls on us to live in a more splendid	373	Letters		26
CREDITOR				
And liv'd accordingly; my creditor	50	Faith		15
CREDITOUR				
My Creditour beleev'd so too.	50	Faith	W	16
CREED				
We forfeit all our Creed.	86	Lent		30
them say their Prayers first, or the Creed, and ten Commandments,	245	Priest 12		35
as thus, in the Creed:	256	Priest 21		6
CREEP				
Thus we creep on,	79	Employm.2	W	29
Whose flat delights on earth do creep and grow;	111	Vanitie 2		2
That these two words might creep & grow	175	The Odour		14
Yet I creep	179	Discipline		15
Yet then I found, that thou didst creep	202	love	W	16
though he even creep into it, and though it smell never so lothsomly.	249	Priest 14		5
now they creep in a Vessel of Metheglin, and still they will be	376	Letters		27
CREEP'ST				
Thou creep'st into my breast;	52	H.Commun.		8
CREEPING				
are of this dark, and creeping disposition, but for example sake,	265	Priest 26		2
CREEPS				
Scarce a good joy creeps through the chink:	60	Whitsunday		22
But then a thought creeps in,	127	Giddinesse		6
It moves, it creeps, it aims at thee:	149	Longing		38
that creeps upon Gods earth, no not tho' the advice step so far,	378	Letters		12
CREPT				
First, Beautie crept into a rose,	110	The Quip		5
CREST				
They are hells land-marks, Satans double crest:	196	Ch.-Milit.		219
CRIE				
If those take up thy day, the sunne will crie	9	Ch.-Porch		81
If those bee all thy day, the sunne will crie	9	Ch.-Porch	W	81
My silence rather doth augment their crie;	29	Sacrifice		93
Heark how they crie aloud still, Crucifie:	29	Sacrifice		97
It is not fit he live a day, they crie,	29	Sacrifice		98
Yet still they shout, and crie, and stop their eares,	30	Sacrifice		105
Who Crucifie him, crie with one strong shout.	32	Sacrifice		186
To crie to thee,	80	Deniall		17
With full crie of affections, quite astray;	80	Christmas		3
But thou dost still lament, and pine, and crie;	112	Dawning		7
Which crie and follow. Thou hast made poore sand	118	Providence		47
Wherefore I crie, and crie again;	124	Gratefulnes		25
Yet heard a crie	142	Pilgrimage		32
To weep or crie?	143	Complaining		14
Should crie so loud, untill the trump were drown'd,	152	The Jews		10
And by that crie of her deare Lord obtain,	152	The Jews		11
CRIED				
Though my sinnes against me cried,	146	Praise 2		13
CRIES				
God holds his peace at man, and man cries out:	32	Sacrifice		187
To thee my cries,	148	Longing		3
If ever Voice was hoarse with Cries,	213	Convert	D	2
CRIME (see also crymes)				
And spreads the plaister equall to the crime:	44	H. Bapt.1		11
Spredding the plaister equall to the crime:	44	H. Bapt.1	W	11
They quickly go and come with lesser crime:	154	Glimpse		9
or hainousness of the crime may be, he is carefull to see condign	254	Priest 20		26
CRIMES				
Fed with the exhalation of our crimes,	64	Ch.-monum.		5
His ancient justice overflows our crimes.	128	Bunch Gr.		14
Amaze poore mortals, and object their crimes.	132	The Storm		6
Amuse poore mortals, and object their crimes.	132	The Storm	V	6
He took fine vizards to conceal his crimes:	195	Ch.-Milit.		186
Both for their vertuous actions and their crimes.	197	Ch.-Milit.		262
CRINGINGS				
and cringings, that they shall ever be despised.	226	Priest 2		35
CRIPPLE				
He that mockes a cripple, ought to be whole.	340	Proverbs		565
CRITICKS				
Criticks are like brushers of Noblemens cloaths.	360	Proverbs	D	1157
CROCODILE				
Most things move th' under-jaw; the Crocodile not.	121	Providence		139
Most things move th' underchaw; the Crocodile not.	121	Providence	V	139
His highest was an ox or crocodile,	193	Ch.-Milit.		122

	PAGE	TITLE		LINE
CRUCIFIE				
Heark how they crie aloud still, Crucifie:	29	Sacrifice		97
Who Crucifie him, crie with one strong shout.	32	Sacrifice		186
CRUELL				
To hunt his cruell food through ev'ry vein.	37	The Agonie		12
Cruelty is more cruell, if we defer the pain.	359	Proverbs	D	1110
CRUELTY				
Yet since in frailty, cruelty, shrowd turns,	32	Sacrifice	W	177
his cruelty shall come.	222	Psalm VII	D	60
Cruelty is more cruell, if we defer the pain.	359	Proverbs	D	1110
CRUMBLE				
O crumble not away thy souls fair heap.	9	Ch.-Porch		70
CRUMBLED				
Be crumbled into dust. Mark here below	65	Ch.-monum.		22
CRUMBLING				
Whereas the other way of crumbling a text into small parts,	235	Priest 7		6
CRUMME				
A crumme of dust from heav'n to hell?	55	Temper 1		14
Thy pile of dust, wherein each crumme	149	Longing		41
Pickt here and there a crumme, and would not die;	154	Glimpse		17
CRUMS				
the one for smalnesse, as crums, and scattered corn, and the like;	241	Priest 10		28
CRUSH				
Where rude unhallow'd steps do crush and grinde	140	Ch.-rents		8
These contrarieties crush me: these crosse actions	165	The Crosse		32
These arms shall crush thee. Spare not, do thy worst.	169	Dial.-Anth		8
CRUSHT				
A prisoner crusht with gluttonie.	96	Charms & K	W	14
And crusht the building: and it's partly true,	127	Giddinesse		15
CRUST				
pork, sausages, pulse, and cake, and py-crust, and the like:	293	Cornaro		13
CRUTCHES				
One foote is better then two crutches.	346	Proverbs		769
all the world would turne Carpenters (to make them crutches).	355	Proverbs		1020
CRY (see also crie)				
Mine owne deare people, cry, away, away,	29	Sacrifice		102
They bow their knees to me, and cry, Hail king:	32	Sacrifice		173
Cry out, Get hence,	136	Ephes.		14
Or cry no more.	136	Ephes.		15
my cry to thee, I pray.	218	Psalm V	D	4
For God himself hath heard my cry;	220	Psalm VI	D	21
CRY'D				
I fell, and cry'd, Alas my King!	142	Pilgrimage		27
And straight he turn'd, and to his brethren cry'd,	151	The Bag		30
I struck the board, and cry'd, No more.	153	The Collar		1
I cry'd unto the Lord, he heard	216	Psalm III	D	9
CRYES				
And heal my troubled breast which cryes,	150	Longing		83
In Penitential Cryes.	214	Convert	D	15
Cover your selfe with your shield, and care not for cryes.	326	Proverbs		161
CRYING				
Out-crying my requests, drowning my tears;	66	Ch.-lock		3
Both knees and heart, in crying night and day,	80	Deniall		13
Both hart & knees, in crying night and day,	80	Deniall	W	13
And then not heare it crying! all day long	80	Deniall		18
The pigeons feed their tender off-spring, crying,	118	Providence		62
Clinging and crying, crying without cease,	205	Persever.	W	15
CRYMES				
Whither my many crymes and use of sinn	205	Persever.	W	11
CRYSTALL				
I am no Crystall, what shall I?	136	Ephes.		30
CULTIVATION				
untoiled places in my countrey, to cultivation and good husbandrie.	302	Cornaro		16
CUNNING				
As cunning fencers suffer heat to tire.	19	Ch.-Porch		316
The cunning workman never doth refuse	20	Ch.-Porch		353
One cunning bosome-sinne blows quite away.	46	Sinne 1		14
O what a cunning guest	126	Confession		1
Yet have I often seen, by cunning hand	161	Priesthood		13
To second thee against there cunning hate.	211	Bohemia	D	22
being cunning to make use of another, and spare themselves:	265	Priest 26		34
he every where understands the cunning hypocrite who by the world is	319	Valdesso	V	20
CUNNINGLY				
By noon most cunningly did steal away,	94	Life		5
CUNTRIES				
come agents hither from the low-Cuntries to treat of divers matters,	368	Letters		5
CUNTRY				
Leave not thine owne deere-cuntry-cleanlines	21	Ch.-Porch	W	367
CUP				
Stay at the third cup, or forgo the place.	8	Ch.-Porch		47
O let this cup passe, if it be thy pleasure:	27	Sacrifice		23
Why he'l not lose a cup of drink for thee:	100	Miserie		8
A friend did steal into my cup for good,	130	Love unkn.		43
My head with oyl, my cup with wine	173	23 Psalme		19
In a cup	182	Banquet		38
(The marks of future bane) shall fill our cup	197	Ch.-Milit.		239
CUPBOARD				
The whole is, either our cupboard of food,	91	Man		29
Thy cupboard serves the world: the meat is set,	118	Providence		49
A narrow cupboard for my griefs and doubts,	164	Grief		11

	PAGE	TITLE		LINE
CUPID				
Out-strip their Cupid easily in flight?	206	walton 1		9
CURBE				
To curbe some Rebell teares, which faine would flow, ...	213	Bohemia	D	58
CURBS				
Then he that curbs them, being but one to five:	89	The Pearl		29
The other curbs sinnes stealing pace and theft.	117	Providence		36
CURE				
Whom oil and balsames kill, what salve can cure?	24	Ch.-Porch		447
Whom oil and mercies kill, what salve can cure?	24	Ch.-Porch	W	447
That as each beast his cure doth know, ...	39	Good Fri.		19
Herbs gladly cure our flesh; because that they	91	Man		23
A rose, besides his beautie, is a cure.	119	Providence		78
The lemmons juice and rinde cure mutually.	120	Providence		131
In Christ two natures met to be thy cure.	147	Offering		6
Cure Tarantulas raging pains.	186	Dooms-day		12
when any of his cure is sick, or afflicted with losse of friend,	249	Priest 15		13
neighbour Phisician, and entertaines him for the Cure of his Parish.	261	Priest 23		1
for this is to cure like a Parson, and this raiseth the action from	262	Priest 23		10
directly (for disputation is no Cure for Atheisme) he scatters in his	281	Priest 34		15
Hee that bewailes himselfe hath the cure in his hands. . . .	336	Proverbs		441
Who paies the Physitian, does the cure.	350	Proverbs		879
CUR'D				
My coat, the type of love, which once cur'd those	34	Sacrifice		242
Fractures well cur'd make us more strong.	49	Repentance		36
That apprehension cur'd so well my foot, ...	50	Faith		11
CURED				
seem to some incredible) I was perfectly cured of all my infirmities.	292	Cornaro		37
I by the grace of God cured my self, onely with returning to my	296	Cornaro		24
and when he hath cured him, commends this also to him, if he will	297	Cornaro		17
Diseases of the eye are to bee cured with the elbow. . . .	327	Proverbs		203
Diseases of the eyes are to bee cured with the elbow. . . .	326	Proverbs	V	203
An ill wound is cured, not an ill name.	329	Proverbs		245
By suppers more have beene killed then Galen ever cured. . .	330	Proverbs		272
By suppers more are killed then Galen ever cured.	330	Proverbs	V	272
Frenzy, Heresie, and Jealovsie, seldome cured.	357	Proverbs	D	1049
Some evils are cured by contempt.	357	Proverbs	D	1052
CURES				
Cures both a fever and lethargicknesse.	19	Ch.-Porch		336
Cures both a fever and a drowsines.	19	Ch.-Porch	W	336
And after death for cures.	94	Life		15
some in Noble houses, some in Parishes residing on their Cures.	226	Priest 2		2
and wishing them ever to do the Cures with their own hands, . .	247	Priest 14		19
and smallage made into a Poultis, have done great and rare cures.	262	Priest 23		8
The Royall Crowne cures not the head-ach.	340	Proverbs		576
CURING				
Curing all wounds, but mine; all, but my fears:	27	Sacrifice		27
a curing, and healing of all wounds and sores with her owne hands;	239	Priest 10		14
if curing poor people, hee supplies them with Receipts, . . .	247	Priest 14		16
In curing of any, the Parson and his Family use to premise prayers,	262	Priest 23		9
yet he looks not in this point of Curing beyond his own Parish,	262	Priest 23		13
and greatly to be esteemed for the knowing & curing of diseases,	298	Cornaro		4
CURIOSITY				
Curiosity in prying into high speculative and unprofitable questions,	238	Priest 9		18
CURIOUS				
The curious unthrift makes his cloth too wide, ...	13	Ch.-Porch		179
The marbles neat and curious veins:	67	Ch.-floore		14
My friend may spit upon my curious floore:	93	Unkindness		11
And ruffle all their curious knots and store.	97	Afflict.5		22
The wanton lover in a curious strain	115	Dulnesse		5
And curious vertues both of herbs and stones?	119	Providence		74
Thy curious art in marshalling thy goods.	119	Providence		94
But trimm'd with curious lace, ...	131	Mans medly		16
With curious questions and divisions?	134	Divinitie		12
And force of fire, what curious things are made	161	Priesthood		14
What cordials make this curious broth, ...	175	The Odour		9
Thence into Greece she fled, where curious Arts	191	Ch.-Milit.	W	49
Are given over, for their curious arts, ...	194	Ch.-Milit.		152
Thy curious vertues much more visibly:	211	Bohemia	D	14
there needs not many and curious things, but onely that a man should	299	Cornaro		8
CURIOUSNESSE				
Much curiousnesse is a perpetuall wooing	14	Ch.-Porch		191
CURL				
Curl o're again.	115	Dulnesse		8
CURLE				
Glitter, and curle, and winde as they:	74	The Starre		26
CURLED				
And with quaint metaphors her curled hair	115	Dulnesse		7
CURLING				
Curling with metaphors a plain intention, ...	102	Jordan 2		5
CURRANT				
For this French sluttery which so currant goes:	21	Ch.-Porch	W	368
But though the streams of thy bloud were currant through darknesse,	288	Priest		32
CURRENT				
His blouds sweet current much more loud to be.	66	Ch.-lock		12
CURRES				
Brabling Curres never want torne eares.	322	Proverbs		52
Brawling Curres never want sore eares.	322	Proverbs	V	52
CURSE				
So sits the earths great curse in Adams fall	32	Sacrifice		165
Wert fain to take our flesh and curse, ...	103	Prayer 2		15

CURSE (cont'd)	PAGE	TITLE		LINE
Which thou dost curse.	148	Longing		9
Thy curse being laid on him, makes thee accurst.	169	Dial.-Anth		6
CURSED				
So in the Old Testament Elisha cursed the children, 2 Kings 2. 24.	285	Priest 36		26
CURSING				
have the Ministers power of Blessing only, but also of cursing.	285	Priest 36		25
both of Blessing, & cursing are expounded in the Common-Prayer-book:	286	Priest 36		3
CURST				
A curst Cow hath short hornes.	339	Proverbs		531
CURTAIN				
Night draws the curtain, which the sunne withdraws;	91	Man		32
CURTAINS				
That thou within his curtains drawn canst see:	100	Miserie		16
CURTESIE				
Curtesie on one side only lasts not long.	348	Proverbs		809
CUSTOMARY				
if there be any extraordinary addition to the customary exercises,	235	Priest 8		34
CUSTOME				
things is bad, but it is the custome and habit that names a glutton.	266	Priest 26		17
first, the custome, and knowledg of their own body, and what it can	266	Priest 26		37
either for fear or shame, break his custome, he shall do passing ill:	273	Priest 31		30
If there be any ill in the custome, that may be severed from	283	Priest 35		32
Another old Custome there is of saying, when light is brought in,	284	Priest 35		22
my Physicians nothing thereof, as is the custome of sick people.	292	Cornaro		30
that Custome was turned into Nature, and therefore it was agreeable	295	Cornaro		28
A Cake and an ill custome must be broken.	322	Proverbs		27
A caske and an ill custome must both of them be broken. . .	322	Proverbs	V	27
The command of custome is great.	341	Proverbs		590
CUSTOMERS				
the Market day comes, or a shopkeeper, when customers use to come in.	235	Priest 8		19
CUSTOMES				
The Countrey Parson is a Lover of old Customes, if they be good,	283	Priest 35		27
With customes wee live well, but Lawes undoe us.	353	Proverbs		973
CUSTOMS				
our Colledge Customs allow not that, and I shou'd account my self	373	Letters		2
CUT				
Thy pow'r doth cut.	26	The Altar		8
Cut me not off for my most foul transgression:	49	Repentance		15
Were cut and martyr'd by the fault	59	Whitsunday		19
But Grace shor'd these, and cut that as it grew.	84	The World		15
Which with the edge of wit they cut and carve.	134	Divinitie		7
Doe winde a rope about, and cut my heart:	165	The Crosse		33
Who were cut short in Alexanders stemme.	192	Ch.-Milit.		74
even as a piece of wood, which they may cut, or hack, or throw into	265	Priest 26		26
because this will cut off all causes of diseases, so that he shall	297	Cornaro		20
Many kisse the hand they wish cut off.	330	Proverbs		283
CUTS				
Cuts through the working waves, that he may fetch	85	Vanitie 1		9
The tongue is not steele, yet it cuts.	349	Proverbs		838
France is a meddow that cuts thrice a yeere.	350	Proverbs		892
CUTTING				
Since by thy cutting he grows better.	122	Time		12
cutting out the Kingdome into Portions, which every yeer he surveys	277	Priest 32		7
CUTTINGS				
Such cuttings rather heal then REND:	133	Paradise		14
CYENS				
Our cyens have purloin'd, and left you drie:	152	The Jews		2
DABO				
Better is one Accipe, then twice to say, Dabo tibi. . . .	358	Proverbs	D	1079
DAIES				
The worky-daies are the back-part;	75	Sunday		11
Reckon right, and February hath one and thirty daies. . . .	328	Proverbs		229
Sweet discourse makes short daies and nights.	345	Proverbs		727
DAIES'				
The six-daies world transposing in an houre, ...	51	Prayer 1		7
The six-daies world-transposing in an houre, ...	51	Prayer 1	V	7
DAILY (see also dayly)				
Which I do give them daily, unto death.	28	Sacrifice		70
Daily didst punish sinne, ...	43	East.wings	W	13
Quitting with daily labour all My pleasure, ...	85	Coloss.		9
My searches are my daily bread;	162	The Search		3
he may say as He did, I sate daily with you teaching in the Temple.	228	Priest 3		1
(though that indeed be very admirable) as at their daily temperance,	237	Priest 9		31
thoughts to God, nor sanctifying their labour with daily prayer;	248	Priest 14		2
what means of Piety, whether daily prayers be used, Grace, . .	251	Priest 17		22
I daily behold a kinde of immortalitie in the succession of my	303	Cornaro		1
Because such are daily exposed to a thousand dangers and deaths,	303	Cornaro		14
thousand dangers and deaths, as daily experience sheweth, and I also,	303	Cornaro		15
those many Love-poems, that are daily writ and consecrated to Venus;	363	Letters		7
passing daily our neighboring Sea, wondrously sound through all our	442	Oration		23
DAINTIE				
A daintie lodging me assign'd.	65	Ch.-mus.		4
The bird that sees a daintie bowre	101	Miserie		55
DAINTIES				
The smacks of dainties and their exaltation:	89	The Pearl	W	27
God, in whom all dainties are.	179	Invitation		6
or for quality is licorous after dainties, is a glutton; . .	266	Priest 26		8
or studying dainties too much, they cannot wel dispatch) nor of their	266	Priest 26		15
The dainties of the great are the teares of the poore. . . .	352	Proverbs		937
He that is at ease seekes dainties.	353	Proverbs		985

DALLY	PAGE	TITLE	LINE
Dally not with mony or women.	326	Proverbs	150
DALTON'S			
with Daltons Justice of Peace, and the Abridgements of the Statutes,	260	Priest 23	2
DAMASK			
the Parson useth damask or white Roses for the one, and plantaine,	261	Priest 23	34
DAME			
None is so wastefull as the scraping dame.	13	Ch.-Porch	173
DAMNATION			
Doth make thee parcell-devil in damnation.	16	Ch.-Porch	258
They drink with greedinesse a full damnation.	24	Ch.-Porch	448
Who gives to man, as he sees fit Salvation. / Damnation. . .	170	Water-crs.	10
DAMP			
O what a damp and shade	183	A Parodie	11
DANBY			
On Henry Danvers earl of Danby. EPITAPH	208	H. Danvers D	T
DANCE			
It cannot vault, or dance, or play;	70	Quidditie	5
All are not merry that dance lightly.	348	Proverbs	808
Knowledge makes one laugh, but wealth makes one dance. . . .	352	Proverbs	957
DANCES			
To make a purchase there: he sees their dances, ...	85	Vanitie 1	5
DANCETH			
Hee that lives in hope danceth without musick.	354	Proverbs	1006
DANCING			
a hatchet, a bushell, leaven, boyes piping and dancing; . .	257	Priest 21	13
DANGER			
Our flesh and frailtie, death and danger.	50	Faith	24
My nature on him, with the danger	50	Faith W	24
Her own destruction and his danger wears.	85	Vanitie 1	14
His own destruction and his danger wears.	85	Vanitie 1 V	14
he often overturnes things, when they are thought past danger;	271	Priest 30	21
regular life can hardly be altered without exceeding great danger.	295	Cornaro	18
A woman and a glasse are ever in danger.	329	Proverbs	244
He that is not in the warres is not out of danger. . . .	354	Proverbs	999
Without danger we cannot get beyond danger.	354	Proverbs	1010
Danger it selfe the best remedy for danger.	357	Proverbs D	1054
DANGEROUS			
that Sermons are dangerous things, that none goes out of Church as he	233	Priest 7	19
because diseases of exinanition are more dangerous, then diseases	267	Priest 26	14
since this is at the best but uncertain, dangerous, and very rare,	300	Cornaro	20
they are equally exempt with God, that is dangerous and too farre.	316	Valdesso	33
It's a dangerous fire begins in the bed-straw.	357	Proverbs D	1070
DANGERS			
to expose himself to so many dangers of diseases and death, . .	300	Cornaro	23
Because such are daily exposed to a thousand dangers and deaths,	303	Cornaro	14
DANTING			
Danting the stoutest hearts, the proudest wits.	141	Justice 2	12
DANVERS			
On Sir John Danvers.	208	J. Danvers D	T
What makes a Danvers	208	J. Danvers D	5
On Henry Danvers earl of Danby. EPITAPH	208	H. Danvers D	T
To Sir J. D.	363	Letters	T
To the truly Noble Sir J. D.	366	Letters	T
for I am enjoined to write to you by Sir John Danvers, to which mine	367	Letters	28
To Sir John Danvers. This Week hath loaded me with your Favours;	369	Letters	T
Herberts reasons for Arth. Woodenoths Living with Sir John Danvers.	380	Woodnoth	T
Lastlie I besech Sir John Danvers that he would be pleased to be	382	G.H.'s Will	31
To Mrs Danvers five pound, To Amy Danvers thirty shillings, . .	383	G.H.'s Will	9
To Amy Danvers thirty shillings, To Mrs Anne Danvers twenty . .	383	G.H.'s Will	9
To Mrs Anne Danvers twenty shillings, To Mrs Mary Danvers twenty	383	G.H.'s Will	10
To Mrs Mary Danvers twenty shillings, To Mrs Michel twenty shillings,	383	G.H.'s Will	11
To Mrs Elizabeth Danvers Mr Henry Danvers wife twenty shillings,	383	G.H.'s Will	12
DANVERS'			
Sir John Danvers' earthly part	208	J. Danvers D	9
To Mrs Elizabeth Danvers Mr Henry Danvers wife twenty shillings,	383	G.H.'s Will	12
DARE			
How dare those eyes upon a Bible look, ...	6	Ch.-Porch	11
Dare to be true. Nothing can need a ly:	9	Ch.-Porch	77
If they dare try, a glorious life, or grave.	10	Ch.-Porch	90
Dare to look in thy chest; for 'tis thine own:	12	Ch.-Porch	147
But shreds of holinesse, that dare not venture	38	The Sinner	6
But now (alas!) I dare not; for our King, ...	78	Ang.&Sts.	16
But now alas I dare not; for my King, ...	78	Ang.&Sts. W	16
Therefore we dare not from his garland steal, ...	78	Ang.&Sts.	24
Wherefore I dare not, I, put forth my hand	161	Priesthood	31
What covert dare eclipse thy face?	163	The Search	31
Happy are they that dare	185	The Elixer W	22
How shall we dare to appear before thy face, who are contrary	288	Priest	9
Saviour prayed with doubtfulnesse, is more then I can or dare say;	315	Valdesso	10
I dare no longer be silent, least while I think I am modest,	364	Letters	7
hath guided me hitherto, and of atchieving my (I dare say) holy ends.	364	Letters	19
I dare say she would make good her promise of taking five or six	367	Letters	2
DARES			
Catch not at quarrels. He that dares not speak	15	Ch.-Porch	217
Dares to assault thee, and besiege thy doore.	132	The Storm	12
DARING			
Look on his daring brightnes, may	203	Even-song W	7
DARK			
Lest on their double-dark souls either shine:	31	Sacrifice	139
As he that sees a dark and shadie grove, ...	43	H. Bapt.1	1

DARK (cont'd)	PAGE	TITLE		LINE
His goodnesse sets not, but in dark can runne:	72	Constancie		23
The week were dark, but for thy light:	75	Sunday		6
The week were dark, but that thy light	75	Sunday	W	6
To digge thee out of thy dark cave and grot:	77	Avarice		8
Since my dark soul and brutish is thy right,	81	Christmas		11
But man is close, reserv'd, and dark to thee:	82	Ungratef.		25
O dark instructions; ev'n as dark as day!	135	Divinitie		19
In that dark state of tears: to all, that so	169	The Answer		12
If that bee dark we can not see:	203	Even-song	W	14
And thou more dark then either.	203	Even-song	W	16
Yet Thou art not so dark, since I know this,	203	Even-song	W	17
ignorant and silly souls, even the dark and deep points of Religion.	256	Priest 21		20
As in cases of an obscure and dark nature, not easily determinable	260	Priest 23		20
whose natures, at least in the beginning, are dark and obscure:	264	Priest 26		8
not because they are all that are of this dark, and creeping	265	Priest 26		2
the person here described to be in the dark, ought to use the first,	312	Valdesso	V	25
No day so clear but hath dark clouds.	359	Proverbs	D	1123
A man's destiny is alwayes dark.	362	Proverbs	D	1180
DARKENESSE				
he is not afraid of the pestilence that walketh in darkenesse,	238	Priest 9		7
DARKER				
The sunn is darker then a Tree,	203	Even-song	W	15
DARKNED				
That which before was darkned clean	51	Faith		37
His darkned fame	93	Unkindness	W	8
and darkned by the Adversaries, and their great stumbling-block.	305	Valdesso		2
DARKNES				
Thus also sinn and darknes constantly	198	Ch.-Milit.	W	272
But thou art Light & darknes both togeather:	203	Even-song	W	13
But that my darknes may touch thine:	203	Even-song	W	18
Since Light thy Darknes is.	203	Even-song	W	20
Splendour from darknes. So close sits the crowne	212	Bohemia	D	37
DARKNESSE				
And now with darknesse closest wearie eyes,	64	Even-song		18
Defects and darknesse in my breast,	174	Aaron		7
Goshen was darknesse, Egypt full of lights,	191	Ch.-Milit.		43
Till such a darknesse do the world invade	196	Ch.-Milit.		230
Thus also Sinne and Darknesse follow still	198	Ch.-Milit.		272
Till your bright gift my darknesse did abate.	209	L. Bacon	D	8
with the unfruitfull works of darknesse, he disableth himself	227	Priest 3		26
for we are darknesse, and weaknesse, and filthinesse, and shame.	288	Priest		10
But though the streams of thy bloud were currant through darknesse,	288	Priest		33
DARLING				
All, Emblems, which thy Darling doth improve.	190	Ch.-Milit.	W	16
DART				
Lord, if thou must needs use thy dart,	56	Temper 2		3
Pluck out thy dart,	150	Longing		82
DARTS				
five shields, wherewith the Godly receive the darts of the wicked;	269	Priest 28		19
DASH				
To bear her filth; and that her sinnes did dash	173	Marie Magd		14
Whose pow'r shall dash and break them all	216	Psalm II	D	23
Follow not truth too near the heels, lest it dash out thy teeth.	360	Proverbs	D	1138
DASHING				
A sick toss'd vessel, dashing on each thing;	102	Miserie		76
DATA				
the one being gratia gratis data, the other gratia gratum faciens,	319	Valdesso		8
DATE				
And then this day, my life shall date.	42	Easter	W	30
DATES				
And dates her letters from thy face,	109	Brit. Ch.		5
DAUGHTER				
Marry your sonne when you will; your daughter when you can.	326	Proverbs		149
The sonne full and tattered, the daughter empty and fine.	328	Proverbs		214
shee had never sought her daughter there.	344	Proverbs		696
DAUGHTERS				
Marry your daughters betimes, lest they marry themselves.	361	Proverbs	D	1171
DAVID				
Though David had his Jonathan, Christ his John.	17	Ch.-Porch		276
or as David says, to be even a door-keeper in the house of God.	270	Priest 29		11
And David (though David) studied all the day long in it:	306	Valdesso		20
Therefore David desireth God in the 119 Psalme, to open his eyes that	309	Valdesso		25
yet you may say with David, That God who hath delivered me out	374	Letters		6
only for the success (as assistance of Sir John) doe as David did:	380	Woodnoth		23
David built the temple as much as Solomon because he desired it,	381	Woodnoth		19
Doe this & be a man as David, after Gods hart.	381	Woodnoth		21
DAVID'S				
Like David's tree, planted beside	213	L' Envoy	D	2
Wherefore as David's Adultery cannot be excused, so need	316	Valdesso		6
DAWN				
bidding the dispersed Hebrews attend to the word till the day dawn,	318	Valdesso		18
DAWNING				
The Dawning.	112	Dawning		T
DAY				
If those take up thy day, the sunne will crie	9	Ch.-Porch		81
If those bee all thy day, the sunne will crie	9	Ch.-Porch	W	81
As the day lessens, and his life with it.	13	Ch.-Porch		160
As all the day thou mayst hold out to go.	14	Ch.-Porch		186
That all the day thou mayst hold out to go.	14	Ch.-Porch	W	186
Twice on the day his due is understood;	22	Ch.-Porch		391

DAY (cont'd)	PAGE	TITLE		LINE
Twice on that day his due is understood;	22	Ch.-Porch	W	391
With saints on earth, shall one day with them shine.	24	Ch.-Porch		438
Summe up at night, what thou hast done by day;	24	Ch.-Porch		451
Summe up at night, what thou hast done that day;	24	Ch.-Porch	W	451
Had to this day been an Egyptian slave.	27	Sacrifice		10
It is not fit he live a day, they crie,	29	Sacrifice		98
With noises confused frighting the day:	29	Sacrifice		103
Is best to celebrate this most high day.	41	Easter		12
But thou wast up by break of day,	42	Easter		21
Can there be any day but this,	42	Easter		27
Teach it to sing thy praise, this day,	42	Easter	W	29
And then this day, my life shall date.	42	Easter	W	30
And sing this day thy victories:	43	East.wings		9
And sing this day thy sacrifice,	43	East.wings	W	9
And feel this day thy victorie:	43	East.wings		18
Each day doth round about us see.	48	Repentance		8
I and this day,	49	Repentance		23
And ev'ry day a new Creatour art.	56	Temper 2		8
Restore this day, for thy great name,	60	Whitsunday		27
O raise me then! poore bees, that work all day,	61	Praise 1		17
Spin all the day:	61	Praise 1	W	18
Kill me not ev'ry day,	62	Afflict.2		1
Then we must needs for that day make a match.	62	Mattens		4
Who gave me eyes, and light, and power this day,	63	Even-song		2
Thou dost inclose us, till the day	64	Even-song		22
The day or night: that is the gale, this th' harbour;	64	Even-song		26
Nor can it entertain the day	70	Quidditie		7
At the next Session-day.	71	Humilitie		32
Misuse them all the day:	71	Frailtie	W	6
At close tentations: when the day is done,	72	Constancie		22
O day most calm, most bright,	75	Sunday		1
O day so calm, so bright:	75	Sunday	W	1
This day my Saviour rose,	76	Sunday		36
And did unhinge that day.	76	Sunday		49
The brightnesse of that day	76	Sunday		50
Thou art a day of mirth:	76	Sunday		57
Both knees and heart, in crying night and day,	80	Deniall		13
Both hart & knees, in crying night and day,	80	Deniall	W	13
And then not heare it crying! all day long	80	Deniall		18
Christmas-Day.	80	Christmas	W	T
All after pleasures as I rid one day,	80	Christmas		1
All after pleasures riding on a Day.	80	Christmas	W	1
Out-sing the day-light houres.	81	Christmas		22
Then we will sing, and shine all our own day,	81	Christmas		31
It's true, we cannot reach Christs forti'th day;	87	Lent		31
Sweet day, so cool, so calm, so bright,	87	Vertue		1
And day by day	90	Afflict.4		27
My God, I heard this day,	90	Man		1
I made a posie, while the day ran by:	94	Life		1
Making my minde to smell my fatall day;	94	Life		11
Maketh two nights to ev'ry day.	96	Charms & K		8
Doubles the night, & trips by day.	96	Charms & K	W	8
My God, I read this day,	97	Afflict.5		1
All day exchanging mirth and breath	98	Mortific.		15
Harmonious peace must rock them all the day:	105	Conscience		9
My spirit gaspeth night and day.	107	Home		4
With one small sigh thou gav'st me th' other day	108	Home		43
The last and lov'd, though dreadfull day.	108	Home		58
The merrie world did on a day	110	The Quip		1
Foolish soul who sinn'd to day?	113	Businesse		2
And make a twist checker'd with night and day!	118	Providence		58
I challenge here the brightest day,	126	Confession		28
Now all day spares.	127	Giddinesse		12
To him I brought a dish of fruit one day,	129	Love unkn.		6
Each day, each houre, each moment of the week,	131	Love unkn.		69
O dark instructions; ev'n as dark as day!	135	Divinitie		19
All day complain.	136	Ephes.		21
Perhaps thou com'st sometimes, and for a day;	137	Familie		23
My tears and prayers night and day do wooe,	139	Artillerie		19
To day.	150	Longing		78
Resolv'd to light; and so one day	151	The Bag		11
My heart was meaning all the day,	168	a true Hymn		2
I shall be one day better then before:	169	Dial.-Anth		9
Thus we prevent the last great day,	171	Self-cond.		19
And got the day.	172	The Glance		16
Runnes over day and night.	173	23 Psalme		20
With these all day I do perfume my minde,	175	The Odour		6
As at dooms-day;	186	Death		18
Dooms-day.	186	Dooms-day		T
Make this the day.	186	Dooms-day		8
To make good that which ev'ry day he winnes.	193	Ch.-Milit.		126
As Rome will one day finde unto her cost.	194	Ch.-Milit.		160
The Day is spent, & hath his will on mee:	203	Even-song	W	1
That I who cannot now by day	203	Even-song	W	6
Than that, which one day Worms may chance refuse?	206	walton 1		14
His meditation day and night:	214	Psalm I	D	7
this day have I begotten thee:	216	Psalm II	D	18
which in the day of wrath hath not one dramme of comfort for us.	227	Priest 3		20
so as a Market-man is, when the Market day comes, or a shopkeeper,	235	Priest 8		18
His thoughts are full of making the best of the day, and contriving	235	Priest 8		20

DAY (cont'd)	PAGE	TITLE		LINE
he makes a peculiar one for a blessing on the exercises of the day,	235	Priest 8		22
he sets himself to the Consideration of the duties of the day,	235	Priest 8		33
The rest of the day he spends either in reconciling neighbours that	236	Priest 8		10
both sutable to the joy of the day, and without hinderance to publick	236	Priest 8		19
As he opened the day with prayer, so he closeth it, humbly beseeching	236	Priest 8		26
night and day against the proper and peculiar temptations of his	238	Priest 9		1
nor of the sicknesse that destroyeth at noone day, [Ghostly pride	238	Priest 9		8
wife is either religious, or night and day he is winning her to it.	239	Priest 10		10
and veal, if he addes any thing for a great day, or a stranger,	241	Priest 10		17
as Sunday is his day of joy, so Friday his day of Humiliation,	241	Priest 10		36
so Friday his day of Humiliation, which he celebrates not only	241	Priest 10		37
first, of eating lesse that day, then on other dayes;	242	Priest 10		3
and not the fish, is to keep the fasting day naturally.	242	Priest 10		15
he bethinketh himselfe what good deeds he can do that day,	244	Priest 12		17
counting that day lost, wherein he hath not exercised his Charity.	244	Priest 12		17
not suffering any that day that hee receives, to want a good meal	245	Priest 12		8
which they put on as their holy-day cloathes, and come to Church in	247	Priest 14		9
and come to Church in frame, but commonly the next day put off both.	247	Priest 14		10
when on the Lords day they do unnecessary servile work,	248	Priest 14		2
touching the last day, so neither touching the intermediate days	250	Priest 16		21
or at some other time of the day, propounds among his Brethren what	253	Priest 19		13
or holy-day, and exposing to them the uncertainty of humane affairs,	253	Priest 19		31
all together choosing some fitt day to carry it themselves,	253	Priest 19		38
God dishonoured every day, and man afflicted.	267	Priest 27		32
that all Christians should pray twice a day, every day of the week,	272	Priest 31		22
pray twice a day, every day of the week, and four times on Sunday,	272	Priest 31		22
that the godly petitioner upon some emergent interruption in the day,	272	Priest 31		30
he hath shew'd the unlawfulness of spending the day in dressing,	277	Priest 32		29
they are Circumcised to this day, and expect the promises	282	Priest 34		1
wher-ever spoken this day throughout the universall Church.	289	Priest		15
by any of these inconveniences, except it were for one onely day.	294	Cornaro		10
and especially since the power of my stomack every day decreased.	295	Cornaro		33
On the twelfth day, a pain of the side took me, which held me two	296	Cornaro		17
although after the fifteenth day it grew lesse and lesse.	296	Cornaro		21
save now and then a little indisposition for a day or two.	296	Cornaro		31
And David (though David) studied all the day long in it:	306	Valdesso		20
And Joshua was to meditate therein Day and Night.	306	Valdesso		21
building it all upon the word untill the day starre arise,	318	Valdesso		8
bidding the dispersed Hebrews attend to the word till the day dawn,	318	Valdesso		18
Every day brings his bread with it.	321	Proverbs		5
Not a long day, but a good heart rids worke.	321	Proverbs		24
The longest Day hath an Eveninge.	322	Proverbs	V	51
Every ill man hath his ill day.	324	Proverbs		92
Praise day at night, and life at the end.	324	Proverbs		97
To a fair day open the window, but make you ready as to a foule.	325	Proverbs		119
I wept when I was borne, and every day shewes why.	327	Proverbs		199
A blustering night, a faire day.	331	Proverbs		307
Though you rise early, yet the day comes	332	Proverbs		333
The morning Sunne never lasts a day.	334	Proverbs		375
Hee that knowes what may bee gained in a day never steales.	336	Proverbs		445
He that contemplates hath a day without night.	341	Proverbs		601
The evening praises the day, and the morning a host.	342	Proverbs		635
The evening praises the day, and the morning a frost.	342	Proverbs	V	635
He that passeth a winters day escapes an enemy.	349	Proverbs		864
One faire day in winter makes not birds merrie.	353	Proverbs		977
Who will make a doore of gold must knock a naile every day.	354	Proverbs		1004
Between the businesse of life and the day of death,	356	Proverbs	D	40
What one day gives us, another takes away from us.	359	Proverbs	D	1111
No day so clear but hath dark clouds.	359	Proverbs	D	1123
We must love, as looking one day to hate.	359	Proverbs	D	1126
A fair day in winter is the mother of a storme.	360	Proverbs	D	1145
but that every day, I may step one step towards my journies end;	364	Letters		27
also I ride to Newmarket, and there lie a day or two for fresh Air;	365	Letters		7
Volumes of Divinity, which yet every day swell, and grow bigger.	365	Letters		14
Buckingham was observed on Christmas day to bee so devout as to come	368	Letters		17
yet have I sent it thither by a faithful Messenger this day:	369	Letters		17
DAY-LIGHT				
Out-sing the day-light houres.	81	Christmas		22
DAYE'S				
Which this dayes favour did beget?	64	Even-song		11
For whereas before the measure of my whole dayes meat, viz.	296	Cornaro		9
DAYES				
In three dayes raz'd, and raised as before.	28	Sacrifice		66
My dayes were straw'd with flow'rs and happinesse;	47	Afflict.1		21
My dayes were strowd with flow'rs and happinesse;	47	Afflict.1	W	21
The other dayes and thou	75	Sunday		8
The other dayes fill up the spare	75	Sunday		24
And where the week-dayes trail on ground,	76	Sunday		58
Sweet spring, full of sweet dayes and roses,	88	Vertue		9
Sweet were the dayes, when thou didst lodge with Lot,	99	Decay		1
And length of dayes lengthen the rod.	123	Time		22
As if thy blessings had spare dayes:	124	Gratefulnes		30
Poets have wrong'd poore storms: such dayes are best;	132	The Storm		17
Sev'n whole dayes, not one in seven,	146	Praise 2		17
My busie heart shall spin it all my dayes:	157	Praise 3		3
And all my sowre-sweet dayes	171	Bittersweet		7
Shall measure all my dayes;	173	23 Psalme		22
he spends his dayes in fasting and prayer, and blesseth God	237	Priest 9		18
it not enough for him to observe the fasting dayes of the Church,	237	Priest 9		22
and devotion, some other dayes for fasting, and hours for prayers;	237	Priest 9		25

DAYES (cont'd)	PAGE	TITLE		LINE
The Parson in his house observes fasting dayes;	241	Priest 10		36
Now fasting dayes containe a treble obligation;	242	Priest 10		2
first, of eating lesse that day, then on other dayes;	242	Priest 10		3
and fasting dayes were fully performed by keeping of the two former,	242	Priest 10		8
and offering to have them taught on holy-dayes by his servants.	248	Priest 14		37
and Baptizeth not willingly, but on Sundayes, or great dayes.	258	Priest 22		3
or Sundayes before the Communion, or on the Eves of all those dayes.	258	Priest 22		29
their parents and kindred snatcht away in the midst of their dayes,	291	Cornaro		10
I found within a few dayes, that I was exceedingly helped,	292	Cornaro		35
what case I was, they concluded that I would die within three dayes.	295	Cornaro		3
This addition after ten dayes wrought so much upon me, that	296	Cornaro		14
came a terrible fever, which continued thirtie five dayes and nights;	296	Cornaro		20
was but a little excesse, in a few dayes had so soon overthrown me.	297	Cornaro		6
orderly life is the most sure way & ground of health and long dayes,	297	Cornaro		13
and that at length they shut up their dayes like a Lamp,	298	Cornaro		17
That God in the dayes of the Gospell will not give an outward Law	310	Valdesso		4
DAYES'				
The brags of life are but a nine dayes wonder;	69	Content		21
DAYLY				
Thou dying dayly, praise thee to thy losse.	73	Afflict.3		18
Except thou make us dayly, we shall spurn	127	Giddinesse		27
While his conquests dayly spread;	199	L'Envoy		8
and the dayly prayers enjoyned him by auctority, which he observeth	237	Priest 9		22
and the dayly importunitie of my friends, to adde something to my	295	Cornaro		20
DAYS				
or in time of divine service on other holy days, except in the cases	248	Priest 14		4
catechizing, singing of Psalms at their work, and on holy days;	248	Priest 14		34
so neither touching the intermediate days of Conversion.	250	Priest 16		22
other good books, how Sundayes, holy-days, and fasting days are kept.	251	Priest 17		24
Misery and sin fill our days:	288	Priest		11
DAZELETH				
since there is a two-fold brightnesse which dazeleth the eyes of men,	442	Oration		33
DAZLE				
which are two great lights able to dazle the eyes of the mis-led,	263	Priest 24		19
DEAD				
Against their Maker: they do wish me dead,	26	Sacrifice		6
Onely let others say, when I am dead,	34	Sacrifice		251
Who dead men raises.	49	Repentance		35
My stock lies dead, and no increase	60	Grace		1
Makes them not dead:	98	Mortific.		10
Dead with eclipses, when we speak of thee:	101	Miserie		34
This was not quick enough, and that was dead.	102	Jordan 2		10
Tombes for the dead, not temples fit for thee:	107	Sion		20
He may attain to, after he is dead.	131	Mans medly		24
I passe away and leave it dead?	135	Ephes.		6
More dead to me!	149	Longing		34
But now both sinne is dead,	150	Longing		67
I am to grief alive, to them as dead.	165	The Crosse		24
Dead to the world, keep house unknown.	166	The Flower		14
Harmonious bells below, raising the dead	174	Aaron		3
A noise of passions ringing me for dead	174	Aaron		8
Another musick, making live not dead,	174	Aaron		13
My onely musick, striking me ev'n dead;	174	Aaron		18
My doctrine tun'd by Christ, (who is not dead,	174	Aaron		23
That thy death is also dead,	199	L'Envoy		7
That allso made thee dead.	201	H. Commun.	W	30
Theire dead, and Time shal be no more:	208	H. Danvers	D	4
or from God by a child born, or dead, or any other accident,	236	Priest 8		1
whereupon all gave me for dead.	296	Cornaro		23
That the life which I live at this age, is not a dead, dumpish,	303	Cornaro		10
He that hath lost his credit is dead to the world.	333	Proverbs		357
Giving is dead, restoring very sicke.	340	Proverbs		573
Speake not of a dead man at the table.	343	Proverbs		672
The Mr. absent, and the house dead.	352	Proverbs		940
Saint Luke was a Saint and a Physitian, yet is dead.	354	Proverbs		1008
A dead Bee maketh no Hony.	358	Proverbs	D	1098
for he asks counsell of the Dead (i.e. books).	361	Proverbs	D	1158
DEADING				
and the stupifying and deading of all the clamorous powers	227	Priest 3		6
DEADLY				
O what a deadly cold	184	A Parodie		26
DEAFE				
Who is so deafe, as he that will not heare?	323	Proverbs		79
Who is so deafe, as he who will not heare?	323	Proverbs	V	79
The deafe gaines the injury.	351	Proverbs		927
DEAL				
To deal in holy Writ.	160	Priesthood		12
in all things wherein they deal, may be more lively and vigorous.	299	Cornaro		20
DEALE				
To deale with brimstone, that untamed stench	212	Bohemia	D	53
The tooth-ach is more ease then to deale with ill people.	340	Proverbs		558
DEALES				
He that deales in the world needes foure seeves.	351	Proverbs		899
DEALING				
There is no dealing with thy mighty passion:	36	Reprisall		2
There is no dealing with thee in that Art:	201	love	W	2
it being the Life of buying, and selling, and dealing in the world;	228	Priest 3		3
DEALS				
God then deals blessings: If a king did so,	22	Ch.-Porch		389
When he deals with any that is heavy, and carnall;	267	Priest 26		17

	PAGE	TITLE		LINE
DEALT				
Who hath dealt his mercies so, ...	92	Antiphon 2		4
DEAR (see also deere)				
When my dear Friend, could write no more, ...	439	Walton 6		1
Grant this dear Father, for thy Son's sake, our only Saviour:	290	Priest		13
my meaning (dear Mother) is in these Sonnets, to declare my . .	363	Letters		10
To my dear brother, Mr. Henry Herbert, at Paris.	366	Letters		26
I have wrote to my dear sick Sister this week already, and therefore	367	Letters		21
you and my dear Mother and Sister to pardon me, for my Cambridge	369	Letters		17
and now the only thing I long for, is to hear of my dear sick Sister;	371	Letters		7
For my dear sick Sister.	371	Letters		T
dear Mother, I alwaies fear'd sickness more then death, . .	373	Letters		7
of the Body, dear Madam, remember the holy Martyrs of God, . .	373	Letters		35
Dear Madam, pardon my boldness, and, accept the good meaning of,	374	Letters		30
To my very dear brother Sir Henry Herbert, at Court. . . .	376	Letters		24
Blessed be My God & Dear Master, the Spring & Fountain of all	379	Letters		16
DEARE				
Have got to be a deare fool for an houre.	16	Ch.-Porch		246
Therefore my soul melts, and my hearts deare treasure	27	Sacrifice		21
Mine owne deare people, cry, away, away, ...	29	Sacrifice		102
Weep not, deare friends, since I for both have wept	31	Sacrifice		149
O my deare Saviour, Victorie!	36	Thanksgvng		48
Is in my deare Redeemers pierced side.	44	H. Bapt.1		6
Ah my deare God! though I am clean forgot, ...	48	Afflict.1		65
Ah my deare King! though I am clean forgot, ...	48	Afflict.1	W	65
Deare flesh, while I do pray, learn here thy stemme	65	Ch.-monum.		17
Deare earth, fine grasse or hay;	71	Frailtie		6
There when I came, whom found I but my deare, ...	81	Christmas		5
But his deare God? who yet his glorious law	85	Vanitie 1		23
Welcome deare feast of Lent: who loves not thee, ...	86	Lent		1
Farewell deare flowers, sweetly your time ye spent, ...	94	Life		13
I and deare prayer would together dwell, ...	103	Prayer 2		23
The bloudie crosse of my deare Lord	106	Conscience		23
Is not so deare to thee as one good grone.	106	Sion		18
He did, he came: O my Redeemer deare, ...	108	Home		25
I joy, deare Mother, when I view	109	Brit. Ch.		1
Deare Friend, sit down, the tale is long and sad:	129	Love unkn.		1
I would say thorns. Deare, could my heart not break, ...	130	Love unkn.		52
Where Pagans tread. O Mother deare and kinde, ...	140	Ch.-rents		24
Of my deare God with all my power & might.	143	Holdfast		2
And by that crie of her deare Lord obtain, ...	152	The Jews		11
Much wrastling, many a combate, this deare end, ...	164	The Crosse		8
Ah my deare Father, ease my smart!	165	The Crosse		31
For he hath sold for money his deare Lord, ...	171	Self-cond.		17
Ah my deare angrie Lord, ...	171	Bittersweet		1
Deare soul, she knew who did vouchsafe and deigne	173	Marie Magd		13
Perfect and light in my deare breast, ...	174	Aaron		22
Welcome deare;	181	Banquet		2
I the unkinde, ungratefull? Ah my deare, ...	189	Love 3		9
My deare, then I will serve.	189	Love 3		16
How deare to me, O God, thy counsels are!	191	Ch.-Milit.		47
How deare to me, O God, thy counsels are!	192	Ch.-Milit.		99
How deare to me, O God, thy counsels are!	194	Ch.-Milit.		155
How deare to me, O God, thy counsels are!	196	Ch.-Milit.		209
How deare to me, O God, thy counsels are!	198	Ch.-Milit.		278
My deare and deserving Brother, your Valdesso I now returne with many	304	Valdesso		1
he every where beares towards our deare [great] Master and Lord,	305	Valdesso		4
To buy deare is not bounty.	326	Proverbs		156
Good cheape is deare.	329	Proverbs		261
Anothers bread costs deare.	332	Proverbs		324
A pleasure long expected is deare enough sold.	350	Proverbs		868
Hee payes too deare for honey that licks it from thorns. . .	350	Proverbs	V	880
properly belonge to me unto my deare wife excepting onely these	382	G.H.'s Will		6
fell to me by the death of my deare Neece Mrs Dorothy Vaughan whereof	382	G.H.'s Will		9
of this parish to be devided according to my deare wives discretion.	382	G.H.'s Will		17
your Excellencies to bee more deare unto us, in that you are	442	Oration		20
DEARELY				
The cheapest sinnes most dearely punisht are;	9	Ch.-Porch		67
His dearely-earned pearl, which God did hide	85	Vanitie 1		10
how much more dearely should a Physician be esteemed, who not onely	298	Cornaro		8
Weigh justly and sell dearely.	338	Proverbs		500
Weight justly and sell dearely.	338	Proverbs	V	500
DEARELY-EARNED				
His dearely-earned pearl, which God did hide	85	Vanitie 1		10
DEARER				
for it sets a dearer price on every thing.	361	Proverbs	D	1178
DEAREST				
My dearest Lord, expecting till the grief	81	Christmas		6
Come dearest Lord, passe not this holy season, ...	109	Home		73
But dearest Mother, (what those misse), ...	110	Brit. Ch.		25
DEARLY				
About some land, which he had dearly bought	40	Redemption		7
DEARTH				
For sinn would faine remove the dearth	59	Whitsunday	W	19
Nothing but drought and dearth, but bush and brake, ...	108	Home		49
Drought never brought dearth.	346	Proverbs		749
It's a wicked thing to make a dearth ones garner.	351	Proverbs		898
DEARTHS				
at hard times, and dearths, he even parts his Living, and life among	245	Priest 12		9
Dearths foreseene come not.	335	Proverbs		407

DEATH	PAGE	TITLE		LINE
As swords cause death, so may a little sting.	20	Ch.-Porch	W	352
For thirtie pence he did my death devise,	27	Sacrifice		17
Which I do give them daily, unto death.	28	Sacrifice		70
And now I am deliver'd unto death,	31	Sacrifice		145
Alas! what have I stollen from you? Death.	34	Sacrifice		231
A servile death in servile companie:	34	Sacrifice		235
Nay, after death their spite shall further go;	34	Sacrifice		245
Nay, after death their spite shall farther go;	34	Sacrifice	W	245
For by thy death I die for thee.	36	Reprisall		8
Shall all thy death?	38	Good Fri.		8
That, as his death calcined thee to dust,	41	Easter		5
Fretting to death our other parts.	49	Repentance	W	30
Our flesh and frailtie, death and danger.	50	Faith		24
Working against the states of death and hell.	58	H.Script.1		12
Death is still working like a mole,	60	Grace		13
Thou Lord of life; since thy one death for me	62	Afflict.2		2
Yet as in sleep we see foul death, and live:	63	Sinne 2		9
Sometimes Death, puffing at the doore,	67	Ch.-floore		16
And after death the fumes that spring	69	Content		22
To endlesse death: but thou dost pull	75	Sunday		16
This fully tc us, till death blow	82	Ungratef.		16
This to us fully, till death blow	82	Ungratef.	W	16
Ev'n unto death: since he di'd for my good,	83	Sighs & Gr.		23
For thou hast life and death at thy command;	83	Sighs & Gr.		26
Then Sinne combin'd with Death in a firm band	84	The World		16
To finde out death, but missest life at hand.	86	Vanitie 1		28
And after death for cures.	94	Life		15
Which do consigne and send them unto death.	98	Mortific.		6
Convey them quickly, who are bound for death.	98	Mortific.		12
Which shall befriend him at the house of death.	98	Mortific.		18
Which shall befriend him at the houre of death.	98	Mortific.	W	18
Unto the coffin, that attends his death.	98	Mortific.		24
Which shall convey him to the house of death.	98	Mortific.		30
Which shall convey him to the place of death.	98	Mortific.	W	30
That all these dyings may be life in death.	99	Mortific.		36
Besides, thy death and bloud	104	Obedience		26
And feel his death, but not his victorie.	112	Dawning		8
'Twixt his sinnes and Saviours death?	114	Businesse		30
Brings thy Saviours death no gain?	114	Businesse		36
Thy bloudy death and undeserv'd, makes thee	115	Dulnesse		11
But after death out of his grave	125	Peace		27
For death is drie as dust. Yet if ye part,	135	Ephes.		10
After so foul a journey death is fair,	142	Pilgrimage		35
For death each houre environs and surrounds.	145	Discharge		36
And such a Life, as killeth death.	156	The Call		4
Since thou in death wast none of thine,	157	Clasping		17
Alas, poore Death, where is thy glorie?	169	Dial.-Anth		1
Poore death! and who was hurt thereby?	169	Dial.-Anth		5
Ev'n in death,	180	Invitation		29
After death can never die.	180	Invitation		30
Hearken under pain of death,	182	Banquet		52
Death.	185	Death		T
Death, thou wast once an uncouth hideous thing,	185	Death		1
But since our Saviours death did put some bloud	186	Death		13
That thy death is also dead,	199	L'Envoy		7
Hell, Death & Divel come short of mee.	202	love	W	24
Love neere his death desir'd to end	439	Walton 5	V	11
For who in death remember Thee?	220	Psalm VI	D	11
The fatal instruments of death	222	Psalm VII	D	45
that when death takes him, as the Jewes and Judas did Christ,	227	Priest 3		32
against all temptations, even to death it selfe, he plainly,	250	Priest 15		4
so that then where sin abounded, not death, but grace superabounded;	288	Priest		25
there would be no help for me, but Death, shortly to be expected.	292	Cornaro		15
and therefore out of an hope of avoiding death and pain,	292	Cornaro		21
to expose himself to so many dangers of diseases and death,	300	Cornaro		23
yeares old, all the time we live after, is rather death then life.	300	Cornaro		30
and, though subject to death, yet continually afraid of it:	303	Cornaro		17
For death to all young men is a terrible thing, as also to those that	303	Cornaro		18
by the regularitie of my life I have shut out death all other wayes.	303	Cornaro		28
And that is a fair and desirable death, which Nature brings by way	303	Cornaro		28
but he might have been justly put to death for it by the Magistrate,	316	Valdesso		25
Hee puls with a long rope, that waits for anothers death.	322	Proverbs		25
Hee puls with a long rope, who looks for anothers death.	322	Proverbs	V	25
In life you lov'd me not, in death you bewaile me.	328	Proverbs		218
Peace, and Patience, and death with repentance.	332	Proverbs		319
Thou hast death in thy house, and dost bewaile anothers.	334	Proverbs		376
Life without a friend is death without a witnesse.	334	Proverbs		385
A faire death honours the whole life.	339	Proverbs		522
Old men, when they scorne young, make much of death.	341	Proverbs		597
When age is jocond it makes sport for death.	342	Proverbs		637
He that feares death lives not.	347	Proverbs		781
Hee hath not liv'd, that lives not after death.	350	Proverbs		873
Death keepes no Calender.	351	Proverbs		908
Old men go to Death, Death comes to Young men.	356	Proverbs	D	1
Between the businesse of life and the day of death,	356	Proverbs	D	40
After Death the Doctor.	356	Proverbs	D	1037
The death of wolves is the safety of the sheep.	358	Proverbs	D	1086
The death of a young wolfe doth never come too soon.	360	Proverbs	D	1131
I alwaies fear'd sickness more then death, because sickness hath made	373	Letters		8
London which fell to me by the death of my deare Neece Mrs Dorothy	382	G.H.'s Will		9

	PAGE	TITLE		LINE
DECEITFULL				
of themselves in time of eating, which because it is deceitfull;	267	Priest 26		3
DECEITS				
Or if such deceits there be,	177	The Rose		9
DECEIVE				
Even there, where they deceive?	201	H. Commun.	W	36
Deceive not thy Physitian, Confessor, nor Lawyer.	324	Proverbs		105
Hee that will deceive the fox, must rise betimes.	333	Proverbs		351
Hee that would deceive the fox, must rise betimes.	333	Proverbs	V	351
To deceive ones selfe is very easie.	342	Proverbs		632
I have not deceived their expectation, let not them deceive mine:	364	Letters		24
DECEIV'D				
I was deceiv'd:	142	Pilgrimage		30
And coin large hopes; but, that I was deceiv'd:	155	Assurance		10
DECEIVED				
I have not deceived their expectation, let not them deceive mine:	364	Letters		24
DECEIVES				
He that once deceives is ever suspected.	335	Proverbs		417
Who so once deceives is ever suspected.	335	Proverbs	V	417
DECENT				
that all things there be decent, and befitting his Name by which it	246	Priest 13		2
kept sweet and clean, in a strong and decent chest, with a Chalice,	246	Priest 13		19
so vertuous, so decent, and so holy, it is worthy by all means to be	300	Cornaro		4
DECENTLY				
The first whereof is, Let all things be done decently, and in order:	246	Priest 13		27
DECIDES				
he never decides it alone, but sends for three or four of the ablest	260	Priest 23		8
DECK				
Furnish & deck my soul, that thou mayst have	81	Christmas		13
DECKING				
Decking the sense, as if it were to sell.	102	Jordan 2		6
DECLARATION				
a plain and evident declaration of the meaning of the text;	235	Priest 7		2
DECLARE				
I will declare the Lords decree,	215	Psalm II	D	15
I will declare the causes which moved me to forsake Intemperance,	291	Cornaro		15
to declare my resolution to be, that my poor Abilities in Poetry,	363	Letters		10
DECLINE				
Why should I justice now decline?	141	Justice 2		23
Thy anger comes, and I decline:	166	The Flower		31
That to decline,	188	Judgement		12
so that they neither decline to the right hand, nor to the left.	230	Priest 5		22
DECREASE				
Nay, it shall ev'ry yeare decrease and fade;	196	Ch.-Milit.		229
DECREASED				
and especially since the power of my stomack every day decreased.	295	Cornaro		33
DECREASING				
and strength decreasing, my stint of meat and drink should be	295	Cornaro		30
DECREE				
I threatned to observe the strict decree	143	Holdfast		1
I threatned to observe the sweet decree	143	Holdfast	V	1
And wrap their policies in thy decree,	190	Ch.-Milit.		6
I will declare the Lords decree,	215	Psalm II	D	15
DECREED				
The decreed burden of each mortall Saint:	33	Sacrifice		199
and hath so decreed in his heart, that he will keep himself a virgin,	237	Priest 9		17
DECREES				
To shew their face, since crosse to thy decrees:	38	The Sinner		7
Not the decrees of power, but bands of love.	190	Ch.-Milit.		10
DECRETALS				
which depend almost wholly on their Canon law and Decretals,	319	Valdesso	V	29
DEDICATION				
The Temple. Sacred Poems and Private Ejaculations. Dedication.	5	Dedication		T
DEED				
And goodnesse of the deed.	86	Lent		27
And here present it as my speciall deed.	104	Obedience		10
Where in the deed there was an intimation	105	Obedience		33
And heart unto this deed, when he hath read;	105	Obedience		38
And heart unto this deed, when he doth read	105	Obedience	W	38
A single deed is small renown.	128	Bunch Gr.		12
The deed and storie	143	Complaining		7
Love will do the deed:	179	Discipline		18
Marketh that deed for thine:	184	The Elixer	W	12
resolves with himself never to omit any present good deed of charity,	240	Priest 10		6
surely it were a great good deed, and I would have her conveyed	375	Letters		31
DEEDE				
An ill deede cannot bring honour.	348	Proverbs		806
The best of the sport is to doe the deede, and say nothing.	348	Proverbs		812
The Italians are wise before the deede,	352	Proverbs		947
the Germanes in the deede, the French after the deede.	352	Proverbs		947
DEEDES				
and syncere Religion, such as are Prayer, Fasting, Almes-deedes, &c.	312	Valdesso		21
Fine words dresse ill deedes.	337	Proverbs		479
Words are women, deedes are men.	349	Proverbs		843
DEEDS				
By great deeds shew, that thou canst little do;	15	Ch.-Porch		220
I, who am Truth, turn into truth their deeds:	32	Sacrifice		179
When all thy deeds, whose brunt thou feel'st alone,	69	Content		29
Brave language, braver deeds:	71	Frailtie		14
Of thoughts, and words, and deeds.	81	Christmas		18
Yet ill deeds loyter not: for they supplie	122	Sinnes rd.		16

DEEDS (cont'd)	PAGE	TITLE		LINE
Who brought his doctrins & his deeds from Rome	195	Ch.-Milit.	W	201
The pattern, but not so in vertuous deeds;	196	Ch.-Milit.		222
Good deeds, and good breeding, are his two great stocks for his	240	Priest 10		10
he bethinketh himselfe what good deeds he can do that day,	244	Priest 12		16
may have wherewithall to serve God the better, and to do good deeds.	248	Priest 14		8
paymaster, rewarding all good deeds to their full proportion.	254	Priest 20		21
But though the Parson sets forward all Charitable deeds,	262	Priest 23		12
DEEM				
As the old heathen would deem prodigies.	194	Ch.-Milit.		154
DEEP				
Deep drawn in pain,	162	The Search		18
Or, since thy wayes are deep, and still the same,	206	Walton 1		10
where the well is deep, and we have nothing of our selves to draw	228	Priest 4		35
that the auditors may plainly perceive that every word is hart-deep.	233	Priest 7		32
that they dive not too deep into worldly affairs, plunging themselves	247	Priest 14		24
ignorant and silly souls, even the dark and deep points of Religion.	256	Priest 21		20
and hath taken so deep roote, that it seems the very life	287	Priest 37		9
they were possessed with a deep Melancholie (a thing usuall	294	Cornaro		18
DEEPE				
A great ship askes deepe waters.	336	Proverbs		449
DEEPER				
Deeper then they, in words, and works, and thoughts.	173	Marie Magd		12
seasoned with pleasantnesse, both enter sooner, and roote deeper.	268	Priest 27		5
DEEPLY				
Is deeply carved there: but th' other week	112	JESU		2
DEERE				
A kinde of thing that's for it self too deere.	13	Ch.-Porch		178
If yet thou love game at so deere a rate,	14	Ch.-Porch		199
But if thou want it, buy it not too deere.	16	Ch.-Porch		244
Leave not thine owne deere-cuntry-cleanlines	21	Ch.-Porch	W	367
The Warrier his deere skarres no more resounds,	191	Ch.-Milit.		63
To my deere brother, Sir Henry Herbert, at Court.	377	Letters		31
DEERE-CUNTRY-CLEANLINES				
Leave not thine owne deere-cuntry-cleanlines	21	Ch.-Porch	W	367
DEERELY				
Learn this, that hath old gamesters deerely cost:	14	Ch.-Porch		200
Learn this, it hath old gamesters deerely cost:	14	Ch.-Porch	W	200
DEFACE				
Wine above all things doth Gods stamp deface.	8	Ch.-Porch		48
Sinn onely, which did all deface	200	H. Commun.	W	23
DEFAMED				
whom the Law would have defamed, except he also do it out of rancour.	287	Priest 37		29
executioners, and the Law gives a malefactour to all to be defamed.	287	Priest 37		31
DEFAMES				
so neither is he that defames him, whom the Law would have defamed,	287	Priest 37		28
DEFAMING				
therfore one anothers company, much lesse defaming one another.	260	Priest 23		28
DEFEAT				
Whom others faults do not defeat;	73	Constancie		29
it were in another's power to defeat my charity, and evill shold be	376	Letters		9
DEFECT				
as he finds any defect in these, hee first considers with himselfe,	251	Priest 17		25
DEFECTIVE				
Yet doubtlesse the best faith in us is defective, and arrives	319	Valdesso		10
DEFECTS				
And make up our defects with his sweet art.	42	Easter		18
Defects and darknesse in my breast,	174	Aaron		7
having observed some defects in the Ministry, he then either in	253	Priest 19		12
and overweigh the defects (as I conceive) towards the publishing	305	Valdesso		13
DEFEND				
so must they fight for, and defend them, when occasion calls.	277	Priest 32		20
that Proverb, wherewith Gluttons use to defend themselves, to wit,	293	Cornaro		8
But all these things could not defend me against their importunities.	296	Cornaro		5
But it is one thing not to judge, another to defend them.	316	Valdesso		14
DEFER				
Cruelty is more cruell, if we defer the pain.	359	Proverbs	D	1110
DEFERR				
If thou deferr this light, then shadow mee:	203	Even-song	W	9
which while they deferr, both sides suffer;	259	Priest 22		4
& therfore deferr it untill they heare farther from the States.	368	Letters		15
DEFERRE				
Deferre not the least vertue: lifes poore span	24	Ch.-Porch		459
Deferre no time;	80	Deniall		27
Wilt thou deferre	149	Longing		39
DEFERRED				
Children and youths are usually deferred too long, under pretence	258	Priest 22		37
which she hath hitherto deferred to do, not of her self,	367	Letters		3
DEFERRINGS				
Thy long deferrings wound me to the quick,	107	Home		3
DEFIE				
He makes flat warre with God, and doth defie	8	Ch.-Porch		53
And yet thy wounds still my attempts defie,	36	Reprisall		7
DEFILE				
Turn out these wranglers, which defile thy seat:	136	Familie		7
DEFIL'D				
To make him clean, who could not be defil'd?	173	Marie Magd		8
DEFINE				
Doth define,	180	Invitation		8
DEFINITION				
This definition is evident, and containes the direct steps	225	Priest 1		2

DEFINITION (cont'd)	PAGE	TITLE		LINE
Wherein is contained the complete definition of a Minister. . . .	225	Priest 1		14
DEFINITIONS				
Have thicken'd it with definitions?	134	Divinitie		10
hath exactly sifted the definitions of all vertues, and vices;	264	Priest 26		32
DEFIXED				
his minde being defixed on it with those nailes wherewith his Master	267	Priest 27		29
DEFORMITIE				
Makes all their beautie his deformitie.	23	Ch.-Porch		420
DEFRAUDING				
Defrauding thee, who gavest two for one.	82	Ungratef.		30
DEFRAY				
And to defray his journey from the east.	196	Ch.-Milit.		214
DEGENERATE				
which is not easily despised, except it degenerate to pride.	268	Priest 28		26
DEGREE				
Scorn no mans love, though of a mean degree;	20	Ch.-Porch		349
As larks, doe by degree, ...	43	East.wings	W	8
And share in my degree.	95	Submission		8
Starres have their storms, ev'n in a high degree, ...	132	The Storm		7
To some degree of spicinesse to thee!	175	The Odour		15
In some degree.	202	Trin.Sun.	W	4
or at least in that degree it ought to be, since he found himselfe	279	Priest 33		11
The first degree of folly is to hold ones selfe wise, ...	337	Proverbs		460
The first degree of folly is to thinke ourselves wise, ...	337	Proverbs	V	460
DEGREES				
And by degrees	79	Employm.2	W	24
DEIGNE				
Then we are shooters both, and thou dost deigne	139	Artillerie		25
Deare soul, she knew who did vouchsafe and deigne	173	Marie Magd		13
DEITIE				
That I did thrust into the Deitie, ...	28	Sacrifice		62
DEITIES				
Fresh and fine deities. They were at great cost, ...	193	Ch.-Milit.		109
From Egypt he tock pettie deities, ...	195	Ch.-Milit.		177
DEITY				
in their seasons argues a Deity.	347	Proverbs		773
DEJECT				
is to win their hearts, and to oppose them therin is to deject them.	283	Priest 35		31
DELAIES				
But with delaies.	57	Employm. 1		16
DELAY				
Sting my delay, ...	61	Praise 1		18
My soul doth love thee, yet it loves delay.	96	Justice 1		11
And then when after much delay, ...	164	The Crosse		7
Make no delay.	186	Dooms-day		2
DELAYED				
and the more the promise is delayed, the more he reads it, . . .	310	Valdesso		29
DELAYES				
But mend mine own without delayes.	36	Thanksgvng		34
But mend my own without delayes.	36	Thanksgvng	W	34
Without delayes, ...	41	Easter		2
What if I say thou seek'st delayes;	61	Grace	W	20
DELICATE				
especially to pious minds, which are ever tender, and delicate.	273	Priest 31		14
DELICATES				
Is in the midst of delicates to need, ...	165	The Crosse		29
DELICIOUS				
I did conceit a most delicious feast;	50	Faith		6
DELIGHT				
And turn delight into a sacrifice.	6	Ch.-Porch		6
The sonne, in whom thou dost delight to be?	33	Sacrifice		214
All my delight, so all my smart:	62	Afflict.2		13
Th' indorsement of supreme delight, ...	75	Sunday		3
Revenging the delight.	86	Lent		24
As our delight, or as our treasure:	91	Man		28
And serve the swine: there, there is his delight:	101	Miserie		44
All thy delight in me fulfill!	104	Obedience		17
What delight or hope remains?	114	Dialogue		8
Whither away delight?	154	Glimpse		1
Me thinks delight should have	154	Glimpse		6
If earth in earth delight.	161	Priesthood		24
I felt a sugred strange delight, ...	171	The Glance		5
And one aspect of thine spend in delight	172	The Glance		22
Your delight, ...	180	Invitation		23
Thy delight	181	Banquet		5
Or say, or dictate, this is my delight.	183	The Posie		8
Then tell me, what is that supreme delight?	188	Heaven		13
But in God's Law sets his delight, ...	214	Psalm I	D	5
cannot in sins delight:	218	Psalm V	D	10
that they get a delight in it, and enter favour with God, . . .	239	Priest 10		28
wherein the Catechized will at length finde delight, and by which	256	Priest 21		18
Could men finde out this delight, they would seldome be from home;	275	Priest 32		35
I am not wearie of life, which I passe with great delight. . . .	301	Cornaro		3
neither omit I any thing that may either teach, or delight me.	302	Cornaro		5
Now lest there should be any delight wanting to my old age, . . .	302	Cornaro		37
DELIGHTED				
I am delighted with their musick and fashion, and I my self also sing	303	Cornaro		6
DELIGHTFULL				
inward heats, drank delightfull wines, and that in great quantitie,	292	Cornaro		29
parted with rills of running water, which truely is very delightfull.	301	Cornaro		16

	PAGE	TITLE		LINE
DELIGHTFULL (cont'd)				
The memorie whereof is exceeding delightfull to me.	301	Cornaro		33
DELIGHTS				
Out of my stock of naturall delights,	46	Afflict.1		5
Thus are we to delights: but we are all	48	Repentance		9
Of strange delights, where we may wish & take.	58	H.Script.1		7
This may allure us with delights;	82	Ungratef.		22
Thine own delights thou didst to us impart:	97	Afflict.5		8
Whose flat delights on earth do creep and grow;	111	Vanitie 2		2
Where are no sorrows, but delights more true,	167	Dotage		17
This worlds delights before true Christian joy,	170	Self-cond.		8
Such delights I meant to say;	177	The Rose		10
In delights of earth was drown'd;	182	Banquet		33
O who will show me those delights on high?	188	Heaven		1
which exceedingly delights him as by way of exercise upon himself,	255	Priest 21		11
is observeable, that God delights to have men feel, and acknowledg,	271	Priest 30		19
recounting the delights and pleasures in this age of eighty three,	300	Cornaro		31
when I was given to disorder and all the delights that could be.	302	Cornaro		11
But this chiefly delights me, that my advice hath taken effect in	302	Cornaro		14
These are the delights and solaces of my old age, which is altogether	302	Cornaro		22
DELINQUENT				
he forbears not in any wise to use the delinquent as before,	263	Priest 25		26
the punishment to a better subduing, and humbling of the delinquent;	263	Priest 25		32
yea though they be tenants, or otherwise ingaged to the delinquent:	270	Priest 29		21
if the punished delinquent shall be much troubled for his sins,	288	Priest 37		2
DELINQUENT'S				
by all means, that the delinquents returne is to his advantage.	264	Priest 25		1
DELIVER				
Deliver us to laws; they send us bound	45	Sinne 1		3
O lett my Soule, whose keyes I must deliver	203	Even-song	W	21
O Lord deliver mee!	220	Psalm VII	D	4
the cause with him, whom he makes to deliver their opinion first;	260	Priest 23		10
doth forsake and persecute them, and there is none to deliver them.	281	Priest 34		12
that in their full strength they may deliver thy message reverently,	289	Priest		28
and deliver your Letter, yet have I sent it thither by a faithful	369	Letters		15
will also deliver me out of the hands of this uncircumcised	374	Letters		7
trouble not your selves, God is at hand to deliver us from all, or,	374	Letters		30
DELIVERANCE				
Wrought our deliverance from th' infernall pit,	54	Love 1		12
of my deliverance:	216	Psalm III	D	6
from the certainty both of deliverance, and reward, if we faint not;	249	Priest 15		25
DELIVER'D				
And now I am deliver'd unto death,	31	Sacrifice		145
Yea, have not oft deliver'd him	221	Psalm VII	D	13
DELIVERED				
he saith, he had delivered them to Satan, that they might learn	286	Priest 36		1
That God who hath delivered me out of the paws of the Lyon and Bear,	374	Letters		6
you bee like great Alexander, unlesse Historie delivered his actions?	443	Oration		3
DELIVERY				
of whose rude delivery my hast makes mee ashamed, only my comfort is	369	Letters		2
DELUDES				
Then chafing said, This man deludes:	123	Time		28
DELUGE				
Oceans of Ink; for, as the Deluge did	206	Walton 2		2
A Deluge on my sensual Flame,	214	Convert	D	9
DEMAIN				
With a great stable or demain:	70	Quidditie		8
With my great stable or demain:	70	Quidditie	W	8
DEMAND				
I did demand; he thus began:	125	Peace		21
now to the answering of this demand of the Kings these Agents pretend	368	Letters		14
DEMANDED				
when the Parson once demanded after other questions about mans	257	Priest 21		2
DEMANDEST				
When thou demandest but a heart,	82	Ungratef.		26
DEMANDING				
demanding an account, but not by the way of an account.	239	Priest 9		2
DEMANDS				
Or else the chilnesse of my faint demands.	66	Ch.-lock		4
Hee that demands misseth not, unlesse his demands be foolish.	333	Proverbs		359
DEMEAN				
To which, besides their own demean,	165	The Flower		3
DEMONSTRATIONS				
Plain demonstrations, evident and cleare,	167	Dotage		10
DEN				
Preferring, like brute beasts, a lothsome den	167	Dotage		15
Prayers chas'd syllogismes into their den,	191	Ch.-Milit.		55
DENIALL				
Deniall.	79	Deniall		T
DENIE				
So they in me denie themselves all pitie:	31	Sacrifice		143
Or fight, or travell, or denie	45	Nature		2
Which to himself he did denie:	63	Even-song		6
And centre both to me denie	162	The Search		7
Neither can any man denie this, who will narrowly consider it.	297	Cornaro		14
I denie not but that Physicians are necessarie, and greatly to be	298	Cornaro		3
DENI'D				
Yet still askt pardon, and was not deni'd.	129	Love unkn.		21
DENIES				
Whose sparkling light accesse denies:	82	Ungratef.		14
Nature denies;	136	Ephes.		32

DENIES (cont'd)	PAGE	TITLE	LINE
Who qives to all, denies all.	322	Proverbs	38
DENOUNCED			
which some observing who heard the interdiction denounced to him,	368	Letters	37
DENY			
That Flesh is there, mine eyes deny:	201	H. Commun. W	31
and vanities of the world, which he is to deny, and not augment.	240	Priest 10	4
and put them to great shame, who deny the Scripture to be perfect.	247	Priest 13	2
and then who can deny the stretched out arme of a mighty God?	282	Priest 34	6
DENYING			
having forms or vizars of godlinesse, but denying the power thereof.	319	Valdesso V	27
DEPART			
For when thou dost depart from hence,	56	Temper 2	11
Yet, if thou wilt from thence depart,	74	The Starre	5
Give up the whole, and with the whole depart?	144	Discharge	8
Thou cam'st but now; wilt thou so soon depart,	154	Glimpse	2
Quite under ground; as flowers depart	166	The Flower	10
Till all depart: so went the Church her way,	191	Ch.-Milit.	33
But now from me depart away,	220	Psalm VI D	19
will they last the longer, and when they depart, returne the sooner.	280	Priest 34	30
DEPARTED			
I never since departed from my setled course of Sobrietie,	293	Cornaro	25
DEPARTS			
but always in the close, before he departs from them:	248	Priest 14	16
DEPARTURE			
which if you can sent to Sir Francis before his departure,	369	Letters	26
whether my peace be yet made with her concerning my unkind departure.	371	Letters	9
that I loved her even in my departure, in looking to her Son,	371	Letters	12
DEPEND			
And I depend on thee;	183	A Parodie	5
making a hook of his Charity, causeth them still to depend on him;	244	Priest 12	32
So that if a farmer should depend upon God all the yeer,	271	Priest 30	28
or if he depend on God further, even till he imbarn his corn,	271	Priest 30	31
and indeed, to depend, and fear continually.	271	Priest 30	36
if our corporall life depend on the harmonie of humours & elements,	297	Cornaro	7
which depend almost wholly on their Canon law and Decretals,	319	Valdesso V	28
DEPENDANCE			
and not break off their acts of dependance, how faire soever	271	Priest 30	27
but to continue his dependance on God, not onely before the corne is	271	Priest 30	34
DEPOS'D			
They had depos'd each one.	70	Humilitie	24
DEPRIVES			
Who likes not the drinke, God deprives him of bread.	334	Proverbs	394
DEPTHS			
Fathom'd the depths of seas, of states, and kings,	37	The Agonie	2
Of future depths, but drink the cleare and good.	145	Discharge	28
DEPUTED			
I was one of those that was deputed for the managing of that work,	302	Cornaro	17
DEPUTIES			
he constituted Deputies in his place, and these are Priests.	225	Priest 1	8
DEPUTY			
A Pastor is the Deputy of Christ for the reducing of Man	225	Priest 1	1
DERIDE			
There they deride me, they abuse me all:	31	Sacrifice	154
the Lord himself shall them deride:	215	Psalm II D	10
some scoffing ruffian, who is likely to deride him for his paines:	273	Priest 31	29
DERIDED			
even for those that derided him then, and still despise him.	288	Priest	29
DESCEND			
Descend and fall, and thou dost flow.	137	The Size	6
And interchangeably descend,	141	Justice 2	17
He did descend, undressing all the way.	151	The Bag	12
to descend yet more particularly, if a man hath wherewithall to buy	265	Priest 26	27
be amisse in this exceeding usefull point to descend to particulars:	275	Priest 32	18
DESCENDED			
Where is that fire which once descended	59	Whitsunday	5
DESCENT			
And true descent; that when thou shalt grow fat,	65	Ch.-monum.	18
In their descent and being; to our minde	91	Man	35
DESCRIBED			
and which are described in this Book, he must be despised;	268	Priest 28	13
the person here described to be in the dark, ought to use the first,	312	Valdesso V	24
DESCRIBING			
in describing the one (which is indeed the bent of my Discourse)	226	Priest 2	17
DESCRY (see also discry)			
DESERT (wasteland)			
but to them an unpenetrable rock, an unaccessible desert.	282	Priest 34	4
DESERT			
After my sinnes! look not on my desert,	83	Sighs & Gr.	2
Entred for both, farre above their desert!	105	Obedience	45
With my glorie and desert,	115	Dialogue	30
If comforts fell according to desert,	138	The Size	39
As thy due desert.	147	Offering	30
But thou art my desert:	156	Assurance	25
And all this not for my desert,	172	23 Psalme	11
DESERTS			
If my deserts were masters of mine eyes:	136	Ephes.	34
And single things grow fruitfull by deserts.	147	Offering	10
DESERVE			
My sinnes deserve the condemnation.	36	Reprisall	4
Lord thou dost deserve much more.	93	Antiphon 2 W	19

	PAGE	TITLE		LINE
DESIRING (cont'd)				
But sensuall men (as most are) desiring to satisfie their Appetite,	298	Cornaro		23
DESIROUS				
Being desirous (thorow the Mercy of GOD) to please Him, . .	224	Priest		1
I was desirous to putt a good mind into the way of charity, . .	375	Letters		7
DESISTS				
long God knocks at our harts, before he be heard, & yet desists not.	381	Woodnoth		3
DESK				
especially that the Pulpit, and Desk, and Communion Table, . .	246	Priest 13		6
DESOLATION				
But lends to us, shall be our desolation.	197	Ch.-Milit.		258
Lendeth to us, shall be our desolation.	197	Ch.-Milit.	W	258
Chapt. 10. after he had complained of the desolation of Israel,	234	Priest 7		4
DESPAIR				
Away despair; my gracious Lord doth heare.	151	The Bag		1
Any thing to me. Heark despair, away.	152	The Bag		42
DESPAIRE				
till either they despise that Love, or despaire of his Mercy:	283	Priest 34		23
DESPAIRED				
Nothing is to be presumed on, or despaired of.	356	Proverbs	D	56
DESPAIRS				
To cold despairs, and gnawing pensivenesse?	155	Assurance		16
DESPERATE				
Is of the two the far more desperate.	210	Paradox	D	30
DESPERATION				
The gloomy cave of Desperation	141	Pilgrimage		4
But if he sees them neerer desperation, then Atheisme; . . .	283	Priest 34		5
DESPISE				
Lord, in my silence how do I despise	71	Frailtie		1
who may not despise my poor labours, but add to those points,	224	Priest		14
to the Apostles rule, he endeavours that none shall despise him;	268	Priest 28		17
at least of those, who are apt to despise:	268	Priest 28		25
till either they despise that Love, or despaire of his Mercy:	283	Priest 34		23
even for those that derided him then, and still despise him.	288	Priest		30
the second to professe it, the third to despise counsell. . .	337	Proverbs		460
DESPISED				
and cringings, that they shall ever be despised.	226	Priest 2		36
and which are described in this Book, he must be despised; . .	268	Priest 28		13
which is not easily despised, except it degenerate to pride.	268	Priest 28		26
DESPISES				
then when any despises him, he takes it either in an humble way,	269	Priest 28		5
DESPISETH				
yet hee is no little foole that despiseth it.	327	Proverbs		206
DESPISING				
but the despising of Love must needs be without it. . . .	283	Priest 34		24
DESPITEFULNESSE				
The Jews accuse me with despitefulnesse;	29	Sacrifice		85
DESTILL'D				
An herb destill'd, and drunk, may dwell next doore, ...	61	Praise 1		13
DESTINIE				
These three make up some Christians destinie:	58	H.Script.2		8
DESTINY				
A man's destiny is alwayes dark.	362	Proverbs	D	1180
DESTITUTE				
That he was fain, when thou wert destitute, ...	77	Avarice		7
how destitute she is, and that in this necessary time of education.	376	Letters		12
DESTROY				
As gunnes destroy, so may a little sling.	20	Ch.-Porch		352
But thou wilt sinne and grief destroy;	49	Repentance		31
Save that, and me; or sin for both destroy.	56	Temper 2		4
While blustring windes destroy the wanton bowres, ...	97	Afflict.5		21
At least in lump: for such doth oft destroy;	138	The Size		27
They would great frosts and snows destroy:	138	The Size		40
Thousands of souls it hath and doth destroy	170	Self-cond.		11
My soul hath felt, ev'n able to destroy, ...	172	The Glance		10
Doth destroy, ...	180	Invitation		20
That though our Saviour did destroy the game, ...	194	Ch.-Milit.		146
Destroy them, Lord, and by their own	219	Psalm V	D	29
it is no wonder that order should preserve, and disorder destroy.	297	Cornaro		9
DESTROY'D				
I have abus'd thy stock, destroy'd thy woods, ...	83	Sighs & Gr.		9
DESTROYED				
the womans oyntment in the Gospell, or sees Jerusalem destroyed.	283	Priest 34		3
DESTROYES				
which it hath escaped, he destroyes it sometimes in the very Haven;	271	Priest 30		23
But Intemperance destroyes most healthy and flourishing . .	292	Cornaro		9
DESTROYETH				
nor of the sicknesse that destroyeth at noone day, [Ghostly pride	238	Priest 9		8
DESTROYING				
That by destroying that which ty'd thy purse, ...	103	Prayer 2		17
DESTROYS				
then God sends such weather, as lays the corn, and destroys it:	271	Priest 30		31
DESTRUCTION				
Her own destruction and his danger wears.	85	Vanitie 1		14
His own destruction and his danger wears.	85	Vanitie 1	V	14
without any resistance, even in resistance, to the same destruction.	269	Priest 28		23
The other concerning the destruction of Jerusalem;	282	Priest 34		27
DETAIN				
Although the Crosse could not Christ here detain, ...	439	Walton 5		1
that if the poorest man of the Parish detain but a pin unjustly from	260	Priest 23		14

	PAGE	TITLE		LINE
DIALOGUES				
some dialogues in Plato were worth the reading, where the singular	256	Priest 21		27
DIAMOND				
The clearest diamond: let them do their best,	126	Confession		29
My Lord. A diamond to mee you sent,	209	L. Bacon	D	1
DICTATE				
Or say, or dictate, this is my delight.	183	The Posie		8
DICTIONARY				
but a dictionary, and may be considered alike in all the Scripture.	235	Priest 7		9
DID				
Did with his liquour slide into his veins.	7	Ch.-Porch		34
God then deals blessings: If a king did so,	22	Ch.-Porch		389
They may weep out the stains by them did rise:	23	Ch.-Porch		417
Whose parts are as thy hand did frame;	26	The Altar		3
Mine own Apostle, who the bag did beare,	27	Sacrifice		13
Though he had all I had, did not forbeare	27	Sacrifice		14
For thirtie pence he did my death devise,	27	Sacrifice		17
Who at three hundred did the ointment prize,	27	Sacrifice		18
That I did thrust into the Deitie,	28	Sacrifice		62
Which Angels did desire to have the grace,	32	Sacrifice		182
Whom Angels did desire to have the grace,	32	Sacrifice	W	182
Alas! I did so, when I left my crown	34	Sacrifice		222
Alas! I did so, when I lost my crown	34	Sacrifice	W	222
But more with malice: yet, when they did call,	34	Sacrifice		238
Did set again abroach; then let him say	37	The Agonie		15
If ever he did taste the like.	37	The Agonie		16
What ever sinne did this pure rock commit,	41	Sepulchre		10
And missing this, most falsly did arraigne thee;	41	Sepulchre		14
My tender age in sorrow did beginne:	43	East.wings		11
Thy glorious houshold-stuffe did me entwine,	46	Afflict.1		9
Thy glorious houshold-stuffe did me bewitch	46	Afflict.1	W	9
But with my yeares sorrow did twist and grow,	47	Afflict.1		23
But with my yeares sorrows did twist and grow,	47	Afflict.1	W	23
Sorrow was all my soul; I did not know	47	Afflict.1	W	29
Till grief did tell me roundly, that I lived.	47	Afflict.1		30
That I did live, but by a pang of woe.	47	Afflict.1	W	30
As we did rise, we die together.	49	Repentance		24
I did conceit a most delicious feast;	50	Faith		6
I had it straight, and did as truly eat,	50	Faith		7
As ever did a welcome guest.	50	Faith		8
I did beleeve that I did nothing owe,	50	Faith		14
Vanisht away, when Faith did change the scene:	51	Faith		39
For sure when Adam did not know	53	H.Commun.		33
And praise him who did make and mend our eies.	54	Love 2		14
That th' earth did like a heav'n appeare;	59	Whitsunday		10
The sunne, which once did shine alone,	59	Whitsunday		13
Of those, who did themselves through their side wound,	59	Whitsunday		20
Did not excite thee, we should wholly sink.	60	Whitsunday		24
He did not heav'n and earth create,	63	Mattens		15
Which to himself he did denie:	63	Even-song		6
Which this dayes favour did beget?	64	Even-song		11
Did through my bodie wound my minde,	65	Ch.-mus.		2
did play their part	66	Ch.-lock	W	4
The angrie Lion did present his paw,	70	Humilitie		9
Humilitie did reach to Fortitude.	70	Humilitie		12
Did weep so fast, that the tears trickling down	71	Humilitie		26
My foot did tread,	71	Frailtie		18
My heart did heave, and there came forth, O God!	73	Afflict.3		1
And did inclose this light for his:	76	Sunday		37
Our great Redeemer did remove	76	Sunday		44
Did th' earth and all things with it move.	76	Sunday		46
And did unhinge that day.	76	Sunday		49
In whom the Lord of hosts did pitch his tent!	77	Anagram		2
When th' elements did for place contest	79	Employm.2		11
Did flie asunder:	80	Deniall		7
Suckt all thy magazens: my head did ake,	83	Sighs & Gr.		10
That her fine cobwebs did support the frame,	84	The World		3
His dearely-earned pearl, which God did hide	85	Vanitie 1		10
Did both conduct and teach me, how by it	89	The Pearl		39
Us did make,	92	Antiphon 2		11
His bloud did spill	94	Unkindness		23
But time did becken to the flowers, and they	94	Life		4
By noon most cunningly did steal away,	94	Life		5
Who did so sweetly deaths sad taste convey,	94	Life		10
And pilfring what I once did give,	95	Submission		11
As we at first did board with thee,	97	Afflict.5		11
Did crown his heart and face.	102	Miserie		72
Such was their lustre, they did so excell,	102	Jordan 2		2
Thousands of notions in my brain did runne,	102	Jordan 2		7
So did I weave my self into the sense.	103	Jordan 2		14
Did not affect thee much, was not thy aim;	106	Sion		8
The bloud did make, which thou didst waste?	107	Home		8
The help did in thy bosome lie.	107	Home		16
He did, he came: O my Redeemer deare,	108	Home		25
The merrie world did on a day	110	The Quip		1
Who did leave his Fathers throne,	113	Businesse		17
He so farre thy good did plot,	113	Businesse		23
Did he die, or did he not?	113	Businesse		25
That as I did freely part	115	Dialogue		29
Then an old prayer-book I did present:	121	Hope		3
I did expect a ring.	121	Hope		8

DID (cont'd)

	PAGE	TITLE	LINE
No marvell Sir, he did replie,	122	Time	3
Perhaps some such of old did passe,	122	Time	7
Thy word our hearts and hands did crave,	123	Gratefulnes	10
Did take.	124	Gratefulnes	24
A hollow winde did seem to answer, No:	124	Peace	5
I did; and going did a rainbow note:	124	Peace	7
Did break and scatter.	124	Peace	12
Then went I to a garden, and did spy	125	Peace	13
I did demand; he thus began:	125	Peace	21
He sweetly liv'd; yet sweetnesse did not save	125	Peace	25
It prosper'd strangely, and did soon disperse	125	Peace	31
Did alter with his minde;	127	Giddinesse	18
Joy, I did lock thee up: but some bad man	128	Bunch Gr.	1
I did toward Canaan draw; but now I am	128	Bunch Gr.	6
I did towards Canaan draw; but now I am	128	Bunch Gr. V	6
Who of the laws sowre juice sweet wine did make,	128	Bunch Gr.	27
Lookt on a servant, who did know his eye	129	Love unkn.	9
And threw it in a font, wherein did fall	129	Love unkn.	13
Indeed 'tis true. I did and do commit	129	Love unkn.	19
Thinking with that, which I did thus present,	129	Love unkn.	31
To warm his love, which I did fear grew cold.	129	Love unkn.	32
But as my heart did tender it, the man	129	Love unkn.	33
A friend did steal into my cup for good,	130	Love unkn.	43
Did oft possesse me, so that when I pray'd,	130	Love unkn.	58
Though my lips went, my heart did stay behinde.	130	Love unkn.	59
The Font did onely, what was old, renew:	130	Love unkn.	64
The Thorns did quicken, what was grown too dull:	130	Love unkn.	66
All did but strive to mend, what you had marr'd.	130	Love unkn.	67
I did behave me carelesly,	133	The Method	15
When I did pray.	133	The Method	16
Me thoughts a starre did shoot into my lap.	139	Artillerie	2
This, this hath done it, this did bite the root	140	Ch.-rents	5
Did once perceive, it blew them under foot,	140	Ch.-rents	7
Did once perceive, it blew thee under foot,	140	Ch.-rents V	7
Thought to let out, the bleeding did you good,	140	Ch.-rents	14
Did worm and work within you more and more,	140	Ch.-rents	17
Then did your sev'rall parts unloose and start:	140	Ch.-rents	21
Did show and shape thy looks to me,	141	Justice 2	4
He that did but look up, was proud and bold.	141	Justice 2	6
Did like some torturing engine show;	141	Justice 2	10
Did like some tottering engine show;	141	Justice 2 V	10
Thy hand above did burn and glow,	141	Justice 2	11
Did not thy heart	144	Discharge	7
That God did make	144	Discharge	17
The God of power, as he did ride	151	The Bag	9
He did descend, undressing all the way.	151	The Bag	12
He smil'd and said as he did go,	151	The Bag	17
He did repair unto an inne.	151	The Bag	20
He did endure to cancell sinne:	151	The Bag	22
Before my sighs did drie it: there was corn	153	The Collar	11
Before my tears did drown it.	153	The Collar	12
When as my fears foretold this, did replie,	154	Glimpse	19
And hold my hand, while I did write.	156	Assurance	30
The windes their stint: and yet when I did call,	158	Praise 3	23
Did weep to heav'n, they found a bottle there	158	Praise 3	27
(Which there did hang like streamers neare the top	158	Praise 3	33
I live to shew his power, who once did bring	159	Jos.coat	13
As if to meet thee they did know,	162	The Search	11
Which my fierce youth did bandie, fall and flow	169	The Answer	3
Did before dimme and choke,	171	Self-cond.	21
To look upon me, who before did lie	171	The Glance	3
Sprung from thine eye, did work within my soul,	172	The Glance	14
She being stain'd her self, why did she strive	173	Marie Magd	7
Deare soul, she knew who did vouchsafe and deigne	173	Marie Magd	13
To bear her filth; and that her sinnes did dash	173	Marie Magd	14
Then did I wash you with my tears, and more,	176	Forerunners	16
Where we did finde	186	Death	10
But since our Saviours death did put some bloud	186	Death	13
Love took my hand, and smiling did reply,	189	Love 3	11
So I did sit and eat.	189	Love 3	18
Spices come from the East; so did thy Spouse,	190	Ch.-Milit.	13
Where th' Ark did rest, there Abraham began	190	Ch.-Milit.	19
When it grew loose, the Jews did hope in vain	190	Ch.-Milit.	23
To Egypt first she came, where they did prove	191	Ch.-Milit.	37
The ten Commandments there did flourish more	191	Ch.-Milit.	39
Though Greece took horse as soon as Egypt did,	191	Ch.-Milit.	57
In both of these Prowesse and Arts did tame	192	Ch.-Milit.	75
Or strength in th' other, did erect her throne.	192	Ch.-Milit.	78
And did this mysterie wrap up and fold	192	Ch.-Milit.	94
Sinne did set out of Eastern Babylon,	193	Ch.-Milit.	103
At first he got to Egypt, and did sow	193	Ch.-Milit.	107
Gardens of Gods, which ev'ry yeare did grow,	193	Ch.-Milit.	108
That though our Saviour did destroy the game,	194	Ch.-Milit.	146
Yet did a rogue with hope of carnall joy	194	Ch.-Milit.	149
So now being Priest he plainly did professe	195	Ch.-Milit.	173
He did surname his palace, Babylon.	195	Ch.-Milit.	182
Such force as once did captivate the Jews;	195	Ch.-Milit.	192
But did bewitch, and finely work each nation	195	Ch.-Milit.	193
But did bewitch both kings & many a nation	195	Ch.-Milit. W	193
It did not fit his gravitie to stirre,	195	Ch.-Milit.	197

DID (cont'd)	PAGE	TITLE		LINE
Then what was in their tongue, did overcome;	196	Ch.-Milit.		202
And having conquer'd, did so strangely rule,	196	Ch.-Milit.		203
That the whole world did seem but the Popes mule.	196	Ch.-Milit.		204
As new and old Rome did one Empire twist;	196	Ch.-Milit.		205
When th' one did set, the other did take place,	196	Ch.-Milit.		217
At Christs last coming, as his first did finde:	196	Ch.-Milit.		231
For gold and grace did never yet agree:	197	Ch.-Milit.		251
So also did the Church by going west	198	Ch.-Milit.		275
Sinn onely, which did all deface	200	H. Commun.	W	23
Then flesh did lend thee, back agen.	202	love	W	18
Did not confess in the first Theefe	202	Trin.Sun.	W	12
Are so, as for the present, I did move	204	Persever.	W	3
Wherewith whole showls of Martyrs once did burn,	206	Walton 1		2
Oceans of Ink; for, as the Deluge did	206	Walton 2		2
Till your bright gift my darknesse did abate.	209	L. Bacon	D	8
If ever Tears did flow from Eyes,	213	Convert	D	1
My Eyes, from whence these Tears did spring,	214	Convert	D	6
Frail Beauty's Charms to Heav'n did raise,	214	Convert	D	13
in that a Priest may do that which Christ did, and by his auctority,	225	Priest 1		17
in that a Priest is to do that which Christ did, and after his	225	Priest 1		18
as the Jewes and Judas did Christ, he may say as He did,	227	Priest 3		33
he may say as He did, I sate daily with you teaching in the Temple.	227	Priest 3		33
or offer up such sacrifices as they did of old, which was of beasts	232	Priest 6		4
How did he put the Romans in all his prayers? Rom. 1. 9.	234	Priest 7		11
or over-nourishing things, as the Israelites did eate sowre herbs:	242	Priest 10		4
and oftentimes, as Nathan did, in the person of another,	248	Priest 14		21
Did you see God make it?	256	Priest 21		8
Socrates did thus in Philosophy, who held that the seeds of all	256	Priest 21		20
And I conceive, our Saviour did this for three reasons:	261	Priest 23		17
that so the body may joyn in the grief, as it did in the sin;	279	Priest 33		28
as he did our Saviour, and the Angels minister to us their owne food,	280	Priest 34		5
as they remember themselves were, when affliction did blow the Coals.	280	Priest 34		21
if the Ministration of condemnation did bless, how shall	285	Priest 36		19
So did St. Paul, 2 Tim. 4. 14. and 1 Tim. 1. 20.	285	Priest 36		31
then did the Lord of life, unable of himselfe to die, contrive to do	288	Priest		27
so man did eat Angels food:	290	Priest		9
which did not onely begin, but had already gone farre in me,	291	Cornaro		17
followed my Appetite, and did eat meats pleasing to my taste;	292	Cornaro		27
and windes and labours did little hurt him, because in his meats	294	Cornaro		7
all these did hurt me little, whereas they hurt them very much who	294	Cornaro		14
neither did I know well, what I did or said.	296	Cornaro		17
so did Plato also, and Isocrates, and Tullie, and many others	298	Cornaro		38
ever outrunning the Teacher, as it did when Peter taught Cornelius:	310	Valdesso		8
not to the point it should, which if it did, it would doe more,	319	Valdesso		11
but, since I know I did not, and that your share continues,	372	Letters		16
That you did not only entertain my proposals, but advance them,	375	Letters		2
of taking her, as once you did, surely it were a great good deed,	375	Letters		31
only for the success (as assistance of Sir John) doe as David did:	380	Woodnoth		23
DID'ST				
which Thou did'st preordain.	221	Psalm VII	D	24
then did'st thou place us in Paradise, and wert proceeding still	288	Priest		14
DIDST				
By thy eternall glorie didst outgo me?	37	Reprisall		10
Remember that thou once didst write in stone.	38	The Sinner		14
Thou didst so punish sinne,	43	East.wings		13
Daily didst punish sinne,	43	East.wings	W	13
Thou didst lay hold, and antedate	44	H. Bapt.2		4
When first thou didst entice to thee my heart,	46	Afflict.1		1
Thou didst betray me to a lingring book,	47	Afflict.1		39
Thou often didst with Academick praise	47	Afflict.1		45
Inherent in them, thou didst make the sunne	51	Faith		34
On thy Apostles? thou didst then	59	Whitsunday		6
Such glorious gifts thou didst bestow,	59	Whitsunday		9
Affront those joyes, wherewith thou didst endow,	71	Frailtie		19
Before didst bow.	74	The Starre		20
Surely thou didst so little contribute	77	Avarice		5
Lord, thou didst make me, yet thou woundest me;	95	Justice 1		2
Thine own delights thou didst to us impart:	97	Afflict.5		8
When we grew wanton, thou didst use displeasure	97	Afflict.5		9
Sweet were the dayes, when thou didst lodge with Lot,	99	Decay		1
The bloud did make, which thou didst waste?	107	Home		8
Sure thou didst put a minde there, if I could	116	Dulnesse		23
When that lay gather'd, thou didst broach the mountains:	120	Providence		114
But thou didst reckon, when at first	123	Gratefulnes		9
And didst allow us all our noise:	124	Gratefulnes		18
Where thou didst lately so triumph and shine,	140	Ch.-rents		2
For where before thou still didst call on me,	141	Justice 2		19
If, though thou didst not beat thy future brow,	144	Discharge		23
Thou didst note my working breast,	146	Praise 2		7
Thou didst cleare me;	146	Praise 2		14
Thou didst heare me.	146	Praise 2		16
Lord Jesu, thou didst bow	149	Longing		31
Lord, didst thou leave thy throne,	150	Longing		61
While thou didst wink and wouldst not see.	153	The Collar		26
Thou didst at once thy self indite,	156	Assurance		29
For thou didst suffer to restore	157	Clasping		14
Yet then as mine didst me restore.	157	Clasping		18
And bloudie battell which thou once didst trie)	158	Praise 3		35
Early didst thou arise to plant this vine,	190	Ch.-Milit.		11
Thou didst rise early for to plant this vine,	190	Ch.-Milit.	W	11

DIMME (cont'd)	PAGE	TITLE		LINE
Did before dimme and choke,	171	Self-cond.		21
DIMNESSE				
Chasing the fathers dimnesse, carri'd farre	168	The Sonne		8
DINE				
Thou must go sleep, or dine.	101	Miserie		54
Nay, thou dost make me sit and dine,	173	23 Psalme		17
and goes with him to the other, and all dine or sup together.	284	Priest 35		21
DINES				
Hee that dines and leaves, layes the cloth twice.	333	Proverbs		347
DINING				
So a man dining, eats at first lawfully;	264	Priest 26		22
DINNER				
and sutably to their needs, then so much given in meat at dinner.	243	Priest 11		17
So that if after dinner they are not fit (or un-weeldy) either	266	Priest 26		31
Not that all must presently work after dinner;	266	Priest 26		33
At dinner my man appeares.	322	Proverbs		37
DINNERS				
Hunger makes dinners, pastime suppers.	348	Proverbs		819
DIOCESAN				
so especially to his Diocesan, honouring him both in word,	253	Priest 19		7
DIOCESE				
use of them, as of Clergy councels, for the benefit of the Diocese.	253	Priest 19		11
DIPPING				
by dipping, and seasoning all our words and sentences in our hearts,	233	Priest 7		28
DIPT				
And have good cause: there it was dipt and di'd,	129	Love unkn.		16
DIRECT				
Direct my prayers to thy Throne,	218	Psalm V	D	7
and containes the direct steps of Pastorall Duty and Auctority.	225	Priest 1		3
unto God, and as his grace shall direct him, so let him proceed.	237	Priest 9		6
therefore I desire him to send me a direct answer in his next Letter.	370	Letters		25
DIRECTED				
being directed by them in the way I ought to hold, I understood,	292	Cornaro		23
DIRECTLY				
then without opposing directly (for disputation is no Cure	281	Priest 34		14
DIRECTNESSE				
and secret of governing to preserve a directnesse, and open	240	Priest 10		34
DIRT (see also durt)				
Look on meat, think it dirt, then eat a bit;	11	Ch.-Porch		131
Give him his dirt to wallow in all night:	101	Miserie		46
They rushed in, and cast them in the dirt	140	Ch.-rents		23
Scorns his first bed of dirt, and means the sky;	169	The Answer		9
DIRTIE				
Man found thee poore and dirtie in a mine.	77	Avarice		4
As dirtie hands foul all they touch,	101	Miserie		37
DIRTY				
Take heed of foul dirty wayes, and long sicknesse.	360	Proverbs	D	1153
DISABILITY				
then their present exile, and disability to live in their Countrey.	282	Priest 34		10
DISABLE				
And Power it self disable.	86	Lent		18
none must eat so as to disable themselves from a fit discharging	266	Priest 26		29
DISABLED				
I am in all a weak disabled thing,	165	The Crosse		17
DISABLETH				
of darknesse, he disableth himself of authority to reprove them:	227	Priest 3		26
DISAFFECTED				
and generally intimateth to the disaffected, or sick person,	250	Priest 15		5
DISAGREE				
When doctrines disagree.	86	Lent		9
DISAGREEABLE				
diligently what meats were agreeable unto me, and what disagreeable:	293	Cornaro		6
DISALLOWED				
1 Sam. 1. 18. though it came from a man disallowed by God:	285	Priest 36		22
DISANULL				
Wouldst thou his laws of fasting disanull?	138	The Size		15
DISAPPOINTED				
thy Counsels, disappointed thy Purposes, and sold our God,	288	Priest		16
DISARMED				
and disarmed with sedentary lives, are to know the use of their Arms:	277	Priest 32		18
A disarmed peace is weake.	342	Proverbs		628
DISBAND				
Yea, when both rocks and all things shall disband,	156	Assurance		34
DISBANDED				
Disbanded humours, sorrows troops of Sinn	204	The Knell	W	11
DISBURSE				
Since we are ever ready to disburse,	78	Ang.&Sts.		29
More then a thousand sunnes disburse in light,	172	The Glance		23
DISBURSMENTS				
even as Princes have theirs, besides their publick disbursments.	236	Priest 8		17
DISCERN				
Which dissolution sure doth best discern,	65	Ch.-monum.		10
DISCERNED				
is in some sort true because they are spiritually discerned,	315	Valdesso		31
DISCHARGE				
The Discharge.	144	Discharge		T
To discharge what is behinde.	199	L'Envoy		16
but also for the discharge of the Church-wardens, who being	259	Priest 22		24
hands (as he sent the fish with mony to S. Peter,) to discharge it:	304	Valdesso		11

	PAGE	TITLE	LINE
DISCHARG'D			
For this thy love? have I discharg'd the debt,	64	Even-song	10
who have already abundantly discharg'd that part, having both ordered	373	Letters	11
DISCHARGED			
and fraile man, discharged the publick duties of the Congregation.	236	Priest 8	9
All those that are crost are discharged already the rest are to be	383	G.H.'s Will	3
DISCHARGETH			
stead to his Parish, and dischargeth God what he can of his promises.	254	Priest 20	9
DISCHARGING			
This is in some sort a discharging of God;	254	Priest 20	18
to disable themselves from a fit discharging either of Divine duties,	266	Priest 26	30
DISCIPLES			
Yet my Disciples sleep: I cannot gain	27	Sacrifice	29
All my Disciples flie; fear puts a barre	28	Sacrifice	49
DISCIPLINE			
Discipline.	178	Discipline	T
indeed the whole order and discipline of the Parish is put into their	269	Priest 29	29
DISCLAIM			
I disclaim the whole designe:	115	Dialogue	23
DISCLAIMS			
Sinne disclaims and I resigne.	115	Dialogue	24
DISCLOSE			
Purgings enmitie disclose,	178	The Rose	19
Who after him should braver truths disclose.	194	Ch.-Milit.	138
thy perfect way disclose.	219	Psalm V D	24
they may disclose anothers fault, finds it somwhat difficult how	286	Priest 37	32
DISCLOSING			
and forbid all disclosing of faults, many an evill may not only be,	286	Priest 37	34
DISCOLOUR			
They would discolour thy most bloudy sweat.	62	Afflict.2	10
And through their glasse discolour thee!	141	Justice 2	5
DISCOMFORT			
and the infection of his flock, and the discomfort, discredit,	287	Priest 37	4
that if one only came, the comfort intended would prove a discomfort.	375	Letters	17
DISCOMMODITIE			
those that pleased my taste brought me commoditie or discommoditie;	293	Cornaro	7
DISCOMMODITIES			
and other like discommodities of the bodie, and troubles	294	Cornaro	13
DISCONTENT			
There is some rub, some discontent,	133	The Method	3
A mans discontent is his worst evill.	331	Proverbs	298
DISCONTENTED			
Discontented.	80	Deniall	25
A discontented man knowes not where to sit easie.	333	Proverbs	345
DISCORD			
There can no discord but in ceasing be.	136	Ephes.	22
DISCOURSE			
Carve, or discourse; do not a famine fear.	11	Ch.-Porch	129
In thy discourse, if thou desire to please:	18	Ch.-Porch	289
Since we are ever ready to discourse,	78	Ang.&Sts. V	29
to whom this discourse ariseth not) some live in the Universities,	225	Priest 2	22
is indeed the bent of my Discourse) the other will be manifest.	226	Priest 2	18
Then turning the discourse to his Majesty, And he is a great God,	234	Priest 7	31
where he takes occasion to discourse of such things as are both	236	Priest 8	21
finds the persons of the house imployed, so he formes his discourse.	247	Priest 14	12
and therefore he lays his discourse so, that he comes to the point	248	Priest 14	20
if he perceive in company any discourse tending to ill,	252	Priest 18	16
an aim and mark of the whole discourse, whither to drive	256	Priest 21	31
as also by discourse with men of that profession, whom he hath ever	260	Priest 23	3
that to put men to discourse of that, wherin they are most eminent,	260	Priest 23	6
and to give him power so to fit his discourse to them, that it may	262	Priest 24	23
for Atheisme) he scatters in his discourse three sorts of arguments;	281	Priest 34	15
and woven into his discourse, at severall times and occasions,	283	Priest 34	4
make others faults their entertainment and discourse, and that even	286	Priest 37	31
All the discourse from this line [place] till the end of this Chapter	311	Valdesso	20
And so his whole discourse and sevenfold observation falls	318	Valdesso	25
Sweet discourse makes short daies and nights.	345	Proverbs	727
DISCOURSERS			
are in Orders, they may be received for Companions, or discoursers;	226	Priest 2	24
DISCOURSES			
for people are very attentive at such discourses, and think it	233	Priest 7	9
Such discourses shew very Holy.	234	Priest 7	36
his wife among her neighbours is the beginner of good discourses,	240	Priest 10	28
After these discourses, if they be poor and needy, whom he thus finds	248	Priest 14	9
Besides these occasionall discourses, the Parson questions what order	248	Priest 14	31
but with these he mingles other discourses for conversation sake,	249	Priest 14	11
or that overtake him, hee begins good discourses, such as may edify,	251	Priest 17	4
which may make his other discourses more welcome, and lesse tedious.	251	Priest 17	6
and ingagement of their discourses for no price sooner,	252	Priest 18	21
and intermingles some mirth in his discourses occasionally,	268	Priest 27	7
DISCOURSING			
Then cease discoursing soul, till thine own ground,	69	Content	33
DISCOURTESIE			
Errour a fault, and truth discourtesie.	18	Ch.-Porch	308
DISCOV'RIES			
Western discov'ries of posteritie.	168	The Sonne	10
DISCOVER			
when it is a fault to discover anothers fault, or when not;	230	Priest 5	25
which will discover it selfe by spitting, and rheume, or flegme.	242	Priest 10	24
but when one is asked a question, he must discover what he is.	257	Priest 21	20
loosely and wildely, and then the Answerer will discover what hee is.	259	Priest 22	9

DISTASTE	PAGE	TITLE		LINE
Into a blacknesse and distaste?	108	Home		40
DISTEMPER'D				
Yet speak they louder then distemper'd fears.	137	Familie		19
DISTILLS (see also destill'd)				
Each Cloud distills thy praise, and doth forbid	206	Walton 2		4
DISTINCTION				
This Liberty he compasseth by one distinction, and that is,	272	Priest 31		20
Here the Parson interposeth with his distinction, and shews	273	Priest 31		4
that the distinction is of singular use and comfort, especially	273	Priest 31		12
This distinction may runne through all Christian duties,	274	Priest 31		1
so it be understood with the former distinction, for Fomes is	308	Valdesso		15
DISTINGUISH				
When any one can distinguish the Sacramentall from common bread,	258	Priest 22		34
The best salve for the whole Chapter, is to distinguish Judgment:	316	Valdesso		34
DISTINGUISHED				
Distinguished, our habitation;	92	Man		39
DISTINGUISHETH				
he so distinguisheth, that he keeps his money for the poor,	243	Priest 11		8
Yet in all his Charity, he distinguisheth, giving them most,	245	Priest 12		15
yet in this he distinguisheth;	248	Priest 14		16
But the Parson distinguisheth according to his double aime,	267	Priest 26		15
The ballance distinguisheth not betweene gold and lead.	342	Proverbs		629
DISTRACTED				
But oh the folly of distracted men,	167	Dotage		13
Happier the hands fetter'd then the head distracted.	341	Proverbs	V	582
DISTRESS				
when I was in distress.	217	Psalm IV	D	4
a shield in their distress.	219	Psalm V	D	44
DISTRESSE				
That thy distresse through all may runne,	39	Good Fri.		15
And Mother of my God, in my distresse.	78	Ang.&Sts.		10
DISTRESSED				
or any ways distressed, fails not to afford his best comforts,	249	Priest 15		15
DISTRIBUTES				
but generally he distributes it thus, To his Children he shewes more	241	Priest 10		9
DISTRIBUTION				
Mercy in releeving the poor by a liberall distribution and largesse,	284	Priest 35		8
DISTRUST				
Yett in thy pursing still thy self distrust	13	Ch.-Porch	W	163
Away distrust:	145	Discharge		54
being no reason, why any should distrust Saint Luke, or Tertullian,	282	Priest 34		20
Distrust, Hope: Of these none can free themselves of themselves,	308	Valdesso		8
DISTRUSTFULLY				
as neither to labour anxiously, nor distrustfully, nor profanely.	247	Priest 14		27
then distrustfully, when they doubt Gods providence, thinking that	247	Priest 14		29
DISTRUSTS				
Impudent sinning, witchcrafts, and distrusts	197	Ch.-Milit.		238
DISTURB				
Disturb the work. O make me not their sport,	155	Glimpse		29
DISTURBANCE				
without disturbance, or interruption of publick divine offices.	236	Priest 8		25
so that men must eat neither to the disturbance of their health,	266	Priest 26		14
DITCH				
He that by being at church escapes the ditch,	24	Ch.-Porch		435
And while he digs out thee, falls in the ditch.	77	Avarice		14
He asked him again, what he would do, if he were in a ditch?	257	Priest 21		5
whether he could get out of the ditch alone, or whether he needed	257	Priest 21		9
DITCHES				
To feel those tempests, which fly over ditches.	11	Ch.-Porch		112
DITTIE				
Now prophesie who strikes thee, is their dittie.	31	Sacrifice		142
Beasts fain would sing; birds dittie to their notes;	117	Providence		9
He will be pleased with that dittie;	176	Forerunners		11
Be my dittie,	182	Banquet		50
DITTIES				
Or a fir'd beacon frighteth from his ditties.	16	Ch.-Porch		250
DIURNALL				
The first Is straight, and our diurnall friend,	84	Coloss.		3
DIVE				
And not his feet? Though we could dive	173	Marie Magd		10
that they dive not too deep into worldly affairs, plunging themselves	247	Priest 14		24
The Philosophy of Princes is to dive into the Secrets of men,	361	Proverbs	D	1165
DIVEL				
And when the Divel shakes the tree,	184	The Elixer	W	12
Hell, Death & Divel come short of mee.	202	love	W	24
DIVELL				
Of Divell, Jessuitt & Spaine,	213	L' Envoy	D	9
when the Divell for a time leaves us, as he did our Saviour,	280	Priest 34		5
and the Divell in Capuch (or cape of the cloak).	358	Proverbs	D	1082
The Divell divides the world between Atheisme and Superstition	359	Proverbs	D	1107
The Divell never assailes a man, except he find him	361	Proverbs	D	1176
DIVER				
The nimble Diver with his side	85	Vanitie 1		8
DIVERS				
From all these places, but at divers times,	195	Ch.-Milit.		185
but after divers gentle admonitions, if they persevere,	232	Priest 6		12
as divers have done lately, to our Countrey's advantage.	278	Priest 32		10
for though the temptations may be diverse in divers Christians,	279	Priest 33		1
because divers worthy young men have obliged me unto it.	291	Cornaro		8
(having a most cold & moist stomack) I fell into divers diseases,	291	Cornaro		21

	PAGE	TITLE	LINE
DIVERS (cont'd)			
Divers reasons they brought, as, that old age could not be sustained	295	Cornaro	21
and divers labours, which suit not with an orderly life:	299	Cornaro	14
my gardens, and those divers, parted with rills of running water,	301	Cornaro	15
and the faith of miracles are divers guifts, and of a different	319	Valdesso	7
come agents hither from the low-Cuntries to treat of divers matters,	368	Letters	5
MS. that there are divers moneys of mine in Mr Stephens hands	383	G.H.'s Will	22
DIVERSE			
yet as diverse, not as repugnant:	229	Priest 4	15
for though the temptations may be diverse in divers Christians,	279	Priest 33	1
These in diverse cases ought, and were of old forborn for a time.	312	Valdesso V	27
DIVERSION			
reserving so much of the affaires, as serve for a diversion for him;	238	Priest 9	38
it judiciously, or breaks it off seasonably by some diversion.	252	Priest 18	18
Nature serving Grace both in comfort of diversion, and the benefit	261	Priest 23	12
DIVERSITIE			
especially since there is a greater diversitie of tempers,	297	Cornaro	31
DIVERSITIES			
Their Diversities.	225	Priest 2	T
DIVERSITY			
to find out variety of thanks for the diversity of your favours,	363	Letters	15
DIVERSLY			
but diversly clothed, illustrated, and inlarged.	230	Priest 5	2
DIVERT			
since this place being civil may divert me too much from Divinity,	370	Letters	20
DIVERTED			
may be prevented, or diverted by reasonable imployment.	274	Priest 32	23
DIVES			
Who dives on further may find Hell.	97	Charms & K W	22
then he dives unto the boundlesse Ocean of Gods Love,	283	Priest 34	7
DIVEST (see also devest)			
DIVIDE (see also devided)			
Sometimes thou dost divide thy gifts to man,	120	Providence	125
Do seem to equally divide,	138	The Size	35
but, wou'd you divide and choose too?	373	Letters	1
DIVIDED			
Feares are divided in the midst.	342	Proverbs	639
DIVIDES			
The Divell divides the world between Atheisme and Superstition	359	Proverbs	D 1107
DIVINE			
My face they cover, though it be divine.	31	Sacrifice	137
Love is that liquour sweet and most divine,	37	The Agonie	17
To sing thy praises, make them lesse divine.	101	Miserie	40
To be exact, transcendent, and divine;	117	Providence	30
Ev'n taken inwardly, and most divine	130	Love unkn.	44
Are the more foul, the more thou wert divine.	140	Ch.-rents	4
Such as is, and makes divine!	181	Banquet	9
Makes drudgerie divine:	185	The Elixer	18
But his heavenly and divine,	208	J. Danvers D	11
Thy teares not needing. For that hand Divine	213	Bohemia D	63
when he is to read divine services, composeth himselfe to all	231	Priest 6	1
instructed his people how to carry themselves in divine service,	231	Priest 6	22
Then having read divine Service twice fully, and preached in	236	Priest 8	7
without disturbance, or interruption of publick divine offices.	236	Priest 8	25
or in time of divine service on other holy days, except in the cases	248	Priest 14	3
and a recreation to more divine studies, Nature serving Grace both in	261	Priest 23	11
to disable themselves from a fit discharging either of Divine duties,	266	Priest 26	30
either of Abstinence a morall vertue, or Mortification a divine.	267	Priest 26	17
to church, or for disorderly carriage in time of divine service.	270	Priest 29	6
that this suit and contention was raised by the Divine Providence,	294	Cornaro	24
amongst all divine and spirituall exercises and duties,	311	Valdesso V	3
like to that of the Jewes, which they added to their divine law.	320	Valdesso	4
Divine ashes are better then earthly meale.	344	Proverbs	684
Divine grace was never slow.	345	Proverbs	710
DIVINER			
But thy diviner world of grace	56	Temper 2	6
DIVINES			
Must all be vail'd, while he that reades, divines,	56	Jordan 1	9
How the godly are exempt from Laws is a known point among Divines,	316	Valdesso	31
Divines hold, that justifying faith, and the faith of miracles are	319	Valdesso	6
DIVINITIE			
Divinitie.	134	Divinitie	T
DIVINITIE'S			
Divinities transcendent skie:	134	Divinitie	6
DIVINITY			
and body of Divinity, which is the storehouse of his Sermons,	230	Priest 5	1
the Church Catechisme, to which all divinity may easily be reduced.	230	Priest 5	9
nature is towards Philosophy, the Catechism is towards Divinity.	256	Priest 21	27
As for better Books of Divinity, they are not in this Consideration,	276	Priest 32	35
Just so it is in Divinity, and that not without manifest reason:	278	Priest 33	32
how he that would beleeve a Divinity, if he had been at the Creation	281	Priest 34	28
though unused a proof of Divinity taken from thence, that	281	Priest 34	33
which evidently argue Christs Divinity by their success:	282	Priest 34	23
saw not more Divinity, then he that reads the womans oyntment in	283	Priest 34	1
how I am now setting foot into Divinity, to lay the platform of my	364	Letters	12
what is that to those infinite Volumes of Divinity, which yet every	365	Letters	14
First, the Bulk of Divinity.	365	Letters	16
since this place being civil may divert me too much from Divinity,	370	Letters	20
DIVISIONS			
With curious questions and divisions?	134	Divinitie	12
As neither good, nor one: so oft divisions	147	Offering	14

DO (see also doe)

	PAGE	TITLE		LINE
Who fears to do ill, sets himself to task:	11	Ch.-Porch		125
Who fears to do well, sure should wear a mask.	11	Ch.-Porch		126
Carve, or discourse; do not a famine fear.	11	Ch.-Porch		129
About thy neck do drown thee? raise thy head;	13	Ch.-Porch		170
Do fortunes seek, when worth and service fail,	14	Ch.-Porch		182
Say not then, This with that lace will do well;	14	Ch.-Porch		189
By great deeds shew, that thou canst little do;	15	Ch.-Porch		220
And do them not: that shall thy wisdome be;	15	Ch.-Porch		221
When basenesse is exalted, do not bate	17	Ch.-Porch		265
When base men are exalted, do not bate	17	Ch.-Porch	W	265
What to ask further. Doubts well rais'd do lock	18	Ch.-Porch		299
What to ask farther. Doubts well rais'd do lock	18	Ch.-Porch	W	299
And give men turns of speech: do not forestall	18	Ch.-Porch		303
Sundaies observe: think when the bells do chime,	22	Ch.-Porch		387
God calleth preaching folly. Do not grudge	23	Ch.-Porch		429
Though God do hedge us in, yet who is holy?	24	Ch.-Porch		450
And in the morning, what thou hast to do.	24	Ch.-Porch		452
If thou do ill; the joy fades, not the pains:	24	Ch.-Porch		461
Against their Maker: they do wish me dead,	26	Sacrifice		6
How with their lanterns do they seek the sunne!	27	Sacrifice		35
Why, he that built the world can do much more:	28	Sacrifice		67
Which I do give them daily, unto death.	28	Sacrifice		70
Herod and all his bands do set me light,	29	Sacrifice		77
Herod in judgement sits, while I do stand;	29	Sacrifice		81
In him to do themselves a courtesie:	30	Sacrifice		114
Then for thy passion - I will do for that -	36	Thanksgvng		49
Into the conquest. Though I can do nought	37	Reprisall		14
Into thy conquest, though I can do nought	37	Reprisall	W	14
Yet do we still persist as we began,	41	Sepulchre		21
O blessed streams! either ye do prevent	44	H. Bapt.1		7
That thou hast ought to do with me.	45	Nature		3
Now I am here, what thou wilt do with me	48	Afflict.1		55
I do confesse	49	Repentance		16
May no lines passe, except they do their dutie	56	Jordan 1		4
This verse marks that, and both do make a motion	58	H.Script.2		5
Then as dispersed herbs do watch a potion,	58	H.Script.2		7
Thy words do finde me out, & parallels bring,	58	H.Script.2		11
Starres are poore books, & oftentimes do misse:	58	H.Script.2		13
I will do more.	61	Praise 1		8
He may do more.	61	Praise 1		12
They can do more.	61	Praise 1		16
As if that thou hadst nothing els to do?	62	Mattens		12
Do end in bubbles, balls of winde;	64	Even-song		14
Deare flesh, while I do pray, learn here thy stemme	65	Ch.-monum.		17
Sure I shall do so, and much more:	66	Ch.-mus.		10
So I do lay the want of my desire,	66	Ch.-lock		7
And sanctif'd me to do good;	68	Trin.Sun.		3
Peace mutt'ring thoughts, and do not grudge to keep	68	Content		1
Do not thy self or friends importune.	69	Content		34
Lord, in my silence how do I despise	71	Frailtie		1
Whom others faults do not defeat;	73	Constancie		29
Do I forbear to crave your speciall aid:	78	Ang.&Sts.		7
Whom we do all joyntly adore and praise,	78	Ang.&Sts.		17
Who do not so;	78	Ang.&Sts.		28
Before we do our wares unfold:	79	Employm.2		28
O do not use me	83	Sighs & Gr.		1
O do not bruise me!	83	Sighs & Gr.		6
O do not urge me!	83	Sighs & Gr.		7
O do not scourge me!	83	Sighs & Gr.		12
O do not blinde me!	83	Sighs & Gr.		13
O do not grinde me!	83	Sighs & Gr.		18
O do not fill me	83	Sighs & Gr.		19
O do not kill me!	83	Sighs & Gr.		24
My words & thoughts do both expresse this notion,	84	Coloss.		1
In both let's do our best.	87	Lent		36
While they do wound and prick my soul.	90	Afflict.4		12
While they do wound and pinke my soul.	90	Afflict.4	W	12
For us the windes do blow,	91	Man		25
And we do crouch.	93	Antiphon 2		18
I do resume my sight,	95	Submission		10
Do not so well agree.	95	Submission		16
Onely do thou lend me a hand,	95	Submission		19
For, I do praise thee, yet I praise thee not:	96	Justice 1		8
I would do well, yet sinne the hand hath got:	96	Justice 1		10
When waves do rise, and tempests rage.	97	Afflict.5		6
Which do consigne and send them unto death.	98	Mortific.		6
And calls for musick, while his veins do swell,	98	Mortific.		14
Till all do melt, and drown his breath	98	Mortific.		27
Do pinch and straiten thee, and use much art	99	Decay		14
As flames do work and winde, when they ascend,	103	Jordan 2		13
By it do all things live their measur'd houre:	103	Prayer 2		10
By it do all things live their silly houre:	103	Prayer 2	W	10
If this poore paper do as much as they.	104	Obedience		5
To which I do agree,	104	Obedience		9
Peace pratler, do not lowre:	105	Conscience		1
I do but taste it, straight it cleanseth me,	106	Conscience		15
My flesh and bones and joynts do pray:	109	Home		74
Whose flat delights on earth do creep and grow;	111	Vanitie 2		2
Heark and beware, lest what you now do measure	111	Vanitie 2		5
Do not by hanging down break from the hand,	112	Dawning		11

DO (cont'd)

	PAGE	TITLE		LINE
Do amount to, onely he,	114	Dialogue		14
Why do I languish thus, drooping and dull,	115	Dulnesse		1
To hold my quill? shall they not do thee right?	116	Providence		4
And hold it fast, as children do their fathers,	118	Providence		46
Others do sleep, and envie not their cheer.	118	Providence		56
Rain, do not hurt my flowers; but gently spend	120	Providence		117
My hands do joyn to finish the inventions.	122	Sinnes rd.		12
My hands do joyn to finish the inventions:	122	Sinnes rd.		13
Twentie for one too sharp do finde it.	122	Time		6
What do I here before his doore?	123	Time		29
For they that taste it do rehearse,	125	Peace		33
With so much earnestnesse you do pursue,	125	Peace		41
The clearest diamond: let them do their best,	126	Confession		29
Indeed 'tis true. I did and do commit	129	Love unkn.		19
My heart, that brought it (do you understand?)	130	Love unkn.		36
Heark, how the birds do sing,	131	Mans medly		1
And woods do ring.	131	Mans medly		2
Both frosts and thoughts do nip,	131	Mans medly		28
Do flie and flow,	132	The Storm		2
What do I see	133	The Method		13
Who do not their own motions heare?	134	The Method		19
Do as ye would be done unto.	135	Divinitie		18
What do these loud complaints and pulling fears,	136	Familie		3
What do these loud complaints and puling fears,	136	Familie	V	3
But little do reserve themselves for more:	138	The Size		20
Do seem to equally divide,	138	The Size		35
Which thou hast open'd: do not spread thy robe	138	The Size		43
Do as thou usest, disobey,	139	Artillerie		6
For I will do, or suffer what I ought.	139	Artillerie		16
My tears and prayers night and day do wooe,	139	Artillerie		19
Much more oblig'd to do thy will,	139	Artillerie		22
Where rude unhallow'd steps do crush and grinde	140	Ch.-rents		8
Do not beguile my heart,	143	Complaining		1
And do encroach upon deaths side.	145	Discharge		35
On future grief, do not remove it thence,	145	Discharge		43
Do not forecast.	145	Discharge		52
Since many gifts do challenge many hearts!	147	Offering		8
Thousands of things do thee employ	158	Praise 3		19
I do not greatly wonder at the sight,	161	Priesthood		23
In praising might, the poore do by submission	161	Priesthood		41
East and West touch, the poles do kisse,	163	The Search		43
What I would do for thee, if once my grones	165	The Crosse		15
These arms shall crush thee. Spare not, do thy worst.	169	Dial.-Anth		8
If troubles overtake thee, do not wail:	170	Water-crs.		4
Sure I will do the like.	171	Bittersweet		4
But lives in me while I do rest)	174	Aaron		24
So do these words a sweet content,	174	The Odour		4
With these all day I do perfume my minde,	175	The Odour		6
Love will do the deed:	179	Discipline		18
Ah Lord! do not withdraw,	183	A Parodie		16
And what I do in any thing,	184	The Elixer		3
To do it as for thee:	184	The Elixer		4
For we do now behold thee gay and glad,	186	Death		17
What others mean to do, I know not well;	187	Judgement		6
Much more do Common-weals acknowledge thee,	190	Ch.-Milit.		5
Onely the West and Rome do keep them free	194	Ch.-Milit.		157
Europe alone and Rome do keep them free	194	Ch.-Milit.	W	157
Till such a darknesse do the world invade	196	Ch.-Milit.		230
Thus do both lights, as well in Church as Sunne,	197	Ch.-Milit.		270
do thou to us afford.	217	Psalm IV	D	24
Thou hat'st those that unjustly do:	218	Psalm V	D	13
their flattering tongues do fain.	219	Psalm V	D	28
Let them that do thy name adore	219	Psalm V	D	39
he do devour my soul:	221	Psalm VII	D	6
that do his justice slight.	222	Psalm VII	D	40
if a man do not all which is here expressed, hee presently sinns,	224	Priest		10
in that a Priest may do that which Christ did, and by his auctority,	225	Priest 1		16
in that a Priest is to do that which Christ did, and after his	225	Priest 1		18
he that ruleth, let him do it with diligence, &c.	226	Priest 2		7
as many of them do, and because they have different Names,	226	Priest 2		20
They who do not thus, while they remember their earthly Lord,	226	Priest 2		31
they remember their earthly Lord, do much forget their heavenly;	226	Priest 2		32
Countrey people (as indeed all honest men) do much esteem their word,	228	Priest 3		2
that if any do Gods will, he shall know of the Doctrine,	228	Priest 4		28
do not know the Scriptures, because they feel them not,	228	Priest 4		30
or kneel, to do all in a strait, and steady posture, as attending	231	Priest 6		26
but even to let the world sinke, so they do their duty;	232	Priest 6		17
Oh let us all take heed what we do, God sees us, he sees whether I	234	Priest 7		27
to his earthly, having no title to either, except he do good to both.	239	Priest 10		22
and somtimes giving them a little mony to do it of themselves,	239	Priest 10		27
which happily for his other children he is not able to do.	239	Priest 10		33
prentices (in case he think fit to do so) he takes care not to put	239	Priest 10		34
servants, both because they do best, and because what they do,	240	Priest 10		15
both because they do best, and because what they do, is blessed,	240	Priest 10		16
and doing that which either he could not do, or was not fit for him	241	Priest 10		32
or was not fit for him to do, by taking both sorts of food into them,	241	Priest 10		33
do as it were dresse and prepare both for man in themselves,	241	Priest 10		33
For it is as unnatural to do any thing, that leads me to a sicknesse,	242	Priest 10		36
some of his Parish, hee taketh his times to do the like to the rest;	243	Priest 11		18
and others spurred to do well, that they may enjoy the like	243	Priest 11		27

DO (cont'd)	PAGE	TITLE	LINE
he bethinketh himselfe what good deeds he can do that day,	244	Priest 12	17
and wishing them ever to do the Cures with their own hands,	247	Priest 14	19
it is a good and just thing for every one to do their own busines.	247	Priest 14	22
when on the Lords day they do unnecessary servile work,	248	Priest 14	2
may have wherewithall to serve God the better, and to do good deeds.	248	Priest 14	8
he also urgeth them to do some pious charitable works, as a necessary	249	Priest 15	32
but the earnestnesse to do all the good he can, moves him to say thus	251	Priest 17	32
such as are every way fitting to do his Countrey true and laudable	252	Priest 19	28
To do otherwise, is deceit;	252	Priest 19	29
that we should do whatsoever things are honest, or just,	253	Priest 19	23
as an obligation to do good, rather then to those that are further,	253	Priest 19	26
telling him when he hath forgotten it, This I do, because at such,	254	Priest 20	17
He asked him again, what he would do, if he were in a ditch?	257	Priest 21	4
and to do such things of legall opposition either in the presenting,	263	Priest 25	23
but proceeding on, comes to do unlawfully, even before he is aware;	264	Priest 26	23
if I do not give every thing its end, I abuse the Creature,	265	Priest 26	9
and those more which concerne me, I either do nothing, or pinch,	265	Priest 26	17
and that pleasantnesse of disposition is a great key to do good;	268	Priest 27	1
contempt shall proceed so far as to do any thing punishable by law,	268	Priest 28	31
punishable by law, as contempt is apt to do, if it be not thwarted,	268	Priest 28	32
in a doctrinall way, saying to the contemner, Alas, why do you thus?	269	Priest 28	12
of his Conscience, whereas they are to do it by Command, and by Oath.	269	Priest 29	31
urges the best unto it, shewing that they do not loose, or go lesse,	270	Priest 29	9
the greatest honor of this world, to do God and his chosen service;	270	Priest 29	10
Do well, and right, and let the world sinke.	270	Priest 29	23
so that though the corn do grow, and be preserved in that act by his	271	Priest 30	15
and when for all that they do come, he be a little affected	273	Priest 31	18
either for fear or shame, break his custome, he shall do passing ill:	273	Priest 31	31
For when men have nothing to do, then they fall to drink,	274	Priest 32	11
say they, we have nothing to do, lets go to the Tavern,	274	Priest 32	13
and who is ready to ask, if he shall mend shoos, or what he shall do?	275	Priest 32	8
and house-keeper hath his hands full, if he do what he ought to do.	275	Priest 32	20
and house-keeper hath his hands full, if he do what he ought to do.	275	Priest 32	21
of his affairs, that hee may have wherewithall to do good.	275	Priest 32	30
inabling him with power to do good, and to restrain all those,	276	Priest 32	14
the Baptist squared out to every one (even to Souldiers) what to do.	277	Priest 32	24
and particularly do it, then he that is generally learned,	278	Priest 33	28
lest their quiet betray them (as it is apt to do) to a coldnesse,	280	Priest 34	18
sea rage so much as it can, and all things do what they can, and all,	281	Priest 34	22
but is rather glad of catching opportunities to do them.	284	Priest 35	26
do so either out of niceness, because they like the salutations,	285	Priest 36	4
for we must not do evill, that good may come of it.	287	Priest 37	7
may talk, so they do it not with sport, but commiseration;)	287	Priest 37	13
whom the Law would have defamed, except he also do it out of rancour.	287	Priest 37	29
it is a duty rather, which may do much good, and save much harme.	288	Priest 37	1
did the Lord of life, unable of himselfe to die, contrive to do it.	288	Priest	28
and do so for thy blessed Son's sake, in whose sweet and pleasing	289	Priest	34
and saw that it was no hard thing to do so, but the proper duty	292	Cornaro	32
which excesse of joy neither could do me any hurt.	294	Cornaro	30
lesse then otherwise they should do) then alwayes to live under bit	298	Cornaro	28
All these things I do at my ease, and at fit seasons, and in mine own	301	Cornaro	9
By doing nothing we learne to do ill.	346	Proverbs	757
Wee leave more to do when wee dye, then wee have done.	353	Proverbs	972
The words ending in Ique do mocke the Physician	357	Proverbs	D 1044
He that will do thee a good turne, either he will be gon or dye.	358	Proverbs	D 1083
Those that God loves, do not live long.	358	Proverbs	D 1094
We do it soon enough, if that we do be well.	359	Proverbs	D 1109
of thanks for the diversity of your favours, if I sought to do so;	363	Letters	16
neither do I make any question, but that you have performed your	363	Letters	23
on Fridayes and Saturdayes, I must do so, which yet sometimes I fast.	365	Letters	5
by the Patents of your perpetual favour to do so still,	365	Letters	25
which she hath hitherto deferred to do, not of her self,	367	Letters	4
opinion of him, that if he can do me a courtesie, he will of himself;	369	Letters	22
it will do well, for it expresseth the Universities inclination	369	Letters	26
So that now if they do not well the falt cannot be charg'd on you;	373	Letters	15
you take her not, I am thinking to do it, even beyond my strengthe;	375	Letters	35
be none of the Court-stile, yet doubtless Madam, can do you no hurt:	377	Letters	3
but he told her Grace, that he would by no meanes do so, urging,	379	Letters	7
DO'ST			
Thou do'st no more, then doth the grave:	202	love	W 22
DOCTOR			
After Death the Doctor.	356	Proverbs	D 1037
DOCTORS			
he takes place next the Doctors, is at all their Assemblies	370	Letters	1
DOCTRINALL			
or else in a doctrinall way, saying to the contemner, Alas,	269	Priest 28	12
But the use of the Doctrinall part is more, in regard it presents us	310	Valdesso	32
DOCTRINE			
Comforts not me, and doth my doctrine stain:	27	Sacrifice	31
Doctrine and life, colours and light, in one	68	Windows	11
But all the doctrine, which he taught and gave,	135	Divinitie	13
My doctrine tun'd by Christ, (who is not dead,	174	Aaron	23
which Christ did, and after his manner, both for Doctrine and Life.	225	Priest 1	19
he shall know of the Doctrine, John 7. and assuring himself,	228	Priest 4	29
there are such conceits, there is no room for his doctrine to enter.	243	Priest 11	24
He exacts of all the Doctrine of the Catechisme;	255	Priest 21	22
familiar things hee might make his Doctrine slip the more easily into	261	Priest 23	19
chiefly considered) might have every where monuments of his Doctrine,	261	Priest 23	22
that God cannot be wanting to them in Doctrine, to whom he is so	263	Priest 24	20
As when the people hungred and thirsted after our Saviours Doctrine,	267	Priest 26	23

DOCTRINE (cont'd)	PAGE	TITLE		LINE
Now because the onely opposer to this Doctrine is the Gallant,	275	Priest 32		6
The Doctrine of the last passage must be warily understood.	308	Valdesso		1
The Doctrine of this Consideration cleareth that of the precedent	310	Valdesso		26
but the truth of the Doctrine would be examined, however it may passe	312	Valdesso		1
This doctrine however true in substance, yet needeth [requireth]	314	Valdesso		1
this cannot stand, and it is ill Doctrine in a common-wealth.	316	Valdesso		17
DOCTRINES				
When doctrines disagree.	86	Lent		9
Through th' old sinnes and new doctrines of our land.	161	Priesthood		33
for life, Doctrines for knowledge, Examples for illustration,	228	Priest 4		24
In the Scripture are Doctrines, these ever teach more and more.	310	Valdesso		13
DOCTRINS				
Who brought his doctrins & his deeds from Rome	195	Ch.-Milit.	W	201
The waight was such they left the doctrins there	196	Ch.-Milit.	W	203
if there be any of his parish that hold strange Doctrins,	262	Priest 24		20
DOE				
If it concurr with vertue: doe thy best	7	Ch.-Porch	W	21
Some great estates provide, but doe not breed	10	Ch.-Porch		103
Be sure to doe it, though it be but small:	11	Ch.-Porch		116
Doe all things like a man, not sneakingly:	11	Ch.-Porch		121
But not their harts, as I by proofe doe try.	30	Sacrifice	W	123
Sinn being gone o doe thou fill	39	Good Fri.	W	29
As larks, doe by degree,	43	East.wings	W	8
You doe prevent most sins & for the rest	44	H. Bapt.1	W	6
And mend as rising starres & rivers doe.	44	H. Bapt.1	W	9
It may doe more.	61	Praise 1	W	16
Who doe no more.	61	Praise 1	W	20
Arise sad heart; if thou doe not withstand,	112	Dawning	V	9
Doe winde a rope about, and cut my heart:	165	The Crosse		33
How neatly doe we give one onely name	168	The Sonne		5
All things I doe to thee	184	The Elixer	W	2
Or whether Bread doe fly away	200	H. Commun.	W	8
Doe owe the symbole of their certainty.	439	Walton 5		8
Doe ruine thee; or if the teares	208	H. Danvers	D	6
Wheare health hath nought to doe;	210	Paradox	D	14
Not from excesse, and therefore doe we spende	210	Paradox	D	21
That which wee doe not neede:	210	Paradox	D	22
And starres alone unto the pitch doe runne	211	Bohemia	D	4
Mee thinkes, in that Dutch optick I doe see	211	Bohemia	D	13
Addes to the union, as lights doe gather	212	Bohemia	D	36
errand I come, let me hold my peace, and doe thou speak thy selfe;	233	Priest 7		36
his flock by themselves, whom his Sermons cannot, or doe not reach.	236	Priest 8		13
therefore doe thou fulfill what thou didst appoint;	257	Priest 22		33
because I would doe nothing negligently that you commit unto mee;	304	Valdesso		5
for which I doe so love him, that were there nothing else,	305	Valdesso		6
And in so doing they doe not sever their trust from God.	307	Valdesso		2
so are wee to doe with the Scriptures and this is the use	310	Valdesso		30
us not with the same thing only when it is read as the promises doe,	310	Valdesso		34
and that no other sin or vertue hath any thing to doe with us;	311	Valdesso		24
but because he cannot doe all, God often chuseth which he shall doe,	313	Valdesso		21
God often chuseth which he shall doe, and that by restraining him	313	Valdesso		22
and that by restraining him from what he would not have him doe.	313	Valdesso		23
when they doe amisse, and they are to be judged according	316	Valdesso		18
Neither doe I doubt but if Abraham had lived in our Kingdome under	316	Valdesso		22
How many places doe the Fathers bring about Untill against	318	Valdesso		9
I doe not then bid him goe away but rather stay longer,	318	Valdesso		15
that I may speak with him or doe some thing else when I doe come.	318	Valdesso		16
that I may speak with him or doe some thing else when I doe come.	318	Valdesso		17
point it should, which if it did, it would doe more, then it does.	319	Valdesso		11
Who would doe ill ne're wants occasion.	324	Proverbs		116
It costs more to doe ill then to doe well.	329	Proverbs		262
should doe what he doth not.	340	Proverbs		559
must doe what he doth not.	340	Proverbs	V	559
Better suffer ill, then doe ill.	346	Proverbs		770
The best of the sport is to doe the deede, and say nothing.	348	Proverbs		812
If thou thy selfe canst doe it, attend no others helpe or hand.	348	Proverbs		813
Doe what thou oughtest, and come what come can.	348	Proverbs		818
It's more paine to doe nothing then something.	350	Proverbs		884
Thornes whiten yet doe nothing.	352	Proverbs		943
which he refusing to doe hath given her occasion to protest shee will	368	Letters		21
am glad that although you offer more, yet you will doe, as you write,	375	Letters		7
them know your love, for which both they shall, and I doe, thank you.	375	Letters		22
having none to doe it but her school-mistresse, and you know what	375	Letters		25
doe that which GOD shall put into your hart, and the LORD bless all	375	Letters		33
I forgett all thinges, so I may doe them good who want it.	376	Letters		6
So I doe my part to them, lett them think of me what they will	376	Letters		6
a long time, to doe the place good, & have endeavoured many wayes,	378	Letters		6
(& promising to get her Son to doe as much) with some little Apology	379	Letters		3
I heard from you, that I long to heare both how you and your's doe:	379	Letters		24
only for the success (as assistance of Sir John) doe as David did:	380	Woodnoth		23
that (which you are thinking to doe) to blessed Mary Magd. & Paul,	381	Woodnoth		4
6. you doe not want all success.	381	Woodnoth		7
& if upon your withdrawing it shold doe so, it would trouble your	381	Woodnoth		12
To desire good & endeavour it when we can doe no more, is to doe it.	381	Woodnoth		15
To desire good & endeavour it when we can doe no more, is to doe it.	381	Woodnoth		16
Doe this & be a man as David, after Gods hart.	381	Woodnoth		20
work rather then doe nothing.	381	Woodnoth		24
body to Almightie God that made them doe thus dispose of my goods.	382	G.H.'s Will		2
we have as much failed, as your Excellencies doe excel, in both.	442	Oration		34
Yet doe not yee contemne these our slight glories, which wee raise	442	Oration		38

	PAGE	TITLE	LINE
DOORE (cont'd)			
That ev'ry man may revell at his doore,	87	Lent	46
And thou within them starve at doore.	93	Unkindness	14
What do I here before his doore?	123	Time	29
Perpetuall knockings at thy doore,	124	Gratefulnes	13
Dares to assault thee, and besiege thy doore.	132	The Storm	12
When sawcie mirth shall knock or call at doore,	136	Ephes.	13
Humble Obedience neare the doore doth stand,	137	Familie	13
Will use me in this kinde, the doore	152	The Bag	38
What is thy aim? wouldst thou unlock the doore	155	Assurance	15
Can hale or draw it out of doore.	158	Praise 3	16
Let a bleak palenesse chalk the doore,	177	Forerunners	35
Onely, most noble Lord, shutt not the doore	209	L. Bacon D	9
The Devill is not alwaies at one doore.	322	Proverbs	31
The back-doore robs the house.	337	Proverbs	474
When you enter into a house, leave the anger ever at the doore.	350	Proverbs	896
An old mans staffe is the rapper of deaths doore.	351	Proverbs	916
When a Lackey comes to hells doore, the devills locke the gates.	353	Proverbs	984
Who will make a doore of gold must knock a naile every day.	354	Proverbs	1004
DOORES			
He breaks up house, turns out of doores his minde.	12	Ch.-Porch	150
Those doores being shut, all by the eare comes in.	23	Ch.-Porch	418
As Sampson bore the doores away,	76	Sunday	47
Of stews and brothels onely knew the doores,	176	Forerunners	15
Knocking at all doores, ever as she went.	190	Ch.-Milit.	30
Statesmen within, without doores cloisterers:	195	Ch.-Milit.	200
Fine dressing is a foule house swept before the doores.	329	Proverbs	243
The greatest step is that out of doores.	337	Proverbs	461
give all my goods both within doores and without doores both monneys	382	G.H.'s Will	3
goods both within doores and without doores both monneys and bookes	382	G.H.'s Will	4
DORE			
On Sunday heavens dore stands ope;	76	Sunday W	33
DORES			
Noble houskeepers neede no dores.	324	Proverbs	91
to be without dores with him, is no ill company.	381	Woodnoth	3
DOROTHY			
death of my deare Neece Mrs Dorothy Vaughan whereof two hundred	382	G.H.'s Will	10
DOST			
When thou dost tell anothers jest, therein	9	Ch.-Porch	61
When thou dost purpose ought within thy power,	11	Ch.-Porch	115
Dost lose? rise up: dost winne? rise in that state.	14	Ch.-Porch	201
The shrine is that which thou dost venerate;	17	Ch.-Porch	267
For so thou dost thy self and him a pleasure:	18	Ch.-Porch	296
Judas, dost thou betray me with a kisse?	28	Sacrifice	41
The sonne, in whom thou dost delight to be?	33	Sacrifice	214
My God, my God, why dost thou part from me?	35	Thanksgvng	9
If thou dost give me wealth, I will restore	35	Thanksgvng	19
If thou dost give me honour, men shall see,	35	Thanksgvng	21
Thus dost thou make proud knowledge bend & crouch	50	Faith	31
Thus dost thou make proud knowledge bow & crouch	50	Faith W	31
To me dost now thy self convey;	52	H.Commun.	4
Wilt thou meet arms with man, that thou dost stretch	55	Temper 1	13
Thou suddenly dost raise and race,	56	Temper 2	7
For when thou dost depart from hence,	56	Temper 2	11
For as thou dost impart thy grace,	57	Employm. 1	9
O come! for thou dost know the way.	61	Grace	21
Thou dost inclose us, till the day	64	Even-song	22
Yet in thy temple thou dost him afford	67	Windows	3
But when thou dost anneal in glasse thy storie,	67	Windows	6
To endlesse death: but thou dost pull	75	Sunday	16
Therefore thou dost not show	82	Ungratef.	15
Lord thou dost deserve much more.	93	Antiphon 2 W	19
Lord, thou dost wound me, yet thou dost relieve me:	95	Justice 1	3
Lord, thou dost kill me, yet thou dost reprieve me.	95	Justice 1	5
A poore mans rod, when thou dost ride,	96	Charms & K	3
But now thou dost thy self immure and close	99	Decay	11
Not a fair look, but thou dost call it foul:	105	Conscience	2
Not a sweet dish, but thou dost call it sowre:	105	Conscience	3
While thou dost ever, ever stay:	107	Home	2
But thou dost still lament, and pine, and crie;	112	Dawning	7
Arise sad heart; if thou dost not withstand,	112	Dawning	9
The very dust, where thou dost tread and go,	115	Dulnesse	15
Who dost so strongly and so sweetly move,	117	Providence	31
How finely dost thou times and seasons spin,	118	Providence	57
If they seek fine things, thou dost make them run	120	Providence	106
For their offence; and then dost turn their speed	120	Providence	107
Sometimes thou dost divide thy gifts to man,	120	Providence	125
Sweet Peace, where dost thou dwell? I humbly crave,	124	Peace	1
When thou dost greater judgements SPARE,	133	Paradise	10
Quickly effect, what thou dost move;	133	The Method	6
Descend and fall, and thou dost flow.	137	The Size	6
And work up to thee; yet thou dost refuse.	139	Artillerie	20
Then we are shooters both, and thou dost deigne	139	Artillerie	25
Why dost thou prie,	144	Discharge	2
Lord thou dost convert,	147	Offering	27
Which thou dost curse.	148	Longing	9
And dost dispose	148	Longing	15
And fall to nothing: thou dost reigne,	150	Longing	56
And thou with me dost thee restore.	157	Clasping	8
When thou dost favour any action,	158	Praise 3	7
When thou dost blesse, hath twelve: one wheel doth rise	158	Praise 3	11

DOST (cont'd)	PAGE	TITLE		LINE
But when thou dost on businesse blow,	158	Praise 3		13
Blest Order, which in power dost so excell,	160	Priesthood		1
Lord, dost thou some new fabrick mold,	162	The Search		25
When thou dost turn, and wilt be neare;	163	The Search		53
When thou dost turn,	166	The Flower		34
Thou who dost dwell and linger here below,	170	Water-crs.		1
Since thou dost love, yet strike;	171	Bittersweet		2
Nay, thou dost make me sit and dine,	173	23 Psalme		17
Because thou dost abide with me,	183	A Parodie		4
Yet when thou dost suppresse	183	A Parodie		6
And when thou dost but shine lesse cleare,	183	A Parodie		19
Thou com'st and dost relieve.	184	A Parodie		30
My God, thou dost prepare for them a way	197	Ch.-Milit.		249
Thou dost come first to them, that showes	200	H. Commun.	W	14
If thou dost find an house built to thy mind	207	Walton 4		1
Why dost thou preach my Laws, and takest my Covenant in thy mouth?	226	Priest 2		13
Thou hast death in thy house, and dost bewaile anothers.	334	Proverbs		376
DOTAGE				
Dotage.	167	Dotage		T
DOTH				
Beware of lust: it doth pollute and foul	6	Ch.-Porch		7
But gladly welcome what he doth afford;	7	Ch.-Porch		15
The drunkard forfets Man, and doth devest	7	Ch.-Porch		35
Wine above all things doth Gods stamp deface.	8	Ch.-Porch		48
He makes flat warre with God, and doth defie	8	Ch.-Porch		53
Thou liv'st by rule. What doth not so, but man?	12	Ch.-Porch		134
Salute thy self: see what thy soul doth wear.	12	Ch.-Porch		146
In clothes, cheap handsomnesse doth bear the bell.	14	Ch.-Porch		187
Onely a herauld, who that way doth passe,	14	Ch.-Porch		197
That temper gives them theirs, and yet doth take	16	Ch.-Porch		254
Doth ratably thy fortunes marre or make.	16	Ch.-Porch		256
Doth make thee parcell-devil in damnation.	16	Ch.-Porch		258
Truth dwels not in the clouds: that Bow doth hit	19	Ch.-Porch	W	317
Doth often aim at, never hit the sphere.	19	Ch.-Porch		318
The cunning workman never doth refuse	20	Ch.-Porch		353
All forrain wisdome doth amount to this,	20	Ch.-Porch		355
A joy for it worth worlds. Thus hell doth jest	23	Ch.-Porch		412
If well; the pain doth fade, the joy remains.	24	Ch.-Porch		462
Thy pow'r doth cut.	26	The Altar		8
Without me each one, who doth now me brave,	27	Sacrifice		9
Comforts not me, and doth my doctrine stain:	27	Sacrifice		31
My silence rather doth augment their crie;	29	Sacrifice		93
My dove doth back into my bosome flie,	29	Sacrifice		94
But I the Prince of peace; peace that doth passe	30	Sacrifice		118
All understanding, more then heav'n doth glasse:	30	Sacrifice		119
For these are all the grapes Sion doth bear,	31	Sacrifice		162
In healing not my self, there doth consist	34	Sacrifice		225
Your safetie in my sicknesse doth subsist:	34	Sacrifice		227
The honour doth belong to thee.	35	Thanksgvng		22
That honour doth belong to thee.	35	Thanksgvng	W	22
The which to measure it doth more behove:	37	The Agonie		5
That as each beast his cure doth know,	39	Good Fri.		19
One box doth lie both ink and sinne:	39	Good Fri.		24
Thus doth thy power crosse-bias me, not making	48	Afflict.1		53
Each day doth round about us see.	48	Repentance		8
One size doth all conditions fit.	50	Faith		28
While mortall love doth all the title gain!	54	Love 1		5
Doth warm our hands, and make them write of love.	54	Love 1		14
If what my soul doth feel sometimes,	55	Temper 1		3
If as a flowre doth spread and die,	57	Employm. 1		1
As is the dust, to which that life doth tend,	57	Employm. 1		15
Seeing not onely how each verse doth shine,	58	H.Script.2		3
Unto a third, that ten leaves off doth lie:	58	H.Script.2		6
Doth my dull husbandrie improve:	60	Grace		2
The dew doth ev'ry morning fall;	60	Grace		9
Saying to man, It doth suffice:	64	Even-song		19
Which dissolution sure doth best discern,	65	Ch.-monum.		10
More rev'rend grows, & more doth win:	67	Windows		9
Doth vanish like a flaring thing,	68	Windows		14
Doth vanish like a flaming thing,	68	Windows	V	14
To court each place or fortune that doth fall,	68	Content		7
Mark how the fire in flints doth quiet lie,	68	Content		9
Mark how the fire in Flint doth quiet lie,	68	Content	W	9
This soul doth span the world, and hang content	69	Content		17
In all, I think my foot doth ever tread	71	Frailtie		7
And ever as I walk my foot doth tredd	71	Frailtie	W	7
That which was dust before, doth quickly rise,	71	Frailtie		15
He that doth still and strongly good pursue,	72	Constancie		2
Nor seeks, nor shunnes them; but doth calmly stay,	72	Constancie		12
What place or person calls for, he doth pay.	72	Constancie		15
But though men fail him, yet his part doth play.	73	Constancie		30
Thy torch doth show the way.	75	Sunday		7
The which he doth not fill.	75	Sunday		21
On which heav'ens kingdome arch'd doth stand:	75	Sunday	W	23
How well her name an Army doth present,	77	Anagram		1
Who blows it not, nor doth controll	79	Employm.2		8
The other Hid and doth obliquely bend.	84	Coloss.		4
That none doth build a stately habitation,	90	Man		2
The earth doth rest, heav'n move, and fountains flow.	91	Man		26
He treads down that which doth befriend him,	92	Man		45

DOTH (cont'd)

	PAGE	TITLE		LINE
My soul doth love thee, yet it loves delay.	96	Justice 1		11
Who goes to bed and doth not pray,	96	Charms & K		7
The powder doth forget the dust.	96	Charms & K		14
In shallow waters heav'n doth show;	97	Charms & K		17
How soon doth man decay!	98	Mortific.		1
Doth closet up it self, and still retreat,	99	Decay		18
His house still burns, and yet he still doth sing,	100	Miserie		4
What strange pollutions doth he wed,	100	Miserie		13
Holds them unto it, and doth cover	100	Miserie		27
He doth not like this vertue, no;	101	Miserie		45
For this he wondrous well doth know	101	Miserie	W	45
But Man doth know	101	Miserie		59
On it my heart doth bleed	104	Obedience		6
As many lines, as there doth need	104	Obedience		7
And heart unto this deed, when he doth read	105	Obedience	W	38
Musick to thee doth howl.	105	Conscience		4
Great God doth fight, he doth submit.	106	Sion		16
Come Lord, my head doth burn, my heart is sick,	107	Home		1
When she doth write.	109	Brit. Ch.		6
Of dressing, that her hair doth lie	110	Brit. Ch.		20
That those thy form doth show,	115	Dulnesse		14
Man is the worlds high Priest: he doth present	117	Providence		13
He that to praise and laud thee doth refrain,	117	Providence		17
Doth not refrain unto himself alone,	117	Providence		18
And doth commit a world of sinne in one.	117	Providence		20
Nothing ingendred doth prevent his meat:	118	Providence		53
So both the flower doth stay, and hony run.	118	Providence		68
Nothing wears clothes, but Man; nothing doth need	120	Providence		109
The whey of milk doth loose, the milk doth binde.	120	Providence		132
Who wants the place, where God doth dwell,	123	Time		23
He doth not crave lesse time, but more.	123	Time		30
Doth shut them out, so that they cannot enter;	126	Confession		20
Doth give a hold and handle to affliction.	126	Confession		24
But he doth bid us take his bloud for wine.	135	Divinitie		21
To take and taste what he doth there designe,	135	Divinitie		23
Then weep mine eyes, the God of love doth grieve:	135	Ephes.		7
Almightie God doth grieve, he puts on sense:	136	Ephes.		16
But to my Gods too; he doth grone.	136	Ephes.		18
What doth this noise of thoughts within my heart	136	Familie		1
Humble Obedience neare the doore doth stand,	137	Familie		13
Nothing more quick when she doth go.	137	Familie		16
This is thy house, with these it doth abound:	137	Familie		21
At least in lump: for such doth oft destroy;	138	The Size		27
Doth tice us on to hopes of more,	138	The Size		29
A worm doth sit, whose many feet and hair	140	Ch.-rents		3
Why doth my Mother blush? is she the rose,	140	Ch.-rents		11
Dropping from heav'n, which doth both cleanse and close	147	Offering		20
Behold, thy dust doth stirre,	149	Longing		37
Away despair; my gracious Lord doth heare.	151	The Bag		1
He doth preserve it: he doth steer,	151	The Bag		3
Must let thee go, return when it doth knock.	154	Glimpse		22
Yet to be thine, doth me restore;	157	Clasping		4
When thou dost blesse, hath twelve: one wheel doth rise	158	Praise 3		11
Blest Order, which in power doth so excell,	160	Priesthood	V	1
Onely, since God doth often vessels make	161	Priesthood		34
Doth flatter power. Lest good come short of ill	161	Priesthood		40
For as thy absence doth excell	163	The Search		57
So doth thy nearenesse bear the bell,	163	The Search		59
Save in the sight thereof, where strength doth sting.	165	The Crosse		18
Ev'n when my will doth studie thy renown:	165	The Crosse		20
Nor doth my flower	166	The Flower		26
God doth supplie the want.	168	a true Hymn		18
And setling to a cloud, doth live and die	169	The Answer		11
He that doth love, and love amisse	170	Self-cond.		7
Thousands of souls it hath and doth destroy	170	Self-cond.		11
And he that doth me feed:	172	23 Psalme		2
Or if I stray, he doth convert	172	23 Psalme		9
How sweetly doth My Master sound! My Master!	174	The Odour		1
As plainly as that above doth show;	175	The Foil		3
So this flower doth judge and sentence	178	The Rose		25
Doth define,	180	Invitation		8
Doth arraigne,	180	Invitation		14
And on sinne doth cast the fright.	180	Invitation		18
Doth destroy,	180	Invitation		20
Sweetly he doth meet my taste.	182	Banquet		39
Doth me invade!	183	A Parodie		12
While Sinne doth rave,	183	A Parodie		22
Doth me infold!	184	A Parodie		27
For that which God doth touch and own	185	The Elixer		23
Thy flock doth stray.	187	Dooms-day		20
Go where it doth deserve.	189	Love 3		14
Which doth not meet with an eternall thought.	190	Ch.-Milit.		8
But above all, thy Church and Spouse doth prove	190	Ch.-Milit.		9
All, Emblems, which thy Darling doth improve.	190	Ch.-Milit.	W	16
And such poore game. Thence he to Greece doth passe,	193	Ch.-Milit.		123
And such small game. Thence he to Greece doth passe,	193	Ch.-Milit.	W	123
Thou do'st no more, then doth the grave:	202	love	W	22
The Bell doth tolle	204	The Knell	W	1
Doth wishly look	204	The Knell	W	3
As a burst fouling-peece doth save the birds	204	Persever.	W	7

DOTH (cont'd)	PAGE	TITLE		LINE
Besides their other flames? Doth Poetry	206	Walton 1		3
Why doth that fire, which by thy power and might	206	Walton 1		12
Cover the Earth, so doth thy Majesty:	206	Walton 2		3
Each Cloud distills thy praise, and doth forbid	206	Walton 2		4
Whose fire is wild, and doth not upward go	206	Walton 2		10
In his progenie doth shine.	208	J. Danvers	D	12
Doth for two clods of earth ten spheres controule,	211	Bohemia	D	8
Of thousand harts: that face doth figure thee	212	Bohemia	D	33
Yet hast thou more dominions: God doth give	212	Bohemia	D	41
that doth my head advance.	216	Psalm III	D	8
But know the Lord himself doth chuse	217	Psalm IV	D	11
For God doth righteous men esteem,	219	Psalm V	D	41
My beauty wears and doth decay	220	Psalm VI	D	17
God is my shield, who doth preserve	222	Psalm VII	D	37
The Parson doth not so, but orders his Life in such a fashion,	227	Priest 3		31
As he doth not so study others, as to neglect the grace of God in	229	Priest 4		19
so doth he assure himself, that God in all ages hath had his	229	Priest 4		21
and that as one Countrey doth not bear all things, that there may be	229	Priest 4		23
This he doth, first, as being truly touched and amazed	231	Priest 6		5
other spirituall wickednesses in high places doth the Parson fear,	238	Priest 9		20
means to continue so, he doth at least, as much as hath been said.	238	Priest 9		25
which doth lesse obstruct, then flesh moderately taken;	243	Priest 10		3
Yet doth hee oftenest invite those, whom hee sees take best courses,	243	Priest 11		24
himselfe what good deeds he can do that day, and presently doth them;	244	Priest 12		17
so doth he also to those at his door, whom God puts in his way,	245	Priest 12		19
So doth hee also before giving make them say their Prayers first,	245	Priest 12		34
And all this he doth, not as out of necessity, or as putting	246	Priest 13		23
Neither in this doth he forbear, though there be company by:	248	Priest 14		25
and so much the rather doth he so, as his accesse to the poor is more	249	Priest 14		7
The like he doth in the morning, using pleasantly the outlandish	251	Priest 17		13
But this he doth discretely, with mollifying, and suppling words;	252	Priest 18		7
And this hee doth, not onely for the benefit of the work,	259	Priest 22		23
he doth not onely prefer home-bred things before them, but condemns	261	Priest 23		36
neither doth he esteem him for an enemy, but as a brother still,	263	Priest 25		29
The Countrey Parson doth often, both publickly, and privately	269	Priest 29		26
so that corne doth not grow by any other vertue, then by that which	271	Priest 30		4
Now this he doth, that men should perpetuate, and not break off their	271	Priest 30		26
childe, or servant, as a Gardiner doth in a choice tree.	275	Priest 32		34
And it fares in this as it doth in Physick:	278	Priest 33		25
The like he doth in other Christian vertues, as of Faith,	279	Priest 33		33
God doth forsake and persecute them, and there is none to deliver	281	Priest 34		11
either he doth it as they are Creatures, dust and ashes;	283	Priest 34		10
the Gospel doth not, which hath so much advanced Charity,	287	Priest 37		22
Neither doth thy love yet stay here!	289	Priest		3
who onely doth wondrous things.	289	Priest		8
comforts and condoles, doth perform an acceptable thing to thee;	298	Cornaro		7
who not onely as a friend doth visit thee, but help thee!	298	Cornaro		9
and also doth preserve even ill tempers in good health,	298	Cornaro		14
Neither doth it hinder, that Plato sayes, That they who are employed	299	Cornaro		11
of Gods Worke in his heart through the Word, doth amisse;	309	Valdesso		31
The Authour doth still discover too slight a regard of the Scripture,	317	Valdesso		22
doth not bid them then cast away the word, or leave it off:	318	Valdesso		19
God complaines not, but doth what is fitting.	327	Proverbs		182
Giving much to the poore, doth inrich a mans store.	327	Proverbs		191
It takes much from the account, to which his sin doth amount.	327	Proverbs		192
Working and making a fire doth discretion require.	328	Proverbs		225
The wise hand doth not all that the foolish mouth speakes.	329	Proverbs		246
While the discreet advise, the foole doth his busines.	330	Proverbs		273
Hee that doth what hee will, doth not what he ought.	333	Proverbs		350
Who doth his owne businesse, foules not his hands.	335	Proverbs		419
The first service a child doth his father is to make him foolish,	337	Proverbs		463
should doe what he doth not.	340	Proverbs		559
must doe what he doth not.	340	Proverbs	V	559
The wine in the bottell doth not quench thirst.	342	Proverbs		616
He that doth what he should not, shall feele what he would not.	347	Proverbs		783
Who praiseth Saint Peter, doth not blame Saint Paul.	349	Proverbs		859
The yeare doth nothing else but open and shut.	351	Proverbs		901
Hee a beast doth die, that hath done no good to his country.	354	Proverbs		993
One month doth nothing without another.	355	Proverbs		1028
One mouth doth nothing without another.	355	Proverbs	V	1028
Silke doth quench the fire in the Kitchin.	356	Proverbs	D	1043
The death of a young wolfe doth never come too soon.	360	Proverbs	D	1131
but my next neighbour doth me more harm	361	Proverbs	D	1173
in the choice of whom their judgement doth even now appeare.	442	Oration		27
DOUBLE (see also dubble)				
Lest on their double-dark souls either shine:	31	Sacrifice		139
And then amerc'd them, double gifts to bring	71	Humilitie		31
That Life hath with the sun a double motion.	84	Coloss.		2
Take up the second, then thy double line	97	Afflict.5		16
To double-moat thee with his grace,	110	Brit. Ch.		29
But as his joyes are double;	131	Mans medly		25
To turn his double pains to double praise.	132	Mans medly		36
On double pleasures: leave thy cold dispute	153	The Collar		20
They are hells land-marks, Satans double crest:	196	Ch.-Milit.		219
But the Parson having a double aime, and making a hook of his	244	Priest 12		31
these two rules comprize and include the double object of our duty,	246	Priest 13		29
But the Parson distinguisheth according to his double aime,	267	Priest 26		15
that there is a double state of a Christian even in this Life,	280	Priest 34		1
Health and sicknesse surely are mens double enemies.	354	Proverbs		1011

	PAGE	TITLE		LINE
DOUBLE-DARK				
Lest on their double-dark souls either shine:	31	Sacrifice		139
DOUBLE-MOAT				
To double-moat thee with his grace,	110	Brit. Ch.		29
DOUBLES				
Doubles each lash: and yet their bitternesse	30	Sacrifice		126
Doubles the night, & trips by day.	96	Charms & K	W	8
but an ill man doubles his fault.	343	Proverbs		655
but an ill, it doubles his fault.	343	Proverbs	V	655
He doubles it to take away the scruple of those that might say,	374	Letters		22
DOUBLING				
With doubling knees and weary bones,	148	Longing		2
doubling his regards, and shewing by all means, that the delinquents	263	Priest 25		34
that if any course could be taken of doubling my Annuity now,	367	Letters		8
DOUBLY				
the holy spirit indeed sometime doubly teaching both in penning	317	Valdesso		30
DOUBT				
Wee doubt much whether you	211	Paradox	D	40
setting aside his care of his Flock, were a madnesse to doubt of.	234	Priest 7		17
when they doubt Gods providence, thinking that their own labour is	247	Priest 14		29
I will not doubt to go without staying to pray there (but onely,	273	Priest 31		34
especially since it may be a just doubt, whether, considering	282	Priest 34		7
Feare is given to Christ, but not doubt, and upon good ground.	315	Valdesso		12
Neither doe I doubt but if Abraham had lived in our Kingdome under	316	Valdesso		22
As for my assistance, doubt not, through Gods blessing,	379	Letters		17
DOUBTED				
having doubted sometimes, whether his repentance were true,	279	Priest 33		10
Neither is it to be doubted, but that he shall ever after live free	297	Cornaro		19
of which is doubted whether it have some further meaning.	368	Letters		18
DOUBTFULL				
the Fathers forbid us to judge of the doubtfull actions of Saints in	316	Valdesso		12
The perswasion of the fortunate swaies the doubtfull.	342	Proverbs		630
DOUBTFULNESSE				
To say our Saviour prayed with doubtfulnesse, is more then I can	315	Valdesso		9
DOUBTING				
not so much doubting a God, as that he is theirs;	283	Priest 34		6
DOUBTLESS				
be none of the Court-stile, yet doubtless Madam, can do you no hurt:	377	Letters		2
DOUBTLESSE				
Doubtlesse our plagues and plentie, peace and warres	119	Providence		79
Doubtlesse, but in the way of punishment,	155	Assurance		4
Doubtlesse, neither starre nor flower	181	Banquet		19
Doubtlesse they are Parsons of the families they live in,	226	Priest 2		21
and doubtlesse the Holy Scripture intends thus much, when it	257	Priest 21		10
doubtlesse then also mens affections and words must turne,	288	Priest 37		4
Yet doubtlesse the best faith in us is defective, and arrives	319	Valdesso		10
DOUBTS				
What to ask further. Doubts well rais'd do lock	18	Ch.-Porch		299
What to ask farther. Doubts well rais'd do lock	18	Ch.-Porch	W	299
A narrow cupboard for my griefs and doubts,	164	Grief		11
He that knowes nothing, doubts nothing.	349	Proverbs		861
DOVE				
But who does hawk at eagles with a dove?	29	Sacrifice		91
My dove doth back into my bosome flie,	29	Sacrifice		94
Listen sweet Dove unto my song,	59	Whitsunday		1
Come blessed Dove charm'd with my song,	59	Whitsunday	W	1
And shall the dew out-strip thy dove?	60	Grace		10
Their follies with the wing of thy milde Dove,	100	Miserie		28
Their follies with the wings of thy milde Dove,	100	Miserie	W	28
And art thou grieved, sweet and sacred Dove,	135	Ephes.		1
Is your dove,	180	Invitation		26
Of Noahs shadie vine, chaste as the dove;	190	Ch.-Milit.		15
As well as any she? Cannot thy Dove	206	Walton 1		8
DOWN (noun)				
Making our pillows either down, or dust.	186	Death		24
DOWN				
And tumble up and down what thou find'st there.	12	Ch.-Porch		148
Thy drops of bloud must pay down all his fear:	17	Ch.-Porch		274
Be down, then winde up both; since we shall be	24	Ch.-Porch		455
Now heal thy self, Physician; now come down.	34	Sacrifice		221
So many joyes I writ down for my part,	46	Afflict.1		3
The starres were coming down to know	59	Whitsunday		11
Hung down his head, and wisht for night,	59	Whitsunday		14
When they shall bow, and kneel, and fall down flat	65	Ch.-monum.		15
Did weep so fast, that the tears trickling down	71	Humilitie		26
But thy silk twist let down from heav'n to me,	89	The Pearl		38
He treads down that which doth befriend him,	92	Man		45
The sunne holds down his head for shame,	101	Miserie		33
When I beheld it trickling down thy face,	107	Home		9
Do not by hanging down break from the hand,	112	Dawning		11
I sat me down to spell them, and perceived	112	JESU		8
He builds a house, which quickly down must go,	127	Giddinesse		13
Their storie pennes and sets us down.	128	Bunch Gr.		11
Deare Friend, sit down, the tale is long and sad:	129	Love unkn.		1
Down with thy knees, up with thy voice.	134	The Method		30
Wherefore sit down, good heart;	138	The Size		37
Bow down thine eare!	149	Longing		21
Which bounds on thee, and will not down thy throat:	156	Assurance		40
Thrown down I fall into a bed, and rest:	159	Jos.coat		2
And with the other throwest down to hell	160	Priesthood		3
Taking me up to throw me down:	165	The Crosse		22

DREAM (cont'd)	PAGE	TITLE	LINE
In hope of great things. Call to minde thy dream, ...	138	The Size	44
DREAM'D			
that Hermogenes never dream'd of, and therefore he could give no	233	Priest 7	25
DREAMED			
tell me what I dreamed last night.	332	Proverbs	336
DREAMES			
Into the hands of senceles Dreames	203	Even-song W	22
DREAMS			
Shadows well mounted, dreams in a career, ...	167	Dotage	4
well and quietly any where, and my dreams are fair and pleasant.	302	Cornaro	13
DREGS			
In so much dregs the quintessence is small:	38	The Sinner	9
Will pour full joyes to thee, but dregs to those, ...	213	Bohemia D	65
DRESSE			
Dresse and undresse thy soul: mark the decay	24	Ch.-Porch	453
They dresse themselves and come to thee.	108	Home	52
Who cannot dresse it well, want wit, not words.	167	The Sonne	4
Whose native beauty needs not dresse or lace	212	Bohemia D	30
do as it were dresse and prepare both for man in themselves,	241	Priest 10	34
to dresse and prune them, and take as much joy in a straight-growing	275	Priest 32	32
Dresse a stick, and it seemes a youth.	324	Proverbs	101
Fine words dresse ill deedes.	337	Proverbs	479
DRESS'D			
And be dispos'd, and dress'd, and tun'd by thee, ...	118	Providence	38
opportunities of having his meat dress'd and other services done	237	Priest 9	9
DRESSED			
Some fruit for him that dressed me.	79	Employm.2	25
DRESSING			
By dressing, mistressing, and complement.	9	Ch.-Porch	80
Of dressing, that her hair doth lie	110	Brit. Ch.	20
he hath shew'd the unlawfulness of spending the day in dressing,	277	Priest 32	29
Fine dressing is a foule house swept before the doores. . .	329	Proverbs	243
DREST			
Praying's the end of preaching. O be drest;	23	Ch.-Porch	410
Heaven in ordinarie, man well drest, ...	51	Prayer 1	11
my soule tc thee, that being drest	80	Christmas W	13
They appeare trim and drest	85	Vanitie 1	20
And drest his herse, while he has breath	99	Mortific.	33
Thus are true Aarons drest.	174	Aaron	5
Poore priest thus am I drest.	174	Aaron	10
In him I am well drest.	174	Aaron	15
And be in him new drest.	174	Aaron	20
Come people; Aaron's drest.	174	Aaron	25
Brought you to Church well drest and clad:	176	Forerunners	17
God is here prepar'd and drest, ...	179	Invitation	4
A garden must be lookt unto and drest as the body.	325	Proverbs	129
Though a lie be well drest, it is ever overcome.	325	Proverbs	133
He that riseth first, is first drest.	327	Proverbs	202
The body is more drest then the soule.	351	Proverbs	919
The body is sooner drest then the soule.	351	Proverbs	920
DREW			
Love bade me welcome: yet my soul drew back, ...	188	Love 3	1
Drew nearer to me, sweetly questioning, ...	188	Love 3	5
Still eastward go; because it drew more neare	198	Ch.-Milit.	276
DRIE			
He clave the stonie rock, when they were drie;	30	Sacrifice	122
And with his buriall-linen drie thine eyes:	112	Dawning	14
For death is drie as dust. Yet if ye part, ...	135	Ephes.	10
But runnes, although I be not drie;	136	Ephes.	29
Our cyens have purloin'd, and left you drie:	152	The Jews	2
Our sinnes have purloin'd, and left you drie:	152	The Jews V	2
Before my sighs did drie it: there was corn	153	The Collar	11
My weary weeping eyes too drie for me, ...	164	Grief	6
DRIES			
Nothing dries sooner then a teare.	343	Proverbs	659
DRINK			
Drink not the third glasse, which thou canst not tame, ...	7	Ch.-Porch	25
They drink with greedinesse a full damnation.	24	Ch.-Porch	448
Below, our drink; above, our meat;	92	Man	40
Why he'l not lose a cup of drink for thee:	100	Miserie	8
What is this weary world; this meat and drink, ...	108	Home	37
Is clothing, meat and trencher, drink and kan, ...	120	Providence	127
Is clothing, meat and trencher, drink and Can, ...	120	Providence V	127
But as birds drink, and straight lift up their head, ...	131	Mans medly	21
Of better drink	131	Mans medly	23
Of future depths, but drink the cleare and good.	145	Discharge	28
And drink this, ...	180	Invitation	11
Which before ye drink is bloud.	180	Invitation	12
where both the people and the drink being cold and flegmatick,	242	Priest 10	20
For when men have nothing to do, then they fall to drink, to steal,	274	Priest 32	11
with a full stomack, but so as I might well both eat and drink more.	293	Cornaro	19
power causeth that the meat and drink that is taken in fit measure,	293	Cornaro	27
power of health consists most in the proportion of meat and drink.	293	Cornaro	33
that old age could not be sustained with so little meat and drink;	295	Cornaro	23
but also to gather strength, which could not be but by meat & drink.	295	Cornaro	25
my stint of meat and drink should be diminished, rather then	295	Cornaro	30
and the measure of my drink, which before was foureteen ounces,	296	Cornaro	12
hidden properties it hath, what meat and drink agrees best with it:	297	Cornaro	28
moment (as I shewed before) if a man be temperate in meat and drink;	299	Cornaro	17
No man that follcwes it, is bound to eat and drink so little as I:	300	Cornaro	7

DRINK (cont'd)	PAGE	TITLE		LINE
quantitie of any meat or drink (though most agreeable to them)	300	Cornaro		12
So that he which is offended with no kinde of meat and drink,	300	Cornaro		15
When a dog is a drowning, every one offers him drink.	323	Proverbs		77
Where the drink goes in, there the wit goes out.	327	Proverbs		187
DRINKE				
as that it is not meate or drinke that hinders them from working.	266	Priest 26		35
Gossips are frogs, they drinke and talke.	330	Proverbs		275
Let none say, I will not drinke water.	331	Proverbs		310
If you could runne, as you drinke, you might catch a hare.	334	Proverbs		373
Who likes not the drinke, God deprives him of bread.	334	Proverbs		394
and his horse drinke at every water,	336	Proverbs		434
but he will drinke when and what he pleaseth.	342	Proverbs		623
DRINKES				
The Chollerick drinkes, the Melancholick eates,	351	Proverbs		924
DRINKING				
but especially that of drinking, because it is the most popular vice;	227	Priest 3		23
when the appetites of the body in eating, drinking, sleep,	230	Priest 5		29
DRINKS				
But who drinks on, to hell may go.	97	Charms & K		18
which is said of hurtfull meats, extends to hurtfull drinks also.	266	Priest 26		28
I forsook all these kinde of meats and drinks, and chose that wine	293	Cornaro		16
because in his meats and drinks he kept a due moderation;	294	Cornaro		8
DRIVE				
They drive them soon away;	71	Humilitie		30
and drive it to practice, turning it to reformation of life,	255	Priest 21		6
whither to drive the Answerer, which the Questionist must have in his	256	Priest 21		31
DRIVEN				
Of earth is driven by winds away,	215	Psalm I	D	15
within a few moneths I should be driven to that exigent,	292	Cornaro		14
DRIVES				
Drives all at last. Therefore I gladly trust	64	Ch.-monum.		6
DRIVEST				
Thou drivest from his seat.	200	H. Commun.	W	24
DRIVING				
and driving of their generall Schoole rules ever to the smallest	265	Priest 26		36
DROOPING (see also drope)				
Why do I languish thus, drooping and dull,	115	Dulnesse		1
DROOPINGS				
as knowing that nature will not bear everlasting droopings,	267	Priest 27		34
DROP				
And drop away,	49	Repentance		29
Drop from above!	60	Grace		4
Drop from abcve!	60	Grace		8
Drop from above.	60	Grace		12
Drop from above.	60	Grace		16
Drop from abcve.	60	Grace		20
Drop from above.	61	Grace	W	20
Drop from above.	61	Grace		24
I saw a vine drop grapes with J and C	116	Love-joy		2
Trees after bearing drop their leaves for soil:	119	Providence		70
But after thou hadst slipt a drop	158	Praise 3		31
My comforts drop and melt away like snow:	169	The Answer		1
DROPE				
And drope away,	49	Repentance	V	29
DROPP				
On men dropp blessings as I fly.	79	Employm.2	W	25
DROPPING				
Dropping from heav'n, which doth both cleanse and close	147	Offering		20
DROPPINGS				
For future times, the droppings of the stock	154	Glimpse		24
DROPS				
Thy drops of bloud must pay down all his fear:	17	Ch.-Porch		274
Drops bloud (the onely beads) my words to measure:	27	Sacrifice		22
These drops being temper'd with a sinners tears,	27	Sacrifice		25
Whose drops of bloud paid the full price,	76	Sunday		54
Your hony drops: presse not to smell them here:	120	Providence		118
Our Scripture-dew drops fast:	128	Bunch Gr.		16
Thy fruite shall with there drops contend;	213	L' Envoy	D	4
DROSSE				
Thou art the man, and man but drosse to thee.	77	Avarice		12
He that loseth gold, though drosse,	114	Businesse		31
DROUGHT				
Whose leaves first sheltred man from drought & dew,	84	The World		12
Nothing but drought and dearth, but bush and brake,	108	Home		49
Drought never brought dearth.	346	Proverbs		749
DROWN				
About thy neck do drown thee? raise thy head;	13	Ch.-Porch		170
Or else give tears to drown them, as they grow.	44	H. Bapt.1		9
Till all do melt, and drown his breath	98	Mortific.		27
Before my tears did drown it.	153	The Collar		12
And in them may drown a friend:	187	Dooms-day		22
DROWN'D				
Should crie so loud, untill the trump were drown'd,	152	The Jews		10
In delights of earth was drown'd;	182	Banquet		33
DROWNED				
and so not be drowned altogether in the works of their vocation,	261	Priest 23		24
but take heede, lest you bee drowned.	326	Proverbs		167
Good swimmers at length are drcwned.	347	Proverbs		801
DROWNETH				
Here is joy that drowneth quite	180	Invitation		22

DROWNING	PAGE	TITLE	LINE
Out-crying my requests, drowning my tears;	66	Ch.-lock	3
the improvement of his grounds, by drowning, or draining,	275	Priest 32	24
When a dog is a drowning, every one offers him drink.	323	Proverbs	77
DROWNS			
Awake sad heart, whom sorrow ever drowns;	112	Dawning	1
And drowns the song.	132	The Storm	14
DROWSIE			
One houre of watching; but their drowsie brain	27	Sacrifice	30
DROWSINES			
Cures both a fever and a drowsines.	19	Ch.-Porch W	336
DRUDGERIE			
Makes drudgerie divine:	185	The Elixer	18
DRUDGERY			
things of ordinary use are not only to serve in the way of drudgery,	257	Priest 21	14
DRUG			
But with a richer drug, then scalding water,	130	Love unkn.	40
DRUGS			
to know what herbs may be used in stead of drugs of the same nature,	261	Priest 23	30
DRUMME			
Who without spear, or sword, or other drumme	195	Ch.-Milit.	201
DRUNK			
An herb destill'd, and drunk, may dwell next doore,	61	Praise 1	13
Which at a board, while many drunk bare wine,	130	Love unkn.	42
Weep what ye have drunk amisse,	180	Invitation	10
DRUNKARD			
The drunkard forfets Man, and doth devest	7	Ch.-Porch	35
DRUNKARD'S			
A drunkards purse is a bottle.	325	Proverbs	143
DRUNKARDS			
There are more Physitians in health then drunkards.	351	Proverbs	903
DRUNKE			
Wine that cost nothing is digested before it be drunke.	352	Proverbs	932
DRUNKEN			
He that is drunken, may his mother kill	7	Ch.-Porch	31
DRUNKENNESS			
comes with sleep, be sins of gluttony, drunkenness, sloath, lust,	230	Priest 5	30
DRY (see also drie)			
Show that thy brests can not be dry,	59	Whitsunday W	21
When th' earth was dry, thou mad'st a sea of wet:	120	Providence	113
Most herbs that grow in brooks, are hot and dry.	120	Providence	129
Dry dust, which sheds no tears, but may extort.	186	Death	12
Sure, Lord, there is enough in thee to dry	206	Walton 2	1
Great God will surely dry those teares,	213	L' Envoy D	5
if a peece of dry flesh at my table be more unpleasant to me,	242	Priest 10	13
without which supply the corne would instantly dry up, as a river	271	Priest 30	7
Dry feet, warme head, bring safe to bed.	335	Proverbs	402
One paire of eares drawes dry a hundred tongues.	339	Proverbs	526
Dry bread at home is better then rost meate abroad.	344	Proverbs	681
Slander is a shipwrack by a dry Tempest.	356	Proverbs D	135
DRYED			
But I fear the heat of my late Ague hath dryed up those springs,	363	Letters	4
DUBBLE			
then I leave to my servant Elizabeth her dubble wages given her,	382	G.H.'s Will	22
DUBIOUS			
BRIEFE NOTES relating to the dubious and offensive places in	306	Valdesso	T
DUCHES'S			
by moving the Duches's heart, to an exceeding cheerfulness,	379	Letters	1
DUCHESS'S			
your relation of my Lady Duchess's forwardnes in our church building.	377	Letters	19
DUE			
Thy need, thine honour, and thy friend his due.	12	Ch.-Porch	152
Restore to God his due in tithe and time:	22	Ch.-Porch	385
Twice on the day his due is understood;	22	Ch.-Porch	391
Twice on that day his due is understood;	22	Ch.-Porch W	391
To thee of all kings onely due)	35	Thanksgvng	2
Each seventh note by right is due to thee.	38	The Sinner	4
Unpinne, or wrench from giving all their due.	72	Constancie	5
Should creatures want for want of heed their due?	119	Providence	86
Are both thy due: but I a silly flie,	143	Complaining	8
As thy due desert.	147	Offering	30
To fetch the bodie; both being due to grief.	159	Jos.coat	9
may go the right way, and thither onely, where they are onely due.	245	Priest 12	34
by a due blessing of God for their safe arrival, and saying grace	251	Priest 17	8
and being there, makes due use of them, as of Clergy councels,	253	Priest 19	10
the Parson having a due respect both to the person, and to the cause,	268	Priest 28	33
because in his meats and drinks he kept a due moderation;	294	Cornaro	8
Hee that looseth his due, gets no thankes.	333	Proverbs	363
three pound more besides that which is due to her, to Ann I leave	382	G.H.'s Will	23
pound MS. that the five pound due to Mrs Judeth Spenser is to be payd	383	G.H.'s Will	20
DUKES			
and among our Dukes, Landus, and Donatus, and many others	299	Cornaro	2
DULL			
Doth my dull husbandrie improve:	60	Grace	2
Whom, if we were not very dull,	75	Sunday	18
Why do I languish thus, drooping and dull,	115	Dulnesse	1
Thy sithe is dull; whet it for shame.	122	Time	2
It must be he. Your heart was dull, I fear.	130	Love unkn.	56
The Thorns did quicken, what was grown too dull:	130	Love unkn.	66
But if the young Gallant think these Courses dull, and phlegmatick,	278	Priest 32	4

	PAGE	TITLE	LINE
DULLER			
As if a starre were duller then a clod,	134	Divinitie	3
DULNESSE			
Dulnesse.	115	Dulnesse	T
Must dulnesse turn me to a clod?	176	Forerunners	5
is this my pleasure made lesse by the decaying dulnesse of my senses,	302	Cornaro	8
DULY			
if not duly once a month, yet at least five or six times in the year;	259	Priest 22	20
DUMB			
or, that my love is as dumb as my papers;	371	Letters	26
DUMBE			
That dumbe inclosure maketh love	98	Mortific.	23
Because the search was dumbe before:	162	The Search	23
For my rough sorrows: cease, be dumbe and mute,	164	Grief	14
DUMPISH			
which I live at this age, is not a dead, dumpish, and sowre life;	303	Cornaro	10
DUNG			
That feeds on dung, is coloured thereby.	15	Ch.-Porch	234
Sheep eat the grasse, and dung the ground for more:	119	Providence	69
Let foolish lovers, if they will love dung,	177	Forerunners	25
DUNGEON			
Thy house would but a dungeon prove,	60	Grace	6
Thy great house would a dungeon prove,	60	Grace W	6
DURST			
And the late reformation never durst	196	Ch.-Milit.	226
DURT			
for the foulnesse, as wash, and durt, and things thereinto fallen;	241	Priest 10	29
Hee that falles into the durt,	335	Proverbs	409
DURTIE			
He that hath little is the lesse durtie.	336	Proverbs	436
DUST			
That, as his death calcined thee to dust,	41	Easter	5
To hide my dust, then thee to hold.	45	Nature	18
What though my bodie runne to dust?	51	Faith	41
And thrown it on that dust which thou hast made,	54	Love 1	4
And thrown it in that dust which thou hast made,	54	Love 1 W	4
Our eies shall see thee, which before saw dust;	54	Love 2	9
Dust blown by wit, till that they both were blinde:	54	Love 2	10
A crumme of dust from heav'n to hell?	55	Temper 1	14
Whether I flie with angels, fall with dust,	55	Temper 1	25
Whether I Angell it, or fall to dust.	55	Temper 1 W	25
As is the dust, to which that life doth tend,	57	Employm. 1	15
May take acquaintance of this heap of dust;	64	Ch.-monum.	3
Comparing dust with dust, and earth with earth.	65	Ch.-monum.	11
To sever the good fellowship of dust,	65	Ch.-monum.	13
That flesh is but the glasse, which holds the dust	65	Ch.-monum.	20
Be crumbled into dust. Mark here below	65	Ch.-monum.	22
Be broken into dust. Mark here below	65	Ch.-monum. W	22
Blows all the dust about the floore:	67	Ch.-floore	17
But is fair dust!	71	Frailtie	4
That which was dust before, doth quickly rise,	71	Frailtie	15
First with thy fire-work burn to dust	74	The Starre	9
O that thou shouldst give dust a tongue	80	Deniall	16
The dust into our eyes:	82	Ungratef.	17
But I am frailtie, and already dust;	83	Sighs & Gr.	17
The powder doth forget the dust.	96	Charms & K	14
The powder does forget the dust.	96	Charms & K W	14
The very dust, where thou dost tread and go,	115	Dulnesse	15
For death is drie as dust. Yet if ye part,	135	Ephes.	10
Thy clay that weeps, thy dust that calls.	143	Complaining	5
Behold, thy dust doth stirre,	149	Longing	37
Thy pile of dust, wherein each crumme	149	Longing	41
Flesh being turn'd to dust, and bones to sticks.	186	Death	8
Dry dust, which sheds no tears, but may extort.	186	Death	12
Making our pillows either down, or dust.	186	Death	24
Summon all the dust to rise,	186	Dooms-day	3
Dust, alas, no musick feels,	186	Dooms-day	9
Guiltie of dust and sinne.	188	Love 3	2
The great heart stoops, and taketh from the dust	192	Ch.-Milit.	67
His dust who under thee must sleepe	208	H. Danvers D	2
Tread down my life, and in the dust	221	Psalm VII D	19
but reverend, and clean, without spots, or dust, or smell;	228	Priest 3	11
that the Church be swept, and kept cleane without dust, or Cobwebs,	246	Priest 13	9
either he doth it as they are Creatures, dust and ashes;	283	Priest 34	10
Hee that blowes in the dust fills his eyes with it.	340	Proverbs	570
DUSTIE			
Written in dustie heraldrie and lines;	65	Ch.-monum.	9
DUTCH			
Mee thinkes, in that Dutch optick I doe see	211	Bohemia D	13
DUTIE			
May no lines passe, except they do their dutie	56	Jordan 1	4
Each thing is full of dutie:	92	Man	37
DUTIES			
he sets himself to the Consideration of the duties of the day,	235	Priest 8	33
and fraile man, discharged the publick duties of the Congregation.	236	Priest 8	10
and without hinderance to publick duties, either to entertaine some	236	Priest 8	19
with prayers, and catechizing, and all religious duties.	239	Priest 10	14
be as they ought, for those great duties that are performed in them.	246	Priest 13	7
to disable themselves from a fit discharging either of Divine duties,	266	Priest 26	30
fit discharging either of Divine duties, or duties of their calling.	266	Priest 26	30
and taint his other duties of piety, which none can perform so wel in	273	Priest 31	2

DUTIES (cont'd)	PAGE	TITLE		LINE
This distinction may runne through all Christian duties,	274	Priest 31		2
but to labour still to be as fervent in Christian Duties,	280	Priest 34		20
amongst all divine and spirituall exercises and duties,	311	Valdesso	V	3
while applying himselfe to the [unquestioned] duties of true Piety,	312	Valdesso		20
or necessary duties, and occasions of our calling and condition	314	Valdesso		17
in a strict performance of a few cheap and easie duties of religion,	319	Valdesso	V	25
Your poor Colony of Servants present their humble duties.	377	Letters		13
we for your gracious acceptance of these poore duties wish,	443	Oration		6
DUTY				
and containes the direct steps of Pastorall Duty and Auctority.	225	Priest 1		3
may be plainly gathered both the Dignity thereof, and the Duty:	225	Priest 1		16
The Duty, in that a Priest is to do that which Christ did,	225	Priest 1		18
whose duty and obligation being the same to the Houses they live in,	226	Priest 2		16
neglect their duty, and shall be so farre from that which they seek	226	Priest 2		34
between fear and zeal, pausing yet pressing, he performes his duty.	231	Priest 6		20
but even to let the world sinke, so they do their duty;	232	Priest 6		17
and were it not his duty to have them so, it were his profit,	240	Priest 10		14
these two rules comprize and include the double object of our duty,	246	Priest 13		30
Likewise in any other Countrey-duty, he considers what is the end	253	Priest 19		3
he fulfills the duty, and debt of neighbourhood to all the Parishes	253	Priest 19		21
things are otherwise equall, therefore he satisfies this duty also.	253	Priest 19		28
for there being three points of his duty, the one, to infuse	255	Priest 21		2
and doing their duty faithfully, they will soon discover:	266	Priest 26		3
that so they may know their duty, and keep their oath the better;	270	Priest 29		16
is additionary, not necessary, and the other duty overweighs it:	273	Priest 31		37
This is the duty of each to other, which they ought to fulfill:	277	Priest 32		21
The neglect of this duty in Ministers themselves, hath made	286	Priest 36		11
such offenders, that it is a duty rather, which may do much good,	288	Priest 37		1
saw that it was no hard thing to do so, but the proper duty of man;	292	Cornaro		33
I remember my most humble duty to my Mother.	367	Letters		20
I remember my most humble duty to my Mother, who cannot think me	371	Letters		1
DWARFE				
A Dwarfe on a Gyants shoulder sees further of the two.	322	Proverbs		50
A Dwarfe on a Gyants shoulder sees farther then they two.	322	Proverbs	V	50
DWELL				
Thousands of toyes dwell there, yet out of doore	40	Sepulchre		7
Consuming agues dwell in ev'ry vein,	47	Afflict.1		27
An herb destill'd, and drunk, may dwell next doore,	61	Praise 1		13
But he that means to dwell therein.	90	Man		3
So brave a Palace built; O dwell in it,	92	Man		50
That it may dwell with thee at last!	92	Man		51
In small draughts Heav'en does shine & dwell:	97	Charms & K	W	21
I and deare prayer would together dwell,	103	Prayer 2		23
Who wants the place, where God doth dwell,	123	Time		23
Sweet Peace, where dost thou dwell? I humbly crave,	124	Peace		1
Peace at the root must dwell.	125	Peace		16
Dwell in my head & eyes: come clouds, & rain:	164	Grief		2
Thou who dost dwell and linger here below,	170	Water-crs.		1
With me, in me, live and dwell:	181	Banquet		3
No evil, Lord, shall dwell with thee,	218	Psalm V	D	11
which while they dwell in their bookes, they will never finde;	266	Priest 26		2
either blessing God, that he will be pleased to dwell among men;	273	Priest 31		25
he adviseth to insist and dwell chiefly on the two noble branches	278	Priest 32		1
God intends that to be as a sacred Temple for himself to dwell in,	374	Letters		10
DWELLEST				
For where thou dwellest all is neat.	136	Familie		8
DWELLETH				
One ague dwelleth in my bones,	165	The Crosse		13
DWELLS				
True beautie dwells on high: ours is a flame	177	Forerunners		28
DWELS				
Truth dwels not in the clouds: the bow that's there	19	Ch.-Porch		317
Truth dwels not in the clouds: that Bow doth hit	19	Ch.-Porch	W	317
DWELT				
At Salem dwelt, who liv'd with good increase	125	Peace		23
But th' Empire dwelt in Greece, to comfort them	192	Ch.-Milit.		73
DY				
For when he sees my waies, I dy:	63	Even-song		7
to let the fervency of the supplicant hang and dy between speaking,	231	Priest 6		18
yet often dy with the Sermon, especially with Countrey people;	233	Priest 7		14
And is in contention for them whither to live, or dy;	234	Priest 7		15
but he would chuse to dy in Spain (where they say	357	Proverbs	D	1047
He that is once borne, once must dy.	358	Proverbs	D	1087
DYDE				
If thou hadst dyde for Bread.	201	H. Commun.	W	27
For who can tell, though thou hast dyde to winn	205	Persever.	W	9
DYE				
They dye in holes where glory never shone.	20	Ch.-Porch	W	348
But that which made my soule to dye	201	H. Commun.	W	28
The Wolfe must dye in his owne skinne.	349	Proverbs		849
Wee leave more to do when wee dye, then wee have done.	353	Proverbs		972
He that will do thee a good turne, either he will be gon or dye.	358	Proverbs	D	1083
DY'D				
Of him, who dy'd to part	74	The Starre		23
DYED				
For both God is there also, and those for whom God dyed:	249	Priest 14		7
DYES				
Which dyes.	150	Longing		84
DYET				
A little with quiet is the onely dyet.	332	Proverbs		327

	PAGE	TITLE		LINE
DYET (cont'd)				
an ill dyet was the mother.	357	Proverbs	D	1048
so that I am fain to dyet in my Chamber at mine own cost;	365	Letters		2
DYING				
Thou dying dayly, praise thee to thy losse.	73	Afflict.3		18
Thy dying head upon the tree:	149	Longing		32
(As dying things are wont) untill it flew	192	Ch.-Milit.		80
and cheerfull dying under persecuting Emperours, (though that indeed	237	Priest 9		30
Labour as long liv'd, pray as ever dying.	337	Proverbs		480
Labour as long liv'd, pray as alwayes dying.	337	Proverbs	V	480
DYINGS				
That all these dyings may be life in death.	99	Mortific.		36
DYM				
And to my dym and sinful eyes	219	Psalm V	D	23
EACH				
Let not each fansy make thee to detest	7	Ch.-Porch	W	19
Let not each motion make thee to detest	7	Ch.-Porch	WC	19
Ballance each dramme of reason, like a potion.	19	Ch.-Porch		322
If thou observest strangers in each fit,	21	Ch.-Porch		365
Wherefore each part	26	The Altar		9
Without me each one, who doth now me brave,	27	Sacrifice		9
Doubles each lash: and yet their bitternesse	30	Sacrifice		126
Which each one calls for so with utmost breath,	31	Sacrifice		146
The decreed burden of each mortall Saint:	33	Sacrifice		199
Each seventh note by right is due to thee.	38	The Sinner		4
And each grief tell?	38	Good Fri.		4
Or shall each leaf,	38	Good Fri.		9
Then let each houre	39	Good Fri.		13
That as each beast his cure doth know,	39	Good Fri.		19
Each sinne may so.	39	Good Fri.		20
Each day doth round about us see.	48	Repentance		8
Seeing not onely how each verse doth shine,	58	H.Script.2		3
And digs my grave at each remove:	60	Grace		14
Die over each houre of Methusalems stay.	62	Afflict.2		5
And th' other black and grave, wherewith each one	67	Ch.-floore		4
To court each place or fortune that doth fall,	68	Content		7
To court each place or fortune that does fall,	68	Content	W	7
Where in each rocm of the well-furnisht tent	69	Content		19
Where in each room of that well-furnisht tent	69	Content	W	19
Of that brave gift, each one began to fume,	70	Humilitie		19
They had depos'd each one.	70	Humilitie		24
That, as each beast his manger knows,	76	Sunday		38
Each took his way; some would to pleasures go,	80	Deniall		8
Each part may call the farthest, brother:	91	Man		16
Each part may call the furthest, brother:	91	Man	V	16
Each thing is full of dutie:	92	Man		37
A sick toss'd vessel, dashing on each thing;	102	Miserie		76
And quickly gain, for each inch lost, an ell.	103	Prayer 2		24
Rivers run, and springs each one	113	Businesse		3
Thou art in all things one, in each thing many:	118	Providence		43
Each creature hath a wisdome for his good.	118	Providence		61
Each thing that is, although in use and name	121	Providence		149
To honour thee; and so each hymne thy fame	121	Providence		151
In those chests, boxes; in each box, a till:	126	Confession		5
Each sev'rall houre.	127	Giddinesse		4
Surely if each one saw anothers heart,	127	Giddinesse		21
So now each Christian hath his journeys spann'd:	128	Bunch Gr.		10
Each day, each houre, each moment of the week,	131	Love unkn.		69
For death each houre environs and surrounds.	145	Discharge		36
Thy pile of dust, wherein each crumme	149	Longing		41
What fine varietie each tongue affords:	167	The Sonne		2
The sphere of vertue, and each shining grace	175	The Foil		2
Each one whispring, Live ye brother?	186	Dooms-day		6
Known also to each minute cf an houre:	190	Ch.-Milit.		4
But did bewitch, and finely work each nation	195	Ch.-Milit.		193
Each with his rodd.	204	The Knell	W	12
Each breast does feel, no braver fuel choose	206	Walton 1		13
Each Cloud distills thy praise, and doth forbid	206	Walton 2		4
Each little comforte much affects our hartes,	210	Paradox	D	33
Strive each to play their Part.	213	Convert	D	5
This is the duty of each tc other, which they ought to fulfill:	277	Priest 32		21
EAGER				
Who think me eager, hot, and undertaking,	169	The Answer		6
EAGERNES				
This letter runs to you with much eagernes, for I am enjoined	367	Letters		27
EAGLE				
and his soul fervent, active, young, and lusty as an eagle.	237	Priest 9		27
EAGLE'S				
The ignorant hath an Eagles wings, and an Owles eyes.	351	Proverbs		902
EAGLES				
But who does hawk at eagles with a dove?	29	Sacrifice		91
EAGLES'				
There hands shall clipp the Eagles winges, & chase	212	Bohemia	D	47
EAR (corn)				
Two sparrows on one Ear of Corn make an ill agreement.	358	Proverbs	D	1074
EAR				
Lord to my words encline thine ear,	218	Psalm V	D	1
passing frcm the ear to the heart, from the heart to the life	289	Priest		30
EARE				
Those doores being shut, all by the eare comes in.	23	Ch.-Porch		418
And in the eare, not conscience ring.	68	Windows		15

EARE (cont'd)	PAGE	TITLE		LINE
May our requests thine eare invade!	103	Prayer 2		3
And should Gcds eare	134	The Method		17
And should Gods eare,	134	The Method		25
Bow down thine eare!	149	Longing		21
Consider, Iord; Lord, bow thine eare,	149	Longing		29
Lord heare! Shall he that made the eare,	149	Longing		35
the choyce of his wife was made rather by his eare, then by his eye;	238	Priest 9		27
It's a bold mouse that nestles in the catts eare.	344	Proverbs		693
EARES (corn)				
But he a few green eares:	121	Hope		6
EARES				
Yet still they shout, and crie, and stop their eares,	30	Sacrifice		105
The sound of glorie ringing in our eares:	46	Sinne 1		10
I know it is my sinne, which locks thine eares,	66	Ch.-lock		1
I know it is my sinne, which stops thine eares,	66	Ch.-lock	W	1
The fearfull Hare her eares, which by their law	70	Humilitie		11
The fearfull Hare her eares, which by the law	70	Humilitie	W	11
Thy silent eares;	79	Deniall		2
May our requests thine eares invade!	103	Prayer 2	W	3
I have both lost mine eyes and eares.	105	Conscience		6
About her eares:	110	Brit. Ch.		21
As if there were no rule or eares?	136	Familie		4
plunging themselves over head and eares into carking, and caring;	247	Priest 14		25
Brabling Curres never want torne eares.	322	Proverbs		52
Brawling Curres never want sore eares.	322	Proverbs	V	52
Little pitchers have wide eares.	334	Proverbs		380
The resolved minde hath nc eares.	337	Proverbs		464
Discreet women have neither eyes nor eares.	337	Proverbs		482
One paire of eares drawes dry a hundred tongues.	339	Proverbs		526
Citties are taken by the eares.	353	Proverbs		970
neighboring Sea, wondrously sound through all our Coasts, and eares.	442	Oration		24
EARING				
much as the usuall seasons of summer and winter, earing and harvest.	281	Priest 34		24
EARL				
On Henry Danvers earl of Danby. EPITAPH	208	H. Danvers	D	T
EARLY				
Thou, whose sweet youth and early hopes inhance	6	Ch.-Porch		1
Early didst thou arise to plant this vine,	190	Ch.-Milit.		11
Thou didst rise early for to plant this vine,	190	Ch.-Milit.	W	11
Though you rise early, yet the day comes	332	Proverbs		333
EARNED				
His dearely-earned pearl, which God did hide	85	Vanitie 1		10
EARNEST				
Thy sorrows were in earnest; no faint proffer,	104	Obedience		28
True earnest sorrows, rooted miseries,	167	Dotage		7
Who griefs in earnest, joyes in jest pursue;	167	Dotage		14
which though earnest, yet often dy with the Sermon, especially	233	Priest 7		14
hear Sermons against both, and himselfe condemn both in good earnest:	264	Priest 26		16
Leave jesting whiles it pleaseth, lest it turne to earnest.	324	Proverbs		104
more constant and the more earnest for you to the God of all	372	Letters		23
EARNESTLY				
or rather increaseth, I wish earnestly that I were again with you:	372	Letters		17
EARNESTNESS				
that where is much earnestness, there is somewhat worth hearing;	232	Priest 7		32
ease of your pains, with that earnestness, that becomes your griefs,	371	Letters		29
EARNESTNESSE				
With so much earnestnesse you do pursue,	125	Peace		41
both by earnestnesse of speech, it being naturall to men to think,	232	Priest 7		31
but the earnestnesse to do all the good he can, moves him to say thus	251	Priest 17		32
EARS				
Spies are the ears and eyes of Princes.	357	Proverbs	D	1067
EARTH				
Because no knowledg, is not earth but mudd.	7	Ch.-Porch	W	36
With his poore clod of earth the spacious sky.	8	Ch.-Porch		54
And say withall, Earth to earth I commit.	11	Ch.-Porch		132
But say withall, Earth to earth I commit.	11	Ch.-Porch	W	132
With saints on earth, shall cne day with them shine.	24	Ch.-Porch		438
Who grasp the earth and heaven with my fist,	30	Sacrifice		130
Who graspes the earth and heaven in his fist,	30	Sacrifice	W	130
From th' earth unto my brows, and bear the thrall:	32	Sacrifice		167
There the circumference earth is, heav'n the centre.	38	The Sinner		8
There the circumference earth is, heav'n the centure.	38	The Sinner	W	8
Long since on earth, to take possession.	40	Redemption		8
So many hearts on earth, and yet not one	40	Sepulchre		3
Such starres I ccunted mine: both heav'n and earth	46	Afflict.1		11
The Christian plummet sounding heav'n and earth;	51	Prayer 1		4
Our innocent earth to heaven.	53	H.Commun.		32
And leave th' earth to their food.	53	H.Commun.		40
The earth is not too low,	53	Antiphon 1		5
That th' earth did like a heav'n appeare;	59	Whitsunday		10
But wee are falne from Heaven to Earth,	59	Whitsunday	W	13
Lord once more shake the Heaven & earth	59	Whitsunday	W	17
He did not heav'n and earth create,	63	Mattens		15
Comparing dust with dust, and earth with earth.	65	Ch.-monum.		11
Deare earth, fine grasse or hay;	71	Frailtie		6
Thy life on earth was grief, and thou art still	73	Afflict.3		13
Did th' earth and all things with it move.	76	Sunday		46
Till that we both, being toss'd from earth,	77	Sunday		62
What's done on earth, we shall not fare the worse,	78	Ang.&Sts.		27
What's done on earth, we shall nct feare the worse,	78	Ang.&Sts.	V	27

EARTH (cont'd)	PAGE	TITLE		LINE
The earth sat still,	79	Employm.2		14
One life is wrapt In flesh, and tends to earth.	84	Coloss.		5
The bridall of the earth and skie:	87	Vertue		2
The earth doth rest, heav'n move, and fountains flow.	91	Man		26
Earth resteth, Heaven moveth, fountains flow,	91	Man	W	26
To see what help in th' earth or skie:	107	Home		14
Whose flat delights on earth do creep and grow;	111	Vanitie 2		2
Take up thine eyes, which feed on earth;	112	Dawning		2
As if I were all earth?	115	Dulnesse		2
When th' earth was dry, thou mad'st a sea of wet:	120	Providence		113
Sponges, non-sense and sense; mines, th' earth & plants.	121	Providence		136
Through all the earth:	125	Peace		32
We are the earth; and they,	126	Confession		13
With th' one hand touching heav'n, with th' other earth.	131	Mans medly		12
It quits the earth, and mounting more and more,	132	The Storm		11
And I but earth and clay: should I presume	160	Priesthood		8
Of wretched earth. Where once I scorn'd to stand,	161	Priesthood		15
That earth is fitted by the fire and trade	161	Priesthood		16
Come from the earth, from whence those vessels come;	161	Priesthood		20
If earth in earth delight.	161	Priesthood		24
My knees pierce th' earth, mine eies the skie;	162	The Search		5
And on earth	182	Banquet		32
In delights of earth was drown'd;	182	Banquet		33
From Heaven, through Earth, to Hell.	202	Trin.Sun.	W	14
Fouling her nest, my earth invade,	203	Even-song	W	11
Cover the Earth, so doth thy Majesty:	206	Walton 2		3
The Water, and the Earth both unto thee	439	Walton 5		7
No Earth can bee thy Jointure. For the sunne	211	Bohemia	D	3
Doth for two clods of earth ten spheres controule,	211	Bohemia	D	8
Of earth is driven by winds away,	215	Psalm I	D	15
The Kings and Potentates of earth	215	Psalm II	D	3
be learned, ye that judge the earth:	216	Psalm II	D	26
Christ being not to continue on earth, but after hee had fulfilled	225	Priest 1		7
the sun in heaven, or the fire on earth, by reason of their fierce,	271	Priest 30		10
when we had sinned beyond any help in heaven or earth, then thou	288	Priest		26
Blessed be the God of Heaven and Earth!	289	Priest		8
word of God, as their Joy, and Crowne, and their Treasure on earth.	317	Valdesso		34
All our pompe the earth covers.	345	Proverbs		716
As the Earth is but a point in respect of the heavens, so are earthly	372	Letters		29
that creeps upon Gods earth, no not tho' the advice step so far,	378	Letters		12
EARTH'S				
This is Earth's language, for if Heaven come in,	10	Ch.-Porch	W	90
So sits the earths great curse in Adams fall	32	Sacrifice		165
Least that the Night, earths gloomy shade	203	Even-song	W	10
Thou shalt possess earth's farthest bounds	216	Psalm II	D	21
EARTHEN				
To pick out treasures from an earthen pot.	23	Ch.-Porch		430
EARTHINESS				
hath no such earthiness in it, but it may very well be joined	370	Letters		22
EARTHLY				
If souls be made of earthly mold,	111	Vanitie 2		11
Then silly soul take heed; for earthly joy	111	Vanitie 2		17
An earthly globe,	138	The Size		45
Sir John Danvers' earthly part	208	J. Danvers	D	9
while they remember their earthly Lord, do much forget their	226	Priest 2		32
Countrey, the other to his earthly, having no title to either,	239	Priest 10		22
Divine ashes are better then earthly meale.	344	Proverbs		684
of the heavens, so are earthly Troubles compar'd to heavenly Joyes;	372	Letters		30
Your last Letter gave me Earthly preferment, and kept Heavenly	372	Letters		34
EARTHQUAKES				
Rending with earthquakes the partition-wall:	190	Ch.-Milit.		26
EASE				
Usefulnesse comes by labour, wit by ease;	18	Ch.-Porch		291
And could see little, to regard his ease,	49	Faith		3
Thou hast restor'd us to this ease	53	H.Commun.		37
Ease, Power, and Love; I value prayer so,	103	Prayer 2		20
That to my broken heart he was I ease you,	112	JESU		9
Ah my deare Father, ease my smart!	165	The Crosse		31
into Covetousnesse, Love of pleasure, or ease, or the like.	238	Priest 9		24
All these things I do at my ease, and at fit seasons, and in mine own	301	Cornaro		9
Thinke of ease, but worke on.	327	Proverbs		178
Great paines quickly find ease.	339	Proverbs		534
The tooth-ach is more ease then to deale with ill people.	340	Proverbs		558
He that is at ease seekes dainties.	353	Proverbs		985
If you would bee at ease, all the world is not.	355	Proverbs		1019
incessantly begging some ease of your pains, with that earnestness,	371	Letters		29
EASETH				
if poor, and he able, he easeth them therein.	244	Priest 12		25
or easeth him in his Tithes, telling him when he hath forgotten it,	254	Priest 20		16
EASIE				
So loose or easie, that a ruffling winde	72	Constancie		7
Of what an easie quick accesse,	103	Prayer 2		1
Hard things are glorious; easie things good cheap.	119	Providence		97
coming cheap, and easie, and arising from the improvement of things,	241	Priest 10		23
whereas on Sundays it is easie for them to compose themselves	247	Priest 14		7
a most plain and easie framing the question, even containing in	256	Priest 21		34
Yet is it easie for any Scholer to attaine to such a measure	261	Priest 23		2
For home-bred medicines are both more easie for the Parsons purse,	261	Priest 23		31
and not to let go the raines as soon as the horse goes easie.	280	Priest 34		16
Order makes arts easie, and armies victorious, and retains	297	Cornaro		9

EASIE (cont'd)	PAGE	TITLE		LINE
which is both easie for common-weals-men, and very convenient,	299	Cornaro		17
especially since it is easie and most agreeable to the nature of Man.	300	Cornaro		5
not the qualitie for his rule, which is very easie to be observed.	300	Cornaro		16
in a strict performance of a few cheap and easie duties of religion,	319	Valdesso	V	25
A discontented man knowes not where to sit easie.	333	Proverbs		345
To deceive ones selfe is very easie.	342	Proverbs		632
A gentle heart is tyed with an easie thread.	345	Proverbs		726
EASIER				
'Tis easier to build two chimneys, then to maintaine one.	350	Proverbs		893
Heresie may be easier kept out, then shooke off.	357	Proverbs	D	1059
EASILY				
Out-strip their Cupid easily in flight?	206	Walton 1		9
the Church Catechisme, to which all divinity may easily be reduced.	230	Priest 5		9
sake, and to make his higher purposes slip the more easily.	249	Priest 14		12
and dark nature, not easily determinable by Lawyers themselves;	260	Priest 23		20
hee might make his Doctrine slip the more easily into the hearts even	261	Priest 23		19
or known commonly, the beginnings of them are not easily observable:	264	Priest 26		19
which is not easily despised, except it degenerate to pride.	268	Priest 28		26
But this is easily answered:	287	Priest 37		24
Intemperance was not such an evil, but it might easily be remedied;	291	Cornaro		6
fitted my stomack, and in such measure, as easily might be digested:	293	Cornaro		17
without such observation, as is not easily to be made upon others;	297	Cornaro		30
(though most agreeable to them) then their stomack can easily digest:	300	Cornaro		13
that I can easily get on horseback without the advantage	300	Cornaro		35
Wood halfe burnt is easily kindled.	341	Proverbs		606
yet it would easily tyre me, to find out variety of thanks	363	Letters		14
how easily is that answered, when we consider that the Blessings in	373	Letters		27
EASINESSE				
To shew that state dislikes not easinesse.	103	Prayer 2		4
EAST				
That brought the wise men of the East from farre.	28	Sacrifice		51
The Sunne arising in the East,	42	Easter		23
Though he give light, & th' East perfume;	42	Easter		24
Is thy great arm which spans the east and west,	103	Prayer 2		8
East and West touch, the poles do kisse,	163	The Search		43
From the first man in th' East, to fresh and new	168	The Sonne		9
Spices come from the East; so did thy Spouse,	190	Ch.-Milit.		13
And to defray his journey from the east.	196	Ch.-Milit.		214
They are Sinnes nipples, feeding th' east and west.	196	Ch.-Milit.		220
And met in th' east their first and ancient sound,	197	Ch.-Milit.		268
But as the Sunne still goes both west and east;	198	Ch.-Milit.		274
EASTER				
Easter.	41	Easter		T
Easter-wings.	43	East.wings		T
And Easter intimate, enlarge the thing,	86	Lent		26
as, at Easter, Christmasse, Whitsuntide, afore and after Harvest,	259	Priest 22		21
The Jewes spend at Easter, the Mores at marriages,	329	Proverbs		242
EASTER-WINGS				
Easter-wings.	43	East.wings		T
EASTERN				
Among the eastern nations for a time,	191	Ch.-Milit.		35
Sinne did set out of Eastern Babylon,	193	Ch.-Milit.		103
EASTWARD				
Still eastward go; because it drew more neare	198	Ch.-Milit.		276
EASY (see also easie)				
will make the Consideration easy, and very observeable:	320	Valdesso		5
EAT				
Look on meat, think it dirt, then eat a bit;	11	Ch.-Porch		131
Will no more talk all, then eat all the feast.	18	Ch.-Porch		306
I had it straight, and did as truly eat,	50	Faith		7
The beasts say, Eat me: but, if beasts must teach,	117	Providence		21
The tongue is yours to eat, but mine to praise.	117	Providence		22
Some creatures have in winter what to eat;	118	Providence		55
Sheep eat the grasse, and dung the ground for more:	119	Providence		69
Now eat his bread in peace,	127	Giddinesse		10
Wouldst thou both eat thy cake, and have it?	138	The Size		18
So I did sit and eat.	189	Love 3		18
Begging his food of that which he may eat,	193	Ch.-Milit.		113
so that to eat little, and that unpleasant, is the naturall rule	242	Priest 10		10
then some fish there, certainly to eat the flesh, and not the fish,	242	Priest 10		14
so that men must eat neither to the disturbance of their health,	266	Priest 26		13
But to eat to ones hurt, comprehends, besides the hurt,	266	Priest 26		20
none must eat so as to disable themselves from a fit discharging	266	Priest 26		29
in eating, that he can eat more, then afterwards he finds true:)	267	Priest 26		3
so man did eat Angels food:	290	Priest		9
followed my Appetite, and did eat meats pleasing to my taste;	292	Cornaro		27
with a full stomack, but so as I might well both eat and drink more.	293	Cornaro		19
the one whereof was, He that will eat much, let him eat little;	295	Cornaro		34
the one whereof was, He that will eat much, let him eat little;	295	Cornaro		35
so that we can eat but a very little, wherewith she is very well	299	Cornaro		28
ought not to eat, but such meats as are agreeable to his disease,	299	Cornaro		30
No man that followes it, is bound to eat and drink so little as I:	300	Cornaro		6
No man is forbidden to eat fruit or fish, which I eat not:	300	Cornaro		7
No man is forbidden to eat fruit or fish, which I eat not:	300	Cornaro		8
For I eat little, because a little sufficeth my weak stomack:	300	Cornaro		8
Threatned men eat bread, says the Spaniard.	358	Proverbs	D	1081
Hee that makes himself a sheep, shall be eat by the wolfe.	358	Proverbs	D	1089
Now this Lent I am forbid utterly to eat any Fish, so that I am fain	365	Letters		2
EATE				
or over-nourishing things, as the Israelites did eate sowre herbs:	242	Priest 10		4

EFFECT (cont'd)	PAGE	TITLE		LINE
that my advice hath taken effect in the reducing of many rude	302	Cornaro		14
That which two will, takes effect.	345	Proverbs		705
The effect speakes, the tongue needes not.	345	Proverbs		709
EFFECTED				
Which they effected, none could them withstand.	84	The World		18
14. which we see even miraculously effected in these new discoveryes,	282	Priest 34		33
EFFECTING				
mens Covetousnesse, and Ambitions to the effecting of his word.	282	Priest 34		34
EFFECTS				
This he effects either by bounty, or perswasion, or by authority,	244	Priest 12		21
For contrarie causes have contrarie effects, and the faults cf Nature	292	Cornaro		10
EFFECTUALL				
understand he meaneth only the effectuall operation or illumination	308	Valdesso		31
EFFECTUALLY				
that it may effectually pierce their hearts, and convert them.	262	Priest 24		24
effectually applying Gods favour to the blessed, by the interesting	286	Priest 36		8
EFFICACIE				
So great is the power and efficacie of that Temperance which ever	302	Cornaro		21
EFFICACY				
promises to every one in particular with such syncerity and efficacy,	309	Valdesso		5
EGGE				
He that steals an egge, will steal an oxe.	358	Proverbs	D	1090
It is very hard to shave an egge.	359	Proverbs	D	1128
EGGES				
of my bread, and egges, and flesh, and broth, was twelve ounces	296	Cornaro		10
EGYPT				
To Egypt first she came, where they did prove	191	Ch.-Milit.		37
Goshen was darknesse, Egypt full of lights,	191	Ch.-Milit.		43
Though Greece took horse as soon as Egypt did,	191	Ch.-Milit.		57
And Rome as both; yet Egypt faster rid,	191	Ch.-Milit.		58
At first he got to Egypt, and did sow,	193	Ch.-Milit.		107
Thus Sinne in Egypt sneaked for a while;	193	Ch.-Milit.		121
So trimme, as Greece and Egypt? yet their hearts	194	Ch.-Milit.		151
So spruse, as Greece and Egypt? yet their hearts	194	Ch.-Milit.	W	151
From Egypt he tock pettie deities,	195	Ch.-Milit.		177
From Egypt Anchorisme and retirednesse,	195	Ch.-Milit.		187
EGYPTIAN				
Had to this day been an Egyptian slave.	27	Sacrifice		10
I have deserv'd that an Egyptian night	83	Sighs & Gr.		14
EIE				
With bushie groves, pricking the lookers eie,	51	Faith		38
He scarce allow'd me half an eie.	111	The Quip		15
EIES				
Thy friend put in thy bosome: wear his eies	17	Ch.-Porch		271
And love's a weight to hearts, to eies a signe.	22	Ch.-Porch		399
In time of service seal up both thine eies,	23	Ch.-Porch		415
Who by my spittle gave the blinde man eies,	31	Sacrifice		134
Who by my spittle gave that blinde man eies,	31	Sacrifice	W	134
Our eies shall see thee, which before saw dust;	54	Love 2		9
And praise him who did make and mend our eies.	54	Love 2		14
My knees pierce th' earth, mine eies the skie;	162	The Search		5
EIGHT				
although I was now seventie eight yeares old, and my bodie spent	296	Cornaro		26
EIGHTIE				
me contrariwise, at the age of eightie and one, strong and lustie;	291	Cornaro		11
EIGHTY				
recounting the delights and pleasures in this age of eighty three,	300	Cornaro		32
EITHER				
For churches are either our heav'n or hell.	23	Ch.-Porch		426
For churches either are our heav'n or hell.	23	Ch.-Porch	W	426
Lest on their double-dark souls either shine:	31	Sacrifice		139
O blessed streams! either ye do prevent	44	H. Bapt.1		7
If either Innocence or Fervencie	66	Ch.-lock	W	4
The gentle rising, which on either hand	67	Ch.-floore		7
From either pole unto the centre:	69	Content		18
From either pole unto the centure:	69	Content	W	18
And hollow room on either hand.	75	Sunday	W	25
The whole is, either our cupboard of food,	91	Man		29
If either will convert us, we are thine:	97	Afflict.5		14
And sev'rall baits in either kinde	97	Afflict.5		17
Yet either this,	101	Miserie		41
The fight is hard on either part.	106	Sion		15
For all they either painted are,	109	Brit. Ch.		11
For either thy command, or thy permission	117	Providence		33
Either grief will not come: or if it must,	145	Discharge		51
Either the league was broke, or neare it;	155	Assurance		11
Making our pillows either down, or dust.	186	Death		24
Either t' his publick foot or private tricks.	195	Ch.-Milit.		196
And thou more dark then either.	203	Even-song	W	16
On either hand	204	The Knell	W	4
entertained to that end, either by an open, or implicite Covenant.	226	Priest 2		22
serves either positively as it is, or else to illustrate some other	228	Priest 4		16
possible reverence, by no means enduring either talking, or sleeping,	231	Priest 6		23
it is either for want of health, or against some great Festivall,	232	Priest 7		22
none goes out of Church as he came in, but either better, or worse;	233	Priest 7		20
exercises, either from the time of the year, or from the State,	235	Priest 8		34
Almighty God, and blessing the people either openly, or to himselfe.	236	Priest 8		6
The rest of the day he spends either in reconciling neighbours that	236	Priest 8		11
either to entertaine some of his neighbours, or to be entertained	236	Priest 8		19
and accordingly either meets with their vices, or advanceth their	239	Priest 10		9

EITHER (cont'd)	PAGE	TITLE		LINE
His wife is either religious, or night and day he is winning her	239	Priest 10		10
which skill either she brought with her, or he takes care she shall	239	Priest 10		15
to his earthly, having no title to either, except he do good to both.	239	Priest 10		22
for all in his house are either teachers or learners, or both,	240	Priest 10		21
and doing that which either he could not do, or was not fit for him	241	Priest 10		32
draught of beer, then if it had taken before either fish, or rootes,	242	Priest 10		24
This he effects either by bounty, or perswasion, or by authority,	244	Priest 12		21
and even in those wrongs which either in tithing, or otherwise are	250	Priest 16		13
First, what disorders there are either in Apparell, or Diet,	251	Priest 17		19
either by the wickedness or quarrelsomnesse thereof, he either	252	Priest 18		16
he either prevents it judiciously, or breaks it off seasonably	252	Priest 18		17
unto him in any difficulty, either in his studies or in his Parish.	253	Priest 19		8
some defects in the Ministry, he then either in Sermon, if he preach,	253	Priest 19		12
if God have sent any calamity either by fire, or famine, . .	253	Priest 19		29
making together a summe either to be sent, or, which were more	253	Priest 19		36
Wherefore there is nothing done either wel or ill, whereof he is	254	Priest 20		10
they come home, either commend or reprove, either reward or punish.	255	Priest 21		28
they come home, either commend or reprove, either reward or punish.	255	Priest 21		29
So, where the Apothecary useth either for loosing, Rubarb, . .	261	Priest 23		33
and to do such things of legall opposition either in the presenting,	263	Priest 25		24
either spends not at all, or not in some proportion to Gods blessing	265	Priest 26		5
and those more which concerne me, I either do nothing, or pinch,	265	Priest 26		16
and I either provide too little for them, or that which is . .	265	Priest 26		20
He that either for quantity eats more then his health or imployments	266	Priest 26		6
offensively to the Company, either in his order, or length of eating,	266	Priest 26		10
to disable themselves from a fit discharging either of Divine duties,	266	Priest 26		30
that if after dinner they are not fit (or un-weeldy) either to pray,	266	Priest 26		31
disposition I am, either hungry or not, according as I feele my self,	267	Priest 26		8
feele my self, either I take my wonted proportion, or diminish of it.	267	Priest 26		9
either of Abstinence a morall vertue, or Mortification a divine.	267	Priest 26		16
that are reproved, but never contempt either in them, or others.	268	Priest 28		30
the Parson think it in his discretion either unfit, or bootelesse	269	Priest 28		4
he takes it either in an humble way, saying nothing at all; . .	269	Priest 28		6
it according as he sees fit, either for reward or punishment.	270	Priest 30		31
certainly it should be either the sun in heaven, or the fire	271	Priest 30		10
either blessing God, that he will be pleased to dwell among men;	273	Priest 31		24
if he now, shall either for fear or shame, break his custome,	273	Priest 31		30
All are either to have a Calling, or prepare for it: . . .	275	Priest 32		11
Wherefore all are either presently to enter into a Calling, . .	275	Priest 32		14
Men are either single, or marryed:	275	Priest 32		19
the Village or Parish which either he lives in, or is neer unto it,	276	Priest 32		2
and either helps them in particular, or hath generall Propositions	276	Priest 32		3
kindle them rather to redeem the Dignity either from true faults,	276	Priest 32		24
for single men, they are either Heirs, or younger Brothers: . .	276	Priest 32		25
morning that hee is at home hee must either ride the Great Horse,	277	Priest 32		16
we are assaulted with temptations either from within or from without.	280	Priest 34		4
either they think, that there is none that can or will look after	281	Priest 34		7
he sees not how a house could be either built without a builder,	281	Priest 34		18
either he doth it as they are Creatures, dust and ashes; . .	283	Priest 34		10
till either they despise that Love, or despaire of his Mercy:	283	Priest 34		23
do so either out of niceness, because they like the salutations,	285	Priest 36		4
Faults are either notorious, or private.	287	Priest 37		11
Again notorious faults are either such as are made known by common	287	Priest 37		12
passed judgment, & been corrected either by whipping, or imprisoning,	287	Priest 37		15
neither omit I any thing that may either teach, or delight me.	302	Cornaro		5
He that will do thee a good turne, either he will be gon or dye.	358	Proverbs	D	1083
Either wealth is much increased, or moderation is much decayed.	360	Proverbs	D	1139
then either of them both.	361	Proverbs	D	1173
either void of knowledge, or of the fear of God.	361	Proverbs	D	1176
either by engaging my future Annuity, or any other way, . .	365	Letters		20
as that either his subjects only should practise it, or at least that	368	Letters		11
therefore, if either Age or Sickness lead you to those Joyes?	372	Letters		31
consider all that can happen to you are either afflictions of Estate,	373	Letters		21
no obligation lying upon you either for the execution or benefitt	380	Woodnoth		26
by the way of supporting either it (in regard of the citty) or your	380	Woodnoth		27
7. Though you want all success either in inclining or restraining,	381	Woodnoth		14
glorious shew is there, either of garments, or of any thing else?	442	Oration		31
EJACULATION				
the reading of the Scripture with some short inward ejaculation,	229	Priest 4		2
EJACULATIONS				
The Temple. Sacred Poems and Private Ejaculations. Dedication.	5	Dedication		T
ELBOW				
Diseases of the eye are to bee cured with the elbow. . . .	327	Proverbs		203
Diseases of the eyes are to bee cured with the elbow. . . .	326	Proverbs	V	203
ELDER				
speech now to the younger sort, then to the elder, now to the poor,	233	Priest 7		4
of the elder, the substance.	255	Priest 21		23
that those of the elder sort, who are not well grounded, . .	255	Priest 21		30
And Elder, camomill, mallowes, comphrey and smallage made into	262	Priest 23		7
ELDEST				
not sparing the eldest, but giving him the prerogative of his Fathers	239	Priest 10		31
I will tell you what I wrote to our eldest brother, when he urged one	375	Letters		10
ELECTED				
Thou hast elected us, thou hast called us, thou hast justified us,	290	Priest		2
ELEMENT				
it is his predominant element.	244	Priest 12		7
ELEMENTARY				
holy Scriptures have not only an Elementary use, but a use . .	306	Valdesso		18
H. Scriptures (as I wrote before) have not only an Elementary use,	309	Valdesso		21

ELEMENTS	PAGE	TITLE	LINE
Onely thy grace, which with these elements comes, ...	52	H.Commun.	19
Though elements change, and heaven move, ...	56	Temper 2	14
To spell his elements, and finde his birth	65	Ch.-monum.	8
When th' elements did for place contest	79	Employm.2	11
The elements are let loose to fight, ...	90	Afflict.4	17
There are but twc devouring elements, fire, and water, he hath both	234	Priest 7	33
the Church-Wardens, that the elements be of the best, not cheape,	258	Priest 22	22
if our corporall life depend on the harmonie of humours & elements,	297	Cornaro	8
ELEPHANT			
Most things sleep lying; th' Elephant leans or stands.	121	Providence	140
Most things sleep lying; th' Elephant leane or stand.	121	Providence V	140
ELEVEN			
I finde eleven grand-children of mine, all the sonnes of one father	303	Cornaro	2
ELEVENTH			
that some are called at the eleventh houre, and therefore hee still	250	Priest 16	19
ELISHA			
So in the Old Testament Elisha cursed the children, 2 Kings 2. 24.	285	Priest 36	26
ELIXER			
The Elixer.	184	The Elixer	T
ELIZABETH			
the Professours whereof were much imployed by Queen Elizabeth,	277	Priest 32	32
then I leave to my servant Elizabeth her dubble wages given her,	382	G.H.'s Will	22
George Herbert (testes Nathaniell Bostocke, Elizabeth Burden)	382	G.H.'s Will	34
To Mrs Elizabeth Danvers Mr Henry Danvers wife twenty shillings,	383	G.H.'s Will	12
To Mr Bostocke forty shillings To Elizabeth Burthen thirty shillings	383	G.H.'s Will	15
ELL			
Make not an ell, by trifling in thy wo.	24	Ch.-Porch	460
And quickly gain, for each inch lost, an ell.	103	Prayer 2	24
ELLES			
In an hundred elles of contention, there is not an inch of love.	348	Proverbs	817
ELLS			
Ill comes in by ells, and goes out by inches.	327	Proverbs	194
ELOQUENCE			
Nor yet thy eloquence here keep him still, ...	439	Walton 5	3
Love and businesse teach eloquence.	345	Proverbs	704
ELOQUENT			
he is not witty, or learned, or eloquent, but Holy.	233	Priest 7	24
ELS			
Or els they breed them tender, make them need	10	Ch.-Porch	105
Then live, and use it: els, it is not true	12	Ch.-Porch	154
To all things els. Wealth is the conjurers devil;	13	Ch.-Porch	165
As if that thou hadst nothing els to do?	62	Mattens	12
if there be any body els that owe me any thing else of old debt I	383	G.H.'s Will	26
ELSE			
I him obey, who all things else command:	29	Sacrifice	83
Or else give tears to drown them, as they grow.	44	H. Bapt.1	9
Or else the chilnesse of my faint demands.	66	Ch.-lock	4
Which else shows watrish, bleak, & thin.	67	Windows	10
Or else undrest.	109	Brit. Ch.	12
positively as it is, or else to illustrate some other knowledge.	228	Priest 4	17
or else if the thing will admit interpretation;	252	Priest 18	10
an illustrating the thing by something else, which he knows,	256	Priest 21	37
or else in a slighting way, shewing that reproaches touch him no	269	Priest 28	6
or else in a doctrinall way, saying to the contemner, Alas, . .	269	Priest 28	11
or else to examine with care, and advice, what they are fittest for,	275	Priest 32	15
all those, who else might both trouble him and the whole State.	276	Priest 32	15
Or else, though there be a great Governour of all things, . .	281	Priest 34	9
not any sin else, but is within his Love;	283	Priest 34	24
Or else, because they think it empty and superfluous.	285	Priest 36	8
or else such as have passed judgment, & been corrected either	287	Priest 37	14
From this ill temper there remained little else to be expected of me,	291	Cornaro	24
I doe so love him, that were there nothing else, I would Print it,	305	Valdesso	7
in the Church of God there is one fundamentall, but else variety.	312	Valdesso	3
that I may speak with him or doe some thing else when I doe come.	318	Valdesso	17
The yeare doth nothing else but open and shut.	351	Proverbs	901
but every thing else in this world.	358	Proverbs D	1077
and hath nothing else to answer your infinite kindnesses, . .	363	Letters	19
spend her eyesight on a piece of paper, or else I had wrote to her;	371	Letters	14
any body els that owe me any thing else of old debt I forgive them.	383	G.H.'s Will	26
glorious shew is there, either of garments, or of any thing else?	442	Oration	32
ELSEWHERE			
Go seek elsewhere.	124	Peace	6
and with more safety then elsewhere, where both the people . .	242	Priest 10	19
and also elsewhere, when they see any remarkable point of Education	276	Priest 32	29
words about the H. Scripture suite with what he writes elsewhere,	306	Valdesso	16
but it is sutable to what the Author holds elsewhere, for he	311	Valdesso	22
EMBALME			
Bedew, embalme, and overrunne my heart, ...	171	The Glance	7
EMBELLISHED			
The wood was all embellished	106	Sion	4
EMBELLISHMENT			
Perhaps with more embellishment can say, ...	177	Forerunners	33
EMBLEMS			
All, Emblems, which thy Darling doth improve.	190	Ch.-Milit. W	16
EMBOLDENING			
not for emboldening the unruly, but for the comfort of the weak,	242	Priest 10	33
EMBOSOMES			
Embosomes in us, mellowing the ground	85	Vanitie 1	24
EMBRACE			
Embrace their activenesse, not vanities.	21	Ch.-Porch	363

	PAGE	TITLE		LINE
EMBRACE (cont'd)				
Then for yourselves not us embrace	211	Paradox	D	37
all who have the care of themselves, to embrace it with open arms?	303	Cornaro		32
A man is to embrace all good, but because he cannot doe all,	313	Valdesso		21
for respect to you, embrace all that is cheerefull, joyous,	442	Oration		7
EMBRACED				
The thrusting away of his arme makes us onely not embraced.	283	Priest 34		26
then a Temperate Life, Temperance by all means is to be embraced.	298	Cornaro		2
that in stead of a Physician a regular life is to be embraced,	298	Cornaro		12
so decent, and so holy, it is worthy by all means to be embraced;	300	Cornaro		5
EMBRACETH				
Losse embraceth shame.	341	Proverbs		603
EMBROIDER'D				
Embroider'd lyes, nothing between two dishes;	167	Dotage		5
EMBROYDERIES				
Nor solid work, as false embroyderies;	111	Vanitie 2		4
EMERGENT				
that the godly petitioner upon some emergent interruption in the day,	272	Priest 31		30
EMINENCY				
is a common temptation to men of any eminency, especially being	238	Priest 9		17
for this argues a height and eminency of mind, which is not easily	268	Priest 28		25
EMINENT				
of that, wherin they are most eminent, is the most gainfull way	260	Priest 23		6
he may go to Court, as the eminent place both of good and ill.	277	Priest 32		5
to publish it, for these three eminent things observable therein:	304	Valdesso		19
These three things are very eminent in the Author, and overweigh	305	Valdesso		12
EMPEROUR				
He was a God, now he's an Emperour.	194	Ch.-Milit.		140
And in old Rome a mightie Emperour;	195	Ch.-Milit.		172
EMPEROURS				
and cheerfull dying under persecuting Emperours, (though that indeed	237	Priest 9		30
EMPIRE				
But th' Empire dwelt in Greece, to comfort them	192	Ch.-Milit.		73
Many a rent and struggling th' Empire knew,	192	Ch.-Milit.		79
That as before Empire and Arts made way,	192	Ch.-Milit.		83
Spain in the Empire shar'd with Germanie,	192	Ch.-Milit.		89
As new and old Rome did one Empire twist;	196	Ch.-Milit.		205
And where of old the Empire and the Arts	197	Ch.-Milit.		263
This is thy empire yet: till better season	213	Bohemia	D	60
EMPLOY (see also imploy)				
Thousands of things do thee employ	158	Praise 3		19
Should all my life employ, and busie me.	175	The Odour		30
which they can better employ to their own advantage, and sutably	243	Priest 11		16
EMPLOYED				
That they who are employed in the common wealth, cannot live	299	Cornaro		12
EMPLOYMENT				
Chase brave employment with a naked sword	10	Ch.-Porch	W	88
Employment.	57	Employm. 1		T
Employment.	78	Employm.2		T
preserve themselves from diseases, which hinder publick employment;	299	Cornaro		19
quickly make good my wish but that my employment does fix me here,	372	Letters		19
EMPLOYMENTS				
Chase brave employments with a naked sword	10	Ch.-Porch		88
EMPTIE				
Emptie vessels sound most.	342	Proverbs		643
EMPTI'D				
A part whereof my Saviour empti'd hath,	83	Sighs & Gr.		22
EMPTINESSE				
Chases in Arras, guilded emptinesse,	167	Dotage		3
EMPTY				
And are like empty vessels under sail.	14	Ch.-Porch		184
As empty boldnesse: therefore first assay	15	Ch.-Porch		207
they would have fainted, had they returned empty, He suffered it not;	267	Priest 26		24
Or else, because they think it empty and superfluous.	285	Priest 36		8
that as the rain returns not empty, so neither may thy word,	289	Priest		31
Empty Chambers make foolish maides.	322	Proverbs		29
The sonne full and tattered, the daughter empty and fine.	328	Proverbs		214
ENABLED (see also inable)				
as being persons enabled by that Name to take moveable goods,	270	Priest 29		1
ENACT				
Enact good cheer?	138	The Size		16
ENCHANTED (see also inchanted)				
Is it no verse, except enchanted groves	56	Jordan 1		6
ENCHANTING				
With her enchanting voice.	170	Self-cond.		12
Lovely enchanting language, sugar-cane,	176	Forerunners		19
ENCLINE				
Lord to my words encline thine ear,	218	Psalm V	D	1
ENCLOSE (see also inclose)				
ENCOMPASS				
His favour shall encompass them,	219	Psalm V	D	43
ENCOUNTER				
Encounter Moses strong complaints and mone:	99	Decay		4
Setting affliction to encounter pleasure;	194	Ch.-Milit.		148
Setting afflictions to encounter pleasure;	194	Ch.-Milit.	W	148
bring strangers to him, he may be the better armed to encounter them.	274	Priest 32		8
ENCOUNTERS				
He that goeth farre hath many encounters.	341	Proverbs		608
ENCOURAGED				
that so both they may be encouraged to persevere, and others spurred	243	Priest 11		26

	PAGE	TITLE		LINE
ENCOURAGEMENT				
is the encouragement of learning all the year after, except my cousin	375	Letters		28
ENCOURAGEMENTS				
sets up as many encouragements to goodnesse as he can, both in	244	Priest 11		3
ENCOURAGING				
encouraging also the servants to learn to read, and offering to have	248	Priest 14		36
ENCROACH (see also incroach)				
And do encroach upon deaths side.	145	Discharge		35
ENCUMBRANCE (see also incumbrances)				
END				
Praying's the end of preaching. O be drest;	23	Ch.-Porch		410
Do end in bubbles, balls of winde;	64	Even-song		14
And us in th' end.	92	Antiphon 2		9
Unto my friends intent and end.	93	Unkindness		4
O sacred Providence, who from end to end	116	Providence		1
More favour then you wot of. Mark the end.	130	Love unkn.		63
And such beginnings touch their END.	133	Paradise		15
End as the night, whose sable hue	135	Ephes.		11
Which have the face of fire, but end in rest.	139	Artillerie		8
Can both the way and end be tears?	142	Pilgrimage		28
And draw the bottome out an end.	145	Discharge		45
No end?	148	Longing		6
Now love and truth will end in man.	156	Assurance		42
Much wrastling, many a combate, this deare end,	164	The Crosse		8
When Love being weary made an end	439	Walton 5		11
Love neere his death desir'd to end	439	Walton 5	V	11
The Flemmish rivers: in the end	213	L' Envoy	D	3
they live in, and are entertained to that end, either by an open,	226	Priest 2		22
To this end, besides his ordinary prayers, he makes a peculiar one	235	Priest 8		21
as that they make not that the end of their labour, but that they may	248	Priest 14		7
To this end he hath throughly digested all the points of consolation,	249	Priest 15		17
he considers what is the end of any Command, and then he suits things	253	Priest 19		4
and then he suits things faithfully according to that end.	253	Priest 19		5
To this end, he hath gotten to himself some insight in things	259	Priest 23		33
because wealth is given to that end to supply our occasions.	265	Priest 26		8
if I do not give every thing its end, I abuse the Creature,	265	Priest 26		9
To this end he represents to his flock, that God hath and exerciseth	270	Priest 30		32
that after many troubles and griefs I should quickly come to an end;	291	Cornaro		26
and abhorring from so sudden an end, and finding my self continually	292	Cornaro		18
increased so much in them, that it brought them to a sudden end.	294	Cornaro		20
For in the end I got the victorie, to my great honour, and no lesse	294	Cornaro		28
they live disorderly, yet continue in health to their lives end:	300	Cornaro		19
are so ordered, that they all meet and end in a fair plot of ground;	301	Cornaro		22
Yet I am sure, that my end is farre from me:	303	Cornaro		25
that Temperance which I have found so good, I here make an end.	303	Cornaro		35
this line [place] till the end of this Chapter may seeme strange,	311	Valdesso		20
Praise day at night, and life at the end.	324	Proverbs		97
At the games end we shall see who gaines.	339	Proverbs		538
He that can make a fire well, can end a quarrell.	340	Proverbs		557
God is at the end, when we thinke he is furthest off it.	341	Proverbs		598
and a latin-bred woman, seldome end well.	349	Proverbs		866
We must recoile a little, to the end we may leap the better.	359	Proverbs	D	1121
Love without end, hath no end, says the Spaniard: (meaning,	361	Proverbs	D	1160
Stay a while, that we may make an end the sooner.	361	Proverbs	D	1161
but that every day, I may step one step towards my journies end;	364	Letters		28
what I desire, and to what end, not vain pleasures, nor to a vain	365	Letters		19
and to what end, not vain pleasures, nor to a vain end.	365	Letters		20
but, their Fiery-tryals have had an end:	374	Letters		1
our observation, to the end, wee might the more by love grow on,	442	Oration		16
ENDEAR (see also indear)				
ENDEAVOUR				
Though many sunnes to shine endeavour?	42	Easter		28
he is to endeavour by all means to be a Knight or Burgess there;	277	Priest 32		9
Wherefore in case a Christian endeavour to weep, and cannot,	279	Priest 33		18
To desire good & endeavour it when we can doe no more, is to doe it.	381	Woodnoth		15
ENDEAVOURED				
& have endeavoured many wayes, to find out a man for it.	378	Letters		6
ENDEAVOURETH				
the Parson endeavoureth to be in Gods stead, knowing that Countrey	254	Priest 20		30
ENDEAVOURING				
endeavouring to disorder the Christian, and put him out of his	272	Priest 31		33
ENDEAVOURS				
to the Apostles rule, he endeavours that none shall despise him;	268	Priest 28		17
which endeavours to preserve a man as much as she can, teacheth us	299	Cornaro		25
ENDING				
The words ending in Ique do mocke the Physician	357	Proverbs	D	1044
ENDLESSE				
To endlesse death: but thou dost pull	75	Sunday		16
Ev'n endlesse tears	136	Ephes.		26
ENDORSEMENT (see also indorsement)				
ENDOW				
Affront those joyes, wherewith thou didst endow,	71	Frailtie		19
ENDOWMENTS				
Wealth, fame, endowments, vertues, all should go;	103	Prayer 2		22
ENDS				
Fathers first enter bonds to natures ends;	17	Ch.-Porch		281
Such a Truth, as ends all strife:	156	The Call		3
I shake my head, and all the thoughts and ends,	169	The Answer		2
if it were not begun on particular ends, it would last).	361	Proverbs	D	1160
hath guided me hitherto, and of atchieving my (I dare say) holy ends.	364	Letters		19

	PAGE	TITLE		LINE
ENDURE				
Of thicker stuffe, which would endure a shake.	15	Ch.-Porch		226
None shall in hell such bitter pangs endure,	24	Ch.-Porch		445
He did endure to cancell sinne:	151	The Bag		22
That thou didst all those pains endure	200	H. Commun.	W	20
live regularly, because they must often endure heats, and colds,	299	Cornaro		13
ENDUR'D				
Wounds willingly endur'd to work his blisse,	192	Ch.-Milit.		65
and have endur'd such other Tortures, as the very mention of them	373	Letters		36
ENDURED				
For having endured many heats & colds, and other like discommodities	294	Cornaro		12
ENDURES				
Therefore hee endures not that any of his Flock should go to Law;	259	Priest 23		31
He that endures is not overcome.	349	Proverbs		854
An Asse endures his burden, but not more then his burden.	358	Proverbs	D	1080
ENDURING				
possible reverence, by no means enduring either talking, or sleeping,	231	Priest 6		23
ENEMIE				
Much lesse make any one thine enemie.	20	Ch.-Porch		351
Much lesse make any one thy enemie.	20	Ch.-Porch	W	351
Lest the enemie should winne?	181	Banquet		18
Then let mine enemie prevail	221	Psalm VII	D	15
He that cockers his child, provides for his enemie.	347	Proverbs		789
ENEMIES				
Leaving his blindnesse to mine enemies:	31	Sacrifice		135
Leaving his blindnesse to my enemies:	31	Sacrifice	W	135
ten thousand enemies:	216	Psalm III	D	14
because of all mine Enemies;	220	Psalm VI	D	18
against these ghostly enemies he girdeth up his loynes,	238	Priest 9		4
like mortall enemies, may sometimes disquiet him likewise;	238	Priest 9		9
and not as enemies, neither avoyding therfore one anothers company,	260	Priest 23		26
for his enemies he died;	288	Priest		29
Health and sicknesse surely are mens double enemies.	354	Proverbs		1011
with which you use to conquer your enemies, and assume more mild	442	Oration		3
ENEMIES'				
Ev'n in my enemies sight:	173	23 Psalme		18
Ev'n in mine enemies sight:	173	23 Psalme	V	18
ENEMY				
when the baits which the enemy lays in company, are discovered	252	Priest 18		14
neither doth he esteem him for an enemy, but as a brother still,	263	Priest 25		29
not the evill which takes hold of them, and is farr the worse enemy.	269	Priest 28		25
One enemy is too much.	339	Proverbs		523
He that passeth a winters day escapes an enemy.	349	Proverbs		864
Wine is a turne-coate (first a friend, then an enemy).	351	Proverbs		929
The War is not don so long as my Enemy lives.	357	Proverbs	D	1051
and a reconciled Enemy.	360	Proverbs	D	1154
Trust no friend with that you need fear him if he were your enemy.	361	Proverbs	D	1169
ENFOLD (see also infold)				
ENFORCE				
Good cable, to enforce and draw,	153	The Collar		24
ENFORCETH				
Enforceth tears. Your heart was foul, I fear.	129	Love unkn.		18
ENGAGING (see also ingaging)				
either by engaging my future Annuity, or any other way,	365	Letters		20
ENGENDER (see also ingendred)				
ENGINE				
Wit's an unruly engine, wildly striking	16	Ch.-Porch		241
Engine against th' Almightie, sinners towre,	51	Prayer 1		5
Engine against th' Almightie, sinners fort,	51	Prayer 1	W	5
Did like some torturing engine show;	141	Justice 2		10
Did like some tottering engine show;	141	Justice 2	V	10
ENGINEER				
Sometimes a friend, sometimes the engineer.	16	Ch.-Porch		242
ENGLAND				
O England! full of sinne, but most of sloth;	10	Ch.-Porch		91
O England, full of all sinn, most of sloth,	10	Ch.-Porch	W	91
But England in the higher victorie:	192	Ch.-Milit.		90
Shall both in France and England domineer:	197	Ch.-Milit.		246
All the Armes of England will not arme feare.	345	Proverbs		722
but upon the want of those Books which were not to be got in England;	367	Letters		5
who writt a poem heere in England & presented it to the King,	368	Letters		30
ENGLISH				
One thing is evident, that an English body, and a Students body,	243	Priest 10		1
by Lud. Cornarus, Translated into English by Mr. George Herbert.	291	Cornaro		T
meet with a witty French speech, try to speak the like in English:	366	Letters		11
ENGRAVE				
Engrave thy rev'rend law and fear;	45	Nature		14
Gladly engrave thy love in steel,	55	Temper 1		2
ENGRAVEN				
On whose meridian was engraven,	138	The Size		46
ENGROSS (see also ingrosse)				
ENHANCE (see also inhanse)				
ENJOINED (see also injoyned)				
for I am enjoined to write to you by Sir John Danvers, to which mine	367	Letters		28
ENJOY				
Mark all his wandrings, and enjoy his frets;	19	Ch.-Porch		315
Light to the minde: what shall the will enjoy?	188	Heaven		15
others spurred to do well, that they may enjoy the like courtesie.	243	Priest 11		27
I enjoy also my gardens, and those divers, parted with rills	301	Cornaro		15
Some times of the yeare I enjoy the pleasure of the Euganean hills,	301	Cornaro		17
that I may enjoy the sight & communication of my friends,	301	Cornaro		35

ENJOY (cont'd)	PAGE	TITLE		LINE
Goods are theirs that enjoy them.	349	Proverbs		850
ENJOYES				
and the world his that enjoyes it.	337	Proverbs		476
ENJOYNED				
and the dayly prayers enjoyned him by auctority, which he observeth	237	Priest 9		23
ENLARGE (see also inlarged)				
And Easter intimate, enlarge the thing, ...	86	Lent		26
that he may enlarge the glory cf God to the company he is in,	251	Priest 17		8
well spoken, or done, he takes occasion to commend, and enlarge it;	252	Priest 18		5
ENLARGED				
O thou that hast enlarged me	217	Psalm IV	D	3
With some of these heads enlarged, and woven into his discourse,	283	Priest 34		3
ENLARGETH				
But when he enlargeth he goes too farre.	315	Valdesso		35
ENLIGHTENS				
but enlightens us with new Considerations the more we read it.	310	Valdesso		34
ENMITIE				
But yet their friendship is my enmitie:	29	Sacrifice		75
Purgings enmitie disclose, ...	178	The Rose		19
Enmitie forbearance urgeth.	178	The Rose		20
ENOUGH (see alsc inough)				
Ah! was it not enough that thou	37	Reprisall		9
Thy praise enough? thou art heav'ns Lidger here, ...	58	H.Script.1	W	11
This was not quick enough, and that was dead.	102	Jordan 2		10
All countreys have enough to serve their need:	120	Providence		105
But who hath praise enough? nay who hath any?	121	Providence		141
Where shall I get me eyes enough to weep, ...	140	Ch.-rents		25
They ask enough; why shouldst thou further go?	145	Discharge		26
Sure, Lord, there is enough in thee to dry	206	Walton 2		1
He therefore thinkes it not enough for him to observe the fasting	237	Priest 9		21
their understandings being ripe enough for ill things, and why	259	Priest 22		1
The saying of the Catechism is necessary, but not enough; . .	259	Priest 22		7
the Gallant, who is witty enough to abuse both others, and himself,	275	Priest 32		6
And with this exposition the Chapter is cleare enough, but the truth	311	Valdesso		31
because the Scripture invites enough, for it invites us to all good,	313	Valdesso		19
Hee that lives well is learned enough.	323	Proverbs		86
Hee who lives well is learned enough.	323	Proverbs	V	86
Hee is rich enough that wants nothing.	335	Proverbs		403
One father is encugh to governe one hundred sons, ...	335	Proverbs		404
but an 100 sons are not enough to govern one Father.	335	Proverbs	V	404
Hee commands enough that obeyes a wise man.	339	Proverbs		547
A pittifull looke askes enough.	347	Proverbs		790
A pleasure long expected is deare enough sold.	350	Proverbs		868
We do it soon enough, if that we do be well.	359	Proverbs	D	1109
be any truth in me, I find it little enough to keep me in health.	364	Letters		32
I shall never find time and paper enough, yet am I Your readiest	370	Letters		32
ENQUIRING				
Busie enquiring heart, what wouldst thou know?	144	Discharge		1
ENRICH (see alsc inrich)				
Enrich my heart, mouth, hands in me, ...	68	Trin.Sun.		7
ENRICHING				
Enriching all the place.	81	Christmas		20
ENROIL				
To enroll thee:	146	Praise 2		26
ENSUE (see also insuing)				
ENTANGLED (see also intangled)				
I was entangled in the world of strife, ...	47	Afflict.1		41
ENTER (see also entred)				
Look to thy mouth; diseases enter there.	11	Ch.-Porch		127
Fathers first enter bonds to natures ends;	17	Ch.-Porch		281
Enter thy pay, ...	90	Afflict.4		26
Doth shut them out, so that they cannot enter;	126	Confession		20
Or, if they enter, cannot rest, ...	126	Confession		21
To enter combate with us, and contest	139	Artillerie		26
and enter favour with God, who weighs even childrens actions,	239	Priest 10		28
there are such conceits, there is no room for his doctrine to enter.	243	Priest 11		24
Wherfore neither disdaineth he to enter into the poorest Cottage,	249	Priest 14		4
are to enter into this great work, he takes the more pains with them,	258	Priest 22		30
seasoned with pleasantnesse, both enter sooner, and roote deeper.	268	Priest 27		4
Wherefore all are either presently to enter into a Calling, . .	275	Priest 32		14
That they who in these two things that enter in at the mouth,	294	Cornaro		4
Bells call others, but themselves enter not into the Church.	340	Proverbs		571
He that will enter into Paradise, must have a good key. . .	350	Proverbs		895
When you enter into a house, leave the anger ever at the doore.	350	Proverbs		896
Gifts enter every where without a wimble.	352	Proverbs		955
ENTER'D				
Then enter'd Sinne, and with that Sycomore, ...	84	The World		11
after I enter'd into a Benefice, I should be most glad to entertain	367	Letters		9
ENTERPRIZE				
An examin'd enterprize goes on boldly.	342	Proverbs		618
ENTERS				
When once thy foot enters the church, be bare.	22	Ch.-Porch		403
Yet grief knows all, and enters when he will.	126	Confession		6
he enters into the secrets of God treasured in the holy Scripture.	229	Priest 4		29
resolves whenever he enters into a Church, to kneel down, . . .	273	Priest 31		23
ENTERTAIN				
Onely these stones in quiet entertain thee, ...	41	Sepulchre		15
Nor can it entertain the day	70	Quidditie		7
as joyfull a ccuntenance, as if he were to entertain some great Lord.	253	Priest 19		20
into a Benefice, I should be most glad to entertain it, and both pay	367	Letters		10

ERE (cont'd)	PAGE	TITLE		LINE
Follow the Church & sunn where ere they fly.	198	Ch.-Milit.	W	273
Hee that's fed at anothers hand may stay long ere he be full.	336	Proverbs		439
Who is fed by anothers hand stays long ere he be full.	336	Proverbs	V	439
He that gives all ere hee dies provides to suffer.	349	Proverbs	V	855
ERECT				
Or strength in th' other, did erect her throne.	192	Ch.-Milit.		78
ERGO				
And Ergo was transform'd into Amen.	191	Ch.-Milit.		56
ERRADICATE				
Some men plant an opinion they seem to erradicate.	361	Proverbs	D	1164
ERRAND				
Oh my Master, on whose errand I come, let me hold my peace,	233	Priest 7		35
Send a wise man on an errand, and say nothing unto him.	328	Proverbs		217
ERRE				
That I not onely may not erre	184	The Elixer	W	3
But these erre greatly, as I will shew by my self, recounting	300	Cornaro		30
Talke much and erre much, saies the Spanyard.	343	Proverbs		649
ERRED				
If the wise erred not, it would goe hard with fooles.	338	Proverbs		510
If wise men erred not, it would goe hard with fooles.	338	Proverbs	V	510
ERROUR				
Errour a fault, and truth discourtesie.	18	Ch.-Porch		308
When sinne and errour	141	Justice 2		3
Shew a good man his errour and he turnes it to a vertue,	343	Proverbs		655
ER'ST				
that er'st so sorely vexed me,	220	Psalm VI	D	26
ES				
After, where ES, and next where U was graved.	112	JESU		6
ESCAPE (see also scapes)				
Or if some yeares with it escape,	73	Afflict.3		10
It's an ill councell that hath no escape.	345	Proverbs		715
ESCAPED				
which it hath escaped, he destroyes it sometimes in the very Haven;	271	Priest 30		23
The escaped mouse ever feeles the taste of the bait.	344	Proverbs		679
I escaped the Thunder, and fell into the Lightning.	358	Proverbs	D	1084
is not altogether escaped.	359	Proverbs	D	1120
ESCAPES				
He that by being at church escapes the ditch,	24	Ch.-Porch		435
Nothing escapes them both; all must appeare,	118	Providence		37
He that passeth a winters day escapes an enemy.	349	Proverbs		864
ESCURIALL				
thou art to me the Escuriall.	335	Proverbs		413
ESPECIALLY				
but especially that of drinking, because it is the most popular vice;	227	Priest 3		23
as of those of antient times, so especially of the late ones;	233	Priest 7		8
yet often dy with the Sermon, especially with Countrey people;	233	Priest 7		15
temptation to men of any eminency, especially being single men.	238	Priest 9		17
especially the 101 Psalm, which is expressed in a fayre table,	240	Priest 10		25
especially, since of the two commands, we are more injoyned to be	245	Priest 12		27
and uniform, especially that the Pulpit, and Desk, and Communion	246	Priest 13		5
necessary evidence and fruit of their faith, at that time especially:	249	Priest 15		33
so especially to his Diocesan, honouring him both in word,	253	Priest 19		7
Especially, if God have sent any calamity either by fire,	253	Priest 19		28
especially since many remove from Parish to Parish, who like	255	Priest 21		19
in vertue the answer also, especially to the more ignorant.	256	Priest 21		36
Especially at Communion times he is in a great confusion,	257	Priest 22		28
especially let his Method of Phisick be diligently perused,	261	Priest 23		7
be preferred, especially since in disobeying there is scandall also:	263	Priest 24		10
especially canvasing those, whose natures are most stealing,	264	Priest 26		32
especially if they carry their eyes ever open, and fix them on their	266	Priest 26		4
must not work, especially Students, and those that are weakly,)	266	Priest 26		34
especially in his own Parish he suffers it not to his utmost power;	268	Priest 28		18
use and comfort, especially to pious minds, which are ever tender,	273	Priest 31		13
the casting of it on mean persons, especially in some Shires:	276	Priest 32		21
especially, the Statutes at large.	276	Priest 32		34
being usefull to all Countreys, and the other especially to Ilands.	278	Priest 32		3
especially since it may be a just doubt, whether, considering	282	Priest 34		7
Especially, blesse this portion here assembled together,	289	Priest		24
and especially since the power of my stomack every day decreased.	295	Cornaro		32
especially since there is a greater diversitie of tempers,	297	Cornaro		30
especially since in observing it, there needs not many and curious	299	Cornaro		7
especially since it is easie and most agreeable to the nature of Man.	300	Cornaro		5
which are all in their perfect vigour, but especially my Taste;	302	Cornaro		9
Scripture suite with what he writes elsewhere, especially Consid. 32.	306	Valdesso		16
especially considering the time and place where he lived.	311	Valdesso	V	7
especially at this time, being more beggarly now than I have been	375	Letters		36
especially no obligation lying upon you either for the execution	380	Woodnoth		25
ESPIE				
And then the heav'n espie.	184	The Elixer		12
ESPIED				
Of theeves and murderers: there I him espied,	40	Redemption		13
Till they fell out: which when the beasts espied,	70	Humilitie		21
ESSENCE				
that the essence of repentance, that it may be alike in all Gods	279	Priest 33		20
ESSENTIALL				
The two former obligations are much more essentiall to a true fast,	242	Priest 10		7
and essentiall to a Christian, that he cannot without this maintain	272	Priest 31		24
EST				
godly in some sort exempt from Lawes, for Lex iusto non est posita:	315	Valdesso		33

	PAGE	TITLE		LINE
ESTABLISHED				
mouth of two or three witnesses the truth may be more established.	232	Priest 7		30
in the mouth of two or three witnesses every word may be established;	283	Priest 34		20
ESTABLISHETH				
that it rather establisheth it, since they that have nothing,	275	Priest 32		4
ESTABLISHING				
or in cases of high consequence, as establishing of inheritances:	260	Priest 23		22
ESTATE				
Give one estate, as one life. None is bound	17	Ch.-Porch		285
A tithe purloin'd cankers the whole estate.	22	Ch.-Porch		386
Mend my estate in any wayes,	61	Praise 1		3
Indeed mans whole estate	63	Mattens		13
Look back upon thine own estate,	170	Self-cond.		4
That your estate	210	Paradox	D	29
or afflicted with losse of friend, or estate, or any ways distressed,	249	Priest 15		14
as he that eats more then his estate will bear, is a Prodigall;	266	Priest 26		9
they cannot wel dispatch) nor of their estate, nor of their brethren.	266	Priest 26		16
by this also, in what estate I am, may be discovered, because	302	Cornaro		27
Hee that lies long a bed, his estate feeles it.	327	Proverbs		179
Estate in twc parishes is bread in two wallets.	328	Proverbs		231
that if he will not give her halfe her estate to live on by her selfe	368	Letters		24
consider all that can happen to you are either afflictions of Estate,	373	Letters		21
For those of Estate? of what poor regard ought they to be,	373	Letters		22
ESTATES				
Some great estates provide, but doe not breed	10	Ch.-Porch		103
Complies and suits with all estates;	69	Content		14
Flyes of estates and sunne-shine. But to all,	169	The Answer		5
ESTEEM				
For God doth righteous men esteem,	219	Psalm V	D	41
Countrey people (as indeed all honest men) do much esteem their word,	228	Priest 3		2
neither doth he esteem him for an enemy, but as a brother still,	263	Priest 25		29
plain the Authour had a very reverend esteem of the holy Scripture,	311	Valdesso	V	6
God in all ages have ever held in so pretious esteem the word of God,	317	Valdesso		33
whome I esteem to be God's faithfull & diligent Servant,	378	Letters		14
now Constancy is such & of great esteem with all.	380	Woodnoth		15
ESTEEMED				
language, he shall be esteemed as ordinary complementers;	286	Priest 36		21
a reverence, and makes him esteemed according to his Profession.	286	Priest 36		25
and greatly to be esteemed for the knowing & curing of diseases,	298	Cornaro		4
how much more dearely should a Physician be esteemed, who not onely	298	Cornaro		9
ESTEEMES				
He greatly esteemes also of cases of conscience, wherein he is much	230	Priest 5		19
ESTEEMING				
esteeming that this private praying is a more voluntary act in them,	241	Priest 10		4
he goe into the world, esteeming it absurd, that he should exceed,	241	Priest 10		20
esteeming that there is no spice comparable, for herbs,	262	Priest 23		1
ESTEEMS				
The great and nationall sin of this Land he esteems to be Idlenesse;	274	Priest 32		9
ESTIMATICN				
our Credit and estimaticn calls on us to live in a more splendid	373	Letters		26
ESTRANGING				
some small and temporary estranging may corroborate the punishment	263	Priest 25		30
&C				
Ephes. 4. 30. Grieve not the Holy Spirit, &c.	135	Ephes.		T
or he that teacheth, on teaching, &c.	226	Priest 2		7
he that ruleth, let him do it with diligence, &c.	226	Priest 2		8
&c. The third means is a diligent Collation of Scripture	229	Priest 4		4
so that while they answer, As it was in the beginning, &c.	231	Priest 6		34
that thou would'st rent the Heavens, that thou wouldst come down, &c.	234	Priest 7		3
Oh Lord, I know that the way of man is not in himself, &c.	234	Priest 7		6
speciall grace of faith, patience, meeknesse, love, obedience, &c.	238	Priest 9		33
alwayes cleer, and evident, as Adultery, Murder, Hatred, Lying, &c.	264	Priest 26		7
the one in, The Grace of our Lord Jesus Christ, &c.	286	Priest 36		4
The Peace of God, &c.	286	Priest 36		5
in whose sweet and pleasing words, we say, Our Father, &c.	289	Priest		35
the defects (as I conceive) towards the publishing thereof, &c.	305	Valdesso		14
by the generall Providence of God, as Socrates and Aristides, &c.	308	Valdesso		13
and syncere Religion, such as are Prayer, Fasting, Almes-deedes, &c.	312	Valdesso		21
Of the first sort are repentance, prayers, fasting, Psalmes, &c.	312	Valdesso	V	27
Jacula Prudentum Or Outlandish Proverbs, Sentences, &c	356	Proverbs	D	T
Neither hath she any to repair unto at good times, as Christmas, &c.	375	Letters		27
ETERNALL				
By thy eternall glorie didst outgo me?	37	Reprisall		10
Angels and grace, eternall hopes and fears.	46	Sinne 1		12
This book of starres lights to eternall blisse.	58	H.Script.2		14
This book of starres can spell eternall blisse.	58	H.Script.2	W	14
Lord, how can man preach thy eternall word?	67	Windows		1
Of the eternall glorious King.	76	Sunday		32
To gain at harvest an eternall Treasure.	85	Coloss.		10
Which doth not meet with an eternall thought.	190	Ch.-Milit.		8
Which does nct meet with an eternall thought.	190	Ch.-Milit.	W	8
ETERNALLY				
Who cannot live lesse then eternally:	29	Sacrifice		99
ETERNITIE				
A full eternitie: thou art a masse	58	H.Script.1		6
Which ev'n eternitie excludes!	123	Time		26
Ev'n eternitie is too short	146	Praise 2		27
ETERNITY				
Eternity into one Bedd.	213	L' Envoy	D	14
EUGANEAN				
Some times of the yeare I enjoy the pleasure of the Euganean hills,	301	Cornaro		17

	PAGE	TITLE	LINE
EUROPE			
And much of Asia and Europe fast asleep,	140	Ch.-rents	27
Europe alone and Rome do keep them free	194	Ch.-Milit. W	157
EVASION			
To use their temperance, seeking no evasion,	86	Lent	14
EVE			
Promising is the eve of giving.	349	Proverbs	847
Say to pleasure, Gentle Eve, I will none of your apple.	360	Proverbs D	1140
EV'N			
Ev'n with the yeare: but age, if it will hit,	13	Ch.-Porch	158
My poore soul, ev'n sick of love:	72	Frailtie	21
Till ev'n his beams sing, and my musick shine.	81	Christmas	34
Ev'n unto death: since he di'd for my good,	83	Sighs & Gr.	23
Yet are we bid, Be holy ev'n as he.	87	Lent	35
So our clay hearts, ev'n when we crouch	101	Miserie	39
And ev'n my verse, when by the ryme and reason	109	Home	75
That ev'n her face by kissing shines,	110	Brit. Ch.	17
Ev'n all to pieces: which I went to seek:	112	JESU	4
Lovers are still pretending, & ev'n wrongs	116	Dulnesse	19
Check the proud sea, ev'n when it swells and gathers.	118	Providence	48
Ev'n poysons praise thee. Should a thing be lost?	119	Providence	85
Ev'n pleasures here increase the wrong,	123	Time	21
Which ev'n eternitie excludes!	123	Time	26
Ev'n God himself, being pressed for my sake.	128	Bunch Gr.	28
I bath'd it often, ev'n with holy bloud,	130	Love unkn.	41
Ev'n taken inwardly, and most divine	130	Love unkn.	44
When with my pleasures ev'n my rest was gone?	130	Love unkn.	53
Yet ev'n the greatest griefs	132	Mans medly	31
Starres have their storms, ev'n in a high degree,	132	The Storm	7
Ev'n fruitfull trees more fruitfull ARE.	133	Paradise	12
O dark instructions; ev'n as dark as day!	135	Divinitie	19
Ev'n endlesse tears	136	Ephes.	26
Then I refuse not ev'n with bloud	139	Artillerie	14
Thy promise now hath ev'n set thee thy laws.	139	Artillerie	24
And ev'n all Africk; would at least I might	140	Ch.-rents	28
Nay, ev'n to trust in him, was also his:	143	Holdfast	6
Ev'n eternitie is too short	146	Praise 2	27
Ev'n when the boat seems most to reel.	151	The Bag	4
Sure it would carrie with it ev'n my heart,	159	Jos.coat	7
Ev'n when my will doth studie thy renown:	165	The Crosse	20
So that, ev'n when my hopes seem to be sped,	165	The Crosse	23
And ev'n in Paradise to be a weed.	165	The Crosse	30
Are thy returns! ev'n as the flowers in spring;	165	The Flower	2
Fetching their proofs ev'n from the very bone;	167	Dotage	11
Before a court, ev'n that above so cleare,	167	Dotage	16
Shines bright and cleare, ev'n unto condemnation,	171	Self-cond.	23
Vouchsaf'd ev'n in the midst of youth and night	171	The Glance	2
My soul hath felt, ev'n able to destroy,	172	The Glance	10
Ev'n in my enemies sight:	173	23 Psalme	18
Ev'n in mine enemies sight:	173	23 Psalme V	18
Ev'n God himself: wherefore she was not loth,	173	Marie Magd	15
My onely musick, striking me ev'n dead;	174	Aaron	18
My minde ev'n thrust into them both:	175	The Odour	7
And ev'n in my unworthinesse pleasing,	175	The Odour	22
Ev'n all my heart, and what is lodged there:	176	Forerunners	8
My god must have my best, ev'n all I had.	176	Forerunners	18
Ev'n in death,	180	Invitation	29
Seest and rulest all things ev'n as one:	190	Ch.-Milit.	2
They have their times of Gospel, ev'n as we.	197	Ch.-Milit.	248
They have their time of Gospel, ev'n as we.	197	Ch.-Milit. W	248
EVEN			
Since, if my soul make even with the week,	38	The Sinner	3
Even-song.	63	Even-song	T
O brook not this, lest if what even now	71	Frailtie	17
Who rides his sure and even trot,	72	Constancie	9
Thy even praise can neither rise, nor fall.	118	Providence	42
And clean and fair, as I one even-tide	129	Love unkn.	23
Thou said'st but even now,	155	Assurance	7
Even there, where they deceive?	201	H. Commun. W	36
Even-song.	203	Even-song W	T
even so farre as reproofe to their very face, when occasion cals,	226	Priest 2	30
even to a wondring, that the world should so much value wealth,	227	Priest 3	19
mind breaking out, and dilating it selfe even to his body, cloaths,	228	Priest 3	12
He condescends even to the knowledge of tillage, and pastorage,	228	Priest 4	18
which if it be necessary even in temporall things, how much more in	228	Priest 4	33
or spitting even in the midst of their answer, but gently	231	Priest 6	31
but even to let the world sinke, so they do their duty;	232	Priest 6	16
them to be so, when God is so neer them, and even over their heads.	233	Priest 7	11
he himself were with Saint Paul even sacrificed upon the service	234	Priest 7	8
even as Princes have theirs, besides their publick disbursments.	236	Priest 8	17
with God, who weighs even childrens actions, 1 Kings 14. 12, 13.	239	Priest 10	29
Even the wals are not idle, but something is written, or painted	240	Priest 10	23
and dearths, he even parts his Living, and life among them,	245	Priest 12	10
even in externall and indifferent things, what course is to be taken;	246	Priest 13	33
though he even creep into it, and though it smell never so lothsomly.	249	Priest 14	5
such as are from Gods generall providence extended even to lillyes;	249	Priest 15	20
against all temptations, even to death it selfe, he plainly,	250	Priest 15	3
and even in those wrongs which either in tithing, or otherwise are	250	Priest 16	12
spirits, and possesse them even before they themselves heed it.	252	Priest 18	7
refreshment, gladly betakes it selfe, even to the losse of honour.	252	Priest 18	23
ever reputed, even among the Heathen, as an obligation to do good,	253	Priest 19	26

EVEN (cont'd)	PAGE	TITLE		LINE
with comparisons, and making much even of a word of truth from him.	256	Priest 21		15
ignorant and silly souls, even the dark and deep points of Religion.	256	Priest 21		20
even containing in vertue the answer also, especially to the more	256	Priest 21		35
made the answer so plaine, that he was even ashamed of his ignorance;	257	Priest 21		6
and cleansed, and serve for lights even of Heavenly Truths. . . .	257	Priest 21		15
This practice exceeds even Sermons in teaching:	257	Priest 21		20
he shews them how to go to Law, even as Brethren, and not as enemies,	260	Priest 23		26
even as our Saviour made plants and seeds to teach the people:	261	Priest 23		13
Doctrine slip the more easily into the hearts even of the meanest.	261	Priest 23		19
up their minds to better things, even in the midst of their pains.	261	Priest 23		25
there are some persons, who abstain not even from known sins;	264	Priest 26		10
to that which is presently unlawfull, even in one continued action.	264	Priest 26		22
but proceeding on, comes to do unlawfully, even before he is aware;	264	Priest 26		23
when his storing, which was even now good, passeth from good to bad.	264	Priest 26		30
things that they buy, even as a piece of wood, which they may cut,	265	Priest 26		25
even somtimes to a forgetting of themselves, knowing that there is	267	Priest 26		20
which carries a reverence with it, even above contempt. . .	268	Priest 28		21
even of the best in the Parish, when occasion requires: . .	268	Priest 28		27
without any resistance, even in resistance, to the same destruction.	269	Priest 28		22
since even by the Common Statute-Law they are taken for a kinde	269	Priest 29		33
or as David says, to be even a door-keeper in the house of God.	270	Priest 29		11
God further, even till he imbarn his corn, and then think all sure;	271	Priest 30		32
So that even in Paradise man had a calling, and how much more out	274	Priest 32		21
Christian soules, and raise them to their height, even to heaven;	275	Priest 32		32
even as John the Baptist squared out to every one (even to Souldiers)	277	Priest 32		22
the Baptist squared out to every one (even to Souldiers) what to do.	277	Priest 32		23
all other things shall be added, even it selfe is a Sermon. . .	278	Priest 33		14
military state of a Christian life, but even in the peaceable also;	279	Priest 33		3
an act of the mind, not of the Body, even as the Originall signifies;	279	Priest 33		15
that there is a double state of a Christian even in this Life,	280	Priest 34		2
and the Angels minister to us their owne food, even joy, and peace;	280	Priest 34		7
dishes at table, which even their present health otherwise admits;	280	Priest 34		23
with all those furnitures which even their present plenty of wealth	280	Priest 34		25
Matthew 24. 14. which we see even miraculously effected in these new	282	Priest 34		32
love for love, even the son of his love out of his bosome of love.	283	Priest 34		16
so that even ill Priests may blesse.	285	Priest 36		23
the clean contrary, even from superstition to coldnes, and Atheism.	286	Priest 36		17
and that even some good men think, so they speak truth, . .	286	Priest 37		31
and forbear to speak of that, which even God himself hath forgotten.	288	Priest 37		5
even for those that derided him then, and still despise him.	288	Priest		29
even to me, pardoning my sins, and bidding me go feed the people	289	Priest		5
For Temperance preserves even old men and sickly men sound: . .	292	Cornaro		8
Moreover I say, that even bruises and squats, and falls, . .	294	Cornaro		33
and also doth preserve even ill tempers in good health, . .	298	Cornaro		14
that they prolong their life even to a hundred yeares and more,	298	Cornaro		15
circumspection) but still even to the most learned and perfect	309	Valdesso		23
because even the godly are chastized but not punished) for evill	311	Valdesso		28
So that the Word hath the precedence even of Revelations and Visions.	318	Valdesso		24
I even study Thrift, and yet I am scarce able with much ado to make	365	Letters		9
for I would have you, even in speeches, to observe so much, . .	366	Letters		9
that I loved her even in my departure, in looking to her Son,	371	Letters		12
as if they not only not desir'd, but, even fear'd to be blessed.	373	Letters		34
you take her not, I am thinking to do it, even beyond my strengthe;	375	Letters		35
a much better Paymaster then my self, even him, whome we both serve:	378	Letters		3
before lower, even where to continue in the lower is no sinn.	380	Woodnoth		4
yet useth his Restraining grace, even in the most wicked: . .	381	Woodnoth		9
in the choice of whom their judgement doth even now appeare.	442	Oration		27
EVEN-SONG				
Even-song.	63	Even-song		T
Even-song.	203	Even-song	W	T
EVEN-TIDE				
And clean and fair, as I one even-tide	129	Love unkn.		23
EV'NING				
As I one ev'ning sat before my cell, ...	139	Artillerie		1
EVENING				
as about prayers morning and evening on their knees, reading	248	Priest 14		32
Evening words are not like to morning.	323	Proverbs		65
In the morning mountaines, in the evening fountaines. . . .	337	Proverbs		473
The evening praises the day, and the morning a host. . . .	342	Proverbs		635
The evening praises the day, and the morning a frost. . . .	342	Proverbs	V	635
EVENINGE				
The longest Day hath an Eveninge.	322	Proverbs	V	51
EVENT				
and the event confirmed it.	285	Priest 36		31
or conditionally he prayed as man, though as God he knew the event.	315	Valdesso		11
EVENTS				
Thine clad with simplenesse, and sad events;	71	Frailtie		11
Tragedie with old Age, by reason of the sad events which it contains.	302	Cornaro		32
E'RE				
Wisedome's a trimmer thing, then shop e're gave.	14	Ch.-Porch		188
Which way so-e're I look, I see.	108	Home		50
He chid the Church away, where e're he came, ...	193	Ch.-Milit.		105
EVER				
Was ever grief like mine?	26	Sacrifice		4
Was ever grief like mine?	26	Sacrifice		8
Was ever grief like mine?	27	Sacrifice		12
Was ever grief like mine?	27	Sacrifice		16
Was ever grief like mine?	27	Sacrifice		20
Was ever grief like mine?	27	Sacrifice		24
Was ever grief like mine?	27	Sacrifice		28

EVER (cont'd)	PAGE	TITLE		LINE
Was ever grief like mine?	27	Sacrifice		32
Was ever grief like mine?	27	Sacrifice		36
Was ever grief like mine?	27	Sacrifice		40
Was ever grief like mine?	28	Sacrifice		44
Was ever grief like mine?	28	Sacrifice		48
Was ever grief like mine?	28	Sacrifice		52
Was ever grief like mine?	28	Sacrifice		56
Was ever grief like mine?	28	Sacrifice		60
Was ever grief like mine?	28	Sacrifice		64
Was ever grief like mine?	28	Sacrifice		68
Was ever grief like mine?	28	Sacrifice		72
Was ever grief like mine?	29	Sacrifice		76
Was ever grief like mine?	29	Sacrifice		80
Was ever grief like mine?	29	Sacrifice		84
Was ever grief like mine?	29	Sacrifice		88
Was ever grief like mine?	29	Sacrifice		92
Was ever grief like mine?	29	Sacrifice		96
Was ever grief like mine?	29	Sacrifice		100
Was ever grief like mine?	29	Sacrifice		104
Was ever grief like mine?	30	Sacrifice		108
Was ever grief like mine?	30	Sacrifice		112
Was ever grief like mine?	30	Sacrifice		116
Was ever grief like mine?	30	Sacrifice		120
Was ever grief like mine?	30	Sacrifice		124
Was ever grief like mine?	30	Sacrifice		128
Was ever grief like mine?	30	Sacrifice		132
Was ever grief like mine?	31	Sacrifice		136
Was ever grief like mine?	31	Sacrifice		140
Was ever grief like mine?	31	Sacrifice		144
Was ever grief like mine?	31	Sacrifice		148
Was ever grief like mine?	31	Sacrifice		152
Was ever grief like mine?	31	Sacrifice		156
Was ever grief like mine?	31	Sacrifice		160
Was ever grief like mine?	31	Sacrifice		164
Was ever grief like mine?	32	Sacrifice		168
Was ever grief like mine?	32	Sacrifice		172
What ever scoffes or scornfulnesse can bring,	32	Sacrifice		174
What ever scoffes & scornfulnesse can bring,	32	Sacrifice	W	174
Was ever grief like mine?	32	Sacrifice		176
Was ever grief like mine?	32	Sacrifice		180
Was ever grief like mine?	32	Sacrifice		184
Was ever grief like mine?	32	Sacrifice		188
Was ever grief like mine?	32	Sacrifice		192
Was ever grief like mine?	33	Sacrifice		196
Was ever grief like mine?	33	Sacrifice		200
Was ever grief like mine?	33	Sacrifice		204
Was ever grief like mine?	33	Sacrifice		208
Was ever grief like mine?	33	Sacrifice		212
Was ever grief like mine?	33	Sacrifice		220
Was ever grief like mine?	34	Sacrifice		224
Was ever grief like mine?	34	Sacrifice		228
Was ever grief like mine?	34	Sacrifice		232
Was ever grief like mine?	34	Sacrifice		236
Was ever grief like mine?	34	Sacrifice		240
Was ever grief like mine?	34	Sacrifice		244
Was ever grief like mine?	34	Sacrifice		248
If ever he did taste the like.	37	The Agonie		16
What ever sinne did this pure rock commit,	41	Sepulchre		10
There is but one, and that one ever.	42	Easter		30
What ever future sinnes should me miscall,	44	H. Bapt.1		13
As ever did a welcome guest.	50	Faith		8
My soul might ever feel!	55	Temper 1		4
But that from them joyes purle for ever	59	Whitsunday	W	22
Hath ever found a happie fortune.	69	Content		36
In all, I think my foot doth ever tread	71	Frailtie		7
And ever as I walk my foot doth tredd	71	Frailtie	W	7
Since we are ever ready to disburse,	78	Ang.&Sts.		29
Since we are ever ready to discourse,	78	Ang.&Sts.	V	29
Ever in warres.	79	Employm.2		17
Then should I ever laden be,	79	Employm.2		23
But we are ever young or old;	79	Employm.2	W	26
Thy root is ever in its grave,	87	Vertue		7
Thy root is ever in his grave,	87	Vertue	V	7
My Saviours bloud: when ever at his board	106	Conscience		14
And ever as they mount, like larks they sing;	107	Sion		23
While thou dost ever, ever stay:	107	Home		2
The word is, Stay, sayes ever, Come.	109	Home		76
Awake sad heart, whom sorrow ever drowns;	112	Dawning		1
Who in heart not ever kneels,	114	Businesse		37
As fair as ever, and as fit to use;	118	Providence		67
What? shall I ever sigh and pine?	153	The Collar		3
Straight as a line, and ever tends to thee,	185	A Wreath		6
Echo. Ever.	188	Heaven		20
Knocking at all doores, ever as she went.	190	Ch.-Milit.		30
Usher'd the Gospel ever in mens hearts,	197	Ch.-Milit.		264
Like Comick Lovers ever one way runn:	198	Ch.-Milit.	W	271
And wake with thee for ever.	203	Even-song	W	24
If ever Tears did flow from Eyes,	213	Convert	D	1
If ever Voice was hoarse with Cries,	213	Convert	D	2
If ever Heart was sore with Sighs;	213	Convert	D	3

EVER (cont'd)	PAGE	TITLE		LINE
and them for ever bless.	219	Psalm V	D	42
but just men ever guide:	221	Psalm VII	D	34
And ever praise the Glorious name	222	Psalm VII	D	63
and cringings, that they shall ever be despised.	226	Priest 2		36
Wherefore he ever begins the reading of the Scripture with some short	229	Priest 4		1
it is an honest joy ever after to looke upon his well spent houres.	230	Priest 5		6
that God hath ever had his people, that have glorified him as wel	231	Priest 6		35
have glorified him as wel as now, and that he shall have so for ever.	232	Priest 6		1
he is ever very well supplyed by some able man who treads in his	232	Priest 7		25
for particulars ever touch, and awake more then generalls.	233	Priest 7		5
and that our feet may be like hindes feet ever climbing up higher,	236	Priest 8		29
that it is ever attempting, or doing one mischief or other.	238	Priest 9		14
When-ever hee gives any thing, and sees them labour in thanking	245	Priest 12		30
and wishing them ever to do the Cures with their own hands,	247	Priest 14		19
in their vocation, and himself be ever the more welcome to them.	248	Priest 14		12
way or other, he ever reproves them, that he may keep himself pure,	248	Priest 14		23
from his promises, from the examples of all Saints, that ever were;	249	Priest 15		22
but is himselfe where ever he is.	251	Priest 17		1
The Countrey Parson, where ever he is, keeps Gods watch;	252	Priest 18		1
and Neighbourhood being ever reputed, even among the Heathen,	253	Priest 19		25
as parrats, without ever piercing into the sense of it.	256	Priest 21		4
whom he hath ever some cases to ask, when he meets with them;	260	Priest 23		4
Yet when ever any controversie is brought to him, he never decides it	260	Priest 23		7
whom yet he ever exhorts not to exceed his bounds, but in tickle	260	Priest 23		35
having ever besides two great helps and powerfull perswaders on his	263	Priest 24		15
punishing of any, as the vulgar ever consters for signes of ill will;	263	Priest 25		25
of their generall Schoole rules ever to the smallest actions of Life;	266	Priest 26		1
especially if they carry their eyes ever open, and fix them on their	266	Priest 26		4
the Godly have ever added some houres of prayer, as at nine,	272	Priest 31		25
especially to pious minds, which are ever tender, and delicate.	273	Priest 31		14
hath ever so many sermons ready penn'd, as he hath victories.	278	Priest 33		24
for no perfect Artist ever yet hated his owne worke.	283	Priest 34		12
O almighty and ever-living Lord God!	288	Priest		7
O brand it in our foreheads for ever:	288	Priest		19
we magnifie thee for ever!	289	Priest		11
wher-ever spoken this day throughout the universall Church.	289	Priest		14
God, be ascribed all Honour, and Glory, and Praise, ever.	290	Priest		16
but that he shall ever after live free from diseases, if he will keep	297	Cornaro		19
Then, I am ever cheerfull, merrie, and well-contented, free from all	300	Cornaro		37
and ever I learn somewhat which is worthy of my knowledge:	302	Cornaro		2
the power and efficacie of that Temperance which ever accompanied me.	302	Cornaro		21
because I have now a clearer voice, then ever I had in my life.	303	Cornaro		7
neither can they ever be exhausted, (as Pictures may be by a plenarie	309	Valdesso		22
observed, who workes by his Word, and ever in the reading of it.	310	Valdesso		1
and ever outrunning the Teacher, as it did when Peter taught	310	Valdesso		7
In the Scripture are Doctrines, these ever teach more and more.	310	Valdesso		13
In the Scripture are Promises, these ever comfort more and more.	310	Valdesso		14
I ever tooke that for a weaknesse in the great Patriark:	316	Valdesso		1
the Saints of God in all ages have ever held in so pretious esteem	317	Valdesso		33
Though a lie be well drest, it is ever overcome.	325	Proverbs		133
from him that saies nothing, for ever.	326	Proverbs		164
Ever since we weare cloathes, we know not one another.	326	Proverbs		168
Truth and oyle are ever above.	328	Proverbs		234
A woman and a glasse are ever in danger.	329	Proverbs		244
By suppers more have beene killed then Galen ever cured.	330	Proverbs		272
By suppers more are killed then Galen ever cured.	330	Proverbs	V	272
Mills and wives ever want.	334	Proverbs		388
He that once deceives is ever suspected.	335	Proverbs		417
Who so once deceives is ever suspected.	335	Proverbs	V	417
Labour as long liv'd, pray as ever dying.	337	Proverbs		480
The Catt sees not the mouse ever.	341	Proverbs		592
The escaped mouse ever feeles the taste of the bait.	344	Proverbs		679
A shippe and a woman are ever repairing.	347	Proverbs		780
He that once hitts, is ever bending.	347	Proverbs		785
Hee that is throwne would ever wrestle.	347	Proverbs		797
Hee lookes not well to himselfe that lookes not ever.	349	Proverbs		835
The Reverend are ever before.	350	Proverbs		891
When you enter into a house, leave the anger ever at the doore.	350	Proverbs		896
Wine ever paies for his lodging.	352	Proverbs		930
A man well mounted is ever Cholerick.	355	Proverbs		1025
in Poetry, shall be all, and ever consecrated to Gods glory.	363	Letters		12
so that I am fain ever and anon, to buy somewhat tending towards my	364	Letters		33
Now I write to you, Sir, because to you I have ever opened my heart;	365	Letters		23
mee in your letters, for I am your ever loving brother, G. HERBERT.	366	Letters		22
and for ever after cease my clamorous and greedy bookish requests.	367	Letters		11
So prayes Your ever loving brother, G. HERBERT.	376	Letters		21
every good worke, to the joy of your ever loving brother, G. HERBERT.	377	Letters		28
yet I shall ever put your care of Leighton, upon my accompt,	378	Letters		3
upon my accompt, & give you my self for it, to be yours for ever.	378	Letters		5
all your Addresses, & for ought I see, they are ever to be liked.	378	Letters		17
EVER-LIVING				
O almighty and ever-living Lord God!	288	Priest		7
EVERLASTING				
Unto thy self in everlasting pleasure.	82	Ungratef.		12
as knowing that nature will not bear everlasting droopings,	267	Priest 27		34
EVERMORE				
Of heav'nly blessings issue evermore:	32	Sacrifice		171
Working and winding slily evermore,	84	The World		13
Wherein she thenceforth evermore	173	Marie Magd		5
Yea, shout for joy for evermore,	219	Psalm V	D	37

EV'RY	PAGE	TITLE	LINE
Think not thy fame at ev'ry twitch will break:	15	Ch.-Porch	219
If that thy fame with ev'ry toy be pos'd,	15	Ch.-Porch	223
My musick shall finde thee, and ev'ry string	36	Thanksgvng	39
To hunt his cruell food through ev'ry vein.	37	The Agonie	12
Consuming agues dwell in ev'ry vein,	47	Afflict.1	27
I was blown through with ev'ry storm and winde.	47	Afflict.1	36
Faith cleaves unto it, counting evr'y grain	51	Faith	42
Let all the world in ev'ry corner sing,	53	Antiphon 1	1
Let all the world in ev'ry corner sing,	53	Antiphon 1	7
Let all the world in ev'ry corner sing,	53	Antiphon 1	13
Make one place ev'ry where.	55	Temper 1	28
And ev'ry day a new Creatour art.	56	Temper 2	8
Suck ev'ry letter, and a hcny gain,	58	H.Script.1	2
Subject to ev'ry mounters bended knee.	58	H.Script.1	14
And comments on thee: for in ev'ry thing	58	H.Script.2	10
And more then fancy: for in ev'ry thing	58	H.Script.2 W	10
The dew doth ev'ry morning fall;	60	Grace	9
Kill me not ev'ry day,	62	Afflict.2	1
Gad not abroad at ev'ry quest and call	68	Content	5
Where ev'ry one is king, and hath his crown,	77	Ang.&Sts.	4
To ev'ry Corporation.	86	Lent	6
That ev'ry man may revell at his doore,	87	Lent	46
For Man is ev'ry thing,	91	Man	7
Then he'l take notice of: in ev'ry path	92	Man	44
Maketh two nights to ev'ry day.	96	Charms & K	8
And strengthen it in ev'ry age,	97	Afflict.5	5
Marking his grave, and thawing ev'ry yeare,	98	Mortific.	26
And peace, which ev'ry where	125	Peace	40
That ev'ry part	150	Longing	75
That nature hath produc'd. Let ev'ry vein	164	Grief	4
For ev'ry mans peculiar book?	187	Judgement	5
Gardens of Gods, which ev'ry yeare did grow,	193	Ch.-Milit.	108
To make good that which ev'ry day he winnes.	193	Ch.-Milit.	126
Nay, it shall ev'ry yeare decrease and fade;	196	Ch.-Milit.	229
EVERY			
Man breaks the fence, and every ground will plough.	7	Ch.-Porch	22
Whose every parcell under-writes a law.	12	Ch.-Porch	142
Shine like the sunne in every corner: see	20	Ch.-Porch	345
Which spread their forces into every part,	52	H.Commun.	11
Anneal'd on every bunch. One standing by	116	Love-joy	3
At every word,	153	The Collar	34
Wherfore he hath one Comment at least upon every book of Scripture,	229	Priest 4	28
is full of such composures, yet every mans own is fittest, readyest,	230	Priest 5	4
For every one hath not digested, when it is a sin to take something	230	Priest 5	23
as attending to what is done in the Church, and every one, man,	231	Priest 6	27
that the auditors may plainly perceive that every word is hart-deep.	233	Priest 7	32
And every one is more awaked, when we come, and say, Thou art	236	Priest 8	14
and pulse of every person in his house, and accordingly either meets	239	Priest 10	8
and how every one profits, comparing this yeer with the last:	240	Priest 10	37
and proper texts of Scripture every where painted, and that all	246	Priest 13	11
it is a good and just thing for every one to do their own busines.	247	Priest 14	22
but such as are every way fitting to do his Countrey true	252	Priest 19	28
infuse a competent knowledge of salvation in every one of his Flock;	255	Priest 21	3
that the same common truths may be every where professed,	255	Priest 21	18
who held that the seeds of all truths lay in every body,	256	Priest 21	22
The time of every ones first receiving is not so much by yeers,	258	Priest 22	32
chiefly considered) might have every where monuments of his Doctrine,	261	Priest 23	21
if I do not give every thing its end, I abuse the Creature,	265	Priest 26	9
God dishonoured every day, and man afflicted.	267	Priest 27	32
and exerciseth a threefold power in every thing which concernes man.	271	Priest 30	1
sustaining pcwer he preserves and actuates every thing in his being;	271	Priest 30	4
pray twice a day, every day of the week, and four times on Sunday,	272	Priest 31	22
he first represents to every body the necessity of a vocation.	274	Priest 32	17
every gift or ability is a talent to be accounted for, and to be	274	Priest 32	24
for every one to imploy himselfe to the advancement of his affairs,	275	Priest 32	28
Hee considers every one there, and either helps them in particular,	276	Priest 32	3
the Kingdome into Portions, which every yeer he surveys peece-meal.	277	Priest 32	8
every morning that hee is at home hee must either ride the Great	277	Priest 32	15
as John the Baptist squared out to every one (even to Souldiers) what	277	Priest 32	23
it is a continued Creation, and a creation every moment.	281	Priest 34	31
in the mouth of two or three witnesses every word may be established;	283	Priest 34	19
they break forth like mighty waters on every side.	290	Priest	8
for this had every way great force for the recovering and preserving	292	Cornaro	5
and especially since the pcwer of my stomack every day decreased.	295	Cornaro	33
Every one by long experience may know the qualities of his own	297	Cornaro	26
which he every where beares towards our deare [great] Master	305	Valdesso	4
concluding every Consideration almost with his holy Name,	305	Valdesso	5
applying the generall promises to every one in particular with such	309	Valdesso	4
By the Saints of the world he every where understands the cunning	319	Valdesso V	19
Every day brings his bread with it.	321	Proverbs	5
Every thing is of use to a houskeeper.	323	Proverbs	70
Every thing new is fine.	323	Proverbs	76
When a dog is a drowning, every one offers him drink.	323	Proverbs	77
Every ill man hath his ill day.	324	Proverbs	92
Every one stretcheth his legges according to his coverlet.	325	Proverbs	147
None is a foole alwaies, every one sometimes.	326	Proverbs	163
I wept when I was borne, and every day shewes why.	327	Proverbs	199
Every path hath a puddle.	328	Proverbs	215
Goe not for every griefe to the Physitian,	331	Proverbs	290
nor for every quarrell to the Lawyer,	331	Proverbs	290

EXACT (cont'd)	PAGE	TITLE		LINE
The Countrey Parson is exceeding exact in his Life, being holy,	227	Priest 3		1
and the exact temperance of our Lord Jesus, with other exemplary	237	Priest 9		34
The Parson is very exact in the governing of his house,	239	Priest 10		6
nothing holp me, but that exact rule which I had so long continued.	296	Cornaro		29
EXACTLY				
ability of a Parson to lead his people exactly in the wayes of Truth,	230	Priest 5		21
and exactly contain, even in externall and indifferent things,	246	Priest 13		33
hath exactly sifted the definitions of all vertues, and vices;	264	Priest 26		31
for there the particulars are exactly discussed, which are brought	277	Priest 32		13
and flesh, and broth, was twelve ounces exactly weighed;	296	Cornaro		11
EXACTNESSE				
for exactnesse lyes in particulars.	275	Priest 32		18
EXACTS				
exacts of them all possible reverence, by no means enduring either	231	Priest 6		22
If his Parish be rich, he exacts this of them;	244	Priest 12		24
thanking of him, he exacts of them to let him alone, and say rather,	245	Priest 12		31
He exacts of all the Doctrine of the Catechisme;	255	Priest 21		22
Wherefore he exacts of all to bee present at the perambulation,	284	Priest 35		10
EXALT				
To a brave soul: Exalt the poore,	61	Praise 1		15
EXALTATION				
The smacks of dainties and their exaltation:	89	The Pearl	W	27
so it may be a fruit of it, and an exaltation. 1 John 5. 14.	319	Valdesso		14
EXALTED				
When basenesse is exalted, do not bate	17	Ch.-Porch		265
When base men are exalted, do not bate	17	Ch.-Porch	W	265
Exalted Manna, gladnesse of the best,	51	Prayer 1		10
Flesh (though exalted) keeps his grass	201	H. Commun.	W	38
Thou hast exalted thy mercy above all things;	288	Priest		22
EXALTS				
And exalts you to the skie:	180	Invitation		27
EXAMIN'D				
An examin'd enterprize goes on boldly.	342	Proverbs		618
EXAMINATION				
referreth the whole matter to the examination, and punishment	268	Priest 28		34
EXAMINE				
knowledg of Religion, may examine their grounds, renew their vowes,	255	Priest 21		33
or else to examine with care, and advice, what they are fittest for,	275	Priest 32		15
EXAMINED				
the Parson hath diligently examined these two with himselfe,	262	Priest 24		32
having for his owne use examined the nature of it, is able	279	Priest 33		8
it were the Authors opinion, yet the truth of it would be examined.	307	Valdesso		22
but the truth of the Doctrine would be examined, however it may passe	312	Valdesso		1
this were the Authors opinion, yet the truth of it would be examined.	319	Valdesso	V	16
EXAMINES				
Examines me with a censorious hand:	29	Sacrifice		82
EXAMPLE				
Till he the thing and the example weigh:	72	Constancie		13
Besides his example, he having often instructed his people how	231	Priest 6		21
but for example sake, and because they are most common,	265	Priest 26		3
I bring this example, because men usually think, that servants	265	Priest 26		23
that so the sentence lighting upon one, the example may reach to all.	269	Priest 28		2
As for example: It is necessary, that all Christians should pray	272	Priest 31		21
As for example: A godly man, not out of superstition,	273	Priest 31		21
after the example of devout Cornelius.	312	Valdesso		21
Infants manners are moulded more by the example of Parents,	357	Proverbs	D	1060
whose Example and Care of them will justifie you both to the world	373	Letters		16
EXAMPLES				
for knowledge, Examples for illustration, and Promises for comfort:	228	Priest 4		25
from his promises, from the examples of all Saints, that ever were;	249	Priest 15		21
except you wink, you cannot but see many brave examples.	366	Letters		7
EXCEED				
Never exceed thy income. Youth may make	13	Ch.-Porch		157
it absurd, that he should exceed, who teacheth others temperance.	241	Priest 10		21
of questions in the one, so they farre exceed them in the other.	257	Priest 21		23
whom yet he ever exhorts not to exceed his bounds, but in tickle	260	Priest 23		35
so it exceed not bounds, for every one to imploy himselfe	275	Priest 32		28
how shall not the ministration of the spirit exceed in blessing?	285	Priest 36		20
EXCEEDING				
The Countrey Parson is exceeding exact in his Life, being holy,	227	Priest 3		1
which will make them appear exceeding reverend, and holy.	234	Priest 7		24
This way he findes exceeding usefull, and winning;	236	Priest 8		15
as being immoderately taken, it is exceeding obstructive.	243	Priest 10		4
But it will not be amisse in this exceeding usefull point to descend	275	Priest 32		18
and with an exceeding great victory, which in the Creation needed	283	Priest 34		15
and fashionableness is so exceeding unbefitting a Minister,	285	Priest 36		7
which is so exceeding useful, and hath taken so deep roote,	287	Priest 37		8
regular life can hardly be altered without exceeding great danger.	295	Cornaro		18
The memorie whereof is exceeding delightfull to me.	301	Cornaro		33
that I take it exceeding kindly of you.	378	Letters		11
to an exceeding cheerfulness, in signing 100 lib. with her own hands	379	Letters		1
whose exceeding glory is equally round with the world it selfe:	442	Oration		10
EXCEEDINGLY				
which exceedingly delights him as by way of exercise upon himself,	255	Priest 21		11
that I was exceedingly helped, and by continuance thereof,	292	Cornaro		35
whereupon also I joyed exceedingly;	294	Cornaro		29
but you joyed me exceedingly with your relation of my Lady Duchess's	377	Letters		19
EXCEEDS				
Who made the arbour: this exceeds her wit.	101	Miserie		58
But as in vice the copie still exceeds	196	Ch.-Milit.		221

EXCEEDS (cont'd)	PAGE	TITLE	LINE
The Parson exceeds not an hour in preaching, because all ages have	235	Priest 7	10
This practice exceeds even Sermons in teaching:	257	Priest 21	20
EXCEL			
we have as much failed, as your Excellencies doe excel, in both.	442	Oration	34
EXCELL			
Such was their lustre, they did so excell,	102	Jordan 2	2
Blest Order, which in power dost so excell,	160	Priesthood	1
Blest Order, which in power doth so excell,	160	Priesthood V	1
For as thy absence doth excell	163	The Search	57
That they in merit shall excell.	187	Judgement	10
EXCELLED			
And herein St Paul excelled in all his Epistles.	234	Priest 7	11
EXCELLENCIES			
The accession of which new title to your Excellencies, all the Muses	442	Oration	1
your Excellencies to bee more deare unto us, in that you are	442	Oration	20
we have as much failed, as your Excellencies doe excel, in both.	442	Oration	34
perpetuall povertie, but when your Excellencies appeare.	442	Oration	38
let the first be the care of your Excellencies;	443	Oration	5
EXCELLENCY			
Let there be no kind of excellency which it is possible for you	366	Letters	13
EXCELLENT			
making use of that excellent statute, which bindes all Parishes	244	Priest 12	23
and ripenesse of judgement for so excellent a Place, not to refuse,	276	Priest 32	17
of excellent wit and noble disposition, overthrown and undone	291	Cornaro	2
as also of excellent Artificers in Architecture, painting,	301	Cornaro	36
Most Excellent and most magnificent Lords:	441	Oration	23
Wherefore most Excellent, most Illustrious Lords, since you are so	442	Oration	27
EXCELLENTLY			
So that they excellently score out the way, and fully, and exactly	246	Priest 13	32
and expresse so clearely and excellently the intent of the Gospell in	304	Valdesso	21
A house and a woman sute excellently.	337	Proverbs	468
EXCELLING			
I conferre often with worthie men, excelling in wit, learning,	301	Cornaro	4
EXCEPT			
Who cannot wish, except I give them bread:	26	Sacrifice	7
May no lines passe, except they do their dutie	56	Jordan 1	4
Is it no verse, except enchanted groves	56	Jordan 1	6
Except thou make us dayly, we shall spurn	127	Giddinesse	27
Except life catch & hold those fast.	202	Trin.Sun. W	10
to his earthly, having no title to either, except he do good to both.	239	Priest 10	22
except the evidence of the misery bring testimony with it.	245	Priest 12	22
except in the cases of extreme poverty, and in the seasons	248	Priest 14	4
except the person bee so poor, that he is not able to reward	262	Priest 23	13
except some small and temporary estranging may corroborate	263	Priest 25	30
which is not easily despised, except it degenerate to pride.	268	Priest 28	26
except besides his office, he add a tincture of private malice in	287	Priest 37	26
whom the Law would have defamed, except he also do it out of rancour.	287	Priest 37	29
by any of these inconveniences, except it were for one onely day.	294	Cornaro	10
except there be a restraining motion (as S. Paul had when hee would	313	Valdesso	15
Knowledge is folly, except grace guide it.	329	Proverbs	248
This world is nothing except it tend to another.	334	Proverbs	382
Count not fowre except you have them in a wallett.	352	Proverbs	962
The Divell never assailes a man, except he find him	361	Proverbs D	1176
except you wink, you cannot but see many brave examples.	366	Letters	6
except my cousin Bett take pitty of her, which yet at that distance	375	Letters	29
EXCEPTING			
to me unto my deare wife excepting onely these legacies hereafter	382	G.H.'s Will	6
to be devided betweene them excepting some legacies of my deceased	382	G.H.'s Will	14
EXCESSE			
Bid him but temper his excesse;	100	Miserie	9
Not from excesse, and therefore doe we spende	210	Paradox D	21
which excesse of joy neither could do me any hurt.	294	Cornaro	29
though it was but a little excesse, in a few dayes had so soon	297	Cornaro	5
EXCESSES			
keep a fit proportion, shall receive little hurt from other excesses.	294	Cornaro	5
EXCESSIVE			
Who with excessive pride	85	Vanitie 1	13
EXCHANGE			
Nor the Exchange, or busie Hall;	70	Quidditie	10
EXCHANGING			
All day exchanging mirth and breath	98	Mortific.	15
Fain put thee on, exchanging my lay-sword	160	Priesthood	5
EXCITE			
Did not excite thee, we should wholly sink.	60	Whitsunday	24
or painted there, which may excite the reader to a thought of piety;	240	Priest 10	24
EXCITER			
And the Parson is a lover of and exciter to justice in all things,	277	Priest 32	22
EXCITING			
but for an exciting of others by their sight, to the acknowledging	282	Priest 34	15
EXCITINGS			
the one, in wanting many excitings of grace;	259	Priest 22	5
EXCLUDE			
Hath still sow'd fig-leaves to exclude thy light:	83	Sighs & Gr.	16
I here exclude the wrangler from thy treasure.	104	Obedience	15
EXCLUDED			
Yet thy brave beames excluded from their right	211	Bohemia D	10
EXCLUDES			
Which ev'n eternitie excludes!	123	Time	26
For mine excludes both measure, tune, and time.	164	Grief	18

	PAGE	TITLE	LINE
EXCUSE			
It gets thee nothing, and hath no excuse.	8	Ch.-Porch	56
It gets thee nothing, and has no excuse.	8	Ch.-Porch W	56
Without excuse or cloke.	171	Self-cond.	24
to those busnesses which justly excuse him from writing at this time,	367	Letters	30
EXCUSED			
Wherefore as David's Adultery cannot be excused, so need	316	Valdesso	6
Sister this week already, and therefore now I hope may be excused.	367	Letters	22
EXCUSES			
A little given seasonably excuses a great gift.	349	Proverbs	834
EXECUTE			
To execute their call,	70	Humilitie	6
EXECUTION			
lying upon you either for the execution or benefitt of a trade,	380	Woodnoth	26
EXECUTIONER			
An executioner at best;	123	Time	15
As the executioner is not uncharitable, that takes away the life	287	Priest 37	25
EXECUTIONERS			
all are executioners, and the Law gives a malefactour to all to be	287	Priest 37	30
EXECUTOR			
A fat house-keeper makes a leane Executor.	322	Proverbs V	28
that Mr Woodnoth should be mine Executor to whome I bequeath twenty	382	G.H.'s Will	28
EXECUTORS			
A fat house-keeper makes leane Executors.	322	Proverbs	28
EXEMPLARY			
with other exemplary vertues of that sort, and to keep them on in	237	Priest 9	34
EXEMPT			
So likewise are the godly in some sort exempt from Lawes,	315	Valdesso	32
How the godly are exempt from Laws is a known point among Divines,	316	Valdesso	31
but when he sayes they are equally exempt with God, that is dangerous	316	Valdesso	32
EXEMPTION			
miseries have a naturall priviledge, and exemption from all law.	245	Priest 12	30
The exemption from both, is by the Grace of God.	308	Valdesso	5
EXERCISE			
where he shall not exercise what he is, unlesse he forsake his	226	Priest 2	26
which exceedingly delights him as by way of exercise upon himself,	255	Priest 21	12
the obscurity in some points being the exercise of the Church,	263	Priest 24	5
The Church needing both an evidence, and an exercise.	263	Priest 24	7
Great Horse, or exercise some of his Military gestures [Postures].	277	Priest 32	16
EXERCISED			
counting that day lost, wherein he hath not exercised his Charity.	244	Priest 12	18
EXERCISES			
he makes a peculiar one for a blessing on the exercises of the day,	235	Priest 8	22
if there be any extraordinary addition to the customary exercises,	235	Priest 8	34
to harden himselfe, and to further his exercises of Mortification.	284	Priest 35	36
amongst all divine and spirituall exercises and duties,	311	Valdesso V	3
or justify himselfe before God, by any acts or exercises of Religion;	312	Valdesso	16
EXERCISETH			
that God hath and exerciseth a threefold power in every thing which	270	Priest 30	33
EXHALATION			
Fed with the exhalation of our crimes,	64	Ch.-monum.	5
As a young exhalation, newly waking,	169	The Answer	8
EXHALATIONS			
Sowre exhalations, and dishonest rheumes,	86	Lent	23
EXHAUSTED			
neither can they ever be exhausted, (as Pictures may be by a plenarie	309	Valdesso	22
EXHORT			
When we exhort people to continue in their vocation, it is in	381	Woodnoth	23
EXHORTATION			
afterward they will attend it of themselves without his exhortation.	318	Valdesso	22
EXHORTATIONS			
for them also men heed, and remember better then exhortations;	233	Priest 7	14
or in exhortations to some of his flock by themselves, whom his	236	Priest 8	12
and these exhortations he cals his privy purse, even as Princes have	236	Priest 8	16
turning it to reformation of life, by pithy and lively exhortations;	255	Priest 21	7
and lively exhortations, not on the Sunday of the Communion only	258	Priest 22	26
EXHORTS			
he hath so done, then he assumes the Parson, and exhorts to Charity.	260	Priest 23	17
whom yet he ever exhorts not to exceed his bounds, but in tickle	260	Priest 23	35
EXIGENT			
and Satan, who knows the exigent, blows the fire, endeavouring	272	Priest 31	33
within a few moneths I should be driven to that exigent,	292	Cornaro	14
EXILE			
then their present exile, and disability to live in their Countrey.	282	Priest 34	10
EXINANITION			
which also in diseases of exinanition (as consumptions) must be	242	Priest 10	31
because diseases of exinanition are more dangerous, then diseases	267	Priest 26	14
EXPATIATE			
Began to spread and to expatiate there:	130	Love unkn.	39
EXPECT			
I did expect a ring.	121	Hope	8
Circumcised to this day, and expect the promises of the Scripture;	282	Priest 34	1
Beare with evill, and expect good.	338	Proverbs	511
Suffer and expect, sustine, abstine.	343	Proverbs V	701
Suffer and expect.	344	Proverbs	702
therfore Expect a harvest. 3. To Change shewes not well & you are	380	Woodnoth	11
EXPECTATION			
My expectation.	141	Pilgrimage	2
I have not deceived their expectation, let not them deceive mine:	364	Letters	24
EXPECTED			
From this ill temper there remained little else to be expected of me,	291	Cornaro	25

EXPRESSIONS (cont'd)	PAGE	TITLE		LINE
With kinde Expressions to his friend, ...	439	Walton 5	V	12
EXTEND				
Thou wouldst extend me to some good, ...	57	Employm. 1		2
But it extend, ...	145	Discharge		44
to extend themselves to all that mirth, which the present occasion	280	Priest 34		26
is ashamed in small things, will extend his pusillanimity to greater.	284	Priest 35		34
EXTENDED				
such as are from Gods generall providence extended even to lillyes;	249	Priest 15		20
EXTENDS				
which is said of hurtfull meats, extends to hurtfull drinks also.	266	Priest 26		27
EXTENSION				
But the extension and the room, ...	57	Employm. 1		6
EXTENT				
O rack me not to such a vast extent;	55	Temper 1		9
EXTERNALL				
even in externall and indifferent things, what course is to be taken;	246	Priest 13		33
EXTINGUISHED				
the naturall concupiscence is not quite extinguished, but the heate	308	Valdesso		17
EXTIRPATE				
Sinne being not able to extirpate quite	194	Ch.-Milit.		161
EXTOLL				
To extoll thee.	146	Praise 2		28
EXTOLLETH				
Extolleth many wayes, yet this one more.	121	Providence		152
EXTORT				
Dry dust, which sheds no tears, but may extort.	186	Death		12
EXTRACT				
The spirit and good extract of my heart	38	The Sinner		10
EXTRAORDINARY				
and if there be any extraordinary addition to the customary . .	235	Priest 8		33
EXTREAM				
and my bodie spent with extream leannesse, and the season . .	296	Cornaro		27
EXTREAMLY				
Away thy blessings, and extreamly flout thee, ...	23	Ch.-Porch		413
Our blessings from us, and extreamly flout thee, ...	23	Ch.-Porch	W	413
My minde would be extreamly stirr'd	95	Submission		3
EXTREME				
except in the cases of extreme poverty, and in the seasons . .	248	Priest 14		4
but that I have both time and work to be Your extreme Servant,	370	Letters		15
EXTREMELY				
and it is this, I want Books extremely;	364	Letters		11
EXTREMITIE				
Before I were by frosts extremitie	57	Employm. 1		3
EXULT				
all we and our whole Kingdome exult with joy, to bee united with that	442	Oration		14
EY'D				
Both their full-ey'd aspects, and secret glances.	85	Vanitie 1		7
Thy full-ey'd love!	172	The Glance		20
But quick-ey'd Love, observing me grow slack	188	Love 3		3
In the kingdome of blind men the one ey'd is king.	337	Proverbs		469
Perversnes makes one squint ey'd.	342	Proverbs		634
EYE (see also eie)				
That thou shouldst it so eye, and wooe, ...	62	Mattens		10
But when it would appeare to others eye, ...	68	Content		11
Taught me to live here so, That still one eye	85	Coloss.		7
Bids the rash gazer wipe his eye:	87	Vertue		6
To all expressions both of hand and eye, ...	88	The Pearl		15
As on a window late I cast mine eye, ...	116	Love-joy		1
Lookt on a servant, who did know his eye	129	Love unkn.		9
More attributes? Am I all throat or eye, ...	143	Complaining		13
And turn, and leer, and with a licorous eye	144	Discharge		3
From thy right eye, ...	158	Praise 3		32
Call home thine eye (that busie wanderer)	170	Self-cond.		5
When first thy sweet and gracious eye	171	The Glance		1
Sprung from thine eye, did work within my soul, ...	172	The Glance		14
On it may stay his eye;	184	The Elixer		10
To which he lent a corner of his eye.	195	Ch.-Milit.		170
and thither lift mine eye.	218	Psalm V	D	8
and busy cast of his eye on his auditors, with letting them know,	233	Priest 7		1
the choyce of his wife was made rather by his eare, then by his eye;	238	Priest 9		27
The Parson's eye.	264	Priest 26		T
Jest not with the eye or with Religion.	326	Proverbs		157
The eye and Religion can beare no jesting.	326	Proverbs		158
Diseases of the eye are to bee cured with the elbow.	327	Proverbs		203
The eye will have his part.	337	Proverbs		466
The masters eye fattens the horse, and his foote the ground.	338	Proverbs		486
Love makes a good eye squint.	339	Proverbs		543
One eye of the masters sees more, then ten of the servants. . .	344	Proverbs		687
Religion, Credit, and the Eye are not to be touched.	349	Proverbs		837
Warre and Physicke are governed by the eye.	351	Proverbs		906
The eye is bigger then the belly.	355	Proverbs		1018
He that hath but one eye, must bee afraid to lose it.	358	Proverbs	D	1088
things inwardly good to have an eye to the world may be pharisaicall:	380	Woodnoth		16
EYES				
Turn their eyes hither, who shall make a gain:	5	Dedication		5
How dare those eyes upon a Bible look, ...	6	Ch.-Porch		11
Oh all ye, who passe by, whose eyes and minde	26	Sacrifice		1
To me, who took eyes that I might you finde:	26	Sacrifice		3
When backward on my sins I turne mine eyes	43	H. Bapt.1	W	1
So when I view my sinnes, mine eyes remove	43	H. Bapt.1		3

EYES (cont'd)	PAGE	TITLE		LINE
That mends the lookers eyes: this is the well	58	H.Script.1		9
I cannot ope mine eyes,	62	Mattens		1
Who gave me eyes, and light, and power this day,	63	Even-song		2
And now with darknesse closest wearie eyes,	64	Even-song		18
Is styled honour, riches, or fair eyes;	71	Frailtie		3
And prick mine eyes.	71	Frailtie		16
Troubling mine eyes.	71	Frailtie	W	16
The dust into our eyes:	82	Ungratef.		17
Therefore not sealed, but with open eyes	89	The Pearl		32
Therefore not seeled, but with open eyes	89	The Pearl	W	32
His eyes dismount the highest starre:	91	Man		21
And both mine eyes are thine,	95	Submission		2
Since thou hast both mine eyes.	95	Submission		20
Shall ne're be troubled with ill eyes.	96	Charms & K		2
Shall ne're be troubled with sore eyes.	96	Charms & K	W	2
Who looks on ground with humble eyes,	96	Charms & K		11
Schooling his eyes;	98	Mortific.		22
Oh foolish man! where are thine eyes?	101	Miserie		49
If I but lift mine eyes, my suit is made:	103	Prayer 2		5
I have both lost mine eyes and eares.	105	Conscience		6
To whom the starres shine not so fair, as eyes;	111	Vanitie 2		3
Take up thine eyes, which feed on earth;	112	Dawning		2
And with his buriall-linen drie thine eyes:	112	Dawning		14
Then weep mine eyes, the God of love doth grieve:	135	Ephes.		7
If my deserts were masters of mine eyes:	136	Ephes.		34
Where shall I get me eyes enough to weep,	140	Ch.-rents		25
As many eyes as starres? since it is night,	140	Ch.-rents		26
With sick and famisht eyes,	148	Longing		1
Well may he close his eyes, but not his heart.	151	The Bag		6
But when mine eyes	158	Praise 3		26
Dwell in my head & eyes: come clouds, & rain:	164	Grief		2
Suck up a river to supply mine eyes,	164	Grief		5
My weary weeping eyes too drie for me,	164	Grief		6
Give up your feet and running to mine eyes,	164	Grief		15
Where I wipe mine eyes, and see	182	Banquet		45
Till it stirre, and rubbe the eyes;	186	Dooms-day		4
Who made the eyes but I?	189	Love 3		12
And blending these he carri'd all mens eyes,	195	Ch.-Milit.		189
That Flesh is there, mine eyes deny:	201	H. Commun.	W	31
Why should I Womens eyes for Chrystal take?	206	Walton 2		8
But veywe yourselves, & inward turn your eyes;	210	Paradox	D	27
If ever Tears did flow from Eyes,	213	Convert	D	1
Let now my Eyes, my Voice, my Heart,	213	Convert	D	4
My Eyes, from whence these Tears did spring,	214	Convert	D	6
And to my dym and sinful eyes	219	Psalm V	D	23
open mine eyes, that I may see the wondrous things of thy Law.	229	Priest 4		3
and eyes, and using all other gestures which may expresse a hearty,	231	Priest 6		3
beseeching the Father of lights to open their eyes, and to give him	262	Priest 24		22
which are two great lights able to dazle the eyes of the mis-led,	263	Priest 24		19
especially if they carry their eyes ever open, and fix them on their	266	Priest 26		4
Hee that saw Christ open a blind mans eyes, saw not more Divinity,	283	Priest 34		1
of Popery should open the eyes of one to understand and expresse	304	Valdesso		20
to open his eyes that he might see the wondrous things of his Lawes,	309	Valdesso		25
Who hath none to still him, may weepe out his eyes.	321	Proverbs		17
Diseases of the eyes are to bee cured with the elbow.	326	Proverbs	V	203
The hearts letter is read in the eyes.	328	Proverbs		220
Neither eyes on letters, nor hands in coffers.	330	Proverbs		288
The buyer needes a hundred eyes, the seller not one.	334	Proverbs		390
Discreet women have neither eyes nor eares.	337	Proverbs		482
Hee that blowes in the dust fills his eyes with it.	340	Proverbs		570
To whirle the eyes too much shewes a Kites braine.	345	Proverbs		717
The ignorant hath an Eagles wings, and an Owles eyes.	351	Proverbs		902
The eyes have one language every where.	352	Proverbs		959
Spies are the ears and eyes of Princes.	357	Proverbs	D	1067
since there is a two-fold brightnesse which dazeleth the eyes of men,	442	Oration		33
EYESIGHT				
she is not disposed to spend her eyesight on a piece of paper,	371	Letters		14
FABRICK				
For all thy frame and fabrick is within.	106	Sion		12
Lord, dost thou some new fabrick mold,	162	The Search		25
FABRICKS				
and antiquities, publick fabricks, temples, and fortifications:	302	Cornaro		4
FACE				
Sure to be crosse he would shift feet and face.	7	Ch.-Porch		24
My face they cover, though it be divine.	31	Sacrifice		137
As Moses face was vailed, so is mine,	31	Sacrifice		138
As Moses face was vailed, so was mine,	31	Sacrifice	W	138
The souldiers also spit upon that face,	32	Sacrifice		181
The souldiers also spit upon my Face,	32	Sacrifice	W	181
To shew their face, since crosse to thy decrees:	38	The Sinner		7
And made her youth and fiercenesse seek thy face.	46	Afflict.1		18
If still the sunne should hide his face,	60	Grace		5
If the Sunn still should hide his face,	60	Grace	W	5
Where beams surround my Saviours face,	74	The Starre		2
Among the beams, which crown the face	74	The Starre		22
Make up one man; whose face thou art,	75	Sunday		9
Nay, thou hast got the face of man; for we	77	Avarice		10
See the smooth face of God, without a frown	77	Ang.&Sts.		2
A face not fearing light:	86	Lent		21
Unto my face:	90	Afflict.4		15

FACE (cont'd)	PAGE	TITLE		LINE
Did crown his heart and face.	102	Miserie		72
When I behold it trickling down thy face, ...	107	Home		9
And dates her letters from thy face, ...	109	Brit. Ch.		5
That ev'n her face by kissing shines, ...	110	Brit. Ch.		17
Yet active strength: whose long and bonie face	138	The Size		33
Which have the face of fire, but end in rest.	139	Artillerie		8
At which the Church falling upon her face	152	The Jews		9
What covert dare eclipse thy face?	163	The Search		31
Into thy face;	186	Death		14
Where first the Church should raise her down-cast face. . .	192	Ch.-Milit.		86
Adoring garlick with an humble face, ...	193	Ch.-Milit.		112
With Glory may attaine thy Face.	202	Trin.Sun.	W	6
With face and hands clinging unto thy brest, ...	205	Persever.	W	14
In the best face but filth, when, Lord, in thee	206	Walton 2		13
When sense is made by Comments. But that face	212	Bohemia	D	29
Of thousand harts: that face doth figure thee	212	Bohemia	D	33
Those ravening Harpyes, which peck at thy face, ...	212	Bohemia	D	48
are like the chaff, which from the face	215	Psalm I	D	14
even so farre as reproofe to their very face, when occasion cals,	226	Priest 2		30
How shall we dare to appear before thy face, who are contrary	288	Priest		9
One hand washeth another, and both the face.	329	Proverbs		239
Who spits against heaven, it falls in his face.	333	Proverbs		346
The wind in ones face makes one wise.	345	Proverbs		721
FACES				
Yet with two faces, as their Janus was;	196	Ch.-Milit.		207
or you hear as you ought, he sees hearts, as we see faces: . .	234	Priest 7		28
since there is a greater diversitie of tempers, then of faces.	297	Cornaro		31
FACIENS				
the other gratia gratum faciens, this being given only to the godly,	319	Valdesso		8
FACT				
and they are to be judged according to the outward fact, . .	316	Valdesso		19
is a judgment of authority (upon a fact) and there is a judgment	316	Valdesso		35
FACTION				
combin'd in one great faction rise.	215	Psalm II	D	4
FACTIOUS				
But that my Inke was factious for this side.	209	L. Bacon	D	12
FACULTY				
in her sensitive faculty, will runne out more or lesse in her	238	Priest 9		11
FADE				
If well; the pain doth fade, the joy remains.	24	Ch.-Porch		462
Sprung from that beautie which can never fade;	54	Love 1		2
Sprung from the beautie which can never fade;	54	Love 1	W	2
Nay, it shall ev'ry yeare decrease and fade;	196	Ch.-Milit.		229
His leaf shall never fade, and all	214	Psalm I	D	11
FADED				
Your colour faded, and calamities	140	Ch.-rents		18
FADES				
If thou do ill; the joy fades, not the pains:	24	Ch.-Porch		461
FAIL				
Do fortunes seek, when worth and service fail, ...	14	Ch.-Porch		182
But though men fail him, yet his part doth play.	73	Constancie		30
As if thy love could fail or change.	108	Home		28
And flesh would fail, ...	136	Ephes.		33
Christ keepeth now, who cannot fail or fall.	143	Holdfast		14
Wherefore if thou canst fail, ...	156	Assurance		31
Though I fail, I weep:	179	Discipline		13
If all fail, then he keeps good correspondence with some neighbour	260	Priest 23		36
that if all fail, yet I am able to stand on mine own legs. . .	370	Letters		10
FAILED				
we have as much failed, as your Excellencies doe excel, . .	442	Oration		34
FAILS				
fails not to afford his best comforts, and rather goes to them,	249	Priest 15		15
This last rule joyned with the first, never fails. . . .	267	Priest 26		6
FAIN				
That he was fain, when thou wert destitute, ...	77	Avarice		7
Wert fain to take our flesh and curse, ...	103	Prayer 2		15
Beasts fain would sing; birds dittie to their notes;	117	Providence		9
But robs a thousand who would praise thee fain, ...	117	Providence		19
Who fain would have you be new, tender, quick.	131	Love unkn.		70
With thine own clay. But I would parley fain:	139	Artillerie		27
Fain would I here have made abode, ...	142	Pilgrimage		9
In thy just censures; fain would I draw nigh, ...	160	Priesthood		4
Fain put thee on, exchanging my lay-sword	160	Priesthood		5
Somewhat it fain would say:	168	a true Hymn		3
their flattering tongues do fain.	219	Psalm V	D	28
and shall I then be fain alwayes to borrow Books, and build . .	364	Letters		13
so that I am fain ever and anon, to buy somewhat tending towards my	364	Letters		33
so that I am fain to dyet in my Chamber at mine own cost; . .	365	Letters		2
FAINE				
For sinn would faine remove the dearth	59	Whitsunday	W	19
To curbe some Rebell teares, which faine would flow, ...	213	Bohemia	D	58
FAINT				
My crosse I bear my self, untill I faint:	33	Sacrifice		197
Or else the chilnesse of my faint demands.	66	Ch.-lock		4
A faint desire, ...	79	Employm.2		9
Thy sorrows were in earnest; no faint proffer, ...	104	Obedience		28
To make me sigh, and seek, and faint, and die, ...	164	The Crosse		2
from the certainty both of deliverance, and reward, if we faint not;	249	Priest 15		26
FAINTED				
so long at it, that they would have fainted, had they returned empty,	267	Priest 26		24

FAINTINGS	PAGE	TITLE	LINE
And in my faintings I presume your love	129	Love unkn.	2
FAIR (see also fayre)			
O crumble not away thy souls fair heap.	9	Ch.-Porch	70
If studious, copie fair, what time hath blurr'd;	10	Ch.-Porch	86
And then as farre as fair behaviour may,	20	Ch.-Porch	359
Copie thy fair, though bloudie hand?	35	Thanksgvng	16
Thy wormwood turn to health, windes to fair weather:	49	Repentance	21
Is styled honour, riches, or fair eyes;	71	Frailtie	3
But is fair dust!	71	Frailtie	4
At some fair oak, or bush, or cave, or well:	99	Decay	7
Not a fair look, but thou dost call it foul:	105	Conscience	2
To whom the starres shine not so fair, as eyes;	111	Vanitie 2	3
Can praise his fairest fair;	115	Dulnesse	6
As fair as ever, and as fit to use;	118	Providence	67
And clean and fair, as I one even-tide	129	Love unkn.	23
To th' Isle of spices, is't not fair?	137	The Size	12
After so foul a journey death is fair,	142	Pilgrimage	35
That all was not so fair, as I conceiv'd,	155	Assurance	8
Of some fair church to show the sore	158	Praise 3	34
Many a spring I shoot up fair,	166	The Flower	24
Thou art grown fair and full of grace,	186	Death	15
are so ordered, that they all meet and end in a fair plot of ground;	301	Cornaro	22
well and quietly any where, and my dreams are fair and pleasant.	302	Cornaro	13
And that is a fair and desirable death, which Nature brings by way	303	Cornaro	28
To a fair day open the window, but make you ready as to a foule.	325	Proverbs	119
New things are fair.	359	Proverbs	D 1117
No love is foule, nor prison fair.	359	Proverbs	D 1122
A fair day in winter is the mother of a storme.	360	Proverbs	D 1145
FAIRE (noun)			
Men speake of the faire, as things went with them there.	326	Proverbs	151
Buy at a faire, but sell at home.	326	Proverbs	160
FAIRE			
of dependance, how faire soever the opportunities present themselves.	271	Priest 30	27
So that if a Farmer hath both a faire harvest, and that also well	271	Priest 30	38
A faire wife and a frontire Castle breede quarrels.	324	Proverbs	103
A blustering night, a faire day.	331	Proverbs	307
Faire shooting never kild bird.	335	Proverbs	405
Never was strumpet faire.	336	Proverbs	431
Faire is not faire, but that which pleaseth.	338	Proverbs	492
A faire death honours the whole life.	339	Proverbs	522
Faire words make mee looke to my purse.	339	Proverbs	548
Of faire things, the Autumne is faire.	340	Proverbs	572
Soft and faire goes farre.	347	Proverbs	772
Faire language grates not the tongue.	347	Proverbs	799
No prison is faire, nor love foule.	348	Proverbs	829
No prison is faire, & no love foule.	348	Proverbs	V 829
One faire day in winter makes not birds merrie.	353	Proverbs	977
FAIRER			
What is fairer then a rose?	178	The Rose	17
Fairer & richer. Now wee know, what's thine,	211	Bohemia	D 18
FAIREST			
Can praise his fairest fair;	115	Dulnesse	6
by his governing power, the fairest harvests come to nothing.	271	Priest 30	18
besides that they are in the fairest place of this learned Citie	301	Cornaro	10
FAIRLY			
Before thy journey fairly part with all.	13	Ch.-Porch	162
Say that fairly I refuse,	178	The Rose	31
and not as many who think they have done fairly, if they leave them	376	Letters	15
FAITH			
Of faith, but furie: yet at their commands	28	Sacrifice	46
My faith in me.	44	H. Bapt.2	5
Faith.	49	Faith	T
And bring by Faith all things to him?	49	Faith	4
Faith makes me any thing, or all	50	Faith	17
Faith sets me higher in his glorie.	50	Faith	20
Faith puts me there with him, who sweetly took	50	Faith	23
Where now by Faith all arms are of a length;	50	Faith	27
Vanisht away, when Faith did change the scene:	51	Faith	39
Faith cleaves unto it, counting evr'y grain	51	Faith	42
With faith, with hope, with charitie;	68	Trin.Sun.	8
Reason triumphs, and faith lies by.	134	Divinitie	8
Faith needs no staffe of flesh, but stoutly can	135	Divinitie	27
This Anchor keeps my faith, that, me secure.	439	Walton 6	4
prophecy, let us prophecy according to the proportion of faith;	226	Priest 2	6
were with Saint Paul even sacrificed upon the service of their faith.	234	Priest 7	9
and by the vertue of the shield of faith, he is not afraid	238	Priest 9	6
could out of humility, produce any speciall grace of faith, patience,	238	Priest 9	32
The life of faith, James 2. 26.	244	Priest 12	11
as a necessary evidence and fruit of their faith, at that time	249	Priest 15	33
or led by sense, more then by faith, by present rewards,	254	Priest 20	32
useth all possible diligence to reduce them to the common Faith.	262	Priest 24	21
The like he doth in other Christian vertues, as of Faith, and Love,	279	Priest 33	34
Infidelity, Faith; Distrust, Hope: Of these none can free themselves	308	Valdesso	8
for he maintaines that it is Faith and Infidelity that shall judge us	311	Valdesso	22
will better appear by his 98 Consideration of faith and good works.	312	Valdesso	V 5
that justifying faith, and the faith of miracles are divers guifts,	319	Valdesso	6
and the faith of miracles are divers guifts, and of a different	319	Valdesso	6
Yet doubtlesse the best faith in us is defective, and arrives	319	Valdesso	10
And miracle-working as it may be severed from justifying faith,	319	Valdesso	13
The 98. Consid. about being justified by faith, or by good works,	319	Valdesso	V 17

FAITH (cont'd)	PAGE	TITLE		LINE
Love askes faith, and faith firmenesse.	339	Proverbs		544
FAITHFUL				
yet have I sent it thither by a faithful Messenger this day:	369	Letters		16
Your most faithful Servant in Christ Jesu, GEORGE HERBERT.	377	Letters		9
FAITHFULL				
Unto an honest faithfull grave;	186	Death		23
whome I esteem to be God's faithfull & diligent Servant,	378	Letters		14
FAITHFULLEST				
for I am sure you love Your faithfullest Servant, GEORGE HERBERT.	365	Letters		26
FAITHFULLY				
is to feed my Flocke diligently and faithfully, since our Saviour	224	Priest		5
of the house best, and then hee faithfully, and boldly applyeth it;	251	Priest 17		27
and then he suits things faithfully according to that end.	253	Priest 19		5
and doing their duty faithfully, they will soon discover:	266	Priest 26		3
deliver thy message reverently, readily, faithfully, & fruitfully.	289	Priest		29
FALL				
Whether thy stock of credit swell, or fall.	20	Ch.-Porch		346
Which he might fall in by companions, gains.	24	Ch.-Porch		436
So sits the earths great curse in Adams fall	32	Sacrifice		165
Then shall the fall further the flight in me.	43	East.wings		10
Then shall my fall further the flight in me.	43	East.wings	W	10
From what life feeleth, Adams fall.	48	Repentance		12
And where sinne placeth me in Adams fall,	50	Faith		19
And where sinne places me in Adams fall,	50	Faith	W	19
Sometimes to hell I fall.	55	Temper 1		8
Whether I flie with angels, fall with dust,	55	Temper 1		25
Whether I Angell it, or fall to dust.	55	Temper 1	W	25
The dew doth ev'ry morning fall;	60	Grace		9
When they shall bow, and kneel, and fall down flat	65	Ch.-monum.		15
That thou mayst fit thy self against thy fall.	65	Ch.-monum.		24
To court each place or fortune that doth fall,	68	Content		7
To court each place or fortune that does fall,	68	Content	W	7
The dew shall weep thy fall to night;	87	Vertue		3
Thy horse shal never fall or tire.	96	Charms & K	W	4
Grace turnes the Optick, then they fall.	97	Charms & K	W	18
And measure not their fall.	100	Miserie		24
Such as springs use that fall, and windes that blow.	117	Providence		16
Thy even praise can neither rise, nor fall.	118	Providence		42
And fall, like rheumes, upon the tendrest parts.	126	Confession		12
And threw it in a font, wherein did fall	129	Love unkn.		13
Descend and fall, and thou dost flow.	137	The Size		6
Christ keepeth now, who cannot fail or fall.	143	Holdfast		14
Let what will fall:	144	Discharge		9
And make me giddie; Lord, I fall,	148	Longing		11
And fall to nothing: thou dost reigne,	150	Longing		56
Thrown down I fall into a bed, and rest:	159	Jos.coat		2
Which my fierce youth did bandie, fall and flow	169	The Answer		3
Till thy conquests and his fall	199	L'Envoy		13
Till thy conquest and his fall	199	L'Envoy	V	13
His fall can tell,	202	Trin.Sun.	W	13
To them that fall,	203	Trin.Sun.	W	16
bad councels let them fall:	219	Psalm V	D	30
but that they still fall from all compromises that have been made.	260	Priest 23		24
For when men have nothing to do, then they fall to drink, to steal,	274	Priest 32		11
curing of diseases, into which they often fall, who live disorderly:	298	Cornaro		5
cannot fall into diseases, and but very seldome into indispositions;	299	Cornaro		36
to avoiding of costlier matters, if I should fall absolutely sick:	365	Letters		8
I have another judge, to whom I stand or fall.	376	Letters		8
If there fall out yet any rubb, you shall heare of me;	377	Letters		22
FALLEN				
for the foulnesse, as wash, and durt, and things thereinto fallen;	241	Priest 10		29
and now we are fallen to the clean contrary, even from superstition	286	Priest 36		16
When the tree is fallen, all goe with their hatchet.	340	Proverbs		566
He that is fallen cannot helpe him that is downe.	346	Proverbs		753
FALLES				
Hee that stumbles and falles not, mends his pace.	321	Proverbs		7
The ill that comes out of our mouth falles into our bosome.	328	Proverbs		221
Hee that falles into the durt,	335	Proverbs		409
Wealth is like rheume, it falles on the weakest parts.	337	Proverbs		475
All that shakes falles not.	355	Proverbs		1022
FALLING				
Rising and falling with your wings:	65	Ch.-mus.		6
A falling starr has lost his place:	97	Charms & K	W	19
At which the Church falling upon her face	152	The Jews		9
FALLS				
Which falls in Autumne, score a grief?	38	Good Fri.		10
And while he digs out thee, falls in the ditch.	77	Avarice		14
Which falls by night, and poure it out for you!	140	Ch.-rents		30
According as the weather falls.	143	Complaining		10
presently falls to work, and seems to himselfe so as a Market-man is,	235	Priest 8		17
those that are tempted, whatsoever is unruly, falls upon two heads;	281	Priest 34		7
that even bruises and squats, and falls, which often kill others,	294	Cornaro		33
so his whole discourse and sevenfold observation falls to the ground.	318	Valdesso		26
Who spits against heaven, it falls in his face.	333	Proverbs		346
FALNE				
But wee are falne from Heaven to Earth,	59	Whitsunday	W	13
FALS				
In the mouth of a bad dog fals often a good bone.	358	Proverbs	D	1093
FALSE				
The Priest and rulers all false witnesse seek	28	Sacrifice		57

	PAGE	TITLE	LINE
FALSE (cont'd)			
The Priests and rulers all false witnesse seek	28	Sacrifice W	57
Who sayes that fictions onely and false hair	56	Jordan 1	1
Nor solid work, as false embroyderies;	111	Vanitie 2	4
False glozing pleasures, casks of happinesse,	167	Dotage	1
False gain before the true,	171	Self-cond.	15
The bloody man, the false one too,	218	Psalm V D	15
I am false to my reason which should guide me, I offend the supreme	265	Priest 26	10
This upon triall I found most false:	293	Cornaro	10
FALSIFYED			
For though these testimonies also may be falsifyed, yet considering	245	Priest 12	23
FALSLY			
And missing this, most falsly did arraigne thee;	41	Sepulchre	14
And falsly boast,	183	A Parodie	23
FALT			
So that now if they do not well the falt cannot be charg'd on you;	373	Letters	15
FAME			
She loseth three for one; her soul, rest, fame.	13	Ch.-Porch	174
Think not thy fame at ev'ry twitch will break:	15	Ch.-Porch	219
If that thy fame with ev'ry toy be pos'd,	15	Ch.-Porch	223
I will tear thence his love and fame.	35	Thanksgvng	26
I will ripp out his love and fame.	35	Thanksgvng W	26
I will teare out his love and fame.	35	Thanksgvng WC	26
Thy nourisht fame is weak or strong.	69	Content	32
His blasted fame	93	Unkindness	8
His darkned fame	93	Unkindness W	8
Wealth, fame, endowments, vertues, all should go;	103	Prayer 2	22
To honour thee; and so each hymne thy fame	121	Providence	151
Thou art requited; for his Fame,	209	H. Danvers D	8
And with that Ring thy fame shall wedd	213	L' Envoy D	13
to goodnesse as he can, both in honour, and profit, and fame;	244	Priest 11	4
are either such as are made known by common fame (and of these,	287	Priest 37	12
There are many waies to fame.	339	Proverbs	539
Fame is sowne in this age, that it may be reaped in the following;	443	Oration	3
FAME'S			
A toy shunn'd cleanly is fames interest.	15	Ch.-Porch W	228
FAMILIAR			
This familiar illustration made the answer so plaine, that he was	257	Priest 21	5
that by familiar things hee might make his Doctrine slip the more	261	Priest 23	18
easie for the Parsons purse, and more familiar for all mens bodyes.	261	Priest 23	32
FAMILIE			
Into thy familie.	46	Afflict.1 W	10
The Familie.	136	Familie	T
But, Lord, the house and familie are thine,	136	Familie	5
But all my wealth, and familie might combine	164	The Crosse	5
FAMILIES			
Doubtlesse they are Parsons of the families they live in,	226	Priest 2	22
and retains and confirms kingdomes, cities, and families in peace.	297	Cornaro	11
FAMILY			
the hour calls, with his family attending him, he goes to Church,	236	Priest 8	3
a providing for her family in such sort, as that neither they want	239	Priest 10	18
so that his family is a Schoole of Religion, and they all account,	240	Priest 10	21
which is expressed in a fayre table, as being the rule of a family.	240	Priest 10	27
and besides the common prayers of the family, he straitly requires	241	Priest 10	1
which when they leave the family, they carry with them.	241	Priest 10	6
or other relations give him any authority over the Family,	251	Priest 17	17
and so shuts them out of his family, esteeming that there is no spice	261	Priest 23	38
the Parson and his Family use to premise prayers, for this is to cure	262	Priest 23	9
both in present for his family, and in future for his children,	264	Priest 26	27
the improvement of his family, by bringing them up in the fear	275	Priest 32	22
But his family is his best care, to labour Christian soules,	275	Priest 32	30
the house-keepers Family be so small, and his dexterity so great,	275	Priest 32	37
When God is made master of a family, he orders the disorderly.	353	Proverbs	983
I was in hope I should my self carry all sickness out of your family:	372	Letters	16
having both ordered your Family, and so brought up your Children that	373	Letters	12
and make your family, a housefull of GOD's servants.	376	Letters	20
FAMINE			
Carve, or discourse; do not a famine fear.	11	Ch.-Porch	129
any calamity either by fire, or famine, to any neighbouring Parish,	253	Priest 19	29
Under water, famine; under snow, bread.	339	Proverbs	516
FAMISHT			
With sick and famisht eyes,	148	Longing	1
FAMOUS			
Where is thy famous force, thy ancient sting?	169	Dial.-Anth	2
This is the famous stone	185	The Elixer	21
FANCIE'S			
And so I came to Fancies medow strow'd	142	Pilgrimage V	7
FANCIES			
'Tis a thinne webbe, which poysonous fancies make:	15	Ch.-Porch	224
Wit fancies beautie, beautie raiseth wit:	54	Love 1	9
FANCY (see also phansies)			
And more then fancy: for in ev'ry thing	58	H.Script.2 W	10
FANSY			
Let not each fansy make thee to detest	7	Ch.-Porch W	19
FAR (see also farr,farre)			
Is of the two the far more desperate.	210	Paradox D	30
before hee proceede to disinheriting, or perhaps never goes so far;	250	Priest 16	18
if the contempt shall proceed so far as to do any thing punishable	268	Priest 28	31
our Saviours selling is so far from crossing Saint Pauls working,	275	Priest 32	3
These are so far from deterring any good man from the place,	276	Priest 32	22
is a Physitian so far as he meetes with the same disease,	278	Priest 33	27

FAR (cont'd)	PAGE	TITLE		LINE
so that they are so far from craving this benefit from their ghostly	286	Priest 36		13
of Conversation, hath proceeded thus far in the discussing of it.	287	Priest 37		10
So that it is so far from being a fault to discover such offenders,	287	Priest 37		38
I humbly thank him, & am so far from giving you cause, to apology,	378	Letters		9
Gods earth, no not tho' the advice step so far, as to be reproof:	378	Letters		13
FARE				
What's done on earth, we shall not fare the worse,	78	Ang.&Sts.		27
When God vouchsafeth to become our fare,	161	Priesthood		27
Save your cost, and mend your fare.	179	Invitation		3
His fare is plain, and common, but wholsome, what hee hath,	241	Priest 10		15
so that any simple fare is more savourie to me now, then heretofore,	302	Cornaro		9
FARES				
And it fares in this as it doth in Physick:	278	Priest 33		25
Ther's no great banquet but some fares ill.	343	Proverbs		668
first, how her health fares, next, whether my peace be yet made	371	Letters		8
FAREWELL				
Farewell deare flowers, sweetly your time ye spent,	94	Life		13
Farewell sweet phrases, lovely metaphors.	176	Forerunners		13
FARMER				
So that if a farmer should depend upon God all the yeer,	271	Priest 30		28
So that if a Farmer hath both a faire harvest, and that also well	271	Priest 30		38
FARMES				
They that hold the greatest farmes, pay the least rent	359	Proverbs	D	1100
FARR				
Guiltles so farr;	66	Ch.-lock	W	10
or, So farr indeed what you say is true, and well said;	252	Priest 18		11
not the evill which takes hold of them, and is farr the worse enemy.	269	Priest 28		25
but difficulties are so farr from cooling christians, that they whett	376	Letters		11
FARRE				
And then as farre as fair behaviour may,	20	Ch.-Porch		359
That brought the wise men of the East from farre.	28	Sacrifice		51
Perhaps my God, though he be farre before,	87	Lent		40
Nothing hath got so farre,	91	Man		19
Entred for both, farre above their desert!	105	Obedience		45
He so farre thy good did plot,	113	Businesse		23
Thus farre Time heard me patiently:	123	Time		27
Oh, what a thing is man! how farre from power,	127	Giddinesse		1
Chasing the fathers dimnesse, carri'd farre	168	The Sonne		8
And can hit from farre.	179	Discipline		24
God, to show how farre his love	181	Banquet		28
Farre from court,	182	Banquet		41
To thee, who art more farre above deceit,	185	A Wreath		7
it is a good strife to go as farre as wee can in pleasing of him,	224	Priest		12
even so farre as reproofe to their very face, when occasion cals,	226	Priest 2		30
and shall be so farre from that which they seek with their	226	Priest 2		34
of questions in the one, so they farre exceed them in the other.	257	Priest 21		23
the Countrey Parson proceeds so farre as to call in Authority,	263	Priest 25		22
he is so farre from condemning such assemblies, that he rather	284	Priest 35		13
but had already gone farre in me, first caused me to leave	291	Cornaro		18
whereas my life seemed as farre from it by Nature, as it was neare it	291	Cornaro		27
as farre as I can conjecture, very apt and well given both	303	Cornaro		4
Yet I am sure, that my end is farre from me:	303	Cornaro		25
But when he enlargeth he goes too farre.	315	Valdesso		35
they are equally exempt with God, that is dangerous and too farre.	316	Valdesso		33
They that know one another salute a farre off.	327	Proverbs		185
He that lives well sees a farre off.	333	Proverbs		352
Water a farre off quencheth not fire.	334	Proverbs		398
Farre shooting never kild bird.	335	Proverbs	V	405
Health and mony goe farre.	336	Proverbs		447
The Lame goes as farre as your staggerer.	339	Proverbs		517
He that goeth farre hath many encounters.	341	Proverbs		608
Soft and faire goes farre.	347	Proverbs		772
FARTHER				
What to ask farther. Doubts well rais'd do lock	18	Ch.-Porch	W	299
Nay, after death their spite shall farther go;	34	Sacrifice	W	245
Farther from it then when I bent my bow;	165	The Crosse		26
A Dwarfe on a Gyants shoulder sees farther then they two.	322	Proverbs	V	50
& therfore deferr it untill they heare farther from the States.	368	Letters		15
FARTHEST				
Each part may call the farthest, brother:	91	Man		16
Unto the farthest old meridian.	192	Ch.-Milit.		98
Thou shalt possess earth's farthest bounds	216	Psalm II	D	21
FARTHING				
The miserable man makes a peny of a farthing,	328	Proverbs		211
and the liberall of a farthing sixe pence.	328	Proverbs		211
but the liberall makes of a farthing sixe pence.	328	Proverbs	V	211
Hee that hath patience hath fatt thrushes for a farthing.	336	Proverbs		430
FASHION				
Some mark a partridge, never their childes fashion:	10	Ch.-Porch		99
As if I us'd them but for fashion.	36	Thanksgvng		36
His words and works and fashion too	72	Constancie		19
That winding is their fashion	74	The Starre		27
Then Pleasure came, who liking not the fashion,	84	The World		6
Or some such words in fashion;	104	Obedience		14
but orders his Life in such a fashion, that when death takes him,	227	Priest 3		32
also are to be done not in a hudling, or slubbering fashion, gaping,	231	Priest 6		31
and obsolete, and not the fashion, he reformes, and teaches them,	284	Priest 35		31
I am delighted with their musick and fashion, and I my self also sing	303	Cornaro		6
whether it be in knowledge, or in fashion, or in words;	366	Letters		8
Credit and estimation calls on us to live in a more splendid fashion?	373	Letters		27

	PAGE	TITLE		LINE
FATHER'S (cont'd)				
Unto my fathers hands and sight	152	The Bag		33
Chasing the fathers dimnesse, carri'd farre	168	The Sonne		8
but giving him the prerogative of his Fathers profession,	239	Priest 10		32
and unbefitting the reverence of their Fathers calling,	240	Priest 10		1
and with pulling, gets the apple out of his Fathers hand:	272	Priest 30		10
Therefore they are to mark their Fathers discretion in ordering his	276	Priest 32		28
No love to a Fathers.	325	Proverbs		121
FATHERS				
Fathers first enter bonds to natures ends;	17	Ch.-Porch		281
And hold it fast, as children do their fathers,	118	Providence		46
and not to think, that when they have read the Fathers, or Schoolmen,	226	Priest 2		11
The fourth means are Commenters and fathers, who have handled	229	Priest 4		17
The Countrey Parson hath read the Fathers also, and the Schoolmen,	229	Priest 5		31
as to all the Fathers of the Church, so especially to his Diocesan,	253	Priest 19		6
He instructeth the God-fathers, and God-mothers, that it is no	258	Priest 22		10
And if temporall Fathers blesse their children, how much more may,	285	Priest 36		14
their children, how much more may, and ought Spirituall Fathers?	285	Priest 36		15
appears Rom. 12. 14. how much more those, who are spiritual Fathers?	286	Priest 36		28
yet I remember the Fathers forbid us to judge of the doubtfull	316	Valdesso		12
How many places doe the Fathers bring about Untill against	318	Valdesso		9
FATHOM'D				
Fathom'd the depths of seas, of states, and kings,	37	The Agonie		2
FATS				
This broth of smells, that feeds and fats my minde.	175	The Odour		10
FATT				
Hee that hath patience hath fatt thrushes for a farthing.	336	Proverbs		430
The fatt man knoweth not, what the leane thinketh.	341	Proverbs		605
FATTENS				
The masters eye fattens the horse, and his foote the ground.	338	Proverbs		486
FAULT (see also falt,faut)				
A fault, which needs it most, grows two thereby.	9	Ch.-Porch		78
Errour a fault, and truth discourtesie.	18	Ch.-Porch		308
Then turn thy fault and his into confession:	24	Ch.-Porch	W	441
Were cut and martyr'd by the fault	59	Whitsunday		19
Wilt thou not then my fault reprove?	61	Grace	W	20
Many a fault more then my lease will bear;	129	Love unkn.		20
when it is a fault to discover anothers fault, or when not;	230	Priest 5		25
that there is no help for a fault done, but confession.	240	Priest 10		35
they may disclose anothers fault, finds it somwhat difficult how	286	Priest 37		32
So that it is so far from being a fault to discover such offenders,	287	Priest 37		38
The fault of the horse is put on the saddle.	329	Proverbs		240
The fault is as great as hee that is faulty.	333	Proverbs		369
He that commits a fault, thinkes every one speakes of it.	340	Proverbs		554
He that's foolish in the fault,	340	Proverbs		555
but an ill man doubles his fault.	343	Proverbs		655
but an ill, it doubles his fault.	343	Proverbs	V	655
Every one puts his fault on the Times.	343	Proverbs		675
All are presumed good, till they are found in a fault.	352	Proverbs		944
not well, I had rather the fault should lie on me, than on them;	364	Letters		29
FAULTIE				
The absent partie is still faultie.	332	Proverbs		318
FAULTS				
Then turn thy faults and his into confession:	24	Ch.-Porch		441
Whom others faults do not defeat;	73	Constancie		29
As may our faults controll:	87	Lent		45
Would thou hadst no faults or fears!	113	Businesse		7
They vent the wares, and passe them with their faults,	122	Sinnes rd.		9
Wherefore my faults and sinnes,	126	Confession		25
But when I thought to sleep out all these faults	130	Love unkn.		49
Why kept she not her tears for her own faults,	173	Marie Magd		9
There thou shalt finde my faults are thine.	188	Judgement		15
These three rules generally comprehend the faults of eating,	266	Priest 26		12
not onely taken a particular Survey of the faults of his own Parish,	274	Priest 32		5
kindle them rather to redeem the Dignity either from true faults,	276	Priest 32		24
make others faults their entertainment and discourse, and that even	286	Priest 37		30
and forbid all disclosing of faults, many an evill may not only be,	286	Priest 37		34
if it be unlawful to open faults, no benefit or advantage can make it	287	Priest 37		5
Faults are either notorious, or private.	287	Priest 37		11
Again notorious faults are either such as are made known by common	287	Priest 37		12
and the faults of Nature are often amended by Art, as barren grounds	292	Cornaro		11
FAULTY				
and this as the more faulty in him, so the more glorious in God.	283	Priest 34		21
The fault is as great as hee that is faulty.	333	Proverbs		369
The faulty stands on his guard.	347	Proverbs		793
FAUTS				
They vent the wares, and passe them with their fauts	122	Sinnes rd.	V	9
Why kept she not her tears for her own fauts,	173	Marie Magd	V	9
FAVOUR				
God reckons for him, counts the favour his:	21	Ch.-Porch		381
Which this dayes favour did beget?	64	Even-song		11
But brings a favour from above;	64	Even-song		31
Leading to this favour:	115	Dialogue		18
More favour then you wot of. Mark the end.	130	Love unkn.		63
Yet thy favour	148	Offering		37
When thou dost favour any action,	158	Praise 3		7
Which favour winnes,	162	The Search		26
His favour shall encompass them,	219	Psalm V	D	43
and enter favour with God, who weighs even childrens actions,	239	Priest 10		28
so that to favour them therein is to win their hearts, and to oppose	283	Priest 35		30
effectually applying Gods favour to the blessed, by the interesting	286	Priest 36		8

	PAGE	TITLE		LINE
FAVOUR (cont'd)				
I shall finde no little comfort in the favour of Jesus Christ.	303	Cornaro		24
Without favour none will know you, ...	326	Proverbs		159
Favour will as surely perish as life.	357	Proverbs	D	1055
They favour learning whose actions are worthy of a learned pen.	357	Proverbs	D	1061
by the Patents of your perpetual favour to do so still, . .	365	Letters		25
occasion for you to amplify your favour to mee in pardoning Your most	369	Letters		4
FAVOURS				
That so thy favours granting my request, ...	80	Deniall		28
In vies of favours whether partie gains, ...	88	The Pearl		13
and wert proceeding still on in thy Favours, untill we interrupted	288	Priest		16
to find out variety of thanks for the diversity of your favours,	363	Letters		16
for, since your favours come a Horse-back, there is reason, . .	363	Letters		22
for your favours are so ancient, that they prevent my memory,	367	Letters		14
because my recompenses of your favours consist in this only.	367	Letters		32
This Week hath loaded me with your Favours;	369	Letters		10
not but that I joy in your favours, but that you may see, . .	370	Letters		9
I thank you for your infinite favours, I fear only that I have	370	Letters		11
though for the reckoning of your favours, I shall never find time	370	Letters		31
& to rise with his favours, can not but be not only allowable	381	Woodnoth		26
FAWNING				
Whom neither force nor fawning can	72	Constancie		4
FAYRE				
In a fayre bodie	208	J. Danvers	D	7
A fayre mind.	208	J. Danvers	D	8
which is expressed in a fayre table, as being the rule of a family.	240	Priest 10		26
FEAR				
Cowards tell lies, and those that fear the rod;	9	Ch.-Porch		75
Carve, or discourse; do not a famine fear.	11	Ch.-Porch		129
Thy drops of bloud must pay down all his fear:	17	Ch.-Porch		274
And make thy self all reverence and fear.	22	Ch.-Porch		406
All my Disciples flie; fear puts a barre	28	Sacrifice		49
Engrave thy rev'rend law and fear;	45	Nature		14
No place for grief or fear.	46	Afflict.1		16
A kinde of tune, which all things heare and fear;	51	Prayer 1		8
And I hope and fear.	55	Temper 1		20
The humble soul compos'd of love and fear	86	Lent		7
Then to serve thee in fear.	100	Miserie		12
The help stands close, and keeps the fear in view.	119	Providence		88
And calls him coward, who for fear of sinne	127	Giddinesse		7
Enforceth tears. Your heart was foul, I fear.	129	Love unkn.		18
To warm his love, which I did fear grew cold.	129	Love unkn.		32
The offerers heart. Your heart was hard, I fear.	130	Love unkn.		37
It must be he. Your heart was dull, I fear.	130	Love unkn.		56
Inclose me still for fear I START.	133	Paradise		7
As men, for fear the starres should sleep and nod, ...	134	Divinitie		1
Grasp not at much, for fear thou losest all.	138	The Size		38
But all I fear is lest thy heart displease, ...	147	Offering		13
Bringing nor man, nor arms, nor fear, ...	151	The Bag		28
And, that I had great cause to fear it.	155	Assurance		12
Well may I walk, not fear:	173	23 Psalme		14
So Thou art still my God, be out of fear.	176	Forerunners		10
Taste and fear not: God is here	180	Invitation		16
Serve our great God in fear, rejoyce, ...	216	Psalm II	D	27
Aided by him, I will not fear	216	Psalm III	D	13
will worship thee in fear.	218	Psalm V	D	20
a grave livelinesse, between fear and zeal, pausing yet pressing,	231	Priest 6		19
other spirituall wickednesses in high places doth the Parson fear,	238	Priest 9		21
a trayning up of her children and mayds in the fear of God, . .	239	Priest 10		13
his servants between love, and fear, according as hee findes them;	241	Priest 10		8
and indeed, to depend, and fear continually.	271	Priest 30		36
if he now, shall either for fear or shame, break his custome,	273	Priest 31		30
by bringing them up in the fear and nurture of the Lord; . .	275	Priest 32		23
But if they shall fear, that at such, or such a time their peace	280	Priest 34		32
not onely a shamefull thing to fear that which cannot be avoided;	303	Cornaro		22
Fear keepes and looks to the vineyard, and not the owner. . .	358	Proverbs	D	1072
Presents of love fear not to be ill taken of strangers. . .	361	Proverbs	D	1162
Trust no friend with that you need fear him if he were your enemy.	361	Proverbs	D	1169
either void of knowledge, or of the fear of God.	361	Proverbs	D	1176
But I fear the heat of my late Ague hath dryed up those springs,	363	Letters		4
I fear only that I have omitted some fitting circumstance, . .	370	Letters		11
but you are freed from that fear, who have already abundantly	373	Letters		11
let such thoughts as these, moderate your present fear and sorrow;	374	Letters		4
FEAR'D				
I alwaies fear'd sickness more then death, because sickness hath made	373	Letters		8
as if they not only not desir'd, but, even fear'd to be blessed.	373	Letters		34
FEARE				
Before that I could feare.	46	Afflict.1	W	16
What's done on earth, we shall not feare the worse, ...	78	Ang.&Sts.	V	27
You allwayes feare to feele those smarts	210	Paradox	D	31
as this is the true reason of his inward feare, so he is content	231	Priest 6		11
Feare is given to Christ, but not doubt, and upon good ground.	315	Valdesso		11
Hee that lives ill, feare followes him.	324	Proverbs		110
Feare keepes the garden better then the gardiner.	330	Proverbs		268
Feare nothing but sinne.	331	Proverbs		299
To have money is a feare, not to have it a griefe.	341	Proverbs		591
To have money is a feare, to want it is a griefe.	341	Proverbs	V	591
All the Armes of England will not arme feare.	345	Proverbs		722
Ships feare fire more then water.	351	Proverbs		909
Paines to get, care to keep, feare to lose.	353	Proverbs		975
Feare, the Bedle of the Law.	357	Proverbs	D	1056

FEARE (cont'd)	PAGE	TITLE		LINE
your selves, wee justly feare that there is nothing here answerable	442	Oration		29
FEARES				
The parter of my wrangling feares,	75	Sunday	W	4
The partner of my wrangling feares,	75	Sunday	WC	4
Your feares in number more, your joyes are lesse.	210	Paradox	D	36
The scalded dog feares cold water.	321	Proverbs		13
The scalded head feares cold water.	321	Proverbs	V	13
Let not him that feares feathers come among wild-foule.	322	Proverbs		48
Hee that hath right, feares; he that hath wrong, hopes.	336	Proverbs		429
He that hopes not for good, feares not evill.	340	Proverbs		563
Feares are divided in the midst.	342	Proverbs		639
He that feares leaves, let him not goe into the wood.	346	Proverbs		768
He that feares death lives not.	347	Proverbs		781
FEARFULL				
The fearfull Hare her eares, which by their law	70	Humilitie		11
The fearfull Hare her eares, which by the law	70	Humilitie	W	11
And therfore St. Peter used that fearfull imprecation to Simon Magus,	285	Priest 36		29
FEARING				
Lets his soul runne for nought, as little fearing.	8	Ch.-Porch		59
A face not fearing light:	86	Lent		21
Which using, and not fearing skill in th' one,	192	Ch.-Milit.		77
fearing lest I should be overthrown, they were possessed with a deep	294	Cornaro		17
FEARS				
Who fears to do ill, sets himself to task:	11	Ch.-Porch		125
Who fears to do well, sure should wear a mask.	11	Ch.-Porch		126
Curing all wounds, but mine; all, but my fears:	27	Sacrifice		27
Putting my life among their sinnes and fears,	30	Sacrifice		106
Angels and grace, eternall hopes and fears.	46	Sinne 1		12
My breast was full of fears	79	Deniall		4
By listning to thy chatting fears	105	Conscience		5
Would thou hadst no faults or fears!	113	Businesse		7
And he of all things fears two deaths alone.	131	Mans medly		30
What do these loud complaints and pulling fears,	136	Familie		3
What do these loud complaints and puling fears,	136	Familie	V	3
Yet speak they louder then distemper'd fears.	137	Familie		19
I see no fears:	141	Justice 2		14
Of swarming fears,	142	Pilgrimage		26
And when Justice call'd for fears,	146	Praise 2		23
Call in thy deaths head there: tie up thy fears.	153	The Collar		29
When as my fears foretold this, did replie,	154	Glimpse		19
that he fears I have not fully resolved of the matter, since this	370	Letters		18
FEAST				
Will no more talk all, then eat all the feast.	18	Ch.-Porch		306
Can not make up so brave a feast	42	Easter	W	25
I did conceit a most delicious feast;	50	Faith		6
Thou art both Judge and Saviour, feast and rod,	83	Sighs & Gr.		27
Welcome deare feast of Lent: who loves not thee,	86	Lent		1
Thraldome from those, who would not at a feast	107	Home		21
Thy creatures leap not, but expresse a feast,	121	Providence		133
Come, my Light, my Feast, my Strength:	156	The Call		5
Such a Light, as shows a feast:	156	The Call		6
Such a Feast, as mends in length:	156	The Call		7
And the feast,	179	Invitation		5
for thou art not only the feast, but the way to it.	258	Priest 22		1
The Feast indeed requires sitting, because it is a Feast;	259	Priest 22		12
The Feast indeed requires sitting, because it is a Feast;	259	Priest 22		13
Contentiousnesse in a feast of Charity is more scandall then any	259	Priest 22		18
A cherefull looke makes a dish a feast.	323	Proverbs		62
A cherefull looke makes one dish a feast.	323	Proverbs	V	62
Who letts his wife goe to every feast,	336	Proverbs		434
He that is angry at a feast is rude.	340	Proverbs		564
Warre is deaths feast.	348	Proverbs		822
FEASTERS				
himself an unworthy one, and therefore differs from other Feasters:	259	Priest 22		16
FEASTING				
Feasting all comers by twelve chosen men.	59	Whitsunday		8
FEATHER				
A feather in hand is better then a bird in the ayre.	340	Proverbs		578
FEATHERS				
God gave thy soul brave wings; put not those feathers	9	Ch.-Porch		83
Let not him that feares feathers come among wild-foule.	322	Proverbs		48
Words and feathers the wind carries away.	359	Proverbs	D	1103
FEBRUARY				
Reckon right, and February hath one and thirty daies.	328	Proverbs		229
February makes a bridge and March breakes it.	346	Proverbs		739
when the Ambassadours were made Masters of Arts. 27. Feb. 1622	441	Oration		T
FED				
With Manna, Angels food, I fed them all:	34	Sacrifice		239
Fed with the exhalation of our crimes,	64	Ch.-monum.		5
And now Lord, thou hast fed us with the bread of life:	290	Priest		8
Hee that's fed at anothers hand may stay long ere he be full.	336	Proverbs		439
Who is fed by anothers hand stays long ere he be full.	336	Proverbs	V	439
FEE				
And two deaths had been thy fee.	113	Businesse		22
Onely the present is thy part and fee.	144	Discharge		21
To make my hopes my torture, and the fee	165	The Crosse		27
Go birds of spring: let winter have his fee,	177	Forerunners		34
FEEBLE				
My feeble spirit, unable to look right,	80	Deniall		23
In some one corner of a feeble heart:	99	Decay		12

	PAGE	TITLE		LINE
FEED				
He pares his apple, that will cleanly feed.	9	Ch.-Porch		64
Tast all, but feed not. if thy stomach call	11	Ch.-Porch	W	128
Feed no man in his sinnes: for adulation	16	Ch.-Porch		257
And pipes that feed the presse, and make it runne;	88	The Pearl		2
And feed the swine, with all his mind & might:	101	Miserie	W	44
Take up thine eyes, which feed on earth;	112	Dawning		2
Where all may reach: no beast but knows his feed.	118	Providence		50
The pigeons feed their tender off-spring, crying,	118	Providence		62
And he that doth me feed:	172	23 Psalme		2
Where I both feed and rest;	172	23 Psalme		6
is to feed my Flocke diligently and faithfully, since our Saviour	224	Priest		4
not keep an uniform diet, but to feed variously, now more,	267	Priest 26		11
he pares the apple, and gives them the clean to feed on.	284	Priest 35		1
pardoning my sins, and bidding me go feed the people of thy love.	289	Priest		6
Unsound minds like unsound Bodies, if you feed, you poyson.	358	Proverbs	D	1076
FEEDE				
Old praise dies, unlesse you feede it.	344	Proverbs		699
FEEDER				
So that at once both feeder, dish, and meat	161	Priesthood		21
FEEDING				
They are Sinnes nipples, feeding th' east and west.	196	Ch.-Milit.		220
FEEDS				
That feeds on dung, is coloured thereby.	15	Ch.-Porch		234
My soul's a shepherd too; a flock it feeds	81	Christmas		17
Feeds not, but addes to the desire of meat.	154	Glimpse		12
This broth of smells, that feeds and fats my minde.	175	The Odour		10
him with those mouths, which he continually fils, and feeds:	269	Priest 28		11
FEEL				
To feel those tempests, which fly over ditches.	11	Ch.-Porch		112
Why should I feel another mans mistakes	18	Ch.-Porch		309
Such sorrow as, if sinfull man could feel,	33	Sacrifice		209
Or feel his part, he would not cease to kneel,	33	Sacrifice		210
Or feel his share, he would not cease to kneel,	33	Sacrifice	W	210
And fathers smile for you, to feel his frown:	34	Sacrifice		223
And feel this day thy victorie:	43	East.wings		18
If what my soul doth feel sometimes,	55	Temper 1		3
My soul might ever feel!	55	Temper 1		4
And feel his death, but not his victorie.	112	Dawning		8
Left all joyes to feel all smart -	115	Dialogue		31
What wonders shall we feel, when we shall see	172	The Glance		19
Each breast does feel, no braver fuel choose	206	Walton 1		13
because they feel them not, and because they are not understood	228	Priest 4		31
is observeable, that God delights to have men feel, and acknowledg,	271	Priest 30		19
by Temperance and the Grace of God I feel not those perturbations	302	Cornaro		24
FEEL'ST				
When all thy deeds, whose brunt thou feel'st alone,	69	Content		29
FEELE				
And fathers smile to feele for you his frown:	34	Sacrifice	W	223
You allwayes feare to feele those smarts	210	Paradox	D	31
according as I feele my self, either I take my wonted proportion,	267	Priest 26		8
He that doth what he should not, shall feele what he would not.	347	Proverbs		783
FEELES				
Hee that lies long a bed, his estate feeles it.	327	Proverbs		179
The escaped mouse ever feeles the taste of the bait.	344	Proverbs		679
feeles it all the winter after.	354	Proverbs		992
FEELETH				
From what life feeleth, Adams fall.	48	Repentance		12
FEELING				
and therefore as feeling their own sweat, and consequently knowing	227	Priest 3		13
the feeling of themselves in time of eating, which because it is	267	Priest 26		2
and feeling when I go to meat in what disposition I am,	267	Priest 26		7
FEELINGLY				
and much more feelingly, and judiciously, then he writes his rules	278	Priest 33		20
FEELS				
Which my God feels as bloud; but I, as wine.	37	The Agonie		18
Neither sinne nor Saviour feels.	114	Businesse		38
Dust, alas, no musick feels,	186	Dooms-day		9
FEET				
Sure to be crosse he would shift feet and face.	7	Ch.-Porch		24
A worm doth sit, whose many feet and hair	140	Ch.-rents		3
By these thy feet, at which my heart	150	Longing		80
I throw me at his feet.	161	Priesthood		36
Give up your feet and running to mine eyes,	164	Grief		15
When blessed Marie wip'd her Saviours feet,	173	Marie Magd		1
And not his feet? Though we could dive	173	Marie Magd		10
and that our feet may be like hindes feet ever climbing up higher,	236	Priest 8		29
A coole mouth, and warme feet, live long.	321	Proverbs		21
Better the feet slip then the tongue.	322	Proverbs		53
To steale the Hog, and give the feet for almes.	329	Proverbs		237
Dry feet, warme head, bring safe to bed.	335	Proverbs		402
To seek in a Sheep five feet when there is but four.	359	Proverbs	D	1112
FEETE				
Where your will is ready, your feete are light.	336	Proverbs		448
When your will is ready, the feete are swift.	336	Proverbs	V	448
All feete tread not in one shoe.	338	Proverbs		497
FELICITIE				
And necessarily must the felicitie of so great Princes redound also	442	Oration		25
FELL				
He that first fell from his great birth	59	Whitsunday	W	15
Till they fell out: which when the beasts espied,	70	Humilitie		21

FEW (cont'd)	PAGE	TITLE		LINE
or the Philosophers stone, sought of many, and found of few.	298	Cornaro		21
onely upon a hope of an happie issue, which yet befalls verie few.	300	Cornaro		24
whose holinesse consists in a few ceremonious and superstitious	319	Valdesso	V	23
in a strict performance of a few cheap and easie duties of religion,	319	Valdesso	V	25
Justice pleaseth few in their owne house.	334	Proverbs		396
The soule needs few things, the body many.	342	Proverbs		640
nor to bewail that so few are writ, that look towards God and Heaven.	363	Letters		8
FICKLE				
Praise none too much, for all are fickle.	347	Proverbs		774
FICTION				
Smooth open hearts no fastning have; but fiction	126	Confession		23
FICTIONS				
Who sayes that fictions onely and false hair	56	Jordan 1		1
FIDDLE				
In the house of a Fidler, all fiddle.	328	Proverbs		223
FIDLER				
In the house of a Fidler, all fiddle.	328	Proverbs		223
FIE				
Fie, thou wilt soil thy broider'd coat,	176	Forerunners		23
FIELD				
in the field, his seed-corn, and tares;	261	Priest 23		23
First, a blessing of God for the fruits of the field:	284	Priest 35		4
Dogs are fine in the field.	352	Proverbs		941
FIELDS				
but preferrs her garden and fields before all outlandish gums.	262	Priest 23		4
on both sides whereof are great and fruitfull fields, well manured	301	Cornaro		25
FIER				
Whose fier, like there malice, nought can quench.	212	Bohemia	D	54
FIERCE				
But as I rav'd and grew more fierce and wilde	153	The Collar		33
Which my fierce youth did bandie, fall and flow	169	The Answer		3
or the fire on earth, by reason of their fierce, strong,	271	Priest 30		11
The Lyon is not so fierce as they paint him.	330	Proverbs		289
FIERCENESSE				
Be calm in arguing: for fiercenesse makes	18	Ch.-Porch		307
And made her youth and fiercenesse seek thy face.	46	Afflict.1		18
FIERY				
but, their Fiery-tryals have had an end:	374	Letters		1
FIERY-TRYALS				
but, their Fiery-tryals have had an end:	374	Letters		1
FIFTEENE				
bequeath twenty pound whereof fifteene pound shal be bestowed uppon	382	G.H.'s Will		29
FIFTEENTH				
although after the fifteenth day it grew lesse and lesse.	296	Cornaro		21
FIFTH				
[afflicted] from the thirtie fifth yeare of my age to the fortieth,	292	Cornaro		1
FIFTY				
forty shillings To Mrs Mary Lawly fifty shillings To Mr Gardiner tenn	383	G.H.'s Will		19
FIG				
Hath still sow'd fig-leaves to exclude thy light:	83	Sighs & Gr.		16
FIG-LEAVES				
Hath still sow'd fig-leaves to exclude thy light:	83	Sighs & Gr.		16
FIGHT				
Who teach all hands to warre, fingers to fight,	29	Sacrifice		78
Thy sorrows in, and bloudie fight;	39	Good Fri.		22
Or fight, or travell, or denie	45	Nature		2
The elements are let loose to fight,	90	Afflict.4		17
The fight is hard on either part.	106	Sion		15
Great God doth fight, he doth submit.	106	Sion		16
Now he will fight it out, and to the warres;	127	Giddinesse		9
Sorrowes & griefs, to fight with them a bout	211	Bohemia	D	20
Husbandman labours for them, so must they fight for, and defend them,	277	Priest 32		20
FIGHTING				
On painting and fighting looke aloofe.	329	Proverbs		247
FIGHTS				
A full belly neither fights nor flies well.	324	Proverbs		88
FIGURE				
Of thousand harts: that face doth figure thee	212	Bohemia	D	33
FIGURES				
The man reply'd; It figures JESUS CHRIST.	116	Love-joy		8
FILL				
Spit out thy flegme, and fill thy brest with glorie:	10	Ch.-Porch		92
The way to make thy sonne rich, is to fill	11	Ch.-Porch		109
Least gaining gaine on thee, & fill thy hart	13	Ch.-Porch	W	164
Sinne being gone, oh fill the place,	39	Good Fri.		29
Sinn being gone o doe thou fill	39	Good Fri.	W	29
Which in thy garland I should fill, were mine	57	Employm. 1		7
The which he doth not fill.	75	Sunday		21
The other dayes fill up the spare	75	Sunday		24
O do not fill me	83	Sighs & Gr.		19
He knows it, fill the glasse.	100	Miserie		6
And threatned man, that he should fill the space.	119	Providence		84
And with their words and posies windows fill:	182	The Posie		2
(The marks of future bane) shall fill our cup	197	Ch.-Milit.		239
Misery and sin fill our days:	288	Priest		11
when you are a hammer, strike your fill.	332	Proverbs		338
you could not fill all to your mind.	343	Proverbs	V	700
FILL'D				
with perfect joy be fill'd.	219	Psalm V	D	36

	PAGE	TITLE	LINE
FILLETH			
is not that which filleth the heart with joy and peace in believing;	309	Valdesso	2
FILLS			
Bitternesse fills our bowels; all our hearts	49	Repentance	27
While grace fills up uneven nature.	50	Faith	32
Fills my soul,	181	Banquet	8
One graine fills not a sacke, but helpes his fellowes.	328	Proverbs	226
A little and good fills the trencher.	338	Proverbs	505
Hee that blowes in the dust fills his eyes with it.	340	Proverbs	570
FILS			
that he fils up that which is behinde of the afflictions of Christ in	225	Priest 1	11
him with those mouths, which he continually fils, and feeds:	269	Priest 28	11
FILTH			
To bear her filth; and that her sinnes did dash	173	Marie Magd	14
In the best face but filth, when, Lord, in thee	206	Walton 2	13
or in a corner (for filth).	330	Proverbs	286
The filth under the white snow, the sunne discovers.	338	Proverbs	495
FILTHINESSE			
Profanenesse, filthinesse, abusivenesse.	16	Ch.-Porch	236
for we are darknesse, and weaknesse, and filthinesse, and shame.	288	Priest	11
FINALL			
Have one beginning and one finall summe:	161	Priesthood	22
FIND			
Who dives on further may find Hell.	97	Charms & K W	22
Open the bones, and you shall nothing find	206	Walton 2	12
If thou chance for to find	207	Walton 3	1
If thou dost find an house built to thy mind	207	Walton 4	1
Find a treasure	208	J. Danvers D	3
Would you find?	208	J. Danvers D	6
For there he shall find his flock most naturally as they are,	247	Priest 14	6
and find some poore afflicted soul, and there be bountifull,	281	Priest 34	2
and find sparkes of such thoughts now and then to break forth,	281	Priest 34	13
Stay a little and news will find you.	332	Proverbs	330
Great paines quickly find ease.	339	Proverbs	534
There is a remedy for every thing, could men find it.	360	Proverbs D	1142
all his life, could he find it.	360	Proverbs D	1143
The Divell never assailes a man, except he find him	361	Proverbs D	1176
to find out variety of thanks for the diversity of your favours,	363	Letters	15
unto you, since I find you so willing to yield to my requests;	363	Letters	21
be any truth in me, I find it little enough to keep me in health.	364	Letters	31
As I shal find occasion, you shal receive them by peeces;	366	Letters	3
shee desires no more) shee will find friends to compell him to it.	368	Letters	25
I cannot yet find leisure to write to my Lord, or Sir Benjamin	370	Letters	29
I shall never find time and paper enough, yet am I Your readiest	370	Letters	31
I never find Blessed be the Rich;	373	Letters	30
if at length they may find out some thing not unworthy of those hands	376	Letters	29
& have endeavoured many wayes, to find out a man for it.	378	Letters	7
FIND'ST			
And tumble up and down what thou find'st there.	12	Ch.-Porch	148
The letter of the word, find'st no fit heart	41	Sepulchre	19
FINDE			
A verse may finde him, who a sermon flies,	6	Ch.-Porch	5
Short of his canne and bodie; must I finde	8	Ch.-Porch	39
Who cannot rest till hee good-fellows finde,	12	Ch.-Porch	149
To compasse this. Finde out mens wants and will,	19	Ch.-Porch	328
To me, who took eyes that I might you finde:	26	Sacrifice	3
Canst thou finde hell about my lips? and misse	28	Sacrifice	42
My musick shall finde thee, and ev'ry string	36	Thanksgvng	39
I have consider'd it, and finde	36	Reprisall	1
I finde there quarries of pil'd vanities,	38	The Sinner	5
Thy words do finde me out, & parallels bring,	58	H.Script.2	11
To spell his elements, and finde his birth	65	Ch.-monum.	8
I took up in the next inne I could finde.	80	Christmas	4
I will go searching, till I finde a sunne	81	Christmas	27
And strip the creature naked, till he finde	85	Vanitie 1	16
To finde out death, but missest life at hand.	86	Vanitie 1	28
Finde their acquaintance there.	91	Man	24
Finde where it lies.	116	Dulnesse	24
Twentie for one too sharp do finde it.	122	Time	6
That I may climbe and finde relief.	144	Complaining	20
Untill thou finde and use it to thy good:	147	Offering	23
Finde nests.	149	Longing	54
Which when we once can finde and prove,	167	The Flower	45
That I might finde	175	The Odour	8
Where we did finde	186	Death	10
There thou shalt finde my faults are thine.	188	Judgement	15
As Rome will one day finde unto her cost.	194	Ch.-Milit.	160
At Christs last coming, as his first did finde:	196	Ch.-Milit.	231
For sins make all equall, whom they finde together;	227	Priest 3	28
If he chance to finde any reading in anothers Bible, he provides him	254	Priest 20	11
If he finde another giving a poor man a penny, he gives him a tester	254	Priest 20	13
wherein the Catechized will at length finde delight, and by which	256	Priest 21	18
which while they dwell in their bookes, they will never finde;	266	Priest 26	2
Could men finde out this delight, they would seldome be from home;	275	Priest 32	34
But they who finde benefit in these meats, may, yea ought to use	300	Cornaro	10
I finde eleven grand-children of mine, all the sonnes of one father	303	Cornaro	2
I shall finde no little comfort in the favour of Jesus Christ.	303	Cornaro	23
Astrologie is true, but the Astrologers cannot finde it.	342	Proverbs	641
FINDES			
A pain in that, wherein he findes a pleasure?	8	Ch.-Porch	40
A pain in that, whereof he findes a pleasure?	8	Ch.-Porch W	40

FINDES (cont'd)	PAGE	TITLE		LINE
Findes his crackt name at length in the church-glasse.	14	Ch.-Porch		198
Findes himself there, and seeks to rise.	96	Charms & K		12
He that findes a silver vein,	114	Businesse		34
In the Scriptures hee findes four things;	228	Priest 4		24
This way he findes exceeding usefull, and winning;	236	Priest 8		15
but findes opportunities of having his meat dress'd and other	237	Priest 9		8
his servants between love, and fear, according as hee findes them;	241	Priest 10		8
Those that he findes religiously imployed, hee both commends them	247	Priest 14		13
as if hee findes them reading, hee furnisheth them with good bocks;	247	Priest 14		15
Those that the Parson findes idle, or ill imployed, he chides	248	Priest 14		13
hee findes some way of releeving it, and reducing the Manna,	254	Priest 19		2
Neither findes he any issue in this, but to throw himself down	257	Priest 22		31
Those that he findes in the peaceable state, he adviseth to be very	280	Priest 34		14
Those that the Parson findes in the military state, he fortifyes,	281	Priest 34		5
FINDETH				
he findeth to be as necessary, and as difficult at least,	237	Priest 9		36
FINDING				
for them often, and in finding out Courtesies to place on them;	262	Priest 24		26
and finding my self continually oppressed with pain and sicknesse,	292	Cornaro		18
FINDS				
and finds no sure abiding place.	215	Psalm I	D	16
Commandments, and as he finds them perfect, rewards them the more.	245	Priest 12		36
and then as hee finds the persons of the house imployed,	247	Priest 14		11
Those that he finds busie in the works of their calling,	247	Priest 14		20
poor and needy, whom he thus finds labouring, he gives them somewhat;	248	Priest 14		10
as he finds any defect in these, hee first considers with himselfe,	251	Priest 17		25
in eating, that he can eat more, then afterwards he finds true:)	267	Priest 26		4
those whom the Parson finds loose, and not ingaged into some	277	Priest 32		25
finds it somwhat difficult how to proceed in this point.	286	Priest 37		32
Hee that lookes not before, finds himselfe behind.	327	Proverbs		200
Good finds good.	337	Proverbs		456
A poore beauty finds more lovers then husbands.	337	Proverbs		481
One slumber finds another.	339	Proverbs		528
No barber shaves so close but another finds worke.	343	Proverbs		667
As God where he finds no roome for his Inclining grace,	381	Woodnoth		7
FINE				
The fine may spare these well, yet not go lesse.	16	Ch.-Porch		238
Fine nets and stratagems to catch us in,	45	Sinne 1		7
Fine nets and casualties to catch us in,	45	Sinne 1	W	7
I looked on thy furniture so fine,	46	Afflict.1		7
And made it fine to me:	46	Afflict.1		8
Not in rich furniture, or fine aray,	52	H.Commun.		1
Deare earth, fine grasse or hay;	71	Frailtie		6
The other fine,	71	Frailtie		12
Whence com'st thou, that thou art so fresh and fine?	77	Avarice		2
That her fine cobwebs did support the frame,	84	The World		3
And those things most, which are most pure and fine:	101	Miserie		38
A fine aspect in fit aray,	109	Brit. Ch.		7
To answer these fine things shall come;	111	The Quip		22
If they seek fine things, thou dost make them run	120	Providence		106
And jagg'd his seamlesse coat, had that been fine,	134	Divinitie		11
Verses, ye are too fine a thing, too wise	164	Grief		13
What fine varietie each tongue affords:	167	The Sonne		2
And if I please him, I write fine and wittie.	176	Forerunners		12
Makes that and th' action fine.	185	The Elixer		20
Fresh and fine deities. They were at great cost,	193	Ch.-Milit.		109
He took fine vizards to conceal his crimes:	195	Ch.-Milit.		186
and sightly Communion Cloth of fine linnen, with an handsome,	246	Priest 13		16
Every thing new is fine.	323	Proverbs		76
To fine folkes a little ill finely wrapt.	324	Proverbs		117
The sonne full and tattered, the daughter empty and fine.	328	Proverbs		214
Fine dressing is a foule house swept before the doores.	329	Proverbs		243
Hee that makes a thing too fine, breakes it.	336	Proverbs		440
Fine words dresse ill deedes.	337	Proverbs		479
Dogs are fine in the field.	352	Proverbs		941
The house is a fine house, when good folke are within.	352	Proverbs		952
The house is a fine house, when good folks are within.	352	Proverbs	V	952
FINELY				
Boldnesse guilds finely, and will set it forth.	15	Ch.-Porch		210
How finely dost thou times and seasons spin,	118	Providence		57
But did bewitch, and finely work each nation	195	Ch.-Milit.		193
To fine folkes a little ill finely wrapt.	324	Proverbs		117
FINEM				
for so he useth the same word in Consideration 68 ad finem.	317	Valdesso	V	8
FINENESSE				
The finenesse which a hymne or psalme affords,	168	a true Hymn		9
for they are not sensible of finenesse:	248	Priest 14		18
FINEST				
you may understand what it is) is the finest place in the University,	369	Letters		31
FINGER				
Finger not my treasure.	114	Dialogue		12
Give a clowne your finger, and he will take your hand.	324	Proverbs		111
Honour without profit is a ring on the finger.	328	Proverbs		230
God strikes with his finger, and not with all his arme.	359	Proverbs	D	1114
FINGERS				
Who teach all hands to warre, fingers to fight,	29	Sacrifice		78
And not of thee, through whom my fingers bend	116	Providence		3
The Germans wit is in his fingers.	322	Proverbs		36
The Germans wit lies in his fingers.	322	Proverbs	V	36
Who remove stones, bruise their fingers.	322	Proverbs		40

	PAGE	TITLE		LINE
FINISH				
My hands do joyn to finish the inventions.	122	Sinnes rd.		12
My hands do joyn to finish the inventions:	122	Sinnes rd.		13
FINISH'D				
Finish'd and fixt the old religion.	190	Ch.-Milit.		22
FINISHED				
But now I die; now all is finished.	34	Sacrifice		249
FINISHT				
After the house is finisht, leave it.	326	Proverbs		172
FINITE				
I am but finite, yet thine infinitely.	139	Artillerie		32
FIRE (see also fier)				
Another chafe, may warm him at his fire,	19	Ch.-Porch		314
And there in hymnes send back thy fire again:	54	Love 2		8
Where is that fire which once descended	59	Whitsunday		5
But balls of wilde-fire to my troubled minde.	64	Even-song		16
But as cold hands are angrie with the fire,	66	Ch.-lock		5
Yet as cold hands are angrie with the fire,	66	Ch.-lock	W	5
Mark how the fire in flints doth quiet lie,	68	Content		9
Mark how the fire in Flint doth quiet lie,	68	Content	W	9
First with thy fire-work burn to dust	74	The Starre		9
Then forcing thee, by fire he made thee bright:	77	Avarice		9
Of mortall fire:	79	Employm.2		7
What willing nature speaks, what forc'd by fire;	88	The Pearl		6
But he to wear them. Nothing useth fire,	120	Providence		110
My words take fire from my inflamed thoughts.	122	Sinnes rd.		6
My words take fire from my inflamed thoughts.	122	Sinnes rd.		7
Which have the face of fire, but end in rest.	139	Artillerie		8
The cloud his bow, the fire his spear,	151	The Bag		14
But thou art fire, sacred and hallow'd fire;	160	Priesthood		7
And force of fire, what curious things are made	161	Priesthood		14
That earth is fitted by the fire and trade	161	Priesthood		16
Steele & a flint strike fire,	202	Trin.Sun.	W	7
Why doth that fire, which by thy power and might	206	Walton 1		12
Whose fire is wild, and doth not upward go	206	Walton 2		10
When the Apostles would have called down fire from Heaven,	229	Priest 4		13
and fervency, and need a mountaine of fire to kindle them;	233	Priest 7		17
There are but two devouring elements, fire, and water, he hath both	234	Priest 7		33
And he himselfe is a consuming fire, Hebrews 12.	234	Priest 7		35
if God have sent any calamity either by fire, or famine,	253	Priest 19		29
or throw into the fire, and so they pay them their wages,	265	Priest 26		26
the sun in heaven, or the fire on earth, by reason of their fierce,	271	Priest 30		10
yet when God pleased, the sun stood stil, the fire burned not.	271	Priest 30		12
be housed, a fire hath broken forth, and suddenly consumed them.	271	Priest 30		24
God sends a fire, and consumes all that he hath:	271	Priest 30		33
blows the fire, endeavouring to disorder the Christian,	272	Priest 31		33
Gods Spirit will mortify and try them as gold in the fire.	314	Valdesso		22
A crooked log makes a strait fire.	322	Proverbs		45
Well may hee smell fire, whose gowne burnes.	325	Proverbs		138
A gentlemans grayhound, and a salt-box; seeke them at the fire.	327	Proverbs		205
Working and making a fire doth discretion require.	328	Proverbs		225
The child saies nothing, but what it heard by the fire.	331	Proverbs		300
Litle stickes kindle the fire; great ones put it out.	332	Proverbs		323
Water a farre off quencheth not fire.	334	Proverbs		398
Water, fire, and souldiers, quickly make roome.	338	Proverbs		514
He that can make a fire well, can end a quarrell.	340	Proverbs		557
To take the nuts from the fire with the dogges foot.	341	Proverbs		584
A litle wind kindles; much puts out the fire.	344	Proverbs		680
Greene wood makes a hott fire.	349	Proverbs		862
Ships feare fire more then water.	351	Proverbs		909
Silkes and Satins put out the fire in the chimney.	351	Proverbs		912
Silkes and Satins put out the fire of the chimney.	351	Proverbs	V	912
You cannot make the fire so low but it will get out.	353	Proverbs		965
Silke doth quench the fire in the Kitchin.	356	Proverbs	D	1043
It's a dangerous fire begins in the bed-straw.	357	Proverbs	D	1070
To play at Chesse when the house is on fire.	360	Proverbs	D	1136
FIRE-WORK				
First with thy fire-work burn to dust	74	The Starre		9
FIR'D				
Or a fir'd beacon frighteth from his ditties.	16	Ch.-Porch		250
FIRES				
Attract the lesser to it: let those fires,	54	Love 2		2
Then have we too our guardian fires and clouds;	128	Bunch Gr.		15
That from small fires comes oft no small mishap.	139	Artillerie		4
Foolish night-fires, womens and childrens wishes,	167	Dotage		2
FIRM				
Which looks so firm and strong,	66	Ch.-floore		2
Then Sinne combin'd with Death in a firm band	84	The World		16
That planted Paradise was not so firm,	97	Afflict.5		2
seats whole, firm, and uniform, especially that the Pulpit,	246	Priest 13		5
FIRMENESSE				
Love askes faith, and faith firmenesse.	339	Proverbs		544
FIRST				
Lord, my first fruits present themselves to thee;	5	Dedication		1
Need or Incontinency: the first way	7	Ch.-Porch	W	16
As empty boldnesse: therefore first assay	15	Ch.-Porch		207
Fathers first enter bonds to natures ends;	17	Ch.-Porch		281
First to bee Slovens, & forsake their nose.	21	Ch.-Porch	W	370
Thus Adam my first breathing rendereth:	28	Sacrifice		71
Or, since one starre show'd thy first breath,	38	Good Fri.		7
Your first acquaintance might discredit all.	44	H. Bapt.1		14

FIRST (cont'd)

	PAGE	TITLE		LINE
My soul bid nothing, but keep hir first wealth:	44	H. Bapt.2	W	13
Parents first season us: then schoolmasters	45	Sinne 1		2
When first thou didst entice to thee my heart,	46	Afflict.1		1
At first thou gav'st me milk and sweetnesses;	47	Afflict.1		19
Which shall consume the world, first make it tame;	54	Love 2		3
He that first fell from his great birth	59	Whitsunday	W	15
First with thy fire-work burn to dust	74	The Starre		9
That as the first affrights,	82	Ungratef.		21
Whose leaves first sheltred man from drought & dew,	84	The World		12
The first Is straight, and our diurnall friend,	84	Coloss.		3
In friendship, first I think, if that agree,	93	Unkindness		2
At first we liv'd in pleasure;	97	Afflict.5		7
As we at first did board with thee,	97	Afflict.5		11
Some Angels us'd the first; if our relief	97	Afflict.5		15
When boyes go first to bed,	98	Mortific.		7
Indeed at first Man was a treasure,	102	Miserie		67
When first my lines of heav'nly joyes made mention,	102	Jordan 2		1
When first my verse of heav'nly joyes made mention,	102	Jordan 2	W	1
First, Beautie crept into a rose,	110	The Quip		5
And first I found the corner, where was J,	112	JESU		5
The first puts on with speed and expedition;	117	Providence		35
But thou didst reckon, when at first	123	Gratefulnes		9
Seek pardon first, and God will say,	134	The Method		31
Could not that wisdome, which first broacht the wine,	134	Divinitie		9
First Peace and Silence all disputes controll,	137	Familie		9
When God at first made man,	159	The Pulley		1
So strength first made a way;	160	The Pulley		6
From the first man in th' East, to fresh and new	168	The Sonne		9
Scorns his first bed of dirt, and means the sky;	169	The Answer		9
When first thy sweet and gracious eye	171	The Glance		1
If thy first glance so powerfull be,	172	The Glance		17
First, there is no pleasure here:	177	The Rose		5
From my first entrance in,	188	Love 3		4
To Egypt first she came, where they did prove	191	Ch.-Milit.		37
Where first the Church should raise her down-cast face.	192	Ch.-Milit.		86
At first he got to Egypt, and did sow	193	Ch.-Milit.		107
The latter Church is to the first a debter.	196	Ch.-Milit.		224
The second Temple could not reach the first:	196	Ch.-Milit.		225
At Christs last coming, as his first did finde:	196	Ch.-Milit.		231
By carrying first their gold from them away:	197	Ch.-Milit.		250
And met in th' east their first and ancient sound,	197	Ch.-Milit.		268
First I am sure, whether bread stay	200	H. Commun.	W	7
Thou dost come first to them, that showes	200	H. Commun.	W	14
Did not confess in the first Theefe	202	Trin.Sun.	W	12
For first, Man fell from God by disobedience.	225	Priest 1		4
and in the first to the Colossians plainly avoucheth, that he fils up	225	Priest 1		10
And first, because Countrey people live hardly, and therefore	227	Priest 3		12
the means he useth are first, a holy Life, remembring what his Master	228	Priest 4		27
first, as being truly touched and amazed with the Majesty of God,	231	Priest 6		5
that being first affected himself, hee may affect also his people,	231	Priest 6		12
But it is gained first, by choosing texts of Devotion,	233	Priest 7		26
who first shed teares over Jerusalem, and afterwards blood.	234	Priest 7		21
first, a plain and evident declaration of the meaning of the text;	235	Priest 7		1
at his first entrance humbly adoring, and worshipping the invisible	236	Priest 8		4
but only by those means, by which at first it was obtained.	237	Priest 9		21
first, a trayning up of her children and mayds in the fear of God,	239	Priest 10		12
His children he first makes Christians, and then Commonwealths-men;	239	Priest 10		20
for the first, Poultry; for the second, swine.	241	Priest 10		30
first, of eating lesse that day, then on other dayes;	242	Priest 10		2
He first considers his own Parish, and takes care, that there be	244	Priest 12		18
So doth hee also before giving make them say their Prayers first,	245	Priest 12		35
Therefore first he takes order, that all things be in good repair;	246	Priest 13		3
The first whereof is, Let all things be done decently, and in order:	246	Priest 13		27
the first being for the honour of God;	246	Priest 13		30
first he blesseth it, and then as hee finds the persons of the house	247	Priest 14		11
first, that they dive not too deep into worldly affairs,	247	Priest 14		23
ill imployed, he chides not at first, for that were neither civill,	248	Priest 14		14
First, what disorders there are either in Apparell, or Diet,	251	Priest 17		18
hee first considers with himselfe, what kind of remedy fits	251	Priest 17		25
And first, he is just to his Countrey;	252	Priest 19		25
he first gives himself liberally, and then incites them to give;	253	Priest 19		35
Catechizing is the first point, and but by Catechizing,	255	Priest 21		7
not himself, but is first a Sermon to himself, and then to others;	255	Priest 21		14
First, for the authority of the work;	255	Priest 21		26
First, an aim and mark of the whole discourse, whither to drive	256	Priest 21		30
Baptisme often (being the first step into their great and glorious	258	Priest 22		18
he first takes order with the Church-Wardens, that the elements be	258	Priest 22		21
The time of every ones first receiving is not so much by yeers,	258	Priest 22		32
the cause with him, whom he makes to deliver their opinion first;	260	Priest 23		11
first, that by familiar things hee might make his Doctrine slip	261	Priest 23		18
The first means he useth is Prayer, beseeching the Father of lights	262	Priest 24		21
So a man dining, eats at first lawfully;	264	Priest 26		22
first, for covetousnes, he lays this ground:	265	Priest 26		4
first, the custome, and knowledg of their own body, and what it can	266	Priest 26		37
This last rule joyned with the first, never fails.	267	Priest 26		6
This he procures, first by his holy and unblameable life;	268	Priest 28		20
The first is a sustaining power;	271	Priest 30		1
First, that this interruption proceed not out of slacknes,	273	Priest 31		15
he first represents to every body the necessity of a vocation.	274	Priest 32		17
first, the improvement of his family, by bringing them up in the fear	275	Priest 32		22

FIT (cont'd)	PAGE	TITLE	LINE
which grass will bane, or which not, how is he fit to be a shepherd?	230	Priest 5	32
At night he thinks it a very fit time, both sutable to the joy	236	Priest 8	18
not his affection found out a fit wife for him, whose humble,	238	Priest 9	28
He afterwards turnes his care to fit all their dispositions with some	239	Priest 10	30
binding them prentices (in case he think fit to do so) he takes care	239	Priest 10	34
or was not fit for him to do, by taking both sorts of food into them,	241	Priest 10	32
both for man in themselves, by growing them selves fit for his table.	241	Priest 10	35
That there be fit, and proper texts of Scripture every where painted,	246	Priest 13	11
of particularizing in these things, hee were not fit to be a Parson:	249	Priest 14	1
he gives him a tester for it, if the giver be fit to receive it;	254	Priest 20	14
and to give him power so to fit his discourse to them, that it may	262	Priest 24	23
to disable themselves from a fit discharging either of Divine duties,	266	Priest 26	29
that if after dinner they are not fit (or un-weeldy) either to pray,	266	Priest 26	31
but that God often changeth it according as he sees fit,	270	Priest 30	31
or at midnight, or as they think fit, & see cause, or rather as Gods	272	Priest 31	27
that ingenuous and fit imployment is never wanting to those that seek	275	Priest 32	9
to enter into a Calling, if they be fit for it, and it for them;	275	Priest 32	15
I thought fit to discover in a short Treatise, that Intemperance was	291	Cornaro	5
power causeth that the meat and drink that is taken in fit measure,	293	Cornaro	27
keep a fit proportion, shall receive little hurt from other excesses.	294	Cornaro	4
things I do at my ease, and at fit seasons, and in mine own houses;	301	Cornaro	9
you could not fit all to your mind.	344	Proverbs	701
and that the Horse is every way fit for me, and I will strive	364	Letters	1
FITLY			
Thy justice me most fitly payes:	96	Justice 1	7
Speake fitly, or be silent wisely.	342	Proverbs	625
FITS			
what kind of remedy fits the temper of the house best, and then hee	251	Priest 17	26
FITT			
all together choosing some fitt day to carry it themselves,	253	Priest 19	38
Love makes one fitt for any work.	343	Proverbs	646
FITTED			
That earth is fitted by the fire and trade	161	Priesthood	16
Prepar'd and fitted to receive thy love.	190	Ch.-Milit.	16
and chose that wine that fitted my stomack, and in such measure,	293	Cornaro	16
Things well fitted abide.	337	Proverbs	483
FITTER			
And a much fitter stone	45	Nature	17
a slighter forme of Catechizing, fitter for country people;	230	Priest 5	16
the place was moorish and unhealthy, fitter for beasts then men.	301	Cornaro	27
FITTEST			
Since bloud is fittest, Lord, to write	39	Good Fri.	21
is full of such composures, yet every mans own is fittest, readyest,	230	Priest 5	4
establisheth it, since they that have nothing, are fittest to work.	275	Priest 32	5
what they are fittest for, and to prepare for that with all	275	Priest 32	16
FITTING			
and that there be a fitting, and sightly Communion Cloth of fine	246	Priest 13	16
but such as are every way fitting to do his Countrey true	252	Priest 19	28
propounds among his Brethren what were fitting to be done.	253	Priest 19	14
God complaines not, but doth what is fitting.	327	Proverbs	182
I fear only that I have omitted some fitting circumstance,	370	Letters	12
FITTS			
A piece of a Churchyard fitts every body.	355	Proverbs	1027
FIVE			
For he, that needs five thousand pound to live,	10	Ch.-Porch	107
Is full as poore as he, that needs but five.	10	Ch.-Porch	108
Then he that curbs them, being but one to five:	89	The Pearl	29
The noblest sence of five.	201	H. Commun. W	33
if not duly once a month, yet at least five or six times in the year;	259	Priest 22	21
These are the five shields, wherewith the Godly receive the darts	269	Priest 28	19
came a terrible fever, which continued thirtie five dayes and nights;	296	Cornaro	20
because that after one is once sixtie five yeares old, all the time	300	Cornaro	29
To seek in a Sheep five feet when there is but four.	359	Proverbs D	1112
And yet if a Book of four or five Shillings come in my way,	365	Letters	11
she would make good her promise of taking five or six pound upon her,	367	Letters	3
this whole sum of five hundred pounds I bequeath unto my Neeces	382	G.H.'s Will	12
uppon Leighton Church, the other five pound I give to himselfe.	382	G.H.'s Will	30
To Mrs Danvers five pound, To Amy Danvers thirty shillings,	383	G.H.'s Will	9
shillings To Mrs Judith Spencer five pound To Mary Owens forty	383	G.H.'s Will	18
Gardiner tenn pound MS. that the five pound due to Mrs Judeth Spenser	383	G.H.'s Will	20
FIX			
O fix thy chair of grace, that all my powers	56	Temper 2	9
May also fix their reverence:	56	Temper 2	10
and fix them on their charge, and not on their preferment.	266	Priest 26	4
quickly make good my wish but that my employment does fix me here,	372	Letters	19
FIXE			
I pass the shades, & fixe upon the true	43	H. Bapt.1 W	4
FIXT			
Finish'd and fixt the old religion.	190	Ch.-Milit.	22
FLAGON			
and decent chest, with a Chalice, and Cover, and a Stoop, or Flagon;	246	Priest 13	19
FLAME			
Immortall Heat, O let thy greater flame	54	Love 2	1
My thoughts are working like a busie flame,	122	Sinnes rd.	3
Surpasse in brightnesse any flame.	135	Divinitie	16
A sonne is light and fruit; a fruitfull flame	168	The Sonne	7
True beautie dwells on high: ours is a flame	177	Forerunners	28
Which soon was blown to such a mightie flame,	194	Ch.-Milit.	145
A Deluge on my sensual Flame,	214	Convert D	9

	PAGE	TITLE		LINE
FLAMES				
As flames do work and winde, when they ascend,	103	Jordan 2		13
Mark well my furnace! O what flames,	149	Longing		26
Besides their other flames? Doth Poetry	206	Walton 1		3
Henceforth in Sacred Flames shall Burn,	214	Convert	D	19
FLAMING				
Doth vanish like a flaming thing,	68	Windows	V	14
And spacious fornace flaming, and thereon	129	Love unkn.		26
FLARING				
Doth vanish like a flaring thing,	68	Windows		14
FLAT				
He makes flat warre with God, and doth defie	8	Ch.-Porch		53
All that they leave: this is flat povertie.	10	Ch.-Porch		106
All that is left: this is flat povertie.	10	Ch.-Porch	W	106
Thou art joyes handsell: heav'n lies flat in thee,	58	H.Script.1		13
Sinne is flat opposite to th' Almighty, seeing	63	Sinne 2		4
When they shall bow, and kneel, and fall down flat	65	Ch.-monum.		15
Whose flat delights on earth do creep and grow;	111	Vanitie 2		2
FLATTER				
Doth flatter power. Lest good come short of ill	161	Priesthood		40
FLATTERER'S				
A flatterers throat is an open Sepulcher.	341	Proverbs		588
FLATTERING				
their flattering tongues do fain.	219	Psalm V	D	28
FLEA				
You cannot flea a stone.	346	Proverbs		764
FLEAS				
Hee that lies with the dogs, riseth with fleas.	332	Proverbs		343
FLED				
The most of me to heav'n is fled:	109	Home		68
Out of the caldron getting, soon I fled	130	Love unkn.		46
Whither, O, whither art thou fled,	162	The Search		1
Is some starre (fled from the sphere)	181	Banquet		10
Religion thence fled into Greece, where arts	191	Ch.-Milit.		49
Thence into Greece she fled, where curious Arts	191	Ch.-Milit.	W	49
FLEDGE				
When they are fledge, that need may teach them flying.	118	Providence		64
The shells of fledge souls left behinde,	186	Death		11
FLEE (see also flea)				
Then shall Religion to America flee:	197	Ch.-Milit.		247
FLEET				
The fleet Astronomer can bore,	85	Vanitie 1		1
FLEGMATICK				
where both the people and the drink being cold and flegmatick,	242	Priest 10		20
the Flegmatick sleepes.	351	Proverbs		924
FLEGME				
Spit out thy flegme, and fill thy brest with glorie:	10	Ch.-Porch		92
which will discover it selfe by spitting, and rheume, or flegme.	242	Priest 10		25
FLEMMISH				
The Flemmish rivers: in the end	213	L' Envoy	D	3
FLESH				
My soule is full of shame, my flesh of wound:	33	Sacrifice	W	217
My flesh get on; yet let her sister	44	H. Bapt.2		12
The growth of flesh is but a blister;	44	H. Bapt.2		14
My flesh began unto my soul in pain,	47	Afflict.1		25
Our flesh and frailtie, death and danger.	50	Faith		24
Reserving all for flesh again.	51	Faith		44
My rebel-flesh, and carrying thy name,	52	H.Commun.		17
Before that sinne turn'd flesh to stone,	53	H.Commun.		29
Here I intombe my flesh, that it betimes	64	Ch.-monum.		2
Deare flesh, while I do pray, learn here thy stemme	65	Ch.-monum.		17
That flesh is but the glasse, which holds the dust	65	Ch.-monum.		20
One life is wrapt In flesh, and tends to earth.	84	Coloss.		5
My stuffe is flesh, not brasse; my senses live,	89	The Pearl		27
Herbs gladly cure our flesh; because that they	91	Man		23
All things unto our flesh are kinde	91	Man		34
A lump of flesh, without a foot or wing	102	Miserie		74
Wert fain to take our flesh and curse,	103	Prayer 2		15
My flesh and bones and joynts do pray:	109	Home		74
Would thou hadst no flesh and bones!	113	Businesse		13
To assume thy flesh and bone;	113	Businesse		18
But I am lost in flesh, whose sugred lyes	116	Dulnesse		21
Frogs marry fish and flesh; bats, bird and beast;	121	Providence		135
In flesh he dies.	131	Mans medly		14
Faith needs no staffe of flesh, but stoutly can	135	Divinitie		27
And flesh would fail,	136	Ephes.		33
And in the flesh condemn'd it as unfit,	138	The Size		26
As flesh may be;	175	The Odour		13
Flesh assumes,	181	Banquet		23
Flesh being turn'd to dust, and bones to sticks.	186	Death		8
That thy flesh hath lost his food,	199	L'Envoy		9
My flesh, & fleshly villany,	201	H. Commun.	W	29
That Flesh is there, mine eyes deny:	201	H. Commun.	W	31
And what shold flesh but flesh discry,	201	H. Commun.	W	32
Flesh (though exalted) keeps his grass	201	H. Commun.	W	38
Thy flesh the least that I request.	201	H. Commun.	W	44
More spotted then my flesh can bee.	202	love	W	9
Then flesh did lend thee, back agen.	202	love	W	18
Now the great combat of our flesh & reason	204	The Knell	W	8
up that which is behinde of the afflictions of Christ in his flesh,	225	Priest 1		12
of eating no flesh, which is but the determination of the second rule	242	Priest 10		5

FLESH (cont'd)	PAGE	TITLE		LINE
unpleasant, is the naturall rule of fasting, although it be flesh.	242	Priest 10		11
if a peece of dry flesh at my table be more unpleasant to me,	242	Priest 10		13
then some fish there, certainly to eat the flesh, and not the fish,	242	Priest 10		14
that the prohibiting of flesh came from hot Countreys, where both	242	Priest 10		16
from hot Countreys, where both flesh alone, and much more with wine,	242	Priest 10		17
and where flesh may be much better spared, and with more safety then	242	Priest 10		18
cold and flegmatick, the eating of flesh is an antidote to both.	242	Priest 10		21
that a weak stomack being prepossessed with flesh, shall much better	242	Priest 10		22
which doth lesse obstruct, then flesh moderately taken;	243	Priest 10		3
He took flesh, he wept, he died;	288	Priest		28
and egges, and flesh, and broth, was twelve ounces exactly weighed;	296	Cornaro		10
All flesh is not venison.	358	Proverbs	D	1096
FLESHE'S				
Fleshes stubbornnesse may have	187	Dooms-day		17
FLESHLY				
Our souls and fleshly hearts;	52	H.Commun.		15
My flesh, & fleshly villany,	201	H. Commun.	W	29
FLESHY				
Our souls and fleshy hearts;	52	H.Commun.	V	15
FLEW				
(As dying things are wont) untill it flew	192	Ch.-Milit.		80
FLIE				
Flie idlenesse, which yet thou canst not flie	9	Ch.-Porch		79
All my Disciples flie; fear puts a barre	28	Sacrifice		49
My dove doth back into my bosome flie,	29	Sacrifice		94
Whom devils flie, thus is he toss'd of men:	32	Sacrifice		191
No room for me, and flie away.	39	Good Fri.		28
More backward still, and to that water flie,	43	H. Bapt.1		4
His praise may thither flie:	53	Antiphon 1		4
Whether I flie with angels, fall with dust,	55	Temper 1		25
Till it get wing, and flie away with thee.	59	Whitsunday		4
Will thither flie;	61	Praise 1		6
To flie home like a laden bee	74	The Starre		30
Flie hand in hand to heav'n!	77	Sunday		63
Did flie asunder:	80	Deniall		7
I flie to thee, and fully understand	89	The Pearl		33
Let them unto their kindred flie:	111	Vanitie 2		14
Do flie and flow,	132	The Storm		2
Are both thy due: but I a silly flie,	143	Complaining		8
Hony of roses, whither wilt thou flie?	176	Forerunners		20
For with it alone I flie	182	Banquet		43
Yet as the Church shall thither westward flie,	197	Ch.-Milit.		259
Into a mouth shut flies flie not.	328	Proverbs		219
The blind eate many a flie.	340	Proverbs		556
You must loose a flie to catch a trout.	348	Proverbs		827
If you must flie, flie well.	355	Proverbs		1021
yet I had rather flie to my old ward, that if any course could be	367	Letters		7
FLIES (see also flyes)				
A verse may finde him, who a sermon flies,	6	Ch.-Porch		5
Flies have their table spread, ere they appeare.	118	Providence		54
In soul he mounts and flies,	131	Mans medly		13
It runnes, it flies:	158	Praise 3		8
Flies are busiest about leane horses.	323	Proverbs		73
A full belly neither fights nor flies well.	324	Proverbs		88
To a boyling pot flies come not.	325	Proverbs		123
Into a mouth shut flies flie not.	328	Proverbs		219
Vertue flies from the heart of a Mercenary man.	360	Proverbs	D	1133
FLIGHT				
Then shall the fall further the flight in me.	43	East.wings		10
Then shall my fall further the flight in me.	43	East.wings	W	10
Affliction shall advance the flight in me.	43	East.wings		20
Motion, and heat, let's take our flight	74	The Starre		18
Thy flight is higher, as thy birth.	76	Sunday		59
By flight of sinne.	125	Peace		36
Yet as the sunne, though forward be his flight,	190	Ch.-Milit.		31
Out-strip their Cupid easily in flight?	206	Walton 1		9
FLING				
I am the floore, the sink, where they it fling:	32	Sacrifice		175
FLINT				
Mark how the fire in Flint doth quiet lie,	68	Content	W	9
Steele & a flint strike fire,	202	Trin.Sun.	W	7
FLINTS				
Mark how the fire in flints doth quiet lie,	68	Content		9
FLOAT (see also floting)				
FLOCK				
My soul's a shepherd too; a flock it feeds	81	Christmas		17
Shepherd and flock shall sing, and all my powers	81	Christmas		21
Thy mercies thither flock and flow:	82	Ungratef.		20
Of flock and fold.	125	Peace		24
Thy flock doth stray.	187	Dooms-day		20
setting aside his care of his Flock, were a madnesse to doubt of.	234	Priest 7		17
never was there such care of a flock expressed, save in the great	234	Priest 7		20
and with edification to his flock, humbly beseeching his Master,	235	Priest 8		25
or in exhortations to some of his flock by themselves, whom his	236	Priest 8		12
For there he shall find his flock most naturally as they are,	247	Priest 14		6
The Countrey Parson is not only a father to his flock, but also	250	Priest 16		7
infuse a competent knowledge of salvation in every one of his Flock;	255	Priest 21		3
or carelesness of his flock, and accordingly applies himselfe	258	Priest 22		25
Therefore hee endures not that any of his Flock should go to Law;	259	Priest 23		31
if there be any of his flock sick, hee is their Physician,	260	Priest 23		29

FLOCK (cont'd)	PAGE	TITLE		LINE
and considering his Flock, discovers two sorts of vices, . .	264	Priest 26		4
To this end he represents to his flock, that God hath and exerciseth	270	Priest 30		33
as he discovers any of his Flock to be in one or the other state,	280	Priest 34		13
dishonor of God, and the infection of his flock, and the discomfort,	287	Priest 37		4
If all fooles wore white Caps, wee should seeme a flock of geese.	338	Proverbs		513
FLOCKE				
is to feed my Flocke diligently and faithfully, since our Saviour	224	Priest		4
FLOCKT				
Whereupon men flockt thither, and built houses with happy successe.	301	Cornaro		29
FLOOD				
Convert & colour all the other flood	204	The Knell	W	14
FLOORE				
Which it would poure on thee, upon the floore.	7	Ch.-Porch		28
Some said, that I the Temple to the floore	28	Sacrifice		65
I am the floore, the sink, where they it fling:	32	Sacrifice		175
On the same floore, ...	61	Praise 1		14
The Church-floore.	66	Ch.-floore		T
Mark you the floore? that square & speckled stone, ...	66	Ch.-floore		1
Blows all the dust about the floore:	67	Ch.-floore		17
To raze the building to the very floore:	84	The World		17
My friend may spit upon my curious floore:	93	Unkindness		11
as walls plaistered, windows glazed, floore paved, seats whole, firm,	246	Priest 13		5
FLOTING				
As was and is thy floting Ark; whose stay	97	Afflict.5		3
FLOUD				
As a floud the lower grounds.	180	Invitation		24
when he cannot more, as he that weeps a floud of tears. . .	279	Priest 33		31
FLOURISH				
The ten Commandments there did flourish more	191	Ch.-Milit.		39
in his own country he would have to flourish in this land of light,	304	Valdesso		14
FLOURISHED				
When Solomons temple stood and flourished!	106	Sion		2
FLOURISHING				
Intemperance destroyes most healthy and flourishing constitutions:	292	Cornaro		9
FLOURS				
Yet though my flours be lost, they say	42	Easter	W	27
FLOUT				
Away thy blessings, and extreamly flout thee, ...	23	Ch.-Porch		413
Our blessings from us, and extreamly flout thee, ...	23	Ch.-Porch	W	413
Servants and abjects flout me; they are wittie:	31	Sacrifice		141
Now come again, said I, and flout me.	108	Home		46
FLOUTED				
Shall I be scourged, flouted, boxed, sold?	35	Thanksgvng		7
FLOW				
That as sinne came, so Sacraments might flow:	34	Sacrifice		247
Thy mercies thither flock and flow:	82	Ungratef.		20
The earth doth rest, heav'n move, and fountains flow. . . .	91	Man		26
Earth resteth, Heaven moveth, fountains flow, ...	91	Man	W	26
The spring, whence all things flow:	101	Miserie		60
Do flie and flow, ...	132	The Storm		2
Descend and fall, and thou dost flow.	137	The Size		6
Which my fierce youth did bandie, fall and flow	169	The Answer		3
To curbe some Rebell teares, which faine would flow, ...	213	Bohemia	D	58
If ever Tears did flow from Eyes, ...	213	Convert	D	1
Shall flow no more - until they bring	214	Convert	D	8
FLOW'RS				
My dayes were straw'd with flow'rs and happinesse;	47	Afflict.1		21
My dayes were strowd with flow'rs and happinesse;	47	Afflict.1	W	21
FLOW'D				
Then beautie flow'd, then wisdome, honour, pleasure:	160	The Pulley		7
FLOW'R				
With thy quick flow'r, thy momentarie bloom;	48	Repentance		3
FLOWER (see also flours)				
Shall thy strokes be my stroking? thorns, my flower?	35	Thanksgvng		13
All worship is prerogative, and a flower	78	Ang.&Sts.		21
Their masters flower, but leave it, having done, ...	118	Providence		66
So both the flower doth stay, and hony run.	118	Providence		68
A gallant flower, ...	125	Peace		14
With many a flower:	142	Pilgrimage		8
The Flower.	165	The Flower		T
Fast in thy Paradise, where no flower can wither!	166	The Flower		23
Nor doth my flower	166	The Flower		26
So this flower doth judge and sentence	178	The Rose		25
Doubtlesse, neither starre nor flower	181	Banquet		19
One flower makes no garland.	339	Proverbs		521
FLOWERS				
I got me flowers to straw thy way;	42	Easter		19
As watring pots give flowers their lives.	90	Afflict.4		10
But time did becken to the flowers, and they	94	Life		4
Farewell deare flowers, sweetly your time ye spent, ...	94	Life		13
With flowers and carvings, mysticall and rare:	106	Sion		5
Rain, do not hurt my flowers; but gently spend	120	Providence		117
No flowers, no garlands gay? all blasted?	153	The Collar		15
Flowers look about, and die not in their prime.	154	Glimpse		10
Are thy returns! ev'n as the flowers in spring;	165	The Flower		2
Quite under ground; as flowers depart	166	The Flower		10
To make us see we are but flowers that glide:	167	The Flower		44
Flowers, and gummes, and powders giving	181	Banquet		16
Then shall thy Glory, fresh as flowers	213	L' Envoy	D	7
Benefits please like flowers while they are fresh.	356	Proverbs	D	40

	PAGE	TITLE		LINE
FLOWRE				
That all may gladly board thee, as a flowre.	21	Ch.-Porch		368
I had prepared many a flowre	42	Easter	W	19
If as a flowre doth spread and die,	57	Employm. 1		1
FLOWRES				
Nor flowres to make that, nor the husbandrie	57	Employm. 1		19
FLOWS				
From thee all pitie flows.	148	Longing		13
FLUNG				
My hill was further: so I flung away,	142	Pilgrimage		31
FLY (see also flie)				
To feel those tempests, which fly over ditches.	11	Ch.-Porch		112
Make not thy sport, abuses: for the fly	15	Ch.-Porch		233
Till I get wing to fly away with thee.	59	Whitsunday	W	4
On men dropp blessings as I fly.	79	Employm.2	W	25
Follow the Church & sunn where ere they fly.	198	Ch.-Milit.	W	273
Or whether Bread doe fly away	200	H. Commun.	W	8
Fly the pleasure that bites to morrow.	336	Proverbs		444
FLYES				
Not flyes, but I shall bee his prey	61	Praise 1	W	19
Flyes of estates and sunne-shine. But to all,	169	The Answer		5
FLYING				
When they are fledge, that need may teach them flying.	118	Providence		64
FOAM (see also fome)				
FODDER				
Man might not of his fodder misse.	76	Sunday		39
if they keep and fodder well their cattel, they must have milk,	270	Priest 30		27
FOE				
And to his foe;	92	Antiphon 2		6
that was my causeless foe:	221	Psalm VII	D	14
FOES				
Who sought for help, never malicious foes:	34	Sacrifice		243
Number according to thy foes?	38	Good Fri.		6
That when sinne spies so many foes,	39	Good Fri.		25
To sell my life unto my friends or foes:	88	The Pearl		19
He our foes in pieces brake;	93	Antiphon 2		13
Yet use I not my foes, as I use thee.	94	Unkindness		25
Where yet both Sinne and Satan, thy old foes,	99	Decay		13
Who would, to be thy foes.	100	Miserie		30
His life from foes.	125	Peace		26
His utter foes?	134	The Method		28
Gave you a colour once; which when your foes	140	Ch.-rents		13
What is objected by my foes.	155	Assurance		24
And in this league, which now my foes invade,	156	Assurance		26
Who, that they might subdue, made all their foes.	191	Ch.-Milit.		62
Who had subdued all the world for foes.	191	Ch.-Milit.	W	62
And if in comming to thy foes	200	H. Commun.	W	13
And meet theire tast, who are thy bitter foes.	213	Bohemia	D	66
How are my foes increased, Lord?	216	Psalm III	D	1
because of all my foes:	219	Psalm V	D	22
And now my foes the Lord will blame	220	Psalm VI	D	25
FOES'				
against my foes disdain:	221	Psalm VII	D	22
FOIL				
The Foil.	175	The Foil		T
God hath made starres the foil	176	The Foil		5
FOILE				
A foile to sett of worth, & make it rare.	211	Bohemia	D	16
FOLD				
The great shepherd of the fold	92	Antiphon 2		10
Of flock and fold.	125	Peace		24
To fetch a sacrifice out of my fold,	129	Love unkn.		30
And did this mysterie wrap up and fold	192	Ch.-Milit.		94
Let not Sinne devoure thy fold,	199	L'Envoy		5
save in the great shepherd of the fold, who first shed teares over	234	Priest 7		21
since there is a two-fold brightnesse which dazeleth the eyes of men,	442	Oration		33
FOLDS				
Who hath made of two folds one.	93	Antiphon 2		23
Which hath made of two folds one.	93	Antiphon 2	W	23
FOLKE				
The house is a fine house, when good folke are within.	352	Proverbs		952
FOLKES				
To fine folkes a little ill finely wrapt.	324	Proverbs		117
FOLKS				
With sick folks, women, those whom passions sway,	73	Constancie		27
The house is a fine house, when good folks are within.	352	Proverbs	V	952
Take heed of mad folks in a narrow place.	360	Proverbs	D	1149
FOLLIE				
Let follie speak in her own native tongue.	177	Forerunners		27
FOLLIES				
Their follies with the wing of thy milde Dove,	100	Miserie		28
Their follies with the wings of thy milde Dove,	100	Miserie	W	28
Who may thy follies span?	102	Miserie	W	66
FOLLOW				
Whom all his passions follow, as he goes.	15	Ch.-Porch		216
I follow straight without complaints or grief,	94	Life		16
Follow my resigning.	115	Dialogue		28
Which crie and follow. Thou hast made poore sand	118	Providence		47
Thus also Sinne and Darknesse follow still	198	Ch.-Milit.		272
Follow the Church & sunn where ere they fly.	198	Ch.-Milit.	W	273
I am to follow our Saviours rule, and to take my brother aside,	248	Priest 14		27

FOLLOW (cont'd)	PAGE	TITLE		LINE
I am then to follow the Apostles rule, 1 Timothy 5. 20. and to rebuke	248	Priest 14		29
But after I had resolved to follow Temperance and Reason, . . .	292	Cornaro		31
age and constitution with them who follow their youthfull appetites,	303	Cornaro		12
as also to those that live in sinne, and follow their appetites:	303	Cornaro		19
Hee that sendes a foole, means to follow him.	322	Proverbs		51
Follow not truth too near the heels, lest it dash out thy teeth.	360	Proverbs	D	1138
had taken ill courses, Follow your Book, and you shall want nothing:	364	Letters		21
FOLLOWED				
followed my Appetite, and did eat meats pleasing to my taste;	292	Cornaro		27
FOLLOWERS				
Money wants no followers.	362	Proverbs	D	1182
FOLLOWES				
In judging, he followes that, which is altogether right; . . .	260	Priest 23		13
No man that followes it, is bound to eat and drink so little as I:	300	Cornaro		6
Hee that lives ill, feare followes him.	324	Proverbs		110
He that followes the Lord hopes to goe before.	354	Proverbs		994
FOLLOWETH				
or otherwise afflicted, he followeth the Churches counsell, namely,	249	Priest 15		28
FOLLOWING				
and as following the Apostles two great and admirable Rules in things	246	Priest 13		25
to the dubious and offensive places in the following CONSIDERATIONS.	306	Valdesso		T
Fame is sowne in this age, that it may be reaped in the following;	443	Oration		4
FOLLOWS				
Who follows all things, forfeiteth his will.	21	Ch.-Porch		364
and what follows after, as also the scope of the Holy Ghost.	229	Priest 4		11
and, it follows in the next verse:	374	Letters		27
FOLLY (see also follie)				
Nothing with labour, folly long a-doing.	14	Ch.-Porch		192
God calleth preaching folly. Do not grudge	23	Ch.-Porch		429
The Jews refused thunder; and we, folly.	24	Ch.-Porch		449
Folly, and worse then folly, lust:	74	The Starre		10
Folly and Sinne play all his game.	100	Miserie		3
Folly and Sinne play out his game.	100	Miserie	W	3
But oh the folly of distracted men, ...	167	Dotage		13
Knowledge is folly, except grace guide it.	329	Proverbs		248
If folly were griefe every house would weepe.	334	Proverbs		370
The first degree of folly is to hold ones selfe wise, . . .	337	Proverbs		460
The first degree of folly is to thinke ourselves wise, . . .	337	Proverbs	V	460
There is no jollitie but hath a smack of folly.	338	Proverbs		493
Folly growes without watering.	341	Proverbs		581
The chiefe disease that raignes this yeare is folly. . . .	346	Proverbs		765
FOME				
I ranne; but all I brought, was fome.	64	Even-song		12
FOMES				
distinction, for Fomes is not taken away, but Accensio Fomitis;	308	Valdesso		15
FOMITIS				
distinction, for Fomes is not taken away, but Accensio Fomitis;	308	Valdesso		16
FOND				
Hath some fond lover tic'd thee to thy bane?	176	Forerunners		21
My Heart, that gave fond Thoughts their Food, ...	214	Convert	D	16
FONT				
And threw it in a font, wherein did fall	129	Love unkn.		13
The Font did onely, what was old, renew:	130	Love unkn.		64
and Font be as they ought, for those great duties that are performed	246	Priest 13		6
FOOD				
For all the week thy food so oft he gave thee.	22	Ch.-Porch		392
Thy cheere is mended; bate not of the food, ...	22	Ch.-Porch		393
With Manna, Angels food, I fed them all:	34	Sacrifice		239
To hunt his cruell food through ev'ry vein.	37	The Agonie		12
Turning my purge to food, thou throwest me	48	Afflict.1		51
And leave th' earth to their food.	53	H.Commun.		40
The whole is, either our cupboard of food, ...	91	Man		29
When they are callow; but withdraw their food	118	Providence		63
Begging his food of that which he may eat, ...	193	Ch.-Milit.		113
That thy flesh hath lost his food, ...	199	L'Envoy		9
Shall they be food & strength & might	201	H. Commun.	W	35
My Heart, that gave fond Thoughts their Food, ...	214	Convert	D	16
by taking both sorts of food into them, do as it were dresse	241	Priest 10		33
vessels, and there is nothing that is food, and not phisick,	243	Priest 10		2
but rather made food miraculously, then suffered so good desires	267	Priest 26		25
and the Angels minister to us their owne food, even joy, . .	280	Priest 34		6
is a great Blessing, and as great as food, for which we give thanks:	284	Priest 35		27
so man did eat Angels food:	290	Priest		9
that the food I was to use, was such as belonged to sickly . .	292	Cornaro		24
FOOL				
Throughout the world. Fool not: for all may have, ...	10	Ch.-Porch		89
Have got to be a deare fool for an houre.	16	Ch.-Porch		246
FOOLE				
He hath great neede of a foole, that plaies the foole himselfe.	322	Proverbs		46
Hee that sendes a foole, means to follow him.	322	Proverbs		51
Play with a foole at home, ...	325	Proverbs		146
None is a foole alwaies, every one sometimes.	326	Proverbs		163
yet hee is no little foole that despiseth it.	327	Proverbs		206
A foole knowes more in his house, then a wise man in anothers.	329	Proverbs		257
While the discreet advise, the foole doth his busines. . . .	330	Proverbs		273
The foole askes much, but hee is more foole that grants it. . .	330	Proverbs		282
Hee is a foole that thinks not that another thinks. . . .	330	Proverbs		287
and hee that hath one son makes him a foole.	336	Proverbs		433
One foole makes a hundred.	339	Proverbs		525
A foole may throw a stone into a well, ...	339	Proverbs		527

FOOLE (cont'd)	PAGE	TITLE		LINE
He is a foole that makes a wedge of his fist.	341	Proverbs		585
If fooles should not foole it, they shall lose their season.	343	Proverbs	V	702
If fooles should not foole it, they should loose their season.	344	Proverbs		703
None is so wise, but the foole overtakes him.	345	Proverbs		734
None is so wise, but that the foole overtakes him.	345	Proverbs	V	734
A white wall is the paper cf a foole.	349	Proverbs		839
He that sends a foole expects one.	349	Proverbs		851
Every one hath a foole in his sleeve.	350	Proverbs		881
Better be a foole then a knave.	352	Proverbs		961
FOOL'D				
But sinne hath fool'd him. Now he is	102	Miserie		73
FOOLERIE				
In us the same transplanted foolerie.	193	Ch.-Milit.		120
FOOLES				
If all fooles had bables, wee should want fuell.	323	Proverbs		63
Were there nc focles, badd ware would not passe.	323	Proverbs		66
We are fooles one to another.	334	Proverbs		381
Fooles bite one another, but wise-men agree together.	336	Proverbs		452
If the wise erred not, it would goe hard with fooles.	338	Proverbs		510
If wise men erred not, it would goe hard with fooles.	338	Proverbs	V	510
If all fooles wore white Caps, wee should seeme a flock of geese.	338	Proverbs		513
To the counsell cf fooles a woodden bell.	339	Proverbs		535
If fooles should not foole it, they shall lose their season.	343	Proverbs	V	702
If fooles should not foole it, they should loose their season.	344	Proverbs		703
Fooles give to please all but their owne.	345	Proverbs		735
Children when they are little make parents fooles,	352	Proverbs		939
Children when they are little make their parents fooles,	352	Proverbs	V	939
Lawyers houses are built on the heads of fooles.	352	Proverbs		951
FOOLISH				
But know, that nothing can so foolish be,	15	Ch.-Porch		206
Man is a foolish thing, a foolish thing,	100	Miserie		2
Oh foolish man! where are thine eyes?	101	Miserie		49
Foolish soul who sinn'd to day?	113	Businesse		2
Foolish soul, Who di'd for thee?	113	Businesse		16
Then burn thy Epicycles, foolish man;	135	Divinitie		25
Weep foolish heart,	135	Ephes.		8
Now foolish thcught go on,	156	Assurance		37
Foolish night-fires, womens and childrens wishes,	167	Dotage		2
Let foolish lovers, if they will love dung,	177	Forerunners		25
My Voice, that oft with foolish Lays,	214	Convert	D	11
and reverend, not with light colours, or foolish anticks.	246	Priest 13		13
O let not our foolish and unworthy hearts rob us of the continuance	289	Priest		19
Empty Chambers make foolish maides.	322	Proverbs		29
The wise hand doth not all that the foolish mouth speakes.	329	Proverbs		246
Hee that demands misseth not, unlesse his demands be foolish.	333	Proverbs		359
The first service a child doth his father is to make him foolish.	337	Proverbs		463
He that's foclish in the fault,	340	Proverbs		555
Foolish tongues talke by the dozen.	343	Proverbs		645
The least foolish is wise.	351	Proverbs		910
not with a foolish vanting of yourself when there is no caus,	366	Letters		16
FOOLISHLY				
Though foolishly he lost the same,	43	East.wings		2
FOOLISHNESSE				
My foolishnesse;	49	Repentance		17
How canst thou brook his foolishnesse?	100	Miserie		7
FOOLS				
As mens returns, what would become of fools?	147	Offering		2
nor fools stand in thy sight.	218	Psalm V	D	12
FOORDS				
What are two shallow foords, two little spouts	164	Grief		9
for to the sea he made havens, and to rivers foords.	331	Proverbs		315
for to the sea he made heavens, and to rivers foords.	331	Proverbs	V	315
FOOT				
When once thy foot enters the church, be bare.	22	Ch.-Porch		403
That apprehension cur'd so well my foot,	50	Faith		11
In all, I think my foot doth ever tread	71	Frailtie		7
And ever as I walk my foot doth tredd	71	Frailtie	W	7
My foot did tread,	71	Frailtie		18
For head with foot hath private amitie,	91	Man		17
A lump of flesh, without a foot or wing	102	Miserie		74
And till they foot and clutch their prey,	126	Confession		15
Did once perceive, it blew them under foot,	140	Ch.-rents		7
Did once perceive, it blew thee under foot,	140	Ch.-rents	V	7
Love is swift of foot;	179	Discipline		21
Letting, while one foot stept, the other stay	191	Ch.-Milit.		34
Either t' his publick foot or private tricks.	195	Ch.-Milit.		196
self to this course of life, that I never went a foot out of the way.	292	Cornaro		34
of the ground, and sometimes I go up high stairs and hills cn foot.	300	Cornaro		36
He that hath one foot in the straw, hath another in the spittle.	336	Proverbs		438
To take the nuts from the fire with the dogges foot.	341	Proverbs		584
Wisedome hath one foot on Land, and another on Sea.	341	Proverbs		611
To go upon the Franciscans Hackney (i.e. on foot).	356	Proverbs	D	1035
come a Horse-back, there is reason, that my desires should go a-foot;	363	Letters		23
how I am now setting foot into Divinity, to lay the platform of my	364	Letters		12
FOOTE				
Better thy foote slip then thy tongue.	322	Proverbs	V	53
Better a bare foote then none.	323	Proverbs		78
The masters eye fattens the horse, and his foote the ground.	338	Proverbs		486
One foote is better then two crutches.	346	Proverbs		769

FOOTED	PAGE	TITLE		LINE
Sure-footed griefs, solid calamities,	167	Dotage		9
FOR				
Yet not mine neither: for from thee they came,	5	Dedication		2
Thy rate and price, and mark thee for a treasure;	6	Ch.-Porch		2
The price of thee, and mark thee for a treasure;	6	Ch.-Porch	W	2
Lets his soul runne for nought, as little fearing.	8	Ch.-Porch		59
For we have wit to mark them, and to spare.	9	Ch.-Porch		69
Against thee: for his light was onely lent.	9	Ch.-Porch		82
Throughout the world. Fool not: for all may have,	10	Ch.-Porch		89
This is Earth's language, for if Heaven come in,	10	Ch.-Porch	W	90
For he, that needs five thousand pound to live,	10	Ch.-Porch		107
For wealth without contentment, climbes a hill	11	Ch.-Porch		111
Think the king sees thee still; for his King does.	11	Ch.-Porch		122
Dare to look in thy chest; for 'tis thine own:	12	Ch.-Porch		147
Take starres for money; starres not to be told	13	Ch.-Porch		171
She loseth three for one; her soul, rest, fame.	13	Ch.-Porch		174
A kinde of thing that's for it self too deere.	13	Ch.-Porch		178
Would have their tale beleeved for their oathes,	14	Ch.-Porch		183
Play not for gain, but sport. Who playes for more	14	Ch.-Porch		193
For wit is newes onely to ignorance.	15	Ch.-Porch		230
Make not thy sport, abuses: for the fly	15	Ch.-Porch		233
Have got to be a deare fool for an houre.	16	Ch.-Porch		246
Feed no man in his sinnes: for adulation	16	Ch.-Porch		257
Envie not greatnesse: for thou mak'st thereby	16	Ch.-Porch		259
The place its honour, for the persons sake.	17	Ch.-Porch		266
To work for two, who brought himself to thrall.	17	Ch.-Porch		286
To work for two, that brought himself to thrall.	17	Ch.-Porch	W	286
For so thou dost thy self and him a pleasure:	18	Ch.-Porch		296
Be calm in arguing: for fiercenesse makes	18	Ch.-Porch		307
Mark what another sayes: for many are	19	Ch.-Porch		319
Who say, I care not, those I give for lost;	20	Ch.-Porch		347
Who say, I care not, I give those for gone;	20	Ch.-Porch	W	347
(Love is a present for a mightie king)	20	Ch.-Porch		350
Love is a present for the greatest king.	20	Ch.-Porch	W	350
For this French sluttery which so currant goes:	21	Ch.-Porch	W	368
Onely thy single market-money for it.	21	Ch.-Porch		375
God reckons for him, counts the favour his:	21	Ch.-Porch		381
Open for thee; or both may come too late.	21	Ch.-Porch		384
Open for thee; or they may come too late.	21	Ch.-Porch	W	384
For all the week thy food so oft he gave thee.	22	Ch.-Porch		392
Pray with the most: for where most pray, is heaven.	22	Ch.-Porch		402
God is more there, then thou: for thou art there	22	Ch.-Porch		404
Stay not for th' other pin: why thou hast lost	23	Ch.-Porch		411
A joy for it worth worlds. Thus hell doth jest	23	Ch.-Porch		412
For churches are either our heav'n or hell.	23	Ch.-Porch		426
For churches either are our heav'n or hell.	23	Ch.-Porch	W	426
Judge not the preacher; for he is thy Judge:	23	Ch.-Porch		427
And love him for his Master: his condition,	24	Ch.-Porch		443
For thirtie pence he did my death devise,	27	Sacrifice		17
A Balsome are for both the Hemispheres:	27	Sacrifice		26
For it was their own cause who killed me:	30	Sacrifice		115
For it was their own case who killed me:	30	Sacrifice	W	115
Which each one calls for so with utmost breath,	31	Sacrifice		146
Weep not, deare friends, since I for both have wept	31	Sacrifice		149
Your tears for your own fortunes should be kept:	31	Sacrifice		151
Yet for twelve heav'nly legions I could call:	31	Sacrifice		155
For these are all the grapes Sion doth bear,	31	Sacrifice		162
Then Simon bears it for me by constraint,	33	Sacrifice		198
The greater world o' th' two; for that came in	33	Sacrifice		206
The greater world o' th' two; for that comes in	33	Sacrifice	W	206
And fathers smile for you, to feel his frown:	34	Sacrifice		223
And fathers smile to feele for you his frown:	34	Sacrifice	W	223
As he that for some robberie suffereth.	34	Sacrifice		230
Who sought for help, never malicious foes:	34	Sacrifice		243
For they will pierce my side, I full well know;	34	Sacrifice		246
Oh King of wounds! how shall I grieve for thee,	35	Thanksgvng		3
King of all wounds, how shall I grieve for thee,	35	Thanksgvng	W	3
As for thy passion - But of that anon,	35	Thanksgvng		29
For thy predestination I'le contrive,	36	Thanksgvng		31
As if I us'd them but for fashion.	36	Thanksgvng		36
Then for thy passion - I will do for that -	36	Thanksgvng		49
For though I die for thee, I am behinde;	36	Reprisall		3
For by thy death I die for thee.	36	Reprisall		8
No room for me, and flie away.	39	Good Fri.		28
For by the writings all may see	39	Good Fri.	W	31
No lodging for thee, but a cold hard stone?	40	Sepulchre		2
For they can lodge transgressions by the score:	40	Sepulchre		6
Awake, my lute, and struggle for thy part	41	Easter		7
For, if I imp my wing on thine,	43	East.wings		19
You doe prevent most sins & for the rest	44	H. Bapt.1	W	6
So many joyes I writ down for my part,	46	Afflict.1		3
No place for grief or fear.	46	Afflict.1		16
And made a partie unawares for wo.	47	Afflict.1		24
And more; for my friends die:	47	Afflict.1		32
Yet, for I threatned oft the siege to raise,	47	Afflict.1		43
For sure then I should grow	48	Afflict.1		58
Cut me not off for my most foul transgression:	49	Repentance		15
For if thou stay,	49	Repentance		22
When thou for sinne rebukest man,	49	Repentance		25
Thy wrath for sinne, as when mans sight was dimme,	49	Faith		2

FOR (cont'd)

	PAGE	TITLE		LINE
Reserving all for flesh again.	51	Faith		44
Thou, who for me wast sold,	52	H.Commun.	V	3
For so thou should'st without me still have been,	52	H.Commun.		5
For sure when Adam did not know	53	H.Commun.		33
The world's toc little for thy tent,	55	Temper 1		11
A grave too big for me.	55	Temper 1		12
Yet take thy way; for sure thy way is best:	55	Temper 1		21
Save that, and me; or sin for both destroy.	56	Temper 2		4
For when thou dost depart from hence,	56	Temper 2		11
Riddle who list, for me, and pull for Prime:	57	Jordan 1		12
For as thou dost impart thy grace,	57	Employm. 1		9
Precious for any grief in any part;	58	H.Script.1		3
And comments on thee: for in ev'ry thing	58	H.Script.2		10
And more then fancy: for in ev'ry thing	58	H.Script.2	W	10
Hung down his head, and wisht for night,	59	Whitsunday		14
When he beheld twelve sunnes for one	59	Whitsunday		15
For sinn would faine remove the dearth	59	Whitsunday	W	19
And lay it on thy husbandry, for shift.	59	Whitsunday	W	20
But that from them joyes purle for ever	59	Whitsunday	W	22
Restore this day, for thy great name,	60	Whitsunday		27
The dew, for which grasse cannot call,	60	Grace		11
O come! for thou dost know the way.	61	Grace		21
To a brave soul: for to a poore,	61	Praise 1	W	15
O raise me then: for if a Spider may	61	Praise 1	W	17
Thou Lord of life; since thy one death for me	62	Afflict.2		2
Then we must needs for that day make a match.	62	Mattens		4
For when he sees my waies, I dy:	63	Even-song		7
For this thy love? have I discharg'd the debt,	64	Even-song		10
These laugh at Jeat and Marble put for signes,	65	Ch.-monum.		12
Comfort, I'le die; for if you poste from me,	66	Ch.-mus.		9
Comfort, I'le die; for if you part from me,	66	Ch.-mus.	W	9
Yet heare, O God, onely for his blouds sake	66	Ch.-lock		9
Which pleads for me:	66	Ch.-lock		10
For though sinnes plead too, yet like stones they make	66	Ch.-lock		11
For I confesse my heavie score,	68	Trin.Sun.		5
(For he would not) as they beheld the grace	70	Humilitie		18
For which ye wrangle, made them turn their frown	71	Humilitie		28
What place or person calls for, he doth pay.	72	Constancie		15
For above all things he abhorres deceit:	72	Constancie		18
Allows for that, and keeps his constant way:	73	Constancie		28
For thou canst make a debter,	74	The Starre		7
The week were dark, but for thy light:	75	Sunday		6
Make bracelets for the spouse & wife	76	Sunday	W	31
And did inclose this light for his:	76	Sunday		37
And made a garden there for those	76	Sunday		41
Who want herbs for their wound.	76	Sunday		42
And fit for Paradise.	76	Sunday		56
Nay, thou hast got the face of man; for we	77	Avarice		10
The great restorative for all decay	78	Ang.&Sts.		12
But now (alas!) I dare not; for our King,	78	Ang.&Sts.		16
But now alas I dare not; for my King,	78	Ang.&Sts.	W	16
To make a posie for inferiour power.	78	Ang.&Sts.		25
To make a garland for inferiour power.	78	Ang.&Sts.	W	25
When th' elements did for place contest	79	Employm.2		11
Some fruit for him that dressed me.	79	Employm.2		25
My God, no hymne for thee?	81	Christmas		16
Then we will chide the sunne for letting night	81	Christmas		23
For by that powder thou wilt make us see.	82	Ungratef.		18
For by this powder thou wilt make us see.	82	Ungratef.	W	18
For we have all of us just such another.	82	Ungratef.		24
Defrauding thee, who gavest two for one.	82	Ungratef.		30
And not refuse me: for thou onely art	83	Sighs & Gr.		4
For what account can thy ill steward make?	83	Sighs & Gr.		8
For thou hast other vessels full of bloud,	83	Sighs & Gr.		21
Ev'n unto death: since he di'd for my good,	83	Sighs & Gr.		23
For thou hast life and death at thy command;	83	Sighs & Gr.		26
For thou must die.	87	Vertue		4
Then shall those powers, which work for grief,	90	Afflict.4		25
For Man is ev'ry thing,	91	Man		7
For head with foot hath private amitie,	91	Man		17
For us the windes do blow,	91	Man		25
For us was sold.	92	Antiphon 2		12
Sues for my heart, I thee displace,	94	Unkindness		19
Fit, while ye liv'd, for smell or ornament,	94	Life		14
And after death for cures.	94	Life		15
For missing my designe.	95	Submission		4
For, I do praise thee, yet I praise thee not:	96	Justice 1		8
Ten still, if sermons go for gains.	96	Charms & K		16
Ten, if a Sermon goe for gains.	96	Charms & K	W	16
Convey them quickly, who are bound for death.	98	Mortific.		12
And calls for musick, while his veins do swell,	98	Mortific.		14
Why he'l not lose a cup of drink for thee:	100	Miserie		8
For one poore minute, stumble at a pinne:	100	Miserie		20
The sunne holds down his head for shame,	101	Miserie		33
For this he wondrous well doth know	101	Miserie	W	45
And for our sakes in person sinne reprove,	103	Prayer 2		16
Thou mightst make way for liberalitie!	103	Prayer 2		18
And quickly gain, for each inch lost, an ell.	103	Prayer 2		24
Entred for both, farre above their desert!	105	Obedience		45
No room for pratlers there.	105	Conscience		10

FOR (cont'd)

	PAGE	TITLE	LINE
Besides my physick, know there's some for thee:	106	Conscience	20
For those that trouble me:	106	Conscience	22
For all thy frame and fabrick is within.	106	Sion	12
Tombes for the dead, not temples fit for thee:	107	Sion	20
The note is sad, yet musick for a king.	107	Sion	24
Leave one poore apple for thy love?	107	Home	22
And for their old acquaintance plead.	109	Home	70
For all they either painted are,	109	Brit. Ch.	11
For her reward.	110	Brit. Ch.	18
But thou shalt answer, Lord, for me.	110	The Quip	8
But thou shalt answer, Lord, for me.	110	The Quip	12
But thou shalt answer, Lord, for me.	111	The Quip	16
But thou shalt answer, Lord, for me.	111	The Quip	20
And write for sweet, prove a most sowre displeasure.	111	Vanitie 2	6
To purchase heaven for repenting,	111	Vanitie 2	9
For they can never be at rest,	111	Vanitie 2	15
Then silly soul take heed; for earthly joy	111	Vanitie 2	17
Foolish soul, Who di'd for thee?	113	Businesse	16
If he had not liv'd for thee,	113	Businesse	20
If he had not di'd for thee,	113	Businesse	26
Who for man was sold, can see;	114	Dialogue	15
So the way to fit me for it,	115	Dialogue	19
Look onely; for to love thee, who can be,	116	Dulnesse	27
The sacrifice for all; while they below	117	Providence	14
For me and all my fellows praise to thee:	117	Providence	26
For either thy command, or thy permission	117	Providence	33
For thou art infinite in one and all.	118	Providence	44
Each creature hath a wisdome for his good.	118	Providence	61
Bees work for man; and yet they never bruise	118	Providence	65
Sheep eat the grasse, and dung the ground for more:	119	Providence	69
Trees after bearing drop their leaves for soil:	119	Providence	70
Is there an herb for that? O that thy care	119	Providence	75
Should creatures want for want of heed their due?	119	Providence	86
For their offence; and then dost turn their speed	120	Providence	107
It go for one, hath many wayes in store	121	Providence	150
Yet ill deeds loyter not: for they supplie	122	Sinnes rd.	16
Thy sithe is dull; whet it for shame.	122	Time	2
Twentie for one too sharp do finde it.	122	Time	6
For where thou onely wert before	123	Time	14
Whom when for Peace	125	Peace	20
For they that taste it do rehearse,	125	Peace	33
And grows for you;	125	Peace	38
They are too subtill for the subt'llest hearts;	126	Confession	11
For since confession pardon winnes,	126	Confession	27
And calls him coward, who for fear of sinne	127	Giddinesse	7
For as the Jews of old by Gods command	128	Bunch Gr.	8
Ev'n God himself, being pressed for my sake.	128	Bunch Gr.	28
I hold for two lives, and both lives in me.	129	Love unkn.	5
A friend did steal into my cup for good,	130	Love unkn.	43
For I had giv'n the key to none, but one:	130	Love unkn.	55
For ought I heare, your Master shows to you	130	Love unkn.	62
Inclose me still for fear I START.	133	Paradise	7
For since thy God refuseth still,	133	The Method	2
For he is Power: and sure he would;	133	The Method	7
For he is Love.	133	The Method	8
As men, for fear the starres should sleep and nod,	134	Divinitie	1
But he doth bid us take his bloud for wine.	135	Divinitie	21
Grieved for me? the God of strength and power	135	Ephes.	4
Griev'd for a worm, which when I tread,	135	Ephes.	5
For death is drie as dust. Yet if ye part,	135	Ephes.	10
If a cleare spring for me no time forbears,	136	Ephes.	28
Lord, pardon, for thy sonne makes good	136	Ephes.	35
For where thou dwellest all is neat.	136	Familie	8
Perhaps thou com'st sometimes, and for a day;	137	Familie	23
And for the future time art heir	137	The Size	11
But little do reserve themselves for more:	138	The Size	20
At least in lump: for such doth oft destroy;	138	The Size	27
And for the present health restore.	138	The Size	30
Grasp not at much, for fear thou losest all.	138	The Size	38
For we should count, Since the last joy.	138	The Size	41
For I will do, or suffer what I ought.	139	Artillerie	16
Which falls by night, and poure it out for you!	140	Ch.-rents	30
For where before thou still didst call on me,	141	Justice 2	19
Against me there is none, but for me much.	141	Justice 2	24
What Adam had, and forfeited for all,	143	Holdfast	13
The crop is his, for he hath sown.	144	Discharge	15
And well it was for thee, when this befell,	144	Discharge	16
For thou canst tell,	144	Discharge	19
Dig not for wo	145	Discharge	29
In times to come; for it will grow.	145	Discharge	30
This houre is mine: if for the next I care,	145	Discharge	33
For death each houre environs and surrounds.	145	Discharge	36
And care for future chances, cannot go	145	Discharge	38
And when Justice call'd for fears,	146	Praise 2	23
Search well and see; for hearts have many holes.	147	Offering	4
(For this heart is none)	148	Offering	33
For many weeks of lingring pain and smart	154	Glimpse	4
But one half houre of comfort for my heart?	154	Glimpse	5
For future times, the droppings of the stock	154	Glimpse	24
To hide thy shame: for thou hast cast a bone	156	Assurance	39

FOR (cont'd)

	PAGE	TITLE	LINE
What for it self love once began,	156	Assurance	41
For thou didst suffer to restore	157	Clasping	14
And when it stops for want of store,	157	Praise 3	4
(As we have boxes for the poore)	158	Praise 3	28
For well he knows, if but one grief and smart	159	Jos.coat	5
For if I should (said he)	160	The Pulley	11
For that of th' holy word.	160	Priesthood	6
Of skilfull artists, for the boards of those	161	Priesthood	17
Of lowly matter for high uses meet,	161	Priesthood	35
For some mean stuffe whereon to show his skill:	161	Priesthood	38
Against, but for me.	163	The Search	52
For as thy absence doth excell	163	The Search	57
My weary weeping eyes too drie for me,	164	Grief	6
A narrow cupboard for my griefs and doubts,	164	Grief	11
For my rough sorrows: cease, be dumbe and mute,	164	Grief	14
And keep your measures for some lovers lute,	164	Grief	16
For mine excludes both measure, tune, and time.	164	Grief	18
What I would do for thee, if once my grones	165	The Crosse	15
Could be allow'd for harmonie)	165	The Crosse	16
Thou hast a garden for us, where to bide.	167	The Flower	46
For what Christ once in humblenesse began,	168	The Sonne	13
For who can look for lesse, that loveth Life. / Strife.	170	Water-crs.	5
For choosing Barabbas a murderer	170	Self-cond.	2
For he hath sold for money his deare Lord,	171	Self-cond.	17
And all this not for my desert,	172	23 Psalme	11
But for his holy name.	172	23 Psalme	12
For thou art with me; and thy rod	173	23 Psalme	15
And wore them for a jewell on her head,	173	Marie Magd	3
Why kept she not her tears for her own faults,	173	Marie Magd	9
Why kept she not her tears for her own fauts,	173	Marie Magd V	9
A noise of passions ringing me for dead	174	Aaron	8
For pardon of my imperfection	175	The Odour	19
For when My Master, which alone is sweet,	175	The Odour	21
For, Thou art still my God, is all that ye	177	Forerunners	32
For they all produce repentance,	178	The Rose	27
For my answer is a rose.	178	The Rose	32
For my hearts desire	178	Discipline	5
For with love	179	Discipline	19
For it seems but just and right	180	Invitation	34
For thy neatnesse passeth sight,	181	Banquet	4
For with it alone I flie	182	Banquet	43
What I seek, for what I sue;	182	Banquet	46
Who hath done so much for me.	182	Banquet	48
To do it as for thee:	184	The Elixer	4
He that does ought for thee,	184	The Elixer W	12
Marketh that deed for thine:	184	The Elixer W	12
Which with his tincture (for thy sake)	184	The Elixer	15
Which with this tincture (for thy sake)	184	The Elixer V	15
Who sweeps a room, as for thy laws,	185	The Elixer	19
Who sweeps a chamber, for thy laws,	185	The Elixer W	19
For that which God doth touch and own	185	The Elixer	23
Cannot for lesse be told.	185	The Elixer	24
Wherein I die, not live: for life is straight,	185	A Wreath	5
For this poore wreath, give thee a crown of praise.	185	A Wreath	12
For we consider'd thee as at some six	186	Death	5
Much in request, much sought for, as a good.	186	Death	16
Much in request, much long'd for as a good.	186	Death W	16
For we do now behold thee gay and glad,	186	Death	17
For ev'ry mans peculiar book?	187	Judgement	5
But I resolve, when thou shalt call for mine,	188	Judgement	11
Thou didst rise early for to plant this vine,	190	Ch.-Milit. W	11
Among the eastern nations for a time,	191	Ch.-Milit.	35
Nilus for monsters brought forth Israelites.	191	Ch.-Milit.	44
For things misshapen, things of highest use.	191	Ch.-Milit.	46
Who had subdued all the world for foes.	191	Ch.-Milit. W	62
Him in his members, who for him was slain.	192	Ch.-Milit.	70
(For no lesse Harbingers would serve then they)	192	Ch.-Milit.	84
Who for a God clearely a sallet lost.	193	Ch.-Milit.	110
Thus Sinne in Egypt sneaked for a while;	193	Ch.-Milit.	121
Here Sinne took heart, and for a garden-bed	193	Ch.-Milit.	127
Where some poore truths were shuffled for a bait	193	Ch.-Milit.	136
Are given over, for their curious arts,	194	Ch.-Milit.	152
Shipping the vices onely for our sphere.	196	Ch.-Milit. W	204
My God, thou dost prepare for them a way	197	Ch.-Milit.	249
For gold and grace did never yet agree:	197	Ch.-Milit.	251
Both for their vertuous actions and their crimes.	197	Ch.-Milit.	262
For thy poore creature there	200	H. Commun. W	6
Is more, but for mee still.	200	H. Commun. W	18
If thou hadst dyde for Bread.	201	H. Commun. W	27
Thou art too hard for me in Love:	201	love W	1
For I decay not hee.	203	Even-song W	4
And wake with thee for ever.	203	Even-song W	24
For some relief.	204	The Knell W	18
Are so, as for the present, I did move	204	Persever. W	3
For who can tell, though thou hast dyde to winn	205	Persever. W	9
Oceans of Ink; for, as the Deluge did	206	Walton 2	2
Why should I Womens eyes for Chrystal take?	206	Walton 2	8
If thou chance for to find	207	Walton 3	1
Are shed for him, dissolve thy frame,	209	H. Danvers D	7
Thou art requited; for his Fame,	209	H. Danvers D	8

FOR (cont'd)

	PAGE	TITLE		LINE
Another Monument for Thee.	209	H. Danvers	D	10
Gifts speake their Givers. For as those Refractions, ...	209	L. Bacon	D	3
But that my Inke was factious for this side.	209	L. Bacon	D	12
Then for yourselves not us embrace	211	Paradox	D	37
For though you vysit us, & wayle our case, ...	211	Paradox	D	39
No Earth can bee thy Jointure. For the sunne	211	Bohemia	D	3
Doth for two clods of earth ten spheres controule, ...	211	Bohemia	D	8
There is thy best Throne. For afflictions are	211	Bohemia	D	15
Children for kingdomes to thee; they shall live	212	Bohemia	D	42
But joyes are stord for thee: thou shalt returne	212	Bohemia	D	55
Thy teares not needing. For that hand Divine	213	Bohemia	D	63
For God himself vouchsafes to know	215	Psalm I	D	21
Against me, saying, For my soul	216	Psalm III	D	3
for God sustain'd me still.	216	Psalm III	D	12
For thou upon the cheek-bone smit'st	217	Psalm III	D	19
For that, O Lord, with perfect joy	218	Psalm IV	D	25
For thy protection, Lord, alone	218	Psalm IV	D	31
for in the morn will I	218	Psalm V	D	6
For wickedness their insides are, ...	219	Psalm V	D	25
Yea, shout for joy for evermore, ...	219	Psalm V	D	37
For God doth righteous men esteem, ...	219	Psalm V	D	41
and them for ever bless.	219	Psalm V	D	42
O pity me! for I (O Lord)	219	Psalm VI	D	3
O heal me, for my bones are vex'd, ...	220	Psalm VI	D	5
my Soul for thy great mercy save;	220	Psalm VI	D	10
For who in death remember Thee?	220	Psalm VI	D	11
For God himself hath heard my cry;	220	Psalm VI	D	21
For their sakes, Lord, return on high, ...	221	Psalm VII	D	27
for others ruine wrought:	222	Psalm VII	D	54
But I for all his righteousness	222	Psalm VII	D	61
Ours (like himselfe) o'recomes; for his wit's more	438	Lat.Trans.		3
(thorow the Mercy of GOD) to please Him, for whom I am, and live,	224	Priest		2
as farre as wee can in pleasing of him, who hath done so much for us.	224	Priest		13
A Pastor is the Deputy of Christ for the reducing of Man . .	225	Priest 1		1
For first, Man fell from God by disobedience.	225	Priest 1		4
Christ is the glorious instrument of God for the revoking of Man.	225	Priest 1		5
of Christ in his flesh, for his Bodie's sake, which is the Church.	225	Priest 1		12
which Christ did, and after his manner, both for Doctrine and Life.	225	Priest 1		19
For, Unto the ungodly, saith God, Why dost thou preach my Laws,	226	Priest 2		13
are in Orders, they may be received for Companions, or discoursers;	226	Priest 2		24
They who for the hope of promotion neglect any necessary admonition,	226	Priest 2		36
of himself, for all the purposes which God hath ordained him.	227	Priest 3		9
which in the day of wrath hath not one dramme of comfort for us.	227	Priest 3		21
For sins make all equall, whom they finde together;	227	Priest 3		27
Neither is it for the servant of Christ to haunt Innes, . . .	227	Priest 3		29
As for oaths, and apparell, the disorders thereof are also very	228	Priest 3		8
Precepts for life, Doctrines for knowledge, Examples	228	Priest 4		24
for life, Doctrines for knowledge, Examples for illustration,	228	Priest 4		25
for knowledge, Examples for illustration, and Promises for comfort:	228	Priest 4		25
But for the understanding of these;	228	Priest 4		26
For all Truth being consonant to it self, and all being penn'd by one	229	Priest 4		5
place with place must be a singular help for the right understanding	229	Priest 4		8
For the Law required one thing, and the Gospel another: . . .	229	Priest 4		14
the servants of God, for the planting both of love, and humility.	229	Priest 4		26
For though the world is full of such composures, yet every mans own	230	Priest 5		3
For it being indifferent in it selfe to choose any Method, . .	230	Priest 5		9
a slighter forme of Catechizing, fitter for country people; . .	230	Priest 5		16
For every one hath not digested, when it is a sin to take something	230	Priest 5		23
when it is a sin to take something for mony lent, or when not;	230	Priest 5		24
have glorified him as wel as now, and that he shall have so for ever.	232	Priest 6		1
it is either for want of health, or against some great Festivall,	232	Priest 7		22
or for the variety of the hearers, that he may be heard at his	232	Priest 7		23
This is for you, and This is for you;	233	Priest 7		5
for particulars ever touch, and awake more then generalls. . .	233	Priest 7		5
for people are very attentive at such discourses, and think it	233	Priest 7		9
for them also men heed, and remember better then exhortations;	233	Priest 7		13
for thou art Love, and when thou teachest, all are Scholers.	233	Priest 7		36
For there is no greater sign of holinesse, then the procuring,	234	Priest 7		9
And ceased not to give thanks for the Ephesians, Eph. 1. 16.	234	Priest 7		13
And for the Corinthians, chap. 1. 4.	234	Priest 7		13
And for the Philippians made request with joy, ch. 1. 4. . .	234	Priest 7		14
And is in contention for them whither to live, or dy; . . .	234	Priest 7		15
for if we be here, hee must be here, since we are here by him,	234	Priest 7		29
he makes a peculiar one for a blessing on the exercises of the day,	235	Priest 8		22
then he turnes to request for his people, that the Lord would be	235	Priest 8		27
and blesseth God for the gift of continency, knowing that it can no	237	Priest 9		19
therefore thinkes it not enough for him to observe the fasting dayes	237	Priest 9		22
and devotion, some other dayes for fasting, and hours for prayers;	237	Priest 9		25
for the humane soule being bounded, and kept in, in her sensitive	238	Priest 9		10
for then commonly the stream of temptations is turned another way,	238	Priest 9		22
not his affection found out a fit wife for him, whose humble,	238	Priest 9		28
reserving so much of the affaires, as serve for a diversion for him;	238	Priest 9		38
governing of his house, making it a copy and modell for his Parish.	239	Priest 10		7
a providing for her family in such sort, as that neither they want	239	Priest 10		17
which happily for his other children he is not able to do. . .	239	Priest 10		32
such as are tavernes for men, and lace-making for women; . .	240	Priest 10		2
for the most part, serve but the vices and vanities of the world,	240	Priest 10		3
in consideration of providing a stock for his children; . .	240	Priest 10		7
is placed surer for his childrens advantage, then if it were given	240	Priest 10		8
and good breeding, are his two great stocks for his children;	240	Priest 10		10

FOR (cont'd)

	PAGE	TITLE	LINE
his profit, for none are so well served, as by religious servants,	240	Priest 10	14
Those that can read, are allowed times for it, and those that cannot,	240	Priest 10	19
for all in his house are either teachers or learners, or both,	240	Priest 10	20
that there is no help for a fault done, but confession.	240	Priest 10	35
for he hath no mony for such things, charity being his only perfume,	241	Priest 10	13
and veal, if he addes any thing for a great day, or a stranger,	241	Priest 10	17
he goes no further for any entertainment, lest he goe into the world,	241	Priest 10	19
for there being two things, which as they are, are unuseful to man,	241	Priest 10	26
are unuseful to man, the one for smalnesse, as crums, and scattered	241	Priest 10	27
the other for the foulnesse, as wash, and durt, and things thereinto	241	Priest 10	28
God hath provided Creatures for both;	241	Priest 10	30
for the first, Poultry; for the second, swine.	241	Priest 10	30
for the second, swine. These save man the labour, and doing that	241	Priest 10	31
or was not fit for him to do, by taking both sorts of food into them,	241	Priest 10	32
do as it were dresse and prepare both for man in themselves,	241	Priest 10	34
both for man in themselves, by growing them selves fit for his table.	241	Priest 10	35
For since fasting in Scripture language is an afflicting of our	242	Priest 10	11
For it is certaine, that a weak stomack being prepossessed	242	Priest 10	21
or roots, and that for quantity little, for quality unpleasant.	242	Priest 10	27
For meat was made for man, not man for meat.	242	Priest 10	32
For meat was made for man, not man for meat.	242	Priest 10	33
not for emboldening the unruly, but for the comfort of the weak,	242	Priest 10	33
but for the comfort of the weak, that not onely sicknesse breaks	242	Priest 10	34
For it is as unnatural to do any thing, that leads me to a sicknesse,	242	Priest 10	36
that he keeps his money for the poor, and his table for those that	243	Priest 11	8
his money for the poor, and his table for those that are above Alms.	243	Priest 11	9
them close by him, and carving for them, both for his own humility,	243	Priest 11	12
and carving for them, both for his own humility, and their comfort,	243	Priest 11	12
there are such conceits, there is no room for his doctrine to enter.	243	Priest 11	24
For though he desire, that all should live well, and vertuously,	243	Priest 11	27
and vertuously, not for any reward of his, but for vertues sake;	243	Priest 11	28
and vertuously, not for any reward of his, but for vertues sake;	243	Priest 11	29
although we should love him onely for his own sake, yet out of his	243	Priest 11	31
pity hath set forth heaven for a reward to draw men to Piety,	243	Priest 11	32
For many and wonderfull things are spoken of thee, thou great Vertue.	244	Priest 12	7
for this in time will lose the name and effect of Charity	244	Priest 12	26
for then they will reckon upon it, as on a debt;	244	Priest 12	27
for that also is some kind of obligation;	245	Priest 12	19
For though these testimonies also may be falsifyed, yet considering	245	Priest 12	23
For other givings are lay, and secular, but this is to give like	245	Priest 12	37
be as they ought, for those great duties that are performed in them.	246	Priest 13	7
and a Bason for Almes and offerings;	246	Priest 13	20
of well minded people, and to lay up treasure for the sick and needy.	246	Priest 13	22
For these two rules comprize and include the double object of our	246	Priest 13	28
the first being for the honour of God;	246	Priest 13	30
the second for the benefit of our neighbor.	246	Priest 13	31
For there he shall find his flock most naturally as they are,	247	Priest 14	5
whereas on Sundays it is easie for them to compose themselves	247	Priest 14	7
for it is a good and just thing for every one to do their own	247	Priest 14	22
it is a good and just thing for every one to do their own busines.	247	Priest 14	22
he adviseth them so to labour for wealth and maintenance,	248	Priest 14	6
he chides not at first, for that were neither civill, nor profitable;	248	Priest 14	14
for if he be a plaine countryman, he reproves him plainly;	248	Priest 14	16
for they are not sensible of finenesse:	248	Priest 14	17
for as when the offence is particular, and against mee,	248	Priest 14	26
For both God is there also, and those for whom God dyed:	249	Priest 14	6
For both God is there also, and those for whom God dyed:	249	Priest 14	7
but with these he mingles other discourses for conversation sake,	249	Priest 14	11
rather goes to them, then sends for the afflicted, though they can,	249	Priest 15	16
For by this means, when any sinns, he hateth him not as an officer,	250	Priest 16	10
by a due blessing of God for their safe arrival, and saying grace	251	Priest 17	9
if hee be to stay for a time, hee considers diligently the state	251	Priest 17	17
and ingagement of their discourses for no price sooner,	252	Priest 18	21
and therefore not for him, who is hearty, and true in all his wayes,	253	Priest 19	1
use of them, as of Clergy councels, for the benefit of the Diocese.	253	Priest 19	11
about him, performing for them any Ministeriall office, which is	253	Priest 19	16
For the Apostles rule Philip. 4. being admirable, and large,	253	Priest 19	22
he gives him a tester for it, if the giver be fit to receive it;	254	Priest 20	14
for there being three points of his duty, the one, to infuse	255	Priest 21	1
of preaching to himself, for the advancing of his own mortification;	255	Priest 21	13
for in preaching to others, he forgets not himself, but is first	255	Priest 21	13
partly for obedience to Authority, partly for uniformity sake,	255	Priest 21	17
partly for uniformity sake, that the same common truths may be every	255	Priest 21	18
First, for the authority of the work;	255	Priest 21	26
for many say the Catechisme by rote, as parrats, without ever	256	Priest 21	3
for he could not but say, he would hast out of it as fast as he	257	Priest 21	6
and cleansed, and serve for lights even of Heavenly Truths.	257	Priest 21	15
For questions cannot inflame or ravish, that must be done by a set,	257	Priest 21	24
with himself, how or what behaviour to assume for so holy things.	257	Priest 22	28
for thou art not only the feast, but the way to it.	257	Priest 22	34
where God is thanked for calling us to the knowledg of his grace,	258	Priest 22	6
and his Saints, and by way of undertaking for a Christian soul.	258	Priest 22	14
for if wise men have thought it the best way of preserving a state	258	Priest 22	15
it is the safest course for Christians also to meditate on their	258	Priest 22	17
not on the Sunday of the Communion only (for then it is too late)	258	Priest 22	27
of devotion to the Sacrament, but it is for want of Instruction;	258	Priest 22	38
their understandings being ripe enough for ill things, and why	259	Priest 22	1
being ripe enough for ill things, and why not then for better?	259	Priest 22	2
as to a great purchase for their children, and servants;	259	Priest 22	3
For the manner of receiving, as the Parson useth all reverence	259	Priest 22	10

FOR (cont'd)

FOR (cont'd)

	PAGE	TITLE	LINE
For the temptations with which a good man is beset, and the ways	278	Priest 33	14
there were no such Physician as he, both for skill and tendernesse.	278	Priest 33	32
for though the temptations may be diverse in divers Christians,	278	Priest 33	33
freed for a while from temptation, in a quiet sweetnesse seeks how	279	Priest 33	4
having for his owne use examined the nature of it, is able	279	Priest 33	8
himselfe sometimes to weepe more for the losse of some temporall	279	Priest 33	12
then for offending God, he came at length to this resolution,	279	Priest 33	13
This Instruction and comfort the Parson getting for himself,	279	Priest 33	32
when the Divell for a time leaves us, as he did our Saviour,	280	Priest 34	5
for with such sacrifices God is well pleased.	281	Priest 34	3
then without opposing directly (for disputation is no Cure	281	Priest 34	14
(for disputation is no Cure for Atheisme) he scatters in his	281	Priest 34	15
For Nature, he sees not how a house could be either built without	281	Priest 34	18
For Preservation is a Creation;	281	Priest 34	30
Secondly, for the Law, there may be so evident, though unused a proof	281	Priest 34	32
in all Lands, was intended not only for a punishment to them;	282	Priest 34	14
but for an exciting of others by their sight, to the acknowledging	282	Priest 34	15
Thirdly, for Grace. Besides the continuall succession (since	282	Priest 34	18
on our Saviour, for which he told, that it should never be forgotten,	282	Priest 34	25
for no perfect Artist ever yet hated his owne worke.	283	Priest 34	12
gave them love for love, even the son of his love out of his bosome	283	Priest 34	16
First, a blessing of God for the fruits of the field:	284	Priest 35	4
is a great Blessing, and as great as food, for which we give thanks:	284	Priest 35	27
As for those that are ashamed to use this forme, as being old,	284	Priest 35	29
of Christs Cross, or for any shame to leave that which is good.	284	Priest 35	33
for it was not the person, but Priesthood, that blessed;	285	Priest 36	22
which though our Saviour reproved as unfitting for his particular,	285	Priest 36	27
and ingaging of Gods own power and institution for a blessing.	286	Priest 36	10
For if he absolutely shut up mens mouths, and forbid all disclosing	286	Priest 37	33
for we must not do evill, that good may come of it.	287	Priest 37	6
by those, which are branded for rogues, that they may be known;	287	Priest 37	20
For in infamy, all are executioners, and the Law gives a malefactour	287	Priest 37	30
for all are honest, till the contrary be proved.	287	Priest 37	34
if the punished delinquent shall be much troubled for his sins,	288	Priest 37	3
for we are darknesse, and weaknesse, and filthinesse, and shame.	288	Priest	10
and sold our God, our glorious, our gracious God for an apple.	288	Priest	18
O brand it in our foreheads for ever:	288	Priest	18
for an apple once we lost our God, and still lose him for no more;	288	Priest	19
for an apple once we lost our God, and still lose him for no more;	288	Priest	20
for money, for meat, for diet:	288	Priest	20
for his enemies he died;	288	Priest	29
even for those that derided him then, and still despise him.	288	Priest	29
for, this word of thy rich peace, and reconciliation, thou hast	289	Priest	3
we magnifie thee for ever!	289	Priest	11
so neither may thy word, but accomplish that for which it is given.	289	Priest	32
and do so for thy blessed Son's sake, in whose sweet and pleasing	289	Priest	34
Thou was born for us, and thou livedst and diedst for us:	290	Priest	4
Thou was born for us, and thou livedst and diedst for us:	290	Priest	5
the measure of thy love, who hast done for us as much as may be.	290	Priest	12
Grant this dear Father, for thy Son's sake, our only Saviour:	290	Priest	13
For when they saw their parents and kindred snatcht away in the midst	291	Cornaro	8
For by it, and my ill constitution, (having a most cold & moist	291	Cornaro	20
the Physicians told me that yet there was one help for me,	292	Cornaro	4
for this had every way great force for the recovering and preserving	292	Cornaro	5
For Temperance preserves even old men and sickly men sound:	292	Cornaro	7
For contrarie causes have contrarie effects, and the faults of Nature	292	Cornaro	10
to that exigent, that there would be no help for me, but Death,	292	Cornaro	15
for strong and very cool wines pleased my taste best, as also melons,	293	Cornaro	11
For although the power of health consists most in the proportion	293	Cornaro	32
by any of these inconveniences, except it were for one onely day.	294	Cornaro	10
For having endured many heats & colds, and other like discommodities	294	Cornaro	11
For when my brother and others of my kindred saw some great powerfull	294	Cornaro	15
For in the end I got the victorie, to my great honour, and no lesse	294	Cornaro	27
for riding in a coach in great haste, it happened that the coach was	294	Cornaro	36
and then was dragged for a good space by the furie of the horses,	294	Cornaro	38
considering what an orderly life I had led for many yeares together,	295	Cornaro	7
and that I had for many yeares continued in good health,	295	Cornaro	26
For whereas before the measure of my whole dayes meat, viz.	296	Cornaro	8
whereupon all gave me for dead.	296	Cornaro	23
save now and then a little indisposition for a day or two.	296	Cornaro	31
For the Temperance of so many yeares spent all ill humours,	296	Cornaro	32
For there is no malignitie of old age in the humours of my bodie,	296	Cornaro	36
whereof the one kept me well for many yeares;	297	Cornaro	5
For indeed no man can be a perfect Physician to another,	297	Cornaro	24
and greatly to be esteemed for the knowing & curing of diseases,	298	Cornaro	4
For if a friend who visits thee in thy sicknesse, and onely comforts	298	Cornaro	6
this I answer, that Galen kept it, and held it for the best Physick:	298	Cornaro	38
For I answer, That those inconveniences are of no great moment (as I	299	Cornaro	15
which is both easie for common-weals-men, and very convenient,	299	Cornaro	17
For suddenly it takes away our appetite, so that we can eat	299	Cornaro	27
For if he should keep his former proportion, Nature, which is	299	Cornaro	32
and the cause being taken away, there is no place for the effect.	300	Cornaro	2
For I eat little, because a little sufficeth my weak stomack:	300	Cornaro	8
and not the qualitie for his rule, which is very easie to be	300	Cornaro	15
the place was moorish and unhealthy, fitter for beasts then men.	301	Cornaro	27
I was one of those that was deputed for the managing of that work,	302	Cornaro	17
which it most suits withall for variety and pleasantnesse;	302	Cornaro	31
For when I come home, I finde eleven grand-children of mine,	303	Cornaro	2
very apt and well given both for learning and behaviour.	303	Cornaro	5
For death to all young men is a terrible thing, as also to those that	303	Cornaro	18

FOR (cont'd)

	PAGE	TITLE		LINE
for I know that (setting casualties aside) I shall not die	303	Cornaro		25
First for your sake, because I would doe nothing negligently that you	304	Valdesso		4
Secondly for the Authors sake, whom I conceive to have been a true	304	Valdesso		6
Thirdly for the Churches sake, to whom by Printing it I would have	304	Valdesso		8
to publish it, for these three eminent things observable therein:	304	Valdesso		18
for which I doe so love him, that were there nothing else,	305	Valdesso		6
But I like none of it, for it slights the Scripture too much:	306	Valdesso		17
Hee that trusts in the Kings word for any thing trusts in the King.	307	Valdesso		4
for I can no more free my selfe from actuall sinnes after Baptisme,	308	Valdesso		3
distinction, for Fomes is not taken away, but Accensio Fomitis;	308	Valdesso		15
As for the Text, They shall be all taught of God, it being Scripture	310	Valdesso		2
yet Peter was to be sent for, and those that have inspirations must	310	Valdesso		10
For as the servant leaves not the letter when he hath read it,	310	Valdesso		27
he himselfe allowes it for a holy conversation and refreshment.	311	Valdesso		2
and meditation of holy Scriptures for the first and principall,	311	Valdesso	V	5
for he maintaines that it is Faith and Infidelity that shall judge us	311	Valdesso		22
chastized but not punished) for evill doing nor rewarded for weldoing	311	Valdesso		28
not punished) for evill doing nor rewarded for weldoing or living,	311	Valdesso		29
or living, for all the point lies in believing or not believing.	311	Valdesso		29
the Doctrine would be examined, however it may passe for his opinion:	312	Valdesso		1
These in diverse cases ought, and were of old forborn for a time.	312	Valdesso	V	28
indifferent things there is roome for motions [notions] and expecting	313	Valdesso		12
for it invites us to all good, according to that singular place,	313	Valdesso		19
For as for these, pious persons ought alwaies to avoid them:	314	Valdesso		19
godly in some sort exempt from Lawes, for Lex iusto non est posita:	315	Valdesso		33
[the law is not made for a righteous man:]	315	Valdesso		34
For first concerning Abraham and Sara, I ever tooke that	315	Valdesso		35
I ever tooke that for a weaknesse in the great Patriark:	316	Valdesso		1
For otherwise any Malefactor may pretend motions, which is	316	Valdesso		20
but he might have been justly put to death for it by the Magistrate,	316	Valdesso		25
The best salve for the whole Chapter, is to distinguish Judgment:	316	Valdesso		34
for as a Magistrate judgeth in his tribunall, so a Scholar judgeth in	317	Valdesso		1
for so he useth the same word in Consideration 68 ad finem.	317	Valdesso	V	8
for the most of his Considerations being grounded upon some text	317	Valdesso		35
and not used it for a time onely, and then cast it away,	318	Valdesso		3
As for the text of S. Pet. 2 Ep. 1. 19. which he makes the ground	318	Valdesso		6
or by good works, or condemned for unbelief, or evil works,	319	Valdesso	V	17
the world is counted a very Saint, for his outward shew of holinesse:	319	Valdesso	V	21
For at least some of the Papists are come now, to what the Pharisees	320	Valdesso		5
Looke not for muske in a dogges kennell.	321	Proverbs		23
Hee puls with a long rope, that waits for anothers death.	322	Proverbs		25
Hee puls with a long rope, who looks for anothers death.	322	Proverbs	V	25
For washing his hands, none sels his lands.	323	Proverbs		54
Who hath a Wolfe for his mate, needes a Dog for his man.	323	Proverbs		57
Vertue and a Trade are the best portion for Children.	324	Proverbs		107
Cover your selfe with your shield, and care not for cryes.	326	Proverbs		161
from him that saies nothing, for ever.	326	Proverbs		164
The tree that growes slowly, keepes it selfe for another.	327	Proverbs		198
Who must account for himselfe and others, must know both.	328	Proverbs		209
men for one pleasure a thousand griefes prove.	328	Proverbs		228
To steale the Hog, and give the feet for almes.	329	Proverbs		237
Chuse not an house neere an Inne (viz. for noise)	330	Proverbs		286
or in a corner (for filth).	330	Proverbs		286
Goe not for every griefe to the Physitian,	331	Proverbs		290
nor for every quarrell to the Lawyer,	331	Proverbs		290
nor for every thirst to the pot.	331	Proverbs		290
Hee that burnes his house warmes himselfe for once.	331	Proverbs		303
for to the sea he made havens, and to rivers foords.	331	Proverbs		315
for to the sea he made heavens, and to rivers foords.	331	Proverbs	V	315
Hee that hath a Fox for his mate,	335	Proverbs		428
Hee that hath patience hath fatt thrushes for a farthing.	336	Proverbs		430
To weepe for joy is a kinde of Manna.	337	Proverbs		462
For want of a naile the shoe is lost,	338	Proverbs		499
for want of a shoe the horse is lost,	338	Proverbs		499
for want of a horse the rider is lost.	338	Proverbs		499
All things in their beeing are good for something.	339	Proverbs		520
Great trees are good for nothing but shade.	339	Proverbs		546
He that hopes not for good, feares not evill.	340	Proverbs		563
A wise man needes not blush for changing his purpose.	342	Proverbs		613
When age is jocond it makes sport for death.	342	Proverbs		637
Send not a Catt for Lard.	342	Proverbs		644
Love makes one fitt for any work.	343	Proverbs		646
An idle head is a boxe for the winde.	343	Proverbs		651
A wise man cares not for what he cannot have.	343	Proverbs		662
A hatt is not made for one shower.	343	Proverbs		673
God provides for him that trusteth.	345	Proverbs		728
Every one is witty for his owne purpose.	346	Proverbs		754
Praise none too much, for all are fickle.	347	Proverbs		774
Hee that marries for wealth sells his liberty.	347	Proverbs		784
He that cockers his child, provides for his enemie.	347	Proverbs		789
At Court, every one for himselfe.	347	Proverbs		795
Hee payes too deare for honey that licks it from thorns.	350	Proverbs	V	880
Wine ever paies for his lodging.	352	Proverbs		930
Manie things are lost for want of asking.	353	Proverbs		968
For a morning raine leave not your journey.	353	Proverbs		976
Chuse none for thy servant who have served thy betters.	354	Proverbs		1014
Were it not for the bone in the legge,	355	Proverbs		1020
Danger it selfe the best remedy for danger.	357	Proverbs	D	1054
For the same man to be an heretick	357	Proverbs	D	1058
He that hath time and looks for better time,	359	Proverbs	D	1102

FOR (cont'd)

	PAGE	TITLE	LINE
There is a remedy for every thing, could men find it.	360	Proverbs	D 1142
for he asks counsell of the Dead (i.e. books).	361	Proverbs	D 1158
There is no body will go to hell for company.	361	Proverbs	D 1177
for it sets a dearer price on every thing.	361	Proverbs	D 1178
For my own part, my meaning (dear Mother) is in these Sonnets,	363	Letters	9
to find out variety of thanks for the diversity of your favours,	363	Letters	15
And therefore let it be sufficient for me, that the same heart,	363	Letters	17
for, since your favours come a Horse-back, there is reason, . .	363	Letters	22
and that the Horse is every way fit for me, and I will strive	364	Letters	1
for, since, I hope, I have not deceived their expectation, . .	364	Letters	23
for infirmities are both painful and costly.	364	Letters	34
for in our publick Halls, you know, is nothing but Fish . .	365	Letters	3
also I ride to Newmarket, and there lie a day or two for fresh Air;	365	Letters	7
or five Shillings come in my way, I buy it, though I fast for it;	365	Letters	12
for I am sure you love Your faithfullest Servant, GEORGE HERBERT.	365	Letters	25
for it hath been my fortune of late to have such sudden warning,	365	Letters	31
for I would have you, even in speeches, to observe so much, . .	366	Letters	9
be no kind of excellency which it is possible for you to attain to,	366	Letters	14
mee in your letters, for I am your ever loving brother, G. HERBERT.	366	Letters	21
that he hath bought a parcel of Books for me, and that they are	366	Letters	30
for that which surmounts, though your noble disposition is infinitely	367	Letters	5
and both pay for the surplusage of these Books, and for ever after	367	Letters	10
and for ever after cease my clamorous and greedy bookish requests.	367	Letters	11
for your favours are so ancient, that they prevent my memory,	367	Letters	14
Letter in yours, for it was because I know your Lodging, but not his.	367	Letters	24
for I am enjoined to write to you by Sir John Danvers, to which mine	367	Letters	27
for though it is likely that the time after the Holydaye will bee	368	Letters	2
& shee being at London sent for him (as shee sayes) to make peace	368	Letters	20
estate to live on by her selfe (for shee desires no more) shee will	368	Letters	24
is that this is but an occasion for you to amplify your favour to mee	369	Letters	3
for my Cambridge necessities are stronger to tye me here, . .	369	Letters	18
Nethersole for me; he and I are ancient acquaintance, and I have	369	Letters	21
will do well, for it expresseth the Universities inclination to me;	369	Letters	26
it is no matter, for the Gentleman needs no incitation to love me.	369	Letters	28
for the Orator writes all the University Letters, makes all . .	369	Letters	33
I thank you for your infinite favours, I fear only that I have	370	Letters	11
if it had to others, yet to me it should not, for ought I yet knew;	370	Letters	24
of the Pedler and the Pack on London-bridge, for there he assigns me.	370	Letters	28
though for the reckoning of your favours, I shall never find time	370	Letters	30
and now the only thing I long for, is to hear of my dear sick Sister;	371	Letters	7
Is it not too much for me?	371	Letters	11
For my dear sick Sister.	371	Letters	T
that my solliciting him has been much, and my tears many for you;	372	Letters	3
constant and the more earnest for you to the God of all Consolation.	372	Letters	23
of all Comfort, who is not willing to behold any sorrow but for sin.	372	Letters	26
What hath Affliction grievous in it more then for a moment? . .	372	Letters	27
Letter gave me Earthly preferment, and kept Heavenly for your self:	373	Letters	1
for, I have alwaies observ'd the thred of Life to be like other	373	Letters	4
bottom is wound up and laid ready for work in the New Jerusalem.	373	Letters	6
For my self, dear Mother, I alwaies fear'd sickness more then death,	373	Letters	7
me unable to perform those Offices for which I came into the world,	373	Letters	9
And, for temporal Afflictions! I beseech you consider all that can	373	Letters	20
For those of Estate? of what poor regard ought they to be, . .	373	Letters	22
and, Blessed be the Mourners, for they shall be comforted. . .	373	Letters	32
And for afflictions of the Body, dear Madam, remember the holy	373	Letters	34
for those Afflictions of the Soul, consider that God intends that	374	Letters	8
God intends that to be as a sacred Temple for himself to dwell in,	374	Letters	10
and will not allow any room there for such an in-mate as Grief;	374	Letters	11
all your Care on the Lord, for he careth for you. (1 Pet. 5.7.)	374	Letters	16
entertains our Care for us that we may the more quietly intend his	374	Letters	18
at all times rejoyce in the Lord, who taketh care for us: . .	374	Letters	26
be careful for nothing. What can be said more comfortably? . .	374	Letters	28
For concerning your offer of receiving one, I will tell you what I	375	Letters	9
the fruit of my observation, for they have lived so lovingly, lying,	375	Letters	18
to let them know your love, for which both they shall, and I doe,	375	Letters	22
greatest charitie of all, for she is youngest, and least looked unto;	375	Letters	24
For the time of breeding is the time of doing children good;	376	Letters	13
upon my accompt, & give you my self for it, to be yours for ever.	378	Letters	5
& have endeavoured many wayes, to find out a man for it. . .	378	Letters	7
gratious Lord God, is pleased to give me you for the Man, I desired,	378	Letters	8
for which I humbly thank him, & am so far from giving you cause,	378	Letters	9
all your Addresses, & for ought I see, they are ever to be liked.	378	Letters	17
the chiefest also, so also have I required Mr W. for his part.	378	Letters	24
I thanke you heartily for Leighton, your care, your Counsell,	379	Letters	13
And as I am glad for the thing, so no less glad for the Heart,	379	Letters	14
so no less glad for the Heart, that God has given you & yours,	379	Letters	15
As for my assistance, doubt not, through Gods blessing, . .	379	Letters	17
& for my power, I have sent my Letters, to your Brother, . .	379	Letters	18
Mr Herberts reasons for Arth. Woodenoths Living with Sir John	380	Woodnoth	T
the one for the nature thereof (as your trade) the other only	380	Woodnoth	21
(as your trade) the other only for the success (as assistance of Sir	380	Woodnoth	22
no obligation lying upon you either for the execution or benefitt	380	Woodnoth	26
As God where he finds no roome for his Inclining grace, . .	381	Woodnoth	8
temple as much as Solomon because he desired it, & prepared for it.	381	Woodnoth	20
For any scruple of leaving your trade, throw it away. . . .	381	Woodnoth	22
of Philosophie, for respect to you, embrace all that is cheerefull,	442	Oration	7
For, what could have happened more pleasing to us, then the accesse	442	Oration	8
For amongst us what glorious shew is there, either of garments,	442	Oration	31
we for your gracious acceptance of these poore duties wish, . .	443	Oration	5

	PAGE	TITLE		LINE
FORBARE				
discover some care, which I forbare not in the midst of my griefes;	304	Valdesso		3
FORBEAR				
Do I forbear to crave your speciall aid:	78	Ang.&Sts.		7
I had a motion to forbear,	134	The Method		23
Neither in this doth he forbear, though there be company by:	248	Priest 14		25
and forbear to speak of that, which even God himself hath forgotten.	288	Priest 37		5
to be in the dark, ought to use the first, and to forbear the second;	312	Valdesso	V	25
FORBEARANCE				
Enmitie forbearance urgeth.	178	The Rose		20
FORBEARE				
Though he had all I had, did not forbeare	27	Sacrifice		14
Forbeare not sowing because of birds.	343	Proverbs		670
FORBEARS				
Who hath these, those ill forbears.	113	Businesse		8
If a cleare spring for me no time forbears,	136	Ephes.		28
He that forbears	153	The Collar		30
he forbears not in any wise to use the delinquent as before,	263	Priest 25		25
FORBID				
May yet forbid the banes and bliss.	205	Persever.	W	12
Each Cloud distills thy praise, and doth forbid	206	Walton 2		4
and forbid all disclosing of faults, many an evill may not only be,	286	Priest 37		34
yet I remember the Fathers forbid us to judge of the doubtfull	316	Valdesso		12
Now this Lent I am forbid utterly to eat any Fish, so that I am fain	365	Letters		2
upon this he was forbid Court & kingdome, yet was seene lately neere	368	Letters		35
FORBIDDEN				
No man is forbidden to eat fruit or fish, which I eat not:	300	Cornaro		7
FORBORN				
This was not so well said, as it might have been forborn;	252	Priest 18		9
These in diverse cases ought, and were of old forborn for a time.	312	Valdesso	V	28
FORCE				
Meeting sinnes force and art.	52	H.Commun.		12
Whom neither force nor fawning can	72	Constancie		4
Hath a strange force:	132	The Storm		10
What open force, or hidden CHARM	133	Paradise		4
All sorts of wounds; of such strange force it is.	147	Offering		21
And force of fire, what curious things are made	161	Priesthood		14
Where is thy famous force, thy ancient sting?	169	Dial.-Anth		2
Such force as once did captivate the Jews;	195	Ch.-Milit.		192
for this had every way great force for the recovering and preserving	292	Cornaro		5
I began to consider the force of Temperance, and to think thus	293	Cornaro		1
yet these forenamed things have also their force.	293	Cornaro		34
There is great force hidden in a sweet command.	341	Proverbs		589
The sight of a man hath the force of a Lyon.	342	Proverbs		617
FORC'D				
What willing nature speaks, what forc'd by fire;	88	The Pearl		6
FORCES				
Which spread their forces into every part,	52	H.Commun.		11
FORCETH				
Sinne is that presse and vice, which forceth pain	37	The Agonie		11
FORCING				
Then forcing thee, by fire he made thee bright:	77	Avarice		9
Cold sinne still forcing it, till it return,	99	Decay		19
FORD (see also foords)				
FORE				
are to prepare in all the fore-mentioned points against the time	276	Priest 32		26
FORE-MENTIONED				
are to prepare in all the fore-mentioned points against the time	276	Priest 32		26
FORECAST				
Do not forecast.	145	Discharge		52
FOREHEAD				
Unfold thy forehead gather'd into frowns:	112	Dawning		3
FOREHEADS				
O brand it in our foreheads for ever:	288	Priest		18
FOREIGN (see also forrain)				
FOREMOST (see also formost)				
FORENAMED				
yet these forenamed things have also their force.	293	Cornaro		34
FORERUNNERS				
The Forerunners.	176	Forerunners		T
FORESEE				
will appear if the Pious soul foresee and prevent such interruptions,	273	Priest 31		17
FORESEENE				
Dearths foreseene come not.	335	Proverbs		407
Deaths foreseene come not.	335	Proverbs	V	407
FORESTALL				
And give men turns of speech: do not forestall	18	Ch.-Porch		303
Wilt thou forestall it, and now grieve to morrow,	145	Discharge		48
FORETELL				
He grew a gallant, and would needs foretell	193	Ch.-Milit.		129
Whereby one may foretell, what sinnes next yeare	197	Ch.-Milit.		245
FORETOLD				
When as my fears foretold this, did replie,	154	Glimpse		19
Saints his Brethren, and this is foretold, that it shall be so still,	268	Priest 28		15
FORFEIT				
We forfeit all our Creed.	86	Lent		30
Forfeit their Paradise by their pride.	167	The Flower		49
And as malefactors may lose & forfeit their goods, or life;	287	Priest 37		32
FORFEITED				
What Adam had, and forfeited for all,	143	Holdfast		13

	PAGE	TITLE	LINE
FORFEITETH			
Who breaks his own bond, forfeiteth himself:	11	Ch.-Porch	119
Who follows all things, forfeiteth his will.	21	Ch.-Porch	364
FORFETS			
The drunkard forfets Man, and doth devest	7	Ch.-Porch	35
FORGET			
The powder doth forget the dust.	96	Charms & K	14
The powder does forget the dust.	96	Charms & K W	14
they remember their earthly Lord, do much forget their heavenly;	226	Priest 2	33
to a reverence, which they forget againe, when they come to pray,	231	Priest 6	15
knowing that there is one, who when they forget, remembers for them;	267	Priest 26	21
FORGETFULNESS			
Think not my silence forgetfulness;	371	Letters	25
FORGETS			
he forgets not himself, but is first a Sermon to himself, . . .	255	Priest 21	14
FORGETT			
I forgett all thinges, so I may doe them good who want it. . . .	376	Letters	5
FORGETTING			
even somtimes to a forgetting of themselves, knowing that there is	267	Priest 26	20
FORGIVE			
O Lord hear, O Lord forgive!	289	Priest	33
any body els that owe me any thing else of old debt I forgive them.	383	G.H.'s Will	27
FORGIVENESSE			
and the forgivenesse of sins, Matthew 6. 14. Luke 7. 47. . . .	244	Priest 12	9
FORGIVES			
as a child, and forgives, so hee may have any signe of amendment;	250	Priest 16	14
FORGO			
Stay at the third cup, or forgo the place.	8	Ch.-Porch	47
Wherefore I all forgo:	105	Obedience	31
FORGOT			
Ah my deare God! though I am clean forgot, ...	48	Afflict.1	65
Ah my deare King! though I am clean forgot, ...	48	Afflict.1 W	65
A thing forgot, ...	89	Afflict.4	3
That his own self he forgot.	113	Businesse	24
When I had forgot my birth, ...	182	Banquet	31
FORGOTTEN			
him in his Tithes, telling him when he hath forgotten it, This I do,	254	Priest 20	16
that it should never be forgotten, but with the Gospel it selfe be	282	Priest 34	25
and forbear to speak of that, which even God himself hath forgotten.	288	Priest 37	6
The river past, and God forgotten.	327	Proverbs	207
FORM			
That those thy form doth show, ...	115	Dulnesse	14
I have resolved to set down the Form and Character of a true Pastour,	224	Priest	6
because to answer in form may still admit ignorance:	259	Priest 22	7
this unusuall form begets a reverence, and makes him esteemed	286	Priest 36	24
FORME			
By outward forme and showe, ...	210	Paradox D	26
expounding of our Catechisme must needs be the most usefull forme.	230	Priest 5	15
a slighter forme of Catechizing, fitter for country people; . .	230	Priest 5	16
As for those that are ashamed to use this forme, as being old,	284	Priest 35	30
to Blesse the people, and the forme thereof is prescribed, Numb. 6.	285	Priest 36	17
FORM'D			
Lord, who hast form'd me out of mud, ...	68	Trin.Sun.	1
FORMER			
Thou, whom the former precepts have	25	Superlim	1
The two former obligations are much more essentiall to a true fast,	242	Priest 10	7
and fasting dayes were fully performed by keeping of the two former,	242	Priest 10	9
but only the two former, which also in diseases of exinanition	242	Priest 10	31
onely with returning to my former course of Diet, although I was now	296	Cornaro	25
For if he should keep his former proportion, Nature, which is	299	Cornaro	33
In former time it was not so, because the place was moorish . .	301	Cornaro	26
so it be understood with the former distinction, for Fomes is	308	Valdesso	15
of this Consideration cleareth that of the precedent [former].	310	Valdesso	27
perhaps he meant all of this later not of the former. . . .	317	Valdesso	5
wherein consisteth the making good of my former education, . .	364	Letters	17
FORMES			
finds the persons of the house imployed, so he formes his discourse.	247	Priest 14	12
and complements, and formes of worldly language better; . . .	285	Priest 36	5
The formes both of Blessing, & cursing are expounded in . .	286	Priest 36	2
FORMOST			
In a retreat the lame are formost.	350	Proverbs	883
FORMS			
And giving all things their set forms and houres, ...	137	Familie	11
both of them having forms or vizars of godlinesse, but denying	319	Valdesso V	26
FORNACE			
And spacious fornace flaming, and thereon	129	Love unkn.	26
FORO			
that is in humano foro & secundum praesumptionem legalem, . .	316	Valdesso	28
FORRAIN			
All forrain wisdome doth amount to this, ...	20	Ch.-Porch	355
All forrain of that name; but scorn their ill:	21	Ch.-Porch	362
Let forrain nations of their language boast, ...	167	The Sonne	1
FORRAINE			
is the key of Commerce, and discovers the Rules of forraine Nations.	277	Priest 32	33
FORRESTS			
Castles are Forrests of stones.	352	Proverbs	936
FORSAKE			
First to bee Slovens, & forsake their nose.	21	Ch.-Porch W	370
Of what is fit, and not. Forsake thy cage, ...	153	The Collar	21
exercise what he is, unlesse he forsake his plough, and look back.	226	Priest 2	27
God doth forsake and persecute them, and there is none to deliver	281	Priest 34	11

FORSAKE (cont'd)	PAGE	TITLE		LINE
I will declare the causes which moved me to forsake Intemperance,	291	Cornaro		15
but lest in any thing I forsake that Temperance which I have found so	303	Cornaro		34
FORSOOK				
I forsook all these kinde of meats and drinks, and chose that wine	293	Cornaro		15
FORT				
Engine against th' Almightie, sinners fort,	51	Prayer 1	W	5
FORTH				
Boldnesse guilds finely, and will set it forth.	15	Ch.-Porch		210
Thus trimmed forth they bring me to the rout,	32	Sacrifice		185
My heart did heave, and there came forth, O God!	73	Afflict.3		1
Which spit it forth like the Sicilian hill.	122	Sinnes rd.		8
And made it bring forth grapes good store.	128	Bunch Gr.		25
May oft break forth, and never break the lock.	154	Glimpse		25
Wherefore I dare not, I, put forth my hand	161	Priesthood		31
Nilus for monsters brought forth Israelites.	191	Ch.-Milit.		44
Had he only brought them forth,	208	J. Danvers	D	13
To serve it forth, & being stript of all	212	Bohemia	D	31
but shall bring forth a lye.	222	Psalm VII	D	52
of his infinite pity hath set forth heaven for a reward to draw men	243	Priest 11		31
be housed, a fire hath broken forth, and suddenly consumed them.	271	Priest 30		25
and find sparkes of such thoughts now and then to break forth,	281	Priest 34		14
they break forth like mighty waters on every side.	290	Priest		7
and setting his merit forth so piously, for which I doe so love him,	305	Valdesso		6
untill shee had brought forth her first borne Sonne, as if afterwards	318	Valdesso		13
The thorne comes forth with his point forwards.	329	Proverbs		238
FORTHWITH				
Forthwith he waxeth wo and wan:	49	Repentance		26
FORTI'TH				
It's true, we cannot reach Christs forti'th day;	87	Lent		31
FORTIETH				
[afflicted] from the thirtie fifth yeare of my age to the fortieth,	292	Cornaro		2
FORTIFICATION				
on the two noble branches therof, of Fortification, and Navigation;	278	Priest 32		2
FORTIFICATIONS				
and antiquities, publick fabricks, temples, and fortifications:	302	Cornaro		4
FORTIFIES				
is delayed, the more he reads it, and fortifies himselfe with it;	310	Valdesso		30
FORTIFYES				
military state, he fortifyes, and strengthens with his utmost skill.	281	Priest 34		5
FORTITUDE				
Humilitie did reach to Fortitude.	70	Humilitie		12
and Christian fortitude in the cold midnight stormes of persecution	237	Priest 9		37
FORTNIGHT				
the midst of much business, and all in a Fortnight, not long since.	371	Letters		4
FORTUNATE				
The perswasion of the fortunate swaies the doubtfull.	342	Proverbs		630
FORTUNE				
Yet wedding marrs thy fortune, fast & pray:	7	Ch.-Porch	W	14
To court each place or fortune that doth fall,	68	Content		7
To court each place or fortune that does fall,	68	Content	W	7
Hath ever found a happie fortune.	69	Content		36
Love built a stately house; where Fortune came,	84	The World		1
He that hath no ill fortune is troubled with good.	333	Proverbs		358
Not only ought fortune to be pictured on a wheel,	358	Proverbs	D	1077
Fortune to one is Mother, to another is Step-mother.	359	Proverbs	D	1118
Great Fortune brings with it Great misfortune.	360	Proverbs	D	1144
for it hath been my fortune of late to have such sudden warning,	365	Letters		31
FORTUNE'S				
And what is fortunes. Thou hast singled out	211	Bohemia	D	19
FORTUNES				
Do fortunes seek, when worth and service fail,	14	Ch.-Porch		182
Doth ratably thy fortunes marre or make.	16	Ch.-Porch		256
Your tears for your own fortunes should be kept:	31	Sacrifice		151
Playntes to bad fortunes dew:	211	Paradox	D	38
FORTY				
I have forty businesses in my hands, your Courtesie will pardon	371	Letters		18
George Herbert one hundred pound To Mrs Beatrice Herbert forty pound,	383	G.H.'s Will		8
To Mr Bostocke forty shillings To Elizabeth Burthen thirty shillings	383	G.H.'s Will		15
Spencer five pound To Mary Owens forty shillings To Mrs Mary Lawly	383	G.H.'s Will		18
FORWARD				
Man had straight forward gone	75	Sunday		15
Yet as the sunne, though forward be his flight,	190	Ch.-Milit.		31
And so forward, requiring answers to all these, and helping	256	Priest 21		12
But though the Parson sets forward all Charitable deeds,	262	Priest 23		12
in that I apprehend what my Friends would have been forward to say,	364	Letters		20
FORWARDNES				
your relation of my Lady Duchess's forwardnes in our church building.	377	Letters		20
FORWARDNESS				
To shew a forwardness in religious works is a good testimony	377	Letters		25
FORWARDS				
The thorne comes forth with his point forwards.	329	Proverbs		238
FOUGHT				
The man, who once against thee fought.	37	Reprisall		16
FOUL (noun)				
Religion a stalking horse to shoot other foul.	357	Proverbs	D	1069
FOUL (see also fowle)				
Beware of lust: it doth pollute and foul	6	Ch.-Porch		7
Though it be cold, hard, foul, from loving man	41	Sepulchre		23
Cut me not off for my most foul transgression:	49	Repentance		15
We paint the devil foul, yet he	63	Sinne 2		2

FOUL (cont'd)	PAGE	TITLE		LINE
Yet as in sleep we see foul death, and live:	63	Sinne 2		9
We sullied by our foul offence:	76	Sunday		51
As dirtie hands foul all they touch,	101	Miserie		37
Not a fair look, but thou dost call it foul:	105	Conscience		2
Enforceth tears. Your heart was foul, I fear.	129	Love unkn.		18
Are the more foul, the more thou wert divine.	140	Ch.-rents		4
After so foul a journey death is fair,	142	Pilgrimage		35
I am both foul and brittle; much unfit	160	Priesthood		11
As if grief were not foul, nor vertue winning.	176	The Foil		8
Whose house is foul, while he adores his broom?	193	Ch.-Milit.		118
Take heed of foul dirty wayes, and long sicknesse.	360	Proverbs	D	1153
FOULE (noun)				
Where all the beasts and Foule by their command	70	Humilitie	W	3
FOULE				
Thy ancient baptism which when I was foule	202	love	W	11
Let not him that feares feathers come among wild-foule.	322	Proverbs		48
To a fair day open the window, but make you ready as to a foule.	325	Proverbs		119
Fine dressing is a foule house swept before the doores.	329	Proverbs		243
A holy habit clenseth not a foule soule.	343	Proverbs		669
No prison is faire, nor love foule.	348	Proverbs		829
No prison is faire, & no love foule.	348	Proverbs	V	829
No love is foule, nor prison fair.	359	Proverbs	D	1122
FOULED				
and those not torne, or fouled, but whole and clean, and well bound;	246	Priest 13		15
FOULES				
Who doth his owne businesse, foules not his hands.	335	Proverbs		419
FOULING				
Fouling her nest, my earth invade,	203	Even-song	W	11
As a burst fouling-peece doth save the birds	204	Persever.	W	7
FOULING-PEECE				
As a burst fouling-peece doth save the birds	204	Persever.	W	7
FOULNESSE				
the other for the foulnesse, as wash, and durt, and things thereinto	241	Priest 10		29
FOULS				
The Italian says, None fouls his hands in his own businesse:	275	Priest 32		27
FOUND				
And Prophets once to see, but found no place:	32	Sacrifice		183
Till I have found therein thy love,	36	Thanksgvng		46
Till I have found thy love therin,	36	Thanksgvng	W	46
He that by seeking hath himself once found,	69	Content		35
Hath ever found a happie fortune.	69	Content		36
Man found thee poore and dirtie in a mine.	77	Avarice		4
There when I came, whom found I but my deare,	81	Christmas		5
Till it found out how to consume thy goods:	83	Sighs & Gr.		11
What hath not man sought out and found,	85	Vanitie 1		22
What hath not man wrought out and found,	85	Vanitie 1	V	22
Both th' old discoveries, and the new-found seas,	88	The Pearl		7
One might have sought and found thee presently	99	Decay		6
And first I found the corner, where was J,	112	JESU		5
Indeed 'tis true. I found a callous matter	130	Love unkn.		38
Indeed it's true. I found a callcus matter	130	Love unkn.	V	38
I found that some had stuff'd the bed with thoughts,	130	Love unkn.		51
Hath found the art	132	Mans medly		35
And where these are not found,	137	Familie		22
Was all I found.	142	Pilgrimage		24
Did weep to heav'n, they found a bottle there	158	Praise 3		27
And both would runne untill they found a biere	159	Jos.coat		8
And so found me on the ground.	182	Banquet		36
Yet then I found, that thou didst creep	202	love	W	16
not his affection found out a fit wife for him, whose humble,	238	Priest 9		28
by questions well ordered he found Philosophy in silly Trades-men.	256	Priest 21		23
which by mine own experience I have found hurtfull, then from those	266	Priest 26		25
since he found himselfe sometimes to weepe more for the losse of some	279	Priest 33		11
And consequently he found, that the essence of repentance,	279	Priest 33		20
Which acts of repentance are and must be found in all Gods servants:	279	Priest 33		26
The fruit of this blessing good Hannah found, and received with great	285	Priest 36		21
as I too wel by experience found.	292	Cornaro		7
I found within a few dayes, that I was exceedingly helped,	292	Cornaro		34
This upon triall I found most false:	293	Cornaro		10
and yet all these I found hurtfull.	293	Cornaro		14
This I found by experience, when I was seventie yeares old:	294	Cornaro		35
qualities to me, if I had not found them out by long experience?	297	Cornaro		35
or the Philosophers stone, sought of many, and found of few.	298	Cornaro		21
sheweth, and I also, when I was a young man, too well found.	303	Cornaro		16
in any thing I forsake that Temperance which I have found so good,	303	Cornaro		35
In a great River great fish are found,	326	Proverbs		167
Love is not found in the market.	334	Proverbs		401
All are presumed good, till they are found in a fault.	352	Proverbs		944
and if there be any such which you have found useful to yourself,	366	Letters		4
FOUNDATION				
Or with a stone! yet make no good foundation.	120	Providence		124
pains with them, that hee may lay the foundation of future Blessings.	258	Priest 22		31
The third means is the observation what is the main foundation,	262	Priest 24		29
be fain alwayes to borrow Books, and build on anothers foundation?	364	Letters		14
this (which is now, when I must lay the foundation of my whole life).	365	Letters		18
FOUNDATIONS				
exercise of the Church, the light in the foundations being the guide;	263	Priest 24		6
FOUNTAIN				
instantly dry up, as a river would if the fountain were stopped.	271	Priest 30		7
be My God & Dear Master, the Spring & Fountain of all Goodness.	379	Letters		17

	PAGE	TITLE		LINE
FOUNTAINES				
In the morninq mountaines, in the evening fountaines.	337	Proverbs		473
FOUNTAINS				
Walk'd with a staffe to heav'n, and traced fountains: . . .	37	The Agonie		3
The earth doth rest, heav'n move, and fountains flow. . . .	91	Man		26
Earth resteth, Heaven moveth, fountains flow, ...	91	Man	W	26
The windes grew gard'ners, and the clouds good fountains. . .	120	Providence		116
where also I have fountains and gardens, and a very convenient house.	301	Cornaro		18
FOUR (see alsc fowre)				
In the Scriptures hee findes four things;	228	Priest 4		24
but sends for three or four of the ablest of the Parish to hear	260	Priest 23		9
every day of the week, and four times on Sunday, if they be well.	272	Priest 31		22
To seek in a Sheep five feet when there is but four. . . .	359	Proverbs	D	1112
And yet if a Book of four or five Shillings come in my way, . .	365	Letters		11
FOURE				
With but foure words, my words, Thy will be done.	165	The Crosse		36
About foure yeares since, I was led by the advice of Physicians,	295	Cornaro		19
A horse stumbles that hath foure legges.	346	Proverbs		740
God keepe me from foure houses, ...	348	Proverbs		816
He that deales in the world needes foure seeves.	351	Proverbs		899
To Sara thirteene shillings foure pence, Alsoe my will and pleasure	382	G.H.'s Will		27
FOURETEEN				
of my drink, which before was foureteen ounces, I made now sixteen.	296	Cornaro		13
FOURTH				
The fourth means are Commenters and fathers, who have handled	229	Priest 4		17
FOURTHLY				
Fourthly, by frequent wishes of the peoples good, and joying therein,	234	Priest 7		6
Fourthly, That all the books appointed by Authority be there,	246	Priest 13		13
Fourthly, he fulfills the duty, and debt of neighbourhood to all	253	Priest 19		20
Fourthly, that those who are well grown in the knowledg of Religion,	255	Priest 21		32
Fourthly, touching the frequency of the Communion, the Parson	259	Priest 22		19
Fourthly, Mercy in releeving the poor by a liberall distribution	284	Priest 35		7
FOURTIE				
Cannot on fourtie: he's a man of pleasure, ...	13	Ch.-Porch		177
Although there were some fourtie heav'ns, or more, ...	55	Temper 1		5
FOWL (see alsc foul,foule)				
FOWLE				
So Blackamoores repute us fowle, and wee	210	Paradox	D	9
FOWLER				
the longer he stayes there, the fowler he is.	335	Proverbs		409
FOWLS				
Where all the beasts and fowls by their command	70	Humilitie		3
FOWRE				
Count not fowre except you have them in a wallett.	352	Proverbs		962
FOX				
And if the Fox had liv'd to rule their side, ...	70	Humilitie		23
At Length the Fox turnes Monk.	323	Proverbs		72
At length the Fox is brought to the Furrier.	323	Proverbs		81
The Fox, when hee cannot reach the grapes, ...	325	Proverbs		130
The Fox knowes much, but more he that catcheth him. . . .	330	Proverbs		280
Hee that will deceive the fox, must rise betimes.	333	Proverbs		351
Hee that would deceive the fox, must rise betimes.	333	Proverbs	V	351
Hee that hath a Fox for his mate, ...	335	Proverbs		428
Though the Fox run, the chicken hath wings.	339	Proverbs		549
Amiens was taken by the Fox, and retaken by the Lion. . . .	356	Proverbs	D	1036
FOXE				
When the Foxe preacheth, beware your geese.	332	Proverbs		337
FOXE'S				
On Justice was bestow'd the Foxes brain, ...	70	Humilitie		15
FRACTURES				
Fractures well cur'd make us more strong.	49	Repentance		36
FRAGMENTS				
I like not in him, as my fragments will expresse, when you read them;	304	Valdesso		17
FRAGRANCIE				
An orientall fragrancie, My Master.	174	The Odour		5
FRAIL				
Yet since mans scepters are as frail as reeds, ...	32	Sacrifice		177
Since the condition of this world is frail, ...	170	Water-crs.		2
Frail Beauty's Charms to Heav'n did raise, ...	214	Convert	D	13
FRAILE				
and fraile man, discharged the publick duties of the Congregation.	236	Priest 8		9
FRAILTIE				
Frailtie gets pardon by submissivenesse;	8	Ch.-Porch		51
Our flesh and frailtie, death and danger.	50	Faith		24
Frailtie.	71	Frailtie		T
But I am frailtie, and already dust;	83	Sighs & Gr.		17
FRAILTIES				
Though man frailties hath, ...	179	Discipline		30
he condescends to humane frailties both in himselfe and others;	268	Priest 27		6
FRAILTY				
Yet since in frailty, cruelty, shrowd turns, ...	32	Sacrifice	W	177
FRAME				
Whose parts are as thy hand did frame;	26	The Altar		3
Meets in this frame, ...	26	The Altar		11
Immortall Love, authour of this great frame, ...	54	Love 1		1
Ties the whole frame, is Love	67	Ch.-floore		11
That her fine cobwebs did support the frame, ...	84	The World		3
For all thy frame and fabrick is within.	106	Sion		12
Oh loose this frame, this knot of man untie!	109	Home		61
A great affliction broke the little frame, ...	112	JESU		3
And bring my minde in frame:	172	23 Psalme		10

	PAGE	TITLE		LINE
FRESH				
Whence com'st thou, that thou art so fresh and fine?	77	Avarice		2
How fresh, O Lord, how sweet and clean	165	The Flower		1
From the first man in th' East, to fresh and new	168	The Sonne		9
Fresh and fine deities. They were at great cost,	193	Ch.-Milit.		109
Then shall thy Glory, fresh as flowers	213	L' Envoy	D	7
and so by continuall, and fresh bounties, unexpected to them,	245	Priest 12		1
Benefits please like flowers while they are fresh.	356	Proverbs	D	40
also I ride to Newmarket, and there lie a day or two for fresh Air;	365	Letters		7
FRESHER				
And made you look much fresher then before.	140	Ch.-rents		15
FRESHLY				
Grieve over freshly all thy pain?	145	Discharge		50
FRET				
Then to have hellish moths still gnaw and fret	69	Content		27
FRETS				
Mark all his wandrings, and enjoy his frets;	19	Ch.-Porch		315
FRETTING				
Fretting to death our other parts.	49	Repentance	W	30
But when debates and fretting jealousies	140	Ch.-rents		16
FRIAR (see also frier)				
FRIDAY				
Good Friday.	38	Good Fri.		T
so Friday his day of Humiliation, which he celebrates not only	241	Priest 10		37
He that sings on friday, will weepe on Sunday.	335	Proverbs		411
the next Friday it is tryed, and accordingly you shall hear.	371	Letters		17
FRIDAYES				
twice a Week, on Fridayes and Saturdayes, I must do so,	365	Letters		5
FRIEND (see also frend)				
Thy need, thine honour, and thy friend his due.	12	Ch.-Porch		152
Sometimes a friend, sometimes the engineer.	16	Ch.-Porch		242
Thy friend put in thy bosome: wear his eies	17	Ch.-Porch		271
If truth be with thy friend, be with them both:	19	Ch.-Porch		323
My bosome friend, if he blaspheme thy name,	35	Thanksgvng		25
Thus thinne and lean without a fence or friend,	47	Afflict.1		35
Dispatches from their friend.	52	H.Commun.		24
Writ by a friend, and with his bloud;	75	Sunday		4
The first Is straight, and our diurnall friend,	84	Coloss.		3
To his friend,	92	Antiphon 2		5
I would not use a friend, as I use Thee.	93	Unkindness		5
If any touch my friend, or his good name,	93	Unkindness		6
I could not use a friend, as I use Thee.	93	Unkindness		10
My friend may spit upon my curious floore:	93	Unkindness		11
I cannot use a friend, as I use Thee.	93	Unkindness		15
When that my friend pretendeth to a place,	94	Unkindness		16
Nor would I use a friend, as I use Thee.	94	Unkindness		20
Yet can a friend what thou hast done fulfill?	94	Unkindness		21
But while I bustled, I might heare a friend	103	Jordan 2		15
Deare Friend, sit down, the tale is long and sad:	129	Love unkn.		1
A friend did steal into my cup for good,	130	Love unkn.		43
Who took the debt upon him. Truly, Friend,	130	Love unkn.		61
Save one good Angell, which a friend had ti'd	142	Pilgrimage		17
Much troubled, till I heard a friend expresse,	143	Holdfast		11
And in them may drown a friend:	187	Dooms-day		22
Of kinde Expressions to his friend,	439	Walton 5		12
With kinde Expressions to his friend,	439	Walton 5	V	12
How sweet a friend was he, who being griev'd	439	Walton 5		15
When my dear Friend, could write no more,	439	walton 6		1
of his cure is sick, or afflicted with losse of friend, or estate,	249	Priest 15		14
is an occasion, my friend is an occasion, my Table is an occasion,	265	Priest 26		14
For if a friend who visits thee in thy sicknesse, and onely comforts	298	Cornaro		6
who not onely as a friend doth visit thee, but help thee!	298	Cornaro		9
by MR. GEORGE HERBERT to his friend the Translator of this Book.	304	Valdesso		T
When a friend askes, there is no to morrow.	322	Proverbs		32
Old wine, and an old friend, are good provisions.	325	Proverbs		136
The bit that one eates, no friend makes.	325	Proverbs		142
Milke saies to wine, welcome friend.	327	Proverbs		184
The best mirrour is an old friend.	331	Proverbs		296
Life without a friend is death without a witnesse.	334	Proverbs		385
An old friend, a new house.	334	Proverbs		400
An old friend is a new house.	334	Proverbs	V	400
When a knave is in a plumtree he hath neither friend nor kin.	338	Proverbs		507
Before you make a friend, eate a bushell of salt with him.	342	Proverbs		624
A kinsman, a friend, or whom you intreate,	347	Proverbs		794
The Rich knowes not who is his friend.	349	Proverbs		865
He quits his place well, that leaves his friend there.	350	Proverbs		875
Wine is a turne-coate (first a friend, then an enemy).	351	Proverbs		929
Trust no friend with that you need fear him if he were your enemy.	361	Proverbs	D	1169
Some had rather lose their friend then their Jest.	361	Proverbs	D	1170
FRIEND'S				
And are her sureties, ere they are a friends.	17	Ch.-Porch		282
Unto my friends intent and end.	93	Unkindness		4
FRIENDLINESS				
and their comfort, who are much cheered with such friendliness.	243	Priest 11		13
There is much preaching in this friendliness.	284	Priest 35		22
FRIENDS				
Thy children, kindred, friends upon thee call;	13	Ch.-Porch		161
Wisdome picks friends; civilitie playes the rest.	15	Ch.-Porch		227
Both friends should die, then hinder them to live.	17	Ch.-Porch		280
Betwixt my friends and me. They leave the starre,	28	Sacrifice		50
Betwixt my friends and me. They leave that starre,	28	Sacrifice	W	50

FRIENDS (cont'd)	PAGE	TITLE		LINE
Weep not, deare friends, since I for both have wept	31	Sacrifice		149
And more; for my friends die:	47	Afflict.1		32
Do not thy self or friends importune.	69	Content		34
To sell my life unto my friends or foes:	88	The Pearl		19
Or if hereafter any of my friends	152	The Bag		37
Like leaves about me: or like summer friends,	169	The Answer		4
Having observed in my time many of my friends, of excellent wit	291	Cornaro		1
have been an ornament to the world, and a comfort to their friends:	291	Cornaro		5
and the dayly importunitie of my friends, to adde something to my	295	Cornaro		20
to avoid obstinacie, and gratifie my friends, at length I yeelded,	296	Cornaro		7
that I may enjoy the sight & communication of my friends,	301	Cornaro		35
Many friends in generall, one in speciall.	330	Proverbs		281
Law sutes consume time, and mony, and rest, and friends.	347	Proverbs		776
It is good to have some friends both in heaven and hell.	359	Proverbs	D	1127
I wrong both my self, and also the confidence my Friends have in me;	364	Letters		8
in that I apprehend what my Friends would have been forward to say,	364	Letters		20
and I love my friends so well, as that if all things proved not well,	364	Letters		28
shee desires no more) shee will find friends to compell him to it.	368	Letters		25
FRIENDSHIP				
But love is lost, the way of friendship's gone,	17	Ch.-Porch		275
But love is lost, the art of friendship's gone,	17	Ch.-Porch	W	275
But yet their friendship is my enmitie:	29	Sacrifice		75
In friendship, first I think, if that agree,	93	Unkindness		2
FRIER				
The Frier preached against stealing,	345	Proverbs		737
FRIGHT				
O dreadfull Justice, what a fright and terrour	141	Justice 2		1
And on sinne doth cast the fright.	180	Invitation		18
FRIGHTETH				
Or a fir'd beacon frighteth from his ditties.	16	Ch.-Porch		250
FRIGHTING				
With noises confused frighting the day:	29	Sacrifice		103
FROGS				
Frogs marry fish and flesh; bats, bird and beast;	121	Providence		135
Gossips are frogs, they drinke and talke.	330	Proverbs		275
FROM				
Yet not mine neither: for from thee they came,	5	Dedication		2
Redeem truth from his jawes: if souldier,	10	Ch.-Porch		87
Redeem truth from his chawes: if souldier,	10	Ch.-Porch	W	87
This losse springs chiefly from our education.	10	Ch.-Porch		97
From his Ecliptick line: becken the skie.	12	Ch.-Porch		137
Or a fir'd beacon frighteth from his ditties.	16	Ch.-Porch		250
Nothing from thine: in service, care, or coldnesse	16	Ch.-Porch		255
Rather then shew his cards.) Steal from his treasure	18	Ch.-Porch		298
Our blessings from us, and extreamly flout thee,	23	Ch.-Porch	W	413
To pick out treasures from an earthen pot.	23	Ch.-Porch		430
That brought the wise men of the East from farre.	28	Sacrifice		51
Then from one ruler to another bound	28	Sacrifice		53
From th' earth unto my brows, and bear the thrall:	32	Sacrifice		167
They strike my head, the rock from whence all store	32	Sacrifice		170
Alas! what have I stollen from you? Death.	34	Sacrifice		231
My God, my God, why dost thou part from me?	35	Thanksgvng		9
Though it be cold, hard, foul, from loving man	41	Sepulchre		23
And stop our sinnes from growing thick and wide,	44	H. Bapt.1		8
Thine own gift good, yet me from my wayes taking.	48	Afflict.1		54
From what life feeleth, Adams fall.	48	Repentance		12
Thou, who from me wast sold,	52	H.Commun.		3
Dispatches from their friend.	52	H.Commun.		24
He might to heav'n from Paradise go,	53	H.Commun.		35
As from one room t' another.	53	H.Commun.		36
Sprung from that beautie which can never fade;	54	Love 1		2
Sprung from the beautie which can never fade;	54	Love 1	W	2
Wrought our deliverance from th' infernall pit,	54	Love 1		12
A crumme of dust from heav'n to hell?	55	Temper 1		14
For when thou dost depart from hence,	56	Temper 2		11
But wee are falne from Heaven to Earth,	59	Whitsunday	W	13
He that first fell from his great birth	59	Whitsunday	W	15
But that from them joyes purle for ever	59	Whitsunday	W	22
Drop from above!	60	Grace		4
Drop from above!	60	Grace		8
Drop from above.	60	Grace		12
Drop from above.	60	Grace		16
Drop from above.	60	Grace		20
Drop from above.	61	Grace	W	20
Drop from above.	61	Grace		24
But brings a favour from above;	64	Even-song		31
How tame these ashes are, how free from lust,	65	Ch.-monum.		23
Comfort, I'le die; for if you poste from me,	66	Ch.-mus.		9
Comfort, I'le die; for if you part from me,	66	Ch.-mus.	W	9
Lord, who hast rais'd me from the mudd	68	Trin.Sun.	WC	1
From either pole unto the centre:	69	Content		18
From either pole unto the center:	69	Content	W	18
From private bodies, make as big a thunder,	69	Content		23
As those which rise from a huge King.	69	Content		24
Unpinne, or wrench from giving all their due.	72	Constancie		5
When the wide world runnes bias, from his will	73	Constancie		32
Bright spark; shot from a brighter place,	74	The Starre		1
Yet, if thou wilt from thence depart,	74	The Starre		5
So disengag'd from sinne and sicknesse,	74	The Starre		13
Leaping with thee from sev'n to sev'n,	77	Sunday		61

FROM (cont'd)	PAGE	TITLE		LINE
Till that we both, being toss'd from earth,	77	Sunday		62
Of his rich crown, from whcm lyes no appeal	78	Ang.&Sts.		22
Of his great crown, from whom lyes no appeal	78	Ang.&Sts.	W	22
Therefore we dare not from his garland steal,	78	Ang.&Sts.		24
Hast thou redeem'd us from the grave!	82	Ungratef.		2
Whose leaves first sheltred man from drought & dew,	84	The World		12
He views their stations, walks from doore to doore,	85	Vanitie 1		3
On purpose from the ventrous wretch;	85	Vanitie 1		11
What reason hath from nature borrowed,	88	The Pearl		3
What reason hath from nature purchased,	88	The Pearl	W	3
But thy silk twist let down from heav'n to me,	89	The Pearl		38
From the least spot or thought of blame.	93	Unkindness		9
Take one from ten, and what remains?	96	Charms & K		15
When clothes are taken from a chest of sweets	98	Mortific.		2
When cloths are taken from a chest of sweets	98	Mortific.	V	2
I here exclude the wrangler from thy treasure.	104	Obedience		15
I here shutt out the wrangler from thy treasure.	104	Obedience	W	15
Thraldome from those, who would not at a feast	107	Home		21
And dates her letters from thy face,	109	Brit. Ch.		5
Do not by hanging down break from the hand,	112	Dawning		11
O sacred Providence, who from end to end	116	Providence		1
To be commerce and trade from sunne to sunne.	120	Providence		108
My words take fire from my inflamed thoughts.	122	Sinnes rd.		6
My words take fire from my inflamed thoughts.	122	Sinnes rd.		7
While it detains us from our God.	123	Time		20
His life from foes.	125	Peace		26
Oh, what a thing is man! how farre from power,	127	Giddinesse		1
From setled peace and rest!	127	Giddinesse		2
A stream of bloud, which issu'd from the side	129	Love unkn.		14
Who was to take it from me, slipt his hand,	130	Love unkn.		34
Was cleare as heav'n, from whence it came.	135	Divinitie		14
That from small fires comes oft no small mishap.	139	Artillerie		4
Expell good motions from thy breast,	139	Artillerie		7
Lifting to heaven from this well of tears.	141	Justice 2		18
Dropping from heav'n, which doth both cleanse and close	147	Offering		20
From thee all pitie flows.	148	Longing		13
Were from my self, I had not half a word,	155	Assurance		22
From thy right eye,	158	Praise 3		32
Come from the earth, from whence those vessels come;	161	Priesthood		20
Thy distance from me; see my charge,	163	The Search		47
Farther from it then when I bent my bow;	165	The Crosse		26
Further from it then when I bent my bow;	165	The Crosse	V	26
Fetching their proofs ev'n from the very bone;	167	Dotage		11
From the first man in th' East, to fresh and new	168	The Sonne		9
Of sov'raigne tears, springing from true remorse:	170	Water-crs.		8
Sprung from thine eye, did work within my soul,	172	The Glance		14
And can hit from farre.	179	Discipline		24
O what sweetnesse from the bowl	181	Banquet		7
Is some starre (fled from the sphere)	181	Banquet		10
Farre from court,	182	Banquet		41
From my first entrance in,	188	Love 3		4
Almightie Lord, who from thy glorious throne	190	Ch.-Milit.		1
Spices come from the East; so did thy Spouse,	190	Ch.-Milit.		13
To bring the other Ark from Canaan.	190	Ch.-Milit.		20
From Greece to Rome she went, subduing those	191	Ch.-Milit.	W	61
The great heart stoops, and taketh from the dust	192	Ch.-Milit.		67
From times great Chronicle, and hither sent.	192	Ch.-Milit.		96
From Greece he went to Rome: and as before	194	Ch.-Milit.		139
From this contagious infidelitie.	194	Ch.-Milit.		158
From Egypt he took pettie deities,	195	Ch.-Milit.		177
From Greece oracular infallibilities,	195	Ch.-Milit.		178
And from old Rome the libertie of pleasure,	195	Ch.-Milit.		179
From all these places, but at divers times,	195	Ch.-Milit.		185
From Egypt Anchorisme and retirednesse,	195	Ch.-Milit.		187
Learning from Greece, from old Rome statelinesse:	195	Ch.-Milit.		188
Who brought his doctrins & his deeds from Rome	195	Ch.-Milit.	W	201
And to defray his journey from the east.	196	Ch.-Milit.		214
By carrying first their gold from them away:	197	Ch.-Milit.		250
Thou drivest from his seat.	200	H. Commun.	W	24
Thou took'st that pledg from mee:	201	H. Commun.	W	45
From Heaven, through Earth, to Hell.	202	Trin.Sun.	W	14
This holy Cable's from all storms secure.	439	Walton 5	V	10
How know you that our teares proceed from woe	210	Paradox	D	15
And not from better fate,	210	Paradox	D	16
From wante of breath proceede,	210	Paradox	D	20
Not from excesse, and therefore doe we spende	210	Paradox	D	21
And though starres shott from heaven loose their light,	211	Bohemia	D	9
Yet thy brave beames excluded from their right	211	Bohemia	D	10
Splendour from darknes. So close sits the crowne	212	Bohemia	D	37
Call thee from out of that surrounded land,	213	Bohemia	D	61
From Holland saile into the Maine:	213	L' Envoy	D	10
If ever Tears did flow from Eyes,	213	Convert	D	1
My Eyes, from whence these Tears did spring,	214	Convert	D	6
are like the chaff, which from the face	215	Psalm I	D	14
and from us cast their cords away.	215	Psalm II	D	8
and straight ye perish from the way:	216	Psalm II	D	30
me from his holy hill:	216	Psalm III	D	10
save me, my God, from thrall:	217	Psalm III	D	18
But now from me depart away,	220	Psalm VI	D	19
Yea, he my prayer from on high	220	Psalm VI	D	23

FROM (cont'd)	PAGE	TITLE	LINE
From all that persecute my life, ...	220	Psalm VII D	3
Remote from ours, then Spaine frcm Britains shoare. . . .	438	Lat.Trans.	4
For first, Man fell from God by disobedience.	225	Priest 1	4
and shall be so farre from that which they seek with their . .	226	Priest 2	34
When the Apostles would have called down fire from Heaven, . .	229	Priest 4	13
him then weary, and so he grows from not relishing, to loathing.	235	Priest 7	14
exercises, either from the time of the year, or from the State,	235	Priest 8	34
the time of the year, or from the State, or from God by a child born,	235	Priest 8	35
or from the State, or from God by a child born, or dead, . .	235	Priest 8	35
keepes the imagination from roving, puts on the whole Armour of God,	238	Priest 9	4
and arising from the improvement of things, which otherwise would be	241	Priest 10	23
that the prohibiting of flesh came from hot Ccuntreys, where both	242	Priest 10	16
miseries have a naturall priviledge, and exemption from all law.	245	Priest 12	30
but always in the close, before he departs from them: . . .	248	Priest 14	16
such as are from Gods generall prcvidence extended even to lillyes;	249	Priest 15	19
frcm his particular, to his Church;	249	Priest 15	20
from his promises, from the examples of all Saints, that ever were;	249	Priest 15	21
from Christ himself, perfecting our Redemption no other way,	249	Priest 15	22
from the Benefit of affliction, which softens, and works the stubborn	249	Priest 15	23
from the certainty both of deliverance, and reward, if we faint not;	249	Priest 15	25
from the miserable ccmparison of the moment of griefs here . .	249	Priest 15	26
so the hunger and thirst after it may come rather from themselves,	250	Priest 15	6
after it may come rather from themselves, then from his perswasion.	250	Priest 15	6
by withdrawing his bounty and courtesie from the parties offending,	254	Priest 20	23
especially since many remove from Parish to Parish, who like	255	Priest 21	19
with comparisons, and making much even of a word of truth from him.	256	Priest 21	15
When any one can distinguish the Sacramentall from common bread,	258	Priest 22	34
himself an unworthy one, and therefore differs from other Feasters:	259	Priest 22	16
poorest man of the Parish detain but a pin unjustly from the richest,	260	Priest 23	15
but that they still fall from all compromises that have been made.	260	Priest 23	24
and this raiseth the action frcm the Shop, to the Church. . .	262	Priest 23	11
The Countrey Parson at spare times from action, standing on a hill,	264	Priest 26	3
there are some persons, who abstain not even from known sins;	264	Priest 26	10
to themselves, and witty to others who shall reprove them from it.	264	Priest 26	14
because of the suddain passing from that which was just now lawfull,	264	Priest 26	20
when his storing, which was even now good, passeth from good to bad.	264	Priest 26	30
I am more bound to abstain from those, which by mine own experience I	266	Priest 26	24
then from those which by a Common tradition, and vulgar knowledge are	266	Priest 26	25
so as to disable themselves frcm a fit discharging either of Divine	266	Priest 26	29
as that it is not meate or drinke that hinders them from working.	266	Priest 26	36
or if he have any leisure to lcok off from thence, he meets . .	267	Priest 27	30
hath the place its dignity frcm the Ecclesiasticall Laws only,	269	Priest 29	32
(who playes his part sometimes in drawing Gods Servants from him,	272	Priest 31	17
The reason of this assertion is taken from the nature of man,	274	Priest 32	18
our Saviours selling is so far from crossing Saint Pauls working,	275	Priest 32	3
Could men finde out this delight, they would seldome be from home;	275	Priest 32	35
These are so far frcm deterring any good man from the place,	276	Priest 32	22
These are so far from deterring any good man from the place,	276	Priest 32	23
kindle them rather to redeem the Dignity either from true faults,	276	Priest 32	24
which are brought from thence to the House but in generall. . .	277	Priest 32	13
freed for a while from temptation, in a quiet sweetnesse seeks how	279	Priest 33	5
we are assaulted with temptations either from within or from without.	280	Priest 34	4
the first taken from Nature, the second from the Law, the third from	281	Priest 34	16
taken from Nature, the second from the Law, the third frcm Grace.	281	Priest 34	16
taken from Nature, the second frcm the Law, the third from Grace.	281	Priest 34	17
though unused a proof of Divinity taken from thence, that . .	281	Priest 34	33
the custome, that may be severed from the good, he pares the apple,	283	Priest 35	32
and those that withdraw, and sever themselves from it, he mislikes,	284	Priest 35	11
he is so farre from condemning such assemblies, that he rather	284	Priest 35	13
1 Sam. 1. 18. though it came from a man disallowed by God: . .	285	Priest 36	22
Now blessing differs from prayer, in assurance, because it is	286	Priest 36	6
so that they are so far frcm craving this benefit from their ghostly	286	Priest 36	13
they are so far from craving this benefit from their ghostly Father,	286	Priest 36	13
the clean contrary, even from superstition to coldnes, and Atheism.	286	Priest 36	17
So that it is so far from being a fault to discover such offenders,	287	Priest 37	38
passing from the ear to the heart, from the heart to the life	289	Priest	30
the ear to the heart, from the heart to the life and conversation:	289	Priest	30
From this ill temper there remained little else to be expected of me,	291	Cornaro	24
whereas my life seemed as farre from it by Nature, as it was neare it	291	Cornaro	27
was thus affected [afflicted] from the thirtie fifth yeare of my age	292	Cornaro	1
and abhorring from so sudden an end, and finding my self continually	292	Cornaro	18
a yeare I was not onely freed from all those evils which had so long	293	Cornaro	20
because frcm the time that I was made whole, I never since departed	293	Cornaro	24
I never since departed from my setled course of Sobrietie, . .	293	Cornaro	25
from hatred and melancholie, and other perturbations of the minde,	293	Cornaro	35
keep a fit proportion, shall receive little hurt from other excesses.	294	Cornaro	5
a temperate life, can receive little hurt from other inconveniences.	295	Cornaro	15
but that he shall ever after live free from diseases, if he will keep	297	Cornaro	19
both that they may preserve themselves from diseases, which hinder	299	Cornaro	19
and I abstain from fruit, and fish, and the like, because they hurt	300	Cornaro	9
and well-contented, free from all troubles and troublesome thoughts;	300	Cornaro	37
Yet I am sure, that my end is farre from me:	303	Cornaro	25
but not as a naked Word severed from God, but as the Word of God:	307	Valdesso	1
And in so doing they doe not sever their trust from God. . .	307	Valdesso	2
for I can no more free my selfe from actuall sinnes after Baptisme,	308	Valdesso	3
The exemption from both, is by the Grace of God.	308	Valdesso	5
or relation from others, is not that which filleth the heart with joy	309	Valdesso	1
All the discourse from this line [place] till the end of this Chapter	311	Valdesso	20
and that by restraining him from what he would not have him doe.	313	Valdesso	22
So likewise are the godly in some sort exempt from Lawes, . .	315	Valdesso	33

FROM (cont'd)	PAGE	TITLE		LINE
How the godly are exempt from Laws is a known point among Divines,	316	Valdesso		31
And miracle-working as it may be severed from justifying faith,	319	Valdesso		13
All came from, and will goe to others.	322	Proverbs		41
From a chollerick man withdraw a little;	326	Proverbs		164
from him that saies nothing, for ever.	326	Proverbs		164
It takes much from the account, to which his sin doth amount.	327	Proverbs		192
Hee wrongs not an old man that steales his supper from him. . .	331	Proverbs		311
A rugged stone growes smooth from hand to hand.	332	Proverbs		316
He that would be well, needs not goe from his owne house. . .	336	Proverbs		442
To take the nuts from the fire with the dogges foot. . . .	341	Proverbs		584
God keepe me from foure houses, ...	348	Proverbs		816
Hee payes too deare for honey that licks it from thorns. . .	350	Proverbs	V	880
What one day gives us, another takes away from us. . . .	359	Proverbs	D	1111
Vertue flies from the heart of a Mercenary man.	360	Proverbs	D	1133
I understand by a Letter from my Brother Henry, that he hath bought	366	Letters		29
upon condition that I should surcease from all title to it, . .	367	Letters		9
to those busnesses which justly excuse him from writing at this time,	367	Letters		31
there are come agents hither from the low-Cuntries to treat of divers	368	Letters		5
& therfore deferr it untill they heare farther from the States.	368	Letters		15
spirituall livings into their owne hands, & taking it from the Popes:	368	Letters		28
I have sent you here inclosed a Letter from our Master in my behalf,	369	Letters		25
I long to hear from Sir Francis, I pray Sir send the Letter you	370	Letters		5
Sir send the Letter you receive from him to me as soon as you can,	370	Letters		6
since this place being civil may divert me too much from Divinity,	370	Letters		20
At my last parting from you, I was the better content because I was	372	Letters		14
but you are freed from that fear, who have already abundantly	373	Letters		11
trouble not your selves, God is at hand to deliver us from all, or,	374	Letters		30
but difficulties are so farr from cooling christians, that they whett	376	Letters		11
I humbly thank him, & am so far from giving you cause, to apology,	378	Letters		9
I refuse not advice from the meanest, that creeps upon Gods earth,	378	Letters		11
much less can I disesteem it from you, whome I esteem to be God's	378	Letters		14
a Letter, from My Brother, Sir Henry H: of the blessed Success,	378	Letters		30
It is so long since I heard from you, that I long to heare both how	379	Letters		23
therefore entertaine it accordingly from Your very affectionate bro;	379	Letters		26
slight glories, which wee raise from bookes, and painefull industrie.	443	Oration		1
FRONTIRE				
A faire wife and a frontire Castle breede quarrels.	324	Proverbs		103
FROST				
As frost-nipt sunnes look sadly.	81	Christmas		30
What frost to that? what pole is not the zone, ...	166	The Flower		32
The evening praises the day, and the morning a frost. . . .	342	Proverbs	V	635
He that is surprized with the first frost	354	Proverbs		992
FROST-NIPT				
As frost-nipt sunnes look sadly.	81	Christmas		30
FROST'S				
Before I were by frosts extremitie	57	Employm. 1		3
FROSTS				
With showres and frosts, with love & aw, ...	85	Vanitie 1		25
The healthy frosts with summer-fruits compare.	119	Providence		100
Both frosts and thoughts do nip, ...	131	Mans medly		28
They would great frosts and snows destroy:	138	The Size		40
The late-past frosts tributes of pleasure bring.	165	The Flower		4
The late-past frosts tributes of pleasures bring.	165	The Flower	V	4
The first and last frosts are the worst.	352	Proverbs		954
FROTH				
The stormie working soul spits lies and froth.	9	Ch.-Porch		76
FROWN				
And fathers smile for you, to feel his frown:	34	Sacrifice		223
And fathers smile to feele for you his frown:	34	Sacrifice	W	223
For which ye wrangle, made them turn their frown	71	Humilitie		28
See the smooth face of God, without a frown	77	Ang.&Sts.		2
And the least frown of thine is shown?	166	The Flower		35
FROWNE				
About thy temples that the furious frowne	212	Bohemia	D	38
FROWNS				
Unfold thy forehead gather'd into frowns:	112	Dawning		3
FRUIT				
Man stole the fruit, but I must climbe the tree;	33	Sacrifice		202
Or cannot leaves, but fruit, be signe	38	Good Fri.		11
To fruit or shade: at least some bird would trust	48	Afflict.1		59
The fruit of this, the next worlds bud, ...	75	Sunday		2
Some fruit for him that dressed me.	79	Employm.2		25
And more: He is a tree, yet bears no fruit;	91	Man		8
And more: He is a tree, yet bears more fruit;	91	Man	W	8
I have their fruit and more.	128	Bunch Gr.		23
To him I brought a dish of fruit one day, ...	129	Love unkn.		6
Quitting the fruit, seiz'd on my heart alone, ...	129	Love unkn.		12
To thee both fruit and order OW.	132	Paradise		3
Can blast my fruit, or bring me HARM, ...	133	Paradise		5
What I have lost with cordiall fruit?	153	The Collar		9
Not so, my heart: but there is fruit, ...	153	The Collar		17
A sonne is light and fruit; a fruitfull flame	168	The Sonne		7
Thou saist, this fruit is mine.	184	The Elixer	W	12
with timely fruit still laden stand:	214	Psalm I	D	10
as a necessary evidence and fruit of their faith, at that time	249	Priest 15		33
when they meet with good fruit, get a graffe of the tree, . . .	276	Priest 32		32
The fruit of this blessing good Hannah found, and received with great	285	Priest 36		20
cool wines pleased my taste best, as also melons, and other fruit;	293	Cornaro		12
No man is forbidden to eat fruit or fish, which I eat not: . . .	300	Cornaro		7
and I abstain from fruit, and fish, and the like, because they hurt	300	Cornaro		9

FURTHER (cont'd)	PAGE	TITLE		LINE
May at his perill further go.	25	Superlim		8
Nay, after death their spite shall further go;	34	Sacrifice		245
Then shall the fall further the flight in me.	43	East.wings		10
Then shall my fall further the flight in me.	43	East.wings	W	10
Who dives on further may find Hell.	97	Charms & K	W	22
My hill was further: so I flung away,	142	Pilgrimage		31
They ask enough; why shouldst thou further go?	145	Discharge		26
Further from it then when I bent my bow;	165	The Crosse	V	26
he goes no further for any entertainment, lest he goe into the world,	241	Priest 10		19
and instructs them further in that skill, shewing them how acceptable	247	Priest 14		17
rather then to those that are further, where things are otherwise	253	Priest 19		27
or if he depend on God further, even till he imbarn his corn,	271	Priest 30		32
their peace and mirth have carryed them further then this moderation,	280	Priest 34		34
to harden himselfe, and to further his exercises of Mortification.	284	Priest 35		36
A Dwarfe on a Gyants shoulder sees further of the two.	322	Proverbs		50
of which is doubted whether it have some further meaning.	368	Letters		19
FURTHERS				
and furthers them when hee is gone, in their imployment;	247	Priest 14		14
FURTHEST				
Each part may call the furthest, brother:	91	Man	V	16
aim in all things, how I may help others to the furthest of my power.	301	Cornaro		8
God is at the end, when we thinke he is furthest off it.	341	Proverbs		598
FURY (see also furie)				
FUTURE				
What ever future sinnes should me miscall,	44	H. Bapt.1		13
By way of imprest, all my future mone.	62	Afflict.2		15
Gods works are wide, and let in future times;	128	Bunch Gr.		13
And for the future time art heir	137	The Size		11
If, though thou didst not beat thy future brow,	144	Discharge		23
Of future depths, but drink the cleare and good.	145	Discharge		28
And care for future chances, cannot go	145	Discharge		38
On future grief, do not remove it thence,	145	Discharge		43
For future times, the droppings of the stock	154	Glimpse		24
(The marks of future bane) shall fill our cup	197	Ch.-Milit.		239
by present rewards, or punishments, more then by future.	254	Priest 20		33
pains with them, that hee may lay the foundation of future Blessings.	258	Priest 22		31
and in future for his children, hardly perceives when his storing	264	Priest 26		27
to lay the platform of my future life, and shall I then be fain	364	Letters		12
either by engaging my future Annuity, or any other way,	365	Letters		21
And above all, If any care of future things molest you?	374	Letters		13
GAD				
Gad not abroad at ev'ry quest and call	68	Content		5
GAIN (see also gayning)				
Turn their eyes hither, who shall make a gain:	5	Dedication		5
Lust and wine plead a pleasure, avarice gain:	8	Ch.-Porch		57
Lust and wine plead a pleasure, cheating gain:	8	Ch.-Porch	W	57
Lest gaining gain on thee, and make thee dimme	13	Ch.-Porch		164
Play not for gain, but sport. Who playes for more	14	Ch.-Porch		193
Fast when thou wilt; but then 'tis gain, not losse.	22	Ch.-Porch		396
Yet my Disciples sleep: I cannot gain	27	Sacrifice		29
While mortall love doth all the title gain!	54	Love 1		5
While mortall love does all the title gain!	54	Love 1	W	5
Suck ev'ry letter, and a hony gain,	58	H.Script.1		2
To gain at harvest an eternall Treasure.	85	Coloss.		10
To gain thy thirds and little part.	99	Decay		15
And quickly gain, for each inch lost, an ell.	103	Prayer 2		24
Brings thy Saviours death no gain?	114	Businesse		36
False gain before the true,	171	Self-cond.		15
Yet that he might the better gain all nations,	195	Ch.-Milit.		183
GAINE				
Least gaining gaine on thee, & fill thy hart	13	Ch.-Porch	W	164
That wee may gaine by crosses.	53	H.Commun.	W	40
Lord that I may the Sunns perfection gaine	57	Employm. 1	W	23
Bee there, to thy truth, & my gaine	200	H. Commun.	W	11
shewing that they do not loose, or go lesse, but gaine by it;	270	Priest 29		10
Sometimes the best gaine is to lose.	328	Proverbs		224
If you loose your time, you cannot get mony nor gaine.	332	Proverbs		320
To gaine teacheth how to spend.	337	Proverbs		455
Every one fastens where there is gaine.	338	Proverbs		496
It's an ill aire where wee gaine nothing.	350	Proverbs		872
GAIN'D				
When I had gain'd the brow and top,	142	Pilgrimage		22
The sky his azure mantle gain'd.	151	The Bag		15
GAINED				
None but the wise or strong had gained it:	50	Faith		26
But it is gained first, by choosing texts of Devotion,	233	Priest 7		26
and cannot be gained, but that they still fall from all compromises	260	Priest 23		24
which gained me this experience, that I perceived, that they had no	293	Cornaro		38
Hee that knowes what may bee gained in a day never steales.	336	Proverbs		445
GAINES				
of making the best of the day, and contriving it to his best gaines.	235	Priest 8		21
A Marchant that gaines not, looseth.	322	Proverbs		47
He that looseth is Marchant as well as he that gaines.	339	Proverbs		518
At the games end we shall see who gaines.	339	Proverbs		538
He that gaines well and spends well, needes no count booke.	349	Proverbs		853
He that gaines well and spends well, needes no count books.	349	Proverbs	V	853
The deafe gaines the injury.	351	Proverbs		927
GAINFULL				
this life, who hath promised, that Godlinesse shall be gainfull:	254	Priest 20		20
they are most eminent, is the most gainfull way of Conversation.	260	Priest 23		7

GAINFULLEST	PAGE	TITLE		LINE
is the finest place in the University, though not the gainfullest;	369	Letters		31
GAINING				
Lest gaining gain on thee, and make thee dimme	13	Ch.-Porch		164
Least gaining gaine on thee, & fill thy hart	13	Ch.-Porch	W	164
Sure thou wilt joy, by gaining me	74	The Starre		29
GAINS				
Which he might fall in by companions, gains.	24	Ch.-Porch		436
In vies of favours whether partie gains,	88	The Pearl		13
Ten still, if sermons go for gains.	96	Charms & K		16
Ten, if a Sermon goe for gains.	96	Charms & K	W	16
Cannot give the name of gains	114	Dialogue		6
What the gains in having thee	114	Dialogue		13
This breathing would with gains by sweetning me	175	The Odour		26
GALE				
The day or night: that is the gale, this th' harbour;	64	Even-song		26
A gale to bring me sooner to my blisse.	73	Afflict.3		12
GALEN				
This Galen confirms, when he sayes, that immoderate heats and colds,	294	Cornaro		6
this I answer, that Galen kept it, and held it for the best Physick:	298	Cornaro		38
By suppers more have beene killed then Galen ever cured.	330	Proverbs		272
By suppers more are killed then Galen ever cured.	330	Proverbs	V	272
GALL				
But hony is their gall, brightnesse their night:	30	Sacrifice		111
They gave me vineger mingled with gall,	34	Sacrifice		237
They give me vineger mingled with gall,	34	Sacrifice	W	237
GALLANT				
Then march on gallant: get substantiall worth.	15	Ch.-Porch		209
A gallant flower,	125	Peace		14
He grew a gallant, and would needs foretell	193	Ch.-Milit.		129
Now because the onely opposer to this Doctrine is the Gallant,	275	Priest 32		6
But if the young Gallant think these Courses dull, and phlegmatick,	278	Priest 32		4
GALLANTS				
If reason move not Gallants, quit the room,	8	Ch.-Porch		43
GAME				
If yet thou love game at so deere a rate,	14	Ch.-Porch		199
Game is a civil gunpowder, in peace	14	Ch.-Porch		203
The world is theirs; they two play out the game,	54	Love 1		10
Folly and Sinne play all his game.	100	Miserie		3
Folly and Sinne play out his game.	100	Miserie	W	3
And such poore game. Thence he to Greece doth passe,	193	Ch.-Milit.		123
And such small game. Thence he to Greece doth passe,	193	Ch.-Milit.	W	123
That though our Saviour did destroy the game,	194	Ch.-Milit.		146
GAME'S				
At the games end we shall see who gaines.	339	Proverbs		538
GAMESTERS				
Learn this, that hath old gamesters deerely cost:	14	Ch.-Porch		200
Learn this, it hath old gamesters deerely cost:	14	Ch.-Porch	W	200
GAMING				
Gaming, women, and wine, while they laugh they make men pine.	341	Proverbs		604
GAMINGS				
to whore, to scoffe, to revile, to all sorts of gamings.	274	Priest 32		12
GAMSTERS				
Gamsters and race-horses never last long.	346	Proverbs		751
GAPE				
The dishes of thy ballance seem'd to gape,	141	Justice 2		7
GAPING				
or slubbering fashion, gaping, or scratching the head, or spitting	231	Priest 6		31
GARD'NER				
Thou art a gard'ner now, and more,	123	Time		16
GARD'NERS				
The windes grew gard'ners, and the clouds good fountains.	120	Providence		116
GARDEN				
Or that the garden, this the grove.	64	Even-song		28
In Gods rich garden: that is bare,	75	Sunday		27
And made a garden there for those	76	Sunday		41
He was a garden in a Paradise:	102	Miserie		70
Then went I to a garden, and did spy	125	Peace		13
Take of this grain, which in my garden grows,	125	Peace		37
Thou hast a garden for us, where to bide.	167	The Flower		46
Strength levels grounds, Art makes a garden there;	192	Ch.-Milit.		87
Here Sinne took heart, and for a garden-bed	193	Ch.-Milit.		127
And Paris garden. Then let there perfume	212	Bohemia	D	51
but clean, whole, and sweet, as sweet as his garden can make;	241	Priest 10		13
or a stranger, his garden or orchard supplyes it, or his barne,	241	Priest 10		18
stead of drugs of the same nature, and to make the garden the shop:	261	Priest 23		30
but preferrs her garden and fields before all outlandish gums.	262	Priest 23		4
A garden must be lookt unto and drest as the body.	325	Proverbs		129
Feare keepes the garden better then the gardiner.	330	Proverbs		268
The market is the best garden.	346	Proverbs		743
You may be on land, yet not in a garden.	353	Proverbs		964
Hee that is in a Taverne thinkes he is in a vine-garden.	353	Proverbs		989
GARDEN-BED				
Here Sinne took heart, and for a garden-bed	193	Ch.-Milit.		127
GARDENS				
In cities, theatres, gardens, parks, and courts:	40	Redemption		11
In grottos, gardens, Palaces & Courts	40	Redemption	W	11
Gardens of Gods, which ev'ry yeare did grow,	193	Ch.-Milit.		108
monuments of his Doctrine, remembring in gardens, his mustard-seed,	261	Priest 23		22
I enjoy also my gardens, and those divers, parted with rills	301	Cornaro		15
where also I have fountains and gardens, and a very convenient house.	301	Cornaro		18

GARDENS (cont'd)	PAGE	TITLE		LINE
I survey palaces, gardens, and antiquities, publick fabricks,	302	Cornaro		3
The charges of building and making of gardens are unknowne.	335	Proverbs		412
GARDINER				
childe, or servant, as a Gardiner doth in a choice tree.	275	Priest 32		34
Feare keepes the garden better then the gardiner.	330	Proverbs		268
Lawly fifty shillings To Mr Gardiner tenn pound MS. that the five	383	G.H.'s Will		20
GARLAND				
Which in thy garland I should fill, were mine	57	Employm. 1		7
And garland-streams.	74	The Starre		32
Therefore we dare not from his garland steal,	78	Ang.&Sts.		24
To make a garland for inferiour power.	78	Ang.&Sts.	W	25
A wreathed garland of deserved praise,	185	A Wreath		1
One flower makes no garland.	339	Proverbs		521
GARLAND-STREAMS				
And garland-streams.	74	The Starre		32
GARLANDS				
No flowers, no garlands gay? all blasted?	153	The Collar		15
GARLICK				
Adoring garlick with an humble face,	193	Ch.-Milit.		112
GARMENTS				
They part my garments, and by lot dispose	34	Sacrifice		241
His skinne, his garments bloudie be.	37	The Agonie		10
glorious shew is there, either of garments, or of any thing else?	442	Oration		32
GARNER				
None saies his Garner is full.	343	Proverbs		657
It's a wicked thing to make a dearth ones garner.	351	Proverbs		898
GARRISONS				
He left behinde him garrisons of sinnes	193	Ch.-Milit.		125
GASPETH				
My spirit gaspeth night and day.	107	Home		4
GATE				
Let thy almes go before, and keep heav'ns gate	21	Ch.-Porch		383
All equall are within the churches gate.	22	Ch.-Porch		408
A narrow way and little gate	44	H. Bapt.2		2
On Sunday heavens gate stands ope;	76	Sunday		33
GATES				
If thou wilt die, the gates of hell are broad:	9	Ch.-Porch		71
Of life, just at the gates of life and blisse?	28	Sacrifice		43
Take up within a cloisters gates.	69	Content		16
When a Lackey comes to hells doore, the devills locke the gates.	353	Proverbs		984
GATHER				
If all the hope and comfort that I gather,	155	Assurance		21
Addes to the unicn, as lights doe gather	212	Bohemia	D	36
but also to gather strength, which could not be but by meat & drink.	295	Cornaro		24
GATHER'D				
Unfold thy forehead gather'd into frowns:	112	Dawning		3
When that lay gather'd, thou didst broach the mountains:	120	Providence		114
GATHERED				
of the Priesthood may be plainly gathered both the Dignity thereof,	225	Priest 1		15
Call me not an olive, till thou see me gathered.	331	Proverbs		301
GATHERS				
Check the proud sea, ev'n when it swells and gathers.	118	Providence		48
out of which he gathers, in case he be ignorant himself,	260	Priest 23		11
He that speakes sowes, and he that holds his peace, gathers.	336	Proverbs		435
He that speakes sowes, and he that hears, gathers.	336	Proverbs	V	435
GAVE				
God gave thy soul brave wings; put not those feathers	9	Ch.-Porch		83
God gave them to thee under lock and key.	12	Ch.-Porch		144
Wisedome's a trimmer thing, then shop e're gave.	14	Ch.-Porch		188
For all the week thy food so oft he gave thee.	22	Ch.-Porch		392
They use that power against me, which I gave:	27	Sacrifice		11
Who by my spittle gave the blinde man eies,	31	Sacrifice		134
Who by my spittle gave that blinde man eies,	31	Sacrifice	W	134
Then with the reed they gave to me before,	32	Sacrifice		169
Then with the reed they gave mee heertofore,	32	Sacrifice	W	169
They gave me vineger mingled with gall,	34	Sacrifice		237
Who gave me eyes, and light, and power this day,	63	Even-song		2
Who gave me sight alone,	63	Even-song		5
Gave them about to all.	70	Humilitie		8
But since thy breath gave me both life and shape,	73	Afflict.3		7
I gave to Hope a watch of mine: but he	121	Hope		1
An anchor gave to me.	121	Hope		2
With that I gave a viall full of tears:	121	Hope		5
But all the doctrine, which he taught and gave,	135	Divinitie		13
Gave you a colour once; which when your foes	140	Ch.-rents		13
Here he gave up his life to pay our score.	151	The Bag		24
Gave her the highest place in all mens hearts.	191	Ch.-Milit.		50
He gave the Seale, and so left o're.	439	Walton 5		14
He gave his soul, and so gave o're.	439	Walton 5	V	14
He gave this Seal, and, so gave ore.	439	walton 6		2
My Heart, that gave fond Thoughts their Food,	214	Convert	D	16
gave them love fcr love, even the son of his love out of his bosome	283	Priest 34		16
whereupon all gave me for dead.	296	Cornaro		22
I gave the mouse a hole, and she is become my heire.	324	Proverbs		94
who because of his importunities gave him a reward, but not so great	368	Letters		32
Your last Letter gave me Earthly preferment, and kept Heavenly	372	Letters		34
GAV'ST				
At first thou gav'st me milk and sweetnesses;	47	Afflict.1		19
With one small sigh thou gav'st me th' other day	108	Home		43

	PAGE	TITLE	LINE
GAVEST			
Defrauding thee, who gavest two for one.	82	Ungratef.	30
GAY			
No point of honour, or gay suit,	69	Quidditie	2
Full of glorie and gay weeds,	71	Frailtie	13
That was requir'd to make us gay,	76	Sunday	55
Neither too mean, nor yet too gay,	109	Brit. Ch.	8
No flowers, no garlands gay? all blasted?	153	The Collar	15
Grow green and gay,	162	The Search	10
For we do now behold thee gay and glad,	186	Death	17
GAYNESSES			
and such like Gaynesses, which will please a young man well.	370	Letters	4
GAYNING			
Learne weeping, and thou shalt laugh gayning.	325	Proverbs	127
GAZE			
and of theirs also who gaze upon them when they come in,	232	Priest 6	10
GAZER			
Bids the rash gazer wipe his eye:	87	Vertue	6
GAZING			
talking, or sleeping, or gazing, or leaning, or halfe-kneeling,	231	Priest 6	24
GEERE			
And all in sport to geere at me.	110	The Quip	4
GEESE			
When the Foxe preacheth, beware your geese.	332	Proverbs	337
If all fooles wore white Caps, wee should seeme a flock of geese.	338	Proverbs	513
To seek these things is lost labour; Geese in an oyle pot,	361	Proverbs	D 1163
GENERALL			
Besides this generall provision, he hath other times of opening his	245	Priest 12	6
These are the Parsons generall aims in his Circuit;	249	Priest 14	10
such as are from Gods generall providence extended even to lillyes;	249	Priest 15	19
and driving of their generall Schoole rules ever to the smallest	265	Priest 26	36
knows well, that both for the generall ignominy which is cast upon	268	Priest 28	10
but a generall also of the diseases of the time, that so,	274	Priest 32	5
or hath generall Propositions to the whole Towne or Hamlet,	276	Priest 32	4
which are brought from thence to the House but in generall.	277	Priest 32	14
The other in generall, in the Commination.	286	Priest 36	5
only by the generall Providence of God, as Socrates and Aristides,	308	Valdesso	12
A generall apprehension, or assent to the promises of the Gospell	308	Valdesso	34
revealing and applying the generall promises to every one in	309	Valdesso	4
difficulty of applying their generall rules to particular actions,	319	Valdesso	V 32
Many friends in generall, one in speciall.	330	Proverbs	281
GENERALLS			
for particulars ever touch, and awake more then generalls.	233	Priest 7	6
GENERALLY			
but generally he distributes it thus, To his Children he shewes more	241	Priest 10	8
and generally intimateth to the disaffected, or sick person,	250	Priest 15	4
These three rules generally comprehend the faults of eating,	266	Priest 26	12
The Countrey Parson is generally sad, because hee knows nothing	267	Priest 27	27
do it, then he that is generally learned, and was never sick.	278	Priest 33	29
and which are such, as that men generally account me happie.	300	Cornaro	33
of kindred bredd up, (which generally is very true,) yet I care not;	376	Letters	5
GENERATION			
that that generation should not passe, till all were fulfilled,	282	Priest 34	28
and ranked backbiters among the generation of the wicked,	287	Priest 37	24
GENTILE			
Though the Mastiffe be gentile, yet bite him not by the lippe.	325	Proverbs	V 132
GENTILES			
But to the Gentiles he bore crosse and all,	190	Ch.-Milit.	25
GENTILITY			
Gentility is nothing but Ancient Riches.	356	Proverbs	D 1033
GENTLE			
If stonie hearts will melt with gentle love.	29	Sacrifice	90
The gentle rising, which on either hand	67	Ch.-floore	7
Give me the pliant minde, whose gentle measure	69	Content	13
Times gentle admonition:	94	Life	9
A slender thread a gentle guest will tie.	154	Glimpse	20
Onely take this gentle rose,	177	The Rose	15
Take the gentle path.	178	Discipline	4
but after divers gentle admonitions, if they persevere,	232	Priest 6	13
and so between gentle reasoning, and pitying, he overcomes the evill:	269	Priest 28	14
but if after gentle, and neighbourly admonitions they still persist	270	Priest 29	19
and also an honourable Imployment of a Gentle, or Noble-man in	276	Priest 32	13
The gentle Hawke halfe mans her selfe.	322	Proverbs	30
A gentle houswife marres the houshold.	322	Proverbs	44
Though the Mastiffe be gentle, yet bite him not by the lippe.	325	Proverbs	132
Love makes all hard hearts gentle.	339	Proverbs	542
A gentle heart is tyed with an easie thread.	345	Proverbs	726
Say to pleasure, Gentle Eve, I will none of your apple.	360	Proverbs	D 1140
GENTLEMAN			
Hee that would be a Gentleman, let him goe to an assault.	350	Proverbs	878
it is no matter, for the Gentleman needs no incitation to love me.	369	Letters	28
GENTLEMAN'S			
A gentlemans grayhound, and a salt-box; seeke them at the fire.	327	Proverbs	205
GENTLEMEN			
For all Gentlemen, that are now weakned, and disarmed with sedentary	277	Priest 32	17
GENTLENESSE			
And vying malice with my gentlenesse,	29	Sacrifice	86
In the husband wisedome, in the wife gentlenesse.	343	Proverbs	658
GENTLY			
Nor wisdome neither: therefore gently move.	18	Ch.-Porch	312
Great is my sinne. Oh! gently treat	48	Repentance	2

GENTLY (cont'd)	PAGE	TITLE	LINE
Rain, do not hurt my flowers; but gently spend	120	Providence	117
Then to the streams that gently passe:	172	23 Psalme	7
of their answer, but gently and pausably, thinking what they say;	231	Priest 6	32
GENTRIE			
Thy Gentrie bleats, as if thy native cloth	10	Ch.-Porch	93
GENTRY			
If there be any of the gentry or nobility of the Parish, . .	232	Priest 6	7
GEORGE			
The AUTHOUR, Mr. G. H.	223	Priest	T
untill the Book grow to a compleat Pastorall. GEO. HERBERT. . .	224	Priest	17
by Lud. Cornarus, Translated into English by Mr. George Herbert.	291	Cornaro	T
A Copy of a letter written by MR. GEORGE HERBERT to his friend	304	Valdesso	T
OUTLANDISH PROVERBS SELECTED By Mr. G. H.	319	Proverbs	T
Selected By Mr George Herbert, Late Orator	356	Proverbs D	T
and after my manner, Your most obedient Servant, GEORGE HERBERT.	364	Letters	5
for I am sure you love Your faithfullest Servant, GEORGE HERBERT.	365	Letters	27
mee in your letters, for I am your ever loving brother, G. HERBERT.	366	Letters	23
and yet still grow upon Your humblest Servant, GEORGE HERBERT.	367	Letters	17
favour to mee in pardoning Your most indebted kinsman GEORGE HERBERT.	369	Letters	6
I have both time and work to be Your extreme Servant, GEORGE HERBERT.	370	Letters	16
and paper enough, yet am I Your readiest Servant, GEORGE HERBERT.	370	Letters	34
will pardon the haste of Your humblest Servant, GEORGE HERBERT.	371	Letters	21
most heartily, affectionate Brother, and Servant, GEORGE HERBERT.	372	Letters	10
accept the good meaning of, Your most obedient Son, GEORGE HERBERT.	374	Letters	33
So prayes Your ever loving brother, G. HERBERT.	376	Letters	22
Your most faithful Servant in Christ Jesu, GEORGE HERBERT. . .	377	Letters	11
every good worke, to the joy of your ever loving brother, G. HERBERT.	377	Letters	29
great Joy of Your Brother & Servant in Christ Jesus GEORGE HERBERT.	378	Letters	29
G. HERBERT. Bemerton. My wife's and neeces' service to you. . .	379	Letters	28
The Will of George Herbert	382	G.H.'s Will	T
I George Herbert commending my soule and body to Almightie God that	382	G.H.'s Will	1
George Herbert (testes Nathaniell Bostocke, Elizabeth Burden)	382	G.H.'s Will	33
To Mr George Herbert one hundred pound To Mrs Beatrice Herbert forty	383	G.H.'s Will	7
The Oration of Master George Herbert, Orator of the Universitie	441	Oration	T
GERMAN'S			
The Germans wit is in his fingers.	322	Proverbs	36
The Germans wit lies in his fingers.	322	Proverbs V	36
GERMANES			
the Germanes in the deede, the French after the deede. . . .	352	Proverbs	947
GERMANIE			
At length to Germanie, still westward bending, ...	192	Ch.-Milit.	81
Spain in the Empire shar'd with Germanie, ...	192	Ch.-Milit.	89
GERMANY			
Or let him travel into Germany, and France, and observing . .	278	Priest 32	8
GERSON			
And Gerson, a spirituall man, wisheth all to incline rather to too	267	Priest 26	12
GESTURES			
and using all other gestures which may expresse a hearty, . .	231	Priest 6	3
Great Horse, or exercise some of his Military gestures [Postures].	277	Priest 32	17
GET			
Never was scraper brave man. Get to live;	12	Ch.-Porch	153
Then march on gallant: get substantiall worth.	15	Ch.-Porch	209
Get a sharp wife, a servant that will lowre.	15	Ch.-Porch	213
Get a good stock of these, then draw the card	18	Ch.-Porch	293
My severall sinnes their sorrows get;	39	Good Fri.	18
My flesh get on; yet let her sister	44	H. Bapt.2	12
Which when I could not get, I thought it here:	50	Faith	10
Yet can these not get over to my soul, ...	52	H.Commun.	13
Till it get wing, and flie away with thee.	59	Whitsunday	4
Till I get wing to fly away with thee.	59	Whitsunday W	4
Get me a standing there, and place	74	The Starre	21
Away; I must get up and see.	108	Home	34
Know their home, and get them gone:	113	Businesse	4
Get without repining;	115	Dialogue	26
Springs vent their streams, and by expense get store: . . .	119	Providence	71
When yet some places could no moisture get, ...	120	Providence	115
An answer get.	132	The Storm	16
Cry out, Get hence, ...	136	Ephes.	14
Where shall I get me eyes enough to weep, ...	140	Ch.-rents	25
Unlesse they get new conduits, new supplies	164	Grief	7
whose aim and labour must be not only to get knowledg, but to subdue	226	Priest 2	9
coveteousnesse, neither being greedy to get, nor nigardly to keep,	227	Priest 3	17
that they get a delight in it, and enter favour with God, . . .	239	Priest 10	28
I am inclined, as not to get out of that sicknesse, when I am in it,	242	Priest 10	37
if he once get the skill of it, will draw out of ignorant and silly	256	Priest 21	19
whether he could get out of the ditch alone, or whether he needed	257	Priest 21	8
we must not be idle, but labour to get more, that we may give more,	275	Priest 32	1
with good fruit, get a graffe of the tree, inriching their Orchard,	276	Priest 32	32
that I can easily get on horseback without the advantage . .	300	Cornaro	35
Make hast to an ill way that you may get out of it. . . .	325	Proverbs	124
If you loose your time, you cannot get mony nor gaine. . . .	332	Proverbs	320
Little dogs start the Hare, the great get her.	341	Proverbs	593
You cannot make the fire so low but it will get out. . . .	353	Proverbs	965
Paines to get, care to keep, feare to lose.	353	Proverbs	975
Without danger we cannot get beyond danger.	354	Proverbs	1010
If gold knew what gold is, gold would get gold I wis. . . .	354	Proverbs	1012
I hope I shall get this place without all your London helps,	370	Letters	7
her own hands (& promising to get her Son to doe as much) with some	379	Letters	3
GETS			
Frailtie gets pardon by submissivenesse;	8	Ch.-Porch	51

GIVE (cont'd)	PAGE	TITLE	LINE
If thou shalt give me wit, it shall appeare,	36	Thanksgvng	43
May give a disentangled state and free:	36	Reprisall	6
Though he give light, & th' East perfume;	42	Easter	24
You give us teares to wash them: lett those beams	44	H. Bapt.1 W	7
Or else give tears to drown them, as they grow.	44	H. Bapt.1	9
Give me my captive soul, or take	52	H.Commun.	25
(Thy workmanship) and give thee share in neither.	54	Love 1	8
Lord place me in thy consort; give one strain	57	Employm. 1	23
Give mee his speed.	57	Employm. 1 W	24
And give new wheels to our disorder'd clocks.	64	Even-song	24
Give me the pliant minde, whose gentle measure	69	Content	13
O that thou shouldst give dust a tongue	80	Deniall	16
Give to thy Mother, what thou wouldst allow	86	Lent	5
As watring pots give flowers their lives.	90	Afflict.4	10
And pilfring what I once did give,	95	Submission	11
They quarrell thee, and would give over	100	Miserie	25
Give him his dirt to wallow in all night:	101	Miserie	46
Cannot give the name of gains	114	Dialogue	6
O give me quicknesse, that I may with mirth	115	Dulnesse	3
To honour thee: and so I give thee praise	121	Providence	147
Give one thing more, a gratefull heart.	123	Gratefulnes	2
They never cool, much lesse give out.	126	Confession	16
Doth give a hold and handle to affliction.	126	Confession	24
Give up the whole, and with the whole depart?	144	Discharge	8
May give savour	148	Offering	38
And give me up to night?	154	Glimpse	3
All things concurre to give it a perfection.	158	Praise 3	9
O who will give me tears? Come all ye springs,	164	Grief	1
Give up your feet and running to mine eyes,	164	Grief	15
How neatly doe we give one onely name	168	The Sonne	5
And give it his perfection.	184	The Elixer	8
Of praise deserved, unto thee I give,	185	A Wreath	2
I give to thee, who knowest all my wayes,	185	A Wreath	3
Give me simplicitie, that I may live,	185	A Wreath	9
Know them and practise them: then shall I give	185	A Wreath	11
For this poore wreath, give thee a crown of praise.	185	A Wreath	12
What wretchednesse can give him any room,	193	Ch.-Milit.	117
Give me not that I had before,	201	H. Commun. W	46
Or give mee that, so I have more	201	H. Commun. W	47
My God, give mee all Thee.	201	H. Commun. W	48
Yet hast thou more dominions: God doth give	212	Bohemia D	41
resort to give Thee praise;	221	Psalm VII D	26
never dream'd of, and therefore he could give no precepts thereof.	233	Priest 7	25
And ceased not to give thanks for the Ephesians, Eph. 1. 16.	234	Priest 7	12
if God give any thing above those, and not spent in them,	240	Priest 10	11
he chooseth rather to give the poor money, which they can better	243	Priest 11	15
but allows by no means to give without testimony, as he obeys	245	Priest 12	25
givings are lay, and secular, but this is to give like a Priest.	245	Priest 12	38
or other relations give him any authority over the Family,	251	Priest 17	16
he first gives himself liberally, and then incites them to give;	253	Priest 19	36
who like Christian Souldiers are to give the word, and to satisfie	255	Priest 21	20
and to give him power so to fit his discourse to them, that it may	262	Priest 24	23
if I do not give every thing its end, I abuse the Creature,	265	Priest 26	9
and to give one instance for all, if God have given me servants,	265	Priest 26	19
yet if God give him not the Grace to use, and utter this well,	272	Priest 30	2
and he will give him the gold for it, which the Child utterly	272	Priest 30	11
to get more, that we may give more, according to St. Pauls rule,	275	Priest 32	1
is a great Blessing, and as great as food, for which we give thanks:	284	Priest 35	27
if he will give his minde to those things which he should,	297	Cornaro	22
I give my self to the reading of some learned book, and afterwards	301	Cornaro	6
the experience of so many yeares have learned to give way to Reason:	303	Cornaro	21
the dayes of the Gospell will not give an outward Law of Ceremonies	310	Valdesso	5
If yee would know a knave, give him a staffe.	321	Proverbs	19
He that gives thee a Capon, give him the leg and the wing.	324	Proverbs	109
Give a clowne your finger, and he will take your hand.	324	Proverbs	111
To a gratefull man give mony when he askes.	324	Proverbs	115
To steale the Hog, and give the feet for almes.	329	Proverbs	237
He that's long a giving, knowes not how to give.	338	Proverbs	494
Give loosers leave to talke.	341	Proverbs	602
Fooles give to please all but their owne.	345	Proverbs	735
Give not S. Peter so much, to leave Saint Paul nothing.	346	Proverbs	763
He can give little to his servant, that lickes his knife.	349	Proverbs	846
The healthfull man can give counsell to the sick.	360	Proverbs D	1130
to threaten him that if he will not give her halfe her estate to live	368	Letters	23
since if we had Riches we are commanded to give them away:	373	Letters	24
upon my accompt, & give you my self for it, to be yours for ever.	378	Letters	4
gratious Lord God, is pleased to give me you for the Man, I desired,	378	Letters	8
I give all my goods both within doores and without doores both	382	G.H.'s Will	3
uppon Leighton Church, the other five pound I give to himselfe.	382	G.H.'s Will	30
of monyes wherof he is to give as I know he will a Just account:	383	G.H.'s Will	25
GIV'N			
Lose all mine own? God hath giv'n me a measure	8	Ch.-Porch	38
Write, So much giv'n to God; thou shalt be heard.	21	Ch.-Porch	382
If thou hast giv'n it me, 'tis here.	36	Thanksgvng	44
Which by consent was giv'n to Mansuetude.	70	Humilitie	10
Thou that hast giv'n so much to me,	123	Gratefulnes	1
All thou hast giv'n him heretofore	123	Gratefulnes	7
For I had giv'n the key to none, but one:	130	Love unkn.	55
And having giv'n the rest before,	151	The Bag	23
But he hath spoil'd the race; and giv'n to anguish	159	Jos.coat	10

GIV'N (cont'd)	PAGE	TITLE		LINE
So much desir'd, is giv'n, to take away	164	The Crosse		9
GIVEN				
To take all that is given; whether wealth,	20	Ch.-Porch		356
Are given over, for their curious arts,	194	Ch.-Milit.		152
according to the grace that is given to us, whether prophecy,	226	Priest 2		5
childrens advantage, then if it were given to the Chamber of London.	240	Priest 10		9
and sutably to their needs, then so much given in meat at dinner.	243	Priest 11		17
To Charity is given the covering of sins, 1 Pet. 4. 8.	244	Priest 12		8
what scandall is, when given or taken;	263	Priest 24		8
because wealth is given to that end to supply our occasions.	265	Priest 26		8
if God have given me servants, and I either provide too little	265	Priest 26		20
when we have sold all, and given it to the poor, we must not be idle,	274	Priest 32		33
so neither may thy word, but accomplish that for which it is given.	289	Priest		33
Thou hast given us the blessings of this life, and of a better.	290	Priest		5
But some, too much given to Appetite, object, That a long life is no	300	Cornaro		27
That I have both given God a Temple, and men to worship him in it:	301	Cornaro		31
when I was given to disorder and all the delights that could be.	302	Cornaro		10
very apt and well given both for learning and behaviour.	303	Cornaro		5
Feare is given to Christ, but not doubt, and upon good ground.	315	Valdesso		12
this being given only to the godly, and the other sometimes	319	Valdesso		9
A gift much expected is paid, not given.	340	Proverbs		574
A little given seasonably excuses a great gift.	349	Proverbs		834
which he refusing to doe hath given her occasion to protest shee will	368	Letters		22
grumblingly said that if he had given it to the pope he should have	368	Letters		33
in the holy Scripture, are never given to the rich, but to the poor.	373	Letters		29
blessed Success, that God had given us, by moving the Duches's heart,	379	Letters		1
liked our Book well, & has given order to the Tenants, at Leighton,	379	Letters		8
glad for the Heart, that God has given you & yours, to pious works.	379	Letters		15
then I leave to my servant Elizabeth her dubble wages given her,	382	G.H.'s Will		22
GIVER				
he gives him a tester for it, if the giver be fit to receive it;	254	Priest 20		14
GIVERS				
Gifts speake their Givers. For as those Refractions,	209	L. Bacon	D	3
GIVES				
That temper gives them theirs, and yet doth take	16	Ch.-Porch		254
Like season'd timber, never gives;	88	Vertue		14
Would show a root, that gives expressions!	119	Providence		76
Such a Way, as gives us breath:	156	The Call		2
Who gives to man, as he sees fit Salvation. / Damnation.	170	Water-crs.		10
Onely God, who gives perfumes,	181	Banquet		22
Listens behinde him, and gives them some light,	191	Ch.-Milit.	W	32
As God gives thee store,	207	Walton 3		5
Acquitts yourselves and gives the sicke all greife.	209	Paradox	D	6
and apply our powers to the service of him, that gives them.	232	Priest 6		6
Therefore he gives her respect both afore her servants,	238	Priest 9		36
But he gives no set pension to any;	244	Priest 12		25
When-ever hee gives any thing, and sees them labour in thanking	245	Priest 12		30
poor and needy, whom he thus finds labouring, he gives them somewhat;	248	Priest 14		10
yet hee gives him not over, but is long before hee proceede	250	Priest 16		16
he first gives himself liberally, and then incites them to give;	253	Priest 19		35
he gives him a tester for it, if the giver be fit to receive it;	254	Priest 20		13
he gives him those freer rules:	267	Priest 26		18
he pares the apple, and gives them the clean to feed on.	284	Priest 35		1
when the other gives him just opportunity, by speaking any good,	286	Priest 36		23
executioners, and the Law gives a malefactour to all to be defamed.	287	Priest 37		30
gives true strength to the bodie, all superfluities passing away	293	Cornaro		27
Who gives to all, denies all.	322	Proverbs		38
He that gives thee a Capon, give him the leg and the wing.	324	Proverbs		109
If the old dog barke he gives counsell.	327	Proverbs		197
The hard gives more then he that hath nothing.	329	Proverbs		259
Hee that gives thee a bone, would not have thee die.	333	Proverbs		355
The good mother sayes not, Will you? but gives.	337	Proverbs		467
He that will not have peace, God gives him warre.	345	Proverbs		729
He that lends, gives.	347	Proverbs		787
He that gives all before hee dies provides to suffer.	349	Proverbs		855
He that gives all ere hee dies provides to suffer.	349	Proverbs	V	855
To a close shorne sheepe, God gives wind by measure.	349	Proverbs		867
He that gives me small gifts would have me live.	354	Proverbs		1000
What one day gives us, another takes away from us.	359	Proverbs	D	1111
God gives his wrath by weight, and without weight his mercy.	359	Proverbs	D	1115
as God gives me higher thoughts, & to rise with his favours,	381	Woodnoth		25
GIVETH				
and live, and who giveth mee my Desires and Performances;	224	Priest		2
He that preacheth giveth almes.	347	Proverbs		788
GIVING				
The Second Thanks-giving.	36	Reprisall	W	T
Going about the world, and giving light.	59	Whitsunday		16
Unpinne, or wrench from giving all their due.	72	Constancie		5
And giving all things their set forms and houres,	137	Familie		11
Flowers, and gummes, and powders giving	181	Banquet		16
Giving new names and numbers to the yeare.	192	Ch.-Milit.		72
Giving the Church a crown to keep her state,	192	Ch.-Milit.		91
Into my hart with joye, giving more rest	202	love	W	17
yet never so giving over the raines, but that he sometimes looks how	239	Priest 9		1
and somtimes giving them a little mony to do it of themselves,	239	Priest 10		27
but giving him the prerogative of his Fathers profession,	239	Priest 10		31
giving some corn outright, and selling other at under rates;	245	Priest 12		10
he distinguisheth, giving them most, who live best, and take most	245	Priest 12		15
So doth hee also before giving make them say their Prayers first,	245	Priest 12		35
and at going to bed by giving the Host notice, that he will have	251	Priest 17		10

GIVING (cont'd)	PAGE	TITLE	LINE
If he finde another giving a poor man a penny, he gives him a tester	254	Priest 20	13
these privately, giving age honour, according to the Apostles rule,	255	Priest 21	24
the other of not giving scandall, that ought not to be preferred,	263	Priest 24	10
giving us one world in our selves, and another to serve us:	288	Priest	13
Great almes-giving lessens no mans living.	327	Proverbs	190
Giving much to the poore, doth inrich a mans store.	327	Proverbs	191
He that's long a giving, knowes not how to give.	338	Proverbs	494
Giving is dead, restoring very sicke.	340	Proverbs	573
Promising is the eve of giving.	349	Proverbs	847
I humbly thank him, & am so far from giving you cause, to apology,	378	Letters	9
GIVINGS			
For other givings are lay, and secular, but this is to give like	245	Priest 12	37
GLAD			
Need & bee glad, & wish thy presence still:	19	Ch.-Porch W	326
And now wearie of sport, glad to ingrosse	33	Sacrifice	193
True Christians should be glad of an occasion	86	Lent	13
Glad heart rejoyce.	134	The Method	32
For we do now behold thee gay and glad,	186	Death	17
in a Triumphant way, being glad, and joyfull, that hee is made	269	Priest 28	16
but is rather glad of catching opportunities to do them.	284	Priest 35	26
into a Benefice, I should be most glad to entertain it, and both pay	367	Letters	10
and am glad that although you offer more, yet you will doe,	375	Letters	6
I was glad of your Cambridge newes, but you joyed me exceedingly	377	Letters	18
I am glad I used you in it, and you have no cause to be sorry,	377	Letters	20
And as I am glad for the thing, so no less glad for the Heart,	379	Letters	14
so no less glad for the Heart, that God has given you & yours,	379	Letters	15
GLADLY			
But gladly welcome what he doth afford;	7	Ch.-Porch	15
That all may gladly board thee, as a flowre.	21	Ch.-Porch	368
Gladly engrave thy love in steel,	55	Temper 1	2
Drives all at last. Therefore I gladly trust	64	Ch.-monum.	6
My vows to thee most gladly, blessed Maid,	78	Ang.&Sts.	9
A willing shiner, that shall shine as gladly,	81	Christmas	29
Gladly had man ador'd the sunne,	82	Ungratef.	4
Herbs gladly cure our flesh; because that they	91	Man	23
refreshment, gladly betakes it selfe, even to the losse of honour.	252	Priest 18	22
GLADNESSE			
Exalted Manna, gladnesse of the best,	51	Prayer 1	10
Into gladnesse	147	Offering	26
GLADSOME			
The gladsome burden of a mortall saint.	33	Sacrifice W	199
The gladsome burthen of a mortall saint.	33	Sacrifice WC	199
At length I got unto the gladsome hill,	142	Pilgrimage	19
GLANCE			
The Glance.	171	The Glance	T
If thy first glance so powerfull be,	172	The Glance	17
GLANCES			
Both their full-ey'd aspects, and secret glances.	85	Vanitie 1	7
GLASSE			
Drink not the third glasse, which thou canst not tame,	7	Ch.-Porch	25
Stay at the third glasse: if thou lose thy hold,	8	Ch.-Porch	41
Findes his crackt name at length in the church-glasse.	14	Ch.-Porch	198
All understanding, more then heav'n doth glasse:	30	Sacrifice	119
Ladies, look here; this is the thankfull glasse,	58	H.Script.1	8
That flesh is but the glasse, which holds the dust	65	Ch.-monum.	20
He is a brittle crazie glasse:	67	Windows	2
But when thou dost anneal in glasse thy storie,	67	Windows	6
He knows it, fill the glasse.	100	Miserie	6
Light without winde is glasse: warm without weight	120	Providence	101
And through their glasse discolour thee!	141	Justice 2	5
The glasse was full and more.	158	Praise 3	36
Having a glasse of blessings standing by;	159	The Pulley	2
A man that looks on glasse,	184	The Elixer	9
Being in this their old crackt looking-glasse.	196	Ch.-Milit.	208
Whose house is of glasse, must not throw stones at another.	327	Proverbs	196
A woman and a glasse are ever in danger.	329	Proverbs	244
The more women looke in their glasse,	329	Proverbs	250
What your glasse telles you, will not be told by Councell.	329	Proverbs	255
GLAZED			
as walls plaistered, windows glazed, floore paved, seats whole,	246	Priest 13	4
GLIDE			
To make us see we are but flowers that glide:	167	The Flower	44
GLIMPSE			
To raise him to the glimpse of blisse:	102	Miserie	75
The Glimpse.	154	Glimpse	T
GLISTERS			
All is not gold that glisters.	331	Proverbs	306
GLITTER			
Glitter, and curle, and winde as they:	74	The Starre	26
GLITTERING			
Can blow away, or glittering look it blinde:	72	Constancie	8
GLOBE			
An earthly globe,	138	The Size	45
This spacious globe: Angels must have their joy,	158	Praise 3	21
GLOOMY			
The gloomy cave of Desperation	141	Pilgrimage	4
Least that the Night, earths gloomy shade	203	Even-song W	10
GLORIE			
Boast not thereof; nor make thy shame thy glorie.	8	Ch.-Porch	50
Spit out thy flegme, and fill thy brest with glorie:	10	Ch.-Porch	92

GLORIE (cont'd)	PAGE	TITLE		LINE
A grain of glorie mixt with humblenesse	19	Ch.-Porch		335
And side with thy triumphant glorie?	35	Thanksgvng		12
By thy eternall glorie didst outgo me?	37	Reprisall		10
The sound of glorie ringing in our eares:	46	Sinne 1		10
Faith sets me higher in his glorie.	50	Faith		20
The greater shall our glorie be.	57	Employm. 1		10
And the configurations of their glorie!	58	H.Script.2		2
The holy Preachers; then the light and glorie	67	Windows		8
Full of glorie and gay weeds,	71	Frailtie		13
But on thy glorie! then thou wilt reform	83	Sighs & Gr.		3
But Love and Grace took Glorie by the hand,	84	The World		19
When glorie swells the heart, and moldeth it	88	The Pearl		14
That both grace and glorie tend	92	Antiphon 2		7
Glorie and grace	102	Miserie		71
Lord with what glorie wast thou serv'd of old,	106	Sion		1
Yet all this glorie, all this pomp and state	106	Sion		7
The mean, thy praise and glorie is,	110	Brit. Ch.		26
Then came brave Glorie puffing by	111	The Quip		13
With my glorie and desert,	115	Dialogue		30
Glorie and honour are set by till it	132	The Storm		15
Thou art the Lord of glorie;	143	Complaining		6
King of Glorie, King of Peace,	146	Praise 2		1
In his majestick robes of glorie,	151	The Bag		10
We him in glorie call, The Sonne of Man.	168	The Sonne		14
Alas, poore Death, where is thy glorie?	169	Dial.-Anth		1
Before the Lord of glorie;	170	Self-cond.		3
Onely whereas the Ark in glorie shone,	190	Ch.-Milit.		27
Glorie was his chief instrument of old:	194	Ch.-Milit.		143
King of glorie, King of peace,	199	L'Envoy		1
same order and habit, of which wee all in this Kingdome glorie to be.	442	Oration		22
GLORIES				
Their beauteous glories. Onely shreds of thee,	140	Ch.-rents		9
Yet doe not yee contemne these our slight glories, which wee raise	443	Oration		1
GLORIFIE				
awake all my powers to glorifie thee!	289	Priest		10
GLORIFIED				
that have glorified him as wel as now, and that he shall have so	231	Priest 6		35
to let him alone, and say rather, God be praised, God be glorified;	245	Priest 12		33
hast called us, thou hast justified us, sanctified, and glorified us:	290	Priest		4
GLORIOUS				
If they dare try, a glorious life, or grave.	10	Ch.-Porch		90
Thy glorious houshold-stuffe did me entwine,	46	Afflict.1		9
Thy glorious houshold-stuffe did me bewitch	46	Afflict.1	W	9
And then appear'd a glorious skie.	51	Faith		40
How hath man parcel'd out thy glorious name,	54	Love 1		3
Thou standing by: and though thy glorious name	54	Love 1		11
Such glorious gifts thou didst bestow,	59	Whitsunday		9
This glorious and transcendent place,	67	Windows		4
Of the eternall glorious King.	76	Sunday		32
Oh glorious spirits, who after all your bands	77	Ang.&Sts.		1
O Thou, whose glorious, yet contracted light,	81	Christmas		9
But his deare God? who yet his glorious law	85	Vanitie 1		23
Hard things are glorious; easie things good cheap.	119	Providence		97
Almightie Lord, who from thy glorious throne	190	Ch.-Milit.		1
But all was glorious cheating, brave deceit,	193	Ch.-Milit.		135
If glorious bodies pass the sight	201	H. Commun.	W	34
And wedd my soule in glorious paradise;	205	Persever.	W	10
And ever praise the Glorious name	222	Psalm VII	D	63
Christ is the glorious instrument of God for the revoking of Man.	225	Priest 1		5
step into their great and glorious calling) and upon what termes,	258	Priest 22		19
and this as the more faulty in him, so the more glorious in God.	283	Priest 34		21
and sold our God, our glorious, our gracious God for an apple.	288	Priest		17
three Persons, but one most glorious, incomprehensible God,	290	Priest		15
therfore God is styled with that glorious title, Long Suffering.	381	Woodnoth		6
For amongst us what glorious shew is there, either of garments,	442	Oration		31
GLORY				
They dye in holes where glory never shone.	20	Ch.-Porch	W	348
But Love took Grace & Glory by the hand,	84	Sighs & Gr.	W	19
With Glory may attaine thy Face.	202	Trin.Sun.	W	6
Betwixt us & the people: when as glory	212	Bohemia	D	25
Then shall thy Glory, fresh as flowers	213	L' Envoy	D	7
Thou art my glory, Lord, and he	216	Psalm III	D	7
my glory into shame?	217	Psalm IV	D	8
and high thy Glory raise.	221	Psalm VII	D	28
himself, but that all may be done with reverence to his glory,	235	Priest 8		25
that he may enlarge the glory of God to the company he is in,	251	Priest 17		8
Majesty, and Power, and Brightnesse, and Glory!	288	Priest		8
and hast made our salvation, not our punishment, thy glory:	288	Priest		24
God, be ascribed all Honour, and Glory, and Praise, ever.	290	Priest		16
It adds to the glory both of soule and body.	327	Proverbs		193
in Poetry, shall be all, and ever consecrated to Gods glory.	363	Letters		12
into your hart, and the LORD bless all your purposes to his glory.	375	Letters		34
blow and bear fruit in your Soul, to his glory, your own good,	377	Letters		6
whose exceeding glory is equally round with the world it selfe:	442	Oration		10
GLORYES				
and he gloryes, never was there such care of a flock expressed,	234	Priest 7		20
GLOVE				
Who sings thy praise? onely a skarf or glove	54	Love 1		13
If thou hadst lost a glove or ring,	133	The Method		11

GO (cont'd)	PAGE	TITLE		LINE
But then he shews them how to go to Law, even as Brethren,	260	Priest 23		26
and feeling when I go to meat in what disposition I am,	267	Priest 26		7
shewing that they do not loose, or go lesse, but gaine by it;	270	Priest 29		9
but to go on as cheerfully, as if he had not been interrupted.	273	Priest 31		11
I will not doubt to go without staying to pray there (but onely,	273	Priest 31		34
we have nothing to do, lets go to the Tavern, or to the stews,	274	Priest 32		13
Sometimes he may go to Court, as the eminent place both of good	277	Priest 32		5
and not to let go the raines as soon as the horse goes easie.	280	Priest 34		15
So let them go, and find some poore afflicted soul, and there be	281	Priest 34		2
pardoning my sins, and bidding me go feed the people of thy love.	289	Priest		6
of the ground, and sometimes I go up high stairs and hills on foot.	300	Cornaro		36
Would you know what mony is, Go borrow some.	334	Proverbs		374
Old men go to Death, Death comes to Young men.	356	Proverbs	D	1
To go where the King goes afoot (i.e. to the stool).	356	Proverbs	D	1034
To go upon the Franciscans Hackney (i.e. on foot).	356	Proverbs	D	1035
There is no body will go to hell for company.	361	Proverbs	D	1177
come a Horse-back, there is reason, that my desires should go a-foot;	363	Letters		23
neither can I so much as go to Bugden, and deliver your Letter,	369	Letters		15
GOATE				
The goate must browse where she is tyed.	323	Proverbs		56
GOD				
Whom God in Baptisme washt with his own blood.	6	Ch.-Porch		8
It spoils an Angel: robs thee of thy God.	6	Ch.-Porch	W	10
Much lesse towards God, whose lust is all their book?	6	Ch.-Porch		12
If thou chuse bravely & rely on God	7	Ch.-Porch	W	17
If God had laid all common, certainly	7	Ch.-Porch		19
God hath impal'd us, on the contrarie	7	Ch.-Porch		21
And God will show thee how to take the towne,	7	Ch.-Porch	W	22
Lose all mine own? God hath giv'n me a measure	8	Ch.-Porch		38
He makes flat warre with God, and doth defie	8	Ch.-Porch		53
Lie not; but let thy heart be true to God,	9	Ch.-Porch		73
God gave thy soul brave wings; put not those feathers	9	Ch.-Porch		83
God gave them to thee under lock and key.	12	Ch.-Porch		144
God made me one man; love makes me no more,	17	Ch.-Porch		287
Joyn hands with God to make a man to live.	21	Ch.-Porch		376
God reckons for him, counts the favour his:	21	Ch.-Porch		381
Write, So much giv'n to God; thou shalt be heard.	21	Ch.-Porch		382
Restore to God his due in tithe and time:	22	Ch.-Porch		385
God then deals blessings: If a king did so,	22	Ch.-Porch		389
Thwart not th' Almighty God: O be not crosse.	22	Ch.-Porch		395
Thwart not the mighty God: O be not crosse.	22	Ch.-Porch	W	395
God is more there, then thou: for thou art there	22	Ch.-Porch		404
God calleth preaching folly. Do not grudge	23	Ch.-Porch		429
God takes a text, and preacheth patience.	23	Ch.-Porch		432
God sent him, whatsoe're he be: O tarry,	24	Ch.-Porch		442
Though God do hedge us in, yet who is holy?	24	Ch.-Porch		450
God holds his peace at man, and man cries out:	32	Sacrifice		187
But, O my God, my God! why leav'st thou me,	33	Sacrifice		213
My God, my God -	33	Sacrifice		215
My God, my God, why dost thou part from me?	35	Thanksgvng		9
And prove one God, one harmonie.	36	Thanksgvng		42
Alas, my God, I know not what.	36	Thanksgvng		50
Which my God feels as bloud; but I, as wine.	37	The Agonie		18
Write thee great God, and me a childe:	44	H. Bapt.2		7
Ah my deare God! though I am clean forgot,	48	Afflict.1		65
My God, accept of my confession.	49	Repentance		18
My God and King.	53	Antiphon 1		2
My God and King.	53	Antiphon 1		8
My God and King.	53	Antiphon 1		14
Will great God measure with a wretch?	55	Temper 1		15
Who plainly say, My God, My King.	57	Jordan 1		15
The same sweet God of love and light:	60	Whitsunday		26
My God, what is a heart?	62	Mattens		5
My God, what is a heart,	62	Mattens		9
But God more care of us hath had:	63	Sinne 2		6
Blest be the God of love,	63	Even-song		1
But much more blest be God above,	63	Even-song		4
My God, thou art all love.	64	Even-song		29
Yet say sometimes, God help poore Kings.	65	Ch.-mus.		8
Yet heare, O God, onely for his blouds sake	66	Ch.-lock		9
My God, a verse is not a crown,	69	Quidditie		1
To God, his neighbour, and himself most true:	72	Constancie		3
My heart did heave, and there came forth, O God!	73	Afflict.3		1
See the smooth face of God, without a frown	77	Ang.&Sts.		2
And Mother of my God, in my distresse.	78	Ang.&Sts.		10
Come, come, my God, O come,	80	Deniall		14
My God, no hymne for thee?	81	Christmas		16
And thought his god most brave;	82	Ungratef.		5
The mightie God, but I a sillie worm;	83	Sighs & Gr.		5
Into the bitter box; but O my God,	83	Sighs & Gr.		29
My God, relieve me!	83	Sighs & Gr.		30
Coloss. 3. 3. Our life is hid with Christ in God.	84	Coloss.		T
His dearely-earned pearl, which God did hide	85	Vanitie 1		10
But his deare God? who yet his glorious law	85	Vanitie 1		23
Perhaps my God, though he be farre before,	87	Lent		40
Oh help, my God! let not their plot	90	Afflict.4		19
My God, I heard this day,	90	Man		1
Since then, my God, thou hast	92	Man		49
Praised be the God of love,	92	Antiphon 2		1
Praised be the God alone,	93	Antiphon 2		22

GOD (cont'd)

	PAGE	TITLE		LINE
O write in brasse, My God upon a tree	94	Unkindness		22
My God, I read this day,	97	Afflict.5		1
My God, so temper joy and wo,	97	Afflict.5		23
Is my God this way? no, they would reply:	99	Decay		8
My God, Man cannot praise thy name:	101	Miserie		31
And all the bloud of God to run in vain.	102	Miserie		64
My God, I mean my self.	102	Miserie		78
My God, if writings may	104	Obedience		1
Great God doth fight, he doth submit.	106	Sion		16
My God, what is this world to me?	108	Home		32
Blessed be God, whose love it was	110	Brit. Ch.		28
Sorrie I am, my God, sorrie I am,	122	Sinnes rd.		1
Sorrie I am, my God, sorrie I am.	122	Sinnes rd.		18
While it detains us from our God.	123	Time		20
Who wants the place, where God doth dwell,	123	Time		23
Blessed be God, who prosper'd Noahs vine,	128	Bunch Gr.		24
Ev'n God himself, being pressed for my sake.	128	Bunch Gr.		28
For since thy God refuseth still,	133	The Method		2
Is God lesse free?	134	The Method		20
Seek pardon first, and God will say,	134	The Method		31
Love God, and love your neighbour. Watch and pray.	135	Divinitie		17
Grieved for me? the God of strength and power	135	Ephes.		4
Then weep mine eyes, the God of love doth grieve:	135	Ephes.		7
Almightie God doth grieve, he puts on sense:	136	Ephes.		16
Is more then God was, who was hungrie here.	138	The Size		14
But turning to my God, whose ministers	139	Artillerie		11
Of my deare God with all my power & might.	143	Holdfast		2
Yet I might trust in God to be my light.	143	Holdfast		4
That God did make	144	Discharge		17
God chains the dog till night: wilt loose the chain,	145	Discharge		46
My God hath promis'd; he is just.	145	Discharge		55
The God of power, as he did ride	151	The Bag		9
Betwixt my God and me; that I allow	155	Assurance		9
When God at first made man,	159	The Pulley		1
When almost all was out, God made a stay,	160	The Pulley		8
And rest in Nature, not the God of Nature:	160	The Pulley		14
But th' holy men of God such vessels are,	161	Priesthood		25
When God vouchsafeth to become our fare,	161	Priesthood		27
Who bring my God to me!	161	Priesthood		30
Onely, since God doth often vessels make	161	Priesthood		34
Where is my God? what hidden place	163	The Search		29
Alas, my God!	164	Grief		19
God doth supplie the want.	168	a true Hymn		18
O, could I love! and stops: God writeth, Loved,	168	a true Hymn		20
The God of love my shepherd is,	172	23 Psalme		1
Ev'n God himself: wherefore she was not loth,	173	Marie Magd		15
God hath made starres the foil	176	The Foil		5
Yet have they left me, Thou art still my God.	176	Forerunners		6
So Thou art still my God, be out of fear.	176	Forerunners		10
My god must have my best, ev'n all I had.	176	Forerunners		18
For, Thou art still my God, is all that ye	177	Forerunners		32
O my God,	178	Discipline		3
Thou art God:	179	Discipline		31
God is here prepar'd and drest,	179	Invitation		4
God, in whom all dainties are.	179	Invitation		6
Taste and fear not: God is here	180	Invitation		16
Onely God, who gives perfumes,	181	Banquet		22
God, to show how farre his love	181	Banquet		28
God took bloud, and needs would be	182	Banquet		34
Teach me, my God and King,	184	The Elixer		1
For that which God doth touch and own	185	The Elixer		23
How deare to me, O God, thy counsels are!	191	Ch.-Milit.		47
How deare to me, O God, thy counsels are!	192	Ch.-Milit.		99
Who for a God clearely a sallet lost.	193	Ch.-Milit.		110
Who makes a root his God, how low is he,	193	Ch.-Milit.		115
If God and man be sever'd infinitely!	193	Ch.-Milit.		116
He was a God, now he's an Emperour.	194	Ch.-Milit.		140
How deare to me, O God, thy counsels are!	194	Ch.-Milit.		155
How deare to me, O God, thy counsels are!	196	Ch.-Milit.		209
My God, thou dost prepare for them a way	197	Ch.-Milit.		249
How deare to me, O God, thy counsels are!	198	Ch.-Milit.		278
Blessed be God alone,	199	L'Envoy		17
My God, give mee all Thee.	201	H. Commun.	W	48
Who God & Saints and Angels loose at last.	203	Trin.Sun.	W	17
O help my God!	204	The Knell	W	9
My God, the poore expressions of my Love	204	Persever.	W	1
My God, where is that ancient heat towards thee,	206	Walton 1		1
As God gives thee store,	207	Walton 3		5
Serve thou the more God and the poore;	207	Walton 4		3
Yet hast thou more dominions: God doth give	212	Bohemia	D	41
Great God will surely dry those teares,	213	L' Envoy	D	5
For God himself vouchsafes to know	215	Psalm I	D	21
But I by God am seated King,	215	Psalm II	D	13
Serve our great God in fear, rejoyce,	216	Psalm II	D	27
no help in God there is.	216	Psalm III	D	4
for God sustain'd me still.	216	Psalm III	D	12
save me, my God, from thrall:	217	Psalm III	D	18
offer to God on high	217	Psalm IV	D	18
My King, my God, vouchsafe to hear	218	Psalm V	D	3
Thou art a God whose puritie	218	Psalm V	D	9

GOD (cont'd)	PAGE	TITLE		LINE
For God doth righteous men esteem,	219	Psalm V	D	41
Return, O God! and rescue me,	220	Psalm VI	D	9
For God himself hath heard my cry;	220	Psalm VI	D	21
Save me, my Lord, my God, because	220	Psalm VII	D	1
O God consider me	221	Psalm VII	D	30
Thou art that righteous God by whom	221	Psalm VII	D	35
God is my shield, who doth preserve	222	Psalm VII	D	37
Being desirous (thorow the Mercy of GOD) to please Him,	224	Priest		1
and displeases God, but that it is a good strife to go as farre	224	Priest		11
the Deputy of Christ for the reducing of Man to the Obedience of God.	225	Priest 1		2
For first, Man fell from God by disobedience.	225	Priest 1		4
Christ is the glorious instrument of God for the revoking of Man.	225	Priest 1		5
Unto the ungodly, saith God, Why dost thou preach my Laws,	226	Priest 2		13
of himself, for all the purposes which God hath ordained him.	227	Priest 3		9
as to neglect the grace of God in himself, and what the Holy Spirit	229	Priest 4		20
that God in all ages hath had his servants, to whom he hath revealed	229	Priest 4		21
so neither hath God opened, or will open all to one, that there may	229	Priest 4		25
that there may be a traffick in knowledg between the servants of God,	229	Priest 4		26
he enters into the secrets of God treasured in the holy Scripture.	229	Priest 4		30
and admirable benefit to the Church of God, and a thing required	230	Priest 5		13
as being truly touched and amazed with the Majesty of God,	231	Priest 6		6
that God hath ever had his people, that have glorified him as wel	231	Priest 6		34
and neglect the present service of God, he by no means suffers it,	232	Priest 6		12
and obligation of his calling, being to obey God rather then men.	232	Priest 6		19
Herein also he serves himselfe of the judgements of God,	233	Priest 7		7
them to be so, when God is so neer them, and even over their heads.	233	Priest 7		10
is careless before his Judg, and that the word of God shal judge us.	233	Priest 7		21
by turning often, and making many Apostrophes to God, as,	233	Priest 7		33
of the desolation of Israel, turnes to God suddenly, Oh Lord,	234	Priest 7		5
by an often urging of the presence, and majesty of God, by these,	234	Priest 7		25
heed what we do, God sees us, he sees whether I speak as I ought,	234	Priest 7		27
the discourse to his Majesty, And he is a great God, and terrible,	234	Priest 7		31
and that the good God would pardon all those, who come with lesse	235	Priest 8		30
or from the State, or from God by a child born, or dead,	235	Priest 8		35
and presence of Almighty God, and blessing the people either openly,	236	Priest 8		5
Let him communicate the thing often by prayer unto God,	237	Priest 9		6
and blesseth God for the gift of continency, knowing that it can no	237	Priest 9		19
puts on the whole Armour of God, and by the vertue of the shield	238	Priest 9		5
that (the good instrument of God to bring women to heaven) a wise	238	Priest 9		30
a trayning up of her children and mayds in the fear of God,	239	Priest 10		13
and enter favour with God, who weighs even childrens actions,	239	Priest 10		28
that mony thus lent to God, is placed surer for his childrens	240	Priest 10		8
if God give any thing above those, and not spent in them,	240	Priest 10		11
not spent in them, he blesseth God, and lays it out as he sees cause.	240	Priest 10		12
God hath provided Creatures for both;	241	Priest 10		30
and therefore as God, although we should love him onely for his own	243	Priest 11		30
name and effect of Charity with the poor people, though not with God:	244	Priest 12		27
hee wins them to praise God more, to live more religiously,	245	Priest 12		2
at his door, whom God puts in his way, and makes his neighbours.	245	Priest 12		20
to let him alone, and say rather, God be praised, God be glorified;	245	Priest 12		32
and include the double object of our duty, God, and our neighbour;	246	Priest 13		30
the first being for the honour of God;	246	Priest 13		31
shewing them how acceptable such works are to God, and wishing them	247	Priest 14		18
never raising their thoughts to God, nor sanctifying their labour	248	Priest 14		1
but that they may have wherewithall to serve God the better,	248	Priest 14		8
and against God, I am then to follow the Apostles rule,	248	Priest 14		29
For both God is there also, and those for whom God dyed:	249	Priest 14		6
For both God is there also, and those for whom God dyed:	249	Priest 14		7
that he may enlarge the glory of God to the company he is in,	251	Priest 17		8
by a due blessing of God for their safe arrival, and saying grace	251	Priest 17		9
if God have sent any calamity either by fire, or famine,	253	Priest 19		29
that the Blessing of God to them ought to make them the more	254	Priest 19		5
stead to his Parish, and dischargeth God what he can of his promises.	254	Priest 20		9
This is in some sort a discharging of God;	254	Priest 20		18
but in the other God is his own immediate paymaster, rewarding all	254	Priest 20		20
Did you see God make it?	256	Priest 21		8
You said, God made the world;	256	Priest 21		11
Who is God? And so forward, requiring answers to all these,	256	Priest 21		12
in a great confusion, as being not only to receive God, but to break,	257	Priest 22		30
where God is thanked for calling us to the knowledg of his grace,	258	Priest 22		5
He instructeth the God-fathers, and God-mothers, that it is no	258	Priest 22		10
and God-mothers, that it is no complementall or light thing	258	Priest 22		10
as being done both in the presence of God, and his Saints,	258	Priest 22		13
wherein the manifold wisedome of God is wonderfully to be seen,	261	Priest 23		28
that God cannot be wanting to them in Doctrine, to whom he is so	263	Priest 24		20
squeeze blood undecently to the station wherein God hath placed me,	265	Priest 26		18
if God have given me servants, and I either provide too little	265	Priest 26		20
God dishonoured every day, and man afflicted.	267	Priest 27		32
because this hath been the portion of God his Master, and of Gods	268	Priest 28		14
the greatest honor of this world, to do God and his chosen service;	270	Priest 29		11
or as David says, to be even a door-keeper in the house of God.	270	Priest 29		12
for their obligation to God, and their own soul, is above any	270	Priest 29		22
but that God often changeth it according as he sees fit,	270	Priest 30		31
that God hath and exerciseth a threefold power in every thing which	270	Priest 30		33
yet when God pleased, the sun stood stil, the fire burned not.	271	Priest 30		12
is observeable, that God delights to have men feel, and acknowledg,	271	Priest 30		19
So that if a farmer should depend upon God all the yeer,	271	Priest 30		28
then God sends such weather, as lays the corn, and destroys it:	271	Priest 30		30
or if he depend on God further, even till he imbarn his corn,	271	Priest 30		32
God sends a fire, and consumes all that he hath:	271	Priest 30		33

GOD (cont'd)	PAGE	TITLE		LINE
but to continue his dependance on God, not onely before the corne is	271	Priest 30		35
by which God turnes all outward blessings to inward advantages.	271	Priest 30		37
yet if God give him not the Grace to use, and utter this well,	272	Priest 30		2
sit down at this world, God bids him sell it, and purchase a better:	272	Priest 30		7
perplexing them in the service of God) stands fast in the Liberty	272	Priest 31		18
God knows the occasion as wel as he, and He is as a gracious Father,	273	Priest 31		7
either blessing God, that he will be pleased to dwell among men;	273	Priest 31		24
throw it away, and be most confident, that God is not displeased.	273	Priest 31		38
wherein God hath placed two great Instruments, Reason in the soul,	274	Priest 32		19
riches are the blessing of God, and the great Instrument of doing	274	Priest 32		29
that if the Kingdome of God be first sought, all other things shall	278	Priest 33		13
when the servant of God, freed for a while from temptation,	279	Priest 33		4
from temptation, in a quiet sweetnesse seeks how to please his God.	279	Priest 33		6
and one of the first steps of pleasing God, having for his owne use	279	Priest 33		8
then for offending God, he came at length to this resolution,	279	Priest 33		13
the chiefe thing, which God in Scriptures requires, is the heart,	279	Priest 33		16
and turning unto God in truth of heart, and newnesse of life:	279	Priest 33		24
for with such sacrifices God is well pleased.	281	Priest 34		4
God doth forsake and persecute them, and there is none to deliver	281	Priest 34		11
and then who can deny the stretched out arme of a mighty God?	282	Priest 34		6
that this very thing was intended by God, that the Jewes should be	282	Priest 34		12
of others by their sight, to the acknowledging of God, and his power,	282	Priest 34		16
God turning mens Covetousnesse, and Ambitions to the effecting of his	282	Priest 34		33
not so much doubting a God, as that he is theirs;	283	Priest 34		6
If God hate them, either he doth it as they are Creatures,	283	Priest 34		9
and this as the more faulty in him, so the more glorious in God.	283	Priest 34		22
that God loves them, till either they despise that Love,	283	Priest 34		22
First, a blessing of God for the fruits of the field:	284	Priest 35		4
when light is brought in, God send us the light of heaven;	284	Priest 35		23
or praying to God at all times, but is rather glad of catching	284	Priest 35		25
1 Sam. 1. 18. though it came from a man disallowed by God:	285	Priest 36		22
The Peace of God, &c.	286	Priest 36		5
interesting of that dignity wherewith God hath invested the Priest,	286	Priest 36		9
(which cannot be applyed without notice) to the dishonor of God,	287	Priest 37		3
and forbear to speak of that, which even God himself hath forgotten.	288	Priest 37		5
O almighty and ever-living Lord God!	288	Priest		7
disappointed thy Purposes, and sold our God, our glorious,	288	Priest		17
and sold our God, our glorious, our gracious God for an apple.	288	Priest		17
for an apple once we lost our God, and still lose him for no more;	288	Priest		19
Blessed be the God of Heaven and Earth!	289	Priest		8
Blessed be God! and the Father of all mercy!	290	Priest		1
but one most glorious, incomprehensible God, be ascribed all Honour,	290	Priest		15
I by the grace of God cured my self, onely with returning to my	296	Cornaro		24
that under God nothing holp me, but that exact rule which I had so	296	Cornaro		28
That I have both given God a Temple, and men to worship him in it:	301	Cornaro		31
by Temperance and the Grace of God I feel not those perturbations	302	Cornaro		24
the Authors sake, whom I conceive to have been a true servant of God;	304	Valdesso		7
and God hath put this into your hands (as he sent the fish with mony	304	Valdesso		10
that God in the midst of Popery should open the eyes of one	304	Valdesso		19
of perfection, and are able to make the man of God perfect, 2 Tim. 3.	306	Valdesso		19
All the Saints of God may be said in some sence to have put	306	Valdesso		28
but not as a naked Word severed from God, but as the Word of God:	307	Valdesso		1
And in so doing they doe not sever their trust from God.	307	Valdesso		2
But by trusting in the word of God they trust in God.	307	Valdesso		3
The exemption from both, is by the Grace of God.	308	Valdesso		6
none can free themselves of themselves, but only by the Grace of God:	308	Valdesso		9
only by the generall Providence of God, as Socrates and Aristides,	308	Valdesso		13
Therefore David desireth God in the 119 Psalme, to open his eyes that	309	Valdesso		25
They shall be all taught of God, it being Scripture cannot be spoken	310	Valdesso		2
That God in the dayes of the Gospell will not give an outward Law	310	Valdesso		4
in the Church of God there is one fundamentall, but else variety.	312	Valdesso		2
that is, to oblige God, or justify himselfe before God,	312	Valdesso		15
or justify himselfe before God, by any acts or exercises of Religion;	312	Valdesso		15
but that he ought to pray God affectionately and fervently to send	312	Valdesso		16
to relieve my Neighbour, God hath already reveled his Will about it.	313	Valdesso		14
God often chuseth which he shall doe, and that by restraining him	313	Valdesso		21
or conditionally he prayed as man, though as God he knew the event.	315	Valdesso		11
be evident to others, as well as to themselves, that God moved them.	316	Valdesso		20
but when he sayes they are equally exempt with God, that is dangerous	316	Valdesso		32
since the Saints of God in all ages have ever held in so pretious	317	Valdesso		32
God in all ages have ever held in so pretious esteem the word of God,	317	Valdesso		33
MAN Proposeth, God disposeth.	321	Proverbs		1
MAN purposethe God disposeth.	321	Proverbs	V	1
God sends cold according to Clcathes.	322	Proverbs		33
Hee looseth nothing, that looseth not God.	322	Proverbs		35
God oft hath a great share in a little house.	323	Proverbs		60
God heales, and the Physitian hath the thankes.	326	Proverbs		169
God complaines not, but doth what is fitting.	327	Proverbs		182
The river past, and God forgotten.	327	Proverbs		207
God strikes not with both hands,	331	Proverbs		315
When God will, no winde but brings raine.	332	Proverbs		332
He that sowes trusts in God.	332	Proverbs		342
God comes to see without a bell.	334	Proverbs		384
Who likes not the drinke, God deprives him of bread.	334	Proverbs		394
In time comes he whom God sends.	334	Proverbs		397
To a good spender God is the Treasurer.	339	Proverbs		530
Helpe thy selfe, and God will helpe thee.	339	Proverbs		537
God is at the end, when we thinke he is furthest off it.	341	Proverbs		598
No sooner is a Temple built to God	343	Proverbs		674
When God will punish, hee will first take away the understanding.	344	Proverbs		688

GOD (cont'd)

	PAGE	TITLE	LINE
The tree that God plants, no winde hurts it.	344	Proverbs	691
God provides for him that trusteth.	345	Proverbs	728
He that will not have peace, God gives him warre.	345	Proverbs	729
Where there is peace, God is.	345	Proverbs	733
God, and Parents, and our Master, can never be requited.	348	Proverbs	805
God keepe me from foure houses,	348	Proverbs	816
To a close shorne sheepe, God gives wind by measure.	349	Proverbs	867
Though God take the sunne out of the Heaven,	353	Proverbs	980
When God is made master of a family, he orders the disorderly.	353	Proverbs	983
The world is now adayes, God save the Conquerour.	358	Proverbs	D 1075
Those that God loves, do not live long.	358	Proverbs	D 1094
(applyed to rich men that are unthankful to God).	359	Proverbs	D 1100
God strikes with his finger, and not with all his arme.	359	Proverbs	D 1114
God gives his wrath by weight, and without weight his mercy.	359	Proverbs	D 1115
either void of knowledge, or of the fear of God.	361	Proverbs	D 1176
nor to bewail that so few are writ, that look towards God and Heaven.	363	Letters	9
it is true (God knows) I am weak, yet not so, but that every day,	364	Letters	26
with our good and gracious God, incessantly begging some ease of your	371	Letters	28
God who knows and sees this Writing, knows also that my solliciting	372	Letters	1
constant and the more earnest for you to the God of all Consolation.	372	Letters	23
and comfort your self in the God of all Comfort, who is not willing	372	Letters	25
but, Oh God! how easily is that answered, when we consider that	373	Letters	27
And yet, Oh God! most carry themselves so, as if they not only	373	Letters	33
remember the holy Martyrs of God, how they have been burnt	373	Letters	35
and yours (which praised be God are less) are not like to continue	374	Letters	2
That God who hath delivered me out of the paws of the Lyon and Bear,	374	Letters	6
consider that God intends that to be as a sacred Temple for himself	374	Letters	9
admirable thing is this, that God puts his shoulder to our burthen;	374	Letters	17
trouble not your selves, God is at hand to deliver us from all, or,	374	Letters	29
doe that which GOD shall put into your hart, and the LORD bless all	375	Letters	33
the good GOD bless you more and more;	376	Letters	19
God knowes, I have desired a long time, to doe the place good,	378	Letters	5
And now My gratious Lord God, is pleased to give me you for the Man,	378	Letters	8
Now God the Father of our Lord Jesus Christ bless you more & more,	378	Letters	24
blessed Success, that God had given us, by moving the Duches's heart,	378	Letters	31
God Almighty prosper the Work.	379	Letters	10
glad for the Heart, that God has given you & yours, to pious works.	379	Letters	15
Blessed be My God & Dear Master, the Spring & Fountain of all	379	Letters	16
In the name of God.	380	Woodnoth	2
putt your self into the hands of God (whose the success of things is)	380	Woodnoth	24
of want of success consider how long God knocks at our harts,	381	Woodnoth	2
if God had done that (which you are thinking to doe) to blessed Mary	381	Woodnoth	4
therfore God is styled with that glorious title, Long Suffering.	381	Woodnoth	6
As God where he finds no roome for his Inclining grace,	381	Woodnoth	7
as God gives me higher thoughts, & to rise with his favours,	381	Woodnoth	25
my soule and body to Almightie God that made them doe thus dispose	382	G.H.'s Will	2

GOD-FATHERS

	PAGE	TITLE	LINE
He instructeth the God-fathers, and God-mothers, that it is no	258	Priest 22	10

GOD-MOTHERS

	PAGE	TITLE	LINE
and God-mothers, that it is no complementall or light thing	258	Priest 22	10

GOD'S

	PAGE	TITLE	LINE
Wine above all things doth Gods stamp deface.	8	Ch.-Porch	48
And if Gods image move thee not, let thine.	10	Ch.-Porch	102
Man is Gods image; but a poore man is	21	Ch.-Porch	379
He that loves Gods abode, and to combine	24	Ch.-Porch	437
As those, who mock at Gods way of salvation.	24	Ch.-Porch	446
Gods breath in man returning to his birth,	51	Prayer 1	2
In Gods rich garden: that is bare,	75	Sunday	27
In Gods rich Paradice.	75	Sunday	W 28
As Gods afflictions into man,	126	Confession	9
For as the Jews of old by Gods command	128	Bunch Gr.	8
Gods works are wide, and let in future times;	128	Bunch Gr.	13
And should Gods eare	134	The Method	17
And should Gods eare,	134	The Method	25
But to my Gods too; he doth grone.	136	Ephes.	18
Gods promises have made thee mine;	141	Justice 2	22
Thy life is Gods, thy time to come is gone,	144	Discharge	11
Of all Gods mercies, is my posie still.	183	The Posie	12
But in God's Law sets his delight,	214	Psalm I	D 5
that if any do Gods will, he shall know of the Doctrine,	228	Priest 4	28
raise up their mindes to apprehend Gods good blessing to our Church,	236	Priest 8	23
and tracker of Gods wayes, sets up as many encouragements	244	Priest 11	2
when they doubt Gods providence, thinking that their own labour is	247	Priest 14	29
but he holds the Rule, that Nothing is little in Gods service:	249	Priest 14	2
such as are from Gods generall providence extended even to lillyes;	249	Priest 15	19
and waits, least hee should determine Gods houre of coming;	250	Priest 16	20
The Countrey Parson, where ever he is, keeps Gods watch;	252	Priest 18	1
This is called keeping Gods watch, when the baits which the enemy	252	Priest 18	13
This is to be on Gods side, and be true to his party.	252	Priest 18	15
The Parson in Gods stead.	254	Priest 20	T
The Countrey Parson is in Gods stead to his Parish, and dischargeth	254	Priest 20	8
the Parson endeavoureth to be in Gods stead, knowing that Countrey	254	Priest 20	30
or not in some proportion to Gods blessing upon him, is covetous.	265	Priest 26	6
his Master, and of Gods Saints his Brethren, and this is foretold,	268	Priest 28	14
which continually breake Gods Laws, and dishonour him with those	269	Priest 28	10
labours to reduce them to see Gods hand in all things,	270	Priest 30	29
By Gods governing power he preserves and orders the references	271	Priest 30	13
in this, how Gods goodnesse strives with mans refractorinesse;	272	Priest 30	5
as they think fit, & see cause, or rather as Gods spirit leads them.	272	Priest 31	27
but of reverence to Gods house, resolves whenever he enters into	273	Priest 31	23

GOD'S (cont'd)	PAGE	TITLE		LINE
that it may be alike in all Gods children (which as concerning	279	Priest 33		21
Which acts of repentance are and must be found in all Gods servants:	279	Priest 33		26
then he dives unto the boundlesse Ocean of Gods Love, ...	283	Priest 34		7
hath two pledges of Gods Love, that in the mouth of two or three	283	Priest 34		18
effectually applying Gods favour to the blessed, by the interesting	286	Priest 36		8
and ingaging of Gods own power and institution for a blessing.	286	Priest 36		10
and observation of Gods Kingdome within us, and the working thereof,	305	Valdesso		10
as to neglect the Consideration of Gods Worke in his heart through	309	Valdesso		30
and Gods worke within us still observed, who workes by his Word,	309	Valdesso		32
and those that have inspirations must still use Peter, Gods Word:	310	Valdesso		10
Gods Spirit will mortify and try them as gold in the fire. . .	314	Valdesso		21
that the world pierceth not godly mens actions no more then Gods,	315	Valdesso		30
And that the best of Gods Servants should have weaknesses is no way	316	Valdesso		2
weaknesses is no way repugnant to the way of Gods Spirit in them,	316	Valdesso		3
have made it appeare, that it was done by Gods immediate precept.	316	Valdesso		26
Gods Mill grinds slow, but sure.	346	Proverbs		747
in Poetry, shall be all, and ever consecrated to Gods glory.	363	Letters		12
and make your family, a housefull of GOD's servants. . . .	376	Letters		20
and you have no cause to be sorry, since it is GOD's business.	377	Letters		21
that creeps upon Gods earth, no not tho' the advice step so far,	378	Letters		12
whome I esteem to be God's faithfull & diligent Servant, . .	378	Letters		14
doubt not, through Gods blessing, but it shall be to the full;	379	Letters		18
In Gods accepting you have done the good you intended, & whom serve	381	Woodnoth		17
Doe this & be a man as David, after Gods hart.	381	Woodnoth		21
the one are Gods servants, the other the commonwealths, . .	381	Woodnoth		28
GODLINESSE				
this life, who hath promised, that Godlinesse shall be gainfull:	254	Priest 20		19
both of them having forms or vizars of godlinesse, but denying	319	Valdesso	V	26
GODLY				
and with truly godly zeal, without hatred to the person, . .	254	Priest 20		27
five shields, wherewith the Godly receive the darts of the wicked;	269	Priest 28		19
the Godly have ever added some houres of prayer, as at nine,	272	Priest 31		25
that the godly petitioner upon some emergent interruption in the day,	272	Priest 31		29
A godly man, not out of superstition, but of reverence to Gods house,	273	Priest 31		22
with such syncerity and efficacy, that it makes him godly, righteous,	309	Valdesso		6
because even the godly are chastized but not punished) for evill	311	Valdesso		28
that restraining motions are much more frequent to the godly,	313	Valdesso		18
that the world pierceth not godly mens actions no more then Gods,	315	Valdesso		30
So likewise are the godly in some sort exempt from Lawes, . .	315	Valdesso		32
the Scriptures, or to themselves being still men, though godly men.	316	Valdesso		5
allowing no Jurisdiction over the godly, this cannot stand, . .	316	Valdesso		16
The godly are punishable as others, when they doe amisse, . .	316	Valdesso		17
How the godly are exempt from Laws is a known point among Divines,	316	Valdesso		30
this being given only to the godly, and the other sometimes . .	319	Valdesso		9
GODS				
Where now we shall be better Gods then he.	82	Ungratef.		6
Gardens of Gods, which ev'ry yeare did grow, ...	193	Ch.-Milit.		108
(who playes his part sometimes in drawing Gods Servants from him,	272	Priest 31		16
these Belly-gods say, that an orderly life is so hard a thing that it	298	Cornaro		36
GODWARD				
hee considers diligently the state thereof to Godward, and that in	251	Priest 17		18
GOE				
If rottenness have more, lett Heaven goe.	7	Ch.-Porch	W	24
As that thy self alone to hell shalt goe.	13	Ch.-Porch	W	168
I goe to Church; make me an Angel, I	61	Praise 1	W	5
Ten, if a Sermon goe for gains.	96	Charms & K	W	16
any entertainment, lest he goe into the world, esteeming it absurd,	241	Priest 10		20
that they oftentimes goe out of church, before he hath blessed them.	286	Priest 36		14
I doe not then bid him goe away but rather stay longer, . .	318	Valdesso		15
All came from, and will goe to others.	322	Proverbs		41
He that will learne to pray, let him goe to Sea.	323	Proverbs		84
He who will learne to pray, let him goe to Sea.	323	Proverbs	V	84
Whether shall the Oxe goe, where he shall not labour? . . .	324	Proverbs		98
Advise none to marry or to goe to warre.	329	Proverbs		236
Advise none to marry nor to goe to warre.	329	Proverbs	V	236
In the world who can not swimme, goe to the bottome. . . .	330	Proverbs	V	285
Goe not for every griefe to the Physitian, ...	331	Proverbs		290
Who letts his wife goe to every feast, ...	336	Proverbs		434
He that would be well, needs not goe from his owne house. . .	336	Proverbs		442
Health and mony goe farre.	336	Proverbs		447
If the wise erred not, it would goe hard with fooles. . . .	338	Proverbs		510
If wise men erred not, it would goe hard with fooles. . . .	338	Proverbs	V	510
When the tree is fallen, all goe with their hatchet. . . .	340	Proverbs		566
Ty it well, and let it goe.	342	Proverbs		642
You cannot make a wind-mill goe with a paire of bellowes. . .	344	Proverbs		676
Prosperity lets goe the bridle.	345	Proverbs		736
He that feares leaves, let him not goe into the wood. . . .	346	Proverbs		768
Hee that would be a Gentleman, let him goe to an assault. . .	350	Proverbs		878
He that followes the Lord hopes to goe before.	354	Proverbs		994
GOES				
Whom all his passions follow, as he goes.	15	Ch.-Porch		216
For this French sluttery which so currant goes:	21	Ch.-Porch	W	368
And bear the bundle, wheresoe're it goes:	88	The Pearl		17
Who goes to bed and doth not pray, ...	96	Charms & K		7
Who goes to bed and does not pray, ...	96	Charms & K	W	7
She wholly goes on th' other side, ...	110	Brit. Ch.		23
Just as I went, None goes that way	142	Pilgrimage		33
But as the Sunne still goes both west and east;	198	Ch.-Milit.		274
While Prince to Spaine, and King to Cambridge goes, ...	438	Lat.Trans.		1
coherence thereof, touching what goes before, and what follows after,	229	Priest 4		11

GOES (cont'd)	PAGE	TITLE		LINE
that none goes out of Church as he came in, but either better,	233	Priest 7		19
he goes to Church, at his first entrance humbly adoring, . . .	236	Priest 8		3
he goes no further for any entertainment, lest he goe into the world,	241	Priest 10		19
best comforts, and rather goes to them, then sends for the afflicted,	249	Priest 15		16
before hee proceede to disinheriting, or perhaps never goes so far;	250	Priest 16		18
Wherefore the Parson strongly opposeth this sin, whersoever he goes.	274	Priest 32		15
and not to let go the raines as soon as the horse goes easie.	280	Priest 34		16
that can or will look after things, but all goes by chance, or wit:	281	Priest 34		9
and goes with him to the other, and all dine or sup together.	284	Priest 35		20
But when he enlargeth he goes too farre.	315	Valdesso		35
Hee that goes barefoot, must not plant thornes.	323	Proverbs		82
Where the drink goes in, there the wit goes out.	327	Proverbs		187
Ill comes in by ells, and goes out by inches.	327	Proverbs		194
The beast that goes alwaies never wants blowes.	329	Proverbs		260
In the world who knowes not to swimme, goes to the bottome. . . .	330	Proverbs		285
The Lame goes as farre as your staggerer.	339	Proverbs		517
An examin'd enterprize goes on boldly.	342	Proverbs		618
That's the best gowne that goes up and downe the house. . . .	346	Proverbs		742
The higher the Ape goes, the more he shewes his taile.	346	Proverbs		745
Soft and faire goes farre.	347	Proverbs		772
Hee goes not out of his way, that goes to a good Inne.	348	Proverbs		831
Hee that goes to bed thirsty riseth healthy.	354	Proverbs		1003
To go where the King goes afoot (i.e. to the stool).	356	Proverbs	D	1034
He that is afraid of leaves, goes not to the wood.	358	Proverbs	D	1092
Concerning the Orators place all goes well yet, the next Friday it is	371	Letters		16
GOEST				
Yet still thou goest on, ...	64	Even-song		17
Whether goest, griefe? where I am wont.	324	Proverbs		96
GOETH				
Though he alight sometimes, still goeth on.	20	Ch.-Porch		340
Who goeth in the way which Christ hath gone, ...	87	Lent		37
Who goeth in that way which Christ hath gone, ...	87	Lent	V	37
Who goeth in the way that Christ hath gone, ...	87	Lent	W	37
He that goeth farre hath many encounters.	341	Proverbs		608
GOING				
Going about the world, and giving light.	59	Whitsunday		16
I did; and going did a rainbow note:	124	Peace		7
So also did the Church by going west	198	Ch.-Milit.		275
and at going to bed by giving the Host notice, that he will have	251	Priest 17		10
sweet usage of them, both in going to, and sending for them often,	262	Priest 24		26
The Mill gets by going.	325	Proverbs		122
GOLD				
Gold thou mayst safely touch; but if it stick	13	Ch.-Porch		167
What skills it, if a bag of stones or gold	13	Ch.-Porch		169
His life may make thee gold, and much more just.	41	Easter		6
Nor in a wedge of gold, ...	52	H.Commun.		2
But since those pipes of gold, which brought	59	Whitsunday		17
Silver, or gold, or precious stone, ...	62	Mattens		6
Thou art the holy mine, whence came the gold, ...	78	Ang.&Sts.		11
Thou art the sacred mine, whence came the gold, ...	78	Ang.&Sts.	W	11
Would he have gold? I lend it instantly;	93	Unkindness		12
Who shuts his hand, hath lost his gold:	96	Charms & K		5
Where most things were of purest gold;	106	Sion		3
Let them love gold;	111	Vanitie 2		12
He that loseth gold, though drosse, ...	114	Businesse		31
Here I was robb'd of all my gold, ...	142	Pilgrimage		16
Between his soul and gold, and hath preferr'd	171	Self-cond.		14
That turneth all to gold:	185	The Elixer		22
By carrying first their gold from them away:	197	Ch.-Milit.		250
For gold and grace did never yet agree:	197	Ch.-Milit.		251
who hath in his hand an apple, and a piece of Gold under it;	272	Priest 30		8
and he will give him the gold for it, which the Child utterly	272	Priest 30		11
Gods Spirit will mortify and try them as gold in the fire. . .	314	Valdesso		22
All is not gold that glisters.	331	Proverbs		306
No lock will hold against the power of gold.	332	Proverbs		317
No Lockes can hold against gold.	332	Proverbs	V	317
Hee that labours and thrives spins gold.	332	Proverbs		341
The ballance distinguisheth not betweene gold and lead. . . .	342	Proverbs		629
That is gold which is worth gold.	349	Proverbs		841
Who will make a doore of gold must knock a naile every day. . .	354	Proverbs		1004
If gold knew what gold is, gold would get gold I wis. . . .	354	Proverbs		1012
GOLDEN				
And spread thy golden wings in me;	59	Whitsunday		2
Display thy golden wings in me;	59	Whitsunday	W	2
GOLIAH				
that if any of yours shou'd prove a Goliah-like trouble, . . .	374	Letters		5
GOLIAH-LIKE				
that if any of yours shou'd prove a Goliah-like trouble, . . .	374	Letters		5
GON				
He that will do thee a good turne, either he will be gon or dye.	358	Proverbs	D	1083
GONE				
Are gone to grasse, and in the pasture lost.	10	Ch.-Porch		96
But love is lost, the way of friendship's gone, ...	17	Ch.-Porch		275
But love is lost, the art of friendship's gone, ...	17	Ch.-Porch	W	275
Who say, I care not, I give those for gone;	20	Ch.-Porch	W	347
One half of me being gone, the rest I give	35	Thanksgvng		27
One half of me being gone, the rest I'le give	35	Thanksgvng	W	27
Sinne being gone, oh fill the place, ...	39	Good Fri.		29
Sinn being gone o doe thou fill	39	Good Fri.	W	29
They told me there, that he was lately gone	40	Redemption		6

GONE (cont'd)	PAGE	TITLE		LINE
Man had straight forward gone	75	Sunday		15
The man is gone,	79	Employm.2		27
Who goeth in the way which Christ hath gone,	87	Lent		37
Who goeth in that way which Christ hath gone,	87	Lent	V	37
Who goeth in the way that Christ hath gone,	87	Lent	W	37
He is to Sinai gone, as we heard tell:	99	Decay		9
My thoughts and joyes are all packt up and gone,	109	Home		69
Know their home, and get them gone:	113	Businesse		4
When with my pleasures ev'n my rest was gone?	130	Love unkn.		53
Thy life is Gods, thy time to come is gone,	144	Discharge		11
Could have recover'd greennesse? It was gone	166	The Flower		9
Souls joy, when thou art gone,	183	A Parodie		1
Till all be gone. so went the Church her way,	191	Ch.-Milit.	W	33
the way that right'ous men have gone:	215	Psalm I	D	22
and furthers them when hee is gone, in their imployment;	247	Priest 14		14
but had already gone farre in me, first caused me to leave	291	Cornaro		18
Thursday come, and the week's gone.	341	Proverbs		587
GOOD				
Ryme thee to good, and make a bait of pleasure.	6	Ch.-Porch		4
Hee that has all ill, & can have no good	7	Ch.-Porch	W	35
Who lives by rule then, keeps good companie.	12	Ch.-Porch		138
Who cannot rest till hee good-fellows finde,	12	Ch.-Porch		149
Is a good spurre. Correct thy passions spite;	16	Ch.-Porch		263
Get a good stock of these, then draw the card	18	Ch.-Porch		293
Kindnesse, good parts, great places are the way	19	Ch.-Porch		327
A good digestion turneth all to health:	20	Ch.-Porch		358
Keep all thy native good, and naturalize	21	Ch.-Porch		361
Give to all something; to a good poore man,	21	Ch.-Porch		377
The worst speak something good: if all want sense,	23	Ch.-Porch		431
The spirit and good extract of my heart	38	The Sinner		10
Good Friday.	38	Good Fri.		T
O my chief good,	38	Good Fri.		1
Since nothing Lord can bee so good	39	Good Fri.	W	21
Sure there is room within our hearts good store;	40	Sepulchre		5
Thine own gift good, yet me from my wayes taking.	48	Afflict.1		54
Is all good structure in a winding stair?	56	Jordan 1		3
Thou wouldst extend me to some good,	57	Employm. 1		2
Such are thy secrets, which my life makes good,	58	H.Script.2		9
Scarce a good joy creeps through the chink:	60	Whitsunday		22
Hath some good in him, all agree.	63	Sinne 2		3
It wants the good of vertue, and of being.	63	Sinne 2		5
To sever the good fellowship of dust,	65	Ch.-monum.		13
And sanctif'd me to do good;	68	Trin.Sun.		3
Nor a good sword, nor yet a lute:	69	Quidditie		4
Nor a good sword, not yet a lute:	69	Quidditie	W	4
He that doth still and strongly good pursue,	72	Constancie		2
Life is a businesse, not good cheer;	79	Employm.2		16
As good go any where, they say,	80	Deniall		11
Ev'n unto death: since he di'd for my good,	83	Sighs & Gr.		23
When good is seasonable;	86	Lent		15
Spoil the good use; lest by that argument	86	Lent		29
Spoil our good use; lest by that argument	86	Lent	W	29
Or of it self, like a good huswife, spunne	88	The Pearl		4
Nothing we see, but means our good,	91	Man		27
If any touch my friend, or his good name,	93	Unkindness		6
Onely to purchase my good-will:	94	Unkindness		24
I took, without more thinking, in good part	94	Life		8
Since if my sent be good, I care not, if	94	Life		17
Of that good companie.	101	Miserie	W	48
Show'd a strange love to all our good:	104	Obedience		27
Is not so deare to thee as one good grone.	106	Sion		18
He so farre thy good did plot,	113	Businesse		23
Each creature hath a wisdome for his good.	118	Providence		61
Hard things are glorious; easie things good cheap.	119	Providence		97
The windes grew gard'ners, and the clouds good fountains.	120	Providence		116
Or with a stone! yet make no good foundation.	120	Providence		124
At length I met a rev'rend good old man,	125	Peace		19
At Salem dwelt, who liv'd with good increase	125	Peace		23
And made it bring forth grapes good store.	128	Bunch Gr.		25
And have good cause: there it was dipt and di'd,	129	Love unkn.		16
A friend did steal into my cup for good,	130	Love unkn.		43
Lord, pardon, for thy sonne makes good	136	Ephes.		35
Enact good cheer?	138	The Size		16
Exact good cheer?	138	The Size	V	16
Wherefore sit down, good heart;	138	The Size		37
Expell good motions from thy breast,	139	Artillerie		7
Dread Lord, said I, so oft my good;	139	Artillerie		13
Thought to let out, the bleeding did you good,	140	Ch.-rents		14
Save one good Angell, which a friend had ti'd	142	Pilgrimage		17
Of future depths, but drink the cleare and good.	145	Discharge		28
Yet one, if good, may title to a number;	147	Offering		9
As neither good, nor one: so oft divisions	147	Offering		14
Untill thou finde and use it to thy good:	147	Offering		23
Were sinne alive, good cause there were	150	Longing		65
Good cable, to enforce and draw,	153	The Collar		24
And so take up at use good store:	159	Praise 3		40
Doth flatter power. Lest good come short of ill	161	Priesthood		40
Good men ye be, to leave me my best room,	176	Forerunners		7
Naming you not to your good:	180	Invitation		9
Still are good,	181	Banquet		26

GOOD (cont'd)

	PAGE	TITLE		LINE
Much in request, much sought for, as a good.	186	Death		16
Much in request, much long'd for as a good.	186	Death	W	16
Breaking her peace, and tainting her good name.	193	Ch.-Milit.		106
To make good that which ev'ry day he winnes.	193	Ch.-Milit.		126
And make that name good by their transmigrations;	195	Ch.-Milit.		184
The hast of thy good will.	200	H. Commun.	W	15
Creatures are good, & have their place	200	H. Commun.	W	22
Be good to the Poor,	207	Walton 3		4
(Till now averse to all that's Good)	214	Convert	D	17
of good men shall the wicked come.	215	Psalm I	D	20
will shew us good? But, Lord,	217	Psalm IV	D	22
He judgeth both the good, and those	222	Psalm VII	D	39
but that it is a good strife to go as farre as wee can in pleasing	224	Priest		11
or a good proportion of all, out of all which he hath compiled	229	Priest 5		32
by frequent wishes of the peoples good, and joying therein,	234	Priest 7		7
of holinesse, then the procuring, and rejoycing in anothers good.	234	Priest 7		10
and that the good God would pardon all those, who come with lesse	235	Priest 8		30
raise up their mindes to apprehend Gods good blessing to our Church,	236	Priest 8		23
He knew that (the good instrument of God to bring women to heaven)	238	Priest 9		30
and out of liberality, make her fruitfull in all good works.	238	Priest 9		33
to his earthly, having no title to either, except he do good to both.	239	Priest 10		23
resolves with himself never to omit any present good deed of charity,	240	Priest 10		6
Good deeds, and good breeding, are his two great stocks for his	240	Priest 10		10
and good breeding, are his two great stocks for his children;	240	Priest 10		10
his wife among her neighbours is the beginner of good discourses,	240	Priest 10		28
but an old good servant boards a child.	241	Priest 10		11
and common, but wholsome, what hee hath, is little, but very good;	241	Priest 10		16
men to Piety, and is content, if at least so, they will become good:	244	Priest 11		1
if not the best way, yet any way, make his Parish good.	244	Priest 11		5
he bethinketh himselfe what good deeds he can do that day,	244	Priest 12		16
hee receives, to want a good meal suting to the joy of the occasion.	245	Priest 12		8
Therefore first he takes order, that all things be in good repair;	246	Priest 13		4
an handsome, and seemly Carpet of good and costly Stuffe, or Cloth,	246	Priest 13		17
as if hee findes them reading, hee furnisheth them with good books;	247	Priest 14		16
for it is a good and just thing for every one to do their own	247	Priest 14		22
may have wherewithall to serve God the better, and to do good deeds.	248	Priest 14		8
make them understand the great good use of this antient and pious	249	Priest 15		30
or that overtake him, hee begins good discourses, such as may edify,	251	Priest 17		4
reading of Scriptures, and other good books, how Sundayes,	251	Priest 17		23
but the earnestnesse to do all the good he can, moves him to say thus	251	Priest 17		32
he keeps good Correspondence with all the neighbouring Pastours round	253	Priest 19		15
or lovely, or of good report, if there be any vertue, or any praise;	253	Priest 19		24
as an obligation to do good, rather then to those that are further,	253	Priest 19		27
such gifts, he sends him a good book, or easeth him in his Tithes,	254	Priest 20		15
paymaster, rewarding all good deeds to their full proportion.	254	Priest 20		21
the secret of whose good consists in this, that at Sermons,	257	Priest 21		18
then he keeps good correspondence with some neighbour Phisician,	260	Priest 23		37
hear Sermons against both, and himselfe condemn both in good earnest:	264	Priest 26		16
when his storing, which was even now good, passeth from good to bad.	264	Priest 26		30
made food miraculously, then suffered so good desires to miscarry.	267	Priest 26		25
and that pleasantnesse of disposition is a great key to do good;	268	Priest 27		1
blessing of God, and the great Instrument of doing admirable good;	274	Priest 32		29
of his affairs, that hee may have wherewithall to do good.	275	Priest 32		30
his beck throughout the Kingdome, accountable for the publick good;	276	Priest 32		12
inabling him with power to do good, and to restrain all those,	276	Priest 32		14
These are so far from deterring any good man from the place,	276	Priest 32		23
when they see any remarkable point of Education or good husbandry,	276	Priest 32		30
when they meet with good fruit, get a graffe of the tree,	276	Priest 32		32
he may go to Court, as the eminent place both of good and ill.	277	Priest 32		6
For the temptations with which a good man is beset, and the ways	278	Priest 33		15
Parson is a Lover of old Customes, if they be good, and harmlesse;	283	Priest 35		28
the custome, that may be severed from the good, he pares the apple,	283	Priest 35		32
that his Parish at good times invite one another to their houses,	284	Priest 35		17
of Christs Cross, or for any shame to leave that which is good.	284	Priest 35		33
The fruit of this blessing good Hannah found, and received with great	285	Priest 36		20
by speaking any good, this unusuall form begets a reverence,	286	Priest 36		24
and that even some good men think, so they speak truth,	286	Priest 37		31
for we must not do evill, that good may come of it.	287	Priest 37		7
so may they their good name, and the possession thereof,	287	Priest 37		32
it is a duty rather, which may do much good, and save much harme.	288	Priest 37		1
as barren grounds are made fruitfull by good husbandry.	292	Cornaro		12
That which savours, is good and nourisheth, be consonant to truth.	293	Cornaro		9
hurt those bodies, which were kept in good order by a moderate Diet:	294	Cornaro		2
and then was dragged for a good space by the furie of the horses,	294	Cornaro		38
and that I had for many yeares continued in good health,	295	Cornaro		27
neither the good humours to be corrupted, or contract any ill	296	Cornaro		34
and also doth preserve even ill tempers in good health,	298	Cornaro		15
But I drained the ground, and made the aire good:	301	Cornaro		28
untoiled places in my countrey, to cultivation and good husbandrie.	302	Cornaro		16
in any thing I forsake that Temperance which I have found so good,	303	Cornaro		35
The Authors good meaning in this, will better appear by his 98	312	Valdesso	V	4
will better appear by his 98 Consideration of faith and good works.	312	Valdesso	V	5
but in things good, as to relieve my Neighbour, God hath already	313	Valdesso		13
for it invites us to all good, according to that singular place,	313	Valdesso		19
A man is to embrace all good, but because he cannot doe all,	313	Valdesso		21
Feare is given to Christ, but not doubt, and upon good ground.	315	Valdesso		12
how this opinion could befall so good a man as it seems Valdesso was,	317	Valdesso		31
justified by faith, or by good works, or condemned for unbelief,	319	Valdesso	V	17
A handfull of good life is better then a bushell of learning.	321	Proverbs		3
A good bargaine is a pick-purse.	321	Proverbs		12

GOOD (cont'd)

	PAGE	TITLE	LINE
Not a long day, but a good heart rids worke.	321	Proverbs	24
In a good house all is quickly ready.	323	Proverbs	58
Never had ill workeman good tooles.	323	Proverbs	67
Good is to bee sought out, and evill attended.	324	Proverbs	112
A good pay-master starts not at assurances.	324	Proverbs	113
Keepe good men company, and you shall be of the number.	325	Proverbs	120
Water trotted is as good as oates.	325	Proverbs	131
Old wine, and an old friend, are good provisions.	325	Proverbs	136
Good is the mora that makes all sure.	325	Proverbs	145
Good words are worth much, and cost little.	326	Proverbs	155
Hell is full of good meanings and wishings.	326	Proverbs	170
Evils have their comfort, good none can support	328	Proverbs	208
In good yeares corne is hay, in ill yeares straw is corne.	328	Proverbs	216
Good cheape is deare.	329	Proverbs	261
Good words quench more then a bucket of water.	329	Proverbs	263
An ill agreement is better then a good judgement.	329	Proverbs	264
Better good afarre off, then evill at hand.	330	Proverbs	267
A mountaine and a river are good neighbours.	330	Proverbs	274
Good service is a great inchantment.	331	Proverbs	291
That is not good language which all understand not.	331	Proverbs	302
He that hath no ill fortune is troubled with good.	333	Proverbs	358
Hee that makes a good warre makes a good peace.	335	Proverbs	420
shall neither have good wife nor good horse.	336	Proverbs	434
Good is good, but better carries it.	337	Proverbs	454
Good finds good.	337	Proverbs	456
The good mother sayes not, Will you? but gives.	337	Proverbs	467
Little journeys and good cost bring safe home.	338	Proverbs	502
A little and good fills the trencher.	338	Proverbs	505
Beare with evill, and expect good.	338	Proverbs	511
A jade eates as much as a good horse.	339	Proverbs	519
All things in their beeing are good for something.	339	Proverbs	520
On a good bargaine thinke twice.	339	Proverbs	529
To a good spender God is the Treasurer.	339	Proverbs	530
Love makes a good eye squint.	339	Proverbs	543
Great trees are good for nothing but shade.	339	Proverbs	546
He that hath no good trade, it is to his losse.	340	Proverbs	560
He that hopes not for good, feares not evill.	340	Proverbs	563
Good & quickly seldome meete.	341	Proverbs	580
A good payer is master of anothers purse.	341	Proverbs	595
A good Judge conceives quickly, judges slowly.	341	Proverbs	599
The thought hath good leggs, and the quill a good tongue.	342	Proverbs	612
In every Art it is good to have a master.	342	Proverbs	619
Shew a good man his errour and he turnes it to a vertue,	343	Proverbs	655
It's not good fishing before the net.	343	Proverbs	663
When my house burnes, it's not good playing at Chesse.	343	Proverbs	666
the rich in keeping, the good in learning.	344	Proverbs	678
Long jesting was never good.	344	Proverbs	694
If a good man thrive, all thrive with him.	344	Proverbs	695
Good workemen are seldome rich.	346	Proverbs	756
A good heart cannot lye.	347	Proverbs	800
Good swimmers at length are drowned.	347	Proverbs	801
Good land, evill way.	347	Proverbs	802
It's good walking with a horse in ones hand.	348	Proverbs	804
Set good against evill.	348	Proverbs	823
Hee that brings good newes knockes hard.	348	Proverbs	824
Hee goes not out of his way, that goes to a good Inne.	348	Proverbs	831
It's good tying the sack before it be full.	349	Proverbs	842
Good newes may bee told at any time, but ill in the morning.	350	Proverbs	877
Amongst good men two men suffice.	350	Proverbs	885
He that will enter into Paradise, must have a good key.	350	Proverbs	895
Good horses make short miles.	352	Proverbs	935
All are presumed good, till they are found in a fault.	352	Proverbs	944
The house is a fine house, when good folke are within.	352	Proverbs	952
The house is a fine house, when good folks are within.	352	Proverbs	V 952
To live peaceably with all breedes good blood.	353	Proverbs	963
Hee a beast doth die, that hath done no good to his country.	354	Proverbs	993
He that dies without the company of good men	354	Proverbs	995
puts not himselfe into a good way.	354	Proverbs	995
and a good subject, is incompossible.	357	Proverbs	D 1058
He that will do thee a good turne, either he will be gon or dye.	358	Proverbs	D 1083
In the mouth of a bad dog fals often a good bone.	358	Proverbs	D 1093
Of a pigs taile you can never make a good shaft.	359	Proverbs	D 1104
It is good to have some friends both in heaven and hell.	359	Proverbs	D 1127
It is good to hold the asse by the bridle.	360	Proverbs	D 1129
wherein consisteth the making good of my former education,	364	Letters	17
it is their ordinary speech, and now let them make it good;	364	Letters	23
of all good which you see in Frenchmen, whether it be in knowledge,	366	Letters	7
so shall you play a good marchant, by transporting French commodities	366	Letters	11
and have a good conceit of your wit, mark what I say, have a good	366	Letters	15
of your wit, mark what I say, have a good conceit of your wit;	366	Letters	15
I dare say she would make good her promise of taking five or six	367	Letters	2
Good Sir, make it plain to her, that I loved her even in my	371	Letters	11
with our good and gracious God, incessantly begging some ease of your	371	Letters	28
would quickly make good my wish but that my employment does fix me	372	Letters	18
and, accept the good meaning of, Your most obedient Son,	374	Letters	31
but advance them, was lovingly done, and like a good brother.	375	Letters	3
I was desirous to putt a good mind into the way of charity,	375	Letters	8
Neither hath she any to repair unto at good times, as Christmas,	375	Letters	27
surely it were a great good deed, and I would have her conveyed	375	Letters	31
I forgett all thinges, so I may doe them good who want it.	376	Letters	6

GOOD (cont'd)	PAGE	TITLE	LINE
power to defeat my charity, and evill shold be stronger then good:	376	Letters	10
For the time of breeding is the time of doing children good;	376	Letters	14
done fairly, if they leave them a good portion after their decease.	376	Letters	16
the good GOD bless you more and more;	376	Letters	19
Wherefore the Lord make good the blessing of your Mother upon you,	377	Letters	4
to his glory, your own good, and the great joy of Madam, . .	377	Letters	6
forwardness in religious works is a good testimony of a good spirit.	377	Letters	25
and make you abound in every good worke, to the joy of your ever	377	Letters	27
a long time, to doe the place good, & have endeavoured many wayes,	378	Letters	6
Higher opportunities of doeing good are to be preferred before lower,	380	Woodnoth	3
therfore your choice at first was good	380	Woodnoth	6
are lovely, & of good report if there be any vertue or any praise.	380	Woodnoth	14
As in things inwardly good to have an eye to the world may be	380	Woodnoth	16
To desire good & endeavour it when we can doe no more, is to doe it.	381	Woodnoth	15
In Gods accepting you have done the good you intended, & whom serve	381	Woodnoth	18
GOOD-FELLOWS			
Who cannot rest till hee good-fellows finde, ...	12	Ch.-Porch	149
GOOD-WILL			
Onely to purchase my good-will:	94	Unkindness	24
GOODNESS			
What a trouble hath your Goodness brought on you, by admitting our	376	Letters	26
be My God & Dear Master, the Spring & Fountain of all Goodness.	379	Letters	17
GOODNESSE			
His goodnesse sets not, but in dark can runne:	72	Constancie	23
And goodnesse of the deed.	86	Lent	27
If goodnesse leade him not, yet wearinesse	160	The Pulley	19
And being craftier much then Goodnesse was, ...	193	Ch.-Milit.	124
sets up as many encouragements to goodnesse as he can, both in	244	Priest 11	3
in this, how Gods goodnesse strives with mans refractorinesse;	272	Priest 30	5
GOODS			
If thou be single, all thy goods and ground	17	Ch.-Porch	283
Thou shalt recover all thy goods in kinde, ...	54	Love 2	11
Till it found out how to consume thy goods:	83	Sighs & Gr.	11
To both our goods, if he to it will stand.	105	Obedience	40
Thy curious art in marshalling thy goods.	119	Providence	94
as being persons enabled by that Name to take moveable goods,	270	Priest 29	2
sued at the Law concerning such goods for the use and profit of their	270	Priest 29	3
or if the goods be housed, a fire hath broken forth, and suddenly	271	Priest 30	24
And as malefactors may lose & forfeit their goods, or life; . .	287	Priest 37	32
Goods are theirs that enjoy them.	349	Proverbs	850
body to Almightie God that made them doe thus dispose of my goods.	382	G.H.'s Will	3
I give all my goods both within doores and without doores both	382	G.H.'s Will	3
GOOSE			
and had a goose in his sleeve.	345	Proverbs	737
GORDIAN			
Who can these Gordian knots undo?	135	Divinitie	20
GOSHEN			
Goshen was darknesse, Egypt full of lights, ...	191	Ch.-Milit.	43
GOSPEL			
And tune mens hearts against the Gospel came:	192	Ch.-Milit.	76
And cleanse mens hearts against the Gospel came:	192	Ch.-Milit. W	76
They have their times of Gospel, ev'n as we.	197	Ch.-Milit.	248
They have their time of Gospel, ev'n as we.	197	Ch.-Milit. W	248
Usher'd the Gospel ever in mens hearts, ...	197	Ch.-Milit.	264
For the Law required one thing, and the Gospel another: . .	229	Priest 4	15
Parson considering that repentance is the great vertue of the Gospel,	279	Priest 33	7
There are two Prophesies in the Gospel, which evidently argue Christs	282	Priest 34	22
but with the Gospel it selfe be preached to all ages, Matth. 26. 13.	282	Priest 34	26
To these might be added the Preaching of the Gospel in all Nations,	282	Priest 34	32
the Gospel doth not, which hath so much advanced Charity, . .	287	Priest 37	22
GOSPELL			
Besides the continuall succession (since the Gospell) of holy men,	282	Priest 34	19
then he that reads the womans oyntment in the Gospell, or sees	283	Priest 34	2
in this land of light, and region of the Gospell, among his chosen.	304	Valdesso	15
excellently the intent of the Gospell in the acceptation of Christs	304	Valdesso	22
testifying, and applying the revealed truth of the Gospell; . .	308	Valdesso	32
or assent to the promises of the Gospell by heare-say, or relation	309	Valdesso	1
That God in the dayes of the Gospell will not give an outward Law	310	Valdesso	5
it is Faith and Infidelity that shall judge us now since the Gospell,	311	Valdesso	23
GOSSIPS			
Gossips are frogs, they drinke and talke.	330	Proverbs	275
GOT			
Have got to be a deare fool for an houre.	16	Ch.-Porch	246
I got me flowers to straw thy way;	42	Easter	19
I got me boughs off many a tree:	42	Easter	20
When I got health, thou took'st away my life, ...	47	Afflict.1	31
But I have got his sonne, and he hath none.	63	Even-song	8
To this great kingdome, which thou now hast got, ...	77	Avarice	6
Nay, thou hast got the face of man; for we	77	Avarice	10
He sayes, in things which use hath justly got, ...	86	Lent	10
Nothing hath got so farre, ...	91	Man	19
I would do well, yet sinne the hand hath got:	96	Justice 1	10
When I had got these parcels, instantly	112	JESU	7
Which many wondring at, got some of those	125	Peace	29
So to cares cops I came, and there got through	142	Pilgrimage	11
At length I got unto the gladsome hill, ...	142	Pilgrimage	19
Hath got a tongue!	150	Longing	76
Whose streams we got by the Apostles sluce, ...	152	The Jews	3
And got the day.	172	The Glance	16
At first he got to Egypt, and did sow	193	Ch.-Milit.	107

	PAGE	TITLE		LINE
GOT (cont'd)				
For in the end I got the victorie, to my great honour, and no lesse	294	Cornaro		28
A penny spar'd is twice got.	338	Proverbs		506
but upon the want of those Books which were not to be got in England;	367	Letters		5
GOTTEN				
That thou hast gotten. Surely use alone	12	Ch.-Porch		155
he hath gotten to himself some insight in things ordinarily incident	259	Priest 23		33
A City that parlies is half gotten.	358	Proverbs	D	1097
GOUT				
Nor his long journey, nor his gout and furre.	195	Ch.-Milit.		198
Nor his long journey, nor his gout or furre.	195	Ch.-Milit.	W	198
and the beginning of the Gout, with almost a continuall fever	291	Cornaro		23
GOVERN				
To guide and govern it to my relief,	73	Afflict.3		3
much as she can, teacheth us how to govern our selves in sicknesse:	299	Cornaro		26
but an 100 sons are not enough to govern one Father.	335	Proverbs	V	404
GOVERNE				
One father is enough to governe one hundred sons,	335	Proverbs		404
GOVERNED				
Warre and Physicke are governed by the eye.	351	Proverbs		906
GOVERNING				
The Parson is very exact in the governing of his house,	239	Priest 10		6
and secret of governing to preserve a directnesse, and open	240	Priest 10		33
the second a governing power;	271	Priest 30		2
By Gods governing power he preserves and orders the references	271	Priest 30		13
and other accidents by his governing power, the fairest harvests come	271	Priest 30		17
GOVERNMENT				
Is thy chief government, to manage woe,	212	Bohemia	D	57
and halfe at least of the government of the house, reserving so much	238	Priest 9		37
I doubt but if Abraham had lived in our Kingdome under government,	316	Valdesso		23
GOVERNOUR				
though there be a great Governour of all things, yet to them he is	281	Priest 34		10
GOVERNOURS				
In great pedigrees there are Governours and Chandlers.	328	Proverbs		222
GOWN				
And wrap me in a gown.	47	Afflict.1		40
A gown and pen became him wondrous well:	194	Ch.-Milit.		167
GOWNE				
Well may hee smell fire, whose gowne burnes.	325	Proverbs		138
The gowne is his that weares it,	337	Proverbs		476
That's the best gowne that goes up and downe the house.	346	Proverbs		742
GRACE				
Which Angels did desire to have the grace,	32	Sacrifice		182
Whom Angels did desire to have the grace,	32	Sacrifice	W	182
And keep possession with thy grace;	39	Good Fri.		30
Angels and grace, eternall hopes and fears.	46	Sinne 1		12
While grace fills up uneven nature.	50	Faith		32
Onely thy grace, which with these elements comes,	52	H.Commun.		19
But thy diviner world of grace	56	Temper 2		6
O fix thy chair of grace, that all my powers	56	Temper 2		9
For as thou dost impart thy grace,	57	Employm. 1		9
Grace.	60	Grace		T
Thy works nights captives: O let grace	60	Grace		7
Let grace work too, and on my soul	60	Grace		15
Let suppling grace, to crosse his art,	60	Grace		19
O lett thy grace, to crosse his art,	60	Grace	W	19
To be a window, through thy grace.	67	Windows		5
(For he would not) as they beheld the grace	70	Humilitie		18
The pasture is thy word: the streams, thy grace	81	Christmas		19
But Love took Grace & Glory by the hand,	84	Sighs & Gr.	W	19
But Grace shor'd these, and cut that as it grew.	84	The World		15
But Love and Grace took Glorie by the hand,	84	The World		19
Betwixt this world and that of grace.	90	Afflict.4		6
That both grace and glorie tend	92	Antiphon 2		7
But when thy grace	94	Unkindness		18
Grace turnes the Optick, then they fall.	97	Charms & K	W	18
The Courtier getts it, that has grace.	97	Charms & K	W	20
Glorie and grace	102	Miserie		71
To double-moat thee with his grace,	110	Brit. Ch.		29
The sphere of vertue, and each shining grace	175	The Foil		2
To the throne of grace.	179	Discipline		16
Thou art grown fair and full of grace,	186	Death		15
Ah, what a thing is man devoid of grace,	193	Ch.-Milit.		111
Confronting equally the law and grace.	196	Ch.-Milit.		218
For gold and grace did never yet agree:	197	Ch.-Milit.		251
Thou wilt revenge their quarrell, making grace	197	Ch.-Milit.		255
Nature & Grace	202	Trin.Sun.	W	5
when I his grace implore:	217	Psalm IV	D	14
and on his grace rely.	217	Psalm IV	D	20
But in th' abundance of thy Grace	218	Psalm V	D	17
shall I in vain thy Grace implore?	220	Psalm VI	D	8
according to the grace that is given to us, whether prophecy,	226	Priest 2		4
as to neglect the grace of God in himself, and what the Holy Spirit	229	Priest 4		20
unto God, and as his grace shall direct him, so let him proceed.	237	Priest 9		6
could out of humility, produce any speciall grace of faith, patience,	238	Priest 9		32
and saying grace at meat, and at going to bed by giving the Host	251	Priest 17		9
whether daily prayers be used, Grace, reading of Scriptures,	251	Priest 17		23
but to throw himself down at the throne of grace, saying,	257	Priest 22		32
where God is thanked for calling us to the knowledg of his grace,	258	Priest 22		6
the one, in wanting many excitings of grace;	259	Priest 22		5
Nature serving Grace both in comfort of diversion, and the benefit	261	Priest 23		11

GRATES	PAGE	TITLE		LINE
Faire language grates not the tongue.	347	Proverbs		799
GRATIA				
the one being gratia gratis data, the other gratia gratum faciens,	319	Valdesso		8
the other gratia gratum faciens, this being given only to the godly,	319	Valdesso		8
GRATIFIE				
to avoid obstinacie, and gratifie my friends, at length I yeelded,	296	Cornaro		6
GRATIOUS				
O gratious Lord how shall I know	200	H. Commun.	W	1
And now My gratious Lord God, is pleased to give me you for the Man,	378	Letters		7
GRATIS				
the one being gratia gratis data, the other gratia gratum faciens,	319	Valdesso		8
GRATUM				
the other gratia gratum faciens, this being given only to the godly,	319	Valdesso		8
GRAVE (serious)				
And th' other black and grave, wherewith each one	67	Ch.-floore		4
His grave aspect had more of heav'n then hell:	194	Ch.-Milit.		168
His grave aspect was liker heav'n then hell:	194	Ch.-Milit.	W	168
just, prudent, temperate, bold, grave in all his wayes. . .	227	Priest 3		2
speaking, but with a grave livelinesse, between fear and zeal,	231	Priest 6		19
This he thinks naturall, and sweet, and grave.	235	Priest 7		5
where painted, and that all the painting be grave, and reverend,	246	Priest 13		12
GRAVE				
If they dare try, a glorious life, or grave.	10	Ch.-Porch		90
A grave too big for me.	55	Temper 1		12
And digs my grave at each remove:	60	Grace		14
Untill the grave increase our cold.	79	Employm.2		30
A better lodging then a rack or grave.	81	Christmas		14
Hast thou redeem'd us from the grave!	82	Ungratef.		2
Thy root is ever in its grave, ...	87	Vertue		7
Thy root is ever in his grave, ...	87	Vertue	V	7
Marking his grave, and thawing ev'ry yeare, ...	98	Mortific.		26
Christ left his grave-clothes, that we might, when grief . .	112	Dawning		15
Christ left his grave-cloths, that we might, when grief . .	112	Dawning	V	15
He makes a grave; as if the thing had sense, ...	119	Providence		83
But after death out of his grave	125	Peace		27
Unto an honest faithfull grave;	186	Death		23
Read that lesson to the grave.	187	Dooms-day		18
Thou do'st no more, then doth the grave:	202	love	W	22
or who shall praise Thee in the grave?	220	Psalm VI	D	12
the carnall and wilfull man with the worm of the grave in this world,	272	Priest 30		13
whereas he thinks it not onely a grave, and reverend thing, . .	285	Priest 36		3
streams of thy bloud were currant through darknesse, grave, and hell;	288	Priest		33
GRAVE-CLOTHES				
Christ left his grave-clothes, that we might, when grief . .	112	Dawning		15
GRAVE-CLOTHS				
Christ left his grave-cloths, that we might, when grief . .	112	Dawning	V	15
GRAVED				
After, where ES, and next where U was graved.	112	JESU		6
GRAVES				
They step into their voluntarie graves, ...	98	Mortific.		8
Let the graves make their confession, ...	187	Dooms-day		15
Untill the graves againe restore	208	H. Danvers	D	3
GRAVITIE				
It did not fit his gravitie to stirre, ...	195	Ch.-Milit.		197
who are come to the gravitie, and ripenesse of judgement for so	276	Priest 32		16
and wee also putting off that countenance and gravitie, . .	442	Oration		5
GRAVITY				
hath neither in it sweetnesse, nor gravity, nor variety, . .	235	Priest 7		8
GRAYHOUND				
A gentlemans grayhound, and a salt-box; seeke them at the fire.	327	Proverbs		205
GRAZE				
While ye graze without your bounds:	180	Invitation		21
GREAT				
Studie this art, make it thy great designe;	10	Ch.-Porch		101
Some great estates provide, but doe not breed	10	Ch.-Porch		103
And rots to nothing at the next great thaw.	12	Ch.-Porch		140
By great deeds shew, that thou canst little do;	15	Ch.-Porch		220
But the great souldiers honour was compos'd	15	Ch.-Porch		225
Towards great persons use respective boldnesse:	16	Ch.-Porch		253
Towards great persons use respectfull boldnesse:	16	Ch.-Porch	W	253
Calmnesse is great advantage: he that lets	19	Ch.-Porch		313
Kindnesse, good parts, great places are the way	19	Ch.-Porch		327
And readie Paschal Lambe of this great week:	28	Sacrifice		59
Then they accuse me of great blasphemie, ...	28	Sacrifice		61
So sits the earths great curse in Adams fall	32	Sacrifice		165
I straight return'd, and knowing his great birth, ...	40	Redemption		9
Sought him accordingly in great resorts;	40	Redemption		10
Write thee great God, and me a childe:	44	H. Bapt.2		7
Lord, I confesse my sinne is great;	48	Repentance		1
Great is my sinne. Oh! gently treat	48	Repentance		2
As a great Clerk, and reach the highest stature.	50	Faith		30
Immortall Love, authour of this great frame, ...	54	Love 1		1
Will great God measure with a wretch?	55	Temper 1		15
At thy great doom.	57	Employm. 1		8
I am no link of thy great chain, ...	57	Employm. 1		21
He that first fell from his great birth	59	Whitsunday	W	15
Restore this day, for thy great name, ...	60	Whitsunday		27
Thy great house would a dungeon prove, ...	60	Grace	W	6
With a great stable or demain:	70	Quidditie		8
With my great stable or demain:	70	Quidditie	W	8

GREAT (cont'd)

	PAGE	TITLE		LINE
Who, when great trials come, ...	72	Constancie		11
Our great Redeemer did remove	76	Sunday		44
To this great kingdome, which thou now hast got, ...	77	Avarice		6
The great restorative for all decay	78	Ang.&Sts.		12
Of his great crown, from whom lyes no appeal	78	Ang.&Sts.	W	22
The great shepherd of the fold	92	Antiphon 2		10
Perhaps great places and thy praise	95	Submission		15
List, ye may heare great Aarons bell.	99	Decay		10
Of thy great love once spread, as in an urn	99	Decay		17
Is thy great arm which spans the east and west, ...	103	Prayer 2		8
So great are thy perfections, ...	104	Obedience		24
Great God doth fight, he doth submit.	106	Sion		16
A great affliction broke the little frame, ...	112	JESU		3
Thou art in small things great, not small in any:	118	Providence		41
The great prey on the lesse, they on some weed.	118	Providence		52
Of a great rock: I well remember all, ...	129	Love unkn.		15
Was in great letters set AFFLICTION.	129	Love unkn.		28
Great joyes are all at once;	138	The Size		19
They would great frosts and snows destroy:	138	The Size		40
In hope of great things. Call to minde thy dream, ...	138	The Size		44
Like two great pits;	141	Justice 2		8
Which by the springs accesse grew much more great.	154	Glimpse		15
And, that I had great cause to fear it.	155	Assurance		12
But since those great ones, be they ne're so great, ...	161	Priesthood		19
Thus we prevent the last great day, ...	171	Self-cond.		19
Holy Macarius and great Anthonie	191	Ch.-Milit.		41
The great heart stoops, and taketh from the dust	192	Ch.-Milit.		67
From times great Chronicle, and hither sent.	192	Ch.-Milit.		96
Fresh and fine deities. They were at great cost, ...	193	Ch.-Milit.		109
To this great lotterie, and all would pull.	193	Ch.-Milit.		134
Great waves of trouble combating my brest:	202	love	W	14
Now the great combat of our flesh & reason	204	The Knell	W	8
'Twas more secure in great Loves Common-weal	439	Walton 5		17
Great God will surely dry those teares, ...	213	L' Envoy	D	5
This oure great Sublunary Ball, ...	213	L' Envoy	D	12
combin'd in one great faction rise.	215	Psalm II	D	4
Serve our great God in fear, rejoyce, ...	216	Psalm II	D	27
my Soul for thy great mercy save;	220	Psalm VI	D	10
and makes great use of them in teaching, because people by what they	228	Priest 4		19
or against some great Festivall, that he may the better celebrate it,	232	Priest 7		22
that he himself hath often urged with no great success, . . .	232	Priest 7		28
scatteringly in the Sermon, carry great holiness in them. . .	234	Priest 7		1
save in the great shepherd of the fold, who first shed teares over	234	Priest 7		21
the discourse to his Majesty, And he is a great God, and terrible,	234	Priest 7		31
and terrible, as great in mercy, so great in judgement: . .	234	Priest 7		32
is another great stumbling block to the holinesse of Scholars.	238	Priest 9		19
and good breeding, are his two great stocks for his children;	240	Priest 10		10
and veal, if he addes any thing for a great day, or a stranger,	241	Priest 10		17
providence and thrift of the great householder of the world:	241	Priest 10		25
are two great obstructed vessels, and there is nothing that is food,	243	Priest 10		1
For many and wonderfull things are spoken of thee, thou great Vertue.	244	Priest 12		8
as at great Festivals, and Communions;	245	Priest 12		7
be as they ought, for those great duties that are performed in them.	246	Priest 13		7
and at great festivalls strawed, and stuck with boughs, . . .	246	Priest 13		9
and as following the Apostles two great and admirable Rules in things	246	Priest 13		26
and put them to great shame, who deny the Scripture to be perfect.	247	Priest 13		1
If it once have the honour of that Name, it grows great instantly.	249	Priest 14		3
labouring to make them understand the great good use of this antient	249	Priest 15		30
And of this he makes great use.	250	Priest 16		10
Wherein a pleasantness of disposition is of great use, men being	252	Priest 18		19
as joyfull a countenance, as if he were to entertain some great Lord.	253	Priest 19		20
Especially at Communion times he is in a great confusion, . . .	257	Priest 22		29
and Baptizeth not willingly, but on Sundayes, or great dayes.	258	Priest 22		3
Hee says that prayer with great devotion, where God is thanked	258	Priest 22		5
thing to sustain that place, but a great honour, and no less burden,	258	Priest 22		12
a state to reduce it to its principles by which it grew great;	258	Priest 22		17
(being the first step into their great and glorious calling) and upon	258	Priest 22		19
are to enter into this great work, he takes the more pains with them,	258	Priest 22		30
as to a great purchase for their children, and servants; . .	259	Priest 22		3
and smallage made into a Poultis, have done great and rare cures.	262	Priest 23		8
having ever besides two great helps and powerfull perswaders on his	263	Priest 24		15
which are two great lights able to dazle the eyes of the mis-led,	263	Priest 24		19
and that pleasantnesse of disposition is a great key to do good;	268	Priest 27		1
what a great Charge lyes upon them, and that indeed the whole order	269	Priest 29		27
considering the great Consequence of their place, and more of their	270	Priest 29		17
he wisheth them by no means to spare any, though never so great;	270	Priest 29		19
Countrey Parson considering the great aptnesse Countrey people have	270	Priest 30		24
he may behave himself so as befits so great a presence; . . .	273	Priest 31		27
duties, and it is a great stay and setling to religious souls.	274	Priest 31		2
The great and nationall sin of this Land he esteems to be Idlenesse;	274	Priest 32		8
great in it selfe, and great in Consequence:	274	Priest 32		9
great in it selfe, and great in Consequence:	274	Priest 32		10
wherein God hath placed two great Instruments, Reason in the soul,	274	Priest 32		19
blessing of God, and the great Instrument of doing admirable good;	274	Priest 32		29
and his dexterity so great, that he have leisure to look out,	276	Priest 32		1
and it is a great advantage to know the practice of the Land;	277	Priest 32		3
morning that hee is at home hee must either ride the Great Horse,	277	Priest 32		16
Parson considering that repentance is the great vertue of the Gospel,	279	Priest 33		7
though there be a great Governour of all things, yet to them he is	281	Priest 34		10
all the great wonders of old live in them, and then who can deny	282	Priest 34		5

	PAGE	TITLE		LINE
GREAT (cont'd)				
and with an exceeding great victory, which in the Creation needed	283	Priest 34		15
Light is a great Blessing, and as great as food, for which we give	284	Priest 35		27
is a great Blessing, and as great as food, for which we give thanks:	284	Priest 35		27
and received with great joy, 1 Sam. 1. 18. though it came from a man	285	Priest 36		21
that if a Minister talke with a great man in the ordinary course	286	Priest 36		20
they had a great desire to know the way of my life, and how I came	291	Cornaro		11
for this had every way great force for the recovering and preserving	292	Cornaro		5
and that in great quantitie, telling my Physicians nothing thereof,	292	Cornaro		29
of the minde, which have a great power over our constitutions.	293	Cornaro		36
that they had no great power tc hurt those bodies, which were kept in	294	Cornaro		1
others of my kindred saw some great powerfull men pick quarrels	294	Cornaro		16
that I might know what great power a sober and temperate life hath	294	Cornaro		25
the end I got the victorie, to my great honour, and no lesse profit:	294	Cornaro		28
for riding in a coach in great haste, it happened that the coach was	294	Cornaro		36
be much troubled, or make a great concourse, refused both remedies,	295	Cornaro		10
regular life can hardly be altered without exceeding great danger.	295	Cornaro		18
clearely be perceived, how great is the power of order and disorder;	297	Cornaro		3
of how great moment ten yeares are in mature age, wherein wisdome	298	Cornaro		29
That those inconveniences are of no great moment (as I shewed before)	299	Cornaro		16
I am not wearie of life, which I passe with great delight.	301	Cornaro		3
on both sides whereof are great and fruitfull fields, well manured	301	Cornaro		24
and husbandrie, whereof in this age there is great plentie.	302	Cornaro		1
heat of summer (which in Italie is very great) receiving not any hurt	302	Cornaro		19
So great is the power and efficacie of that Temperance which ever	302	Cornaro		20
and darkned by the Adversaries, and their great stumbling-block.	305	Valdesso		2
the great honour and reverence, which he every where beares towards	305	Valdesso		3
he every where beares towards our deare [great] Master and Lord,	305	Valdesso		4
I ever tooke that for a weaknesse in the great Patriark:	316	Valdesso		1
Things needing great Consideration. Mat. 24. 15.	317	Valdesso		25
Building and marrying of Children are great wasters.	321	Proverbs		11
Great strokes make not sweete musick.	322	Proverbs		26
He hath great neede of a foole, that plaies the foole himselfe.	322	Proverbs		46
God oft hath a great share in a little house.	323	Proverbs		60
In a great River great fish are found,	326	Proverbs		167
Great almes-giving lessens no mans living.	327	Proverbs		190
In great pedigrees there are Governours and Chandlers.	328	Proverbs		222
It is a great victory that comes without blood.	328	Proverbs		227
Good service is a great inchantment.	331	Proverbs		291
There would bee no great ones if there were no little ones.	331	Proverbs		292
There would bee no great ones if there were no mean ones.	331	Proverbs	V	292
Litle sticks kindle the fire; great ones put it out.	332	Proverbs		323
Pardons and pleasantnesse are great revenges of slanders.	333	Proverbs		365
Pardons and pleasantnesse are great Revengers of slanders.	333	Proverbs	V	365
The fault is as great as hee that is faulty.	333	Proverbs		369
A great ship askes deepe waters.	336	Proverbs		449
Great paines quickly find ease.	339	Proverbs		534
Great trees are good for nothing but shade.	339	Proverbs		546
There is great force hidden in a sweet command.	341	Proverbs		589
The command of custome is great.	341	Proverbs		590
Little dogs start the Hare, the great get her.	341	Proverbs		593
Ther's no great banquet but some fares ill.	343	Proverbs		668
If great men would have care of little ones,	344	Proverbs		697
Great businesses turne on a little pinne.	345	Proverbs		720
To a great night, a great Lanthorne.	345	Proverbs		731
A great dowry is a bed full of brables.	346	Proverbs		758
A little given seasonably excuses a great gift.	349	Proverbs		834
The little cannot bee great, unlesse he devoure many.	351	Proverbs		922
The dainties of the great are the teares of the poore.	352	Proverbs		937
when they are great they make them mad.	352	Proverbs		939
The great put the little on the hooke.	352	Proverbs		945
The great would have none great and the little all little.	352	Proverbs		946
Little losses amaze, great tame.	354	Proverbs		1013
A man of a great memory without learning	358	Proverbs	D	1085
Great Fortune brings with it Great misfortune.	360	Proverbs	D	1144
He is a great Necromancer,	361	Proverbs	D	1158
Great deservers grow Intolerable presumers.	361	Proverbs	D	1167
but not so great as he expected & therfore he grumblingly said that	368	Letters		32
yet you will pardon my haste, which is very great, though never so,	370	Letters		13
surely it were a great good deed, and I would have her conveyed	375	Letters		31
and the great joy of Madam, Your most faithful Servant in Christ	377	Letters		7
& the great Joy of Your Brother & Servant in Christ Jesus GEORGE	378	Letters		27
now Constancy is such & of great esteem with all.	380	Woodnoth		15
with that bloud, which useth to infuse so great and worthie Spirits.	442	Oration		15
must the felicitie of so great Princes redound also to those	442	Oration		25
since you are so great both in your Princes, and your selves,	442	Oration		28
How could you bee like great Alexander, unlesse Historie delivered	443	Oration		2
GREATER				
Thy self the worse, and so the distance greater.	16	Ch.-Porch		260
The greater world o' th' two; for that came in	33	Sacrifice		206
The greater world o' th' two; for that comes in	33	Sacrifice	W	206
Immortall Heat, O let thy greater flame	54	Love 2		1
The greater shall our glorie be.	57	Employm. 1		10
Lesser pains scape greater ones.	113	Businesse		14
When thou dost greater judgements SPARE,	133	Paradise		10
Of a lesse wcrld? the greater is but small,	164	Grief		10
But seems to yeeld Christ hath the greater wounds,	191	Ch.-Milit.		64
But seems to yeeld Christ had the greater wounds,	191	Ch.-Milit.	W	64
The question is, whose love the greater showes:	438	Lat.Trans.		2
For there is no greater sign of holinesse, then the procuring,	234	Priest 7		9
is ashamed in small things, will extend his pusillanimity to greater.	284	Priest 35		35

GREATER (cont'd)	PAGE	TITLE		LINE
that the hurt of too much meat is greater, then the commoditie	296	Cornaro		3
especially since there is a greater diversitie of tempers, . . .	297	Cornaro		31
lest they take a greater quantitie of any meat or drink (though most	300	Cornaro		12
The noise is greater then the nuts.	358	Proverbs	D	1073
if he had given it to the pope he should have had a greater reward.	368	Letters		34
GREATEST				
Love is a present for the greatest king.	20	Ch.-Porch	W	350
Most true to those, who are my greatest grief:	27	Sacrifice		39
Yet ev'n the greatest griefs	132	Mans medly		31
The greatest and hardest preparation is within:	226	Priest 2		12
herein is the greatest ability of a Parson to lead his people exactly	230	Priest 5		20
they all account, that to teach the ignorant is the greatest almes.	240	Priest 10		23
it being the greatest honor of this world, to do God and his chosen	270	Priest 29		10
The greatest step is that out of doores.	337	Proverbs		461
the Catholick Religion is professed with greatest strictness).	357	Proverbs	D	1047
They that hold the greatest farmes, pay the least rent	359	Proverbs	D	1100
whom to receive were the greatest charitie of all, for she is	375	Letters		24
GREATLY				
I do not greatly wonder at the sight, ...	161	Priesthood		23
He greatly esteemes also of cases of conscience, wherein he is much	230	Priest 5		18
and greatly to be esteemed for the knowing & curing of diseases,	298	Cornaro		4
But these erre greatly, as I will shew by my self, recounting	300	Cornaro		30
GREATNESS				
or if the poor Church-wardens be affrighted with their greatness,	232	Priest 6		15
GREATNESSE				
Envie not greatnesse: for thou mak'st thereby	16	Ch.-Porch		259
The greatnesse shew'd the owner. So I went	129	Love unkn.		29
there is nothing here answerable to the greatnesse of your presence.	442	Oration		30
GREECE				
Religion thence fled into Greece, where arts	191	Ch.-Milit.		49
Thence into Greece she fled, where curious Arts	191	Ch.-Milit.	W	49
Though Greece took horse as soon as Egypt did, ...	191	Ch.-Milit.		57
Before the other. Greece being past her prime, ...	191	Ch.-Milit.		60
From Greece to Rome she went, subduing those	191	Ch.-Milit.	W	61
But th' Empire dwelt in Greece, to comfort them	192	Ch.-Milit.		73
And such poore game. Thence he to Greece doth passe, ...	193	Ch.-Milit.		123
And such small game. Thence he to Greece doth passe, ...	193	Ch.-Milit.	W	123
From Greece he went to Rome: and as before	194	Ch.-Milit.		139
So trimme, as Greece and Egypt? yet their hearts	194	Ch.-Milit.		151
So spruse, as Greece and Egypt? yet their hearts	194	Ch.-Milit.	W	151
As Sinne in Greece a Prophet was before, ...	195	Ch.-Milit.		171
From Greece oracular infallibilities, ...	195	Ch.-Milit.		178
Learning from Greece, from old Rome statelinesse:	195	Ch.-Milit.		188
GREEDIE				
Content thee, greedie heart.	137	The Size		1
GREEDINESSE				
They drink with greedinesse a full damnation.	24	Ch.-Porch		448
GREEDY				
coveteousnesse, neither being greedy to get, nor nigardly to keep,	227	Priest 3		17
To a greedy eating horse a short halter.	359	Proverbs	D	1106
and for ever after cease my clamorous and greedy bookish requests.	367	Letters		12
GREEK				
And if a Greek Pcet of old was praised, that at the age of 73 yeares	302	Cornaro		33
GREEN				
But he a few green eares:	121	Hope		6
Grow green and gay, ...	162	The Search		10
GREENE				
Greene wood makes a hott fire.	349	Proverbs		862
GREENNESSE				
Could have recover'd greennesse? It was gone	166	The Flower		9
GREESE				
As Amber-greese leaves a rich sent	174	The Odour		2
GREIFE				
Acquitts yourselves and gives the sicke all greife.	209	Paradox	D	6
GREIVED				
or in a sad way, greived at his own, and others sins, which . . .	269	Priest 28		9
GREW				
But Grace shor'd these, and cut that as it grew.	84	The World		15
When we grew wanton, thou didst use displeasure	97	Afflict.5		9
The windes grew gard'ners, and the clouds good fountains. . .	120	Providence		116
As Babel grew, before there were dissensions.	122	Sinnes rd.		15
To warm his love, which I did fear grew cold.	129	Love unkn.		32
But as I rav'd and grew more fierce and wilde	153	The Collar		33
Which by the springs accesse grew much more great.	154	Glimpse		15
And surging griefs, when they grew bold, controll, ...	172	The Glance		15
When it grew loose, the Jews did hope in vain	190	Ch.-Milit.		23
The Shepherds hook grew to a scepter here, ...	192	Ch.-Milit.		71
He grew a gallant, and would needs foretell	193	Ch.-Milit.		129
Pleasure succeeded straight, when that grew cold.	194	Ch.-Milit.		144
Whereby he grew apace and scorn'd to use	195	Ch.-Milit.		191
a state to reduce it to its principles by which it grew great;	258	Priest 22		17
I grew fully perswaded, that all my griefs arose out of Intemperance:	292	Cornaro		19
although after the fifteenth day it grew lesse and lesse. . . .	296	Cornaro		21
GREW'ST				
Thou grew'st soft and moist with tears, ...	146	Praise 2		21
GRIEF (see also greife,griefe)				
Was ever grief like mine?	26	Sacrifice		4
Was ever grief like mine?	26	Sacrifice		8
Was ever grief like mine?	27	Sacrifice		12
Was ever grief like mine?	27	Sacrifice		16

GRIEF (cont'd)

	PAGE	TITLE	LINE
Was ever grief like mine?	27	Sacrifice	20
Was ever grief like mine?	27	Sacrifice	24
Was ever grief like mine?	27	Sacrifice	28
Was ever grief like mine?	27	Sacrifice	32
Was ever grief like mine?	27	Sacrifice	36
Most true to those, who are my greatest grief:	27	Sacrifice	39
Was ever grief like mine?	27	Sacrifice	40
Was ever grief like mine?	28	Sacrifice	44
Was ever grief like mine?	28	Sacrifice	48
Was ever grief like mine?	28	Sacrifice	52
Was ever grief like mine?	28	Sacrifice	56
Was ever grief like mine?	28	Sacrifice	60
Was ever grief like mine?	28	Sacrifice	64
Was ever grief like mine?	28	Sacrifice	68
Was ever grief like mine?	28	Sacrifice	72
Was ever grief like mine?	29	Sacrifice	76
Was ever grief like mine?	29	Sacrifice	80
Was ever grief like mine?	29	Sacrifice	84
Was ever grief like mine?	29	Sacrifice	88
Was ever grief like mine?	29	Sacrifice	92
Was ever grief like mine?	29	Sacrifice	96
Was ever grief like mine?	29	Sacrifice	100
Was ever grief like mine?	29	Sacrifice	104
Was ever grief like mine?	30	Sacrifice	108
Was ever grief like mine?	30	Sacrifice	112
Was ever grief like mine?	30	Sacrifice	116
Was ever grief like mine?	30	Sacrifice	120
Was ever grief like mine?	30	Sacrifice	124
Windes up my grief to a mysteriousnesse:	30	Sacrifice	127
Was ever grief like mine?	30	Sacrifice	128
Was ever grief like mine?	30	Sacrifice	132
Was ever grief like mine?	31	Sacrifice	136
Was ever grief like mine?	31	Sacrifice	140
Was ever grief like mine?	31	Sacrifice	144
Was ever grief like mine?	31	Sacrifice	148
Was ever grief like mine?	31	Sacrifice	152
Was ever grief like mine?	31	Sacrifice	156
Was ever grief like mine?	31	Sacrifice	160
Was ever grief like mine?	31	Sacrifice	164
Was ever grief like mine?	32	Sacrifice	168
Was ever grief like mine?	32	Sacrifice	172
Was ever grief like mine?	32	Sacrifice	176
Was ever grief like mine?	32	Sacrifice	180
Was ever grief like mine?	32	Sacrifice	184
Was ever grief like mine?	32	Sacrifice	188
Was ever grief like mine?	32	Sacrifice	192
Was ever grief like mine?	33	Sacrifice	196
Was ever grief like mine?	33	Sacrifice	200
Was ever grief like mine?	33	Sacrifice	204
Was ever grief like mine?	33	Sacrifice	208
Was ever grief like mine?	33	Sacrifice	212
Never was grief like mine.	33	Sacrifice	216
Was ever grief like mine?	33	Sacrifice	220
Was ever grief like mine?	34	Sacrifice	224
Was ever grief like mine?	34	Sacrifice	228
Was ever grief like mine?	34	Sacrifice	232
Was ever grief like mine?	34	Sacrifice	236
Was ever grief like mine?	34	Sacrifice	240
Was ever grief like mine?	34	Sacrifice	244
Was ever grief like mine?	34	Sacrifice	248
Never was grief like mine.	34	Sacrifice	252
Oh King of grief! (a title strange, yet true,	35	Thanksgvng	1
King of all Grief (a title strange, yet true,	35	Thanksgvng W	1
Who in all grief preventest me?	35	Thanksgvng	4
Was such a grief as cannot be.	35	Thanksgvng	10
And each grief tell?	38	Good Fri.	4
Which falls in Autumne, score a grief?	38	Good Fri.	10
Of my whole life one grief devoure;	39	Good Fri.	14
No place for grief or fear.	46	Afflict.1	16
Till grief did tell me roundly, that I lived.	47	Afflict.1	30
But thou wilt sinne and grief destroy;	49	Repentance	31
Precious for any grief in any part;	58	H.Script.1	3
Thou art my grief alone,	62	Afflict.2	11
By that I knew that thou wast in the grief,	73	Afflict.3	2
Thy life on earth was grief, and thou art still	73	Afflict.3	13
My dearest Lord, expecting till the grief	81	Christmas	6
Then shall those powers, which work for grief,	90	Afflict.4	25
I follow straight without complaints or grief,	94	Life	16
There is but joy and grief;	97	Afflict.5	13
Christ left his grave-clothes, that we might, when grief	112	Dawning	15
Christ left his grave-cloths, that we might, when grief	112	Dawning V	15
Is this same grief! within my heart I made	126	Confession	2
Yet grief knows all, and enters when he will.	126	Confession	6
I sinne not to my grief alone,	136	Ephes.	17
Lord, I adjudge my self to tears and grief,	136	Ephes.	25
Have I no parts but those of grief?	143	Complaining	15
On future grief, do not remove it thence,	145	Discharge	43
Either grief will not come: or if it must,	145	Discharge	51
In bitter grief: yet am I stil'd	150	Longing	59
Thou knowst how grief and sinne	155	Glimpse	28

GRIEF (cont'd)	PAGE	TITLE		LINE
For well he knows, if but one grief and smart	159	Jos.coat		5
To fetch the bodie; both being due to grief.	159	Jos.coat		9
Since then my grief must be as large,	163	The Search		45
Grief.	164	Grief		T
My grief hath need of all the watry things,	164	Grief		3
Whose grief allows him musick and a ryme:	164	Grief		17
I am to grief alive, to them as dead.	165	The Crosse		24
Grief melts away	165	The Flower		5
As if grief were not foul, nor vertue winning.	176	The Foil		8
And streams of grief	204	The Knell	W	15
that so the body may joyn in the grief, as it did in the sin;	279	Priest 33		28
can bring little grief or hurt to those that are temperate.	294	Cornaro		34
In all which time I felt no grief, save now and then a little	296	Cornaro		30
of the radicall moisture, without grief or perturbation of humours.	298	Cornaro		18
and will not allow any room there for such an in-mate as Grief;	374	Letters		11
GRIEF'S				
Couldst thou not griefs sad conquests me allow,	37	Reprisall		11
GRIEFE				
if he resent it to a mislike, but not a griefe.	273	Priest 31		20
Whether goest, griefe? where I am wont.	324	Proverbs		96
Where there is no honour, there is no griefe.	327	Proverbs		186
Goe not for every griefe to the Physitian,	331	Proverbs		290
If you would know secrets, looke them in griefe or pleasure.	333	Proverbs		367
If folly were griefe every house would weepe.	334	Proverbs		370
To have money is a feare, not to have it a griefe.	341	Proverbs		591
To have money is a feare, to want it is a griefe.	341	Proverbs	V	591
He that talkes much of his happinesse summons griefe.	349	Proverbs		856
He who talkes much of his happinesse summons griefe.	349	Proverbs	V	856
GRIEFES				
discover some care, which I forbare not in the midst of my griefes;	304	Valdesso		4
men for one pleasure a thousand griefes prove.	328	Proverbs		228
All griefes with bread are lesse.	334	Proverbs		377
All griefes with bread are lesse, or Nor woe to want.	334	Proverbs	V	377
GRIEFS				
Which is thy best stake, when griefs make thee tame.	9	Ch.-Porch		66
Yet ev'n the greatest griefs	132	Mans medly		31
Joyes oft are there, and griefs as oft as joyes;	137	Familie		17
But griefs without a noise:	137	Familie		18
When griefs prevail;	137	The Size		10
What griefs, what shames!	149	Longing		28
My joyes to weep, and now my griefs to sing.	159	Jos.coat		14
A narrow cupboard for my griefs and doubts,	164	Grief		11
Sure-footed griefs, solid calamities,	167	Dotage		9
Who griefs in earnest, joyes in jest pursue;	167	Dotage		14
And surging griefs, when they grew bold, controll,	172	The Glance		15
To set off vertues; griefs to set off sinning:	176	The Foil		6
Colour'd griefs indeed there are,	177	The Rose		6
Sorrowes & griefs, to fight with them a bout	211	Bohemia	D	20
comparison of the moment of griefs here with the weight of joyes	249	Priest 15		27
that after many troubles and griefs I should quickly come to an end;	291	Cornaro		25
I grew fully perswaded, that all my griefs arose out of Intemperance:	292	Cornaro		20
with that earnestness, that becomes your griefs, and my love.	372	Letters		1
GRIEVE				
Oh King of wounds! how shall I grieve for thee,	35	Thanksgvng		3
King of all wounds, how shall I grieve for thee,	35	Thanksgvng	W	3
A point of honour, now to grieve in me,	73	Afflict.3		15
But when I thus dispute and grieve,	95	Submission		9
Ephes. 4. 30. Grieve not the Holy Spirit, &c.	135	Ephes.		T
Then weep mine eyes, the God of love doth grieve:	135	Ephes.		7
Almightie God doth grieve, he puts on sense:	136	Ephes.		16
Wilt thou forestall it, and now grieve to morrow,	145	Discharge		48
Grieve over freshly all thy pain?	145	Discharge		50
That Sinne sayes true: but while I grieve,	184	A Parodie		29
GRIEV'D				
Griev'd for a worm, which when I tread,	135	Ephes.		5
How sweet a friend was he, who being griev'd	439	Walton 5		15
GRIEVED				
And art thou grieved, sweet and sacred Dove,	135	Ephes.		1
Grieved for me? the God of strength and power	135	Ephes.		4
GRIEVES				
and he is sorry, he grieves, and he gloryes, never was there such	234	Priest 7		19
Truly it grieves me to think of the child, how destitute she is,	376	Letters		12
GRIEVOUS				
What hath Affliction grievous in it more then for a moment?	372	Letters		26
GRIND				
The mill cannot grind with the water that's past.	326	Proverbs		153
GRINDE				
O do not grinde me!	83	Sighs & Gr.		18
But where one man would have me grinde it,	122	Time		5
Where rude unhallow'd steps do crush and grinde	140	Ch.-rents		8
GRINDS				
Gods Mill grinds slow, but sure.	346	Proverbs		747
GROANE				
You neither groane nor weepe	209	Paradox	D	2
GROANING				
With groaning I am wearied,	220	Psalm VI	D	13
GRONE				
And though my hard heart scarce to thee can grone,	38	The Sinner		13
Is not so deare to thee as one good grone.	106	Sion		18
What have I left, that I should stay and grone?	109	Home		67

GROW (cont'd)	PAGE	TITLE		LINE
But with my yeares sorrows did twist and grow,	47	Afflict.1	W	23
For sure then I should grow	48	Afflict.1		58
His praises there may grow.	53	Antiphon 1		6
They grow unruly, and sit in thy bowers.	56	Temper 2		12
By sight of sinne we should grow mad.	63	Sinne 2		8
And true descent; that when thou shalt grow fat,	65	Ch.-monum.		18
Then should thy praises with me grow,	95	Submission		7
Whose flat delights on earth do creep and grow;	111	Vanitie 2		2
Still mock me, and grow bold:	116	Dulnesse		22
Most herbs that grow in brooks, are hot and dry.	120	Providence		129
I blesse thee, Lord, because I GROW	132	Paradise		1
And in thy lookings stretch and grow?	144	Discharge		5
In times to come; for it will grow.	145	Discharge		30
I grow too wide,	145	Discharge		34
And single things grow fruitfull by deserts.	147	Offering		10
Thy beggars grow; rid them away	150	Longing		77
Grow green and gay,	162	The Search		10
But while I grow in a straight line,	166	The Flower		29
Where of all plants afflictions soonest grow;	170	Water-crs.		3
That these two words might creep & grow	175	The Odour		14
Will not grow bright and clean.	184	The Elixer		16
Will not to Heaven grow.	184	The Elixer	W	16
Some in noisome vapours grow	187	Dooms-day		23
But quick-ey'd Love, observing me grow slack	188	Love 3		3
Gardens of Gods, which ev'ry yeare did grow,	193	Ch.-Milit.		108
which I have observed, untill the Book grow to a compleat Pastorall.	224	Priest		16
that we may grow therein, and that our feet may be like hindes feet	236	Priest 8		28
so that corne doth not grow by any other vertue, then by that which	271	Priest 30		4
so that though the corn do grow, and be preserved in that act by his	271	Priest 30		15
When all sinnes grow old, coveteousnesse is young.	321	Proverbs		18
When all sinnes grow old, coveteousnesse grows young.	321	Proverbs	V	18
Great deservers grow Intolerable presumers.	361	Proverbs	D	1167
Volumes of Divinity, which yet every day swell, and grow bigger.	365	Letters		15
and yet still grow upon Your humblest Servant, GEORGE HERBERT.	367	Letters		15
things may grow worse by your withdrawing which grow not better	381	Woodnoth		10
worse by your withdrawing which grow not better by your presence.	381	Woodnoth		11
wee might the more by love grow on, both the Spanish and Brittish	442	Oration		17
GROWE				
Light burthens, long borne, growe heavie.	321	Proverbs		15
GROWES				
Hee that gets out of debt, growes rich.	321	Proverbs		9
Vertue never growes old.	323	Proverbs		64
The tree that growes slowly, keepes it selfe for another.	327	Proverbs		198
A rugged stone growes smooth from hand to hand.	332	Proverbs		316
Folly growes without watering.	341	Proverbs		581
GROWING				
And stop our sinnes from growing thick and wide,	44	H. Bapt.1		8
Offring at heav'n, growing and groning thither:	166	The Flower		25
both for man in themselves, by growing them selves fit for his table.	241	Priest 10		34
growing with the growth of his Parish.	255	Priest 21		15
and take as much joy in a straight-growing childe, or servant,	275	Priest 32		33
GROWN				
Is saplesse grown,	45	Nature		16
But wee strangers grown, o Lord,	53	H.Commun.	W	37
The Caldron suppled, what was grown too hard:	130	Love unkn.		65
The Thorns did quicken, what was grown too dull:	130	Love unkn.		66
That thou art grown	150	Longing		63
Thou art grown fair and full of grace,	186	Death		15
that those who are well grown in the knowledg of Religion,	255	Priest 21		32
GROWS				
Then thou art modest, and the wine grows bold.	8	Ch.-Porch		42
A fault, which needs it most, grows two thereby.	9	Ch.-Porch		78
Courtesie grows in court; news in the citie.	18	Ch.-Porch		292
Courtesie grows at Court; news in the citie.	18	Ch.-Porch	W	292
More rev'rend grows, & more doth win:	67	Windows		9
When man grows staid and wise,	98	Mortific.		19
When age grows low and weak,	98	Mortific.		25
I see the world grows old, when as the heat	99	Decay		16
Since by thy cutting he grows better.	122	Time		12
Take of this grain, which in my garden grows,	125	Peace		37
And grows for you;	125	Peace		38
But cooling by the way, grows pursie and slow,	169	The Answer		10
him then weary, and so he grows from not relishing, to loathing.	235	Priest 7		14
If it once have the honour of that Name, it grows great instantly.	249	Priest 14		3
When all sinnes grow old, coveteousnesse grows young.	321	Proverbs	V	18
Power seldome grows old at Court.	357	Proverbs	D	1053
GROWTH				
And growth of it: if with thy watch, that too	24	Ch.-Porch		454
The growth of flesh is but a blister;	44	H. Bapt.2		14
growing with the growth of his Parish.	255	Priest 21		15
yet if he suite not other things to the growth, as seasons,	271	Priest 30		16
GRUDGE				
God calleth preaching folly. Do not grudge	23	Ch.-Porch		429
Peace mutt'ring thoughts, and do not grudge to keep	68	Content		1
GRUDGING				
Not grudging, that thy lust hath bounds and staies.	7	Ch.-Porch		16
GRUMBLE				
And grumble oft, that they have more in me	89	The Pearl		28
GRUMBLINGLY				
as he expected & therfore he grumblingly said that if he had given it	368	Letters		33

HABITS	PAGE	TITLE		LINE
Secondly, among Habits, some oppose Theologicall vertues,	308	Valdesso		6
Other Habits oppose morall vertues, as Prodigality opposes	308	Valdesso		10
HABITT				
(Whom Schollers Habitt & Obscurity	209	L. Bacon	D	6
HABITUALL				
but habituall, for I can no more free my selfe from actuall sinnes	308	Valdesso		3
HACK				
which they may cut, or hack, or throw into the fire, and so they pay	265	Priest 26		26
HACKNEY				
To go upon the Franciscans Hackney (i.e. on foot).	356	Proverbs	D	1035
HAD				
If God had laid all common, certainly	7	Ch.-Porch		19
Though David had his Jonathan, Christ his John.	17	Ch.-Porch		276
Had to this day been an Egyptian slave.	27	Sacrifice		10
Though he had all I had, did not forbeare	27	Sacrifice		14
About some land, which he had dearly bought	40	Redemption		7
I had prepared many a flowre	42	Easter	W	19
Are blowne away, as if they nere had bin.	46	Sinne 1	W	14
I had my wish and way:	47	Afflict.1		20
Before I had the power to change my life.	47	Afflict.1		42
Hungrie I was, and had no meat:	50	Faith		5
I had it straight, and did as truly eat,	50	Faith		7
If blisse had lien in art or strength,	50	Faith		25
None but the wise or strong had gained it:	50	Faith		26
When creatures had no reall light	51	Faith		33
But God more care of us hath had:	63	Sinne 2		6
And if the Fox had liv'd to rule their side,	70	Humilitie		23
They had depos'd each one.	70	Humilitie		24
Hadst thou not had thy part,	73	Afflict.3		5
Sure the unruly sigh had broke my heart.	73	Afflict.3		6
Man had straight forward gone	75	Sunday		15
O that I had the wing and thigh	79	Employm.2	W	21
Gladly had man ador'd the sunne,	82	Ungratef.		4
Till she had weakned all by alteration:	84	The World		8
Surveys, as if he had design'd.	85	Vanitie 1		4
I often blotted what I had begunne;	102	Jordan 2		9
I heard in Musick you had skill.	110	The Quip		11
When I had got these parcels, instantly	112	JESU		7
Had he life, or had he none?	113	Businesse		19
If he had not liv'd for thee,	113	Businesse		20
And two deaths had been thy fee.	113	Businesse		22
If he had not di'd for thee,	113	Businesse		26
He makes a grave; as if the thing had sense,	119	Providence		83
As if thy blessings had spare dayes:	124	Gratefulnes		30
Will more complie, then help. A Lord I had,	129	Love unkn.		3
Which I had lost, I hasted to my bed.	130	Love unkn.		48
I found that some had stuff'd the bed with thoughts,	130	Love unkn.		51
Full well I understood, who had been there:	130	Love unkn.		54
For I had giv'n the key to none, but one:	130	Love unkn.		55
All did but strive to mend, what you had marr'd.	130	Love unkn.		67
I had a motion to forbear,	134	The Method		23
And jagg'd his seamlesse coat, had that been fine,	134	Divinitie		11
As if they had a part?	136	Familie		2
I, who had heard of musick in the spheres,	139	Artillerie		9
Save one good Angell, which a friend had ti'd	142	Pilgrimage		17
When I had gain'd the brow and top,	142	Pilgrimage		22
What Adam had, and forfeited for all,	143	Holdfast		13
O that within us hearts had propagation,	147	Offering		7
Had I many,	148	Offering		31
Had I any,	148	Offering		32
He had new clothes a making here below.	151	The Bag		18
And, that I had great cause to fear it.	155	Assurance		12
Could poyson, if it had a tongue, expresse?	155	Assurance		14
Were from my self, I had not half a word,	155	Assurance		22
That which had but two legs before,	158	Praise 3		10
Among my many had his full career,	159	Jos.coat		6
Untill I had some place, where I might sing,	164	The Crosse		3
Had the malicious and ill-meaning harm	172	The Glance		11
(Whose precepts she had trampled on before)	173	Marie Magd		2
As she had brought wherewith to stain,	173	Marie Magd		16
My god must have my best, ev'n all I had.	176	Forerunners		18
When I had forgot my birth,	182	Banquet		31
Then the ten bitter plagues had done before.	191	Ch.-Milit.		40
Who had subdued all the world for foes.	191	Ch.-Milit.	W	62
But seems to yeeld Christ had the greater wounds,	191	Ch.-Milit.	W	64
And not go lesse then she had done of late.	192	Ch.-Milit.		92
His grave aspect had more of heav'n then hell:	194	Ch.-Milit.		168
Give me not that I had before,	201	H. Commun.	W	46
Had he only brought them forth,	208	J. Danvers	D	13
Know that much had been his worth;	208	J. Danvers	D	14
Perhaps some other subject I had tryed	209	L. Bacon	D	11
Worthy had bin, thou hadst not lost thine owne:	211	Bohemia	D	2
but after hee had fulfilled the work of Reconciliation,	225	Priest 1		7
that God in all ages hath had his servants, to whom he hath revealed	229	Priest 4		22
that God hath ever had his people, that have glorified him as wel	231	Priest 6		35
Chapt. 10. after he had complained of the desolation of Israel,	234	Priest 7		4
performed by keeping of the two former, had not Authority interposed:	242	Priest 10		9
draught of beer, then if it had taken before either fish, or rootes,	242	Priest 10		23
it about with him as fully, as if he had begot his whole Parish.	250	Priest 16		9
they would have fainted, had they returned empty, He suffered it not;	267	Priest 26		24

HAD (cont'd)	PAGE	TITLE		LINE
but to go on as cheerfully, as if he had not been interrupted.	273	Priest 31		11
So that even in Paradise man had a calling, and how much more out	274	Priest 32		21
And if the same person had been sick of all diseases, and were	278	Priest 33		30
if he had been at the Creation of all things, should lesse beleeve	281	Priest 34		28
who had withstood his preaching, The Lord (saith he) reward him	285	Priest 36		33
he saith, he had delivered them to Satan, that they might learn	286	Priest 36		1
which before their offence and Judgment they had in all mens brests:	287	Priest 37		34
when we had sinned beyond any help in heaven or earth, then thou	288	Priest		26
if they had lived, would have been an ornament to the world,	291	Cornaro		3
they had a great desire to know the way of my life, and how I came	291	Cornaro		11
but had already gone farre in me, first caused me to leave	291	Cornaro		18
for this had every way great force for the recovering and preserving	292	Cornaro		5
This they had told me before:	292	Cornaro		26
But after I had resolved to follow Temperance and Reason,	292	Cornaro		31
If Temperance had so much power as to bring me health;	293	Cornaro		3
was not onely freed from all those evils which had so long beset me,	293	Cornaro		21
that they had no great power to hurt those bodies, which were kept in	294	Cornaro		1
considering what an orderly life I had led for many yeares together,	295	Cornaro		7
and that I had for many yeares continued in good health,	295	Cornaro		26
nothing holp me, but that exact rule which I had so long continued.	296	Cornaro		29
although it was a sore evil, yet had no power to kill me.	297	Cornaro		2
was but a little excesse, in a few dayes had so soon overthrown me.	297	Cornaro		6
qualities to me, if I had not found them out by long experience?	297	Cornaro		35
because I have now a clearer voice, then ever I had in my life.	303	Cornaro		8
if I had my wish, would I change age and constitution with them who	303	Cornaro		11
Cornelius had revelation, yet Peter was to be sent for,	310	Valdesso		9
that it is plain the Authour had a very reverend esteem of the holy	311	Valdesso	V	6
restraining motion (as S. Paul had when hee would have preached in	313	Valdesso		16
Neither doe I doubt but if Abraham had lived in our Kingdome under	316	Valdesso		23
and had killed his sonne Isaac, but he might have been justly put	316	Valdesso		24
He had done justly, and yet he had been punished justly,	316	Valdesso		27
and yet he had been punished justly, that is in humano foro &	316	Valdesso		27
untill shee had brought forth her first borne Sonne, as if afterwards	318	Valdesso		13
forth her first borne Sonne, as if afterwards he had knowne her:	318	Valdesso		13
If all fooles had bables, wee should want fuell.	323	Proverbs		63
Never had ill workeman good tooles.	323	Proverbs		67
I had rather ride on an asse that carries me,	329	Proverbs		258
I had rather aske of my sire browne bread,	330	Proverbs		269
If the mother had not beene in the oven,	344	Proverbs		696
shee had never sought her daughter there.	344	Proverbs		696
Had you the world on your Chesse-bord,	344	Proverbs		701
and had a gocse in his sleeve.	345	Proverbs		737
Some had rather lose their friend then their Jest.	361	Proverbs	D	1170
Though I had the best wit in the World, yet it would easily tyre me,	363	Letters		14
been forward to say, if I had taken ill courses, Follow your Book,	364	Letters		21
not well, I had rather the fault should lie on me, than on them;	364	Letters		29
yet I had rather flie to my old ward, that if any course could be	367	Letters		6
he grumblingly said that if he had given it to the pope he should	368	Letters		33
if he had given it to the pope he should have had a greater reward.	368	Letters		34
or if it had to others, yet to me it should not, for ought I yet	370	Letters		23
spend her eyesight on a piece of paper, or else I had wrote to her;	371	Letters		14
since if we had Riches we are commanded to give them away:	373	Letters		23
but, their Fiery-tryals have had an end:	374	Letters		1
As I had written thus much, I received a Letter, from My Brother,	378	Letters		30
blessed Success, that God had given us, by moving the Duches's heart,	379	Letters		1
some little Apology that she had done nothing in it (as my Brother	379	Letters		4
if God had done that (which you are thinking to doe) to blessed Mary	381	Woodnoth		4
to doe) to blessed Mary Magd. & Paul, heaven had wanted chief saints:	381	Woodnoth		5
HADST				
As if that thou hadst nothing els to do?	62	Mattens		12
Hadst thou not had thy part,	73	Afflict.3		5
If thou hadst let us runne,	82	Ungratef.		3
Thou hadst but two rich cabinets of treasure,	82	Ungratef.	W	7
Would thou hadst no faults or fears!	113	Businesse		7
Would thou hadst no flesh and bones!	113	Businesse		13
Thou hadst di'd most wretchedly;	113	Businesse		21
Thou hadst liv'd in miserie.	113	Businesse		27
If thou hadst lost a glove or ring,	133	The Method		11
But after thou hadst slipt a drop	158	Praise 3		31
If thou hadst dyde for Bread.	201	H. Commun.	W	27
Worthy had bin, thou hadst not lost thine owne:	211	Bohemia	D	2
HAIL				
They bow their knees to me, and cry, Hail king:	32	Sacrifice		173
HAINOUSNESS				
or hainousness of the crime may be, he is carefull to see condign	254	Priest 20		26
HAIR				
A man so wrung with pains, that all his hair,	37	The Agonie		9
Who sayes that fictions onely and false hair	56	Jordan 1		1
When th' hair is sweet through pride or lust,	96	Charms & K		13
Of dressing, that her hair doth lie	110	Brit. Ch.		20
And with quaint metaphors her curled hair	115	Dulnesse		7
A worm doth sit, whose many feet and hair	140	Ch.-rents		3
No hair so small but hath his shadow.	359	Proverbs	D	1124
HALE				
Can hale or draw it out of doore.	158	Praise 3		16
When all things pull & hale, that they may bring	212	Bohemia	D	27
HALF				
Not half so sweet as my sweet sacrifice:	27	Sacrifice		19
One half of me being gone, the rest I give	35	Thanksgvng		27
One half of me being gone, the rest I'le give	35	Thanksgvng	W	27

HALF (cont'd)	PAGE	TITLE		LINE
He scarce allow'd me half an eie.	111	The Quip		15
Partakes already half of hell.	123	Time		24
But one half houre of comfort for my heart?	154	Glimpse		5
But one half houre of comfort to my heart?	154	Glimpse	V	5
Were from my self, I had not half a word,	155	Assurance		22
Not half a letter to oppose	155	Assurance		23
I half beleeve,	184	A Parodie		28
Half that we have	186	Death		22
A City that parlies is half gotten.	358	Proverbs	D	1097
yet I am scarce able with much ado to make one half years allowance,	365	Letters		10
HALFE				
Hee that desires is more then halfe the way.	10	Ch.-Porch	W	90
or halfe-kneeling, or any undutifull behaviour in them,	231	Priest 6		24
and halfe at least of the government of the house, reserving so much	238	Priest 9		37
Pleasing ware is halfe sould.	321	Proverbs		14
The gentle Hawke halfe mans her selfe.	322	Proverbs		30
Health without money is halfe an ague.	338	Proverbs		509
Wood halfe burnt is easily kindled.	341	Proverbs		606
To a crafty man, a crafty and an halfe.	347	Proverbs		796
Halfe the world knowes not how the other halfe lives.	351	Proverbs		907
Halfe the world knowes not how the other halfe lies.	351	Proverbs	V	907
Life is halfe spent before we know what it is.	351	Proverbs		917
that if he will not give her halfe her estate to live on by her selfe	368	Letters		24
Brugensis uppon the Scripture and his halfe yeares wages aforehand,	382	G.H.'s Will		19
Bostocke St. Augustines workes and his halfe yeares wages aforehand,	382	G.H.'s Will		21
HALFE-KNEELING				
or halfe-kneeling, or any undutifull behaviour in them,	231	Priest 6		24
HALL				
The souldiers lead me to the common hall;	31	Sacrifice		153
Nor the Exchange, or busie Hall;	70	Quidditie		10
that he will have prayers in the hall, wishing him to informe his	251	Priest 17		11
HALLOW'D				
But thou art fire, sacred and hallow'd fire;	160	Priesthood		7
HALLS				
Closets are halls to them; and hearts, high-wayes.	126	Confession		18
for in our publick Halls, you know, is nothing but Fish	365	Letters		3
HALT				
Though I halt in pace,	179	Discipline		14
HALTER				
Mention not a halter in the house of him that was hanged.	343	Proverbs		671
To a greedy eating horse a short halter.	359	Proverbs	D	1106
The horse that drawes after him his halter,	359	Proverbs	D	1120
HAMLET				
or hath generall Propositions to the whole Towne or Hamlet,	276	Priest 32		5
HAMLETS				
not onely in the citie, but also in villages and hamlets.	299	Cornaro		4
HAMMER				
when you are a hammer, strike your fill.	332	Proverbs		338
HAMMERING				
Sinne is still hammering my heart	60	Grace		17
HAMPER'D				
As an intangled, hamper'd thing.	109	Home		64
HAND				
Whose parts are as thy hand did frame;	26	The Altar		3
Examines me with a censorious hand:	29	Sacrifice		82
Copie thy fair, though bloudie hand?	35	Thanksgvng		16
Who takes thee by the hand, that thou likewise	41	Easter		3
The gentle rising, which on either hand	67	Ch.-floore		7
I saw the Vertues sitting hand in hand	70	Humilitie		1
And hollow room on either hand.	75	Sunday	W	25
Flie hand in hand to heav'n!	77	Sunday		63
If any one our Masters hand can show.	78	Ang.&Sts.		30
But Love took Grace & Glory by the hand,	84	Sighs & Gr.	W	19
Cordiall and Corrosive: put not thy hand	83	Sighs & Gr.		28
But Love and Grace took Glorie by the hand,	84	The World		19
To finde out death, but missest life at hand.	86	Vanitie 1		28
May turn, and take me by the hand, and more	87	Lent		41
To all expressions both of hand and eye,	88	The Pearl		15
I know all these, and have them in my hand:	89	The Pearl		31
And wither'd in my hand.	94	Life		6
My hand was next to them, and then my heart:	94	Life		7
Onely do thou lend me a hand,	95	Submission		19
I would do well, yet sinne the hand hath got:	96	Justice 1		10
Who shuts his hand, hath lost his gold:	96	Charms & K		5
The best of men, turn but thy hand	100	Miserie		19
As I have mine, may set his hand	105	Obedience		37
Do not by hanging down break from the hand,	112	Dawning		11
And put the penne alone into his hand,	117	Providence		7
The trees say, Pull me: but the hand you stretch,	117	Providence		23
Tempests are calm to thee; they know thy hand,	118	Providence		45
Who was to take it from me, slipt his hand,	130	Love unkn.		34
With th' one hand touching heav'n, with th' other earth.	131	Mans medly		12
Then let me want thy hand & ART.	133	Paradise		9
Thy hand above did burn and glow,	141	Justice 2		11
Thy hand is white,	141	Justice 2		15
And hold my hand, while I did write.	156	Assurance		30
That with th' one hand thou liftest to the sky,	160	Priesthood		2
Yet have I often seen, by cunning hand	161	Priesthood		13
Wherefore I dare not, I, put forth my hand	161	Priesthood		31
And thrust a Testament into thy hand:	188	Judgement		13

HANDS (cont'd)	PAGE	TITLE		LINE
God strikes not with both hands,	331	Proverbs		315
Who doth his owne businesse, foules not his hands.	335	Proverbs		419
Hee that bewailes himselfe hath the cure in his hands.	336	Proverbs		441
Happier are the hands compast with yron,	341	Proverbs		582
Happier the hands fetter'd then the head distracted.	341	Proverbs	V	582
of a monke on all hands.	351	Proverbs	V	900
ado to make one half years allowance, shake hands with the other:	365	Letters		11
resuming the donation of spirituall livings into their owne hands,	368	Letters		28
I have forty businesses in my hands, your Courtesie will pardon	371	Letters		18
also deliver me out of the hands of this uncircumcised Philistin.	374	Letters		8
one of our neeces into your hands but barely what I wrote I meant,	375	Letters		5
find out some thing not unworthy of those hands at which they aim.	377	Letters		1
in signing 100 lib. with her own hands (& promising to get her Son	379	Letters		2
putt your self into the hands of God (whose the success of things is)	380	Woodnoth		24
the success of things is) & not into the hands of men or mens trades:	380	Woodnoth		25
pounds in Mr Thomas Lawleys hands a Merchant of London which fell	382	G.H.'s Will		8
are divers moneys of mine in Mr Stephens hands Stationer of London,	383	G.H.'s Will		23
HANDSELL				
Thou art joyes handsell: heav'n lies flat in thee,	58	H.Script.1		13
HANDSOM				
No Church-yard is so handsom,	353	Proverbs		969
HANDSOME				
Onely there was a handsome picture by,	194	Ch.-Milit.		169
with an handsome, and seemly Carpet of good and costly Stuffe,	246	Priest 13		17
He that is not handsome at 20, nor strong at 30, nor rich at 40,	333	Proverbs		349
nor wise at 50, will never bee handsome, strong, rich, or wise.	333	Proverbs		349
HANDSOMNESSE				
In clothes, cheap handsomnesse doth bear the bell.	14	Ch.-Porch		187
HANG				
Lo, here I hang, charg'd with a world of sinne,	33	Sacrifice		205
This soul doth span the world, and hang content	69	Content		17
That it may hang and move	74	The Starre		15
(Which there did hang like streamers neare the top	158	Praise 3		33
to let the fervency of the supplicant hang and dy between speaking,	231	Priest 6		18
thy blessings hang in clusters, they come trooping upon us!	290	Priest		6
All keyes hang not on one girdle.	345	Proverbs		719
HANGED				
Mention not a halter in the house of him that was hanged.	343	Proverbs		671
HANGING				
Do not by hanging down break from the hand,	112	Dawning		11
HANGS				
It hangs, it clogs:	158	Praise 3		14
Onely my soule hangs on thy promisses	205	Persever.	W	13
Warre makes theeves, and peace hangs them.	337	Proverbs		471
HANNAH				
The fruit of this blessing good Hannah found, and received with great	285	Priest 36		21
HAPPEN				
there may happen somtimes some cases, wherein he chooseth to permit	260	Priest 23		18
you consider all that can happen to you are either afflictions	373	Letters		21
HAPPENED				
it happened that the coach was overturned, and then was dragged	294	Cornaro		37
what could have happened more pleasing to us, then the accesse	442	Oration		8
HAPPENS				
Now it so happens, that the godly petitioner upon some emergent	272	Priest 31		29
But it happens, that neer the place where he is to pray,	273	Priest 31		27
as usually happens in old mens bodies, which live without rule.	296	Cornaro		35
HAPPIE				
Yet lest perchance I should too happie be	48	Afflict.1		49
Hath ever found a happie fortune.	69	Content		36
The other winds towards Him, whose happie birth	84	Coloss.		6
How happie were my part,	105	Obedience		41
Happie is he, whose heart	132	Mans medly		34
onely upon a hope of an happie issue, which yet befalls verie few.	300	Cornaro		24
and which are such, as that men generally account me happie.	300	Cornaro		33
why should I be accounted lesse happie, or lesse my self,	302	Cornaro		35
Since therefore a temperate life is so happie and pleasant a thing;	303	Cornaro		30
Happie is hee that chastens himselfe.	325	Proverbs		137
HAPPIER				
Happier are the hands compast with yron,	341	Proverbs		582
Happier the hands fetter'd then the head distracted.	341	Proverbs	V	582
HAPPILY				
which happily for his other children he is not able to do.	239	Priest 10		32
which if it happily take effect, he then comes on the faster,	263	Priest 25		32
happily also with this (as his thoughts are fruitfull) intending	304	Valdesso		12
so though you incline not, happily you restraine.	381	Woodnoth		10
HAPPINESSE				
Pick quarrels with their onely happinesse:	29	Sacrifice		87
My dayes were straw'd with flow'rs and happinesse;	47	Afflict.1		21
My dayes were strowd with flow'rs and happinesse;	47	Afflict.1	W	21
False glozing pleasures, casks of happinesse,	167	Dotage		1
He that talkes much of his happinesse summons griefe.	349	Proverbs		856
He who talkes much of his happinesse summons griefe.	349	Proverbs	V	856
HAPPY				
Then may the beasts draw thee to happy light.	16	Ch.-Porch		264
And happy thou,	144	Discharge		22
Happy are they that dare	185	The Elixer	W	22
he shall be like an happy tree,	214	Psalm I	D	8
Whereupon men flockt thither, and built houses with happy successe.	301	Cornaro		29
There is an hour wherein a man might be happy	360	Proverbs	D	1143
Can I be so happy, as to hear of both these that they succeed well?	371	Letters		10

	PAGE	TITLE		LINE
HAPPY (cont'd)				
and I shou'd account my self most happy if I might change with you;	373	Letters		3
Happy is he, whose bottom is wound up and laid ready for work in	373	Letters		6
HARBINGERS				
The harbingers are come. See, see their mark;	176	Forerunners		1
(For no lesse Harbingers would serve then they)	192	Ch.-Milit.		84
HARBOUR				
The day or night: that is the gale, this th' harbour;	64	Even-song		26
HARD				
Of my hard heart	26	The Altar		10
And though my hard heart scarce to thee can grone,	38	The Sinner		13
No lodging for thee, but a cold hard stone?	40	Sepulchre		2
Where our hard hearts have took up stones to brain thee,	41	Sepulchre		13
Though it be cold, hard, foul, from loving man	41	Sepulchre		23
The fight is hard on either part.	106	Sion		15
Is no hard rate.	111	Vanitie 2		10
Hard things are glorious; easie things good cheap.	119	Providence		97
The offerers heart. Your heart was hard, I fear.	130	Love unkn.		37
The Caldron suppled, what was grown too hard:	130	Love unkn.		65
More bowels have, then such hard things.	136	Ephes.		24
Thus hard to me?	150	Longing		64
All the hard weather,	166	The Flower		13
Thou art too hard for me in Love:	201	love	W	1
who by hard usage increase their travell, the Countrey Parson is very	227	Priest 3		14
and heavy, and hard to raise to a poynt of Zeal, and fervency,	233	Priest 7		16
But specially, at hard times, and dearths, he even parts his Living,	245	Priest 12		9
and saw that it was no hard thing to do so, but the proper duty	292	Cornaro		32
that an orderly life is so hard a thing that it cannot be kept.	298	Cornaro		37
Things hard to bee understood.	317	Valdesso		25
Hee that eats the hard shall eate the ripe.	328	Proverbs		210
The hard gives more then he that hath nothing.	329	Proverbs		259
If the wise erred not, it would goe hard with fooles.	338	Proverbs		510
If wise men erred not, it would goe hard with fooles.	338	Proverbs	V	510
Love makes all hard hearts gentle.	339	Proverbs		542
'Tis hard to be wretched, but worse to be knowne so.	340	Proverbs		577
but the Devill builds a Chappell hard by.	343	Proverbs		674
Hee that brings good newes knockes hard.	348	Proverbs		824
It is very hard to shave an egge.	359	Proverbs	D	1128
perhaps they will say, you are sickly, you must not study too hard;	364	Letters		26
HARDEN				
should a Christian Souldier take such occasions to harden himselfe,	284	Priest 35		36
HARDEST				
The greatest and hardest preparation is within:	226	Priest 2		12
HARDLY				
Sometimes I hardly reach a score,	55	Temper 1		7
Can on anothers hardly rest.	68	Content		4
because Countrey people live hardly, and therefore as feeling their	227	Priest 3		12
his children, hardly perceives when his storing becomes unlawfull:	264	Priest 26		27
an orderly and regular life can hardly be altered without exceeding	295	Cornaro		17
which, but in that age, can hardly be perfected.	298	Cornaro		31
with it you will hardly know your selfe.	326	Proverbs	V	159
and perhaps a little more mild, but you will hardly perceive it.	366	Letters		25
HARDNESSE				
Unto a hardnesse, void of love:	60	Grace		18
HARDNESSES				
To supple hardnesses. But at the length	130	Love unkn.		45
HARE				
The fearfull Hare her eares, which by their law	70	Humilitie		11
The fearfull Hare her eares, which by the law	70	Humilitie	W	11
If you could runne, as you drinke, you might catch a hare.	334	Proverbs		373
Little dogs start the Hare, the great get her.	341	Proverbs		593
HARKEN (see also heark)				
The Lord will harken unto me	217	Psalm IV	D	13
Harken to reason or shee will bee heard.	323	Proverbs		74
HARLEY				
To Sir Robert Harley, at Brampton.	367	Letters		T
HARM				
Can blast my fruit, or bring me HARM,	133	Paradise		5
Had the malicious and ill-meaning harm	172	The Glance		11
but my next neighbour doth me more harm	361	Proverbs	D	1173
HARME				
it is a duty rather, which may do much good, and save much harme.	288	Priest 37		2
HARMLESSE				
Parson is a Lover of old Customes, if they be good, and harmlesse;	283	Priest 35		28
HARMONIE				
And prove one God, one harmonie.	36	Thanksgvng		42
Could be allow'd for harmonie)	165	The Crosse		16
if our corporall life depend on the harmonie of humours & elements,	297	Cornaro		7
HARMONIOUS				
Harmonious peace must rock them all the day:	105	Conscience		9
Harmonious bells below, raising the dead	174	Aaron		3
HARMONIOUSLY				
As larks, harmoniously,	43	East.wings		8
HARP				
And harp on thee.	141	Justice 2		21
HARPYES				
Those ravening Harpyes, which peck at thy face,	212	Bohemia	D	48
HARQUEBUZE				
Spectacles are deaths Harquebuze.	352	Proverbs		950
HARSH				
How harsh are thorns to pears! and yet they make	120	Providence		121

	PAGE	TITLE		LINE
HART				
Least gaining gaine on thee, & fill thy hart	13	Ch.-Porch	W	164
A hart can never come too late.	42	Easter	W	28
Which of them soonest should attaine my hart.	66	Ch.-lock	W	4
Both hart & knees, in crying night and day,	80	Deniall	W	13
They and my hart may chime,	80	Deniall	W	29
At th' hart of others, hit their own.	96	Charms & K	W	10
Into my hart with joye, giving more rest	202	love	W	17
that the auditors may plainly perceive that every word is hart-deep.	233	Priest 7		32
doe that which GOD shall put into your hart, and the LORD bless all	375	Letters		33
Doe this & be a man as David, after Gods hart.	381	Woodnoth		21
HART-DEEP				
that the auditors may plainly perceive that every word is hart-deep.	233	Priest 7		32
HARTES				
Each little comforte much affects our hartes,	210	Paradox	D	33
HARTS				
But not their harts, as I by proofe doe try.	30	Sacrifice	W	123
Of thousand harts: that face doth figure thee	212	Bohemia	D	33
of want of success consider how long God knocks at our harts,	381	Woodnoth		2
HARVEST				
To gain at harvest an eternall Treasure.	85	Coloss.		10
Have I no harvest but a thorn	153	The Collar		7
of extreme poverty, and in the seasons of Seed-time, and Harvest.	248	Priest 14		5
Whitsuntide, afore and after Harvest, and the beginning of Lent.	259	Priest 22		22
So that if a Farmer hath both a faire harvest, and that also well	272	Priest 30		1
much as the usuall seasons of summer and winter, earing and harvest.	281	Priest 34		25
therfore Expect a harvest. 3. To Change shewes not well & you are	380	Woodnoth		11
poore duties wish, and vow unto you of the last a plenteous Harvest.	443	Oration		7
HARVESTS				
We talk of harvests; there are no such things,	108	Home		55
by his governing power, the fairest harvests come to nothing.	271	Priest 30		18
HAS				
Hee that has all ill, & can have no good	7	Ch.-Porch	W	35
It gets thee nothing, and has no excuse.	8	Ch.-Porch	W	56
Yet publick has more promises, more love:	22	Ch.-Porch	W	398
But Man has caught and kept it, as his prey.	91	Man	W	20
A falling starr has lost his place:	97	Charms & K	W	19
The Courtier getts it, that has grace.	97	Charms & K	W	20
And drest his herse, while he has breath	99	Mortific.		33
To passe it self and all it has to thee.	104	Obedience	W	8
Hee that has one,	203	Trin.Sun.	W	18
Has all.	203	Trin.Sun.	W	19
knows also that my sclliciting him has been much, and my tears many	372	Letters		3
liked our Book well, & has given order to the Tenants, at Leighton,	379	Letters		8
glad for the Heart, that God has given you & yours, to pious works.	379	Letters		15
HAST (haste)				
and Masters should make hast in this, as to a great purchase	259	Priest 22		3
a tincture of private malice in the joy, and hast of acting his part;	287	Priest 37		27
Make hast to an ill way that you may get out of it.	325	Proverbs		124
Hast comes not alone.	348	Proverbs		826
Who hath no hast in his businesse,	354	Proverbs		997
of whose rude delivery my hast makes mee ashamed, only my comfort is	369	Letters		2
HAST				
Thou hast run all thy race, ere thou beginn.	10	Ch.-Porch	W	90
Thou hast two scenses, if thy stomack call;	11	Ch.-Porch		128
That thou hast gotten. Surely use alone	12	Ch.-Porch		155
But may be wittie, if thou hast the vein.	16	Ch.-Porch		240
Hast thou the knack? pamper it not with liking:	16	Ch.-Porch		243
Stay not for th' other pin: why thou hast lost	23	Ch.-Porch		411
Summe up at night, what thou hast done by day;	24	Ch.-Porch		451
Summe up at night, what thou hast done that day;	24	Ch.-Porch	W	451
And in the morning, what thou hast to do.	24	Ch.-Porch		452
Shall I weep bloud? why, thou hast wept such store	35	Thanksgvng		5
If thou hast giv'n it me, 'tis here.	36	Thanksgvng		44
Thou hast an ancient claime to mee.	39	Good Fri.	W	32
That thou hast ought to do with me.	45	Nature		3
Lord, with what care hast thou begirt us round!	45	Sinne 1		1
Which thou hast pour'd into my soul;	49	Repentance		20
Thou hast restor'd us to this ease	53	H.Commun.		37
Since thou hast taught us by thy word,	53	H.Commun.	W	39
And thrown it on that dust which thou hast made,	54	Love 1		4
And thrown it in that dust which thou hast made,	54	Love 1	W	4
Lord, who hast form'd me out of mud,	68	Trin.Sun.		1
Lord, who hast made me living mudd,	68	Trin.Sun.	W	1
Lord, who hast rais'd me from the mudd	68	Trin.Sun.	WC	1
And hast redeem'd me through thy bloud,	68	Trin.Sun.		2
To this great kingdome, which thou now hast got,	77	Avarice		6
Nay, thou hast got the face of man; for we	77	Avarice		10
Hast thou redeem'd us from the grave!	82	Ungratef.		2
Thou hast but two rare cabinets full of treasure,	82	Ungratef.		7
Thou hast unlockt them both,	82	Ungratef.		9
Thou hast layd open both,	82	Ungratef.	W	9
For thou hast other vessels full of bloud,	83	Sighs & Gr.		21
For thou hast life and death at thy command;	83	Sighs & Gr.		26
Since then, my God, thou hast	92	Man		49
Yet can a friend what thou hast done fulfill?	94	Unkindness		21
Since thou hast both mine eyes.	95	Submission		20
How hast thou lost them in a croud of cares?	101	Miserie		50
Hast thou tears, or hast thou none?	113	Businesse		5
If, poore soul, thou hast no tears,	113	Businesse		6
Hast thou sighs, or hast thou not?	113	Businesse		11

HAST (cont'd)	PAGE	TITLE		LINE
If thou hast no sighs or grones,	113	Businesse		12
Onely to Man thou hast made known thy wayes,	117	Providence		6
Which crie and follow. Thou hast made poore sand	118	Providence		47
Thou hast hid metals: man may take them thence;	119	Providence		81
Thou that hast giv'n so much to me,	123	Gratefulnes		1
All thou hast giv'n him heretofore	123	Gratefulnes		7
Nay thou hast made a sigh and grone	124	Gratefulnes		19
Not that thou hast not still above	124	Gratefulnes		21
If thou hast wherewithall to spice a draught,	137	The Size		9
Which thou hast open'd: do not spread thy robe	138	The Size		43
Hast thou not made thy counts, and summ'd up all?	144	Discharge		6
Thou hast granted my request,	146	Praise 2		5
Thou hast heard me:	146	Praise 2		6
Thou hast spar'd me.	146	Praise 2		8
What hast thou there? a heart? but is it pure?	147	Offering		3
What thou hast kept,	147	Offering		29
Hast thou left all things to their course,	149	Longing		44
Hast thou not heard, that my Lord JESUS di'd?	151	The Bag		7
And thou hast hands.	153	The Collar		18
To hide thy shame: for thou hast cast a bone	156	Assurance		39
Thou hast a garden for us, where to bide.	167	The Flower		46
The hast of thy good will.	200	H. Commun.	W	15
For who can tell, though thou hast dyde to winn	205	Persever.	W	9
And what is fortunes. Thou hast singled out	211	Bohemia	D	19
Yet hast thou more dominions: God doth give	212	Bohemia	D	41
And thou hast brok th' ungodly's teeth:	217	Psalm III	D	21
O thou that hast enlarged me	217	Psalm IV	D	3
he could not but say, he would hast out of it as fast as he could.	257	Priest 21		7
Thou hast exalted thy mercy above all things;	288	Priest		22
and hast made our salvation, not our punishment, thy glory:	288	Priest		23
and reconciliation, thou hast committed, not to Thunder,	289	Priest		4
which thou hast made a Land of light, a store-house of thy treasures	289	Priest		18
but pardon our sins, and perfect what thou hast begun.	289	Priest		21
Thou hast elected us, thou hast called us, thou hast justified us,	290	Priest		2
Thou hast elected us, thou hast called us, thou hast justified us,	290	Priest		3
thou hast called us, thou hast justified us, sanctified,	290	Priest		3
Thou hast given us the blessings of this life, and of a better.	290	Priest		5
And now Lord, thou hast fed us with the bread of life:	290	Priest		8
the measure of thy love, who hast done for us as much as may be.	290	Priest		12
Thou hast death in thy house, and dost bewaile anothers.	334	Proverbs		376
HASTE (see also hast)				
Who would not haste, nay give, to see the show?	22	Ch.-Porch		390
Alas! what haste they make to be undone!	27	Sacrifice		34
I never saw thing make such haste.	107	Home		10
if I am to visit the sick in haste, and my neerest way ly through	273	Priest 31		33
for riding in a coach in great haste, it happened that the coach was	294	Cornaro		36
circumstance, yet you will pardon my haste, which is very great,	370	Letters		13
your Courtesie will pardon the haste of Your humblest Servant,	371	Letters		19
HASTED				
Which I had lost, I hasted to my bed.	130	Love unkn.		48
HASTENS				
Who hastens a glutton choakes him.	349	Proverbs		858
HAT (see also hatt)				
HATCH				
Untill their cockatrice they hatch and bring:	122	Sinnes rd.		4
HATCHET				
To whom thy sithe a hatchet was,	122	Time		9
when it condescends to the naming of a plough, a hatchet, a bushell,	257	Priest 21		12
When the tree is fallen, all goe with their hatchet.	340	Proverbs		566
HATCHING				
Hatching my tender heart so long,	59	Whitsunday		3
HATE				
Thou who condemnest Jewish hate,	170	Self-cond.		1
To second thee against there cunning hate.	211	Bohemia	D	22
If God hate them, either he doth it as they are Creatures,	283	Priest 34		9
because notwithstanding his infinite hate of sinne, his Love overcame	283	Priest 34		14
his infinite hate of sinne, his Love overcame that hate;	283	Priest 34		15
We must love, as looking one day to hate.	359	Proverbs	D	1126
HATED				
and will not be perswaded, but being not invited, they are hated.	243	Priest 11		22
for no perfect Artist ever yet hated his owne worke.	283	Priest 34		12
HAT'ST				
Thou hat'st those that unjustly do:	218	Psalm V	D	13
HATETH				
he hateth him not as an officer, but pityes him as a Father:	250	Priest 16		11
HATH				
Not grudging, that thy lust hath bounds and staies.	7	Ch.-Porch		16
Continence hath his joy: weigh both; and so	7	Ch.-Porch		17
A Virgin-bed, which hath a speciall Crowne	7	Ch.-Porch	W	20
God hath impal'd us, on the contrarie	7	Ch.-Porch		21
Bigge with his sister: he hath lost the reins,	7	Ch.-Porch		32
Bigge with his sister: he hath lost his reins,	7	Ch.-Porch	W	32
All worldly right, save what he hath by beast.	7	Ch.-Porch		36
Lose all mine own? God hath giv'n me a measure	8	Ch.-Porch		38
It gets thee nothing, and hath no excuse.	8	Ch.-Porch		56
If studious, copie fair, what time hath blurr'd;	10	Ch.-Porch		86
Whom when he thinks he hath, the devil hath him.	13	Ch.-Porch		166
Perhaps his wives too, and whom she hath bore:	14	Ch.-Porch		195
Learn this, that hath old gamesters deerely cost:	14	Ch.-Porch		200
Learn this, it hath old gamesters deerely cost:	14	Ch.-Porch	W	200

HATH (cont'd)

	PAGE	TITLE		LINE
Yet publick hath more promises, more love:	22	Ch.-Porch		398
Preachers conclude with, hath not lost his pains.	24	Ch.-Porch		434
No workmans tool hath touch'd the same.	26	The Altar		4
My heart hath store, write there, where in	39	Good Fri.		23
Which holds thee now? Who hath indited it	41	Sepulchre		11
And in this shew, what Christ hath done.	51	Faith		36
This shadowes out what Christ hath done.	51	Faith	W	36
And hath the privie key,	52	H.Commun.		21
How hath man parcel'd out thy glorious name,	54	Love 1		3
O let me, when thy roof my soul hath hid,	55	Temper 1		17
Hath some good in him, all agree.	63	Sinne 2		3
But God more care of us hath had:	63	Sinne 2		6
But I have got his sonne, and he hath none.	63	Even-song		8
He that by seeking hath himself once found,	69	Content		35
Hath ever found a happie fortune.	69	Content		36
Christ hath took in this piece of ground,	76	Sunday		40
Where ev'ry one is king, and hath his crown,	77	Ang.&Sts.		4
Hath still sow'd fig-leaves to exclude thy light:	83	Sighs & Gr.		16
A part wherecf my Saviour empti'd hath,	83	Sighs & Gr.		22
That Life hath with the sun a double motion.	84	Coloss.		2
What hath not man sought out and found,	85	Vanitie 1		22
What hath not man wrought out and found,	85	Vanitie 1	V	22
He sayes, in things which use hath justly got,	86	Lent		10
Who goeth in the way which Christ hath gone,	87	Lent		37
Who goeth in that way which Christ hath gone,	87	Lent	V	37
Who goeth in the way that Christ hath gone,	87	Lent	W	37
What reason hath from nature borrowed,	88	The Pearl		3
What reason hath from nature purchased,	88	The Pearl	W	3
What house more stately hath there been,	90	Man		4
For head with foot hath private amitie,	91	Man		17
Nothing hath got so farre,	91	Man		19
But Man hath caught and kept it, as his prey.	91	Man		20
Both are our cleanlinesse. Hath one such beautie?	92	Man		41
Oh mightie love! Man is one world, and hath	92	Man		47
Who hath dealt his mercies so,	92	Antiphon 2		4
Who hath made of two folds one.	93	Antiphon 2		23
Which hath made cf two folds one.	93	Antiphon 2	W	23
I would do well, yet sinne the hand hath got:	96	Justice 1		10
Who shuts his hand, hath lost his gold:	96	Charms & K		5
Who opens it, hath it twice told.	96	Charms & K		6
Hath put together a solemnitie,	99	Mortific.		32
But sinne hath fool'd him. Now he is	102	Miserie		73
To passe it self and all it hath to thee.	104	Obedience		8
And heart unto this deed, when he hath read;	105	Obedience		38
Hath kiss'd so long her painted shrines,	110	Brit. Ch.		16
Who hath these, those ill forbears.	113	Businesse		8
And hath any space of breath	114	Businesse		29
He that sinnes, hath he no losse?	114	Businesse		33
Each creature hath a wisdome for his good.	118	Providence		61
Who hath the vertue to expresse the rare	119	Providence		73
And if an herb hath power, what have the starres?	119	Providence		77
And onely he hath fuell in desire.	120	Providence		112
But who hath praise enough? nay who hath any?	121	Providence		141
It go for one, hath many wayes in store	121	Providence		150
Christs coming hath made man thy debter,	122	Time		11
When he a torture hath design'd.	126	Confession		10
Hath let thee out again:	128	Bunch Gr.		2
So now each Christian hath his journeys spann'd:	128	Bunch Gr.		10
But can he want the grape, who hath the wine?	128	Bunch Gr.		22
But can he want the grape, who hath the vine?	128	Bunch Gr.	V	22
All creatures have their joy: and man hath his.	131	Mans medly		3
He hath two winters, other things but one:	131	Mans medly		27
Hath found the art	132	Mans medly		35
Hath a strange force:	132	The Storm		10
Thy promise now hath ev'n set thee thy laws.	139	Artillerie		24
This, this hath done it, this did bite the root	140	Ch.-rents		5
The crop is his, for he hath sown.	144	Discharge		15
My God hath promis'd; he is just.	145	Discharge		55
Is all lockt? hath a sinners plea	149	Longing		47
Hath interlin'd.	149	Longing		52
Which hath been broken now so long,	150	Longing		74
Hath got a tongue!	150	Longing		76
When thou dost blesse, hath twelve: one wheel doth rise	158	Praise 3		11
Sorrow hath chang'd its note: such is his will,	159	Jos.coat		3
But he hath spoil'd the race; and giv'n to anguish	159	Jos.coat		10
My grief hath need of all the watry things,	164	Grief		3
That nature hath produc'd. Let ev'ry vein	164	Grief		4
Hath made a Jewish choice:	170	Self-cond.		9
Thousands of souls it hath and doth destroy	170	Self-cond.		11
He that hath made a sorrie wedding	171	Self-cond.		13
Between his soul and gold, and hath preferr'd	171	Self-cond.		14
Hath done what he condemnes in reading:	171	Self-cond.		16
For he hath sold for money his deare Lord,	171	Self-cond.		17
My soul hath felt, ev'n able to destroy,	172	The Glance		10
God hath made starres the foil	176	The Foil		5
Hath some fond lover tic'd thee to thy bane?	176	Forerunners		21
Though man frailties hath,	179	Discipline		30
Or hath sweetnesse in the bread	181	Banquet		13
Hath the power	181	Banquet		20
Who hath done so much for me.	182	Banquet		48

HATH (cont'd)

	PAGE	TITLE		LINE
Such power hath mightie Baptisme to produce	191	Ch.-Milit.		45
But seems to yeeld Christ hath the greater wounds, . . .	191	Ch.-Milit.		64
Spain hath done one; when Arts perform the other, ...	197	Ch.-Milit.		265
That thy flesh hath lost his food, ...	199	L'Envoy		9
The Day is spent, & hath his will on mee:	203	Even-song	W	1
Hath soild with Black) the colour of my state, ...	209	L. Bacon	D	7
Wheare health hath nought to doe;	210	Paradox	D	14
Since that mirth hath	210	Paradox	D	17
Nor hath in way of sinners stood, ...	214	Psalm I	D	3
For God himself hath heard my cry;	220	Psalm VI	D	21
But in the pit which he hath made	222	Psalm VII	D	55
since our Saviour hath made that the argument of a Pastour's love,	224	Priest		5
as farre as wee can in pleasing of him, who hath done so much for us.	224	Priest		12
therefore he hath throughly studied these, that he may be an absolute	227	Priest 3		7
of himself, for all the purposes which God hath ordained him.	227	Priest 3		10
which in the day of wrath hath not one dramme of comfort for us.	227	Priest 3		21
These he hath digested severally.	228	Priest 4		26
that God in all ages hath had his servants, to whom he hath revealed	229	Priest 4		22
his servants, to whom he hath revealed his Truth, as well as to him;	229	Priest 4		22
so neither hath God opened, or will open all to one, that there may	229	Priest 4		25
Wherfore he hath one Comment at least upon every book of Scripture,	229	Priest 4		27
The Countrey Parson hath read the Fathers also, and the Schoolmen,	229	Priest 5		31
out of all which he hath compiled a book, and body of Divinity,	229	Priest 5		33
Yet hath the Parson, besides this laborious work, a slighter forme	230	Priest 5		15
For every one hath not digested, when it is a sin to take something	230	Priest 5		23
Wherefore the Parson hath throughly canvassed al the particulars	230	Priest 5		33
that God hath ever had his people, that have glorified him as wel	231	Priest 6		34
who treads in his steps, and will not throw down what he hath built;	232	Priest 7		27
that he himself hath often urged with no great success, . .	232	Priest 7		28
are but two devouring elements, fire, and water, he hath both in him;	234	Priest 7		33
and the like, hath neither in it sweetnesse, nor gravity, . .	235	Priest 7		8
the afternoone, he thinks he hath in some measure, according to poor,	236	Priest 8		8
he hath not a woman in his house, but findes opportunities of having	237	Priest 9		7
but hath power over his own will, and hath so decreed in his heart,	237	Priest 9		16
and hath so decreed in his heart, that he will keep himself a virgin,	237	Priest 9		17
Other temptations he hath, which, like mortall enemies, . .	238	Priest 9		9
means to continue so, he doth at least, as much as hath been said.	238	Priest 9		25
for he hath no mony for such things, charity being his only perfume,	241	Priest 10		13
and common, but wholsome, what hee hath, is little, but very good;	241	Priest 10		16
God hath provided Creatures for both;	241	Priest 10		30
hee hath them all with him, because countrey people are very	243	Priest 11		19
yet out of his infinite pity hath set forth heaven for a reward	243	Priest 11		31
counting that day lost, wherein he hath not exercised his Charity.	244	Priest 12		18
this generall provision, he hath other times of opening his hand;	245	Priest 12		6
The Countrey Parson hath a speciall care of his Church, . .	246	Priest 13		1
he hath a Poor-mans Box conveniently seated, to receive the charity	246	Priest 13		20
To this end he hath throughly digested all the points of consolation,	249	Priest 15		17
and then when he hath affrighted them with this, exposing . .	253	Priest 19		33
him in his Tithes, telling him when he hath forgotten it, This I do,	254	Priest 20		16
this life, who hath promised, that Godlinesse shall be gainfull:	254	Priest 20		19
Baptisme being a blessing, that the word hath not the like. . .	258	Priest 22		7
the Sacrament, hath the confidence of a Guest, and hee that kneels,	259	Priest 22		14
he hath gotten to himself some insight in things ordinarily incident	259	Priest 23		33
whom he hath ever some cases to ask, when he meets with them;	260	Priest 23		4
but when he hath so done, then he assumes the Parson, and exhorts	260	Priest 23		16
Wherefore the Parson hath diligently examined these two . .	262	Priest 24		31
be a rule to it selfe, whether it hath a rule, whether having a rule,	263	Priest 24		2
These and the like points hee hath accurately digested, . .	263	Priest 24		14
hath exactly sifted the definitions of all vertues, and vices;	264	Priest 26		31
in perverting that order which he hath set both to things, . .	265	Priest 26		11
squeeze blood undecently to the station wherein God hath placed me,	265	Priest 26		18
if a man hath wherewithall to buy a spade, and yet hee chuseth rather	265	Priest 26		28
which out of his choysest judgment hee hath resolved to observe,	268	Priest 28		12
because this hath been the portion of God his Master, and of Gods	268	Priest 28		14
in the world as he was, hath this undoubted pledge of his salvation.	269	Priest 28		18
Neither hath the place its dignity from the Ecclesiasticall Laws	269	Priest 29		32
that God hath and exerciseth a threefold power in every thing which	270	Priest 30		33
As when a Merchant hath a ship come home after many a storme,	271	Priest 30		22
which it hath escaped, he destroyes it sometimes in the very Haven;	271	Priest 30		23
be housed, a fire hath broken forth, and suddenly consumed them.	271	Priest 30		24
God sends a fire, and consumes all that he hath:	271	Priest 30		33
So that if a Farmer hath both a faire harvest, and that also well	271	Priest 30		38
who hath in his hand an apple, and a piece of Gold under it;	272	Priest 30		8
God) stands fast in the Liberty wherewith Christ hath made us free.	272	Priest 31		19
The Countrey Parson hath not onely taken a particular Survey	274	Priest 32		4
wherein God hath placed two great Instruments, Reason in the soul,	274	Priest 32		19
He that hath or can have yet no imployment, if he truly, . .	275	Priest 32		12
The marryed and house-keeper hath his hands full, if he do what he	275	Priest 32		20
or hath generall Propositions to the whole Towne or Hamlet, . .	276	Priest 32		4
No Common-wealth in the world hath a braver [better] Institution then	276	Priest 32		9
who hath so many dispersed Officers at his beck throughout . .	276	Priest 32		10
after he hath shew'd the unlawfulness of spending the day in	277	Priest 32		28
Hee that hath considered how to carry himself at table about his	278	Priest 33		18
hath ever so many sermons ready penn'd, as he hath victories.	278	Priest 33		23
hath ever so many sermons ready penn'd, as he hath victories.	278	Priest 33		24
He that hath been sick of a Consumption, and knows what recovered	278	Priest 33		25
He hath one argument unanswerable.	283	Priest 34		9
hath two pledges of Gods Love, that in the mouth of two or three	283	Priest 34		18
where he knowes there hath been or is a little difference, . . .	284	Priest 35		19
interesting of that dignity wherewith God hath invested the Priest,	286	Priest 36		9

HATH (cont'd)

	PAGE	TITLE		LINE
duty in Ministers themselves, hath made the people also neglect it;	286	Priest 36		12
that they oftentimes goe out of church, before he hath blessed them.	286	Priest 36		14
and hath taken so deep roote, that it seems the very life	287	Priest 37		8
of Conversation, hath proceeded thus far in the discussing of it.	287	Priest 37		10
which hath so much advanced Charity, and ranked backbiters among	287	Priest 37		22
and Charity to the publick hath the precedence of private charity.	287	Priest 37		37
and forbear to speak of that, which even God himself hath forgotten.	288	Priest 37		5
power a sober and temperate life hath over our bodies and mindes,	294	Cornaro		25
and when he hath cured him, commends this also to him, if he will	297	Cornaro		17
and what hidden properties it hath, what meat and drink agrees best	297	Cornaro		28
shall he use in diseases, which being in health he hath anticipated?	299	Cornaro		24
whether he hath lived heretofore orderly or disorderly,	299	Cornaro		29
and drink, hath the quantitie, and not the qualitie for his rule,	300	Cornaro		15
that my advice hath taken effect in the reducing of many rude	302	Cornaro		14
and God hath put this into your hands (as he sent the fish with mony	304	Valdesso		10
For as the servant leaves not the letter when he hath read it,	310	Valdesso		28
and that no cther sin or vertue hath any thing to doe with us;	311	Valdesso		24
to relieve my Neighbour, God hath already reveled his Will about it.	313	Valdesso		14
So that the Word hath the precedence even of Revelations and Visions.	318	Valdesso		24
Who hath none to still him, may weepe out his eyes.	321	Proverbs		17
He hath great neede of a foole, that plaies the foole himselfe.	322	Proverbs		46
The longest Day hath an Eveninge.	322	Proverbs	V	51
Who hath a Wolfe for his mate, needes a Dog for his man.	323	Proverbs		57
God oft hath a great share in a little house.	323	Proverbs		60
Every ill man hath his ill day.	324	Proverbs		92
Who hath no more bread then neede, must not keepe a dog.	325	Proverbs		128
A wicked mans gift hath a touch of his master.	326	Proverbs		162
God heales, and the Physitian hath the thankes.	326	Proverbs		169
Every path hath a puddle.	328	Proverbs		215
Reckon right, and February hath one and thirty daies.	328	Proverbs		229
He that riseth betimes hath some thing in his head.	329	Proverbs		235
The hard gives more then he that hath nothing.	329	Proverbs		259
He is not poore that hath little, but he that desireth much.	331	Proverbs		309
He that hath a mouth of his owne,	333	Proverbs		353
He that hath lost his credit is dead to the world.	333	Proverbs		357
He that hath no ill fortune is troubled with good.	333	Proverbs		358
He that hath no hony in his pot, let him have it in his mouth.	333	Proverbs		360
Who hath bitter in his mouth, spits not all sweet.	335	Proverbs		422
He that hath children, all his morsels are not his owne.	335	Proverbs		423
He who hath children, all his morsels are not his owne.	335	Proverbs	V	423
He that hath the spice, may season as he list.	335	Proverbs		424
He who hath the spice, may season as he pleaseth.	335	Proverbs	V	424
He that hath a head of waxe must not walke in the sunne.	335	Proverbs		425
He that hath love in his brest, hath spurres in his sides.	335	Proverbs		426
Hee that hath a Fox for his mate,	335	Proverbs		428
hath neede of a net at his girdle.	335	Proverbs		428
Hee that hath right, feares; he that hath wrong, hopes.	336	Proverbs		429
Hee that hath patience hath fatt thrushes for a farthing.	336	Proverbs		430
Hee that hath one hogge makes him fat,	336	Proverbs		433
and hee that hath one son makes him a foole.	336	Proverbs		433
Hee who hath but one sonne makes him fat,	336	Proverbs	V	433
He that hath little is the lesse durtie.	336	Proverbs		436
He that hath one foot in the straw, hath another in the spittle.	336	Proverbs		438
Hee that bewailes himselfe hath the cure in his hands.	336	Proverbs		441
The resolved minde hath no eares.	337	Proverbs		464
The resolved minde hath no cares.	337	Proverbs	V	464
There is no jollitie but hath a smack of folly.	338	Proverbs		493
When a knave is in a plumtree he hath neither friend nor kin.	338	Proverbs		507
A curst Cow hath short hornes.	339	Proverbs		531
Though the Fox run, the chicken hath wings.	339	Proverbs		549
Hee that should have what hee hath not,	340	Proverbs		559
Hee that would have what hee hath not,	340	Proverbs	V	559
He that hath no good trade, it is to his losse.	340	Proverbs		560
He that hath hornes in his bosom,	340	Proverbs		567
He that contemplates hath a day without night.	341	Proverbs		601
He that goeth farre hath many encounters.	341	Proverbs		608
Wisedome hath one foot on Land, and another on Sea.	341	Proverbs		611
The thought hath good leggs, and the quill a good tongue.	342	Proverbs		612
The sight of a man hath the force of a Lyon.	342	Proverbs		617
It's an ill councell that hath no escape.	345	Proverbs		715
A horse stumbles that hath foure legges.	346	Proverbs		740
Hee that hath a wife and children wants not businesse.	347	Proverbs		778
A small heart hath small desires.	348	Proverbs		807
He that hath not the craft, let him shut up shop.	349	Proverbs		860
Hee hath not liv'd, that lives not after death.	350	Proverbs		873
Every one hath a foole in his sleeve.	350	Proverbs		881
The Court hath no Almanack.	350	Proverbs		894
Hee hath no leisure who useth it not.	351	Proverbs		897
The ignorant hath an Eagles wings, and an Owles eyes.	351	Proverbs		902
Hee that learnes a trade hath a purchase made.	353	Proverbs		978
Hee that hath charge of soules transports them not in bundles.	353	Proverbs		986
Hee a beast doth die, that hath done no good to his country.	354	Proverbs		993
Who hath no head, needes no hatt.	354	Proverbs		996
Who hath no head, needes no heart.	354	Proverbs	V	996
Who hath no hast in his businesse,	354	Proverbs		997
knowes nothing sure but what hee hath laid out.	354	Proverbs		1001
He that hath lands hath quarrells.	354	Proverbs		1002
hath a rock and a spindle, and no staffe to spin.	358	Proverbs	D	1085
He that hath but one eye, must bee afraid to lose it.	358	Proverbs	D	1088
He that hath time and looks for better time,	359	Proverbs	D	1102

HATH (cont'd)	PAGE	TITLE		LINE
The Bathe of the Blackamoor hath sworne not to whiten.	359	Proverbs	D	1105
No day so clear but hath dark clouds.	359	Proverbs	D	1123
No hair so small but hath his shadow.	359	Proverbs	D	1124
The mouse that hath but one hole is quickly taken.	360	Proverbs	D	1135
Love without end, hath no end, says the Spaniard: (meaning,	361	Proverbs	D	1160
But I fear the heat of my late Ague hath dryed up those springs,	363	Letters		4
and hath nothing else to answer your infinite kindnesses,	363	Letters		18
education, of obeying that Spirit which hath guided me hitherto,	364	Letters		18
for it hath been my fortune of late to have such sudden warning,	365	Letters		31
that he hath bought a parcel of Books for me, and that they are	366	Letters		30
which she hath hitherto deferred to do, not of her self,	367	Letters		3
which he refusing to doe hath given her occasion to protest shee will	368	Letters		22
There is a Spanish Lawyer hath written a treatise concerning	368	Letters		26
This Week hath loaded me with your Favours;	369	Letters		10
long in Latin, and my Lincoln journey hath set me much behind hand:	369	Letters		14
hath no such earthiness in it, but it may very well be joined	370	Letters		22
What hath Affliction grievous in it more then for a moment?	372	Letters		26
because sickness hath made me unable to perform those Offices	373	Letters		9
That God who hath delivered me out of the paws of the Lyon and Bear,	374	Letters		6
Neither hath she any to repair unto at good times, as Christmas,	375	Letters		27
as being now a father, "the best-bredd child hath the best portion".	376	Letters		18
What a trouble hath your Goodness brought on you, by admitting our	376	Letters		26
HATRED				
without hatred to the person, hungreth and thirsteth after righteous	254	Priest 20		28
alwayes cleer, and evident, as Adultery, Murder, Hatred, Lying, &c.	264	Priest 26		7
for this may produce hatred in those that are reproved,	268	Priest 28		29
from hatred and melancholie, and other perturbations of the minde,	293	Cornaro		35
HATT				
Pull downe your hatt on the winds side.	332	Proverbs		334
A hatt is not made for one shower.	343	Proverbs		673
Who hath no head, needes no hatt.	354	Proverbs		996
HAUNT				
Neither is it for the servant of Christ to haunt Innes,	227	Priest 3		30
HAVE				
If rottennesse have more, let Heaven go.	7	Ch.-Porch		18
Man would have been th' incloser: but since now	7	Ch.-Porch		20
If rottenness have more, lett Heaven goe.	7	Ch.-Porch	W	24
Hee that has all ill, & can have no good	7	Ch.-Porch	W	35
For we have wit to mark them, and to spare.	9	Ch.-Porch		69
Pride and full sinnes have made the way a road.	9	Ch.-Porch		72
Throughout the world. Fool not: for all may have,	10	Ch.-Porch		89
Would have their tale beleeved for their oathes,	14	Ch.-Porch		183
Have got to be a deare fool for an houre.	16	Ch.-Porch		246
Let thy mindes sweetnesse have his operation	21	Ch.-Porch		371
Let vain or busie thoughts have there no part:	23	Ch.-Porch		421
Let vain & busie thoughts have there no part:	23	Ch.-Porch	W	421
Thou, whom the former precepts have	25	Superlim		1
I suffer binding, who have loos'd their bands:	28	Sacrifice		47
Weep not, deare friends, since I for both have wept	31	Sacrifice		149
Which Angels did desire to have the grace,	32	Sacrifice		182
Whom Angels did desire to have the grace,	32	Sacrifice	W	182
Alas! what have I stollen from you? Death.	34	Sacrifice		231
When with the other I have done.	35	Thanksgvng		30
Shall have his attribute to sing;	36	Thanksgvng		40
Till I have found therein thy love,	36	Thanksgvng		46
Till I have found thy love therin,	36	Thanksgvng	W	46
I have consider'd it, and finde	36	Reprisall		1
Philosophers have measur'd mountains,	37	The Agonie		1
What I have treasur'd in my memorie!	38	The Sinner		2
Where our hard hearts have took up stones to brain thee,	41	Sepulchre		13
Besides what I might have	46	Afflict.1		4
For so thou should'st without me still have been,	52	H.Commun.		5
A fervent sigh might well have blown	53	H.Commun.		31
Thou shalt have more.	61	Praise 1		4
Who have a work, as well as they,	61	Praise 1		19
But I have got his sonne, and he hath none.	63	Even-song		8
What have I brought thee home	64	Even-song		9
For this thy love? have I discharg'd the debt,	64	Even-song		10
Of winde to thee whom I have crost,	64	Even-song		15
To kisse those heaps, which now they have in trust?	65	Ch.-monum.		16
Then to have hellish moths still gnaw and fret	69	Content		27
Have with our stamp and seal transferr'd our right:	77	Avarice		11
Furnish & deck my soul, that thou mayst have	81	Christmas		13
Shall stay, till we have done;	81	Christmas		28
For we have all of us just such another.	82	Ungratef.		24
Sinnes have their box apart,	82	Ungratef.		29
I have abus'd thy stock, destroy'd thy woods,	83	Sighs & Gr.		9
I have deserv'd that an Egyptian night	83	Sighs & Gr.		14
My musick shows ye have your closes,	88	Vertue		11
All these stand open, or I have the keyes:	88	The Pearl		9
Have done these twentie hundred yeares, and more:	89	The Pearl		25
Have done these many hundred yeares, and more:	89	The Pearl	W	25
And grumble oft, that they have more in me	89	The Pearl		28
I know all these, and have them in my hand:	89	The Pearl		31
And at what rate and price I have thy love;	89	The Pearl		35
The starres have us to bed;	91	Man		31
Both are our cleanlines: if one have beauty,	92	Man	W	41
We have none,	93	Antiphon 2		20
Wee have no store.	93	Antiphon 2	W	21
Would he have gold? I lend it instantly;	93	Unkindness		12

HAVE (cont'd)

	PAGE	TITLE	LINE
One might have sought and found thee presently	99	Decay	6
They would not have their actions scann'd,	100	Miserie	21
As I have mine, may set his hand	105	Obedience	37
I have both lost mine eyes and eares.	105	Conscience	6
That I have physick to expell thee.	105	Conscience	12
What have I left, that I should stay and grone?	109	Home	67
And then they have their answer home.	111	The Quip	24
Of Joy and Charitie. Sir, you have not miss'd,	116	Love-joy	7
While all things have their will, yet none but thine.	117	Providence	32
Birds teach us hawking; fishes have their net:	118	Providence	51
Flies have their table spread, ere they appeare.	118	Providence	54
Some creatures have in winter what to eat;	118	Providence	55
And if an herb hath power, what have the starres?	119	Providence	77
The common all men have; that which is rare,	119	Providence	98
Men therefore seek to have, and care to keep.	119	Providence	99
All countreys have enough to serve their need:	120	Providence	105
All things that are, though they have sev'rall wayes,	121	Providence	145
And when they once have perfected their draughts,	122	Sinnes rd.	5
But where one man would have me grinde it,	122	Time	5
Gift upon gift, much would have more,	124	Gratefulnes	15
No smith can make such locks, but they have keyes:	126	Confession	17
Smooth open hearts no fastning have; but fiction	126	Confession	23
Then have we too our guardian fires and clouds;	128	Bunch Gr.	15
We have our sands and serpents, tents and shrowds;	128	Bunch Gr.	17
I have their fruit and more.	128	Bunch Gr.	23
And have, of whom some grounds which may improve,	129	Love unkn.	4
And have good cause: there it was dipt and di'd,	129	Love unkn.	16
Who fain would have you be new, tender, quick.	131	Love unkn.	70
All creatures have their joy: and man hath his.	131	Mans medly	3
In th' other Angels have a right by birth:	131	Mans medly	9
Starres have their storms, ev'n in a high degree,	132	The Storm	7
Poets have wrong'd poore storms: such dayes are best;	132	The Storm	17
Late when I would have something done,	134	The Method	22
And trip at night, have spheres suppli'd;	134	Divinitie	2
Have thicken'd it with definitions?	134	Divinitie	10
More bowels have, then such hard things.	136	Ephes.	24
Modest and moderate joyes to those, that have	137	The Size	2
What though some have a fraught	137	The Size	7
Wouldst thou both eat thy cake, and have it?	138	The Size	18
Those have their hopes; these what they have renounce,	138	The Size	21
Which have the face of fire, but end in rest.	139	Artillerie	8
But I have also starres and shooters too,	139	Artillerie	17
Gods promises have made thee mine;	141	Justice 2	22
Fain would I here have made abode,	142	Pilgrimage	9
But to have nought is ours, not to confesse	143	Holdfast	9
That we have nought. I stood amaz'd at this,	143	Holdfast	10
Have I no parts but those of grief?	143	Complaining	15
Search well and see; for hearts have many holes.	147	Offering	4
Thy lusts have made, and not thy lusts alone;	147	Offering	15
Thy passions also have their set partitions.	147	Offering	16
Where all things have their leafe assign'd:	149	Longing	50
If ye have any thing to send or write,	152	The Bag	31
(I have no bag, but here is room):	152	The Bag	32
Our cyens have purloin'd, and left you drie:	152	The Jews	2
Our sinnes have purloin'd, and left you drie:	152	The Jews V	2
Have I no harvest but a thorn	153	The Collar	7
What I have lost with cordiall fruit?	153	The Collar	9
Have I no bayes to crown it?	153	The Collar	14
Which pettie thoughts have made, and made to thee	153	The Collar	23
Me thinks delight should have	154	Glimpse	6
If I have more to spinne,	155	Glimpse	26
That thou mayst yet have more.	157	Praise 3	6
This spacious globe: Angels must have their joy,	158	Praise 3	21
I have not lost one single tear:	158	Praise 3	25
(As we have boxes for the poore)	158	Praise 3	28
Yet have I often seen, by cunning hand	161	Priesthood	13
Have one beginning and one finall summe:	161	Priesthood	22
To have my aim, and yet to be	165	The Crosse	25
Who would have thought my shrivel'd heart	166	The Flower	8
Could have recover'd greennesse? It was gone	166	The Flower	9
To see their mother-root, when they have blown;	166	The Flower	11
Show me, and set me, I have one reply,	169	The Answer	13
Go spell and reade how I have kill'd thy King.	169	Dial.-Anth	4
In both I have the best.	172	23 Psalme	8
I have, another heart and breast,	174	Aaron	12
Without whom I could have no rest:	174	Aaron	14
But must they have my brain? must they dispark	176	Forerunners	3
Yet have they left me, Thou art still my God.	176	Forerunners	6
My god must have my best, ev'n all I had.	176	Forerunners	18
Go birds of spring: let winter have his fee,	177	Forerunners	34
Who have pass'd my right away.	177	The Rose	12
Weep what ye have drunk amisse,	180	Invitation	10
Lord I have invited all,	180	Invitation	31
And then what life I have,	183	A Parodie	21
Half that we have	186	Death	22
Fleshes stubbornnesse may have	187	Dooms-day	17
Truth Lord, but I have marr'd them: let my shame	189	Love 3	13
When Italie of us shall have her will,	197	Ch.-Milit.	243
They have their times of Gospel, ev'n as we.	197	Ch.-Milit.	248
They have their time of Gospel, ev'n as we.	197	Ch.-Milit. W	248

HAVE (cont'd)	PAGE	TITLE		LINE
They have their period also and set times	197	Ch.-Milit.		261
That when they have accomplished the round,	197	Ch.-Milit.		267
That when they have accomplished their round,	197	Ch.-Milit.	W	267
Creatures are good, & have their place	200	H. Commun.	W	22
Or give mee that, so I have more	201	H. Commun.	W	47
Let mee but once the conquest have	202	love	W	19
I and the Sunn have runn our races,	203	Even-song	W	2
Reade him there, and I have done.	208	J. Danvers	D	16
the way that right'ous men have gone:	215	Psalm I	D	22
this day have I begotten thee:	216	Psalm II	D	18
Have mercy on me Lord, and hear	217	Psalm IV	D	5
Thou in the morn shalt have my mone,	218	Psalm V	D	5
they vainly have rebell'd:	219	Psalm V	D	34
If I have done this thing, O Lord,	221	Psalm VII	D	9
If I have ill rewarded him	221	Psalm VII	D	11
Yea, have not oft deliver'd him	221	Psalm VII	D	13
I have resolved to set down the Form and Character of a true Pastour,	224	Priest		6
and Character of a true Pastour, that I may have a Mark to aim at:	224	Priest		7
which I have observed, untill the Book grow to a compleat Pastorall.	224	Priest		15
and not to think, that when they have read the Fathers, or Schoolmen,	226	Priest 2		11
and because they have different Names, think their Office different.	226	Priest 2		20
the well is deep, and we have nothing of our selves to draw with?	228	Priest 4		35
When the Apostles would have called down fire from Heaven,	229	Priest 4		12
who have handled the places controverted, which the Parson by no	229	Priest 4		18
that have glorified him as wel as now, and that he shall have so	231	Priest 6		35
have glorified him as wel as now, and that he shall have so for ever.	232	Priest 6		1
because all ages have thought that a competency, and he that profits	235	Priest 7		11
even as Princes have theirs, besides their publick disbursments.	236	Priest 8		17
where he may have occasion to converse with women, and that among	237	Priest 9		2
and were it not his duty to have them so, it were his profit,	240	Priest 10		14
and till they have learned them, makes them kneel by him;	241	Priest 10		3
But evident miseries have a naturall priviledge, and exemption from	245	Priest 12		29
but that they may have wherewithall to serve God the better,	248	Priest 14		7
and offering to have them taught on holy-dayes by his servants.	248	Priest 14		37
If it once have the honour of that Name, it grows great instantly.	249	Priest 14		3
as a child, and forgives, so hee may have any signe of amendment;	250	Priest 16		15
that he will have prayers in the hall, wishing him to informe his	251	Priest 17		11
This was not so well said, as it might have been forborn;	252	Priest 18		9
if God have sent any calamity either by fire, or famine,	253	Priest 19		29
When once all have learned the words of the Catechisme,	256	Priest 21		1
which the Questionist must have in his mind before any question be	256	Priest 21		32
for if wise men have thought it the best way of preserving a state	258	Priest 22		15
but that they still fall from all compromises that have been made.	260	Priest 23		25
but to have the skill of healing a wound, or helping the sick.	260	Priest 23		31
if neither himselfe, nor his wife have the skil, and his means serve,	260	Priest 23		33
(whom he chiefly considered) might have every where monuments of his	261	Priest 23		21
and smallage made into a Poultis, have done great and rare cures.	262	Priest 23		8
if God have given me servants, and I either provide too little	265	Priest 26		20
which by mine own experience I have found hurtfull, then from those	266	Priest 26		25
so long at it, that they would have fainted, had they returned empty,	267	Priest 26		23
or if he have any leisure to look off from thence, he meets	267	Priest 27		30
the great aptnesse Countrey people have to think that all things come	270	Priest 30		25
and that if they sow and soyle their grounds, they must have corn;	270	Priest 30		27
keep and fodder well their cattel, they must have milk, and Calves;	270	Priest 30		28
is observeable, that God delights to have men feel, and acknowledg,	271	Priest 30		19
the Godly have ever added some houres of prayer, as at nine,	272	Priest 31		25
For when men have nothing to do, then they fall to drink,	274	Priest 32		10
say they, we have nothing to do, lets go to the Tavern,	274	Priest 32		12
Yet is it also a debt to our Countrey to have a Calling,	274	Priest 32		26
reason crosseth not our Saviours precept of selling what we have,	274	Priest 32		32
because when we have sold all, and given it to the poor,	274	Priest 32		33
establisheth it, since they that have nothing, are fittest to work.	275	Priest 32		5
All are either to have a Calling, or prepare for it:	275	Priest 32		11
He that hath or can have yet no imployment, if he truly,	275	Priest 32		12
of his affairs, that hee may have wherewithall to do good.	275	Priest 32		30
that he have leisure to look out, the Village or Parish which either	276	Priest 32		1
as divers have done lately, to our Countrey's advantage.	278	Priest 32		10
such a time their peace and mirth have carryed them further then this	280	Priest 34		33
sacrificed lest his Children should have transgressed in their mirth:	281	Priest 34		1
weather be what it will, still we have bread, though sometimes more,	281	Priest 34		25
that the Atheist, or Epicurian can have nothing to contradict.	281	Priest 34		34
they have their Law and Language bearing witnesse to them,	281	Priest 34		35
who have born witness to the truth, (there being no reason,	282	Priest 34		19
Neither have the Ministers power of Blessing only, but also	285	Priest 36		24
or else such as have passed judgment, & been corrected either	287	Priest 37		14
whom the Law would have defamed, except he also do it out of rancour.	287	Priest 37		29
would have been an ornament to the world, and a comfort to their	291	Cornaro		3
because divers worthy young men have obliged me unto it.	291	Cornaro		8
a sober life, expressing also the means which I have used therein.	291	Cornaro		16
For contrarie causes have contrarie effects, and the faults of Nature	292	Cornaro		10
yet these forenamed things have also their force.	293	Cornaro		34
of the minde, which have a great power over our constitutions.	293	Cornaro		36
whom that matter ought to have affected most, received no	294	Cornaro		21
What Physician could have discovered these hidden qualities to me,	297	Cornaro		34
since none can have a better Physician then himself, nor better	297	Cornaro		37
Many have thought that this could be done by Aurum potabile,	298	Cornaro		19
are not almost all the learned books that we have, written by their	298	Cornaro		33
Wherefore since many have cbserved a regular life, both of old times	299	Cornaro		5
joy and peace have taken up their standing in my heart.	301	Cornaro		2
When I cannot have their companie, I give my self to the reading	301	Cornaro		5

HAVE (cont'd)

	PAGE	TITLE		LINE
where also I have fountains and gardens, and a very convenient house.	301	Cornaro		18
That I have both given God a Temple, and men to worship him in it:	301	Cornaro		31
at these yeares (viz. 83) I have made a most pleasant comedie,	302	Cornaro		28
or lesse my self, who being ten yeares older have made a Comedie?	302	Cornaro		35
because I have now a clearer voice, then ever I had in my life.	303	Cornaro		7
the experience of so many yeares have learned to give way to Reason:	303	Cornaro		20
by the regularitie of my life I have shut out death all other wayes.	303	Cornaro		27
but that I should wish all who have the care of themselves,	303	Cornaro		31
in any thing I forsake that Temperance which I have found so good,	303	Cornaro		34
the Authors sake, whom I conceive to have been a true servant of God;	304	Valdesso		6
Churches sake, to whom by Printing it I would have you consecrate it.	304	Valdesso		9
in his own country he would have to flourish in this land of light,	304	Valdesso		14
holy Scriptures have not only an Elementary use, but a use	306	Valdesso		18
of God may be said in some sence to have put confidence in Scripture,	306	Valdesso		28
H. Scriptures (as I wrote before) have not only an Elementary use,	309	Valdesso		20
but such a one as shall still have the assistance of the holy spirit	310	Valdesso		6
and those that have inspirations must still use Peter, Gods Word:	310	Valdesso		10
motion (as S. Paul had when hee would have preached in Asia),	313	Valdesso		16
and that by restraining him from what he would not have him doe.	313	Valdesso		23
because the anointing which we have received, and abideth in us,	314	Valdesso	V	6
the best of Gods Servants should have weaknesses is no way repugnant	316	Valdesso		2
but he might have been justly put to death for it by the Magistrate,	316	Valdesso		24
unlesse he could have made it appeare, that it was done by Gods	316	Valdesso		26
the Saints of God in all ages have ever held in so pretious esteem	317	Valdesso		33
but however he would have them attend to it till that time,	318	Valdesso		20
Humble Hearts have humble desires.	321	Proverbs		6
you can have but water of it.	327	Proverbs		180
Evils have their comfort, good none can support	328	Proverbs		208
Better spare to have of thine own, then aske of other men.	330	Proverbs		266
By suppers more have beene killed then Galen ever cured.	330	Proverbs		272
Aske much to have a little.	332	Proverbs		322
Hee that gives thee a bone, would not have thee die.	333	Proverbs		355
He that hath no hony in his pot, let him have it in his mouth.	333	Proverbs		360
All things have their place, knew wee how to place them.	334	Proverbs		379
Little pitchers have wide eares.	334	Proverbs		380
shall neither have good wife nor good horse.	336	Proverbs		434
The eye will have his part.	337	Proverbs		466
Discreet women have neither eyes nor eares.	337	Proverbs		482
When children stand quiet, they have done some ill.	338	Proverbs		504
Hee that should have what hee hath not,	340	Proverbs		559
Hee that would have what hee hath not,	340	Proverbs	V	559
To have money is a feare, not to have it a griefe.	341	Proverbs		591
To have money is a feare, to want it is a griefe.	341	Proverbs	V	591
In every Art it is good to have a master.	342	Proverbs		619
A wise man cares not for what he cannot have.	343	Proverbs		662
More have repented speech then silence.	344	Proverbs		682
If great men would have care of little ones,	344	Proverbs		697
He that will not have peace, God gives him warre.	345	Proverbs		729
The Cow knowes not what her taile is worth, till she have lost it.	350	Proverbs		870
He that will enter into Paradise, must have a good key.	350	Proverbs		895
The great would have none great and the little all little.	352	Proverbs		946
The best bred have the best portion.	352	Proverbs		953
The best bred have the best portions.	352	Proverbs	V	953
Princes have no way.	352	Proverbs		956
The eyes have one language every where.	352	Proverbs		959
It is better to have wings then hornes.	352	Proverbs		960
Count not fowre except you have them in a wallett.	352	Proverbs		962
Wee leave more to do when wee dye, then wee have done.	353	Proverbs		972
When all men have what belongs to them, it cannot bee much.	353	Proverbs		979
yet we must have patience.	353	Proverbs		980
He that gives me small gifts would have me live.	354	Proverbs		1000
Chuse none for thy servant who have served thy betters.	354	Proverbs		1014
(applyed to those that have a blow).	356	Proverbs	D	1040
It is good to have some friends both in heaven and hell.	359	Proverbs	D	1127
The wolfe eats oft of the sheep that have been warn'd.	360	Proverbs	D	1134
Take heed of credit decaid, and people that have nothing.	360	Proverbs	D	1150
leaving the secrets of nature to those that have spare time.	361	Proverbs	D	1165
States have their conversions and periods	361	Proverbs	D	1166
the same heart, which you have won long since, is still true to you,	363	Letters		18
but that you have performed your kindness to the full, and that	363	Letters		24
I wrong both my self, and also the confidence my Friends have in me;	364	Letters		9
in that I apprehend what my Friends would have been forward to say,	364	Letters		20
I have not deceived their expectation, let not them deceive mine:	364	Letters		24
Now I write to you, Sir, because to you I have ever opened my heart;	365	Letters		23
and have reason, by the Patents of your perpetual favour to do so	365	Letters		24
for it hath been my fortune of late to have such sudden warning,	365	Letters		31
that I have not leazure to impart unto you some of those observations	365	Letters		32
of those observations which I have framed to myself in conversation;	366	Letters		1
and whereof I would not have you ignorant.	366	Letters		2
and if there be any such which you have found useful to yourself,	366	Letters		4
for I would have you, even in speeches, to observe so much,	366	Letters		9
and have a good conceit of your wit, mark what I say, have a good	366	Letters		14
of your wit, mark what I say, have a good conceit of your wit;	366	Letters		15
when I have more time, you shall hear more;	366	Letters		20
Now though they have hitherto travelled upon your charge,	366	Letters		31
burden to you, since I can never answer what I have already received;	367	Letters		14
I have wrote to my dear sick Sister this week already, and therefore	367	Letters		20
injuries which they are thought to have offerd to our Merchants	368	Letters		6
at the Indies, wherein they have satisfied the King reasonably.	368	Letters		7
untill they have satisfied him also concerning the fishing which	368	Letters		9

HAVE (cont'd)	PAGE	TITLE	LINE
demand of the Kings these Agents pretend they have no commission,	368	Letters	14
of which is doubted whether it have some further meaning.	368	Letters	18
if he had given it to the pope he should have had a greater reward.	368	Letters	34
I wish I could have come in person to thank you, but it is	369	Letters	11
yet have I sent it thither by a faithful Messenger this day:	369	Letters	16
If I could possibly have come, none should have done my message	369	Letters	19
could possibly have come, none should have done my message to Sir Fr:	369	Letters	20
and I have a strong opinion of him, that if he can do me a courtesie,	369	Letters	22
I have sent you here inclosed a Letter from our Master in my behalf,	369	Letters	24
I fear only that I have omitted some fitting circumstance,	370	Letters	11
but that I have both time and work to be Your extreme Servant,	370	Letters	13
that he fears I have not fully resolved of the matter, since this	370	Letters	19
but, I have wrote him back, that this dignity, hath no such	370	Letters	21
I have received the things you sent me, safe;	371	Letters	6
I have forty businesses in my hands, your Courtesie will pardon	371	Letters	18
have so much power or boldness as to oppose the hope of our Joyes	372	Letters	28
consider what advantage you have over Youth and Health,	372	Letters	32
I have alwaies observ'd the thred of Life to be like other threds	373	Letters	4
who have already abundantly discharg'd that part, having both ordered	373	Letters	11
up your Children that they have attain'd to the years of Discretion,	373	Letters	13
that are to come, you have strong preservatives against all disquiet.	373	Letters	19
so that the best use of them is, having, not to have them.	373	Letters	25
how they have been burnt by thousands, and have endur'd such other	373	Letters	36
and have endur'd such other Tortures, as the very mention of them	373	Letters	36
but, their Fiery-tryals have had an end:	374	Letters	1
I wrote to him that I would have both or neither;	375	Letters	12
Since that I have seen the fruit of my observation, for they have	375	Letters	17
the fruit of my observation, for they have lived so lovingly, lying,	375	Letters	18
and would not have to part them yet, till I take some opportunity	375	Letters	20
it were a great good deed, and I would have her conveyed to you.	375	Letters	32
being more beggarly now than I have been these many years,	375	Letters	36
which to me that have nothing yett, is very much.	376	Letters	2
I have another judge, to whom I stand or fall.	376	Letters	7
and not as many who think they have done fairly, if they leave them	376	Letters	15
and you have no cause to be sorry, since it is GOD's business.	377	Letters	21
Although you have a much better Paymaster then my self,	378	Letters	2
God knowes, I have desired a long time, to doe the place good,	378	Letters	5
& have endeavoured many wayes, to find out a man for it.	378	Letters	6
the chiefest also, so also have I required Mr W. for his part.	378	Letters	23
& for my power, I have sent my Letters, to your Brother,	379	Letters	19
sent my Letters, to your Brother, investing him, in all that I have.	379	Letters	20
you have bin at charges:	380	Woodnoth	8
you have stockd the grounds:	380	Woodnoth	9
you have layed out thoughts & prayers you have sowed.	380	Woodnoth	9
you have layed out thoughts & prayers you have sowed.	380	Woodnoth	10
As in things inwardly good to have an eye to the world may be	380	Woodnoth	16
Complaine not of the want of success, when you have the fruit of it.	381	Woodnoth	17
In Gods accepting you have done the good you intended, & whom serve	381	Woodnoth	17
what could have happened more pleasing to us, then the accesse	442	Oration	8
we have as much failed, as your Excellencies doe excel,	442	Oration	34
HAVEN			
These seas are tears, and heav'n the haven.	138	The Size	47
which it hath escaped, he destroyes it sometimes in the very Haven;	271	Priest 30	24
HAVENS			
for to the sea he made havens, and to rivers foords.	331	Proverbs	315
HAVING			
Having been tenant long to a rich Lord,	40	Redemption	1
Having a new at his expence,	76	Sunday	53
Were but worth the having,	114	Dialogue	2
What the gains in having thee	114	Dialogue	13
Their masters flower, but leave it, having done,	118	Providence	66
And having giv'n the rest before,	151	The Bag	23
Having a glasse of blessings standing by;	159	The Pulley	2
As having keyes unto thy love,	162	The Search	15
I tun'd another (having store)	162	The Search	21
I turn'd another (having store)	162	The Search V	21
Here is love, which having breath	180	Invitation	28
Having rais'd me to look up,	182	Banquet	37
And having conquer'd, did so strangely rule,	196	Ch.-Milit.	203
Rom. 12. 6. Having gifts differing, according to the grace that is	226	Priest 2	4
and by having fellowship, with the unfruitfull works of darknesse,	227	Priest 3	25
he having often instructed his people how to carry themselves in	231	Priest 6	21
Then having read divine Service twice fully, and preached in	236	Priest 8	6
but findes opportunities of having his meat dress'd and other	237	Priest 9	8
in his heart, having no necessity, but hath power over his own will,	237	Priest 9	16
to his earthly, having no title to either, except he do good to both.	239	Priest 10	22
Therefore having seasoned them with all Piety, not only of words in	239	Priest 10	23
Having then invited some of his Parish, hee taketh his times to do	243	Priest 11	17
But the Parson having a double aime, and making a hook of his	244	Priest 12	31
as having continuall use of them, such as are from Gods generall	249	Priest 15	18
having observed some defects in the Ministry, he then either in	253	Priest 19	12
who having not received yet, are to enter into this great work,	258	Priest 22	29
reading one Book of Phisick, having one Herball by him.	261	Priest 23	5
whether having a rule, it ought not to be guided by it;	263	Priest 24	2
having ever besides two great helps and powerfull perswaders on his	263	Priest 24	15
the Parson having a due respect both to the person, and to the cause,	268	Priest 28	33
the one in having no calling, the other in walking carelesly in our	274	Priest 32	16
So that the Parson having studied, and mastered all his lusts	278	Priest 33	22
having for his owne use examined the nature of it, is able	279	Priest 33	8
having doubted sometimes, whether his repentance were true,	279	Priest 33	10

HAVING (cont'd)	PAGE	TITLE		LINE
Now the Parson having a Spirituall Judgement, according as he	280	Priest 34		12
Having observed in my time many of my friends, of excellent wit	291	Cornaro		1
(having a most cold & moist stomack) I fell into divers diseases,	291	Cornaro		20
having tried all remedies fruitlesly, the Physicians told me that yet	292	Cornaro		2
For having endured many heats & colds, and other like discommodities	294	Cornaro		12
both of them having forms or vizars of godlinesse, but denying	319	Valdesso	V	26
having both ordered your Family, and so brought up your Children that	373	Letters		12
so that the best use of them is, having, not to have them.	373	Letters		24
having none to doe it but her school-mistresse, and you know what	375	Letters		25
these many years, as having spent two hundred pounds in building;	376	Letters		1
but a Trade having two things, the one imployment, the other profitt,	381	Woodnoth		30
having lately receaved an hundred and two pounds besides some	383	G.H.'s Will		23
HAWK				
But who does hawk at eagles with a dove?	29	Sacrifice		91
No hawk, or banquet, or renown,	69	Quidditie		3
A servile hawk: low without losse, a spade.	120	Providence		104
HAWKE				
Nor hawke, nor banquet, nor renowne,	69	Quidditie	W	3
The gentle Hawke halfe mans her selfe.	322	Proverbs		30
HAWKING				
Birds teach us hawking; fishes have their net:	118	Providence		51
HAY				
Deare earth, fine grasse or hay;	71	Frailtie		6
But when we leave our corn and hay:	108	Home		56
In good yeares corne is hay, in ill yeares straw is corne.	328	Proverbs		216
HAYS				
Then I bequeath to Mr Hays the Comment of Lucas Brugensis uppon	382	G.H.'s Will		18
HAZARDS				
thy conflicts, and seemingly hazards, didst thou arise triumphant,	289	Priest		1
HE (see also hee)				
But gladly welcome what he doth afford;	7	Ch.-Porch		15
O what were man, might he himself misplace!	7	Ch.-Porch		23
Sure to be crosse he would shift feet and face.	7	Ch.-Porch		24
He that is drunken, may his mother kill	7	Ch.-Porch		31
Bigge with his sister: he hath lost the reins,	7	Ch.-Porch		32
Bigge with his sister: he hath lost his reins,	7	Ch.-Porch	W	32
All worldly right, save what he hath by beast.	7	Ch.-Porch		36
A pain in that, wherein he findes a pleasure?	8	Ch.-Porch		40
A pain in that, whereof he findes a pleasure?	8	Ch.-Porch	W	40
But he that boasts, shuts that out of his storie.	8	Ch.-Porch		52
He makes flat warre with God, and doth defie	8	Ch.-Porch		53
He pares his apple, that will cleanly feed.	9	Ch.-Porch		64
For he, that needs five thousand pound to live,	10	Ch.-Porch		107
Is full as poore as he, that needs but five.	10	Ch.-Porch		108
What nature made a ship, he makes a shelf.	11	Ch.-Porch		120
He breaks up house, turns out of doores his minde.	12	Ch.-Porch		150
Whom when he thinks he hath, the devil hath him.	13	Ch.-Porch		166
Cannot on fourtie: he's a man of pleasure,	13	Ch.-Porch		177
Then he can lose with pleasure, stakes his heart;	14	Ch.-Porch		194
Command thy self in chief. He lifes warre knows,	15	Ch.-Porch		215
Whom all his passions follow, as he goes.	15	Ch.-Porch		216
Catch not at quarrels. He that dares not speak	15	Ch.-Porch		217
Then he's the sport: the mirth then in him rests,	16	Ch.-Porch		251
Still in thy heart, that he may see what's there.	17	Ch.-Porch		272
My childrens right, nor ought he take it: rather	17	Ch.-Porch		279
Calmnesse is great advantage: he that lets	19	Ch.-Porch		313
Shoots higher much then he that means a tree.	19	Ch.-Porch		334
Though he alight sometimes, still goeth on.	20	Ch.-Porch		340
The meanest tool, that he may chance to use.	20	Ch.-Porch		354
Till thou change names, and be where he began.	21	Ch.-Porch		378
For all the week thy food so oft he gave thee.	22	Ch.-Porch		392
Judge not the preacher; for he is thy Judge:	23	Ch.-Porch		427
He that gets patience, and the blessing which	24	Ch.-Porch		433
He that by being at church escapes the ditch,	24	Ch.-Porch		435
Which he might fall in by companions, gains.	24	Ch.-Porch		436
He that loves Gods abode, and to combine	24	Ch.-Porch		437
God sent him, whatsoe're he be: O tarry,	24	Ch.-Porch		442
Though he had all I had, did not forbeare	27	Sacrifice		14
For thirtie pence he did my death devise,	27	Sacrifice		17
Why, he that built the world can do much more:	28	Sacrifice		67
They binde, and leade me unto Herod: he	29	Sacrifice		73
It is not fit he live a day, they crie,	29	Sacrifice		98
And a seditious murderer he was:	30	Sacrifice		117
He clave the stonie rock, when they were drie;	30	Sacrifice		122
And never yet, whom he would punish, miss'd:	30	Sacrifice	W	131
That he before me well nigh suffereth:	31	Sacrifice		147
Whom devils flie, thus is he toss'd of men:	32	Sacrifice		191
Or feel his part, he would not cease to kneel,	33	Sacrifice		210
Or feel his share, he would not cease to kneel,	33	Sacrifice	W	210
Till all were melted, though he were all steel:	33	Sacrifice		211
As he that for some robberie suffereth.	34	Sacrifice		230
My bosome friend, if he blaspheme thy name,	35	Thanksgvng		25
Unto mount Olivet; there shall he see	37	The Agonie		8
If ever he did taste the like.	37	The Agonie		16
All come to lodge there, he may say,	39	Good Fri.	W	27
They told me there, that he was lately gone	40	Redemption		6
About some land, which he had dearly bought	40	Redemption		7
Though he give light, & th' East perfume;	42	Easter		24
Though foolishly he lost the same,	43	East.wings		2
Till he became	43	East.wings		4

HE (cont'd)

	PAGE	TITLE		LINE
As he that sees a dark and shadie grove,	43	H. Bapt.1		1
As he that Heaven beyond much thicket spyes	43	H. Bapt.1	W	3
Forthwith he waxeth wo and wan:	49	Repentance		26
He might to heav'n from Paradise go,	53	H.Commun.		35
Shall he thy stature spell?	55	Temper 1		16
Must all be vail'd, while he that reades, divines,	56	Jordan 1		9
When he beheld twelve sunnes for one	59	Whitsunday		15
He that first fell from his great birth	59	Whitsunday	W	15
He may do more.	61	Praise 1		12
He did not heav'n and earth create,	63	Mattens		15
We paint the devil foul, yet he	63	Sinne 2		2
Which to himself he did denie:	63	Even-song		6
For when he sees my waies, I dy:	63	Even-song		7
But I have got his sonne, and he hath none.	63	Even-song		8
But while he thinks to spoil the room, he sweeps.	67	Ch.-floore		18
He is a brittle crazie glasse:	67	Windows		2
He lies warm, and without adventure.	69	Content		20
He that by seeking hath himself once found,	69	Content		35
(For he would not) as they beheld the grace	70	Humilitie		18
He that doth still and strongly good pursue,	72	Constancie		2
Till he the thing and the example weigh:	72	Constancie		13
What place or person calls for, he doth pay.	72	Constancie		15
For above all things he abhorres deceit:	72	Constancie		18
Who, when he is to treat	73	Constancie		26
The which he doth not fill.	75	Sunday		21
That he was fain, when thou wert destitute,	77	Avarice		7
Then forcing thee, by fire he made thee bright:	77	Avarice		9
And while he digs out thee, falls in the ditch.	77	Avarice		14
He that is weary, let him sit.	78	Employm.2		1
We sing one common Lord; wherefore he should	81	Christmas		25
Where now we shall be better Gods then he.	82	Ungratef.		6
He cavils instantly.	82	Ungratef.		27
Ev'n unto death: since he di'd for my good,	83	Sighs & Gr.		23
He views their stations, walks from doore to doore,	85	Vanitie 1		3
Surveys, as if he had design'd.	85	Vanitie 1		4
To make a purchase there: he sees their dances,	85	Vanitie 1		5
Cuts through the working waves, that he may fetch	85	Vanitie 1		9
That he might save his life, and also hers,	85	Vanitie 1		12
And strip the creature naked, till he finde	85	Vanitie 1		16
There he imparts to them his minde,	85	Vanitie 1		18
He loves not Temperance, or Authoritie,	86	Lent		2
He sayes, in things which use hath justly got,	86	Lent		10
Yet are we bid, Be holy ev'n as he.	87	Lent		35
Perhaps my God, though he be farre before,	87	Lent		40
Then he that curbs them, being but one to five:	89	The Pearl		29
But he that means to dwell therein.	90	Man		3
And more: He is a tree, yet bears no fruit;	91	Man		8
And more: He is a tree, yet bears more fruit;	91	Man	W	8
He is in little all the sphere.	91	Man		22
Then he'l take notice of: in ev'ry path	92	Man		44
He treads down that which doth befriend him,	92	Man		45
He our foes in pieces brake;	93	Antiphon 2		13
Wherefore since that he is such,	93	Antiphon 2		16
Would he have gold? I lend it instantly;	93	Unkindness		12
Getting a house and home, where he may move	98	Mortific.		20
When he would speak;	98	Mortific.		28
Man, ere he is aware,	99	Mortific.		31
And drest his herse, while he has breath	99	Mortific.		33
He is to Sinai gone, as we heard tell:	99	Decay		9
His house still burns, and yet he still doth sing,	100	Miserie		4
He knows it, fill the glasse.	100	Miserie		6
Why he'l not lose a cup of drink for thee:	100	Miserie		8
Not he: he knows, where he can better be,	100	Miserie		10
As he will swear,	100	Miserie		11
What strange pollutions doth he wed,	100	Miserie		13
And make his own? as if none knew, but he.	100	Miserie		14
He doth not like this vertue, no;	101	Miserie		45
For this he wondrous well doth know	101	Miserie	W	45
And yet as though he knew it not,	102	Miserie		61
He was a garden in a Paradise:	102	Miserie		70
But sinne hath fool'd him. Now he is	102	Miserie		73
He that will passe his land,	105	Obedience		36
And heart unto this deed, when he hath read;	105	Obedience		38
And heart unto this deed, when he doth read	105	Obedience	W	38
To both our goods, if he to it will stand.	105	Obedience		40
Great God doth fight, he doth submit.	106	Sion		16
There lay thy sonne: and must he leave that nest,	107	Home		19
He did, he came: O my Redeemer deare,	108	Home		25
What tune is this, poore man? said he:	110	The Quip		10
In silks that whistled, who but he?	111	The Quip		14
He scarce allow'd me half an eie.	111	The Quip		15
And he would needs a comfort be,	111	The Quip		18
That to my broken heart he was I ease you,	112	JESU		9
Had he life, or had he none?	113	Businesse		19
If he had not liv'd for thee,	113	Businesse		20
He so farre thy good did plot,	113	Businesse		23
That his own self he forgot.	113	Businesse		24
Did he die, or did he not?	113	Businesse		25
If he had not di'd for thee,	113	Businesse		26
He that loseth gold, though drosse,	114	Businesse		31

HE (cont'd)

	PAGE	TITLE	LINE
Tells to all he meets, his crosse:	114	Businesse	32
He that sinnes, hath he no losse?	114	Businesse	33
He that findes a silver vein,	114	Businesse	34
Do amount to, onely he,	114	Dialogue	14
Man is the worlds high Priest: he doth present	117	Providence	13
He that to praise and laud thee doth refrain,	117	Providence	17
But at his perill: when he digs the place,	119	Providence	82
He makes a grave; as if the thing had sense,	119	Providence	83
And threatned man, that he should fill the space.	119	Providence	84
But he to wear them. Nothing useth fire,	120	Providence	110
And onely he hath fuell in desire.	120	Providence	112
None can expresse thy works, but he that knows them:	121	Providence	142
And so complete, but onely he that owes them.	121	Providence	144
I gave to Hope a watch of mine: but he	121	Hope	1
And he an optick sent.	121	Hope	4
But he a few green eares:	121	Hope	6
No marvell Sir, he did replie,	122	Time	3
Since by thy cutting he grows better.	122	Time	12
He doth not crave lesse time, but more.	123	Time	30
He makes thy gifts occasion more,	123	Gratefulnes	5
And sayes, If he in this be crost,	123	Gratefulnes	6
I did demand; he thus began:	125	Peace	21
He sweetly liv'd; yet sweetnesse did not save	125	Peace	25
Yet grief knows all, and enters when he will.	126	Confession	6
When he a torture hath design'd.	126	Confession	10
He is some twentie sev'rall men at least	127	Giddinesse	3
One while he counts of heav'n, as of his treasure:	127	Giddinesse	5
Now he will fight it out, and to the warres;	127	Giddinesse	9
And snudge in quiet: now he scorns increase;	127	Giddinesse	11
He builds a house, which quickly down must go,	127	Giddinesse	13
But can he want the grape, who hath the wine?	128	Bunch Gr.	22
But can he want the grape, who hath the vine?	128	Bunch Gr. V	22
And in the middle plac'd my heart. But he	129	Love unkn.	7
It must be he. Your heart was dull, I fear.	130	Love unkn.	56
In soul he mounts and flies,	131	Mans medly	13
In flesh he dies.	131	Mans medly	14
He wears a stuffe whose thread is course and round,	131	Mans medly	15
Not, that he may not here	131	Mans medly	19
So must he sip and think	131	Mans medly	22
So he must sip and think	131	Mans medly V	22
He may attain to, after he is dead.	131	Mans medly	24
He hath two winters, other things but one:	131	Mans medly	27
And he of all things fears two deaths alone.	131	Mans medly	30
Could he but take them right, and in their wayes.	132	Mans medly	33
Happie is he, whose heart	132	Mans medly	34
For he is Power: and sure he would;	133	The Method	7
For he is Love.	133	The Method	8
But all the doctrine, which he taught and gave,	135	Divinitie	13
But he doth bid us take his bloud for wine.	135	Divinitie	21
Bid what he please; yet I am sure,	135	Divinitie	22
To take and taste what he doth there designe,	135	Divinitie	23
Almightie God doth grieve, he puts on sense:	136	Ephes.	16
But to my Gods too; he doth grone.	136	Ephes.	18
He that did but look up, was proud and bold.	141	Justice 2	6
Then I confesse, that he my succour is:	143	Holdfast	8
He is thy night at noon: he is at night	144	Discharge	13
The crop is his, for he hath sown.	144	Discharge	15
Man and the present fit: if he provide,	145	Discharge	31
He breaks the square.	145	Discharge	32
He that would know	145	Discharge	37
My God hath promis'd; he is just.	145	Discharge	55
Lord heare! Shall he that made the eare,	149	Longing	35
He doth preserve it: he doth steer,	151	The Bag	3
Well may he close his eyes, but not his heart.	151	The Bag	6
The God of power, as he did ride	151	The Bag	9
He did descend, undressing all the way.	151	The Bag	12
And when they ask'd, what he would wear;	151	The Bag	16
He smil'd and said as he did go,	151	The Bag	17
He had new clothes a making here below.	151	The Bag	18
When he was come, as travellers are wont,	151	The Bag	19
He did repair unto an inne.	151	The Bag	20
He did endure to cancell sinne:	151	The Bag	22
Here he gave up his life to pay our score.	151	The Bag	24
But as he was returning, there came one	151	The Bag	25
He, who came hither all alone,	151	The Bag	27
And straight he turn'd, and to his brethren cry'd,	151	The Bag	30
Shall still be open; what he sends	152	The Bag	39
He that forbears	153	The Collar	30
For well he knows, if but one grief and smart	159	Jos.coat	5
But he hath spoil'd the race; and giv'n to anguish	159	Jos.coat	10
Let us (said he) poure on him all we can:	159	The Pulley	3
For if I should (said he)	160	The Pulley	11
He would adore my gifts in stead of me,	160	The Pulley	13
That I am he	166	The Flower	41
He who craves all the minde,	168	a true Hymn	11
Who gives to man, as he sees fit Salvation. / Damnation.	170	Water-crs.	10
He that doth love, and love amisse	170	Self-cond.	7
He that hath made a sorrie wedding	171	Self-cond.	13
Hath done what he condemnes in reading:	171	Self-cond.	16
For he hath sold for money his deare Lord,	171	Self-cond.	17

HE (cont'd)

	PAGE	TITLE		LINE
And he that doth me feed:	172	23 Psalme		2
While he is mine, and I am his,	172	23 Psalme		3
He leads me to the tender grasse,	172	23 Psalme		5
Or if I stray, he doth convert	172	23 Psalme		9
He will be pleased with that dittie;	176	Forerunners		11
Sweetly he doth meet my taste.	182	Banquet		39
Or if he pleaseth, through it passe,	184	The Elixer		11
He that does ought for thee,	184	The Elixer	W	12
Love said, you shall be he.	189	Love 3		8
But to the Gentiles he bore crosse and all,	190	Ch.-Milit.		25
He chid the Church away, where e're he came,	193	Ch.-Milit.		105
At first he got to Egypt, and did sow	193	Ch.-Milit.		107
Begging his food of that which he may eat,	193	Ch.-Milit.		113
Starving the while he worshippeth his meat!	193	Ch.-Milit.		114
Who makes a root his God, how low is he,	193	Ch.-Milit.		115
Whose house is foul, while he adores his broom?	193	Ch.-Milit.		118
And such poore game. Thence he to Greece doth passe,	193	Ch.-Milit.		123
And such small game. Thence he to Greece doth passe,	193	Ch.-Milit.	W	123
He left behinde him garrisons of sinnes	193	Ch.-Milit.		125
To make good that which ev'ry day he winnes.	193	Ch.-Milit.		126
Rich shrines and oracles he purchased:	193	Ch.-Milit.		128
He grew a gallant, and would needs foretell	193	Ch.-Milit.		129
Nay, he became a poet, and would serve	193	Ch.-Milit.		131
From Greece he went to Rome: and as before	194	Ch.-Milit.		139
He was a God, now he's an Emperour.	194	Ch.-Milit.		140
I saw him in his studie, where he sate	194	Ch.-Milit.		165
To which he lent a corner of his eye.	195	Ch.-Milit.		170
So now being Priest he plainly did professe	195	Ch.-Milit.		173
From Egypt he took pettie deities,	195	Ch.-Milit.		177
He did surname his palace, Babylon.	195	Ch.-Milit.		182
Yet that he might the better gain all nations,	195	Ch.-Milit.		183
He took fine vizards to conceal his crimes:	195	Ch.-Milit.		186
And blending these he carri'd all mens eyes,	195	Ch.-Milit.		189
Whereby he grew apace and scorn'd to use	195	Ch.-Milit.		191
Therefore he sent out able ministers,	195	Ch.-Milit.		199
Of his two thrones he made the latter best,	196	Ch.-Milit.		213
He that is one,	202	Trin.Sun.	W	1
Though nail'd unto 't, but he ascends again,	439	Walton 5		2
When nail'd unto 't, but he ascends again	439	Walton 5	V	2
He writ; when 's hand could write no more,	439	Walton 5		13
He gave the Seale, and so left o're.	439	Walton 5		14
He gave his soul, and so gave o're.	439	Walton 5	V	14
How sweet a friend was he, who being griev'd	439	Walton 5		15
He gave this Seal, and, so gave ore.	439	walton 6		2
Had he only brought them forth,	208	J. Danvers	D	13
he shall be like an happy tree,	214	Psalm I	D	8
shall prosper that he takes in hand.	214	Psalm I	D	12
But He, that sits in Heaven, shall laugh,	215	Psalm II	D	9
Then shall He speak to them in wrath,	215	Psalm II	D	11
He said to me, Thou art my Son,	216	Psalm II	D	17
O kiss the Son, lest he be wrath,	216	Psalm II	D	29
Thou art my glory, Lord, and he	216	Psalm III	D	7
I cry'd unto the Lord, he heard	216	Psalm III	D	9
Yea, he my prayer from on high	220	Psalm VI	D	23
he do devour my soul:	221	Psalm VII	D	6
He judgeth both the good, and those	222	Psalm VII	D	39
Exploits of mischief he conceives,	222	Psalm VII	D	51
But in the pit which he hath made	222	Psalm VII	D	55
shall he himself be caught.	222	Psalm VII	D	56
he constituted Deputies in his place, and these are Priests.	225	Priest 1		8
that he fils up that which is behinde of the afflictions of Christ in	225	Priest 1		11
or he that teacheth, on teaching, &c.	226	Priest 2		7
he that ruleth, let him do it with diligence, &c.	226	Priest 2		7
he cannot agree to come into any house, where he shall not exercise	226	Priest 2		25
where he shall not exercise what he is, unlesse he forsake his	226	Priest 2		26
exercise what he i , unlesse he forsake his plough, and look back.	226	Priest 2		26
therefore he hath throughly studied these, that he may be an absolute	227	Priest 3		7
that he may be an absolute Master and commander of himself,	227	Priest 3		8
Yet in these points he labours most in those things which are most	227	Priest 3		10
into which if he come, he prostitutes himself both to shame,	227	Priest 3		24
into which if he come, he prostitutes himself both to shame, and sin,	227	Priest 3		25
of darknesse, he disableth himself of authority to reprove them:	227	Priest 3		26
he may say as He did, I sate daily with you teaching in the Temple.	227	Priest 3		33
as knowing, that if he be not so, he wil quickly be discovered,	228	Priest 3		6
that if he be not so, he wil quickly be discovered, and disregarded:	228	Priest 3		6
He condescends even to the knowledge of tillage, and pastorage,	228	Priest 4		17
There he sucks, and lives.	228	Priest 4		23
These he hath digested severally.	228	Priest 4		26
the means he useth are first, a holy Life, remembring what his Master	228	Priest 4		27
he shall know of the Doctrine, John 7. and assuring himself,	228	Priest 4		29
Wherefore he ever begins the reading of the Scripture with some short	229	Priest 4		1
As he doth not so study others, as to neglect the grace of God in	229	Priest 4		19
so doth he assure himself, that God in all ages hath had his	229	Priest 4		21
his servants, to whom he hath revealed his Truth, as well as to him;	229	Priest 4		22
Wherfore he hath one Comment at least upon every book of Scripture,	229	Priest 4		27
he enters into the secrets of God treasured in the holy Scripture.	229	Priest 4		29
out of all which he hath compiled a book, and body of Divinity,	229	Priest 5		33
the storehouse of his Sermons, and which he preacheth all his Life;	230	Priest 5		2
This Body he made by way of expounding the Church Catechisme,	230	Priest 5		7
according as his audience is, so he useth one, or other;	230	Priest 5		17

HE (cont'd)

	PAGE	TITLE	LINE
He greatly esteemes also of cases of conscience, wherein he is much	230	Priest 5	18
esteemes also of cases of conscience, wherein he is much versed.	230	Priest 5	19
which grass will bane, or which not, how is he fit to be a shepherd?	230	Priest 5	32
at least all those which he observeth are most incident to his	230	Priest 5	35
when he is to read divine services, composeth himselfe to all	231	Priest 6	1
This he doth, first, as being truly touched and amazed . . .	231	Priest 6	5
amazed with the Majesty of God, before whom he then presents himself;	231	Priest 6	6
whose sins he then beares, and brings with his own to the heavenly	231	Priest 6	8
so he is content to expresse this outwardly to the utmost of his	231	Priest 6	11
between fear and zeal, pausing yet pressing, he performes his duty.	231	Priest 6	20
he having often instructed his people how to carry themselves in	231	Priest 6	21
have glorified him as wel as now, and that he shall have so for ever.	232	Priest 6	1
he by no means suffers it, but after divers gentle admonitions,	232	Priest 6	12
admonitions, if they persevere, he causes them to be presented:	232	Priest 6	13
he presents them himself, only protesting to them, that not any ill	232	Priest 6	17
if he at any time intermit, it is either for want of health,	232	Priest 7	21
that he may the better celebrate it, or for the variety . .	232	Priest 7	23
of the hearers, that he may be heard at his returne more attentively.	232	Priest 7	24
When he intermits, he is ever very well supplyed by some able man who	232	Priest 7	25
he is ever very well supplyed by some able man who treads in his	232	Priest 7	25
who treads in his steps, and will not throw down what he hath built;	232	Priest 7	27
whom also he intreats to press some point, that he himself hath often	232	Priest 7	27
that he himself hath often urged with no great success, . .	232	Priest 7	28
When he preacheth, he procures attention by all possible art,	232	Priest 7	30
he procures attention by all possible art, both by earnestnesse	232	Priest 7	30
with letting them know, that he observes who marks, and who not;	233	Priest 7	2
Herein also he serves himselfe of the judgements of God, . .	233	Priest 7	6
Sometimes he tells them stories, and sayings of others, . .	233	Priest 7	11
He often tels them, that Sermons are dangerous things, that none goes	233	Priest 7	18
that none goes out of Church as he came in, but either better,	233	Priest 7	20
he is not witty, or learned, or eloquent, but Holy. . . .	233	Priest 7	23
never dream'd of, and therefore he could give no precepts thereof.	233	Priest 7	25
Chapt. 10. after he had complained of the desolation of Israel,	234	Priest 7	4
though he himself were with Saint Paul even sacrificed upon . .	234	Priest 7	7
How did he put the Romans in all his prayers? Rom. 1. 9. . .	234	Priest 7	11
he joyes, and he is sorry, he grieves, and he gloryes, never was	234	Priest 7	19
and he is sorry, he grieves, and he gloryes, never was there such	234	Priest 7	19
and he gloryes, never was there such care of a flock expressed,	234	Priest 7	19
he sees whether I speak as I ought, or you hear as you ought,	234	Priest 7	27
or you hear as you ought, he sees hearts, as we see faces: . .	234	Priest 7	28
he is among us; for if we be here, hee must be here, since we are	234	Priest 7	28
the discourse to his Majesty, And he is a great God, and terrible,	234	Priest 7	31
are but two devouring elements, fire, and water, he hath both in him;	234	Priest 7	33
And he himselfe is a consuming fire, Hebrews 12.	234	Priest 7	35
This he thinks naturall, and sweet, and grave.	235	Priest 7	4
and he that profits not in that time, will lesse afterwards,	235	Priest 7	12
him then weary, and so he grows from not relishing, to loathing.	235	Priest 7	14
as soon as he awakes on Sunday morning, presently falls to work,	235	Priest 8	16
he makes a peculiar one for a blessing on the exercises of the day,	235	Priest 8	21
him unworthy of that Majesty before which he is to present himself,	235	Priest 8	24
that how or whenever he punish him, it be not in his Ministry:	235	Priest 8	26
then he turnes to request for his people, that the Lord would be	235	Priest 8	27
he sets himself to the Consideration of the duties of the day,	235	Priest 8	32
he contrives how and in what manner to induce it to the best	236	Priest 8	1
he goes to Church, at his first entrance humbly adoring, . .	236	Priest 8	3
the afternoone, he thinks he hath in some measure, according to poor,	236	Priest 8	8
The rest of the day he spends either in reconciling neighbours that	236	Priest 8	10
This way he findes exceeding usefull, and winning; . . .	236	Priest 8	15
and these exhortations he cals his privy purse, even as Princes have	236	Priest 8	16
At night he thinks it a very fit time, both sutable to the joy	236	Priest 8	18
where he takes occasion to discourse of such things as are both	236	Priest 8	21
As he opened the day with prayer, so he closeth it, humbly beseeching	236	Priest 8	25
so he closeth it, humbly beseeching the Almighty to pardon and accept	236	Priest 8	26
where he may have occasion to converse with women, and that among	237	Priest 9	2
like circumstances considered, he is rather married then unmarried.	237	Priest 9	4
If he be unmarried, and keepe house, he hath not a woman in his	237	Priest 9	7
he hath not a woman in his house, but findes opportunities of having	237	Priest 9	7
If he be unmarryed, and sojourne, he never talkes with any woman	237	Priest 9	10
he never talkes with any woman alone, but in the audience of others,	237	Priest 9	11
He is very circumspect in all companyes, both of his behaviour,	237	Priest 9	13
If he stand steadfast in his heart, having no necessity, . .	237	Priest 9	16
that he will keep himself a virgin, he spends his dayes in fasting	237	Priest 9	18
he spends his dayes in fasting and prayer, and blesseth God . .	237	Priest 9	18
He therefore thinkes it not enough for him to observe the fasting	237	Priest 9	21
which he observeth out of humble conformity, and obedience; . .	237	Priest 9	23
He often readeth the Lives of the Primitive Monks, Hermits, . .	237	Priest 9	27
he findeth to be as necessary, and as difficult at least, . .	237	Priest 9	36
He keepeth his watch and ward, night and day against the proper	237	Priest 9	38
against these ghostly enemies he girdeth up his loynes, . .	238	Priest 9	4
he is not afraid of the pestilence that walketh in darkenesse,	238	Priest 9	6
Other temptations he hath, which, like mortall enemies, . .	238	Priest 9	9
and that much more being single, then if he were marryed; . .	238	Priest 9	22
means to continue so, he doth at least, as much as hath been said.	238	Priest 9	25
If he be married, the choyce of his wife was made rather by his eare,	238	Priest 9	26
and liberall disposition he preferred before beauty, riches,	238	Priest 9	29
He knew that (the good instrument of God to bring women to heaven)	238	Priest 9	30
so is he to his wife also, counting nothing so much his owne,	238	Priest 9	34
counting nothing so much his owne, as that he may be unjust unto it.	238	Priest 9	35
Therefore he gives her respect both afore her servants, . .	238	Priest 9	36
but that he sometimes looks how things go, demanding an account,	239	Priest 9	1

HE (cont'd)

	PAGE	TITLE	LINE
He knows the temper, and pulse of every person in his house,	239	Priest 10	7
wife is either religious, or night and day he is winning her to it.	239	Priest 10	10
stead of the qualities of the world, he requires onely three of her;	239	Priest 10	11
or he takes care she shall learn it of some religious neighbour.	239	Priest 10	16
His children he first makes Christians, and then Commonwealths-men;	239	Priest 10	20
the one he owes to his heavenly Countrey, the other to his earthly,	239	Priest 10	21
to his earthly, having no title to either, except he do good to both.	239	Priest 10	22
He afterwards turnes his care to fit all their dispositions with some	239	Priest 10	29
which happily for his other children he is not able to do. . .	239	Priest 10	33
binding them prentices (in case he think fit to do so) he takes care	239	Priest 10	34
(in case he think fit to do so) he takes care not to put them into	239	Priest 10	34
and vanities of the world, which he is to deny, and not augment.	240	Priest 10	4
he resolves with himself never to omit any present good deed	240	Priest 10	5
not spent in them, he blesseth God, and lays it out as he sees cause.	240	Priest 10	12
he teacheth them, that three things make a compleate servant,	240	Priest 10	17
He suffers not a ly or equivocation by any means in his house,	240	Priest 10	32
He himselfe, or his Wife, takes account of Sermons, and how every one	240	Priest 10	36
he straitly requires of all to pray by themselves before they sleep	241	Priest 10	1
He keeps his servants between love, and fear, according as hee findes	241	Priest 10	7
but generally he distributes it thus, To his Children he shewes more	241	Priest 10	8
To his Children he shewes more love then terrour, to his servants	241	Priest 10	9
for he hath no mony for such things, charity being his only perfume,	241	Priest 10	13
being his only perfume, which deserves cost when he can spare it.	241	Priest 10	14
and veal, if he addes any thing for a great day, or a stranger,	241	Priest 10	17
he goes no further for any entertainment, lest he goe into the world,	241	Priest 10	19
any entertainment, lest he goe into the world, esteeming it absurd,	241	Priest 10	20
it absurd, that he should exceed, who teacheth others temperance.	241	Priest 10	20
But those which his home produceth, he refuseth not, as coming cheap,	241	Priest 10	22
Wherein he admires and imitates the wonderfull providence and thrift	241	Priest 10	24
and doing that which either he could not do, or was not fit for him	241	Priest 10	32
which he celebrates not only with abstinence of diet, but also	241	Priest 10	37
the Parson, if he be in full health, keeps the three obligations,	242	Priest 10	26
he cannot keep the last obligation, nor suffer others in his house	242	Priest 10	29
he so distinguisheth, that he keeps his money for the poor, . .	243	Priest 11	7
that he keeps his money for the poor, and his table for those that	243	Priest 11	8
whom he sometimes purposely takes home with him, setting them close	243	Priest 11	10
he chooseth rather to give the poor money, which they can better	243	Priest 11	14
For though he desire, that all should live well, and vertuously,	243	Priest 11	28
sets up as many encouragements to goodnesse as he can, both in	244	Priest 11	3
that he may, if not the best way, yet any way, make his Parish good.	244	Priest 11	4
When he riseth in the morning, he bethinketh himselfe what good deeds	244	Priest 12	15
he bethinketh himselfe what good deeds he can do that day, . .	244	Priest 12	16
counting that day lost, wherein he hath not exercised his Charity.	244	Priest 12	18
He first considers his own Parish, and takes care, that there be	244	Priest 12	18
This he effects either by bounty, or perswasion, or by authority,	244	Priest 12	21
If his Parish be rich, he exacts this of them;	244	Priest 12	24
if poor, and he able, he easeth them therein.	244	Priest 12	25
But he gives no set pension to any;	244	Priest 12	25
and repine as much, as he that is disseized of his own inheritance.	244	Priest 12	30
this generall provision, he hath other times of opening his hand;	245	Priest 12	6
and dearths, he even parts his Living, and life among them, . .	245	Priest 12	10
of the pulpit, and never leaving them, till he obtaine his desire.	245	Priest 12	14
Yet in all his Charity, he distinguisheth, giving them most,	245	Priest 12	15
consideration of his own Parish, he inlargeth himself, if he be able,	245	Priest 12	18
he inlargeth himself, if he be able, to the neighbour-hood; . .	245	Priest 12	18
so doth he also to those at his door, whom God puts in his way,	245	Priest 12	20
But these he helps not without some testimony, except the evidence	245	Priest 12	21
as he obeys Authority in the one, so that being once satisfied,	245	Priest 12	26
once satisfied, he allows his Charity some blindnesse in the other;	245	Priest 12	26
thanking of him, he exacts of them to let him alone, and say rather,	245	Priest 12	31
Commandments, and as he finds them perfect, rewards them the more.	245	Priest 12	36
Therefore first he takes order, that all things be in good repair;	246	Priest 13	3
he hath a Poor-mans Box conveniently seated, to receive the charity	246	Priest 13	20
And all this he doth, not as out of necessity, or as putting	246	Priest 13	23
For there he shall find his flock most naturally as they are,	247	Priest 14	5
When he comes to any house, first he blesseth it, and then as hee	247	Priest 14	10
first he blesseth it, and then as hee finds the persons of the house	247	Priest 14	11
finds the persons of the house imployed, so he formes his discourse.	247	Priest 14	12
Those that he findes religiously imployed, hee both commends them	247	Priest 14	13
Those that he finds busie in the works of their calling, . .	247	Priest 14	20
finds busie in the works of their calling, he commendeth them also:	247	Priest 14	21
But then he admonisheth them of two things;	247	Priest 14	23
he adviseth them so to labour for wealth and maintenance, . .	248	Priest 14	5
poor and needy, whom he thus finds labouring, he gives them somewhat;	248	Priest 14	9
poor and needy, whom he thus finds labouring, he gives them somewhat;	248	Priest 14	10
ill imployed, he chides not at first, for that were neither civill,	248	Priest 14	14
but always in the close, before he departs from them: . . .	248	Priest 14	15
yet in this he distinguisheth;	248	Priest 14	16
for if he be a plaine countryman, he reproves him plainly; . .	248	Priest 14	16
for if he be a plaine countryman, he reproves him plainly; . .	248	Priest 14	17
and therefore he lays his discourse so, that he comes to the point	248	Priest 14	20
that he comes to the point very leasurely, and oftentimes, .	248	Priest 14	20
way or other, he ever reproves them, that he may keep himself pure,	248	Priest 14	23
that he may keep himself pure, and not be intangled in others sinnes.	248	Priest 14	23
Neither in this doth he forbear, though there be company by:	248	Priest 14	25
and sometimes he hears the children read himselfe, and blesseth them,	248	Priest 14	35
but he holds the Rule, that Nothing is little in Gods service:	249	Priest 14	1
Wherfore neither disdaineth he to enter into the poorest Cottage,	249	Priest 14	4
though he even creep into it, and though it smell never so lothsomly.	249	Priest 14	5
and so much the rather doth he so, as his accesse to the poor is more	249	Priest 14	7

HE (cont'd)

	PAGE	TITLE	LINE
but with these he mingles other discourses for conversation sake,	249	Priest 14	10
To this end he hath throughly digested all the points of consolation,	249	Priest 15	17
or otherwise afflicted, he followeth the Churches counsell, namely,	249	Priest 15	28
he also urgeth them to do some pious charitable works, as a necessary	249	Priest 15	32
he plainly, and generally intimateth to the disaffected,	250	Priest 15	4
it about with him as fully, as if he had begot his whole Parish.	250	Priest 16	9
And of this he makes great use.	250	Priest 16	10
he hateth him not as an officer, but pityes him as a Father:	250	Priest 16	11
a just occasion calleth him out of his Parish (which he diligently,	250	Priest 17	24
but is himselfe where ever he is.	251	Priest 17	1
Therefore those he meets on the way he blesseth audibly,	251	Priest 17	2
and with those he overtakes or that overtake him, hee begins good	251	Priest 17	3
And when he comes to his Inn, he refuseth not to joyne,	251	Priest 17	7
he refuseth not to joyne, that he may enlarge the glory of God	251	Priest 17	7
that he may enlarge the glory of God to the company he is in,	251	Priest 17	7
that he may enlarge the glory of God to the company he is in,	251	Priest 17	8
that he will have prayers in the hall, wishing him to informe his	251	Priest 17	10
The like he doth in the morning, using pleasantly the outlandish	251	Priest 17	13
When he comes to any other house, where his kindred, or other	251	Priest 17	15
as he finds any defect in these, hee first considers with himselfe,	251	Priest 17	25
but the earnestnesse to do all the good he can, moves him to say thus	251	Priest 17	32
The Countrey Parson, where ever he is, keeps Gods watch;	252	Priest 18	1
or done in the Company where he is, but comes under his Test	252	Priest 18	3
well spoken, or done, he takes occasion to commend, and enlarge it;	252	Priest 18	4
he presently lays hold of it, least the poyson steal into some young	252	Priest 18	5
But this he doth discretely, with mollifying, and suppling words;	252	Priest 18	7
if he perceive in company any discourse tending to ill,	252	Priest 18	15
he either prevents it judiciously, or breaks it off seasonably	252	Priest 18	17
And first, he is just to his Countrey;	252	Priest 19	25
as when he is set at an armour, or horse, he borrowes them	252	Priest 19	26
he borrowes them not to serve the turne, nor provides slight,	252	Priest 19	26
he considers what is the end of any Command, and then he suits things	253	Priest 19	3
and then he suits things faithfully according to that end.	253	Priest 19	4
he carryes himself very respectively, as to all the Fathers	253	Priest 19	5
He observes Visitations, and being there, makes due use of them,	253	Priest 19	9
And therefore before he comes, having observed some defects in	253	Priest 19	11
some defects in the Ministry, he then either in Sermon, if he preach,	253	Priest 19	12
either in Sermon, if he preach, or at some other time of the day,	253	Priest 19	13
he keeps good Correspondence with all the neighbouring Pastours round	253	Priest 19	15
Likewise he welcomes to his house any Minister, how poor or mean	253	Priest 19	18
as joyfull a countenance, as if he were to entertain some great Lord.	253	Priest 19	20
he fulfills the duty, and debt of neighbourhood to all the Parishes	253	Priest 19	20
things are otherwise equall, therefore he satisfies this duty also.	253	Priest 19	28
or famine, to any neighbouring Parish, then he expects no Briefe;	253	Priest 19	30
and then when he hath affrighted them with this, exposing	253	Priest 19	33
he first gives himself liberally, and then incites them to give;	253	Priest 19	35
not the lesse, lest he cast their neighbours poverty on them also.	254	Priest 19	6
stead to his Parish, and dischargeth God what he can of his promises.	254	Priest 20	9
done either wel or ill, whereof he is not the rewarder, or punisher.	254	Priest 20	11
If he chance to finde any reading in anothers Bible, he provides him	254	Priest 20	11
finde any reading in anothers Bible, he provides him one of his own.	254	Priest 20	12
If he finde another giving a poor man a penny, he gives him a tester	254	Priest 20	13
he gives him a tester for it, if the giver be fit to receive it;	254	Priest 20	13
or if he be of a condition above such gifts, he sends him a good	254	Priest 20	14
such gifts, he sends him a good book, or easeth him in his Tithes,	254	Priest 20	15
him in his Tithes, telling him when he hath forgotten it, This I do,	254	Priest 20	16
he is carefull to see condign punishment inflicted, and with truly	254	Priest 20	26
he forgets not himself, but is first a Sermon to himself,	255	Priest 21	14
He useth, and preferreth the ordinary Church-Catechism,	255	Priest 21	16
He exacts of all the Doctrine of the Catechisme;	255	Priest 21	22
Those he Catechizeth publickly, these privately, giving age honour,	255	Priest 21	24
He requires all to be present at Catechizing:	255	Priest 21	25
he thinks it the most usefull way that a Pastor can take,	256	Priest 21	1
if he once get the skill of it, will draw out of ignorant and silly	256	Priest 21	19
accordingly by questions well ordered he found Philosophy in silly	256	Priest 21	22
which he knows, making what hee knows to serve him in that which he	256	Priest 21	38
making what hee knows to serve him in that which he knows not:	257	Priest 21	1
He asked him again, what he would do, if he were in a ditch?	257	Priest 21	4
made the answer so plaine, that he was even ashamed of his ignorance;	257	Priest 21	6
for he could not but say, he would hast out of it as fast as he	257	Priest 21	6
he could not but say, he would hast out of it as fast as he could.	257	Priest 21	7
Then he proceeded to ask, whether he could get out of the ditch	257	Priest 21	8
whether he could get out of the ditch alone, or whether he needed	257	Priest 21	8
or whether he needed a helper, and who was that helper.	257	Priest 21	9
but when one is asked a question, he must discover what he is.	257	Priest 21	19
but when one is asked a question, he must discover what he is.	257	Priest 21	20
Especially at Communion times he is in a great confusion,	257	Priest 22	29
Neither findes he any issue in this, but to throw himself down	257	Priest 22	31
he requires the presence of all, and Baptizeth not willingly,	258	Priest 22	2
He willingly and cheerfully crosseth the child, and thinketh	258	Priest 22	7
He instructeth the God-fathers, and God-mothers, that it is no	258	Priest 22	9
He adviseth all to call to minde their Baptism often;	258	Priest 22	14
he first takes order with the Church-Wardens, that the elements be	258	Priest 22	21
he takes the more pains with them, that hee may lay the foundation	258	Priest 22	30
all reverence himself, so he administers to none but to the reverent.	259	Priest 22	11
he hath gotten to himself some insight in things ordinarily incident	259	Priest 23	33
whom he hath ever some cases to ask, when he meets with them;	260	Priest 23	4
whom he hath ever some cases to ask, when he meets with them;	260	Priest 23	5
he never decides it alone, but sends for three or four of the ablest	260	Priest 23	8
the cause with him, whom he makes to deliver their opinion first;	260	Priest 23	10

HE (cont'd)

	PAGE	TITLE	LINE
out of which he gathers, in case he be ignorant himself,	260	Priest 23	11
of which he gathers, in case he be ignorant himself, what to hold;	260	Priest 23	11
In judging, he followes that, which is altogether right;	260	Priest 23	13
pin unjustly from the richest, he absolutely restores it as a Judge;	260	Priest 23	15
but when he hath so done, then he assumes the Parson, and exhorts	260	Priest 23	16
he hath so done, then he assumes the Parson, and exhorts to Charity.	260	Priest 23	16
wherein he chooseth to permit his Parishioners rather to make use	260	Priest 23	18
But then he shews them how to go to Law, even as Brethren,	260	Priest 23	25
Now as the Parson is in Law, so is he in sicknesse also:	260	Priest 23	28
he asks no other, but to have the skill of healing a wound,	260	Priest 23	31
whom yet he ever exhorts not to exceed his bounds, but in tickle	260	Priest 23	35
then he keeps good correspondence with some neighbour Phisician,	260	Priest 23	36
let Fernelius be the Phisick Authour, for he writes briefly, neatly,	261	Priest 23	6
for he was the true householder, who bringeth out of his treasure	261	Priest 23	14
that labouring people (whom he chiefly considered) might have every	261	Priest 23	20
Thirdly, that he might set a Copy for Parsons.	261	Priest 23	26
he doth not onely prefer home-bred things before them, but condemns	261	Priest 23	36
yet he looks not in this point of Curing beyond his own Parish,	262	Priest 23	12
the person bee so poor, that he is not able to reward the Phisician:	262	Priest 23	14
for as hee is Charitable, so he is just also.	262	Priest 23	15
Now it is a justice and debt to the Common-wealth he lives in,	262	Priest 23	16
The first means he useth is Prayer, beseeching the Father of lights	262	Priest 24	21
as if he be a Papist, the Church is the hinge he turnes on;	262	Priest 24	30
be wanting to them in Doctrine, to whom he is so gracious in Life.	263	Priest 24	21
he forbears not in any wise to use the delinquent as before,	263	Priest 25	25
neither doth he esteem him for an enemy, but as a brother still,	263	Priest 25	29
he then comes on the faster, and makes so much the more of him,	263	Priest 25	33
and makes so much the more of him, as before he alienated himselfe;	263	Priest 25	34
but proceeding on, comes to do unlawfully, even before he is aware;	264	Priest 26	24
for example sake, and because they are most common, he thus thinks:	265	Priest 26	4
first, for covetousnes, he lays this ground:	265	Priest 26	4
in perverting that order which he hath set both to things,	265	Priest 26	11
rather to use his neighbours, and wear out that, he is covetous.	265	Priest 26	30
He that either for quantity eats more then his health or imployments	266	Priest 26	6
as he that eats more then his estate will bear, is a Prodigall;	266	Priest 26	9
in eating, that he can eat more, then afterwards he finds true:)	267	Priest 26	3
in eating, that he can eat more, then afterwards he finds true:)	267	Priest 26	4
When he deals with any that is heavy, and carnall;	267	Priest 26	17
he gives him those freer rules:	267	Priest 26	18
but when he meets with a refined, and heavenly disposition,	267	Priest 26	18
he carryes them higher, even somtimes to a forgetting of themselves,	267	Priest 26	19
they would have fainted, had they returned empty, He suffered it not;	267	Priest 26	24
or if he have any leisure to look off from thence, he meets	267	Priest 27	30
he meets continually with two most sad spectacles, Sin,	267	Priest 27	30
he somtimes refresheth himselfe, as knowing that nature will not bear	267	Priest 27	33
Wherefore he condescends to humane frailties both in himselfe	268	Priest 27	5
and which are described in this Book, he must be despised;	268	Priest 28	13
to the Apostles rule, he endeavours that none shall despise him;	268	Priest 28	17
especially in his own Parish he suffers it not to his utmost power;	268	Priest 28	18
This he procures, first by his holy and unblameable life;	268	Priest 28	20
he that wil be respected, must respect;	268	Priest 28	23
he takes it either in an humble way, saying nothing at all;	269	Priest 28	5
then a stone thrown against heaven, where he is, and lives;	269	Priest 28	8
him with those mouths, which he continually fils, and feeds:	269	Priest 28	11
he that throws a stone at another, hits himselfe;	269	Priest 28	13
and so between gentle reasoning, and pitying, he overcomes the evill:	269	Priest 28	15
and being in the world as he was, hath this undoubted pledge of his	269	Priest 28	17
he wisheth them by no means to spare any, though never so great;	270	Priest 29	18
but that God often changeth it according as he sees fit,	270	Priest 30	31
To this end he represents to his flock, that God hath and exerciseth	270	Priest 30	32
By his sustaining power he preserves and actuates every thing in his	271	Priest 30	3
then by that which he continually supplyes, as the corn needs it;	271	Priest 30	5
By Gods governing power he preserves and orders the references	271	Priest 30	13
yet if he suite not other things to the growth, as seasons,	271	Priest 30	16
and therefore he often overturnes things, when they are thought past	271	Priest 30	20
which it hath escaped, he destroyes it sometimes in the very Haven;	271	Priest 30	23
Now this he doth, that men should perpetuate, and not break off their	271	Priest 30	25
or if he depend on God further, even till he imbarn his corn,	271	Priest 30	31
God further, even till he imbarn his corn, and then think all sure;	271	Priest 30	32
God sends a fire, and consumes all that he hath:	271	Priest 30	33
For that he ought not to break off, but to continue his dependance	271	Priest 30	34
and he will give him the gold for it, which the Child utterly	272	Priest 30	10
This Liberty he compasseth by one distinction, and that is,	272	Priest 31	19
that he cannot without this maintain himself in a Christian state.	272	Priest 31	24
God knows the occasion as wel as he, and He is as a gracious Father,	273	Priest 31	8
and He is as a gracious Father, who more accepts a common course	273	Priest 31	8
And of this he is so to assure himself, as to admit no scruple,	273	Priest 31	10
but to go on as cheerfully, as if he had not been interrupted.	273	Priest 31	11
and prevent such interruptions, what he may, before they come,	273	Priest 31	17
they do come, he be a little affected therewith, but not afflicted,	273	Priest 31	19
if he resent it to a mislike, but not a griefe.	273	Priest 31	20
resolves whenever he enters into a Church, to kneel down,	273	Priest 31	23
either blessing God, that he will be pleased to dwell among men;	273	Priest 31	24
that whenever he repaires to his house, he may behave himself so	273	Priest 31	26
he may behave himself so as befits so great a presence;	273	Priest 31	26
that neer the place where he is to pray, he spyes some scoffing	273	Priest 31	28
he spyes some scoffing ruffian, who is likely to deride him for his	273	Priest 31	28
if he now, shall either for fear or shame, break his custome,	273	Priest 31	30
either for fear or shame, break his custome, he shall do passing ill:	273	Priest 31	30
so much the rather ought he to proceed, as that by this he may take	273	Priest 31	31

HE (cont'd)

	PAGE	TITLE	LINE
as that by this he may take into his Prayer humiliation also.	273	Priest 31	32
bring strangers to him, he may be the better armed to encounter them.	274	Priest 32	7
The great and nationall sin of this Land he esteems to be Idlenesse;	274	Priest 32	9
Wherefore the Parson strongly opposeth this sin, whersoever he goes.	274	Priest 32	15
he first represents to every body the necessity of a vocation.	274	Priest 32	17
when the evills which he is now subject unto, may be prevented,	274	Priest 32	23
and who is ready to ask, if he shall mend shoos, or what he shall do?	275	Priest 32	8
He that hath or can have yet no imployment, if he truly, . .	275	Priest 32	12
have yet no imployment, if he truly, and seriously prepare for it,	275	Priest 32	13
and seriously prepare for it, he is safe and within bounds. . .	275	Priest 32	13
and house-keeper hath his hands full, if he do what he ought to do.	275	Priest 32	20
and house-keeper hath his hands full, if he do what he ought to do.	275	Priest 32	21
that he have leisure to look out, the Village or Parish which either	276	Priest 32	1
the Village or Parish which either he lives in, or is neer unto it,	276	Priest 32	2
or Noble-man in the Country he lives in, inabling him with power	276	Priest 32	13
Sometimes he may go to Court, as the eminent place both of good	277	Priest 32	5
At other times he is to travell over the King's Dominions, . .	277	Priest 32	6
the Kingdome intc Portions, which every yeer he surveys peece-meal.	277	Priest 32	8
he is to endeavour by all means to be a Knight or Burgess there;	277	Priest 32	9
And when he is there, he must not only be a morning man, . .	277	Priest 32	11
he must not only be a morning man, but at Committees also; . .	277	Priest 32	11
after he hath shew'd the unlawfulness of spending the day in	277	Priest 32	28
he first commends the study of the Civill Law, as a brave, .	277	Priest 32	30
he commends the Mathematicks, as the only wonder-working knowledg,	277	Priest 32	34
he adviseth to insist and dwell chiefly on the two noble branches	277	Priest 32	36
where can he busie himself better, then in those new Plantations,	278	Priest 32	5
and the ways which he used to overcome them, being told to another,	278	Priest 33	16
at table about his appetite, if he tell this to another, preacheth;	278	Priest 33	19
judiciously, then he writes his rules of temperance out of bookes.	278	Priest 33	20
hath ever so many sermons ready penn'd, as he hath victories.	278	Priest 33	24
He that hath been sick of a Consumption, and knows what recovered	278	Priest 33	25
is a Physitian so far as he meetes with the same disease, . .	278	Priest 33	27
do it, then he that is generally learned, and was never sick.	278	Priest 33	29
of all diseases, and were recovered of all by things that he knew;	278	Priest 33	31
there were no such Physician as he, both for skill and tendernesse.	278	Priest 33	32
since he found himselfe sometimes to weepe more for the losse of some	279	Priest 33	11
he came at length to this resolution, that repentance is an act	279	Priest 33	13
And consequently he found, that the essence of repentance, . .	279	Priest 33	20
so that he as truly repents, who performes the other acts . .	279	Priest 33	29
when he cannot more, as he that weeps a floud of tears. . .	279	Priest 33	30
when he cannot more, as he that weeps a floud of tears. . .	279	Priest 33	31
getting for himself, when he tels it to others, becomes a Sermon.	279	Priest 33	32
The like he doth in other Christian vertues, as of Faith, . .	279	Priest 33	33
wherein (as Saint Paul implyes that he ought, Romans 2.) hee first	279	Priest 33	35
as he did our Saviour, and the Angels minister to us their owne food,	280	Priest 34	5
his preaching, but afterwards also, as Mat. 22. 35. He was tempted:	280	Priest 34	9
And Luke 10. 21. He rejoyced in Spirit:	280	Priest 34	10
according as he discovers any of his Flock to be in one or the other	280	Priest 34	12
to be in one or the other state, so he applies himselfe to them.	280	Priest 34	13
Those that he findes in the peaceable state, he adviseth to be very	280	Priest 34	14
he adviseth to be very vigilant, and not to let go the raines as soon	280	Priest 34	15
Particularly, he counselleth them to two things:	280	Priest 34	16
military state, he fortifyes, and strengthens with his utmost skill.	281	Priest 34	5
Governour of all things, yet to them he is lost, as if they said,	281	Priest 34	10
disputation is no Cure for Atheisme) he scatters in his discourse	281	Priest 34	15
he sees not how a house could be either built without a builder,	281	Priest 34	18
He conceives not possibly, how the windes should blow so much as they	281	Priest 34	20
He conceives not possibly, how he that would beleeve a Divinity,	281	Priest 34	27
how he that would beleeve a Divinity, if he had been at the Creation	281	Priest 34	27
if he had been at the Creation of all things, should lesse beleeve	281	Priest 34	28
should be his proof, and witnesses, as he calls them, Isaiah 43. 12.	282	Priest 34	13
on our Saviour, for which he told, that it should never be forgotten,	282	Priest 34	25
then he that reads the womans oyntment in the Gospell, or sees	283	Priest 34	1
But if he sees them neerer desperation, then Atheisme; . . .	283	Priest 34	5
not so much doubting a God, as that he is theirs;	283	Priest 34	6
then he dives unto the boundlesse Ocean of Gods Love, . . .	283	Priest 34	7
He hath one argument unanswerable.	283	Priest 34	9
either he doth it as they are Creatures, dust and ashes; . .	283	Priest 34	10
As Creatures, he must needs love them;	283	Priest 34	11
As sinfull, he must much mcre love them;	283	Priest 34	13
which way soever he turnes, hath two pledges of Gods Love, . .	283	Priest 34	18
he pares the apple, and gives them the clean to feed on. . .	283	Priest 35	32
Particularly, he loves Procession, and maintains it, because there	284	Priest 35	1
Wherefore he exacts of all to bee present at the perambulation,	284	Priest 35	9
sever themselves from it, he mislikes, and reproves as uncharitable,	284	Priest 35	11
he is so farre from condemning such assemblies, that he rather	284	Priest 35	13
that he rather procures them to be often, as knowing that absence	284	Priest 35	14
wherefore he likes well, that his Parish at good times invite one	284	Priest 35	17
times invite one another to their houses, and he urgeth them to it:	284	Priest 35	18
where he knowes there hath been or is a little difference, . .	284	Priest 35	19
neither is he affraid of praising, or praying to God at all times,	284	Priest 35	24
and not the fashion, he reformes, and teaches them, that at Baptisme	284	Priest 35	31
He that is ashamed in small things, will extend his pusillanimity	284	Priest 35	33
whereas he thinks it not onely a grave, and reverend thing, . .	285	Priest 36	2
shew all humility before his Passion, yet he allows in his Apostles.	285	Priest 36	28
his preaching, The Lord (saith he) reward him according to his works.	285	Priest 36	33
of Hymeneus and Alexander, he saith, he had delivered them to Satan,	286	Priest 36	1
he saith, he had delivered them to Satan, that they might learn	286	Priest 36	1
that they oftentimes goe out of church, before he hath blessed them.	286	Priest 36	14
language, he shall be esteemed as ordinary complementers; . .	286	Priest 36	21

HE (cont'd)	PAGE	TITLE		LINE
but if he often interpose a Blessing, when the other gives him just	286	Priest 36		22
For if he absolutely shut up mens mouths, and forbid all disclosing	286	Priest 37		33
he add a tincture of private malice in the joy, and hast of acting	287	Priest 37		26
so neither is he that defames him, whom the Law would have defamed,	287	Priest 37		28
whom the Law would have defamed, except he also do it out of rancour.	287	Priest 37		29
He took flesh, he wept, he died;	288	Priest		28
for his enemies he died;	288	Priest		29
This Galen confirms, when he sayes, that immoderate heats and colds,	294	Cornaro		6
because in his meats and drinks he kept a due moderation;	294	Cornaro		8
the one whereof was, He that will eat much, let him eat little;	295	Cornaro		34
because by eating little he prolongs his life.	295	Cornaro		35
when he cometh to visit his patient, prescribes this Physick first,	297	Cornaro		15
prescribes this Physick first, That he use a moderate diet:	297	Cornaro		16
and when he hath cured him, commends this also to him, if he will	297	Cornaro		17
hath cured him, commends this also to him, if he will live in health.	297	Cornaro		18
but that he shall ever after live free from diseases, if he will keep	297	Cornaro		19
after live free from diseases, if he will keep such a course of life;	297	Cornaro		20
of diseases, so that he shall need neither Physick nor Physician:	297	Cornaro		21
if he will give his minde to those things which he should,	297	Cornaro		22
if he will give his minde to those things which he should,	297	Cornaro		23
he will prove himself a Physician, and that a very compleat one:	297	Cornaro		23
He which lives a regular life, eating alwayes light meats,	299	Cornaro		22
what diet shall he use in diseases, which being in health he hath	299	Cornaro		24
shall he use in diseases, which being in health he hath anticipated?	299	Cornaro		24
whether he hath lived heretofore orderly or disorderly,	299	Cornaro		29
heretofore orderly or disorderly, when he is sick, ought not to eat,	299	Cornaro		30
and that in much smaller quantitie then when he was well.	299	Cornaro		32
For if he should keep his former proportion, Nature, which is	299	Cornaro		32
That he which lives a temperate life, cannot fall into diseases,	299	Cornaro		35
So that he which is offended with no kinde of meat and drink,	300	Cornaro		14
of old was praised, that at the age of 73 yeares he writ a Tragedie;	302	Cornaro		34
hath put this into your hands (as he sent the fish with mony to S.	304	Valdesso		11
being obscured in his own country he would have to flourish in this	304	Valdesso		14
Christs righteousnesse (as he sheweth through all his Considerations)	304	Valdesso		22
which he every where beares towards our deare [great] Master	305	Valdesso		4
and the working thereof, of which he was a very diligent observer.	305	Valdesso		11
words about the H. Scripture suite with what he writes elsewhere,	306	Valdesso		15
Where he sayes the Inflammation of the naturall, he sayes aptly,	308	Valdesso		13
he sayes aptly, so it be understood with the former distinction,	308	Valdesso		14
He often useth this manner of speech Beleeving by Revelation,	308	Valdesso		29
whereby I understand he meaneth only the effectuall operation	308	Valdesso		30
As if he should say:	308	Valdesso		33
to open his eyes that he might see the wondrous things of his Lawes,	309	Valdesso		26
wondrous things of his Lawes, and that he would make them his study.	309	Valdesso		26
same Psalme it is evident, that he was not meanly conversant in them.	309	Valdesso		28
Indeed he that shall so attend to the bark of the letter,	309	Valdesso		29
For as the servant leaves not the letter when he hath read it,	310	Valdesso		27
is delayed, the more he reads it, and fortifies himselfe with it;	310	Valdesso		29
he himselfe allowes it for a holy conversation and refreshment.	311	Valdesso		1
he nameth the reading and meditation of holy Scriptures for the first	311	Valdesso	V	4
especially considering the time and place where he lived.	311	Valdesso	V	8
for he maintaines that it is Faith and Infidelity that shall judge us	311	Valdesso		22
Therefore he saith here, we shall not be punished (which word I like	311	Valdesso		26
He meaneth (I suppose) that a man presume not to merit,	312	Valdesso		14
but that he ought to pray God affectionately and fervently to send	312	Valdesso		16
but because he cannot doe all, God often chuseth which he shall doe,	313	Valdesso		21
God often chuseth which he shall doe, and that by restraining him	313	Valdesso		22
and that by restraining him from what he would not have him doe.	313	Valdesso		23
He meanes a mans fre-will is only in outward, not in spirituall	313	Valdesso		33
holy Scripture, he meaneth that we should not use it as the onely,	314	Valdesso	V	4
or conditionally he prayed as man, though as God he knew the event.	315	Valdesso		11
But when he enlargeth he goes too farre.	315	Valdesso		34
But when he enlargeth he goes too farre.	315	Valdesso		35
when he professed himselfe a Pharisee, which strictly he was not,	316	Valdesso		7
which strictly he was not, though in the point of Resurrection he	316	Valdesso		8
though in the point of Resurrection he agreed with them,	316	Valdesso		9
when he useth the word Jurisdiction, allowing no Jurisdiction over	316	Valdesso		15
but he might have been justly put to death for it by the Magistrate,	316	Valdesso		24
unlesse he could have made it appeare, that it was done by Gods	316	Valdesso		25
He had done justly, and yet he had been punished justly,	316	Valdesso		27
and yet he had been punished justly, that is in humano foro &	316	Valdesso		27
but when he sayes they are equally exempt with God, that is dangerous	316	Valdesso		32
perhaps he meant all of this later not of the former.	317	Valdesso		4
for so he useth the same word in Consideration 68 ad finem.	317	Valdesso	V	8
Besides he opposeth the teaching of the spirit to the teaching	317	Valdesso		26
shewes that he was continually conversant in it, and not used it	318	Valdesso		2
it for a time onely, and then cast it away, as he sayes strangely.	318	Valdesso		3
text of S. Pet. 2 Ep. 1. 19. which he makes the ground of his [this]	318	Valdesso		7
forth her first borne Sonne, as if afterwards he had knowne her:	318	Valdesso		13
but however he would have them attend to it till that time,	318	Valdesso		20
is observeable that in that very place he preferres the Word before	318	Valdesso		22
By the Saints of the world he every where understands the cunning	319	Valdesso	V	19
he meaneth not the very Ceremonies of the Jewes, which no Christian	319	Valdesso		34
He that studies his content, wants it.	321	Proverbs		4
He that will take the bird, must not skare it.	322	Proverbs		42
He lives unsafely, that lookes too neere on things.	322	Proverbs		43
He hath great neede of a foole, that plaies the foole himselfe.	322	Proverbs		46
Who is so deafe, as he that will not heare?	323	Proverbs		79
Who is so deafe, as he who will not heare?	323	Proverbs	V	79
He that is warme, thinkes all so.	323	Proverbs		80

HE (cont'd)

	PAGE	TITLE		LINE
He that will learne to pray, let him goe to Sea.	323	Proverbs		84
He who will learne to pray, let him goe to Sea.	323	Proverbs	V	84
Whether shall the Oxe goe, where he shall not labour?	324	Proverbs		98
He that gives thee a Capon, give him the leg and the wing.	324	Proverbs		109
Give a clowne your finger, and he will take your hand.	324	Proverbs		111
To a gratefull man give mony when he askes.	324	Proverbs		115
and he will play with you in the market.	325	Proverbs		146
He that staies does the businesse.	327	Proverbs		188
If the old dog barke he gives counsell.	327	Proverbs		197
He that plaies his mony ought not to value it.	327	Proverbs		201
He that riseth first, is first drest.	327	Proverbs		202
He that riseth betimes hath some thing in his head.	329	Proverbs		235
The hard gives more then he that hath nothing.	329	Proverbs		259
Let an ill man lie in thy straw, and he lookes to be thy heire.	330	Proverbs		271
The Fox knowes much, but more he that catcheth him.	330	Proverbs		280
He will burne his house, to warme his hands.	331	Proverbs		304
He is not poore that hath little, but he that desireth much.	331	Proverbs		309
for to the sea he made havens, and to rivers foords.	331	Proverbs		315
for to the sea he made heavens, and to rivers foords.	331	Proverbs	V	315
He that makes his bed ill, lies there.	332	Proverbs		340
He that sowes trusts in God.	332	Proverbs		342
He that is not handsome at 20, nor strong at 30, nor rich at 40,	333	Proverbs		349
Hee that doth what hee will, doth not what he ought.	333	Proverbs		350
He that lives well sees a farre off.	333	Proverbs		352
He that hath a mouth of his owne,	333	Proverbs		353
He that will be served must bee patient.	333	Proverbs		354
He that chastens one, chastens 20.	333	Proverbs		356
He that hath lost his credit is dead to the world.	333	Proverbs		357
He that hath no ill fortune is troubled with good.	333	Proverbs		358
He that hath no hony in his pot, let him have it in his mouth.	333	Proverbs		360
He that takes not up a pin, slights his wife.	333	Proverbs		361
He that owes nothing, if he makes not mouthes at us, is courteous.	333	Proverbs		362
He that beleeveth all, misseth;	333	Proverbs		364
The horse thinkes one thing, and he that sadles him another.	334	Proverbs		387
He carries well, to whom it waighes not.	334	Proverbs		391
In time comes he whom God sends.	334	Proverbs		397
the longer he stayes there, the fowler he is.	335	Proverbs		409
He that blames would buy.	335	Proverbs		410
He that sings on friday, will weepe on Sunday.	335	Proverbs		411
He that seekes trouble never misses.	335	Proverbs		416
He that once deceives is ever suspected.	335	Proverbs		417
He that hath children, all his morsels are not his owne.	335	Proverbs		423
He who hath children, all his morsels are not his owne.	335	Proverbs	V	423
He that hath the spice, may season as he list.	335	Proverbs		424
He who hath the spice, may season as he pleaseth.	335	Proverbs	V	424
He that hath a head of waxe must not walke in the sunne.	335	Proverbs		425
He that hath love in his brest, hath spurres in his sides.	335	Proverbs		426
Hee that hath right, feares; he that hath wrong, hopes.	336	Proverbs		429
He that measures not himselfe, is measured.	336	Proverbs		432
He that speakes sowes, and he that holds his peace, gathers.	336	Proverbs		435
He that speakes sowes, and he that hears, gathers.	336	Proverbs	V	435
He that hath little is the lesse durtie.	336	Proverbs		436
He that lives most dies most.	336	Proverbs		437
He that hath one foot in the straw, hath another in the spittle.	336	Proverbs		438
Hee that's fed at anothers hand may stay long ere he be full.	336	Proverbs		439
Who is fed by anothers hand stays long ere he be full.	336	Proverbs	V	439
He that would be well, needs not goe from his owne house.	336	Proverbs		442
The dog gnawes the bone because he cannot swallow it.	337	Proverbs		457
He that's long a giving, knowes not how to give.	338	Proverbs		494
When a knave is in a plumtree he hath neither friend nor kin.	338	Proverbs		507
He that tells a secret is anothers servant.	338	Proverbs		512
He that looseth is Marchant as well as he that gaines.	339	Proverbs		518
He plaies well that winnes.	339	Proverbs		550
He that commits a fault, thinkes every one speakes of it.	340	Proverbs		554
He that's foolish in the fault,	340	Proverbs		555
He that can make a fire well, can end a quarrell.	340	Proverbs		557
should doe what he doth not.	340	Proverbs		559
must doe what he doth not.	340	Proverbs	V	559
He that hath no good trade, it is to his losse.	340	Proverbs		560
He that lives not well one yeare, sorrowes seven after.	340	Proverbs		562
He that hopes not for good, feares not evill.	340	Proverbs		563
He that is angry at a feast is rude.	340	Proverbs		564
He that mockes a cripple, ought to be whole.	340	Proverbs		565
He that hath hornes in his bosom,	340	Proverbs		567
He that burnes most shines most.	340	Proverbs		568
He that trusts in a lie, shall perish in truth.	340	Proverbs		569
He that trusts in a lie, shall perish by the truth.	340	Proverbs	V	569
He is a foole that makes a wedge of his fist.	341	Proverbs		585
God is at the end, when we thinke he is furthest off it.	341	Proverbs		598
He that contemplates hath a day without night.	341	Proverbs		601
He that goeth farre hath many encounters.	341	Proverbs		608
but he will drinke when and what he pleaseth.	342	Proverbs		623
Shew a good man his errour and he turnes it to a vertue,	343	Proverbs		655
A wise man cares not for what he cannot have.	343	Proverbs		662
He cannot be vertuous that is not rigorous.	343	Proverbs		664
He complaines wrongfully of the sea	345	Proverbs		706
He complaines wrongfully on the sea	345	Proverbs	V	706
He is onely bright that shines by himselfe.	345	Proverbs		707
He that will not have peace, God gives him warre.	345	Proverbs		729
The higher the Ape goes, the more he shewes his taile.	346	Proverbs		745

HE (cont'd)	PAGE	TITLE		LINE
He that is fallen cannot helpe him that is downe.	346	Proverbs		753
He that feares leaves, let him not goe into the wood.	346	Proverbs		768
He that feares death lives not.	347	Proverbs		781
He that pitties another, remembers himselfe.	347	Proverbs		782
He that doth what he should not, shall feele what he would not.	347	Proverbs		783
He that once hitts, is ever bending.	347	Proverbs		785
He that serves, must serve.	347	Proverbs		786
He that lends, gives.	347	Proverbs		787
He that preacheth giveth almes.	347	Proverbs		788
He that cockers his child, provides for his enemie.	347	Proverbs		789
He that serves well needes not ask his wages.	347	Proverbs		798
He warmes too neere that burnes.	348	Proverbs		815
He thinkes not well, that thinkes not againe.	349	Proverbs		836
He can give little to his servant, that lickes his knife. . .	349	Proverbs		846
He that sends a foole expects one.	349	Proverbs		851
He that can stay obtaines.	349	Proverbs		852
He that gaines well and spends well, needes no count booke. . .	349	Proverbs		853
He that gaines well and spends well, needes no count books. . .	349	Proverbs	V	853
He that endures is not overcome.	349	Proverbs		854
He that gives all before hee dies provides to suffer. . . .	349	Proverbs		855
He that gives all ere hee dies provides to suffer.	349	Proverbs	V	855
He that talkes much of his happinesse summons griefe. . . .	349	Proverbs		856
He who talkes much of his happinesse summons griefe. . . .	349	Proverbs	V	856
He that hath not the craft, let him shut up shop.	349	Proverbs		860
He that knowes nothing, doubts nothing.	349	Proverbs		861
He that marries late, marries ill.	349	Proverbs		863
He that passeth a winters day escapes an enemy.	349	Proverbs		864
He quits his place well, that leaves his friend there. . . .	350	Proverbs		875
He that will enter into Paradise, must have a good key. . .	350	Proverbs		895
He that deales in the world needes foure seeves.	351	Proverbs		899
The little cannot bee great, unlesse he devoure many. . . .	351	Proverbs		922
Conversation makes one what he is.	351	Proverbs		926
The Citizen is at his businesse before he rise.	352	Proverbs		958
When God is made master of a family, he orders the disorderly.	353	Proverbs		983
He that is at ease seekes dainties.	353	Proverbs		985
Hee that is in a Taverne thinkes he is in a vine-garden. . .	353	Proverbs		989
He that praiseth himselfe spattereth himselfe.	353	Proverbs		990
He that is surprized with the first frost	354	Proverbs		992
He that followes the Lord hopes to goe before.	354	Proverbs		994
He that dies without the company of good men	354	Proverbs		995
He that is not in the warres is not out of danger.	354	Proverbs		999
He that gives me small gifts would have me live.	354	Proverbs		1000
He that is his owne Counsellor	354	Proverbs		1001
He that hath lands hath quarrells.	354	Proverbs		1002
He that trusts much Obliges much, says the Spaniard. . . .	357	Proverbs	D	1045
He that thinks amiss, concludes worse.	357	Proverbs	D	1046
but he would chuse to dy in Spain (where they say	357	Proverbs	D	1047
He that will do thee a good turne, either he will be gon or dye.	358	Proverbs	D	1083
He that is once borne, once must dy.	358	Proverbs	D	1087
He that hath but one eye, must bee afraid to lose it. . . .	358	Proverbs	D	1088
He that steals an egge, will steal an oxe.	358	Proverbs	D	1090
He that will be surety, shall pay.	358	Proverbs	D	1091
He that is afraid of leaves, goes not to the wood.	358	Proverbs	D	1092
Still fisheth he that catcheth one.	358	Proverbs	D	1095
He that hath time and looks for better time, ...	359	Proverbs	D	1102
time comes that he repents himself of time.	359	Proverbs	D	1102
but sometimes he can hurt.	359	Proverbs	D	1119
all his life, could he find it.	360	Proverbs	D	1143
He is a great Necromancer, ...	361	Proverbs	D	1158
for he asks counsell of the Dead (i.e. books).	361	Proverbs	D	1158
Trust no friend with that you need fear him if he were your enemy.	361	Proverbs	D	1169
The Divell never assailes a man, except he find him	361	Proverbs	D	1176
that he hath bought a parcel of Books for me, and that they are	366	Letters		30
but yet he will heare of no other affaires, untill they have	368	Letters		8
which he refusing to doe hath given her occasion to protest shee will	368	Letters		21
& to threaten him that if he will not give her halfe her estate	368	Letters		23
but not so great as he expected & therfore he grumblingly said that	368	Letters		32
great as he expected & therfore he grumblingly said that if he had	368	Letters		33
therfore he grumblingly said that if he had given it to the pope he	368	Letters		33
if he had given it to the pope he should have had a greater reward.	368	Letters		34
upon this he was forbid Court & kingdome, yet was seene lately neere	368	Letters		34
denounced to him, told the King & so he is committed to prison.	368	Letters		37
he and I are ancient acquaintance, and I have a strong opinion	369	Letters		21
opinion of him, that if he can do me a courtesie, he will of himself;	369	Letters		22
opinion of him, that if he can do me a courtesie, he will of himself;	369	Letters		23
he takes place next the Doctors, is at all their Assemblies . .	370	Letters		1
that he fears I have not fully resolved of the matter, since this	370	Letters		18
much from Divinity, at which, not without cause, he thinks, I aim;	370	Letters		21
of the Pedler and the Pack on London-bridge, for there he assigns me.	370	Letters		28
Happy is he, whose bottom is wound up and laid ready for work in	373	Letters		6
Cast thy Care on the Lord and he shall nourish thee. (Psal. 55.)	374	Letters		14
all your Care on the Lord, for he careth for you. (1 Pet. 5.7.)	374	Letters		16
He doubles it to take away the scruple of those that might say,	374	Letters		22
wrote to our eldest brother, when he urged one upon me, and but one,	375	Letters		10
but he told her Grace, that he would by no meanes do so, . .	379	Letters		6
but he told her Grace, that he would by no meanes do so, urging,	379	Letters		7
long God knocks at our harts, before he be heard, & yet desists not.	381	Woodnoth		2
As God where he finds no roome for his Inclining grace, . .	381	Woodnoth		7
David built the temple as much as Solomon because he desired it,	381	Woodnoth		20
I besech Sir John Danvers that he would be pleased to be Overseer	382	G.H.'s Will		31

HE (cont'd)	PAGE	TITLE		LINE
some Remainders of monyes wherof he is to give as I know he will	383	G.H.'s Will		25
of monyes wherof he is to give as I know he will a Just account:	383	G.H.'s Will		25
HEAD				
About thy neck do drown thee? raise thy head;	13	Ch.-Porch		170
The Princes of my people make a head	26	Sacrifice		5
Then on my head a crown of thorns I wear:	31	Sacrifice		161
Upon my head: so I remove it all	32	Sacrifice		166
They strike my head, the rock from whence all store	32	Sacrifice		170
My wo, mans weal: and now I bow my head.	34	Sacrifice		250
Hung down his head, and wisht for night,	59	Whitsunday		14
Upon their head.	71	Frailtie		8
If not upon his head, yet in his hands:	77	Ang.&Sts.		5
Suckt all thy magazens: my head did ake,	83	Sighs & Gr.		10
I know the wayes of Learning; both the head	88	The Pearl		1
For head with foot hath private amitie,	91	Man		17
Musick and light attend our head.	91	Man		33
At th' head of others, hit their own.	96	Charms & K		10
No man shall beat into his head,	100	Miserie		15
The sunne holds down his head for shame,	101	Miserie		33
His head to shoot and ake.	101	Miserie		48
His head to shoot and shake.	101	Miserie	V	48
Much lesse those joyes which trample on his head.	102	Jordan 2		12
Come Lord, my head doth burn, my heart is sick,	107	Home		1
Poore silly soul, whose hope and head lies low;	111	Vanitie 2		1
But as birds drink, and straight lift up their head,	131	Mans medly		21
Break all thy spheres, and save thy head.	135	Divinitie		26
Thy dying head upon the tree:	149	Longing		32
That wants his head;	150	Longing		69
Call in thy deaths head there: tie up thy fears.	153	The Collar		29
Dwell in my head & eyes: come clouds, & rain:	164	Grief		2
I shake my head, and all the thoughts and ends,	169	The Answer		2
My head with oyl, my cup with wine	173	23 Psalme		19
And wore them for a jewell on her head,	173	Marie Magd		3
Holinesse on the head,	174	Aaron		1
Profanenesse in my head,	174	Aaron		6
Onely another head	174	Aaron		11
Christ is my onely head,	174	Aaron		16
So holy in my head,	174	Aaron		21
White is their colour, and behold my head.	176	Forerunners		2
Made a head	181	Banquet		14
Making a Head & spring against thy Reason.	213	Bohemia	D	59
that doth my head advance.	216	Psalm III	D	8
To his own head his wickedness	222	Psalm VII	D	57
or scratching the head, or spitting even in the midst of their	231	Priest 6		31
plunging themselves over head and eares into carking, and caring;	247	Priest 14		25
whereby my head and whole bodie was sore hurt, and also one of my	294	Cornaro		39
The scalded head feares cold water.	321	Proverbs	V	13
He that riseth betimes hath some thing in his head.	329	Proverbs		235
Hee that strikes with his tongue, must ward with his head.	331	Proverbs		313
Bee not a Baker, if your head be of butter.	332	Proverbs		321
The comforters head never akes.	334	Proverbs		392
Dry feet, warme head, bring safe to bed.	335	Proverbs		402
his head akes not at the matter.	335	Proverbs		421
He that hath a head of waxe must not walke in the sunne.	335	Proverbs		425
Councell breakes not the head.	336	Proverbs		443
let him not put them on his head.	340	Proverbs		567
The Royall Crowne cures not the head-ach.	340	Proverbs		576
It's better to be the head of a Lyzard, then the tayle of a Lyon.	340	Proverbs		579
It's better to be the head of a mouse, then the tayle of a Lyon.	340	Proverbs	V	579
Happier the hands fetter'd then the head distracted.	341	Proverbs	V	582
A pittifull mother makes a scald head.	343	Proverbs		647
An idle head is a boxe for the winde.	343	Proverbs		651
When a man sleepes, his head is in his stomach.	353	Proverbs		981
Who hath no head, needes no hatt.	354	Proverbs		996
Who hath no head, needes no heart.	354	Proverbs	V	996
HEAD-ACH				
The Royall Crowne cures not the head-ach.	340	Proverbs		576
HEAD'S				
The tongue talkes at the heads cost.	331	Proverbs		312
HEADS				
them to be so, when God is so neer them, and even over their heads.	233	Priest 7		11
those that are tempted, whatsoever is unruly, falls upon two heads;	281	Priest 34		7
With some of these heads enlarged, and woven into his discourse,	283	Priest 34		3
Lawyers houses are built on the heads of fooles.	352	Proverbs		951
to me as soon as you can, that I may work the heads to my purpose.	370	Letters		7
HEAL				
Now heal thy self, Physician; now come down.	34	Sacrifice		221
Such cuttings rather heal then REND:	133	Paradise		14
Seek out this All-heal, and seek no repose,	147	Offering		22
And heal my troubled breast which cryes,	150	Longing		83
O heal me, for my bones are vex'd,	220	Psalm VI	D	5
HEALES				
God heales, and the Physitian hath the thankes.	326	Proverbs		169
HEALING				
In healing not my self, there doth consist	34	Sacrifice		225
and healing of all wounds and sores with her owne hands;	239	Priest 10		14
but to have the skill of healing a wound, or helping the sick.	260	Priest 23		32
HEALTH				
A good digestion turneth all to health:	20	Ch.-Porch		358
Childhood is health.	44	H. Bapt.2		15

HEALTH (cont'd)	PAGE	TITLE		LINE
When I got health, thou took'st away my life,	47	Afflict.1		31
Thy wormwood turn to health, windes to fair weather:	49	Repentance		21
Thou art all health, health thriving, till it make	58	H.Script.1		5
The hills with health abound; the vales with store;	119	Providence		95
And for the present health restore.	138	The Size		30
Your health and beautie both began to break.	140	Ch.-rents		20
But I health, not physick choose:	178	The Rose		29
Wheare health hath nought to doe;	210	Paradox	D	14
it is either for want of health, or against some great Festivall,	232	Priest 7		22
the Parson, if he be in full health, keeps the three obligations,	242	Priest 10		26
when they overdo it, to the loss of their quiet, and health:	247	Priest 14		28
for quantity eats more then his health or imployments will bear,	266	Priest 26		7
so that men must eat neither to the disturbance of their health,	266	Priest 26		14
as if they were Masters of their health, and so they will stand	266	Priest 26		19
Yet Phisicians bid those that would live in health, not keep	267	Priest 26		10
dishes at table, which even their present health otherwise admits;	280	Priest 34		23
O Lord, make it health and strength unto us;	290	Priest		10
every way great force for the recovering and preserving of Health,	292	Cornaro		6
If Temperance had so much power as to bring me health;	293	Cornaro		3
For although the power of health consists most in the proportion	293	Cornaro		33
and that I had for many yeares continued in good health,	295	Cornaro		27
orderly life is the most sure way & ground of health and long dayes,	297	Cornaro		12
hath cured him, commends this also to him, if he will live in health.	297	Cornaro		18
But that a man may preserve himself in health, I advise,	298	Cornaro		11
and also doth preserve even ill tempers in good health,	298	Cornaro		15
shall he use in diseases, which being in health he hath anticipated?	299	Cornaro		24
they live disorderly, yet continue in health to their lives end:	300	Cornaro		18
I am continually in health, and I am so nimble, that I can easily get	300	Cornaro		34
all the sonnes of one father and mother, all in perfect health;	303	Cornaro		4
Health and mony goe farre.	336	Proverbs		447
Poverty is the mother of health.	337	Proverbs		472
Health without money is halfe an ague.	338	Proverbs		509
A little labour, much health.	344	Proverbs		689
There are more Physitians in health then drunkards.	351	Proverbs		903
The chiefe boxe of health is time.	351	Proverbs		911
Health and sicknesse surely are mens double enemies.	354	Proverbs		1011
be any truth in me, I find it little enough to keep me in health.	364	Letters		32
I am fain ever and anon, to buy somewhat tending towards my health;	364	Letters		34
first, how her health fares, next, whether my peace be yet made	371	Letters		8
consider what advantage you have over Youth and Health,	372	Letters		33
HEALTHFULL				
and by these hee keeps his body tame, serviceable, and healthfull;	237	Priest 9		26
The healthfull man can give counsell to the sick.	360	Proverbs	D	1130
HEALTHS				
Slight those who say amidst their sickly healths,	12	Ch.-Porch		133
HEALTHY				
The healthy frosts with summer-fruits compare.	119	Providence		100
Intemperance destroyes most healthy and flourishing constitutions:	292	Cornaro		9
Hee that goes to bed thirsty riseth healthy.	354	Proverbs		1003
HEAP				
O crumble not away thy souls fair heap.	9	Ch.-Porch		70
May take acquaintance of this heap of dust;	64	Ch.-monum.		3
Although thy heap be kept	154	Glimpse		23
HEAPS				
To kisse those heaps, which now they have in trust?	65	Ch.-monum.		16
HEAR				
Lord hear me when I call on Thee,	217	Psalm IV	D	1
Have mercy on me Lord, and hear	217	Psalm IV	D	5
My King, my God, vouchsafe to hear	218	Psalm V	D	3
whether I speak as I ought, or you hear as you ought, he sees hearts,	234	Priest 7		28
as they hear the answers prove, may when they come home,	255	Priest 21		27
three or four of the ablest of the Parish to hear the cause with him,	260	Priest 23		9
and yet hear Sermons against both, and himselfe condemn both in good	264	Priest 26		15
or hear them read often, as also the visitation Articles,	270	Priest 29		14
O Lord hear, O Lord forgive!	289	Priest		33
when I have more time, you shall hear more;	366	Letters		20
I long to hear from Sir Francis, I pray Sir send the Letter you	370	Letters		5
and now the only thing I long for, is to hear of my dear sick Sister;	371	Letters		7
Can I be so happy, as to hear of both these that they succeed well?	371	Letters		10
the next Friday it is tryed, and accordingly you shall hear.	371	Letters		17
HEARD				
That suites him best, of whom thy speech is heard.	18	Ch.-Porch		294
Write, So much giv'n to God; thou shalt be heard.	21	Ch.-Porch		382
At length I heard a ragged noise and mirth	40	Redemption		12
Church-bels beyond the starres heard, the souls bloud,	51	Prayer 1		13
And spinning phansies, she was heard to say,	84	The World		2
My God, I heard this day,	90	Man		1
He is to Sinai gone, as we heard tell:	99	Decay		9
I heard in Musick you had skill.	110	The Quip		11
Thus farre Time heard me patiently:	123	Time		27
When suddenly I heard one say,	139	Artillerie		5
I, who had heard of musick in the spheres,	139	Artillerie		9
Yet heard a crie	142	Pilgrimage		32
Much troubled, till I heard a friend expresse,	143	Holdfast		11
Thou hast heard me:	146	Praise 2		6
Hast thou not heard, that my Lord JESUS di'd?	151	The Bag		7
Me thoughts I heard one calling, childe:	154	The Collar		35
Who heard thee say it. O most gracious Lord,	155	Assurance		20
I cry'd unto the Lord, he heard	216	Psalm III	D	9
For God himself hath heard my cry;	220	Psalm VI	D	21

HEARD (cont'd)	PAGE	TITLE		LINE
of the hearers, that he may be heard at his returne more attentively.	232	Priest 7		24
Harken to reason or shee will bee heard.	323	Proverbs		74
The groundsell speakes not save what it heard at the hinges.	331	Proverbs		295
The child saies nothing, but what it heard by the fire.	331	Proverbs		300
which some observing who heard the interdiction denounced to him,	368	Letters		36
It is so long since I heard from you, that I long to heare both how	379	Letters		23
long God knocks at our harts, before he be heard, & yet desists not.	381	Woodnoth		2
HEARDST				
Thou heardst my call, and more.	158	Praise 3		24
HEARE				
Yet Lord restore thine image, heare my call:	38	The Sinner		12
A kinde of tune, which all things heare and fear;	51	Prayer 1		8
Yet heare, O God, onely for his blouds sake	66	Ch.-lock		9
And then not heare it crying! all day long	80	Deniall		18
List, ye may heare great Aarons bell.	99	Decay		10
But while I bustled, I might heare a friend	103	Jordan 2		15
Thou canst no more not heare, then thou canst die.	103	Prayer 2		6
O heare betimes, lest thy relenting	111	Vanitie 2		7
Who sweetly temper'st all. If we could heare	118	Providence		39
But you shall heare. After my heart was well,	129	Love unkn.		22
For ought I heare, your Master shows to you	130	Love unkn.		62
Who do not their own motions heare?	134	The Method		19
Who heare not him, but quickly heare	134	The Method		27
Thou didst heare me.	146	Praise 2		16
Bowels of pitie, heare!	149	Longing		19
And heare!	149	Longing		30
Lord heare! Shall he that made the eare,	149	Longing		35
Not heare?	149	Longing		36
Lord JESU, heare my heart,	150	Longing		73
My love, my sweetnesse, heare!	150	Longing		79
Away despair; my gracious Lord doth heare.	151	The Bag		1
Yet I heare tell,	187	Judgement		7
or assent to the promises of the Gospell by heare-say, or relation	309	Valdesso		1
Who is so deafe, as he that will not heare?	323	Proverbs		79
Who is so deafe, as he who will not heare?	323	Proverbs	V	79
but yet he will heare of no other affaires, untill they have	368	Letters		8
& therfore deferr it untill they heare farther from the States.	368	Letters		15
If there fall out yet any rubb, you shall heare of me;	377	Letters		22
I heard from you, that I long to heare both how you and your's doe:	379	Letters		23
HEARE-SAY				
or assent to the promises of the Gospell by heare-say, or relation	309	Valdesso		1
HEARER				
in his discourses occasionally, according to the pulse of the hearer.	268	Priest 27		8
HEARERS				
or for the variety of the hearers, that he may be heard at his	232	Priest 7		24
Were there no hearers, there would be no backbiters.	323	Proverbs		69
HEARING				
But no hearing.	80	Deniall		15
But no hearing.	80	Deniall		20
Yet no hearing.	80	Deniall	W	20
that where is much earnestness, there is somewhat worth hearing;	232	Priest 7		33
In vaine is the mill-clacke, if the Miller his hearing lack.	332	Proverbs		328
HEARK				
Heark how they crie aloud still, Crucifie:	29	Sacrifice		97
Heark and beware, lest what you now do measure	111	Vanitie 2		5
Heark, how the birds do sing,	131	Mans medly		1
Any thing to me. Heark despair, away.	152	The Bag		42
HEARKEN (see also harken)				
Hearken unto a Verser, who may chance	6	Ch.-Porch		3
Hearken under pain of death,	182	Banquet		52
O Lord, hearken, and do so for thy blessed Son's sake, in whose sweet	289	Priest		33
HEARS				
and humble supplication hears.	220	Psalm VI	D	24
and sometimes he hears the children read himselfe, and blesseth them,	248	Priest 14		35
He that speakes sowes, and he that hears, gathers.	336	Proverbs	V	435
HEARSE (see also herse)				
HEART (see also hart)				
Lie not; but let thy heart be true to God,	9	Ch.-Porch		73
Then he can lose with pleasure, stakes his heart;	14	Ch.-Porch		194
Still in thy heart, that he may see what's there.	17	Ch.-Porch		272
And send them to thine heart; that spying sinne,	23	Ch.-Porch		416
And send them to thy heart; that spying sinne,	23	Ch.-Porch	W	416
Christ purg'd his temple; so must thou thy heart.	23	Ch.-Porch		423
Made of a heart, and cemented with teares:	26	The Altar		2
A HEART alone	26	The Altar		5
Of my hard heart	26	The Altar		10
The spirit and good extract of my heart	38	The Sinner		10
And though my hard heart scarce to thee can grone,	38	The Sinner		13
My heart hath store, write there, where in	39	Good Fri.		23
The letter of the word, find'st no fit heart	41	Sepulchre		19
Rise heart; thy Lord is risen. Sing his praise	41	Easter		1
Consort both heart and lute, and twist a song	42	Easter		13
O tame my heart;	45	Nature		4
O smooth my rugged heart, and there	45	Nature		13
When first thou didst entice to thee my heart,	46	Afflict.1		1
The soul in paraphrase, heart in pilgrimage,	51	Prayer 1		3
But above all, the heart	53	Antiphon 1		11
Bear all the sway, possessing heart and brain,	54	Love 1		7
Which just now took up all my heart?	56	Temper 2		2
Oh Book! infinite sweetnesse! let my heart	58	H.Script.1		1

HEART (cont'd)

	PAGE	TITLE		LINE
Hatching my tender heart so long,	59	Whitsunday		3
Sinne is still hammering my heart	60	Grace		17
My God, what is a heart?	62	Mattens		5
My God, what is a heart,	62	Mattens		9
Could build so strong in a weak heart.	67	Ch.-floore		20
Enrich my heart, mouth, hands in me,	68	Trin.Sun.		7
My heart did heave, and there came forth, O God!	73	Afflict.3		1
Sure the unruly sigh had broke my heart.	73	Afflict.3		6
Take a bad lodging in my heart;	74	The Starre		6
Sinne and my heart:	74	The Starre		24
Then was my heart broken, as was my verse:	79	Deniall		3
Both knees and heart, in crying night and day,	80	Deniall		13
My heart was in my knee,	80	Deniall		19
When thou demandest but a heart,	82	Ungratef.		26
When glorie swells the heart, and moldeth it	88	The Pearl		14
Wounding my heart	90	Afflict.4		8
Sues for my heart, I thee displace,	94	Unkindness		19
My hand was next to them, and then my heart:	94	Life		7
In some one corner of a feeble heart:	99	Decay		12
Did crown his heart and face.	102	Miserie		72
On it my heart doth bleed	104	Obedience		6
And heart unto this deed, when he hath read;	105	Obedience		38
And heart unto this deed, when he doth read	105	Obedience	W	38
If some kinde man would thrust his heart	105	Obedience		42
There thou art struggling with a peevish heart,	106	Sion		13
Come Lord, my head doth burn, my heart is sick,	107	Home		1
Awake sad heart, whom sorrow ever drowns;	112	Dawning		1
And with a thankfull heart his comforts take.	112	Dawning		6
Arise sad heart; if thou dost not withstand,	112	Dawning		9
Arise sad heart; if thou doe not withstand,	112	Dawning	V	9
JESU is in my heart, his sacred name	112	JESU		1
That to my broken heart he was I ease you,	112	JESU		9
Who in heart not ever kneels,	114	Businesse		37
Ah! no more: thou break'st my heart.	115	Dialogue		32
Give one thing more, a gratefull heart.	123	Gratefulnes		2
Till I a thankfull heart obtain	124	Gratefulnes		27
But such a heart, whose pulse may be	124	Gratefulnes		31
Is this same grief! within my heart I made	126	Confession		2
Surely if each one saw anothers heart,	127	Giddinesse		21
And in the middle plac'd my heart. But he	129	Love unkn.		7
Quitting the fruit, seiz'd on my heart alone,	129	Love unkn.		12
Enforceth tears. Your heart was foul, I fear.	129	Love unkn.		18
But you shall heare. After my heart was well,	129	Love unkn.		22
But as my heart did tender it, the man	129	Love unkn.		33
And threw my heart into the scalding pan;	130	Love unkn.		35
My heart, that brought it (do you understand?)	130	Love unkn.		36
The offerers heart. Your heart was hard, I fear.	130	Love unkn.		37
I would say thorns. Deare, could my heart not break,	130	Love unkn.		52
It must be he. Your heart was dull, I fear.	130	Love unkn.		56
Though my lips went, my heart did stay behinde.	130	Love unkn.		59
Happie is he, whose heart	132	Mans medly		34
Poore heart, lament.	133	The Method		1
Glad heart rejoyce.	134	The Method		32
Weep foolish heart,	135	Ephes.		8
What doth this noise of thoughts within my heart	136	Familie		1
Content thee, greedie heart.	137	The Size		1
Wherefore sit down, good heart;	138	The Size		37
Where lay my heart; and climbing still,	142	Pilgrimage		21
Yet taking heart I rose, and then perceiv'd	142	Pilgrimage		29
Do not beguile my heart,	143	Complaining		1
Busie enquiring heart, what wouldst thou know?	144	Discharge		1
Did not thy heart	144	Discharge		7
And the cream of all my heart	146	Praise 2		11
In my heart, though not in heaven,	146	Praise 2		19
What hast thou there? a heart? but is it pure?	147	Offering		3
Yet one pure heart is nothing to bestow:	147	Offering		5
But all I fear is lest thy heart displease,	147	Offering		13
These parcell out thy heart: recover these,	147	Offering		17
(For this heart is none)	148	Offering		33
My heart is wither'd like a ground	148	Longing		8
Lord JESU, heare my heart,	150	Longing		73
By these thy feet, at which my heart	150	Longing		80
Well may he close his eyes, but not his heart.	151	The Bag		6
Look, you may put it very neare my heart.	152	The Bag		36
Not so, my heart: but there is fruit,	153	The Collar		17
But one half houre of comfort for my heart?	154	Glimpse		5
But one half houre of comfort to my heart?	154	Glimpse	V	5
In hope of thee my heart	154	Glimpse		16
Yet if the heart that wept	154	Glimpse		21
Come, my Joy, my Love, my Heart:	156	The Call		9
Such a Heart, as joyes in love.	156	The Call		12
My busie heart shall spin it all my dayes:	157	Praise 3		3
Wherefore I sing. Yet since my heart,	159	Praise 3		37
Sure it would carrie with it ev'n my heart,	159	Jos.coat		7
Doe winde a rope about, and cut my heart:	165	The Crosse		33
Who would have thought my shrivel'd heart	166	The Flower		8
My heart was meaning all the day,	168	a true Hymn		2
Whereas if th' heart be moved,	168	a true Hymn		16
As when th' heart sayes (sighing to be approved)	168	a true Hymn		19
Bedew, embalme, and overrunne my heart,	171	The Glance		7

HEART (cont'd)	PAGE	TITLE		LINE
I have, another heart and breast,	174	Aaron		12
My alone onely heart and breast,	174	Aaron		17
Ev'n all my heart, and what is lodged there:	176	Forerunners		8
And with it perfumes my heart.	181	Banquet		24
Able a heart of iron to appall,	187	Judgement		3
The great heart stoops, and taketh from the dust	192	Ch.-Milit.		67
Here Sinne took heart, and for a garden-bed	193	Ch.-Milit.		127
If ever Heart was sore with Sighs;	213	Convert	D	3
Let now my Eyes, my Voice, my Heart,	213	Convert	D	4
My Heart, that gave fond Thoughts their Food,	214	Convert	D	16
those that in heart are right:	222	Psalm VII	D	38
lifting up his heart and hands, and eyes, and using all other	231	Priest 6		3
If he stand steadfast in his heart, having no necessity,	237	Priest 9		16
and hath so decreed in his heart, that he will keep himself a virgin,	237	Priest 9		17
are principally these two, Spirituall pride, and Impurity of heart:	238	Priest 9		3
of affliction, which softens, and works the stubborn heart of man;	249	Priest 15		24
in my heart) because this kinde of Prayer is additionary,	273	Priest 31		36
which God in Scriptures requires, is the heart, and the spirit,	279	Priest 33		16
and turning unto God in truth of heart, and newnesse of life:	279	Priest 33		25
passing from the ear to the heart, from the heart to the life	289	Priest		30
the ear to the heart, from the heart to the life and conversation:	289	Priest		30
joy and peace have taken up their standing in my heart.	301	Cornaro		2
is not that which filleth the heart with joy and peace in believing;	309	Valdesso		2
the Consideration of Gods Worke in his heart through the Word,	309	Valdesso		31
Not a long day, but a good heart rids worke.	321	Proverbs		24
(to wit - with a moderate and contented heart).	328	Proverbs		208
then a heart with thoughts.	341	Proverbs		582
A gentle heart is tyed with an easie thread.	345	Proverbs		726
A good heart cannot lye.	347	Proverbs		800
A small heart hath small desires.	348	Proverbs		807
Who hath no head, needes no heart.	354	Proverbs	V	996
Vertue flies from the heart of a Mercenary man.	360	Proverbs	D	1133
for me, that the same heart, which you have won long since,	363	Letters		17
Now I write to you, Sir, because to you I have ever opened my heart;	365	Letters		24
businesses may stop my hand, yet my heart, a much better member,	371	Letters		27
by moving the Duches's heart, to an exceeding cheerfulness,	379	Letters		1
so no less glad for the Heart, that God has given you & yours,	379	Letters		15
HEART'S				
Therefore my soul melts, and my hearts deare treasure	27	Sacrifice		21
For my hearts desire	178	Discipline		5
The hearts letter is read in the eyes.	328	Proverbs		220
HEARTILY				
justly value Your most truly, most heartily, affectionate Brother,	372	Letters		7
I thanke you heartily for Leighton, your care, your Counsell,	379	Letters		13
HEARTLESSE				
O cheer and tune my heartlesse breast,	80	Deniall		26
HEARTS				
And love's a weight to hearts, to eies a signe.	22	Ch.-Porch		399
If stonie hearts will melt with gentle love.	29	Sacrifice		90
But surely not their hearts, as I well trie:	30	Sacrifice		123
But surely not their hearts, as I will trie:	30	Sacrifice	V	123
So many hearts on earth, and yet not one	40	Sepulchre		3
Sure there is room within our hearts good store;	40	Sepulchre		5
Where our hard hearts have took up stones to brain thee,	41	Sepulchre		13
Bitternesse fills our bowels; all our hearts	49	Repentance		27
Our souls and fleshly hearts;	52	H.Commun.		15
Our souls and fleshy hearts;	52	H.Commun.	V	15
And kindle in our hearts such true desires,	54	Love 2		4
Then shall our hearts pant thee; then shall our brain	54	Love 2		6
So our clay hearts, ev'n when we crouch	101	Miserie		39
Thy word our hearts and hands did crave,	123	Gratefulnes		10
They are too subtill for the subt'llest hearts;	126	Confession		11
Closets are halls to them; and hearts, high-wayes.	126	Confession		18
Smooth open hearts no fastning have; but fiction	126	Confession		23
Danting the stoutest hearts, the proudest wits.	141	Justice 2		12
Search well and see; for hearts have many holes.	147	Offering		4
O that within us hearts had propagation,	147	Offering		7
Since many gifts do challenge many hearts!	147	Offering		8
O that I might some other hearts convert,	159	Praise 3		39
Stonie hearts will bleed.	179	Discipline		20
Gave her the highest place in all mens hearts.	191	Ch.-Milit.		50
And tune mens hearts against the Gospel came:	192	Ch.-Milit.		76
And cleanse mens hearts against the Gospel came:	192	Ch.-Milit.	W	76
So trimme, as Greece and Egypt? yet their hearts	194	Ch.-Milit.		151
So spruse, as Greece and Egypt? yet their hearts	194	Ch.-Milit.	W	151
Usher'd the Gospel ever in mens hearts,	197	Ch.-Milit.		264
Within your chamber try your hearts,	217	Psalm IV	D	17
the hearts and reins are try'd.	221	Psalm VII	D	36
and seasoning all our words and sentences in our hearts,	233	Priest 7		29
or you hear as you ought, he sees hearts, as we see faces:	234	Priest 7		28
that they may come with holy hearts, and awfull mindes into	235	Priest 8		29
all those, who come with lesse prepared hearts then they ought.	235	Priest 8		31
Doctrine slip the more easily into the hearts even of the meanest.	261	Priest 23		19
that it may effectually pierce their hearts, and convert them.	262	Priest 24		24
so that to favour them therein is to win their hearts, and to oppose	283	Priest 35		30
not our foolish and unworthy hearts rob us of the continuance of this	289	Priest		20
have the assistance of the holy spirit applying it to our hearts,	310	Valdesso		7
Humble Hearts have humble desires.	321	Proverbs		6
Love makes all hard hearts gentle.	339	Proverbs		542
but you married men laugh till your hearts ake.	361	Proverbs	D	1175

	PAGE	TITLE		LINE
HEARTY				
and using all other gestures which may expresse a hearty,	231	Priest 6		4
and therefore not for him, who is hearty, and true in all his wayes,	253	Priest 19		1
HEAT				
As cunning fencers suffer heat to tire.	19	Ch.-Porch		316
Immortall Heat, O let thy greater flame	54	Love 2		1
Motion, and heat, let's take our flight	74	The Starre		18
I see the world grows old, when as the heat	99	Decay		16
Clouds cool by heat, and baths by cooling boil.	119	Providence		72
A neighbour spring to cool his inward heat;	154	Glimpse		14
My God, where is that ancient heat towards thee,	206	Walton 1		1
other hurtfull things also, as too much heat and cold, wearinesse,	293	Cornaro		31
or that cinnamon should heat me more then pepper?	297	Cornaro		33
places two whole moneths in the heat of summer (which in Italie is	302	Cornaro		18
There is no heat of affection but is joyned	357	Proverbs	D	1050
But I fear the heat of my late Ague hath dryed up those springs,	363	Letters		4
HEATE				
is not quite extinguished, but the heate of it asswaged.	308	Valdesso		17
HEATHEN				
As the old heathen would deem prodigies.	194	Ch.-Milit.		154
Why are the Heathen swell'd with rage,	215	Psalm II	D	1
the Heathen shall thy portion be.	216	Psalm II	D	20
ever reputed, even among the Heathen, as an obligation to do good,	253	Priest 19		26
Of these the heathen freed themselves, only by the generall	308	Valdesso		12
HEATS				
What heats abound!	149	Longing		27
and, when I felt inward heats, drank delightfull wines,	292	Cornaro		28
that immoderate heats and colds, and windes and labours did little	294	Cornaro		6
For having endured many heats & colds, and other like discommodities	294	Cornaro		12
live regularly, because they must often endure heats, and colds,	299	Cornaro		13
HEAV'EN				
In small draughts Heav'en does shine & dwell:	97	Charms & K	W	21
HEAV'EN'S				
On which heav'ens kingdome arch'd doth stand:	75	Sunday	W	23
HEAV'N'S				
Let thy almes go before, and keep heav'ns gate	21	Ch.-Porch		383
Thy praise too much? thou art heav'ns Lidger here,	58	H.Script.1		11
Thy praise enough? thou art heav'ns Lidger here,	58	H.Script.1	W	11
On which heav'ns palace arched lies:	75	Sunday		23
Into these lines; till in heav'ns court of rolls	105	Obedience		43
HEAV'NLY				
Yet for twelve heav'nly legions I could call:	31	Sacrifice		155
Of heav'nly blessings issue evermore:	32	Sacrifice		171
Of heav'nly blessings issue to the poore:	32	Sacrifice	W	171
And as of old, the law by heav'nly art	41	Sepulchre		17
By this thy heav'nly bloud;	53	H.Commun.		38
When first my lines of heav'nly joyes made mention,	102	Jordan 2		1
When first my verse of heav'nly joyes made mention,	102	Jordan 2	W	1
But Man alone, to show his heav'nly breed:	120	Providence		111
HEAV'NS				
Which is above the heav'ns, whose spring and rent	44	H. Bapt.1		5
Which is above the heav'ns, whose spring and vent	44	H. Bapt.1	V	5
The heav'ns are not too high,	53	Antiphon 1		3
Although there were some fourtie heav'ns, or more,	55	Temper 1		5
Although there were a hundred heav'ns, or more,	55	Temper 1	W	5
HEAVE				
My heart did heave, and there came forth, O God!	73	Afflict.3		1
Like moles within us, heave, and cast about:	126	Confession		14
HEAV'N				
Think heav'n a better bargain, then to give	21	Ch.-Porch		374
For churches are either our heav'n or hell.	23	Ch.-Porch		426
For churches either are our heav'n or hell.	23	Ch.-Porch	W	426
All understanding, more then heav'n doth glasse:	30	Sacrifice		119
Walk'd with a staffe to heav'n, and traced fountains:	37	The Agonie		3
There the circumference earth is, heav'n the centre.	38	The Sinner		8
There the circumference earth is, heav'n the centure.	38	The Sinner	W	8
Such starres I counted mine: both heav'n and earth	46	Afflict.1		11
That I can walk to heav'n well neare.	50	Faith		12
The Christian plummet sounding heav'n and earth;	51	Prayer 1		4
He might to heav'n from Paradise go,	53	H.Commun.		35
A crumme of dust from heav'n to hell?	55	Temper 1		14
Thou art joyes handsell: heav'n lies flat in thee,	58	H.Script.1		13
That th' earth did like a heav'n appeare;	59	Whitsunday		10
He did not heav'n and earth create,	63	Mattens		15
Commodious to conquer heav'n and thee	72	Frailtie		23
Flie hand in hand to heav'n!	77	Sunday		63
But thy silk twist let down from heav'n to me,	89	The Pearl		38
Till I reach heav'n, and much more thee.	90	Afflict.4		30
The earth doth rest, heav'n move, and fountains flow.	91	Man		26
In shallow waters heav'n doth show;	97	Charms & K		17
The most of me to heav'n is fled:	109	Home		68
One while he counts of heav'n, as of his treasure:	127	Giddinesse		5
With th' one hand touching heav'n, with th' other earth.	131	Mans medly		12
Just so the other heav'n they also serve,	134	Divinitie		5
Was cleare as heav'n, from whence it came.	135	Divinitie		14
To heav'n alone both go, and leade.	135	Divinitie		28
These seas are tears, and heav'n the haven.	138	The Size		47
Dropping from heav'n, which doth both cleanse and close	147	Offering		20
Did weep to heav'n, they found a bottle there	158	Praise 3		27
Offring at heav'n, growing and groning thither:	166	The Flower		25
Still upwards bent, as if heav'n were mine own,	166	The Flower		30

HEAV'N (cont'd)	PAGE	TITLE		LINE
In heav'n above.	172	The Glance		24
And then the heav'n espie.	184	The Elixer		12
His grave aspect had more of heav'n then hell:	194	Ch.-Milit.		168
His grave aspect was liker heav'n then hell:	194	Ch.-Milit.	W	168
As is the moon and sunne to heav'n and light.	196	Ch.-Milit.		216
Frail Beauty's Charms to Heav'n did raise,	214	Convert	D	13
HEAVEN				
If rottennesse have more, let Heaven go.	7	Ch.-Porch		18
If rottenness have more, lett Heaven goe.	7	Ch.-Porch	W	24
This is Earth's language, for if Heaven come in,	10	Ch.-Porch	W	90
Pray with the most: for where most pray, is heaven.	22	Ch.-Porch		402
Who grasp the earth and heaven with my fist,	30	Sacrifice		130
Who graspes the earth and heaven in his fist,	30	Sacrifice	W	130
In heaven at his manour I him sought:	40	Redemption		5
As he that Heaven beyond much thicket spyes	43	H. Bapt.1	W	3
Heaven in ordinarie, man well drest,	51	Prayer 1		11
Our innocent earth to heaven.	53	H.Commun.		32
Though elements change, and heaven move,	56	Temper 2		14
But wee are falne from Heaven to Earth,	59	Whitsunday	W	13
Lord once more shake the Heaven & earth	59	Whitsunday	W	17
Knocking at heaven with thy brow:	75	Sunday		10
Earth resteth, Heaven moveth, fountains flow,	91	Man	W	26
To purchase heaven for repenting,	111	Vanitie 2		9
Lifting to heaven from this well of tears.	141	Justice 2		18
In my heart, though not in heaven,	146	Praise 2		19
And up to heaven in an houre;	166	The Flower		17
Will not to Heaven grow.	184	The Elixer	W	16
Heaven.	188	Heaven		T
From Heaven, through Earth, to Hell.	202	Trin.Sun.	W	14
And though starres shott from heaven loose their light,	211	Bohemia	D	9
But He, that sits in Heaven, shall laugh,	215	Psalm II	D	9
to be received up into heaven, he constituted Deputies in his place,	225	Priest 1		8
When the Apostles would have called down fire from Heaven,	229	Priest 4		13
instrument of God to bring women to heaven) a wise and loving husband	238	Priest 9		31
of his infinite pity hath set forth heaven for a reward to draw men	243	Priest 11		32
touch him no more, then a stone thrown against heaven, where he is,	269	Priest 28		8
certainly it should be either the sun in heaven, or the fire	271	Priest 30		10
Christian soules, and raise them to their height, even to heaven;	275	Priest 32		32
when light is brought in, God send us the light of heaven;	284	Priest 35		24
when we had sinned beyond any help in heaven or earth, then thou	288	Priest		26
Blessed be the God of Heaven and Earth!	289	Priest		8
Who spits against heaven, it falls in his face.	333	Proverbs		346
Though God take the sunne out of the Heaven,	353	Proverbs		980
It is good to have some friends both in heaven and hell.	359	Proverbs	D	1127
Princes are venison in Heaven.	360	Proverbs	D	1156
nor to bewail that so few are writ, that look towards God and Heaven.	363	Letters		9
no such earthiness in it, but it may very well be joined with Heaven;	370	Letters		23
to doe) to blessed Mary Magd. & Paul, heaven had wanted chief saints:	381	Woodnoth		5
HEAVEN'S				
You know the way to heavens doore.	66	Ch.-mus.		12
On Sunday heavens gate stands ope;	76	Sunday		33
On Sunday heavens dore stands ope;	76	Sunday	W	33
HEAVENLY				
But his heavenly and divine,	208	J. Danvers	D	11
they remember their earthly Lord, do much forget their heavenly;	226	Priest 2		33
and brings with his own to the heavenly altar to be bathed,	231	Priest 6		9
the one he owes to his heavenly Countrey, the other to his earthly,	239	Priest 10		21
and cleansed, and serve for lights even of Heavenly Truths.	257	Priest 21		15
with a refined, and heavenly disposition, he carryes them higher,	267	Priest 26		19
of the heavens, so are earthly Troubles compar'd to heavenly Joyes;	372	Letters		31
Letter gave me Earthly preferment, and kept Heavenly for your self:	373	Letters		1
one to the other, that ye may be a heavenly comfort, to his prayse,	378	Letters		26
HEAVENS				
Waters above the Heavens. O sweet streams	44	H. Bapt.1	W	5
So Isa. 64. Oh that thou would'st rent the Heavens, that thou wouldst	234	Priest 7		3
for to the sea he made heavens, and to rivers foords.	331	Proverbs	V	315
As the Earth is but a point in respect of the heavens, so are earthly	372	Letters		30
HEAVIE				
For I confesse my heavie score,	68	Trin.Sun.		5
And truly brasse and stones are heavie things,	107	Sion		19
Light burthens, long borne, growe heavie.	321	Proverbs		15
Light burdens, long borne, are heavie.	321	Proverbs	V	15
HEAVIEST				
Every one thinkes his sacke heaviest.	346	Proverbs		748
HEAVY				
which are thick, and heavy, and hard to raise to a poynt of Zeal,	233	Priest 7		16
When he deals with any that is heavy, and carnall;	267	Priest 26		17
HEBREW				
By Hebrew piety, he meaneth not the very Ceremonies of the Jewes,	319	Valdesso		34
HEBREWS				
And he himselfe is a consuming fire, Hebrews 12.	234	Priest 7		35
there is not onely milke there, but strong meat also. Heb. 5. 14.	317	Valdesso		24
Peter bidding the dispersed Hebrews attend to the word till the day	318	Valdesso		18
HECTIQUE				
(as Hectique, Paralitique, Apoplectique. Lethargique).	357	Proverbs	D	1044
HEDGE				
Though God do hedge us in, yet who is holy?	24	Ch.-Porch		450
A better hedge, and need lesse reparation.	120	Providence		122
Love your neighbour, yet pull not downe your hedge.	325	Proverbs		141
Love your neighbour, but pull not downe your hedge.	325	Proverbs	V	141

HEE

	PAGE	TITLE		LINE
Hee'le make thy wife a blessing not a rodd.	7	Ch.-Porch	W	18
Hee that has all ill, & can have no good	7	Ch.-Porch	W	35
Hee that desires is more then halfe the way.	10	Ch.-Porch	W	90
And though hee bee a ship, is his owne shelf.	11	Ch.-Porch	W	120
Who cannot rest till hee good-fellows finde,	12	Ch.-Porch		149
Though hee bring light & th' other sents:	42	Easter	W	24
Hee that has one,	203	Trin.Sun.	W	18
For I decay not hee.	203	Even-song	W	4
Shine then more bright then hee.	203	Even-song	W	8
Meane while, if hee (which all thinges weares)	208	H. Danvers	D	5
since hee shoots higher that threatens the Moon, then hee that aims	224	Priest		8
shoots higher that threatens the Moon, then hee that aims at a Tree.	224	Priest		9
all which is here expressed, hee presently sinns, and displeases God,	224	Priest		11
but after hee had fulfilled the work of Reconciliation,	225	Priest 1		7
In the Scriptures hee findes four things;	228	Priest 4		24
hee may affect also his people, knowing that no Sermon moves them so	231	Priest 6		13
for if we be here, hee must be here, since we are here by him,	234	Priest 7		29
and by these hee keeps his body tame, serviceable, and healthfull;	237	Priest 9		26
As hee is just in all things, so is he to his wife also,	238	Priest 9		34
the seldomer, according as hee is satisfied of his Wifes discretion.	239	Priest 9		4
his servants between love, and fear, according as hee findes them;	241	Priest 10		8
and common, but wholsome, what hee hath, is little, but very good;	241	Priest 10		16
some of his Parish, hee taketh his times to do the like to the rest;	243	Priest 11		18
hee hath them all with him, because countrey people are very	243	Priest 11		19
Yet doth hee oftenest invite those, whom hee sees take best courses,	243	Priest 11		24
whom hee sees take best courses, that so both they may be encouraged	243	Priest 11		25
hee wins them to praise God more, to live more religiously,	245	Priest 12		2
not suffering any that day that hee receives, to want a good meal	245	Priest 12		8
When-ever hee gives any thing, and sees them labour in thanking	245	Priest 12		30
So doth hee also before giving make them say their Prayers first,	245	Priest 12		34
and then as hee finds the persons of the house imployed,	247	Priest 14		11
hee both commends them much, and furthers them when hee is gone,	247	Priest 14		13
and furthers them when hee is gone, in their imployment;	247	Priest 14		14
as if hee findes them reading, hee furnisheth them with good books;	247	Priest 14		15
hee supplies them with Receipts, and instructs them further in that	247	Priest 14		16
of particularizing in these things, hee were not fit to be a Parson:	249	Priest 14		1
his owne person, hee considers the offender as a child, and forgives,	250	Priest 16		14
as a child, and forgives, so hee may have any signe of amendment;	250	Priest 16		14
yet hee gives him not over, but is long before hee proceede	250	Priest 16		16
but is long before hee proceede to disinheriting, or perhaps never	250	Priest 16		17
at the eleventh houre, and therefore hee still expects, and waits,	250	Priest 16		19
and waits, least hee should determine Gods houre of coming;	250	Priest 16		20
which as hee cannot, touching the last day, so neither touching	250	Priest 16		21
or that overtake him, hee begins good discourses, such as may edify,	251	Priest 17		3
if hee be to stay for a time, hee considers diligently the state	251	Priest 17		17
hee considers diligently the state thereof to Godward, and that in	251	Priest 17		17
hee first considers with himselfe, what kind of remedy fits	251	Priest 17		25
of the house best, and then hee faithfully, and boldly applyeth it;	251	Priest 17		27
hee findes some way of releeving it, and reducing the Manna,	254	Priest 19		2
making what hee knows to serve him in that which he knows not:	256	Priest 21		38
Hee admits no vaine or idle names, but such as are usuall	258	Priest 22		3
Hee says that prayer with great devotion, where God is thanked	258	Priest 22		5
hee considers and looks into the ignorance, or carelesness of his	258	Priest 22		23
pains with them, that hee may lay the foundation of future Blessings.	258	Priest 22		31
and the difference, hee ought to receive, of what age soever.	258	Priest 22		36
loosely and wildely, and then the Answerer will discover what hee is.	259	Priest 22		10
Hee that comes to the Sacrament, hath the confidence of a Guest,	259	Priest 22		14
and hee that kneels, confesseth himself an unworthy one,	259	Priest 22		15
but hee that sits, or lies, puts up to an Apostle:	259	Priest 22		17
And this hee doth, not onely for the benefit of the work,	259	Priest 22		23
Therefore hee endures not that any of his Flock should go to Law;	259	Priest 23		31
any of his flock sick, hee is their Physician, or at least his Wife,	260	Priest 23		29
hee keepes some young practicioner in his house for the benefit	260	Priest 23		33
that by familiar things hee might make his Doctrine slip the more	261	Priest 23		18
for as hee is Charitable, so he is just also.	262	Priest 23		15
These and the like points hee hath accurately digested,	263	Priest 24		14
and yet hee chuseth rather to use his neighbours, and wear out that,	265	Priest 26		29
and hee that eats offensively to the Company, either in his order,	266	Priest 26		10
because hee knows nothing but the Crosse of Christ, his minde being	267	Priest 27		27
which out of his choysest judgment hee hath resolved to observe,	268	Priest 28		12
and joyfull, that hee is made conformable to his Master;	269	Priest 28		16
of his affairs, that hee may have wherewithall to do good.	275	Priest 32		30
Hee considers every one there, and either helps them in particular,	276	Priest 32		3
But if hee may bee of the Commission of Peace, there is nothing	276	Priest 32		7
every morning that hee is at home hee must either ride the Great	277	Priest 32		15
morning that hee is at home hee must either ride the Great Horse,	277	Priest 32		15
Hee that hath considered how to carry himself at table about his	278	Priest 33		18
Romans 2.) hee first preacheth to himselfe, and then to others.	279	Priest 33		36
Hee that saw Christ open a blind mans eyes, saw not more Divinity,	282	Priest 34		38
hee takes one of the parties, and goes with him to the other,	284	Priest 35		20
Hee that trusts in the Kings word for any thing trusts in the King.	307	Valdesso		3
hee in the meane while applying himselfe to the [unquestioned] duties	312	Valdesso		19
motion (as S. Paul had when hee would have preached in Asia),	313	Valdesso		16
By occasions (I suppose) hee meaneth the ordinary, or necessary	314	Valdesso		16
Hee begins to die, that quits his desires.	321	Proverbs		2
Hee that stumbles and falles not, mends his pace.	321	Proverbs		7
Hee that gets out of debt, growes rich.	321	Proverbs		9
Hee puls with a long rope, that waits for anothers death.	322	Proverbs		25
Hee puls with a long rope, who looks for anothers death.	322	Proverbs	V	25
Hee looseth nothing, that looseth not God.	322	Proverbs		35

HEE (cont'd)

	PAGE	TITLE		LINE
Hee that sendes a foole, means to follow him.	322	Proverbs		51
Hee stands not surely, that never slips.	323	Proverbs		68
Hee stands not surely, that never slipte.	323	Proverbs	V	68
Hee that goes barefoot, must not plant thornes.	323	Proverbs		82
Hee that lives well is learned enough.	323	Proverbs		86
Hee who lives well is learned enough.	323	Proverbs	V	86
Hee that lives ill, feare followes him.	324	Proverbs		110
The Fox, when hee cannot reach the grapes,	325	Proverbs		130
Happie is hee that chastens himselfe.	325	Proverbs		137
Well may hee smell fire, whose gowne burnes.	325	Proverbs		138
Hee that lies long a bed, his estate feeles it.	327	Proverbs		179
Hee that lookes not before, finds himselfe behind.	327	Proverbs		200
yet hee is no little foole that despiseth it.	327	Proverbs		206
Hee that eats the hard shall eate the ripe.	328	Proverbs		210
The foole askes much, but hee is more foole that grants it.	330	Proverbs		282
Hee is a foole that thinks not that another thinks.	330	Proverbs		287
Hee that burnes his house warmes himselfe for once.	331	Proverbs		303
Hee will spend a whole yeares rent at one meales meate.	331	Proverbs		305
Hee wrongs not an old man that steales his supper from him.	331	Proverbs		311
Hee that strikes with his tongue, must ward with his head.	331	Proverbs		313
Hee that strikes with his tongue, must ward with his hand.	331	Proverbs	V	313
Hee that labours and thrives spins gold.	332	Proverbs		341
Hee that lies with the dogs, riseth with fleas.	332	Proverbs		343
Hee that repaires not a part, builds all.	333	Proverbs		344
Hee that repaires not a part, at length must all.	333	Proverbs	V	344
Hee that dines and leaves, layes the cloth twice.	333	Proverbs		347
Hee that doth what hee will, doth not what he ought.	333	Proverbs		350
Hee that will deceive the fox, must rise betimes.	333	Proverbs		351
Hee that would deceive the fox, must rise betimes.	333	Proverbs	V	351
Hee that gives thee a bone, would not have thee die.	333	Proverbs		355
Hee that demands misseth not, unlesse his demands be foolish.	333	Proverbs		359
Hee that looseth his due, gets no thankes.	333	Proverbs		363
hee that beleeveth nothing, hitts not.	333	Proverbs		364
the time comes that hee will repay thee.	333	Proverbs		368
The fault is as great as hee that is faulty.	333	Proverbs		369
Hee that would bee well old, must bee old betimes.	334	Proverbs		371
Hee is rich enough that wants nothing.	335	Proverbs		403
Hee that falles into the durt,	335	Proverbs		409
Hee that comes of a hen must scrape.	335	Proverbs		415
Hee that comes after must scrape.	335	Proverbs	V	415
Hee that makes a good warre makes a good peace.	335	Proverbs		420
Hee that workes after his owne manner,	335	Proverbs		421
Hee that respects not, is not respected.	335	Proverbs		427
Hee that hath a Fox for his mate,	335	Proverbs		428
Hee that hath right, feares; he that hath wrong, hopes.	336	Proverbs		429
Hee that hath patience hath fatt thrushes for a farthing.	336	Proverbs		430
Hee that hath one hogge makes him fat,	336	Proverbs		433
and hee that hath one son makes him a foole.	336	Proverbs		433
Hee who hath but one sonne makes him fat,	336	Proverbs	V	433
Hee that's fed at anothers hand may stay long ere he be full.	336	Proverbs		439
Hee that makes a thing too fine, breakes it.	336	Proverbs		440
Hee that bewailes himselfe hath the cure in his hands.	336	Proverbs		441
Hee that knowes what may bee gained in a day never steales.	336	Proverbs		445
Hee commands enough that obeyes a wise man.	339	Proverbs		547
Hee that should have what hee hath not,	340	Proverbs		559
Hee that would have what hee hath not,	340	Proverbs	V	559
Hee that blowes in the dust fills his eyes with it.	340	Proverbs		570
When God will punish, hee will first take away the understanding.	344	Proverbs		688
Hee that hath a wife and children wants not businesse.	347	Proverbs		778
Hee that marries for wealth sells his liberty.	347	Proverbs		784
Hee that is throwne would ever wrestle.	347	Proverbs		797
Hee that brings good newes knockes hard.	348	Proverbs		824
Hee is not free that drawes his chaine.	348	Proverbs		830
Hee goes not out of his way, that goes to a good Inne.	348	Proverbs		831
Hee lookes not well to himselfe that lookes not ever.	349	Proverbs		835
Hee that keepes his owne makes warre.	349	Proverbs		848
He that gives all before hee dies provides to suffer.	349	Proverbs		855
He that gives all ere hee dies provides to suffer.	349	Proverbs	V	855
Hee that loves the tree, loves the branch.	349	Proverbs		857
Hee hath not liv'd, that lives not after death.	350	Proverbs		873
Hee that would be a Gentleman, let him goe to an assault.	350	Proverbs		878
Hee payes too deare for honey that licks it from thorns.	350	Proverbs	V	880
Hee hath no leisure who useth it not.	351	Proverbs		897
Hee that learnes a trade hath a purchase made.	353	Proverbs		978
When one is on horsebacke hee knowes all things.	353	Proverbs		982
Hee that hath charge of soules transports them not in bundles.	353	Proverbs		986
Hee that tells his wife newes is but newly married.	353	Proverbs		987
Hee that is in a towne in May loseth his spring.	353	Proverbs		988
Hee that is in a Taverne thinkes he is in a vine-garden.	353	Proverbs		989
Hee that is a master must serve (another).	354	Proverbs		991
Hee a beast doth die, that hath done no good to his country.	354	Proverbs		993
knowes nothing sure but what hee hath laid out.	354	Proverbs		1001
Hee that goes to bed thirsty riseth healthy.	354	Proverbs		1003
Hee that lives in hope danceth without musick.	354	Proverbs		1006
Hee that wipes the childs nose, kisseth the mothers cheeke.	355	Proverbs		1032
Hee that makes himself a sheep, shall be eat by the wolfe.	358	Proverbs	D	1089

HEED

	PAGE	TITLE		LINE
Then silly soul take heed; for earthly joy	111	Vanitie 2		17
Should creatures want for want of heed their due?	119	Providence		86
Away; take heed:	153	The Collar		27

HEED (cont'd)	PAGE	TITLE	LINE
for them also men heed, and remember better then exhortations;	233	Priest 7	13
Oh let us all take heed what we do, God sees us, he sees whether I	234	Priest 7	26
spirits, and possesse them even before they themselves heed it.	252	Priest 18	7
to take heed, lest their quiet betray them (as it is apt to do)	280	Priest 34	17
yet all must [needs] take heed, lest they take a greater quantitie	300	Cornaro	11
Take heed of the wrath of a mighty man, ...	360	Proverbs	D 1148
Take heed of mad folks in a narrow place.	360	Proverbs	D 1149
Take heed of credit decaid, and people that have nothing. . .	360	Proverbs	D 1150
Take heed of a young wench, ...	360	Proverbs	D 1151
Take heed of a person marked, and a Widdow thrice married. . .	360	Proverbs	D 1152
Take heed of foul dirty wayes, and long sicknesse. . . .	360	Proverbs	D 1153
Take heed of winde that comes in at a hole, ...	360	Proverbs	D 1154
Take heed of a step-mother; the very name of her sufficeth. . .	360	Proverbs	D 1155
only hereafter I will take heed how I propose my desires unto you,	363	Letters	20
HEEDE			
but take heede, lest you bee drowned.	326	Proverbs	167
Take heede of still waters, the quick passe away.	326	Proverbs	171
Take heede of the viniger of sweet wine.	336	Proverbs	451
Too much taking heede is losse.	350	Proverbs	889
Take heede of an oxe before, of an horse behind, ...	351	Proverbs	900
HEELS			
Follow not truth too near the heels, lest it dash out thy teeth.	360	Proverbs	D 1138
HEERE			
There is a Frenchman who writt a poem heere in England & presented it	368	Letters	30
HEERTOFORE			
Then with the reed they gave mee heertofore, ...	32	Sacrifice	W 169
HEIGHT (see also hight)			
O let thy height of mercie then	49	Repentance	13
Speed without pains, a horse: tall without height, ...	120	Providence	103
When height of malice, and prodigious lusts, ...	197	Ch.-Milit.	237
for this argues a height and eminency of mind, which is not easily	268	Priest 28	25
Christian soules, and raise them to their height, even to heaven;	275	Priest 32	32
HEIGHTEN			
Heighten a spirit to sound out thy praise	206	walton 1	7
HEINOUS (see also hainousness)			
HEIR			
And for the future time art heir	137	The Size	11
HEIRE			
I gave the mouse a hole, and she is become my heire. . . .	324	Proverbs	94
Let an ill man lie in thy straw, and he lookes to be thy heire.	330	Proverbs	271
HEIRS			
for single men, they are either Heirs, or younger Brothers: . . .	276	Priest 32	25
The Heirs are to prepare in all the fore-mentioned points against	276	Priest 32	26
HELD			
Humilitie, who held the plume, at this	71	Humilitie	25
who held that the seeds of all truths lay in every body, . .	256	Priest 21	21
a pain of the side took me, which held me two and twentie houres.	296	Cornaro	18
this I answer, that Galen kept it, and held it for the best Physick:	298	Cornaro	38
of God in all ages have ever held in so pretious esteem the word	317	Valdesso	33
HELL			
If thou wilt die, the gates of hell are broad:	9	Ch.-Porch	71
As that thy self alone to hell shalt goe.	13	Ch.-Porch	W 168
A joy for it worth worlds. Thus hell doth jest	23	Ch.-Porch	412
For churches are either our heav'n or hell.	23	Ch.-Porch	426
For churches either are our heav'n or hell.	23	Ch.-Porch	W 426
None shall in hell such bitter pangs endure, ...	24	Ch.-Porch	445
Canst thou finde hell about my lips? and misse	28	Sacrifice	42
Sometimes to hell I fall.	55	Temper 1	8
A crumme of dust from heav'n to hell?	55	Temper 1	14
Working against the states of death and hell.	58	H.Script.1	12
Without thy help, leads us his way to Hell.	59	Whitsunday	W 16
But who drinks on, to hell may go.	97	Charms & K	18
Who dives on further may find Hell.	97	Charms & K	W 22
Partakes already half of hell.	123	Time	24
And with the other throwest down to hell	160	Priesthood	3
Killing and quickning, bringing down to hell	166	The Flower	16
His grave aspect had more of heav'n then hell:	194	Ch.-Milit.	168
His grave aspect was liker heav'n then hell:	194	Ch.-Milit.	W 168
Old and new Babylon are to hell and night, ...	196	Ch.-Milit.	215
Hell, Death & Divel come short of mee.	202	love	W 24
From Heaven, through Earth, to Hell.	202	Trin.Sun.	W 14
At once to Hell, without a baiting while	212	Bohemia	D 49
streams of thy bloud were currant through darknesse, grave, and hell;	288	Priest	33
Hell is full of good meanings and wishings.	326	Proverbs	170
It is good to have some friends both in heaven and hell. . .	359	Proverbs	D 1127
When war begins, then hell openeth.	360	Proverbs	D 1141
There is no body will go to hell for company.	361	Proverbs	D 1177
HELL'S			
They are hells land-marks, Satans double crest:	196	Ch.-Milit.	219
When a Lackey comes to hells doore, the devills locke the gates.	353	Proverbs	984
HELLISH			
Then to have hellish moths still gnaw and fret	69	Content	27
HELP			
Who sought for help, never malicious foes:	34	Sacrifice	243
Lett Prayer help our losses, ...	53	H.Commun.	W 38
Without thy help, leads us his way to Hell.	59	Whitsunday	W 16
I go to Church; help me to wings, and I	61	Praise 1	5
Yet say sometimes, God help poore Kings.	65	Ch.-mus.	8
Oh help, my God! let not their plot	90	Afflict.4	19
To see what help in th' earth or skie:	107	Home	14

HELP (cont'd)	PAGE	TITLE		LINE
But there was none; at least no help without:	107	Home		15
The help did in thy bosome lie.	107	Home		16
The help stands close, and keeps the fear in view.	119	Providence		88
Cold fruits warm kernells help against the winde.	120	Providence		130
Will more complie, then help. A Lord I had,	129	Love unkn.		3
To thee help appertains.	149	Longing		43
Cast down, yet help afford;	171	Bittersweet		3
Help our decay.	187	Dooms-day		26
Lord help thy servant whose perplexed Soule	204	The Knell	W	2
O help my God!	204	The Knell	W	9
Shal help another, but my judgment bee;	204	Persever.	W	6
no help in God there is.	216	Psalm III	D	4
place with place must be a singular help for the right understanding	229	Priest 4		8
that there is no help for a fault done, but confession.	240	Priest 10		35
not to exceed his bounds, but in tickle cases to call in help.	260	Priest 23		36
as they may be an help, and a recreation to more divine studies,	261	Priest 23		10
when we had sinned beyond any help in heaven or earth, then thou	288	Priest		26
and withall help many others, who will take this into consideration,	291	Cornaro		13
the Physicians told me that yet there was one help for me,	292	Cornaro		3
to that exigent, that there would be no help for me, but Death,	292	Cornaro		15
beleeve that old wine should hurt my stomack, and new should help it;	297	Cornaro		33
who not onely as a friend doth visit thee, but help thee!	298	Cornaro		9
aim in all things, how I may help others to the furthest of my power.	301	Cornaro		8
By renouncing the help of humane learning in the studying	314	Valdesso	V	3
I need not their help, to reprove the vanity of those many	363	Letters		6
HELPE				
Lyes round about us to helpe out the story,	212	Bohemia	D	26
if we believe not, no vertue shall helpe us.	311	Valdesso		26
Helpe thy selfe, and God will helpe thee.	339	Proverbs		537
He that is fallen cannot helpe him that is downe.	346	Proverbs		753
If thou thy selfe canst doe it, attend no others helpe or hand.	348	Proverbs		813
HELPED				
that I was exceedingly helped, and by continuance thereof,	292	Cornaro		35
HELPER				
or whether he needed a helper, and who was that helper.	257	Priest 21		9
or whether he needed a helper, and who was that helper.	257	Priest 21		10
HELPES				
One graine fills not a sacke, but helpes his fellowes.	328	Proverbs		226
HELPING				
and helping and cherishing the Answerer, by making the Question very	256	Priest 21		13
but to have the skill of healing a wound, or helping the sick.	260	Priest 23		32
Three helping one another, beare the burthen of sixe.	325	Proverbs		135
HELPS				
But these he helps not without some testimony, except the evidence	245	Priest 12		21
having ever besides two great helps and powerfull perswaders on his	263	Priest 24		15
and either helps them in particular, or hath generall Propositions	276	Priest 32		4
Musick helps not the tooth-ach.	339	Proverbs		532
I hope I shall get this place without all your London helps,	370	Letters		8
HEMISPHERES				
A Balsome are for both the Hemispheres:	27	Sacrifice		26
HEN				
Hee that comes of a hen must scrape.	335	Proverbs		415
HENCE				
That three yeares hence, if I survive,	36	Thanksgvng		32
For when thou dost depart from hence,	56	Temper 2		11
This world of wo? hence all ye clouds, away,	108	Home		33
Cry out, Get hence,	136	Ephes.		14
Or ten yeares hence,	186	Death		6
Hence it comes, that a Physician, when he cometh to visit his	297	Cornaro		15
HENCEFORTH				
Henceforth repose; your work is done.	64	Even-song		20
Henceforth shall only pierce the Skies,	214	Convert	D	14
Henceforth in Sacred Flames shall Burn,	214	Convert	D	19
HENRY				
On Henry Danvers earl of Danby. EPITAPH	208	H. Danvers	D	T
To my dear brother, Mr. Henry Herbert, at Paris.	366	Letters		27
I understand by a Letter from my Brother Henry, that he hath bought	366	Letters		29
To my very dear brother Sir Henry Herbert, at Court.	376	Letters		25
To my deere brother, Sir Henry Herbert, at Court.	377	Letters		32
Sir Henry H: of the blessed Success, that God had given us,	378	Letters		31
To Sir Henry Herbert.	379	Letters		T
To Mrs Elizabeth Danvers Mr Henry Danvers wife twenty shillings,	383	G.H.'s Will		12
HER (see also hir)				
She loseth three for one; her soul, rest, fame.	13	Ch.-Porch		174
And are her sureties, ere they are a friends.	17	Ch.-Porch		282
She and her children shall be thine.	35	Thanksgvng		24
My flesh get on; yet let her sister	44	H. Bapt.2		12
My soul bid nothing, but preserve her wealth:	44	H. Bapt.2		13
And made her youth and fiercenesse seek thy face.	46	Afflict.1		18
Her houshold to me, and I should be just.	48	Afflict.1		60
All her invention on thine Altar lay,	54	Love 2		7
While that my soul repairs to her devotion,	64	Ch.-monum.		1
The fearfull Hare her eares, which by their law	70	Humilitie		11
The fearfull Hare her eares, which by the law	70	Humilitie	W	11
How well her name an Army doth present,	77	Anagram		1
That her fine cobwebs did support the frame,	84	The World		3
Her own destruction and his danger wears.	85	Vanitie 1		14
Who made the arbour: this exceeds her wit.	101	Miserie		58
Cavill, and claim her part and measure,	104	Obedience		12
That my free soul may use her wing,	109	Home		62

HER (cont'd)

	PAGE	TITLE		LINE
Beautie in thee takes up her place,	109	Brit. Ch.		4
And dates her letters from thy face,	109	Brit. Ch.		5
By her preferr'd,	110	Brit. Ch.		15
Hath kiss'd so long her painted shrines,	110	Brit. Ch.		16
That ev'n her face by kissing shines,	110	Brit. Ch.		17
For her reward.	110	Brit. Ch.		18
Of dressing, that her hair doth lie	110	Brit. Ch.		20
About her eares:	110	Brit. Ch.		21
While she avoids her neighbours pride,	110	Brit. Ch.		22
And with quaint metaphors her curled hair	115	Dulnesse		7
At which the Church falling upon her face	152	The Jews		9
And by that crie of her deare Lord obtain,	152	The Jews		11
With her enchanting voice.	170	Self-cond.		12
When blessed Marie wip'd her Saviours feet,	173	Marie Magd		1
And wore them for a jewell on her head,	173	Marie Magd		3
She being stain'd her self, why did she strive	173	Marie Magd		7
Why kept she not her tears for her own faults,	173	Marie Magd		9
Why kept she not her tears for her own fauts,	173	Marie Magd	V	9
To bear her filth; and that her sinnes did dash	173	Marie Magd		14
Let follie speak in her own native tongue.	177	Forerunners		27
Till all depart: so went the Church her way,	191	Ch.-Milit.		33
Till all be gone. so went the Church her way,	191	Ch.-Milit.	W	33
Gave her the highest place in all mens hearts.	191	Ch.-Milit.		50
And spent her period and prefixed time	191	Ch.-Milit.		59
Spending her period and prefixed time	191	Ch.-Milit.	W	59
Before the other. Greece being past her prime,	191	Ch.-Milit.		60
Or strength in th' other, did erect her throne.	192	Ch.-Milit.		78
Where first the Church should raise her down-cast face.	192	Ch.-Milit.		86
Giving the Church a crown to keep her state,	192	Ch.-Milit.		91
Both where and when the Church began her race,	192	Ch.-Milit.		102
Breaking her peace, and tainting her good name.	193	Ch.-Milit.		106
As Rome will one day finde unto her cost.	194	Ch.-Milit.		160
By letting in them both, pollutes her streams:	197	Ch.-Milit.		242
By letting in them both pollute her streams:	197	Ch.-Milit.	W	242
When Italie of us shall have her will,	197	Ch.-Milit.		243
And all her calender of sinnes fulfill;	197	Ch.-Milit.		244
To pay our debts, and leave her ancient place	197	Ch.-Milit.	W	256
So Sinne shall trace and dog her instantly:	197	Ch.-Milit.		260
Fouling her nest, my earth invade,	203	Even-song	W	11
Wear Venus Livery? only serve her turn?	206	Walton 1		4
in her sensitive faculty, will runne out more or lesse in her	238	Priest 9		11
sensitive faculty, will runne out more or lesse in her intellectuall.	238	Priest 9		11
and out of liberality, make her fruitfull in all good works.	238	Priest 9		33
Therefore he gives her respect both afore her servants,	238	Priest 9		36
wife is either religious, or night and day he is winning her to it.	239	Priest 10		11
stead of the qualities of the world, he requires onely three of her;	239	Priest 10		12
a trayning up of her children and mayds in the fear of God,	239	Priest 10		12
and healing of all wounds and sores with her owne hands;	239	Priest 10		15
which skill either she brought with her, or he takes care she shall	239	Priest 10		16
a providing for her family in such sort, as that neither they want	239	Priest 10		17
want a competent sustentation, nor her husband be brought in debt.	239	Priest 10		19
his wife among her neighbours is the beginner of good discourses,	240	Priest 10		27
but preferrs her garden and fields before all outlandish gums.	262	Priest 23		4
Joseph knew her not, untill shee had brought forth her first borne	318	Valdesso		12
untill shee had brought forth her first borne Sonne, as if afterwards	318	Valdesso		13
forth her first borne Sonne, as if afterwards he had knowne her:	318	Valdesso		14
The gentle Hawke halfe mans her selfe.	322	Proverbs		30
The bird loves her nest.	323	Proverbs		75
Shee spins well that breedes her children.	325	Proverbs		144
Shee spins well that breedes her child.	325	Proverbs	V	144
A journying woman speakes much of all, and all of her.	330	Proverbs		279
Little dogs start the Hare, the great get her.	341	Proverbs		593
shee had never sought her daughter there.	344	Proverbs		696
The Cow knowes not what her taile is worth, till she have lost it.	350	Proverbs		870
An old cat sports not with her prey.	355	Proverbs		1030
Take heed of a step-mother; the very name of her sufficeth.	360	Proverbs	D	1155
dare say she would make good her promise of taking five or six pound	367	Letters		2
she would make good her promise of taking five or six pound upon her,	367	Letters		3
not of her self, but upon the want of those Books which were	367	Letters		4
he refusing to doe hath given her occasion to protest shee will never	368	Letters		22
to threaten him that if he will not give her halfe her estate to live	368	Letters		24
that if he will not give her halfe her estate to live on by her selfe	368	Letters		24
halfe her estate to live on by her selfe (for shee desires no more)	368	Letters		24
first, how her health fares, next, whether my peace be yet made	371	Letters		8
whether my peace be yet made with her concerning my unkind departure.	371	Letters		9
make it plain to her, that I loved her even in my departure,	371	Letters		11
that I loved her even in my departure, in looking to her Son,	371	Letters		12
loved her even in my departure, in looking to her Son, and my charge.	371	Letters		12
she is not disposed to spend her eyesight on a piece of paper,	371	Letters		13
spend her eyesight on a piece of paper, or else I had wrote to her;	371	Letters		14
To his Mother, in her sickness.	372	Letters		T
having none to doe it but her school-mistresse, and you know what	375	Letters		25
except my cousin Bett take pitty of her, which yet at that distance	375	Letters		29
If you could think of taking her, as once you did, surely it were	375	Letters		31
it were a great good deed, and I would have her conveyed to you.	375	Letters		32
Yet, truly if you take her not, I am thinking to do it,	375	Letters		35
of your Mother upon you, and cause all her wishes, diligence,	377	Letters		5
in signing 100 lib. with her own hands (& promising to get her Son	379	Letters		2
own hands (& promising to get her Son to doe as much) with some	379	Letters		3
but he told her Grace, that he would by no meanes do so,	379	Letters		6

	PAGE	TITLE	LINE
HER (cont'd)			
then I leave to my servant Elizabeth her dubble wages given her,	382	G.H.'s Will	22
then I leave to my servant Elizabeth her dubble wages given her,	382	G.H.'s Will	23
three pound more besides that which is due to her, to Ann I leave	382	G.H.'s Will	23
HERALDRIE			
Written in dustie heraldrie and lines;	65	Ch.-monum.	9
HERAULD			
Onely a herauld, who that way doth passe,	14	Ch.-Porch	197
HERB			
An herb destill'd, and drunk, may dwell next doore,	61	Praise 1	13
Is there an herb for that? O that thy care	119	Providence	75
And if an herb hath power, what have the starres?	119	Providence	77
HERBALL			
reading one Book of Phisick, having one Herball by him.	261	Priest 23	5
HERBERT			
untill the Book grow to a compleat Pastorall. GEO. HERBERT.	224	Priest	17
by Lud. Cornarus, Translated into English by Mr. George Herbert.	291	Cornaro	T
a letter written by MR. GEORGE HERBERT to his friend the Translator	304	Valdesso	T
Selected By Mr George Herbert, Late Orator	356	Proverbs D	T
and after my manner, Your most obedient Servant, GEORGE HERBERT.	364	Letters	5
for I am sure you love Your faithfullest Servant, GEORGE HERBERT.	365	Letters	27
mee in your letters, for I am your ever loving brother, G. HERBERT.	366	Letters	23
To my dear brother, Mr. Henry Herbert, at Paris.	366	Letters	27
and yet still grow upon Your humblest Servant, GEORGE HERBERT.	367	Letters	17
favour to mee in pardoning Your most indebted kinsman GEORGE HERBERT.	369	Letters	6
I have both time and work to be Your extreme Servant, GEORGE HERBERT.	370	Letters	16
and paper enough, yet am I Your readiest Servant, GEORGE HERBERT.	370	Letters	34
will pardon the haste of Your humblest Servant, GEORGE HERBERT.	371	Letters	21
most heartily, affectionate Brother, and Servant, GEORGE HERBERT.	372	Letters	10
accept the good meaning of, Your most obedient Son, GEORGE HERBERT.	374	Letters	33
So prayes Your ever loving brother, G. HERBERT.	376	Letters	22
To my very dear brother Sir Henry Herbert, at Court.	376	Letters	25
Your most faithful Servant in Christ Jesu, GEORGE HERBERT.	377	Letters	11
every good worke, to the joy of your ever loving brother, G. HERBERT.	377	Letters	29
To my deere brother, Sir Henry Herbert, at Court.	377	Letters	32
great Joy of Your Brother & Servant in Christ Jesus GEORGE HERBERT.	378	Letters	29
To Sir Henry Herbert.	379	Letters	T
G. HERBERT. Bemerton. My wife's and neeces' service to you.	379	Letters	28
The Will of George Herbert	382	G.H.'s Will	T
I George Herbert commending my soule and body to Almightie God that	382	G.H.'s Will	1
George Herbert (testes Nathaniell Bostocke, Elizabeth Burden)	382	G.H.'s Will	33
To Mr George Herbert one hundred pound To Mrs Beatrice Herbert forty	383	G.H.'s Will	7
George Herbert one hundred pound To Mrs Beatrice Herbert forty pound,	383	G.H.'s Will	8
To Mrs Jane Herbert tenn pound, To Mrs Danvers five pound,	383	G.H.'s Will	8
The Oration of Master George Herbert, Orator of the Universitie	441	Oration	T
HERBERT'S			
Mr Herberts reasons for Arth. Woodenoths Living with Sir John	380	Woodnoth	T
HERBS			
Then as dispersed herbs do watch a potion,	58	H.Script.2	7
Who want herbs for their wound.	76	Sunday	42
Herbs gladly cure our flesh; because that they	91	Man	23
And curious vertues both of herbs and stones?	119	Providence	74
Most herbs that grow in brooks, are hot and dry.	120	Providence	129
Yet can I mark how herbs below	162	The Search	9
or over-nourishing things, as the Israelites did eate sowre herbs:	242	Priest 10	5
and the knowing of herbs may be done at such times, as they may be	261	Priest 23	9
to know what herbs may be used in stead of drugs of the same nature,	261	Priest 23	29
esteeming that there is no spice comparable, for herbs, to rosemary,	262	Priest 23	1
Vertue now is in herbs and stones and words onely.	337	Proverbs	478
Vertue now is in stones, herbs & words only.	337	Proverbs V	478
HERCULES			
of his praise, no, not, as in past ages, those Pillars of Hercules.	442	Oration	13
HERE (see also heere)			
Write on the others, Here lies such a one.	20	Ch.-Porch	342
Avoid, profanenesse; come not here:	25	Superlim	5
Lo, here I hang, charg'd with a world of sinne,	33	Sacrifice	205
Shall not perceive, that I am here.	36	Thanksgvng	38
If thou hast giv'n it me, 'tis here.	36	Thanksgvng	44
Now I am here, what thou wilt do with me	48	Afflict.1	55
Which when I could not get, I thought it here:	50	Faith	10
Ladies, look here; this is the thankfull glasse,	58	H.Script.1	8
Thy praise too much? thou art heav'ns Lidger here,	58	H.Script.1	11
Thy praise enough? thou art heav'ns Lidger here,	58	H.Script.1 W	11
If they might mend their wages, and serve here.	59	Whitsunday	12
Here I intombe my flesh, that it betimes	64	Ch.-monum.	2
Deare flesh, while I do pray, learn here thy stemme	65	Ch.-monum.	17
Be crumbled into dust. Mark here below	65	Ch.-monum.	22
Be broken into dust. Mark here below	65	Ch.-monum. W	22
Spoil'd all the train: then saying, Here it is	71	Humilitie	27
The sunne still shineth there or here,	79	Employm.2	18
Taught me to live here so, That still one eye	85	Coloss.	7
Here below,	92	Antiphon 2	2
And here above:	92	Antiphon 2	3
Here will I smell my remnant out, and tie	94	Life	2
And here present it as my speciall deed.	104	Obedience	10
I here exclude the wrangler from thy treasure.	104	Obedience	15
I here shutt out the wrangler from thy treasure.	104	Obedience W	15
Makes beauties here;	115	Dulnesse	16
Wherefore, most sacred Spirit, I here present	117	Providence	25
Your hony drops: presse not to smell them here:	120	Providence	118
Ev'n pleasures here increase the wrong,	123	Time	21

	PAGE	TITLE		LINE
HERS				
That he might save his life, and also hers,	85	Vanitie 1		12
HERSE				
And drest his herse, while he has breath	99	Mortific.		33
HIBBERT				
Gifford tenn shillings To Anne Hibbert tenn shillings To William	383	G.H.'s Will		17
HID				
O let me, when thy roof my soul hath hid,	55	Temper 1		17
Coloss. 3. 3. Our life is hid with Christ in God.	84	Coloss.		T
The other Hid and doth obliquely bend.	84	Coloss.		4
Thou hast hid metals: man may take them thence;	119	Providence		81
Love and a Cough cannot be hid.	322	Proverbs		49
HIDDEN				
What open force, or hidden CHARM	133	Paradise		4
Where is my God? what hidden place	163	The Search		29
and what hidden properties it hath, what meat and drink agrees best	297	Cornaro		27
What Physician could have discovered these hidden qualities to me,	297	Cornaro		34
There is great force hidden in a sweet command.	341	Proverbs		589
HIDE				
To hide my dust, then thee to hold.	45	Nature		18
If still the sunne should hide his face,	60	Grace		5
If the Sunn still should hide his face,	60	Grace	W	5
His dearely-earned pearl, which God did hide	85	Vanitie 1		10
To hide thy shame: for thou hast cast a bone	156	Assurance		39
nor can I hide his sacred will.	215	Psalm II	D	16
You cannot hide an eele in a sacke.	346	Proverbs		762
You cannot hide a needle in a sacke.	346	Proverbs	V	762
HIDEOUS				
Death, thou wast once an uncouth hideous thing,	185	Death		1
HIDES				
The corne hides it self in the snow, as an old man in furrs.	329	Proverbs		241
HIGH				
Pitch thy behaviour low, thy projects high;	19	Ch.-Porch		331
Because the raging waters still are high:	29	Sacrifice		95
A king my title is, prefixt on high;	34	Sacrifice		233
Is best to celebrate this most high day.	41	Easter		12
The heav'ns are not too high,	53	Antiphon 1		3
Should aim and shoot at that which Is on high:	85	Coloss.		8
If born on high,	111	Vanitie 2		13
Man is the worlds high Priest: he doth present	117	Providence		13
And so my sinnes ascend three stories high,	122	Sinnes rd.		14
Closets are halls to them; and hearts, high-wayes.	126	Confession		18
Starres have their storms, ev'n in a high degree,	132	The Storm		7
Look high and low;	144	Discharge		4
And rule on high,	150	Longing		57
So high a torture? Is such poyson bought?	155	Assurance		3
Of lowly matter for high uses meet,	161	Priesthood		35
True beautie dwells on high: ours is a flame	177	Forerunners		28
But these are high perfections:	185	The Elixer	W	21
O who will show me those delights on high?	188	Heaven		1
offer to God on high	217	Psalm IV	D	18
Yea, he my prayer from on high	220	Psalm VI	D	23
For their sakes, Lord, return on high,	221	Psalm VII	D	27
and high thy Glory raise.	221	Psalm VII	D	28
of him that is on high.	222	Psalm VII	D	64
which also I will set as high as I can, since hee shoots higher that	224	Priest		8
Curiosity in prying into high speculative and unprofitable questions,	238	Priest 9		18
other spirituall wickednesses in high places doth the Parson fear,	238	Priest 9		20
or in cases of high consequence, as establishing of inheritances:	260	Priest 23		21
of the ground, and sometimes I go up high stairs and hills on foot.	300	Cornaro		36
It is high time now that I should be no more a burden to you,	367	Letters		12
HIGH-WAYES				
Closets are halls to them; and hearts, high-wayes.	126	Confession		18
HIGHER				
Shoots higher much then he that means a tree.	19	Ch.-Porch		334
Faith sets me higher in his glorie.	50	Faith		20
Let not thy higher Court remove,	56	Temper 2		15
Thy flight is higher, as thy birth.	76	Sunday		59
But England in the higher victorie:	192	Ch.-Milit.		90
since hee shoots higher that threatens the Moon, then hee that aims	224	Priest		9
and that our feet may be like hindes feet ever climbing up higher,	236	Priest 8		30
may be like hindes feet ever climbing up higher, and higher unto him.	236	Priest 8		30
Parson considering that virginity is a higher state then Matrimony,	236	Priest 9		32
or untimely desire of promotion to an higher state, or place,	238	Priest 9		15
if they be of higher quality, they commonly are quick, and sensible,	248	Priest 14		18
sake, and to make his higher purposes slip the more easily.	249	Priest 14		12
he carryes them higher, even somtimes to a forgetting of themselves,	267	Priest 26		19
The higher the Ape goes, the more he shewes his taile.	346	Proverbs		745
Amen 1. Higher opportunities of doeing good are to be preferred	380	Woodnoth		3
but to chuse a higher work, as God gives me higher thoughts,	381	Woodnoth		25
as God gives me higher thoughts, & to rise with his favours,	381	Woodnoth		25
HIGHEST				
It is thy highest art	45	Nature		5
As a great Clerk, and reach the highest stature.	50	Faith		30
May guard it safe beyond the highest starr.	66	Ch.-lock	W	12
Ordain'd the highest to be best;	79	Employm.2		13
His eyes dismount the highest starre:	91	Man		21
For things misshapen, things of highest use.	191	Ch.-Milit.		46
Gave her the highest place in all mens hearts.	191	Ch.-Milit.		50
His highest was an ox or crocodile,	193	Ch.-Milit.		122
When winds and waves rise highest, I am sure,	439	Walton 6		3

HIGHEST (cont'd)	PAGE	TITLE		LINE
but tremble in your highest mirth.	216	Psalm II	D	28
And because the two highest points of Life, wherein a Christian is	227	Priest 3		3
and that the Ministry requires the best and highest things,	236	Priest 9		33
HIGHLY				
The Countrey Parson values Catechizing highly:	255	Priest 21		1
the Priests Benedicite, and his holy water were over highly valued;	286	Priest 36		16
HIGHT				
In hight of their transgression,	219	Psalm V	D	31
HILL				
For wealth without contentment, climbes a hill	11	Ch.-Porch		111
Which spit it forth like the Sicilian hill.	122	Sinnes rd.		8
And meet the rest on Sions hill.	138	The Size		24
I travell'd on, seeing the hill, where lay	141	Pilgrimage		1
At length I got unto the gladsome hill,	142	Pilgrimage		19
My hill was further: so I flung away,	142	Pilgrimage		31
on Sion His most Holy hill,	215	Psalm II	D	14
me from his holy hill:	216	Psalm III	D	10
times from action, standing on a hill, and considering his Flock,	264	Priest 26		4
Praise a hill, but keepe below.	338	Proverbs		488
HILLS				
She on the hills, which wantonly	110	Brit. Ch.		13
The hills with health abound; the vales with store;	119	Providence		95
of the ground, and sometimes I go up high stairs and hills on foot.	300	Cornaro		36
Some times of the yeare I enjoy the pleasure of the Euganean hills,	301	Cornaro		17
HIM				
A verse may finde him, who a sermon flies,	6	Ch.-Porch		5
Whom when he thinks he hath, the devil hath him.	13	Ch.-Porch		166
Then he's the sport: the mirth then in him rests,	16	Ch.-Porch		251
That suites him best, of whom thy speech is heard.	18	Ch.-Porch		294
For so thou dost thy self and him a pleasure:	18	Ch.-Porch		296
Another chafe, may warm him at his fire,	19	Ch.-Porch		314
God reckons for him, counts the favour his:	21	Ch.-Porch		381
If thou mislike him, thou conceiv'st him not.	23	Ch.-Porch		428
How know'st thou, but thy sinnes made him miscarrie?	24	Ch.-Porch		440
God sent him, whatsoe're he be: O tarry,	24	Ch.-Porch		442
And love him for his Master: his condition,	24	Ch.-Porch		443
Though it be ill, makes him no ill Physician.	24	Ch.-Porch		444
'Gainst him, who seeks not life, but is the meek	28	Sacrifice		58
I him obey, who all things else command:	29	Sacrifice		83
In him to do themselves a courtesie:	30	Sacrifice		114
They buffet him, and box him as they list,	30	Sacrifice	W	129
Who Crucifie him, crie with one strong shout.	32	Sacrifice		186
Who would know Sinne, let him repair	37	The Agonie		7
Who knows not Love, let him assay	37	The Agonie		13
Did set again abroach; then let him say	37	The Agonie		15
And make a suit unto him, to afford	40	Redemption		3
In heaven at his manour I him sought:	40	Redemption		5
Sought him accordingly in great resorts;	40	Redemption		10
Sought him in Citties, Theaters, resorts	40	Redemption	W	10
Of theeves and murderers: there I him espied,	40	Redemption		13
With him mayst rise:	41	Easter		4
And bring by Faith all things to him?	49	Faith		4
Faith puts me there with him, who sweetly took	50	Faith		23
My nature on him, with the danger	50	Faith	W	24
And praise him who did make and mend our eies.	54	Love 2		14
Yet studies them, not him by whom they be.	63	Mattens		16
Hath some good in him, all agree.	63	Sinne 2		3
Yet in thy temple thou dost him afford	67	Windows		3
But though men fail him, yet his part doth play.	73	Constancie		30
Of him, who dy'd to part	74	The Starre		23
He that is weary, let him sit.	78	Employm.2		1
With him, whose will	79	Employm.2		12
Some fruit for him that dressed me.	79	Employm.2		25
Of pleasures brought me to him, readie there	81	Christmas		7
The other winds towards Him, whose happie birth	84	Coloss.		6
Is much more sure to meet with him, then one	87	Lent		38
He treads down that which doth befriend him,	92	Man		45
When sicknesse makes him pale and wan.	92	Man		46
Another to attend him.	92	Man		48
Him we touch;	93	Antiphon 2		14
And him we take.	93	Antiphon 2		15
Which shall befriend him at the house of death.	98	Mortific.		18
Which shall befriend him at the houre of death.	98	Mortific.	W	18
Which shall convey him to the house of death.	98	Mortific.		30
Which shall convey him to the place of death.	98	Mortific.	W	30
Bid him but temper his excesse;	100	Miserie		9
Man cannot serve thee; let him go,	101	Miserie		43
Give him his dirt to wallow in all night:	101	Miserie		46
Making him free	101	Miserie	W	47
But sinne hath fool'd him. Now he is	102	Miserie		73
To raise him to the glimpse of blisse:	102	Miserie		75
Thy Saviour comes, and with him mirth:	112	Dawning		4
And made him Secretarie of thy praise.	117	Providence		8
Are rul'd by him, and taught to serve his trade.	119	Providence		92
All thou hast giv'n him heretofore	123	Gratefulnes		7
And calls him coward, who for fear of sinne	127	Giddinesse		7
But much more him I must adore,	128	Bunch Gr.		26
To him I brought a dish of fruit one day,	129	Love unkn.		6
Who took the debt upon him. Truly, Friend,	130	Love unkn.		61
Wherefore be cheer'd, and praise him to the full	130	Love unkn.		68

HIM (cont'd)

	PAGE	TITLE	LINE
Who heare not him, but quickly heare	134	The Method	27
Then will I trust, said I, in him alone.	143	Holdfast	5
Nay, ev'n to trust in him, was also his:	143	Holdfast	6
That ran upon him with a spear.	151	The Bag	26
Who changeth all things, as him pleaseth best.	159	Jos.coat	4
Let us (said he) poure on him all we can:	159	The Pulley	3
Yet let him keep the rest,	160	The Pulley	16
Let him be rich and wearie, that at least,	160	The Pulley	18
If goodnesse leade him not, yet wearinesse	160	The Pulley	19
May tosse him to my breast.	160	The Pulley	20
As serve him up, who all the world commands:	161	Priesthood	26
Their hands convey him, who conveys their hands.	161	Priesthood	28
Whose grief allows him musick and a ryme:	164	Grief	17
We turn upon him in a sense most true:	168	The Sonne	12
We him in glorie call, The Sonne of Man.	168	The Sonne	14
Thy curse being laid on him, makes thee accurst.	169	Dial.-Anth	6
That so in purenesse thou mayst him adore,	170	Water-crs.	9
To make him clean, who could not be defil'd?	173	Marie Magd	8
In him I am well drest.	174	Aaron	15
And be in him new drest.	174	Aaron	20
And if I please him, I write fine and wittie.	176	Forerunners	12
And hurt thy self, and him that sings the note.	176	Forerunners	24
Him I view,	182	Banquet	47
Listens behinde him, and allows some light,	191	Ch.-Milit.	32
Listens behinde him, and gives them some light,	191	Ch.-Milit. W	32
Him in his members, who for him was slain.	192	Ch.-Milit.	70
What wretchednesse can give him any room,	193	Ch.-Milit.	117
He left behinde him garrisons of sinnes	193	Ch.-Milit.	125
To credit him, and to discredit those	193	Ch.-Milit.	137
To credit him, and so discredit those	193	Ch.-Milit. W	137
Who after him should braver truths disclose.	194	Ch.-Milit.	138
Nero and others lodg'd him bravely there,	194	Ch.-Milit.	141
Put him in trust to rule the Romane sphere.	194	Ch.-Milit.	142
I saw him in his studie, where he sate	194	Ch.-Milit.	165
A gown and pen became him wondrous well:	194	Ch.-Milit.	167
Choke him, let him say no more,	199	L'Envoy	11
Choke him, let him speak no more,	199	L'Envoy W	11
Nor yet thy eloquence here keep him still,	439	Walton 5	3
Reade him there, and I have done.	208	J. Danvers D	16
Are shed for him, dissolve thy frame,	209	H. Danvers D	7
Aided by him, I will not fear	216	Psalm III D	13
O learn to stand in awe of him,	217	Psalm IV D	15
If I have ill rewarded him	221	Psalm VII D	11
Yea, have not oft deliver'd him	221	Psalm VII D	13
Let him pursue and take my soul,	221	Psalm VII D	17
yea, let him to the Clay	221	Psalm VII D	18
His arrows are ordain'd 'gainst him	222	Psalm VII D	47
of him that is on high.	222	Psalm VII D	64
Being desirous (thorow the Mercy of GOD) to please Him,	224	Priest	2
That the way to please him, is to feed my Flocke diligently	224	Priest	4
it is a good strife to go as farre as wee can in pleasing of him,	224	Priest	12
he that ruleth, let him do it with diligence, &c.	226	Priest 2	7
of himself, for all the purposes which God hath ordained him.	227	Priest 3	10
that when death takes him, as the Jewes and Judas did Christ,	227	Priest 3	32
neither will they beleeve him in the pulpit, whom they cannot trust	228	Priest 3	7
the grace of God in himself, and what the Holy Spirit teacheth him;	229	Priest 4	21
his servants, to whom he hath revealed his Truth, as well as to him;	229	Priest 4	23
yet every mans own is fittest, readyest, and most savory to him.	230	Priest 5	5
that have glorified him as wel as now, and that he shall have so	231	Priest 6	35
and apply our powers to the service of him, that gives them.	232	Priest 6	6
that not any ill will draws him to it, but the debt and obligation	232	Priest 6	18
and sayings of others, according as his text invites him;	233	Priest 7	13
since we are here by him, and without him could not be here.	234	Priest 7	30
are but two devouring elements, fire, and water, he hath both in him;	234	Priest 7	34
the same affection which made him not profit before, making him then	235	Priest 7	13
making him then weary, and so he grows from not relishing,	235	Priest 7	14
That nothing befall him unworthy of that Majesty before which he is	235	Priest 8	23
that how or whenever he punish him, it be not in his Ministry:	235	Priest 8	27
the hour calls, with his family attending him, he goes to Church,	236	Priest 8	3
may be like hindes feet ever climbing up higher, and higher unto him.	236	Priest 8	30
Let him communicate the thing often by prayer unto God,	237	Priest 9	5
unto God, and as his grace shall direct him, so let him proceed.	237	Priest 9	6
unto God, and as his grace shall direct him, so let him proceed.	237	Priest 9	7
therefore thinkes it not enough for him to observe the fasting dayes	237	Priest 9	22
and the dayly prayers enjoyned him by auctority, which he observeth	237	Priest 9	23
like mortall enemies, may sometimes disquiet him likewise;	238	Priest 9	10
not his affection found out a fit wife for him, whose humble,	238	Priest 9	28
reserving so much of the affaires, as serve for a diversion for him;	239	Priest 9	1
but giving him the prerogative of his Fathers profession,	239	Priest 10	31
and till they have learned them, makes them kneel by him;	241	Priest 10	4
or was not fit for him to do, by taking both sorts of food into them,	241	Priest 10	32
whom he sometimes purposely takes home with him, setting them close	243	Priest 11	11
takes home with him, setting them close by him, and carving for them,	243	Priest 11	11
hee hath them all with him, because countrey people are very	243	Priest 11	20
although we should love him onely for his own sake, yet out of his	243	Priest 11	30
making a hook of his Charity, causeth them still to depend on him;	244	Priest 12	32
and sees them labour in thanking of him, he exacts of them to let him	245	Priest 12	31
thanking of him, he exacts of them to let him alone, and say rather,	245	Priest 12	32
for if he be a plaine countryman, he reproves him plainly;	248	Priest 14	17
our Saviours rule, and to take my brother aside, and reprove him;	248	Priest 14	28

HIM (cont'd)	PAGE	TITLE	LINE
the afflicted, though they can, and otherwise ought to come to him.	249	Priest 15	17
carrying it about with him as fully, as if he had begot his whole	250	Priest 16	9
he hateth him not as an officer, but pityes him as a Father:	250	Priest 16	11
he hateth him not as an officer, but pityes him as a Father:	250	Priest 16	12
yet hee gives him not over, but is long before hee proceede . .	250	Priest 16	17
when a just occasion calleth him out of his Parish (which he	250	Priest 17	23
being all his joy, and thought) leaveth not his Ministry behind him;	251	Priest 17	1
and with those he overtakes or that overtake him, hee begins good	251	Priest 17	3
wishing him to informe his guests thereof, that if any be willing	251	Priest 17	11
or other relations give him any authority over the Family, . .	251	Priest 17	16
to do all the good he can, moves him to say thus and thus. . .	251	Priest 17	32
and therefore not for him, who is hearty, and true in all his wayes,	253	Priest 19	1
as being the servant of him, in whom there was no guile. . .	253	Priest 19	2
to his Diocesan, honouring him both in word, and behaviour, . .	253	Priest 19	7
and resorting unto him in any difficulty, either in his studies or in	253	Priest 19	8
Correspondence with all the neighbouring Pastours round about him,	253	Priest 19	16
and debt of neighbourhood to all the Parishes which are neer him.	253	Priest 19	22
finde any reading in anothers Bible, he provides him one of his own.	254	Priest 20	12
he gives him a tester for it, if the giver be fit to receive it;	254	Priest 20	13
such gifts, he sends him a good book, or easeth him in his Tithes,	254	Priest 20	15
or easeth him in his Tithes, telling him when he hath forgotten it,	254	Priest 20	16
him in his Tithes, telling him when he hath forgotten it, This I do,	254	Priest 20	16
which exceedingly delights him as by way of exercise upon himself,	255	Priest 21	11
with comparisons, and making much even of a word of truth from him.	256	Priest 21	15
making what hee knows to serve him in that which he knows not:	256	Priest 21	38
He asked him again, what he would do, if he were in a ditch?	257	Priest 21	4
as being not only to receive God, but to break, and administer him.	257	Priest 22	30
in any Controversie, that they should resort to him as their Judge.	259	Priest 23	33
Yet when ever any controversie is brought to him, he never decides it	260	Priest 23	8
three or four of the ablest of the Parish to hear the cause with him,	260	Priest 23	10
neighbour Phisician, and entertaines him for the Cure of his Parish.	261	Priest 23	1
as may be of much use to him both for himself, and others. . .	261	Priest 23	3
reading one Book of Phisick, having one Herball by him. . .	261	Priest 23	5
Now both the reading of him, and the knowing of herbs may be done	261	Priest 23	9
and to give him power so to fit his discourse to them, that it may	262	Priest 24	23
in his behaviour and carriage towards him, not avoyding his company,	263	Priest 25	27
neither doth he esteem him for an enemy, but as a brother still,	263	Priest 25	29
and makes so much the more of him, as before he alienated himselfe;	263	Priest 25	34
or not in some proportion to Gods blessing upon him, is covetous.	265	Priest 26	7
he gives him those freer rules:	267	Priest 26	18
to the Apostles rule, he endeavours that none shall despise him;	268	Priest 28	17
then when any despises him, he takes it either in an humble way,	269	Priest 28	5
shewing that reproaches touch him no more, then a stone thrown	269	Priest 28	7
and dishonour him with those mouths, which he continually fils,	269	Priest 28	10
yet if God give him not the Grace to use, and utter this well,	272	Priest 30	2
sit down at this world, God bids him sell it, and purchase a better:	272	Priest 30	7
his Father bids him throw it away, and he will give him the gold	272	Priest 30	10
and he will give him the gold for it, which the Child utterly	272	Priest 30	11
(who playes his part sometimes in drawing Gods Servants from him,	272	Priest 31	17
and put him out of his station, and to inlarge the perplexity,	272	Priest 31	34
omission thereof upon just occasion ought by no means to trouble him.	273	Priest 31	7
or beseeching him, that whenever he repaires to his house, . .	273	Priest 31	25
some scoffing ruffian, who is likely to deride him for his paines:	273	Priest 31	29
when his occasions carry him abroad, or bring strangers to him,	274	Priest 32	7
or bring strangers to him, he may be the better armed to encounter	274	Priest 32	7
inabling him with power to do good, and to restrain all those,	276	Priest 32	14
all those, who else might both trouble him and the whole State.	276	Priest 32	15
When none of these occasions call him abroad, every morning that hee	277	Priest 32	15
Or let him travel into Germany, and France, and observing . .	278	Priest 32	8
and knows what recovered him, is a Physitian so far as he meetes	278	Priest 33	26
and the spirit, and to worship him in truth, and spirit. . .	279	Priest 33	17
and this as the more faulty in him, so the more glorious in God.	283	Priest 34	21
and goes with him to the other, and all dine or sup together.	284	Priest 35	20
his preaching, The Lord (saith he) reward him according to his works.	285	Priest 36	34
when the other gives him just opportunity, by speaking any good,	286	Priest 36	23
a reverence, and makes him esteemed according to his Profession.	286	Priest 36	24
so neither is he that defames him, whom the Law would have defamed,	287	Priest 37	28
for an apple once we lost our God, and still lose him for no more;	288	Priest	19
even for those that derided him then, and still despise him.	288	Priest	30
and windes and labours did little hurt him, because in his meats	294	Cornaro	7
the one whereof was, He that will eat much, let him eat little;	295	Cornaro	34
and when he hath cured him, commends this also to him, if he will	297	Cornaro	17
hath cured him, commends this also to him, if he will live in health.	297	Cornaro	18
That I have both given God a Temple, and men to worship him in it:	301	Cornaro	32
there are some things which I like not in him, as my fragments will	304	Valdesso	16
for which I doe so love him, that were there nothing else, . .	305	Valdesso	7
with such syncerity and efficacy, that it makes him godly, righteous,	309	Valdesso	6
hath read it, but keepes it by him, and reads it againe and againe,	310	Valdesso	28
God affectionately and fervently to send him the light of his spirit,	312	Valdesso	17
which may be unto him as the sunne to a Travellour in his journey,	312	Valdesso	18
and that by restraining him from what he would not have him doe.	313	Valdesso	22
and that by restraining him from what he would not have him doe.	313	Valdesso	23
in the point of Resurrection he agreed with them, and they with him.	316	Valdesso	10
I doe not then bid him goe away but rather stay longer, . .	318	Valdesso	15
that I may speak with him or doe some thing else when I doe come.	318	Valdesso	16
All is well with him, who is beloved of his neighbours. . .	321	Proverbs	10
All is well to him, that is loved of his neighbours. . . .	321	Proverbs V	10
Who hath none to still him, may weepe out his eyes. . . .	321	Proverbs	17
If yee would know a knave, give him a staffe.	321	Proverbs	19
Let not him that feares feathers come among wild-foule. . .	322	Proverbs	48

HIM (cont'd)	PAGE	TITLE		LINE
Hee that sendes a foole, means to follow him.	322	Proverbs		51
When a dog is a drowning, every one offers him drink.	323	Proverbs		77
He that will learne to pray, let him goe to Sea.	323	Proverbs		84
He who will learne to pray, let him goe to Sea.	323	Proverbs	V	84
He that gives thee a Capon, give him the leg and the wing.	324	Proverbs		109
Hee that lives ill, feare follcwes him.	324	Proverbs		110
Though the Mastiffe be gentle, yet bite him not by the lippe.	325	Proverbs		132
Though the Mastiffe be gentile, yet bite him not by the lippe.	325	Proverbs	V	132
from him that saies nothing, for ever.	326	Proverbs		164
Send a wise man on an errand, and say nothing unto him.	328	Proverbs		217
The Fox knowes much, but more he that catcheth him.	330	Proverbs		280
The Lyon is not so fierce as they paint him.	330	Proverbs		289
Hee wrongs not an old man that steales his supper from him.	331	Proverbs		311
He that hath no hony in his pot, let him have it in his mouth.	333	Proverbs		360
The horse thinkes one thing, and he that sadles him another.	334	Proverbs		387
Who likes not the drinke, God deprives him of bread.	334	Proverbs		394
Hee that hath one hogge makes him fat,	336	Proverbs		433
and hee that hath one son makes him a foole.	336	Proverbs		433
Hee who hath but one sonne makes him fat,	336	Proverbs	V	433
The first service a child doth his father is to make him foolish.	337	Proverbs		463
let him be wise in the punishment.	340	Proverbs		555
let him not put them on his head.	340	Proverbs		567
Before you make a friend, eate a bushell of salt with him.	342	Proverbs		624
Mention not a halter in the house of him that was hanged.	343	Proverbs		671
If a good man thrive, all thrive with him.	344	Proverbs		695
God provides for him that trusteth.	345	Proverbs		728
He that will not have peace, God gives him warre.	345	Proverbs		729
To him that will, waies are not wanting.	345	Proverbs		730
None is so wise, but the foole overtakes him.	345	Proverbs		734
None is so wise, but that the foole overtakes him.	345	Proverbs	V	734
He that is fallen cannot helpe him that is downe.	346	Proverbs		753
Of him that speakes ill, consider the life more then the words.	346	Proverbs		761
Of him that speakes ill, consider the life more then the word.	346	Proverbs	V	761
He that feares leaves, let him not goe into the wood.	346	Proverbs		768
Who hastens a glutton choakes him.	349	Proverbs		858
He that hath not the craft, let him shut up shop.	349	Proverbs		860
Hee that would be a Gentleman, let him goe to an assault.	350	Proverbs		878
but the patient owes nothing to him but a little mony.	351	Proverbs		921
mountaines to him seeme valleys.	354	Proverbs		997
The horse that drawes after him his halter,	359	Proverbs	D	1120
Wo be to him that reads but one book.	360	Proverbs	D	1146
Trust no friend with that you need fear him if he were your enemy.	361	Proverbs	D	1169
The Divell never assailes a man, except he find him	361	Proverbs	D	1176
to those busnesses which justly excuse him from writing at this time,	367	Letters		31
untill they have satisfied him also concerning the fishing which	368	Letters		9
that the Hollanders should pay him tribute out of their fishing.	368	Letters		13
& shee being at London sent for him (as shee sayes) to make peace	368	Letters		20
being at London sent for him (as shee sayes) to make peace with him,	368	Letters		21
given her occasion to protest shee will never speake with him againe,	368	Letters		23
& to threaten him that if he will not give her halfe her estate	368	Letters		23
shee desires no more) shee will find friends to compell him to it.	368	Letters		25
who because of his importunities gave him a reward, but not so great	368	Letters		32
which some observing who heard the interdiction denounced to him,	368	Letters		37
and I have a strong opinion of him, that if he can do me a courtesie,	369	Letters		22
Sir send the Letter you receive from him to me as soon as you can,	370	Letters		6
but, I have wrote him back, that this dignity, hath no such	370	Letters		21
and therefore I desire him to send me a direct answer in his next	370	Letters		25
knows also that my solliciting him has been much, and my tears many	372	Letters		2
I wrote to him that I would have both or neither;	375	Letters		12
a much better Paymaster then my self, even him, whome we both serve:	378	Letters		3
for which I humbly thank him, & am so far from giving you cause,	378	Letters		9
sent my Letters, to your Brother, investing him, in all that I have.	379	Letters		20
to be without dores with him, is no ill company.	381	Woodnoth		3
HIMSELF				
O what were man, might he himself misplace!	7	Ch.-Porch		23
Is outlawd by himself: all kinde of ill	7	Ch.-Porch		33
Is outlawd by himself: all kinds of ill	7	Ch.-Porch	W	33
Who breaks his own bond, forfeiteth himself:	11	Ch.-Porch		119
Who fears to do ill, sets himself to task:	11	Ch.-Porch		125
Who keeps no guard upon himself, is slack,	12	Ch.-Porch		139
And spares himself, but would his taylor chide.	13	Ch.-Porch		180
To work for two, who brought himself to thrall.	17	Ch.-Porch		286
To work for two, that brought himself to thrall.	17	Ch.-Porch	W	286
Which to himself he did denie:	63	Even-song		6
He that by seeking hath himself once found,	69	Content		35
To God, his neighbour, and himself most true:	72	Constancie		3
Himself the candle hold.	81	Christmas		26
Findes himself there, and seeks to rise.	96	Charms & K		12
Doth not refrain unto himself alone,	117	Providence		18
Ev'n God himself, being pressed for my sake.	128	Bunch Gr.		28
Ev'n God himself: wherefore she was not loth,	173	Marie Magd		15
For God himself vouchsafes to know	215	Psalm I	D	21
the Lord himself shall them deride:	215	Psalm II	D	10
But know the Lord himself doth chuse	217	Psalm IV	D	11
For God himself hath heard my cry;	220	Psalm VI	D	21
shall he himself be caught.	222	Psalm VII	D	56
that he may be an absolute Master and commander of himself,	227	Priest 3		9
into which if he come, he prostitutes himself both to shame, and sin,	227	Priest 3		25
of darknesse, he disableth himself of authority to reprove them:	227	Priest 3		27
know of the Doctrine, John 7. and assuring himself, that wicked men,	228	Priest 4		30

HIMSELF (cont'd)	PAGE	TITLE	LINE
as to neglect the grace of God in himself, and what the Holy Spirit	229	Priest 4	20
so doth he assure himself, that God in all ages hath had his	229	Priest 4	21
amazed with the Majesty of God, before whom he then presents himself;	231	Priest 6	6
yet not as himself alone, but as presenting with himself the whole	231	Priest 6	7
but as presenting with himself the whole Congregation, whose sins he	231	Priest 6	7
that being first affected himself, hee may affect also his people,	231	Priest 6	13
he presents them himself, only protesting to them, that not any ill	232	Priest 6	17
that he himself hath often urged with no great success, . .	232	Priest 7	28
Oh Lord, I know that the way of man is not in himself, &c. . .	234	Priest 7	6
though he himself were with Saint Paul even sacrificed upon . .	234	Priest 7	7
him unworthy of that Majesty before which he is to present himself,	235	Priest 8	24
he sets himself to the Consideration of the duties of the day,	235	Priest 8	32
and very looks, knowing himself to be both suspected, and envyed.	237	Priest 9	15
that he will keep himself a virgin, he spends his dayes in fasting	237	Priest 9	18
he resolves with himself never to omit any present good deed	240	Priest 10	5
but resolved to himself, hee wins them to praise God more, . .	245	Priest 12	2
consideration of his own Parish, he inlargeth himself, if he be able,	245	Priest 12	18
in their vocation, and himself be ever the more welcome to them.	248	Priest 14	12
that he may keep himself pure, and not be intangled in others sinnes.	248	Priest 14	24
from Christ himself, perfecting our Redemption no other way,	249	Priest 15	22
he carryes himself very respectively, as to all the Fathers . .	253	Priest 19	5
he first gives himself liberally, and then incites them to give;	253	Priest 19	35
which exceedingly delights him as by way of exercise upon himself,	255	Priest 21	12
and by way of preaching to himself, for the advancing of his own	255	Priest 21	12
he forgets not himself, but is first a Sermon to himself, . .	255	Priest 21	14
not himself, but is first a Sermon to himself, and then to others;	255	Priest 21	15
is at a stand with himself, how or what behaviour to assume for so	257	Priest 22	27
but to throw himself down at the throne of grace, saying, . .	257	Priest 22	31
as the Parson useth all reverence himself, so he administers to none	259	Priest 22	11
confesseth himself an unworthy one, and therefore differs from other	259	Priest 22	15
he hath gotten to himself some insight in things ordinarily incident	259	Priest 23	34
of which he gathers, in case he be ignorant himself, what to hold;	260	Priest 23	11
permit his Parishioners rather to make use of the Law, then himself:	260	Priest 23	19
as may be of much use to him both for himself, and others. . .	261	Priest 23	3
hand to sickle, shall then secure himself, and think all cock-sure;	271	Priest 30	30
that he cannot without this maintain himself in a Christian state.	272	Priest 31	25
or by oversleeping himself at night, omits his additionary prayer.	272	Priest 31	31
And of this he is so to assure himself, as to admit no scruple,	273	Priest 31	10
he may behave himself so as befits so great a presence; . .	273	Priest 31	26
enough to abuse both others, and himself, and who is ready to ask,	275	Priest 32	7
and ordering his land to the best advantage both of himself,	275	Priest 32	26
where can he busie himself better, then in those new Plantations,	278	Priest 32	5
hath considered how to carry himself at table about his appetite,	278	Priest 33	18
This Instruction and comfort the Parson getting for himself,	279	Priest 33	32
But the Parson first values the gift in himself, and then teacheth	286	Priest 36	18
and forbear to speak of that, which even God himself hath forgotten.	288	Priest 37	5
he will prove himself a Physician, and that a very compleat one:	297	Cornaro	23
no man can be a perfect Physician to another, but to himself onely.	297	Cornaro	25
since none can have a better Physician then himself, nor better	298	Cornaro	1
But that a man may preserve himself in health, I advise, . .	298	Cornaro	11
man should begin and by little and little accustome himself unto it.	299	Cornaro	9
to expose himself to so many dangers of diseases and death, . .	300	Cornaro	22
Hee that makes himself a sheep, shall be eat by the wolfe. . .	358	Proverbs	D 1089
time comes that he repents himself of time.	359	Proverbs	D 1102
and it is the part of a poor spirit to undervalue himself and blush.	366	Letters	19
opinion of him, that if he can do me a courtesie, he will of himself;	369	Letters	23
God intends that to be as a sacred Temple for himself to dwell in,	374	Letters	10
HIMSELFE			
Ours (like himselfe) o'recomes; for his wit's more	438	Lat.Trans.	3
read divine services, composeth himselfe to all possible reverence;	231	Priest 6	2
Herein also he serves himselfe of the judgements of God, . .	233	Priest 7	6
And he himselfe is a consuming fire, Hebrews 12.	234	Priest 7	35
and seems to himselfe so as a Market-man is, when the Market day	235	Priest 8	17
Almighty God, and blessing the people either openly, or to himselfe.	236	Priest 8	6
but assures himselfe, that mony thus lent to God, is placed surer	240	Priest 10	7
He himselfe, or his Wife, takes account of Sermons, and how every one	240	Priest 10	36
he bethinketh himselfe what good deeds he can do that day, . .	244	Priest 12	16
and sometimes he hears the children read himselfe, and blesseth them,	248	Priest 14	35
and in regard of himselfe, it is more humiliation. . . .	249	Priest 14	9
but also professeth himselfe throughly of the opinion, carrying it	250	Priest 16	8
but is himselfe where ever he is.	251	Priest 17	1
hee first considers with himselfe, what kind of remedy fits . .	251	Priest 17	26
being himselfe in white, he requires the presence of all, . .	258	Priest 22	1
and accordingly applies himselfe with Catechizings, and lively	258	Priest 22	25
But if neither himselfe, nor his wife have the skil, and his means	260	Priest 23	33
the Parson hath diligently examined these twc with himselfe,	262	Priest 24	32
and makes so much the more of him, as before he alienated himselfe;	263	Priest 25	34
hear Sermons against both, and himselfe condemn both in good earnest:	264	Priest 26	16
he somtimes refresheth himselfe, as knowing that nature will not bear	267	Priest 27	33
he condescends to humane frailties both in himselfe and others;	268	Priest 27	6
he that throws a stone at another, hits himselfe;	269	Priest 28	14
If himselfe reforme any thing, it is out of the overflowing of his	269	Priest 29	29
for every one to imploy himselfe to the advancement of his affairs,	275	Priest 32	29
since he found himselfe sometimes to weepe more for the losse of some	279	Priest 33	12
Romans 2.) hee first preacheth to himselfe, and then to others.	279	Priest 33	36
to be in one or the other state, so he applies himselfe to them.	280	Priest 34	14
should a Christian Souldier take such occasions to harden himselfe,	284	Priest 35	36
which our Saviour himselfe used, Marke 10. 16, cannot bee vain	285	Priest 36	10
did the Lord of life, unable of himselfe to die, contrive to do it.	288	Priest	28
is delayed, the more he reads it, and fortifies himselfe with it;	310	Valdesso	30

HIMSELFE (cont'd)	PAGE	TITLE		LINE
he himselfe allowes it for a holy conversation and refreshment.	311	Valdesso		1
or justify himselfe before God, by any acts or exercises of Religion;	312	Valdesso		15
hee in the meane while applying himselfe to the [unquestioned] duties	312	Valdesso		19
when he professed himselfe a Pharisee, which strictly he was not,	316	Valdesso		8
He hath great neede of a foole, that plaies the foole himselfe.	322	Proverbs		46
Happie is hee that chastens himselfe.	325	Proverbs		137
Hee that lookes not before, finds himselfe behind.	327	Proverbs		200
Who must account for himselfe and others, must know both.	328	Proverbs		209
A well-bred youth neither speakes of himselfe,	330	Proverbs		278
Hee that burnes his house warmes himselfe for once.	331	Proverbs		303
He that measures not himselfe, is measured.	336	Proverbs		432
Hee that bewailes himselfe hath the cure in his hands.	336	Proverbs		441
None is offended but by himselfe.	343	Proverbs		656
He is onely bright that shines by himselfe.	345	Proverbs		707
He that pitties another, remembers himselfe.	347	Proverbs		782
At Court, every one for himselfe.	347	Proverbs		795
Hee lookes not well to himselfe that lookes not ever.	349	Proverbs		835
A Tyrant is most tyrant to himselfe.	350	Proverbs		888
He that praiseth himselfe spattereth himselfe.	353	Proverbs		990
puts not himselfe into a good way.	354	Proverbs		995
which the King would so appropriate to himselfe, as that either his	368	Letters		11
uppon Leighton Church, the other five pound I give to himselfe.	382	G.H.'s Will		31
HINDER				
Both friends should die, then hinder them to live.	17	Ch.-Porch		280
outlandish proverb, that Prayers and Provender never hinder journey.	251	Priest 17		15
Neither doth it hinder, that Plato sayes, That they who are employed	299	Cornaro		11
preserve themselves from diseases, which hinder publick employment;	299	Cornaro		19
Prayers and provender hinder no journey.	330	Proverbs		277
Prayers and provender never hinder any journey.	330	Proverbs	V	277
HINDERANCE				
in keeping his word, though it be to his own hinderance, as knowing,	228	Priest 3		5
and without hinderance to publick duties, either to entertaine some	236	Priest 8		19
and the discomfort, discredit, & hinderance of the Pastor.	287	Priest 37		4
HINDERS				
And struggling hinders more.	158	Praise 3		18
as that it is not meate or drinke that hinders them from working.	266	Priest 26		36
HINDES'				
and that our feet may be like hindes feet ever climbing up higher,	236	Priest 8		29
HINDRED				
and fever (which was certainly expected) might be hindred.	295	Cornaro		6
HINGE				
as if he be a Papist, the Church is the hinge he turnes on;	262	Priest 24		30
HINGES				
The groundsell speakes not save what it heard at the hinges.	331	Proverbs		295
HIR				
My soul bid nothing, but keep hir first wealth:	44	H. Bapt.2	W	13
Hir waters alsoe and desired Bathe.	210	Paradox	D	18
HIRE				
A poore mans rod if thou wilt hire	96	Charms & K	W	3
HIS				
Whom God in Baptisme washt with his own blood.	6	Ch.-Porch		8
Continence hath his joy: weigh both; and so	7	Ch.-Porch		17
He that is drunken, may his mother kill	7	Ch.-Porch		31
Bigge with his sister: he hath lost the reins,	7	Ch.-Porch		32
Bigge with his sister: he hath lost his reins,	7	Ch.-Porch	W	32
Did with his liquour slide into his veins.	7	Ch.-Porch		34
Short of his canne and bodie; must I finde	8	Ch.-Porch		39
But he that boasts, shuts that out of his storie.	8	Ch.-Porch		52
With his poore clod of earth the spacious sky.	8	Ch.-Porch		54
Take not his name, who made thy mouth, in vain:	8	Ch.-Porch		55
But the cheap swearer through his open sluce	8	Ch.-Porch		58
Lets his soul runne for nought, as little fearing.	8	Ch.-Porch		59
He pares his apple, that will cleanly feed.	9	Ch.-Porch		64
Against thee: for his light was onely lent.	9	Ch.-Porch		82
Redeem truth from his jawes: if souldier,	10	Ch.-Porch		87
Redeem truth from his chawes: if souldier,	10	Ch.-Porch	W	87
His minde with rest, before his trunk with riches:	11	Ch.-Porch		110
His minde with rest, before his trunks with riches:	11	Ch.-Porch	W	110
But if thy sonne can make ten pound his measure,	11	Ch.-Porch		113
Then all thou addest may be call'd his treasure.	11	Ch.-Porch		114
Who breaks his own bond, forfeiteth himself:	11	Ch.-Porch		119
And though hee bee a ship, is his owne shelf.	11	Ch.-Porch	W	120
Think the king sees thee still; for his King does.	11	Ch.-Porch		122
From his Ecliptick line: becken the skie.	12	Ch.-Porch		137
He breaks up house, turns out of doores his minde.	12	Ch.-Porch		150
Thy need, thine honour, and thy friend his due.	12	Ch.-Porch		152
Shoots a bow short, and lessens still his stake,	13	Ch.-Porch		159
As the day lessens, and his life with it.	13	Ch.-Porch		160
The curious unthrift makes his cloth too wide,	13	Ch.-Porch		179
And spares himself, but would his taylor chide.	13	Ch.-Porch		180
Then he can lose with pleasure, stakes his heart;	14	Ch.-Porch		194
Perhaps his wives too, and whom she hath bore:	14	Ch.-Porch		195
Findes his crackt name at length in the church-glasse.	14	Ch.-Porch		198
Whom all his passions follow, as he goes.	15	Ch.-Porch		216
Or a fir'd beacon frighteth from his ditties.	16	Ch.-Porch		250
And the sad man is cock of all his jests.	16	Ch.-Porch		252
Feed no man in his sinnes: for adulation	16	Ch.-Porch		257
And not the beast, that bears it on his back.	17	Ch.-Porch		268
Thy friend put in thy bosome: wear his eies	17	Ch.-Porch		271
If cause require, thou art his sacrifice;	17	Ch.-Porch		273

HIS (cont'd)

	PAGE	TITLE		LINE
Thy drops of bloud must pay down all his fear:	17	Ch.-Porch		274
Though David had his Jonathan, Christ his John.	17	Ch.-Porch		276
(But a proud ignorance will lose his rest,	18	Ch.-Porch		297
Rather then shew his cards.) Steal from his treasure	18	Ch.-Porch		298
More, then his sicknesses or povertie?	18	Ch.-Porch		310
Another chafe, may warm him at his fire,	19	Ch.-Porch		314
Mark all his wandrings, and enjoy his frets;	19	Ch.-Porch		315
Who follows all things, forfeiteth his will.	21	Ch.-Porch		364
Let thy mindes sweetnesse have his operation	21	Ch.-Porch		371
God reckons for him, counts the favour his:	21	Ch.-Porch		381
Restore to God his due in tithe and time:	22	Ch.-Porch		385
Twice on the day his due is understood;	22	Ch.-Porch		391
Twice on that day his due is understood;	22	Ch.-Porch	W	391
Onely by his permission. Then beware,	22	Ch.-Porch		405
Makes all their beautie his deformitie.	23	Ch.-Porch		420
Turns all their beauty to his uglines.	23	Ch.-Porch	W	420
Christ purg'd his temple; so must thou thy heart.	23	Ch.-Porch		423
Preachers conclude with, hath not lost his pains.	24	Ch.-Porch		434
Then turn thy faults and his into confession:	24	Ch.-Porch		441
Then turn thy fault and his into confession:	24	Ch.-Porch	W	441
And love him for his Master: his condition,	24	Ch.-Porch		443
May at his perill further go.	25	Superlim		8
Herod and all his bands do set me light,	29	Sacrifice		77
Who graspes the earth and heaven in his fist,	30	Sacrifice	W	130
Leaving his blindnesse to mine enemies:	31	Sacrifice		135
Leaving his blindnesse to my enemies:	31	Sacrifice	W	135
God holds his peace at man, and man cries out:	32	Sacrifice		187
Or feel his part, he would not cease to kneel,	33	Sacrifice		210
Or feel his share, he would not cease to kneel,	33	Sacrifice	W	210
And fathers smile for you, to feel his frown:	34	Sacrifice		223
And fathers smile to feele for you his frown:	34	Sacrifice	W	223
I will tear thence his love and fame.	35	Thanksgvng		26
I will ripp out his love and fame.	35	Thanksgvng	W	26
I will teare out his love and fame.	35	Thanksgvng	WC	26
Shall have his attribute to sing;	36	Thanksgvng		40
A man so wrung with pains, that all his hair,	37	The Agonie		9
His skinne, his garments bloudie be.	37	The Agonie		10
To hunt his cruell food through ev'ry vein.	37	The Agonie		12
That as each beast his cure doth know,	39	Good Fri.		19
In heaven at his manour I him sought:	40	Redemption		5
I straight return'd, and knowing his great birth,	40	Redemption		9
Rise heart; thy Lord is risen. Sing his praise	41	Easter		1
That, as his death calcined thee to dust,	41	Easter		5
His life may make thee gold, and much more just.	41	Easter		6
The crosse taught all wood to resound his name,	41	Easter		9
His stretched sinews taught all strings, what key	41	Easter		11
And make up our defects with his sweet art.	42	Easter		18
Full of his praises,	49	Repentance		34
And could see little, to regard his ease,	49	Faith		3
Faith sets me higher in his glorie.	50	Faith		20
Gods breath in man returning to his birth,	51	Prayer 1		2
His praise may thither flie:	53	Antiphon 1		4
His praises there may grow.	53	Antiphon 1		6
Give mee his speed.	57	Employm. 1	W	24
Hung down his head, and wisht for night,	59	Whitsunday		14
He that first fell from his great birth	59	Whitsunday	W	15
Without thy help, leads us his way to Hell.	59	Whitsunday	W	16
Unto his ancient and miraculous right.	60	Whitsunday		28
If still the sunne should hide his face,	60	Grace		5
If the Sunn still should hide his face,	60	Grace	W	5
Let suppling grace, to crosse his art,	60	Grace		19
O lett thy grace, to crosse his art,	60	Grace	W	19
His arm is short; yet with a sling	61	Praise 1		11
Not flyes, but I shall bee his prey	61	Praise 1	W	19
But I have got his sonne, and he hath none.	63	Even-song		8
To spell his elements, and finde his birth	65	Ch.-monum.		8
Yet heare, O God, onely for his blouds sake	66	Ch.-lock		9
His blouds sweet current much more loud to be.	66	Ch.-lock		12
Who cannot on his own bed sweetly sleep,	68	Content		3
The angrie Lion did present his paw,	70	Humilitie		9
The jealous Turkie brought his corall-chain;	70	Humilitie		13
And challenge it, as proper to his place,	70	Humilitie		20
To God, his neighbour, and himself most true:	72	Constancie		3
Who rides his sure and even trot,	72	Constancie		9
His words and works and fashion too	72	Constancie		19
His goodnesse sets not, but in dark can runne:	72	Constancie		23
And is their vertue; Vertue is his Sunne.	72	Constancie		25
Allows for that, and keeps his constant way:	73	Constancie		28
But though men fail him, yet his part doth play.	73	Constancie		30
When the wide world runnes bias, from his will	73	Constancie		32
To writhe his limbes, and share, not mend the ill.	73	Constancie		33
To writhe his limbes, and thare, not mend the ill.	73	Constancie	V	33
Writ by a friend, and with his bloud;	75	Sunday		4
And did inclose this light for his:	76	Sunday		37
That, as each beast his manger knows,	76	Sunday		38
Man might not of his fodder misse.	76	Sunday		39
With the same shake, which at his passion	76	Sunday		45
Having a new at his expence,	76	Sunday		53
Man calleth thee his wealth, who made thee rich;	77	Avarice		13
In whom the Lord of hosts did pitch his tent!	77	Anagram		2

HIS (cont'd)

	PAGE	TITLE		LINE
Where ev'ry one is king, and hath his crown,	77	Ang.&Sts.		4
If not upon his head, yet in his hands:	77	Ang.&Sts.		5
And where his pleasure no injunction layes,	78	Ang.&Sts.		19
Of his rich crown, from whcm lyes no appeal	78	Ang.&Sts.		22
Of his great crown, from whom lyes no appeal	78	Ang.&Sts.	W	22
Therefore we dare not from his garland steal,	78	Ang.&Sts.		24
Lets his own ashes choke his scul.	79	Employm.2		10
Each took his way; some would to pleasures go,	80	Deniall		8
Take up his place and right:	81	Christmas		24
His beams shall cheer my breast, and both so twine,	81	Christmas		33
Till ev'n his beams sing, and my musick shine.	81	Christmas		34
And thought his god most brave;	82	Ungratef.		5
In his poore cabinet of bone	82	Ungratef.		28
And thred the spheres with his quick-piercing minde:	85	Vanitie 1		2
The nimble Diver with his side	85	Vanitie 1		8
His dearely-earned pearl, which God did hide	85	Vanitie 1		10
That he might save his life, and also hers,	85	Vanitie 1		12
Her own destruction and his danger wears.	85	Vanitie 1		14
His own destruction and his danger wears.	85	Vanitie 1	V	14
There he imparts to them his minde,	85	Vanitie 1		18
But his deare God? who yet his glorious law	85	Vanitie 1		23
That ev'ry man may revell at his doore,	87	Lent		46
Not in his parlour; banquetting the poore,	87	Lent		47
And among those his soul.	87	Lent		48
Bids the rash gazer wipe his eye:	87	Vertue		6
Thy root is ever in his grave,	87	Vertue	V	7
As the sunne scatters by his light	90	Afflict.4		23
But Man hath caught and kept it, as his prey.	91	Man		20
But Man has caught and kept it, as his prey.	91	Man	W	20
His eyes dismount the highest starre:	91	Man		21
Who hath dealt his mercies so,	92	Antiphon 2		4
To his friend,	92	Antiphon 2		5
And to his foe;	92	Antiphon 2		6
If any touch my friend, or his good name,	93	Unkindness		6
His blasted fame	93	Unkindness		8
His darkned fame	93	Unkindness	W	8
His bloud did spill	94	Unkindness		23
Who shuts his hand, hath lost his gold:	96	Charms & K		5
A falling starr has lost his place:	97	Charms & K	W	19
And calls for musick, while his veins do swell,	98	Mortific.		14
Within the circle of his breath,	98	Mortific.		21
Schooling his eyes;	98	Mortific.		22
Unto the coffin, that attends his death.	98	Mortific.		24
Marking his grave, and thawing ev'ry yeare,	98	Mortific.		26
Till all do melt, and drown his breath	98	Mortific.		27
And drest his herse, while he has breath	99	Mortific.		33
Folly and Sinne play all his game.	100	Miserie		3
Folly and Sinne play out his game.	100	Miserie	W	3
His house still burns, and yet he still doth sing,	100	Miserie		4
How canst thou brook his foolishnesse?	100	Miserie		7
Bid him but temper his excesse;	100	Miserie		9
And make his own? as if none knew, but he.	100	Miserie		14
No man shall beat into his head,	100	Miserie		15
That thou within his curtains drawn canst see:	100	Miserie		16
The sunne holds down his head for shame,	101	Miserie		33
And serve the swine: there, there is his delight:	101	Miserie		44
And feed the swine, with all his mind & might:	101	Miserie	W	44
Give him his dirt to wallow in all night:	101	Miserie		46
They will be kind, and all his pains requite,	101	Miserie	W	46
His head to shoot and ake.	101	Miserie		48
His head to shoot and shake.	101	Miserie	V	48
Wonders and sings, but not his power	101	Miserie		57
His knowledge winks, and lets his humours reigne;	102	Miserie		62
They make his life a constant blot,	102	Miserie		63
Did crown his heart and face.	102	Miserie		72
Nay, his own shelf:	102	Miserie		77
Much lesse those joyes which trample on his head.	102	Jordan 2		12
He that will passe his land,	105	Obedience		36
As I have mine, may set his hand	105	Obedience		37
If some kinde man would thrust his heart	105	Obedience		42
My Saviours bloud: when ever at his board	106	Conscience		14
To double-moat thee with his grace,	110	Brit. Ch.		29
With his train-bands and mates agree	110	The Quip		2
And with a thankfull heart his comforts take.	112	Dawning		6
And feel his death, but not his victorie.	112	Dawning		8
And with his buriall-linen drie thine eyes:	112	Dawning		14
Christ left his grave-clothes, that we might, when grief	112	Dawning		15
Christ left his grave-cloths, that we might, when grief	112	Dawning	V	15
JESU is in my heart, his sacred name	112	JESU		1
Who did leave his Fathers throne,	113	Businesse		17
That his own self he forgot.	113	Businesse		24
'Twixt his sinnes and Saviours death?	114	Businesse		30
Tells to all he meets, his crosse:	114	Businesse		32
Can praise his fairest fair;	115	Dulnesse		6
And put the penne alone into his hand,	117	Providence		7
Where all may reach: no beast but knows his feed.	118	Providence		50
Nothing ingendred doth prevent his meat:	118	Providence		53
Each creature hath a wisdome for his good.	118	Providence		61
A rose, besides his beautie, is a cure.	119	Providence		78
But at his perill: when he digs the place,	119	Providence		82

HIS (cont'd)	PAGE	TITLE	LINE
Are rul'd by him, and taught to serve his trade.	119	Providence	92
But Man alone, to show his heav'nly breed:	120	Providence	111
And in his blessing thou art blest:	123	Time	13
What do I here before his doore?	123	Time	29
His life from foes.	125	Peace	26
But after death out of his grave	125	Peace	27
One while he counts of heav'n, as of his treasure:	127	Giddinesse	5
Now eat his bread in peace,	127	Giddinesse	10
His minde is so.	127	Giddinesse	16
O what a sight were Man, if his attires	127	Giddinesse	17
Did alter with his minde;	127	Giddinesse	18
And like a Dolphins skinne, his clothes combin'd	127	Giddinesse	19
With his desires!	127	Giddinesse	20
So now each Christian hath his journeys spann'd:	128	Bunch Gr.	10
His ancient justice overflows our crimes.	128	Bunch Gr.	14
Lookt on a servant, who did know his eye	129	Love unkn.	9
To warm his love, which I did fear grew cold.	129	Love unkn.	32
Who was to take it from me, slipt his hand,	130	Love unkn.	34
All creatures have their joy: and man hath his.	131	Mans medly	3
But as his joyes are double;	131	Mans medly	25
So is his trouble.	131	Mans medly	26
And bite his lip;	131	Mans medly	29
To turn his double pains to double praise.	132	Mans medly	36
Which cools his will.	133	The Method	4
His utter foes?	134	The Method	28
Which knows his way without a guide:	134	Divinitie	4
And jagg'd his seamlesse coat, had that been fine,	134	Divinitie	11
But he doth bid us take his bloud for wine.	135	Divinitie	21
Wouldst thou his laws of fasting disanull?	138	The Size	15
Nay, ev'n to trust in him, was also his:	143	Holdfast	6
That all things were more ours by being his.	143	Holdfast	12
And is his right.	144	Discharge	12
The crop is his, for he hath sown.	144	Discharge	15
Thy businesse his, and in thy life partake:	144	Discharge	18
If it be his once, all is well.	144	Discharge	20
That wants his head;	150	Longing	69
Storms are the triumph of his art:	151	The Bag	5
Well may he close his eyes, but not his heart.	151	The Bag	6
In his majestick robes of glorie,	151	The Bag	10
The starres his tire of light and rings obtain'd,	151	The Bag	13
The cloud his bow, the fire his spear,	151	The Bag	14
The sky his azure mantle gain'd.	151	The Bag	15
Here he gave up his life to pay our score.	151	The Bag	24
Receiv'd the blow upon his side,	151	The Bag	29
And straight he turn'd, and to his brethren cry'd,	151	The Bag	30
Not to his hurt. Sighs will convey	152	The Bag	41
To suit and serve his need,	153	The Collar	31
Deserves his load.	153	The Collar	32
A neighbour spring to cool his inward heat;	154	Glimpse	14
But constant to his part	154	Glimpse	18
Such a Strength, as makes his guest.	156	The Call	8
Devils their rod, the sea his shore,	158	Praise 3	22
Sorrow hath chang'd its note: such is his will,	159	Jos.coat	3
Among my many had his full career,	159	Jos.coat	6
I live to shew his power, who once did bring	159	Jos.coat	13
Perceiving that alone of all his treasure	160	The Pulley	9
I throw me at his feet.	161	Priesthood	36
For some mean stuffe whereon to show his skill:	161	Priesthood	38
To make his verse, or write a hymne in kinde.	168	a true Hymn	15
Scorns his first bed of dirt, and means the sky;	169	The Answer	9
Between his soul and gold, and hath preferr'd	171	Self-cond.	14
For he hath sold for money his deare Lord,	171	Self-cond.	17
His swing and sway:	172	The Glance	12
While he is mine, and I am his,	172	23 Psalme	3
But for his holy name.	172	23 Psalme	12
Shewing his steps should be the street,	173	Marie Magd	4
And not his feet? Though we could dive	173	Marie Magd	10
Go birds of spring: let winter have his fee,	177	Forerunners	34
Who can scape his bow?	179	Discipline	25
God, to show how farre his love	181	Banquet	28
Let the wonder of his pitie	182	Banquet	49
And give it his perfection.	184	The Elixer	8
On it may stay his eye;	184	The Elixer	10
Which with his tincture (for thy sake)	184	The Elixer	15
Yet as the sunne, though forward be his flight,	190	Ch.-Milit.	31
The Warrier his deere skarres no more resounds,	191	Ch.-Milit.	63
Wounds willingly endur'd to work his blisse,	192	Ch.-Milit.	65
Who by an ambush lost his Paradise.	192	Ch.-Milit.	66
Quitting his spear, lest it should pierce again	192	Ch.-Milit.	69
Him in his members, who for him was slain.	192	Ch.-Milit.	70
Begging his food of that which he may eat,	193	Ch.-Milit.	113
Starving the while he worshippeth his meat!	193	Ch.-Milit.	114
Who makes a root his God, how low is he,	193	Ch.-Milit.	115
Whose house is foul, while he adores his broom?	193	Ch.-Milit.	118
His highest was an ox or crocodile,	193	Ch.-Milit.	122
His pills of sublimate in that conserve.	193	Ch.-Milit.	132
Glorie was his chief instrument of old:	194	Ch.-Milit.	143
I saw him in his studie, where he sate	194	Ch.-Milit.	165
His grave aspect had more of heav'n then hell:	194	Ch.-Milit.	168
His grave aspect was liker heav'n then hell:	194	Ch.-Milit. W	168

HIS (cont'd)

	PAGE	TITLE		LINE
To which he lent a corner of his eye.	195	Ch.-Milit.		170
The rather since his scatter'd jugglings were	195	Ch.-Milit.		175
Then in memoriall of his ancient throne	195	Ch.-Milit.		181
He did surname his palace, Babylon.	195	Ch.-Milit.		182
He took fine vizards to conceal his crimes:	195	Ch.-Milit.		186
While Truth sat by, counting his victories:	195	Ch.-Milit.		190
Either t' his publick foot or private tricks.	195	Ch.-Milit.		196
It did not fit his gravitie to stirre,	195	Ch.-Milit.		197
Nor his long journey, nor his gout and furre.	195	Ch.-Milit.		198
Nor his long journey, nor his gout or furre.	195	Ch.-Milit.	W	198
Who brought his doctrins & his deeds from Rome	195	Ch.-Milit.	W	201
Of his two thrones he made the latter best,	196	Ch.-Milit.		213
And to defray his journey from the east.	196	Ch.-Milit.		214
So though Sinne made his latter seat the better,	196	Ch.-Milit.		223
So though Sinne made his later seat the better,	196	Ch.-Milit.	W	223
At Christs last coming, as his first did finde:	196	Ch.-Milit.		231
While his conquests dayly spread;	199	L'Envoy		8
That thy flesh hath lost his food,	199	L'Envoy		9
But reserve his breath in store,	199	L'Envoy		12
Or reserve his breath in store,	199	L'Envoy	W	12
Till thy conquests and his fall	199	L'Envoy		13
Till thy conquest and his fall	199	L'Envoy	V	13
Make his sighs to use it all,	199	L'Envoy		14
Thou drivest from his seat.	200	H. Commun.	W	24
Flesh (though exalted) keeps his grass	201	H. Commun.	W	38
His fall can tell,	202	Trin.Sun.	W	13
The Day is spent, & hath his will on mee:	203	Even-song	W	1
Look on his daring brightnes, may	203	Even-song	W	7
Each with his rodd.	204	The Knell	W	12
Love neere his death desir'd to end	439	Walton 5	V	11
Of kinde Expressions to his friend,	439	Walton 5		12
With kinde Expressions to his friend,	439	Walton 5	V	12
He gave his soul, and so gave o're.	439	Walton 5	V	14
His letters were broke rudely up, believ'd	439	Walton 5		16
But his heavenly and divine,	208	J. Danvers	D	11
In his progenie doth shine.	208	J. Danvers	D	12
Know that much had been his worth;	208	J. Danvers	D	14
His dust who under thee must sleepe	208	H. Danvers	D	2
Thou art requited; for his Fame,	209	H. Danvers	D	8
His Vertues, and his Worth shal bee	209	H. Danvers	D	9
But in God's Law sets his delight,	214	Psalm I	D	5
His meditation day and night:	214	Psalm I	D	7
His leaf shall never fade, and all	214	Psalm I	D	11
and 'gainst his Christ, presume to say,	215	Psalm II	D	6
on Sion His most Holy hill,	215	Psalm II	D	14
nor can I hide his sacred will.	215	Psalm II	D	16
When once his anger burns, thrice blest	216	Psalm II	D	31
me from his holy hill:	216	Psalm III	D	10
when I his grace implore:	217	Psalm IV	D	14
and on his grace rely.	217	Psalm IV	D	20
His favour shall encompass them,	219	Psalm V	D	43
his mallice to controul.	221	Psalm VII	D	8
that do his justice slight.	222	Psalm VII	D	40
the Lord will whet his Sword:	222	Psalm VII	D	42
His bow is bent, his quiver is	222	Psalm VII	D	43
His arrows are ordain'd 'gainst him	222	Psalm VII	D	47
with his iniquitie:	222	Psalm VII	D	50
To his own head his wickedness	222	Psalm VII	D	57
And on his own accursed pate	222	Psalm VII	D	59
his cruelty shall come.	222	Psalm VII	D	60
But I for all his righteousness	222	Psalm VII	D	61
Ours (like himselfe) o'recomes; for his wit's more	438	Lat.Trans.		3
The Countrey PARSON HIS CHARACTER, AND Rule of Holy Life.	223	Priest		T
he constituted Deputies in his place, and these are Priests.	225	Priest 1		8
And therefore St. Paul in the beginning of his Epistles,	225	Priest 1		10
up that which is behinde of the afflictions of Christ in his flesh,	225	Priest 1		12
of Christ in his flesh, for his Bodie's sake, which is the Church.	225	Priest 1		12
that which Christ did, and by his auctority, and as his Vicegerent.	225	Priest 1		17
which Christ did, and after his manner, both for Doctrine and Life.	225	Priest 1		19
as a Parsons to his Parish, in describing the one (which is indeed	226	Priest 2		17
exercise what he is, unlesse he forsake his plough, and look back.	226	Priest 2		27
The Countrey Parson is exceeding exact in his Life, being holy,	227	Priest 3		1
just, prudent, temperate, bold, grave in all his wayes.	227	Priest 3		3
most in those things which are most apt to scandalize his Parish.	227	Priest 3		11
but in all his words and actions slighting, and disesteeming it,	227	Priest 3		18
or Ale-houses, to the dishonour of his person and office.	227	Priest 3		31
but orders his Life in such a fashion, that when death takes him,	227	Priest 3		31
therfore the Parson is very strict in keeping his word,	228	Priest 3		5
in keeping his word, though it be to his own hinderance, as knowing,	228	Priest 3		5
him in the pulpit, whom they cannot trust in his Conversation.	228	Priest 3		8
and his apparrell plaine, but reverend, and clean, without spots,	228	Priest 3		10
the purity of his mind breaking out, and dilating it selfe even	228	Priest 3		12
mind breaking out, and dilating it selfe even to his body, cloaths,	228	Priest 3		13
But the chief and top of his knowledge consists in the book of books,	228	Priest 4		21
remembring what his Master saith, that if any do Gods will,	228	Priest 4		28
that God in all ages hath had his servants, to whom he hath revealed	229	Priest 4		22
his servants, to whom he hath revealed his Truth, as well as to him;	229	Priest 4		22
and his own meditations, he enters into the secrets of God treasured	229	Priest 4		29
which is the storehouse of his Sermons, and which he preacheth all	230	Priest 5		1
the storehouse of his Sermons, and which he preacheth all his Life;	230	Priest 5		2

HIS (cont'd)

	PAGE	TITLE	LINE
this being to be done in his younger and preparatory times,	230	Priest 5	5
it is an honest joy ever after to looke upon his well spent houres.	230	Priest 5	7
according as his audience is, so he useth one, or other;	230	Priest 5	17
or somtimes both, if his audience be intermixed.	230	Priest 5	18
greatest ability of a Parson to lead his people exactly in the wayes	230	Priest 5	21
least all those which he observeth are most incident to his Parish.	230	Priest 5	35
lifting up his heart and hands, and eyes, and using all other	231	Priest 6	3
and brings with his own to the heavenly altar to be bathed,	231	Priest 6	9
as this is the true reason of his inward feare, so he is content	231	Priest 6	11
he is content to expresse this outwardly to the utmost of his power;	231	Priest 6	12
hee may affect also his people, knowing that no Sermon moves them so	231	Priest 6	13
Accordingly his voyce is humble, his words treatable, and slow;	231	Priest 6	16
Accordingly his voyce is humble, his words treatable, and slow;	231	Priest 6	17
between fear and zeal, pausing yet pressing, he performes his duty.	231	Priest 6	20
Besides his example, he having often instructed his people how	231	Priest 6	21
he having often instructed his people how to carry themselves in	231	Priest 6	21
that God hath ever had his people, that have glorified him as wel	231	Priest 6	35
notwithstanding his instruction that they ought not to be so,	232	Priest 6	15
but the debt and obligation of his calling, being to obey God rather	232	Priest 6	19
Parson preacheth constantly, the pulpit is his joy and his throne:	232	Priest 7	21
of the hearers, that he may be heard at his returne more attentively.	232	Priest 7	24
is ever very well supplyed by some able man who treads in his steps,	232	Priest 7	26
and busy cast of his eye on his auditors, with letting them know,	233	Priest 7	1
and with particularizing of his speech now to the younger sort,	233	Priest 7	3
and those most, which are nearest to his Parish;	233	Priest 7	9
and sayings of others, according as his text invites him;	233	Priest 7	12
that none is careless before his Judg, and that the word of God shal	233	Priest 7	21
but the character of his Sermon is Holiness;	233	Priest 7	23
And herein St Paul excelled in all his Epistles.	234	Priest 7	11
How did he put the Romans in all his prayers? Rom. 1. 9.	234	Priest 7	12
setting aside his care of his Flock, were a madnesse to doubt of.	234	Priest 7	16
setting aside his care of his Flock, were a madnesse to doubt of.	234	Priest 7	17
Then turning the discourse to his Majesty, And he is a great God,	234	Priest 7	31
His voyce is as the sound of many waters, Revelations 1.	234	Priest 7	34
His thoughts are full of making the best of the day, and contriving	235	Priest 8	19
of making the best of the day, and contriving it to his best gaines.	235	Priest 8	20
besides his ordinary prayers, he makes a peculiar one for a blessing	235	Priest 8	21
himself, but that all may be done with reverence to his glory,	235	Priest 8	25
and with edification to his flock, humbly beseeching his Master,	235	Priest 8	25
humbly beseeching his Master, that how or whenever he punish him,	235	Priest 8	26
that how or whenever he punish him, it be not in his Ministry:	235	Priest 8	27
then he turnes to request for his people, that the Lord would be	235	Priest 8	28
the hour calls, with his family attending him, he goes to Church,	236	Priest 8	3
at his first entrance humbly adoring, and worshipping the invisible	236	Priest 8	4
or in exhortations to some of his flock by themselves, whom his	236	Priest 8	12
his flock by themselves, whom his Sermons cannot, or doe not reach.	236	Priest 8	13
and these exhortations he cals his privy purse, even as Princes have	236	Priest 8	16
either to entertaine some of his neighbours, or to be entertained	236	Priest 8	20
But yet as the temper of his body may be, or as the temper of his	237	Priest 9	1
or as the temper of his Parish may be, where he may have occasion	237	Priest 9	2
unto God, and as his grace shall direct him, so let him proceed.	237	Priest 9	6
he hath not a woman in his house, but findes opportunities of having	237	Priest 9	8
findes opportunities of having his meat dress'd and other services	237	Priest 9	9
services done by men-servants at home, and his linnen washed abroad.	237	Priest 9	10
is very circumspect in all companyes, both of his behaviour, speech,	237	Priest 9	14
If he stand steadfast in his heart, having no necessity,	237	Priest 9	16
but hath power over his own will, and hath so decreed in his heart,	237	Priest 9	17
and hath so decreed in his heart, that he will keep himself a virgin,	237	Priest 9	17
he spends his dayes in fasting and prayer, and blesseth God	237	Priest 9	18
and by these hee keeps his body tame, serviceable, and healthfull;	237	Priest 9	26
and his soul fervent, active, young, and lusty as an eagle.	237	Priest 9	27
He keepeth his watch and ward, night and day against the proper	238	Priest 9	1
day against the proper and peculiar temptations of his state of Life,	238	Priest 9	2
against these ghostly enemies he girdeth up his loynes,	238	Priest 9	4
the choyce of his wife was made rather by his eare, then by his eye;	238	Priest 9	26
the choyce of his wife was made rather by his eare, then by his eye;	238	Priest 9	27
his judgement, not his affection found out a fit wife for him,	238	Priest 9	27
not his affection found out a fit wife for him, whose humble,	238	Priest 9	27
so is he to his wife also, counting nothing so much his owne,	238	Priest 9	34
counting nothing so much his owne, as that he may be unjust unto it.	238	Priest 9	35
the seldomer, according as hee is satisfied of his Wifes discretion.	239	Priest 9	4
The Parson in his house.	239	Priest 10	T
The Parson is very exact in the governing of his house,	239	Priest 10	6
governing of his house, making it a copy and modell for his Parish.	239	Priest 10	7
and pulse of every person in his house, and accordingly either meets	239	Priest 10	8
His wife is either religious, or night and day he is winning her	239	Priest 10	10
His children he first makes Christians, and then Commonwealths-men;	239	Priest 10	19
the one he owes to his heavenly Countrey, the other to his earthly,	239	Priest 10	21
Countrey, the other to his earthly, having no title to either,	239	Priest 10	22
and sending his charity by them to the poor, and somtimes giving them	239	Priest 10	26
He afterwards turnes his care to fit all their dispositions with some	239	Priest 10	30
but giving him the prerogative of his Fathers profession,	239	Priest 10	32
which happily for his other children he is not able to do.	239	Priest 10	32
in consideration of providing a stock for his children;	240	Priest 10	7
is placed surer for his childrens advantage, then if it were given	240	Priest 10	8
and good breeding, are his two great stocks for his children;	240	Priest 10	10
and good breeding, are his two great stocks for his children;	240	Priest 10	11
His servants are all religious, and were it not his duty to have them	240	Priest 10	13
and were it not his duty to have them so, it were his profit,	240	Priest 10	13
to have them so, it were his profit, for none are so well served,	240	Priest 10	14

HIS (cont'd)

	PAGE	TITLE	LINE
for all in his house are either teachers or learners, or both,	240	Priest 10	20
so that his family is a Schoole of Religion, and they all account,	240	Priest 10	21
his wife among her neighbours is the beginner of good discourses,	240	Priest 10	27
his children among children, his servants among other servants;	240	Priest 10	28
his children among children, his servants among other servants;	240	Priest 10	29
He suffers not a ly or equivocation by any means in his house,	240	Priest 10	32
so that all his house knowes, that there is no help for a fault done,	240	Priest 10	35
He himselfe, or his Wife, takes account of Sermons, and how every one	240	Priest 10	36
He keeps his servants between love, and fear, according as hee findes	241	Priest 10	7
To his Children he shewes more love then terrour, to his servants	241	Priest 10	9
more love then terrour, to his servants more terrour then love;	241	Priest 10	10
The furniture of his house is very plain, but clean, whole, . .	241	Priest 10	11
but clean, whole, and sweet, as sweet as his garden can make;	241	Priest 10	12
charity being his only perfume, which deserves cost when he can spare	241	Priest 10	14
His fare is plain, and common, but wholsome, what hee hath, . .	241	Priest 10	15
or a stranger, his garden or orchard supplyes it, or his barne,	241	Priest 10	18
his garden or orchard supplyes it, or his barne, and back-side:	241	Priest 10	18
But those which his home produceth, he refuseth not, as coming cheap,	241	Priest 10	22
both for man in themselves, by growing them selves fit for his table.	241	Priest 10	35
The Parson in his house observes fasting dayes;	241	Priest 10	35
as Sunday is his day of joy, so Friday his day of Humiliation,	241	Priest 10	36
so Friday his day of Humiliation, which he celebrates not only	241	Priest 10	37
If his body be weak and obstructed, as most Students are, . .	242	Priest 10	28
nor suffer others in his house that are so, to keep it; . .	242	Priest 10	30
and of Courtesie to his other parishioners, he so distinguisheth,	243	Priest 11	7
that he keeps his money for the poor, and his table for those that	243	Priest 11	8
his money for the poor, and his table for those that are above Alms.	243	Priest 11	8
Not but that the poor are welcome also to his table, whom he	243	Priest 11	10
and carving for them, both for his own humility, and their comfort,	243	Priest 11	12
Having then invited some of his Parish, hee taketh his times to do	243	Priest 11	18
some of his Parish, hee taketh his times to do the like to the rest;	243	Priest 11	18
there are such conceits, there is no room for his doctrine to enter.	243	Priest 11	24
and vertuously, not for any reward of his, but for vertues sake;	243	Priest 11	29
although we should love him onely for his own sake, yet out of his	243	Priest 11	31
yet out of his infinite pity hath set forth heaven for a reward	243	Priest 11	31
if not the best way, yet any way, make his Parish good. . .	244	Priest 11	5
it is his predominant element.	244	Priest 12	6
Wherefore all his works rellish of Charity.	244	Priest 12	15
counting that day lost, wherein he hath not exercised his Charity.	244	Priest 12	18
He first considers his own Parish, and takes care, that there be	244	Priest 12	19
or idle person in his Parish, but that all bee in a competent way	244	Priest 12	20
If his Parish be rich, he exacts this of them;	244	Priest 12	24
and repine as much, as he that is disseized of his own inheritance.	244	Priest 12	30
and making a hook of his Charity, causeth them still to depend	244	Priest 12	31
this generall provision, he hath other times of opening his hand;	245	Priest 12	6
and dearths, he even parts his Living, and life among them, . .	245	Priest 12	10
and when his own stock serves not, working those that are able	245	Priest 12	11
of the pulpit, and never leaving them, till he obtaine his desire.	245	Priest 12	14
Yet in all his Charity, he distinguisheth, giving them most,	245	Priest 12	15
So is his charity in effect a Sermon.	245	Priest 12	16
After the consideration of his own Parish, he inlargeth himself,	245	Priest 12	17
so doth he also to those at his door, whom God puts in his way,	245	Priest 12	20
at his door, whom God puts in his way, and makes his neighbours.	245	Priest 12	20
at his door, whom God puts in his way, and makes his neighbours.	245	Priest 12	21
once satisfied, he allows his Charity some blindnesse in the other;	245	Priest 12	27
The Countrey Parson hath a speciall care of his Church, . .	246	Priest 13	1
things there be decent, and befitting his Name by which it is called.	246	Priest 13	2
to visite in person, now one quarter of his Parish, now another.	247	Priest 14	5
For there he shall find his flock most naturally as they are,	247	Priest 14	6
finds the persons of the house imployed, so he formes his discourse.	247	Priest 14	12
and opens not only his mouth, but his purse to their relief,	248	Priest 14	11
but his purse to their relief, that so they go on more cheerfully in	248	Priest 14	11
and therefore he lays his discourse so, that he comes to the point	248	Priest 14	20
and offering to have them taught on holy-dayes by his servants.	248	Priest 14	37
as his accesse to the poor is more comfortable, then to the rich;	249	Priest 14	8
These are the Parsons generall aims in his Circuit; . . .	249	Priest 14	10
sake, and to make his higher purposes slip the more easily. . .	249	Priest 14	12
when any of his cure is sick, or afflicted with losse of friend,	249	Priest 15	13
fails not to afford his best comforts, and rather goes to them,	249	Priest 15	15
from his particular, to his Church;	249	Priest 15	20
from his promises, from the examples of all Saints, that ever were;	249	Priest 15	21
Besides this, in his visiting the sick, or otherwise afflicted,	249	Priest 15	28
after it may come rather from themselves, then from his perswasion.	250	Priest 15	6
The Countrey Parson is not only a father to his flock, but also	250	Priest 16	7
it about with him as fully, as if he had begot his whole Parish.	250	Priest 16	9
or otherwise are done to his owne person, hee considers the offender	250	Priest 16	13
a just occasion calleth him out of his Parish (which he diligently,	250	Priest 17	24
his Parish being all his joy, and thought) leaveth not his Ministry	250	Priest 17	25
being all his joy, and thought) leaveth not his Ministry behind him;	251	Priest 17	1
which may make his other discourses more welcome, and lesse tedious.	251	Priest 17	5
And when he comes to his Inn, he refuseth not to joyne, . .	251	Priest 17	7
wishing him to informe his guests thereof, that if any be willing	251	Priest 17	11
where his kindred, or other relations give him any authority over	251	Priest 17	16
in the Company where he is, but comes under his Test and censure:	252	Priest 18	3
This is to be on Gods side, and be true to his party. . . .	252	Priest 18	15
The Countrey Parson is sincere and upright in all his relations.	252	Priest 19	24
And first, he is just to his Countrey;	252	Priest 19	25
are every way fitting to do his Countrey true and laudable service,	252	Priest 19	28
and true in all his wayes, as being the servant of him, . .	253	Priest 19	1
so especially to his Diocesan, honouring him both in word, . .	253	Priest 19	7

HIS (cont'd)	PAGE	TITLE	LINE
unto him in any difficulty, either in his studies or in his Parish.	253	Priest 19	9
propounds among his Brethren what were fitting to be done. . .	253	Priest 19	14
Ministeriall office, which is not to the prejudice of his own Parish.	253	Priest 19	17
Likewise he welcomes to his house any Minister, how poor or mean	253	Priest 19	18
but taking his Parish together the next Sunday, or holy-day,	253	Priest 19	31
and his owne lesse charged, hee findes some way of releeving it,	254	Priest 19	2
representing to his people, that the Blessing of God to them ought	254	Priest 19	4
The Countrey Parson is in Gods stead to his Parish, and dischargeth	254	Priest 20	8
stead to his Parish, and dischargeth God what he can of his promises.	254	Priest 20	9
finde any reading in anothers Bible, he provides him one of his own.	254	Priest 20	12
or easeth him in his Tithes, telling him when he hath forgotten it,	254	Priest 20	16
but in the other God is his own immediate paymaster, rewarding all	254	Priest 20	20
is rather by withdrawing his bounty and courtesie from the parties	254	Priest 20	23
for there being three points of his duty, the one, to infuse	255	Priest 21	2
infuse a competent knowledge of salvation in every one of his Flock;	255	Priest 21	3
of preaching to himself, for the advancing of his own mortification;	255	Priest 21	13
growing with the growth of his Parish.	255	Priest 21	15
the Questionist must have in his mind before any question be	256	Priest 21	32
made the answer so plaine, that he was even ashamed of his ignorance;	257	Priest 21	6
which the Parson so much commends to all his fellow-labourers;	257	Priest 21	17
where God is thanked for calling us to the knowledg of his grace,	258	Priest 22	6
and his Saints, and by way of undertaking for a Christian soul.	258	Priest 22	13
or carelesness of his flock, and accordingly applies himselfe	258	Priest 22	24
The Countrey Parson desires to be all to his Parish, and not onely	259	Priest 23	29
Therefore hee endures not that any of his Flock should go to Law;	259	Priest 23	31
wherein he chooseth to permit his Parishioners rather to make use	260	Priest 23	19
if there be any of his flock sick, hee is their Physician, . .	260	Priest 23	29
or at least his Wife, of whom in stead of the qualities of the world,	260	Priest 23	30
if neither himselfe, nor his wife have the skil, and his means serve,	260	Priest 23	33
and his means serve, hee keepes some young practicioner in his house	260	Priest 23	33
keepes some young practicioner in his house for the benefit of his	260	Priest 23	34
some young practicioner in his house for the benefit of his Parish,	260	Priest 23	35
whom yet he ever exhorts not to exceed his bounds, but in tickle	260	Priest 23	35
neighbour Phisician, and entertaines him for the Cure of his Parish.	261	Priest 23	1
especially let his Method of Phisick be diligently perused, . .	261	Priest 23	7
householder, who bringeth out of his treasure things new and old;	261	Priest 23	15
familiar things hee might make his Doctrine slip the more easily into	261	Priest 23	19
chiefly considered) might have every where monuments of his Doctrine,	261	Priest 23	21
his Doctrine, remembring in gardens, his mustard-seed, and lillyes;	261	Priest 23	22
in the field, his seed-corn, and tares;	261	Priest 23	23
and so shuts them out of his family, esteeming that there is no spice	261	Priest 23	38
his wife seeks not the city, but preferrs her garden and fields	262	Priest 23	3
the Parson and his Family use to premise prayers, for this is to cure	262	Priest 23	9
yet he looks not in this point of Curing beyond his own Parish,	262	Priest 23	13
not to incroach on others Professions, but to live on his own.	262	Priest 23	17
if there be any of his parish that hold strange Doctrins, . .	262	Priest 24	19
and to give him power so to fit his discourse to them, that it may	262	Priest 24	23
ever besides two great helps and powerfull perswaders on his side;	263	Priest 24	16
in his behaviour and carriage towards him, not avoyding his company,	263	Priest 25	26
not avoyding his company, or doing any thing of aversenesse,	263	Priest 25	27
doubling his regards, and shewing by all means, that the delinquents	263	Priest 25	34
by all means, that the delinquents returne is to his advantage.	264	Priest 25	2
and considering his Flock, discovers two sorts of vices, . .	264	Priest 26	4
the bounds of the action, nor when his eating begins to be unlawfull.	264	Priest 26	25
So a man storing up mony for his necessary provisions, both in	264	Priest 26	26
both in present for his family, and in future for his children,	264	Priest 26	27
and in future for his children, hardly perceives when his storing	264	Priest 26	27
his children, hardly perceives when his storing becomes unlawfull:	264	Priest 26	28
yet is there a period for his storing, and a point, or center,	264	Priest 26	29
or center, when his storing, which was even now good, passeth from	264	Priest 26	29
Wherefore the Parson being true to his businesse, hath exactly sifted	264	Priest 26	31
and yet hee chuseth rather to use his neighbours, and wear out that,	265	Priest 26	29
for quantity eats more then his health or imployments will bear,	266	Priest 26	7
as he that eats more then his estate will bear, is a Prodigall;	266	Priest 26	9
offensively to the Company, either in his order, or length of eating,	266	Priest 26	10
his reason is, because diseases of exinanition are more dangerous,	267	Priest 26	13
But the Parson distinguisheth according to his double aime, . .	267	Priest 26	15
his minde being defixed on it with those nailes wherewith his Master	267	Priest 27	28
minde being defixed on it with those nailes wherewith his Master was:	267	Priest 27	29
and intermingles some mirth in his discourses occasionally, . .	268	Priest 27	7
which out of his choysest judgment hee hath resolved to observe,	268	Priest 28	11
because this hath been the portion of God his Master, and of Gods	268	Priest 28	14
his Master, and of Gods Saints his Brethren, and this is foretold,	268	Priest 28	15
especially in his own Parish he suffers it not to his utmost power;	268	Priest 28	18
This he procures, first by his holy and unblameable life; . .	268	Priest 28	20
the Parson think it in his discretion either unfit, or bootelesse	269	Priest 28	4
or in a sad way, greived at his own, and others sins, which . .	269	Priest 28	9
and joyfull, that hee is made conformable to his Master; . .	269	Priest 28	17
in the world as he was, hath this undoubted pledge of his salvation.	269	Priest 28	18
The Parson with his Church-Wardens.	269	Priest 29	T
and privately instruct his Church-Wardens, what a great Charge lyes	269	Priest 29	27
it is out of the overflowing of his Conscience, whereas they are	269	Priest 29	30
the greatest honor of this world, to do God and his chosen service;	270	Priest 29	11
To this end he represents to his flock, that God hath and exerciseth	270	Priest 30	32
By his sustaining power he preserves and actuates every thing in his	271	Priest 30	3
sustaining power he preserves and actuates every thing in his being;	271	Priest 30	4
and be preserved in that act by his sustaining power, yet if he suite	271	Priest 30	15
and other accidents by his governing power, the fairest harvests come	271	Priest 30	17
and reverence his power, and therefore he often overturnes things,	271	Priest 30	20
that is his time of interposing:	271	Priest 30	21

HIS (cont'd)

	PAGE	TITLE	LINE
God further, even till he imbarn his corn, and then think all sure;	271	Priest 30	32
but to continue his dependance on God, not onely before the corne is	271	Priest 30	34
and utter this well, all his advantages are to his losse. . .	272	Priest 30	3
Better were his corne burnt, then not spiritually improved. . .	272	Priest 30	4
who hath in his hand an apple, and a piece of Gold under it;	272	Priest 30	8
and with pulling, gets the apple out of his Fathers hand: . .	272	Priest 30	9
his Father bids him throw it away, and he will give him the gold	272	Priest 30	10
wiles of Satan (who playes his part sometimes in drawing Gods	272	Priest 31	16
or by oversleeping himself at night, omits his additionary prayer.	272	Priest 31	31
Upon this his mind begins to be perplexed, and troubled, . .	272	Priest 31	32
and put him out of his station, and to inlarge the perplexity,	272	Priest 31	34
and taint his other duties of piety, which none can perform so wel in	273	Priest 31	1
Here the Parson interposeth with his distinction, and shews . .	273	Priest 31	4
that whenever he repaires to his house, he may behave himself so	273	Priest 31	26
some scoffing ruffian, who is likely to deride him for his paines:	273	Priest 31	29
either for fear or shame, break his custome, he shall do passing ill:	273	Priest 31	30
as that by this he may take into his Prayer humiliation also.	273	Priest 31	32
not onely taken a particular Survey of the faults of his own Parish,	274	Priest 32	5
when his occasions carry him abroad, or bring strangers to him,	274	Priest 32	6
The marryed and house-keeper hath his hands full, if he do what he	275	Priest 32	20
For there are two branches of his affaires;	275	Priest 32	21
the improvement of his family, by bringing them up in the fear	275	Priest 32	22
and secondly, the improvement of his grounds, by drowning, . .	275	Priest 32	24
and ordering his land to the best advantage both of himself,	275	Priest 32	25
his land to the best advantage both of himself, and his neighbours.	275	Priest 32	26
The Italian says, None fouls his hands in his own businesse:	275	Priest 32	27
for every one to imploy himselfe to the advancement of his affairs,	275	Priest 32	29
But his family is his best care, to labour Christian soules,	275	Priest 32	30
and his dexterity so great, that he have leisure to look out,	275	Priest 32	37
which either he lives in, or is neer unto it, is his imployment.	276	Priest 32	2
hath so many dispersed Officers at his beck throughout the Kingdome,	276	Priest 32	11
to mark their Fathers discretion in ordering his House and Affairs;	276	Priest 32	28
and to transplant it in time to his own home, with the same care	276	Priest 32	31
Great Horse, or exercise some of his Military gestures [Postures].	277	Priest 32	16
hath considered how to carry himself at table about his appetite,	278	Priest 33	19
judiciously, then he writes his rules of temperance out of bookes.	278	Priest 33	21
and mastered all his lusts and affections within, and the whole Army	278	Priest 33	22
from temptation, in a quiet sweetnesse seeks how to please his God.	279	Priest 33	6
having for his owne use examined the nature of it, is able . .	279	Priest 33	8
whether his repentance were true, or at least in that degree it ought	279	Priest 33	10
not only in the beginning of his preaching, but afterwards also,	280	Priest 34	9
And they must be likewise in all that are his.	280	Priest 34	11
according as he discovers any of his Flock to be in one or the other	280	Priest 34	13
who sacrificed lest his Children should have transgressed in their	281	Priest 34	1
military state, he fortifyes, and strengthens with his utmost skill.	281	Priest 34	6
for Atheisme) he scatters in his discourse three sorts of arguments;	281	Priest 34	15
intended by God, that the Jewes should be his proof, and witnesses,	282	Priest 34	12
to the acknowledging of God, and his power, Psalm 59. 11. . .	282	Priest 34	16
mens Covetousnesse, and Ambitions to the effecting of his word.	282	Priest 34	34
and woven into his discourse, at severall times and occasions,	283	Priest 34	4
of Gods Love, and the unspeakeable riches of his loving kindnesse.	283	Priest 34	8
for no perfect Artist ever yet hated his owne worke. . . .	283	Priest 34	12
because notwithstanding his infinite hate of sinne, his Love overcame	283	Priest 34	14
his infinite hate of sinne, his Love overcame that hate; . .	283	Priest 34	14
love for love, even the son of his love out of his bosome of love.	283	Priest 34	17
the one in his being, the other in his sinfull being: . . .	283	Priest 34	20
till either they despise that Love, or despaire of his Mercy:	283	Priest 34	23
not any sin else, but is within his Love;	283	Priest 34	24
The thrusting away of his arme makes us onely not embraced. . .	283	Priest 34	26
Now Love is his business, and aime;	284	Priest 35	16
that his Parish at good times invite one another to their houses,	284	Priest 35	17
is ashamed in small things, will extend his pusillanimity to greater.	284	Priest 35	34
to harden himselfe, and to further his exercises of Mortification.	284	Priest 35	36
that Blessing the people is in so little use with his brethren:	285	Priest 36	2
which though our Saviour reproved as unfitting for his particular,	285	Priest 36	27
who was to shew all humility before his Passion, yet he allows in his	285	Priest 36	28
shew all humility before his Passion, yet he allows in his Apostles.	285	Priest 36	28
who had withstood his preaching, The Lord (saith he) reward him	285	Priest 36	33
his preaching, The Lord (saith he) reward him according to his works.	285	Priest 36	34
the Priests Benedicite, and his holy water were over highly valued;	286	Priest 36	15
values the gift in himself, and then teacheth his parish to value it.	286	Priest 36	19
a reverence, and makes him esteemed according to his Profession.	286	Priest 36	25
but also spread in his Parish, without any remedy (which cannot be	287	Priest 37	1
dishonor of God, and the infection of his flock, and the discomfort,	287	Priest 37	3
except besides his office, he add a tincture of private malice in	287	Priest 37	26
a tincture of private malice in the joy, and hast of acting his part;	287	Priest 37	28
if the punished delinquent shall be much troubled for his sins,	288	Priest 37	3
for his enemies he died;	288	Priest	29
who continueth to pour his benefits upon us.	290	Priest	2
because in his meats and drinks he kept a due moderation; . .	294	Cornaro	8
because by eating little he prolongs his life.	295	Cornaro	35
when he cometh to visit his patient, prescribes this Physick first,	297	Cornaro	16
if he will give his minde to those things which he should, . .	297	Cornaro	22
one by long experience may know the qualities of his own nature,	297	Cornaro	27
but such meats as are agreeable to his disease, and that in much	299	Cornaro	31
For if he should keep his former proportion, Nature, which is	299	Cornaro	33
and not the qualitie for his rule, which is very easie to be	300	Cornaro	15
written by MR. GEORGE HERBERT to his friend the Translator of this	304	Valdesso	T
happily also with this (as his thoughts are fruitfull) intending	304	Valdesso	12
are fruitfull) intending the honour of his servant the Author,	304	Valdesso	13

HIS (cont'd)

	PAGE	TITLE		LINE
who being obscured in his own country he would have to flourish in	304	Valdesso		14
in this land of light, and region of the Gospell, among his chosen.	304	Valdesso		15
(as he sheweth through all his Considerations) a thing strangely	305	Valdesso		1
concluding every Consideration almost with his holy Name,	305	Valdesso		5
and setting his merit forth so piously, for which I doe so love him,	305	Valdesso		6
that it makes him godly, righteous, and sober all his life long;	309	Valdesso		6
to open his eyes that he might see the wondrous things of his Lawes,	309	Valdesso		25
to open his eyes that he might see the wondrous things of his Lawes,	309	Valdesso		26
wondrous things of his Lawes, and that he would make them his study.	309	Valdesso		27
the Consideration of Gods Worke in his heart through the Word,	309	Valdesso		30
observed, who workes by his Word, and ever in the reading of it.	310	Valdesso		1
the Doctrine would be examined, however it may passe for his opinion:	312	Valdesso		1
will better appear by his 98 Consideration of faith and good works.	312	Valdesso	V	5
God affectionately and fervently to send him the light of his spirit,	312	Valdesso		17
which may be unto him as the sunne to a Travellour in his journey,	312	Valdesso		18
to relieve my Neighbour, God hath already reveled his Will about it.	313	Valdesso		14
reviling also of Ananias seemes, by his owne recalling, an oversight;	316	Valdesso		11
and had killed his sonne Isaac, but he might have been justly put	316	Valdesso		24
for as a Magistrate judgeth in his tribunall, so a Scholar judgeth in	317	Valdesso		2
so a Scholar judgeth in his study, and censureth this or that;	317	Valdesso		2
Yet his owne practice seemes to confute his opinion, for the most	317	Valdesso		35
for the most of his Considerations being grounded upon some text	318	Valdesso		1
said of this Chapter but that his opinion of the scripture is	318	Valdesso		5
2 Ep. 1. 19. which he makes the ground of his [this] Consideration,	318	Valdesso		7
afterward they will attend it of themselves without his exhortation.	318	Valdesso		22
And so his whole discourse and sevenfold observation falls	318	Valdesso		25
the world is counted a very Saint, for his outward shew of holinesse:	319	Valdesso	V	21
Hee begins to die, that quits his desires.	321	Proverbs		2
He that studies his content, wants it.	321	Proverbs		4
Every day brings his bread with it.	321	Proverbs		5
Hee that stumbles and falles not, mends his pace.	321	Proverbs		7
All is well with him, who is beloved of his neighbours.	321	Proverbs		10
All is well to him, that is loved of his neighbours.	321	Proverbs	V	10
Who hath none to still him, may weepe out his eyes.	321	Proverbs		17
The Germans wit is in his fingers.	322	Proverbs		36
The Germans wit lies in his fingers.	322	Proverbs	V	36
For washing his hands, none sels his lands.	323	Proverbs		54
Who hath a Wolfe for his mate, needes a Dog for his man.	323	Proverbs		57
Every ill man hath his ill day.	324	Proverbs		92
Every one stretcheth his legges according to his coverlet.	325	Proverbs		147
A wicked mans gift hath a touch of his master.	326	Proverbs		162
Hee that lies long a bed, his estate feeles it.	327	Proverbs		179
It takes much from the account, to which his sin doth amount.	327	Proverbs		192
The Smith and his penny both are black.	327	Proverbs		195
He that plaies his mony ought not to value it.	327	Proverbs		201
One graine fills not a sacke, but helpes his fellowes.	328	Proverbs		226
He that riseth betimes hath some thing in his head.	329	Proverbs		235
The thorne comes forth with his point forwards.	329	Proverbs		238
A foole knowes more in his house, then a wise man in anothers.	329	Proverbs		257
While the discreet advise, the foole doth his busines.	330	Proverbs		273
A mans discontent is his worst evill.	331	Proverbs		298
Hee that burnes his house warmes himselfe for once.	331	Proverbs		303
He will burne his house, to warme his hands.	331	Proverbs		304
Hee wrongs not an old man that steales his supper from him.	331	Proverbs		311
Hee that strikes with his tongue, must ward with his head.	331	Proverbs		313
Hee that strikes with his tongue, must ward with his hand.	331	Proverbs	V	313
In vaine is the mill-clacke, if the Miller his hearing lack.	332	Proverbs		328
at his time, and not till then.	332	Proverbs		333
He that makes his bed ill, lies there.	332	Proverbs		340
Who spits against heaven, it falls in his face.	333	Proverbs		346
Who eates his cock alone must saddle his horse alone.	333	Proverbs		348
Who eates his cake alone must saddle his horse alone.	333	Proverbs	V	348
He that hath a mouth of his owne,	333	Proverbs		353
He that hath lost his credit is dead to the world.	333	Proverbs		357
Hee that demands misseth not, unlesse his demands be foolish.	333	Proverbs		359
He that hath no hony in his pot, let him have it in his mouth.	333	Proverbs		360
He that takes not up a pin, slights his wife.	333	Proverbs		361
Hee that looseth his due, gets no thankes.	333	Proverbs		363
A married man turns his staffe into a stake.	333	Proverbs		366
An ill labourer quarrells with his tooles.	335	Proverbs		408
Who doth his owne businesse, foules not his hands.	335	Proverbs		419
Hee that workes after his owne manner,	335	Proverbs		421
his head akes not at the matter.	335	Proverbs		421
Who hath bitter in his mouth, spits not all sweet.	335	Proverbs		422
He that hath children, all his morsels are not his owne.	335	Proverbs		423
He who hath children, all his morsels are not his owne.	335	Proverbs	V	423
He that hath love in his brest, hath spurres in his sides.	335	Proverbs		426
Hee that hath a Fox for his mate,	335	Proverbs		428
hath neede of a net at his girdle.	335	Proverbs		428
Who letts his wife goe to every feast,	336	Proverbs		434
and his horse drinke at every water,	336	Proverbs		434
He that speakes sowes, and he that holds his peace, gathers.	336	Proverbs		435
Hee that bewailes himselfe hath the cure in his hands.	336	Proverbs		441
He that would be well, needs not goe from his owne house.	336	Proverbs		442
The first service a child doth his father is to make him foolish.	337	Proverbs		463
The eye will have his part.	337	Proverbs		466
The gowne is his that weares it,	337	Proverbs		476
and the world his that enjoyes it.	337	Proverbs		476
The masters eye fattens the horse, and his foote the ground.	338	Proverbs		486
Love rules his kingdome without a sword.	339	Proverbs		541

HIT (cont'd)	PAGE	TITLE		LINE
At th' hart of others, hit their own.	96	Charms & K	W	10
And can hit from farre.	179	Discipline		24
HITHER				
Turn their eyes hither, who shall make a gain:	5	Dedication		5
Hither sometimes Sinne steals, and stains	67	Ch.-floore		13
He, who came hither all alone,	151	The Bag		27
Come ye hither all, whose taste	179	Invitation		1
Come ye hither all, whom wine	180	Invitation		7
Come ye hither all, whom pain	180	Invitation		13
Come ye hither all, whcm joy	180	Invitation		19
Come ye hither all, whose love	180	Invitation		25
From times great Chronicle, and hither sent.	192	Ch.-Milit.		96
there, transplant them hither, as divers have done lately,	278	Priest 32		9
you that there are come agents hither from the low-Cuntries to treat	368	Letters		5
HITHERTO				
education, of obeying that Spirit which hath guided me hitherto,	364	Letters		18
Now though they have hitherto travelled upon your charge,	366	Letters		31
which she hath hitherto deferred to do, not of her self,	367	Letters		3
that she had done nothing in it (as my Brother writes) hitherto.	379	Letters		5
HITS				
he that throws a stone at another, hits himselfe;	269	Priest 28		14
HITTS				
hee that beleeveth nothing, hitts not.	333	Proverbs		364
He that once hitts, is ever bending.	347	Proverbs		785
HIVE				
Unto that hive of beams	74	The Starre		31
That hive of sweetnesse, tc remove	107	Home		20
HOARSE				
My throat, my soul is hoarse;	148	Longing		7
If ever Voice was hoarse with Cries,	213	Convert	D	2
HOG				
To steale the Hog, and give the feet for almes.	329	Proverbs		237
HOGGE				
Hee that hath one hogge makes him fat,	336	Proverbs		433
HOGS				
fat Hogs among Jews, and Wine in a fishing net.	361	Proverbs	D	1163
HOLD				
Stay at the third glasse: if thou lose thy hold,	8	Ch.-Porch		41
As all the day thou mayst hold out to go.	14	Ch.-Porch		186
That all the day thou mayst hold out to go.	14	Ch.-Porch	W	186
That if I chance to hold my peace,	26	The Altar		13
See, they lay hold on me, not with the hands	28	Sacrifice		45
To hold thee.	41	Sepulchre		20
Thou didst lay hold, and antedate	44	H. Bapt.2		4
To hide my dust, then thee to hold.	45	Nature		18
Himself the candle hold.	81	Christmas		26
To hold my quill? shall they not do thee right?	116	Providence		4
And hold it fast, as children do their fathers,	118	Providence		46
Doth give a hold and handle to affliction.	126	Confession		24
I hold for two lives, and both lives in me.	129	Love unkn.		5
And hold my hand, while I did write.	156	Assurance		30
To hold the Ark, although it seem to shake	161	Priesthood		32
Except life catch & hold those fast.	202	Trin.Sun.	W	10
errand I come, let me hold my peace, and doe thou speak thy selfe;	233	Priest 7		35
he presently lays hold of it, least the poyson steal into some young	252	Priest 18		5
That position will not hold in Christianity, because it contains	256	Priest 21		24
of which he gathers, in case he be ignorant himself, what to hold;	260	Priest 23		12
if there be any of his parish that hold strange Doctrins,	262	Priest 24		20
they resist not the evill which takes hold of them, and is farr	269	Priest 28		24
being directed by them in the way I ought to hold, I understood,	292	Cornaro		24
Divines hold, that justifying faith, and the faith of miracles are	319	Valdesso		6
Mend your cloathes, and you may hold out this yeare.	324	Proverbs		100
No lock will hold against the power of gold.	332	Proverbs		317
No Lockes can hold against gold.	332	Proverbs	V	317
When you are an Anvill, hold you still;	332	Proverbs		338
The first degree of folly is to hold ones selfe wise,	337	Proverbs		460
Three can hold their peace, if two be away.	345	Proverbs		714
They that hold the greatest farmes, pay the least rent	359	Proverbs	D	1100
It is good to hold the asse by the bridle.	360	Proverbs	D	1129
HOLDETH				
Pilate a stranger holdeth off; but they,	29	Sacrifice		101
HOLDFAST				
The Holdfast.	143	Holdfast		T
HOLDING				
holding that rule, that to put men to discourse of that,	260	Priest 23		5
HOLDS				
God holds his peace at man, and man cries out:	32	Sacrifice		187
Which holds thee now? Who hath indited it	41	Sepulchre		11
To captivate strong holds to thee.	45	Nature		6
That flesh is but the glasse, which holds the dust	65	Ch.-monum.		20
Holds them unto it, and doth cover	100	Miserie		27
The sunne holds down his head for shame,	101	Miserie		33
but he holds the Rule, that Nothing is little in Gods service:	249	Priest 14		1
but it is sutable to what the Author holds elsewhere, for he	311	Valdesso		22
He that speakes sowes, and he that holds his peace, gathers.	336	Proverbs		435
HOLE				
I gave the mouse a hole, and she is become my heire.	324	Proverbs		94
The hole calls the thiefe.	327	Proverbs		204
The mouse that hath but one hole is quickly taken.	360	Proverbs	D	1135
Take heed of winde that comes in at a hole,	360	Proverbs	D	1154

HONOUR (cont'd)	PAGE	TITLE		LINE
To set thy honour up, as our designe.	164	The Crosse		6
my slaughter'd hcnour lay.	221	Psalm VII	D	20
increase of means, or honour, be a sin of covetousnes or ambition,	230	Priest 5		27
liberall disposition he preferred before beauty, riches, or honour.	238	Priest 9		29
encouragements to goodnesse as he can, both in honour, and profit,	244	Priest 11		4
the first being for the honour of God;	246	Priest 13		31
If it once have the honour of that Name, it grows great instantly.	249	Priest 14		3
refreshment, gladly betakes it selfe, even to the losse of honour.	252	Priest 18		23
these privately, giving age honour, according to the Apostles rule,	255	Priest 21		24
thing to sustain that place, but a great honour, and no less burden,	258	Priest 22		12
incomprehensible God, be ascribed all Honour, and Glory, . .	290	Priest		16
the end I got the victorie, to my great honour, and no lesse profit:	294	Cornaro		28
are fruitfull) intending the hcnour of his servant the Author,	304	Valdesso		13
the great honour and reverence, which he every where beares towards	305	Valdesso		3
Print it, that with it the honour of my Lord might be published.	305	Valdesso		8
Where there is no honour, there is no griefe.	327	Proverbs		186
Honour without profit is a ring on the finger.	328	Proverbs		230
Honour and profit lie not in one sacke.	328	Proverbs		232
We cannot come to honour under a Coverlet.	339	Proverbs		533
No profit to hcnour, no honour to Religion.	346	Proverbs		759
An ill deede cannot bring honour.	348	Proverbs		806
Modesty sets off one newly come to honour.	357	Proverbs	D	1062
HONOURABLE				
may then by an honourable way take occasion to be better instructed.	255	Priest 21		31
and also an honourable Imployment of a Gentle, or Noble-man in	276	Priest 32		12
To the Right Honourable the Lady Anne, Countess of Pembr. and Montg.	376	Letters		T
HONOURING				
to his Diocesan, honouring him both in word, and behaviour, . .	253	Priest 19		7
HONOURS				
A faire death honours the whole life.	339	Proverbs		522
HONY				
But hony is their gall, brightnesse their night:	30	Sacrifice		111
Neither bring hcny with the bees, ...	57	Employm. 1		18
Suck ev'ry letter, and a hony gain, ...	58	H.Script.1		2
So both the flower doth stay, and hony run.	118	Providence		68
Your hony drops: presse not to smell them here:	120	Providence		118
Hony of roses, whither wilt thou flie?	176	Forerunners		20
He that hath no hony in his pot, let him have it in his mouth.	333	Proverbs		360
Every bees hony is sweet.	341	Proverbs		609
A dead Bee maketh no Hony.	358	Proverbs	D	1098
HOOD				
he inlargeth himself, if he be able, to the neighbour-hood; . .	245	Priest 12		18
of Charity, and Neighbour-hood, he first gives himself liberally,	253	Priest 19		35
HOOK				
The Shepherds hock grew to a scepter here, ...	192	Ch.-Milit.		71
Strugling on th' hook.	204	The Knell	W	6
and making a hook of his Charity, causeth them still to depend	244	Priest 12		31
HOOKE				
The great put the little on the hooke.	352	Proverbs		945
HOOPES				
but to put bounds, and hoopes to their joyes:	280	Priest 34		29
HOPE				
And I hope and fear.	55	Temper 1		20
With faith, with hope, with charitie;	68	Trin.Sun.		8
Of an untrained hope or passion.	68	Content		6
Of an untrained hope & passion.	68	Content	V	6
Of an untrained hope and passion.	68	Content	W	6
More plentifull then hope.	76	Sunday		35
More plentifull and hope.	76	Sunday	W	35
Allureth all in hope to be	110	Brit. Ch.		14
Poore silly soul, whose hope and head lies low;	111	Vanitie 2		1
What delight or hope remains?	114	Dialogue		8
Hope.	121	Hope		T
I gave to Hope a watch of mine: but he	121	Hope		1
Lay out thy joy, yet hope to save it?	138	The Size		17
In hope of great things. Call to minde thy dream, ...	138	The Size		44
Where lay my hope, ...	142	Pilgrimage		20
In hope of thee my heart	154	Glimpse		16
If all the hope and comfort that I gather, ...	155	Assurance		21
When it grew loose, the Jews did hope in vain	190	Ch.-Milit.		23
Yet did a rogue with hope of carnall joy	194	Ch.-Milit.		149
And hope, that may teach it to shine, ...	203	Even-song	W	19
They who for the hope of promotion neglect any necessary admonition,	226	Priest 2		36
and therefore out of an hope of avoiding death and pain, . .	292	Cornaro		21
onely upon a hope of an happie issue, which yet befalls verie few.	300	Cornaro		23
but also I hope, when I shall come to that point, I shall finde no	303	Cornaro		23
Distrust, Hope: Of these none can free themselves of themselves,	308	Valdesso		8
Hope is the poore mans bread.	337	Proverbs		477
Hee that lives in hope danceth without musick.	354	Proverbs		1006
since, I hope, I have not deceived their expectation, let not them	364	Letters		23
Sister this week already, and therefore now I hope may be excused.	367	Letters		22
I hope I shall get this place without all your London helps,	370	Letters		7
but I hope I shall shortly, though for the reckoning of your favours,	370	Letters		30
better content because I was in hope I should my self carry all	372	Letters		15
much power or boldness as to oppose the hope of our Joyes hereafter!	372	Letters		28
HOPES				
Thou, whose sweet youth and early hopes inhance	6	Ch.-Porch		1
Spend not on hopes. They that by pleading clothes	14	Ch.-Porch		181
Angels and grace, eternall hopes and fears.	46	Sinne 1		12
Thus argu'd into hopes, my thoughts reserved	46	Afflict.1		15

HOW (cont'd)

	PAGE	TITLE		LINE
How shall I count what thee befell,	38	Good Fri.		3
Lord, how couldst thou so much appease	49	Faith		1
How hath man parcel'd out thy glorious name,	54	Love 1		3
How should I praise thee, Lord! how should my rymes	55	Temper 1		1
Oh that I knew how all thy lights combine,	58	H.Script.2		1
Seeing not onely how each verse doth shine,	58	H.Script.2		3
How tame these ashes are, how free from lust,	65	Ch.-monum.		23
Lord, how can man preach thy eternall word?	67	Windows		1
Mark how the fire in flints doth quiet lie,	68	Content		9
Mark how the fire in Flint doth quiet lie,	68	Content	W	9
Lord, in my silence how do I despise	71	Frailtie		1
How well her name an Army doth present,	77	Anagram		1
Till it found out how to consume thy goods:	83	Sighs & Gr.		11
How many drammes of spirit there must be	88	The Pearl		18
Did both conduct and teach me, how by it	89	The Pearl		39
Then how are all things neat?	92	Man		42
How know I, if thou shouldst me raise,	95	Submission		13
How soon doth man decay!	98	Mortific.		1
How soon does man decay	98	Mortific.	W	1
How canst thou brook his foolishnesse?	100	Miserie		7
How shall infection	101	Miserie		35
How hast thou lost them in a croud of cares?	101	Miserie		50
Whisper, How wide is all this long pretence!	103	Jordan 2		16
Whisper, How wide is all this preparation	103	Jordan 2	W	16
My blessed Lord, art thou! how suddenly	103	Prayer 2		2
Art thou, my blessed King? how suddenly	103	Prayer 2	W	2
How happie were my part,	105	Obedience		41
How canst thou stay, considering the pace	107	Home		7
How finely dost thou times and seasons spin,	118	Providence		57
How harsh are thorns to pears! and yet they make	120	Providence		121
How smooth are silks compared with a stake,	120	Providence		123
See how thy beggar works on thee	123	Gratefulnes		3
Oh, what a thing is man! how farre from power,	127	Giddinesse		1
Heark, how the birds do sing,	131	Mans medly		1
Not to relieve? how can it be,	150	Longing		62
Thou knowst how grief and sinne	155	Glimpse		28
Yet can I mark how herbs below	162	The Search		9
Yet can I mark how starres above	162	The Search		13
How fresh, O Lord, how sweet and clean	165	The Flower		1
How neatly doe we give one onely name	168	The Sonne		5
Go spell and reade how I have kill'd thy King.	169	Dial.-Anth		4
How sweetly doth My Master sound! My Master!	174	The Odour		1
God, to show how farre his love	181	Banquet		28
Almightie Judge, how shall poore wretches brook	187	Judgement		1
How deare to me, O God, thy counsels are!	191	Ch.-Milit.		47
How deare to me, O God, thy counsels are!	192	Ch.-Milit.		99
Who makes a root his God, how low is he,	193	Ch.-Milit.		115
How deare to me, O God, thy counsels are!	194	Ch.-Milit.		155
How deare to me, O God, thy counsels are!	196	Ch.-Milit.		209
How deare to me, O God, thy counsels are!	198	Ch.-Milit.		278
O gratious Lord how shall I know	200	H. Commun.	W	1
How sweet a friend was he, who being griev'd	439	Walton 5		15
How know you that our teares proceed from woe	210	Paradox	D	15
How know you that the sighes we send	210	Paradox	D	19
How are my foes increased, Lord?	216	Psalm III	D	1
How long will ye, vain men, convert	217	Psalm IV	D	7
How long will ye seek after lies,	217	Psalm IV	D	9
But, Lord, how long so much perplex'd	220	Psalm VI	D	7
how much more in things of another world, where the well is deep,	228	Priest 4		34
which grass will bane, or which not, how is he fit to be a shepherd?	230	Priest 5		32
having often instructed his people how to carry themselves in divine	231	Priest 6		21
How did he put the Romans in all his prayers? Rom. 1. 9.	234	Priest 7		11
how full of affections? he joyes, and he is sorry, he grieves,	234	Priest 7		18
that how or whenever he punish him, it be not in his Ministry:	235	Priest 8		26
he contrives how and in what manner to induce it to the best	236	Priest 8		1
but that he sometimes looks how things go, demanding an account,	239	Priest 9		2
and how every one profits, comparing this yeer with the last:	240	Priest 10		37
shewing them how acceptable such works are to God, and wishing them	247	Priest 14		18
antient and pious ordinance, and how necessary it is in some cases:	249	Priest 15		31
how comfortable, and Soveraigne a Medicine it is to all sin-sick	250	Priest 15		1
and other good books, how Sundayes, holy-days, and fasting days are	251	Priest 17		24
how poor or mean soever, with as joyfull a countenance,	253	Priest 19		19
How came this world to be as it is?	256	Priest 21		6
with himself, how or what behaviour to assume for so holy things.	257	Priest 22		27
But then he shews them how to go to Law, even as Brethren,	260	Priest 23		25
as what the Church is, how it began, how it proceeded, whether it be	263	Priest 24		1
how it began, how it proceeded, whether it be a rule to it selfe,	263	Priest 24		1
and how then should the best be so, at least in fundamentall things,	263	Priest 24		4
of dependance, how faire soever the opportunities present themselves.	271	Priest 30		27
in this, how Gods goodnesse strives with mans refractorinesse;	272	Priest 30		5
and how much more out of Paradise, when the evills which he is now	274	Priest 32		22
Hee that hath considered how to carry himself at table about his	278	Priest 33		18
from temptation, in a quiet sweetnesse seeks how to please his God.	279	Priest 33		5
he sees not how a house could be either built without a builder,	281	Priest 34		18
how the windes should blow so much as they can, and the sea rage so	281	Priest 34		20
how he that would beleeve a Divinity, if he had been at the Creation	281	Priest 34		27
their children, how much more may, and ought Spirituall Fathers?	285	Priest 36		14
how shall not the ministration of the spirit exceed in blessing?	285	Priest 36		19
as appears Rom. 12. 14. how much more those, who are spirituall	286	Priest 36		27
finds it somwhat difficult how to proceed in this point.	286	Priest 37		33

HOW (cont'd)	PAGE	TITLE		LINE
How shall we dare to appear before thy face, who are contrary	288	Priest		8
a great desire tc know the way of my life, and how I came to be so.	291	Cornaro		12
how much more to preserve it!	293	Cornaro		3
clearely be perceived, how great is the power of order and disorder;	297	Cornaro		3
how much more dearely should a Physician be esteemed, who not onely	298	Cornaro		8
of how great moment ten yeares are in mature age, wherein wisdome	298	Cornaro		29
much as she can, teacheth us hcw to govern our selves in sicknesse:	299	Cornaro		26
aim in all things, how I may help others to the furthest of my power.	301	Cornaro		8
I know how inconsiderate that age is, and, though subject to death,	303	Cornaro		16
How the godly are exempt from Laws is a known point among Divines,	316	Valdesso		30
I wonder how this opinion could befall so good a man as it seems	317	Valdesso		31
How many places doe the Fathers bring about Untill against	318	Valdesso		9
how that which is to come will be drawne on.	332	Proverbs		329
All things have their place, knew wee how to place them.	334	Proverbs		379
To gaine teacheth how to spend.	337	Proverbs		455
He that's long a giving, knowes not how to give.	338	Proverbs		494
Halfe the world knowes not how the other halfe lives.	351	Proverbs		907
Halfe the world knowes not how the other halfe lies.	351	Proverbs	V	907
only hereafter I will take heed how I propose my desires unto you,	363	Letters		20
how I am now setting foot into Divinity, to lay the platform of my	364	Letters		11
first, how her health fares, next, whether my peace be yet made	371	Letters		8
my absence by how much it naturally augmenteth suspicion,	372	Letters		21
how easily is that answered, when we consider that the Blessings in	373	Letters		27
how they have been burnt by thousands, and have endur'd such other	373	Letters		36
how destitute she is, and that in this necessary time of education.	376	Letters		12
I heard frcm you, that I long to heare both how you and your's doe:	379	Letters		24
of want of success consider how long God knocks at our harts,	381	Woodnoth		1
by which we well know how to convince the sterne, and more austere	442	Oration		6
How could you bee like great Alexander, unlesse Historie delivered	443	Oration		2
HOWARD				
Sir Charles Howard & his Lady are at much difference, & shee being	368	Letters		19
HOWEVER				
that wicked men, however learned, do not know the Scriptures,	228	Priest 4		30
However, he resolves with himself never to omit any present good deed	240	Priest 10		5
However, one way or other, he ever reproves them, that he may keep	248	Priest 14		23
the Doctrine would be examined, however it may passe for his opinion:	312	Valdesso		1
This doctrine however true in substance, yet needeth [requireth]	314	Valdesso		1
but however he would have them attend to it till that time,	318	Valdesso		20
However, I need not their help, to reprove the vanity of those many	363	Letters		6
HOWL				
Musick to thee doth howl.	105	Conscience		4
HOWRE				
so devout as to come to the Chappell an howre before prayers began,	368	Letters		17
HOWSHOULD				
both monneys and bookes and howshould stuffe whether in my possession	382	G.H.'s Will		4
HUDLING				
which answers also are to be done not in a hudling, or slubbering	231	Priest 6		30
HUE				
Sweet rose, whose hue angrie and brave	87	Vertue		5
Thy perfect lineaments, and hue	109	Brit. Ch.		2
End as the night, whose sable hue	135	Ephes.		11
HUGE				
As those which rise from a huge King.	69	Content		24
HUMANE				
Parson hath throughly canvassed al the particulars of humane actions,	230	Priest 5		34
for the humane soule being bounded, and kept in, in her sensitive	238	Priest 9		10
and exposing to them the uncertainty of humane affairs,	253	Priest 19		32
Wherefore he condescends to humane frailties both in himselfe	268	Priest 27		5
By renouncing the help of humane learning in the studying	314	Valdesso	V	3
HUMANO				
that is in humano foro & secundum praesumptionem legalem,	316	Valdesso		28
HUMBLE				
So shalt thou humble and magnanimous be:	19	Ch.-Porch		332
The humble scul compos'd of love and fear	86	Lent		7
Who looks on ground with humble eyes,	96	Charms & K		11
Humble Obedience neare the doore doth stand,	137	Familie		13
Thy board is full, yet humble guests	149	Longing		53
Adoring garlick with an humble face,	193	Ch.-Milit.		112
Against this meane & humble Blackamore.	209	L. Bacon	D	10
and humble supplication hears.	220	Psalm VI	D	24
Accordingly his voyce is humble, his words treatable, and slow;	231	Priest 6		17
which he observeth out of humble conformity, and obedience;	237	Priest 9		24
whose humble, and liberall disposition he preferred before beauty,	238	Priest 9		28
the other an humble, and ingenuous search of truth;	263	Priest 24		17
he takes it either in an humble way, saying nothing at all;	269	Priest 28		6
Humble Hearts have humble desires.	321	Proverbs		6
I remember my most humble duty to my Mother.	367	Letters		20
I remember my most humble duty to my Mother, who cannot think me	371	Letters		1
Your poor Colony of Servants present their humble duties.	377	Letters		13
HUMBLENESSE				
A grain of glorie mixt with humblenesse	19	Ch.-Porch		335
For what Christ once in humblenesse began,	168	The Sonne		13
With pensive humblenesse would live and tread:	173	Marie Magd		6
in Catechizing there is an humblenesse very sutable to Christian	255	Priest 21		10
HUMBLEST				
and yet still grow upon Your humblest Servant, GEORGE HERBERT.	367	Letters		16
your Courtesie will pardon the haste of Your humblest Servant,	371	Letters		20
HUMBLING				
the punishment to a better subduing, and humbling of the delinquent;	263	Priest 25		32

HUMBLY	PAGE	TITLE	LINE
Sweet Peace, where dost thou dwell? I humbly crave, . . .	124	Peace	1
humbly beseeching his Master, that how or whenever he punish him,	235	Priest 8	26
at his first entrance humbly adoring, and worshipping the invisible	236	Priest 8	4
humbly beseeching the Almighty to pardon and accept our poor	236	Priest 8	26
for which I humbly thank him, & am so far from giving you cause,	378	Letters	9
HUMILIATION			
so Friday his day of Humiliation, which he celebrates not only	241	Priest 10	37
and in regard of himselfe, it is more humiliation.	249	Priest 14	9
as that by this he may take into his Prayer humiliation also.	273	Priest 31	32
acts of humiliation, and acts of confidence and joy;	312	Valdesso V	23
HUMILITIE			
Humilitie:	67	Ch.-floore	6
Humilitie.	70	Humilitie	T
Humilitie, who sat the lowest there	70	Humilitie	5
Humilitie did reach to Fortitude.	70	Humilitie	12
Humilitie, who held the plume, at this	71	Humilitie	25
So in one word our Lords humilitie	168	The Sonne	11
HUMILITY			
the servants of God, for the planting both of love, and humility.	229	Priest 4	27
To put on the profound humility, and the exact temperance of our Lord	237	Priest 9	33
women to heaven) a wise and loving husband could out of humility,	238	Priest 9	31
and carving for them, both for his own humility, and their comfort,	243	Priest 11	12
who was to shew all humility before his Passion, yet he allows in his	285	Priest 36	28
HUMOUR			
no inconvenience thereby, because that humour abounded not in me.	294	Cornaro	22
HUMOURS			
Lose not thy self, nor give thy humours way:	12	Ch.-Porch	143
His knowledge winks, and lets his humours reigne;	102	Miserie	62
Disbanded humours, sorrows trocps of Sinn	204	The Knell W	11
without difficultie, and no ill humours being ingendred in the body.	293	Cornaro	29
and purging, that the store of humours, and inflammation, . . .	295	Cornaro	5
which must needs so temper the humours of the bodie, that they could	295	Cornaro	8
For the Temperance of so many yeares spent all ill humours, . . .	296	Cornaro	33
neither the good humours to be corrupted, or contract any ill	296	Cornaro	34
For there is no malignitie of old age in the humours of my bodie,	296	Cornaro	37
if our corporall life depend on the harmonie of humours & elements,	297	Cornaro	8
of the radicall moisture, without grief or perturbation of humours.	298	Cornaro	19
HUNDRED			
Who at three hundred did the ointment prize, ...	27	Sacrifice	18
Comes to about the many hundred part.	38	The Sinner W	11
We count three hundred, but we misse:	42	Easter	29
Although there were a hundred heav'ns, or more, ...	55	Temper 1 W	5
Have done these twentie hundred yeares, and more:	89	The Pearl	25
Have done these many hundred yeares, and more:	89	The Pearl W	25
that they prolong their life even to a hundred yeares and more,	298	Cornaro	16
The buyer needes a hundred eyes, the seller not one.	334	Proverbs	390
One father is enough to governe one hundred sons, ...	335	Proverbs	404
but not a hundred sons one father.	335	Proverbs	404
A hundred loade of thought will not pay one of debts.	335	Proverbs	414
One foole makes a hundred.	339	Proverbs	525
One paire of eares drawes dry a hundred tongues.	339	Proverbs	526
which a hundred wise men cannot pull out.	339	Proverbs	527
One father is more then a hundred Schoolemasters.	344	Proverbs	686
In an hundred elles of contention, there is not an inch of love.	348	Proverbs	817
these many years, as having spent two hundred pounds in building;	376	Letters	1
First there is seaven hundred pounds in Mr Thomas Lawleys hands	382	G.H.'s Will	8
Dorothy Vaughan whereof two hundred pounds belongs to my two Neeces	382	G.H.'s Will	10
this whole sum of five hundred pounds I bequeath unto my Neeces	382	G.H.'s Will	12
To Mrss Magdalen Vaughan one hundred pound, To Mrs Catharine Vaughan	383	G.H.'s Will	5
To Mrs Catharine Vaughan One hundred pound, To Mr George Herbert one	383	G.H.'s Will	6
To Mr George Herbert one hundred pound To Mrs Beatrice Herbert forty	383	G.H.'s Will	7
having lately receaved an hundred and two pounds besides some	383	G.H.'s Will	24
HUNDREDTH			
Comes to about the many hundredth part.	38	The Sinner	11
HUNG			
Hung down his head, and wisht for night, ...	59	Whitsunday	14
Like a nipt blossome, hung	80	Deniall	24
HUNGER			
that so the hunger and thirst after it may come rather from . .	250	Priest 15	5
Hunger makes dinners, pastime suppers.	348	Proverbs	819
HUNGRED			
As when the people hungred and thirsted after our Saviours Doctrine,	267	Priest 26	22
HUNGRETH			
to the person, hungreth and thirsteth after righteous punishment	254	Priest 20	28
HUNGRIE			
Hungrie I was, and had no meat:	50	Faith	5
Is more then God was, who was hungrie here.	138	The Size	14
HUNGRY			
disposition I am, either hungry cr not, according as I feele my self,	267	Priest 26	8
HUNT			
To hunt his cruell food through ev'ry vein.	37	The Agonie	12
Lord, hunt me not, ...	89	Afflict.4	2
HUNTING			
In war, hunting, and love, ...	328	Proverbs	228
HURL'D			
Man is out of order hurl'd, ...	187	Dooms-day	27
HURT			
Theirs, who shall hurt themselves or me, refrain.	5	Dedication	6
Rain, do not hurt my flowers; but gently spend	120	Providence	117
Not to his hurt. Sighs will convey	152	The Bag	41

HURT (cont'd)	PAGE	TITLE	LINE
Poore death! and who was hurt thereby?	169	Dial.-Anth	5
And hurt thy self, and him that sings the note.	176	Forerunners	24
But to eat to ones hurt, comprehends, besides the hurt, . .	266	Priest 26	21
comprehends, besides the hurt, an act against reason, because it is	266	Priest 26	21
an act against reason, because it is unnaturall to hurt ones self;	266	Priest 26	22
you hurt your selfe, not me;	269	Priest 28	13
that they had no great power to hurt those bodies, which were kept in	294	Cornaro	2
keep a fit proportion, shall receive little hurt from other excesses.	294	Cornaro	5
and windes and labours did little hurt him, because in his meats	294	Cornaro	7
all these did hurt me little, whereas they hurt them very much who	294	Cornaro	14
whereas they hurt them very much who live intemperately. . .	294	Cornaro	14
which excesse of joy neither could do me any hurt.	294	Cornaro	30
neither melancholie, nor any other passion can hurt a temperate life.	294	Cornaro	31
can bring little grief or hurt to those that are temperate. . .	294	Cornaro	34
whereby my head and whole bodie was sore hurt, and also one of my	294	Cornaro	39
a temperate life, can receive little hurt from other inconveniences.	295	Cornaro	15
that the hurt of too much meat is greater, then the commoditie	296	Cornaro	2
Who would beleeve that old wine should hurt my stomack, . .	297	Cornaro	32
I abstain from fruit, and fish, and the like, because they hurt me.	300	Cornaro	10
is very great) receiving not any hurt or inconvenience thereby:	302	Cornaro	20
if we believe, no sinne shall hurt us;	311	Valdesso	25
but sometimes he can hurt.	359	Proverbs D	1119
be none of the Court-stile, yet doubtless Madam, can do you no hurt:	377	Letters	3
HURTFULL			
Yet of hurtfull things, I am more bound to abstain from those,	266	Priest 26	23
which by mine own experience I have found hurtfull, then from those	266	Priest 26	25
That which is said of hurtfull meats, extends to hurtfull drinks	266	Priest 26	27
which is said of hurtfull meats, extends to hurtfull drinks also.	266	Priest 26	27
and yet all these I found hurtfull.	293	Cornaro	14
Yet with this diet I avoided other hurtfull things also, . .	293	Cornaro	30
HURTS			
As hurts not others, but may make thee better, ...	16	Ch.-Porch	262
The tree that God plants, no winde hurts it.	344	Proverbs	691
HUSBAND			
That thou canst speak, at once; but husband it, ...	18	Ch.-Porch	302
women to heaven) a wise and loving husband could out of humility,	238	Priest 9	31
want a competent sustentation, nor her husband be brought in debt.	239	Priest 10	19
The wrongs of a Husband or Master are not reproached. . . .	325	Proverbs	139
In the husband wisedome, in the wife gentlenesse.	343	Proverbs	658
If the husband be not at home, there is nobodie.	354	Proverbs	1016
HUSBANDMAN			
and as the Husbandman labours for them, so must they fight for,	277	Priest 32	19
HUSBANDRIE			
Nor flowres to make that, nor the husbandrie	57	Employm. 1	19
Doth my dull husbandrie improve:	60	Grace	2
and husbandrie, whereof in this age there is great plentie. . .	301	Cornaro	37
untoiled places in my countrey, to cultivation and good husbandrie.	302	Cornaro	16
HUSBANDRY			
And lay it on thy husbandry, for shift.	59	Whitsunday W	20
when they see any remarkable point of Education or good husbandry,	276	Priest 32	30
as barren grounds are made fruitfull by good husbandry. . .	292	Cornaro	12
HUSBANDS			
A poore beauty finds more lovers then husbands.	337	Proverbs	481
HUSWIFE			
Or of it self, like a good huswife, spunne	88	The Pearl	4
HYMENEUS			
And again, of Hymeneus and Alexander, he saith, he had delivered them	285	Priest 36	34
HYMNE			
My God, no hymne for thee?	81	Christmas	16
To honour thee; and so each hymne thy fame	121	Providence	151
Then bring thy gift; and let thy hymne be this;	147	Offering	24
A true Hymne.	168	a true Hymn	T
The finenesse which a hymne or psalme affords, ...	168	a true Hymn	9
To make his verse, or write a hymne in kinde.	168	a true Hymn	15
HYMNES			
And there in hymnes send back thy fire again:	54	Love 2	8
In all my other hymnes, but in this twice.	121	Providence	148
HYPOCRISIE			
Simpring is but a lay-hypocrisie:	11	Ch.-Porch	123
HYPOCRITE			
where understands the cunning hypocrite who by the world is counted	319	Valdesso V	20
HYSSOPE			
And surely hyssope, valerian, mercury, adders tongue, yerrow,	262	Priest 23	5
I			
Which would throw me there, if I keep the round.	7	Ch.-Porch	30
Shall I, to please anothers wine-sprung minde, ...	8	Ch.-Porch	37
Short of his canne and bodie; must I finde	8	Ch.-Porch	39
Were I an Epicure, I could bate swearing.	8	Ch.-Porch	60
And say withall, Earth to earth I commit.	11	Ch.-Porch	132
But say withall, Earth to earth I commit.	11	Ch.-Porch W	132
I care not though the cloth of state should be	17	Ch.-Porch	269
Love is a personall debt. I cannot give	17	Ch.-Porch	278
Why should I feel another mans mistakes	18	Ch.-Porch	309
In love I should: but anger is not love, ...	18	Ch.-Porch	311
Who say, I care not, those I give for lost;	20	Ch.-Porch	347
Who say, I care not, I give those for gone;	20	Ch.-Porch W	347
That if I chance to hold my peace, ...	26	The Altar	13
To me, who took eyes that I might you finde:	26	Sacrifice	3
Who cannot wish, except I give them bread:	26	Sacrifice	7
They use that power against me, which I gave:	27	Sacrifice	11

I (cont'd)

	PAGE	TITLE		LINE
Though he had all I had, did not forbeare	27	Sacrifice		14
Yet my Disciples sleep: I cannot gain	27	Sacrifice		29
I suffer binding, who have loos'd their bands:	28	Sacrifice		47
What I taught: Comments would the text confound.	28	Sacrifice		55
That I did thrust into the Deitie,	28	Sacrifice		62
Some said, that I the Temple to the floore	28	Sacrifice		65
Which I do give them daily, unto death.	28	Sacrifice		70
Herod in judgement sits, while I do stand;	29	Sacrifice		81
I him obey, who all things else command:	29	Sacrifice		83
I answer nothing, but with patience prove	29	Sacrifice		89
But I the Prince of peace; peace that doth passe	30	Sacrifice		118
Why, Caesar is their onely King, not I:	30	Sacrifice		121
But surely not their hearts, as I well trie:	30	Sacrifice		123
But surely not their hearts, as I will trie:	30	Sacrifice	V	123
But not their harts, as I by proofe doe try.	30	Sacrifice	W	123
And never yet, whom I would punish, miss'd:	30	Sacrifice		131
And now I am deliver'd unto death,	31	Sacrifice		145
Weep not, deare friends, since I for both have wept	31	Sacrifice		149
Yet for twelve heav'nly legions I could call:	31	Sacrifice		155
Then on my head a crown of thorns I wear:	31	Sacrifice		161
Though I my vine planted and watred there:	31	Sacrifice		163
Upon my head: so I remove it all	32	Sacrifice		166
I am the floore, the sink, where they it fling:	32	Sacrifice		175
I, who am Truth, turn into truth their deeds:	32	Sacrifice		179
I, who am Truth, turn into truth their scorns:	32	Sacrifice	W	179
With stronger blows strike mee as I come out:	32	Sacrifice	W	187
My crosse I bear my self, untill I faint:	33	Sacrifice		197
Man stole the fruit, but I must climbe the tree;	33	Sacrifice		202
Lo, here I hang, charg'd with a world of sinne,	33	Sacrifice		205
Bywords, but this by sorrow I must win:	33	Sacrifice		207
Reproches, which are free, while I am bound.	33	Sacrifice		219
Alas! I did so, when I left my crown	34	Sacrifice		222
Alas! I did so, when I lost my crown	34	Sacrifice	W	222
Betwixt two theeves I spend my utmost breath,	34	Sacrifice		229
Alas! what have I stollen from you? Death.	34	Sacrifice		231
With Manna, Angels food, I fed them all:	34	Sacrifice		239
For they will pierce my side, I full well know;	34	Sacrifice		246
But now I die; now all is finished.	34	Sacrifice		249
My wo, mans weal: and now I bow my head.	34	Sacrifice		250
Onely let others say, when I am dead,	34	Sacrifice		251
Oh King of wounds! how shall I grieve for thee,	35	Thanksgvng		3
King of all wounds, how shall I grieve for thee,	35	Thanksgvng	W	3
Shall I weep bloud? why, thou hast wept such store	35	Thanksgvng		5
Shall I be scourged, flouted, boxed, sold?	35	Thanksgvng		7
Shall I then sing, skipping, thy dolefull storie,	35	Thanksgvng		11
Shall I then sing, neglecting thy sad storie,	35	Thanksgvng	W	11
But how then shall I imitate thee, and	35	Thanksgvng		15
Surely I will revenge me on thy love,	35	Thanksgvng		17
If thou dost give me wealth, I will restore	35	Thanksgvng		19
I will not marry; or, if she be mine,	35	Thanksgvng		23
I will tear thence his love and fame.	35	Thanksgvng		26
I will ripp out his love and fame.	35	Thanksgvng	W	26
I will teare out his love and fame.	35	Thanksgvng	WC	26
One half of me being gone, the rest I give	35	Thanksgvng		27
One half of me being gone, the rest I'le give	35	Thanksgvng	W	27
When with the other I have done.	35	Thanksgvng		30
For thy predestination I'le contrive,	36	Thanksgvng		31
That three yeares hence, if I survive,	36	Thanksgvng		32
I'le build a spittle, or mend common wayes,	36	Thanksgvng		33
Then I will use the works of thy creation,	36	Thanksgvng		35
Then will I use the works of thy creation,	36	Thanksgvng	W	35
As if I us'd them but for fashion.	36	Thanksgvng		36
The world and I will quarrell; and the yeare	36	Thanksgvng		37
Shall not perceive, that I am here.	36	Thanksgvng		38
Nay, I will reade thy book, and never move	36	Thanksgvng		45
Nay, I will reade thy book, and never linn	36	Thanksgvng	W	45
Till I have found therein thy love,	36	Thanksgvng		46
Till I have found thy love therin,	36	Thanksgvng	W	46
Thy art of love, which I'le turn back on thee:	36	Thanksgvng		47
Then for thy passion - I will do for that -	36	Thanksgvng		49
Alas, my God, I know not what.	36	Thanksgvng		50
I have consider'd it, and finde	36	Reprisall		1
For though I die for thee, I am behinde;	36	Reprisall		3
O make me innocent, that I	36	Reprisall		5
For by thy death I die for thee.	36	Reprisall		8
Yet by confession will I come	37	Reprisall		13
Into the conquest. Though I can do nought	37	Reprisall		14
Into thy conquest, though I can do nought	37	Reprisall	W	14
Against thee, in thee I will overcome	37	Reprisall		15
Which my God feels as bloud; but I, as wine.	37	The Agonie		18
Lord, how I am all ague, when I seek	38	The Sinner		1
What I have treasur'd in my memorie!	38	The Sinner		2
I finde there quarries of pil'd vanities,	38	The Sinner		5
How shall I measure out thy bloud?	38	Good Fri.		2
How shall I count what thee befell,	38	Good Fri.		3
Shall I thy woes	38	Good Fri.		5
Not thriving, I resolved to be bold,	40	Redemption		2
In heaven at his manour I him sought:	40	Redemption		5
I straight return'd, and knowing his great birth,	40	Redemption		9
At length I heard a ragged noise and mirth	40	Redemption		12

I (cont'd)	PAGE	TITLE		LINE
Of theeves and murderers: there I him espied,	40	Redemption		13
I got me flowers to straw thy way;	42	Easter		19
I had prepared many a flowre	42	Easter	W	19
I got me boughs off many a tree:	42	Easter		20
That I became	43	East.wings		14
Till I became	43	East.wings	W	14
For, if I imp my wing on thine,	43	East.wings		19
When backward on my sins I turne mine eyes	43	H. Bapt.1	W	1
So when I view my sinnes, mine eyes remove	43	H. Bapt.1		3
I pass the shades, & fixe upon the true	43	H. Bapt.1	W	4
Full of rebellion, I would die,	45	Nature		1
I thought the service brave:	46	Afflict.1		2
So many joyes I writ down for my part,	46	Afflict.1		3
Besides what I might have	46	Afflict.1		4
I looked on thy furniture so fine,	46	Afflict.1		7
I looked on thy furniture so rich,	46	Afflict.1	W	7
Such starres I counted mine: both heav'n and earth	46	Afflict.1		11
What pleasures could I want, whose King I served,	46	Afflict.1		13
Thus argu'd into hopes, I was preserved	46	Afflict.1	W	15
Before that I could feare.	46	Afflict.1	W	16
I had my wish and way:	47	Afflict.1		20
Sorrow was all my soul; I scarce beleeved,	47	Afflict.1		29
Sorrow was all my soul; I did not know	47	Afflict.1	W	29
Till grief did tell me roundly, that I lived.	47	Afflict.1		30
That I did live, but by a pang of woe.	47	Afflict.1	W	30
When I got health, thou took'st away my life,	47	Afflict.1		31
Was of more use then I.	47	Afflict.1		34
I was blown through with ev'ry storm and winde.	47	Afflict.1		36
I was entangled in the world of strife,	47	Afflict.1		41
Before I had the power to change my life.	47	Afflict.1		42
Yet, for I threatned oft the siege to raise,	47	Afflict.1		43
I took thy sweetned pill, till I came neare;	47	Afflict.1		47
I took thy sweetned pill, till I came where	47	Afflict.1	W	47
I could not go away, nor persevere.	47	Afflict.1		48
Yet lest perchance I should too happie be	48	Afflict.1		49
Now I am here, what thou wilt do with me	48	Afflict.1		55
I reade, and sigh, and wish I were a tree;	48	Afflict.1		57
For sure then I should grow	48	Afflict.1		58
Her houshold to me, and I should be just.	48	Afflict.1		60
Yet, though thou troublest me, I must be meek;	48	Afflict.1		61
Well, I will change the service, and go seek	48	Afflict.1		63
Ah my deare God! though I am clean forgot,	48	Afflict.1		65
Ah my deare King! though I am clean forgot,	48	Afflict.1	W	65
Let me not love thee, if I love thee not.	48	Afflict.1		66
Lord, I confesse my sinne is great;	48	Repentance		1
I do confesse	49	Repentance		16
I and this day,	49	Repentance		23
Hungrie I was, and had no meat:	50	Faith		5
I did conceit a most delicious feast;	50	Faith		6
I had it straight, and did as truly eat,	50	Faith		7
Which when I could not get, I thought it here:	50	Faith		10
That I can walk to heav'n well neare.	50	Faith		12
I owed thousands and much more:	50	Faith		13
I did beleeve that I did nothing owe,	50	Faith		14
That I beleeve is in the sacred storie:	50	Faith		18
If I go lower in the book,	50	Faith		21
Which I can go to, when I please,	53	H.Commun.		39
How should I praise thee, Lord! how should my rymes	55	Temper 1		1
Sometimes I peere above them all;	55	Temper 1		6
Sometimes I hardly reach a score,	55	Temper 1		7
Sometimes to hell I fall.	55	Temper 1		8
And I hope and fear.	55	Temper 1		20
Whether I flie with angels, fall with dust,	55	Temper 1		25
Whether I Angell it, or fall to dust.	55	Temper 1	W	25
Thy hands made both, and I am there:	55	Temper 1		26
I envie no mans nightingale or spring;	57	Jordan 1		13
Before I were by frosts extremitie	57	Employm. 1		3
Which in thy garland I should fill, were mine	57	Employm. 1		7
All things are busie; onely I	57	Employm. 1		17
I am no link of thy great chain,	57	Employm. 1		21
Lord that I may the Sunns perfection gaine	57	Employm. 1	W	23
Oh that I knew how all thy lights combine,	58	H.Script.2		1
Till I get wing to fly away with thee.	59	Whitsunday	W	4
What if I say thou seek'st delayes;	61	Grace	W	20
Remove me, where I need not say,	61	Grace		23
That I can raise:	61	Praise 1		2
I go to Church; help me to wings, and I	61	Praise 1		5
I goe to Church; make me an Angel, I	61	Praise 1	W	5
Or, if I mount unto the skie,	61	Praise 1		7
Or, if I steale up to the skie,	61	Praise 1	W	7
I will do more.	61	Praise 1		8
Not flyes, but I shall bee his prey	61	Praise 1	W	19
Though I in broken pay	62	Afflict.2		4
I cannot ope mine eyes,	62	Mattens		1
That this new light, which now I see,	63	Mattens		18
Then by a sunne-beam I will climbe to thee.	63	Mattens		20
O that I could a sinne once see!	63	Sinne 2		1
For when he sees my waies, I dy:	63	Even-song		7
But I have got his sonne, and he hath none.	63	Even-song		8
What have I brought thee home	64	Even-song		9

I (cont'd)

	PAGE	TITLE		LINE
For this thy love? have I discharg'd the debt,	64	Even-song		10
I ranne; but all I brought, was fome.	64	Even-song		12
Of winde to thee whom I have crost,	64	Even-song		15
I muse, which shows more love,	64	Even-song		25
And in this love, more then in bed, I rest.	64	Even-song		32
Here I intombe my flesh, that it betimes	64	Ch.-monum.		2
Drives all at last. Therefore I gladly trust	64	Ch.-monum.		6
Deare flesh, while I do pray, learn here thy stemme	65	Ch.-monum.		17
Sweetest of sweets, I thank you: when displeasure	65	Ch.-mus.		1
Now I in you without a bodie move,	65	Ch.-mus.		5
Comfort, I'le die; for if you poste from me,	66	Ch.-mus.		9
Comfort, I'le die; for if you part from me,	66	Ch.-mus.	W	9
Sure I shall do so, and much more:	66	Ch.-mus.		10
But if I travell in your companie,	66	Ch.-mus.		11
I know it is my sinne, which locks thine eares,	66	Ch.-lock		1
I know it is my sinne, which stops thine eares,	66	Ch.-lock	W	1
So I do lay the want of my desire,	66	Ch.-lock		7
For I confesse my heavie score,	68	Trin.Sun.		5
And I will strive to sinne no more.	68	Trin.Sun.		6
That I may runne, rise, rest with thee.	68	Trin.Sun.		9
That I may runne, rise, rest in thee.	68	Trin.Sun.	W	9
But it is that which while I use	70	Quidditie		11
I am with thee, and Most take all.	70	Quidditie		12
I saw the Vertues sitting hand in hand	70	Humilitie		1
Lord, in my silence how do I despise	71	Frailtie		1
I surname them guilded clay,	71	Frailtie		5
In all, I think my foot doth ever tread	71	Frailtie		7
And ever as I walk my foot doth tredd	71	Frailtie	W	7
But when I view abroad both Regiments;	71	Frailtie		9
By that I knew that thou wast in the grief,	73	Afflict.3		2
That so among the rest I may	74	The Starre		25
I know thy parentage is base and low:	77	Avarice		3
Do I forbear to crave your speciall aid:	78	Ang.&Sts.		7
I would addresse	78	Ang.&Sts.		8
Chiefly to thee would I my soul unfold:	78	Ang.&Sts.		15
But now (alas!) I dare not; for our King,	78	Ang.&Sts.		16
But now alas I dare not; for my King,	78	Ang.&Sts.	W	16
Oh that I were an Orenge-tree,	79	Employm.2		21
O that I had the wing and thigh	79	Employm.2	W	21
Then should I ever laden be,	79	Employm.2		23
Then would I mount up instantly	79	Employm.2	W	23
On men dropp blessings as I fly.	79	Employm.2	W	25
All after pleasures as I rid one day,	80	Christmas		1
My horse and I, both tir'd, bodie and minde,	80	Christmas		2
I took up in the next inne I could finde.	80	Christmas		4
There when I came, whom found I but my deare,	81	Christmas		5
The shepherds sing; and shall I silent be?	81	Christmas		15
I will go searching, till I finde a sunne	81	Christmas		27
The mightie God, but I a sillie worm;	83	Sighs & Gr.		5
I have abus'd thy stock, destroy'd thy woods,	83	Sighs & Gr.		9
I have deserv'd that an Egyptian night	83	Sighs & Gr.		14
But I am frailtie, and already dust;	83	Sighs & Gr.		17
I am a scandall to the Church, and not	86	Lent		11
I know the wayes of Learning; both the head	88	The Pearl		1
All these stand open, or I have the keyes:	88	The Pearl		9
Yet I love thee.	88	The Pearl		10
I know the wayes of Honour, what maintains	88	The Pearl		11
Yet I love thee.	88	The Pearl		20
I know the wayes of Pleasure, the sweet strains,	89	The Pearl		21
I know the projects of unbridled store:	89	The Pearl		26
I know the projects of unbundled store:	89	The Pearl	V	26
Yet I love thee.	89	The Pearl		30
I know all these, and have them in my hand:	89	The Pearl		31
I flie to thee, and fully understand	89	The Pearl		33
And at what rate and price I have thy love;	89	The Pearl		35
And while I live, trie out their right.	90	Afflict.4		18
Till I reach heav'n, and much more thee.	90	Afflict.4		30
My God, I heard this day,	90	Man		1
In friendship, first I think, if that agree,	93	Unkindness		2
Which I intend,	93	Unkindness		3
I would not use a friend, as I use Thee.	93	Unkindness		5
I could not use a friend, as I use Thee.	93	Unkindness		10
Would he have gold? I lend it instantly;	93	Unkindness		12
I cannot use a friend, as I use Thee.	93	Unkindness		15
I quit my interest, and leave it free:	94	Unkindness		17
Sues for my heart, I thee displace,	94	Unkindness		19
Nor would I use a friend, as I use Thee.	94	Unkindness		20
Yet use I not my foes, as I use thee.	94	Unkindness		25
I made a posie, while the day ran by:	94	Life		1
Here will I smell my remnant out, and tie	94	Life		2
I took, without more thinking, in good part	94	Life		8
I follow straight without complaints or grief,	94	Life		16
Since if my sent be good, I care not, if	94	Life		17
But when I thus dispute and grieve,	95	Submission		9
I do resume my sight,	95	Submission		10
And pilfring what I once did give,	95	Submission		11
How know I, if thou shouldst me raise,	95	Submission		13
That I should then raise thee?	95	Submission		14
Wherefore unto my gift I stand;	95	Submission		17
I will no more advise:	95	Submission		18

I (cont'd)

	PAGE	TITLE		LINE
I cannot skill of these thy wayes.	95	Justice 1		1
Lord, thou relievest, yet I die by thee:	95	Justice 1		4
But when I mark my life and praise,	96	Justice 1		6
For, I do praise thee, yet I praise thee not:	96	Justice 1		8
I would do well, yet sinne the hand hath got:	96	Justice 1		10
I cannot skill of these my wayes.	96	Justice 1		12
My God, I read this day,	97	Afflict.5		1
I see the world grows old, when as the heat	99	Decay		16
My God, I mean my self.	102	Miserie		78
That I sought out quaint words, and trim invention;	102	Jordan 2		3
Off'ring their service, if I were not sped:	102	Jordan 2		8
I often blotted what I had begunne;	102	Jordan 2		9
So did I weave my self into the sense.	103	Jordan 2		14
So I bespoke me much insinuation:	103	Jordan 2	W	14
But while I bustled, I might heare a friend	103	Jordan 2		15
If I but lift mine eyes, my suit is made:	103	Prayer 2		5
Ease, Power, and Love; I value prayer so,	103	Prayer 2		20
That were I to leave all but one,	103	Prayer 2		21
I and deare prayer would together dwell,	103	Prayer 2		23
To which I do agree,	104	Obedience		9
I here exclude the wrangler from thy treasure.	104	Obedience		15
I here shutt out the wrangler from thy treasure.	104	Obedience	W	15
Wherefore I all forgo:	105	Obedience		31
To one word onely I say, No:	105	Obedience		32
As I have mine, may set his hand	105	Obedience		37
I have both lost mine eyes and eares.	105	Conscience		6
Pratler, no more, I say:	105	Conscience		7
If thou persistest, I will tell thee,	105	Conscience		11
That I have physick to expell thee.	105	Conscience		12
I do but taste it, straight it cleanseth me,	106	Conscience		15
When I behold it trickling down thy face,	107	Home		9
I never saw thing make such haste.	107	Home		10
Yet if thou stayest still, why must I stay?	108	Home		31
Away; I must get up and see.	108	Home		34
What is this woman-kinde, which I can wink	108	Home		39
I blasted all the joyes about me:	108	Home		44
Now come again, said I, and flout me.	108	Home		46
Which way so-e're I look, I see.	108	Home		50
What have I left, that I should stay and grone?	109	Home		67
I joy, deare Mother, when I view	109	Brit. Ch.		1
To meet together, where I lay,	110	The Quip		3
Which when I pluckt not, Sir, said she,	110	The Quip		6
Tell me, I pray, Whose hands are those?	110	The Quip		7
I heard in Musick you had skill.	110	The Quip		11
Speak not at large, say, I am thine:	111	The Quip		23
Ev'n all to pieces: which I went to seek:	112	JESU		4
And first I found the corner, where was J,	112	JESU		5
When I had got these parcels, instantly	112	JESU		7
I sat me down to spell them, and perceived	112	JESU		8
That to my broken heart he was I ease you,	112	JESU		9
Quickly should I then controll	114	Dialogue		3
If I say, Thou shalt be mine;	114	Dialogue		11
But as I can see no merit,	115	Dialogue		17
I disclaim the whole designe:	115	Dialogue		23
Sinne disclaims and I resigne.	115	Dialogue		24
That is all, if that I could	115	Dialogue		25
That as I did freely part	115	Dialogue		29
Why do I languish thus, drooping and dull,	115	Dulnesse		1
As if I were all earth?	115	Dulnesse		2
O give me quicknesse, that I may with mirth	115	Dulnesse		3
But I am lost in flesh, whose sugred lyes	116	Dulnesse		21
Sure thou didst put a minde there, if I could	116	Dulnesse		23
I may but look towards thee:	116	Dulnesse		26
As on a window late I cast mine eye,	116	Love-joy		1
I saw a vine drop grapes with J and C	116	Love-joy		2
Ask'd what it meant. I, (who am never loth	116	Love-joy		4
Strongly and sweetly movest, shall I write,	116	Providence		2
Wherefore, most sacred Spirit, I here present	117	Providence		25
And just it is that I should pay the rent,	117	Providence		27
And as thy house is full, so I adore	119	Providence		93
To honour thee: and so I give thee praise	121	Providence		147
I gave to Hope a watch of mine: but he	121	Hope		1
Then an old prayer-book I did present:	121	Hope		3
With that I gave a viall full of tears:	121	Hope		5
Ah Loyterer! I'le no more, no more I'le bring:	121	Hope		7
I did expect a ring.	121	Hope		8
Sorrie I am, my God, sorrie I am,	122	Sinnes rd.		1
Sorrie I am, my God, sorrie I am.	122	Sinnes rd.		18
Meeting with Time, Slack thing, said I,	122	Time		1
What do I here before his doore?	123	Time		29
Wherefore I crie, and crie again;	124	Gratefulnes		25
Till I a thankfull heart obtain	124	Gratefulnes		27
Sweet Peace, where dost thou dwell? I humbly crave,	124	Peace		1
I sought thee in a secret cave,	124	Peace		3
I did; and going did a rainbow note:	124	Peace		7
Surely, thought I,	124	Peace		8
I will search out the matter.	124	Peace		10
But while I lookt, the clouds immediately	124	Peace		11
Then went I to a garden, and did spy	125	Peace		13
The Crown Imperiall: Sure, said I,	125	Peace		15

I (cont'd)

	PAGE	TITLE		LINE
But when I digg'd, I saw a worm devoure	125	Peace		17
At length I met a rev'rend good old man,	125	Peace		19
I did demand; he thus began:	125	Peace		21
Is this same grief! within my heart I made	126	Confession		2
Lord, I acknowledge; take thy plagues away:	126	Confession		26
I challenge here the brightest day,	126	Confession		28
Joy, I did lock thee up: but some bad man	128	Bunch Gr.		1
And now, me thinks, I am where I began	128	Bunch Gr.		3
I did toward Canaan draw; but now I am	128	Bunch Gr.		6
I did towards Canaan draw; but now I am	128	Bunch Gr.	V	6
Of mine inheritance? Lord, if I must borrow,	128	Bunch Gr.		20
I have their fruit and more.	128	Bunch Gr.		23
But much more him I must adore,	128	Bunch Gr.		26
And in my faintings I presume your love	129	Love unkn.		2
Will more complie, then help. A Lord I had,	129	Love unkn.		3
I hold for two lives, and both lives in me.	129	Love unkn.		5
To him I brought a dish of fruit one day,	129	Love unkn.		6
(I sigh to say)	129	Love unkn.		8
Then I my self. The servant instantly	129	Love unkn.		11
Of a great rock: I well remember all,	129	Love unkn.		15
Enforceth tears. Your heart was foul, I fear.	129	Love unkn.		18
Indeed 'tis true. I did and do commit	129	Love unkn.		19
And clean and fair, as I one even-tide	129	Love unkn.		23
(I sigh to tell)	129	Love unkn.		24
Walkt by my self abroad, I saw a large	129	Love unkn.		25
The greatnesse shew'd the owner. So I went	129	Love unkn.		29
Thinking with that, which I did thus present,	129	Love unkn.		31
To warm his love, which I did fear grew cold.	129	Love unkn.		32
The offerers heart. Your heart was hard, I fear.	130	Love unkn.		37
Indeed 'tis true. I found a callous matter	130	Love unkn.		38
Indeed it's true. I found a callous matter	130	Love unkn.	V	38
I bath'd it often, ev'n with holy bloud,	130	Love unkn.		41
Out of the caldron getting, soon I fled	130	Love unkn.		46
Which I had lost, I hasted to my bed.	130	Love unkn.		48
But when I thought to sleep out all these faults	130	Love unkn.		49
(I sigh to speak)	130	Love unkn.		50
I found that some had stuff'd the bed with thoughts,	130	Love unkn.		51
I would say thorns. Deare, could my heart not break,	130	Love unkn.		52
Full well I understood, who had been there:	130	Love unkn.		54
For I had giv'n the key to none, but one:	130	Love unkn.		55
It must be he. Your heart was dull, I fear.	130	Love unkn.		56
Did oft possesse me, so that when I pray'd,	130	Love unkn.		58
For ought I heare, your Master shows to you	130	Love unkn.		62
I blesse thee, Lord, because I GROW	132	Paradise		1
Inclose me still for fear I START.	133	Paradise		7
What do I see	133	The Method		13
I did behave me carelesly,	133	The Method		15
When I did pray.	133	The Method		16
Late when I would have something done,	134	The Method		22
I had a motion to forbear,	134	The Method		23
Yet I went on.	134	The Method		24
Bid what he please; yet I am sure,	135	Divinitie		22
When I am sowre,	135	Ephes.		2
Griev'd for a worm, which when I tread,	135	Ephes.		5
I passe away and leave it dead?	135	Ephes.		6
I sinne not to my grief alone,	136	Ephes.		17
Lord, I adjudge my self to tears and grief,	136	Ephes.		25
But runnes, although I be not drie;	136	Ephes.		29
I am no Crystall, what shall I?	136	Ephes.		30
Yet if I wail not still, since still to wail	136	Ephes.		31
As I one ev'ning sat before my cell,	139	Artillerie		1
I rose, and shook my clothes, as knowing well,	139	Artillerie		3
When suddenly I heard one say,	139	Artillerie		5
I, who had heard of musick in the spheres,	139	Artillerie		9
The starres and all things are; If I refuse,	139	Artillerie		12
Dread Lord, said I, so oft my good;	139	Artillerie		13
Then I refuse not ev'n with bloud	139	Artillerie		14
For I will do, or suffer what I ought.	139	Artillerie		16
But I have also starres and shooters too,	139	Artillerie		17
Not, but I am (I must say still)	139	Artillerie		21
With thine own clay. But I would parley fain:	139	Artillerie		27
Yet if thou shunnest, I am thine:	139	Artillerie		29
I must be so, if I am mine.	139	Artillerie		30
I am but finite, yet thine infinitely.	139	Artillerie		32
And those all bitten, in thy chair I see.	140	Ch.-rents		10
And those all sitten in thy chair I see.	140	Ch.-rents	V	10
Where shall I get me eyes enough to weep,	140	Ch.-rents		25
And ev'n all Africk; would at least I might	140	Ch.-rents		28
I see no fears:	141	Justice 2		14
Now I still touch	141	Justice 2		20
Why should I justice now decline?	141	Justice 2		23
I travell'd on, seeing the hill, where lay	141	Pilgrimage		1
I left on th' one, and on the other side	142	Pilgrimage		5
And so I came to phansies medow strow'd	142	Pilgrimage		7
And so I came to Fancies medow strow'd	142	Pilgrimage	V	7
Fain would I here have made abode,	142	Pilgrimage		9
But I was quicken'd by my houre.	142	Pilgrimage		10
So to cares cops I came, and there got through	142	Pilgrimage		11
Here I was robb'd of all my gold,	142	Pilgrimage		16
At length I got unto the gladsome hill,	142	Pilgrimage		19

I (cont'd)

	PAGE	TITLE	LINE
When I had gain'd the brow and top,	142	Pilgrimage	22
Was all I found.	142	Pilgrimage	24
I fell, and cry'd, Alas my King!	142	Pilgrimage	27
Yet taking heart I rose, and then perceiv'd	142	Pilgrimage	29
I was deceiv'd:	142	Pilgrimage	30
My hill was further: so I flung away,	142	Pilgrimage	31
Just as I went, None goes that way	142	Pilgrimage	33
And lives: If that be all, said I,	142	Pilgrimage	34
I threatned to observe the strict decree	143	Holdfast	1
I threatned to observe the sweet decree	143	Holdfast V	1
But I was told by one, it could not be;	143	Holdfast	3
Yet I might trust in God to be my light.	143	Holdfast	4
Then will I trust, said I, in him alone.	143	Holdfast	5
Then I confesse, that he my succour is:	143	Holdfast	8
That we have nought. I stood amaz'd at this,	143	Holdfast	10
Much troubled, till I heard a friend expresse,	143	Holdfast	11
Because I am	143	Complaining	4
Are both thy due: but I a silly flie,	143	Complaining	8
More attributes? Am I all throat or eye,	143	Complaining	13
Have I no parts but those of grief?	143	Complaining	15
That I may climbe and finde relief.	144	Complaining	20
This houre is mine: if for the next I care,	145	Discharge	33
I grow too wide,	145	Discharge	34
I will love thee:	146	Praise 2	2
I will move thee.	146	Praise 2	4
I will sing thee,	146	Praise 2	10
I will bring thee.	146	Praise 2	12
I will praise thee.	146	Praise 2	18
I can raise thee.	146	Praise 2	20
But all I fear is lest thy heart displease,	147	Offering	13
Had I many,	148	Offering	31
Had I any,	148	Offering	32
And make me giddie; Lord, I fall,	148	Longing	11
Thou tarriest, while I die,	150	Longing	55
While I remain	150	Longing	58
In bitter grief: yet am I stil'd	150	Longing	59
(I have no bag, but here is room):	152	The Bag	32
That I shall minde, what you impart;	152	The Bag	35
I will present, and somewhat more,	152	The Bag	40
I struck the board, and cry'd, No more.	153	The Collar	1
I will abroad.	153	The Collar	2
What? shall I ever sigh and pine?	153	The Collar	3
Shall I be still in suit?	153	The Collar	6
Have I no harvest but a thorn	153	The Collar	7
What I have lost with cordiall fruit?	153	The Collar	9
Have I no bayes to crown it?	153	The Collar	14
I will abroad.	153	The Collar	28
But as I rav'd and grew more fierce and wilde	153	The Collar	33
Me thoughts I heard one calling, childe:	154	The Collar	35
And I reply'd, My Lord.	154	The Collar	36
If I have more to spinne,	155	Glimpse	26
That all was not so fair, as I conceiv'd,	155	Assurance	8
Betwixt my God and me; that I allow	155	Assurance	9
And coin large hopes; but, that I was deceiv'd:	155	Assurance	10
And, that I had great cause to fear it.	155	Assurance	12
Wouldst thou raise devils? I see, I know,	155	Assurance	17
I writ thy purpose long ago.	155	Assurance	18
But I will to my Father,	155	Assurance	19
If all the hope and comfort that I gather,	155	Assurance	21
Were from my self, I had not half a word,	155	Assurance	22
And hold my hand, while I did write.	156	Assurance	30
Then can thy truth and I: but while rocks stand,	156	Assurance	32
Lord, thou art mine, and I am thine,	157	Clasping	1
If mine I am: and thine much more,	157	Clasping	2
Then I or ought, or can be mine.	157	Clasping	3
So that again I now am mine,	157	Clasping	5
If I without thee would be mine,	157	Clasping	9
I neither should be mine nor thine.	157	Clasping	10
Lord, I am thine, and thou art mine:	157	Clasping	11
I may presume thee mine, then thine.	157	Clasping	13
Lord, I will mean and speak thy praise,	157	Praise 3	1
Then will I wring it with a sigh or grone,	157	Praise 3	5
The windes their stint: and yet when I did call,	158	Praise 3	23
I have not lost one single tear:	158	Praise 3	25
Wherefore I sing. Yet since my heart,	159	Praise 3	37
O that I might some other hearts convert,	159	Praise 3	39
Wounded I sing, tormented I indite,	159	Jos.coat	1
Thrown down I fall into a bed, and rest:	159	Jos.coat	2
I live to shew his power, who once did bring	159	Jos.coat	13
For if I should (said he)	160	The Pulley	11
In thy just censures; fain would I draw nigh,	160	Priesthood	4
And I but earth and clay: should I presume	160	Priesthood	8
I am both foul and brittle; much unfit	160	Priesthood	11
Yet have I often seen, by cunning hand	161	Priesthood	13
Of wretched earth. Where once I scorn'd to stand,	161	Priesthood	15
I do not greatly wonder at the sight,	161	Priesthood	23
Wherefore I dare not, I, put forth my hand	161	Priesthood	31
I throw me at his feet.	161	Priesthood	36
There will I lie, untill my Maker seek	161	Priesthood	37
Yet can I mark how herbs below	162	The Search	9

I (cont'd)

	PAGE	TITLE	LINE
While I decay.	162	The Search	12
Yet can I mark how starres above	162	The Search	13
While poore I pine.	162	The Search	16
I sent a sigh to seek thee out,	162	The Search	17
I tun'd another (having store)	162	The Search	21
I turn'd another (having store)	162	The Search V	21
And I will passe.	163	The Search	36
Untill I had some place, where I might sing,	164	The Crosse	3
And serve thee; and not onely I,	164	The Crosse	4
What I would do for thee, if once my grones	165	The Crosse	15
I am in all a weak disabled thing,	165	The Crosse	17
I am to grief alive, to them as dead.	165	The Crosse	24
Farther from it then when I bent my bow;	165	The Crosse	26
Further from it then when I bent my bow;	165	The Crosse V	26
O that I once past changing were,	166	The Flower	22
Many a spring I shoot up fair,	166	The Flower	24
My sinnes and I joining together:	166	The Flower	28
But while I grow in a straight line,	166	The Flower	29
Thy anger comes, and I decline:	166	The Flower	31
And now in age I bud again,	166	The Flower	36
After so many deaths I live and write;	166	The Flower	37
I once more smell the dew and rain,	166	The Flower	38
That I am he	166	The Flower	41
I like our language, as our men and coast:	167	The Sonne	3
O, could I love! and stops: God writeth, Loved,	168	a true Hymn	20
I shake my head, and all the thoughts and ends,	169	The Answer	2
Show me, and set me, I have one reply,	169	The Answer	13
Which they that know the rest, know more then I.	169	The Answer	14
Go spell and reade how I have kill'd thy King.	169	Dial.-Anth	4
I shall be one day better then before:	169	Dial.-Anth	9
Sure I will do the like.	171	Bittersweet	4
I will complain, yet praise;	171	Bittersweet	5
I will bewail, approve:	171	Bittersweet	6
I will lament, and love.	171	Bittersweet	8
I felt a sugred strange delight,	171	The Glance	5
While he is mine, and I am his,	172	23 Psalme	3
What can I want or need?	172	23 Psalme	4
Where I both feed and rest;	172	23 Psalme	6
In both I have the best.	172	23 Psalme	8
Or if I stray, he doth convert	172	23 Psalme	9
Well may I walk, not fear:	173	23 Psalme	14
Poore priest thus am I drest.	174	Aaron	10
I have, another heart and breast,	174	Aaron	12
Without whom I could have no rest:	174	Aaron	14
In him I am well drest.	174	Aaron	15
That to the old man I may rest,	174	Aaron	19
But lives in me while I do rest)	174	Aaron	24
With these all day I do perfume my minde,	175	The Odour	6
That I might finde	175	The Odour	8
My Master, shall I speak? O that to thee	175	The Odour	11
I passe not, I, what of the rest become,	176	Forerunners	9
And if I please him, I write fine and wittie.	176	Forerunners	12
Then did I wash you with my tears, and more,	176	Forerunners	16
My god must have my best, ev'n all I had.	176	Forerunners	18
Yet if you go, I passe not; take your way:	177	Forerunners	31
Such delights I meant to say;	177	The Rose	10
But I will not much oppose	177	The Rose	13
But I health, not physick choose:	178	The Rose	29
Onely though I you oppose,	178	The Rose	30
Say that fairly I refuse,	178	The Rose	31
I aspire	178	Discipline	7
I affect to own,	178	Discipline	10
Though I fail, I weep:	179	Discipline	13
Though I halt in pace,	179	Discipline	14
Yet I creep	179	Discipline	15
Lord I have invited all,	180	Invitation	31
And I shall	180	Invitation	32
When I had forgot my birth,	182	Banquet	31
But I still being low and short,	182	Banquet	40
For with it alone I flie	182	Banquet	43
Where I wipe mine eyes, and see	182	Banquet	45
What I seek, for what I sue;	182	Banquet	46
Him I view,	182	Banquet	47
This by my picture, in my book I write:	183	The Posie	6
Whether I sing,	183	The Posie	7
And I alone,	183	A Parodie	2
And I depend on thee;	183	A Parodie	5
And then what life I have,	183	A Parodie	21
That I may seek, but thou art lost;	183	A Parodie	24
I half beleeve,	184	A Parodie	28
That Sinne sayes true: but while I grieve,	184	A Parodie	29
All things I doe to thee	184	The Elixer W	2
And what I do in any thing,	184	The Elixer	3
That I not onely may not erre	184	The Elixer W	3
Of praise deserved, unto thee I give,	185	A Wreath	2
I give to thee, who knowest all my wayes,	185	A Wreath	3
My crooked winding wayes, wherein I live,	185	A Wreath	4
Wherein I die, not live: for life is straight,	185	A Wreath	5
Give me simplicitie, that I may live,	185	A Wreath	9
So live and like, that I may know thy wayes,	185	A Wreath	10

I (cont'd)

	PAGE	TITLE		LINE
Know them and practise them: then shall I give	185	A Wreath		11
What others mean to do, I know not well;	187	Judgement		6
Yet I heare tell,	187	Judgement		7
But I resolve, when thou shalt call for mine,	188	Judgement		11
Echo. I.	188	Heaven		2
If I lack'd any thing.	188	Love 3		6
A guest, I answer'd, worthy to be here:	189	Love 3		7
I the unkinde, ungratefull? Ah my deare,	189	Love 3		9
I cannot look on thee.	189	Love 3		10
Who made the eyes but I?	189	Love 3		12
Truth Lord, but I have marr'd them: let my shame	189	Love 3		13
My deare, then I will serve.	189	Love 3		16
So I did sit and eat.	189	Love 3		18
I saw him in his studie, where he sate	194	Ch.-Milit.		165
O gratious Lord how shall I know	200	H. Commun.	W	1
First I am sure, whether bread stay	200	H. Commun.	W	7
Then of this also I am sure	200	H. Commun.	W	19
I could beleeve an Impanation	201	H. Commun.	W	25
Thy flesh the least that I request.	201	H. Commun.	W	44
Give me not that I had before,	201	H. Commun.	W	46
Or give mee that, so I have more	201	H. Commun.	W	47
That is thy Master-peece I see	201	love	W	3
When I contrive & plott to prove	201	love	W	4
Sometimes, when as I wash, I say	202	love	W	7
And shrodely, as I think, Lord wash my soule	202	love	W	8
Thy ancient baptism which when I was foule	202	love	W	11
I took a time when thou didst sleep	202	love	W	13
I thought it brave to praise thee then,	202	love	W	15
Yet then I found, that thou didst creep	202	love	W	16
Whereas if I orecome thee & thy Love	202	love	W	23
I and the Sunn have runn our races,	203	Even-song	W	2
I went the slower, yet more paces,	203	Even-song	W	3
For I decay not hee.	203	Even-song	W	4
That I who cannot now by day	203	Even-song	W	6
Yet Thou art not so dark, since I know this,	203	Even-song	W	17
O lett my Soule, whose keyes I must deliver	203	Even-song	W	21
Are so, as for the present, I did move	204	Persever.	W	3
Why should I Womens eyes for Chrystal take?	206	Walton 2		8
When winds and waves rise highest, I am sure,	439	walton 6		3
Reade him there, and I have done.	208	J. Danvers	D	16
And I to you a Blackamore present.	209	L. Bacon	D	2
Perhaps some other subject I had tryed	209	L. Bacon	D	11
Mee thinkes, in that Dutch optick I doe see	211	Bohemia	D	13
But I by God am seated King,	215	Psalm II	D	13
I will declare the Lords decree,	215	Psalm II	D	15
nor can I hide his sacred will.	215	Psalm II	D	16
this day have I begotten thee:	216	Psalm II	D	18
Make thy request, and I will grant	216	Psalm II	D	19
I cry'd unto the Lord, he heard	216	Psalm III	D	9
I laid me down and slept, I wak'd;	216	Psalm III	D	11
Aided by him, I will not fear	216	Psalm III	D	13
Lord hear me when I call on Thee,	217	Psalm IV	D	1
when I was in distress.	217	Psalm IV	D	4
the Prayer that I frame:	217	Psalm IV	D	6
when I his grace implore:	217	Psalm IV	D	14
Therefore will I lie down in peace,	218	Psalm IV	D	29
my cry to thee, I pray.	218	Psalm V	D	4
for in the morn will I	218	Psalm V	D	6
will I to thee draw near:	218	Psalm V	D	18
O pity me! for I (O Lord)	219	Psalm VI	D	3
shall I in vain thy Grace implore?	220	Psalm VI	D	8
With groaning I am wearied,	220	Psalm VI	D	13
all night I make my Couch to swim;	220	Psalm VI	D	14
I put my trust in Thee:	220	Psalm VII	D	2
If I have done this thing, O Lord,	221	Psalm VII	D	9
if I so guilty be:	221	Psalm VII	D	10
If I have ill rewarded him	221	Psalm VII	D	11
But I for all his righteousness	222	Psalm VII	D	61
(thorow the Mercy of GOD) to please Him, for whom I am, and live,	224	Priest		2
I have resolved to set down the Form and Character of a true Pastour,	224	Priest		6
and Character of a true Pastour, that I may have a Mark to aim at:	224	Priest		7
which also I will set as high as I can, since hee shoots higher that	224	Priest		8
Not that I think, if a man do not all which is here expressed,	224	Priest		10
which I have observed, untill the Book grow to a compleat Pastorall.	224	Priest		15
he may say as He did, I sate daily with you teaching in the Temple.	227	Priest 3		33
open mine eyes, that I may see the wondrous things of thy Law.	229	Priest 4		3
Oh my Master, on whose errand I come, let me hold my peace,	233	Priest 7		35
Oh Lord, I know that the way of man is not in himself, &c.	234	Priest 7		5
he sees whether I speak as I ought, or you hear as you ought,	234	Priest 7		27
to which I am inclined, as not to get out of that sicknesse,	242	Priest 10		37
as not to get out of that sicknesse, when I am in it, by any diet.	242	Priest 10		38
I am to follow our Saviours rule, and to take my brother aside,	248	Priest 14		26
I am then to follow the Apostles rule, 1 Timothy 5. 20. and to rebuke	248	Priest 14		29
telling him when he hath forgotten it, This I do, because at such,	254	Priest 20		17
And I conceive, our Saviour did this for three reasons:	261	Priest 23		17
if I do not give every thing its end, I abuse the Creature,	265	Priest 26		9
I abuse the Creature, I am false to my reason which should guide me,	265	Priest 26		9
I am false to my reason which should guide me, I offend the supreme	265	Priest 26		10
I offend the supreme Judg, in perverting that order which he hath set	265	Priest 26		10
and those more which concerne me, I either do nothing, or pinch,	265	Priest 26		16

I (cont'd)

	PAGE	TITLE	LINE
undecently to the station wherein God hath placed me, I am Covetous.	265	Priest 26	18
and I either provide too little for them, or that which is . .	265	Priest 26	20
sometimes too salt, and so not competent nourishment, I am Covetous.	265	Priest 26	23
I bring this example, because men usually think, that servants	265	Priest 26	23
I am more bound to abstain from those, which by mine own experience I	266	Priest 26	23
which by mine own experience I have found hurtfull, then from those	266	Priest 26	25
and feeling when I go to meat in what disposition I am, . .	267	Priest 26	7
and feeling when I go to meat in what disposition I am, . .	267	Priest 26	8
according as I feele my self, either I take my wonted proportion,	267	Priest 26	8
feele my self, either I take my wonted proportion, or diminish of it.	267	Priest 26	9
if I am to visit the sick in haste, and my neerest way ly through	273	Priest 31	33
I will not doubt to go without staying to pray there (but onely,	273	Priest 31	34
as I passe, in my heart) because this kinde of Prayer is additionary,	273	Priest 31	35
if any scruple arise, I will throw it away, and be most confident,	273	Priest 31	38
beyond any help in heaven or earth, then thou saidest, Lo, I come!	288	Priest	27
teach thou me, that I may teach them:	289	Priest	26
I thought fit to discover in a short Treatise, that Intemperance was	291	Cornaro	5
which I undertake the more willingly, because divers worthy young men	291	Cornaro	7
a great desire to know the way of my life, and how I came to be so.	291	Cornaro	12
that I may satisfie their honest desire, and withall help many	291	Cornaro	13
I will declare the causes which moved me to forsake Intemperance,	291	Cornaro	14
a sober life, expressing also the means which I have used therein.	291	Cornaro	16
I say therefore, that the infirmities, which did not onely begin,	291	Cornaro	17
first caused me to leave Intemperance, to which I was much addicted:	291	Cornaro	19
(having a most cold & moist stomack) I fell into divers diseases,	291	Cornaro	21
that after many troubles and griefs I should quickly come to an end;	291	Cornaro	26
When therefore I was thus affected [afflicted] from the thirtie fifth	292	Cornaro	1
there was one help for me, if I could constantly pursue it, to wit,	292	Cornaro	4
as I too wel by experience found.	292	Cornaro	7
that unlesse I speedily used that remedy, within a few moneths I	292	Cornaro	13
within a few moneths I should be driven to that exigent, . .	292	Cornaro	14
I grew fully perswaded, that all my griefs arose out of Intemperance:	292	Cornaro	19
hope of avoiding death and pain, I resolved to live a temperate life.	292	Cornaro	22
being directed by them in the way I ought to hold, I understood,	292	Cornaro	23
in the way I ought to hold, I understood, that the food I was to use,	292	Cornaro	24
that the food I was to use, was such as belonged to sickly . .	292	Cornaro	24
But I, then not liking that kinde of Diet, followed my Appetite,	292	Cornaro	26
and, when I felt inward heats, drank delightfull wines, . .	292	Cornaro	28
But after I had resolved to follow Temperance and Reason, . .	292	Cornaro	31
I so addicted my self to this course of life, that I never went	292	Cornaro	33
self to this course of life, that I never went a foot out of the way.	292	Cornaro	34
I found within a few dayes, that I was exceedingly helped, . .	292	Cornaro	34
that I was exceedingly helped, and by continuance thereof, . .	292	Cornaro	35
may seem to some incredible) I was perfectly cured of all my	292	Cornaro	37
I began to consider the force of Temperance, and to think thus	293	Cornaro	1
Wherefore I began to search out most diligently what meats were	293	Cornaro	4
And I purposed to try, whether those that pleased my taste brought me	293	Cornaro	6
This upon triall I found most false:	293	Cornaro	10
and yet all these I found hurtfull.	293	Cornaro	14
I forsook all these kinde of meats and drinks, and chose that wine	293	Cornaro	15
with a full stomack, but so as I might well both eat and drink more.	293	Cornaro	19
within lesse then a yeare I was not onely freed from all those evils	293	Cornaro	20
but also afterwards I fell not into that yearely disease, . .	293	Cornaro	22
whereinto I was wont, when I pleased my Sense & Appetite. . .	293	Cornaro	23
because from the time that I was made whole, I never since departed	293	Cornaro	25
I never since departed from my setled course of Sobrietie, . .	293	Cornaro	25
Yet with this diet I avoided other hurtfull things also, . .	293	Cornaro	30
I preserved me also, asmuch as I could, from hatred and melancholie,	293	Cornaro	34
I preserved me also, asmuch as I could, from hatred and melancholie,	293	Cornaro	35
Yet could I not so avoid all these, but that now and then I fell into	293	Cornaro	37
I not so avoid all these, but that now and then I fell into them;	293	Cornaro	38
that I perceived, that they had no great power to hurt those bodies,	294	Cornaro	1
So that I can truly say, That they who in these two things that enter	294	Cornaro	3
fearing lest I should be overthrown, they were possessed with a deep	294	Cornaro	17
But I, whom that matter ought to have affected most, received no	294	Cornaro	20
I began to perswade my self, that this suit and contention was raised	294	Cornaro	23
that I might know what great power a sober and temperate life hath	294	Cornaro	24
and that at length I should be a conquerour, as also a little after	294	Cornaro	26
For in the end I got the victorie, to my great honour, and no lesse	294	Cornaro	28
whereupon also I joyed exceedingly;	294	Cornaro	29
Moreover I say, that even bruises and squats, and falls, . .	294	Cornaro	33
This I found by experience, when I was seventie yeares old: . .	294	Cornaro	35
when the Physicians saw in what case I was, they concluded that I	295	Cornaro	2
what case I was, they concluded that I would die within three dayes.	295	Cornaro	3
But I, considering what an orderly life I had led for many yeares	295	Cornaro	7
considering what an orderly life I had led for many yeares together,	295	Cornaro	7
and so without other remedie or inconvenience I recovered; . .	295	Cornaro	13
Whence I conclude, That they that live a temperate life, . .	295	Cornaro	14
I was led by the advice of Physicians, and the dayly importunitie	295	Cornaro	19
On the other side I argued, that Nature was contented with a little,	295	Cornaro	25
and that I had for many yeares continued in good health, . .	295	Cornaro	26
at length I yeelded, and permitted the quantitie of meat to be	296	Cornaro	7
I increased it to the quantitie of two ounces more; . . .	296	Cornaro	11
of my drink, which before was foureteen ounces, I made now sixteen.	296	Cornaro	13
of a cheerfull and merrie man I became melancholie and cholerick;	296	Cornaro	15
neither did I know well, what I did or said.	296	Cornaro	17
Besides all this, I could not sleep, no not a quarter of an houre:	296	Cornaro	21
I by the grace of God cured my self, onely with returning to my	296	Cornaro	24
although I was now seventie eight yeares old, and my bodie spent	296	Cornaro	25
And I am confident, that under God nothing holp me, but that exact	296	Cornaro	28

I (cont'd)

	PAGE	TITLE	LINE
nothing holp me, but that exact rule which I had so long continued.	296	Cornaro	29
In all which time I felt nc grief, save now and then a little	296	Cornaro	30
which I contracted by breaking my diet, although it was a sore evil,	297	Cornaro	1
Whence I conclude, That an orderly life is the most sure way & ground	297	Cornaro	11
qualities to me, if I had not found them out by long experience?	297	Cornaro	35
Whereupon I conclude, since none can have a better Physician then	297	Cornaro	37
I denie not but that Physicians are necessarie, and greatly to be	298	Cornaro	3
I advise, that in stead of a Physician a regular life is to be	298	Cornaro	11
And that I may say nothing of cther things, are not almost all	298	Cornaro	32
To this I answer, that Galen kept it, and held it for the best	298	Cornaro	37
For I answer, That those inconveniences are of no great moment (as I	299	Cornaro	15
are of no great moment (as I shewed before) if a man be temperate	299	Cornaro	16
I answer first; Nature, which endeavours to preserve a man as much	299	Cornaro	25
Secondly, I answer better, That he which lives a temperate life,	299	Cornaro	35
No man that followes it, is bound to eat and drink so little as I:	300	Cornaro	7
No man is forbidden to eat fruit or fish, which I eat not: . .	300	Cornaro	8
For I eat little, because a little sufficeth my weak stomack:	300	Cornaro	8
and I abstain from fruit, and fish, and the like, because they hurt	300	Cornaro	9
as I will shew by my self, recounting the delights and pleasures in	300	Cornaro	30
in this age of eighty three, which now I take, and which are such,	300	Cornaro	32
I am continually in health, and I am so nimble, that I can easily get	300	Cornaro	34
and I am so nimble, that I can easily get on horseback without	300	Cornaro	34
that I can easily get on horseback without the advantage . .	300	Cornaro	34
of the ground, and sometimes I go up high stairs and hills cn foot.	300	Cornaro	36
Then, I am ever cheerfull, merrie, and well-contented, free from all	300	Cornaro	37
I am not wearie of life, which I passe with great delight. . .	301	Cornaro	2
I am not wearie of life, which I passe with great delight. . .	301	Cornaro	3
I conferre often with worthie men, excelling in wit, learning,	301	Cornaro	3
When I cannot have their companie, I give my self to the reading	301	Cornaro	5
I give my self to the reading of some learned book, and afterwards	301	Cornaro	6
aim in all things, how I may help others to the furthest of my power.	301	Cornaro	8
All these things I do at my ease, and at fit seasons, and in mine own	301	Cornaro	9
I enjoy also my gardens, and those divers, parted with rills	301	Cornaro	15
Some times of the yeare I enjoy the pleasure of the Euganean hills,	301	Cornaro	17
where also I have fountains and gardens, and a very convenient house.	301	Cornaro	18
At other times, I repair to a village of mine, seated in the valley;	301	Cornaro	19
But I drained the ground, and made the aire good:	301	Cornaro	28
So that I can truly say, That I have both given God a Temple,	301	Cornaro	31
That I have both given God a Temple, and men to worship him in it:	301	Cornaro	31
Sometimes I ride to some of the neighbour-cities, that I may enjoy	301	Cornaro	34
that I may enjoy the sight & communication of my friends, . .	301	Cornaro	35
I view their pieces, I compare them with those of Antiquitie;	302	Cornaro	1
and ever I learn somewhat which is worthy of my knowledge: . .	302	Cornaro	2
I survey palaces, gardens, and antiquities, publick fabricks,	302	Cornaro	3
neither omit I any thing that may either teach, or delight me.	302	Cornaro	4
I am much pleased also in my travells, with the beauty of situation.	302	Cornaro	5
when I was given to disorder and all the delights that could be.	302	Cornaro	10
I sleep well and quietly any where, and my dreams are fair . .	302	Cornaro	12
I was one of those that was deputed for the managing of that work,	302	Cornaro	16
by Temperance and the Grace of God I feel not those perturbations	302	Cornaro	24
by this also, in what estate I am, may be discovered, because	302	Cornaro	27
at these yeares (viz. 83) I have made a most pleasant comedie,	302	Cornaro	28
why should I be accounted lesse happie, or lesse my self, . .	302	Cornaro	34
I daily behold a kinde of immortalitie in the succession of my	303	Cornaro	1
For when I come home, I finde eleven grand-children of mine,	303	Cornaro	2
I finde eleven grand-children of mine, all the sonnes of one father	303	Cornaro	2
as farre as I can conjecture, very apt and well given both . .	303	Cornaro	4
I am delighted with their musick and fashion, and I my self also sing	303	Cornaro	6
with their musick and fashion, and I my self also sing often;	303	Cornaro	6
because I have now a clearer voice, then ever I had in my life.	303	Cornaro	7
because I have now a clearer voice, then ever I had in my life.	303	Cornaro	8
it is evident, That the life which I live at this age, is not a dead,	303	Cornaro	9
if I had my wish, would I change age and constitution with them who	303	Cornaro	11
would I change age and constitution with them who follow their	303	Cornaro	11
as daily experience sheweth, and I also, when I was a young man,	303	Cornaro	15
sheweth, and I also, when I was a young man, too well found.	303	Cornaro	15
I know how inconsiderate that age is, and, though subject to death,	303	Cornaro	16
whereas I by the experience of so many yeares have learned to give	303	Cornaro	20
but also I hope, when I shall come to that point, I shall finde no	303	Cornaro	23
when I shall come to that point, I shall finde no little comfort in	303	Cornaro	23
I shall finde no little comfort in the favour of Jesus Christ.	303	Cornaro	23
Yet I am sure, that my end is farre from me:	303	Cornaro	24
for I know that (setting casualties aside) I shall not die . .	303	Cornaro	25
(setting casualties aside) I shall not die but by a pure resolution:	303	Cornaro	26
by the regularitie of my life I have shut out death all other wayes.	303	Cornaro	27
but that I should wish all who have the care of themselves, . .	303	Cornaro	31
but lest in any thing I forsake that Temperance which I have found so	303	Cornaro	34
in any thing I forsake that Temperance which I have found so good,	303	Cornaro	34
that Temperance which I have found so good, I here make an end.	303	Cornaro	35
your Valdesso I now returne with many thanks, and some notes,	304	Valdesso	1
discover some care, which I forbare not in the midst of my griefes;	304	Valdesso	3
because I would doe nothing negligently that you commit unto mee;	304	Valdesso	4
the Authors sake, whom I conceive to have been a true servant of God;	304	Valdesso	6
and to such, and all that is theirs, I owe diligence; . . .	304	Valdesso	8
Churches sake, to whom by Printing it I would have you consecrate it.	304	Valdesso	9
there are some things which I like not in him, as my fragments will	304	Valdesso	16
neverthelesse I wish you by all meanes to publish it, for these three	304	Valdesso	18
for which I doe so love him, that were there nothing else, . .	305	Valdesso	6
I would Print it, that with it the honour of my Lord might be	305	Valdesso	7
and overweigh the defects (as I conceive) towards the publishing	305	Valdesso	13

I (cont'd)

	PAGE	TITLE	LINE
But I like none of it, for it slights the Scripture too much:	306	Valdesso	16
for I can no more free my selfe from actuall sinnes after Baptisme,	308	Valdesso	3
then I could of Originall before, and without Baptisme.	308	Valdesso	4
whereby I understand he meaneth only the effectuall operation	308	Valdesso	30
this I call beleeving by Revelation, and not by Relation.	309	Valdesso	6
I much mislike the Comparison of Images, and H. Scripture,	309	Valdesso	18
The H. Scriptures (as I wrote before) have not only an Elementary	309	Valdesso	20
not be punished (which word I like here better then chastizement,	311	Valdesso	27
He meaneth (I suppose) that a man presume not to merit,	312	Valdesso	14
and I conceive that restraining motions are much more frequent	313	Valdesso	17
By occasions (I suppose) hee meaneth the ordinary, or necessary	314	Valdesso	16
Saviour prayed with doubtfulnesse, is more then I can or dare say;	315	Valdesso	10
I ever tooke that for a weaknesse in the great Patriark:	316	Valdesso	1
yet I remember the Fathers forbid us to judge of the doubtfull	316	Valdesso	11
Neither doe I doubt but if Abraham had lived in our Kingdome under	316	Valdesso	22
I wonder how this opinion could befall so good a man as it seems	317	Valdesso	31
if I bid a man stay in a place untill I come, I doe not then bid him	318	Valdesso	14
if I bid a man stay in a place untill I come, I doe not then bid him	318	Valdesso	15
I doe not then bid him goe away but rather stay longer,	318	Valdesso	15
that I may speak with him or doe some thing else when I doe come.	318	Valdesso	16
that I may speak with him or doe some thing else when I doe come.	318	Valdesso	17
I gave the mouse a hole, and she is become my heire.	324	Proverbs	94
Whether goest, griefe? where I am wont.	324	Proverbs	96
I wept when I was borne, and every day shewes why.	327	Proverbs	199
I had rather ride on an asse that carries me,	329	Proverbs	258
I had rather aske of my sire browne bread,	330	Proverbs	269
Let none say, I will not drinke water.	331	Proverbs	310
Since you know all, and I nothing,	332	Proverbs	336
tell me what I dreamed last night.	332	Proverbs	336
I was taken by a morsell, saies the fish.	342	Proverbs	627
Shew me a lyer, and I'le shew thee a theefe.	343	Proverbs	652
If gold knew what gold is, gold would get gold I wis.	354	Proverbs	1012
I escaped the Thunder, and fell into the Lightning.	358	Proverbs	D 1084
Say to pleasure, Gentle Eve, I will none of your apple.	360	Proverbs	D 1140
But I fear the heat of my late Ague hath dryed up those springs,	363	Letters	4
I need not their help, to reprove the vanity of those many	363	Letters	6
Though I had the best wit in the World, yet it would easily tyre me,	363	Letters	14
of thanks for the diversity of your favours, if I sought to do so;	363	Letters	16
but, I profess it not:	363	Letters	16
only hereafter I will take heed how I propose my desires unto you,	363	Letters	20
unto you, since I find you so willing to yield to my requests;	363	Letters	21
neither do I make any question, but that you have performed your	363	Letters	24
and I will strive to imitate the compleatness of your love,	364	Letters	2
I dare no longer be silent, least while I think I am modest,	364	Letters	7
be silent, least while I think I am modest, I wrong both my self,	364	Letters	7
I wrong both my self, and also the confidence my Friends have in me;	364	Letters	8
wherefore I will open my case unto you, which I think deserves	364	Letters	9
my case unto you, which I think deserves the reading at the least;	364	Letters	10
and it is this, I want Books extremely;	364	Letters	10
how I am now setting foot into Divinity, to lay the platform of my	364	Letters	11
and shall I then be fain alwayes to borrow Books, and build	364	Letters	13
nor can I write coldly in that, wherein consisteth the making good	364	Letters	16
hath guided me hitherto, and of atchieving my (I dare say) holy ends.	364	Letters	19
in that I apprehend what my Friends would have been forward to say,	364	Letters	20
been forward to say, if I had taken ill courses, Follow your Book,	364	Letters	21
since, I hope, I have not deceived their expectation, let not them	364	Letters	23
I have not deceived their expectation, let not them deceive mine:	364	Letters	24
it is true (God knows) I am weak, yet not so, but that every day,	364	Letters	26
but that every day, I may step one step towards my journies end;	364	Letters	27
and I love my friends so well, as that if all things proved not well,	364	Letters	28
not well, I had rather the fault should lie on me, than on them;	364	Letters	29
be any truth in me, I find it little enough to keep me in health.	364	Letters	31
You know I was sick last Vacation, neither am I yet recovered,	364	Letters	32
neither am I yet recovered, so that I am fain ever and anon,	364	Letters	33
so that I am fain ever and anon, to buy somewhat tending towards my	364	Letters	33
Now this Lent I am forbid utterly to eat any Fish, so that I am fain	365	Letters	1
so that I am fain to dyet in my Chamber at mine own cost;	365	Letters	2
on Fridayes and Saturdayes, I must do so, which yet sometimes I fast.	365	Letters	5
on Fridayes and Saturdayes, I must do so, which yet sometimes I fast.	365	Letters	6
Sometimes also I ride to Newmarket, and there lie a day or two	365	Letters	6
to avoiding of costlier matters, if I should fall absolutely sick:	365	Letters	8
I protest and vow, I even study Thrift, and yet I am scarce able	365	Letters	9
I even study Thrift, and yet I am scarce able with much ado to make	365	Letters	9
and yet I am scarce able with much ado to make one half years	365	Letters	9
or five Shillings come in my way, I buy it, though I fast for it;	365	Letters	12
the time when I desire this (which is now, when I must lay	365	Letters	17
this (which is now, when I must lay the foundation of my whole life).	365	Letters	18
Thirdly, what I desire, and to what end, not vain pleasures,	365	Letters	19
or any other way, I desire you, Sir, to be my Mediator to them in my	365	Letters	21
Now I write to you, Sir, because to you I have ever opened my heart;	365	Letters	23
for I am sure you love Your faithfullest Servant, GEORGE HERBERT.	365	Letters	25
The disease which I am troubled with now is the shortness of time,	365	Letters	30
that I have not leazure to impart unto you some of those observations	365	Letters	32
of those observations which I have framed to myself in conversation;	366	Letters	1
and whereof I would not have you ignorant.	366	Letters	2
As I shal find occasion, you shal receive them by peeces;	366	Letters	3
for I would have you, even in speeches, to observe so much,	366	Letters	9
of your wit, mark what I say, have a good conceit of your wit;	366	Letters	15
But I am out of my time:	366	Letters	19
when I have more time, you shall hear more;	366	Letters	20

I (cont'd)

	PAGE	TITLE	LINE
mee in your letters, for I am your ever loving brother, G. HERBERT.	366	Letters	21
I understand by a Letter from my Brother Henry, that he hath bought	366	Letters	29
I dare say she wculd make good her promise of taking five or six	367	Letters	2
yet I had rather flie to my old ward, that if any course could be	367	Letters	6
upon condition that I should surcease from all title to it, . .	367	Letters	8
after I enter'd into a Benefice, I should be most glad to entertain	367	Letters	9
into a Benefice, I should be most glad to entertain it, and both pay	367	Letters	10
It is high time now that I should be no more a burden to you,	367	Letters	13
burden to you, since I can never answer what I have already received;	367	Letters	13
burden to you, since I can never answer what I have already received;	367	Letters	14
I remember my most humble duty to my Mother.	367	Letters	20
I have wrote to my dear sick Sister this week already, and therefore	367	Letters	20
Sister this week already, and therefore now I hope may be excused.	367	Letters	22
I pray Sir, pardon my boldness of inclosing my Brothers Letter in	367	Letters	23
Letter in yours, for it was because I know your Lodging, but not his.	367	Letters	24
for I am enjoined to write to you by Sir John Danvers, to which mine	367	Letters	27
& therfore I am not over much beholding to those busnesses which	367	Letters	29
These are the things I am to acquaint you with, of whose rude	369	Letters	1
I wish I could have come in person to thank you, but it is . .	369	Letters	10
I wish I could have come in person to thank you, but it is . .	369	Letters	11
I am to make an Oration to the whole University of an hour long in	369	Letters	12
neither can I so much as go to Bugden, and deliver your Letter,	369	Letters	15
yet have I sent it thither by a faithful Messenger this day:	369	Letters	16
I beseech you all, you and my dear Mother and Sister to pardon me,	369	Letters	17
If I could possibly have come, none should have done my message	369	Letters	19
he and I are ancient acquaintance, and I have a strong opinion	369	Letters	21
and I have a strong opinion of him, that if he can do me a courtesie,	369	Letters	22
I have sent you here inclosed a Letter from our Master in my behalf,	369	Letters	24
I long to hear from Sir Francis, I pray Sir send the Letter you	370	Letters	5
I pray Sir send the Letter you receive from him to me as soon as you	370	Letters	5
to me as scon as you can, that I may work the heads to my purpose.	370	Letters	6
I hope I shall get this place without all your London helps,	370	Letters	7
of which I am very proud, not but that I joy in your favours,	370	Letters	8
not but that I joy in your favours, but that you may see, . .	370	Letters	9
that if all fail, yet I am able to stand on mine own legs. . .	370	Letters	10
I thank you for your infinite favours, I fear only that I have	370	Letters	11
I fear only that I have omitted some fitting circumstance, . .	370	Letters	11
but that I have both time and work to be Your extreme Servant,	370	Letters	13
I understand by Sir Francis Nethersols Letter, that he fears I have	370	Letters	18
that he fears I have not fully resolved of the matter, since this	370	Letters	19
much from Divinity, at which, not without cause, he thinks, I aim;	370	Letters	21
but, I have wrote him back, that this dignity, hath no such . .	370	Letters	21
if it had to others, yet to me it should not, for ought I yet knew;	370	Letters	24
and therefore I desire him to send me a direct answer in his next	370	Letters	25
I pray Sir therefore, cause this inclosed to be carried to his	370	Letters	26
brothers house of his own name (as I think) at the sign of the Pedler	370	Letters	27
I cannot yet find leisure to write to my Lord, or Sir Benjamin	370	Letters	29
but I hope I shall shortly, though for the reckoning of your favours,	370	Letters	30
I shall never find time and paper enough, yet am I Your readiest	370	Letters	31
and paper encugh, yet am I Your readiest Servant, GEORGE HERBERT.	370	Letters	32
I remember my most humble duty to my Mother, who cannot think me	371	Letters	1
since I rode 200 mile to see a Sister, in a way I knew not, . .	371	Letters	2
to see a Sister, in a way I knew not, in the midst of much business,	371	Letters	3
I have received the things you sent me, safe;	371	Letters	6
and now the only thing I lcng for, is to hear of my dear sick Sister;	371	Letters	7
Can I be so happy, as to hear of both these that they succeed well?	371	Letters	9
that I loved her even in my departure, in looking to her Son,	371	Letters	12
I suppose she is not disposed to spend her eyesight on a piece	371	Letters	13
spend her eyesight on a piece of paper, or else I had wrote to her;	371	Letters	14
when I shall understand that a Letter will be seasonable, . .	371	Letters	14
I have forty businesses in my hands, your Courtesie will pardon	371	Letters	17
I was the better content because I was in hope I should my self carry	372	Letters	14
I was the better content because I was in hope I should my self carry	372	Letters	15
content because I was in hope I should my self carry all sickness	372	Letters	15
but, since I know I did not, and that your share continues, . .	372	Letters	16
or rather increaseth, I wish earnestly that I were again with you:	372	Letters	17
or rather increaseth, I wish earnestly that I were again with you:	372	Letters	18
I beseech you to be chearful, and comfort your self in the God of all	372	Letters	24
and I shou'd acccunt my self most happy if I might change with you;	373	Letters	2
and I shou'd account my self most happy if I might change with you;	373	Letters	3
I have alwaies observ'd the thred of Life to be like other threds	373	Letters	4
I alwaies fear'd sickness more then death, because sickness hath made	373	Letters	8
me unable to perform those Offices for which I came into the world,	373	Letters	9
I beseech you consider all that can happen to you are either	373	Letters	20
I never find Blessed be the Rich;	373	Letters	29
I beseech you let such thoughts as these, moderate your present fear	374	Letters	3
Rejoyce in the Lord alwaies, and again I say rejoyce. . . .	374	Letters	21
yes, I say again rejoyce;	374	Letters	23
when I wrote, to putt one of our neeces into your hands but barely	375	Letters	4
one of our neeces into your hands but barely what I wrote I meant,	375	Letters	5
one of our neeces into your hands but barely what I wrote I meant,	375	Letters	6
I was desirous to putt a good mind into the way of charity, . .	375	Letters	7
a good mind into the way of charity, and that was all I intended.	375	Letters	9
I will tell you what I wrote to our eldest brother, when he urged one	375	Letters	10
I wrote to him that I would have both or neither;	375	Letters	12
Therefore I considered that if one only came, the comfort intended	375	Letters	16
Since that I have seen the fruit of my observation, for they have	375	Letters	17
working, still together, that I take a comfort therein; . .	375	Letters	20
till I take some opportunity to let them know your love, . .	375	Letters	21
them know your lcve, for which both they shall, and I doe, thank you.	375	Letters	22

I (cont'd)	PAGE	TITLE		LINE
it were a great good deed, and I would have her conveyed to you.	375	Letters		32
But I judge you not:	375	Letters		32
you take her not, I am thinking to do it, even beyond my strengthe;	375	Letters		35
being more beggarly now than I have been these many years,	375	Letters		36
But though I both consider this, and your observation, also,	376	Letters		3
of kindred bredd up, (which generally is very true,) yet I care not;	376	Letters		5
I forgett all thinges, so I may doe them good who want it.	376	Letters		5
I forgett all thinges, so I may doe them good who want it.	376	Letters		6
So I doe my part to them, lett them think of me what they will	376	Letters		6
I have another judge, to whom I stand or fall.	376	Letters		7
I have another judge, to whom I stand or fall.	376	Letters		8
Yf I should regard such things, it were in another's power to defeat	376	Letters		8
which I commend to you as being now a father, "the best-bredd child	376	Letters		17
I was glad of your Cambridge newes, but you joyed me exceedingly	377	Letters		18
I am glad I used you in it, and you have no cause to be sorry,	377	Letters		20
yet I shall ever put your care of Leighton, upon my accompt,	378	Letters		3
God knowes, I have desired a long time, to doe the place good,	378	Letters		5
to give me you for the Man, I desired, for which I humbly thank him,	378	Letters		8
for which I humbly thank him, & am so far from giving you cause,	378	Letters		9
that I take it exceeding kindly of you.	378	Letters		11
I refuse not advice from the meanest, that creeps upon Gods earth,	378	Letters		11
much less can I disesteem it from you, whome I esteem to be God's	378	Letters		13
whome I esteem to be God's faithfull & diligent Servant,	378	Letters		14
you any other wayes, as neyther I my self desire to be considered.	378	Letters		16
Particularly, I like all your Addresses, & for ought I see,	378	Letters		16
all your Addresses, & for ought I see, they are ever to be liked.	378	Letters		17
the chiefest also, so also have I required Mr W. for his part.	378	Letters		23
As I had written thus much, I received a Letter, from My Brother,	378	Letters		30
I thanke you heartily for Leighton, your care, your Counsell,	379	Letters		13
And as I am glad for the thing, so no less glad for the Heart,	379	Letters		14
& for my power, I have sent my Letters, to your Brother,	379	Letters		19
sent my Letters, to your Brother, investing him, in all that I have.	379	Letters		20
It is so long since I heard from you, that I long to heare both how	379	Letters		23
I heard from you, that I long to heare both how you and your's doe:	379	Letters		23
the other profitt, the work I may change, the profitt, I am master	381	Woodnoth		31
other profitt, the work I may change, the profitt, I am master of.	381	Woodnoth		32
I George Herbert commending my soule and body to Almightie God that	382	G.H.'s Will		1
I give all my goods both within doores and without doores both	382	G.H.'s Will		3
whole sum of five hundred pounds I bequeath unto my Neeces equally	382	G.H.'s Will		12
Then I bequeath twenty pounds unto the poore of this parish to be	382	G.H.'s Will		16
Then I bequeath to Mr Hays the Comment of Lucas Brugensis uppon	382	G.H.'s Will		18
then I bequeath to Mr Bostocke St. Augustines workes and his halfe	382	G.H.'s Will		20
then I leave to my servant Elizabeth her dubble wages given her,	382	G.H.'s Will		22
besides that which is due to her, to Ann I leave thirty shillings:	382	G.H.'s Will		24
should be mine Executor to whome I bequeath twenty pound whereof	382	G.H.'s Will		28
uppon Leighton Church, the other five pound I give to himselfe.	382	G.H.'s Will		30
Lastlie I besech Sir John Danvers that he would be pleased to be	382	G.H.'s Will		31
of monyes wherof he is to give as I know he will a Just account:	383	G.H.'s Will		25
any body els that owe me any thing else of old debt I forgive them.	383	G.H.'s Will		27
ICE				
Trust not one nights ice.	336	Proverbs		453
IDLE				
Canst be idle? canst thou play,	113	Businesse		1
But if yet thou idle be,	113	Businesse		15
Even the wals are not idle, but something is written, or painted	240	Priest 10		23
or idle person in his Parish, but that all bee in a competent way	244	Priest 12		20
Those that the Parson findes idle, or ill imployed, he chides	248	Priest 14		13
Hee admits no vaine or idle names, but such as are usuall	258	Priest 22		4
the Common-wealth, that none should be idle, but all busied.	274	Priest 32		28
given it to the poor, we must not be idle, but labour to get more,	275	Priest 32		1
Bee not idle and you shall not bee longing.	331	Proverbs		308
An idle head is a boxe for the winde.	343	Proverbs		651
An Idle youth, a needy Age.	356	Proverbs	D	1042
IDLENES				
people to continue in their vocation, it is in opposition to idlenes.	381	Woodnoth		24
IDLENESS				
or breeding up children to no Calling, but in idleness, or the like.	251	Priest 17		21
And because Idleness is twofold, the one in having no calling,	274	Priest 32		15
IDLENESSE				
Flie idlenesse, which yet thou canst not flie	9	Ch.-Porch		79
which otherwise they would reckon upon, and turn to idlenesse.	245	Priest 12		5
The great and nationall sin of this Land he esteems to be Idlenesse;	274	Priest 32		9
with some idlenesse of brain, says the Spaniard.	357	Proverbs	D	1050
IDOL				
The Temple where an Idol stood,	214	Convert	D	18
IDOL'S				
And be that Idol's URN.	214	Convert	D	20
IE				
To go where the King goes afoot (i.e. to the stool).	356	Proverbs	D	1034
To go upon the Franciscans Hackney (i.e. on foot).	356	Proverbs	D	1035
for he asks counsell of the Dead (i.e. books).	361	Proverbs	D	1158
IF (see also yf)				
Abstaine or wedd: if thou canst not abstaine	7	Ch.-Porch	W	13
If this seeme Monkish; think which brings most paine	7	Ch.-Porch	W	15
If thou chuse bravely & rely on God	7	Ch.-Porch	W	17
If rottennesse have more, let Heaven go.	7	Ch.-Porch		18
If God had laid all common, certainly	7	Ch.-Porch		19
If it concurr with vertue: doe thy best	7	Ch.-Porch	W	21
If rottenness have more, lett Heaven goe.	7	Ch.-Porch	W	24
Which would throw me there, if I keep the round.	7	Ch.-Porch		30

IF (cont'd)

	PAGE	TITLE		LINE
Stay at the third glasse: if thou lose thy hold,	8	Ch.-Porch		41
If reason move not Gallants, quit the room,	8	Ch.-Porch		43
Yet, if thou sinne in wine or wantonnesse,	8	Ch.-Porch		49
If thou wilt die, the gates of hell are broad:	9	Ch.-Porch		71
If those take up thy day, the sunne will crie	9	Ch.-Porch		81
If those bee all thy day, the sunne will crie	9	Ch.-Porch	W	81
If studious, copie fair, what time hath blurr'd;	10	Ch.-Porch		86
Redeem truth from his jawes: if souldier,	10	Ch.-Porch		87
Redeem truth from his chawes: if souldier,	10	Ch.-Porch	W	87
If they dare try, a glorious life, or grave.	10	Ch.-Porch		90
If thou art nothing, think what thou wouldst bee	10	Ch.-Porch	W	90
But if thou coole, then take some shame to thee	10	Ch.-Porch	W	90
This is Earth's language, for if Heaven come in,	10	Ch.-Porch	W	90
Thy Gentrie bleats, as if thy native cloth	10	Ch.-Porch		93
And if Gods image move thee not, let thine.	10	Ch.-Porch		102
But if thy sonne can make ten pound his measure,	11	Ch.-Porch		113
Thou hast two sconses, if thy stomack call;	11	Ch.-Porch		128
Tast all, but feed not. if thy stomach call	11	Ch.-Porch	W	128
Entice the trusty sunne, if that you can,	12	Ch.-Porch		136
Entice the trusty sunne, if that thou can,	12	Ch.-Porch	W	136
Ev'n with the yeare: but age, if it will hit,	13	Ch.-Porch		158
Which if it cleave to coine, one common rust	13	Ch.-Porch	W	165
Gold thou mayst safely touch; but if it stick	13	Ch.-Porch		167
What skills it, if a bag of stones or gold	13	Ch.-Porch		169
If yet thou love game at so deere a rate,	14	Ch.-Porch		199
If that thy fame with ev'ry toy be pos'd,	15	Ch.-Porch		223
But may be wittie, if thou hast the vein.	16	Ch.-Porch		240
But if thou want it, buy it not too deere.	16	Ch.-Porch		244
If cause require, thou art his sacrifice;	17	Ch.-Porch		273
Yet be not surety, if thou be a father.	17	Ch.-Porch		277
If thou be single, all thy goods and ground	17	Ch.-Porch		283
In thy discourse, if thou desire to please:	18	Ch.-Porch		289
If thou be Master-gunner, spend not all	18	Ch.-Porch		301
As if thou mad'st thy will. A civil guest	18	Ch.-Porch		305
If truth be with thy friend, be with them both:	19	Ch.-Porch		323
If thou observest strangers in each fit,	21	Ch.-Porch		365
As if none could bee brave, but who profess	21	Ch.-Porch	W	369
God then deals blessings: If a king did so,	22	Ch.-Porch		389
If thou mislike him, thou conceiv'st him not.	23	Ch.-Porch		428
The worst speak something good: if all want sense,	23	Ch.-Porch		431
And growth of it: if with thy watch, that too	24	Ch.-Porch		454
If thou do ill; the joy fades, not the pains:	24	Ch.-Porch		461
If well; the pain doth fade, the joy remains.	24	Ch.-Porch		462
That if I chance to hold my peace,	26	The Altar		13
O let this cup passe, if it be thy pleasure:	27	Sacrifice		23
If stonie hearts will melt with gentle love.	29	Sacrifice		90
Such sorrow as, if sinfull man could feel,	33	Sacrifice		209
If thou dost give me wealth, I will restore	35	Thanksgvng		19
If thou dost give me honour, men shall see,	35	Thanksgvng		21
I will not marry; or, if she be mine,	35	Thanksgvng		23
My bosome friend, if he blaspheme thy name,	35	Thanksgvng		25
That three yeares hence, if I survive,	36	Thanksgvng		32
As if I us'd them but for fashion.	36	Thanksgvng		36
If thou shalt give me wit, it shall appeare,	36	Thanksgvng		43
If thou hast giv'n it me, 'tis here.	36	Thanksgvng		44
If ever he did taste the like.	37	The Agonie		16
Since, if my soul make even with the week,	38	The Sinner		3
If they should offer to contest	42	Easter		25
For, if I imp my wing on thine,	43	East.wings		19
If thou shalt let this venome lurk,	45	Nature		7
Are blowne away, as if they nere had bin.	46	Sinne 1	W	14
Let me not love thee, if I love thee not.	48	Afflict.1		66
If life be told	48	Repentance		11
For if thou stay,	49	Repentance		22
If I go lower in the book,	50	Faith		21
If blisse had lien in art or strength,	50	Faith		25
If what my soul doth feel sometimes,	55	Temper 1		3
Lord, if thou must needs use thy dart,	56	Temper 2		3
If as a flowre doth spread and die,	57	Employm. 1		1
If they might mend their wages, and serve here.	59	Whitsunday		12
And if wee can stay there, it's well.	59	Whitsunday	W	14
And if the braves of conqu'ring sinne	60	Whitsunday		23
If still the sunne should hide his face,	60	Grace		5
If the Sunn still should hide his face,	60	Grace	W	5
What if I say thou seek'st delayes;	61	Grace	W	20
Or if to me thou wilt not move,	61	Grace		22
Or, if I mount unto the skie,	61	Praise 1		7
Or, if I steale up to the skie,	61	Praise 1	W	7
O raise me then: for if a Spider may	61	Praise 1	W	17
If all mens tears were let	62	Afflict.2		6
Wherein if they were set,	62	Afflict.2		9
As if that thou hadst nothing els to do?	62	Mattens		12
If apparitions make us sad,	63	Sinne 2		7
Comfort, I'le die; for if you poste from me,	66	Ch.-mus.		9
Comfort, I'le die; for if you part from me,	66	Ch.-mus.	W	9
But if I travell in your companie,	66	Ch.-mus.		11
If either Innocence or Fervencie	66	Ch.-lock	W	4
And if the Fox had liv'd to rule their side,	70	Humilitie		23
O brook not this, lest if what even now	71	Frailtie		17
O brook not this, lest if that, which just now	71	Frailtie	W	17

IF (cont'd)

	PAGE	TITLE		LINE
Or if some yeares with it escape,	73	Afflict.3		10
Yet, if thou wilt from thence depart,	74	The Starre		5
Whom, if we were not very dull,	75	Sunday		18
If not upon his head, yet in his hands:	77	Ang.&Sts.		5
Although then others court you, if ye know	78	Ang.&Sts.		26
If any one our Masters hand can show.	78	Ang.&Sts.		30
If thou hadst let us runne,	82	Ungratef.		3
Surveys, as if he had design'd.	85	Vanitie 1		4
Parrats may thank us, if they are not mute,	91	Man		11
Both are our cleanlines: if one have beauty,	92	Man	W	41
In friendship, first I think, if that agree,	93	Unkindness		2
If any touch my friend, or his good name,	93	Unkindness		6
Since if my sent be good, I care not, if	94	Life		17
How know I, if thou shouldst me raise,	95	Submission		13
A poore mans rod if thou wilt hire	96	Charms & K	W	3
Ten still, if sermons go for gains.	96	Charms & K		16
Ten, if a Sermon goe for gains.	96	Charms & K	W	16
If either will convert us, we are thine:	97	Afflict.5		14
Some Angels us'd the first; if our relief	97	Afflict.5		15
And make his own? as if none knew, but he.	100	Miserie		14
Decking the sense, as if it were to sell.	102	Jordan 2		6
Praising the sense, as if it were to sell.	102	Jordan 2	W	6
Off'ring their service, if I were not sped:	102	Jordan 2		8
If I but lift mine eyes, my suit is made:	103	Prayer 2		5
My God, if writings may	104	Obedience		1
If this poore paper do as much as they.	104	Obedience		5
If that hereafter Pleasure	104	Obedience		11
As if this passed with a reservation,	104	Obedience		13
To both our goods, if he to it will stand.	105	Obedience		40
If some kinde man would thrust his heart	105	Obedience		42
If thou persistest, I will tell thee,	105	Conscience		11
Yet if thou talkest still,	106	Conscience		19
As if thy love could fail or change.	108	Home		28
Yet if thou stayest still, why must I stay?	108	Home		31
If souls be made of earthly mold,	111	Vanitie 2		11
If born on high,	111	Vanitie 2		13
Arise sad heart; if thou dost not withstand,	112	Dawning		9
Arise sad heart; if thou doe not withstand,	112	Dawning	V	9
If, poore soul, thou hast no tears,	113	Businesse		6
If thou hast no sighs or grones,	113	Businesse		12
But if yet thou idle be,	113	Businesse		15
If he had not liv'd for thee,	113	Businesse		20
If he had not di'd for thee,	113	Businesse		26
Sweetest Saviour, if my soul	114	Dialogue		1
If I say, Thou shalt be mine;	114	Dialogue		11
That is all, if that I could	115	Dialogue		25
As if I were all earth?	115	Dulnesse		2
Sure thou didst put a minde there, if I could	116	Dulnesse		23
The beasts say, Eat me: but, if beasts must teach,	117	Providence		21
Who sweetly temper'st all. If we could heare	118	Providence		39
And if an herb hath power, what have the starres?	119	Providence		77
He makes a grave; as if the thing had sense,	119	Providence		83
If they seek fine things, thou dost make them run	120	Providence		106
To show thou art not bound, as if thy lot	121	Providence		137
If it at length deserve some blame:	122	Time		4
And sayes, If he in this be crost,	123	Gratefulnes		6
As if thy blessings had spare dayes:	124	Gratefulnes		30
And ask'd, if Peace were there.	124	Peace		4
Or, if they enter, cannot rest,	126	Confession		21
As if a whirlwinde blew	127	Giddinesse		14
O what a sight were Man, if his attires	127	Giddinesse		17
Surely if each one saw anothers heart,	127	Giddinesse		21
Of mine inheritance? Lord, if I must borrow,	128	Bunch Gr.		20
Yet if we rightly measure,	131	Mans medly		4
If as the windes and waters here below	132	The Storm		1
If thou hadst lost a glove or ring,	133	The Method		11
As if a starre were duller then a clod,	134	Divinitie		3
For death is drie as dust. Yet if ye part,	135	Ephes.		10
If a cleare spring for me no time forbears,	136	Ephes.		28
Yet if I wail not still, since still to wail	136	Ephes.		31
If my deserts were masters of mine eyes:	136	Ephes.		34
As if they had a part?	136	Familie		2
As if there were no rule or eares?	136	Familie		4
If thou hast wherewithall to spice a draught,	137	The Size		9
If comforts fell according to desert,	138	The Size		39
The starres and all things are; If I refuse,	139	Artillerie		12
Yet if thou shunnest, I am thine:	139	Artillerie		29
I must be so, if I am mine.	139	Artillerie		30
And lives: If that be all, said I,	142	Pilgrimage		34
If it be his once, all is well.	144	Discharge		20
If, though thou didst not beat thy future brow,	144	Discharge		23
Man and the present fit: if he provide,	145	Discharge		31
This houre is mine: if for the next I care,	145	Discharge		33
Either grief will not come: or if it must,	145	Discharge		51
Come, bring thy gift. If blessings were as slow	147	Offering		1
Yet one, if good, may title to a number;	147	Offering		9
If ye have any thing to send or write,	152	The Bag		31
Or if hereafter any of my friends	152	The Bag		37
Yet if the heart that wept	154	Glimpse		21
If I have more to spinne,	155	Glimpse		26

IF (cont'd)

	PAGE	TITLE		LINE
Could poyson, if it had a tongue, expresse?	155	Assurance		14
If all the hope and comfort that I gather,	155	Assurance		21
Wherefore if thou canst fail,	156	Assurance		31
If mine I am: and thine much more,	157	Clasping		2
If I without thee would be mine,	157	Clasping		9
For well he knows, if but one grief and smart	159	Jos.coat		5
For if I should (said he)	160	The Pulley		11
If goodnesse leade him not, yet wearinesse	160	The Pulley		19
If earth in earth delight.	161	Priesthood		24
As if to meet thee they did know,	162	The Search		11
What I would do for thee, if once my grones	165	The Crosse		15
As if there were no such cold thing.	165	The Flower		7
Thy word is all, if we could spell.	166	The Flower		21
Still upwards bent, as if heav'n were mine own,	166	The Flower		30
If truly said, they may take part	168	a true Hymn		7
If the words onely ryme,	168	a true Hymn		13
Whereas if th' heart be moved,	168	a true Hymn		16
If troubles overtake thee, do not wail:	170	Water-crs.		4
If thy first glance so powerfull be,	172	The Glance		17
Or if I stray, he doth convert	172	23 Psalme		9
If we could see below	175	The Foil		1
As if grief were not foul, nor vertue winning.	176	The Foil		8
And if I please him, I write fine and wittie.	176	Forerunners		12
Let foolish lovers, if they will love dung,	177	Forerunners		25
Yet if you go, I passe not; take your way:	177	Forerunners		31
As if they could beautie spare.	177	The Rose		8
Or if such deceits there be,	177	The Rose		9
If then all that worldlings prize	178	The Rose		21
Or if he pleaseth, through it passe,	184	The Elixer		11
If I lack'd any thing.	188	Love 3		6
If God and man be sever'd infinitely!	193	Ch.-Milit.		116
And if in comming to thy foes	200	H. Commun.	W	13
Or if that thou two stations makest	200	H. Commun.	W	16
If thou hadst dyde for Bread.	201	H. Commun.	W	27
If glorious bodies pass the sight	201	H. Commun.	W	34
If thou subdue mortalitie	202	love	W	21
Whereas if I orecome thee & thy Love	202	love	W	23
If thou deferr this light, then shadow mee:	203	Even-song	W	9
As if shades knew not Thee.	203	Even-song	W	12
If that bee dark we can not see:	203	Even-song	W	14
If thou chance for to find	207	Walton 3		1
If thou dost find an house built to thy mind	207	Walton 4		1
Meane while, if hee (which all thinges weares)	208	H. Danvers	D	5
Doe ruine thee; or if the teares	208	H. Danvers	D	6
Bright soule, of whome if any countrey knowne	211	Bohemia	D	1
If ever Tears did flow from Eyes,	213	Convert	D	1
If ever Voice was hoarse with Cries,	213	Convert	D	2
If ever Heart was sore with Sighs;	213	Convert	D	3
If I have done this thing, O Lord,	221	Psalm VII	D	9
if I so guilty be:	221	Psalm VII	D	10
If I have ill rewarded him	221	Psalm VII	D	11
if a man do not all which is here expressed, hee presently sinns,	224	Priest		10
into which if he come, he prostitutes himself both to shame,	227	Priest 3		24
as knowing, that if he be not so, he wil quickly be discovered,	228	Priest 3		6
that if any do Gods will, he shall know of the Doctrine,	228	Priest 4		28
which if it be necessary even in temporall things, how much more in	228	Priest 4		33
or somtimes both, if his audience be intermixed.	230	Priest 5		18
Now if a shepherd know not which grass will bane, or which not,	230	Priest 5		31
If there be any of the gentry or nobility of the Parish,	232	Priest 6		7
admonitions, if they persevere, he causes them to be presented:	232	Priest 6		13
or if the poor Church-wardens be affrighted with their greatness,	232	Priest 6		14
if he at any time intermit, it is either for want of health,	232	Priest 7		21
for if we be here, hee must be here, since we are here by him,	234	Priest 7		29
and if there be any extraordinary addition to the customary	235	Priest 8		33
If he be unmarried, and keepe house, he hath not a woman in his	237	Priest 9		7
If he be unmarryed, and sojourne, he never talkes with any woman	237	Priest 9		10
If he stand steadfast in his heart, having no necessity,	237	Priest 9		16
and that much more being single, then if he were marryed;	238	Priest 9		22
If the Parson be unmarryed, and means to continue so, he doth	238	Priest 9		24
If he be marryed, the choyce of his wife was made rather by his eare,	238	Priest 9		26
childrens advantage, then if it were given to the Chamber of London.	240	Priest 10		9
if God give any thing above those, and not spent in them,	240	Priest 10		11
and veal, if he addes any thing for a great day, or a stranger,	241	Priest 10		17
if a peece of dry flesh at my table be more unpleasant to me,	242	Priest 10		12
draught of beer, then if it had taken before either fish, or rootes,	242	Priest 10		23
the Parson, if he be in full health, keeps the three obligations,	242	Priest 10		26
If his body be weak and obstructed, as most Students are,	242	Priest 10		28
men to Piety, and is content, if at least so, they will become good:	243	Priest 11		32
that he may, if not the best way, yet any way, make his Parish good.	244	Priest 11		4
If his Parish be rich, he exacts this of them;	244	Priest 12		24
if poor, and he able, he easeth them therein.	244	Priest 12		24
and if it be taken away, though justly, they will murmur,	244	Priest 12		28
he inlargeth himself, if he be able, to the neighbour-hood;	245	Priest 12		18
as if hee findes them reading, hee furnisheth them with good books;	247	Priest 14		15
if curing poor people, hee supplies them with Receipts,	247	Priest 14		16
as if it were in their own hands to thrive, or not to thrive.	247	Priest 14		30
if they be poor and needy, whom he thus finds labouring,	248	Priest 14		9
for if he be a plaine countryman, he reproves him plainly;	248	Priest 14		16
if they be of higher quality, they commonly are quick, and sensible,	248	Priest 14		18
If the Parson were ashamed of particularizing in these things,	248	Priest 14		38

IF (cont'd)

	PAGE	TITLE	LINE
If it once have the honour of that Name, it grows great instantly.	249	Priest 14	2
from the certainty both of deliverance, and reward, if we faint not;	249	Priest 15	25
it about with him as fully, as if he had begot his whole Parish.	250	Priest 16	9
that if any be willing to partake, they may resort thither.	251	Priest 17	12
if hee be to stay for a time, hee considers diligently the state	251	Priest 17	17
If it be well spoken, or done, he takes occasion to commend,	252	Priest 18	4
if ill, he presently lays hold of it, least the poyson steal into	252	Priest 18	5
or else if the thing will admit interpretation;	252	Priest 18	10
if he perceive in company any discourse tending to ill,	252	Priest 18	15
either in Sermon, if he preach, or at some other time of the day,	253	Priest 19	13
as joyfull a countenance, as if he were to entertain some great Lord.	253	Priest 19	19
or of good report, if there be any vertue, or any praise;	253	Priest 19	24
if God have sent any calamity either by fire, or famine,	253	Priest 19	29
if any neighbouring village be overburdened with poore,	254	Priest 19	1
If he chance to finde any reading in anothers Bible, he provides him	254	Priest 20	11
If he finde another giving a poor man a penny, he gives him a tester	254	Priest 20	13
he gives him a tester for it, if the giver be fit to receive it;	254	Priest 20	14
or if he be of a condition above such gifts, he sends him a good	254	Priest 20	14
if he once get the skill of it, will draw out of ignorant and silly	256	Priest 21	18
He asked him again, what he would do, if he were in a ditch?	257	Priest 21	4
for if wise men have thought it the best way of preserving a state	258	Priest 22	15
If there be any, who having not received yet, are to enter into this	258	Priest 22	29
if not duly once a month, yet at least five or six times in the year;	259	Priest 22	20
if there be but three Communions, neither can all the people so order	259	Priest 22	25
so that if the poorest man of the Parish detain but a pin unjustly	260	Priest 23	14
if there be any of his flock sick, hee is their Physician,	260	Priest 23	29
But if neither himselfe, nor his wife have the skil, and his means	260	Priest 23	32
If all fail, then he keeps good correspondence with some neighbour	260	Priest 23	36
if there be any of his parish that hold strange Doctrins,	262	Priest 24	19
as if he be a Papist, the Church is the hinge he turnes on;	262	Priest 24	29
if a Schismatick, scandall. Wherefore the Parson hath diligently	262	Priest 24	30
which if it happily take effect, he then comes on the faster,	263	Priest 25	32
if I do not give every thing its end, I abuse the Creature,	265	Priest 26	9
if in all these, and those more which concerne me, I either do	265	Priest 26	16
if God have given me servants, and I either provide too little	265	Priest 26	20
if a man hath wherewithall to buy a spade, and yet hee chuseth rather	265	Priest 26	28
especially if they carry their eyes ever open, and fix them on their	266	Priest 26	4
as if they were Masters of their health, and so they will stand	266	Priest 26	19
So that if after dinner they are not fit (or un-weeldy) either	266	Priest 26	31
or if he have any leisure to look off from thence, he meets	267	Priest 27	30
if the contempt shall proceed so far as to do any thing punishable	268	Priest 28	30
if it be not thwarted, the Parson having a due respect both	268	Priest 28	32
But if the Contempt be not punishable by Law, or being so,	269	Priest 28	3
If himselfe reforme any thing, it is out of the overflowing of his	269	Priest 29	29
but if after gentle, and neighbourly admonitions they still persist	270	Priest 29	19
and that if they sow and soyle their grounds, they must have corn;	270	Priest 30	26
if they keep and fodder well their cattel, they must have milk,	270	Priest 30	27
instantly dry up, as a river would if the fountain were stopped.	271	Priest 30	7
that if anything could presume of an inevitable course,	271	Priest 30	8
yet if he suite not other things to the growth, as seasons,	271	Priest 30	16
or if the goods be housed, a fire hath broken forth, and suddenly	271	Priest 30	24
So that if a farmer should depend upon God all the yeer,	271	Priest 30	28
or if he depend on God further, even till he imbarn his corn,	271	Priest 30	31
So that if a Farmer hath both a faire harvest, and that also well	271	Priest 30	38
yet if God give him not the Grace to use, and utter this well,	272	Priest 30	2
every day of the week, and four times on Sunday, if they be well.	272	Priest 31	23
but to go on as cheerfully, as if he had not been interrupted.	273	Priest 31	11
which will appear if the Pious soul foresee and prevent such	273	Priest 31	16
if he resent it to a mislike, but not a griefe.	273	Priest 31	20
if he now, shall either for fear or shame, break his custome,	273	Priest 31	29
if I am to visit the sick in haste, and my neerest way ly through	273	Priest 31	33
So that if any scruple arise, I will throw it away, and be most	273	Priest 31	37
and who is ready to ask, if he shall mend shoos, or what he shall do?	275	Priest 32	8
But if it should be, the Assertion stands thus:	275	Priest 32	10
have yet no imployment, if he truly, and seriously prepare for it,	275	Priest 32	13
to enter into a Calling, if they be fit for it, and it for them;	275	Priest 32	15
and house-keeper hath his hands full, if he do what he ought to do.	275	Priest 32	20
But if after all this care well dispatched, the house-keepers Family	275	Priest 32	36
But if hee may bee of the Commission of Peace, there is nothing	276	Priest 32	7
But if the young Gallant think these Courses dull, and phlegmatick,	278	Priest 32	3
that if the Kingdome of God be first sought, all other things shall	278	Priest 33	13
at table about his appetite, if he tell this to another, preacheth;	278	Priest 33	19
And if the same person had been sick of all diseases, and were	278	Priest 33	29
If we would judg ourselves, we should not be judged;	280	Priest 34	30
and if we would bound our selves, we should not be bounded.	280	Priest 34	31
But if they shall fear, that at such, or such a time their peace	280	Priest 34	32
he is lost, as if they said, God doth forsake and persecute them,	281	Priest 34	10
If the Parson suspect the first, and find sparkes of such thoughts	281	Priest 34	12
if he had been at the Creation of all things, should lesse beleeve	281	Priest 34	28
Wherefore if the Jewes live, all the great wonders of old live in	282	Priest 34	4
But if he sees them neerer desperation, then Atheisme;	283	Priest 34	5
If God hate them, either he doth it as they are Creatures,	283	Priest 34	9
Parson is a Lover of old Customes, if they be good, and harmlesse;	283	Priest 35	27
If there be any ill in the custome, that may be severed from	283	Priest 35	31
with reconciling of differences at that time, if there be any:	284	Priest 35	7
and if they will not reforme, presents them.	284	Priest 35	12
And if temporall Fathers blesse their children, how much more may,	285	Priest 36	14
if the Ministration of condemnation did bless, how shall	285	Priest 36	18
that if a Minister talke with a great man in the ordinary course	286	Priest 36	20
but if he often interpose a Blessing, when the other gives him just	286	Priest 36	22

IF (cont'd)

	PAGE	TITLE	LINE
if all men are to blesse upon occasion, as appears Rom. 12. 14. how	286	Priest 36	26
For if he absolutely shut up mens mouths, and forbid all disclosing	286	Priest 37	33
if it be unlawful to open faults, no benefit or advantage can make it	287	Priest 37	5
if the punished delinquent shall be much troubled for his sins,	288	Priest 37	2
if they had lived, would have been an ornament to the world,	291	Cornaro	3
there was one help for me, if I could constantly pursue it, to wit,	292	Cornaro	4
If Temperance had so much power as to bring me health;	293	Cornaro	2
If the world consist of order, if our corporall life depend	297	Cornaro	6
if our corporall life depend on the harmonie of humours & elements,	297	Cornaro	7
hath cured him, commends this also to him, if he will live in health.	297	Cornaro	18
after live free from diseases, if he will keep such a course of life;	297	Cornaro	20
if he will give his minde to those things which he should,	297	Cornaro	22
qualities to me, if I had not found them out by long experience?	297	Cornaro	35
For if a friend who visits thee in thy sicknesse, and onely comforts	298	Cornaro	6
But surely there is no such matter, if Temperance be wanting.	298	Cornaro	21
of no great moment (as I shewed before) if a man be temperate in meat	299	Cornaro	16
For if he should keep his former proportion, Nature, which is	299	Cornaro	32
And if a Greek Poet of old was praised, that at the age of 73 yeares	302	Cornaro	33
if I had my wish, would I change age and constitution with them who	303	Cornaro	11
As if he should say:	308	Valdesso	33
as if they were both but Alphabets and after a time to be left.	309	Valdesso	19
if we make another sence of that Text, wee shall overthrow all means,	310	Valdesso	11
if we believe, no sinne shall hurt us;	311	Valdesso	24
if we believe not, no vertue shall helpe us.	311	Valdesso	25
Neither doe I doubt but if Abraham had lived in our Kingdome under	316	Valdesso	22
as if it were but childrens meat, whereas there is not onely milke	317	Valdesso	23
forth her first borne Sonne, as if afterwards he had knowne her:	318	Valdesso	13
if I bid a man stay in a place untill I come, I doe not then bid him	318	Valdesso	14
not to the point it should, which if it did, it would doe more,	319	Valdesso	11
If yee would know a knave, give him a staffe.	321	Proverbs	19
If all fooles had bables, wee should want fuell.	323	Proverbs	63
Welcome evill, if thou commest alone.	325	Proverbs	140
If the old dog barke he gives counsell.	327	Proverbs	197
There would bee no great ones if there were no little ones.	331	Proverbs	292
There would bee no great ones if there were no mean ones.	331	Proverbs	V 292
There were no ill language, if it were not ill taken.	331	Proverbs	294
If you loose your time, you cannot get mony nor gaine.	332	Proverbs	320
Bee not a Baker, if your head be of butter.	332	Proverbs	321
In vaine is the mill-clacke, if the Miller his hearing lack.	332	Proverbs	328
if you will know the truth of the thing.	332	Proverbs	331
He that owes nothing, if he makes not mouthes at us, is courteous.	333	Proverbs	362
If you would know secrets, looke them in griefe or pleasure.	333	Proverbs	367
If folly were griefe every house would weepe.	334	Proverbs	370
If you could runne, as you drinke, you might catch a hare.	334	Proverbs	373
If the wise erred not, it would goe hard with fooles.	338	Proverbs	510
If wise men erred not, it would goe hard with fooles.	338	Proverbs	V 510
If all fooles wore white Caps, wee should seeme a flock of geese.	338	Proverbs	513
If the staffe be crooked, the shadow cannot be straight.	341	Proverbs	583
If a good man thrive, all thrive with him.	344	Proverbs	695
If the mother had not beene in the oven,	344	Proverbs	696
If great men would have care of little ones,	344	Proverbs	697
If things were to be done twice, all would be wise.	344	Proverbs	700
If all things might be done twice, all would be wise.	343	Proverbs	V 700
If fooles should not foole it, they shall lose their season.	343	Proverbs	V 702
If fooles should not foole it, they should loose their season.	344	Proverbs	703
Three can hold their peace, if two be away.	345	Proverbs	714
take not to serve you, if you will be served neately.	347	Proverbs	794
If thou thy selfe canst doe it, attend no others helpe or hand.	348	Proverbs	813
If gold knew what gold is, gold would get gold I wis.	354	Proverbs	1012
If the husband be not at home, there is nobodie.	354	Proverbs	1016
If you would bee at ease, all the world is not.	355	Proverbs	1019
If you must flie, flie well.	355	Proverbs	1021
If the braine sowes not corne, it plants thistles.	355	Proverbs	1024
Unsound minds like unsound Bodies, if you feed, you poyson.	358	Proverbs	D 1076
We do it soon enough, if that we do be well.	359	Proverbs	D 1109
Cruelty is more cruell, if we defer the pain.	359	Proverbs	D 1110
if it were not begun on particular ends, it would last).	361	Proverbs	D 1160
Trust no friend with that you need fear him if he were your enemy.	361	Proverbs	D 1169
of thanks for the diversity of your favours, if I sought to do so;	363	Letters	16
been forward to say, if I had taken ill courses, Follow your Book,	364	Letters	21
as that if all things proved not well, I had rather the fault should	364	Letters	28
if there be any truth in me, I find it little enough to keep me in	364	Letters	31
to avoiding of costlier matters, if I should fall absolutely sick:	365	Letters	8
And yet if a Book of four or five Shillings come in my way,	365	Letters	11
If then, Sir, there be any course, either by engaging my future	365	Letters	20
and if there be any such which you have found useful to yourself,	366	Letters	4
yet if my Sister were acquainted that they are ready, I dare say she	367	Letters	1
that if any course could be taken of doubling my Annuity now,	367	Letters	7
& to threaten him that if he will not give her halfe her estate	368	Letters	23
therfore he grumblingly said that if he had given it to the pope he	368	Letters	33
If I could possibly have come, none should have done my message	369	Letters	19
opinion of him, that if he can do me a courtesie, he will of himself;	369	Letters	22
which if you can sent to Sir Francis before his departure,	369	Letters	25
yet if you cannot send it with much convenience, it is no matter,	369	Letters	27
that if all fail, yet I am able to stand on mine own legs.	370	Letters	9
or if it had to others, yet to me it should not, for ought I yet	370	Letters	23
therefore, if either Age or Sickness lead you to those Joyes?	372	Letters	31
and I shou'd account my self most happy if I might change with you;	373	Letters	3
So that now if they do not well the falt cannot be charg'd on you;	373	Letters	14
since if we had Riches we are commanded to give them away:	373	Letters	23

IF (cont'd)	PAGE	TITLE		LINE
most carry themselves so, as if they not only not desir'd, but,	373	Letters		33
that if any of yours shou'd prove a Goliah-like trouble,	374	Letters		4
And above all, If any care of future things molest you?	374	Letters		12
Therefore I considered that if one only came, the comfort intended	375	Letters		16
If you could think of taking her, as once you did, surely it were	375	Letters		30
Yet, truly if you take her not, I am thinking to do it,	375	Letters		34
done fairly, if they leave them a good portion after their decease.	376	Letters		15
if at length they may find out some thing not unworthy of those hands	376	Letters		29
If there fall out yet any rubb, you shall heare of me;	377	Letters		22
If so, let this of Leighton Church the care, be amongst the chiefest	378	Letters		22
are lovely, & of good report if there be any vertue or any praise.	380	Woodnoth		14
if God had done that (which you are thinking to doe) to blessed Mary	381	Woodnoth		4
& if upon your withdrawing it shold doe so, it would trouble your	381	Woodnoth		11
if there be any body els that owe me any thing else of old debt I	383	G.H.'s Will		26
IGNOMINY				
knows well, that both for the generall ignominy which is cast upon	268	Priest 28		10
IGNORANCE				
For wit is newes onely to ignorance.	15	Ch.-Porch		230
(But a proud ignorance will lose his rest,	18	Ch.-Porch		297
made the answer so plaine, that he was even ashamed of his ignorance;	257	Priest 21		6
hee considers and looks into the ignorance, or carelesness of his	258	Priest 22		24
because to answer in form may still admit ignorance:	259	Priest 22		8
IGNORANT				
they were reproved, as ignorant of what spirit they were.	229	Priest 4		14
they all account, that to teach the ignorant is the greatest almes.	240	Priest 10		23
will draw out of ignorant and silly souls, even the dark and deep	256	Priest 21		19
in vertue the answer also, especially to the more ignorant.	256	Priest 21		36
of which he gathers, in case he be ignorant himself, what to hold;	260	Priest 23		11
The ignorant hath an Eagles wings, and an Owles eyes.	351	Proverbs		902
and whereof I would not have you ignorant.	366	Letters		2
ILANDS				
being usefull to all Countreys, and the other especially to Ilands.	278	Priest 32		3
ILE				
At Purgatory, there inchanted Ile,	212	Bohemia	D	50
ILL				
Is outlawd by himself: all kinde of ill	7	Ch.-Porch		33
Is outlawd by himself: all kinds of ill	7	Ch.-Porch	W	33
Hee that has all ill, & can have no good	7	Ch.-Porch	W	35
Into a bed, to sleep out all ill weathers.	9	Ch.-Porch		84
Who fears to do ill, sets himself to task:	11	Ch.-Porch		125
All forrain of that name; but scorn their ill:	21	Ch.-Porch		362
Though it be ill, makes him no ill Physician.	24	Ch.-Porch		444
If thou do ill; the joy fades, not the pains:	24	Ch.-Porch		461
Behither ill.	44	H. Bapt.2		10
To writhe his limbes, and share, not mend the ill.	73	Constancie		33
To writhe his limbes, and thare, not mend the ill.	73	Constancie	V	33
And in thy members suffer ill.	73	Afflict.3		16
For what account can thy ill steward make?	83	Sighs & Gr.		8
Shall ne're be troubled with ill eyes.	96	Charms & K		2
Who hath these, those ill forbears.	113	Businesse		8
And by their breathing ventilate the ill.	122	Sinnes rd.		10
Yet ill deeds loyter not: for they supplie	122	Sinnes rd.		16
Doth flatter power. Lest good come short of ill	161	Priesthood		40
Had the malicious and ill-meaning harm	172	The Glance		11
If I have ill rewarded him	221	Psalm VII	D	11
They say, it is an ill Mason that refuseth any stone:	228	Priest 4		15
that not any ill will draws him to it, but the debt and obligation	232	Priest 6		18
that the Parson findes idle, or ill imployed, he chides not at first,	248	Priest 14		14
if ill, he presently lays hold of it, least the poyson steal into	252	Priest 18		5
if he perceive in company any discourse tending to ill,	252	Priest 18		16
Wherefore there is nothing done either wel or ill, whereof he is	254	Priest 20		10
not cheape, or course, much lesse ill-tasted, or unwholsome.	258	Priest 22		23
their understandings being ripe enough for ill things, and why	259	Priest 22		1
punishing of any, as the vulgar ever consters for signes of ill will;	263	Priest 25		25
whom anothers ill mastereth, and leadeth captive without any	269	Priest 28		21
and neighbourly admonitions they still persist in ill, to present	270	Priest 29		20
either for fear or shame, break his custome, he shall do passing ill:	273	Priest 31		31
he may go to Court, as the eminent place both of good and ill.	277	Priest 32		6
If there be any ill in the custome, that may be severed from	283	Priest 35		31
so that even ill Priests may blesse.	285	Priest 36		23
and my ill constitution, (having a most cold & moist stomack) I fell	291	Cornaro		20
From this ill temper there remained little else to be expected of me,	291	Cornaro		24
without difficultie, and no ill humours being ingendred in the body.	293	Cornaro		29
watching, ill aire, overmuch use of the benefit of marriage.	293	Cornaro		31
For the Temperance of so many yeares spent all ill humours,	296	Cornaro		32
or contract any ill qualitie, as usually happens in old mens bodies,	296	Cornaro		35
and also doth preserve even ill tempers in good health,	298	Cornaro		14
although they see themselves ill handled by their intemperance,	298	Cornaro		25
An old man of an ill constitution, but living orderly, is more sure	300	Cornaro		25
this cannot stand, and it is ill Doctrine in a common-wealth.	316	Valdesso		16
The Wolfe knowes, what the ill beast thinkes.	321	Proverbs		16
A Cake and an ill custome must be broken.	322	Proverbs		27
A caske and an ill custome must both of them be broken.	322	Proverbs	V	27
Ill ware is never cheape.	323	Proverbs		61
Never had ill workeman good tooles.	323	Proverbs		67
Ill vessells seldome miscarry.	324	Proverbs		87
Every ill man hath his ill day.	324	Proverbs		92
Ill natures, the more you aske them, the more they stick.	324	Proverbs		106
Hee that lives ill, feare followes him.	324	Proverbs		110
Who would doe ill ne're wants occasion.	324	Proverbs		116

	PAGE	TITLE	LINE
IMPUTE			
Impute a lustre, and allow them bright;	51	Faith	35
IN-MATE			
and will not allow any room there for such an in-mate as Grief;	374	Letters	11
INABLE			
and inable all my powers, that in their full strength they may	289	Priest	27
INABLING			
inabling him with power to do good, and to restrain all those,	276	Priest 32	14
INACCESSIBLE (see also unaccessible)			
INCARNATION			
The Trinitie, and Incarnation:	82	Ungratef.	8
At the rate of an Incarnation	201	H. Commun. W	26
INCENSE			
festivalls strawed, and stuck with boughs, and perfumed with incense.	246	Priest 13	10
INCESSANT			
To which the blast of deaths incessant motion, ...	64	Ch.-monum.	4
INCESSANTLY			
incessantly begging some ease of your pains, with that earnestness,	371	Letters	28
INCH			
And quickly gain, for each inch lost, an ell.	103	Prayer 2	24
My inch of life: or let thy gracious power	144	Complaining	18
In an hundred elles of contention, there is not an inch of love.	348	Proverbs	817
INCHANTED			
At Purgatory, there inchanted Ile, ...	212	Bohemia D	50
INCHANTMENT			
Good service is a great inchantment.	331	Proverbs	291
INCHES			
Ill comes in by ells, and goes out by inches.	327	Proverbs	194
INCIDENT			
least all those which he observeth are most incident to his Parish.	230	Priest 5	35
himself some insight in things ordinarily incident and controverted,	259	Priest 23	34
INCITATION			
it is no matter, for the Gentleman needs no incitation to love me.	369	Letters	29
INCITES			
he first gives himself liberally, and then incites them to give;	253	Priest 19	36
INCLINATION			
will do well, for it expresseth the Universities inclination to me;	369	Letters	27
INCLINE (see also encline)			
wisheth all to incline rather to too much, then to too little;	267	Priest 26	12
so though you incline not, happily you restraine.	381	Woodnoth	9
INCLINED			
to which I am inclined, as not to get out of that sicknesse,	242	Priest 10	37
INCLINING			
As God where he finds no roome for his Inclining grace, . .	381	Woodnoth	8
7. Though you want all success either in inclining or restraining,	381	Woodnoth	14
INCLOSE			
Thou dost inclose us, till the day	64	Even-song	22
And did inclose this light for his:	76	Sunday	37
Inclose me still for fear I START.	133	Paradise	7
INCLOSED			
I have sent you here inclosed a Letter from our Master in my behalf,	369	Letters	24
cause this inclosed to be carried to his brothers house of his own	370	Letters	26
INCLOSER			
Man would have been th' incloser: but since now	7	Ch.-Porch	20
INCLOSING			
pardon my boldness of inclosing my Brothers Letter in yours,	367	Letters	23
INCLOSURE			
That dumbe inclosure maketh love	98	Mortific.	23
While the inclosure is thine ARM?	133	Paradise	6
INCLUDE			
these two rules comprize and include the double object of our duty,	246	Priest 13	29
INCOME			
Never exceed thy income. Youth may make	13	Ch.-Porch	157
INCOMPOSSIBLE			
and a good subject, is incompossible.	357	Proverbs D	1058
INCOMPREHENSIBLE			
but one most glorious, incomprehensible God, be ascribed all Honour,	290	Priest	15
INCONSIDERATE			
I know how inconsiderate that age is, and, though subject to death,	303	Cornaro	16
INCONTINENCY			
Need or Incontinency: the first way	7	Ch.-Porch W	16
INCONVENIENCE			
received no inconvenience thereby, because that humour abounded	294	Cornaro	21
and so without other remedie or inconvenience I recovered; . .	295	Cornaro	13
is very great) receiving not any hurt or inconvenience thereby:	302	Cornaro	20
INCONVENIENCES			
and therefore never was sick by any of these inconveniences,	294	Cornaro	9
a temperate life, can receive little hurt from other inconveniences.	295	Cornaro	15
That those inconveniences are of no great moment (as I shewed before)	299	Cornaro	15
INCREASE			
Blowing up houses with their whole increase.	14	Ch.-Porch	204
My stock lies dead, and no increase	60	Grace	1
Untill the grave increase our cold.	79	Employm.2	30
Unlesse Authoritie, which should increase	86	Lent	16
Ev'n pleasures here increase the wrong, ...	123	Time	21
At Salem dwelt, who liv'd with good increase	125	Peace	23
And snudge in quiet: now he scorns increase;	127	Giddinesse	11
who by hard usage increase their travell, the Countrey Parson is very	227	Priest 3	15
affections of the soul in desiring and procuring increase of means,	230	Priest 5	27
Keep not ill men company, lest you increase the number. . .	331	Proverbs	314

	PAGE	TITLE	LINE
INCREASED			
How are my foes increased, Lord?	216	Psalm III	D 1
(a thing usuall to disorderly lives) which increased so much in them,	294	Cornaro	19
stint of meat and drink should be diminished, rather then increased;	295	Cornaro	31
and permitted the quantitie of meat to be increased, yet but two	296	Cornaro	8
I increased it to the quantitie of two ounces more;	296	Cornaro	11
Either wealth is much increased, or moderation is much decayed.	360	Proverbs	D 1139
INCREASETH			
or rather increaseth, I wish earnestly that I were again with you:	372	Letters	17
INCREASING			
to reason, that my yeares increasing, and strength decreasing,	295	Cornaro	29
INCREDIBLE			
yeare (although it may seem to some incredible) I was perfectly cured	292	Cornaro	37
INCROACH			
not to incroach on others Professions, but to live on his own.	262	Priest 23	16
INCUMBRANCES			
other threds or skenes of silk, full of snarles and incumbrances:	373	Letters	5
INCURABLE			
evils which had so long beset me, and were almost become incurable;	293	Cornaro	22
INDEARE			
That washes what it shows. Who can indeare	58	H.Script.1	10
Which might the more indeare it to be thine.	190	Ch.-Milit.	12
INDEBTED			
favour to mee in pardoning Your most indebted kinsman GEORGE HERBERT.	369	Letters	5
INDECENT (see also undecent)			
INDEED			
Indeed mans whole estate	63	Mattens	13
Indeed at first Man was a treasure,	102	Miserie	67
Indeed 'tis true. I did and do commit	129	Love unkn.	19
Indeed 'tis true. I found a callous matter	130	Love unkn.	38
Indeed it's true. I found a callous matter	130	Love unkn.	V 38
Indeed a slack and sleepie state of minde	130	Love unkn.	57
And shows it so? Indeed Christs precious bloud	140	Ch.-rents	12
There is a balsome, or indeed a bloud,	147	Offering	19
Indeed the world's thy book,	149	Longing	49
Colour'd griefs indeed there are,	177	The Rose	6
Sweetly there indeed it lies,	178	The Rose	23
in describing the one (which is indeed the bent of my Discourse)	226	Priest 2	18
because Countrey people (as indeed all honest men) do much esteem	228	Priest 3	2
And indeed, herein is the greatest ability of a Parson to lead his	230	Priest 5	20
(though that indeed be very admirable) as at their daily temperance,	237	Priest 9	30
or, So farr indeed what you say is true, and well said;	252	Priest 18	11
The Feast indeed requires sitting, because it is a Feast;	259	Priest 22	12
It is true indeed, they are long a knowing it, being partiall	264	Priest 26	12
and that indeed the whole order and discipline of the Parish is put	269	Priest 29	28
and indeed, to depend, and fear continually.	271	Priest 30	36
For indeed no man can be a perfect Physician to another,	297	Cornaro	24
Indeed he that shall so attend to the bark of the letter,	309	Valdesso	29
the holy spirit indeed sometime doubly teaching both in penning	317	Valdesso	30
and indeed in common sence, if I bid a man stay in a place untill I	318	Valdesso	14
yea, indeed of all, both Courtly, Militarie, Academicall.	441	Oration	27
INDIAN			
Sometimes unite. The Indian nut alone	120	Providence	126
INDIAS			
both Indias to his Spaine, knowes no limits of his praise,	442	Oration	11
INDIES			
which they are thought to have offerd to our Merchants at the Indies,	368	Letters	7
INDIFFERENT			
For it being indifferent in it selfe to choose any Method,	230	Priest 5	9
even in externall and indifferent things, what course is to be taken;	246	Priest 13	33
whether things once indifferent, being made by the precept	263	Priest 24	12
being made by the precept of Authority more then indifferent,	263	Priest 24	13
In indifferent things there is roome for motions [notions]	313	Valdesso	12
INDIFFERENTS			
To such indifferents chained be,	134	The Method	18
INDISPOSITION			
save now and then a little indisposition for a day or two.	296	Cornaro	31
INDISPOSITIONS			
cannot fall into diseases, and but very seldome into indispositions;	299	Cornaro	36
INDITE			
Thou didst at once thy self indite,	156	Assurance	29
Wounded I sing, tormented I indite,	159	Jos.coat	1
INDITED			
Which holds thee now? Who hath indited it	41	Sepulchre	11
INDORSEMENT			
Th' indorsement of supreme delight,	75	Sunday	3
INDUCE			
contrives how and in what manner to induce it to the best advantage.	236	Priest 8	2
INDUSTRIE			
slight glories, which wee raise from bookes, and painefull industrie.	443	Oration	1
INDUSTRIOUS			
but that an industrious, and judicious comparing of place with place	229	Priest 4	7
INEVITABLE			
that things are not set in such an inevitable order, but that God	270	Priest 30	30
that if anything could presume of an inevitable course,	271	Priest 30	9
INFALLIBILITIES			
From Greece oracular infallibilities,	195	Ch.-Milit.	178
INFAMY			
because infamy is a part of the sentence against malefactours,	287	Priest 37	18
For in infamy, all are executioners, and the Law gives a malefactour	287	Priest 37	30

	PAGE	TITLE		LINE
INTERMIT				
if he at any time intermit, it is either for want of health,	232	Priest 7		21
INTERMITS				
When he intermits, he is ever very well supplyed by some able man who	232	Priest 7		25
INTERMIXED				
or somtimes both, if his audience be intermixed.	230	Priest 5		18
INTERPOSE				
but if he often interpose a Blessing, when the other gives him just	286	Priest 36		22
INTERPOSED				
performed by keeping of the two former, had not Authority interposed:	242	Priest 10		10
a space ought to be interposed.	356	Proverbs	D	40
INTERPOSETH				
Here the Parson interposeth with his distinction, and shews	273	Priest 31		3
INTERPOSING				
interposing sometimes some short, and honest refreshments,	251	Priest 17		4
that is his time of interposing:	271	Priest 30		21
INTERPRETATION				
or else if the thing will admit interpretation;	252	Priest 18		10
INTERRUPTED				
but to go on as cheerfully, as if he had not been interrupted.	273	Priest 31		12
untill we interrupted thy Counsels, disappointed thy Purposes,	288	Priest		16
INTERRUPTION				
without disturbance, or interruption of publick divine offices.	236	Priest 8		25
that the godly petitioner upon some emergent interruption in the day,	272	Priest 31		30
common course of devotion, then dislikes an occasionall interruption.	273	Priest 31		10
that this interruption proceed not out of slacknes, or coldness,	273	Priest 31		15
Secondly, that this interruption proceede not out of shame.	273	Priest 31		21
INTERRUPTIONS				
will appear if the Pious soul foresee and prevent such interruptions,	273	Priest 31		17
INTIMATE				
And Easter intimate, enlarge the thing,	86	Lent		26
INTIMATED				
By which is intimated, that the hurt of too much meat is greater,	296	Cornaro		2
INTIMATETH				
and generally intimateth to the disaffected, or sick person,	250	Priest 15		4
INTIMATION				
Where in the deed there was an intimation	105	Obedience		33
INTO				
And turn delight into a sacrifice.	6	Ch.-Porch		6
Did with his liquour slide into his veins.	7	Ch.-Porch		34
Into a bed, to sleep out all ill weathers.	9	Ch.-Porch		84
Transfus'd a sheepishnesse into thy storie:	10	Ch.-Porch		94
And change thy temperance into braverie.	15	Ch.-Porch		222
Take all into thee; then with equall care	19	Ch.-Porch		321
Then turn thy faults and his into confession:	24	Ch.-Porch		441
Then turn thy fault and his into confession:	24	Ch.-Porch	W	441
That I did thrust into the Deitie,	28	Sacrifice		62
My dove doth back into my bosome flie,	29	Sacrifice		94
I, who am Truth, turn into truth their deeds:	32	Sacrifice		179
I, who am Truth, turn into truth their scorns:	32	Sacrifice	W	179
Into the conquest. Though I can do nought	37	Reprisall		14
Into thy conquest, though I can do nought	37	Reprisall	W	14
Vanish into a winde,	45	Nature		11
Into thy familie.	46	Afflict.1	W	10
Thus argu'd into hopes, my thoughts reserved	46	Afflict.1		15
Thus argu'd into hopes, I was preserved	46	Afflict.1	W	15
Into more sicknesses.	48	Afflict.1		52
Which thou hast pour'd into my soul;	49	Repentance		20
Thou creep'st into my breast;	52	H.Commun.		8
Which spread their forces into every part,	52	H.Commun.		11
Melt into blessings all the sky,	59	Whitsunday	W	23
Into one common sewer, sea, and brine;	62	Afflict.2		7
Be crumbled into dust. Mark here below	65	Ch.-monum.		22
Be broken into dust. Mark here below	65	Ch.-monum.	W	22
All being brought into a summe,	72	Constancie		14
Wrapt in nights mantle, stole into a manger;	81	Christmas		10
The dust into our eyes:	82	Ungratef.		17
Into the bitter box; but O my God,	83	Sighs & Gr.		29
They step into their voluntarie graves,	98	Mortific.		8
No man shall beat into his head,	100	Miserie		15
So did I weave my self into the sense.	103	Jordan 2		14
Into these lines; till in heav'ns court of rolls	105	Obedience		43
Into a blacknesse and distaste?	108	Home		40
First, Beautie crept into a rose,	110	The Quip		5
Unfold thy forehead gather'd into frowns:	112	Dawning		3
And put the penne alone into his hand,	117	Providence		7
Into a piece of timber work and winde,	126	Confession		8
As Gods afflictions into man,	126	Confession		9
And threw my heart into the scalding pan;	130	Love unkn.		35
A friend did steal into my cup for good,	130	Love unkn.		43
Your sinnes expresse; melt into dew.	135	Ephes.		12
Let th' upper springs into the low	137	The Size		5
Me thoughts a starre did shoot into my lap.	139	Artillerie		2
Turned your ruddie into pale and bleak:	140	Ch.-rents		19
Into gladnesse	147	Offering		26
Thrown down I fall into a bed, and rest:	159	Jos.coat		2
Contract into a span.	159	The Pulley		5
Into a grone;	162	The Search		22
My minde ev'n thrust into them both:	175	The Odour		7
To runne into an action;	184	The Elixer		6
Into thy face;	186	Death		14

	PAGE	TITLE		LINE
INTRENCHING				
Thy will such an intrenching is,	163	The Search		37
INVADE				
May our requests thine eare invade!	103	Prayer 2		3
May our requests thine eares invade!	103	Prayer 2	W	3
And in this league, which now my foes invade,	156	Assurance		26
Doth me invade!	183	A Parodie		12
Till such a darknesse do the world invade	196	Ch.-Milit.		230
Fouling her nest, my earth invade,	203	Even-song	W	11
INVENT				
Bitterly spitefull thought! Couldst thou invent	155	Assurance		2
INVENTION				
Which siding with invention, they together	54	Love 1		6
All her invention on thine Altar lay,	54	Love 2		7
Invention	102	Jordan 2	W	T
That I sought out quaint words, and trim invention;	102	Jordan 2		3
Invention rest,	183	The Posie		9
Such poor invention burns in their low mind	206	Walton 2		9
INVENTIONS				
My hands do joyn to finish the inventions.	122	Sinnes rd.		12
My hands do joyn to finish the inventions:	122	Sinnes rd.		13
INVESTED				
interesting of that dignity wherewith God hath invested the Priest,	286	Priest 36		9
INVESTING				
sent my Letters, to your Brother, investing him, in all that I have.	379	Letters		19
INVISIBLE				
and worshipping the invisible majesty, and presence of Almighty God,	236	Priest 8		5
INVITATION				
The Invitation.	179	Invitation		T
INVITE				
Still invite, still call to thee:	180	Invitation		33
Yet doth hee oftenest invite those, whom hee sees take best courses,	243	Priest 11		25
that his Parish at good times invite one another to their houses,	284	Priest 35		17
INVITED				
Lord I have invited all,	180	Invitation		31
both is to be done, the better sort invited, and meaner relieved,	243	Priest 11		14
Having then invited some of his Parish, hee taketh his times to do	243	Priest 11		17
and will not be perswaded, but being not invited, they are hated.	243	Priest 11		21
INVITES				
and sayings of others, according as his text invites him;	233	Priest 7		12
but invites and urges the best unto it, shewing that they do	270	Priest 29		8
because the Scripture invites enough, for it invites us to all good,	313	Valdesso		19
for it invites us to all good, according to that singular place,	313	Valdesso		19
INVITING				
motions are much more frequent to the godly, then inviting motions;	313	Valdesso		18
INWARD				
The inward walls and Sommers cleft and tore:	84	The World		14
A neighbour spring to cool his inward heat;	154	Glimpse		14
As well show inward warblinge as decay.	210	Paradox	D	24
But veywe yourselves, & inward turn your eyes;	210	Paradox	D	27
the reading of the Scripture with some short inward ejaculation,	229	Priest 4		2
as this is the true reason of his inward feare, so he is content	231	Priest 6		11
by reason of continuall inward, or outward temptations,	238	Priest 9		13
by which God turnes all outward blessings to inward advantages.	271	Priest 30		38
and, when I felt inward heats, drank delightfull wines,	292	Cornaro		28
INWARDLY				
Ev'n taken inwardly, and most divine	130	Love unkn.		44
As in things inwardly good to have an eye to the world may be	380	Woodnoth		16
IQUE				
The words ending in Ique do mocke the Physician	357	Proverbs	D	1044
IRON (see also yron)				
Able a heart of iron to appall,	187	Judgement		3
IRRADIATIONS				
Some such irradiations scatteringly in the Sermon, carry great	233	Priest 7		37
'S				
Cannot on fourtie: he's a man of pleasure,	13	Ch.-Porch		177
A kinde of thing that's for it self too deere.	13	Ch.-Porch		178
Wisedome's a trimmer thing, then shop e're gave.	14	Ch.-Porch		188
All things are bigge with jest: nothing that's plain,	16	Ch.-Porch		239
Wit's an unruly engine, wildly striking	16	Ch.-Porch		241
Then he's the sport: the mirth then in him rests,	16	Ch.-Porch		251
Still in thy heart, that he may see what's there.	17	Ch.-Porch		272
But love is lost, the way of friendship's gone,	17	Ch.-Porch		275
But love is lost, the art of friendship's gone,	17	Ch.-Porch	W	275
Truth dwels not in the clouds: the bow that's there	19	Ch.-Porch		317
And love's a weight to hearts, to eies a signe.	22	Ch.-Porch		399
Praying's the end of preaching. O be drest;	23	Ch.-Porch		410
The world's too little for thy tent,	55	Temper 1		11
And if wee can stay there, it's well.	59	Whitsunday	W	14
Thou knowst my tallies; and when there's assign'd	73	Afflict.3		8
So much breath to a sigh, what's then behinde?	73	Afflict.3		9
Motion, and heat, let's take our flight	74	The Starre		18
What's done on earth, we shall not fare the worse,	78	Ang.&Sts.		27
What's done on earth, we shall not feare the worse,	78	Ang.&Sts.	V	27
My soul's a shepherd too; a flock it feeds	81	Christmas		17
So that we need not say, Where's this command?	86	Vanitie 1		26
It's true, we cannot reach Christs forti'th day;	87	Lent		31
In both let's do our best.	87	Lent		36
Besides my physick, know there's some for thee:	106	Conscience		20
And crusht the building: and it's partly true,	127	Giddinesse		15
But where's the cluster? where's the taste	128	Bunch Gr.		19

'S (cont'd)	PAGE	TITLE		LINE
Indeed it's true. I found a callous matter	130	Love unkn.	V	38
But stay! what's there?	134	The Method		21
Indeed the world's thy book,	149	Longing		49
Come people; Aaron's drest.	174	Aaron		25
Love's a man of warre,	179	Discipline		22
He was a God, now he's an Emperour.	194	Ch.-Milit.		140
And then, my Labour's not lost.	207	Walton 3		6
This holy Cable's of all storms secure.	439	Walton 5		10
This holy Cable's from all storms secure.	439	Walton 5	V	10
He writ; when 's hand could write no more,	439	Walton 5		13
Ther's no monument to a sonne,	208	J. Danvers	D	15
Fairer & richer. Now wee know, what's thine,	211	Bohemia	D	18
(Till now averse to all that's Good)	214	Convert	D	17
And peace-meal rent it, while there's none	221	Psalm VII	D	7
Ours (like himselfe) o'recomes; for his wit's more	438	Lat.Trans.		3
The mill cannot grind with the water that's past.	326	Proverbs		153
A diligent Scholler, and the Master's paid.	327	Proverbs		183
It's no sure rule to fish with a cros-bow.	331	Proverbs		293
Hee that's fed at anothers hand may stay long ere he be full.	336	Proverbs		439
He that's long a giving, knowes not how to give.	338	Proverbs		494
It's a poore stake that cannot stand one yeare in the ground.	340	Proverbs		553
He that's foolish in the fault,	340	Proverbs		555
It's better to be the head of a Lyzard, then the tayle of a Lyon.	340	Proverbs		579
It's better to be the head of a mouse, then the tayle of a Lyon.	340	Proverbs	V	579
Thursday come, and the week's gone.	341	Proverbs		587
It's not good fishing before the net.	343	Proverbs		663
When my house burnes, it's not good playing at Chesse.	343	Proverbs		666
Ther's no great banquet but some fares ill.	343	Proverbs		668
It's a bold mouse that nestles in the catts eare.	344	Proverbs		693
It's a proud horse that will not carry his owne provender.	345	Proverbs		712
It's an ill councell that hath no escape.	345	Proverbs		715
That's the best gowne that goes up and downe the house.	346	Proverbs		742
It's a poore sport that's not worth the candle.	346	Proverbs		752
It's absurd to warme one in his armour.	347	Proverbs		775
It's good walking with a horse in ones hand.	348	Proverbs		804
It's good tying the sack before it be full.	349	Proverbs		842
It's an ill aire where wee gaine nothing.	350	Proverbs		872
It's more paine to doe nothing then something.	350	Proverbs		884
It's a wicked thing to make a dearth ones garner.	351	Proverbs		898
There's no such conquering weapon as the necessity of conquering.	357	Proverbs	D	1064
It's a dangerous fire begins in the bed-straw.	357	Proverbs	D	1070
IS (see also 'tis)				
It makes thy soule a blott: it is a rodd	6	Ch.-Porch	W	8
Much lesse towards God, whose lust is all their book?	6	Ch.-Porch		12
When once it is within thee; but before	7	Ch.-Porch		26
It is most just to throw that on the ground,	7	Ch.-Porch		29
He that is drunken, may his mother kill	7	Ch.-Porch		31
Is outlawd by himself: all kinde of ill	7	Ch.-Porch		33
Is outlawd by himself: all kinds of ill	7	Ch.-Porch	W	33
Because no knowledg, is not earth but mudd.	7	Ch.-Porch	W	36
Which is thy best stake, when griefs make thee tame.	9	Ch.-Porch		66
Because to shun them also is so cheap:	9	Ch.-Porch		68
Hee that desires is more then halfe the way.	10	Ch.-Porch	W	90
This is Earth's language, for if Heaven come in,	10	Ch.-Porch	W	90
Some ship them over, and the thing is done.	10	Ch.-Porch		100
All that they leave: this is flat povertie.	10	Ch.-Porch		106
All that is left: this is flat povertie.	10	Ch.-Porch	W	106
Is full as poore as he, that needs but five.	10	Ch.-Porch		108
The way to make thy sonne rich, is to fill	11	Ch.-Porch		109
And though hee bee a ship, is his owne shelf.	11	Ch.-Porch	W	120
Simpring is but a lay-hypocrisie:	11	Ch.-Porch		123
Who carves, is kind to two; who talks, to all.	11	Ch.-Porch		130
Who keeps no guard upon himself, is slack,	12	Ch.-Porch		139
Man is a shop of rules, a well truss'd pack,	12	Ch.-Porch		141
Then live, and use it: els, it is not true	12	Ch.-Porch		154
To all things els. Wealth is the conjurers devil;	13	Ch.-Porch		165
None is so wastefull as the scraping dame.	13	Ch.-Porch		173
Much curiousnesse is a perpetuall wooing	14	Ch.-Porch		191
Game is a civil gunpowder, in peace	14	Ch.-Porch		203
Be sweet to all. Is thy complexion sowre?	15	Ch.-Porch		211
Plainly and home, is coward of the two.	15	Ch.-Porch		218
A toy shunn'd cleanly is fames interest.	15	Ch.-Porch	W	228
For wit is newes onely to ignorance.	15	Ch.-Porch		230
That feeds on dung, is coloured thereby.	15	Ch.-Porch		234
A sad wise valour is the brave complexion,	16	Ch.-Porch		247
The gigler is a milk-maid, whom infection,	16	Ch.-Porch		249
And the sad man is cock of all his jests.	16	Ch.-Porch		252
Is a good spurre. Correct thy passions spite;	16	Ch.-Porch		263
When basenesse is exalted, do not bate	17	Ch.-Porch		265
The shrine is that which thou dost venerate;	17	Ch.-Porch		267
But love is lost, the way of friendship's gone,	17	Ch.-Porch		275
But love is lost, the art of friendship's gone,	17	Ch.-Porch	W	275
Love is a personall debt. I cannot give	17	Ch.-Porch		278
Give one estate, as one life. None is bound	17	Ch.-Porch		285
All such is courteous, usefull, new, or wittie.	18	Ch.-Porch		290
That suites him best, of whom thy speech is heard.	18	Ch.-Porch		294
In love I should: but anger is not love,	18	Ch.-Porch		311
Calmnesse is great advantage: he that lets	19	Ch.-Porch		313
(Love is a present for a mightie king)	20	Ch.-Porch		350
Love is a present for the greatest king.	20	Ch.-Porch	W	350

IS (cont'd)

	PAGE	TITLE		LINE
To take all that is given; whether wealth,	20	Ch.-Porch		356
Man is Gods image; but a poore man is	21	Ch.-Porch		379
Twice on the day his due is understood;	22	Ch.-Porch		391
Twice on that day his due is understood;	22	Ch.-Porch	W	391
Thy cheere is mended; bate not of the food,	22	Ch.-Porch		393
Where it is warmest. Leave thy six and seven;	22	Ch.-Porch		401
Pray with the most: for where most pray, is heaven.	22	Ch.-Porch		402
God is more there, then thou: for thou art there	22	Ch.-Porch		404
Judge not the preacher; for he is thy Judge:	23	Ch.-Porch		427
Though God do hedge us in, yet who is holy?	24	Ch.-Porch		450
Is such a stone,	26	The Altar		6
'Gainst him, who seeks not life, but is the meek	28	Sacrifice		58
But yet their friendship is my enmitie:	29	Sacrifice		75
To whose powre Thunder is but weake and slight:	29	Sacrifice	W	79
It is not fit he live a day, they crie,	29	Sacrifice		98
But hony is their gall, brightnesse their night:	30	Sacrifice		111
Why, Caesar is their onely King, not I:	30	Sacrifice		121
As Moses face was vailed, so is mine,	31	Sacrifice		138
Now prophesie who strikes thee, is their dittie.	31	Sacrifice		142
Whom devils flie, thus is he toss'd of men:	32	Sacrifice		191
My soule is full of shame, my flesh of wound:	33	Sacrifice	W	217
A king my title is, prefixt on high;	34	Sacrifice		233
But now I die; now all is finished.	34	Sacrifice		249
'Tis but to tell the tale is told.	35	Thanksgvng		8
There is no dealing with thy mighty passion:	36	Reprisall		2
There is no medling with thy mighty passion:	36	Reprisall	W	2
Sinne is that presse and vice, which forceth pain	37	The Agonie		11
Love is that liquour sweet and most divine,	37	The Agonie		17
Each seventh note by right is due to thee.	38	The Sinner		4
There the circumference earth is, heav'n the centre.	38	The Sinner		8
There the circumference earth is, heav'n the centure.	38	The Sinner	W	8
In so much dregs the quintessence is small:	38	The Sinner		9
Since bloud is fittest, Lord, to write	39	Good Fri.		21
Who straight, Your suit is granted, said, & died.	40	Redemption		14
Sure there is room within our hearts good store;	40	Sepulchre		5
Rise heart; thy Lord is risen. Sing his praise	41	Easter		1
Is best to celebrate this most high day.	41	Easter		12
Or since all musick is but three parts vied	42	Easter		15
There is but one, and that one ever.	42	Easter		30
Which is above the heav'ns, whose spring and rent	44	H. Bapt.1		5
Which is above the heav'ns, whose spring and vent	44	H. Bapt.1	V	5
Is in my deare Redeemers pierced side.	44	H. Bapt.1		6
Is all the passage, on my infancie	44	H. Bapt.2		3
The growth of flesh is but a blister;	44	H. Bapt.2		14
Childhood is health.	44	H. Bapt.2		15
It is thy highest art	45	Nature		5
Is saplesse grown,	45	Nature		16
Lord, I confesse my sinne is great;	48	Repentance		1
Great is my sinne. Oh! gently treat	48	Repentance		2
Is one undressing,	48	Repentance		5
Mans age is two houres work, or three:	48	Repentance		7
There is a rare outlandish root,	50	Faith		9
That I beleeve is in the sacred storie:	50	Faith		18
The earth is not too low,	53	Antiphon 1		5
The world is theirs; they two play out the game,	54	Love 1		10
Yet take thy way; for sure thy way is best:	55	Temper 1		21
This is but tuning of my breast,	55	Temper 1		23
It cannot be. Where is that mightie joy,	56	Temper 2		1
Become a verse? Is there in truth no beautie?	56	Jordan 1		2
Is all good structure in a winding stair?	56	Jordan 1		3
Is it no verse, except enchanted groves	56	Jordan 1		6
The measure of our joyes is in this place,	57	Employm. 1		11
As is the dust, to which that life doth tend,	57	Employm. 1		15
But all my companie is a weed.	57	Employm. 1		22
Ladies, look here; this is the thankfull glasse,	58	H.Script.1		8
That mends the lookers eyes: this is the well	58	H.Script.1		9
Where is that fire which once descended	59	Whitsunday		5
Death is still working like a mole,	60	Grace		13
Sinne is still hammering my heart	60	Grace		17
To write a verse or two is all the praise,	61	Praise 1		1
Man is all weaknesse; there is no such thing	61	Praise 1		9
His arm is short; yet with a sling	61	Praise 1		11
Is more then all my deaths can be,	62	Afflict.2		3
My God, what is a heart?	62	Mattens		5
My God, what is a heart,	62	Mattens		9
Sinne is flat opposite to th' Almighty, seeing	63	Sinne 2		4
Henceforth repose; your work is done.	64	Even-song		20
The day or night: that is the gale, this th' harbour;	64	Even-song		26
That is the walk, and this the arbour;	64	Even-song		27
That flesh is but the glasse, which holds the dust	65	Ch.-monum.		20
O what a state is this, which never knew	65	Ch.-mus.	W	8
I know it is my sinne, which locks thine eares,	66	Ch.-lock		1
I know it is my sinne, which stops thine eares,	66	Ch.-lock	W	1
Is Patience:	66	Ch.-floore		3
Is checker'd all along,	67	Ch.-floore		5
Is Confidence:	67	Ch.-floore		9
Ties the whole frame, is Love	67	Ch.-floore		11
But all is cleansed when the marble weeps.	67	Ch.-floore		15
He is a brittle crazie glasse:	67	Windows		2
Is wantonnesse in contemplation.	68	Content		8

IS (cont'd)

IS (cont'd)

	PAGE	TITLE	LINE
Which now is pinion'd with mortalitie,	109	Home	63
The most of me to heav'n is fled:	109	Home	68
The word is, Stay, sayes ever, Come.	109	Home	76
Shows who is best.	109	Brit. Ch.	9
She in the valley is so shie	110	Brit. Ch.	19
The mean, thy praise and glorie is,	110	Brit. Ch.	26
What tune is this, poore man? said he:	110	The Quip	10
Is no hard rate.	111	Vanitie 2	10
Is but a bubble, and makes thee a boy.	111	Vanitie 2	18
JESU is in my heart, his sacred name	112	JESU	1
Is deeply carved there: but th' other week	112	JESU	2
And to my whole is JESU.	112	JESU	10
Windes still work: it is their plot,	113	Businesse	9
What, (childe), is the ballance thine,	114	Dialogue	9
Is beyond my savour.	115	Dialogue	20
As the reason then is thine;	115	Dialogue	21
So the way is none of mine:	115	Dialogue	22
That is all, if that I could	115	Dialogue	25
Man is the worlds high Priest: he doth present	117	Providence	13
The tongue is yours to eat, but mine to praise.	117	Providence	22
Is mine to write, as it is yours to raise.	117	Providence	24
And just it is that I should pay the rent,	117	Providence	27
Thy cupboard serves the world: the meat is set,	118	Providence	49
Is there an herb for that? O that thy care	119	Providence	75
A rose, besides his beautie, is a cure.	119	Providence	78
Are there much surer then our art is sure.	119	Providence	80
Is by a ship the speedier passage made.	119	Providence	90
And as thy house is full, so I adore	119	Providence	93
The common all men have; that which is rare,	119	Providence	98
Light without winde is glasse: warm without weight	120	Providence	101
Is wooll and furres: cool without closenesse, shade:	120	Providence	102
Is wooll and furre: cool without closenesse, shade:	120	Providence V	102
Is clothing, meat and trencher, drink and kan,	120	Providence	127
Is clothing, meat and trencher, drink and Can,	120	Providence V	127
Each thing that is, although in use and name	121	Providence	149
Thy sithe is dull; whet it for shame.	122	Time	2
Which now is but a pruning-knife.	122	Time	10
And this is that makes life so long,	123	Time	19
Is lost.	123	Gratefulnes	8
This is the lace of Peaces coat:	124	Peace	9
Is onely there.	125	Peace	42
Is this same grief! within my heart I made	126	Confession	2
Oh, what a thing is man! how farre from power,	127	Giddinesse	1
He is some twentie sev'rall men at least	127	Giddinesse	3
His minde is so.	127	Giddinesse	16
A single deed is small renown.	128	Bunch Gr.	12
Deare Friend, sit down, the tale is long and sad:	129	Love unkn.	1
Better then you know me, or (which is one)	129	Love unkn.	10
Better then you knew me, or (which is one)	129	Love unkn. V	10
Rather hereafter, then in present, is.	131	Mans medly	6
He wears a stuffe whose thread is course and round,	131	Mans medly	15
He may attain to, after he is dead.	131	Mans medly	24
So is his trouble.	131	Mans medly	26
Happie is he, whose heart	132	Mans medly	34
While the inclosure is thine ARM?	133	Paradise	6
There is some rub, some discontent,	133	The Method	3
For he is Power: and sure he would;	133	The Method	7
For he is Love.	133	The Method	8
Is God lesse free?	134	The Method	20
Is all that saves, and not obscure.	135	Divinitie	24
For death is drie as dust. Yet if ye part,	135	Ephes.	10
For where thou dwellest all is neat.	136	Familie	8
What is so shrill as silent tears?	137	Familie	20
This is thy house, with these it doth abound:	137	Familie	21
To th' Isle of spices, is't not fair?	137	The Size	12
Is more then God was, who was hungrie here.	138	The Size	14
Is not a corpulent, but a thinne and spare,	138	The Size	32
There is no articling with thee:	139	Artillerie	31
Why doth my Mother blush? is she the rose,	140	Ch.-rents	11
As many eyes as starres? since it is night,	140	Ch.-rents	26
Thy hand is white,	141	Justice 2	15
Against me there is none, but for me much.	141	Justice 2	24
After so foul a journey death is fair,	142	Pilgrimage	35
We must confesse that nothing is our own.	143	Holdfast	7
Then I confesse, that he my succour is:	143	Holdfast	8
But to have nought is ours, not to confesse	143	Holdfast	9
That which is past who can recall?	144	Discharge	10
Thy life is Gods, thy time to come is gone,	144	Discharge	11
And is his right.	144	Discharge	12
He is thy night at noon: he is at night	144	Discharge	13
The crop is his, for he hath sown.	144	Discharge	15
If it be his once, all is well.	144	Discharge	20
Onely the present is thy part and fee.	144	Discharge	21
This houre is mine: if for the next I care,	145	Discharge	33
And while it cometh, it is almost past.	145	Discharge	53
My God hath promis'd; he is just.	145	Discharge	55
Small it is, in this poore sort	146	Praise 2	25
Ev'n eternitie is too short	146	Praise 2	27
What hast thou there? a heart? but is it pure?	147	Offering	3
Yet one pure heart is nothing to bestow:	147	Offering	5

IS (cont'd)

	PAGE	TITLE	LINE
But all I fear is lest thy heart displease,	147	Offering	13
There is a balsome, or indeed a bloud,	147	Offering	19
All sorts of wounds; of such strange force it is.	147	Offering	21
(For this heart is none)	148	Offering	33
My throat, my soul is hoarse;	148	Longing	7
My heart is wither'd like a ground	148	Longing	8
Is all lockt? hath a sinners plea	149	Longing	47
Thy board is full, yet humble guests	149	Longing	53
But now both sinne is dead,	150	Longing	67
(I have no bag, but here is room):	152	The Bag	32
Is the yeare onely lost to me?	153	The Collar	13
Not so, my heart: but there is fruit,	153	The Collar	17
Of what is fit, and not. Forsake thy cage,	153	The Collar	21
So high a torture? Is such poyson bought?	155	Assurance	3
What is thy aim? wouldst thou unlock the doore	155	Assurance	15
What is objected by my foes.	155	Assurance	24
Sorrow hath chang'd its note: such is his will,	159	Jos.coat	3
That earth is fitted by the fire and trade	161	Priesthood	16
Then is my time. The distance of the meek	161	Priesthood	39
Where is my God? what hidden place	163	The Search	29
Is it thy will?	163	The Search	32
Thy will such an intrenching is,	163	The Search	37
Thy will such a strange distance is,	163	The Search	41
As is thy space,	163	The Search	46
Of a lesse world? the greater is but small,	164	Grief	10
What is this strange and uncouth thing?	164	The Crosse	1
So much desir'd, is giv'n, to take away	164	The Crosse	9
Is in the midst of delicates to need,	165	The Crosse	29
This or that is:	166	The Flower	20
Thy word is all, if we could spell.	166	The Flower	21
What frost to that? what pole is not the zone,	166	The Flower	32
And the least frown of thine is shown?	166	The Flower	35
A sonne is light and fruit; a fruitfull flame	168	The Sonne	7
Is, when the soul unto the lines accords.	168	a true Hymn	10
Justly complains, that somewhat is behinde	168	a true Hymn	14
Alas, poore Death, where is thy glorie?	169	Dial.-Anth	1
Where is thy famous force, thy ancient sting?	169	Dial.-Anth	2
Since the condition of this world is frail,	170	Water-crs.	2
The world an ancient murderer is;	170	Self-cond.	10
And is a Judas-Jew.	171	Self-cond.	18
The God of love my shepherd is,	172	23 Psalme	1
While he is mine, and I am his,	172	23 Psalme	3
Unto a place where is no rest.	174	Aaron	9
Christ is my onely head,	174	Aaron	16
My doctrine tun'd by Christ, (who is not dead,	174	Aaron	23
For when My Master, which alone is sweet,	175	The Odour	21
That call is but the breathing of the sweet.	175	The Odour	25
White is their colour, and behold my head.	176	Forerunners	2
Ev'n all my heart, and what is lodged there:	176	Forerunners	8
True beautie dwells on high: ours is a flame	177	Forerunners	28
For, Thou art still my God, is all that ye	177	Forerunners	32
First, there is no pleasure here:	177	The Rose	5
What is fairer then a rose?	178	The Rose	17
What is sweeter? yet it purgeth.	178	The Rose	18
And repentance is a purge.	178	The Rose	28
For my answer is a rose.	178	The Rose	32
Unto thine is bent:	178	Discipline	6
Love is swift of foot;	179	Discipline	21
Is your waste;	179	Invitation	2
God is here prepar'd and drest,	179	Invitation	4
Which before ye drink is bloud.	180	Invitation	12
Taste and fear not: God is here	180	Invitation	16
Here is joy that drowneth quite	180	Invitation	22
Is your dove,	180	Invitation	26
Here is love, which having breath	180	Invitation	28
Where is all, there all should be.	180	Invitation	36
Such as is, and makes divine!	181	Banquet	9
Is some starre (fled from the sphere)	181	Banquet	10
Here, as broken, is presented.	181	Banquet	30
Of all thy mercies, is my posie still.	182	The Posie	4
Or say, or dictate, this is my delight.	183	The Posie	8
Of all Gods mercies, is my posie still.	183	The Posie	12
Thou saist, this fruit is mine.	184	The Elixer W	12
This is the famous stone	185	The Elixer	21
Wherein I die, not live: for life is straight,	185	A Wreath	5
Man is out of order hurl'd,	187	Dooms-day	27
Then tell me, what is that supreme delight?	188	Heaven	13
Ah, what a thing is man devoid of grace,	193	Ch.-Milit.	111
Who makes a root his God, how low is he,	193	Ch.-Milit.	115
Whose house is foul, while he adores his broom?	193	Ch.-Milit.	118
And this is all the Rock, whereof they boast,	194	Ch.-Milit.	159
As is the moon and sunne to heav'n and light.	196	Ch.-Milit.	216
The latter Church is to the first a debter.	196	Ch.-Milit.	224
To these diminishings, as is between	196	Ch.-Milit.	233
Bragging that thy bloud is cold,	199	L'Envoy	6
That thy death is also dead,	199	L'Envoy	7
And thy Crosse is common wood.	199	L'Envoy	10
To discharge what is behinde.	199	L'Envoy	16
Is more, but for mee still.	200	H. Commun. W	18
That Flesh is there, mine eyes deny:	201	H. Commun. W	31

IS (cont'd)

	PAGE	TITLE		LINE
This gift of all gifts is the best,	201	H. Commun.	W	43
There is no dealing with thee in that Art:	201	love	W	2
That is thy Master-peece I see	201	love	W	3
He that is one,	202	Trin.Sun.	W	1
Is none.	202	Trin.Sun.	W	2
The Day is spent, & hath his will on mee:	203	Even-song	W	1
The sunn is darker then a Tree,	203	Even-song	W	15
Since Light thy Darknes is.	203	Even-song	W	20
Now is the season	204	The Knell	W	7
But kill the man, is seald with thee.	204	Persever.	W	8
My God, where is that ancient heat towards thee,	206	Walton 1		1
Sure, Lord, there is enough in thee to dry	206	Walton 2		1
A pair of Cheeks of them, is thy abuse.	206	Walton 2		7
Whose fire is wild, and doth not upward go	206	Walton 2		10
My labour is not lost.	207	Walton 4		4
Here is copied out by art;	208	J. Danvers	D	10
Your state, to ours, is contrary;	210	Paradox	D	7
Is of the two the far more desperate.	210	Paradox	D	30
There is thy best Throne. For afflictions are	211	Bohemia	D	15
And what is fortunes. Thou hast singled out	211	Bohemia	D	19
When sense is made by Comments. But that face	212	Bohemia	D	29
Is selfe-sufficient to bee the thrall	212	Bohemia	D	32
Is thy chief government, to manage woe,	212	Bohemia	D	57
This is thy empire yet: till better season	213	Bohemia	D	60
Blest is the man that never would	214	Psalm I	D	1
Of earth is driven by winds away,	215	Psalm I	D	15
no help in God there is.	216	Psalm III	D	4
my Soul is troubled very sore;	220	Psalm VI	D	6
God is my shield, who doth preserve	222	Psalm VII	D	37
His bow is bent, his quiver is	222	Psalm VII	D	43
of him that is on high.	222	Psalm VII	D	64
The question is, whose love the greater showes:	438	Lat.Trans.		2
is to feed my Flocke diligently and faithfully, since our Saviour	224	Priest		4
if a man do not all which is here expressed, hee presently sinns,	224	Priest		10
but that it is a good strife to go as farre as wee can in pleasing	224	Priest		11
A Pastor is the Deputy of Christ for the reducing of Man	225	Priest 1		1
This definition is evident, and containes the direct steps	225	Priest 1		2
Christ is the glorious instrument of God for the revoking of Man.	225	Priest 1		5
that he fils up that which is behinde of the afflictions of Christ in	225	Priest 1		12
of Christ in his flesh, for his Bodie's sake, which is the Church.	225	Priest 1		13
Wherein is contained the complete definition of a Minister.	225	Priest 1		13
in that a Priest is to do that which Christ did, and after his	225	Priest 1		18
some live there in office, whose rule is that of the Apostle;	226	Priest 2		3
according to the grace that is given to us, whether prophecy,	226	Priest 2		5
the Fathers, or Schoolmen, a Minister is made, and the thing done.	226	Priest 2		11
The greatest and hardest preparation is within:	226	Priest 2		13
in describing the one (which is indeed the bent of my Discourse)	226	Priest 2		18
but after a man is once Minister, he cannot agree to come into any	226	Priest 2		25
where he shall not exercise what he is, unlesse he forsake his	226	Priest 2		26
The Countrey Parson is exceeding exact in his Life, being holy,	227	Priest 3		1
points of Life, wherein a Christian is most seen, are Patience,	227	Priest 3		4
the Countrey Parson is very circumspect in avoiding all	227	Priest 3		15
Secondly because Luxury is a very visible sinne, the Parson is very	227	Priest 3		22
the Parson is very carefull to avoid all the kinds thereof,	227	Priest 3		22
but especially that of drinking, because it is the most popular vice;	227	Priest 3		24
Neither is it for the servant of Christ to haunt Innes,	227	Priest 3		29
therfore the Parson is very strict in keeping his word,	228	Priest 3		4
The Parsons yea is yea, and nay nay;	228	Priest 3		10
The Countrey Parson is full of all knowledg.	228	Priest 4		14
They say, it is an ill Mason that refuseth any stone:	228	Priest 4		15
and there is no knowledg, but, in a skilfull hand, serves either	228	Priest 4		15
serves either positively as it is, or else to illustrate some other	228	Priest 4		17
The second means is prayer, which if it be necessary even in	228	Priest 4		33
where the well is deep, and we have nothing of our selves to draw	228	Priest 4		35
The third means is a diligent Collation of Scripture with Scripture.	229	Priest 4		4
therefore the spirit of both is to be considered, and weighed.	229	Priest 4		16
which is the storehouse of his Sermons, and which he preacheth all	230	Priest 5		1
For though the world is full of such composures, yet every mans own	230	Priest 5		3
is full of such composures, yet every mans own is fittest, readyest,	230	Priest 5		4
it is an honest joy ever after to looke upon his well spent houres.	230	Priest 5		6
that is best to be chosen, of which there is likelyest to be most	230	Priest 5		10
is best to be chosen, of which there is likelyest to be most use.	230	Priest 5		11
according as his audience is, so he useth one, or other;	230	Priest 5		17
esteemes also of cases of conscience, wherein he is much versed.	230	Priest 5		19
herein is the greatest ability of a Parson to lead his people exactly	230	Priest 5		20
when it is a sin to take something for mony lent, or when not;	230	Priest 5		24
when it is a fault to discover anothers fault, or when not;	230	Priest 5		25
which grass will bane, or which not, how is he fit to be a shepherd?	230	Priest 5		32
when he is to read divine services, composeth himselfe to all	231	Priest 6		1
as this is the true reason of his inward feare, so he is content	231	Priest 6		10
so he is content to expresse this outwardly to the utmost of his	231	Priest 6		11
Accordingly his voyce is humble, his words treatable, and slow;	231	Priest 6		16
as attending to what is done in the Church, and every one,	231	Priest 6		27
This is that which the Apostle cals a reasonable service,	232	Priest 6		2
Parson preacheth constantly, the pulpit is his joy and his throne:	232	Priest 7		21
it is either for want of health, or against some great Festivall,	232	Priest 7		21
he is ever very well supplyed by some able man who treads in his	232	Priest 7		25
that where is much earnestness, there is somewhat worth hearing;	232	Priest 7		32
that where is much earnestness, there is somewhat worth hearing;	232	Priest 7		33
This is for you, and This is for you;	233	Priest 7		4

IS (cont'd)

	PAGE	TITLE	LINE
This is for you, and This is for you;	233	Priest 7	5
them to be so, when God is so neer them, and even over their heads.	233	Priest 7	10
that none is careless before his Judg, and that the word of God shal	233	Priest 7	20
but the character of his Sermon is Holiness;	233	Priest 7	23
he is not witty, or learned, or eloquent, but Holy.	233	Priest 7	23
But it is gained first, by choosing texts of Devotion,	233	Priest 7	26
that the auditors may plainly perceive that every word is hart-deep.	233	Priest 7	32
Oh Lord, I know that the way of man is not in himself, &c.	234	Priest 7	6
For there is no greater sign of holinesse, then the procuring,	234	Priest 7	9
And is in contention for them whither to live, or dy;	234	Priest 7	15
What an admirable Epistle is the second to the Corinthians?	234	Priest 7	18
he joyes, and he is sorry, he grieves, and he gloryes, never was	234	Priest 7	19
he is among us; for if we be here, hee must be here, since we are	234	Priest 7	28
the discourse to his Majesty, And he is a great God, and terrible,	234	Priest 7	31
His voyce is as the sound of many waters, Revelations 1.	234	Priest 7	34
And he himselfe is a consuming fire, Hebrews 12.	234	Priest 7	35
and seems to himselfe so as a Market-man is, when the Market day	235	Priest 8	18
him unworthy of that Majesty before which he is to present himself,	235	Priest 8	24
And every one is more awaked, when we come, and say, Thou art	236	Priest 8	14
that order is kept in the one, and peace in the other, without	236	Priest 8	24
Parson considering that virginity is a higher state then Matrimony,	236	Priest 9	31
the best and highest things, is rather unmarryed, then marryed.	236	Priest 9	33
like circumstances considered, he is rather married then unmarried.	237	Priest 9	4
He is very circumspect in all companyes, both of his behaviour,	237	Priest 9	13
he is not afraid of the pestilence that walketh in darkenesse,	238	Priest 9	6
Originall concupisence is such an active thing, by reason	238	Priest 9	12
that it is ever attempting, or doing one mischief or other.	238	Priest 9	13
is a common temptation to men of any eminency, especially being	238	Priest 9	16
is another great stumbling block to the holinesse of Scholars.	238	Priest 9	19
for then commonly the stream of temptations is turned another way,	238	Priest 9	23
As hee is just in all things, so is he to his wife also,	238	Priest 9	34
so is he to his wife also, counting nothing so much his owne,	238	Priest 9	34
the seldomer, according as hee is satisfied of his Wifes discretion.	239	Priest 9	4
The Parson is very exact in the governing of his house,	239	Priest 10	6
His wife is either religious, or night and day he is winning her	239	Priest 10	10
wife is either religious, or night and day he is winning her to it.	239	Priest 10	10
which happily for his other children he is not able to do.	239	Priest 10	33
and vanities of the world, which he is to deny, and not augment.	240	Priest 10	4
is placed surer for his childrens advantage, then if it were given	240	Priest 10	8
they do best, and because what they do, is blessed, and prospers.	240	Priest 10	16
so that his family is a Schoole of Religion, and they all account,	240	Priest 10	21
they all account, that to teach the ignorant is the greatest almes.	240	Priest 10	23
the wals are not idle, but something is written, or painted there,	240	Priest 10	24
which is expressed in a fayre table, as being the rule of a family.	240	Priest 10	26
his wife among her neighbours is the beginner of good discourses,	240	Priest 10	28
that there is no help for a fault done, but confession.	240	Priest 10	35
esteeming that this private praying is a more voluntary act in them,	241	Priest 10	4
The furniture of his house is very plain, but clean, whole,	241	Priest 10	11
His fare is plain, and common, but wholsome, what hee hath,	241	Priest 10	15
and common, but wholsome, what hee hath, is little, but very good;	241	Priest 10	16
as Sunday is his day of joy, so Friday his day of Humiliation,	241	Priest 10	36
which is but the determination of the second rule by Authority	242	Priest 10	5
unpleasant, is the naturall rule of fasting, although it be flesh.	242	Priest 10	10
since fasting in Scripture language is an afflicting of our souls,	242	Priest 10	12
and not the fish, is to keep the fasting day naturally.	242	Priest 10	14
And it is observable, that the prohibiting of flesh came from hot	242	Priest 10	15
is apt to nourish more then in cold regions, and where flesh may be	242	Priest 10	17
cold and flegmatick, the eating of flesh is an antidote to both.	242	Priest 10	21
For it is certaine, that a weak stomack being prepossessed	242	Priest 10	21
For it is as unnatural to do any thing, that leads me to a sicknesse,	242	Priest 10	36
One thing is evident, that an English body, and a Students body,	242	Priest 10	38
vessels, and there is nothing that is food, and not phisick,	243	Priest 10	2
as being immoderately taken, it is exceeding obstructive.	243	Priest 10	4
But since both is to be done, the better sort invited, and meaner	243	Priest 11	13
there are such conceits, there is no room for his doctrine to enter.	243	Priest 11	23
for a reward to draw men to Piety, and is content, if at least so,	243	Priest 11	32
Parson, who is a diligent observer, and tracker of Gods wayes,	244	Priest 11	2
The Countrey Parson is full of Charity;	244	Priest 12	6
it is his predominant element.	244	Priest 12	6
To Charity is given the covering of sins, 1 Pet. 4. 8.	244	Priest 12	8
In brief, it is the body of Religion, John 13. 35.	244	Priest 12	13
and repine as much, as he that is disseized of his own inheritance.	244	Priest 12	30
So is his charity in effect a Sermon.	245	Priest 12	16
for that also is some kind of obligation;	245	Priest 12	19
givings are lay, and secular, but this is to give like a Priest.	245	Priest 12	38
things there be decent, and befitting his Name by which it is called.	246	Priest 13	3
The first whereof is, Let all things be done decently, and in order:	246	Priest 13	27
even in externall and indifferent things, what course is to be taken;	247	Priest 13	1
whereas on Sundays it is easie for them to compose themselves	247	Priest 14	7
and furthers them when hee is gone, in their imployment;	247	Priest 14	14
for it is a good and just thing for every one to do their own	247	Priest 14	22
thinking that their own labour is the cause of their thriving,	247	Priest 14	30
for as when the offence is particular, and against mee,	248	Priest 14	26
so when the offence is publicke, and against God, I am then to follow	248	Priest 14	28
1 Timothy 5. 20. and to rebuke openly that which is done openly.	248	Priest 14	30
the Parson questions what order is kept in the house, as about	248	Priest 14	31
but he holds the Rule, that Nothing is little in Gods service:	249	Priest 14	2
For both God is there also, and those for whom God dyed:	249	Priest 14	6
as his accesse to the poor is more comfortable, then to the rich;	249	Priest 14	8
and in regard of himselfe, it is more humiliation.	249	Priest 14	9

IS (cont'd)

	PAGE	TITLE	LINE
when any of his cure is sick, or afflicted with losse of friend,	249	Priest 15	13
antient and pious ordinance, and how necessary it is in some cases:	249	Priest 15	31
comfortable, and Soveraigne a Medicine it is to all sin-sick souls;	250	Priest 15	2
The Countrey Parson is not only a father to his flock, but also	250	Priest 16	7
but is long before hee proceede to disinheriting, or perhaps never	250	Priest 16	17
but is himselfe where ever he is.	251	Priest 17	1
but is himselfe where ever he is.	251	Priest 17	2
that he may enlarge the glory of God to the company he is in,	251	Priest 17	8
The Countrey Parson, where ever he is, keeps Gods watch;	252	Priest 18	1
that is, there is nothing spoken, or done in the Company where he is,	252	Priest 18	2
there is nothing spoken, or done in the Company where he is,	252	Priest 18	2
or done in the Company where he is, but comes under his Test	252	Priest 18	3
Your meaning is not thus, but thus;	252	Priest 18	11
or, So farr indeed what you say is true, and well said;	252	Priest 18	12
This is called keeping Gods watch, when the baits which the enemy	252	Priest 18	13
This is to be on Gods side, and be true to his party.	252	Priest 18	15
Wherein a pleasantness of disposition is of great use, men being	252	Priest 18	19
The Countrey Parson is sincere and upright in all his relations.	252	Priest 19	24
And first, he is just to his Countrey;	252	Priest 19	25
as when he is set at an armour, or horse, he borrowes them	252	Priest 19	26
To do otherwise, is deceit;	252	Priest 19	29
and therefore not for him, who is hearty, and true in all his wayes,	253	Priest 19	1
he considers what is the end of any Command, and then he suits things	253	Priest 19	4
Ministeriall office, which is not to the prejudice of his own Parish.	253	Priest 19	17
The Countrey Parson is in Gods stead to his Parish, and dischargeth	254	Priest 20	8
Wherefore there is nothing done either wel or ill, whereof he is	254	Priest 20	10
done either wel or ill, whereof he is not the rewarder, or punisher.	254	Priest 20	11
This is in some sort a discharging of God;	254	Priest 20	18
but in the other God is his own immediate paymaster, rewarding all	254	Priest 20	20
is rather by withdrawing his bounty and courtesie from the parties	254	Priest 20	22
he is carefull to see condign punishment inflicted, and with truly	254	Priest 20	26
Catechizing is the first point, and but by Catechizing,	255	Priest 21	7
whereas in Sermons there is a kinde of state, in Catechizing there is	255	Priest 21	9
in Catechizing there is an humblenesse very sutable to Christian	255	Priest 21	10
not himself, but is first a Sermon to himself, and then to others;	255	Priest 21	14
How came this world to be as it is?	256	Priest 21	7
Is this the nature of beliefe?	256	Priest 21	9
Is not Christianity full of such things, as are not to be seen,	256	Priest 21	10
Who is God? And so forward, requiring answers to all these,	256	Priest 21	12
And this is an admirable way of teaching, wherein the Catechized will	256	Priest 21	17
but after that the Catechisme is once learn'd, that which nature is	256	Priest 21	25
that which nature is towards Philosophy, the Catechism is towards	256	Priest 21	26
nature is towards Philosophy, the Catechism is towards Divinity.	256	Priest 21	26
since man is so miserable, what is to be done?	257	Priest 21	3
This is the skill, and doubtlesse the Holy Scripture intends thus	257	Priest 21	10
This is the Practice which the Parson so much commends to all his	257	Priest 21	16
but when one is asked a question, he must discover what he is.	257	Priest 21	19
but when one is asked a question, he must discover what he is.	257	Priest 21	20
is at a stand with himself, how or what behaviour to assume for so	257	Priest 22	27
Especially at Communion times he is in a great confusion,	257	Priest 22	29
where God is thanked for calling us to the knowledg of his grace,	258	Priest 22	5
that it is no complementall or light thing to sustain that place,	258	Priest 22	10
it is the safest course for Christians also to meditate on their	258	Priest 22	17
of the Communion only (for then it is too late) but the Sunday,	258	Priest 22	27
The time of every ones first receiving is not so much by yeers,	258	Priest 22	32
of devotion to the Sacrament, but it is for want of Instruction;	258	Priest 22	38
The saying of the Catechism is necessary, but not enough;	259	Priest 22	6
loosely and wildely, and then the Answerer will discover what hee is.	259	Priest 22	10
The Feast indeed requires sitting, because it is a Feast;	259	Priest 22	13
Contentiousnesse in a feast of Charity is more scandall then any	259	Priest 22	18
they are most eminent, is the most gainfull way of Conversation.	260	Priest 23	6
Yet when ever any controversie is brought to him, he never decides it	260	Priest 23	8
In judging, he followes that, which is altogether right;	260	Priest 23	13
Now as the Parson is in Law, so is he in sicknesse also:	260	Priest 23	28
any of his flock sick, hee is their Physician, or at least his Wife,	260	Priest 23	29
Yet is it easie for any Scholer to attaine to such a measure	261	Priest 23	1
This is done by seeing one Anatomy, reading one Book of Phisick,	261	Priest 23	4
wherein the manifold wisedome of God is wonderfully to be seen,	261	Priest 23	28
which is, to know what herbs may be used in stead of drugs	261	Priest 23	29
esteeming that there is no spice comparable, for herbs,	262	Priest 23	1
for this is to cure like a Parson, and this raiseth the action from	262	Priest 23	10
the person bee so poor, that he is not able to reward the Phisician:	262	Priest 23	14
for as hee is Charitable, so he is just also.	262	Priest 23	15
Now it is a justice and debt to the Common-wealth he lives in,	262	Priest 23	15
And justice is the ground of Charity.	262	Priest 23	17
The first means he useth is Prayer, beseeching the Father of lights	262	Priest 24	22
The second means is a very loving, and sweet usage of them,	262	Priest 24	25
The third means is the observation what is the main foundation,	262	Priest 24	28
as if he be a Papist, the Church is the hinge he turnes on;	262	Priest 24	30
these two with himselfe, as what the Church is, how it began,	262	Priest 24	32
what scandall is, when given or taken;	263	Priest 24	8
be preferred, especially since in disobeying there is scandall also:	263	Priest 24	11
be wanting to them in Doctrine, to whom he is so gracious in Life.	263	Priest 24	21
by all means, that the delinquents returne is to his advantage.	264	Priest 25	2
It is true indeed, they are long a knowing it, being partiall	264	Priest 26	12
and the reason hereof is, because the natures of these vices being	264	Priest 26	17
to that which is presently unlawfull, even in one continued action.	264	Priest 26	21
but proceeding on, comes to do unlawfully, even before he is aware;	264	Priest 26	24
yet is there a period for his storing, and a point, or center,	264	Priest 26	28
or not in some proportion to Gods blessing upon him, is covetous.	265	Priest 26	7

IS (cont'd)

	PAGE	TITLE		LINE
which is alreadie burdened with a disease, would be wholly oppressed.	299	Cornaro		33
and the cause being taken away, there is no place for the effect.	300	Cornaro		2
Wherefore since an orderly life is so profitable, so vertuous,	300	Cornaro		3
so decent, and so holy, it is worthy by all means to be embraced;	300	Cornaro		4
especially since it is easie and most agreeable to the nature of Man.	300	Cornaro		5
No man that follcwes it, is bound to eat and drink so little as I:	300	Cornaro		6
No man is forbidden to eat fruit or fish, which I eat not:	300	Cornaro		7
So that he which is offended with no kinde of meat and drink,	300	Cornaro		14
not the qualitie for his rule, which is very easie to be observed.	300	Cornaro		16
Because since this is at the best but uncertain, dangerous,	300	Cornaro		19
It is not the part of a wise man, to expose himself to so many	300	Cornaro		22
is more sure of life, then the most strong young man who lives	300	Cornaro		25
That a long life is no such desirable thing, because that after one	300	Cornaro		28
because that after one is once sixtie five yeares old, all the time	300	Cornaro		29
yeares old, all the time we live after, is rather death then life.	300	Cornaro		29
parted with rills of running water, which truely is very delightfull.	301	Cornaro		16
which is therefore very pleasant, because many wayes thither are so	301	Cornaro		20
in the midst whereof is a Church suitable to the condition	301	Cornaro		22
This place is washed with the river Brenta;	301	Cornaro		23
By this means the place is come to that perfection we now see it is:	301	Cornaro		30
By this means the place is come to that perfection we now see it is:	301	Cornaro		31
The memorie whereof is exceeding delightfull to me.	301	Cornaro		33
and husbandrie, whereof in this age there is great plentie.	301	Cornaro		37
and ever I learn somewhat which is worthy of my knowledge:	302	Cornaro		2
Neither is this my pleasure made lesse by the decaying dulnesse of my	302	Cornaro		7
so that any simple fare is more savourie to me now, then heretofore,	302	Cornaro		9
heat of summer (which in Italie is very great) receiving not any hurt	302	Cornaro		19
So great is the power and efficacie of that Temperance which ever	302	Cornaro		20
which is altogether to be preferred before others youth:	302	Cornaro		23
By which it is evident, That the life which I live at this age,	303	Cornaro		9
That the life which I live at this age, is not a dead, dumpish,	303	Cornaro		10
I know how inconsiderate that age is, and, though subject to death,	303	Cornaro		17
For death to all young men is a terrible thing, as also to those that	303	Cornaro		18
Yet I am sure, that my end is farre from me:	303	Cornaro		25
And that is a fair and desirable death, which Nature brings by way	303	Cornaro		28
Since therefore a temperate life is so happie and pleasant a thing;	303	Cornaro		30
and to such, and all that is theirs, I owe diligence;	304	Valdesso		7
It is true, there are some things which I like not in him,	304	Valdesso		15
that it is not to be understood of actuall sinnes, but habituall,	308	Valdesso		2
The exemption from both, is by the Grace of God.	308	Valdesso		5
distinction, for Fomes is not taken away, but Accensio Fomitis;	308	Valdesso		15
the naturall concupiscence is not quite extinguished, but the heate	308	Valdesso		16
is not that which filleth the heart with joy and peace in believing;	309	Valdesso		2
learned and perfect in them, there is somewhat to be learned more:	309	Valdesso		24
Although by other words of the same Psalme it is evident,	309	Valdesso		28
but the meaning is this, That God in the dayes of the Gospell will	310	Valdesso		4
there the case is plaine, Cornelius had revelation, yet Peter was	310	Valdesso		9
and the more the promise is delayed, the more he reads it,	310	Valdesso		29
wee to doe with the Scriptures and this is the use of the promises	310	Valdesso		31
But the use of the Doctrinall part is more, in regard it presents us	310	Valdesso		32
us not with the same thing only when it is read as the promises doe,	310	Valdesso		34
so that it is plain the Authour had a very reverend esteem	311	Valdesso	V	6
but it is sutable to what the Author holds elsewhere, for he	311	Valdesso		21
for he maintaines that it is Faith and Infidelity that shall judge us	311	Valdesso		22
And with this exposition the Chapter is cleare enough, but the truth	311	Valdesso		31
in the Church of God there is one fundamentall, but else variety.	312	Valdesso		2
(I suppose) that a man presume not to merit, that is, to oblige God,	312	Valdesso		15
In indifferent things there is roome for motions [notions]	313	Valdesso		12
A man is to embrace all good, but because he cannot doe all,	313	Valdesso		20
He meanes a mans fre-will is only in outward, not in spirituall	313	Valdesso		33
Saviour prayed with doubtfulnesse, is more then I can or dare say;	315	Valdesso		9
Feare is given tc Christ, but not doubt, and upon good ground.	315	Valdesso		12
This Chapter is considerable. The intent of it, that the world	315	Valdesso		29
is in some sort true because they are spiritually discerned,	315	Valdesso		30
[the law is not made for a righteous man:]	315	Valdesso		34
Gods Servants should have weaknesses is no way repugnant to the way	316	Valdesso		3
which is a mcdest admonition.	316	Valdesso		13
But it is one thing not to judge, another to defend them.	316	Valdesso		13
this cannot stand, and it is ill Doctrine in a common-wealth.	316	Valdesso		16
may pretend motions, which is unsufferable in a Common-wealth.	316	Valdesso		21
that is in humano foro & secundum praesumptionem legalem,	316	Valdesso		28
How the godly are exempt from Laws is a known point among Divines,	316	Valdesso		31
they are equally exempt with God, that is dangerous and too farre.	316	Valdesso		32
The best salve for the whole Chapter, is to distinguish Judgment:	316	Valdesso		34
There is a judgment of authority (upon a fact) and there is	316	Valdesso		35
of authority (upon a fact) and there is a judgment of the Learned;	317	Valdesso		1
whereas there is not onely milke there, but strong meat also.	317	Valdesso		23
There is no more to be said of this Chapter but that his opinion	318	Valdesso		5
this Chapter but that his opinion of the scripture is unsufferable.	318	Valdesso		6
it all upon the word untill the day starre arise, it is nothing.	318	Valdesso		9
of the blessed Virgin out of that text Mat. 1. 25. where it is said,	318	Valdesso		12
Nay it is observeable that in that very place he preferres the Word	318	Valdesso		22
Yet doubtlesse the best faith in us is defective, and arrives	319	Valdesso		10
the cunning hypocrite who by the world is counted a very Saint,	319	Valdesso	V	20
This is true onley of the Popish Cases of Conscience, which depend	319	Valdesso	V	28
A handfull of good life is better then a bushell of learning.	321	Proverbs		3
All is well with him, who is beloved of his neighbours.	321	Proverbs		10
All is well to him, that is loved of his neighbours.	321	Proverbs	V	10
A good bargaine is a pick-purse.	321	Proverbs		12
Pleasing ware is halfe sould.	321	Proverbs		14

IS (cont'd)

	PAGE	TITLE		LINE
When all sinnes grow old, coveteousnesse is young.	321	Proverbs		18
The Devill is not alwaies at one doore.	322	Proverbs		31
When a friend askes, there is no to morrow.	322	Proverbs		32
The Germans wit is in his fingers.	322	Proverbs		36
A Lyons skin is never cheape.	323	Proverbs		55
The goate must browse where she is tyed.	323	Proverbs		56
In a good house all is quickly ready.	323	Proverbs		58
Ill ware is never cheape.	323	Proverbs		61
Every thing is of use to a houskeeper.	323	Proverbs		70
When prayers are done, my Lady is ready.	323	Proverbs		71
Every thing new is fine.	323	Proverbs		76
When a dog is a drowning, every one offers him drink.	323	Proverbs		77
Who is so deafe, as he that will not heare?	323	Proverbs		79
Who is so deafe, as he who will not heare?	323	Proverbs	V	79
He that is warme, thinkes all so.	323	Proverbs		80
At length the Fox is brought to the Furrier.	323	Proverbs		81
Hee that lives well is learned enough.	323	Proverbs		86
Hee who lives well is learned enough.	323	Proverbs	V	86
An old wise mans shaddow is better then a young buzzards sword.	324	Proverbs		90
I gave the mouse a hole, and she is become my heire.	324	Proverbs		94
Where you thinke there is bacon, there is no Chimney.	324	Proverbs		99
The Chicken is the Countries, but the Citie eates it.	324	Proverbs		108
Good is to bee sought out, and evill attended.	324	Proverbs		112
Water trotted is as good as oates.	325	Proverbs		131
Though a lie be well drest, it is ever overcome.	325	Proverbs		133
Happie is hee that chastens himselfe.	325	Proverbs		137
A drunkards purse is a bottle.	325	Proverbs		143
Good is the mora that makes all sure.	325	Proverbs		145
The best remedy against an ill man is much ground betweene both.	326	Proverbs		152
Corne is cleaned with winde, and the soule with chastnings.	326	Proverbs		154
To buy deare is not bounty.	326	Proverbs		156
None is a foole alwaies, every one sometimes.	326	Proverbs		163
Hell is full of good meanings and wishings.	326	Proverbs		170
After the house is finisht, leave it.	326	Proverbs		172
God complaines not, but doth what is fitting.	327	Proverbs		182
Where there is nc honour, there is no griefe.	327	Proverbs		186
Whose house is of glasse, must not throw stones at another.	327	Proverbs		196
He that riseth first, is first drest.	327	Proverbs		202
A childs service is little,	327	Proverbs		206
yet hee is no little foole that despiseth it.	327	Proverbs		206
The honey is sweet, but the Bee stings.	328	Proverbs		212
In good yeares corne is hay, in ill yeares straw is corne.	328	Proverbs		216
The hearts letter is read in the eyes.	328	Proverbs		220
Sometimes the best gaine is to lose.	328	Proverbs		224
It is a great victory that comes without blood.	328	Proverbs		227
Honour without profit is a ring on the finger.	328	Proverbs		230
Estate in twc parishes is bread in two wallets.	328	Proverbs		231
A naughty child is better sick then whole.	328	Proverbs		233
The fault of the horse is put on the saddle.	329	Proverbs		240
Fine dressing is a foule house swept before the doores.	329	Proverbs		243
An ill wound is cured, not an ill name.	329	Proverbs		245
Knowledge is folly, except grace guide it.	329	Proverbs		248
Punishment is lame, but it comes.	329	Proverbs		249
A long tongue is a signe of a short hand.	329	Proverbs		251
The worst of law is, that one suit breedes twenty.	329	Proverbs		253
Providence is better then a rent.	329	Proverbs		254
Good cheape is deare.	329	Proverbs		261
An ill agreement is better then a good judgement.	329	Proverbs		264
There is more talke then trouble.	330	Proverbs		265
nor being spoken to is silent.	330	Proverbs		278
The foole askes much, but hee is more foole that grants it.	330	Proverbs		282
Hee is a foole that thinks not that another thinks.	330	Proverbs		287
The Lyon is not so fierce as they paint him.	330	Proverbs		289
Good service is a great inchantment.	331	Proverbs		291
The best mirrour is an old friend.	331	Proverbs		296
A mans discontent is his worst evill.	331	Proverbs		298
That is not good language which all understand not.	331	Proverbs		302
All is not gold that glisters.	331	Proverbs		306
He is not poore that hath little, but he that desireth much.	331	Proverbs		309
The absent partie is still faultie.	332	Proverbs		318
A little with quiet is the onely dyet.	332	Proverbs		327
In vaine is the mill-clacke, if the Miller his hearing lack.	332	Proverbs		328
and by that which is past, see	332	Proverbs		329
how that which is to come will be drawne on.	332	Proverbs		329
As the yeere is, your pot must seeth.	332	Proverbs		335
He that is not handsome at 20, nor strong at 30, nor rich at 40,	333	Proverbs		349
He that hath lost his credit is dead to the world.	333	Proverbs		357
He that hath no ill fortune is troubled with good.	333	Proverbs		358
He that owes nothing, if he makes not mouthes at us, is courteous.	333	Proverbs		362
The fault is as great as hee that is faulty.	333	Proverbs		369
Would you know what mony is, Gc borrow some.	334	Proverbs		374
This world is nothing except it tend to another.	334	Proverbs		382
Life without a friend is death without a witnesse.	334	Proverbs		385
Step after step the ladder is ascended.	334	Proverbs		393
An old friend is a new house.	334	Proverbs	V	400
Love is not found in the market.	334	Proverbs		401
Hee is rich enough that wants nothing.	335	Proverbs		403
One father is enough to governe one hundred sons,	335	Proverbs		404
the longer he stayes there, the fowler he is.	335	Proverbs		409
He that once deceives is ever suspected.	335	Proverbs		417

IS (cont'd)

	PAGE	TITLE		LINE
Who so once deceives is ever suspected.	335	Proverbs	V	417
Hee that respects not, is not respected.	335	Proverbs		427
He that measures not himselfe, is measured.	336	Proverbs		432
He that hath little is the lesse durtie.	336	Proverbs		436
Who is fed by anothers hand stays long ere he be full.	336	Proverbs	V	439
Where your will is ready, your feete are light.	336	Proverbs		448
When your will is ready, the feete are swift.	336	Proverbs	V	448
Woe to the house where there is no chiding.	336	Proverbs		450
Good is good, but better carries it.	336	Proverbs		454
Building is a sweet impoverishing.	337	Proverbs		459
The first degree of folly is to hold ones selfe wise,	337	Proverbs		460
The first degree of folly is to thinke ourselves wise,	337	Proverbs	V	460
The greatest step is that out of doores.	337	Proverbs		461
To weepe for joy is a kinde of Manna.	337	Proverbs		462
The first service a child doth his father is to make him foolish.	337	Proverbs		463
In the kingdome of a cheater the wallet is carried before.	337	Proverbs		465
In the kingdome of blind men the one ey'd is king.	337	Proverbs		469
Poverty is the mother of health.	337	Proverbs		472
Wealth is like rheume, it falles on the weakest parts.	337	Proverbs		475
The gowne is his that weares it,	337	Proverbs		476
Hope is the poore mans bread.	337	Proverbs		477
Vertue now is in herbs and stones and words onely.	337	Proverbs		478
Vertue now is in stones, herbs & words only.	337	Proverbs	V	478
Faire is not faire, but that which pleaseth.	338	Proverbs		492
There is no jollitie but hath a smack of folly.	338	Proverbs		493
Every one fastens where there is gaine.	338	Proverbs		496
For want of a naile the shoe is lost,	338	Proverbs		499
for want of a shoe the horse is lost,	338	Proverbs		499
for want of a horse the rider is lost.	338	Proverbs		499
A penny spar'd is twice got.	338	Proverbs		506
When a knave is in a plumtree he hath neither friend nor kin.	338	Proverbs		507
Health without money is halfe an ague.	338	Proverbs		509
He that tells a secret is anothers servant.	338	Proverbs		512
He that looseth is Marchant as well as he that gaines.	339	Proverbs		518
One enemy is too much.	339	Proverbs		523
Living well is the best revenge.	339	Proverbs		524
To a good spender God is the Treasurer.	339	Proverbs		530
Love is the true price of love.	339	Proverbs		540
A scepter is one thing, and a ladle another.	339	Proverbs		545
The shortest answer is doing.	340	Proverbs		552
The tooth-ach is more ease then to deale with ill people.	340	Proverbs		558
He that hath no good trade, it is to his losse.	340	Proverbs		560
He that is angry at a feast is rude.	340	Proverbs		564
When the tree is fallen, all goe with their hatchet.	340	Proverbs		566
Of faire things, the Autumne is faire.	340	Proverbs		572
Giving is dead, restoring very sicke.	340	Proverbs		573
A gift much expected is paid, not given.	340	Proverbs		574
A feather in hand is better then a bird in the ayre.	340	Proverbs		578
He is a foole that makes a wedge of his fist.	341	Proverbs		585
Valour that parlies is neare yeelding.	341	Proverbs		586
A flatterers throat is an open Sepulcher.	341	Proverbs		588
There is great force hidden in a sweet command.	341	Proverbs		589
The command of custome is great.	341	Proverbs		590
To have money is a feare, not to have it a griefe.	341	Proverbs		591
To have money is a feare, to want it is a griefe.	341	Proverbs	V	591
A good payer is master of anothers purse.	341	Proverbs		595
The thread breakes, where it is weakest.	341	Proverbs		596
God is at the end, when we thinke he is furthest off it.	341	Proverbs		598
Wood halfe burnt is easily kindled.	341	Proverbs		606
Every bees hony is sweet.	341	Proverbs		609
The slothful is the servant of the counters.	341	Proverbs		610
The slothful is the servant of the vertuous.	341	Proverbs	V	610
Time is the Rider that breakes youth.	342	Proverbs		615
In every Art it is good to have a master.	342	Proverbs		619
A disarmed peace is weake.	342	Proverbs		628
To bee beloved is above all bargaines.	342	Proverbs		631
To deceive ones selfe is very easie.	342	Proverbs		632
When age is jocond it makes sport for death.	342	Proverbs		637
Astrologie is true, but the Astrologers cannot finde it.	342	Proverbs		641
An idle head is a boxe for the winde.	343	Proverbs		651
A beane in liberty is better then a comfit in prison.	343	Proverbs		653
None is borne Master.	343	Proverbs		654
None is offended but by himselfe.	343	Proverbs		656
None saies his Garner is full.	343	Proverbs		657
He cannot be vertuous that is not rigorous.	343	Proverbs		664
A hatt is not made for one shower.	343	Proverbs		673
No sooner is a Temple built to God	343	Proverbs		674
Every one is weary, the poore in seeking,	344	Proverbs		678
Dry bread at home is better then rost meate abroad.	344	Proverbs		681
One father is more then a hundred Schoolemasters.	344	Proverbs		686
Knowledge is no burthen.	344	Proverbs		692
He is onely bright that shines by himselfe.	345	Proverbs		707
A valiant mans looke is more then a cowards sword.	345	Proverbs		708
A gentle heart is tyed with an easie thread.	345	Proverbs		726
To a child all weather is cold.	345	Proverbs		732
Where there is peace, God is.	345	Proverbs		733
None is so wise, but the foole overtakes him.	345	Proverbs		734
None is so wise, but that the foole overtakes him.	345	Proverbs	V	734
The best smell is bread, the best savour, salt,	346	Proverbs		741
The market is the best garden.	346	Proverbs		743

IS (cont'd)

	PAGE	TITLE		LINE
Night is the mother of Councels.	346	Proverbs		746
He that is fallen cannot helpe him that is downe.	346	Proverbs		753
Every one is witty for his owne purpose.	346	Proverbs		754
A great dowry is a bed full of brables.	346	Proverbs		758
The chiefe disease that raignes this yeare is folly.	346	Proverbs		765
One foote is better then two crutches.	346	Proverbs		769
He that once hitts, is ever bending.	347	Proverbs		785
Service is no Inheritance.	347	Proverbs		792
Hee that is throwne would ever wrestle.	347	Proverbs		797
Weening is not measure.	348	Proverbs		811
The best of the sport is to doe the deede, and say nothing.	348	Proverbs		812
In an hundred elles of contention, there is not an inch of love.	348	Proverbs		817
Warre is deaths feast.	348	Proverbs		822
No prison is faire, nor love foule.	348	Proverbs		829
No prison is faire, & no love foule.	348	Proverbs	V	829
Hee is not free that drawes his chaine.	348	Proverbs		830
The tongue is not steele, yet it cuts.	349	Proverbs		838
A white wall is the paper of a foole.	349	Proverbs		839
That is gold which is worth gold.	349	Proverbs		841
Poverty is no sinne.	349	Proverbs		844
A stone in a well is not lost.	349	Proverbs		845
Promising is the eve of giving.	349	Proverbs		847
He that endures is not overcome.	349	Proverbs		854
The Rich knowes not who is his friend.	349	Proverbs		865
A pleasure long expected is deare enough sold.	350	Proverbs		868
The Cow knowes not what her taile is worth, till she have lost it.	350	Proverbs		870
That which sufficeth is not little.	350	Proverbs		876
One houres sleepe before midnight is worth three after.	350	Proverbs		882
A Tyrant is most tyrant to himselfe.	350	Proverbs		888
Too much taking heede is losse.	350	Proverbs		889
France is a meddow that cuts thrice a yeere.	350	Proverbs		892
The wife is the key of the house.	351	Proverbs		904
The Law is not the same at morning and at night.	351	Proverbs		905
The least foolish is wise.	351	Proverbs		910
The chiefe boxe of health is time.	351	Proverbs		911
The first blow is as much as two.	351	Proverbs		913
The life of man is a winter way.	351	Proverbs		914
The way is an ill neighbour.	351	Proverbs		915
An old mans staffe is the rapper of deaths doore.	351	Proverbs		916
Life is halfe spent before we know what it is.	351	Proverbs		917
The body is more drest then the soule.	351	Proverbs		919
The body is sooner drest then the soule.	351	Proverbs		920
Conversation makes one what he is.	351	Proverbs		926
Wine is a turne-coate (first a friend, then an enemy).	351	Proverbs		929
Wine that cost nothing is digested before it be drunke.	352	Proverbs		932
Armour is light at table.	352	Proverbs		934
Every mile is two in winter.	352	Proverbs		949
The house is a fine house, when good folke are within.	352	Proverbs		952
The house is a fine house, when good folks are within.	352	Proverbs	V	952
The Citizen is at his businesse before he rise.	352	Proverbs		958
It is better to have wings then hornes.	352	Proverbs		960
An Oxe is taken by the horns, and a Man by the tongue.	353	Proverbs		967
No Church-yard is so handsom,	353	Proverbs		969
When a man sleepes, his head is in his stomach.	353	Proverbs		981
When one is on horsebacke hee knowes all things.	353	Proverbs		982
When God is made master of a family, he orders the disorderly.	353	Proverbs		983
He that is at ease seekes dainties.	353	Proverbs		985
Hee that tells his wife newes is but newly married.	353	Proverbs		987
Hee that is in a towne in May loseth his spring.	353	Proverbs		988
Hee that is in a Taverne thinkes he is in a vine-garden.	353	Proverbs		989
Hee that is a master must serve (another).	354	Proverbs		991
He that is surprized with the first frost	354	Proverbs		992
He that is not in the warres is not out of danger.	354	Proverbs		999
He that is his owne Counsellor	354	Proverbs		1001
A trade is better then service.	354	Proverbs		1005
To review ones store is to mow twice.	354	Proverbs		1007
Saint Luke was a Saint and a Physitian, yet is dead.	354	Proverbs		1008
If gold knew what gold is, gold would get gold I wis.	354	Proverbs		1012
Service without reward is punishment.	354	Proverbs		1015
If the husband be not at home, there is nobodie.	354	Proverbs		1016
An oath that is not to bee made is not to be kept.	354	Proverbs		1017
The eye is bigger then the belly.	355	Proverbs		1018
If you would bee at ease, all the world is not.	355	Proverbs		1019
A man well mounted is ever Cholerick.	355	Proverbs		1025
Every one is a master and servant.	355	Proverbs		1026
Nothing is to be presumed on, or despaired of.	356	Proverbs	D	56
Slander is a shipwrack by a dry Tempest.	356	Proverbs	D	135
Gentility is nothing but Ancient Riches.	356	Proverbs	D	1033
Ready mony is a ready Medicine.	356	Proverbs	D	1038
It is the Philosophy of the Distaffe.	356	Proverbs	D	1039
It is a sheep of Berry, it is marked on the nose	356	Proverbs	D	1040
the Catholick Religion is professed with greatest strictness).	357	Proverbs	D	1047
There is no heat of affection but is joyned	357	Proverbs	D	1050
The War is not don so long as my Enemy lives.	357	Proverbs	D	1051
Heresie is the school of pride.	357	Proverbs	D	1057
and a good subject, is incompossible.	357	Proverbs	D	1058
No naked man is sought after to be rifled.	357	Proverbs	D	1063
The life of spies is to know, not bee known.	357	Proverbs	D	1068
The noise is greater then the nuts.	358	Proverbs	D	1073
The world is now adayes, God save the Conquerour.	358	Proverbs	D	1075

IS (cont'd)

	PAGE	TITLE	LINE
Better is one Accipe, then twice to say, Dabo tibi.	358	Proverbs	D 1079
The death of wolves is the safety of the sheep.	358	Proverbs	D 1086
He that is once borne, once must dy.	358	Proverbs	D 1087
He that is afraid of leaves, goes not to the wood.	358	Proverbs	D 1092
All flesh is not venison.	358	Proverbs	D 1096
A City that parlies is half gotten.	358	Proverbs	D 1097
Cruelty is more cruell, if we defer the pain.	359	Proverbs	D 1110
To seek in a Sheep five feet when there is but four.	359	Proverbs	D 1112
Fortune to one is Mother, to another is Step-mother.	359	Proverbs	D 1118
There is no man, though never so little,	359	Proverbs	D 1119
is not altogether escaped.	359	Proverbs	D 1120
No love is foule, nor prison fair.	359	Proverbs	D 1122
It is good to have some friends both in heaven and hell.	359	Proverbs	D 1127
It is very hard to shave an egge.	359	Proverbs	D 1128
It is good to hold the asse by the bridle.	360	Proverbs	D 1129
The rage of a wild boar is able to spoil more then one wood.	360	Proverbs	D 1132
The mouse that hath but one hole is quickly taken.	360	Proverbs	D 1135
To play at Chesse when the house is on fire.	360	Proverbs	D 1136
The itch of disputing is the scab of the Church.	360	Proverbs	D 1137
Either wealth is much increased, or moderation is much decayed.	360	Proverbs	D 1139
There is a remedy for every thing, could men find it.	360	Proverbs	D 1142
There is an hour wherein a man might be happy	360	Proverbs	D 1143
A fair day in winter is the mother of a storme.	360	Proverbs	D 1145
He is a great Necromancer,	361	Proverbs	D 1158
A man is known to be mortal by two things, Sleep and Lust.	361	Proverbs	D 1159
To seek these things is lost labour; Geese in an oyle pot,	361	Proverbs	D 1163
The Philosophy of Princes is to dive into the Secrets of men,	361	Proverbs	D 1165
Here is a talk of the Turk and the Pope,	361	Proverbs	D 1173
There is no body will go to hell for company.	361	Proverbs	D 1177
The vertue of a coward is suspition.	362	Proverbs	D 1179
A man's destiny is alwayes dark.	362	Proverbs	D 1180
Every man's censure is first moulded in his own nature.	362	Proverbs	D 1181
Whatever is made by the hand of man,	362	Proverbs	D 1184
my meaning (dear Mother) is in these Sonnets, to declare my	363	Letters	10
is still true to you, and hath nothing else to answer your infinite	363	Letters	18
come a Horse-back, there is reason, that my desires should go a-foot;	363	Letters	23
and that the Horse is every way fit for me, and I will strive	364	Letters	1
and it is this, I want Books extremely;	364	Letters	10
What Trades-man is there who will set up without his Tools?	364	Letters	14
it is a most serious Case, nor can I write coldly in that,	364	Letters	15
This also is aggravated, in that I apprehend what my Friends would	364	Letters	19
it is their ordinary speech, and now let them make it good;	364	Letters	22
it is true (God knows) I am weak, yet not so, but that every day,	364	Letters	26
in our publick Halls, you know, is nothing but Fish and Whit-meats:	365	Letters	4
what is that to those infinite Volumes of Divinity, which yet every	365	Letters	13
the time when I desire this (which is now, when I must lay	365	Letters	17
The disease which I am troubled with now is the shortness of time,	365	Letters	30
be no kind of excellency which it is possible for you to attain to,	366	Letters	13
that is, be proud, not with a foolish vanting of yourself when there	366	Letters	16
not with a foolish vanting of yourself when there is no caus,	366	Letters	17
and it is the part of a poor spirit to undervalue himself and blush.	366	Letters	18
P.S. My brother is somewhat of the same temper, and perhaps a little	366	Letters	24
though your noble disposition is infinitely free, yet I had rather	367	Letters	6
It is high time now that I should be no more a burden to you,	367	Letters	12
Now his desire is to acquaint you with those passages of newes which	367	Letters	32
for though it is likely that the time after the Holydaye will bee	368	Letters	2
of which is doubted whether it have some further meaning.	368	Letters	18
There is a Spanish Lawyer hath written a treatise concerning	368	Letters	25
There is a Frenchman who writt a poem heere in England & presented it	368	Letters	30
denounced to him, told the King & so he is committed to prison.	368	Letters	37
only my comfort is that this is but an occasion for you to amplify	369	Letters	3
I could have come in person to thank you, but it is not possible;	369	Letters	11
it is no matter, for the Gentleman needs no incitation to love me.	369	Letters	28
you may understand what it is) is the finest place in the University,	369	Letters	30
you may understand what it is) is the finest place in the University,	369	Letters	31
be about 30 l. per an. but the commodiousness is beyond the Revenue;	369	Letters	33
is at all their Assemblies and Meetings, and sits above the Proctors,	370	Letters	1
is Regent or Non-regent at his pleasure, and such like Gaynesses,	370	Letters	2
yet you will pardon my haste, which is very great, though never so,	370	Letters	13
and now the only thing I long for, is to hear of my dear sick Sister;	371	Letters	7
Is it not too much for me?	371	Letters	10
I suppose she is not disposed to spend her eyesight on a piece	371	Letters	13
I shall understand that a Letter will be seasonable, my Pen is ready.	371	Letters	15
the next Friday it is tryed, and accordingly you shall hear.	371	Letters	17
or, that my love is as dumb as my papers;	371	Letters	25
yet my heart, a much better member, is alwayes with you:	371	Letters	27
and which is more, with our good and gracious God, incessantly	371	Letters	28
of all Comfort, who is not willing to behold any sorrow but for sin.	372	Letters	25
As the Earth is but a point in respect of the heavens, so are earthly	372	Letters	29
Happy is he, whose bottom is wound up and laid ready for work in	373	Letters	6
whose bottom is wound up and laid ready for work in the New	373	Letters	6
so that the best use of them is, having, not to have them.	373	Letters	24
how easily is that answered, when we consider that the Blessings in	373	Letters	27
What an admirable thing is this, that God puts his shoulder to our	374	Letters	17
so that it is not left to us to rejoyce or not rejoyce:	374	Letters	24
Let your moderation appear to all men, the Lord is at hand:	374	Letters	28
trouble not your selves, God is at hand to deliver us from all, or,	374	Letters	29
It is true there is a third sister, whom to receive were the greatest	375	Letters	23
greatest charitie of all, for she is youngest, and least looked unto;	375	Letters	24
is the encouragement of learning all the year after, except my cousin	375	Letters	28

JEWES (cont'd)	PAGE	TITLE	LINE
Wherefore if the Jewes live, all the great wonders of old live in	282	Priest 34	5
intended by God, that the Jewes should be his proof, and witnesses,	282	Priest 34	12
he meaneth not the very Ceremonies of the Jewes, which no Christian	320	Valdesso	1
like to that of the Jewes, which they added to their divine law.	320	Valdesso	3
The Jewes spend at Easter, the Mores at marriages, ...	329	Proverbs	242
JEWISH			
Thou who condemnest Jewish hate, ...	170	Self-cond.	1
Hath made a Jewish choice:	170	Self-cond.	9
JEWS			
The Jews refused thunder; and we, folly.	24	Ch.-Porch	449
The Jews accuse me with despitefulnesse;	29	Sacrifice	85
For as the Jews of old by Gods command	128	Bunch Gr.	8
The Jews.	152	The Jews	T
When it grew loose, the Jews did hope in vain	190	Ch.-Milit.	23
Such force as once did captivate the Jews;	195	Ch.-Milit.	192
But in the Jews and us deserveth tears.	196	Ch.-Milit.	228
fat Hogs among Jews, and Wine in a fishing net.	361	Proverbs D	1163
JOB'S			
then to take Jobs admirable Course, who sacrificed lest his Children	280	Priest 34	34
JOCOND			
When age is jocond it makes sport for death.	342	Proverbs	637
JOGS			
While this member jogs the other, ...	186	Dooms-day	5
JOHN			
Though David had his Jonathan, Christ his John.	17	Ch.-Porch	276
On Sir John Danvers.	208	J. Danvers D	T
Sir John Danvers' earthly part	208	J. Danvers D	9
know of the Doctrine, John 7. and assuring himself, that wicked men,	228	Priest 4	29
In brief, it is the body of Religion, John 13. 35.	244	Priest 12	14
even as John the Baptist squared out to every one (even to Souldiers)	277	Priest 32	23
so it may be a fruit of it, and an exaltation. 1 John 5. 14.	319	Valdesso	14
for I am enjoined to write to you by Sir John Danvers, to which mine	367	Letters	28
To Sir John Danvers. This Week hath loaded me with your Favours;	369	Letters	T
Herberts reasons for Arth. Woodenoths Living with Sir John Danvers.	380	Woodnoth	T
only for the success (as assistance of Sir Jchn) doe as David did:	380	Woodnoth	23
To John twentie shillings, all these are over and above their wages,	382	G.H.'s Will	25
Lastlie I besech Sir John Danvers that he would be pleased to be	382	G.H.'s Will	31
JOHN'S			
yerrow, melilot, and Saint Johns wort made into a salve; . .	262	Priest 23	6
thing to advize you now, & before you took Sir Johns affairs.	380	Woodnoth	8
JOIN'D			
Which then join'd with you still meet in my brest	44	H. Bapt.1 W	8
JOINED (see also joyn)			
no such earthiness in it, but it may very well be joined with Heaven;	370	Letters	23
JOINING			
My sinnes and I joining together:	166	The Flower	28
JOINT (see also joynt)			
JOINTURE			
No Earth can bee thy Jointure. For the sunne	211	Bohemia D	3
JOLLITIE			
There is no jollitie but hath a smack of folly.	338	Proverbs	493
JONATHAN			
Though David had his Jonathan, Christ his John.	17	Ch.-Porch	276
JORDAN			
Jordan.	56	Jordan 1	T
Jordan.	102	Jordan 2	T
JOSEPH			
wherewith also a carefull Joseph might meet.	281	Priest 34	27
Joseph knew her not, untill shee had brought forth her first borne	318	Valdesso	12
JOSEPH'S			
Josephs coat.	159	Jos.coat	T
JOSEPHUS'S			
Which Josephus's History confirmeth, and the continuance of which	282	Priest 34	29
JOSHUA			
And Joshua was to meditate therein Day and Night.	306	Valdesso	21
And Joshua was to meditate therein Day and Night. Josh. the 1.	306	Valdesso	21
JOURNEY			
Before thy journey fairly part with all.	13	Ch.-Porch	162
Those are at home; these journey still, ...	138	The Size	23
After so foul a journey death is fair, ...	142	Pilgrimage	35
Nor his long journey, nor his gout and furre.	195	Ch.-Milit.	198
Nor his long journey, nor his gout or furre.	195	Ch.-Milit. W	198
And to defray his journey from the east.	196	Ch.-Milit.	214
The Parson in Journey.	250	Priest 17	T
outlandish proverb, that Prayers and Provender never hinder journey.	251	Priest 17	15
which may be unto him as the sunne to a Travellour in his journey,	312	Valdesso	19
Prayers and provender hinder no journey.	330	Proverbs	277
Prayers and provender never hinder any journey.	330	Proverbs V	277
In a long journey straw waighs.	348	Proverbs	820
For a morning raine leave not your journey.	353	Proverbs	976
long in Latin, and my Lincoln journey hath set me much behind hand:	369	Letters	14
JOURNEYING			
And travell'd westward also: journeying on	193	Ch.-Milit.	104
JOURNEYS			
So now each Christian hath his journeys spann'd:	128	Bunch Gr.	10
In sports and journeys men are knowne.	334	Proverbs	399
Little journeys and good cost bring safe home.	338	Proverbs	502
JOURNIE'S			
but that every day, I may step one step towards my journies end;	364	Letters	28

	PAGE	TITLE		LINE
JOURNYING				
A journying woman speakes much of all, and all of her.	330	Proverbs		279
JOY				
Continence hath his joy: weigh both; and so	7	Ch.-Porch		17
To the one joy of doing kindnesses.	19	Ch.-Porch		330
To that one joy of doing kindnesses.	19	Ch.-Porch	W	330
A joy for it worth worlds. Thus hell doth jest	23	Ch.-Porch		412
If thou do ill; the joy fades, not the pains:	24	Ch.-Porch		461
If well; the pain doth fade, the joy remains.	24	Ch.-Porch		462
That so the broken bones may joy,	49	Repentance		32
Softnesse, and peace, and joy, and love, and blisse,	51	Prayer 1		9
It cannot be. Where is that mightie joy,	56	Temper 2		1
Scarce a good joy creeps through the chink:	60	Whitsunday		22
Sure thou wilt joy, by gaining me	74	The Starre		29
There is but joy and grief;	97	Afflict.5		13
My God, so temper joy and wo,	97	Afflict.5		23
I joy, deare Mother, when I view	109	Brit. Ch.		1
Then silly soul take heed; for earthly joy	111	Vanitie 2		17
Love-joy.	116	Love-joy		T
Of Joy and Charitie. Sir, you have not miss'd,	116	Love-joy		7
Joy, I did lock thee up: but some bad man	128	Bunch Gr.		1
Let me as well take up their joy, as sorrow.	128	Bunch Gr.		21
All creatures have their joy: and man hath his.	131	Mans medly		3
Mans joy and pleasure	131	Mans medly		5
Lay out thy joy, yet hope to save it?	138	The Size		17
Thy Saviour sentenc'd joy,	138	The Size		25
For we should count, Since the last joy.	138	The Size		41
Come, my Joy, my Love, my Heart:	156	The Call		9
Such a Joy, as none can move:	156	The Call		10
This spacious globe: Angels must have their joy,	158	Praise 3		21
My joy, my life, my crown!	168	a true Hymn		1
With onely this, My joy, my life, my crown.	168	a true Hymn		5
This worlds delights before true Christian joy,	170	Self-cond.		8
But still thy sweet originall joy	172	The Glance		13
Come ye hither all, whom joy	180	Invitation		19
Here is joy that drowneth quite	180	Invitation		22
Souls joy, when thou art gone,	183	A Parodie		1
Echo. Joy.	188	Heaven		16
Light, joy, and leisure; but shall they persever?	188	Heaven		19
Yet did a rogue with hope of carnall joy	194	Ch.-Milit.		149
For that, O Lord, with perfect joy	218	Psalm IV	D	25
with perfect joy be fill'd.	219	Psalm V	D	36
Yea, shout for joy for evermore,	219	Psalm V	D	37
it is an honest joy ever after to looke upon his well spent houres.	230	Priest 5		6
Parson preacheth constantly, the pulpit is his joy and his throne:	232	Priest 7		21
And for the Philippians made request with joy, ch. 1. 4.	234	Priest 7		14
both sutable to the joy of the day, and without hinderance to publick	236	Priest 8		19
as Sunday is his day of joy, so Friday his day of Humiliation,	241	Priest 10		37
hee receives, to want a good meal suting to the joy of the occasion.	245	Priest 12		9
and joy, and peace it administers against all temptations,	250	Priest 15		3
his Parish being all his joy, and thought) leaveth not his Ministry	250	Priest 17		25
and take as much joy in a straight-growing childe, or servant,	275	Priest 32		33
and the Angels minister to us their owne food, even joy, and peace;	280	Priest 34		7
and received with great joy, 1 Sam. 1. 18. though it came from a man	285	Priest 36		21
he add a tincture of private malice in the joy, and hast of acting	287	Priest 37		27
which excesse of joy neither could do me any hurt.	294	Cornaro		30
joy and peace have taken up their standing in my heart.	301	Cornaro		1
is not that which filleth the heart with joy and peace in believing;	309	Valdesso		2
acts of humiliation, and acts of confidence and joy;	312	Valdesso	V	24
held in so pretious esteem the word of God, as their Joy, and Crowne,	317	Valdesso		34
To weepe for joy is a kinde of Manna.	337	Proverbs		462
not but that I joy in your favours, but that you may see,	370	Letters		9
and the great joy of Madam, Your most faithful Servant in Christ	377	Letters		7
every good worke, to the joy of your ever loving brother, G. HERBERT.	377	Letters		27
& the great Joy of Your Brother & Servant in Christ Jesus GEORGE	378	Letters		27
all we and our whole Kingdome exult with joy, to bee united with that	442	Oration		14
JOY'D				
Then worldlings joy'd with all their store	218	Psalm IV	D	27
JOYE				
Into my hart with joye, giving more rest	202	love	W	17
JOYE'S				
Thou art joyes handsell: heav'n lies flat in thee,	58	H.Script.1		13
One of Joyes coats, ticing it with relief	159	Jos.coat		11
JOYED				
whereupon also I joyed exceedingly;	294	Cornaro		29
but you joyed me exceedingly with your relation of my Lady Duchess's	377	Letters		18
JOYES				
And winne thy selfe: Compare the joyes & so	7	Ch.-Porch	W	23
And meet them there. All worldly joyes go lesse	19	Ch.-Porch		329
And meet them there. All wordly joyes go lesse	19	Ch.-Porch	W	329
So many joyes I writ down for my part,	46	Afflict.1		3
Where joyes my fellows were?	46	Afflict.1		14
The measure of our joyes is in this place,	57	Employm. 1		11
But that from them joyes purle for ever	59	Whitsunday	W	22
Affront those joyes, wherewith thou didst endow,	71	Frailtie		19
The joyes of Company or Contemplation	89	The Pearl	W	29
When first my lines of heav'nly joyes made mention,	102	Jordan 2		1
When first my verse of heav'nly joyes made mention,	102	Jordan 2	W	1
Much lesse those joyes which trample on his head.	102	Jordan 2		12
I blasted all the joyes about me:	108	Home		44
My thoughts and joyes are all packt up and gone,	109	Home		69

JOYES (cont'd)	PAGE	TITLE		LINE
Left all joyes to feel all smart -	115	Dialogue		31
Thy joyes.	124	Gratefulnes		20
But as his joyes are double;	131	Mans medly		25
Joyes oft are there, and griefs as oft as joyes;	137	Familie		17
Modest and moderate joyes to those, that have	137	The Size		2
Great joyes are all at cnce;	138	The Size		19
Such a Heart, as joyes in love.	156	The Call		12
My joyes to weep, and now my griefs to sing.	159	Jos.coat		14
Who griefs in earnest, joyes in jest pursue;	167	Dotage		14
Worldly joyes to be a scourge:	178	The Rose		26
None but gross jcyes you move:	210	Paradox	D	34
Your feares in number more, your joyes are lesse.	210	Paradox	D	36
But joyes are stord for thee: thou shalt returne	212	Bohemia	D	55
Will pour full joyes to thee, but dregs to those,	213	Bohemia	D	65
he joyes, and he is sorry, he grieves, and he gloryes, never was	234	Priest 7		19
of the moment cf griefs here with the weight of joyes hereafter.	249	Priest 15		27
but to put bounds, and hoopes to their joyes:	280	Priest 34		29
much power or boldness as to oppose the hope of our Joyes hereafter!	372	Letters		29
of the heavens, so are earthly Troubles compar'd to heavenly Joyes;	372	Letters		31
therefore, if either Age or Sickness lead you to those Joyes?	372	Letters		32
or on the Joyes that are to come, you have strong preservatives	373	Letters		18
JOYFUL				
in that still joyful bee.	219	Psalm V	D	40
JOYFULL				
with as joyfull a countenance, as if he were to entertain some great	253	Priest 19		19
and joyfull, that hee is made conformable to his Master;	269	Priest 28		16
JOYING				
and joying therein, though he himself were with Saint Paul even	234	Priest 7		7
JOYN				
Joyn hands with God to make a man to live.	21	Ch.-Porch		376
Yet in their being joyn with one advise	121	Providence		146
My hands do joyn to finish the inventions.	122	Sinnes rd.		12
My hands do joyn to finish the inventions:	122	Sinnes rd.		13
that so the body may joyn in the grief, as it did in the sin;	279	Priest 33		27
To which joyn that of St. peter, Casting all your Care on the Lord,	374	Letters		15
JOYNE				
he refuseth not to joyne, that he may enlarge the glory of God	251	Priest 17		7
JOYNED				
This last rule joyned with the first, never fails.	267	Priest 26		5
There is no heat of affection but is joyned	357	Proverbs	D	1050
JOYNT				
was sore hurt, and also one of my arms and legges put out of joynt.	295	Cornaro		1
JOYNTLY				
Against the beasts: so joyntly bandying,	71	Humilitie		29
Against the beasts: so joyntly banding,	71	Humilitie	V	29
Whom we do all joyntly adore and praise,	78	Ang.&Sts.		17
JOYNTS				
My flesh and bones and joynts do pray:	109	Home		74
JOYOUS				
for respect to you, embrace all that is cheerefull, joyous, pleasing.	442	Oration		8
JUDAS				
Judas, dost thou betray me with a kisse?	28	Sacrifice		41
And is a Judas-Jew.	171	Self-cond.		18
admonition, cr reproofe, sell (with Judas) their Lord and Master.	226	Priest 2		38
as the Jewes and Judas did Christ, he may say as He did,	227	Priest 3		33
JUDAS-JEW				
And is a Judas-Jew.	171	Self-cond.		18
JUDG				
that none is careless before his Judg, and that the word of God shal	233	Priest 7		21
I offend the supreme Judg, in perverting that order which he hath set	265	Priest 26		11
If we would judg ourselves, we should not be judged;	280	Priest 34		30
Worldly learned men cannot judg spirituall mens actions,	317	Valdesso		5
JUDGE				
Judge not the preacher; for he is thy Judge:	23	Ch.-Porch		427
Thou art both Judge and Saviour, feast and rod,	83	Sighs & Gr.		27
And judge our selves. That light, which sin & passion	171	Self-cond.		20
So this flower doth judge and sentence	178	The Rose		25
Almightie Judge, how shall poore wretches brook	187	Judgement		1
And judge of things but Mediocritie.	210	Paradox	D	12
Cease then to judge calamityes	210	Paradox	D	25
be learned, ye that judge the earth:	216	Psalm II	D	26
The Lord shall judge the people all:	221	Psalm VII	D	29
is careless before his Judg, and that the word of God shal judge us.	233	Priest 7		21
in any Controversie, that they should resort to him as their Judge.	259	Priest 23		33
pin unjustly from the richest, he absolutely restores it as a Judge;	260	Priest 23		16
it is Faith and Infidelity that shall judge us now since the Gospell,	311	Valdesso		23
I remember the Fathers forbid us to judge of the doubtfull actions	316	Valdesso		12
But it is one thing not to judge, another to defend them.	316	Valdesso		14
A good Judge conceives quickly, judges slowly.	341	Proverbs		599
judge me then by those waters, and not by my ink, and then you shall	372	Letters		3
But I judge you not:	375	Letters		32
I have another judge, to whom I stand or fall.	376	Letters		8
JUDGE'S				
able to stand the Judges doom:	215	Psalm I	D	18
JUDG'D				
Most surely judg'd, make thy accounts agree.	24	Ch.-Porch		456
JUDGED				
If we would judg ourselves, we should not be judged;	280	Priest 34		31
and they are to be judged according to the outward fact,	316	Valdesso		18

JUST (cont'd)	PAGE	TITLE	LINE
when the other gives him just opportunity, by speaking any good,	286	Priest 36	23
So may a warre be just on both sides, and was just in the Canaanites	316	Valdesso	29
on both sides, and was just in the Canaanites and Israelites both.	316	Valdesso	29
when there is no caus, but by setting a just price of your qualities:	366	Letters	18
of monyes wherof he is to give as I know he will a Just account:	383	G.H.'s Will	25
JUSTICE			
On Justice was bestow'd the Foxes brain,	70	Humilitie	15
Justice.	95	Justice 1	T
Thy justice me most fitly payes:	96	Justice 1	7
And calling Justice, all things burn.	99	Decay	20
His ancient justice overflows our crimes.	128	Bunch Gr.	14
Justice.	141	Justice 2	T
O dreadfull Justice, what a fright and terrour	141	Justice 2	1
Why should I justice now decline?	141	Justice 2	23
Art thou all justice, Lord?	143	Complaining	11
And when Justice call'd for fears,	146	Praise 2	23
that do his justice slight.	222	Psalm VII D	40
with Daltons Justice of Peace, and the Abridgements of the Statutes,	260	Priest 23	2
Now it is a justice and debt to the Common-wealth he lives in,	262	Priest 23	15
And justice is the ground of Charity.	262	Priest 23	17
since there is a Justice in the least things, and for the least there	265	Priest 26	32
Besides, they are to read Books of Law, and Justice;	276	Priest 32	34
And the Parson is a lover of and exciter to justice in all things,	277	Priest 32	22
Secondly, justice in the Preservation of bounds:	284	Priest 35	4
Justice pleaseth few in their owne house.	334	Proverbs	396
JUSTICES			
a braver [better] Institution then that of Justices of the Peace:	276	Priest 32	9
JUSTIFIE			
Example and Care of them will justifie you both to the world and your	373	Letters	16
JUSTIFIED			
thou hast called us, thou hast justified us, sanctified,	290	Priest	3
The 98. Consid. about being justified by faith, or by good works,	319	Valdesso V	16
JUSTIFY			
or justify himselfe before God, by any acts or exercises of Religion;	312	Valdesso	15
JUSTIFYING			
that justifying faith, and the faith of miracles are divers guifts,	319	Valdesso	6
And miracle-working as it may be severed from justifying faith,	319	Valdesso	13
JUSTLY			
He sayes, in things which use hath justly got,	86	Lent	10
Justly complains, that somewhat is behinde	168	a true Hymn	14
and if it be taken away, though justly, they will murmur,	244	Priest 12	29
but he might have been justly put to death for it by the Magistrate,	316	Valdesso	25
He had done justly, and yet he had been punished justly,	316	Valdesso	27
and yet he had been punished justly, that is in humano foro &	316	Valdesso	28
Weigh justly and sell dearely.	338	Proverbs	500
Weight justly and sell dearely.	338	Proverbs V	500
beholding to those busnesses which justly excuse him from writing	367	Letters	30
and then you shall justly value Your most truly, most heartily,	372	Letters	4
your selves, wee justly feare that there is nothing here answerable	442	Oration	29
KAN			
Is clothing, meat and trencher, drink and kan,	120	Providence	127
KEEL			
Though windes and waves assault my keel,	151	The Bag	2
KEEN			
What edge so keen,	163	The Search	54
KEEP			
Which would throw me there, if I keep the round.	7	Ch.-Porch	30
Then keep such companie; make them thy allay:	15	Ch.-Porch	212
Keep all thy native good, and naturalize	21	Ch.-Porch	361
Let thy almes go before, and keep heav'ns gate	21	Ch.-Porch	383
And keep possession with thy grace;	39	Good Fri.	30
The Place, & keep possession still.	39	Good Fri. W	30
My soul bid nothing, but keep hir first wealth:	44	H. Bapt.2 W	13
No doore can keep them out:	53	Antiphon 1	10
But keep a standing Majestie in me.	56	Temper 2	16
Keep open house, richly attended,	59	Whitsunday	7
Peace mutt'ring thoughts, and do not grudge to keep	68	Content	1
Men therefore seek to have, and care to keep.	119	Providence	99
More skill in musick, and keep better time.	154	Glimpse	7
Yet let him keep the rest,	160	The Pulley	16
But keep them with repining restlesnesse:	160	The Pulley	17
And keep your measures for some lovers lute,	164	Grief	16
Dead to the world, keep house unknown.	166	The Flower	14
Giving the Church a crown to keep her state,	192	Ch.-Milit.	91
Onely the West and Rome do keep them free	194	Ch.-Milit.	157
Europe alone and Rome do keep them free	194	Ch.-Milit. W	157
But keep a constant Pole.	201	H. Commun. W	42
Nor yet thy eloquence here keep him still,	439	Walton 5	3
shall me in safety keep.	218	Psalm IV D	32
but to keep up with the Lord and Lady of the house, and to preserve	226	Priest 2	28
nor nigardly to keep, nor troubled to lose any worldly wealth;	227	Priest 3	17
that he will keep himself a virgin, he spends his dayes in fasting	237	Priest 9	18
and to keep them on in the sunshine, and noone of prosperity,	237	Priest 9	35
and not the fish, is to keep the fasting day naturally.	242	Priest 10	15
he cannot keep the last obligation, nor suffer others in his house	242	Priest 10	29
nor suffer others in his house that are so, to keep it;	242	Priest 10	30
but as desiring to keep the middle way between superstition,	246	Priest 13	24
that he may keep himself pure, and not be intangled in others sinnes.	248	Priest 14	24
live in health, not keep an uniform diet, but to feed variously,	267	Priest 26	10
that so they may know their duty, and keep their oath the better;	270	Priest 29	16

	PAGE	TITLE	LINE
KEEP (cont'd)			
if they keep and fodder well their cattel, they must have milk,	270	Priest 30	27
keep a fit proportion, shall receive little hurt from other excesses.	294	Cornaro	4
after live free from diseases, if he will keep such a course of life;	297	Cornaro	20
For if he should keep his former proportion, Nature, which is	299	Cornaro	33
Keep not ill men company, lest you increase the number.	331	Proverbs	314
Paines to get, care to keep, feare to lose.	353	Proverbs	975
be any truth in me, I find it little enough to keep me in health.	364	Letters	32
KEEPE			
Sacred Marble, safely keepe	208	H. Danvers D	1
he be unmarried, and keepe house, he hath not a woman in his house,	237	Priest 9	7
Keepe good men company, and you shall be of the number.	325	Proverbs	120
Who hath no more bread then neede, must not keepe a dog.	325	Proverbs	128
Praise a hill, but keepe below.	338	Proverbs	488
Praise the Sea, but keepe on land.	338	Proverbs	489
God keepe me from foure houses,	348	Proverbs	816
KEEPER			
or as David says, to be even a door-keeper in the house of God.	270	Priest 29	12
The marryed and house-keeper hath his hands full, if he do what he	275	Priest 32	20
built without a builder, or kept in repaire without a house-keeper.	281	Priest 34	19
A fat house-keeper makes leane Executors.	322	Proverbs	28
A fat house-keeper makes a leane Executor.	322	Proverbs V	28
KEEPER'S			
the house-keepers Family be so small, and his dexterity so great,	275	Priest 32	37
KEEPES			
keepes the imagination from roving, puts on the whole Armour of God,	238	Priest 9	4
hee keepes some young practicioner in his house for the benefit	260	Priest 23	34
hath read it, but keepes it by him, and reads it againe and againe,	310	Valdesso	28
The tree that growes slowly, keepes it selfe for another.	327	Proverbs	198
Feare keepes the garden better then the gardiner.	330	Proverbs	268
One sword keepes another in the sheath.	345	Proverbs	723
Hee that keepes his owne makes warre.	349	Proverbs	848
Death keepes no Calender.	351	Proverbs	908
The singing man keepes his shop in his throate.	351	Proverbs	918
Fear keepes and looks to the vineyard, and not the owner.	358	Proverbs D	1072
KEEP'ST			
Thou shutt'st the doore, and keep'st within;	60	Whitsunday	21
KEEPETH			
Christ keepeth now, who cannot fail or fall.	143	Holdfast	14
He keepeth his watch and ward, night and day against the proper	237	Priest 9	38
KEEPING			
Who by not keeping once, became a debter;	152	The Jews	5
And now by keeping lose the letter:	152	The Jews	6
therfore the Parson is very strict in keeping his word,	228	Priest 3	4
and fasting dayes were fully performed by keeping of the two former,	242	Priest 10	9
This is called keeping Gods watch, when the baits which the enemy	252	Priest 18	13
the rich in keeping, the good in learning.	344	Proverbs	678
KEEPS			
Who lives by rule then, keeps good companie.	12	Ch.-Porch	138
Who keeps no guard upon himself, is slack,	12	Ch.-Porch	139
Allows for that, and keeps his constant way:	73	Constancie	28
The help stands close, and keeps the fear in view.	119	Providence	88
And keeps thee present, leaving th' old	162	The Search	27
Flesh (though exalted) keeps his grass	201	H. Commun. W	38
This Anchor keeps my faith, that, me secure.	439	Walton 6	4
and by these hee keeps his body tame, serviceable, and healthfull;	237	Priest 9	26
He keeps his servants between love, and fear, according as hee findes	241	Priest 10	7
if he be in full health, keeps the three obligations, eating fish,	242	Priest 10	26
that he keeps his money for the poor, and his table for those that	243	Priest 11	8
The Countrey Parson, where ever he is, keeps Gods watch;	252	Priest 18	1
he keeps good Correspondence with all the neighbouring Pastours round	253	Priest 19	15
then he keeps good correspondence with some neighbour Phisician,	260	Priest 23	37
KENNELL			
Looke not for muske in a dogges kennell.	321	Proverbs	23
KEPT			
Your tears for your own fortunes should be kept:	31	Sacrifice	151
But Man hath caught and kept it, as his prey.	91	Man	20
But Man has caught and kept it, as his prey.	91	Man W	20
What thou hast kept,	147	Offering	29
Although thy heap be kept	154	Glimpse	23
Why kept she not her tears for her own faults,	173	Marie Magd	9
Why kept she not her tears for her own fauts,	173	Marie Magd V	9
In water kept, maugre the powers	213	L' Envoy D	8
that order is kept in the one, and peace in the other, without	236	Priest 8	24
humane soule being bounded, and kept in, in her sensitive faculty,	238	Priest 9	11
that the Church be swept, and kept cleane without dust, or Cobwebs,	246	Priest 13	8
and all kept sweet and clean, in a strong and decent chest,	246	Priest 13	18
the Parson questions what order is kept in the house, as about	248	Priest 14	32
other good books, how Sundayes, holy-days, and fasting days are kept.	251	Priest 17	24
In this course the order of the Catechisme would be kept,	256	Priest 21	5
built without a builder, or kept in repaire without a house-keeper.	281	Priest 34	19
hurt those bodies, which were kept in good order by a moderate Diet:	294	Cornaro	2
because in his meats and drinks he kept a due moderation;	294	Cornaro	8
whereof the one kept me well for many yeares;	297	Cornaro	4
that an orderly life is so hard a thing that it cannot be kept.	298	Cornaro	37
this I answer, that Galen kept it, and held it for the best Physick:	298	Cornaro	38
An oath that is not to bee made is not to be kept.	354	Proverbs	1017
Heresie may be easier kept out, then shooke off.	357	Proverbs D	1059
Letter gave me Earthly preferment, and kept Heavenly for your self:	372	Letters	34
Offices for which I came into the world, and must yet be kept in it;	373	Letters	10

KINDLE (cont'd)	PAGE	TITLE		LINE
that they kindle them rather to redeem the Dignity either from true	276	Priest 32		23
Litle stickes kindle the fire; great ones put it out.	332	Proverbs		323
KINDLED				
Wood halfe burnt is easily kindled.	341	Proverbs		606
KINDLES				
A litle wind kindles; much puts out the fire.	344	Proverbs		680
KINDLY				
that I take it exceeding kindly of you.	378	Letters		11
KINDNESS				
but that you have performed your kindness to the full, and that	364	Letters		1
KINDNESSE				
Kindnesse, good parts, great places are the way	19	Ch.-Porch		327
of Gods Love, and the unspeakeable riches of his loving kindnesse.	283	Priest 34		8
KINDNESSES				
To the one joy of doing kindnesses.	19	Ch.-Porch		330
To that one joy of doing kindnesses.	19	Ch.-Porch	W	330
doing kindnesses, but receiving none;	268	Priest 28		24
and hath nothing else to answer your infinite kindnesses,	363	Letters		19
KINDRED				
Thy children, kindred, friends upon thee call;	13	Ch.-Porch		161
Let them unto their kindred flie:	111	Vanitie 2		14
where his kindred, or other relations give him any authority over	251	Priest 17		16
For when they saw their parents and kindred snatcht away in the midst	291	Cornaro		9
when my brother and others of my kindred saw some great powerfull men	294	Cornaro		16
of the unthankfulness of kindred bredd up, (which generally is very	376	Letters		4
either it (in regard of the citty) or your self or your kindred.	380	Woodnoth		28
KINDS				
Is outlawd by himself: all kinds of ill	7	Ch.-Porch	W	33
the Parson is very carefull to avoid all the kinds thereof,	227	Priest 3		23
KING				
Think the king sees thee still; for his King does.	11	Ch.-Porch		122
(Love is a present for a mightie king)	20	Ch.-Porch		350
Love is a present for the greatest king.	20	Ch.-Porch	W	350
God then deals blessings: If a king did so,	22	Ch.-Porch		389
Why, Caesar is their onely King, not I:	30	Sacrifice		121
They bow their knees to me, and cry, Hail king:	32	Sacrifice		173
A king my title is, prefixt on high;	34	Sacrifice		233
Oh King of grief! (a title strange, yet true,	35	Thanksgvng		1
King of all Grief (a title strange, yet true,	35	Thanksgvng	W	1
Oh King of wounds! how shall I grieve for thee,	35	Thanksgvng		3
King of all wounds, how shall I grieve for thee,	35	Thanksgvng	W	3
What pleasures could I want, whose King I served,	46	Afflict.1		13
Ah my deare King! though I am clean forgot,	48	Afflict.1	W	65
My God and King.	53	Antiphon 1		2
My God and King.	53	Antiphon 1		8
My God and King.	53	Antiphon 1		14
Who plainly say, My God, My King.	57	Jordan 1		15
As Prince or King:	61	Praise 1		10
As those which rise from a huge King.	69	Content		24
Of the eternall glorious King.	76	Sunday		32
Of the Immortal onely King.	76	Sunday	W	32
Where ev'ry one is king, and hath his crown,	77	Ang.&Sts.		4
But now (alas!) I dare not; for our King,	78	Ang.&Sts.		16
But now alas I dare not; for my King,	78	Ang.&Sts.	W	16
Art thou, my blessed King? how suddenly	103	Prayer 2	W	2
The note is sad, yet musick for a king.	107	Sion		24
I fell, and cry'd, Alas my King!	142	Pilgrimage		27
King of Glorie, King of Peace,	146	Praise 2		1
Go spell and reade how I have kill'd thy King.	169	Dial.-Anth		4
Teach me, my God and King,	184	The Elixer		1
Moses pursu'd this: but King Solomon	190	Ch.-Milit.		21
King of glorie, King of peace,	199	L'Envoy		1
A slow behaviour to the style of king,	212	Bohemia	D	28
But I by God am seated King,	215	Psalm II	D	13
My King, my God, vouchsafe to hear	218	Psalm V	D	3
While Prince to Spaine, and King to Cambridge goes,	438	Lat.Trans.		1
For it is both a security to the King, who hath so many dispersed	276	Priest 32		10
Hee that trusts in the Kings word for any thing trusts in the King.	307	Valdesso		4
In the kingdome of blind men the one ey'd is king.	337	Proverbs		469
To go where the King goes afoot (i.e. to the stool).	356	Proverbs	D	1034
at the Indies, wherein they have satisfied the King reasonably.	368	Letters		8
which the King would so appropriate to himselfe, as that either his	368	Letters		10
this passeth in Spaine freely with consent of King & counsell.	368	Letters		29
who writt a poem heere in England & presented it to the King,	368	Letters		31
yet was seene lately neere the king, which some observing who heard	368	Letters		36
denounced to him, told the King & so he is committed to prison.	368	Letters		37
makes all the Orations, be it to King, Prince, or whatever comes	369	Letters		34
then the accesse of the Officers of the Catholike King?	442	Oration		10
KING'S				
At other times he is to travell over the King's Dominions,	277	Priest 32		7
Hee that trusts in the Kings word for any thing trusts in the King.	307	Valdesso		4
answering of this demand of the Kings these Agents pretend they have	368	Letters		14
KINGDOM				
blesse it in this thy own Kingdom, which thou hast made a Land	289	Priest		18
KINGDOME				
On which heav'ens kingdome arch'd doth stand:	75	Sunday	W	23
To this great kingdome, which thou now hast got,	77	Avarice		6
hath so many dispersed Officers at his beck throughout the Kingdome,	276	Priest 32		11
cutting out the Kingdome into Portions, which every yeer he surveys	277	Priest 32		7
that if the Kingdome of God be first sought, all other things shall	278	Priest 33		13

KINGDOME (cont'd)	PAGE	TITLE		LINE
and observation of Gods Kingdome within us, and the working thereof,	305	Valdesso		10
I doubt but if Abraham had lived in our Kingdome under government,	316	Valdesso		23
In the kingdome of a cheater the wallet is carried before.	337	Proverbs		465
In the kingdome of blind men the one ey'd is king.	337	Proverbs		469
Love rules his kingdome without a sword.	339	Proverbs		541
upon this he was forbid Court & kingdome, yet was seene lately neere	368	Letters		35
all we and our whole Kingdome exult with joy, to bee united with that	442	Oration		14
same order and habit, of which wee all in this Kingdome glorie to be.	442	Oration		21
KINGDOMES				
Children for kingdomes to thee; they shall live	212	Bohemia	D	42
and armies victorious, and retains and confirms kingdomes, cities,	297	Cornaro		10
KINGS				
To thee of all kings onely due)	35	Thanksgvng		2
Fathom'd the depths of seas, of states, and kings,	37	The Agonie		2
Yet say sometimes, God help poore Kings.	65	Ch.-mus.		8
But did bewitch both kings & many a nation	195	Ch.-Milit.	W	193
The Kings and Potentates of earth	215	Psalm II	D	3
Now therefore, O ye Kings, be wise,	216	Psalm II	D	25
with God, who weighs even childrens actions, 1 Kings 14. 12, 13.	239	Priest 10		29
2 Kings 2. 24. which though our Saviour reproved as unfitting for his	285	Priest 36		26
concerning the lawfulnes of kings resuming the donation of spirituall	368	Letters		27
KINSMAN				
A kinsman, a friend, or whom you intreate,	347	Proverbs		794
favour to mee in pardoning Your most indebted kinsman GEORGE HERBERT.	369	Letters		5
KISS				
O kiss the Son, lest he be wrath,	216	Psalm II	D	29
KISSE				
Judas, dost thou betray me with a kisse?	28	Sacrifice		41
To kisse those heaps, which now they have in trust?	65	Ch.-monum.		16
East and West touch, the poles do kisse,	163	The Search		43
Many kisse the hand they wish cut off.	330	Proverbs		283
KISS'D				
Hath kiss'd so long her painted shrines,	110	Brit. Ch.		16
KISSETH				
Hee that wipes the childs nose, kisseth the mothers cheeke.	355	Proverbs		1032
KISSING				
That ev'n her face by kissing shines,	110	Brit. Ch.		17
KITCHIN				
A little Kitchin makes a large house.	337	Proverbs		470
Silke doth quench the fire in the Kitchin.	356	Proverbs	D	1043
KITE'S				
To whirle the eyes too much shewes a Kites braine.	345	Proverbs		717
KNACK				
Hast thou the knack? pamper it not with liking:	16	Ch.-Porch		243
KNAVE				
If yee would know a knave, give him a staffe.	321	Proverbs		19
When a knave is in a plumtree he hath neither friend nor kin.	338	Proverbs		507
Better be a foole then a knave.	352	Proverbs		961
KNEE				
Subject to ev'ry mounters bended knee.	58	H.Script.1		14
My heart was in my knee,	80	Deniall		19
KNEEL				
Or feel his part, he would not cease to kneel,	33	Sacrifice		210
Or feel his share, he would not cease to kneel,	33	Sacrifice	W	210
When they shall bow, and kneel, and fall down flat	65	Ch.-monum.		15
or stand, or kneel, to do all in a strait, and steady posture,	231	Priest 6		26
and till they have learned them, makes them kneel by him;	241	Priest 10		4
resolves whenever he enters into a Church, to kneel down, and pray,	273	Priest 31		24
KNEELING				
Kneeling ne're spoil'd silk stocking: quit thy state.	22	Ch.-Porch		407
or halfe-kneeling, or any undutifull behaviour in them,	231	Priest 6		24
but man's unpreparednesse asks kneeling.	259	Priest 22		13
KNEELS				
Who in heart not ever kneels,	114	Businesse		37
But thy trumpet: then it kneels,	186	Dooms-day		10
and hee that kneels, confesseth himself an unworthy one,	259	Priest 22		15
KNEES				
They bow their knees to me, and cry, Hail king:	32	Sacrifice		173
All knees shall bow to thee; all wits shall rise,	54	Love 2		13
Both knees and heart, in crying night and day,	80	Deniall		13
Both hart & knees, in crying night and day,	80	Deniall	W	13
Down with thy knees, up with thy voice.	134	The Method		30
With doubling knees and weary bones,	148	Longing		2
My knees pierce th' earth, mine eies the skie;	162	The Search		5
as about prayers morning and evening on their knees, reading	248	Priest 14		33
KNELL				
That musick summons to the knell,	98	Mortific.		17
The Knell.	204	The Knell	W	T
KNEW				
Oh that I knew how all thy lights combine,	58	H.Script.2		1
O what a state is this, which never knew	65	Ch.-mus.	W	8
By that I knew that thou wast in the grief,	73	Afflict.3		2
And make his own? as if none knew, but he.	100	Miserie		14
And yet as though he knew it not,	102	Miserie		61
Better then you knew me, or (which is one)	129	Love unkn.	V	10
Deare soul, she knew who did vouchsafe and deigne	173	Marie Magd		13
Of stews and brothels onely knew the doores,	176	Forerunners		15
Many a rent and struggling th' Empire knew,	192	Ch.-Milit.		79
And knew it not, yet cleansed mee.	202	love	W	12
As if shades knew not Thee.	203	Even-song	W	12

KNEW (cont'd)	PAGE	TITLE		LINE
He knew that (the good instrument of God to bring women to heaven)	238	Priest 9		30
of all diseases, and were recovered of all by things that he knew;	278	Priest 33		31
or conditionally he prayed as man, though as God he knew the event.	315	Valdesso		11
Joseph knew her not, untill shee had brought forth her first borne	318	Valdesso		12
All things have their place, knew wee how to place them. . . .	334	Proverbs		379
If gold knew what gold is, gold would get gold I wis.	354	Proverbs		1012
if it had to others, yet to me it should not, for ought I yet knew;	370	Letters		24
to see a Sister, in a way I knew not, in the midst of much business,	371	Letters		3
and age, and knew none but one who could be no company to them.	375	Letters		15
KNIFE				
My mirth and edge was lost; a blunted knife	47	Afflict.1		33
Which now is but a pruning-knife.	122	Time		10
And with thy knife but prune and PARE, ...	133	Paradise		11
He can give little to his servant, that lickes his knife. . . .	349	Proverbs		846
KNIGHT				
he is to endeavour by all means to be a Knight or Burgess there;	277	Priest 32		10
KNITS				
Constancie knits the bones, and makes us stowre, ...	11	Ch.-Porch		117
Constancie knits the bones, and makes us sowre, ...	11	Ch.-Porch	W	117
KNIVES				
My thoughts are all a case of knives, ...	90	Afflict.4		7
KNOCK				
Without a knock it never shone.	68	Content		12
When sawcie mirth shall knock or call at doore, ...	136	Ephes.		13
Must let thee go, return when it doth knock.	154	Glimpse		22
Who will make a doore of gold must knock a naile every day. . . .	354	Proverbs		1004
KNOCKES				
Hee that brings good newes knockes hard.	348	Proverbs		824
KNOCKING				
Knocking at heaven with thy brow:	75	Sunday		10
There it stands knocking, to thy musicks wrong, ...	132	The Storm		13
Knocking at all doores, ever as she went.	190	Ch.-Milit.		30
KNOCKINGS				
Perpetuall knockings at thy doore, ...	124	Gratefulnes		13
KNOCKS				
of want of success consider how long God knocks at our harts,	381	Woodnoth		2
KNOT				
Which on the world a true-love-knot may tie, ...	88	The Pearl		16
Who art my life: dissolve the knot, ...	90	Afflict.4		22
Oh loose this frame, this knot of man untie!	109	Home		61
knot-grasse for the other, and that with better successe. . . .	261	Priest 23		35
who tying, as with a knot, both Indias to his Spaine, knowes no	442	Oration		11
KNOT-GRASSE				
knot-grasse for the other, and that with better successe. . . .	261	Priest 23		35
KNOTS				
Charms and Knots.	96	Charms & K		T
And ruffle all their curious knots and store.	97	Afflict.5		22
Who can these Gordian knots undo?	135	Divinitie		20
their Canon law and Decretals, knots of their own tying and untying:	319	Valdesso	V	29
KNOW				
Old courtiers know this; therefore set out so, ...	14	Ch.-Porch		185
But know, that nothing can so foolish be, ...	15	Ch.-Porch		206
Entice all neatly to what they know best;	18	Ch.-Porch		295
For they will pierce my side, I full well know;	34	Sacrifice		246
Alas, my God, I know not what.	36	Thanksgvng		50
Who would know Sinne, let him repair	37	The Agonie		7
That as each beast his cure doth know, ...	39	Good Fri.		19
Sorrow was all my soul; I did not know	47	Afflict.1	W	29
For sure when Adam did not know	53	H.Commun.		33
The starres were coming down to know	59	Whitsunday		11
O come! for thou dost know the way.	61	Grace		21
Teach me thy love to know;	63	Mattens		17
And wanton in thy cravings, thou mayst know, ...	65	Ch.-monum.		19
You know the way to heavens doore.	66	Ch.-mus.		12
I know it is my sinne, which locks thine eares, ...	66	Ch.-lock		1
I know it is my sinne, which stops thine eares, ...	66	Ch.-lock	W	1
I know thy parentage is base and low:	77	Avarice		3
Although then others court you, if ye know	78	Ang.&Sts.		26
Because this box we know;	82	Ungratef.		23
I know the wayes of Learning; both the head	88	The Pearl		1
I know the wayes of Honour, what maintains	88	The Pearl		11
I know the wayes of Pleasure, the sweet strains, ...	89	The Pearl		21
I know the projects of unbridled store:	89	The Pearl		26
I know the projects of unbundled store:	89	The Pearl	V	26
I know all these, and have them in my hand:	89	The Pearl		31
How know I, if thou shouldst me raise, ...	95	Submission		13
For this he wondrous well doth know	101	Miserie	W	45
But Man doth know	101	Miserie		59
Besides my physick, know there's some for thee:	106	Conscience		20
Know their home, and get them gone:	113	Businesse		4
Tempests are calm to thee; they know thy hand, ...	118	Providence		45
And none can know thy works, which are so many, ...	121	Providence		143
Let me once know.	124	Peace		2
Lookt on a servant, who did know his eye	129	Love unkn.		9
Better then you know me, or (which is one)	129	Love unkn.		10
Busie enquiring heart, what wouldst thou know?	144	Discharge		1
He that would know	145	Discharge		37
Wouldst thou raise devils? I see, I know, ...	155	Assurance		17
As if to meet thee they did know, ...	162	The Search		11
Which they that know the rest, know more then I.	169	The Answer		14

KNOW (cont'd)	PAGE	TITLE		LINE
So live and like, that I may know thy wayes,	185	A Wreath		10
Know them and practise them: then shall I give	185	A Wreath		11
What others mean to do, I know not well;	187	Judgement		6
Thou Echo, thou art mortall, all men know.	188	Heaven		3
And know you not, sayes Love, who bore the blame?	189	Love 3		15
O gratious Lord how shall I know	200	H. Commun.	W	1
Yet Thou art not so dark, since I know this,	203	Even-song	W	17
Which know not thee, suck in thy beames	203	Even-song	W	23
Know that much had been his worth;	208	J. Danvers	D	14
How know you that our teares proceed from woe	210	Paradox	D	15
How know you that the sighes we send	210	Paradox	D	19
Fairer & richer. Now wee know, what's thine,	211	Bohemia	D	18
For God himself vouchsafes to know	215	Psalm I	D	21
But know the Lord himself doth chuse	217	Psalm IV	D	11
he shall know of the Doctrine, John 7. and assuring himself,	228	Priest 4		29
do not know the Scriptures, because they feel them not,	228	Priest 4		30
Now if a shepherd know not which grass will bane, or which not,	230	Priest 5		31
on his auditors, with letting them know, that he observes who marks,	233	Priest 7		2
Oh Lord, I know that the way of man is not in himself, &c.	234	Priest 7		5
to know what herbs may be used in stead of drugs of the same nature,	261	Priest 23		29
who when they know a sin evidently, they commit it not.	264	Priest 26		11
that so they may know their duty, and keep their oath the better;	270	Priest 29		15
and it is a great advantage to know the practice of the Land;	277	Priest 32		4
and disarmed with sedentary lives, are to know the use of their Arms:	277	Priest 32		18
thinke this superstitious, neither know superstition, nor themselves.	284	Priest 35		29
known by common fame (and of these, those that know them, may talk,	287	Priest 37		13
and more, they may discover them to those that know them not:	287	Priest 37		17
they had a great desire to know the way of my life, and how I came	291	Cornaro		12
as all that know me, can testifie:	294	Cornaro		11
that I might know what great power a sober and temperate life hath	294	Cornaro		25
neither did I know well, what I did or said.	296	Cornaro		17
one by long experience may know the qualities of his own nature,	297	Cornaro		26
I know how inconsiderate that age is, and, though subject to death,	303	Cornaro		16
for I know that (setting casualties aside) I shall not die	303	Cornaro		25
If yee would know a knave, give him a staffe.	321	Proverbs		19
You cannot know wine by the barrell.	321	Proverbs		20
Without favour none will know you,	326	Proverbs		159
and with it you will not know your selfe.	326	Proverbs		159
with it you will hardly know your selfe.	326	Proverbs	V	159
Ever since we weare cloathes, we know not one another.	326	Proverbs		168
They that know one another salute a farre off.	327	Proverbs		185
Who must account for himselfe and others, must know both.	328	Proverbs		209
if you will know the truth of the thing.	332	Proverbs		331
Since you know all, and I nothing,	332	Proverbs		336
If you would know secrets, looke them in griefe or pleasure.	333	Proverbs		367
Would you know what mony is, Go borrow some.	334	Proverbs		374
There needs a long time to know the worlds pulse.	350	Proverbs		886
Life is halfe spent before we know what it is.	351	Proverbs		917
Yeeres know more then bookes.	351	Proverbs		928
Wee know not who lives or dies.	353	Proverbs		966
The life of spies is to know, not bee known.	357	Proverbs	D	1068
You know Sir, how I am now setting foot into Divinity, to lay	364	Letters		11
You know Sir, it is their ordinary speech, and now let them make it	364	Letters		22
You know I was sick last Vacation, neither am I yet recovered,	364	Letters		32
in our publick Halls, you know, is nothing but Fish and Whit-meats:	365	Letters		4
Letter in yours, for it was because I know your Lodging, but not his.	367	Letters		24
but, since I know I did not, and that your share continues,	372	Letters		16
and know, that if any of yours shou'd prove a Goliah-like trouble,	374	Letters		4
till I take some opportunity to let them know your love,	375	Letters		21
school-mistresse, and you know what those mercenary creatures are.	375	Letters		26
you know, is the encouragement of learning all the year after,	375	Letters		28
of monyes wherof he is to give as I know he will a Just account:	383	G.H.'s Will		25
by which we well know how to convince the sterne, and more austere	442	Oration		6
KNOWE				
Then you shall fully knowe	210	Paradox	D	28
KNOWES				
so that all his house knowes, that there is no help for a fault done,	240	Priest 10		35
where he knowes there hath been or is a little difference,	284	Priest 35		19
The Wolfe knowes, what the ill beast thinkes.	321	Proverbs		16
A foole knowes more in his house, then a wise man in anothers.	329	Proverbs		257
The Fox knowes much, but more he that catcheth him.	330	Proverbs		280
In the world who knowes not to swimme, goes to the bottome.	330	Proverbs		285
A discontented man knowes not where to sit easie.	333	Proverbs		345
Hee that knowes what may bee gained in a day never steales.	336	Proverbs		445
The wearer knowes, where the shoe wrings.	338	Proverbs		491
He that's long a giving, knowes not how to give.	338	Proverbs		494
He that knowes nothing, doubts nothing.	349	Proverbs		861
The Rich knowes not who is his friend.	349	Proverbs		865
The Cow knowes not what her taile is worth, till she have lost it.	350	Proverbs		870
None knowes the weight of anothers burthen.	350	Proverbs		880
Halfe the world knowes not how the other halfe lives.	351	Proverbs		907
Halfe the world knowes not how the other halfe lies.	351	Proverbs	V	907
When one is on horsebacke hee knowes all things.	353	Proverbs		982
knowes nothing sure but what hee hath laid out.	354	Proverbs		1001
A woman conceales what shee knowes not.	355	Proverbs		1031
God knowes, I have desired a long time, to doe the place good,	378	Letters		5
both Indias to his Spaine, knowes no limits of his praise, no,	442	Oration		12
KNOW'ST				
How know'st thou, but thy sinnes made him miscarrie?	24	Ch.-Porch		440
Thou and alone thou know'st.	183	A Parodie		25

LANGUAGE (ccnt'd)	PAGE	TITLE	LINE
There were no ill language, if it were not ill taken.	331	Proverbs	294
That is not good language which all understand not.	331	Proverbs	302
Faire language grates not the tongue.	347	Proverbs	799
The eyes have one language every where.	352	Proverbs	959
LANGUISH			
Let me not languish then, and spend	57	Employm. 1	13
Why do I languish thus, drooping and dull,	115	Dulnesse	1
To linger in me, and together languish.	159	Jos.coat	12
LANTERNS			
How with their lanterns do they seek the sunne!	27	Sacrifice	35
LANTHORNE			
To a great night, a great Lanthorne.	345	Proverbs	731
LAP			
Me thoughts a starre did shoot into my lap.	139	Artillerie	2
LARD			
Send not a Catt for Lard.	342	Proverbs	644
LARGE			
But that which shews them large, shews them unfit.	41	Sepulchre	9
Speak not at large, say, I am thine:	111	The Quip	23
Walkt by my self abroad, I saw a large	129	Love unkn.	25
Loose as the winde, as large as store.	153	The Collar	5
And coin large hopes; but, that I was deceiv'd:	155	Assurance	10
Since then my grief must be as large,	163	The Search	45
and large, that we should do whatsoever things are honest,	253	Priest 19	23
especially, the Statutes at large.	276	Priest 32	35
A little Kitchin makes a large hcuse.	337	Proverbs	470
LARGER			
And to use a larger measure	177	The Rose	3
LARGESSE			
Mercy in releeving the poor by a liberall distribution and largesse,	284	Priest 35	8
LARKS			
As larks, harmoniously,	43	East.wings	8
As larks, doe by degree,	43	East.wings W	8
And ever as they mount, like larks they sing;	107	Sion	23
LASH			
Doubles each lash: and yet their bitternesse	30	Sacrifice	126
LAST			
Beforehand, and anticipate their last houre.	21	Ch.-Porch	370
Drives all at last. Therefore I gladly trust	64	Ch.-monum.	6
At the last houre:	78	Ang.&Sts.	23
That it may dwell with thee at last!	92	Man	51
The last and lov'd, though dreadfull day.	108	Home	58
Alas! our murmurings come not last.	128	Bunch Gr.	18
For we should count, Since the last joy.	138	The Size	41
Thus we prevent the last great day,	171	Self-cond.	19
Wine becomes a wing at last.	182	Banquet	42
At Christs last coming, as his first did finde:	196	Ch.-Milit.	231
Who God & Saints and Angels loose at last.	203	Trin.Sun. W	17
and how every one profits, comparing this yeer with the last:	240	Priest 10	38
are much more essentiall to a true fast, then the third and last;	242	Priest 10	8
he cannot keep the last obligation, nor suffer others in his house	242	Priest 10	29
touching the last day, so neither touching the intermediate days	250	Priest 16	21
This last rule joyned with the first, never fails.	267	Priest 26	5
so will they last the longer, and when they depart, returne	280	Priest 34	29
The Doctrine of the last passage must be warily understood.	308	Valdesso	1
tell me what I dreamed last night.	332	Proverbs	336
both would last long.	344	Proverbs	697
Gamsters and race-horses never last long.	346	Proverbs	751
The first and last frosts are the worst.	352	Proverbs	954
if it were not begun on particular ends, it would last).	361	Proverbs D	1160
You know I was sick last Vacation, neither am I yet recovered,	364	Letters	32
At my last parting from you, I was the better content because I was	372	Letters	14
Your last Letter gave me Earthly preferment, and kept Heavenly	372	Letters	34
as to you deserving them, Wee at last salute you Masters of Arts;	441	Oration	27
poore duties wish, and vow unto you of the last a plenteous Harvest.	443	Oration	6
LASTLIE			
Lastlie I besech Sir John Danvers that he would be pleased to be	382	G.H.'s Will	31
LASTLY			
Lastly, by an oftèn urging of the presence, and majesty of God,	234	Priest 7	24
or Lastly, when the persons in difference are of a contentious	260	Priest 23	22
Lastly, if the contempt shall proceed so far as to do any thing	268	Priest 28	30
or lastly, in a Triumphant way, being glad, and joyfull,	269	Priest 28	15
Lastly, riches are the blessing of God, and the great Instrument	274	Priest 32	28
and lastly, the trouble of it:	276	Priest 32	22
Lastly, for those Afflictions of the Soul, consider that God intends	374	Letters	8
LASTS			
The morning Sunne never lasts a day.	334	Proverbs	375
Nothing lasts but the Church.	343	Proverbs	661
Curtesie on one side only lasts not long.	348	Proverbs	809
The ofspring of those that are very young, or very old, lasts not.	350	Proverbs	887
LATE			
Open for thee; or both may come too late.	21	Ch.-Porch	384
Open for thee; or they may come too late.	21	Ch.-Porch W	384
'Tis angels musick; therefore come not late.	22	Ch.-Porch	388
A hart can never come too late.	42	Easter W	28
May come too late!	111	Vanitie 2	8
As on a window late I cast mine eye,	116	Love-joy	1
Late when I would have something done,	134	The Method	22
The late-past frosts tributes of pleasure bring.	165	The Flower	4
The late-past frosts tributes of pleasures bring.	165	The Flower V	4

LAYES (noun)	PAGE	TITLE		LINE
Why are not Sonnets made of thee? and layes	206	Walton 1		5
LAYES				
And where his pleasure no injunction layes, ...	78	Ang.&Sts.		19
Begins at home, and layes the burden there, ...	86	Lent		8
Hee that dines and leaves, layes the cloth twice.	333	Proverbs		347
LAYS (noun)				
My Voice, that oft with foolish Lays, ...	214	Convert	D	11
LAYS				
not spent in them, he blesseth God, and lays it out as he sees cause.	240	Priest 10		12
and therefore he lays his discourse so, that he comes to the point	248	Priest 14		20
he presently lays hold of it, least the poyson steal into some young	252	Priest 18		5
when the baits which the enemy lays in company, are discovered	252	Priest 18		14
first, for covetousnes, he lays this ground:	265	Priest 26		4
Secondly, for Gluttony, The Parson lays this ground:	266	Priest 26		6
then God sends such weather, as lays the corn, and destroys it:	271	Priest 30		31
LAZY				
who cannot think me lazy, since I rode 200 mile to see a Sister,	371	Letters		2
L'				
L' Envoy.	199	L'Envoy		T
L' Envoy.	213	L' Envoy	D	T
LEAD (noun)				
The ballance distinguisheth not betweene gold and lead. . . .	342	Proverbs		629
LEAD				
The souldiers lead me to the common hall;	31	Sacrifice		153
Lord lead me in thy righteousness, ...	219	Psalm V	D	21
greatest ability of a Parson to lead his people exactly in the wayes	230	Priest 5		21
therefore, if either Age or Sickness lead you to those Joyes?	372	Letters		31
LEADE				
They leade me; urging, that it was not sound	28	Sacrifice		54
They binde, and leade me unto Herod: he	29	Sacrifice		73
They leade me in once more, and putting then	32	Sacrifice		189
Mine own clothes on, they leade me out agen.	32	Sacrifice		190
To heav'n alone both go, and leade.	135	Divinitie		28
If goodnesse leade him not, yet wearinesse	160	The Pulley		19
To leade them unto life and rest.	174	Aaron		4
the presuming upon it ought not to leade us to a disorderly life.	300	Cornaro		21
LEADETH				
and leadeth captive without any resistance, even in resistance,	269	Priest 28		22
LEADING				
Leading to this favour:	115	Dialogue		18
LEADS				
That leads the van, and swallows up the cities.	16	Ch.-Porch		248
Without thy help, leads us his way to Hell.	59	Whitsunday	W	16
Leads to the Quire above, ...	67	Ch.-floore		8
He leads me to the tender grasse, ...	172	23 Psalme		5
do any thing, that leads me to a sicknesse, to which I am inclined,	242	Priest 10		36
as they think fit, & see cause, or rather as Gods spirit leads them.	272	Priest 31		28
LEAF				
Or shall each leaf, ...	38	Good Fri.		9
His leaf shall never fade, and all	214	Psalm I	D	11
LEAFE				
Where all things have their leafe assign'd:	149	Longing		50
LEAGUE				
Either the league was broke, or neare it;	155	Assurance		11
And in this league, which now my foes invade, ...	156	Assurance		26
But also mine; as when the league was made	156	Assurance		28
LEAN				
Thus thinne and lean without a fence or friend, ...	47	Afflict.1		35
LEANE				
Most things sleep lying; th' Elephant leane or stand.	121	Providence	V	140
A fat house-keeper makes leane Executors.	322	Proverbs		28
A fat house-keeper makes a leane Executor.	322	Proverbs	V	28
Flies are busiest about leane horses.	323	Proverbs		73
The fatt man knoweth not, what the leane thinketh.	341	Proverbs		605
LEANING				
or gazing, or leaning, or halfe-kneeling, or any undutifull behaviour	231	Priest 6		24
LEANNESSE				
and my bodie spent with extream leannesse, and the season . . .	296	Cornaro		27
LEANS				
Most things sleep lying; th' Elephant leans or stands. . . .	121	Providence		140
LEAP				
Thy creatures leap not, but expresse a feast, ...	121	Providence		133
We must recoile a little, to the end we may leap the better.	359	Proverbs	D	1121
LEAPING				
Leaping the wall that parts	52	H.Commun.		14
Leaping with thee from sev'n to sev'n, ...	77	Sunday		61
LEAPT				
They leapt upon the throne;	70	Humilitie		22
LEARN				
Learn this, that hath old gamesters deerely cost:	14	Ch.-Porch		200
Learn this, it hath old gamesters deerely cost:	14	Ch.-Porch	W	200
My bodie to this school, that it may learn	65	Ch.-monum.		7
Deare flesh, while I do pray, learn here thy stemme	65	Ch.-monum.		17
O learn to stand in awe of him, ...	217	Psalm IV	D	15
or he takes care she shall learn it of some religious neighbour.	239	Priest 10		16
encouraging also the servants to learn to read, and offering to have	248	Priest 14		36
had delivered them to Satan, that they might learn not to Blaspheme.	286	Priest 36		2
and ever I learn somewhat which is worthy of my knowledge: . .	302	Cornaro		2
LEARN'D				
Therefore this care may be learn'd there, and then woven into	234	Priest 7		23

LEARN'D (cont'd)	PAGE	TITLE		LINE
but after that the Catechisme is once learn'd, that which nature is	256	Priest 21		25
LEARNE				
He that will learne to pray, let him goe to Sea.	323	Proverbs		84
He who will learne to pray, let him goe to Sea.	323	Proverbs	V	84
Learne weeping, and thou shalt laugh gayning.	325	Proverbs		127
By doing nothing we learne to do ill.	346	Proverbs		757
In doing we learne.	347	Proverbs		803
LEARNED				
be learned, ye that judge the earth:	216	Psalm II	D	26
that wicked men, however learned, do not know the Scriptures,	228	Priest 4		30
he is not witty, or learned, or eloquent, but Holy.	233	Priest 7		24
and till they have learned them, makes them kneel by him;	241	Priest 10		3
When once all have learned the words of the Catechisme,	256	Priest 21		1
do it, then he that is generally learned, and was never sick.	278	Priest 33		29
are not almost all the learned books that we have, written by their	298	Cornaro		33
I give my self to the reading of some learned book, and afterwards	301	Cornaro		6
that they are in the fairest place of this learned Citie of Padua,	301	Cornaro		11
the experience of so many yeares have learned to give way to Reason:	303	Cornaro		20
but still even to the most learned and perfect in them,	309	Valdesso		23
learned and perfect in them, there is somewhat to be learned more:	309	Valdesso		24
of authority (upon a fact) and there is a judgment of the Learned;	317	Valdesso		1
Worldly learned men cannot judg spirituall mens actions,	317	Valdesso		5
Hee that lives well is learned enough.	323	Proverbs		86
Hee who lives well is learned enough.	323	Proverbs	V	86
They favour learning whose actions are worthy of a learned pen.	357	Proverbs	D	1061
LEARNERS				
for all in his house are either teachers or learners, or both,	240	Priest 10		21
LEARNES				
Hee that learnes a trade hath a purchase made.	353	Proverbs		978
LEARNING				
I know the wayes of Learning; both the head	88	The Pearl		1
Learning was pos'd, Philosophie was set,	191	Ch.-Milit.		51
Learning from Greece, from old Rome statelinesse:	195	Ch.-Milit.		188
excelling in wit, learning, behaviour, and other vertues.	301	Cornaro		4
very apt and well given both for learning and behaviour.	303	Cornaro		5
renouncing the help of humane learning in the studying to understand	314	Valdesso	V	3
A handfull of good life is better then a bushell of learning.	321	Proverbs		3
the rich in keeping, the good in learning.	344	Proverbs		678
They favour learning whose actions are worthy of a learned pen.	357	Proverbs	D	1061
A man of a great memory without learning	358	Proverbs	D	1085
The love of money and the love of learning rarely meet.	361	Proverbs	D	1168
is the encouragement of learning all the year after, except my cousin	375	Letters		28
LEASE				
A new small-rented lease, and cancell th' old.	40	Redemption		4
Many a fault more then my lease will bear;	129	Love unkn.		20
LEAST (see also lest)				
Least gaining gaine on thee, & fill thy hart	13	Ch.-Porch	W	164
A stumbler stumbles least in rugged way.	15	Ch.-Porch		214
Laugh not too much: the wittie man laughs least:	15	Ch.-Porch		229
Deferre not the least vertue: lifes poore span	24	Ch.-Porch		459
To fruit or shade: at least some bird would trust	48	Afflict.1		59
Least want of Graces seeme thy thrift:	59	Whitsunday	W	18
O make mee wholy guiltles, or at least	66	Ch.-lock	W	9
From the least spot or thought of blame.	93	Unkindness		9
But there was none; at least no help without:	107	Home		15
He is some twentie sev'rall men at least	127	Giddinesse		3
At least those beams of truth, which onely save,	135	Divinitie		15
At least in lump: for such doth oft destroy;	138	The Size		27
And ev'n all Africk; would at least I might	140	Ch.-rents		28
Let him be rich and wearie, that at least,	160	The Pulley		18
And the least frown of thine is shown?	166	The Flower		35
Lesse then the least	182	The Posie		3
Lesse then the least	183	The Posie		11
Thy flesh the least that I request.	201	H. Commun.	W	44
Least that the Night, earths gloomy shade	203	Even-song	W	10
Wherfore he hath one Comment at least upon every book of Scripture,	229	Priest 4		28
at least all those which he observeth are most incident to his	230	Priest 5		34
and as difficult at least, as to be cloathed with perfect patience,	237	Priest 9		36
means to continue so, he doth at least, as much as hath been said.	238	Priest 9		25
and halfe at least of the government of the house, reserving so much	238	Priest 9		37
men to Piety, and is content, if at least so, they will become good:	244	Priest 11		1
and waits, least hee should determine Gods houre of coming;	250	Priest 16		20
least the poyson steal into some young and unwary spirits,	252	Priest 18		5
if not duly once a month, yet at least five or six times in the year;	259	Priest 22		20
or at least his Wife, of whom in stead of the qualities of the world,	260	Priest 23		30
at least in fundamentall things, the obscurity in some points being	263	Priest 24		4
whose natures, at least in the beginning, are dark and obscure:	264	Priest 26		8
since there is a Justice in the least things, and for the least there	265	Priest 26		32
in the least things, and for the least there shall be a judgment.	265	Priest 26		33
at least of those, who are apt to despise:	268	Priest 28		24
whereas now, of any place, they are least there.	275	Priest 32		36
Judges and Magistrates, to attend them, at least in their Shire;	277	Priest 32		3
or at least in that degree it ought to be, since he found himselfe	279	Priest 33		11
a wonder sent to Posterity, least they complaine of want of wonders.	282	Priest 34		35
For at least some of the Papists are come now, to what the Pharisees	320	Valdesso		6
The least foolish is wise.	351	Proverbs		910
They that hold the greatest farmes, pay the least rent	359	Proverbs	D	1100
be silent, least while I think I am modest, I wrong both my self,	364	Letters		7
my case unto you, which I think deserves the reading at the least;	364	Letters		10
or at least that the Hollanders should pay him tribute out of their	368	Letters		12

LEAST (cont'd)	PAGE	TITLE		LINE
greatest charitie of all, for she is youngest, and least looked unto;	375	Letters		24
LEASURE				
when they are at leasure, make others faults their entertainment	286	Priest 37		30
LEASURELY				
that he comes to the point very leasurely, and oftentimes,	248	Priest 14		21
LEAVE (noun)				
Give loosers leave to talke.	341	Proverbs		602
LEAVE				
All that they leave: this is flat povertie.	10	Ch.-Porch		106
Leave not thine owne deere-cuntry-cleanlines	21	Ch.-Porch	W	367
Where it is warmest. Leave thy six and seven;	22	Ch.-Porch		401
Betwixt my friends and me. They leave the starre,	28	Sacrifice		50
Betwixt my friends and me. They leave that starre,	28	Sacrifice	W	50
They leave thee.	40	Sepulchre		8
And leave th' earth to their food.	53	H.Commun.		40
I quit my interest, and leave it free:	94	Unkindness		17
That were I to leave all but one,	103	Prayer 2		21
There lay thy sonne: and must he leave that nest,	107	Home		19
Leave one poore apple for thy love?	107	Home		22
But when we leave our corn and hay:	108	Home		56
Who did leave his Fathers throne,	113	Businesse		17
Their masters flower, but leave it, having done,	118	Providence		66
I passe away and leave it dead?	135	Ephes.		6
Lord, didst thou leave thy throne,	150	Longing		61
On double pleasures: leave thy cold dispute	153	The Collar		20
Good men ye be, to leave me my best room,	176	Forerunners		7
But will ye leave me thus? when ye before	176	Forerunners		14
And wilt thou leave the Church, and love a stie?	176	Forerunners		22
But leave me to my load:	183	A Parodie		10
To pay our debts, and leave our ancient place	197	Ch.-Milit.		256
To pay our debts, and leave her ancient place	197	Ch.-Milit.	W	256
which when they leave the family, they carry with them.	241	Priest 10		6
of Christs Cross, or for any shame to leave that which is good.	284	Priest 35		33
first caused me to leave Intemperance, to which I was much addicted:	291	Cornaro		19
doth not bid them then cast away the word, or leave it off:	318	Valdesso		19
Leave jesting whiles it pleaseth, lest it turne to earnest.	324	Proverbs		104
After the house is finisht, leave it.	326	Proverbs		172
Marry a widdow before she leave mourning.	329	Proverbs		252
Although the sun shine, leave not thy cloake at home.	332	Proverbs		326
Give not S. Peter so much, to leave Saint Paul nothing.	346	Proverbs		763
When you enter into a house, leave the anger ever at the doore.	350	Proverbs		896
Wee leave more to do when wee dye, then wee have done.	353	Proverbs		972
For a morning raine leave not your journey.	353	Proverbs		976
done fairly, if they leave them a good portion after their decease.	376	Letters		15
then I leave to my servant Elizabeth her dubble wages given her,	382	G.H.'s Will		22
besides that which is due to her, to Ann I leave thirty shillings:	382	G.H.'s Will		24
LEAVEN				
And all our lump to leaven;	53	H.Commun.		30
a hatchet, a bushell, leaven, boyes piping and dancing;	257	Priest 21		12
LEAVES (noun)				
And leaves thee not a word;	106	Conscience		16
As Amber-greese leaves a rich sent	174	The Odour		2
For as the servant leaves not the letter when he hath read it,	310	Valdesso		27
He quits his place well, that leaves his friend there.	350	Proverbs		875
LEAVES				
Or cannot leaves, but fruit, be signe	38	Good Fri.		11
Unto a third, that ten leaves off doth lie:	58	H.Script.2		6
Hath still sow'd fig-leaves to exclude thy light:	83	Sighs & Gr.		16
Whose leaves first sheltred man from drought & dew,	84	The World		12
Trees after bearing drop their leaves for soil:	119	Providence		70
And bottome of the leaves: which when the winde	140	Ch.-rents		6
Like leaves about me: or like summer friends,	169	The Answer		4
That some will turn thee to some leaves therein	187	Judgement		8
Wert thou not born among the trees and leaves?	188	Heaven		5
Wert thou not born among the woods and leaves?	188	Heaven	W	5
Echo. Leaves.	188	Heaven		6
And are there any leaves, that still abide?	188	Heaven		7
And are there any leaves, which still abide?	188	Heaven	W	7
What leaves are they? impart the matter wholly.	188	Heaven		9
Are holy leaves the Echo then of blisse?	188	Heaven		11
when the Divell for a time leaves us, as he did our Saviour,	280	Priest 34		5
Hee that dines and leaves, layes the cloth twice.	333	Proverbs		347
He that feares leaves, let him not goe into the wood.	346	Proverbs		768
He that is afraid of leaves, goes not to the wood.	358	Proverbs	D	1092
LEAV'ST				
But, O my God, my God! why leav'st thou me,	33	Sacrifice		213
LEAVETH				
being all his joy, and thought) leaveth not his Ministry behind him;	250	Priest 17		25
LEAVING				
Leaving his blindnesse to mine enemies:	31	Sacrifice		135
Leaving his blindnesse to my enemies:	31	Sacrifice	W	135
Leaving within me sinne:	52	H.Commun.		6
And keeps thee present, leaving th' old	162	The Search		27
Tak'st all the Lodging, leaving none	200	H. Commun.	W	5
of the pulpit, and never leaving them, till he obtaine his desire.	245	Priest 12		14
leaving anger, and retorting, and revenge to the children	269	Priest 28		20
leaving the secrets of nature to those that have spare time.	361	Proverbs	D	1165
For any scruple of leaving your trade, throw it away.	381	Woodnoth		22
LEAZURE				
that I have not leazure to impart unto you some of those observations	365	Letters		32

LED	PAGE	TITLE	LINE
That led me to the wilde of passion, which	142	Pilgrimage	13
by what they understand, are best led to what they understand not.	228	Priest 4	20
that Countrey people are drawne, or led by sense, more then by faith,	254	Priest 20	31
which are two great lights able to dazle the eyes of the mis-led,	263	Priest 24	19
considering what an orderly life I had led for many yeares together,	295	Cornaro	7
I was led by the advice of Physicians, and the dayly importunitie	295	Cornaro	19
LEER			
And turn, and leer, and with a licorous eye	144	Discharge	3
LEFT (direction)			
Lay hands on all: they are thy right and left.	117	Providence	34
so that they neither decline to the right hand, nor to the left.	230	Priest 5	22
LEFT			
All that is left: this is flat povertie.	10	Ch.-Porch W	106
And cordiall left to repair mans decay:	31	Sacrifice	159
Alas! I did so, when I left my crown	34	Sacrifice	222
What have I left, that I should stay and grone?	109	Home	67
Christ left his grave-clothes, that we might, when grief	112	Dawning	15
Christ left his grave-cloths, that we might, when grief	112	Dawning V	15
Left all joyes to feel all smart -	115	Dialogue	31
I left on th' one, and on the other side	142	Pilgrimage	5
Hast thou left all things to their course,	149	Longing	44
Our cyens have purloin'd, and left you drie:	152	The Jews	2
Our sinnes have purloin'd, and left you drie:	152	The Jews V	2
Yet have they left me, Thou art still my God.	176	Forerunners	6
The shells of fledge souls left behinde,	186	Death	11
He left behinde him garrisons of sinnes	193	Ch.-Milit.	125
The waight was such they left the doctrins there	196	Ch.-Milit. W	203
He gave the Seale, and so left o're.	439	Walton 5	14
as if they were both but Alphabets and after a time to be left.	309	Valdesso	20
so that it is not left to us to rejoyce or not rejoyce:	374	Letters	24
side are the names of those to whome my deceased Neece left legacyes.	383	G.H.'s Will	2
LEG			
He that gives thee a Capon, give him the leg and the wing.	324	Proverbs	109
LEGACIES			
unto my deare wife excepting onely these legacies hereafter insuing.	382	G.H.'s Will	7
betweene them excepting some legacies of my deceased Neece which are	382	G.H.'s Will	14
LEGACYES			
side are the names of those to whome my deceased Neece left legacyes.	383	G.H.'s Will	2
LEGAL			
[according to the common and legal proceedings among men.]	316	Valdesso	28
LEGALEM			
that is in humano foro & secundum praesumptionem legalem,	316	Valdesso	28
LEGALL			
and to do such things of legall opposition either in the presenting,	263	Priest 25	23
LEGGE			
and onely commanded that my arm and legge should be set,	295	Cornaro	11
Were it not for the bone in the legge,	355	Proverbs	1020
LEGGES			
was sore hurt, and also one of my arms and legges put out of joynt.	295	Cornaro	1
Every one stretcheth his legges according to his coverlet.	325	Proverbs	147
A horse stumbles that hath foure legges.	346	Proverbs	740
LEGGS			
The thought hath good leggs, and the quill a good tongue.	342	Proverbs	612
LEGIONS			
Yet for twelve heav'nly legions I could call:	31	Sacrifice	155
LEGS			
That which had but two legs before,	158	Praise 3	10
Legs are but stumps, and Pharaohs wheels but logs,	158	Praise 3	17
that if all fail, yet I am able to stand on mine own legs.	370	Letters	10
LEIGHTON			
yet I shall ever put your care of Leighton, upon my accompt,	378	Letters	4
let this of Leighton Church the care, be amongst the chiefest also,	378	Letters	22
& has given order to the Tenants, at Leighton, to make payment of it.	379	Letters	9
I thanke you heartily for Leighton, your care, your Counsell,	379	Letters	13
pound whereof fifteene pound shal be bestowed uppon Leighton Church,	382	G.H.'s Will	30
LEISURE (see also leasure,leazure)			
Echo. Leisure.	188	Heaven	18
Light, joy, and leisure; but shall they persever?	188	Heaven	19
or if he have any leisure to look off from thence, he meets	267	Priest 27	30
that he have leisure to look out, the Village or Parish which either	276	Priest 32	1
Hee hath no leisure who useth it not.	351	Proverbs	897
I cannot yet find leisure to write to my Lord, or Sir Benjamin	370	Letters	29
LEMMON'S			
The lemmons juice and rinde cure mutually.	120	Providence	131
LEND			
Would he have gold? I lend it instantly;	93	Unkindness	12
Onely do thou lend me a hand,	95	Submission	19
Some to windes their bodie lend,	187	Dooms-day	21
Some to windes their bodies lend,	187	Dooms-day W	21
Then flesh did lend thee, back agen.	202	love W	18
LENDETH			
Lendeth to us, shall be our desolation.	197	Ch.-Milit. W	258
LENDS			
But lends to us, shall be our desolation.	197	Ch.-Milit.	258
He that lends, gives.	347	Proverbs	787
LENGTH			
Findes his crackt name at length in the church-glasse.	14	Ch.-Porch	198
At length I heard a ragged noise and mirth	40	Redemption	12
Sweeten at length this bitter bowl,	49	Repentance	19
Where now by Faith all arms are of a length;	50	Faith	27

LESSE (cont'd)	PAGE	TITLE		LINE
within lesse then one yeare (although it may seem to some incredible)	292	Cornaro		36
within lesse then a yeare I was not onely freed from all those evils	293	Cornaro		20
the end I got the victorie, to my great honour, and no lesse profit:	294	Cornaro		28
although after the fifteenth day it grew lesse and lesse.	296	Cornaro		21
(though they live ten yeares lesse then otherwise they should do)	298	Cornaro		27
Neither is this my pleasure made lesse by the decaying dulnesse of my	302	Cornaro		7
why should I be accounted lesse happie, or lesse my self,	302	Cornaro		34
or lesse my self, who being ten yeares older have made a Comedie?	302	Cornaro		35
the lesse they looke to their house.	329	Proverbs		250
All griefes with bread are lesse.	334	Proverbs		377
All griefes with bread are lesse, or Nor woe to want.	334	Proverbs	V	377
He that hath little is the lesse durtie.	336	Proverbs		436
LESSENS				
Shoots a bow short, and lessens still his stake,	13	Ch.-Porch		159
As the day lessens, and his life with it.	13	Ch.-Porch		160
Great almes-giving lessens no mans living.	327	Proverbs		190
LESSER				
Attract the lesser to it: let those fires,	54	Love 2		2
Lesser pains scape greater ones.	113	Businesse		14
They quickly go and come with lesser crime:	154	Glimpse		9
LESSON				
It blots thy lesson written in thy soul;	6	Ch.-Porch		9
Read that lesson to the grave.	187	Dooms-day		18
LEST				
Lest gaining gain on thee, and make thee dimme	13	Ch.-Porch		164
Lesse at thine own things laugh; lest in the jest	15	Ch.-Porch		231
Lest on their double-dark souls either shine:	31	Sacrifice		139
Lest sinne take courage and return,	39	Good Fri.		31
Yet lest perchance I should too happie be	48	Afflict.1		49
O brook not this, lest if what even now	71	Frailtie		17
O brook not this, lest if that, which just now	71	Frailtie	W	17
Spoil the good use; lest by that argument	86	Lent		29
Spoil our good use; lest by that argument	86	Lent	W	29
Heark and beware, lest what you now do measure	111	Vanitie 2		5
O heare betimes, lest thy relenting	111	Vanitie 2		7
But all I fear is lest thy heart displease,	147	Offering		13
Doth flatter power. Lest good come short of ill	161	Priesthood		40
Lest the enemie should winne?	181	Banquet		18
Lest want of aw	183	A Parodie		17
Lest at length they plead possession:	187	Dooms-day		16
Quitting his spear, lest it should pierce again	192	Ch.-Milit.		69
O kiss the Son, lest he be wrath,	216	Psalm II	D	29
Lest like a Lion swollen with rage	221	Psalm VII	D	5
any entertainment, lest he goe into the world, esteeming it absurd,	241	Priest 10		20
not the lesse, lest he cast their neighbours poverty on them also.	254	Priest 19		6
lest their quiet betray them (as it is apt to do) to a coldnesse,	280	Priest 34		17
who sacrificed lest his Children should have transgressed in their	281	Priest 34		1
fearing lest I should be overthrown, they were possessed with a deep	294	Cornaro		17
lest they take a greater quantitie of any meat or drink (though most	300	Cornaro		12
Now lest there should be any delight wanting to my old age,	302	Cornaro		37
but lest in any thing I forsake that Temperance which I have found so	303	Cornaro		34
Leave jesting whiles it pleaseth, lest it turne to earnest.	324	Proverbs		104
but take heede, lest you bee drowned.	326	Proverbs		167
Keep not ill men company, lest you increase the number.	331	Proverbs		314
Follow not truth too near the heels, lest it dash out thy teeth.	360	Proverbs	D	1138
Marry your daughters betimes, lest they marry themselves.	361	Proverbs	D	1171
LET				
If rottennesse have more, let Heaven go.	7	Ch.-Porch		18
Let not each fansy make thee to detest	7	Ch.-Porch	W	19
Let not each motion make thee to detest	7	Ch.-Porch	WC	19
Let not a common ruine thee intombe:	8	Ch.-Porch		45
Lie not; but let thy heart be true to God,	9	Ch.-Porch		73
Some till their ground, but let weeds chcke their sonne:	10	Ch.-Porch		98
And if Gods image move thee not, let thine.	10	Ch.-Porch		102
Let thy minde still be bent, still plotting where,	20	Ch.-Porch		337
Let thy mindes sweetnesse have his operation	21	Ch.-Porch		371
Let thy almes go before, and keep heav'ns gate	21	Ch.-Porch		383
We all are but cold suitours; let us move	22	Ch.-Porch		400
Let vain or busie thoughts have there no part:	23	Ch.-Porch		421
Let vain & busie thoughts have there no part:	23	Ch.-Porch	W	421
O let thy blessed SACRIFICE be mine,	26	The Altar		15
O let thy onely SACRIFICE be mine,	26	The Altar	W	15
O let this cup passe, if it be thy pleasure:	27	Sacrifice		23
Onely let others say, when I am dead,	34	Sacrifice		251
Who would know Sinne, let him repair	37	The Agonie		7
Who knows not Love, let him assay	37	The Agonie		13
Did set again abroach; then let him say	37	The Agonie		15
Then let each houre	39	Good Fri.		13
Or rather let	39	Good Fri.		17
O let thy blessed Spirit bear a part,	42	Easter		17
O let me rise	43	East.wings		7
Let me combine	43	East.wings		17
O let me still	44	H. Bapt.2		6
Let me be soft and supple to thy will,	44	H. Bapt.2		8
My flesh get on; yet let her sister	44	H. Bapt.2		12
If thou shalt let this venome lurk,	45	Nature		7
Let me not love thee, if I love thee not.	48	Afflict.1		66
O let thy height of mercie then	49	Repentance		13
Let all the world in ev'ry corner sing,	53	Antiphon 1		1
Let all the world in ev'ry corner sing,	53	Antiphon 1		7

LET (cont'd)	PAGE	TITLE		LINE
Let all the world in ev'ry corner sing,	53	Antiphon 1		13
Immortall Heat, O let thy greater flame	54	Love 2		1
Attract the lesser to it: let those fires,	54	Love 2		2
O let me, when thy roof my soul hath hid,	55	Temper 1		17
O let me roost and nestle there:	55	Temper 1		18
Let not thy higher Court remove,	56	Temper 2		15
Shepherds are honest people; let them sing:	57	Jordan 1		11
Nor let them punish me with losse of ryme,	57	Jordan 1		14
Nor let them punish me with losse of time,	57	Jordan 1	V	14
Let me not languish then, and spend	57	Employm. 1		13
Oh Book! infinite sweetnesse! let my heart	58	H.Script.1		1
O let thy graces without cease	60	Grace		3
Thy works nights captives: O let grace	60	Grace		7
Let grace work too, and on my soul	60	Grace		15
Let suppling grace, to crosse his art,	60	Grace		19
If all mens tears were let	62	Afflict.2		6
Which can let loose to a crown, and yet with pleasure	69	Content		15
Motion, and heat, let's take our flight	74	The Starre		18
O let me take thee at the bound,	76	Sunday		60
He that is weary, let him sit.	78	Employm.2		1
If thou hadst let us runne,	82	Ungratef.		3
In both let's do our best.	87	Lent		36
But thy silk twist let down from heav'n to me,	89	The Pearl		38
The elements are let loose to fight,	90	Afflict.4		17
Oh help, my God! let not their plot	90	Afflict.4		19
But let the poore,	93	Unkindness		13
Thy words were then, Let me alone.	99	Decay		5
Lord, let the Angels praise thy name.	100	Miserie		1
Man cannot serve thee; let him go,	101	Miserie		43
There let them shine,	101	Miserie		53
Let it not thee displease,	104	Obedience		4
O let thy sacred will	104	Obedience		16
Let me not think an action mine own way,	104	Obedience		18
Lord, let it now by way of purchase go.	105	Obedience		35
Let them love gold;	111	Vanitie 2		12
Let them unto their kindred flie:	111	Vanitie 2		14
Let me once know.	124	Peace		2
The clearest diamond: let them do their best,	126	Confession		29
Hath let thee out again:	128	Bunch Gr.		2
Gods works are wide, and let in future times;	128	Bunch Gr.		13
Let me as well take up their joy, as sorrow.	128	Bunch Gr.		21
Then let me want thy hand & ART.	133	Paradise		9
Let th' upper springs into the low	137	The Size		5
Thought to let out, the bleeding did you good,	140	Ch.-rents		14
Let not thy wrathfull power	144	Complaining		16
My inch of life: or let thy gracious power	144	Complaining		18
Let what will fall:	144	Discharge		9
Then bring thy gift; and let thy hymne be this;	147	Offering		24
Let not the winde	149	Longing		22
Then let me tell thee a strange storie.	151	The Bag		8
To let me bloud, and not restore	153	The Collar		8
Must let thee go, return when it doth knock.	154	Glimpse		22
Let us (said he) poure on him all we can:	159	The Pulley		3
Let the worlds riches, which dispersed lie,	159	The Pulley		4
Yet let him keep the rest,	160	The Pulley		16
Let him be rich and wearie, that at least,	160	The Pulley		18
O let not that of any thing;	163	The Search		33
Let rather brasse,	163	The Search		34
Be not Almightie, let me say,	163	The Search		51
That nature hath produc'd. Let ev'ry vein	164	Grief		4
Let forrain nations of their language boast,	167	The Sonne		1
Let losers talk: yet thou shalt die;	169	Dial.-Anth		7
Let foolish lovers, if they will love dung,	177	Forerunners		25
Let follie speak in her own native tongue.	177	Forerunners		27
Go birds of spring: let winter have his fee,	177	Forerunners		34
Let a bleak palenesse chalk the doore,	177	Forerunners		35
Then let wrath remove;	179	Discipline		17
Let the wonder of his pitie	182	Banquet		49
Let the wonder of this pitie	182	Banquet	V	49
Let wits contest,	182	The Posie		1
Let the graves make their confession,	187	Dooms-day		15
Let that be scann'd.	188	Judgement		14
Truth Lord, but I have marr'd them: let my shame	189	Love 3		13
Let not Sinne devoure thy fold,	199	L'Envoy		5
Choke him, let him say no more,	199	L'Envoy		11
Choke him, let him speak no more,	199	L'Envoy	W	11
Let mee but once the conquest have	202	love	W	19
Let the world reel, we and all ours stand sure,	439	Walton 5		9
And Paris garden. Then let there perfume	212	Bohemia	D	51
Let now my Eyes, my Voice, my Heart,	213	Convert	D	4
Let us in sunder break their bonds,	215	Psalm II	D	7
bad councels let them fall:	219	Psalm V	D	30
But let all those that trust in thee	219	Psalm V	D	35
Let them that do thy name adore	219	Psalm V	D	39
Then let mine enemie prevail	221	Psalm VII	D	15
Let him pursue and take my soul,	221	Psalm VII	D	17
yea, let him to the Clay	221	Psalm VII	D	18
prophecy, let us prophecy according to the proportion of faith;	226	Priest 2		5
or ministry, let us wait on our ministring;	226	Priest 2		6
he that ruleth, let him do it with diligence, &c.	226	Priest 2		7

LET (cont'd)	PAGE	TITLE		LINE
Let not Chaplains think themselves so free, as many of them do,	226	Priest 2		19
Neither let any think this a slight thing.	230	Priest 5		23
as to let the fervency of the supplicant hang and dy between	231	Priest 6		18
but even to let the world sinke, so they do their duty;	232	Priest 6		16
errand I come, let me hold my peace, and doe thou speak thy selfe;	233	Priest 7		35
Oh let us all take heed what we do, God sees us, he sees whether I	234	Priest 7		26
Let him communicate the thing often by prayer unto God,	237	Priest 9		5
unto God, and as his grace shall direct him, so let him proceed.	237	Priest 9		6
thanking of him, he exacts of them to let him alone, and say rather,	245	Priest 12		32
The first whereof is, Let all things be done decently, and in order:	246	Priest 13		27
The second, Let all things be done to edification, 1 Cor. 14.	246	Priest 13		28
And let Fernelius be the Phisick Authour, for he writes briefly,	261	Priest 23		5
especially let his Method of Phisick be diligently perused,	261	Priest 23		7
Do well, and right, and let the world sinke.	270	Priest 29		23
Or let him travel into Germany, and France, and observing	278	Priest 32		8
and not to let go the raines as soon as the horse goes easie.	280	Priest 34		15
So let them go, and find some poore afflicted soul, and there be	281	Priest 34		2
Let the weather be what it will, still we have bread, though	281	Priest 34		25
O let not our foolish and unworthy hearts rob us of the continuance	289	Priest		19
the one whereof was, He that will eat much, let him eat little;	295	Cornaro		34
Let no man here object unto me, That there are many, who,	300	Cornaro		17
Let not him that feares feathers come among wild-foule.	322	Proverbs		48
He that will learne to pray, let him goe to Sea.	323	Proverbs		84
He who will learne to pray, let him goe to Sea.	323	Proverbs	V	84
Let an ill man lie in thy straw, and he lookes to be thy heire.	330	Proverbs		271
Let none say, I will not drinke water.	331	Proverbs		310
He that hath no hony in his pot, let him have it in his mouth.	333	Proverbs		360
let him be wise in the punishment.	340	Proverbs		555
let him not put them on his head.	340	Proverbs		567
Ty it well, and let it goe.	342	Proverbs		642
let it not come betweene the spindle and the distaffe.	343	Proverbs		665
Let all live as they would die.	345	Proverbs		725
He that feares leaves, let him not goe into the wood.	346	Proverbs		768
He that hath not the craft, let him shut up shop.	349	Proverbs		860
Hee that would be a Gentleman, let him goe to an assault.	350	Proverbs		878
And therefore let it be sufficient for me, that the same heart,	363	Letters		17
it is their ordinary speech, and now let them make it good;	364	Letters		23
I have not deceived their expectation, let not them deceive mine:	364	Letters		24
Let there be no kind of excellency which it is possible for you	366	Letters		13
I beseech you let such thoughts as these, moderate your present fear	374	Letters		3
Let me commend only one place more to you (Philip. 4. 4.) St. Paul	374	Letters		20
Let your moderation appear to all men, the Lord is at hand:	374	Letters		27
till I take some opportunity to let them know your love,	375	Letters		21
let this of Leighton Church the care, be amongst the chiefest also,	378	Letters		22
let the first be the care of your Excellencies;	443	Oration		4
LETHARGICKNESSE				
Cures both a fever and lethargicknesse.	19	Ch.-Porch		336
LETHARGIQUE				
(as Hectique, Paralitique, Apoplectique. Lethargique).	357	Proverbs	D	1044
LETS				
Lets his soul runne for nought, as little fearing.	8	Ch.-Porch		59
Calmnesse is great advantage: he that lets	19	Ch.-Porch		313
Beleeves so too, and lets me go.	50	Faith		16
Lets his own ashes choke his soul.	79	Employm.2		10
His knowledge winks, and lets his humours reigne;	102	Miserie		62
we have nothing to do, lets go to the Tavern, or to the stews,	274	Priest 32		13
Prosperity lets goe the bridle.	345	Proverbs		736
A little lett lets an ill workeman.	346	Proverbs		755
LETT				
If rottenness have more, lett Heaven goe.	7	Ch.-Porch	W	24
You give us teares to wash them: lett those beams	44	H. Bapt.1	W	7
Lett Prayer help our losses,	53	H.Commun.	W	38
O lett thy grace, to crosse his art,	60	Grace	W	19
Lett in the Light to all their actions	185	The Elixer	W	23
Lett two of those alone	203	Trin.Sun.	W	15
O lett my Soule, whose keyes I must deliver	203	Even-song	W	21
A little lett lets an ill workeman.	346	Proverbs		755
I doe my part to them, lett them think of me what they will or can.	376	Letters		7
LETTER				
The letter of the word, find'st no fit heart	41	Sepulchre		19
Suck ev'ry letter, and a hony gain,	58	H.Script.1		2
And now by keeping lose the letter:	152	The Jews		6
Not half a letter to oppose	155	Assurance		23
It is a letter sealed, and sent, which to the bearer is but paper,	282	Priest 34		36
Considerations A Copy of a letter written by MR. GEORGE HERBERT	304	Valdesso		T
Indeed he that shall so attend to the bark of the letter,	309	Valdesso		30
For as the servant leaves not the letter when he hath read it,	310	Valdesso		27
The hearts letter is read in the eyes.	328	Proverbs		220
I understand by a Letter from my Brother Henry, that he hath bought	366	Letters		29
pardon my boldness of inclosing my Brothers Letter in yours,	367	Letters		24
This letter runs to you with much eagernes, for I am enjoined	367	Letters		27
and deliver your Letter, yet have I sent it thither by a faithful	369	Letters		16
I have sent you here inclosed a Letter from our Master in my behalf,	369	Letters		24
I pray Sir send the Letter you receive from him to me as soon as you	370	Letters		5
I understand by Sir Francis Nethersols Letter, that he fears I have	370	Letters		18
therefore I desire him to send me a direct answer in his next Letter.	370	Letters		25
when I shall understand that a Letter will be seasonable,	371	Letters		15
Your last Letter gave me Earthly preferment, and kept Heavenly	372	Letters		34
As I had written thus much, I received a Letter, from My Brother,	378	Letters		30
It is the whole amount of this letter, and therefore entertaine it	379	Letters		25

	PAGE	TITLE		LINE
LETTERS				
And dates her letters from thy face,	109	Brit. Ch.		5
To be the bodie and the letters both	116	Love-joy		6
Was in great letters set AFFLICTION.	129	Love unkn.		28
His letters were broke rudely up, believ'd	439	Walton 5		16
The same is to be observed in writing Letters also.	286	Priest 36		26
Neither eyes on letters, nor hands in coffers.	330	Proverbs		288
and write you freely to mee in your letters, for I am your ever	366	Letters		21
for the Orator writes all the University Letters, makes all	369	Letters		34
& for my power, I have sent my Letters, to your Brother,	379	Letters		19
LETTICE				
in like manner, raw lettice, fish, pork, sausages, pulse,	293	Cornaro		12
LETTING				
Then we will chide the sunne for letting night	81	Christmas		23
Letting, while one foot stept, the other stay	191	Ch.-Milit.		34
By letting in them both, pollutes her streams:	197	Ch.-Milit.		242
By letting in them both pollute her streams:	197	Ch.-Milit.	W	242
on his auditors, with letting them know, that he observes who marks,	233	Priest 7		1
a venture two remedies might be used, letting of bloud, and purging,	295	Cornaro		4
LETTS				
Who letts his wife goe to every feast,	336	Proverbs		434
LEVELS				
Strength levels grounds, Art makes a garden there;	192	Ch.-Milit.		87
LEVY				
by the same law they are to levy penalties for negligence in	270	Priest 29		5
LEWD				
But words suffice not, where are lewd intentions:	122	Sinnes rd.		11
LEX				
godly in some sort exempt from Lawes, for Lex iusto non est posita:	315	Valdesso		33
LIB				
in signing 100 lib. with her own hands (& promising to get her Son	379	Letters		2
LIBERALITIE				
Thou mightst make way for liberalitie!	103	Prayer 2		18
LIBERALITY				
and out of liberality, make her fruitfull in all good works.	238	Priest 9		33
LIBERALL				
and liberall disposition he preferred before beauty, riches,	238	Priest 9		28
some poore afflicted soul, and there be bountifull, and liberall;	281	Priest 34		3
Mercy in releeving the poor by a liberall distribution and largesse,	284	Priest 35		8
and the liberall of a farthing sixe pence.	328	Proverbs		211
but the liberall makes of a farthing sixe pence.	328	Proverbs	V	211
Poore and liberall, rich and coveteous.	332	Proverbs		339
The coveteous spends more then the liberall.	344	Proverbs		683
LIBERALLY				
he first gives himself liberally, and then incites them to give;	253	Priest 19		35
LIBERTIE				
And from old Rome the libertie of pleasure,	195	Ch.-Milit.		179
LIBERTY				
Many think they are at more liberty then they are, as if they were	266	Priest 26		19
The Parson in Liberty.	272	Priest 31		T
of God) stands fast in the Liberty wherewith Christ hath made us	272	Priest 31		18
This Liberty he compasseth by one distinction, and that is,	272	Priest 31		19
not to take the full compasse, and liberty of their Peace:	280	Priest 34		22
A beane in liberty is better then a comfit in prison.	343	Proverbs		653
Hee that marries for wealth sells his liberty.	347	Proverbs		784
LIBRARY				
The Parson's Library.	278	Priest 33		T
The Countrey Parson's Library is a holy Life:	278	Priest 33		11
LICK				
With these two poore ones lick up all the dew,	140	Ch.-rents		29
LICKES				
He can give little to his servant, that lickes his knife.	349	Proverbs		846
LICKS				
The dog that licks ashes, trust not with meale.	334	Proverbs		389
Hee payes too deare for honey that licks it from thorns.	350	Proverbs	V	880
LICOROUS				
And turn, and leer, and with a licorous eye	144	Discharge		3
or for quality is licorous after dainties, is a glutton;	266	Priest 26		8
LIDGER				
Thy praise too much? thou art heav'ns Lidger here,	58	H.Script.1		11
Thy praise enough? thou art heav'ns Lidger here,	58	H.Script.1	W	11
LIE (noun)				
Lie not; but let thy heart be true to God,	9	Ch.-Porch		73
Though a lie be well drest, it is ever overcome.	325	Proverbs		133
He that trusts in a lie, shall perish in truth.	340	Proverbs		569
He that trusts in a lie, shall perish by the truth.	340	Proverbs	V	569
LIE				
One box doth lie both ink and sinne:	39	Good Fri.		24
Unto a third, that ten leaves off doth lie:	58	H.Script.2		6
Mark how the fire in flints doth quiet lie,	68	Content		9
Mark how the fire in Flint doth quiet lie,	68	Content	W	9
A box where sweets compacted lie;	88	Vertue		10
The help did in thy bosome lie.	107	Home		16
Of dressing, that her hair doth lie	110	Brit. Ch.		20
That vertues lie therein,	125	Peace	V	34
Let the worlds riches, which dispersed lie,	159	The Pulley		4
There will I lie, untill my Maker seek	161	Priesthood		37
To look upon me, who before did lie	171	The Glance		3
Therefore will I lie down in peace,	218	Psalm IV	D	29
Honour and profit lie not in one sacke.	328	Proverbs		232
Let an ill man lie in thy straw, and he lookes to be thy heire.	330	Proverbs		271

LIE (cont'd)	PAGE	TITLE		LINE
not well, I had rather the fault should lie on me, than on them;	364	Letters		29
also I ride to Newmarket, and there lie a day or two for fresh Air;	365	Letters		7
LIEN				
If blisse had lien in art or strength,	50	Faith		25
LIES (noun)				
Cowards tell lies, and those that fear the rod;	9	Ch.-Porch		75
The stormie working soul spits lies and froth.	9	Ch.-Porch		76
In this world of sugred lies,	177	The Rose		2
How long will ye seek after lies,	217	Psalm IV	D	9
LIES				
Write on the others, Here lies such a one.	20	Ch.-Porch		342
Thou art joyes handsell: heav'n lies flat in thee,	58	H.Script.1		13
My stock lies dead, and no increase	60	Grace		1
He lies warm, and without adventure.	69	Content		20
The burden of the week lies there,	75	Sunday		12
On which heav'ns palace arched lies:	75	Sunday		23
Poore silly soul, whose hope and head lies low;	111	Vanitie 2		1
Finde where it lies.	116	Dulnesse		24
That vertue lies therein,	125	Peace		34
Reason triumphs, and faith lies by.	134	Divinitie		8
Lies all the yeare,	150	Longing		81
And therein my answer lies.	177	The Rose		16
Sweetly there indeed it lies,	178	The Rose		23
The beauty lies in the discovery.	206	Walton 2		14
but hee that sits, or lies, puts up to an Apostle:	259	Priest 22		17
or living, for all the point lies in believing or not believing.	311	Valdesso		30
The Germans wit lies in his fingers.	322	Proverbs	V	36
In spending lies the advantage.	323	Proverbs		85
Hee that lies long a bed, his estate feeles it.	327	Proverbs		179
He that makes his bed ill, lies there.	332	Proverbs		340
Hee that lies with the dogs, riseth with fleas.	332	Proverbs		343
Reason lies betweene the spurre and the bridle.	345	Proverbs		711
Halfe the world knowes not how the other halfe lies.	351	Proverbs	V	907
LIFE				
If they dare try, a glorious life, or grave.	10	Ch.-Porch		90
As the day lessens, and his life with it.	13	Ch.-Porch		160
Give one estate, as one life. None is bound	17	Ch.-Porch		285
Of life, just at the gates of life and blisse?	28	Sacrifice		43
'Gainst him, who seeks not life, but is the meek	28	Sacrifice		58
Putting my life among their sinnes and fears,	30	Sacrifice		106
All spite in one, counting my life their losse,	33	Sacrifice		194
The tree of life to all, but onely me:	33	Sacrifice		203
Of my whole life one grief devoure;	39	Good Fri.		14
His life may make thee gold, and much more just.	41	Easter		6
And then this day, my life shall date.	42	Easter	W	30
You taught the book of life my name, that so	44	H. Bapt.1		12
When I got health, thou took'st away my life,	47	Afflict.1		31
Before I had the power to change my life.	47	Afflict.1		42
Whose life still pressing	48	Repentance		4
If life be told	48	Repentance		11
From what life feeleth, Adams fall.	48	Repentance		12
A life as barren to thy praise,	57	Employm. 1		14
As is the dust, to which that life doth tend,	57	Employm. 1		15
Such are thy secrets, which my life makes good,	58	H.Script.2		9
Thou Lord of life; since thy one death for me	62	Afflict.2		2
Making thy life to shine within	67	Windows		7
Doctrine and life, colours and light, in one	68	Windows		11
The brags of life are but a nine dayes wonder;	69	Content		21
But since thy breath gave me both life and shape,	73	Afflict.3		7
Thy life on earth was grief, and thou art still	73	Afflict.3		13
The Sundaies of mans life,	76	Sunday		29
Life is a businesse, not good cheer;	79	Employm.2		16
For thou hast life and death at thy command;	83	Sighs & Gr.		26
Coloss. 3. 3. Our life is hid with Christ in God.	84	Coloss.		T
That Life hath with the sun a double motion.	84	Coloss.		2
One life is wrapt In flesh, and tends to earth.	84	Coloss.		5
That he might save his life, and also hers,	85	Vanitie 1		12
To finde out death, but missest life at hand.	86	Vanitie 1		28
To sell my life unto my friends or foes:	88	The Pearl		19
Nothing performs the task of life:	90	Afflict.4		16
Who art my life: dissolve the knot,	90	Afflict.4		22
Life.	94	Life		T
My life within this band.	94	Life		3
But when I mark my life and praise,	96	Justice 1		6
That all these dyings may be life in death.	99	Mortific.		36
They make his life a constant blot,	102	Miserie		63
Had he life, or had he none?	113	Businesse		19
Thou art my lovelinesse, my life, my light,	115	Dulnesse		9
Who above all things lov'd this life;	122	Time		8
And this is that makes life so long,	123	Time		19
His life frcm foes.	125	Peace		26
To this life things of sense	131	Mans medly		7
My inch of life: or let thy gracious power	144	Complaining		18
Thy life is Gods, thy time to come is gone,	144	Discharge		11
Thy businesse his, and in thy life partake:	144	Discharge		18
Here he gave up his life to pay our score.	151	The Bag		24
My lines and life are free; free as the rode,	153	The Collar		4
Come, my Way, my Truth, my Life:	156	The Call		1
And such a Life, as killeth death.	156	The Call		4
My joy, my life, my crown!	168	a true Hymn		1

LIFE (cont'd)	PAGE	TITLE		LINE
With onely this, My joy, my life, my crown.	168	a true Hymn		5
For who can look for lesse, that loveth Life. / Strife.	170	Water-crs.		5
To leade them unto life and rest.	174	Aaron		4
Should all my life employ, and busie me.	175	The Odour		30
And take up my lines and life:	182	Banquet		51
And then what life I have,	183	A Parodie		21
Wherein I die, not live: for life is straight,	185	A Wreath		5
After the losse of life and sense,	186	Death		7
Except life catch & hold those fast.	202	Trin.Sun.	W	10
From all that persecute my life,	220	Psalm VII	D	3
Tread down my life, and in the dust	221	Psalm VII	D	19
The Countrey PARSON HIS CHARACTER, AND Rule of Holy Life.	223	Priest		T
which Christ did, and after his manner, both for Doctrine and Life.	225	Priest 1		19
The Parsons Life.	227	Priest 3		T
The Countrey Parson is exceeding exact in his Life, being holy,	227	Priest 3		1
And because the two highest points of Life, wherein a Christian is	227	Priest 3		3
but orders his Life in such a fashion, that when death takes him,	227	Priest 3		32
do much esteem their word, it being the Life of buying, and selling,	228	Priest 3		3
the storehouse and magazene of life and comfort, the holy Scriptures.	228	Priest 4		22
Precepts for life, Doctrines for knowledge, Examples	228	Priest 4		24
he useth are first, a holy Life, remembring what his Master saith,	228	Priest 4		28
the storehouse of his Sermons, and which he preacheth all his Life;	230	Priest 5		2
The Parson's state of Life.	236	Priest 9		T
day against the proper and peculiar temptations of his state of Life,	238	Priest 9		2
The life of faith, James 2. 26.	244	Priest 12		11
The blessings of this life, Proverbs 22. 9. Psalm 41. 2.	244	Priest 12		12
parts his Living, and life among them, giving some corn outright,	245	Priest 12		10
as concerning this life, who hath promised, that Godlinesse shall be	254	Priest 20		19
turning it to reformation of life, by pithy and lively exhortations;	255	Priest 21		7
the one, a strict religious life;	263	Priest 24		16
be wanting to them in Doctrine, to whom he is so gracious in Life.	263	Priest 24		21
of their generall Schoole rules ever to the smallest actions of Life;	266	Priest 26		1
This he procures, first by his holy and unblameable life;	268	Priest 28		21
The Countrey Parson's Library is a holy Life:	278	Priest 33		11
Neither is this true onely in the military state of a Christian life,	279	Priest 33		3
and turning unto God in truth of heart, and newnesse of life:	279	Priest 33		25
that there is a double state of a Christian even in this Life,	280	Priest 34		2
that it seems the very life and substance of Conversation,	287	Priest 37		9
that takes away the life of the condemned, except besides his office,	287	Priest 37		26
And as malefactors may lose & forfeit their goods, or life;	287	Priest 37		32
then did the Lord of life, unable of himselfe to die, contrive to do	288	Priest		27
the ear to the heart, from the heart to the life and conversation:	289	Priest		30
Thou hast given us the blessings of this life, and of a better.	290	Priest		5
And now Lord, thou hast fed us with the bread of life:	290	Priest		9
they had a great desire to know the way of my life, and how I came	291	Cornaro		12
and live a sober life, expressing also the means which I have used	291	Cornaro		16
whereas my life seemed as farre from it by Nature, as it was neare it	291	Cornaro		26
if I could constantly pursue it, to wit, A sober and orderly life:	292	Cornaro		5
preserving of Health, as a disorderly life to the overthrowing of it;	292	Cornaro		6
hope of avoiding death and pain, I resolved to live a temperate life.	292	Cornaro		22
I so addicted my self to this course of life, that I never went	292	Cornaro		33
power a sober and temperate life hath over our bodies and mindes,	294	Cornaro		25
neither melancholie, nor any other passion can hurt a temperate life.	294	Cornaro		32
considering what an orderly life I had led for many yeares together,	295	Cornaro		7
That they that live a temperate life, can receive little hurt from	295	Cornaro		15
That an orderly and regular life can hardly be altered without	295	Cornaro		17
because by eating little he prolongs his life.	295	Cornaro		35
if our corporall life depend on the harmonie of humours & elements,	297	Cornaro		7
That an orderly life is the most sure way & ground of health and long	297	Cornaro		12
after live free from diseases, if he will keep such a course of life;	297	Cornaro		20
nor better Physick then a Temperate Life, Temperance by all means is	298	Cornaro		2
that in stead of a Physician a regular life is to be embraced,	298	Cornaro		12
and procure that they prolong their life even to a hundred yeares	298	Cornaro		15
ill handled by their intemperance, yet shunne a sober life:	298	Cornaro		26
that an orderly life is so hard a thing that it cannot be kept.	298	Cornaro		36
Wherefore since many have observed a regular life, both of old times	299	Cornaro		5
and divers labours, which suit not with an orderly life:	299	Cornaro		15
He which lives a regular life, eating alwayes light meats,	299	Cornaro		22
That he which lives a temperate life, cannot fall into diseases,	299	Cornaro		35
Wherefore since an orderly life is so profitable, so vertuous,	300	Cornaro		3
the presuming upon it ought not to leade us to a disorderly life.	300	Cornaro		21
is more sure of life, then the most strong young man who lives	300	Cornaro		25
That a long life is no such desirable thing, because that after one	300	Cornaro		28
yeares old, all the time we live after, is rather death then life.	300	Cornaro		30
I am not wearie of life, which I passe with great delight.	301	Cornaro		3
because I have now a clearer voice, then ever I had in my life.	303	Cornaro		8
it is evident, That the life which I live at this age, is not a dead,	303	Cornaro		9
which I live at this age, is not a dead, dumpish, and sowre life;	303	Cornaro		10
that by the regularitie of my life I have shut out death all other	303	Cornaro		27
Since therefore a temperate life is so happie and pleasant a thing;	303	Cornaro		30
the many pious rules of ordering our life, about mortification,	305	Valdesso		9
that it makes him godly, righteous, and sober all his life long;	309	Valdesso		6
necessary duties, and occasions of our calling and condition of life;	314	Valdesso		18
A handfull of good life is better then a bushell of learning.	321	Proverbs		3
Praise day at night, and life at the end.	324	Proverbs		97
In life you lov'd me not, in death you bewaile me.	328	Proverbs		218
Life without a friend is death without a witnesse.	334	Proverbs		385
A faire death honours the whole life.	339	Proverbs		522
Of him that speakes ill, consider the life more then the words.	346	Proverbs		761
Of him that speakes ill, consider the life more then the word.	346	Proverbs	V	761

LIFE (cont'd)	PAGE	TITLE		LINE
The life of man is a winter way.	351	Proverbs		914
Life is halfe spent before we know what it is.	351	Proverbs		917
Between the businesse of life and the day of death,	356	Proverbs	D	40
Favour will as surely perish as life.	357	Proverbs	D	1055
The life of spies is to know, not bee known.	357	Proverbs	D	1068
all his life, could he find it.	360	Proverbs	D	1143
to lay the platform of my future life, and shall I then be fain	364	Letters		12
this (which is now, when I must lay the foundation of my whole life).	365	Letters		18
alwaies observ'd the thred of Life to be like other threds or skenes	373	Letters		4
that whether you turn your thoughts on the life past, or on the Joyes	373	Letters		18
as the course of our life & the changes thereof, we are to regard	380	Woodnoth		18
LIFE'S				
Command thy self in chief. He lifes warre knows,	15	Ch.-Porch		215
Deferre not the least vertue: lifes poore span	24	Ch.-Porch		459
LIFT				
Another lift like this will make	52	H.Commun.		27
If I but lift mine eyes, my suit is made:	103	Prayer 2		5
But as birds drink, and straight lift up their head,	131	Mans medly		21
and thither lift mine eye.	218	Psalm V	D	8
but sometimes lift up their minds to better things, even in the midst	261	Priest 23		25
LIFTEST				
That with th' one hand thou liftest to the sky,	160	Priesthood		2
LIFTING				
Lifting to heaven from this well of tears.	141	Justice 2		18
lifting up his heart and hands, and eyes, and using all other	231	Priest 6		2
LIGHT (weight)				
Herod and all his bands do set me light,	29	Sacrifice		77
that it is no complementall or light thing to sustain that place,	258	Priest 22		11
regular life, eating alwayes light meats, and in a little quantitie,	299	Cornaro		23
Light burthens, long borne, growe heavie.	321	Proverbs		15
Light burdens, long borne, are heavie.	321	Proverbs	V	15
Where your will is ready, your feete are light.	336	Proverbs		448
Armour is light at table.	352	Proverbs		934
LIGHT				
Against thee: for his light was onely lent.	9	Ch.-Porch		82
Then may the beasts draw thee to happy light.	16	Ch.-Porch		264
Used, and wished, are the whole worlds light:	30	Sacrifice		110
Though he give light, & th' East perfume;	42	Easter		24
Though hee bring light & th' other sents:	42	Easter	W	24
When creatures had no reall light	51	Faith		33
Going about the world, and giving light.	59	Whitsunday		16
The same sweet God of love and light:	60	Whitsunday		26
That this new light, which now I see,	63	Mattens		18
Who gave me eyes, and light, and power this day,	63	Even-song		2
The holy Preachers; then the light and glorie	67	Windows		8
Doctrine and life, colours and light, in one	68	Windows		11
Then with thy light refine,	74	The Starre		11
Then with our trinitie of light,	74	The Starre		17
The week were dark, but for thy light:	75	Sunday		6
The week were dark, but that thy light	75	Sunday	W	6
And did inclose this light for his:	76	Sunday		37
O Thou, whose glorious, yet contracted light,	81	Christmas		9
Out-sing the day-light houres.	81	Christmas		22
Whose sparkling light accesse denies:	82	Ungratef.		14
Hath still sow'd fig-leaves to exclude thy light:	83	Sighs & Gr.		16
A face not fearing light:	86	Lent		21
As the sunne scatters by his light	90	Afflict.4		23
Musick and light attend our head.	91	Man		33
Thou art my lovelinesse, my life, my light,	115	Dulnesse		9
Light without winde is glasse: warm without weight	120	Providence		101
Yet I might trust in God to be my light.	143	Holdfast		4
Resolv'd to light; and so one day	151	The Bag		11
The starres his tire of light and rings obtain'd,	151	The Bag		13
Come, my Light, my Feast, my Strength:	156	The Call		5
Such a Light, as shows a feast:	156	The Call		6
And relish versing: O my onely light,	166	The Flower		39
A sonne is light and fruit; a fruitfull flame	168	The Sonne		7
And judge our selves. That light, which sin & passion	171	Self-cond.		20
More then a thousand sunnes disburse in light,	172	The Glance		23
Light and perfections on the breast,	174	Aaron		2
Perfect and light in my deare breast,	174	Aaron		22
But borrow'd thence to light us thither.	177	Forerunners		29
As thy eclipsed light.	183	A Parodie		15
Lett in the Light to all their actions	185	The Elixer	W	23
Echo. Light.	188	Heaven		14
Light to the minde: what shall the will enjoy?	188	Heaven		15
Light, joy, and leisure; but shall they persever?	188	Heaven		19
Trimme as the light, sweet as the laden boughs	190	Ch.-Milit.		14
The course was westward, that the sunne might light	190	Ch.-Milit.		17
Listens behinde him, and allows some light,	191	Ch.-Milit.		32
Listens behinde him, and gives them some light,	191	Ch.-Milit.	W	32
As is the moon and sunne to heav'n and light.	196	Ch.-Milit.		216
Light one another, and together runne.	198	Ch.-Milit.		271
If thou deferr this light, then shadow mee:	203	Even-song	W	9
But thou art Light & darknes both togeather:	203	Even-song	W	13
Since Light thy Darknes is.	203	Even-song	W	20
And though starres shott from heaven loose their light,	211	Bohemia	D	9
Thy countenances cheering light	217	Psalm IV	D	23
and reverend, not with light colours, or foolish anticks.	246	Priest 13		13
exercise of the Church, the light in the foundations being the guide;	263	Priest 24		6

	PAGE	TITLE	LINE
LIGHT (cont'd)			
when light is brought in, God send us the light of heaven;	284	Priest 35	23
Light is a great Blessing, and as great as food, for which we give	284	Priest 35	26
which thou hast made a Land of light, a store-house of thy treasures	289	Priest	18
in his own country he would have to flourish in this land of light,	304	Valdesso	15
God affectionately and fervently to send him the light of his spirit,	312	Valdesso	17
LIGHTING			
that so the sentence lighting upon one, the example may reach to all.	269	Priest 28	2
LIGHTLY			
All are not merry that dance lightly.	348	Proverbs	808
LIGHTNING			
I escaped the Thunder, and fell into the Lightning.	358	Proverbs	D 1084
LIGHTS			
Oh that I knew how all thy lights combine,	58	H.Script.2	1
This book of starres lights to eternall blisse.	58	H.Script.2	14
Goshen was darknesse, Egypt full of lights,	191	Ch.-Milit.	43
Thus do both lights, as well in Church as Sunne,	197	Ch.-Milit.	270
Addes to the union, as lights doe gather	212	Bohemia	D 36
and cleansed, and serve for lights even of Heavenly Truths.	257	Priest 21	15
beseeching the Father of lights to open their eyes, and to give him	262	Priest 24	22
which are two great lights able to dazle the eyes of the mis-led,	263	Priest 24	19
LIKE (verb)			
I like our language, as our men and coast:	167	The Sonne	3
So live and like, that I may know thy wayes,	185	A Wreath	10
out of niceness, because they like the salutations, and complements,	285	Priest 36	5
there are some things which I like not in him, as my fragments will	304	Valdesso	16
But I like none of it, for it slights the Scripture too much:	306	Valdesso	16
not be punished (which word I like here better then chastizement,	311	Valdesso	27
Particularly, I like all your Addresses, & for ought I see,	378	Letters	16
LIKE			
Doe all things like a man, not sneakingly:	11	Ch.-Porch	121
And are like empty vessels under sail.	14	Ch.-Porch	184
Pick out of mirth, like stones out of thy ground,	16	Ch.-Porch	235
Ballance each dramme of reason, like a potion.	19	Ch.-Porch	322
Shine like the sunne in every corner: see	20	Ch.-Porch	345
Was ever grief like mine?	26	Sacrifice	4
Was ever grief like mine?	26	Sacrifice	8
Was ever grief like mine?	27	Sacrifice	12
Was ever grief like mine?	27	Sacrifice	16
Was ever grief like mine?	27	Sacrifice	20
Was ever grief like mine?	27	Sacrifice	24
Was ever grief like mine?	27	Sacrifice	28
Was ever grief like mine?	27	Sacrifice	32
Was ever grief like mine?	27	Sacrifice	36
Was ever grief like mine?	27	Sacrifice	40
Was ever grief like mine?	28	Sacrifice	44
Was ever grief like mine?	28	Sacrifice	48
Was ever grief like mine?	28	Sacrifice	52
Was ever grief like mine?	28	Sacrifice	56
Was ever grief like mine?	28	Sacrifice	60
Was ever grief like mine?	28	Sacrifice	64
Was ever grief like mine?	28	Sacrifice	68
Was ever grief like mine?	28	Sacrifice	72
Was ever grief like mine?	29	Sacrifice	76
Was ever grief like mine?	29	Sacrifice	80
Was ever grief like mine?	29	Sacrifice	84
Was ever grief like mine?	29	Sacrifice	88
Was ever grief like mine?	29	Sacrifice	92
Was ever grief like mine?	29	Sacrifice	96
Was ever grief like mine?	29	Sacrifice	100
Was ever grief like mine?	29	Sacrifice	104
Was ever grief like mine?	30	Sacrifice	108
Was ever grief like mine?	30	Sacrifice	112
Was ever grief like mine?	30	Sacrifice	116
Was ever grief like mine?	30	Sacrifice	120
Was ever grief like mine?	30	Sacrifice	124
Was ever grief like mine?	30	Sacrifice	128
Was ever grief like mine?	30	Sacrifice	132
Was ever grief like mine?	31	Sacrifice	136
Was ever grief like mine?	31	Sacrifice	140
Was ever grief like mine?	31	Sacrifice	144
Was ever grief like mine?	31	Sacrifice	148
Was ever grief like mine?	31	Sacrifice	152
Was ever grief like mine?	31	Sacrifice	156
Was ever grief like mine?	31	Sacrifice	160
Was ever grief like mine?	31	Sacrifice	164
Was ever grief like mine?	32	Sacrifice	168
Was ever grief like mine?	32	Sacrifice	172
Was ever grief like mine?	32	Sacrifice	176
Was ever grief like mine?	32	Sacrifice	180
Was ever grief like mine?	32	Sacrifice	184
Was ever grief like mine?	32	Sacrifice	188
Was ever grief like mine?	32	Sacrifice	192
Was ever grief like mine?	33	Sacrifice	196
Was ever grief like mine?	33	Sacrifice	200
Was ever grief like mine?	33	Sacrifice	204
Was ever grief like mine?	33	Sacrifice	208
Was ever grief like mine?	33	Sacrifice	212
Never was grief like mine.	33	Sacrifice	216
Was ever grief like mine?	33	Sacrifice	220
Was ever grief like mine?	34	Sacrifice	224

LIKE (cont'd)

	PAGE	TITLE		LINE
Was ever grief like mine?	34	Sacrifice		228
Was ever grief like mine?	34	Sacrifice		232
Was ever grief like mine?	34	Sacrifice		236
Was ever grief like mine?	34	Sacrifice		240
Was ever grief like mine?	34	Sacrifice		244
Was ever grief like mine?	34	Sacrifice		248
Never was grief like mine.	34	Sacrifice		252
If ever he did taste the like.	37	The Agonie		16
Another lift like this will make	52	H.Commun.		27
That th' earth did like a heav'n appeare;	59	Whitsunday		10
Death is still working like a mole,	60	Grace		13
For though sinnes plead too, yet like stones they make	66	Ch.-lock		11
Doth vanish like a flaring thing,	68	Windows		14
Doth vanish like a flaming thing,	68	Windows	V	14
To flie home like a laden bee	74	The Starre		30
My bent thoughts, like a brittle bow,	80	Deniall		6
Like a nipt blossome, hung	80	Deniall		24
Like season'd timber, never gives;	88	Vertue		14
Or of it self, like a good huswife, spunne	88	The Pearl		4
Successive nights, like rolling waves,	98	Mortific.		11
He doth not like this vertue, no;	101	Miserie		45
My thoughts must work, but like a noiselesse sphere;	105	Conscience		8
And ever as they mount, like larks they sing;	107	Sion		23
My thoughts are working like a busie flame,	122	Sinnes rd.		3
Which spit it forth like the Sicilian hill.	122	Sinnes rd.		8
And like a master in my trade,	126	Confession		4
And fall, like rheumes, upon the tendrest parts.	126	Confession		12
Like moles within us, heave, and cast about:	126	Confession		14
And like a Dolphins skinne, his clothes combin'd	127	Giddinesse		19
Like a pretender, not a bride.	138	The Size		36
Which when your neighbours saw, like a north-winde,	140	Ch.-rents		22
Like two great pits;	141	Justice 2		8
Did like some torturing engine show;	141	Justice 2		10
Did like some tottering engine show;	141	Justice 2	V	10
Thy scales like buckets, which attend	141	Justice 2		16
My heart is wither'd like a ground	148	Longing		8
(Which there did hang like streamers neare the top	158	Praise 3		33
Wing'd like an arrow: but my scout	162	The Search		19
Like snow in May,	165	The Flower		6
Preferring, like brute beasts, a lothsome den	167	Dotage		15
My comforts drop and melt away like snow:	169	The Answer		1
Like leaves about me: or like summer friends,	169	The Answer		4
Sure I will do the like.	171	Bittersweet		4
In tears like seas, our sinnes are pil'd	173	Marie Magd		11
Religion, like a pilgrime, westward bent,	190	Ch.-Milit.		29
Like Comick Lovers ever one way runn:	198	Ch.-Milit.	W	271
Of th' universe, like as the windes, & name	212	Bohemia	D	44
Whose fier, like there malice, nought can quench.	212	Bohemia	D	54
Like David's tree, planted beside	213	L' Envoy	D	2
he shall be like an happy tree,	214	Psalm I	D	8
are like the chaff, which from the face	215	Psalm I	D	14
like vessels made of brittle clay.	216	Psalm II	D	24
Lest like a Lion swollen with rage	221	Psalm VII	D	5
Ours (like himselfe) o'recomes; for his wit's more	438	Lat.Trans.		3
And the like in other answers.	232	Priest 6		1
of the presence, and majesty of God, by these, or such like speeches.	234	Priest 7		26
and object, and the like, hath neither in it sweetnesse,	235	Priest 7		7
and that our feet may be like hindes feet ever climbing up higher,	236	Priest 8		29
and other like circumstances considered, he is rather married then	237	Priest 9		4
like mortall enemies, may sometimes disquiet him likewise;	238	Priest 9		9
into Covetousnesse, Love of pleasure, or ease, or the like.	238	Priest 9		24
the one for smalnesse, as crums, and scattered corn, and the like;	241	Priest 10		28
some of his Parish, hee taketh his times to do the like to the rest;	243	Priest 11		18
others spurred to do well, that they may enjoy the like courtesie.	243	Priest 11		27
givings are lay, and secular, but this is to give like a Priest.	245	Priest 12		38
when they set themselves to work like brute beasts, never raising	247	Priest 14		32
The like he doth in the morning, using pleasantly the outlandish	251	Priest 17		13
or breeding up children to no Calling, but in idleness, or the like.	251	Priest 17		22
who like Christian Souldiers are to give the word, and to satisfie	255	Priest 21		20
Baptisme being a blessing, that the word hath not the like.	258	Priest 22		7
for this is to cure like a Parson, and this raiseth the action from	262	Priest 23		10
These and the like points hee hath accurately digested,	263	Priest 24		14
The like he doth in other Christian vertues, as of Faith,	279	Priest 33		33
& been corrected either by whipping, or imprisoning, or the like.	287	Priest 37		16
they break forth like mighty waters on every side.	290	Priest		7
in like manner, raw lettice, fish, pork, sausages, pulse,	293	Cornaro		12
pork, sausages, pulse, and cake, and py-crust, and the like:	293	Cornaro		13
and other like discommodities of the bodie, and troubles	294	Cornaro		12
and that at length they shut up their dayes like a Lamp,	298	Cornaro		17
I abstain from fruit, and fish, and the like, because they hurt me.	300	Cornaro		9
like to that of the Jewes, which they added to their divine law.	320	Valdesso		3
Evening words are not like to morning.	323	Proverbs		65
Wealth is like rheume, it falles on the weakest parts.	337	Proverbs		475
Disgraces are like cherries, one drawes another.	338	Proverbs		487
Benefits please like flowers while they are fresh.	356	Proverbs	D	40
Unsound minds like unsound Bodies, if you feed, you poyson.	358	Proverbs	D	1076
Criticks are like brushers of Noblemens cloaths.	360	Proverbs	D	1157
Souldiers in peace are like chimneys in summer.	361	Proverbs	D	1172
meet with a witty French speech, try to speak the like in English:	366	Letters		11
and such like Gaynesses, which will please a young man well.	370	Letters		3

	PAGE	TITLE	LINE
LIKE (cont'd)			
observ'd the thred of Life to be like other threds or skenes of silk,	373	Letters	4
yours (which praised be God are less) are not like to continue long.	374	Letters	2
that if any of yours shou'd prove a Goliah-like trouble,	374	Letters	5
but advance them, was lovingly done, and like a good brother.	375	Letters	3
How could you bee like great Alexander, unlesse Historie delivered	443	Oration	2
LIKED			
all your Addresses, & for ought I see, they are ever to be liked.	378	Letters	18
She liked our Book well, & has given order to the Tenants,	379	Letters	8
LIKELY			
some scoffing ruffian, who is likely to deride him for his paines:	273	Priest 31	29
for though it is likely that the time after the Holydaye will bee	368	Letters	2
LIKELYEST			
is best to be chosen, of which there is likelyest to be most use.	230	Priest 5	11
LIKER			
His grave aspect was liker heav'n then hell:	194	Ch.-Milit. W	168
LIKES			
wherefore he likes well, that his Parish at good times invite one	284	Priest 35	17
And the Parson likes this very well;	284	Priest 35	24
Who likes not the drinke, God deprives him of bread.	334	Proverbs	394
LIKEWISE			
Who takes thee by the hand, that thou likewise	41	Easter	3
like mortall enemies, may sometimes disquiet him likewise;	238	Priest 9	10
Likewise in any other Countrey-duty, he considers what is the end	253	Priest 19	3
Likewise he welcomes to his house any Minister, how poor or mean	253	Priest 19	18
So likewise there are some persons, who abstain not even from known	264	Priest 26	9
And they must be likewise in all that are his.	280	Priest 34	11
So likewise are the godly in some sort exempt from Lawes,	315	Valdesso	32
LIKING			
Hast thou the knack? pamper it not with liking:	16	Ch.-Porch	243
Then Pleasure came, who liking not the fashion,	84	The World	6
then not liking that kinde of Diet, followed my Appetite,	292	Cornaro	26
LILLIES			
Roses and Lillies speak thee; and to make	206	Walton 2	6
LILLYES			
such as are from Gods generall providence extended even to lillyes;	249	Priest 15	20
his Doctrine, remembring in gardens, his mustard-seed, and lillyes;	261	Priest 23	23
LIMBE			
Full of proportions, one limbe to another,	91	Man	14
LIMBES			
To writhe his limbes, and share, not mend the ill.	73	Constancie	33
To writhe his limbes, and thare, not mend the ill.	73	Constancie V	33
LIME			
Lime begg'd of old, (they say),	154	Glimpse	13
LIMITS			
both Indias to his Spaine, knowes no limits of his praise, no,	442	Oration	12
LINCOLN			
long in Latin, and my Lincoln journey hath set me much behind hand:	369	Letters	14
LINE			
From his Ecliptick line: becken the skie.	12	Ch.-Porch	137
Take up the second, then thy double line	97	Afflict.5	16
But while I grow in a straight line,	166	The Flower	29
Straight as a line, and ever tends to thee,	185	A Wreath	6
Constantines British line meant this of old,	192	Ch.-Milit.	93
All the discourse from this line [place] till the end of this Chapter	311	Valdesso	20
LINEAMENTS			
Thy perfect lineaments, and hue	109	Brit. Ch.	2
LINEN			
And with his buriall-linen drie thine eyes:	112	Dawning	14
LINES			
The holy lines cannot be understood.	6	Ch.-Porch	10
May no lines passe, except they do their dutie	56	Jordan 1	4
And sudden arbours shadow course-spunne lines?	56	Jordan 1	7
Written in dustie heraldrie and lines;	65	Ch.-monum.	9
When first my lines of heav'nly joyes made mention,	102	Jordan 2	1
As many lines, as there doth need	104	Obedience	7
As many lines, as it does need	104	Obedience W	7
Into these lines; till in heav'ns court of rolls	105	Obedience	43
Where are my lines then? my approaches? views?	116	Dulnesse	17
My lines and life are free; free as the rode,	153	The Collar	4
Is, when the soul unto the lines accords.	168	a true Hymn	10
And take up my lines and life:	182	Banquet	51
Which warme these lines, & serve them up to thee	204	Persever. W	2
LINGER			
To linger in me, and together languish.	159	Jos.coat	12
Thou who dost dwell and linger here below,	170	Water-crs.	1
LINGRING			
Thou didst betray me to a lingring book,	47	Afflict.1	39
For many weeks of lingring pain and smart	154	Glimpse	4
LINK			
I am no link of thy great chain,	57	Employm. 1	21
LINN			
Nay, I will reade thy book, and never linn	36	Thanksgvng W	45
LINNEN			
services done by men-servants at home, and his linnen washed abroad.	237	Priest 9	10
and sightly Communion Cloth of fine linnen, with an handsome,	246	Priest 13	17
LION (see also lyon)			
The angrie Lion did present his paw,	70	Humilitie	9
Lest like a Lion swollen with rage	221	Psalm VII D	5
Amiens was taken by the Fox, and retaken by the Lion.	356	Proverbs D	1036

LITTLE (cont'd)	PAGE	TITLE		LINE
He that hath little is the lesse durtie.	336	Proverbs		436
A little Kitchin makes a large house.	337	Proverbs		470
Little wealth, little care.	338	Proverbs		501
Little journeys and good cost bring safe home.	338	Proverbs		502
A little and good fills the trencher.	338	Proverbs		505
Little dogs start the Hare, the great get her.	341	Proverbs		593
A little labour, much health.	344	Proverbs		689
If great men would have care of little ones,	344	Proverbs		697
Great businesses turne on a little pinne.	345	Proverbs		720
A little lett lets an ill workeman.	346	Proverbs		755
Of a little thing a little displeaseth.	348	Proverbs		814
A little given seasonably excuses a great gift.	349	Proverbs		834
He can give little to his servant, that lickes his knife.	349	Proverbs		846
That which sufficeth is not little.	350	Proverbs		876
but the patient owes nothing to him but a little mony.	351	Proverbs		921
The little cannot bee great, unlesse he devoure many.	351	Proverbs		922
Children when they are little make parents fooles,	352	Proverbs		939
Children when they are little make their parents fooles,	352	Proverbs	V	939
The great put the little on the hooke.	352	Proverbs		945
The great would have none great and the little all little.	352	Proverbs		946
Little losses amaze, great tame.	354	Proverbs		1013
There is no man, though never so little,	359	Proverbs	D	1119
We must recoile a little, to the end we may leap the better.	359	Proverbs	D	1121
be any truth in me, I find it little enough to keep me in health.	364	Letters		31
and perhaps a little more mild, but you will hardly perceive it.	366	Letters		25
Son to doe as much) with some little Apology that she had done	379	Letters		3
LIVD				
And livd accordingly with no new score,	50	Faith	W	15
LIVE				
For he, that needs five thousand pound to live,	10	Ch.-Porch		107
Never was scraper brave man. Get to live;	12	Ch.-Porch		153
Then live, and use it: els, it is not true	12	Ch.-Porch		154
Who cannot live on twentie pound a yeare,	13	Ch.-Porch		176
Both friends should die, then hinder them to live.	17	Ch.-Porch		280
Active and stirring spirits live alone.	20	Ch.-Porch		341
Joyn hands with God to make a man to live.	21	Ch.-Porch		376
It is not fit he live a day, they crie,	29	Sacrifice		98
Who cannot live lesse then eternally:	29	Sacrifice		99
Unto some Chappell, die or live.	35	Thanksgvng		28
That I did live, but by a pang of woe.	47	Afflict.1	W	30
Yet as in sleep we see foul death, and live:	63	Sinne 2		9
We both together sweetly live and love,	65	Ch.-mus.		7
Taught me to live here so, That still one eye	85	Coloss.		7
My stuffe is flesh, not brasse; my senses live,	89	The Pearl		27
And while I live, trie out their right.	90	Afflict.4		18
By it do all things live their measur'd houre:	103	Prayer 2		10
By it do all things live their silly houre:	103	Prayer 2	W	10
And live apart.	127	Giddinesse		24
And weeping live:	135	Ephes.		9
And live on score:	138	The Size		22
That live or die	143	Complaining		9
And all thy promises live and bide.	150	Longing		68
I live to shew his power, who once did bring	159	Jos.coat		13
After so many deaths I live and write;	166	The Flower		37
And setling to a cloud, doth live and die	169	The Answer		11
With pensive humblenesse would live and tread:	173	Marie Magd		6
Another musick, making live not dead,	174	Aaron		13
With me, in me, live and dwell:	181	Banquet		3
My crooked winding wayes, wherein I live,	185	A Wreath		4
Wherein I die, not live: for life is straight,	185	A Wreath		5
Give me simplicitie, that I may live,	185	A Wreath		9
So live and like, that I may know thy wayes,	185	A Wreath		10
Each one whispring, Live ye brother?	186	Dooms-day		6
Children for kingdomes to thee; they shall live	212	Bohemia	D	42
and live, and who giveth mee my Desires and Performances;	224	Priest		2
to whom this discourse ariseth not) some live in the Universities,	225	Priest 2		22
Of those that live in the Universities, some live there in office,	226	Priest 2		2
some live there in office, whose rule is that of the Apostle;	226	Priest 2		3
Those that live in Noble Houses are called Chaplains, whose duty	226	Priest 2		15
whose duty and obligation being the same to the Houses they live in,	226	Priest 2		17
Doubtlesse they are Parsons of the families they live in,	226	Priest 2		22
because Countrey people live hardly, and therefore as feeling their	227	Priest 3		12
And is in contention for them whither to live, or dy;	234	Priest 7		15
For though he desire, that all should live well, and vertuously,	243	Priest 11		28
to live more religiously, and to take more paines in their vocation,	245	Priest 12		2
giving them most, who live best, and take most paines, and are most	245	Priest 12		15
not to incroach on others Professions, but to live on his own.	262	Priest 23		17
Yet Phisicians bid those that would live in health, not keep	267	Priest 26		10
The Jewes yet live, and are known:	281	Priest 34		35
Wherefore if the Jewes live, all the great wonders of old live in	282	Priest 34		5
all the great wonders of old live in them, and then who can deny	282	Priest 34		5
then their present exile, and disability to live in their Countrey.	282	Priest 34		10
and live a sober life, expressing also the means which I have used	291	Cornaro		16
hope of avoiding death and pain, I resolved to live a temperate life.	292	Cornaro		22
whereas they hurt them very much who live intemperately.	294	Cornaro		15
That they that live a temperate life, can receive little hurt from	295	Cornaro		14
as usually happens in old mens bodies, which live without rule.	296	Cornaro		36
hath cured him, commends this also to him, if he will live in health.	297	Cornaro		18
but that he shall ever after live free from diseases, if he will keep	297	Cornaro		19
curing of diseases, into which they often fall, who live disorderly:	298	Cornaro		5

LIVE (cont'd)	PAGE	TITLE		LINE
please the Appetite (though they live ten yeares lesse then otherwise	298	Cornaro		27
otherwise they should do) then alwayes to live under bit and bridle.	298	Cornaro		28
cannot live regularly, because they must often endure heats,	299	Cornaro		12
though they live disorderly, yet continue in health to their lives	300	Cornaro		18
yeares old, all the time we live after, is rather death then life.	300	Cornaro		29
it is evident, That the life which I live at this age, is not a dead,	303	Cornaro		9
as also to those that live in sinne, and follow their appetites:	303	Cornaro		19
A coole mouth, and warme feet, live long.	321	Proverbs		21
Let all live as they would die.	345	Proverbs		725
To live peaceably with all breedes good blood.	353	Proverbs		963
With customes wee live well, but Lawes undoe us.	353	Proverbs		973
He that gives me small gifts would have me live.	354	Proverbs		1000
A man would live in Italy (a place of pleasure)	357	Proverbs	D	1047
Those that God loves, do not live long.	358	Proverbs	D	1094
You live in a brave nation, where, except you wink, you cannot	366	Letters		5
give her halfe her estate to live on by her selfe (for shee desires	368	Letters		24
Credit and estimation calls on us to live in a more splendid fashion?	373	Letters		26
LIV'D				
And liv'd accordingly; my creditor	50	Faith		15
And if the Fox had liv'd to rule their side, ...	70	Humilitie		23
Fit, while ye liv'd, for smell or ornament, ...	94	Life		14
At first we liv'd in pleasure;	97	Afflict.5		7
If he had not liv'd for thee, ...	113	Businesse		20
Thou hadst liv'd in miserie.	113	Businesse		27
At Salem dwelt, who liv'd with good increase	125	Peace		23
He sweetly liv'd; yet sweetnesse did not save	125	Peace		25
Labour as long liv'd, pray as ever dying.	337	Proverbs		480
Labour as long liv'd, pray as alwayes dying.	337	Proverbs	V	480
Hee hath not liv'd, that lives not after death.	350	Proverbs		873
LIVED				
Till grief did tell me roundly, that I lived.	47	Afflict.1		30
if they had lived, would have been an ornament to the world,	291	Cornaro		3
Paul the third, and Cardinal Bembo, who therefore lived so long;	299	Cornaro		2
whether he hath lived heretofore orderly or disorderly, . .	299	Cornaro		29
especially considering the time and place where he lived. . .	311	Valdesso	V	8
I doubt but if Abraham had lived in our Kingdome under government,	316	Valdesso		23
the fruit of my observation, for they have lived so lovingly, lying,	375	Letters		18
LIVEDST				
Thou was born for us, and thou livedst and diedst for us: . .	290	Priest		4
LIVELIER				
So all within be livelier then before.	177	Forerunners		36
LIVELINESSE				
speaking, but with a grave livelinesse, between fear and zeal,	231	Priest 6		19
LIVELY				
turning it to reformation of life, by pithy and lively exhortations;	255	Priest 21		7
and lively exhortations, not on the Sunday of the Communion only	258	Priest 22		26
in all things wherein they deal, may be more lively and vigorous.	299	Cornaro		21
but cheerfull, lively, and pleasant.	303	Cornaro		11
LIVERY				
With livery-graces furnishing thy men.	59	Whitsunday	W	8
Wear Venus Livery? only serve her turn?	206	walton 1		4
LIVERY-GRACES				
With livery-graces furnishing thy men.	59	Whitsunday	W	8
LIVES				
Who lives by rule then, keeps good companie.	12	Ch.-Porch		138
Then chiefly lives.	88	Vertue		16
As watring pots give flowers their lives.	90	Afflict.4		10
Two lives worse then ten deaths be.	113	Businesse		28
I hold for two lives, and both lives in me.	129	Love unkn.		5
And lives: If that be all, said I, ...	142	Pilgrimage		34
But lives in me while I do rest)	174	Aaron		24
There he sucks, and lives.	228	Priest 4		23
He often readeth the Lives of the Primitive Monks, Hermits, . .	237	Priest 9		28
Now it is a justice and debt to the Common-wealth he lives in,	262	Priest 23		16
then a stone thrown against heaven, where he is, and lives; . .	269	Priest 28		8
the Village or Parish which either he lives in, or is neer unto it,	276	Priest 32		2
or Noble-man in the Country he lives in, inabling him with power	276	Priest 32		14
and disarmed with sedentary lives, are to know the use of their Arms:	277	Priest 32		18
(a thing usuall to disorderly lives) which increased so much in them,	294	Cornaro		19
He which lives a regular life, eating alwayes light meats, . .	299	Cornaro		22
That he which lives a temperate life, cannot fall into diseases,	299	Cornaro		35
sure of life, then the most strong young man who lives disorderly.	300	Cornaro		26
He lives unsafely, that lookes too neere on things. . . .	322	Proverbs		43
Hee that lives well is learned enough.	323	Proverbs		86
Hee who lives well is learned enough.	323	Proverbs	V	86
Hee that lives ill, feare followes him.	324	Proverbs		110
He that lives well sees a farre off.	333	Proverbs		352
He that lives most dies most.	336	Proverbs		437
He that lives not well one yeare, sorrowes seven after. . .	340	Proverbs		562
He that feares death lives not.	347	Proverbs		781
Hee hath not liv'd, that lives not after death.	350	Proverbs		873
Halfe the world knowes not how the other halfe lives. . . .	351	Proverbs		907
Wee know not who lives or dies.	353	Proverbs		966
Hee that lives in hope danceth without musick.	354	Proverbs		1006
The War is not don so long as my Enemy lives.	357	Proverbs	D	1051
LIVES'				
they live disorderly, yet continue in health to their lives end:	300	Cornaro		19
LIV'ST				
Thou liv'st by rule. What doth not so, but man?	12	Ch.-Porch		134
Thou liv'st by rule. What does not so, but man?	12	Ch.-Porch	W	134

LONG (cont'd)	PAGE	TITLE		LINE
Having been tenant long to a rich Lord,	40	Redemption		1
Long since on earth, to take possession.	40	Redemption		8
Pleasant and long:	42	Easter		14
Hatching my tender heart so long,	59	Whitsunday		3
And long since wed	71	Frailtie		20
And then not heare it crying! all day long	80	Deniall		18
And knoweth long before,	85	Vanitie 1		6
Whisper, How wide is all this long pretence!	103	Jordan 2		16
Thy long deferrings wound me to the quick,	107	Home		3
Hath kiss'd so long her painted shrines,	110	Brit. Ch.		16
And long may be.	110	Brit. Ch.		27
And this is that makes life so long,	123	Time		19
Deare Friend, sit down, the tale is long and sad:	129	Love unkn.		1
Yet active strength: whose long and bonie face	138	The Size		33
A long it was and weary way.	141	Pilgrimage		3
Which hath been broken now so long,	150	Longing		74
I writ thy purpose long ago.	155	Assurance		18
Nor his long journey, nor his gout and furre.	195	Ch.-Milit.		198
Nor his long journey, nor his gout or furre.	195	Ch.-Milit.	W	198
How long will ye, vain men, convert	217	Psalm IV	D	7
How long will ye seek after lies,	217	Psalm IV	D	9
But, Lord, how long so much perplex'd	220	Psalm VI	D	7
but is long before hee proceede to disinheriting, or perhaps never	250	Priest 16		17
Children and youths are usually deferred too long, under pretence	258	Priest 22		37
they are long a knowing it, being partiall to themselves,	264	Priest 26		12
and tarryed so long at it, that they would have fainted,	267	Priest 26		23
still striving & prospering so long within us, untill our obedience	290	Priest		11
was not onely freed from all those evils which had so long beset me,	293	Cornaro		21
nothing holp me, but that exact rule which I had so long continued.	296	Cornaro		29
orderly life is the most sure way & ground of health and long dayes,	297	Cornaro		13
Every one by long experience may know the qualities of his own	297	Cornaro		26
qualities to me, if I had not found them out by long experience?	297	Cornaro		35
Paul the third, and Cardinal Bembo, who therefore lived so long;	299	Cornaro		2
That a long life is no such desirable thing, because that after one	300	Cornaro		28
And David (though David) studied all the day long in it:	306	Valdesso		20
that it makes him godly, righteous, and sober all his life long;	309	Valdesso		6
Light burthens, long borne, growe heavie.	321	Proverbs		15
Light burdens, long borne, are heavie.	321	Proverbs	V	15
A coole mouth, and warme feet, live long.	321	Proverbs		21
Not a long day, but a good heart rids worke.	321	Proverbs		24
Hee puls with a long rope, that waits for anothers death.	322	Proverbs		25
Hee puls with a long rope, who locks for anothers death.	322	Proverbs	V	25
Autumnall Agues are long, or mortall.	326	Proverbs		148
Hee that lies long a bed, his estate feeles it.	327	Proverbs		179
A long tongue is a signe of a short hand.	329	Proverbs		251
Hee that's fed at anothers hand may stay long ere he be full.	336	Proverbs		439
Who is fed by anothers hand stays long ere he be full.	336	Proverbs	V	439
Labour as long liv'd, pray as ever dying.	337	Proverbs		480
Labour as long liv'd, pray as alwayes dying.	337	Proverbs	V	480
He that's long a giving, knowes not how to give.	338	Proverbs		494
Short boughs, long vintage.	338	Proverbs		508
Long jesting was never good.	344	Proverbs		694
both would last long.	344	Proverbs		697
Gamsters and race-horses never last long.	346	Proverbs		751
Curtesie on one side only lasts not long.	348	Proverbs		809
In a long journey straw waighs.	348	Proverbs		820
They talke of Christmas so long, that it comes.	349	Proverbs		840
A pleasure long expected is deare enough sold.	350	Proverbs		868
There needs a long time to know the worlds pulse.	350	Proverbs		886
The War is not don so long as my Enemy lives.	357	Proverbs	D	1051
Those that God loves, do not live long.	358	Proverbs	D	1094
Take heed of foul dirty wayes, and long sicknesse.	360	Proverbs	D	1153
the same heart, which you have won long since, is still true to you,	363	Letters		18
to make an Oration to the whole University of an hour long in Latin,	369	Letters		13
the midst of much business, and all in a Fortnight, not long since.	371	Letters		4
yours (which praised be God are less) are not like to continue long.	374	Letters		3
God knowes, I have desired a long time, to doe the place good,	378	Letters		6
I heard from you, that I long to heare both how you and your's doe:	379	Letters		23
of want of success consider how long God knocks at our harts,	381	Woodnoth		2
therfore God is styled with that glorious title, Long Suffering.	381	Woodnoth		6
Long since, all we and our whole Kingdome exult with joy,	442	Oration		13
LONG'D				
Much in request, much long'd for as a good.	186	Death	W	16
LONGER				
so will they last the longer, and when they depart, returne	280	Priest 34		29
I doe not then bid him goe away but rather stay longer,	318	Valdesso		16
the longer he stayes there, the fowler he is.	335	Proverbs		409
I dare no longer be silent, least while I think I am modest,	364	Letters		7
LONGEST				
Must bear the longest part.	53	Antiphon 1		12
The longest Day hath an Eveninge.	322	Proverbs	V	51
LONGING				
Longing.	148	Longing		T
Bee not idle and you shall not bee longing.	331	Proverbs		308
LOOK				
How dare those eyes upon a Bible look,	6	Ch.-Porch		11
Look to thy mouth; diseases enter there.	11	Ch.-Porch		127
Look on meat, think it dirt, then eat a bit;	11	Ch.-Porch		131
Dare to look in thy chest; for 'tis thine own:	12	Ch.-Porch		147
To couzin thee. Look to thy actions well:	23	Ch.-Porch		425

LOOK (cont'd)	PAGE	TITLE		LINE
Look not on pleasures as they come, but go.	24	Ch.-Porch		458
Arise, arise, they come. Look how they runne!	27	Sacrifice		33
Ladies, look here; this is the thankfull glasse,	58	H.Script.1		8
Can blow away, or glittering look it blinde:	72	Constancie		8
And turn us round to look on one,	75	Sunday		17
We could not choose but look on still;	75	Sunday		19
My feeble spirit, unable to look right,	80	Deniall		23
As frost-nipt sunnes look sadly.	81	Christmas		30
After my sinnes! look not on my desert,	83	Sighs & Gr.		2
Not a fair look, but thou dost call it foul:	105	Conscience		2
Which way so-e're I look, I see.	108	Home		50
I may but look towards thee:	116	Dulnesse		26
Look onely; for to love thee, who can be,	116	Dulnesse		27
Wouldst thou not look?	133	The Method		12
And made you look much fresher then before.	140	Ch.-rents		15
He that did but look up, was proud and bold.	141	Justice 2		6
Look high and low;	144	Discharge		4
Look on my sorrows round!	149	Longing		25
Yet a meek look	149	Longing		51
Look, you may put it very neare my heart.	152	The Bag		36
Flowers look about, and die not in their prime.	154	Glimpse		10
For who can look for lesse, that loveth Life. / Strife.	170	Water-crs.		5
Look back upon thine own estate,	170	Self-cond.		4
To look upon me, who before did lie	171	The Glance		3
When thou shalt look us out of pain,	172	The Glance		21
Blushing woes, that look as cleare	177	The Rose		7
Not a word or look	178	Discipline		9
Having rais'd me to look up,	182	Banquet		37
Thy dreadfull look,	187	Judgement		2
I cannot look on thee.	189	Love 3		10
Look on his daring brightnes, may	203	Even-song	W	7
Doth wishly look	204	The Knell	W	3
exercise what he is, unlesse he forsake his plough, and look back.	226	Priest 2		27
or if he have any leisure to look off from thence, he meets	267	Priest 27		30
that he have leisure to look out, the Village or Parish which either	276	Priest 32		1
that there is none that can or will look after things, but all goes	281	Priest 34		8
nor to bewail that so few are writ, that look towards God and Heaven.	363	Letters		9
LOOKE				
it is an honest joy ever after to looke upon his well spent houres.	230	Priest 5		7
Looke not for muske in a dogges kennell.	321	Proverbs		23
A cherefull looke makes a dish a feast.	323	Proverbs		62
A cherefull looke makes one dish a feast.	323	Proverbs	V	62
On painting and fighting looke aloofe.	329	Proverbs		247
The more women looke in their glasse,	329	Proverbs		250
the lesse they looke to their house.	329	Proverbs		250
If you would know secrets, looke them in griefe or pleasure.	333	Proverbs		367
Faire words make mee looke to my purse.	339	Proverbs		548
A valiant mans looke is more then a cowards sword.	345	Proverbs		708
A pittifull looke askes enough.	347	Proverbs		790
LOOKED				
I looked on thy furniture so fine,	46	Afflict.1		7
I looked on thy furniture so rich,	46	Afflict.1	W	7
or put into the stocks, that they may be looked upon.	287	Priest 37		21
greatest charitie of all, for she is youngest, and least looked unto;	375	Letters		24
LOOKER'S				
With bushie groves, pricking the lookers eie,	51	Faith		38
That mends the lookers eyes: this is the well	58	H.Script.1		9
LOOKES				
He lives unsafely, that lookes too neere on things.	322	Proverbs		43
Hee that lookes not before, finds himselfe behind.	327	Proverbs		200
Let an ill man lie in thy straw, and he lookes to be thy heire.	330	Proverbs		271
Hee lookes not well to himselfe that lookes not ever.	349	Proverbs		835
entreating that you would a while lay aside those warlike lockes,	442	Oration		3
LOOKING				
Looking on this side, & beyond us all:	48	Repentance	W	9
Being in this their old crackt looking-glasse.	196	Ch.-Milit.		208
We must love, as looking one day to hate.	359	Proverbs	D	1126
loved her even in my departure, in looking to her Son, and my charge.	371	Letters		12
LOOKING-GLASSE				
Being in this their old crackt looking-glasse.	196	Ch.-Milit.		208
LOOKINGS				
And in thy lookings stretch and grow?	144	Discharge		5
LOOKS				
Stayes not, but looks beyond it on the skie;	43	H. Bapt.1		2
Which looks so firm and strong,	66	Ch.-floore		2
Who looks on ground with humble eyes,	96	Charms & K		11
Outlandish looks may not compare:	109	Brit. Ch.		10
Did show and shape thy looks to me,	141	Justice 2		4
A man that looks on glasse,	184	The Elixer		9
speech, and very looks, knowing himself to be both suspected,	237	Priest 9		15
but that he sometimes looks how things go, demanding an account,	239	Priest 9		2
hee considers and looks into the ignorance, or carelesness of his	258	Priest 22		24
yet he looks not in this point of Curing beyond his own Parish,	262	Priest 23		12
Hee puls with a long rope, who looks for anothers death.	322	Proverbs	V	25
Fear keepes and looks to the vineyard, and not the owner.	358	Proverbs	D	1072
He that hath time and looks for better time,	359	Proverbs	D	1102
LOOKT				
When man was lost, thy pitie lookt about	107	Home		13
But while I lookt, the clouds immediately	124	Peace		11
Lookt on a servant, who did know his eye	129	Love unkn.		9

LORD (cont'd)

	PAGE	TITLE		LINE
But thou shalt answer, Lord, for me.	111	The Quip		16
But thou shalt answer, Lord, for me.	111	The Quip		20
Lord, cleare thy gift, that with a constant wit	116	Dulnesse		25
Lord, I acknowledge; take thy plagues away:	126	Confession		26
Lord, mend or rather make us: one creation	127	Giddinesse		25
Of mine inheritance? Lord, if I must borrow,	128	Bunch Gr.		20
Will more complie, then help. A Lord I had,	129	Love unkn.		3
I blesse thee, Lord, because I GROW	132	Paradise		1
Lord, I adjudge my self to tears and grief,	136	Ephes.		25
Lord, pardon, for thy sonne makes good	136	Ephes.		35
But, Lord, the house and familie are thine,	136	Familie		5
Dread Lord, said I, so oft my good;	139	Artillerie		13
Thou art the Lord of glorie;	143	Complaining		6
Art thou all justice, Lord?	143	Complaining		11
Lord thou dost convert,	147	Offering		27
And make me giddie; Lord, I fall,	148	Longing		11
Lord of my scul, love of my minde,	149	Longing		20
Consider, Lord; Lord, bow thine eare,	149	Longing		29
Lord Jesu, thou didst bow	149	Longing		31
Lord heare! Shall he that made the eare,	149	Longing		35
Lord, didst thou leave thy throne,	150	Longing		61
Lord JESU, heare my heart,	150	Longing		73
Away despair; my gracious Lord doth heare.	151	The Bag		1
Hast thou not heard, that my Lord JESUS di'd?	151	The Bag		7
And by that crie of her deare Lord obtain,	152	The Jews		11
And I reply'd, My Lord.	154	The Collar		36
Who heard thee say it. O most gracious Lord,	155	Assurance		20
Lord, thou art mine, and I am thine,	157	Clasping		1
Lord, I am thine, and thou art mine:	157	Clasping		11
Lord, I will mean and speak thy praise,	157	Praise 3		1
My Lord, my Love?	162	The Search		2
Lord, dost thou some new fabrick mold,	162	The Search		25
Lord, see my case.	163	The Search		48
How fresh, O Lord, how sweet and clean	165	The Flower		1
These are thy wonders, Lord of power,	166	The Flower		15
These are thy wonders, Lord of love,	167	The Flower		43
Before the Lord of glorie;	170	Self-cond.		3
For he hath sold for money his deare Lord,	171	Self-cond.		17
Ah my deare angrie Lord,	171	Bittersweet		1
Lord I have invited all,	180	Invitation		31
Ah Lord! do not withdraw,	183	A Parodie		16
Lord teach mee to referr	184	The Elixer	W	1
Lord, thy broken consort raise,	187	Dooms-day		29
Truth Lord, but I have marr'd them: let my shame	189	Love 3		13
Almightie Lord, who from thy glorious throne	190	Ch.-Milit.		1
O gratious Lord how shall I know	200	H. Commun.	W	1
Thou still, O Lord, outstrippest mee.	201	love	W	6
And shrodely, as I think, Lord wash my soule	202	love	W	8
Lord make my Losses up, & sett mee free:	203	Even-song	W	5
Lord help thy servant whose perplexed Soule	204	The Knell	W	2
Lord make thy Blood	204	The Knell	W	13
Sure, Lord, there is enough in thee to dry	206	Walton 2		1
To praise, and on thee, Lord, some Ink bestow.	206	Walton 2		11
In the best face but filth, when, Lord, in thee	206	Walton 2		13
My Lord. A diamond to mee you sent,	209	L. Bacon	D	1
Onely, most noble Lord, shutt not the doore	209	L. Bacon	D	9
And taking councels 'gainst the Lord,	215	Psalm II	D	5
the Lord himself shall them deride:	215	Psalm II	D	10
How are my foes increased, Lord?	216	Psalm III	D	1
But thou, O Lord, art still the shield	216	Psalm III	D	5
Thou art my glory, Lord, and he	216	Psalm III	D	7
I cry'd unto the Lord, he heard	216	Psalm III	D	9
Arise, O Lord, and rescue me;	217	Psalm III	D	17
Belongs, O Lord, thy blessing shall	217	Psalm III	D	23
Lord hear me when I call on Thee,	217	Psalm IV	D	1
Lord of my righteousness:	217	Psalm IV	D	2
Have mercy on me Lord, and hear	217	Psalm IV	D	5
But know the Lord himself doth chuse	217	Psalm IV	D	11
The Lord will harken unto me	217	Psalm IV	D	13
will shew us good? But, Lord,	217	Psalm IV	D	22
For that, O Lord, with perfect joy	218	Psalm IV	D	25
For thy protection, Lord, alone	218	Psalm IV	D	31
Lord to my words encline thine ear,	218	Psalm V	D	1
No evil, Lord, shall dwell with thee,	218	Psalm V	D	11
Lord lead me in thy righteousness,	219	Psalm V	D	21
Destroy them, Lord, and by their own	219	Psalm V	D	29
o Lord, reject them all,	219	Psalm V	D	32
Rebuke me not in wrath, O Lord,	219	Psalm VI	D	1
O pity me! for I (O Lord)	219	Psalm VI	D	3
But, Lord, how long so much perplex'd	220	Psalm VI	D	7
the Lord vouchsafes to weigh my tears;	220	Psalm VI	D	22
And now my foes the Lord will blame	220	Psalm VI	D	25
Save me, my Lord, my God, because	220	Psalm VII	D	1
O Lord deliver mee!	220	Psalm VII	D	4
If I have done this thing, O Lord,	221	Psalm VII	D	9
Arise in wrath, O Lord, advance	221	Psalm VII	D	21
For their sakes, Lord, return on high,	221	Psalm VII	D	27
The Lord shall judge the people all:	221	Psalm VII	D	29
The wicked's malice, Lord, confound,	221	Psalm VII	D	33
the Lord will whet his Sword:	222	Psalm VII	D	42

LORD (cont'd)	PAGE	TITLE		LINE
the Lord will magnifie:	222	Psalm VII	D	62
The Lord prosper the intention to my selfe, and others,	224	Priest		13
but to keep up with the Lord and Lady of the house, and to preserve	226	Priest 2		28
while they remember their earthly Lord, do much forget their	226	Priest 2		32
admonition, or reproofe, sell (with Judas) their Lord and Master.	226	Priest 2		38
as, Lord, open mine eyes, that I may see the wondrous things of thy	229	Priest 4		3
as, Oh Lord blesse my people, and teach them this point;	233	Priest 7		33
God suddenly, Oh Lord, I know that the way of man is not in himself,	234	Priest 7		5
that the Lord would be pleased to sanctifie them all, that they may	235	Priest 8		28
and the exact temperance of our Lord Jesus, with other exemplary	237	Priest 9		34
yet seasonably, and discreetly, by taking aside the Lord, or Lady;	251	Priest 17		28
as joyfull a countenance, as if he were to entertain some great Lord.	253	Priest 19		20
saying, Lord, thou knowest what thou didst, when thou appointedst it	257	Priest 22		32
by bringing them up in the fear and nurture of the Lord;	275	Priest 32		23
his preaching, The Lord (saith he) reward him according to his works.	285	Priest 36		33
the one in, The Grace of our Lord Jesus Christ, &c.	286	Priest 36		4
O almighty and ever-living Lord God!	288	Priest		7
But thou Lord, art patience, and pity, and sweetnesse, and love;	288	Priest		20
then did the Lord of life, unable of himselfe to die, contrive to do	288	Priest		27
And now, O Lord! in the power of thy Victories, and in the wayes	289	Priest		11
Ride on Lord, because of the word of truth, and meeknesse,	289	Priest		22
Lord Jesu! teach thou me, that I may teach them:	289	Priest		26
O Lord hear, O Lord forgive!	289	Priest		33
O Lord, hearken, and do so for thy blessed Son's sake, in whose sweet	289	Priest		33
O Lord! thy blessings hang in clusters, they come trooping upon us!	290	Priest		6
And now Lord, thou hast fed us with the bread of life:	290	Priest		8
O Lord, blesse it: O Lord, make it health and strength unto us;	290	Priest		9
O Lord, make it health and strength unto us;	290	Priest		10
he every where beares towards our deare [great] Master and Lord,	305	Valdesso		5
Print it, that with it the honour of my Lord might be published.	305	Valdesso		8
He that followes the Lord hopes to goe before.	354	Proverbs		994
My Lord of Buckingham was observed on Christmas day to bee so devout	368	Letters		16
I cannot yet find leisure to write to my Lord, or Sir Benjamin	370	Letters		29
Cast thy Care on the Lord and he shall nourish thee. (Psal. 55.)	374	Letters		14
Casting all your Care on the Lord, for he careth for you. (1 Pet.	374	Letters		16
Rejoyce in the Lord alwaies, and again I say rejoyce.	374	Letters		21
at all times rejoyce in the Lord, who taketh care for us:	374	Letters		26
Let your moderation appear to all men, the Lord is at hand:	374	Letters		28
into your hart, and the LORD bless all your purposes to his glory.	375	Letters		33
Wherefore the Lord make good the blessing of your Mother upon you,	377	Letters		3
The LORD bless you, and make you abound in every good worke,	377	Letters		26
And now My gratious Lord God, is pleased to give me you for the Man,	378	Letters		8
Now God the Father of our Lord Jesus Christ bless you more & more,	378	Letters		24
poore of the parish twenty pound To my Lord of Cherbury tenn pound,	383	G.H.'s Will		14
LORD'S				
So in one word our Lords humilitie	168	The Sonne		11
I will declare the Lords decree,	215	Psalm II	D	15
when on the Iords day they do unnecessary servile work,	248	Priest 14		2
LORDS				
Thy hands both made us, and also made us Lords of all thy creatures;	288	Priest		13
offering of yourself to move my Lords of Manchester and Boollingbrook	377	Letters		23
Most Excellent and most magnificent Lords:	441	Oration		23
most Illustrious Lords, since you are so great both in your Princes,	442	Oration		28
LORDSHIP				
Convey a Lordship any way	104	Obedience		2
Convey a Lordship any waies.	104	Obedience	V	2
LOSE (see also loose)				
Lose all mine own? God hath giv'n me a measure	8	Ch.-Porch		38
Stay at the third glasse: if thou lose thy hold,	8	Ch.-Porch		41
Lose not thy self, nor give thy humours way:	12	Ch.-Porch		143
Then he can lose with pleasure, stakes his heart;	14	Ch.-Porch		194
Dost lose? rise up: dost winne? rise in that state.	14	Ch.-Porch		201
(But a proud ignorance will lose his rest,	18	Ch.-Porch		297
Why he'l not lose a cup of drink for thee:	100	Miserie		8
Will lose a pleasure.	127	Giddinesse		8
And now by keeping lose the letter:	152	The Jews		6
nor nigardly to keep, nor troubled to lose any worldly wealth;	227	Priest 3		17
for this in time will lose the name and effect of Charity	244	Priest 12		26
And as malefactors may lose & forfeit their goods, or life;	287	Priest 37		32
for an apple once we lost our God, and still lose him for no more;	288	Priest		19
Sometimes the best gaine is to lose.	328	Proverbs		224
If fooles should not foole it, they shall lose their season.	343	Proverbs	V	702
Paines to get, care to keep, feare to lose.	353	Proverbs		975
All covet, all lose.	358	Proverbs	D	1078
He that hath but one eye, must bee afraid to lose it.	358	Proverbs	D	1088
Some had rather lose their friend then their Jest.	361	Proverbs	D	1170
LOSERS				
So both should losers be.	160	The Pulley		15
Let losers talk: yet thou shalt die;	169	Dial.-Anth		7
LOSEST				
Grasp not at much, for fear thou losest all.	138	The Size		38
LOSETH				
She loseth three for one; her soul, rest, fame.	13	Ch.-Porch		174
He that loseth gold, though drosse,	114	Businesse		31
Hee that is in a towne in May loseth his spring.	353	Proverbs		988
LOSING				
Who strive to sit out losing hands, are lost.	14	Ch.-Porch		202
LOSS				
both to their own loss, and of theirs also who gaze upon them when	232	Priest 6		10
when they overdo it, to the loss of their quiet, and health:	247	Priest 14		28

	PAGE	TITLE		LINE
LOSSE				
This losse springs chiefly from our education.	10	Ch.-Porch		97
Slight not the smallest losse, whether it be	20	Ch.-Porch		343
Fast when thou wilt; but then 'tis gain, not losse.	22	Ch.-Porch		396
All spite in one, counting my life their losse,	33	Sacrifice		194
Nor let them punish me with losse of ryme,	57	Jordan 1		14
Nor let them punish me with losse of time,	57	Jordan 1	V	14
Thou dying dayly, praise thee to thy losse.	73	Afflict.3		18
He that sinnes, hath he no losse?	114	Businesse		33
A servile hawk: low without losse, a spade.	120	Providence		104
After the losse of life and sense,	186	Death		7
Plato and Aristotle were at a losse,	191	Ch.-Milit.		53
of his cure is sick, or afflicted with losse of friend, or estate,	249	Priest 15		14
refreshment, gladly betakes it selfe, even to the losse of honour.	252	Priest 18		23
and utter this well, all his advantages are to his losse.	272	Priest 30		3
sometimes to weepe more for the losse of some temporall things,	279	Priest 33		12
He that hath no good trade, it is to his losse.	340	Proverbs		560
Losse embraceth shame.	341	Proverbs		603
Too much taking heede is losse.	350	Proverbs		889
LOSSES				
Lett Prayer help our losses,	53	H.Commun.	W	38
Lord make my Losses up, & sett mee free:	203	Even-song	W	5
Little losses amaze, great tame.	354	Proverbs		1013
LOST				
Bigge with his sister: he hath lost the reins,	7	Ch.-Porch		32
Bigge with his sister: he hath lost his reins,	7	Ch.-Porch	W	32
Are gone to grasse, and in the pasture lost.	10	Ch.-Porch		96
A mast'ring minde; so both are lost thereby:	10	Ch.-Porch		104
Who strive to sit out losing hands, are lost.	14	Ch.-Porch		202
But love is lost, the way of friendship's gone,	17	Ch.-Porch		275
But love is lost, the art of friendship's gone,	17	Ch.-Porch	W	275
Who say, I care not, those I give for lost;	20	Ch.-Porch		347
Stay not for th' other pin: why thou hast lost	23	Ch.-Porch		411
Preachers conclude with, hath not lost his pains.	24	Ch.-Porch		434
Alas! I did so, when I lost my crown	34	Sacrifice	W	222
Yet though my flours be lost, they say	42	Easter	W	27
Though foolishly he lost the same,	43	East.wings		2
My mirth and edge was lost; a blunted knife	47	Afflict.1		33
Onely thy Chronicle is lost; and yet	69	Content		25
Who shuts his hand, hath lost his gold:	96	Charms & K		5
A falling starr has lost his place:	97	Charms & K	W	19
How hast thou lost them in a croud of cares?	101	Miserie		50
And quickly gain, for each inch lost, an ell.	103	Prayer 2		24
I have both lost mine eyes and eares.	105	Conscience		6
When man was lost, thy pitie lookt about	107	Home		13
But I am lost in flesh, whose sugred lyes	116	Dulnesse		21
Ev'n poysons praise thee. Should a thing be lost?	119	Providence		85
Is lost.	123	Gratefulnes		8
Which I had lost, I hasted to my bed.	130	Love unkn.		48
If thou hadst lost a glove or ring,	133	The Method		11
What I have lost with cordiall fruit?	153	The Collar		9
Is the yeare onely lost to me?	153	The Collar		13
I have not lost one single tear:	158	Praise 3		25
That I may seek, but thou art lost;	183	A Parodie		24
Who by an ambush lost his Paradise.	192	Ch.-Milit.		66
Who for a God clearely a sallet lost.	193	Ch.-Milit.		110
That thy flesh hath lost his food,	199	L'Envoy		9
And then, my Labour's not lost.	207	Walton 3		6
My labour is not lost.	207	Walton 4		4
Worthy had bin, thou hadst not lost thine owne:	211	Bohemia	D	2
from the improvement of things, which otherwise would be lost.	241	Priest 10		24
counting that day lost, wherein he hath not exercised his Charity.	244	Priest 12		18
Governour of all things, yet to them he is lost, as if they said,	281	Priest 34		10
for an apple once we lost our God, and still lose him for no more;	288	Priest		19
He that hath lost his credit is dead to the world.	333	Proverbs		357
For want of a naile the shoe is lost,	338	Proverbs		499
for want of a shoe the horse is lost,	338	Proverbs		499
for want of a horse the rider is lost.	338	Proverbs		499
A stone in a well is not lost.	349	Proverbs		845
The Cow knowes not what her taile is worth, till she have lost it.	350	Proverbs		870
Manie things are lost for want of asking.	353	Proverbs		968
To seek these things is lost labour; Geese in an oyle pot,	361	Proverbs	D	1163
LOT				
They part my garments, and by lot dispose	34	Sacrifice		241
Sweet were the dayes, when thou didst lodge with Lot,	99	Decay		1
To show thou art not bound, as if thy lot	121	Providence		137
LOTH				
Ask'd what it meant. I, (who am never loth	116	Love-joy		4
Ev'n God himself: wherefore she was not loth,	173	Marie Magd		15
LOTHSOME				
Preferring, like brute beasts, a lothsome den	167	Dotage		15
LOTHSOMLY				
though he even creep into it, and though it smell never so lothsomly.	249	Priest 14		6
LOTTERIE				
To this great lotterie, and all would pull.	193	Ch.-Milit.		134
LOUD				
His blouds sweet current much more loud to be.	66	Ch.-lock		12
What do these loud complaints and pulling fears,	136	Familie		3
What do these loud complaints and puling fears,	136	Familie	V	3
Should crie so loud, untill the trump were drown'd,	152	The Jews		10

LOUDER	PAGE	TITLE		LINE
Yet speak they louder then distemper'd fears.	137	Familie		19
LOUR (see also lowre)				
LOUT (see also lowt)				
LOVE				
If yet thou love game at so deere a rate,	14	Ch.-Porch		199
But love is lost, the way of friendship's gone,	17	Ch.-Porch		275
But love is lost, the art of friendship's gone,	17	Ch.-Porch	W	275
Love is a personall debt. I cannot give	17	Ch.-Porch		278
Submit to love; but yet not more then all.	17	Ch.-Porch		284
God made me one man; love makes me no more,	17	Ch.-Porch		287
In love I should: but anger is not love,	18	Ch.-Porch		311
In love or honour: take account of all;	20	Ch.-Porch		344
Scorn no mans love, though of a mean degree;	20	Ch.-Porch		349
(Love is a present for a mightie king)	20	Ch.-Porch		350
Love is a present for the greatest king.	20	Ch.-Porch	W	350
Or love, or language; nothing comes amisse:	20	Ch.-Porch		357
Yet publick hath more promises, more love:	22	Ch.-Porch		398
Yet publick has more promises, more love:	22	Ch.-Porch	W	398
And love's a weight to hearts, to eies a signe.	22	Ch.-Porch		399
And love him for his Master: his condition,	24	Ch.-Porch		443
If stonie hearts will melt with gentle love.	29	Sacrifice		90
My coat, the type of love, which once cur'd those	34	Sacrifice		242
Surely I will revenge me on thy love,	35	Thanksgvng		17
I will tear thence his love and fame.	35	Thanksgvng		26
I will ripp out his love and fame.	35	Thanksgvng	W	26
I will teare out his love and fame.	35	Thanksgvng	WC	26
Till I have found therein thy love,	36	Thanksgvng		46
Till I have found thy love therin,	36	Thanksgvng	W	46
Thy art of lcve, which I'le turn back on thee:	36	Thanksgvng		47
Yet few there are that sound them; Sinne and Love.	37	The Agonie		6
Who knows not Love, let him assay	37	The Agonie		13
Love is that liquour sweet and most divine,	37	The Agonie		17
Let me not love thee, if I love thee not.	48	Afflict.1		66
Softnesse, and peace, and joy, and love, and blisse,	51	Prayer 1		9
Love 1.	54	Love 1		T
Immortall Love, authour of this great frame,	54	Love 1		1
While mortall love doth all the title gain!	54	Love 1		5
While mortall love does all the title gain!	54	Love 1	W	5
Doth warm our hands, and make them write of love.	54	Love 1		14
Love 2.	54	Love 2		T
Gladly engrave thy love in steel,	55	Temper 1		2
Thy power and love, my love and trust	55	Temper 1		27
The same sweet God of love and light:	60	Whitsunday		26
Unto a hardnesse, void of love:	60	Grace		18
Teach me thy love to know;	63	Mattens		17
Blest be the God of love,	63	Even-song		1
For this thy love? have I discharg'd the debt,	64	Even-song		10
I muse, which shows more love,	64	Even-song		25
My God, thou art all love.	64	Even-song		29
And in this love, more then in bed, I rest.	64	Even-song		32
We both together sweetly live and love,	65	Ch.-mus.		7
Ties the whole frame, is Lcve	67	Ch.-floore		11
My poore soul, ev'n sick of love:	72	Frailtie		21
After thy love.	74	The Starre		16
But Love took Grace & Glory by the hand,	84	Sighs & Gr.	W	19
Love built a stately house; where Fortune came,	84	The World		1
But Love and Grace took Glorie by the hand,	84	The World		19
With showres and frosts, with love & aw,	85	Vanitie 1		25
The humble soul compos'd of love and fear	86	Lent		7
Yet I love thee.	88	The Pearl		10
Which on the world a true-love-knot may tie,	88	The Pearl		16
Yet I love thee.	88	The Pearl		20
What mirth and musick mean; what love and wit	89	The Pearl		24
Yet I love thee.	89	The Pearl		30
And at what rate and price I have thy love;	89	The Pearl		35
Oh mightie lcve! Man is one world, and hath	92	Man		47
Praised be the God of love,	92	Antiphon 2		1
It is my honour and my love to free	93	Unkindness		7
My soul doth love thee, yet it loves delay.	96	Justice 1		11
That dumbe inclosure maketh love	98	Mortific.		23
Of thy great love once spread, as in an urn	99	Decay		17
The bargain made to serve thee: but thy love	100	Miserie		26
There is in love a sweetnesse readie penn'd:	103	Jordan 2		17
Of what unmeasurable love	103	Prayer 2		13
Ease, Power, and Love; I value prayer so,	103	Prayer 2		20
But as thy love shall sway,	104	Obedience		19
Show'd a strange love to all our good:	104	Obedience		27
Leave one poore apple for thy love?	107	Home		22
As if thy love could fail or change.	108	Home		28
Blessed be God, whose love it was	110	Brit. Ch.		28
Let them love gold;	111	Vanitie 2		12
Look onely; for to love thee, who can be,	116	Dulnesse		27
Love-joy.	116	Love-joy		T
We all acknowledge both thy power and love	117	Providence		29
But that these ccuntrey-aires thy love	124	Gratefulnes		23
Love unknown.	129	Love unkn.		T
And in my faintings I presume your love	129	Love unkn.		2
To warm his love, which I did fear grew cold.	129	Love unkn.		32
For he is Love.	133	The Method		8
Love God, and love your neighbour. Watch and pray.	135	Divinitie		17

LOVE (cont'd)

	PAGE	TITLE		LINE
And crosse thy love?	135	Ephes.		3
Then weep mine eyes, the God of love doth grieve:	135	Ephes.		7
I will love thee:	146	Praise 2		2
And that love may never cease,	146	Praise 2		3
Lord of my scul, love of my minde,	149	Longing		20
My love, my sweetnesse, heare!	150	Longing		79
What for it self love once began,	156	Assurance		41
Now love and truth will end in man.	156	Assurance		42
Come, my Joy, my Love, my Heart:	156	The Call		9
Such a Love, as none can part:	156	The Call		11
Such a Heart, as joyes in love.	156	The Call		12
My Lord, my Love?	162	The Search		2
As having keyes unto thy love,	162	The Search		15
These are thy wonders, Lord of love,	167	The Flower		43
O, could I love! and stops: God writeth, Loved,	168	a true Hymn		20
He that doth love, and love amisse	170	Self-cond.		7
Since thou dost love, yet strike;	171	Bittersweet		2
I will lament, and love.	171	Bittersweet		8
Thy full-ey'd love!	172	The Glance		20
The God of love my shepherd is,	172	23 Psalme		1
Surely thy sweet and wondrous love	173	23 Psalme		21
And wilt thou leave the Church, and love a stie?	176	Forerunners		22
Let foolish lovers, if they will love dung,	177	Forerunners		25
Love will do the deed:	179	Discipline		18
For with love	179	Discipline		19
Love is swift of foot;	179	Discipline		21
Love's a man of warre,	179	Discipline		22
Come ye hither all, whose love	180	Invitation		25
Here is love, which having breath	180	Invitation		28
God, to show how farre his love	181	Banquet		28
Strive in this, and love the strife.	182	Banquet		54
Love.	188	Love 3		T
Love bade me welcome: yet my soul drew back,	188	Love 3		1
But quick-ey'd Love, observing me grow slack	188	Love 3		3
Love said, you shall be he.	189	Love 3		8
Love took my hand, and smiling did reply,	189	Love 3		11
And know you not, sayes Love, who bore the blame?	189	Love 3		15
You must sit down, sayes Love, and taste my meat:	189	Love 3		17
Not the decrees of power, but bands of love.	190	Ch.-Milit.		10
Prepar'd and fitted to receive thy love.	190	Ch.-Milit.		16
Wonders of anger once, but now of love.	191	Ch.-Milit.		38
Thee to love, in thee to sleep.	199	L'Envoy		4
Love.	201	love	W	T
Thou art too hard for me in Love:	201	love	W	1
Whereas if I orecome thee & thy Love	202	love	W	23
My God, the poore expressions of my Love	204	Persever.	W	1
Upon thine Altar burnt? Cannot thy love	206	Walton 1		6
When Love being weary made an end	439	Walton 5		11
Love neere his death desir'd to end	439	Walton 5	V	11
the righteous man to love.	217	Psalm IV	D	12
The question is, whose love the greater showes:	438	Lat.Trans.		2
since our Saviour hath made that the argument of a Pastour's love,	224	Priest		6
the servants of God, for the planting both of love, and humility.	229	Priest 4		27
for thou art Love, and when thou teachest, all are Scholers.	233	Priest 7		36
into Covetousnesse, Love of pleasure, or ease, or the like.	238	Priest 9		23
speciall grace of faith, patience, meeknesse, love, obedience, &c.	238	Priest 9		32
He keeps his servants between love, and fear, according as hee findes	241	Priest 10		7
To his Children he shewes more love then terrour, to his servants	241	Priest 10		9
more love then terrour, to his servants more terrour then love;	241	Priest 10		10
although we should love him onely for his own sake, yet out of his	243	Priest 11		30
and Love, and the Cases of Conscience belonging thereto,	279	Priest 33		34
then he dives unto the boundlesse Ocean of Gods Love,	283	Priest 34		8
As Creatures, he must needs love them;	283	Priest 34		11
As sinfull, he must much more love them;	283	Priest 34		13
his infinite hate of sinne, his Love overcame that hate;	283	Priest 34		14
gave them love for love, even the son of his love out of his bosome	283	Priest 34		16
love for love, even the son of his love out of his bosome of love.	283	Priest 34		17
hath two pledges of Gods Love, that in the mouth of two or three	283	Priest 34		18
till either they despise that Love, or despaire of his Mercy:	283	Priest 34		23
not any sin else, but is within his Love;	283	Priest 34		24
but the despising of Love must needs be without it.	283	Priest 34		25
as knowing that absence breedes strangeness, but presence love.	284	Priest 35		16
Now Love is his business, and aime;	284	Priest 35		16
But thou Lord, art patience, and pity, and sweetnesse, and love;	288	Priest		21
many waters could not quench thy love!	288	Priest		31
Neither doth thy love yet stay here!	289	Priest		3
pardoning my sins, and bidding me go feed the people of thy love.	289	Priest		7
and in the wayes of thy Ordinances, and in the truth of thy Love, Lo,	289	Priest		13
and unworthy hearts rob us of the continuance of this thy sweet love:	289	Priest		21
untill our obedience reach the measure of thy love, who hast done	290	Priest		12
for which I doe so love him, that were there nothing else,	305	Valdesso		7
Love and a Cough cannot be hid.	322	Proverbs		49
No love to a Fathers.	325	Proverbs		121
Love your neighbour, yet pull not downe your hedge.	325	Proverbs		141
Love your neighbour, but pull not downe your hedge.	325	Proverbs	V	141
In war, hunting, and love,	328	Proverbs		228
Love is not found in the market.	334	Proverbs		401
He that hath love in his brest, hath spurres in his sides.	335	Proverbs		426
Love is the true price of love.	339	Proverbs		540
Love rules his kingdome without a sword.	339	Proverbs		541

LOVE (cont'd)	PAGE	TITLE		LINE
Love makes all hard hearts gentle.	339	Proverbs		542
Love makes a good eye squint.	339	Proverbs		543
Love askes faith, and faith firmenesse.	339	Proverbs		544
Love makes one fitt for any work.	343	Proverbs		646
Love and businesse teach eloquence.	345	Proverbs		704
the best love that of children.	346	Proverbs		741
In an hundred elles of contention, there is not an inch of love.	348	Proverbs		817
No prison is faire, nor love foule.	348	Proverbs		829
No prison is faire, & no love foule.	348	Proverbs	V	829
No love is foule, nor prison fair.	359	Proverbs	D	1122
We must love, as looking one day to hate.	359	Proverbs	D	1126
Love without end, hath no end, says the Spaniard: (meaning, . .	361	Proverbs	D	1160
Presents of love fear not to be ill taken of strangers. . .	361	Proverbs	D	1162
The love of money and the love of learning rarely meet. . .	361	Proverbs	D	1168
to reprove the vanity of those many Love-poems, that are daily writ	363	Letters		7
and I will strive to imitate the compleatness of your love, . .	364	Letters		3
and I love my friends so well, as that if all things proved not well,	364	Letters		28
for I am sure you love Your faithfullest Servant, GEORGE HERBERT.	365	Letters		25
yet his love expects them not but first certifies you that there are	368	Letters		3
it is no matter, for the Gentleman needs no incitation to love me.	369	Letters		29
or, that my love is as dumb as my papers;	371	Letters		25
with that earnestness, that becomes your griefs, and my love.	372	Letters		1
till I take some opportunity to let them know your love, . .	375	Letters		22
wee might the more by love grow on, both the Spanish and Brittish	442	Oration		17
LOVE-JOY				
Love-joy.	116	Love-joy		T
LOVE-POEMS				
to reprove the vanity of those many Love-poems, that are daily writ	363	Letters		7
LOVE'S				
'Twas more secure in great Loves Common-weal	439	Walton 5		17
LOV'D				
The last and lov'd, though dreadfull day.	108	Home		58
Who above all things lov'd this life;	122	Time		8
In life you lov'd me not, in death you bewaile me. . . .	328	Proverbs		218
LOVED				
O, could I love! and stops: God writeth, Loved, ...	168	a true Hymn		20
All is well to him, that is loved of his neighbours. . . .	321	Proverbs	V	10
that I loved her even in my departure, in looking to her Son,	371	Letters		12
LOVELINESSE				
Thou art my lovelinesse, my life, my light, ...	115	Dulnesse		9
LOVELY				
Farewell sweet phrases, lovely metaphors.	176	Forerunners		13
Lovely enchanting language, sugar-cane, ...	176	Forerunners		19
or pure, or lovely, or of good report, if there be any vertue,	253	Priest 19		24
but things that are lovely, & of good report if there be any vertue	380	Woodnoth		14
LOVER				
The wanton lover in a curious strain	115	Dulnesse		5
Hath some fond lover tic'd thee to thy bane?	176	Forerunners		21
And the Parson is a lover of and exciter to justice in all things,	277	Priest 32		22
The Countrey Parson is a Lover of old Customes, if they be good,	283	Priest 35		27
LOVER'S				
Must purling streams refresh a lovers loves?	56	Jordan 1		8
And keep your measures for some lovers lute, ...	164	Grief		16
LOVERS				
Lovers are still pretending, & ev'n wrongs	116	Dulnesse		19
Let foolish lovers, if they will love dung, ...	177	Forerunners		25
Like Comick Lovers ever one way runn:	198	Ch.-Milit.	W	271
A poore beauty finds more lovers then husbands.	337	Proverbs		481
LOVES				
He that loves Gods abode, and to combine	24	Ch.-Porch		437
Must purling streams refresh a lovers loves?	56	Jordan 1		8
Welcome deare feast of Lent: who loves not thee, ...	86	Lent		1
He loves not Temperance, or Authoritie, ...	86	Lent		2
My soul doth love thee, yet it loves delay.	96	Justice 1		11
that God loves them, till either they despise that Love, . .	283	Priest 34		22
Particularly, he loves Procession, and maintains it, because there	284	Priest 35		2
The bird loves her nest.	323	Proverbs		75
Hee that loves the tree, loves the branch.	349	Proverbs		857
Those that God loves, do not live long.	358	Proverbs	D	1094
LOVETH				
For who can look for lesse, that loveth Life. / Strife. . .	170	Water-crs.		5
LOVING				
Though it be cold, hard, foul, from loving man	41	Sepulchre		23
women to heaven) a wise and loving husband could out of humility,	238	Priest 9		31
the nature of man, loving refreshment, gladly betakes it selfe,	252	Priest 18		22
The second means is a very loving, and sweet usage of them, . .	262	Priest 24		25
of Gods Love, and the unspeakeable riches of his loving kindnesse.	283	Priest 34		8
Charity in loving walking, and neighbourly accompanying one another,	284	Priest 35		5
mee in your letters, for I am your ever loving brother, G. HERBERT.	366	Letters		22
So prayes Your ever loving brother, G. HERBERT.	376	Letters		21
every good worke, to the joy of your ever loving brother, G. HERBERT.	377	Letters		28
LOVINGLY				
but advance them, was lovingly done, and like a good brother.	375	Letters		3
the fruit of my observation, for they have lived so lovingly, lying,	375	Letters		18
You write very lovingly that all your things are mine. . . .	378	Letters		21
LOW				
Pitch thy behaviour low, thy projects high;	19	Ch.-Porch		331
The earth is not too low, ...	53	Antiphon 1		5
I know thy parentage is base and low:	77	Avarice		3
When age grows low and weak, ...	98	Mortific.		25

LOW (cont'd)	PAGE	TITLE	LINE
Poore silly soul, whose hope and head lies low;	111	Vanitie 2	1
A servile hawk: low without losse, a spade.	120	Providence	104
Let th' upper springs into the low	137	The Size	5
Look high and low;	144	Discharge	4
Brought thee low, ...	179	Discipline	27
But I still being low and short, ...	182	Banquet	40
Nothing can be sc low, ...	184	The Elixer W	14
Who makes a root his God, how low is he, ...	193	Ch.-Milit.	115
Such poor invention burns in their low mind	206	Walton 2	9
few bring covetousness thus low, or consider it so narrowly,	265	Priest 26	31
You cannot make the fire so low but it will get out.	353	Proverbs	965
come agents hither from the low-Cuntries to treat of divers matters,	368	Letters	5
LOW-CUNTRIES			
come agents hither from the low-Cuntries to treat of divers matters,	368	Letters	5
LOWER			
If I go lower in the book, ...	50	Faith	21
What can be lower then the common manger?	50	Faith	22
As a floud the lower grounds.	180	Invitation	24
be vilified or debased, by being cast on the lower ranke of people;	270	Priest 29	8
Higher opportunities of doeing good are to be preferred before lower,	380	Woodnoth	4
before lower, even where to continue in the lower is no sinn.	380	Woodnoth	4
LOWEST			
Humilitie, who sat the lowest there	70	Humilitie	5
LOWLY			
Of lowly matter for high uses meet, ...	161	Priesthood	35
LOWRE			
Get a sharp wife, a servant that will lowre.	15	Ch.-Porch	213
Peace pratler, dc not lowre:	105	Conscience	1
LOWT			
A sleepy master makes his servant a Lowt.	346	Proverbs	766
LOYNES			
against these ghostly enemies he girdeth up his loynes, . . .	238	Priest 9	4
LOYTER			
Yet ill deeds loyter not: for they supplie	122	Sinnes rd.	16
LOYTERER			
Ah Loyterer! I'le no more, no more I'le bring:	121	Hope	7
LUCAS			
to Mr Hays the Comment of Lucas Brugensis uppon the Scripture	382	G.H.'s Will	19
LUD			
Written by Lud. Cornarus, Translated into English by Mr. George	291	Cornaro	T
LUKE			
and the forgivenesse of sins, Matthew 6. 14. Luke 7. 47. . . .	244	Priest 12	10
And Luke 10. 21. He rejoyced in Spirit:	280	Priest 34	10
being no reason, why any should distrust Saint Luke, or Tertullian,	282	Priest 34	21
generation should not passe, till all were fulfilled, Luke 21. 32.	282	Priest 34	29
Saint Luke was a Saint and a Physitian, yet is dead. . . .	354	Proverbs	1008
LULLINGS			
The lullings and the relishes of it;	89	The Pearl	22
LUMP			
And all our lump to leaven;	53	H.Commun.	30
A lump of flesh, without a foot or wing	102	Miserie	74
At least in lump: for such doth oft destroy;	138	The Size	27
LURK			
If thou shalt let this venome lurk, ...	45	Nature	7
LUST			
Beware of lust: it doth pollute and foul	6	Ch.-Porch	7
Beware of Lust (startle not) o beware	6	Ch.-Porch W	7
Much lesse towards God, whose lust is all their book? . . .	6	Ch.-Porch	12
Not grudging, that thy lust hath bounds and staies. . . .	7	Ch.-Porch	16
Lust and wine plead a pleasure, avarice gain:	8	Ch.-Porch	57
Lust and wine plead a pleasure, cheating gain:	8	Ch.-Porch W	57
Who wert disseized by usurping lust:	54	Love 2	12
How tame these ashes are, how free from lust, ...	65	Ch.-monum.	23
Folly, and worse then folly, lust:	74	The Starre	10
Should thicken all my powers; because my lust	83	Sighs & Gr.	15
When th' hair is sweet through pride or lust, ...	96	Charms & K	13
A sad repentance, not the spoils of lust:	192	Ch.-Milit.	68
sloath, lust, and when not, and so in many circumstances of actions.	230	Priest 5	30
A man is known tc be mortal by two things, Sleep and Lust. . .	361	Proverbs D	1159
LUSTIE			
me contrariwise, at the age of eightie and one, strong and lustie;	291	Cornaro	11
LUSTRE			
Impute a lustre, and allow them bright;	51	Faith	35
Impart a lustre, and allow them bright;	51	Faith W	35
Such was their lustre, they did so excell, ...	102	Jordan 2	2
Maintaine there Lustre still, & shining cleere	211	Bohemia D	11
LUSTS			
As may consume our lusts, and make thee way.	54	Love 2	5
Thy lusts have made, and not thy lusts alone;	147	Offering	15
When height of malice, and prodigious lusts, ...	197	Ch.-Milit.	237
to get knowledg, but to subdue and mortifie all lusts and affections:	226	Priest 2	10
Mortification in regard of lusts and affections, and the stupifying	227	Priest 3	6
and mastered all his lusts and affections within, and the whole Army,	278	Priest 33	22
LUSTY			
and his soul fervent, active, young, and lusty as an eagle. . .	237	Priest 9	27
LUTE			
Awake, my lute, and struggle for thy part	41	Easter	7
Consort both heart and lute, and twist a song	42	Easter	13
Nor a good sword, nor yet a lute:	69	Quidditie	4
Nor a good sword, not yet a lute:	69	Quidditie W	4

LUTE (cont'd)	PAGE	TITLE		LINE
Trees would be tuning on their native lute	117	Providence		10
Oh take thy lute, and tune it to a strain,	136	Ephes.		19
And keep your measures for some lovers lute,	164	Grief		16
Awake therefore, my Lute, and my Viol!	289	Priest		9
LUTER'S				
The Apothecaries morter spoiles the Luters musick.	351	Proverbs		925
LUXURY				
Secondly because Luxury is a very visible sinne, the Parson is very	227	Priest 3		22
LY (noun)				
Dare to be true. Nothing can need a ly:	9	Ch.-Porch		77
He suffers not a ly or equivocation by any means in his house,	240	Priest 10		32
LY				
and my neerest way ly through the Church, I will not doubt to go	273	Priest 31		34
LYE				
thou slay'st the men that lye:	218	Psalm V	D	14
but shall bring forth a lye.	222	Psalm VII	D	52
Better speake truth rudely, then lye covertly.	346	Proverbs		767
A good heart cannot lye.	347	Proverbs		800
LYER				
Shew me a lyer, and I'le shew thee a theefe.	343	Proverbs		652
LYERS				
Debters are lyers.	326	Proverbs		165
LYES (noun)				
But I am lost in flesh, whose sugred lyes	116	Dulnesse		21
Embroider'd lyes, nothing between two dishes;	167	Dotage		5
LYES				
Of his rich crown, from whom lyes no appeal	78	Ang.&Sts.		22
Of his great crown, from whom lyes no appeal	78	Ang.&Sts.	W	22
Lyes round about us to helpe out the story,	212	Bohemia	D	26
as it lyes entire, and unbroken in the Scripture it self.	235	Priest 7		4
what a great Charge lyes upon them, and that indeed the whole order	269	Priest 29		28
for exactnesse lyes in particulars.	275	Priest 32		19
LYEST				
Thou lyest warme, and wilt not rise,	101	Miserie	W	51
LYING				
Most things sleep lying; th' Elephant leans or stands.	121	Providence		140
Most things sleep lying; th' Elephant leane or stand.	121	Providence	V	140
alwayes cleer, and evident, as Adultery, Murder, Hatred, Lying, &c.	264	Priest 26		7
for they have lived so lovingly, lying, eating, walking,	375	Letters		19
especially no obligation lying upon you either for the execution	380	Woodnoth		26
LYON				
The Lyon is not so fierce as they paint him.	330	Proverbs		289
It's better to be the head of a Lyzard, then the tayle of a Lyon.	340	Proverbs		579
It's better to be the head of a mouse, then the tayle of a Lyon.	340	Proverbs	V	579
The sight of a man hath the force of a Lyon.	342	Proverbs		617
Beate the dog before the Lyon.	348	Proverbs		825
That God who hath delivered me out of the paws of the Lyon and Bear,	374	Letters		7
LYON'S				
A Lyons skin is never cheape.	323	Proverbs		55
LYZARD				
It's better to be the head of a Lyzard, then the tayle of a Lyon.	340	Proverbs		579
MACARIUS				
Holy Macarius and great Anthonie	191	Ch.-Milit.		41
MAD				
By sight of sinne we should grow mad.	63	Sinne 2		8
when they are great they make them mad.	352	Proverbs		939
Take heed of mad folks in a narrow place.	360	Proverbs	D	1149
MADAM				
Madam! As the Earth is but a point in respect of the heavens,	372	Letters		29
of the Body, dear Madam, remember the holy Martyrs of God,	373	Letters		35
Dear Madam, pardon my boldness, and, accept the good meaning of,	374	Letters		30
be none of the Court-stile, yet doubtless Madam, can do you no hurt:	377	Letters		3
and the great joy of Madam, Your most faithful Servant in Christ	377	Letters		8
Madam, Your poor Colony of Servants present their humble duties.	377	Letters		13
MADE				
Take not his name, who made thy mouth, in vain:	8	Ch.-Porch		55
Pride and full sinnes have made the way a road.	9	Ch.-Porch		72
What nature made a ship, he makes a shelf.	11	Ch.-Porch		120
God made me one man; love makes me no more,	17	Ch.-Porch		287
How know'st thou, but thy sinnes made him miscarrie?	24	Ch.-Porch		440
Made of a heart, and cemented with teares:	26	The Altar		2
And made it fine to me:	46	Afflict.1		8
And made it rich to me:	46	Afflict.1	W	8
And made her youth and fiercenesse seek thy face.	46	Afflict.1		18
And made a partie unawares for wo.	47	Afflict.1		24
And thrown it on that dust which thou hast made,	54	Love 1		4
And thrown it in that dust which thou hast made,	54	Love 1	W	4
Thy hands made both, and I am there:	55	Temper 1		26
Lord, who hast made me living mudd,	68	Trin.Sun.	W	1
For which ye wrangle, made them turn their frown	71	Humilitie		28
And made a garden there for those	76	Sunday		41
Then forcing thee, by fire he made thee bright:	77	Avarice		9
Man calleth thee his wealth, who made thee rich;	77	Avarice		13
And made them jewels to betroth	82	Ungratef.		10
Who hath made of two folds one.	93	Antiphon 2		23
Which hath made of two folds one.	93	Antiphon 2	W	23
I made a posie, while the day ran by:	94	Life		1
The bargain made to serve thee: but thy love	100	Miserie		26
Made in the tree, where she was wont to sit,	101	Miserie		56
Who made the arbour: this exceeds her wit.	101	Miserie		58

MADE (cont'd)	PAGE	TITLE		LINE
When first my lines of heav'nly joyes made mention,	102	Jordan 2		1
When first my verse of heav'nly joyes made mention,	102	Jordan 2	W	1
If I but lift mine eyes, my suit is made:	103	Prayer 2		5
If souls be made of earthly mold,	111	Vanitie 2		11
Onely to Man thou hast made known thy wayes,	117	Providence		6
And made him Secretarie of thy praise.	117	Providence		8
Which crie and follow. Thou hast made poore sand	118	Providence		47
Is by a ship the speedier passage made.	119	Providence		90
Christs coming hath made man thy debter,	122	Time		11
Nay thou hast made a sigh and grone	124	Gratefulnes		19
Is this same grief! within my heart I made	126	Confession		2
And made it bring forth grapes good store.	128	Bunch Gr.		25
And made you look much fresher then before.	140	Ch.-rents		15
Gods promises have made thee mine;	141	Justice 2		22
Fain would I here have made abode,	142	Pilgrimage		9
Hast thou not made thy counts, and summ'd up all?	144	Discharge		6
Thy lusts have made, and not thy lusts alone;	147	Offering		15
Lord heare! Shall he that made the eare,	149	Longing		35
Which pettie thoughts have made, and made to thee	153	The Collar		23
Who by thy coming may be made a court!	155	Glimpse		30
But also mine; as when the league was made	156	Assurance		28
When God at first made man,	159	The Pulley		1
So strength first made a way;	160	The Pulley		6
When almost all was out, God made a stay,	160	The Pulley		8
And force of fire, what curious things are made	161	Priesthood		14
Hath made a Jewish choice:	170	Self-cond.		9
He that hath made a sorrie wedding	171	Self-cond.		13
Passing all cordials made by any art,	171	The Glance		6
God hath made starres the foil	176	The Foil		5
Made a head	181	Banquet		14
Who made the eyes but I?	189	Love 3		12
Made Pharaoh Moses, changing th' historie.	191	Ch.-Milit.		42
Who, that they might subdue, made all their foes.	191	Ch.-Milit.		62
That as before Empire and Arts made way,	192	Ch.-Milit.		83
Of his two thrones he made the latter best,	196	Ch.-Milit.		213
So though Sinne made his latter seat the better,	196	Ch.-Milit.		223
So though Sinne made his later seat the better,	196	Ch.-Milit.	W	223
But that which made my soule to dye	201	H. Commun.	W	28
That also made thee dead.	201	H. Commun.	W	30
Why are not Sonnets made of thee? and layes	206	Walton 1		5
When Love being weary made an end	439	Walton 5		11
When sense is made by Comments. But that face	212	Bohemia	D	29
like vessels made of brittle clay.	216	Psalm II	D	24
But in the pit which he hath made	222	Psalm VII	D	55
since our Saviour hath made that the argument of a Pastour's love,	224	Priest		5
the Fathers, or Schoolmen, a Minister is made, and the thing done.	226	Priest 2		12
This Body he made by way of expounding the Church Catechisme,	230	Priest 5		7
And for the Philippians made request with joy, ch. 1. 4.	234	Priest 7		14
the same affection which made him not profit before, making him then	235	Priest 7		13
the choyce of his wife was made rather by his eare, then by his eye;	238	Priest 9		26
For meat was made for man, not man for meat.	242	Priest 10		32
Was it made, or came it by chance?	256	Priest 21		7
Who made it? Did you see God make it?	256	Priest 21		8
You said, God made the world;	256	Priest 21		11
This familiar illustration made the answer so plaine, that he was	257	Priest 21		5
but that they still fall from all compromises that have been made.	260	Priest 23		25
even as our Saviour made plants and seeds to teach the people:	261	Priest 23		13
yerrow, melilot, and Saint Johns wort made into a salve;	262	Priest 23		6
comphrey and smallage made into a Poultis, have done great and rare	262	Priest 23		8
being made by the precept of Authority more then indifferent,	263	Priest 24		12
but rather made food miraculously, then suffered so good desires	267	Priest 26		25
and joyfull, that hee is made conformable to his Master;	269	Priest 28		16
God) stands fast in the Liberty wherewith Christ hath made us free.	272	Priest 31		19
whereas there are usually three Objections made against the Place;	276	Priest 32		19
duty in Ministers themselves, hath made the people also neglect it;	286	Priest 36		12
notorious faults are either such as are made known by common fame	287	Priest 37		12
Thy hands both made us, and also made us Lords of all thy creatures;	288	Priest		12
Thy hands both made us, and also made us Lords of all thy creatures;	288	Priest		13
and hast made our salvation, not our punishment, thy glory:	288	Priest		23
which thou hast made a Land of light, a store-house of thy treasures	289	Priest		18
as barren grounds are made fruitfull by good husbandry.	292	Cornaro		12
because from the time that I was made whole, I never since departed	293	Cornaro		25
of my drink, which before was foureteen ounces, I made now sixteen.	296	Cornaro		13
without such observation, as is not easily to be made upon others;	297	Cornaro		30
But I drained the ground, and made the aire good:	301	Cornaro		28
Neither is this my pleasure made lesse by the decaying dulnesse of my	302	Cornaro		7
at these yeares (viz. 83) I have made a most pleasant comedie,	302	Cornaro		28
or lesse my self, who being ten yeares older have made a Comedie?	302	Cornaro		36
[the law is not made for a righteous man:]	315	Valdesso		34
unlesse he could have made it appeare, that it was done by Gods	316	Valdesso		26
A Horse made, and a man to make.	321	Proverbs		22
for to the sea he made havens, and to rivers foords.	331	Proverbs		315
for to the sea he made heavens, and to rivers foords.	331	Proverbs	V	315
A hatt is not made for one shower.	343	Proverbs		673
Chuse a horse made, and a wife to make.	350	Proverbs		871
Hee that learnes a trade hath a purchase made.	353	Proverbs		978
When God is made master of a family, he orders the disorderly.	353	Proverbs		983
An oath that is not to bee made is not to be kept.	354	Proverbs		1017
Civill Wars of France made	361	Proverbs	D	1174
Whatever is made by the hand of man,	362	Proverbs	D	1184

MADE (cont'd)	PAGE	TITLE		LINE
whether my peace be yet made with her concerning my unkind departure.	371	Letters		8
because sickness hath made me unable to perform those Offices	373	Letters		9
and body to Almightie God that made them doe thus dispose of my	382	G.H.'s Will		2
of Cambridge, when the Ambassadours were made Masters of Arts.	441	Oration		T
MAD'ST				
As if thou mad'st thy will. A civil guest	18	Ch.-Porch		305
When th' earth was dry, thou mad'st a sea of wet:	120	Providence		113
didst thou arise triumphant, and therein mad'st us victorious.	289	Priest		2
MADNESSE				
setting aside his care of his Flock, were a madnesse to doubt of.	234	Priest 7		17
MAGAZENE				
the storehouse and magazene of life and comfort, the holy Scriptures.	228	Priest 4		22
MAGAZENS				
Suckt all thy magazens: my head did ake, ...	83	Sighs & Gr.		10
MAGDALEN				
To Mrss Magdalen Vaughan one hundred pound, To Mrs Catharine Vaughan	383	G.H.'s Will		5
MAGDALENE				
Marie Magdalene.	173	Marie Magd		T
that (which you are thinking to doe) to blessed Mary Magd. & Paul,	381	Woodnoth		5
MAGISTRATE				
Art thou a Magistrate? then be severe:	10	Ch.-Porch		85
but he might have been justly put to death for it by the Magistrate,	316	Valdesso		25
for as a Magistrate judgeth in his tribunall, so a Scholar judgeth in	317	Valdesso		1
men cannot judg spirituall mens actions, but the Magistrate may.	317	Valdesso		6
MAGISTRATES				
both an honor which they owe to the Reverend Judges and Magistrates,	277	Priest 32		2
The case of ministers and magistrates is another thing, . .	381	Woodnoth		27
MAGNANIMITY				
and Pusillanimity, Magnanimity: Of these the heathen freed . .	308	Valdesso		11
MAGNANIMOUS				
So shalt thou humble and magnanimous be:	19	Ch.-Porch		332
MAGNIFICENT				
Most Excellent and most magnificent Lords:	441	Oration		23
MAGNIFIE				
the Lord will magnifie:	222	Psalm VII	D	62
we magnifie thee for ever!	289	Priest		11
MAGUS				
And therfore St. Peter used that fearfull imprecation to Simon Magus,	285	Priest 36		30
MAHOMETAN				
To such Mahometan stupidities, ...	194	Ch.-Milit.		153
MAID (see also mayds)				
The gigler is a milk-maid, whom infection, ...	16	Ch.-Porch		249
My vows to thee most gladly, blessed Maid, ...	78	Ang.&Sts.		9
MAIDES				
Empty Chambers make foolish maides.	322	Proverbs		29
MAIN				
Both the main sale, and the commodities;	89	The Pearl		34
The third means is the observation what is the main foundation,	262	Priest 24		28
MAINE				
From Holland saile into the Maine:	213	L' Envoy	D	10
MAINTAIN				
that he cannot without this maintain himself in a Christian state.	272	Priest 31		24
MAINTAINE				
Maintaine there Lustre still, & shining cleere	211	Bohemia	D	11
excellent statute, which bindes all Parishes to maintaine their own.	244	Priest 12		23
'Tis easier to build two chimneys, then to maintaine one. . .	350	Proverbs		893
MAINTAINES				
for he maintaines that it is Faith and Infidelity that shall judge us	311	Valdesso		22
MAINTAINS				
I know the wayes of Honour, what maintains	88	The Pearl		11
and maintains it, because there are contained therein 4 manifest	284	Priest 35		2
MAINTENANCE				
he adviseth them so to labour for wealth and maintenance, . .	248	Priest 14		6
have attain'd to the years of Discretion, and competent Maintenance.	373	Letters		14
MAIST				
Of better lodging thou maist be possest.	80	Christmas	W	14
MAJESTICK				
In his majestick robes of glorie, ...	151	The Bag		10
Shine on, Majestick soule, abide	213	L' Envoy	D	1
MAJESTIE				
But keep a standing Majestie in me.	56	Temper 2		16
MAJESTY				
Cover the Earth, so doth thy Majesty:	206	Walton 2		3
Because against thy Majesty	219	Psalm V	D	33
as being truly touched and amazed with the Majesty of God, . .	231	Priest 6		6
by an often urging of the presence, and majesty of God, by these,	234	Priest 7		25
Then turning the discourse to his Majesty, And he is a great God,	234	Priest 7		31
befall him unworthy of that Majesty before which he is to present	235	Priest 8		23
and worshipping the invisible majesty, and presence of Almighty God,	236	Priest 8		5
Majesty, and Power, and Brightnesse, and Glory!	288	Priest		7
MAJESTYE				
And show thy undivided Majestye	212	Bohemia	D	34
MAKE				
And make us strive, who shall sing best thy name.	5	Dedication		4
Turn their eyes hither, who shall make a gain:	5	Dedication		5
Ryme thee to good, and make a bait of pleasure.	6	Ch.-Porch		4
Hee'le make thy wife a blessing not a rodd.	7	Ch.-Porch	W	18
Let not each fansy make thee to detest	7	Ch.-Porch	W	19
Let not each motion make thee to detest	7	Ch.-Porch	WC	19
Boast not thereof; nor make thy shame thy glorie.	8	Ch.-Porch		50

MAKE (cont'd)

	PAGE	TITLE		LINE
Which is thy best stake, when griefs make thee tame.	9	Ch.-Porch		66
Desire and shame, will make thy labour, play:	10	Ch.-Porch	W	90
Studie this art, make it thy great designe;	10	Ch.-Porch		101
Or els they breed them tender, make them need	10	Ch.-Porch		105
The way to make thy sonne rich, is to fill	11	Ch.-Porch		109
But if thy sonne can make ten pound his measure,	11	Ch.-Porch		113
Never exceed thy income. Youth may make	13	Ch.-Porch		157
Lest gaining gain on thee, and make thee dimme	13	Ch.-Porch		164
Then keep such companie; make them thy allay:	15	Ch.-Porch		212
'Tis a thinne webbe, which poysonous fancies make:	15	Ch.-Porch		224
Make not thy sport, abuses: for the fly	15	Ch.-Porch		233
Doth ratably thy fortunes marre or make.	16	Ch.-Porch		256
Doth make thee parcell-devil in damnation.	16	Ch.-Porch		258
As hurts not others, but may make thee better,	16	Ch.-Porch		262
Till labour come, and make my weaknesse score.	17	Ch.-Porch		288
Much lesse make any one thine enemie.	20	Ch.-Porch		351
Much lesse make any one thy enemie.	20	Ch.-Porch	W	351
Joyn hands with God to make a man to live.	21	Ch.-Porch		376
And make thy self all reverence and fear.	22	Ch.-Porch		406
Most surely judg'd, make thy accounts agree.	24	Ch.-Porch		456
Make not an ell, by trifling in thy wo.	24	Ch.-Porch		460
The Princes of my people make a head	26	Sacrifice		5
Alas! what haste they make to be undone!	27	Sacrifice		34
O make me innocent, that I	36	Reprisall		5
Since, if my soul make even with the week,	38	The Sinner		3
And make a suit unto him, to afford	40	Redemption		3
His life may make thee gold, and much more just.	41	Easter		6
And make up our defects with his sweet art.	42	Easter		18
Can not make up so brave a feast	42	Easter	W	25
Or make a new one, since the old	45	Nature		15
Fractures well cur'd make us more strong.	49	Repentance		36
Thus dost thou make proud knowledge bend & crouch	50	Faith		31
Thus dost thou make proud knowledge bow & crouch	50	Faith	W	31
Inherent in them, thou didst make the sunne	51	Faith		34
Another lift like this will make	52	H.Commun.		27
Doth warm our hands, and make them write of love.	54	Love 1		14
Which shall consume the world, first make it tame;	54	Love 2		3
As may consume our lusts, and make thee way.	54	Love 2		5
And praise him who did make and mend our eies.	54	Love 2		14
To make the musick better.	55	Temper 1		24
Make one place ev'ry where.	55	Temper 1		28
Nor flowres to make that, nor the husbandrie	57	Employm. 1		19
Thou art all health, health thriving, till it make	58	H.Script.1		5
This verse marks that, and both do make a motion	58	H.Script.2		5
These three make up some Christians destinie:	58	H.Script.2		8
And in another make me understood.	58	H.Script.2		12
I goe to Church; make me an Angel, I	61	Praise 1	W	5
Then we must needs for that day make a match.	62	Mattens		4
If apparitions make us sad,	63	Sinne 2		7
O make mee wholy guiltles, or at least	66	Ch.-lock	W	9
For though sinnes plead too, yet like stones they make	66	Ch.-lock		11
From private bodies, make as big a thunder,	69	Content		23
For thou canst make a debter,	74	The Starre		7
And make it better.	74	The Starre		8
And make it shine:	74	The Starre		12
Make up one man; whose face thou art,	75	Sunday		9
Make bracelets to adorn the wife	76	Sunday		31
Make bracelets for the spouse & wife	76	Sunday	W	31
That was requir'd to make us gay,	76	Sunday		55
To make a posie for inferiour power.	78	Ang.&Sts.		25
To make a garland for inferiour power.	78	Ang.&Sts.	W	25
For by that powder thou wilt make us see.	82	Ungratef.		18
For by this powder thou wilt make us see.	82	Ungratef.	W	18
For what account can thy ill steward make?	83	Sighs & Gr.		8
Began to make Balcones, Terraces,	84	The World		7
To make a purchase there: he sees their dances,	85	Vanitie 1		5
The obligation in us, make it lesse,	86	Lent		17
And pipes that feed the presse, and make it runne;	88	The Pearl		2
Us did make,	92	Antiphon 2		11
Lord, make me coy and tender to offend:	93	Unkindness		1
Lord, thou didst make me, yet thou woundest me;	95	Justice 1		2
To make us thine: yet that we might not part,	97	Afflict.5		10
And make his own? as if none knew, but he.	100	Miserie		14
To sing thy praises, make them lesse divine.	101	Miserie		40
These Preachers make	101	Miserie		47
They make his life a constant blot,	102	Miserie		63
Thou mightst make way for liberalitie!	103	Prayer 2		18
And make the purchase spread	105	Obedience		39
Some wood and nails to make a staffe or bill	106	Conscience		21
The bloud did make, which thou didst waste?	107	Home		8
I never saw thing make such haste.	107	Home		10
And, to be short, make an oration.	111	The Quip		19
And make a twist checker'd with night and day!	118	Providence		58
If they seek fine things, thou dost make them run	120	Providence		106
How harsh are thorns to pears! and yet they make	120	Providence		121
Or with a stone! yet make no good foundation.	120	Providence		124
Much better tunes, then grones can make;	124	Gratefulnes		22
Make bread of it: and that repose	125	Peace		39
No smith can make such locks, but they have keyes:	126	Confession		17
Lord, mend or rather make us: one creation	127	Giddinesse		25

MAKE (cont'd)

	PAGE	TITLE		LINE
Except thou make us dayly, we shall spurn	127	Giddinesse		27
Who of the laws sowre juice sweet wine did make,	128	Bunch Gr.		27
Make their pretence:	131	Mans medly		8
But not to make a constant stay.	137	Familie		24
That God did make	144	Discharge		17
And make me giddie; Lord, I fall,	148	Longing		11
Disturb the work. O make me not their sport,	155	Glimpse		29
And make their ruine praise thy power.	156	Assurance		36
Spin out thy thread, and make thereof a coat	156	Assurance		38
O be mine still! still make me thine!	157	Clasping		19
Or rather make no Thine and Mine!	157	Clasping		20
Who make the bravest shows.	161	Priesthood		18
Onely, since God doth often vessels make	161	Priesthood		34
To make me sigh, and seek, and faint, and die,	164	The Crosse		2
To make my hopes my torture, and the fee	165	The Crosse		27
To make us see we are but flowers that glide:	167	The Flower		44
To make his verse, or write a hymne in kinde.	168	a true Hymn		15
Nay, thou dost make me sit and dine,	173	23 Psalme		17
To make him clean, who could not be defil'd?	173	Marie Magd		8
What cordials make this curious broth,	175	The Odour		9
Make Sinne appeare;	183	A Parodie		18
But still to make thee prepossest,	184	The Elixer		7
Make no delay.	186	Dooms-day		2
Make this the day.	186	Dooms-day		8
O make no stay!	187	Dooms-day		14
Let the graves make their confession,	187	Dooms-day		15
To make good that which ev'ry day he winnes.	193	Ch.-Milit.		126
To make a jest of Christs three offices:	195	Ch.-Milit.		174
And make that name good by their transmigrations;	195	Ch.-Milit.		184
Unto the brimme, and make cur measure up;	197	Ch.-Milit.		240
With the one make warre to cease;	199	L'Envoy		2
With the one make warrs to cease;	199	L'Envoy	W	2
Make his sighs tc use it all,	199	L'Envoy		14
Lord make my Losses up, & sett mee free:	203	Even-song	W	5
Lord make thy Blood	204	The Knell	W	13
Roses and Lillies speak thee; and to make	206	Walton 2		6
A foile to sett of worth, & make it rare.	211	Bohemia	D	16
Make thy request, and I will grant	216	Psalm II	D	19
are all that make the Son their stay.	216	Psalm II	D	32
all night I make my Couch to swim;	220	Psalm VI	D	14
For sins make all equall, whom they finde together;	227	Priest 3		27
who somtimes make it a piece of state not to come at the beginning	232	Priest 6		8
which will make them appear exceeding reverend, and holy.	234	Priest 7		24
and out of liberality, make her fruitfull in all good works.	238	Priest 9		33
he teacheth them, that three things make a compleate servant, Truth,	240	Priest 10		17
but clean, whole, and sweet, as sweet as his garden can make;	241	Priest 10		13
if not the best way, yet any way, make his Parish good.	244	Priest 11		5
So doth hee also before giving make them say their Prayers first,	245	Priest 12		35
as that they make not that the end of their labour, but that they may	248	Priest 14		6
sake, and to make his higher purposes slip the more easily.	249	Priest 14		11
labouring to make them understand the great good use of this antient	249	Priest 15		30
which may make his other discourses more welcome, and lesse tedious.	251	Priest 17		5
the Blessing of God to them ought to make them the more charitable,	254	Priest 19		5
Did you see God make it?	256	Priest 21		8
and Masters should make hast in this, as to a great purchase	259	Priest 22		3
he chooseth to permit his Parishioners rather to make use of the Law,	260	Priest 23		19
by familiar things hee might make his Doctrine slip the more easily	261	Priest 23		18
stead of drugs of the same nature, and to make the garden the shop:	261	Priest 23		30
being cunning to make use of another, and spare themselves:	265	Priest 26		34
make others faults their entertainment and discourse, and that even	286	Priest 37		30
unlawful to open faults, no benefit or advantage can make it lawfull:	287	Priest 37		6
O make it a word of power and peace, to convert those who are not yet	289	Priest		15
O make thy word a swift word, passing from the ear to the heart,	289	Priest		29
O Lord, make it health and strength unto us;	290	Priest		10
be much troubled, or make a great concourse, refused both remedies,	295	Cornaro		9
that Temperance which I have found so good, I here make an end.	303	Cornaro		35
of perfection, and are able to make the man of God perfect, 2 Tim. 3.	306	Valdesso		19
wondrous things cf his Lawes, and that he would make them his study.	309	Valdesso		27
if we make another sence of that Text, wee shall overthrow all means,	310	Valdesso		11
for unbelief, or evil works, make plain the Authors meaning.	319	Valdesso	V	18
will make the Consideration easy, and very observeable:	320	Valdesso		5
A Horse made, and a man to make.	321	Proverbs		22
Great strokes make not sweete musick.	322	Proverbs		26
Empty Chambers make foolish maides.	322	Proverbs		29
To a fair day open the window, but make you ready as to a foule.	325	Proverbs		119
Make hast to an ill way that you may get out of it.	325	Proverbs		124
Almes never make poore. Or thus,	327	Proverbs		189
Sit in your place and none can make you rise.	334	Proverbs		372
The first service a child doth his father is to make him foolish.	337	Proverbs		463
Water, fire, and souldiers, quickly make roome.	338	Proverbs		514
Faire words make mee looke to my purse.	339	Proverbs		548
He that can make a fire well, can end a quarrell.	340	Proverbs		557
Two ill meales make the third a glutton.	340	Proverbs		575
Old men, when they scorne young, make much of death.	341	Proverbs		597
Gaming, women, and wine, while they laugh they make men pine.	341	Proverbs		604
Before you make a friend, eate a bushell of salt with him.	342	Proverbs		624
Some make a conscience of spitting in the Church,	343	Proverbs		650
You cannot make a wind-mill goe with a paire of bellowes.	344	Proverbs		676
Three women make a market.	345	Proverbs		713
Chuse a horse made, and a wife to make.	350	Proverbs		871

MALICE (cont'd)	PAGE	TITLE		LINE
And yet as the malice of the person, or hainousness of the crime may	254	Priest 20		25
he add a tincture of private malice in the joy, and hast of acting	287	Priest 37		27
MALICIOUS				
Who sought for help, never malicious foes:	34	Sacrifice		243
Had the malicious and ill-meaning harm	172	The Glance		11
MALICIOUSNESSE				
Not out of envie or maliciousnesse	78	Ang.&Sts.		6
MALIGNITIE				
For there is no malignitie of old age in the humours of my bodie,	296	Cornaro		36
MALLICE				
his mallice to controul.	221	Psalm VII	D	8
MALLOWES				
camomill, mallowes, comphrey and smallage made into a Poultis,	262	Priest 23		7
MAN				
Man would have been th' incloser: but since now	7	Ch.-Porch		20
Man breaks the fence, and every ground will plough.	7	Ch.-Porch		22
O what were man, might he himself misplace!	7	Ch.-Porch		23
The drunkard forfets Man, and doth devest	7	Ch.-Porch		35
Doe all things like a man, not sneakingly:	11	Ch.-Porch		121
Thou liv'st by rule. What doth not so, but man?	12	Ch.-Porch		134
Thou liv'st by rule. What does not so, but man?	12	Ch.-Porch	W	134
Man is a shop of rules, a well truss'd pack,	12	Ch.-Porch		141
Never was scraper brave man. Get to live;	12	Ch.-Porch		153
Cannot on fourtie: he's a man of pleasure,	13	Ch.-Porch		177
Laugh not too much: the wittie man laughs least:	15	Ch.-Porch		229
And the sad man is cock of all his jests.	16	Ch.-Porch		252
Feed no man in his sinnes: for adulation	16	Ch.-Porch		257
God made me one man; love makes me no more,	17	Ch.-Porch		287
Joyn hands with God to make a man to live.	21	Ch.-Porch		376
Give to all something; to a good poore man,	21	Ch.-Porch		377
Man is Gods image; but a poore man is	21	Ch.-Porch		379
In brief, acquit thee bravely; play the man.	24	Ch.-Porch		457
Who by my spittle gave the blinde man eies,	31	Sacrifice		134
Who by my spittle gave that blinde man eies,	31	Sacrifice	W	134
God holds his peace at man, and man cries out:	32	Sacrifice		187
Man stole the fruit, but I must climbe the tree;	33	Sacrifice		202
Such sorrow as, if sinfull man could feel,	33	Sacrifice		209
The man, who once against thee fought.	37	Reprisall		16
A man so wrung with pains, that all his hair,	37	The Agonie		9
Though it be cold, hard, foul, from loving man	41	Sepulchre		23
Lord, who createdst man in wealth and store,	43	East.wings		1
When thou for sinne rebukest man,	49	Repentance		25
Gods breath in man returning to his birth,	51	Prayer 1		2
Heaven in ordinarie, man well drest,	51	Prayer 1		11
How hath man parcel'd out thy glorious name,	54	Love 1		3
Wilt thou meet arms with man, that thou dost stretch	55	Temper 1		13
Man is all weaknesse; there is no such thing	61	Praise 1		9
Saying to man, It doth suffice:	64	Even-song		19
Lord, how can man preach thy eternall word?	67	Windows		1
Who is the honest man?	72	Constancie		1
This is the Mark-man, safe and sure,	73	Constancie		34
Make up one man; whose face thou art,	75	Sunday		9
Man had straight forward gone	75	Sunday		15
Man might not of his fodder misse.	76	Sunday		39
Man found thee poore and dirtie in a mine.	77	Avarice		4
Nay, thou hast got the face of man; for we	77	Avarice		10
Thou art the man, and man but drosse to thee.	77	Avarice		12
Man calleth thee his wealth, who made thee rich;	77	Avarice		13
Man is no starre, but a quick coal	79	Employm.2		6
The man is gone,	79	Employm.2		27
To Man of all beasts be not thou a stranger:	81	Christmas		12
Gladly had man ador'd the sunne,	82	Ungratef.		4
But man is close, reserv'd, and dark to thee:	82	Ungratef.		25
Whose leaves first sheltred man from drought & dew,	84	The World		12
What hath not man sought out and found,	85	Vanitie 1		22
What hath not man wrought out and found,	85	Vanitie 1	V	22
Poore man, thou searchest round	86	Vanitie 1		27
That ev'ry man may revell at his doore,	87	Lent		46
Man.	90	Man		T
That no man builds a stately habitation,	90	Man	W	2
Or can be, then is Man? to whose creation	90	Man		5
For Man is ev'ry thing,	91	Man		7
Man is all symmetrie,	91	Man		13
But Man hath caught and kept it, as his prey.	91	Man		20
But Man has caught and kept it, as his prey.	91	Man	W	20
More servants wait on Man,	92	Man		43
Oh mightie love! Man is one world, and hath	92	Man		47
How soon doth man decay!	98	Mortific.		1
How soon does man decay	98	Mortific.	W	1
When man grows staid and wise,	98	Mortific.		19
Man, ere he is aware,	99	Mortific.		31
Man is a foolish thing, a foolish thing,	100	Miserie		2
Man is but grasse,	100	Miserie		5
No man shall beat into his head,	100	Miserie		15
My God, Man cannot praise thy name:	101	Miserie		31
Man cannot serve thee; let him go,	101	Miserie		43
Oh foolish man! where are thine eyes?	101	Miserie		49
But Man doth know	101	Miserie		59
Ah wretched man	102	Miserie	W	65
Indeed at first Man was a treasure,	102	Miserie		67

MAN (cont'd)

	PAGE	TITLE		LINE
Lord, what is man to thee,	104	Obedience		21
If some kinde man would thrust his heart	105	Obedience		42
When man was lost, thy pitie lookt about	107	Home		13
Oh loose this frame, this knot of man untie!	109	Home		61
What tune is this, poore man? said he:	110	The Quip		10
Who for man was sold, can see;	114	Dialogue		15
The man reply'd; It figures JESUS CHRIST.	116	Love-joy		8
Onely to Man thou hast made known thy wayes,	117	Providence		6
Are brought to Man, while they are lame and mute.	117	Providence		12
Man is the worlds high Priest: he doth present	117	Providence		13
Bees work for man; and yet they never bruise	118	Providence		65
Thou hast hid metals: man may take them thence;	119	Providence		81
And threatned man, that he should fill the space.	119	Providence		84
Nothing wears clothes, but Man; nothing doth need	120	Providence		109
But Man alone, to show his heav'nly breed:	120	Providence		111
Sometimes thou dost divide thy gifts to man,	120	Providence		125
But where one man would have me grinde it,	122	Time		5
Christs coming hath made man thy debter,	122	Time		11
Then chafing said, This man deludes:	123	Time		28
At length I met a rev'rend good old man,	125	Peace		19
As Gods afflictions into man,	126	Confession		9
Oh, what a thing is man! how farre from power,	127	Giddinesse		1
O what a sight were Man, if his attires	127	Giddinesse		17
Joy, I did lock thee up: but some bad man	128	Bunch Gr.		1
But as my heart did tender it, the man	129	Love unkn.		33
All creatures have their joy: and man hath his.	131	Mans medly		3
Man ties them both alone,	131	Mans medly		10
Which needs not man, be ty'd to those	134	The Method		26
Then burn thy Epicycles, foolish man;	135	Divinitie		25
Man and the present fit: if he provide,	145	Discharge		31
Bringing nor man, nor arms, nor fear,	151	The Bag		28
Now love and truth will end in man.	156	Assurance		42
When God at first made man,	159	The Pulley		1
From the first man in th' East, to fresh and new	168	The Sonne		9
We him in glorie call, The Sonne of Man.	168	The Sonne		14
Who gives to man, as he sees fit Salvation. / Damnation.	170	Water-crs.		10
That to the old man I may rest,	174	Aaron		19
Love's a man of warre,	179	Discipline		22
Though man frailties hath,	179	Discipline		30
A man that looks on glasse,	184	The Elixer		9
Man is out of order hurl'd,	187	Dooms-day		27
Ah, what a thing is man devoid of grace,	193	Ch.-Milit.		111
If God and man be sever'd infinitely!	193	Ch.-Milit.		116
To be a Church-man too, and wear a Mitre:	194	Ch.-Milit.		163
But kill the man, is seald with thee.	204	Persever.	W	8
Blest is the man that never would	214	Psalm I	D	1
the righteous man to love.	217	Psalm IV	D	12
The bloody man, the false one too,	218	Psalm V	D	15
if a man do not all which is here expressed, hee presently sinns,	224	Priest		10
the Deputy of Christ for the reducing of Man to the Obedience of God.	225	Priest 1		1
For first, Man fell from God by disobedience.	225	Priest 1		4
Christ is the glorious instrument of God for the revoking of Man.	225	Priest 1		6
but after a man is once Minister, he cannot agree to come into any	226	Priest 2		25
and every one, man, and child, answering aloud both Amen,	231	Priest 6		27
is ever very well supplyed by some able man who treads in his steps,	232	Priest 7		26
Oh Lord, I know that the way of man is not in himself, &c.	234	Priest 7		6
and seems to himselfe so as a Market-man is, when the Market day	235	Priest 8		18
and fraile man, discharged the publick duties of the Congregation.	236	Priest 8		9
every one is more awaked, when we come, and say, Thou art the man.	236	Priest 8		15
which as they are, are unuseful to man, the one for smalnesse,	241	Priest 10		27
These save man the labour, and doing that which either he could	241	Priest 10		31
do as it were dresse and prepare both for man in themselves,	241	Priest 10		34
For meat was made for man, not man for meat.	242	Priest 10		32
of affliction, which softens, and works the stubborn heart of man;	249	Priest 15		25
whither the nature of man, loving refreshment, gladly betakes it	252	Priest 18		22
If he finde another giving a poor man a penny, he gives him a tester	254	Priest 20		13
since man is so miserable, what is to be done?	257	Priest 21		3
so that if the poorest man of the Parish detain but a pin unjustly	260	Priest 23		14
A man may be both Covetous, and Intemperate, and yet hear Sermons	264	Priest 26		14
So a man dining, eats at first lawfully;	264	Priest 26		22
So a man storing up mony for his necessary provisions, both in	264	Priest 26		25
but in brief, a poor man is an occasion, my countrey is an occasion,	265	Priest 26		13
if a man hath wherewithall to buy a spade, and yet hee chuseth rather	265	Priest 26		28
a spirituall man, wisheth all to incline rather to too much,	267	Priest 26		12
God dishonoured every day, and man afflicted.	267	Priest 27		32
and exerciseth a threefold power in every thing which concernes man.	271	Priest 30		1
Man would sit down at this world, God bids him sell it,	272	Priest 30		6
So is the carnall and wilfull man with the worm of the grave in this	272	Priest 30		13
A godly man, not out of superstition, but of reverence to Gods house,	273	Priest 31		22
The reason of this assertion is taken from the nature of man,	274	Priest 32		19
So that even in Paradise man had a calling, and how much more out	274	Priest 32		21
or Noble-man in the Country he lives in, inabling him with power	276	Priest 32		13
These are so far from deterring any good man from the place,	276	Priest 32		23
he must not only be a morning man, but at Committees also;	277	Priest 32		12
For the temptations with which a good man is beset, and the ways	278	Priest 33		15
So that man, which way soever he turnes, hath two pledges of Gods	283	Priest 34		17
1 Sam. 1. 18. though it came from a man disallowed by God:	285	Priest 36		22
that if a Minister talke with a great man in the ordinary course	286	Priest 36		20
and turne quite another man, doubtlesse then also mens affections	288	Priest 37		3
so man did eat Angels food:	290	Priest		9

MAN (cont'd)	PAGE	TITLE		LINE
saw that it was no hard thing to do so, but the proper duty of man;	292	Cornaro		33
of a cheerfull and merrie man I became melancholie and cholerick;	296	Cornaro		15
Neither can any man denie this, who will narrowly consider it.	297	Cornaro		14
For indeed no man can be a perfect Physician to another,	297	Cornaro		24
But that a man may preserve himself in health, I advise,	298	Cornaro		11
but onely that a man should begin and by little and little accustome	299	Cornaro		8
moment (as I shewed before) if a man be temperate in meat and drink;	299	Cornaro		16
which endeavcurs to preserve a man as much as she can, teacheth us	299	Cornaro		25
So that a sick man, whether he hath lived heretofore orderly	299	Cornaro		29
especially since it is easie and most agreeable to the nature of Man.	300	Cornaro		6
No man that follcwes it, is bound to eat and drink so little as I:	300	Cornaro		6
No man is forbidden to eat fruit or fish, which I eat not:	300	Cornaro		7
Let no man here object unto me, That there are many, who,	300	Cornaro		17
It is not the part of a wise man, to expose himself to so many	300	Cornaro		22
An old man of an ill constitution, but living orderly, is more sure	300	Cornaro		24
sure of life, then the most strong young man who lives disorderly.	300	Cornaro		26
sheweth, and I also, when I was a young man, too well found.	303	Cornaro		16
of perfection, and are able to make the man of God perfect, 2 Tim. 3.	306	Valdesso		19
He meaneth (I suppose) that a man presume not to merit,	312	Valdesso		14
A man is to embrace all good, but because he cannot doe all,	313	Valdesso		20
or conditionally he prayed as man, though as God he knew the event.	315	Valdesso		11
[the law is not made for a righteous man:]	315	Valdesso		34
how this opinion could befall so good a man as it seems Valdesso was,	317	Valdesso		32
if I bid a man stay in a place untill I come, I doe not then bid him	318	Valdesso		14
MAN Proposeth, God disposeth.	321	Proverbs		1
MAN purposethe God disposeth.	321	Proverbs	V	1
A Horse made, and a man to make.	321	Proverbs		22
At dinner my man appeares.	322	Proverbs		37
Who hath a Wolfe for his mate, needes a Dog for his man.	323	Proverbs		57
Every ill man hath his ill day.	324	Proverbs		92
To a gratefull man give mony when he askes.	324	Proverbs		115
The best remedy against an ill man is much ground betweene both.	326	Proverbs		152
From a chollerick man withdraw a little;	326	Proverbs		164
The miserable man makes a peny of a farthing,	328	Proverbs		211
Send a wise man on an errand, and say nothing unto him.	328	Proverbs		217
The corne hides it self in the snow, as an old man in furrs.	329	Proverbs		241
A foole knowes more in his house, then a wise man in anothers.	329	Proverbs		257
Let an ill man lie in thy straw, and he lookes to be thy heire.	330	Proverbs		271
Hee wrongs not an old man that steales his supper from him.	331	Proverbs		311
A discontented man knowes not where to sit easie.	333	Proverbs		345
A married man turns his staffe into a stake.	333	Proverbs		366
Pension never inriched young man.	339	Proverbs		515
The cholerick man never wants woe.	339	Proverbs		536
Hee commands enough that obeyes a wise man.	339	Proverbs		547
The fatt man knoweth not, what the leane thinketh.	341	Proverbs		605
A wise man needes not blush for changing his purpose.	342	Proverbs		613
The sight of a man hath the force of a Lyon.	342	Proverbs		617
Shew a good man his errour and he turnes it to a vertue,	343	Proverbs		655
but an ill man doubles his fault.	343	Proverbs		655
A wise man cares not for what he cannot have.	343	Proverbs		662
Speake not of a dead man at the table.	343	Proverbs		672
If a good man thrive, all thrive with him.	344	Proverbs		695
Though you see a Church-man ill, yet continue in the Church still.	344	Proverbs		698
To a crafty man, a crafty and an halfe.	347	Proverbs		796
The life of man is a winter way.	351	Proverbs		914
The singing man keepes his shop in his throate.	351	Proverbs		918
An Oxe is taken by the horns, and a Man by the tongue.	353	Proverbs		967
Take an oxe by his hornes & a man by his tongue.	353	Proverbs	V	967
that a man would desire straight to bee buried there.	353	Proverbs		969
Once a yeare a man may say: On his conscience.	353	Proverbs		971
When a man sleepes, his head is in his stomach.	353	Proverbs		981
A man well mounted is ever Cholerick.	355	Proverbs		1025
A man would live in Italy (a place of pleasure)	357	Proverbs	D	1047
For the same man to be an heretick	357	Proverbs	D	1058
No naked man is sought after to be rifled.	357	Proverbs	D	1063
A man of a great memory without learning	358	Proverbs	D	1085
There is no man, though never so little,	359	Proverbs	D	1119
The healthfull man can give counsell to the sick.	360	Proverbs	D	1130
Vertue flies frcm the heart of a Mercenary man.	360	Proverbs	D	1133
There is an hour wherein a man might be happy	360	Proverbs	D	1143
Take heed of the wrath of a mighty man,	360	Proverbs	D	1148
A man is known to be mortal by two things, Sleep and Lust.	361	Proverbs	D	1159
The Divell never assailes a man, except he find him	361	Proverbs	D	1176
Whatever is made by the hand of man,	362	Proverbs	D	1184
by the hand of man may be overturned.	362	Proverbs	D	1184
What Trades-man is there who will set up without his Tools?	364	Letters		14
and such like Gaynesses, which will please a young man well.	370	Letters		4
& have endeavoured many wayes, to find out a man for it.	378	Letters		7
gratious Lord God, is pleased to give me you for the Man, I desired,	378	Letters		8
Doe this & be a man as David, after Gods hart.	381	Woodnoth		21
MAN'S				
Why should I feel another mans mistakes	18	Ch.-Porch		309
Scorn no mans love, though of a mean degree;	20	Ch.-Porch		349
And cordiall left to repair mans decay:	31	Sacrifice		159
Yet since mans scepters are as frail as reeds,	32	Sacrifice		177
My wo, mans weal: and now I bow my head.	34	Sacrifice		250
Mans age is two houres work, or three:	48	Repentance		7
Thy wrath for sinne, as when mans sight was dimme,	49	Faith		2
I envie no mans nightingale or spring;	57	Jordan 1		13
Indeed mans whcle estate	63	Mattens		13

MAN'S (cont'd)	PAGE	TITLE		LINE
The Sundaies of mans life,	76	Sunday		29
A poore mans rod, when thou dost ride,	96	Charms & K		3
A poore mans rod if thou wilt hire	96	Charms & K	W	3
Mans medley.	131	Mans medly		T
Mans joy and pleasure	131	Mans medly		5
For ev'ry mans peculiar book?	187	Judgement		5
When written Truths shall censure mans devise.	194	Ch.-Milit.	W	160
is full of such composures, yet every mans own is fittest, readyest,	230	Priest 5		4
he hath a Poor-mans Box conveniently seated, to receive the charity	246	Priest 13		21
the Parson once demanded after other questions about mans misery;	257	Priest 21		2
but man's unpreparednesse asks kneeling.	259	Priest 22		13
in this, how Gods goodnesse strives with mans refractorinesse;	272	Priest 30		6
Hee that saw Christ open a blind mans eyes, saw not more Divinity,	283	Priest 34		1
He meanes a mans fre-will is only in outward, not in spirituall	313	Valdesso		33
An old wise mans shaddow is better then a young buzzards sword.	324	Proverbs		90
A wicked mans gift hath a touch of his master.	326	Proverbs		162
Great almes-giving lessens no mans living.	327	Proverbs		190
Giving much to the poore, doth inrich a mans store.	327	Proverbs		191
A mans discontent is his worst evill.	331	Proverbs		298
Hope is the poore mans bread.	337	Proverbs		477
A valiant mans looke is more then a cowards sword.	345	Proverbs		708
A poore mans Cow dies, a rich mans child.	350	Proverbs		869
An old mans staffe is the rapper of deaths doore.	351	Proverbs		916
A man's destiny is alwayes dark.	362	Proverbs	D	1180
Every man's censure is first moulded in his own nature.	362	Proverbs	D	1181
MANAGE				
Is thy chief government, to manage woe,	212	Bohemia	D	57
MANAGING				
of advancing the publick Stock, and managing Commons, or Woods,	276	Priest 32		6
I was one of those that was deputed for the managing of that work,	302	Cornaro		17
MANCHESTER				
yourself to move my Lords of Manchester and Boollingbrook is very	377	Letters		23
MANGER				
What can be lower then the common manger?	50	Faith		22
That, as each beast his manger knows,	76	Sunday		38
Wrapt in nights mantle, stole into a manger;	81	Christmas		10
MANIE				
Manie things are lost for want of asking.	353	Proverbs		968
MANIFEST				
is indeed the bent of my Discourse) the other will be manifest.	226	Priest 2		19
and apparell, the disorders thereof are also very manifest.	228	Priest 3		9
The reason of the ground is manifest, because wealth is given to that	265	Priest 26		7
Just so it is in Divinity, and that not without manifest reason:	278	Priest 33		33
because there are contained therein 4 manifest advantages.	284	Priest 35		3
By which it is manifest, That neither melancholie, nor any other	294	Cornaro		30
as is manifest by experience, is a naturall Physick most agreeable	298	Cornaro		13
MANIFOLD				
wherein the manifold wisedome of God is wonderfully to be seen,	261	Priest 23		27
Countrey Parson observing the manifold wiles of Satan (who playes his	272	Priest 31		15
MANNA				
With Manna, Angels food, I fed them all:	34	Sacrifice		239
Exalted Manna, gladnesse of the best,	51	Prayer 1		10
and reducing the Manna, and bread of Charity to some equality,	254	Priest 19		3
To weepe for joy is a kinde of Manna.	337	Proverbs		462
MANNER				
which Christ did, and after his manner, both for Doctrine and Life.	225	Priest 1		19
contrives how and in what manner to induce it to the best advantage.	236	Priest 8		2
and then also in a serious manner, never jestingly or sportfully.	237	Priest 9		13
For the manner of receiving, as the Parson useth all reverence	259	Priest 22		10
in like manner, raw lettice, fish, pork, sausages, pulse,	293	Cornaro		12
He often useth this manner of speech Beleeving by Revelation,	308	Valdesso		29
Hee that workes after his owne manner,	335	Proverbs		421
in some proportion, and after my manner, Your most obedient Servant,	364	Letters		3
MANNERS				
Infants manners are moulded more by the example of Parents,	357	Proverbs	D	1060
MANOUR				
In heaven at his manour I him sought:	40	Redemption		5
MANS				
The gentle Hawke halfe mans her selfe.	322	Proverbs		30
MANSUETUDE				
Which by consent was giv'n to Mansuetude.	70	Humilitie		10
MANTLE				
Wrapt in nights mantle, stole into a manger;	81	Christmas		10
The sky his azure mantle gain'd.	151	The Bag		15
MANUFACTURES				
the Artifices, and Manufactures there, transplant them hither,	278	Priest 32		9
MANURED				
and fruitfull fields, well manured and adorned with many habitations.	301	Cornaro		25
MANY (see also manie)				
Many affecting wit beyond their power,	16	Ch.-Porch		245
Mark what another sayes: for many are	19	Ch.-Porch		319
Shame tears my soul, my bodie many a wound;	33	Sacrifice		217
Comes to about the many hundredth part.	38	The Sinner		11
Comes to about the many hundred part.	38	The Sinner	W	11
That when sinne spies so many foes,	39	Good Fri.		25
So many hearts on earth, and yet not one	40	Sepulchre		3
I had prepared many a flowre	42	Easter	W	19
I got me boughs off many a tree:	42	Easter		20
Though many sunnes to shine endeavour?	42	Easter		28
So many joyes I writ down for my part,	46	Afflict.1		3

MANY (cont'd)

	PAGE	TITLE		LINE
But rev'rend laws, and many a proclamation	84	The World		9
How many drammes of spirit there must be	88	The Pearl		18
Have done these many hundred yeares, and more:	89	The Pearl	W	25
As many lines, as there doth need	104	Obedience		7
As many lines, as it does need	104	Obedience	W	7
So many yeares baptiz'd, and not appeare?	108	Home		27
Thou art in all things one, in each thing many:	118	Providence		43
And none can know thy works, which are so many,	121	Providence		143
It go for one, hath many wayes in store	121	Providence		150
Extolleth many wayes, yet this one more.	121	Providence		152
Which many wondring at, got some of those	125	Peace		29
Closets; and in them many a chest;	126	Confession		3
Many a fault more then my lease will bear;	129	Love unkn.		20
Which at a board, while many drunk bare wine,	130	Love unkn.		42
A worm doth sit, whose many feet and hair	140	Ch.-rents		3
As many eyes as starres? since it is night,	140	Ch.-rents		26
With many a flower:	142	Pilgrimage		8
With that abash'd and struck with many a sting	142	Pilgrimage		25
Search well and see; for hearts have many holes.	147	Offering		4
Since many gifts do challenge many hearts!	147	Offering		8
And thou mayst offer many gifts in one.	147	Offering		18
Had I many,	148	Offering		31
Both then, and after, many a brunt	151	The Bag		21
For many weeks of lingring pain and smart	154	Glimpse		4
Among my many had his full career,	159	Jos.coat		6
Much wrastling, many a combate, this deare end,	164	The Crosse		8
Many a spring I shoot up fair,	166	The Flower		24
After so many deaths I live and write;	166	The Flower		37
Since that time many a bitter storm	172	The Glance		9
Many a rent and struggling th' Empire knew,	192	Ch.-Milit.		79
But did bewitch both kings & many a nation	195	Ch.-Milit.	W	193
Whither my many crymes and use of sinn	205	Persever.	W	11
many are they that rise	216	Psalm III	D	2
Many there are that say, O who	217	Psalm IV	D	21
as many of them do, and because they have different Names,	226	Priest 2		20
lust, and when not, and so in many circumstances of actions.	230	Priest 5		30
by turning often, and making many Apostrophes to God, as,	233	Priest 7		33
His voyce is as the sound of many waters, Revelations 1.	234	Priest 7		34
These and many other spirituall wickednesses in high places doth	238	Priest 9		20
sets up as many encouragements to goodnesse as he can, both in	244	Priest 11		3
For many and wonderfull things are spoken of thee, thou great Vertue.	244	Priest 12		7
so also when after many admonitions, any continue to be refractory,	250	Priest 16		15
especially since many remove from Parish to Parish, who like	255	Priest 21		19
for many say the Catechisme by rote, as parrats, without ever	256	Priest 21		3
the one, in wanting many excitings of grace;	259	Priest 22		5
Many think they are at more liberty then they are, as if they were	266	Priest 26		18
As when a Merchant hath a ship come home after many a storme,	271	Priest 30		22
who hath so many dispersed Officers at his beck throughout	276	Priest 32		10
hath ever so many sermons ready penn'd, as he hath victories.	278	Priest 33		24
then in their Countrey under so many miracles were a stranger thing,	282	Priest 34		9
many an evill may not only be, but also spread in his Parish,	287	Priest 37		1
many waters could not quench thy love!	288	Priest		30
Having observed in my time many of my friends, of excellent wit	291	Cornaro		1
and withall help many others, who will take this into consideration,	291	Cornaro		14
then that after many troubles and griefs I should quickly come	291	Cornaro		25
For having endured many heats & colds, and other like discommodities	294	Cornaro		12
considering what an orderly life I had led for many yeares together,	295	Cornaro		7
and that I had for many yeares continued in good health,	295	Cornaro		26
For the Temperance of so many yeares spent all ill humours,	296	Cornaro		32
whereof the one kept me well for many yeares;	297	Cornaro		5
and long dayes, and the true and onely medicine of many diseases.	297	Cornaro		13
Many have thought that this could be done by Aurum potabile,	298	Cornaro		19
or the Philosophers stone, sought of many, and found of few.	298	Cornaro		20
and Isocrates, and Tullie, and many others of the Ancients;	298	Cornaro		39
and many others of inferiour condition, not onely in the citie,	299	Cornaro		3
Wherefore since many have observed a regular life, both of old times	299	Cornaro		5
there needs not many and curious things, but onely that a man should	299	Cornaro		8
Let no man here object unto me, That there are many, who,	300	Cornaro		17
to expose himself to so many dangers of diseases and death,	300	Cornaro		23
because many wayes thither are so ordered, that they all meet and end	301	Cornaro		21
and fruitfull fields, well manured and adorned with many habitations.	301	Cornaro		25
taken effect in the reducing of many rude and untoiled places in my	302	Cornaro		15
whereas I by the experience of so many yeares have learned to give	303	Cornaro		20
Many things more might be said in commendation hereof:	303	Cornaro		33
your Valdesso I now returne with many thanks, and some notes,	304	Valdesso		2
the many pious rules of ordering our life, about mortification,	305	Valdesso		9
This place together with many other, as namely Consid. 71. upon Our	307	Valdesso		16
whence come so many Books of severall mens opinions:	317	Valdesso		3
How many places doe the Fathers bring about Untill against	318	Valdesso		9
Many friends in generall, one in speciall.	330	Proverbs		281
Many kisse the hand they wish cut off.	330	Proverbs		283
There are many waies to fame.	339	Proverbs		539
when there are many to strike on one Anvile.	340	Proverbs		551
The blind eate many a flie.	340	Proverbs		556
He that goeth farre hath many encounters.	341	Proverbs		608
The soule needs few things, the body many.	342	Proverbs		640
The soule needs some things, the body many.	342	Proverbs	V	640
So many men in Court and so many strangers.	350	Proverbs		874
The little cannot bee great, unlesse he devoure many.	351	Proverbs		922
to reprove the vanity of those many Love-poems, that are daily writ	363	Letters		7

MANY (cont'd)	PAGE	TITLE	LINE
except you wink, you cannot but see many brave examples.	366	Letters	6
that my solliciting him has been much, and my tears many for you;	372	Letters	3
being more beggarly now than I have been these many years,	376	Letters	1
and not as many who think they have done fairly, if they leave them	376	Letters	15
& have endeavoured many wayes, to find out a man for it.	378	Letters	7
After many singular honors, remarkable commands, most noble	441	Oration	24
MARBLE			
These laugh at Jeat and Marble put for signes,	65	Ch.-monum.	12
But all is cleansed when the marble weeps.	67	Ch.-floore	15
The South with marble; North with furres & woods.	119	Providence	96
Sacred Marble, safely keepe	208	H. Danvers D	1
MARBLE'S			
The marbles neat and curious veins:	67	Ch.-floore	14
MARBLES			
Marbles can weep; and surely strings	136	Ephes.	23
MARCH (verb)			
Then march on gallant: get substantiall worth.	15	Ch.-Porch	209
MARCH			
The March sunne raises but dissolves not.	342	Proverbs	614
February makes a bridge and March breakes it.	346	Proverbs	739
MARCHANT			
A Marchant that gaines not, looseth.	322	Proverbs	47
He that looseth is Marchant as well as he that gaines.	339	Proverbs	518
so shall you play a good marchant, by transporting French commodities	366	Letters	12
MARGERET			
to Margeret twenty shillings: To William Twenty Nobles,	382	G.H.'s Will	24
MARIE			
Marie Magdalene.	173	Marie Magd	T
When blessed Marie wip'd her Saviours feet,	173	Marie Magd	1
MARINER			
The windes, who think they rule the mariner,	119	Providence	91
MARK			
Thy rate and price, and mark thee for a treasure;	6	Ch.-Porch	2
The price of thee, and mark thee for a treasure;	6	Ch.-Porch W	2
For we have wit to mark them, and to spare.	9	Ch.-Porch	69
Some mark a partridge, never their childes fashion:	10	Ch.-Porch	99
Mark all his wandrings, and enjoy his frets;	19	Ch.-Porch	315
Mark what ancther sayes: for many are	19	Ch.-Porch	319
Dresse and undresse thy soul: mark the decay	24	Ch.-Porch	453
Be crumbled into dust. Mark here below	65	Ch.-monum.	22
Be broken into dust. Mark here below	65	Ch.-monum. W	22
Mark you the floore? that square & speckled stone,	66	Ch.-floore	1
Mark how the fire in flints doth quiet lie,	68	Content	9
Mark how the fire in Flint doth quiet lie,	68	Content W	9
This is the Mark-man, safe and sure,	73	Constancie	34
But when I mark my life and praise,	96	Justice 1	6
More favour then you wot of. Mark the end.	130	Love unkn.	63
Mark well my furnace! O what flames,	149	Longing	26
Yet can I mark how herbs below	162	The Search	9
Yet can I mark how starres above	162	The Search	13
The harbingers are come. See, see their mark;	176	Forerunners	1
and Character of a true Pastour, that I may have a Mark to aim at:	224	Priest	7
an aim and mark of the whole discourse, whither to drive	256	Priest 21	31
Therefore they are to mark their Fathers discretion in ordering his	276	Priest 32	28
of your wit, mark what I say, have a good conceit of your wit;	366	Letters	15
MARK-MAN			
This is the Mark-man, safe and sure,	73	Constancie	34
MARKE			
Saviour himselfe used, Marke 10. 16, cannot bee vain and superfluous.	285	Priest 36	11
MARKED			
It is a sheep of Berry, it is marked on the nose	356	Proverbs D	1040
Take heed of a person marked, and a Widdow thrice married.	360	Proverbs D	1152
MARKET			
Onely thy single market-money for it.	21	Ch.-Porch	375
and seems to himselfe so as a Market-man is, when the Market day	235	Priest 8	18
so as a Market-man is, when the Market day comes, or a shopkeeper,	235	Priest 8	18
and he will play with you in the market.	325	Proverbs	146
Love is not found in the market.	334	Proverbs	401
Three women make a market.	345	Proverbs	713
The market is the best garden.	346	Proverbs	743
Old Camels carry young Camels skins to the Market.	359	Proverbs D	1101
MARKET-MAN			
and seems to himselfe so as a Market-man is, when the Market day	235	Priest 8	18
MARKET-MONEY			
Onely thy single market-money for it.	21	Ch.-Porch	375
MARKETH			
Marketh that deed for thine:	184	The Elixer W	12
MARKING			
Marking his grave, and thawing ev'ry yeare,	98	Mortific.	26
MARKS			
Who marks in church-time others symmetrie,	23	Ch.-Porch	419
Who marks in church-time others comlines,	23	Ch.-Porch W	419
This verse marks that, and both do make a motion	58	H.Script.2	5
They are hells land-marks, Satans double crest:	196	Ch.-Milit.	219
(The marks of future bane) shall fill our cup	197	Ch.-Milit.	239
with letting them know, that he observes who marks, and who not;	233	Priest 7	2
MARRE			
Doth ratably thy fortunes marre or make.	16	Ch.-Porch	256
MARR'D			
All did but strive to mend, what you had marr'd.	130	Love unkn.	67

MARR'D (cont'd)	PAGE	TITLE	LINE
Truth Lord, but I have marr'd them: let my shame	189	Love 3	13
MARRES			
A gentle houswife marres the houshold.	322	Proverbs	44
To speake of an Usurer at the table marres the wine.	353	Proverbs	974
MARRIAGE			
watching, ill aire, overmuch use of the benefit of marriage.	293	Cornaro	32
MARRIAGES			
The Jewes spend at Easter, the Mores at marriages,	329	Proverbs	242
MARRIED			
like circumstances considered, he is rather married then unmarried.	237	Priest 9	4
A married man turns his staffe into a stake.	333	Proverbs	366
Hee that tells his wife newes is but newly married.	353	Proverbs	987
Take heed of a person marked, and a Widdow thrice married.	360	Proverbs	D 1152
but you married men laugh till your hearts ake.	361	Proverbs	D 1175
MARRIES			
Hee that marries for wealth sells his liberty.	347	Proverbs	784
He that marries late, marries ill.	349	Proverbs	863
MARRS			
Yet wedding marrs thy fortune, fast & pray:	7	Ch.-Porch	W 14
MARRY			
I will not marry; or, if she be mine,	35	Thanksgvng	23
Frogs marry fish and flesh; bats, bird and beast;	121	Providence	135
Marry your sonne when you will; your daughter when you can.	326	Proverbs	149
Advise none to marry or to goe to warre.	329	Proverbs	236
Advise none to marry nor to goe to warre.	329	Proverbs	V 236
Marry a widdow before she leave mourning.	329	Proverbs	252
Marry your daughters betimes, lest they marry themselves.	361	Proverbs	D 1171
MARRYED			
the best and highest things, is rather unmarryed, then marryed.	237	Priest 9	1
and that much more being single, then if he were marryed;	238	Priest 9	22
If he be marryed, the choyce of his wife was made rather by his eare,	238	Priest 9	26
Men are either single, or marryed:	275	Priest 32	19
The marryed and house-keeper hath his hands full, if he do what he	275	Priest 32	20
MARRYING			
Building and marrying of Children are great wasters.	321	Proverbs	11
MARSHALLING			
Thy curious art in marshalling thy goods.	119	Providence	94
MARTYR'D			
Were cut and martyr'd by the fault	59	Whitsunday	19
MARTYRS			
Wherewith whole showls of Martyrs once did burn,	206	Walton 1	2
remember the holy Martyrs of God, how they have been burnt	373	Letters	35
MARVELL			
No marvell Sir, he did replie,	122	Time	3
MARY			
Anagram MARY / ARMY.	77	Anagram	T
that (which you are thinking to doe) to blessed Mary Magd. & Paul,	381	Woodnoth	5
To Mrs Mary Danvers twenty shillings, To Mrs Michel twenty shillings,	383	G.H.'s Will	11
Burthen thirty shillings To Mary Gifford tenn shillings To Anne	383	G.H.'s Will	16
Judith Spencer five pound To Mary Owens forty shillings To Mrs Mary	383	G.H.'s Will	18
Owens forty shillings To Mrs Mary Lawly fifty shillings To Mr	383	G.H.'s Will	19
due to Mrs Judeth Spenser is to be payd to Mrs Mary Lawly at Chelsey	383	G.H.'s Will	21
MASK			
Who fears to do well, sure should wear a mask.	11	Ch.-Porch	126
MASON			
They say, it is an ill Mason that refuseth any stone:	228	Priest 4	15
MASSE			
A full eternitie: thou art a masse	58	H.Script.1	6
MASTER			
If thou be Master-gunner, spend not all	18	Ch.-Porch	301
And love him for his Master: his condition,	24	Ch.-Porch	443
Some other master out.	48	Afflict.1	64
And like a master in my trade,	126	Confession	4
For ought I heare, your Master shows to you	130	Love unkn.	62
How sweetly doth My Master sound! My Master!	174	The Odour	1
An orientall fragrancie, My Master.	174	The Odour	5
My Master, shall I speak? O that to thee	175	The Odour	11
For when My Master, which alone is sweet,	175	The Odour	21
That is thy Master-peece I see	201	love	W 3
admonition, or reproofe, sell (with Judas) their Lord and Master.	226	Priest 2	38
that he may be an absolute Master and commander of himself,	227	Priest 3	8
remembring what his Master saith, that if any do Gods will,	228	Priest 4	28
or, Oh my Master, on whose errand I come, let me hold my peace,	233	Priest 7	35
humbly beseeching his Master, that how or whenever he punish him,	235	Priest 8	26
or Master and Mistres of the house, and shewing them cleerly,	251	Priest 17	29
minde being defixed on it with those nailes wherewith his Master was:	267	Priest 27	29
because this hath been the portion of God his Master, and of Gods	268	Priest 28	14
and joyfull, that hee is made conformable to his Master;	269	Priest 28	17
he every where beares towards our deare [great] Master and Lord,	305	Valdesso	4
A good pay-master starts not at assurances.	324	Proverbs	113
The wrongs of a Husband or Master are not reproached.	325	Proverbs	139
A wicked mans gift hath a touch of his master.	326	Proverbs	162
A diligent Scholler, and the Master's paid.	327	Proverbs	183
A good payer is master of anothers purse.	341	Proverbs	595
In every Art it is good to have a master.	342	Proverbs	619
None is borne Master.	343	Proverbs	654
A sleepy master makes his servant a Lowt.	346	Proverbs	766
God, and Parents, and our Master, can never be requited.	348	Proverbs	805
When God is made master of a family, he orders the disorderly.	353	Proverbs	983
Hee that is a master must serve (another).	354	Proverbs	991

MASTER (cont'd)	PAGE	TITLE		LINE
Every one is a master and servant.	355	Proverbs		1026
A master of straw eates a servant of steele.	355	Proverbs		1029
I have sent you here inclosed a Letter from our Master in my behalf,	369	Letters		25
Blessed be My God & Dear Master, the Spring & Fountain of all	379	Letters		16
other profitt, the work I may change, the profitt, I am master of.	381	Woodnoth		32
The Oration of Master George Herbert, Orator of the Universitie	441	Oration		T
MASTER-GUNNER				
If thou be Master-gunner, spend not all	18	Ch.-Porch		301
MASTER-PEECE				
That is thy Master-peece I see	201	love	W	3
MASTER'S				
If any one our Masters hand can show.	78	Ang.&Sts.		30
Their masters flower, but leave it, having done,	118	Providence		66
to be accounted for, and to be improved to our Masters Advantage.	274	Priest 32		25
The masters eye fattens the horse, and his foote the ground.	338	Proverbs		486
One eye of the masters sees more, then ten of the servants.	344	Proverbs		687
MASTERED				
and mastered all his lusts and affections within, and the whole Army	278	Priest 33		22
MASTERETH				
whom anothers ill mastereth, and leadeth captive without any	269	Priest 28		21
MAST'RING				
A mast'ring minde; so both are lost thereby:	10	Ch.-Porch		104
MASTERS				
If my deserts were masters of mine eyes:	136	Ephes.		34
that Parents, and Masters, as they hear the answers prove,	255	Priest 21		27
and Masters should make hast in this, as to a great purchase	259	Priest 22		2
as if they were Masters of their health, and so they will stand	266	Priest 26		19
and this they are not masters of.	266	Priest 26		23
since we are not Masters of our bodies, this sufficeth.	279	Priest 33		19
of Cambridge, when the Ambassadours were made Masters of Arts.	441	Oration		T
as to you deserving them, Wee at last salute you Masters of Arts;	441	Oration		27
MASTERS'				
& therfore not relinquishable without their masters consent.	381	Woodnoth		29
MASTIFFE				
Though the Mastiffe be gentle, yet bite him not by the lippe.	325	Proverbs		132
Though the Mastiffe be gentile, yet bite him not by the lippe.	325	Proverbs	V	132
MATCH				
Then we must needs for that day make a match.	62	Mattens		4
MATE				
Who hath a Wolfe for his mate, needes a Dog for his man.	323	Proverbs		57
Hee that hath a Fox for his mate,	335	Proverbs		428
and will not allow any room there for such an in-mate as Grief;	374	Letters		11
MATES				
With his train-bands and mates agree	110	The Quip		2
MATHEMATICKS				
he commends the Mathematicks, as the only wonder-working knowledg,	277	Priest 32		34
MATRIMONY				
Parson considering that virginity is a higher state then Matrimony,	236	Priest 9		32
MATTENS				
Mattens.	62	Mattens		T
MATTER				
I will search out the matter.	124	Peace		10
Indeed 'tis true. I found a callous matter	130	Love unkn.		38
Indeed it's true. I found a callous matter	130	Love unkn.	V	38
Of lowly matter for high uses meet,	161	Priesthood		35
What leaves are they? impart the matter wholly.	188	Heaven		9
Upon the matter 'twill thy conquest prove:	202	love	W	20
referreth the whole matter to the examination, and punishment	268	Priest 28		34
whom that matter ought to have affected most, received no	294	Cornaro		20
But surely there is no such matter, if Temperance be wanting.	298	Cornaro		21
his head akes not at the matter.	335	Proverbs		421
it is no matter, for the Gentleman needs no incitation to love me.	369	Letters		28
that he fears I have not fully resolved of the matter, since this	370	Letters		19
MATTERS				
all which tend to avoiding of costlier matters, if I should fall	365	Letters		8
come agents hither from the low-Cuntries to treat of divers matters,	368	Letters		5
MATTHEW				
The Pearl. Matthew 13.	88	The Pearl		T
and the forgivenesse of sins, Matthew 6. 14. Luke 7. 47.	244	Priest 12		10
And the reward of the next, Matth. 25. 35.	244	Priest 12		13
his preaching, but afterwards also, as Mat. 22. 35. He was tempted:	280	Priest 34		9
but with the Gospel it selfe be preached to all ages, Matth. 26. 13.	282	Priest 34		26
Matthew 24. 14. which we see even miraculously effected in these new	282	Priest 34		32
Things needing great Consideration. Mat. 24. 15.	317	Valdesso		26
of the blessed Virgin out of that text Mat. 1. 25. where it is said,	318	Valdesso		12
MATURE				
of how great moment ten yeares are in mature age, wherein wisdome	298	Cornaro		29
MAUGRE				
In water kept, maugre the powers	213	L' Envoy	D	8
MAY (noun)				
There was no moneth but May.	47	Afflict.1		22
Like snow in May,	165	The Flower		6
Hee that is in a towne in May loseth his spring.	353	Proverbs		988
MAY (see also maist)				
Hearken unto a Verser, who may chance	6	Ch.-Porch		3
A verse may finde him, who a sermon flies,	6	Ch.-Porch		5
He that is drunken, may his mother kill	7	Ch.-Porch		31
Throughout the world. Fool not: for all may have,	10	Ch.-Porch		89
Then all thou addest may be call'd his treasure.	11	Ch.-Porch		114
Never exceed thy income. Youth may make	13	Ch.-Porch		157

MAY (cont'd)

	PAGE	TITLE		LINE
The fine may spare these well, yet not go lesse.	16	Ch.-Porch		238
But may be wittie, if thou hast the vein.	16	Ch.-Porch		240
As hurts not others, but may make thee better,	16	Ch.-Porch		262
Then may the beasts draw thee to happy light.	16	Ch.-Porch		264
Still in thy heart, that he may see what's there.	17	Ch.-Porch		272
Another chafe, may warm him at his fire,	19	Ch.-Porch		314
Be usefull where thou livest, that they may	19	Ch.-Porch		325
And when, and how the businesse may be done.	20	Ch.-Porch		338
As gunnes destroy, so may a little sling.	20	Ch.-Porch		352
As swords cause death, so may a little sting.	20	Ch.-Porch	W	352
The meanest tool, that he may chance to use.	20	Ch.-Porch		354
And then as farre as fair behaviour may,	20	Ch.-Porch		359
That all may gladly board thee, as a flowre.	21	Ch.-Porch		368
Open for thee; or both may come too late.	21	Ch.-Porch		384
Open for thee; or they may come too late.	21	Ch.-Porch	W	384
Because 'tis better, and perhaps may save thee.	22	Ch.-Porch		394
They may weep out the stains by them did rise:	23	Ch.-Porch		417
May at his perill further go.	25	Superlim		8
These stones to praise thee may not cease.	26	The Altar		14
That all together may accord in thee,	36	Thanksgvng		41
May give a disentangled state and free:	36	Reprisall		6
That thy distresse through all may runne,	39	Good Fri.		15
Each sinne may so.	39	Good Fri.		20
All come to lodge there, sinne may say,	39	Good Fri.		27
All come to lodge there, he may say,	39	Good Fri.	W	27
For by the writings all may see	39	Good Fri.	W	31
His life may make thee gold, and much more just.	41	Easter		6
That so the broken bones may joy,	49	Repentance		32
A peasant may beleeve as much	50	Faith		29
But as th' outworks, they may controll	52	H.Commun.		16
That wee may gaine by crosses.	53	H.Commun.	W	40
His praise may thither flie:	53	Antiphon 1		4
His praises there may grow.	53	Antiphon 1		6
As may consume our lusts, and make thee way.	54	Love 2		5
May also fix their reverence:	56	Temper 2		10
May no lines passe, except they do their dutie	56	Jordan 1		4
Lord that I may the Sunns perfection gaine	57	Employm. 1	W	23
Of strange delights, where we may wish & take.	58	H.Script.1		7
So wee may cease to suck: to praise thee, never.	59	Whitsunday	W	24
He may do more.	61	Praise 1		12
An herb destill'd, and drunk, may dwell next doore,	61	Praise 1		13
It may doe more.	61	Praise 1	W	16
O raise me then: for if a Spider may	61	Praise 1	W	17
May both the work and workman show:	63	Mattens		19
May take acquaintance of this heap of dust;	64	Ch.-monum.		3
My bodie to this school, that it may learn	65	Ch.-monum.		7
May guard it safe beyond the highest starr.	66	Ch.-lock	W	12
That I may runne, rise, rest with thee.	68	Trin.Sun.		9
That I may runne, rise, rest in thee.	68	Trin.Sun.	W	9
Thy name in books, which may not rent:	69	Content		28
Thy name in books, which may not vent:	69	Content	W	28
It may a Babel prove	72	Frailtie		22
That it may hang and move	74	The Starre		15
That so among the rest I may	74	The Starre		25
They and my minde may chime,	80	Deniall		29
They and my hart may chime,	80	Deniall	W	29
They and my soule may chime,	80	Deniall	WC	29
This may allure us with delights;	82	Ungratef.		22
Cuts through the working waves, that he may fetch	85	Vanitie 1		9
May turn, and take me by the hand, and more	87	Lent		41
May strengthen my decayes.	87	Lent		42
As may our faults controll:	87	Lent		45
As may all vice controll:	87	Lent	W	45
That ev'ry man may revell at his doore,	87	Lent		46
Which on the world a true-love-knot may tie,	88	The Pearl		16
With all the circumstances that may move:	89	The Pearl		36
Parrats may thank us, if they are not mute,	91	Man		11
Each part may call the farthest, brother:	91	Man		16
Each part may call the furthest, brother:	91	Man	V	16
That it may dwell with thee at last!	92	Man		51
That, as the world serves us, we may serve thee,	92	Man		53
So we may bee to Thee.	92	Man	W	54
My friend may spit upon my curious floore:	93	Unkindness		11
But who drinks on, to hell may go.	97	Charms & K		18
Who dives on further may find Hell.	97	Charms & K	W	22
That thy bright beams may tame thy bow.	97	Afflict.5		24
Getting a house and home, where he may move	98	Mortific.		20
That all these dyings may be life in death.	99	Mortific.		36
List, ye may heare great Aarons bell.	99	Decay		10
Who may thy follies span?	102	Miserie	W	66
May our requests thine eare invade!	103	Prayer 2		3
May our requests thine eares invade!	103	Prayer 2	W	3
My God, if writings may	104	Obedience		1
As I have mine, may set his hand	105	Obedience		37
Some may dream merrily, but when they wake,	108	Home		51
That my free soul may use her wing,	109	Home		62
Outlandish looks may not compare:	109	Brit. Ch.		10
And long may be.	110	Brit. Ch.		27
May come too late!	111	Vanitie 2		8
Christs resurrection thine may be:	112	Dawning		10

MAY (cont'd)

	PAGE	TITLE	LINE
O give me quicknesse, that I may with mirth	115	Dulnesse	3
I may but lock towards thee:	116	Dulnesse	26
Where all may reach: no beast but knows his feed.	118	Providence	50
When they are fledge, that need may teach them flying.	118	Providence	64
Thou hast hid metals: man may take them thence;	119	Providence	81
But such a heart, whose pulse may be	124	Gratefulnes	31
And have, of whom some grounds which may improve,	129	Love unkn.	4
Not, that he may not here	131	Mans medly	19
He may attain to, after he is dead.	131	Mans medly	24
May be reliefs,	132	Mans medly	32
Which may with thee	136	Ephes.	20
That I may climbe and finde relief.	144	Complaining	20
And that love may never cease,	146	Praise 2	3
Yet one, if good, may title to a number;	147	Offering	9
In publick judgements one may be a nation,	147	Offering	11
May give savour	148	Offering	38
Well may he close his eyes, but not his heart.	151	The Bag	6
Look, you may put it very neare my heart.	152	The Bag	36
May oft break forth, and never break the lock.	154	Glimpse	25
Who by thy coming may be made a court!	155	Glimpse	30
I may presume thee mine, then thine.	157	Clasping	13
May tosse him to my breast.	160	The Pulley	20
If truly said, they may take part	168	a true Hymn	7
That choice may be thy storie.	170	Self-cond.	6
Well may I walk, not fear:	173	23 Psalme	14
That to the old man I may rest,	174	Aaron	19
As flesh may be;	175	The Odour	13
That I may seek, but thou art lost;	183	A Parodie	24
That I not onely may not erre	184	The Elixer W	3
On it may stay his eye;	184	The Elixer	10
All may of thee partake:	184	The Elixer	13
Give me simplicitie, that I may live,	185	A Wreath	9
So live and like, that I may know thy wayes,	185	A Wreath	10
Dry dust, which sheds no tears, but may extort.	186	Death	12
Fleshes stubbornnesse may have	187	Dooms-day	17
And in them may drown a friend:	187	Dooms-day	22
Who may with thee compare?	191	Ch.-Milit.	48
Who may with thee compare?	192	Ch.-Milit.	100
Begging his food of that which he may eat,	193	Ch.-Milit.	113
Who may with thee compare?	194	Ch.-Milit.	156
Who may with thee compare?	196	Ch.-Milit.	210
Whereby one may foretell, what sinnes next yeare	197	Ch.-Milit.	245
Judgement may meet them both & search them round.	197	Ch.-Milit.	269
Who may with thee compare?	198	Ch.-Milit.	279
Something that may be conquest on my part	201	love W	5
With Glory may attaine thy Face.	202	Trin.Sun. W	6
Look on his daring brightnes, may	203	Even-song W	7
But that my darknes may touch thine:	203	Even-song W	18
And hope, that may teach it to shine,	203	Even-song W	19
That they may bee	204	The Knell W	16
May yet forbid the banes and bliss.	205	Persever. W	12
Than that, which one day Worms may chance refuse?	206	Walton 1	14
Search and you may	208	J. Danvers D	2
So by the Other, you may read in mee	209	L. Bacon D	5
So tremblinge may	210	Paradox D	23
When all things pull & hale, that they may bring	212	Bohemia D	27
and Character of a true Pastour, that I may have a Mark to aim at:	224	Priest	7
who may not despise my poor labours, but add to those points,	224	Priest	14
Out of this Chartre of the Priesthood may be plainly gathered both	225	Priest 1	15
in that a Priest may do that which Christ did, and by his auctority,	225	Priest 1	16
are in Orders, they may be received for Companions, or discoursers;	226	Priest 2	24
that he may be an absolute Master and commander of himself,	227	Priest 3	8
he may say as He did, I sate daily with you teaching in the Temple.	227	Priest 3	33
open mine eyes, that I may see the wondrous things of thy Law.	229	Priest 4	3
To this may be added the consideration of any text with the coherence	229	Priest 4	9
one Countrey doth not bear all things, that there may be a Commerce;	229	Priest 4	24
that there may be a traffick in knowledg between the servants of God,	229	Priest 4	25
the Church Catechisme, to which all divinity may easily be reduced.	230	Priest 5	9
and using all other gestures which may expresse a hearty,	231	Priest 6	4
hee may affect also his people, knowing that no Sermon moves them so	231	Priest 6	13
that he may the better celebrate it, or for the variety	232	Priest 7	23
of the hearers, that he may be heard at his returne more attentively.	232	Priest 7	24
mouth of two or three witnesses the truth may be more established.	232	Priest 7	29
so that the auditors may plainly perceive that every word is	233	Priest 7	31
Therefore this care may be learn'd there, and then woven into	234	Priest 7	22
but a dictionary, and may be considered alike in all the Scripture.	235	Priest 7	9
himself, but that all may be done with reverence to his glory,	235	Priest 8	24
that they may come with holy hearts, and awfull mindes into	235	Priest 8	29
that we may grow therein, and that our feet may be like hindes feet	236	Priest 8	28
and that our feet may be like hindes feet ever climbing up higher,	236	Priest 8	29
But yet as the temper of his body may be, or as the temper of his	237	Priest 9	1
or as the temper of his Parish may be, where he may have occasion	237	Priest 9	2
where he may have occasion to converse with women, and that among	237	Priest 9	2
like mortall enemies, may sometimes disquiet him likewise;	238	Priest 9	9
counting nothing so much his owne, as that he may be unjust unto it.	238	Priest 9	35
or painted there, which may excite the reader to a thought of piety;	240	Priest 10	24
and where flesh may be much better spared, and with more safety then	242	Priest 10	18
To all this may be added, not for emboldening the unruly,	242	Priest 10	33
that so both they may be encouraged to persevere, and others spurred	243	Priest 11	26
others spurred to do well, that they may enjoy the like courtesie.	243	Priest 11	27

MAY (cont'd)

	PAGE	TITLE	LINE
that he may, if not the best way, yet any way, make his Parish good.	244	Priest 11	4
For though these testimonies also may be falsifyed, yet considering	245	Priest 12	23
that so the thanks may go the right way, and thither onely, . .	245	Priest 12	33
but that they may have wherewithall to serve God the better,	248	Priest 14	7
that he may keep himself pure, and not be intangled in others sinnes.	248	Priest 14	24
so the hunger and thirst after it may come rather from themselves,	250	Priest 15	6
as a child, and forgives, so hee may have any signe of amendment;	250	Priest 16	15
good discourses, such as may edify, interposing sometimes some short,	251	Priest 17	4
which may make his other discourses more welcome, and lesse tedious.	251	Priest 17	5
that he may enlarge the glory of God to the company he is in,	251	Priest 17	7
that if any be willing to partake, they may resort thither. . .	251	Priest 17	12
none knowing whose turne may be next, and then when he hath . .	253	Priest 19	33
or hainousness of the crime may be, he is carefull to see condign	254	Priest 20	26
that the same common truths may be every where professed, . .	255	Priest 21	18
answers prove, may when they come home, either commend or reprove,	255	Priest 21	28
may then by an honourable way take occasion to be better instructed.	255	Priest 21	30
knowledg of Religion, may examine their grounds, renew their vowes,	255	Priest 21	33
the singular dexterity of Socrates in this kind may be observed,	256	Priest 21	29
in this, that at Sermons, and Prayers, men may sleep or wander;	257	Priest 21	19
pains with them, that hee may lay the foundation of future Blessings.	258	Priest 22	31
particularly, the rule may be this:	258	Priest 22	33
because to answer in form may still admit ignorance: . . .	259	Priest 22	7
there may happen somtimes some cases, wherein he chooseth to permit	260	Priest 23	17
as may be of much use to him both for himself, and others. . .	261	Priest 23	3
and the knowing of herbs may be done at such times, as they may be	261	Priest 23	9
as they may be an help, and a recreation to more divine studies,	261	Priest 23	10
to know what herbs may be used in stead of drugs of the same nature,	261	Priest 23	29
that it may effectually pierce their hearts, and convert them.	262	Priest 24	24
some small and temporary estranging may corroborate the punishment	263	Priest 25	31
A man may be both Covetous, and Intemperate, and yet hear Sermons	264	Priest 26	14
even as a piece of wood, which they may cut, or hack, or throw into	265	Priest 26	26
for this may produce hatred in those that are reproved, . .	268	Priest 28	29
that so the sentence lighting upon one, the example may reach to all.	269	Priest 28	2
that so they may know their duty, and keep their oath the better;	270	Priest 29	15
and prevent such interruptions, what he may, before they come,	273	Priest 31	18
he may behave himself so as befits so great a presence; . .	273	Priest 31	26
as that by this he may take into his Prayer humiliation also.	273	Priest 31	32
This distinction may runne through all Christian duties, . .	274	Priest 31	1
bring strangers to him, he may be the better armed to encounter them.	274	Priest 32	7
may be prevented, or diverted by reasonable imployment. . .	274	Priest 32	23
to get more, that we may give more, according to St. Pauls rule,	275	Priest 32	1
of his affairs, that hee may have wherewithall to do good. . .	275	Priest 32	30
But if hee may bee of the Commission of Peace, there is nothing	276	Priest 32	7
Sometimes he may go to Court, as the eminent place both of good	277	Priest 32	5
but also as they may be handled, a religious imployment? . .	278	Priest 32	7
for though the temptations may be diverse in divers Christians,	279	Priest 33	1
that it may be alike in all Gods children (which as concerning	279	Priest 33	21
that so the body may joyn in the grief, as it did in the sin;	279	Priest 33	27
there may be so evident, though unused a proof of Divinity taken from	281	Priest 34	32
especially since it may be a just doubt, whether, considering	282	Priest 34	7
in the mouth of two or three witnesses every word may be established;	283	Priest 34	19
And all may certainly conclude, that God loves them, till either they	283	Priest 34	22
the custome, that may be severed from the good, he pares the apple,	283	Priest 35	32
their children, how much more may, and ought Spirituall Fathers?	285	Priest 36	15
so that even ill Priests may blesse.	285	Priest 36	24
they may disclose anothers fault, finds it somwhat difficult how	286	Priest 37	32
many an evill may not only be, but also spread in his Parish,	287	Priest 37	1
for we must not do evill, that good may come of it. . . .	287	Priest 37	7
those that know them, may talk, so they do it not with sport,	287	Priest 37	13
Of these also men may talk, and more, they may discover them to those	287	Priest 37	16
and more, they may discover them to those that know them not:	287	Priest 37	17
by those, which are branded for rogues, that they may be known;	287	Priest 37	20
or put into the stocks, that they may be looked upon. . . .	287	Priest 37	21
But some may say, though the Law allow this, the Gospel doth not,	287	Priest 37	21
And as malefactors may lose & forfeit their goods, or life; . .	287	Priest 37	31
so may they their good name, and the possession thereof, . .	287	Priest 37	32
it is a duty rather, which may do much good, and save much harme.	288	Priest 37	1
teach thou me, that I may teach them:	289	Priest	26
that in their full strength they may deliver thy message reverently,	289	Priest	28
so neither may thy word, but accomplish that for which it is given.	289	Priest	32
the measure of thy love, who hast done for us as much as may be.	290	Priest	12
that I may satisfie their honest desire, and withall help many	291	Cornaro	13
lesse then one yeare (although it may seem to some incredible) I was	292	Cornaro	37
By this it may clearely be perceived, how great is the power of order	297	Cornaro	3
Every one by long experience may know the qualities of his own	297	Cornaro	26
But that a man may preserve himself in health, I advise, . .	298	Cornaro	11
And that I may say nothing of other things, are not almost all	298	Cornaro	32
and later yeares, it is no such thing which may not be performed;	299	Cornaro	6
both that they may preserve themselves from diseases, which hinder	299	Cornaro	18
in all things wherein they deal, may be more lively and vigorous.	299	Cornaro	20
But some may say, He which lives a regular life, eating alwayes light	299	Cornaro	22
they who finde benefit in these meats, may, yea ought to use them:	300	Cornaro	11
aim in all things, how I may help others to the furthest of my power.	301	Cornaro	8
that I may enjoy the sight & communication of my friends, . .	301	Cornaro	35
neither omit I any thing that may either teach, or delight me.	302	Cornaro	5
may be discovered, because at these yeares (viz. 83) I have made	302	Cornaro	27
All the Saints of God may be said in some sence to have put . .	306	Valdesso	28
(as Pictures may be by a plenarie circumspection) but still even	309	Valdesso	22
this line [place] till the end of this Chapter may seeme strange,	311	Valdesso	21
the Doctrine would be examined, however it may passe for his opinion:	312	Valdesso	1

MAY (cont'd)	PAGE	TITLE		LINE
which may be unto him as the sunne to a Travellour in his journey,	312	Valdesso		18
For otherwise any Malefactor may pretend motions, which is . .	316	Valdesso		21
So may a warre be just on both sides, and was just in the Canaanites	316	Valdesso		29
men cannot judg spirituall mens actions, but the Magistrate may.	317	Valdesso		6
that I may speak with him or doe some thing else when I doe come.	318	Valdesso		16
And miracle-working as it may be severed from justifying faith,	319	Valdesso		12
so it may be a fruit of it, and an exaltation. 1 John 5. 14.	319	Valdesso		13
Who hath none to still him, may weepe out his eyes.	321	Proverbs		17
Mend your cloathes, and you may hold out this yeare.	324	Proverbs		100
Make hast to an ill way that you may get out of it.	325	Proverbs		124
Well may hee smell fire, whose gowne burnes.	325	Proverbs		138
He that hath the spice, may season as he list.	335	Proverbs		424
He who hath the spice, may season as he pleaseth.	335	Proverbs	V	424
Hee that's fed at anothers hand may stay long ere he be full.	336	Proverbs		439
Hee that knowes what may bee gained in a day never steales. . .	336	Proverbs		445
A foole may throw a stone into a well, ...	339	Proverbs		527
You may bring a horse to the river, ...	342	Proverbs		623
Good newes may bee told at any time, but ill in the morning.	350	Proverbs		877
You may be on land, yet not in a garden.	353	Proverbs		964
Once a yeare a man may say: On his conscience.	353	Proverbs		971
Heresie may be easier kept out, then shooke off.	357	Proverbs	D	1059
We must recoile a little, to the end we may leap the better.	359	Proverbs	D	1121
Stay a while, that we may make an end the sooner.	361	Proverbs	D	1161
by the hand of man may be overturned.	362	Proverbs	D	1184
but that every day, I may step one step towards my journies end;	364	Letters		27
Sister this week already, and therefore now I hope may be excused.	367	Letters		22
The Orators place (that you may understand what it is) is the finest	369	Letters		30
to me as soon as you can, that I may work the heads to my purpose.	370	Letters		6
that I joy in your favours, but that you may see, that if all fail,	370	Letters		9
since this place being civil may divert me too much from Divinity,	370	Letters		20
no such earthiness in it, but it may very well be joined with Heaven;	370	Letters		22
though businesses may stop my hand, yet my heart, a much better	371	Letters		26
yet you may say with David, That God who hath delivered me out	374	Letters		6
entertains our Care for us that we may the more quietly intend his	374	Letters		19
I forgett all thinges, so I may doe them good who want it. . .	376	Letters		6
if at length they may find out some thing not unworthy of those hands	376	Letters		29
one to the other, that ye may be a heavenly comfort, to his prayse,	378	Letters		26
things inwardly good to have an eye to the world may be pharisaicall:	380	Woodnoth		16
things may grow worse by your withdrawing which grow not better	381	Woodnoth		10
the other profitt, the work I may change, the profitt, I am master	381	Woodnoth		31
that you may well conceive, your Excellencies to bee more deare unto	442	Oration		19
Fame is sowne in this age, that it may be reaped in the following;	443	Oration		3
MAYDS				
a trayning up of her children and mayds in the fear of God, . .	239	Priest 10		13
MAYST				
Mayst rule it, as thou list; and poure the shame, ...	7	Ch.-Porch		27
Gold thou mayst safely touch; but if it stick	13	Ch.-Porch		167
As all the day thou mayst hold out to go.	14	Ch.-Porch		186
That all the day thou mayst hold out to go.	14	Ch.-Porch	W	186
With him mayst rise:	41	Easter		4
And wanton in thy cravings, thou mayst know, ...	65	Ch.-monum.		19
That thou mayst fit thy self against thy fall.	65	Ch.-monum.		24
Furnish & deck my soul, that thou mayst have	81	Christmas		13
Thou mayst as well my actions guide, as see.	104	Obedience		25
And thou mayst offer many gifts in one.	147	Offering		18
That thou mayst yet have more.	157	Praise 3		6
That so in purenesse thou mayst him adore, ...	170	Water-crs.		9
ME (see also mee)				
And must return. Accept of them and me, ...	5	Dedication		3
Theirs, who shall hurt themselves or me, refrain.	5	Dedication		6
Which would throw me there, if I keep the round.	7	Ch.-Porch		30
Lose all mine own? God hath giv'n me a measure	8	Ch.-Porch		38
God made me one man; love makes me no more, ...	17	Ch.-Porch		287
To worldly things are sharp, but to me blinde;	26	Sacrifice		2
To me, who took eyes that I might you finde:	26	Sacrifice		3
Against their Maker: they do wish me dead, ...	26	Sacrifice		6
Without me each one, who doth now me brave, ...	27	Sacrifice		9
They use that power against me, which I gave:	27	Sacrifice		11
To sell me also, and to put me there:	27	Sacrifice		15
Comforts not me, and doth my doctrine stain:	27	Sacrifice		31
With clubs and staves they seek me, as a thief, ...	27	Sacrifice		37
Judas, dost thou betray me with a kisse?	28	Sacrifice		41
See, they lay hold on me, not with the hands	28	Sacrifice		45
Betwixt my friends and me. They leave the starre, ...	28	Sacrifice		50
Betwixt my friends and me. They leave that starre, ...	28	Sacrifice	W	50
They leade me; urging, that it was not sound	28	Sacrifice		54
Then they accuse me of great blasphemie, ...	28	Sacrifice		61
Then they condemne me all with that same breath, ...	28	Sacrifice		69
They binde, and leade me unto Herod: he	29	Sacrifice		73
Sends me to Pilate. This makes them agree;	29	Sacrifice		74
Herod and all his bands do set me light, ...	29	Sacrifice		77
Examines me with a censorious hand:	29	Sacrifice		82
The Jews accuse me with despitefulnesse;	29	Sacrifice		85
For it was their own cause who killed me:	30	Sacrifice		115
For it was their own case who killed me:	30	Sacrifice	W	115
Ah! how they scourge me! yet my tendernesse	30	Sacrifice		125
They buffet me, and box me as they list, ...	30	Sacrifice		129
Behold, they spit on me in scornfull wise, ...	31	Sacrifice		133
Servants and abjects flout me; they are wittie:	31	Sacrifice		141
So they in me denie themselves all pitie:	31	Sacrifice		143

ME (cont'd)

	PAGE	TITLE		LINE
That he before me well nigh suffereth:	31	Sacrifice		147
The souldiers lead me to the common hall;	31	Sacrifice		153
There they deride me, they abuse me all:	31	Sacrifice		154
Then with a scarlet robe they me aray;	31	Sacrifice		157
Then with the reed they gave to me before,	32	Sacrifice		169
They bow their knees to me, and cry, Hail king:	32	Sacrifice		173
Thus trimmed forth they bring me to the rout,	32	Sacrifice		185
They leade me in once more, and putting then	32	Sacrifice		189
Mine own clothes on, they leade me out agen.	32	Sacrifice		190
They carrie me to my most bitter crosse:	33	Sacrifice		195
Then Simon bears it for me by constraint,	33	Sacrifice		198
The tree of life to all, but onely me:	33	Sacrifice		203
But, O my God, my God! why leav'st thou me,	33	Sacrifice		213
They gave me vineger mingled with gall,	34	Sacrifice		237
They give me vineger mingled with gall,	34	Sacrifice	W	237
Who in all grief preventest me?	35	Thanksgvng		4
My God, my God, why dost thou part from me?	35	Thanksgvng		9
Surely I will revenge me on thy love,	35	Thanksgvng		17
If thou dost give me wealth, I will restore	35	Thanksgvng		19
If thou dost give me honour, men shall see,	35	Thanksgvng		21
One half of me being gone, the rest I give	35	Thanksgvng		27
One half of me being gone, the rest I'le give	35	Thanksgvng	W	27
If thou shalt give me wit, it shall appeare,	36	Thanksgvng		43
If thou hast giv'n it me, 'tis here.	36	Thanksgvng		44
O make me innocent, that I	36	Reprisall		5
By thy eternall glorie didst outgo me?	37	Reprisall		10
Couldst thou not griefs sad conquests me allow,	37	Reprisall		11
But in all vict'ries overthrow me?	37	Reprisall		12
No room for me, and flie away.	39	Good Fri.		28
They told me there, that he was lately gone	40	Redemption		6
I got me flowers to straw thy way;	42	Easter		19
I got me boughs off many a tree:	42	Easter		20
O let me rise	43	East.wings		7
Then shall the fall further the flight in me.	43	East.wings		10
Then shall my fall further the flight in me.	43	East.wings	W	10
Let me combine	43	East.wings		17
Affliction shall advance the flight in me.	43	East.wings		20
What ever future sinnes should me miscall,	44	H. Bapt.1		13
My faith in me.	44	H. Bapt.2		5
O let me still	44	H. Bapt.2		6
Write thee great God, and me a childe:	44	H. Bapt.2		7
Let me be soft and supple to thy will,	44	H. Bapt.2		8
That thou hast ought to do with me.	45	Nature		3
And made it fine to me:	46	Afflict.1		8
And made it rich to me:	46	Afflict.1	W	8
Thy glorious houshold-stuffe did me entwine,	46	Afflict.1		9
Thy glorious houshold-stuffe did me bewitch	46	Afflict.1	W	9
And 'tice me unto thee.	46	Afflict.1		10
Payd me my wages in a world of mirth.	46	Afflict.1		12
At first thou gav'st me milk and sweetnesses;	47	Afflict.1		19
Till grief did tell me roundly, that I lived.	47	Afflict.1		30
Thou didst betray me to a lingring book,	47	Afflict.1		39
And wrap me in a gown.	47	Afflict.1		40
Turning my purge to food, thou throwest me	48	Afflict.1		51
Thus doth thy power crosse-bias me, not making	48	Afflict.1		53
Thine own gift good, yet me from my wayes taking.	48	Afflict.1		54
Now I am here, what thou wilt do with me	48	Afflict.1		55
Her houshold to me, and I should be just.	48	Afflict.1		60
Yet, though thou troublest me, I must be meek;	48	Afflict.1		61
Let me not love thee, if I love thee not.	48	Afflict.1		66
Cut me not off for my most foul transgression:	49	Repentance		15
Beleeves so too, and lets me go.	50	Faith		16
Faith makes me any thing, or all	50	Faith		17
And where sinne placeth me in Adams fall,	50	Faith		19
And where sinne places me in Adams fall,	50	Faith	W	19
Faith sets me higher in his glorie.	50	Faith		20
Faith puts me there with him, who sweetly took	50	Faith		23
Thou, who from me wast sold,	52	H.Commun.		3
Thou, who for me wast sold,	52	H.Commun.	V	3
To me dost now thy self convey;	52	H.Commun.		4
For so thou should'st without me still have been,	52	H.Commun.		5
Leaving within me sinne:	52	H.Commun.		6
Give me my captive soul, or take	52	H.Commun.		25
O rack me not to such a vast extent;	55	Temper 1		9
A grave too big for me.	55	Temper 1		12
O let me, when thy roof my soul hath hid,	55	Temper 1		17
O let me roost and nestle there:	55	Temper 1		18
Stretch or contract me thy poore debter:	55	Temper 1		22
Save that, and me; or sin for both destroy.	56	Temper 2		4
But keep a standing Majestie in me.	56	Temper 2		16
Riddle who list, for me, and pull for Prime:	57	Jordan 1		12
Nor let them punish me with losse of ryme,	57	Jordan 1		14
Nor let them punish me with losse of time,	57	Jordan 1	V	14
Thou wouldst extend me to some good,	57	Employm. 1		2
Let me not languish then, and spend	57	Employm. 1		13
Lord place me in thy consort; give one strain	57	Employm. 1		23
Thy words do finde me out, & parallels bring,	58	H.Script.2		11
And in another make me understood.	58	H.Script.2		12
And spread thy golden wings in me;	59	Whitsunday		2
Display thy golden wings in me;	59	Whitsunday	W	2

ME (cont'd)

	PAGE	TITLE		LINE
Or if to me thou wilt not move,	61	Grace		22
Remove me, where I need not say,	61	Grace		23
I go to Church; help me to wings, and I	61	Praise 1		5
I goe to Church; make me an Angel, I	61	Praise 1	W	5
O raise me then! poore bees, that work all day,	61	Praise 1		17
O raise me then: for if a Spider may	61	Praise 1	W	17
Kill me not ev'ry day,	62	Afflict.2		1
Thou Lord of life; since thy one death for me	62	Afflict.2		2
Teach me thy love to know;	63	Mattens		17
Who gave me eyes, and light, and power this day,	63	Even-song		2
Who gave me sight alone,	63	Even-song		5
You took me thence, and in your house of pleasure	65	Ch.-mus.		3
A daintie lodging me assign'd.	65	Ch.-mus.		4
Comfort, I'le die; for if you poste from me,	66	Ch.-mus.		9
Comfort, I'le die; for if you part from me,	66	Ch.-mus.	W	9
Which pleads for me:	66	Ch.-lock		10
Lord, who hast form'd me out of mud,	68	Trin.Sun.		1
Lord, who hast made me living mudd,	68	Trin.Sun.	W	1
Lord, who hast rais'd me from the mudd	68	Trin.Sun.	WC	1
And hast redeem'd me through thy bloud,	68	Trin.Sun.		2
And sanctif'd me to do good;	68	Trin.Sun.		3
Enrich my heart, mouth, hands in me,	68	Trin.Sun.		7
Give me the pliant minde, whose gentle measure	69	Content		13
Planted in me.	72	Frailtie		24
But since thy breath gave me both life and shape,	73	Afflict.3		7
A gale to bring me sooner to my blisse.	73	Afflict.3		12
A point of honour, now to grieve in me,	73	Afflict.3		15
Get me a standing there, and place	74	The Starre		21
Sure thou wilt joy, by gaining me	74	The Starre		29
O let me take thee at the bound,	76	Sunday		60
Some fruit for him that dressed me.	79	Employm.2		25
Of pleasures brought me to him, readie there	81	Christmas		7
O do not use me	83	Sighs & Gr.		1
And not refuse me: for thou onely art	83	Sighs & Gr.		4
O do not bruise me!	83	Sighs & Gr.		6
O do not urge me!	83	Sighs & Gr.		7
O do not scourge me!	83	Sighs & Gr.		12
O do not blinde me!	83	Sighs & Gr.		13
O do not grinde me!	83	Sighs & Gr.		18
O do not fill me	83	Sighs & Gr.		19
O do not kill me!	83	Sighs & Gr.		24
But O reprieve me!	83	Sighs & Gr.		25
My God, relieve me!	83	Sighs & Gr.		30
Taught me to live here so, That still one eye	85	Coloss.		7
The Church is so to me.	86	Lent		12
May turn, and take me by the hand, and more	87	Lent		41
And grumble oft, that they have more in me	89	The Pearl		28
But thy silk twist let down from heav'n to me,	89	The Pearl		38
Did both conduct and teach me, how by it	89	The Pearl		39
Lord, hunt me not,	89	Afflict.4		2
Kill them and me,	90	Afflict.4		20
With care and courage building me,	90	Afflict.4		29
Lord, make me coy and tender to offend:	93	Unkindness		1
Some place and power on me?	95	Submission		6
Then should thy praises with me grow,	95	Submission		7
How know I, if thou shouldst me raise,	95	Submission		13
Onely do thou lend me a hand,	95	Submission		19
Lord, thou didst make me, yet thou woundest me;	95	Justice 1		2
Lord, thou dost wound me, yet thou dost relieve me:	95	Justice 1		3
Lord, thou dost kill me, yet thou dost reprieve me.	95	Justice 1		5
Thy justice me most fitly payes:	96	Justice 1		7
Thy words were then, Let me alone.	99	Decay		5
So I bespoke me much insinuation:	103	Jordan 2	W	14
All thy delight in me fulfill!	104	Obedience		17
Let me not think an action mine own way,	104	Obedience		18
I do but taste it, straight it cleanseth me,	106	Conscience		15
For those that trouble me:	106	Conscience		22
Thy long deferrings wound me to the quick,	107	Home		3
O show thy self to me,	107	Home		5
Or take me up to thee!	107	Home		6
O show thy self to me,	107	Home		11
Or take me up to thee!	107	Home		12
O show thy self to me,	107	Home		17
Or take me up to thee!	107	Home		18
O show thy self to me,	107	Home		23
Or take me up to thee!	107	Home		24
O show thy self to me,	108	Home		29
Or take me up to thee!	108	Home		30
My God, what is this world to me?	108	Home		32
O show thy self to me,	108	Home		35
Or take me up to thee!	108	Home		36
O show thy self to me,	108	Home		41
Or take me up to thee!	108	Home		42
With one small sigh thou gav'st me th' other day	108	Home		43
I blasted all the joyes about me:	108	Home		44
Now come again, said I, and flout me.	108	Home		46
O show thy self to me,	108	Home		47
Or take me up to thee!	108	Home		48
O show thy self to me,	108	Home		53
Or take me up to thee!	108	Home		54

ME (cont'd)

	PAGE	TITLE	LINE
O show thy self to me,	108	Home	59
Or take me up to thee!	108	Home	60
O show thy self to me,	109	Home	65
Or take me up to thee!	109	Home	66
The most of me to heav'n is fled:	109	Home	68
O show thy self to me,	109	Home	71
Or take me up to thee!	109	Home	72
O show thy self to me,	109	Home	77
Or take me up to thee!	109	Home	78
And all in sport to geere at me.	110	The Quip	4
Tell me, I pray, Whose hands are those?	110	The Quip	7
But thou shalt answer, Lord, for me.	110	The Quip	8
But thou shalt answer, Lord, for me.	110	The Quip	12
He scarce allow'd me half an eie.	111	The Quip	15
But thou shalt answer, Lord, for me.	111	The Quip	16
But thou shalt answer, Lord, for me.	111	The Quip	20
I sat me down to spell them, and perceived	112	JESU	8
That transferr'd th' accounts to me.	114	Dialogue	16
So the way to fit me for it,	115	Dialogue	19
O give me quicknesse, that I may with mirth	115	Dulnesse	3
Beautie alone to me:	115	Dulnesse	10
Still mock me, and grow bold:	116	Dulnesse	22
To spend my judgement), said, It seem'd to me	116	Love-joy	5
The beasts say, Eat me: but, if beasts must teach,	117	Providence	21
The trees say, Pull me: but the hand you stretch,	117	Providence	23
For me and all my fellows praise to thee:	117	Providence	26
Because the benefit accrues to me.	117	Providence	28
An anchor gave to me.	121	Hope	2
But where one man would have me grinde it,	122	Time	5
Thus farre Time heard me patiently:	123	Time	27
Thou that hast giv'n so much to me,	123	Gratefulnes	1
Not thankfull, when it pleaseth me;	124	Gratefulnes	29
Let me once know.	124	Peace	2
And now, me thinks, I am where I began	128	Bunch Gr.	3
Let me as well take up their joy, as sorrow.	128	Bunch Gr.	21
I hold for two lives, and both lives in me.	129	Love unkn.	5
Better then you know me, or (which is one)	129	Love unkn.	10
Better then you knew me, or (which is one)	129	Love unkn. V	10
Who was to take it from me, slipt his hand,	130	Love unkn.	34
Did oft possesse me, so that when I pray'd,	130	Love unkn.	58
Can blast my fruit, or bring me HARM,	133	Paradise	5
Inclose me still for fear I START.	133	Paradise	7
Be to me rather sharp and TART,	133	Paradise	8
Then let me want thy hand & ART.	133	Paradise	9
I did behave me carelesly,	133	The Method	15
Grieved for me? the God of strength and power	135	Ephes.	4
If a cleare spring for me no time forbears,	136	Ephes.	28
Me thoughts a starre did shoot into my lap.	139	Artillerie	2
Where shall I get me eyes enough to weep,	140	Ch.-rents	25
Did show and shape thy looks to me,	141	Justice 2	4
For where before thou still didst call on me,	141	Justice 2	19
Against me there is none, but for me much.	141	Justice 2	24
That led me to the wilde of passion, which	142	Pilgrimage	13
My power and wisdome. Put me not to shame,	143	Complaining	3
Thou hast heard me:	146	Praise 2	6
Thou hast spar'd me.	146	Praise 2	8
Though my sinnes against me cried,	146	Praise 2	13
Thou didst cleare me;	146	Praise 2	14
Thou didst heare me.	146	Praise 2	16
And make me giddie; Lord, I fall,	148	Longing	11
More dead to me!	149	Longing	34
To succour me,	149	Longing	40
Thus hard to me?	150	Longing	64
Then let me tell thee a strange storie.	151	The Bag	8
(Beleeve me), it shall safely come.	152	The Bag	34
Will use me in this kinde, the doore	152	The Bag	38
Any thing to me. Heark despair, away.	152	The Bag	42
To let me bloud, and not restore	153	The Collar	8
Is the yeare onely lost to me?	153	The Collar	13
Me thoughts I heard one calling, childe:	154	The Collar	35
And give me up to night?	154	Glimpse	3
Me thinks delight should have	154	Glimpse	6
Disturb the work. O make me not their sport,	155	Glimpse	29
Betwixt my God and me; that I allow	155	Assurance	9
Yet to be thine, doth me restore;	157	Clasping	4
And thou with me dost thee restore.	157	Clasping	8
Not thee, but me, and to be mine:	157	Clasping	15
Yet then as mine didst me restore.	157	Clasping	18
O be mine still! still make me thine!	157	Clasping	19
To linger in me, and together languish.	159	Jos.coat	12
He would adore my gifts in stead of me,	160	The Pulley	13
Who bring my God to me!	161	Priesthood	30
I throw me at his feet.	161	Priesthood	36
And centre both to me denie	162	The Search	7
Thy distance from me; see my charge,	163	The Search	47
Turn, and restore me:	163	The Search	50
Be not Almightie, let me say,	163	The Search	51
Against, but for me.	163	The Search	52
O who will give me tears? Come all ye springs,	164	Grief	1
My weary weeping eyes too drie for me,	164	Grief	6

ME (cont'd)

	PAGE	TITLE		LINE
To make me sigh, and seek, and faint, and die,	164	The Crosse		2
Thou turnest th' edge of all things on me still,	165	The Crosse		21
Taking me up to throw me down:	165	The Crosse		22
These contrarieties crush me: these crosse actions	165	The Crosse		32
Like leaves about me: or like summer friends,	169	The Answer		4
Who think me eager, hot, and undertaking,	169	The Answer		6
Show me, and set me, I have one reply,	169	The Answer		13
To look upon me, who before did lie	171	The Glance		3
And he that doth me feed:	172	23 Psalme		2
He leads me to the tender grasse,	172	23 Psalme		5
For thou art with me; and thy rod	173	23 Psalme		15
Nay, thou dost make me sit and dine,	173	23 Psalme		17
A noise of passions ringing me for dead	174	Aaron		8
My onely musick, striking me ev'n dead;	174	Aaron		18
But lives in me while I do rest)	174	Aaron		24
And tell me more:	175	The Odour		18
This breathing would with gains by sweetning me	175	The Odour		26
Should all my life employ, and busie me.	175	The Odour		30
Must dulnesse turn me to a clod?	176	Forerunners		5
Yet have they left me, Thou art still my God.	176	Forerunners		6
Good men ye be, to leave me my best room,	176	Forerunners		7
But will ye leave me thus? when ye before	176	Forerunners		14
Presse me not to take more pleasure	177	The Rose		1
There are no such things to me,	177	The Rose		11
Needs must work on me.	179	Discipline		28
With me, in me, live and dwell:	181	Banquet		3
Spilt with me,	182	Banquet		35
And so found me on the ground.	182	Banquet		36
Having rais'd me to look up,	182	Banquet		37
Who hath done so much for me.	182	Banquet		48
Because thou dost abide with me,	183	A Parodie		4
But leave me to my load:	183	A Parodie		10
Doth me invade!	183	A Parodie		12
Doth me infold!	184	A Parodie		27
Teach me, my God and King,	184	The Elixer		1
Give me simplicitie, that I may live,	185	A Wreath		9
O who will show me those delights on high?	188	Heaven		1
Then tell me, what is that supreme delight?	188	Heaven		13
Love bade me welcome: yet my soul drew back,	188	Love 3		1
But quick-ey'd Love, observing me grow slack	188	Love 3		3
Drew nearer to me, sweetly questioning,	188	Love 3		5
How deare to me, O God, thy counsels are!	191	Ch.-Milit.		47
How deare to me, O God, thy counsels are!	192	Ch.-Milit.		99
How deare to me, O God, thy counsels are!	194	Ch.-Milit.		155
How deare to me, O God, thy counsels are!	196	Ch.-Milit.		209
How deare to me, O God, thy counsels are!	198	Ch.-Milit.		278
Give me not that I had before,	201	H. Commun.	W	46
Thou art too hard for me in Love:	201	love	W	1
This Anchor keeps my faith, that, me secure.	439	walton 6		4
He said to me, Thou art my Son,	216	Psalm II	D	17
Against me, saying, For my soul	216	Psalm III	D	3
me from his holy hill:	216	Psalm III	D	10
I laid me down and slept, I wak'd;	216	Psalm III	D	11
for God sustain'd me still.	216	Psalm III	D	12
that can against me rise.	216	Psalm III	D	16
Arise, O Lord, and rescue me;	217	Psalm III	D	17
save me, my God, from thrall:	217	Psalm III	D	18
Lord hear me when I call on Thee,	217	Psalm IV	D	1
O thou that hast enlarged me	217	Psalm IV	D	3
Have mercy on me Lord, and hear	217	Psalm IV	D	5
The Lord will harken unto me	217	Psalm IV	D	13
shall more replenish me,	218	Psalm IV	D	26
shall me in safety keep.	218	Psalm IV	D	32
Lord lead me in thy righteousness,	219	Psalm V	D	21
Rebuke me not in wrath, O Lord,	219	Psalm VI	D	1
nor in thine anger chasten me:	219	Psalm VI	D	2
O pity me! for I (O Lord)	219	Psalm VI	D	3
O heal me, for my bones are vex'd,	220	Psalm VI	D	5
Return, O God! and rescue me,	220	Psalm VI	D	9
But now from me depart away,	220	Psalm VI	D	19
that er'st so sorely vexed me,	220	Psalm VI	D	26
Save me, my Lord, my God, because	220	Psalm VII	D	1
that was at peace with me:	221	Psalm VII	D	12
O God consider me	221	Psalm VII	D	30
that persecuteth me.	222	Psalm VII	D	48
errand I come, let me hold my peace, and doe thou speak thy selfe;	233	Priest 7		35
if a peece of dry flesh at my table be more unpleasant to me,	242	Priest 10		13
do any thing, that leads me to a sicknesse, to which I am inclined,	242	Priest 10		36
I am false to my reason which should guide me, I offend the supreme	265	Priest 26		10
in all these, and those more which concerne me, I either do nothing,	265	Priest 26		16
squeeze blood undecently to the station wherein God hath placed me,	265	Priest 26		18
if God have given me servants, and I either provide too little	265	Priest 26		20
you hurt your selfe, not me;	269	Priest 28		13
even to me, pardoning my sins, and bidding me go feed the people	289	Priest		5
pardoning my sins, and bidding me go feed the people of thy love.	289	Priest		6
teach thou me, that I may teach them:	289	Priest		26
because divers worthy young men have obliged me unto it.	291	Cornaro		8
of their dayes, and me contrariwise, at the age of eightie and one,	291	Cornaro		10
I will declare the causes which moved me to forsake Intemperance,	291	Cornaro		15
but had already gone farre in me, first caused me to leave	291	Cornaro		18

ME (cont'd)	PAGE	TITLE	LINE
first caused me to leave Intemperance, to which I was much addicted:	291	Cornaro	19
From this ill temper there remained little else to be expected of me,	291	Cornaro	25
the Physicians told me that yet there was one help for me,	292	Cornaro	3
the Physicians told me that yet there was one help for me,	292	Cornaro	4
to that exigent, that there would be no help for me, but Death,	292	Cornaro	15
This they had told me before:	292	Cornaro	26
If Temperance had so much power as to bring me health;	293	Cornaro	3
to search out most diligently what meats were agreeable unto me,	293	Cornaro	5
those that pleased my taste brought me commoditie or discommoditie;	293	Cornaro	7
was not onely freed from all those evils which had so long beset me,	293	Cornaro	21
I preserved me also, asmuch as I could, from hatred and melancholie,	293	Cornaro	35
which gained me this experience, that I perceived, that they had no	294	Cornaro	1
as all that know me, can testifie:	294	Cornaro	11
all these did hurt me little, whereas they hurt them very much who	294	Cornaro	14
of my kindred saw some great powerfull men pick quarrels against me,	294	Cornaro	17
no inconvenience thereby, because that humour abounded not in me.	294	Cornaro	22
which excesse of joy neither could do me any hurt.	294	Cornaro	30
But my experience taught me another thing also, to wit,	295	Cornaro	16
But all these things could not defend me against their importunities.	296	Cornaro	5
This addition after ten dayes wrought so much upon me, that	296	Cornaro	14
so that all things were troublesome to me:	296	Cornaro	16
a pain of the side took me, which held me two and twentie houres.	296	Cornaro	18
whereupon all gave me for dead.	296	Cornaro	23
that under God nothing holp me, but that exact rule which I had so	296	Cornaro	29
although it was a sore evil, yet had no power to kill me.	297	Cornaro	2
whereof the one kept me well for many yeares;	297	Cornaro	4
was but a little excesse, in a few dayes had so soon overthrown me.	297	Cornaro	6
or that cinnamon should heat me more then pepper?	297	Cornaro	33
What Physician could have discovered these hidden qualities to me,	297	Cornaro	35
I abstain from fruit, and fish, and the like, because they hurt me.	300	Cornaro	10
Let no man here object unto me, That there are many, who,	300	Cornaro	17
and which are such, as that men generally account me happie.	300	Cornaro	33
being so built by me according to the rules of Architecture,	301	Cornaro	12
The memorie whereof is exceeding delightfull to me.	301	Cornaro	33
neither omit I any thing that may either teach, or delight me.	302	Cornaro	5
so that any simple fare is more savourie to me now, then heretofore,	302	Cornaro	10
To change my bed, troubles me not;	302	Cornaro	12
But this chiefly delights me, that my advice hath taken effect in	302	Cornaro	14
the power and efficacie of that Temperance which ever accompanied me.	302	Cornaro	21
whence it seems to me, not onely a shamefull thing to fear that which	303	Cornaro	21
Yet I am sure, that my end is farre from me:	303	Cornaro	25
In life you lov'd me not, in death you bewaile me.	328	Proverbs	218
I had rather ride on an asse that carries me,	329	Proverbs	258
then a horse that throwes me.	329	Proverbs	258
Call me not an olive, till thou see me gathered.	331	Proverbs	301
tell me what I dreamed last night.	332	Proverbs	336
thou art to me the Escuriall.	335	Proverbs	413
Shew me a lyer, and I'le shew thee a theefe.	343	Proverbs	652
God keepe me from foure houses,	348	Proverbs	816
He that gives me small gifts would have me live.	354	Proverbs	1000
but my next neighbour doth me more harm	361	Proverbs	D 1173
yet it would easily tyre me, to find out variety of thanks	363	Letters	15
And therefore let it be sufficient for me, that the same heart,	363	Letters	17
and that the Horse is every way fit for me, and I will strive	364	Letters	2
I wrong both my self, and also the confidence my Friends have in me;	364	Letters	9
education, of obeying that Spirit which hath guided me hitherto,	364	Letters	18
not well, I had rather the fault should lie on me, than on them;	364	Letters	29
if there be any truth in me, I find it little enough to keep me in	364	Letters	31
be any truth in me, I find it little enough to keep me in health.	364	Letters	32
such which you have found useful to yourself, communicate them to me.	366	Letters	5
that he hath bought a parcel of Books for me, and that they are	366	Letters	30
This Week hath loaded me with your Favours;	369	Letters	10
long in Latin, and my Lincoln journey hath set me much behind hand:	369	Letters	14
you and my dear Mother and Sister to pardon me, for my Cambridge	369	Letters	18
for my Cambridge necessities are stronger to tye me here,	369	Letters	19
Nethersole for me; he and I are ancient acquaintance, and I have	369	Letters	21
opinion of him, that if he can do me a courtesie, he will of himself;	369	Letters	22
yet your appearing in it, affects me strangely.	369	Letters	24
will do well, for it expresseth the Universities inclination to me;	369	Letters	27
it is no matter, for the Gentleman needs no incitation to love me.	369	Letters	29
Sir send the Letter you receive from him to me as soon as you can,	370	Letters	6
since this place being civil may divert me too much from Divinity,	370	Letters	20
if it had to others, yet to me it should not, for ought I yet knew;	370	Letters	24
therefore I desire him to send me a direct answer in his next Letter.	370	Letters	25
of the Pedler and the Pack on London-bridge, for there he assigns me.	370	Letters	29
who cannot think me lazy, since I rode 200 mile to see a Sister,	371	Letters	2
I have received the things you sent me, safe;	371	Letters	6
Is it not too much for me?	371	Letters	11
judge me then by those waters, and not by my ink, and then you shall	372	Letters	3
quickly make good my wish but that my employment does fix me here,	372	Letters	19
Your last Letter gave me Earthly preferment, and kept Heavenly	372	Letters	34
because sickness hath made me unable to perform those Offices	373	Letters	9
That God who hath delivered me out of the paws of the Lyon and Bear,	374	Letters	6
will also deliver me out of the hands of this uncircumcised	374	Letters	7
Let me commend only one place more to you (Philip. 4. 4.) St. Paul	374	Letters	20
wrote to our eldest brother, when he urged one upon me, and but one,	375	Letters	11
which to me that have nothing yett, is very much.	376	Letters	2
I doe my part to them, lett them think of me what they will or can.	376	Letters	7
Truly it grieves me to think of the child, how destitute she is,	376	Letters	12
but you joyed me exceedingly with your relation of my Lady Duchess's	377	Letters	18

ME (cont'd)	PAGE	TITLE	LINE
If there fall out yet any rubb, you shall heare of me;	377	Letters	22
gratious Lord God, is pleased to give me you for the Man, I desired,	378	Letters	8
from giving you cause, to apolcgy, about your counselling me herein:	378	Letters	10
as God gives me higher thoughts, & to rise with his favours,	381	Woodnoth	25
possession that properly belonge to me unto my deare wife excepting	382	G.H.'s Will	6
Merchant of London which fell to me by the death of my deare Neece	382	G.H.'s Will	9
there be any body els that owe me any thing else of old debt I	383	G.H.'s Will	26
MEADOW (see alsc meddow)			
MEAL			
And peace-meal rent it, while there's none	221	Psalm VII D	7
hee receives, to want a good meal suting to the joy of the occasion.	245	Priest 12	8
the Kingdome into Portions, which every yeer he surveys peece-meal.	277	Priest 32	8
MEALE			
The dog that licks ashes, trust not with meale.	334	Proverbs	389
Divine ashes are better then earthly meale.	344	Proverbs	684
MEALE'S			
Hee will spend a whole yeares rent at one meales meate.	331	Proverbs	305
MEALES			
Two ill meales make the third a glutton.	340	Proverbs	575
MEAN (medium)			
The mean, thy praise and glorie is,	110	Brit. Ch.	26
In the mean time, I beseech you to be chearful, and comfort your self	372	Letters	23
In the mean time a Priests blessing, though it be none	377	Letters	1
MEAN (verb)			
What mirth and musick mean; what love and wit	89	The Pearl	24
My prayers mean thee, yet my prayers stray:	96	Justice 1	9
My God, I mean my self.	102	Miserie	78
Lord, I will mean and speak thy praise,	157	Praise 3	1
What others mean to do, I know not well;	187	Judgement	6
MEAN			
Not of rich arras, but mean tapestrie.	17	Ch.-Porch	270
Scorn no mans love, though of a mean degree;	20	Ch.-Porch	349
Neither too mean, nor yet too gay,	109	Brit. Ch.	8
For some mean stuffe whereon to show his skill:	161	Priesthood	38
Nothing can be so mean,	184	The Elixer	14
how poor or mean soever, with as joyfull a countenance,	253	Priest 19	19
the casting of it on mean persons, especially in some Shires:	276	Priest 32	21
There would bee no great ones if there were no mean ones.	331	Proverbs V	292
MEANE (medium)			
Meane while, if hee (which all thinges weares)	208	H. Danvers D	5
hee in the meane while applying himselfe to the [unquestioned] duties	312	Valdesso	19
MEANE (verb)			
Speake not of my debts, unlesse you meane to pay them.	354	Proverbs	998
MEANE			
Against this meane & humble Blackamore.	209	L. Bacon D	10
MEANER			
and meaner relieved, he chooseth rather to give the poor money,	243	Priest 11	14
MEANES			
neverthelesse I wish you by all meanes to publish it, for these three	304	Valdesso	18
He meanes a mans fre-will is only in outward, not in spirituall	313	Valdesso	33
but he told her Grace, that he would by no meanes do so, urging,	379	Letters	7
MEANEST			
The meanest tool, that he may chance to use.	20	Ch.-Porch	354
Doctrine slip the more easily into the hearts even of the meanest.	261	Priest 23	20
I refuse not advice from the meanest, that creeps upon Gods earth,	378	Letters	12
MEANETH			
whereby I understand he meaneth only the effectuall operation	308	Valdesso	30
He meaneth (I suppose) that a man presume not to merit,	312	Valdesso	14
holy Scripture, he meaneth that we should not use it as the onely,	314	Valdesso V	4
By occasions (I suppose) hee meaneth the ordinary, or necessary	314	Valdesso	16
he meaneth not the very Ceremonies of the Jewes, which no Christian	319	Valdesso	34
MEANING			
My heart was meaning all the day,	168	a true Hymn	2
Had the malicious and ill-meaning harm	172	The Glance	11
a plain and evident declaration of the meaning of the text;	235	Priest 7	2
Your meaning is not thus, but thus;	252	Priest 18	11
but the meaning is this, That God in the dayes of the Gospell will	310	Valdesso	4
The Authors good meaning in this, will better appear by his 98	312	Valdesso V	4
for unbelief, or evil works, make plain the Authors meaning.	319	Valdesso V	18
Love without end, hath no end, says the Spaniard: (meaning,	361	Proverbs D	1160
my meaning (dear Mother) is in these Sonnets, to declare my	363	Letters	10
of which is doubted whether it have some further meaning.	368	Letters	19
and, accept the good meaning of, Your most obedient Son,	374	Letters	31
Yet truly it was none of my meaning, when I wrote, to putt one of our	375	Letters	4
MEANINGS			
Hell is full of good meanings and wishings.	326	Proverbs	170
MEANLY			
same Psalme it is evident, that he was not meanly conversant in them.	309	Valdesso	28
MEANS (verb)			
Shoots higher much then he that means a tree.	19	Ch.-Porch	334
Which knoweth not, what means, to Morrow.	65	Ch.-mus. W	8
But he that means to dwell therein.	90	Man	3
Nothing we see, but means our good,	91	Man	27
Scorns his first bed of dirt, and means the sky;	169	The Answer	9
the Parson be unmarryed, and means to continue so, he doth at least,	238	Priest 9	25
Hee that sendes a foole, means to follow him.	322	Proverbs	51
MEANS			
By all means use sometimes to be alone.	12	Ch.-Porch	145
By no means runne in debt: take thine own measure.	13	Ch.-Porch	175
In Almes regard thy means, and others merit.	21	Ch.-Porch	373

MEE (cont'd)	PAGE	TITLE		LINE
Hell, Death & Divel come short of mee.	202	love	W	24
The Day is spent, & hath his will on mee:	203	Even-song	W	1
Lord make my Losses up, & sett mee free:	203	Even-song	W	5
If thou deferr this light, then shadow mee:	203	Even-song	W	9
Or rather as thou movedst mee.	204	Persever.	W	4
My Lord. A diamond to mee you sent,	209	L. Bacon	D	1
So by the Other, you may read in mee	209	L. Bacon	D	5
Mee thinkes, in that Dutch optick I doe see	211	Bohemia	D	13
O Lord deliver mee!	220	Psalm VII	D	4
and live, and who giveth mee my Desires and Performances;	224	Priest		2
is particular, and against mee, I am to follow our Saviours rule,	248	Priest 14		26
because I would doe nothing negligently that you commit unto mee;	304	Valdesso		5
Faire words make mee looke to my purse.	339	Proverbs		548
and write you freely to mee in your letters, for I am your ever	366	Letters		21
of whose rude delivery my hast makes mee ashamed, only my comfort is	369	Letters		2
for you to amplify your favour to mee in pardoning Your most indebted	369	Letters		4
move my Lords of Manchester and Boollingbrook is very welcome to mee.	377	Letters		24
MEEK				
'Gainst him, who seeks not life, but is the meek	28	Sacrifice		58
Yet, though thou troublest me, I must be meek;	48	Afflict.1		61
Yet a meek look	149	Longing		51
Then is my time. The distance of the meek	161	Priesthood		39
but, Blessed be the Meek, and Blessed be the Poor, and,	373	Letters		31
MEEKNESSE				
any speciall grace of faith, patience, meeknesse, love, obedience,	238	Priest 9		32
because of the word of truth, and meeknesse, and righteousnesse;	289	Priest		23
MEET				
And meet them there. All worldly joyes go lesse	19	Ch.-Porch		329
And meet them there. All wordly joyes go lesse	19	Ch.-Porch	W	329
Which then join'd with you still meet in my brest	44	H. Bapt.1	W	8
Wilt thou meet arms with man, that thou dost stretch	55	Temper 1		13
And meet my ryme.	80	Deniall	W	30
Is much more sure to meet with him, then one	87	Lent		38
To meet together, where I lay,	110	The Quip		3
And meet the rest on Sions hill.	138	The Size		24
When wit contrives to meet with thee,	155	Assurance		5
Of lowly matter for high uses meet,	161	Priesthood		35
As if to meet thee they did know,	162	The Search		11
And parallels meet.	163	The Search		44
Shall call and meet,	175	The Odour		23
(As sweet things traffick when they meet)	175	The Odour		27
Sweetly he doth meet my taste.	182	Banquet		39
Which doth not meet with an eternall thought.	190	Ch.-Milit.		8
Which does not meet with an eternall thought.	190	Ch.-Milit.	W	8
Judgement may meet them both & search them round.	197	Ch.-Milit.		269
And meet theire tast, who are thy bitter foes.	213	Bohemia	D	66
when they meet with good fruit, get a graffe of the tree,	276	Priest 32		32
wherewith also a carefull Joseph might meet.	281	Priest 34		27
are so ordered, that they all meet and end in a fair plot of ground;	301	Cornaro		21
and we meet with two sorts of these Saints of the world;	319	Valdesso	V	21
The love of money and the love of learning rarely meet.	361	Proverbs	D	1168
as when you meet with a witty French speech, try to speak the like in	366	Letters		10
MEETE				
Good & quickly seldome meete.	341	Proverbs		580
MEETES				
is a Physitian so far as he meetes with the same disease,	278	Priest 33		27
MEETING				
Meeting sinnes force and art.	52	H.Commun.		12
And spoil the meeting. What shall point out them,	65	Ch.-monum.		14
Meeting with Time, Slack thing, said I,	122	Time		1
MEETINGS				
is at all their Assemblies and Meetings, and sits above the Proctors,	370	Letters		2
MEETS				
Meets in this frame,	26	The Altar		11
And now thy Architecture meets with sinne;	106	Sion		11
Tells to all he meets, his crosse:	114	Businesse		32
and accordingly either meets with their vices, or advanceth their	239	Priest 10		9
Therefore those he meets on the way he blesseth audibly,	251	Priest 17		2
whom he hath ever some cases to ask, when he meets with them;	260	Priest 23		5
but when he meets with a refined, and heavenly disposition,	267	Priest 26		18
he meets continually with two most sad spectacles, Sin,	267	Priest 27		31
MELANCHOLICK				
The Chollerick drinkes, the Melancholick eates,	351	Proverbs		924
MELANCHOLIE				
from hatred and melancholie, and other perturbations of the minde,	293	Cornaro		35
were possessed with a deep Melancholie (a thing usuall to disorderly	294	Cornaro		18
That neither melanchclie, nor any other passion can hurt a temperate	294	Cornaro		31
of a cheerfull and merrie man I became melancholie and cholerick;	296	Cornaro		15
MELILOT				
yerrow, melilot, and Saint Johns wort made into a salve;	262	Priest 23		6
MELLOWING				
Embosomes in us, mellowing the ground	85	Vanitie 1		24
MELONS				
cool wines pleased my taste best, as also melons, and other fruit;	293	Cornaro		12
MELT				
If stonie hearts will melt with gentle love.	29	Sacrifice		90
Melt and dissolve my rage.	47	Afflict.1		46
Melt & consume	49	Repentance	W	28
Melt into blessings all the sky,	59	Whitsunday	W	23
Till all do melt, and drown his breath	98	Mortific.		27

MELT (cont'd)	PAGE	TITLE		LINE
Your sinnes expresse; melt into dew.	135	Ephes.		12
My comforts drop and melt away like snow:	169	The Answer		1
As we sugar melt in wine?	181	Banquet		12
MELTED				
Till all were melted, though he were all steel:	33	Sacrifice		211
Melted there,	181	Banquet		11
MELTING				
some being of a more melting temper then others) consisteth in a true	279	Priest 33		22
MELTS				
Therefore my soul melts, and my hearts deare treasure	27	Sacrifice		21
Who never melts or thaws	72	Constancie		21
Grief melts away	165	The Flower		5
MEMBER				
While this member jogs the other,	186	Dooms-day		5
yet my heart, a much better member, is alwayes with you:	371	Letters		27
MEMBERS				
And in thy members suffer ill.	73	Afflict.3		16
Him in his members, who for him was slain.	192	Ch.-Milit.		70
MEMORIALL				
Then in memoriall of his ancient throne	195	Ch.-Milit.		181
MEMORIE				
What I have treasur'd in my memorie!	38	The Sinner		2
Another in my soul (the memorie	165	The Crosse		14
The memorie whereof is exceeding delightfull to me.	301	Cornaro		32
MEMORY				
A man of a great memory without learning	358	Proverbs	D	1085
that they prevent my memory, and yet still grow upon Your humblest	367	Letters		15
MEN				
When base men are exalted, do not bate	17	Ch.-Porch	W	265
And give men turns of speech: do not forestall	18	Ch.-Porch		303
That brought the wise men of the East from farre.	28	Sacrifice		51
Whom devils flie, thus is he toss'd of men:	32	Sacrifice		191
If thou dost give me honour, men shall see,	35	Thanksgvng		21
Compassionate short-breathed men.	49	Repentance		14
Who dead men raises.	49	Repentance		35
Feasting all comers by twelve chosen men.	59	Whitsunday		8
With livery-graces furnishing thy men.	59	Whitsunday	W	8
But though men fail him, yet his part doth play.	73	Constancie		30
On men dropp blessings as I fly.	79	Employm.2	W	25
The best of men, turn but thy hand	100	Miserie		19
The common all men have; that which is rare,	119	Providence		98
Men therefore seek to have, and care to keep.	119	Providence		99
He is some twentie sev'rall men at least	127	Giddinesse		3
As men, for fear the starres should sleep and nod,	134	Divinitie		1
But th' holy men of God such vessels are,	161	Priesthood		25
But oh the folly of distracted men,	167	Dotage		13
I like our language, as our men and coast:	167	The Sonne		3
Good men ye be, to leave me my best room,	176	Forerunners		7
Thou Echo, thou art mortall, all men know.	188	Heaven		3
of good men shall the wicked come.	215	Psalm I	D	20
the way that right'ous men have gone:	215	Psalm I	D	22
How long will ye, vain men, convert	217	Psalm IV	D	7
thou slay'st the men that lye:	218	Psalm V	D	14
For God doth righteous men esteem,	219	Psalm V	D	41
but just men ever guide:	221	Psalm VII	D	34
Countrey people (as indeed all honest men) do much esteem their word,	228	Priest 3		2
John 7. and assuring himself, that wicked men, however learned,	228	Priest 4		30
and obligation of his calling, being to obey God rather then men.	232	Priest 6		19
it being naturall to men to think, that where is much earnestness,	232	Priest 7		32
for them also men heed, and remember better then exhortaticns;	233	Priest 7		13
and that among suspicious men, and other like circumstances	237	Priest 9		3
his meat dress'd and other services done by men-servants at home,	237	Priest 9		9
is a common temptation to men of any eminency, especially being	238	Priest 9		17
temptation to men of any eminency, especially being single men.	238	Priest 9		17
His children he first makes Christians, and then Commonwealths-men;	239	Priest 10		21
such as are tavernes for men, and lace-making for women;	240	Priest 10		2
pity hath set forth heaven for a reward to draw men to Piety,	243	Priest 11		32
men being willing to sell the interest, and ingagement of their	252	Priest 18		19
by questions well ordered he found Philosophy in silly Trades-men.	256	Priest 21		23
in this, that at Sermons, and Prayers, men may sleep or wander;	257	Priest 21		18
for if wise men have thought it the best way of preserving a state	258	Priest 22		15
as also by discourse with men of that profession, whom he hath ever	260	Priest 23		3
that to put men to discourse of that, wherin they are most eminent,	260	Priest 23		5
because men usually think, that servants for their mony are as other	265	Priest 26		24
so that men must eat neither to the disturbance of their health,	266	Priest 26		13
not onely because all men shun the company of perpetuall severity,	268	Priest 27		2
is observeable, that God delights to have men feel, and acknowledg,	271	Priest 30		19
that men should perpetuate, and not break off their acts	271	Priest 30		26
either blessing God, that he will be pleased to dwell among men;	273	Priest 31		25
For when men have nothing to do, then they fall to drink,	274	Priest 32		10
Men are either single, or marryed:	275	Priest 32		19
Could men finde out this delight, they would seldome be from home;	275	Priest 32		34
Now, for single men, they are either Heirs, or younger Brothers:	276	Priest 32		25
Besides the continuall succession (since the Gospell) of holy men,	282	Priest 34		19
if all men are to blesse upon occasion, as appears Rom. 12. 14. how	286	Priest 36		26
and that even some good men think, so they speak truth,	286	Priest 37		31
Of these also men may talk, and more, they may discover them to those	287	Priest 37		16
therefore we sons of men are not consumed.	288	Priest		22
not to Thunder, or Angels, but to silly and sinfull men:	289	Priest		5
because divers worthy young men have obliged me unto it.	291	Cornaro		8

MEN (cont'd)	PAGE	TITLE		LINE
For Temperance preserves even old men and sickly men sound: . .	292	Cornaro		8
of my kindred saw some great powerfull men pick quarrels against me,	294	Cornaro		16
of old age in the humours of my bodie, which commonly kills men.	296	Cornaro		37
But sensuall men (as most are) desiring to satisfie their Appetite,	298	Cornaro		23
which is both easie for common-weals-men, and very convenient,	299	Cornaro		17
and which are such, as that men generally account me happie.	300	Cornaro		33
I conferre often with worthie men, excelling in wit, learning,	301	Cornaro		4
the place was moorish and unhealthy, fitter for beasts then men.	301	Cornaro		27
Whereupon men flcckt thither, and built houses with happy successe.	301	Cornaro		29
That I have both given God a Temple, and men to worship him in it:	301	Cornaro		32
For death to all young men is a terrible thing, as also to those that	303	Cornaro		18
the Scriptures, or to themselves being still men, though godly men.	316	Valdesso		4
the Scriptures, cr to themselves being still men, though godly men.	316	Valdesso		5
[according to the common and legal proceedings among men.] . .	316	Valdesso		28
Worldly learned men cannot judg spirituall mens actions, . .	317	Valdesso		5
Keepe good men company, and you shall be of the number. . .	325	Proverbs		120
Men speake of the faire, as things went with them there. . .	326	Proverbs		151
men for one pleasure a thousand griefes prove.	328	Proverbs		228
There are more men threatned then stricken.	329	Proverbs		256
Better spare to have of thine own, then aske of other men. . .	330	Proverbs		266
Keep not ill men company, lest you increase the number. . .	331	Proverbs		314
In sports and journeys men are knowne.	334	Proverbs		399
Fooles bite one another, but wise-men agree together. . . .	336	Proverbs		452
In the kingdome of blind men the one ey'd is king. . . .	337	Proverbs		469
If wise men erred not, it would goe hard with fooles. . . .	338	Proverbs	V	510
which a hundred wise men cannot pull out.	339	Proverbs		527
Old men, when they scorne young, make much of death. . . .	341	Proverbs		597
Gaming, women, and wine, while they laugh they make men pine.	341	Proverbs		604
If great men would have care of little ones, ...	344	Proverbs		697
Words are women, deedes are men.	349	Proverbs		843
So many men in Court and so many strangers.	350	Proverbs		874
Amongst good men two men suffice.	350	Proverbs		885
When all men have what belongs to them, it cannot bee much. . .	353	Proverbs		979
He that dies without the company of good men	354	Proverbs		995
Old men go to Death, Death comes to Young men.	356	Proverbs	D	1
Threatned men eat bread, says the Spaniard.	358	Proverbs	D	1081
(applyed to rich men that are unthankful to God).	359	Proverbs	D	1100
There is a remedy for every thing, could men find it. . . .	360	Proverbs	D	1142
Some men plant an opinion they seem to erradicate. . . .	361	Proverbs	D	1164
The Philosophy of Princes is to dive into the Secrets of men,	361	Proverbs	D	1165
but you married men laugh till your hearts ake.	361	Proverbs	D	1175
Let your moderation appear to all men, the Lord is at hand: . .	374	Letters		28
the success of things is) & not into the hands of men or mens trades:	380	Woodnoth		25
since there is a two-fold brightnesse which dazeleth the eyes of men,	442	Oration		34
MEN-SERVANTS				
his meat dress'd and other services done by men-servants at home,	237	Priest 9		9
MEN'S				
To compasse this. Finde out mens wants and will, ...	19	Ch.-Porch		328
If all mens tears were let	62	Afflict.2		6
Neither ought other mens abuse of Lent	86	Lent		28
As mens returns, what would become of fools?	147	Offering		2
Gave her the highest place in all mens hearts.	191	Ch.-Milit.		50
And tune mens hearts against the Gospel came:	192	Ch.-Milit.		76
And cleanse mens hearts against the Gospel came:	192	Ch.-Milit.	W	76
And blending these he carri'd all mens eyes, ...	195	Ch.-Milit.		189
Usher'd the Gospel ever in mens hearts, ...	197	Ch.-Milit.		264
easie for the Parsons purse, and more familiar for all mens bodyes.	261	Priest 23		32
God turning mens Covetousnesse, and Ambitions to the effecting of his	282	Priest 34		34
For if he absolutely shut up mens mouths, and forbid all disclosing	286	Priest 37		34
which before their offence and Judgment they had in all mens brests:	287	Priest 37		34
doubtlesse then also mens affections and words must turne, . .	288	Priest 37		4
as usually happens in old mens bodies, which live without rule.	296	Cornaro		35
that the world pierceth not godly mens actions no more then Gods,	315	Valdesso		30
whence come so many Books of severall mens opinions:	317	Valdesso		4
Worldly learned men cannot judg spirituall mens actions, . .	317	Valdesso		6
Health and sicknesse surely are mens double enemies. . . .	354	Proverbs		1011
the success of things is) & not into the hands of men or mens trades:	380	Woodnoth		25
MENACES				
Quickly reformed all with menaces.	84	Sighs & Gr.	W	10
Reformed all at length with menaces.	84	The World		10
MEND				
I'le build a spittle, or mend common wayes, ...	36	Thanksgvng		33
But mend mine own without delayes.	36	Thanksgvng		34
But mend my own without delayes.	36	Thanksgvng	W	34
And mend as rising starres & rivers doe.	44	H. Bapt.1	W	9
And praise him who did make and mend our eies.	54	Love 2		14
If they might mend their wages, and serve here.	59	Whitsunday		12
Mend my estate in any wayes, ...	61	Praise 1		3
And mend it still;	66	Ch.-lock		6
To writhe his limbes, and share, not mend the ill. . . .	73	Constancie		33
To writhe his limbes, and thare, not mend the ill. . . .	73	Constancie	V	33
And mend my ryme.	80	Deniall		30
Lord, mend or rather make us: one creation	127	Giddinesse		25
All did but strive to mend, what you had marr'd.	130	Love unkn.		67
A speaking sweet, mend by reflection, ...	175	The Odour		17
Save your cost, and mend your fare.	179	Invitation		3
and who is ready to ask, if he shall mend shoos, or what he shall do?	275	Priest 32		8
Mend your cloathes, and you may hold out this yeare. . . .	324	Proverbs		100
MENDED				
Thy cheere is mended; bate not of the food, ...	22	Ch.-Porch		393

	PAGE	TITLE		LINE
MENDING				
Mending it still;	66	Ch.-lock	W	6
MENDS				
That mends the lookers eyes: this is the well	58	H.Script.1		9
Such a Feast, as mends in length:	156	The Call		7
Hee that stumbles and falles not, mends his pace.	321	Proverbs		7
MENTION				
When first my lines of heav'nly joyes made mention, ...	102	Jordan 2		1
When first my verse of heav'nly joyes made mention, ...	102	Jordan 2	W	1
Mention not a halter in the house of him that was hanged. . .	343	Proverbs		671
other Tortures, as the very mention of them might beget amazement;	373	Letters		37
MENTIONED				
are to prepare in all the fore-mentioned points against the time	276	Priest 32		26
MERCENARY				
Vertue flies from the heart of a Mercenary man.	360	Proverbs	D	1133
school-mistresse, and you know what those mercenary creatures are.	375	Letters		26
MERCHANT (see also marchant)				
As when a Merchant hath a ship come home after many a storme,	271	Priest 30		22
in Mr Thomas Lawleys hands a Merchant of London which fell to me	382	G.H.'s Will		8
MERCHANTS				
which they are thought to have offerd to our Merchants at the Indies,	368	Letters		7
MERCIE				
O let thy height of mercie then	49	Repentance		13
MERCIES				
Whom oil and mercies kill, what salve can cure?	24	Ch.-Porch	W	447
Thy mercies thither flock and flow:	82	Ungratef.		20
Who hath dealt his mercies so, ...	92	Antiphon 2		4
Of all thy mercies, is my posie still.	182	The Posie		4
Of all Gods mercies, is my posie still.	183	The Posie		12
made a Land of light, a store-house of thy treasures and mercies:	289	Priest		19
MERCURY				
And surely hyssope, valerian, mercury, adders tongue, yerrow,	262	Priest 23		5
MERCY				
Have mercy on me Lord, and hear	217	Psalm IV	D	5
my Soul for thy great mercy save;	220	Psalm VI	D	10
Being desirous (thorow the Mercy of GOD) to please Him, . .	224	Priest		1
and terrible, as great in mercy, so great in judgement: . .	234	Priest 7		32
till either they despise that Love, or despaire of his Mercy:	283	Priest 34		23
Mercy in releeving the poor by a liberall distribution and largesse,	284	Priest 35		7
Thou hast exalted thy mercy above all things;	288	Priest		23
and the Father of all mercy!	290	Priest		1
God gives his wrath by weight, and without weight his mercy.	359	Proverbs	D	1115
MERES				
Nor can they change their bounds & meres, ...	201	H. Commun.	W	41
MERIDIAN				
On whose meridian was engraven, ...	138	The Size		46
Unto the farthest old meridian.	192	Ch.-Milit.		98
MERIT				
In Almes regard thy means, and others merit.	21	Ch.-Porch		373
But as I can see no merit, ...	115	Dialogue		17
That they in merit shall excell.	187	Judgement		10
and setting his merit forth so piously, for which I doe so love him,	305	Valdesso		6
He meaneth (I suppose) that a man presume not to merit, . .	312	Valdesso		14
MERRIE				
The merrie world did on a day	110	The Quip		1
that of a cheerfull and merrie man I became melancholie . .	296	Cornaro		15
I am ever cheerfull, merrie, and well-contented, free from all	300	Cornaro		37
One faire day in winter makes not birds merrie.	353	Proverbs		977
MERRILY				
Some may dream merrily, but when they wake, ...	108	Home		51
MERRIMENT				
have made a most pleasant comedie, full of honest wit and merriment:	302	Cornaro		29
MERRY				
nor when they are among them that are merry, to extend themselves	280	Priest 34		26
All are not merry that dance lightly.	348	Proverbs		808
MESSAGE				
that in their full strength they may deliver thy message reverently,	289	Priest		28
could possibly have come, none should have done my message to Sir Fr:	369	Letters		20
MESSENGER				
Stay till the lame messenger come, ...	332	Proverbs		331
yet have I sent it thither by a faithful Messenger this day:	369	Letters		16
MESSENGERS				
To rules of reason, holy messengers, ...	45	Sinne 1		4
MET				
All worldly thoughts are but theeves met together	23	Ch.-Porch		424
At length I met a rev'rend good old man, ...	125	Peace		19
In Christ two natures met to be thy cure.	147	Offering		6
And met in th' east their first and ancient sound, ...	197	Ch.-Milit.		268
METALS				
Thou hast hid metals: man may take them thence;	119	Providence		81
METAPHORS				
Curling with metaphors a plain intention, ...	102	Jordan 2		5
And with quaint metaphors her curled hair	115	Dulnesse		7
Farewell sweet phrases, lovely metaphors.	176	Forerunners		13
METHEGLIN				
now they creep in a Vessel of Metheglin, and still they will be	376	Letters		28
METHOD				
The Method.	133	The Method		T
For it being indifferent in it selfe to choose any Method, . .	230	Priest 5		10
The Parsons Method in handling of a text consists of two parts;	234	Priest 7		36
especially let his Method of Phisick be diligently perused, . .	261	Priest 23		7

	PAGE	TITLE		LINE
METHUSALEM'S				
Die over each houre of Methusalems stay.	62	Afflict.2		5
MICHAELMAS				
presently after Michaelmas, I am to make an Oration to the whole	369	Letters		12
MICHEL				
To Mrs Michel twenty shillings, To Mrs Elizabeth Danvers Mr Henry	383	G.H.'s Will		11
MIDDLE				
And in the middle plac'd my heart. But he	129	Love unkn.		7
but as desiring to keep the middle way between superstition,	246	Priest 13		24
MIDNIGHT				
and Christian fortitude in the cold midnight stormes of persecution	237	Priest 9		38
or at three, or at midnight, or as they think fit, & see cause,	272	Priest 31		27
One houres sleepe before midnight is worth three after.	350	Proverbs		882
MIDPRAYERS				
their poor neighbours, but at midprayers, both to their own loss,	232	Priest 6		10
MIDST				
Which want provision in the midst of all.	164	Grief		12
Is in the midst of delicates to need,	165	The Crosse		29
Vouchsaf'd ev'n in the midst of youth and night	171	The Glance		2
or spitting even in the midst of their answer, but gently	231	Priest 6		32
most naturally as they are, wallowing in the midst of their affairs:	247	Priest 14		7
up their minds to better things, even in the midst of their pains.	261	Priest 23		25
their parents and kindred snatcht away in the midst of their dayes,	291	Cornaro		10
in the midst whereof is a Church suitable to the condition	301	Cornaro		22
discover some care, which I forbare not in the midst of my griefes;	304	Valdesso		4
that God in the midst of Popery should open the eyes of one	304	Valdesso		20
Feares are divided in the midst.	342	Proverbs		639
I knew not, in the midst of much business, and all in a Fortnight,	371	Letters		3
MIGHT (noun)				
And onely am the Lord of hosts and might:	29	Sacrifice		79
And feed the swine, with all his mind & might:	101	Miserie	W	44
Of my deare God with all my power & might.	143	Holdfast		2
In praising might, the poore do by submission	161	Priesthood		41
Shall they be food & strength & might	201	H. Commun.	W	35
Why doth that fire, which by thy power and might	206	Walton 1		12
MIGHT				
O what were man, might he himself misplace!	7	Ch.-Porch		23
Which he might fall in by companions, gains.	24	Ch.-Porch		436
To me, who took eyes that I might you finde:	26	Sacrifice		3
That as sinne came, so Sacraments might flow:	34	Sacrifice		247
Your first acquaintance might discredit all.	44	H. Bapt.1		14
Besides what I might have	46	Afflict.1		4
A fervent sigh might well have blown	53	H.Commun.		31
He might to heav'n from Paradise go,	53	H.Commun.		35
My soul might ever feel!	55	Temper 1		4
If they might mend their wages, and serve here.	59	Whitsunday		12
Man might not of his fodder misse.	76	Sunday		39
That he might save his life, and also hers,	85	Vanitie 1		12
To make us thine: yet that we might not part,	97	Afflict.5		10
One might have sought and found thee presently	99	Decay		6
But while I bustled, I might heare a friend	103	Jordan 2		15
Of what we might not take, or be withstood.	104	Obedience		30
Christ left his grave-clothes, that we might, when grief	112	Dawning		15
Christ left his grave-cloths, that we might, when grief	112	Dawning	V	15
And ev'n all Africk; would at least I might	140	Ch.-rents		28
Yet I might trust in God to be my light.	143	Holdfast		4
Oh that some Angel might a trumpet sound;	152	The Jews		8
That your sweet sap might come again!	152	The Jews		12
O that I might some other hearts convert,	159	Praise 3		39
That to thy chests there might be coming in	159	Praise 3		41
That to thy chest there might be coming in	159	Praise 3	V	41
My slender compositions might consume.	160	Priesthood		10
Untill I had some place, where I might sing,	164	The Crosse		3
But all my wealth, and familie might combine	164	The Crosse		5
That I might finde	175	The Odour		8
That these two words might creep & grow	175	The Odour		14
Which might the more indeare it to be thine.	190	Ch.-Milit.		12
The course was westward, that the sunne might light	190	Ch.-Milit.		17
Who, that they might subdue, made all their foes.	191	Ch.-Milit.		62
So they might still, and point us out the place	192	Ch.-Milit.		85
Yet that he might the better gain all nations,	195	Ch.-Milit.		183
This was not so well said, as it might have been forborn;	252	Priest 18		9
that by familiar things hee might make his Doctrine slip the more	261	Priest 23		18
(whom he chiefly considered) might have every where monuments of his	261	Priest 23		21
Thirdly, that he might set a Copy for Parsons.	261	Priest 23		26
all those, who else might both trouble him and the whole State.	276	Priest 32		15
wherewith also a carefull Joseph might meet.	281	Priest 34		27
To these might be added the Preaching of the Gospel in all Nations,	282	Priest 34		31
had delivered them to Satan, that they might learn not to Blaspheme.	286	Priest 36		2
Intemperance was not such an evil, but it might easily be remedied;	291	Cornaro		6
fitted my stomack, and in such measure, as easily might be digested:	293	Cornaro		17
with a full stomack, but so as I might well both eat and drink more.	293	Cornaro		19
that I might know what great power a sober and temperate life hath	294	Cornaro		24
Neverthelesse at a venture two remedies might be used, letting	295	Cornaro		4
and fever (which was certainly expected) might be hindred.	295	Cornaro		6
that the patient might be proportionable to the agent, and especially	295	Cornaro		31
Many things more might be said in commendation hereof:	303	Cornaro		33
Print it, that with it the honour of my Lord might be published.	305	Valdesso		8
to open his eyes that he might see the wondrous things of his Lawes,	309	Valdesso		26
Much more might be said, but this sufficeth, he himselfe allowes it	311	Valdesso		1
but he might have been justly put to death for it by the Magistrate,	316	Valdesso		24

MIGHT (cont'd)	PAGE	TITLE		LINE
If you could runne, as you drinke, you might catch a hare.	334	Proverbs		373
If all things might be done twice, all would be wise.	343	Proverbs	V	700
There is an hour wherein a man might be happy	360	Proverbs	D	1143
and I shou'd account my self most happy if I might change with you;	373	Letters		3
other Tortures, as the very mention of them might beget amazement;	373	Letters		37
He doubles it to take away the scruple of those that might say,	374	Letters		23
wee might the more by love grow on, both the Spanish and Brittish	442	Oration		17
MIGHTIE				
(Love is a present for a mightie king)	20	Ch.-Porch		350
It cannot be. Where is that mightie joy,	56	Temper 2		1
The mightie God, but I a sillie worm;	83	Sighs & Gr.		5
Oh mightie love! Man is one world, and hath	92	Man		47
Such power hath mightie Baptisme to produce	191	Ch.-Milit.		45
Which soon was blown to such a mightie flame,	194	Ch.-Milit.		145
And in old Rome a mightie Emperour;	195	Ch.-Milit.		172
MIGHTST				
Thou mightst make way for liberalitie!	103	Prayer 2		18
MIGHTY				
Thwart not the mighty God: O be not crosse.	22	Ch.-Porch	W	395
There is no dealing with thy mighty passion:	36	Reprisall		2
There is no medling with thy mighty passion:	36	Reprisall	W	2
and then who can deny the stretched out arme of a mighty God?	282	Priest 34		6
they break forth like mighty waters on every side.	290	Priest		7
Take heed of the wrath of a mighty man,	360	Proverbs	D	1148
MILD				
and perhaps a little more mild, but you will hardly perceive it.	366	Letters		25
to conquer your enemies, and assume more mild and gracious aspects;	442	Oration		4
MILDE				
Small to my self, to others milde,	44	H. Bapt.2		9
Their follies with the wing of thy milde Dove,	100	Miserie		28
Their follies with the wings of thy milde Dove,	100	Miserie	W	28
MILE				
Every mile is two in winter.	352	Proverbs		949
since I rode 200 mile to see a Sister, in a way I knew not,	371	Letters		2
MILES				
Good horses make short miles.	352	Proverbs		935
MILITANT				
The Church Militant.	190	Ch.-Milit.		T
MILITARIE				
yea, indeed of all, both Courtly, Militarie, Academicall.	441	Oration		28
MILITARY				
Great Horse, or exercise some of his Military gestures [Postures].	277	Priest 32		16
Neither is this true onely in the military state of a Christian life,	279	Priest 33		3
a Christian even in this Life, the one military, the other peaceable.	280	Priest 34		2
The military is, when we are assaulted with temptations either from	280	Priest 34		3
Those that the Parson findes in the military state, he fortifyes,	281	Priest 34		5
MILK				
The gigler is a milk-maid, whom infection,	16	Ch.-Porch		249
At first thou gav'st me milk and sweetnesses;	47	Afflict.1		19
The whey of milk doth loose, the milk doth binde.	120	Providence		132
keep and fodder well their cattel, they must have milk, and Calves;	270	Priest 30		28
MILK-MAID				
The gigler is a milk-maid, whom infection,	16	Ch.-Porch		249
MILKE				
whereas there is not onely milke there, but strong meat also.	317	Valdesso		24
Milke saies to wine, welcome friend.	327	Proverbs		184
MILKIE				
The milkie way, the bird of Paradise,	51	Prayer 1		12
MILL				
The Mill gets by going.	325	Proverbs		122
The mill cannot grind with the water that's past.	326	Proverbs		153
In vaine is the mill-clacke, if the Miller his hearing lack.	332	Proverbs		328
You cannot make a wind-mill goe with a paire of bellowes.	344	Proverbs		676
Gods Mill grinds slow, but sure.	346	Proverbs		747
MILL-CLACKE				
In vaine is the mill-clacke, if the Miller his hearing lack.	332	Proverbs		328
MILLER				
In vaine is the mill-clacke, if the Miller his hearing lack.	332	Proverbs		328
MILLION				
a million of Atheists, and 30000 Witches.	361	Proverbs	D	1174
MILLIONS				
Bibles laid open, millions of surprises,	45	Sinne 1		8
MILLS				
Mills and wives ever want.	334	Proverbs		388
MIND				
And feed the swine, with all his mind & might:	101	Miserie	W	44
Such poor invention burns in their low mind	206	Walton 2		9
A new House to thy mind,	207	Walton 3		2
If thou dost find an house built to thy mind	207	Walton 4		1
A fayre mind.	208	J. Danvers	D	8
the purity of his mind breaking out, and dilating it selfe even	228	Priest 3		12
Questionist must have in his mind before any question be propounded,	256	Priest 21		32
for this argues a height and eminency of mind, which is not easily	268	Priest 28		26
Upon this his mind begins to be perplexed, and troubled,	272	Priest 31		32
that repentance is an act of the mind, not of the Body,	279	Priest 33		14
you could not fill all to your mind.	343	Proverbs	V	700
you could not fit all to your mind.	344	Proverbs		701
can happen to you are either afflictions of Estate, or Body, or Mind.	373	Letters		22
I was desirous to putt a good mind into the way of charity,	375	Letters		8

MINDE	PAGE	TITLE		LINE
Shall I, to please anothers wine-sprung minde,	8	Ch.-Porch		37
A mast'ring minde; so both are lost thereby:	10	Ch.-Porch		104
His minde with rest, before his trunk with riches:	11	Ch.-Porch		110
His minde with rest, before his trunks with riches:	11	Ch.-Porch	W	110
He breaks up house, turns out of doores his minde.	12	Ch.-Porch		150
To stuffe thy minde with solid braverie;	15	Ch.-Porch		208
Let thy minde still be bent, still plotting where,	20	Ch.-Porch		337
Oh all ye, who passe by, whose eyes and minde	26	Sacrifice		1
But balls of wilde-fire to my troubled minde.	64	Even-song		16
Did through my bodie wound my minde,	65	Ch.-mus.		2
Give me the pliant minde, whose gentle measure	69	Content		13
They and my minde may chime,	80	Deniall		29
My horse and I, both tir'd, bodie and minde,	80	Christmas		2
And thred the spheres with his quick-piercing minde:	85	Vanitie 1		2
There he imparts to them his minde,	85	Vanitie 1		18
In their descent and being; to our minde	91	Man		35
Making my minde to smell my fatall day;	94	Life		11
My minde would be extreamly stirr'd	95	Submission		3
Furnish thy table to thy minde.	97	Afflict.5		18
That thou shouldst minde a rotten tree?	104	Obedience		22
Sure thou didst put a minde there, if I could	116	Dulnesse		23
His minde is so.	127	Giddinesse		16
Did alter with his minde;	127	Giddinesse		18
Indeed a slack and sleepie state of minde	130	Love unkn.		57
In hope of great things. Call to minde thy dream,	138	The Size		44
Lord of my soul, love of my minde,	149	Longing		20
That I shall minde, what you impart;	152	The Bag		35
He who craves all the minde,	168	a true Hymn		11
And bring my minde in frame:	172	23 Psalme		10
With these all day I do perfume my minde,	175	The Odour		6
My minde ev'n thrust into them both:	175	The Odour		7
This broth of smells, that feeds and fats my minde.	175	The Odour		10
Light to the minde: what shall the will enjoy?	188	Heaven		15
He adviseth all to call to minde their Baptism often;	258	Priest 22		14
his minde being defixed on it with those nailes wherewith his Master	267	Priest 27		28
and other perturbations of the minde, which have a great power over	293	Cornaro		36
and troubles of the minde, all these did hurt me little,	294	Cornaro		13
if he will give his minde to those things which he should,	297	Cornaro		22
as also that their minde, in all things wherein they deal,	299	Cornaro		20
the Grace of God I feel not those perturbations of bodie and minde,	302	Cornaro		25
The resolved minde hath no eares.	337	Proverbs		464
The resolved minde hath no cares.	337	Proverbs	V	464
MINDE'S				
Let thy mindes sweetnesse have his operation	21	Ch.-Porch		371
MINDED				
to receive the charity of well minded people, and to lay up treasure	246	Priest 13		22
MINDES				
and awfull mindes into the Congregation, and that the good God would	235	Priest 8		29
and to raise up their mindes to apprehend Gods good blessing to our	236	Priest 8		23
power a sober and temperate life hath over our bodies and mindes,	294	Cornaro		26
MINDS				
Bodyes & Minds are different Spheres	201	H. Commun.	W	40
but sometimes lift up their minds to better things, even in the midst	261	Priest 23		25
use and comfort, especially to pious minds, which are ever tender,	273	Priest 31		13
at severall times and occasions, the Parson setleth wavering minds.	283	Priest 34		5
Unsound minds like unsound Bodies, if you feed, you poyson.	358	Proverbs	D	1076
MINE (noun)				
Man found thee poore and dirtie in a mine.	77	Avarice		4
Thou art the holy mine, whence came the gold,	78	Ang.&Sts.		11
Thou art the sacred mine, whence came the gold,	78	Ang.&Sts.	W	11
MINE (see also myne)				
Yet not mine neither: for from thee they came,	5	Dedication		2
Lose all mine own? God hath giv'n me a measure	8	Ch.-Porch		38
O let thy blessed SACRIFICE be mine,	26	The Altar		15
O let thy onely SACRIFICE be mine,	26	The Altar	W	15
Was ever grief like mine?	26	Sacrifice		4
Was ever grief like mine?	26	Sacrifice		8
Was ever grief like mine?	27	Sacrifice		12
Mine own Apostle, who the bag did beare,	27	Sacrifice		13
Was ever grief like mine?	27	Sacrifice		16
Was ever grief like mine?	27	Sacrifice		20
Was ever grief like mine?	27	Sacrifice		24
Curing all wounds, but mine; all, but my fears:	27	Sacrifice		27
Was ever grief like mine?	27	Sacrifice		28
Was ever grief like mine?	27	Sacrifice		32
Was ever grief like mine?	27	Sacrifice		36
Was ever grief like mine?	27	Sacrifice		40
Was ever grief like mine?	28	Sacrifice		44
Was ever grief like mine?	28	Sacrifice		48
Was ever grief like mine?	28	Sacrifice		52
Was ever grief like mine?	28	Sacrifice		56
Was ever grief like mine?	28	Sacrifice		60
Was ever grief like mine?	28	Sacrifice		64
Was ever grief like mine?	28	Sacrifice		68
Was ever grief like mine?	28	Sacrifice		72
Was ever grief like mine?	29	Sacrifice		76
Was ever grief like mine?	29	Sacrifice		80
Was ever grief like mine?	29	Sacrifice		84
Was ever grief like mine?	29	Sacrifice		88
Was ever grief like mine?	29	Sacrifice		92

MIRACULOUSLY (cont'd)	PAGE	TITLE		LINE
14. which we see even miraculously effected in these new discoveryes,	282	Priest 34		33
MIRROUR				
The best mirrour is an old friend.	331	Proverbs		296
MIRTH				
Pick out of tales the mirth, but not the sinne.	9	Ch.-Porch		63
Thy person share, and thou thy mirth inhanse.	15	Ch.-Porch	W	232
Pick out of mirth, like stones out of thy ground, ...	16	Ch.-Porch		235
Then he's the sport: the mirth then in him rests, ...	16	Ch.-Porch		251
At length I heard a ragged noise and mirth	40	Redemption		12
Payd me my wages in a world of mirth.	46	Afflict.1		12
My mirth and edge was lost; a blunted knife	47	Afflict.1		33
Thou art a day of mirth:	76	Sunday		57
What mirth and musick mean; what love and wit	89	The Pearl		24
All day exchanging mirth and breath	98	Mortific.		15
Thy Saviour comes, and with him mirth:	112	Dawning		4
O give me quicknesse, that I may with mirth	115	Dulnesse		3
A secret vertue bringing peace and mirth	125	Peace		35
When sawcie mirth shall knock or call at doore, ...	136	Ephes.		13
A mirth but open'd and seal'd up again;	172	The Glance		18
Since that mirth hath	210	Paradox	D	17
but tremble in your highest mirth.	216	Psalm II	D	28
of their discourses for no price sooner, then that of mirth;	252	Priest 18		21
The Parson in mirth.	267	Priest 27		T
and intermingles some mirth in his discourses occasionally, . .	268	Priest 27		7
to extend themselves to all that mirth, which the present occasion	280	Priest 34		27
or such a time their peace and mirth have carryed them further then	280	Priest 34		33
sacrificed lest his Children should have transgressed in their mirth:	281	Priest 34		2
MIS				
which are two great lights able to dazle the eyes of the mis-led,	263	Priest 24		19
MIS-LED				
which are two great lights able to dazle the eyes of the mis-led,	263	Priest 24		19
MISCALL				
What ever future sinnes should me miscall, ...	44	H. Bapt.1		13
MISCARRIE				
How know'st thou, but thy sinnes made him miscarrie?	24	Ch.-Porch		440
MISCARRY				
made food miraculously, then suffered so good desires to miscarry.	267	Priest 26		26
Ill vessells seldome miscarry.	324	Proverbs		87
MISCHIEF				
Exploits of mischief he conceives, ...	222	Psalm VII	D	51
that it is ever attempting, or doing one mischief or other. . .	238	Priest 9		14
MISDOUBT				
Yet in thy thriving still misdoubt some evil;	13	Ch.-Porch		163
MISERABLE				
from the miserable comparison of the moment of griefs here . .	249	Priest 15		26
since man is so miserable, what is to be done?	257	Priest 21		3
The miserable man makes a peny of a farthing, ...	328	Proverbs		211
MISERIE				
Now thou wouldst taste our miserie.	97	Afflict.5		12
Miserie.	100	Miserie		T
Thou hadst liv'd in miserie.	113	Businesse		27
MISERIES				
True earnest sorrows, rooted miseries, ...	167	Dotage		7
Then miseries are here!	167	Dotage		18
But evident miseries have a naturall priviledge, and exemption from	245	Priest 12		29
MISERY				
Which misery cannot untwist but rather	212	Bohemia	D	35
except the evidence of the misery bring testimony with it. . .	245	Priest 12		22
the Parson once demanded after other questions about mans misery;	257	Priest 21		2
he meets continually with two most sad spectacles, Sin, and Misery;	267	Priest 27		32
Misery and sin fill our days:	288	Priest		11
MISFORTUNE				
Great Fortune brings with it Great misfortune.	360	Proverbs	D	1144
MISHAP				
That from small fires comes oft no small mishap.	139	Artillerie		4
MISLIKE				
If thou mislike him, thou conceiv'st him not.	23	Ch.-Porch		428
if he resent it to a mislike, but not a griefe.	273	Priest 31		20
I much mislike the Comparison of Images, and H. Scripture, . .	309	Valdesso		18
MISLIKES				
sever themselves from it, he mislikes, and reproves as uncharitable,	284	Priest 35		11
MISPLACE				
O what were man, might he himself misplace!	7	Ch.-Porch		23
MISSE				
Canst thou finde hell about my lips? and misse	28	Sacrifice		42
We count three hundred, but we misse:	42	Easter		29
Starres are poore books, & oftentimes do misse:	58	H.Script.2		13
Man might not of his fodder misse.	76	Sunday		39
But dearest Mother, (what those misse), ...	110	Brit. Ch.		25
MISS'D				
And never yet, whom I would punish, miss'd:	30	Sacrifice		131
And never yet, whom he would punish, miss'd:	30	Sacrifice	W	131
Of Joy and Charitie. Sir, you have not miss'd, ...	116	Love-joy		7
MISSES				
He that seekes trouble never misses.	335	Proverbs		416
MISSEST				
To finde out death, but missest life at hand.	86	Vanitie 1		28
MISSETH				
Hee that demands misseth not, unlesse his demands be foolish.	333	Proverbs		359
He that beleeveth all, misseth;	333	Proverbs		364

MONETHS	PAGE	TITLE		LINE
within a few moneths I should be driven to that exigent,	292	Cornaro		14
those fenny places two whole moneths in the heat of summer (which in	302	Cornaro		18
MONEY (see also mony)				
Makes money not a contemptible stone.	12	Ch.-Porch		156
Take starres for money; starres not to be told	13	Ch.-Porch		171
Onely thy single market-money for it.	21	Ch.-Porch		375
Money, thou bane of blisse, & sourse of wo,	77	Avarice		1
Then Money came, and chinking still,	110	The Quip		9
For he hath sold for money his deare Lord,	171	Self-cond.		17
None will beleeve this now, though money be	193	Ch.-Milit.		119
that he keeps his money for the poor, and his table for those that	243	Priest 11		8
he chooseth rather to give the poor money, which they can better	243	Priest 11		15
for money, for meat, for diet:	288	Priest		20
Patience, time and money accommodate all things.	338	Proverbs		498
Health without money is halfe an ague.	338	Proverbs		509
To have money is a feare, not to have it a griefe.	341	Proverbs		591
To have money is a feare, to want it is a griefe.	341	Proverbs	V	591
The love of money and the love of learning rarely meet.	361	Proverbs	D	1168
Much money makes a Countrey poor,	361	Proverbs	D	1178
Money wants no followers.	362	Proverbs	D	1182
MONEYS				
MS. that there are divers moneys of mine in Mr Stephens hands	383	G.H.'s Will		22
MONK				
At Length the Fox turnes Monk.	323	Proverbs		72
MONKE				
of a monke on all sides.	351	Proverbs		900
of a monke on all hands.	351	Proverbs	V	900
MONKISH				
If this seeme Monkish; think which brings most paine	7	Ch.-Porch	W	15
MONKS				
He often readeth the Lives of the Primitive Monks, Hermits,	237	Priest 9		28
MONNEYS				
doores and without doores both monneys and bookes and howshould	382	G.H.'s Will		4
MONSTERS				
Nilus for monsters brought forth Israelites.	191	Ch.-Milit.		44
MONTGOMERY				
Honourable the Lady Anne, Countess of Pembr. and Montg. at court.	376	Letters		T
MONTH (see also moneth)				
if not duly once a month, yet at least five or six times in the year;	259	Priest 22		20
One month doth nothing without another.	355	Proverbs		1028
does fix me here, it being now but a month to our Commencement:	372	Letters		20
MONUMENT				
Ther's no monument to a sonne,	208	J. Danvers	D	15
Another Monument for Thee.	209	H. Danvers	D	10
MONUMENTS				
Church-monuments.	64	Ch.-monum.		T
chiefly considered) might have every where monuments of his Doctrine,	261	Priest 23		21
MONY				
and consequently knowing the price of mony, are offended much	227	Priest 3		14
when it is a sin to take something for mony lent, or when not;	230	Priest 5		24
and somtimes giving them a little mony to do it of themselves,	239	Priest 10		27
that mony thus lent to God, is placed surer for his childrens	240	Priest 10		8
for he hath no mony for such things, charity being his only perfume,	241	Priest 10		13
So a man storing up mony for his necessary provisions, both in	264	Priest 26		26
that servants for their mony are as other things that they buy,	265	Priest 26		24
imprecation to Simon Magus, Act. 8. Thy mony perish with thee:	285	Priest 36		30
put this into your hands (as he sent the fish with mony to S. Peter,)	304	Valdesso		11
To a gratefull man give mony when he askes.	324	Proverbs		115
Dally not with mony or women.	326	Proverbs		150
He that plaies his mony ought not to value it.	327	Proverbs		201
If you loose your time, you cannot get mony nor gaine.	332	Proverbs		320
Would you know what mony is, Go borrow some.	334	Proverbs		374
Mony refused looseth its brightnesse.	336	Proverbs		446
Health and mony goe farre.	336	Proverbs		447
Law sutes consume time, and mony, and rest, and friends.	347	Proverbs		776
but the patient owes nothing to him but a little mony.	351	Proverbs		921
Ready mony is a ready Medicine.	356	Proverbs	D	1038
MONYES				
besides some Remainders of monyes wherof he is to give as I know	383	G.H.'s Will		25
MOON				
As is the moon and sunne to heav'n and light.	196	Ch.-Milit.		216
since hee shoots higher that threatens the Moon, then hee that aims	224	Priest		9
MOONS				
And both with moons and tides.	91	Man		18
MOOR (see also mores)				
MOORISH				
because the place was moorish and unhealthy, fitter for beasts then	301	Cornaro		27
MORA				
Good is the mora that makes all sure.	325	Proverbs		145
MORALITY				
there are other Cases of Conscience grounded on Piety and Morality,	319	Valdesso	V	31
MORALL				
either of Abstinence a morall vertue, or Mortification a divine.	267	Priest 26		16
Other Habits oppose morall vertues, as Prodigality opposes	308	Valdesso		10
MORE				
If rottennesse have more, let Heaven go.	7	Ch.-Porch		18
If rottenness have more, lett Heaven goe.	7	Ch.-Porch	W	24
Hee that desires is more then halfe the way.	10	Ch.-Porch	W	90
Play not for gain, but sport. Who playes for more	14	Ch.-Porch		193
Submit to love; but yet not more then all.	17	Ch.-Porch		284

MORE (cont'd)

	PAGE	TITLE		LINE
God made me one man; love makes me no more,	17	Ch.-Porch		287
Will no more talk all, then eat all the feast.	18	Ch.-Porch		306
More, then his sicknesses or povertie?	18	Ch.-Porch		310
No more then passion when shee talkes of it.	19	Ch.-Porch	W	318
Yet publick hath more promises, more love:	22	Ch.-Porch		398
Yet publick has more promises, more love:	22	Ch.-Porch	W	398
God is more there, then thou: for thou art there	22	Ch.-Porch		404
Why, he that built the world can do much more:	28	Sacrifice		67
All understanding, more then heav'n doth glasse:	30	Sacrifice		119
They leade me in once more, and putting then	32	Sacrifice		189
But more with malice: yet, when they did call,	34	Sacrifice		238
The which to measure it doth more behove:	37	The Agonie		5
His life may make thee gold, and much more just.	41	Easter		6
Decaying more and more,	43	East.wings		3
More backward still, and to that water flie,	43	H. Bapt.1		4
And more; for my friends die:	47	Afflict.1		32
Was of more use then I.	47	Afflict.1		34
Into more sicknesses.	48	Afflict.1		52
Fractures well cur'd make us more strong.	49	Repentance		36
I owed thousands and much more:	50	Faith		13
Although there were some fourtie heav'ns, or more,	55	Temper 1		5
Although there were a hundred heav'ns, or more,	55	Temper 1	W	5
And more then fancy: for in ev'ry thing	58	H.Script.2	W	10
Lord once more shake the Heaven & earth	59	Whitsunday	W	17
Thou shalt have more.	61	Praise 1		4
I will do more.	61	Praise 1		8
He may do more.	61	Praise 1		12
They can do more.	61	Praise 1		16
It may doe more.	61	Praise 1	W	16
And much, much more.	61	Praise 1		20
Who doe no more.	61	Praise 1	W	20
Is more then all my deaths can be,	62	Afflict.2		3
But God more care of us hath had:	63	Sinne 2		6
But much more blest be God above,	63	Even-song		4
I muse, which shows more love,	64	Even-song		25
And in this love, more then in bed, I rest.	64	Even-song		32
Sure I shall do so, and much more:	66	Ch.-mus.		10
His blouds sweet current much more loud to be.	66	Ch.-lock		12
More rev'rend grows, & more doth win:	67	Windows		9
And I will strive to sinne no more.	68	Trin.Sun.		6
More plentifull then hope.	76	Sunday		35
More plentifull and hope.	76	Sunday	W	35
Is much more sure to meet with him, then one	87	Lent		38
May turn, and take me by the hand, and more	87	Lent		41
Have done these twentie hundred yeares, and more:	89	The Pearl		25
Have done these many hundred yeares, and more:	89	The Pearl	W	25
And grumble oft, that they have more in me	89	The Pearl		28
Till I reach heav'n, and much more thee.	90	Afflict.4		30
What house more stately hath there been,	90	Man		4
And more: He is a tree, yet bears no fruit;	91	Man		8
And more: He is a tree, yet bears more fruit;	91	Man	W	8
A beast, yet is, or should be more:	91	Man		9
More servants wait on Man,	92	Man		43
Lord, thy praises should be more.	93	Antiphon 2		19
Lord thou dost deserve much more.	93	Antiphon 2	W	19
I took, without more thinking, in good part	94	Life		8
I will no more advise:	95	Submission		18
We are the trees, whom shaking fastens more,	97	Afflict.5		20
Thou canst no more not heare, then thou canst die.	103	Prayer 2		6
Pratler, no more, I say:	105	Conscience		7
Ah! no more: thou break'st my heart.	115	Dialogue		32
Sheep eat the grasse, and dung the ground for more:	119	Providence		69
Extolleth many wayes, yet this one more.	121	Providence		152
Ah Loyterer! I'le no more, no more I'le bring:	121	Hope		7
Thou art a gard'ner now, and more,	123	Time		16
He doth not crave lesse time, but more.	123	Time		30
Give one thing more, a gratefull heart.	123	Gratefulnes		2
He makes thy gifts occasion more,	123	Gratefulnes		5
Gift upon gift, much would have more,	124	Gratefulnes		15
I have their fruit and more.	128	Bunch Gr.		23
But much more him I must adore,	128	Bunch Gr.		26
Will more complie, then help. A Lord I had,	129	Love unkn.		3
Many a fault more then my lease will bear;	129	Love unkn.		20
More favour then you wot of. Mark the end.	130	Love unkn.		63
It quits the earth, and mounting more and more,	132	The Storm		11
Ev'n fruitfull trees more fruitfull ARE.	133	Paradise		12
Then once more pray:	134	The Method		29
Or cry no more.	136	Ephes.		15
More bowels have, then such hard things.	136	Ephes.		24
Then whom in waiting nothing seems more slow,	137	Familie		15
Nothing more quick when she doth go.	137	Familie		16
Title to more hereafter when they part,	137	The Size		3
Is more then God was, who was hungrie here.	138	The Size		14
But little do reserve themselves for more:	138	The Size		20
Doth tice us on to hopes of more,	138	The Size		29
Much more oblig'd to do thy will,	139	Artillerie		22
Are the more foul, the more thou wert divine.	140	Ch.-rents		4
Did worm and work within you more and more,	140	Ch.-rents		17
That all things were more ours by being his.	143	Holdfast		12
More attributes? Am I all throat or eye,	143	Complaining		13

MORE (cont'd)

	PAGE	TITLE		LINE
More free.	148	Longing		18
More dead to me!	149	Longing		34
I will present, and somewhat more,	152	The Bag		40
I struck the board, and cry'd, No more.	153	The Collar		1
But as I rav'd and grew more fierce and wilde	153	The Collar		33
More skill in musick, and keep better time.	154	Glimpse		7
Which by the springs accesse grew much more great.	154	Glimpse		15
If I have more to spinne,	155	Glimpse		26
And what to this? what more	155	Assurance		13
If mine I am: and thine much more,	157	Clasping		2
And with advantage mine the more.	157	Clasping		6
So mine thou art, that something more	157	Clasping		12
And with advantage mine the more,	157	Clasping		16
That thou mayst yet have more.	157	Praise 3		6
To twentie then, or more.	158	Praise 3		12
And struggling hinders more.	158	Praise 3		18
Thou heardst my call, and more.	158	Praise 3		24
That would contain much more.	158	Praise 3		30
The glasse was full and more.	158	Praise 3		36
Both all my praise, and more!	159	Praise 3		42
I once more smell the dew and rain,	166	The Flower		38
Who would be more,	167	The Flower		47
Where are no sorrows, but delights more true,	167	Dotage		17
Which they that know the rest, know more then I.	169	The Answer		14
Thou so much worse, that thou shalt be no more.	169	Dial.-Anth		10
More then a thousand sunnes disburse in light,	172	The Glance		23
And tell me more:	175	The Odour		18
Then did I wash you with my tears, and more,	176	Forerunners		16
Perhaps with more embellishment can say,	177	Forerunners		33
Presse me not to take more pleasure	177	The Rose		1
To thee, who art more farre above deceit,	185	A Wreath		7
Much more do Common-weals acknowledge thee,	190	Ch.-Milit.		5
Which might the more indeare it to be thine.	190	Ch.-Milit.		12
The ten Commandments there did flourish more	191	Ch.-Milit.		39
The Warrier his deere skarres no more resounds,	191	Ch.-Milit.		63
His grave aspect had more of heav'n then hell:	194	Ch.-Milit.		168
We are more poore, and they more rich by this.	197	Ch.-Milit.		254
Still eastward go; because it drew more neare	198	Ch.-Milit.		276
Choke him, let him say no more,	199	L'Envoy		11
Choke him, let him speak no more,	199	L'Envoy	W	11
Is more, but for mee still.	200	H. Commun.	W	18
Or give mee that, so I have more	201	H. Commun.	W	47
More spotted then my flesh can bee.	202	love	W	9
Into my hart with joye, giving more rest	202	love	W	17
Thou do'st no more, then doth the grave:	202	love	W	22
I went the slower, yet more paces,	203	Even-song	W	3
Shine then more bright then hee.	203	Even-song	W	8
And thou more dark then either.	203	Even-song	W	16
Serve thou the more God and the poore;	207	Walton 4		3
He writ; when 's hand could write no more,	439	Walton 5		13
'Twas more secure in great Loves Common-weal	439	Walton 5		17
When my dear Friend, could write no more,	439	walton 6		1
Theire dead, and Time shal be no more:	208	H. Danvers	D	4
Are quit with them and more.	210	Paradox	D	10
Is of the two the far more desperate.	210	Paradox	D	30
Your feares in number more, your joyes are lesse.	210	Paradox	D	36
Thy curious vertues much more visibly:	211	Bohemia	D	14
Yet hast thou more dominions: God doth give	212	Bohemia	D	41
Shall flow no more - until they bring	214	Convert	D	8
and sin not any more.	217	Psalm IV	D	16
shall more replenish me,	218	Psalm IV	D	26
Ours (like himselfe) o'recomes; for his wit's more	438	Lat.Trans.		3
how much more in things of another world, where the well is deep,	228	Priest 4		34
of the hearers, that he may be heard at his returne more attentively.	232	Priest 7		24
mouth of two or three witnesses the truth may be more established.	232	Priest 7		30
for particulars ever touch, and awake more then generalls.	233	Priest 7		6
And every one is more awaked, when we come, and say, Thou art	236	Priest 8		14
sensitive faculty, will runne out more or lesse in her intellectuall.	238	Priest 9		11
and that much more being single, then if he were marryed;	238	Priest 9		21
esteeming that this private praying is a more voluntary act in them,	241	Priest 10		5
To his Children he shewes more love then terrour, to his servants	241	Priest 10		9
more love then terrour, to his servants more terrour then love;	241	Priest 10		10
The two former obligations are much more essentiall to a true fast,	242	Priest 10		7
if a peece of dry flesh at my table be more unpleasant to me,	242	Priest 10		13
and much more with wine, is apt to nourish more then in cold regions,	242	Priest 10		17
is apt to nourish more then in cold regions, and where flesh may be	242	Priest 10		17
and with more safety then elsewhere, where both the people	242	Priest 10		19
hee wins them to praise God more, to live more religiously,	245	Priest 12		2
to live more religiously, and to take more paines in their vocation,	245	Priest 12		2
and to take more paines in their vocation, as not knowing when they	245	Priest 12		3
the two commands, we are more injoyned to be charitable, then wise.	245	Priest 12		28
Commandments, and as he finds them perfect, rewards them the more.	245	Priest 12		37
that so they go on more cheerfully in their vocation, and himself be	248	Priest 14		12
in their vocation, and himself be ever the more welcome to them.	248	Priest 14		13
as his accesse to the poor is more comfortable, then to the rich;	249	Priest 14		8
and in regard of himselfe, it is more humiliation.	249	Priest 14		9
sake, and to make his higher purposes slip the more easily.	249	Priest 14		12
which may make his other discourses more welcome, and lesse tedious.	251	Priest 17		6
which were more comfortable, all together choosing some fitt day	253	Priest 19		37
the Blessing of God to them ought to make them the more charitable,	254	Priest 19		5

MORE (cont'd)	PAGE	TITLE		LINE
or led by sense, more then by faith, by present rewards, . . .	254	Priest 20		31
by present rewards, or punishments, more then by future. . .	254	Priest 20		32
in vertue the answer also, especially to the more ignorant. . .	256	Priest 21		36
he takes the more pains with them, that hee may lay the foundation	258	Priest 22		30
in a feast of Charity is more scandall then any posture. . .	259	Priest 22		18
and so the thing passeth with more authority, and lesse envy.	260	Priest 23		12
and a recreation to more divine studies, Nature serving Grace both in	261	Priest 23		10
hee might make his Doctrine slip the more easily into the hearts even	261	Priest 23		19
For home-bred medicines are both more easie for the Parsons purse,	261	Priest 23		31
easie for the Parsons purse, and more familiar for all mens bodyes.	261	Priest 23		32
being made by the precept of Authority more then indifferent,	263	Priest 24		13
and makes so much the more of him, as before he alienated himselfe;	263	Priest 25		34
in all these, and those more which concerne me, I either do nothing,	265	Priest 26		16
More particularly, and to give one instance for all, if God have	265	Priest 26		19
to descend yet more particularly, if a man hath wherewithall to buy	265	Priest 26		27
He that either for quantity eats more then his health or imployments	266	Priest 26		7
as he that eats more then his estate will bear, is a Prodigall;	266	Priest 26		9
Many think they are at more liberty then they are, as if they were	266	Priest 26		18
I am more bound to abstain from those, which by mine own experience I	266	Priest 26		24
in eating, that he can eat more, then afterwards he finds true:)	267	Priest 26		3
not keep an uniform diet, but to feed variously, now more, now lesse:	267	Priest 26		11
because diseases of exinanition are more dangerous, then diseases	267	Priest 26		14
and much more for those rules, which out of his choysest judgment hee	268	Priest 28		11
this is foretold, that it shall be so still, until things be no more.	268	Priest 28		16
shewing that reproaches touch him no more, then a stone thrown	269	Priest 28		7
and more of their oath, he wisheth them by no means to spare any,	270	Priest 29		17
who more accepts a common course of devotion, then dislikes . .	273	Priest 31		8
and how much more out of Paradise, when the evills which he is now	274	Priest 32		22
we must not be idle, but labour to get more, that we may give more,	275	Priest 32		1
to get more, that we may give more, according to St. Pauls rule,	275	Priest 32		1
and much more feelingly, and judiciously, then he writes his rules	278	Priest 33		20
himselfe sometimes to weepe more for the losse of some temporall	279	Priest 33		12
some being of a more melting temper then others) consisteth in a true	279	Priest 33		22
when he cannot more, as he that weeps a floud of tears. . .	279	Priest 33		31
still we have bread, though sometimes more, somtimes lesse; . .	281	Priest 34		26
and more, it is a continued Creation, and a creation every moment.	281	Priest 34		30
or Tertullian, or Chrysostome, more then Tully, Virgill, or Livy;)	282	Priest 34		21
saw not more Divinity, then he that reads the womans oyntment in	283	Priest 34		1
As sinfull, he must much more love them;	283	Priest 34		13
and this as the more faulty in him, so the more glorious in God.	283	Priest 34		21
no more then to be a spirituall Father was appropriated to them.	285	Priest 36		12
their children, how much more may, and ought Spirituall Fathers?	285	Priest 36		14
as appears Rom. 12. 14. how much more those, who are spiritual	286	Priest 36		28
and more, they may discover them to those that know them not:	287	Priest 37		17
for an apple once we lost our God, and still lose him for no more;	288	Priest		20
which I undertake the more willingly, because divers worthy young men	291	Cornaro		7
how much more to preserve it!	293	Cornaro		3
with a full stomack, but so as I might well both eat and drink more.	293	Cornaro		19
But mine own experience confirmeth this more;	294	Cornaro		11
The meat which remaineth, profits more then that which is eaten.	296	Cornaro		1
I increased it to the quantitie of two ounces more;	296	Cornaro		12
or that cinnamon should heat me more then pepper?	297	Cornaro		33
how much more dearely should a Physician be esteemed, who not onely	298	Cornaro		8
that they prolong their life even to a hundred yeares and more,	298	Cornaro		16
in all things wherein they deal, may be more lively and vigorous.	299	Cornaro		21
is more sure of life, then the most strong young man who lives	300	Cornaro		25
so that any simple fare is more savourie to me now, then heretofore,	302	Cornaro		9
Many things more might be said in commendation hereof: . . .	303	Cornaro		33
for I can no more free my selfe from actuall sinnes after Baptisme,	308	Valdesso		3
learned and perfect in them, there is somewhat to be learned more:	309	Valdesso		24
In the Scripture are Doctrines, these ever teach more and more.	310	Valdesso		13
In the Scripture are Promises, these ever comfort more and more.	310	Valdesso		14
and the more the promise is delayed, the more he reads it, . .	310	Valdesso		29
is delayed, the more he reads it, and fortifies himselfe with it;	310	Valdesso		29
But the use of the Doctrinall part is more, in regard it presents us	310	Valdesso		32
but enlightens us with new Considerations the more we read it.	310	Valdesso		35
Much more might be said, but this sufficeth, he himselfe allowes it	311	Valdesso		1
that restraining motions are much more frequent to the godly,	313	Valdesso		18
Saviour prayed with doubtfulnesse, is more then I can or dare say;	315	Valdesso		9
that the world pierceth not godly mens actions no more then Gods,	315	Valdesso		30
There is no more to be said of this Chapter but that his opinion	318	Valdesso		5
point it should, which if it did, it would doe more, then it does.	319	Valdesso		12
Ill natures, the more you aske them, the more they stick. . .	324	Proverbs		106
Who hath no more bread then neede, must not keepe a dog. . .	325	Proverbs		128
The more women looke in their glasse, ...	329	Proverbs		250
There are more men threatned then stricken.	329	Proverbs		256
A foole knowes more in his house, then a wise man in anothers.	329	Proverbs		257
The hard gives more then he that hath nothing.	329	Proverbs		259
It costs more to doe ill then to doe well.	329	Proverbs		262
Good words quench more then a bucket of water.	329	Proverbs		263
Soft words quench more then cold water.	329	Proverbs	V	263
There is more talke then trouble.	330	Proverbs		265
By suppers more have beene killed then Galen ever cured. . .	330	Proverbs		272
By suppers more are killed then Galen ever cured.	330	Proverbs	V	272
Much spends the traveller, more then the abider.	330	Proverbs		276
The Fox knowes much, but more he that catcheth him. . . .	330	Proverbs		280
The foole askes much, but hee is more foole that grants it. . .	330	Proverbs		282
A poore beauty finds more lovers then husbands.	337	Proverbs		481
Gluttony kills more then the sword.	338	Proverbs		503
The tooth-ach is more ease then to deale with ill people. . .	340	Proverbs		558

MORE (cont'd)	PAGE	TITLE		LINE
The table robbes more then a thiefe.	342	Proverbs		636
More have repented speech then silence.	344	Proverbs		682
The coveteous spends more then the liberall.	344	Proverbs		683
Beauty drawes more then oxen.	344	Proverbs		685
One father is more then a hundred Schoolemasters.	344	Proverbs		686
One eye of the masters sees more, then ten of the servants.	344	Proverbs		687
A valiant mans looke is more then a cowards sword.	345	Proverbs		708
The higher the Ape goes, the more he shewes his taile.	346	Proverbs		745
Of him that speakes ill, consider the life more then the words.	346	Proverbs		761
Of him that speakes ill, consider the life more then the word.	346	Proverbs	V	761
Nature drawes more then ten teemes.	347	Proverbs		777
It's more paine to doe nothing then something.	350	Proverbs		884
There are more Physitians in health then drunkards.	351	Proverbs		903
Ships feare fire more then water.	351	Proverbs		909
The body is more drest then the soule.	351	Proverbs		919
Yeeres know more then bookes.	351	Proverbs		928
Wee leave more to do when wee dye, then wee have done.	353	Proverbs		972
Infants manners are moulded more by the example of Parents,	357	Proverbs	D	1060
An Asse endures his burden, but not more then his burden.	358	Proverbs	D	1080
Cruelty is more cruell, if we defer the pain.	359	Proverbs	D	1110
The rage of a wild boar is able to spoil more then one wood.	360	Proverbs	D	1132
but my next neighbour doth me more harm	361	Proverbs	D	1173
when I have more time, you shall hear more;	366	Letters		20
and perhaps a little more mild, but you will hardly perceive it.	366	Letters		25
It is high time now that I should be no more a burden to you,	367	Letters		13
selfe (for shee desires no more) shee will find friends to compell	368	Letters		25
and which is more, with our good and gracious God, incessantly	371	Letters		28
much shall it make my prayers the more constant and the more earnest	372	Letters		22
my prayers the more constant and the more earnest for you to the God	372	Letters		22
What hath Affliction grievous in it more then for a moment?	372	Letters		27
I alwaies fear'd sickness more then death, because sickness hath made	373	Letters		8
Credit and estimation calls on us to live in a more splendid fashion?	373	Letters		27
our Care for us that we may the more quietly intend his service.	374	Letters		19
Let me commend only one place more to you (Philip. 4. 4.) St. Paul	374	Letters		20
What can be said more comfortably?	374	Letters		29
neeces into your hands but barely what I wrote I meant, and no more;	375	Letters		6
and am glad that although you offer more, yet you will doe,	375	Letters		7
being more beggarly now than I have been these many years,	375	Letters		36
the good GOD bless you more and more;	376	Letters		19
Now God the Father of our Lord Jesus Christ bless you more & more,	378	Letters		25
To desire good & endeavour it when we can doe no more, is to doe it.	381	Woodnoth		16
three pound more besides that which is due to her, to Ann I leave	382	G.H.'s Will		23
to conquer your enemies, and assume more mild and gracious aspects;	442	Oration		4
and more austere sort of Philosophie, for respect to you,	442	Oration		6
what could have happened more pleasing to us, then the accesse	442	Oration		8
wee might the more by love grow on, both the Spanish and Brittish	442	Oration		17
your Excellencies to bee more deare unto us, in that you are	442	Oration		20
MOREOVER				
Moreover I say, that even bruises and squats, and falls,	294	Cornaro		33
Moreover, by this also, in what estate I am, may be discovered,	302	Cornaro		27
MORES				
The Jewes spend at Easter, the Mores at marriages,	329	Proverbs		242
MORN				
Thou in the morn shalt have my mone,	218	Psalm V	D	5
for in the morn will I	218	Psalm V	D	6
MORNE				
Laden with comforts thence, where now to morne	212	Bohemia	D	56
MORNING				
And in the morning, what thou hast to do.	24	Ch.-Porch		452
The dew doth ev'ry morning fall;	60	Grace		9
My morning-soul and sacrifice:	62	Mattens		3
as soon as he awakes on Sunday morning, presently falls to work,	235	Priest 8		17
and preached in the morning, and catechized in the afternoone,	236	Priest 8		7
and stir out in the morning, and knows what prayers they say,	241	Priest 10		2
When he riseth in the morning, he bethinketh himselfe what good deeds	244	Priest 12		16
as about prayers morning and evening on their knees, reading	248	Priest 14		32
The like he doth in the morning, using pleasantly the outlandish	251	Priest 17		13
he must not only be a morning man, but at Committees also;	277	Priest 32		12
every morning that hee is at home hee must either ride the Great	277	Priest 32		15
Evening words are not like to morning.	323	Proverbs		65
The morning Sunne never lasts a day.	334	Proverbs		375
In the morning mountaines, in the evening fountaines.	337	Proverbs		473
In every countrey the sun rises in the morning.	342	Proverbs		621
The evening praises the day, and the morning a host.	342	Proverbs		635
The evening praises the day, and the morning a frost.	342	Proverbs	V	635
A morning sunne, and a wine-bred child,	349	Proverbs		866
Good newes may bee told at any time, but ill in the morning.	350	Proverbs		877
The Law is not the same at morning and at night.	351	Proverbs		905
For a morning raine leave not your journey.	353	Proverbs		976
MORNING-SOUL				
My morning-soul and sacrifice:	62	Mattens		3
MORROW				
Which knoweth not, what means, to Morrow.	65	Ch.-mus.	W	8
Which knoweth not, what means, too Morrow.	65	Ch.-mus.	W	9
Wilt thou forestall it, and now grieve to morrow,	145	Discharge		48
When a friend askes, there is no to morrow.	322	Proverbs		32
Fly the pleasure that bites to morrow.	336	Proverbs		444
MORSELL				
An upbraided morsell never choaked any.	335	Proverbs		406
I was taken by a morsell, saies the fish.	342	Proverbs		627

	PAGE	TITLE		LINE
MORSELS				
He that hath children, all his morsels are not his owne.	335	Proverbs		423
He who hath children, all his morsels are not his owne.	335	Proverbs	V	423
MORTAL				
A man is known to be mortal by two things, Sleep and Lust.	361	Proverbs	D	1159
MORTALITIE				
Which now is pinion'd with mortalitie,	109	Home		63
If thou subdue mortalitie	202	love	W	21
MORTALL				
The decreed burden of each mortall Saint:	33	Sacrifice		199
The gladsome burden of a mortall saint.	33	Sacrifice	W	199
The gladsome burthen of a mortall saint.	33	Sacrifice	WC	199
While mortall love doth all the title gain!	54	Love 1		5
While mortall love does all the title gain!	54	Love 1	W	5
Of mortall fire:	79	Employm.2		7
Alas poore mortall, void of storie,	169	Dial.-Anth		3
Thou Echo, thou art mortall, all men know.	188	Heaven		3
like mortall enemies, may sometimes disquiet him likewise;	238	Priest 9		9
Autumnall Agues are long, or mortall.	326	Proverbs		148
MORTALS				
Amaze poore mortals, and object their crimes.	132	The Storm		6
Amuse poore mortals, and object their crimes.	132	The Storm	V	6
MORTER				
The Apothecaries morter spoiles the Luters musick.	351	Proverbs		925
MORTIFICATION				
Mortification.	98	Mortific.		T
wherein a Christian is most seen, are Patience, and Mortification;	227	Priest 3		4
Mortification in regard of lusts and affections, and the stupifying	227	Priest 3		5
with confession of sins, and all acts of Mortification.	242	Priest 10		1
of preaching to himself, for the advancing of his own mortification;	255	Priest 21		13
either of Abstinence a morall vertue, or Mortification a divine.	267	Priest 26		16
to harden himselfe, and to further his exercises of Mortification.	284	Priest 35		37
about mortification, and observation of Gods Kingdome within us,	305	Valdesso		10
MORTIFICATIONS				
and mortifications in the times of peace and prosperity.	237	Priest 9		32
MORTIFIE				
to get knowledg, but to subdue and mortifie all lusts and affections:	226	Priest 2		10
MORTIFY				
Gods Spirit will mortify and try them as gold in the fire.	314	Valdesso		21
MOSES				
Moses pursu'd this: but King Solomon	190	Ch.-Milit.		21
Made Pharaoh Moses, changing th' historie.	191	Ch.-Milit.		42
MOSES'				
As Moses face was vailed, so is mine,	31	Sacrifice		138
As Moses face was vailed, so was mine,	31	Sacrifice	W	138
Encounter Moses strong complaints and mone:	99	Decay		4
MOST				
If this seeme Monkish; think which brings most paine	7	Ch.-Porch	W	15
It is most just to throw that on the ground,	7	Ch.-Porch		29
The cheapest sinnes most dearely punisht are;	9	Ch.-Porch		67
A fault, which needs it most, grows two thereby.	9	Ch.-Porch		78
O England! full of sinne, but most of sloth;	10	Ch.-Porch		91
O England, full of all sinn, most of sloth,	10	Ch.-Porch	W	91
Not that they all are so; but that the most	10	Ch.-Porch		95
Not that they are all so; but that the most	10	Ch.-Porch	W	95
Pray with the most: for where most pray, is heaven.	22	Ch.-Porch		402
Resort to sermons, but to prayers most:	23	Ch.-Porch		409
Most surely judg'd, make thy accounts agree.	24	Ch.-Porch		456
Most true to those, who are my greatest grief:	27	Sacrifice		39
They carrie me to my most bitter crosse:	33	Sacrifice		195
Love is that liquour sweet and most divine,	37	The Agonie		17
And missing this, most falsly did arraigne thee;	41	Sepulchre		14
Is best to celebrate this most high day.	41	Easter		12
Most poore:	43	East.wings		5
Most thinne.	43	East.wings		15
You doe prevent most sins & for the rest	44	H. Bapt.1	W	6
Cut me not off for my most foul transgression:	49	Repentance		15
I did conceit a most delicious feast;	50	Faith		6
With an exact and most particular trust,	51	Faith		43
Op'ning the souls most subtile rooms;	52	H.Commun.		22
They would discolour thy most bloudy sweat.	62	Afflict.2		10
I am with thee, and Most take all.	70	Quidditie		12
To God, his neighbour, and himself most true:	72	Constancie		3
O day most calm, most bright,	75	Sunday		1
My vows to thee most gladly, blessed Maid,	78	Ang.&Sts.		9
To be all passengers most sweet relief?	81	Christmas		8
And thought his god most brave;	82	Ungratef.		5
By noon most cunningly did steal away,	94	Life		5
Thy justice me most fitly payes:	96	Justice 1		7
And those things most, which are most pure and fine:	101	Miserie		38
Where most things were of purest gold;	106	Sion		3
The most of me to heav'n is fled:	109	Home		68
And write for sweet, prove a most sowre displeasure.	111	Vanitie 2		6
Thou hadst di'd most wretchedly;	113	Businesse		21
Wherefore, most sacred Spirit, I here present	117	Providence		25
Since where are poysons, antidotes are most:	119	Providence		87
Most herbs that grow in brooks, are hot and dry.	120	Providence		129
Most things move th' under-jaw; the Crocodile not.	121	Providence		139
Most things move th' underchaw; the Crocodile not.	121	Providence	V	139
Most things sleep lying; th' Elephant leans or stands.	121	Providence		140
Most things sleep lying; th' Elephant leane or stand.	121	Providence	V	140

MOST (cont'd)

	PAGE	TITLE		LINE
Ev'n taken inwardly, and most divine	130	Love unkn.		44
Ev'n when the boat seems most to reel.	151	The Bag		4
Who heard thee say it. O most gracious Lord,	155	Assurance		20
O what pure things, most pure must those things be,	161	Priesthood		29
We turn upon him in a sense most true:	168	The Sonne		12
Cheat the most subtill nations. Who so coy,	194	Ch.-Milit.		150
Onely, most noble Lord, shutt not the doore	209	L. Bacon	D	9
on Sion His most Holy hill,	215	Psalm II	D	14
And toward thy most Holy place	218	Psalm V	D	19
points of Life, wherein a Christian is most seen, are Patience,	227	Priest 3		4
Yet in these points he labours most in those things which are most	227	Priest 3		10
most in those things which are most apt to scandalize his Parish.	227	Priest 3		11
but especially that of drinking, because it is the most popular vice;	227	Priest 3		24
yet every mans own is fittest, readyest, and most savory to him.	230	Priest 5		5
is best to be chosen, of which there is likelyest to be most use.	230	Priest 5		11
expounding of our Catechisme must needs be the most usefull forme.	230	Priest 5		14
least all those which he observeth are most incident to his Parish.	230	Priest 5		35
and those most, which are nearest to his Parish;	233	Priest 7		8
for the most part, serve but the vices and vanities of the world,	240	Priest 10		3
it consisteth most of mutton, beefe, and veal, if he addes any thing	241	Priest 10		16
as most Students are, he cannot keep the last obligation,	242	Priest 10		28
And obstructions are the cause of most diseases.	243	Priest 10		5
he distinguisheth, giving them most, who live best, and take most	245	Priest 12		15
who live best, and take most paines, and are most charged:	245	Priest 12		16
For there he shall find his flock most naturally as they are,	247	Priest 14		6
them cleerly, that they respect them most, who wish them best,	251	Priest 17		30
he thinks it the most usefull way that a Pastor can take,	256	Priest 21		2
a most plain and easie framing the question, even containing in	256	Priest 21		34
of that, wherin they are most eminent, is the most gainfull way	260	Priest 23		6
they are most eminent, is the most gainfull way of Conversation.	260	Priest 23		7
be diligently perused, as being the practicall part, and of most use.	261	Priest 23		8
whose natures are most stealing, and beginnings uncertaine.	264	Priest 26		33
for example sake, and because they are most common, he thus thinks:	265	Priest 26		3
he meets continually with two most sad spectacles, Sin,	267	Priest 27		31
throw it away, and be most confident, that God is not displeased.	273	Priest 31		38
The Countrey Parson perceiving, that most, when they are at leasure,	286	Priest 37		29
three Persons, but one most glorious, incomprehensible God,	290	Priest		15
(having a most cold & moist stomack) I fell into divers diseases,	291	Cornaro		20
But Intemperance destroyes most healthy and flourishing	292	Cornaro		9
Wherefore I began to search out most diligently what meats were	293	Cornaro		4
This upon triall I found most false:	293	Cornaro		10
although the power of health consists most in the proportion of meat	293	Cornaro		33
whom that matter ought to have affected most, received no	294	Cornaro		21
and the season of the yeare was winter and most cold aire.	296	Cornaro		28
That an orderly life is the most sure way & ground of health and long	297	Cornaro		12
is a naturall Physick most agreeable to us, and also doth preserve	298	Cornaro		14
But sensuall men (as most are) desiring to satisfie their Appetite,	298	Cornaro		23
wherein wisdome and all kinde of vertues is most vigorous;	298	Cornaro		30
especially since it is easie and most agreeable to the nature of Man.	300	Cornaro		5
of any meat or drink (though most agreeable to them) then their	300	Cornaro		13
sure of life, then the most strong young man who lives disorderly.	300	Cornaro		26
are verie beautifull and convenient above most in this age,	301	Cornaro		12
at these yeares (viz. 83) I have made a most pleasant comedie,	302	Cornaro		28
which it most suits withall for variety and pleasantnesse;	302	Cornaro		31
their youthfull appetites, although they be of a most strong temper:	303	Cornaro		13
circumspection) but still even to the most learned and perfect in	309	Valdesso		23
for the most of his Considerations being grounded upon some text	317	Valdesso		35
generall rules to particular actions, which are a most noble study.	319	Valdesso	V	33
He that lives most dies most.	336	Proverbs		437
He that burnes most shines most.	340	Proverbs		568
Emptie vessels sound most.	342	Proverbs		643
A Tyrant is most tyrant to himselfe.	350	Proverbs		888
and after my manner, Your most obedient Servant, GEORGE HERBERT.	364	Letters		4
it is a most serious Case, nor can I write coldly in that,	364	Letters		16
into a Benefice, I should be most glad to entertain it, and both pay	367	Letters		10
I remember my most humble duty to my Mother.	367	Letters		20
favour to mee in pardoning Your most indebted kinsman GEORGE HERBERT.	369	Letters		5
I remember my most humble duty to my Mother, who cannot think me	371	Letters		1
and then you shall justly value Your most truly, most heartily,	372	Letters		6
justly value Your most truly, most heartily, affectionate Brother,	372	Letters		7
and I shou'd account my self most happy if I might change with you;	373	Letters		3
most carry themselves so, as if they not only not desir'd,	373	Letters		33
accept the good meaning of, Your most obedient Son, GEORGE HERBERT.	374	Letters		32
Your most faithful Servant in Christ Jesu, GEORGE HERBERT.	377	Letters		9
yet useth his Restraining grace, even in the most wicked:	381	Woodnoth		9
Most Excellent and most magnificent Lords:	441	Oration		23
commands, most noble Ambassages, and other titles most pleasing,	441	Oration		25
and other titles most pleasing, as well to us remembring,	441	Oration		25
The praises also and vertues of the most renowned Princesse Isabel,	442	Oration		22
Wherefore most Excellent, most Illustrious Lords, since you are so	442	Oration		27
most Illustrious Lords, since you are so great both in your Princes,	442	Oration		27

MOTH

	PAGE	TITLE		LINE
Where never yet came moth.	100	Miserie		18

MOTHER

	PAGE	TITLE		LINE
He that is drunken, may his mother kill	7	Ch.-Porch		31
And Mother of my God, in my distresse.	78	Ang.&Sts.		10
Give to thy Mother, what thou wouldst allow	86	Lent		5
I joy, deare Mother, when I view	109	Brit. Ch.		1
But dearest Mother, (what those misse),	110	Brit. Ch.		25
Why doth my Mother blush? is she the rose,	140	Ch.-rents		11

MOTHER (cont'd)	PAGE	TITLE	LINE
Where Pagans tread. O Mother deare and kinde,	140	Ch.-rents	24
To see their mother-root, when they have blown;	166	The Flower	11
all the sonnes of one father and mother, all in perfect health;	303	Cornaro	4
The good mother sayes not, Will you? but gives.	337	Proverbs	467
Poverty is the mother of health.	337	Proverbs	472
A pittifull mother makes a scald head.	343	Proverbs	647
If the mother had not beene in the oven,	344	Proverbs	696
Night is the mother of Councels.	346	Proverbs	746
an ill dyet was the mother.	357	Proverbs	D 1048
Fortune to one is Mother, to another is Step-mother.	359	Proverbs	D 1118
A fair day in winter is the mother of a storme.	360	Proverbs	D 1145
Take heed of a step-mother; the very name of her sufficeth.	360	Proverbs	D 1155
my meaning (dear Mother) is in these Sonnets, to declare my	363	Letters	10
I remember my most humble duty to my Mother.	367	Letters	20
you and my dear Mother and Sister to pardon me, for my Cambridge	369	Letters	17
I remember my most humble duty to my Mother, who cannot think me	371	Letters	1
To his Mother, in her sickness.	372	Letters	T
dear Mother, I alwaies fear'd sickness more then death,	373	Letters	7
Wherefore the Lord make good the blessing of your Mother upon you,	377	Letters	4
MOTHER-ROOT			
To see their mother-root, when they have blown;	166	The Flower	11
MOTHER'S			
Hee that wipes the childs nose, kisseth the mothers cheeke.	355	Proverbs	1032
MOTHERS			
Mothers are kinde, because thou art,	148	Longing	14
and God-mothers, that it is no complementall or light thing	258	Priest 22	10
MOTHS			
Then to have hellish moths still gnaw and fret	69	Content	27
MOTION			
Let not each motion make thee to detest	7	Ch.-Porch	WC 19
This verse marks that, and both do make a motion	58	H.Script.2	5
To which the blast of deaths incessant motion,	64	Ch.-monum.	4
Motion, and heat, let's take our flight	74	The Starre	18
That Life hath with the sun a double motion.	84	Coloss.	2
I had a motion to forbear,	134	The Method	23
except there be a restraining motion (as S. Paul had when hee would	313	Valdesso	16
MOTIONS			
Quick thoughts and motions at a small expense,	86	Lent	20
And all their motions upward be;	107	Sion	22
Who do not their own motions heare?	134	The Method	19
Expell good motions from thy breast,	139	Artillerie	7
things there is roome for motions [notions] and expecting of them;	313	Valdesso	12
and I conceive that restraining motions are much more frequent	313	Valdesso	17
motions are much more frequent to the godly, then inviting motions;	313	Valdesso	18
For otherwise any Malefactor may pretend motions, which is	316	Valdesso	21
MOULDED			
Infants manners are moulded more by the example of Parents,	357	Proverbs	D 1060
Every man's censure is first moulded in his own nature.	362	Proverbs	D 1181
MOUNT			
Unto mount Olivet; there shall he see	37	The Agonie	8
Or, if I mount unto the skie,	61	Praise 1	7
Then would I mcunt up instantly	79	Employm.2	W 23
And ever as they mount, like larks they sing;	107	Sion	23
MOUNTAINE			
and fervency, and need a mountaine of fire to kindle them;	233	Priest 7	17
A mountaine and a river are good neighbours.	330	Proverbs	274
MOUNTAINES			
In the morning mountaines, in the evening fountaines.	337	Proverbs	473
mountaines tc him seeme valleys.	354	Proverbs	997
MOUNTAINS			
Philosophers have measur'd mountains,	37	The Agonie	1
When that lay gather'd, thou didst broach the mountains:	120	Providence	114
Or steel, or mountains be thy ring,	163	The Search	35
MOUNTED			
Shadows well mcunted, dreams in a career,	167	Dotage	4
A man well mounted is ever Cholerick.	355	Proverbs	1025
MOUNTER'S			
Subject to ev'ry mounters bended knee.	58	H.Script.1	14
MOUNTING			
It quits the earth, and mounting more and more,	132	The Storm	11
MOUNTS			
In soul he mcunts and flies,	131	Mans medly	13
MOURNERS			
and, Blessed be the Mourners, for they shall be comforted.	373	Letters	32
MOURNING			
Marry a widdow before she leave mourning.	329	Proverbs	252
MOUSE			
I gave the mouse a hole, and she is become my heire.	324	Proverbs	94
It's better to be the head of a mouse, then the tayle of a Lyon.	340	Proverbs	V 579
The Catt sees not the mouse ever.	341	Proverbs	592
The escaped mouse ever feeles the taste of the bait.	344	Proverbs	679
It's a bold mouse that nestles in the catts eare.	344	Proverbs	693
The mouse that hath but one hole is quickly taken.	360	Proverbs	D 1135
MOUTH			
Take not his name, who made thy mouth, in vain:	8	Ch.-Porch	55
Thy mouth to it, thy actions to them both:	9	Ch.-Porch	74
Look to thy mouth; diseases enter there.	11	Ch.-Porch	127
Enrich my heart, mouth, hands in me,	68	Trin.Sun.	7
Thy mouth was open, but thou couldst not sing.	185	Death	4
preach my Laws, and takest my Covenant in thy mouth? Psal. 50. 16.	226	Priest 2	14

MOUTH (cont'd)	PAGE	TITLE		LINE
that so in the mouth of two or three witnesses the truth may be more	232	Priest 7		29
and opens not only his mouth, but his purse to their relief,	248	Priest 14		11
that in the mouth of two or three witnesses every word may be	283	Priest 34		19
That they who in these two things that enter in at the mouth,	294	Cornaro		4
A coole mouth, and warme feet, live long.	321	Proverbs		21
Into a mouth shut flies flie not.	328	Proverbs		219
The ill that comes out of our mouth falles into our bosome.	328	Proverbs		221
The wise hand doth not all that the foolish mouth speakes.	329	Proverbs		246
He that hath a mouth of his owne,	333	Proverbs		353
He that hath no hony in his pot, let him have it in his mouth.	333	Proverbs		360
Who hath bitter in his mouth, spits not all sweet.	335	Proverbs		422
One mouth doth nothing without another.	355	Proverbs	V	1028
In the mouth of a bad dog fals often a good bone.	358	Proverbs	D	1093
MOUTHES				
He that owes nothing, if he makes not mouthes at us, is courteous.	333	Proverbs		362
MOUTHS				
their mouths no truth retain.	219	Psalm V	D	26
in our hearts, before they come into our mouths, truly affecting,	233	Priest 7		30
and dishonour him with those mouths, which he continually fils,	269	Priest 28		11
For if he absolutely shut up mens mouths, and forbid all disclosing	286	Priest 37		34
MOVE				
If reason move not Gallants, quit the room,	8	Ch.-Porch		43
And if Gods image move thee not, let thine.	10	Ch.-Porch		102
Nor wisdome neither: therefore gently move.	18	Ch.-Porch		312
We all are but cold suitours; let us move	22	Ch.-Porch		400
Nay, I will reade thy book, and never move	36	Thanksgvng		45
Though elements change, and heaven move,	56	Temper 2		14
Or if to me thou wilt not move,	61	Grace		22
Now I in you without a bodie move,	65	Ch.-mus.		5
That it may hang and move	74	The Starre		15
Did th' earth and all things with it move.	76	Sunday		46
('Tis your own case) ye never move a wing.	78	Ang.&Sts.		20
'tis your own case, ye never move your wing.	78	Ang.&Sts.	W	20
With all the circumstances that may move:	89	The Pearl		36
The earth doth rest, heav'n move, and fountains flow.	91	Man		26
Getting a house and home, where he may move	98	Mortific.		20
Who dost so strongly and so sweetly move,	117	Providence		31
Most things move th' under-jaw; the Crocodile not.	121	Providence		139
Most things move th' underchaw; the Crocodile not.	121	Providence	V	139
Sure they would move	132	The Storm		4
Quickly effect, what thou dost move;	133	The Method		6
I will move thee.	146	Praise 2		4
Such a Joy, as none can move:	156	The Call		10
Are so, as for the present, I did move	204	Persever.	W	3
None but gross joyes you move:	210	Paradox	D	34
and your offering of yourself to move my Lords of Manchester	377	Letters		23
MOVEABLE				
as being persons enabled by that Name to take moveable goods,	270	Priest 29		2
MOVED				
Whereas if th' heart be moved,	168	a true Hymn		16
I will declare the causes which moved me to forsake Intemperance,	291	Cornaro		15
be evident to others, as well as to themselves, that God moved them.	316	Valdesso		20
MOVEDST				
Or rather as thou movedst mee.	204	Persever.	W	4
MOVES				
It moves, it creeps, it aims at thee:	149	Longing		38
knowing that no Sermon moves them so much to a reverence,	231	Priest 6		14
to do all the good he can, moves him to say thus and thus.	251	Priest 17		32
MOVEST				
Strongly and sweetly movest, shall I write,	116	Providence		2
MOVETH				
Earth resteth, Heaven moveth, fountains flow,	91	Man	W	26
MOVING				
moving and ravishing texts, whereof the Scriptures are full.	233	Priest 7		27
by moving the Duches's heart, to an exceeding cheerfulness,	379	Letters		1
MOW				
To review ones store is to mow twice.	354	Proverbs		1007
MR				
The AUTHOUR, Mr. G. H.	223	Priest		T
by Lud. Cornarus, Translated into English by Mr. George Herbert.	291	Cornaro		T
A Copy of a letter written by MR. GEORGE HERBERT to his friend	304	Valdesso		T
OUTLANDISH PROVERBS SELECTED By Mr. G. H.	319	Proverbs		T
The Mr. absent, and the house dead.	352	Proverbs		940
Selected By Mr George Herbert, Late Orator	356	Proverbs	D	T
To my dear brother, Mr. Henry Herbert, at Paris.	366	Letters		27
To Mr. Nicholas Ferrar.	378	Letters		T
the chiefest also, so also have I required Mr W. for his part.	378	Letters		23
Mr Herberts reasons for Arth. Woodenoths Living with Sir John	380	Woodnoth		T
there is seaven hundred pounds in Mr Thomas Lawleys hands a Merchant	382	G.H.'s Will		8
Then I bequeath to Mr Hays the Comment of Lucas Brugensis uppon	382	G.H.'s Will		18
then I bequeath to Mr Bostocke St. Augustines workes and his halfe	382	G.H.'s Will		20
my will and pleasure is that Mr Woodnoth should be mine Executor	382	G.H.'s Will		28
To Mr George Herbert one hundred pound To Mrs Beatrice Herbert forty	383	G.H.'s Will		6
To Mrs Elizabeth Danvers Mr Henry Danvers wife twenty shillings,	383	G.H.'s Will		12
To Mr Bostocke forty shillings To Elizabeth Burthen thirty shillings	383	G.H.'s Will		14
To Mrs Mary Lawly fifty shillings To Mr Gardiner tenn pound MS. that	383	G.H.'s Will		19
are divers moneys of mine in Mr Stephens hands Stationer of London,	383	G.H.'s Will		22
MRS				
the death of my deare Neece Mrs Dorothy Vaughan whereof two hundred	382	G.H.'s Will		10
To Mrs Catharine Vaughan One hundred pound, To Mr George Herbert one	383	G.H.'s Will		6

MRS (cont'd)	PAGE	TITLE	LINE
George Herbert one hundred pound To Mrs Beatrice Herbert forty pound,	383	G.H.'s Will	7
To Mrs Jane Herbert tenn pound, To Mrs Danvers five pound,	383	G.H.'s Will	8
To Mrs Danvers five pound, To Amy Danvers thirty shillings,	383	G.H.'s Will	9
To Mrs Anne Danvers twenty shillings, To Mrs Mary Danvers twenty	383	G.H.'s Will	10
To Mrs Mary Danvers twenty shillings, To Mrs Michel twenty shillings,	383	G.H.'s Will	10
To Mrs Michel twenty shillings, To Mrs Elizabeth Danvers Mr Henry	383	G.H.'s Will	11
To Mrs Elizabeth Danvers Mr Henry Danvers wife twenty shillings,	383	G.H.'s Will	12
To William Scuce twenty shillings To Mrs Judith Spencer five pound	383	G.H.'s Will	18
To Mary Owens forty shillings To Mrs Mary Lawly fifty shillings To Mr	383	G.H.'s Will	19
pound MS. that the five pound due to Mrs Judeth Spenser is to be payd	383	G.H.'s Will	20
due to Mrs Judeth Spenser is to be payd to Mrs Mary Lawly at Chelsey	383	G.H.'s Will	21
MRSS			
To Mrss Magdalen Vaughan one hundred pound, To Mrs Catharine Vaughan	383	G.H.'s Will	5
MS			
To Mr Gardiner tenn pound MS. that the five pound due to Mrs	383	G.H.'s Will	20
MS. that there are divers moneys of mine in Mr Stephens hands	383	G.H.'s Will	22
MUCH			
Much lesse towards God, whose lust is all their book?	6	Ch.-Porch	12
Much curiousnesse is a perpetuall wooing	14	Ch.-Porch	191
Laugh not too much: the wittie man laughs least:	15	Ch.-Porch	229
Shoots higher much then he that means a tree.	19	Ch.-Porch	334
Much lesse make any one thine enemie.	20	Ch.-Porch	351
Much lesse make any one thy enemie.	20	Ch.-Porch W	351
Write, So much giv'n to God; thou shalt be heard.	21	Ch.-Porch	382
Why, he that built the world can do much more:	28	Sacrifice	67
In so much dregs the quintessence is small:	38	The Sinner	9
His life may make thee gold, and much more just.	41	Easter	6
As he that Heaven beyond much thicket spyes	43	H. Bapt.1 W	3
And a much fitter stone	45	Nature	17
Lord, how couldst thou so much appease	49	Faith	1
I owed thousands and much more:	50	Faith	13
A peasant may beleeve as much	50	Faith	29
Thy praise too much? thou art heav'ns Lidger here,	58	H.Script.1	11
And much, much more.	61	Praise 1	20
But much more blest be God above,	63	Even-song	4
Sure I shall do so, and much more:	66	Ch.-mus.	10
His blouds sweet current much more loud to be.	66	Ch.-lock	12
So much breath to a sigh, what's then behinde?	73	Afflict.3	9
Is much more sure to meet with him, then one	87	Lent	38
Till I reach heav'n, and much more thee.	90	Afflict.4	30
Till then, afford us so much wit;	92	Man	52
Lord thou dost deserve much more.	93	Antiphon 2 W	19
Do pinch and straiten thee, and use much art	99	Decay	14
Much lesse those joyes which trample on his head.	102	Jordan 2	12
So I bespoke me much insinuation:	103	Jordan 2 W	14
If this poore paper do as much as they.	104	Obedience	5
Did not affect thee much, was not thy aim;	106	Sion	8
Are there much surer then our art is sure.	119	Providence	80
Thou that hast giv'n so much to me,	123	Gratefulnes	1
Gift upon gift, much would have more,	124	Gratefulnes	15
Much better tunes, then grones can make;	124	Gratefulnes	22
With so much earnestnesse you do pursue,	125	Peace	41
They never cool, much lesse give out.	126	Confession	16
But much more him I must adore,	128	Bunch Gr.	26
And much affect thee, as tempestuous times	132	The Storm	5
Grasp not at much, for fear thou losest all.	138	The Size	38
Much more oblig'd to do thy will,	139	Artillerie	22
And made you look much fresher then before.	140	Ch.-rents	15
And much of Asia and Europe fast asleep,	140	Ch.-rents	27
Against me there is none, but for me much.	141	Justice 2	24
With much ado.	142	Pilgrimage	12
Much troubled, till I heard a friend expresse,	143	Holdfast	11
Which by the springs accesse grew much more great.	154	Glimpse	15
If mine I am: and thine much more,	157	Clasping	2
That would contain much more.	158	Praise 3	30
I am both foul and brittle; much unfit	160	Priesthood	11
And then when after much delay,	164	The Crosse	7
Much wrastling, many a combate, this deare end,	164	The Crosse	8
So much desir'd, is giv'n, to take away	164	The Crosse	9
Thou so much worse, that thou shalt be no more.	169	Dial.-Anth	10
But I will not much oppose	177	The Rose	13
Who hath done so much for me.	182	Banquet	48
Much in request, much sought for, as a good.	186	Death	16
Much in request, much long'd for as a good.	186	Death W	16
Much more do Common-weals acknowledge thee,	190	Ch.-Milit.	5
Much about one and the same time and place,	192	Ch.-Milit.	101
And being craftier much then Goodnesse was,	193	Ch.-Milit.	124
Know that much had been his worth;	208	J. Danvers D	14
Each little comforte much affects our hartes,	210	Paradox D	33
Wee doubt much whether you	211	Paradox D	40
Thy curious vertues much more visibly:	211	Bohemia D	14
But, Lord, how long so much perplex'd	220	Psalm VI D	7
as farre as wee can in pleasing of him, who hath done so much for us.	224	Priest	13
they remember their earthly Lord, do much forget their heavenly;	226	Priest 2	32
are offended much with any, who by hard usage increase their travell,	227	Priest 3	14
that the world should so much value wealth, which in the day of wrath	227	Priest 3	20
Countrey people (as indeed all honest men) do much esteem their word,	228	Priest 3	2
how much more in things of another world, where the well is deep,	228	Priest 4	34
esteemes also of cases of conscience, wherein he is much versed.	230	Priest 5	19
knowing that no Sermon moves them so much to a reverence,	231	Priest 6	14

MUCH (cont'd)	PAGE	TITLE		LINE
that where is much earnestness, there is somewhat worth hearing;	232	Priest 7		32
and wondreth not so much at their patient suffering, and cheerfull	237	Priest 9		29
and that much more being single, then if he were marryed;	238	Priest 9		21
means to continue so, he doth at least, as much as hath been said.	238	Priest 9		25
counting nothing so much his owne, as that he may be unjust unto it.	238	Priest 9		35
reserving so much of the affaires, as serve for a diversion for him;	238	Priest 9		38
The two former obligations are much more essentiall to a true fast,	242	Priest 10		7
and much more with wine, is apt to nourish more then in cold regions,	242	Priest 10		17
and where flesh may be much better spared, and with more safety then	242	Priest 10		18
shall much better brooke and bear a draught of beer, then if it had	242	Priest 10		22
and their comfort, who are much cheered with such friendliness.	243	Priest 11		13
and sutably to their needs, then so much given in meat at dinner.	243	Priest 11		17
and repine as much, as he that is disseized of his own inheritance.	244	Priest 12		29
hee both commends them much, and furthers them when hee is gone,	247	Priest 14		14
and so much the rather doth he so, as his accesse to the poor is more	249	Priest 14		7
with comparisons, and making much even of a word of truth from him.	256	Priest 21		15
and doubtlesse the Holy Scripture intends thus much, when it	257	Priest 21		11
which the Parson so much commends to all his fellow-labourers;	257	Priest 21		16
not cheape, or course, much lesse ill-tasted, or unwholsome.	258	Priest 22		23
The time of every ones first receiving is not so much by yeers,	258	Priest 22		32
therfore one anothers company, much lesse defaming one another.	260	Priest 23		27
as may be of much use to him both for himself, and others.	261	Priest 23		3
and makes so much the more of him, as before he alienated himselfe;	263	Priest 25		33
or studying dainties too much, they cannot wel dispatch) nor of their	266	Priest 26		15
wisheth all to incline rather to too much, then to too little;	267	Priest 26		13
and much more for those rules, which out of his choysest judgment hee	268	Priest 28		11
so much the rather ought he to proceed, as that by this he may take	273	Priest 31		31
and how much more out of Paradise, when the evills which he is now	274	Priest 32		22
and take as much joy in a straight-growing childe, or servant,	275	Priest 32		33
the Professours whereof were much imployed by Queen Elizabeth,	277	Priest 32		32
and much more feelingly, and judiciously, then he writes his rules	278	Priest 33		20
and can much better, and particularly do it, then he that is	278	Priest 33		28
how the windes should blow so much as they can, and the sea rage so	281	Priest 34		21
and the sea rage so much as it can, and all things do what they can,	281	Priest 34		21
by taking away so much as the usuall seasons of summer and winter,	281	Priest 34		24
not so much doubting a God, as that he is theirs;	283	Priest 34		6
As sinfull, he must much more love them;	283	Priest 34		13
because Countrey people are much addicted to them, so that to favour	283	Priest 35		29
There is much preaching in this friendliness.	284	Priest 35		21
their children, how much more may, and ought Spirituall Fathers?	285	Priest 36		14
as appears Rom. 12. 14. how much more those, who are spiritual	286	Priest 36		28
which hath so much advanced Charity, and ranked backbiters among	287	Priest 37		23
it is a duty rather, which may do much good, and save much harme.	288	Priest 37		1
if the punished delinquent shall be much troubled for his sins,	288	Priest 37		3
the measure of thy love, who hast done for us as much as may be.	290	Priest		12
first caused me to leave Intemperance, to which I was much addicted:	291	Cornaro		19
If Temperance had so much power as to bring me health;	293	Cornaro		3
how much more to preserve it!	293	Cornaro		3
other hurtfull things also, as too much heat and cold, wearinesse,	293	Cornaro		31
whereas they hurt them very much who live intemperately.	294	Cornaro		14
(a thing usuall to disorderly lives) which increased so much in them,	294	Cornaro		19
that they could not be much troubled, or make a great concourse,	295	Cornaro		9
the one whereof was, He that will eat much, let him eat little;	295	Cornaro		34
that the hurt of too much meat is greater, then the commoditie	296	Cornaro		3
This addition after ten dayes wrought so much upon me, that	296	Cornaro		14
how much more dearely should a Physician be esteemed, who not onely	298	Cornaro		8
which endeavours to preserve a man as much as she can, teacheth us	299	Cornaro		26
and that in much smaller quantitie then when he was well.	299	Cornaro		31
But some, too much given to Appetite, object, That a long life is no	300	Cornaro		27
I am much pleased also in my travells, with the beauty of situation.	302	Cornaro		5
But I like none of it, for it slights the Scripture too much:	306	Valdesso		17
I much mislike the Comparison of Images, and H. Scripture,	309	Valdesso		18
Much more might be said, but this sufficeth, he himselfe allowes it	311	Valdesso		1
that restraining motions are much more frequent to the godly,	313	Valdesso		17
The best remedy against an ill man is much ground betweene both.	326	Proverbs		152
Good words are worth much, and cost little.	326	Proverbs		155
Giving much to the poore, doth inrich a mans store.	327	Proverbs		191
It takes much from the account, to which his sin doth amount.	327	Proverbs		192
Much spends the traveller, more then the abider.	330	Proverbs		276
A journying woman speakes much of all, and all of her.	330	Proverbs		279
The Fox knowes much, but more he that catcheth him.	330	Proverbs		280
The foole askes much, but hee is more foole that grants it.	330	Proverbs		282
He is not poore that hath little, but he that desireth much.	331	Proverbs		309
Aske much to have a little.	332	Proverbs		322
A jade eates as much as a good horse.	339	Proverbs		519
One enemy is too much.	339	Proverbs		523
A gift much expected is paid, not given.	340	Proverbs		574
Old men, when they scorne young, make much of death.	341	Proverbs		597
Talke much and erre much, saies the Spanyard.	343	Proverbs		649
A little wind kindles; much puts out the fire.	344	Proverbs		680
A little labour, much health.	344	Proverbs		689
To whirle the eyes too much shewes a Kites braine.	345	Proverbs		717
Give not S. Peter so much, to leave Saint Paul nothing.	346	Proverbs		763
Praise none too much, for all are fickle.	347	Proverbs		774
He that talkes much of his happinesse summons griefe.	349	Proverbs		856
He who talkes much of his happinesse summons griefe.	349	Proverbs	V	856
Too much taking heede is losse.	350	Proverbs		889
The first blow is as much as two.	351	Proverbs		913
When all men have what belongs to them, it cannot bee much.	353	Proverbs		979
He that trusts much Obliges much, says the Spaniard.	357	Proverbs	D	1045

MUCH (cont'd)	PAGE	TITLE		LINE
Either wealth is much increased, or moderation is much decayed.	360	Proverbs	D	1139
Much money makes a Countrey poor,	361	Proverbs	D	1178
and yet I am scarce able with much ado to make one half years	365	Letters		10
to observe so much, as when you meet with a witty French speech,	366	Letters		10
This letter runs to you with much eagernes, for I am enjoined	367	Letters		27
& therfore I am not over much beholding to those busnesses which	367	Letters		30
Sir Charles Howard & his Lady are at much difference, & shee being	368	Letters		20
long in Latin, and my Lincoln journey hath set me much behind hand:	369	Letters		14
neither can I so much as go to Bugden, and deliver your Letter,	369	Letters		15
yet if you cannot send it with much convenience, it is no matter,	369	Letters		28
since this place being civil may divert me too much from Divinity,	370	Letters		20
I knew not, in the midst of much business, and all in a Fortnight,	371	Letters		3
Is it not too much for me?	371	Letters		11
yet my heart, a much better member, is alwayes with you:	371	Letters		27
knows also that my solliciting him has been much, and my tears many	372	Letters		3
my absence by how much it naturally augmenteth suspicion,	372	Letters		21
by so much shall it make my prayers the more constant and the more	372	Letters		21
have so much power or boldness as to oppose the hope of our Joyes	372	Letters		28
which to me that have nothing yett, is very much.	376	Letters		3
Although you have a much better Paymaster then my self,	378	Letters		2
much less can I disesteem it from you, whome I esteem to be God's	378	Letters		13
As I had written thus much, I received a Letter, from My Brother,	378	Letters		30
to get her Son to doe as much) with some little Apology that	379	Letters		3
David built the temple as much as Solomon because he desired it,	381	Woodnoth		19
we have as much failed, as your Excellencies doe excel,	442	Oration		34
MUD				
Lord, who hast form'd me out of mud,	68	Trin.Sun.		1
MUDD				
Because no knowledg, is not earth but mudd.	7	Ch.-Porch	W	36
Lord, who hast made me living mudd,	68	Trin.Sun.	W	1
Lord, who hast rais'd me from the mudd	68	Trin.Sun.	WC	1
MUDDE				
Raise not the mudde	145	Discharge		27
MULE				
That the whole world did seem but the Popes mule.	196	Ch.-Milit.		204
MULTIPLIED				
And multiplied;	42	Easter		16
MULTIPLY				
to multiply, and build up this knowledge to a spirituall Temple;	255	Priest 21		4
MURDER				
Of murder?	41	Sepulchre		12
alwayes cleer, and evident, as Adultery, Murder, Hatred, Lying, &c.	264	Priest 26		7
MURDERER				
They choose a murderer, and all agree	30	Sacrifice		113
And a seditious murderer he was:	30	Sacrifice		117
For choosing Barabbas a murderer	170	Self-cond.		2
The world an ancient murderer is;	170	Self-cond.		10
MURDERERS				
Of theeves and murderers: there I him espied,	40	Redemption		13
MURMUR				
though justly, they will murmur, and repine as much, as he that is	244	Priest 12		29
MURMURINGS				
Alas! our murmurings come not last.	128	Bunch Gr.		18
MUSE				
I muse, which shows more love,	64	Even-song		25
Sharpen their Muse:	116	Dulnesse		20
But not of speech in starres, began to muse:	139	Artillerie		10
MUSES				
by which Scholars say, the Muses use to take up their habitations.	363	Letters		5
title to your Excellencies, all the Muses and Graces congratulate;	442	Oration		1
MUSICIANS				
in the house of those that are skill'd in Musick, all are Musicians;	240	Priest 10		31
MUSICK				
'Tis angels musick; therefore come not late.	22	Ch.-Porch		388
My musick shall finde thee, and ev'ry string	36	Thanksgvng		39
Or since all musick is but three parts vied	42	Easter		15
To make the musick better.	55	Temper 1		24
Church-musick.	65	Ch.-mus.		T
Till ev'n his beams sing, and my musick shine.	81	Christmas		34
My musick shows ye have your closes,	88	Vertue		11
What mirth and musick mean; what love and wit	89	The Pearl		24
Musick and light attend our head.	91	Man		33
And calls for musick, while his veins do swell,	98	Mortific.		14
That musick summons to the knell,	98	Mortific.		17
Musick to thee doth howl.	105	Conscience		4
The note is sad, yet musick for a king.	107	Sion		24
I heard in Musick you had skill.	110	The Quip		11
Thy skill and art, what musick would it be!	118	Providence		40
I, who had heard of musick in the spheres,	139	Artillerie		9
More skill in musick, and keep better time.	154	Glimpse		7
Whose grief allows him musick and a ryme:	164	Grief		17
Another musick, making live not dead,	174	Aaron		13
My onely musick, striking me ev'n dead;	174	Aaron		18
Dust, alas, no musick feels,	186	Dooms-day		9
And the musick shall be praise.	187	Dooms-day		30
so that as in the house of those that are skill'd in Musick,	240	Priest 10		30
stonecutting, musick, and husbandrie, whereof in this age there is	301	Cornaro		37
I am delighted with their musick and fashion, and I my self also sing	303	Cornaro		6
Great strokes make not sweete musick.	322	Proverbs		26
Musick helps not the tooth-ach.	339	Proverbs		532

	PAGE	TITLE	LINE
MUSICK (cont'd)			
The Apothecaries morter spoiles the Luters musick.	351	Proverbs	925
Hee that lives in hope danceth without musick.	354	Proverbs	1006
MUSICK'S			
There it stands knocking, to thy musicks wrong,	132	The Storm	13
MUSKE			
Looke not for muske in a dogges kennell.	321	Proverbs	23
MUST			
And must return. Accept of them and me,	5	Dedication	3
Short of his canne and bodie; must I finde	8	Ch.-Porch	39
Thy drops of bloud must pay down all his fear:	17	Ch.-Porch	274
Christ purg'd his temple; so must thou thy heart.	23	Ch.-Porch	423
Man stole the fruit, but I must climbe the tree;	33	Sacrifice	202
Bywords, but this by sorrow I must win:	33	Sacrifice	207
Yet, though thou troublest me, I must be meek;	48	Afflict.1	61
In weaknesse must be stout.	48	Afflict.1	62
The church with psalms must shout,	53	Antiphon 1	9
Must bear the longest part.	53	Antiphon 1	12
Must bear the chiefest part.	53	Antiphon 1 V	12
Lord, if thou must needs use thy dart,	56	Temper 2	3
Must purling streams refresh a lovers loves?	56	Jordan 1	8
Must all be vail'd, while he that reades, divines,	56	Jordan 1	9
Then we must needs for that day make a match.	62	Mattens	4
For thou must die.	87	Vertue	4
And thou must die.	87	Vertue	8
And all must die.	88	Vertue	12
How many drammes of spirit there must be	88	The Pearl	18
Thou must go sleep, or dine.	101	Miserie	54
My thoughts must work, but like a noiselesse sphere;	105	Conscience	8
Harmonious peace must rock them all the day:	105	Conscience	9
There lay thy sonne: and must he leave that nest,	107	Home	19
Yet if thou stayest still, why must I stay?	108	Home	31
Away; I must get up and see.	108	Home	34
The beasts say, Eat me: but, if beasts must teach,	117	Providence	21
Nothing escapes them both; all must appeare,	118	Providence	37
Of what strange length must that needs be,	123	Time	25
Peace at the root must dwell.	125	Peace	16
He builds a house, which quickly down must go,	127	Giddinesse	13
Of mine inheritance? Lord, if I must borrow,	128	Bunch Gr.	20
But much more him I must adore,	128	Bunch Gr.	26
It must be he. Your heart was dull, I fear.	130	Love unkn.	56
So must he sip and think	131	Mans medly	22
So he must sip and think	131	Mans medly V	22
Not, but I am (I must say still)	139	Artillerie	21
I must be so, if I am mine.	139	Artillerie	30
We must confesse that nothing is our own.	143	Holdfast	7
Either grief will not come: or if it must,	145	Discharge	51
Must let thee go, return when it doth knock.	154	Glimpse	22
This spacious globe: Angels must have their joy,	158	Praise 3	21
O what pure things, most pure must those things be,	161	Priesthood	29
Since then my grief must be as large,	163	The Search	45
But must they have my brain? must they dispark	176	Forerunners	3
Must dulnesse turn me to a clod?	176	Forerunners	5
My god must have my best, ev'n all I had.	176	Forerunners	18
Needs must work on me.	179	Discipline	28
You must sit down, sayes Love, and taste my meat:	189	Love 3	17
They who rely on them must reckon twice	194	Ch.-Milit. W	160
Yet must there such proportions be assign'd	196	Ch.-Milit.	232
Yet must there such proportion be assign'd	196	Ch.-Milit. W	232
O lett my Soule, whose keyes I must deliver	203	Even-song W	21
His dust who under thee must sleepe	208	H. Danvers D	2
whose aim and labour must be not only to get knowledg, but to subdue	226	Priest 2	9
comparing of place with place must be a singular help for the right	229	Priest 4	8
expounding of our Catechisme must needs be the most usefull forme.	230	Priest 5	14
for if we be here, hee must be here, since we are here by him,	234	Priest 7	29
And this must bee done the oftner, or the seldomer, according as hee	239	Priest 9	3
also in diseases of exinanition (as consumptions) must be broken:	242	Priest 10	32
which the Questionist must have in his mind before any question be	256	Priest 21	32
but when one is asked a question, he must discover what he is.	257	Priest 21	20
cannot inflame or ravish, that must be done by a set, and laboured,	257	Priest 21	24
but the Questions must be propounded loosely and wildely,	259	Priest 22	8
so that men must eat neither to the disturbance of their health,	266	Priest 26	13
none must eat so as to disable themselves from a fit discharging	266	Priest 26	29
Not that all must presently work after dinner;	266	Priest 26	32
(For they rather must not work, especially Students, and those that	266	Priest 26	33
but that they must rise so, as that it is not meate or drinke that	266	Priest 26	35
and which are described in this Book, he must be despised;	268	Priest 28	13
he that wil be respected, must respect;	268	Priest 28	23
and that if they sow and soyle their grounds, they must have corn;	270	Priest 30	27
keep and fodder well their cattel, they must have milk, and Calves;	270	Priest 30	28
given it to the poor, we must not be idle, but labour to get more,	274	Priest 32	33
he must not only be a morning man, but at Committees also;	277	Priest 32	11
morning that hee is at home hee must either ride the Great Horse,	277	Priest 32	15
Husbandman labours for them, so must they fight for, and defend them,	277	Priest 32	19
Which acts of repentance are and must be found in all Gods servants:	279	Priest 33	26
And they must be likewise in all that are his.	280	Priest 34	11
As Creatures, he must needs love them;	283	Priest 34	11
As sinfull, he must much more love them;	283	Priest 34	13
but the despising of Love must needs be without it.	283	Priest 34	25
for we must not do evill, that good may come of it.	287	Priest 37	6
doubtlesse then also mens affections and words must turne,	288	Priest 37	4

MUST (cont'd)	PAGE	TITLE		LINE
which must needs so temper the humours of the bodie, that they could	295	Cornaro		8
live regularly, because they must often endure heats, and colds,	299	Cornaro		13
yet all must [needs] take heed, lest they take a greater quantitie	300	Cornaro		11
The Doctrine of the last passage must be warily understood. . .	308	Valdesso		1
and those that have inspirations must still use Peter, Gods Word:	310	Valdesso		10
A Cake and an ill custome must be broken.	322	Proverbs		27
A caske and an ill custome must both of them be broken. . .	322	Proverbs	V	27
He that will take the bird, must not skare it.	322	Proverbs		42
The goate must browse where she is tyed.	323	Proverbs		56
Hee that goes barefoot, must not plant thornes.	323	Proverbs		82
Who hath no more bread then neede, must not keepe a dog. . .	325	Proverbs		128
A garden must be lookt unto and drest as the body. . . .	325	Proverbs		129
Whose house is of glasse, must not throw stones at another. . .	327	Proverbs		196
Who must account for himselfe and others, must know both. . .	328	Proverbs		209
Hee that strikes with his tongue, must ward with his head. . .	331	Proverbs		313
Hee that strikes with his tongue, must ward with his hand. . .	331	Proverbs	V	313
As the yeere is, your pot must seeth.	332	Proverbs		335
Hee that repaires not a part, at length must all.	333	Proverbs	V	344
Who eates his cock alone must saddle his horse alone. . . .	333	Proverbs		348
Who eates his cake alone must saddle his horse alone. . . .	333	Proverbs	V	348
Hee that will deceive the fox, must rise betimes.	333	Proverbs		351
Hee that would deceive the fox, must rise betimes. . . .	333	Proverbs	V	351
must not say to another; Blow.	333	Proverbs		353
He that will be served must bee patient.	333	Proverbs		354
Hee that would bee well old, must bee old betimes. . . .	334	Proverbs		371
Hee that comes of a hen must scrape.	335	Proverbs		415
Hee that comes after must scrape.	335	Proverbs	V	415
He that hath a head of waxe must not walke in the sunne. . .	335	Proverbs		425
You must strike in measure, ...	340	Proverbs		551
must doe what he doth not.	340	Proverbs	V	559
He that serves, must serve.	347	Proverbs		786
Who will sell the Cow, must say the word.	347	Proverbs		791
You must loose a flie to catch a trout.	348	Proverbs		827
The Wolfe must dye in his owne skinne.	349	Proverbs		849
He that will enter into Paradise, must have a good key. . .	350	Proverbs		895
yet we must have patience.	353	Proverbs		980
Hee that is a master must serve (another).	354	Proverbs		991
Who will make a doore of gold must knock a naile every day. . .	354	Proverbs		1004
If you must flie, flie well.	355	Proverbs		1021
He that is once borne, once must dy.	358	Proverbs	D	1087
He that hath but one eye, must bee afraid to lose it. . . .	358	Proverbs	D	1088
We must recoile a little, to the end we may leap the better.	359	Proverbs	D	1121
We must love, as looking one day to hate.	359	Proverbs	D	1126
perhaps they will say, you are sickly, you must not study too hard;	364	Letters		25
on Fridayes and Saturdayes, I must do so, which yet sometimes I fast.	365	Letters		5
this (which is now, when I must lay the foundation of my whole life).	365	Letters		18
Offices for which I came into the world, and must yet be kept in it;	373	Letters		10
whatsoever befals us we must alwaies, at all times rejoyce in	374	Letters		25
that he would by no meanes do so, urging, that Charity must be free.	379	Letters		8
And necessarily must the felicitie of so great Princes redound also	442	Oration		25
MUSTARD				
his Doctrine, remembring in gardens, his mustard-seed, and lillyes;	261	Priest 23		22
MUSTARD-SEED				
his Doctrine, remembring in gardens, his mustard-seed, and lillyes;	261	Priest 23		22
MUTE				
Parrats may thank us, if they are not mute, ...	91	Man		11
Are brought to Man, while they are lame and mute.	117	Providence		12
For my rough sorrows: cease, be dumbe and mute, ...	164	Grief		14
MUTTER				
Unto the service mutter an assent, ...	117	Providence		15
MUTT'RING				
Peace mutt'ring thoughts, and do not grudge to keep	68	Content		1
And still it runneth mutt'ring up and down	168	a true Hymn		4
MUTTON				
it consisteth most of mutton, beefe, and veal, if he addes any thing	241	Priest 10		17
MUTUALLY				
The lemmons juice and rinde cure mutually.	120	Providence		131
MY				
Lord, my first fruits present themselves to thee;	5	Dedication		1
But, This with my discretion will be brave.	14	Ch.-Porch		190
My childrens right, nor ought he take it: rather	17	Ch.-Porch		279
Till labour come, and make my weaknesse score.	17	Ch.-Porch		288
Of my hard heart	26	The Altar		10
That if I chance to hold my peace, ...	26	The Altar		13
The Princes of my people make a head	26	Sacrifice		5
For thirtie pence he did my death devise, ...	27	Sacrifice		17
Not half so sweet as my sweet sacrifice:	27	Sacrifice		19
Therefore my soul melts, and my hearts deare treasure . . .	27	Sacrifice		21
Drops bloud (the onely beads) my words to measure:	27	Sacrifice		22
Curing all wounds, but mine; all, but my fears:	27	Sacrifice		27
Yet my Disciples sleep: I cannot gain	27	Sacrifice		29
Comforts not me, and doth my doctrine stain:	27	Sacrifice		31
Most true to those, who are my greatest grief:	27	Sacrifice		39
Canst thou finde hell about my lips? and misse	28	Sacrifice		42
All my Disciples flie; fear puts a barre	28	Sacrifice		49
Betwixt my friends and me. They leave the starre, ...	28	Sacrifice		50
Betwixt my friends and me. They leave that starre, ...	28	Sacrifice	W	50
Thus Adam my first breathing rendereth:	28	Sacrifice		71
But yet their friendship is my enmitie:	29	Sacrifice		75
And vying malice with my gentlenesse, ...	29	Sacrifice		86

MY (cont'd)

	PAGE	TITLE		LINE
My silence rather doth augment their crie;	29	Sacrifice		93
My dove doth back into my bosome flie,	29	Sacrifice		94
Putting my life among their sinnes and fears,	30	Sacrifice		106
And therefore wish my bloud on them and theirs:	30	Sacrifice		107
Ah! how they scourge me! yet my tendernesse	30	Sacrifice		125
Windes up my grief to a mysteriousnesse:	30	Sacrifice		127
Who grasp the earth and heaven with my fist,	30	Sacrifice		130
Who by my spittle gave the blinde man eies,	31	Sacrifice		134
Who by my spittle gave that blinde man eies,	31	Sacrifice	W	134
Leaving his blindnesse to my enemies:	31	Sacrifice	W	135
My face they cover, though it be divine.	31	Sacrifice		137
When all my tears were bloud, the while you slept:	31	Sacrifice		150
Which shews my bloud to be the onely way,	31	Sacrifice		158
Then on my head a crown of thorns I wear:	31	Sacrifice		161
Though I my vine planted and watred there:	31	Sacrifice		163
Upon my head: so I remove it all	32	Sacrifice		166
From th' earth unto my brows, and bear the thrall:	32	Sacrifice		167
They strike my head, the rock from whence all store	32	Sacrifice		170
The souldiers also spit upon my Face,	32	Sacrifice	W	181
All spite in one, counting my life their losse,	33	Sacrifice		194
They carrie me to my most bitter crosse:	33	Sacrifice		195
My crosse I bear my self, untill I faint:	33	Sacrifice		197
But, O my God, my God! why leav'st thou me,	33	Sacrifice		213
My God, my God -	33	Sacrifice		215
Shame tears my soul, my bodie many a wound;	33	Sacrifice		217
My soule is full of shame, my flesh of wound:	33	Sacrifice	W	217
Alas! I did so, when I left my crown	34	Sacrifice		222
Alas! I did so, when I lost my crown	34	Sacrifice	W	222
In healing not my self, there doth consist	34	Sacrifice		225
Your safetie in my sicknesse doth subsist:	34	Sacrifice		227
Betwixt two theeves I spend my utmost breath,	34	Sacrifice		229
A king my title is, prefixt on high;	34	Sacrifice		233
Yet by my subjects am condemn'd to die	34	Sacrifice		234
They part my garments, and by lot dispose	34	Sacrifice		241
My coat, the type of love, which once cur'd those	34	Sacrifice		242
For they will pierce my side, I full well know;	34	Sacrifice		246
My wo, mans weal: and now I bow my head.	34	Sacrifice		250
My God, my God, why dost thou part from me?	35	Thanksgvng		9
Shall thy strokes be my stroking? thorns, my flower?	35	Thanksgvng		13
Thy rod, my posie? crosse, my bower?	35	Thanksgvng		14
My bosome friend, if he blaspheme thy name,	35	Thanksgvng		25
But mend my own without delayes.	35	Thanksgvng		31
My musick shall finde thee, and ev'ry string	36	Thanksgvng	W	34
O my deare Saviour, Victorie!	36	Thanksgvng		39
Alas, my God, I know not what.	36	Thanksgvng		48
My sinnes deserve the condemnation.	36	Reprisall		4
And yet thy wounds still my attempts defie,	36	Reprisall		7
Which my God feels as bloud; but I, as wine.	37	The Agonie		18
What I have treasur'd in my memorie!	38	The Sinner		2
Since, if my soul make even with the week,	38	The Sinner		3
The spirit and good extract of my heart	38	The Sinner		10
Yet Lord restore thine image, heare my call:	38	The Sinner		12
And though my hard heart scarce to thee can grone,	38	The Sinner		13
O my chief good,	38	Good Fri.		1
Of my whole life one grief devoure;	39	Good Fri.		14
And be my sunne.	39	Good Fri.		16
My severall sinnes their sorrows get;	39	Good Fri.		18
My heart hath store, write there, where in	39	Good Fri.		23
Awake, my lute, and struggle for thy part	41	Easter		7
Yet though my flours be lost, they say	42	Easter	W	27
And then this day, my life shall date.	42	Easter	W	30
Then shall my fall further the flight in me.	43	East.wings	W	10
My tender age in sorrow did beginne:	43	East.wings		11
For, if I imp my wing on thine,	43	East.wings		19
When backward on my sins I turne mine eyes	43	H. Bapt.1	W	1
And then beyond them all my Baptisme view	43	H. Bapt.1	W	2
So when I view my sinnes, mine eyes remove	43	H. Bapt.1		3
Is in my deare Redeemers pierced side.	44	H. Bapt.1		6
Which then join'd with you still meet in my brest	44	H. Bapt.1	W	8
In you Redemption measures all my time,	44	H. Bapt.1		10
You taught the book of life my name, that so	44	H. Bapt.1		12
Is all the passage, on my infancie	44	H. Bapt.2		3
My faith in me.	44	H. Bapt.2		5
Small to my self, to others milde,	44	H. Bapt.2		9
My flesh get on; yet let her sister	44	H. Bapt.2		12
My soul bid nothing, but preserve her wealth:	44	H. Bapt.2		13
My soul bid nothing, but keep hir first wealth:	44	H. Bapt.2	W	13
O tame my heart;	45	Nature		4
My soul will turn to bubbles straight,	45	Nature		9
My soul will bee all bubble straight,	45	Nature	W	9
O smooth my rugged heart, and there	45	Nature		13
To hide my dust, then thee to hold.	45	Nature		18
When first thou didst entice to thee my heart,	46	Afflict.1		1
So many joyes I writ down for my part,	46	Afflict.1		3
Out of my stock of naturall delights,	46	Afflict.1		5
Payd me my wages in a world of mirth.	46	Afflict.1		12
Where joyes my fellows were?	46	Afflict.1		14
Thus argu'd into hopes, my thoughts reserved	46	Afflict.1		15
Therefore my sudden soul caught at the place,	46	Afflict.1		17
I had my wish and way:	47	Afflict.1		20

MY (cont'd)

MY (cont'd)

	PAGE	TITLE		LINE
That zele and purenes circling my request	66	Ch.-lock	W	11
Purge all my sinnes done heretofore:	68	Trin.Sun.		4
For I confesse my heavie score,	68	Trin.Sun.		5
Enrich my heart, mouth, hands in me,	68	Trin.Sun.		7
My God, a verse is not a crown,	69	Quidditie		1
With my great stable or demain:	70	Quidditie	W	8
Lord, in my silence how do I despise	71	Frailtie		1
In all, I think my foot doth ever tread	71	Frailtie		7
And ever as I walk my foot doth tredd	71	Frailtie	W	7
My foot did tread,	71	Frailtie		18
My poore soul, ev'n sick of love:	72	Frailtie		21
My heart did heave, and there came forth, O God!	73	Afflict.3		1
To guide and govern it to my relief,	73	Afflict.3		3
Sure the unruly sigh had broke my heart.	73	Afflict.3		6
Thou knowst my tallies; and when there's assign'd	73	Afflict.3		8
A gale to bring me sooner to my blisse.	73	Afflict.3		12
Where beams surround my Saviours face,	74	The Starre		2
Take a bad lodging in my heart;	74	The Starre		6
Sinne and my heart:	74	The Starre		24
The parter of my wrangling feares,	75	Sunday	W	4
The partner of my wrangling feares,	75	Sunday	WC	4
This day my Saviour rose,	76	Sunday		36
My vows to thee most gladly, blessed Maid,	78	Ang.&Sts.		9
And Mother of my God, in my distresse.	78	Ang.&Sts.		10
Chiefly to thee would I my soul unfold:	78	Ang.&Sts.		15
But now alas I dare not; for my King,	78	Ang.&Sts.	W	16
My soul would stirre	78	Employm.2		2
When my devotions could not pierce	79	Deniall		1
Then was my heart broken, as was my verse:	79	Deniall		3
My breast was full of fears	79	Deniall		4
My bent thoughts, like a brittle bow,	80	Deniall		6
Come, come, my God, O come,	80	Deniall		14
My heart was in my knee,	80	Deniall		19
Therefore my soul lay out of sight,	80	Deniall		21
My feeble spirit, unable to lock right,	80	Deniall		23
O cheer and tune my heartlesse breast,	80	Deniall		26
That so thy favours granting my request,	80	Deniall		28
They and my minde may chime,	80	Deniall		29
They and my hart may chime,	80	Deniall	W	29
They and my soule may chime,	80	Deniall	WC	29
And mend my ryme.	80	Deniall		30
And meet my ryme.	80	Deniall	W	30
My horse and I, both tir'd, bodie and minde,	80	Christmas		2
There when I came, whom found I but my deare,	81	Christmas		5
My dearest Lord, expecting till the grief	81	Christmas		6
Since my dark soul and brutish is thy right,	81	Christmas		11
Furnish & deck my soul, that thou mayst have	81	Christmas		13
my soule to thee, that being drest	80	Christmas	W	13
My God, no hymne for thee?	81	Christmas		16
My soul's a shepherd too; a flock it feeds	81	Christmas		17
Shepherd and flock shall sing, and all my powers	81	Christmas		21
His beams shall cheer my breast, and both so twine,	81	Christmas		33
Till ev'n his beams sing, and my musick shine.	81	Christmas		34
After my sinnes! look not on my desert,	83	Sighs & Gr.		2
Suckt all thy magazens: my head did ake,	83	Sighs & Gr.		10
Should thicken all my powers; because my lust	83	Sighs & Gr.		15
A part whereof my Saviour empti'd hath,	83	Sighs & Gr.		22
Ev'n unto death: since he di'd for my good,	83	Sighs & Gr.		23
Into the bitter box; but O my God,	83	Sighs & Gr.		29
My God, relieve me!	83	Sighs & Gr.		30
My words & thoughts do both expresse this notion,	84	Coloss.		1
Quitting with daily labour all My pleasure,	85	Coloss.		9
Perhaps my God, though he be farre before,	87	Lent		40
May strengthen my decayes.	87	Lent		42
My musick shows ye have your closes,	88	Vertue		11
To sell my life unto my friends or foes:	88	The Pearl		19
My stuffe is flesh, not brasse; my senses live,	89	The Pearl		27
I know all these, and have them in my hand:	89	The Pearl		31
Yet through the labyrinths, not my groveling wit,	89	The Pearl		37
Yet through these labyrinths, not my groveling wit,	89	The Pearl	W	37
My thoughts are all a case of knives,	90	Afflict.4		7
Wounding my heart	90	Afflict.4		8
While they do wound and prick my soul.	90	Afflict.4		12
While they do wound and pinke my soul.	90	Afflict.4	W	12
All my attendants are at strife,	90	Afflict.4		13
Unto my face:	90	Afflict.4		15
Oh help, my God! let not their plot	90	Afflict.4		19
Who art my life: dissolve the knot,	90	Afflict.4		22
Labour thy praise, and my relief;	90	Afflict.4		28
My God, I heard this day,	90	Man		1
Since then, my God, thou hast	92	Man		49
Unto my friends intent and end.	93	Unkindness		4
If any touch my friend, or his good name,	93	Unkindness		6
It is my honour and my love to free	93	Unkindness		7
My friend may spit upon my curious floore:	93	Unkindness		11
When that my friend pretendeth to a place,	94	Unkindness		16
I quit my interest, and leave it free:	94	Unkindness		17
Sues for my heart, I thee displace,	94	Unkindness		19
O write in brasse, My God upon a tree	94	Unkindness		22
Onely to purchase my good-will:	94	Unkindness		24

MY (cont'd)

	PAGE	TITLE		LINE
Yet use I not my foes, as I use thee.	94	Unkindness		25
Here will I smell my remnant out, and tie	94	Life		2
My life within this band.	94	Life		3
And wither'd in my hand.	94	Life		6
My hand was next to them, and then my heart:	94	Life		7
Making my minde to smell my fatall day;	94	Life		11
Since if my sent be good, I care not, if	94	Life		17
But that thou art my wisdome, Lord,	95	Submission		1
My minde would be extreamly stirr'd	95	Submission		3
For missing my designe.	95	Submission		4
And share in my degree.	95	Submission		8
I do resume my sight,	95	Submission		10
Wherefore unto my gift I stand;	95	Submission		17
But when I mark my life and praise,	96	Justice 1		6
My prayers mean thee, yet my prayers stray:	96	Justice 1		9
My soul doth love thee, yet it loves delay.	96	Justice 1		11
I cannot skill of these my wayes.	96	Justice 1		12
My God, I read this day,	97	Afflict.5		1
My God, so temper joy and wo,	97	Afflict.5		23
Is my God this way? no, they would reply:	99	Decay		8
My God, Man cannot praise thy name:	101	Miserie		31
A ring, whose posie was, My pleasure:	102	Miserie		69
My God, I mean my self.	102	Miserie		78
When first my lines of heav'nly joyes made mention,	102	Jordan 2		1
When first my verse of heav'nly joyes made mention,	102	Jordan 2	W	1
My thoughts began to burnish, sprout, and swell,	102	Jordan 2		4
My thoughts began to burnish, spredd, and swell,	102	Jordan 2	W	4
Thousands of notions in my brain did runne,	102	Jordan 2		7
So did I weave my self into the sense.	103	Jordan 2		14
My blessed Lord, art thou! how suddenly	103	Prayer 2		2
Art thou, my blessed King? how suddenly	103	Prayer 2	W	2
If I but lift mine eyes, my suit is made:	103	Prayer 2		5
My God, if writings may	104	Obedience		1
On it my heart doth bleed	104	Obedience		6
And here present it as my speciall deed.	104	Obedience		10
Yet since thou canst not choose but see my actions;	104	Obedience		23
Thou mayst as well my actions guide, as see.	104	Obedience		25
How happie were my part,	105	Obedience		41
My thoughts must work, but like a noiselesse sphere;	105	Conscience		8
My Saviours bloud: when ever at his board	106	Conscience		14
And at my actions carp, or catch.	106	Conscience		18
Besides my physick, know there's some for thee:	106	Conscience		20
The bloudie crosse of my deare Lord	106	Conscience		23
Is both my physick and my sword.	106	Conscience		24
Come Lord, my head doth burn, my heart is sick,	107	Home		1
My spirit gaspeth night and day.	107	Home		4
He did, he came: O my Redeemer deare,	108	Home		25
My God, what is this world to me?	108	Home		32
That my free soul may use her wing,	109	Home		62
My thoughts and joyes are all packt up and gone,	109	Home		69
My flesh and bones and joynts do pray:	109	Home		74
And ev'n my verse, when by the ryme and reason	109	Home		75
JESU is in my heart, his sacred name	112	JESU		1
That to my broken heart he was I ease you,	112	JESU		9
And to my whole is JESU.	112	JESU		10
Sweetest Saviour, if my soul	114	Dialogue		1
But when all my care and pains	114	Dialogue		5
Finger not my treasure.	114	Dialogue		12
Is beyond my savour.	115	Dialogue		20
And my clay my creature would	115	Dialogue		27
Follow my resigning.	115	Dialogue		28
With my glorie and desert,	115	Dialogue		30
Ah! no more: thou break'st my heart.	115	Dialogue		32
Thou art my lovelinesse, my life, my light,	115	Dulnesse		9
Where are my lines then? my approaches? views?	116	Dulnesse		17
Where are my window-songs?	116	Dulnesse		18
To spend my judgement), said, It seem'd to me	116	Love-joy		5
And not of thee, through whom my fingers bend	116	Providence		3
To hold my quill? shall they not do thee right?	116	Providence		4
For me and all my fellows praise to thee:	117	Providence		26
Rain, do not hurt my flowers; but gently spend	120	Providence		117
In all my other hymnes, but in this twice.	121	Providence		148
Sorrie I am, my God, sorrie I am,	122	Sinnes rd.		1
That my offences course it in a ring.	122	Sinnes rd.		2
My thoughts are working like a busie flame,	122	Sinnes rd.		3
My words take fire from my inflamed thoughts.	122	Sinnes rd.		6
My words take fire from my inflamed thoughts.	122	Sinnes rd.		7
My hands do joyn to finish the inventions.	122	Sinnes rd.		12
My hands do joyn to finish the inventions:	122	Sinnes rd.		13
And so my sinnes ascend three stories high,	122	Sinnes rd.		14
New thoughts of sinning: wherefore, to my shame,	122	Sinnes rd.		17
Sorrie I am, my God, sorrie I am.	122	Sinnes rd.		18
Take of this grain, which in my garden grows,	125	Peace		37
Is this same grief! within my heart I made	126	Confession		2
And like a master in my trade,	126	Confession		4
Wherefore my faults and sinnes,	126	Confession		25
They shall be thick and cloudie to my breast.	126	Confession		30
One aire of thoughts usurps my brain.	128	Bunch Gr.		5
Ev'n God himself, being pressed for my sake.	128	Bunch Gr.		28
And in my faintings I presume your love	129	Love unkn.		2

MY (cont'd)

	PAGE	TITLE	LINE
And in the middle plac'd my heart. But he	129	Love unkn.	7
Then I my self. The servant instantly	129	Love unkn.	11
Quitting the fruit, seiz'd on my heart alone,	129	Love unkn.	12
Many a fault more then my lease will bear;	129	Love unkn.	20
But you shall heare. After my heart was well,	129	Love unkn.	22
Walkt by my self abroad, I saw a large	129	Love unkn.	25
To fetch a sacrifice out of my fold,	129	Love unkn.	30
But as my heart did tender it, the man	129	Love unkn.	33
And threw my heart into the scalding pan;	130	Love unkn.	35
My heart, that brought it (do you understand?)	130	Love unkn.	36
A friend did steal into my cup for good,	130	Love unkn.	43
Unto my house, where to repair the strength	130	Love unkn.	47
Which I had lost, I hasted to my bed.	130	Love unkn.	48
I would say thorns. Deare, could my heart not break,	130	Love unkn.	52
When with my pleasures ev'n my rest was gone?	130	Love unkn.	53
Though my lips went, my heart did stay behinde.	130	Love unkn.	59
But all my scores were by another paid,	130	Love unkn.	60
My sighs and tears as busie were above;	132	The Storm	3
Can blast my fruit, or bring me HARM,	133	Paradise	5
I sinne not to my grief alone,	136	Ephes.	17
But to my Gods too; he doth grone.	136	Ephes.	18
Lord, I adjudge my self to tears and grief,	136	Ephes.	25
If my deserts were masters of mine eyes:	136	Ephes.	34
My want of tears with store of bloud.	136	Ephes.	36
What doth this noise of thoughts within my heart	136	Familie	1
As I one ev'ning sat before my cell,	139	Artillerie	1
Me thoughts a starre did shoot into my lap.	139	Artillerie	2
I rose, and shook my clothes, as knowing well,	139	Artillerie	3
But turning to my God, whose ministers	139	Artillerie	11
Dread Lord, said I, so oft my good;	139	Artillerie	13
To wash away my stubborn thought:	139	Artillerie	15
My tears and prayers night and day do wooe,	139	Artillerie	19
Shunne not my arrows, and behold my breast.	139	Artillerie	28
Why doth my Mother blush? is she the rose,	140	Ch.-rents	11
My expectation.	141	Pilgrimage	2
But I was quicken'd by my houre.	142	Pilgrimage	10
Here I was robb'd of all my gold,	142	Pilgrimage	16
Close to my side.	142	Pilgrimage	18
Where lay my hope,	142	Pilgrimage	20
Where lay my heart; and climbing still,	142	Pilgrimage	21
I fell, and cry'd, Alas my King!	142	Pilgrimage	27
My hill was further: so I flung away,	142	Pilgrimage	31
Of my deare God with all my power & might.	143	Holdfast	2
Yet I might trust in God to be my light.	143	Holdfast	4
Then I confesse, that he my succour is:	143	Holdfast	8
Do not beguile my heart,	143	Complaining	1
My power and wisdome. Put me not to shame,	143	Complaining	3
Afflict my houre,	144	Complaining	17
My inch of life: or let thy gracious power	144	Complaining	18
Contract my houre,	144	Complaining	19
My God hath promis'd; he is just.	145	Discharge	55
Thou hast granted my request,	146	Praise 2	5
Thou didst note my working breast,	146	Praise 2	7
Wherefore with my utmost art	146	Praise 2	9
And the cream of all my heart	146	Praise 2	11
Though my sinnes against me cried,	146	Praise 2	13
In my heart, though not in heaven,	146	Praise 2	19
Since my sadnesse	147	Offering	25
And be my salvation.	148	Offering	42
To thee my cries,	148	Longing	3
To thee my grones,	148	Longing	4
To thee my sighs, my tears ascend:	148	Longing	5
My throat, my soul is hoarse;	148	Longing	7
My heart is wither'd like a ground	148	Longing	8
My thoughts turn round,	148	Longing	10
Lord of my soul, love of my minde,	149	Longing	20
Scatter my words, and in the same	149	Longing	23
Look on my sorrows round!	149	Longing	25
Mark well my furnace! O what flames,	149	Longing	26
And in thy boscme poure my tears,	150	Longing	71
Lord JESU, heare my heart,	150	Longing	73
My love, my sweetnesse, heare!	150	Longing	79
By these thy feet, at which my heart	150	Longing	80
And heal my troubled breast which cryes,	150	Longing	83
Away despair; my gracious Lord doth heare.	151	The Bag	1
Though windes and waves assault my keel,	151	The Bag	2
Hast thou not heard, that my Lord JESUS di'd?	151	The Bag	7
Unto my fathers hands and sight	152	The Bag	33
Look, you may put it very neare my heart.	152	The Bag	36
Or if hereafter any of my friends	152	The Bag	37
Oh that my prayers! mine, alas!	152	The Jews	7
My lines and life are free; free as the rode,	153	The Collar	4
Before my sighs did drie it: there was corn	153	The Collar	11
Before my tears did drown it.	153	The Collar	12
Not so, my heart: but there is fruit,	153	The Collar	17
And I reply'd, My Lord.	154	The Collar	36
But one half houre of comfort for my heart?	154	Glimpse	5
But one half houre of comfort to my heart?	154	Glimpse V	5
In hope of thee my heart	154	Glimpse	16
When as my fears foretold this, did replie,	154	Glimpse	19

MY (cont'd)

	PAGE	TITLE	LINE
Betwixt my God and me; that I allow	155	Assurance	9
But I will tc my Father,	155	Assurance	19
Were from my self, I had nct half a word,	155	Assurance	22
What is objected by my foes.	155	Assurance	24
But thou art my desert:	156	Assurance	25
And in this league, which now my foes invade,	156	Assurance	26
And hold my hand, while I did write.	156	Assurance	30
Then shalt thou be my rock and tower,	156	Assurance	35
Come, my Way, my Truth, my Life:	156	The Call	1
Come, my Light, my Feast, my Strength:	156	The Call	5
Come, my Joy, my Love, my Heart:	156	The Call	9
My busie heart shall spin it all my dayes:	157	Praise 3	3
Thou heardst my call, and more.	158	Praise 3	24
Wherefore I sing. Yet since my heart,	159	Praise 3	37
Both all my praise, and more!	159	Praise 3	42
Among my many had his full career,	159	Jos.coat	6
Sure it would carrie with it ev'n my heart,	159	Jos.coat	7
My joyes to weep, and now my griefs to sing.	159	Jos.coat	14
Bestow this jewell also on my creature,	160	The Pulley	12
He would adore my gifts in stead of me,	160	The Pulley	13
May tosse him to my breast.	160	The Pulley	20
Fain put thee on, exchanging my lay-sword	160	Priesthood	5
My slender compositions might consume.	160	Priesthood	10
Who bring my God to me!	161	Priesthood	30
Wherefore I dare not, I, put forth my hand	161	Priesthood	31
There will I lie, untill my Maker seek	161	Priesthood	37
Then is my time. The distance of the meek	161	Priesthood	39
My Lord, my Love?	162	The Search	2
My searches are my daily bread;	162	The Search	3
My knees pierce th' earth, mine eies the skie;	162	The Search	5
Wing'd like an arrow: but my scout	162	The Search	19
Where is my God? what hidden place	163	The Search	29
Since then my grief must be as large,	163	The Search	45
Thy distance from me; see my charge,	163	The Search	47
Lord, see my case.	163	The Search	48
Dwell in my head & eyes: come clouds, & rain:	164	Grief	2
My grief hath need of all the watry things,	164	Grief	3
My weary weeping eyes too drie for me,	164	Grief	6
To bear them out, and with my state agree.	164	Grief	8
A narrow cupboard for my griefs and doubts,	164	Grief	11
For my rough sorrows: cease, be dumbe and mute,	164	Grief	14
Alas, my God!	164	Grief	19
But all my wealth, and familie might combine	164	The Crosse	5
My power to serve thee; to unbend	164	The Crosse	10
All my abilities, my designes confound,	164	The Crosse	11
And lay my threatnings bleeding on the ground.	164	The Crosse	12
One ague dwelleth in my bones,	165	The Crosse	13
Another in my soul (the memorie	165	The Crosse	14
What I would do for thee, if once my grones	165	The Crosse	15
Besides, things sort not to my will,	165	The Crosse	19
Ev'n when my will doth studie thy renown:	165	The Crosse	20
So that, ev'n when my hopes seem to be sped,	165	The Crosse	23
To have my aim, and yet to be	165	The Crosse	25
Farther from it then when I bent my bow;	165	The Crosse	26
Further frcm it then when I bent my bow;	165	The Crosse V	26
To make my hopes my torture, and the fee	165	The Crosse	27
Of all my woes another wo,	165	The Crosse	28
Ah my deare Father, ease my smart!	165	The Crosse	31
Doe winde a rope about, and cut my heart:	165	The Crosse	33
With but foure words, my wcrds, Thy will be done.	165	The Crosse	36
Who would have thought my shrivel'd heart	166	The Flower	8
Nor doth my flower	166	The Flower	26
My sinnes and I joining together:	166	The Flower	28
And relish versing: O my onely light,	166	The Flower	39
My joy, my life, my crown!	168	a true Hymn	1
My heart was meaning all the day,	168	a true Hymn	2
With onely this, My joy, my life, my crown.	168	a true Hymn	5
My comforts drop and melt away like snow:	169	The Answer	1
I shake my head, and all the thoughts and ends,	169	The Answer	2
Which my fierce youth did bandie, fall and flow	169	The Answer	3
But in my prosecutions slack and small;	169	The Answer	7
Ah my deare angrie Lord,	171	Bittersweet	1
And all my sowre-sweet dayes	171	Bittersweet	7
Bedew, embalme, and overrunne my heart,	171	The Glance	7
My soul hath felt, ev'n able to destroy,	172	The Glance	10
Sprung from thine eye, did work within my soul,	172	The Glance	14
The God of love my shepherd is,	172	23 Psalme	1
And bring my minde in frame:	172	23 Psalme	10
And all this not for my desert,	172	23 Psalme	11
Ev'n in my enemies sight:	173	23 Psalme	18
My head with oyl, my cup with wine	173	23 Psalme	19
Shall measure all my dayes;	173	23 Psalme	22
So neither shall my praise.	173	23 Psalme	24
Profanenesse in my head,	174	Aaron	6
Defects and darknesse in my breast,	174	Aaron	7
Christ is my onely head,	174	Aaron	16
My alone onely heart and breast,	174	Aaron	17
My onely musick, striking me ev'n dead;	174	Aaron	18
So holy in my head,	174	Aaron	21
Perfect and light in my deare breast,	174	Aaron	22

MY (cont'd)

	PAGE	TITLE		LINE
My doctrine tun'd by Christ, (who is not dead,	174	Aaron		23
How sweetly doth My Master sound! My Master!	174	The Odour		1
An orientall fragrancie, My Master.	174	The Odour		5
With these all day I do perfume my minde,	175	The Odour		6
My minde ev'n thrust into them both:	175	The Odour		7
This broth of smells, that feeds and fats my minde.	175	The Odour		10
My Master, shall I speak? O that to thee	175	The Odour		11
My servant were a little so,	175	The Odour		12
For pardon of my imperfection	175	The Odour		19
For when My Master, which alone is sweet,	175	The Odour		21
And ev'n in my unworthinesse pleasing,	175	The Odour		22
My servant, as thee not displeasing,	175	The Odour		24
Should all my life employ, and busie me.	175	The Odour		30
White is their colour, and behold my head.	176	Forerunners		2
But must they have my brain? must they dispark	176	Forerunners		3
Yet have they left me, Thou art still my God.	176	Forerunners		6
Good men ye be, to leave me my best room,	176	Forerunners		7
Ev'n all my heart, and what is lodged there:	176	Forerunners		8
So Thou art still my God, be out of fear.	176	Forerunners		10
Then did I wash you with my tears, and more,	176	Forerunners		16
My god must have my best, ev'n all I had.	176	Forerunners		18
For, Thou art still my God, is all that ye	177	Forerunners		32
Then my strict, yet welcome size.	177	The Rose		4
Who have pass'd my right away.	177	The Rose		12
And therein my answer lies.	177	The Rose		16
For my answer is a rose.	178	The Rose		32
O my God,	178	Discipline		3
For my hearts desire	178	Discipline		5
In my sight,	180	Invitation		35
Fills my soul,	181	Banquet		8
And with it perfumes my heart.	181	Banquet		24
When I had forgot my birth,	182	Banquet		31
Sweetly he doth meet my taste.	182	Banquet		39
Be my dittie,	182	Banquet		50
And take up my lines and life:	182	Banquet		51
Of all thy mercies, is my posie still.	182	The Posie		4
This on my ring,	183	The Posie		5
This by my picture, in my book I write:	183	The Posie		6
Or say, or dictate, this is my delight.	183	The Posie		8
Of all Gods mercies, is my posie still.	183	The Posie		12
And in my powers not stirre abroad,	183	A Parodie		9
But leave me to my load:	183	A Parodie		10
Teach me, my God and King,	184	The Elixer		1
I give to thee, who knowest all my wayes,	185	A Wreath		3
My crooked winding wayes, wherein I live,	185	A Wreath		4
There thou shalt finde my faults are thine.	188	Judgement		15
Love bade me welcome: yet my soul drew back,	188	Love 3		1
From my first entrance in,	188	Love 3		4
I the unkinde, ungratefull? Ah my deare,	189	Love 3		9
Love took my hand, and smiling did reply,	189	Love 3		11
Truth Lord, but I have marr'd them: let my shame	189	Love 3		13
My deare, then I will serve.	189	Love 3		16
You must sit down, sayes Love, and taste my meat:	189	Love 3		17
My God, thou dost prepare for them a way	197	Ch.-Milit.		249
Bee there, to thy truth, & my gaine	200	H. Commun.	W	11
But that which made my soule to dye	201	H. Commun.	W	28
My flesh, & fleshly villany,	201	H. Commun.	W	29
Into my soule this cannot pass	201	H. Commun.	W	37
My God, give mee all Thee.	201	H. Commun.	W	48
Something that may be conquest on my part	201	love	W	5
And shrodely, as I think, Lord wash my soule	202	love	W	8
More spotted then my flesh can bee.	202	love	W	9
But then there comes into my way	202	love	W	10
Great waves of trouble combating my brest:	202	love	W	14
Into my hart with joye, giving more rest	202	love	W	17
Lord make my Losses up, & sett mee free:	203	Even-song	W	5
Fouling her nest, my earth invade,	203	Even-song	W	11
But that my darknes may touch thine:	203	Even-song	W	18
O lett my Soule, whose keyes I must deliver	203	Even-song	W	21
O help my God!	204	The Knell	W	9
My God, the poore expressions of my Love	204	Persever.	W	1
But what shall issue, whither these my words	204	Persever.	W	5
Shal help another, but my judgment bee;	204	Persever.	W	6
And wedd my soule in glorious paradise;	205	Persever.	W	10
Whither my many crymes and use of sinn	205	Persever.	W	11
Onely my soule hangs on thy promisses	205	Persever.	W	13
Thou art my rock, thou art my rest.	205	Persever.	W	16
My God, where is that ancient heat towards thee,	206	Walton 1		1
To my Successor.	207	Walton 3		T
And then, my Labour's not lost.	207	Walton 3		6
To my Successor.	207	Walton 4		T
My labour is not lost.	207	Walton 4		4
When my dear Friend, could write no more,	439	walton 6		1
This Anchor keeps my faith, that, me secure.	439	walton 6		4
My Lord. A diamond to mee you sent,	209	L. Bacon	D	1
Hath soild with Black) the colour of my state,	209	L. Bacon	D	7
Till your bright gift my darknesse did abate.	209	L. Bacon	D	8
But that my Inke was factious for this side.	209	L. Bacon	D	12
Let now my Eyes, my Voice, my Heart,	213	Convert	D	4
My Eyes, from whence these Tears did spring,	214	Convert	D	6

MY (cont'd)

	PAGE	TITLE		LINE
A Deluge on my sensual Flame,	214	Convert	D	9
And wash away my Shame.	214	Convert	D	10
My Voice, that oft with foolish Lays,	214	Convert	D	11
My Heart, that gave fond Thoughts their Food,	214	Convert	D	16
He said to me, Thou art my Son,	216	Psalm II	D	17
How are my foes increased, Lord?	216	Psalm III	D	1
Against me, saying, For my soul	216	Psalm III	D	3
of my deliverance:	216	Psalm III	D	6
Thou art my glory, Lord, and he	216	Psalm III	D	7
that doth my head advance.	216	Psalm III	D	8
save me, my God, from thrall:	217	Psalm III	D	18
Lord of my righteousness:	217	Psalm IV	D	2
my glory into shame?	217	Psalm IV	D	8
and take my restful sleep:	218	Psalm IV	D	30
Lord to my words encline thine ear,	218	Psalm V	D	1
my meditation weigh:	218	Psalm V	D	2
My King, my God, vouchsafe to hear	218	Psalm V	D	3
my cry to thee, I pray.	218	Psalm V	D	4
Thou in the morn shalt have my mone,	218	Psalm V	D	5
Direct my prayers to thy Throne,	218	Psalm V	D	7
because of all my foes:	219	Psalm V	D	22
And to my dym and sinful eyes	219	Psalm V	D	23
O heal me, for my bones are vex'd,	220	Psalm VI	D	5
my Soul is troubled very sore;	220	Psalm VI	D	6
my Soul for thy great mercy save;	220	Psalm VI	D	10
all night I make my Couch to swim;	220	Psalm VI	D	14
And water with salt tears my Bed,	220	Psalm VI	D	15
my sight with sorrow waxeth dim.	220	Psalm VI	D	16
My beauty wears and doth decay	220	Psalm VI	D	17
For God himself hath heard my cry;	220	Psalm VI	D	21
the Lord vouchsafes to weigh my tears;	220	Psalm VI	D	22
Yea, he my prayer from on high	220	Psalm VI	D	23
And now my foes the Lord will blame	220	Psalm VI	D	25
Save me, my Lord, my God, because	220	Psalm VII	D	1
I put my trust in Thee:	220	Psalm VII	D	2
From all that persecute my life,	220	Psalm VII	D	3
he do devour my soul:	221	Psalm VII	D	6
that was my causeless foe:	221	Psalm VII	D	14
Let him pursue and take my soul,	221	Psalm VII	D	17
Tread down my life, and in the dust	221	Psalm VII	D	19
my slaughter'd honour lay.	221	Psalm VII	D	20
against my foes disdain:	221	Psalm VII	D	22
According to my righteousness,	221	Psalm VII	D	31
God is my shield, who doth preserve	222	Psalm VII	D	37
and live, and who giveth mee my Desires and Performances;	224	Priest		2
and considering with my self, That the way to please him,	224	Priest		3
is to feed my Flocke diligently and faithfully, since our Saviour	224	Priest		4
The Lord prosper the intention to my selfe, and others,	224	Priest		13
who may not despise my poor labours, but add to those points,	224	Priest		14
Why dost thou preach my Laws, and takest my Covenant in thy mouth?	226	Priest 2		14
preach my Laws, and takest my Covenant in thy mouth? Psal. 50. 16.	226	Priest 2		14
(which is indeed the bent of my Discourse) the other will be	226	Priest 2		18
as, Oh Lord blesse my people, and teach them this point;	233	Priest 7		34
or, Oh my Master, on whose errand I come, let me hold my peace,	233	Priest 7		34
errand I come, let me hold my peace, and doe thou speak thy selfe;	233	Priest 7		35
if a peece of dry flesh at my table be more unpleasant to me,	242	Priest 10		13
our Saviours rule, and to take my brother aside, and reprove him;	248	Priest 14		27
I am false to my reason which should guide me, I offend the supreme	265	Priest 26		10
is an occasion, my countrey is an occasion, my friend is an occasion,	265	Priest 26		14
is an occasion, my friend is an occasion, my Table is an occasion,	265	Priest 26		14
is an occasion, my Table is an occasion, my apparell is an occasion:	265	Priest 26		15
according as I feele my self, either I take my wonted proportion,	267	Priest 26		8
feele my self, either I take my wonted proportion, or diminish of it.	267	Priest 26		9
and my neerest way ly through the Church, I will not doubt to go	273	Priest 31		33
in my heart) because this kinde of Prayer is additionary,	273	Priest 31		35
pardoning my sins, and bidding me go feed the people of thy love.	289	Priest		6
Awake therefore, my Lute, and my Viol!	289	Priest		9
awake all my powers to glorifie thee!	289	Priest		10
and inable all my powers, that in their full strength they may	289	Priest		27
Having observed in my time many of my friends, of excellent wit	291	Cornaro		1
they had a great desire to know the way of my life, and how I came	291	Cornaro		12
and my ill constitution, (having a most cold & moist stomack) I fell	291	Cornaro		20
whereas my life seemed as farre from it by Nature, as it was neare it	291	Cornaro		26
[afflicted] from the thirtie fifth yeare of my age to the fortieth,	292	Cornaro		2
weighing their reasons with my self, and abhorring from so sudden	292	Cornaro		17
and finding my self continually oppressed with pain and sicknesse,	292	Cornaro		18
I grew fully perswaded, that all my griefs arose out of Intemperance:	292	Cornaro		20
followed my Appetite, and did eat meats pleasing to my taste;	292	Cornaro		27
followed my Appetite, and did eat meats pleasing to my taste;	292	Cornaro		28
telling my Physicians nothing thereof, as is the custome of sick	292	Cornaro		29
I so addicted my self to this course of life, that I never went	292	Cornaro		33
seem to some incredible) I was perfectly cured of all my infirmities.	292	Cornaro		38
to consider the force of Temperance, and to think thus with my self:	293	Cornaro		2
whether those that pleased my taste brought me commoditie	293	Cornaro		7
for strong and very cool wines pleased my taste best, as also melons,	293	Cornaro		11
and chose that wine that fitted my stomack, and in such measure,	293	Cornaro		16
whereinto I was wont, when I pleased my Sense & Appetite.	293	Cornaro		23
I never since departed from my setled course of Sobrietie,	293	Cornaro		26
For when my brother and others of my kindred saw some great powerfull	294	Cornaro		15
For when my brother and others of my kindred saw some great powerfull	294	Cornaro		16

MY (cont'd)

	PAGE	TITLE	LINE
I began to perswade my self, that this suit and contention was raised	294	Cornaro	23
the end I got the victorie, to my great honour, and no lesse profit:	294	Cornaro	28
whereby my head and whole bodie was sore hurt, and also one of my	294	Cornaro	39
was sore hurt, and also one of my arms and legges put out of joynt.	294	Cornaro	39
and onely commanded that my arm and legge should be set,	295	Cornaro	11
my arm and legge should be set, and my whole bodie anointed with oyl:	295	Cornaro	11
But my experience taught me another thing also, to wit,	295	Cornaro	16
and the dayly importunitie of my friends, to adde something to my	295	Cornaro	20
of my friends, to adde something to my usuall stint and measure.	295	Cornaro	21
to reason, that my yeares increasing, and strength decreasing,	295	Cornaro	29
my stint of meat and drink should be diminished, rather then	295	Cornaro	30
and especially since the power of my stomack every day decreased.	295	Cornaro	32
to avoid obstinacie, and gratifie my friends, at length I yeelded,	296	Cornaro	6
For whereas before the measure of my whole dayes meat, viz.	296	Cornaro	9
of my bread, and egges, and flesh, and broth, was twelve ounces	296	Cornaro	9
and the measure of my drink, which before was foureteen ounces,	296	Cornaro	12
I by the grace of God cured my self, onely with returning to my	296	Cornaro	24
onely with returning to my former course of Diet, although I was now	296	Cornaro	25
and my bodie spent with extream leannesse, and the season	296	Cornaro	26
For there is no malignitie of old age in the humours of my bodie,	296	Cornaro	37
which I contracted by breaking my diet, although it was a sore evil,	297	Cornaro	1
Who would beleeve that old wine should hurt my stomack,	297	Cornaro	32
For I eat little, because a little sufficeth my weak stomack:	300	Cornaro	8
as I will shew by my self, recounting the delights and pleasures in	300	Cornaro	30
joy and peace have taken up their standing in my heart.	301	Cornaro	2
I give my self to the reading of some learned book, and afterwards	301	Cornaro	6
making it my aim in all things, how I may help others to the furthest	301	Cornaro	7
aim in all things, how I may help others to the furthest of my power.	301	Cornaro	8
All these things I do at my ease, and at fit seasons, and in mine own	301	Cornaro	9
I enjoy also my gardens, and those divers, parted with rills	301	Cornaro	15
that I may enjoy the sight & communication of my friends,	301	Cornaro	35
and ever I learn somewhat which is worthy of my knowledge:	302	Cornaro	3
I am much pleased also in my travells, with the beauty of situation.	302	Cornaro	6
Neither is this my pleasure made lesse by the decaying dulnesse of my	302	Cornaro	7
is this my pleasure made lesse by the decaying dulnesse of my senses,	302	Cornaro	8
which are all in their perfect vigour, but especially my Taste;	302	Cornaro	9
To change my bed, troubles me not;	302	Cornaro	12
well and quietly any where, and my dreams are fair and pleasant.	302	Cornaro	13
that my advice hath taken effect in the reducing of many rude	302	Cornaro	14
in the reducing of many rude and untoiled places in my countrey,	302	Cornaro	15
These are the delights and solaces of my old age, which is altogether	302	Cornaro	22
or lesse my self, who being ten yeares older have made a Comedie?	302	Cornaro	35
Now lest there should be any delight wanting to my old age,	302	Cornaro	37
behold a kinde of immortalitie in the succession of my posteritie.	303	Cornaro	2
with their musick and fashion, and I my self also sing often;	303	Cornaro	6
because I have now a clearer voice, then ever I had in my life.	303	Cornaro	8
if I had my wish, would I change age and constitution with them who	303	Cornaro	11
Yet I am sure, that my end is farre from me:	303	Cornaro	25
because that by the regularitie of my life I have shut out death all	303	Cornaro	27
My deare and deserving Brother, your Valdesso I now returne with many	304	Valdesso	1
discover some care, which I forbare not in the midst of my griefes;	304	Valdesso	4
I like not in him, as my fragments will expresse, when you read them;	304	Valdesso	16
Print it, that with it the honour of my Lord might be published.	305	Valdesso	8
for I can no more free my selfe from actuall sinnes after Baptisme,	308	Valdesso	3
as to relieve my Neighbour, God hath already reveled his Will about	313	Valdesso	13
At dinner my man appeares.	322	Proverbs	37
When prayers are done, my Lady is ready.	323	Proverbs	71
I gave the mouse a hole, and she is become my heire.	324	Proverbs	94
I had rather aske of my sire browne bread,	330	Proverbs	269
then borrow of my neighbour white.	330	Proverbs	269
Your pot broken seemes better then my whole one.	330	Proverbs	270
My house, my house, though thou art small,	335	Proverbs	413
Faire words make mee looke to my purse.	339	Proverbs	548
When my house burnes, it's not good playing at Chesse.	343	Proverbs	666
Speake not of my debts, unlesse you meane to pay them.	354	Proverbs	998
The War is not don so long as my Enemy lives.	357	Proverbs	D 1051
but my next neighbour doth me more harm	361	Proverbs	D 1173
But I fear the heat of my late Ague hath dryed up those springs,	363	Letters	4
For my own part, my meaning (dear Mother) is in these Sonnets,	363	Letters	9
my meaning (dear Mother) is in these Sonnets, to declare my	363	Letters	10
to declare my resolution to be, that my poor Abilities in Poetry,	363	Letters	11
my resolution to be, that my poor Abilities in Poetry, shall be all,	363	Letters	11
only hereafter I will take heed how I propose my desires unto you,	363	Letters	21
unto you, since I find you so willing to yield to my requests;	363	Letters	22
come a Horse-back, there is reason, that my desires should go a-foot;	363	Letters	23
in some proportion, and after my manner, Your most obedient Servant,	364	Letters	3
I wrong both my self, and also the confidence my Friends have in me;	364	Letters	8
wherefore I will open my case unto you, which I think deserves	364	Letters	9
to lay the platform of my future life, and shall I then be fain	364	Letters	12
Pardon my boldness Sir, it is a most serious Case, nor can I write	364	Letters	15
wherein consisteth the making good of my former education,	364	Letters	17
hath guided me hitherto, and of atchieving my (I dare say) holy ends.	364	Letters	19
in that I apprehend what my Friends would have been forward to say,	364	Letters	20
but that every day, I may step one step towards my journies end;	364	Letters	27
and I love my friends so well, as that if all things proved not well,	364	Letters	28
I am fain ever and anon, to buy somewhat tending towards my health;	364	Letters	34
so that I am fain to dyet in my Chamber at mine own cost;	365	Letters	3
And yet if a Book of four or five Shillings come in my way,	365	Letters	12
pardon my boldness, and consider but these three things.	365	Letters	15
this (which is now, when I must lay the foundation of my whole life).	365	Letters	18

MY (cont'd)

	PAGE	TITLE	LINE
either by engaging my future Annuity, or any other way, . .	365	Letters	21
I desire you, Sir, to be my Mediator to them in my behalf. . .	365	Letters	22
Now I write to you, Sir, because to you I have ever opened my heart;	365	Letters	24
for it hath been my fortune of late to have such sudden warning,	365	Letters	31
But I am out of my time:	366	Letters	19
P.S. My brother is somewhat of the same temper, and perhaps a little	366	Letters	24
To my dear brother, Mr. Henry Herbert, at Paris.	366	Letters	26
I understand by a Letter from my Brother Henry, that he hath bought	366	Letters	29
yet if my Sister were acquainted that they are ready, I dare say she	367	Letters	1
yet I had rather flie to my old ward, that if any course could be	367	Letters	7
that if any course could be taken of doubling my Annuity now,	367	Letters	8
and for ever after cease my clamorous and greedy bookish requests.	367	Letters	11
that they prevent my memory, and yet still grow upon Your humblest	367	Letters	15
I remember my most humble duty to my Mother.	367	Letters	20
I have wrote to my dear sick Sister this week already, and therefore	367	Letters	21
pardon my boldness of inclosing my Brothers Letter in yours,	367	Letters	23
because my recompenses of your favours consist in this only.	367	Letters	31
My Lord of Buckingham was observed on Christmas day to bee so devout	368	Letters	16
of whose rude delivery my hast makes mee ashamed, only my comfort is	369	Letters	2
only my comfort is that this is but an occasion for you to amplify	369	Letters	3
long in Latin, and my Lincoln journey hath set me much behind hand:	369	Letters	14
you and my dear Mother and Sister to pardon me, for my Cambridge	369	Letters	17
for my Cambridge necessities are stronger to tye me here, . .	369	Letters	18
could possibly have come, none should have done my message to Sir Fr:	369	Letters	20
I have sent you here inclosed a Letter from our Master in my behalf,	369	Letters	25
to me as soon as you can, that I may work the heads to my purpose.	370	Letters	7
circumstance, yet you will pardon my haste, which is very great,	370	Letters	12
I cannot yet find leisure to write to my Lord, or Sir Benjamin	370	Letters	29
I remember my most humble duty to my Mother, who cannot think me	371	Letters	1
and now the only thing I long for, is to hear of my dear sick Sister;	371	Letters	7
whether my peace be yet made with her concerning my unkind departure.	371	Letters	8
whether my peace be yet made with her concerning my unkind departure.	371	Letters	9
that I loved her even in my departure, in looking to her Son,	371	Letters	12
loved her even in my departure, in looking to her Son, and my charge.	371	Letters	13
I shall understand that a Letter will be seasonable, my Pen is ready.	371	Letters	15
I have forty businesses in my hands, your Courtesie will pardon	371	Letters	18
For my dear sick Sister.	371	Letters	T
Think not my silence forgetfulness;	371	Letters	25
or, that my love is as dumb as my papers;	371	Letters	25
or, that my love is as dumb as my papers;	371	Letters	26
though businesses may stop my hand, yet my heart, a much better	371	Letters	26
businesses may stop my hand, yet my heart, a much better member,	371	Letters	27
with that earnestness, that becomes your griefs, and my love.	372	Letters	1
knows also that my solliciting him has been much, and my tears many	372	Letters	2
that my solliciting him has been much, and my tears many for you;	372	Letters	3
and not by my ink, and then you shall justly value Your most truly,	372	Letters	4
At my last parting from you, I was the better content because I was	372	Letters	14
because I was in hope I should my self carry all sickness out of your	372	Letters	15
would quickly make good my wish but that my employment does fix me	372	Letters	18
quickly make good my wish but that my employment does fix me here,	372	Letters	19
my absence by how much it naturally augmenteth suspicion, . .	372	Letters	20
by so much shall it make my prayers the more constant and the more	372	Letters	22
and I shou'd account my self most happy if I might change with you;	373	Letters	3
For my self, dear Mother, I alwaies fear'd sickness more then death,	373	Letters	7
Dear Madam, pardon my boldness, and, accept the good meaning of,	374	Letters	31
That you did not only entertain my proposals, but advance them,	375	Letters	2
Yet truly it was none of my meaning, when I wrote, to putt one of our	375	Letters	4
when he urged one upon me, and but one, and that at my choice.	375	Letters	11
Since that I have seen the fruit of my observation, for they have	375	Letters	18
except my cousin Bett take pitty of her, which yet at that distance	375	Letters	29
you take her not, I am thinking to do it, even beyond my strengthe;	375	Letters	35
So I doe my part to them, lett them think of me what they will	376	Letters	6
it were in another's power to defeat my charity, and evill shold be	376	Letters	9
My wife's and neeces' service.	376	Letters	23
To my very dear brother Sir Henry Herbert, at Court. . . .	376	Letters	24
exceedingly with your relation of my Lady Duchess's forwardnes in our	377	Letters	19
offering of yourself to move my Lords of Manchester and Boollingbrook	377	Letters	23
To my deere brother, Sir Henry Herbert, at Court.	377	Letters	31
Although you have a much better Paymaster then my self, . .	378	Letters	2
your care of Leighton, upon my accompt, & give you my self for it,	378	Letters	4
upon my accompt, & give you my self for it, to be yours for ever.	378	Letters	4
And now My gratious Lord God, is pleased to give me you for the Man,	378	Letters	7
you any other wayes, as neyther I my self desire to be considered.	378	Letters	16
a Letter, from My Brother, Sir Henry H: of the blessed Success,	378	Letters	31
that she had done nothing in it (as my Brother writes) hitherto.	379	Letters	4
She referred it also to My Brother, to name at first, what the summe	379	Letters	5
Blessed be My God & Dear Master, the Spring & Fountain of all	379	Letters	16
As for my assistance, doubt not, through Gods blessing, . .	379	Letters	17
& for my power, I have sent my Letters, to your Brother, . .	379	Letters	18
& for my power, I have sent my Letters, to your Brother, . .	379	Letters	19
My wife's and neeces' service to you.	379	Letters	30
I George Herbert commending my soule and body to Almightie God that	382	G.H.'s Will	1
body to Almightie God that made them doe thus dispose of my goods.	382	G.H.'s Will	3
I give all my goods both within doores and without doores both	382	G.H.'s Will	3
and howshould stuffe whether in my possession or out of my possession	382	G.H.'s Will	5
in my possession or out of my possession that properly belonge	382	G.H.'s Will	5
that properly belonge to me unto my deare wife excepting onely these	382	G.H.'s Will	6
which fell to me by the death of my deare Neece Mrs Dorothy Vaughan	382	G.H.'s Will	9
whereof two hundred pounds belongs to my two Neeces that survive	382	G.H.'s Will	11
belongs to my two Neeces that survive and the rest unto my selfe,	382	G.H.'s Will	12

MY (cont'd)	PAGE	TITLE		LINE
hundred pounds I bequeath unto my Neeces equally to be devided	382	G.H.'s Will		13
them excepting some legacies of my deceased Neece which are to be	382	G.H.'s Will		14
of this parish to be devided according to my deare wives discretion.	382	G.H.'s Will		17
then I leave to my servant Elizabeth her dubble wages given her,	382	G.H.'s Will		22
Alsoe my will and pleasure is that Mr Woodnoth should be mine	382	G.H.'s Will		27
side are the names of those to whome my deceased Neece left legacyes.	383	G.H.'s Will		1
poore of the parish twenty pound To my Lord of Cherbury tenn pound,	383	G.H.'s Will		14
MYNE				
But thou wast up before myne houre	42	Easter	W	21
MYSELF				
of those observations which I have framed to myself in conversation;	366	Letters		1
MYSTERIE				
And did this mysterie wrap up and fold	192	Ch.-Milit.		94
MYSTERIOUSNESSE				
Windes up my grief to a mysteriousnesse:	30	Sacrifice		127
MYSTICALL				
The churches mysticall repast.	25	Superlim		4
With flowers and carvings, mysticall and rare:	106	Sion		5
NAIL				
No, not a tooth or nail to scratch, ...	106	Conscience		17
NAILE				
For want of a naile the shoe is lost, ...	338	Proverbs		499
Who will make a doore of gold must knock a naile every day. . .	354	Proverbs		1004
NAIL'D				
Christs hands, though nail'd, wrought our salvation, ...	76	Sunday		48
Though nail'd unto 't, but he ascends again, ...	439	Walton 5		2
When nail'd unto 't, but he ascends again	439	Walton 5	V	2
NAILES				
minde being defixed on it with those nailes wherewith his Master was:	267	Priest 27		29
NAILING				
By nailing Christ to fasten it again.	190	Ch.-Milit.		24
NAILS				
Sharp nails pierce this, but sharper that confound;	33	Sacrifice		218
Thy whips, thy nails, thy wounds, thy woes, ...	39	Good Fri.		26
Some wood and nails to make a staffe or bill	106	Conscience		21
NAKED				
Chase brave emplcyments with a naked sword	10	Ch.-Porch		88
Chase brave employment with a naked sword	10	Ch.-Porch	W	88
And strip the creature naked, till he finde	85	Vanitie 1		16
but not as a naked Word severed from God, but as the Word of God:	306	Valdesso		29
No naked man is sought after to be rifled.	357	Proverbs	D	1063
NAME				
And make us strive, who shall sing best thy name.	5	Dedication		4
Take not his name, who made thy mouth, in vain:	8	Ch.-Porch		55
Play not away the vertue of that name, ...	9	Ch.-Porch		65
Findes his crackt name at length in the church-glasse.	14	Ch.-Porch		198
All forrain of that name; but scorn their ill:	21	Ch.-Porch		362
To praise thy Name:	26	The Altar		12
My bosome friend, if he blaspheme thy name, ...	35	Thanksgvng		25
The crosse taught all wood to resound his name, ...	41	Easter		9
You taught the book of life my name, that so	44	H. Bapt.1		12
My rebel-flesh, and carrying thy name, ...	52	H.Commun.		17
How hath man parcel'd out thy glorious name, ...	54	Love 1		3
Thou standing by: and though thy glorious name	54	Love 1		11
Restore this day, for thy great name, ...	60	Whitsunday		27
Thy name in books, which may not rent:	69	Content		28
Thy name in books, which may not vent:	69	Content	W	28
How well her name an Army doth present, ...	77	Anagram		1
If any touch my friend, or his good name, ...	93	Unkindness		6
Lord, let the Angels praise thy name.	100	Miserie		1
My God, Man cannot praise thy name:	101	Miserie		31
JESU is in my heart, his sacred name	112	JESU		1
Cannot give the name of gains	114	Dialogue		6
Each thing that is, although in use and name	121	Providence		149
Thy name!	149	Longing		24
How neatly doe we give one onely name	168	The Sonne		5
But for his holy name.	172	23 Psalme		12
Breaking her peace, and tainting her good name.	193	Ch.-Milit.		106
And make that name good by their transmigrations;	195	Ch.-Milit.		184
Will not a verse run smooth that bears thy name?	206	walton 1		11
Of th' universe, like as the windes, & name	212	Bohemia	D	44
Let them that do thy name adore	219	Psalm V	D	39
And ever praise the Glorious name	222	Psalm VII	D	63
for this in time will lose the name and effect of Charity . .	244	Priest 12		26
things there be decent, and befitting his Name by which it is called.	246	Priest 13		2
If it once have the honour of that Name, it grows great instantly.	249	Priest 14		3
as being persons enabled by that Name to take moveable goods,	270	Priest 29		2
so may they their good name, and the possession thereof, . .	287	Priest 37		33
concluding every Consideration almost with his holy Name, . .	305	Valdesso		6
An ill wound is cured, not an ill name.	329	Proverbs		245
Take heed of a step-mother; the very name of her sufficeth. . .	360	Proverbs	D	1155
to his brothers house of his own name (as I think) at the sign	370	Letters		27
it also to My Brother, to name at first, what the summe should be,	379	Letters		6
In the name of God.	380	Woodnoth		2
NAMELY				
counsell, namely, in perswading them to particular confession,	249	Priest 15		29
together with many other, as namely Consid. 71. upon Our Father;	307	Valdesso		16
NAMES				
Till thou change names, and be where he began.	21	Ch.-Porch		378
Giving new names and numbers to the yeare.	192	Ch.-Milit.		72

NAMES (cont'd)	PAGE	TITLE	LINE
and because they have different Names, think their Office different.	226	Priest 2	20
Hee admits no vaine or idle names, but such as are usuall	258	Priest 22	4
things is bad, but it is the custome and habit that names a glutton.	266	Priest 26	18
payd out of it unto some whose names shal be annexed unto this bill.	382	G.H.'s Will	15
On the other side are the names of those to whome my deceased Neece	383	G.H.'s Will	1
NAMETH			
he nameth the reading and meditation of holy Scriptures for the first	311	Valdesso V	4
NAMING			
Naming you not to your good:	180	Invitation	9
when it condescends to the naming of a plough, a hatchet,	257	Priest 21	12
NARROW			
A narrow way and little gate	44	H. Bapt.2	2
A narrow cupboard for my griefs and doubts,	164	Grief	11
Take heed of mad folks in a narrow place.	360	Proverbs D	1149
NARROWLY			
or consider it so narrowly, which yet ought to be done,	265	Priest 26	31
Neither can any man denie this, who will narrowly consider it.	297	Cornaro	14
NATHAN			
and oftentimes, as Nathan did, in the person of another,	248	Priest 14	21
NATHANIELL			
George Herbert (testes Nathaniell Bostocke, Elizabeth Burden)	382	G.H.'s Will	34
NATION			
In publick judgements one may be a nation,	147	Offering	11
Poore nation, whose sweet sap, and juice	152	The Jews	1
But did bewitch, and finely work each nation	195	Ch.-Milit.	193
But did bewitch both kings & many a nation	195	Ch.-Milit. W	193
To go to them, while that which now their nation	197	Ch.-Milit.	257
Of Pastors (intending mine own Nation only, and also therein setting	225	Priest 2	20
considering the stubbornnesse of the Nation, their living then in	282	Priest 34	8
You live in a brave nation, where, except you wink, you cannot	366	Letters	6
both the Spanish and Brittish Nation serve and worship James.	442	Oration	18
NATIONALL			
The great and nationall sin of this Land he esteems to be Idlenesse;	274	Priest 32	8
NATIONS			
Let forrain nations of their language boast,	167	The Sonne	1
Among the eastern nations for a time,	191	Ch.-Milit.	35
Cheat the most subtill nations. Who so coy,	194	Ch.-Milit.	150
Yet that he might the better gain all nations,	195	Ch.-Milit.	183
is the key of Commerce, and discovers the Rules of forraine Nations.	277	Priest 32	33
To these might be added the Preaching of the Gospel in all Nations,	282	Priest 34	32
NATIVE			
Thy Gentrie bleats, as if thy native cloth	10	Ch.-Porch	93
Keep all thy native good, and naturalize	21	Ch.-Porch	361
Trees would be tuning on their native lute	117	Providence	10
Let follie speak in her own native tongue.	177	Forerunners	27
Whose native beauty needs not dresse or lace	212	Bohemia D	30
NATIVITIES			
then by stars at their nativities.	357	Proverbs D	1060
NATURALIZE			
Keep all thy native good, and naturalize	21	Ch.-Porch	361
NATURALL			
Out of my stock of naturall delights,	46	Afflict.1	5
it being naturall to men to think, that where is much earnestness,	232	Priest 7	32
This he thinks naturall, and sweet, and grave.	235	Priest 7	5
unpleasant, is the naturall rule of fasting, although it be flesh.	242	Priest 10	11
But evident miseries have a naturall priviledge, and exemption from	245	Priest 12	29
have to think that all things come by a kind of naturall course;	270	Priest 30	26
is a naturall Physick most agreeable to us, and also doth preserve	298	Cornaro	13
Where he sayes the Inflammation of the naturall, he sayes aptly,	308	Valdesso	14
the naturall concupiscence is not quite extinguished, but the heate	308	Valdesso	16
as well as naturall bodies.	361	Proverbs D	1166
NATURALLY			
and not the fish, is to keep the fasting day naturally.	242	Priest 10	15
For there he shall find his flock most naturally as they are,	247	Priest 14	6
my absence by how much it naturally augmenteth suspicion,	372	Letters	21
so in things naturally visible & apparent, as the course of our life	380	Woodnoth	17
NATURE			
What nature made a ship, he makes a shelf.	11	Ch.-Porch	120
Nature.	45	Nature	T
My nature on him, with the danger	50	Faith W	24
While grace fills up uneven nature.	50	Faith	32
What reason hath from nature borrowed,	88	The Pearl	3
What reason hath from nature purchased,	88	The Pearl W	3
What willing nature speaks, what forc'd by fire;	88	The Pearl	6
Nature denies;	136	Ephes.	32
And rest in Nature, not the God of Nature:	160	The Pulley	14
That nature hath produc'd. Let ev'ry vein	164	Grief	4
Nature & Grace	202	Trin.Sun. W	5
the Apostles two great and admirable Rules in things of this nature:	246	Priest 13	26
whither the nature of man, loving refreshment, gladly betakes it	252	Priest 18	22
Is this the nature of beliefe?	256	Priest 21	10
not hold in Christianity, because it contains things above nature:	256	Priest 21	25
that which nature is towards Philosophy, the Catechism is towards	256	Priest 21	26
As in cases of an obscure and dark nature, not easily determinable	260	Priest 23	20
Nature serving Grace both in comfort of diversion, and the benefit	261	Priest 23	11
to know what herbs may be used in stead of drugs of the same nature,	261	Priest 23	30
as knowing that nature will not bear everlasting droopings,	267	Priest 27	34
The reason of this assertion is taken from the nature of man,	274	Priest 32	19
having for his owne use examined the nature of it, is able	279	Priest 33	8
the first taken from Nature, the second from the Law, the third from	281	Priest 34	16

NEEDES (cont'd)	PAGE	TITLE	LINE
Who hath no head, needes no heart.	354	Proverbs V	996
NEEDETH			
in substance, yet needeth [requireth] discreet, and wary explaining.	314	Valdesso	1
NEEDING			
To cold complexions needing it.	78	Employm.2	5
Thy teares not needing. For that hand Divine	213	Bohemia D	63
The Church needing both an evidence, and an exercise.	263	Priest 24	7
Things needing great Consideration. Mat. 24. 15.	317	Valdesso	25
NEEDLE			
Boat, cable, sail and needle, all in one.	120	Providence	128
By the needle you shall draw the thread,	332	Proverbs	329
You cannot hide a needle in a sacke.	346	Proverbs V	762
NEEDS			
A fault, which needs it most, grows two thereby.	9	Ch.-Porch	78
For he, that needs five thousand pound to live,	10	Ch.-Porch	107
Is full as poore as he, that needs but five.	10	Ch.-Porch	108
Lord, if thou must needs use thy dart,	56	Temper 2	3
Then we must needs for that day make a match.	62	Mattens	4
Coppy out that: there needs no alteration.	103	Jordan 2 W	18
And he would needs a comfort be,	111	The Quip	18
Of what strange length must that needs be,	123	Time	25
Which needs not man, be ty'd to those	134	The Method	26
Faith needs no staffe of flesh, but stoutly can	135	Divinitie	27
Needs must wcrk cn me.	179	Discipline	28
God took bloud, and needs would be	182	Banquet	34
He grew a gallant, and would needs foretell	193	Ch.-Milit.	129
Whose native beauty needs not dresse or lace	212	Bohemia D	30
expounding of our Catechisme must needs be the most usefull forme.	230	Priest 5	14
and sutably to their needs, then so much given in meat at dinner.	243	Priest 11	16
the faults of eating, and the truth of them needs no proofe:	266	Priest 26	13
then by that which he continually supplyes, as the corn needs it;	271	Priest 30	6
As Creatures, he must needs love them;	283	Priest 34	11
but the despising of Love must needs be without it.	283	Priest 34	25
which must needs so temper the humours of the bodie, that they could	295	Cornaro	8
which yet needs not onely to be sustained, but also to gather	295	Cornaro	23
there needs not many and curious things, but onely that a man should	299	Cornaro	8
yet all must [needs] take heed, lest they take a greater quantitie	300	Cornaro	11
He that would be well, needs not goe from his owne house.	336	Proverbs	442
The soule needs few things, the body many.	342	Proverbs	640
The soule needs some things, the body many.	342	Proverbs V	640
There needs a long time to know the worlds pulse.	350	Proverbs	886
it is no matter, for the Gentleman needs no incitation to love me.	369	Letters	29
NEEDY			
of well minded people, and to lay up treasure for the sick and needy.	246	Priest 13	22
if they be poor and needy, whom he thus finds labouring,	248	Priest 14	9
An Idle youth, a needy Age.	356	Proverbs D	1042
NEER			
them to be so, when God is so neer them, and even over their heads.	233	Priest 7	10
and debt of neighbourhood to all the Parishes which are neer him.	253	Priest 19	22
that neer the place where he is to pray, he spyes some scoffing	273	Priest 31	28
which either he lives in, or is neer unto it, is his imployment.	276	Priest 32	2
NEERE			
Love neere his death desir'd to end	439	Walton 5 V	11
He lives unsafely, that lookes too neere on things.	322	Proverbs	43
Chuse not an house neere an Inne (viz. for noise)	330	Proverbs	286
He warmes too neere that burnes.	348	Proverbs	815
yet was seene lately neere the king, which some observing who heard	368	Letters	35
NEERER			
But if he sees them neerer desperation, then Atheisme;	283	Priest 34	5
NEEREST			
and my neerest way ly through the Church, I will not doubt to go	273	Priest 31	34
NEGLECT			
neglect their duty, and shall be so farre from that which they seek	226	Priest 2	33
They who for the hope of promotion neglect any necessary admcnition,	226	Priest 2	37
as to neglect the grace of God in himself, and what the Holy Spirit	229	Priest 4	20
and neglect the present service of God, he by no means suffers it,	232	Priest 6	11
whose neglect in this point is intolerable, and a shamefull wrong	277	Priest 32	26
The neglect of this duty in Ministers themselves, hath made	286	Priest 36	11
duty in Ministers themselves, hath made the people also neglect it;	286	Priest 36	12
as to neglect the Consideration of Gods Worke in his heart through	309	Valdesso	30
NEGLECTING			
Shall I then sing, neglecting thy sad storie,	35	Thanksgvng W	11
of the tree, inriching their Orchard, and neglecting their House.	276	Priest 32	33
NEGLIGENCE			
Law they are to levy penalties for negligence in resorting to church,	270	Priest 29	5
NEGLIGENTLY			
because I would doe nothing negligently that you commit unto mee;	304	Valdesso	5
NEIGHBOR			
the second for the benefit of our neighbor.	246	Priest 13	31
NEIGHBORING			
passing daily our neighboring Sea, wondrously sound through all our	442	Oration	23
NEIGHBOUR			
To God, his neighbour, and himself most true:	72	Constancie	3
Love God, and love your neighbour. Watch and pray.	135	Divinitie	17
A neighbour spring to cool his inward heat;	154	Glimpse	14
or he takes care she shall learn it of some religious neighbour.	239	Priest 10	17
he inlargeth himself, if he be able, to the neighbour-hood;	245	Priest 12	18
and include the double object of our duty, God, and our neighbour;	246	Priest 13	30
of Charity, and Neighbour-hood, he first gives himself liberally,	253	Priest 19	35
then he keeps good correspondence with some neighbour Phisician,	260	Priest 23	37

NEIGHBOUR (cont'd)	PAGE	TITLE		LINE
Sometimes I ride to some of the neighbour-cities, that I may enjoy	301	Cornaro		34
as to relieve my Neighbour, God hath already reveled his Will about	313	Valdesso		14
Love your neighbour, yet pull not downe your hedge.	325	Proverbs		141
Love your neighbour, but pull not downe your hedge.	325	Proverbs	V	141
then borrow of my neighbour white.	330	Proverbs		269
The way is an ill neighbour.	351	Proverbs		915
but my next neighbour doth me more harm	361	Proverbs	D	1173
NEIGHBOUR-CITIES				
Sometimes I ride to some of the neighbour-cities, that I may enjoy	301	Cornaro		34
NEIGHBOUR-HOOD				
he inlargeth himself, if he be able, to the neighbour-hood;	245	Priest 12		18
of Charity, and Neighbour-hood, he first gives himself liberally,	253	Priest 19		35
NEIGHBOUR'S				
While she avoids her neighbours pride,	110	Brit. Ch.		22
and yet hee chuseth rather to use his neighbours, and wear out that,	265	Priest 26		29
NEIGHBOURHOOD				
and debt of neighbourhood to all the Parishes which are neer him.	253	Priest 19		21
and Neighbourhood being ever reputed, even among the Heathen,	253	Priest 19		25
NEIGHBOURING				
Correspondence with all the neighbouring Pastours round about him,	253	Priest 19		16
or famine, to any neighbouring Parish, then he expects no Briefe;	253	Priest 19		30
if any neighbouring village be overburdened with poore,	254	Priest 19		1
NEIGHBOURLY				
and neighbourly admonitions they still persist in ill, to present	270	Priest 29		19
and neighbourly accompanying one another, with reconciling	284	Priest 35		6
NEIGHBOURS				
Which when your neighbours saw, like a north-winde,	140	Ch.-rents		22
not to come at the beginning of service with their poor neighbours,	232	Priest 6		9
day he spends either in reconciling neighbours that are at variance,	236	Priest 8		11
either to entertaine some of his neighbours, or to be entertained	236	Priest 8		20
his wife among her neighbours is the beginner of good discourses,	240	Priest 10		28
at his door, whom God puts in his way, and makes his neighbours.	245	Priest 12		21
his land to the best advantage both of himself, and his neighbours.	275	Priest 32		26
All is well with him, who is beloved of his neighbours.	321	Proverbs		10
All is well to him, that is loved of his neighbours.	321	Proverbs	V	10
A mountaine and a river are good neighbours.	330	Proverbs		274
NEIGHBOURS'				
not the lesse, lest he cast their neighbours poverty on them also.	254	Priest 19		6
NEITHER (see also neyther)				
Yet not mine neither: for from thee they came,	5	Dedication		2
Nor wisdome neither: therefore gently move.	18	Ch.-Porch		312
(Thy workmanship) and give thee share in neither.	54	Love 1		8
Neither bring hony with the bees,	57	Employm. 1		18
Whom neither force nor fawning can	72	Constancie		4
Neither ought other mens abuse of Lent	86	Lent		28
Neither too mean, nor yet too gay,	109	Brit. Ch.		8
Neither sinne nor Saviour feels.	114	Businesse		38
Thy even praise can neither rise, nor fall.	118	Providence		42
As neither good, nor one: so oft divisions	147	Offering		14
I neither should be mine nor thine.	157	Clasping		10
So neither shall my praise.	173	23 Psalme		24
So neither shall thy praise.	173	23 Psalme	V	24
Doubtlesse, neither starre nor flower	181	Banquet		19
You neither groane nor weepe	209	Paradox	D	2
coveteousnesse, neither being greedy to get, nor nigardly to keep,	227	Priest 3		16
Neither is it for the servant of Christ to haunt Innes,	227	Priest 3		29
neither will they beleeve him in the pulpit, whom they cannot trust	228	Priest 3		7
so neither hath God opened, or will open all to one, that there may	229	Priest 4		24
so that they neither decline to the right hand, nor to the left.	230	Priest 5		22
Neither let any think this a slight thing.	230	Priest 5		23
yet not so slow neither, as to let the fervency of the supplicant	231	Priest 6		17
and the like, hath neither in it sweetnesse, nor gravity,	235	Priest 7		8
as that neither they want a competent sustentation, nor her husband	239	Priest 10		18
they so labour, as neither to labour anxiously, nor distrustfully,	247	Priest 14		26
he chides not at first, for that were neither civill, nor profitable;	248	Priest 14		14
Neither in this doth he forbear, though there be company by:	248	Priest 14		25
Wherfore neither disdaineth he to enter into the poorest Cottage,	249	Priest 14		4
so neither touching the intermediate days of Conversion.	250	Priest 16		21
Neither findes he any issue in this, but to throw himself down	257	Priest 22		30
neither can all the people so order their affairs as to receive just	259	Priest 22		26
neither avoyding therfore one anothers company, much lesse defaming	260	Priest 23		26
But if neither himselfe, nor his wife have the skil, and his means	260	Priest 23		32
neither doth he esteem him for an enemy, but as a brother still,	263	Priest 25		29
so that men must eat neither to the disturbance of their health,	266	Priest 26		14
Neither hath the place its dignity from the Ecclesiasticall Laws	269	Priest 29		32
Neither is this true onely in the military state of a Christian life,	279	Priest 33		2
neither is he affraid of praising, or praying to God at all times,	284	Priest 35		24
thinke this superstitious, neither know superstition, nor themselves.	284	Priest 35		28
Neither have the Ministers power of Blessing only, but also	285	Priest 36		24
so neither is he that defames him, whom the Law would have defamed,	287	Priest 37		28
Neither doth thy love yet stay here!	289	Priest		3
so neither may thy word, but accomplish that for which it is given.	289	Priest		32
which excesse of joy neither could do me any hurt.	294	Cornaro		30
That neither melancholie, nor any other passion can hurt a temperate	294	Cornaro		31
neither did I know well, what I did or said.	296	Cornaro		16
neither the good humours to be corrupted, or contract any ill	296	Cornaro		34
Neither can any man denie this, who will narrowly consider it.	297	Cornaro		14
Neither is it to be doubted, but that he shall ever after live free	297	Cornaro		18
of diseases, so that he shall need neither Physick nor Physician:	297	Cornaro		21
Neither doth it hinder, that Plato sayes, That they who are employed	299	Cornaro		11

NEITHER (cont'd)	PAGE	TITLE		LINE
neither omit I any thing that may either teach, or delight me.	302	Cornaro		4
Neither is this my pleasure made lesse by the decaying dulnesse of my	302	Cornaro		7
Neither, if I had my wish, would I change age and constitution	303	Cornaro		11
neither can they ever be exhausted, (as Pictures may be by a plenarie	309	Valdesso		21
nor Paul's neither, when he professed himselfe a Pharisee,	316	Valdesso		7
Neither doe I doubt but if Abraham had lived in our Kingdome under	316	Valdesso		22
A full belly neither fights nor flies well.	324	Proverbs		88
A well-bred youth neither speakes of himselfe,	330	Proverbs		278
Neither bribe nor loose thy right.	330	Proverbs		284
Neither eyes on letters, nor hands in coffers.	330	Proverbs		288
shall neither have good wife nor good horse.	336	Proverbs		434
Discreet women have neither eyes nor eares.	337	Proverbs		482
When a knave is in a plumtree he hath neither friend nor kin.	338	Proverbs		507
Neither praise nor dispraise thy selfe,	347	Proverbs		771
neither do I make any question, but that you have performed your	363	Letters		23
neither am I yet recovered, so that I am fain ever and anon,	364	Letters		33
neither can I so much as go to Bugden, and deliver your Letter,	369	Letters		15
I wrote to him that I would have both or neither;	375	Letters		12
Neither hath she any to repair unto at good times, as Christmas,	375	Letters		26
& neither to scandalize them, nor wound our owne reputation.	380	Woodnoth		19
NERE				
Are blowne away, as if they nere had bin.	46	Sinne 1	W	14
NERO				
Nero and others lodg'd him bravely there,	194	Ch.-Milit.		141
NEST				
The callow principles within their nest:	85	Vanitie 1		17
There lay thy sonne: and must he leave that nest,	107	Home		19
Till they regain their ancient nest.	111	Vanitie 2		16
Fouling her nest, my earth invade,	203	Even-song	W	11
The bird loves her nest.	323	Proverbs		75
NESTLE				
O let me roost and nestle there:	55	Temper 1		18
NESTLES				
It's a bold mouse that nestles in the catts eare.	344	Proverbs		693
NESTS				
Finde nests.	149	Longing		54
NET				
Birds teach us hawking; fishes have their net:	118	Providence		51
Sophisters taken in a fishers net.	191	Ch.-Milit.		52
hath neede of a net at his girdle.	335	Proverbs		428
It's not good fishing before the net.	343	Proverbs		663
fat Hogs among Jews, and Wine in a fishing net.	361	Proverbs	D	1163
NETHERSOL'S				
I understand by Sir Francis Nethersols Letter, that he fears I have	370	Letters		18
NETHERSOLE				
Nethersole for me; he and I are ancient acquaintance, and I have	369	Letters		21
NETS				
Fine nets and stratagems to catch us in,	45	Sinne 1		7
Fine nets and casualties to catch us in,	45	Sinne 1	W	7
NE'RE				
Kneeling ne're spoil'd silk stocking: quit thy state.	22	Ch.-Porch		407
Shall ne're be troubled with ill eyes.	96	Charms & K		2
Shall ne're be troubled with sore eyes.	96	Charms & K	W	2
But since those great ones, be they ne're so great,	161	Priesthood		19
Who would doe ill ne're wants occasion.	324	Proverbs		116
NEVER				
Some mark a partridge, never their childes fashion:	10	Ch.-Porch		99
Never was scraper brave man. Get to live;	12	Ch.-Porch		153
Never exceed thy income. Youth may make	13	Ch.-Porch		157
Doth often aim at, never hit the sphere.	19	Ch.-Porch		318
They dye in holes where glory never shone.	20	Ch.-Porch	W	348
The cunning workman never doth refuse	20	Ch.-Porch		353
Who never thought that any robberie:	28	Sacrifice		63
And never yet, whom I would punish, miss'd:	30	Sacrifice		131
And never yet, whom he would punish, miss'd:	30	Sacrifice	W	131
Never was grief like mine.	33	Sacrifice		216
Who sought for help, never malicious foes:	34	Sacrifice		243
Never was grief like mine.	34	Sacrifice		252
Nay, I will reade thy book, and never move	36	Thanksgvng		45
Nay, I will reade thy book, and never linn	36	Thanksgvng	W	45
A hart can never come too late.	42	Easter	W	28
Sprung from that beautie which can never fade;	54	Love 1		2
Sprung from the beautie which can never fade;	54	Love 1	W	2
So wee may cease to suck: to praise thee, never.	59	Whitsunday	W	24
O what a state is this, which never knew	65	Ch.-mus.	W	8
Without a knock it never shone.	68	Content		12
It never was in France or Spain;	70	Quidditie		6
Who never melts or thaws	72	Constancie		21
('Tis your own case) ye never move a wing.	78	Ang.&Sts.		20
'tis your own case, ye never move your wing.	78	Ang.&Sts.	W	20
And never want	79	Employm.2		24
Like season'd timber, never gives;	88	Vertue		14
Thy horse shal never fall or tire.	96	Charms & K	W	4
Where never yet came moth.	100	Miserie		18
I never saw thing make such haste.	107	Home		10
For they can never be at rest,	111	Vanitie 2		15
Ask'd what it meant. I, (who am never loth	116	Love-joy		4
Bees work for man; and yet they never bruise	118	Providence		65
They never cool, much lesse give out.	126	Confession		16
And that love may never cease,	146	Praise 2		3

NEVER (cont'd)	PAGE	TITLE		LINE
May oft break forth, and never break the lock.	154	Glimpse		25
Yet never prove.	162	The Search		4
And as it never shall remove,	173	23 Psalme		23
After death can never die.	180	Invitation		30
And the late reformation never durst	196	Ch.-Milit.		226
For gold and grace did never yet agree:	197	Ch.-Milit.		251
Never to thee aspire,	202	Trin.Sun.	W	9
The world anew: the sunne shall never rise	212	Bohemia	D	45
Blest is the man that never would	214	Psalm I	D	1
His leaf shall never fade, and all	214	Psalm I	D	11
that Hermogenes never dream'd of, and therefore he could give no	233	Priest 7		25
never was there such care of a flock expressed, save in the great	234	Priest 7		20
he never talkes with any woman alone, but in the audience of others,	237	Priest 9		11
and then also in a serious manner, never jestingly or sportfully.	237	Priest 9		13
yet never so giving over the raines, but that he sometimes looks how	239	Priest 9		1
he resolves with himself never to omit any present good deed	240	Priest 10		5
of the pulpit, and never leaving them, till he obtaine his desire.	245	Priest 12		14
never raising their thoughts to God, nor sanctifying their labour	248	Priest 14		1
though he even creep into it, and though it smell never so lothsomly.	249	Priest 14		6
before hee proceede to disinheriting, or perhaps never goes so far;	250	Priest 16		18
outlandish proverb, that Prayers and Provender never hinder journey.	251	Priest 17		15
he never decides it alone, but sends for three or four of the ablest	260	Priest 23		8
which while they dwell in their bookes, they will never finde;	266	Priest 26		2
This last rule joyned with the first, never fails.	267	Priest 26		6
that are reproved, but never contempt either in them, or others.	268	Priest 28		30
he wisheth them by no means to spare any, though never so great;	270	Priest 29		19
ingenuous and fit imployment is never wanting to those that seek it.	275	Priest 32		10
do it, then he that is generally learned, and was never sick.	278	Priest 33		29
that it should never be forgotten, but with the Gospel it selfe be	282	Priest 34		25
self to this course of life, that I never went a foot out of the way.	292	Cornaro		34
taking care never to rise with a full stomack, but so as I might well	293	Cornaro		18
I never since departed from my setled course of Sobrietie,	293	Cornaro		25
and therefore never was sick by any of these inconveniences,	294	Cornaro		9
Brabling Curres never want torne eares.	322	Proverbs		52
Brawling Curres never want sore eares.	322	Proverbs	V	52
A Lyons skin is never cheape.	323	Proverbs		55
A bad dog never sees the Wolfe.	323	Proverbs		59
Ill ware is never cheape.	323	Proverbs		61
Vertue never growes old.	323	Proverbs		64
Never had ill workeman good tooles.	323	Proverbs		67
Hee stands not surely, that never slips.	323	Proverbs		68
Hee stands not surely, that never slipte.	323	Proverbs	V	68
Almes never make poore. Or thus,	327	Proverbs		189
The beast that goes alwaies never wants blowes.	329	Proverbs		260
Prayers and provender never hinder any journey.	330	Proverbs	V	277
nor wise at 50, will never bee handsome, strong, rich, or wise.	333	Proverbs		349
The morning Sunne never lasts a day.	334	Proverbs		375
The comforters head never akes.	334	Proverbs		392
Faire shooting never kild bird.	335	Proverbs		405
Farre shooting never kild bird.	335	Proverbs	V	405
An upbraided morsell never choaked any.	335	Proverbs		406
He that seekes trouble never misses.	335	Proverbs		416
Never was strumpet faire.	336	Proverbs		431
Hee that knowes what may bee gained in a day never steales.	336	Proverbs		445
Pension never inriched young man.	339	Proverbs		515
The cholerick man never wants woe.	339	Proverbs		536
The offender never pardons.	340	Proverbs		561
Long jesting was never good.	344	Proverbs		694
shee had never sought her daughter there.	344	Proverbs		696
Divine grace was never slow.	345	Proverbs		710
Drought never brought dearth.	346	Proverbs		749
Gamsters and race-horses never last long.	346	Proverbs		751
God, and Parents, and our Master, can never be requited.	348	Proverbs		805
Of a pigs taile you can never make a good shaft.	359	Proverbs	D	1104
There is no man, though never so little,	359	Proverbs	D	1119
A wolfe will never make war against another wolfe.	359	Proverbs	D	1125
The death of a young wolfe doth never come too soon.	360	Proverbs	D	1131
The Divell never assailes a man, except he find him	361	Proverbs	D	1176
burden to you, since I can never answer what I have already received;	367	Letters		13
given her occasion to protest shee will never speake with him againe,	368	Letters		22
though never so, but that I have both time and work to be Your	370	Letters		13
I shall never find time and paper enough, yet am I Your readiest	370	Letters		31
in the holy Scripture, are never given to the rich, but to the poor.	373	Letters		29
I never find Blessed be the Rich;	373	Letters		30
NEVERTHELESS				
Nevertheless, few bring covetousness thus low, or consider it so	265	Priest 26		30
Nevertheless, I by the grace of God cured my self, onely	296	Cornaro		24
NEVERTHELESSE				
Neverthelesse, there may happen somtimes some cases, wherein he	260	Priest 23		17
Neverthelesse, he somtimes refresheth himselfe, as knowing that	267	Priest 27		33
Neverthelesse, according to the Apostles rule, he endeavours that	268	Priest 28		16
Neverthelesse, if the punished delinquent shall be much troubled	288	Priest 37		2
Neverthelesse at a venture two remedies might be used, letting	295	Cornaro		3
Neverthelesse, I denie not but that Physicians are necessarie,	298	Cornaro		3
neverthelesse I wish you by all meanes to publish it, for these three	304	Valdesso		17
NEW				
All such is courteous, usefull, new, or wittie.	18	Ch.-Porch		290
A new small-rented lease, and cancell th' old.	40	Redemption		4
Or make a new one, since the old	45	Nature		15
And livd accordingly with no new score,	50	Faith	W	15

NEW (cont'd)	PAGE	TITLE		LINE
And ev'ry day a new Creatour art.	56	Temper 2		8
That this new light, which now I see,	63	Mattens		18
And give new wheels to our disorder'd clocks.	64	Even-song		24
Having a new at his expence,	76	Sunday		53
Both th' old discoveries, and the new-found seas,	88	The Pearl		7
New thoughts of sinning: wherefore, to my shame,	122	Sinnes rd.		17
But quickly seek some new adventure.	126	Confession		22
Who fain would have you be new, tender, quick.	131	Love unkn.		70
He had new clothes a making here below.	151	The Bag		18
Through th' old sinnes and new doctrines of our land.	161	Priesthood		33
Lord, dost thou some new fabrick mold,	162	The Search		25
Unlesse they get new conduits, new supplies	164	Grief		7
From the first man in th' East, to fresh and new	168	The Sonne		9
And be in him new drest.	174	Aaron		20
And so this new commerce and sweet	175	The Odour		29
When souls shall wear their new aray,	186	Death		19
Giving new names and numbers to the yeare.	192	Ch.-Milit.		72
As new and old Rome did one Empire twist;	196	Ch.-Milit.		205
Old and new Babylon are to hell and night,	196	Ch.-Milit.		215
A new House to thy mind,	207	Walton 3		2
To conquere new ones, & shall share the frame	212	Bohemia	D	43
householder, who bringeth out of his treasure things new and old;	261	Priest 23		15
the old things of Philosophy, and the new of Grace;	261	Priest 23		16
busie himself better, then in those new Plantations, and discoveryes,	278	Priest 32		5
14. which we see even miraculously effected in these new discoveryes,	282	Priest 34		33
and suffered not any new of that kinde to arise, neither the good	296	Cornaro		33
And that new one, which I contracted by breaking my diet,	297	Cornaro		1
beleeve that old wine should hurt my stomack, and new should help it;	297	Cornaro		32
but enlightens us with new Considerations the more we read it.	310	Valdesso		34
Every thing new is fine.	323	Proverbs		76
An old friend, a new house.	334	Proverbs		400
An old friend is a new house.	334	Proverbs	V	400
Of a new Prince, new bondage.	359	Proverbs	D	1116
New things are fair.	359	Proverbs	D	1117
bottom is wound up and laid ready for work in the New Jerusalem.	373	Letters		7
The accession of which new title to your Excellencies, all the Muses	442	Oration		1
NEW-FOUND				
Both th' old discoveries, and the new-found seas,	88	The Pearl		7
NEWES				
For wit is newes onely to ignorance.	15	Ch.-Porch		230
Hee that brings good newes knockes hard.	348	Proverbs		824
Good newes may bee told at any time, but ill in the morning.	350	Proverbs		877
Hee that tells his wife newes is but newly married.	353	Proverbs		987
to acquaint you with those passages of newes which this time affords;	368	Letters		1
I was glad of your Cambridge newes, but you joyed me exceedingly	377	Letters		18
NEWLY				
As a young exhalation, newly waking,	169	The Answer		8
Hee that tells his wife newes is but newly married.	353	Proverbs		987
Modesty sets off one newly come to honour.	357	Proverbs	D	1062
NEWMARKET				
Sometimes also I ride to Newmarket, and there lie a day or two	365	Letters		7
NEWNESSE				
and turning unto God in truth of heart, and newnesse of life:	279	Priest 33		25
NEWS				
Courtesie grows in court; news in the citie.	18	Ch.-Porch		292
Courtesie grows at Court; news in the citie.	18	Ch.-Porch	W	292
It is no office, art, or news,	70	Quidditie		9
Stay a little and news will find you.	332	Proverbs		330
NEXT				
And rots to nothing at the next great thaw.	12	Ch.-Porch		140
An herb destill'd, and drunk, may dwell next doore,	61	Praise 1		13
At the next Session-day.	71	Humilitie		32
The fruit of this, the next worlds bud,	75	Sunday		2
I took up in the next inne I could finde.	80	Christmas		4
My hand was next to them, and then my heart:	94	Life		7
After, where ES, and next where U was graved.	112	JESU		6
This houre is mine: if for the next I care,	145	Discharge		33
Whereby one may foretell, what sinnes next yeare	197	Ch.-Milit.		245
And the reward of the next, Matth. 25. 35.	244	Priest 12		13
and come to Church in frame, but commonly the next day put off both.	247	Priest 14		10
but taking his Parish together the next Sunday, or holy-day,	253	Priest 19		31
none knowing whose turne may be next, and then when he hath	253	Priest 19		33
of the grave in this world, and the worm of Conscience in the next.	272	Priest 30		14
but my next neighbour doth me more harm	361	Proverbs	D	1173
he takes place next the Doctors, is at all their Assemblies	370	Letters		1
therefore I desire him to send me a direct answer in his next Letter.	370	Letters		25
next, whether my peace be yet made with her concerning my unkind	371	Letters		8
the next Friday it is tryed, and accordingly you shall hear.	371	Letters		17
and, it follcws in the next verse:	374	Letters		27
NEYTHER				
you any other wayes, as neyther I my self desire to be considered.	378	Letters		16
NICENESS				
do so either out of niceness, because they like the salutations,	285	Priest 36		4
NICHOLAS				
To Mr. Nicholas Ferrar.	378	Letters		T
NIECE (see also neece)				
NIGARDLY				
nor nigardly to keep, nor troubled to lose any worldly wealth;	227	Priest 3		17
NIGH				
That he before me well nigh suffereth:	31	Sacrifice		147

NO (cont'd)	PAGE	TITLE		LINE
Scorn no mans love, though of a mean degree;	20	Ch.-Porch		349
Let vain or busie thoughts have there no part:	23	Ch.-Porch		421
Let vain & busie thoughts have there no part:	23	Ch.-Porch	W	421
Though it be ill, makes him no ill Physician.	24	Ch.-Porch		444
No workmans tool hath touch'd the same.	26	The Altar		4
And Prophets once to see, but found no place:	32	Sacrifice		183
There is no dealing with thy mighty passion:	36	Reprisall		2
There is no medling with thy mighty passion:	36	Reprisall	W	2
No room for me, and flie away.	39	Good Fri.		28
No lodging for thee, but a cold hard stone?	40	Sepulchre		2
The letter of the word, find'st no fit heart	41	Sepulchre		19
No place for grief or fear.	46	Afflict.1		16
There was no moneth but May.	47	Afflict.1		22
Hungrie I was, and had no meat:	50	Faith		5
And livd accordingly with no new score,	50	Faith	W	15
When creatures had no reall light	51	Faith		33
No doore can keep them out:	53	Antiphon 1		10
Become a verse? Is there in truth no beautie?	56	Jordan 1		2
May no lines passe, except they do their dutie	56	Jordan 1		4
Is it no verse, except enchanted groves	56	Jordan 1		6
I envie no mans nightingale or spring;	57	Jordan 1		13
I am no link of thy great chain,	57	Employm. 1		21
My stock lies dead, and no increase	60	Grace		1
Man is all weaknesse; there is no such thing	61	Praise 1		9
Who doe no more.	61	Praise 1	W	20
And I will strive to sinne no more.	68	Trin.Sun.		6
No point of honour, or gay suit,	69	Quidditie		2
No hawk, or banquet, or renown,	69	Quidditie		3
It is no office, art, or news,	70	Quidditie		9
Since there is no place so alone,	75	Sunday		20
Bids no such thing:	78	Ang.&Sts.		18
And where his pleasure no injunction layes,	78	Ang.&Sts.		19
Of his rich crown, from whom lyes no appeal	78	Ang.&Sts.		22
Of his great crown, from whom lyes no appeal	78	Ang.&Sts.	W	22
Man is no starre, but a quick coal	79	Employm.2		6
But no hearing.	80	Deniall		15
But no hearing.	80	Deniall		20
Yet no hearing.	80	Deniall	W	20
Deferre no time;	80	Deniall		27
My God, no hymne for thee?	81	Christmas		16
To use their temperance, seeking no evasion,	86	Lent		14
That no man builds a stately habitation,	90	Man	W	2
And more: He is a tree, yet bears no fruit;	91	Man		8
And we no store.	93	Antiphon 2		21
Wee have no store.	93	Antiphon 2	W	21
I will no more advise:	95	Submission		18
Is my God this way? no, they would reply:	99	Decay		8
No man shall beat into his head,	100	Miserie		15
He doth not like this vertue, no;	101	Miserie		45
No, not to purchase the whole pack of starres:	101	Miserie		52
Coppy out that: there needs no alteration.	103	Jordan 2	W	18
Thou canst no more not heare, then thou canst die.	103	Prayer 2		6
Thy sorrows were in earnest; no faint proffer,	104	Obedience		28
To one word onely I say, No:	105	Obedience		32
Pratler, no more, I say:	105	Conscience		7
No room for pratlers there.	105	Conscience		10
No, not a tooth or nail to scratch,	106	Conscience		17
But there was none; at least no help without:	107	Home		15
We talk of harvests; there are no such things,	108	Home		55
There is no fruitfull yeare, but that which brings	108	Home		57
Is no hard rate.	111	Vanitie 2		10
If, poore soul, thou hast no tears,	113	Businesse		6
Would thou hadst no faults or fears!	113	Businesse		7
If thou hast no sighs or grones,	113	Businesse		12
Would thou hadst no flesh and bones!	113	Businesse		13
He that sinnes, hath he no losse?	114	Businesse		33
Brings thy Saviours death no gain?	114	Businesse		36
But as I can see no merit,	115	Dialogue		17
Ah! no more: thou break'st my heart.	115	Dialogue		32
Where all may reach: no beast but knows his feed.	118	Providence		50
When yet some places could no moisture get,	120	Providence		115
Or with a stone! yet make no good foundation.	120	Providence		124
Ah Loyterer! I'le no more, no more I'le bring:	121	Hope		7
No marvell Sir, he did replie,	122	Time		3
And in no quiet canst thou be,	124	Gratefulnes		26
A hollow winde did seem to answer, No:	124	Peace		5
No scrue, no piercer can	126	Confession		7
No smith can make such locks, but they have keyes:	126	Confession		17
Smooth open hearts no fastning have; but fiction	126	Confession		23
There would be no commerce,	127	Giddinesse		22
No sale or bargain passe: all would disperse,	127	Giddinesse		23
Travell'd, and saw no town;	128	Bunch Gr.		9
Faith needs no staffe of flesh, but stoutly can	135	Divinitie		27
Or cry no more.	136	Ephes.		15
There can no discord but in ceasing be.	136	Ephes.		22
If a cleare spring for me no time forbears,	136	Ephes.		28
I am no Crystall, what shall I?	136	Ephes.		30
As if there were no rule or eares?	136	Familie		4
That from small fires comes oft no small mishap.	139	Artillerie		4
There is no articling with thee:	139	Artillerie		31

NO (cont'd)

	PAGE	TITLE		LINE
I see no fears:	141	Justice 2		14
Have I no parts but those of grief?	143	Complaining		15
Seek out this All-heal, and seek no repose,	147	Offering		22
No end?	148	Longing		6
No key?	149	Longing		48
(I have no bag, but here is room):	152	The Bag		32
I struck the board, and cry'd, No more.	153	The Collar		1
Have I no harvest but a thorn	153	The Collar		7
Have I no bayes to crown it?	153	The Collar		14
No flowers, no garlands gay? all blasted?	153	The Collar		15
No such rank poyson can there be.	155	Assurance		6
Or rather make no Thine and Mine!	157	Clasping		20
As if there were no such cold thing.	165	The Flower		7
Fast in thy Paradise, where no flower can wither!	166	The Flower		23
Where are no sorrows, but delights more true,	167	Dotage		17
Thou so much worse, that thou shalt be no more.	169	Dial.-Anth		10
Unto a place where is no rest.	174	Aaron		9
Without whom I could have no rest:	174	Aaron		14
First, there is no pleasure here:	177	The Rose		5
There are no such things to me,	177	The Rose		11
No stormie night	183	A Parodie		13
Dry dust, which sheds no tears, but may extort.	186	Death		12
Make no delay.	186	Dooms-day		2
Dust, alas, no musick feels,	186	Dooms-day		9
O make no stay!	187	Dooms-day		14
Echo. No.	188	Heaven		4
The Warrier his deere skarres no more resounds,	191	Ch.-Milit.		63
(For no lesse Harbingers would serve then they)	192	Ch.-Milit.		84
Choke him, let him say no more,	199	L'Envoy		11
Choke him, let him speak no more,	199	L'Envoy	W	11
There is no dealing with thee in that Art:	201	love	W	2
Thou do'st no more, then doth the grave:	202	love	W	22
Each breast does feel, no braver fuel choose	206	Walton 1		13
He writ; when 's hand could write no more,	439	Walton 5		13
When my dear Friend, could write no more,	439	walton 6		1
Ther's no monument to a sonne,	208	J. Danvers	D	15
Theire dead, and Time shal be no more:	208	H. Danvers	D	4
No Earth can bee thy Jointure. For the sunne	211	Bohemia	D	3
Shall flow no more - until they bring	214	Convert	D	8
and finds no sure abiding place.	215	Psalm I	D	16
no help in God there is.	216	Psalm III	D	4
No evil, Lord, shall dwell with thee,	218	Psalm V	D	11
their mouths no truth retain.	219	Psalm V	D	26
and there is no knowledg, but, in a skilfull hand, serves either	228	Priest 4		16
the places controverted, which the Parson by no means refuseth.	229	Priest 4		19
knowing that no Sermon moves them so much to a reverence,	231	Priest 6		14
possible reverence, by no means enduring either talking, or sleeping,	231	Priest 6		23
he by no means suffers it, but after divers gentle admonitions,	232	Priest 6		12
that he himself hath often urged with no great success,	232	Priest 7		28
never dream'd of, and therefore he could give no precepts thereof.	233	Priest 7		26
For there is no greater sign of holinesse, then the procuring,	234	Priest 7		9
in his heart, having no necessity, but hath power over his own will,	237	Priest 9		16
knowing that it can no way be preserved, but only by those means,	237	Priest 9		20
to his earthly, having no title to either, except he do good to both.	239	Priest 10		22
that there is no help for a fault done, but confession.	240	Priest 10		35
for he hath no mony for such things, charity being his only perfume,	241	Priest 10		13
he goes no further for any entertainment, lest he goe into the world,	241	Priest 10		19
secondly, of eating no pleasing, or over-nourishing things,	242	Priest 10		3
of eating no flesh, which is but the determination of the second rule	242	Priest 10		5
there are such conceits, there is no room for his doctrine to enter.	243	Priest 11		24
But he gives no set pension to any;	244	Priest 12		25
but allows by no means to give without testimony, as he obeys	245	Priest 12		25
perfecting our Redemption no other way, then by sorrow;	249	Priest 15		23
or breeding up children to no Calling, but in idleness,	251	Priest 17		21
and ingagement of their discourses for no price sooner,	252	Priest 18		21
as being the servant of him, in whom there was no guile.	253	Priest 19		2
or famine, to any neighbouring Parish, then he expects no Briefe;	253	Priest 19		30
Hee admits no vaine or idle names, but such as are usuall	258	Priest 22		3
that it is no complementall or light thing to sustain that place,	258	Priest 22		10
and no less burden, as being done both in the presence of God,	258	Priest 22		12
he asks no other, but to have the skill of healing a wound,	260	Priest 23		31
esteeming that there is no spice comparable, for herbs,	262	Priest 23		1
the faults of eating, and the truth of them needs no proofe:	266	Priest 26		13
this is foretold, that it shall be so still, until things be no more.	268	Priest 28		16
for that, where contempt is, there is no room for instruction.	268	Priest 28		19
shewing that reproaches touch him no more, then a stone thrown	269	Priest 28		7
he wisheth them by no means to spare any, though never so great;	270	Priest 29		18
omission thereof upon just occasion ought by no means to trouble him.	273	Priest 31		7
assure himself, as to admit no scruple, but to go on as cheerfully,	273	Priest 31		11
the one in having no calling, the other in walking carelesly in our	274	Priest 32		16
He that hath or can have yet no imployment, if he truly,	275	Priest 32		12
No Common-wealth in the world hath a braver [better] Institution then	276	Priest 32		8
for there is no School to a Parliament.	277	Priest 32		10
there were no such Physician as he, both for skill and tendernesse.	278	Priest 33		31
directly (for disputation is no Cure for Atheisme) he scatters	281	Priest 34		14
(there being no reason, why any should distrust Saint Luke,	282	Priest 34		20
for no perfect Artist ever yet hated his owne worke.	283	Priest 34		12
no more then to be a spirituall Father was appropriated to them.	285	Priest 36		12
unlawful to open faults, no benefit or advantage can make it lawfull:	287	Priest 37		6
for an apple once we lost our God, and still lose him for no more;	288	Priest		20

NO (cont'd)

	PAGE	TITLE		LINE
nor no pit overwhelme it.	288	Priest		31
to that exigent, that there would be no help for me, but Death,	292	Cornaro		15
and saw that it was no hard thing to do so, but the proper duty	292	Cornaro		32
without difficultie, and no ill humours being ingendred in the body.	293	Cornaro		29
that they had no great power to hurt those bodies, which were kept in	294	Cornaro		1
received no inconvenience thereby, because that humour abounded	294	Cornaro		21
the end I got the victorie, to my great honour, and no lesse profit:	294	Cornaro		28
Besides all this, I could not sleep, no not a quarter of an houre:	296	Cornaro		22
In all which time I felt no grief, save now and then a little	296	Cornaro		30
For there is no malignitie of old age in the humours of my bodie,	296	Cornaro		36
although it was a sore evil, yet had no power to kill me.	297	Cornaro		2
it is no wonder that order should preserve, and disorder destroy.	297	Cornaro		8
For indeed no man can be a perfect Physician to another,	297	Cornaro		24
But surely there is no such matter, if Temperance be wanting.	298	Cornaro		21
and later yeares, it is no such thing which may not be performed;	299	Cornaro		6
That those inconveniences are of no great moment (as I shewed before)	299	Cornaro		16
and the cause being taken away, there is no place for the effect.	300	Cornaro		2
No man that follcwes it, is bound to eat and drink so little as I:	300	Cornaro		6
No man is forbidden to eat fruit or fish, which I eat not:	300	Cornaro		7
So that he which is offended with no kinde of meat and drink,	300	Cornaro		14
Let no man here cbject unto me, That there are many, who,	300	Cornaro		17
That a long life is no such desirable thing, because that after one	300	Cornaro		28
I shall finde no little comfort in the favour of Jesus Christ.	303	Cornaro		23
for I can no more free my selfe from actuall sinnes after Baptisme,	308	Valdesso		3
and that no other sin or vertue hath any thing to doe with us;	311	Valdesso		24
if we believe, no sinne shall hurt us;	311	Valdesso		25
if we believe not, no vertue shall helpe us.	311	Valdesso		25
that the world pierceth not godly mens actions no more then Gods,	315	Valdesso		30
Gods Servants should have weaknesses is no way repugnant to the way	316	Valdesso		3
allowing no Jurisdiction over the godly, this cannot stand,	316	Valdesso		15
There is no more to be said of this Chapter but that his opinion	318	Valdesso		5
a few cheap and easie duties of religion, with no less superstition;	319	Valdesso	V	25
the very Ceremonies of the Jewes, which no Christian observes now;	320	Valdesso		1
When a friend askes, there is no to morrow.	322	Proverbs		32
Were there no fooles, badd ware would not passe.	323	Proverbs		66
Were there no hearers, there would be no backbiters.	323	Proverbs		69
Noble houskeepers neede no dores.	324	Proverbs		91
Where you thinke there is baccn, there is no Chimney.	324	Proverbs		99
No Alchymy to saving.	324	Proverbs		114
No love to a Fathers.	325	Proverbs		121
Who hath no more bread then neede, must not keepe a dog.	325	Proverbs		128
The bit that one eates, no friend makes.	325	Proverbs		142
The eye and Religion can beare no jesting.	326	Proverbs		158
Where there is no honour, there is no griefe.	327	Proverbs		186
Great almes-giving lessens no mans living.	327	Proverbs		190
yet hee is no little foole that despiseth it.	327	Proverbs		206
Prayers and provender hinder no journey.	330	Proverbs		277
There would bee no great ones if there were no little ones.	331	Proverbs		292
There would bee no great ones if there were no mean ones.	331	Proverbs	V	292
It's no sure rule to fish with a cros-bow.	331	Proverbs		293
There were no ill language, if it were not ill taken.	331	Proverbs		294
Say no ill of the yeere, till it be past.	331	Proverbs		297
No lock will hold against the power of gold.	332	Proverbs		317
No Lockes can hold against gcld.	332	Proverbs	V	317
When God will, no winde but brings raine.	332	Proverbs		332
He that hath no ill fortune is troubled with good.	333	Proverbs		358
He that hath no hony in his pot, let him have it in his mouth.	333	Proverbs		360
Hee that looseth his due, gets no thankes.	333	Proverbs		363
Woe to the house where there is no chiding.	336	Proverbs		450
The resolved minde hath no eares.	337	Proverbs		464
The resolved minde hath no cares.	337	Proverbs	V	464
Talking payes no toll.	338	Proverbs		485
There is no jollitie but hath a smack of folly.	338	Proverbs		493
One flower makes no garland.	339	Proverbs		521
He that hath no good trade, it is to his losse.	340	Proverbs		560
No barber shaves so close but another finds worke.	343	Proverbs		667
Ther's no great banquet but some fares ill.	343	Proverbs		668
No sooner is a Temple built to God	343	Proverbs		674
The tree that God plants, no winde hurts it.	344	Proverbs		691
Knowledge is no burthen.	344	Proverbs		692
It's an ill councell that hath no escape.	345	Proverbs		715
No profit to honour, no honour to Religion.	346	Proverbs		759
Service is no Inheritance.	347	Proverbs		792
If thou thy selfe canst doe it, attend no others helpe or hand.	348	Proverbs		813
No prison is faire, nor love foule.	348	Proverbs		829
No prison is faire, & no love foule.	348	Proverbs	V	829
Poverty is no sinne.	349	Proverbs		844
He that gaines well and spends well, needes no count booke.	349	Proverbs		853
He that gaines well and spends well, needes no count books.	349	Proverbs	V	853
Craft against craft makes no living.	350	Proverbs		890
The Court hath no Almanack.	350	Proverbs		894
Hee hath no leisure who useth it not.	351	Proverbs		897
Death keepes no Calender.	351	Proverbs		908
Princes have no way.	352	Proverbs		956
No Church-yard is so handsom,	353	Proverbs		969
Hee a beast doth die, that hath done no good to his country.	354	Proverbs		993
Who hath no head, needes no hatt.	354	Proverbs		996
Who hath no head, needes no heart.	354	Proverbs	V	996
Who hath no hast in his businesse,	354	Proverbs		997
There is no heat of affection but is joyned	357	Proverbs	D	1050

NO (cont'd)	PAGE	TITLE	LINE
No naked man is sought after to be rifled.	357	Proverbs	D 1063
There's no such conquering weapon as the necessity of conquering.	357	Proverbs	D 1064
No tye can oblige the perfidious.	357	Proverbs	D 1066
hath a rock and a spindle, and no staffe to spin.	358	Proverbs	D 1085
A dead Bee maketh no Hony.	358	Proverbs	D 1098
There is no man, though never so little, ...	359	Proverbs	D 1119
No love is foule, nor prison fair.	359	Proverbs	D 1122
No day so clear but hath dark clouds.	359	Proverbs	D 1123
No hair so small but hath his shadow.	359	Proverbs	D 1124
Love without end, hath no end, says the Spaniard: (meaning, . .	361	Proverbs	D 1160
Trust no friend with that you need fear him if he were your enemy.	361	Proverbs	D 1169
There is no body will go to hell for company.	361	Proverbs	D 1177
Money wants no fcllowers.	362	Proverbs	D 1182
I dare no longer be silent, least while I think I am modest,	364	Letters	7
Let there be no kind of excellency which it is possible for you	366	Letters	13
not with a foolish vanting of yourself when there is no caus,	366	Letters	17
It is high time now that I should be no more a burden to you,	367	Letters	13
but yet he will heare of no other affaires, untill they have	368	Letters	8
demand of the Kings these Agents pretend they have no commission,	368	Letters	14
on by her selfe (for shee desires no more) shee will find friends	368	Letters	24
it is no matter, for the Gentleman needs no incitation to love me.	369	Letters	28
it is no matter, for the Gentleman needs no incitation to love me.	369	Letters	29
hath no such earthiness in it, but it may very well be joined	370	Letters	22
neeces into your hands but barely what I wrote I meant, and no more;	375	Letters	6
and age, and knew none but one who could be no company to them.	375	Letters	15
be none of the Court-stile, yet doubtless Madam, can do you no hurt:	377	Letters	3
and you have no cause to be sorry, since it is GOD's business.	377	Letters	21
Gods earth, no not tho' the advice step so far, as to be reproof:	378	Letters	12
but he told her Grace, that he would by no meanes do so, urging,	379	Letters	7
so no less glad for the Heart, that God has given you & yours,	379	Letters	14
before lower, even where to continue in the lower is no sinn.	380	Woodnoth	4
especially no obligation lying upcn you either for the execution	380	Woodnoth	25
to be without dores with him, is no ill company.	381	Woodnoth	3
As God where he finds no roome for his Inclining grace, . .	381	Woodnoth	7
To desire good & endeavour it when we can doe no more, is to doe it.	381	Woodnoth	16
both Indias to his Spaine, knowes no limits of his praise, no,	442	Oration	12
knowes no limits of his praise, no, not, as in past ages, . .	442	Oration	12
NOAH'S			
Blessed be God, who prosper'd Noahs vine, ...	128	Bunch Gr.	24
Of Noahs shadie vine, chaste as the dove;	190	Ch.-Milit.	15
NOBILITY			
If there be any of the gentry or nobility of the Parish, . .	232	Priest 6	7
NOBLE			
Onely, most noble Lord, shutt not the doore	209	L. Bacon D	9
some in Noble houses, some in Parishes residing on their Cures.	226	Priest 2	1
Those that live in Noble Houses are called Chaplains, whose duty	226	Priest 2	15
or Noble-man in the Country he lives in, inabling him with power	276	Priest 32	13
to insist and dwell chiefly on the two noble branches therof,	278	Priest 32	1
which are not only a noble, but also as they may be handled,	278	Priest 32	6
of excellent wit and noble disposition, overthrown and undone	291	Cornaro	2
generall rules to particular actions, which are a most noble study.	319	Valdesso V	33
Noble houskeepers neede no dores.	324	Proverbs	91
Serve a noble disposition, though poore, ...	333	Proverbs	368
A noble plant suites not with a stubborne ground.	342	Proverbs	622
Noble Sir, pardon my boldness, and consider but these three things.	365	Letters	15
To the truly Noble Sir J. D.	366	Letters	T
though your noble disposition is infinitely free, yet I had rather	367	Letters	6
Noble Sir, I thank you for your infinite favours, I fear only that I	370	Letters	10
or, Blessed be the Noble;	373	Letters	30
commands, most noble Ambassages, and other titles most pleasing,	441	Oration	25
NOBLE-MAN			
or Noble-man in the Country he lives in, inabling him with power	276	Priest 32	13
NOBLEMEN'S			
Criticks are like brushers of Noblemens cloaths.	360	Proverbs	D 1157
NOBLES			
To William Twenty Nobles, To John twentie shillings, all these are	382	G.H.'s Will	25
NOBLEST			
The noblest sence of five.	201	H. Commun. W	33
NOBODIE			
If the husband be not at home, there is nobodie.	354	Proverbs	1016
NOD			
As men, for fear the starres should sleep and nod, ...	134	Divinitie	1
NOISE			
At length I heard a ragged noise and mirth	40	Redemption	12
And didst allow us all our noise:	124	Gratefulnes	18
What doth this ncise of thoughts within my heart	136	Familie	1
But griefs without a noise:	137	Familie	18
A noise of passions ringing me for dead	174	Aaron	8
Chuse not an house neere an Inne (viz. for noise)	330	Proverbs	286
The noise is greater then the nuts.	358	Proverbs	D 1073
NOISELESSE			
My thoughts must work, but like a noiselesse sphere;	105	Conscience	8
NOISES			
With noises confused frighting the day:	29	Sacrifice	103
NOISOME			
Some in noiscme vapours grcw	187	Dooms-day	23
NOISCMNESSE			
Slovens take up their stock of noisomnesse	21	Ch.-Porch	369
NON			
Sponges, non-sense and sense; mines, th' earth & plants. . .	121	Providence	136

NON (cont'd)	PAGE	TITLE		LINE
godly in some sort exempt from Lawes, for Lex iusto non est posita:	315	Valdesso		33
is Regent or Non-regent at his pleasure, and such like Gaynesses,	370	Letters		3
NON-REGENT				
is Regent or Non-regent at his pleasure, and such like Gaynesses,	370	Letters		3
NON-SENSE				
Sponges, non-sense and sense; mines, th' earth & plants.	121	Providence		136
NONE				
None is so wastefull as the scraping dame.	13	Ch.-Porch		173
Give one estate, as one life. None is bound	17	Ch.-Porch		285
Strike off all scores; none are so cleare as they.	20	Ch.-Porch		360
As if none could bee brave, but who profess	21	Ch.-Porch	W	369
None shall in hell such bitter pangs endure,	24	Ch.-Porch		445
None of my books will show:	48	Afflict.1		56
None but the wise or strong had gained it:	50	Faith		26
But I have got his sonne, and he hath none.	63	Even-song		8
Where all my debts are payd, none can accrue	65	Ch.-mus.	W	8
Whom none can work or wooe	72	Constancie		16
Which they effected, none could them withstand.	84	The World		18
That none doth build a stately habitation,	90	Man		2
We have none,	93	Antiphon 2		20
And make his own? as if none knew, but he.	100	Miserie		14
Or none thy portion is.	101	Miserie		42
But there was none; at least no help without:	107	Home		15
And none but thee.	110	Brit. Ch.		30
Hast thou tears, or hast thou none?	113	Businesse		5
Had he life, or had he none?	113	Businesse		19
So the way is none of mine:	115	Dialogue		22
While all things have their will, yet none but thine.	117	Providence		32
None can expresse thy works, but he that knows them:	121	Providence		142
And none can know thy works, which are so many,	121	Providence		143
For I had giv'n the key to none, but one:	130	Love unkn.		55
Against me there is none, but for me much.	141	Justice 2		24
Just as I went, None goes that way	142	Pilgrimage		33
(For this heart is none)	148	Offering		33
And none of mine:	148	Offering		35
Such a Joy, as none can move:	156	The Call		10
Such a Love, as none can part:	156	The Call		11
Since thou in death wast none of thine,	157	Clasping		17
None will beleeve this now, though money be	193	Ch.-Milit.		119
Tak'st all the Lodging, leaving none	200	H. Commun.	W	5
Is none.	202	Trin.Sun.	W	2
None but gross joyes you move:	210	Paradox	D	34
And peace-meal rent it, while there's none	221	Psalm VII	D	7
that none goes out of Church as he came in, but either better,	233	Priest 7		19
that none is careless before his Judg, and that the word of God shal	233	Priest 7		20
his profit, for none are so well served, as by religious servants,	240	Priest 10		14
none knowing whose turne may be next, and then when he hath	253	Priest 19		32
all reverence himself, so he administers to none but to the reverent.	259	Priest 22		11
none must eat so as to disable themselves from a fit discharging	266	Priest 26		29
to the Apostles rule, he endeavours that none shall despise him;	268	Priest 28		17
doing kindnesses, but receiving none;	268	Priest 28		24
which none can perform so wel in trouble, as in calmness.	273	Priest 31		2
the Common-wealth, that none should be idle, but all busied.	274	Priest 32		27
The Italian says, None fouls his hands in his own businesse:	275	Priest 32		27
When none of these occasions call him abroad, every morning that hee	277	Priest 32		14
that there is none that can or will look after things, but all goes	281	Priest 34		8
doth forsake and persecute them, and there is none to deliver them.	281	Priest 34		12
since none can have a better Physician then himself, nor better	297	Cornaro		37
But I like none of it, for it slights the Scripture too much:	306	Valdesso		16
Of these none can free themselves of themselves, but only	308	Valdesso		8
Who hath none to still him, may weepe out his eyes.	321	Proverbs		17
For washing his hands, none sels his lands.	323	Proverbs		54
Better a bare foote then none.	323	Proverbs		78
Without favour none will know you,	326	Proverbs		159
None is a foole alwaies, every one sometimes.	326	Proverbs		163
Evils have their comfort, good none can support	328	Proverbs		208
Advise none to marry or to goe to warre.	329	Proverbs		236
Advise none to marry nor to goe to warre.	329	Proverbs	V	236
Let none say, I will not drinke water.	331	Proverbs		310
Sit in your place and none can make you rise.	334	Proverbs		372
None is borne Master.	343	Proverbs		654
None is offended but by himselfe.	343	Proverbs		656
None saies his Garner is full.	343	Proverbs		657
None is so wise, but the foole overtakes him.	345	Proverbs		734
None is so wise, but that the foole overtakes him.	345	Proverbs	V	734
Praise none too much, for all are fickle.	347	Proverbs		774
None knowes the weight of anothers burthen.	350	Proverbs		880
The great would have none great and the little all little.	352	Proverbs		946
Chuse none for thy servant who have served thy betters.	354	Proverbs		1014
Say to pleasure, Gentle Eve, I will none of your apple.	360	Proverbs	D	1140
could possibly have come, none should have done my message to Sir Fr:	369	Letters		20
Yet truly it was none of my meaning, when I wrote, to putt one of our	375	Letters		4
and age, and knew none but one who could be no company to them.	375	Letters		15
having none to doe it but her school-mistresse, and you know what	375	Letters		25
though it be none of the Court-stile, yet doubtless Madam,	377	Letters		2
NOON				
By noon most cunningly did steal away,	94	Life		5
He is thy night at noon: he is at night	144	Discharge		13
Thy noon alone.	144	Discharge		14

	PAGE	TITLE		LINE
NOONE				
and noone of prosperity, he findeth to be as necessary,	237	Priest 9		35
nor of the sicknesse that destroyeth at noone day, [Ghostly pride	238	Priest 9		8
NOR				
Boast not thereof; nor make thy shame thy glorie.	8	Ch.-Porch		50
Lose not thy self, nor give thy humours way:	12	Ch.-Porch		143
My childrens right, nor ought he take it: rather	17	Ch.-Porch		279
Nor wisdome neither: therefore gently move.	18	Ch.-Porch		312
I could not go away, nor persevere.	47	Afflict.1		48
Nor in a wedge of gold,	52	H.Commun.		2
Nor let them punish me with losse of ryme,	57	Jordan 1		14
Nor let them punish me with losse of time,	57	Jordan 1	V	14
Nor flowres to make that, nor the husbandrie	57	Employm. 1		19
Nor hawke, nor banquet, nor renowne,	69	Quidditie	W	3
Nor a good sword, nor yet a lute:	69	Quidditie		4
Nor a good sword, not yet a lute:	69	Quidditie	W	4
Nor can it entertain the day	70	Quidditie		7
Nor the Exchange, or busie Hall;	70	Quidditie		10
Whom neither force nor fawning can	72	Constancie		4
Nor seeks, nor shunnes them; but doth calmly stay,	72	Constancie		12
Who blows it not, nor doth controll	79	Employm.2		8
Nor would I use a friend, as I use Thee.	94	Unkindness		20
Nor any sorrow tell them that they sinne,	100	Miserie		22
Neither too mean, nor yet too gay,	109	Brit. Ch.		8
Nor solid work, as false embroyderies;	111	Vanitie 2		4
Neither sinne nor Saviour feels.	114	Businesse		38
Thy even praise can neither rise, nor fall.	118	Providence		42
As neither good, nor one: so oft divisions	147	Offering		14
Bringing nor man, nor arms, nor fear,	151	The Bag		28
I neither should be mine nor thine.	157	Clasping		10
Nor doth my flower	166	The Flower		26
As if grief were not foul, nor vertue winning.	176	The Foil		8
Doubtlesse, neither starre nor flower	181	Banquet		19
Nor his long journey, nor his gout and furre.	195	Ch.-Milit.		198
Nor his long journey, nor his gout or furre.	195	Ch.-Milit.	W	198
Nor can they change their bounds & meres,	201	H. Commun.	W	41
Nor yet thy eloquence here keep him still,	439	Walton 5		3
Nor canst thou be content, unlesse thou to	439	Walton 5		5
You neither groane nor weepe	209	Paradox	D	2
Nor hath in way of sinners stood,	214	Psalm I	D	3
nor sitten in the scorners chair.	214	Psalm I	D	4
Nor in the safe society	215	Psalm I	D	19
nor can I hide his sacred will.	215	Psalm II	D	16
Nor all the people round about,	216	Psalm III	D	15
nor fools stand in thy sight.	218	Psalm V	D	12
nor in thine anger chasten me:	219	Psalm VI	D	2
nor nigardly to keep, nor troubled to lose any worldly wealth;	227	Priest 3		17
so that they neither decline to the right hand, nor to the left.	230	Priest 5		22
hath neither in it sweetnesse, nor gravity, nor variety,	235	Priest 7		8
nor gravity, nor variety, since the words apart are not Scripture,	235	Priest 7		8
nor of the sicknesse that destroyeth at noone day, [Ghostly pride	238	Priest 9		7
want a competent sustentation, nor her husband be brought in debt.	239	Priest 10		19
nor suffer others in his house that are so, to keep it;	242	Priest 10		29
as neither to labour anxiously, nor distrustfully, nor profanely.	247	Priest 14		26
as neither to labour anxiously, nor distrustfully, nor profanely.	247	Priest 14		27
thoughts to God, nor sanctifying their labour with daily prayer;	248	Priest 14		1
he chides not at first, for that were neither civill, nor profitable;	248	Priest 14		15
them not to serve the turne, nor provides slight, and unusefull,	252	Priest 19		27
nor the Church-Wardens so well take notice who receive thrice,	259	Priest 22		27
if neither himselfe, nor his wife have the skil, and his means serve,	260	Priest 23		33
the bounds of the action, nor when his eating begins to be unlawfull.	264	Priest 26		25
of their health, nor of their affairs, (which being overburdened,	266	Priest 26		14
they cannot wel dispatch) nor of their estate, nor of their brethren.	266	Priest 26		16
nor to store their house with all those furnitures which even their	280	Priest 34		24
nor when they are among them that are merry, to extend themselves	280	Priest 34		26
thinke this superstitious, neither know superstition, nor themselves.	284	Priest 35		29
nor no pit overwhelme it.	288	Priest		31
neither melancholie, nor any other passion can hurt a temperate life.	294	Cornaro		31
of diseases, so that he shall need neither Physick nor Physician:	297	Cornaro		22
nor better Physick then a Temperate Life, Temperance by all means is	298	Cornaro		1
not punished) for evill doing nor rewarded for weldoing or living,	311	Valdesso		29
nor Paul's neither, when he professed himselfe a Pharisee,	316	Valdesso		7
A full belly neither fights nor flies well.	324	Proverbs		88
Deceive not thy Physitian, Confessor, nor Lawyer.	324	Proverbs		105
Advise none to marry nor to goe to warre.	329	Proverbs	V	236
nor being spoken to is silent.	330	Proverbs		278
Neither bribe nor loose thy right.	330	Proverbs		284
Neither eyes on letters, nor hands in coffers.	330	Proverbs		288
nor for every quarrell to the Lawyer,	331	Proverbs		290
nor for every thirst to the pot.	331	Proverbs		290
If you loose your time, you cannot get mony nor gaine.	332	Proverbs		320
He that is not handsome at 20, nor strong at 30, nor rich at 40,	333	Proverbs		349
nor wise at 50, will never bee handsome, strong, rich, or wise.	333	Proverbs		349
All griefes with bread are lesse, or Nor woe to want.	334	Proverbs	V	377
shall neither have good wife nor good horse.	336	Proverbs		434
Discreet women have neither eyes nor eares.	337	Proverbs		482
When a knave is in a plumtree he hath neither friend nor kin.	338	Proverbs		507
Neither praise nor dispraise thy selfe,	347	Proverbs		771
No prison is faire, nor love foule.	348	Proverbs		829
No love is foule, nor prison fair.	359	Proverbs	D	1122
nor to bewail that so few are writ, that look towards God and Heaven.	363	Letters		8

NOT (con't'd)

	PAGE	TITLE		LINE
Judge not the preacher; for he is thy Judge:	23	Ch.-Porch		427
If thou mislike him, thou conceiv'st him not.	23	Ch.-Porch		428
God calleth preaching folly. Do not grudge	23	Ch.-Porch		429
Preachers conclude with, hath not lost his pains.	24	Ch.-Porch		434
Jest not at preachers language, or expression:	24	Ch.-Porch		439
Look not on pleasures as they come, but go.	24	Ch.-Porch		458
Deferre not the least vertue: lifes poore span	24	Ch.-Porch		459
Make not an ell, by trifling in thy wo.	24	Ch.-Porch		460
If thou do ill; the joy fades, not the pains:	24	Ch.-Porch		461
Avoid, profanenesse; come not here:	25	Superlim		5
These stones to praise thee may not cease.	26	The Altar		14
Though he had all I had, did not forbeare	27	Sacrifice		14
Not half so sweet as my sweet sacrifice:	27	Sacrifice		19
Comforts not me, and doth my doctrine stain:	27	Sacrifice		31
See, they lay hold on me, not with the hands	28	Sacrifice		45
They leade me; urging, that it was not sound	28	Sacrifice		54
'Gainst him, who seeks not life, but is the meek	28	Sacrifice		58
It is not fit he live a day, they crie,	29	Sacrifice		98
Why, Caesar is their onely King, not I:	30	Sacrifice		121
But surely not their hearts, as I well trie:	30	Sacrifice		123
But surely not their hearts, as I will trie:	30	Sacrifice	V	123
But not their harts, as I by proofe doe try.	30	Sacrifice	W	123
Weep not, deare friends, since I for both have wept	31	Sacrifice		149
Or feel his part, he would not cease to kneel,	33	Sacrifice		210
Or feel his share, he would not cease to kneel,	33	Sacrifice	W	210
In healing not my self, there doth consist	34	Sacrifice		225
I will not marry; or, if she be mine,	35	Thanksgvng		23
Shall not perceive, that I am here.	36	Thanksgvng		38
Alas, my God, I know not what.	36	Thanksgvng		50
Ah! was it not enough that thou	37	Reprisall		9
Couldst thou not griefs sad conquests me allow,	37	Reprisall		11
Who knows not Love, let him assay	37	The Agonie		13
But shreds of holinesse, that dare not venture	38	The Sinner		6
Not thriving, I resolved to be bold,	40	Redemption		2
So many hearts on earth, and yet not one	40	Sepulchre		3
Can not make up so brave a feast	42	Easter	W	25
Stayes not, but looks beyond it on the skie;	43	H. Bapt.1		2
Sorrow was all my soul; I did not know	47	Afflict.1	W	29
Not simpring all mine age,	47	Afflict.1		44
Not simpring all my age,	47	Afflict.1	W	44
I could not go away, nor persevere.	47	Afflict.1		48
Thus doth thy power crosse-bias me, not making	48	Afflict.1		53
Let me not love thee, if I love thee not.	48	Afflict.1		66
Cut me not off for my most foul transgression:	49	Repentance		15
Which when I could not get, I thought it here:	50	Faith		10
Not in rich furniture, or fine aray,	52	H.Commun.		1
Yet can these not get over to my soul,	52	H.Commun.		13
For sure when Adam did not know	53	H.Commun.		33
The heav'ns are not too high,	53	Antiphon 1		3
The earth is not too low,	53	Antiphon 1		5
O rack me not to such a vast extent;	55	Temper 1		9
Let not thy higher Court remove,	56	Temper 2		15
Not to a true, but painted chair?	56	Jordan 1		5
Let me not languish then, and spend	57	Employm. 1		13
Seeing not onely how each verse doth shine,	58	H.Script.2		3
Show that thy brests can not be dry,	59	Whitsunday	W	21
Did not excite thee, we should wholly sink.	60	Whitsunday		24
Wilt thou not then my fault reprove?	61	Grace	W	20
Or if to me thou wilt not move,	61	Grace		22
Remove me, where I need not say,	61	Grace		23
Not flyes, but I shall bee his prey	61	Praise 1	W	19
Kill me not ev'ry day,	62	Afflict.2		1
Thou Lord conceal it not: and as thou art	62	Afflict.2		12
He did not heav'n and earth create,	63	Mattens		15
Yet studies them, not him by whom they be.	63	Mattens		16
Not one poore minute scapes thy breast,	64	Even-song		30
Which knoweth not, what means, to Morrow.	65	Ch.-mus.	W	8
Which knoweth not, what means, too Morrow.	65	Ch.-mus.	W	9
Not on my sinnes, or coldnesse, but thy will.	66	Ch.-lock		8
And in the eare, not conscience ring.	68	Windows		15
Peace mutt'ring thoughts, and do not grudge to keep	68	Content		1
Gad not abroad at ev'ry quest and call	68	Content		5
Thy name in books, which may not rent:	69	Content		28
Thy name in books, which may not vent:	69	Content	W	28
Do not thy self or friends importune.	69	Content		34
My God, a verse is not a crown,	69	Quidditie		1
Nor a good sword, not yet a lute:	69	Quidditie	W	4
(For he would not) as they beheld the grace	70	Humilitie		18
O brook not this, lest if what even now	71	Frailtie		17
O brook not this, lest if that, which just now	71	Frailtie	W	17
Whose honestie is not	72	Constancie		6
His goodnesse sets not, but in dark can runne:	72	Constancie		23
Whom others faults do not defeat;	73	Constancie		29
To writhe his limbes, and share, not mend the ill.	73	Constancie		33
To writhe his limbes, and thare, not mend the ill.	73	Constancie	V	33
Hadst thou not had thy part,	73	Afflict.3		5
Teaches it not to stumble.	75	Sunday	W	7
Whom, if we were not very dull,	75	Sunday		18
We could not choose but look on still;	75	Sunday		19
The which he doth not fill.	75	Sunday		21

NOT (cont'd)

	PAGE	TITLE		LINE
Man might not of his fodder misse.	76	Sunday		39
If not upon his head, yet in his hands:	77	Ang.&Sts.		5
Not out of envie or maliciousnesse	78	Ang.&Sts.		6
But now (alas!) I dare not; for our King,	78	Ang.&Sts.		16
But now alas I dare not; for my King,	78	Ang.&Sts.	W	16
Therefore we dare not from his garland steal,	78	Ang.&Sts.		24
What's done on earth, we shall not fare the worse,	78	Ang.&Sts.		27
What's done on earth, we shall not feare the worse,	78	Ang.&Sts.	V	27
Who do not so;	78	Ang.&Sts.		28
Who blows it not, nor doth controll	79	Employm.2		8
Life is a businesse, not good cheer;	79	Employm.2		16
When my devotions could not pierce	79	Deniall		1
And then not heare it crying! all day long	80	Deniall		18
To Man of all beasts be not thou a stranger:	81	Christmas		12
Therefore thou dost not show	82	Ungratef.		15
O do not use me	83	Sighs & Gr.		1
After my sinnes! look not on my desert,	83	Sighs & Gr.		2
And not refuse me: for thou onely art	83	Sighs & Gr.		4
O do not bruise me!	83	Sighs & Gr.		6
O do not urge me!	83	Sighs & Gr.		7
O do not scourge me!	83	Sighs & Gr.		12
O do not blinde me!	83	Sighs & Gr.		13
O do not grinde me!	83	Sighs & Gr.		18
O do not fill me	83	Sighs & Gr.		19
O do not kill me!	83	Sighs & Gr.		24
Cordiall and Corrosive: put not thy hand	83	Sighs & Gr.		28
Then Pleasure came, who liking not the fashion,	84	The World		6
What hath not man sought out and found,	85	Vanitie 1		22
What hath not man wrought out and found,	85	Vanitie 1	V	22
So that we need not say, Where's this command?	86	Vanitie 1		26
Welcome deare feast of Lent: who loves not thee,	86	Lent		1
He loves not Temperance, or Authoritie,	86	Lent		2
I am a scandall to the Church, and not	86	Lent		11
A face not fearing light:	86	Lent		21
Not in his parlour; banquetting the poore,	87	Lent		47
My stuffe is flesh, not brasse; my senses live,	89	The Pearl		27
Therefore not sealed, but with open eyes	89	The Pearl		32
Therefore not seeled, but with open eyes	89	The Pearl	W	32
Yet through the labyrinths, not my groveling wit,	89	The Pearl		37
Yet through these labyrinths, not my groveling wit,	89	The Pearl	W	37
Lord, hunt me not,	89	Afflict.4		2
Oh help, my God! let not their plot	90	Afflict.4		19
Parrats may thank us, if they are not mute,	91	Man		11
I would not use a friend, as I use Thee.	93	Unkindness		5
I could not use a friend, as I use Thee.	93	Unkindness		10
Yet use I not my foes, as I use thee.	94	Unkindness		25
Since if my sent be good, I care not, if	94	Life		17
Were it not better to bestow	95	Submission		5
Do not so well agree.	95	Submission		16
For, I do praise thee, yet I praise thee not:	96	Justice 1		8
Who goes to bed and doth not pray,	96	Charms & K		7
Who goes to bed and does not pray,	96	Charms & K	W	7
That planted Paradise was not so firm,	97	Afflict.5		2
To make us thine: yet that we might not part,	97	Afflict.5		10
Makes them not dead:	98	Mortific.		10
Advise with Abraham, when thy power could not	99	Decay		3
Why he'l not lose a cup of drink for thee:	100	Miserie		8
Not he: he knows, where he can better be,	100	Miserie		10
They would not have their actions scann'd,	100	Miserie		21
And measure not their fall.	100	Miserie		24
Not suff'ring those	100	Miserie		29
He doth not like this vertue, no;	101	Miserie		45
Thou pull'st the rug, and wilt not rise,	101	Miserie		51
Thou lyest warme, and wilt not rise,	101	Miserie	W	51
No, not to purchase the whole pack of starres:	101	Miserie		52
Wonders and sings, but not his power	101	Miserie		57
And yet as though he knew it not,	102	Miserie		61
Off'ring their service, if I were not sped:	102	Jordan 2		8
This was not quick enough, and that was dead.	102	Jordan 2		10
To shew that state dislikes not easinesse.	103	Prayer 2		4
Thou canst no more not heare, then thou canst die.	103	Prayer 2		6
We cannot ask the thing, which is not there,	103	Prayer 2		11
Art thou possest, who, when thou couldst not die,	103	Prayer 2		14
Let it not thee displease,	104	Obedience		4
Let me not think an action mine own way,	104	Obedience		18
Yet since thou canst not choose but see my actions;	104	Obedience		23
Of what we might not take, or be withstood.	104	Obedience		30
Peace pratler, do not lowre:	105	Conscience		1
Not a fair look, but thou dost call it foul:	105	Conscience		2
Not a sweet dish, but thou dost call it sowre:	105	Conscience		3
And leaves thee not a word;	106	Conscience		16
No, not a tooth or nail to scratch,	106	Conscience		17
Did not affect thee much, was not thy aim;	106	Sion		8
Is not so deare to thee as one good grone.	106	Sion		18
Tombes for the dead, not temples fit for thee:	107	Sion		20
Thraldome from those, who would not at a feast	107	Home		21
So many yeares baptiz'd, and not appeare?	108	Home		27
Come dearest Lord, passe not this holy season,	109	Home		73
Outlandish looks may not compare:	109	Brit. Ch.		10
Which when I pluckt not, Sir, said she,	110	The Quip		6

NOT (cont'd)

	PAGE	TITLE	LINE
Speak not at large, say, I am thine:	111	The Quip	23
To whom the starres shine not so fair, as eyes;	111	Vanitie 2	3
And feel his death, but not his victorie.	112	Dawning	8
Arise sad heart; if thou dost not withstand,	112	Dawning	9
Arise sad heart; if thou doe not withstand,	112	Dawning V	9
Do not by hanging down break from the hand,	112	Dawning	11
Draws tears, or bloud, not want an handkerchief.	112	Dawning	16
Hast thou sighs, or hast thou not?	113	Businesse	11
If he had not liv'd for thee,	113	Businesse	20
Did he die, or did he not?	113	Businesse	25
If he had not di'd for thee,	113	Businesse	26
Who in heart not ever kneels,	114	Businesse	37
Finger not my treasure.	114	Dialogue	12
Of Joy and Charitie. Sir, you have not miss'd,	116	Love-joy	7
And not of thee, through whom my fingers bend	116	Providence	3
To hold my quill? shall they not do thee right?	116	Providence	4
Doth not refrain unto himself alone,	117	Providence	18
Thou art in small things great, not small in any:	118	Providence	41
Others do sleep, and envie not their cheer.	118	Providence	56
Rain, do not hurt my flowers; but gently spend	120	Providence	117
Your hony drops: presse not to smell them here:	120	Providence	118
Thy creatures leap not, but expresse a feast,	121	Providence	133
To show thou art not bound, as if thy lot	121	Providence	137
Most things move th' under-jaw; the Crocodile not.	121	Providence	139
Most things move th' underchaw; the Crocodile not.	121	Providence V	139
But words suffice not, where are lewd intentions:	122	Sinnes rd.	11
Yet ill deeds loyter not: for they supplie	122	Sinnes rd.	16
He doth not crave lesse time, but more.	123	Time	30
This not withstanding, thou wentst on,	124	Gratefulnes	17
Not that thou hast not still above	124	Gratefulnes	21
Not thankfull, when it pleaseth me;	124	Gratefulnes	29
He sweetly liv'd; yet sweetnesse did not save	125	Peace	25
Will not suffice our turn:	127	Giddinesse	26
Alas! our murmurings come not last.	128	Bunch Gr.	18
Yet still askt pardon, and was not deni'd.	129	Love unkn.	21
I would say thorns. Deare, could my heart not break,	130	Love unkn.	52
After the trimming, not the stuffe and ground.	131	Mans medly	18
Not, that he may not here	131	Mans medly	19
Wouldst thou not look?	133	The Method	12
Who do not their own motions heare?	134	The Method	19
Which needs not man, be ty'd to those	134	The Method	26
Who heare not him, but quickly heare	134	The Method	27
Could not that wisdome, which first broacht the wine,	134	Divinitie	9
Is all that saves, and not obscure.	135	Divinitie	24
Ephes. 4. 30. Grieve not the Holy Spirit, &c.	135	Ephes.	T
I sinne not to my grief alone,	136	Ephes.	17
But runnes, although I be not drie;	136	Ephes.	29
Yet if I wail not still, since still to wail	136	Ephes.	31
And where these are not found,	137	Familie	22
But not to make a constant stay.	137	Familie	24
To th' Isle of spices, is't not fair?	137	The Size	12
Is not a corpulent, but a thinne and spare,	138	The Size	32
Like a pretender, not a bride.	138	The Size	36
Grasp not at much, for fear thou losest all.	138	The Size	38
Which thou hast open'd: do not spread thy robe	138	The Size	43
But not of speech in starres, began to muse:	139	Artillerie	10
Then I refuse not ev'n with bloud	139	Artillerie	14
Not, but I am (I must say still)	139	Artillerie	21
Shunne not my arrows, and behold my breast.	139	Artillerie	28
But I was told by one, it could not be;	143	Holdfast	3
But to have nought is ours, not to confesse	143	Holdfast	9
Do not beguile my heart,	143	Complaining	1
My power and wisdome. Put me not to shame,	143	Complaining	3
Shows not thy word	143	Complaining	12
Let not thy wrathfull power	144	Complaining	16
Hast thou not made thy counts, and summ'd up all?	144	Discharge	6
Did not thy heart	144	Discharge	7
If, though thou didst not beat thy future brow,	144	Discharge	23
Raise not the mudde	145	Discharge	27
Dig not for wo	145	Discharge	29
On future grief, do not remove it thence,	145	Discharge	43
Either grief will not come: or if it must,	145	Discharge	51
Do not forecast.	145	Discharge	52
Sev'n whole dayes, not one in seven,	146	Praise 2	17
In my heart, though not in heaven,	146	Praise 2	19
Thy lusts have made, and not thy lusts alone;	147	Offering	15
Let not the winde	149	Longing	22
O be not now	149	Longing	33
Not heare?	149	Longing	36
Not to relieve? how can it be,	150	Longing	62
Well may he close his eyes, but not his heart.	151	The Bag	6
Hast thou not heard, that my Lord JESUS di'd?	151	The Bag	7
Not to his hurt. Sighs will convey	152	The Bag	41
Who by not keeping once, became a debter;	152	The Jews	5
To let me bloud, and not restore	153	The Collar	8
Not so, my heart: but there is fruit,	153	The Collar	17
Of what is fit, and not. Forsake thy cage,	153	The Collar	21
While thou didst wink and wouldst not see.	153	The Collar	26
Flowers look about, and die not in their prime.	154	Glimpse	10
Feeds not, but addes to the desire of meat.	154	Glimpse	12

NOT (cont'd)

	PAGE	TITLE	LINE
Pickt here and there a crumme, and would not die;	154	Glimpse	17
Disturb the work. O make me not their sport,	155	Glimpse	29
That all was not so fair, as I conceiv'd,	155	Assurance	8
Were from my self, I had not half a word,	155	Assurance	22
Not half a letter to oppose	155	Assurance	23
Thou art not onely to perform thy part,	156	Assurance	27
And rivers stirre, thou canst not shrink or quail:	156	Assurance	33
Which bounds on thee, and will not down thy throat:	156	Assurance	40
Not thee, but me, and to be mine:	157	Clasping	15
Not all the teams of Albion in a row	158	Praise 3	15
I have not lost one single tear:	158	Praise 3	25
And rest in Nature, not the God of Nature:	160	The Pulley	14
If goodnesse leade him not, yet wearinesse	160	The Pulley	19
I do not greatly wonder at the sight,	161	Priesthood	23
Wherefore I dare not, I, put forth my hand	161	Priesthood	31
O let not that of any thing;	163	The Search	33
Be not Almightie, let me say,	163	The Search	51
And serve thee; and not onely I,	164	The Crosse	4
Besides, things sort not to my will,	165	The Crosse	19
What frost to that? what pole is not the zone,	166	The Flower	32
Who cannot dresse it well, want wit, not words.	167	The Sonne	4
Yet slight not these few words:	168	a true Hymn	6
These arms shall crush thee. Spare not, do thy worst.	169	Dial.-Anth	8
If troubles overtake thee, do not wail:	170	Water-crs.	4
And all this not for my desert,	172	23 Psalme	11
Well may I walk, not fear:	173	23 Psalme	14
To make him clean, who could not be defil'd?	173	Marie Magd	8
Why kept she not her tears for her own faults,	173	Marie Magd	9
Why kept she not her tears for her own fauts,	173	Marie Magd V	9
And not his feet? Though we could dive	173	Marie Magd	10
Ev'n God himself: wherefore she was not loth,	173	Marie Magd	15
Another musick, making live not dead,	174	Aaron	13
My doctrine tun'd by Christ, (who is not dead,	174	Aaron	23
My servant, as thee not displeasing,	175	The Odour	24
As if grief were not foul, nor vertue winning.	176	The Foil	8
I passe not, I, what of the rest become,	176	Forerunners	9
With canvas, not with arras clothe their shame:	177	Forerunners	26
Yet if you go, I passe not; take your way:	177	Forerunners	31
Presse me not to take more pleasure	177	The Rose	1
But I will not much oppose	177	The Rose	13
But I health, not physick choose:	178	The Rose	29
Not a word or look	178	Discipline	9
Naming you not to your good:	180	Invitation	9
Taste and fear not: God is here	180	Invitation	16
And in my powers not stirre abroad,	183	A Parodie	9
Ah Lord! do not withdraw,	183	A Parodie	16
Say, that thou art not here.	183	A Parodie	20
That I not onely may not erre	184	The Elixer W	3
Not rudely, as a beast,	184	The Elixer	5
Will not grow bright and clean.	184	The Elixer	16
Will not to Heaven grow.	184	The Elixer W	16
Wherein I die, not live: for life is straight,	185	A Wreath	5
Thy mouth was open, but thou couldst not sing.	185	Death	4
What others mean to do, I know not well;	187	Judgement	6
Wert thou not born among the trees and leaves?	188	Heaven	5
Wert thou not born among the woods and leaves?	188	Heaven W	5
And know you not, sayes Love, who bore the blame?	189	Love 3	15
Which doth not meet with an eternall thought.	190	Ch.-Milit.	8
Which does not meet with an eternall thought.	190	Ch.-Milit. W	8
Not the decrees of power, but bands of love.	190	Ch.-Milit.	10
A sad repentance, not the spoils of lust:	192	Ch.-Milit.	68
Which using, and not fearing skill in th' one,	192	Ch.-Milit.	77
And not go lesse then she had done of late.	192	Ch.-Milit.	92
Sinne being not able to extirpate quite	194	Ch.-Milit.	161
It did not fit his gravitie to stirre,	195	Ch.-Milit.	197
Yet not as Sinne, but as Religion.	196	Ch.-Milit.	212
The pattern, but not so in vertuous deeds;	196	Ch.-Milit.	222
The second Temple could not reach the first:	196	Ch.-Milit.	225
Let not Sinne devoure thy fold,	199	L'Envoy	5
Concerneth bread not mee.	200	H. Commun. W	9
To' abolish Sinn, not Wheat.	200	H. Commun. W	21
Give me not that I had before,	201	H. Commun. W	46
And knew it not, yet cleansed mee.	202	love W	12
Did not confess in the first Theefe	202	Trin.Sun. W	12
For I decay not hee.	203	Even-song W	4
As if shades knew not Thee.	203	Even-song W	12
If that bee dark we can not see:	203	Even-song W	14
Yet Thou art not so dark, since I know this,	203	Even-song W	17
Which know not thee, suck in thy beames	203	Even-song W	23
Why are not Sonnets made of thee? and layes	206	Walton 1	5
Will not a verse run smooth that bears thy name?	206	Walton 1	11
Whose fire is wild, and doth not upward go	206	Walton 2	10
And then, my Labour's not lost.	207	Walton 3	6
My labour is not lost.	207	Walton 4	4
Although the Crosse could not Christ here detain,	439	Walton 5	1
Passe not by,	208	J. Danvers D	1
Onely, most noble Lord, shutt not the doore	209	L. Bacon D	9
And not from better fate,	210	Paradox D	16
Not from excesse, and therefore doe we spende	210	Paradox D	21
That which wee doe not neede:	210	Paradox D	22

NOT (cont'd)	PAGE	TITLE		LINE
Then for yourselves not us embrace	211	Paradox	D	37
Worthy had bin, thou hadst not lost thine owne:	211	Bohemia	D	2
Whose native beauty needs not dresse or lace	212	Bohemia	D	30
Thou shalt not bee a Queene and conquer there.	212	Bohemia	D	40
Thy teares not needing. For that hand Divine	213	Bohemia	D	63
The wicked are not so, but they	215	Psalm I	D	13
Therefore shall not the wicked be	215	Psalm I	D	17
Aided by him, I will not fear	216	Psalm III	D	13
and sin not any more.	217	Psalm IV	D	16
Rebuke me not in wrath, O Lord, ...	219	Psalm VI	D	1
Yea, have not oft deliver'd him	221	Psalm VII	D	13
Not that I think, if a man do not all which is here expressed,	224	Priest		10
if a man do not all which is here expressed, hee presently sinns,	224	Priest		10
who may not despise my poor labours, but add to those points,	224	Priest		14
Christ being not to continue on earth, but after hee had fulfilled	225	Priest 1		6
to whom this discourse ariseth not) some live in the Universities,	225	Priest 2		22
whose aim and labour must be not only to get knowledg, but to subdue	226	Priest 2		9
and not to think, that when they have read the Fathers, . .	226	Priest 2		10
Let not Chaplains think themselves so free, as many of them do,	226	Priest 2		19
where he shall not exercise what he is, unlesse he forsake his	226	Priest 2		26
Wherfore they are not to be over-submissive, and base, but to keep up	226	Priest 2		27
They who do not thus, while they remember their earthly Lord,	226	Priest 2		32
which in the day of wrath hath not one dramme of comfort for us.	227	Priest 3		21
The Parson doth not so, but orders his Life in such a fashicn,	227	Priest 3		31
as knowing, that if he be not so, he wil quickly be discovered,	228	Priest 3		6
by what they understand, are best led to what they understand not.	228	Priest 4		21
do not know the Scriptures, because they feel them not, . .	228	Priest 4		30
because they feel them not, and because they are not understood	228	Priest 4		31
and because they are not understood but with the same Spirit that	228	Priest 4		32
yet as diverse, not as repugnant:	229	Priest 4		15
As he doth not so study others, as to neglect the grace of God in	229	Priest 4		19
and that as one Countrey doth not bear all things, that there may be	229	Priest 4		23
For every one hath not digested, when it is a sin to take something	230	Priest 5		24
when it is a sin to take something for mony lent, or when not;	230	Priest 5		25
when it is a fault to discover anothers fault, or when not; . .	230	Priest 5		26
or honour, be a sin of covetousnes or ambition, and when not;	230	Priest 5		28
lust, and when not, and so in many circumstances of actions.	230	Priest 5		30
Now if a shepherd know not which grass will bane, or which not,	230	Priest 5		31
which grass will bane, or which not, how is he fit to be a shepherd?	230	Priest 5		32
yet not as himself alone, but as presenting with himself the whole	231	Priest 6		7
yet not so slow neither, as to let the fervency of the supplicant	231	Priest 6		17
which answers also are to be done not in a hudling, or slubbering	231	Priest 6		30
service, Rom. 12. when we speak not as Parrats, without reason,	232	Priest 6		3
who somtimes make it a piece of state not to come at the beginning	232	Priest 6		8
notwithstanding his instruction that they ought not to be so,	232	Priest 6		16
that not any ill will draws him to it, but the debt and obligation	232	Priest 6		18
who treads in his steps, and will not throw down what he hath built;	232	Priest 7		26
with letting them know, that he observes who marks, and who not;	233	Priest 7		2
he is not witty, or learned, or eloquent, but Holy. . . .	233	Priest 7		23
texts of Devotion, not Controversie, moving and ravishing texts,	233	Priest 7		27
Oh Lord, I know that the way of man is not in himself, &c. . .	234	Priest 7		6
And ceased not to give thanks for the Ephesians, Eph. 1. 16.	234	Priest 7		12
since we are here by him, and without him could not be here.	234	Priest 7		30
since the words apart are not Scripture, but a dictionary, . .	235	Priest 7		9
The Parson exceeds not an hour in preaching, because all ages have	235	Priest 7		11
and he that profits not in that time, will lesse afterwards,	235	Priest 7		12
the same affection which made him not profit before, making him then	235	Priest 7		13
him then weary, and so he grows from not relishing, to loathing.	235	Priest 7		14
that how or whenever he punish him, it be not in his Ministry:	235	Priest 8		27
his flock by themselves, whom his Sermons cannot, or doe not reach.	236	Priest 8		13
he hath not a woman in his house, but findes opportunities of having	237	Priest 9		8
He therefore thinkes it not enough for him to observe the fasting	237	Priest 9		21
and wondreth not so much at their patient suffering, and cheerfull	237	Priest 9		29
he is not afraid of the pestilence that walketh in darkenesse,	238	Priest 9		6
not his affection found out a fit wife for him, whose humble,	238	Priest 9		27
demanding an account, but not by the way of an account. . .	239	Priest 9		2
them with all Piety, not only of words in praying, and reading;	239	Priest 10		24
not sparing the eldest, but giving him the prerogative of his Fathers	239	Priest 10		31
which happily for his other children he is not able to do. . .	239	Priest 10		33
think fit to do so) he takes care not to put them into vain trades,	239	Priest 10		34
and vanities of the world, which he is to deny, and not augment.	240	Priest 10		5
give any thing above those, and not spent in them, he blesseth God,	240	Priest 10		11
and were it not his duty to have them so, it were his profit,	240	Priest 10		13
Even the wals are not idle, but something is written, or painted	240	Priest 10		23
He suffers not a ly or equivocation by any means in his house,	240	Priest 10		32
But those which his home produceth, he refuseth not, as coming cheap,	241	Priest 10		22
and doing that which either he could not do, or was not fit for him	241	Priest 10		32
or was not fit for him to do, by taking both sorts of food into them,	241	Priest 10		32
which he celebrates not only with abstinence of diet, but also	241	Priest 10		38
performed by keeping of the twc former, had not Authority interposed:	242	Priest 10		9
and not the fish, is to keep the fasting day naturally. . .	242	Priest 10		14
For meat was made for man, not man for meat.	242	Priest 10		32
not for emboldening the unruly, but for the comfort of the weak,	242	Priest 10		33
that not onely sicknesse breaks these obligations of fasting,	242	Priest 10		34
I am inclined, as not to get out of that sicknesse, when I am in it,	242	Priest 10		37
is nothing that is food, and not phisick, which doth lesse obstruct,	243	Priest 10		2
Not but that the poor are welcome also to his table, whom he	243	Priest 11		9
of such things, and will not be perswaded, but being not invited,	243	Priest 11		21
and will not be perswaded, but being not invited, they are hated.	243	Priest 11		21
and vertuously, not for any reward of his, but for vertues sake;	243	Priest 11		28

NOT (cont'd)

	PAGE	TITLE	LINE
yet that will not be so:	243	Priest 11	29
that he may, if not the best way, yet any way, make his Parish good.	244	Priest 11	4
counting that day lost, wherein he hath not exercised his Charity.	244	Priest 12	18
that there be not a begger, or idle person in his Parish,	244	Priest 12	19
name and effect of Charity with the poor people, though not with God:	244	Priest 12	27
paines in their vocation, as not knowing when they shal be relieved;	245	Priest 12	3
not suffering any that day that hee receives, to want a good meal	245	Priest 12	7
and when his own stock serves not, working those that are able	245	Priest 12	12
But these he helps not without some testimony, except the evidence	245	Priest 12	21
and reverend, not with light colours, or foolish anticks.	246	Priest 13	13
appointed by Authority be there, and those not torne, or fouled,	246	Priest 13	14
not as out of necessity, or as putting a holiness in the things,	246	Priest 13	23
the Cures with their own hands, and not to put them over to servants.	247	Priest 14	20
that they dive not too deep into worldly affairs, plunging themselves	247	Priest 14	24
as if it were in their own hands to thrive, or not to thrive.	247	Priest 14	31
as that they make not that the end of their labour, but that they may	248	Priest 14	6
and opens not cnly his mouth, but his purse to their relief,	248	Priest 14	10
ill imployed, he chides not at first, for that were neither civill,	248	Priest 14	14
for they are not sensible of finenesse:	248	Priest 14	18
that he may keep himself pure, and not be intangled in others sinnes.	248	Priest 14	24
who can read, who not;	248	Priest 14	35
of particularizing in these things, hee were not fit to be a Parson:	249	Priest 14	1
fails not to afford his best comforts, and rather goes to them,	249	Priest 15	15
from the certainty both of deliverance, and reward, if we faint not;	249	Priest 15	26
The Countrey Parson is not only a father to his flock, but also	250	Priest 16	7
he hateth him not as an officer, but pityes him as a Father:	250	Priest 16	11
yet hee gives him not over, but is long before hee proceede	250	Priest 16	17
being all his joy, and thought) leaveth not his Ministry behind him;	251	Priest 17	1
he refuseth not to joyne, that he may enlarge the glory of God	251	Priest 17	7
wish them best, and that not a desire to meddle with others affairs,	251	Priest 17	31
This was not so well said, as it might have been forborn;	252	Priest 18	9
Your meaning is not thus, but thus;	252	Priest 18	11
but this will not stand.	252	Priest 18	12
he borrowes them not to serve the turne, nor provides slight,	252	Priest 19	26
and therefore not for him, who is hearty, and true in all his wayes,	253	Priest 19	1
Ministeriall office, which is not to the prejudice of his own Parish.	253	Priest 19	17
and not the lesse, lest he cast their neighbours poverty on them	254	Priest 19	6
done either wel or ill, whereof he is not the rewarder, or punisher.	254	Priest 20	11
he forgets not himself, but is first a Sermon to himself,	255	Priest 21	14
who are not well grounded, may then by an honourable way take	255	Priest 21	30
Then are there some things to be beleeved that are not seen?	256	Priest 21	9
Is not Christianity full of such things, as are not to be seen,	256	Priest 21	10
full of such things, as are not to be seen, but beleeved?	256	Priest 21	11
That position will not hold in Christianity, because it contains	256	Priest 21	24
making what hee knows to serve him in that which he knows not:	257	Priest 21	1
And the answerer could not tell;	257	Priest 21	4
for he could not but say, he would hast out of it as fast as he	257	Priest 21	7
things of ordinary use are not only to serve in the way of drudgery,	257	Priest 21	14
in a great confusion, as being not only to receive God, but to break,	257	Priest 22	29
for thou art not only the feast, but the way to it.	257	Priest 22	34
the presence of all, and Baptizeth not willingly, but on Sundayes,	258	Priest 22	2
Baptisme being a blessing, that the word hath not the like.	258	Priest 22	7
and thinketh the Ceremony not onely innocent, but reverend.	258	Priest 22	9
that the elements be of the best, not cheape, or course,	258	Priest 22	22
not on the Sunday of the Communion only (for then it is too late)	258	Priest 22	26
who having not received yet, are to enter into this great work,	258	Priest 22	29
The time of every ones first receiving is not so much by yeers,	258	Priest 22	32
being ripe enough for ill things, and why not then for better?	259	Priest 22	2
The saying of the Catechism is necessary, but not enough;	259	Priest 22	7
if not duly once a month, yet at least five or six times in the year;	259	Priest 22	20
not onely for the benefit of the work, but also for the discharge	259	Priest 22	23
who being to present all that receive not thrice a year;	259	Priest 22	25
Church-Wardens so well take notice who receive thrice, and who not.	259	Priest 22	28
to be all to his Parish, and not onely a Pastour, but a Lawyer also,	259	Priest 23	30
Therefore hee endures not that any of his Flock should go to Law;	259	Priest 23	31
and dark nature, not easily determinable by Lawyers themselves;	260	Priest 23	20
and not as enemies, neither avoyding therfore one anothers company,	260	Priest 23	26
whom yet he ever exhorts not to exceed his bounds, but in tickle	260	Priest 23	35
and so not be drowned altogether in the works of their vocation,	261	Priest 23	23
he doth not onely prefer hcme-bred things before them, but condemns	261	Priest 23	37
his wife seeks nct the city, but preferrs her garden and fields	262	Priest 23	4
yet he looks not in this point of Curing beyond his own Parish,	262	Priest 23	12
the person bee so poor, that he is not able to reward the Phisician:	262	Priest 23	14
not to incroach on others Professions, but to live on his own.	262	Priest 23	16
whether having a rule, it ought not to be guided by it;	263	Priest 24	2
the other of not giving scandall, that ought not to be preferred,	263	Priest 24	9
that ought not to be preferred, especially since in disobeying there	263	Priest 24	10
he forbears not in any wise to use the delinquent as before,	263	Priest 25	25
not avoyding his company, cr doing any thing of aversenesse,	263	Priest 25	27
there are some persons, who abstain not even from known sins;	264	Priest 26	10
who when they kncw a sin evidently, they commit it not.	264	Priest 26	12
because the natures of these vices being not evidently discussed,	264	Priest 26	17
or known commonly, the beginnings of them are not easily observable:	264	Priest 26	19
and the beginnings of them are not observed, because of the suddain	264	Priest 26	19
not knowing the bounds of the action, nor when his eating begins	264	Priest 26	24
not because they are all that are of this dark, and creeping	265	Priest 26	1
either spends not at all, or not in some proportion to Gods blessing	265	Priest 26	6
or not in some proportion to Gods blessing upon him, is covetous.	265	Priest 26	6
if I do not give every thing its end, I abuse the Creature,	265	Priest 26	9
sometimes too salt, and so not competent nourishment, I am Covetous.	265	Priest 26	22

NOT (cont'd)

	PAGE	TITLE	LINE
and fix them on their charge, and not on their preferment.	266	Priest 26	5
and this they are not masters of.	266	Priest 26	23
that if after dinner they are not fit (or un-weeldy) either to pray,	266	Priest 26	31
Not that all must presently work after dinner;	266	Priest 26	32
(For they rather must not work, especially Students, and those that	266	Priest 26	33
as that it is not meate or drinke that hinders them from working.	266	Priest 26	35
disposition I am, either hungry or not, according as I feele my self,	267	Priest 26	8
live in health, not keep an uniform diet, but to feed variously,	267	Priest 26	10
they would have fainted, had they returned empty, He suffered it not;	267	Priest 26	24
as knowing that nature will not bear everlasting droopings,	267	Priest 27	34
not onely because all men shun the company of perpetuall severity,	268	Priest 27	1
especially in his own Parish he suffers it not to his utmost power;	268	Priest 28	18
which is not easily despised, except it degenerate to pride.	268	Priest 28	26
if it be not thwarted, the Parson having a due respect both	268	Priest 28	32
But if the Contempt be not punishable by Law, or being so,	269	Priest 28	3
you hurt your selfe, not me;	269	Priest 28	13
they resist not the evill which takes hold of them, and is farr	269	Priest 28	24
Wherefore the Parson suffers not the place to be vilified or debased,	270	Priest 29	7
urges the best unto it, shewing that they do not loose, or go lesse,	270	Priest 29	9
that things are not set in such an inevitable order, but that God	270	Priest 30	30
so that corne doth not grow by any other vertue, then by that which	271	Priest 30	4
yet when God pleased, the sun stood stil, the fire burned not.	271	Priest 30	12
yet if he suite not other things to the growth, as seasons,	271	Priest 30	16
and not break off their acts of dependance, how faire soever	271	Priest 30	26
For that he ought not to break off, but to continue his dependance	271	Priest 30	34
on God, not cnely before the corne is inned, but after also;	271	Priest 30	35
yet if God give him not the Grace to use, and utter this well,	272	Priest 30	2
Better were his corne burnt, then not spiritually improved.	272	Priest 30	4
But these prayers are not necessary, but additionary.	272	Priest 31	28
Christian, that this prayer being additionary, not necessary;	273	Priest 31	5
not commanded, the omission thereof upon just occasion ought by no	273	Priest 31	5
but to go on as cheerfully, as if he had not been interrupted.	273	Priest 31	11
that this interruption proceed not out of slacknes, or coldness,	273	Priest 31	16
he be a little affected therewith, but not afflicted, or troubled;	273	Priest 31	19
if he resent it to a mislike, but not a griefe.	273	Priest 31	20
Secondly, that this interruption proceede not out of shame.	273	Priest 31	21
not out of superstition, but of reverence to Gods house,	273	Priest 31	22
I will not doubt to go without staying to pray there (but onely,	273	Priest 31	34
is additionary, not necessary, and the other duty overweighs it:	273	Priest 31	36
throw it away, and be most confident, that God is not displeased.	274	Priest 31	1
The Countrey Parson hath not onely taken a particular Survey	274	Priest 32	4
nothing to do, lets go to the Tavern, or to the stews, or what not.	274	Priest 32	14
them honestly, and seasonably, when they are not better imployed.	274	Priest 32	31
Now this reason crosseth not our Saviours precept of selling what we	274	Priest 32	32
given it to the poor, we must not be idle, but labour to get more,	274	Priest 32	33
But it will not be amisse in this exceeding usefull point to descend	275	Priest 32	17
so it exceed not bounds, for every one to imploy himselfe	275	Priest 32	28
for so excellent a Place, not to refuse, but rather to procure it.	276	Priest 32	17
they are not in this Consideration, because we are about a Calling,	276	Priest 32	36
he must not cnly be a morning man, but at Committees also;	277	Priest 32	11
and not ingaged into some Profession by their Parents, whose neglect	277	Priest 32	25
which are not only a noble, but also as they may be handled,	278	Priest 32	6
Just so it is in Divinity, and that not without manifest reason:	278	Priest 33	33
an act of the mind, not of the Body, even as the Originall signifies;	279	Priest 33	14
since we are not Masters of our bodies, this sufficeth.	279	Priest 33	19
Not that weeping is not usefull, where it can be, that so the body	279	Priest 33	26
Not that weeping is not usefull, where it can be, that so the body	279	Priest 33	27
but that, so the other acts be, that is not necessary:	279	Priest 33	29
not only in the beginning of his preaching, but afterwards also,	280	Priest 34	8
and not to let go the raines as soon as the horse goes easie.	280	Priest 34	15
not to take the full compasse, and liberty of their Peace:	280	Priest 34	21
not to eate of all those dishes at table, which even their present	280	Priest 34	22
If we would judg ourselves, we should not be judged;	280	Priest 34	31
and if we would bound our selves, we should not be bounded.	280	Priest 34	32
he sees not how a house could be either built without a builder,	281	Priest 34	18
He conceives not possibly, how the windes should blow so much as they	281	Priest 34	20
not only without dissolution of the whole, but also of any part,	281	Priest 34	22
He conceives not possibly, how he that would beleeve a Divinity,	281	Priest 34	27
in all Lands, was intended not only for a punishment to them;	282	Priest 34	14
that that generation should not passe, till all were fulfilled,	282	Priest 34	28
saw not more Divinity, then he that reads the womans oyntment in	283	Priest 34	1
not so much doubting a God, as that he is theirs;	283	Priest 34	6
which in the Creation needed not, gave them love for love,	283	Priest 34	16
not any sin else, but is within his Love;	283	Priest 34	24
The thrusting away of his arme makes us onely not embraced.	283	Priest 34	26
and if they will not reforme, presents them.	284	Priest 35	13
and obsolete, and not the fashion, he reformes, and teaches them,	284	Priest 35	31
that at Baptisme they professed not to be ashamed of Christs Cross,	284	Priest 35	32
whereas he thinks it not onely a grave, and reverend thing,	285	Priest 36	3
Those who use it not, do so either out of niceness, because they like	285	Priest 36	4
unbefitting a Minister, that it deserves reproof, not refutation:	285	Priest 36	8
But this was not proper to Christ, or the Apostles cnly,	285	Priest 36	12
how shall not the ministration of the spirit exceed in blessing?	285	Priest 36	19
for it was not the person, but Priesthood, that blessed;	285	Priest 36	23
had delivered them to Satan, that they might learn not to Blaspheme.	286	Priest 36	2
because it is not performed by way of request, but of confidence,	286	Priest 36	7
many an evill may not only be, but also spread in his Parish,	287	Priest 37	1
for we must not do evill, that good may come of it.	287	Priest 37	6
may talk, so they do it not with sport, but commiseration;)	287	Priest 37	14
and more, they may discover them to those that know them not:	287	Priest 37	17

NOT (cont'd)

	PAGE	TITLE	LINE
the Gospel doth not, which hath so much advanced Charity, . .	287	Priest 37	22
As the executioner is not uncharitable, that takes away the life	287	Priest 37	25
therefore we sons of men are not consumed.	288	Priest	22
and hast made our salvation, not our punishment, thy glory: . .	288	Priest	23
so that then where sin abounded, not death, but grace superabounded;	288	Priest	25
many waters could not quench thy love!	288	Priest	31
thou hast committed, not to Thunder, or Angels, but to silly	289	Priest	4
to convert those who are not yet thine, and to confirme those that	289	Priest	16
O let not our foolish and unworthy hearts rob us of the continuance	289	Priest	19
that as the rain returns not empty, so neither may thy word,	289	Priest	31
that Intemperance was not such an evil, but it might easily be	291	Cornaro	6
which did not onely begin, but had already gone farre in me,	291	Cornaro	18
then not liking that kinde of Diet, followed my Appetite, . .	292	Cornaro	26
within lesse then a yeare I was not onely freed from all those evils	293	Cornaro	20
but also afterwards I fell not into that yearely disease, . .	293	Cornaro	22
Yet could I not so avoid all these, but that now and then I fell into	293	Cornaro	37
no inconvenience thereby, because that humour abounded not in me.	294	Cornaro	22
that they could not be much troubled, or make a great concourse,	295	Cornaro	9
that old age could not be sustained with so little meat and drink;	295	Cornaro	22
which yet needs not onely to be sustained, but also to gather	295	Cornaro	23
but also to gather strength, which could not be but by meat & drink.	295	Cornaro	24
But all these things could not defend me against their importunities.	296	Cornaro	5
Besides all this, I could not sleep, no not a quarter of an houre:	296	Cornaro	22
and suffered not any new of that kinde to arise, neither the good	296	Cornaro	33
without such observation, as is not easily to be made upon others;	297	Cornaro	30
qualities to me, if I had not found them out by long experience?	297	Cornaro	35
I denie not but that Physicians are necessarie, and greatly to be	298	Cornaro	3
who not onely as a friend doth visit thee, but help thee! . .	298	Cornaro	9
But they consider not, of how great moment ten yeares are in mature	298	Cornaro	29
are not almost all the learned books that we have, written by their	298	Cornaro	32
not onely in the citie, but also in villages and hamlets. . .	299	Cornaro	3
and later yeares, it is no such thing which may not be performed;	299	Cornaro	7
there needs not many and curious things, but onely that a man should	299	Cornaro	8
and divers labours, which suit not with an orderly life: . .	299	Cornaro	14
ought not to eat, but such meats as are agreeable to his disease,	299	Cornaro	30
No man is forbidden to eat fruit or fish, which I eat not: . .	300	Cornaro	8
and not the qualitie for his rule, which is very easie to be	300	Cornaro	15
the presuming upon it ought not to leade us to a disorderly life.	300	Cornaro	20
It is not the part of a wise man, to expose himself to so many	300	Cornaro	22
I am not wearie of life, which I passe with great delight. . .	301	Cornaro	3
In former time it was not so, because the place was moorish . .	301	Cornaro	26
To change my bed, troubles me not;	302	Cornaro	12
Italie is very great) receiving not any hurt or inconvenience	302	Cornaro	19
and the Grace of God I feel not those perturbations of bodie	302	Cornaro	24
That the life which I live at this age, is not a dead, dumpish,	303	Cornaro	10
not onely a shamefull thing to fear that which cannot be avoided;	303	Cornaro	21
(setting casualties aside) I shall not die but by a pure resolution:	303	Cornaro	26
discover some care, which I forbare not in the midst of my griefes;	304	Valdesso	3
there are some things which I like not in him, as my fragments will	304	Valdesso	16
holy Scriptures have not only an Elementary use, but a use . .	306	Valdesso	18
but not as a naked Word severed from God, but as the Word of God:	306	Valdesso	29
And in so doing they doe not sever their trust from God. . .	307	Valdesso	2
that it is not to be understood of actuall sinnes, but habituall,	308	Valdesso	2
distinction, for Fomes is not taken away, but Accensio Fomitis;	308	Valdesso	15
the naturall concupiscence is not quite extinguished, but the heate	308	Valdesso	16
not by relation, whereby I understand he meaneth only the effectuall	308	Valdesso	30
and not any private Enthusiasmes, or Revelations:	308	Valdesso	33
is not that which filleth the heart with joy and peace in believing;	309	Valdesso	2
this I call beleeving by Revelation, and not by Relation. . .	309	Valdesso	7
H. Scriptures (as I wrote before) have not only an Elementary use,	309	Valdesso	20
same Psalme it is evident, that he was not meanly conversant in them.	309	Valdesso	28
the dayes of the Gospell will not give an outward Law of Ceremonies	310	Valdesso	5
For as the servant leaves not the letter when he hath read it,	310	Valdesso	27
in regard it presents us not with the same thing only when it is read	310	Valdesso	33
if we believe not, no vertue shall helpe us.	311	Valdesso	25
we shall not be punished (which word I like here better then	311	Valdesso	26
even the godly are chastized but not punished) for evill doing	311	Valdesso	28
or living, for all the point lies in believing or not believing.	311	Valdesso	30
He meaneth (I suppose) that a man presume not to merit, . .	312	Valdesso	14
and that by restraining him from what he would not have him doe.	313	Valdesso	23
meanes a mans fre-will is only in outward, not in spirituall things.	313	Valdesso	33
holy Scripture, he meaneth that we should not use it as the onely,	314	Valdesso V	4
and not those which are in themselves occasions of sinne; . .	314	Valdesso	18
Feare is given to Christ, but not doubt, and upon good ground.	315	Valdesso	12
that the world pierceth not godly mens actions no more then Gods,	315	Valdesso	30
[the law is not made for a righteous man:]	315	Valdesso	34
so need not Abraham's Equivocation, nor Paul's neither, . .	316	Valdesso	7
which strictly he was not, though in the point of Resurrection he	316	Valdesso	8
But it is one thing not to judge, another to defend them. . .	316	Valdesso	14
perhaps he meant all of this later not of the former. . . .	317	Valdesso	5
whereas there is not onely milke there, but strong meat also.	317	Valdesso	24
and not used it for a time onely, and then cast it away, . .	318	Valdesso	3
Joseph knew her not, untill shee had brought forth her first borne	318	Valdesso	12
I doe not then bid him goe away but rather stay longer, . .	318	Valdesso	15
doth not bid them then cast away the word, or leave it off: . .	318	Valdesso	19
and arrives not to the point it should, which if it did, . .	319	Valdesso	11
he meaneth not the very Ceremonies of the Jewes, which no Christian	319	Valdesso	34
Hee that stumbles and falles not, mends his pace.	321	Proverbs	7
Looke not for muske in a dogges kennell.	321	Proverbs	23
Not a long day, but a good heart rids worke.	321	Proverbs	24

NOT (cont'd)

	PAGE	TITLE		LINE
Great strokes make not sweete musick.	322	Proverbs		26
The Devill is not alwaies at one doore.	322	Proverbs		31
Hee looseth nothing, that looseth not God.	322	Proverbs		35
He that will take the bird, must not skare it.	322	Proverbs		42
A Marchant that gaines not, looseth.	322	Proverbs		47
Let not him that feares feathers come among wild-foule.	322	Proverbs		48
Evening words are not like to morning.	323	Proverbs		65
Were there no fooles, badd ware would not passe.	323	Proverbs		66
Hee stands not surely, that never slips.	323	Proverbs		68
Hee stands not surely, that never slipte.	323	Proverbs	V	68
Who is so deafe, as he that will not heare?	323	Proverbs		79
Who is so deafe, as he who will not heare?	323	Proverbs	V	79
Hee that goes barefoot, must not plant thornes.	323	Proverbs		82
They that are booted are not alwaies ready.	323	Proverbs		83
All truths are not to be told.	324	Proverbs		89
Whether shall the Oxe goe, where he shall not labour?	324	Proverbs		98
The tongue walkes where the teeth speede not.	324	Proverbs		102
Deceive not thy Physitian, Confessor, nor Lawyer.	324	Proverbs		105
A good pay-master starts not at assurances.	324	Proverbs		113
A child correct behind and not before.	324	Proverbs		118
A horse and a child correct behind and not before.	324	Proverbs	V	118
To a boyling pot flies come not.	325	Proverbs		123
Who hath no more bread then neede, must not keepe a dog.	325	Proverbs		128
saies they are not ripe.	325	Proverbs		130
Though the Mastiffe be gentle, yet bite him not by the lippe.	325	Proverbs		132
Though the Mastiffe be gentile, yet bite him not by the lippe.	325	Proverbs	V	132
The wrongs of a Husband or Master are not reproached.	325	Proverbs		139
Love your neighbour, yet pull not downe your hedge.	325	Proverbs		141
Love your neighbour, but pull not downe your hedge.	325	Proverbs	V	141
Dally not with mony or women.	326	Proverbs		150
To buy deare is not bounty.	326	Proverbs		156
Jest not with the eye or with Religion.	326	Proverbs		157
and with it you will not know your selfe.	326	Proverbs		159
Cover your selfe with your shield, and care not for cryes.	326	Proverbs		161
Ever since we weare cloathes, we know not one another.	326	Proverbs		168
Our owne actions are our security, not others judgements.	326	Proverbs		173
Our owne actions secure us not others judgements.	326	Proverbs	V	173
One stroke fells not an oke.	327	Proverbs		181
God complaines not, but doth what is fitting.	327	Proverbs		182
Whose house is of glasse, must not throw stones at another.	327	Proverbs		196
Hee that lookes not before, finds himselfe behind.	327	Proverbs		200
He that plaies his mony ought not to value it.	327	Proverbs		201
In life you lov'd me not, in death you bewaile me.	328	Proverbs		218
Into a mouth shut flies flie not.	328	Proverbs		219
One graine fills not a sacke, but helpes his fellowes.	328	Proverbs		226
Honour and profit lie not in one sacke.	328	Proverbs		232
An ill wound is cured, not an ill name.	329	Proverbs		245
The wise hand doth not all that the foolish mouth speakes.	329	Proverbs		246
What your glasse telles you, will not be told by Councell.	329	Proverbs		255
In the world who knowes not to swimme, goes to the bottome.	330	Proverbs		285
In the world who can not swimme, goe to the bottome.	330	Proverbs	V	285
Chuse not an house neere an Inne (viz. for noise)	330	Proverbs		286
Hee is a foole that thinks not that another thinks.	330	Proverbs		287
The Lyon is not so fierce as they paint him.	330	Proverbs		289
Goe not for every griefe to the Physitian,	331	Proverbs		290
There were no ill language, if it were not ill taken.	331	Proverbs		294
The groundsell speakes not save what it heard at the hinges.	331	Proverbs		295
Call me not an olive, till thou see me gathered.	331	Proverbs		301
That is not good language which all understand not.	331	Proverbs		302
All is not gold that glisters.	331	Proverbs		306
Bee not idle and you shall not bee longing.	331	Proverbs		308
He is not poore that hath little, but he that desireth much.	331	Proverbs		309
Let none say, I will not drinke water.	331	Proverbs		310
Hee wrongs not an old man that steales his supper from him.	331	Proverbs		311
Keep not ill men company, lest you increase the number.	331	Proverbs		314
God strikes not with both hands,	331	Proverbs		315
Bee not a Baker, if your head be of butter.	332	Proverbs		321
Although it raine, throw not away thy watering pot.	332	Proverbs		325
Although the sun shine, leave not thy cloake at home.	332	Proverbs		326
at his time, and not till then.	332	Proverbs		333
Hee that repaires not a part, builds all.	333	Proverbs		344
Hee that repaires not a part, at length must all.	333	Proverbs	V	344
A discontented man knowes not where to sit easie.	333	Proverbs		345
He that is not handsome at 20, nor strong at 30, nor rich at 40,	333	Proverbs		349
Hee that doth what hee will, doth not what he ought.	333	Proverbs		350
must not say to another; Blow.	333	Proverbs		353
Hee that gives thee a bone, would not have thee die.	333	Proverbs		355
Hee that demands misseth not, unlesse his demands be foolish.	333	Proverbs		359
He that takes not up a pin, slights his wife.	333	Proverbs		361
He that owes nothing, if he makes not mouthes at us, is courteous.	333	Proverbs		362
hee that beleeveth nothing, hitts not.	333	Proverbs		364
The dog that licks ashes, trust not with meale.	334	Proverbs		389
The buyer needes a hundred eyes, the seller not one.	334	Proverbs		390
He carries well, to whom it waighes not.	334	Proverbs		391
Who likes not the drinke, God deprives him of bread.	334	Proverbs		394
Water a farre off quencheth not fire.	334	Proverbs		398
Love is not found in the market.	334	Proverbs		401
but not a hundred sons one father.	335	Proverbs		404
but an 100 sons are not enough to govern one Father.	335	Proverbs	V	404
Dearths foreseene come not.	335	Proverbs		407

NOT (cont'd)

	PAGE	TITLE		LINE
Deaths foreseene come not.	335	Proverbs	V	407
A hundred loade of thought will not pay one of debts.	335	Proverbs		414
Who doth his owne businesse, foules not his hands.	335	Proverbs		419
his head akes not at the matter.	335	Proverbs		421
Who hath bitter in his mouth, spits not all sweet.	335	Proverbs		422
He that hath children, all his morsels are not his owne.	335	Proverbs		423
He who hath children, all his morsels are not his owne.	335	Proverbs	V	423
He that hath a head of waxe must not walke in the sunne.	335	Proverbs		425
Hee that respects not, is not respected.	335	Proverbs		427
He that measures not himselfe, is measured.	336	Proverbs		432
He that would be well, needs not goe from his owne house.	336	Proverbs		442
Councell breakes not the head.	336	Proverbs		443
Trust not one nights ice.	336	Proverbs		453
The good mother sayes not, Will you? but gives.	337	Proverbs		467
we ought not to trust another.	338	Proverbs		490
Faire is not faire, but that which pleaseth.	338	Proverbs		492
He that's long a giving, knowes not how to give.	338	Proverbs		494
All feete tread not in one shoe.	338	Proverbs		497
If the wise erred not, it would goe hard with fooles.	338	Proverbs		510
If wise men erred not, it would goe hard with fooles.	338	Proverbs	V	510
Musick helps not the tooth-ach.	339	Proverbs		532
Hee that should have what hee hath not,	340	Proverbs		559
should doe what he doth not.	340	Proverbs		559
Hee that would have what hee hath not,	340	Proverbs	V	559
must doe what he doth not.	340	Proverbs	V	559
He that lives not well one yeare, sorrowes seven after.	340	Proverbs		562
He that hopes not for good, feares not evill.	340	Proverbs		563
let him not put them on his head.	340	Proverbs		567
Bells call others, but themselves enter not into the Church.	340	Proverbs		571
A gift much expected is paid, not given.	340	Proverbs		574
The Royall Crowne cures not the head-ach.	340	Proverbs		576
To have money is a feare, not to have it a griefe.	341	Proverbs		591
The Catt sees not the mouse ever.	341	Proverbs		592
The fatt man knoweth not, what the leane thinketh.	341	Proverbs		605
A wise man needes not blush for changing his purpose.	342	Proverbs		613
The March sunne raises but dissolves not.	342	Proverbs		614
The wine in the bottell doth not quench thirst.	342	Proverbs		616
A noble plant suites not with a stubborne ground.	342	Proverbs		622
The ballance distinguisheth not betweene gold and lead.	342	Proverbs		629
The reasons of the poore weigh not.	342	Proverbs		633
Send not a Catt for Lard.	342	Proverbs		644
In a Leopard the spotts are not observed.	343	Proverbs		660
A wise man cares not for what he cannot have.	343	Proverbs		662
It's not good fishing before the net.	343	Proverbs		663
He cannot be vertuous that is not rigorous.	343	Proverbs		664
That which will not be spun,	343	Proverbs		665
let it not come betweene the spindle and the distaffe.	343	Proverbs		665
When my house burnes, it's not good playing at Chesse.	343	Proverbs		666
A holy habit clenseth not a foule soule.	343	Proverbs		669
Forbeare not sowing because of birds.	343	Proverbs		670
Mention not a halter in the house of him that was hanged.	343	Proverbs		671
Speake not of a dead man at the table.	343	Proverbs		672
A hatt is not made for one shower.	343	Proverbs		673
If the mother had not beene in the oven,	344	Proverbs		696
you could not fill all to your mind.	343	Proverbs	V	700
you could not fit all to your mind.	344	Proverbs		701
If fooles should not foole it, they shall lose their season.	343	Proverbs	V	702
If fooles should not foole it, they should loose their season.	344	Proverbs		703
The effect speakes, the tongue needes not.	345	Proverbs		709
It's a proud horse that will not carry his owne provender.	345	Proverbs		712
All keyes hang not on one girdle.	345	Proverbs		719
All the Armes of England will not arme feare.	345	Proverbs		722
He that will not have peace, God gives him warre.	345	Proverbs		729
To him that will, waies are not wanting.	345	Proverbs		730
It's a poore sport that's not worth the candle.	346	Proverbs		752
Give not S. Peter so much, to leave Saint Paul nothing.	346	Proverbs		763
He that feares leaves, let him not goe into the wood.	346	Proverbs		768
Prayse not thyself, thy actions serve the Turne.	347	Proverbs	V	771
Hee that hath a wife and children wants not businesse.	347	Proverbs		778
He that feares death lives not.	347	Proverbs		781
He that doth what he should not, shall feele what he would not.	347	Proverbs		783
take not to serve you, if you will be served neately.	347	Proverbs		794
He that serves well needes not ask his wages.	347	Proverbs		798
Faire language grates not the tongue.	347	Proverbs		799
All are not merry that dance lightly.	348	Proverbs		808
Curtesie on one side only lasts not long.	348	Proverbs		809
Weening is not measure.	348	Proverbs		811
In an hundred elles of contention, there is not an inch of love.	348	Proverbs		817
Hast comes not alone.	348	Proverbs		826
Hee is not free that drawes his chaine.	348	Proverbs		830
Hee goes not out of his way, that goes to a good Inne.	348	Proverbs		831
Hee lookes not well to himselfe that lookes not ever.	349	Proverbs		835
He thinkes not well, that thinkes not againe.	349	Proverbs		836
Religion, Credit, and the Eye are not to be touched.	349	Proverbs		837
The tongue is not steele, yet it cuts.	349	Proverbs		838
A stone in a well is not lost.	349	Proverbs		845
He that endures is not overcome.	349	Proverbs		854
Who praiseth Saint Peter, doth not blame Saint Paul.	349	Proverbs		859
He that hath not the craft, let him shut up shop.	349	Proverbs		860
The Rich knowes not who is his friend.	349	Proverbs		865

NOT (cont'd)	PAGE	TITLE	LINE
The Cow knowes not what her taile is worth, till she have lost it.	350	Proverbs	870
Hee hath not liv'd, that lives not after death.	350	Proverbs	873
That which sufficeth is not little.	350	Proverbs	876
The ofspring of those that are very young, or very old, lasts not.	350	Proverbs	887
Hee hath no leisure who useth it not.	351	Proverbs	897
The Law is not the same at morning and at night.	351	Proverbs	905
Halfe the world knowes not how the other halfe lives.	351	Proverbs	907
Halfe the world knowes not how the other halfe lies.	351	Proverbs	V 907
Sinnes are not knowne till they bee acted.	352	Proverbs	942
Count not fowre except you have them in a wallett.	352	Proverbs	962
You may be on land, yet not in a garden.	353	Proverbs	964
Wee know not who lives or dies.	353	Proverbs	966
For a morning raine leave not your journey.	353	Proverbs	976
One faire day in winter makes not birds merrie.	353	Proverbs	977
Hee that hath charge of soules transports them not in bundles.	353	Proverbs	986
puts not himselfe into a good way.	354	Proverbs	995
Speake not of my debts, unlesse you meane to pay them.	354	Proverbs	998
He that is not in the warres is not out of danger.	354	Proverbs	999
If the husband be not at home, there is nobodie.	354	Proverbs	1016
An oath that is not to bee made is not to be kept.	354	Proverbs	1017
If you would bee at ease, all the world is not.	355	Proverbs	1019
Were it not for the bone in the legge,	355	Proverbs	1020
All that shakes falles not.	355	Proverbs	1022
If the braine sowes not corne, it plants thistles.	355	Proverbs	1024
An old cat sports not with her prey.	355	Proverbs	1030
A woman conceales what shee knowes not.	355	Proverbs	1031
The War is not don so long as my Enemy lives.	357	Proverbs	D 1051
The life of spies is to know, not bee known.	357	Proverbs	D 1068
Fear keepes and looks to the vineyard, and not the owner.	358	Proverbs	D 1072
Not only ought fortune to be pictured on a wheel,	358	Proverbs	D 1077
An Asse endures his burden, but not more then his burden.	358	Proverbs	D 1080
He that is afraid of leaves, goes not to the wood.	358	Proverbs	D 1092
Those that God loves, do not live long.	358	Proverbs	D 1094
All flesh is not venison.	358	Proverbs	D 1096
An old dog barks not in vain.	358	Proverbs	D 1099
The Bathe of the Blackamoor hath sworne not to whiten.	359	Proverbs	D 1105
God strikes with his finger, and not with all his arme.	359	Proverbs	D 1114
is not altogether escaped.	359	Proverbs	D 1120
Follow not truth too near the heels, lest it dash out thy teeth.	360	Proverbs	D 1138
if it were not begun on particular ends, it would last).	361	Proverbs	D 1160
Presents of love fear not to be ill taken of strangers.	361	Proverbs	D 1162
I need not their help, to reprove the vanity of those many	363	Letters	6
but, I profess it not:	363	Letters	16
I have not deceived their expectation, let not them deceive mine:	364	Letters	24
perhaps they will say, you are sickly, you must not study too hard;	364	Letters	26
it is true (God knows) I am weak, yet not so, but that every day,	364	Letters	27
as that if all things proved not well, I had rather the fault should	364	Letters	29
and to what end, not vain pleasures, nor to a vain end.	365	Letters	19
that I have not leazure to impart unto you some of those observations	365	Letters	32
and whereof I would not have you ignorant.	366	Letters	2
which it is possible for you to attain to, which you seek not;	366	Letters	14
not with a foolish vanting of yourself when there is no caus,	366	Letters	16
not of her self, but upon the want of those Books which were	367	Letters	4
but upon the want of those Books which were not to be got in England;	367	Letters	5
Letter in yours, for it was because I know your Lodging, but not his.	367	Letters	25
& therfore I am not over much beholding to those busnesses which	367	Letters	29
yet his love expects them not but first certifies you that there are	368	Letters	4
to threaten him that if he will not give her halfe her estate to live	368	Letters	23
but not so great as he expected & therfore he grumblingly said that	368	Letters	32
I could have come in person to thank you, but it is not possible;	369	Letters	11
is the finest place in the University, though not the gainfullest;	369	Letters	31
not but that I joy in your favours, but that you may see,	370	Letters	8
that he fears I have not fully resolved of the matter, since this	370	Letters	19
much from Divinity, at which, not without cause, he thinks, I aim;	370	Letters	20
if it had to others, yet to me it should not, for ought I yet knew;	370	Letters	24
to see a Sister, in a way I knew not, in the midst of much business,	371	Letters	3
the midst of much business, and all in a Fortnight, not long since.	371	Letters	4
Is it not too much for me?	371	Letters	11
I suppose she is not disposed to spend her eyesight on a piece	371	Letters	13
Think not my silence forgetfulness;	371	Letters	25
and not by my ink, and then you shall justly value Your most truly,	372	Letters	4
but, since I know I did not, and that your share continues,	372	Letters	16
of all Comfort, who is not willing to behold any sorrow but for sin.	372	Letters	25
our Colledge Customs allow not that, and I shou'd account my self	373	Letters	2
So that now if they do not well the falt cannot be charg'd on you;	373	Letters	15
so that the best use of them is, having, not to have them.	373	Letters	25
most carry themselves so, as if they not only not desir'd, but,	373	Letters	33
yours (which praised be God are less) are not like to continue long.	374	Letters	2
and will not allow any room there for such an in-mate as Grief;	374	Letters	10
so that it is not left to us to rejoyce or not rejoyce:	374	Letters	24
trouble not your selves, God is at hand to deliver us from all,	374	Letters	29
That you did not only entertain my proposals, but advance them,	375	Letters	2
and would not have to part them yet, till I take some opportunity	375	Letters	20
But I judge you not:	375	Letters	32
Yet, truly if you take her not, I am thinking to do it,	375	Letters	35
of kindred bredd up, (which generally is very true,) yet I care not;	376	Letters	5
and not as many who think they have done fairly, if they leave them	376	Letters	14
they may find out some thing not unworthy of those hands at which	376	Letters	29
I refuse not advice from the meanest, that creeps upon Gods earth,	378	Letters	11
Gods earth, no not tho' the advice step so far, as to be reproof:	378	Letters	12

NOT (cont'd)	PAGE	TITLE		LINE
not considering you any other wayes, as neyther I my self desire	378	Letters		15
As for my assistance, doubt not, through Gods blessing, . .	379	Letters		17
3. To Change shewes not well & you are by the Apostles rule (Philip	380	Woodnoth		12
by the Apostles rule (Philip 4, 8.) not only to pursue pure things,	380	Woodnoth		13
(whose the success of things is) & not into the hands of men or mens	380	Woodnoth		24
long God knocks at our harts, before he be heard, & yet desists not.	381	Woodnoth		3
6. you doe not want all success.	381	Woodnoth		7
so though you incline not, happily you restraine.	381	Woodnoth		9
worse by your withdrawing which grow not better by your presence.	381	Woodnoth		11
Complaine not of the want of success, when you have the fruit of it.	381	Woodnoth		16
with his favours, can not but be not only allowable but commendable.	381	Woodnoth		26
& therfore not relinquishable without their masters consent.	381	Woodnoth		29
of his praise, no, not, as in past ages, those Pillars of Hercules.	442	Oration		12
Yet doe not yee contemne these our slight glories, which wee raise	442	Oration		38
NOTE				
Each seventh note by right is due to thee.	38	The Sinner		4
The note is sad, yet musick for a king.	107	Sion		24
I did; and going did a rainbow note:	124	Peace		7
Thou didst note my working breast, ...	146	Praise 2		7
Sorrow hath chang'd its note: such is his will, ...	159	Jos.coat		3
And hurt thy self, and him that sings the note.	176	Forerunners		24
See the note upon Consid. 36.	307	Valdesso		22
NOTES				
Beasts fain would sing; birds dittie to their notes;	117	Providence		9
As peculiar notes and strains	186	Dooms-day		11
Briefe Notes on Valdesso's Considerations A Copy of a letter written	304	Valdesso		T
and some notes, in which perhaps you will discover some care,	304	Valdesso		2
BRIEFE NOTES relating to the dubious and offensive places in	306	Valdesso		T
NOTHING				
It gets thee nothing, and hath no excuse.	8	Ch.-Porch		56
It gets thee nothing, and has no excuse.	8	Ch.-Porch	W	56
Dare to be true. Nothing can need a ly:	9	Ch.-Porch		77
If thou art nothing, think what thou wouldst bee	10	Ch.-Porch	W	90
And rots to nothing at the next great thaw.	12	Ch.-Porch		140
Nothing with labour, folly long a-doing.	14	Ch.-Porch		192
But know, that nothing can so foolish be, ...	15	Ch.-Porch		206
All things are bigge with jest: nothing that's plain, ...	16	Ch.-Porch		239
Nothing from thine: in service, care, or coldnesse	16	Ch.-Porch		255
Or love, or language; nothing comes amisse:	20	Ch.-Porch		357
Nothing but holy, pure, and cleare, ...	25	Superlim		6
As nothing but	26	The Altar		7
I answer nothing, but with patience prove	29	Sacrifice		89
Since nothing Lord can bee so good	39	Good Fri.	W	21
And so should perish, but that nothing can, ...	41	Sepulchre		22
My soul bid nothing, but preserve her wealth:	44	H. Bapt.2		13
My soul bid nothing, but keep hir first wealth:	44	H. Bapt.2	W	13
I did beleeve that I did nothing owe, ...	50	Faith		14
As if that thou hadst nothing els to do?	62	Mattens		12
Whom nothing can procure, ...	73	Constancie		31
Nothing their furie can controll, ...	90	Afflict.4		11
Nothing performs the task of life:	90	Afflict.4		16
Nothing hath got so farre, ...	91	Man		19
Nothing we see, but means our good, ...	91	Man		27
Nothing could seem too rich to clothe the sunne, ...	102	Jordan 2		11
Nothing but drought and dearth, but bush and brake, ...	108	Home		49
And nothing wears.	110	Brit. Ch.		24
Nothing escapes them both; all must appeare, ...	118	Providence		37
Nothing ingendred doth prevent his meat:	118	Providence		53
Nothing wears clothes, but Man; nothing doth need	120	Providence		109
But he to wear them. Nothing useth fire, ...	120	Providence		110
Where all the guests sit close, and nothing wants.	121	Providence		134
Then whom in waiting nothing seems more slow, ...	137	Familie		15
Nothing more quick when she doth go.	137	Familie		16
We must confesse that nothing is our own.	143	Holdfast		7
Yet one pure heart is nothing to bestow:	147	Offering		5
And fall to nothing: thou dost reigne, ...	150	Longing		56
Embroider'd lyes, nothing between two dishes;	167	Dotage		5
Nothing can be so mean, ...	184	The Elixer		14
Nothing can be so low, ...	184	The Elixer	W	14
Nothing but bones, ...	185	Death		2
Open the bones, and you shall nothing find	206	Walton 2		12
(Where nothing should be broke) to adde a Seal.	439	Walton 5		18
am nothing but Infirmitie.	219	Psalm VI	D	4
the well is deep, and we have nothing of our selves to draw with?	228	Priest 4		35
That nothing befall him unworthy of that Majesty before which he is	235	Priest 8		23
counting nothing so much his owne, as that he may be unjust unto it.	238	Priest 9		35
vessels, and there is nothing that is food, and not phisick,	243	Priest 10		2
but he holds the Rule, that Nothing is little in Gods service:	249	Priest 14		2
there is nothing spoken, or done in the Company where he is,	252	Priest 18		2
Wherefore there is nothing done either wel or ill, whereof he is	254	Priest 20		10
and those more which concerne me, I either do nothing, or pinch,	265	Priest 26		17
because hee knows nothing but the Crosse of Christ, his minde being	267	Priest 27		28
he takes it either in an humble way, saying nothing at all; . .	269	Priest 28		6
by his governing power, the fairest harvests come to nothing.	271	Priest 30		18
For when men have nothing to do, then they fall to drink, . .	274	Priest 32		10
say they, we have nothing to do, lets go to the Tavern, . .	274	Priest 32		13
establisheth it, since they that have nothing, are fittest to work.	275	Priest 32		5
if hee may bee of the Commission of Peace, there is nothing to that:	276	Priest 32		8
that the Atheist, or Epicurian can have nothing to contradict.	281	Priest 34		34
telling my Physicians nothing thereof, as is the custome of sick	292	Cornaro		30

NOTHING (cont'd)	PAGE	TITLE		LINE
that under God nothing holp me, but that exact rule which I had so	296	Cornaro		29
And that I may say nothing of other things, are not almost all	298	Cornaro		32
because I would doe nothing negligently that you commit unto mee;	304	Valdesso		5
I doe so love him, that were there nothing else, I would Print it,	305	Valdesso		7
it all upon the word untill the day starre arise, it is nothing.	318	Valdesso		9
Hee looseth nothing, that looseth not God.	322	Proverbs		35
from him that saies nothing, for ever.	326	Proverbs		164
Send a wise man on an errand, and say nothing unto him.	328	Proverbs		217
The hard gives more then he that hath nothing.	329	Proverbs		259
Feare nothing but sinne.	331	Proverbs		299
The child saies nothing, but what it heard by the fire.	331	Proverbs		300
Since you know all, and I nothing,	332	Proverbs		336
He that owes nothing, if he makes not mouthes at us, is courteous.	333	Proverbs		362
hee that beleeveth nothing, hitts not.	333	Proverbs		364
This world is nothing except it tend to another.	334	Proverbs		382
Hee is rich enough that wants nothing.	335	Proverbs		403
Great trees are good for nothing but shade.	339	Proverbs		546
Nothing dries sooner then a teare.	343	Proverbs		659
Nothing lasts but the Church.	343	Proverbs		661
By doing nothing we learne to do ill.	346	Proverbs		757
Give not S. Peter so much, to leave Saint Paul nothing.	346	Proverbs		763
The best of the sport is to doe the deede, and say nothing.	348	Proverbs		812
He that knowes nothing, doubts nothing.	349	Proverbs		861
It's an ill aire where wee gaine nothing.	350	Proverbs		872
It's more paine to doe nothing then something.	350	Proverbs		884
The yeare doth nothing else but open and shut.	351	Proverbs		901
but the patient owes nothing to him but a little mony.	351	Proverbs		921
Wine that cost nothing is digested before it be drunke.	352	Proverbs		932
Thornes whiten yet doe nothing.	352	Proverbs		943
knowes nothing sure but what hee hath laid out.	354	Proverbs		1001
One month doth nothing without another.	355	Proverbs		1028
One mouth doth nothing without another.	355	Proverbs	V	1028
Nothing is to be presumed on, or despaired of.	356	Proverbs	D	56
Gentility is nothing but Ancient Riches.	356	Proverbs	D	1033
Nothing secure unlesse suspected.	357	Proverbs	D	1065
Take heed of credit decaid, and people that have nothing.	360	Proverbs	D	1150
and hath nothing else to answer your infinite kindnesses,	363	Letters		18
had taken ill courses, Follow your Book, and you shall want nothing:	364	Letters		22
in our publick Halls, you know, is nothing but Fish and Whit-meats:	365	Letters		4
be careful for nothing. What can be said more comfortably?	374	Letters		28
which to me that have nothing yett, is very much.	376	Letters		2
little Apology that she had done nothing in it (as my Brother writes)	379	Letters		4
work rather then doe nothing.	381	Woodnoth		24
justly feare that there is nothing here answerable to the greatnesse	442	Oration		30
NOTHINGE				
Nothinge can see	210	Paradox	D	11
NOTICE				
Then he'l take notice of: in ev'ry path	92	Man		44
and at going to bed by giving the Host notice, that he will have	251	Priest 17		10
nor the Church-Wardens so well take notice who receive thrice,	259	Priest 22		28
(which cannot be applyed without notice) to the dishonor of God,	287	Priest 37		3
NOTION				
Full of themselves, and answer their own notion.	19	Ch.-Porch		320
My words & thoughts do both expresse this notion,	84	Coloss.		1
NOTIONS				
Thousands of notions in my brain did runne,	102	Jordan 2		7
Those sparkling notions, which therein were bred?	176	Forerunners		4
things there is roome for motions [notions] and expecting of them;	313	Valdesso		12
NOTORIOUS				
Faults are either notorious, or private.	287	Priest 37		11
Again notorious faults are either such as are made known by common	287	Priest 37		11
NOTWITHSTANDING				
notwithstanding his instruction that they ought not to be so,	232	Priest 6		15
because notwithstanding his infinite hate of sinne, his Love overcame	283	Priest 34		14
NOUGHT				
Lets his soul runne for nought, as little fearing.	8	Ch.-Porch		59
Into the conquest. Though I can do nought	37	Reprisall		14
Into thy conquest, though I can do nought	37	Reprisall	W	14
But to have nought is ours, not to confesse	143	Holdfast		9
That we have nought. I stood amaz'd at this,	143	Holdfast		10
Are things of nought.	163	The Search		40
Complying with thy counsels, doing nought	190	Ch.-Milit.		7
Wheare health hath nought to doe;	210	Paradox	D	14
Whose fier, like there malice, nought can quench.	212	Bohemia	D	54
There comes nought out of the sacke but what was there.	348	Proverbs		833
There come nought out of the sacke but what was there.	348	Proverbs	V	833
NOURISH				
is apt to nourish more then in cold regions, and where flesh may be	242	Priest 10		17
Cast thy Care on the Lord and he shall nourish thee. (Psal. 55.)	374	Letters		15
NOURISHETH				
That which savours, is good and nourisheth, be consonant to truth.	293	Cornaro		9
NOURISHING				
or over-nourishing things, as the Israelites did eate sowre herbs:	242	Priest 10		4
NOURISHMENT				
But by the way of nourishment and strength	52	H.Commun.		7
sometimes too salt, and so not competent nourishment, I am Covetous.	265	Priest 26		23
NOURISHT				
Thy nourisht fame is weak or strong.	69	Content		32
NOVELTIES				
that the time after the Holydaye will bee fruitfuller of novelties,	368	Letters		3

NOW

	PAGE	TITLE		LINE
Man would have been th' incloser: but since now	7	Ch.-Porch		20
In conversation boldnesse now bears sway.	15	Ch.-Porch		205
Without me each one, who doth now me brave,	27	Sacrifice		9
Now prophesie who strikes thee, is their dittie.	31	Sacrifice		142
And now I am deliver'd unto death,	31	Sacrifice		145
And now wearie of sport, glad to ingrosse	33	Sacrifice		193
Now heal thy self, Physician; now come down.	34	Sacrifice		221
All that salvation, which ye now resist;	34	Sacrifice		226
But now I die; now all is finished.	34	Sacrifice		249
My wo, mans weal: and now I bow my head.	34	Sacrifice		250
Which holds thee now? Who hath indited it	41	Sepulchre		11
Now I am here, what thou wilt do with me	48	Afflict.1		55
Where now by Faith all arms are of a length;	50	Faith		27
To me dost now thy self convey;	52	H.Commun.		4
Which just ncw took up all my heart?	56	Temper 2		2
That this new light, which now I see,	63	Mattens		18
And now with darknesse closest wearie eyes,	64	Even-song		18
To kisse those heaps, which now they have in trust?	65	Ch.-monum.		16
Now I in you without a bodie move,	65	Ch.-mus.		5
O brook not this, lest if what even now	71	Frailtie		17
O brook not this, lest if that, which just now	71	Frailtie	W	17
While the world now rides by, now lags behinde.	72	Constancie		10
A point of honour, now to grieve in me,	73	Afflict.3		15
To this great kingdome, which thou now hast got,	77	Avarice		6
But now (alas!) I dare not; for our King,	78	Ang.&Sts.		16
But now alas I dare not; for my King,	78	Ang.&Sts.	W	16
Where now we shall be better Gods then he.	82	Ungratef.		6
The Scriptures bid us fast; the Church sayes, now:	86	Lent		4
Once a poore creature, now a wonder,	89	Afflict.4		4
Now thou wouldst taste our miserie.	97	Afflict.5		12
But now thou dost thy self immure and close	99	Decay		11
But sinne hath fool'd him. Now he is	102	Miserie		73
Lord, let it now by way of purchase go.	105	Obedience		35
And now thy Architecture meets with sinne;	106	Sion		11
Now come again, said I, and flout me.	108	Home		46
Which now is pinion'd with mortalitie,	109	Home		63
Heark and beware, lest what you now do measure	111	Vanitie 2		5
Which now is but a pruning-knife.	122	Time		10
Thou art a gard'ner now, and more,	123	Time		16
Now he will fight it out, and to the warres;	127	Giddinesse		9
Now eat his bread in peace,	127	Giddinesse		10
And snudge in quiet: now he scorns increase;	127	Giddinesse		11
Now all day spares.	127	Giddinesse		12
And now, me thinks, I am where I began	128	Bunch Gr.		3
I did toward Canaan draw; but now I am	128	Bunch Gr.		6
I did towards Canaan draw; but now I am	128	Bunch Gr.	V	6
So now each Christian hath his journeys spann'd:	128	Bunch Gr.		10
Thy promise now hath ev'n set thee thy laws.	139	Artillerie		24
But now that Christs pure vail presents the sight,	141	Justice 2		13
Now I still touch	141	Justice 2		20
Why should I justice now decline?	141	Justice 2		23
Christ keepeth now, whc cannot fail or fall.	143	Holdfast		14
Wilt thou forestall it, and now grieve to morrow,	145	Discharge		48
O be not now	149	Longing		33
But now both sinne is dead,	150	Longing		67
Which hath been broken now so long,	150	Longing		74
And now by keeping lose the letter:	152	The Jews		6
Thou cam'st but now; wilt thou so soon depart,	154	Glimpse		2
Thou said'st but even now,	155	Assurance		7
And in this league, which now my foes invade,	156	Assurance		26
Now foolish thought go on,	156	Assurance		37
Now love and truth will end in man.	156	Assurance		42
So that again I now am mine,	157	Clasping		5
My joyes to weep, and now my griefs to sing.	159	Jos.coat		14
And now in age I bud again,	166	The Flower		36
Unto what you now advise:	177	The Rose		14
For we do now behold thee gay and glad,	186	Death		17
Now with the crosse, as with a staffe, alone,	190	Ch.-Milit.		28
Wonders of anger once, but now of love.	191	Ch.-Milit.		38
None will beleeve this now, though money be	193	Ch.-Milit.		119
He was a God, now he's an Emperour.	194	Ch.-Milit.		140
So now being Priest he plainly did professe	195	Ch.-Milit.		173
United now in one both time and sphere.	195	Ch.-Milit.		176
To go to them, while that which now their nation	197	Ch.-Milit.		257
That I who cannot now by day	203	Even-song	W	6
Now is the season	204	The Knell	W	7
Now the great combat of our flesh & reason	204	The Knell	W	8
Fairer & richer. Now wee know, what's thine,	211	Bohemia	D	18
Laden with comforts thence, where now to morne	212	Bohemia	D	56
Which now that moist land to thee beares.	213	L' Envoy	D	6
Let now my Eyes, my Voice, my Heart,	213	Convert	D	4
(Till now averse to all that's Good)	214	Convert	D	17
Now therefore, O ye Kings, be wise,	216	Psalm II	D	25
But now from me depart away,	220	Psalm VI	D	19
And now my foes the Lord will blame	220	Psalm VI	D	25
Wake and confirm that judgment now,	221	Psalm VII	D	23
Now Catechizing being a work of singular, and admirable benefit	230	Priest 5		11
Now if a shepherd know not which grass will bane, or which not,	230	Priest 5		31
that have glorified him as wel as now, and that he shall have so	231	Priest 6		35
and with particularizing of his speech now to the younger sort,	233	Priest 7		3

	PAGE	TITLE	LINE
NUTS			
To take the nuts from the fire with the dogges foot.	341	Proverbs	584
The noise is greater then the nuts.	358	Proverbs	D 1073
OAK (see also oke)			
At some fair oak, or bush, or cave, or well:	99	Decay	7
OATES			
Water trotted is as good as oates.	325	Proverbs	131
OATH			
of his Conscience, whereas they are to do it by Command, and by Oath.	269	Priest 29	31
that so they may know their duty, and keep their oath the better;	270	Priest 29	16
and more of their oath, he wisheth them by no means to spare any,	270	Priest 29	18
An oath that is not to bee made is not to be kept.	354	Proverbs	1017
OATHES			
Omit the oathes, which true wit cannot need:	9	Ch.-Porch	62
Would have their tale beleeved for their oathes,	14	Ch.-Porch	183
OATHS			
As for oaths, and apparell, the disorders thereof are also very	228	Priest 3	8
OBEDIENCE			
Obedience.	104	Obedience	T
Humble Obedience neare the doore doth stand,	137	Familie	13
the Deputy of Christ for the reducing of Man to the Obedience of God.	225	Priest 1	2
and a thing required under Canonicall obedience, the expounding	230	Priest 5	13
which he observeth out of humble conformity, and obedience;	237	Priest 9	24
speciall grace of faith, patience, meeknesse, love, obedience, &c.	238	Priest 9	32
partly for obedience to Authority, partly for uniformity sake,	255	Priest 21	17
untill our obedience reach the measure of thy love, who hast done	290	Priest	11
to answer your infinite kindnesses, but a constancy of obedience;	363	Letters	20
OBEDIENT			
and after my manner, Your most obedient Servant, GEORGE HERBERT.	364	Letters	4
accept the good meaning of, Your most obedient Son, GEORGE HERBERT.	374	Letters	32
OBEY			
I him obey, who all things else command:	29	Sacrifice	83
and obligation of his calling, being to obey God rather then men.	232	Priest 6	19
OBEYED			
the other, in being worse served and obeyed.	259	Priest 22	6
OBEYES			
Hee commands enough that obeyes a wise man.	339	Proverbs	547
OBEYING			
one of obeying Authority, the other of not giving scandall,	263	Priest 24	9
education, of obeying that Spirit which hath guided me hitherto,	364	Letters	18
OBEYS			
as he obeys Authority in the one, so that being once satisfied,	245	Priest 12	26
OBJECT			
Amaze poore mortals, and object their crimes.	132	The Storm	6
Amuse poore mortals, and object their crimes.	132	The Storm	V 6
the subject, and object, and the like, hath neither in it sweetnesse,	235	Priest 7	7
these two rules comprize and include the double object of our duty,	246	Priest 13	29
Let no man here object unto me, That there are many, who,	300	Cornaro	17
to Appetite, object, That a long life is no such desirable thing,	300	Cornaro	27
but they will object again, What becomes of your Annuity?	364	Letters	30
OBJECTED			
What is objected by my foes.	155	Assurance	24
OBJECTIONS			
whereas there are usually three Objections made against the Place;	276	Priest 32	19
OBLATION			
To this poore oblation;	148	Offering	39
OBLIGATION			
The obligation in us, make it lesse,	86	Lent	17
whose duty and obligation being the same to the Houses they live in,	226	Priest 2	16
but the debt and obligation of his calling, being to obey God rather	232	Priest 6	19
Now fasting dayes containe a treble obligation;	242	Priest 10	2
he cannot keep the last obligation, nor suffer others in his house	242	Priest 10	29
for that also is some kind of obligation;	245	Priest 12	19
as an obligation to do good, rather then to those that are further,	253	Priest 19	26
exposing the obligation of Charity, and Neighbour-hood,	253	Priest 19	34
for their obligation to God, and their own soul, is above any	270	Priest 29	22
especially no obligation lying upon you either for the execution	380	Woodnoth	25
OBLIGATIONS			
The two former obligations are much more essentiall to a true fast,	242	Priest 10	7
if he be in full health, keeps the three obligations, eating fish,	242	Priest 10	26
that not onely sicknesse breaks these obligations of fasting,	242	Priest 10	35
to which mine owne obligations were occasion inough, & therfore I am	367	Letters	29
OBLIGE			
that is, to oblige God, or justify himselfe before God,	312	Valdesso	15
No tye can oblige the perfidious.	357	Proverbs	D 1066
OBLIG'D			
Much more oblig'd to do thy will,	139	Artillerie	22
OBLIGED			
because divers worthy young men have obliged me unto it.	291	Cornaro	8
OBLIGES			
He that trusts much Obliges much, says the Spaniard.	357	Proverbs	D 1045
OBLIQUELY			
The other Hid and doth obliquely bend.	84	Coloss.	4
OBSCURE			
Is all that saves, and not obscure.	135	Divinitie	24
As in cases of an obscure and dark nature, not easily determinable	260	Priest 23	20
whether any rule in the world be obscure, and how then should	263	Priest 24	3
whose natures, at least in the beginning, are dark and obscure:	264	Priest 26	9
OBSCURED			
who being obscured in his own country he would have to flourish in	304	Valdesso	13

	PAGE	TITLE	LINE
OBTAIN'D			
The starres his tire of light and rings obtain'd,	151	The Bag	13
OBTAINED			
but only by those means, by which at first it was obtained.	237	Priest 9	21
OBTAINES			
He that can stay obtaines.	349	Proverbs	852
OCCASION			
True Christians should be glad of an occasion	86	Lent	13
He makes thy gifts occasion more,	123	Gratefulnes	5
their very face, when occasion cals, but seasonably and discreetly.	226	Priest 2	31
where he takes occasion to discourse of such things as are both	236	Priest 8	21
where he may have occasion to converse with women, and that among	237	Priest 9	2
hee receives, to want a good meal suting to the joy of the occasion.	245	Priest 12	9
takes occasion sometimes to visite in person, now one quarter of his	247	Priest 14	4
when a just occasion calleth him out of his Parish (which he	250	Priest 17	23
well spoken, or done, he takes occasion to commend, and enlarge it;	252	Priest 18	4
to do his Countrey true and laudable service, when occasion requires.	252	Priest 19	29
may then by an honourable way take occasion to be better instructed.	255	Priest 21	31
their vowes, and by occasicn of both, inlarge their meditations.	255	Priest 21	34
Whosoever when a just occasion cals, either spends not at all,	265	Priest 26	5
but in brief, a poor man is an occasion, my countrey is an occasion,	265	Priest 26	14
is an occasion, my countrey is an occasion, my friend is an occasion,	265	Priest 26	14
is an occasion, my friend is an occasion, my Table is an occasion,	265	Priest 26	15
is an occasion, my Table is an occasion, my apparell is an occasion:	265	Priest 26	15
even of the best in the Parish, when occasion requires:	268	Priest 28	28
the omission thereof upon just occasion ought by no means to trouble	273	Priest 31	6
God knows the occasion as wel as he, and He is as a gracious Father,	273	Priest 31	7
so must they fight for, and defend them, when occasion calls.	277	Priest 32	20
which the present occasion of wit and company otherwise admits;	280	Priest 34	27
if all men are to blesse upon occasion, as appears Rom. 12. 14. how	286	Priest 36	27
Who would doe ill ne're wants occasion.	324	Proverbs	116
As I shal find occasion, you shal receive them by peeces;	366	Letters	3
to which mine owne obligations were occasion inough, & therfore I am	367	Letters	29
refusing to doe hath given her occasion to protest shee will never	368	Letters	22
comfort is that this is but an occasion for you to amplify your	369	Letters	3
OCCASIONALL			
Besides these occasionall discourses, the Parson questions what order	248	Priest 14	31
common course of devotion, then dislikes an occasionall interruption.	273	Priest 31	9
OCCASIONALLY			
and intermingles some mirth in his discourses occasionally,	268	Priest 27	7
OCCASIONS			
because wealth is given to that end to supply our occasions.	265	Priest 26	8
when his occasions carry him abroad, or bring strangers to him,	274	Priest 32	6
When none of these occasions call him abroad, every morning that hee	277	Priest 32	14
at severall times and occasions, the Parson setleth wavering minds.	283	Priest 34	4
should a Christian Souldier take such occasions to harden himselfe,	284	Priest 35	36
By occasions (I suppose) hee meaneth the ordinary, or necessary	314	Valdesso	16
necessary duties, and occasions of our calling and condition of life;	314	Valdesso	17
and not those which are in themselves occasions of sinne;	314	Valdesso	18
but in those other occasions, Gods Spirit will mortify and try them	314	Valdesso	21
OCEAN			
then he dives unto the boundlesse Ocean of Gods Love,	283	Priest 34	7
OCEANS			
Oceans of Ink; for, as the Deluge did	206	Walton 2	2
ODE			
Ode.	92	Antiphon 2 W	T
The Convert. An Ode.	213	Convert D	T
ODIOUS			
Comparisons are odious.	345	Proverbs	718
ODOUR			
When they are ripe, their odour will ascend,	120	Providence	119
The Odour. 2. Cor. 2.	174	The Odour	T
O'			
The greater world o' th' two; for that came in	33	Sacrifice	206
The greater world o' th' two; for that comes in	33	Sacrifice W	206
OFF			
Strike off all scores; none are so cleare as they.	20	Ch.-Porch	360
Pilate a stranger holdeth off; but they,	29	Sacrifice	101
I got me boughs off many a tree:	42	Easter	20
Cut me not off for my most foul transgression:	49	Repentance	15
Unto a third, that ten leaves off doth lie:	58	H.Script.2	6
The pigeons feed their tender off-spring, crying,	118	Providence	62
To set off vertues; griefs to set off sinning:	176	The Foil	6
and come to Church in frame, but commonly the next day put off both.	247	Priest 14	10
it judiciously, cr breaks it off seasonably by some diversion.	252	Priest 18	18
or if he have any leisure to lcok off from thence, he meets	267	Priest 27	30
and not break off their acts of dependance, how faire soever	271	Priest 30	26
For that he ought not to break off, but to continue his dependance	271	Priest 30	34
because this will cut off all causes of diseases, so that he shall	297	Cornaro	20
doth not bid them then cast away the word, or leave it off:	318	Valdesso	19
They that know one another salute a farre off.	327	Proverbs	185
Better good afarre off, then evill at hand.	330	Proverbs	267
Many kisse the hand they wish cut off.	330	Proverbs	283
He that lives well sees a farre off.	333	Proverbs	352
Water a farre off quencheth not fire.	334	Proverbs	398
God is at the end, when we thinke he is furthest off it.	341	Proverbs	598
Better a snotty child, then his nose wip'd off.	348	Proverbs	828
Heresie may be easier kept out, then shooke off.	357	Proverbs	D 1059
Modesty sets off one newly ccme to honour.	357	Proverbs	D 1062
and wee also putting off that countenance and gravitie,	442	Oration	5

	PAGE	TITLE		LINE
OFTEN (cont'd)				
I often blotted what I had begunne;	102	Jordan 2		9
I bath'd it often, ev'n with holy bloud, ...	130	Love unkn.		41
Yet have I often seen, by cunning hand	161	Priesthood		13
Onely, since God doth often vessels make	161	Priesthood		34
he having often instructed his people how to carry themselves in	231	Priest 6		21
that he himself hath often urged with no great success, . .	232	Priest 7		28
yet often dy with the Sermon, especially with Countrey people;	233	Priest 7		14
He often tels them, that Sermons are dangerous things, that none goes	233	Priest 7		18
Thirdly, by turning often, and making many Apostrophes to God,	233	Priest 7		33
by an often urging of the presence, and majesty of God, . .	234	Priest 7		25
Let him communicate the thing often by prayer unto God, . .	237	Priest 9		5
He often readeth the Lives of the Primitive Monks, Hermits, . .	237	Priest 9		28
He adviseth all to call to minde their Baptism often; . . .	258	Priest 22		15
to meditate on their Baptisme often (being the first step into their	258	Priest 22		18
and sending for them often, and in finding out Courtesies to place	262	Priest 24		26
The Countrey Parson doth often, both publickly, and privately	269	Priest 29		26
or hear them read often, as also the visitation Articles, . .	270	Priest 29		14
but that God often changeth it according as he sees fit, . .	270	Priest 30		31
and therefore he often overturnes things, when they are thought past	271	Priest 30		20
that he rather procures them to be often, as knowing that absence	284	Priest 35		15
but if he often interpose a Blessing, when the other gives him just	286	Priest 36		22
of the stomack, and often of the side, and the beginning of the Gout,	291	Cornaro		22
and the faults of Nature are often amended by Art, as barren grounds	292	Cornaro		11
which often kill others, can bring little grief or hurt to those that	294	Cornaro		34
curing of diseases, into which they often fall, who live disorderly:	298	Cornaro		5
live regularly, because they must often endure heats, and colds,	299	Cornaro		13
I conferre often with worthie men, excelling in wit, learning,	301	Cornaro		4
with their musick and fashion, and I my self also sing often;	303	Cornaro		7
He often useth this manner of speech Beleeving by Revelation,	308	Valdesso		29
God often chuseth which he shall doe, and that by restraining him	313	Valdesso		21
In the mouth of a bad dog fals often a good bone.	358	Proverbs	D	1093
OFTENEST				
Yet doth hee oftenest invite those, whom hee sees take best courses,	243	Priest 11		24
OFTENTIMES				
Starres are poore books, & oftentimes do misse:	58	H.Script.2		13
he comes to the point very leasurely, and oftentimes, as Nathan did,	248	Priest 14		21
that they oftentimes goe out of church, before he hath blessed them.	286	Priest 36		14
OFTNER				
And this must bee done the oftner, or the seldomer, according as hee	239	Priest 9		3
O				
Beware of Lust (startle not) o beware	6	Ch.-Porch	W	7
O what were man, might he himself misplace!	7	Ch.-Porch		23
O crumble not away thy souls fair heap.	9	Ch.-Porch		70
O England! full of sinne, but most of sloth;	10	Ch.-Porch		91
O England, full of all sinn, most of sloth, ...	10	Ch.-Porch	W	91
Thwart not th' Almighty God: O be not crosse.	22	Ch.-Porch		395
Thwart not the mighty God: O be not crosse.	22	Ch.-Porch	W	395
Praying's the end of preaching. O be drest;	23	Ch.-Porch		410
God sent him, whatsoe're he be: O tarry, ...	24	Ch.-Porch		442
O let thy blessed SACRIFICE be mine, ...	26	The Altar		15
O let thy onely SACRIFICE be mine, ...	26	The Altar	W	15
O let this cup passe, if it be thy pleasure:	27	Sacrifice		23
O all ye who passe by, behold and see;	33	Sacrifice		201
But, O my God, my God! why leav'st thou me, ...	33	Sacrifice		213
O my deare Saviour, Victorie!	36	Thanksgvng		48
O make me innocent, that I	36	Reprisall		5
O my chief good, ...	38	Good Fri.		1
Sinn being gone o doe thou fill	39	Good Fri.	W	29
O blessed bodie! Whither art thou thrown?	40	Sepulchre		1
O let thy blessed Spirit bear a part, ...	42	Easter		17
O let me rise	43	East.wings		7
Waters above the Heavens. O sweet streams	44	H. Bapt.1	W	5
O blessed streams! either ye do prevent	44	H. Bapt.1		7
O let me still	44	H. Bapt.2		6
O tame my heart;	45	Nature		4
O smooth my rugged heart, and there	45	Nature		13
O let thy height of mercie then	49	Repentance		13
But wee strangers grown, o Lord, ...	53	H.Commun.	W	37
Immortall Heat, O let thy greater flame	54	Love 2		1
O rack me not to such a vast extent;	55	Temper 1		9
O let me, when thy roof my soul hath hid, ...	55	Temper 1		17
O let me roost and nestle there:	55	Temper 1		18
O fix thy chair of grace, that all my powers	56	Temper 2		9
O let thy graces without cease	60	Grace		3
Thy works nights captives: O let grace	60	Grace		7
O lett thy grace, to crosse his art, ...	60	Grace	W	19
O come! for thou dost know the way.	61	Grace		21
O raise me then! poore bees, that work all day, ...	61	Praise 1		17
O raise me then: for if a Spider may	61	Praise 1	W	17
O that I could a sinne once see!	63	Sinne 2		1
O what a state is this, which never knew	65	Ch.-mus.	W	8
Yet heare, O God, onely for his blouds sake	66	Ch.-lock		9
O make mee wholy guiltles, or at least	66	Ch.-lock	W	9
O brook not this, lest if what even now	71	Frailtie		17
O brook not this, lest if that, which just now	71	Frailtie	W	17
My heart did heave, and there came forth, O God!	73	Afflict.3		1
O day most calm, most bright, ...	75	Sunday		1
O day so calm, so bright:	75	Sunday	W	1
O let me take thee at the bound, ...	76	Sunday		60
O that I had the wing and thigh	79	Employm.2	W	21

O (cont'd)

	PAGE	TITLE		LINE
Come, come, my God, O come,	80	Deniall		14
O that thou shouldst give dust a tongue	80	Deniall		16
O cheer and tune my heartlesse breast,	80	Deniall		26
O Thou, whose glorious, yet contracted light,	81	Christmas		9
O do not use me	83	Sighs & Gr.		1
O do not bruise me!	83	Sighs & Gr.		6
O do not urge me!	83	Sighs & Gr.		7
O do not scourge me!	83	Sighs & Gr.		12
O do not blinde me!	83	Sighs & Gr.		13
O do not grinde me!	83	Sighs & Gr.		18
O do not fill me	83	Sighs & Gr.		19
O do not kill me!	83	Sighs & Gr.		24
But O reprieve me!	83	Sighs & Gr.		25
Into the bitter box; but O my God,	83	Sighs & Gr.		29
So brave a Palace built; O dwell in it,	92	Man		50
O write in brasse, My God upon a tree	94	Unkindness		22
O let thy sacred will	104	Obedience		16
O show thy self to me,	107	Home		5
O show thy self to me,	107	Home		11
O show thy self to me,	107	Home		17
O show thy self to me,	107	Home		23
He did, he came: O my Redeemer deare,	108	Home		25
O show thy self to me,	108	Home		29
O show thy self to me,	108	Home		35
O show thy self to me,	108	Home		41
O show thy self to me,	108	Home		47
O show thy self to me,	108	Home		53
O show thy self to me,	108	Home		59
O show thy self to me,	109	Home		65
O show thy self to me,	109	Home		71
O show thy self to me,	109	Home		77
O heare betimes, lest thy relenting	111	Vanitie 2		7
O give me quicknesse, that I may with mirth	115	Dulnesse		3
O sacred Providence, who from end to end	116	Providence		1
Is there an herb for that? O that thy care	119	Providence		75
O what a cunning guest	126	Confession		1
O what a sight were Man, if his attires	127	Giddinesse		17
O dark instructions; ev'n as dark as day!	135	Divinitie		19
Where Pagans tread. O Mother deare and kinde,	140	Ch.-rents		24
O dreadfull Justice, what a fright and terrour	141	Justice 2		1
O that within us hearts had propagation,	147	Offering		7
O accept	147	Offering		28
Mark well my furnace! O what flames,	149	Longing		26
O be not now	149	Longing		33
Disturb the work. O make me not their sport,	155	Glimpse		29
O spitefull bitter thought!	155	Assurance		1
Who heard thee say it. O most gracious Lord,	155	Assurance		20
O be mine still! still make me thine!	157	Clasping		19
O that I might some other hearts convert,	159	Praise 3		39
O what pure things, most pure must those things be,	161	Priesthood		29
Whither, O, whither art thou fled,	162	The Search		1
O let not that of any thing;	163	The Search		33
O take these barres, these lengths away;	163	The Search		49
O who will give me tears? Come all ye springs,	164	Grief		1
How fresh, O Lord, how sweet and clean	165	The Flower		1
O that I once past changing were,	166	The Flower		22
And relish versing: O my onely light,	166	The Flower		39
O, could I love! and stops: God writeth, Loved,	168	a true Hymn		20
My Master, shall I speak? O that to thee	175	The Odour		11
O my God,	178	Discipline		3
O what sweetnesse from the bowl	181	Banquet		7
O what a damp and shade	183	A Parodie		11
O what a deadly cold	184	A Parodie		26
O make no stay!	187	Dooms-day		14
O who will show me those delights on high?	188	Heaven		1
How deare to me, O God, thy counsels are!	191	Ch.-Milit.		47
How deare to me, O God, thy counsels are!	192	Ch.-Milit.		99
How deare to me, O God, thy counsels are!	194	Ch.-Milit.		155
How deare to me, O God, thy counsels are!	196	Ch.-Milit.		209
How deare to me, O God, thy counsels are!	198	Ch.-Milit.		278
O gratious Lord how shall I know	200	H. Commun.	W	1
Thou still, O Lord, outstrippest mee.	201	love	W	6
O lett my Soule, whose keyes I must deliver	203	Even-song	W	21
O help my God!	204	The Knell	W	9
O what a poore thing 'tis to bee a Queene	212	Bohemia	D	23
Now therefore, O ye Kings, be wise,	216	Psalm II	D	25
O kiss the Son, lest he be wrath,	216	Psalm II	D	29
But thou, O Lord, art still the shield	216	Psalm III	D	5
Arise, O Lord, and rescue me;	217	Psalm III	D	17
Belongs, O Lord, thy blessing shall	217	Psalm III	D	23
O thou that hast enlarged me	217	Psalm IV	D	3
O learn to stand in awe of him,	217	Psalm IV	D	15
Many there are that say, O who	217	Psalm IV	D	21
For that, O Lord, with perfect joy	218	Psalm IV	D	25
o Lord, reject them all,	219	Psalm V	D	32
Rebuke me not in wrath, O Lord,	219	Psalm VI	D	1
O pity me! for I (O Lord)	219	Psalm VI	D	3
O heal me, for my bones are vex'd,	220	Psalm VI	D	5
Return, O God! and rescue me,	220	Psalm VI	D	9
O Lord deliver mee!	220	Psalm VII	D	4

O (cont'd)	PAGE	TITLE		LINE
If I have done this thing, O Lord,	221	Psalm VII	D	9
Arise in wrath, O Lord, advance	221	Psalm VII	D	21
O God consider me	221	Psalm VII	D	30
O almighty and ever-living Lord God!	288	Priest		7
O write it! O brand it in our foreheads for ever:	288	Priest		18
O brand it in our foreheads for ever:	288	Priest		18
And now, O Lord! in the power of thy Victories, and in the wayes	289	Priest		11
O make it a word of power and peace, to convert those who are not yet	289	Priest		15
O let not our foolish and unworthy hearts rob us of the continuance	289	Priest		19
O make thy word a swift word, passing from the ear to the heart,	289	Priest		29
O Lord hear, O Lord forgive!	289	Priest		33
O Lord, hearken, and do so for thy blessed Son's sake, in whose sweet	289	Priest		33
O Lord! thy blessings hang in clusters, they come trooping upon us!	290	Priest		6
O Lord, blesse it: O Lord, make it health and strength unto us;	290	Priest		9
O Lord, make it health and strength unto us;	290	Priest		10
OH				
Oh all ye, who passe by, whose eyes and minde	26	Sacrifice		1
Oh King of grief! (a title strange, yet true,	35	Thanksgvng		1
Oh King of wounds! how shall I grieve for thee,	35	Thanksgvng		3
Sinne being gone, oh fill the place,	39	Good Fri.		29
Great is my sinne. Oh! gently treat	48	Repentance		2
Oh Book! infinite sweetnesse! let my heart	58	H.Script.1		1
Oh that I knew how all thy lights combine,	58	H.Script.2		1
Oh glorious spirits, who after all your bands	77	Ang.&Sts.		1
Oh that I were an Orenge-tree,	79	Employm.2		21
Oh help, my God! let not their plot	90	Afflict.4		19
Oh mightie love! Man is one world, and hath	92	Man		47
Oh foolish man! where are thine eyes?	101	Miserie		49
Oh loose this frame, this knot of man untie!	109	Home		61
Oh, what a thing is man! how farre from power,	127	Giddinesse		1
Oh take thy lute, and tune it to a strain,	136	Ephes.		19
Oh that my prayers! mine, alas!	152	The Jews		7
Oh that some Angel might a trumpet sound;	152	The Jews		8
But oh the folly of distracted men,	167	Dotage		13
as, Oh Lord blesse my people, and teach them this point;	233	Priest 7		33
or, Oh my Master, on whose errand I come, let me hold my peace,	233	Priest 7		34
So Isa. 64. Oh that thou would'st rent the Heavens, that thou wouldst	234	Priest 7		2
God suddenly, Oh Lord, I know that the way of man is not in himself,	234	Priest 7		5
Oh let us all take heed what we do, God sees us, he sees whether I	234	Priest 7		26
but, Oh God! how easily is that answered, when we consider that	373	Letters		27
And yet, Oh God! most carry themselves so, as if they not only	373	Letters		32
OIL (see also oyl)				
Whom oil and balsames kill, what salve can cure?	24	Ch.-Porch		447
Whom oil and mercies kill, what salve can cure?	24	Ch.-Porch	W	447
OINTMENT (see also oyntment)				
Who at three hundred did the ointment prize,	27	Sacrifice		18
OKE				
One stroke fells not an oke.	327	Proverbs		181
OLD				
Old courtiers know this; therefore set out so,	14	Ch.-Porch		185
Learn this, that hath old gamesters deerely cost:	14	Ch.-Porch		200
Learn this, it hath old gamesters deerely cost:	14	Ch.-Porch	W	200
A new small-rented lease, and cancell th' old.	40	Redemption		4
And as of old, the law by heav'nly art	41	Sepulchre		17
Or make a new one, since the old	45	Nature		15
To sorrows old,	48	Repentance		10
Wee are born old.	48	Repentance	W	10
In young and old;	78	Ang.&Sts.		13
But we are still too young or old;	79	Employm.2		26
But we are ever young or old;	79	Employm.2	W	26
Both th' old discoveries, and the new-found seas,	88	The Pearl		7
Us of old,	92	Antiphon 2		8
Where yet both Sinne and Satan, thy old foes,	99	Decay		13
I see the world grows old, when as the heat	99	Decay		16
Lord with what glorie wast thou serv'd of old,	106	Sion		1
And for their old acquaintance plead.	109	Home		70
Then an old prayer-book I did present:	121	Hope		3
Perhaps some such of old did passe,	122	Time		7
At length I met a rev'rend good old man,	125	Peace		19
There was a Prince of old	125	Peace		22
For as the Jews of old by Gods command	128	Bunch Gr.		8
The Font did onely, what was old, renew:	130	Love unkn.		64
Wast thou of old,	141	Justice 2		2
Lime begg'd of old, (they say),	154	Glimpse		13
Through th' old sinnes and new doctrines of our land.	161	Priesthood		33
And keeps thee present, leaving th' old	162	The Search		27
That to the old man I may rest,	174	Aaron		19
Finish'd and fixt the old religion.	190	Ch.-Milit.		22
Constantines British line meant this of old,	192	Ch.-Milit.		93
Unto the farthest old meridian.	192	Ch.-Milit.		98
Glorie was his chief instrument of old:	194	Ch.-Milit.		143
As the old heathen would deem prodigies.	194	Ch.-Milit.		154
The old debauched ruffian would turn writer.	194	Ch.-Milit.		164
And in old Rome a mightie Emperour;	195	Ch.-Milit.		172
And from old Rome the libertie of pleasure,	195	Ch.-Milit.		179
Learning from Greece, from old Rome statelinesse:	195	Ch.-Milit.		188
As new and old Rome did one Empire twist;	196	Ch.-Milit.		205
Being in this their old crackt looking-glasse.	196	Ch.-Milit.		208
Old and new Babylon are to hell and night,	196	Ch.-Milit.		215
And where of old the Empire and the Arts	197	Ch.-Milit.		263

ON (cont'd)

ON (cont'd)

	PAGE	TITLE		LINE
For where before thou still didst call on me,	141	Justice 2		19
And harp on thee.	141	Justice 2		21
I travell'd on, seeing the hill, where lay	141	Pilgrimage		1
I left on th' one, and on the other side	142	Pilgrimage		5
A lake of brackish waters on the ground	142	Pilgrimage		23
On future grief, do not remove it thence,	145	Discharge		43
Look on my sorrows round!	149	Longing		25
And rule on high,	150	Longing		57
On double pleasures: leave thy cold dispute	153	The Collar		20
Now foolish thought go on,	156	Assurance		37
Which bounds on thee, and will not down thy throat:	156	Assurance		40
But when thou dost on businesse blow,	158	Praise 3		13
Let us (said he) poure on him all we can:	159	The Pulley		3
Bestow this jewell also on my creature,	160	The Pulley		12
Fain put thee on, exchanging my lay-sword	160	Priesthood		5
And lay my threatnings bleeding on the ground.	164	The Crosse		12
Thou turnest th' edge of all things on me still,	165	The Crosse		21
On whom thy tempests fell all night.	166	The Flower		42
Thy curse being laid on him, makes thee accurst.	169	Dial.-Anth		6
(Whose precepts she had trampled on before)	173	Marie Magd		2
And wore them for a jewell on her head,	173	Marie Magd		3
Holinesse on the head,	174	Aaron		1
Light and perfections on the breast,	174	Aaron		2
True beautie dwells on high: ours is a flame	177	Forerunners		28
That which wrought on thee,	179	Discipline		26
Needs must work on me.	179	Discipline		28
And on sinne doth cast the fright.	180	Invitation		18
And on earth	182	Banquet		32
And so found me on the ground.	182	Banquet		36
This on my ring,	183	The Posie		5
And I depend on thee;	183	A Parodie		5
A man that looks on glasse,	184	The Elixer		9
On it may stay his eye;	184	The Elixer		10
We lookt on this side of thee, shooting short;	186	Death		9
O who will show me those delights on high?	188	Heaven		1
I cannot look on thee.	189	Love 3		10
And travell'd westward also: journeying on	193	Ch.-Milit.		104
And travell'd Westward allso, coasting on,	193	Ch.-Milit.	W	104
They who rely on them must reckon twice	194	Ch.-Milit.	W	160
Religion stands on tip-toe in our land,	196	Ch.-Milit.		235
Something that may be conquest on my part	201	love	W	5
The Day is spent, & hath his will on mee:	203	Even-song	W	1
Look on his daring brightnes, may	203	Even-song	W	7
On either hand	204	The Knell	W	4
Strugling on th' hook.	204	The Knell	W	6
Julips & Cordials when wee call on thee	204	The Knell	W	17
Onely my soule hangs on thy promisses	205	Persever.	W	13
To praise, and on thee, Lord, some Ink bestow.	206	Walton 2		11
On Sir John Danvers.	208	J. Danvers	D	T
On Henry Danvers earl of Danby. EPITAPH	208	H. Danvers	D	T
Shine on, Majestick soule, abide	213	L' Envoy	D	1
Thence wheeling on, it compass shall	213	L' Envoy	D	11
A Deluge on my sensual Flame,	214	Convert	D	9
on Sion His most Holy hill,	215	Psalm II	D	14
Lord hear me when I call on Thee,	217	Psalm IV	D	1
Have mercy on me Lord, and hear	217	Psalm IV	D	5
offer to God on high	217	Psalm IV	D	18
and on his grace rely.	217	Psalm IV	D	20
Yea, he my prayer from on high	220	Psalm VI	D	23
For their sakes, Lord, return on high,	221	Psalm VII	D	27
And on his own accursed pate	222	Psalm VII	D	59
of him that is on high.	222	Psalm VII	D	64
Christ being not to continue on earth, but after hee had fulfilled	225	Priest 1		6
some in Noble houses, some in Parishes residing on their Cures.	226	Priest 2		2
or ministry, let us wait on our ministring;	226	Priest 2		6
or he that teacheth, on teaching, &c.	226	Priest 2		7
other answers, which are on the Clerks and peoples part to answer;	231	Priest 6		29
and busy cast of his eye on his auditors, with letting them know,	233	Priest 7		1
Oh my Master, on whose errand I come, let me hold my peace,	233	Priest 7		35
The Parson on Sundays.	235	Priest 8		T
as soon as he awakes on Sunday morning, presently falls to work,	235	Priest 8		16
he makes a peculiar one for a blessing on the exercises of the day,	235	Priest 8		22
To put on the profound humility, and the exact temperance of our Lord	237	Priest 9		33
and to keep them on in the sunshine, and noone of prosperity,	237	Priest 9		35
puts on the whole Armour of God, and by the vertue of the shield	238	Priest 9		5
first, of eating lesse that day, then on other dayes;	242	Priest 10		3
for then they will reckon upon it, as on a debt;	244	Priest 12		28
making a hook of his Charity, causeth them still to depend on him;	244	Priest 12		32
whereas on Sundays it is easie for them to compose themselves	247	Priest 14		7
which they put on as their holy-day cloathes, and come to Church in	247	Priest 14		8
when on the Lords day they do unnecessary servile work,	248	Priest 14		2
or in time of divine service on other holy days, except in the cases	248	Priest 14		3
that so they go on more cheerfully in their vocation, and himself be	248	Priest 14		12
as about prayers morning and evening on their knees, reading	248	Priest 14		32
catechizing, singing of Psalms at their work, and on holy days;	248	Priest 14		34
and offering to have them taught on holy-dayes by his servants.	248	Priest 14		37
Therefore those he meets on the way he blesseth audibly,	251	Priest 17		2
This is to be on Gods side, and be true to his party.	252	Priest 18		15
not the lesse, lest he cast their neighbours poverty on them also.	254	Priest 19		7
and Baptizeth not willingly, but on Sundayes, or great dayes.	258	Priest 22		3

ON (cont'd)

	PAGE	TITLE		LINE
course for Christians also to meditate on their Baptisme often (being	258	Priest 22		18
not on the Sunday of the Communion only (for then it is too late)	258	Priest 22		26
or Sundayes before the Communion, or on the Eves of all those dayes.	258	Priest 22		28
not to incroach on others Professions, but to live on his own.	262	Priest 23		16
not to incroach on others Professions, but to live on his own.	262	Priest 23		17
for them often, and in finding out Courtesies to place on them;	262	Priest 24		27
as if he be a Papist, the Church is the hinge he turnes on;	262	Priest 24		30
ever besides two great helps and powerfull perswaders on his side;	263	Priest 24		16
he then comes on the faster, and makes so much the more of him,	263	Priest 25		33
times from action, standing on a hill, and considering his Flock,	264	Priest 26		4
but proceeding on, comes to do unlawfully, even before he is aware;	264	Priest 26		23
and fix them on their charge, and not on their preferment.	266	Priest 26		5
his minde being defixed on it with those nailes wherewith his Master	267	Priest 27		29
be vilified or debased, by being cast on the lower ranke of people;	270	Priest 29		8
the sun in heaven, or the fire on earth, by reason of their fierce,	271	Priest 30		10
or if he depend on God further, even till he imbarn his corn,	271	Priest 30		31
but to continue his dependance on God, not onely before the corne is	271	Priest 30		35
every day of the week, and four times on Sunday, if they be well.	272	Priest 31		23
but to go on as cheerfully, as if he had not been interrupted.	273	Priest 31		11
On the other side, if I am to visit the sick in haste, and my neerest	273	Priest 31		33
the casting of it on mean persons, especially in some Shires:	276	Priest 32		21
to insist and dwell chiefly on the two noble branches therof,	278	Priest 32		1
the one concerning the woman that spent the oyntment on our Saviour,	282	Priest 34		24
he pares the apple, and gives them the clean to feed on.	284	Priest 35		1
On the other side, if it be unlawful to open faults, no benefit	287	Priest 37		5
and wert proceeding still on in thy Favours, untill we interrupted	288	Priest		15
Ride on Lord, because of the word of truth, and meeknesse,	289	Priest		22
they break forth like mighty waters on every side.	290	Priest		8
Therefore trusting on experience, I forsook all these kinde of meats	293	Cornaro		15
On the other side I argued, that Nature was contented with a little,	295	Cornaro		25
On the twelfth day, a pain of the side took me, which held me two	296	Cornaro		17
if our corporall life depend on the harmonie of humours & elements,	297	Cornaro		7
that I can easily get on horseback without the advantage	300	Cornaro		35
of the ground, and sometimes I go up high stairs and hills on foot.	300	Cornaro		36
on both sides whereof are great and fruitfull fields, well manured	301	Cornaro		24
Briefe Notes on Valdesso's Considerations A Copy of a letter written	304	Valdesso		T
So may a warre be just on both sides, and was just in the Canaanites	316	Valdesso		29
word of God, as their Joy, and Crowne, and their Treasure on earth.	317	Valdesso		34
which depend almost wholly on their Canon law and Decretals,	319	Valdesso	V	29
there are other Cases of Conscience grounded on Piety and Morality,	319	Valdesso	V	31
He lives unsafely, that lookes too neere on things.	322	Proverbs		43
A Dwarfe on a Gyants shoulder sees further of the two.	322	Proverbs		50
A Dwarfe on a Gyants shoulder sees farther then they two.	322	Proverbs	V	50
Thinke of ease, but worke on.	327	Proverbs		178
Send a wise man on an errand, and say nothing unto him.	328	Proverbs		217
Honour without profit is a ring on the finger.	328	Proverbs		230
The fault of the horse is put on the saddle.	329	Proverbs		240
On painting and fighting looke aloofe.	329	Proverbs		247
I had rather ride on an asse that carries me,	329	Proverbs		258
Neither eyes on letters, nor hands in coffers.	330	Proverbs		288
how that which is to come will be drawne on.	332	Proverbs		329
Pull downe your hatt on the winds side.	332	Proverbs		334
He that sings on friday, will weepe on Sunday.	335	Proverbs		411
Being on sea saile, being on land settle.	335	Proverbs		418
Wealth is like rheume, it falles on the weakest parts.	337	Proverbs		475
Praise the Sea, but keepe on land.	338	Proverbs		489
On a good bargaine thinke twice.	339	Proverbs		529
when there are many to strike on one Anvile.	340	Proverbs		551
let him not put them on his head.	340	Proverbs		567
Wisedome hath one foot on Land, and another on Sea.	341	Proverbs		611
An examin'd enterprize goes on boldly.	342	Proverbs		618
Every one puts his fault on the Times.	343	Proverbs		675
Had you the world on your Chesse-bord,	344	Proverbs		701
He complaines wrongfully on the sea	345	Proverbs	V	706
All keyes hang not on one girdle.	345	Proverbs		719
Great businesses turne on a little pinne.	345	Proverbs		720
The faulty stands on his guard.	347	Proverbs		793
Curtesie on one side only lasts not long.	348	Proverbs		809
of a monke on all sides.	351	Proverbs		900
of a monke on all hands.	351	Proverbs	V	900
The great put the little on the hooke.	352	Proverbs		945
Lawyers houses are built on the heads of fooles.	352	Proverbs		951
You may be on land, yet not in a garden.	353	Proverbs		964
Once a yeare a man may say: On his conscience.	353	Proverbs		971
When one is on horsebacke hee knowes all things.	353	Proverbs		982
Nothing is to be presumed on, or despaired of.	356	Proverbs	D	56
To go upon the Franciscans Hackney (i.e. on foot).	356	Proverbs	D	1035
It is a sheep of Berry, it is marked on the nose	356	Proverbs	D	1040
Two sparrows on one Ear of Corn make an ill agreement.	358	Proverbs	D	1074
Not only ought fortune to be pictured on a wheel,	358	Proverbs	D	1077
To play at Chesse when the house is on fire.	360	Proverbs	D	1136
if it were not begun on particular ends, it would last).	361	Proverbs	D	1160
for it sets a dearer price on every thing.	361	Proverbs	D	1178
be fain alwayes to borrow Books, and build on anothers foundation?	364	Letters		13
not well, I had rather the fault should lie on me, than on them;	364	Letters		29
not well, I had rather the fault should lie on me, than on them;	364	Letters		30
twice a Week, on Fridayes and Saturdayes, I must do so,	365	Letters		5
My Lord of Buckingham was observed on Christmas day to bee so devout	368	Letters		16
give her halfe her estate to live on by her selfe (for shee desires	368	Letters		24
that if all fail, yet I am able to stand on mine own legs.	370	Letters		10

ON (cont'd)	PAGE	TITLE		LINE
(as I think) at the sign of the Pedler and the Pack on London-bridge,	370	Letters		28
she is not disposed to spend her eyesight on a piece of paper,	371	Letters		14
So that now if they do not well the falt cannot be charg'd on you;	373	Letters		15
that whether you turn your thoughts on the life past, or on the Joyes	373	Letters		18
or on the Joyes that are to come, you have strong preservatives	373	Letters		18
our Credit and estimation calls on us to live in a more splendid	373	Letters		26
Cast thy Care on the Lord and he shall nourish thee. (Psal. 55.)	374	Letters		14
Casting all your Care on the Lord, for he careth for you. (1 Pet.	374	Letters		16
What a trouble hath your Goodness brought on you, by admitting our	376	Letters		26
On the other side are the names of those to whome my deceased Neece	383	G.H.'s Will		1
wee might the more by love grow on, both the Spanish and Brittish	442	Oration		17
ONCE				
When once it is within thee; but before	7	Ch.-Porch		26
That thou canst speak, at once; but husband it,	18	Ch.-Porch		302
When once thy foot enters the church, be bare.	22	Ch.-Porch		403
And Prophets once to see, but found no place:	32	Sacrifice		183
They leade me in once more, and putting then	32	Sacrifice		189
My coat, the type of love, which once cur'd those	34	Sacrifice		242
The man, who once against thee fought.	37	Reprisall		16
Remember that thou once didst write in stone.	38	The Sinner		14
Where is that fire which once descended	59	Whitsunday		5
The sunne, which once did shine alone,	59	Whitsunday		13
Lord once more shake the Heaven & earth	59	Whitsunday	W	17
O that I could a sinne once see!	63	Sinne 2		1
Better by worms be all once spent,	69	Content		26
He that by seeking hath himself once found,	69	Content		35
Once a poore creature, now a wonder,	89	Afflict.4		4
And pilfring what I once did give,	95	Submission		11
Of thy great love once spread, as in an urn	99	Decay		17
And when they once have perfected their draughts,	122	Sinnes rd.		5
Let me once know.	124	Peace		2
Then once more pray:	134	The Method		29
Great joyes are all at once;	138	The Size		19
Did once perceive, it blew them under foot,	140	Ch.-rents		7
Did once perceive, it blew thee under foot,	140	Ch.-rents	V	7
Gave you a colour once; which when your foes	140	Ch.-rents		13
If it be his once, all is well.	144	Discharge		20
Who by not keeping once, became a debter;	152	The Jews		5
Thou didst at once thy self indite,	156	Assurance		29
What for it self love once began,	156	Assurance		41
And bloudie battell which thou once didst trie)	158	Praise 3		35
I live to shew his power, who once did bring	159	Jos.coat		13
Of wretched earth. Where once I scorn'd to stand,	161	Priesthood		15
So that at once both feeder, dish, and meat	161	Priesthood		21
What I would do for thee, if once my grones	165	The Crosse		15
O that I once past changing were,	166	The Flower		22
I once more smell the dew and rain,	166	The Flower		38
Which when we once can finde and prove,	167	The Flower		45
For what Christ once in humblenesse began,	168	The Sonne		13
When once those snuffes are ta'ne away,	171	Self-cond.		22
Death, thou wast once an uncouth hideous thing,	185	Death		1
Wonders of anger once, but now of love.	191	Ch.-Milit.		38
Such force as once did captivate the Jews;	195	Ch.-Milit.		192
Let mee but once the conquest have	202	love	W	19
Wherewith whole showls of Martyrs once did burn,	206	Walton 1		2
At once to Hell, without a baiting while	212	Bohemia	D	49
When once his anger burns, thrice blest	216	Psalm II	D	31
but after a man is once Minister, he cannot agree to come into any	226	Priest 2		25
so that being once satisfied, he allows his Charity some blindnesse	245	Priest 12		26
If it once have the honour of that Name, it grows great instantly.	249	Priest 14		2
When once all have learned the words of the Catechisme,	256	Priest 21		1
if he once get the skill of it, will draw out of ignorant and silly	256	Priest 21		19
but after that the Catechisme is once learn'd, that which nature is	256	Priest 21		25
when the Parson once demanded after other questions about mans	257	Priest 21		1
if not duly once a month, yet at least five or six times in the year;	259	Priest 22		20
whether things once indifferent, being made by the precept	263	Priest 24		12
for an apple once we lost our God, and still lose him for no more;	288	Priest		19
because that after one is once sixtie five yeares old, all the time	300	Cornaro		29
Hee that burnes his house warmes himselfe for once.	331	Proverbs		303
He that once deceives is ever suspected.	335	Proverbs		417
Who so once deceives is ever suspected.	335	Proverbs	V	417
He that once hitts, is ever bending.	347	Proverbs		785
Trees eate but once.	352	Proverbs		933
Once a yeare a man may say: On his conscience.	353	Proverbs		971
He that is once borne, once must dy.	358	Proverbs	D	1087
of taking her, as once you did, surely it were a great good deed,	375	Letters		31
ONE				
Which if it cleave to coine, one common rust	13	Ch.-Porch	W	165
One common waight will press downe both, yet so	13	Ch.-Porch	W	167
She loseth three for one; her soul, rest, fame.	13	Ch.-Porch		174
Give one estate, as one life. None is bound	17	Ch.-Porch		285
God made me one man; love makes me no more,	17	Ch.-Porch		287
To the one joy of doing kindnesses.	19	Ch.-Porch		330
To that one joy of doing kindnesses.	19	Ch.-Porch	W	330
Write on the others, Here lies such a one.	20	Ch.-Porch		342
Much lesse make any one thine enemie.	20	Ch.-Porch		351
Much lesse make any one thy enemie.	20	Ch.-Porch	W	351
With saints on earth, shall one day with them shine.	24	Ch.-Porch		438
Without me each one, who doth now me brave,	27	Sacrifice		9
One houre of watching; but their drowsie brain	27	Sacrifice		30

ONE (cont'd)

	PAGE	TITLE		LINE
Then from one ruler to another bound	28	Sacrifice		53
Which each one calls for so with utmost breath,	31	Sacrifice		146
Who Crucifie him, crie with one strong shout.	32	Sacrifice		186
All spite in one, counting my life their losse,	33	Sacrifice		194
That all thy body was one doore.	35	Thanksgvng		6
One half of me being gone, the rest I give	35	Thanksgvng		27
One half of me being gone, the rest I'le give	35	Thanksgvng	W	27
And prove one God, one harmonie.	36	Thanksgvng		42
Or, since one starre show'd thy first breath,	38	Good Fri.		7
Of my whole life one grief devoure;	39	Good Fri.		14
One box doth lie both ink and sinne:	39	Good Fri.		24
So many hearts on earth, and yet not one	40	Sepulchre		3
There is but one, and that one ever.	42	Easter		30
Or make a new one, since the old	45	Nature		15
Yet all these fences with one bosome sinn	46	Sinne 1	W	13
One cunning bosome-sinne blows quite away.	46	Sinne 1		14
Is one undressing,	48	Repentance		5
One size doth all conditions fit.	50	Faith		28
As from one room t' another.	53	H.Commun.		36
Make one place ev'ry where.	55	Temper 1		28
Lord place me in thy consort; give one strain	57	Employm. 1		23
When he beheld twelve sunnes for one	59	Whitsunday		15
Thou Lord of life; since thy one death for me	62	Afflict.2		2
Into one common sewer, sea, and brine;	62	Afflict.2		7
Thy crosse took up in one,	62	Afflict.2		14
Of all these things, or all of them in one?	62	Mattens		8
Not one poore minute scapes thy breast,	64	Even-song		30
And th' other black and grave, wherewith each one	67	Ch.-floore		4
But the sweet cement, which in one sure band	67	Ch.-floore		10
Doctrine and life, colours and light, in one	68	Windows		11
Of that brave gift, each one began to fume,	70	Humilitie		19
They had depos'd each one.	70	Humilitie		24
They who lament one crosse,	73	Afflict.3		17
Make up one man; whose face thou art,	75	Sunday		9
And turn us round to look on one,	75	Sunday		17
Where ev'ry one is king, and hath his crown,	77	Ang.&Sts.		4
If any one our Masters hand can show.	78	Ang.&Sts.		30
All after pleasures as I rid one day,	80	Christmas		1
We sing one common Lord; wherefore he should	81	Christmas		25
And one another pay:	81	Christmas		32
Defrauding thee, who gavest two for one.	82	Ungratef.		30
One life is wrapt In flesh, and tends to earth.	84	Coloss.		5
Taught me to live here so, That still one eye	85	Coloss.		7
Is much more sure to meet with him, then one	87	Lent		38
Then he that curbs them, being but one to five:	89	The Pearl		29
Full of proportions, one limbe to another,	91	Man		14
Both are our cleanlinesse. Hath one such beautie?	92	Man		41
Both are our cleanlines: if one have beauty,	92	Man	W	41
Oh mightie love! Man is one world, and hath	92	Man		47
Who hath made of two folds one.	93	Antiphon 2		23
Which hath made of two folds one.	93	Antiphon 2	W	23
Take one from ten, and what remains?	96	Charms & K		15
One might have sought and found thee presently	99	Decay		6
In some one corner of a feeble heart:	99	Decay		12
For one poore minute, stumble at a pinne:	100	Miserie		20
That were I to leave all but one,	103	Prayer 2		21
To one word onely I say, No:	105	Obedience		32
Is not so deare to thee as one good grone.	106	Sion		18
Leave one poore apple for thy love?	107	Home		22
With one small sigh thou gav'st me th' other day	108	Home		43
Rivers run, and springs each one	113	Businesse		3
When all perfections as but one appeare,	115	Dulnesse		13
Anneal'd on every bunch. One standing by	116	Love-joy		3
And doth commit a world of sinne in one.	117	Providence		20
Thou art in all things one, in each thing many:	118	Providence		43
For thou art infinite in one and all.	118	Providence		44
Boat, cable, sail and needle, all in one.	120	Providence		128
Yet in their being joyn with one advise	121	Providence		146
It go for one, hath many wayes in store	121	Providence		150
Extolleth many wayes, yet this one more.	121	Providence		152
But where one man would have me grinde it,	122	Time		5
Twentie for one too sharp do finde it.	122	Time		6
Give one thing more, a gratefull heart.	123	Gratefulnes		2
One while he counts of heav'n, as of his treasure:	127	Giddinesse		5
Surely if each one saw anothers heart,	127	Giddinesse		21
Lord, mend or rather make us: one creation	127	Giddinesse		25
Sev'n yeares ago: one vogue and vein,	128	Bunch Gr.		4
One aire of thoughts usurps my brain.	128	Bunch Gr.		5
To him I brought a dish of fruit one day,	129	Love unkn.		6
Better then you know me, or (which is one)	129	Love unkn.		10
Better then you knew me, or (which is one)	129	Love unkn.	V	10
And clean and fair, as I one even-tide	129	Love unkn.		23
For I had giv'n the key to none, but one:	130	Love unkn.		55
And makes them one,	131	Mans medly		11
With th' one hand touching heav'n, with th' other earth.	131	Mans medly		12
He hath two winters, other things but one:	131	Mans medly		27
As I one ev'ning sat before my cell,	139	Artillerie		1
When suddenly I heard one say,	139	Artillerie		5
I left on th' one, and on the other side	142	Pilgrimage		5
Save one good Angell, which a friend had ti'd	142	Pilgrimage		17

ONE (cont'd)

	PAGE	TITLE		LINE
But I was told by one, it could not be;	143	Holdfast		3
Sev'n whole dayes, not one in seven,	146	Praise 2		17
Yet one pure heart is nothing to bestow:	147	Offering		5
Yet one, if good, may title to a number;	147	Offering		9
In publick judgements one may be a nation,	147	Offering		11
As neither good, nor one: so oft divisions	147	Offering		14
And thou mayst offer many gifts in one.	147	Offering		18
Resolv'd to light; and so one day	151	The Bag		11
But as he was returning, there came one	151	The Bag		25
Me thoughts I heard one calling, childe:	154	The Collar		35
But one half houre of comfort for my heart?	154	Glimpse		5
But one half houre of comfort to my heart?	154	Glimpse	V	5
When thou dost blesse, hath twelve: one wheel doth rise	158	Praise 3		11
I have not lost one single tear:	158	Praise 3		25
For well he knows, if but one grief and smart	159	Jos.coat		5
One of Joyes coats, ticing it with relief	159	Jos.coat		11
That with th' one hand thou liftest to the sky,	160	Priesthood		2
Have one beginning and one finall summe:	161	Priesthood		22
But all was one.	162	The Search		24
Making two one.	163	The Search		60
One ague dwelleth in my bones,	165	The Crosse		13
How neatly doe we give one onely name	168	The Sonne		5
So in one word our Lords humilitie	168	The Sonne		11
Show me, and set me, I have one reply,	169	The Answer		13
I shall be one day better then before:	169	Dial.-Anth		9
And one aspect of thine spend in delight	172	The Glance		22
And yet in washing one, she washed both.	173	Marie Magd		18
Each one whispring, Live ye brother?	186	Dooms-day		6
Seest and rulest all things ev'n as one:	190	Ch.-Milit.		2
Letting, while one foot stept, the other stay	191	Ch.-Milit.		34
Which using, and not fearing skill in th' one,	192	Ch.-Milit.		77
Much about one and the same time and place,	192	Ch.-Milit.		101
As Rome will one day finde unto her cost.	194	Ch.-Milit.		160
The Churches here, bravely resolv'd one night	194	Ch.-Milit.		162
United now in one both time and sphere.	195	Ch.-Milit.		176
As new and old Rome did one Empire twist;	196	Ch.-Milit.		205
So both together are one Antichrist,	196	Ch.-Milit.		206
When th' one did set, the other did take place,	196	Ch.-Milit.		217
Whereby one may foretell, what sinnes next yeare	197	Ch.-Milit.		245
Spain hath done one; when Arts perform the other,	197	Ch.-Milit.		265
Light one another, and together runne.	198	Ch.-Milit.		271
Like Comick Lovers ever one way runn:	198	Ch.-Milit.	W	271
With the one make warre to cease;	199	L'Envoy		2
With the one make warrs to cease;	199	L'Envoy	W	2
Thrice blessed Three in One.	199	L'Envoy		18
He that is one,	202	Trin.Sun.	W	1
Hee that has one,	203	Trin.Sun.	W	18
Than that, which one day Worms may chance refuse?	206	Walton 1		14
To want one ownce of sleepe,	209	Paradox	D	4
Eternity into one Bedd.	213	L' Envoy	D	14
combin'd in one great faction rise.	215	Psalm II	D	4
The bloody man, the false one too,	218	Psalm V	D	15
in describing the one (which is indeed the bent of my Discourse)	226	Priest 2		18
which in the day of wrath hath not one dramme of comfort for us.	227	Priest 3		21
and all being penn'd by one and the self-same Spirit, it cannot be,	229	Priest 4		6
For the Law required one thing, and the Gospel another:	229	Priest 4		14
and that as one Countrey doth not bear all things, that there may be	229	Priest 4		23
or will open all to one, that there may be a traffick in knowledg	229	Priest 4		25
Wherfore he hath one Comment at least upon every book of Scripture,	229	Priest 4		27
according as his audience is, so he useth one, or other;	230	Priest 5		17
For every one hath not digested, when it is a sin to take something	230	Priest 5		23
as attending to what is done in the Church, and every one, man,	231	Priest 6		27
he makes a peculiar one for a blessing on the exercises of the day,	235	Priest 8		22
And every one is more awaked, when we come, and say, Thou art	236	Priest 8		14
that order is kept in the one, and peace in the other, without	236	Priest 8		24
that it is ever attempting, or doing one mischief or other.	238	Priest 9		14
the one he owes to his heavenly Countrey, the other to his earthly,	239	Priest 10		21
and how every one profits, comparing this yeer with the last:	240	Priest 10		37
are unuseful to man, the one for smalnesse, as crums, and scattered	241	Priest 10		27
One thing is evident, that an English body, and a Students body,	242	Priest 10		38
as he obeys Authority in the one, so that being once satisfied,	245	Priest 12		26
to visite in person, now one quarter of his Parish, now another.	247	Priest 14		5
it is a good and just thing for every one to do their own busines.	247	Priest 14		22
However, one way or other, he ever reproves them, that he may keep	248	Priest 14		23
finde any reading in anothers Bible, he provides him one of his own.	254	Priest 20		12
the one, to infuse a competent knowledge of salvation in every one	255	Priest 21		2
infuse a competent knowledge of salvation in every one of his Flock;	255	Priest 21		3
This order being used to one, would be a little varyed to another.	256	Priest 21		16
but when one is asked a question, he must discover what he is.	257	Priest 21		19
being two things in Sermons, the one Informing, the other Inflaming;	257	Priest 21		22
as Sermons come short of questions in the one, so they farre exceed	257	Priest 21		23
When any one can distinguish the Sacramentall from common bread,	258	Priest 22		34
the one, in wanting many excitings of grace;	259	Priest 22		5
confesseth himself an unworthy one, and therefore differs from other	259	Priest 22		16
neither avoyding therfore one anothers company, much lesse defaming	260	Priest 23		27
therfore one anothers company, much lesse defaming one another.	260	Priest 23		28
This is done by seeing one Anatomy, reading one Book of Phisick,	261	Priest 23		4
reading one Book of Phisick, having one Herball by him.	261	Priest 23		4
reading one Book of Phisick, having one Herball by him.	261	Priest 23		5
and maketh the one serve the other.	261	Priest 23		17

ONE (cont'd)

	PAGE	TITLE		LINE
God is wonderfully to be seen, one thing would be carefully observed;	261	Priest 23		28
the Parson useth damask or white Roses for the one, and plantaine,	261	Priest 23		35
one of obeying Authority, the other of not giving scandall,	263	Priest 24		9
the one, a strict religious life;	263	Priest 24		16
to that which is presently unlawfull, even in one continued action.	264	Priest 26		22
and to give one instance for all, if God have given me servants,	265	Priest 26		19
One act in these things is bad, but it is the custome and habit that	266	Priest 26		17
(for one thinks in eating, that he can eat more, then afterwards he	267	Priest 26		3
For knowing what one usually can well disgest, and feeling when I go	267	Priest 26		6
of themselves, knowing that there is one, who when they forget,	267	Priest 26		21
that so the sentence lighting upon one, the example may reach to all.	269	Priest 28		2
he preserves and orders the references of things one to the other,	271	Priest 30		14
This Liberty he compasseth by one distinction, and that is,	272	Priest 31		19
the one in having no calling, the other in walking carelesly in our	274	Priest 32		16
for every one to imploy himselfe to the advancement of his affairs,	275	Priest 32		28
Hee considers every one there, and either helps them in particular,	276	Priest 32		3
the one, the abuse of it, by taking petty Countrey bribes;	276	Priest 32		19
the Baptist squared out to every one (even to Souldiers) what to do.	277	Priest 32		23
The one being usefull to all Countreys, and the other especially	278	Priest 32		2
and one of the first steps of pleasing God, having for his owne use	279	Priest 33		7
a Christian even in this Life, the one military, the other peaceable.	280	Priest 34		2
as he discovers any of his Flock to be in one or the other state,	280	Priest 34		13
the one concerning the woman that spent the oyntment on our Saviour,	282	Priest 34		24
He hath one argument unanswerable.	283	Priest 34		9
the one in his being, the other in his sinfull being:	283	Priest 34		20
and neighbourly accompanying one another, with reconciling	284	Priest 35		6
that his Parish at good times invite one another to their houses,	284	Priest 35		18
hee takes one of the parties, and goes with him to the other,	284	Priest 35		20
the one in, The Grace of our Lord Jesus Christ, &c.	286	Priest 36		4
giving us one world in our selves, and another to serve us:	288	Priest		13
three Persons, but one most glorious, incomprehensible God,	290	Priest		15
me contrariwise, at the age of eightie and one, strong and lustie;	291	Cornaro		11
the Physicians told me that yet there was one help for me,	292	Cornaro		3
within lesse then one yeare (although it may seem to some incredible)	292	Cornaro		36
by any of these inconveniences, except it were for one onely day.	294	Cornaro		10
was sore hurt, and also one of my arms and legges put out of joynt.	294	Cornaro		39
two Italian Proverbs, the one whereof was, He that will eat much,	295	Cornaro		34
And that new one, which I contracted by breaking my diet,	297	Cornaro		1
whereof the one kept me well for many yeares;	297	Cornaro		4
he will prove himself a Physician, and that a very compleat one:	297	Cornaro		24
Every one by long experience may know the qualities of his own	297	Cornaro		26
Wherefore one to another cannot be a perfect Physician.	297	Cornaro		36
because that after one is once sixtie five yeares old, all the time	300	Cornaro		28
I was one of those that was deputed for the managing of that work,	302	Cornaro		16
all the sonnes of one father and mother, all in perfect health;	303	Cornaro		3
Popery should open the eyes of one to understand and expresse so	304	Valdesso		20
the generall promises to every one in particular with such syncerity	309	Valdesso		4
but such a one as shall still have the assistance of the holy spirit	310	Valdesso		6
in the Church of God there is one fundamentall, but else variety.	312	Valdesso		2
But it is one thing not to judge, another to defend them.	316	Valdesso		14
the one being gratia gratis data, the other gratia gratum faciens,	319	Valdesso		7
one, whose holinesse consists in a few ceremonious and superstitious	319	Valdesso	V	22
The Devill is not alwaies at one doore.	322	Proverbs		31
One sound blow will serve to undo all.	322	Proverbs		34
A cherefull looke makes one dish a feast.	323	Proverbs	V	62
When a dog is a drowning, every one offers him drink.	323	Proverbs		77
Three helping one another, beare the burthen of sixe.	325	Proverbs		135
The bit that one eates, no friend makes.	325	Proverbs		142
Every one stretcheth his legges according to his coverlet.	325	Proverbs		147
None is a foole alwaies, every one sometimes.	326	Proverbs		163
Ever since we weare cloathes, we know not one another.	326	Proverbs		168
One stroke fells not an oke.	327	Proverbs		181
They that know one another salute a farre off.	327	Proverbs		185
One graine fills not a sacke, but helpes his fellowes.	328	Proverbs		226
men for one pleasure a thousand griefes prove.	328	Proverbs		228
Reckon right, and February hath one and thirty daies.	328	Proverbs		229
Honour and profit lie not in one sacke.	328	Proverbs		232
One hand washeth another, and both the face.	329	Proverbs		239
The worst of law is, that one suit breedes twenty.	329	Proverbs		253
Your pot broken seemes better then my whole one.	330	Proverbs		270
Many friends in generall, one in speciall.	330	Proverbs		281
Hee will spend a whole yeares rent at one meales meate.	331	Proverbs		305
He that chastens one, chastens 20.	333	Proverbs		356
We are fooles one to another.	334	Proverbs		381
The horse thinkes one thing, and he that sadles him another.	334	Proverbs		387
The buyer needes a hundred eyes, the seller not one.	334	Proverbs		390
One father is enough to governe one hundred sons,	335	Proverbs		404
but not a hundred sons one father.	335	Proverbs		404
but an 100 sons are not enough to govern one Father.	335	Proverbs	V	404
A hundred loade of thought will not pay one of debts.	335	Proverbs		414
Hee that hath one hogge makes him fat,	336	Proverbs		433
and hee that hath one son makes him a foole.	336	Proverbs		433
Hee who hath but one sonne makes him fat,	336	Proverbs	V	433
He that hath one foot in the straw, hath another in the spittle.	336	Proverbs		438
Fooles bite one another, but wise-men agree together.	336	Proverbs		452
Trust not one nights ice.	336	Proverbs		453
In the kingdome of blind men the one ey'd is king.	337	Proverbs		469
Disgraces are like cherries, one drawes another.	338	Proverbs		487
Every one fastens where there is gaine.	338	Proverbs		496
All feete tread not in one shoe.	338	Proverbs		497

ONE (cont'd)	PAGE	TITLE		LINE
One flower makes no garland.	339	Proverbs		521
One enemy is too much.	339	Proverbs		523
One foole makes a hundred.	339	Proverbs		525
One paire of eares drawes dry a hundred tongues.	339	Proverbs		526
One slumber finds another.	339	Proverbs		528
A scepter is one thing, and a ladle another.	339	Proverbs		545
when there are many to strike on one Anvile.	340	Proverbs		551
It's a poore stake that cannot stand one yeare in the ground.	340	Proverbs		553
He that commits a fault, thinkes every one speakes of it.	340	Proverbs		554
He that lives not well one yeare, sorrowes seven after.	340	Proverbs		562
Wisedome hath one foot on Land, and another on Sea.	341	Proverbs		611
Perversnes makes one squint ey'd.	342	Proverbs		634
Love makes one fitt for any work.	343	Proverbs		646
A hatt is not made for one shower.	343	Proverbs		673
Every one puts his fault on the Times.	343	Proverbs		675
Every one is weary, the poore in seeking,	344	Proverbs		678
One father is more then a hundred Schoolemasters.	344	Proverbs		686
One eye of the masters sees more, then ten of the servants.	344	Proverbs		687
All keyes hang not on one girdle.	345	Proverbs		719
The wind in ones face makes one wise.	345	Proverbs		721
One sword keepes another in the sheath.	345	Proverbs		723
Every one thinkes his sacke heaviest.	346	Proverbs		748
Every one is witty for his owne purpose.	346	Proverbs		754
One foote is better then two crutches.	346	Proverbs		769
It's absurd to warme one in his armour.	347	Proverbs		775
At Court, every one for himselfe.	347	Proverbs		795
Curtesie on one side only lasts not long.	348	Proverbs		809
He that sends a foole expects one.	349	Proverbs		851
Every one hath a foole in his sleeve.	350	Proverbs		881
One houres sleepe before midnight is worth three after.	350	Proverbs		882
'Tis easier to build two chimneys, then to maintaine one.	350	Proverbs		893
Conversation makes one what he is.	351	Proverbs		926
Conversation makes one what they are.	351	Proverbs	V	926
Knowledge makes one laugh, but wealth makes one dance.	352	Proverbs		957
The eyes have one language every where.	352	Proverbs		959
One faire day in winter makes not birds merrie.	353	Proverbs		977
When one is cn horsebacke hee knowes all things.	353	Proverbs		982
Every one is a master and servant.	355	Proverbs		1026
One month doth nothing without another.	355	Proverbs		1028
One mouth doth nothing without another.	355	Proverbs	V	1028
Modesty sets off one newly come to honour.	357	Proverbs	D	1062
Two sparrows on one Ear of Corn make an ill agreement.	358	Proverbs	D	1074
Better is one Accipe, then twice to say, Dabo tibi.	358	Proverbs	D	1079
He that hath but one eye, must bee afraid to lose it.	358	Proverbs	D	1088
Still fisheth he that catcheth one.	358	Proverbs	D	1095
What one day gives us, another takes away from us.	359	Proverbs	D	1111
Fortune to one is Mother, to another is Step-mother.	359	Proverbs	D	1118
We must love, as looking one day to hate.	359	Proverbs	D	1126
The rage of a wild boar is able to spoil more then one wood.	360	Proverbs	D	1132
The mouse that hath but one hole is quickly taken.	360	Proverbs	D	1135
Wo be to him that reads but one book.	360	Proverbs	D	1146
but that every day, I may step one step towards my journies end;	364	Letters		27
yet I am scarce able with much ado to make one half years allowance,	365	Letters		10
Let me commend only one place more to you (Philip. 4. 4.) St. Paul	374	Letters		20
to putt one of our neeces into your hands but barely what I wrote I	375	Letters		5
For concerning your offer of receiving one, I will tell you what I	375	Letters		9
wrote to our eldest brother, when he urged one upon me, and but one,	375	Letters		11
when he urged one upon me, and but one, and that at my choice.	375	Letters		11
and age, and knew none but one who could be no company to them.	375	Letters		15
Therefore I considered that if one cnly came, the comfort intended	375	Letters		16
and it is an outlandish one, which I commend to you as being now	376	Letters		17
severall wayes, one to the other, that ye may be a heavenly comfort,	378	Letters		26
the one for the nature thereof (as your trade) the other only	380	Woodnoth		21
the one are Gods servants, the other the commonwealths,	381	Woodnoth		28
but a Trade having two things, the one imployment, the other profitt,	381	Woodnoth		30
To Mrss Magdalen Vaughan one hundred pound, To Mrs Catharine Vaughan	383	G.H.'s Will		5
To Mrs Catharine Vaughan One hundred pound, To Mr George Herbert one	383	G.H.'s Will		6
To Mr George Herbert one hundred pound To Mrs Beatrice Herbert forty	383	G.H.'s Will		7
ONE'S				
The time of every ones first receiving is not so much by yeers,	258	Priest 22		32
But to eat to ones hurt, comprehends, besides the hurt,	266	Priest 26		21
an act against reason, because it is unnaturall to hurt ones self;	266	Priest 26		22
The first degree of folly is to hold ones selfe wise,	337	Proverbs		460
To deceive ones selfe is very easie.	342	Proverbs		632
The wind in ones face makes one wise.	345	Proverbs		721
It's good walking with a horse in ones hand.	348	Proverbs		804
It's a wicked thing to make a dearth ones garner.	351	Proverbs		898
To review ones store is to mow twice.	354	Proverbs		1007
ONELY				
Against thee: for his light was onely lent.	9	Ch.-Porch		82
Onely a herauld, who that way doth passe,	14	Ch.-Porch		197
For wit is newes onely to ignorance.	15	Ch.-Porch		230
Onely thy single market-money for it.	21	Ch.-Porch		375
Onely by his permission. Then beware,	22	Ch.-Porch		405
O let thy onely SACRIFICE be mine,	26	The Altar	W	15
Drops bloud (the onely beads) my words to measure:	27	Sacrifice		22
And onely am the Lord of hosts and might:	29	Sacrifice		79
Pick quarrels with their onely happinesse:	29	Sacrifice		87
Why, Caesar is their onely King, not I:	30	Sacrifice		121
Which shews my bloud to be the onely way,	31	Sacrifice		158

ONELY (cont'd)

	PAGE	TITLE	LINE
The tree of life to all, but onely me:	33	Sacrifice	203
Onely let others say, when I am dead,	34	Sacrifice	251
To thee of all kings onely due)	35	Thanksgvng	2
Onely these stones in quiet entertain thee,	41	Sepulchre	15
Onely thy grace, which with these elements comes,	52	H.Commun.	19
Who sings thy praise? onely a skarf or glove	54	Love 1	13
Who sayes that fictions onely and false hair	56	Jordan 1	1
All things are busie; onely I	57	Employm. 1	17
Seeing not onely how each verse doth shine,	58	H.Script.2	3
Yet heare, O God, onely for his bloods sake	66	Ch.-lock	9
Onely thy Chronicle is lost; and yet	69	Content	25
The sigh then onely is	73	Afflict.3	11
Of the Immortal onely King.	76	Sunday W	32
And not refuse me: for thou onely art	83	Sighs & Gr.	4
Onely a sweet and vertuous soul,	88	Vertue	13
Reason and speech we onely bring.	91	Man	10
Onely to purchase my good-will:	94	Unkindness	24
Onely do thou lend me a hand,	95	Submission	19
And anchor thou art onely, to confirm	97	Afflict.5	4
Sleep bindes them fast; onely their breath	98	Mortific.	9
Copie out onely that, and save expense.	103	Jordan 2	18
To one word onely I say, No:	105	Obedience	32
Do amount to, onely he,	114	Dialogue	14
Look onely; for to love thee, who can be,	116	Dulnesse	27
Onely to Man thou hast made known thy wayes,	117	Providence	6
And onely he hath fuell in desire.	120	Providence	112
And so complete, but onely he that owes them.	121	Providence	144
For where thou onely wert before	123	Time	14
Is onely there.	125	Peace	42
Onely an open breast	126	Confession	19
The Font did onely, what was old, renew:	130	Love unkn.	64
At least those beams of truth, which onely save,	135	Divinitie	15
Their beauteous glories. Onely shreds of thee,	140	Ch.-rents	9
Onely the present is thy part and fee.	144	Discharge	21
Is the yeare onely lost to me?	153	The Collar	13
Thou art not onely to perform thy part,	156	Assurance	27
Onely, since God doth often vessels make	161	Priesthood	34
And serve thee; and not onely I,	164	The Crosse	4
And relish versing: O my onely light,	166	The Flower	39
How neatly doe we give one onely name	168	The Sonne	5
With onely this, My joy, my life, my crown.	168	a true Hymn	5
If the words onely ryme,	168	a true Hymn	13
Onely another head	174	Aaron	11
Christ is my onely head,	174	Aaron	16
My alone onely heart and breast,	174	Aaron	17
My onely musick, striking me ev'n dead;	174	Aaron	18
Of stews and brothels onely knew the doores,	176	Forerunners	15
Onely take this gentle rose,	177	The Rose	15
Onely though I you oppose,	178	The Rose	30
Onely God, who gives perfumes,	181	Banquet	22
That I not onely may not erre	184	The Elixer W	3
Onely whereas the Ark in glorie shone,	190	Ch.-Milit.	27
Onely the West and Rome do keep them free	194	Ch.-Milit.	157
Onely there was a handsome picture by,	194	Ch.-Milit.	169
Shipping the vices onely for our sphere.	196	Ch.-Milit. W	204
Sinn onely, which did all deface	200	H. Commun. W	23
Onely my soule hangs on thy promisses	205	Persever. W	13
But onely while thou speak'st; This Anchor will.	439	Walton 5	4
Onely, most noble Lord, shutt not the doore	209	L. Bacon D	9
And pace of thy swift vertues; onely they	211	Bohemia D	5
stead of the qualities of the world, he requires onely three of her;	239	Priest 10	12
that not onely sicknesse breaks these obligations of fasting,	242	Priest 10	34
although we should love him onely for his own sake, yet out of his	243	Priest 11	30
may go the right way, and thither onely, where they are onely due.	245	Priest 12	34
and thinketh the Ceremony not onely innocent, but reverend.	258	Priest 22	9
not onely for the benefit of the work, but also for the discharge	259	Priest 22	23
to be all to his Parish, and not onely a Pastour, but a Lawyer also,	259	Priest 23	30
he doth not onely prefer home-bred things before them, but condemns	261	Priest 23	37
not onely because all men shun the company of perpetuall severity,	268	Priest 27	2
on God, not onely before the corne is inned, but after also;	271	Priest 30	35
I will not doubt to go without staying to pray there (but onely,	273	Priest 31	35
The Countrey Parson hath not onely taken a particular Survey	274	Priest 32	4
Now because the onely opposer to this Doctrine is the Gallant,	275	Priest 32	5
Neither is this true onely in the military state of a Christian life,	279	Priest 33	3
The thrusting away of his arme makes us onely not embraced.	283	Priest 34	26
whereas he thinks it not onely a grave, and reverend thing,	285	Priest 36	3
who onely doth wondrous things.	289	Priest	8
which did not onely begin, but had already gone farre in me,	291	Cornaro	18
lesse then a yeare I was not onely freed from all those evils which	293	Cornaro	20
by any of these inconveniences, except it were for one onely day.	294	Cornaro	10
and onely commanded that my arm and legge should be set,	295	Cornaro	10
which yet needs not onely to be sustained, but also to gather	295	Cornaro	23
the quantitie of meat to be increased, yet but two ounces onely.	296	Cornaro	8
onely with returning to my former course of Diet, although I was now	296	Cornaro	24
and long dayes, and the true and onely medicine of many diseases.	297	Cornaro	13
no man can be a perfect Physician to another, but to himself onely.	297	Cornaro	25
and onely comforts and condoles, doth perform an acceptable thing	298	Cornaro	6
who not onely as a friend doth visit thee, but help thee!	298	Cornaro	9
onely by a pure consumption of the radicall moisture, without grief	298	Cornaro	17
not onely in the citie, but also in villages and hamlets.	299	Cornaro	4

ONELY (cont'd)	PAGE	TITLE		LINE
but onely that a man should begin and by little and little accustome	299	Cornaro		8
onely upon a hope of an happie issue, which yet befalls verie few.	300	Cornaro		23
not onely a shamefull thing to fear that which cannot be avoided;	303	Cornaro		21
holy Scripture, he meaneth that we should not use it as the onely,	314	Valdesso	V	5
whereas there is not onely milke there, but strong meat also.	317	Valdesso		24
and not used it for a time onely, and then cast it away,	318	Valdesso		3
A little with quiet is the onely dyet.	332	Proverbs		327
Vertue now is in herbs and stones and words onely.	337	Proverbs		478
He is onely bright that shines by himselfe.	345	Proverbs		707
unto my deare wife excepting onely these legacies hereafter insuing.	382	G.H.'s Will		6
ONES				
Lesser pains scape greater ones.	113	Businesse		14
With these two poore ones lick up all the dew,	140	Ch.-rents		29
But since those great ones, be they ne're so great,	161	Priesthood		19
To conquere new ones, & shall share the frame	212	Bohemia	D	43
as of those of antient times, so especially of the late ones;	233	Priest 7		8
There would bee no great ones if there were no little ones.	331	Proverbs		292
There would bee no great ones if there were no mean ones.	331	Proverbs	V	292
Litle stickes kindle the fire; great ones put it out.	332	Proverbs		323
If great men would have care of little ones,	344	Proverbs		697
ONLEY				
This is true onley of the Popish Cases of Conscience, which depend	319	Valdesso	V	28
ONLY (see also onely)				
Wear Venus Livery? only serve her turn?	206	Walton 1		4
Had he only brought them forth,	208	J. Danvers	D	13
Henceforth shall only pierce the Skies,	214	Convert	D	14
Of Pastors (intending mine own Nation only, and also therein setting	225	Priest 2		20
whose aim and labour must be not only to get knowledg, but to subdue	226	Priest 2		9
only protesting to them, that not any ill will draws him to it,	232	Priest 6		17
but only by those means, by which at first it was obtained.	237	Priest 9		20
them with all Piety, not only of words in praying, and reading;	239	Priest 10		24
charity being his only perfume, which deserves cost when he can spare	241	Priest 10		14
which he celebrates not only with abstinence of diet, but also	241	Priest 10		38
but only the two former, which also in diseases of exinanition	242	Priest 10		30
and opens not only his mouth, but his purse to their relief,	248	Priest 14		11
The Countrey Parson is not only a father to his flock, but also	250	Priest 16		7
things of ordinary use are not only to serve in the way of drudgery,	257	Priest 21		14
in a great confusion, as being not only to receive God, but to break,	257	Priest 22		29
for thou art not only the feast, but the way to it.	257	Priest 22		34
not on the Sunday of the Communion only (for then it is too late)	258	Priest 22		27
hath the place its dignity from the Ecclesiasticall Laws only,	269	Priest 29		33
he must not only be a morning man, but at Committees also;	277	Priest 32		11
as the only wonder-working knowledg, and therefore requiring the best	277	Priest 32		34
which are not only a noble, but also as they may be handled,	278	Priest 32		6
not only in the beginning of his preaching, but afterwards also,	280	Priest 34		8
not only without dissolution of the whole, but also of any part,	281	Priest 34		22
in all Lands, was intended not only for a punishment to them;	282	Priest 34		14
or the Apostles only, no more then to be a spirituall Father was	285	Priest 36		12
Neither have the Ministers power of Blessing only, but also	285	Priest 36		25
many an evill may not only be, but also spread in his Parish,	287	Priest 37		1
Grant this dear Father, for thy Son's sake, our only Saviour:	290	Priest		13
holy Scriptures have not only an Elementary use, but a use	306	Valdesso		18
none can free themselves of themselves, but only by the Grace of God:	308	Valdesso		9
only by the generall Providence of God, as Socrates and Aristides,	308	Valdesso		12
whereby I understand he meaneth only the effectuall operation	308	Valdesso		30
H. Scriptures (as I wrote before) have not only an Elementary use,	309	Valdesso		21
us not with the same thing only when it is read as the promises	310	Valdesso		33
He meanes a mans fre-will is only in outward, not in spirituall	313	Valdesso		33
this being given only to the godly, and the other sometimes	319	Valdesso		9
Vertue now is in stones, herbs & words only.	337	Proverbs	V	478
Curtesie on one side only lasts not long.	348	Proverbs		809
Cities seldome change Religion only.	356	Proverbs	D	71
Not only ought fortune to be pictured on a wheel,	358	Proverbs	D	1077
only hereafter I will take heed how I propose my desires unto you,	363	Letters		20
because my recompenses of your favours consist in this only.	367	Letters		32
as that either his subjects only should practise it, or at least that	368	Letters		11
only my comfort is that this is but an occasion for you to amplify	369	Letters		2
I fear only that I have omitted some fitting circumstance,	370	Letters		11
and now the only thing I long for, is to hear of my dear sick Sister;	371	Letters		7
most carry themselves so, as if they not only not desir'd, but,	373	Letters		33
Let me commend only one place more to you (Philip. 4. 4.) St. Paul	374	Letters		20
That you did not only entertain my proposals, but advance them,	375	Letters		2
Therefore I considered that if one only came, the comfort intended	375	Letters		16
by the Apostles rule (Philip 4, 8.) not only to pursue pure things,	380	Woodnoth		13
thereof (as your trade) the other only for the success (as assistance	380	Woodnoth		22
with his favours, can not but be not only allowable but commendable.	381	Woodnoth		26
OPE				
I cannot ope mine eyes,	62	Mattens		1
On Sunday heavens gate stands ope;	76	Sunday		33
On Sunday heavens dore stands ope;	76	Sunday	W	33
OPEN				
But the cheap swearer through his open sluce	8	Ch.-Porch		58
Open for thee; or both may come too late.	21	Ch.-Porch		384
Open for thee; or they may come too late.	21	Ch.-Porch	W	384
Bibles laid open, millions of surprises,	45	Sinne 1		8
Keep open house, richly attended,	59	Whitsunday		7
Thou hast layd open both,	82	Ungratef.	W	9
All these stand open, or I have the keyes:	88	The Pearl		9
Therefore not sealed, but with open eyes	89	The Pearl		32
Therefore not seeled, but with open eyes	89	The Pearl	W	32

	PAGE	TITLE		LINE
OPPOSITION				
What pride by opposition.	161	Priesthood		42
Of opposition cannot place thee, where	212	Bohemia	D	39
and to do such things of legall opposition either in the presenting,	263	Priest 25		24
people to continue in their vocation, it is in opposition to idlenes.	381	Woodnoth		24
OPPRESSED				
and finding my self continually oppressed with pain and sicknesse,	292	Cornaro		19
which is alreadie burdened with a disease, would be wholly oppressed.	299	Cornaro		34
OPPREST				
And by the others is opprest.	79	Employm.2		15
OPTICK				
Grace turnes the Optick, then they fall.	97	Charms & K	W	18
And he an optick sent.	121	Hope		4
Mee thinkes, in that Dutch optick I doe see	211	Bohemia	D	13
OR				
Theirs, who shall hurt themselves or me, refrain.	5	Dedication		6
Abstain wholly, or wed. Thy bounteous Lord	7	Ch.-Porch		13
Abstaine or wedd: if thou canst not abstaine	7	Ch.-Porch	W	13
Need or Incontinency: the first way	7	Ch.-Porch	W	16
Stay at the third cup, or forgo the place.	8	Ch.-Porch		47
Yet, if thou sinne in wine or wantonnesse,	8	Ch.-Porch		49
If they dare try, a glorious life, or grave.	10	Ch.-Porch		90
Or els they breed them tender, make them need	10	Ch.-Porch		105
Carve, or discourse; do not a famine fear.	11	Ch.-Porch		129
What skills it, if a bag of stones or gold	13	Ch.-Porch		169
Or a fir'd beacon frighteth from his ditties.	16	Ch.-Porch		250
Nothing from thine: in service, care, or coldnesse	16	Ch.-Porch		255
Doth ratably thy fortunes marre or make.	16	Ch.-Porch		256
All such is courteous, usefull, new, or wittie.	18	Ch.-Porch		290
More, then his sicknesses or povertie?	18	Ch.-Porch		310
In love or honour: take account of all;	20	Ch.-Porch		344
Whether thy stock of credit swell, or fall.	20	Ch.-Porch		346
Or love, or language; nothing comes amisse:	20	Ch.-Porch		357
Open for thee; or both may come too late.	21	Ch.-Porch		384
Open for thee; or they may come too late.	21	Ch.-Porch	W	384
Let vain or busie thoughts have there no part:	23	Ch.-Porch		421
For churches are either our heav'n or hell.	23	Ch.-Porch		426
For churches either are our heav'n or hell.	23	Ch.-Porch	W	426
Jest not at preachers language, or expression:	24	Ch.-Porch		439
Or that which groneth to be so,	25	Superlim		7
What ever scoffes or scornfulnesse can bring,	32	Sacrifice		174
Or feel his part, he would not cease to kneel,	33	Sacrifice		210
Or feel his share, he would not cease to kneel,	33	Sacrifice	W	210
I will not marry; or, if she be mine,	35	Thanksgvng		23
Unto some Chappell, die or live.	35	Thanksgvng		28
I'le build a spittle, or mend common wayes,	36	Thanksgvng		33
Or, since one starre show'd thy first breath,	38	Good Fri.		7
Or shall each leaf,	38	Good Fri.		9
Or cannot leaves, but fruit, be signe	38	Good Fri.		11
Or rather let	39	Good Fri.		17
And all the writings blot or burn.	39	Good Fri.		32
Or since all musick is but three parts vied	42	Easter		15
Or else give tears to drown them, as they grow.	44	H. Bapt.1		9
Or fight, or travell, or denie	45	Nature		2
Or make a new one, since the old	45	Nature		15
No place for grief or fear.	46	Afflict.1		16
Thus thinne and lean without a fence or friend,	47	Afflict.1		35
To fruit or shade: at least some bird would trust	48	Afflict.1		59
Mans age is two houres work, or three:	48	Repentance		7
Faith makes me any thing, or all	50	Faith		17
If blisse had lien in art or strength,	50	Faith		25
None but the wise or strong had gained it:	50	Faith		26
Not in rich furniture, or fine aray,	52	H.Commun.		1
Give me my captive soul, or take	52	H.Commun.		25
To sinne, or sinne to smother;	53	H.Commun.		34
Who sings thy praise? onely a skarf or glove	54	Love 1		13
Although there were some fourtie heav'ns, or more,	55	Temper 1		5
Although there were a hundred heav'ns, or more,	55	Temper 1	W	5
Stretch or contract me thy poore debter:	55	Temper 1		22
Whether I Angell it, or fall to dust.	55	Temper 1	W	25
Save that, and me; or sin for both destroy.	56	Temper 2		4
Scatter, or binde them all to bend to thee:	56	Temper 2		13
I envie no mans nightingale or spring;	57	Jordan 1		13
Or if to me thou wilt not move,	61	Grace		22
To write a verse or two is all the praise,	61	Praise 1		1
Or, if I mount unto the skie,	61	Praise 1		7
Or, if I steale up to the skie,	61	Praise 1	W	7
As Prince or King:	61	Praise 1		10
Silver, or gold, or precious stone,	62	Mattens		6
Or starre, or rainbow, or a part	62	Mattens		7
Of all these things, or all of them in one?	62	Mattens		8
The day or night: that is the gale, this th' harbour;	64	Even-song		26
Or that the garden, this the grove.	64	Even-song		28
Sicknes, or shame, or sinn, or sorrow:	65	Ch.-mus.	W	8
Or else the chilnesse of my faint demands.	66	Ch.-lock		4
If either Innocence or Fervencie	66	Ch.-lock	W	4
Not on my sinnes, or coldnesse, but thy will.	66	Ch.-lock		8
O make mee wholy guiltles, or at least	66	Ch.-lock	W	9
Of an untrained hope or passion.	68	Content		6
To court each place or fortune that doth fall,	68	Content		7
To court each place or fortune that does fall,	68	Content	W	7

OR (cont'd)

	PAGE	TITLE	LINE
Thy nourisht fame is weak or strong.	69	Content	32
Do not thy self or friends importune.	69	Content	34
No point of honour, or gay suit,	69	Quidditie	2
No hawk, or banquet, or renown,	69	Quidditie	3
It cannot vault, or dance, or play;	70	Quidditie	5
It never was in France or Spain;	70	Quidditie	6
With a great stable or demain:	70	Quidditie	8
With my great stable or demain:	70	Quidditie W	8
It is no office, art, or news,	70	Quidditie	9
Nor the Exchange, or busie Hall;	70	Quidditie	10
Is styled honour, riches, or fair eyes;	71	Frailtie	3
Deare earth, fine grasse or hay;	71	Frailtie	6
Unpinne, or wrench from giving all their due.	72	Constancie	5
So loose or easie, that a ruffling winde	72	Constancie	7
Can blow away, or glittering look it blinde:	72	Constancie	8
What place or person calls for, he doth pay.	72	Constancie	15
Whom none can work or wooe	72	Constancie	16
To use in any thing a trick or sleight;	72	Constancie	17
Who never melts or thaws	72	Constancie	21
Or if some yeares with it escape,	73	Afflict.3	10
Parted with alleys or with grass	75	Sunday W	27
Or strict commands;	77	Ang.&Sts.	3
Not out of envie or maliciousnesse	78	Ang.&Sts.	6
The sunne still shineth there or here,	79	Employm.2	18
But we are still too young or old;	79	Employm.2	26
But we are ever young or old;	79	Employm.2 W	26
A better lodging then a rack or grave.	81	Christmas	14
He loves not Temperance, or Authoritie,	86	Lent	2
Or of it self, like a good huswife, spunne	88	The Pearl	4
All these stand open, or I have the keyes:	88	The Pearl	9
To sell my life unto my friends or foes:	88	The Pearl	19
The joyes of Company or Contemplation	89	The Pearl W	29
Or can be, then is Man? to whose creation	90	Man	5
A beast, yet is, or should be more:	91	Man	9
As our delight, or as our treasure:	91	Man	28
Or cabinet of pleasure.	91	Man	30
If any touch my friend, or his good name,	93	Unkindness	6
From the least spot or thought of blame.	93	Unkindness	9
Fit, while ye liv'd, for smell or ornament,	94	Life	14
I follow straight without complaints or grief,	94	Life	16
Thy horse shal never fall or tire.	96	Charms & K W	4
When th' hair is sweet through pride or lust,	96	Charms & K	13
A chair or litter shows the biere,	98	Mortific.	29
At some fair oak, or bush, or cave, or well:	99	Decay	7
Or none thy portion is.	101	Miserie	42
Thou must go sleep, or dine.	101	Miserie	54
A lump of flesh, without a foot or wing	102	Miserie	74
Or some such words in fashion;	104	Obedience	14
Or superficiall offer	104	Obedience	29
Of what we might not take, or be withstood.	104	Obedience	30
Of a gift or donation,	105	Obedience	34
No, not a tooth or nail to scratch,	106	Conscience	17
And at my actions carp, or catch.	106	Conscience	18
Some wood and nails to make a staffe or bill	106	Conscience	21
Or take me up to thee!	107	Home	6
Or take me up to thee!	107	Home	12
To see what help in th' earth or skie:	107	Home	14
Or take me up to thee!	107	Home	18
Or take me up to thee!	107	Home	24
As if thy love could fail or change.	108	Home	28
Or take me up to thee!	108	Home	30
Or take me up to thee!	108	Home	36
Or take me up to thee!	108	Home	42
Or take me up to thee!	108	Home	48
Or take me up to thee!	108	Home	54
Or take me up to thee!	108	Home	60
Or take me up to thee!	109	Home	66
Or take me up to thee!	109	Home	72
Or take me up to thee!	109	Home	78
Or else undrest.	109	Brit. Ch.	12
Draws tears, or bloud, not want an handkerchief.	112	Dawning	16
Hast thou tears, or hast thou none?	113	Businesse	5
Would thou hadst no faults or fears!	113	Businesse	7
Be the season cold, or hot:	113	Businesse	10
Hast thou sighs, or hast thou not?	113	Businesse	11
If thou hast no sighs or grones,	113	Businesse	12
Had he life, or had he none?	113	Businesse	19
Did he die, or did he not?	113	Businesse	25
What delight or hope remains?	114	Dialogue	8
For either thy command, or thy permission	117	Providence	33
Or with a stone! yet make no good foundation.	120	Providence	124
Most things sleep lying; th' Elephant leans or stands.	121	Providence	140
Most things sleep lying; th' Elephant leane or stand.	121	Providence V	140
Or, if they enter, cannot rest,	126	Confession	21
No sale or bargain passe: all would disperse,	127	Giddinesse	23
Lord, mend or rather make us: one creation	127	Giddinesse	25
Better then you know me, or (which is one)	129	Love unkn.	10
Better then you knew me, or (which is one)	129	Love unkn. V	10
What open force, or hidden CHARM	133	Paradise	4
Can blast my fruit, or bring me HARM,	133	Paradise	5

OR (cont'd)

	PAGE	TITLE		LINE
If thou hadst lost a glove or ring,	133	The Method		11
When sawcie mirth shall knock or call at doore,	136	Ephes.		13
Or cry no more.	136	Ephes.		15
As if there were no rule or eares?	136	Familie		4
For I will do, or suffer what I ought.	139	Artillerie		16
Christ keepeth now, who cannot fail or fall.	143	Holdfast		14
That live or die	143	Complaining		9
More attributes? Am I all throat or eye,	143	Complaining		13
To weep or crie?	143	Complaining		14
My inch of life: or let thy gracious power	144	Complaining		18
Either grief will not come: or if it must,	145	Discharge		51
There is a balsome, or indeed a bloud,	147	Offering		19
If ye have any thing to send or write,	152	The Bag		31
Or if hereafter any of my friends	152	The Bag		37
Wert thou a winde or wave,	154	Glimpse		8
Either the league was broke, or neare it;	155	Assurance		11
And rivers stirre, thou canst not shrink or quail:	156	Assurance		33
Then I or ought, or can be mine.	157	Clasping		3
Or rather make no Thine and Mine!	157	Clasping		20
Then will I wring it with a sigh or grone,	157	Praise 3		5
To twentie then, or more.	158	Praise 3		12
Can hale or draw it out of doore.	158	Praise 3		16
Or steel, or mountains be thy ring,	163	The Search		35
This or that is:	166	The Flower		20
The finenesse which a hymne or psalme affords,	168	a true Hymn		9
To make his verse, or write a hymne in kinde.	168	a true Hymn		15
Like leaves about me: or like summer friends,	169	The Answer		4
Without excuse or cloke.	171	Self-cond.		24
What can I want or need?	172	23 Psalme		4
Or if I stray, he doth convert	172	23 Psalme		9
Or if such deceits there be,	177	The Rose		9
Not a word or look	178	Discipline		9
Passeth tongue to taste or tell.	181	Banquet		6
Or hath sweetnesse in the bread	181	Banquet		13
Or say, or dictate, this is my delight.	183	The Posie		8
Can so afflict or so affright,	183	A Parodie		14
Or if he pleaseth, through it passe,	184	The Elixer		11
Or ten yeares hence,	186	Death		6
Making our pillows either down, or dust.	186	Death		24
The smallest ant or atome knows thy power,	190	Ch.-Milit.		3
Or strength in th' other, did erect her throne.	192	Ch.-Milit.		78
Or strength in th' other, took possession.	192	Ch.-Milit.	W	78
His highest was an ox or crocodile,	193	Ch.-Milit.		122
Either t' his publick foot or private tricks.	195	Ch.-Milit.		196
Nor his long journey, nor his gout or furre.	195	Ch.-Milit.	W	198
Who without spear, or sword, or other drumme	195	Ch.-Milit.		201
Or reserve his breath in store,	199	L'Envoy	W	12
Or rather so, as thou alone	200	H. Commun.	W	4
Or whether Bread doe fly away	200	H. Commun.	W	8
Or if that thou two stations makest	200	H. Commun.	W	16
Or give mee that, so I have more	201	H. Commun.	W	47
Or rather as thou movedst mee.	204	Persever.	W	4
Or, since thy wayes are deep, and still the same,	206	Walton 1		10
Doe ruine thee; or if the teares	208	H. Danvers	D	6
To comforte us, or to bee comforted.	211	Paradox	D	42
At there owne weapons, without pomp or state	211	Bohemia	D	21
Whose native beauty needs not dresse or lace	212	Bohemia	D	30
or who shall praise Thee in the grave?	220	Psalm VI	D	12
A PRIEST To the TEMPLE, OR, The Countrey PARSON	223	Priest		T
or ministry, let us wait on our ministring;	226	Priest 2		6
or he that teacheth, on teaching, &c.	226	Priest 2		6
when they have read the Fathers, or Schoolmen, a Minister is made,	226	Priest 2		11
entertained to that end, either by an open, or implicite Covenant.	226	Priest 2		23
are in Orders, they may be received for Companions, or discoursers;	226	Priest 2		24
admonition, or reproofe, sell (with Judas) their Lord and Master.	226	Priest 2		37
for the servant of Christ to haunt Innes, or Tavernes, or Ale-houses,	227	Priest 3		30
or Ale-houses, to the dishonour of his person and office.	227	Priest 3		30
but reverend, and clean, without spots, or dust, or smell;	228	Priest 3		11
positively as it is, or else to illustrate some other knowledge.	228	Priest 4		17
or will open all to one, that there may be a traffick in knowledg	229	Priest 4		25
or a good proportion of all, out of all which he hath compiled	229	Priest 5		32
according as his audience is, so he useth one, or other;	230	Priest 5		17
or somtimes both, if his audience be intermixed.	230	Priest 5		17
when it is a sin to take something for mony lent, or when not;	230	Priest 5		25
when it is a fault to discover anothers fault, or when not;	230	Priest 5		25
increase of means, or honour, be a sin of covetousnes or ambition,	230	Priest 5		27
or honour, be a sin of covetousnes or ambition, and when not;	230	Priest 5		27
which grass will bane, or which not, how is he fit to be a shepherd?	230	Priest 5		32
by no means enduring either talking, or sleeping, or gazing,	231	Priest 6		23
talking, or sleeping, or gazing, or leaning, or halfe-kneeling,	231	Priest 6		24
or gazing, or leaning, or halfe-kneeling, or any undutifull behaviour	231	Priest 6		24
or halfe-kneeling, or any undutifull behaviour in them,	231	Priest 6		24
or any undutifull behaviour in them, but causing them,	231	Priest 6		24
when they sit, or stand, or kneel, to do all in a strait,	231	Priest 6		25
or stand, or kneel, to do all in a strait, and steady posture,	231	Priest 6		26
also are to be done not in a hudling, or slubbering fashion, gaping,	231	Priest 6		30
or scratching the head, or spitting even in the midst of their	231	Priest 6		31
or spitting even in the midst of their answer, but gently	231	Priest 6		31
or offer up such sacrifices as they did of old, which was of beasts	232	Priest 6		4
If there be any of the gentry or nobility of the Parish,	232	Priest 6		7

OR (cont'd)

	PAGE	TITLE	LINE
or if the poor Church-wardens be affrighted with their greatness,	232	Priest 6	14
or against some great Festivall, that he may the better celebrate it,	232	Priest 7	22
or for the variety of the hearers, that he may be heard at his	232	Priest 7	23
that so in the mouth of two or three witnesses the truth may be more	232	Priest 7	29
none goes out of Church as he came in, but either better, or worse;	233	Priest 7	20
he is not witty, or learned, or eloquent, but Holy. . . .	233	Priest 7	24
or, Oh my Master, on whose errand I come, let me hold my peace,	233	Priest 7	34
And is in contention for them whither to live, or dy; . . .	234	Priest 7	15
be with them, or Christ, verse 23. which, setting aside his care	234	Priest 7	16
of the presence, and majesty of God, by these, or such like speeches.	234	Priest 7	26
whether I speak as I ought, or you hear as you ought, he sees hearts,	234	Priest 7	27
the Person speaking, or spoken to, the subject, and object, . .	235	Priest 7	7
the Market day comes, or a shopkeeper, when customers use to come in.	235	Priest 8	18
that how or whenever he punish him, it be not in his Ministry:	235	Priest 8	26
the time of the year, or from the State, or from God by a child born,	235	Priest 8	35
or from the State, or from God by a child born, or dead, . .	235	Priest 8	35
or from God by a child born, or dead, or any other accident,	235	Priest 8	35
or any other accident, he contrives how and in what manner to induce	236	Priest 8	1
Almighty God, and blessing the people either openly, or to himselfe.	236	Priest 8	6
or in visiting the sick, or in exhortations to some of his flock	236	Priest 8	12
or in exhortations to some of his flock by themselves, whom his	236	Priest 8	12
his flock by themselves, whom his Sermons cannot, or doe not reach.	236	Priest 8	13
or to be entertained of them, where he takes occasion to discourse	236	Priest 8	20
without disturbance, or interruption of publick divine offices.	236	Priest 8	25
or as the temper of his Parish may be, where he may have occasion	237	Priest 9	1
and then also in a serious manner, never jestingly or sportfully.	237	Priest 9	13
sensitive faculty, will runne out more or lesse in her intellectuall.	238	Priest 9	11
inward, or outward temptations, that it is ever attempting, . .	238	Priest 9	13
that it is ever attempting, or doing one mischief or other. . .	238	Priest 9	14
or untimely desire of promotion to an higher state, or place,	238	Priest 9	14
to an higher state, or place, under colour of accommodation,	238	Priest 9	15
or necessary provision, is a common temptation to men of any	238	Priest 9	16
in high places doth the Parson fear, or experiment, or both;	238	Priest 9	21
into Covetousnesse, Love of pleasure, or ease, or the like. . .	238	Priest 9	24
liberall disposition he preferred before beauty, riches, or honour.	238	Priest 9	29
or the seldomer, according as hee is satisfied of his Wifes . .	239	Priest 9	4
either meets with their vices, or advanceth their vertues. . .	239	Priest 10	9
wife is either religious, or night and day he is winning her to it.	239	Priest 10	10
or he takes care she shall learn it of some religious neighbour.	239	Priest 10	16
servant, Truth, and Diligence, and Neatnesse, or Cleanlinesse.	240	Priest 10	18
for all in his house are either teachers or learners, or both,	240	Priest 10	21
or learners, or both, so that his family is a Schoole of Religion,	240	Priest 10	21
or painted there, which may excite the reader to a thought of piety;	240	Priest 10	24
He suffers not a ly or equivocation by any means in his house,	240	Priest 10	32
He himselfe, or his Wife, takes account of Sermons, and how every one	240	Priest 10	36
for a great day, or a stranger, his garden or orchard supplyes it,	241	Priest 10	18
or a stranger, his garden or orchard supplyes it, or his barne,	241	Priest 10	18
his garden or orchard supplyes it, or his barne, and back-side:	241	Priest 10	18
or was not fit for him to do, by taking both sorts of food into them,	241	Priest 10	32
or over-nourishing things, as the Israelites did eate sowre herbs:	242	Priest 10	3
then if it had taken before either fish, or rootes, or such things;	242	Priest 10	24
which will discover it selfe by spitting, and rheume, or flegme.	242	Priest 10	25
eating fish, or roots, and that for quantity little, for quality	242	Priest 10	27
or idle person in his Parish, but that all bee in a competent way	244	Priest 12	20
This he effects either by bounty, or perswasion, or by authority,	244	Priest 12	22
or perswasion, or by authority, making use of that excellent statute,	244	Priest 12	22
them say their Prayers first, or the Creed, and ten Commandments,	245	Priest 12	35
cleane without dust, or Cobwebs, and at great festivalls strawed,	246	Priest 13	9
and reverend, not with light colours, or foolish anticks. . .	246	Priest 13	13
and those not torne, or fouled, but whole and clean, and well bound;	246	Priest 13	15
of good and costly Stuffe, or Cloth, and all kept sweet and clean,	246	Priest 13	18
and decent chest, with a Chalice, and Cover, and a Stoop, or Flagon;	246	Priest 13	19
or as putting a holiness in the things, but as desiring to keep	246	Priest 13	23
as if it were in their own hands to thrive, or not to thrive.	247	Priest 14	31
or in time of divine service on other holy days, except in the cases	248	Priest 14	3
that the Parson findes idle, or ill imployed, he chides not at first,	248	Priest 14	14
However, one way or other, he ever reproves them, that he may keep	248	Priest 14	23
of his cure is sick, or afflicted with losse of friend, or estate,	249	Priest 15	13
or afflicted with losse of friend, or estate, or any ways distressed,	249	Priest 15	14
or any ways distressed, fails not to afford his best comforts,	249	Priest 15	14
or otherwise afflicted, he followeth the Churches counsell, . .	249	Priest 15	28
or sick person, that so the hunger and thirst after it may come	250	Priest 15	5
or otherwise are done to his owne person, hee considers the offender	250	Priest 16	13
before hee proceede to disinheriting, or perhaps never goes so far;	250	Priest 16	18
and with those he overtakes or that overtake him, hee begins good	251	Priest 17	3
or other relations give him any authority over the Family, . .	251	Priest 17	16
there are either in Apparell, or Diet, or too open a Buttery,	251	Priest 17	19
or Diet, or too open a Buttery, or reading vain books, or swearing,	251	Priest 17	19
or too open a Buttery, or reading vain books, or swearing, . .	251	Priest 17	20
vain books, or swearing, or breeding up children to no Calling,	251	Priest 17	20
or breeding up children to no Calling, but in idleness, . .	251	Priest 17	20
or breeding up children to no Calling, but in idleness, or the like.	251	Priest 17	21
yet seasonably, and discreetly, by taking aside the Lord, or Lady;	251	Priest 17	28
or Master and Mistres of the house, and shewing them cleerly,	251	Priest 17	29
or done in the Company where he is, but comes under his Test	252	Priest 18	2
If it be well spoken, or done, he takes occasion to commend,	252	Priest 18	4
or else if the thing will admit interpretation;	252	Priest 18	10
or, So farr indeed what you say is true, and well said; . .	252	Priest 18	11
either by the wickedness or quarrelsomnesse thereof, he either	252	Priest 18	17
it judiciously, or breaks it off seasonably by some diversion.	252	Priest 18	18

OR (cont'd)	PAGE	TITLE	LINE
set at an armour, or horse, he borrowes them not to serve the turne,	252	Priest 19	26
unto him in any difficulty, either in his studies or in his Parish.	253	Priest 19	9
or at some other time of the day, propounds among his Brethren what	253	Priest 19	13
how poor or mean soever, with as joyfull a countenance,	253	Priest 19	19
that we should do whatsoever things are honest, or just, or pure,	253	Priest 19	24
things are honest, or just, or pure, or lovely, or of good report,	253	Priest 19	24
or pure, or lovely, or of good report, if there be any vertue,	253	Priest 19	24
or lovely, or of good report, if there be any vertue, or any praise;	253	Priest 19	24
or of good report, if there be any vertue, or any praise;	253	Priest 19	25
any calamity either by fire, or famine, to any neighbouring Parish,	253	Priest 19	29
or holy-day, and exposing to them the uncertainty of humane affairs,	253	Priest 19	31
together a summe either to be sent, or, which were more comfortable,	253	Priest 19	37
Wherefore there is nothing done either wel or ill, whereof he is	254	Priest 20	10
done either wel or ill, whereof he is not the rewarder, or punisher.	254	Priest 20	11
or if he be of a condition above such gifts, he sends him a good	254	Priest 20	14
or easeth him in his Tithes, telling him when he hath forgotten it,	254	Priest 20	15
from the parties offending, or by private, or publick reproof,	254	Priest 20	23
or by private, or publick reproof, as the case requires,	254	Priest 20	24
then by causing them to be presented, or otherwise complained of.	254	Priest 20	25
or hainousness of the crime may be, he is carefull to see condign	254	Priest 20	26
that Countrey people are drawne, or led by sense, more then by faith,	254	Priest 20	31
by present rewards, or punishments, more then by future.	254	Priest 20	32
they come home, either commend or reprove, either reward or punish.	255	Priest 21	29
Was it made, or came it by chance?	256	Priest 21	7
or whether he needed a helper, and who was that helper.	257	Priest 21	9
in this, that at Sermons, and Prayers, men may sleep or wander;	257	Priest 21	19
For questions cannot inflame or ravish, that must be done by a set,	257	Priest 21	24
with himself, how or what behaviour to assume for so holy things.	257	Priest 22	27
and Baptizeth not willingly, but on Sundayes, or great dayes.	258	Priest 22	3
Hee admits no vaine or idle names, but such as are usuall	258	Priest 22	4
that it is no complementall or light thing to sustain that place,	258	Priest 22	11
not cheape, or course, much lesse ill-tasted, or unwholsome.	258	Priest 22	22
not cheape, or course, much lesse ill-tasted, or unwholsome.	258	Priest 22	23
or carelesness of his flock, and accordingly applies himselfe	258	Priest 22	24
or Sundayes before the Communion, or on the Eves of all those dayes.	258	Priest 22	28
but hee that sits, or lies, puts up to an Apostle:	259	Priest 22	17
if not duly once a month, yet at least five or six times in the year;	259	Priest 22	21
but sends for three or four of the ablest of the Parish to hear	260	Priest 23	9
or in cases of high consequence, as establishing of inheritances:	260	Priest 23	21
or Lastly, when the persons in difference are of a contentious	260	Priest 23	22
or at least his Wife, of whom in stead of the qualities of the world,	260	Priest 23	30
but to have the skill of healing a wound, or helping the sick.	260	Priest 23	32
Rubarb, or for binding, Bolearmena, the Parson useth damask or white	261	Priest 23	33
the Parson useth damask or white Roses for the one, and plantaine,	261	Priest 23	34
as in their tithes, or otherwise.	262	Priest 24	27
what scandall is, when given or taken;	263	Priest 24	8
more then indifferent, it be in our power to omit or refuse them.	263	Priest 24	13
or punishing of any, as the vulgar ever consters for signes of ill	263	Priest 25	24
or doing any thing of aversenesse, save in the very act	263	Priest 25	27
or known commonly, the beginnings of them are not easily observable:	264	Priest 26	18
and a point, or center, when his storing, which was even now good,	264	Priest 26	29
or not in some proportion to Gods blessing upon him, is covetous.	265	Priest 26	6
I either do nothing, or pinch, and scrape, and squeeze blood	265	Priest 26	17
or that which is unwholsome, being sometimes baned meat,	265	Priest 26	21
which they may cut, or hack, or throw into the fire, and so they pay	265	Priest 26	26
or throw into the fire, and so they pay them their wages,	265	Priest 26	26
or consider it so narrowly, which yet ought to be done,	265	Priest 26	31
for quantity eats more then his health or imployments will bear,	266	Priest 26	7
or for quality is licorous after dainties, is a glutton;	266	Priest 26	8
in his order, or length of eating, is scandalous and uncharitable.	266	Priest 26	11
or studying dainties too much, they cannot wel dispatch) nor of their	266	Priest 26	15
fit discharging either of Divine duties, or duties of their calling.	266	Priest 26	30
that if after dinner they are not fit (or un-weeldy) either to pray,	266	Priest 26	31
not fit (or un-weeldy) either to pray, or work, they are gluttons.	266	Priest 26	32
as that it is not meate or drinke that hinders them from working.	266	Priest 26	35
disposition I am, either hungry or not, according as I feele my self,	267	Priest 26	8
feele my self, either I take my wonted proportion, or diminish of it.	267	Priest 26	9
either of Abstinence a morall vertue, or Mortification a divine.	267	Priest 26	16
or if he have any leisure to look off from thence, he meets	267	Priest 27	30
that are reproved, but never contempt either in them, or others.	268	Priest 28	30
or being so, the Parson think it in his discretion either unfit,	269	Priest 28	3
either unfit, or bootelesse to contend, then when any despises him,	269	Priest 28	4
or else in a slighting way, shewing that reproaches touch him no	269	Priest 28	6
or in a sad way, greived at his own, and others sins, which	269	Priest 28	8
or else in a doctrinall way, saying to the contemner, Alas,	269	Priest 28	11
or lastly, in a Triumphant way, being glad, and joyfull,	269	Priest 28	15
enabled by that Name to take moveable goods, or chattels, and to sue,	270	Priest 29	2
to church, or for disorderly carriage in time of divine service.	270	Priest 29	5
Wherefore the Parson suffers not the place to be vilified or debased,	270	Priest 29	7
shewing that they do not loose, or go lesse, but gaine by it;	270	Priest 29	9
or as David says, to be even a door-keeper in the house of God.	270	Priest 29	11
or hear them read often, as also the visitation Articles,	270	Priest 29	13
yea though they be tenants, or otherwise ingaged to the delinquent:	270	Priest 29	21
it according as he sees fit, either for reward or punishment.	270	Priest 30	32
the sun in heaven, or the fire on earth, by reason of their fierce,	271	Priest 30	10
or if the goods be housed, a fire hath broken forth, and suddenly	271	Priest 30	24
or if he depend on God further, even till he imbarn his corn,	271	Priest 30	31
as at nine, or at three, or at midnight, or as they think fit,	272	Priest 31	26
or at three, or at midnight, or as they think fit, & see cause,	272	Priest 31	26
or at midnight, or as they think fit, & see cause, or rather as Gods	272	Priest 31	27

OR (cont'd)

	PAGE	TITLE	LINE
as they think fit, & see cause, or rather as Gods spirit leads them.	272	Priest 31	27
or by oversleeping himself at night, omits his additionary prayer.	272	Priest 31	30
or coldness, which will appear if the Pious soul foresee and prevent	273	Priest 31	16
he be a little affected therewith, but not afflicted, or troubled;	273	Priest 31	19
or beseeching him, that whenever he repaires to his house,	273	Priest 31	25
if he now, shall either for fear or shame, break his custome,	273	Priest 31	30
or bring strangers to him, he may be the better armed to encounter	274	Priest 32	7
nothing to do, lets go to the Tavern, or to the stews, or what not.	274	Priest 32	13
may be prevented, or diverted by reasonable imployment.	274	Priest 32	23
every gift or ability is a talent to be accounted for, and to be	274	Priest 32	24
and who is ready to ask, if he shall mend shoos, or what he shall do?	275	Priest 32	8
All are either to have a Calling, or prepare for it:	275	Priest 32	11
He that hath or can have yet no imployment, if he truly,	275	Priest 32	12
or else to examine with care, and advice, what they are fittest for,	275	Priest 32	15
Men are either single, or marryed:	275	Priest 32	19
of his grounds, by drowning, or draining, or stocking, or fencing,	275	Priest 32	24
or draining, or stocking, or fencing, and ordering his land	275	Priest 32	25
or fencing, and ordering his land to the best advantage both	275	Priest 32	25
childe, or servant, as a Gardiner doth in a choice tree.	275	Priest 32	33
the Village or Parish which either he lives in, or is neer unto it,	276	Priest 32	2
which either he lives in, or is neer unto it, is his imployment.	276	Priest 32	2
or hath generall Propositions to the whole Towne or Hamlet,	276	Priest 32	4
or hath generall Propositions to the whole Towne or Hamlet,	276	Priest 32	5
and managing Commons, or Woods, according as the place suggests.	276	Priest 32	6
or Noble-man in the Country he lives in, inabling him with power	276	Priest 32	13
to redeem the Dignity either from true faults, or unjust aspersions.	276	Priest 32	24
for single men, they are either Heirs, or younger Brothers:	276	Priest 32	25
when they see any remarkable point of Education or good husbandry,	276	Priest 32	30
he is to endeavour by all means to be a Knight or Burgess there;	277	Priest 32	10
Great Horse, or exercise some of his Military gestures [Postures].	277	Priest 32	16
Or let him travel into Germany, and France, and observing	278	Priest 32	7
whether in private conference, or in the Church, are a Sermon.	278	Priest 33	17
or at least in that degree it ought to be, since he found himselfe	279	Priest 33	11
we are assaulted with temptations either from within or from without.	280	Priest 34	4
as he discovers any of his Flock to be in one or the other state,	280	Priest 34	13
or such a time their peace and mirth have carryed them further then	280	Priest 34	33
that there is none that can or will look after things, but all goes	281	Priest 34	8
that can or will look after things, but all goes by chance, or wit:	281	Priest 34	9
Or else, though there be a great Governour of all things,	281	Priest 34	9
built without a builder, or kept in repaire without a house-keeper.	281	Priest 34	19
that the Atheist, or Epicurian can have nothing to contradict.	281	Priest 34	34
why any should distrust Saint Luke, or Tertullian, or Chrysostome,	282	Priest 34	21
or Tertullian, or Chrysostome, more then Tully, Virgill,	282	Priest 34	21
or Tertullian, or Chrysostome, more then Tully, Virgill, or Livy;)	282	Priest 34	22
the womans oyntment in the Gospell, or sees Jerusalem destroyed.	283	Priest 34	2
or as they are sinfull.	283	Priest 34	11
that in the mouth of two or three witnesses every word may be	283	Priest 34	19
till either they despise that Love, or despaire of his Mercy:	283	Priest 34	23
and largesse, which at that time is, or ought to be used.	284	Priest 35	9
where he knowes there hath been or is a little difference,	284	Priest 35	19
and goes with him to the other, and all dine or sup together.	284	Priest 35	21
or praying to God at all times, but is rather glad of catching	284	Priest 35	25
of Christs Cross, or for any shame to leave that which is good.	284	Priest 35	33
Or else, because they think it empty and superfluous.	285	Priest 36	8
or the Apostles only, no more then to be a spirituall Father was	285	Priest 36	12
unlawful to open faults, no benefit or advantage can make it lawfull:	287	Priest 37	6
Faults are either notorious, or private.	287	Priest 37	11
or else such as have passed judgment, & been corrected either	287	Priest 37	14
& been corrected either by whipping, or imprisoning, or the like.	287	Priest 37	15
& been corrected either by whipping, or imprisoning, or the like.	287	Priest 37	16
or put into the stocks, that they may be looked upon.	287	Priest 37	20
And as malefactors may lose & forfeit their goods, or life;	287	Priest 37	32
when we had sinned beyond any help in heaven or earth, then thou	288	Priest	26
not to Thunder, or Angels, but to silly and sinfull men:	289	Priest	5
those that pleased my taste brought me commoditie or discommoditie;	293	Cornaro	7
can bring little grief or hurt to those that are temperate.	294	Cornaro	34
be much troubled, or make a great concourse, refused both remedies,	295	Cornaro	9
and so without other remedie or inconvenience I recovered;	295	Cornaro	12
neither did I know well, what I did or said.	296	Cornaro	17
save now and then a little indisposition for a day or two.	296	Cornaro	31
or contract any ill qualitie, as usually happens in old mens bodies,	296	Cornaro	34
or that cinnamon should heat me more then pepper?	297	Cornaro	33
of the radicall moisture, without grief or perturbation of humours.	298	Cornaro	18
be done by Aurum potabile, or the Philosophers stone, sought of many,	298	Cornaro	20
whether he hath lived heretofore orderly or disorderly,	299	Cornaro	30
No man is forbidden to eat fruit or fish, which I eat not:	300	Cornaro	7
take a greater quantitie of any meat or drink (though most agreeable	300	Cornaro	12
neither omit I any thing that may either teach, or delight me.	302	Cornaro	5
is very great) receiving not any hurt or inconvenience thereby:	302	Cornaro	20
or lesse my self, who being ten yeares older have made a Comedie?	302	Cornaro	35
only the effectuall operation or illumination of the holy spirit,	308	Valdesso	31
and not any private Enthusiasmes, or Revelations:	308	Valdesso	33
or assent to the promises of the Gospell by heare-say, or relation	308	Valdesso	34
or relation from others, is not that which filleth the heart with joy	309	Valdesso	1
and that no other sin or vertue hath any thing to doe with us;	311	Valdesso	24
not punished) for evill doing nor rewarded for weldoing or living,	311	Valdesso	29
or living, for all the point lies in believing or not believing.	311	Valdesso	30
or justify himselfe before God, by any acts or exercises of Religion;	312	Valdesso	15
or justify himselfe before God, by any acts or exercises of Religion;	312	Valdesso	16
that we should not use it as the onely, or as the principall means;	314	Valdesso V	5

	PAGE	TITLE		LINE
ORATOR'S				
The Orators place (that you may understand what it is) is the finest	369	Letters		30
Concerning the Orators place all goes well yet, the next Friday it is	371	Letters		16
ORCHARD				
or a stranger, his garden or orchard supplyes it, or his barne,	241	Priest 10		18
of the tree, inriching their Orchard, and neglecting their House.	276	Priest 32		33
ORDAIN'D				
Ordain'd the highest to be best;	79	Employm.2		13
His arrows are ordain'd 'gainst him	222	Psalm VII	D	47
ORDAINED				
of himself, for all the purposes which God hath ordained him.	227	Priest 3		10
ORDER				
And order.	41	Sepulchre		16
Setting in order what they tumble:	75	Sunday	W	5
To thee both fruit and order OW.	132	Paradise		3
Then Order plaies the soul;	137	Familie		10
Blest Order, which in power dost so excell,	160	Priesthood		1
Blest Order, which in power doth so excell,	160	Priesthood	V	1
Man is out of order hurl'd,	187	Dooms-day		27
that order is kept in the one, and peace in the other, without	236	Priest 8		24
Therefore first he takes order, that all things be in good repair;	246	Priest 13		3
The first whereof is, Let all things be done decently, and in order:	246	Priest 13		27
on Sundays it is easie for them to compose themselves to order,	247	Priest 14		8
the Parson questions what order is kept in the house, as about	248	Priest 14		31
In this course the order of the Catechisme would be kept,	256	Priest 21		5
This order being used to one, would be a little varyed to another.	256	Priest 21		15
he first takes order with the Church-Wardens, that the elements be	258	Priest 22		21
neither can all the people so order their affairs as to receive just	259	Priest 22		26
in perverting that order which he hath set both to things,	265	Priest 26		11
offensively to the Company, either in his order, or length of eating,	266	Priest 26		11
and that indeed the whole order and discipline of the Parish is put	269	Priest 29		28
that things are not set in such an inevitable order, but that God	270	Priest 30		30
hurt those bodies, which were kept in good order by a moderate Diet:	294	Cornaro		2
clearely be perceived, how great is the power of order and disorder;	297	Cornaro		4
If the world consist of order, if our corporall life depend	297	Cornaro		7
it is no wonder that order should preserve, and disorder destroy.	297	Cornaro		8
Order makes arts easie, and armies victorious, and retains	297	Cornaro		9
liked our Book well, & has given order to the Tenants, at Leighton,	379	Letters		9
in that you are of the same order and habit, of which wee all in this	442	Oration		21
ORDERED				
accordingly by questions well ordered he found Philosophy in silly	256	Priest 21		22
because many wayes thither are so ordered, that they all meet and end	301	Cornaro		21
having both ordered your Family, and so brought up your Children that	373	Letters		12
ORDERING				
and ordering his land to the best advantage both of himself,	275	Priest 32		25
to mark their Fathers discretion in ordering his House and Affairs;	276	Priest 32		28
the many pious rules of ordering our life, about mortification,	305	Valdesso		9
ORDERLY				
if I could constantly pursue it, to wit, A sober and orderly life:	292	Cornaro		5
considering what an orderly life I had led for many yeares together,	295	Cornaro		7
That an orderly and regular life can hardly be altered without	295	Cornaro		17
That an orderly life is the most sure way & ground of health and long	297	Cornaro		12
that an orderly life is so hard a thing that it cannot be kept.	298	Cornaro		36
and divers labours, which suit not with an orderly life:	299	Cornaro		15
whether he hath lived heretofore orderly or disorderly,	299	Cornaro		30
Wherefore since an orderly life is so profitable, so vertuous,	300	Cornaro		3
man of an ill constitution, but living orderly, is more sure of life,	300	Cornaro		25
ORDERS				
Which parts their ranks and orders.	75	Sunday		28
Before they are in Orders, they may be received for Companions,	226	Priest 2		23
but orders his Life in such a fashion, that when death takes him,	227	Priest 3		31
governing power he preserves and orders the references of things one	271	Priest 30		13
When God is made master of a family, he orders the disorderly.	353	Proverbs		983
ORDINANCE				
understand the great good use of this antient and pious ordinance,	249	Priest 15		31
ORDINANCES				
and in the wayes of thy Ordinances, and in the truth of thy Love,	289	Priest		13
ORDINARIE				
Heaven in ordinarie, man well drest,	51	Prayer 1		11
To ordinarie suitours at the doore.	85	Vanitie 1		21
ORDINARILY				
himself some insight in things ordinarily incident and controverted,	259	Priest 23		34
ORDINARY				
besides his ordinary prayers, he makes a peculiar one for a blessing	235	Priest 8		21
and preferreth the ordinary Church-Catechism, partly for obedience	255	Priest 21		16
shewing that things of ordinary use are not only to serve in the way	257	Priest 21		13
talke with a great man in the ordinary course of complementing	286	Priest 36		20
language, he shall be esteemed as ordinary complementers;	286	Priest 36		22
By occasions (I suppose) hee meaneth the ordinary, or necessary	314	Valdesso		16
it is their ordinary speech, and now let them make it good;	364	Letters		22
ORE				
He gave this Seal, and, so gave ore.	439	Walton 6		2
ORECOME				
Whereas if I orecome thee & thy Love	202	love	W	23
ORENGE				
Oh that I were an Orenge-tree,	79	Employm.2		21
ORENGE-TREE				
Oh that I were an Orenge-tree,	79	Employm.2		21
ORIENTALL				
An orientall fragrancie, My Master.	174	The Odour		5

	PAGE	TITLE		LINE
ORIGINALL				
But still thy sweet originall joy	172	The Glance		13
Originall concupisence is such an active thing, by reason	238	Priest 9		12
an act of the mind, not of the Body, even as the Originall signifies;	279	Priest 33		15
then I could of Originall before, and without Baptisme.	308	Valdesso		4
ORNAMENT				
Fit, while ye liv'd, for smell or ornament,	94	Life		14
would have been an ornament to the world, and a comfort to their	291	Cornaro		4
OTHER				
Stay not for th' other pin: why thou hast lost	23	Ch.-Porch		411
When with the other I have done.	35	Thanksgvng		30
Though hee bring light & th' other sents:	42	Easter	W	24
Some other master out.	48	Afflict.1		64
And carrie with them th' other parts.	49	Repentance		30
Fretting to death our other parts.	49	Repentance	W	30
And th' other black and grave, wherewith each one	67	Ch.-floore		4
The other fine,	71	Frailtie		12
The other dayes and thou	75	Sunday		8
The other dayes fill up the spare	75	Sunday		24
But all thy sweets are packt up in the other;	82	Ungratef.		19
For thou hast other vessels full of bloud,	83	Sighs & Gr.		21
The other Hid and doth obliquely bend.	84	Coloss.		4
The other winds towards Him, whose happie birth	84	Coloss.		6
Neither ought other mens abuse of Lent	86	Lent		28
With one small sigh thou gav'st me th' other day	108	Home		43
She wholly goes on th' other side,	110	Brit. Ch.		23
Is deeply carved there: but th' other week	112	JESU		2
The other curbs sinnes stealing pace and theft.	117	Providence		36
In all my other hymnes, but in this twice.	121	Providence		148
In th' other Angels have a right by birth:	131	Mans medly		9
With th' one hand touching heav'n, with th' other earth.	131	Mans medly		12
He hath two winters, other things but one:	131	Mans medly		27
Just so the other heav'n they also serve,	134	Divinitie		5
I left on th' one, and on the other side	142	Pilgrimage		5
O that I might some other hearts convert,	159	Praise 3		39
And with the other throwest down to hell	160	Priesthood		3
While this member jogs the other,	186	Dooms-day		5
To bring the other Ark from Canaan.	190	Ch.-Milit.		20
To bring the other Ark to Canaan.	190	Ch.-Milit.	W	21
Letting, while one foot stept, the other stay	191	Ch.-Milit.		34
Before the other. Greece being past her prime,	191	Ch.-Milit.		60
Before the other two were in their prime.	191	Ch.-Milit.	W	60
Or strength in th' other, did erect her throne.	192	Ch.-Milit.		78
Or strength in th' other, took possession.	192	Ch.-Milit.	W	78
Who without spear, or sword, or other drumme	195	Ch.-Milit.		201
When th' one did set, the other did take place,	196	Ch.-Milit.		217
Spain hath done one; when Arts perform the other,	197	Ch.-Milit.		265
With the other blesse thy sheep,	199	L'Envoy		3
Convert & colour all the other flood	204	The Knell	W	14
Besides their other flames? Doth Poetry	206	Walton 1		3
So by the Other, you may read in mee	209	L. Bacon	D	5
Perhaps some other subject I had tryed	209	L. Bacon	D	11
is indeed the bent of my Discourse) the other will be manifest.	226	Priest 2		18
positively as it is, or else to illustrate some other knowledge.	228	Priest 4		17
according as his audience is, so he useth one, or other;	230	Priest 5		17
and using all other gestures which may expresse a hearty,	231	Priest 6		3
and all other answers, which are on the Clerks and peoples part	231	Priest 6		28
And the like in other answers.	232	Priest 6		1
By these and other means the Parson procures attention;	233	Priest 7		22
Whereas the other way of crumbling a text into small parts,	235	Priest 7		5
or any other accident, he contrives how and in what manner to induce	236	Priest 8		1
is kept in the one, and peace in the other, without disturbance,	236	Priest 8		24
and other like circumstances considered, he is rather married then	237	Priest 9		4
of having his meat dress'd and other services done by men-servants	237	Priest 9		9
and devotion, some other dayes for fasting, and hours for prayers;	237	Priest 9		25
with other exemplary vertues of that sort, and to keep them on in	237	Priest 9		34
Other temptations he hath, which, like mortall enemies,	238	Priest 9		8
that it is ever attempting, or doing one mischief or other.	238	Priest 9		14
These and many other spirituall wickednesses in high places doth	238	Priest 9		20
Countrey, the other to his earthly, having no title to either,	239	Priest 10		22
in visiting other sick children, and tending their wounds,	239	Priest 10		25
which happily for his other children he is not able to do.	239	Priest 10		32
his children among children, his servants among other servants;	240	Priest 10		29
the other for the foulnesse, as wash, and durt, and things thereinto	241	Priest 10		28
first, of eating lesse that day, then on other dayes;	242	Priest 10		3
and of Courtesie to his other parishioners, he so distinguisheth,	243	Priest 11		7
this generall provision, he hath other times of opening his hand;	245	Priest 12		6
giving some corn outright, and selling other at under rates;	245	Priest 12		11
once satisfied, he allows his Charity some blindnesse in the other;	245	Priest 12		27
For other givings are lay, and secular, but this is to give like	245	Priest 12		37
or in time of divine service on other holy days, except in the cases	248	Priest 14		3
However, one way or other, he ever reproves them, that he may keep	248	Priest 14		23
but with these he mingles other discourses for conversation sake,	249	Priest 14		11
perfecting our Redemption no other way, then by sorrow;	249	Priest 15		23
which may make his other discourses more welcome, and lesse tedious.	251	Priest 17		6
When he comes to any other house, where his kindred, or other	251	Priest 17		15
or other relations give him any authority over the Family,	251	Priest 17		16
reading of Scriptures, and other good books, how Sundayes,	251	Priest 17		23
Likewise in any other Countrey-duty, he considers what is the end	253	Priest 19		3
or at some other time of the day, propounds among his Brethren what	253	Priest 19		13
but in the other God is his own immediate paymaster, rewarding all	254	Priest 20		20

OTHER (cont'd)

	PAGE	TITLE		LINE
the other, to multiply, and build up this knowledge to a spirituall	255	Priest 21		4
first point, and but by Catechizing, the other cannot be attained.	255	Priest 21		8
way that a Pastor can take, to go over the same, but in other words:	256	Priest 21		3
the Parson once demanded after other questions about mans misery;	257	Priest 21		2
being two things in Sermons, the one Informing, the other Inflaming;	257	Priest 21		22
of questions in the one, so they farre exceed them in the other.	257	Priest 21		24
the other, in being worse served and obeyed.	259	Priest 22		5
himself an unworthy one, and therefore differs from other Feasters:	259	Priest 22		16
he asks no other, but to have the skill of healing a wound,	260	Priest 23		31
and maketh the one serve the other.	261	Priest 23		17
knot-grasse for the other, and that with better successe.	261	Priest 23		36
the other of not giving scandall, that ought not to be preferred,	263	Priest 24		9
the other an humble, and ingenuous search of truth;	263	Priest 24		16
There are other vices, whose natures, at least in the beginning,	264	Priest 26		7
that servants for their mony are as other things that they buy,	265	Priest 26		24
so that corne doth not grow by any other vertue, then by that which	271	Priest 30		5
he preserves and orders the references of things one to the other,	271	Priest 30		14
yet if he suite not other things to the growth, as seasons,	271	Priest 30		16
and other accidents by his governing power, the fairest harvests come	271	Priest 30		17
and taint his other duties of piety, which none can perform so wel in	273	Priest 31		2
On the other side, if I am to visit the sick in haste, and my neerest	273	Priest 31		33
is additionary, not necessary, and the other duty overweighs it:	273	Priest 31		37
the other in walking carelesly in our calling, he first represents	274	Priest 32		16
the other, the casting of it on mean persons, especially in some	276	Priest 32		20
At other times he is to travell over the King's Dominions,	277	Priest 32		6
This is the duty of each to other, which they ought to fulfill:	277	Priest 32		21
being usefull to all Countreys, and the other especially to Ilands.	278	Priest 32		3
all other things shall be added, even it selfe is a Sermon.	278	Priest 33		14
but that, so the other acts be, that is not necessary:	279	Priest 33		28
who performes the other acts of repentance, when he cannot more,	279	Priest 33		30
The like he doth in other Christian vertues, as of Faith,	279	Priest 33		33
a Christian even in this Life, the one military, the other peaceable.	280	Priest 34		3
as he discovers any of his Flock to be in one or the other state,	280	Priest 34		13
therefore this kind of Punishment was chosen rather then any other.	282	Priest 34		17
The other concerning the destruction of Jerusalem;	282	Priest 34		27
the one in his being, the other in his sinfull being:	283	Priest 34		20
and goes with him to the other, and all dine or sup together.	284	Priest 35		21
The other in generall, in the Commination.	286	Priest 36		5
when the other gives him just opportunity, by speaking any good,	286	Priest 36		23
On the other side, if it be unlawful to open faults, no benefit	287	Priest 37		5
cool wines pleased my taste best, as also melons, and other fruit;	293	Cornaro		12
Yet with this diet I avoided other hurtfull things also,	293	Cornaro		30
and other perturbations of the minde, which have a great power over	293	Cornaro		36
keep a fit proportion, shall receive little hurt from other excesses.	294	Cornaro		5
and other like discommodities of the bodie, and troubles	294	Cornaro		12
neither melancholie, nor any other passion can hurt a temperate life.	294	Cornaro		31
and so without other remedie or inconvenience I recovered;	295	Cornaro		12
a temperate life, can receive little hurt from other inconveniences.	295	Cornaro		15
On the other side I argued, that Nature was contented with a little,	295	Cornaro		25
The other Proverb was, The meat which remaineth, profits more then	296	Cornaro		1
the other, though it was but a little excesse, in a few dayes had so	297	Cornaro		5
And that I may say nothing of other things, are not almost all	298	Cornaro		32
excelling in wit, learning, behaviour, and other vertues.	301	Cornaro		5
At other times, I repair to a village of mine, seated in the valley;	301	Cornaro		19
by the regularitie of my life I have shut out death all other wayes.	303	Cornaro		28
This place together with many other, as namely Consid. 71. upon Our	307	Valdesso		16
Other Habits oppose morall vertues, as Prodigality opposes	308	Valdesso		10
Although by other words of the same Psalme it is evident,	309	Valdesso		27
and that no other sin or vertue hath any thing to doe with us;	311	Valdesso		24
but in those other occasions, Gods Spirit will mortify and try them	314	Valdesso		21
the other gratia gratum faciens, this being given only to the godly,	319	Valdesso		8
being given only to the godly, and the other sometimes to the wicked.	319	Valdesso		9
But there are other Cases of Conscience grounded on Piety	319	Valdesso	V	30
Better spare to have of thine own, then aske of other men.	330	Proverbs		266
Willowes are weak, yet they bind other wood.	341	Proverbs		594
Halfe the world knowes not how the other halfe lives.	351	Proverbs		907
Halfe the world knowes not how the other halfe lies.	351	Proverbs	V	907
Religion a stalking horse to shoot other foul.	357	Proverbs	D	1069
ado to make one half years allowance, shake hands with the other:	365	Letters		11
either by engaging my future Annuity, or any other way, I desire you,	365	Letters		21
but yet he will heare of no other affaires, untill they have	368	Letters		8
observ'd the thred of Life to be like other threds or skenes of silk,	373	Letters		4
and have endur'd such other Tortures, as the very mention of them	373	Letters		37
not considering you any other wayes, as neyther I my self desire	378	Letters		15
severall wayes, one to the other, that ye may be a heavenly comfort,	378	Letters		26
thereof (as your trade) the other only for the success (as assistance	380	Woodnoth		22
the other the commonwealths, & therfore not relinquishable without	381	Woodnoth		28
the one imployment, the other profitt, the work I may change,	381	Woodnoth		31
uppon Leighton Church, the other five pound I give to himselfe.	382	G.H.'s Will		30
On the other side are the names of those to whome my deceased Neece	383	G.H.'s Will		1
and other titles most pleasing, as well to us remembring,	441	Oration		25

OTHER'S

If thou thy selfe canst doe it, attend no others helpe or hand.	348	Proverbs		813

OTHERS

As hurts not others, but may make thee better,	16	Ch.-Porch		262
Write on the others, Here lies such a one.	20	Ch.-Porch		342
Onely let others say, when I am dead,	34	Sacrifice		251
Small to my self, to others milde,	44	H. Bapt.2		9
The sunne to others writeth laws,	72	Constancie		24
Although then others court you, if ye know	78	Ang.&Sts.		26

OTHERS (cont'd)	PAGE	TITLE		LINE
And by the others is opprest.	79	Employm.2		15
At th' head of others, hit their own.	96	Charms & K		10
At th' hart cf others, hit their own.	96	Charms & K	W	10
Others do sleep, and envie not their cheer.	118	Providence		56
And fence a plague, while others sleep and slumber.	147	Offering		12
And fence a plague, whiles others sleep and slumber.	147	Offering	V	12
What others mean to do, I know not well;	187	Judgement		6
Nero and others lodg'd him bravely there,	194	Ch.-Milit.		141
to my selfe, and others, who may not despise my poor labours,	224	Priest		14
As he doth not so study others, as to neglect the grace of God in	229	Priest 4		19
and sayings of others, according as his text invites him;	233	Priest 7		12
with any woman alone, but in the audience of others, and that seldom,	237	Priest 9		12
and others, and halfe at least of the government of the house,	238	Priest 9		37
act in them, then when they are called to others prayers, and that,	241	Priest 10		6
it absurd, that he should exceed, who teacheth others temperance.	241	Priest 10		21
nor suffer others in his house that are so, to keep it;	242	Priest 10		30
and others spurred to do well, that they may enjoy the like	243	Priest 11		26
for in preaching to others, he forgets not himself, but is first	255	Priest 21		14
not himself, but is first a Sermon to himself, and then to others;	255	Priest 21		15
as may be of much use to him both for himself, and others.	261	Priest 23		3
there are others, who when they know a sin evidently, they commit it	264	Priest 26		11
to themselves, and witty to others who shall reprove them from it.	264	Priest 26		13
he condescends to humane frailties both in himselfe and others;	268	Priest 27		6
that are reproved, but never contempt either in them, or others.	268	Priest 28		30
the Gallant, who is witty enough to abuse both others, and himself,	275	Priest 32		7
with the same care as others, when they meet with good fruit,	276	Priest 32		31
examined the nature of it, is able to explaine it after to others.	279	Priest 33		9
a more melting temper then others) consisteth in a true detestation	279	Priest 33		23
getting for himself, when he tels it to others, becomes a Sermon.	279	Priest 33		32
Romans 2.) hee first preacheth to himselfe, and then to others.	279	Priest 33		37
and frequented by others, but to them an unpenetrable rock,	282	Priest 34		3
but for an exciting of others by their sight, to the acknowledging	282	Priest 34		15
and withall help many others, who will take this into consideration,	291	Cornaro		14
For when my brother and others of my kindred saw some great powerfull	294	Cornaro		15
which often kill others, can bring little grief or hurt to those that	294	Cornaro		34
which things in others cannot be known without such observation,	297	Cornaro		29
without such observation, as is not easily to be made upon others;	297	Cornaro		30
and Isocrates, and Tullie, and many others of the Ancients;	298	Cornaro		39
and many others of inferiour condition, not onely in the citie,	299	Cornaro		3
aim in all things, how I may help others to the furthest of my power.	301	Cornaro		8
which is altogether to be preferred before others youth:	302	Cornaro		23
or relation from others, is not that which filleth the heart with joy	309	Valdesso		1
Scriptures for the first and principall, as Consid. 47, and others;	311	Valdesso	V	5
The godly are punishable as others, when they doe amisse,	316	Valdesso		18
unlesse it be evident to others, as well as to themselves,	316	Valdesso		19
the others, in a zeal against these, and in a strict performance	319	Valdesso	V	23
All came from, and will goe to others.	322	Proverbs		41
Who must account for himselfe and others, must know both.	328	Proverbs		209
Bells call others, but themselves enter not into the Church.	340	Proverbs		571
or if it had to others, yet to me it should not, for ought I yet	370	Letters		23
thereof, we are to regard others, & neither to scandalize them,	380	Woodnoth		19
OTHERS'				
By lavishnesse thine own, and others wit,	18	Ch.-Porch		304
In Almes regard thy means, and others merit.	21	Ch.-Porch		373
Who marks in church-time others symmetrie,	23	Ch.-Porch		419
Who marks in church-time others comlines,	23	Ch.-Porch	W	419
But when it would appeare to others eye,	68	Content		11
Are chaw'd by others pens and tongue;	69	Content		30
Are chaw'd by others pen and tongue;	69	Content	W	30
Whom others faults do not defeat;	73	Constancie		29
for others ruine wrought:	222	Psalm VII	D	54
that he may keep himself pure, and not be intangled in others sinnes.	248	Priest 14		24
wish them best, and that not a desire to meddle with others affairs,	251	Priest 17		31
not to incroach on others Professions, but to live on his own.	262	Priest 23		17
at his own, and others sins, which continually breake Gods Laws,	269	Priest 28		9
make others faults their entertainment and discourse, and that even	286	Priest 37		30
Our owne actions are our security, not others judgements.	326	Proverbs		173
Our owne actions secure us not others judgements.	326	Proverbs	V	173
OTHERWISE				
from the improvement of things, which otherwise would be lost.	241	Priest 10		24
which otherwise they would reckon upon, and turn to idlenesse.	245	Priest 12		4
the afflicted, though they can, and otherwise ought to come to him.	249	Priest 15		17
or otherwise afflicted, he followeth the Churches counsell,	249	Priest 15		28
or otherwise are done to his owne person, hee considers the offender	250	Priest 16		13
To do otherwise, is deceit;	252	Priest 19		29
where things are otherwise equall, therefore he satisfies this duty	253	Priest 19		28
then by causing them to be presented, or otherwise complained of.	254	Priest 20		25
as in their tithes, or otherwise.	262	Priest 24		27
yea though they be tenants, or otherwise ingaged to the delinquent:	270	Priest 29		21
dishes at table, which even their present health otherwise admits;	280	Priest 34		23
which even their present plenty of wealth otherwise admits;	280	Priest 34		25
which the present occasion of wit and company otherwise admits;	280	Priest 34		28
live ten yeares lesse then otherwise they should do) then alwayes	298	Cornaro		27
For otherwise any Malefactor may pretend motions, which is	316	Valdesso		21
OUGHT (aught)				
When thou dost purpose ought within thy power,	11	Ch.-Porch		115
That thou hast ought to do with me.	45	Nature		3
For ought I heare, your Master shows to you	130	Love unkn.		62
Then I or ought, or can be mine.	157	Clasping		3
He that does ought for thee,	184	The Elixer	W	12

OUGHT (cont'd)	PAGE	TITLE		LINE
their children, how much more may, and ought Spirituall Fathers?	285	Priest 36		15
if it had to others, yet to me it should not, for ought I yet knew;	370	Letters		24
all your Addresses, & for ought I see, they are ever to be liked.	378	Letters		17
OUGHT (see also aught)				
My childrens right, nor ought he take it: rather	17	Ch.-Porch		279
Neither ought other mens abuse of Lent	86	Lent		28
For I will do, or suffer what I ought.	139	Artillerie		16
and then they are worst, who ought to be best.	227	Priest 3		29
notwithstanding his instruction that they ought not to be so,	232	Priest 6		16
he sees whether I speak as I ought, or you hear as you ought,	234	Priest 7		27
whether I speak as I ought, or you hear as you ought, he sees hearts,	234	Priest 7		28
all those, who ccme with lesse prepared hearts then they ought.	235	Priest 8		32
and Font be as they ought, for those great duties that are performed	246	Priest 13		7
the afflicted, though they can, and otherwise ought to come to him.	249	Priest 15		17
the Blessing of God to them ought to make them the more charitable,	254	Priest 19		5
and the difference, hee ought to receive, of what age soever.	258	Priest 22		36
whether having a rule, it ought not to be guided by it;	263	Priest 24		2
that ought not to be preferred, especially since in disobeying there	263	Priest 24		10
which yet ought to be done, since there is a Justice in the least	265	Priest 26		31
And Scholers ought to be diligent in the observation of these,	265	Priest 26		35
For that he ought not to break off, but to continue his dependance	271	Priest 30		34
omission thereof upon just occasion ought by no means to trouble him.	273	Priest 31		6
so much the rather ought he to proceed, as that by this he may take	273	Priest 31		31
and house-keeper hath his hands full, if he do what he ought to do.	275	Priest 32		21
This is the duty of each to other, which they ought to fulfill:	277	Priest 32		21
or at least in that degree it ought to be, since he found himselfe	279	Priest 33		11
wherein (as Saint Paul implyes that he ought, Romans 2.) hee first	279	Priest 33		36
and largesse, which at that time is, or ought to be used.	284	Priest 35		9
being directed by them in the way I ought to hold, I understood,	292	Cornaro		23
whom that matter ought to have affected most, received no	294	Cornaro		21
ought not to eat, but such meats as are agreeable to his disease,	299	Cornaro		30
they who finde benefit in these meats, may, yea ought to use them:	300	Cornaro		11
the presuming upon it ought not to leade us to a disorderly life.	300	Cornaro		20
but that he ought to pray God affectionately and fervently to send	312	Valdesso		16
to be in the dark, ought to use the first, and to forbear the second;	312	Valdesso	V	25
These in diverse cases ought, and were of old forborn for a time.	312	Valdesso	V	27
Therefore wee ought to proceed, except there be a restraining motion	313	Valdesso		15
For as for these, pious persons ought alwaies to avoid them:	314	Valdesso		20
He that plaies his mony ought not to value it.	327	Proverbs		201
Hee that doth what hee will, doth not what he ought.	333	Proverbs		350
we ought not to trust another.	338	Proverbs		490
He that mockes a cripple, ought to be whole.	340	Proverbs		565
a space ought to be interposed.	356	Proverbs	D	40
Not only ought fortune to be pictured on a wheel,	358	Proverbs	D	1077
of what poor regard ought they to be, since if we had Riches we are	373	Letters		23
OUGHTEST				
Doe what thou oughtest, and come what come can.	348	Proverbs		818
OUNCES (see also ownce)				
the quantitie of meat to be increased, yet but two ounces onely.	296	Cornaro		8
and flesh, and broth, was twelve ounces exactly weighed;	296	Cornaro		10
I increased it to the quantitie of two ounces more;	296	Cornaro		11
of my drink, which before was foureteen ounces, I made now sixteen.	296	Cornaro		13
OUR				
This losse springs chiefly from our education.	10	Ch.-Porch		97
Our blessings from us, and extreamly flout thee,	23	Ch.-Porch	W	413
For churches are either our heav'n or hell.	23	Ch.-Porch		426
For churches either are our heav'n or hell.	23	Ch.-Porch	W	426
Sure there is room within our hearts good store;	40	Sepulchre		5
Where our hard hearts have took up stones to brain thee,	41	Sepulchre		13
And make up our defects with his sweet art.	42	Easter		18
And stop our sinnes from growing thick and wide,	44	H. Bapt.1		8
The sound of glorie ringing in our eares:	46	Sinne 1		10
Without, our shame; within, our consciences;	46	Sinne 1		11
Bitternesse fills our bowels; all our hearts	49	Repentance		27
Fretting to death our other parts.	49	Repentance	W	30
Our flesh and frailtie, death and danger.	50	Faith		24
Our souls and fleshly hearts;	52	H.Commun.		15
Our souls and fleshy hearts;	52	H.Commun.	V	15
And all our lump to leaven;	53	H.Commun.		30
Our innocent earth to heaven.	53	H.Commun.		32
Lett Prayer help our losses,	53	H.Commun.	W	38
Wrought our deliverance from th' infernall pit,	54	Love 1		12
Doth warm our hands, and make them write of love.	54	Love 1		14
And kindle in our hearts such true desires,	54	Love 2		4
As may consume our lusts, and make thee way.	54	Love 2		5
Then shall our hearts pant thee; then shall our brain	54	Love 2		6
Our eies shall see thee, which before saw dust;	54	Love 2		9
And praise him who did make and mend our eies.	54	Love 2		14
The greater shall our glorie be.	57	Employm. 1		10
The measure of our joyes is in this place,	57	Employm. 1		11
That cordiall water to our ground,	59	Whitsunday		18
So devils are our sinnes in perspective.	63	Sinne 2		10
Put our amendment in our way,	64	Even-song		23
And give new wheels to our disorder'd clocks.	64	Even-song		24
Fed with the exhalation of our crimes,	64	Ch.-monum.		5
That measures all our time; which also shall	65	Ch.-monum.		21
Then with our trinitie of light,	74	The Starre		17
Motion, and heat, let's take our flight	74	The Starre		18
The rest of our Creation	76	Sunday		43
Our great Redeemer did remove	76	Sunday		44

OUR (cont'd)

	PAGE	TITLE		LINE
Christs hands, though nail'd, wrought our salvation,	76	Sunday		48
We sullied by our foul offence:	76	Sunday		51
Have with our stamp and seal transferr'd our right:	77	Avarice		11
But now (alas!) I dare not; for our King,	78	Ang.&Sts.		16
If any one our Masters hand can show.	78	Ang.&Sts.		30
Before we do our wares unfold:	79	Employm.2		28
Untill the grave increase our cold.	79	Employm.2		30
Then we will sing, and shine all our own day,	81	Christmas		31
The dust into our eyes:	82	Ungratef.		17
Coloss. 3. 3. Our life is hid with Christ in God.	84	Coloss.		T
The first Is straight, and our diurnall friend,	84	Coloss.		3
Spoil our good use; lest by that argument	86	Lent	W	29
We forfeit all our Creed.	86	Lent		30
We cannot reach our Saviours puritie;	87	Lent		34
In both let's do our best.	87	Lent		36
Yet Lord instruct us to improve our fast	87	Lent		43
As may our faults controll:	87	Lent		45
Herbs gladly cure our flesh; because that they	91	Man		23
Nothing we see, but means our good,	91	Man		27
As our delight, or as our treasure:	91	Man		28
The whole is, either our cupboard of food,	91	Man		29
Musick and light attend our head.	91	Man		33
All things unto our flesh are kinde	91	Man		34
In their descent and being; to our minde	91	Man		35
Waters united are our navigation;	92	Man		38
Distinguished, our habitation;	92	Man		39
Below, our drink; above, our meat;	92	Man		40
Both are our cleanlinesse. Hath one such beautie?	92	Man		41
Both are our cleanlines: if one have beauty,	92	Man	W	41
He our foes in pieces brake;	93	Antiphon 2		13
Now thou wouldst taste our miserie.	97	Afflict.5		12
Some Angels us'd the first; if our relief	97	Afflict.5		15
So our clay hearts, ev'n when we crouch	101	Miserie		39
May our requests thine eare invade!	103	Prayer 2		3
May our requests thine eares invade!	103	Prayer 2	W	3
Blaming the shallownesse of our request.	103	Prayer 2		12
Wert fain to take our flesh and curse,	103	Prayer 2		15
And for our sakes in person sinne reprove,	103	Prayer 2		16
Show'd a strange love to all our good:	104	Obedience		27
To both our goods, if he to it will stand.	105	Obedience		40
But when we leave our corn and hay:	108	Home		56
Doubtlesse our plagues and plentie, peace and warres	119	Providence		79
Are there much surer then our art is sure.	119	Providence		80
An usher to convey our souls	123	Time		17
While it detains us from our God.	123	Time		20
Thy word our hearts and hands did crave,	123	Gratefulnes		10
And didst allow us all our noise:	124	Gratefulnes		18
Will not suffice our turn:	127	Giddinesse		26
Our own salvation.	127	Giddinesse		28
His ancient justice overflows our crimes.	128	Bunch Gr.		14
Then have we too our guardian fires and clouds;	128	Bunch Gr.		15
Our Scripture-dew drops fast:	128	Bunch Gr.		16
We have our sands and serpents, tents and shrowds;	128	Bunch Gr.		17
Alas! our murmurings come not last.	128	Bunch Gr.		18
We must confesse that nothing is our own.	143	Holdfast		7
Here he gave up his life to pay our score.	151	The Bag		24
Our cyens have purloin'd, and left you drie:	152	The Jews		2
Our sinnes have purloin'd, and left you drie:	152	The Jews	V	2
When God vouchsafeth to become our fare,	161	Priesthood		27
Through th' old sinnes and new doctrines of our land.	161	Priesthood		33
To set thy honour up, as our designe.	164	The Crosse		6
I like our language, as our men and coast:	167	The Sonne		3
So in one word our Lords humilitie	168	The Sonne		11
And judge our selves. That light, which sin & passion	171	Self-cond.		20
In tears like seas, our sinnes are pil'd	173	Marie Magd		11
But since our Saviours death did put some bloud	186	Death		13
Making our pillows either down, or dust.	186	Death		24
Help our decay.	187	Dooms-day		26
As well our understanding as our sight.	190	Ch.-Milit.		18
That though our Saviour did destroy the game,	194	Ch.-Milit.		146
Traditions are accounts without our host.	194	Ch.-Milit.	W	160
Shipping the vices onely for our sphere.	196	Ch.-Milit.	W	204
Religion stands on tip-toe in our land,	196	Ch.-Milit.		235
(The marks of future bane) shall fill our cup	197	Ch.-Milit.		239
Unto the brimme, and make our measure up;	197	Ch.-Milit.		240
To pay our debts, and leave our ancient place	197	Ch.-Milit.		256
To pay our debts, and leave her ancient place	197	Ch.-Milit.	W	256
But lends to us, shall be our desolation.	197	Ch.-Milit.		258
Lendeth to us, shall be our desolation.	197	Ch.-Milit.	W	258
I and the Sunn have runn our races,	203	Even-song	W	2
Now the great combat of our flesh & reason	204	The Knell	W	8
How know you that our teares proceed from woe	210	Paradox	D	15
Each little comforte much affects our hartes,	210	Paradox	D	33
For though you vysit us, & wayle our case,	211	Paradox	D	39
Come to our bed	211	Paradox	D	41
Serve our great God in fear, rejoyce,	216	Psalm II	D	27
since our Saviour hath made that the argument of a Pastour's love,	224	Priest		5
or ministry, let us wait on our ministring;	226	Priest 2		6
the well is deep, and we have nothing of our selves to draw with?	228	Priest 4		35
the expounding of our Catechisme must needs be the most usefull	230	Priest 5		14

OUR (cont'd)

	PAGE	TITLE	LINE
but when we use our reason, and apply our powers to the service	232	Priest 6	5
and apply our powers to the service of him, that gives them.	232	Priest 6	6
and seasoning all our words and sentences in our hearts,	233	Priest 7	29
in our hearts, before they come into our mouths, truly affecting,	233	Priest 7	30
raise up their mindes to apprehend Gods good blessing to our Church,	236	Priest 8	23
beseeching the Almighty to pardon and accept our poor services,	236	Priest 8	27
and that our feet may be like hindes feet ever climbing up higher,	236	Priest 8	29
and the exact temperance of our Lord Jesus, with other exemplary	237	Priest 9	34
since fasting in Scripture language is an afflicting of our souls,	242	Priest 10	12
these two rules comprize and include the double object of our duty,	246	Priest 13	30
and include the double object of our duty, God, and our neighbour;	246	Priest 13	30
the second for the benefit of our neighbor.	246	Priest 13	31
I am to follow our Saviours rule, and to take my brother aside,	248	Priest 14	27
perfecting our Redemption no other way, then by sorrow;	249	Priest 15	22
even as our Saviour made plants and seeds to teach the people:	261	Priest 23	13
And I conceive, our Saviour did this for three reasons:	261	Priest 23	17
more then indifferent, it be in our power to omit or refuse them.	263	Priest 24	13
because wealth is given to that end to supply our occasions.	265	Priest 26	8
touching our imployments, none must eat so as to disable themselves	266	Priest 26	28
As when the people hungred and thirsted after our Saviours Doctrine,	267	Priest 26	22
the other in walking carelesly in our calling, he first represents	274	Priest 32	16
to be accounted for, and to be improved to our Masters Advantage.	274	Priest 32	25
Yet is it also a debt to our Countrey to have a Calling,	274	Priest 32	26
Now this reason crosseth not our Saviours precept of selling what we	274	Priest 32	32
So that our Saviours selling is so far from crossing Saint Pauls	275	Priest 32	3
for our Law is Practice.	277	Priest 32	4
as divers have done lately, to our Countrey's advantage.	278	Priest 32	10
since we are not Masters of our bodies, this sufficeth.	279	Priest 33	19
as he did our Saviour, and the Angels minister to us their owne food,	280	Priest 34	6
These two states were in our Saviour, not only in the beginning	280	Priest 34	8
and if we would bound our selves, we should not be bounded.	280	Priest 34	31
the one concerning the woman that spent the oyntment on our Saviour,	282	Priest 34	24
of which our Saviour said, that that generation should not passe,	282	Priest 34	28
which our Saviour himselfe used, Marke 10. 16, cannot bee vain	285	Priest 36	10
2 Kings 2. 24. which though our Saviour reproved as unfitting for his	285	Priest 36	26
the one in, The Grace of our Lord Jesus Christ, &c.	286	Priest 36	4
Misery and sin fill our days:	288	Priest	11
yet art thou our Creatour, and we thy work:	288	Priest	12
giving us one world in our selves, and another to serve us:	288	Priest	14
disappointed thy Purposes, and sold our God, our glorious,	288	Priest	17
and sold our God, our glorious, our gracious God for an apple.	288	Priest	17
O brand it in our foreheads for ever:	288	Priest	18
for an apple once we lost our God, and still lose him for no more;	288	Priest	19
and hast made our salvation, not our punishment, thy glory:	288	Priest	23
O let not our foolish and unworthy hearts rob us of the continuance	289	Priest	19
but pardon our sins, and perfect what thou hast begun.	289	Priest	21
in whose sweet and pleasing words, we say, Our Father, &c.	289	Priest	35
untill our obedience reach the measure of thy love, who hast done	290	Priest	11
Grant this dear Father, for thy Son's sake, our only Saviour:	290	Priest	13
of the minde, which have a great power over our constitutions.	293	Cornaro	37
power a sober and temperate life hath over our bodies and mindes,	294	Cornaro	26
if our corporall life depend on the harmonie of humours & elements,	297	Cornaro	7
and in our age, Paul the third, and Cardinal Bembo, who therefore	299	Cornaro	1
and among our Dukes, Landus, and Donatus, and many others	299	Cornaro	2
much as she can, teacheth us how to govern our selves in sicknesse:	299	Cornaro	26
For suddenly it takes away our appetite, so that we can eat	299	Cornaro	27
he every where beares towards our deare [great] Master and Lord,	305	Valdesso	4
the many pious rules of ordering our life, about mortification,	305	Valdesso	9
together with many other, as namely Consid. 71. upon Our Father;	307	Valdesso	17
but the spirits bearing witnesse with our spirit, revealing	309	Valdesso	3
have the assistance of the holy spirit applying it to our hearts,	310	Valdesso	7
necessary duties, and occasions of our calling and condition of life;	314	Valdesso	17
To say our Saviour prayed with doubtfulnesse, is more then I can	315	Valdesso	9
I doubt but if Abraham had lived in our Kingdome under government,	316	Valdesso	23
are come now, to what the Pharisees were come in our Saviours time.	320	Valdesso	7
Our owne actions are our security, not others judgements.	326	Proverbs	173
Our owne actions secure us not others judgements.	326	Proverbs	V 173
The ill that comes out of our mouth falles into our bosome.	328	Proverbs	221
All our pompe the earth covers.	345	Proverbs	716
God, and Parents, and our Master, can never be requited.	348	Proverbs	805
We Batchelors laugh and shew our teeth,	361	Proverbs	D 1175
for in our publick Halls, you know, is nothing but Fish	365	Letters	3
which they are thought to have offerd to our Merchants at the Indies,	368	Letters	6
also concerning the fishing which the Hollanders use in our coasts,	368	Letters	10
I have sent you here inclosed a Letter from our Master in my behalf,	369	Letters	25
with our good and gracious God, incessantly begging some ease of your	371	Letters	28
does fix me here, it being now but a month to our Commencement:	372	Letters	20
or why should our afflictions here, have so much power or boldness	372	Letters	27
much power or boldness as to oppose the hope of our Joyes hereafter!	372	Letters	28
our Colledge Customs allow not that, and I shou'd account my self	373	Letters	2
our Credit and estimation calls on us to live in a more splendid	373	Letters	26
admirable thing is this, that God puts his shoulder to our burthen;	374	Letters	18
entertains our Care for us that we may the more quietly intend his	374	Letters	18
to putt one of our neeces into your hands but barely what I wrote I	375	Letters	5
I will tell you what I wrote to our eldest brother, when he urged one	375	Letters	10
hath your Goodness brought on you, by admitting our poor services?	376	Letters	27
your relation of my Lady Duchess's forwardnes in our church building.	377	Letters	20
Now God the Father of our Lord Jesus Christ bless you more & more,	378	Letters	24
She liked our Book well, & has given order to the Tenants,	379	Letters	8
as the course of our life & the changes thereof, we are to regard	380	Woodnoth	18

OUT (cont'd)	PAGE	TITLE		LINE
Spin out thy thread, and make thereof a coat	156	Assurance		38
Can hale or draw it out of doore.	158	Praise 3		16
When almost all was out, God made a stay,	160	The Pulley		8
I sent a sigh to seek thee out,	162	The Search		17
To bear them out, and with my state agree.	164	Grief		8
When thou shalt look us out of pain,	172	The Glance		21
So Thou art still my God, be out of fear.	176	Forerunners		10
Man is out of order hurl'd,	187	Dooms-day		27
Parcel'd out to all the world.	187	Dooms-day		28
So they might still, and point us out the place	192	Ch.-Milit.		85
Sinne did set out of Eastern Babylon,	193	Ch.-Milit.		103
Therefore he sent out able ministers,	195	Ch.-Milit.		199
Heighten a spirit to sound out thy praise	206	Walton 1		7
Out-strip their Cupid easily in flight?	206	Walton 1		9
Here is copied out by art;	208	J. Danvers	D	10
Shining and sharp, point out your rare Perfections;	209	L. Bacon	D	4
And what is fortunes. Thou hast singled out	211	Bohemia	D	19
Lyes round about us to helpe out the story,	212	Bohemia	D	26
Call thee from out of that surrounded land,	213	Bohemia	D	61
Out of this Chartre of the Priesthood may be plainly gathered both	225	Priest 1		14
the purity of his mind breaking out, and dilating it selfe even	228	Priest 3		12
out of all which he hath compiled a book, and body of Divinity,	229	Priest 5		33
that none goes out of Church as he came in, but either better,	233	Priest 7		19
some choyce Observations drawn out of the whole text, as it lyes	235	Priest 7		3
which he observeth out of humble conformity, and obedience;	237	Priest 9		23
out of choyce and devotion, some other dayes for fasting,	237	Priest 9		24
sensitive faculty, will runne out more or lesse in her intellectuall.	238	Priest 9		11
not his affection found out a fit wife for him, whose humble,	238	Priest 9		28
women to heaven) a wise and loving husband could out of humility,	238	Priest 9		31
and out of liberality, make her fruitfull in all good works.	238	Priest 9		33
not spent in them, he blesseth God, and lays it out as he sees cause.	240	Priest 10		12
and stir out in the morning, and knows what prayers they say,	241	Priest 10		2
I am inclined, as not to get out of that sicknesse, when I am in it,	242	Priest 10		37
yet out of his infinite pity hath set forth heaven for a reward	243	Priest 11		31
it in the pulpit, and out of the pulpit, and never leaving them,	245	Priest 12		13
not as out of necessity, or as putting a holiness in the things,	246	Priest 13		23
So that they excellently score out the way, and fully, and exactly	246	Priest 13		32
a just occasion calleth him out of his Parish (which he diligently,	250	Priest 17		24
will draw out of ignorant and silly souls, even the dark and deep	256	Priest 21		19
he could not but say, he would hast out of it as fast as he could.	257	Priest 21		7
whether he could get out of the ditch alone, or whether he needed	257	Priest 21		8
out of which he gathers, in case he be ignorant himself,	260	Priest 23		11
householder, who bringeth out of his treasure things new and old;	261	Priest 23		15
and so shuts them out of his family, esteeming that there is no spice	261	Priest 23		38
for them often, and in finding out Courtesies to place on them;	262	Priest 24		27
rather to use his neighbours, and wear out that, he is covetous.	265	Priest 26		29
which out of his choysest judgment hee hath resolved to observe,	268	Priest 28		11
it is out of the overflowing of his Conscience, whereas they are	269	Priest 29		30
and with pulling, gets the apple out of his Fathers hand:	272	Priest 30		9
and put him out of his station, and to inlarge the perplexity,	272	Priest 31		34
that this interruption proceed not out of slacknes, or coldness,	273	Priest 31		16
Secondly, that this interruption proceede not out of shame.	273	Priest 31		21
not out of superstition, but of reverence to Gods house,	273	Priest 31		22
and how much more out of Paradise, when the evills which he is now	274	Priest 32		22
Could men finde out this delight, they would seldome be from home;	275	Priest 32		34
that he have leisure to look out, the Village or Parish which either	276	Priest 32		1
cutting out the Kingdome into Portions, which every yeer he surveys	277	Priest 32		7
even as John the Baptist squared out to every one (even to Souldiers)	277	Priest 32		23
judiciously, then he writes his rules of temperance out of bookes.	278	Priest 33		21
and then who can deny the stretched out arme of a mighty God?	282	Priest 34		6
love for love, even the son of his love out of his bosome of love.	283	Priest 34		17
do so either out of niceness, because they like the salutations,	285	Priest 36		4
that they oftentimes goe out of church, before he hath blessed them.	286	Priest 36		14
whom the Law would have defamed, except he also do it out of rancour.	287	Priest 37		29
I grew fully perswaded, that all my griefs arose out of Intemperance:	292	Cornaro		20
and therefore out of an hope of avoiding death and pain,	292	Cornaro		21
self to this course of life, that I never went a foot out of the way.	292	Cornaro		34
Wherefore I began to search out most diligently what meats were	293	Cornaro		4
was sore hurt, and also one of my arms and legges put out of joynt.	295	Cornaro		1
qualities to me, if I had not found them out by long experience?	297	Cornaro		35
by the regularitie of my life I have shut out death all other wayes.	303	Cornaro		27
Virginity of the blessed Virgin out of that text Mat. 1. 25. where it	318	Valdesso		11
Hee that gets out of debt, growes rich.	321	Proverbs		9
Who hath none to still him, may weepe out his eyes.	321	Proverbs		17
Mend your cloathes, and you may hold out this yeare.	324	Proverbs		100
Good is to bee sought out, and evill attended.	324	Proverbs		112
Make hast to an ill way that you may get out of it.	325	Proverbs		124
Where the drink goes in, there the wit goes out.	327	Proverbs		187
Ill comes in by ells, and goes out by inches.	327	Proverbs		194
The ill that comes out of our mouth falles into our bosome.	328	Proverbs		221
Litle stickes kindle the fire; great ones put it out.	332	Proverbs		323
The greatest step is that out of doores.	337	Proverbs		461
which a hundred wise men cannot pull out.	339	Proverbs		527
A litle wind kindles; much puts out the fire.	344	Proverbs		680
Hee goes not out of his way, that goes to a good Inne.	348	Proverbs		831
There comes nought out of the sacke but what was there.	348	Proverbs		833
There come nought out of the sacke but what was there.	348	Proverbs	V	833
Silkes and Satins put out the fire in the chimney.	351	Proverbs		912
Silkes and Satins put out the fire of the chimney.	351	Proverbs	V	912
You cannot make the fire so low but it will get out.	353	Proverbs		965

OUT (cont'd)	PAGE	TITLE		LINE
Though God take the sunne out of the Heaven,	353	Proverbs		980
He that is not in the warres is not out of danger.	354	Proverbs		999
knowes nothing sure but what hee hath laid out.	354	Proverbs		1001
Heresie may be easier kept out, then shooke off.	357	Proverbs	D	1059
Follow not truth too near the heels, lest it dash out thy teeth.	360	Proverbs	D	1138
to find out variety of thanks for the diversity of your favours,	363	Letters		15
Out of Lent also, twice a Week, on Fridayes and Saturdayes,	365	Letters		4
But I am out of my time:	366	Letters		19
that the Hollanders should pay him tribute out of their fishing.	368	Letters		13
I was in hope I should my self carry all sickness out of your family:	372	Letters		15
That God who hath delivered me out of the paws of the Lyon and Bear,	374	Letters		6
will also deliver me out of the hands of this uncircumcised	374	Letters		7
if at length they may find out some thing not unworthy of those hands	376	Letters		29
If there fall out yet any rubb, you shall heare of me;	377	Letters		22
& have endeavoured many wayes, to find out a man for it.	378	Letters		7
you have layed out thoughts & prayers you have sowed.	380	Woodnoth		10
stuffe whether in my possession or out of my possession that properly	382	G.H.'s Will		5
deceased Neece which are to be payd out of it unto some whose names	382	G.H.'s Will		15
OUT-CRYING				
Out-crying my requests, drowning my tears;	66	Ch.-lock		3
OUT-SING				
Out-sing the day-light houres.	81	Christmas		22
OUT-STRIP				
And shall the dew out-strip thy dove?	60	Grace		10
Out-strip their Cupid easily in flight?	206	walton 1		9
OUTGO				
By thy eternall glorie didst outgo me?	37	Reprisall		10
OUTLANDISH				
There is a rare outlandish root,	50	Faith		9
Outlandish looks may not compare:	109	Brit. Ch.		10
using pleasantly the outlandish proverb, that Prayers and Provender	251	Priest 17		14
but preferrs her garden and fields before all outlandish gums.	262	Priest 23		5
OUTLANDISH PROVERBS SELECTED By Mr. G. H.	319	Proverbs		T
Jacula Prudentum Or Outlandish Proverbs, Sentences, &c	356	Proverbs	D	T
and it is an outlandish one, which I commend to you as being now	376	Letters		17
OUTLAWD				
Is outlawd by himself: all kinde of ill	7	Ch.-Porch		33
Is outlawd by himself: all kinds of ill	7	Ch.-Porch	W	33
OUTRIGHT				
giving some corn outright, and selling other at under rates;	245	Priest 12		11
OUTRUNNING				
and ever outrunning the Teacher, as it did when Peter taught	310	Valdesso		7
OUTSTRIPPEST				
Thou still, O Lord, outstrippest mee.	201	love	W	6
OUTWARD				
To cleare the breast, to suple outward pain.	58	H.Script.1	W	4
By outward forme and showe,	210	Paradox	D	26
inward, or outward temptations, that it is ever attempting,	238	Priest 9		13
but also of company, recreation, and all outward contentments;	241	Priest 10		39
by which God turnes all outward blessings to inward advantages.	271	Priest 30		37
of the Gospell will not give an outward Law of Ceremonies as of old,	310	Valdesso		5
He meanes a mans fre-will is only in outward, not in spirituall	313	Valdesso		33
and they are to be judged according to the outward fact,	316	Valdesso		19
the world is counted a very Saint, for his outward shew of holinesse:	319	Valdesso	V	21
OUTWARDLY				
he is content to expresse this outwardly to the utmost of his power;	231	Priest 6		12
OUTWORKS				
But as th' outworks, they may controll	52	H.Commun.		16
OVEN				
If the mother had not beene in the oven,	344	Proverbs		696
O'RE				
Curl o're again.	115	Dulnesse		8
He gave the Seale, and so left o're.	439	Walton 5		14
He gave his soul, and so gave o're.	439	Walton 5	V	14
OVER (see also ore)				
Some ship them over, and the thing is done.	10	Ch.-Porch		100
To feel those tempests, which fly over ditches.	11	Ch.-Porch		112
Yet can these not get over to my soul,	52	H.Commun.		13
Die over each houre of Methusalems stay.	62	Afflict.2		5
They quarrell thee, and would give over	100	Miserie		25
Grieve over freshly all thy pain?	145	Discharge		50
Runnes over day and night.	173	23 Psalme		20
Are given over, for their curious arts,	194	Ch.-Milit.		152
Wherfore they are not to be over-submissive, and base, but to keep up	226	Priest 2		28
so farre from that which they seek with their over-submissivenesse,	226	Priest 2		35
them to be so, when God is so neer them, and even over their heads.	233	Priest 7		11
who first shed teares over Jerusalem, and afterwards blood.	234	Priest 7		21
but hath power over his own will, and hath so decreed in his heart,	237	Priest 9		17
yet never so giving over the raines, but that he sometimes looks how	239	Priest 9		1
or over-nourishing things, as the Israelites did eate sowre herbs:	242	Priest 10		4
the Cures with their own hands, and not to put them over to servants.	247	Priest 14		20
plunging themselves over head and eares into carking, and caring;	247	Priest 14		25
yet hee gives him not over, but is long before hee proceede	250	Priest 16		17
or other relations give him any authority over the Family,	251	Priest 17		16
way that a Pastor can take, to go over the same, but in other words:	256	Priest 21		2
At other times he is to travell over the King's Dominions,	277	Priest 32		7
the Priests Benedicite, and his holy water were over highly valued;	286	Priest 36		16
of the minde, which have a great power over our constitutions.	293	Cornaro		37
power a sober and temperate life hath over our bodies and mindes,	294	Cornaro		25
allowing no Jurisdiction over the godly, this cannot stand,	316	Valdesso		16

OVER (cont'd)	PAGE	TITLE		LINE
hath bought a parcel of Books for me, and that they are coming over.	366	Letters		31
& therfore I am not over much beholding to those busnesses which	367	Letters		30
consider what advantage you have over Youth and Health, . . .	372	Letters		32
all these are over and above their wages, To Sara thirteene shillings	382	G.H.'s Will		26
OVER-NOURISHING				
or over-nourishing things, as the Israelites did eate sowre herbs:	242	Priest 10		4
OVER-SUBMISSIVE				
Wherfore they are not to be over-submissive, and base, but to keep up	226	Priest 2		28
OVER-SUBMISSIVENESSE				
so farre from that which they seek with their over-submissivenesse,	226	Priest 2		35
OVERBURDENED				
if any neighbouring village be overburdened with poore, . . .	254	Priest 19		1
(which being overburdened, or studying dainties too much, . . .	266	Priest 26		15
OVERCAME				
his infinite hate of sinne, his Love overcame that hate; . . .	283	Priest 34		14
OVERCOME (see also orecome)				
Against thee, in thee I will overcome	37	Reprisall		15
Then what was in their tongue, did overcome;	196	Ch.-Milit.		202
and the ways which he used to overcome them, being told to another,	278	Priest 33		16
Though a lie be well drest, it is ever overcome.	325	Proverbs		133
He that endures is not overcome.	349	Proverbs		854
O'RECOMES				
Ours (like himselfe) o'recomes; for his wit's more	438	Lat.Trans.		3
OVERCOMES				
and so between gentle reasoning, and pitying, he overcomes the evill:	269	Priest 28		15
OVERDO				
labour anxiously, when they overdo it, to the loss of their quiet,	247	Priest 14		28
OVERFLOWING				
it is out of the overflowing of his Conscience, whereas they are	269	Priest 29		30
OVERFLOWS				
His ancient justice overflows our crimes.	128	Bunch Gr.		14
OVERMUCH				
watching, ill aire, overmuch use of the benefit of marriage.	293	Cornaro		31
OVERRUNNE				
Bedew, embalme, and overrunne my heart, ...	171	The Glance		7
OVERSEER				
John Danvers that he would be pleased to be Overseer of this Will.	382	G.H.'s Will		32
OVERSIGHT				
reviling also of Ananias seemes, by his owne recalling, an oversight;	316	Valdesso		11
OVERSLEEPING				
or by oversleeping himself at night, omits his additionary prayer.	272	Priest 31		31
OVERTAKE				
If troubles overtake thee, do not wail:	170	Water-crs.		4
and with those he overtakes or that overtake him, hee begins good	251	Priest 17		3
OVERTAKES				
and with those he overtakes or that overtake him, hee begins good	251	Priest 17		3
None is so wise, but the foole overtakes him.	345	Proverbs		734
None is so wise, but that the foole overtakes him. . . .	345	Proverbs	V	734
OVERTHROW				
But in all vict'ries overthrow me?	37	Reprisall		12
unto mine overthrow.	221	Psalm VII	D	16
sence of that Text, wee shall overthrow all means, save catechizing,	310	Valdesso		11
OVERTHROWING				
preserving of Health, as a disorderly life to the overthrowing of it;	292	Cornaro		7
OVERTHROWN				
shall utterly be overthrown.	215	Psalm I	D	24
wit and noble disposition, overthrown and undone by Intemperance;	291	Cornaro		2
fearing lest I should be overthrown, they were possessed with a deep	294	Cornaro		17
was but a little excesse, in a few dayes had so soon overthrown me.	297	Cornaro		6
OVERTURNED				
it happened that the coach was overturned, and then was dragged	294	Cornaro		37
by the hand of man may be overturned.	362	Proverbs	D	1184
OVERTURNES				
and therefore he often overturnes things, when they are thought past	271	Priest 30		20
OVERWEIGH				
and overweigh the defects (as I conceive) towards the publishing	305	Valdesso		13
OVERWEIGHS				
is additionary, not necessary, and the other duty overweighs it:	273	Priest 31		37
OVERWHELME				
nor no pit overwhelme it.	288	Priest		31
OW				
To thee both fruit and order OW.	132	Paradise		3
OWE				
I did beleeve that I did nothing owe, ...	50	Faith		14
Doe owe the symbole of their certainty.	439	Walton 5		8
for it is both an honor which they owe to the Reverend Judges	277	Priest 32		2
and to such, and all that is theirs, I owe diligence; . . .	304	Valdesso		8
You owe the Church a debt, and God hath put this into your hands	304	Valdesso		9
if there be any body els that owe me any thing else of old debt I	383	G.H.'s Will		26
OWED				
I owed thousands and much more:	50	Faith		13
OWENS				
Spencer five pound To Mary Owens forty shillings To Mrs Mary Lawly	383	G.H.'s Will		18
OWES				
And so complete, but onely he that owes them.	121	Providence		144
the one he owes to his heavenly Countrey, the other to his earthly,	239	Priest 10		21
He that owes nothing, if he makes not mouthes at us, is courteous.	333	Proverbs		362
The Physitian owes all to the patient, ...	351	Proverbs		921
but the patient owes nothing to him but a little mony. . . .	351	Proverbs		921

	PAGE	TITLE	LINE
OWING			
The Countrey Parson owing a debt of Charity to the poor,	243	Priest 11	6
Sleepe without supping, and wake without owing.	324	Proverbs	93
OWLE'S			
The ignorant hath an Eagles wings, and an Owles eyes.	351	Proverbs	902
OWN			
Whom God in Baptisme washt with his own blood.	6	Ch.-Porch	8
Lose all mine own? God hath giv'n me a measure	8	Ch.-Porch	38
Who breaks his own bond, forfeiteth himself:	11	Ch.-Porch	119
Dare to look in thy chest; for 'tis thine own:	12	Ch.-Porch	147
By no means runne in debt: take thine own measure.	13	Ch.-Porch	175
Lesse at thine own things laugh; lest in the jest	15	Ch.-Porch	231
Be not thine own worm: yet such jealousie,	16	Ch.-Porch	261
By lavishnesse thine own, and others wit,	18	Ch.-Porch	304
Full of themselves, and answer their own notion.	19	Ch.-Porch	320
Mine own Apostle, who the bag did beare,	27	Sacrifice	13
For it was their own cause who killed me:	30	Sacrifice	115
For it was their own case who killed me:	30	Sacrifice W	115
Your tears for your own fortunes should be kept:	31	Sacrifice	151
Mine own clothes on, they leade me out agen.	32	Sacrifice	190
But mend mine own without delayes.	36	Thanksgvng	34
But mend my own without delayes.	36	Thanksgvng W	34
Thine own gift good, yet me from my wayes taking.	48	Afflict.1	54
Within the walls of your own breast:	68	Content	2
Who cannot on his own bed sweetly sleep,	68	Content	3
Then cease discoursing soul, till thine own ground,	69	Content	33
('Tis your own case) ye never move a wing.	78	Ang.&Sts.	20
'tis your own case, ye never move your wing.	78	Ang.&Sts. W	20
Lets his own ashes choke his soul.	79	Employm.2	10
Then we will sing, and shine all our own day,	81	Christmas	31
Her own destruction and his danger wears.	85	Vanitie 1	14
His own destruction and his danger wears.	85	Vanitie 1 V	14
At th' head of others, hit their own.	96	Charms & K	10
At th' hart of others, hit their own.	96	Charms & K W	10
Thine own delights thou didst to us impart:	97	Afflict.5	8
And make his own? as if none knew, but he.	100	Miserie	14
Nay, his own shelf:	102	Miserie	77
Let me not think an action mine own way,	104	Obedience	18
That his own self he forgot.	113	Businesse	24
Our own salvation.	127	Giddinesse	28
Who do not their own motions heare?	134	The Method	19
With thine own clay. But I would parley fain:	139	Artillerie	27
We must confesse that nothing is our own.	143	Holdfast	7
To which, besides their own demean,	165	The Flower	3
Still upwards bent, as if heav'n were mine own,	166	The Flower	30
Look back upon thine own estate,	170	Self-cond.	4
Why kept she not her tears for her own faults,	173	Marie Magd	9
Why kept she not her tears for her own fauts,	173	Marie Magd V	9
Let follie speak in her own native tongue.	177	Forerunners	27
I affect to own,	178	Discipline	10
For that which God doth touch and own	185	The Elixer	23
Destroy them, Lord, and by their own	219	Psalm V D	29
To his own head his wickedness	222	Psalm VII D	57
And on his own accursed pate	222	Psalm VII D	59
Of Pastors (intending mine own Nation only, and also therein setting	225	Priest 2	20
and therefore as feeling their own sweat, and consequently knowing	227	Priest 3	13
in keeping his word, though it be to his own hinderance, as knowing,	228	Priest 3	5
and his own meditations, he enters into the secrets of God treasured	229	Priest 4	29
is full of such composures, yet every mans own is fittest, readyest,	230	Priest 5	4
and brings with his own to the heavenly altar to be bathed,	231	Priest 6	9
both to their own loss, and of theirs also who gaze upon them when	232	Priest 6	10
but hath power over his own will, and hath so decreed in his heart,	237	Priest 9	17
and carving for them, both for his own humility, and their comfort,	243	Priest 11	12
which they can better employ to their own advantage, and sutably	243	Priest 11	16
although we should love him onely for his own sake, yet out of his	243	Priest 11	31
He first considers his own Parish, and takes care, that there be	244	Priest 12	19
excellent statute, which bindes all Parishes to maintaine their own.	244	Priest 12	24
and repine as much, as he that is disseized of his own inheritance.	244	Priest 12	30
and when his own stock serves not, working those that are able	245	Priest 12	12
After the consideration of his own Parish, he inlargeth himself,	245	Priest 12	17
and wishing them ever to do the Cures with their own hands,	247	Priest 14	19
it is a good and just thing for every one to do their own busines.	247	Priest 14	22
thinking that their own labour is the cause of their thriving,	247	Priest 14	30
as if it were in their own hands to thrive, or not to thrive.	247	Priest 14	31
Ministeriall office, which is not to the prejudice of his own Parish.	253	Priest 19	17
finde any reading in anothers Bible, he provides him one of his own.	254	Priest 20	12
but in the other God is his own immediate paymaster, rewarding all	254	Priest 20	20
of preaching to himself, for the advancing of his own mortification;	255	Priest 21	13
yet he looks not in this point of Curing beyond his own Parish,	262	Priest 23	13
not to incroach on others Professions, but to live on his own.	262	Priest 23	17
which by mine own experience I have found hurtfull, then from those	266	Priest 26	24
and knowledg of their own body, and what it can well disgest:	267	Priest 26	1
especially in his own Parish he suffers it not to his utmost power;	268	Priest 28	18
or in a sad way, greived at his own, and others sins, which	269	Priest 28	9
obligation to God, and their own soul, is above any temporall tye.	270	Priest 29	22
not onely taken a particular Survey of the faults of his own Parish,	274	Priest 32	5
The Italian says, None fouls his hands in his own businesse:	275	Priest 32	27
and to transplant it in time to his own home, with the same care	276	Priest 32	31
and a shamefull wrong both to the Common-wealth, and their own House:	277	Priest 32	28
and ingaging of Gods own power and institution for a blessing.	286	Priest 36	10
blesse it in this thy own Kingdom, which thou hast made a Land	289	Priest	18

OWN (cont'd)	PAGE	TITLE		LINE
But mine own experience confirmeth this more;	294	Cornaro		10
one by long experience may know the qualities of his own nature,	297	Cornaro		27
things I do at my ease, and at fit seasons, and in mine own houses;	301	Cornaro		10
who being obscured in his own country he would have to flourish in	304	Valdesso		14
their Canon law and Decretals, knots of their own tying and untying:	319	Valdesso	V	29
Better spare to have of thine own, then aske of other men.	330	Proverbs		266
Every man's censure is first moulded in his own nature.	362	Proverbs	D	1181
For my own part, my meaning (dear Mother) is in these Sonnets,	363	Letters		9
so that I am fain to dyet in my Chamber at mine own cost;	365	Letters		3
by transporting French commodities to your own country.	366	Letters		12
that if all fail, yet I am able to stand on mine own legs.	370	Letters		10
to his brothers house of his own name (as I think) at the sign	370	Letters		27
of them will justifie you both to the world and your own Conscience:	373	Letters		17
to his glory, your own good, and the great joy of Madam,	377	Letters		6
in signing 100 lib. with her own hands (& promising to get her Son	379	Letters		2
OWNCE				
To want one ownce of sleepe,	209	Paradox	D	4
OWNE				
And though hee bee a ship, is his owne shelf.	11	Ch.-Porch	W	120
Leave not thine owne deere-cuntry-cleanlines	21	Ch.-Porch	W	367
Mine owne deare people, cry, away, away,	29	Sacrifice		102
Prevent my Sinn to thine owne praise,	61	Grace	W	20
Worthy had bin, thou hadst not lost thine owne:	211	Bohemia	D	2
At there owne weapons, without pomp or state	211	Bohemia	D	21
counting nothing so much his owne, as that he may be unjust unto it.	238	Priest 9		35
and healing of all wounds and sores with her owne hands;	239	Priest 10		15
or otherwise are done to his owne person, hee considers the offender	250	Priest 16		13
and his owne lesse charged, hee findes some way of releeving it,	254	Priest 19		2
having for his owne use examined the nature of it, is able	279	Priest 33		8
and the Angels minister to us their owne food, even joy,	280	Priest 34		6
for no perfect Artist ever yet hated his owne worke.	283	Priest 34		12
reviling also of Ananias seemes, by his owne recalling, an oversight;	316	Valdesso		11
Yet his owne practice seemes to confute his opinion, for the most	317	Valdesso		35
Our owne actions are our security, not others judgements.	326	Proverbs		173
Our owne actions secure us not others judgements.	326	Proverbs	V	173
He that hath a mouth of his owne,	333	Proverbs		353
Justice pleaseth few in their owne house.	334	Proverbs		396
Who doth his owne businesse, foules not his hands.	335	Proverbs		419
Hee that workes after his owne manner,	335	Proverbs		421
He that hath children, all his morsels are not his owne.	335	Proverbs		423
He who hath children, all his morsels are not his owne.	335	Proverbs	V	423
He that would be well, needs not goe from his owne house.	336	Proverbs		442
It's a proud horse that will not carry his owne provender.	345	Proverbs		712
Fooles give to please all but their owne.	345	Proverbs		735
Every one is witty for his owne purpose.	346	Proverbs		754
Hee that keepes his owne makes warre.	349	Proverbs		848
The Wolfe must dye in his owne skinne.	349	Proverbs		849
He that is his owne Counsellor	354	Proverbs		1001
to which mine owne obligations were occasion inough, & therfore I am	367	Letters		28
resuming the donation of spirituall livings into their owne hands,	368	Letters		28
& neither to scandalize them, nor wound our owne reputation.	380	Woodnoth		19
OWNER				
The greatnesse shew'd the owner. So I went	129	Love unkn.		29
The House shewes the owner.	321	Proverbs		8
Fear keepes and looks to the vineyard, and not the owner.	358	Proverbs	D	1072
OX				
His highest was an ox or crocodile,	193	Ch.-Milit.		122
OXE				
Whether shall the Oxe goe, where he shall not labour?	324	Proverbs		98
Take heede of an oxe before, of an horse behind,	351	Proverbs		900
An Oxe is taken by the horns, and a Man by the tongue.	353	Proverbs		967
Take an oxe by his hornes & a man by his tongue.	353	Proverbs	V	967
He that steals an egge, will steal an oxe.	358	Proverbs	D	1090
OXEN				
Beauty drawes more then oxen.	344	Proverbs		685
OYL				
My head with oyl, my cup with wine	173	23 Psalme		19
my arm and legge should be set, and my whole bodie anointed with oyl:	295	Cornaro		12
OYLE				
Truth and oyle are ever above.	328	Proverbs		234
To seek these things is lost labour; Geese in an oyle pot,	361	Proverbs	D	1163
OYNTMENT				
the one concerning the woman that spent the oyntment on our Saviour,	282	Priest 34		24
then he that reads the womans oyntment in the Gospell, or sees	283	Priest 34		2
PACE				
How canst thou stay, considering the pace	107	Home		7
The other curbs sinnes stealing pace and theft.	117	Providence		36
Though I halt in pace,	179	Discipline		14
And pace of thy swift vertues; onely they	211	Bohemia	D	5
Hee that stumbles and falles not, mends his pace.	321	Proverbs		7
PACES				
I went the slower, yet more paces,	203	Even-song	W	3
PACK				
Man is a shop of rules, a well truss'd pack,	12	Ch.-Porch		141
No, not to purchase the whole pack of starres:	101	Miserie		52
(as I think) at the sign of the Pedler and the Pack on London-bridge,	370	Letters		28
PACKT				
But all thy sweets are packt up in the other;	82	Ungratef.		19
My thoughts and joyes are all packt up and gone,	109	Home		69

	PAGE	TITLE	LINE
PADUA			
that they are in the fairest place of this learned Citie of Padua,	301	Cornaro	11
PAGANS			
Where Pagans tread. O Mother deare and kinde,	140	Ch.-rents	24
PAID			
Whose drops of bloud paid the full price,	76	Sunday	54
But all my scores were by another paid,	130	Love unkn.	60
A diligent Scholler, and the Master's paid.	327	Proverbs	183
A gift much expected is paid, not given.	340	Proverbs	574
PAIES			
Who paies the Physitian, does the cure.	350	Proverbs	879
Wine ever paies for his lodging.	352	Proverbs	930
PAIN			
A pain in that, wherein he findes a pleasure?	8	Ch.-Porch	40
A pain in that, whereof he findes a pleasure?	8	Ch.-Porch W	40
If well; the pain doth fade, the joy remains.	24	Ch.-Porch	462
Sinne is that presse and vice, which forceth pain	37	The Agonie	11
My flesh began unto my soul in pain,	47	Afflict.1	25
To cleare the breast, to mollifie all pain.	58	H.Script.1	4
To cleare the breast, to suple outward pain.	58	H.Script.1 W	4
Grieve over freshly all thy pain?	145	Discharge	50
For many weeks of lingring pain and smart	154	Glimpse	4
Deep drawn in pain,	162	The Search	18
When thou shalt look us out of pain,	172	The Glance	21
Come ye hither all, whom pain	180	Invitation	13
Hearken under pain of death,	182	Banquet	52
of their health, and so they will stand to the pain, all is well.	266	Priest 26	20
to wit, into the pain of the stomack, and often of the side,	291	Cornaro	22
and finding my self continually oppressed with pain and sicknesse,	292	Cornaro	19
and therefore out of an hope of avoiding death and pain,	292	Cornaro	21
a pain of the side took me, which held me two and twentie houres.	296	Cornaro	18
Cruelty is more cruell, if we defer the pain.	359	Proverbs D	1110
PAINE			
If this seeme Monkish; think which brings most paine	7	Ch.-Porch W	15
It's more paine to doe nothing then something.	350	Proverbs	884
PAINEFULL			
slight glories, which wee raise from bookes, and painefull industrie.	443	Oration	1
PAINES			
and to take more paines in their vocation, as not knowing when they	245	Priest 12	3
who live best, and take most paines, and are most charged:	245	Priest 12	16
some scoffing ruffian, who is likely to deride him for his paines:	273	Priest 31	29
Great paines quickly find ease.	339	Proverbs	534
Paines to get, care to keep, feare to lose.	353	Proverbs	975
PAINFUL			
for infirmities are both painful and costly.	365	Letters	1
PAINS			
Preachers conclude with, hath not lost his pains.	24	Ch.-Porch	434
If thou do ill; the joy fades, not the pains:	24	Ch.-Porch	461
A man so wrung with pains, that all his hair,	37	The Agonie	9
They will be kind, and all his pains requite,	101	Miserie W	46
Lesser pains scape greater ones.	113	Businesse	14
But when all my care and pains	114	Dialogue	5
Speed without pains, a horse: tall without height,	120	Providence	103
To turn his double pains to double praise.	132	Mans medly	36
Cure Tarantulas raging pains.	186	Dooms-day	12
That thou didst all those pains endure	200	H. Commun. W	20
he takes the more pains with them, that hee may lay the foundation	258	Priest 22	30
up their minds to better things, even in the midst of their pains.	261	Priest 23	26
to requite these pains, he takes place next the Doctors,	370	Letters	1
incessantly begging some ease of your pains, with that earnestness,	371	Letters	29
PAINT			
We paint the devil foul, yet he	63	Sinne 2	2
The Lyon is not so fierce as they paint him.	330	Proverbs	289
PAINTED			
Not to a true, but painted chair?	56	Jordan 1	5
For all they either painted are,	109	Brit. Ch.	11
Hath kiss'd so long her painted shrines,	110	Brit. Ch.	16
or painted there, which may excite the reader to a thought of piety;	240	Priest 10	24
and proper texts of Scripture every where painted, and that all	246	Priest 13	12
PAINTING			
where painted, and that all the painting be grave, and reverend,	246	Priest 13	12
also of excellent Artificers in Architecture, painting, stonecutting,	301	Cornaro	36
On painting and fighting looke aloofe.	329	Proverbs	247
PAIR			
A pair of Cheeks of them, is thy abuse.	206	Walton 2	7
PAIRE			
One paire of eares drawes dry a hundred tongues.	339	Proverbs	526
You cannot make a wind-mill goe with a paire of bellowes.	344	Proverbs	676
PALACE			
On which heav'ns palace arched lies:	75	Sunday	23
And built a braver Palace then before.	84	The World	20
So brave a Palace built; O dwell in it,	92	Man	50
He did surname his palace, Babylon.	195	Ch.-Milit.	182
PALACES			
In grottos, gardens, Palaces & Courts	40	Redemption W	11
I survey palaces, gardens, and antiquities, publick fabricks,	302	Cornaro	3
PALE			
When sicknesse makes him pale and wan.	92	Man	46
Turned your ruddie into pale and bleak:	140	Ch.-rents	19
PALENESSE			
Let a bleak palenesse chalk the doore,	177	Forerunners	35

	PAGE	TITLE		LINE
PAMPER				
Hast thou the knack? pamper it not with liking:	16	Ch.-Porch		243
and pamper their belly, although they see themselves ill handled	298	Cornaro		24
PAN				
And threw my heart into the scalding pan;	130	Love unkn.		35
PANG				
That I did live, but by a pang of woe.	47	Afflict.1	W	30
PANGS				
None shall in hell such bitter pangs endure, ...	24	Ch.-Porch		445
PANT				
Then shall our hearts pant thee; then shall our brain	54	Love 2		6
PAPER				
If this poore paper do as much as they.	104	Obedience		5
Within a sheet of paper, which was rent	192	Ch.-Milit.		95
and sent, which to the bearer is but paper, but to the receiver,	282	Priest 34		37
A white wall is the paper of a foole.	349	Proverbs		839
I shall never find time and paper enough, yet am I Your readiest	370	Letters		32
she is not disposed to spend her eyesight on a piece of paper,	371	Letters		14
PAPERS				
or, that my love is as dumb as my papers;	371	Letters		26
PAPIST				
as if he be a Papist, the Church is the hinge he turnes on; . . .	262	Priest 24		30
PAPISTS				
For at least some of the Papists are come now, to what the Pharisees	320	Valdesso		6
PARADICE				
In Gods rich Paradice.	75	Sunday	W	28
PARADISE				
The milkie way, the bird of Paradise, ...	51	Prayer 1		12
He might to heav'n from Paradise go, ...	53	H.Commun.		35
And fit for Paradise.	76	Sunday		56
That planted Paradise was not so firm, ...	97	Afflict.5		2
He was a garden in a Paradise:	102	Miserie		70
Paradise.	132	Paradise		T
And ev'n in Paradise to be a weed.	165	The Crosse		30
Fast in thy Paradise, where no flower can wither!	166	The Flower		23
Forfeit their Paradise by their pride.	167	The Flower		49
Who by an ambush lost his Paradise.	192	Ch.-Milit.		66
And wedd my soule in glorious paradise;	205	Persever.	W	10
So that even in Paradise man had a calling, and how much more out	274	Priest 32		21
and how much more out of Paradise, when the evills which he is now	274	Priest 32		22
then did'st thou place us in Paradise, and wert proceeding still	288	Priest		15
He that will enter into Paradise, must have a good key. . .	350	Proverbs		895
PARADOX				
A Paradox. That the Sicke are in better State then the Whole.	209	Paradox	D	T
PARALITIQUE				
(as Hectique, Paralitique, Apoplectique. Lethargique).	357	Proverbs	D	1044
PARALLELS				
Thy words do finde me out, & parallels bring, ...	58	H.Script.2		11
And parallels meet.	163	The Search		44
PARAPHRASE				
The soul in paraphrase, heart in pilgrimage, ...	51	Prayer 1		3
PARCEL				
that he hath bought a parcel of Books for me, and that they are	366	Letters		30
PARCEL'D				
How hath man parcel'd out thy glorious name, ...	54	Love 1		3
Parcel'd out to all the world.	187	Dooms-day		28
PARCELL				
Whose every parcell under-writes a law.	12	Ch.-Porch		142
Doth make thee parcell-devil in damnation.	16	Ch.-Porch		258
These parcell out thy heart: recover these, ...	147	Offering		17
PARCELL-DEVIL				
Doth make thee parcell-devil in damnation.	16	Ch.-Porch		258
PARCELS				
When I had got these parcels, instantly	112	JESU		7
PARDON				
Frailtie gets pardon by submissivenesse;	8	Ch.-Porch		51
For since confession pardon winnes, ...	126	Confession		27
Yet still askt pardon, and was not deni'd.	129	Love unkn.		21
Seek pardon first, and God will say, ...	134	The Method		31
Lord, pardon, for thy sonne makes good	136	Ephes.		35
For pardon of my imperfection	175	The Odour		19
and that the good God would pardon all those, who come with lesse	235	Priest 8		30
beseeching the Almighty to pardon and accept our poor services,	236	Priest 8		27
but pardon our sins, and perfect what thou hast begun. . . .	289	Priest		21
Pardon all but thy selfe.	344	Proverbs		677
Pardon my boldness Sir, it is a most serious Case, nor can I write	364	Letters		15
pardon my boldness, and consider but these three things. . .	365	Letters		15
pardon my boldness of inclosing my Brothers Letter in yours,	367	Letters		23
you and my dear Mother and Sister to pardon me, for my Cambridge	369	Letters		18
circumstance, yet you will pardon my haste, which is very great,	370	Letters		12
your Courtesie will pardon the haste of Your humblest Servant,	371	Letters		19
Dear Madam, pardon my boldness, and, accept the good meaning of,	374	Letters		30
PARDONING				
pardoning my sins, and bidding me go feed the people of thy love.	289	Priest		6
amplify your favour to mee in pardoning Your most indebted kinsman	369	Letters		4
PARDONS				
Pardons and pleasantnesse are great revenges of slanders. . .	333	Proverbs		365
Pardons and pleasantnesse are great Revengers of slanders. . .	333	Proverbs	V	365
The offender never pardons.	340	Proverbs		561
PARE				
And with thy knife but prune and PARE, ...	133	Paradise		11

	PAGE	TITLE		LINE
PARENTAGE				
I know thy parentage is base and low:	77	Avarice		3
PARENTS				
Parents first season us: then schoolmasters	45	Sinne 1		2
Secondly, that Parents, and Masters, as they hear the answers prove,	255	Priest 21		27
But Parents, and Masters should make hast in this, as to a great	259	Priest 22		2
and not ingaged into some Profession by their Parents, whose neglect	277	Priest 32		26
For when they saw their parents and kindred snatcht away in the midst	291	Cornaro		9
God, and Parents, and our Master, can never be requited. . . .	348	Proverbs		805
Children when they are little make parents fooles, ...	352	Proverbs		939
Children when they are little make their parents fooles, . .	352	Proverbs	V	939
Infants manners are moulded more by the example of Parents, . .	357	Proverbs	D	1060
PARENTS'				
To parents issue and the sunnes bright starre!	168	The Sonne		6
To parents issue and the sonnes bright starre!	168	The Sonne	V	6
PARES				
He pares his apple, that will cleanly feed.	9	Ch.-Porch		64
he pares the apple, and gives them the clean to feed on. . .	283	Priest 35		32
PARIS				
And Paris garden. Then let there perfume	212	Bohemia	D	51
To my dear brother, Mr. Henry Herbert, at Paris.	366	Letters		27
PARISH				
as a Parsons to his Parish, in describing the one (which is indeed	226	Priest 2		17
most in those things which are most apt to scandalize his Parish.	227	Priest 3		11
least all those which he observeth are most incident to his Parish.	230	Priest 5		35
If there be any of the gentry or nobility of the Parish, . .	232	Priest 6		7
and those most, which are nearest to his Parish;	233	Priest 7		9
or as the temper of his Parish may be, where he may have occasion	237	Priest 9		2
governing of his house, making it a copy and modell for his Parish.	239	Priest 10		7
Having then invited some of his Parish, hee taketh his times to do	243	Priest 11		18
if not the best way, yet any way, make his Parish good. . .	244	Priest 11		5
He first considers his own Parish, and takes care, that there be	244	Priest 12		19
or idle person in his Parish, but that all bee in a competent way	244	Priest 12		20
If his Parish be rich, he exacts this of them;	244	Priest 12		24
After the consideration of his own Parish, he inlargeth himself,	245	Priest 12		18
to visite in person, now one quarter of his Parish, now another.	247	Priest 14		5
it about with him as fully, as if he had begot his whole Parish.	250	Priest 16		10
a just occasion calleth him out of his Parish (which he diligently,	250	Priest 17		24
his Parish being all his joy, and thought) leaveth not his Ministry	250	Priest 17		25
unto him in any difficulty, either in his studies or in his Parish.	253	Priest 19		9
Ministeriall office, which is not to the prejudice of his own Parish.	253	Priest 19		18
or famine, tc any neighbouring Parish, then he expects no Briefe;	253	Priest 19		30
but taking his Parish together the next Sunday, or holy-day,	253	Priest 19		31
The Countrey Parson is in Gods stead to his Parish, and dischargeth	254	Priest 20		8
growing with the growth of his Parish.	255	Priest 21		16
especially since many remove from Parish to Parish, who like	255	Priest 21		19
especially since many remove from Parish to Parish, who like	255	Priest 21		20
The Countrey Parson desires to be all to his Parish, and not onely	259	Priest 23		29
three or four of the ablest of the Parish to hear the cause with him,	260	Priest 23		9
that if the poorest man of the Parish detain but a pin unjustly from	260	Priest 23		14
some young practicioner in his house for the benefit of his Parish,	260	Priest 23		35
neighbour Phisician, and entertaines him for the Cure of his Parish.	261	Priest 23		1
yet he looks not in this point of Curing beyond his own Parish,	262	Priest 23		13
if there be any of his parish that hold strange Doctrins, . .	262	Priest 24		19
especially in his own Parish he suffers it not to his utmost power;	268	Priest 28		18
even of the best in the Parish, when occasion requires: . .	268	Priest 28		28
the whole order and discipline of the Parish is put into their hands.	269	Priest 29		29
the Law concerning such goods for the use and profit of their Parish:	270	Priest 29		4
not onely taken a particular Survey of the faults of his own Parish,	274	Priest 32		5
the Village or Parish which either he lives in, or is neer unto it,	276	Priest 32		2
that his Parish at good times invite one another to their houses,	284	Priest 35		17
values the gift in himself, and then teacheth his parish to value it.	286	Priest 36		19
but also spread in his Parish, without any remedy (which cannot be	287	Priest 37		1
pounds unto the poore of this parish to be devided according to my	382	G.H.'s Will		17
to the poore of the parish twenty pound To my Lord of Cherbury tenn	383	G.H.'s Will		13
PARISHES				
some in Noble houses, some in Parishes residing on their Cures.	226	Priest 2		1
excellent statute, which bindes all Parishes to maintaine their own.	244	Priest 12		23
and debt of neighbourhood to all the Parishes which are neer him.	253	Priest 19		21
Estate in twc parishes is bread in two wallets.	328	Proverbs		231
PARISHIONERS				
and of Courtesie to his other parishioners, he so distinguisheth,	243	Priest 11		7
wherein he chooseth to permit his Parishioners rather to make use	260	Priest 23		19
PARKS				
In cities, theatres, gardens, parks, and courts:	40	Redemption		11
PARLEY				
With thine own clay. But I would parley fain:	139	Artillerie		27
PARLIAMENT				
When there is a Parliament, he is to endeavour by all means to be	277	Priest 32		9
for there is no School to a Parliament.	277	Priest 32		11
PARLIES				
Valour that parlies is neare yeelding.	341	Proverbs		586
A City that parlies is half gotten.	358	Proverbs	D	1097
PARLOUR				
Not in his parlour; banquetting the poore, ...	87	Lent		47
PARODIE				
A Parodie.	183	A Parodie		T
PARRATS				
Parrats may thank us, if they are not mute, ...	91	Man		11
service, Rom. 12. when we speak not as Parrats, without reason,	232	Priest 6		3
as parrats, without ever piercing into the sense of it. . .	256	Priest 21		4

PARSON	PAGE	TITLE	LINE
The Countrey PARSON HIS CHARACTER, AND Rule of Holy Life.	223	Priest	T
The Countrey Parson is exceeding exact in his Life, being holy,	227	Priest 3	1
the Countrey Parson is very circumspect in avoiding all	227	Priest 3	15
the Parson is very carefull to avoid all the kinds thereof,	227	Priest 3	22
The Parson doth not so, but orders his Life in such a fashion,	227	Priest 3	31
therfore the Parson is very strict in keeping his word,	228	Priest 3	4
The Countrey Parson is full of all knowledg.	228	Priest 4	14
the places controverted, which the Parson by no means refuseth.	229	Priest 4	18
The Countrey Parson hath read the Fathers also, and the Schoolmen,	229	Priest 5	31
Yet hath the Parson, besides this laborious work, a slighter forme	230	Priest 5	15
is the greatest ability of a Parson to lead his people exactly in	230	Priest 5	21
Wherefore the Parson hath throughly canvassed al the particulars	230	Priest 5	33
The Parson praying.	231	Priest 6	T
The Countrey Parson, when he is to read divine services,	231	Priest 6	1
The Parson preaching.	232	Priest 7	T
The Countrey Parson preacheth constantly, the pulpit is his joy	232	Priest 7	20
By these and other means the Parson procures attention;	233	Priest 7	22
The Parson exceeds not an hour in preaching, because all ages have	235	Priest 7	10
The Parson on Sundays.	235	Priest 8	T
The Country Parson, as soon as he awakes on Sunday morning,	235	Priest 8	16
The Country Parson considering that virginity is a higher state then	236	Priest 9	31
other spirituall wickednesses in high places doth the Parson fear,	238	Priest 9	21
If the Parson be unmarryed, and means to continue so, he doth	238	Priest 9	24
The Parson in his house.	239	Priest 10	T
The Parson is very exact in the governing of his house,	239	Priest 10	6
The Parson in his house observes fasting dayes;	241	Priest 10	35
To conclude, the Parson, if he be in full health, keeps the three	242	Priest 10	26
The Countrey Parson owing a debt of Charity to the poor,	243	Priest 11	6
Which perswasion the Parson by all means avoyds, knowing that where	243	Priest 11	22
So the Countrey Parson, who is a diligent observer, and tracker	244	Priest 11	1
The Countrey Parson is full of Charity;	244	Priest 12	6
But the Parson having a double aime, and making a hook of his	244	Priest 12	30
The Countrey Parson hath a speciall care of his Church,	246	Priest 13	1
The Parson in Circuit.	247	Priest 14	T
The Countrey Parson upon the afternoons in the weekdays,	247	Priest 14	3
Those that the Parson findes idle, or ill imployed, he chides	248	Priest 14	13
the Parson questions what order is kept in the house, as about	248	Priest 14	31
If the Parson were ashamed of particularizing in these things,	248	Priest 14	38
of particularizing in these things, hee were not fit to be a Parson:	249	Priest 14	1
The Parson Comforting.	249	Priest 15	T
The Countrey Parson, when any of his cure is sick, or afflicted	249	Priest 15	13
The Parson a Father.	250	Priest 16	T
The Countrey Parson is not only a father to his flock, but also	250	Priest 16	7
The Parson in Journey.	250	Priest 17	T
The Countrey Parson, when a just occasion calleth him out of his	250	Priest 17	23
The Parson in Sentinell.	252	Priest 18	T
The Countrey Parson, where ever he is, keeps Gods watch;	252	Priest 18	1
The Parson in reference.	252	Priest 19	T
The Countrey Parson is sincere and upright in all his relations.	252	Priest 19	24
The Parson in Gods stead.	254	Priest 20	T
The Countrey Parson is in Gods stead to his Parish, and dischargeth	254	Priest 20	8
the Parson endeavoureth to be in Gods stead, knowing that Countrey	254	Priest 20	30
The Parson Catechizing.	255	Priest 21	T
The Countrey Parson values Catechizing highly:	255	Priest 21	1
when the Parson once demanded after other questions about mans	257	Priest 21	1
This is the Practice which the Parson so much commends to all his	257	Priest 21	16
The Parson in Sacraments.	257	Priest 22	T
The Countrey Parson being to administer the Sacraments,	257	Priest 22	26
as the Parson useth all reverence himself, so he administers to none	259	Priest 22	11
of the Communion, the Parson celebrates it, if not duly once a month,	259	Priest 22	20
The Countrey Parson desires to be all to his Parish, and not onely	259	Priest 23	29
he hath so done, then he assumes the Parson, and exhorts to Charity.	260	Priest 23	17
Now as the Parson is in Law, so is he in sicknesse also:	260	Priest 23	28
the Parson useth damask or white Roses for the one, and plantaine,	261	Priest 23	34
the Parson and his Family use to premise prayers, for this is to cure	262	Priest 23	9
for this is to cure like a Parson, and this raiseth the action from	262	Priest 23	10
But though the Parson sets forward all Charitable deeds,	262	Priest 23	11
The Parson arguing.	262	Priest 24	T
The Countrey Parson, if there be any of his parish that hold strange	262	Priest 24	19
Wherefore the Parson hath diligently examined these two	262	Priest 24	31
The Parson punishing.	263	Priest 25	T
Whensoever the Countrey Parson proceeds so farre as to call in	263	Priest 25	22
The Countrey Parson at spare times from action, standing on a hill,	264	Priest 26	3
Wherefore the Parson being true to his businesse, hath exactly sifted	264	Priest 26	31
Secondly, for Gluttony, The Parson lays this ground:	266	Priest 26	6
But the Parson distinguisheth according to his double aime,	267	Priest 26	15
The Parson in mirth.	267	Priest 27	T
The Countrey Parson is generally sad, because hee knows nothing	267	Priest 27	27
The Parson in Contempt.	268	Priest 28	T
The Countrey Parson knows well, that both for the generall ignominy	268	Priest 28	9
the Parson having a due respect both to the person, and to the cause,	268	Priest 28	33
the Parson think it in his discretion either unfit, or bootelesse	269	Priest 28	4
The Parson with his Church-Wardens.	269	Priest 29	T
The Countrey Parson doth often, both publickly, and privately	269	Priest 29	26
Wherefore the Parson suffers not the place to be vilified or debased,	270	Priest 29	7
the Parson adviseth them to read, or hear them read often,	270	Priest 29	13
The Countrey Parson considering the great aptnesse Countrey people	270	Priest 30	24
The Parson in Liberty.	272	Priest 31	T
The Countrey Parson observing the manifold wiles of Satan (who playes	272	Priest 31	15
Here the Parson interposeth with his distinction, and shews	273	Priest 31	3

PARSON (cont'd)	PAGE	TITLE		LINE
The Countrey Parson hath not onely taken a particular Survey	274	Priest 32		4
Wherefore the Parson strongly opposeth this sin, whersoever he goes.	274	Priest 32		14
Therfore the Parson unmoved, sheweth, that ingenuous and fit	275	Priest 32		9
And the Parson is a lover of and exciter to justice in all things,	277	Priest 32		22
those whom the Parson finds loose, and not ingaged into some	277	Priest 32		24
So that the Parson having studied, and mastered all his lusts	278	Priest 33		21
Thus the Parson considering that repentance is the great vertue	279	Priest 33		6
This Instruction and comfort the Parson getting for himself,	279	Priest 33		32
The Countrey Parson knows, that there is a double state	280	Priest 34		1
Now the Parson having a Spirituall Judgement, according as he	280	Priest 34		11
Those that the Parson findes in the military state, he fortifyes,	281	Priest 34		5
If the Parson suspect the first, and find sparkes of such thoughts	281	Priest 34		12
at severall times and occasions, the Parson setleth wavering minds.	283	Priest 34		4
The Countrey Parson is a Lover of old Customes, if they be good,	283	Priest 35		27
And the Parson likes this very well;	284	Priest 35		24
The Parson Blessing.	285	Priest 36		T
The Countrey Parson wonders, that Blessing the people is in so little	285	Priest 36		1
But the Parson first values the gift in himself, and then teacheth	286	Priest 36		18
The Countrey Parson perceiving, that most, when they are at leasure,	286	Priest 37		29
Now the Parson taking this point to task, which is so exceeding	287	Priest 37		7
PARSON'S				
as a Parsons to his Parish, in describing the one (which is indeed	226	Priest 2		17
The Parsons Life.	227	Priest 3		T
The Parsons yea is yea, and nay nay;	228	Priest 3		10
The Parsons Knowledg.	228	Priest 4		T
The Parsons Accessary Knowledges.	229	Priest 5		T
The Parson's state of Life.	236	Priest 9		T
The Parson's Courtesie.	243	Priest 11		T
The Parson's Charity.	244	Priest 12		T
The Parson's Church.	246	Priest 13		T
These are the Parsons generall aims in his Circuit;	249	Priest 14		10
The Parsons punishing of sin and vice, is rather by withdrawing his	254	Priest 20		22
The Parson's Completenesse.	259	Priest 23		T
For home-bred medicines are both more easie for the Parsons purse,	261	Priest 23		31
The Parson's eye.	264	Priest 26		T
The Parson's Consideration of Providence.	270	Priest 30		T
The Parson's Surveys.	274	Priest 32		T
The Parson's Library.	278	Priest 33		T
The Countrey Parson's Library is a holy Life:	278	Priest 33		11
The Parson's Dexterity in applying of Remedies.	280	Priest 34		T
The Parson's Condescending.	283	Priest 35		T
PARSONS				
Doubtlesse they are Parsons of the families they live in,	226	Priest 2		21
The Parsons Methcd in handling of a text consists of two parts;	234	Priest 7		36
Thirdly, that he might set a Copy for Parsons.	261	Priest 23		26
Parsons are soules waggoners.	352	Proverbs		938
PART				
Before thy journey fairly part with all.	13	Ch.-Porch		162
Servants and churches also play their part.	14	Ch.-Porch		196
Let vain or busie thoughts have there no part:	23	Ch.-Porch		421
Let vain & busie thoughts have there no part:	23	Ch.-Porch	W	421
Wherefore each part	26	The Altar		9
Or feel his part, he would not cease to kneel,	33	Sacrifice		210
They part my garments, and by lot dispose	34	Sacrifice		241
My God, my God, why dost thou part from me?	35	Thanksgvng		9
Comes to about the many hundredth part.	38	The Sinner		11
Comes to about the many hundred part.	38	The Sinner	W	11
Awake, my lute, and struggle for thy part	41	Easter		7
O let thy blessed Spirit bear a part,	42	Easter		17
So many joyes I writ down for my part,	46	Afflict.1		3
Which spread their forces into every part,	52	H.Commun.		11
Must bear the longest part.	53	Antiphon 1		12
Must bear the chiefest part.	53	Antiphon 1	V	12
Precious for any grief in any part;	58	H.Script.1		3
Or starre, or rainbow, or a part	62	Mattens		7
Comfort, I'le die; for if you part from me,	66	Ch.-mus.	W	9
did play their part	66	Ch.-lock	W	4
But though men fail him, yet his part doth play.	73	Constancie		30
Hadst thou nct had thy part,	73	Afflict.3		5
Of him, who dy'd to part	74	The Starre		23
The worky-daies are the back-part;	75	Sunday		11
A part whereof my Saviour empti'd hath,	83	Sighs & Gr.		22
Yet to go part of that religious way,	87	Lent		32
Each part may call the farthest, brother:	91	Man		16
Each part may call the furthest, brother:	91	Man	V	16
I took, without more thinking, in good part	94	Life		8
To make us thine: yet that we might not part,	97	Afflict.5		10
To gain thy thirds and little part.	99	Decay		15
Cavill, and claim her part and measure,	104	Obedience		12
How happie were my part,	105	Obedience		41
The fight is hard on either part.	106	Sion		15
That as I did freely part	115	Dialogue		29
For death is drie as dust. Yet if ye part,	135	Ephes.		10
As if they had a part?	136	Familie		2
Title to more hereafter when they part,	137	The Size		3
Onely the present is thy part and fee.	144	Discharge		21
To them a part:	148	Longing		16
That ev'ry part	150	Longing		75
But constant to his part	154	Glimpse		18
Thou art not onely to perform thy part,	156	Assurance		27

PART (cont'd)	PAGE	TITLE	LINE
Such a Love, as none can part:	156	The Call	11
If truly said, they may take part	168	a true Hymn	7
Something that may be conquest on my part	201	love W	5
Sir John Danvers' earthly part	208	J. Danvers D	9
Strive each to play their Part.	213	Convert D	5
other answers, which are on the Clerks and peoples part to answer;	231	Priest 6	29
for the most part, serve but the vices and vanities of the world,	240	Priest 10	3
be diligently perused, as being the practicall part, and of most use.	261	Priest 23	8
wiles of Satan (who playes his part sometimes in drawing Gods	272	Priest 31	16
but also of any part, by taking away so much as the usuall seasons	281	Priest 34	23
because infamy is a part of the sentence against malefactours,	287	Priest 37	18
a tincture of private malice in the joy, and hast of acting his part;	287	Priest 37	28
It is not the part of a wise man, to expose himself to so many	300	Cornaro	22
But the use of the Doctrinall part is more, in regard it presents us	310	Valdesso	32
Hee that repaires not a part, builds all.	333	Proverbs	344
Hee that repaires not a part, at length must all.	333	Proverbs V	344
The eye will have his part.	337	Proverbs	466
For my own part, my meaning (dear Mother) is in these Sonnets,	363	Letters	9
and it is the part of a poor spirit to undervalue himself and blush.	366	Letters	18
who have already abundantly discharg'd that part, having both ordered	373	Letters	12
and would not have to part them yet, till I take some opportunity	375	Letters	20
So I doe my part to them, lett them think of me what they will	376	Letters	6
the chiefest also, so also have I required Mr W. for his part.	378	Letters	24
PARTAKE			
Thy businesse his, and in thy life partake:	144	Discharge	18
All may of thee partake:	184	The Elixer	13
that if any be willing to partake, they may resort thither. . . .	251	Priest 17	12
PARTAKES			
Partakes already half of hell.	123	Time	24
PARTED			
Parted with alleys or with grass	75	Sunday W	27
parted with rills of running water, which truely is very delightfull.	301	Cornaro	15
PARTER			
The parter of my wrangling feares, ...	75	Sunday W	4
PARTIALL			
being partiall to themselves, and witty to others who shall reprove	264	Priest 26	13
PARTICIPATION			
the participation of the holy Sacrament, how comfortable, . . .	250	Priest 15	1
PARTICULAR			
With an exact and most particular trust, ...	51	Faith	43
the determination of the second rule by Authority to this particular.	242	Priest 10	6
for as when the offence is particular, and against mee, . . .	248	Priest 14	26
from his particular, to his Church;	249	Priest 15	20
in perswading them to particular confession, labouring to make them	249	Priest 15	29
Parson hath not onely taken a particular Survey of the faults of his	274	Priest 32	4
and either helps them in particular, or hath generall Propositions	276	Priest 32	4
which though our Saviour reproved as unfitting for his particular,	285	Priest 36	27
promises to every one in particular with such syncerity and efficacy,	309	Valdesso	5
difficulty of applying their generall rules to particular actions,	319	Valdesso V	32
if it were not begun on particular ends, it would last). . . .	361	Proverbs D	1160
PARTICULARIZING			
and with particularizing of his speech now to the younger sort,	233	Priest 7	3
If the Parson were ashamed of particularizing in these things,	248	Priest 14	38
PARTICULARLY			
and particularly, as Sunday is his day of joy, so Friday his day	241	Priest 10	36
particularly, the rule may be this:	258	Priest 22	33
Particularly, concerning these two vices, not because they are all	265	Priest 26	1
More particularly, and to give one instance for all, if God have	265	Priest 26	19
to descend yet more particularly, if a man hath wherewithall to buy	265	Priest 26	28
and particularly do it, then he that is generally learned, . . .	278	Priest 33	28
And particularly, having doubted sometimes, whether his repentance	279	Priest 33	9
Particularly, he counselleth them to two things:	280	Priest 34	16
Particularly, he loves Procession, and maintains it, because there	284	Priest 35	1
particularly, blesse it in this thy own Kingdom, which thou hast made	289	Priest	17
Particularly, I like all your Addresses, & for ought I see, . . .	378	Letters	16
PARTICULARS			
Parson hath throughly canvassed al the particulars of humane actions,	230	Priest 5	34
for particulars ever touch, and awake more then generalls. . . .	233	Priest 7	5
be amisse in this exceeding usefull point to descend to particulars:	275	Priest 32	18
for exactnesse lyes in particulars.	275	Priest 32	19
for there the particulars are exactly discussed, which are brought	277	Priest 32	13
PARTIE			
And made a partie unawares for wo.	47	Afflict.1	24
In vies of favours whether partie gains, ...	88	The Pearl	13
The absent partie is still faultie.	332	Proverbs	318
PARTIES			
by withdrawing his bounty and courtesie from the parties offending,	254	Priest 20	23
hee takes one of the parties, and goes with him to the other,	284	Priest 35	20
PARTING			
At my last parting from you, I was the better content because I was	372	Letters	14
PARTITION			
Rending with earthquakes the partition-wall:	190	Ch.-Milit.	26
PARTITION-WALL			
Rending with earthquakes the partition-wall:	190	Ch.-Milit.	26
PARTITIONS			
Thy passions also have their set partitions.	147	Offering	16
PARTLY			
And crusht the building: and it's partly true, ...	127	Giddinesse	15
partly for obedience to Authority, partly for uniformity sake,	255	Priest 21	17
partly for uniformity sake, that the same common truths may be every	255	Priest 21	17

	PAGE	TITLE	LINE
PARTNER			
The partner of my wrangling feares,	75	Sunday WC	4
PARTRIDGE			
Some mark a partridge, never their childes fashion:	10	Ch.-Porch	99
PARTS			
Kindnesse, good parts, great places are the way	19	Ch.-Porch	327
Whose parts are as thy hand did frame;	26	The Altar	3
Or since all musick is but three parts vied	42	Easter	15
And carrie with them th' other parts.	49	Repentance	30
Fretting to death our other parts.	49	Repentance W	30
Leaping the wall that parts	52	H.Commun.	14
Which parts their ranks and orders.	75	Sunday	28
And fall, like rheumes, upon the tendrest parts.	126	Confession	12
Then did your sev'rall parts unloose and start:	140	Ch.-rents	21
Have I no parts but those of grief?	143	Complaining	15
The Parsons Method in handling of a text consists of two parts;	235	Priest 7	1
Whereas the other way of crumbling a text into small parts,	235	Priest 7	6
and dearths, he even parts his Living, and life among them,	245	Priest 12	10
Wealth is like rheume, it falles on the weakest parts.	337	Proverbs	475
PARTY (see also partie)			
This is to be on Gods side, and be true to his party.	252	Priest 18	15
PASCHAL			
And readie Paschal Lambe of this great week:	28	Sacrifice	59
PASS			
I pass the shades, & fixe upon the true	43	H. Bapt.1 W	4
If glorious bodies pass the sight	201	H. Commun. W	34
Into my soule this cannot pass	201	H. Commun. W	37
PASSAGE			
Is all the passage, on my infancie	44	H. Bapt.2	3
Is by a ship the speedier passage made.	119	Providence	90
The Doctrine of the last passage must be warily understood.	308	Valdesso	1
PASSAGES			
to acquaint you with those passages of newes which this time affords;	368	Letters	1
PASSE			
Onely a herauld, who that way doth passe,	14	Ch.-Porch	197
Oh all ye, who passe by, whose eyes and minde	26	Sacrifice	1
O let this cup passe, if it be thy pleasure:	27	Sacrifice	23
But I the Prince of peace; peace that doth passe	30	Sacrifice	118
O all ye who passe by, behold and see;	33	Sacrifice	201
May no lines passe, except they do their dutie	56	Jordan 1	4
To passe it self and all it hath to thee.	104	Obedience	8
To passe it self and all it has to thee.	104	Obedience W	8
He that will passe his land,	105	Obedience	36
Come dearest Lord, passe not this holy season,	109	Home	73
They vent the wares, and passe them with their faults,	122	Sinnes rd.	9
They vent the wares, and passe them with their fauts	122	Sinnes rd. V	9
Perhaps some such of old did passe,	122	Time	7
No sale or bargain passe: all would disperse,	127	Giddinesse	23
I passe away and leave it dead?	135	Ephes.	6
And I will passe.	163	The Search	36
Then to the streams that gently passe:	172	23 Psalme	7
I passe not, I, what of the rest become,	176	Forerunners	9
Yet if you go, I passe not; take your way:	177	Forerunners	31
Or if he pleaseth, through it passe,	184	The Elixer	11
And such poore game. Thence he to Greece doth passe,	193	Ch.-Milit.	123
And such small game. Thence he to Greece doth passe,	193	Ch.-Milit. W	123
Readie to passe to the American strand.	196	Ch.-Milit.	236
Passe not by,	208	J. Danvers D	1
as I passe, in my heart) because this kinde of Prayer is additionary,	273	Priest 31	35
that that generation should not passe, till all were fulfilled,	282	Priest 34	29
I should be a conquerour, as also a little after it came to passe:	294	Cornaro	27
I am not wearie of life, which I passe witn great delight.	301	Cornaro	3
the Doctrine would be examined, however it may passe for his opinion:	312	Valdesso	1
Were there no fooles, badd ware would not passe.	323	Proverbs	66
Take heede of still waters, the quick passe away.	326	Proverbs	171
PASS'D			
Who have pass'd my right away.	177	The Rose	12
PASSED			
As if this passed with a reservation,	104	Obedience	13
or else such as have passed judgment, & been corrected either	287	Priest 37	15
PASSENGERS'			
To be all passengers most sweet relief?	81	Christmas	8
PASSETH			
A toy shunn'd cleanly passeth with the best.	15	Ch.-Porch	228
As passeth thought:	163	The Search	38
For thy neatnesse passeth sight,	181	Banquet	4
Passeth tongue to taste or tell.	181	Banquet	6
and so the thing passeth with more authority, and lesse envy.	260	Priest 23	12
when his storing, which was even now good, passeth from good to bad.	264	Priest 26	30
He that passeth a winters day escapes an enemy.	349	Proverbs	864
this passeth in Spaine freely with consent of King & counsell.	368	Letters	29
PASSING			
Are passing brave.	137	The Size	4
Making a chiming of a passing-bell.	166	The Flower	18
Passing all cordials made by any art,	171	The Glance	6
because of the suddain passing from that which was just now lawfull,	264	Priest 26	20
either for fear or shame, break his custome, he shall do passing ill:	273	Priest 31	31
passing from the ear to the heart, from the heart to the life	289	Priest	30
all superfluities passing away without difficultie, and no ill	293	Cornaro	28
passing daily our neighboring Sea, wondrously sound through all our	442	Oration	23

	PAGE	TITLE		LINE
PASSING-BELL				
Making a chiming of a passing-bell.	166	The Flower		18
PASSION				
No more then passion when shee talkes of it.	19	Ch.-Porch	W	318
As for thy passion - But of that anon,	35	Thanksgvng		29
Then for thy passion - I will do for that -	36	Thanksgvng		49
There is no dealing with thy mighty passion:	36	Reprisall		2
There is no medling with thy mighty passion:	36	Reprisall	W	2
The Passion.	39	Good Fri.	WC	T
The Passion.	40	Redemption	W	T
Of an untrained hope or passion.	68	Content		6
Of an untrained hope & passion.	68	Content	V	6
Of an untrained hope and passion.	68	Content	W	6
With the same shake, which at his passion	76	Sunday		45
But is compos'd of passion.	86	Lent		3
But is a child of passion.	86	Lent	W	3
That led me to the wilde of passion, which	142	Pilgrimage		13
And judge our selves. That light, which sin & passion	171	Self-cond.		20
who was to shew all humility before his Passion, yet he allows in his	285	Priest 36		28
neither melancholie, nor any other passion can hurt a temperate life.	294	Cornaro		31
PASSIONS				
Whom all his passions follcw, as he goes.	15	Ch.-Porch		216
Is a good spurre. Correct thy passions spite;	16	Ch.-Porch		263
With sick folks, women, those whom passions sway,	73	Constancie		27
Thy passions also have their set partitions.	147	Offering		16
A noise of passions ringing me for dead	174	Aaron		8
PAST				
That which is past who can recall?	144	Discharge		10
And while it cometh, it is almost past.	145	Discharge		53
The late-past frosts tributes of pleasure bring.	165	The Flower		4
The late-past frcsts tributes of pleasures bring.	165	The Flower	V	4
O that I once past changing were,	166	The Flower		22
Before the other. Greece being past her prime,	191	Ch.-Milit.		60
he often overturnes things, when they are thought past danger;	271	Priest 30		21
The mill cannot grind with the water that's past.	326	Proverbs		153
The river past, and God forgotten.	327	Proverbs		207
Say no ill of the yeere, till it be past.	331	Proverbs		297
and by that which is past, see	332	Proverbs		329
that whether you turn your thoughts on the life past, or on the Joyes	373	Letters		18
of his praise, nc, not, as in past ages, those Pillars of Hercules.	442	Oration		12
PASTIME				
Hunger makes dinners, pastime suppers.	348	Proverbs		819
PASTOR				
Of a Pastor.	225	Priest 1		T
A Pastor is the Deputy of Christ for the reducing of Man	225	Priest 1		1
he thinks it the most usefull way that a Pastor can take,	256	Priest 21		2
and the discomfort, discredit, & hinderance of the Pastor.	287	Priest 37		5
PASTORAGE				
and pastorage, and makes great use of them in teaching,	228	Priest 4		18
PASTORALL				
which I have observed, untill the Book grow to a compleat Pastorall.	224	Priest		16
and containes the direct steps of Pastorall Duty and Auctority.	225	Priest 1		3
PASTORS				
Of Pastors (intending mine own Nation only, and also therein setting	225	Priest 2		20
PASTOUR				
I have resolved to set down the Form and Character of a true Pastour,	224	Priest		7
to be all to his Parish, and not onely a Pastour, but a Lawyer also,	259	Priest 23		30
PASTOUR'S				
since our Saviour hath made that the argument of a Pastour's love,	224	Priest		6
PASTOURS				
Correspondence with all the neighbouring Pastours round about him,	253	Priest 19		16
PASTURE				
Are gone to grasse, and in the pasture lost.	10	Ch.-Porch		96
The pasture is thy word: the streams, thy grace	81	Christmas		19
PATE				
And on his own accursed pate	222	Psalm VII	D	59
PATENTS				
by the Patents of your perpetual favour to do so still,	365	Letters		24
PATH				
Then he'l take notice of: in ev'ry path	92	Man		44
Take the gentle path.	178	Discipline		4
Every path hath a puddle.	328	Proverbs		215
PATHS				
Allows thee choise of paths: take no by-wayes;	7	Ch.-Porch		14
PATIENCE				
God takes a text, and preacheth patience.	23	Ch.-Porch		432
He that gets patience, and the blessing which	24	Ch.-Porch		433
I answer nothing, but with patience prove	29	Sacrifice		89
Is Patience:	66	Ch.-floore		3
wherein a Christian is most seen, are Patience, and Mortification;	227	Priest 3		4
Patience in regard of afflictions, Mortification in regard of lusts	227	Priest 3		5
as to be cloathed with perfect patience, and Christian fortitude in	237	Priest 9		37
produce any speciall grace of faith, patience, meeknesse,	238	Priest 9		32
But thou Lord, art patience, and pity, and sweetnesse, and love;	288	Priest		21
Peace, and Patience, and death with repentance.	332	Proverbs		319
Hee that hath patience hath fatt thrushes for a farthing.	336	Proverbs		430
Patience, time and money accommodate all things.	338	Proverbs		498
yet we must have patience.	353	Proverbs		980
PATIENT				
and wondreth not so much at their patient suffering, and cheerfull	237	Priest 9		29
that the patient might be proportionable to the agent, and especially	295	Cornaro		31

	PAGE	TITLE		LINE
PATIENT (cont'd)				
when he cometh to visit his patient, prescribes this Physick first,	297	Cornaro		16
He that will be served must bee patient.	333	Proverbs		354
The Physitian owes all to the patient, ...	351	Proverbs		921
but the patient owes nothing to him but a little mony. . . .	351	Proverbs		921
PATIENTLY				
Thus farre Time heard me patiently:	123	Time		27
PATRIARK				
I ever tooke that for a weaknesse in the great Patriark: . .	316	Valdesso		1
PATTERN				
The pattern, but not so in vertuous deeds;	196	Ch.-Milit.		222
PAUL				
And therefore St. Paul in the beginning of his Epistles, . .	225	Priest 1		9
he himself were with Saint Paul even sacrificed upon the service	234	Priest 7		8
And herein St Paul excelled in all his Epistles.	234	Priest 7		11
wherein (as Saint Paul implyes that he ought, Romans 2.) hee first	279	Priest 33		35
So did St. Paul, 2 Tim. 4. 14. and 1 Tim. 1. 20.	285	Priest 36		31
and in our age, Paul the third, and Cardinal Bembo, who therefore	299	Cornaro		1
be a restraining motion (as S. Paul had when hee would have preached	313	Valdesso		16
Give not S. Peter so much, to leave Saint Paul nothing. . .	346	Proverbs		763
Who praiseth Saint Peter, doth not blame Saint Paul. . . .	349	Proverbs		859
only one place more to you (Philip. 4. 4.) St. Paul saith there:	374	Letters		21
that (which you are thinking to doe) to blessed Mary Magd. & Paul,	381	Woodnoth		5
PAUL'S				
according to St. Pauls rule, Ephes. 4. 28. 1 Thes. 4. 11, 12.	275	Priest 32		2
our Saviours selling is so far from crossing Saint Pauls working,	275	Priest 32		4
nor Paul's neither, when he professed himselfe a Pharisee, . .	316	Valdesso		7
PAUSABLY				
of their answer, but gently and pausably, thinking what they say;	231	Priest 6		32
PAUSING				
between fear and zeal, pausing yet pressing, he performes his duty.	231	Priest 6		20
PAVED				
as walls plaistered, windows glazed, floore paved, seats whole, firm,	246	Priest 13		5
PAW				
The angrie Lion did present his paw, ...	70	Humilitie		9
PAWS				
That God who hath delivered me out of the paws of the Lyon and Bear,	374	Letters		7
PAY (see also paies)				
Thy drops of bloud must pay down all his fear:	17	Ch.-Porch		274
Though I in broken pay	62	Afflict.2		4
What place or person calls for, he doth pay.	72	Constancie		15
And one another pay:	81	Christmas		32
Enter thy pay, ...	90	Afflict.4		26
And just it is that I should pay the rent, ...	117	Providence		27
Here he gave up his life to pay our score.	151	The Bag		24
To pay our debts, and leave our ancient place	197	Ch.-Milit.		256
To pay our debts, and leave her ancient place	197	Ch.-Milit.	W	256
throw into the fire, and so they pay them their wages, all is well.	265	Priest 26		26
A good pay-master starts not at assurances.	324	Proverbs		113
A hundred loade of thought will not pay one of debts. . . .	335	Proverbs		414
Speake not of my debts, unlesse you meane to pay them. . . .	354	Proverbs		998
He that will be surety, shall pay.	358	Proverbs	D	1091
They that hold the greatest farmes, pay the least rent . . .	359	Proverbs	D	1100
and both pay for the surplusage of these Books, and for ever after	367	Letters		10
that the Hollanders should pay him tribute out of their fishing.	368	Letters		12
PAY-MASTER				
A good pay-master starts not at assurances.	324	Proverbs		113
PAYD				
Payd me my wages in a world of mirth.	46	Afflict.1		12
Where all my debts are payd, none can accrue	65	Ch.-mus.	W	8
deceased Neece which are to be payd out of it unto some whose names	382	G.H.'s Will		15
those that are crost are discharged already the rest are to be payd.	383	G.H.'s Will		4
due to Mrs Judeth Spenser is to be payd to Mrs Mary Lawly at Chelsey	383	G.H.'s Will		21
PAYER				
A good payer is master of anothers purse.	341	Proverbs		595
PAYES				
Thy justice me most fitly payes:	96	Justice 1		7
Talking payes no toll.	338	Proverbs		485
Hee payes too deare for honey that licks it from thorns. . .	350	Proverbs	V	880
PAYMASTER				
but in the other God is his own immediate paymaster, rewarding all	254	Priest 20		21
Although you have a much better Paymaster then my self, . .	378	Letters		2
PAYMENT				
& has given order to the Tenants, at Leighton, to make payment of it.	379	Letters		9
PEACE				
Game is a civil gunpowder, in peace	14	Ch.-Porch		203
That if I chance to hold my peace, ...	26	The Altar		13
But I the Prince of peace; peace that doth passe	30	Sacrifice		118
God holds his peace at man, and man cries out:	32	Sacrifice		187
Softnesse, and peace, and joy, and love, and blisse, . . .	51	Prayer 1		9
Peace mutt'ring thoughts, and do not grudge to keep . . .	68	Content		1
Peace pratler, do not lowre:	105	Conscience		1
Harmonious peace must rock them all the day:	105	Conscience		9
Doubtlesse our plagues and plentie, peace and warres . . .	119	Providence		79
Peace.	124	Peace		T
Sweet Peace, where dost thou dwell? I humbly crave, . . .	124	Peace		1
And ask'd, if Peace were there.	124	Peace		4
Peace at the root must dwell.	125	Peace		16
Whom when for Peace	125	Peace		20
A secret vertue bringing peace and mirth	125	Peace		35
And peace, which ev'ry where	125	Peace		40

PEACE (cont'd)	PAGE	TITLE		LINE
From setled peace and rest!	127	Giddinesse		2
Now eat his bread in peace,	127	Giddinesse		10
First Peace and Silence all disputes controll,	137	Familie		9
King of Glorie, King of Peace,	146	Praise 2		1
Breaking her peace, and tainting her good name.	193	Ch.-Milit.		106
King of glorie, King of peace,	199	L'Envoy		1
Therefore will I lie down in peace,	218	Psalm IV	D	29
And peace-meal rent it, while there's none	221	Psalm VII	D	7
that was at peace with me:	221	Psalm VII	D	12
errand I come, let me hold my peace, and doe thou speak thy selfe;	233	Priest 7		35
is kept in the one, and peace in the other, without disturbance,	236	Priest 8		24
and mortifications in the times of peace and prosperity.	237	Priest 9		33
and peace it administers against all temptations, even to death it	250	Priest 15		3
with Daltons Justice of Peace, and the Abridgements of the Statutes,	260	Priest 23		2
But if hee may bee of the Commission of Peace, there is nothing	276	Priest 32		7
a braver [better] Institution then that of Justices of the Peace:	276	Priest 32		9
and the Angels minister to us their owne food, even joy, and peace;	280	Priest 34		7
not to take the full compasse, and liberty of their Peace:	280	Priest 34		22
or such a time their peace and mirth have carryed them further then	280	Priest 34		33
The Peace of God, &c.	286	Priest 36		5
for, this word of thy rich peace, and reconciliation, thou hast	289	Priest		4
O make it a word of power and peace, to convert those who are not yet	289	Priest		16
and retains and confirms kingdomes, cities, and families in peace.	297	Cornaro		11
joy and peace have taken up their standing in my heart.	301	Cornaro		2
is not that which filleth the heart with joy and peace in believing;	309	Valdesso		2
Peace, and Patience, and death with repentance.	332	Proverbs		319
Cloath thee in war, arme thee in peace.	334	Proverbs		386
Hee that makes a good warre makes a good peace.	335	Proverbs		420
He that speakes sowes, and he that holds his peace, gathers.	336	Proverbs		435
Warre makes theeves, and peace hangs them.	337	Proverbs		471
A disarmed peace is weake.	342	Proverbs		628
Three can hold their peace, if two be away.	345	Proverbs		714
He that will not have peace, God gives him warre.	345	Proverbs		729
Where there is peace, God is.	345	Proverbs		733
Souldiers in peace are like chimneys in summer.	361	Proverbs	D	1172
being at London sent for him (as shee sayes) to make peace with him,	368	Letters		21
whether my peace be yet made with her concerning my unkind departure.	371	Letters		8
repose, peace with all but Booke-wormes, perpetuall povertie,	442	Oration		36
PEACE-MEAL				
And peace-meal rent it, while there's none	221	Psalm VII	D	7
PEACE'S				
This is the lace of Peaces coat:	124	Peace		9
PEACEABLE				
military state of a Christian life, but even in the peaceable also;	279	Priest 33		4
a Christian even in this Life, the one military, the other peaceable.	280	Priest 34		3
The Peaceable is, when the Divell for a time leaves us,	280	Priest 34		5
Those that he findes in the peaceable state, he adviseth to be very	280	Priest 34		14
PEACEABLY				
To live peaceably with all breedes good blood.	353	Proverbs		963
PEACOCK'S				
At length the Crow bringing the Peacocks plume,	70	Humilitie		17
PEARL				
His dearely-earned pearl, which God did hide	85	Vanitie 1		10
The Pearl. Matthew 13.	88	The Pearl		T
PEARS				
How harsh are thorns to pears! and yet they make	120	Providence		121
PEASANT				
A peasant may beleeve as much	50	Faith		29
PECK				
Those ravening Harpyes, which peck at thy face,	212	Bohemia	D	48
PECULIAR				
As peculiar notes and strains	186	Dooms-day		11
For ev'ry mans peculiar book?	187	Judgement		5
he makes a peculiar one for a blessing on the exercises of the day,	235	Priest 8		22
and day against the proper and peculiar temptations of his state	238	Priest 9		1
PEDIGREES				
In great pedigrees there are Governours and Chandlers.	328	Proverbs		222
PEDLER				
(as I think) at the sign of the Pedler and the Pack on London-bridge,	370	Letters		28
PEECE				
That is thy Master-peece I see	201	love	W	3
As a burst fouling-peece doth save the birds	204	Persever.	W	7
if a peece of dry flesh at my table be more unpleasant to me,	242	Priest 10		12
the Kingdome intc Portions, which every yeer he surveys peece-meal.	277	Priest 32		8
PEECE-MEAL				
the Kingdome into Portions, which every yeer he surveys peece-meal.	277	Priest 32		8
PEECES				
As I shal find occasion, you shal receive them by peeces;	366	Letters		3
PEERE				
Sometimes I peere above them all;	55	Temper 1		6
PEEVISH				
There thou art struggling with a peevish heart,	106	Sion		13
PEGS				
What both the stops and pegs of pleasure bee:	89	The Pearl	W	28
PEMBROKE				
Honourable the Lady Anne, Countess of Pembr. and Montg. at court.	376	Letters		T
PEN				
Are chaw'd by others pen and tongue;	69	Content	W	30
A gown and pen became him wondrous well:	194	Ch.-Milit.		167
They favour learning whose actions are worthy of a learned pen.	357	Proverbs	D	1061

PEN (cont'd)	PAGE	TITLE		LINE
I shall understand that a Letter will be seasonable, my Pen is ready.	371	Letters		15
PENALTIES				
the same Law they are to levy penalties for negligence in resorting	270	Priest 29		5
PENCE				
For thirtie pence he did my death devise,	27	Sacrifice		17
and the liberall of a farthing sixe pence.	328	Proverbs		211
but the liberall makes of a farthing sixe pence.	328	Proverbs	V	211
To Sara thirteene shillings foure pence, Alsoe my will and pleasure	382	G.H.'s Will		27
PENDANT				
Then those same pendant profits, which the spring	86	Lent		25
PENITENTIAL				
In Penitential Cryes.	214	Convert	D	15
PENNE				
And put the penne alone into his hand,	117	Providence		7
PENN'D				
There is in love a sweetnesse readie penn'd:	103	Jordan 2		17
and all being penn'd by one and the self-same Spirit, it cannot be,	229	Priest 4		6
hath ever so many sermons ready penn'd, as he hath victories.	278	Priest 33		24
PENNES				
Their storie pennes and sets us down.	128	Bunch Gr.		11
PENNING				
indeed sometime doubly teaching both in penning and in applying.	317	Valdesso		30
PENNY				
If he finde another giving a poor man a penny, he gives him a tester	254	Priest 20		13
The Smith and his penny both are black.	327	Proverbs		195
A penny spar'd is twice got.	338	Proverbs		506
PENS				
Are chaw'd by others pens and tongue;	69	Content		30
PENSION				
But he gives no set pension to any;	244	Priest 12		26
Pension never inriched young man.	339	Proverbs		515
PENSIVE				
With pensive humblenesse would live and tread:	173	Marie Magd		6
PENSIVENESSE				
To cold despairs, and gnawing pensivenesse?	155	Assurance		16
PENY				
The miserable man makes a peny of a farthing,	328	Proverbs		211
PEOPLE				
The Princes of my people make a head	26	Sacrifice		5
Mine owne deare people, cry, away, away,	29	Sacrifice		102
Shepherds are honest people; let them sing:	57	Jordan 1		11
Come people; Aaron's drest.	174	Aaron		25
Betwixt us & the people: when as glory	212	Bohemia	D	25
the people vain exploits devise?	215	Psalm II	D	2
Nor all the people round about,	216	Psalm III	D	15
upon thy people be.	217	Psalm III	D	24
So shall the people round about	221	Psalm VII	D	25
The Lord shall judge the people all:	221	Psalm VII	D	29
because Countrey people live hardly, and therefore as feeling their	227	Priest 3		12
because Countrey people (as indeed all honest men) do much esteem	228	Priest 3		2
because people by what they understand, are best led to what they	228	Priest 4		19
a slighter forme of Catechizing, fitter for country people;	230	Priest 5		16
ability of a Parson to lead his people exactly in the wayes of Truth,	230	Priest 5		21
hee may affect also his people, knowing that no Sermon moves them so	231	Priest 6		13
having often instrücted his people how to carry themselves in divine	231	Priest 6		21
that God hath ever had his people, that have glorified him as wel	231	Priest 6		35
for people are very attentive at such discourses, and think it	233	Priest 7		9
yet often dy with the Sermon, especially with Countrey people;	233	Priest 7		15
as, Oh Lord blesse my people, and teach them this point;	233	Priest 7		34
then he turnes to request for his people, that the Lord would be	235	Priest 8		28
Almighty God, and blessing the people either openly, or to himselfe.	236	Priest 8		6
where both the people and the drink being cold and flegmatick,	242	Priest 10		20
because countrey people are very observant of such things,	243	Priest 11		20
time will lose the name and effect of Charity with the poor people,	244	Priest 12		27
to receive the charity of well minded people, and to lay up treasure	246	Priest 13		22
if curing poor people, hee supplies them with Receipts,	247	Priest 14		16
representing to his people, that the Blessing of God to them ought	254	Priest 19		4
knowing that Ccuntrey people are drawne, or led by sense,	254	Priest 20		31
neither can all the people so order their affairs as to receive just	259	Priest 22		26
even as our Saviour made plants and seeds to teach the people:	261	Priest 23		14
that labouring people (whom he chiefly considered) might have every	261	Priest 23		20
Country people are full of these petty injustices, being cunning	265	Priest 26		33
As when the people hungred and thirsted after our Saviours Doctrine,	267	Priest 26		22
be vilified or debased, by being cast on the lower ranke of people;	270	Priest 29		8
the great aptnesse Countrey people have to think that all things	270	Priest 30		25
because Countrey people are much addicted to them, so that to favour	283	Priest 35		29
that Blessing the people is in so little use with his brethren:	285	Priest 36		1
the Priests cf the Old Testament were commanded to Blesse the people,	285	Priest 36		16
duty in Ministers themselves, hath made the people also neglect it;	286	Priest 36		12
pardoning my sins, and bidding me go feed the people of thy love.	289	Priest		6
my Physicians nothing thereof, as is the custome of sick people.	292	Cornaro		30
The tooth-ach is more ease then to deale with ill people.	340	Proverbs		558
and the tumult of the people.	360	Proverbs	D	1148
Take heed of credit decaid, and people that have nothing.	360	Proverbs	D	1150
But perhaps being above the Common people, our Credit and estimation	373	Letters		26
When we exhort people to continue in their vocation, it is in	381	Woodnoth		23
PEOPLE'S				
by frequent wishes of the peoples good, and joying therein,	234	Priest 7		7
PEOPLES'				
other answers, which are on the Clerks and peoples part to answer;	231	Priest 6		29

PEPPER	PAGE	TITLE		LINE
or that cinnamon should heat me more then pepper?	297	Cornaro		34
PER				
yet that will be about 30 l. per an. but the commodiousness is beyond	369	Letters		32
PERAMBULATION				
Wherefore he exacts of all to bee present at the perambulation,	284	Priest 35		10
PERCEIVE				
Shall not perceive, that I am here.	36	Thanksgvng		38
Did once perceive, it blew them under foot,	140	Ch.-rents		7
Did once perceive, it blew thee under foot,	140	Ch.-rents	V	7
that the auditors may plainly perceive that every word is hart-deep.	233	Priest 7		32
if he perceive in company any discourse tending to ill,	252	Priest 18		16
and perhaps a little more mild, but you will hardly perceive it.	366	Letters		25
PERCEIV'D				
Yet taking heart I rose, and then perceiv'd	142	Pilgrimage		29
PERCEIVED				
I sat me down to spell them, and perceived	112	JESU		8
that I perceived, that they had no great power to hurt those bodies,	294	Cornaro		1
By this it may clearely be perceived, how great is the power of order	297	Cornaro		3
PERCEIVES				
his children, hardly perceives when his storing becomes unlawfull:	264	Priest 26		27
PERCEIVING				
Perceiving that alone of all his treasure	160	The Pulley		9
The Countrey Parson perceiving, that most, when they are at leasure,	286	Priest 37		29
PERCHANCE				
Yet lest perchance I should too happie be	48	Afflict.1		49
PERFECT				
Thou art all brightnesse, perfect puritie;	101	Miserie		32
Thy perfect lineaments, and hue	109	Brit. Ch.		2
Perfect and light in my deare breast,	174	Aaron		22
For that, O Lord, with perfect joy	218	Psalm IV	D	25
thy perfect way disclose.	219	Psalm V	D	24
with perfect joy be fill'd.	219	Psalm V	D	36
as to be cloathed with perfect patience, and Christian fortitude in	237	Priest 9		37
Commandments, and as he finds them perfect, rewards them the more.	245	Priest 12		36
and put them to great shame, who deny the Scripture to be perfect.	247	Priest 13		2
for no perfect Artist ever yet hated his owne worke.	283	Priest 34		12
but pardon our sins, and perfect what thou hast begun.	289	Priest		21
For indeed no man can be a perfect Physician to another,	297	Cornaro		24
Wherefore one to another cannot be a perfect Physician.	297	Cornaro		36
which are all in their perfect vigour, but especially my Taste;	302	Cornaro		8
all the sonnes of one father and mother, all in perfect health;	303	Cornaro		4
of perfection, and are able to make the man of God perfect, 2 Tim. 3.	306	Valdesso		19
but still even to the most learned and perfect in them,	309	Valdesso		23
PERFECTED				
And when they once have perfected their draughts,	122	Sinnes rd.		5
which, but in that age, can hardly be perfected.	298	Cornaro		31
PERFECTING				
perfecting our Redemption no other way, then by sorrow;	249	Priest 15		22
PERFECTION				
Lord that I may the Sunns perfection gaine	57	Employm. 1	W	23
Presume on thy perfection?	101	Miserie		36
All things concurre to give it a perfection.	158	Praise 3		9
Perfection	184	The Elixer	W	T
And give it his perfection.	184	The Elixer		8
By this means the place is come to that perfection we now see it is:	301	Cornaro		30
but a use of perfection, and are able to make the man of God perfect,	306	Valdesso		18
but a use of perfection, neither can they ever be exhausted,	309	Valdesso		21
PERFECTIONS				
So great are thy perfections,	104	Obedience		24
When all perfections as but one appeare,	115	Dulnesse		13
Light and perfections on the breast,	174	Aaron		2
But these are high perfections:	185	The Elixer	W	21
Shining and sharp, point out your rare Perfections;	209	L. Bacon	D	4
PERFECTLY				
seem to some incredible) I was perfectly cured of all my infirmities.	292	Cornaro		37
PERFIDIOUS				
No tye can oblige the perfidious.	357	Proverbs	D	1066
PERFORM				
Thou art not onely to perform thy part,	156	Assurance		27
Spain hath dcne one; when Arts perform the other,	197	Ch.-Milit.		265
which none can perform so wel in trouble, as in calmness.	273	Priest 31		2
comforts and condoles, doth perform an acceptable thing to thee;	298	Cornaro		7
sickness hath made me unable to perform those Offices for which I	373	Letters		9
PERFORMANCE				
and in a strict performance of a few cheap and easie duties	319	Valdesso	V	24
PERFORMANCES				
and live, and who giveth mee my Desires and Performances;	224	Priest		3
PERFORMED				
and fasting dayes were fully performed by keeping of the two former,	242	Priest 10		9
be as they ought, for those great duties that are performed in them.	246	Priest 13		7
because it is not performed by way of request, but of confidence,	286	Priest 36		7
and later yeares, it is no such thing which may not be performed;	299	Cornaro		7
but that you have performed your kindness to the full, and that	363	Letters		24
PERFORMES				
between fear and zeal, pausing yet pressing, he performes his duty.	231	Priest 6		20
who performes the other acts of repentance, when he cannot more,	279	Priest 33		30
PERFORMING				
about him, performing for them any Ministeriall office, which is	253	Priest 19		16
PERFORMS				
Nothing performs the task of life:	90	Afflict.4		16

	PAGE	TITLE		LINE
PERFUME				
Though he give light, & th' East perfume;	42	Easter		24
With these all day I do perfume my minde,	175	The Odour		6
And Paris garden. Then let there perfume	212	Bohemia	D	51
charity being his only perfume, which deserves cost when he can spare	241	Priest 10		14
PERFUMED				
festivalls strawed, and stuck with boughs, and perfumed with incense.	246	Priest 13		10
PERFUMES				
Onely God, who gives perfumes,	181	Banquet		22
And with it perfumes my heart.	181	Banquet		24
PERHAPS				
Perhaps his wives too, and whom she hath bore:	14	Ch.-Porch		195
Because 'tis better, and perhaps may save thee.	22	Ch.-Porch		394
Perhaps my God, though he be farre before,	87	Lent		40
Perhaps great places and thy praise	95	Submission		15
Perhaps some such of old did passe,	122	Time		7
Perhaps thou com'st sometimes, and for a day;	137	Familie		23
Perhaps with more embellishment can say,	177	Forerunners		33
Perhaps some other subject I had tryed	209	L. Bacon	D	11
before hee proceede to disinheriting, or perhaps never goes so far;	250	Priest 16		18
in which perhaps you will discover some care, which I forbare not in	304	Valdesso		3
perhaps he meant all of this later not of the former.	317	Valdesso		4
But perhaps they will say, you are sickly, you must not study too	364	Letters		25
and perhaps a little more mild, but you will hardly perceive it.	366	Letters		25
But perhaps being above the Common people, our Credit and estimation	373	Letters		25
PERILL				
May at his perill further go.	25	Superlim		8
But at his perill: when he digs the place,	119	Providence		82
PERIOD				
And spent her period and prefixed time	191	Ch.-Milit.		59
Spending her period and prefixed time	191	Ch.-Milit.	W	59
They have their period also and set times	197	Ch.-Milit.		261
yet is there a period for his storing, and a point, or center,	264	Priest 26		28
PERIODS				
States have their conversions and periods	361	Proverbs	D	1166
PERIRRHANTERIUM				
The Church-porch. Perirrhanterium.	6	Ch.-Porch		T
PERISH				
And so should perish, but that nothing can,	41	Sepulchre		22
and straight ye perish from the way:	216	Psalm II	D	30
imprecation to Simon Magus, Act. 8. Thy mony perish with thee:	285	Priest 36		30
He that trusts in a lie, shall perish in truth.	340	Proverbs		569
He that trusts in a lie, shall perish by the truth.	340	Proverbs	V	569
Favour will as surely perish as life.	357	Proverbs	D	1055
PERMISSICN				
Onely by his permission. Then beware,	22	Ch.-Porch		405
For either thy command, or thy permission	117	Providence		33
PERMIT				
wherein he chooseth to permit his Parishioners rather to make use	260	Priest 23		18
PERMITTED				
and permitted the quantitie of meat to be increased, yet but two	296	Cornaro		7
PERPETUAL				
by the Patents of your perpetual favour to do so still,	365	Letters		24
PERPETUALL				
Much curiousnesse is a perpetuall wooing	14	Ch.-Porch		191
Perpetuall knockings at thy doore,	124	Gratefulnes		13
not onely because all men shun the company of perpetuall severity,	268	Priest 27		2
perpetuall povertie, but when your Excellencies appeare.	442	Oration		37
PERPETUATE				
that men should perpetuate, and not break off their acts	271	Priest 30		26
PERPLEX'D				
But, Lord, how long so much perplex'd	220	Psalm VI	D	7
PERPLEXED				
Lord help thy servant whose perplexed Soule	204	The Knell	W	2
Upon this his mind begins to be perplexed, and troubled,	272	Priest 31		32
and shews the perplexed Christian, that this prayer being	273	Priest 31		4
PERPLEXING				
sometimes in perplexing them in the service of God) stands fast in	272	Priest 31		17
PERPLEXITY				
out of his station, and to inlarge the perplexity, untill it spread,	273	Priest 31		1
PERQUISITES				
Augmented with thy graces perquisites.	46	Afflict.1	W	6
PERSECUTE				
From all that persecute my life,	220	Psalm VII	D	3
God doth forsake and persecute them, and there is none to deliver	281	Priest 34		11
PERSECUTETH				
that persecuteth me.	222	Psalm VII	D	48
PERSECUTING				
and cheerfull dying under persecuting Emperours, (though that indeed	237	Priest 9		30
PERSECUTION				
fortitude in the cold midnight stormes of persecution and adversity.	237	Priest 9		38
PERSEVER				
Light, joy, and leisure; but shall they persever?	188	Heaven		19
PERSEVERANCE				
Perseverance.	204	Persever.	W	T
PERSEVERE				
I could not go away, nor persevere.	47	Afflict.1		48
admonitions, if they persevere, he causes them to be presented:	232	Priest 6		13
that so both they may be encouraged to persevere, and others spurred	243	Priest 11		26
PERSIST				
Yet do we still persist as we began,	41	Sepulchre		21

	PAGE	TITLE	LINE
PHYSITIAN			
is a Physitian sc far as he meetes with the same disease, . . .	278	Priest 33	27
Deceive not thy Physitian, Confessor, nor Lawyer.	324	Proverbs	105
God heales, and the Physitian hath the thankes.	326	Proverbs	169
Goe not for every griefe to the Physitian, ...	331	Proverbs	290
An old Physitian, and a young Lawyer.	343	Proverbs	648
Who paies the Physitian, does the cure.	350	Proverbs	879
The Physitian owes all to the patient, ...	351	Proverbs	921
Saint Luke was a Saint and a Physitian, yet is dead.	354	Proverbs	1008
PHYSITIANS			
There are more Physitians in health then drunkards.	351	Proverbs	903
PICK			
Pick out of tales the mirth, but not the sinne.	9	Ch.-Porch	63
Pick out of mirth, like stones out of thy ground, ...	16	Ch.-Porch	235
To pick out treasures from an earthen pot.	23	Ch.-Porch	430
Pick quarrels with their onely happinesse:	29	Sacrifice	87
of my kindred saw some great powerfull men pick quarrels against me,	294	Cornaro	16
A good bargaine is a pick-purse.	321	Proverbs	12
PICK-PURSE			
A good bargaine is a pick-purse.	321	Proverbs	12
PICKS			
Wisdome picks friends; civilitie playes the rest.	15	Ch.-Porch	227
PICKT			
Pickt here and there a crumme, and would not die;	154	Glimpse	17
PICTURE			
This by my picture, in my book I write:	183	The Posie	6
Onely there was a handsome picture by, ...	194	Ch.-Milit.	169
PICTURED			
Not only ought fortune to be pictured on a wheel, ...	358	Proverbs	D 1077
PICTURES			
(as Pictures may be by a plenarie circumspection) but still even	309	Valdesso	22
PIECE (see also peece)			
All of a piece, and all are cleare and straight.	72	Constancie	20
Christ hath took in this piece of ground, ...	76	Sunday	40
Into a piece of timber work and winde, ...	126	Confession	8
who somtimes make it a piece of state not to come at the beginning	232	Priest 6	8
things that they buy, even as a piece of wood, which they may cut,	265	Priest 26	25
who hath in his hand an apple, and a piece of Gold under it;	272	Priest 30	8
A piece of a Churchyard fitts every body.	355	Proverbs	1027
she is not disposed to spend her eyesight on a piece of paper,	371	Letters	14
PIECES			
Broken in pieces all asunder, ...	89	Afflict.4	1
He our foes in pieces brake;	93	Antiphon 2	13
Ev'n all to pieces: which I went to seek:	112	JESU	4
I view their pieces, I compare them with those of Antiquitie;	302	Cornaro	1
PIECRUST (see also py-crust)			
PIERCE			
Sharp nails pierce this, but sharper that confound;	33	Sacrifice	218
For they will pierce my side, I full well know;	34	Sacrifice	246
When my devotions could not pierce	79	Deniall	1
My knees pierce th' earth, mine eies the skie;	162	The Search	5
Quitting his spear, lest it should pierce again	192	Ch.-Milit.	69
Henceforth shall only pierce the Skies, ...	214	Convert	D 14
that it may effectually pierce their hearts, and convert them.	262	Priest 24	24
PIERCED			
Is in my deare Redeemers pierced side.	44	H. Bapt.1	6
PIERCER			
No scrue, no piercer can	126	Confession	7
PIERCETH			
that the world pierceth not godly mens actions no more then Gods,	315	Valdesso	30
PIERCING			
Reversed thunder, Christ-side-piercing spear, ...	51	Prayer 1	6
And thred the spheres with his quick-piercing minde:	85	Vanitie 1	2
What point so piercing can appeare	163	The Search	55
as parrats, without ever piercing into the sense of it. . . .	256	Priest 21	4
PIETY			
Therefore having seasoned them with all Piety, not only of words in	239	Priest 10	24
or painted there, which may excite the reader to a thought of piety;	240	Priest 10	25
pity hath set forth heaven for a reward to draw men to Piety,	243	Priest 11	32
Secondly, what means of Piety, whether daily prayers be used,	251	Priest 17	22
and taint his other duties of piety, which none can perform so wel in	273	Priest 31	2
while applying himselfe to the [unquestioned] duties of true Piety,	312	Valdesso	20
there are other Cases of Conscience grounded on Piety and Morality,	319	Valdesso	V 31
By Hebrew piety, he meaneth not the very Ceremonies of the Jewes,	319	Valdesso	34
PIG'S			
Of a pigs taile you can never make a good shaft.	359	Proverbs	D 1104
PIGEONS			
The pigeons feed their tender off-spring, crying, ...	118	Providence	62
PIKE			
And taste that juice, which on the crosse a pike	37	The Agonie	14
PILATE			
Sends me to Pilate. This makes them agree;	29	Sacrifice	74
Pilate a stranger holdeth cff; but they, ...	29	Sacrifice	101
PILE			
Thy pile of dust, wherein each crumme	149	Longing	41
PIL'D			
I finde there quarries of pil'd vanities, ...	38	The Sinner	5
In tears like seas, our sinnes are pil'd	173	Marie Magd	11
PILFRING			
And pilfring what I once did give, ...	95	Submission	11

	PAGE	TITLE		LINE
PITYES				
he hateth him not as an officer, but pityes him as a Father:	250	Priest 16		12
PITYING				
and so between gentle reasoning, and pitying, he overcomes the evill:	269	Priest 28		15
PLACE				
Stay at the third cup, or forgo the place.	8	Ch.-Porch		47
The place its honour, for the persons sake.	17	Ch.-Porch		266
And Prophets once to see, but found no place:	32	Sacrifice		183
Sinne being gone, oh fill the place,	39	Good Fri.		29
The Place, & keep possession still.	39	Good Fri.	W	30
No place for grief or fear.	46	Afflict.1		16
Therefore my sudden soul caught at the place,	46	Afflict.1		17
Make one place ev'ry where.	55	Temper 1		28
The measure of our joyes is in this place,	57	Employm. 1		11
Lord place me in thy consort; give one strain	57	Employm. 1		23
This glorious and transcendent place,	67	Windows		4
To court each place or fortune that doth fall,	68	Content		7
To court each place or fortune that does fall,	68	Content	W	7
And challenge it, as proper to his place,	70	Humilitie		20
What place or person calls for, he doth pay.	72	Constancie		15
Bright spark; shot from a brighter place,	74	The Starre		1
Unto the place where thou	74	The Starre		19
Get me a standing there, and place	74	The Starre		21
Since there is no place so alone,	75	Sunday		20
When th' elements did for place contest	79	Employm.2		11
Enriching all the place.	81	Christmas		20
Take up his place and right:	81	Christmas		24
Quitting their place	90	Afflict.4		14
When that my friend pretendeth to a place,	94	Unkindness		16
Some place and power on me?	95	Submission		6
A falling starr has lost his place:	97	Charms & K	W	19
Which shall convey him to the place of death.	98	Mortific.	W	30
Beautie in thee takes up her place,	109	Brit. Ch.		4
Beautie in thee takes up the place,	109	Brit. Ch.	V	4
But at his perill: when he digs the place,	119	Providence		82
Who wants the place, where God doth dwell,	123	Time		23
And should take place	131	Mans medly		17
Brave rose, (alas!) where art thou? in the place	140	Ch.-rents	V	1
A wasted place, but sometimes rich.	142	Pilgrimage		15
Where is my God? what hidden place	163	The Search		29
Untill I had some place, where I might sing,	164	The Crosse		3
Unto a place where is no rest.	174	Aaron		9
This were the better skie, the brighter place.	175	The Foil		4
Gave her the highest place in all mens hearts.	191	Ch.-Milit.		50
So they might still, and point us out the place	192	Ch.-Milit.		85
Much about one and the same time and place,	192	Ch.-Milit.		101
When th' one did set, the other did take place,	196	Ch.-Milit.		217
To pay our debts, and leave our ancient place	197	Ch.-Milit.		256
To pay our debts, and leave her ancient place	197	Ch.-Milit.	W	256
To time and place, where judgement shall appeare.	198	Ch.-Milit.		277
Creatures are good, & have their place	200	H. Commun.	W	22
Of opposition cannot place thee, where	212	Bohemia	D	39
and finds no sure abiding place.	215	Psalm I	D	16
And toward thy most Holy place	218	Psalm V	D	19
he constituted Deputies in his place, and these are Priests.	225	Priest 1		9
and judicious comparing of place with place must be a singular help	229	Priest 4		8
to an higher state, or place, under colour of accommodation,	238	Priest 9		15
that it is no complementall or light thing to sustain that place,	258	Priest 22		11
for them often, and in finding out Courtesies to place on them;	262	Priest 24		27
Neither hath the place its dignity from the Ecclesiasticall Laws	269	Priest 29		32
Wherefore the Parson suffers not the place to be vilified or debased,	270	Priest 29		7
considering the great Consequence of their place, and more of their	270	Priest 29		17
that neer the place where he is to pray, he spyes some scoffing	273	Priest 31		28
whereas now, of any place, they are least there.	275	Priest 32		36
and managing Commons, or Woods, according as the place suggests.	276	Priest 32		6
and ripenesse of judgement for so excellent a Place, not to refuse,	276	Priest 32		17
whereas there are usually three Objections made against the Place;	276	Priest 32		19
These are so far from deterring any good man from the place,	276	Priest 32		23
he may go to Court, as the eminent place both of good and ill.	277	Priest 32		6
then did'st thou place us in Paradise, and wert proceeding still	288	Priest		15
and the cause being taken away, there is no place for the effect.	300	Cornaro		2
in whose place, joy and peace have taken up their standing in my	301	Cornaro		1
that they are in the fairest place of this learned Citie of Padua,	301	Cornaro		11
the midst whereof is a Church suitable to the condition of the place.	301	Cornaro		23
This place is washed with the river Brenta;	301	Cornaro		23
because the place was moorish and unhealthy, fitter for beasts then	301	Cornaro		26
By this means the place is come to that perfection we now see it is:	301	Cornaro		30
This place together with many other, as namely Consid. 71. upon Our	307	Valdesso		16
especially considering the time and place where he lived.	311	Valdesso	V	8
the discourse from this line [place] till the end of this Chapter may	311	Valdesso		20
invites us to all good, according to that singular place, Phil. 4. 8.	313	Valdesso		20
if I bid a man stay in a place untill I come, I doe not then bid him	318	Valdesso		15
is observeable that in that very place he preferres the Word before	318	Valdesso		22
Sit in your place and none can make you rise.	334	Proverbs		372
All things have their place, knew wee how to place them.	334	Proverbs		379
He quits his place well, that leaves his friend there.	350	Proverbs		875
A man would live in Italy (a place of pleasure)	357	Proverbs	D	1047
Take heed of mad folks in a narrow place.	360	Proverbs	D	1149
The Orators place (that you may understand what it is) is the finest	369	Letters		30
you may understand what it is) is the finest place in the University,	369	Letters		31
he takes place next the Doctors, is at all their Assemblies	370	Letters		1

PLACE (cont'd)	PAGE	TITLE		LINE
I hope I shall get this place without all your London helps,	370	Letters		7
since this place being civil may divert me too much from Divinity,	370	Letters		19
Concerning the Orators place all goes well yet, the next Friday it is	371	Letters		16
Let me commend only one place more to you (Philip. 4. 4.) St. Paul	374	Letters		20
a long time, to doe the place good, & have endeavoured many wayes,	378	Letters		6
PLAC'D				
And in the middle plac'd my heart. But he	129	Love unkn.		7
PLACED				
is placed surer for his childrens advantage, then if it were given	240	Priest 10		8
squeeze blood undecently to the station wherein God hath placed me,	265	Priest 26		18
wherein God hath placed two great Instruments, Reason in the soul,	274	Priest 32		19
PLACES				
Kindnesse, good parts, great places are the way	19	Ch.-Porch		327
And where sinne places me in Adams fall,	50	Faith	W	19
Perhaps great places and thy praise	95	Submission		15
When yet some places could no moisture get,	120	Providence		115
From all these places, but at divers times,	195	Ch.-Milit.		185
who have handled the places controverted, which the Parson by no	229	Priest 4		18
other spirituall wickednesses in high places doth the Parson fear,	238	Priest 9		20
their Countrey also is known, the places, and rivers travelled unto,	282	Priest 34		2
in the reducing of many rude and untoiled places in my countrey,	302	Cornaro		15
and abode in those fenny places two whole moneths in the heat	302	Cornaro		18
to the dubious and offensive places in the following CONSIDERATIONS.	306	Valdesso		T
How many places doe the Fathers bring about Untill against	318	Valdesso		9
PLACETH				
And where sinne placeth me in Adams fall,	50	Faith		19
PLAGUE				
And fence a plague, while others sleep and slumber.	147	Offering		12
And fence a plague, whiles others sleep and slumber.	147	Offering	V	12
To a plague and publick wo.	187	Dooms-day		24
PLAGUES				
Doubtlesse our plagues and plentie, peace and warres	119	Providence		79
Lord, I acknowledge; take thy plagues away:	126	Confession		26
Then the ten bitter plagues had done before.	191	Ch.-Milit.		40
PLAIES				
Then Order plaies the soul;	137	Familie		10
He hath great neede of a foole, that plaies the foole himselfe.	322	Proverbs		46
He that plaies his mony ought not to value it.	327	Proverbs		201
He plaies well that winnes.	339	Proverbs		550
PLAIN				
All things are bigge with jest: nothing that's plain,	16	Ch.-Porch		239
Curling with metaphors a plain intention,	102	Jordan 2		5
Plain demonstrations, evident and cleare,	167	Dotage		10
a plain and evident declaration of the meaning of the text;	235	Priest 7		1
The furniture of his house is very plain, but clean, whole,	241	Priest 10		12
His fare is plain, and common, but wholsome, what hee hath,	241	Priest 10		15
a most plain and easie framing the question, even containing in	256	Priest 21		34
so that it is plain the Authour had a very reverend esteem	311	Valdesso	V	6
for unbelief, or evil works, make plain the Authors meaning.	319	Valdesso	V	18
make it plain to her, that I loved her even in my departure,	371	Letters		11
PLAINE				
and his apparrell plaine, but reverend, and clean, without spots,	228	Priest 3		10
for if he be a plaine countryman, he reproves him plainly;	248	Priest 14		17
by making the Question very plaine with comparisons, and making much	256	Priest 21		14
This familiar illustration made the answer so plaine, that he was	257	Priest 21		6
there the case is plaine, Cornelius had revelation, yet Peter was	310	Valdesso		9
PLAINLY				
Plainly and home, is coward of the two.	15	Ch.-Porch		218
Who plainly say, My God, My King.	57	Jordan 1		15
As plainly as that above doth show;	175	The Foil		3
So now being Priest he plainly did professe	195	Ch.-Milit.		173
and in the first to the Colossians plainly avoucheth, that he fils up	225	Priest 1		11
Chartre of the Priesthood may be plainly gathered both the Dignity	225	Priest 1		15
so that the auditors may plainly perceive that every word is	233	Priest 7		31
for if he be a plaine countryman, he reproves him plainly;	248	Priest 14		17
he plainly, and generally intimateth to the disaffected,	250	Priest 15		4
PLAINNESSE				
to preserve a directnesse, and open plainnesse in all things;	240	Priest 10		34
PLAISTER				
And spreads the plaister equall to the crime:	44	H. Bapt.1		11
Spredding the plaister equall to the crime:	44	H. Bapt.1	W	11
PLAISTERED				
as walls plaistered, windows glazed, floore paved, seats whole,	246	Priest 13		4
PLANT				
That busie plant!	79	Employm.2		22
To plant and set.	125	Peace		30
Early didst thou arise to plant this vine,	190	Ch.-Milit.		11
Thou didst rise early for to plant this vine,	190	Ch.-Milit.	W	11
Hee that goes barefoot, must not plant thornes.	323	Proverbs		82
A noble plant suites not with a stubborne ground.	342	Proverbs		622
Some men plant an opinion they seem to erradicate.	361	Proverbs	D	1164
PLANTAINE				
damask or white Roses for the one, and plantaine, shepherds purse,	261	Priest 23		35
PLANTATIONS				
busie himself better, then in those new Plantations, and discoveryes,	278	Priest 32		6
PLANTED				
Though I my vine planted and watred there:	31	Sacrifice		163
Planted in me.	72	Frailtie		24
That planted Paradise was not so firm,	97	Afflict.5		2
Like David's tree, planted beside	213	L' Envoy	D	2

	PAGE	TITLE		LINE
PLANTED (cont'd)				
Which, planted by the waters, shall	214	Psalm I	D	9
PLANTING				
the servants of God, for the planting both of love, and humility.	229	Priest 4		27
PLANTS				
Sponges, non-sense and sense; mines, th' earth & plants. . .	121	Providence		136
Where of all plants afflictions soonest grow;	170	Water-crs.		3
even as our Saviour made plants and seeds to teach the people:	261	Priest 23		13
The tree that God plants, no winde hurts it.	344	Proverbs		691
If the braine sowes not corne, it plants thistles.	355	Proverbs		1024
PLATFORM				
to lay the platform of my future life, and shall I then be fain	364	Letters		12
PLATO				
Plato and Aristotle were at a losse, ...	191	Ch.-Milit.		53
some dialogues in Plato were worth the reading, where the singular	256	Priest 21		27
so did Plato also, and Isocrates, and Tullie, and many others	298	Cornaro		38
that Plato sayes, That they who are employed in the common wealth,	299	Cornaro		11
PLAY (see also plaies)				
Play not away the vertue of that name, ...	9	Ch.-Porch		65
Desire and shame, will make thy labour, play:	10	Ch.-Porch	W	90
Play not for gain, but sport. Who playes for more	14	Ch.-Porch		193
Servants and churches also play their part.	14	Ch.-Porch		196
In brief, acquit thee bravely; play the man.	24	Ch.-Porch		457
The world is theirs; they two play out the game, ...	54	Love 1		10
Both to be busie, and to play.	63	Even-song		3
did play their part	66	Ch.-lock	W	4
It cannot vault, or dance, or play;	70	Quidditie		5
But though men fail him, yet his part doth play.	73	Constancie		30
Folly and Sinne play all his game.	100	Miserie		3
Folly and Sinne play out his game.	100	Miserie	W	3
Canst be idle? canst thou play, ...	113	Businesse		1
Comparisons go play, wit use thy will:	183	The Posie		10
Strive each to play their Part.	213	Convert	D	5
Play with a foole at home, ...	325	Proverbs		146
and he will play with you in the market.	325	Proverbs		146
To play at Chesse when the house is on fire.	360	Proverbs	D	1136
so shall you play a good marchant, by transporting French commodities	366	Letters		11
PLAYES				
Play not for gain, but sport. Who playes for more	14	Ch.-Porch		193
Wisdome picks friends; civilitie playes the rest.	15	Ch.-Porch		227
the manifold wiles of Satan (who playes his part sometimes in drawing	272	Priest 31		16
PLAYING				
When my house burnes, it's not good playing at Chesse.	343	Proverbs		666
PLAYNTES				
Playntes to bad fortunes dew:	211	Paradox	D	38
PLEA				
Is all lockt? hath a sinners plea	149	Longing		47
PLEAD				
Lust and wine plead a pleasure, avarice gain:	8	Ch.-Porch		57
Lust and wine plead a pleasure, cheating gain:	8	Ch.-Porch	W	57
For though sinnes plead too, yet like stones they make	66	Ch.-lock		11
And for their old acquaintance plead.	109	Home		70
Lest at length they plead possession:	187	Dooms-day		16
PLEADING				
Spend not on hopes. They that by pleading clothes	14	Ch.-Porch		181
PLEADS				
Which pleads for me:	66	Ch.-lock		10
PLEAS'D				
The sonne, in whom thou art well pleas'd to be?	33	Sacrifice	W	214
PLEASANT				
Pleasant and long:	42	Easter		14
and pleasant, and to raise up their mindes to apprehend Gods good	236	Priest 8		22
which is therefore very pleasant, because many wayes thither are so	301	Cornaro		20
well and quietly any where, and my dreams are fair and pleasant.	302	Cornaro		13
at these yeares (viz. 83) I have made a most pleasant comedie,	302	Cornaro		29
but cheerfull, lively, and pleasant.	303	Cornaro		11
Since therefore a temperate life is so happie and pleasant a thing;	303	Cornaro		30
PLEASANTLY				
using pleasantly the outlandish proverb, that Prayers and Provender	251	Priest 17		14
PLEASANTNESS				
Wherein a pleasantness of disposition is of great use, men being	252	Priest 18		19
PLEASANTNESSE				
and that pleasantnesse of disposition is a great key to do good;	268	Priest 27		1
instructions seasoned with pleasantnesse, both enter sooner,	268	Priest 27		4
which it most suits withall for variety and pleasantnesse; . .	302	Cornaro		31
Pardons and pleasantnesse are great revenges of slanders. . .	333	Proverbs		365
Pardons and pleasantnesse are great Revengers of slanders. . .	333	Proverbs	V	365
PLEASE				
Shall I, to please anothers wine-sprung minde, ...	8	Ch.-Porch		37
In thy discourse, if thou desire to please:	18	Ch.-Porch		289
Which I can go to, when I please, ...	53	H.Commun.		39
Whither the buyer and the seller please;	104	Obedience		3
Bid what he please; yet I am sure, ...	135	Divinitie		22
And if I please him, I write fine and wittie.	176	Forerunners		12
Being desirous (thorow the Mercy of GOD) to please Him, . .	224	Priest		1
That the way to please him, is to feed my Flocke diligently .	224	Priest		4
from temptation, in a quiet sweetnesse seeks how to please his God.	279	Priest 33		5
It is better to please the Appetite (though they live ten yeares	298	Cornaro		26
Fooles give to please all but their owne.	345	Proverbs		735
Benefits please like flowers while they are fresh. . . .	356	Proverbs	D	40
and such like Gaynesses, which will please a young man well.	370	Letters		4

PLEASE (cont'd)	PAGE	TITLE		LINE
or whom would you please?	381	Woodnoth		19
PLEASED				
He will be pleased with that dittie;	176	Forerunners		11
that the Lord would be pleased to sanctifie them all, that they may	235	Priest 8		28
yet when God pleased, the sun stood stil, the fire burned not.	271	Priest 30		12
either blessing God, that he will be pleased to dwell among men;	273	Priest 31		25
for with such sacrifices God is well pleased.	281	Priest 34		4
whether those that pleased my taste brought me commoditie	293	Cornaro		7
for strong and very cool wines pleased my taste best, as also melons,	293	Cornaro		11
whereinto I was wont, when I pleased my Sense & Appetite.	293	Cornaro		23
I am much pleased also in my travells, with the beauty of situation.	302	Cornaro		6
gratious Lord God, is pleased to give me you for the Man, I desired,	378	Letters		8
John Danvers that he would be pleased to be Overseer of this Will.	382	G.H.'s Will		32
PLEASETH				
Not thankfull, when it pleaseth me;	124	Gratefulnes		29
Who changeth all things, as him pleaseth best.	159	Jos.coat		4
Or if he pleaseth, through it passe,	184	The Elixer		11
Leave jesting whiles it pleaseth, lest it turne to earnest.	324	Proverbs		104
Justice pleaseth few in their owne house.	334	Proverbs		396
He who hath the spice, may season as he pleaseth.	335	Proverbs	V	424
Faire is not faire, but that which pleaseth.	338	Proverbs		492
but he will drinke when and what he pleaseth.	342	Proverbs		623
The first dish pleaseth all.	346	Proverbs		744
PLEASING				
Both want, and wish thy pleasing presence still.	19	Ch.-Porch		326
And ev'n in my unworthinesse pleasing,	175	The Odour		22
But allso pleasing bee.	184	The Elixer	W	4
it is a good strife to go as farre as wee can in pleasing of him,	224	Priest		12
secondly, of eating no pleasing, or over-nourishing things,	242	Priest 10		3
and one of the first steps of pleasing God, having for his owne use	279	Priest 33		8
thy blessed Son's sake, in whose sweet and pleasing words, we say,	289	Priest		35
followed my Appetite, and did eat meats pleasing to my taste;	292	Cornaro		28
Pleasing ware is halfe sould.	321	Proverbs		14
and other titles most pleasing, as well to us remembring,	441	Oration		25
for respect to you, embrace all that is cheerefull, joyous, pleasing.	442	Oration		8
what could have happened more pleasing to us, then the accesse	442	Oration		9
PLEASURE				
Ryme thee to good, and make a bait of pleasure.	6	Ch.-Porch		4
A pain in that, wherein he findes a pleasure?	8	Ch.-Porch		40
A pain in that, whereof he findes a pleasure?	8	Ch.-Porch	W	40
Lust and wine plead a pleasure, avarice gain:	8	Ch.-Porch		57
Lust and wine plead a pleasure, cheating gain:	8	Ch.-Porch	W	57
Cannot on fourtie: he's a man of pleasure,	13	Ch.-Porch		177
Then he can lose with pleasure, stakes his heart;	14	Ch.-Porch		194
For so thou dost thy self and him a pleasure:	18	Ch.-Porch		296
O let this cup passe, if it be thy pleasure:	27	Sacrifice		23
You took me thence, and in your house of pleasure	65	Ch.-mus.		3
Which can let loose to a crown, and yet with pleasure	69	Content		15
And where his pleasure no injunction layes,	78	Ang.&Sts.		19
Unto thy self in everlasting pleasure.	82	Ungratef.		12
Then Pleasure came, who liking not the fashion,	84	The World		6
Quitting with daily labour all My pleasure,	85	Coloss.		9
I know the wayes of Pleasure, the sweet strains,	89	The Pearl		21
What both the steps and pegs of pleasure bee:	89	The Pearl	W	28
Or cabinet of pleasure.	91	Man		30
At first we liv'd in pleasure;	97	Afflict.5		7
A ring, whose posie was, My pleasure:	102	Miserie		69
If that hereafter Pleasure	104	Obedience		11
Will lose a pleasure.	127	Giddinesse		8
Mans joy and pleasure	131	Mans medly		5
Then beautie flow'd, then wisdome, honour, pleasure:	160	The Pulley		7
The late-past frosts tributes of pleasure bring.	165	The Flower		4
Presse me not to take more pleasure	177	The Rose		1
First, there is no pleasure here:	177	The Rose		5
But are their cares and businesse with the pleasure?	188	Judgement	V	17
But are there cares and businesse with the pleasure?	188	Heaven		17
Pleasure succeeded straight, when that grew cold.	194	Ch.-Milit.		144
Setting affliction to encounter pleasure;	194	Ch.-Milit.		148
Setting afflictions to encounter pleasure;	194	Ch.-Milit.	W	148
And from old Rome the libertie of pleasure,	195	Ch.-Milit.		179
and the pleasure that comes with sleep, be sins of gluttony,	230	Priest 5		29
into Covetousnesse, Love of pleasure, or ease, or the like.	238	Priest 9		24
Some times of the yeare I enjoy the pleasure of the Euganean hills,	301	Cornaro		17
Neither is this my pleasure made lesse by the decaying dulnesse of my	302	Cornaro		7
men for one pleasure a thousand griefes prove.	328	Proverbs		228
If you would know secrets, looke them in griefe or pleasure.	333	Proverbs		367
Fly the pleasure that bites to morrow.	336	Proverbs		444
A pleasure long expected is deare enough sold.	350	Proverbs		868
A man would live in Italy (a place of pleasure)	357	Proverbs	D	1047
Say to pleasure, Gentle Eve, I will none of your apple.	360	Proverbs	D	1140
is Regent or Non-regent at his pleasure, and such like Gaynesses,	370	Letters		3
Alsoe my will and pleasure is that Mr Woodnoth should be mine	382	G.H.'s Will		27
PLEASURES				
Whose twigs are pleasures, & they whip thee bare,	6	Ch.-Porch	W	9
When wanton pleasures becken us to thrall.	11	Ch.-Porch		118
Bring not thy plough, thy plots, thy pleasures thither.	23	Ch.-Porch		422
Look not on pleasures as they come, but go.	24	Ch.-Porch		458
What pleasures could I want, whose King I served,	46	Afflict.1		13
Each took his way; some would to pleasures go,	80	Deniall		8
All after pleasures as I rid one day,	80	Christmas		1

POINT (cont'd)	PAGE	TITLE		LINE
yet is there a period for his storing, and a point, or center,	264	Priest 26		29
be amisse in this exceeding usefull point to descend to particulars:	275	Priest 32		18
when they see any remarkable point of Education or good husbandry,	276	Priest 32		30
whose neglect in this point is intolerable, and a shamefull wrong	277	Priest 32		26
finds it somwhat difficult how to proceed in this point.	286	Priest 37		33
Now the Parson taking this point to task, which is so exceeding	287	Priest 37		8
when I shall come to that point, I shall finde no little comfort in	303	Cornaro		23
or living, for all the point lies in believing or not believing.	311	Valdesso		30
though in the point of Resurrection he agreed with them,	316	Valdesso		9
How the godly are exempt from Laws is a known point among Divines,	316	Valdesso		31
and arrives not to the point it should, which if it did,	319	Valdesso		11
The thorne comes forth with his point forwards.	329	Proverbs		238
As the Earth is but a point in respect of the heavens, so are earthly	372	Letters		29
POINTS				
my poor labours, but add to those points, which I have observed,	224	Priest		15
And because the two highest points of Life, wherein a Christian is	227	Priest 3		3
Yet in these points he labours most in those things which are most	227	Priest 3		10
To this end he hath throughly digested all the points of consolation,	249	Priest 15		18
diligently the state thereof to Godward, and that in two points:	251	Priest 17		18
for there being three points of his duty, the one, to infuse	255	Priest 21		2
ignorant and silly souls, even the dark and deep points of Religion.	256	Priest 21		20
Yet the skill consists but in these three points:	256	Priest 21		30
the obscurity in some points being the exercise of the Church,	263	Priest 24		5
These and the like points hee hath accurately digested,	263	Priest 24		14
prepare in all the fore-mentioned points against the time of their	276	Priest 32		27
POISE				
Thine the poise and measure?	114	Dialogue		10
POISON (see also poyson)				
POLE				
From either pole unto the centre:	69	Content		18
From either pole unto the centure:	69	Content	W	18
What frost to that? what pole is not the zone,	166	The Flower		32
But keep a constant Pole.	201	H. Commun.	W	42
POLES				
Beyond the utmost starres and poles.	123	Time		18
East and West touch, the poles do kisse,	163	The Search		43
POLICIE				
In laws and policie; what the starres conspire,	88	The Pearl		5
POLICIES				
And wrap their policies in thy decree,	190	Ch.-Milit.		6
POLLUTE				
Beware of lust: it doth pollute and foul	6	Ch.-Porch		7
By letting in them both pollute her streams:	197	Ch.-Milit.	W	242
POLLUTES				
By letting in them both, pollutes her streams:	197	Ch.-Milit.		242
POLLUTIONS				
What strange pollutions doth he wed,	100	Miserie		13
POMANDER				
Then should the Pomander, which was before	175	The Odour		16
POMANDERS				
But as Pomanders and wood	181	Banquet		25
POMP				
Yet all this glorie, all this pomp and state	106	Sion		7
At there owne weapons, without pomp or state	211	Bohemia	D	21
POMPE				
All our pompe the earth covers.	345	Proverbs		716
POOR				
Such poor invention burns in their low mind	206	Walton 2		9
Be good to the Poor,	207	Walton 3		4
who may not despise my poor labours, but add to those points,	224	Priest		14
not to come at the beginning of service with their poor neighbours,	232	Priest 6		9
or if the poor Church-wardens be affrighted with their greatness,	232	Priest 6		14
then to the elder, now to the poor, and now to the rich.	233	Priest 7		4
he thinks he hath in some measure, according to poor, and fraile man,	236	Priest 8		9
beseeching the Almighty to pardon and accept our poor services,	236	Priest 8		27
and sending his charity by them to the poor, and somtimes giving them	239	Priest 10		26
The Countrey Parson owing a debt of Charity to the poor,	243	Priest 11		7
that he keeps his money for the poor, and his table for those that	243	Priest 11		8
Not but that the poor are welcome also to his table, whom he	243	Priest 11		9
he chooseth rather to give the poor money, which they can better	243	Priest 11		15
if poor, and he able, he easeth them therein.	244	Priest 12		24
time will lose the name and effect of Charity with the poor people,	244	Priest 12		27
he hath a Poor-mans Box conveniently seated, to receive the charity	246	Priest 13		21
if curing poor people, hee supplies them with Receipts,	247	Priest 14		16
if they be poor and needy, whom he thus finds labouring,	248	Priest 14		9
as his accesse to the poor is more comfortable, then to the rich;	249	Priest 14		8
how poor or mean soever, with as joyfull a countenance,	253	Priest 19		19
If he finde another giving a poor man a penny, he gives him a tester	254	Priest 20		13
except the person bee so poor, that he is not able to reward	262	Priest 23		14
but in brief, a poor man is an occasion, my countrey is an occasion,	265	Priest 26		13
when we have sold all, and given it to the poor, we must not be idle,	274	Priest 32		33
Mercy in releeving the poor by a liberall distribution and largesse,	284	Priest 35		8
Much money makes a Countrey poor,	361	Proverbs	D	1178
my resolution to be, that my poor Abilities in Poetry, shall be all,	363	Letters		11
and it is the part of a poor spirit to undervalue himself and blush.	366	Letters		18
of what poor regard ought they to be, since if we had Riches we are	373	Letters		22
in the holy Scripture, are never given to the rich, but to the poor.	373	Letters		29
Blessed be the Meek, and Blessed be the Poor, and, Blessed be	373	Letters		31
hath your Goodness brought on you, by admitting our poor services?	376	Letters		27
Your poor Colony of Servants present their humble duties.	377	Letters		13

POT (cont'd)	PAGE	TITLE		LINE
Although it raine, throw not away thy watering pot.	332	Proverbs		325
As the yeere is, your pot must seeth.	332	Proverbs		335
He that hath no hony in his pot, let him have it in his mouth.	333	Proverbs		360
To seek these things is lost labour; Geese in an oyle pot, . .	361	Proverbs	D	1163
POTABILE				
Many have thought that this could be done by Aurum potabile,	298	Cornaro		20
POTENTATES				
The Kings and Potentates of earth	215	Psalm II	D	3
POTION				
Ballance each dramme of reason, like a potion.	19	Ch.-Porch		322
Then as dispersed herbs do watch a potion, ...	58	H.Script.2		7
POTS				
As watring pots give flowers their lives.	90	Afflict.4		10
POULTIS				
comphrey and smallage made into a Poultis, have done great and rare	262	Priest 23		8
POULTRY				
for the first, Poultry; for the second, swine.	241	Priest 10		30
POUND (verb)				
Whether you boyle snow or pound it, ...	327	Proverbs		180
POUND				
For he, that needs five thousand pound to live, ...	10	Ch.-Porch		107
But if thy sonne can make ten pound his measure, ...	11	Ch.-Porch		113
Who cannot live on twentie pound a yeare, ...	13	Ch.-Porch		176
she would make good her promise of taking five or six pound upon her,	367	Letters		3
three pound more besides that which is due to her, to Ann I leave	382	G.H.'s Will		23
Executor to whome I bequeath twenty pound whereof fifteene pound shal	382	G.H.'s Will		29
twenty pound whereof fifteene pound shal be bestowed uppon Leighton	382	G.H.'s Will		29
uppon Leighton Church, the other five pound I give to himselfe.	382	G.H.'s Will		30
To Mrss Magdalen Vaughan one hundred pound, To Mrs Catharine Vaughan	383	G.H.'s Will		5
To Mrs Catharine Vaughan One hundred pound, To Mr George Herbert one	383	G.H.'s Will		6
Mr George Herbert one hundred pound To Mrs Beatrice Herbert forty	383	G.H.'s Will		7
George Herbert one hundred pound To Mrs Beatrice Herbert forty pound,	383	G.H.'s Will		8
To Mrs Jane Herbert tenn pound, To Mrs Danvers five pound, . .	383	G.H.'s Will		8
To Mrs Danvers five pound, To Amy Danvers thirty shillings, . .	383	G.H.'s Will		9
poore of the parish twenty pound To my Lord of Cherbury tenn pound,	383	G.H.'s Will		14
To Mrs Judith Spencer five pound To Mary Owens forty shillings	383	G.H.'s Will		18
fifty shillings To Mr Gardiner tenn pound MS. that the five pound due	383	G.H.'s Will		20
tenn pound MS. that the five pound due to Mrs Judeth Spenser is	383	G.H.'s Will		20
POUNDS				
these many years, as having spent two hundred pounds in building;	376	Letters		1
First there is seaven hundred pounds in Mr Thomas Lawleys hands	382	G.H.'s Will		8
Vaughan whereof two hundred pounds belongs to my two Neeces that	382	G.H.'s Will		10
this whole sum of five hundred pounds I bequeath unto my Neeces	382	G.H.'s Will		12
Then I bequeath twenty pounds unto the poore of this parish to be	382	G.H.'s Will		16
receaved an hundred and two pounds besides some Remainders of monyes	383	G.H.'s Will		24
POUR (see also powre)				
Will pour full joyes to thee, but dregs to those, ...	213	Bohemia	D	65
who continueth to pour his benefits upon us.	290	Priest		2
POURE				
Mayst rule it, as thou list; and poure the shame, ...	7	Ch.-Porch		27
Which it would poure on thee, upon the floore.	7	Ch.-Porch		28
Which falls by night, and poure it out for you!	140	Ch.-rents		30
And in thy bosome poure my tears, ...	150	Longing		71
Let us (said he) poure on him all we can:	159	The Pulley		3
POUR'D				
Which thou hast pour'd into my soul;	49	Repentance		20
POVERTIE				
All that they leave: this is flat povertie.	10	Ch.-Porch		106
All that is left: this is flat povertie.	10	Ch.-Porch	W	106
More, then his sicknesses or povertie?	18	Ch.-Porch		310
Religion alwaies sides with povertie.	197	Ch.-Milit.		252
Religion alway sides with povertie.	197	Ch.-Milit.	W	252
perpetuall povertie, but when your Excellencies appeare. . . .	442	Oration		37
POVERTY				
except in the cases of extreme poverty, and in the seasons . .	248	Priest 14		4
not the lesse, lest he cast their neighbours poverty on them also.	254	Priest 19		7
Poverty is the mother of health.	337	Proverbs		472
Poverty is no sinne.	349	Proverbs		844
POWDER				
For by that powder thou wilt make us see.	82	Ungratef.		18
For by this powder thou wilt make us see.	82	Ungratef.	W	18
The powder doth forget the dust.	96	Charms & K		14
The powder does forget the dust.	96	Charms & K	W	14
POWDERS				
Flowers, and gummes, and powders giving	181	Banquet		16
POW'R				
Thy pow'r doth cut.	26	The Altar		8
Whose pow'r shall dash and break them all	216	Psalm II	D	23
POWER				
When thou dost purpose ought within thy power, ...	11	Ch.-Porch		115
Many affecting wit beyond their power, ...	16	Ch.-Porch		245
They use that power against me, which I gave:	27	Sacrifice		11
Before I had the power to change my life.	47	Afflict.1		42
Thus doth thy power crosse-bias me, not making	48	Afflict.1		53
Thy power and love, my love and trust	55	Temper 1		27
Who gave me eyes, and light, and power this day, ...	63	Even-song		2
To make a posie for inferiour power.	78	Ang.&Sts.		25
To make a garland for inferiour power.	78	Ang.&Sts.	W	25
And Power it self disable.	86	Lent		18
Some place and power on me?	95	Submission		6

PRAISE (cont'd)	PAGE	TITLE		LINE
And ever praise the Glorious name	222	Psalm VII	D	63
hee wins them to praise God more, to live more religiously,	245	Priest 12		2
or of good report, if there be any vertue, or any praise;	253	Priest 19		25
We praise thee! we blesse thee!	289	Priest		10
God, be ascribed all Honour, and Glory, and Praise, ever.	290	Priest		16
Praise day at night, and life at the end.	324	Proverbs		97
Praise a hill, but keepe below.	338	Proverbs		488
Praise the Sea, but keepe on land.	338	Proverbs		489
True praise rootes and spreedes.	342	Proverbs		638
Old praise dies, unlesse you feede it.	344	Proverbs		699
Neither praise nor dispraise thy selfe,	347	Proverbs		771
Praise none too much, for all are fickle.	347	Proverbs		774
are lovely, & of good report if there be any vertue or any praise.	380	Woodnoth		15
both Indias to his Spaine, knowes no limits of his praise, no,	442	Oration		12
PRAISED				
Praised be the God of love,	92	Antiphon 2		1
Praised be the God alone,	93	Antiphon 2		22
to let him alone, and say rather, God be praised, God be glorified;	245	Priest 12		32
And if a Greek Poet of old was praised, that at the age of 73 yeares	302	Cornaro		33
and yours (which praised be God are less) are not like to continue	374	Letters		2
PRAISES				
Full of his praises,	49	Repentance		34
His praises there may grow.	53	Antiphon 1		6
Lord, thy praises should be more.	93	Antiphon 2		19
Then should thy praises with me grow,	95	Submission		7
To sing thy praises, make them lesse divine.	101	Miserie		40
The evening praises the day, and the morning a host.	342	Proverbs		635
The evening praises the day, and the morning a frost.	342	Proverbs	V	635
The praises also and vertues of the most renowned Princesse Isabel,	442	Oration		22
PRAISETH				
Who praiseth Saint Peter, doth not blame Saint Paul.	349	Proverbs		859
He that praiseth himselfe spattereth himselfe.	353	Proverbs		990
PRAISING				
Praising the sense, as if it were to sell.	102	Jordan 2	W	6
In praising might, the poore do by submission	161	Priesthood		41
neither is he affraid of praising, or praying to God at all times,	284	Priest 35		25
PRATLER				
Peace pratler, do not lowre:	105	Conscience		1
Pratler, no more, I say:	105	Conscience		7
PRATLERS				
No room for pratlers there.	105	Conscience		10
PRAY				
Yet wedding marrs thy fortune, fast & pray:	7	Ch.-Porch	W	14
Pray with the most: for where most pray, is heaven.	22	Ch.-Porch		402
Deare flesh, while I do pray, learn here thy stemme	65	Ch.-monum.		17
Who goes to bed and doth not pray,	96	Charms & K		7
Who goes to bed and does not pray,	96	Charms & K	W	7
My flesh and bones and joynts do pray:	109	Home		74
Tell me, I pray, Whose hands are those?	110	The Quip		7
When I did pray.	133	The Method		16
Then once more pray:	134	The Method		29
Love God, and love your neighbour. Watch and pray.	135	Divinitie		17
my cry to thee, I pray.	218	Psalm V	D	4
when they come to pray, as a devout behaviour in the very act	231	Priest 6		15
he straitly requires of all to pray by themselves before they sleep	241	Priest 10		1
that if after dinner they are not fit (or un-weeldy) either to pray,	266	Priest 26		32
that all Christians should pray twice a day, every day of the week,	272	Priest 31		22
to kneel down, and pray, either blessing God, that he will be pleased	273	Priest 31		24
that neer the place where he is to pray, he spyes some scoffing	273	Priest 31		28
I will not doubt to go without staying to pray there (but onely,	273	Priest 31		35
but that he ought to pray God affectionately and fervently to send	312	Valdesso		16
He that will learne to pray, let him goe to Sea.	323	Proverbs		84
He who will learne to pray, let him goe to Sea.	323	Proverbs	V	84
Labour as long liv'd, pray as ever dying.	337	Proverbs		480
Labour as long liv'd, pray as alwayes dying.	337	Proverbs	V	480
I pray Sir, pardon my boldness of inclosing my Brothers Letter in	367	Letters		23
I pray Sir send the Letter you receive from him to me as soon as you	370	Letters		5
I pray Sir therefore, cause this inclosed to be carried to his	370	Letters		26
PRAY'D				
Did oft possesse me, so that when I pray'd,	130	Love unkn.		58
PRAYED				
To say our Saviour prayed with doubtfulnesse, is more then I can	315	Valdesso		9
or conditionally he prayed as man, though as God he knew the event.	315	Valdesso		11
PRAYER				
Though private prayer be a brave designe,	22	Ch.-Porch		397
Prayer.	51	Prayer 1		T
Prayer the Churches banquet, Angels age,	51	Prayer 1		1
Prayer.	52	H.Commun.	W	T
Lett Prayer help our losses,	53	H.Commun.	W	38
Prayer.	66	Ch.-lock	W	T
Prayer.	103	Prayer 2		T
Ease, Power, and Love; I value prayer so,	103	Prayer 2		20
I and deare prayer would together dwell,	103	Prayer 2		23
Then an old prayer-book I did present:	121	Hope		3
the Prayer that I frame:	217	Psalm IV	D	6
Yea, he my prayer from on high	220	Psalm VI	D	23
The second means is prayer, which if it be necessary even in	228	Priest 4		33
As he opened the day with prayer, so he closeth it, humbly beseeching	236	Priest 8		26
Let him communicate the thing often by prayer unto God,	237	Priest 9		6
he spends his dayes in fasting and prayer, and blesseth God	237	Priest 9		19

PRAYER (cont'd)	PAGE	TITLE		LINE
thoughts to God, nor sanctifying their labour with daily prayer;	248	Priest 14		2
Hee says that prayer with great devotion, where God is thanked	258	Priest 22		5
The first means he useth is Prayer, beseeching the Father of lights	262	Priest 24		22
the Godly have ever added some houres of prayer, as at nine,	272	Priest 31		26
or by oversleeping himself at night, omits his additionary prayer.	272	Priest 31		31
Christian, that this prayer being additionary, not necessary;	273	Priest 31		5
as that by this he may take into his Prayer humiliation also.	273	Priest 31		32
in my heart) because this kinde of Prayer is additionary, . .	273	Priest 31		36
both of Blessing, & cursing are expounded in the Common-Prayer-book:	286	Priest 36		3
Now blessing differs from prayer, in assurance, because it is	286	Priest 36		6
The Authour's Prayer before Sermon.	288	Priest		T
A Prayer after Sermon.	290	Priest		T
and syncere Religion, such as are Prayer, Fasting, Almes-deedes,	312	Valdesso		21
PRAYER-BOOK				
Then an old prayer-book I did present:	121	Hope		3
PRAYERS				
Resort to sermons, but to prayers most:	23	Ch.-Porch		409
My prayers mean thee, yet my prayers stray:	96	Justice 1		9
My tears and prayers night and day do wooe, ...	139	Artillerie		19
Oh that my prayers! mine, alas!	152	The Jews		7
Prayers chas'd syllogismes into their den, ...	191	Ch.-Milit.		55
Direct my prayers to thy Throne, ...	218	Psalm V	D	7
How did he put the Romans in all his prayers? Rom. 1. 9. . .	234	Priest 7		12
besides his ordinary prayers, he makes a peculiar one for a blessing	235	Priest 8		21
and the dayly prayers enjoyned him by auctority, which he observeth	237	Priest 9		23
and devotion, some other dayes for fasting, and hours for prayers;	237	Priest 9		25
and constant prayers, and mortifications in the times of peace	237	Priest 9		32
children and mayds in the fear of God, with prayers, and catechizing,	239	Priest 10		13
and besides the common prayers of the family, he straitly requires	240	Priest 10		38
and knows what prayers they say, and till they have learned them,	241	Priest 10		3
act in them, then when they are called to others prayers, and that,	241	Priest 10		6
So doth hee also before giving make them say their Prayers first,	245	Priest 12		35
as about prayers morning and evening on their knees, reading	248	Priest 14		32
that he will have prayers in the hall, wishing him to informe his	251	Priest 17		11
outlandish proverb, that Prayers and Provender never hinder journey.	251	Priest 17		14
what means of Piety, whether daily prayers be used, Grace, . .	251	Priest 17		22
in this, that at Sermons, and Prayers, men may sleep or wander;	257	Priest 21		18
the Parson and his Family use to premise prayers, for this is to cure	262	Priest 23		10
But these prayers are not necessary, but additionary. . . .	272	Priest 31		28
Of the first sort are repentance, prayers, fasting, Psalmes,	312	Valdesso	V	26
When prayers are done, my Lady is ready.	323	Proverbs		71
Prayers and provender hinder no journey.	330	Proverbs		277
Prayers and provender never hinder any journey.	330	Proverbs	V	277
so devout as to come to the Chappell an howre before prayers began,	368	Letters		18
by so much shall it make my prayers the more constant and the more	372	Letters		22
diligence, prayers and tears, to bud, blow and bear fruit in your	377	Letters		5
you have layed out thoughts & prayers you have sowed. . . .	380	Woodnoth		10
PRAYES				
Who still is right, and prayes to be so still.	73	Constancie		35
So prayes Your ever loving brother, G. HERBERT.	376	Letters		20
PRAYING				
Praying's the end of preaching. O be drest;	23	Ch.-Porch		410
The Parson praying.	231	Priest 6		T
they come to pray, as a devout behaviour in the very act of praying.	231	Priest 6		16
them with all Piety, not only of words in praying, and reading;	239	Priest 10		24
esteeming that this private praying is a more voluntary act in them,	241	Priest 10		4
or praying to God at all times, but is rather glad of catching	284	Priest 35		25
eating, walking, praying, working, still together, that I take	375	Letters		19
PRAYSE				
Prayse not thyself, thy actions serve the Turne.	347	Proverbs	V	771
to his prayse, & the great Joy of Your Brother & Servant in Christ	378	Letters		27
PREACH				
Lord, how can man preach thy eternall word?	67	Windows		1
Why dost thou preach my Laws, and takest my Covenant in thy mouth?	226	Priest 2		14
either in Sermon, if he preach, or at some other time of the day,	253	Priest 19		13
PREACHED				
and preached in the morning, and catechized in the afternoone,	236	Priest 8		7
but with the Gospel it selfe be preached to all ages, Matth. 26. 13.	282	Priest 34		26
motion (as S. Paul had when hee would have preached in Asia),	313	Valdesso		16
The Frier preached against stealing, ...	345	Proverbs		737
PREACHER				
Judge not the preacher; for he is thy Judge:	23	Ch.-Porch		427
so in the house of a Preacher, all are preachers.	240	Priest 10		31
PREACHER'S				
The holy Preachers; then the light and glorie	67	Windows		8
PREACHERS				
Preachers conclude with, hath not lost his pains.	24	Ch.-Porch		434
These Preachers make	101	Miserie		47
so in the house of a Preacher, all are preachers.	240	Priest 10		31
PREACHERS'				
Jest not at preachers language, or expression:	24	Ch.-Porch		439
PREACHETH				
God takes a text, and preacheth patience.	23	Ch.-Porch		432
the storehouse of his Sermons, and which he preacheth all his Life;	230	Priest 5		2
The Countrey Parson preacheth constantly, the pulpit is his joy	232	Priest 7		20
When he preacheth, he procures attention by all possible art,	232	Priest 7		30
at table about his appetite, if he tell this to another, preacheth;	278	Priest 33		19
Romans 2.) hee first preacheth to himselfe, and then to others.	279	Priest 33		36
When the Foxe preacheth, beware your geese.	332	Proverbs		337
He that preacheth giveth almes.	347	Proverbs		788

	PAGE	TITLE		LINE
PREPARED (cont'd)				
temple as much as Solomon because he desired it, & prepared for it.	381	Woodnoth		20
PREPOSSESSED				
that a weak stomack being prepossessed with flesh, shall much better	242	Priest 10		22
PREPOSSEST				
But still to make thee prepossest, ...	184	The Elixer		7
PREROGATIVE				
All worship is prerogative, and a flower	78	Ang.&Sts.		21
but giving him the prerogative of his Fathers profession, . .	239	Priest 10		31
PRESCRIBED				
to Blesse the people, and the forme thereof is prescribed, Numb. 6.	285	Priest 36		17
PRESCRIBES				
prescribes this Physick first, That he use a moderate diet: . .	297	Cornaro		16
PRESENCE				
Both want, and wish thy pleasing presence still.	19	Ch.-Porch		326
Need & bee glad, & wish thy presence still:	19	Ch.-Porch	W	326
by an often urging of the presence, and majesty of God, . .	234	Priest 7		25
and presence of Almighty God, and blessing the people either openly,	236	Priest 8		5
he requires the presence of all, and Baptizeth not willingly,	258	Priest 22		2
as being done both in the presence of God, and his Saints, . .	258	Priest 22		13
he may behave himself so as befits so great a presence; . .	273	Priest 31		27
as knowing that absence breedes strangeness, but presence love.	284	Priest 35		16
worse by your withdrawing which grow not better by your presence.	381	Woodnoth		11
there is nothing here answerable to the greatnesse of your presence.	442	Oration		30
PRESENT				
Lord, my first fruits present themselves to thee;	5	Dedication		1
(Love is a present for a mightie king)	20	Ch.-Porch		350
Love is a present for the greatest king.	20	Ch.-Porch	W	350
The angrie Lion did present his paw, ...	70	Humilitie		9
How well her name an Army doth present, ...	77	Anagram		1
And here present it as my speciall deed.	104	Obedience		10
Man is the wcrlds high Priest: he doth present	117	Providence		13
Wherefore, most sacred Spirit, I here present	117	Providence		25
Then an old prayer-book I did present:	121	Hope		3
Thinking with that, which I did thus present, ...	129	Love unkn.		31
Rather hereafter, then in present, is.	131	Mans medly		6
And for the present health restore.	138	The Size		30
Onely the present is thy part and fee.	144	Discharge		21
What present things requir'd of thee.	144	Discharge		25
Man and the present fit: if he provide, ...	145	Discharge		31
Things present shrink and die: but they that spend . . .	145	Discharge		41
I will present, and somewhat more, ...	152	The Bag		40
And keeps thee present, leaving th' old	162	The Search		27
Are so, as for the present, I did move	204	Persever.	W	3
And I to you a Blackamore present.	209	L. Bacon	D	2
and neglect the present service of God, he by no means suffers it,	232	Priest 6		11
him unworthy of that Majesty before which he is to present himself,	235	Priest 8		24
resolves with himself never to omit any present good deed of charity,	240	Priest 10		6
more then by faith, by present rewards, or punishments, . .	254	Priest 20		32
He requires all to be present at Catechizing:	255	Priest 21		26
who being to present all that receive not thrice a year; . .	259	Priest 22		25
both in present for his family, and in future for his children,	264	Priest 26		26
neighbourly admonitions they still persist in ill, to present them;	270	Priest 29		20
of dependance, how faire soever the opportunities present themselves.	271	Priest 30		27
dishes at table, which even their present health otherwise admits;	280	Priest 34		23
furnitures which even their present plenty of wealth otherwise	280	Priest 34		25
which the present occasion of wit and company otherwise admits;	280	Priest 34		27
then their present exile, and disability to live in their Countrey.	282	Priest 34		10
Wherefore he exacts of all to bee present at the perambulaticn,	284	Priest 35		10
let such thoughts as these, moderate your present fear and sorrow;	374	Letters		4
Your poor Colony of Servants present their humble duties. . .	377	Letters		13
PRESENTED				
Presented tokens of submission.	70	Humilitie		4
Here, as broken, is presented.	181	Banquet		30
admonitions, if they persevere, he causes them to be presented:	232	Priest 6		14
then by causing them to be presented, or otherwise complained of.	254	Priest 20		25
who writt a poem heere in England & presented it to the King,	368	Letters		31
PRESENTING				
but as presenting with himself the whole Congregation, whose sins he	231	Priest 6		7
and to do such things of legall opposition either in the presenting,	263	Priest 25		24
and still they will be presenting or wishing to see, if at length	376	Letters		28
PRESENTLY				
One might have sought and found thee presently	99	Decay		6
all which is here expressed, hee presently sinns, and displeases God,	224	Priest		11
presently falls to work, and seems to himselfe so as a Market-man is,	235	Priest 8		17
himselfe what good deeds he can do that day, and presently doth them;	244	Priest 12		17
he presently lays hold of it, least the poyson steal into some young	252	Priest 18		5
to that which is presently unlawfull, even in one continued action.	264	Priest 26		21
Not that all must presently work after dinner;	266	Priest 26		33
Wherefore all are either presently to enter into a Calling, . .	275	Priest 32		14
presently after Michaelmas, I am to make an Cration to the whole	369	Letters		12
PRESENTS				
As thy discoverie presents.	42	Easter	W	26
When by the beasts the presents tendred were, ...	70	Humilitie		7
But now that Christs pure vail presents the sight, ...	141	Justice 2		13
amazed with the Majesty of God, before whom he then presents himself;	231	Priest 6		6
he presents them himself, only protesting to them, that not any ill	232	Priest 6		17
and if they will not reforme, presents them.	284	Priest 35		13
in regard it presents us not with the same thing only when it is read	310	Valdesso		33
Presents of love fear not to be ill taken of strangers. . .	361	Proverbs	D	1162

PREVENT (cont'd)	PAGE	TITLE		LINE
Thus we prevent the last great day,	171	Self-cond.		19
will appear if the Pious soul foresee and prevent such interruptions,	273	Priest 31		17
that they prevent my memory, and yet still grow upon Your humblest	367	Letters		15
PREVENTED				
may be prevented, or diverted by reasonable imployment.	274	Priest 32		23
PREVENTEST				
Who in all grief preventest me?	35	Thanksgvng		4
PREVENTS				
he either prevents it judiciously, or breaks it off seasonably	252	Priest 18		17
PREY				
Not flyes, but I shall bee his prey	61	Praise 1	W	19
But Man hath caught and kept it, as his prey.	91	Man		20
But Man has caught and kept it, as his prey.	91	Man	W	20
The great prey on the lesse, they on some weed.	118	Providence		52
And till they foot and clutch their prey,	126	Confession		15
All beasts of prey are strong or treacherous.	355	Proverbs		1023
An old cat sports not with her prey.	355	Proverbs		1030
PRICE				
Thy rate and price, and mark thee for a treasure;	6	Ch.-Porch		2
The price of thee, and mark thee for a treasure;	6	Ch.-Porch	W	2
Whose drops of bloud paid the full price,	76	Sunday		54
And at what rate and price I have thy love;	89	The Pearl		35
and consequently knowing the price of mony, are offended much	227	Priest 3		14
and ingagement of their discourses for no price sooner,	252	Priest 18		21
Love is the true price of love.	339	Proverbs		540
for it sets a dearer price on every thing.	361	Proverbs	D	1178
when there is no caus, but by setting a just price of your qualities:	366	Letters		18
PRICK				
And prick mine eyes.	71	Frailtie		16
While they do wound and prick my soul.	90	Afflict.4		12
PRICKING				
With bushie groves, pricking the lookers eie,	51	Faith		38
PRIDE				
Pride and full sinnes have made the way a road.	9	Ch.-Porch		72
Who with excessive pride	85	Vanitie 1		13
When th' hair is sweet through pride or lust,	96	Charms & K		13
While she avoids her neighbours pride,	110	Brit. Ch.		22
The rock of Pride.	142	Pilgrimage		6
What pride by opposition.	161	Priesthood		42
Forfeit their Paradise by their pride.	167	The Flower		49
and in sore anger vex their pride.	215	Psalm II	D	12
are principally these two, Spirituall pride, and Impurity of heart:	238	Priest 9		3
that destroyeth at noone day, [Ghostly pride and self-conceite.]	238	Priest 9		8
which is not easily despised, except it degenerate to pride.	268	Priest 28		27
Heresie is the school of pride.	357	Proverbs	D	1057
PRIE				
Why dost thou prie,	144	Discharge		2
PRIEST				
The Priest and rulers all false witnesse seek	28	Sacrifice		57
Man is the worlds high Priest: he doth present	117	Providence		13
Poore priest thus am I drest.	174	Aaron		10
So now being Priest he plainly did professe	195	Ch.-Milit.		173
A PRIEST To the TEMPLE, OR, The Countrey PARSON	223	Priest		T
in that a Priest may do that which Christ did, and by his auctority,	225	Priest 1		16
in that a Priest is to do that which Christ did, and after his	225	Priest 1		18
givings are lay, and secular, but this is to give like a Priest.	245	Priest 12		38
interesting of that dignity wherewith God hath invested the Priest,	286	Priest 36		10
PRIEST'S				
the Priests Benedicite, and his holy water were over highly valued;	286	Priest 36		15
In the mean time a Priests blessing, though it be none	377	Letters		1
PRIESTHOOD				
The Priesthood.	160	Priesthood		T
Out of this Chartre of the Priesthood may be plainly gathered both	225	Priest 1		14
they wrong the Priesthood, neglect their duty, and shall be so farre	226	Priest 2		33
for it was not the person, but Priesthood, that blessed;	285	Priest 36		23
PRIESTS				
The Priests and rulers all false witnesse seek	28	Sacrifice	W	57
he constituted Deputies in his place, and these are Priests.	225	Priest 1		9
the Priests of the Old Testament were commanded to Blesse the people,	285	Priest 36		15
so that even ill Priests may blesse.	285	Priest 36		24
PRIME				
Riddle who list, for me, and pull for Prime:	57	Jordan 1		12
Flowers look about, and die not in their prime.	154	Glimpse		10
Before the other. Greece being past her prime,	191	Ch.-Milit.		60
Before the other two were in their prime.	191	Ch.-Milit.	W	60
PRIMITIVE				
He often readeth the Lives of the Primitive Monks, Hermits,	237	Priest 9		28
PRINCE				
But I the Prince of peace; peace that doth passe	30	Sacrifice		118
As Prince or King:	61	Praise 1		10
There was a Prince of old	125	Peace		22
While Prince to Spaine, and King to Cambridge goes,	438	Lat.Trans.		1
Of a new Prince, new bondage.	359	Proverbs	D	1116
be it to King, Prince, or whatever comes to the University;	369	Letters		35
PRINCES				
The Princes of my people make a head	26	Sacrifice		5
All poste to Rome: Princes submit their necks	195	Ch.-Milit.		195
even as Princes have theirs, besides their publick disbursments.	236	Priest 8		17
Princes have no way.	352	Proverbs		956
Spies are the ears and eyes of Princes.	357	Proverbs	D	1067

PROCURES (cont'd)	PAGE	TITLE	LINE
that he rather procures them to be often, as knowing that absence	284	Priest 35	14
PROCURING			
affections of the soul in desiring and procuring increase of means,	230	Priest 5	27
of holinesse, then the procuring, and rejoycing in anothers good.	234	Priest 7	10
PRODIGALITY			
Habits oppose morall vertues, as Prodigality opposes Moderation;	308	Valdesso	10
PRODIGALL			
as he that eats more then his estate will bear, is a Prodigall;	266	Priest 26	9
PRODIGIES			
As the old heathen would deem prodigies.	194	Ch.-Milit.	154
PRODIGIOUS			
When height of malice, and prodigious lusts, ...	197	Ch.-Milit.	237
PRODUCE			
For they all produce repentance, ...	178	The Rose	27
Such power hath mightie Baptisme to produce	191	Ch.-Milit.	45
could out of humility, produce any speciall grace of faith, patience,	238	Priest 9	31
for this may produce hatred in those that are reproved, . .	268	Priest 28	29
PRODUC'D			
That nature hath produc'd. Let ev'ry vein	164	Grief	4
PRODUCETH			
But those which his home produceth, he refuseth not, as coming cheap,	241	Priest 10	22
PROFANELY			
as neither to labour anxiously, nor distrustfully, nor profanely.	247	Priest 14	27
Then they labour profanely, when they set themselves to work like	247	Priest 14	32
PROFANENESSE			
Profanenesse, filthinesse, abusivenesse.	16	Ch.-Porch	236
Avoid, profanenesse; come not here:	25	Superlim	5
Profanenesse in my head, ...	174	Aaron	6
PROFESS			
As if none could bee brave, but who profess	21	Ch.-Porch W	369
but, I profess it not:	363	Letters	16
PROFESSE			
So now being Priest he plainly did professe	195	Ch.-Milit.	173
the second to professe it, the third to despise counsell. . .	337	Proverbs	460
PROFESSED			
that the same common truths may be every where professed, . . .	255	Priest 21	19
that at Baptisme they professed not to be ashamed of Christs Cross,	284	Priest 35	32
when he professed himselfe a Pharisee, which strictly he was not,	316	Valdesso	8
the Catholick Religion is professed with greatest strictness).	357	Proverbs D	1047
PROFESSETH			
therefore St. Paul in the beginning of his Epistles, professeth this:	225	Priest 1	10
but also professeth himselfe throughly of the opinion, carrying it	250	Priest 16	8
PROFESSION			
but giving him the prerogative of his Fathers profession, . . .	239	Priest 10	32
as also by discourse with men of that profession, whom he hath ever	260	Priest 23	4
both for the generall ignominy which is cast upon the profession,	268	Priest 28	10
and not ingaged into some Profession by their Parents, whose neglect	277	Priest 32	25
a reverence, and makes him esteemed according to his Profession.	286	Priest 36	25
PROFESSIONS			
not to incroach on others Professions, but to live on his own.	262	Priest 23	17
PROFESSOURS			
the Professours whereof were much imployed by Queen Elizabeth,	277	Priest 32	31
PROFFER			
Thy sorrows were in earnest; no faint proffer, ...	104	Obedience	28
PROFIT			
the same affection which made him not profit before, making him then	235	Priest 7	13
to have them so, it were his profit, for none are so well served,	240	Priest 10	14
to goodnesse as he can, both in honour, and profit, and fame;	244	Priest 11	4
the Law concerning such goods for the use and profit of their Parish:	270	Priest 29	4
the end I got the victorie, to my great honour, and no lesse profit:	294	Cornaro	29
Honour without profit is a ring on the finger.	328	Proverbs	230
Honour and profit lie not in one sacke.	328	Proverbs	232
No profit to honour, no honour to Religion.	346	Proverbs	759
PROFITABLE			
he takes occasion to discourse of such things as are both profitable,	236	Priest 8	22
he chides not at first, for that were neither civill, nor profitable;	248	Priest 14	15
Wherefore since an orderly life is so profitable, so vertuous,	300	Cornaro	3
PROFITS			
Then those same pendant profits, which the spring	86	Lent	25
and he that profits not in that time, will lesse afterwards,	235	Priest 7	12
and how every one profits, comparing this yeer with the last:	240	Priest 10	37
The meat which remaineth, profits more then that which is eaten.	296	Cornaro	1
PROFITT			
the one imployment, the other profitt, the work I may change,	381	Woodnoth	31
other profitt, the work I may change, the profitt, I am master of.	381	Woodnoth	32
PROFOUND			
To put on the profound humility, and the exact temperance of our Lord	237	Priest 9	33
PROGENIE			
In his progenie doth shine.	208	J. Danvers D	12
PROHIBITING			
that the prohibiting of flesh came from hot Countreys, where both	242	Priest 10	16
PROJECTS			
Pitch thy behaviour low, thy projects high;	19	Ch.-Porch	331
I know the projects of unbridled store:	89	The Pearl	26
I know the projects of unbundled store:	89	The Pearl V	26
PROLONG			
and procure that they prolong their life even to a hundred yeares	298	Cornaro	15
PROLONGS			
because by eating little he prolongs his life.	295	Cornaro	35

PROMISE	PAGE	TITLE		LINE
Thy promise now hath ev'n set thee thy laws.	139	Artillerie		24
there being a promise, that if the Kingdome of God be first sought,	278	Priest 33		13
and the more the promise is delayed, the more he reads it, . .	310	Valdesso		29
say she would make good her promise of taking five or six pound upon	367	Letters		2
PROMIS'D				
My God hath promis'd; he is just.	145	Discharge		55
PROMISED				
this life, who hath promised, that Godlinesse shall be gainfull:	254	Priest 20		19
PROMISES				
Yet publick hath more promises, more love:	22	Ch.-Porch		398
Yet publick has more promises, more love:	22	Ch.-Porch	W	398
Gods promises have made thee mine;	141	Justice 2		22
And all thy promises live and bide.	150	Longing		68
for knowledge, Examples for illustration, and Promises for comfort:	228	Priest 4		25
from his promises, from the examples of all Saints, that ever were;	249	Priest 15		21
stead to his Parish, and dischargeth God what he can of his promises.	254	Priest 20		9
Circumcised to this day, and expect the promises of the Scripture;	282	Priest 34		1
or assent to the promises of the Gospell by heare-say, or relation	309	Valdesso		1
and applying the generall promises to every one in particular	309	Valdesso		4
In the Scripture are Promises, these ever comfort more and more.	310	Valdesso		14
the Scriptures and this is the use of the promises of the Scriptures.	310	Valdesso		31
us not with the same thing only when it is read as the promises doe,	310	Valdesso		34
PROMISING				
Promising is the eve of giving.	349	Proverbs		847
lib. with her own hands (& promising to get her Son to doe as much)	379	Letters		3
PROMISSES				
Onely my soule hangs on thy promisses	205	Persever.	W	13
PROMOTION				
They who for the hope of promotion neglect any necessary admonition,	226	Priest 2		36
or untimely desire of promotion to an higher state, or place,	238	Priest 9		15
PROOF				
though unused a proof of Divinity taken from thence, that . . .	281	Priest 34		33
intended by God, that the Jewes should be his proof, and witnesses,	282	Priest 34		12
PROOFE				
But not their harts, as I by proofe doe try.	30	Sacrifice	W	123
the faults of eating, and the truth of them needs no proofe:	266	Priest 26		13
PROOFS				
Fetching their proofs ev'n from the very bone;	167	Dotage		11
PROPAGATION				
O that within us hearts had propagation, ...	147	Offering		7
PROPER				
And challenge it, as proper to his place, ...	70	Humilitie		20
night and day against the proper and peculiar temptations of his	238	Priest 9		1
and proper texts of Scripture every where painted, and that all	246	Priest 13		11
But this was not proper to Christ, or the Apostles only, . .	285	Priest 36		12
saw that it was no hard thing to do so, but the proper duty of man;	292	Cornaro		32
PROPERLY				
Are properly a crosse felt by thy sonne, ...	165	The Crosse		35
or out of my possession that properly belonge to me unto my deare	382	G.H.'s Will		6
PROPERTIES				
and what hidden properties it hath, what meat and drink agrees best	297	Cornaro		27
PROPHECY				
whether prophecy, let us prophecy according to the proportion	226	Priest 2		5
prophecy, let us prophecy according to the proportion of faith;	226	Priest 2		5
PROPHESIE				
Now prophesie who strikes thee, is their dittie.	31	Sacrifice		142
Now a prophesie is a wonder sent to Posterity, least they complaine	282	Priest 34		35
PROPHESIES				
There are two Prophesies in the Gospel, which evidently argue Christs	282	Priest 34		22
PROPHET				
As Sinne in Greece a Prophet was before, ...	195	Ch.-Milit.		171
PROPHETESSE				
a prophetesse, and a Lattin bred woman.	360	Proverbs	D	1151
PROPHETS				
And Prophets once to see, but found no place:	32	Sacrifice		183
The Prophets are admirable in this.	234	Priest 7		1
PROPORTION				
Yet must there such proportion be assign'd	196	Ch.-Milit.	W	232
prophecy, let us prophecy according to the proportion of faith;	226	Priest 2		6
or a good proportion of all, out of all which he hath compiled	229	Priest 5		33
paymaster, rewarding all good deeds to their full proportion.	254	Priest 20		21
or not in some proportion to Gods blessing upon him, is covetous.	265	Priest 26		6
feele my self, either I take my wonted proportion, or diminish of it.	267	Priest 26		9
power of health consists most in the proportion of meat and drink.	293	Cornaro		33
keep a fit proportion, shall receive little hurt from other excesses.	294	Cornaro		5
then the commoditie of meat taken in a moderate proportion. . .	296	Cornaro		4
For if he should keep his former proportion, Nature, which is	299	Cornaro		33
of your love, with being in some proportion, and after my manner,	364	Letters		3
PROPORTIONABLE				
that the patient might be proportionable to the agent, and especially	295	Cornaro		31
PROPORTIONS				
Full of proportions, one limbe to another, ...	91	Man		14
Yet must there such proportions be assign'd	196	Ch.-Milit.		232
PROPOSALS				
That you did not only entertain my proposals, but advance them,	375	Letters		2
PROPOSE				
only hereafter I will take heed how I propose my desires unto you,	363	Letters		20
PROPOSETH				
MAN Proposeth, God disposeth.	321	Proverbs		1

PUBLICKE	PAGE	TITLE		LINE
so when the offence is publicke, and against God, I am then to follow	248	Priest 14		28
PUBLICKLY				
Those he Catechizeth publickly, these privately, giving age honour,	255	Priest 21		24
both publickly, and privately instruct his Church-Wardens,	269	Priest 29		26
PUBLISH				
nevertheless I wish you by all meanes to publish it, for these three	304	Valdesso		18
PUBLISHED				
Print it, that with it the honour of my Lord might be published.	305	Valdesso		8
PUBLISHING				
overweigh the defects (as I conceive) towards the publishing thereof,	305	Valdesso		14
PUDDLE				
Every path hath a puddle.	328	Proverbs		215
PUFFING				
Sometimes Death, puffing at the doore,	67	Ch.-floore		16
Then came brave Glorie puffing by	111	The Quip		13
PULING				
What do these loud complaints and puling fears,	136	Familie	V	3
PULL (see also puls)				
Riddle who list, for me, and pull for Prime:	57	Jordan 1		12
To endlesse death: but thou dost pull	75	Sunday		16
The trees say, Pull me: but the hand you stretch,	117	Providence		23
To this great lotterie, and all would pull.	193	Ch.-Milit.		134
When all things pull & hale, that they may bring	212	Bohemia	D	27
Love your neighbour, yet pull not downe your hedge.	325	Proverbs		141
Love your neighbour, but pull not downe your hedge.	325	Proverbs	V	141
Pull downe your hatt on the winds side.	332	Proverbs		334
which a hundred wise men cannot pull out.	339	Proverbs		527
PULL'ST				
Thou pull'st the rug, and wilt not rise,	101	Miserie		51
PULLEY				
The Pulley.	159	The Pulley		T
PULLING				
What do these loud complaints and pulling fears,	136	Familie		3
and with pulling, gets the apple out of his Fathers hand:	272	Priest 30		9
PULPIT				
neither will they beleeve him in the pulpit, whom they cannot trust	228	Priest 3		7
Parson preacheth constantly, the pulpit is his joy and his throne:	232	Priest 7		20
still pressing it in the pulpit, and out of the pulpit,	245	Priest 12		13
it in the pulpit, and out of the pulpit, and never leaving them,	245	Priest 12		13
and uniform, especially that the Pulpit, and Desk, and Communion	246	Priest 13		6
PULPITS				
Pulpits and sundayes, sorrow dogging sinne,	45	Sinne 1		5
PULS				
Hee puls with a long rope, that waits for anothers death.	322	Proverbs		25
Hee puls with a long rope, who looks for anothers death.	322	Proverbs	V	25
PULSE				
But such a heart, whose pulse may be	124	Gratefulnes		31
and pulse of every person in his house, and accordingly either meets	239	Priest 10		8
in his discourses occasionally, according to the pulse of the hearer.	268	Priest 27		7
pork, sausages, pulse, and cake, and py-crust, and the like:	293	Cornaro		13
There needs a long time to know the worlds pulse.	350	Proverbs		886
PUNISH				
And never yet, whom I would punish, miss'd:	30	Sacrifice		131
And never yet, whom he would punish, miss'd:	30	Sacrifice	W	131
Thou didst so punish sinne,	43	East.wings		13
Daily didst punish sinne,	43	East.wings	W	13
Nor let them punish me with losse of ryme,	57	Jordan 1		14
Nor let them punish me with losse of time,	57	Jordan 1	V	14
that how or whenever he punish him, it be not in his Ministry:	235	Priest 8		26
they come home, either commend or reprove, either reward or punish.	255	Priest 21		29
When God will punish, hee will first take away the understanding.	344	Proverbs		688
PUNISHABLE				
contempt shall proceed so far as to do any thing punishable by law,	268	Priest 28		32
But if the Contempt be not punishable by Law, or being so,	269	Priest 28		3
The godly are punishable as others, when they doe amisse,	316	Valdesso		17
PUNISHED				
if the punished delinquent shall be much troubled for his sins,	288	Priest 37		2
we shall not be punished (which word I like here better then	311	Valdesso		27
godly are chastized but not punished) for evill doing nor rewarded	311	Valdesso		28
and yet he had been punished justly, that is in humano foro &	316	Valdesso		27
PUNISHER				
done either wel or ill, whereof he is not the rewarder, or punisher.	254	Priest 20		11
PUNISHING				
The Parsons punishing of sin and vice, is rather by withdrawing his	254	Priest 20		22
and in punishing vice, the Parson endeavoureth to be in Gods stead,	254	Priest 20		30
The Parson punishing.	263	Priest 25		T
or punishing of any, as the vulgar ever conşters for signes of ill	263	Priest 25		24
PUNISHMENT				
Doubtlesse, but in the way of punishment,	155	Assurance		4
he is carefull to see condign punishment inflicted, and with truly	254	Priest 20		27
and thirsteth after righteous punishment of unrighteousnesse.	254	Priest 20		28
doing any thing of aversenesse, save in the very act of punishment:	263	Priest 25		29
estranging may corroborate the punishment to a better subduing,	263	Priest 25		31
to the examination, and punishment of those which are in Authority;	269	Priest 28		1
it according as he sees fit, either for reward or punishment.	270	Priest 30		32
in all Lands, was intended not only for a punishment to them;	282	Priest 34		14
And therefore this kind of Punishment was chosen rather then any	282	Priest 34		17
and hast made our salvation, not our punishment, thy glory:	288	Priest		24
Punishment is lame, but it comes.	329	Proverbs		249
let him be wise in the punishment.	340	Proverbs		555

PUNISHMENT (cont'd)	PAGE	TITLE		LINE
Every sin brings its punishment with it.	346	Proverbs		760
Service without reward is punishment.	354	Proverbs		1015
PUNISHMENTS				
by present rewards, or punishments, more then by future.	254	Priest 20		32
PUNISHT				
The cheapest sinnes most dearely punisht are;	9	Ch.-Porch		67
PURCHASE				
To make a purchase there: he sees their dances,	85	Vanitie 1		5
Onely to purchase my good-will:	94	Unkindness		24
No, not to purchase the whole pack of starres:	101	Miserie		52
Lord, let it now by way of purchase go.	105	Obedience		35
And make the purchase spread	105	Obedience		39
To purchase heaven for repenting,	111	Vanitie 2		9
as to a great purchase for their children, and servants;	259	Priest 22		3
sit down at this world, God bids him sell it, and purchase a better:	272	Priest 30		7
Hee that learnes a trade hath a purchase made.	353	Proverbs		978
PURCHASED				
By any art, yet to be purchased.	13	Ch.-Porch		172
What reason hath from nature purchased,	88	The Pearl	W	3
Rich shrines and oracles he purchased:	193	Ch.-Milit.		128
PURE				
Nothing but holy, pure, and cleare,	25	Superlim		6
What ever sinne did this pure rock commit,	41	Sepulchre		10
And those things most, which are most pure and fine:	101	Miserie		38
Pure red and white.	115	Dulnesse		12
But now that Christs pure vail presents the sight,	141	Justice 2		13
What hast thou there? a heart? but is it pure?	147	Offering		3
Yet one pure heart is nothing to bestow:	147	Offering		5
O what pure things, most pure must those things be,	161	Priesthood		29
that he may keep himself pure, and not be intangled in others sinnes.	248	Priest 14		24
things are honest, or just, or pure, or lovely, or of good report,	253	Priest 19		24
onely by a pure consumption of the radicall moisture, without grief	298	Cornaro		17
(setting casualties aside) I shall not die but by a pure resolution:	303	Cornaro		26
by the Apostles rule (Philip 4, 8.) not only to pursue pure things,	380	Woodnoth		13
PURENES				
That zele and purenes circling my request	66	Ch.-lock	W	11
PURENESSE				
That so in purenesse thou mayst him adore,	170	Water-crs.		9
PURER				
Compare with ancient times and purer yeares;	196	Ch.-Milit.		227
PUREST				
Where most things were of purest gold;	106	Sion		3
PURGATORY				
At Purgatory, there inchanted Ile,	212	Bohemia	D	50
PURGE				
Turning my purge to food, thou throwest me	48	Afflict.1		51
Purge all my sinnes done heretofore:	68	Trin.Sun.		4
They purge the aire without, within the breast.	132	The Storm		18
And repentance is a purge.	178	The Rose		28
PURG'D				
Christ purg'd his temple; so must thou thy heart.	23	Ch.-Porch		423
PURGETH				
What is sweeter? yet it purgeth.	178	The Rose		18
PURGING				
letting of bloud, and purging, that the store of humours,	295	Cornaro		4
PURGINGS				
Purgings enmitie disclose,	178	The Rose		19
PURITIE				
We cannot reach our Saviours puritie;	87	Lent		34
Thou art all brightnesse, perfect puritie;	101	Miserie		32
Thou art a God whose puritie	218	Psalm V	D	9
PURITY				
the purity of his mind breaking out, and dilating it selfe even	228	Priest 3		12
PURLE				
But that from them joyes purle for ever	59	Whitsunday	W	22
PURLING				
Must purling streams refresh a lovers loves?	56	Jordan 1		8
PURLOIN'D				
A tithe purloin'd cankers the whole estate.	22	Ch.-Porch		386
Our cyens have purloin'd, and left you drie:	152	The Jews		2
Our sinnes have purloin'd, and left you drie:	152	The Jews	V	2
PURPOSE				
When thou dost purpose ought within thy power,	11	Ch.-Porch		115
On purpose from the ventrous wretch;	85	Vanitie 1		11
I writ thy purpose long ago.	155	Assurance		18
To this purpose, some dialogues in Plato were worth the reading,	256	Priest 21		27
A wise man needes not blush for changing his purpose.	342	Proverbs		613
Every one is witty for his owne purpose.	346	Proverbs		754
to me as soon as you can, that I may work the heads to my purpose.	370	Letters		7
PURPOSED				
And I purposed to try, whether those that pleased my taste brought me	293	Cornaro		6
PURPOSELY				
whom he sometimes purposely takes home with him, setting them close	243	Priest 11		10
Nay they are purposely recorded in holy Writ.	316	Valdesso		5
PURPOSES				
of himself, for all the purposes which God hath ordained him.	227	Priest 3		9
sake, and to make his higher purposes slip the more easily.	249	Priest 14		12
thy Counsels, disappointed thy Purposes, and sold our God,	288	Priest		17
into your hart, and the LORD bless all your purposes to his glory.	375	Letters		34

	PAGE	TITLE		LINE
PURPOSETHE				
MAN purposethe Gcd disposeth.	321	Proverbs	V	1
PURSE				
That by destroying that which ty'd thy purse, ...	103	Prayer 2		17
and these exhortations he cals his privy purse, even as Princes have	236	Priest 8		16
but his purse to their relief, that so they go on more cheerfully in	248	Priest 14		11
For home-bred medicines are both more easie for the Parsons purse,	261	Priest 23		32
and plantaine, shepherds purse, knot-grasse for the other, . .	261	Priest 23		35
A good bargaine is a pick-purse.	321	Proverbs		12
A drunkards purse is a bottle.	325	Proverbs		143
Faire words make mee looke to my purse.	339	Proverbs		548
A good payer is master of anothers purse.	341	Proverbs		595
PURSES				
The world came both with hands and purses full	193	Ch.-Milit.		133
The world came in with hands and purses full	193	Ch.-Milit.	W	133
PURSIE				
But cooling by the way, grows pursie and slow, ...	169	The Answer		10
PURSING				
Yett in thy pursing still thy self distrust	13	Ch.-Porch	W	163
PURSUE				
He that doth still and strongly good pursue, ...	72	Constancie		2
With so much earnestnesse you do pursue, ...	125	Peace		41
Who griefs in earnest, joyes in jest pursue;	167	Dotage		14
Let him pursue and take my soul, ...	221	Psalm VII	D	17
there was one help for me, if I could constantly pursue it, to wit,	292	Cornaro		4
by the Apostles rule (Philip 4, 8.) not only to pursue pure things,	380	Woodnoth		13
PURSU'D				
Moses pursu'd this: but King Solomon	190	Ch.-Milit.		21
PUSILLANIMITY				
is ashamed in small things, will extend his pusillanimity to greater.	284	Priest 35		34
and Pusillanimity, Magnanimity: Of these the heathen freed . .	308	Valdesso		11
PUT				
God gave thy soul brave wings; put not those feathers	9	Ch.-Porch		83
Thy friend put in thy bosome: wear his eies	17	Ch.-Porch		271
To sell me also, and to put me there:	27	Sacrifice		15
Put our amendment in our way, ...	64	Even-song		23
These laugh at Jeat and Marble put for signes, ...	65	Ch.-monum.		12
Cordiall and Corrosive: put not thy hand	83	Sighs & Gr.		28
Hath put together a solemnitie, ...	99	Mortific.		32
Sure thou didst put a minde there, if I could	116	Dulnesse		23
And put the penne alone into his hand, ...	117	Providence		7
My power and wisdome. Put me not to shame, ...	143	Complaining		3
Look, you may put it very neare my heart.	152	The Bag		36
Fain put thee on, exchanging my lay-sword	160	Priesthood		5
Wherefore I dare not, I, put forth my hand	161	Priesthood		31
But since our Saviours death did put some bloud	186	Death		13
Put him in trust to rule the Romane sphere.	194	Ch.-Milit.		142
And put them all to utter shame, ...	220	Psalm VI	D	27
I put my trust in Thee:	220	Psalm VII	D	2
How did he put the Romans in all his prayers? Rom. 1. 9. . .	234	Priest 7		11
To put on the profound humility, and the exact temperance of our Lord	237	Priest 9		33
think fit to do so) he takes care not to put them into vain trades,	239	Priest 10		34
and put them to great shame, who deny the Scripture to be perfect.	247	Priest 13		1
which they put on as their holy-day cloathes, and come to Church in	247	Priest 14		8
and come to Church in frame, but commonly the next day put off both.	247	Priest 14		10
the Cures with their own hands, and not to put them over to servants.	247	Priest 14		20
that to put men to discourse of that, wherin they are most eminent,	260	Priest 23		5
the whole order and discipline of the Parish is put into their hands.	269	Priest 29		29
and being ready to put hand to sickle, shall then secure himself,	271	Priest 30		29
and put him out of his station, and to inlarge the perplexity,	272	Priest 31		34
but to put bounds, and hoopes to their joyes:	280	Priest 34		28
or put into the stocks, that they may be looked upon. . . .	287	Priest 37		20
was sore hurt, and also one of my arms and legges put out of joynt.	295	Cornaro		1
and God hath put this into your hands (as he sent the fish with mony	304	Valdesso		10
of God may be said in some sence to have put confidence in Scripture,	306	Valdesso		29
but he might have been justly put to death for it by the Magistrate,	316	Valdesso		25
The fault of the horse is put on the saddle.	329	Proverbs		240
Litle stickes kindle the fire; great ones put it out.	332	Proverbs		323
let him not put them on his head.	340	Proverbs		567
Silkes and Satins put out the fire in the chimney.	351	Proverbs		912
Silkes and Satins put out the fire of the chimney.	351	Proverbs	V	912
The great put the little on the hooke.	352	Proverbs		945
doe that which GOD shall put into your hart, and the LORD bless all	375	Letters		33
yet I shall ever put your care of Leighton, upon my accompt,	378	Letters		3
PUTS				
All my Disciples flie; fear puts a barre	28	Sacrifice		49
Faith puts me there with him, who sweetly took	50	Faith		23
The first puts on with speed and expedition;	117	Providence		35
Almightie God doth grieve, he puts on sense:	136	Ephes.		16
puts on the whole Armour of God, and by the vertue of the shield	238	Priest 9		5
at his door, whom God puts in his way, and makes his neighbours.	245	Priest 12		20
but hee that sits, or lies, puts up to an Apostle:	259	Priest 22		17
Every one puts his fault on the Times.	343	Proverbs		675
A litle wind kindles; much puts out the fire.	344	Proverbs		680
puts not himselfe into a good way.	354	Proverbs		995
admirable thing is this, that God puts his shoulder to our burthen;	374	Letters		17
PUTT				
to putt one of our neeces into your hands but barely what I wrote I	375	Letters		4
I was desirous to putt a good mind into the way of charity, . . .	375	Letters		8
putt your self into the hands of God (whose the success of things is)	380	Woodnoth		23

	PAGE	TITLE		LINE
PUTTING				
Putting my life among their sinnes and fears,	30	Sacrifice		106
They leade me in once more, and putting then	32	Sacrifice		189
or as putting a holiness in the things, but as desiring to keep	246	Priest 13		23
and wee also putting off that countenance and gravitie,	442	Oration		5
PY				
pork, sausages, pulse, and cake, and py-crust, and the like:	293	Cornaro		13
PY-CRUST				
pork, sausages, pulse, and cake, and py-crust, and the like:	293	Cornaro		13
QUAIL				
And rivers stirre, thou canst not shrink or quail:	156	Assurance		33
QUAINT				
That I sought out quaint words, and trim invention;	102	Jordan 2		3
And with quaint metaphors her curled hair	115	Dulnesse		7
QUALITIE				
or contract any ill qualitie, as usually happens in old mens bodies,	296	Cornaro		35
and not the qualitie for his rule, which is very easie to be	300	Cornaro		15
QUALITIES				
In stead of the qualities of the world, he requires onely three	239	Priest 10		11
of whom in stead of the qualities of the world, he asks no other,	260	Priest 23		31
one by long experience may know the qualities of his own nature,	297	Cornaro		27
What Physician could have discovered these hidden qualities to me,	297	Cornaro		35
when there is no caus, but by setting a just price of your qualities:	366	Letters		18
QUALITY				
or roots, and that for quantity little, for quality unpleasant.	242	Priest 10		27
if they be of higher quality, they commonly are quick, and sensible,	248	Priest 14		18
or for quality is licorous after dainties, is a glutton;	266	Priest 26		8
QUANTITIE				
as belonged to sickly constitutions, and that in a small quantitie.	292	Cornaro		25
and that in great quantitie, telling my Physicians nothing thereof,	292	Cornaro		29
and permitted the quantitie of meat to be increased, yet but two	296	Cornaro		7
I increased it to the quantitie of two ounces more;	296	Cornaro		11
and in a little quantitie, what diet shall he use in diseases,	299	Cornaro		23
and that in much smaller quantitie then when he was well.	299	Cornaro		32
lest they take a greater quantitie of any meat or drink (though most	300	Cornaro		12
and drink, hath the quantitie, and not the qualitie for his rule,	300	Cornaro		15
QUANTITIES				
And thy small quantities my length;	52	H.Commun.		10
QUANTITY				
or roots, and that for quantity little, for quality unpleasant.	242	Priest 10		27
He that either for quantity eats more then his health or imployments	266	Priest 26		7
As for the quantity, touching our imployments, none must eat so	266	Priest 26		28
QUARRELL				
The world and I will quarrell; and the yeare	36	Thanksgvng		37
They quarrell thee, and would give over	100	Miserie		25
Thou wilt revenge their quarrell, making grace	197	Ch.-Milit.		255
nor for every quarrell to the Lawyer,	331	Proverbs		290
He that can make a fire well, can end a quarrell.	340	Proverbs		557
QUARRELLS				
An ill labourer quarrells with his tooles.	335	Proverbs		408
He that hath lands hath quarrells.	354	Proverbs		1002
QUARRELS				
Catch not at quarrels. He that dares not speak	15	Ch.-Porch		217
Pick quarrels with their onely happinesse:	29	Sacrifice		87
of my kindred saw some great powerfull men pick quarrels against me,	294	Cornaro		16
A faire wife and a frontire Castle breede quarrels.	324	Proverbs		103
QUARRELSCMNESSE				
either by the wickedness or quarrelsomnesse thereof, he either	252	Priest 18		17
QUARRIES				
I finde there quarries of pil'd vanities,	38	The Sinner		5
QUARTER				
to visite in person, now one quarter of his Parish, now another.	247	Priest 14		5
Besides all this, I could not sleep, no not a quarter of an houre:	296	Cornaro		22
QUEEN				
the Professours whereof were much imployed by Queen Elizabeth,	277	Priest 32		32
QUEENE				
To the Queene of Bohemia.	211	Bohemia	D	T
O what a poore thing 'tis to bee a Queene	212	Bohemia	D	23
Thou shalt not bee a Queene and conquer there.	212	Bohemia	D	40
QUENCH				
Whose fier, like there malice, nought can quench.	212	Bohemia	D	54
many waters could not quench thy love!	288	Priest		31
Good words quench more then a bucket of water.	329	Proverbs		263
Soft words quench more then cold water.	329	Proverbs	V	263
The wine in the bottell doth not quench thirst.	342	Proverbs		616
Silke doth quench the fire in the Kitchin.	356	Proverbs	D	1043
QUENCHETH				
Water a farre off quencheth not fire.	334	Proverbs		398
QUEST				
Gad not abroad at ev'ry quest and call	68	Content		5
QUESTION				
The question is, whose love the greater showes:	438	Lat.Trans.		2
by making the Question very plaine with comparisons, and making much	256	Priest 21		14
Questionist must have in his mind before any question be propounded,	256	Priest 21		33
a most plain and easie framing the question, even containing in	256	Priest 21		35
but when one is asked a question, he must discover what he is.	257	Priest 21		19
neither do I make any question, but that you have performed your	363	Letters		24
QUESTIONING				
Drew nearer to me, sweetly questioning,	188	Love 3		5
QUESTIONIST				
which the Questionist must have in his mind before any question be	256	Priest 21		32

QUESTIONS	PAGE	TITLE	LINE
With curious questions and divisions?	134	Divinitie	12
Curiosity in prying into high speculative and unprofitable questions,	238	Priest 9	18
the Parson questions what order is kept in the house, as about	248	Priest 14	31
and accordingly by questions well ordered he found Philosophy in	256	Priest 21	22
upon which and to which the questions are to be chained.	256	Priest 21	34
the Parson once demanded after other questions about mans misery;	257	Priest 21	2
as Sermons come short of questions in the one, so they farre exceed	257	Priest 21	23
For questions cannot inflame or ravish, that must be done by a set,	257	Priest 21	24
but the Questions must be propounded loosely and wildely,	259	Priest 22	8
QUICK			
Unto thy hands, it woundeth to the quick.	13	Ch.-Porch	168
With thy quick flow'r, thy momentarie bloom;	48	Repentance	3
Man is no starre, but a quick coal	79	Employm.2	6
And thred the spheres with his quick-piercing minde:	85	Vanitie 1	2
Quick thoughts and motions at a small expense,	86	Lent	20
The quick returns of courtesie and wit:	88	The Pearl	12
This was not quick enough, and that was dead.	102	Jordan 2	10
Of what an easie quick accesse,	103	Prayer 2	1
But grones are quick, and full of wings,	107	Sion	21
Thy long deferrings wound me to the quick,	107	Home	3
Then came quick Wit and Conversation,	111	The Quip	17
Who fain would have you be new, tender, quick.	131	Love unkn.	70
Nothing more quick when she doth go.	137	Familie	16
But quick-ey'd Love, observing me grow slack	188	Love 3	3
if they be of higher quality, they commonly are quick, and sensible,	248	Priest 14	19
Quick beleevers neede broad shoulders.	322	Proverbs	39
Take heede of still waters, the quick passe away.	326	Proverbs	171
QUICK-EY'D			
But quick-ey'd Love, observing me grow slack	188	Love 3	3
QUICK-PIERCING			
And thred the spheres with his quick-piercing minde:	85	Vanitie 1	2
QUICKEN			
The Thorns did quicken, what was grown too dull:	130	Love unkn.	66
QUICKEN'D			
But I was quicken'd by my houre.	142	Pilgrimage	10
QUICKLY			
That which was dust before, doth quickly rise,	71	Frailtie	15
Quickly reformed all with menaces.	84	Sighs & Gr.W	10
But Wisdome quickly swept them all away.	84	The World	5
Convey them quickly, who are bound for death.	98	Mortific.	12
And quickly gain, for each inch lost, an ell.	103	Prayer 2	24
Quickly should I then controll	114	Dialogue	3
But quickly seek some new adventure.	126	Confession	22
He builds a house, which quickly down must go,	127	Giddinesse	13
Quickly effect, what thou dost move;	133	The Method	6
Who heare not him, but quickly heare	134	The Method	27
They quickly go and come with lesser crime:	154	Glimpse	9
that if he be not so, he wil quickly be discovered, and disregarded:	228	Priest 3	6
that after many troubles and griefs I should quickly come to an end;	291	Cornaro	26
In a good house all is quickly ready.	323	Proverbs	58
Water, fire, and souldiers, quickly make roome.	338	Proverbs	514
Great paines quickly find ease.	339	Proverbs	534
Good & quickly seldome meete.	341	Proverbs	580
A good Judge conceives quickly, judges slowly.	341	Proverbs	599
The mouse that hath but one hole is quickly taken.	360	Proverbs D	1135
would quickly make good my wish but that my employment does fix me	372	Letters	18
QUICKNESSE			
Touch it with thy celestiall quicknesse,	74	The Starre	14
O give me quicknesse, that I may with mirth	115	Dulnesse	3
QUICKNING			
Killing and quickning, bringing down to hell	166	The Flower	16
QUIDDITIE			
The Quidditie.	69	Quidditie	T
QUIET			
Onely these stones in quiet entertain thee,	41	Sepulchre	15
Mark how the fire in flints doth quiet lie,	68	Content	9
Mark how the fire in Flint doth quiet lie,	68	Content W	9
And in no quiet canst thou be,	124	Gratefulnes	26
And snudge in quiet: now he scorns increase;	127	Giddinesse	11
when they overdo it, to the loss of their quiet, and health:	247	Priest 14	28
from temptation, in a quiet sweetnesse seeks how to please his God.	279	Priest 33	5
lest their quiet betray them (as it is apt to do) to a coldnesse,	280	Priest 34	17
A little with quiet is the onely dyet.	332	Proverbs	327
When children stand quiet, they have done some ill.	338	Proverbs	504
QUIETLY			
I sleep well and quietly any where, and my dreams are fair	302	Cornaro	13
our Care for us that we may the more quietly intend his service.	374	Letters	19
QUIETNES			
But yet the Arts in quietnes and silence here are reverenced,	442	Oration	35
QUILL			
To hold my quill? shall they not do thee right?	116	Providence	4
The thought hath good leggs, and the quill a good tongue.	342	Proverbs	612
QUINTESSENCE			
In so much dregs the quintessence is small:	38	The Sinner	9
QUIP			
The Quip.	110	The Quip	T
QUIRE			
Leads to the Quire above,	67	Ch.-floore	8
QUIT			
If reason move not Gallants, quit the room,	8	Ch.-Porch	43

	PAGE	TITLE		LINE
QUIT (cont'd)				
And to instruct them, will not quit the cost.	20	Ch.-Porch		348
Kneeling ne're spoil'd silk stocking: quit thy state.	22	Ch.-Porch		407
I quit my interest, and leave it free:	94	Unkindness		17
Are quit with them and more.	210	Paradox	D	10
QUITE				
One cunning bosome-sinne blows quite away.	46	Sinne 1		14
With full crie of affections, quite astray;	80	Christmas		3
Quite under ground; as flowers depart	166	The Flower		10
Here is joy that drowneth quite	180	Invitation		22
Sinne being not able to extirpate quite	194	Ch.-Milit.		161
and turne quite another man, doubtlesse then also mens affections	288	Priest 37		3
the naturall concupiscence is not quite extinguished, but the heate	308	Valdesso		17
QUITS				
It quits the earth, and mounting more and more,	132	The Storm		11
Hee begins to die, that quits his desires.	321	Proverbs		2
He quits his place well, that leaves his friend there.	350	Proverbs		875
QUITT'ST				
Wherefore thou quitt'st thy ancient claim:	106	Sion		10
QUITTING				
Quitting the furre	78	Employm.2		4
Quitting with daily labour all My pleasure,	85	Coloss.		9
Quitting their place	90	Afflict.4		14
Quitting the fruit, seiz'd on my heart alone,	129	Love unkn.		12
Quitting his spear, lest it should pierce again	192	Ch.-Milit.		69
QUIVER				
His bow is bent, his quiver is	222	Psalm VII	D	43
RACE				
Thou hast run all thy race, ere thou beginn.	10	Ch.-Porch	W	90
Thou suddenly dost raise and race,	56	Temper 2		7
But he hath spoil'd the race; and giv'n to anguish	159	Jos.coat		10
Both where and when the Church began her race,	192	Ch.-Milit.		102
Gamsters and race-horses never last long.	346	Proverbs		751
RACE-HORSES				
Gamsters and race-horses never last long.	346	Proverbs		751
RACES				
I and the Sunn have runn our races,	203	Even-song	W	2
RACK				
O rack me not to such a vast extent;	55	Temper 1		9
A better lodging then a rack or grave.	81	Christmas		14
RADICALL				
onely by a pure consumption of the radicall moisture, without grief	298	Cornaro		18
RAGE				
Melt and dissolve my rage.	47	Afflict.1		46
When waves do rise, and tempests rage.	97	Afflict.5		6
Why are the Heathen swell'd with rage,	215	Psalm II	D	1
Lest like a Lion swollen with rage	221	Psalm VII	D	5
and the sea rage so much as it can, and all things do what they can,	281	Priest 34		21
The rage of a wild boar is able to spoil more then one wood.	360	Proverbs	D	1132
RAGGED				
At length I heard a ragged noise and mirth	40	Redemption		12
RAGING				
Because the raging waters still are high:	29	Sacrifice		95
Cure Tarantulas raging pains.	186	Dooms-day		12
RAIGNES				
The chiefe disease that raignes this yeare is folly.	346	Proverbs		765
RAIN				
Rain, do not hurt my flowers; but gently spend	120	Providence		117
Dwell in my head & eyes: come clouds, & rain:	164	Grief		2
I once more smell the dew and rain,	166	The Flower		38
that as the rain returns not empty, so neither may thy word,	289	Priest		31
RAINBOW				
Or starre, or rainbow, or a part	62	Mattens		7
I did; and going did a rainbow note:	124	Peace		7
RAINE				
Although it raine, throw not away thy watering pot.	332	Proverbs		325
When God will, no winde but brings raine.	332	Proverbs		332
For a morning raine leave not your journey.	353	Proverbs		976
RAINES				
yet never so giving over the raines, but that he sometimes looks how	239	Priest 9		1
and not to let go the raines as soon as the horse goes easie.	280	Priest 34		15
RAISE				
About thy neck do drown thee? raise thy head;	13	Ch.-Porch		170
Yet, for I threatned oft the siege to raise,	47	Afflict.1		43
Thou suddenly dost raise and race,	56	Temper 2		7
That I can raise:	61	Praise 1		2
O raise me then! poore bees, that work all day,	61	Praise 1		17
O raise me then: for if a Spider may	61	Praise 1	W	17
How know I, if thou shouldst me raise,	95	Submission		13
That I should then raise thee?	95	Submission		14
To raise him to the glimpse of blisse:	102	Miserie		75
Is mine to write, as it is yours to raise.	117	Providence		24
Raise not the mudde	145	Discharge		27
I can raise thee.	146	Praise 2		20
And it raise	148	Offering		40
Wouldst thou raise devils? I see, I know,	155	Assurance		17
Lord, thy broken consort raise,	187	Dooms-day		29
Where first the Church should raise her down-cast face.	192	Ch.-Milit.		86
Frail Beauty's Charms to Heav'n did raise,	214	Convert	D	13
and high thy Glory raise.	221	Psalm VII	D	28
and heavy, and hard to raise to a poynt of Zeal, and fervency,	233	Priest 7		16

RAISE (cont'd)	PAGE	TITLE		LINE
and to raise up their mindes to apprehend Gods good blessing to our	236	Priest 8		22
Christian soules, and raise them to their height, even to heaven;	275	Priest 32		31
slight glories, which wee raise from bookes, and painefull industrie.	443	Oration		1
RAIS'D				
What to ask further. Doubts well rais'd do lock	18	Ch.-Porch		299
What to ask farther. Doubts well rais'd do lock	18	Ch.-Porch	W	299
Lord, who hast rais'd me from the mudd	68	Trin.Sun.	WC	1
Having rais'd me to look up,	182	Banquet		37
RAISED				
In three dayes raz'd, and raised as before.	28	Sacrifice		66
that this suit and contention was raised by the Divine Providence,	294	Cornaro		24
RAISES				
Who dead men raises.	49	Repentance		35
The March sunne raises but dissolves not.	342	Proverbs		614
RAISETH				
Wit fancies beautie, beautie raiseth wit:	54	Love 1		9
Which as it riseth, raiseth thee:	112	Dawning		12
and this raiseth the action from the Shop, to the Church.	262	Priest 23		10
RAISING				
Harmonious bells below, raising the dead	174	Aaron		3
never raising their thoughts to God, nor sanctifying their labour	248	Priest 14		1
RAN				
I made a posie, while the day ran by:	94	Life		1
That ran upon him with a spear.	151	The Bag		26
Thus both the Church and Sunne together ran	192	Ch.-Milit.		97
RANCOUR				
whom the Law would have defamed, except he also do it out of rancour.	287	Priest 37		29
RANK				
No such rank poyson can there be.	155	Assurance		6
RANKE				
be vilified or debased, by being cast on the lower ranke of people;	270	Priest 29		8
RANKED				
and ranked backbiters among the generation of the wicked,	287	Priest 37		23
RANKS				
In sev'rall ranks upon an azure throne,	70	Humilitie		2
Which parts their ranks and orders.	75	Sunday		28
RANNE				
I ranne; but all I brought, was fome.	64	Even-song		12
RANTS				
With Vows and Rants, and sensless Praise,	214	Convert	D	12
RAPPER				
An old mans staffe is the rapper of deaths doore.	351	Proverbs		916
RARE				
There is a rare outlandish root,	50	Faith		9
Lord, with what bountie and rare clemencie	82	Ungratef.		1
Thou hast but two rare cabinets full of treasure,	82	Ungratef.		7
With flowers and carvings, mysticall and rare:	106	Sion		5
Who hath the vertue to expresse the rare	119	Providence		73
The common all men have; that which is rare,	119	Providence		98
Shining and sharp, point out your rare Perfections;	209	L. Bacon	D	4
A foile to sett of worth, & make it rare.	211	Bohemia	D	16
and smallage made into a Poultis, have done great and rare cures.	262	Priest 23		8
and very rare, the presuming upon it ought not to leade us	300	Cornaro		20
RARELY				
The love of money and the love of learning rarely meet.	361	Proverbs	D	1168
RARITIES				
A box of jewels, shop of rarities,	102	Miserie		68
RASH				
Bids the rash gazer wipe his eye:	87	Vertue		6
RATABLY				
Doth ratably thy fortunes marre or make.	16	Ch.-Porch		256
RATE				
Thy rate and price, and mark thee for a treasure;	6	Ch.-Porch		2
If yet thou love game at so deere a rate,	14	Ch.-Porch		199
And at what rate and price I have thy love;	89	The Pearl		35
Is no hard rate.	111	Vanitie 2		10
At the rate of an Incarnation	201	H. Commun.	W	26
RATES				
giving some corn outright, and selling other at under rates;	245	Priest 12		11
RATHER				
My childrens right, nor ought he take it: rather	17	Ch.-Porch		279
Rather then shew his cards.) Steal from his treasure	18	Ch.-Porch		298
My silence rather doth augment their crie;	29	Sacrifice		93
Or rather let	39	Good Fri.		17
Whereas my birth and spirit rather took	47	Afflict.1		37
Lord, mend or rather make us: one creation	127	Giddinesse		25
Rather hereafter, then in present, is.	131	Mans medly		6
Be to me rather sharp and TART,	133	Paradise		8
Such cuttings rather heal then REND:	133	Paradise		14
Or rather make no Thine and Mine!	157	Clasping		20
Let rather brasse,	163	The Search		34
But rather turn the pipe, and waters course	170	Water-crs.		6
The rather since his scatter'd jugglings were	195	Ch.-Milit.		175
Or rather so, as thou alone	200	H. Commun.	W	4
Or rather as thou movedst mee.	204	Persever.	W	4
Which misery cannot untwist but rather	212	Bohemia	D	35
and obligation of his calling, being to obey God rather then men.	232	Priest 6		19
the best and highest things, is rather unmarryed, then marryed.	236	Priest 9		33
like circumstances considered, he is rather married then unmarried.	237	Priest 9		4
the choyce of his wife was made rather by his eare, then by his eye;	238	Priest 9		26

	PAGE	TITLE		LINE
RATHER (cont'd)				
he chooseth rather to give the poor money, which they can better	243	Priest 11		15
he exacts of them to let him alone, and say rather, God be praised,	245	Priest 12		32
and so much the rather doth he so, as his accesse to the poor is more	249	Priest 14		7
best comforts, and rather goes to them, then sends for the afflicted,	249	Priest 15		15
so the hunger and thirst after it may come rather from themselves,	250	Priest 15		6
rather then to those that are further, where things are otherwise	253	Priest 19		27
is rather by withdrawing his bounty and courtesie from the parties	254	Priest 20		22
he chooseth to permit his Parishioners rather to make use of the Law,	260	Priest 23		19
and yet hee chuseth rather to use his neighbours, and wear out that,	265	Priest 26		29
(For they rather must not work, especially Students, and those that	266	Priest 26		33
wisheth all to incline rather to too much, then to too little;	267	Priest 26		12
but rather made food miraculously, then suffered so good desires	267	Priest 26		25
as they think fit, & see cause, or rather as Gods spirit leads them.	272	Priest 31		27
so much the rather ought he to proceed, as that by this he may take	273	Priest 31		31
that it rather establisheth it, since they that have nothing,	275	Priest 32		4
for so excellent a Place, not to refuse, but rather to procure it.	276	Priest 32		18
that they kindle them rather to redeem the Dignity either from true	276	Priest 32		23
therefore this kind of Punishment was chosen rather then any other.	282	Priest 34		17
and the rather, because Countrey people are much addicted to them,	283	Priest 35		28
that he rather procures them to be often, as knowing that absence	284	Priest 35		14
but is rather glad of catching opportunities to do them.	284	Priest 35		26
Rather should a Christian Souldier take such occasions to harden	284	Priest 35		35
such offenders, that it is a duty rather, which may do much good,	288	Priest 37		1
stint of meat and drink should be diminished, rather then increased;	295	Cornaro		31
yeares old, all the time we live after, is rather death then life.	300	Cornaro		29
I doe not then bid him goe away but rather stay longer,	318	Valdesso		16
I had rather ride on an asse that carries me,	329	Proverbs		258
I had rather aske of my sire browne bread,	330	Proverbs		269
Some had rather lose their friend then their Jest.	361	Proverbs	D	1170
not well, I had rather the fault should lie on me, than on them;	364	Letters		29
yet I had rather flie to my old ward, that if any course could be	367	Letters		7
or rather increaseth, I wish earnestly that I were again with you:	372	Letters		17
work rather then doe nothing.	381	Woodnoth		24
RAVE				
While Sinne doth rave,	183	A Parodie		22
RAV'D				
But as I rav'd and grew more fierce and wilde	153	The Collar		33
RAVENING				
Those ravening Harpyes, which peck at thy face,	212	Bohemia	D	48
RAVISH				
For questions cannot inflame or ravish, that must be done by a set,	257	Priest 21		24
RAVISHING				
moving and ravishing texts, whereof the Scriptures are full.	233	Priest 7		27
RAW				
in like manner, raw lettice, fish, pork, sausages, pulse,	293	Cornaro		12
RAZE				
To raze the building to the very floore:	84	The World		17
RAZ'D				
In three dayes raz'd, and raised as before.	28	Sacrifice		66
REACH				
As a great Clerk, and reach the highest stature.	50	Faith		30
Sometimes I hardly reach a score,	55	Temper 1		7
Humilitie did reach to Fortitude.	70	Humilitie		12
It's true, we cannot reach Christs forti'th day;	87	Lent		31
We cannot reach our Saviours puritie;	87	Lent		34
Till I reach heav'n, and much more thee.	90	Afflict.4		30
Where all may reach: no beast but knows his feed.	118	Providence		50
The second Temple could not reach the first:	196	Ch.-Milit.		225
his flock by themselves, whom his Sermons cannot, or doe not reach.	236	Priest 8		13
that so the sentence lighting upon one, the example may reach to all.	269	Priest 28		2
untill our obedience reach the measure of thy love, who hast done	290	Priest		11
The Fox, when hee cannot reach the grapes,	325	Proverbs		130
REACHETH				
Two reacheth thee	202	Trin.Sun.	W	3
READ				
My God, I read this day,	97	Afflict.5		1
And heart unto this deed, when he hath read;	105	Obedience		38
And heart unto this deed, when he doth read	105	Obedience	W	38
Read that lesson to the grave.	187	Dooms-day		18
So by the Other, you may read in mee	209	L. Bacon	D	5
and not to think, that when they have read the Fathers, or Schoolmen,	226	Priest 2		11
The Countrey Parson hath read the Fathers also, and the Schoolmen,	229	Priest 5		31
when he is to read divine services, composeth himselfe to all	231	Priest 6		1
Then having read divine Service twice fully, and preached in	236	Priest 8		6
Those that can read, are allowed times for it, and those that cannot,	240	Priest 10		19
who can read, who not;	248	Priest 14		34
and sometimes he hears the children read himselfe, and blesseth them,	248	Priest 14		35
encouraging also the servants to learn to read, and offering to have	248	Priest 14		37
the Parson adviseth them to read, or hear them read often,	270	Priest 29		13
or hear them read often, as also the visitation Articles,	270	Priest 29		14
Besides, they are to read Books of Law, and Justice;	276	Priest 32		34
I like not in him, as my fragments will expresse, when you read them;	304	Valdesso		17
For as the servant leaves not the letter when he hath read it,	310	Valdesso		28
us not with the same thing only when it is read as the promises doe,	310	Valdesso		34
but enlightens us with new Considerations the more we read it.	310	Valdesso		35
The hearts letter is read in the eyes.	328	Proverbs		220
READE				
Nay, I will reade thy book, and never move	36	Thanksgvng		45
Nay, I will reade thy book, and never linn	36	Thanksgvng	W	45
I reade, and sigh, and wish I were a tree;	48	Afflict.1		57

READE (cont'd)

	PAGE	TITLE		LINE
Who reade a chapter when they rise,	96	Charms & K		1
Go spell and reade how I have kill'd thy King.	169	Dial.-Anth		4
Reade him there, and I have done.	208	J. Danvers	D	16
READER				
The Authour to the Reader.	224	Priest		T
or painted there, which may excite the reader to a thought of piety;	240	Priest 10		25
READES				
Must all be vail'd, while he that reades, divines,	56	Jordan 1		9
READETH				
He often readeth the Lives of the Primitive Monks, Hermits,	237	Priest 9		28
READIE				
And readie Paschal Lambe of this great week:	28	Sacrifice		59
Of pleasures brought me to him, readie there	81	Christmas		7
There is in love a sweetnesse readie penn'd:	103	Jordan 2		17
Readie to take them in; yet of a size	158	Praise 3		29
Readie to passe to the American strand.	196	Ch.-Milit.		236
READIEST				
and paper enough, yet am I Your readiest Servant, GEORGE HERBERT.	370	Letters		33
READILY				
they may deliver thy message reverently, readily, faithfully,	289	Priest		28
READING				
Hath done what he condemnes in reading:	171	Self-cond.		16
Wherefore he ever begins the reading of the Scripture with some short	229	Priest 4		1
them with all Piety, not only of words in praying, and reading;	239	Priest 10		24
as if hee findes them reading, hee furnisheth them with good books;	247	Priest 14		15
and evening on their knees, reading of Scripture, catechizing,	248	Priest 14		33
or too open a Buttery, or reading vain books, or swearing,	251	Priest 17		20
Grace, reading of Scriptures, and other good books, how Sundayes,	251	Priest 17		23
If he chance to finde any reading in anothers Bible, he provides him	254	Priest 20		12
some dialogues in Plato were worth the reading, where the singular	256	Priest 21		28
and by reading some initiatory treatises in the Law, with Daltons	260	Priest 23		1
reading one Book of Phisick, having one Herball by him.	261	Priest 23		4
Now both the reading of him, and the knowing of herbs may be done	261	Priest 23		9
I give my self to the reading of some learned book, and afterwards	301	Cornaro		6
observed, whc workes by his Word, and ever in the reading of it.	310	Valdesso		1
he nameth the reading and meditation of holy Scriptures for the first	311	Valdesso	V	4
my case unto you, which I think deserves the reading at the least;	364	Letters		10
READS				
then he that reads the womans oyntment in the Gospell, or sees	283	Priest 34		1
and reads it againe and againe, and the more the promise is delayed,	310	Valdesso		28
is delayed, the more he reads it, and fortifies himselfe with it;	310	Valdesso		30
Wo be to him that reads but one book.	360	Proverbs	D	1146
READY				
Knoweth the ready way,	52	H.Commun.		20
But thou art ready there to catch	62	Mattens		2
Since we are ever ready to disburse,	78	Ang.&Sts.		29
Since we are ever ready to discourse,	78	Ang.&Sts.	V	29
and being ready to put hand to sickle, shall then secure himself,	271	Priest 30		29
and himself, and who is ready to ask, if he shall mend shoos,	275	Priest 32		7
hath ever so many sermons ready penn'd, as he hath victories.	278	Priest 33		24
In a good house all is quickly ready.	323	Proverbs		58
When prayers are done, my Lady is ready.	323	Proverbs		71
They that are booted are not alwaies ready.	323	Proverbs		83
To a fair day open the window, but make you ready as to a foule.	325	Proverbs		119
Where your will is ready, your feete are light.	336	Proverbs		448
When your will is ready, the feete are swift.	336	Proverbs	V	448
Ready mony is a ready Medicine.	356	Proverbs	D	1038
yet if my Sister were acquainted that they are ready, I dare say she	367	Letters		2
I shall understand that a Letter will be seasonable, my Pen is ready.	371	Letters		16
bottom is wound up and laid ready for work in the New Jerusalem.	373	Letters		6
READYEST				
yet every mans own is fittest, readyest, and most savory to him.	230	Priest 5		4
REALL				
When creatures had no reall light	51	Faith		33
REAPED				
Fame is sowne in this age, that it may be reaped in the following;	443	Oration		4
REARES				
A broken ALTAR, Lord, thy servant reares,	26	The Altar		1
REASON				
If reason move not Gallants, quit the room,	8	Ch.-Porch		43
Ballance each dramme of reason, like a potion.	19	Ch.-Porch		322
To rules of reason, holy messengers,	45	Sinne 1		4
What reason hath from nature borrowed,	88	The Pearl		3
What reason hath from nature purchased,	88	The Pearl	W	3
Reason and speech we onely bring.	91	Man		10
And ev'n my verse, when by the ryme and reason	109	Home		75
As the reason then is thine;	115	Dialogue		21
Reason triumphs, and faith lies by.	134	Divinitie		8
Now the great combat of our flesh & reason	204	The Knell	W	8
Making a Head & spring against thy Reason.	213	Bohemia	D	59
as this is the true reason of his inward feare, so he is content	231	Priest 6		11
without reason, or offer up such sacrifices as they did of old,	232	Priest 6		4
sacrifices as they did of old, which was of beasts devoyd of reason;	232	Priest 6		5
but when we use our reason, and apply our powers to the service	232	Priest 6		5
by reason of continuall inward, or outward temptations,	238	Priest 9		13
and the reason hereof is, because the natures of these vices being	264	Priest 26		16
The reason of the ground is manifest, because wealth is given to that	265	Priest 26		7
I am false to my reason which should guide me, I offend the supreme	265	Priest 26		10
that order which he hath set both to things, and to reason.	265	Priest 26		12
an act against reason, because it is unnaturall to hurt ones self;	266	Priest 26		22

RECEIVING (cont'd)	PAGE	TITLE		LINE
For the manner of receiving, as the Parson useth all reverence	259	Priest 22		10
doinq kindnesses, but receiving none;	268	Priest 28		24
in Italie is very great) receiving not any hurt or inconvenience	302	Cornaro		19
For concerning your offer of receiving one, I will tell you what I	375	Letters		9
RECKON				
But thou didst reckon, when at first	123	Gratefulnes		9
They who rely on them must reckon twice	194	Ch.-Milit.	W	160
for then they will reckon upon it, as on a debt;	244	Priest 12		28
which otherwise they would reckon upon, and turn to idlenesse.	245	Priest 12		5
Reckon right, and February hath one and thirty daies. . . .	328	Proverbs		229
RECKONING				
though for the reckoning of your favours, I shall never find time	370	Letters		31
RECKONS				
God reckons for him, counts the favour his:	21	Ch.-Porch		381
RECOILE				
We must recoile a little, to the end we may leap the better.	359	Proverbs	D	1121
RECOMPENSES				
because my recompenses of your favours consist in this only.	367	Letters		31
RECONCILED				
and a reconciled Enemy.	360	Proverbs	D	1154
RECONCILIATION				
but after hee had fulfilled the work of Reconciliation, . .	225	Priest 1		7
this word of thy rich peace, and reconciliation, thou hast committed,	289	Priest		4
RECONCILING				
day he spends either in reconciling neighbours that are at variance,	236	Priest 8		11
with reconciling of differences at that time, if there be any:	284	Priest 35		6
RECORDED				
Nay they are purposely recorded in holy Writ.	316	Valdesso		5
RECOUNTING				
recounting the delights and pleasures in this age of eighty three,	300	Cornaro		31
RECOVER				
Thou shalt recover all thy goods in kinde, ...	54	Love 2		11
These parcell out thy heart: recover these, ...	147	Offering		17
Recover all thy sigh-blown age	153	The Collar		19
RECOVER'D				
Could have recover'd greennesse? It was gone	166	The Flower		9
RECOVERED				
and knows what recovered him, is a Physitian so far as he meetes	278	Priest 33		26
of all diseases, and were recovered of all by things that he knew;	278	Priest 33		30
and so without other remedie or inconvenience I recovered; . .	295	Cornaro		13
neither am I yet recovered, so that I am fain ever and anon,	364	Letters		33
RECOVERING				
every way great force for the recovering and preserving of Health,	292	Cornaro		5
RECREATION				
but also of company, recreation, and all outward contentments;	241	Priest 10		39
and a recreation to more divine studies, Nature serving Grace both in	261	Priest 23		10
RED				
Pure red and white.	115	Dulnesse		12
Brought back to the Red Sea, the sea of shame.	128	Bunch Gr.		7
REDEEM				
Redeem truth from his jawes: if souldier, ...	10	Ch.-Porch		87
Redeem truth from his chawes: if souldier, ...	10	Ch.-Porch	W	87
that they kindle them rather to redeem the Dignity either from true	276	Priest 32		24
REDEEM'D				
And hast redeem'd me through thy bloud, ...	68	Trin.Sun.		2
Hast thou redeem'd us from the grave!	82	Ungratef.		2
REDEEMER				
Our great Redeemer did remove	76	Sunday		44
He did, he came: O my Redeemer deare, ...	108	Home		25
REDEEMER'S				
Is in my deare Redeemers pierced side.	44	H. Bapt.1		6
REDEMPTION				
Redemption.	40	Redemption		T
In you Redemption measures all my time, ...	44	H. Bapt.1		10
perfecting our Redemption no other way, then by sorrow; . .	249	Priest 15		23
REDOUND				
the felicitie of so great Princes redound also to those servants,	442	Oration		25
REDUCE				
way of preserving a state to reduce it to its principles by which	258	Priest 22		16
useth all possible diligence to reduce them to the common Faith.	262	Priest 24		21
labours to reduce them to see Gods hand in all things, . . .	270	Priest 30		29
REDUCED				
the Church Catechisme, to which all divinity may easily be reduced.	230	Priest 5		9
REDUCING				
the Deputy of Christ for the reducing of Man to the Obedience of God.	225	Priest 1		1
and reducing the Manna, and bread of Charity to some equality,	254	Priest 19		3
advice hath taken effect in the reducing of many rude and untoiled	302	Cornaro		15
REED				
Then with the reed they gave to me before, ...	32	Sacrifice		169
Then with the reed they gave mee heertofore, ...	32	Sacrifice	W	169
To my poore reed.	57	Employm. 1		24
REEDS				
Yet since mans scepters are as frail as reeds, ...	32	Sacrifice		177
All Scepters, Reeds: Cloths, Scarlet: Crowns are Thorns: . .	32	Sacrifice	W	178
REEL				
Ev'n when the boat seems most to reel.	151	The Bag		4
Let the world reel, we and all ours stand sure, ...	439	Walton 5		9
REFERENCE				
The Parson in reference.	252	Priest 19		T

REGARD (cont'd)	PAGE	TITLE		LINE
the way of supporting either it (in regard of the citty) or your self	380	Woodnoth		27
REGARDS				
doubling his regards, and shewing by all means, that the delinquents	264	Priest 25		1
REGENERATION				
there is an humblenesse very sutable to Christian regeneration,	255	Priest 21		11
REGENT				
is Regent or Non-regent at his pleasure, and such like Gaynesses,	370	Letters		3
REGIMENTS				
But when I view abroad both Regiments;	71	Frailtie		9
REGION				
in this land of light, and region of the Gospell, among his chosen.	304	Valdesso		15
REGIONS				
is apt to nourish more then in cold regions, and where flesh may be	242	Priest 10		18
REGULAR				
That an orderly and regular life can hardly be altered without	295	Cornaro		17
that in stead of a Physician a regular life is to be embraced,	298	Cornaro		12
Wherefore since many have observed a regular life, both of old times	299	Cornaro		5
He which lives a regular life, eating alwayes light meats, . .	299	Cornaro		22
REGULARITIE				
because that by the regularitie of my life I have shut out death all	303	Cornaro		27
REGULARLY				
cannot live regularly, because they must often endure heats,	299	Cornaro		12
REHEARSE				
Can thy strange wayes rehearse?	102	Miserie		66
For they that taste it do rehearse, ...	125	Peace		33
REIGN (see also raignes)				
REIGNE				
His knowledge winks, and lets his humours reigne;	102	Miserie		62
And fall to nothing: thou dost reigne, ...	150	Longing		56
REINS (see also rains)				
Bigge with his sister: he hath lost the reins, ...	7	Ch.-Porch		32
Bigge with his sister: he hath lost his reins, ...	7	Ch.-Porch	W	32
And laid the reins	149	Longing		45
the hearts and reins are try'd.	221	Psalm VII	D	36
REJECT				
O Lord, reject them all, ...	219	Psalm V	D	32
REJOYCE				
Glad heart rejoyce.	134	The Method		32
Serve our great God in fear, rejoyce, ...	216	Psalm II	D	27
Rejoyce in the Lord alwaies, and again I say rejoyce.	374	Letters		21
Rejoyce in the Lord alwaies, and again I say rejoyce.	374	Letters		22
of those that might say, What shall we rejoyce in afflictions?	374	Letters		23
yes, I say again rejoyce;	374	Letters		24
so that it is not left to us to rejoyce or not rejoyce: . .	374	Letters		24
so that it is not left to us to rejoyce or not rejoyce: . .	374	Letters		25
at all times rejoyce in the Lord, who taketh care for us: . .	374	Letters		26
REJOYCED				
And Luke 10. 21. He rejoyced in Spirit:	280	Priest 34		10
REJOYCING				
of holinesse, then the procuring, and rejoycing in anothers good.	234	Priest 7		10
RELATING				
BRIEFE NOTES relating to the dubious and offensive places in	306	Valdesso		T
RELATION				
not by relation, whereby I understand he meaneth only the effectuall	308	Valdesso		30
or relation from others, is not that which filleth the heart with joy	309	Valdesso		1
this I call beleeving by Revelation, and not by Relation. . .	309	Valdesso		7
me exceedingly with your relation of my Lady Duchess's forwardnes	377	Letters		19
RELATIONS				
or other relations give him any authority over the Family, . .	251	Priest 17		16
The Countrey Parson is sincere and upright in all his relations.	252	Priest 19		25
RELEASE				
Till thy release appeare.	75	Sunday		14
RELEEVING				
hee findes some way of releeving it, and reducing the Manna,	254	Priest 19		3
Mercy in releeving the poor by a liberall distribution and largesse,	284	Priest 35		8
RELENTEDST				
Thou relentedst:	146	Praise 2		22
RELENTING				
O heare betimes, lest thy relenting	111	Vanitie 2		7
RELIEF				
Who am the way of truth, the true relief;	27	Sacrifice		38
Who am the way & Truth, the true relief;	27	Sacrifice	W	38
To guide and govern it to my relief, ...	73	Afflict.3		3
To be all passengers most sweet relief?	81	Christmas		8
Labour thy praise, and my relief;	90	Afflict.4		28
Some Angels us'd the first; if our relief	97	Afflict.5		15
Without relief.	136	Ephes.		27
That I may climbe and finde relief.	144	Complaining		20
One of Joyes coats, ticing it with relief	159	Jos.coat		11
For some relief.	204	The Knell	W	18
but his purse to their relief, that so they go on more cheerfully in	248	Priest 14		11
RELIEFS				
May be reliefs, ...	132	Mans medly		32
RELIEVE (see also releeving)				
My God, relieve me!	83	Sighs & Gr.		30
Lord, thou dost wound me, yet thou dost relieve me:	95	Justice 1		3
Not to relieve? how can it be, ...	150	Longing		62
Thou com'st and dost relieve.	184	A Parodie		30
as to relieve my Neighbour, God hath already reveled his Will about	313	Valdesso		13

	PAGE	TITLE		LINE
RELIEVED				
and meaner relieved, he chooseth rather to give the poor money,	243	Priest 11		14
paines in their vocation, as not knowing when they shal be relieved;	245	Priest 12		4
RELIEVEST				
Lord, thou relievest, yet I die by thee:	95	Justice 1		4
RELIGION				
Finish'd and fixt the old religion.	190	Ch.-Milit.		22
Religion, like a pilgrime, westward bent, ...	190	Ch.-Milit.		29
Religion thence fled into Greece, where arts	191	Ch.-Milit.		49
Religion went to Rome, subduing those, ...	191	Ch.-Milit.		61
Then showres Religion, and makes all to bear.	192	Ch.-Milit.		88
Yet not as Sinne, but as Religion.	196	Ch.-Milit.		212
Religion stands on tip-toe in our land, ...	196	Ch.-Milit.		235
Then shall Religion to America flee:	197	Ch.-Milit.		247
Religion alwaies sides with povertie.	197	Ch.-Milit.		252
Religion alway sides with povertie.	197	Ch.-Milit.	W	252
After religion, he teacheth them, that three things make a compleate	240	Priest 10		17
so that his family is a Schoole of Religion, and they all account,	240	Priest 10		22
In brief, it is the body of Religion, John 13. 35. . . .	244	Priest 12		13
that those who are well grown in the knowledg of Religion, . .	255	Priest 21		33
ignorant and silly souls, even the dark and deep points of Religion.	256	Priest 21		20
or justify himselfe before God, by any acts or exercises of Religion;	312	Valdesso		16
duties of true Piety, and syncere Religion, such as are Prayer,	312	Valdesso		20
There are two sorts of acts in religion;	312	Valdesso	V	23
in a strict performance of a few cheap and easie duties of religion,	319	Valdesso	V	25
Jest not with the eye or with Religion.	326	Proverbs		157
The eye and Religion can beare no jesting.	326	Proverbs		158
No profit to honour, no honour to Religion.	346	Proverbs		759
Religion, Credit, and the Eye are not to be touched. . . .	349	Proverbs		837
Cities seldome change Religion only.	356	Proverbs	D	71
the Catholick Religion is professed with greatest strictness).	357	Proverbs	D	1047
Religion a stalking horse to shoot other foul.	357	Proverbs	D	1069
RELIGIOUS				
Yet to go part of that religious way, ...	87	Lent		32
His wife is either religious, or night and day he is winning her	239	Priest 10		10
with prayers, and catechizing, and all religious duties. . .	239	Priest 10		14
or he takes care she shall learn it of some religious neighbour.	239	Priest 10		17
His servants are all religious, and were it not his duty to have them	240	Priest 10		13
so well served, as by religious servants, both because they do best,	240	Priest 10		15
the one, a strict religious life;	263	Priest 24		16
duties, and it is a great stay and setling to religious souls.	274	Priest 31		2
but also as they may be handled, a religious imployment? . .	278	Priest 32		7
To shew a forwardness in religious works is a good testimony	377	Letters		25
RELIGIOUSLY				
to live more religiously, and to take more paines in their vocation,	245	Priest 12		3
Those that he findes religiously imployed, hee both commends them	247	Priest 14		13
RELINQUISHABLE				
& therfore not relinquishable without their masters consent.	381	Woodnoth		29
RELISH				
And relish versing: O my onely light, ...	166	The Flower		39
RELISHES				
The lullings and the relishes of it;	89	The Pearl		22
The gustos and the relishes of it;	89	The Pearl	W	22
RELISHING				
him then weary, and so he grows from not relishing, to loathing.	235	Priest 7		15
RELLISH				
Wherefore all his works rellish of Charity.	244	Priest 12		15
RELY				
If thou chuse bravely & rely on God	7	Ch.-Porch	W	17
They who rely on them must reckon twice	194	Ch.-Milit.	W	160
and on his grace rely.	217	Psalm IV	D	20
is the main foundation, and pillar of their cause, whereon they rely;	262	Priest 24		29
REMAIN				
While I remain	150	Longing		58
REMAINDERS				
and two pounds besides some Remainders of monyes wherof he is to give	383	G.H.'s Will		24
REMAINED				
From this ill temper there remained little else to be expected of me,	291	Cornaro		24
REMAINETH				
The meat which remaineth, profits more then that which is eaten.	296	Cornaro		1
REMAINS				
If well; the pain doth fade, the joy remains.	24	Ch.-Porch		462
Take one from ten, and what remains?	96	Charms & K		15
What delight or hope remains?	114	Dialogue		8
what remains, but that I should wish all who have the care . .	303	Cornaro		31
REMARKABLE				
when they see any remarkable point of Education or good husbandry,	276	Priest 32		29
many singular honors, remarkable commands, most noble Ambassages,	441	Oration		24
REMEDIE				
and so without other remedie or inconvenience I recovered; . . .	295	Cornaro		12
REMEDIED				
Intemperance was not such an evil, but it might easily be remedied;	291	Cornaro		7
REMEDIES				
The Parson's Dexterity in applying of Remedies.	280	Priest 34		T
having tried all remedies fruitlesly, the Physicians told me that yet	292	Cornaro		2
Neverthelesse at a venture two remedies might be used, letting	295	Cornaro		4
refused both remedies, and onely commanded that my arm and legge	295	Cornaro		10
REMEDY				
what kind of remedy fits the temper of the house best, and then hee	251	Priest 17		26
without any remedy (which cannot be applyed without notice) . .	287	Priest 37		2
that unlesse I speedily used that remedy, within a few moneths I	292	Cornaro		13

REMEDY (cont'd)	PAGE	TITLE		LINE
The best remedy against an ill man is much ground betweene both.	326	Proverbs		152
Danger it selfe the best remedy for danger.	357	Proverbs	D	1054
There is a remedy for every thing, could men find it.	360	Proverbs	D	1142
REMEMBER				
Remember that thou once didst write in stone.	38	The Sinner		14
Of a great rock: I well remember all,	129	Love unkn.		15
For who in death remember Thee?	220	Psalm VI	D	11
while they remember their earthly Lord, do much forget their	226	Priest 2		32
for them also men heed, and remember better then exhortations;	233	Priest 7		13
but stories and sayings they will well remember.	233	Priest 7		18
as they remember themselves were, when affliction did blow the Coals.	280	Priest 34		20
yet I remember the Fathers forbid us to judge of the doubtfull	316	Valdesso		11
I remember my most humble duty to my Mother.	367	Letters		20
I remember my most humble duty to my Mother, who cannot think me	371	Letters		1
remember the holy Martyrs of God, how they have been burnt	373	Letters		35
remember those admirable words of the Psalmist:	374	Letters		13
REMEMBERS				
knowing that there is one, who when they forget, remembers for them;	267	Priest 26		21
He that pitties another, remembers himselfe.	347	Proverbs		782
REMEMBRING				
remembring what his Master saith, that if any do Gods will,	228	Priest 4		28
monuments of his Doctrine, remembring in gardens, his mustard-seed,	261	Priest 23		22
most pleasing, as well to us remembring, as to you deserving them,	441	Oration		26
REMNANT				
Here will I smell my remnant out, and tie	94	Life		2
REMORSE				
A throbbing conscience spurred by remorse	132	The Storm		9
Of sov'raigne tears, springing from true remorse:	170	Water-crs.		8
REMOTE				
Remote from ours, then Spaine from Britains shoare.	438	Lat.Trans.		4
REMOVE				
Upon my head: so I remove it all	32	Sacrifice		166
So when I view my sinnes, mine eyes remove	43	H. Bapt.1		3
Let not thy higher Court remove,	56	Temper 2		15
For sinn would faine remove the dearth	59	Whitsunday	W	19
And digs my grave at each remove:	60	Grace		14
Remove me, where I need not say,	61	Grace		23
Our great Redeemer did remove	76	Sunday		44
That hive of sweetnesse, to remove	107	Home		20
On future grief, do not remove it thence,	145	Discharge		43
And as it never shall remove,	173	23 Psalme		23
Then let wrath remove;	179	Discipline		17
especially since many remove from Parish to Parish, who like	255	Priest 21		19
Who remove stones, bruise their fingers.	322	Proverbs		40
REMOVED				
Till both removed to the western clime.	191	Ch.-Milit.		36
REMOVES				
Catching the sense at two removes?	56	Jordan 1		10
REND				
Such cuttings rather heal then REND:	133	Paradise		14
RENDERETH				
Thus Adam my first breathing rendereth:	28	Sacrifice		71
RENDING				
Rending with earthquakes the partition-wall:	190	Ch.-Milit.		26
RENEW				
The Font did onely, what was old, renew:	130	Love unkn.		64
examine their grounds, renew their vowes, and by occasion of both,	255	Priest 21		33
RENOUNCE				
Those have their hopes; these what they have renounce,	138	The Size		21
RENOUNCING				
and renouncing sin, and turning unto God in truth of heart,	279	Priest 33		24
By renouncing the help of humane learning in the studying	314	Valdesso	V	3
RENOWN				
No hawk, or banquet, or renown,	69	Quidditie		3
To thy renown: but all their hands and throats	117	Providence		11
A single deed is small renown.	128	Bunch Gr.		12
Ev'n when my will doth studie thy renown:	165	The Crosse		20
RENOWNE				
Nor hawke, nor banquet, nor renowne,	69	Quidditie	W	3
RENOWNED				
The praises also and vertues of the most renowned Princesse Isabel,	442	Oration		23
RENT (lease)				
And just it is that I should pay the rent,	117	Providence		27
Providence is better then a rent.	329	Proverbs		254
Hee will spend a whole yeares rent at one meales meate.	331	Proverbs		305
They that hold the greatest farmes, pay the least rent	359	Proverbs	D	1100
RENT				
Which is above the heav'ns, whose spring and rent	44	H. Bapt.1		5
Thy name in books, which may not rent:	69	Content		28
Many a rent and struggling th' Empire knew,	192	Ch.-Milit.		79
Within a sheet of paper, which was rent	192	Ch.-Milit.		95
And peace-meal rent it, while there's none	221	Psalm VII	D	7
So Isa. 64. Oh that thou would'st rent the Heavens, that thou wouldst	234	Priest 7		2
RENTED				
A new small-rented lease, and cancell th' old.	40	Redemption		4
RENTS				
Church-rents and schismes.	140	Ch.-rents		T
REPAIR				
And cordiall left to repair mans decay:	31	Sacrifice		159
Who would know Sinne, let him repair	37	The Agonie		7

REPROOF (cont'd)	PAGE	TITLE		LINE
or by private, or publick reproof, as the case requires,	254	Priest 20		24
by a bold and impartial reproof, even of the best in the Parish,	268	Priest 28		27
unbefitting a Minister, that it deserves reproof, not refutation:	285	Priest 36		8
Gods earth, no not tho' the advice step so far, as to be reproof:	378	Letters		13
REPROOFE				
even so farre as reproofe to their very face, when occasion cals,	226	Priest 2		30
admonition, or reproofe, sell (with Judas) their Lord and Master.	226	Priest 2		37
REPROVE				
Wilt thou not then my fault reprove?	61	Grace	W	20
And for our sakes in person sinne reprove,	103	Prayer 2		16
of darknesse, he disableth himself of authority to reprove them:	227	Priest 3		27
in the person of another, making them to reprove themselves.	248	Priest 14		22
our Saviours rule, and to take my brother aside, and reprove him;	248	Priest 14		28
they come home, either commend or reprove, either reward or punish.	255	Priest 21		29
to themselves, and witty to others who shall reprove them from it.	264	Priest 26		14
to reprove the vanity of those many Love-poems, that are daily writ	363	Letters		6
REPROVED				
they were reproved, as ignorant of what spirit they were.	229	Priest 4		13
for this may produce hatred in those that are reproved,	268	Priest 28		29
which though our Saviour reproved as unfitting for his particular,	285	Priest 36		27
REPROVES				
for if he be a plaine countryman, he reproves him plainly;	248	Priest 14		17
way or other, he ever reproves them, that he may keep himself pure,	248	Priest 14		23
he mislikes, and reproves as uncharitable, and unneighbourly;	284	Priest 35		12
REPUGNANT				
yet as diverse, not as repugnant:	229	Priest 4		15
have weaknesses is no way repugnant to the way of Gods Spirit in	316	Valdesso		3
REPUTATION				
& neither to scandalize them, nor wound our owne reputation.	380	Woodnoth		20
REPUTE				
So Blackamoores repute us fowle, and wee	210	Paradox	D	9
REPUTED				
and Neighbourhood being ever reputed, even among the Heathen,	253	Priest 19		26
by a Common tradition, and vulgar knowledge are reputed to be so.	266	Priest 26		26
REQUEST				
That zele and purenes circling my request	66	Ch.-lock	W	11
That so thy favours granting my request,	80	Deniall		28
Blaming the shallownesse of our request.	103	Prayer 2		12
Thou hast granted my request,	146	Praise 2		5
Much in request, much sought for, as a good.	186	Death		16
Much in request, much long'd for as a good.	186	Death	W	16
Thy flesh the least that I request.	201	H. Commun.	W	44
Make thy request, and I will grant	216	Psalm II	D	19
And for the Philippians made request with joy, ch. 1. 4.	234	Priest 7		14
then he turnes to request for his people, that the Lord would be	235	Priest 8		27
because it is not performed by way of request, but of confidence,	286	Priest 36		7
REQUESTS				
Out-crying my requests, drowning my tears;	66	Ch.-lock		3
May our requests thine eare invade!	103	Prayer 2		3
May our requests thine eares invade!	103	Prayer 2	W	3
unto you, since I find you so willing to yield to my requests;	363	Letters		22
and for ever after cease my clamorous and greedy bookish requests.	367	Letters		12
REQUIRE				
If cause require, thou art his sacrifice;	17	Ch.-Porch		273
Working and making a fire doth discretion require.	328	Proverbs		225
All things require skill, but an appetite.	334	Proverbs		378
REQUIR'D				
That was requir'd to make us gay,	76	Sunday		55
What present things requir'd of thee.	144	Discharge		25
REQUIRED				
For the Law required one thing, and the Gospel another:	229	Priest 4		14
and a thing required under Canonicall obedience, the expounding	230	Priest 5		13
the chiefest also, so also have I required Mr W. for his part.	378	Letters		23
REQUIRES				
and that the Ministry requires the best and highest things,	236	Priest 9		33
stead of the qualities of the world, he requires onely three of her;	239	Priest 10		12
he straitly requires of all to pray by themselves before they sleep	241	Priest 10		1
to do his Countrey true and laudable service, when occasion requires.	252	Priest 19		29
as the case requires, then by causing them to be presented,	254	Priest 20		24
He requires all to be present at Catechizing:	255	Priest 21		25
he requires the presence of all, and Baptizeth not willingly,	258	Priest 22		2
The Feast indeed requires sitting, because it is a Feast;	259	Priest 22		12
of diversion, and the benefit of application when need requires;	261	Priest 23		12
even of the best in the Parish, when occasion requires:	268	Priest 28		28
the chiefe thing, which God in Scriptures requires, is the heart,	279	Priest 33		16
REQUIRETH				
in substance, yet needeth [requireth] discreet, and wary explaining.	314	Valdesso		1
REQUIRING				
requiring answers to all these, and helping and cherishing	256	Priest 21		12
wonder-working knowledg, and therefore requiring the best spirits.	277	Priest 32		35
REQUITE				
They will be kind, and all his pains requite,	101	Miserie	W	46
to requite these pains, he takes place next the Doctors,	369	Letters		35
REQUITED				
Thou art requited; for his Fame,	209	H. Danvers	D	8
God, and Parents, and our Master, can never be requited.	348	Proverbs		805
RESCUE				
Arise, O Lord, and rescue me;	217	Psalm III	D	17
Return, O God! and rescue me,	220	Psalm VI	D	9

	PAGE	TITLE	LINE
REV'REND (cont'd)			
But rev'rend laws, and many a proclamation	84	The World	9
At length I met a rev'rend good old man,	125	Peace	19
REVEREND			
and also therein setting aside the Reverend Prelates of the Church,	225	Priest 2	21
and his apparrell plaine, but reverend, and clean, without spots,	228	Priest 3	11
which will make them appear exceeding reverend, and holy.	234	Priest 7	24
that all the painting be grave, and reverend, not with light colours,	246	Priest 13	12
and thinketh the Ceremony not onely innocent, but reverend.	258	Priest 22	9
both an honor which they owe to the Reverend Judges and Magistrates,	277	Priest 32	2
it not onely a grave, and reverend thing, but a beneficial also.	285	Priest 36	3
plain the Authour had a very reverend esteem of the holy Scripture,	311	Valdesso V	6
The Reverend are ever before.	350	Proverbs	891
REVERENT			
all reverence himself, so he administers to none but to the reverent.	259	Priest 22	12
REVERENTLY			
that in their full strength they may deliver thy message reverently,	289	Priest	28
REVERSED			
Reversed thunder, Christ-side-piercing spear,	51	Prayer 1	6
REVIEW			
To review ones store is to mow twice.	354	Proverbs	1007
REVILE			
to whore, to scoffe, to revile, to all sorts of gamings.	274	Priest 32	12
REVILES			
For while they resist the person that reviles, they resist	269	Priest 28	24
REVILING			
The reviling also of Ananias seemes, by his owne recalling,	316	Valdesso	10
REVOKING			
Christ is the glorious instrument of God for the revoking of Man.	225	Priest 1	6
REWARD			
For her reward.	110	Brit. Ch.	18
and vertuously, not for any reward of his, but for vertues sake;	243	Priest 11	29
pity hath set forth heaven for a reward to draw men to Piety,	243	Priest 11	32
And the reward of the next, Matth. 25. 35.	244	Priest 12	12
from the certainty both of deliverance, and reward, if we faint not;	249	Priest 15	25
they come home, either commend or reprove, either reward or punish.	255	Priest 21	29
the person bee so poor, that he is not able to reward the Phisician:	262	Priest 23	14
it according as he sees fit, either for reward or punishment.	270	Priest 30	32
his preaching, The Lord (saith he) reward him according to his works.	285	Priest 36	33
Service without reward is punishment.	354	Proverbs	1015
who because of his importunities gave him a reward, but not so great	368	Letters	32
if he had given it to the pope he should have had a greater reward.	368	Letters	34
REWARDED			
If I have ill rewarded him	221	Psalm VII D	11
not punished) for evill doing nor rewarded for weldoing or living,	311	Valdesso	29
REWARDER			
done either wel or ill, whereof he is not the rewarder, or punisher.	254	Priest 20	11
REWARDING			
paymaster, rewarding all good deeds to their full proportion.	254	Priest 20	21
Thus both in rewarding vertue, and in punishing vice, the Parson	254	Priest 20	29
REWARDS			
Commandments, and as he finds them perfect, rewards them the more.	245	Priest 12	37
more then by faith, by present rewards, or punishments,	254	Priest 20	32
RHENISH			
Which mingles water with thy Rhenish wine	213	Bohemia D	64
RHEUME			
which will discover it selfe by spitting, and rheume, or flegme.	242	Priest 10	25
Wealth is like rheume, it falles on the weakest parts.	337	Proverbs	475
RHEUMES			
Sowre exhalations, and dishonest rheumes,	86	Lent	23
And fall, like rheumes, upon the tendrest parts.	126	Confession	12
RHUBARB (see also rubarb)			
RHUME			
To a salt rhume	49	Repentance WC	29
RHYME (see also ryme)			
RICH			
The way to make thy sonne rich, is to fill	11	Ch.-Porch	109
Not of rich arras, but mean tapestrie.	17	Ch.-Porch	270
Having been tenant long to a rich Lord,	40	Redemption	1
I looked on thy furniture so rich,	46	Afflict.1 W	7
And made it rich to me:	46	Afflict.1 W	8
Not in rich furniture, or fine aray,	52	H.Commun.	1
In Gods rich garden: that is bare,	75	Sunday	27
In Gods rich Paradice.	75	Sunday W	28
Man calleth thee his wealth, who made thee rich;	77	Avarice	13
Of his rich crown, from whom lyes no appeal	78	Ang.&Sts.	22
Thou hadst but two rich cabinets of treasure,	82	Ungratef. W	7
Nothing could seem too rich to clothe the sunne,	102	Jordan 2	11
A wasted place, but sometimes rich.	142	Pilgrimage	15
Let him be rich and wearie, that at least,	160	The Pulley	18
As Amber-greese leaves a rich sent	174	The Odour	2
Rich shrines and oracles he purchased:	193	Ch.-Milit.	128
We are more poore, and they more rich by this.	197	Ch.-Milit.	254
then to the elder, now to the poor, and now to the rich.	233	Priest 7	4
If his Parish be rich, he exacts this of them;	244	Priest 12	24
as his accesse to the poor is more comfortable, then to the rich;	249	Priest 14	8
for, this word of thy rich peace, and reconciliation, thou hast	289	Priest	4
Hee that gets out of debt, growes rich.	321	Proverbs	9
A snow yeare, a rich yeare.	325	Proverbs	125
Poore and liberall, rich and coveteous.	332	Proverbs	339
He that is not handsome at 20, nor strong at 30, nor rich at 40,	333	Proverbs	349

RIGHT (cont'd)	PAGE	TITLE		LINE
Hee that hath right, feares; he that hath wrong, hopes.	336	Proverbs		429
To the Right Honourable the Lady Anne, Countess of Pembr. and Montg.	376	Letters		T
RIGHT'OUS				
the way that right'ous men have gone:	215	Psalm I	D	22
RIGHTEOUS				
the righteous man to love.	217	Psalm IV	D	12
For God doth righteous men esteem,	219	Psalm V	D	41
Thou art that righteous God by whom	221	Psalm VII	D	35
and thirsteth after righteous punishment of unrighteousnesse.	254	Priest 20		28
that it makes him godly, righteous, and sober all his life long;	309	Valdesso		6
[the law is not made for a righteous man:]	315	Valdesso		34
RIGHTEOUSNESS				
Lord of my righteousness:	217	Psalm IV	D	2
The sacrifice of righteousness,	217	Psalm IV	D	19
Lord lead me in thy righteousness,	219	Psalm V	D	21
According to my righteousness,	221	Psalm VII	D	31
But I for all his righteousness	222	Psalm VII	D	61
RIGHTEOUSNESSE				
because of the word of truth, and meeknesse, and righteousnesse;	289	Priest		23
the acceptation of Christs righteousnesse (as he sheweth through all	304	Valdesso		22
RIGHTLY				
Yet if we rightly measure,	131	Mans medly		4
RIGOROUS				
He cannot be vertuous that is not rigorous.	343	Proverbs		664
RILLS				
parted with rills of running water, which truely is very delightfull.	301	Cornaro		16
RINDE				
The lemmons juice and rinde cure mutually.	120	Providence		131
RING (sound)				
And in the eare, not conscience ring.	68	Windows		15
And woods do ring.	131	Mans medly		2
RING				
A ring, whose posie was, My pleasure:	102	Miserie		69
I did expect a ring.	121	Hope		8
That my offences course it in a ring.	122	Sinnes rd.		2
If thou hadst lost a glove or ring,	133	The Method		11
Or steel, or mountains be thy ring,	163	The Search		35
This on my ring,	183	The Posie		5
And with that Ring thy fame shall wedd	213	L' Envoy	D	13
Honour without profit is a ring on the finger.	328	Proverbs		230
RINGING				
The sound of glorie ringing in our eares:	46	Sinne 1		10
A noise of passions ringing me for dead	174	Aaron		8
RINGS				
The starres his tire of light and rings obtain'd,	151	The Bag		13
RIPE				
When they are ripe, their odour will ascend,	120	Providence		119
Anguish in grain, vexations ripe and blown,	167	Dotage		8
their understandings being ripe enough for ill things, and why	259	Priest 22		1
saies they are not ripe.	325	Proverbs		130
Hee that eats the hard shall eate the ripe.	328	Proverbs		210
RIPENESSE				
and ripenesse of judgement for so excellent a Place, not to refuse,	276	Priest 32		17
RIPP				
I will ripp out his love and fame.	35	Thanksgvng	W	26
RISE				
Dost lose? rise up: dost winne? rise in that state.	14	Ch.-Porch		201
They may weep out the stains by them did rise:	23	Ch.-Porch		417
Rise heart; thy Lord is risen. Sing his praise	41	Easter		1
With him mayst rise:	41	Easter		4
O let me rise	43	East.wings		7
As we did rise, we die together.	49	Repentance		24
All knees shall bow to thee; all wits shall rise,	54	Love 2		13
That I may runne, rise, rest with thee.	68	Trin.Sun.		9
That I may runne, rise, rest in thee.	68	Trin.Sun.	W	9
As those which rise from a huge King.	69	Content		24
That which was dust before, doth quickly rise,	71	Frailtie		15
Who reade a chapter when they rise,	96	Charms & K		1
Findes himself there, and seeks to rise.	96	Charms & K		12
When waves do rise, and tempests rage.	97	Afflict.5		6
Thou pull'st the rug, and wilt not rise,	101	Miserie		51
Thou lyest warme, and wilt not rise,	101	Miserie	W	51
Thy even praise can neither rise, nor fall.	118	Providence		42
When thou dost blesse, hath twelve: one wheel doth rise	158	Praise 3		11
Summon all the dust to rise,	186	Dooms-day		3
Thou didst rise early for to plant this vine,	190	Ch.-Milit.	W	11
When winds and waves rise highest, I am sure,	439	Walton 6		3
The world anew: the sunne shall never rise	212	Bohemia	D	45
combin'd in one great faction rise.	215	Psalm II	D	4
many are they that rise	216	Psalm III	D	2
that can against me rise.	216	Psalm III	D	16
but that they must rise so, as that it is not meate or drinke that	266	Priest 26		35
taking care never to rise with a full stomack, but so as I might well	293	Cornaro		18
Though you rise early, yet the day comes	332	Proverbs		333
Hee that will deceive the fox, must rise betimes.	333	Proverbs		351
Hee that would deceive the fox, must rise betimes.	333	Proverbs	V	351
Sit in your place and none can make you rise.	334	Proverbs		372
The Citizen is at his businesse before he rise.	352	Proverbs		958
& to rise with his favours, can not but be not only allowable	381	Woodnoth		26

	PAGE	TITLE		LINE
RISEN				
Rise heart; thy Lord is risen. Sing his praise	41	Easter		1
RISES				
In every countrey the sun rises in the morning.	342	Proverbs		621
RISETH				
Which as it riseth, raiseth thee:	112	Dawning		12
When he riseth in the morning, he bethinketh himselfe what good deeds	244	Priest 12		15
He that riseth first, is first drest.	327	Proverbs		202
He that riseth betimes hath some thing in his head.	329	Proverbs		235
Hee that lies with the dogs, riseth with fleas.	332	Proverbs		343
Hee that goes to bed thirsty riseth healthy.	354	Proverbs		1003
RISING				
And mend as rising starres & rivers doe.	44	H. Bapt.1	W	9
Rising and falling with your wings:	65	Ch.-mus.		6
The gentle rising, which on either hand	67	Ch.-floore		7
RIVER				
Suck up a river to supply mine eyes,	164	Grief		5
instantly dry up, as a river would if the fountain were stopped.	271	Priest 30		7
This place is washed with the river Brenta;	301	Cornaro		24
In a great River great fish are found,	326	Proverbs		167
The river past, and God forgotten.	327	Proverbs		207
A mountaine and a river are good neighbours.	330	Proverbs		274
You may bring a horse to the river,	342	Proverbs		623
RIVERS				
And mend as rising starres & rivers doe.	44	H. Bapt.1	W	9
Rivers run, and springs each one	113	Businesse		3
And rivers stirre, thou canst not shrink or quail:	156	Assurance		33
The Flemmish rivers: in the end	213	L' Envoy	D	3
the places, and rivers travelled unto, and frequented by others,	282	Priest 34		3
for to the sea he made havens, and to rivers foords.	331	Proverbs		315
for to the sea he made heavens, and to rivers foords.	331	Proverbs	V	315
Rivers neede a spring.	341	Proverbs		600
ROAD (see also rode)				
Pride and full sinnes have made the way a road.	9	Ch.-Porch		72
ROAST (see also rost)				
ROB				
We think we rob them, but we think amisse:	197	Ch.-Milit.		253
our foolish and unworthy hearts rob us of the continuance of this thy	289	Priest		20
ROBBE				
yet robbe the Altar.	343	Proverbs		650
ROBB'D				
Here I was robb'd of all my gold,	142	Pilgrimage		16
ROBBERIE				
Who never thought that any robberie:	28	Sacrifice		63
As he that for some robberie suffereth.	34	Sacrifice		230
ROBBES				
The table robbes more then a thiefe.	342	Proverbs		636
ROBE				
Then with a scarlet robe they me aray;	31	Sacrifice		157
Wherefore that robe we cast away,	76	Sunday		52
Which thou hast open'd: do not spread thy robe	138	The Size		43
ROBERT				
To Sir Robert Harley, at Brampton.	367	Letters		T
ROBES				
In his majestick robes of glorie,	151	The Bag		10
ROBS				
It spoils an Angel: robs thee of thy God.	6	Ch.-Porch	W	10
But robs a thousand who would praise thee fain,	117	Providence		19
The back-doore robs the house.	337	Proverbs		474
ROCK (verb)				
Harmonious peace must rock them all the day:	105	Conscience		9
ROCK				
He clave the stonie rock, when they were drie;	30	Sacrifice		122
They strike my head, the rock from whence all store	32	Sacrifice		170
What ever sinne did this pure rock commit,	41	Sepulchre		10
Of a great rock: I well remember all,	129	Love unkn.		15
The rock of Pride.	142	Pilgrimage		6
Then shalt thou be my rock and tower,	156	Assurance		35
And this is all the Rock, whereof they boast,	194	Ch.-Milit.		159
Thou art my rock, thou art my rest.	205	Persever.	W	16
but to them an unpenetrable rock, an unaccessible desert.	282	Priest 34		4
hath a rock and a spindle, and no staffe to spin.	358	Proverbs	D	1085
ROCKS				
Then can thy truth and I: but while rocks stand,	156	Assurance		32
Yea, when both rocks and all things shall disband,	156	Assurance		34
ROD				
Cowards tell lies, and those that fear the rod;	9	Ch.-Porch		75
Thy rod, my posie? crosse, my bower?	35	Thanksgvng		14
Making a scepter of the rod:	73	Afflict.3		4
Thou art both Judge and Saviour, feast and rod,	83	Sighs & Gr.		27
A poore mans rod, when thou dost ride,	96	Charms & K		3
A poore mans rod if thou wilt hire	96	Charms & K	W	3
And length of dayes lengthen the rod.	123	Time		22
Devils their rod, the sea his shore,	158	Praise 3		22
For thou art with me; and thy rod	173	23 Psalme		15
Throw away thy rod,	178	Discipline		1
Throw away thy rod;	179	Discipline		29
RODD				
It makes thy soule a blott: it is a rodd	6	Ch.-Porch	W	8
Hee'le make thy wife a blessing not a rodd.	7	Ch.-Porch	W	18
Each with his rodd.	204	The Knell	W	12

	PAGE	TITLE	LINE
RODE (road)			
My lines and life are free; free as the rode, ...	153	The Collar	4
RODE (see also rid)			
since I rode 200 mile to see a Sister, in a way I knew not, . . .	371	Letters	2
ROGUE			
Yet did a rogue with hope of carnall joy	194	Ch.-Milit.	149
ROGUES			
by those, which are branded for rogues, that they may be known;	287	Priest 37	20
that Rogues should be known, and Charity to the publick hath	287	Priest 37	36
ROLLING			
Successive nights, like rolling waves, ...	98	Mortific.	11
ROLLS			
Into these lines; till in heav'ns court of rolls	105	Obedience	43
ROMANE			
Put him in trust to rule the Romane sphere.	194	Ch.-Milit.	142
ROMANS			
Rom. 12. 6. Having gifts differing, according to the grace that is	226	Priest 2	4
service, Rom. 12. when we speak not as Parrats, without reason,	232	Priest 6	3
How did he put the Romans in all his prayers? Rom. 1. 9. . .	234	Priest 7	12
The fulfilling of the Law, Romans 13. 10.	244	Priest 12	11
Romans 2.) hee first preacheth to himselfe, and then to others.	279	Priest 33	36
as appears Rom. 12. 14. how much more those, who are spiritual	286	Priest 36	27
and ranked backbiters among the generation of the wicked, Rom. 1. 30.	287	Priest 37	24
Scripture are Promises, these ever comfort more and more. Rom. 15. 4.	310	Valdesso	15
ROME			
And Rome as both; yet Egypt faster rid, ...	191	Ch.-Milit.	58
Religion went to Rome, subduing those, ...	191	Ch.-Milit.	61
From Greece to Rome she went, subduing those	191	Ch.-Milit. W	61
From Greece he went to Rome: and as before	194	Ch.-Milit.	139
Onely the West and Rome do keep them free	194	Ch.-Milit.	157
Europe alone and Rome do keep them free	194	Ch.-Milit. W	157
As Rome will one day finde unto her cost.	194	Ch.-Milit.	160
And in old Rome a mightie Emperour;	195	Ch.-Milit.	172
And from old Rome the libertie of pleasure, ...	195	Ch.-Milit.	179
Learning from Greece, from old Rome statelinesse:	195	Ch.-Milit.	188
All poste to Rome: Princes submit their necks	195	Ch.-Milit.	195
Who brought his doctrins & his deeds from Rome	195	Ch.-Milit. W	201
As new and old Rome did one Empire twist;	196	Ch.-Milit.	205
ROOF			
O let me, when thy roof my soul hath hid, ...	55	Temper 1	17
ROOM			
If reason move not Gallants, quit the room, ...	8	Ch.-Porch	43
No room for me, and flie away.	39	Good Fri.	28
Sure there is room within our hearts good store;	40	Sepulchre	5
As from one room t' another.	53	H.Commun.	36
But the extension and the room, ...	57	Employm. 1	6
But while he thinks to spoil the room, he sweeps.	67	Ch.-floore	18
Where in each room of the well-furnisht tent	69	Content	19
Where in each room of that well-furnisht tent	69	Content W	19
And hollow room with vanities.	75	Sunday	25
And hollow room on either hand.	75	Sunday W	25
No room for pratlers there.	105	Conscience	10
(I have no bag, but here is room):	152	The Bag	32
Good men ye be, to leave me my best room, ...	176	Forerunners	7
Who sweeps a room, as for thy laws, ...	185	The Elixer	19
What wretchednesse can give him any room, ...	193	Ch.-Milit.	117
there are such conceits, there is no room for his doctrine to enter.	243	Priest 11	24
for that, where contempt is, there is no room for instruction.	268	Priest 28	19
and will not allow any room there for such an in-mate as Grief;	374	Letters	11
ROOME			
indifferent things there is roome for motions [notions] and expecting	313	Valdesso	12
Water, fire, and souldiers, quickly make roome.	338	Proverbs	514
As God where he finds no roome for his Inclining grace, . . .	381	Woodnoth	8
ROOMS			
Op'ning the souls most subtile rooms;	52	H.Commun.	22
Tears sullying thy transparent rooms, ...	124	Gratefulnes	14
ROOST			
O let me roost and nestle there:	55	Temper 1	18
ROOT			
There is a rare outlandish root, ...	50	Faith	9
Thy root is ever in its grave, ...	87	Vertue	7
Thy root is ever in his grave, ...	87	Vertue V	7
Would show a root, that gives expressions!	119	Providence	76
Peace at the root must dwell.	125	Peace	16
This, this hath done it, this did bite the root	140	Ch.-rents	5
To see their mother-root, when they have blown;	166	The Flower	11
Who makes a root his God, how low is he, ...	193	Ch.-Milit.	115
ROOTE			
seasoned with pleasantnesse, both enter sooner, and roote deeper.	268	Priest 27	5
and hath taken so deep roote, that it seems the very life . .	287	Priest 37	9
ROOTED			
True earnest sorrows, rooted miseries, ...	167	Dotage	7
ROOTES			
then if it had taken before either fish, or rootes, or such things;	242	Priest 10	24
True praise rootes and spreedes.	342	Proverbs	638
ROOTS			
eating fish, or roots, and that for quantity little, for quality	242	Priest 10	27
ROPE			
Thy rope of sands, ...	153	The Collar	22
Doe winde a rope about, and cut my heart:	165	The Crosse	33
Hee puls with a long rope, that waits for anothers death. . .	322	Proverbs	25

ROPE (cont'd)	PAGE	TITLE		LINE
Hee puls with a long rope, who looks for anothers death.	322	Proverbs	V	25
ROSE (verb)				
This day my Saviour rose,	76	Sunday		36
I rose, and shook my clothes, as knowing well,	139	Artillerie		3
Yet taking heart I rose, and then perceiv'd	142	Pilgrimage		29
ROSE				
Sweet rose, whose hue angrie and brave	87	Vertue		5
First, Beautie crept into a rose,	110	The Quip		5
A rose, besides his beautie, is a cure.	119	Providence		78
Brave rose, (alas!) where art thou? in the chair	140	Ch.-rents		1
Brave rose, (alas!) where art thou? in the place	140	Ch.-rents	V	1
Why doth my Mother blush? is she the rose,	140	Ch.-rents		11
The Rose.	177	The Rose		T
Onely take this gentle rose,	177	The Rose		15
What is fairer then a rose?	178	The Rose		17
Be contracted to a rose;	178	The Rose		22
For my answer is a rose.	178	The Rose		32
ROSEMARY				
there is no spice comparable, for herbs, to rosemary, time, savoury,	262	Priest 23		2
ROSES				
Sweet spring, full of sweet dayes and roses,	88	Vertue		9
Hony of roses, whither wilt thou flie?	176	Forerunners		20
Roses and Lillies speak thee; and to make	206	Walton 2		6
the Parson useth damask or white Roses for the one, and plantaine,	261	Priest 23		34
ROST				
Dry bread at home is better then rost meate abroad.	344	Proverbs		681
ROTE				
for many say the Catechisme by rote, as parrats, without ever	256	Priest 21		4
ROTS				
And rots to nothing at the next great thaw.	12	Ch.-Porch		140
ROTTEN				
That thou shouldst minde a rotten tree?	104	Obedience		22
ROTTENNESS				
If rottenness have more, lett Heaven goe.	7	Ch.-Porch	W	24
ROTTENNESSE				
If rottennesse have more, let Heaven go.	7	Ch.-Porch		18
ROUGH				
For my rough sorrows: cease, be dumbe and mute,	164	Grief		14
ROUND				
Which would throw me there, if I keep the round.	7	Ch.-Porch		30
Lord, with what care hast thou begirt us round!	45	Sinne 1		1
Each day doth round about us see.	48	Repentance		8
And turn us round to look on one,	75	Sunday		17
Poore man, thou searchest round	86	Vanitie 1		27
Sinnes round.	122	Sinnes rd.		T
A boyling caldron, round about whose verge	129	Love unkn.		27
He wears a stuffe whose thread is course and round,	131	Mans medly		15
My thoughts turn round,	148	Longing		10
Look on my sorrows round!	149	Longing		25
That when they have accomplished the round,	197	Ch.-Milit.		267
That when they have accomplished their round,	197	Ch.-Milit.	W	267
Judgement may meet them both & search them round.	197	Ch.-Milit.		269
Lyes round about us to helpe out the story,	212	Bohemia	D	26
Nor all the people round about,	216	Psalm III	D	15
So shall the people round about	221	Psalm VII	D	25
Correspondence with all the neighbouring Pastours round about him,	253	Priest 19		16
whose exceeding glory is equally round with the world it selfe:	442	Oration		10
ROUNDLY				
Till grief did tell me roundly, that I lived.	47	Afflict.1		30
ROUT				
Thus trimmed forth they bring me to the rout,	32	Sacrifice		185
ROVING				
keepes the imagination from roving, puts on the whole Armour of God,	238	Priest 9		5
ROW				
Among thy trees, which in a ROW	132	Paradise		2
Not all the teams of Albion in a row	158	Praise 3		15
ROWS				
They are the rows of fruitfull trees	75	Sunday	W	26
ROYALL				
The Royall Crowne cures not the head-ach.	340	Proverbs		576
RUB				
There is some rub, some discontent,	133	The Method		3
RUBARB				
the Apothecary useth either for loosing, Rubarb, or for binding,	261	Priest 23		33
RUBB				
If there fall out yet any rubb, you shall heare of me;	377	Letters		22
RUBBE				
Till it stirre, and rubbe the eyes;	186	Dooms-day		4
RUDDER				
Resigning up the rudder to thy skill.	104	Obedience		20
RUDDIE				
Turned your ruddie into pale and bleak:	140	Ch.-rents		19
RUDDYARD				
yet find leisure to write to my Lord, or Sir Benjamin Ruddyard;	370	Letters		30
RUDE				
Where rude unhallow'd steps do crush and grinde	140	Ch.-rents		8
effect in the reducing of many rude and untoiled places in my	302	Cornaro		15
He that is angry at a feast is rude.	340	Proverbs		564
of whose rude delivery my hast makes mee ashamed, only my comfort is	369	Letters		2

	PAGE	TITLE	LINE
RUDELY			
Not rudely, as a beast, ...	184	The Elixer	5
His letters were broke rudely up, believ'd	439	Walton 5	16
Better speake truth rudely, then lye covertly.	346	Proverbs	767
RUFFIAN			
The old debauched ruffian would turn writer.	194	Ch.-Milit.	164
he spyes some scoffing ruffian, who is likely to deride him for his	273	Priest 31	29
RUFFLE			
And ruffle all their curious knots and store.	97	Afflict.5	22
RUFFLING			
So loose or easie, that a ruffling winde	72	Constancie	7
RUG			
Thou pull'st the rug, and wilt not rise, ...	101	Miserie	51
RUGGED			
A stumbler stumbles least in rugged way.	15	Ch.-Porch	214
O smooth my rugged heart, and there	45	Nature	13
A rugged stone growes smooth from hand to hand.	332	Proverbs	316
RUINE			
Let not a common ruine thee intombe:	8	Ch.-Porch	45
And make their ruine praise thy power.	156	Assurance	36
Doe ruine thee; or if the teares	208	H. Danvers D	6
for others ruine wrought:	222	Psalm VII D	54
RULE			
Mayst rule it, as thou list; and poure the shame, ...	7	Ch.-Porch	27
Thou liv'st by rule. What doth not so, but man?	12	Ch.-Porch	134
Thou liv'st by rule. What does not so, but man?	12	Ch.-Porch W	134
Houses are built by rule, and common-wealths.	12	Ch.-Porch	135
Who lives by rule then, keeps good companie.	12	Ch.-Porch	138
And if the Fox had liv'd to rule their side, ...	70	Humilitie	23
The windes, who think they rule the mariner, ...	119	Providence	91
As if there were no rule or eares?	136	Familie	4
And rule on high, ...	150	Longing	57
Put him in trust to rule the Romane sphere.	194	Ch.-Milit.	142
And having conquer'd, did so strangely rule, ...	196	Ch.-Milit.	203
Are thy dominion. Those that rule in clay	211	Bohemia D	6
The Countrey PARSON HIS CHARACTER, AND Rule of Holy Life. . .	223	Priest	T
some live there in office, whose rule is that of the Apostle;	226	Priest 2	3
which is expressed in a fayre table, as being the rule of a family.	240	Priest 10	26
the determination of the second rule by Authority to this particular.	242	Priest 10	6
unpleasant, is the naturall rule of fasting, although it be flesh.	242	Priest 10	11
I am to follow our Saviours rule, and to take my brother aside,	248	Priest 14	27
I am then to follow the Apostles rule, 1 Timothy 5. 20. and to rebuke	248	Priest 14	29
but he holds the Rule, that Nothing is little in Gods service:	249	Priest 14	2
For the Apostles rule Philip. 4. being admirable, and large,	253	Priest 19	22
giving age honour, according to the Apostles rule, 1 Tim. 5. 1.	255	Priest 21	25
particularly, the rule may be this:	258	Priest 22	33
holding that rule, that to put men to discourse of that, . . .	260	Priest 23	5
whether it be a rule to it selfe, whether it hath a rule, . . .	263	Priest 24	1
be a rule to it selfe, whether it hath a rule, whether having a rule,	263	Priest 24	2
whether having a rule, it ought not to be guided by it; . .	263	Priest 24	2
whether any rule in the world be obscure, and how then should	263	Priest 24	3
This last rule joyned with the first, never fails.	267	Priest 26	5
according to the Apostles rule, he endeavours that none shall despise	268	Priest 28	17
Now the Canons being the Church-wardens rule, the Parson adviseth	270	Priest 29	13
according to St. Pauls rule, Ephes. 4. 28. 1 Thes. 4. 11, 12.	275	Priest 32	2
nothing holp me, but that exact rule which I had so long continued.	296	Cornaro	29
as usually happens in old mens bodies, which live without rule.	296	Cornaro	36
and not the qualitie for his rule, which is very easie to be	300	Cornaro	15
It's no sure rule to fish with a cros-bow.	331	Proverbs	293
But take this rule, and it is an outlandish one, which I commend	376	Letters	16
by the Apostles rule. 1 Cor.	380	Woodnoth	5
well & you are by the Apostles rule (Philip 4, 8.) not only to pursue	380	Woodnoth	12
RUL'D			
Are rul'd by him, and taught to serve his trade.	119	Providence	92
RULER			
Then from one ruler to another bound	28	Sacrifice	53
RULERS			
The Priest and rulers all false witnesse seek	28	Sacrifice	57
The Priests and rulers all false witnesse seek	28	Sacrifice W	57
RULES			
Man is a shop of rules, a well truss'd pack, ...	12	Ch.-Porch	141
To rules of reason, holy messengers, ...	45	Sinne 1	4
the Apostles two great and admirable Rules in things of this nature:	246	Priest 13	26
For these two rules comprize and include the double object of our	246	Priest 13	29
driving of their generall Schoole rules ever to the smallest actions	266	Priest 26	1
These three rules generally comprehend the faults of eating,	266	Priest 26	12
To guide them in this, there are three rules:	266	Priest 26	37
he gives him those freer rules:	267	Priest 26	18
and much more for those rules, which out of his choysest judgment hee	268	Priest 28	11
is the key of Commerce, and discovers the Rules of forraine Nations.	277	Priest 32	33
judiciously, then he writes his rules of temperance out of bookes.	278	Priest 33	21
being so built by me according to the rules of Architecture,	301	Cornaro	13
the many pious rules of ordering our life, about mortification,	305	Valdesso	9
difficulty of applying their generall rules to particular actions,	319	Valdesso V	32
Love rules his kingdome without a sword.	339	Proverbs	541
RULEST			
Seest and rulest all things ev'n as one:	190	Ch.-Milit.	2
RULETH			
he that ruleth, let him do it with diligence, &c.	226	Priest 2	7
RULING			
In ruling all	158	Praise 3	20

	PAGE	TITLE		LINE
RUN				
Thou hast run all thy race, ere thou beginn.	10	Ch.-Porch	W	90
And all the bloud of God to run in vain.	102	Miserie		64
Rivers run, and springs each one	113	Businesse		3
So both the flower doth stay, and hony run.	118	Providence		68
If they seek fine things, thou dost make them run	120	Providence		106
Will not a verse run smooth that bears thy name?	206	Walton 1		11
Though the Fox run, the chicken hath wings.	339	Proverbs		549
RUNN				
Like Comick lovers ever one way runn:	198	Ch.-Milit.	W	271
I and the Sunn have runn our races,	203	Even-song	W	2
RUNNE				
Lets his soul runne for nought, as little fearing.	8	Ch.-Porch		59
By no means runne in debt: take thine own measure.	13	Ch.-Porch		175
In time they'l runne thee out of all thy wit.	21	Ch.-Porch		366
Arise, arise, they come. Look how they runne!	27	Sacrifice		33
That thy distresse through all may runne,	39	Good Fri.		15
What though my bodie runne to dust?	51	Faith		41
That I may runne, rise, rest with thee.	68	Trin.Sun.		9
That I may runne, rise, rest in thee.	68	Trin.Sun.	W	9
His goodnesse sets not, but in dark can runne:	72	Constancie		23
If thou hadst let us runne,	82	Ungratef.		3
And pipes that feed the presse, and make it runne;	88	The Pearl		2
Thousands of notions in my brain did runne,	102	Jordan 2		7
And both would runne untill they found a biere	159	Jos.coat		8
To runne into an action;	184	The Elixer		6
Light one another, and together runne.	198	Ch.-Milit.		271
And starres alone unto the pitch doe runne	211	Bohemia	D	4
sensitive faculty, will runne out more or lesse in her intellectuall.	238	Priest 9		11
This distinction may runne through all Christian duties,	274	Priest 31		1
If you could runne, as you drinke, you might catch a hare.	334	Proverbs		373
RUNNES				
When the wide world runnes bias, from his will	73	Constancie		32
But runnes, although I be not drie;	136	Ephes.		29
It runnes, it flies:	158	Praise 3		8
Though press'd, runnes thin;	159	Praise 3		38
Runnes over day and night.	173	23 Psalme		20
RUNNETH				
And still it runneth mutt'ring up and down	168	a true Hymn		4
RUNNING				
Give up your feet and running to mine eyes,	164	Grief		15
parted with rills of running water, which truely is very delightfull.	301	Cornaro		16
RUNS				
This letter runs to you with much eagernes, for I am enjoined	367	Letters		27
RUSHED				
They rushed in, and cast them in the dirt	140	Ch.-rents		23
RUST				
Which if it cleave to coine, one common rust	13	Ch.-Porch	W	165
RYME				
Ryme thee to good, and make a bait of pleasure.	6	Ch.-Porch		4
Nor let them punish me with losse of ryme,	57	Jordan 1		14
And mend my ryme.	80	Deniall		30
And meet my ryme.	80	Deniall	W	30
And ev'n my verse, when by the ryme and reason	109	Home		75
Whose grief allows him musick and a ryme:	164	Grief		17
If the words onely ryme,	168	a true Hymn		13
RYMES				
How should I praise thee, Lord! how should my rymes	55	Temper 1		1
S				
put this into your hands (as he sent the fish with mony to S. Peter,)	304	Valdesso		11
there be a restraining motion (as S. Paul had when hee would have	313	Valdesso		16
As for the text of S. Pet. 2 Ep. 1. 19. which he makes the ground	318	Valdesso		7
So S. Peter bidding the dispersed Hebrews attend to the word till	318	Valdesso		17
Give not S. Peter so much, to leave Saint Paul nothing.	346	Proverbs		763
SABLE				
End as the night, whose sable hue	135	Ephes.		11
SACK				
It's good tying the sack before it be full.	349	Proverbs		842
SACKE				
One graine fills not a sacke, but helpes his fellowes.	328	Proverbs		226
Honour and profit lie not in one sacke.	328	Proverbs		232
Every one thinkes his sacke heaviest.	346	Proverbs		748
You cannot hide an eele in a sacke.	346	Proverbs		762
You cannot hide a needle in a sacke.	346	Proverbs	V	762
There comes nought out of the sacke but what was there.	348	Proverbs		833
There come nought out of the sacke but what was there.	348	Proverbs	V	833
SACRAMENT				
the participation of the holy Sacrament, how comfortable,	250	Priest 15		1
under pretence of devotion to the Sacrament, but it is for want	258	Priest 22		38
Hee that comes to the Sacrament, hath the confidence of a Guest,	259	Priest 22		14
SACRAMENTALL				
When any one can distinguish the Sacramentall from common bread,	258	Priest 22		34
SACRAMENTS				
That as sinne came, so Sacraments might flow:	34	Sacrifice		247
The Parson in Sacraments.	257	Priest 22		T
The Countrey Parson being to administer the Sacraments,	257	Priest 22		26
SACRED				
The Temple. Sacred Poems and Private Ejaculations. Dedication.	5	Dedication		T
That I beleeve is in the sacred storie:	50	Faith		18
Thou art the sacred mine, whence came the gold,	78	Ang.&Sts.	W	11
O let thy sacred will	104	Obedience		16

SACRED (cont'd)	PAGE	TITLE		LINE
JESU is in my heart, his sacred name	112	JESU		1
O sacred Providence, who from end to end	116	Providence		1
Wherefore, most sacred Spirit, I here present	117	Providence		25
And art thou grieved, sweet and sacred Dove,	135	Ephes.		1
But thou art fire, sacred and hallow'd fire;	160	Priesthood		7
Sacred Martle, safely keepe	208	H. Danvers	D	1
Henceforth in Sacred Flames shall Burn,	214	Convert	D	19
nor can I hide his sacred will.	215	Psalm II	D	16
altar to be bathed, and washed in the sacred Laver of Christs blood.	231	Priest 6		10
that God intends that to be as a sacred Temple for himself to dwell	374	Letters		10
SACRIFICE				
And turn delight into a sacrifice.	6	Ch.-Porch		6
If cause require, thou art his sacrifice;	17	Ch.-Porch		273
O let thy blessed SACRIFICE be mine,	26	The Altar		15
O let thy onely SACRIFICE be mine,	26	The Altar	W	15
The sacrifice.	26	Sacrifice		T
Not half so sweet as my sweet sacrifice:	27	Sacrifice		19
And sing this day thy sacrifice,	43	East.wings	W	9
My morning-soul and sacrifice:	62	Mattens		3
The sacrifice for all; while they below	117	Providence		14
To fetch a sacrifice out of my fold,	129	Love unkn.		30
The sacrifice of righteousness,	217	Psalm IV	D	19
SACRIFICED				
were with Saint Paul even sacrificed upon the service of their	234	Priest 7		8
who sacrificed lest his Children should have transgressed in their	281	Priest 34		1
SACRIFICES				
or offer up such sacrifices as they did of old, which was of beasts	232	Priest 6		4
for with such sacrifices God is well pleased.	281	Priest 34		4
SAD				
A sad wise valour is the brave complexion,	16	Ch.-Porch		247
And the sad man is cock of all his jests.	16	Ch.-Porch		252
Shall I then sing, neglecting thy sad storie,	35	Thanksgvng	W	11
Couldst thou not griefs sad conquests me allow,	37	Reprisall		11
If apparitions make us sad,	63	Sinne 2		7
Thine clad with simplenesse, and sad events;	71	Frailtie		11
Who did so sweetly deaths sad taste convey,	94	Life		10
The note is sad, yet musick for a king.	107	Sion		24
Awake sad heart, whom sorrow ever drowns;	112	Dawning		1
Arise sad heart; if thou dost not withstand,	112	Dawning		9
Arise sad heart; if thou dce not withstand,	112	Dawning	V	9
Deare Friend, sit down, the tale is long and sad:	129	Love unkn.		1
The sad effect of sadder grones:	185	Death		3
A sad repentance, not the spoils of lust:	192	Ch.-Milit.		68
The Countrey Parson is generally sad, because hee knows nothing	267	Priest 27		27
he meets continually with two most sad spectacles, Sin,	267	Priest 27		31
or in a sad way, greived at his own, and others sins, which	269	Priest 28		9
Tragedie with old Age, by reason of the sad events which it contains.	302	Cornaro		32
SADDER				
The sad effect of sadder grones:	185	Death		3
SADDLE				
The fault of the horse is put on the saddle.	329	Proverbs		240
Who eates his cock alone must saddle his horse alone.	333	Proverbs		348
Who eates his cake alone must saddle his horse alone.	333	Proverbs	V	348
SADLES				
The horse thinkes one thing, and he that sadles him another.	334	Proverbs		387
SADLY				
As frost-nipt sunnes look sadly.	81	Christmas		30
SADNESS				
or, allow that any sadness shall be his Competitor.	374	Letters		12
SADNESSE				
Since my sadnesse	147	Offering		25
SAFE				
May guard it safe beyond the highest starr.	66	Ch.-lock	W	12
This is the Mark-man, safe and sure,	73	Constancie		34
Nor in the safe society	215	Psalm I	D	19
by a due blessing of God for their safe arrival, and saying grace	251	Priest 17		9
and that alsc well inned, and imbarned, and continuing safe there;	272	Priest 30		2
and seriously prepare for it, he is safe and within bounds.	275	Priest 32		13
Dry feet, warme head, bring safe to bed.	335	Proverbs		402
Little journeys and good cost bring safe home.	338	Proverbs		502
I have received the things you sent me, safe;	371	Letters		6
SAFELY				
Gold thou mayst safely touch; but if it stick	13	Ch.-Porch		167
(Beleeve me), it shall safely come.	152	The Bag		34
Sacred Marble, safely keepe	208	H. Danvers	D	1
SAFEST				
it is the safest course for Christians also to meditate on their	258	Priest 22		17
SAFETIE				
Your safetie in my sicknesse doth subsist:	34	Sacrifice		227
SAFETY				
shall me in safety keep.	218	Psalm IV	D	32
and with more safety then elsewhere, where both the people	242	Priest 10		19
The death of wolves is the safety of the sheep.	358	Proverbs	D	1086
SAID				
Some said, that I the Temple to the floore	28	Sacrifice		65
Who straight, Your suit is granted, said, & died.	40	Redemption		14
Now come again, said I, and flout me.	108	Home		46
Which when I pluckt not, Sir, said she,	110	The Quip		6
What tune is this, poore man? said he:	110	The Quip		10
To spend my judgement), said, It seem'd to me	116	Love-joy		5

	PAGE	TITLE		LINE
SAID (cont'd)				
Meeting with Time, Slack thing, said I,	122	Time		1
Then chafing said, This man deludes:	123	Time		28
The Crown Imperiall: Sure, said I,	125	Peace		15
Dread Lord, said I, so oft my good;	139	Artillerie		13
And lives: If that be all, said I,	142	Pilgrimage		34
Then will I trust, said I, in him alone.	143	Holdfast		5
He smil'd and said as he did go,	151	The Bag		17
Let us (said he) poure on him all we can:	159	The Pulley		3
For if I should (said he)	160	The Pulley		11
If truly said, they may take part	168	a true Hymn		7
Love said, you shall be he.	189	Love 3		8
He said to me, Thou art my Son,	216	Psalm II	D	17
means to continue so, he doth at least, as much as hath been said.	238	Priest 9		25
This was not so well said, as it might have been forborn;	252	Priest 18		9
or, So farr indeed what you say is true, and well said;	252	Priest 18		12
You said, God made the world;	256	Priest 21		11
That which is said of hurtfull meats, extends to hurtfull drinks	266	Priest 26		27
he is lost, as if they said, God doth forsake and persecute them,	281	Priest 34		11
of which our Saviour said, that that generation should not passe,	282	Priest 34		28
neither did I know well, what I did or said.	296	Cornaro		17
Many things more might be said in commendation hereof:	303	Cornaro		33
All the Saints of God may be said in some sence to have put	306	Valdesso		28
Much more might be said, but this sufficeth, he himselfe allowes it	311	Valdesso		1
There is no more to be said of this Chapter but that his opinion	318	Valdesso		5
of the blessed Virgin out of that text Mat. 1. 25. where it is said,	318	Valdesso		12
as he expected & therfore he grumblingly said that if he had given it	368	Letters		33
What can be said more comfortably?	374	Letters		29
SAID'ST				
Thou said'st but even now,	155	Assurance		7
SAIDEST				
had sinned beyond any help in heaven or earth, then thou saidest, Lo,	288	Priest		27
SAIES				
saies they are not ripe.	325	Proverbs		130
from him that saies nothing, for ever.	326	Proverbs		164
Milke saies to wine, welcome friend.	327	Proverbs		184
The child saies nothing, but what it heard by the fire.	331	Proverbs		300
I was taken by a morsell, saies the fish.	342	Proverbs		627
Talke much and erre much, saies the Spanyard.	343	Proverbs		649
None saies his Garner is full.	343	Proverbs		657
SAIL				
And are like empty vessels under sail.	14	Ch.-Porch		184
Boat, cable, sail and needle, all in one.	120	Providence		128
Of cloves and nutmegs, and in cinamon sail;	137	The Size		8
SAILE				
From Holland saile into the Maine:	213	L' Envoy	D	10
Being on sea saile, being on land settle.	335	Proverbs		418
SAINT (see also s,st)				
The decreed burden of each mortall Saint:	33	Sacrifice		199
The gladsome burden of a mortall saint.	33	Sacrifice	W	199
The gladsome burthen of a mortall saint.	33	Sacrifice	WC	199
though he himself were with Saint Paul even sacrificed upon	234	Priest 7		8
yerrow, melilot, and Saint Johns wort made into a salve;	262	Priest 23		6
our Saviours selling is so far from crossing Saint Pauls working,	275	Priest 32		3
wherein (as Saint Paul implyes that he ought, Romans 2.) hee first	279	Priest 33		35
being no reason, why any should distrust Saint Luke, or Tertullian,	282	Priest 34		21
the cunning hypocrite who by the world is counted a very Saint,	319	Valdesso	V	20
Give not S. Peter so much, to leave Saint Paul nothing.	346	Proverbs		763
Who praiseth Saint Peter, doth not blame Saint Paul.	349	Proverbs		859
Saint Luke was a Saint and a Physitian, yet is dead.	354	Proverbs		1008
Such a Saint, such an offering.	359	Proverbs	D	1108
James is the protecting Saint unto us both;	442	Oration		19
SAINTS				
With saints on earth, shall one day with them shine.	24	Ch.-Porch		438
To all Angels and Saints.	77	Ang.&Sts.		T
Who God & Saints and Angels loose at last.	203	Trin.Sun.	W	17
from his promises, from the examples of all Saints, that ever were;	249	Priest 15		21
and his Saints, and by way of undertaking for a Christian soul.	258	Priest 22		13
his Master, and of Gods Saints his Brethren, and this is foretold,	268	Priest 28		14
All the Saints of God may be said in some sence to have put	306	Valdesso		28
us to judge of the doubtfull actions of Saints in the Scriptures;	316	Valdesso		12
since the Saints of God in all ages have ever held in so pretious	317	Valdesso		32
By the Saints of the world he every where understands the cunning	319	Valdesso	V	19
and we meet with two sorts of these Saints of the world;	319	Valdesso	V	22
to doe) to blessed Mary Magd. & Paul, heaven had wanted chief saints:	381	Woodnoth		5
SAIST				
Thou saist, this fruit is mine.	184	The Elixer	W	12
SAITH				
Unto the ungodly, saith God, Why dost thou preach my Laws,	226	Priest 2		13
remembring what his Master saith, that if any do Gods will,	228	Priest 4		28
his preaching, The Lord (saith he) reward him according to his works.	285	Priest 36		33
of Hymeneus and Alexander, he saith, he had delivered them to Satan,	286	Priest 36		1
Therefore he saith here, we shall not be punished (which word I like	311	Valdesso		26
only one place more to you (Philip. 4. 4.) St. Paul saith there:	374	Letters		21
SAKE				
The place its honour, for the persons sake.	17	Ch.-Porch		266
Yet heare, O God, onely for his blouds sake	66	Ch.-lock		9
Ev'n God himself, being pressed for my sake.	128	Bunch Gr.		28
Which with his tincture (for thy sake)	184	The Elixer		15
Which with this tincture (for thy sake)	184	The Elixer	V	15
of Christ in his flesh, for his Bodie's sake, which is the Church.	225	Priest 1		13

SAKE (cont'd)	PAGE	TITLE		LINE
and vertuously, not for any reward of his, but for vertues sake;	243	Priest 11		29
although we should love him onely for his own sake, yet out of his	243	Priest 11		31
but with these he mingles other discourses for conversation sake,	249	Priest 14		11
partly for uniformity sake, that the same common truths may be every	255	Priest 21		18
but for example sake, and because they are most common, . .	265	Priest 26		3
and do so for thy blessed Son's sake, in whose sweet and pleasing	289	Priest		34
Grant this dear Father, for thy Son's sake, our only Saviour:	290	Priest		13
First for your sake, because I would doe nothing negligently that you	304	Valdesso		4
Secondly for the Authors sake, whom I conceive to have been a true	304	Valdesso		6
Thirdly for the Churches sake, to whom by Printing it I would have	304	Valdesso		8
SAKES				
And for our sakes in person sinne reprove, ...	103	Prayer 2		16
For their sakes, Lord, return on high, ...	221	Psalm VII	D	27
SALE				
Both the main sale, and the commodities;	89	The Pearl		34
No sale or bargain passe: all would disperse, ...	127	Giddinesse		23
SALEM				
At Salem dwelt, who liv'd with good increase	125	Peace		23
SALLET				
Who for a God clearely a sallet lost.	193	Ch.-Milit.		110
SALT				
To a salt rhume	49	Repentance	WC	29
And water with salt tears my Bed, ...	220	Psalm VI	D	15
baned meat, sometimes too salt, and so not competent nourishment,	265	Priest 26		22
Of all smells, bread: of all tasts, salt.	326	Proverbs		166
A gentlemans grayhound, and a salt-box; seeke them at the fire.	327	Proverbs		205
Before you make a friend, eate a bushell of salt with him. . .	342	Proverbs		624
The best smell is bread, the best savour, salt, ...	346	Proverbs		741
SALT-BOX				
A gentlemans grayhound, and a salt-box; seeke them at the fire.	327	Proverbs		205
SALUTATIONS				
out of niceness, because they like the salutations, and complements,	285	Priest 36		5
SALUTE				
Salute thy self: see what thy soul doth wear.	12	Ch.-Porch		146
They that know one another salute a farre off.	327	Proverbs		185
as to you deserving them, Wee at last salute you Masters of Arts;	441	Oration		27
SALVATION				
As those, who mock at Gods way of salvation.	24	Ch.-Porch		446
All that salvation, which ye now resist;	34	Sacrifice		226
Christs hands, though nail'd, wrought our salvation, ...	76	Sunday		48
Our own salvation.	127	Giddinesse		28
And be my salvation.	148	Offering		42
Who gives to man, as he sees fit Salvation. / Damnation. . .	170	Water-crs.		10
Salvation unto thee	217	Psalm III	D	22
infuse a competent knowledge of salvation in every one of his Flock;	255	Priest 21		3
in the world as he was, hath this undoubted pledge of his salvation.	269	Priest 28		18
and hast made our salvation, not our punishment, thy glory: . .	288	Priest		23
SALVE				
Whom oil and balsames kill, what salve can cure?	24	Ch.-Porch		447
Whom oil and mercies kill, what salve can cure?	24	Ch.-Porch	W	447
yerrow, melilot, and Saint Johns wort made into a salve; . .	262	Priest 23		7
The best salve for the whole Chapter, is to distinguish Judgment:	316	Valdesso		34
SALVES				
Accordingly, for salves, his wife seeks not the city, but preferrs	262	Priest 23		3
SAME				
No workmans tool hath touch'd the same.	26	The Altar		4
Then they condemne me all with that same breath, ...	28	Sacrifice		69
Who bore the same.	41	Easter		10
Though foolishly he lost the same, ...	43	East.wings		2
Lord, though we change, thou art the same;	60	Whitsunday		25
The same sweet God of love and light:	60	Whitsunday		26
On the same floore, ...	61	Praise 1		14
With the same shake, which at his passion	76	Sunday.		45
Whereas they were supported by the same:	84	The World		4
Then those same pendant profits, which the spring	86	Lent		25
Is this same grief! within my heart I made	126	Confession		2
Scatter my words, and in the same	149	Longing		23
Much about one and the same time and place, ...	192	Ch.-Milit.		101
In us the same transplanted foolerie.	193	Ch.-Milit.		120
Or, since thy wayes are deep, and still the same, ...	206	Walton 1		10
whose duty and obligation being the same to the Houses they live in,	226	Priest 2		16
they are not understood but with the same Spirit that writ them.	228	Priest 4		32
and all being penn'd by one and the self-same Spirit, it cannot be,	229	Priest 4		6
the same affection which made him not profit before, making him then	235	Priest 7		13
working those that are able to the same charity, still pressing it in	245	Priest 12		12
that the same common truths may be every where professed, . .	255	Priest 21		18
way that a Pastor can take, to go over the same, but in other words:	256	Priest 21		3
to know what herbs may be used in stead of drugs of the same nature,	261	Priest 23		30
without any resistance, even in resistance, to the same destruction.	269	Priest 28		23
and by the same Law they are to levy penalties for negligence in	270	Priest 29		4
with the same care as others, when they meet with good fruit,	276	Priest 32		31
is a Physitian so far as he meetes with the same disease, . .	278	Priest 33		27
And if the same person had been sick of all diseases, and were	278	Priest 33		30
yet the victory is alike in all, being by the self-same Spirit.	279	Priest 33		2
The same is to be observed in writing Letters also. . . .	286	Priest 36		25
Although by other words of the same Psalme it is evident, . .	309	Valdesso		28
in regard it presents us not with the same thing only when it is read	310	Valdesso		33
for so he useth the same word in Consideration 68 ad finem. . .	317	Valdesso	V	8
The Law is not the same at morning and at night.	351	Proverbs		905
For the same man to be an heretick	357	Proverbs	D	1058

SAVE (cont'd)	PAGE	TITLE	LINE
it is a duty rather, which may do much good, and save much harme.	288	Priest 37	1
The world is now adayes, God save the Conquerour.	358	Proverbs	D 1075
SAVES			
Is all that saves, and not obscure.	135	Divinitie	24
SAVING			
No Alchymy to saving.	324	Proverbs	114
SAVIOUR			
O my deare Saviour, Victorie!	36	Thanksgvng	48
This day my Savicur rose,	76	Sunday	36
A part whereof my Saviour empti'd hath,	83	Sighs & Gr.	22
Thou art both Judge and Saviour, feast and rod,	83	Sighs & Gr.	27
Thy Saviour comes, and with him mirth:	112	Dawning	4
Neither sinne nor Saviour feels.	114	Businesse	38
Sweetest Saviour, if my soul	114	Dialogue	1
Thy Saviour sentenc'd joy,	138	The Size	25
That though our Saviour did destroy the game,	194	Ch.-Milit.	146
since our Saviour hath made that the argument of a Pastour's love,	224	Priest	5
even as our Saviour made plants and seeds to teach the people:	261	Priest 23	13
And I conceive, our Saviour did this for three reasons:	261	Priest 23	17
as he did our Saviour, and the Angels minister to us their owne food,	280	Priest 34	6
These two states were in our Saviour, not only in the beginning	280	Priest 34	8
the one concerning the woman that spent the oyntment on our Saviour,	282	Priest 34	25
of which our Saviour said, that that generation should not passe,	282	Priest 34	28
which our Saviour himselfe used, Marke 10. 16, cannot bee vain	285	Priest 36	10
Kings 2. 24. which though our Saviour reproved as unfitting for his	285	Priest 36	27
Blessed Saviour! many waters could not quench thy love!	288	Priest	30
Grant this dear Father, for thy Son's sake, our only Saviour:	290	Priest	13
To say our Saviour prayed with doubtfulnesse, is more then I can	315	Valdesso	9
SAVIOUR'S			
Where beams surround my Saviours face,	74	The Starre	2
We cannot reach our Saviours puritie;	87	Lent	34
My Saviours bloud: when ever at his board	106	Conscience	14
'Twixt his sinnes and Saviours death?	114	Businesse	30
Brings thy Saviours death no gain?	114	Businesse	36
When blessed Marie wip'd her Saviours feet,	173	Marie Magd	1
But since our Saviours death did put some bloud	186	Death	13
I am to follow our Saviours rule, and to take my brother aside,	248	Priest 14	27
As when the people hungred and thirsted after our Saviours Doctrine,	267	Priest 26	22
this reason crosseth not our Saviours precept of selling what we	274	Priest 32	32
So that our Saviours selling is so far from crossing Saint Pauls	275	Priest 32	3
are come now, to what the Pharisees were come in our Saviours time.	320	Valdesso	7
SAVORY			
yet every mans own is fittest, readyest, and most savory to him.	230	Priest 5	5
SAVOUR			
Is beyond my savour.	115	Dialogue	20
May give savour	148	Offering	38
The best smell is bread, the best savour, salt,	346	Proverbs	741
SAVOURIE			
so that any simple fare is more savourie to me now, then heretofore,	302	Cornaro	10
SAVOURS			
to wit, That which savours, is good and nourisheth, be consonant	293	Cornaro	9
SAVOURY			
is no spice comparable, for herbs, to rosemary, time, savoury, mints;	262	Priest 23	2
SAW			
Our eies shall see thee, which before saw dust;	54	Love 2	9
I saw the Vertues sitting hand in hand	70	Humilitie	1
I never saw thing make such haste.	107	Home	10
I saw a vine drop grapes with J and C	116	Love-joy	2
But when I digg'd, I saw a worm devoure	125	Peace	17
Surely if each one saw anothers heart,	127	Giddinesse	21
Travell'd, and saw no town;	128	Bunch Gr.	9
Walkt by my self abroad, I saw a large	129	Love unkn.	25
Which when your neighbours saw, like a north-winde,	140	Ch.-rents	22
I saw him in his studie, where he sate	194	Ch.-Milit.	165
Hee that saw Christ open a blind mans eyes, saw not more Divinity,	282	Priest 34	38
saw not more Divinity, then he that reads the womans oyntment in	283	Priest 34	1
For when they saw their parents and kindred snatcht away in the midst	291	Cornaro	9
and saw that it was no hard thing to do so, but the proper duty	292	Cornaro	32
brother and others of my kindred saw some great powerfull men pick	294	Cornaro	16
when the Physicians saw in what case I was, they concluded that I	295	Cornaro	2
SAWCIE			
When sawcie mirth shall knock or call at doore,	136	Ephes.	13
SAY (see also saies)			
And say withall, Earth to earth I commit.	11	Ch.-Porch	132
But say withall, Earth to earth I commit.	11	Ch.-Porch W	132
Slight those who say amidst their sickly healths,	12	Ch.-Porch	133
Say not then, This with that lace will do well;	14	Ch.-Porch	189
Who say, I care not, those I give for lost;	20	Ch.-Porch	347
Who say, I care not, I give those for gone;	20	Ch.-Porch W	347
Onely let others say, when I am dead,	34	Sacrifice	251
Did set again abroach; then let him say	37	The Agonie	15
All come to lodge there, sinne may say,	39	Good Fri.	27
All come to lodge there, he may say,	39	Good Fri. W	27
Yet though my flours be lost, they say	42	Easter W	27
Who plainly say, My God, My King.	57	Jordan 1	15
What if I say thou seek'st delayes;	61	Grace W	20
Remove me, where I need not say,	61	Grace	23
Yet say sometimes, God help poore Kings.	65	Ch.-mus.	8
As good go any where, they say,	80	Deniall	11
And spinning phansies, she was heard to say,	84	The World	2

SAY (cont'd)	PAGE	TITLE		LINE
So that we need not say, Where's this command?	86	Vanitie 1		26
To one word onely I say, No:	105	Obedience		32
Pratler, no more, I say:	105	Conscience		7
Speak not at large, say, I am thine:	111	The Quip		23
If I say, Thou shalt be mine;	114	Dialogue		11
The beasts say, Eat me: but, if beasts must teach,	117	Providence		21
The trees say, Pull me: but the hand you stretch,	117	Providence		23
(I sigh to say)	129	Love unkn.		8
I would say thorns. Deare, could my heart not break,	130	Love unkn.		52
Seek pardon first, and God will say,	134	The Method		31
When suddenly I heard one say,	139	Artillerie		5
Not, but I am (I must say still)	139	Artillerie		21
Lime begg'd of old, (they say),	154	Glimpse		13
Who heard thee say it. O most gracious Lord,	155	Assurance		20
Be not Almightie, let me say,	163	The Search		51
We say amisse,	166	The Flower		19
Somewhat it fain would say:	168	a true Hymn		3
Perhaps with more embellishment can say,	177	Forerunners		33
Such delights I meant to say;	177	The Rose		10
Say that fairly I refuse,	178	The Rose		31
Or say, or dictate, this is my delight.	183	The Posie		8
Say, that thou art not here.	183	A Parodie		20
Choke him, let him say no more,	199	L'Envoy		11
Sometimes, when as I wash, I say	202	love	W	7
and 'gainst his Christ, presume to say,	215	Psalm II	D	6
Many there are that say, O who	217	Psalm IV	D	21
he may say as He did, I sate daily with you teaching in the Temple.	227	Priest 3		33
They say, it is an ill Mason that refuseth any stone:	228	Priest 4		14
of their answer, but gently and pausably, thinking what they say;	231	Priest 6		33
truly affecting, and cordially expressing all that we say;	233	Priest 7		31
every one is more awaked, when we come, and say, Thou art the man.	236	Priest 8		14
and knows what prayers they say, and till they have learned them,	241	Priest 10		3
he exacts of them to let him alone, and say rather, God be praised,	245	Priest 12		32
So doth hee also before giving make them say their Prayers first,	245	Priest 12		35
to do all the good he can, moves him to say thus and thus.	251	Priest 17		32
or, So farr indeed what you say is true, and well said;	252	Priest 18		12
for many say the Catechisme by rote, as parrats, without ever	256	Priest 21		3
for he could not but say, he would hast out of it as fast as he	257	Priest 21		7
Come, say they, we have nothing to do, lets go to the Tavern,	274	Priest 32		12
But some may say, though the Law allow this, the Gospel doth not,	287	Priest 37		21
in whose sweet and pleasing words, we say, Our Father, &c.	289	Priest		35
I say therefore, that the infirmities, which did not onely begin,	291	Cornaro		17
So that I can truly say, That they who in these two things that enter	294	Cornaro		3
Moreover I say, that even bruises and squats, and falls,	294	Cornaro		33
because they say, It is better to please the Appetite (though they	298	Cornaro		26
And that I may say nothing of other things, are not almost all	298	Cornaro		32
these Belly-gods say, that an orderly life is so hard a thing that it	298	Cornaro		36
But some may say, He which lives a regular life, eating alwayes light	299	Cornaro		22
So that I can truly say, That I have both given God a Temple,	301	Cornaro		31
As if he should say:	308	Valdesso		34
or assent to the promises of the Gospell by heare-say, or relation	309	Valdesso		1
To say our Saviour prayed with doubtfulnesse, is more then I can	315	Valdesso		9
Saviour prayed with doubtfulnesse, is more then I can or dare say;	315	Valdesso		10
Send a wise man on an errand, and say nothing unto him.	328	Proverbs		217
Say no ill of the yeere, till it be past.	331	Proverbs		297
Let none say, I will not drinke water.	331	Proverbs		310
must not say to another; Blow.	333	Proverbs		353
Who will sell the Cow, must say the word.	347	Proverbs		791
The best of the sport is to doe the deede, and say nothing.	348	Proverbs		812
Once a yeare a man may say: On his conscience.	353	Proverbs		971
but he would chuse to dy in Spain (where they say	357	Proverbs	D	1047
Better is one Accipe, then twice to say, Dabo tibi.	358	Proverbs	D	1079
Say to pleasure, Gentle Eve, I will none of your apple.	360	Proverbs	D	1140
by which Scholars say, the Muses use to take up their habitations.	363	Letters		5
hath guided me hitherto, and of atchieving my (I dare say) holy ends.	364	Letters		19
in that I apprehend what my Friends would have been forward to say,	364	Letters		21
But perhaps they will say, you are sickly, you must not study too	364	Letters		25
of your wit, mark what I say, have a good conceit of your wit;	366	Letters		15
I dare say she would make good her promise of taking five or six	367	Letters		2
yet you may say with David, That God who hath delivered me out	374	Letters		6
Rejoyce in the Lord alwaies, and again I say rejoyce.	374	Letters		22
He doubles it to take away the scruple of those that might say,	374	Letters		23
yes, I say again rejoyce;	374	Letters		24
SAYES				
Mark what another sayes: for many are	19	Ch.-Porch		319
Who sayes that fictions onely and false hair	56	Jordan 1		1
The Scriptures bid us fast; the Church sayes, now:	86	Lent		4
He sayes, in things which use hath justly got,	86	Lent		10
The word is, Stay, sayes ever, Come.	109	Home		76
And sayes, If he in this be crost,	123	Gratefulnes		6
Sayes, Come?	149	Longing		42
As when th' heart sayes (sighing to be approved)	168	a true Hymn		19
That Sinne sayes true: but while I grieve,	184	A Parodie		29
And know you not, sayes Love, who bore the blame?	189	Love 3		15
You must sit down, sayes Love, and taste my meat:	189	Love 3		17
This Galen confirms, when he sayes, that immoderate heats and colds,	294	Cornaro		6
that Plato sayes, That they who are employed in the common wealth,	299	Cornaro		11
Where he sayes the Inflammation of the naturall, he sayes aptly,	308	Valdesso		13
he sayes aptly, so it be understood with the former distinction,	308	Valdesso		14
but when he sayes they are equally exempt with God, that is dangerous	316	Valdesso		32

SAYES (cont'd)	PAGE	TITLE		LINE
it for a time onely, and then cast it away, as he sayes strangely.	318	Valdesso		4
The good mother sayes not, Will you? but gives.	337	Proverbs		467
being at London sent for him (as shee sayes) to make peace with him,	368	Letters		21
SAYING				
Saying to man, It doth suffice:	64	Even-song		19
Spoil'd all the train: then saying, Here it is	71	Humilitie		27
Against me, saying, For my soul	216	Psalm III	D	3
and saying grace at meat, and at going to bed by giving the Host	251	Priest 17		9
but to throw himself down at the throne of grace, saying, Lord,	257	Priest 22		32
The saying of the Catechism is necessary, but not enough; . .	259	Priest 22		6
he takes it either in an humble way, saying nothing at all; . .	269	Priest 28		6
or else in a doctrinall way, saying to the contemner, Alas, . .	269	Priest 28		12
Another old Custome there is of saying, when light is brought in,	284	Priest 35		23
SAYINGS				
and sayings of others, according as his text invites him; . .	233	Priest 7		12
but stories and sayings they will well remember.	233	Priest 7		18
SAYS				
Hee says that prayer with great devotion, where God is thanked	258	Priest 22		5
or as David says, to be even a door-keeper in the house of God.	270	Priest 29		11
The Italian says, None fouls his hands in his own businesse:	275	Priest 32		27
He that trusts much Obliges much, says the Spaniard. . . .	357	Proverbs	D	1045
with some idlenesse of brain, says the Spaniard.	357	Proverbs	D	1050
Threatned men eat bread, says the Spaniard.	358	Proverbs	D	1081
Love without end, hath no end, says the Spaniard: (meaning, . .	361	Proverbs	D	1160
SCAB				
The itch of disputing is the scab of the Church.	360	Proverbs	D	1137
SCAB'D				
A scab'd horse cannot abide the comb.	359	Proverbs	D	1113
SCALD				
A pittifull mother makes a scald head.	343	Proverbs		647
SCALDED				
The scalded dog feares cold water.	321	Proverbs		13
The scalded head feares cold water.	321	Proverbs	V	13
SCALDING				
And threw my heart into the scalding pan;	130	Love unkn.		35
But with a richer drug, then scalding water, ...	130	Love unkn.		40
SCALES				
Thy scales like buckets, which attend	141	Justice 2		16
SCANDALIZE				
most in those things which are most apt to scandalize his Parish.	227	Priest 3		11
& neither to scandalize them, nor wound our owne reputation.	380	Woodnoth		19
SCANDALL				
I am a scandall to the Church, and not	86	Lent		11
in a feast of Charity is more scandall then any posture. . .	259	Priest 22		18
if a Schismatick, scandall. Wherefore the Parson hath diligently	262	Priest 24		31
So for Scandall: what scandall is, when given or taken; . .	263	Priest 24		7
what scandall is, when given or taken;	263	Priest 24		8
the other of not giving scandall, that ought not to be preferred,	263	Priest 24		10
be preferred, especially since in disobeying there is scandall also:	263	Priest 24		11
SCANDALOUS				
in his order, or length of eating, is scandalous and uncharitable.	266	Priest 26		11
SCANN'D				
They would not have their actions scann'd, ...	100	Miserie		21
Let that be scann'd.	188	Judgement		14
SCANT				
Although the verse be somewhat scant, ...	168	a true Hymn		17
SCAPE				
Lesser pains scape greater ones.	113	Businesse		14
The beam and scape	141	Justice 2		9
Who can scape his bow?	179	Discipline		25
SCAPES				
Not one poore minute scapes thy breast, ...	64	Even-song		30
SCAR (see also skarres)				
SCARCE				
And though my hard heart scarce to thee can grone, ...	38	The Sinner		13
Sorrow was all my soul; I scarce beleeved, ...	47	Afflict.1		29
Scarce a good joy creeps through the chink:	60	Whitsunday		22
Scarce knows the way;	98	Mortific.		4
He scarce allow'd me half an eie.	111	The Quip		15
and yet I am scarce able with much ado to make one half years	365	Letters		9
SCARED				
Welcome sweet and scared cheer, ...	181	Banquet		1
SCARF (see also skarf)				
SCARLET				
Then with a scarlet robe they me aray;	31	Sacrifice		157
All Scepters, Reeds: Cloths, Scarlet: Crowns are Thorns: . .	32	Sacrifice	W	178
SCATTER				
Scatter, or binde them all to bend to thee:	56	Temper 2		13
Did break and scatter.	124	Peace		12
Scatter my words, and in the same	149	Longing		23
SCATTER'D				
With scatter'd smart, ...	90	Afflict.4		9
The rather since his scatter'd jugglings were	195	Ch.-Milit.		175
SCATTERED				
the one for smalnesse, as crums, and scattered corn, and the like;	241	Priest 10		28
SCATTERINGLY				
Some such irradiations scatteringly in the Sermon, carry great	233	Priest 7		37
SCATTERS				
As the sunne scatters by his light	90	Afflict.4		23
is no Cure for Atheisme) he scatters in his discourse three sorts	281	Priest 34		15

	PAGE	TITLE		LINE
SCRUPLE (cont'd)				
He doubles it to take away the scruple of those that might say,	374	Letters		22
For any scruple of leaving your trade, throw it away. . . .	381	Woodnoth		22
SCUCE				
tenn shillings To William Scuce twenty shillings To Mrs Judith	383	G.H.'s Will		17
SCUMME				
These are the scumme, with which course wits abound:	16	Ch.-Porch		237
SCYTHE (see also sithe)				
SEA				
Into one common sewer, sea, and brine;	62	Afflict.2		7
All Solomons sea of brasse and world of stone	106	Sion		17
Of all the creatures both in sea and land	117	Providence		5
Check the proud sea, ev'n when it swells and gathers.	118	Providence		48
The sea, which seems to stop the traveller, ...	119	Providence		89
When th' earth was dry, thou mad'st a sea of wet:	120	Providence		113
Brought back to the Red Sea, the sea of shame.	128	Bunch Gr.		7
Devils their rod, the sea his shore, ...	158	Praise 3		22
That habitable sea, & brinish strand, ...	213	Bohemia	D	62
and the sea rage so much as it can, and all things do what they can,	281	Priest 34		21
He that will learne to pray, let him goe to Sea.	323	Proverbs		84
He who will learne to pray, let him goe to Sea.	323	Proverbs	V	84
for to the sea he made havens, and to rivers foords.	331	Proverbs		315
for to the sea he made heavens, and to rivers foords.	331	Proverbs	V	315
There are three waies, the Universities, the Sea, the Court.	334	Proverbs		383
Being on sea saile, being on land settle.	335	Proverbs		418
Praise the Sea, but keepe on land.	338	Proverbs		489
Wisedome hath one foot on Land, and another on Sea.	341	Proverbs		611
He complaines wrongfully of the sea	345	Proverbs		706
He complaines wrongfully on the sea	345	Proverbs	V	706
passing daily our neighboring Sea, wondrously sound through all our	442	Oration		24
SEAL				
In time of service seal up both thine eies, ...	23	Ch.-Porch		415
Have with our stamp and seal transferr'd our right:	77	Avarice		11
This certain Anchor adde a Seal, and so	439	Walton 5		6
(Where nothing should be broke) to adde a Seal.	439	Walton 5		18
He gave this Seal, and, so gave ore.	439	Walton 6		2
SEALD				
But kill the man, is seald with thee.	204	Persever.	W	8
SEALE				
He gave the Seale, and so left o're.	439	Walton 5		14
SEAL'D				
A mirth but open'd and seal'd up again;	172	The Glance		18
SEALED				
Therefore not sealed, but with open eyes	89	The Pearl		32
It is a letter sealed, and sent, which to the bearer is but paper,	282	Priest 34		36
SEAM				
Then close again the seam, ...	138	The Size		42
SEAMLESSE				
And jagg'd his seamlesse coat, had that been fine, ...	134	Divinitie		11
SEARCH				
I will search out the matter.	124	Peace		10
Go search this thing, ...	133	The Method		9
Search well and see; for hearts have many holes.	147	Offering		4
The Search.	162	The Search		T
Because the search was dumbe before:	162	The Search		23
Judgement may meet them both & search them round.	197	Ch.-Milit.		269
Search and you may	208	J. Danvers	D	2
the other an humble, and ingenuous search of truth; . . .	263	Priest 24		17
Wherefore I began to search out most diligently what meats were	293	Cornaro		4
SEARCHES				
My searches are my daily bread;	162	The Search		3
SEARCHEST				
Poore man, thou searchest round	86	Vanitie 1		27
SEARCHING				
I will go searching, till I finde a sunne	81	Christmas		27
SEAS				
Fathom'd the depths of seas, of states, and kings, ...	37	The Agonie		2
Both th' old discoveries, and the new-found seas, ...	88	The Pearl		7
These seas are tears, and heav'n the haven.	138	The Size		47
In tears like seas, our sinnes are pil'd	173	Marie Magd		11
SEASON				
Parents first season us: then schoolmasters	45	Sinne 1		2
Come dearest Lord, passe not this holy season, ...	109	Home		73
Be the season cold, or hot:	113	Businesse		10
Now is the season	204	The Knell	W	7
This is thy empire yet: till better season	213	Bohemia	D	60
and the season of the yeare was winter and most cold aire. . .	296	Cornaro		27
He that hath the spice, may season as he list.	335	Proverbs		424
He who hath the spice, may season as he pleaseth.	335	Proverbs	V	424
If fooles should not foole it, they shall lose their season.	343	Proverbs	V	702
If fooles should not foole it, they should loose their season.	344	Proverbs		703
SEASONABLE				
When good is seasonable;	86	Lent		15
when I shall understand that a Letter will be seasonable, . .	371	Letters		15
SEASONABLY				
their very face, when occasion cals, but seasonably and discreetly.	226	Priest 2		31
yet seasonably, and discreetly, by taking aside the Lord, . .	251	Priest 17		28
it judiciously, or breaks it off seasonably by some diversion.	252	Priest 18		18
them honestly, and seasonably, when they are not better imployed.	274	Priest 32		30
A little given seasonably excuses a great gift.	349	Proverbs		834

	PAGE	TITLE		LINE
SEASON'D				
Like season'd timber, never gives;	88	Vertue		14
SEASONED				
Therefore having seasoned them with all Piety, not only of words in	239	Priest 10		23
instructions seasoned with pleasantnesse, both enter sooner,	268	Priest 27		4
SEASONING				
and seasoning all our words and sentences in our hearts,	233	Priest 7		29
SEASONS				
How finely dost thou times and seasons spin,	118	Providence		57
of extreme poverty, and in the seasons of Seed-time, and Harvest.	248	Priest 14		4
if he suite not other things to the growth, as seasons, and weather,	271	Priest 30		16
by taking away so much as the usuall seasons of summer and winter,	281	Priest 34		24
things I do at my ease, and at fit seasons, and in mine own houses;	301	Cornaro		9
in their seasons argues a Deity.	347	Proverbs		773
SEAT				
Turn out these wranglers, which defile thy seat:	136	Familie		7
So though Sinne made his latter seat the better,	196	Ch.-Milit.		223
So though Sinne made his later seat the better,	196	Ch.-Milit.	W	223
Thou drivest from his seat.	200	H. Commun.	W	24
SEATED				
But I by God am seated King,	215	Psalm II	D	13
he hath a Poor-mans Box conveniently seated, to receive the charity	246	Priest 13		21
but being seated in the Countrey, and doing their duty faithfully,	266	Priest 26		2
At other times, I repair to a village of mine, seated in the valley;	301	Cornaro		20
SEATS				
windows glazed, floore paved, seats whole, firm, and uniform,	246	Priest 13		5
SEAVEN				
First there is seaven hundred pounds in Mr Thomas Lawleys hands	382	G.H.'s Will		7
SECOND				
The Second Thanks-giving.	36	Reprisall	W	T
Take up the second, then thy double line	97	Afflict.5		16
The second Temple could not reach the first:	196	Ch.-Milit.		225
To second thee against there cunning hate.	211	Bohemia	D	22
The second means is prayer, which if it be necessary even in	228	Priest 4		33
What an admirable Epistle is the second to the Corinthians?	234	Priest 7		18
for the second, swine. These save man the labour, and doing that	241	Priest 10		31
but the determination of the second rule by Authority to this	242	Priest 10		6
The second, Let all things be done to edification, 1 Cor. 14.	246	Priest 13		28
the second for the benefit of our neighbor.	246	Priest 13		31
The second means is a very loving, and sweet usage of them,	262	Priest 24		25
The second, the feeling of themselves in time of eating,	267	Priest 26		1
the second a governing power;	271	Priest 30		2
taken from Nature, the second from the Law, the third from Grace.	281	Priest 34		16
to be in the dark, ought to use the first, and to forbear the second;	312	Valdesso	V	26
the second to professe it, the third to despise counsell.	337	Proverbs		460
SECONDLY				
Secondly, Christ is the glorious instrument of God for the revoking	225	Priest 1		5
Secondly because Luxury is a very visible sinne, the Parson is very	227	Priest 3		21
Secondly, as this is the true reason of his inward feare,	231	Priest 6		10
Secondly, by dipping, and seasoning all our words and sentences in	233	Priest 7		28
and secondly, some choyce Observations drawn out of the whole text,	235	Priest 7		2
Secondly, a curing, and healing of all wounds and sores with her owne	239	Priest 10		14
secondly, of eating no pleasing, or over-nourishing things,	242	Priest 10		3
Secondly, that the Church be swept, and kept cleane without dust,	246	Priest 13		8
Secondly, he adviseth them so to labour for wealth and maintenance,	248	Priest 14		5
Secondly, what means of Piety, whether daily prayers be used,	251	Priest 17		22
Secondly, he carryes himself very respectively, as to all the Fathers	253	Priest 19		5
Secondly, that Parents, and Masters, as they hear the answers prove,	255	Priest 21		27
Secondly, a most plain and easie framing the question, even	256	Priest 21		34
Secondly, hee considers and looks into the ignorance, or carelesness	258	Priest 22		23
Secondly, that labouring people (whom he chiefly considered) might	261	Priest 23		20
Secondly, for Gluttony, The Parson lays this ground:	266	Priest 26		5
Secondly, by a courteous carriage, & winning behaviour:	268	Priest 28		22
Secondly, that this interruption proceede not out of shame.	273	Priest 31		20
and secondly, the improvement of his grounds, by drowning,	275	Priest 32		23
Secondly, he commends the Mathematicks, as the only wonder-working	277	Priest 32		34
Secondly, not to take the full compasse, and liberty of their Peace:	280	Priest 34		21
Secondly, for the Law, there may be so evident, though unused a proof	281	Priest 34		32
Secondly, justice in the Preservation of bounds:	284	Priest 35		4
Secondly, I answer better, That he which lives a temperate life,	299	Cornaro		34
Secondly for the Authors sake, whom I conceive to have been a true	304	Valdesso		6
Secondly, the great honour and reverence, which he every where beares	305	Valdesso		3
Secondly, among Habits, some oppose Theologicall vertues,	308	Valdesso		6
Secondly, when he useth the word Jurisdiction, allowing no	316	Valdesso		14
Secondly, the time when I desire this (which is now, when I must lay	365	Letters		17
SECRET				
Both their full-ey'd aspects, and secret glances.	85	Vanitie 1		7
I sought thee in a secret cave,	124	Peace		3
A secret vertue bringing peace and mirth	125	Peace		35
and secret of governing to preserve a directnesse, and open	240	Priest 10		33
the secret of whose good consists in this, that at Sermons,	257	Priest 21		17
He that tells a secret is anothers servant.	338	Proverbs		512
SECRETARIE				
And made him Secretarie of thy praise.	117	Providence		8
SECRETS				
Such are thy secrets, which my life makes good,	58	H.Script.2		9
he enters into the secrets of God treasured in the holy Scripture.	229	Priest 4		30
If you would know secrets, looke them in griefe or pleasure.	333	Proverbs		367
The Philosophy of Princes is to dive into the Secrets of men,	361	Proverbs	D	1165
leaving the secrets of nature to those that have spare time.	361	Proverbs	D	1165

	PAGE	TITLE		LINE
SECULAR				
givings are lay, and secular, but this is to give like a Priest.	245	Priest 12		38
SECUNDUM				
that is in humano foro & secundum praesumptionem legalem, . . .	316	Valdesso		28
SECURE				
This holy Cable's of all storms secure.	439	Walton 5		10
This holy Cable's from all storms secure.	439	Walton 5	V	10
'Twas more secure in great Loves Common-weal	439	Walton 5		17
This Anchor keeps my faith, that, me secure.	439	walton 6		4
hand to sickle, shall then secure himself, and think all cock-sure;	271	Priest 30		30
Our owne actions secure us not others judgements.	326	Proverbs	V	173
Nothing secure unlesse suspected.	357	Proverbs	D	1065
SECURITY				
For it is both a security to the King, who hath so many dispersed	276	Priest 32		10
Our owne actions are our security, not others judgements. . .	326	Proverbs		173
SEDENTARY				
and disarmed with sedentary lives, are to know the use of their Arms:	277	Priest 32		18
SEDITIOUS				
And a seditious murderer he was:	30	Sacrifice		117
SEE				
Salute thy self: see what thy soul doth wear.	12	Ch.-Porch		146
Still in thy heart, that he may see what's there.	17	Ch.-Porch		272
Shine like the sunne in every corner: see	20	Ch.-Porch		345
Who would not haste, nay give, to see the show?	22	Ch.-Porch		390
See, they lay hold on me, not with the hands	28	Sacrifice		45
See how spite cankers things. These words aright	30	Sacrifice		109
And Prophets once to see, but found no place:	32	Sacrifice		183
O all ye who passe by, behold and see;	33	Sacrifice		201
If thou dost give me honour, men shall see, ...	35	Thanksgvng		21
Unto mount Olivet; there shall he see	37	The Agonie		8
For by the writings all may see	39	Good Fri.	W	31
Each day doth round about us see.	48	Repentance		8
And could see little, to regard his ease, ...	49	Faith		3
Our eies shall see thee, which before saw dust;	54	Love 2		9
That this new light, which now I see, ...	63	Mattens		18
O that I could a sinne once see!	63	Sinne 2		1
Yet as in sleep we see foul death, and live:	63	Sinne 2		9
See the smooth face of God, without a frown	77	Ang.&Sts.		2
For by that powder thou wilt make us see.	82	Ungratef.		18
For by this powder thou wilt make us see.	82	Ungratef.	W	18
Nothing we see, but means our good, ...	91	Man		27
I see the world grows old, when as the heat	99	Decay		16
That thou within his curtains drawn canst see:	100	Miserie		16
Yet since thou canst not choose but see my actions;	104	Obedience		23
Thou mayst as well my actions guide, as see.	104	Obedience		25
To see what help in th' earth or skie:	107	Home		14
Away; I must get up and see.	108	Home		34
Which way so-e're I look, I see.	108	Home		50
Who for man was sold, can see;	114	Dialogue		15
But as I can see no merit, ...	115	Dialogue		17
See how thy beggar works on thee	123	Gratefulnes		3
What do I see	133	The Method		13
And those all bitten, in thy chair I see.	140	Ch.-rents		10
And those all sitten in thy chair I see.	140	Ch.-rents	V	10
I see no fears:	141	Justice 2		14
Thou couldst well see	144	Discharge		24
Search well and see; for hearts have many holes.	147	Offering		4
While thou didst wink and wouldst not see.	153	The Collar		26
Wouldst thou raise devils? I see, I know, ...	155	Assurance		17
Thy distance from me; see my charge, ...	163	The Search		47
Lord, see my case.	163	The Search		48
To see their mother-root, when they have blown;	166	The Flower		11
To make us see we are but flowers that glide:	167	The Flower		44
What wonders shall we feel, when we shall see	172	The Glance		19
If we could see below	175	The Foil		1
The harbingers are come. See, see their mark;	176	Forerunners		1
Where I wipe mine eyes, and see	182	Banquet		45
In all things thee to see, ...	184	The Elixer		2
That is thy Master-peece I see	201	love	W	3
If that bee dark we can not see:	203	Even-song	W	14
See, they breake in	204	The Knell	W	10
Nothinge can see	210	Paradox	D	11
Mee thinkes, in that Dutch optick I doe see	211	Bohemia	D	13
open mine eyes, that I may see the wondrous things of thy Law.	229	Priest 4		3
or you hear as you ought, he sees hearts, as we see faces: . .	234	Priest 7		28
he is carefull to see condign punishment inflicted, and with truly	254	Priest 20		26
Did you see God make it?	256	Priest 21		8
labours to reduce them to see Gods hand in all things, . . .	270	Priest 30		29
as they think fit, & see cause, or rather as Gods spirit leads them.	272	Priest 31		27
when they see any remarkable point of Education or good husbandry,	276	Priest 32		29
Matthew 24. 14. which we see even miraculously effected in these new	282	Priest 34		32
although they see themselves ill handled by their intemperance,	298	Cornaro		24
By this means the place is come to that perfection we now see it is:	301	Cornaro		31
See the note upon Consid. 36.	307	Valdesso		22
to open his eyes that he might see the wondrous things of his Lawes,	309	Valdesso		26
Better to be blinde, then to see ill.	325	Proverbs		126
Call me not an olive, till thou see me gathered.	331	Proverbs		301
and by that which is past, see	332	Proverbs		329
God comes to see without a bell.	334	Proverbs		384
At the games end we shall see who gaines.	339	Proverbs		538
Though you see a Church-man ill, yet continue in the Church still.	344	Proverbs		698

SELF	PAGE	TITLE		LINE
Lose not thy self, nor give thy humours way:	12	Ch.-Porch		143
Salute thy self: see what thy soul doth wear.	12	Ch.-Porch		146
Yett in thy pursing still thy self distrust	13	Ch.-Porch	W	163
As that thy self alone to hell shalt goe.	13	Ch.-Porch	W	168
A kinde of thing that's for it self too deere.	13	Ch.-Porch		178
Command thy self in chief. He lifes warre knows,	15	Ch.-Porch		215
Thy self the worse, and so the distance greater.	16	Ch.-Porch		260
For so thou dost thy self and him a pleasure:	18	Ch.-Porch		296
And make thy self all reverence and fear.	22	Ch.-Porch		406
Thy self in church; approach, and taste	25	Superlim		3
My crosse I bear my self, untill I faint:	33	Sacrifice		197
Now heal thy self, Physician; now come down.	34	Sacrifice		221
In healing not my self, there doth consist	34	Sacrifice		225
Small to my self, to others milde,	44	H. Bapt.2		9
To me dost now thy self convey;	52	H.Commun.		4
That thou mayst fit thy self against thy fall.	65	Ch.-monum.		24
Content and warm t' it self alone:	68	Content		10
Do not thy self or friends importune.	69	Content		34
Unto thy self in everlasting pleasure.	82	Ungratef.		12
And Power it self disable.	86	Lent		18
Or of it self, like a good huswife, spunne	88	The Pearl		4
But now thou dost thy self immure and close	99	Decay		11
Doth closet up it self, and still retreat,	99	Decay		18
My God, I mean my self.	102	Miserie		78
So did I weave my self into the sense.	103	Jordan 2		14
To passe it self and all it hath to thee.	104	Obedience		8
To passe it self and all it has to thee.	104	Obedience	W	8
O show thy self to me,	107	Home		5
O show thy self to me,	107	Home		11
O show thy self to me,	107	Home		17
O show thy self to me,	107	Home		23
O show thy self to me,	108	Home		29
O show thy self to me,	108	Home		35
O show thy self to me,	108	Home		41
O show thy self to me,	108	Home		47
O show thy self to me,	108	Home		53
O show thy self to me,	108	Home		59
O show thy self to me,	109	Home		65
O show thy self to me,	109	Home		71
O show thy self to me,	109	Home		77
That his own self he forgot.	113	Businesse		24
Then I my self. The servant instantly	129	Love unkn.		11
Walkt by my self abroad, I saw a large	129	Love unkn.		25
Lord, I adjudge my self to tears and grief,	136	Ephes.		25
Were from my self, I had not half a word,	155	Assurance		22
Thou didst at once thy self indite,	156	Assurance		29
What for it self love once began,	156	Assurance		41
Self-condemnation.	170	Self-cond.		T
She being stain'd her self, why did she strive	173	Marie Magd		7
And hurt thy self, and him that sings the note.	176	Forerunners		24
and considering with my self, That the way to please him,	224	Priest		3
For all Truth being consonant to it self, and all being penn'd by one	229	Priest 4		6
and all being penn'd by one and the self-same Spirit, it cannot be,	229	Priest 4		6
as it lyes entire, and unbroken in the Scripture it self.	235	Priest 7		4
that destroyeth at noone day, [Ghostly pride and self-conceite.]	238	Priest 9		8
an act against reason, because it is unnaturall to hurt ones self;	266	Priest 26		22
according as I feele my self, either I take my wonted proportion,	267	Priest 26		8
yet the victory is alike in all, being by the self-same Spirit.	279	Priest 33		2
weighing their reasons with my self, and abhorring from so sudden	292	Cornaro		17
and finding my self continually oppressed with pain and sicknesse,	292	Cornaro		18
I so addicted my self to this course of life, that I never went	292	Cornaro		33
to consider the force of Temperance, and to think thus with my self:	293	Cornaro		2
I began to perswade my self, that this suit and contention was raised	294	Cornaro		23
I by the grace of God cured my self, onely with returning to my	296	Cornaro		24
as I will shew by my self, recounting the delights and pleasures in	300	Cornaro		31
I give my self to the reading of some learned book, and afterwards	301	Cornaro		6
or lesse my self, who being ten yeares older have made a Comedie?	302	Cornaro		35
with their musick and fashion, and I my self also sing often;	303	Cornaro		6
The corne hides it self in the snow, as an old man in furrs.	329	Proverbs		241
I wrong both my self, and also the confidence my Friends have in me;	364	Letters		8
not of her self, but upon the want of those Books which were	367	Letters		4
because I was in hope I should my self carry all sickness out of your	372	Letters		15
and comfort your self in the God of all Comfort, who is not willing	372	Letters		24
Letter gave me Earthly preferment, and kept Heavenly for your self:	373	Letters		1
and I shou'd account my self most happy if I might change with you;	373	Letters		3
For my self, dear Mother, I alwaies fear'd sickness more then death,	373	Letters		7
Although you have a much better Paymaster then my self,	378	Letters		3
upon my accompt, & give you my self for it, to be yours for ever.	378	Letters		5
you any other wayes, as neyther I my self desire to be considered.	378	Letters		16
putt your self into the hands of God (whose the success of things is)	380	Woodnoth		23
either it (in regard of the citty) or your self or your kindred.	380	Woodnoth		28
SELF-CONCEITE				
that destroyeth at noone day, [Ghostly pride and self-conceite.]	238	Priest 9		8
SELF-CONDEMNATION				
Self-condemnation.	170	Self-cond.		T
SELF-SAME				
and all being penn'd by one and the self-same Spirit, it cannot be,	229	Priest 4		6
yet the victory is alike in all, being by the self-same Spirit.	279	Priest 33		2
SELFE				
And winne thy selfe: Compare the joyes & so	7	Ch.-Porch	W	23

	PAGE	TITLE		LINE
SENDING (cont'd)				
and sending for them often, and in finding out Courtesies to place	262	Priest 24		26
SENDS				
Sends me to Pilate. This makes them agree;	29	Sacrifice		74
Shall still be open; what he sends	152	The Bag		39
rather goes to them, then sends for the afflicted, though they can,	249	Priest 15		16
such gifts, he sends him a good book, or easeth him in his Tithes,	254	Priest 20		15
but sends for three or four of the ablest of the Parish to hear	260	Priest 23		9
then God sends such weather, as lays the corn, and destroys it:	271	Priest 30		30
God sends a fire, and consumes all that he hath:	271	Priest 30		33
God sends cold according to Cloathes.	322	Proverbs		33
In time comes he whom God sends.	334	Proverbs		397
He that sends a foole expects one.	349	Proverbs		851
SENSE (see also sence)				
The worst speak something good: if all want sense,	23	Ch.-Porch		431
Catching the sense at two removes?	56	Jordan 1		10
Decking the sense, as if it were to sell.	102	Jordan 2		6
Praising the sense, as if it were to sell.	102	Jordan 2	W	6
So did I weave my self into the sense.	103	Jordan 2		14
He makes a grave; as if the thing had sense,	119	Providence		83
Sponges, non-sense and sense; mines, th' earth & plants.	121	Providence		136
To this life things cf sense	131	Mans medly		7
Almightie God doth grieve, he puts on sense:	136	Ephes.		16
Their thoughts and sense	145	Discharge		42
We turn upon him in a sense most true:	168	The Sonne		12
After the losse of life and sense,	186	Death		7
When sense is made by Comments. But that face	212	Bohemia	D	29
that Countrey people are drawne, or led by sense, more then by faith,	254	Priest 20		31
as parrats, without ever piercing into the sense of it.	256	Priest 21		4
whereinto I was wont, when I pleased my Sense & Appetite.	293	Cornaro		23
tender in knowledge, sense, and age, and knew none but one who could	375	Letters		14
SENSES				
My stuffe is flesh, not brasse; my senses live,	89	The Pearl		27
is this my pleasure made lesse by the decaying dulnesse of my senses,	302	Cornaro		8
SENSIBLE				
for they are not sensible of finenesse:	248	Priest 14		18
they commonly are quick, and sensible, and very tender of reprocf:	248	Priest 14		19
SENSITIVE				
in her sensitive faculty, will runne out more or lesse in her	238	Priest 9		11
SENSLESS				
With Vows and Rants, and sensless Praise,	214	Convert	D	12
SENSUAL				
A Deluge on my sensual Flame,	214	Convert	D	9
SENSUALL				
But sensuall men (as most are) desiring to satisfie their Appetite,	298	Cornaro		23
SENT (noun)				
Since if my sent be good, I care not, if	94	Life		17
As Amber-greese leaves a rich sent	174	The Odour		2
SENT				
God sent him, whatsoe're he be: O tarry,	24	Ch.-Porch		442
And he an optick sent.	121	Hope		4
I sent a sigh to seek thee out,	162	The Search		17
From times great Chronicle, and hither sent.	192	Ch.-Milit.		96
Therefore he sent out able ministers,	195	Ch.-Milit.		199
My Lord. A diamond to mee you sent,	209	L. Bacon	D	1
if God have sent any calamity either by fire, or famine,	253	Priest 19		29
making together a summe either to be sent, or, which were more	253	Priest 19		37
Now a prophesie is a wonder sent to Posterity, least they complaine	282	Priest 34		35
It is a letter sealed, and sent, which to the bearer is but paper,	282	Priest 34		37
put this into your hands (as he sent the fish with mony to S. Peter,)	304	Valdesso		11
yet Peter was to be sent for, and those that have inspiraticns must	310	Valdesso		9
& shee being at London sent for him (as shee sayes) to make peace	368	Letters		20
yet have I sent it thither by a faithful Messenger this day:	369	Letters		16
I have sent you here inclosed a Letter from our Master in my behalf,	369	Letters		24
which if you can sent to Sir Francis before his departure,	369	Letters		25
I have received the things you sent me, safe;	371	Letters		6
&. for my power, I have sent my Letters, to your Brother,	379	Letters		19
SENTED				
Yet being bruis'd are better sented:	181	Banquet		27
SENTENCE				
So this flower doth judge and sentence	178	The Rose		25
that so the sentence lighting upon one, the example may reach to all.	269	Priest 28		2
because infamy is a part of the sentence against malefactours,	287	Priest 37		18
SENTENC'D				
Thy Saviour sentenc'd joy,	138	The Size		25
SENTENCES				
and seasoning all our words and sentences in our hearts,	233	Priest 7		29
Jacula Prudentum Or Outlandish Proverbs, Sentences, &c	356	Proverbs	D	T
SENTINELL				
The Parson in Sentinell.	252	Priest 18		T
SENTS				
Though hee bring light & th' other sents:	42	Easter	W	24
And Spanish sents, wisely layd up, presume	212	Bohemia	D	52
SEPT				
I conceive) towards the publishing thereof, &c. Bemmorton Sept. 29.	305	Valdesso		15
SEPULCHER				
Their throat an open Sepulcher,	219	Psalm V	D	27
A flatterers throat is an open Sepulcher.	341	Proverbs		588
SEPULCHRE				
Sepulchre.	40	Sepulchre		T

	PAGE	TITLE	LINE
SERIOUS			
and then also in a serious manner, never jestingly or sportfully.	237	Priest 9	13
it is a most serious Case, nor can I write coldly in that, . . .	364	Letters	16
SERIOUSLY			
and seriously prepare for it, he is safe and within bounds. . .	275	Priest 32	13
SERMON			
A verse may finde him, who a sermon flies, ...	6	Ch.-Porch	5
Ten, if a Sermon goe for gains.	96	Charms & K W	16
knowing that no Sermon moves them so much to a reverence, . .	231	Priest 6	14
yet often dy with the Sermon, especially with Countrey people;	233	Priest 7	15
but the character of his Sermon is Holiness;	233	Priest 7	23
Some such irradiations scatteringly in the Sermon, carry great	234	Priest 7	1
So is his charity in effect a Sermon.	245	Priest 12	17
some defects in the Ministry, he then either in Sermon, if he preach,	253	Priest 19	13
not himself, but is first a Sermon to himself, and then to others;	255	Priest 21	14
all other things shall be added, even it selfe is a Sermon. . .	278	Priest 33	14
whether in private conference, or in the Church, are a Sermon.	278	Priest 33	18
getting for himself, when he tels it to others, becomes a Sermon.	279	Priest 33	33
The Authour's Prayer before Sermon.	288	Priest	T
A Prayer after Sermon.	290	Priest	T
SERMONS			
Resort to sermons, but to prayers most:	23	Ch.-Porch	409
Ten still, if sermons go for gains.	96	Charms & K	16
which is the storehouse of his Sermons, and which he preacheth all	230	Priest 5	1
that Sermons are dangerous things, that none goes out of Church as he	233	Priest 7	19
and then woven into Sermons, which will make them appear exceeding	234	Priest 7	23
his flock by themselves, whom his Sermons cannot, or doe not reach.	236	Priest 8	13
or his Wife, takes account of Sermons, and how every one profits,	240	Priest 10	37
whereas in Sermons there is a kinde of state, in Catechizing there is	255	Priest 21	9
secret of whose good consists in this, that at Sermons, and Prayers,	257	Priest 21	18
This practice exceeds even Sermons in teaching:	257	Priest 21	21
but there being two things in Sermons, the one Informing, . .	257	Priest 21	21
as Sermons come short of questions in the one, so they farre exceed	257	Priest 21	22
and yet hear Sermons against both, and himselfe condemn both in good	264	Priest 26	15
hath ever so many sermons ready penn'd, as he hath victories.	278	Priest 33	24
SERPENTS			
We have our sands and serpents, tents and shrowds;	128	Bunch Gr.	17
SERVANT			
Get a sharp wife, a servant that will lowre.	15	Ch.-Porch	213
A broken ALTAR, Lord, thy servant reares, ...	26	The Altar	1
Lookt on a servant, who did know his eye	129	Love unkn.	9
Then I my self. The servant instantly	129	Love unkn.	11
My servant were a little so, ...	175	The Odour	12
My servant, as thee not displeasing, ...	175	The Odour	24
A servant with this clause	185	The Elixer	17
Lord help thy servant whose perplexed Soule	204	The Knell W	2
Neither is it for the servant of Christ to haunt Innes, . .	227	Priest 3	29
he teacheth them, that three things make a compleate servant, Truth,	240	Priest 10	18
but an old good servant boards a child.	241	Priest 10	11
as being the servant of him, in whom there was no guile. . .	253	Priest 19	2
childe, or servant, as a Gardiner doth in a choice tree. . .	275	Priest 32	33
when the servant of God, freed for a while from temptation, . .	279	Priest 33	4
assembled together, with thy unworthy Servant speaking unto them:	289	Priest	25
the Authors sake, whom I conceive to have been a true servant of God;	304	Valdesso	7
are fruitfull) intending the honour of his servant the Author,	304	Valdesso	13
For as the servant leaves not the letter when he hath read it,	310	Valdesso	27
He that tells a secret is anothers servant.	338	Proverbs	512
The slothful is the servant of the counters.	341	Proverbs	610
The slothful is the servant of the vertuous.	341	Proverbs V	610
A sleepy master makes his servant a Lowt.	346	Proverbs	766
He can give little to his servant, that lickes his knife. . .	349	Proverbs	846
Chuse none for thy servant who have served thy betters. . .	354	Proverbs	1014
Every one is a master and servant.	355	Proverbs	1026
A master of straw eates a servant of steele.	355	Proverbs	1029
and after my manner, Your most obedient Servant, GEORGE HERBERT.	364	Letters	4
for I am sure you love Your faithfullest Servant, GEORGE HERBERT.	365	Letters	26
and yet still grow upon Your humblest Servant, GEORGE HERBERT.	367	Letters	16
but that I have both time and work to be Your extreme Servant,	370	Letters	15
and paper enough, yet am I Your readiest Servant, GEORGE HERBERT.	370	Letters	33
your Courtesie will pardon the haste of Your humblest Servant,	371	Letters	20
most heartily, affectionate Brother, and Servant, GEORGE HERBERT.	372	Letters	9
Your most faithful Servant in Christ Jesu, GEORGE HERBERT. . .	377	Letters	9
whome I esteem to be God's faithfull & diligent Servant, . .	378	Letters	15
great Joy of Your Brother & Servant in Christ Jesus GEORGE HERBERT.	378	Letters	28
then I leave to my servant Elizabeth her dubble wages given her,	382	G.H.'s Will	22
SERVANT'S			
One eye of the masters sees more, then ten of the servants. . .	344	Proverbs	687
SERVANTS			
Servants and churches also play their part.	14	Ch.-Porch	196
Servants and abjects flout me; they are wittie:	31	Sacrifice	141
More servants wait on Man, ...	92	Man	43
And both thy servants be.	92	Man	54
Born where thy servants both artilleries use.	139	Artillerie	18
that God in all ages hath had his servants, to whom he hath revealed	229	Priest 4	22
that there may be a traffick in knowledg between the servants of God,	229	Priest 4	26
his meat dress'd and other services done by men-servants at home,	237	Priest 9	9
Therefore he gives her respect both afore her servants, . . .	238	Priest 9	36
His servants are all religious, and were it not his duty to have them	240	Priest 10	13
so well served, as by religious servants, both because they do best,	240	Priest 10	15
his children among children, his servants among other servants;	240	Priest 10	29
He keeps his servants between love, and fear, according as hee findes	241	Priest 10	7

SERVANTS (cont'd)	PAGE	TITLE		LINE
more love then terrour, to his servants more terrour then love;	241	Priest 10		10
the Cures with their own hands, and not to put them over to servants.	247	Priest 14		20
encouraging also the servants to learn to read, and offering to have	248	Priest 14		36
and offering to have them taught on holy-dayes by his servants.	248	Priest 14		38
as to a great purchase for their children, and servants;	259	Priest 22		4
if God have given me servants, and I either provide too little	265	Priest 26		20
that servants for their mony are as other things that they buy,	265	Priest 26		24
(who playes his part sometimes in drawing Gods Servants from him,	272	Priest 31		17
Which acts of repentance are and must be found in all Gods servants:	279	Priest 33		26
And that the best of Gods Servants should have weaknesses is no way	316	Valdesso		2
and make your family, a housefull of GOD's servants.	376	Letters		20
Your poor Colony of Servants present their humble duties.	377	Letters		13
the one are Gods servants, the other the commonwealths,	381	Woodnoth		28
the felicitie of so great Princes redound also to those servants,	442	Oration		26
SERVE				
If they might mend their wages, and serve here.	59	Whitsunday		12
Amounts (and richly) to serve thee:	63	Mattens		14
That, as the world serves us, we may serve thee,	92	Man		53
Then to serve thee in fear.	100	Miserie		12
The bargain made to serve thee: but thy love	100	Miserie		26
Man cannot serve thee; let him go,	101	Miserie		43
And serve the swine: there, there is his delight:	101	Miserie		44
Are rul'd by him, and taught to serve his trade.	119	Providence		92
All countreys have enough to serve their need:	120	Providence		105
Just so the other heav'n they also serve,	134	Divinitie		5
To suit and serve his need,	153	The Collar		31
As serve him up, who all the world commands:	161	Priesthood		26
And serve thee; and not onely I,	164	The Crosse		4
My power to serve thee; to unbend	164	The Crosse		10
To serve thy sinnes, and furnish thee with store	170	Water-crs.		7
My deare, then I will serve.	189	Love 3		16
(For no lesse Harbingers would serve then they)	192	Ch.-Milit.		84
Nay, he became a poet, and would serve	193	Ch.-Milit.		131
Which warme these lines, & serve them up to thee	204	Persever.	W	2
Wear Venus Livery? only serve her turn?	206	Walton 1		4
Serve thou the more God and the poore;	207	Walton 4		3
To serve it forth, & being stript of all	212	Bohemia	D	31
Serve our great God in fear, rejoyce,	216	Psalm II	D	27
reserving so much of the affaires, as serve for a diversion for him;	238	Priest 9		38
serve but the vices and vanities of the world, which he is to deny,	240	Priest 10		3
but that they may have wherewithall to serve God the better,	248	Priest 14		8
he borrowes them not to serve the turne, nor provides slight,	252	Priest 19		26
making what hee knows to serve him in that which he knows not:	256	Priest 21		38
things of ordinary use are not only to serve in the way of drudgery,	257	Priest 21		14
and cleansed, and serve for lights even of Heavenly Truths.	257	Priest 21		15
and his means serve, hee keepes some young practicioner in his house	260	Priest 23		33
and maketh the one serve the other.	261	Priest 23		17
giving us one world in our selves, and another to serve us:	288	Priest		14
One sound blow will serve to undo all.	322	Proverbs		34
Serve a noble disposition, though poore,	333	Proverbs		368
thy actions serve the turne.	347	Proverbs		771
Prayse not thyself, thy actions serve the Turne.	347	Proverbs	V	771
He that serves, must serve.	347	Proverbs		786
take not to serve you, if you will be served neately.	347	Proverbs		794
Hee that is a master must serve (another).	354	Proverbs		991
a much better Paymaster then my self, even him, whome we both serve:	378	Letters		3
Gods accepting you have done the good you intended, & whom serve you?	381	Woodnoth		18
both the Spanish and Brittish Nation serve and worship James.	442	Oration		18
SERV'D				
Lord with what glorie wast thou serv'd of old,	106	Sion		1
SERVED				
What pleasures could I want, whose King I served,	46	Afflict.1		13
his profit, for none are so well served, as by religious servants,	240	Priest 10		15
the other, in being worse served and obeyed.	259	Priest 22		6
He that will be served must bee patient.	333	Proverbs		354
take not to serve you, if you will be served neately.	347	Proverbs		794
Chuse none for thy servant who have served thy betters.	354	Proverbs		1014
SERVES				
That, as the world serves us, we may serve thee,	92	Man		53
Thy cupboard serves the world: the meat is set,	118	Providence		49
serves either positively as it is, or else to illustrate some other	228	Priest 4		16
Herein also he serves himselfe of the judgements of God,	233	Priest 7		6
and when his own stock serves not, working those that are able	245	Priest 12		12
He that serves, must serve.	347	Proverbs		786
He that serves well needes not ask his wages.	347	Proverbs		798
SERVICE				
Do fortunes seek, when worth and service fail,	14	Ch.-Porch		182
Nothing from thine: in service, care, or coldnesse	16	Ch.-Porch		255
In time of service seal up both thine eies,	23	Ch.-Porch		415
I thought the service brave:	46	Afflict.1		2
Well, I will change the service, and go seek	48	Afflict.1		63
Off'ring their service, if I were not sped:	102	Jordan 2		8
Unto the service mutter an assent,	117	Providence		15
instructed his people how to carry themselves in divine service,	231	Priest 6		22
This is that which the Apostle cals a reasonable service,	232	Priest 6		3
and apply our powers to the service of him, that gives them.	232	Priest 6		6
not to come at the beginning of service with their poor neighbours,	232	Priest 6		9
and neglect the present service of God, he by no means suffers it,	232	Priest 6		12
were with Saint Paul even sacrificed upon the service of their faith.	234	Priest 7		8
Then having read divine Service twice fully, and preached in	236	Priest 8		7

	PAGE	TITLE	LINE
SERVICE (cont'd)			
or in time of divine service on other holy days, except in the cases	248	Priest 14	3
but he holds the Rule, that Nothing is little in Gods service:	249	Priest 14	2
are every way fitting to do his Countrey true and laudable service,	252	Priest 19	29
to church, or for disorderly carriage in time of divine service.	270	Priest 29	6
the greatest honor of this world, to do God and his chosen service;	270	Priest 29	11
sometimes in perplexing them in the service of God) stands fast in	272	Priest 31	18
A childs service is little,	327	Proverbs	206
Good service is a great inchantment.	331	Proverbs	291
The first service a child doth his father is to make him foolish.	337	Proverbs	463
Service is no Inheritance.	347	Proverbs	792
A trade is better then service.	354	Proverbs	1005
Service without reward is punishment.	354	Proverbs	1015
our Care for us that we may the more quietly intend his service.	374	Letters	19
My wife's and neeces' service.	376	Letters	23
My wife's and neeces' service to you.	379	Letters	30
SERVICEABLE			
and by these hee keeps his body tame, serviceable, and healthfull;	237	Priest 9	26
SERVICES			
when he is to read divine services, composeth himselfe to all	231	Priest 6	1
beseeching the Almighty to pardon and accept our poor services,	236	Priest 8	28
his meat dress'd and other services done by men-servants at home,	237	Priest 9	9
hath your Goodness brought on you, by admitting our poor services?	376	Letters	27
SERVILE			
A servile death in servile companie:	34	Sacrifice	235
A servile hawk: low without losse, a spade.	120	Providence	104
when on the Lords day they do unnecessary servile work,	248	Priest 14	3
SERVING			
Nature serving Grace both in comfort of diversion, and the benefit	261	Priest 23	11
SESSION			
At the next Session-day.	71	Humilitie	32
SESSION-DAY			
At the next Session-day.	71	Humilitie	32
SESSIONS			
and above all things, they are to frequent Sessions and Sizes;	277	Priest 32	1
SET			
Old courtiers know this; therefore set out so,	14	Ch.-Porch	185
Boldnesse guilds finely, and will set it forth.	15	Ch.-Porch	210
Herod and all his bands do set me light,	29	Sacrifice	77
Did set again abroach; then let him say	37	The Agonie	15
And tune together in a well-set song,	49	Repentance	33
Wherein if they were set,	62	Afflict.2	9
As I have mine, may set his hand	105	Obedience	37
Thy cupboard serves the world: the meat is set,	118	Providence	49
To plant and set.	125	Peace	30
Was in great letters set AFFLICTION.	129	Love unkn.	28
Glorie and honour are set by till it	132	The Storm	15
And giving all things their set forms and houres,	137	Familie	11
Thy promise now hath ev'n set thee thy laws.	139	Artillerie	24
Thy passions also have their set partitions.	147	Offering	16
To set thy honour up, as our designe.	164	The Crosse	6
Show me, and set me, I have one reply,	169	The Answer	13
To set off vertues; griefs to set off sinning:	176	The Foil	6
Learning was pos'd, Philosophie was set,	191	Ch.-Milit.	51
Sinne did set out of Eastern Babylon,	193	Ch.-Milit.	103
When th' one did set, the other did take place,	196	Ch.-Milit.	217
They have their period also and set times	197	Ch.-Milit.	261
I have resolved to set down the Form and Character of a true Pastour,	224	Priest	6
which also I will set as high as I can, since hee shoots higher that	224	Priest	8
out of his infinite pity hath set forth heaven for a reward to draw	243	Priest 11	31
But he gives no set pension to any;	244	Priest 12	25
when they set themselves to work like brute beasts, never raising	247	Priest 14	32
as when he is set at an armour, or horse, he borrowes them	252	Priest 19	26
cannot inflame or ravish, that must be done by a set, and laboured,	257	Priest 21	25
Thirdly, that he might set a Copy for Parsons.	261	Priest 23	26
in perverting that order which he hath set both to things,	265	Priest 26	12
that things are not set in such an inevitable order, but that God	270	Priest 30	30
and onely commanded that my arm and legge should be set,	295	Cornaro	11
those ten yeares, which they set at naught in regard of their belly?	298	Cornaro	34
shall overthrow all means, save catechizing, and set up Enthusiasmes.	310	Valdesso	12
Set good against evill.	348	Proverbs	823
What Trades-man is there who will set up without his Tools?	364	Letters	15
long in Latin, and my Lincoln journey hath set me much behind hand:	369	Letters	14
SETLED			
From setled peace and rest!	127	Giddinesse	2
I never since departed from my setled course of Sobrietie,	293	Cornaro	26
SETLETH			
at severall times and occasions, the Parson setleth wavering minds.	283	Priest 34	5
SETLING			
And setling to a cloud, doth live and die	169	The Answer	11
duties, and it is a great stay and setling to religious souls.	274	Priest 31	2
SETS			
Who fears to do ill, sets himself to task:	11	Ch.-Porch	125
Faith sets me higher in his glorie.	50	Faith	20
His goodnesse sets not, but in dark can runne:	72	Constancie	23
Their storie pennes and sets us down.	128	Bunch Gr.	11
But in God's Law sets his delight,	214	Psalm I	D 5
he sets himself to the Consideration of the duties of the day,	235	Priest 8	32
sets up as many encouragements to goodnesse as he can, both in	244	Priest 11	2
But though the Parson sets forward all Charitable deeds,	262	Priest 23	12
Modesty sets off one newly come to honour.	357	Proverbs	D 1062

SETS (cont'd)	PAGE	TITLE		LINE
for it sets a dearer price on every thing.	361	Proverbs	D	1178
SETT				
Lord make my Losses up, & sett mee free:	203	Even-song	W	5
A foile to sett of worth, & make it rare.	211	Bohemia	D	16
SETTETH				
Who turnes a trencher, setteth free	96	Charms & K	W	14
SETTING				
Setting in order what they tumble:	75	Sunday	W	5
Setting affliction to encounter pleasure;	194	Ch.-Milit.		148
Setting afflictions to encounter pleasure;	194	Ch.-Milit.	W	148
and also therein setting aside the Reverend Prelates of the Church,	225	Priest 2		21
setting aside his care of his Flock, were a madnesse to doubt of.	234	Priest 7		16
takes home with him, setting them close by him, and carving for them,	243	Priest 11		11
for I know that (setting casualties aside) I shall not die . .	303	Cornaro		25
and setting his merit forth so piously, for which I doe so love him,	305	Valdesso		6
how I am now setting foot into Divinity, to lay the platform of my	364	Letters		11
when there is no caus, but by setting a just price of your qualities:	366	Letters		17
SETTLE (see also setled)				
Being on sea saile, being on land settle.	335	Proverbs		418
SEV'N				
Leaping with thee from sev'n to sev'n, ...	77	Sunday		61
Sev'n yeares ago: one vogue and vein, ...	128	Bunch Gr.		4
Sev'n whole dayes, not one in seven, ...	146	Praise 2		17
SEVEN (see also seaven)				
Where it is warmest. Leave thy six and seven;	22	Ch.-Porch		401
Sev'n whole dayes, not one in seven, ...	146	Praise 2		17
He that lives not well one yeare, sorrowes seven after. . .	340	Proverbs		562
SEVENFOLD				
so his whole discourse and sevenfold observation falls to the ground.	318	Valdesso		26
SEVENTH				
Each seventh note by right is due to thee.	38	The Sinner		4
SEVENTIE				
This I found by experience, when I was seventie yeares old: . .	294	Cornaro		36
although I was now seventie eight yeares old, and my bodie spent	296	Cornaro		26
SEVER				
To sever the good fellowship of dust, ...	65	Ch.-monum.		13
and those that withdraw, and sever themselves from it, he mislikes,	284	Priest 35		11
And in so doing they doe not sever their trust from God. . .	307	Valdesso		2
SEV'RALL				
In sev'rall ranks upon an azure throne, ...	70	Humilitie		2
And sev'rall baits in either kinde	97	Afflict.5		17
All things that are, though they have sev'rall wayes, . . .	121	Providence		145
He is some twentie sev'rall men at least	127	Giddinesse		3
Each sev'rall houre.	127	Giddinesse		4
Then did your sev'rall parts unloose and start:	140	Ch.-rents		21
SEVERALL				
(All in a shipwrack shift their severall way)	8	Ch.-Porch		44
My severall sinnes their sorrows get;	39	Good Fri.		18
After the severall knowledg of these, he adviseth to insist and dwell	277	Priest 32		36
at severall times and occasions, the Parson setleth wavering minds.	283	Priest 34		4
whence come so many Books of severall mens opinions: . . .	317	Valdesso		4
& so turn you all, in your severall wayes, one to the other,	378	Letters		25
SEVERALLY				
These he hath digested severally.	228	Priest 4		26
SEVERE				
Art thou a Magistrate? then be severe:	10	Ch.-Porch		85
To wear thy habit, the severe attire	160	Priesthood		9
SEVER'D				
If God and man be sever'd infinitely!	193	Ch.-Milit.		116
SEVERED				
the custome, that may be severed from the good, he pares the apple,	283	Priest 35		32
but not as a naked Word severed from God, but as the Word of God:	307	Valdesso		1
And miracle-working as it may be severed from justifying faith,	319	Valdesso		13
SEVERITY				
not onely because all men shun the company of perpetuall severity,	268	Priest 27		3
SEWER				
Into one common sewer, sea, and brine;	62	Afflict.2		7
SHADDOW				
An old wise mans shaddow is better then a young buzzards sword.	324	Proverbs		90
SHADE				
To fruit or shade: at least some bird would trust	48	Afflict.1		59
Is wooll and furres: cool without closenesse, shade:	120	Providence		102
Is wooll and furre: cool without closenesse, shade:	120	Providence	V	102
O what a damp and shade	183	A Parodie		11
Least that the Night, earths gloomy shade	203	Even-song	W	10
Great trees are good for nothing but shade.	339	Proverbs		546
SHADES				
I pass the shades, & fixe upon the true	43	H. Bapt.1	W	4
As if shades knew not Thee.	203	Even-song	W	12
SHADIE				
As he that sees a dark and shadie grove, ...	43	H. Bapt.1		1
Yea, in deaths shadie black abode	173	23 Psalme		13
Of Noahs shadie vine, chaste as the dove;	190	Ch.-Milit.		15
SHADOW				
And sudden arbours shadow course-spunne lines?	56	Jordan 1		7
If thou deferr this light, then shadow mee:	203	Even-song	W	9
If the staffe be crooked, the shadow cannot be straight. . .	341	Proverbs		583
No hair so small but hath his shadow.	359	Proverbs	D	1124
SHADOWES				
This shadowes out what Christ hath done.	51	Faith	W	36

SHALL (cont'd)

	PAGE	TITLE		LINE
Which shall convey him to the house of death.	98	Mortific.		30
Which shall convey him to the place of death.	98	Mortific.	W	30
No man shall beat into his head,	100	Miserie		15
How shall infection	101	Miserie		35
But as thy love shall sway,	104	Obedience		19
And the receit shall be	106	Conscience		13
To answer these fine things shall come;	111	The Quip		22
Strongly and sweetly movest, shall I write,	116	Providence		2
To hold my quill? shall they not do thee right?	116	Providence		4
They shall be thick and cloudie to my breast.	126	Confession		30
Except thou make us dayly, we shall spurn	127	Giddinesse		27
But you shall heare. After my heart was well,	129	Love unkn.		22
When sawcie mirth shall knock or call at doore,	136	Ephes.		13
I am no Crystall, what shall I?	136	Ephes.		30
Where shall I get me eyes enough to weep,	140	Ch.-rents		25
Lord heare! Shall he that made the eare,	149	Longing		35
(Beleeve me), it shall safely come.	152	The Bag		34
That I shall minde, what you impart;	152	The Bag		35
Shall still be open; what he sends	152	The Bag		39
What? shall I ever sigh and pine?	153	The Collar		3
Shall I be still in suit?	153	The Collar		6
The wheel shall go, so that thy stay be short.	155	Glimpse		27
Yea, when both rocks and all things shall disband,	156	Assurance		34
My busie heart shall spin it all my dayes:	157	Praise 3		3
These arms shall crush thee. Spare not, do thy worst.	169	Dial.-Anth		8
I shall be one day better then before:	169	Dial.-Anth		9
What wonders shall we feel, when we shall see	172	The Glance		19
Shall measure all my dayes;	173	23 Psalme		22
And as it never shall remove,	173	23 Psalme		23
So neither shall my praise.	173	23 Psalme		24
So neither shall thy praise.	173	23 Psalme	V	24
My Master, shall I speak? O that to thee	175	The Odour		11
Shall call and meet,	175	The Odour		23
And I shall	180	Invitation		32
Know them and practise them: then shall I give	185	A Wreath		11
When souls shall wear their new aray,	186	Death		19
And all thy bones with beautie shall be clad.	186	Death		20
And the musick shall be praise.	187	Dooms-day		30
Almightie Judge, how shall poore wretches brook	187	Judgement		1
That they in merit shall excell.	187	Judgement		10
Light to the minde: what shall the will enjoy?	188	Heaven		15
Light, joy, and leisure; but shall they persever?	188	Heaven		19
Love said, you shall be he.	189	Love 3		8
When written Truths shall censure mans devise.	194	Ch.-Milit.	W	160
Nay, it shall ev'ry yeare decrease and fade;	196	Ch.-Milit.		229
(The marks of future bane) shall fill our cup	197	Ch.-Milit.		239
When Sein shall swallow Tiber, and the Thames	197	Ch.-Milit.		241
When Italie of us shall have her will,	197	Ch.-Milit.		243
Shall both in France and England domineer:	197	Ch.-Milit.		246
Then shall Religion to America flee:	197	Ch.-Milit.		247
But lends to us, shall be our desolation.	197	Ch.-Milit.		258
Lendeth to us, shall be our desolation.	197	Ch.-Milit.	W	258
Yet as the Church shall thither westward flie,	197	Ch.-Milit.		259
So Sinne shall trace and dog her instantly:	197	Ch.-Milit.		260
The Church shall come, & Sinne the Church shall smother:	197	Ch.-Milit.		266
To time and place, where judgement shall appeare.	198	Ch.-Milit.		277
O gratious Lord how shall I know	200	H. Commun.	W	1
Shall they be food & strength & might	201	H. Commun.	W	35
But what shall issue, whither these my words	204	Persever.	W	5
Open the bones, and you shall nothing find	206	Walton 2		12
Then you shall fully knowe	210	Paradox	D	28
Children for kingdomes to thee; they shall live	212	Bohemia	D	42
To conquere new ones, & shall share the frame	212	Bohemia	D	43
The world anew: the sunne shall never rise	212	Bohemia	D	45
But it shall spy some of there victories.	212	Bohemia	D	46
There hands shall clipp the Eagles winges, & chase	212	Bohemia	D	47
Thy fruite shall with there drops contend;	213	L' Envoy	D	4
Then shall thy Glory, fresh as flowers	213	L' Envoy	D	7
Thence wheeling on, it compass shall	213	L' Envoy	D	11
And with that Ring thy fame shall wedd	213	L' Envoy	D	13
Shall flow no more - until they bring	214	Convert	D	8
Henceforth shall only pierce the Skies,	214	Convert	D	14
Henceforth in Sacred Flames shall Burn,	214	Convert	D	19
he shall be like an happy tree,	214	Psalm I	D	8
Which, planted by the waters, shall	214	Psalm I	D	9
His leaf shall never fade, and all	214	Psalm I	D	11
shall prosper that he takes in hand.	214	Psalm I	D	12
Therefore shall not the wicked be	215	Psalm I	D	17
of good men shall the wicked come.	215	Psalm I	D	20
shall utterly be overthrown.	215	Psalm I	D	24
But He, that sits in Heaven, shall laugh,	215	Psalm II	D	9
the Lord himself shall them deride:	215	Psalm II	D	10
Then shall He speak to them in wrath,	215	Psalm II	D	11
the Heathen shall thy portion be.	216	Psalm II	D	20
Whose pow'r shall dash and break them all	216	Psalm II	D	23
Belongs, O Lord, thy blessing shall	217	Psalm III	D	23
shall more replenish me,	218	Psalm IV	D	26
shall me in safety keep.	218	Psalm IV	D	32
No evil, Lord, shall dwell with thee,	218	Psalm V	D	11
shall be abhorr'd by thee.	218	Psalm V	D	16

	PAGE	TITLE		LINE
SHALL (cont'd)				
His favour shall encompass them,	219	Psalm V	D	43
shall I in vain thy Grace implore?	220	Psalm VI	D	8
or who shall praise Thee in the grave?	220	Psalm VI	D	12
So shall the people round about	221	Psalm VII	D	25
The Lord shall judge the people all:	221	Psalm VII	D	29
but shall bring forth a lye.	222	Psalm VII	D	52
shall he himself be caught.	222	Psalm VII	D	56
shall be returned home:	222	Psalm VII	D	58
his cruelty shall come.	222	Psalm VII	D	60
where he shall not exercise what he is, unlesse he forsake his	226	Priest 2		26
and shall be so farre from that which they seek with their	226	Priest 2		34
and cringings, that they shall ever be despised.	226	Priest 2		36
he shall know of the Doctrine, John 7. and assuring himself,	228	Priest 4		29
have glorified him as wel as now, and that he shall have so for ever.	232	Priest 6		1
unto God, and as his grace shall direct him, so let him proceed.	237	Priest 9		6
or he takes care she shall learn it of some religious neighbour.	239	Priest 10		16
shall much better brooke and bear a draught of beer, then if it had	242	Priest 10		22
For there he shall find his flock most naturally as they are,	247	Priest 14		5
this life, who hath promised, that Godlinesse shall be gainfull:	254	Priest 20		20
to themselves, and witty to others who shall reprove them from it.	264	Priest 26		13
in the least things, and for the least there shall be a judgment.	265	Priest 26		33
this is foretold, that it shall be so still, until things be no more.	268	Priest 28		15
to the Apostles rule, he endeavours that none shall despise him;	268	Priest 28		17
if the contempt shall proceed so far as to do any thing punishable	268	Priest 28		31
hand to sickle, shall then secure himself, and think all cock-sure;	271	Priest 30		29
if he now, shall either for fear or shame, break his custome,	273	Priest 31		30
either for fear or shame, break his custome, he shall do passing ill:	273	Priest 31		31
and who is ready to ask, if he shall mend shoos, or what he shall do?	275	Priest 32		8
all other things shall be added, even it selfe is a Sermon.	278	Priest 33		14
But if they shall fear, that at such, or such a time their peace	280	Priest 34		32
how shall not the ministration of the spirit exceed in blessing?	285	Priest 36		19
language, he shall be esteemed as ordinary complementers;	286	Priest 36		21
if the punished delinquent shall be much troubled for his sins,	288	Priest 37		2
How shall we dare to appear before thy face, who are contrary	288	Priest		8
and thy right hand shall teach thee terrible things.	289	Priest		23
keep a fit proportion, shall receive little hurt from other excesses.	294	Cornaro		5
but that he shall ever after live free from diseases, if he will keep	297	Cornaro		19
of diseases, so that he shall need neither Physick nor Physician:	297	Cornaro		21
what diet shall he use in diseases, which being in health he hath	299	Cornaro		23
when I shall come to that point, I shall finde no little comfort in	303	Cornaro		23
I shall finde no little comfort in the favour of Jesus Christ.	303	Cornaro		23
(setting casualties aside) I shall not die but by a pure resolution:	303	Cornaro		26
Indeed he that shall so attend to the bark of the letter,	309	Valdesso		29
They shall be all taught of God, it being Scripture cannot be spoken	310	Valdesso		2
but such a one as shall still have the assistance of the holy spirit	310	Valdesso		6
sence of that Text, wee shall overthrow all means, save catechizing,	310	Valdesso		11
it is Faith and Infidelity that shall judge us now since the Gospell,	311	Valdesso		23
if we believe, no sinne shall hurt us;	311	Valdesso		25
if we believe not, no vertue shall helpe us.	311	Valdesso		26
we shall not be punished (which word I like here better then	311	Valdesso		26
God often chuseth which he shall doe, and that by restraining him	313	Valdesso		22
Whether shall the Oxe goe, where he shall not labour?	324	Proverbs		98
Keepe good men company, and you shall be of the number.	325	Proverbs		120
Hee that eats the hard shall eate the ripe.	328	Proverbs		210
Bee not idle and you shall not bee longing.	331	Proverbs		308
By the needle you shall draw the thread,	332	Proverbs		329
shall neither have good wife nor good horse.	336	Proverbs		434
At the games end we shall see who gaines.	339	Proverbs		538
He that trusts in a lie, shall perish in truth.	340	Proverbs		569
He that trusts in a lie, shall perish by the truth.	340	Proverbs	V	569
If fooles should not foole it, they shall lose their season.	343	Proverbs	V	702
He that doth what he should not, shall feele what he would not.	347	Proverbs		783
Hee that makes himself a sheep, shall be eat by the wolfe.	358	Proverbs	D	1089
He that will be surety, shall pay.	358	Proverbs	D	1091
in Poetry, shall be all, and ever consecrated to Gods glory.	363	Letters		11
and shall I then be fain alwayes to borrow Books, and build	364	Letters		13
had taken ill courses, Follow your Book, and you shall want nothing:	364	Letters		22
so shall you play a good marchant, by transporting French commodities	366	Letters		11
when I have more time, you shall hear more;	366	Letters		20
I hope I shall get this place without all your London helps,	370	Letters		7
but I hope I shall shortly, though for the reckoning of your favours,	370	Letters		30
I shall never find time and paper enough, yet am I Your readiest	370	Letters		31
when I shall understand that a Letter will be seasonable,	371	Letters		15
the next Friday it is tryed, and accordingly you shall hear.	371	Letters		17
and then you shall justly value Your most truly, most heartily,	372	Letters		4
by so much shall it make my prayers the more constant and the more	372	Letters		22
and, Blessed be the Mourners, for they shall be comforted.	373	Letters		32
or, allow that any sadness shall be his Competitor.	374	Letters		12
Cast thy Care on the Lord and he shall nourish thee. (Psal. 55.)	374	Letters		14
of those that might say, What shall we rejoyce in afflictions?	374	Letters		23
to let them know your love, for which both they shall, and I doe,	375	Letters		22
doe that which GOD shall put into your hart, and the LORD bless all	375	Letters		33
If there fall out yet any rubb, you shall heare of me;	377	Letters		22
yet I shall ever put your care of Leighton, upon my accompt,	378	Letters		3
doubt not, through Gods blessing, but it shall be to the full;	379	Letters		18
SHALLOW				
In shallow waters heav'n doth show;	97	Charms & K		17
What are two shallow foords, two little spouts	164	Grief		9
SHALLOWNESSE				
Blaming the shallownesse of our request.	103	Prayer 2		12

	PAGE	TITLE		LINE
SHALLT				
Will canker both, yett thou alone shallt smart:	13	Ch.-Porch	W	166
SHALT				
As that thy self alone to hell shalt goe.	13	Ch.-Porch	W	168
So shalt thou humble and magnanimous be:	19	Ch.-Porch		332
Write, So much giv'n to God; thou shalt be heard.	21	Ch.-Porch		382
If thou shalt give me wit, it shall appeare,	36	Thanksgvng		43
If thou shalt let this vencme lurk,	45	Nature		7
Thou shalt recover all thy goods in kinde,	54	Love 2		11
Thou shalt have more.	61	Praise 1		4
And true descent; that when thou shalt grow fat,	65	Ch.-mcnum.		18
But thou shalt answer, Lord, for me.	110	The Quip		8
But thou shalt answer, Lord, for me.	110	The Quip		12
But thou shalt answer, Lord, for me.	111	The Quip		16
But thou shalt answer, Lord, for me.	111	The Quip		20
If I say, Thou shalt be mine;	114	Dialogue		11
Then shalt thou be my rock and tower,	156	Assurance		35
Let losers talk: yet thou shalt die;	169	Dial.-Anth		7
Thou so much worse, that thou shalt be no more.	169	Dial.-Anth		10
When thou shalt look us out of pain,	172	The Glance		21
When thou shalt call	187	Judgement		4
But I resolve, when thou shalt call for mine,	188	Judgement		11
There thou shalt finde my faults are thine.	188	Judgement		15
Thou shalt not bee a Queene and conquer there.	212	Bohemia	D	40
But joyes are stord for thee: thou shalt returne	212	Bohemia	D	55
Thou shalt possess earth's farthest bounds	216	Psalm II	D	21
Thou in the morn shalt have my mone,	218	Psalm V	D	5
Learne weeping, and thou shalt laugh gayning.	325	Proverbs		127
SHAME				
Mayst rule it, as thou list; and poure the shame,	7	Ch.-Porch		27
Boast not thereof; nor make thy shame thy glorie.	8	Ch.-Porch		50
But if thou coole, then take some shame to thee	10	Ch.-Porch	W	90
Desire and shame, will make thy labour, play:	10	Ch.-Porch	W	90
Shame tears my soul, my bodie many a wound;	33	Sacrifice		217
My soule is full of shame, my flesh of wound:	33	Sacrifice	W	217
And still with sicknesses and shame	43	East.wings		12
Yet thou with sicknesses and shame	43	East.wings	W	12
Without, our shame; within, our consciences;	46	Sinne 1		11
Affright both sinne and shame.	52	H.Commun.		18
Sicknes, or shame, or sinn, or sorrow:	65	Ch.-mus.	W	8
The sunne holds down his head for shame,	101	Miserie		33
New thoughts of sinning: wherefore, to my shame,	122	Sinnes rd.		17
Thy sithe is dull; whet it for shame.	122	Time		2
Brought back to the Red Sea, the sea of shame.	128	Bunch Gr.		7
My power and wisdome. Put me not to shame,	143	Complaining		3
To hide thy shame: for thou hast cast a bone	156	Assurance		39
With canvas, not with arras clothe their shame:	177	Forerunners		26
Truth Lord, but I have marr'd them: let my shame	189	Love 3		13
And wash away my Shame.	214	Convert	D	10
my glory into shame?	217	Psalm IV	D	8
And put them all to utter shame,	220	Psalm VI	D	27
into which if he come, he prostitutes himself both to shame, and sin,	227	Priest 3		25
and put them to great shame, who deny the Scripture to be perfect.	247	Priest 13		1
Secondly, that this interruption proceede not out of shame.	273	Priest 31		21
if he now, shall either for fear or shame, break his custome,	273	Priest 31		30
of Christs Cross, or for any shame to leave that which is good.	284	Priest 35		33
for we are darknesse, and weaknesse, and filthinesse, and shame.	288	Priest		11
Losse embraceth shame.	341	Proverbs		603
SHAMEFULL				
and a shamefull wrong both to the Common-wealth, and their own House:	277	Priest 32		27
not onely a shamefull thing to fear that which cannot be avoided;	303	Cornaro		22
SHAMES				
What griefs, what shames!	149	Longing		28
SHAPE				
But since thy breath gave me both life and shape,	73	Afflict.3		7
Did show and shape thy looks to me,	141	Justice 2		4
SHARE				
Thy person share, and the conceit advance.	15	Ch.-Porch		232
Thy person share, and thou thy mirth inhanse.	15	Ch.-Porch	W	232
Share in the conquest, and confesse a troth.	19	Ch.-Porch		324
Or feel his share, he would not cease to kneel,	33	Sacrifice	W	210
(Thy workmanship) and give thee share in neither.	54	Love 1		8
To writhe his limbes, and share, not mend the ill.	73	Constancie		33
And share in my degree.	95	Submission		8
To conquere new ones, & shall share the frame	212	Bohemia	D	43
in councels of th' ungodly share,	214	Psalm I	D	2
God oft hath a great share in a little house.	323	Proverbs		60
know I did not, and that your share continues, or rather increaseth,	372	Letters		17
SHAR'D				
Spain in the Empire shar'd with Germanie,	192	Ch.-Milit.		89
SHARP				
Get a sharp wife, a servant that will lowre.	15	Ch.-Porch		213
To worldly things are sharp, but to me blinde;	26	Sacrifice		2
Sharp nails pierce this, but sharper that confound;	33	Sacrifice		218
Twentie for one too sharp do finde it.	122	Time		6
Be to me rather sharp and TART,	133	Paradise		8
Shining and sharp, point out your rare Perfections;	209	L. Bacon	D	4
SHARPEN				
Sharpen their Muse:	116	Dulnesse		20
SHARPER				
Sharp nails pierce this, but sharper that confound;	33	Sacrifice		218

	PAGE	TITLE		LINE
SHARPNES				
Such sharpnes shows the sweetest FREND:	133	Paradise		13
SHAVE				
It is very hard to shave an egge.	359	Proverbs	D	1128
SHAVES				
No barber shaves so close but another finds worke.	343	Proverbs		667
SHE				
She loseth three for one; her soul, rest, fame.	13	Ch.-Porch		174
Perhaps his wives too, and whom she hath bore:	14	Ch.-Porch		195
I will not marry; or, if she be mine,	35	Thanksgvng		23
She and her children shall be thine.	35	Thanksgvng		24
And spinning phansies, she was heard to say,	84	The World		2
Till she had weakned all by alteration:	84	The World		8
Made in the tree, where she was wont to sit,	101	Miserie		56
When she doth write.	109	Brit. Ch.		6
She on the hills, which wantonly	110	Brit. Ch.		13
She in the valley is so shie	110	Brit. Ch.		19
While she avoids her neighbours pride,	110	Brit. Ch.		22
She wholly goes on th' other side,	110	Brit. Ch.		23
Which when I pluckt not, Sir, said she,	110	The Quip		6
Nothing more quick when she doth go.	137	Familie		16
Why doth my Mother blush? is she the rose,	140	Ch.-rents		11
(Whose precepts she had trampled on before)	173	Marie Magd		2
Wherein she thenceforth evermore	173	Marie Magd		5
She being stain'd her self, why did she strive	173	Marie Magd		7
Why kept she not her tears for her own faults,	173	Marie Magd		9
Why kept she not her tears for her own fauts,	173	Marie Magd	V	9
Deare soul, she knew who did vouchsafe and deigne	173	Marie Magd		13
Ev'n God himself: wherefore she was not loth,	173	Marie Magd		15
As she had brought wherewith to stain,	173	Marie Magd		16
And yet in washing one, she washed both.	173	Marie Magd		18
Knocking at all doores, ever as she went.	190	Ch.-Milit.		30
To Egypt first she came, where they did prove	191	Ch.-Milit.		37
Thence into Greece she fled, where curious Arts	191	Ch.-Milit.	W	49
From Greece to Rome she went, subduing those	191	Ch.-Milit.	W	61
And not go lesse then she had done of late.	192	Ch.-Milit.		92
As well as any she? Cannot thy Dove	206	Walton 1		8
which skill either she brought with her, or he takes care she shall	239	Priest 10		16
or he takes care she shall learn it of some religious neighbour.	239	Priest 10		16
which endeavours to preserve a man as much as she can, teacheth us	299	Cornaro		26
we can eat but a very little, wherewith she is very well contented:	299	Cornaro		28
The goate must browse where she is tyed.	323	Proverbs		56
I gave the mouse a hole, and she is become my heire.	324	Proverbs		94
Marry a widdow before she leave mourning.	329	Proverbs		252
The Cow knowes not what her taile is worth, till she have lost it.	350	Proverbs		870
I dare say she would make good her promise of taking five or six	367	Letters		2
which she hath hitherto deferred to do, not of her self,	367	Letters		3
I suppose she is not disposed to spend her eyesight on a piece	371	Letters		13
greatest charitie of all, for she is youngest, and least looked unto;	375	Letters		24
Neither hath she any to repair unto at good times, as Christmas,	375	Letters		27
how destitute she is, and that in this necessary time of education.	376	Letters		12
with some little Apology that she had done nothing in it (as my	379	Letters		4
She referred it also to My Brother, to name at first, what the summe	379	Letters		5
She liked our Bock well, & has given order to the Tenants,	379	Letters		8
SHEATH				
One sword keepes another in the sheath.	345	Proverbs		723
SHED				
Are shed for him, dissolve thy frame,	209	H. Danvers	D	7
who first shed teares over Jerusalem, and afterwards blood.	234	Priest 7		21
SHEDS				
Dry dust, which sheds no tears, but may extort.	186	Death		12
SHEE				
No more then passion when shee talkes of it.	19	Ch.-Porch	W	318
untill shee had brought forth her first borne Sonne, as if afterwards	318	Valdesso		12
Harken to reason or shee will bee heard.	323	Proverbs		74
Shee spins well that breedes her children.	325	Proverbs		144
Shee spins well that breedes her child.	325	Proverbs	V	144
shee had never sought her daughter there.	344	Proverbs		696
A woman conceales what shee knowes not.	355	Proverbs		1031
& shee being at London sent for him (as shee sayes) to make peace	368	Letters		20
being at London sent for him (as shee sayes) to make peace with him,	368	Letters		21
given her occasicn to protest shee will never speake with him againe,	368	Letters		22
to live on by her selfe (for shee desires no more) shee will find	368	Letters		24
selfe (for shee desires no more) shee will find friends to compell	368	Letters		25
SHEEP				
Sheep eat the grasse, and dung the ground for more:	119	Providence		69
With the other blesse thy sheep,	199	L'Envoy		3
It is a sheep of Berry, it is marked on the nose	356	Proverbs	D	1040
The death of wolves is the safety of the sheep.	358	Proverbs	D	1086
Hee that makes himself a sheep, shall be eat by the wolfe.	358	Proverbs	D	1089
To seek in a Sheep five feet when there is but four.	359	Proverbs	D	1112
The wolfe eats oft of the sheep that have been warn'd.	360	Proverbs	D	1134
SHEEPE				
The crow bewailes the sheepe, and then eates it.	337	Proverbs		458
To a close shorne sheepe, God gives wind by measure.	349	Proverbs		867
SHEEPISHNESSE				
Transfus'd a sheepishnesse into thy storie:	10	Ch.-Porch		94
SHEET				
Within a sheet of paper, which was rent	192	Ch.-Milit.		95
SHEETS				
Those clouts are little winding sheets,	98	Mortific.		5

	PAGE	TITLE		LINE
SHELF				
What nature made a ship, he makes a shelf.	11	Ch.-Porch		120
And though hee bee a ship, is his owne shelf.	11	Ch.-Porch	W	120
Nay, his own shelf:	102	Miserie		77
SHELLS				
The shells of fledge souls left behinde,	186	Death		11
SHELTRED				
Whose leaves first sheltred man from drought & dew,	84	The World		12
SHEPHERD				
My soul's a shepherd too; a flock it feeds	81	Christmas		17
Shepherd and flock shall sing, and all my powers	81	Christmas		21
The great shepherd of the fold	92	Antiphon 2		10
The God of love my shepherd is,	172	23 Psalme		1
Now if a shepherd know not which grass will bane, or which not,	230	Priest 5		31
which grass will bane, or which not, how is he fit to be a shepherd?	230	Priest 5		33
save in the great shepherd of the fold, who first shed teares over	234	Priest 7		21
SHEPHERD'S				
The Shepherds hook grew to a scepter here,	192	Ch.-Milit.		71
and plantaine, shepherds purse, knot-grasse for the other,	261	Priest 23		35
SHEPHERDS				
Shepherds are honest people; let them sing:	57	Jordan 1		11
The shepherds sing; and shall I silent be?	81	Christmas		15
SHEW				
By great deeds shew, that thou canst little do;	15	Ch.-Porch		220
Rather then shew his cards.) Steal from his treasure	18	Ch.-Porch		298
To shew their face, since crosse to thy decrees:	38	The Sinner		7
And in this shew, what Christ hath done.	51	Faith		36
To shew that state dislikes not easinesse.	103	Prayer 2		4
I live to shew his power, who once did bring	159	Jos.coat		13
will shew us good? But, Lord,	217	Psalm IV	D	22
Such discourses shew very Holy.	234	Priest 7		36
who was to shew all humility before his Passion, yet he allows in his	285	Priest 36		28
as I will shew by my self, recounting the delights and pleasures in	300	Cornaro		30
the world is counted a very Saint, for his outward shew of holinesse:	319	Valdesso	V	21
Shew me a lyer, and I'le shew thee a theefe.	343	Proverbs		652
Shew a good man his errour and he turnes it to a vertue,	343	Proverbs		655
We Batchelors laugh and shew our teeth,	361	Proverbs	D	1175
To shew a forwardness in religious works is a good testimony	377	Letters		24
For amongst us what glorious shew is there, either of garments,	442	Oration		31
SHEW'D				
The greatnesse shew'd the owner. So I went	129	Love unkn.		29
after he hath shew'd the unlawfulness of spending the day in	277	Priest 32		28
SHEWED				
are of no great moment (as I shewed before) if a man be temperate	299	Cornaro		16
SHEWES				
To his Children he shewes more love then terrour, to his servants	241	Priest 10		9
shewes that he was continually conversant in it, and not used it	318	Valdesso		2
The House shewes the owner.	321	Proverbs		8
I wept when I was borne, and every day shewes why.	327	Proverbs		199
To whirle the eyes too much shewes a Kites braine.	345	Proverbs		717
The higher the Ape goes, the more he shewes his taile.	346	Proverbs		745
3. To Change shewes not well & you are by the Apostles rule (Philip	380	Woodnoth		12
SHEWETH				
sheweth, that ingenuous and fit imployment is never wanting to those	275	Priest 32		9
thousand dangers and deaths, as daily experience sheweth, and I also,	303	Cornaro		15
Christs righteousnesse (as he sheweth through all his Considerations)	305	Valdesso		1
SHEWING				
Shewing his steps should be the street,	173	Marie Magd		4
shewing them how acceptable such works are to God, and wishing them	247	Priest 14		18
of the house, and shewing them cleerly, that they respect them most,	251	Priest 17		29
shewing that things of ordinary use are not only to serve in the way	257	Priest 21		13
and shewing by all means, that the delinquents returne is to his	264	Priest 25		1
shewing that reproaches touch him no more, then a stone thrown	269	Priest 28		7
urges the best unto it, shewing that they do not loose, or go lesse,	270	Priest 29		9
SHEWS				
Which shews my bloud to be the onely way,	31	Sacrifice		158
But that which shews them large, shews them unfit.	41	Sepulchre		9
But then he shews them how to go to Law, even as Brethren,	260	Priest 23		25
and shews the perplexed Christian, that this prayer being	273	Priest 31		4
SHIE				
She in the valley is so shie	110	Brit. Ch.		19
SHIELD				
But thou, O Lord, art still the shield	216	Psalm III	D	5
a shield in their distress.	219	Psalm V	D	44
God is my shield, who doth preserve	222	Psalm VII	D	37
and by the vertue of the shield of faith, he is not afraid	238	Priest 9		6
Cover your selfe with your shield, and care not for cryes.	326	Proverbs		161
SHIELDS				
These are the five shields, wherewith the Godly receive the darts	269	Priest 28		19
SHIFT				
Sure to be crosse he would shift feet and face.	7	Ch.-Porch		24
(All in a shipwrack shift their severall way)	8	Ch.-Porch		44
And lay it on thy husbandry, for shift.	59	Whitsunday	W	20
SHIFTEST				
Were worse then ours; sometimes thou shiftest hands.	121	Providence		138
SHILLINGS				
And yet if a Book of four or five Shillings come in my way,	365	Letters		12
yea, sometimes of Ten Shillings:	365	Letters		13
besides that which is due to her, to Ann I leave thirty shillings:	382	G.H.'s Will		24
to Margeret twenty shillings: To William Twenty Nobles,	382	G.H.'s Will		24
To John twentie shillings, all these are over and above their wages,	382	G.H.'s Will		25

	PAGE	TITLE		LINE
SHILLINGS (cont'd)				
To Sara thirteene shillings foure pence, Alsoe my will and pleasure	382	G.H.'s Will		27
To Amy Danvers thirty shillings, To Mrs Anne Danvers twenty . .	383	G.H.'s Will		10
To Mrs Anne Danvers twenty shillings, To Mrs Mary Danvers twenty	383	G.H.'s Will		10
To Mrs Mary Danvers twenty shillings, To Mrs Michel twenty shillings,	383	G.H.'s Will		11
To Mrs Michel twenty shillings, To Mrs Elizabeth Danvers Mr Henry	383	G.H.'s Will		12
To Mrs Elizabeth Danvers Mr Henry Danvers wife twenty shillings,	383	G.H.'s Will		13
To Mr Bostocke forty shillings To Elizabeth Burthen thirty shillings	383	G.H.'s Will		15
To Elizabeth Burthen thirty shillings To Mary Gifford tenn shillings	383	G.H.'s Will		16
To Mary Gifford tenn shillings To Anne Hibbert tenn shillings	383	G.H.'s Will		16
shillings To Anne Hibbert tenn shillings To William Scuce twenty	383	G.H.'s Will		17
To William Scuce twenty shillings To Mrs Judith Spencer five	383	G.H.'s Will		17
pound To Mary Owens forty shillings To Mrs Mary Lawly fifty shillings	383	G.H.'s Will		19
shillings To Mrs Mary Lawly fifty shillings To Mr Gardiner tenn pound	383	G.H.'s Will		19
SHINE				
Shine like the sunne in every corner: see	20	Ch.-Porch		345
With saints on earth, shall one day with them shine.	24	Ch.-Porch		438
Lest on their double-dark souls either shine:	31	Sacrifice		139
Though many sunnes to shine endeavour?	42	Easter		28
Seeing not onely how each verse doth shine, ...	58	H.Script.2		3
The sunne, which once did shine alone, ...	59	Whitsunday		13
Making thy life to shine within	67	Windows		7
And make it shine:	74	The Starre		12
A willing shiner, that shall shine as gladly, ...	81	Christmas		29
Then we will sing, and shine all our own day, ...	81	Christmas		31
Till ev'n his beams sing, and my musick shine.	81	Christmas		34
In small draughts Heav'en does shine & dwell:	97	Charms & K	W	21
There let them shine, ...	101	Miserie		53
To whom the starres shine not so fair, as eyes;	111	Vanitie 2		3
Where thou didst lately so triumph and shine, ...	140	Ch.-rents		2
Simper and shine, ...	162	The Search		14
Flyes of estates and sunne-shine. But to all, ...	169	The Answer		5
And when thou dost but shine lesse cleare, ...	183	A Parodie		19
Shine then more bright then hee.	203	Even-song	W	8
And hope, that may teach it to shine, ...	203	Even-song	W	19
In his progenie doth shine.	208	J. Danvers	D	12
Through that black tiffany thy vertues shine	211	Bohemia	D	17
Shine on, Majestick soule, abide	213	L' Envoy	D	1
Although the sun shine, leave not thy cloake at home.	332	Proverbs		326
SHINER				
A willing shiner, that shall shine as gladly, ...	81	Christmas		29
SHINES				
That ev'n her face by kissing shines, ...	110	Brit. Ch.		17
Shines bright and cleare, ev'n unto condemnation, ...	171	Self-cond.		23
He that burnes most shines most.	340	Proverbs		568
He is onely bright that shines by himselfe.	345	Proverbs		707
SHINETH				
The sunne still shineth there or here, ...	79	Employm.2		18
SHINING				
The sphere of vertue, and each shining grace	175	The Foil		2
Shining and sharp, point out your rare Perfections;	209	L. Bacon	D	4
Maintaine there Lustre still, & shining cleere	211	Bohemia	D	11
SHIP				
Some ship them over, and the thing is done.	10	Ch.-Porch		100
What nature made a ship, he makes a shelf.	11	Ch.-Porch		120
And though hee bee a ship, is his owne shelf.	11	Ch.-Porch	W	120
Is by a ship the speedier passage made.	119	Providence		90
As when a Merchant hath a ship come home after many a storme,	271	Priest 30		22
To a crazy ship all winds are contrary.	334	Proverbs		395
A great ship askes deepe waters.	336	Proverbs		449
SHIPPE				
A shippe and a woman are ever repairing.	347	Proverbs		780
SHIPPING				
Shipping the vices onely for our sphere.	196	Ch.-Milit.	W	204
SHIPS				
Ships feare fire more then water.	351	Proverbs		909
SHIPWRACK				
(All in a shipwrack shift their severall way)	8	Ch.-Porch		44
that twice suffers shipwrack.	345	Proverbs		706
who twice suffers shipwrack.	345	Proverbs	V	706
Slander is a shipwrack by a dry Tempest.	356	Proverbs	D	135
SHIRE				
Judges and Magistrates, to attend them, at least in their Shire;	277	Priest 32		3
SHIRES				
the casting of it on mean persons, especially in some Shires:	276	Priest 32		21
SHOALS (see also showls)				
SHOARE				
Remote from ours, then Spaine from Britains shoare.	438	Lat.Trans.		4
SHOE (see also shoos)				
The wearer knowes, where the shoe wrings.	338	Proverbs		491
All feete tread not in one shoe.	338	Proverbs		497
For want of a naile the shoe is lost, ...	338	Proverbs		499
for want of a shoe the horse is lost, ...	338	Proverbs		499
SHOLD				
And what shold flesh but flesh discry, ...	201	H. Commun.	W	32
power to defeat my charity, and evill shold be stronger then good:	376	Letters		10
& if upon your withdrawing it shold doe so, it would trouble your	381	Woodnoth		12
SHONE				
They dye in holes where glory never shone.	20	Ch.-Porch	W	348
Without a knock it never shone.	68	Content		12
Onely whereas the Ark in glorie shone, ...	190	Ch.-Milit.		27

SHOULD (cont'd)	PAGE	TITLE		LINE
or that cinnamon should heat me more then pepper?	297	Cornaro		33
how much more dearely should a Physician be esteemed, who not onely	298	Cornaro		8
lesse then otherwise they should do) then alwayes to live under	298	Cornaro		27
but onely that a man should begin and by little and little accustome	299	Cornaro		9
For if he should keep his former proportion, Nature, which is	299	Cornaro		32
why should I be accounted lesse happie, or lesse my self,	302	Cornaro		34
Now lest there should be any delight wanting to my old age,	302	Cornaro		37
but that I should wish all who have the care of themselves,	303	Cornaro		31
God in the midst of Popery should open the eyes of one to understand	304	Valdesso		20
As if he should say:	308	Valdesso		34
holy Scripture, he meaneth that we should not use it as the onely,	314	Valdesso	V	4
that the best of Gods Servants should have weaknesses is no way	316	Valdesso		2
and arrives not to the point it should, which if it did,	319	Valdesso		11
If all fooles had bables, wee should want fuell.	323	Proverbs		63
If all fooles wore white Caps, wee should seeme a flock of geese.	338	Proverbs		513
Hee that should have what hee hath not,	340	Proverbs		559
should doe what he doth not.	340	Proverbs		559
If fooles should not foole it, they shall lose their season.	343	Proverbs	V	702
If fooles should not foole it, they should loose their season.	344	Proverbs		703
He that doth what he should not, shall feele what he would not.	347	Proverbs		783
come a Horse-back, there is reason, that my desires should go a-foot;	363	Letters		23
not well, I had rather the fault should lie on me, than on them;	364	Letters		29
to avoiding of costlier matters, if I should fall absolutely sick:	365	Letters		8
upon condition that I should surcease from all title to it,	367	Letters		8
into a Benefice, I should be most glad to entertain it, and both pay	367	Letters		10
It is high time now that I should be no more a burden to you,	367	Letters		13
as that either his subjects only should practise it, or at least that	368	Letters		12
or at least that the Hollanders should pay him tribute out of their	368	Letters		12
if he had given it to the pope he should have had a greater reward.	368	Letters		34
could possibly have come, none should have done my message to Sir Fr:	369	Letters		20
if it had to others, yet to me it should not, for ought I yet knew;	370	Letters		24
content because I was in hope I should my self carry all sickness out	372	Letters		15
or why should our afflictions here, have so much power or boldness	372	Letters		27
Yf I should regard such things, it were in another's power to defeat	376	Letters		8
to name at first, what the summe should be, but he told her Grace,	379	Letters		6
pleasure is that Mr Woodnoth should be mine Executor to whome I	382	G.H.'s Will		28
SHOULDER				
A Dwarfe on a Gyants shoulder sees further of the two.	322	Proverbs		50
A Dwarfe on a Gyants shoulder sees farther then they two.	322	Proverbs	V	50
admirable thing is this, that God puts his shoulder to our burthen;	374	Letters		18
SHOULDERS				
Quick beleevers neede broad shoulders.	322	Proverbs		39
SHOULD'ST				
For so thou should'st without me still have been,	52	H.Commun.		5
SHOULDST				
That thou shouldst it so eye, and wooe,	62	Mattens		10
O that thou shouldst give dust a tongue	80	Deniall		16
How know I, if thou shouldst me raise,	95	Submission		13
That thou shouldst minde a rotten tree?	104	Obedience		22
They ask enough; why shouldst thou further go?	145	Discharge		26
SHOUT				
Yet still they shout, and crie, and stop their eares,	30	Sacrifice		105
Who Crucifie him, crie with one strong shout.	32	Sacrifice		186
The church with psalms must shout,	53	Antiphon 1		9
Yea, shout for joy for evermore,	219	Psalm V	D	37
SHOW (see also shew)				
And God will show thee how to take the towne,	7	Ch.-Porch	W	22
Who would not haste, nay give, to see the show?	22	Ch.-Porch		390
None of my books will show:	48	Afflict.1		56
Show that thy brests can not be dry,	59	Whitsunday	W	21
May both the work and workman show:	63	Mattens		19
Thy torch doth show the way.	75	Sunday		7
If any one our Masters hand can show.	78	Ang.&Sts.		30
Therefore thou dost not show	82	Ungratef.		15
In shallow waters heav'n doth show;	97	Charms & K		17
O show thy self to me,	107	Home		5
O show thy self to me,	107	Home		11
O show thy self to me,	107	Home		17
O show thy self to me,	107	Home		23
O show thy self to me,	108	Home		29
O show thy self to me,	108	Home		35
O show thy self to me,	108	Home		41
O show thy self to me,	108	Home		47
O show thy self to me,	108	Home		53
O show thy self to me,	108	Home		59
O show thy self to me,	109	Home		65
O show thy self to me,	109	Home		71
O show thy self to me,	109	Home		77
That those thy form doth show,	115	Dulnesse		14
Would show a root, that gives expressions!	119	Providence		76
But Man alone, to show his heav'nly breed:	120	Providence		111
To show thou art not bound, as if thy lot	121	Providence		137
Did show and shape thy looks to me,	141	Justice 2		4
Did like some torturing engine show;	141	Justice 2		10
Did like some tottering engine show;	141	Justice 2	V	10
Of some fair church to show the sore	158	Praise 3		34
For some mean stuffe whereon to show his skill:	161	Priesthood		38
Show me, and set me, I have one reply,	169	The Answer		13
As plainly as that above doth show;	175	The Foil		3
God, to show how farre his love	181	Banquet		28

SHUTT	PAGE	TITLE		LINE
I here shutt out the wrangler from thy treasure.	104	Obedience	W	15
Onely, most noble Lord, shutt not the doore	209	L. Bacon	D	9
SHUTT'ST				
Thou shutt'st the doore, and keep'st within;	60	Whitsunday		21
SHY (see also shie)				
SICILIAN				
Which spit it forth like the Sicilian hill.	122	Sinnes rd.		8
SICK				
My poore soul, ev'n sick of love:	72	Frailtie		21
With sick folks, women, those whom passions sway,	73	Constancie		27
A sick toss'd vessel, dashing on each thing;	102	Miserie		76
Come Lord, my head doth burn, my heart is sick,	107	Home		1
With sick and famisht eyes,	148	Longing		1
or in visiting the sick, or in exhortations to some of his flock	236	Priest 8		12
in visiting other sick children, and tending their wounds,	239	Priest 10		25
of well minded people, and to lay up treasure for the sick and needy.	246	Priest 13		22
when any of his cure is sick, or afflicted with losse of friend,	249	Priest 15		13
Besides this, in his visiting the sick, or otherwise afflicted,	249	Priest 15		28
comfortable, and Soveraigne a Medicine it is to all sin-sick souls;	250	Priest 15		2
or sick person, that so the hunger and thirst after it may come	250	Priest 15		5
if there be any of his flock sick, hee is their Physician,	260	Priest 23		29
but to have the skill of healing a wound, or helping the sick.	260	Priest 23		32
if I am to visit the sick in haste, and my neerest way ly through	273	Priest 31		33
He that hath been sick of a Consumption, and knows what recovered	278	Priest 33		26
do it, then he that is generally learned, and was never sick.	278	Priest 33		29
And if the same person had been sick of all diseases, and were	278	Priest 33		30
my Physicians nothing thereof, as is the custome of sick people.	292	Cornaro		30
and therefore never was sick by any of these inconveniences,	294	Cornaro		9
So that a sick man, whether he hath lived heretofore orderly	299	Cornaro		29
heretofore orderly or disorderly, when he is sick, ought not to eat,	299	Cornaro		30
A naughty child is better sick then whole.	328	Proverbs		233
The healthfull man can give counsell to the sick.	360	Proverbs	D	1130
You know I was sick last Vacation, neither am I yet recovered,	364	Letters		32
to avoiding of costlier matters, if I should fall absolutely sick:	365	Letters		8
I have wrote to my dear sick Sister this week already, and therefore	367	Letters		21
and now the only thing I long for, is to hear of my dear sick Sister;	371	Letters		7
For my dear sick Sister.	371	Letters		T
SICKE				
A Paradox. That the Sicke are in better State then the Whole.	209	Paradox	D	T
Acquitts yourselves and gives the sicke all greife.	209	Paradox	D	6
The sicke are in themselves a State	210	Paradox	D	13
Giving is dead, restoring very sicke.	340	Proverbs		573
SICKLE				
and being ready to put hand to sickle, shall then secure himself,	271	Priest 30		29
SICKLINESSE				
sicknesse breaks these obligations of fasting, but sicklinesse also.	242	Priest 10		35
SICKLY				
Slight those who say amidst their sickly healths,	12	Ch.-Porch		133
For Temperance preserves even old men and sickly men sound:	292	Cornaro		8
was such as belonged to sickly constitutions, and that in a small	292	Cornaro		25
perhaps they will say, you are sickly, you must not study too hard;	364	Letters		25
SICKNES				
Sicknes, or shame, or sinn, or sorrow:	65	Ch.-mus.	W	8
SICKNESS				
To his Mother, in her sickness.	372	Letters		T
I was in hope I should my self carry all sickness out of your family:	372	Letters		15
therefore, if either Age or Sickness lead you to those Joyes?	372	Letters		31
I alwaies fear'd sickness more then death, because sickness hath made	373	Letters		8
because sickness hath made me unable to perform those Offices	373	Letters		8
SICKNESSE				
Your safetie in my sicknesse doth subsist:	34	Sacrifice		227
So disengag'd from sinne and sicknesse,	74	The Starre		13
When sicknesse makes him pale and wan.	92	Man		46
nor of the sicknesse that destroyeth at noone day, [Ghostly pride	238	Priest 9		7
that not onely sicknesse breaks these obligations of fasting,	242	Priest 10		35
do any thing, that leads me to a sicknesse, to which I am inclined,	242	Priest 10		37
I am inclined, as not to get out of that sicknesse, when I am in it,	242	Priest 10		38
Now as the Parson is in Law, so is he in sicknesse also:	260	Priest 23		29
and finding my self continually oppressed with pain and sicknesse,	292	Cornaro		19
For if a friend who visits thee in thy sicknesse, and onely comforts	298	Cornaro		6
much as she can, teacheth us how to govern our selves in sicknesse:	299	Cornaro		27
Health and sicknesse surely are mens double enemies.	354	Proverbs		1011
Take heed of foul dirty wayes, and long sicknesse.	360	Proverbs	D	1153
SICKNESSES				
More, then his sicknesses or povertie?	18	Ch.-Porch		310
And still with sicknesses and shame	43	East.wings		12
Yet thou with sicknesses and shame	43	East.wings	W	12
Sicknesses cleave my bones;	47	Afflict.1		26
Into more sicknesses.	48	Afflict.1		52
SIDE				
For they will pierce my side, I full well know;	34	Sacrifice		246
And side with thy triumphant glorie?	35	Thanksgvng		12
Is in my deare Redeemers pierced side.	44	H. Bapt.1		6
Looking on this side, & beyond us all:	48	Repentance	W	9
Reversed thunder, Christ-side-piercing spear,	51	Prayer 1		6
Of those, who did themselves through their side wound,	59	Whitsunday		20
And if the Fox had liv'd to rule their side,	70	Humilitie		23
The nimble Diver with his side	85	Vanitie 1		8
She wholly goes on th' other side,	110	Brit. Ch.		23
A stream of bloud, which issu'd from the side	129	Love unkn.		14

	PAGE	TITLE	LINE
SIDE (cont'd)			
I left on th' one, and on the other side	142	Pilgrimage	5
Close to my side.	142	Pilgrimage	18
And do encroach upon deaths side.	145	Discharge	35
Receiv'd the blow upon his side,	151	The Bag	29
We lookt on this side of thee, shooting short;	186	Death	9
But that my Inke was factious for this side.	209	L. Bacon D	12
his garden or orchard supplyes it, or his barne, and back-side:	241	Priest 10	19
This is to be on Gods side, and be true to his party.	252	Priest 18	15
ever besides two great helps and powerfull perswaders on his side;	263	Priest 24	16
On the other side, if I am to visit the sick in haste, and my neerest	273	Priest 31	33
On the other side, if it be unlawful to open faults, no benefit	287	Priest 37	5
they break forth like mighty waters on every side.	290	Priest	8
of the stomack, and often of the side, and the beginning of the Gout,	291	Cornaro	22
On the other side I argued, that Nature was contented with a little,	295	Cornaro	25
a pain of the side took me, which held me two and twentie houres.	296	Cornaro	18
Pull downe your hatt on the winds side.	332	Proverbs	334
Curtesie on one side only lasts not long.	348	Proverbs	809
On the other side are the names of those to whome my deceased Neece	383	G.H.'s Will	1
SIDES			
Religion alwaies sides with povertie.	197	Ch.-Milit.	252
Religion alway sides with povertie.	197	Ch.-Milit. W	252
which while they deferr, both sides suffer;	259	Priest 22	4
on both sides whereof are great and fruitfull fields, well manured	301	Cornaro	24
So may a warre be just on both sides, and was just in the Canaanites	316	Valdesso	29
He that hath love in his brest, hath spurres in his sides.	335	Proverbs	426
of a monke on all sides.	351	Proverbs	900
SIDING			
Which siding with invention, they together	54	Love 1	6
SIEGE			
Yet, for I threatned oft the siege to raise,	47	Afflict.1	43
SIEVE (see also seeves)			
SIFTED			
hath exactly sifted the definitions of all vertues, and vices;	264	Priest 26	31
SIGH			
I reade, and sigh, and wish I were a tree;	48	Afflict.1	57
A fervent sigh might well have blown	53	H.Commun.	31
Sure the unruly sigh had broke my heart.	73	Afflict.3	6
So much breath to a sigh, what's then behinde?	73	Afflict.3	9
The sigh then onely is	73	Afflict.3	11
With one small sigh thou gav'st me th' other day	108	Home	43
Nay thou hast made a sigh and grone	124	Gratefulnes	19
(I sigh to say)	129	Love unkn.	8
(I sigh to tell)	129	Love unkn.	24
(I sigh to speak)	130	Love unkn.	50
What? shall I ever sigh and pine?	153	The Collar	3
Recover all thy sigh-blown age	153	The Collar	19
Then will I wring it with a sigh or grone,	157	Praise 3	5
I sent a sigh to seek thee out,	162	The Search	17
To make me sigh, and seek, and faint, and die,	164	The Crosse	2
SIGH-BLOWN			
Recover all thy sigh-blown age	153	The Collar	19
SIGHES			
How know you that the sighes we send	210	Paradox D	19
SIGHING			
As when th' heart sayes (sighing to be approved)	168	a true Hymn	19
SIGHS			
Sighs and Grones.	83	Sighs & Gr.	T
Hast thou sighs, or hast thou not?	113	Businesse	11
If thou hast no sighs or grones,	113	Businesse	12
My sighs and tears as busie were above;	132	The Storm	3
To thee my sighs, my tears ascend:	148	Longing	5
Not to his hurt. Sighs will convey	152	The Bag	41
Before my sighs did drie it: there was corn	153	The Collar	11
Make his sighs to use it all,	199	L'Envoy	14
If ever Heart was sore with Sighs;	213	Convert D	3
SIGHT			
Thy wrath for sinne, as when mans sight was dimme,	49	Faith	2
By sight of sinne we should grow mad.	63	Sinne 2	8
Who gave me sight alone,	63	Even-song	5
Therefore my soul lay out of sight,	80	Deniall	21
I do resume my sight,	95	Submission	10
O what a sight were Man, if his attires	127	Giddinesse	17
But now that Christs pure vail presents the sight,	141	Justice 2	13
Unto my fathers hands and sight	152	The Bag	33
I do not greatly wonder at the sight,	161	Priesthood	23
Save in the sight thereof, where strength doth sting.	165	The Crosse	18
Ev'n in my enemies sight:	173	23 Psalme	18
Ev'n in mine enemies sight:	173	23 Psalme V	18
Bringing all your sinnes to sight:	180	Invitation	15
In my sight,	180	Invitation	35
For thy neatnesse passeth sight,	181	Banquet	4
As well our understanding as our sight.	190	Ch.-Milit.	18
If glorious bodies pass the sight	201	H. Commun. W	34
nor fools stand in thy sight.	218	Psalm V D	12
my sight with sorrow waxeth dim.	220	Psalm VI D	16
but for an exciting of others by their sight, to the acknowledging	282	Priest 34	15
that I may enjoy the sight & communication of my friends,	301	Cornaro	35
preferres the Word before the sight of the Transfiguration of Christ.	318	Valdesso	23
The sight of a man hath the force of a Lyon.	342	Proverbs	617

SIN (cont'd)	PAGE	TITLE		LINE
so that then where sin abounded, not death, but grace superabounded;	288	Priest		24
and that no other sin or vertue hath any thing to doe with us;	311	Valdesso		24
It takes much from the account, to which his sin doth amount.	327	Proverbs		192
Every sin brings its punishment with it.	346	Proverbs		760
of all Comfort, who is not willing to behold any sorrow but for sin.	372	Letters		26
SIN-SICK				
comfortable, and Soveraigne a Medicine it is to all sin-sick souls;	250	Priest 15		2
SINAI				
He is to Sinai gone, as we heard tell:	99	Decay		9
SINCE				
Man would have been th' incloser: but since now	7	Ch.-Porch		20
Be down, then winde up both; since we shall be	24	Ch.-Porch		455
Weep not, deare friends, since I for both have wept	31	Sacrifice		149
Yet since mans scepters are as frail as reeds,	32	Sacrifice		177
Yet since in frailty, cruelty, shrowd turns,	32	Sacrifice	W	177
Since, if my soul make even with the week,	38	The Sinner		3
To shew their face, since crosse to thy decrees:	38	The Sinner		7
Or, since one starre show'd thy first breath,	38	Good Fri.		7
Since bloud is fittest, Lord, to write	39	Good Fri.		21
Since nothing Lord can bee so good	39	Good Fri.	W	21
Long since on earth, to take possession.	40	Redemption		8
Or since all musick is but three parts vied	42	Easter		15
Since, Lord, to thee	44	H. Bapt.2		1
Or make a new one, since the old	45	Nature		15
Since thou hast taught us by thy word,	53	H.Commun.	W	39
But since those pipes of gold, which brought	59	Whitsunday		17
Thou Lord of life; since thy one death for me	62	Afflict.2		2
And long since wed	71	Frailtie		20
But since thy breath gave me both life and shape,	73	Afflict.3		7
Since there is no place so alone,	75	Sunday		20
Since we are ever ready to disburse,	78	Ang.&Sts.		29
Since we are ever ready to discourse,	78	Ang.&Sts.	V	29
Since my dark soul and brutish is thy right,	81	Christmas		11
Ev'n unto death: since he di'd for my good,	83	Sighs & Gr.		23
Since then, my God, thou hast	92	Man		49
Wherefore since that he is such,	93	Antiphon 2		16
Since if my sent be good, I care not, if	94	Life		17
Since thou hast both mine eyes.	95	Submission		20
Since then these three wait on thy throne,	103	Prayer 2		19
Yet since thou canst not choose but see my actions;	104	Obedience		23
Since where are poysons, antidotes are most:	119	Providence		87
Since by thy cutting he grows better.	122	Time		12
For since confession pardon winnes,	126	Confession		27
For since thy God refuseth still,	133	The Method		2
Yet if I wail not still, since still to wail	136	Ephes.		31
For we should count, Since the last joy.	138	The Size		41
As many eyes as starres? since it is night,	140	Ch.-rents		26
Since many gifts do challenge many hearts!	147	Offering		8
Since my sadnesse	147	Offering		25
Since this being mine, brings with it thine,	157	Clasping		7
Since thou in death wast none of thine,	157	Clasping		17
Wherefore I sing. Yet since my heart,	159	Praise 3		37
But since those great ones, be they ne're so great,	161	Priesthood		19
Onely, since God doth often vessels make	161	Priesthood		34
Since then my grief must be as large,	163	The Search		45
And yet since these thy contradictions	165	The Crosse		34
Since the condition of this world is frail,	170	Water-crs.		2
Since thou dost love, yet strike;	171	Bittersweet		2
Since that time many a bitter storm	172	The Glance		9
But since our Saviours death did put some bloud	186	Death		13
The rather since his scatter'd jugglings were	195	Ch.-Milit.		175
Yet Thou art not so dark, since I know this,	203	Even-song	W	17
Since Light thy Darknes is.	203	Even-song	W	20
Or, since thy wayes are deep, and still the same,	206	Walton 1		10
Since that mirth hath	210	Paradox	D	17
since our Saviour hath made that the argument of a Pastour's love,	224	Priest		5
since hee shoots higher that threatens the Moon, then hee that aims	224	Priest		8
since we are here by him, and without him could not be here.	234	Priest 7		29
since the words apart are not Scripture, but a dictionary,	235	Priest 7		8
For since fasting in Scripture language is an afflicting of our	242	Priest 10		11
But since both is to be done, the better sort invited, and meaner	243	Priest 11		13
since of the two commands, we are more injoyned to be charitable,	245	Priest 12		28
especially since many remove from Parish to Parish, who like	255	Priest 21		19
since man is so miserable, what is to be done?	257	Priest 21		2
be preferred, especially since in disobeying there is scandall also:	263	Priest 24		11
since there is a Justice in the least things, and for the least there	265	Priest 26		32
since even by the Common Statute-Law they are taken for a kinde	269	Priest 29		33
establisheth it, since they that have nothing, are fittest to work.	275	Priest 32		4
since he found himselfe sometimes to weepe more for the losse of some	279	Priest 33		11
since we are not Masters of our bodies, this sufficeth.	279	Priest 33		19
especially since it may be a just doubt, whether, considering	282	Priest 34		7
Besides the continuall succession (since the Gospell) of holy men,	282	Priest 34		19
I never since departed from my setled course of Sobrietie,	293	Cornaro		25
About foure yeares since, I was led by the advice of Physicians,	295	Cornaro		19
and especially since the power of my stomack every day decreased.	295	Cornaro		32
especially since there is a greater diversitie of tempers,	297	Cornaro		30
since none can have a better Physician then himself, nor better	297	Cornaro		37
Wherefore since many have observed a regular life, both of old times	299	Cornaro		5
especially since in observing it, there needs not many and curious	299	Cornaro		7
Wherefore since an orderly life is so profitable, so vertuous,	300	Cornaro		3

SINCE (cont'd)	PAGE	TITLE		LINE
especially since it is easie and most agreeable to the nature of Man.	300	Cornaro		5
Because since this is at the best but uncertain, dangerous,	300	Cornaro		19
Since therefore a temperate life is so happie and pleasant a thing;	303	Cornaro		30
it is Faith and Infidelity that shall judge us now since the Gospell,	311	Valdesso		23
since the Saints of God in all ages have ever held in so pretious	317	Valdesso		32
Ever since we weare cloathes, we know not one another.	326	Proverbs		168
Since you know all, and I nothing,	332	Proverbs		336
the same heart, which you have won long since, is still true to you,	363	Letters		18
unto you, since I find you so willing to yield to my requests;	363	Letters		21
for, since your favours come a Horse-back, there is reason,	363	Letters		22
for, since, I hope, I have not deceived their expectation,	364	Letters		23
burden to you, since I can never answer what I have already received;	367	Letters		13
since this place being civil may divert me too much from Divinity,	370	Letters		19
since I rode 200 mile to see a Sister, in a way I knew not,	371	Letters		2
the midst of much business, and all in a Fortnight, not long since.	371	Letters		4
but, since I know I did not, and that your share continues,	372	Letters		16
since if we had Riches we are commanded to give them away:	373	Letters		23
Since that I have seen the fruit of my observation, for they have	375	Letters		17
and you have no cause to be sorry, since it is GOD's business.	377	Letters		21
It is so long since I heard from you, that I long to heare both how	379	Letters		23
Long since, all we and our whole Kingdome exult with joy,	442	Oration		13
since you are so great both in your Princes, and your selves,	442	Oration		28
since there is a two-fold brightnesse which dazeleth the eyes of men,	442	Oration		32
SINCERE (see also syncere)				
The Countrey Parson is sincere and upright in all his relations.	252	Priest 19		24
SINEWS				
His stretched sinews taught all strings, what key	41	Easter		11
SINFUL				
And to my dym and sinful eyes	219	Psalm V	D	23
SINFULL				
Such sorrow as, if sinfull man could feel,	33	Sacrifice		209
or as they are sinfull.	283	Priest 34		11
As sinfull, he must much more love them;	283	Priest 34		13
the one in his being, the other in his sinfull being:	283	Priest 34		20
not to Thunder, or Angels, but to silly and sinfull men:	289	Priest		5
SING				
And make us strive, who shall sing best thy name.	5	Dedication		4
Shall I then sing, skipping, thy dolefull storie,	35	Thanksgvng		11
Shall I then sing, neglecting thy sad storie,	35	Thanksgvng	W	11
Shall have his attribute to sing;	36	Thanksgvng		40
Rise heart; thy Lord is risen. Sing his praise	41	Easter		1
Teach it to sing thy praise, this day,	42	Easter	W	29
And sing this day thy victories:	43	East.wings		9
And sing this day thy sacrifice,	43	East.wings	W	9
Let all the world in ev'ry corner sing,	53	Antiphon 1		1
Let all the world in ev'ry corner sing,	53	Antiphon 1		7
Let all the world in ev'ry corner sing,	53	Antiphon 1		13
Shepherds are honest people; let them sing:	57	Jordan 1		11
The shepherds sing; and shall I silent be?	81	Christmas		15
Shepherd and flock shall sing, and all my powers	81	Christmas		21
Out-sing the day-light houres.	81	Christmas		22
We sing one common Lord; wherefore he should	81	Christmas		25
Then we will sing, and shine all our own day,	81	Christmas		31
Till ev'n his beams sing, and my musick shine.	81	Christmas		34
His house still burns, and yet he still doth sing,	100	Miserie		4
To sing thy praises, make them lesse divine.	101	Miserie		40
And ever as they mount, like larks they sing;	107	Sion		23
Beasts fain would sing; birds dittie to their notes;	117	Providence		9
Heark, how the birds do sing,	131	Mans medly		1
I will sing thee,	146	Praise 2		10
Wherefore I sing. Yet since my heart,	159	Praise 3		37
Wounded I sing, tormented I indite,	159	Jos.coat		1
My joyes to weep, and now my griefs to sing.	159	Jos.coat		14
Untill I had some place, where I might sing,	164	The Crosse		3
Whether I sing,	183	The Posie		7
Thy mouth was open, but thou couldst not sing.	185	Death		4
Where treach'rous Syrens us'd to sing,	214	Convert	D	7
with their musick and fashion, and I my self also sing often;	303	Cornaro		7
SINGING				
catechizing, singing of Psalms at their work, and on holy days;	248	Priest 14		33
The singing man keepes his shop in his throate.	351	Proverbs		918
SINGLE				
If thou be single, all thy goods and ground	17	Ch.-Porch		283
Onely thy single market-money for it.	21	Ch.-Porch		375
A single deed is small renown.	128	Bunch Gr.		12
And single things grow fruitfull by deserts.	147	Offering		10
I have not lost one single tear:	158	Praise 3		25
temptation to men of any eminency, especially being single men.	238	Priest 9		17
and that much more being single, then if he were marryed;	238	Priest 9		22
Men are either single, or marryed:	275	Priest 32		19
Now, for single men, they are either Heirs, or younger Brothers:	276	Priest 32		25
SINGLED				
And what is fortunes. Thou hast singled out	211	Bohemia	D	19
SINGS				
Who sings thy praise? onely a skarf or glove	54	Love 1		13
Wonders and sings, but not his power	101	Miserie		57
And hurt thy self, and him that sings the note.	176	Forerunners		24
He that sings on friday, will weepe on Sunday.	335	Proverbs		411
SINGULAR				
place with place must be a singular help for the right understanding	229	Priest 4		8

SINGULAR (cont'd)	PAGE	TITLE		LINE
Now Catechizing being a work of singular, and admirable benefit	230	Priest 5		12
where the singular dexterity of Socrates in this kind may be	256	Priest 21		28
that the distinction is of singular use and comfort, especially	273	Priest 31		13
invites us to all good, according to that singular place, Phil. 4. 8.	313	Valdesso		20
After many singular honors, remarkable commands, most noble	441	Oration		24
SINK				
Sink not in spirit: who aimeth at the sky,	19	Ch.-Porch		333
I am the floore, the sink, where they it fling:	32	Sacrifice		175
Did not excite thee, we should wholly sink.	60	Whitsunday		24
SINKE				
but even to let the world sinke, so they do their duty;	232	Priest 6		16
Do well, and right, and let the world sinke.	270	Priest 29		23
SINN				
O England, full of all sinn, most of sloth,	10	Ch.-Porch	W	91
Sinn being gone o doe thou fill	39	Good Fri.	W	29
Yet all these fences with one bosome sinn	46	Sinne 1	W	13
For sinn would faine remove the dearth	59	Whitsunday	W	19
Prevent my Sinn to thine owne praise,	61	Grace	W	20
Sicknes, or shame, or sinn, or sorrow:	65	Ch.-mus.	W	8
Thus also sinn and darknes constantly	198	Ch.-Milit.	W	272
To' abolish Sinn, not Wheat.	200	H. Commun.	W	21
Sinn onely, which did all deface	200	H. Commun.	W	23
Disbanded humours, sorrows troops of Sinn	204	The Knell	W	11
Whither my many crymes and use of sinn	205	Persever.	W	11
before lower, even where to continue in the lower is no sinn.	380	Woodnoth		4
SINNE				
Yet, if thou sinne in wine or wantonnesse,	8	Ch.-Porch		49
Pick out of tales the mirth, but not the sinne.	9	Ch.-Porch		63
O England! full of sinne, but most of sloth;	10	Ch.-Porch		91
And send them to thine heart; that spying sinne,	23	Ch.-Porch		416
And send them to thy heart; that spying sinne,	23	Ch.-Porch	W	416
Lo, here I hang, charg'd with a world of sinne,	33	Sacrifice		205
That as sinne came, so Sacraments might flow:	34	Sacrifice		247
Yet few there are that sound them; Sinne and Love.	37	The Agonie		6
Who would know Sinne, let him repair	37	The Agonie		7
Sinne is that presse and vice, which forceth pain	37	The Agonie		11
Each sinne may so.	39	Good Fri.		20
One box doth lie both ink and sinne:	39	Good Fri.		24
That when sinne spies so many foes,	39	Good Fri.		25
All come to lodge there, sinne may say,	39	Good Fri.		27
Sinne being gone, oh fill the place,	39	Good Fri.		29
Lest sinne take courage and return,	39	Good Fri.		31
What ever sinne did this pure rock commit,	41	Sepulchre		10
Thou didst so punish sinne,	43	East.wings		13
Daily didst punish sinne,	43	East.wings	W	13
Sinne.	45	Sinne 1		T
Pulpits and sundayes, sorrow dogging sinne,	45	Sinne 1		5
One cunning bosome-sinne blows quite away.	46	Sinne 1		14
Lord, I confesse my sinne is great;	48	Repentance		1
Great is my sinne. Oh! gently treat	48	Repentance		2
When thou for sinne rebukest man,	49	Repentance		25
But thou wilt sinne and grief destroy;	49	Repentance		31
Thy wrath for sinne, as when mans sight was dimme,	49	Faith		2
And where sinne placeth me in Adams fall,	50	Faith		19
And where sinne places me in Adams fall,	50	Faith	W	19
Leaving within me sinne:	52	H.Commun.		6
Affright both sinne and shame.	52	H.Commun.		18
Before that sinne turn'd flesh to stone,	53	H.Commun.		29
To sinne, or sinne to smother;	53	H.Commun.		34
And if the braves of conqu'ring sinne	60	Whitsunday		23
Sinne is still hammering my heart	60	Grace		17
Sinne.	63	Sinne 2		T
O that I could a sinne once see!	63	Sinne 2		1
Sinne is flat opposite to th' Almighty, seeing	63	Sinne 2		4
By sight of sinne we should grow mad.	63	Sinne 2		8
I know it is my sinne, which locks thine eares,	66	Ch.-lock		1
I know it is my sinne, which stops thine eares,	66	Ch.-lock	W	1
Hither sometimes Sinne steals, and stains	67	Ch.-floore		13
And I will strive to sinne no more.	68	Trin.Sun.		6
So disengag'd from sinne and sicknesse,	74	The Starre		13
Sinne and my heart:	74	The Starre		24
Then enter'd Sinne, and with that Sycomore,	84	The World		11
Then Sinne combin'd with Death in a firm band	84	The World		16
By starving sinne and taking such repast,	87	Lent		44
I would do well, yet sinne the hand hath got:	96	Justice 1		10
Where yet both Sinne and Satan, thy old foes,	99	Decay		13
Cold sinne still forcing it, till it return,	99	Decay		19
Folly and Sinne play all his game.	100	Miserie		3
Folly and Sinne play out his game.	100	Miserie	W	3
Nor any sorrow tell them that they sinne,	100	Miserie		22
But sinne hath fool'd him. Now he is	102	Miserie		73
And for our sakes in person sinne reprove,	103	Prayer 2		16
And now thy Architecture meets with sinne;	106	Sion		11
Neither sinne nor Saviour feels.	114	Businesse		38
Sinne disclaims and I resigne.	115	Dialogue		24
And doth commit a world of sinne in one.	117	Providence		20
By flight of sinne.	125	Peace		36
And calls him coward, who for fear of sinne	127	Giddinesse		7
I sinne not to my grief alone,	136	Ephes.		17
When sinne and errour	141	Justice 2		3

SINNE (cont'd)	PAGE	TITLE		LINE
Were sinne alive, good cause there were	150	Longing		65
But now both sinne is dead,	150	Longing		67
He did endure to cancell sinne:	151	The Bag		22
Thou knowst how grief and sinne	155	Glimpse		28
Weltring in sinne;	171	The Glance		4
And on sinne doth cast the fright.	180	Invitation		18
To subdue the smell of sinne;	181	Banquet		15
Make Sinne appeare;	183	A Parodie		18
While Sinne doth rave,	183	A Parodie		22
That Sinne sayes true: but while I grieve,	184	A Parodie		29
So void of sinne,	187	Judgement		9
Guiltie of dust and sinne.	188	Love 3		2
Sinne did set out of Eastern Babylon,	193	Ch.-Milit.		103
Thus Sinne in Egypt sneaked for a while;	193	Ch.-Milit.		121
Here Sinne took heart, and for a garden-bed	193	Ch.-Milit.		127
Sinne being not able to extirpate quite	194	Ch.-Milit.		161
As Sinne in Greece a Prophet was before,	195	Ch.-Milit.		171
Thus Sinne triumphs in Western Babylon;	196	Ch.-Milit.		211
Yet not as Sinne, but as Religion.	196	Ch.-Milit.		212
So though Sinne made his latter seat the better,	196	Ch.-Milit.		223
So though Sinne made his later seat the better,	196	Ch.-Milit.	W	223
So Sinne shall trace and dog her instantly:	197	Ch.-Milit.		260
The Church shall come, & Sinne the Church shall smother:	197	Ch.-Milit.		266
Thus also Sinne and Darknesse follow still	198	Ch.-Milit.		272
Let not Sinne devoure thy fold,	199	L'Envoy		5
Secondly because Luxury is a very visible sinne, the Parson is very	227	Priest 3		22
because notwithstanding his infinite hate of sinne, his Love overcame	283	Priest 34		14
as also to those that live in sinne, and follow their appetites:	303	Cornaro		19
if we believe, no sinne shall hurt us;	311	Valdesso		25
and not those which are in themselves occasions of sinne;	314	Valdesso		19
Feare nothing but sinne.	331	Proverbs		299
Poverty is no sinne.	349	Proverbs		844
SINNE'S				
Meeting sinnes force and art.	52	H.Commun.		12
The other curbs sinnes stealing pace and theft.	117	Providence		36
Sinnes round.	122	Sinnes rd.		T
They are Sinnes nipples, feeding th' east and west.	196	Ch.-Milit.		220
SINN'D				
Foolish soul who sinn'd to day?	113	Businesse		2
SINNED				
when we had sinned beyond any help in heaven or earth, then thou	288	Priest		26
SINNER				
The Sinner.	38	The Sinner		T
Then of a sinner thou art rid,	55	Temper 1		19
SINNER'S				
These drops being temper'd with a sinners tears,	27	Sacrifice		25
Is all lockt? hath a sinners plea	149	Longing		47
SINNERS				
Nor hath in way of sinners stood,	214	Psalm I	D	3
SINNERS'				
Engine against th' Almightie, sinners towre,	51	Prayer 1		5
Engine against th' Almightie, sinners fort,	51	Prayer 1	W	5
SINNES				
The cheapest sinnes most dearely punisht are;	9	Ch.-Porch		67
Pride and full sinnes have made the way a road.	9	Ch.-Porch		72
Feed no man in his sinnes: for adulation	16	Ch.-Porch		257
How know'st thou, but thy sinnes made him miscarrie?	24	Ch.-Porch		440
Putting my life among their sinnes and fears,	30	Sacrifice		106
My sinnes deserve the condemnation.	36	Reprisall		4
My severall sinnes their sorrows get;	39	Good Fri.		18
So when I view my sinnes, mine eyes remove	43	H. Bapt.1		3
And stop our sinnes from growing thick and wide,	44	H. Bapt.1		8
What ever future sinnes should me miscall,	44	H. Bapt.1		13
So devils are our sinnes in perspective.	63	Sinne 2		10
Not on my sinnes, or coldnesse, but thy will.	66	Ch.-lock		8
For though sinnes plead too, yet like stones they make	66	Ch.-lock		11
Purge all my sinnes done heretofore:	68	Trin.Sun.		4
Sinnes have their box apart,	82	Ungratef.		29
After my sinnes! look not on my desert,	83	Sighs & Gr.		2
'Twixt his sinnes and Saviours death?	114	Businesse		30
He that sinnes, hath he no losse?	114	Businesse		33
And so my sinnes ascend three stories high,	122	Sinnes rd.		14
Wherefore my faults and sinnes,	126	Confession		25
Your sinnes expresse; melt into dew.	135	Ephes.		12
Though my sinnes against me cried,	146	Praise 2		13
Our sinnes have purloin'd, and left you drie:	152	The Jews	V	2
Through th' old sinnes and new doctrines of our land.	161	Priesthood		33
Unto their sinnes?	162	The Search		28
My sinnes and I joining together:	166	The Flower		28
To serve thy sinnes, and furnish thee with store	170	Water-crs.		7
In tears like seas, our sinnes are pil'd	173	Marie Magd		11
To bear her filth; and that her sinnes did dash	173	Marie Magd		14
Bringing all your sinnes to sight:	180	Invitation		15
He left behinde him garrisons of sinnes	193	Ch.-Milit.		125
And all her calender of sinnes fulfill;	197	Ch.-Milit.		244
Whereby one may foretell, what sinnes next yeare	197	Ch.-Milit.		245
that he may keep himself pure, and not be intangled in others sinnes.	248	Priest 14		24
that it is not to be understood of actuall sinnes, but habituall,	308	Valdesso		2
for I can no more free my selfe from actuall sinnes after Baptisme,	308	Valdesso		4
When all sinnes grow old, coveteousnesse is young.	321	Proverbs		18

SINNES (cont'd)	PAGE	TITLE	LINE
When all sinnes grow old, coveteousnesse grows young.	321	Proverbs V	18
Sinnes are not knowne till they bee acted.	352	Proverbs	942
SINNING			
New thoughts of sinning: wherefore, to my shame,	122	Sinnes rd.	17
To set off vertues; griefs to set off sinning:	176	The Foil	6
Impudent sinning, witchcrafts, and distrusts	197	Ch.-Milit.	238
SINNS			
all which is here expressed, hee presently sinns, and displeases God,	224	Priest	11
For by this means, when any sinns, he hateth him not as an officer,	250	Priest 16	11
SINS			
When backward on my sins I turne mine eyes	43	H. Bapt.1 W	1
You doe prevent most sins & for the rest	44	H. Bapt.1 W	6
cannot in sins delight:	218	Psalm V D	10
For sins make all equall, whom they finde together;	227	Priest 3	27
the pleasure that comes with sleep, be sins of gluttony, drunkenness,	230	Priest 5	29
whose sins he then beares, and brings with his own to the heavenly	231	Priest 6	8
with confession of sins, and all acts of Mortification.	242	Priest 10	1
To Charity is given the covering of sins, 1 Pet. 4. 8.	244	Priest 12	9
and the forgivenesse of sins, Matthew 6. 14. Luke 7. 47.	244	Priest 12	9
there are some persons, who abstain not even from known sins;	264	Priest 26	10
at his own, and others sins, which continually breake Gods Laws,	269	Priest 28	9
if the punished delinquent shall be much troubled for his sins,	288	Priest 37	3
pardoning my sins, and bidding me go feed the people of thy love.	289	Priest	6
but pardon our sins, and perfect what thou hast begun.	289	Priest	21
SION			
For these are all the grapes Sion doth bear,	31	Sacrifice	162
Sion.	106	Sion	T
on Sion His most Holy hill,	215	Psalm II D	14
SION'S			
And meet the rest on Sions hill.	138	The Size	24
SIP			
So must he sip and think	131	Mans medly	22
So he must sip and think	131	Mans medly V	22
SIR			
Which when I pluckt not, Sir, said she,	110	The Quip	6
Of Joy and Charitie. Sir, you have not miss'd,	116	Love-joy	7
No marvell Sir, he did replie,	122	Time	3
On Sir John Danvers.	208	J. Danvers D	T
Sir John Danvers' earthly part	208	J. Danvers D	9
To Sir J. D.	363	Letters	T
You know Sir, how I am now setting foot into Divinity, to lay	364	Letters	11
Pardon my boldness Sir, it is a most serious Case, nor can I write	364	Letters	15
You know Sir, it is their ordinary speech, and now let them make it	364	Letters	22
Sir, if there be any truth in me, I find it little enough to keep me	364	Letters	31
alas Sir, what is that to those infinite Volumes of Divinity,	365	Letters	13
Noble Sir, pardon my boldness, and consider but these three things.	365	Letters	15
If then, Sir, there be any course, either by engaging my future	365	Letters	20
I desire you, Sir, to be my Mediator to them in my behalf.	365	Letters	21
Now I write to you, Sir, because to you I have ever opened my heart;	365	Letters	23
To the truly Noble Sir J. D.	366	Letters	T
I pray Sir, pardon my boldness of inclosing my Brothers Letter in	367	Letters	23
To Sir Robert Harley, at Brampton.	367	Letters	T
for I am enjoined to write to you by Sir John Danvers, to which mine	367	Letters	28
Sir Charles Howard & his Lady are at much difference, & shee being	368	Letters	19
To Sir John Danvers. This Week hath loaded me with your Favours;	369	Letters	T
could possibly have come, none should have done my message to Sir Fr:	369	Letters	20
which if you can sent to Sir Francis before his departure,	369	Letters	25
I long to hear from Sir Francis, I pray Sir send the Letter you	370	Letters	5
I pray Sir send the Letter you receive from him to me as soon as you	370	Letters	5
Noble Sir, I thank you for your infinite favours, I fear only that I	370	Letters	10
I understand by Sir Francis Nethersols Letter, that he fears I have	370	Letters	18
I pray Sir therefore, cause this inclosed to be carried to his	370	Letters	26
yet find leisure to write to my Lord, or Sir Benjamin Ruddyard;	370	Letters	29
Good Sir, make it plain to her, that I loved her even in my	371	Letters	11
To my very dear brother Sir Henry Herbert, at Court.	376	Letters	25
To my deere brother, Sir Henry Herbert, at Court.	377	Letters	32
Sir Henry H: of the blessed Success, that God had given us,	378	Letters	31
To Sir Henry Herbert.	379	Letters	T
Herberts reasons for Arth. Woodenoths Living with Sir John Danvers.	380	Woodnoth	T
thing to advize you now, & before you took Sir Johns affairs.	380	Woodnoth	8
only for the success (as assistance of Sir John) doe as David did:	380	Woodnoth	23
Lastlie I besech Sir John Danvers that he would be pleased to be	382	G.H.'s Will	31
SIRE			
I had rather aske of my sire browne bread,	330	Proverbs	269
SIRENS (see also syrens)			
SISTER			
Bigge with his sister: he hath lost the reins,	7	Ch.-Porch	32
Bigge with his sister: he hath lost his reins,	7	Ch.-Porch W	32
My flesh get on; yet let her sister	44	H. Bapt.2	12
yet if my Sister were acquainted that they are ready, I dare say she	367	Letters	1
I have wrote to my dear sick Sister this week already, and therefore	367	Letters	21
you and my dear Mother and Sister to pardon me, for my Cambridge	369	Letters	17
since I rode 200 mile to see a Sister, in a way I knew not,	371	Letters	2
and now the only thing I long for, is to hear of my dear sick Sister;	371	Letters	7
For my dear sick Sister.	371	Letters	T
It is true there is a third sister, whom to receive were the greatest	375	Letters	23
SIT			
Who strive to sit out losing hands, are lost.	14	Ch.-Porch	202
They grow unruly, and sit in thy bowers.	56	Temper 2	12
He that is weary, let him sit.	78	Employm.2	1

SIT (cont'd)	PAGE	TITLE		LINE
Struggle with Jacob, sit with Gideon,	99	Decay		2
Made in the tree, where she was wont to sit,	101	Miserie		56
Where all the guests sit close, and nothing wants.	121	Providence		134
Deare Friend, sit down, the tale is long and sad:	129	Love unkn.		1
Wherefore sit down, good heart;	138	The Size		37
A worm doth sit, whose many feet and hair	140	Ch.-rents		3
Nay, thou dost make me sit and dine,	173	23 Psalme		17
You must sit down, sayes Love, and taste my meat:	189	Love 3		17
So I did sit and eat.	189	Love 3		18
in them, but causing them, when they sit, or stand, or kneel,	231	Priest 6		25
The third is the observation with what appetite they sit down.	267	Priest 26		5
Man would sit down at this world, God bids him sell it,	272	Priest 30		6
A discontented man knowes not where to sit easie.	333	Proverbs		345
Sit in your place and none can make you rise.	334	Proverbs		372
SITHE				
Thy sithe is dull; whet it for shame.	122	Time		2
To whom thy sithe a hatchet was,	122	Time		9
SITS				
Herod in judgement sits, while I do stand;	29	Sacrifice		81
So sits the earths great curse in Adams fall	32	Sacrifice		165
Splendour from darknes. So close sits the crowne	212	Bohemia	D	37
But He, that sits in Heaven, shall laugh,	215	Psalm II	D	9
but hee that sits, or lies, puts up to an Apostle:	259	Priest 22		17
and sits above the Proctors, is Regent or Non-regent at his pleasure,	370	Letters		2
SITTEN				
And those all sitten in thy chair I see.	140	Ch.-rents	V	10
nor sitten in the scorners chair.	214	Psalm I	D	4
SITTING				
I saw the Vertues sitting hand in hand	70	Humilitie		1
The Feast indeed requires sitting, because it is a Feast;	259	Priest 22		12
SITUATION				
I am much pleased also in my travells, with the beauty of situation.	302	Cornaro		6
SIX				
Where it is warmest. Leave thy six and seven;	22	Ch.-Porch		401
The six-daies world transposing in an houre,	51	Prayer 1		7
The six-daies world-transposing in an houre,	51	Prayer 1	V	7
For we consider'd thee as at some six	186	Death		5
if not duly once a month, yet at least five or six times in the year;	259	Priest 22		21
she would make good her promise of taking five or six pound upon her,	367	Letters		3
SIX-DAIES'				
The six-daies world transposing in an houre,	51	Prayer 1		7
The six-daies world-transposing in an houre,	51	Prayer 1	V	7
SIXE				
Three helping one another, beare the burthen of sixe.	325	Proverbs		135
and the liberall of a farthing sixe pence.	328	Proverbs		211
but the liberall makes of a farthing sixe pence.	328	Proverbs	V	211
SIXTEEN				
of my drink, which before was foureteen ounces, I made now sixteen.	296	Cornaro		13
SIXTIE				
because that after one is once sixtie five yeares old, all the time	300	Cornaro		29
SIZE				
One size doth all conditions fit.	50	Faith		28
The Size.	137	The Size		T
Readie to take them in; yet of a size	158	Praise 3		29
Then my strict, yet welcome size.	177	The Rose		4
SIZES				
Afflictions sorted, anguish of all sizes,	45	Sinne 1		6
and above all things, they are to frequent Sessions and Sizes;	277	Priest 32		1
SKARE				
He that will take the bird, must not skare it.	322	Proverbs		42
SKARF				
Who sings thy praise? onely a skarf or glove	54	Love 1		13
SKARRES				
The Warrier his deere skarres no more resounds,	191	Ch.-Milit.		63
SKENES				
observ'd the thred of Life to be like other threds or skenes of silk,	373	Letters		5
SKIE				
From his Ecliptick line: becken the skie.	12	Ch.-Porch		137
Stayes not, but looks beyond it on the skie;	43	H. Bapt.1		2
And then appear'd a glorious skie.	51	Faith		40
Or, if I mount unto the skie,	61	Praise 1		7
Or, if I steale up to the skie,	61	Praise 1	W	7
The bridall of the earth and skie:	87	Vertue		2
To see what help in th' earth or skie:	107	Home		14
Divinities transcendent skie:	134	Divinitie		6
My knees pierce th' earth, mine eies the skie;	162	The Search		5
This were the better skie, the brighter place.	175	The Foil		4
And exalts ycu tc the skie:	180	Invitation		27
To the skie:	182	Banquet		44
SKIES				
Henceforth shall only pierce the Skies,	214	Convert	D	14
SKIL				
if neither himselfe, nor his wife have the skil, and his means serve,	260	Priest 23		33
SKILFULL				
Of skilfull artists, for the boards of those	161	Priesthood		17
but, in a skilfull hand, serves either positively as it is,	228	Priest 4		16
SKILL				
I cannot skill of these thy wayes.	95	Justice 1		1
I cannot skill of these my wayes.	96	Justice 1		12
Resigning up the rudder to thy skill.	104	Obedience		20

	PAGE	TITLE		LINE
SKILL (cont'd)				
I heard in Musick you had skill.	110	The Quip		11
Thy skill and art, what musick would it be!	118	Providence		40
More skill in musick, and keep better time.	154	Glimpse		7
For some mean stuffe whereon to show his skill:	161	Priesthood		38
Which using, and not fearing skill in th' one,	192	Ch.-Milit.		77
The Church and Sunne with all their power and skill.	198	Ch.-Milit.		273
which skill either she brought with her, or he takes care she shall	239	Priest 10		15
and instructs them further in that skill, shewing them how acceptable	247	Priest 14		17
if he once get the skill of it, will draw out of ignorant and silly	256	Priest 21		19
Yet the skill consists but in these three points:	256	Priest 21		30
This is the skill, and doubtlesse the Holy Scripture intends thus	257	Priest 21		10
but to have the skill of healing a wound, or helping the sick.	260	Priest 23		31
there were no such Physician as he, both for skill and tendernesse.	278	Priest 33		32
military state, he fortifyes, and strengthens with his utmost skill.	281	Priest 34		6
All things require skill, but an appetite.	334	Proverbs		378
Skill and confidence are an unconquered army.	342	Proverbs		626
SKILL'D				
so that as in the house of those that are skill'd in Musick,	240	Priest 10		30
SKILLS				
What skills it, if a bag of stones or gold	13	Ch.-Porch		169
SKIN				
A Lyons skin is never cheape.	323	Proverbs		55
SKINNE				
His skinne, his garments bloudie be.	37	The Agonie		10
And like a Dolphins skinne, his clothes combin'd	127	Giddinesse		19
The Wolfe must dye in his owne skinne.	349	Proverbs		849
SKINS				
Old Camels carry young Camels skins to the Market.	359	Proverbs	D	1101
SKIPPING				
Shall I then sing, skipping, thy dolefull storie,	35	Thanksgvng		11
SKY (see also skie)				
With his poore clod of earth the spacious sky.	8	Ch.-Porch		54
Sink not in spirit: who aimeth at the sky,	19	Ch.-Porch		333
Melt into blessings all the sky,	59	Whitsunday	W	23
The sky his azure mantle gain'd.	151	The Bag		15
That with th' one hand thou liftest to the sky,	160	Priesthood		2
Scorns his first bed of dirt, and means the sky;	169	The Answer		9
SLACK				
Who keeps no guard upon himself, is slack,	12	Ch.-Porch		139
Meeting with Time, Slack thing, said I,	122	Time		1
Indeed a slack and sleepie state of minde	130	Love unkn.		57
But in my prosecutions slack and small;	169	The Answer		7
But quick-ey'd Love, observing me grow slack	188	Love 3		3
SLACKNES				
that this interruption proceed not out of slacknes, or coldness,	273	Priest 31		16
SLACKNESSE				
Slacknesse breeds worms; but the sure traveller,	20	Ch.-Porch		339
SLAIN				
Him in his members, who for him was slain.	192	Ch.-Milit.		70
SLANDER				
Slander is a shipwrack by a dry Tempest.	356	Proverbs	D	135
SLANDERS				
Pardons and pleasantnesse are great revenges of slanders.	333	Proverbs		365
Pardons and pleasantnesse are great Revengers of slanders.	333	Proverbs	V	365
SLAUGHTER'D				
my slaughter'd honour lay.	221	Psalm VII	D	20
SLAVE				
Had to this day been an Egyptian slave.	27	Sacrifice		10
SLAY'ST				
thou slay'st the men that lye:	218	Psalm V	D	14
SLEEP				
Into a bed, to sleep out all ill weathers.	9	Ch.-Porch		84
Yet my Disciples sleep: I cannot gain	27	Sacrifice		29
Yet as in sleep we see foul death, and live:	63	Sinne 2		9
Who cannot on his own bed sweetly sleep,	68	Content		3
Sleep bindes them fast; onely their breath	98	Mortific.		9
Thou must go sleep, or dine.	101	Miserie		54
Others do sleep, and envie not their cheer.	118	Providence		56
Most things sleep lying; th' Elephant leans or stands.	121	Providence		140
Most things sleep lying; th' Elephant leane or stand.	121	Providence	V	140
But when I thought to sleep out all these faults	130	Love unkn.		49
As men, for fear the starres should sleep and nod,	134	Divinitie		1
And fence a plague, while others sleep and slumber.	147	Offering		12
And fence a plague, whiles others sleep and slumber.	147	Offering	V	12
Therefore we can go die as sleep, and trust	186	Death		21
Thee to love, in thee to sleep.	199	L'Envoy		4
I took a time when thou didst sleep	202	love	W	13
and take my restful sleep:	218	Psalm IV	D	30
drinking, sleep, and the pleasure that comes with sleep,	230	Priest 5		29
and the pleasure that comes with sleep, be sins of gluttony,	230	Priest 5		29
requires of all to pray by themselves before they sleep at night,	241	Priest 10		2
in this, that at Sermons, and Prayers, men may sleep or wander;	257	Priest 21		19
Besides all this, I could not sleep, no not a quarter of an houre:	296	Cornaro		22
I sleep well and quietly any where, and my dreams are fair	302	Cornaro		12
A man is known to be mortal by two things, Sleep and Lust.	361	Proverbs	D	1159
SLEEPE				
His dust who under thee must sleepe	208	H. Danvers	D	2
To want one ownce of sleepe,	209	Paradox	D	4
Sleepe without supping, and wake without owing.	324	Proverbs		93
One houres sleepe before midnight is worth three after.	350	Proverbs		882

	PAGE	TITLE		LINE
SLEEPES				
the Flegmatick sleepes.	351	Proverbs		924
When a man sleepes, his head is in his stomach.	353	Proverbs		981
SLEEPIE				
Indeed a slack and sleepie state of minde	130	Love unkn.		57
SLEEPING				
by no means enduring either talking, or sleeping, or gazing,	231	Priest 6		23
SLEEPY				
A sleepy master makes his servant a Lowt.	346	Proverbs		766
SLEEVE				
and had a goose in his sleeve.	345	Proverbs		737
Every one hath a foole in his sleeve.	350	Proverbs		881
SLEIGHT				
To use in any thing a trick or sleight;	72	Constancie		17
SLENDER				
A slender thread a gentle guest will tie.	154	Glimpse		20
My slender compositions might consume.	160	Priesthood		10
SLEPT				
When all my tears were bloud, the while you slept:	31	Sacrifice		150
I laid me down and slept, I wak'd;	216	Psalm III	D	11
SLIDE				
Did with his liquour slide into his veins.	7	Ch.-Porch		34
SLIGHT				
Slight those who say amidst their sickly healths, ...	12	Ch.-Porch		133
Slight not the smallest losse, whether it be	20	Ch.-Porch		343
To whose powre Thunder is but weake and slight:	29	Sacrifice	W	79
Yet slight not these few words:	168	a true Hymn		6
that do his justice slight.	222	Psalm VII	D	40
Neither let any think this a slight thing.	230	Priest 5		23
them not to serve the turne, nor provides slight, and unusefull,	252	Priest 19		27
The Authour doth still discover too slight a regard of the Scripture,	317	Valdesso		22
Yet doe not yee contemne these our slight glories, which wee raise	442	Oration		38
SLIGHTER				
a slighter forme of Catechizing, fitter for country people; . .	230	Priest 5		16
SLIGHTING				
but in all his words and actions slighting, and disesteeming it,	227	Priest 3		18
or else in a slighting way, shewing that reproaches touch him no	269	Priest 28		7
SLIGHTS				
But I like none of it, for it slights the Scripture too much:	306	Valdesso		17
He that takes not up a pin, slights his wife.	333	Proverbs		361
SLILY				
Working and winding slily evermore, ...	84	The World		13
SLING				
As gunnes destroy, so may a little sling.	20	Ch.-Porch		352
His arm is short; yet with a sling	61	Praise 1		11
SLIP				
sake, and to make his higher purposes slip the more easily. . .	249	Priest 14		12
hee might make his Doctrine slip the more easily into the hearts	261	Priest 23		19
Better the feet slip then the tongue.	322	Proverbs		53
Better thy foote slip then thy tongue.	322	Proverbs	V	53
SLIPS				
Hee stands not surely, that never slips.	323	Proverbs		68
SLIPT				
Who was to take it from me, slipt his hand, ...	130	Love unkn.		34
But after thou hadst slipt a drop	158	Praise 3		31
SLIPTE				
Hee stands not surely, that never slipte.	323	Proverbs	V	68
SLOATH				
be sins of gluttony, drunkenness, sloath, lust, and when not,	230	Priest 5		30
SLOTH				
O England! full of sinne, but most of sloth;	10	Ch.-Porch		91
O England, full of all sinn, most of sloth, ...	10	Ch.-Porch	W	91
SLOTHFUL				
The slothful is the servant of the counters.	341	Proverbs		610
The slothful is the servant of the vertuous.	341	Proverbs	V	610
SLOVENLINESSE				
and slovenlinesse, and as following the Apostles two great . .	246	Priest 13		25
SLOVENS				
Slovens take up their stock of noisomnesse	21	Ch.-Porch		369
First to bee Slovens, & forsake their nose.	21	Ch.-Porch	W	370
SLOW				
Then whom in waiting nothing seems more slow, ...	137	Familie		15
Come, bring thy gift. If blessings were as slow	147	Offering		1
But cooling by the way, grows pursie and slow, ...	169	The Answer		10
A slow behaviour to the style of king, ...	212	Bohemia	D	28
Accordingly his voyce is humble, his words treatable, and slow;	231	Priest 6		17
yet not so slow neither, as to let the fervency of the supplicant	231	Priest 6		17
Divine grace was never slow.	345	Proverbs		710
Gods Mill grinds slow, but sure.	346	Proverbs		747
SLOWER				
I went the slower, yet more paces, ...	203	Even-song	W	3
SLOWLY				
The tree that growes slowly, keepes it selfe for another. . .	327	Proverbs		198
A good Judge conceives quickly, judges slowly.	341	Proverbs		599
SLUBBERING				
also are to be done not in a hudling, or slubbering fashion, gaping,	231	Priest 6		30
SLUCE				
But the cheap swearer through his open sluce	8	Ch.-Porch		58
Whose streams we got by the Apostles sluce, ...	152	The Jews		3
SLUMBER				
And fence a plague, while others sleep and slumber. . . .	147	Offering		12

	PAGE	TITLE		LINE
SLUMBER (cont'd)				
And fence a plague, whiles others sleep and slumber.	147	Offering	V	12
One slumber finds another.	339	Proverbs		528
SLUTTERY				
For this French sluttery which so currant goes:	21	Ch.-Porch	W	368
SLUTTISH				
Whereas in fulnesse there are sluttish fumes,	86	Lent		22
SMACK				
There is no jollitie but hath a smack of folly.	338	Proverbs		493
SMACKS				
The smacks of dainties and their exaltation:	89	The Pearl	W	27
SMALL				
Be sure to doe it, though it be but small:	11	Ch.-Porch		116
In so much dregs the quintessence is small:	38	The Sinner		9
A new small-rented lease, and cancell th' old.	40	Redemption		4
Small to my self, to others milde,	44	H. Bapt.2		9
And thy small quantities my length;	52	H.Commun.		10
Quick thoughts and motions at a small expense,	86	Lent		20
In small draughts Heav'en does shine & dwell:	97	Charms & K	W	21
Though it be small,	100	Miserie		23
With one small sigh thou gav'st me th' other day	108	Home		43
Thou art in small things great, not small in any:	118	Providence		41
A single deed is small renown.	128	Bunch Gr.		12
That from small fires comes oft no small mishap.	139	Artillerie		4
Small it is, in this poore sort	146	Praise 2		25
Of a lesse world? the greater is but small,	164	Grief		10
But in my prosecutions slack and small;	169	The Answer		7
And such small game. Thence he to Greece doth passe,	193	Ch.-Milit.	W	123
Whereas the other way of crumbling a text into small parts,	235	Priest 7		6
except some small and temporary estranging may corroborate	263	Priest 25		30
the house-keepers Family be so small, and his dexterity so great,	275	Priest 32		37
He that is ashamed in small things, will extend his pusillanimity	284	Priest 35		34
as belonged to sickly constitutions, and that in a small quantitie.	292	Cornaro		25
My house, my house, though thou art small,	335	Proverbs		413
A small heart hath small desires.	348	Proverbs		807
He that gives me small gifts would have me live.	354	Proverbs		1000
No hair so small but hath his shadow.	359	Proverbs	D	1124
SMALL-RENTED				
A new small-rented lease, and cancell th' old.	40	Redemption		4
SMALLAGE				
comphrey and smallage made into a Poultis, have done great and rare	262	Priest 23		8
SMALLER				
and that in much smaller quantitie then when he was well.	299	Cornaro		32
SMALLEST				
Slight not the smallest losse, whether it be	20	Ch.-Porch		343
The smallest ant or atome knows thy power,	190	Ch.-Milit.		3
of their generall Schoole rules ever to the smallest actions of Life;	266	Priest 26		1
SMALNESSE				
are unuseful to man, the one for smalnesse, as crums, and scattered	241	Priest 10		27
SMART				
Will canker both, yett thou alone shallt smart:	13	Ch.-Porch	W	166
All my delight, so all my smart:	62	Afflict.2		13
With scatter'd smart,	90	Afflict.4		9
Left all joyes to feel all smart -	115	Dialogue		31
For many weeks of lingring pain and smart	154	Glimpse		4
For well he knows, if but one grief and smart	159	Jos.coat		5
Ah my deare Father, ease my smart!	165	The Crosse		31
SMARTS				
You allwayes feare to feele those smarts	210	Paradox	D	31
SMELL				
Here will I smell my remnant out, and tie	94	Life		2
Making my minde to smell my fatall day;	94	Life		11
Fit, while ye liv'd, for smell or ornament,	94	Life		14
Your hony drops: presse not to smell them here:	120	Providence		118
I once more smell the dew and rain,	166	The Flower		38
To subdue the smell of sinne;	181	Banquet		15
but reverend, and clean, without spots, or dust, or smell;	228	Priest 3		11
though he even creep into it, and though it smell never so lothsomly.	249	Priest 14		5
Well may hee smell fire, whose gowne burnes.	325	Proverbs		138
The best smell is bread, the best savour, salt,	346	Proverbs		741
SMELLS				
This broth of smells, that feeds and fats my minde.	175	The Odour		10
Of all smells, bread: of all tasts, salt.	326	Proverbs		166
SMILE				
And fathers smile for you, to feel his frown:	34	Sacrifice		223
And fathers smile to feele for you his frown:	34	Sacrifice	W	223
SMIL'D				
He smil'd and said as he did go,	151	The Bag		17
SMILING				
Love took my hand, and smiling did reply,	189	Love 3		11
SMIT'ST				
For thou upon the cheek-bone smit'st	217	Psalm III	D	19
SMITH				
No smith can make such locks, but they have keyes:	126	Confession		17
The Smith and his penny both are black.	327	Proverbs		195
SMOKE				
To smoke & fume	49	Repentance	W	29
SMOOTH				
O smooth my rugged heart, and there	45	Nature		13
See the smooth face of God, without a frown	77	Ang.&Sts.		2
How smooth are silks compared with a stake,	120	Providence		123

SMOOTH (cont'd)	PAGE	TITLE		LINE
Smooth open hearts no fastning have; but fiction	126	Confession		23
Will not a verse run smooth that bears thy name?	206	Walton 1		11
A rugged stone growes smooth from hand to hand.	332	Proverbs		316
SMOTHER				
To sinne, or sinne to smother;	53	H.Commun.		34
The Church shall come, & Sinne the Church shall smother:	197	Ch.-Milit.		266
SNARLES				
other threds or skenes of silk, full of snarles and incumbrances:	373	Letters		5
SNATCHT				
saw their parents and kindred snatcht away in the midst of their	291	Cornaro		9
SNEAKED				
Thus Sinne in Egypt sneaked for a while;	193	Ch.-Milit.		121
SNEAKINGLY				
Doe all things like a man, not sneakingly:	11	Ch.-Porch		121
SNOTTY				
Better a snotty child, then his nose wip'd off.	348	Proverbs		828
SNOW				
Like snow in May,	165	The Flower		6
My comforts drop and melt away like snow:	169	The Answer		1
A snow yeare, a rich yeare.	325	Proverbs		125
Whether you boyle snow or pound it,	327	Proverbs		180
The corne hides it self in the snow, as an old man in furrs.	329	Proverbs		241
The filth under the white snow, the sunne discovers.	338	Proverbs		495
Under water, famine; under snow, bread.	339	Proverbs		516
SNOWS				
They would great frosts and snows destroy:	138	The Size		40
SNUDGE				
And snudge in quiet: now he scorns increase;	127	Giddinesse		11
SNUFFES				
When once those snuffes are ta'ne away,	171	Self-cond.		22
SO				
Continence hath his joy: weigh both; and so	7	Ch.-Porch		17
And winne thy selfe: Compare the joyes & so	7	Ch.-Porch	W	23
Because to shun them also is so cheap:	9	Ch.-Porch		68
Not that they all are so; but that the most	10	Ch.-Porch		95
Not that they are all so; but that the most	10	Ch.-Porch	W	95
A mast'ring minde; so both are lost thereby:	10	Ch.-Porch		104
Thou liv'st by rule. What doth not so, but man?	12	Ch.-Porch		134
Thou liv'st by rule. What does not so, but man?	12	Ch.-Porch	W	134
One common waight will press downe both, yet so	13	Ch.-Porch	W	167
None is so wastefull as the scraping dame.	13	Ch.-Porch		173
Old courtiers know this; therefore set out so,	14	Ch.-Porch		185
If yet thou love game at so deere a rate,	14	Ch.-Porch		199
But know, that nothing can so foolish be,	15	Ch.-Porch		206
Thy self the worse, and so the distance greater.	16	Ch.-Porch		260
For so thou dost thy self and him a pleasure:	18	Ch.-Porch		296
So shalt thou humble and magnanimous be:	19	Ch.-Porch		332
As gunnes destroy, so may a little sling.	20	Ch.-Porch		352
As swords cause death, so may a little sting.	20	Ch.-Porch	W	352
Strike off all scores; none are so cleare as they.	20	Ch.-Porch		360
For this French sluttery which so currant goes:	21	Ch.-Porch	W	368
Write, So much giv'n to God; thou shalt be heard.	21	Ch.-Porch		382
God then deals blessings: If a king did so,	22	Ch.-Porch		389
For all the week thy food so oft he gave thee.	22	Ch.-Porch		392
Christ purg'd his temple; so must thou thy heart.	23	Ch.-Porch		423
Or that which groneth to be so,	25	Superlim		7
Not half so sweet as my sweet sacrifice:	27	Sacrifice		19
As Moses face was vailed, so is mine,	31	Sacrifice		138
As Moses face was vailed, so was mine,	31	Sacrifice	W	138
So they in me denie themselves all pitie:	31	Sacrifice		143
Which each one calls for so with utmost breath,	31	Sacrifice		146
So sits the earths great curse in Adams fall	32	Sacrifice		165
Upon my head: so I remove it all	32	Sacrifice		166
Alas! I did so, when I left my crown	34	Sacrifice		222
Alas! I did so, when I lost my crown	34	Sacrifice	W	222
That as sinne came, so Sacraments might flow:	34	Sacrifice		247
A man so wrung with pains, that all his hair,	37	The Agonie		9
In so much dregs the quintessence is small:	38	The Sinner		9
Each sinne may so.	39	Good Fri.		20
Since nothing Lord can bee so good	39	Good Fri.	W	21
That when sinne spies so many foes,	39	Good Fri.		25
So many hearts on earth, and yet not one	40	Sepulchre		3
Was writ in stone; so thou, which also art	41	Sepulchre		18
And so should perish, but that nothing can,	41	Sepulchre		22
Can not make up so brave a feast	42	Easter	W	25
Thou didst so punish sinne,	43	East.wings		13
So when I view my sinnes, mine eyes remove	43	H. Bapt.1		3
You taught the book of life my name, that so	44	H. Bapt.1		12
So many joyes I writ down for my part,	46	Afflict.1		3
I looked on thy furniture so fine,	46	Afflict.1		7
I looked on thy furniture so rich,	46	Afflict.1	W	7
That so the broken bones may joy,	49	Repentance		32
Lord, how couldst thou so much appease	49	Faith		1
That apprehension cur'd so well my foot,	50	Faith		11
Beleeves so too, and lets me go.	50	Faith		16
My Creditour beleev'd so too.	50	Faith	W	16
For so thou should'st without me still have been,	52	H.Commun.		5
Hatching my tender heart so long,	59	Whitsunday		3
So wee may cease to suck: to praise thee, never.	59	Whitsunday	W	24
All my delight, so all my smart:	62	Afflict.2		13

SO (cont'd)	PAGE	TITLE		LINE
That thou shouldst it so eye, and wooe,	62	Mattens		10
So devils are our sinnes in perspective.	63	Sinne 2		10
Sure I shall do so, and much more:	66	Ch.-mus.		10
So I do lay the want of my desire,	66	Ch.-lock		7
Guiltles so farr;	66	Ch.-lock	W	10
Which looks so firm and strong,	66	Ch.-floore		2
Could build so strong in a weak heart.	67	Ch.-floore		20
Did weep so fast, that the tears trickling down	71	Humilitie		26
Against the beasts: so joyntly bandying,	71	Humilitie		29
Against the beasts: so joyntly banding,	71	Humilitie	V	29
So loose or easie, that a ruffling winde	72	Constancie		7
Who still is right, and prayes to be so still.	73	Constancie		35
So much breath to a sigh, what's then behinde?	73	Afflict.3		9
So well as there?	74	The Starre		4
So disengag'd from sinne and sicknesse,	74	The Starre		13
That so among the rest I may	74	The Starre		25
O day so calm, so bright:	75	Sunday	W	1
Since there is no place so alone,	75	Sunday		20
Whence com'st thou, that thou art so fresh and fine?	77	Avarice		2
Surely thou didst so little contribute	77	Avarice		5
Who do not so;	78	Ang.&Sts.		28
So we freeze on,	79	Employm.2		29
That so thy favours granting my request,	80	Deniall		28
His beams shall cheer my breast, and both so twine,	81	Christmas		33
Taught me to live here so, That still one eye	85	Coloss.		7
So that we need not say, Where's this command?	86	Vanitie 1		26
The Church is so to me.	86	Lent		12
Sweet day, so cool, so calm, so bright,	87	Vertue		1
Nothing hath got so farre,	91	Man		19
So brave a Palace built; O dwell in it,	92	Man		50
Till then, afford us so much wit;	92	Man		52
So we may bee to Thee.	92	Man	W	54
Who hath dealt his mercies so,	92	Antiphon 2		4
Who did so sweetly deaths sad taste convey,	94	Life		10
Do not so well agree.	95	Submission		16
That planted Paradise was not so firm,	97	Afflict.5		2
My God, so temper joy and wo,	97	Afflict.5		23
Yet Lord, instruct us so to die,	99	Mortific.		35
So our clay hearts, ev'n when we crouch	101	Miserie		39
Such was their lustre, they did so excell,	102	Jordan 2		2
So did I weave my self into the sense.	103	Jordan 2		14
So I bespoke me much insinuation:	103	Jordan 2	W	14
Ease, Power, and Love; I value prayer so,	103	Prayer 2		20
So great are thy perfections,	104	Obedience		24
Is not so deare to thee as one good grone.	106	Sion		18
So many yeares baptiz'd, and not appeare?	108	Home		27
That chains us by the teeth so fast?	108	Home		38
Which way so-e're I look, I see.	108	Home		50
Hath kiss'd so long her painted shrines,	110	Brit. Ch.		16
She in the valley is so shie	110	Brit. Ch.		19
To whom the starres shine not so fair, as eyes;	111	Vanitie 2		3
He so farre thy good did plot,	113	Businesse		23
To thy wretch so full of stains;	114	Dialogue		7
So the way to fit me for it,	115	Dialogue		19
So the way is none of mine:	115	Dialogue		22
Who dost so strongly and so sweetly move,	117	Providence		31
So both the flower doth stay, and hony run.	118	Providence		68
And as thy house is full, so I adore	119	Providence		93
And none can know thy works, which are so many,	121	Providence		143
And so complete, but onely he that owes them.	121	Providence		144
To honour thee: and so I give thee praise	121	Providence		147
To honour thee; and so each hymne thy fame	121	Providence		151
And so my sinnes ascend three stories high,	122	Sinnes rd.		14
And this is that makes life so long,	123	Time		19
Thou that hast giv'n so much to me,	123	Gratefulnes		1
What show'd so well.	125	Peace		18
With so much earnestnesse you do pursue,	125	Peace		41
Doth shut them out, so that they cannot enter;	126	Confession		20
His minde is so.	127	Giddinesse		16
So now each Christian hath his journeys spann'd:	128	Bunch Gr.		10
The greatnesse shew'd the owner. So I went	129	Love unkn.		29
Did oft possesse me, so that when I pray'd,	130	Love unkn.		58
So must he sip and think	131	Mans medly		22
So he must sip and think	131	Mans medly	V	22
So is his trouble.	131	Mans medly		26
Just so the other heav'n they also serve,	134	Divinitie		5
What is so shrill as silent tears?	137	Familie		20
Dread Lord, said I, so oft my good;	139	Artillerie		13
I must be so, if I am mine.	139	Artillerie		30
Where thou didst lately so triumph and shine,	140	Ch.-rents		2
And shows it so? Indeed Christs precious bloud	140	Ch.-rents		12
And so I came to phansies medow strow'd	142	Pilgrimage		7
And so I came to Fancies medow strow'd	142	Pilgrimage	V	7
So to cares cops I came, and there got through	142	Pilgrimage		11
My hill was further: so I flung away,	142	Pilgrimage		31
After so foul a journey death is fair,	142	Pilgrimage		35
As neither good, nor one: so oft divisions	147	Offering		14
Which hath been broken now so long,	150	Longing		74
Resolv'd to light; and so one day	151	The Bag		11
Should crie so loud, untill the trump were drown'd,	152	The Jews		10

SO (cont'd)

	PAGE	TITLE		LINE
Not so, my heart: but there is fruit,	153	The Collar		17
Thou cam'st but now; wilt thou so soon depart,	154	Glimpse		2
The wheel shall go, so that thy stay be short.	155	Glimpse		27
So high a torture? Is such poyson bought?	155	Assurance		3
That all was not so fair, as I conceiv'd,	155	Assurance		8
So that again I now am mine,	157	Clasping		5
So mine thou art, that something more	157	Clasping		12
And so take up at use good store:	159	Praise 3		40
So strength first made a way;	160	The Pulley		6
So both should losers be.	160	The Pulley		15
Blest Order, which in power dost so excell,	160	Priesthood		1
Blest Order, which in power doth so excell,	160	Priesthood	V	1
But since those great ones, be they ne're so great,	161	Priesthood		19
So that at once both feeder, dish, and meat	161	Priesthood		21
What edge so keen,	163	The Search		54
What point so piercing can appeare	163	The Search		55
So doth thy nearenesse bear the bell,	163	The Search		59
So much desir'd, is giv'n, to take away	164	The Crosse		9
So that, ev'n when my hopes seem to be sped,	165	The Crosse		23
After so many deaths I live and write;	166	The Flower		37
Before a court, ev'n that above so cleare,	167	Dotage		16
So in one word our Lords humilitie	168	The Sonne		11
In that dark state of tears: to all, that so	169	The Answer		12
Thou so much worse, that thou shalt be no more.	169	Dial.-Anth		10
That so in purenesse thou mayst him adore,	170	Water-crs.		9
If thy first glance so powerfull be,	172	The Glance		17
So neither shall my praise.	173	23 Psalme		24
So neither shall thy praise.	173	23 Psalme	V	24
So to bring in wherewith to wash:	173	Marie Magd		17
So holy in my head,	174	Aaron		21
So do these words a sweet content,	174	The Odour		4
My servant were a little so,	175	The Odour		12
And so this new commerce and sweet	175	The Odour		29
So Thou art still my God, be out of fear.	176	Forerunners		10
So all within be livelier then before.	177	Forerunners		36
So this flower doth judge and sentence	178	The Rose		25
And so found me on the ground.	182	Banquet		36
Who hath done so much for me.	182	Banquet		48
Can so afflict or so affright,	183	A Parodie		14
Nothing can be so mean,	184	The Elixer		14
Nothing can be so low,	184	The Elixer	W	14
So live and like, that I may know thy wayes,	185	A Wreath		10
So void of sinne,	187	Judgement		9
So I did sit and eat.	189	Love 3		18
Spices come from the East; so did thy Spouse,	190	Ch.-Milit.		13
Till all depart: so went the Church her way,	191	Ch.-Milit.		33
Till all be gone. so went the Church her way,	191	Ch.-Milit.	W	33
So they might still, and point us out the place	192	Ch.-Milit.		85
To credit him, and so discredit those	193	Ch.-Milit.	W	137
Cheat the most subtill nations. Who so coy,	194	Ch.-Milit.		150
So trimme, as Greece and Egypt? yet their hearts	194	Ch.-Milit.		151
So spruse, as Greece and Egypt? yet their hearts	194	Ch.-Milit.	W	151
So now being Priest he plainly did professe	195	Ch.-Milit.		173
And having conquer'd, did so strangely rule,	196	Ch.-Milit.		203
So both together are one Antichrist,	196	Ch.-Milit.		206
The pattern, but not so in vertuous deeds;	196	Ch.-Milit.		222
So though Sinne made his latter seat the better,	196	Ch.-Milit.		223
So though Sinne made his later seat the better,	196	Ch.-Milit.	W	223
So Sinne shall trace and dog her instantly:	197	Ch.-Milit.		260
So also did the Church by going west	198	Ch.-Milit.		275
Whether in these gifts thou bee so	200	H. Commun.	W	2
Or rather so, as thou alone	200	H. Commun.	W	4
Or give mee that, so I have more	201	H. Commun.	W	47
Yet Thou art not so dark, since I know this,	203	Even-song	W	17
Are so, as for the present, I did move	204	Persever.	W	3
Cover the Earth, so doth thy Majesty:	206	Walton 2		3
This certain Anchor adde a Seal, and so	439	Walton 5		6
He gave the Seale, and so left o're.	439	Walton 5		14
He gave his soul, and so gave o're.	439	Walton 5	V	14
He gave this Seal, and, so gave ore.	439	Walton 6		2
So by the Other, you may read in mee	209	L. Bacon	D	5
So Blackamoores repute us fowle, and wee	210	Paradox	D	9
So tremblinge may	210	Paradox	D	23
Splendour from darknes. So close sits the crowne	212	Bohemia	D	37
The wicked are not so, but they	215	Psalm I	D	13
But, Lord, how long so much perplex'd	220	Psalm VI	D	7
that er'st so sorely vexed me,	220	Psalm VI	D	26
if I so guilty be:	221	Psalm VII	D	10
So shall the people round about	221	Psalm VII	D	25
as farre as wee can in pleasing of him, who hath done so much for us.	224	Priest		13
Let not Chaplains think themselves so free, as many of them do,	226	Priest 2		19
even so farre as reproofe to their very face, when occasion cals,	226	Priest 2		30
and shall be so farre from that which they seek with their	226	Priest 2		34
that the world should so much value wealth, which in the day of wrath	227	Priest 3		20
The Parson doth not so, but orders his Life in such a fashion,	227	Priest 3		31
as knowing, that if he be not so, he wil quickly be discovered,	228	Priest 3		6
As he doth not so study others, as to neglect the grace of God in	229	Priest 4		19
so doth he assure himself, that God in all ages hath had his	229	Priest 4		21
so neither hath God opened, or will open all to one, that there may	229	Priest 4		24
according as his audience is, so he useth one, or other;	230	Priest 5		17

SO (cont'd)

	PAGE	TITLE	LINE
so that they neither decline to the right hand, nor to the left.	230	Priest 5	21
lust, and when not, and so in many circumstances of actions.	230	Priest 5	30
so he is content to expresse this outwardly to the utmost of his	231	Priest 6	11
knowing that no Sermon moves them so much to a reverence,	231	Priest 6	14
yet not so slow neither, as to let the fervency of the supplicant	231	Priest 6	17
so that while they answer, As it was in the beginning, &c.	231	Priest 6	33
have glorified him as wel as now, and that he shall have so for ever.	232	Priest 6	1
notwithstanding his instruction that they ought not to be so,	232	Priest 6	16
but even to let the world sinke, so they do their duty;	232	Priest 6	16
that so in the mouth of two or three witnesses the truth may be more	232	Priest 7	29
as of those of antient times, so especially of the late ones;	233	Priest 7	7
and think it behoves them to be so, when God is so neer them,	233	Priest 7	10
them to be so, when God is so neer them, and even over their heads.	233	Priest 7	10
so that the auditors may plainly perceive that every word is	233	Priest 7	31
So Isa. 64. Oh that thou would'st rent the Heavens, that thou wouldst	234	Priest 7	2
and terrible, as great in mercy, so great in judgement:	234	Priest 7	32
him then weary, and so he grows from not relishing, to loathing.	235	Priest 7	14
and seems to himselfe so as a Market-man is, when the Market day	235	Priest 8	18
so he closeth it, humbly beseeching the Almighty to pardon and accept	236	Priest 8	26
unto God, and as his grace shall direct him, so let him proceed.	237	Priest 9	6
and hath so decreed in his heart, that he will keep himself a virgin,	237	Priest 9	17
and wondreth not so much at their patient suffering, and cheerfull	237	Priest 9	29
the Parson be unmarryed, and means to continue so, he doth at least,	238	Priest 9	25
so is he to his wife also, counting nothing so much his owne,	238	Priest 9	34
counting nothing so much his owne, as that he may be unjust unto it.	238	Priest 9	35
reserving so much of the affaires, as serve for a diversion for him;	238	Priest 9	38
yet never so giving over the raines, but that he sometimes looks how	239	Priest 9	1
(in case he think fit to do so) he takes care not to put them	239	Priest 10	34
and were it not his duty to have them so, it were his profit,	240	Priest 10	14
his profit, for none are so well served, as by religious servants,	240	Priest 10	14
so that his family is a Schoole of Religion, and they all account,	240	Priest 10	21
so that as in the house of those that are skill'd in Musick,	240	Priest 10	29
so in the house of a Preacher, all are preachers.	240	Priest 10	31
so that all his house knowes, that there is no help for a fault done,	240	Priest 10	34
so Friday his day of Humiliation, which he celebrates not only	241	Priest 10	37
so that to eat little, and that unpleasant, is the naturall rule	242	Priest 10	10
nor suffer others in his house that are so, to keep it;	242	Priest 10	30
he so distinguisheth, that he keeps his money for the poor,	243	Priest 11	7
and sutably to their needs, then so much given in meat at dinner.	243	Priest 11	17
so that in the compasse of the year, hee hath them all with him,	243	Priest 11	19
that so both they may be encouraged to persevere, and others spurred	243	Priest 11	25
yet that will not be so:	243	Priest 11	29
men to Piety, and is content, if at least so, they will become good:	244	Priest 11	1
So the Countrey Parson, who is a diligent observer, and tracker	244	Priest 11	1
and so by continuall, and fresh bounties, unexpected to them,	244	Priest 12	32
So is his charity in effect a Sermon.	245	Priest 12	16
so doth he also to those at his door, whom God puts in his way,	245	Priest 12	19
so that being once satisfied, he allows his Charity some blindnesse	245	Priest 12	26
that so the thanks may go the right way, and thither onely,	245	Priest 12	33
So doth hee also before giving make them say their Prayers first,	245	Priest 12	34
So that they excellently score out the way, and fully, and exactly	246	Priest 13	32
finds the persons of the house imployed, so he formes his discourse.	247	Priest 14	12
but that they so labour, as neither to labour anxiously,	247	Priest 14	26
he adviseth them so to labour for wealth and maintenance,	248	Priest 14	5
that so they go on more cheerfully in their vocation, and himself be	248	Priest 14	11
and therefore he lays his discourse so, that he comes to the point	248	Priest 14	20
so when the offence is publicke, and against God, I am then to follow	248	Priest 14	28
though he even creep into it, and though it smell never so lothsomly.	249	Priest 14	6
and so much the rather doth he so, as his accesse to the poor is more	249	Priest 14	7
that so the hunger and thirst after it may come rather from	250	Priest 15	5
as a child, and forgives, so hee may have any signe of amendment;	250	Priest 16	14
so also when after many admonitions, any continue to be refractory,	250	Priest 16	15
before hee proceede to disinheriting, or perhaps never goes so far;	250	Priest 16	18
so neither touching the intermediate days of Conversion.	250	Priest 16	21
This was not so well said, as it might have been forborn;	252	Priest 18	9
or, So farr indeed what you say is true, and well said;	252	Priest 18	11
so especially to his Diocesan, honouring him both in word,	253	Priest 19	6
So, if any neighbouring village be overburdened with poore,	254	Priest 19	1
And so forward, requiring answers to all these, and helping	256	Priest 21	12
since man is so miserable, what is to be done?	257	Priest 21	3
This familiar illustration made the answer so plaine, that he was	257	Priest 21	6
Practice which the Parson so much commends to all his	257	Priest 21	16
of questions in the one, so they farre exceed them in the other.	257	Priest 21	23
with himself, how or what behaviour to assume for so holy things.	257	Priest 22	28
The time of every ones first receiving is not so much by yeers,	258	Priest 22	32
all reverence himself, so he administers to none but to the reverent.	259	Priest 22	11
neither can all the people so order their affairs as to receive just	259	Priest 22	26
nor the Church-Wardens so well take notice who receive thrice,	259	Priest 22	28
and so the thing passeth with more authority, and lesse envy.	260	Priest 23	12
so that if the poorest man of the Parish detain but a pin unjustly	260	Priest 23	14
but when he hath so done, then he assumes the Parson, and exhorts	260	Priest 23	16
Now as the Parson is in Law, so is he in sicknesse also:	260	Priest 23	28
and so not be drowned altogether in the works of their vocation,	261	Priest 23	23
So, where the Apothecary useth either for loosing, Rubarb,	261	Priest 23	32
and so shuts them out of his family, esteeming that there is no spice	261	Priest 23	38
except the person bee so poor, that he is not able to reward	262	Priest 23	14
for as hee is Charitable, so he is just also.	262	Priest 23	15
and to give him power so to fit his discourse to them, that it may	262	Priest 24	23
and how then should the best be so, at least in fundamentall things,	263	Priest 24	4
So for Scandall: what scandall is, when given or taken;	263	Priest 24	7

SO (cont'd)

	PAGE	TITLE	LINE
be wanting to them in Doctrine, to whom he is so gracious in Life.	263	Priest 24	21
the Countrey Parson proceeds so farre as to call in Authority,	263	Priest 25	22
and makes so much the more of him, as before he alienated himselfe;	263	Priest 25	33
So likewise there are some persons, who abstain not even from known	264	Priest 26	9
So a man dining, eats at first lawfully;	264	Priest 26	22
So a man storing up mony for his necessary provisions, both in	264	Priest 26	25
sometimes too salt, and so not competent nourishment, I am Covetous.	265	Priest 26	22
throw into the fire, and so they pay them their wages, all is well.	265	Priest 26	26
or consider it so narrowly, which yet ought to be done,	265	Priest 26	31
so that men must eat neither to the disturbance of their health,	266	Priest 26	13
of their health, and so they will stand to the pain, all is well.	266	Priest 26	20
by a Common tradition, and vulgar knowledge are reputed to be so.	266	Priest 26	27
none must eat so as to disable themselves from a fit discharging	266	Priest 26	29
So that if after dinner they are not fit (or un-weeldy) either	266	Priest 26	31
but that they must rise so, as that it is not meate or drinke that	266	Priest 26	35
and tarryed so long at it, that they would have fainted,	267	Priest 26	23
made food miraculously, then suffered so good desires to miscarry.	267	Priest 26	25
this is foretold, that it shall be so still, until things be no more.	268	Priest 28	15
if the contempt shall proceed so far as to do any thing punishable	268	Priest 28	31
that so the sentence lighting upon one, the example may reach to all.	269	Priest 28	1
or being so, the Parson think it in his discretion either unfit,	269	Priest 28	3
and so between gentle reasoning, and pitying, he overcomes the evill:	269	Priest 28	14
that so they may know their duty, and keep their oath the better;	270	Priest 29	15
he wisheth them by no means to spare any, though never so great;	270	Priest 29	19
so that corne doth not grow by any other vertue, then by that which	271	Priest 30	4
so that though the corn do grow, and be preserved in that act by his	271	Priest 30	14
So that if a farmer should depend upon God all the yeer,	271	Priest 30	28
So that if a Farmer hath both a faire harvest, and that also well	271	Priest 30	38
So is the carnall and wilfull man with the worm of the grave in this	272	Priest 30	12
This is so necessary, and essentiall to a Christian, that he cannot	272	Priest 31	23
Now it so happens, that the godly petitioner upon some emergent	272	Priest 31	29
which none can perform so wel in trouble, as in calmness.	273	Priest 31	2
And of this he is so to assure himself, as to admit no scruple,	273	Priest 31	10
he may behave himself so as befits so great a presence;	273	Priest 31	26
he may behave himself so as befits so great a presence;	273	Priest 31	27
so much the rather ought he to proceed, as that by this he may take	273	Priest 31	31
So that if any scruple arise, I will throw it away, and be most	273	Priest 31	37
diseases of the time, that so, when his occasions carry him abroad,	274	Priest 32	6
So that even in Paradise man had a calling, and how much more out	274	Priest 32	21
So that our Saviours selling is so far from crossing Saint Pauls	275	Priest 32	3
so it exceed not bounds, for every one to imploy himselfe	275	Priest 32	28
the house-keepers Family be so small, and his dexterity so great,	275	Priest 32	37
and his dexterity so great, that he have leisure to look out,	276	Priest 32	1
who hath so many dispersed Officers at his beck throughout	276	Priest 32	10
and ripenesse of judgement for so excellent a Place, not to refuse,	276	Priest 32	17
These are so far from deterring any good man from the place,	276	Priest 32	22
Husbandman labours for them, so must they fight for, and defend them,	277	Priest 32	19
So that the Parson having studied, and mastered all his lusts	278	Priest 33	21
hath ever so many sermons ready penn'd, as he hath victories.	278	Priest 33	24
is a Physitian so far as he meetes with the same disease,	278	Priest 33	27
Just so it is in Divinity, and that not without manifest reason:	278	Priest 33	32
that so the body may joyn in the grief, as it did in the sin;	279	Priest 33	27
but that, so the other acts be, that is not necessary:	279	Priest 33	28
so that he as truly repents, who performes the other acts	279	Priest 33	29
to be in one or the other state, so he applies himselfe to them.	280	Priest 34	13
so will they last the longer, and when they depart, returne	280	Priest 34	29
So let them go, and find some poore afflicted soul, and there be	281	Priest 34	2
how the windes should blow so much as they can, and the sea rage so	281	Priest 34	20
and the sea rage so much as it can, and all things do what they can,	281	Priest 34	21
by taking away so much as the usuall seasons of summer and winter,	281	Priest 34	24
there may be so evident, though unused a proof of Divinity taken from	281	Priest 34	32
living then in their Countrey under so many miracles were a stranger	282	Priest 34	9
not so much doubting a God, as that he is theirs;	283	Priest 34	6
So that man, which way soever he turnes, hath two pledges of Gods	283	Priest 34	17
and this as the more faulty in him, so the more glorious in God.	283	Priest 34	21
so that to favour them therein is to win their hearts, and to oppose	283	Priest 35	29
he is so farre from condemning such assemblies, that he rather	284	Priest 35	13
that Blessing the people is in so little use with his brethren:	285	Priest 36	2
do so either out of niceness, because they like the salutations,	285	Priest 36	4
which conformity and fashionableness is so exceeding unbefitting	285	Priest 36	7
But that which the Apostles used so diligently in their writings,	285	Priest 36	9
so that even ill Priests may blesse.	285	Priest 36	23
So in the Old Testament Elisha cursed the children, 2 Kings 2. 24.	285	Priest 36	25
So did St. Paul, 2 Tim. 4. 14. and 1 Tim. 1. 20.	285	Priest 36	31
so that they are so far from craving this benefit from their ghostly	286	Priest 36	12
so that they are so far from craving this benefit from their ghostly	286	Priest 36	13
men think, so they speak truth, they may disclose anothers fault,	286	Priest 37	31
which is so exceeding useful, and hath taken so deep roote,	287	Priest 37	8
and hath taken so deep roote, that it seems the very life	287	Priest 37	9
may talk, so they do it not with sport, but commiseration;)	287	Priest 37	13
which hath so much advanced Charity, and ranked backbiters among	287	Priest 37	23
so neither is he that defames him, whom the Law would have defamed,	287	Priest 37	28
so may they their good name, and the possession thereof,	287	Priest 37	32
So that it is so far from being a fault to discover such offenders,	287	Priest 37	37
So that it is so far from being a fault to discover such offenders,	287	Priest 37	38
so that then where sin abounded, not death, but grace superabounded;	288	Priest	24
so neither may thy word, but accomplish that for which it is given.	289	Priest	31
and do so for thy blessed Son's sake, in whose sweet and pleasing	289	Priest	34
so man did eat Angels food:	290	Priest	9
still striving & prospering so long within us, untill our obedience	290	Priest	11

SO (cont'd)

	PAGE	TITLE		LINE
a great desire to know the way of my life, and how I came to be so.	291	Cornaro		12
and abhorring from so sudden an end, and finding my self continually	292	Cornaro		18
and saw that it was no hard thing to do so, but the proper duty	292	Cornaro		32
I so addicted my self to this course of life, that I never went	292	Cornaro		33
If Temperance had so much power as to bring me health; . . .	293	Cornaro		3
with a full stomack, but so as I might well both eat and drink more.	293	Cornaro		19
was not onely freed from all those evils which had so long beset me,	293	Cornaro		21
Yet could I not so avoid all these, but that now and then I fell into	293	Cornaro		37
So that I can truly say, That they who in these two things that enter	294	Cornaro		3
(a thing usuall to disorderly lives) which increased so much in them,	294	Cornaro		19
which must needs so temper the humours of the bodie, that they could	295	Cornaro		8
and so without other remedie or inconvenience I recovered; . .	295	Cornaro		12
that old age could not be sustained with so little meat and drink;	295	Cornaro		22
This addition after ten dayes wrought so much upon me, that . .	296	Cornaro		14
so that all things were troublesome to me:	296	Cornaro		16
nothing holp me, but that exact rule which I had so long continued.	296	Cornaro		29
For the Temperance of so many yeares spent all ill humours, . .	296	Cornaro		32
was but a little excesse, in a few dayes had so soon overthrown me.	297	Cornaro		6
of diseases, so that he shall need neither Physick nor Physician:	297	Cornaro		21
that an orderly life is so hard a thing that it cannot be kept.	298	Cornaro		36
so did Plato also, and Isocrates, and Tullie, and many others	298	Cornaro		38
Paul the third, and Cardinal Bembo, who therefore lived so long;	299	Cornaro		2
so that we can eat but a very little, wherewith she is very well	299	Cornaro		27
So that a sick man, whether he hath lived heretofore orderly	299	Cornaro		29
Wherefore since an orderly life is so profitable, so vertuous,	300	Cornaro		3
since an orderly life is so profitable, so vertuous, so decent,	300	Cornaro		3
so vertuous, so decent, and so holy, it is worthy by all means to be	300	Cornaro		4
so decent, and so holy, it is worthy by all means to be embraced;	300	Cornaro		4
No man that followes it, is bound to eat and drink so little as I:	300	Cornaro		7
So that he which is offended with no kinde of meat and drink,	300	Cornaro		14
to expose himself to so many dangers of diseases and death, . .	300	Cornaro		22
and I am so nimble, that I can easily get on horseback without	300	Cornaro		34
being so built by me according to the rules of Architecture,	301	Cornaro		12
because many wayes thither are so ordered, that they all meet and end	301	Cornaro		21
In former time it was not so, because the place was moorish . .	301	Cornaro		26
So that I can truly say, That I have both given God a Temple,	301	Cornaro		31
so that any simple fare is more savourie to me now, then heretofore,	302	Cornaro		9
So great is the power and efficacie of that Temperance which ever	302	Cornaro		20
whereas I by the experience of so many yeares have learned to give	303	Cornaro		20
Since therefore a temperate life is so happie and pleasant a thing;	303	Cornaro		30
in any thing I forsake that Temperance which I have found so good,	303	Cornaro		35
one to understand and expresse so clearely and excellently the intent	304	Valdesso		21
and setting his merit forth so piously, for which I doe so love him,	305	Valdesso		6
for which I doe so love him, that were there nothing else, . .	305	Valdesso		7
And in so doing they doe not sever their trust from God. . .	307	Valdesso		1
so it be understood with the former distinction, for Fomes is	308	Valdesso		14
Indeed he that shall so attend to the bark of the letter, . .	309	Valdesso		29
so are wee to doe with the Scriptures and this is the use . .	310	Valdesso		30
so that it is plain the Authour had a very reverend esteem . .	311	Valdesso	V	6
So likewise are the godly in some sort exempt from Lawes, . .	315	Valdesso		32
so need not Abraham's Equivocation, nor Paul's neither, .	316	Valdesso		6
So may a warre be just on both sides, and was just in the Canaanites	316	Valdesso		29
so a Scholar judgeth in his study, and censureth this or that;	317	Valdesso		2
whence come so many Books of severall mens opinions: . . .	317	Valdesso		3
for so he useth the same word in Consideration 68 ad finem. . .	317	Valdesso	V	8
how this opinion could befall so good a man as it seems Valdesso	317	Valdesso		31
God in all ages have ever held in so pretious esteem the word of God,	317	Valdesso		33
So S. Peter bidding the dispersed Hebrews attend to the word till	318	Valdesso		17
So that the Word hath the precedence even of Revelations and Visions.	318	Valdesso		24
And so his whole discourse and sevenfold observation falls . .	318	Valdesso		25
so it may be a fruit of it, and an exaltation. 1 John 5. 14.	319	Valdesso		13
Who is so deafe, as he that will not heare?	323	Proverbs		79
Who is so deafe, as he who will not heare?	323	Proverbs	V	79
He that is warme, thinkes all so.	323	Proverbs		80
The Lyon is not so fierce as they paint him.	330	Proverbs		289
Who so once deceives is ever suspected.	335	Proverbs	V	417
'Tis hard to be wretched, but worse to be knowne so.	340	Proverbs		577
No barber shaves so close but another finds worke.	343	Proverbs		667
None is so wise, but the foole overtakes him.	345	Proverbs		734
None is so wise, but that the foole overtakes him.	345	Proverbs	V	734
Give not S. Peter so much, to leave Saint Paul nothing. . .	346	Proverbs		763
They talke of Christmas so long, that it comes.	349	Proverbs		840
So many men in Court and so many strangers.	350	Proverbs		874
You cannot make the fire so low but it will get out.	353	Proverbs		965
No Church-yard is so handsom, ...	353	Proverbs		969
The War is not don so long as my Enemy lives.	357	Proverbs	D	1051
There is no man, though never so little, ...	359	Proverbs	D	1119
No day so clear but hath dark clouds.	359	Proverbs	D	1123
No hair so small but hath his shadow.	359	Proverbs	D	1124
nor to bewail that so few are writ, that look towards God and Heaven.	363	Letters		8
of thanks for the diversity of your favours, if I sought to do so;	363	Letters		16
unto you, since I find you so willing to yield to my requests;	363	Letters		21
it is true (God knows) I am weak, yet not so, but that every day,	364	Letters		27
and I love my friends so well, as that if all things proved not well,	364	Letters		28
so that I am fain ever and anon, to buy somewhat tending towards my	364	Letters		33
so that I am fain to dyet in my Chamber at mine own cost; . .	365	Letters		2
on Fridayes and Saturdayes, I must do so, which yet sometimes I fast.	365	Letters		5
by the Patents of your perpetual favour to do so still, . .	365	Letters		25
to observe so much, as when you meet with a witty French speech,	366	Letters		10
so shall you play a good marchant, by transporting French commodities	366	Letters		11

SO (cont'd)	PAGE	TITLE		LINE
for your favours are so ancient, that they prevent my memory,	367	Letters		14
which the King would so appropriate to himselfe, as that either his	368	Letters		10
observed on Christmas day to bee so devout as to come to the Chappell	368	Letters		17
but not so great as he expected & therfore he grumblingly said that	368	Letters		32
denounced to him, told the King & so he is committed to prison.	368	Letters		37
neither can I so much as go to Bugden, and deliver your Letter,	369	Letters		15
though never so, but that I have both time and work to be Your	370	Letters		13
Can I be so happy, as to hear of both these that they succeed well?	371	Letters		9
by so much shall it make my prayers the more constant and the more	372	Letters		21
have so much power or boldness as to oppose the hope of our Joyes	372	Letters		28
of the heavens, so are earthly Troubles compar'd to heavenly Joyes;	372	Letters		30
have over Youth and Health, who are now so near those true Comforts.	372	Letters		33
and so brought up your Children that they have attain'd to the years	373	Letters		12
So that now if they do not well the falt cannot be charg'd on you;	373	Letters		14
so that the best use of them is, having, not to have them. . .	373	Letters		24
most carry themselves so, as if they not only not desir'd, . .	373	Letters		33
so that it is not left to us to rejoyce or not rejoyce: . .	374	Letters		24
the fruit of my observation, for they have lived so lovingly, lying,	375	Letters		18
I forgett all thinges, so I may doe them good who want it. . .	376	Letters		6
So I doe my part to them, lett them think of me what they will	376	Letters		6
but difficulties are so farr from cooling christians, that they whett	376	Letters		10
So prayes Your ever loving brother, G. HERBERT.	376	Letters		20
I humbly thank him, & am so far from giving you cause, to apology,	378	Letters		9
Gods earth, no not tho' the advice step so far, as to be reproof:	378	Letters		13
If so, let this of Leighton Church the care, be amongst the chiefest	378	Letters		22
the chiefest also, so also have I required Mr W. for his part.	378	Letters		23
bless you more & more, & so turn you all, in your severall wayes,	378	Letters		25
but he told her Grace, that he would by no meanes do so, urging,	379	Letters		7
so no less glad for the Heart, that God has given you & yours,	379	Letters		14
It is so long since I heard from you, that I long to heare both how	379	Letters		23
so in things naturally visible & apparent, as the course of our life	380	Woodnoth		17
so though you incline not, happily you restraine.	381	Woodnoth		9
& if upon your withdrawing it shold doe so, it would trouble your	381	Woodnoth		12
with that bloud, which useth to infuse so great and worthie Spirits.	442	Oration		15
And necessarily must the felicitie of so great Princes redound also	442	Oration		25
since you are so great both in your Princes, and your selves,	442	Oration		28
SO-E'RE				
Which way so-e're I look, I see.	108	Home		50
SOBER				
and live a sober life, expressing also the means which I have used	291	Cornaro		16
if I could constantly pursue it, to wit, A sober and orderly life:	292	Cornaro		4
might know what great power a sober and temperate life hath over our	294	Cornaro		25
ill handled by their intemperance, yet shunne a sober life: . .	298	Cornaro		25
that it makes him godly, righteous, and sober all his life long;	309	Valdesso		6
SOBRIETIE				
A Treatise of Temperance and Sobrietie:	291	Cornaro		T
I never since departed from my setled course of Sobrietie, . . .	293	Cornaro		26
SOCIETY				
Nor in the safe society	215	Psalm I	D	19
SOCRATES				
Socrates did thus in Philosophy, who held that the seeds of all	256	Priest 21		20
the singular dexterity of Socrates in this kind may be observed,	256	Priest 21		29
by the generall Providence of God, as Socrates and Aristides, &c.	308	Valdesso		13
SOEVER				
how poor or mean soever, with as joyfull a countenance, . . .	253	Priest 19		19
and the difference, hee ought to receive, of what age soever.	258	Priest 22		36
of dependance, how faire soever the opportunities present themselves.	271	Priest 30		27
which way soever he turnes, hath two pledges of Gods Love, . . .	283	Priest 34		18
SOFT				
Let me be soft and supple to thy will, ...	44	H. Bapt.2		8
Thou grew'st soft and moist with tears, ...	146	Praise 2		21
Soft words quench more then cold water.	329	Proverbs	V	263
Soft and faire goes farre.	347	Proverbs		772
SOFTENS				
of affliction, which softens, and works the stubborn heart of man;	249	Priest 15		24
SOFTNESSE				
Softnesse, and peace, and joy, and love, and blisse, ...	51	Prayer 1		9
SOIL (see also soyle)				
Trees after bearing drop their leaves for soil:	119	Providence		70
Fie, thou wilt soil thy broider'd coat, ...	176	Forerunners		23
SOILD				
Hath soild with Black) the colour of my state, ...	209	L. Bacon	D	7
SOJOURNE				
he be unmarryed, and sojourne, he never talkes with any woman alone,	237	Priest 9		11
SOLACES				
These are the delights and solaces of my old age, which is altogether	302	Cornaro		22
SOLD (see also sould)				
Shall I be scourged, flouted, boxed, sold?	35	Thanksgvng		7
Thou, who from me wast sold, ...	52	H.Commun.		3
Thou, who for me wast sold, ...	52	H.Commun.	V	3
For us was sold.	92	Antiphon 2		12
Who for man was sold, can see;	114	Dialogue		15
For he hath sold for money his deare Lord, ...	171	Self-cond.		17
because when we have sold all, and given it to the poor, . . .	274	Priest 32		33
disappointed thy Purposes, and sold our God, our glorious, . . .	288	Priest		17
A pleasure long expected is deare enough sold.	350	Proverbs		868
SOLEMNITIE				
Hath put together a solemnitie, ...	99	Mortific.		32
SOLID				
To stuffe thy minde with solid braverie;	15	Ch.-Porch		208

	PAGE	TITLE		LINE
SOLID (cont'd)				
Nor solid work, as false embroyderies;	111	Vanitie 2		4
Sure-footed griefs, solid calamities,	167	Dotage		9
SOLLICITING				
knows also that my solliciting him has been much, and my tears many	372	Letters		2
SOLOMON				
Moses pursu'd this: but King Solomon	190	Ch.-Milit.		21
David built the temple as much as Solomon because he desired it,	381	Woodnoth		20
SOLOMON'S				
When Solomons temple stood and flourished!	106	Sion		2
All Solomons sea of brasse and world of stone	106	Sion		17
SOME				
But if thou coole, then take some shame to thee	10	Ch.-Porch	W	90
Some till their ground, but let weeds choke their sonne:	10	Ch.-Porch		98
Some mark a partridge, never their childes fashion:	10	Ch.-Porch		99
Some ship them over, and the thing is done.	10	Ch.-Porch		100
Some great estates provide, but doe not breed	10	Ch.-Porch		103
Yet in thy thriving still misdoubt some evil;	13	Ch.-Porch		163
Some said, that I the Temple to the floore	28	Sacrifice		65
As he that for some robberie suffereth.	34	Sacrifice		230
Unto some Chappell, die or live.	35	Thanksgvng		28
About some land, which he had dearly bought	40	Redemption		7
To fruit or shade: at least some bird would trust	48	Afflict.1		59
Some other master out.	48	Afflict.1		64
Although there were some fourtie heav'ns, or more,	55	Temper 1		5
Thou wouldst extend me to some good,	57	Employm. 1		2
These three make up some Christians destinie:	58	H.Script.2		8
Hath some good in him, all agree.	63	Sinne 2		3
Or if some yeares with it escape,	73	Afflict.3		10
Some fruit for him that dressed me.	79	Employm.2		25
Each took his way; some would to pleasures go,	80	Deniall		8
Some to the warres and thunder	80	Deniall		9
Some place and power on me?	95	Submission		6
Some Angels us'd the first; if our relief	97	Afflict.5		15
At some fair oak, or bush, or cave, or well:	99	Decay		7
In some one corner of a feeble heart:	99	Decay		12
Or some such words in fashion;	104	Obedience		14
If some kinde man would thrust his heart	105	Obedience		42
Besides my physick, know there's some for thee:	106	Conscience		20
Some wood and nails to make a staffe or bill	106	Conscience		21
Some may dream merrily, but when they wake,	108	Home		51
The great prey on the lesse, they on some weed.	118	Providence		52
Some creatures have in winter what to eat;	118	Providence		55
When yet some places could no moisture get,	120	Providence		115
If it at length deserve some blame:	122	Time		4
Perhaps some such of old did passe,	122	Time		7
Which many wondring at, got some of those	125	Peace		29
But quickly seek some new adventure.	126	Confession		22
He is some twentie sev'rall men at least	127	Giddinesse		3
Joy, I did lock thee up: but some bad man	128	Bunch Gr.		1
And have, of whom some grounds which may improve,	129	Love unkn.		4
I found that some had stuff'd the bed with thoughts,	130	Love unkn.		51
There is some rub, some discontent,	133	The Method		3
Though some of them repine.	136	Familie		6
What though some have a fraught	137	The Size		7
Did like some torturing engine show;	141	Justice 2		10
Did like some tottering engine show;	141	Justice 2	V	10
Some call the wold;	142	Pilgrimage		14
Some call the world;	142	Pilgrimage	V	14
Some call the would;	142	Pilgrimage	V	14
Oh that some Angel might a trumpet sound;	152	The Jews		8
Of some fair church to show the sore	158	Praise 3		34
O that I might some other hearts convert,	159	Praise 3		39
For some mean stuffe whereon to show his skill:	161	Priesthood		38
Lord, dost thou some new fabrick mold,	162	The Search		25
And keep your measures for some lovers lute,	164	Grief		16
Untill I had scme place, where I might sing,	164	The Crosse		3
To some degree of spicinesse to thee!	175	The Odour		15
Hath some fond lover tic'd thee to thy bane?	176	Forerunners		21
Is some starre (fled from the sphere)	181	Banquet		10
For we consider'd thee as at some six	186	Death		5
But since our Saviours death did put some bloud	186	Death		13
Some to windes their bodie lend,	187	Dooms-day		21
Some to windes their bodies lend,	187	Dooms-day	W	21
Some in noisome vapours grow	187	Dooms-day		23
That some will turn thee to some leaves therein	187	Judgement		8
Listens behinde him, and allows some light,	191	Ch.-Milit.		32
Listens behinde him, and gives them some light,	191	Ch.-Milit.	W	32
Where some poore truths were shuffled for a bait	193	Ch.-Milit.		136
In some degree.	202	Trin.Sun.	W	4
For some relief.	204	The Knell	W	18
To praise, and on thee, Lord, some Ink bestow.	206	Walton 2		11
Perhaps some other subject I had tryed	209	L. Bacon	D	11
But it shall spy some of there victories.	212	Bohemia	D	46
To curbe some Rebell teares, which faine would flow,	213	Bohemia	D	58
to whom this discourse ariseth not) some live in the Universities,	225	Priest 2		22
some in Noble houses, some in Parishes residing on their Cures.	226	Priest 2		1
some live there in office, whose rule is that of the Apostle;	226	Priest 2		3
Some in a preparatory way, whose aim and labour must be not only	226	Priest 2		8
positively as it is, or else to illustrate some other knowledge.	228	Priest 4		17
the reading of the Scripture with some short inward ejaculation,	229	Priest 4		2

SOME (cont'd)

	PAGE	TITLE		LINE
or against some great Festivall, that he may the better celebrate it,	232	Priest 7		22
is ever very well supplyed by some able man who treads in his steps,	232	Priest 7		25
whom also he intreats to press some point, that he himself hath often	232	Priest 7		27
Some such irradiations scatteringly in the Sermon, carry great	233	Priest 7		37
some choyce Observations drawn out of the whole text, as it lyes	235	Priest 7		3
the afternoone, he thinks he hath in some measure, according to poor,	236	Priest 8		8
or in exhortaticns to some of his flock by themselves, whom his	236	Priest 8		12
either to entertaine some of his neighbours, or to be entertained	236	Priest 8		20
and devotion, scme other dayes for fasting, and hours for prayers;	237	Priest 9		25
or he takes care she shall learn it of some religious neighbour.	239	Priest 10		17
turnes his care to fit all their dispositions with some calling,	239	Priest 10		30
unpleasant to me, then some fish there, certainly to eat the flesh,	242	Priest 10		13
Having then invited some of his Parish, hee taketh his times to do	243	Priest 11		18
giving some corn outright, and selling other at under rates;	245	Priest 12		10
for that also is some kind of obligation;	245	Priest 12		19
But these he helps not without some testimony, except the evidence	245	Priest 12		21
once satisfied, he allows his Charity some blindnesse in the other;	245	Priest 12		27
antient and pious ordinance, and how necessary it is in some cases:	249	Priest 15		32
he also urgeth them to do some pious charitable works, as a necessary	249	Priest 15		32
that some are called at the eleventh houre, and therefore hee still	250	Priest 16		18
interposing sometimes some short, and honest refreshments, . .	251	Priest 17		5
least the poyson steal into some young and unwary spirits, . .	252	Priest 18		6
it judiciously, or breaks it off seasonably by some diversion.	252	Priest 18		18
having observed some defects in the Ministry, he then either in	253	Priest 19		12
or at some other time of the day, propounds among his Brethren what	253	Priest 19		13
as joyfull a countenance, as if he were to entertain some great Lord.	253	Priest 19		20
all together choosing some fitt day to carry it themselves, . .	253	Priest 19		38
hee findes some way of releeving it, and reducing the Manna,	254	Priest 19		2
and bread of Charity to some equality, representing to his people,	254	Priest 19		4
This is in some sort a discharging of God;	254	Priest 20		18
Then are there some things to be beleeved that are not seen?	256	Priest 21		9
some dialogues in Plato were worth the reading, where the singular	256	Priest 21		27
he hath gotten to himself some insight in things ordinarily incident	259	Priest 23		34
and by reading some initiatory treatises in the Law, with Daltons	260	Priest 23		1
whom he hath ever some cases to ask, when he meets with them;	260	Priest 23		4
there may happen somtimes some cases, wherein he chooseth to permit	260	Priest 23		18
hee keepes some young practicioner in his house for the benefit	260	Priest 23		34
then he keeps good correspondence with some neighbour Phisician,	260	Priest 23		37
the obscurity in some points being the exercise of the Church,	263	Priest 24		5
except some small and temporary estranging may corroborate . .	263	Priest 25		30
There are some vices, whose natures are alwayes cleer, and evident,	264	Priest 26		6
So likewise there are some persons, who abstain not even from known	264	Priest 26		10
or not in some proportion to Gods blessing upon him, is covetous.	265	Priest 26		6
and intermingles some mirth in his discourses occasionally, . .	268	Priest 27		6
the Godly have ever added some houres of prayer, as at nine,	272	Priest 31		26
that the godly petitioner upon some emergent interruption in the day,	272	Priest 31		30
he spyes some scoffing ruffian, who is likely to deride him for his	273	Priest 31		28
the casting of it on mean persons, especially in some Shires:	276	Priest 32		21
Great Horse, or exercise scme of his Military gestures [Postures].	277	Priest 32		16
and not ingaged into some Profession by their Parents, whose neglect	277	Priest 32		25
sometimes to weepe more for the losse of some temporall things,	279	Priest 33		12
some being of a more melting temper then others) consisteth in a true	279	Priest 33		22
and find some pocre afflicted soul, and there be bountifull,	281	Priest 34		2
With some of these heads enlarged, and woven into his discourse,	283	Priest 34		3
and that even some good men think, so they speak truth, . .	286	Priest 37		31
But some may say, though the Law allow this, the Gospel doth not,	287	Priest 37		21
yeare (although it may seem to some incredible) I was perfectly cured	292	Cornaro		37
and others of my kindred saw some great powerfull men pick quarrels	294	Cornaro		16
But some may say, He which lives a regular life, eating alwayes light	299	Cornaro		22
But some, too much given to Appetite, object, That a long life is no	300	Cornaro		27
I give my self to the reading of some learned book, and afterwards	301	Cornaro		6
Some times of the yeare I enjoy the pleasure of the Euganean hills,	301	Cornaro		16
Sometimes I ride to some of the neighbour-cities, that I may enjoy	301	Cornaro		34
and some notes, in which perhaps you will discover some care,	304	Valdesso		2
in which perhaps you will discover some care, which I forbare not in	304	Valdesso		3
there are some things which I like not in him, as my fragments will	304	Valdesso		16
the Saints of God may be said in some sence to have put confidence in	306	Valdesso		28
some oppose Theologicall vertues, as Uncharitablenesse opposes	308	Valdesso		6
is in some sort true because they are spiritually discerned,	315	Valdesso		31
So likewise are the godly in some sort exempt from Lawes, . .	315	Valdesso		32
of his Considerations being grounded upon some text of scripture,	318	Valdesso		1
that I may speak with him or dce some thing else when I doe come.	318	Valdesso		17
For at least some of the Papists are come now, to what the Pharisees	320	Valdesso		6
He that riseth betimes hath some thing in his head.	329	Proverbs		235
Would you know what mony is, Go borrow some.	334	Proverbs		374
When children stand quiet, they have done some ill.	338	Proverbs		504
The soule needs some things, the body many.	342	Proverbs	V	640
Some make a conscience of spitting in the Church, ...	343	Proverbs		650
Ther's no great banquet but some fares ill.	343	Proverbs		668
with some idlenesse of brain, says the Spaniard.	357	Proverbs	D	1050
Some evils are cured by contempt.	357	Proverbs	D	1052
It is good to have some friends both in heaven and hell. . .	359	Proverbs	D	1127
Some men plant an opinion they seem to erradicate. . . .	361	Proverbs	D	1164
Some had rather lose their friend then their Jest. . . .	361	Proverbs	D	1170
of your love, with being in some proportion, and after my manner,	364	Letters		3
not leazure to impart unto you some of those observations which I	366	Letters		1
of which is doubted whether it have some further meaning. . .	368	Letters		18
which some observing who heard the interdiction denounced to him,	368	Letters		36
I fear only that I have omitted some fitting circumstance, . .	370	Letters		12
incessantly begging some ease of your pains, with that earnestness,	371	Letters		29

SOME (cont'd)	PAGE	TITLE	LINE
till I take some opportunity to let them know your love,	375	Letters	21
take pitty of her, which yet at that distance is some difficulty.	375	Letters	30
if at length they may find out some thing not unworthy of those hands	376	Letters	29
her Son to doe as much) with some little Apology that she had done	379	Letters	3
devided betweene them excepting some legacies of my deceased Neece	382	G.H.'s Will	14
are to be payd out of it unto some whose names shal be annexed unto	382	G.H.'s Will	15
hundred and two pounds besides some Remainders of monyes wherof he is	383	G.H.'s Will	24
SOMETHING			
Give to all something; to a good poore man,	21	Ch.-Porch	377
The worst speak something good: if all want sense,	23	Ch.-Porch	431
The land of spices; something understood.	51	Prayer 1	14
Something there was, that sow'd debate:	106	Sion	9
Late when I would have something done,	134	The Method	22
So mine thou art, that something more	157	Clasping	12
Something that may be conquest on my part	201	love W	5
when it is a sin to take something for mony lent, or when not;	230	Priest 5	24
the wals are not idle, but something is written, or painted there,	240	Priest 10	24
an illustrating the thing by something else, which he knows,	256	Priest 21	37
of my friends, to adde something to my usuall stint and measure.	295	Cornaro	21
All things in their beeing are good for something.	339	Proverbs	520
It's more paine to doe nothing then something.	350	Proverbs	884
SOMETIME			
the holy spirit indeed sometime doubly teaching both in penning	317	Valdesso	30
SOMETIMES (see also somtimes)			
By all means use sometimes to be alone.	12	Ch.-Porch	145
Sometimes a friend, sometimes the engineer.	16	Ch.-Porch	242
Though he alight sometimes, still goeth on.	20	Ch.-Porch	340
If what my soul doth feel sometimes,	55	Temper 1	3
Sometimes I peere above them all;	55	Temper 1	6
Sometimes I hardly reach a score,	55	Temper 1	7
Sometimes to hell I fall.	55	Temper 1	8
Yet say sometimes, God help poore Kings.	65	Ch.-mus.	8
Hither sometimes Sinne steals, and stains	67	Ch.-floore	13
Sometimes Death, puffing at the doore,	67	Ch.-floore	16
Which sometimes crosseth thee, thou sometimes it:	106	Sion	14
Sometimes thou dost divide thy gifts to man,	120	Providence	125
Sometimes unite. The Indian nut alone	120	Providence	126
Were worse then ours; sometimes thou shiftest hands.	121	Providence	138
Perhaps thou com'st sometimes, and for a day;	137	Familie	23
A wasted place, but sometimes rich.	142	Pilgrimage	15
Sometimes, when as I wash, I say	202	love W	7
And sometimes offers, sometimes makes a stand	204	The Knell W	5
Sometimes he tells them stories, and sayings of others,	233	Priest 7	11
like mortall enemies, may sometimes disquiet him likewise;	238	Priest 9	9
but that he sometimes looks how things go, demanding an account,	239	Priest 9	2
whom he sometimes purposely takes home with him, setting them close	243	Priest 11	10
takes occasion sometimes to visite in person, now one quarter of his	247	Priest 14	4
and sometimes he hears the children read himselfe, and blesseth them,	248	Priest 14	35
interposing sometimes some short, and honest refreshments,	251	Priest 17	4
but sometimes lift up their minds to better things, even in the midst	261	Priest 23	25
which is unwholsome, being sometimes baned meat, sometimes too salt,	265	Priest 26	22
baned meat, sometimes too salt, and so not competent nourishment,	265	Priest 26	22
which it hath escaped, he destroyes it sometimes in the very Haven;	271	Priest 30	23
of Satan (who playes his part sometimes in drawing Gods Servants from	272	Priest 31	16
sometimes in perplexing them in the service of God) stands fast in	272	Priest 31	17
Sometimes he may go to Court, as the eminent place both of good	277	Priest 32	5
having doubted sometimes, whether his repentance were true,	279	Priest 33	10
since he found himselfe sometimes to weepe more for the losse of some	279	Priest 33	12
still we have bread, though sometimes more, somtimes lesse;	281	Priest 34	26
and sometimes, where he knowes there hath been or is a little	284	Priest 35	19
of the ground, and sometimes I go up high stairs and hills on foot.	300	Cornaro	36
Sometimes I ride to some of the neighbour-cities, that I may enjoy	301	Cornaro	34
being given only to the godly, and the other sometimes to the wicked.	319	Valdesso	9
None is a foole alwaies, every one sometimes.	326	Proverbs	163
Sometimes the best gaine is to lose.	328	Proverbs	224
but sometimes he can hurt.	359	Proverbs	D 1119
on Fridayes and Saturdayes, I must do so, which yet sometimes I fast.	365	Letters	6
Sometimes also I ride to Newmarket, and there lie a day or two	365	Letters	6
yea, sometimes of Ten Shillings:	365	Letters	13
SOMEWHAT (see also somwhat)			
I will present, and somewhat more,	152	The Bag	40
Somewhat it fain would say:	168	a true Hymn	3
Justly complains, that somewhat is behinde	168	a true Hymn	14
Although the verse be somewhat scant,	168	a true Hymn	17
that where is much earnestness, there is somewhat worth hearing;	232	Priest 7	33
poor and needy, whom he thus finds labouring, he gives them somewhat;	248	Priest 14	10
and ever I learn somewhat which is worthy of my knowledge:	302	Cornaro	2
learned and perfect in them, there is somewhat to be learned more:	309	Valdesso	24
I am fain ever and anon, to buy somewhat tending towards my health;	364	Letters	34
P.S. My brother is somewhat of the same temper, and perhaps a little	366	Letters	24
SOMMER			
and also what becomes of you this sommer.	379	Letters	25
SOMMERS			
The inward walls and Sommers cleft and tore:	84	The World	14
SOMTIMES			
or somtimes both, if his audience be intermixed.	230	Priest 5	18
who somtimes make it a piece of state not to come at the beginning	232	Priest 6	8
and somtimes giving them a little mony to do it of themselves,	239	Priest 10	27
there may happen somtimes some cases, wherein he chooseth to permit	260	Priest 23	18
even somtimes to a forgetting of themselves, knowing that there is	267	Priest 26	20

SOMTIMES (cont'd)	PAGE	TITLE		LINE
he somtimes refresheth himselfe, as knowing that nature will not bear	267	Priest 27		33
still we have bread, though sometimes more, somtimes lesse;	281	Priest 34		26
SOMTYMES				
Which wee but somtymes prove:	210	Paradox	D	32
SOMWHAT				
finds it somwhat difficult how to proceed in this point.	286	Priest 37		32
SON				
He said to me, Thou art my Son,	216	Psalm II	D	17
O kiss the Son, lest he be wrath,	216	Psalm II	D	29
are all that make the Son their stay.	216	Psalm II	D	32
love for love, even the son of his love out of his bosome of love.	283	Priest 34		16
and hee that hath one son makes him a foole.	336	Proverbs		433
loved her even in my departure, in looking to her Son, and my charge.	371	Letters		12
accept the good meaning of, Your most obedient Son, GEORGE HERBERT.	374	Letters		32
hands (& promising to get her Son to doe as much) with some little	379	Letters		3
SON'S				
and do so for thy blessed Son's sake, in whose sweet and pleasing	289	Priest		34
Grant this dear Father, for thy Son's sake, our only Saviour:	290	Priest		13
SONG				
Consort both heart and lute, and twist a song	42	Easter		13
And tune together in a well-set song,	49	Repentance		33
Listen sweet Dove unto my song,	59	Whitsunday		1
Come blessed Dove charm'd with my song,	59	Whitsunday	W	1
Even-song.	63	Even-song		T
And drowns the song.	132	The Storm		14
Even-song.	203	Even-song	W	T
SONGS				
Where are my window-songs?	116	Dulnesse		18
SONNE				
Some till their ground, but let weeds choke their sonne:	10	Ch.-Porch		98
The way to make thy sonne rich, is to fill	11	Ch.-Porch		109
But if thy sonne can make ten pound his measure,	11	Ch.-Porch		113
The sonne, in whom thou dost delight to be?	33	Sacrifice		214
The sonne, in whom thou art well pleas'd to be?	33	Sacrifice	W	214
But I have got his sonne, and he hath none.	63	Even-song		8
There lay thy sonne: and must he leave that nest,	107	Home		19
Lord, pardon, for thy sonne makes good	136	Ephes.		35
Are properly a crosse felt by thy sonne,	165	The Crosse		35
The Sonne.	167	The Sonne		T
A sonne is light and fruit; a fruitfull flame	168	The Sonne		7
We him in glorie call, The Sonne of Man.	168	The Sonne		14
Ther's no monument to a sonne,	208	J. Danvers	D	15
and had killed his sonne Isaac, but he might have been justly put	316	Valdesso		24
untill shee had brought forth her first borne Sonne, as if afterwards	318	Valdesso		13
Marry your sonne when you will; your daughter when you can.	326	Proverbs		149
The sonne full and tattered, the daughter empty and fine.	328	Proverbs		214
Hee who hath but one sonne makes him fat,	336	Proverbs	V	433
SONNE'S				
To parents issue and the sonnes bright starre!	168	The Sonne	V	6
SONNES				
all the sonnes of one father and mother, all in perfect health;	303	Cornaro		3
SONNET				
Sonnet 1.	206	Walton 1		T
Sonnet 2.	206	Walton 2		T
SONNETS				
Why are not Sonnets made of thee? and layes	206	Walton 1		5
my meaning (dear Mother) is in these Sonnets, to declare my	363	Letters		10
SONS				
therefore we sons of men are not consumed.	288	Priest		22
One father is enough to governe one hundred sons,	335	Proverbs		404
but not a hundred sons one father.	335	Proverbs		404
but an 100 sons are not enough to govern one Father.	335	Proverbs	V	404
SOON				
They drive them soon away;	71	Humilitie		30
How soon doth man decay!	98	Mortific.		1
How soon does man decay	98	Mortific.	W	1
It prosper'd strangely, and did soon disperse	125	Peace		31
Out of the caldron getting, soon I fled	130	Love unkn.		46
Thou cam'st but now; wilt thou so soon depart,	154	Glimpse		2
Though Greece took horse as soon as Egypt did,	191	Ch.-Milit.		57
Which soon was blown to such a mightie flame,	194	Ch.-Milit.		145
as soon as he awakes on Sunday morning, presently falls to work,	235	Priest 8		16
and doing their duty faithfully, they will soon discover:	266	Priest 26		3
and not to let go the raines as soon as the horse goes easie.	280	Priest 34		16
was but a little excesse, in a few dayes had so soon overthrown me.	297	Cornaro		6
We do it soon enough, if that we do be well.	359	Proverbs	D	1109
The death of a young wolfe doth never come too soon.	360	Proverbs	D	1131
Sir send the Letter you receive from him to me as soon as you can,	370	Letters		6
SOONER				
A gale to bring me sooner to my blisse.	73	Afflict.3		12
and ingagement of their discourses for no price sooner,	252	Priest 18		21
seasoned with pleasantnesse, both enter sooner, and roote deeper.	268	Priest 27		4
will they last the longer, and when they depart, returne the sooner.	280	Priest 34		30
Nothing dries sooner then a teare.	343	Proverbs		659
No sooner is a Temple built to God	343	Proverbs		674
The body is sooner drest then the soule.	351	Proverbs		920
Stay a while, that we may make an end the sooner.	361	Proverbs	D	1161
SOONEST				
Which of them soonest should attaine my hart.	66	Ch.-lock	W	4
Where of all plants afflictions soonest grow;	170	Water-crs.		3

	PAGE	TITLE		LINE
SOPHISTERS				
Sophisters taken in a fishers net.	191	Ch.-Milit.		52
Sophisters taken in a Fishernett.	191	Ch.-Milit.	W	52
SORBON				
But when they were unto the Sorbon come,	196	Ch.-Milit.	W	202
SORE				
Shall ne're be troubled with sore eyes.	96	Charms & K	W	2
Of some fair church to show the sore	158	Praise 3		34
If ever Heart was sore with Sighs;	213	Convert	D	3
and in sore anger vex their pride.	215	Psalm II	D	12
my Soul is troubled very sore;	220	Psalm VI	D	6
whereby my head and whole bodie was sore hurt, and also one of my	294	Cornaro		39
although it was a sore evil, yet had no power to kill me.	297	Cornaro		2
Brawling Curres never want sore eares.	322	Proverbs	V	52
SORELY				
that er'st so sorely vexed me,	220	Psalm VI	D	26
SORES				
and healing of all wounds and sores with her owne hands;	239	Priest 10		15
SORRIE				
Sorrie I am, my God, sorrie I am,	122	Sinnes rd.		1
Sorrie I am, my God, sorrie I am.	122	Sinnes rd.		18
He that hath made a sorrie wedding	171	Self-cond.		13
SORROW				
Bywords, but this by sorrow I must win:	33	Sacrifice		207
Such sorrow as, if sinfull man could feel,	33	Sacrifice		209
My tender age in sorrow did beginne:	43	East.wings		11
Pulpits and sundayes, sorrow dogging sinne,	45	Sinne 1		5
But with my yeares sorrow did twist and grow,	47	Afflict.1		23
Sorrow was all my soul; I scarce beleeved,	47	Afflict.1		29
Sorrow was all my soul; I did not know	47	Afflict.1	W	29
Sicknes, or shame, or sinn, or sorrow:	65	Ch.-mus.	W	8
Nor any sorrow tell them that they sinne,	100	Miserie		22
Awake sad heart, whom sorrow ever drowns;	112	Dawning		1
Let me as well take up their joy, as sorrow.	128	Bunch Gr.		21
And wake thy sorrow?	145	Discharge		47
Sorrow hath chang'd its note: such is his will,	159	Jos.coat		3
my sight with sorrow waxeth dim.	220	Psalm VI	D	16
perfecting our Redemption no other way, then by sorrow;	249	Priest 15		23
of all Comfort, who is not willing to behold any sorrow but for sin.	372	Letters		26
let such thoughts as these, moderate your present fear and sorrow;	374	Letters		4
SORROWES				
Sorrowes & griefs, to fight with them a bout	211	Bohemia	D	20
He that lives not well one yeare, sorrowes seven after.	340	Proverbs		562
SORROWS				
My severall sinnes their sorrows get;	39	Good Fri.		18
Thy sorrows in, and bloudie fight;	39	Good Fri.		22
To write thy sorrows in, as blood	39	Good Fri.	W	22
But with my yeares sorrows did twist and grow,	47	Afflict.1	W	23
To sorrows old,	48	Repentance		10
Thy sorrows were in earnest; no faint proffer,	104	Obedience		28
Look on my sorrows round!	149	Longing		25
For my rough sorrows: cease, be dumbe and mute,	164	Grief		14
True earnest sorrows, rooted miseries,	167	Dotage		7
These are the sorrows here.	167	Dotage		12
Where are no sorrows, but delights more true,	167	Dotage		17
Disbanded humours, sorrows troops of Sinn	204	The Knell	W	11
SORRY (see also sorrie)				
he joyes, and he is sorry, he grieves, and he gloryes, never was	234	Priest 7		19
and you have no cause to be sorry, since it is GOD's business.	377	Letters		21
SORT				
Small it is, in this poore sort	146	Praise 2		25
Besides, things sort not to my will,	165	The Crosse		19
and with particularizing of his speech now to the younger sort,	233	Priest 7		3
with other exemplary vertues of that sort, and to keep them on in	237	Priest 9		35
a providing for her family in such sort, as that neither they want	239	Priest 10		18
both is to be done, the better sort invited, and meaner relieved,	243	Priest 11		14
This is in some sort a discharging of God;	254	Priest 20		18
of the younger sort, the very words;	255	Priest 21		23
that those of the elder sort, who are not well grounded,	255	Priest 21		30
Of the first sort are repentance, prayers, fasting, Psalmes,	312	Valdesso	V	26
is in some sort true because they are spiritually discerned,	315	Valdesso		31
So likewise are the godly in some sort exempt from Lawes,	315	Valdesso		32
and more austere sort of Philosophie, for respect to you,	442	Oration		6
SORTED				
Afflictions sorted, anguish of all sizes,	45	Sinne 1		6
SORTS				
All sorts of wounds; of such strange force it is.	147	Offering		21
by taking both sorts of food into them, do as it were dresse	241	Priest 10		33
discovers two sorts of vices, and two sorts of vicious persons.	264	Priest 26		5
to whore, to scoffe, to revile, to all sorts of gamings.	274	Priest 32		12
for Atheisme) he scatters in his discourse three sorts of arguments;	281	Priest 34		15
There are two sorts of acts in religion;	312	Valdesso	V	23
and we meet with two sorts of these Saints of the world;	319	Valdesso	V	21
Wine makes all sorts of creatures at table.	352	Proverbs		931
SOUGHT				
Who sought for help, never malicious foes:	34	Sacrifice		243
In heaven at his manour I him sought:	40	Redemption		5
Sought him accordingly in great resorts;	40	Redemption		10
Sought him in Citties, Theaters, resorts	40	Redemption	W	10
What hath not man sought out and found,	85	Vanitie 1		22
One might have sought and found thee presently	99	Decay		6

SOUGHT (cont'd)	PAGE	TITLE		LINE
That I sought out quaint words, and trim invention;	102	Jordan 2		3
I sought thee in a secret cave,	124	Peace		3
Much in request, much sought for, as a good.	186	Death		16
that if the Kingdome of God be first sought, all other things shall	278	Priest 33		13
or the Philosophers stone, sought of many, and found of few.	298	Cornaro		20
Good is to bee sought out, and evill attended.	324	Proverbs		112
shee had never sought her daughter there.	344	Proverbs		696
No naked man is sought after to be rifled.	357	Proverbs	D	1063
of thanks for the diversity of your favours, if I sought to do so;	363	Letters		16
SOUL				
It blots thy lesson written in thy soul;	6	Ch.-Porch		9
Lets his soul runne for nought, as little fearing.	8	Ch.-Porch		59
The stormie working soul spits lies and froth.	9	Ch.-Porch		76
God gave thy soul brave wings; put not those feathers	9	Ch.-Porch		83
Salute thy self: see what thy soul doth wear.	12	Ch.-Porch		146
She loseth three for one; her soul, rest, fame.	13	Ch.-Porch		174
Thy clothes being fast, but thy soul loose about thee.	23	Ch.-Porch		414
Dresse and undresse thy soul: mark the decay	24	Ch.-Porch		453
Therefore my soul melts, and my hearts deare treasure	27	Sacrifice		21
Shame tears my soul, my bodie many a wound;	33	Sacrifice		217
Since, if my soul make even with the week,	38	The Sinner		3
My soul bid nothing, but preserve her wealth:	44	H. Bapt.2		13
My soul bid nothing, but keep hir first wealth:	44	H. Bapt.2	W	13
My soul will turn to bubbles straight,	45	Nature		9
My soul will bee all bubble straight,	45	Nature	W	9
Therefore my sudden soul caught at the place,	46	Afflict.1		17
My flesh began unto my soul in pain,	47	Afflict.1		25
Sorrow was all my soul; I scarce beleeved,	47	Afflict.1		29
Sorrow was all my soul; I did not know	47	Afflict.1	W	29
Which thou hast pour'd into my soul;	49	Repentance		20
The soul in paraphrase, heart in pilgrimage,	51	Prayer 1		3
Yet can these not get over to my soul,	52	H.Commun.		13
Give me my captive soul, or take	52	H.Commun.		25
If what my soul doth feel sometimes,	55	Temper 1		3
My soul might ever feel!	55	Temper 1		4
O let me, when thy roof my soul hath hid,	55	Temper 1		17
Let grace work too, and on my soul	60	Grace		15
To a brave soul: Exalt the poore,	61	Praise 1		15
To a brave soul: for to a poore,	61	Praise 1	W	15
My morning-soul and sacrifice:	62	Mattens		3
While that my soul repairs to her devotion,	64	Ch.-monum.		1
This soul doth span the world, and hang content	69	Content		17
Then cease discoursing soul, till thine own ground,	69	Content		33
My poore soul, ev'n sick of love:	72	Frailtie		21
Chiefly to thee would I my soul unfold:	78	Ang.&Sts.		15
My soul would stirre	78	Employm.2		2
Lets his own ashes choke his soul.	79	Employm.2		10
Therefore my soul lay out of sight,	80	Deniall		21
Since my dark soul and brutish is thy right,	81	Christmas		11
Furnish & deck my soul, that thou mayst have	81	Christmas		13
My soul's a shepherd too; a flock it feeds	81	Christmas		17
The humble soul compos'd of love and fear	86	Lent		7
And among those his soul.	87	Lent		48
Onely a sweet and vertuous soul,	88	Vertue		13
While they do wound and prick my soul.	90	Afflict.4		12
While they do wound and pinke my soul.	90	Afflict.4	W	12
My soul doth love thee, yet it loves delay.	96	Justice 1		11
That my free soul may use her wing,	109	Home		62
Poore silly soul, whose hope and head lies low;	111	Vanitie 2		1
Then silly soul take heed; for earthly joy	111	Vanitie 2		17
Foolish soul who sinn'd to day?	113	Businesse		2
If, poore soul, thou hast no tears,	113	Businesse		6
Foolish soul, Who di'd for thee?	113	Businesse		16
Sweetest Saviour, if my soul	114	Dialogue		1
In soul he mounts and flies,	131	Mans medly		13
Then Order plaies the soul;	137	Familie		10
My throat, my soul is hoarse;	148	Longing		7
Lord of my soul, love of my minde,	149	Longing		20
Another in my soul (the memorie	165	The Crosse		14
Is, when the soul unto the lines accords.	168	a true Hymn		10
And all the soul, and strength, and time,	168	a true Hymn		12
Between his soul and gold, and hath preferr'd	171	Self-cond.		14
My soul hath felt, ev'n able to destroy,	172	The Glance		10
Sprung from thine eye, did work within my soul,	172	The Glance		14
Deare soul, she knew who did vouchsafe and deigne	173	Marie Magd		13
Fills my soul,	181	Banquet		8
Love bade me welcome: yet my soul drew back,	188	Love 3		1
He gave his soul, and so gave o're.	439	Walton 5	V	14
Against me, saying, For my soul	216	Psalm III	D	3
my Soul is troubled very sore;	220	Psalm VI	D	6
my Soul for thy great mercy save;	220	Psalm VI	D	10
he do devour my soul:	221	Psalm VII	D	6
Let him pursue and take my soul,	221	Psalm VII	D	17
the stupifying and deading of all the clamorous powers of the soul,	227	Priest 3		7
when the affections of the soul in desiring and procuring increase	230	Priest 5		26
and his soul fervent, active, young, and lusty as an eagle.	237	Priest 9		27
and his Saints, and by way of undertaking for a Christian soul.	258	Priest 22		14
obligation to God, and their own soul, is above any temporall tye.	270	Priest 29		22
will appear if the Pious soul foresee and prevent such interruptions,	273	Priest 31		17
two great Instruments, Reason in the soul, and a hand in the Body,	274	Priest 32		20

	PAGE	TITLE	LINE
SOUTH			
The South with marble; North with furres & woods.	119	Providence	96
SOV'RAIGNE			
Of sov'raigne tears, springing from true remorse:	170	Water-crs.	8
SOVERAIGNE			
comfortable, and Soveraigne a Medicine it is to all sin-sick souls;	250	Priest 15	2
SOW			
At first he got to Egypt, and did sow	193	Ch.-Milit.	107
and that if they sow and soyle their grounds, they must have corn;	270	Priest 30	26
SOW'D			
Hath still sow'd fig-leaves to exclude thy light:	83	Sighs & Gr.	16
Something there was, that sow'd debate:	106	Sion	9
SOWED			
you have layed out thoughts & prayers you have sowed.	380	Woodnoth	10
SOWES			
He that sowes trusts in God.	332	Proverbs	342
He that speakes sowes, and he that holds his peace, gathers.	336	Proverbs	435
He that speakes sowes, and he that hears, gathers.	336	Proverbs	V 435
If the braine sowes not corne, it plants thistles.	355	Proverbs	1024
SOWING			
Forbeare not sowing because of birds.	343	Proverbs	670
SOWN			
The crop is his, for he hath sown.	144	Discharge	15
SOWNE			
Fame is sowne in this age, that it may be reaped in the following;	443	Oration	3
SOWRE			
Constancie knits the bones, and makes us sowre, ...	11	Ch.-Porch	W 117
Be sweet to all. Is thy complexion sowre?	15	Ch.-Porch	211
Sowre exhalations, and dishonest rheumes, ...	86	Lent	23
Not a sweet dish, but thou dost call it sowre:	105	Conscience	3
And write for sweet, prove a most sowre displeasure.	111	Vanitie 2	6
Who of the laws sowre juice sweet wine did make, ...	128	Bunch Gr.	27
When I am sowre, ...	135	Ephes.	2
And all my sowre-sweet dayes	171	Bittersweet	7
or over-nourishing things, as the Israelites did eate sowre herbs:	242	Priest 10	4
which I live at this age, is not a dead, dumpish, and sowre life;	303	Cornaro	10
SOWRE-SWEET			
And all my sowre-sweet dayes	171	Bittersweet	7
SOYLE			
and that if they sow and soyle their grounds, they must have corn;	270	Priest 30	26
SPACE			
A wonder tortur'd in the space	90	Afflict.4	5
And hath any space of breath	114	Businesse	29
And threatned man, that he should fill the space.	119	Providence	84
As is thy space, ...	163	The Search	46
and then was dragged for a good space by the furie of the horses,	294	Cornaro	38
a space ought to be interposed.	356	Proverbs	D 40
SPACIOUS			
With his poore clod of earth the spacious sky.	8	Ch.-Porch	54
But there are two vast, spacious things, ...	37	The Agonie	4
And spacious fornace flaming, and thereon	129	Love unkn.	26
This spacious globe: Angels must have their joy, ...	158	Praise 3	21
The spacious world and Jurie to be seen.	196	Ch.-Milit.	234
SPADE			
A servile hawk: low without losse, a spade.	120	Providence	104
if a man hath wherewithall to buy a spade, and yet hee chuseth rather	265	Priest 26	28
SPAIN			
It never was in France or Spain;	70	Quidditie	6
Spain in the Empire shar'd with Germanie, ...	192	Ch.-Milit.	89
Spain hath done one; when Arts perform the other, ...	197	Ch.-Milit.	265
To build castles in Spain.	356	Proverbs	D 1041
but he would chuse to dy in Spain (where they say	357	Proverbs	D 1047
SPAINE			
Of Divell, Jessuitt & Spaine, ...	213	L' Envoy	D 9
While Prince to Spaine, and King to Cambridge goes, ...	438	Lat.Trans.	1
Remote from ours, then Spaine from Britains shoare.	438	Lat.Trans.	4
this passeth in Spaine freely with consent of King & counsell.	368	Letters	29
both Indias to his Spaine, knowes no limits of his praise, . .	442	Oration	12
SPAN			
Deferre not the least vertue: lifes poore span	24	Ch.-Porch	459
This soul doth span the world, and hang content	69	Content	17
Who may thy follies span?	102	Miserie	W 66
Contract into a span.	159	The Pulley	5
SPANIARD			
He that trusts much Obliges much, says the Spaniard.	357	Proverbs	D 1045
with some idlenesse of brain, says the Spaniard.	357	Proverbs	D 1050
Threatned men eat bread, says the Spaniard.	358	Proverbs	D 1081
Love without end, hath no end, says the Spaniard: (meaning, . .	361	Proverbs	D 1160
SPANISH			
And Spanish sents, wisely layd up, presume	212	Bohemia	D 52
There is a Spanish Lawyer hath written a treatise concerning	368	Letters	26
both the Spanish and Brittish Nation serve and worship James.	442	Oration	17
SPANN'D			
So now each Christian hath his journeys spann'd:	128	Bunch Gr.	10
SPANS			
Is thy great arm which spans the east and west, ...	103	Prayer 2	8
SPANYARD			
Talke much and erre much, saies the Spanyard.	343	Proverbs	649
SPARE			
For we have wit to mark them, and to spare.	9	Ch.-Porch	69
The fine may spare these well, yet not go lesse.	16	Ch.-Porch	238

	PAGE	TITLE		LINE
SPENDS (cont'd)				
The coveteous spends more then the liberall.	344	Proverbs		683
He that gaines well and spends well, needes no count booke.	349	Proverbs		853
He that gaines well and spends well, needes no count books.	349	Proverbs	V	853
SPENSER				
five pound due to Mrs Judeth Spenser is to be payd to Mrs Mary Lawly	383	G.H.'s Will		21
SPENT				
Better by worms be all once spent,	69	Content		26
Farewell deare flowers, sweetly your time ye spent,	94	Life		13
And spent her period and prefixed time	191	Ch.-Milit.		59
The Day is spent, & hath his will on mee:	203	Even-song	W	1
it is an honest joy ever after to looke upon his well spent houres.	230	Priest 5		7
give any thing above those, and not spent in them, he blesseth God,	240	Priest 10		12
the one concerning the woman that spent the oyntment on our Saviour,	282	Priest 34		24
and my bodie spent with extream leannesse, and the season	296	Cornaro		26
For the Temperance of so many yeares spent all ill humours,	296	Cornaro		32
Life is halfe spent before we know what it is.	351	Proverbs		917
these many years, as having spent two hundred pounds in building;	376	Letters		1
SPHERE				
Doth often aim at, never hit the sphere.	19	Ch.-Porch		318
He is in little all the sphere.	91	Man		22
And tacks the centre to the sphere!	103	Prayer 2		9
My thoughts must work, but like a noiselesse sphere;	105	Conscience		8
And yet the sphere	162	The Search		6
The sphere of vertue, and each shining grace	175	The Foil		2
Is some starre (fled from the sphere)	181	Banquet		10
Put him in trust to rule the Romane sphere.	194	Ch.-Milit.		142
United now in one both time and sphere.	195	Ch.-Milit.		176
Shipping the vices onely for our sphere.	196	Ch.-Milit.	W	204
Turne watrish Holland to a chrystalline sphere.	211	Bohemia	D	12
SPHERES				
And thred the spheres with his quick-piercing minde:	85	Vanitie 1		2
And trip at night, have spheres suppli'd;	134	Divinitie		2
Break all thy spheres, and save thy head.	135	Divinitie		26
I, who had heard of musick in the spheres,	139	Artillerie		9
Bodyes & Minds are different Spheres	201	H. Commun.	W	40
Doth for two clods of earth ten spheres controule,	211	Bohemia	D	8
SPICE				
If thou hast wherewithall to spice a draught,	137	The Size		9
esteeming that there is no spice comparable, for herbs,	262	Priest 23		1
He that hath the spice, may season as he list.	335	Proverbs		424
He who hath the spice, may season as he pleaseth.	335	Proverbs	V	424
SPICES				
The land of spices; something understood.	51	Prayer 1		14
To th' Isle of spices, is't not fair?	137	The Size		12
Spices come from the East; so did thy Spouse,	190	Ch.-Milit.		13
As for spices, he doth not onely prefer home-bred things before them,	261	Priest 23		36
SPICINESSE				
To some degree of spicinesse to thee!	175	The Odour		15
SPIDER				
O raise me then: for if a Spider may	61	Praise 1	W	17
SPIES				
That when sinne spies so many foes,	39	Good Fri.		25
Spies are the ears and eyes of Princes.	357	Proverbs	D	1067
The life of spies is to know, not bee known.	357	Proverbs	D	1068
SPILL				
His bloud did spill	94	Unkindness		23
SPILT				
Spilt with me,	182	Banquet		35
SPIN				
Spin all the day:	61	Praise 1	W	18
How finely dost thou times and seasons spin,	118	Providence		57
Spin out thy thread, and make thereof a coat	156	Assurance		38
My busie heart shall spin it all my dayes:	157	Praise 3		3
hath a rock and a spindle, and no staffe to spin.	358	Proverbs	D	1085
SPINDLE				
let it not come betweene the spindle and the distaffe.	343	Proverbs		665
hath a rock and a spindle, and no staffe to spin.	358	Proverbs	D	1085
SPINNE				
If I have more to spinne,	155	Glimpse		26
SPINNING				
And spinning phansies, she was heard to say,	84	The World		2
SPINS				
Shee spins well that breedes her children.	325	Proverbs		144
Shee spins well that breedes her child.	325	Proverbs	V	144
Hee that labours and thrives spins gold.	332	Proverbs		341
SPIRIT				
Sink not in spirit: who aimeth at the sky,	19	Ch.-Porch		333
The spirit and good extract of my heart	38	The Sinner		10
O let thy blessed Spirit bear a part,	42	Easter		17
Whereas my birth and spirit rather took	47	Afflict.1		37
My feeble spirit, unable to look right,	80	Deniall		23
How many drammes of spirit there must be	88	The Pearl		18
My spirit gaspeth night and day.	107	Home		4
Wherefore, most sacred Spirit, I here present	117	Providence		25
Ephes. 4. 30. Grieve not the Holy Spirit, &c.	135	Ephes.		T
Heighten a spirit to sound out thy praise	206	Walton 1		7
they are not understood but with the same Spirit that writ them.	228	Priest 4		32
and all being penn'd by one and the self-same Spirit, it cannot be,	229	Priest 4		6
they were reproved, as ignorant of what spirit they were.	229	Priest 4		14
therefore the spirit of both is to be considered, and weighed.	229	Priest 4		16

SPIRIT (cont'd)	PAGE	TITLE		LINE
the grace of God in himself, and what the Holy Spirit teacheth him;	229	Priest 4		21
as they think fit, & see cause, or rather as Gods spirit leads them.	272	Priest 31		28
yet the victory is alike in all, being by the self-same Spirit.	279	Priest 33		2
is the heart, and the spirit, and to worship him in truth, . .	279	Priest 33		17
and the spirit, and to worship him in truth, and spirit. . .	279	Priest 33		17
And Luke 10. 21. He rejoyced in Spirit:	280	Priest 34		10
how shall not the ministration of the spirit exceed in blessing?	285	Priest 36		20
only the effectuall operation or illumination of the holy spirit,	308	Valdesso		31
but the spirits bearing witnesse with our spirit, revealing . .	309	Valdesso		3
have the assistance of the holy spirit applying it to our hearts,	310	Valdesso		7
God affectionately and fervently to send him the light of his spirit,	312	Valdesso		17
Gods Spirit will mortify and try them as gold in the fire. . .	314	Valdesso		21
weaknesses is no way repugnant to the way of Gods Spirit in them,	316	Valdesso		3
opposeth the teaching of the spirit to the teaching of the scripture,	317	Valdesso		27
spirit to the teaching of the scripture, which the holy spirit wrot.	317	Valdesso		28
Although the holy spirit apply the scripture, yet what the scripture	317	Valdesso		28
the spirit teacheth, the holy spirit indeed sometime doubly teaching	317	Valdesso		29
the holy spirit indeed sometime doubly teaching both in penning	317	Valdesso		30
education, of obeying that Spirit which hath guided me hitherto,	364	Letters		18
and it is the part of a poor spirit to undervalue himself and blush.	366	Letters		18
forwardness in religious works is a good testimony of a good spirit.	377	Letters		26
SPIRITS				
Active and stirring spirits live alone.	20	Ch.-Porch		341
While those to spirits refin'd, at doore attend	52	H.Commun.		23
Oh glorious spirits, who after all your bands	77	Ang.&Sts.		1
least the poyson steal into some young and unwary spirits, . .	252	Priest 18		6
wonder-working knowledg, and therefore requiring the best spirits.	277	Priest 32		36
but the spirits bearing witnesse with our spirit, revealing . .	309	Valdesso		3
with that bloud, which useth to infuse so great and worthie Spirits.	442	Oration		15
SPIRITUAL				
appears Rom. 12. 14. how much more those, who are spiritual Fathers?	286	Priest 36		28
SPIRITUALL				
are principally these two, Spirituall pride, and Impurity of heart:	238	Priest 9		3
These and many other spirituall wickednesses in high places doth	238	Priest 9		20
to multiply, and build up this knowledge to a spirituall Temple;	255	Priest 21		5
a spirituall man, wisheth all to incline rather to too much,	267	Priest 26		12
the third a spirituall power.	271	Priest 30		2
The third power is spirituall, by which God turnes all outward	271	Priest 30		37
Now the Parson having a Spirituall Judgement, according as he	280	Priest 34		12
no more then to be a spirituall Father was appropriated to them.	285	Priest 36		13
their children, how much more may, and ought Spirituall Fathers?	285	Priest 36		15
amongst all divine and spirituall exercises and duties, . .	311	Valdesso	V	3
meanes a mans fre-will is only in outward, not in spirituall things.	313	Valdesso		34
Worldly learned men cannot judg spirituall mens actions, . .	317	Valdesso		5
resuming the donation of spirituall livings into their owne hands,	368	Letters		27
SPIRITUALLY				
Better were his corne burnt, then not spiritually improved. . .	272	Priest 30		4
is in some sort true because they are spiritually discerned,	315	Valdesso		31
SPIT				
Spit out thy flegme, and fill thy brest with glorie:	10	Ch.-Porch		92
Behold, they spit on me in scornfull wise, ...	31	Sacrifice		133
The souldiers also spit upon that face, ...	32	Sacrifice		181
The souldiers also spit upon my Face, ...	32	Sacrifice	W	181
My friend may spit upon my curious floore:	93	Unkindness		11
Which spit it forth like the Sicilian hill.	122	Sinnes rd.		8
SPITE				
Is a good spurre. Correct thy passions spite;	16	Ch.-Porch		263
See how spite cankers things. These words aright	30	Sacrifice		109
All spite in one, counting my life their losse, ...	33	Sacrifice		194
Nay, after death their spite shall further go;	34	Sacrifice		245
Nay, after death their spite shall farther go;	34	Sacrifice	W	245
SPITEFULL				
O spitefull bitter thought!	155	Assurance		1
Bitterly spitefull thought! Couldst thou invent	155	Assurance		2
SPITS				
The stormie working soul spits lies and froth.	9	Ch.-Porch		76
Who spits against heaven, it falls in his face.	333	Proverbs		346
Who hath bitter in his mouth, spits not all sweet.	335	Proverbs		422
SPITTING				
or spitting even in the midst of their answer, but gently . .	231	Priest 6		31
which will discover it selfe by spitting, and rheume, or flegme.	242	Priest 10		25
Some make a conscience of spitting in the Church, ...	343	Proverbs		650
SPITTLE (hospital)				
I'le build a spittle, or mend common wayes, ...	36	Thanksgvng		33
an Usurers, a Taverne, a Spittle, and a Prison.	348	Proverbs		816
SPITTLE				
Who by my spittle gave the blinde man eies, ...	31	Sacrifice		134
Who by my spittle gave that blinde man eies, ...	31	Sacrifice	W	134
He that hath one foot in the straw, hath another in the spittle.	336	Proverbs		438
SPLENDID				
Credit and estimation calls on us to live in a more splendid fashion?	373	Letters		27
SPLENDOR				
what splendor? surely, since there is a two-fold brightnesse which	442	Oration		32
SPLENDOUR				
Splendour from darknes. So close sits the crowne	212	Bohemia	D	37
SPOIL				
And spoil the meeting. What shall point out them, ...	65	Ch.-monum.		14
But while he thinks to spoil the room, he sweeps.	67	Ch.-floore		18
Spoil the good use; lest by that argument	86	Lent		29
Spoil our good use; lest by that argument	86	Lent	W	29

SPOIL (cont'd)	PAGE	TITLE		LINE
The rage of a wild boar is able to spoil more then one wood.	360	Proverbs	D	1132
SPOIL'D				
Kneeling ne're spoil'd silk stocking: quit thy state.	22	Ch.-Porch		407
Spoil'd all the train: then saying, Here it is	71	Humilitie		27
But he hath spoil'd the race; and giv'n to anguish	159	Jos.coat		10
SPOILES				
The Apothecaries morter spoiles the Luters musick.	351	Proverbs		925
SPOILS				
It spoils an Angel: robs thee of thy God.	6	Ch.-Porch	W	10
A sad repentance, not the spoils of lust:	192	Ch.-Milit.		68
SPOKEN				
the Person speaking, or spoken to, the subject, and object,	235	Priest 7		7
For many and wonderfull things are spoken of thee, thou great Vertue.	244	Priest 12		8
there is nothing spoken, or done in the Company where he is,	252	Priest 18		2
If it be well spoken, or done, he takes occasion to commend,	252	Priest 18		4
wher-ever spoken this day throughout the universall Church.	289	Priest		14
being Scripture cannot be spoken to the disparagement of Scripture;	310	Valdesso		3
nor being spoken to is silent.	330	Proverbs		278
SPONGES				
Sponges, non-sense and sense; mines, th' earth & plants.	121	Providence		136
SPORT				
Play not for gain, but sport. Who playes for more	14	Ch.-Porch		193
Make not thy sport, abuses: for the fly	15	Ch.-Porch		233
Then he's the sport: the mirth then in him rests,	16	Ch.-Porch		251
And now wearie of sport, glad to ingrosse	33	Sacrifice		193
And all in sport to geere at me.	110	The Quip		4
Disturb the work. O make me not their sport,	155	Glimpse		29
may talk, so they do it not with sport, but commiseration;)	287	Priest 37		14
When age is jocond it makes sport for death.	342	Proverbs		637
It's a poore sport that's not worth the candle.	346	Proverbs		752
The best of the sport is to doe the deede, and say nothing.	348	Proverbs		812
SPORTFULLY				
and then also in a serious manner, never jestingly or sportfully.	237	Priest 9		13
SPORTING				
and sporting, he first commends the study of the Civill Law,	277	Priest 32		30
SPORTS				
In sports and journeys men are knowne.	334	Proverbs		399
An old cat sports not with her prey.	355	Proverbs		1030
SPOT				
From the least spot or thought of blame.	93	Unkindness		9
SPOTS				
but reverend, and clean, without spots, or dust, or smell;	228	Priest 3		11
SPOTTED				
More spotted then my flesh can bee.	202	love	W	9
SPOTTS				
In a Leopard the spotts are not observed.	343	Proverbs		660
SPOUSE				
Make bracelets for the spouse & wife	76	Sunday	W	31
But above all, thy Church and Spouse doth prove	190	Ch.-Milit.		9
Spices come from the East; so did thy Spouse,	190	Ch.-Milit.		13
SPOUTS				
What are two shallow foords, two little spouts	164	Grief		9
SPRANG				
There sprang twelve stalks of wheat:	125	Peace		28
SPREAD				
Which spread their forces into every part,	52	H.Commun.		11
If as a flowre doth spread and die,	57	Employm. 1		1
And spread thy golden wings in me;	59	Whitsunday		2
Of thy great love once spread, as in an urn	99	Decay		17
And make the purchase spread	105	Obedience		39
Flies have their table spread, ere they appeare.	118	Providence		54
Began to spread and to expatiate there:	130	Love unkn.		39
Which thou hast open'd: do not spread thy robe	138	The Size		43
While his conquests dayly spread;	199	L'Envoy		8
perplexity, untill it spread, and taint his other duties of piety,	273	Priest 31		1
but also spread in his Parish, without any remedy (which cannot be	287	Priest 37		1
SPREADS				
And spreads the plaister equall to the crime:	44	H. Bapt.1		11
SPREDD				
My thoughts began to burnish, spredd, and swell,	102	Jordan 2	W	4
SPREDDING				
Spredding the plaister equall to the crime:	44	H. Bapt.1	W	11
SPREEDES				
True praise rootes and spreedes.	342	Proverbs		638
SPRING				
Which is above the heav'ns, whose spring and rent	44	H. Bapt.1		5
Which is above the heav'ns, whose spring and vent	44	H. Bapt.1	V	5
I envie no mans nightingale or spring;	57	Jordan 1		13
And after death the fumes that spring	69	Content		22
Then those same pendant profits, which the spring	86	Lent		25
Sweet spring, full of sweet dayes and roses,	88	Vertue		9
The spring, whence all things flow:	101	Miserie		60
The pigeons feed their tender off-spring, crying,	118	Providence		62
If a cleare spring for me no time forbears,	136	Ephes.		28
A neighbour spring to cool his inward heat;	154	Glimpse		14
Are thy returns! ev'n as the flowers in spring;	165	The Flower		2
Many a spring I shoot up fair,	166	The Flower		24
Want a spring-showre,	166	The Flower		27
Go birds of spring: let winter have his fee,	177	Forerunners		34
Making a Head & spring against thy Reason.	213	Bohemia	D	59

SPRING (cont'd)	PAGE	TITLE		LINE
My Eyes, from whence these Tears did spring,	214	Convert	D	6
Rivers neede a spring.	341	Proverbs		600
Hee that is in a towne in May loseth his spring.	353	Proverbs		988
be My God & Dear Master, the Spring & Fountain of all Goodness.	379	Letters		16
SPRING-SHOWRE				
Want a spring-showre,	166	The Flower		27
SPRING'S				
Which by the springs accesse grew much more great.	154	Glimpse		15
SPRINGING				
Of sov'raigne tears, springing from true remorse:	170	Water-crs.		8
SPRINGS				
This losse springs chiefly from our education.	10	Ch.-Porch		97
Rivers run, and springs each one	113	Businesse		3
Such as springs use that fall, and windes that blow.	117	Providence		16
Springs vent their streams, and by expense get store:	119	Providence		71
Let th' upper springs into the low	137	The Size		5
O who will give me tears? Come all ye springs,	164	Grief		1
But I fear the heat of my late Ague hath dryed up those springs,	363	Letters		5
SPRINKLED				
Sprinkled and taught, how to behave	25	Superlim		2
SPROUT				
My thoughts began to burnish, sprout, and swell,	102	Jordan 2		4
SPRUCE (see alsc spruse)				
SPRUNG				
Shall I, to please anothers wine-sprung minde,	8	Ch.-Porch		37
Sprung from that beautie which can never fade;	54	Love 1		2
Sprunq from the beautie which can never fade;	54	Love 1	W	2
Sprunq from thine eye, did work within my soul,	172	The Glance		14
Busie in controversies sprung of late.	194	Ch.-Milit.		166
SPRUSE				
So spruse, as Greece and Egypt? yet their hearts	194	Ch.-Milit.	W	151
SPUN				
That which will not be spun,	343	Proverbs		665
SPUNNE				
And sudden arbours shadow course-spunne lines?	56	Jordan 1		7
Or of it self, like a good huswife, spunne	88	The Pearl		4
SPURN				
Except thou make us dayly, we shall spurn	127	Giddinesse		27
SPURRE				
Is a good spurre. Correct thy passions spite;	16	Ch.-Porch		263
Reason lies betweene the spurre and the bridle.	345	Proverbs		711
SPURRED				
A throbbing conscience spurred by remorse	132	The Storm		9
and others spurred to do well, that they may enjoy the like	243	Priest 11		26
SPURRES				
He that hath love in his brest, hath spurres in his sides.	335	Proverbs		426
SPY				
Then went I to a garden, and did spy	125	Peace		13
But it shall spy some of there victories.	212	Bohemia	D	46
SPYES				
As he that Heaven beyond much thicket spyes	43	H. Bapt.1	W	3
he spyes some scoffing ruffian, who is likely to deride him for his	273	Priest 31		28
SPYING				
And send them to thine heart; that spying sinne,	23	Ch.-Porch		416
And send them to thy heart; that spying sinne,	23	Ch.-Porch	W	416
SQUARE				
Mark you the floore? that square & speckled stone,	66	Ch.-floore		1
He breaks the square.	145	Discharge		32
SQUARED				
even as John the Baptist squared out to every one (even to Souldiers)	277	Priest 32		23
SQUATS				
Moreover I say, that even bruises and squats, and falls,	294	Cornaro		33
SQUEEZE				
and squeeze blood undecently to the station wherein God hath placed	265	Priest 26		17
SQUINT				
Love makes a good eye squint.	339	Proverbs		543
Perversnes makes one squint ey'd.	342	Proverbs		634
ST				
And therefore St. Paul in the beginning of his Epistles,	225	Priest 1		9
And herein St Paul excelled in all his Epistles.	234	Priest 7		10
according to St. Pauls rule, Ephes. 4. 28. 1 Thes. 4. 11, 12.	275	Priest 32		2
And therfore St. Peter used that fearfull imprecation to Simon Magus,	285	Priest 36		29
So did St. Paul, 2 Tim. 4. 14. and 1 Tim. 1. 20.	285	Priest 36		31
To which joyn that of St. peter, Casting all your Care on the Lord,	374	Letters		15
only one place more to you (Philip. 4. 4.) St. Paul saith there:	374	Letters		21
then I bequeath to Mr Bostocke St. Augustines workes and his halfe	382	G.H.'s Will		20
STABIE				
With a great stable or demain:	70	Quidditie		8
With my great stable or demain:	70	Quidditie	W	8
STAFFE				
Walk'd with a staffe to heav'n, and traced fountains:	37	The Agonie		3
Some wood and nails to make a staffe or bill	106	Conscience		21
Faith needs no staffe of flesh, but stoutly can	135	Divinitie		27
To guide, thy staffe to bear.	173	23 Psalme		16
Now with the crosse, as with a staffe, alone,	190	Ch.-Milit.		28
If yee would know a knave, give him a staffe.	321	Proverbs		19
A married man turns his staffe into a stake.	333	Proverbs		366
If the staffe be crooked, the shadow cannot be straight.	341	Proverbs		583
An old mans staffe is the rapper of deaths doore.	351	Proverbs		916
hath a rock and a spindle, and no staffe to spin.	358	Proverbs	D	1085

STARRE (cont'd)	PAGE	TITLE		LINE
Or, since one starre show'd thy first breath,	38	Good Fri.		7
Or starre, or rainbow, or a part	62	Mattens		7
The Starre.	74	The Starre		T
Man is no starre, but a quick coal	79	Employm.2		6
His eyes dismount the highest starre:	91	Man		21
As if a starre were duller then a clod,	134	Divinitie		3
Me thoughts a starre did shoot into my lap.	139	Artillerie		2
To parents issue and the sunnes bright starre!	168	The Sonne		6
To parents issue and the sonnes bright starre!	168	The Sonne	V	6
Is some starre (fled from the sphere)	181	Banquet		10
Doubtlesse, neither starre nor flower	181	Banquet		19
building it all upon the word untill the day starre arise,	318	Valdesso		9
STARRES				
Take starres for money; starres not to be told	13	Ch.-Porch		171
And mend as rising starres & rivers doe.	44	H. Bapt.1	W	9
Such starres I counted mine: both heav'n and earth	46	Afflict.1		11
Church-bels beyond the starres heard, the souls bloud,	51	Prayer 1		13
Starres are poore books, & oftentimes do misse:	58	H.Script.2		13
This book of starres lights to eternall blisse.	58	H.Script.2		14
This book of starres can spell eternall blisse.	58	H.Script.2	W	14
The starres were coming down to know	59	Whitsunday		11
Whereas the starres	79	Employm.2		19
In laws and policie; what the starres conspire,	88	The Pearl		5
The starres have us to bed;	91	Man		31
No, not to purchase the whole pack of starres:	101	Miserie		52
To whom the starres shine not so fair, as eyes;	111	Vanitie 2		3
And if an herb hath power, what have the starres?	119	Providence		77
Beyond the utmost starres and poles.	123	Time		18
Starres have their storms, ev'n in a high degree,	132	The Storm		7
As men, for fear the starres should sleep and nod,	134	Divinitie		1
But not of speech in starres, began to muse:	139	Artillerie		10
The starres and all things are; If I refuse,	139	Artillerie		12
But I have also starres and shooters too,	139	Artillerie		17
As many eyes as starres? since it is night,	140	Ch.-rents		26
The starres his tire of light and rings obtain'd,	151	The Bag		13
Yet can I mark how starres above	162	The Search		13
God hath made starres the foil	176	The Foil		5
And starres alone unto the pitch doe runne	211	Bohemia	D	4
And though starres shott from heaven loose their light,	211	Bohemia	D	9
STARS				
then by stars at their nativities.	357	Proverbs	D	1060
START				
Inclose me still for fear I START.	133	Paradise		7
Then did your sev'rall parts unloose and start:	140	Ch.-rents		21
Little dogs start the Hare, the great get her.	341	Proverbs		593
STARTLE				
Beware of Lust (startle not) o beware	6	Ch.-Porch	W	7
STARTS				
A good pay-master starts not at assurances.	324	Proverbs		113
STARVE				
And thou within them starve at doore.	93	Unkindness		14
STARVING				
By starving sinne and taking such repast,	87	Lent		44
Starving the while he worshippeth his meat!	193	Ch.-Milit.		114
STATE				
Dost lose? rise up: dost winne? rise in that state.	14	Ch.-Porch		201
I care not though the cloth of state should be	17	Ch.-Porch		269
Kneeling ne're spoil'd silk stocking: quit thy state.	22	Ch.-Porch		407
May give a disentangled state and free:	36	Reprisall		6
O what a state is this, which never knew	65	Ch.-mus.	W	8
To shew that state dislikes not easinesse.	103	Prayer 2		4
Yet all this glorie, all this pomp and state	106	Sion		7
Indeed a slack and sleepie state of minde	130	Love unkn.		57
A Christians state and case	138	The Size		31
To bear them out, and with my state agree.	164	Grief		8
In that dark state of tears: to all, that so	169	The Answer		12
Giving the Church a crown to keep her state,	192	Ch.-Milit.		91
Hath soild with Black) the colour of my state,	209	L. Bacon	D	7
A Paradox. That the Sicke are in better State then the Whole.	209	Paradox	D	T
Your state, to ours, is contrary;	210	Paradox	D	7
The sicke are in themselves a State	210	Paradox	D	13
At there owne weapons, without pomp or state	211	Bohemia	D	21
When scepters, state, Attendants are the screen	212	Bohemia	D	24
who somtimes make it a piece of state not to come at the beginning	232	Priest 6		8
the time of the year, or from the State, or from God by a child born,	235	Priest 8		35
mindes to apprehend Gods good blessing to our Church, and State;	236	Priest 8		23
The Parson's state of Life.	236	Priest 9		T
Parson considering that virginity is a higher state then Matrimony,	236	Priest 9		32
day against the proper and peculiar temptations of his state of Life,	238	Priest 9		2
or untimely desire of promotion to an higher state, or place,	238	Priest 9		15
hee considers diligently the state thereof to Godward, and that in	251	Priest 17		18
whereas in Sermons there is a kinde of state, in Catechizing there is	255	Priest 21		9
it the best way of preserving a state to reduce it to its principles	258	Priest 22		16
that he cannot without this maintain himself in a Christian state.	272	Priest 31		25
all those, who else might both trouble him and the whole State.	276	Priest 32		16
Neither is this true onely in the military state of a Christian life,	279	Priest 33		3
that there is a double state of a Christian even in this Life,	280	Priest 34		1
as he discovers any of his Flock to be in one or the other state,	280	Priest 34		13
Those that he findes in the peaceable state, he adviseth to be very	280	Priest 34		14
Those that the Parson findes in the military state, he fortifyes,	281	Priest 34		5

	PAGE	TITLE		LINE
STEAD (cont'd)				
The Countrey Parson is in Gods stead to his Parish, and dischargeth	254	Priest 20		8
the Parson endeavoureth to be in Gods stead, knowing that Countrey	254	Priest 20		30
of whom in stead of the qualities of the world, he asks no other,	260	Priest 23		30
to know what herbs may be used in stead of drugs of the same nature,	261	Priest 23		29
that in stead of a Physician a regular life is to be embraced,	298	Cornaro		12
STEADFAST				
If he stand steadfast in his heart, having no necessity,	237	Priest 9		16
STEADIE				
A steadie aiming at a tombe.	48	Repentance		6
STEADY				
and steady posture, as attending to what is done in the Church,	231	Priest 6		26
STEAL				
Rather then shew his cards.) Steal from his treasure	18	Ch.-Porch		298
Therefore we dare not from his garland steal,	78	Ang.&Sts.		24
By noon most cunningly did steal away,	94	Life		5
A friend did steal into my cup for good,	130	Love unkn.		43
least the poyson steal into some young and unwary spirits,	252	Priest 18		6
then they fall to drink, to steal, to whore, to scoffe,	274	Priest 32		11
He that steals an egge, will steal an oxe.	358	Proverbs	D	1090
STEALE				
Or, if I steale up to the skie,	61	Praise 1	W	7
To steale the Hog, and give the feet for almes.	329	Proverbs		237
STEALES				
Hee wrongs not an old man that steales his supper from him.	331	Proverbs		311
Hee that knowes what may bee gained in a day never steales.	336	Proverbs		445
STEALING				
The other curbs sinnes stealing pace and theft.	117	Providence		36
whose natures are most stealing, and beginnings uncertaine.	264	Priest 26		33
The Frier preached against stealing,	345	Proverbs		737
STEALS				
Hither sometimes Sinne steals, and stains	67	Ch.-floore		13
He that steals an egge, will steal an oxe.	358	Proverbs	D	1090
STEALTH				
Although by stealth	44	H. Bapt.2		11
Though that by stealth	44	H. Bapt.2	W	11
STEEL				
Till all were melted, though he were all steel:	33	Sacrifice		211
Gladly engrave thy love in steel,	55	Temper 1		2
Or steel, or mountains be thy ring,	163	The Search		35
STEELE				
Steele & a flint strike fire,	202	Trin.Sun.	W	7
The tongue is not steele, yet it cuts.	349	Proverbs		838
A master of straw eates a servant of steele.	355	Proverbs		1029
STEER				
He doth preserve it: he doth steer,	151	The Bag		3
STEMME				
Deare flesh, while I do pray, learn here thy stemme	65	Ch.-monum.		17
Who were cut short in Alexanders stemme.	192	Ch.-Milit.		74
STENCH				
To deale with brimstone, that untamed stench	212	Bohemia	D	53
STEP (see also stept)				
They step into their voluntarie graves,	98	Mortific.		8
Baptisme often (being the first step into their great and glorious	258	Priest 22		18
Step after step the ladder is ascended.	334	Proverbs		393
The greatest step is that out of doores.	337	Proverbs		461
Fortune to one is Mother, to another is Step-mother.	359	Proverbs	D	1118
Take heed of a step-mother; the very name of her sufficeth.	360	Proverbs	D	1155
but that every day, I may step one step towards my journies end;	364	Letters		27
Gods earth, no not tho' the advice step so far, as to be reproof:	378	Letters		13
STEP-MOTHER				
Fortune to one is Mother, to another is Step-mother.	359	Proverbs	D	1118
Take heed of a step-mother; the very name of her sufficeth.	360	Proverbs	D	1155
STEPHENS'				
are divers moneys of mine in Mr Stephens hands Stationer of London,	383	G.H.'s Will		22
STEPS				
Where rude unhallow'd steps do crush and grinde	140	Ch.-rents		8
Shewing his steps should be the street,	173	Marie Magd		4
and containes the direct steps of Pastorall Duty and Auctority.	225	Priest 1		3
is ever very well supplyed by some able man who treads in his steps,	232	Priest 7		26
and one of the first steps of pleasing God, having for his owne use	279	Priest 33		7
STEPT				
Letting, while one foot stept, the other stay	191	Ch.-Milit.		34
STERNE				
by which we well know how to convince the sterne, and more austere	442	Oration		6
STEWARD				
For what account can thy ill steward make?	83	Sighs & Gr.		8
STEWS				
Of stews and brothels onely knew the doores,	176	Forerunners		15
nothing to do, lets go to the Tavern, or to the stews, or what not.	274	Priest 32		13
STICK				
Gold thou mayst safely touch; but if it stick	13	Ch.-Porch		167
Stick fast therein, but thy transcendent soule	211	Bohemia	D	7
Dresse a stick, and it seemes a youth.	324	Proverbs		101
Presse a stick, and it seemes a youth.	324	Proverbs	V	101
Ill natures, the more you aske them, the more they stick.	324	Proverbs		106
STICKES				
Litle stickes kindle the fire; great ones put it out.	332	Proverbs		323
STICKS				
Flesh being turn'd to dust, and bones to sticks.	186	Death		8
when the answerer sticks, an illustrating the thing by something	256	Priest 21		37

	PAGE	TITLE		LINE
STIE				
And wilt thou leave the Church, and love a stie?	176	Forerunners		22
STIL				
yet when God pleased, the sun stood stil, the fire burned not.	271	Priest 30		12
STILE				
though it be none of the Court-stile, yet doubtless Madam,	377	Letters		2
STIL'D				
In bitter grief: yet am I stil'd	150	Longing		59
STILL				
Think the king sees thee still; for his King does.	11	Ch.-Porch		122
Shoots a bow short, and lessens still his stake,	13	Ch.-Porch		159
Yet in thy thriving still misdoubt some evil;	13	Ch.-Porch		163
Yett in thy pursing still thy self distrust	13	Ch.-Porch	W	163
Still in thy heart, that he may see what's there.	17	Ch.-Porch		272
Both want, and wish thy pleasing presence still.	19	Ch.-Porch		326
Need & bee glad, & wish thy presence still:	19	Ch.-Porch	W	326
Let thy minde still be bent, still plotting where,	20	Ch.-Porch		337
Though he alight sometimes, still goeth on.	20	Ch.-Porch		340
Because the raging waters still are high:	29	Sacrifice		95
Heark how they crie aloud still, Crucifie:	29	Sacrifice		97
Yet still they shout, and crie, and stop their eares,	30	Sacrifice		105
And yet thy wounds still my attempts defie,	36	Reprisall		7
The Place, & keep possession still.	39	Good Fri.	W	30
Yet do we still persist as we began,	41	Sepulchre		21
And still with sicknesses and shame	43	East.wings		12
More backward still, and to that water flie,	43	H. Bapt.1		4
Which then join'd with you still meet in my brest	44	H. Bapt.1	W	8
O let me still	44	H. Bapt.2		6
Whose life still pressing	48	Repentance		4
For so thou should'st without me still have been,	52	H.Commun.		5
If still the sunne should hide his face,	60	Grace		5
If the Sunn still should hide his face,	60	Grace	W	5
Death is still working like a mole,	60	Grace		13
Sinne is still hammering my heart	60	Grace		17
Yet still thou goest on,	64	Even-song		17
And mend it still;	66	Ch.-lock		6
Mending it still;	66	Ch.-lock	W	6
Then to have hellish moths still gnaw and fret	69	Content		27
He that doth still and strongly good pursue,	72	Constancie		2
Who still is right, and prayes to be so still.	73	Constancie		35
Thy life on earth was grief, and thou art still	73	Afflict.3		13
We could not choose but look on still;	75	Sunday		19
The earth sat still,	79	Employm.2		14
The sunne still shineth there or here,	79	Employm.2		18
But we are still too young or old;	79	Employm.2		26
Hath still sow'd fig-leaves to exclude thy light:	83	Sighs & Gr.		16
Taught me to live here so, That still one eye	85	Coloss.		7
Ten still, if sermons go for gains.	96	Charms & K		16
Doth closet up it self, and still retreat,	99	Decay		18
Cold sinne still forcing it, till it return,	99	Decay		19
His house still burns, and yet he still doth sing,	100	Miserie		4
Yet if thou talkest still,	106	Conscience		19
Yet if thou stayest still, why must I stay?	108	Home		31
Then Money came, and chinking still,	110	The Quip		9
But thou dost still lament, and pine, and crie;	112	Dawning		7
Windes still work: it is their plot,	113	Businesse		9
Lovers are still pretending, & ev'n wrongs	116	Dulnesse		19
Still mock me, and grow bold:	116	Dulnesse		22
Not that thou hast not still above	124	Gratefulnes		21
Yet still askt pardon, and was not deni'd.	129	Love unkn.		21
Inclose me still for fear I START.	133	Paradise		7
For since thy God refuseth still,	133	The Method		2
Yet if I wail not still, since still to wail	136	Ephes.		31
Those are at home; these journey still,	138	The Size		23
Not, but I am (I must say still)	139	Artillerie		21
For where before thou still didst call on me,	141	Justice 2		19
Now I still touch	141	Justice 2		20
Where lay my heart; and climbing still,	142	Pilgrimage		21
Shall still be open; what he sends	152	The Bag		39
Shall I be still in suit?	153	The Collar		6
O be mine still! still make me thine!	157	Clasping		19
Conceals thee still?	163	The Search		30
Thou turnest th' edge of all things on me still,	165	The Crosse		21
Still upwards bent, as if heav'n were mine own,	166	The Flower		30
And still it runneth mutt'ring up and down	168	a true Hymn		4
But still thy sweet originall joy	172	The Glance		13
Yet have they left me, Thou art still my God.	176	Forerunners		6
So Thou art still my God, be out of fear.	176	Forerunners		10
For, Thou art still my God, is all that ye	177	Forerunners		32
Still invite, still call to thee:	180	Invitation		33
Still are good,	181	Banquet		26
But I still being low and short,	182	Banquet		40
Of all thy mercies, is my posie still.	182	The Posie		4
Of all Gods mercies, is my posie still.	183	The Posie		12
But still to make thee prepossest,	184	The Elixer		7
And are there any leaves, that still abide?	188	Heaven		7
And are there any leaves, which still abide?	188	Heaven	W	7
At length to Germanie, still westward bending,	192	Ch.-Milit.		81
So they might still, and point us out the place	192	Ch.-Milit.		85
But as in vice the copie still exceeds	196	Ch.-Milit.		221
Thus also Sinne and Darknesse follow still	198	Ch.-Milit.		272

STILL (cont'd)	PAGE	TITLE		LINE
But as the Sunne still goes both west and east;	198	Ch.-Milit.		274
Still eastward go; because it drew more neare	198	Ch.-Milit.		276
Is more, but for mee still.	200	H. Commun.	W	18
Thou still, O Lord, outstrippest mee.	201	love	W	6
Or, since thy wayes are deep, and still the same,	206	Walton 1		10
Nor yet thy eloquence here keep him still,	439	Walton 5		3
Maintaine there Lustre still, & shining cleere	211	Bohemia	D	11
with timely fruit still laden stand:	214	Psalm I	D	10
But thou, O Lord, art still the shield	216	Psalm III	D	5
for God sustain'd me still.	216	Psalm III	D	12
protected still by thee:	219	Psalm V	D	38
in that still joyful bee.	219	Psalm V	D	40
making a hook of his Charity, causeth them still to depend on him;	244	Priest 12		32
still pressing it in the pulpit, and out of the pulpit,	245	Priest 12		13
at the eleventh houre, and therefore hee still expects, and waits,	250	Priest 16		19
because to answer in form may still admit ignorance:	259	Priest 22		8
but that they still fall from all compromises that have been made.	260	Priest 23		24
but as a brother still, except some small and temporary estranging	263	Priest 25		30
this is foretold, that it shall be so still, until things be no more.	268	Priest 28		15
and neighbourly admonitions they still persist in ill, to present	270	Priest 29		20
but to labour still to be as fervent in Christian Duties,	280	Priest 34		19
weather be what it will, still we have bread, though sometimes more,	281	Priest 34		25
and wert proceeding still on in thy Favours, untill we interrupted	288	Priest		15
for an apple once we lost our God, and still lose him for no more;	288	Priest		19
even for those that derided him then, and still despise him.	288	Priest		30
still striving & prospering so long within us, untill our obedience	290	Priest		10
Which benefits also still continue, because from the time that I was	293	Cornaro		24
be by a plenarie circumspection) but still even to the most learned	309	Valdesso		23
the Scriptures still used, and Gods worke within us still observed,	309	Valdesso		32
and Gods worke within us still observed, who workes by his Word,	309	Valdesso		32
but such a one as shall still have the assistance of the holy spirit	310	Valdesso		6
and those that have inspirations must still use Peter, Gods Word:	310	Valdesso		10
the Scriptures, cr to themselves being still men, though godly men.	316	Valdesso		4
The Authour doth still discover too slight a regard of the Scripture,	317	Valdesso		22
Who hath none to still him, may weepe out his eyes.	321	Proverbs		17
Though old and wise, yet still advise.	325	Proverbs		134
Take heede of still waters, the quick passe away.	326	Proverbs		171
The absent partie is still faultie.	332	Proverbs		318
When you are an Anvill, hold you still;	332	Proverbs		338
Though you see a Church-man ill, yet continue in the Church still.	344	Proverbs		698
Still fisheth he that catcheth one.	358	Proverbs	D	1095
is still true to you, and hath nothing else to answer your infinite	363	Letters		18
by the Patents of your perpetual favour to do so still,	365	Letters		25
and yet still grow upon Your humblest Servant, GEORGE HERBERT.	367	Letters		15
working, still together, that I take a comfort therein;	375	Letters		19
and still they will be presenting or wishing to see, if at length	376	Letters		28
STING				
As swords cause death, so may a little sting.	20	Ch.-Porch	W	352
Sting my delay,	61	Praise 1		18
With that abash'd and struck with many a sting	142	Pilgrimage		25
Save in the sight thereof, where strength doth sting.	165	The Crosse		18
Where is thy famous force, thy ancient sting?	169	Dial.-Anth		2
STINGS				
The honey is sweet, but the Bee stings.	328	Proverbs		212
STINT				
The windes their stint: and yet when I did call,	158	Praise 3		23
of my friends, to adde something to my usuall stint and measure.	295	Cornaro		21
my stint of meat and drink should be diminished, rather then	295	Cornaro		30
STIR				
and stir out in the morning, and knows what prayers they say,	241	Priest 10		2
STIRRE				
My soul would stirre	78	Employm.2		2
Behold, thy dust doth stirre,	149	Longing		37
And rivers stirre, thou canst not shrink or quail:	156	Assurance		33
And in my powers not stirre abroad,	183	A Parodie		9
Till it stirre, and rubbe the eyes;	186	Dooms-day		4
It did not fit his gravitie to stirre,	195	Ch.-Milit.		197
STIRR'D				
My minde would be extreamly stirr'd	95	Submission		3
STIRRING				
Active and stirring spirits live alone.	20	Ch.-Porch		341
STOCK				
Get a good stock of these, then draw the card	18	Ch.-Porch		293
The speaker to thee, and preserve thy stock.	18	Ch.-Porch		300
Whether thy stock of credit swell, or fall.	20	Ch.-Porch		346
Slovens take up their stock of noisomnesse	21	Ch.-Porch		369
Out of my stock of naturall delights,	46	Afflict.1		5
My stock lies dead, and no increase	60	Grace		1
I have abus'd thy stock, destroy'd thy woods,	83	Sighs & Gr.		9
The stock and surplus, cause and historie:	88	The Pearl		8
For future times, the droppings of the stock	154	Glimpse		24
in consideration of providing a stock for his children;	240	Priest 10		7
and when his own stock serves not, working those that are able	245	Priest 12		12
or Hamlet, of advancing the publick Stock, and managing Commons,	276	Priest 32		5
STOCKD				
you have stockd the grounds:	380	Woodnoth		9
STOCKING				
Kneeling ne're spoil'd silk stocking: quit thy state.	22	Ch.-Porch		407
or draining, or stocking, or fencing, and ordering his land	275	Priest 32		25

	PAGE	TITLE		LINE
STOCKS				
and good breeding, are his two great stocks for his children;	240	Priest 10		10
or put into the stocks, that they may be looked upon.	287	Priest 37		21
STOLE				
Man stole the fruit, but I must climbe the tree;	33	Sacrifice		202
Wrapt in nights mantle, stole into a manger;	81	Christmas		10
STOLLEN				
Alas! what have I stollen from you? Death.	34	Sacrifice		231
STOMACH				
Tast all, but feed not. if thy stomach call	11	Ch.-Porch	W	128
When a man sleepes, his head is in his stomach.	353	Proverbs		981
STOMACK				
Thou hast two sconses, if thy stomack call;	11	Ch.-Porch		128
that a weak stomack being prepossessed with flesh, shall much better	242	Priest 10		22
(having a most cold & moist stomack) I fell into divers diseases,	291	Cornaro		21
to wit, into the pain of the stomack, and often of the side,	291	Cornaro		22
and chose that wine that fitted my stomack, and in such measure,	293	Cornaro		17
taking care never to rise with a full stomack, but so as I might well	293	Cornaro		18
and especially since the power of my stomack every day decreased.	295	Cornaro		33
Who would beleeve that old wine should hurt my stomack,	297	Cornaro		32
For I eat little, because a little sufficeth my weak stomack:	300	Cornaro		9
(though most agreeable to them) then their stomack can easily digest:	300	Cornaro		13
STONE				
Makes money not a contemptible stone.	12	Ch.-Porch		156
Is such a stone,	26	The Altar		6
Remember that thou once didst write in stone.	38	The Sinner		14
No lodging for thee, but a cold hard stone?	40	Sepulchre		2
Was writ in stone; so thou, which also art	41	Sepulchre		18
And a much fitter stone	45	Nature		17
Before that sinne turn'd flesh to stone,	53	H.Commun.		29
Silver, or gold, or precious stone,	62	Mattens		6
Mark you the floore? that square & speckled stone,	66	Ch.-floore		1
Who by aspersions throw a stone	96	Charms & K		9
All Solomons sea of brasse and world of stone	106	Sion		17
Or with a stone! yet make no good foundation.	120	Providence		124
This is the famous stone	185	The Elixer		21
They say, it is an ill Mason that refuseth any stone:	228	Priest 4		15
touch him no more, then a stone thrown against heaven, where he is,	269	Priest 28		8
he that throws a stone at another, hits himselfe;	269	Priest 28		14
be done by Aurum potabile, or the Philosophers stone, sought of many,	298	Cornaro		20
A rugged stone growes smooth from hand to hand.	332	Proverbs		316
A foole may throw a stone into a well,	339	Proverbs		527
You cannot flea a stone.	346	Proverbs		764
A stone in a well is not lost.	349	Proverbs		845
STONECUTTING				
in Architecture, painting, stonecutting, musick, and husbandrie,	301	Cornaro		37
STONES				
What skills it, if a bag of stones or gold	13	Ch.-Porch		169
Pick out of mirth, like stones out of thy ground,	16	Ch.-Porch		235
These stones to praise thee may not cease.	26	The Altar		14
Where our hard hearts have took up stones to brain thee,	41	Sepulchre		13
Onely these stones in quiet entertain thee,	41	Sepulchre		15
For though sinnes plead too, yet like stones they make	66	Ch.-lock		11
And truly brasse and stones are heavie things,	107	Sion		19
And curious vertues both of herbs and stones?	119	Providence		74
Who remove stones, bruise their fingers.	322	Proverbs		40
Whose house is of glasse, must not throw stones at another.	327	Proverbs		196
Vertue now is in herbs and stones and words onely.	337	Proverbs		478
Vertue now is in stones, herbs & words only.	337	Proverbs	V	478
Castles are Forrests of stones.	352	Proverbs		936
STONIE				
If stonie hearts will melt with gentle love.	29	Sacrifice		90
He clave the stonie rock, when they were drie;	30	Sacrifice		122
Stonie hearts will bleed.	179	Discipline		20
STOOD				
When Solomons temple stood and flourished!	106	Sion		2
That we have nought. I stood amaz'd at this,	143	Holdfast		10
The Temple where an Idol stood,	214	Convert	D	18
Nor hath in way of sinners stood,	214	Psalm I	D	3
yet when God pleased, the sun stood stil, the fire burned not.	271	Priest 30		12
STOOL				
To go where the King goes afoot (i.e. to the stool).	356	Proverbs	D	1034
STOOP (see also stoup)				
and decent chest, with a Chalice, and Cover, and a Stoop, or Flagon;	246	Priest 13		19
STOOPS				
The great heart stoops, and taketh from the dust	192	Ch.-Milit.		67
STOP				
Yet still they shout, and crie, and stop their eares,	30	Sacrifice		105
And stop our sinnes from growing thick and wide,	44	H. Bapt.1		8
The sea, which seems to stop the traveller,	119	Providence		89
though businesses may stop my hand, yet my heart, a much better	371	Letters		26
STOPPED				
instantly dry up, as a river would if the fountain were stopped.	271	Priest 30		7
STOPS				
I know it is my sinne, which stops thine eares,	66	Ch.-lock	W	1
What both the stops and pegs of pleasure bee:	89	The Pearl	W	28
And when it stops for want of store,	157	Praise 3		4
O, could I love! and stops: God writeth, Loved,	168	a true Hymn		20
STOR'D				
with shafts of vengeance stor'd.	222	Psalm VII	D	44

	PAGE	TITLE		LINE
STORD				
But joyes are stord for thee: thou shalt returne	212	Bohemia	D	55
STORE				
They strike my head, the rock from whence all store	32	Sacrifice		170
Shall I weep bloud? why, thou hast wept such store	35	Thanksgvng		5
My heart hath store, write there, where in	39	Good Fri.		23
Sure there is room within our hearts good store;	40	Sepulchre		5
Lord, who createdst man in wealth and store,	43	East.wings		1
I know the projects of unbridled store:	89	The Pearl		26
I know the projects of unbundled store:	89	The Pearl	V	26
Where both their baskets are with all their store,	89	The Pearl	W	26
And we no store.	93	Antiphon 2		21
Wee have no store.	93	Antiphon 2	W	21
And ruffle all their curious knots and store.	97	Afflict.5		22
Springs vent their streams, and by expense get store:	119	Providence		71
The hills with health abound; the vales with store;	119	Providence		95
It go for one, hath many wayes in store	121	Providence		150
And made it bring forth grapes good store.	128	Bunch Gr.		25
My want of tears with store of bloud.	136	Ephes.		36
Loose as the winde, as large as store.	153	The Collar		5
And when it stops for want of store,	157	Praise 3		4
And so take up at use good store:	159	Praise 3		40
I tun'd another (having store)	162	The Search		21
I turn'd another (having store)	162	The Search	V	21
Swelling through store,	167	The Flower		48
To serve thy sinnes, and furnish thee with store	170	Water-crs.		7
But reserve his breath in store,	199	L'Envoy		12
Or reserve his breath in store,	199	L'Envoy	W	12
As God gives thee store,	207	Walton 3		5
Then worldlings joy'd with all their store	218	Psalm IV	D	27
nor to store their house with all those furnitures which even their	280	Priest 34		24
made a Land of light, a store-house of thy treasures and mercies:	289	Priest		19
and purging, that the store of humours, and inflammation,	295	Cornaro		5
Giving much to the poore, doth inrich a mans store.	327	Proverbs		191
To review ones store is to mow twice.	354	Proverbs		1007
STORE-HOUSE				
made a Land of light, a store-house of thy treasures and mercies:	289	Priest		19
STOREHOUSE				
the storehouse and magazene of life and comfort, the holy Scriptures.	228	Priest 4		22
which is the storehouse of his Sermons, and which he preacheth all	230	Priest 5		1
STORIE				
But he that boasts, shuts that out of his storie.	8	Ch.-Porch		52
Transfus'd a sheepishnesse into thy storie:	10	Ch.-Porch		94
Shall I then sing, skipping, thy dolefull storie,	35	Thanksgvng		11
Shall I then sing, neglecting thy sad storie,	35	Thanksgvng	W	11
That I beleeve is in the sacred storie:	50	Faith		18
But all the constellations of the storie.	58	H.Script.2		4
But when thou dost anneal in glasse thy storie,	67	Windows		6
Their storie pennes and sets us down.	128	Bunch Gr.		11
The deed and storie	143	Complaining		7
Then let me tell thee a strange storie.	151	The Bag		8
Alas poore mortall, void of storie,	169	Dial.-Anth		3
That choice may be thy storie.	170	Self-cond.		6
STORIES (levels)				
And so my sinnes ascend three stories high,	122	Sinnes rd.		14
STORIES				
Sometimes he tells them stories, and sayings of others,	233	Priest 7		12
but stories and sayings they will well remember.	233	Priest 7		17
STORING				
So a man storing up mony for his necessary provisions, both in	264	Priest 26		26
his children, hardly perceives when his storing becomes unlawfull:	264	Priest 26		28
yet is there a period for his storing, and a point, or center,	264	Priest 26		29
or center, when his storing, which was even now good, passeth from	264	Priest 26		29
STORM				
I was blown through with ev'ry storm and winde.	47	Afflict.1		36
The Storm.	132	The Storm		T
Since that time many a bitter storm	172	The Glance		9
STORME				
As when a Merchant hath a ship come home after many a storme,	271	Priest 30		23
A fair day in winter is the mother of a storme.	360	Proverbs	D	1145
STORMES				
fortitude in the cold midnight stormes of persecution and adversity.	237	Priest 9		38
STORMIE				
The stormie working soul spits lies and froth.	9	Ch.-Porch		76
No stormie night	183	A Parodie		13
STORMS				
Starres have their storms, ev'n in a high degree,	132	The Storm		7
Poets have wrong'd poore storms: such dayes are best;	132	The Storm		17
Storms are the triumph of his art:	151	The Bag		5
This holy Cable's of all storms secure.	439	Walton 5		10
This holy Cable's from all storms secure.	439	Walton 5	V	10
STORY				
Lyes round about us to helpe out the story,	212	Bohemia	D	26
STOUP				
Making the whole to stoup and bow,	75	Sunday		13
STOUT				
In weaknesse must be stout.	48	Afflict.1		62
STOUTEST				
Danting the stoutest hearts, the proudest wits.	141	Justice 2		12
STOUTLY				
Faith needs no staffe of flesh, but stoutly can	135	Divinitie		27

	PAGE	TITLE		LINE
STOWRE				
Constancie knits the bones, and makes us stowre, ...	11	Ch.-Porch		117
STRAIGHT				
I straight return'd, and knowing his great birth, ...	40	Redemption		9
Who straight, Your suit is granted, said, & died.	40	Redemption		14
My soul will turn to bubbles straight, ...	45	Nature		9
My soul will bee all bubble straight, ...	45	Nature	W	9
I had it straight, and did as truly eat, ...	50	Faith		7
All of a piece, and all are cleare and straight.	72	Constancie		20
Man had straight forward gone	75	Sunday		15
The first Is straight, and our diurnall friend, ...	84	Coloss.		3
I follow straight without complaints or grief, ...	94	Life		16
I do but taste it, straight it cleanseth me, ...	106	Conscience		15
But as birds drink, and straight lift up their head, ...	131	Mans medly		21
And straight he turn'd, and to his brethren cry'd, ...	151	The Bag		30
But while I grow in a straight line, ...	166	The Flower		29
Wherein I die, not live: for life is straight, ...	185	A Wreath		5
Straight as a line, and ever tends to thee, ...	185	A Wreath		6
Pleasure succeeded straight, when that grew cold.	194	Ch.-Milit.		144
and straight ye perish from the way:	216	Psalm II	D	30
and take as much joy in a straight-growing childe, or servant,	275	Priest 32		33
If the staffe be crooked, the shadow cannot be straight. . .	341	Proverbs		583
that a man would desire straight to bee buried there. . . .	353	Proverbs		969
STRAIGHT-GROWING				
and take as much joy in a straight-growing childe, or servant,	275	Priest 32		33
STRAIN				
Lord place me in thy consort; give one strain	57	Employm. 1		23
The wanton lover in a curious strain	115	Dulnesse		5
Oh take thy lute, and tune it to a strain, ...	136	Ephes.		19
STRAINS				
I know the wayes of Pleasure, the sweet strains, ...	89	The Pearl		21
As peculiar notes and strains	186	Dooms-day		11
STRAIT				
or kneel, to do all in a strait, and steady posture, as attending	231	Priest 6		26
A crooked log makes a strait fire.	322	Proverbs		45
STRAITEN				
Do pinch and straiten thee, and use much art	99	Decay		14
STRAITLY				
he straitly requires of all to pray by themselves before they sleep	241	Priest 10		1
STRAND				
Readie to passe to the American strand.	196	Ch.-Milit.		236
That habitable sea, & brinish strand, ...	213	Bohemia	D	62
STRANGE				
Oh King of grief! (a title strange, yet true, ...	35	Thanksgvng		1
King of all Grief (a title strange, yet true, ...	35	Thanksgvng	W	1
Of strange delights, where we may wish & take.	58	H.Script.1		7
What strange pollutions doth he wed, ...	100	Miserie		13
Can thy strange wayes rehearse?	102	Miserie		66
Show'd a strange love to all our good:	104	Obedience		27
After all this canst thou be strange?	108	Home		26
Of what strange length must that needs be, ...	123	Time		25
Hath a strange force:	132	The Storm		10
All sorts of wounds; of such strange force it is.	147	Offering		21
Then let me tell thee a strange storie.	151	The Bag		8
Thy will such a strange distance is, ...	163	The Search		41
What is this strange and uncouth thing?	164	The Crosse		1
I felt a sugred strange delight, ...	171	The Glance		5
if there be any of his parish that hold strange Doctrins, . .	262	Priest 24		20
this line [place] till the end of this Chapter may seeme strange,	311	Valdesso		21
STRANGELY				
It prosper'd strangely, and did soon disperse	125	Peace		31
And having conquer'd, did so strangely rule, ...	196	Ch.-Milit.		203
he sheweth through all his Considerations) a thing strangely buried,	305	Valdesso		1
it for a time onely, and then cast it away, as he sayes strangely.	318	Valdesso		4
yet your appearing in it, affects me strangely.	369	Letters		24
STRANGENESS				
as knowing that absence breedes strangeness, but presence love.	284	Priest 35		15
STRANGER				
Pilate a stranger holdeth off; but they, ...	29	Sacrifice		101
To Man of all beasts be not thou a stranger:	81	Christmas		12
for a great day, or a stranger, his garden or orchard supplyes it,	241	Priest 10		18
then in their Countrey under so many miracles were a stranger thing,	282	Priest 34		9
STRANGERS				
If thou observest strangers in each fit, ...	21	Ch.-Porch		365
But wee strangers grown, O Lord, ...	53	H.Commun.	W	37
or bring strangers to him, he may be the better armed to encounter	274	Priest 32		7
So many men in Court and so many strangers.	350	Proverbs		874
Presents of love fear not to be ill taken of strangers. . .	361	Proverbs	D	1162
STRATAGEMS				
Fine nets and stratagems to catch us in, ...	45	Sinne 1		7
STRAW				
I got me flowers to straw thy way;	42	Easter		19
In good yeares corne is hay, in ill yeares straw is corne. . .	328	Proverbs		216
Let an ill man lie in thy straw, and he lookes to be thy heire.	330	Proverbs		271
He that hath one foot in the straw, hath another in the spittle.	336	Proverbs		438
In a long journey straw waighs.	348	Proverbs		820
A master of straw eates a servant of steele.	355	Proverbs		1029
It's a dangerous fire begins in the bed-straw.	357	Proverbs	D	1070
STRAW'D				
My dayes were straw'd with flow'rs and happinesse;	47	Afflict.1		21

	PAGE	TITLE	LINE
STRAWED			
and at great festivalls strawed, and stuck with boughs, . . .	246	Priest 13	9
STRAY			
My prayers mean thee, yet my prayers stray:	96	Justice 1	9
Or if I stray, he doth convert	172	23 Psalme	9
Thy flock doth stray.	187	Dooms-day	20
STREAM			
A stream of bloud, which issu'd from the side	129	Love unkn.	14
for then commonly the stream of temptations is turned another way,	238	Priest 9	22
STREAMERS			
(Which there did hang like streamers neare the top	158	Praise 3	33
STREAMS			
Waters above the Heavens. O sweet streams	44	H. Bapt.1 W	5
O blessed streams! either ye do prevent	44	H. Bapt.1	7
Must purling streams refresh a lovers loves?	56	Jordan 1	8
And garland-streams.	74	The Starre	32
The pasture is thy word: the streams, thy grace	81	Christmas	19
Springs vent their streams, and by expense get store: . . .	119	Providence	71
Whose streams we got by the Apostles sluce, ...	152	The Jews	3
Then to the streams that gently passe:	172	23 Psalme	7
By letting in them both, pollutes her streams:	197	Ch.-Milit.	242
By letting in them both pollute her streams:	197	Ch.-Milit. W	242
And streams of grief	204	The Knell W	15
But though the streams of thy bloud were currant through darknesse,	288	Priest	32
STREET			
Shewing his steps should be the street, ...	173	Marie Magd	4
STRENGTH			
If blisse had lien in art or strength, ...	50	Faith	25
But by the way of nourishment and strength	52	H.Commun.	7
Unto my house, where to repair the strength	130	Love unkn.	47
Grieved for me? the God of strength and power	135	Ephes.	4
Yet active strength: whose long and bonie face	138	The Size	33
Come, my Light, my Feast, my Strength:	156	The Call	5
Such a Strength, as makes his guest.	156	The Call	8
So strength first made a way;	160	The Pulley	6
To it all strength, all subtilties	163	The Search	39
Save in the sight thereof, where strength doth sting.	165	The Crosse	18
And all the soul, and strength, and time, ...	168	a true Hymn	12
Or strength in th' other, did erect her throne.	192	Ch.-Milit.	78
Or strength in th' other, took possession.	192	Ch.-Milit. W	78
Strength levels grounds, Art makes a garden there;	192	Ch.-Milit.	87
Shall they be food & strength & might	201	H. Commun. W	35
what strength, and joy, and peace it administers against all	250	Priest 15	2
that in their full strength they may deliver thy message reverently,	289	Priest	28
O Lord, make it health and strength unto us;	290	Priest	10
gives true strength to the bodie, all superfluities passing away	293	Cornaro	28
but also to gather strength, which could not be but by meat & drink.	295	Cornaro	24
and strength decreasing, my stint of meat and drink should be	295	Cornaro	29
STRENGTHE			
you take her not, I am thinking to do it, even beyond my strengthe;	375	Letters	35
STRENGTHEN			
May strengthen my decayes.	87	Lent	42
And strengthen it in ev'ry age, ...	97	Afflict.5	5
STRENGTHENS			
military state, he fortifyes, and strengthens with his utmost skill.	281	Priest 34	5
STRETCH			
Wilt thou meet arms with man, that thou dost stretch	55	Temper 1	13
Stretch or contract me thy poore debter:	55	Temper 1	22
The trees say, Pull me: but the hand you stretch, ...	117	Providence	23
And in thy lookings stretch and grow?	144	Discharge	5
STRETCHED			
His stretched sinews taught all strings, what key	41	Easter	11
and then who can deny the stretched out arme of a mighty God?	282	Priest 34	6
STRETCHETH			
Every one stretcheth his legges according to his coverlet. . . .	325	Proverbs	147
STREW (see also straw,strow)			
STRICKEN			
There are more men threatned then stricken.	329	Proverbs	256
STRICT			
Or strict commands;	77	Ang.&Sts.	3
I threatned to observe the strict decree	143	Holdfast	1
Then my strict, yet welcome size.	177	The Rose	4
therfore the Parson is very strict in keeping his word, . . .	228	Priest 3	4
the one, a strict religious life;	263	Priest 24	16
and in a strict performance of a few cheap and easie duties . .	319	Valdesso V	24
STRICTLY			
he diligently, and strictly weigheth, his Parish being all his joy,	250	Priest 17	24
which strictly he was not, though in the point of Resurrection he	316	Valdesso	8
STRICTNESS			
the Catholick Religion is professed with greatest strictness).	357	Proverbs D	1047
STRIFE			
I was entangled in the world of strife, ...	47	Afflict.1	41
All my attendants are at strife, ...	90	Afflict.4	13
Such a Truth, as ends all strife:	156	The Call	3
For who can look for lesse, that loveth Life. / Strife. . . .	170	Water-crs.	5
Strive in this, and love the strife.	182	Banquet	54
but that it is a good strife to go as farre as wee can in pleasing	224	Priest	12
Waight and measure take away strife.	328	Proverbs	213
STRIKE			
Strike off all scores; none are so cleare as they.	20	Ch.-Porch	360
They strike my head, the rock from whence all store	32	Sacrifice	170

	PAGE	TITLE		LINE
STRIKE (cont'd)				
With stronger blows strike mee as I come out:	32	Sacrifice	W	187
Since thou dost love, yet strike;	171	Bittersweet		2
Steele & a flint strike fire,	202	Trin.Sun.	W	7
when you are a hammer, strike your fill.	332	Proverbs		338
You must strike in measure,	340	Proverbs		551
when there are many to strike on one Anvile.	340	Proverbs		551
STRIKES				
Now prophesie who strikes thee, is their dittie.	31	Sacrifice		142
Hee that strikes with his tongue, must ward with his head.	331	Proverbs		313
Hee that strikes with his tongue, must ward with his hand.	331	Proverbs	V	313
God strikes not with both hands,	331	Proverbs		315
God strikes with his finger, and not with all his arme.	359	Proverbs	D	1114
STRIKING				
Wit's an unruly engine, wildly striking	16	Ch.-Porch		241
My onely musick, striking me ev'n dead;	174	Aaron		18
STRING				
My musick shall finde thee, and ev'ry string	36	Thanksgvng		39
Thredded together on times string,	76	Sunday		30
STRINGS				
His stretched sinews taught all strings, what key	41	Easter		11
Marbles can weep; and surely strings	136	Ephes.		23
STRIP				
And shall the dew out-strip thy dove?	60	Grace		10
And strip the creature naked, till he finde	85	Vanitie 1		16
Out-strip their Cupid easily in flight?	206	walton 1		9
STRIPT				
To serve it forth, & being stript of all	212	Bohemia	D	31
STRIVE				
And make us strive, who shall sing best thy name.	5	Dedication		4
Who strive to sit out losing hands, are lost.	14	Ch.-Porch		202
And I will strive to sinne no more.	68	Trin.Sun.		6
All did but strive to mend, what you had marr'd.	130	Love unkn.		67
She being stain'd her self, why did she strive	173	Marie Magd		7
Strive in this, and love the strife.	182	Banquet		54
Strive each to play their Part.	213	Convert	D	5
and I will strive to imitate the compleatness of your love,	364	Letters		2
STRIVES				
in this, how Gods goodnesse strives with mans refractorinesse;	272	Priest 30		5
STRIVING				
still striving & prospering so long within us, untill our obedience	290	Priest		10
STROKE				
One stroke fells not an oke.	327	Proverbs		181
STROKES				
Shall thy strokes be my stroking? thorns, my flower?	35	Thanksgvng		13
Great strokes make not sweete musick.	322	Proverbs		26
STROKING				
Shall thy strokes be my stroking? thorns, my flower?	35	Thanksgvng		13
STRONG				
Who Crucifie him, crie with one strong shout.	32	Sacrifice		186
To captivate strong holds to thee.	45	Nature		6
Fractures well cur'd make us more strong.	49	Repentance		36
None but the wise or strong had gained it:	50	Faith		26
Which looks so firm and strong,	66	Ch.-floore		2
Could build so strong in a weak heart.	67	Ch.-floore		20
A strong regard and aw: but speech alone	68	Windows		13
Thy nourish fame is weak or strong.	69	Content		32
Encounter Moses strong complaints and mone:	99	Decay		4
kept sweet and clean, in a strong and decent chest, with a Chalice,	246	Priest 13		18
by reason of their fierce, strong, and violent natures:	271	Priest 30		11
me contrariwise, at the age of eightie and one, strong and lustie;	291	Cornaro		11
for strong and very cool wines pleased my taste best, as also melons,	293	Cornaro		11
sure of life, then the most strong young man who lives disorderly.	300	Cornaro		26
their youthfull appetites, although they be of a most strong temper:	303	Cornaro		13
whereas there is not onely milke there, but strong meat also.	317	Valdesso		24
He that is not handsome at 20, nor strong at 30, nor rich at 40,	333	Proverbs		349
nor wise at 50, will never bee handsome, strong, rich, or wise.	333	Proverbs		349
All beasts of prey are strong or treacherous.	355	Proverbs		1023
and I have a strong opinion of him, that if he can do me a courtesie,	369	Letters		22
that are to come, you have strong preservatives against all disquiet.	373	Letters		19
STRONGE				
Your stronge beliefe	209	Paradox	D	5
STRONGER				
With stronger blows strike mee as I come out:	32	Sacrifice	W	187
for my Cambridge necessities are stronger to tye me here,	369	Letters		18
power to defeat my charity, and evill shold be stronger then good:	376	Letters		10
STRONGLY				
He that doth still and strongly good pursue,	72	Constancie		2
Strongly and sweetly movest, shall I write,	116	Providence		2
Who dost so strongly and so sweetly move,	117	Providence		31
Wherefore the Parson strongly opposeth this sin, whersoever he goes.	274	Priest 32		14
STROW				
To strow thy way and Victorie,	42	Easter	W	20
STROWD				
My dayes were strowd with flow'rs and happinesse;	47	Afflict.1	W	21
STROW'D				
And so I came to phansies medow strow'd	142	Pilgrimage		7
And so I came to Fancies medow strow'd	142	Pilgrimage	V	7
STRUCK				
With that abash'd and struck with many a sting	142	Pilgrimage		25
I struck the board, and cry'd, No more.	153	The Collar		1

	PAGE	TITLE		LINE
STRUCTURE				
Is all good structure in a winding stair?	56	Jordan 1		3
STRUGGLE				
Awake, my lute, and struggle for thy part	41	Easter		7
Struggle with Jacob, sit with Gideon, ...	99	Decay		2
STRUGGLING				
There thou art struggling with a peevish heart, ...	106	Sion		13
And struggling hinders more.	158	Praise 3		18
Many a rent and struggling th' Empire knew, ...	192	Ch.-Milit.		79
STRUGLING				
Strugling on th' hook.	204	The Knell	W	6
STRUMPET				
Never was strumpet faire.	336	Proverbs		431
STUBBORN				
To wash away my stubborn thought:	139	Artillerie		15
of affliction, which softens, and works the stubborn heart of man;	249	Priest 15		24
STUBBORNE				
A noble plant suites not with a stubborne ground.	342	Proverbs		622
STUBBORNNESSE				
Fleshes stubbornnesse may have	187	Dooms-day		17
considering the stubbornnesse of the Nation, their living then in	282	Priest 34		8
STUCK				
festivalls strawed, and stuck with boughs, and perfumed with incense.	246	Priest 13		10
STUDENT'S				
English body, and a Students body, are two great obstructed vessels,	243	Priest 10		1
STUDENTS				
as most Students are, he cannot keep the last obligation, . .	242	Priest 10		29
must not work, especially Students, and those that are weakly,)	266	Priest 26		34
STUDIE				
Studie this art, make it thy great designe;	10	Ch.-Porch		101
Ev'n when my will doth studie thy renown:	165	The Crosse		20
I saw him in his studie, where he sate	194	Ch.-Milit.		165
STUDIED				
therefore he hath throughly studied these, that he may be an absolute	227	Priest 3		8
So that the Parson having studied, and mastered all his lusts	278	Priest 33		22
And David (though David) studied all the day long in it: . .	306	Valdesso		20
STUDIES				
Yet studies them, not him by whom they be.	63	Mattens		16
unto him in any difficulty, either in his studies or in his Parish.	253	Priest 19		9
and a recreation to more divine studies, Nature serving Grace both in	261	Priest 23		11
He that studies his content, wants it.	321	Proverbs		4
STUDIOUS				
If studious, copie fair, what time hath blurr'd;	10	Ch.-Porch		86
STUDY				
As he doth not so study others, as to neglect the grace of God in	229	Priest 4		19
he first commends the study of the Civill Law, as a brave, . .	277	Priest 32		30
wondrous things of his Lawes, and that he would make them his study.	309	Valdesso		27
so a Scholar judgeth in his study, and censureth this or that;	317	Valdesso		2
generall rules to particular actions, which are a most noble study.	319	Valdesso	V	33
perhaps they will say, you are sickly, you must not study too hard;	364	Letters		26
I even study Thrift, and yet I am scarce able with much ado to make	365	Letters		9
STUDYING				
or studying dainties too much, they cannot wel dispatch) nor of their	266	Priest 26		15
help of humane learning in the studying to understand holy Scripture,	314	Valdesso	V	3
STUFFE				
To stuffe thy minde with solid braverie;	15	Ch.-Porch		208
Of thicker stuffe, which would endure a shake.	15	Ch.-Porch		226
Thy glorious houshold-stuffe did me entwine, ...	46	Afflict.1		9
Thy glorious houshold-stuffe did me bewitch	46	Afflict.1	W	9
The stuffe with thee.	57	Employm. 1		12
My stuffe is flesh, not brasse; my senses live, ...	89	The Pearl		27
He wears a stuffe whose thread is course and round, ...	131	Mans medly		15
After the trimming, not the stuffe and ground.	131	Mans medly		18
For some mean stuffe whereon to show his skill:	161	Priesthood		38
an handsome, and seemly Carpet of good and costly Stuffe, or Cloth,	246	Priest 13		18
both monneys and bookes and howshould stuffe whether in my possession	382	G.H.'s Will		5
STUFF'D				
I found that some had stuff'd the bed with thoughts, ...	130	Love unkn.		51
STUMBLE				
Teaches it not to stumble.	75	Sunday	W	7
For one poore minute, stumble at a pinne:	100	Miserie		20
STUMBLER				
A stumbler stumbles least in rugged way.	15	Ch.-Porch		214
STUMBLES				
A stumbler stumbles least in rugged way.	15	Ch.-Porch		214
Hee that stumbles and falles not, mends his pace.	321	Proverbs		7
A horse stumbles that hath foure legges.	346	Proverbs		740
STUMBLING				
is another great stumbling block to the holinesse of Scholars.	238	Priest 9		19
and darkned by the Adversaries, and their great stumbling-block.	305	Valdesso		3
STUMBLING-BLOCK				
and darkned by the Adversaries, and their great stumbling-block.	305	Valdesso		3
STUMPS				
Legs are but stumps, and Pharachs wheels but logs, ...	158	Praise 3		17
STUPIDITIES				
To such Mahometan stupidities, ...	194	Ch.-Milit.		153
STUPIFYING				
and the stupifying and deading of all the clamorous powers . .	227	Priest 3		6
STY (see also stie)				
STYLE (see also stile)				
A slow behaviour to the style of king, ...	212	Bohemia	D	28

SUCH (cont'd)

	PAGE	TITLE	LINE
All such is courteous, usefull, new, or wittie.	18	Ch.-Porch	290
Write on the others, Here lies such a one.	20	Ch.-Porch	342
None shall in hell such bitter pangs endure,	24	Ch.-Porch	445
Is such a stone,	26	The Altar	6
Such sorrow as, if sinfull man could feel,	33	Sacrifice	209
Shall I weep bloud? why, thou hast wept such store	35	Thanksgvng	5
Was such a grief as cannot be.	35	Thanksgvng	10
Such starres I counted mine: both heav'n and earth	46	Afflict.1	11
And kindle in our hearts such true desires,	54	Love 2	4
O rack me not to such a vast extent;	55	Temper 1	9
Such are thy secrets, which my life makes good,	58	H.Script.2	9
Such glorious gifts thou didst bestow,	59	Whitsunday	9
Man is all weaknesse; there is no such thing	61	Praise 1	9
Bids no such thing:	78	Ang.&Sts.	18
For we have all of us just such another.	82	Ungratef.	24
By starving sinne and taking such repast,	87	Lent	44
Both are our cleanlinesse. Hath one such beautie?	92	Man	41
Wherefore since that he is such,	93	Antiphon 2	16
Such was their lustre, they did so excell,	102	Jordan 2	2
Or some such words in fashion;	104	Obedience	14
I never saw thing make such haste.	107	Home	10
We talk of harvests; there are no such things,	108	Home	55
Such as springs use that fall, and windes that blow.	117	Providence	16
Perhaps some such of old did passe,	122	Time	7
But such a heart, whose pulse may be	124	Gratefulnes	31
No smith can make such locks, but they have keyes:	126	Confession	17
Poets have wrong'd poore storms: such dayes are best;	132	The Storm	17
Such sharpnes shows the sweetest FREND:	133	Paradise	13
Such cuttings rather heal then REND:	133	Paradise	14
And such beginnings touch their END.	133	Paradise	15
To such indifferents chained be,	134	The Method	18
More bowels have, then such hard things.	136	Ephes.	24
At least in lump: for such doth oft destroy;	138	The Size	27
All sorts of wounds; of such strange force it is.	147	Offering	21
So high a torture? Is such poyson bought?	155	Assurance	3
No such rank poyson can there be.	155	Assurance	6
Such a Way, as gives us breath:	156	The Call	2
Such a Truth, as ends all strife:	156	The Call	3
And such a Life, as killeth death.	156	The Call	4
Such a Light, as shows a feast:	156	The Call	6
Such a Feast, as mends in length:	156	The Call	7
Such a Strength, as makes his guest.	156	The Call	8
Such a Joy, as none can move:	156	The Call	10
Such a Love, as none can part:	156	The Call	11
Such a Heart, as joyes in love.	156	The Call	12
Sorrow hath chang'd its note: such is his will,	159	Jos.coat	3
But th' holy men of God such vessels are,	161	Priesthood	25
Thy will such an intrenching is,	163	The Search	37
Thy will such a strange distance is,	163	The Search	41
As if there were no such cold thing.	165	The Flower	7
Or if such deceits there be,	177	The Rose	9
Such delights I meant to say;	177	The Rose	10
There are no such things to me,	177	The Rose	11
Such as is, and makes divine!	181	Banquet	9
Such a sweetnesse to impart:	181	Banquet	21
Such power hath mightie Baptisme to produce	191	Ch.-Milit.	45
And such poore game. Thence he to Greece doth passe,	193	Ch.-Milit.	123
And such small game. Thence he to Greece doth passe,	193	Ch.-Milit. W	123
Which soon was blown to such a mightie flame,	194	Ch.-Milit.	145
To such Mahometan stupidities,	194	Ch.-Milit.	153
Such force as once did captivate the Jews;	195	Ch.-Milit.	192
The waight was such they left the doctrins there	196	Ch.-Milit. W	203
Till such a darknesse do the world invade	196	Ch.-Milit.	230
Yet must there such proportions be assign'd	196	Ch.-Milit.	232
Yet must there such proportion be assign'd	196	Ch.-Milit. W	232
Such poor invention burns in their low mind	206	Walton 2	9
but orders his Life in such a fashion, that when death takes him,	227	Priest 3	32
For though the world is full of such composures, yet every mans own	230	Priest 5	4
or offer up such sacrifices as they did of old, which was of beasts	232	Priest 6	4
for people are very attentive at such discourses, and think it	233	Priest 7	9
Some such irradiations scatteringly in the Sermon, carry great	233	Priest 7	37
never was there such care of a flock expressed, save in the great	234	Priest 7	20
of the presence, and majesty of God, by these, or such like speeches.	234	Priest 7	26
Such discourses shew very Holy.	234	Priest 7	35
he takes occasion to discourse of such things as are both profitable,	236	Priest 8	21
Originall concupisence is such an active thing, by reason	238	Priest 9	12
a providing for her family in such sort, as that neither they want	239	Priest 10	18
such as are tavernes for men, and lace-making for women;	240	Priest 10	2
for he hath no mony for such things, charity being his only perfume,	241	Priest 10	13
then if it had taken before either fish, or rootes, or such things;	242	Priest 10	24
and their comfort, who are much cheered with such friendliness.	243	Priest 11	13
because countrey people are very observant of such things,	243	Priest 11	20
knowing that where there are such conceits, there is no room for his	243	Priest 11	23
shewing them how acceptable such works are to God, and wishing them	247	Priest 14	18
such as are from Gods generall providence extended even to lillyes;	249	Priest 15	19
good discourses, such as may edify, interposing sometimes some short,	251	Priest 17	4
but such as are every way fitting to do his Countrey true	252	Priest 19	27
or if he be of a condition above such gifts, he sends him a good	254	Priest 20	15
This I do, because at such, and such a time you were charitable.	254	Priest 20	17
Is not Christianity full of such things, as are not to be seen,	256	Priest 21	10

	PAGE	TITLE	LINE
SUCH (cont'd)			
admits no vaine or idle names, but such as are usuall and accustomed.	258	Priest 22	4
is it easie for any Scholer to attaine to such a measure of Phisick,	261	Priest 23	2
and the knowing of herbs may be done at such times, as they may be	261	Priest 23	10
and to do such things of legall opposition either in the presenting,	263	Priest 25	23
to be sued at the Law concerning such goods for the use and profit	270	Priest 29	3
that things are not set in such an inevitable order, but that God	270	Priest 30	30
then God sends such weather, as lays the corn, and destroys it:	271	Priest 30	30
will appear if the Pious soul foresee and prevent such interruptions,	273	Priest 31	17
there were no such Physician as he, both for skill and tendernesse.	278	Priest 33	31
that at such, or such a time their peace and mirth have carryed them	280	Priest 34	33
or such a time their peace and mirth have carryed them further then	280	Priest 34	33
for with such sacrifices God is well pleased.	281	Priest 34	4
and find sparkes of such thoughts now and then to break forth,	281	Priest 34	13
he is so farre from condemning such assemblies, that he rather	284	Priest 35	14
should a Christian Souldier take such occasions to harden himselfe,	284	Priest 35	35
notorious faults are either such as are made known by common fame	287	Priest 37	12
or else such as have passed judgment, & been corrected either	287	Priest 37	14
So that it is so far from being a fault to discover such offenders,	287	Priest 37	38
that Intemperance was not such an evil, but it might easily be	291	Cornaro	6
was such as belonged to sickly constitutions, and that in a small	292	Cornaro	24
fitted my stomack, and in such measure, as easily might be digested:	293	Cornaro	17
after live free from diseases, if he will keep such a course of life;	297	Cornaro	20
which things in others cannot be known without such observation,	297	Cornaro	29
But surely there is no such matter, if Temperance be wanting.	298	Cornaro	21
and later yeares, it is no such thing which may not be performed;	299	Cornaro	6
but such meats as are agreeable to his disease, and that in much	299	Cornaro	31
That a long life is no such desirable thing, because that after one	300	Cornaro	28
and which are such, as that men generally account me happie.	300	Cornaro	32
Because such are daily exposed to a thousand dangers and deaths,	303	Cornaro	14
and to such, and all that is theirs, I owe diligence;	304	Valdesso	7
promises to every one in particular with such syncerity and efficacy,	309	Valdesso	5
but such a one as shall still have the assistance of the holy spirit	310	Valdesso	6
and syncere Religion, such as are Prayer, Fasting, Almes-deedes,	312	Valdesso	20
such as are all vain conversations:	314	Valdesso	19
There's no such conquering weapon as the necessity of conquering.	357	Proverbs D	1064
Such a Saint, such an offering.	359	Proverbs D	1108
for it hath been my fortune of late to have such sudden warning,	365	Letters	31
and if there be any such which you have found useful to yourself,	366	Letters	4
and such like Gaynesses, which will please a young man well.	370	Letters	3
hath no such earthiness in it, but it may very well be joined	370	Letters	22
and have endur'd such other Tortures, as the very mention of them	373	Letters	37
I beseech you let such thoughts as these, moderate your present fear	374	Letters	3
and will not allow any room there for such an in-mate as Grief;	374	Letters	11
Yf I should regard such things, it were in another's power to defeat	376	Letters	9
now Constancy is such & of great esteem with all.	380	Woodnoth	15
SUCK			
Suck ev'ry letter, and a hony gain, ...	58	H.Script.1	2
So wee may cease to suck: to praise thee, never.	59	Whitsunday W	24
Their infants, them; and they suck thee	148	Longing	17
Suck up a river to supply mine eyes, ...	164	Grief	5
Which know not thee, suck in thy beames	203	Even-song W	23
SUCKS			
There he sucks, and lives.	228	Priest 4	23
SUCKT			
Suckt all thy magazens: my head did ake, ...	83	Sighs & Gr.	10
SUDDAIN			
because of the suddain passing from that which was just now lawfull,	264	Priest 26	20
SUDDAINLY			
and to confusion suddainly.	220	Psalm VI D	28
SUDDEN			
Therefore my sudden soul caught at the place, ...	46	Afflict.1	17
And sudden arbours shadow course-spunne lines?	56	Jordan 1	7
and abhorring from so sudden an end, and finding my self continually	292	Cornaro	18
increased so much in them, that it brought them to a sudden end.	294	Cornaro	20
for it hath been my fortune of late to have such sudden warning,	365	Letters	32
SUDDENLY			
Thou suddenly dost raise and race, ...	56	Temper 2	7
My blessed Lord, art thou! how suddenly	103	Prayer 2	2
Art thou, my blessed King? how suddenly	103	Prayer 2 W	2
When suddenly I heard one say, ...	139	Artillerie	5
of the desolation of Israel, turnes to God suddenly, Oh Lord,	234	Priest 7	5
be housed, a fire hath broken forth, and suddenly consumed them.	271	Priest 30	25
For suddenly it takes away our appetite, so that we can eat . .	299	Cornaro	27
SUE			
What I seek, for what I sue;	182	Banquet	46
and to sue, and to be sued at the Law concerning such goods . .	270	Priest 29	2
SUED			
and to be sued at the Law concerning such goods for the use . .	270	Priest 29	3
SUES			
Sues for my heart, I thee displace, ...	94	Unkindness	19
SUFFER			
As cunning fencers suffer heat to tire.	19	Ch.-Porch	316
I suffer binding, who have loos'd their bands:	28	Sacrifice	47
And in thy members suffer ill.	73	Afflict.3	16
For I will do, or suffer what I ought.	139	Artillerie	16
For thou didst suffer to restore	157	Clasping	14
nor suffer others in his house that are so, to keep it; . . .	242	Priest 10	29
which while they deferr, both sides suffer;	259	Priest 22	4
Suffer and expect, sustine, abstine.	343	Proverbs V	701
Suffer and expect.	344	Proverbs	702

SUFFER (cont'd)	PAGE	TITLE		LINE
Better suffer ill, then doe ill.	346	Proverbs		770
He that gives all before hee dies provides to suffer.	349	Proverbs		855
He that gives all ere hee dies provides to suffer.	349	Proverbs	V	855
SUFFERED				
they would have fainted, had they returned empty, He suffered it not;	267	Priest 26		24
made food miraculously, then suffered so good desires to miscarry.	267	Priest 26		25
and suffered not any new of that kinde to arise, neither the good	296	Cornaro		33
SUFFERETH				
That he before me well nigh suffereth:	31	Sacrifice		147
As he that for some robberie suffereth.	34	Sacrifice		230
SUFF'RING				
Not suff'ring those	100	Miserie		29
SUFFERING				
and wondreth not so much at their patient suffering, and cheerfull	237	Priest 9		29
not suffering any that day that hee receives, to want a good meal	245	Priest 12		7
therfore God is styled with that glorious title, Long Suffering.	381	Woodnoth		6
SUFFERS				
he by no means suffers it, but after divers gentle admonitions,	232	Priest 6		12
He suffers not a ly or equivocation by any means in his house,	240	Priest 10		32
especially in his own Parish he suffers it not to his utmost power;	268	Priest 28		18
Wherefore the Parson suffers not the place to be vilified or debased,	270	Priest 29		7
that twice suffers shipwrack.	345	Proverbs		706
who twice suffers shipwrack.	345	Proverbs	V	706
SUFFICE				
Saying to man, It doth suffice:	64	Even-song		19
But words suffice not, where are lewd intentions:	122	Sinnes rd.		11
Will not suffice our turn:	127	Giddinesse		26
Amongst good men two men suffice.	350	Proverbs		885
SUFFICETH				
since we are not Masters of our bodies, this sufficeth.	279	Priest 33		19
For I eat little, because a little sufficeth my weak stomack:	300	Cornaro		8
but this sufficeth, he himselfe allowes it for a holy conversation	311	Valdesso		1
That which sufficeth is not little.	350	Proverbs		876
Take heed of a step-mother; the very name of her sufficeth.	360	Proverbs	D	1155
SUFFICIENT				
Is selfe-sufficient to bee the thrall	212	Bohemia	D	32
And therefore let it be sufficient for me, that the same heart,	363	Letters		17
SUGAR				
Lovely enchanting language, sugar-cane,	176	Forerunners		19
As we sugar melt in wine?	181	Banquet		12
SUGAR-CANE				
Lovely enchanting language, sugar-cane,	176	Forerunners		19
SUGGESTIONS				
And in suggestions fume and work,	45	Nature		8
SUGGESTS				
and managing Commons, or Woods, according as the place suggests.	276	Priest 32		7
SUGRED				
But I am lost in flesh, whose sugred lyes	116	Dulnesse		21
I felt a sugred strange delight,	171	The Glance		5
In this world of sugred lies,	177	The Rose		2
SUGRING				
Yet sugring the suspicion.	94	Life		12
SUIT (see also sute)				
And make a suit unto him, to afford	40	Redemption		3
Who straight, Your suit is granted, said, & died.	40	Redemption		14
No point of honour, or gay suit,	69	Quidditie		2
If I but lift mine eyes, my suit is made:	103	Prayer 2		5
Shall I be still in suit?	153	The Collar		6
To suit and serve his need,	153	The Collar		31
that this suit and contention was raised by the Divine Providence,	294	Cornaro		23
and divers labours, which suit not with an orderly life:	299	Cornaro		14
The worst of law is, that one suit breedes twenty.	329	Proverbs		253
SUITABLE				
the midst whereof is a Church suitable to the condition of the place.	301	Cornaro		23
SUITE				
yet if he suite not other things to the growth, as seasons,	271	Priest 30		16
words about the H. Scripture suite with what he writes elsewhere,	306	Valdesso		15
SUITES				
That suites him best, of whom thy speech is heard.	18	Ch.-Porch		294
A noble plant suites not with a stubborne ground.	342	Proverbs		622
SUITOURS				
We all are but cold suitours; let us move	22	Ch.-Porch		400
To ordinarie suitours at the doore.	85	Vanitie 1		21
SUITS				
Complies and suits with all estates;	69	Content		14
and then he suits things faithfully according to that end.	253	Priest 19		4
which it most suits withall for variety and pleasantnesse;	302	Cornaro		31
SULLIED				
We sullied by our foul offence:	76	Sunday		51
SULLYING				
Tears sullying thy transparent rooms,	124	Gratefulnes		14
SUM				
this whole sum of five hundred pounds I bequeath unto my Neeces	382	G.H.'s Will		12
SUMME				
Summe up at night, what thou hast done by day;	24	Ch.-Porch		451
Summe up at night, what thou hast done that day;	24	Ch.-Porch	W	451
All being brought into a summe,	72	Constancie		14
Have one beginning and one finall summe:	161	Priesthood		22
making together a summe either to be sent, or, which were more	253	Priest 19		36
to name at first, what the summe should be, but he told her Grace,	379	Letters		6

	PAGE	TITLE		LINE
SUNNE (cont'd)				
which may be unto him as the sunne to a Travellour in his journey,	312	Valdesso		18
The morning Sunne never lasts a day.	334	Proverbs		375
He that hath a head of waxe must not walke in the sunne.	335	Proverbs		425
The filth under the white snow, the sunne discovers.	338	Proverbs		495
The March sunne raises but dissolves not.	342	Proverbs		614
A morning sunne, and a wine-bred child,	349	Proverbs		866
Though God take the sunne out of the Heaven,	353	Proverbs		980
SUNNE-BEAM				
Then by a sunne-beam I will climbe to thee.	63	Mattens		20
SUNNE-SHINE				
Flyes of estates and sunne-shine. But to all,	169	The Answer		5
SUNNE'S				
To parents issue and the sunnes bright starre!	168	The Sonne		6
SUNNES				
Though many sunnes to shine endeavour?	42	Easter		28
When he beheld twelve sunnes for one	59	Whitsunday		15
As frost-nipt sunnes look sadly.	81	Christmas		30
More then a thousand sunnes disburse in light,	172	The Glance		23
SUNSHINE				
and to keep them on in the sunshine, and noone of prosperity,	237	Priest 9		35
SUP				
and goes with him to the other, and all dine or sup together.	284	Priest 35		21
SUPERABOUNDED				
so that then where sin abounded, not death, but grace superabounded;	288	Priest		25
SUPERFICIALL				
Or superficiall cffer	104	Obedience		29
SUPERFLUITIES				
all superfluities passing away without difficultie, and no ill	293	Cornaro		28
SUPERFLUCUS				
Or else, because they think it empty and superfluous.	285	Priest 36		9
Saviour himselfe used, Marke 10. 16, cannot bee vain and superfluous.	285	Priest 36		11
SUPERINDUCED				
superinduced to the scriptures, like to that of the Jewes,	320	Valdesso		3
SUPERLIMINARE				
Superliminare.	25	Superlim		T
SUPERSTITION				
but as desiring to keep the middle way between superstition,	246	Priest 13		25
not out of superstition, but of reverence to Gods house,	273	Priest 31		22
thinke this superstitious, neither know superstition, nor themselves.	284	Priest 35		29
the clean contrary, even from superstition to coldnes, and Atheism.	286	Priest 36		17
a few cheap and easie duties of religion, with no less superstition;	319	Valdesso	V	26
The Divell divides the world between Atheisme and Superstition	359	Proverbs	D	1107
SUPERSTITIOUS				
and those that thinke this superstitious, neither know superstition,	284	Priest 35		28
consists in a few ceremonious and superstitious observations;	319	Valdesso	V	23
SUPLE				
To cleare the breast, to suple outward pain.	58	H.Script.1	W	4
SUPPER				
Hee wrongs nct an old man that steales his supper from him.	331	Proverbs		311
SUPPERS				
By suppers more have beene killed then Galen ever cured.	330	Proverbs		272
By suppers more are killed then Galen ever cured.	330	Proverbs	V	272
Hunger makes dinners, pastime suppers.	348	Proverbs		819
SUPPING				
Sleepe without supping, and wake without owing.	324	Proverbs		93
SUPPLE (see alsc suple)				
Let me be soft and supple to thy will,	44	H. Bapt.2		8
To supple hardnesses. But at the length	130	Love unkn.		45
SUPPLED				
The Caldron suppled, what was grown too hard:	130	Love unkn.		65
SUPPLICANT				
to let the fervency of the supplicant hang and dy between speaking,	231	Priest 6		18
SUPPLICATICN				
and humble supplication hears.	220	Psalm VI	D	24
SUPPLIE				
Yet ill deeds loyter not: for they supplie	122	Sinnes rd.		16
God doth supplie the want.	168	a true Hymn		18
SUPPLI'D				
And trip at night, have spheres suppli'd;	134	Divinitie		2
SUPPLIES				
Unlesse they get new conduits, new supplies	164	Grief		7
hee supplies them with Receipts, and instructs them further in that	247	Priest 14		16
SUPPLING				
Let suppling grace, to crosse his art,	60	Grace		19
But this he doth discretely, with mollifying, and suppling words;	252	Priest 18		8
SUPPLY				
Suck up a river to supply mine eyes,	164	Grief		5
because wealth is given to that end to supply our occasions.	265	Priest 26		8
without which supply the corne would instantly dry up, as a river	271	Priest 30		6
SUPPLYED				
he is ever very well supplyed by some able man who treads in his	232	Priest 7		25
SUPPLYES				
or a stranger, his garden or orchard supplyes it, or his barne,	241	Priest 10		18
then by that which he continually supplyes, as the corn needs it;	271	Priest 30		5
SUPPORT				
That her fine cobwebs did support the frame,	84	The World		3
Evils have their comfort, good none can support	328	Proverbs		208
SUPPORTED				
Whereas they were supported by the same:	84	The World		4

	PAGE	TITLE	LINE
SUPPORTING			
by the way of supporting either it (in regard of the citty) or your	380	Woodnoth	27
SUPPOSE			
He meaneth (I suppose) that a man presume not to merit, . . .	312	Valdesso	14
By occasions (I suppose) hee meaneth the ordinary, or necessary	314	Valdesso	16
I suppose she is not disposed to spend her eyesight on a piece	371	Letters	13
SUPPRESSE			
Yet when thou dost suppresse	183	A Parodie	6
SUPREME			
Th' indorsement of supreme delight, ...	75	Sunday	3
Of what supreme almightie power	103	Prayer 2	7
Then tell me, what is that supreme delight?	188	Heaven	13
I offend the supreme Judg, in perverting that order which he hath set	265	Priest 26	11
SURCEASE			
upon condition that I should surcease from all title to it, . . .	367	Letters	9
SURE			
Sure to be crosse he would shift feet and face.	7	Ch.-Porch	24
Be sure to doe it, though it be but small:	11	Ch.-Porch	116
Who fears to do well, sure should wear a mask.	11	Ch.-Porch	126
Slacknesse breeds worms; but the sure traveller, ...	20	Ch.-Porch	339
Sure there is room within our hearts good store;	40	Sepulchre	5
For sure then I should grow	48	Afflict.1	58
For sure when Adam did not know	53	H.Commun.	33
Yet take thy way; for sure thy way is best:	55	Temper 1	21
Which dissolution sure doth best discern, ...	65	Ch.-monum.	10
Sure I shall do so, and much more:	66	Ch.-mus.	10
But the sweet cement, which in one sure band	67	Ch.-floore	10
Who rides his sure and even trot, ...	72	Constancie	9
This is the Mark-man, safe and sure, ...	73	Constancie	34
Sure the unruly sigh had broke my heart.	73	Afflict.3	6
Sure thou wilt joy, by gaining me	74	The Starre	29
Is much more sure to meet with him, then one	87	Lent	38
Sure thou didst put a minde there, if I could	116	Dulnesse	23
Are there much surer then our art is sure.	119	Providence	80
The Crown Imperiall: Sure, said I, ...	125	Peace	15
Sure they would move	132	The Storm	4
For he is Power: and sure he would;	133	The Method	7
Bid what he please; yet I am sure, ...	135	Divinitie	22
Sure there was wine	153	The Collar	10
Sure it would carrie with it ev'n my heart, ...	159	Jos.coat	7
Sure-footed griefs, solid calamities, ...	167	Dotage	9
Sure I will do the like.	171	Bittersweet	4
First I am sure, whether bread stay	200	H. Commun. W	7
Then of this also I am sure	200	H. Commun. W	19
Sure, Lord, there is enough in thee to dry	206	Walton 2	1
Let the world reel, we and all ours stand sure, ...	439	Walton 5	9
When winds and waves rise highest, I am sure, ...	439	Walton 6	3
and finds no sure abiding place.	215	Psalm I D	16
hand to sickle, shall then secure himself, and think all cock-sure;	271	Priest 30	30
God further, even till he imbarn his corn, and then think all sure;	271	Priest 30	33
That an orderly life is the most sure way & ground of health and long	297	Cornaro	12
is more sure of life, then the most strong young man who lives	300	Cornaro	25
Yet I am sure, that my end is farre from me:	303	Cornaro	24
Good is the mora that makes all sure.	325	Proverbs	145
It's no sure rule to fish with a cros-bow.	331	Proverbs	293
Gods Mill grinds slow, but sure.	346	Proverbs	747
knowes nothing sure but what hee hath laid out.	354	Proverbs	1001
for I am sure you love Your faithfullest Servant, GEORGE HERBERT.	365	Letters	25
SURE-FOOTED			
Sure-footed griefs, solid calamities, ...	167	Dotage	9
SURELY			
That thou hast gotten. Surely use alone	12	Ch.-Porch	155
Most surely judg'd, make thy accounts agree.	24	Ch.-Porch	456
But surely not their hearts, as I well trie:	30	Sacrifice	123
But surely not their hearts, as I will trie:	30	Sacrifice V	123
Surely I will revenge me on thy love, ...	35	Thanksgvng	17
Surely thou didst so little contribute	77	Avarice	5
Surely, thought I, ...	124	Peace	8
Surely if each one saw anothers heart, ...	127	Giddinesse	21
Marbles can weep; and surely strings	136	Ephes.	23
Surely thine alone.	148	Offering	36
Surely thy sweet and wondrous love	173	23 Psalme	21
Great God will surely dry those teares, ...	213	L' Envoy D	5
And surely hyssope, valerian, mercury, adders tongue, yerrow,	262	Priest 23	5
But surely there is no such matter, if Temperance be wanting.	298	Cornaro	21
and surely this the Author meant by the word Jurisdiction, . . .	317	Valdesso V	7
Hee stands not surely, that never slips.	323	Proverbs	68
Hee stands not surely, that never slipte.	323	Proverbs V	68
Health and sicknesse surely are mens double enemies.	354	Proverbs	1011
Favour will as surely perish as life.	357	Proverbs D	1055
surely it were a great good deed, and I would have her conveyed	375	Letters	31
surely, since there is a two-fold brightnesse which dazeleth the eyes	442	Oration	32
SURER			
Are there much surer then our art is sure.	119	Providence	80
is placed surer for his childrens advantage, then if it were given	240	Priest 10	8
SURETIES			
And are her sureties, ere they are a friends.	17	Ch.-Porch	282
SURETY			
Yet be not surety, if thou be a father.	17	Ch.-Porch	277
He that will be surety, shall pay.	358	Proverbs D	1091

	PAGE	TITLE		LINE
SURGING				
And surging griefs, when they grew bold, controll,	172	The Glance		15
SURMOUNTS				
for that which surmounts, though your noble disposition is infinitely	367	Letters		5
SURNAME				
I surname them guilded clay,	71	Frailtie		5
He did surname his palace, Babylon.	195	Ch.-Milit.		182
SURPASSE				
Surpasse in brightnesse any flame.	135	Divinitie		16
SURPLUS				
The stock and surplus, cause and historie:	88	The Pearl		8
SURPLUSAGE				
and both pay for the surplusage of these Books, and for ever after	367	Letters		11
SURPRISES				
Bibles laid cpen, millions of surprises,	45	Sinne 1		8
SURPRIZED				
He that is surprized with the first frost	354	Proverbs		992
SURRCUND				
Where beams surround my Saviours face,	74	The Starre		2
SURROUNDED				
Call thee frcm out of that surrounded land,	213	Bohemia	D	61
SURROUNDS				
For death each houre environs and surrounds.	145	Discharge		36
SURVEY				
not onely taken a particular Survey of the faults of his own Parish,	274	Priest 32		5
I survey palaces, gardens, and antiquities, publick fabricks,	302	Cornaro		3
SURVEYS				
Surveys, as if he had design'd.	85	Vanitie 1		4
The Parson's Surveys.	274	Priest 32		T
the Kingdome into Portions, which every yeer he surveys peece-meal.	277	Priest 32		8
SURVIVE				
That three yeares hence, if I survive,	36	Thanksgvng		32
belongs to my two Neeces that survive and the rest unto my selfe,	382	G.H.'s Will		11
SUSPECT				
If the Parson suspect the first, and find sparkes of such thoughts	281	Priest 34		12
SUSPECTED				
and very looks, knowing himself to be both suspected, and envyed.	237	Priest 9		15
He that once deceives is ever suspected.	335	Proverbs		417
Who so once deceives is ever suspected.	335	Proverbs	V	417
Nothing secure unlesse suspected.	357	Proverbs	D	1065
SUSPICION				
Yet sugring the suspicion.	94	Life		12
my absence by how much it naturally augmenteth suspicion,	372	Letters		21
SUSPICIOUS				
and that among suspicious men, and other like circumstances	237	Priest 9		3
SUSPITION				
The vertue of a coward is suspition.	362	Proverbs	D	1179
SUSTAIN				
that it is no complementall or light thing to sustain that place,	258	Priest 22		11
SUSTAIN'D				
for God sustain'd me still.	216	Psalm III	D	12
SUSTAINED				
that old age could not be sustained with so little meat and drink;	295	Cornaro		22
which yet needs not onely to be sustained, but also to gather	295	Cornaro		24
SUSTAINING				
The first is a sustaining power;	271	Priest 30		1
By his sustaining power he preserves and actuates every thing in his	271	Priest 30		3
and be preserved in that act by his sustaining power, yet if he suite	271	Priest 30		15
SUSTENTATION				
as that neither they want a competent sustentation, nor her husband	239	Priest 10		19
SUSTINE				
Suffer and expect, sustine, abstine.	343	Proverbs	V	701
SUTABLE				
both sutable to the joy of the day, and without hinderance to publick	236	Priest 8		18
there is an humblenesse very sutable to Christian regeneraticn,	255	Priest 21		10
but it is sutable to what the Author holds elsewhere, for he	311	Valdesso		21
SUTABLY				
and sutably to their needs, then so much given in meat at dinner.	243	Priest 11		16
SUTE				
A house and a woman sute excellently.	337	Proverbs		468
SUTES				
the Christians in sutes.	329	Proverbs		242
Law sutes consume time, and mony, and rest, and friends.	347	Proverbs		776
SUTING				
hee receives, to want a good meal suting to the joy of the occasion.	245	Priest 12		8
SWADDLE				
To swaddle infants, whose young breath	98	Mortific.		3
SWAIES				
The perswasion of the fortunate swaies the doubtfull.	342	Proverbs		630
SWALLOW				
When Sein shall swallow Tiber, and the Thames	197	Ch.-Milit.		241
The dog gnawes the bone because he cannot swallow it.	337	Proverbs		457
SWALLOWS				
That leads the van, and swallows up the cities.	16	Ch.-Porch		248
SWARMING				
Of swarming fears,	142	Pilgrimage		26
SWAY (see also swaies)				
In conversation boldnesse now bears sway.	15	Ch.-Porch		205
Bear all the sway, possessing heart and brain,	54	Love 1		7
With sick folks, women, those whom passions sway,	73	Constancie		27
But as thy lcve shall sway,	104	Obedience		19

SWEETLY (cont'd)	PAGE	TITLE		LINE
Who did so sweetly deaths sad taste convey,	94	Life		10
Farewell deare flowers, sweetly your time ye spent,	94	Life		13
Stronqly and sweetly movest, shall I write,	116	Providence		2
Who dost so stronqly and so sweetly move,	117	Providence		31
Who sweetly temper'st all. If we could heare	118	Providence		39
He sweetly liv'd; yet sweetnesse did not save	125	Peace		25
How sweetly doth My Master sound! My Master!	174	The Odour		1
Sweetly there indeed it lies,	178	The Rose		23
Sweetly he doth meet my taste.	182	Banquet		39
Drew nearer to me, sweetly questioning,	188	Love 3		5
SWEETNED				
I took thy sweetned pill, till I came neare;	47	Afflict.1		47
I took thy sweetned pill, till I came where	47	Afflict.1	W	47
SWEETNESSE				
Let thy mindes sweetnesse have his operation	21	Ch.-Porch		371
The sweetnesse and the praise were thine;	57	Employm. 1		5
Oh Book! infinite sweetnesse! let my heart	58	H.Script.1		1
There is in love a sweetnesse readie penn'd:	103	Jordan 2		17
That hive of sweetnesse, to remove	107	Home		20
He sweetly liv'd; yet sweetnesse did not save	125	Peace		25
My love, my sweetnesse, heare!	150	Longing		79
O what sweetnesse from the bowl	181	Banquet		7
Or hath sweetnesse in the bread	181	Banquet		13
Such a sweetnesse to impart:	181	Banquet		21
and the like, hath neither in it sweetnesse, nor gravity,	235	Priest 7		8
from temptation, in a quiet sweetnesse seeks how to please his God.	279	Priest 33		5
But thou Lord, art patience, and pity, and sweetnesse, and love;	288	Priest		21
SWEETNESSES				
At first thou gav'st me milk and sweetnesses;	47	Afflict.1		19
SWEETNING				
This breathing would with gains by sweetning me	175	The Odour		26
SWEETS				
And brought'st thy sweets along with thee.	42	Easter		22
Bringinge thy sweets along with thee.	42	Easter	W	22
And brought thy sweets along with thee.	42	Easter	WC	22
Sweetest of sweets, I thank you: when displeasure	65	Ch.-mus.		1
But all thy sweets are packt up in the other;	82	Ungratef.		19
A box where sweets compacted lie;	88	Vertue		10
When clothes are taken from a chest of sweets	98	Mortific.		2
When cloths are taken from a chest of sweets	98	Mortific.	V	2
SWELL				
Whether thy stock of credit swell, or fall.	20	Ch.-Porch		346
And calls for musick, while his veins do swell,	98	Mortific.		14
My thoughts began to burnish, sprout, and swell,	102	Jordan 2		4
My thoughts began to burnish, spredd, and swell,	102	Jordan 2	W	4
Volumes of Divinity, which yet every day swell, and grow bigger.	365	Letters		15
SWELL'D				
Why are the Heathen swell'd with rage,	215	Psalm II	D	1
SWELLING				
Swelling through store,	167	The Flower		48
SWELLS				
When glorie swells the heart, and moldeth it	88	The Pearl		14
Check the proud sea, ev'n when it swells and gathers.	118	Providence		48
SWEPT				
But Wisdome quickly swept them all away.	84	The World		5
that the Church be swept, and kept cleane without dust,	246	Priest 13		8
Fine dressing is a foule house swept before the doores.	329	Proverbs		243
SWIFT				
Love is swift of foot;	179	Discipline		21
And pace of thy swift vertues; onely they	211	Bohemia	D	5
O make thy word a swift word, passing from the ear to the heart,	289	Priest		29
When your will is ready, the feete are swift.	336	Proverbs	V	448
SWIM				
all night I make my Couch to swim;	220	Psalm VI	D	14
SWIMME				
In the world who knowes not to swimme, goes to the bottome.	330	Proverbs		285
In the world who can not swimme, goe to the bottome.	330	Proverbs	V	285
SWIMMERS				
Good swimmers at length are drowned.	347	Proverbs		801
SWINE				
And serve the swine: there, there is his delight:	101	Miserie		44
And feed the swine, with all his mind & might:	101	Miserie	W	44
for the second, swine. These save man the labour, and doing that	241	Priest 10		31
SWING				
His swing and sway:	172	The Glance		12
SWOLLEN				
Lest like a Lion swollen with rage	221	Psalm VII	D	5
SWORD				
Chase brave employments with a naked sword	10	Ch.-Porch		88
Chase brave employment with a naked sword	10	Ch.-Porch	W	88
Nor a good sword, nor yet a lute:	69	Quidditie		4
Nor a good sword, not yet a lute:	69	Quidditie	W	4
Is both my physick and my sword.	106	Conscience		24
Fain put thee on, exchanging my lay-sword	160	Priesthood		5
Who without spear, or sword, or other drumme	195	Ch.-Milit.		201
the Lord will whet his Sword:	222	Psalm VII	D	42
An old wise mans shaddow is better then a young buzzards sword.	324	Proverbs		90
In chusing a wife, and buying a sword,	338	Proverbs		490
Gluttony kills more then the sword.	338	Proverbs		503
Love rules his kingdome without a sword.	339	Proverbs		541

SWORD (cont'd)	PAGE	TITLE		LINE
A valiant mans looke is more then a cowards sword.	345	Proverbs		708
One sword keepes another in the sheath.	345	Proverbs		723
SWORDS				
As swords cause death, so may a little sting.	20	Ch.-Porch	W	352
SWORNE				
The Bathe of the Blackamoor hath sworne not to whiten.	359	Proverbs	D	1105
SYCOMORE				
Then enter'd Sinne, and with that Sycomore,	84	The World		11
SYLLOGISMES				
Prayers chas'd syllogismes into their den,	191	Ch.-Milit.		55
SYMBOLE				
Doe owe the symbole of their certainty.	439	Walton 5		8
SYMMETRIE				
Who marks in church-time others symmetrie,	23	Ch.-Porch		419
Man is all symmetrie,	91	Man		13
SYNCERE				
duties of true Piety, and syncere Religion, such as are Prayer,	312	Valdesso		20
SYNCERITY				
promises to every one in particular with such syncerity and efficacy,	309	Valdesso		5
SYRENS				
Where treach'rous Syrens us'd to sing,	214	Convert	D	7
TABLE				
Furnish thy table to thy minde.	97	Afflict.5		18
Flies have their table spread, ere they appeare.	118	Providence		54
which is expressed in a fayre table, as being the rule of a family.	240	Priest 10		26
both for man in themselves, by growing them selves fit for his table.	241	Priest 10		35
if a peece of dry flesh at my table be more unpleasant to me,	242	Priest 10		13
his money for the poor, and his table for those that are above Alms.	243	Priest 11		9
Not but that the poor are welcome also to his table, whom he	243	Priest 11		10
and Desk, and Communion Table, and Font be as they ought,	246	Priest 13		6
is an occasion, my Table is an occasion, my apparell is an occasion:	265	Priest 26		15
hath considered how to carry himself at table about his appetite,	278	Priest 33		19
not to eate of all those dishes at table, which even their present	280	Priest 34		23
The table robbes more then a thiefe.	342	Proverbs		636
Speake not of a dead man at the table.	343	Proverbs		672
Wine makes all scrts of creatures at table.	352	Proverbs		931
Armour is light at table.	352	Proverbs		934
To speake of an Usurer at the table marres the wine.	353	Proverbs		974
TACKS				
And tacks the centre to the sphere!	103	Prayer 2		9
TAIL (see also tayle)				
TAILE				
The higher the Ape goes, the more he shewes his taile.	346	Proverbs		745
The Cow knowes not what her taile is worth, till she have lost it.	350	Proverbs		870
Of a pigs taile you can never make a good shaft.	359	Proverbs	D	1104
TAILOR (see also taylor)				
TAINT				
and taint his other duties of piety, which none can perform so wel in	273	Priest 31		1
TAINTING				
Breaking her peace, and tainting her good name.	193	Ch.-Milit.		106
TAKE				
Allows thee choise of paths: take no by-wayes;	7	Ch.-Porch		14
And God will shew thee how to take the towne,	7	Ch.-Porch	W	22
Take not his name, who made thy mouth, in vain:	8	Ch.-Porch		55
If those take up thy day, the sunne will crie	9	Ch.-Porch		81
But if thou coole, then take some shame to thee	10	Ch.-Porch	W	90
Take starres for money; starres not to be told	13	Ch.-Porch		171
By no means runne in debt: take thine own measure.	13	Ch.-Porch		175
That temper gives them theirs, and yet doth take	16	Ch.-Porch		254
My childrens right, nor ought he take it: rather	17	Ch.-Porch		279
Take all intc thee; then with equall care	19	Ch.-Porch		321
In love or honour: take account of all;	20	Ch.-Porch		344
To take all that is given; whether wealth,	20	Ch.-Porch		356
Slovens take up their stock of noisomnesse	21	Ch.-Porch		369
Lest sinne take courage and return,	39	Good Fri.		31
Long since on earth, to take possession.	40	Redemption		8
Give me my captive soul, or take	52	H.Commun.		25
Yet take thy way; for sure thy way is best:	55	Temper 1		21
Of strange delights, where we may wish & take.	58	H.Script.1		7
May take acquaintance of this heap of dust;	64	Ch.-monum.		3
Take up within a cloisters gates.	69	Content		16
I am with thee, and Most take all.	70	Quidditie		12
Take a bad lodging in my heart;	74	The Starre		6
Motion, and heat, let's take our flight	74	The Starre		18
O let me take thee at the bound,	76	Sunday		60
Take up his place and right:	81	Christmas		24
May turn, and take me by the hand, and more	87	Lent		41
Then he'l take notice of: in ev'ry path	92	Man		44
And him we take.	93	Antiphon 2		15
Take one from ten, and what remains?	96	Charms & K		15
Take up the second, then thy double line	97	Afflict.5		16
Wert fain to take our flesh and curse,	103	Prayer 2		15
Of what we might not take, or be withstood.	104	Obedience		30
Or take me up to thee!	107	Home		6
Or take me up to thee!	107	Home		12
Or take me up to thee!	107	Home		18
Or take me up to thee!	107	Home		24
Or take me up to thee!	108	Home		30
Or take me up to thee!	108	Home		36
Or take me up to thee!	108	Home		42

TAKE (cont'd)

	PAGE	TITLE		LINE
Or take me up to thee!	108	Home		48
Or take me up to thee!	108	Home		54
Or take me up to thee!	108	Home		60
Or take me up to thee!	109	Home		66
Or take me up to thee!	109	Home		72
Or take me up to thee!	109	Home		78
Then silly soul take heed; for earthly joy	111	Vanitie 2		17
Take up thine eyes, which feed on earth;	112	Dawning		2
And with a thankfull heart his comforts take.	112	Dawning		6
Thou hast hid metals: man may take them thence;	119	Providence		81
My words take fire from my inflamed thoughts.	122	Sinnes rd.		6
My words take fire from my inflamed thoughts.	122	Sinnes rd.		7
Did take.	124	Gratefulnes		24
Take of this grain, which in my garden grows,	125	Peace		37
Lord, I acknowledge; take thy plagues away:	126	Confession		26
Let me as well take up their joy, as sorrow.	128	Bunch Gr.		21
Who was to take it from me, slipt his hand,	130	Love unkn.		34
And should take place	131	Mans medly		17
Could he but take them right, and in their wayes.	132	Mans medly		33
But he doth bid us take his bloud for wine.	135	Divinitie		21
To take and taste what he doth there designe,	135	Divinitie		23
Oh take thy lute, and tune it to a strain,	136	Ephes.		19
Away; take heed:	153	The Collar		27
Readie to take them in; yet of a size	158	Praise 3		29
And so take up at use good store:	159	Praise 3		40
O take these barres, these lengths away;	163	The Search		49
So much desir'd, is giv'n, to take away	164	The Crosse		9
If truly said, they may take part	168	a true Hymn		7
And take it in.	171	The Glance		8
Yet if you go, I passe not; take your way:	177	Forerunners		31
Presse me not to take more pleasure	177	The Rose		1
Onely take this gentle rose,	177	The Rose		15
Take the gentle path.	178	Discipline		4
And take up my lines and life:	182	Banquet		51
When th' one did set, the other did take place,	196	Ch.-Milit.		217
Why should I Womens eyes for Chrystal take?	206	Walton 2		8
and take my restful sleep:	218	Psalm IV	D	30
Let him pursue and take my soul,	221	Psalm VII	D	17
when it is a sin to take something for mony lent, or when not;	230	Priest 5		24
Oh let us all take heed what we do, God sees us, he sees whether I	234	Priest 7		26
whom hee sees take best courses, that so both they may be encouraged	243	Priest 11		25
and to take more paines in their vocation, as not knowing when they	245	Priest 12		3
who live best, and take most paines, and are most charged:	245	Priest 12		16
our Saviours rule, and to take my brother aside, and reprove him;	248	Priest 14		27
may then by an honourable way take occasion to be better instructed.	255	Priest 21		31
he thinks it the most usefull way that a Pastor can take,	256	Priest 21		2
nor the Church-Wardens so well take notice who receive thrice,	259	Priest 22		28
which if it happily take effect, he then comes on the faster,	263	Priest 25		32
feele my self, either I take my wonted proportion, or diminish of it.	267	Priest 26		9
as being persons enabled by that Name to take moveable goods,	270	Priest 29		2
as that by this he may take into his Prayer humiliation also.	273	Priest 31		32
and take as much joy in a straight-growing childe, or servant,	275	Priest 32		32
to take heed, lest their quiet betray them (as it is apt to do)	280	Priest 34		17
not to take the full compasse, and liberty of their Peace:	280	Priest 34		21
then to take Jobs admirable Course, who sacrificed lest his Children	280	Priest 34		34
should a Christian Souldier take such occasions to harden himselfe,	284	Priest 35		35
who will take this into consideration, I will declare the causes	291	Cornaro		14
yet all must [needs] take heed, lest they take a greater quantitie	300	Cornaro		11
lest they take a greater quantitie of any meat or drink (though most	300	Cornaro		12
in this age of eighty three, which now I take, and which are such,	300	Cornaro		32
He that will take the bird, must not skare it.	322	Proverbs		42
Give a clowne your finger, and he will take your hand.	324	Proverbs		111
but take heede, lest you bee drowned.	326	Proverbs		167
Take heede of still waters, the quick passe away.	326	Proverbs		171
Waight and measure take away strife.	328	Proverbs		213
Take heede of the viniger of sweet wine.	336	Proverbs		451
To take the nuts from the fire with the dogges foot.	341	Proverbs		584
When God will punish, hee will first take away the understanding.	344	Proverbs		688
take not to serve you, if you will be served neately.	347	Proverbs		794
Take heede of an oxe before, of an horse behind,	351	Proverbs		900
Take an oxe by his hornes & a man by his tongue.	353	Proverbs	V	967
Though God take the sunne cut of the Heaven,	353	Proverbs		980
Take heed of the wrath of a mighty man,	360	Proverbs	D	1148
Take heed of mad folks in a narrow place.	360	Proverbs	D	1149
Take heed of credit decaid, and people that have nothing.	360	Proverbs	D	1150
Take heed of a young wench,	360	Proverbs	D	1151
Take heed of a person marked, and a Widdow thrice married.	360	Proverbs	D	1152
Take heed of foul dirty wayes, and long sicknesse.	360	Proverbs	D	1153
Take heed of winde that comes in at a hole,	360	Proverbs	D	1154
Take heed of a step-mother; the very name of her sufficeth.	360	Proverbs	D	1155
by which Scholars say, the Muses use to take up their habitations.	363	Letters		5
only hereafter I will take heed how I propose my desires unto you,	363	Letters		20
He doubles it to take away the scruple of those that might say,	374	Letters		22
working, still together, that I take a comfort therein;	375	Letters		20
till I take some opportunity to let them know your love,	375	Letters		21
except my cousin Bett take pitty of her, which yet at that distance	375	Letters		29
Yet, truly if you take her not, I am thinking to do it,	375	Letters		34
But take this rule, and it is an outlandish one, which I commend	376	Letters		16
that I take it exceeding kindly of you.	378	Letters		11

	PAGE	TITLE		LINE
TEAR (rip)				
I will tear thence his love and fame.	35	Thanksgvng		26
TEAR				
I have not lcst one single tear:	158	Praise 3		25
TEARE (rip)				
I will teare out his love and fame.	35	Thanksgvng	WC	26
TEARE				
Nothing dries sooner then a teare.	343	Proverbs		659
TEARES				
Made of a heart, and cemented with teares:	26	The Altar		2
You give us teares to wash them: lett those beams	44	H. Bapt.1	W	7
Doe ruine thee; or if the teares	208	H. Danvers	D	6
How know you that our teares proceed from woe	210	Paradox	D	15
To curbe some Rebell teares, which faine would flow,	213	Bohemia	D	58
Thy teares not needing. For that hand Divine	213	Bohemia	D	63
Great God will surely dry those teares,	213	L' Envoy	D	5
who first shed teares over Jerusalem, and afterwards blood.	234	Priest 7		21
The dainties of the great are the teares of the poore.	352	Proverbs		937
TEARS (rip)				
Shame tears my soul, my bodie many a wound;	33	Sacrifice		217
TEARS				
These drops being temper'd with a sinners tears,	27	Sacrifice		25
When all my tears were bloud, the while you slept:	31	Sacrifice		150
Your tears for your own fortunes should be kept:	31	Sacrifice		151
Or else give tears to drown them, as they grow.	44	H. Bapt.1		9
If all mens tears were let	62	Afflict.2		6
Out-crying my requests, drowning my tears;	66	Ch.-lock		3
Did weep so fast, that the tears trickling down	71	Humilitie		26
The Couch of Time, the balme of tears,	75	Sunday	W	2
Draws tears, or bloud, not want an handkerchief.	112	Dawning		16
Hast thou tears, or hast thou none?	113	Businesse		5
If, poore soul, thou hast no tears,	113	Businesse		6
With that I gave a viall full of tears:	121	Hope		5
Tears sullying thy transparent rooms,	124	Gratefulnes		14
Enforceth tears. Your heart was foul, I fear.	129	Love unkn.		18
My sighs and tears as busie were above;	132	The Storm		3
Lord, I adjudge my self to tears and grief,	136	Ephes.		25
Ev'n endlesse tears	136	Ephes.		26
My want of tears with store of bloud.	136	Ephes.		36
What is so shrill as silent tears?	137	Familie		20
These seas are tears, and heav'n the haven.	138	The Size		47
My tears and prayers night and day do wooe,	139	Artillerie		19
Lifting to heaven from this well of tears.	141	Justice 2		18
Can both the way and end be tears?	142	Pilgrimage		28
Thou grew'st soft and moist with tears,	146	Praise 2		21
To thee my sighs, my tears ascend:	148	Longing		5
And in thy bosome poure my tears,	150	Longing		71
Before my tears did drown it.	153	The Collar		12
O who will give me tears? Come all ye springs,	164	Grief		1
In that dark state of tears: to all, that so	169	The Answer		12
Of sov'raigne tears, springing from true remorse:	170	Water-crs.		8
Why kept she not her tears for her own faults,	173	Marie Magd		9
Why kept she not her tears for her own fauts,	173	Marie Magd	V	9
In tears like seas, our sinnes are pil'd	173	Marie Magd		11
Then did I wash you with my tears, and more,	176	Forerunners		16
Dry dust, which sheds no tears, but may extort.	186	Death		12
But in the Jews and us deserveth tears.	196	Ch.-Milit.		228
If ever Tears did flow from Eyes,	213	Convert	D	1
My Eyes, from whence these Tears did spring,	214	Convert	D	6
And water with salt tears my Bed,	220	Psalm VI	D	15
the Lord vouchsafes to weigh my tears;	220	Psalm VI	D	22
when he cannot more, as he that weeps a floud of tears.	279	Priest 33		31
that my solliciting him has been much, and my tears many for you;	372	Letters		3
diligence, prayers and tears, to bud, blow and bear fruit in your	377	Letters		5
TEDIOUS				
which may make his other discourses more welcome, and lesse tedious.	251	Priest 17		6
TEEMES				
Nature drawes more then ten teemes.	347	Proverbs		777
TEETH				
That chains us by the teeth so fast?	108	Home		38
And thou hast brok th' ungodly's teeth:	217	Psalm III	D	21
The tongue walkes where the teeth speede not.	324	Proverbs		102
Follow not truth too near the heels, lest it dash out thy teeth.	360	Proverbs	D	1138
We Batchelors laugh and shew our teeth,	361	Proverbs	D	1175
TELL				
When thou dost tell anothers jest, therein	9	Ch.-Porch		61
Cowards tell lies, and those that fear the rod;	9	Ch.-Porch		75
'Tis but to tell the tale is told.	35	Thanksgvng		8
And each grief tell?	38	Good Fri.		4
Till grief did tell me roundly, that I lived.	47	Afflict.1		30
He is to Sinai gone, as we heard tell:	99	Decay		9
Nor any sorrow tell them that they sinne,	100	Miserie		22
If thou persistest, I will tell thee,	105	Conscience		11
Tell me, I pray, Whose hands are those?	110	The Quip		7
(I sigh to tell)	129	Love unkn.		24
For thou canst tell,	144	Discharge		19
Then let me tell thee a strange storie.	151	The Bag		8
And tell me more:	175	The Odour		18
Passeth tongue to taste or tell.	181	Banquet		6
Yet I heare tell,	187	Judgement		7
Then tell me, what is that supreme delight?	188	Heaven		13

TELL (cont'd)	PAGE	TITLE		LINE
His fall can tell, ...	202	Trin.Sun.	W	13
For who can tell, though thou hast dyde to winn	205	Persever.	W	9
And the answerer could not tell;	257	Priest 21		4
at table about his appetite, if he tell this to another, preacheth;	278	Priest 33		19
tell me what I dreamed last night.	332	Proverbs		336
I will tell you what I wrote to our eldest brother, when he urged one	375	Letters		10
TELLES				
What your glasse telles you, will not be told by Councell. . . .	329	Proverbs		255
TELLING				
him in his Tithes, telling him when he hath forgotten it, This I do,	254	Priest 20		16
telling my Physicians nothing thereof, as is the custome of sick	292	Cornaro		29
TELLS				
Tells to all he meets, his crosse:	114	Businesse		32
Sometimes he tells them stories, and sayings of others, . . .	233	Priest 7		11
He that tells a secret is anothers servant.	338	Proverbs		512
Hee that tells his wife newes is but newly married.	353	Proverbs		987
TELS				
He often tels them, that Sermons are dangerous things, that none goes	233	Priest 7		18
getting for himself, when he tels it to others, becomes a Sermon.	279	Priest 33		32
TEMPER				
That temper gives them theirs, and yet doth take	16	Ch.-Porch		254
The Temper.	55	Temper 1		T
The Christian Temper.	55	Temper 1	W	T
The Temper.	56	Temper 2		T
The Christian Temper.	56	Temper 2	W	T
My God, so temper joy and wo, ...	97	Afflict.5		23
Bid him but temper his excesse;	100	Miserie		9
But yet as the temper of his body may be, or as the temper of his	237	Priest 9		1
or as the temper of his Parish may be, where he may have occasion	237	Priest 9		2
He knows the temper, and pulse of every person in his house,	239	Priest 10		8
what kind of remedy fits the temper of the house best, and then hee	251	Priest 17		26
is a Physitian so far as he meetes with the same disease, and temper;	278	Priest 33		28
some being of a more melting temper then others) consisteth in a true	279	Priest 33		22
From this ill temper there remained little else to be expected of me,	291	Cornaro		24
which must needs so temper the humours of the bodie, that they could	295	Cornaro		8
their youthfull appetites, although they be of a most strong temper:	303	Cornaro		13
P.S. My brother is somewhat of the same temper, and perhaps a little	366	Letters		24
TEMPER'ST				
Who sweetly temper'st all. If we could heare	118	Providence		39
TEMPERANCE				
And change thy temperance into braverie.	15	Ch.-Porch		222
That went to Temperance.	70	Humilitie		14
He loves not Temperance, or Authoritie, ...	86	Lent		2
To use their temperance, seeking no evasion, ...	86	Lent		14
(though that indeed be very admirable) as at their daily temperance,	237	Priest 9		31
and the exact temperance of our Lord Jesus, with other exemplary	237	Priest 9		34
it absurd, that he should exceed, who teacheth others temperance.	241	Priest 10		21
judiciously, then he writes his rules of temperance out of bookes.	278	Priest 33		21
A Treatise of Temperance and Sobrietie:	291	Cornaro		T
For Temperance preserves even old men and sickly men sound: . .	292	Cornaro		8
But after I had resolved to follow Temperance and Reason, . .	292	Cornaro		31
I began to consider the force of Temperance, and to think thus	293	Cornaro		2
If Temperance had so much power as to bring me health; . . .	293	Cornaro		2
For the Temperance of so many yeares spent all ill humours, . .	296	Cornaro		32
then a Temperate Life, Temperance by all means is to be embraced.	298	Cornaro		2
But surely there is no such matter, if Temperance be wanting.	298	Cornaro		22
because Temperance takes away the cause of diseases:	300	Cornaro		1
the power and efficacie of that Temperance which ever accompanied me.	302	Cornaro		21
Because that by Temperance and the Grace of God I feel not those	302	Cornaro		24
in any thing I forsake that Temperance which I have found so good,	303	Cornaro		34
TEMPERATE				
just, prudent, temperate, bold, grave in all his wayes. . . .	227	Priest 3		2
hope of avoiding death and pain, I resolved to live a temperate life.	292	Cornaro		22
know what great power a sober and temperate life hath over our bodies	294	Cornaro		25
neither melancholie, nor any other passion can hurt a temperate life.	294	Cornaro		32
can bring little grief or hurt to those that are temperate. . . .	294	Cornaro		35
That they that live a temperate life, can receive little hurt from	295	Cornaro		15
nor better Physick then a Temperate Life, Temperance by all means is	298	Cornaro		2
moment (as I shewed before) if a man be temperate in meat and drink;	299	Cornaro		16
That he which lives a temperate life, cannot fall into diseases,	299	Cornaro		35
Since therefore a temperate life is so happie and pleasant a thing;	303	Cornaro		30
TEMPER'D				
These drops being temper'd with a sinners tears, ...	27	Sacrifice		25
TEMPERS				
especially since there is a greater diversitie of tempers, . .	297	Cornaro		31
and also doth preserve even ill tempers in good health, . .	298	Cornaro		14
TEMPEST				
Slander is a shipwrack by a dry Tempest.	356	Proverbs	D	135
TEMPESTS				
To feel those tempests, which fly over ditches.	11	Ch.-Porch		112
When waves do rise, and tempests rage.	97	Afflict.5		6
Tempests are calm to thee; they know thy hand, ...	118	Providence		45
On whom thy tempests fell all night.	166	The Flower		42
TEMPESTUOUS				
And much affect thee, as tempestuous times	132	The Storm		5
TEMPLE				
The Temple. Sacred Poems and Private Ejaculations. Dedication.	5	Dedication		T
Christ purg'd his temple; so must thou thy heart.	23	Ch.-Porch		423
Some said, that I the Temple to the floore	28	Sacrifice		65
Yet in thy temple thou dost him afford	67	Windows		3

THANK (cont'd)	PAGE	TITLE	LINE
for which I humbly thank him, & am so far from giving you cause,	378	Letters	9
THANKE			
I thanke you heartily for Leighton, your care, your Counsell,	379	Letters	13
THANKED			
where God is thanked for calling us to the knowledg of his grace,	258	Priest 22	6
THANKES			
God heales, and the Physitian hath the thankes.	326	Proverbs	169
Hee that looseth his due, gets no thankes.	333	Proverbs	363
THANKFULL			
Ladies, look here; this is the thankfull glasse,	58	H.Script.1	8
And with a thankfull heart his comforts take.	112	Dawning	6
Till I a thankfull heart obtain	124	Gratefulnes	27
Not thankfull, when it pleaseth me;	124	Gratefulnes	29
THANKING			
and sees them labour in thanking of him, he exacts of them to let him	245	Priest 12	31
THANKS			
The Second Thanks-giving.	36	Reprisall W	T
And at your lodging with their thanks appeare.	120	Providence	120
And ceased not to give thanks for the Ephesians, Eph. 1. 16.	234	Priest 7	13
that so the thanks may go the right way, and thither onely,	245	Priest 12	33
is a great Blessing, and as great as food, for which we give thanks:	284	Priest 35	28
your Valdesso I now returne with many thanks, and some notes,	304	Valdesso	2
to find out variety of thanks for the diversity of your favours,	363	Letters	15
THANKS-GIVING			
The Second Thanks-giving.	36	Reprisall W	T
THANKSGIVING			
The Thanksgiving.	35	Thanksgvng	T
THARE			
To writhe his limbes, and thare, not mend the ill.	73	Constancie V	33
THAW			
And rots to nothing at the next great thaw.	12	Ch.-Porch	140
THAWING			
Marking his grave, and thawing ev'ry yeare,	98	Mortific.	26
THAWS			
Who never melts or thaws	72	Constancie	21
TH'			
Man would have been th' incloser: but since now	7	Ch.-Porch	20
Thwart not th' Almighty God: O be not crosse.	22	Ch.-Porch	395
Stay not for th' other pin: why thou hast lost	23	Ch.-Porch	411
From th' earth unto my brows, and bear the thrall:	32	Sacrifice	167
The greater world o' th' two; for that came in	33	Sacrifice	206
The greater world o' th' two; for that comes in	33	Sacrifice W	206
A new small-rented lease, and cancell th' old.	40	Redemption	4
Though he give light, & th' East perfume;	42	Easter	24
Though hee bring light & th' other sents:	42	Easter W	24
And carrie with them th' other parts.	49	Repentance	30
Engine against th' Almightie, sinners towre,	51	Prayer 1	5
Engine against th' Almightie, sinners fort,	51	Prayer 1 W	5
But as th' outworks, they may controll	52	H.Commun.	16
And leave th' earth to their food.	53	H.Commun.	40
Wrought our deliverance from th' infernall pit,	54	Love 1	12
That th' earth did like a heav'n appeare;	59	Whitsunday	10
Sinne is flat opposite to th' Almighty, seeing	63	Sinne 2	4
The day or night: that is the gale, this th' harbour;	64	Even-song	26
And th' other black and grave, wherewith each one	67	Ch.-floore	4
Th' indorsement of supreme delight,	75	Sunday	3
Did th' earth and all things with it move.	76	Sunday	46
When th' elements did for place contest	79	Employm.2	11
Both th' old discoveries, and the new-found seas,	88	The Pearl	7
And us in th' end.	92	Antiphon 2	9
At th' head of others, hit their own.	96	Charms & K	10
At th' hart of others, hit their own.	96	Charms & K W	10
When th' hair is sweet through pride or lust,	96	Charms & K	13
To see what help in th' earth or skie:	107	Home	14
With one small sigh thou gav'st me th' other day	108	Home	43
She wholly goes on th' other side,	110	Brit. Ch.	23
Is deeply carved there: but th' other week	112	JESU	2
That transferr'd th' accounts to me.	114	Dialogue	16
When th' earth was dry, thou mad'st a sea of wet:	120	Providence	113
Sponges, non-sense and sense; mines, th' earth & plants.	121	Providence	136
Most things move th' under-jaw; the Crocodile not.	121	Providence	139
Most things move th' underchaw; the Crocodile not.	121	Providence V	139
Most things sleep lying; th' Elephant leans or stands.	121	Providence	140
Most things sleep lying; th' Elephant leane or stand.	121	Providence V	140
In th' other Angels have a right by birth:	131	Mans medly	9
With th' one hand touching heav'n, with th' other earth.	131	Mans medly	12
Let th' upper springs into the low	137	The Size	5
To th' Isle of spices, is't not fair?	137	The Size	12
I left on th' one, and on the other side	142	Pilgrimage	5
That with th' one hand thou liftest to the sky,	160	Priesthood	2
For that of th' holy word.	160	Priesthood	6
But th' holy men of God such vessels are,	161	Priesthood	25
Through th' old sinnes and new doctrines of our land.	161	Priesthood	33
My knees pierce th' earth, mine eies the skie;	162	The Search	5
And keeps thee present, leaving th' old	162	The Search	27
Thou turnest th' edge of all things on me still,	165	The Crosse	21
From the first man in th' East, to fresh and new	168	The Sonne	9
Whereas if th' heart be moved,	168	a true Hymn	16
As when th' heart sayes (sighing to be approved)	168	a true Hymn	19
Makes that and th' action fine.	185	The Elixer	20

TH' (cont'd)	PAGE	TITLE		LINE
Where th' Ark did rest, there Abraham began	190	Ch.-Milit.		19
Made Pharaoh Moses, changing th' historie.	191	Ch.-Milit.		42
But th' Empire dwelt in Greece, to comfort them	192	Ch.-Milit.		73
Which using, and not fearing skill in th' one,	192	Ch.-Milit.		77
Or strength in th' other, did erect her throne.	192	Ch.-Milit.		78
Or strength in th' other, took possession.	192	Ch.-Milit.	W	78
Many a rent and struggling th' Empire knew,	192	Ch.-Milit.		79
When th' one did set, the other did take place,	196	Ch.-Milit.		217
They are Sinnes nipples, feeding th' east and west.	196	Ch.-Milit.		220
And met in th' east their first and ancient sound,	197	Ch.-Milit.		268
Strugling on th' hook.	204	The Knell	W	6
Of th' universe, like as the windes, & name	212	Bohemia	D	44
in councels of th' ungodly share,	214	Psalm I	D	2
And thou hast brok th' ungodly's teeth:	217	Psalm III	D	21
But in th' abundance of thy Grace	218	Psalm V	D	17
THEATERS				
Sought him in Citties, Theaters, resorts	40	Redemption	W	10
THEATRES				
In cities, theatres, gardens, parks, and courts:	40	Redemption		11
THEE				
Lord, my first fruits present themselves to thee;	5	Dedication		1
Yet not mine neither: for from thee they came,	5	Dedication		2
Thy rate and price, and mark thee for a treasure;	6	Ch.-Porch		2
The price of thee, and mark thee for a treasure;	6	Ch.-Porch	W	2
Ryme thee to good, and make a bait of pleasure.	6	Ch.-Porch		4
Whose twigs are pleasures, & they whip thee bare,	6	Ch.-Porch	W	9
It spoils an Angel: robs thee of thy God.	6	Ch.-Porch	W	10
Allows thee choise of paths: take no by-wayes;	7	Ch.-Porch		14
Let not each fansy make thee to detest	7	Ch.-Porch	W	19
Let not each motion make thee to detest	7	Ch.-Porch	WC	19
And God will show thee how to take the towne,	7	Ch.-Porch	W	22
When once it is within thee; but before	7	Ch.-Porch		26
Which it would poure on thee, upon the floore.	7	Ch.-Porch		28
Let not a common ruine thee intombe:	8	Ch.-Porch		45
It gets thee nothing, and hath no excuse.	8	Ch.-Porch		56
It gets thee nothing, and has no excuse.	8	Ch.-Porch	W	56
Which is thy best stake, when griefs make thee tame.	9	Ch.-Porch		66
Against thee: for his light was onely lent.	9	Ch.-Porch		82
But if thou coole, then take some shame to thee	10	Ch.-Porch	W	90
And if Gods image move thee not, let thine.	10	Ch.-Porch		102
Think the king sees thee still; for his King does.	11	Ch.-Porch		122
God gave them to thee under lock and key.	12	Ch.-Porch		144
Thy children, kindred, friends upon thee call;	13	Ch.-Porch		161
Lest gaining gain on thee, and make thee dimme	13	Ch.-Porch		164
Least gaining gaine on thee, & fill thy hart	13	Ch.-Porch	W	164
About thy neck do drown thee? raise thy head;	13	Ch.-Porch		170
Doth make thee parcell-devil in damnation.	16	Ch.-Porch		258
As hurts not others, but may make thee better,	16	Ch.-Porch		262
Then may the beasts draw thee to happy light.	16	Ch.-Porch		264
The speaker to thee, and preserve thy stock.	18	Ch.-Porch		300
Take all into thee; then with equall care	19	Ch.-Porch		321
In time they'l runne thee out of all thy wit.	21	Ch.-Porch		366
Affect in things about thee cleanlinesse,	21	Ch.-Porch		367
That all may gladly board thee, as a flowre.	21	Ch.-Porch		368
Open for thee; or both may come too late.	21	Ch.-Porch		384
Open for thee; or they may come too late.	21	Ch.-Porch	W	384
For all the week thy food so oft he gave thee.	22	Ch.-Porch		392
Because 'tis better, and perhaps may save thee.	22	Ch.-Porch		394
Away thy blessings, and extreamly flout thee,	23	Ch.-Porch		413
Our blessings from us, and extreamly flout thee,	23	Ch.-Porch	W	413
Thy clothes being fast, but thy soul loose about thee.	23	Ch.-Porch		414
To couzin thee. Look to thy actions well:	23	Ch.-Porch		425
In brief, acquit thee bravely; play the man.	24	Ch.-Porch		457
These stones to praise thee may not cease.	26	The Altar		14
Now prophesie who strikes thee, is their dittie.	31	Sacrifice		142
To thee of all kings onely due)	35	Thanksgvng		2
Oh King of wounds! how shall I grieve for thee,	35	Thanksgvng		3
King of all wounds, how shall I grieve for thee,	35	Thanksgvng	W	3
But how then shall I imitate thee, and	35	Thanksgvng		15
All back unto thee by the poore.	35	Thanksgvng		20
All back unto thee in the poore.	35	Thanksgvng	W	20
The honour doth belong to thee.	35	Thanksgvng		22
That honour doth belong to thee.	35	Thanksgvng	W	22
My musick shall finde thee, and ev'ry string	36	Thanksgvng		39
That all together may accord in thee,	36	Thanksgvng		41
Thy art of love, which I'le turn back on thee:	36	Thanksgvng		47
For though I die for thee, I am behinde;	36	Reprisall		3
For by thy death I die for thee.	36	Reprisall		8
Against thee, in thee I will overcome	37	Reprisall		15
The man, who once against thee fought.	37	Reprisall		16
Each seventh note by right is due to thee.	38	The Sinner		4
And though my hard heart scarce to thee can grone,	38	The Sinner		13
How shall I count what thee befell,	38	Good Fri.		3
No lodging for thee, but a cold hard stone?	40	Sepulchre		2
Receive thee?	40	Sepulchre		4
They leave thee.	40	Sepulchre		8
Which holds thee now? Who hath indited it	41	Sepulchre		11
Where our hard hearts have took up stones to brain thee,	41	Sepulchre		13
And missing this, most falsly did arraigne thee;	41	Sepulchre		14
Onely these stones in quiet entertain thee,	41	Sepulchre		15

THEE (cont'd)

THEE (cont'd)

	PAGE	TITLE		LINE
To passe it self and all it has to thee.	104	Obedience	W	8
Lord, what is man to thee,	104	Obedience		21
Musick to thee doth howl.	105	Conscience		4
If thou persistest, I will tell thee,	105	Conscience		11
That I have physick to expell thee.	105	Conscience		12
And leaves thee not a word;	106	Conscience		16
Besides my physick, know there's some for thee:	106	Conscience		20
Did not affect thee much, was not thy aim;	106	Sion		8
Which sometimes crosseth thee, thou sometimes it:	106	Sion		14
Is not so deare to thee as one good grone.	106	Sion		18
Tombes for the dead, not temples fit for thee:	107	Sion		20
Or take me up to thee!	107	Home		6
Or take me up to thee!	107	Home		12
Or take me up to thee!	107	Home		18
Or take me up to thee!	107	Home		24
Or take me up to thee!	108	Home		30
Or take me up to thee!	108	Home		36
Or take me up to thee!	108	Home		42
Or take me up to thee!	108	Home		48
They dresse themselves and come to thee.	108	Home		52
Or take me up to thee!	108	Home		54
Or take me up to thee!	108	Home		60
Or take me up to thee!	109	Home		66
Or take me up to thee!	109	Home		72
Or take me up to thee!	109	Home		78
Beautie in thee takes up her place,	109	Brit. Ch.		4
Beautie in thee takes up the place,	109	Brit. Ch.	V	4
To double-moat thee with his grace,	110	Brit. Ch.		29
And none but thee.	110	Brit. Ch.		30
Is but a bubble, and makes thee a boy.	111	Vanitie 2		18
Which as it riseth, raiseth thee:	112	Dawning		12
Foolish soul, Who di'd for thee?	113	Businesse		16
If he had not liv'd for thee,	113	Businesse		20
If he had not di'd for thee,	113	Businesse		26
What the gains in having thee	114	Dialogue		13
Praise thee brim-full!	115	Dulnesse		4
Thy bloudy death and undeserv'd, makes thee	115	Dulnesse		11
I may but look towards thee:	116	Dulnesse		26
Look onely; for to love thee, who can be,	116	Dulnesse		27
And not of thee, through whom my fingers bend	116	Providence		3
To hold my quill? shall they not do thee right?	116	Providence		4
He that to praise and laud thee doth refrain,	117	Providence		17
But robs a thousand who would praise thee fain,	117	Providence		19
For me and all my fellows praise to thee:	117	Providence		26
And be dispos'd, and dress'd, and tun'd by thee,	118	Providence		38
Tempests are calm to thee; they know thy hand,	118	Providence		45
Ev'n poysons praise thee. Should a thing be lost?	119	Providence		85
To honour thee: and so I give thee praise	121	Providence		147
To honour thee; and so each hymne thy fame	121	Providence		151
See how thy beggar works on thee	123	Gratefulnes		3
Of thee:	124	Gratefulnes		28
I sought thee in a secret cave,	124	Peace		3
Joy, I did lock thee up: but some bad man	128	Bunch Gr.		1
Hath let thee out again:	128	Bunch Gr.		2
And much affect thee, as tempestuous times	132	The Storm		5
Dares to assault thee, and besiege thy doore.	132	The Storm		12
I blesse thee, Lord, because I GROW	132	Paradise		1
To thee both fruit and order OW.	132	Paradise		3
Which may with thee	136	Ephes.		20
Content thee, greedie heart.	137	The Size		1
And work up to thee; yet thou dost refuse.	139	Artillerie		20
Thy promise now hath ev'n set thee thy laws.	139	Artillerie		24
There is no articling with thee:	139	Artillerie		31
Did once perceive, it blew thee under foot,	140	Ch.-rents	V	7
Their beauteous glories. Onely shreds of thee,	140	Ch.-rents		9
And through their glasse discolour thee!	141	Justice 2		5
And harp on thee.	141	Justice 2		21
Gods promises have made thee mine;	141	Justice 2		22
And well it was for thee, when this befell,	144	Discharge		16
What present things requir'd of thee.	144	Discharge		25
I will love thee:	146	Praise 2		2
I will move thee.	146	Praise 2		4
I will sing thee,	146	Praise 2		10
I will bring thee.	146	Praise 2		12
I will praise thee.	146	Praise 2		18
I can raise thee.	146	Praise 2		20
To enroll thee:	146	Praise 2		26
To extoll thee.	146	Praise 2		28
To thee my cries,	148	Longing		3
To thee my grones,	148	Longing		4
To thee my sighs, my tears ascend:	148	Longing		5
From thee all pitie flows.	148	Longing		13
Their infants, them; and they suck thee	148	Longing		17
Their infants, them; and they seek thee	148	Longing	V	17
It moves, it creeps, it aims at thee:	149	Longing		38
To thee help appertains.	149	Longing		43
Then let me tell thee a strange storie.	151	The Bag		8
Which pettie thoughts have made, and made to thee	153	The Collar		23
In hope of thee my heart	154	Glimpse		16
Must let thee go, return when it doth knock.	154	Glimpse		22

THEE (cont'd)

	PAGE	TITLE		LINE
When wit contrives to meet with thee,	155	Assurance		5
Who heard thee say it. O most gracious Lord,	155	Assurance		20
Which bounds on thee, and will not down thy throat:	156	Assurance		40
And thou with me dost thee restore.	157	Clasping		8
If I without thee would be mine,	157	Clasping		9
I may presume thee mine, then thine.	157	Clasping		13
Not thee, but me, and to be mine:	157	Clasping		15
Thousands of things do thee employ	158	Praise 3		19
Fain put thee on, exchanging my lay-sword	160	Priesthood		5
As if to meet thee they did know,	162	The Search		11
I sent a sigh to seek thee out,	162	The Search		17
And keeps thee present, leaving th' old	162	The Search		27
Conceals thee still?	163	The Search		30
And serve thee; and not onely I,	164	The Crosse		4
My power to serve thee; to unbend	164	The Crosse		10
What I would do for thee, if once my grones	165	The Crosse		15
Thy curse being laid on him, makes thee accurst.	169	Dial.-Anth		6
These arms shall crush thee. Spare not, do thy worst.	169	Dial.-Anth		8
If troubles overtake thee, do not wail:	170	Water-crs.		4
To serve thy sinnes, and furnish thee with store	170	Water-crs.		7
My Master, shall I speak? O that to thee	175	The Odour		11
To some degree of spicinesse to thee!	175	The Odour		15
My servant, as thee not displeasing,	175	The Odour		24
Return to thee.	175	The Odour		28
Hath some fond lover tic'd thee to thy bane?	176	Forerunners		21
That which wrought on thee,	179	Discipline		26
Brought thee low,	179	Discipline		27
Still invite, still call to thee:	180	Invitation		33
And I depend on thee;	183	A Parodie		5
In all things thee to see,	184	The Elixer		2
All things I doe to thee	184	The Elixer	W	2
To do it as for thee:	184	The Elixer		4
But still to make thee prepossest,	184	The Elixer		7
He that does ought for thee,	184	The Elixer	W	12
All may of thee partake:	184	The Elixer		13
Of praise deserved, unto thee I give,	185	A Wreath		2
I give to thee, who knowest all my wayes,	185	A Wreath		3
Straight as a line, and ever tends to thee,	185	A Wreath		6
To thee, who art more farre above deceit,	185	A Wreath		7
For this poore wreath, give thee a crown of praise.	185	A Wreath		12
For we consider'd thee as at some six	186	Death		5
We lookt on this side of thee, shooting short;	186	Death		9
For we do now behold thee gay and glad,	186	Death		17
That some will turn thee to some leaves therein	187	Judgement		8
I cannot look on thee.	189	Love 3		10
Much more do Common-weals acknowledge thee,	190	Ch.-Milit.		5
Who may with thee compare?	191	Ch.-Milit.		48
Who may with thee compare?	192	Ch.-Milit.		100
Who may with thee compare?	194	Ch.-Milit.		156
Who may with thee compare?	196	Ch.-Milit.		210
Who may with thee compare?	198	Ch.-Milit.		279
Thee to love, in thee to sleep.	199	L'Envoy		4
Concerneth mee & Thee.	200	H. Commun.	W	12
That allso made thee dead.	201	H. Commun.	W	30
My God, give mee all Thee.	201	H. Commun.	W	48
There is no dealing with thee in that Art:	201	love	W	2
I thought it brave to praise thee then,	202	love	W	15
Then flesh did lend thee, back agen.	202	love	W	18
Whereas if I orecome thee & thy Love	202	love	W	23
Two reacheth thee	202	Trin.Sun.	W	3
Never to thee aspire,	202	Trin.Sun.	W	9
As if shades knew not Thee.	203	Even-song	W	12
Which know not thee, suck in thy beames	203	Even-song	W	23
And wake with thee for ever.	203	Even-song	W	24
Julips & Cordials when wee call on thee	204	The Knell	W	17
Which warme these lines, & serve them up to thee	204	Persever.	W	2
But kill the man, is seald with thee.	204	Persever.	W	8
My God, where is that ancient heat towards thee,	206	Walton 1		1
Why are not Sonnets made of thee? and layes	206	Walton 1		5
Sure, Lord, there is enough in thee to dry	206	Walton 2		1
Roses and Lillies speak thee; and to make	206	Walton 2		6
To praise, and on thee, Lord, some Ink bestow.	206	Walton 2		11
In the best face but filth, when, Lord, in thee	206	Walton 2		13
As God gives thee store,	207	Walton 3		5
The Water, and the Earth both unto thee	439	Walton 5		7
His dust who under thee must sleepe	208	H. Danvers	D	2
Doe ruine thee; or if the teares	208	H. Danvers	D	6
Another Monument for Thee.	209	H. Danvers	D	10
To second thee against there cunning hate.	211	Bohemia	D	22
Of thousand harts: that face doth figure thee	212	Bohemia	D	33
Of opposition cannot place thee, where	212	Bohemia	D	39
Children for kingdomes to thee; they shall live	212	Bohemia	D	42
But joyes are stord for thee: thou shalt returne	212	Bohemia	D	55
Call thee from out of that surrounded land,	213	Bohemia	D	61
Will pour full joyes to thee, but dregs to those,	213	Bohemia	D	65
Which now that moist land to thee beares.	213	L' Envoy	D	6
this day have I begotten thee:	216	Psalm II	D	18
Salvation unto thee	217	Psalm III	D	22
Lord hear me when I call on Thee,	217	Psalm IV	D	1
my cry to thee, I pray.	218	Psalm V	D	4

	PAGE	TITLE		LINE
THEE (cont'd)				
No evil, Lord, shall dwell with thee,	218	Psalm V	D	11
shall be abhorr'd by thee.	218	Psalm V	D	16
will I to thee draw near:	218	Psalm V	D	18
will worship thee in fear.	218	Psalm V	D	20
But let all those that trust in thee	219	Psalm V	D	35
protected still by thee:	219	Psalm V	D	38
For who in death remember Thee?	220	Psalm VI	D	11
or who shall praise Thee in the grave?	220	Psalm VI	D	12
I put my trust in Thee:	220	Psalm VII	D	2
resort to give Thee praise;	221	Psalm VII	D	26
For many and wonderfull things are spoken of thee, thou great Vertue.	244	Priest 12		8
imprecation to Simon Magus, Act. 8. Thy mony perish with thee:	285	Priest 36		30
before thy face, who are contrary to thee, in all we call thee?	288	Priest		9
before thy face, who are contrary to thee, in all we call thee?	288	Priest		10
awake all my powers to glorifie thee!	289	Priest		10
We praise thee! we blesse thee!	289	Priest		10
we blesse thee! we magnifie thee for ever!	289	Priest		11
we magnifie thee for ever!	289	Priest		11
beseeching thee to blesse thy word, wher-ever spoken this day	289	Priest		14
and thy right hand shall teach thee terrible things.	289	Priest		24
To whom with thee, and the Holy Ghost, three Persons, but one most	290	Priest		14
For if a friend who visits thee in thy sicknesse, and onely comforts	298	Cornaro		6
comforts and condoles, doth perform an acceptable thing to thee;	298	Cornaro		8
who not onely as a friend doth visit thee, but help thee!	298	Cornaro		9
who not onely as a friend doth visit thee, but help thee!	298	Cornaro		10
He that gives thee a Capon, give him the leg and the wing.	324	Proverbs		109
Hee that gives thee a bone, would not have thee die.	333	Proverbs		355
the time comes that hee will repay thee.	333	Proverbs		368
Cloath thee in war, arme thee in peace.	334	Proverbs		386
Helpe thy selfe, and God will helpe thee.	339	Proverbs		537
Shew me a lyer, and I'le shew thee a theefe.	343	Proverbs		652
He that will do thee a good turne, either he will be gon or dye.	358	Proverbs	D	1083
Cast thy Care on the Lord and he shall nourish thee. (Psal. 55.)	374	Letters		15
THEEFE				
Did not confess in the first Theefe	202	Trin.Sun.	W	12
Shew me a lyer, and I'le shew thee a theefe.	343	Proverbs		652
When it thunders, the theefe becomes honest.	344	Proverbs		690
THEEVES				
All worldly thoughts are but theeves met together	23	Ch.-Porch		424
Betwixt two theeves I spend my utmost breath,	34	Sacrifice		229
Of theeves and murderers: there I him espied,	40	Redemption		13
Warre makes theeves, and peace hangs them.	337	Proverbs		471
THEFT				
The other curbs sinnes stealing pace and theft.	117	Providence		36
THEIR				
Turn their eyes hither, who shall make a gain:	5	Dedication		5
Much lesse towards God, whose lust is all their book?	6	Ch.-Porch		12
(All in a shipwrack shift their severall way)	8	Ch.-Porch		44
Some till their ground, but let weeds choke their sonne:	10	Ch.-Porch		98
Some mark a partridge, never their childes fashion:	10	Ch.-Porch		99
Slight those who say amidst their sickly healths,	12	Ch.-Porch		133
Would have their tale beleeved for their oathes,	14	Ch.-Porch		183
Servants and churches also play their part.	14	Ch.-Porch		196
Blowing up houses with their whole increase.	14	Ch.-Porch		204
Many affecting wit beyond their power,	16	Ch.-Porch		245
Full of themselves, and answer their own notion.	19	Ch.-Porch		320
All forrain of that name; but scorn their ill:	21	Ch.-Porch		362
Embrace their activenesse, not vanities.	21	Ch.-Porch		363
Slovens take up their stock of noisomnesse	21	Ch.-Porch		369
Beforehand, and anticipate their last houre.	21	Ch.-Porch		370
First to bee Slovens, & forsake their nose.	21	Ch.-Porch	W	370
Makes all their beautie his deformitie.	23	Ch.-Porch		420
Turns all their beauty to his uglines.	23	Ch.-Porch	W	420
Against their Maker: they do wish me dead,	26	Sacrifice		6
One houre of watching; but their drowsie brain	27	Sacrifice		30
How with their lanterns do they seek the sunne!	27	Sacrifice		35
Of faith, but furie: yet at their commands	28	Sacrifice		46
I suffer binding, who have loos'd their bands:	28	Sacrifice		47
But yet their friendship is my enmitie:	29	Sacrifice		75
Pick quarrels with their onely happinesse:	29	Sacrifice		87
My silence rather doth augment their crie:	29	Sacrifice		93
Yet still they shout, and crie, and stop their eares,	30	Sacrifice		105
Putting my life among their sinnes and fears,	30	Sacrifice		106
But hony is their gall, brightnesse their night:	30	Sacrifice		111
For it was their own cause who killed me:	30	Sacrifice		115
For it was their own case who killed me:	30	Sacrifice	W	115
Why, Caesar is their onely King, not I:	30	Sacrifice		121
But surely not their hearts, as I well trie:	30	Sacrifice		123
But surely not their hearts, as I will trie:	30	Sacrifice	V	123
But not their harts, as I by proofe doe try.	30	Sacrifice	W	123
Doubles each lash: and yet their bitternesse	30	Sacrifice		126
Lest on their double-dark souls either shine:	31	Sacrifice		139
Now prophesie who strikes thee, is their dittie.	31	Sacrifice		142
They bow their knees to me, and cry, Hail king:	32	Sacrifice		173
And thorny all their crowns, bloudie their weeds;	32	Sacrifice		178
I, who am Truth, turn into truth their deeds:	32	Sacrifice		179
I, who am Truth, turn into truth their scorns:	32	Sacrifice	W	179
All spite in one, counting my life their losse,	33	Sacrifice		194
Nay, after death their spite shall further go;	34	Sacrifice		245
Nay, after death their spite shall farther go;	34	Sacrifice	W	245

THEIR (cont'd)

	PAGE	TITLE		LINE
To shew their face, since crosse to thy decrees:	38	The Sinner		7
My severall sinnes their sorrows get;	39	Good Fri.		18
Yet all these fences and their whole aray	46	Sinne 1		13
Which spread their forces into every part,	52	H.Commun.		11
Dispatches from their friend.	52	H.Commun.		24
And leave th' earth to their food.	53	H.Commun.		40
May also fix their reverence:	56	Temper 2		10
May no lines passe, except they do their dutie	56	Jordan 1		4
And the configurations of their glorie!	58	H.Script.2		2
If they might mend their wages, and serve here.	59	Whitsunday		12
Of those, who did themselves through their side wound,	59	Whitsunday		20
did play their part	66	Ch.-lock	W	4
And as their wit is, their digestion,	69	Content		31
Where all the beasts and fowls by their command	70	Humilitie		3
Where all the beasts and Foule by their command	70	Humilitie	W	3
To execute their call,	70	Humilitie		6
The fearfull Hare her eares, which by their law	70	Humilitie		11
And if the Fox had liv'd to rule their side,	70	Humilitie		23
For which ye wrangle, made them turn their frown	71	Humilitie		28
Upon their head.	71	Frailtie		8
Unpinne, or wrench from giving all their due.	72	Constancie		5
And is their vertue; Vertue is his Sunne.	72	Constancie		25
That winding is their fashion	74	The Starre		27
Which parts their ranks and orders.	75	Sunday		28
Who want herbs for their wound.	76	Sunday		42
Sinnes have their box apart,	82	Ungratef.		29
He views their stations, walks from doore to doore,	85	Vanitie 1		3
To make a purchase there: he sees their dances,	85	Vanitie 1		5
Both their full-ey'd aspects, and secret glances.	85	Vanitie 1		7
The callow principles within their nest:	85	Vanitie 1		17
Admitted to their bed-chamber, before	85	Vanitie 1		19
To use their temperance, seeking no evasion,	86	Lent		14
Where both their baskets are with all their store,	89	The Pearl	W	26
The smacks of dainties and their exaltation:	89	The Pearl	W	27
As watring pots give flowers their lives.	90	Afflict.4		10
Nothing their furie can controll,	90	Afflict.4		11
Quitting their place	90	Afflict.4		14
And while I live, trie out their right.	90	Afflict.4		18
Oh help, my God! let not their plot	90	Afflict.4		19
Finde their acquaintance there.	91	Man		24
In their descent and being; to our minde	91	Man		35
In their ascent and cause.	91	Man		36
At th' head of others, hit their own.	96	Charms & K		10
At th' hart of others, hit their own.	96	Charms & K	W	10
And ruffle all their curious knots and store.	97	Afflict.5		22
They step into their voluntarie graves,	98	Mortific.		8
Sleep bindes them fast; onely their breath	98	Mortific.		9
They would not have their actions scann'd,	100	Miserie		21
And measure not their fall.	100	Miserie		24
Their follies with the wing of thy milde Dove,	100	Miserie		28
Their follies with the wings of thy milde Dove,	100	Miserie	W	28
Such was their lustre, they did so excell,	102	Jordan 2		2
Off'ring their service, if I were not sped:	102	Jordan 2		8
By it do all things live their measur'd houre:	103	Prayer 2		10
By it do all things live their silly houre:	103	Prayer 2	W	10
Entred for both, farre above their desert!	105	Obedience		45
And all their motions upward be;	107	Sion		22
And for their old acquaintance plead.	109	Home		70
And then they have their answer home.	111	The Quip		24
Let them unto their kindred flie:	111	Vanitie 2		14
Till they regain their ancient nest.	111	Vanitie 2		16
Know their home, and get them gone:	113	Businesse		4
Windes still work: it is their plot,	113	Businesse		9
Sharpen their Muse:	116	Dulnesse		20
Beasts fain would sing; birds dittie to their notes;	117	Providence		9
Trees would be tuning on their native lute	117	Providence		10
To thy renown: but all their hands and throats	117	Providence		11
While all things have their will, yet none but thine.	117	Providence		32
And hold it fast, as children do their fathers,	118	Providence		46
Birds teach us hawking; fishes have their net:	118	Providence		51
Flies have their table spread, ere they appeare.	118	Providence		54
Others do sleep, and envie not their cheer.	118	Providence		56
The pigeons feed their tender off-spring, crying,	118	Providence		62
When they are callow; but withdraw their food	118	Providence		63
Their masters flower, but leave it, having done,	118	Providence		66
Trees after bearing drop their leaves for soil:	119	Providence		70
Springs vent their streams, and by expense get store:	119	Providence		71
Should creatures want for want of heed their due?	119	Providence		86
All countreys have enough to serve their need:	120	Providence		105
For their offence; and then dost turn their speed	120	Providence		107
When they are ripe, their odour will ascend,	120	Providence		119
And at your lodging with their thanks appeare.	120	Providence		120
Yet in their being joyn with one advise	121	Providence		146
Untill their cockatrice they hatch and bring:	122	Sinnes rd.		4
And when they once have perfected their draughts,	122	Sinnes rd.		5
They vent the wares, and passe them with their faults,	122	Sinnes rd.		9
They vent the wares, and passe them with their fauts	122	Sinnes rd.	V	9
And by their breathing ventilate the ill.	122	Sinnes rd.		10
And till they foot and clutch their prey,	126	Confession		15
The clearest diamond: let them do their best,	126	Confession		29

THEIR (cont'd)

	PAGE	TITLE		LINE
Their storie pennes and sets us down.	128	Bunch Gr.		11
Let me as well take up their joy, as sorrow.	128	Bunch Gr.		21
I have their fruit and more.	128	Bunch Gr.		23
All creatures have their joy: and man hath his.	131	Mans medly		3
Make their pretence:	131	Mans medly		8
But as birds drink, and straight lift up their head,	131	Mans medly		21
Could he but take them right, and in their wayes.	132	Mans medly		33
Amaze poore mortals, and object their crimes.	132	The Storm		6
Amuse poore mortals, and object their crimes.	132	The Storm	V	6
Starres have their storms, ev'n in a high degree,	132	The Storm		7
And such beginnings touch their END.	133	Paradise		15
Who do not their own motions heare?	134	The Method		19
And giving all things their set forms and houres,	137	Familie		11
Those have their hopes; these what they have renounce,	138	The Size		21
Their beauteous glories. Onely shreds of thee,	140	Ch.-rents		9
And through their glasse discolour thee!	141	Justice 2		5
Their thoughts and sense	145	Discharge		42
Thy passions also have their set partitions.	147	Offering		16
Their infants, them; and they suck thee	148	Longing		17
Their infants, them; and they seek thee	148	Longing	V	17
Hast thou left all things to their course,	149	Longing		44
Where all things have their leafe assign'd:	149	Longing		50
Flowers look about, and die not in their prime.	154	Glimpse		10
Disturb the work. O make me not their sport,	155	Glimpse		29
And make their ruine praise thy power.	156	Assurance		36
This spacious globe: Angels must have their joy,	158	Praise 3		21
Devils their rod, the sea his shore,	158	Praise 3		22
The windes their stint: and yet when I did call,	158	Praise 3		23
Their hands convey him, who conveys their hands.	161	Priesthood		28
Unto their sinnes?	162	The Search		28
To which, besides their own demean,	165	The Flower		3
To see their mother-root, when they have blown;	166	The Flower		11
Forfeit their Paradise by their pride.	167	The Flower		49
Fetching their proofs ev'n from the very bone;	167	Dotage		11
Let forrain nations of their language boast,	167	The Sonne		1
The harbingers are come. See, see their mark;	176	Forerunners		1
White is their colour, and behold my head.	176	Forerunners		2
With canvas, not with arras clothe their shame:	177	Forerunners		26
All their living,	181	Banquet		17
And with their words and posies windows fill:	182	The Posie		2
Lett in the Light to all their actions	185	The Elixer	W	23
When souls shall wear their new aray,	186	Death		19
Let the graves make their confession,	187	Dooms-day		15
Some to windes their bodie lend,	187	Dooms-day		21
Some to windes their bodies lend,	187	Dooms-day	W	21
But are their cares and businesse with the pleasure?	188	Judgement	V	17
And wrap their policies in thy decree,	190	Ch.-Milit.		6
Prayers chas'd syllogismes into their den,	191	Ch.-Milit.		55
Before the other two were in their prime.	191	Ch.-Milit.	W	60
Who, that they might subdue, made all their foes.	191	Ch.-Milit.		62
Disparking oracles, and all their treasure,	194	Ch.-Milit.		147
So trimme, as Greece and Egypt? yet their hearts	194	Ch.-Milit.		151
So spruse, as Greece and Egypt? yet their hearts	194	Ch.-Milit.	W	151
Are given over, for their curious arts,	194	Ch.-Milit.		152
And make that name good by their transmigrations;	195	Ch.-Milit.		184
All poste to Rome: Princes submit their necks	195	Ch.-Milit.		195
Then what was in their tongue, did overcome;	196	Ch.-Milit.		202
Yet with two faces, as their Janus was;	196	Ch.-Milit.		207
Being in this their old crackt looking-glasse.	196	Ch.-Milit.		208
They have their times of Gospel, ev'n as we.	197	Ch.-Milit.		248
They have their time of Gospel, ev'n as we.	197	Ch.-Milit.	W	248
By carrying first their gold from them away:	197	Ch.-Milit.		250
Thou wilt revenge their quarrell, making grace	197	Ch.-Milit.		255
To go to them, while that which now their nation	197	Ch.-Milit.		257
They have their period also and set times	197	Ch.-Milit.		261
Both for their vertuous actions and their crimes.	197	Ch.-Milit.		262
That when they have accomplished their round,	197	Ch.-Milit.	W	267
And met in th' east their first and ancient sound,	197	Ch.-Milit.		268
The Church and Sunne with all their power and skill.	198	Ch.-Milit.		273
Creatures are good, & have their place	200	H. Commun.	W	22
Nor can they change their bounds & meres,	201	H. Commun.	W	41
Besides their other flames? Doth Poetry	206	Walton 1		3
Out-strip their Cupid easily in flight?	206	Walton 1		9
Such poor invention burns in their low mind	206	Walton 2		9
Doe owe the symbole of their certainty.	439	Walton 5		8
Gifts speake their Givers. For as those Refractions,	209	L. Bacon	D	3
And though starres shott from heaven loose their light,	211	Bohemia	D	9
Yet thy brave beames excluded from their right	211	Bohemia	D	10
Strive each to play their Part.	213	Convert	D	5
My Heart, that gave fond Thoughts their Food,	214	Convert	D	16
Let us in sunder break their bonds,	215	Psalm II	D	7
and from us cast their cords away.	215	Psalm II	D	8
and in sore anger vex their pride.	215	Psalm II	D	12
are all that make the Son their stay.	216	Psalm II	D	32
Then worldlings joy'd with all their store	218	Psalm IV	D	27
For wickedness their insides are,	219	Psalm V	D	25
their mouths no truth retain.	219	Psalm V	D	26
Their throat an open Sepulcher,	219	Psalm V	D	27
their flattering tongues do fain.	219	Psalm V	D	28
Destroy them, Lord, and by their own	219	Psalm V	D	29

THEIR (cont'd)

	PAGE	TITLE		LINE
In hight of their transgression,	219	Psalm V	D	31
a shield in their distress.	219	Psalm V	D	44
For their sakes, Lord, return on high,	221	Psalm VII	D	27
Their Diversities.	225	Priest 2		T
some in Noble houses, some in Parishes residing on their Cures.	226	Priest 2		2
and because they have different Names, think their Office different.	226	Priest 2		21
even so farre as reproofe to their very face, when occasion cals,	226	Priest 2		30
while they remember their earthly Lord, do much forget their	226	Priest 2		32
they remember their earthly Lord, do much forget their heavenly;	226	Priest 2		33
neglect their duty, and shall be so farre from that which they seek	226	Priest 2		34
so farre from that which they seek with their over-submissivenesse,	226	Priest 2		35
admonition, cr reproofe, sell (with Judas) their Lord and Master.	226	Priest 2		38
and therefore as feeling their own sweat, and consequently knowing	227	Priest 3		13
who by hard usage increase their travell, the Countrey Parson is very	227	Priest 3		15
Countrey people (as indeed all honest men) do much esteem their word,	228	Priest 3		2
or spitting even in the midst of their answer, but gently	231	Priest 6		32
not to come at the beginning of service with their poor neighbours,	232	Priest 6		9
both to their own loss, and of theirs also who gaze upon them when	232	Priest 6		10
or if the poor Church-wardens be affrighted with their greatness,	232	Priest 6		15
but even to let the world sinke, so they do their duty;	232	Priest 6		17
them to be so, when God is so neer them, and even over their heads.	233	Priest 7		11
were with Saint Paul even sacrificed upon the service of their faith.	234	Priest 7		8
even as Princes have theirs, besides their publick disbursments.	236	Priest 8		17
and to raise up their mindes tc apprehend Gods good blessing to our	236	Priest 8		22
and wondreth not so much at their patient suffering, and cheerfull	237	Priest 9		29
(though that indeed be very admirable) as at their daily temperance,	237	Priest 9		31
and accordingly either meets with their vices, or advanceth their	239	Priest 10		9
either meets with their vices, or advanceth their vertues.	239	Priest 10		9
and tending their wounds, and sending his charity by them	239	Priest 10		25
turnes his care to fit all their dispositions with some calling,	239	Priest 10		30
and unbefitting the reverence of their Fathers calling,	240	Priest 10		1
and their comfort, who are much cheered with such friendliness.	243	Priest 11		12
which they can better employ to their own advantage, and sutably	243	Priest 11		16
and sutably to their needs, then so much given in meat at dinner.	243	Priest 11		16
but that all bee in a competent way of getting their living.	244	Priest 12		21
excellent statute, which bindes all Parishes to maintaine their own.	244	Priest 12		23
and to take more paines in their vocation, as not knowing when they	245	Priest 12		3
So doth hee also before giving make them say their Prayers first,	245	Priest 12		35
most naturally as they are, wallowing in the midst of their affairs:	247	Priest 14		7
which they put on as their holy-day cloathes, and come to Church in	247	Priest 14		8
and furthers them when hee is gone, in their imployment;	247	Priest 14		14
and wishing them ever to do the Cures with their own hands,	247	Priest 14		19
Those that he finds busie in the works of their calling,	247	Priest 14		21
it is a good and just thing for every one to do their own busines.	247	Priest 14		22
when they overdo it, to the loss of their quiet, and health:	247	Priest 14		28
thinking that their own labour is the cause of their thriving,	247	Priest 14		30
as if it were in their own hands to thrive, or not to thrive.	247	Priest 14		31
never raising their thoughts to God, nor sanctifying their labour	248	Priest 14		1
thoughts to God, nor sanctifying their labour with daily prayer;	248	Priest 14		1
as that they make not that the end of their labour, but that they may	248	Priest 14		7
but his purse to their relief, that so they go on more cheerfully in	248	Priest 14		11
that so they go on more cheerfully in their vocation, and himself be	248	Priest 14		12
as about prayers morning and evening on their knees, reading	248	Priest 14		33
catechizing, singing of Psalms at their work, and on holy days;	248	Priest 14		34
as a necessary evidence and fruit of their faith, at that time	249	Priest 15		33
by a due blessing of God for their safe arrival, and saying grace	251	Priest 17		9
and ingagement of their discourses for no price sooner,	252	Priest 18		20
not the lesse, lest he cast their neighbours poverty on them also.	254	Priest 19		6
paymaster, rewarding all good deeds to their full proportion.	254	Priest 20		21
and to satisfie the Congregation by their Catholick answers.	255	Priest 21		21
knowledg of Religion, may examine their grounds, renew their vowes,	255	Priest 21		33
examine their grounds, renew their vowes, and by occasion of both,	255	Priest 21		33
their vowes, and by occasion of both, inlarge their meditations.	255	Priest 21		34
He adviseth all to call to minde their Baptism often;	258	Priest 22		14
Christians also to meditate on their Baptisme often (being the first	258	Priest 22		18
often (being the first step into their great and glorious calling)	258	Priest 22		19
their understandings being ripe enough for ill things, and why	259	Priest 22		1
as to a great purchase for their children, and servants;	259	Priest 22		3
neither can all the people so order their affairs as to receive just	259	Priest 22		26
in any Controversie, that they should resort to him as their Judge.	259	Priest 23		33
the cause with him, whom he makes to deliver their opinion first;	260	Priest 23		10
any of his flock sick, hee is their Physician, or at least his Wife,	260	Priest 23		29
and so not be drowned altogether in the works of their vocation,	261	Priest 23		24
but sometimes lift up their minds to better things, even in the midst	261	Priest 23		25
up their minds to better things, even in the midst of their pains.	261	Priest 23		26
beseeching the Father of lights to open their eyes, and to give him	262	Priest 24		22
that it may effectually pierce their hearts, and convert them.	262	Priest 24		24
as in their tithes, or otherwise.	262	Priest 24		27
is the main foundation, and pillar of their cause, whereon they rely;	262	Priest 24		29
that servants for their mony are as other things that they buy,	265	Priest 26		24
throw into the fire, and so they pay them their wages, all is well.	265	Priest 26		27
and driving of their generall Schocle rules ever to the smallest	265	Priest 26		36
which while they dwell in their bookes, they will never finde;	266	Priest 26		2
and doing their duty faithfully, they will soon discover:	266	Priest 26		3
especially if they carry their eyes ever open, and fix them on their	266	Priest 26		4
and fix them on their charge, and not on their preferment.	266	Priest 26		5
so that men must eat neither to the disturbance of their health,	266	Priest 26		14
of their health, nor of their affairs, (which being overburdened,	266	Priest 26		14
they cannot wel dispatch) nor of their estate, nor of their brethren.	266	Priest 26		16
as if they were Masters of their health, and so they will stand	266	Priest 26		19

THEIR (cont'd)

	PAGE	TITLE		LINE
fit discharging either of Divine duties, or duties of their calling.	266	Priest 26		30
and knowledg of their own body, and what it can well disgest:	266	Priest 26		37
the whole order and discipline of the Parish is put into their hands.	269	Priest 29		29
the Law concerning such goods for the use and profit of their Parish:	270	Priest 29		4
that so they may know their duty, and keep their oath the better;	270	Priest 29		15
that so they may know their duty, and keep their oath the better;	270	Priest 29		16
considering the great Consequence of their place, and more of their	270	Priest 29		17
and more of their oath, he wisheth them by no means to spare any,	270	Priest 29		18
for their obligation to God, and their own soul, is above any	270	Priest 29		21
obligation to God, and their own soul, is above any temporall tye.	270	Priest 29		22
and that if they sow and soyle their grounds, they must have corn;	270	Priest 30		26
if they keep and fodder well their cattel, they must have milk,	270	Priest 30		28
or the fire on earth, by reason of their fierce, strong, . .	271	Priest 30		11
and not break off their acts of dependance, how faire soever	271	Priest 30		26
Christian soules, and raise them to their height, even to heaven;	275	Priest 32		31
in all the fore-mentioned points against the time of their practice.	276	Priest 32		27
Therefore they are to mark their Fathers discretion in ordering his	276	Priest 32		28
of the tree, inriching their Orchard, and neglecting their House.	276	Priest 32		33
Judges and Magistrates, to attend them, at least in their Shire;	277	Priest 32		3
and disarmed with sedentary lives, are to know the use of their Arms:	277	Priest 32		18
and not ingaged into some Profession by their Parents, whose neglect	277	Priest 32		25
and a shamefull wrong both to the Common-wealth, and their own House:	277	Priest 32		27
and the Angels minister to us their owne food, even joy, . .	280	Priest 34		6
lest their quiet betray them (as it is apt to do) to a coldnesse,	280	Priest 34		17
and carelesnesse in their devotions, but to labour still to be	280	Priest 34		19
not to take the full compasse, and liberty of their Peace: . .	280	Priest 34		22
dishes at table, which even their present health otherwise admits;	280	Priest 34		23
nor to store their house with all those furnitures which even their	280	Priest 34		24
those furnitures which even their present plenty of wealth otherwise	280	Priest 34		25
but to put bounds, and hoopes to their joyes:	280	Priest 34		29
or such a time their peace and mirth have carryed them further then	280	Priest 34		33
sacrificed lest his Children should have transgressed in their mirth:	281	Priest 34		2
they have their Law and Language bearing witnesse to them, . .	281	Priest 34		35
their Countrey also is known, the places, and rivers travelled unto,	282	Priest 34		2
their living then in their Countrey under so many miracles were	282	Priest 34		8
then their present exile, and disability to live in their Countrey.	282	Priest 34		10
And their very dispersion in all Lands, was intended not only	282	Priest 34		13
but for an exciting of others by their sight, to the acknowledging	282	Priest 34		15
which evidently argue Christs Divinity by their success: . .	282	Priest 34		23
so that to favour them therein is to win their hearts, and to oppose	283	Priest 35		30
that his Parish at good times invite one another to their houses,	284	Priest 35		18
But that which the Apostles used so diligently in their writings,	285	Priest 36		10
And if temporall Fathers blesse their children, how much more may,	285	Priest 36		14
they are so far from craving this benefit from their ghostly Father,	286	Priest 36		13
make others faults their entertainment and discourse, and that even	286	Priest 37		30
And as malefactors may lose & forfeit their goods, or life; . .	287	Priest 37		32
so may they their good name, and the possession thereof, . .	287	Priest 37		32
which before their offence and Judgment they had in all mens brests:	287	Priest 37		33
that in their full strength they may deliver thy message reverently,	289	Priest		27
have been an ornament to the world, and a comfort to their friends:	291	Cornaro		4
For when they saw their parents and kindred snatcht away in the midst	291	Cornaro		9
their parents and kindred snatcht away in the midst of their dayes,	291	Cornaro		10
that I may satisfie their honest desire, and withall help many	291	Cornaro		13
weighing their reasons with my self, and abhorring from so sudden	292	Cornaro		17
yet these forenamed things have also their force.	293	Cornaro		34
But all these things could not defend me against their importunities.	296	Cornaro		5
and procure that they prolong their life even to a hundred yeares	298	Cornaro		15
and that at length they shut up their dayes like a Lamp, . .	298	Cornaro		17
But sensuall men (as most are) desiring to satisfie their Appetite,	298	Cornaro		23
and pamper their belly, although they see themselves ill handled	298	Cornaro		24
although they see themselves ill handled by their intemperance,	298	Cornaro		25
written by their Authors in that age, and those ten yeares, . .	298	Cornaro		33
those ten yeares, which they set at naught in regard of their belly?	298	Cornaro		35
as also that their minde, in all things wherein they deal, . .	299	Cornaro		20
(though most agreeable to them) then their stomack can easily digest:	300	Cornaro		13
they live disorderly, yet continue in health to their lives end:	300	Cornaro		19
joy and peace have taken up their standing in my heart. . .	301	Cornaro		2
When I cannot have their companie, I give my self to the reading	301	Cornaro		5
I view their pieces, I compare them with those of Antiquitie;	302	Cornaro		1
which are all in their perfect vigour, but especially my Taste;	302	Cornaro		8
I am delighted with their musick and fashion, and I my self also sing	303	Cornaro		6
age and constitution with them who follow their youthfull appetites,	303	Cornaro		12
as also to those that live in sinne, and follow their appetites:	303	Cornaro		19
and darkned by the Adversaries, and their great stumbling-block.	305	Valdesso		2
And in so doing they doe not sever their trust from God. . .	307	Valdesso		2
held in so pretious esteem the word of God, as their Joy, and Crowne,	317	Valdesso		34
word of God, as their Joy, and Crowne, and their Treasure on earth.	317	Valdesso		34
which depend almost wholly on their Canon law and Decretals,	319	Valdesso	V	29
their Canon law and Decretals, knots of their own tying and untying:	319	Valdesso	V	29
and the difficulty of applying their generall rules to particular	319	Valdesso	V	32
like to that of the Jewes, which they added to their divine law.	320	Valdesso		4
Who remove stones, bruise their fingers.	322	Proverbs		40
Evils have their comfort, good none can support	328	Proverbs		208
The more women looke in their glasse, ...	329	Proverbs		250
the lesse they looke to their house.	329	Proverbs		250
All things have their place, knew wee how to place them. . .	334	Proverbs		379
Justice pleaseth few in their owne house.	334	Proverbs		396
All things in their beeing are good for something. . . .	339	Proverbs		520
When the tree is fallen, all goe with their hatchet. . . .	340	Proverbs		566
If fooles should not foole it, they shall lose their season.	343	Proverbs	V	702

THEIR (cont'd)	PAGE	TITLE		LINE
If fooles should not foole it, they should loose their season.	344	Proverbs		703
Three can hold their peace, if two be away.	345	Proverbs		714
Fooles give to please all but their owne.	345	Proverbs		735
in their seasons argues a Deity.	347	Proverbs		773
Children when they are little make their parents fooles,	352	Proverbs	V	939
then by stars at their nativities.	357	Proverbs	D	1060
States have their conversions and periods	361	Proverbs	D	1166
Some had rather lose their friend then their Jest.	361	Proverbs	D	1170
by which Scholars say, the Muses use to take up their habitations.	363	Letters		6
I need not their help, to reprove the vanity of those many	363	Letters		6
it is their ordinary speech, and now let them make it good;	364	Letters		22
I have not deceived their expectation, let not them deceive mine:	364	Letters		24
that the Hollanders should pay him tribute out of their fishing.	368	Letters		13
resuming the donation of spirituall livings into their owne hands,	368	Letters		28
is at all their Assemblies and Meetings, and sits above the Proctors,	370	Letters		1
but, their Fiery-tryals have had an end:	374	Letters		1
done fairly, if they leave them a good portion after their decease.	376	Letters		16
Your poor Colony of Servants present their humble duties.	377	Letters		13
When we exhort people to continue in their vocation, it is in	381	Woodnoth		23
& therfore not relinquishable without their masters consent.	381	Woodnoth		29
all these are over and above their wages, To Sara thirteene shillings	382	G.H.'s Will		26
in the choice of whom their judgement doth even now appeare.	442	Oration		26
THEIRE				
Theire dead, and Time shal be no more:	208	H. Danvers	D	4
And meet theire tast, who are thy bitter foes.	213	Bohemia	D	66
THEIRS				
Theirs, who shall hurt themselves or me, refrain.	5	Dedication		6
That temper gives them theirs, and yet doth take	16	Ch.-Porch		254
And therefore wish my bloud on them and theirs:	30	Sacrifice		107
The world is theirs; they two play out the game,	54	Love 1		10
As theirs.	150	Longing		72
and of theirs also who gaze upon them when they come in,	232	Priest 6		10
even as Princes have theirs, besides their publick disbursments.	236	Priest 8		17
not so much doubting a God, as that he is theirs;	283	Priest 34		7
and to such, and all that is theirs, I owe diligence;	304	Valdesso		7
Goods are theirs that enjoy them.	349	Proverbs		850
THEM				
And must return. Accept of them and me,	5	Dedication		3
Because to shun them also is so cheap:	9	Ch.-Porch		68
For we have wit to mark them, and to spare.	9	Ch.-Porch		69
Thy mouth to it, thy actions to them both:	9	Ch.-Porch		74
Some ship them over, and the thing is done.	10	Ch.-Porch		100
Or els they breed them tender, make them need	10	Ch.-Porch		105
God gave them to thee under lock and key.	12	Ch.-Porch		144
Then keep such companie; make them thy allay:	15	Ch.-Porch		212
And do them not: that shall thy wisdome be;	15	Ch.-Porch		221
That temper gives them theirs, and yet doth take	16	Ch.-Porch		254
Both friends should die, then hinder them to live.	17	Ch.-Porch		280
If truth be with thy friend, be with them both:	19	Ch.-Porch		323
And meet them there. All worldly joyes go lesse	19	Ch.-Porch		329
And meet them there. All wordly joyes go lesse	19	Ch.-Porch	W	329
And to instruct them, will not quit the cost.	20	Ch.-Porch		348
And send them to thine heart; that spying sinne,	23	Ch.-Porch		416
And send them to thy heart; that spying sinne,	23	Ch.-Porch	W	416
They may weep out the stains by them did rise:	23	Ch.-Porch		417
With saints on earth, shall one day with them shine.	24	Ch.-Porch		438
Who cannot wish, except I give them bread:	26	Sacrifice		7
Which I do give them daily, unto death.	28	Sacrifice		70
Sends me to Pilate. This makes them agree;	29	Sacrifice		74
And therefore wish my bloud on them and theirs:	30	Sacrifice		107
With Manna, Angels food, I fed them all:	34	Sacrifice		239
As if I us'd them but for fashion.	36	Thanksgvng		36
Yet few there are that sound them; Sinne and Love.	37	The Agonie		6
But that which shews them large, shews them unfit.	41	Sepulchre		9
And then beyond them all my Baptisme view	43	H. Bapt.1	W	2
You give us teares to wash them: lett those beams	44	H. Bapt.1	W	7
Or else give tears to drown them, as they grow.	44	H. Bapt.1		9
And carrie with them th' other parts.	49	Repentance		30
Inherent in them, thou didst make the sunne	51	Faith		34
Impute a lustre, and allow them bright;	51	Faith		35
Impart a lustre, and allow them bright;	51	Faith	W	35
Them both to be together.	52	H.Commun.		28
No doore can keep them out:	53	Antiphon 1		10
Doth warm our hands, and make them write of love.	54	Love 1		14
Sometimes I peere above them all;	55	Temper 1		6
Scatter, or binde them all to bend to thee:	56	Temper 2		13
Shepherds are honest people; let them sing:	57	Jordan 1		11
Nor let them punish me with losse of ryme,	57	Jordan 1		14
Nor let them punish me with losse of time,	57	Jordan 1	V	14
But that from them joyes purle for ever	59	Whitsunday	W	22
Of all these things, or all of them in one?	62	Mattens		8
Yet studies them, not him by whom they be.	63	Mattens		16
And spoil the meeting. What shall point out them,	65	Ch.-monum.		14
Which of them socnest should attaine my hart.	66	Ch.-lock	W	4
Gave them about to all.	70	Humilitie		8
For which ye wrangle, made them turn their frown	71	Humilitie		28
They drive them soon away;	71	Humilitie		30
And then amerc'd them, double gifts to bring	71	Humilitie		31
I surname them guilded clay,	71	Frailtie		5
Misuse them all the day:	71	Frailtie	W	6

THEM (cont'd)

	PAGE	TITLE		LINE
Nor seeks, nor shunnes them; but doth calmly stay,	72	Constancie		12
Thou hast unlockt them both,	82	Ungratef.		9
And made them jewels to betroth	82	Ungratef.		10
But Wisdome quickly swept them all away.	84	The World		5
Which they effected, none could them withstand.	84	The World		18
There he imparts to them his minde,	85	Vanitie 1		18
Then he that curbs them, being but one to five:	89	The Pearl		29
I know all these, and have them in my hand:	89	The Pearl		31
Kill them and me,	90	Afflict.4		20
And thou within them starve at doore.	93	Unkindness		14
My hand was next to them, and then my heart:	94	Life		7
Which do consigne and send them unto death.	98	Mortific.		6
Sleep bindes them fast; onely their breath	98	Mortific.		9
Makes them not dead:	98	Mortific.		10
Convey them quickly, who are bound for death.	98	Mortific.		12
Nor any sorrow tell them that they sinne,	100	Miserie		22
Holds them unto it, and doth cover	100	Miserie		27
To sing thy praises, make them lesse divine.	101	Miserie		40
How hast thou lost them in a croud of cares?	101	Miserie		50
There let them shine,	101	Miserie		53
Harmonious peace must rock them all the day:	105	Conscience		9
And scouling on them as they pin'd away,	108	Home		45
Let them love gold;	111	Vanitie 2		12
Let them unto their kindred flie:	111	Vanitie 2		14
I sat me down to spell them, and perceived	112	JESU		8
Know their home, and get them gone:	113	Businesse		4
Nothing escapes them both; all must appeare,	118	Providence		37
When they are fledge, that need may teach them flying.	118	Providence		64
Thou hast hid metals: man may take them thence;	119	Providence		81
If they seek fine things, thou dost make them run	120	Providence		106
But he to wear them. Nothing useth fire,	120	Providence		110
Your hony drops: presse not to smell them here:	120	Providence		118
None can expresse thy works, but he that knows them:	121	Providence		142
And so complete, but onely he that owes them.	121	Providence		144
They vent the wares, and passe them with their faults,	122	Sinnes rd.		9
They vent the wares, and passe them with their fauts	122	Sinnes rd.	V	9
Closets; and in them many a chest;	126	Confession		3
Closets are halls to them; and hearts, high-wayes.	126	Confession		18
Doth shut them out, so that they cannot enter;	126	Confession		20
The clearest diamond: let them do their best,	126	Confession		29
Man ties them both alone,	131	Mans medly		10
And makes them one,	131	Mans medly		11
Could he but take them right, and in their wayes.	132	Mans medly		33
Though some of them repine.	136	Familie		6
Did once perceive, it blew them under foot,	140	Ch.-rents		7
They rushed in, and cast them in the dirt	140	Ch.-rents		23
But through a Church-yard which them bounds.	145	Discharge		40
To them a part:	148	Longing		16
Their infants, them; and they suck thee	148	Longing		17
Their infants, them; and they seek thee	148	Longing	V	17
Thy beggars grow; rid them away	150	Longing		77
Readie to take them in; yet of a size	158	Praise 3		29
But keep them with repining restlesnesse:	160	The Pulley		17
To bear them out, and with my state agree.	164	Grief		8
I am to grief alive, to them as dead.	165	The Crosse		24
And wore them for a jewell on her head,	173	Marie Magd		3
To leade them unto life and rest.	174	Aaron		4
My minde ev'n thrust into them both:	175	The Odour		7
And show them as they are.	185	The Elixer	W	24
Know them and practise them: then shall I give	185	A Wreath		11
And in them may drown a friend:	187	Dooms-day		22
Truth Lord, but I have marr'd them: let my shame	189	Love 3		13
Listens behinde him, and gives them some light,	191	Ch.-Milit.	W	32
But th' Empire dwelt in Greece, to comfort them	192	Ch.-Milit.		73
Onely the West and Rome do keep them free	194	Ch.-Milit.		157
Europe alone and Rome do keep them free	194	Ch.-Milit.	W	157
They who rely on them must reckon twice	194	Ch.-Milit.	W	160
By letting in them both, pollutes her streams:	197	Ch.-Milit.		242
By letting in them both pollute her streams:	197	Ch.-Milit.	W	242
My God, thou dost prepare for them a way	197	Ch.-Milit.		249
By carrying first their gold from them away:	197	Ch.-Milit.		250
We think we rob them, but we think amisse:	197	Ch.-Milit.		253
To go to them, while that which now their nation	197	Ch.-Milit.		257
Judgement may meet them both & search them round.	197	Ch.-Milit.		269
Thou dost come first to them, that showes	200	H. Commun.	W	14
To them that fall,	203	Trin.Sun.	W	16
Which warme these lines, & serve them up to thee	204	Persever.	W	2
A pair of Cheeks of them, is thy abuse.	206	Walton 2		7
Had he only brought them forth,	208	J. Danvers	D	13
Are quit with them and more.	210	Paradox	D	10
Sorrowes & griefs, to fight with them a bout	211	Bohemia	D	20
the Lord himself shall them deride:	215	Psalm II	D	10
Then shall He speak to them in wrath,	215	Psalm II	D	11
Whose pow'r shall dash and break them all	216	Psalm II	D	23
Destroy them, Lord, and by their own	219	Psalm V	D	29
bad councels let them fall:	219	Psalm V	D	30
O Lord, reject them all,	219	Psalm V	D	32
Let them that do thy name adore	219	Psalm V	D	39
and them for ever bless.	219	Psalm V	D	42
His favour shall encompass them,	219	Psalm V	D	43

THEM (cont'd)

	PAGE	TITLE	LINE
And put them all to utter shame, ...	220	Psalm VI D	27
as many of them do, and because they have different Names, . .	226	Priest 2	20
and to preserve a boldness with them and all, even so farre . .	226	Priest 2	29
of darknesse, he disableth himself of authority to reprove them:	227	Priest 3	27
and makes great use of them in teaching, because people by what they	228	Priest 4	19
because they feel them not, and because they are not understood	228	Priest 4	31
they are not understood but with the same Spirit that writ them.	228	Priest 4	32
knowing that no Sermon moves them so much to a reverence, . .	231	Priest 6	14
exacts of them all possible reverence, by no means enduring either	231	Priest 6	22
or any undutifull behaviour in them, but causing them, . . .	231	Priest 6	25
or any undutifull behaviour in them, but causing them, when they sit,	231	Priest 6	25
and apply our powers to the service of him, that gives them.	232	Priest 6	6
and of theirs also who gaze upon them when they come in, . .	232	Priest 6	11
admonitions, if they persevere, he causes them to be presented:	232	Priest 6	13
he presents them himself, only protesting to them, that not any ill	232	Priest 6	17
only protesting to them, that not any ill will draws him to it,	232	Priest 6	18
on his auditors, with letting them know, that he observes who marks,	233	Priest 7	1
and think it behoves them to be so, when God is so neer them,	233	Priest 7	10
them to be so, when God is so neer them, and even over their heads.	233	Priest 7	11
Sometimes he tells them stories, and sayings of others, . .	233	Priest 7	11
for them also men heed, and remember better then exhortations;	233	Priest 7	13
and fervency, and need a mountaine of fire to kindle them; . .	233	Priest 7	17
He often tels them, that Sermons are dangerous things, that none goes	233	Priest 7	18
as, Oh Lord blesse my people, and teach them this point; . .	233	Priest 7	34
scatteringly in the Sermon, carry great holiness in them. . .	234	Priest 7	1
And is in contention for them whither to live, or dy; . . .	234	Priest 7	15
be with them, or Christ, verse 23. which, setting aside his care	234	Priest 7	16
which will make them appear exceeding reverend, and holy. . .	234	Priest 7	24
that the Lord would be pleased to sanctifie them all, that they may	235	Priest 8	28
or to be entertained of them, where he takes occasion to discourse	236	Priest 8	21
our poor services, and to improve them, that we may grow therein,	236	Priest 8	28
but adds to them, out of choyce and devotion, some other dayes	237	Priest 9	24
and to keep them on in the sunshine, and noone of prosperity,	237	Priest 9	35
Therefore having seasoned them with all Piety, not only of words in	239	Priest 10	23
and sending his charity by them to the poor, and somtimes giving them	239	Priest 10	26
and somtimes giving them a little mony to do it of themselves,	239	Priest 10	27
Yet in binding them prentices (in case he think fit to do so) he	239	Priest 10	33
think fit to do so) he takes care not to put them into vain trades,	239	Priest 10	34
give any thing above those, and not spent in them, he blesseth God,	240	Priest 10	12
and were it not his duty to have them so, it were his profit,	240	Priest 10	14
he teacheth them, that three things make a compleate servant,	240	Priest 10	17
and till they have learned them, makes them kneel by him; . .	241	Priest 10	3
and till they have learned them, makes them kneel by him; . .	241	Priest 10	4
esteeming that this private praying is a more voluntary act in them,	241	Priest 10	5
which when they leave the family, they carry with them. . .	241	Priest 10	7
his servants between love, and fear, according as hee findes them;	241	Priest 10	8
by taking both sorts of food into them, do as it were dresse	241	Priest 10	33
both for man in themselves, by growing them selves fit for his table.	241	Priest 10	35
takes home with him, setting them close by him, and carving for them,	243	Priest 11	11
them close by him, and carving for them, both for his own humility,	243	Priest 11	12
hee hath them all with him, because countrey people are very	243	Priest 11	19
himselfe what good deeds he can do that day, and presently doth them;	244	Priest 12	17
If his Parish be rich, he exacts this of them;	244	Priest 12	24
if poor, and he able, he easeth them therein.	244	Priest 12	25
making a hook of his Charity, causeth them still to depend on him;	244	Priest 12	32
and fresh bounties, unexpected to them, but resolved to himself,	245	Priest 12	1
hee wins them to praise God more, to live more religiously, . .	245	Priest 12	2
parts his Living, and life among them, giving some corn outright,	245	Priest 12	10
of the pulpit, and never leaving them, till he obtaine his desire.	245	Priest 12	14
he distinguisheth, giving them most, who live best, and take most	245	Priest 12	15
and sees them labour in thanking of him, he exacts of them to let him	245	Priest 12	31
thanking of him, he exacts of them to let him alone, and say rather,	245	Priest 12	32
So doth hee also before giving make them say their Prayers first,	245	Priest 12	35
Commandments, and as he finds them perfect, rewards them the more.	245	Priest 12	36
Commandments, and as he finds them perfect, rewards them the more.	245	Priest 12	37
be as they ought, for those great duties that are performed in them.	246	Priest 13	8
and put them to great shame, who deny the Scripture to be perfect.	247	Priest 13	1
on Sundays it is easie for them to compose themselves to order,	247	Priest 14	7
hee both commends them much, and furthers them when hee is gone,	247	Priest 14	14
and furthers them when hee is gone, in their imployment; . .	247	Priest 14	14
as if hee findes them reading, hee furnisheth them with good books;	247	Priest 14	15
as if hee findes them reading, hee furnisheth them with good books;	247	Priest 14	16
hee supplies them with Receipts, and instructs them further in that	247	Priest 14	17
and instructs them further in that skill, shewing them how acceptable	247	Priest 14	17
shewing them how acceptable such works are to God, and wishing them	247	Priest 14	18
and wishing them ever to do the Cures with their own hands, . .	247	Priest 14	19
the Cures with their own hands, and not to put them over to servants.	247	Priest 14	20
finds busie in the works of their calling, he commendeth them also:	247	Priest 14	21
But then he admonisheth them of two things;	247	Priest 14	23
he adviseth them so to labour for wealth and maintenance, . .	248	Priest 14	5
poor and needy, whom he thus finds labouring, he gives them somewhat;	248	Priest 14	10
in their vocation, and himself be ever the more welcome to them.	248	Priest 14	13
but always in the close, before he departs from them: . . .	248	Priest 14	16
in the person of another, making them to reprove themselves.	248	Priest 14	22
way or other, he ever reproves them, that he may keep himself pure,	248	Priest 14	23
and blesseth them, encouraging also the servants to learn to read,	248	Priest 14	36
and offering to have them taught on holy-dayes by his servants.	248	Priest 14	37
best comforts, and rather goes to them, then sends for the afflicted,	249	Priest 15	16
as having continuall use of them, such as are from Gods generall	249	Priest 15	19
in perswading them to particular confession, labouring to make them	249	Priest 15	29

THEM (cont'd)

	PAGE	TITLE	LINE
labouring to make them understand the great good use of this antient	249	Priest 15	30
he also urgeth them to do some pious charitable works, as a necessary	249	Priest 15	32
of the house, and shewing them cleerly, that they respect them most,	251	Priest 17	29
them cleerly, that they respect them most, who wish them best,	251	Priest 17	30
who wish them best, and that not a desire to meddle with others	251	Priest 17	30
spirits, and possesse them even before they themselves heed it.	252	Priest 18	7
he borrowes them not to serve the turne, nor provides slight,	252	Priest 19	26
and being there, makes due use of them, as of Clergy councels,	253	Priest 19	10
about him, performing for them any Ministeriall office, which is	253	Priest 19	16
and exposing to them the uncertainty of humane affairs,	253	Priest 19	32
and then when he hath affrighted them with this, exposing	253	Priest 19	34
he first gives himself liberally, and then incites them to give;	253	Priest 19	36
that the Blessing of God to them ought to make them the more	254	Priest 19	5
the Blessing of God to them ought to make them the more charitable,	254	Priest 19	5
not the lesse, lest he cast their neighbours poverty on them also.	254	Priest 19	7
then by causing them to be presented, or otherwise complained of.	254	Priest 20	24
of questions in the one, so they farre exceed them in the other.	257	Priest 21	23
he takes the more pains with them, that hee may lay the foundation	258	Priest 22	31
whom he hath ever some cases to ask, when he meets with them;	260	Priest 23	5
But then he shews them how to go to Law, even as Brethren,	260	Priest 23	25
he doth not onely prefer home-bred things before them, but condemns	261	Priest 23	37
but condemns them for vanities, and so shuts them out of his family,	261	Priest 23	38
and so shuts them out of his family, esteeming that there is no spice	261	Priest 23	38
useth all possible diligence to reduce them to the common Faith.	262	Priest 24	21
and to give him power so to fit his discourse to them, that it may	262	Priest 24	23
that it may effectually pierce their hearts, and convert them.	262	Priest 24	24
means is a very loving, and sweet usage of them, both in going to,	262	Priest 24	25
and sending for them often, and in finding out Courtesies to place	262	Priest 24	26
for them often, and in finding out Courtesies to place on them;	262	Priest 24	27
more then indifferent, it be in our power to omit or refuse them.	263	Priest 24	14
that God cannot be wanting to them in Doctrine, to whom he is so	263	Priest 24	20
to themselves, and witty to others who shall reprove them from it.	264	Priest 26	14
or known commonly, the beginnings of them are not easily observable:	264	Priest 26	18
and the beginnings of them are not observed, because of the suddain	264	Priest 26	19
and I either provide too little for them, or that which is	265	Priest 26	21
throw into the fire, and so they pay them their wages, all is well.	265	Priest 26	27
and fix them on their charge, and not on their preferment.	266	Priest 26	5
the faults of eating, and the truth of them needs no proofe:	266	Priest 26	13
as that it is not meate or drinke that hinders them from working.	266	Priest 26	36
To guide them in this, there are three rules:	266	Priest 26	36
he carryes them higher, even somtimes to a forgetting of themselves,	267	Priest 26	19
knowing that there is one, who when they forget, remembers for them;	267	Priest 26	21
that are reproved, but never contempt either in them, or others.	268	Priest 28	30
they resist not the evill which takes hold of them, and is farr	269	Priest 28	25
what a great Charge lyes upon them, and that indeed the whole order	269	Priest 29	28
the Parson adviseth them to read, or hear them read often,	270	Priest 29	13
or hear them read often, as also the visitation Articles,	270	Priest 29	14
he wisheth them by no means to spare any, though never so great;	270	Priest 29	18
neighbourly admonitions they still persist in ill, to present them;	270	Priest 29	20
labours to reduce them to see Gods hand in all things,	270	Priest 30	29
be housed, a fire hath broken forth, and suddenly consumed them.	271	Priest 30	25
sometimes in perplexing them in the service of God) stands fast in	272	Priest 31	17
as they think fit, & see cause, or rather as Gods spirit leads them.	272	Priest 31	28
bring strangers to him, he may be the better armed to encounter them.	274	Priest 32	8
therfore all are to procure them honestly, and seasonably,	274	Priest 32	30
to enter into a Calling, if they be fit for it, and it for them;	275	Priest 32	15
by bringing them up in the fear and nurture of the Lord;	275	Priest 32	23
Christian soules, and raise them to their height, even to heaven;	275	Priest 32	31
to dresse and prune them, and take as much joy in a straight-growing	275	Priest 32	32
and either helps them in particular, or hath generall Propositions	276	Priest 32	4
that they kindle them rather to redeem the Dignity either from true	276	Priest 32	23
Judges and Magistrates, to attend them, at least in their Shire;	277	Priest 32	3
and as the Husbandman labours for them, so must they fight for,	277	Priest 32	19
so must they fight for, and defend them, when occasion calls.	277	Priest 32	20
To them, after he hath shew'd the unlawfulness of spending the day in	277	Priest 32	28
there, transplant them hither, as divers have done lately,	278	Priest 32	9
and the ways which he used to overcome them, being told to another,	278	Priest 33	16
to be in one or the other state, so he applies himselfe to them.	280	Priest 34	14
Particularly, he counselleth them to two things:	280	Priest 34	17
lest their quiet betray them (as it is apt to do) to a coldnesse,	280	Priest 34	18
nor when they are among them that are merry, to extend themselves	280	Priest 34	26
their peace and mirth have carryed them further then this moderation,	280	Priest 34	34
So let them go, and find some poore afflicted soul, and there be	281	Priest 34	2
Governour of all things, yet to them he is lost, as if they said,	281	Priest 34	10
God doth forsake and persecute them, and there is none to deliver	281	Priest 34	11
doth forsake and persecute them, and there is none to deliver them.	281	Priest 34	12
they have their Law and Language bearing witnesse to them,	281	Priest 34	36
but to them an unpenetrable rock, an unaccessible desert.	282	Priest 34	3
all the great wonders of old live in them, and then who can deny	282	Priest 34	5
should be his proof, and witnesses, as he calls them, Isaiah 43. 12.	282	Priest 34	13
in all Lands, was intended not only for a punishment to them;	282	Priest 34	14
But if he sees them neerer desperation, then Atheisme;	283	Priest 34	5
If God hate them, either he doth it as they are Creatures,	283	Priest 34	10
As Creatures, he must needs love them;	283	Priest 34	12
As sinfull, he must much more love them;	283	Priest 34	13
gave them love for love, even the son of his love out of his bosome	283	Priest 34	16
that God loves them, till either they despise that Love,	283	Priest 34	22
because Countrey people are much addicted to them, so that to favour	283	Priest 35	29
so that to favour them therein is to win their hearts, and to oppose	283	Priest 35	30
is to win their hearts, and to oppose them therin is to deject them.	283	Priest 35	31

THEM (cont'd)

	PAGE	TITLE		LINE
he pares the apple, and gives them the clean to feed on.	284	Priest 35		1
and if they will not reforme, presents them.	284	Priest 35		13
that he rather procures them to be often, as knowing that absence	284	Priest 35		14
times invite one another to their houses, and he urgeth them to it:	284	Priest 35		18
but is rather glad of catching opportunities to do them.	284	Priest 35		26
and teaches them, that at Baptisme they professed not to be ashamed	284	Priest 35		31
no more then to be a spirituall Father was appropriated to them.	285	Priest 36		13
he saith, he had delivered them to Satan, that they might learn	286	Priest 36		1
that they oftentimes goe out of church, before he hath blessed them.	286	Priest 36		15
known by common fame (and of these, those that know them, may talk,	287	Priest 37		13
and more, they may discover them to those that know them not:	287	Priest 37		17
assembled together, with thy unworthy Servant speaking unto them:	289	Priest		26
teach thou me, that I may teach them:	289	Priest		27
being directed by them in the way I ought to hold, I understood,	292	Cornaro		23
I not so avoid all these, but that now and then I fell into them;	293	Cornaro		38
whereas they hurt them very much who live intemperately.	294	Cornaro		14
(a thing usuall to disorderly lives) which increased so much in them,	294	Cornaro		19
increased so much in them, that it brought them to a sudden end.	294	Cornaro		20
qualities to me, if I had not found them out by long experience?	297	Cornaro		35
they who finde benefit in these meats, may, yea ought to use them:	300	Cornaro		11
drink (though most agreeable to them) then their stomack can easily	300	Cornaro		13
I view their pieces, I compare them with those of Antiquitie;	302	Cornaro		1
change age and constitution with them who follow their youthfull	303	Cornaro		12
I like not in him, as my fragments will expresse, when you read them;	304	Valdesso		17
but still even to the most learned and perfect in them,	309	Valdesso		24
wondrous things of his Lawes, and that he would make them his study.	309	Valdesso		27
same Psalme it is evident, that he was not meanly conversant in them.	309	Valdesso		29
things there is roome for motions [notions] and expecting of them;	313	Valdesso		13
For as for these, pious persons ought alwaies to avoid them:	314	Valdesso		20
Gods Spirit will mortify and try them as gold in the fire.	314	Valdesso		21
weaknesses is no way repugnant to the way of Gods Spirit in them,	316	Valdesso		3
though in the point of Resurrection he agreed with them,	316	Valdesso		9
But it is one thing not to judge, another to defend them.	316	Valdesso		14
be evident to others, as well as to themselves, that God moved them.	316	Valdesso		20
doth not bid them then cast away the word, or leave it off:	318	Valdesso		19
but however he would have them attend to it till that time,	318	Valdesso		20
both of them having forms or vizars of godlinesse, but denying	319	Valdesso	V	26
A caske and an ill custome must both of them be broken.	322	Proverbs	V	27
Ill natures, the more you aske them, the more they stick.	324	Proverbs		106
Men speake of the faire, as things went with them there.	326	Proverbs		151
A gentlemans grayhound, and a salt-box; seeke them at the fire.	327	Proverbs		205
If you would know secrets, looke them in griefe or pleasure.	333	Proverbs		367
All things have their place, knew wee how to place them.	334	Proverbs		379
Warre makes theeves, and peace hangs them.	337	Proverbs		471
let him not put them on his head.	340	Proverbs		567
Goods are theirs that enjoy them.	349	Proverbs		850
when they are great they make them mad.	352	Proverbs		939
Count not fowre except you have them in a wallett.	352	Proverbs		962
When all men have what belongs to them, it cannot bee much.	353	Proverbs		979
Hee that hath charge of soules transports them not in bundles.	353	Proverbs		986
Speake not of my debts, unlesse you meane to pay them.	354	Proverbs		998
all the world would turne Carpenters (to make them crutches).	355	Proverbs		1020
then either of them both.	361	Proverbs	D	1173
it is their ordinary speech, and now let them make it good;	364	Letters		23
I have not deceived their expectation, let not them deceive mine:	364	Letters		24
not well, I had rather the fault should lie on me, than on them;	364	Letters		30
I desire you, Sir, to be my Mediator to them in my behalf.	365	Letters		22
As I shal find occasion, you shal receive them by peeces;	366	Letters		3
such which you have found useful to yourself, communicate them to me.	366	Letters		5
yet his love expects them not but first certifies you that there are	368	Letters		4
whose Example and Care of them will justifie you both to the world	373	Letters		16
since if we had Riches we are commanded to give them away:	373	Letters		24
so that the best use of them is, having, not to have them.	373	Letters		24
so that the best use of them is, having, not to have them.	373	Letters		25
other Tortures, as the very mention of them might beget amazement;	373	Letters		37
not only entertain my proposals, but advance them, was lovingly done,	375	Letters		3
and age, and knew none but one who could be no company to them.	375	Letters		15
and would not have to part them yet, till I take some opportunity	375	Letters		21
till I take some opportunity to let them know your love,	375	Letters		21
I forgett all thinges, so I may doe them good who want it.	376	Letters		6
So I doe my part to them, lett them think of me what they will	376	Letters		7
I doe my part to them, lett them think of me what they will or can.	376	Letters		7
are so farr from cooling christians, that they whett them.	376	Letters		11
done fairly, if they leave them a good portion after their decease.	376	Letters		15
& neither to scandalize them, nor wound our owne reputation.	380	Woodnoth		19
body to Almightie God that made them doe thus dispose of my goods.	382	G.H.'s Will		2
equally to be devided betweene them excepting some legacies of my	382	G.H.'s Will		13
any body els that owe me any thing else of old debt I forgive them.	383	G.H.'s Will		27
as to you deserving them, Wee at last salute you Masters of Arts;	441	Oration		26

THEMSELVES

	PAGE	TITLE		LINE
Lord, my first fruits present themselves to thee;	5	Dedication		1
Theirs, who shall hurt themselves or me, refrain.	5	Dedication		6
Full of themselves, and answer their own notion.	19	Ch.-Porch		320
In him to do themselves a courtesie:	30	Sacrifice		114
So they in me denie themselves all pitie:	31	Sacrifice		143
Of those, who did themselves through their side wound,	59	Whitsunday		20
They dresse themselves and come to thee.	108	Home		52
But little do reserve themselves for more:	138	The Size		20
The sicke are in themselves a State	210	Paradox	D	13
Let not Chaplains think themselves so free, as many of them do,	226	Priest 2		19

THEMSELVES (cont'd)	PAGE	TITLE		LINE
instructed his people how to carry themselves in divine service,	231	Priest 6		22
or in exhortations to some of his flock by themselves, whom his	236	Priest 8		13
and somtimes giving them a little mony to do it of themselves,	239	Priest 10		27
requires of all to pray by themselves before they sleep at night,	241	Priest 10		1
do as it were dresse and prepare both for man in themselves,	241	Priest 10		34
on Sundays it is easie for them to compose themselves to order,	247	Priest 14		8
plunging themselves over head and eares into carking, and caring;	247	Priest 14		25
when they set themselves to work like brute beasts, never raising	247	Priest 14		32
in the person of another, making them to reprove themselves.	248	Priest 14		22
so the hunger and thirst after it may come rather from themselves,	250	Priest 15		6
spirits, and possesse them even before they themselves heed it.	252	Priest 18		7
all together choosing some fitt day to carry it themselves,	253	Priest 19		38
and dark nature, not easily determinable by Lawyers themselves;	260	Priest 23		21
being partiall to themselves, and witty to others who shall reprove	264	Priest 26		13
being cunning to make use of another, and spare themselves:	265	Priest 26		35
must eat so as to disable themselves from a fit discharging either	266	Priest 26		29
the feeling of themselves in time of eating, which because it is	267	Priest 26		2
even somtimes to a forgetting of themselves, knowing that there is	267	Priest 26		20
of dependance, how faire soever the opportunities present themselves.	271	Priest 30		28
as they remember themselves were, when affliction did blow the Coals.	280	Priest 34		20
to extend themselves to all that mirth, which the present occasion	280	Priest 34		27
and those that withdraw, and sever themselves from it, he mislikes,	284	Priest 35		11
thinke this superstitious, neither know superstition, nor themselves.	284	Priest 35		29
The neglect of this duty in Ministers themselves, hath made	286	Priest 36		11
that Proverb, wherewith Gluttons use to defend themselves, to wit,	293	Cornaro		9
although they see themselves ill handled by their intemperance,	298	Cornaro		24
both that they may preserve themselves from diseases, which hinder	299	Cornaro		18
but that I should wish all who have the care of themselves,	303	Cornaro		32
Of these none can free themselves of themselves, but only	308	Valdesso		9
Of these the heathen freed themselves, only by the generall	308	Valdesso		12
and not those which are in themselves occasions of sinne;	314	Valdesso		18
the Scriptures, or to themselves being still men, though godly men.	316	Valdesso		4
be evident to others, as well as to themselves, that God moved them.	316	Valdesso		20
afterward they will attend it of themselves without his exhortation.	318	Valdesso		21
Bells call others, but themselves enter not into the Church.	340	Proverbs		571
Marry your daughters betimes, lest they marry themselves.	361	Proverbs	D	1171
most carry themselves so, as if they not only not desir'd,	373	Letters		33
THEN (comparative)				
Hee that desires is more then halfe the way.	10	Ch.-Porch	W	90
Wisedome's a trimmer thing, then shop e're gave.	14	Ch.-Porch		188
Then he can lose with pleasure, stakes his heart;	14	Ch.-Porch		194
Both friends should die, then hinder them to live.	17	Ch.-Porch		280
Submit to love; but yet not more then all.	17	Ch.-Porch		284
Rather then shew his cards.) Steal from his treasure	18	Ch.-Porch		298
Will no more talk all, then eat all the feast.	18	Ch.-Porch		306
More, then his sicknesses or povertie?	18	Ch.-Porch		310
No more then passion when shee talkes of it.	19	Ch.-Porch	W	318
Shoots higher much then he that means a tree.	19	Ch.-Porch		334
Think heav'n a better bargain, then to give	21	Ch.-Porch		374
God is more there, then thou: for thou art there	22	Ch.-Porch		404
Who cannot live lesse then eternally:	29	Sacrifice		99
All understanding, more then heav'n doth glasse:	30	Sacrifice		119
To hide my dust, then thee to hold.	45	Nature		18
Was of more use then I.	47	Afflict.1		34
What can be lower then the common manger?	50	Faith		22
And more then fancy: for in ev'ry thing	58	H.Script.2	W	10
Is more then all my deaths can be,	62	Afflict.2		3
And in this love, more then in bed, I rest.	64	Even-song		32
Then to have hellish moths still gnaw and fret	69	Content		27
Folly, and worse then folly, lust:	74	The Starre		10
More plentifull then hope.	76	Sunday		35
A better lodging then a rack or grave.	81	Christmas		14
Where now we shall be better Gods then he.	82	Ungratef.		6
And built a braver Palace then before.	84	The World		20
Is better then to rest:	87	Lent		33
Is much more sure to meet with him, then one	87	Lent		38
Then he that curbs them, being but one to five:	89	The Pearl		29
Or can be, then is Man? to whose creation	90	Man		5
Then to serve thee in fear.	100	Miserie		12
Thou canst no more not heare, then thou canst die.	103	Prayer 2		6
Two lives worse then ten deaths be.	113	Businesse		28
Are there much surer then our art is sure.	119	Providence		80
Were worse then ours; sometimes thou shiftest hands.	121	Providence		138
Much better tunes, then grones can make;	124	Gratefulnes		22
Will more complie, then help. A Lord I had,	129	Love unkn.		3
Better then you know me, or (which is one)	129	Love unkn.		10
Better then you knew me, or (which is one)	129	Love unkn.	V	10
Then I my self. The servant instantly	129	Love unkn.		11
Many a fault more then my lease will bear;	129	Love unkn.		20
But with a richer drug, then scalding water,	130	Love unkn.		40
More favour then you wot of. Mark the end.	130	Love unkn.		63
Rather hereafter, then in present, is.	131	Mans medly		6
Then let me want thy hand & ART.	133	Paradise		9
Such cuttings rather heal then REND:	133	Paradise		14
As if a starre were duller then a clod,	134	Divinitie		3
More bowels have, then such hard things.	136	Ephes.		24
Then whom in waiting nothing seems more slow,	137	Familie		15
Yet speak they louder then distemper'd fears.	137	Familie		19
Is more then God was, who was hungrie here.	138	The Size		14
Then thou to grant mine: but because	139	Artillerie		23

THEN (cont'd)

	PAGE	TITLE		LINE
And made you look much fresher then before.	140	Ch.-rents		15
Farther from it then when I bent my bow;	165	The Crosse		26
Further from it then when I bent my bow;	165	The Crosse	V	26
Which they that know the rest, know more then I.	169	The Answer		14
I shall be one day better then before:	169	Dial.-Anth		9
More then a thousand sunnes disburse in light,	172	The Glance		23
Deeper then they, in words, and works, and thoughts.	173	Marie Magd		12
Would warm and work it sweeter then before.	175	The Odour		20
So all within be livelier then before.	177	Forerunners		36
Then my strict, yet welcome size.	177	The Rose		4
What is fairer then a rose?	178	The Rose		17
Lesse then the least	182	The Posie		3
Lesse then the least	183	The Posie		11
Then the ten bitter plagues had done before.	191	Ch.-Milit.		40
(For no lesse Harbingers would serve then they)	192	Ch.-Milit.		84
And not go lesse then she had done of late.	192	Ch.-Milit.		92
And being craftier much then Goodnesse was,	193	Ch.-Milit.		124
His grave aspect had more of heav'n then hell:	194	Ch.-Milit.		168
His grave aspect was liker heav'n then hell:	194	Ch.-Milit.	W	168
More spotted then my flesh can bee.	202	love	W	9
Thou do'st no more, then doth the grave:	202	love	W	22
Shine then more bright then hee.	203	Even-song	W	8
The sunn is darker then a Tree,	203	Even-song	W	15
And thou more dark then either.	203	Even-song	W	16
A Paradox. That the Sicke are in better State then the Whole.	209	Paradox	D	T
Then worldlings joy'd with all their store	218	Psalm IV	D	27
Remote from ours, then Spaine from Britains shoare.	438	Lat.Trans.		4
shoots higher that threatens the Moon, then hee that aims at a Tree.	224	Priest		9
and obligation of his calling, being to obey God rather then men.	232	Priest 6		19
for particulars ever touch, and awake more then generalls.	233	Priest 7		6
for them also men heed, and remember better then exhortations;	233	Priest 7		13
all those, who come with lesse prepared hearts then they ought.	235	Priest 8		31
Parson considering that virginity is a higher state then Matrimony,	236	Priest 9		32
like circumstances considered, he is rather married then unmarried.	237	Priest 9		5
and that much more being single, then if he were marryed;	238	Priest 9		22
the choyce of his wife was made rather by his eare, then by his eye;	238	Priest 9		27
His children he first makes Christians, and then Commonwealths-men;	239	Priest 10		20
childrens advantage, then if it were given to the Chamber of London.	240	Priest 10		9
act in them, then when they are called to others prayers, and that,	241	Priest 10		5
To his Children he shewes more love then terrour, to his servants	241	Priest 10		9
more love then terrour, to his servants more terrour then love;	241	Priest 10		10
first, of eating lesse that day, then on other dayes;	242	Priest 10		3
are much more essentiall to a true fast, then the third and last;	242	Priest 10		8
unpleasant to me, then some fish there, certainly to eat the flesh,	242	Priest 10		13
is apt to nourish more then in cold regions, and where flesh may be	242	Priest 10		18
and with more safety then elsewhere, where both the people	242	Priest 10		19
draught of beer, then if it had taken before either fish, or rootes,	242	Priest 10		23
which doth lesse obstruct, then flesh moderately taken;	243	Priest 10		3
and sutably to their needs, then so much given in meat at dinner.	243	Priest 11		17
the two commands, we are more injoyned to be charitable, then wise.	245	Priest 12		29
as his accesse to the poor is more comfortable, then to the rich;	249	Priest 14		8
rather goes to them, then sends for the afflicted, though they can,	249	Priest 15		16
perfecting our Redemption no other way, then by sorrow;	249	Priest 15		23
after it may come rather from themselves, then from his perswasion.	250	Priest 15		6
of their discourses for no price sooner, then that of mirth;	252	Priest 18		21
rather then to those that are further, where things are otherwise	253	Priest 19		27
then by causing them to be presented, or otherwise complained of.	254	Priest 20		24
or led by sense, more then by faith, by present rewards,	254	Priest 20		32
by present rewards, or punishments, more then by future.	254	Priest 20		32
in a feast of Charity is more scandall then any posture.	259	Priest 22		18
permit his Parishioners rather to make use of the Law, then himself:	260	Priest 23		19
being made by the precept of Authority more then indifferent,	263	Priest 24		13
either for quantity eats more then his health or imployments will	266	Priest 26		7
as he that eats more then his estate will bear, is a Prodigall;	266	Priest 26		9
Many think they are at more liberty then they are, as if they were	266	Priest 26		19
then from those which by a Common tradition, and vulgar knowledge are	266	Priest 26		25
in eating, that he can eat more, then afterwards he finds true:)	267	Priest 26		4
wisheth all to incline rather to too much, then to too little;	267	Priest 26		13
of exinanition are more dangerous, then diseases of repletion.	267	Priest 26		14
made food miraculously, then suffered so good desires to miscarry.	267	Priest 26		25
touch him no more, then a stone thrown against heaven, where he is,	269	Priest 28		8
then by that which he continually supplyes, as the corn needs it;	271	Priest 30		5
Better were his corne burnt, then not spiritually improved.	272	Priest 30		4
common course of devotion, then dislikes an occasionall interruption.	273	Priest 31		9
a braver [better] Institution then that of Justices of the Peace:	276	Priest 32		9
busie himself better, then in those new Plantations, and discoveryes,	278	Priest 32		5
do it, then he that is generally learned, and was never sick.	278	Priest 33		28
then for offending God, he came at length to this resolution,	279	Priest 33		13
being of a more melting temper then others) consisteth in a true	279	Priest 33		23
their peace and mirth have carryed them further then this moderation,	280	Priest 34		34
then to take Jobs admirable Course, who sacrificed lest his Children	280	Priest 34		34
then their present exile, and disability to live in their Countrey.	282	Priest 34		10
therefore this kind of Punishment was chosen rather then any other.	282	Priest 34		17
or Tertullian, or Chrysostome, more then Tully, Virgill, or Livy;)	282	Priest 34		21
then he that reads the womans oyntment in the Gospell, or sees	283	Priest 34		1
But if he sees them neerer desperation, then Atheisme;	283	Priest 34		6
no more then to be a spirituall Father was appropriated to them.	285	Priest 36		13
then that after many troubles and griefs I should quickly come	291	Cornaro		25
within lesse then one yeare (although it may seem to some incredible)	292	Cornaro		36
within lesse then a yeare I was not onely freed from all those evils	293	Cornaro		20

THEN (cont'd)

	PAGE	TITLE		LINE
stint of meat and drink should be diminished, rather then increased;	295	Cornaro		31
The meat which remaineth, profits more then that which is eaten.	296	Cornaro		2
then the commoditie of meat taken in a moderate proportion.	296	Cornaro		3
since there is a greater diversitie of tempers, then of faces.	297	Cornaro		31
or that cinnamon should heat me more then pepper?	297	Cornaro		33
since none can have a better Physician then himself, nor better	298	Cornaro		1
nor better Physick then a Temperate Life, Temperance by all means is	298	Cornaro		1
they live ten yeares lesse then otherwise they should do) then	298	Cornaro		27
lesse then otherwise they should do) then alwayes to live under bit	298	Cornaro		28
and that in much smaller quantitie then when he was well.	299	Cornaro		32
(though most agreeable to them) then their stomack can easily digest:	300	Cornaro		13
sure of life, then the most strong young man who lives disorderly.	300	Cornaro		26
yeares old, all the time we live after, is rather death then life.	300	Cornaro		30
the place was moorish and unhealthy, fitter for beasts then men.	301	Cornaro		27
then heretofore, when I was given to disorder and all the delights	302	Cornaro		10
because I have now a clearer voice, then ever I had in my life.	303	Cornaro		7
then I could of Originall before, and without Baptisme.	308	Valdesso		4
not be punished (which word I like here better then chastizement,	311	Valdesso		27
motions are much more frequent to the godly, then inviting motions;	313	Valdesso		18
Saviour prayed with doubtfulnesse, is more then I can or dare say;	315	Valdesso		10
that the world pierceth not godly mens actions no more then Gods,	315	Valdesso		30
point it should, which if it did, it would doe more, then it does.	319	Valdesso		12
A handfull of good life is better then a bushell of learning.	321	Proverbs		3
A Dwarfe on a Gyants shoulder sees farther then they two.	322	Proverbs	V	50
Better the feet slip then the tongue.	322	Proverbs		53
Better thy foote slip then thy tongue.	322	Proverbs	V	53
Better a bare foote then none.	323	Proverbs		78
Better bend then break.	323	Proverbs	V	85
An old wise mans shaddow is better then a young buzzards sword.	324	Proverbs		90
Better to be blinde, then to see ill.	325	Proverbs		126
Who hath no more bread then neede, must not keepe a dog.	325	Proverbs		128
A naughty child is better sick then whole.	328	Proverbs		233
Providence is better then a rent.	329	Proverbs		254
There are more men threatned then stricken.	329	Proverbs		256
A foole knowes more in his house, then a wise man in anothers.	329	Proverbs		257
then a horse that throwes me.	329	Proverbs		258
The hard gives more then he that hath nothing.	329	Proverbs		259
It costs more to doe ill then to doe well.	329	Proverbs		262
Good words quench more then a bucket of water.	329	Proverbs		263
Soft words quench more then cold water.	329	Proverbs	V	263
An ill agreement is better then a good judgement.	329	Proverbs		264
There is more talke then trouble.	330	Proverbs		265
Better spare to have of thine own, then aske of other men.	330	Proverbs		266
Better good afarre off, then evill at hand.	330	Proverbs		267
Feare keepes the garden better then the gardiner.	330	Proverbs		268
then borrow of my neighbour white.	330	Proverbs		269
Your pot broken seemes better then my whole one.	330	Proverbs		270
By suppers more have beene killed then Galen ever cured.	330	Proverbs		272
By suppers more are killed then Galen ever cured.	330	Proverbs	V	272
Much spends the traveller, more then the abider.	330	Proverbs		276
A poore beauty finds more lovers then husbands.	337	Proverbs		481
Gluttony kills more then the sword.	338	Proverbs		503
The tooth-ach is more ease then to deale with ill people.	340	Proverbs		558
A feather in hand is better then a bird in the ayre.	340	Proverbs		578
It's better to be the head of a Lyzard, then the tayle of a Lyon.	340	Proverbs		579
It's better to be the head of a mouse, then the tayle of a Lyon.	340	Proverbs	V	579
then a heart with thoughts.	341	Proverbs		582
Happier the hands fetter'd then the head distracted.	341	Proverbs	V	582
The table robbes more then a thiefe.	342	Proverbs		636
A beane in liberty is better then a comfit in prison.	343	Proverbs		653
Nothing dries sooner then a teare.	343	Proverbs		659
Dry bread at home is better then rost meate abroad.	344	Proverbs		681
More have repented speech then silence.	344	Proverbs		682
The coveteous spends more then the liberall.	344	Proverbs		683
Divine ashes are better then earthly meale.	344	Proverbs		684
Beauty drawes more then oxen.	344	Proverbs		685
One father is more then a hundred Schoolemasters.	344	Proverbs		686
One eye of the masters sees more, then ten of the servants.	344	Proverbs		687
A valiant mans looke is more then a cowards sword.	345	Proverbs		708
Of him that speakes ill, consider the life more then the words.	346	Proverbs		761
Of him that speakes ill, consider the life more then the word.	346	Proverbs	V	761
Better speake truth rudely, then lye covertly.	346	Proverbs		767
One foote is better then two crutches.	346	Proverbs		769
Better suffer ill, then doe ill.	346	Proverbs		770
Nature drawes more then ten teemes.	347	Proverbs		777
Better a snotty child, then his nose wip'd off.	348	Proverbs		828
It's more paine to doe nothing then something.	350	Proverbs		884
'Tis easier to build two chimneys, then to maintaine one.	350	Proverbs		893
There are more Physitians in health then drunkards.	351	Proverbs		903
Ships feare fire more then water.	351	Proverbs		909
The body is more drest then the soule.	351	Proverbs		919
The body is sooner drest then the soule.	351	Proverbs		920
Yeeres know more then bookes.	351	Proverbs		928
It is better to have wings then hornes.	352	Proverbs		960
Better be a foole then a knave.	352	Proverbs		961
Wee leave more to do when wee dye, then wee have done.	353	Proverbs		972
A trade is better then service.	354	Proverbs		1005
The eye is bigger then the belly.	355	Proverbs		1018
Heresie may be easier kept out, then shooke off.	357	Proverbs	D	1059
then by stars at their nativities.	357	Proverbs	D	1060

THEN (cont'd)

	PAGE	TITLE		LINE
The noise is greater then the nuts.	358	Proverbs	D	1073
Better is one Accipe, then twice to say, Dabo tibi.	358	Proverbs	D	1079
An Asse endures his burden, but not more then his burden.	358	Proverbs	D	1080
The rage of a wild boar is able to spoil more then one wood.	360	Proverbs	D	1132
Some had rather lose their friend then their Jest.	361	Proverbs	D	1170
then either of them both.	361	Proverbs	D	1173
What hath Affliction grievous in it more then for a moment?	372	Letters		27
I alwaies fear'd sickness more then death, because sickness hath made	373	Letters		8
power to defeat my charity, and evill shold be stronger then good:	376	Letters		10
Although you have a much better Paymaster then my self,	378	Letters		2
work rather then doe nothing.	381	Woodnoth		24

THEN

	PAGE	TITLE		LINE
Then thou art modest, and the wine grows bold.	8	Ch.-Porch		42
Art thou a Magistrate? then be severe:	10	Ch.-Porch		85
But if thou coole, then take some shame to thee	10	Ch.-Porch	W	90
Then all thou addest may be call'd his treasure.	11	Ch.-Porch		114
Look on meat, think it dirt, then eat a bit;	11	Ch.-Porch		131
Who lives by rule then, keeps good companie.	12	Ch.-Porch		138
Then live, and use it: els, it is not true	12	Ch.-Porch		154
Say not then, This with that lace will do well;	14	Ch.-Porch		189
Then march on gallant: get substantiall worth.	15	Ch.-Porch		209
Then keep such companie; make them thy allay:	15	Ch.-Porch		212
Then he's the sport: the mirth then in him rests,	16	Ch.-Porch		251
Then may the beasts draw thee to happy light.	16	Ch.-Porch		264
Get a good stock of these, then draw the card	18	Ch.-Porch		293
Take all into thee; then with equall care	19	Ch.-Porch		321
And then as farre as fair behaviour may,	20	Ch.-Porch		359
God then deals blessings: If a king did so,	22	Ch.-Porch		389
Fast when thou wilt; but then 'tis gain, not losse.	22	Ch.-Porch		396
Onely by his permission. Then beware,	22	Ch.-Porch		405
Then turn thy faults and his into confession:	24	Ch.-Porch		441
Then turn thy fault and his into confession:	24	Ch.-Porch	W	441
Be down, then winde up both; since we shall be	24	Ch.-Porch		455
Then from one ruler to another bound	28	Sacrifice		53
Then they accuse me of great blasphemie,	28	Sacrifice		61
Then they condemne me all with that same breath,	28	Sacrifice		69
Then with a scarlet robe they me aray;	31	Sacrifice		157
Then on my head a crown of thorns I wear:	31	Sacrifice		161
Then with the reed they gave to me before,	32	Sacrifice		169
Then with the reed they gave mee heertofore,	32	Sacrifice	W	169
They leade me in once more, and putting then	32	Sacrifice		189
Then Simon bears it for me by constraint,	33	Sacrifice		198
Shall I then sing, skipping, thy dolefull storie,	35	Thanksgvng		11
Shall I then sing, neglecting thy sad storie,	35	Thanksgvng	W	11
But how then shall I imitate thee, and	35	Thanksgvng		15
Then I will use the works of thy creation,	36	Thanksgvng		35
Then will I use the works of thy creation,	36	Thanksgvng	W	35
Then for thy passion - I will do for that -	36	Thanksgvng		49
Did set again abroach; then let him say	37	The Agonie		15
Then let each houre	39	Good Fri.		13
And then this day, my life shall date.	42	Easter	W	30
Then shall the fall further the flight in me.	43	East.wings		10
Then shall my fall further the flight in me.	43	East.wings	W	10
And then beyond them all my Baptisme view	43	H. Bapt.1	W	2
Which then join'd with you still meet in my brest	44	H. Bapt.1	W	8
Parents first season us: then schoolmasters	45	Sinne 1		2
For sure then I should grow	48	Afflict.1		58
O let thy height of mercie then	49	Repentance		13
And then appear'd a glorious skie.	51	Faith		40
Then shall our hearts pant thee; then shall our brain	54	Love 2		6
Then of a sinner thou art rid,	55	Temper 1		19
Let me not languish then, and spend	57	Employm. 1		13
Then as dispersed herbs do watch a potion,	58	H.Script.2		7
On thy Apostles? thou didst then	59	Whitsunday		6
Wilt thou not then my fault reprove?	61	Grace	W	20
O raise me then! poore bees, that work all day,	61	Praise 1		17
O raise me then: for if a Spider may	61	Praise 1	W	17
Then we must needs for that day make a match.	62	Mattens		4
Then by a sunne-beam I will climbe to thee.	63	Mattens		20
The holy Preachers; then the light and glorie	67	Windows		8
Then cease discoursing soul, till thine own ground,	69	Content		33
Spoil'd all the train: then saying, Here it is	71	Humilitie		27
And then amerc'd them, double gifts to bring	71	Humilitie		31
So much breath to a sigh, what's then behinde?	73	Afflict.3		9
The sigh then onely is	73	Afflict.3		11
Then with thy light refine,	74	The Starre		11
Then with our trinitie of light,	74	The Starre		17
Then forcing thee, by fire he made thee bright:	77	Avarice		9
Although then others court you, if ye know	78	Ang.&Sts.		26
Then should I ever laden be,	79	Employm.2		23
Then would I mount up instantly	79	Employm.2	W	23
Then was my heart broken, as was my verse:	79	Deniall		3
And then not heare it crying! all day long	80	Deniall		18
Then we will chide the sunne for letting night	81	Christmas		23
Then we will sing, and shine all our own day,	81	Christmas		31
But on thy glorie! then thou wilt reform	83	Sighs & Gr.		3
Then Pleasure came, who liking not the fashion,	84	The World		6
Then enter'd Sinne, and with that Sycomore,	84	The World		11
Then Sinne combin'd with Death in a firm band	84	The World		16
Then those same pendant profits, which the spring	86	Lent		25

THEN (cont'd)

	PAGE	TITLE	LINE
Then chiefly lives.	88	Vertue	16
Then shall those powers, which work for grief,	90	Afflict.4	25
Then how are all things neat?	92	Man	42
Then he'l take notice of: in ev'ry path	92	Man	44
Since then, my God, thou hast	92	Man	49
Till then, afford us so much wit;	92	Man	52
My hand was next to them, and then my heart:	94	Life	7
Then should thy praises with me grow,	95	Submission	7
That I should then raise thee?	95	Submission	14
Grace turnes the Optick, then they fall.	97	Charms & K W	18
Take up the second, then thy double line	97	Afflict.5	16
Affliction then is ours;	97	Afflict.5	19
Thy words were then, Let me alone.	99	Decay	5
Since then these three wait on thy throne,	103	Prayer 2	19
Then Money came, and chinking still,	110	The Quip	9
Then came brave Glorie puffing by	111	The Quip	13
Then came quick Wit and Conversation,	111	The Quip	17
And then they have their answer home.	111	The Quip	24
Then silly soul take heed; for earthly joy	111	Vanitie 2	17
Quickly should I then controll	114	Dialogue	3
As the reason then is thine;	115	Dialogue	21
Where are my lines then? my approaches? views?	116	Dulnesse	17
For their offence; and then dost turn their speed	120	Providence	107
Then an old prayer-book I did present:	121	Hope	3
Then chafing said, This man deludes:	123	Time	28
Then went I to a garden, and did spy	125	Peace	13
But then a thought creeps in,	127	Giddinesse	6
Then have we too our guardian fires and clouds;	128	Bunch Gr.	15
Then once more pray:	134	The Method	29
Then burn thy Epicycles, foolish man;	135	Divinitie	25
Then weep mine eyes, the God of love doth grieve:	135	Ephes.	7
Then Order plaies the soul;	137	Familie	10
Then close again the seam,	138	The Size	42
Then I refuse not ev'n with bloud	139	Artillerie	14
Then we are shooters both, and thou dost deigne	139	Artillerie	25
Then did your sev'rall parts unloose and start:	140	Ch.-rents	21
Yet taking heart I rose, and then perceiv'd	142	Pilgrimage	29
Then will I trust, said I, in him alone.	143	Holdfast	5
Then I confesse, that he my succour is:	143	Holdfast	8
And then again	145	Discharge	49
Then bring thy gift; and let thy hymne be this;	147	Offering	24
Then let me tell thee a strange storie.	151	The Bag	8
Both then, and after, many a brunt	151	The Bag	21
Then can thy truth and I: but while rocks stand,	156	Assurance	32
Then shalt thou be my rock and tower,	156	Assurance	35
Then I or ought, or can be mine.	157	Clasping	3
I may presume thee mine, then thine.	157	Clasping	13
Yet then as mine didst me restore.	157	Clasping	18
Then will I wring it with a sigh or grone,	157	Praise 3	5
To twentie then, or more.	158	Praise 3	12
Then beautie flow'd, then wisdome, honour, pleasure:	160	The Pulley	7
Then is my time. The distance of the meek	161	Priesthood	39
Since then my grief must be as large,	163	The Search	45
And then when after much delay,	164	The Crosse	7
Then miseries are here!	167	Dotage	18
Then to the streams that gently passe:	172	23 Psalme	7
Then should the Pomander, which was before	175	The Odour	16
Then did I wash you with my tears, and more,	176	Forerunners	16
If then all that worldlings prize	178	The Rose	21
Then let wrath remove;	179	Discipline	17
And then what life I have,	183	A Parodie	21
And then the heav'n espie.	184	The Elixer	12
Then deceit seems above simplicitie.	185	A Wreath	8
Know them and practise them: then shall I give	185	A Wreath	11
But thy trumpet: then it kneels,	186	Dooms-day	10
Are holy leaves the Echo then of blisse?	188	Heaven	11
Then tell me, what is that supreme delight?	188	Heaven	13
My deare, then I will serve.	189	Love 3	16
Then showres Religion, and makes all to bear.	192	Ch.-Milit.	88
Then in memoriall of his ancient throne	195	Ch.-Milit.	181
Then what was in their tongue, did overcome;	196	Ch.-Milit.	202
Then shall Religion to America flee:	197	Ch.-Milit.	247
And then bargain with the winde	199	L'Envoy	15
Then of this also I am sure	200	H. Commun. W	19
But then there comes into my way	202	love W	10
I thought it brave to praise thee then,	202	love W	15
Yet then I found, that thou didst creep	202	love W	16
Then flesh did lend thee, back agen.	202	love W	18
Shine then more bright then hee.	203	Even-song W	8
If thou deferr this light, then shadow mee:	203	Even-song W	9
And then, my Labour's not lost.	207	Walton 3	6
Cease then to judge calamityes	210	Paradox D	25
Then you shall fully knowe	210	Paradox D	28
Why then confesse	210	Paradox D	35
Then for yourselves not us embrace	211	Paradox D	37
And Paris garden. Then let there perfume	212	Bohemia D	51
Then shall thy Glory, fresh as flowers	213	L' Envoy D	7
Then shall He speak to them in wrath,	215	Psalm II D	11
Then let mine enemie prevail	221	Psalm VII D	15
and then they are worst, who ought to be best.	227	Priest 3	28

THEN (cont'd)	PAGE	TITLE	LINE
amazed with the Majesty of God, before whom he then presents himself;	231	Priest 6	6
whose sins he then beares, and brings with his own to the heavenly	231	Priest 6	8
speech now to the younger sort, then to the elder, now to the poor,	233	Priest 7	3
of holinesse, then the procuring, and rejoycing in anothers good.	234	Priest 7	9
and then woven into Sermons, which will make them appear exceeding	234	Priest 7	23
Then turning the discourse to his Majesty, And he is a great God,	234	Priest 7	30
making him then weary, and so he grows from not relishing,	235	Priest 7	14
then he turnes to request for his people, that the Lord would be	235	Priest 8	27
Then having read divine Service twice fully, and preached in	236	Priest 8	6
the best and highest things, is rather unmarryed, then marryed.	236	Priest 9	33
and then alsc in a serious manner, never jestingly or sportfully.	237	Priest 9	12
for then commonly the stream of temptations is turned another way,	238	Priest 9	22
Having then invited some of his Parish, hee taketh his times to do	243	Priest 11	17
for then they will reckon upon it, as on a debt;	244	Priest 12	28
and then as hee finds the persons of the house imployed,	247	Priest 14	11
But then he admonisheth them of two things;	247	Priest 14	23
Then they labour anxiously, when they overdo it, to the loss of their	247	Priest 14	27
then distrustfully, when they doubt Gods providence, thinking that	247	Priest 14	29
Then they labour profanely, when they set themselves to work like	247	Priest 14	31
I am then to follow the Apostles rule, 1 Timothy 5. 20. and to rebuke	248	Priest 14	29
of the house best, and then hee faithfully, and boldly applyeth it;	251	Priest 17	27
and then he suits things faithfully according to that end.	253	Priest 19	4
some defects in the Ministry, he then either in Sermon, if he preach,	253	Priest 19	12
or famine, tc any neighbouring Parish, then he expects no Briefe;	253	Priest 19	30
and then when he hath affrighted them with this, exposing	253	Priest 19	33
he first gives himself liberally, and then incites them to give;	253	Priest 19	36
not himself, but is first a Sermon to himself, and then to others;	255	Priest 21	15
may then by an honourable way take occasion to be better instructed.	255	Priest 21	30
Then are there scme things to be beleeved that are not seen?	256	Priest 21	8
Then he proceeded to ask, whether he could get out of the ditch	257	Priest 21	8
of the Communion only (for then it is too late) but the Sunday,	258	Priest 22	27
being ripe enough for ill things, and why not then for better?	259	Priest 22	2
loosely and wildely, and then the Answerer will discover what hee is.	259	Priest 22	9
he hath so done, then he assumes the Parson, and exhorts to Charity.	260	Priest 23	16
But then he shews them how to go to Law, even as Brethren,	260	Priest 23	25
then he keeps good correspondence with some neighbour Phisician,	260	Priest 23	36
and how then should the best be so, at least in fundamentall things,	263	Priest 24	4
he then comes on the faster, and makes so much the more of him,	263	Priest 25	33
then when any despises him, he takes it either in an humble way,	269	Priest 28	5
hand to sickle, shall then secure himself, and think all cock-sure;	271	Priest 30	29
then God sends such weather, as lays the corn, and destroys it:	271	Priest 30	30
God further, even till he imbarn his corn, and then think all sure;	271	Priest 30	32
For when men have nothing to do, then they fall to drink, to steal,	274	Priest 32	11
judiciously, then he writes his rules of temperance out of bookes.	278	Priest 33	20
Romans 2.) hee first preacheth to himselfe, and then to others.	279	Priest 33	36
and find sparkes of such thoughts now and then to break forth,	281	Priest 34	13
then without opposing directly (for disputation is no Cure	281	Priest 34	14
and then who can deny the stretched out arme of a mighty God?	282	Priest 34	6
their living then in their Countrey under so many miracles were	282	Priest 34	8
then he dives unto the boundlesse Ocean of Gods Love,	283	Priest 34	7
values the gift in himself, and then teacheth his parish to value it.	286	Priest 36	19
doubtlesse then also mens affections and words must turne,	288	Priest 37	4
then did'st thou place us in Paradise, and wert proceeding still	288	Priest	14
so that then where sin abounded, not death, but grace superabounded;	288	Priest	24
had sinned beyond any help in heaven or earth, then thou saidest, Lo,	288	Priest	26
then did the Lord of life, unable of himselfe to die, contrive to do	288	Priest	27
even for those that derided him then, and still despise him.	288	Priest	30
then not liking that kinde of Diet, followed my Appetite,	292	Cornaro	26
I not so avoid all these, but that now and then I fell into them;	293	Cornaro	38
and then was dragged for a good space by the furie of the horses,	294	Cornaro	37
save now and then a little indisposition for a day or two.	296	Cornaro	31
Then, I am ever cheerfull, merrie, and well-contented, free from all	300	Cornaro	36
it for a time onely, and then cast it away, as he sayes strangely.	318	Valdesso	3
I doe not then bid him goe away but rather stay longer,	318	Valdesso	15
doth not bid them then cast away the word, or leave it off:	318	Valdesso	19
and then afterward they will attend it of themselves without his	318	Valdesso	21
at his time, and not till then.	332	Proverbs	333
The crow bewailes the sheepe, and then eates it.	337	Proverbs	458
Wine is a turne-coate (first a friend, then an enemy).	351	Proverbs	929
When war begins, then hell openeth.	360	Proverbs	D 1141
and shall I then be fain alwayes to borrow Books, and build	364	Letters	13
If then, Sir, there be any course, either by engaging my future	365	Letters	20
Bee covetous, then, of all good which you see in Frenchmen,	366	Letters	7
judge me then by those waters, and not by my ink, and then you shall	372	Letters	3
and then you shall justly value Your most truly, most heartily,	372	Letters	4
Then I bequeath twenty pounds unto the poore of this parish to be	382	G.H.'s Will	16
Then I bequeath to Mr Hays the Comment of Lucas Brugensis uppon	382	G.H.'s Will	18
then I bequeath to Mr Bostocke St. Augustines workes and his halfe	382	G.H.'s Will	20
then I leave to my servant Elizabeth her dubble wages given her,	382	G.H.'s Will	22
then the accesse of the Officers of the Catholike King?	442	Oration	9
THENCE			
I will tear thence his love and fame.	35	Thanksgvng	26
And thence by kinde	45	Nature	10
You took me thence, and in your house of pleasure	65	Ch.-mus.	3
Yet, if thou wilt from thence depart,	74	The Starre	5
Thou hast hid metals: man may take them thence;	119	Providence	81
On future grief, do not remove it thence,	145	Discharge	43
But borrow'd thence to light us thither.	177	Forerunners	29
Religion thence fled into Greece, where arts	191	Ch.-Milit.	49
Thence into Greece she fled, where curious Arts	191	Ch.-Milit. W	49

	PAGE	TITLE	LINE
THENCE (cont'd)			
And such poore game. Thence he to Greece doth passe,	193	Ch.-Milit.	123
And such small game. Thence he to Greece doth passe,	193	Ch.-Milit. W	123
Laden with comforts thence, where now to morne	212	Bohemia D	56
Thence wheeling on, it compass shall	213	L' Envoy D	11
or if he have any leisure to look off from thence, he meets	267	Priest 27	30
which are brought from thence to the House but in generall.	277	Priest 32	13
though unused a proof of Divinity taken from thence, that	281	Priest 34	33
THENCEFORTH			
Wherein she thenceforth evermore	173	Marie Magd	5
THEOLOGICALL			
some oppose Theologicall vertues, as Uncharitablenesse opposes	308	Valdesso	7
THER			
Ther's no monument to a sonne,	208	J. Danvers D	15
Ther's no great banquet but some fares ill.	343	Proverbs	668
THERE			
Which would throw me there, if I keep the round.	7	Ch.-Porch	30
Look to thy mouth; diseases enter there.	11	Ch.-Porch	127
And tumble up and down what thou find'st there.	12	Ch.-Porch	148
Still in thy heart, that he may see what's there.	17	Ch.-Porch	272
Truth dwels not in the clouds: the bow that's there	19	Ch.-Porch	317
And meet them there. All worldly joyes go lesse	19	Ch.-Porch	329
And meet them there. All wordly joyes go lesse	19	Ch.-Porch W	329
God is more there, then thou: for thou art there	22	Ch.-Porch	404
Let vain or busie thoughts have there no part:	23	Ch.-Porch	421
Let vain & busie thoughts have there no part:	23	Ch.-Porch W	421
To sell me also, and to put me there:	27	Sacrifice	15
There they deride me, they abuse me all:	31	Sacrifice	154
Though I my vine planted and watred there:	31	Sacrifice	163
In healing not my self, there doth consist	34	Sacrifice	225
There is no dealing with thy mighty passion:	36	Reprisall	2
There is no medling with thy mighty passion:	36	Reprisall W	2
But there are two vast, spacious things,	37	The Agonie	4
Yet few there are that sound them; Sinne and Love.	37	The Agonie	6
Unto mount Olivet; there shall he see	37	The Agonie	8
I finde there quarries of pil'd vanities,	38	The Sinner	5
There the circumference earth is, heav'n the centre.	38	The Sinner	8
There the circumference earth is, heav'n the centure.	38	The Sinner W	8
My heart hath store, write there, where in	39	Good Fri.	23
All come to lodge there, sinne may say,	39	Good Fri.	27
All come to lodge there, he may say,	39	Good Fri. W	27
They told me there, that he was lately gone	40	Redemption	6
Of theeves and murderers: there I him espied,	40	Redemption	13
Sure there is room within our hearts good store;	40	Sepulchre	5
Thousands of toyes dwell there, yet out of doore	40	Sepulchre	7
Can there be any day but this,	42	Easter	27
There is but one, and that one ever.	42	Easter	30
O smooth my rugged heart, and there	45	Nature	13
There was no moneth but May.	47	Afflict.1	22
There is a rare outlandish root,	50	Faith	9
Faith puts me there with him, who sweetly took	50	Faith	23
His praises there may grow.	53	Antiphon 1	6
And there in hymnes send back thy fire again:	54	Love 2	8
Although there were some fourtie heav'ns, or more,	55	Temper 1	5
Although there were a hundred heav'ns, or more,	55	Temper 1 W	5
O let me roost and nestle there:	55	Temper 1	18
Thy hands made both, and I am there:	55	Temper 1	26
Become a verse? Is there in truth no beautie?	56	Jordan 1	2
And if wee can stay there, it's well.	59	Whitsunday W	14
Man is all weaknesse; there is no such thing	61	Praise 1	9
But thou art ready there to catch	62	Mattens	2
Humilitie, who sat the lowest there	70	Humilitie	5
My heart did heave, and there came forth, O God!	73	Afflict.3	1
Thou knowst my tallies; and when there's assign'd	73	Afflict.3	8
So well as there?	74	The Starre	4
Get me a standing there, and place	74	The Stàrre	21
The burden of the week lies there,	75	Sunday	12
Since there is no place so alone,	75	Sunday	20
And made a garden there for those	76	Sunday	41
The sunne still shineth there or here,	79	Employm.2	18
There when I came, whom found I but my deare,	81	Christmas	5
Of pleasures brought me to him, readie there	81	Christmas	7
To make a purchase there: he sees their dances,	85	Vanitie 1	5
There he imparts to them his minde,	85	Vanitie 1	18
Begins at home, and layes the burden there,	86	Lent	8
Whereas in fulnesse there are sluttish fumes,	86	Lent	22
How many drammes of spirit there must be	88	The Pearl	18
What house more stately hath there been,	90	Man	4
Finde their acquaintance there.	91	Man	24
Findes himself there, and seeks to rise.	96	Charms & K	12
There is but joy and grief;	97	Afflict.5	13
And serve the swine: there, there is his delight:	101	Miserie	44
There let them shine,	101	Miserie	53
There is in love a sweetnesse readie penn'd:	103	Jordan 2	17
Coppy out that: there needs no alteration.	103	Jordan 2 W	18
We cannot ask the thing, which is not there,	103	Prayer 2	11
As many lines, as there doth need	104	Obedience	7
Where in the deed there was an intimation	105	Obedience	33
No room for pratlers there.	105	Conscience	10
Besides my physick, know there's some for thee:	106	Conscience	20
Something there was, that sow'd debate:	106	Sion	9

THERE (cont'd)

	PAGE	TITLE		LINE
There thou art struggling with a peevish heart,	106	Sion		13
But there was none; at least no help without:	107	Home		15
There lay thy sonne: and must he leave that nest,	107	Home		19
We talk of harvests; there are no such things,	108	Home		55
There is no fruitfull yeare, but that which brings	108	Home		57
Is deeply carved there: but th' other week	112	JESU		2
Sure thou didst put a minde there, if I could	116	Dulnesse		23
Is there an herb for that? O that thy care	119	Providence		75
Are there much surer then our art is sure.	119	Providence		80
As Babel grew, before there were dissensions.	122	Sinnes rd.		15
And ask'd, if Peace were there.	124	Peace		4
There was a Prince of old	125	Peace		22
There sprang twelve stalks of wheat:	125	Peace		28
Is onely there.	125	Peace		42
There would be no commerce,	127	Giddinesse		22
And have good cause: there it was dipt and di'd,	129	Love unkn.		16
Began to spread and to expatiate there:	130	Love unkn.		39
Full well I understood, who had been there:	130	Love unkn.		54
There it stands knocking, to thy musicks wrong,	132	The Storm		13
There is some rub, some discontent,	133	The Method		3
Written above there? Yesterday	133	The Method		14
But stay! what's there?	134	The Method		21
To take and taste what he doth there designe,	135	Divinitie		23
There can no discord but in ceasing be.	136	Ephes.		22
As if there were no rule or eares?	136	Familie		4
Joyes oft are there, and griefs as oft as joyes;	137	Familie		17
There is no articling with thee:	139	Artillerie		31
Against me there is none, but for me much.	141	Justice 2		24
So to cares cops I came, and there got through	142	Pilgrimage		11
What hast thou there? a heart? but is it pure?	147	Offering		3
There is a balsome, or indeed a bloud,	147	Offering		19
Were sinne alive, good cause there were	150	Longing		65
But as he was returning, there came one	151	The Bag		25
Sure there was wine	153	The Collar		10
Before my sighs did drie it: there was corn	153	The Collar		11
Not so, my heart: but there is fruit,	153	The Collar		17
Call in thy deaths head there: tie up thy fears.	153	The Collar		29
Pickt here and there a crumme, and would not die;	154	Glimpse		17
No such rank poyson can there be.	155	Assurance		6
Did weep to heav'n, they found a bottle there	158	Praise 3		27
(Which there did hang like streamers neare the top	158	Praise 3		33
That to thy chests there might be coming in	159	Praise 3		41
That to thy chest there might be coming in	159	Praise 3	V	41
There will I lie, untill my Maker seek	161	Priesthood		37
That thou art there.	162	The Search		8
As if there were no such cold thing.	165	The Flower		7
Ev'n all my heart, and what is lodged there:	176	Forerunners		8
First, there is no pleasure here:	177	The Rose		5
Colour'd griefs indeed there are,	177	The Rose		6
Or if such deceits there be,	177	The Rose		9
There are no such things to me,	177	The Rose		11
Sweetly there indeed it lies,	178	The Rose		23
Where is all, there all should be.	180	Invitation		36
Melted there,	181	Banquet		11
There thou shalt finde my faults are thine.	188	Judgement		15
And are there any leaves, that still abide?	188	Heaven		7
And are there any leaves, which still abide?	188	Heaven	W	7
But are there cares and businesse with the pleasure?	188	Heaven		17
Where th' Ark did rest, there Abraham began	190	Ch.-Milit.		19
The ten Commandments there did flourish more	191	Ch.-Milit.		39
And there the Churches festivall attending:	192	Ch.-Milit.		82
Strength levels grounds, Art makes a garden there;	192	Ch.-Milit.		87
Nero and others lodg'd him bravely there,	194	Ch.-Milit.		141
Onely there was a handsome picture by,	194	Ch.-Milit.		169
The waight was such they left the doctrins there	196	Ch.-Milit.	W	203
Yet must there such proportions be assign'd	196	Ch.-Milit.		232
Yet must there such proportion be assign'd	196	Ch.-Milit.	W	232
For thy poore creature there	200	H. Commun.	W	6
Bee there, to thy truth, & my gaine	200	H. Commun.	W	11
That Flesh is there, mine eyes deny:	201	H. Commun.	W	31
Even there, where they deceive?	201	H. Commun.	W	36
There is no dealing with thee in that Art:	201	love	W	2
But then there comes into my way	202	love	W	10
Sure, Lord, there is enough in thee to dry	206	Walton 2		1
Reade him there, and I have done.	208	J. Danvers	D	16
Maintaine there Lustre still, & shining cleere	211	Bohemia	D	11
There is thy best Throne. For afflictions are	211	Bohemia	D	15
At there owne weapons, without pomp or state	211	Bohemia	D	21
To second thee against there cunning hate.	211	Bohemia	D	22
Thou shalt not bee a Queene and conquer there.	212	Bohemia	D	40
But it shall spy some of there victories.	212	Bohemia	D	46
There hands shall clipp the Eagles winges, & chase	212	Bohemia	D	47
At Purgatory, there inchanted Ile,	212	Bohemia	D	50
And Paris garden. Then let there perfume	212	Bohemia	D	51
Whose fier, like there malice, nought can quench.	212	Bohemia	D	54
Thy fruite shall with there drops contend;	213	L' Envoy	D	4
and there an awful Scepter sway:	216	Psalm II	D	22
no help in God there is.	216	Psalm III	D	4
Many there are that say, O who	217	Psalm IV	D	21
And peace-meal rent it, while there's none	221	Psalm VII	D	7

THERE (cont'd)

	PAGE	TITLE	LINE
some live there in office, whose rule is that of the Apostle;	226	Priest 2	3
and there is no knowledg, but, in a skilfull hand, serves either	228	Priest 4	15
There he sucks, and lives.	228	Priest 4	23
one Countrey doth not bear all things, that there may be a Commerce;	229	Priest 4	24
that there may be a traffick in knowledg between the servants of God,	229	Priest 4	25
is best to be chosen, of which there is likelyest to be most use.	230	Priest 5	11
If there be any of the gentry or nobility of the Parish,	232	Priest 6	7
that where is much earnestness, there is somewhat worth hearing;	232	Priest 7	33
For there is no greater sign of holinesse, then the procuring,	234	Priest 7	9
never was there such care of a flock expressed, save in the great	234	Priest 7	20
Therefore this care may be learn'd there, and then woven into	234	Priest 7	23
There are but two devouring elements, fire, and water, he hath both	234	Priest 7	32
and if there be any extraordinary addition to the customary	235	Priest 8	33
or painted there, which may excite the reader to a thought of piety;	240	Priest 10	24
that there is no help for a fault done, but confession.	240	Priest 10	35
for there being two things, which as they are, are unuseful to man,	241	Priest 10	26
unpleasant to me, then some fish there, certainly to eat the flesh,	242	Priest 10	14
vessels, and there is nothing that is food, and not phisick,	243	Priest 10	2
knowing that where there are such conceits, there is no room for his	243	Priest 11	23
there are such conceits, there is no room for his doctrine to enter.	243	Priest 11	23
that there be not a begger, or idle person in his Parish,	244	Priest 12	19
that all things there be decent, and befitting his Name by which it	246	Priest 13	2
That there be fit, and proper texts of Scripture every where painted,	246	Priest 13	11
That all the books appointed by Authority be there, and those	246	Priest 13	14
and that there be a fitting, and sightly Communion Cloth of fine	246	Priest 13	16
For there he shall find his flock most naturally as they are,	247	Priest 14	5
Neither in this doth he forbear, though there be company by:	248	Priest 14	25
For both God is there also, and those for whom God dyed:	249	Priest 14	6
First, what disorders there are either in Apparell, or Diet,	251	Priest 17	19
there is nothing spoken, or done in the Company where he is,	252	Priest 18	2
as being the servant of him, in whom there was no guile.	253	Priest 19	2
He observes Visitations, and being there, makes due use of them,	253	Priest 19	10
or of good report, if there be any vertue, or any praise;	253	Priest 19	24
Wherefore there is nothing done either wel or ill, whereof he is	254	Priest 20	10
for there being three points of his duty, the one, to infuse	255	Priest 21	2
whereas in Sermons there is a kinde of state, in Catechizing there is	255	Priest 21	9
in Catechizing there is an humblenesse very sutable to Christian	255	Priest 21	10
Then are there some things to be beleeved that are not seen?	256	Priest 21	8
but there being two things in Sermons, the one Informing,	257	Priest 21	21
If there be any, who having not received yet, are to enter into this	258	Priest 22	29
if there be but three Communions, neither can all the people so order	259	Priest 22	25
there may happen somtimes some cases, wherein he chooseth to permit	260	Priest 23	17
if there be any of his flock sick, hee is their Physician,	260	Priest 23	29
esteeming that there is no spice comparable, for herbs,	262	Priest 23	1
if there be any of his parish that hold strange Doctrins,	262	Priest 24	19
whether, there being two precepts, one of obeying Authority,	263	Priest 24	8
be preferred, especially since in disobeying there is scandall also:	263	Priest 24	11
There are some vices, whose natures are alwayes cleer, and evident,	264	Priest 26	5
There are other vices, whose natures, at least in the beginning,	264	Priest 26	7
So likewise there are some persons, who abstain not even from known	264	Priest 26	9
there are others, who when they know a sin evidently, they commit it	264	Priest 26	11
yet is there a period for his storing, and a point, or center,	264	Priest 26	28
since there is a Justice in the least things, and for the least there	265	Priest 26	32
in the least things, and for the least there shall be a judgment.	265	Priest 26	33
To guide them in this, there are three rules:	266	Priest 26	36
of themselves, knowing that there is one, who when they forget,	267	Priest 26	21
for that, where contempt is, there is no room for instruction.	268	Priest 28	19
and that also well inned, and imbarned, and continuing safe there;	272	Priest 30	2
But here there are two Cautions to be added.	273	Priest 31	14
I will not doubt to go without staying to pray there (but onely,	273	Priest 31	35
For there are two branches of his affaires;	275	Priest 32	21
whereas now, of any place, they are least there.	275	Priest 32	36
Hee considers every one there, and either helps them in particular,	276	Priest 32	3
if hee may bee of the Commission of Peace, there is nothing to that:	276	Priest 32	8
And whereas there are usually three Objections made against	276	Priest 32	18
When there is a Parliament, he is to endeavour by all means to be	277	Priest 32	9
he is to endeavour by all means to be a Knight or Burgess there;	277	Priest 32	10
for there is no School to a Parliament.	277	Priest 32	10
And when he is there, he must not only be a morning man,	277	Priest 32	11
for there the particulars are exactly discussed, which are brought	277	Priest 32	12
the Artifices, and Manufactures there, transplant them hither,	278	Priest 32	9
there being a promise, that if the Kingdome of God be first sought,	278	Priest 33	12
there were no such Physician as he, both for skill and tendernesse.	278	Priest 33	31
that there is a double state of a Christian even in this Life,	280	Priest 34	1
some poore afflicted soul, and there be bountifull, and liberall;	281	Priest 34	3
that there is none that can or will look after things, but all goes	281	Priest 34	8
though there be a great Governour of all things, yet to them he is	281	Priest 34	9
doth forsake and persecute them, and there is none to deliver them.	281	Priest 34	11
there may be so evident, though unused a proof of Divinity taken from	281	Priest 34	32
(there being no reason, why any should distrust Saint Luke,	282	Priest 34	20
There are two Prophesies in the Gospel, which evidently argue Christs	282	Priest 34	22
If there be any ill in the custome, that may be severed from	283	Priest 35	31
because there are contained therein 4 manifest advantages.	284	Priest 35	2
with reconciling of differences at that time, if there be any:	284	Priest 35	7
where he knowes there hath been or is a little difference,	284	Priest 35	19
There is much preaching in this friendliness.	284	Priest 35	21
Another old Custome there is of saying, when light is brought in,	284	Priest 35	22
From this ill temper there remained little else to be expected of me,	291	Cornaro	24
the Physicians told me that yet there was one help for me,	292	Cornaro	3
to that exigent, that there would be no help for me, but Death,	292	Cornaro	15

THERE (cont'd)	PAGE	TITLE		LINE
For there is no malignitie of old age in the humours of my bodie,	296	Cornaro		36
especially since there is a greater diversitie of tempers,	297	Cornaro		30
But surely there is no such matter, if Temperance be wanting.	298	Cornaro		21
there needs not many and curious things, but onely that a man should	299	Cornaro		7
and the cause being taken away, there is no place for the effect.	300	Cornaro		2
Let no man here object unto me, That there are many, who,	300	Cornaro		17
and husbandrie, whereof in this age there is great plentie.	301	Cornaro		37
Now lest there should be any delight wanting to my old age,	302	Cornaro		37
there are some things which I like not in him, as my fragments will	304	Valdesso		16
I doe so love him, that were there nothing else, I would Print it,	305	Valdesso		7
learned and perfect in them, there is somewhat to be learned more:	309	Valdesso		24
there the case is plaine, Cornelius had revelation, yet Peter was	310	Valdesso		8
in the Church of God there is one fundamentall, but else variety.	312	Valdesso		2
There are two sorts of acts in religion;	312	Valdesso	V	23
In indifferent things there is roome for motions [notions]	313	Valdesso		12
except there be a restraining motion (as S. Paul had when hee would	313	Valdesso		15
There is a judgment of authority (upon a fact) and there is	316	Valdesso		35
of authority (upon a fact) and there is a judgment of the Learned;	317	Valdesso		1
whereas there is not onely milke there, but strong meat also.	317	Valdesso		23
whereas there is not onely milke there, but strong meat also.	317	Valdesso		24
There is no more to be said of this Chapter but that his opinion	318	Valdesso		5
But there are other Cases of Conscience grounded on Piety	319	Valdesso	V	30
When a friend askes, there is no to morrow.	322	Proverbs		32
Were there no fooles, badd ware would not passe.	323	Proverbs		66
Were there no hearers, there would be no backbiters.	323	Proverbs		69
Where you thinke there is bacon, there is no Chimney.	324	Proverbs		99
Men speake of the faire, as things went with them there.	326	Proverbs		151
Where there is no honour, there is no griefe.	327	Proverbs		186
Where the drink goes in, there the wit goes out.	327	Proverbs		187
In great pedigrees there are Governours and Chandlers.	328	Proverbs		222
There are more men threatned then stricken.	329	Proverbs		256
There is more talke then trouble.	330	Proverbs		265
There would bee no great ones if there were no little ones.	331	Proverbs		292
There would bee no great ones if there were no mean ones.	331	Proverbs	V	292
There were no ill language, if it were not ill taken.	331	Proverbs		294
He that makes his bed ill, lies there.	332	Proverbs		340
There are three waies, the Universities, the Sea, the Court.	334	Proverbs		383
the longer he stayes there, the fowler he is.	335	Proverbs		409
Woe to the house where there is no chiding.	336	Proverbs		450
There is no jollitie but hath a smack of folly.	338	Proverbs		493
Every one fastens where there is gaine.	338	Proverbs		496
There are many waies to fame.	339	Proverbs		539
when there are many to strike on one Anvile.	340	Proverbs		551
There is great force hidden in a sweet command.	341	Proverbs		589
shee had never sought her daughter there.	344	Proverbs		696
Where there is peace, God is.	345	Proverbs		733
In an hundred elles of contention, there is not an inch of love.	348	Proverbs		817
There comes nought out of the sacke but what was there.	348	Proverbs		833
There come nought out of the sacke but what was there.	348	Proverbs	V	833
He quits his place well, that leaves his friend there.	350	Proverbs		875
There needs a long time to know the worlds pulse.	350	Proverbs		886
There are more Physitians in health then drunkards.	351	Proverbs		903
that a man would desire straight to bee buried there.	353	Proverbs		969
If the husband be not at home, there is nobodie.	354	Proverbs		1016
There is no heat of affection but is joyned	357	Proverbs	D	1050
There's no such conquering weapon as the necessity of conquering.	357	Proverbs	D	1064
To seek in a Sheep five feet when there is but four.	359	Proverbs	D	1112
There is no man, though never so little,	359	Proverbs	D	1119
There is a remedy for every thing, could men find it.	360	Proverbs	D	1142
There is an hour wherein a man might be happy	360	Proverbs	D	1143
There is no body will go to hell for company.	361	Proverbs	D	1177
come a Horse-back, there is reason, that my desires should go a-foot;	363	Letters		23
What Trades-man is there who will set up without his Tools?	364	Letters		14
if there be any truth in me, I find it little enough to keep me in	364	Letters		31
also I ride to Newmarket, and there lie a day or two for fresh Air;	365	Letters		7
there be any course, either by engaging my future Annuity,	365	Letters		20
and if there be any such which you have found useful to yourself,	366	Letters		4
Let there be no kind of excellency which it is possible for you	366	Letters		13
not with a foolish vanting of yourself when there is no caus,	366	Letters		17
not but first certifies you that there are come agents hither from	368	Letters		4
There is a Spanish Lawyer hath written a treatise concerning	368	Letters		25
There is a Frenchman who writt a poem heere in England & presented it	368	Letters		30
of the Pedler and the Pack on London-bridge, for there he assigns me.	370	Letters		28
and will not allow any room there for such an in-mate as Grief;	374	Letters		11
only one place more to you (Philip. 4. 4.) St. Paul saith there:	374	Letters		21
It is true there is a third sister, whom to receive were the greatest	375	Letters		23
If there fall out yet any rubb, you shall heare of me;	377	Letters		22
are lovely, & of good report if there be any vertue or any praise.	380	Woodnoth		14
First there is seaven hundred pounds in Mr Thomas Lawleys hands	382	G.H.'s Will		7
MS. that there are divers moneys of mine in Mr Stephens hands	383	G.H.'s Will		22
if there be any body els that owe me any thing else of old debt I	383	G.H.'s Will		26
your selves, wee justly feare that there is nothing here answerable	442	Oration		29
For amongst us what glorious shew is there, either of garments,	442	Oration		31
since there is a two-fold brightnesse which dazeleth the eyes of men,	442	Oration		33
THEREBY				
A fault, which needs it most, grows two thereby.	9	Ch.-Porch		78
A mast'ring minde; so both are lost thereby:	10	Ch.-Porch		104
That feeds on dung, is coloured thereby.	15	Ch.-Porch		234
Envie not greatnesse: for thou mak'st thereby	16	Ch.-Porch		259
Poore death! and who was hurt thereby?	169	Dial.-Anth		5

THESE (cont'd)	PAGE	TITLE		LINE
This is thy house, with these it doth abound:	137	Familie		21
And where these are not found,	137	Familie		22
Those have their hopes; these what they have renounce,	138	The Size		21
Those are at home; these journey still,	138	The Size		23
These seas are tears, and heav'n the haven.	138	The Size		47
With these two poore ones lick up all the dew,	140	Ch.-rents		29
These parcell out thy heart: recover these,	147	Offering		17
These speak and chide,	150	Longing		70
By these thy feet, at which my heart	150	Longing		80
O take these barres, these lengths away;	163	The Search		49
These contrarieties crush me: these crosse actions	165	The Crosse		32
And yet since these thy contradictions	165	The Crosse		34
These are thy wonders, Lord of power,	166	The Flower		15
These are thy wonders, Lord of love,	167	The Flower		43
These are the pleasures here.	167	Dotage		6
These are the sorrows here.	167	Dotage		12
Yet slight not these few words:	168	a true Hymn		6
These arms shall crush thee. Spare not, do thy worst.	169	Dial.-Anth		8
So do these words a sweet content,	174	The Odour		4
With these all day I do perfume my minde,	175	The Odour		6
That these two words might creep & grow	175	The Odour		14
But these are high perfections:	185	The Elixer	W	21
In both of these Prowesse and Arts did tame	192	Ch.-Milit.		75
From all these places, but at divers times,	195	Ch.-Milit.		185
And blending these he carri'd all mens eyes,	195	Ch.-Milit.		189
To these diminishings, as is between	196	Ch.-Milit.		233
Whether in these gifts thou bee so	200	H. Commun.	W	2
Which warme these lines, & serve them up to thee	204	Persever.	W	2
But what shall issue, whither these my words	204	Persever.	W	5
My Eyes, from whence these Tears did spring,	214	Convert	D	6
he constituted Deputies in his place, and these are Priests.	225	Priest 1		9
therefore he hath throughly studied these, that he may be an absolute	227	Priest 3		8
Yet in these points he labours most in those things which are most	227	Priest 3		10
These he hath digested severally.	228	Priest 4		26
But for the understanding of these;	228	Priest 4		27
By these and other means the Parson procures attention;	233	Priest 7		22
of the presence, and majesty of God, by these, or such like speeches.	234	Priest 7		26
and these exhortations he cals his privy purse, even as Princes have	236	Priest 8		16
and by these hee keeps his body tame, serviceable, and healthfull;	237	Priest 9		26
his state of Life, which are principally these two, Spirituall pride,	238	Priest 9		2
against these ghostly enemies he girdeth up his loynes,	238	Priest 9		3
These and many other spirituall wickednesses in high places doth	238	Priest 9		19
These save man the labour, and doing that which either he could	241	Priest 10		31
that not onely sicknesse breaks these obligations of fasting,	242	Priest 10		35
But these he helps not without some testimony, except the evidence	245	Priest 12		21
For though these testimonies also may be falsifyed, yet considering	245	Priest 12		23
yet considering that the Law allows these in case they be true,	245	Priest 12		24
For these two rules comprize and include the double object of our	246	Priest 13		29
After these discourses, if they be poor and needy, whom he thus finds	248	Priest 14		9
Besides these occasionall discourses, the Parson questions what order	248	Priest 14		30
If the Parson were ashamed of particularizing in these things,	249	Priest 14		1
These are the Parsons generall aims in his Circuit;	249	Priest 14		9
but with these he mingles other discourses for conversation sake,	249	Priest 14		10
as he finds any defect in these, hee first considers with himselfe,	251	Priest 17		25
Those he Catechizeth publickly, these privately, giving age honour,	255	Priest 21		24
requiring answers to all these, and helping and cherishing	256	Priest 21		13
Yet the skill consists but in these three points:	256	Priest 21		30
the Parson hath diligently examined these two with himselfe,	262	Priest 24		32
These and the like points hee hath accurately digested,	263	Priest 24		14
because the natures of these vices being not evidently discussed,	264	Priest 26		17
concerning these two vices, not because they are all that are of this	265	Priest 26		1
if in all these, and those more which concerne me, I either do	265	Priest 26		16
Country people are full of these petty injustices, being cunning	265	Priest 26		34
And Scholers ought to be diligent in the observation of these,	265	Priest 26		36
These three rules generally comprehend the faults of eating,	266	Priest 26		12
One act in these things is bad, but it is the custome and habit that	266	Priest 26		17
These are the five shields, wherewith the Godly receive the darts	269	Priest 28		18
But these prayers are not necessary, but additionary.	272	Priest 31		28
These are so far from deterring any good man from the place,	276	Priest 32		22
When none of these occasions call him abroad, every morning that hee	277	Priest 32		14
After the severall knowledg of these, he adviseth to insist and dwell	277	Priest 32		36
But if the young Gallant think these Courses dull, and phlegmatick,	278	Priest 32		4
These two states were in our Saviour, not only in the beginning	280	Priest 34		7
To these might be added the Preaching of the Gospel in all Nations,	282	Priest 34		31
14. which we see even miraculously effected in these new discoveryes,	282	Priest 34		33
With some of these heads enlarged, and woven into his discourse,	283	Priest 34		3
are either such as are made known by common fame (and of these,	287	Priest 37		13
Of these also men may talk, and more, they may discover them to those	287	Priest 37		16
yet by these thy conflicts, and seemingly hazards, didst thou arise	288	Priest		33
and yet all these I found hurtfull.	293	Cornaro		14
I forsook all these kinde of meats and drinks, and chose that wine	293	Cornaro		15
yet these forenamed things have also their force.	293	Cornaro		34
Yet could I not so avoid all these, but that now and then I fell into	293	Cornaro		38
That they who in these two things that enter in at the mouth,	294	Cornaro		4
and therefore never was sick by any of these inconveniences,	294	Cornaro		9
all these did hurt me little, whereas they hurt them very much who	294	Cornaro		14
But all these things could not defend me against their importunities.	296	Cornaro		5
What Physician could have discovered these hidden qualities to me,	297	Cornaro		34
these Belly-gods say, that an orderly life is so hard a thing that it	298	Cornaro		36
But they who finde benefit in these meats, may, yea ought to use	300	Cornaro		10

THESE (cont'd)	PAGE	TITLE		LINE
But these erre greatly, as I will shew by my self, recounting	300	Cornaro		30
All these things I do at my ease, and at fit seasons, and in mine own	301	Cornaro		9
These are the delights and solaces of my old age, which is altogether	302	Cornaro		22
because at these yeares (viz. 83) I have made a most pleasant	302	Cornaro		28
to publish it, for these three eminent things observable therein:	304	Valdesso		18
These three things are very eminent in the Author, and overweigh	305	Valdesso		12
These words about the H. Scripture suite with what he writes	306	Valdesso		15
and Consid. 94. upon these words:	307	Valdesso		17
Of these none can free themselves of themselves, but only	308	Valdesso		8
Of these the heathen freed themselves, only by the generall	308	Valdesso		11
In the Scripture are Doctrines, these ever teach more and more.	310	Valdesso		13
In the Scripture are Promises, these ever comfort more and more.	310	Valdesso		14
These in diverse cases ought, and were of old forborn for a time.	312	Valdesso	V	27
For as for these, pious persons ought alwaies to avoid them:	314	Valdesso		19
and we meet with two sorts of these Saints of the world;	319	Valdesso	V	22
in a zeal against these, and in a strict performance of a few cheap	319	Valdesso	V	24
To seek these things is lost labour; Geese in an oyle pot,	361	Proverbs	D	1163
my meaning (dear Mother) is in these Sonnets, to declare my	363	Letters		10
pardon my boldness, and consider but these three things.	365	Letters		16
and both pay for the surplusage of these Books, and for ever after	367	Letters		11
of this demand of the Kings these Agents pretend they have no	368	Letters		14
These are the things I am to acquaint you with, of whose rude	369	Letters		1
to requite these pains, he takes place next the Doctors,	370	Letters		1
Can I be so happy, as to hear of both these that they succeed well?	371	Letters		10
I beseech you let such thoughts as these, moderate your present fear	374	Letters		3
being more beggarly now than I have been these many years,	376	Letters		1
unto my deare wife excepting onely these legacies hereafter insuing.	382	G.H.'s Will		7
all these are over and above their wages, To Sara thirteene shillings	382	G.H.'s Will		26
Yet doe not yee contemne these our slight glories, which wee raise	442	Oration		38
we for your gracious acceptance of these poore duties wish,	443	Oration		5
THESSALONIANS				
according to St. Pauls rule, Ephes. 4. 28. 1 Thes. 4. 11, 12.	275	Priest 32		2
THEY				
Yet not mine neither: for from thee they came,	5	Dedication		2
Whose twigs are pleasures, & they whip thee bare,	6	Ch.-Porch	W	9
If they dare try, a glorious life, or grave.	10	Ch.-Porch		90
Not that they all are so; but that the most	10	Ch.-Porch		95
Not that they are all so; but that the most	10	Ch.-Porch	W	95
Or els they breed them tender, make them need	10	Ch.-Porch		105
All that they leave: this is flat povertie.	10	Ch.-Porch		106
Spend not on hopes. They that by pleading clothes	14	Ch.-Porch		181
And are her sureties, ere they are a friends.	17	Ch.-Porch		282
Entice all neatly to what they know best;	18	Ch.-Porch		295
Be usefull where thou livest, that they may	19	Ch.-Porch		325
They dye in holes where glory never shone.	20	Ch.-Porch	W	348
Strike off all scores; none are so cleare as they.	20	Ch.-Porch		360
In time they'l runne thee out of all thy wit.	21	Ch.-Porch		366
Open for thee; or they may come too late.	21	Ch.-Porch	W	384
They may weep out the stains by them did rise:	23	Ch.-Porch		417
They drink with greedinesse a full damnation.	24	Ch.-Porch		448
Look not on pleasures as they come, but go.	24	Ch.-Porch		458
Against their Maker: they do wish me dead,	26	Sacrifice		6
They use that power against me, which I gave:	27	Sacrifice		11
Arise, arise, they come. Look how they runne!	27	Sacrifice		33
Alas! what haste they make to be undone!	27	Sacrifice		34
How with their lanterns do they seek the sunne!	27	Sacrifice		35
With clubs and staves they seek me, as a thief,	27	Sacrifice		37
See, they lay hold on me, not with the hands	28	Sacrifice		45
Betwixt my friends and me. They leave the starre,	28	Sacrifice		50
Betwixt my friends and me. They leave that starre,	28	Sacrifice	W	50
They leade me; urging, that it was not sound	28	Sacrifice		54
Then they accuse me of great blasphemie,	28	Sacrifice		61
Then they condemne me all with that same breath,	28	Sacrifice		69
They binde, and leade me unto Herod: he	29	Sacrifice		73
Heark how they crie aloud still, Crucifie:	29	Sacrifice		97
It is not fit he live a day, they crie,	29	Sacrifice		98
Pilate a stranger holdeth off; but they,	29	Sacrifice		101
Yet still they shout, and crie, and stop their eares,	30	Sacrifice		105
They choose a murderer, and all agree	30	Sacrifice		113
He clave the stonie rock, when they were drie;	30	Sacrifice		122
Ah! how they scourge me! yet my tendernesse	30	Sacrifice		125
They buffet me, and box me as they list,	30	Sacrifice		129
They buffet him, and box him as they list,	30	Sacrifice	W	129
Behold, they spit on me in scornfull wise,	31	Sacrifice		133
My face they cover, though it be divine.	31	Sacrifice		137
Servants and abjects flout me; they are wittie:	31	Sacrifice		141
So they in me denie themselves all pitie:	31	Sacrifice		143
There they deride me, they abuse me all:	31	Sacrifice		154
Then with a scarlet robe they me aray;	31	Sacrifice		157
Then with the reed they gave to me before,	32	Sacrifice		169
Then with the reed they gave mee heertofore,	32	Sacrifice	W	169
They strike my head, the rock from whence all store	32	Sacrifice		170
They bow their knees to me, and cry, Hail king:	32	Sacrifice		173
I am the floore, the sink, where they it fling:	32	Sacrifice		175
Thus trimmed forth they bring me to the rout,	32	Sacrifice		185
They leade me in once more, and putting then	32	Sacrifice		189
Mine own clothes on, they leade me out agen.	32	Sacrifice		190
They carrie me to my most bitter crosse:	33	Sacrifice		195
They gave me vineger mingled with gall,	34	Sacrifice		237
They give me vineger mingled with gall,	34	Sacrifice	W	237

THEY (cont'd)

	PAGE	TITLE		LINE
But more with malice: yet, when they did call,	34	Sacrifice		238
They part my garments, and by lot dispose	34	Sacrifice		241
For they will pierce my side, I full well know;	34	Sacrifice		246
They told me there, that he was lately gone	40	Redemption		6
For they can lodge transgressions by the score:	40	Sepulchre		6
They leave thee.	40	Sepulchre		8
If they should offer to contest	42	Easter		25
With thy arising, they presume.	42	Easter		26
Yet though my flours be lost, they say	42	Easter	W	27
Or else give tears to drown them, as they grow.	44	H. Bapt.1		9
Deliver us to laws; they send us bound	45	Sinne 1		3
Are blowne away, as if they nere had bin.	46	Sinne 1	W	14
But as th' outworks, they may controll	52	H.Commun.		16
Which siding with invention, they together	54	Love 1		6
The world is theirs; they two play out the game,	54	Love 1		10
Dust blown by wit, till that they both were blinde:	54	Love 2		10
They grow unruly, and sit in thy bowers.	56	Temper 2		12
May no lines passe, except they do their dutie	56	Jordan 1		4
If they might mend their wages, and serve here.	59	Whitsunday		12
They can do more.	61	Praise 1		16
Who have a work, as well as they,	61	Praise 1		19
What were they all, compar'd to thine?	62	Afflict.2		8
Wherein if they were set,	62	Afflict.2		9
They would discolour thy most bloudy sweat.	62	Afflict.2		10
Yet studies them, not him by whom they be.	63	Mattens		16
When they shall bow, and kneel, and fall down flat	65	Ch.-monum.		15
To kisse those heaps, which now they have in trust?	65	Ch.-monum.		16
For though sinnes plead too, yet like stones they make	66	Ch.-lock		11
When they combine and mingle, bring	68	Windows		12
(For he would not) as they beheld the grace	70	Humilitie		18
Till they fell out: which when the beasts espied,	70	Humilitie		21
They leapt upon the throne;	70	Humilitie		22
They had depos'd each one.	70	Humilitie		24
They drive them soon away;	71	Humilitie		30
They who lament one crosse,	73	Afflict.3		17
Glitter, and curle, and winde as they:	74	The Starre		26
Setting in order what they tumble:	75	Sunday	W	5
They are the fruitfull beds and borders	75	Sunday		26
They are the rows of fruitfull trees	75	Sunday	W	26
As good go any where, they say,	80	Deniall		11
They and my minde may chime,	80	Deniall		29
They and my hart may chime,	80	Deniall	W	29
They and my soule may chime,	80	Deniall	WC	29
Whereas they were supported by the same:	84	The World		4
Which they effected, none could them withstand.	84	The World		18
They appeare trim and drest	85	Vanitie 1		20
And grumble oft, that they have more in me	89	The Pearl		28
While they do wound and prick my soul.	90	Afflict.4		12
While they do wound and pinke my soul.	90	Afflict.4	W	12
Parrats may thank us, if they are not mute,	91	Man		11
They go upon the score.	91	Man		12
Herbs gladly cure our flesh; because that they	91	Man		23
But time did becken to the flowers, and they	94	Life		4
Who reade a chapter when they rise,	96	Charms & K		1
Grace turnes the Optick, then they fall.	97	Charms & K	W	18
They step into their voluntarie graves,	98	Mortific.		8
Is my God this way? no, they would reply:	99	Decay		8
They are of cloth,	100	Miserie		17
They would not have their actions scann'd,	100	Miserie		21
Nor any sorrow tell them that they sinne,	100	Miserie		22
They quarrell thee, and would give over	100	Miserie		25
As dirtie hands foul all they touch,	101	Miserie		37
They will be kind, and all his pains requite,	101	Miserie	W	46
They make his life a constant blot,	102	Miserie		63
Such was their lustre, they did so excell,	102	Jordan 2		2
As flames do work and winde, when they ascend,	103	Jordan 2		13
If this poore paper do as much as they.	104	Obedience		5
They were by winged souls	105	Obedience		44
And ever as they mount, like larks they sing;	107	Sion		23
And scouling on them as they pin'd away,	108	Home		45
Some may dream merrily, but when they wake,	108	Home		51
They dresse themselves and come to thee.	108	Home		52
For all they either painted are,	109	Brit. Ch.		11
And then they have their answer home.	111	The Quip		24
For they can never be at rest,	111	Vanitie 2		15
Till they regain their ancient nest.	111	Vanitie 2		16
To hold my quill? shall they not do thee right?	116	Providence		4
Are brought to Man, while they are lame and mute.	117	Providence		12
The sacrifice for all; while they below	117	Providence		14
Lay hands on all: they are thy right and left.	117	Providence		34
Tempests are calm to thee; they know thy hand,	118	Providence		45
The great prey on the lesse, they on some weed.	118	Providence		52
Flies have their table spread, ere they appeare.	118	Providence		54
When they are callow; but withdraw their food	118	Providence		63
When they are fledge, that need may teach them flying.	118	Providence		64
Bees work for man; and yet they never bruise	118	Providence		65
The windes, who think they rule the mariner,	119	Providence		91
If they seek fine things, thou dost make them run	120	Providence		106
When they are ripe, their odour will ascend,	120	Providence		119
How harsh are thorns to pears! and yet they make	120	Providence		121

THEY (cont'd)

	PAGE	TITLE		LINE
All things that are, though they have sev'rall wayes,	121	Providence		145
Untill their cockatrice they hatch and bring:	122	Sinnes rd.		4
And when they once have perfected their draughts,	122	Sinnes rd.		5
They vent the wares, and passe them with their faults,	122	Sinnes rd.		9
They vent the wares, and passe them with their fauts	122	Sinnes rd.	V	9
Yet ill deeds loyter not: for they supplie	122	Sinnes rd.		16
For they that taste it do rehearse,	125	Peace		33
They are too subtill for the subt'llest hearts;	126	Confession		11
We are the earth; and they,	126	Confession		13
And till they foot and clutch their prey,	126	Confession		15
They never cool, much lesse give out.	126	Confession		16
No smith can make such locks, but they have keyes:	126	Confession		17
Doth shut them out, so that they cannot enter;	126	Confession		20
Or, if they enter, cannot rest,	126	Confession		21
They shall be thick and cloudie to my breast.	126	Confession		30
Sure they would move	132	The Storm		4
They purge the aire without, within the breast.	132	The Storm		18
Just so the other heav'n they also serve,	134	Divinitie		5
Which with the edge of wit they cut and carve.	134	Divinitie		7
As if they had a part?	136	Familie		2
Yet speak they louder then distemper'd fears.	137	Familie		19
Title to more hereafter when they part,	137	The Size		3
Those have their hopes; these what they have renounce,	138	The Size		21
They would great frosts and snows destroy:	138	The Size		40
They rushed in, and cast them in the dirt	140	Ch.-rents		23
They ask enough; why shouldst thou further go?	145	Discharge		26
Things present shrink and die: but they that spend	145	Discharge		41
And alone, when they replied,	146	Praise 2		15
Their infants, them; and they suck thee	148	Longing		17
Their infants, them; and they seek thee	148	Longing	V	17
And when they ask'd, what he would wear;	151	The Bag		16
They quickly go and come with lesser crime:	154	Glimpse		9
Lime begg'd of old, (they say),	154	Glimpse		13
Did weep to heav'n, they found a bottle there	158	Praise 3		27
And both would runne untill they found a biere	159	Jos.coat		8
But since those great ones, be they ne're so great,	161	Priesthood		19
As if to meet thee they did know,	162	The Search		11
Unlesse they get new conduits, new supplies	164	Grief		7
To see their mother-root, when they have blown;	166	The Flower		11
Where they together	166	The Flower		12
If truly said, they may take part	168	a true Hymn		7
Which they that know the rest, know more then I.	169	The Answer		14
And surging griefs, when they grew bold, controll,	172	The Glance		15
Deeper then they, in words, and works, and thoughts.	173	Marie Magd		12
(As sweet things traffick when they meet)	175	The Odour		27
But must they have my brain? must they dispark	176	Forerunners		3
Yet have they left me, Thou art still my God.	176	Forerunners		6
Let foolish lovers, if they will love dung,	177	Forerunners		25
As if they could beautie spare.	177	The Rose		8
For they all produce repentance,	178	The Rose		27
Happy are they that dare	185	The Elixer	W	22
And show them as they are.	185	The Elixer	W	24
Lest at length they plead possession:	187	Dooms-day		16
That they in merit shall excell.	187	Judgement		10
What leaves are they? impart the matter wholly.	188	Heaven		9
Light, joy, and leisure; but shall they persever?	188	Heaven		19
To Egypt first she came, where they did prove	191	Ch.-Milit.		37
Who, that they might subdue, made all their foes.	191	Ch.-Milit.		62
(For no lesse Harbingers would serve then they)	192	Ch.-Milit.		84
So they might still, and point us out the place	192	Ch.-Milit.		85
Fresh and fine deities. They were at great cost,	193	Ch.-Milit.		109
And this is all the Rock, whereof they boast,	194	Ch.-Milit.		159
They who rely on them must reckon twice	194	Ch.-Milit.	W	160
But when they were unto the Sorbon come,	196	Ch.-Milit.	W	202
The waight was such they left the doctrins there	196	Ch.-Milit.	W	203
They are hells land-marks, Satans double crest:	196	Ch.-Milit.		219
They are Sinnes nipples, feeding th' east and west.	196	Ch.-Milit.		220
They have their times of Gospel, ev'n as we.	197	Ch.-Milit.		248
They have their time of Gospel, ev'n as we.	197	Ch.-Milit.	W	248
We are more poore, and they more rich by this.	197	Ch.-Milit.		254
They have their period also and set times	197	Ch.-Milit.		261
That when they have accomplished the round,	197	Ch.-Milit.		267
That when they have accomplished their round,	197	Ch.-Milit.	W	267
Follow the Church & sunn where ere they fly.	198	Ch.-Milit.	W	273
Shall they be food & strength & might	201	H. Commun.	W	35
Even there, where they deceive?	201	H. Commun.	W	36
Nor can they change their bounds & meres,	201	H. Commun.	W	41
See, they breake in	204	The Knell	W	10
That they may bee	204	The Knell	W	16
And pace of thy swift vertues; onely they	211	Bohemia	D	5
When all things pull & hale, that they may bring	212	Bohemia	D	27
Children for kingdomes to thee; they shall live	212	Bohemia	D	42
Shall flow no more - until they bring	214	Convert	D	8
The wicked are not so, but they	215	Psalm I	D	13
many are they that rise	216	Psalm III	D	2
they vainly have rebell'd:	219	Psalm V	D	34
and not to think, that when they have read the Fathers, or Schoolmen,	226	Priest 2		11
whose duty and obligation being the same to the Houses they live in,	226	Priest 2		17
and because they have different Names, think their Office different.	226	Priest 2		20
Doubtlesse they are Parsons of the families they live in,	226	Priest 2		21

THEY (cont'd)

	PAGE	TITLE	LINE
Doubtlesse they are Parsons of the families they live in, . .	226	Priest 2	22
Before they are in Orders, they may be received for Companions,	226	Priest 2	23
are in Orders, they may be received for Companions, or discoursers;	226	Priest 2	24
Wherfore they are not to be over-submissive, and base, but to keep up	226	Priest 2	27
They who do not thus, while they remember their earthly Lord,	226	Priest 2	31
while they remember their earthly Lord, do much forget their	226	Priest 2	32
they wrong the Priesthood, neglect their duty, and shall be so farre	226	Priest 2	33
so farre from that which they seek with their over-submissivenesse,	226	Priest 2	34
and cringings, that they shall ever be despised.	226	Priest 2	35
They who for the hope of promotion neglect any necessary admonition,	226	Priest 2	36
For sins make all equall, whom they finde together; . . .	227	Priest 3	28
and then they are worst, who ought to be best.	227	Priest 3	28
neither will they beleeve him in the pulpit, whom they cannot trust	228	Priest 3	7
him in the pulpit, whom they cannot trust in his Conversation.	228	Priest 3	8
They say, it is an ill Mason that refuseth any stone: . . .	228	Priest 4	14
because people by what they understand, are best led to what they	228	Priest 4	20
by what they understand, are best led to what they understand not.	228	Priest 4	20
because they feel them not, and because they are not understood	228	Priest 4	31
and because they are not understood but with the same Spirit that	228	Priest 4	31
they were reproved, as ignorant of what spirit they were. . .	229	Priest 4	13
they were reproved, as ignorant of what spirit they were. . .	229	Priest 4	14
so that they neither decline to the right hand, nor to the left.	230	Priest 5	22
to a reverence, which they forget againe, when they come to pray,	231	Priest 6	14
when they come to pray, as a devout behaviour in the very act	231	Priest 6	15
in them, but causing them, when they sit, or stand, or kneel,	231	Priest 6	25
of their answer, but gently and pausably, thinking what they say;	231	Priest 6	33
so that while they answer, As it was in the beginning, &c. . .	231	Priest 6	33
they meditate as they speak, that God hath ever had his people,	231	Priest 6	34
or offer up such sacrifices as they did of old, which was of beasts	232	Priest 6	4
and of theirs also who gaze upon them when they come in, . .	232	Priest 6	11
admonitions, if they persevere, he causes them to be presented:	232	Priest 6	13
notwithstanding his instruction that they ought not to be so,	232	Priest 6	15
but even to let the world sinke, so they do their duty; . .	232	Priest 6	16
but stories and sayings they will well remember.	233	Priest 7	18
in our hearts, before they come into our mouths, truly affecting,	233	Priest 7	30
that they may come with holy hearts, and awfull mindes into . .	235	Priest 8	29
all those, who come with lesse prepared hearts then they ought.	235	Priest 8	31
as that neither they want a competent sustentation, nor her husband	239	Priest 10	18
that they get a delight in it, and enter favour with God, . .	239	Priest 10	28
servants, both because they do best, and because what they do,	240	Priest 10	15
both because they do best, and because what they do, is blessed,	240	Priest 10	16
and they all account, that to teach the ignorant is the greatest	240	Priest 10	22
And when they go abroad, his wife among her neighbours is . .	240	Priest 10	27
requires of all to pray by themselves before they sleep at night,	241	Priest 10	2
and knows what prayers they say, and till they have learned them,	241	Priest 10	3
and till they have learned them, makes them kneel by him; . .	241	Priest 10	3
act in them, then when they are called to others prayers, and that,	241	Priest 10	5
which when they leave the family, they carry with them. . .	241	Priest 10	6
which when they leave the family, they carry with them. . .	241	Priest 10	7
for there being two things, which as they are, are unuseful to man,	241	Priest 10	27
which they can better emplcy to their own advantage, and sutably	243	Priest 11	15
and will not be perswaded, but being not invited, they are hated.	243	Priest 11	22
that so both they may be encouraged to persevere, and others spurred	243	Priest 11	26
others spurred to do well, that they may enjoy the like courtesie.	243	Priest 11	27
men to Piety, and is content, if at least so, they will become good:	244	Priest 11	1
for then they will reckon upon it, as on a debt;	244	Priest 12	28
though justly, they will murmur, and repine as much, as he that is	244	Priest 12	29
paines in their vocation, as not knowing when they shal be relieved;	245	Priest 12	4
which otherwise they would reckon upon, and turn to idlenesse.	245	Priest 12	4
yet considering that the Law allows these in case they be true,	245	Priest 12	24
may go the right way, and thither onely, where they are onely due.	245	Priest 12	34
and Font be as they ought, for those great duties that are performed	246	Priest 13	7
So that they excellently score out the way, and fully, and exactly	246	Priest 13	32
For there he shall find his flock most naturally as they are,	247	Priest 14	6
which they put on as their holy-day cloathes, and come to Church in	247	Priest 14	8
that they dive not too deep into worldly affairs, plunging themselves	247	Priest 14	24
but that they so labour, as neither to labour anxiously, . .	247	Priest 14	26
Then they labour anxiously, when they overdo it, to the loss of their	247	Priest 14	27
labour anxiously, when they overdo it, to the loss of their quiet,	247	Priest 14	28
when they doubt Gods providence, thinking that their own labour is	247	Priest 14	29
Then they labour profanely, when they set themselves to work like	247	Priest 14	32
when they set themselves to work like brute beasts, never raising	247	Priest 14	32
when on the Iords day they do unnecessary servile work, . .	248	Priest 14	2
as that they make not that the end of their labour, but that they may	248	Priest 14	6
but that they may have wherewithall to serve God the better,	248	Priest 14	7
if they be poor and needy, whom he thus finds labouring, . .	248	Priest 14	9
that so they go on more cheerfully in their vocation, and himself be	248	Priest 14	11
for they are not sensible of finenesse:	248	Priest 14	17
if they be of higher quality, they commonly are quick, and sensible,	248	Priest 14	18
the afflicted, though they can, and otherwise ought to come to him.	249	Priest 15	16
that if any be willing to partake, they may resort thither. . .	251	Priest 17	12
them cleerly, that they respect them most, who wish them best,	251	Priest 17	30
spirits, and possesse them even before they themselves heed it.	252	Priest 18	7
as they hear the answers prove, may when they come home, . .	255	Priest 21	27
answers prove, may when they come home, either commend or reprove,	255	Priest 21	28
of questions in the one, so they farre exceed them in the other.	257	Priest 21	23
and upon what termes, and with what vowes they were Baptized.	258	Priest 22	20
which while they deferr, both sides suffer;	259	Priest 22	4
in any Controversie, that they should resort to him as their Judge.	259	Priest 23	32
of that, wherin they are most eminent, is the most gainfull way	260	Priest 23	6

THEY (cont'd)

	PAGE	TITLE	LINE
but that they still fall from all compromises that have been made.	260	Priest 23	24
as they may be an help, and a recreation to more divine studies,	261	Priest 23	10
is the main foundation, and pillar of their cause, whereon they rely;	262	Priest 24	29
while they consider, that God cannot be wanting to them in Doctrine,	263	Priest 24	19
who when they know a sin evidently, they commit it not. . .	264	Priest 26	11
they are long a knowing it, being partiall to themselves, . .	264	Priest 26	12
not because they are all that are of this dark, and creeping	265	Priest 26	2
for example sake, and because they are most common, he thus thinks:	265	Priest 26	3
that servants for their mony are as other things that they buy,	265	Priest 26	25
even as a piece of wood, which they may cut, or hack, or throw into	265	Priest 26	25
throw into the fire, and so they pay them their wages, all is well.	265	Priest 26	26
which while they dwell in their bookes, they will never finde;	266	Priest 26	1
which while they dwell in their bookes, they will never finde;	266	Priest 26	2
and doing their duty faithfully, they will soon discover: . .	266	Priest 26	3
especially if they carry their eyes ever open, and fix them on their	266	Priest 26	4
they cannot wel dispatch) nor of their estate, nor of their brethren.	266	Priest 26	16
Many think they are at more liberty then they are, as if they were	266	Priest 26	18
Many think they are at more liberty then they are, as if they were	266	Priest 26	19
as if they were Masters of their health, and so they will stand	266	Priest 26	19
of their health, and so they will stand to the pain, all is well.	266	Priest 26	20
and this they are not masters of.	266	Priest 26	23
So that if after dinner they are not fit (or un-weeldy) either	266	Priest 26	31
not fit (or un-weeldy) either to pray, or work, they are gluttons.	266	Priest 26	32
(For they rather must not work, especially Students, and those that	266	Priest 26	33
but that they must rise so, as that it is not meate or drinke that	266	Priest 26	35
The third is the observation with what appetite they sit down.	267	Priest 26	5
knowing that there is one, who when they forget, remembers for them;	267	Priest 26	21
so long at it, that they would have fainted, had they returned empty,	267	Priest 26	23
they would have fainted, had they returned empty, He suffered it not;	267	Priest 26	24
but also for that when they are in company, instructions seasoned	268	Priest 27	3
For while they resist the person that reviles, they resist . .	269	Priest 28	23
they resist not the evill which takes hold of them, and is farr	269	Priest 28	24
of his Conscience, whereas they are to do it by Command, and by Oath.	269	Priest 29	31
by the Common Statute-Law they are taken for a kinde of Corporation,	269	Priest 29	33
and by the same Law they are to levy penalties for negligence in	270	Priest 29	4
urges the best unto it, shewing that they do not loose, or go lesse,	270	Priest 29	9
that so they may know their duty, and keep their oath the better;	270	Priest 29	15
and neighbourly admonitions they still persist in ill, to present	270	Priest 29	20
yea though they be tenants, or otherwise ingaged to the delinquent:	270	Priest 29	20
and that if they sow and soyle their grounds, they must have corn;	270	Priest 30	26
and that if they sow and soyle their grounds, they must have corn;	270	Priest 30	27
if they keep and fodder well their cattel, they must have milk,	270	Priest 30	27
keep and fodder well their cattel, they must have milk, and Calves;	270	Priest 30	28
he often overturnes things, when they are thought past danger;	271	Priest 30	21
every day of the week, and four times on Sunday, if they be well.	272	Priest 31	23
or at midnight, or as they think fit, & see cause, or rather as Gods	272	Priest 31	27
what he may, before they come, and when for all that they do come,	273	Priest 31	18
and when for all that they do come, he be a little affected . .	273	Priest 31	18
For when men have nothing to do, then they fall to drink, to steal,	274	Priest 32	11
Come, say they, we have nothing to do, lets go to the Tavern,	274	Priest 32	12
them honestly, and seasonably, when they are not better imployed.	274	Priest 32	31
establisheth it, since they that have nothing, are fittest to work.	275	Priest 32	4
to enter into a Calling, if they be fit for it, and it for them;	275	Priest 32	15
what they are fittest for, and to prepare for that with all . .	275	Priest 32	16
Could men finde out this delight, they would seldome be from home;	275	Priest 32	35
whereas now, of any place, they are least there.	275	Priest 32	36
that they kindle them rather to redeem the Dignity either from true	276	Priest 32	23
for single men, they are either Heirs, or younger Brothers: . .	276	Priest 32	25
Therefore they are to mark their Fathers discretion in ordering his	276	Priest 32	27
when they see any remarkable point of Education or good husbandry,	276	Priest 32	29
when they meet with good fruit, get a graffe of the tree, . .	276	Priest 32	32
Besides, they are to read Books of Law, and Justice; . . .	276	Priest 32	33
they are not in this Consideration, because we are about a Calling,	276	Priest 32	35
and above all things, they are to frequent Sessions and Sizes;	277	Priest 32	1
for it is both an honor which they owe to the Reverend Judges	277	Priest 32	2
Husbandman labours for them, so must they fight for, and defend them,	277	Priest 32	20
This is the duty of each to other, which they ought to fulfill:	277	Priest 32	21
but also as they may be handled, a religious imployment? . .	278	Priest 32	7
And they must be likewise in all that are his.	280	Priest 34	11
as they remember themselves were, when affliction did blow the Coals.	280	Priest 34	20
nor when they are among them that are merry, to extend themselves	280	Priest 34	26
so will they last the longer, and when they depart, returne . .	280	Priest 34	29
will they last the longer, and when they depart, returne the sooner.	280	Priest 34	30
But if they shall fear, that at such, or such a time their peace	280	Priest 34	32
either they think, that there is none that can or will look after	281	Priest 34	7
he is lost, as if they said, God doth forsake and persecute them,	281	Priest 34	11
how the windes should blow so much as they can, and the sea rage so	281	Priest 34	21
sea rage so much as it can, and all things do what they can, and all,	281	Priest 34	22
they have their Law and Language bearing witnesse to them, . .	281	Priest 34	35
have their Law and Language bearing witnesse to them, and they to it:	281	Priest 34	36
they are Circumcised to this day, and expect the promises . .	281	Priest 34	36
a wonder sent to Posterity, least they complaine of want of wonders.	282	Priest 34	36
either he doth it as they are Creatures, dust and ashes; . .	283	Priest 34	10
or as they are sinfull.	283	Priest 34	11
till either they despise that Love, or despaire of his Mercy:	283	Priest 34	23
Parson is a Lover of old Customes, if they be good, and harmlesse;	283	Priest 35	28
and if they will not reforme, presents them.	284	Priest 35	12
that at Baptisme they professed not to be ashamed of Christs Cross,	284	Priest 35	32
out of niceness, because they like the salutations, and complements,	285	Priest 36	5
Or else, because they think it empty and superfluous. . . .	285	Priest 36	8

THEY (cont'd)

	PAGE	TITLE		LINE
had delivered them to Satan, that they might learn not to Blaspheme.	286	Priest 36		1
so that they are so far from craving this benefit from their ghostly	286	Priest 36		12
that they oftentimes goe out of church, before he hath blessed them.	286	Priest 36		14
when they are at leasure, make others faults their entertainment	286	Priest 37		29
men think, so they speak truth, they may disclose anothers fault,	286	Priest 37		31
they may disclose anothers fault, finds it somwhat difficult how	286	Priest 37		32
may talk, so they do it not with sport, but commiseration;)	287	Priest 37		13
and more, they may discover them to those that know them not:	287	Priest 37		17
by those, which are branded for rogues, that they may be known;	287	Priest 37		20
or put into the stocks, that they may be looked upon.	287	Priest 37		21
so may they their good name, and the possession thereof,	287	Priest 37		32
which before their offence and Judgment they had in all mens brests:	287	Priest 37		34
that in their full strength they may deliver thy message reverently,	289	Priest		28
thy blessings hang in clusters, they come trooping upon us!	290	Priest		6
they break forth like mighty waters on every side.	290	Priest		7
if they had lived, would have been an ornament to the world,	291	Cornaro		3
For when they saw their parents and kindred snatcht away in the midst	291	Cornaro		9
they had a great desire to know the way of my life, and how I came	291	Cornaro		11
They added withall, that unlesse I speedily used that remedy,	292	Cornaro		12
This they had told me before:	292	Cornaro		26
that they had no great power to hurt those bodies, which were kept in	294	Cornaro		1
That they who in these two things that enter in at the mouth,	294	Cornaro		3
whereas they hurt them very much who live intemperately.	294	Cornaro		14
they were possessed with a deep Melancholie (a thing usuall	294	Cornaro		17
what case I was, they concluded that I would die within three dayes.	295	Cornaro		2
that they could not be much troubled, or make a great concourse,	295	Cornaro		9
That they that live a temperate life, can receive little hurt from	295	Cornaro		14
Divers reasons they brought, as, that old age could not be sustained	295	Cornaro		22
curing of diseases, into which they often fall, who live disorderly:	298	Cornaro		5
and procure that they prolong their life even to a hundred yeares	298	Cornaro		15
and that at length they shut up their dayes like a Lamp,	298	Cornaro		16
although they see themselves ill handled by their intemperance,	298	Cornaro		24
because they say, It is better to please the Appetite (though they	298	Cornaro		26
please the Appetite (though they live ten yeares lesse then otherwise	298	Cornaro		27
ten yeares lesse then otherwise they should do) then alwayes to live	298	Cornaro		27
But they consider not, of how great moment ten yeares are in mature	298	Cornaro		28
those ten yeares, which they set at naught in regard of their belly?	298	Cornaro		34
That they who are employed in the common wealth, cannot live	299	Cornaro		11
live regularly, because they must often endure heats, and colds,	299	Cornaro		13
both that they may preserve themselves from diseases, which hinder	299	Cornaro		18
in all things wherein they deal, may be more lively and vigorous.	299	Cornaro		20
I abstain from fruit, and fish, and the like, because they hurt me.	300	Cornaro		10
But they who finde benefit in these meats, may, yea ought to use	300	Cornaro		10
lest they take a greater quantitie of any meat or drink (though most	300	Cornaro		12
though they live disorderly, yet continue in health to their lives	300	Cornaro		18
besides that they are in the fairest place of this learned Citie	301	Cornaro		10
of Architecture, that they are cool in summer, and warm in winter.	301	Cornaro		13
are so ordered, that they all meet and end in a fair plot of ground;	301	Cornaro		21
their youthfull appetites, although they be of a most strong temper:	303	Cornaro		13
And in so doing they doe not sever their trust from God.	307	Valdesso		2
But by trusting in the word of God they trust in God.	307	Valdesso		3
as if they were both but Alphabets and after a time to be left.	309	Valdesso		19
neither can they ever be exhausted, (as Pictures may be by a plenarie	309	Valdesso		22
They shall be all taught of God, it being Scripture cannot be spoken	310	Valdesso		2
is in some sort true because they are spiritually discerned,	315	Valdesso		31
Nay they are purposely recorded in holy Writ.	316	Valdesso		5
in the point of Resurrection he agreed with them, and they with him.	316	Valdesso		10
when they doe amisse, and they are to be judged according	316	Valdesso		18
and they are to be judged according to the outward fact,	316	Valdesso		18
but when he sayes they are equally exempt with God, that is dangerous	316	Valdesso		32
and then afterward they will attend it of themselves without his	318	Valdesso		21
like to that of the Jewes, which they added to their divine law.	320	Valdesso		4
A Dwarfe on a Gyants shoulder sees farther then they two.	322	Proverbs	V	50
They that are booted are not alwaies ready.	323	Proverbs		83
Ill natures, the more you aske them, the more they stick.	324	Proverbs		106
saies they are not ripe.	325	Proverbs		130
They that know one another salute a farre off.	327	Proverbs		185
the lesse they looke to their house.	329	Proverbs		250
Gossips are frogs, they drinke and talke.	330	Proverbs		275
Many kisse the hand they wish cut off.	330	Proverbs		283
The Lyon is not so fierce as they paint him.	330	Proverbs		289
When children stand quiet, they have done some ill.	338	Proverbs		504
Willowes are weak, yet they bind other wood.	341	Proverbs		594
Old men, when they scorne young, make much of death.	341	Proverbs		597
Gaming, women, and wine, while they laugh they make men pine.	341	Proverbs		604
If fooles should not foole it, they shall lose their season.	343	Proverbs	V	702
If fooles should not foole it, they should loose their season.	344	Proverbs		703
Let all live as they would die.	345	Proverbs		725
Women laugh when they can, and weepe when they will.	348	Proverbs		821
They talke of Christmas so long, that it comes.	349	Proverbs		840
Conversation makes one what they are.	351	Proverbs	V	926
Children when they are little make parents fooles,	352	Proverbs		939
when they are great they make them mad.	352	Proverbs		939
Children when they are little make their parents fooles,	352	Proverbs	V	939
Sinnes are not knowne till they bee acted.	352	Proverbs		942
All are presumed good, till they are found in a fault.	352	Proverbs		944
Benefits please like flowers while they are fresh.	356	Proverbs	D	40
but he would chuse to dy in Spain (where they say	357	Proverbs	D	1047
They favour learning whose actions are worthy of a learned pen.	357	Proverbs	D	1061
They that hold the greatest farmes, pay the least rent	359	Proverbs	D	1100

	PAGE	TITLE		LINE
THEY (cont'd)				
Some men plant an opinion they seem to erradicate.	361	Proverbs	D	1164
Marry your daughters betimes, lest they marry themselves.	361	Proverbs	D	1171
But perhaps they will say, you are sickly, you must not study too	364	Letters		25
but they will object again, What becomes of your Annuity?	364	Letters		30
hath bought a parcel of Books for me, and that they are coming over.	366	Letters		30
Now though they have hitherto travelled upon your charge,	366	Letters		31
yet if my Sister were acquainted that they are ready, I dare say she	367	Letters		1
that they prevent my memory, and yet still grow upon Your humblest	367	Letters		15
as of certaine injuries which they are thought to have offerd to our	368	Letters		6
at the Indies, wherein they have satisfied the King reasonably.	368	Letters		7
untill they have satisfied him also concerning the fishing which	368	Letters		9
demand of the Kings these Agents pretend they have no commission,	368	Letters		14
& therfore deferr it untill they heare farther from the States.	368	Letters		15
Can I be so happy, as to hear of both these that they succeed well?	371	Letters		10
and so brought up your Children that they have attain'd to the years	373	Letters		13
So that now if they do not well the falt cannot be charg'd on you;	373	Letters		15
of what poor regard ought they to be, since if we had Riches we are	373	Letters		23
and, Blessed be the Mourners, for they shall be comforted.	373	Letters		32
most carry themselves so, as if they not only not desir'd, but,	373	Letters		33
how they have been burnt by thousands, and have endur'd such other	373	Letters		36
because they were to come into an unknown country, tender in	375	Letters		13
the fruit of my observation, for they have lived so lovingly, lying,	375	Letters		18
to let them know your love, for which both they shall, and I doe,	375	Letters		22
I doe my part to them, lett them think of me what they will or can.	376	Letters		7
are so farr from cooling christians, that they whett them.	376	Letters		11
and not as many who think they have done fairly, if they leave them	376	Letters		15
done fairly, if they leave them a good portion after their decease.	376	Letters		15
now they creep in a Vessel of Metheglin, and still they will be	376	Letters		27
and still they will be presenting or wishing to see, if at length	376	Letters		28
if at length they may find out some thing not unworthy of those hands	376	Letters		29
find out some thing not unworthy of those hands at which they aim.	377	Letters		1
all your Addresses, & for ought I see, they are ever to be liked.	378	Letters		17
THICK				
And stop our sinnes from growing thick and wide,	44	H. Bapt.1		8
They shall be thick and cloudie to my breast.	126	Confession		30
which are thick, and heavy, and hard to raise to a poynt of Zeal,	233	Priest 7		15
THICKEN				
Should thicken all my powers; because my lust	83	Sighs & Gr.		15
THICKEN'D				
Have thicken'd it with definitions?	134	Divinitie		10
THICKER				
Of thicker stuffe, which would endure a shake.	15	Ch.-Porch		226
THICKET				
As he that Heaven beyond much thicket spyes	43	H. Bapt.1	W	3
THIEF (see also theef)				
With clubs and staves they seek me, as a thief,	27	Sacrifice		37
THIEFE				
The hole calls the thiefe.	327	Proverbs		204
The table robbes more then a thiefe.	342	Proverbs		636
THIGH				
O that I had the wing and thigh	79	Employm.2	W	21
THIN (see also thinne)				
Which else shows watrish, bleak, & thin.	67	Windows		10
Though press'd, runnes thin;	159	Praise 3		38
THINE				
And if Gods image move thee not, let thine.	10	Ch.-Porch		102
Dare to look in thy chest; for 'tis thine own:	12	Ch.-Porch		147
Thy need, thine honour, and thy friend his due.	12	Ch.-Porch		152
By no means runne in debt: take thine own measure.	13	Ch.-Porch		175
Lesse at thine own things laugh; lest in the jest	15	Ch.-Porch		231
Nothing from thine: in service, care, or coldnesse	16	Ch.-Porch		255
Be not thine own worm: yet such jealousie,	16	Ch.-Porch		261
By lavishnesse thine own, and others wit,	18	Ch.-Porch		304
Much lesse make any one thine enemie.	20	Ch.-Porch		351
Leave not thine owne deere-cuntry-cleanlines	21	Ch.-Porch	W	367
In time of service seal up both thine eies,	23	Ch.-Porch		415
And send them to thine heart; that spying sinne,	23	Ch.-Porch		416
And sanctifie this ALTAR to be thine.	26	The Altar		16
She and her children shall be thine.	35	Thanksgvng		24
Yet Lord restore thine image, heare my call:	38	The Sinner		12
For, if I imp my wing on thine,	43	East.wings		19
Thine own gift good, yet me frcm my wayes taking.	48	Afflict.1		54
All her invention on thine Altar lay,	54	Love 2		7
The sweetnesse and the praise were thine;	57	Employm. 1		5
Prevent my Sinn to thine owne praise,	61	Grace	W	20
What were they all, compar'd to thine?	62	Afflict.2		8
I know it is my sinne, which locks thine eares,	66	Ch.-lock		1
I know it is my sinne, which stops thine eares,	66	Ch.-lock	W	1
Then cease discoursing soul, till thine own ground,	69	Content		33
The worlds, and thine:	71	Frailtie		10
Thine clad with simplenesse, and sad events;	71	Frailtie		11
And both mine eyes are thine,	95	Submission		2
Thine own delights thou didst to us impart:	97	Afflict.5		8
To make us thine: yet that we might not part,	97	Afflict.5		10
If either will convert us, we are thine:	97	Afflict.5		14
Oh foolish man! where are thine eyes?	101	Miserie		49
May our requests thine eare invade!	103	Prayer 2		3
May our requests thine eares invade!	103	Prayer 2	W	3
Speak not at large, say, I am thine:	111	The Quip		23
Take up thine eyes, which feed on earth;	112	Dawning		2

	PAGE	TITLE		LINE
THINE (cont'd)				
Christs resurrection thine may be:	112	Dawning		10
And with his buriall-linen drie thine eyes:	112	Dawning		14
What, (childe), is the ballance thine,	114	Dialogue		9
Thine the poise and measure?	114	Dialogue		10
As the reason then is thine;	115	Dialogue		21
While all things have their will, yet none but thine.	117	Providence		32
While the inclosure is thine ARM?	133	Paradise		6
But, Lord, the house and familie are thine,	136	Familie		5
With thine own clay. But I would parley fain:	139	Artillerie		27
Yet if thou shunnest, I am thine:	139	Artillerie		29
I am but finite, yet thine infinitely.	139	Artillerie		32
All were thine	148	Offering		34
Surely thine alone.	148	Offering		36
Bow down thine eare!	149	Longing		21
Consider, Lord; Lord, bow thine eare,	149	Longing		29
Lord, thou art mine, and I am thine,	157	Clasping		1
If mine I am: and thine much more,	157	Clasping		2
Yet to be thine, doth me restore;	157	Clasping		4
Since this being mine, brings with it thine,	157	Clasping		7
I neither should be mine nor thine.	157	Clasping		10
Lord, I am thine, and thou art mine:	157	Clasping		11
I may presume thee mine, then thine.	157	Clasping		13
Since thou in death wast none of thine,	157	Clasping		17
O be mine still! still make me thine!	157	Clasping		19
Or rather make no Thine and Mine!	157	Clasping		20
And the least frown of thine is shown?	166	The Flower		35
Look back upon thine own estate,	170	Self-cond.		4
Call home thine eye (that busie wanderer)	170	Self-cond.		5
Sprung from thine eye, did work within my soul,	172	The Glance		14
And one aspect of thine spend in delight	172	The Glance		22
Unto thine is bent:	178	Discipline		6
Marketh that deed for thine:	184	The Elixer	W	12
There thou shalt finde my faults are thine.	188	Judgement		15
Which might the more indeare it to be thine.	190	Ch.-Milit.		12
But that my darknes may touch thine:	203	Even-song	W	18
Upon thine Altar burnt? Cannot thy love	206	Walton 1		6
Worthy had bin, thou hadst not lost thine owne:	211	Bohemia	D	2
Fairer & richer. Now wee know, what's thine,	211	Bohemia	D	18
Lord to my words encline thine ear,	218	Psalm V	D	1
nor in thine anger chasten me:	219	Psalm VI	D	2
to convert those who are not yet thine, and to confirme those that	289	Priest		16
Better spare to have of thine own, then aske of other men.	330	Proverbs		266
THING				
Some ship them over, and the thing is done.	10	Ch.-Porch		100
A kinde of thing that's for it self too deere.	13	Ch.-Porch		178
Wisedome's a trimmer thing, then shop e're gave.	14	Ch.-Porch		188
Faith makes me any thing, or all	50	Faith		17
And comments on thee: for in ev'ry thing	58	H.Script.2		10
And more then fancy: for in ev'ry thing	58	H.Script.2	W	10
Man is all weaknesse; there is no such thing	61	Praise 1		9
Doth vanish like a flaring thing,	68	Windows		14
Doth vanish like a flaming thing,	68	Windows	V	14
Till he the thing and the example weigh:	72	Constancie		13
To use in any thing a trick or sleight;	72	Constancie		17
Bids no such thing:	78	Ang.&Sts.		18
And Easter intimate, enlarge the thing,	86	Lent		26
A thing forgot,	89	Afflict.4		3
For Man is ev'ry thing,	91	Man		7
Each thing is full of dutie:	92	Man		37
Man is a foolish thing, a foolish thing,	100	Miserie		2
A sick toss'd vessel, dashing on each thing;	102	Miserie		76
We cannot ask the thing, which is not there,	103	Prayer 2		11
I never saw thing make such haste.	107	Home		10
As an intangled, hamper'd thing.	109	Home		64
Thou art in all things one, in each thing many:	118	Providence		43
He makes a grave; as if the thing had sense,	119	Providence		83
Ev'n poysons praise thee. Should a thing be lost?	119	Providence		85
Each thing that is, although in use and name	121	Providence		149
Meeting with Time, Slack thing, said I,	122	Time		1
Give one thing more, a gratefull heart.	123	Gratefulnes		2
Oh, what a thing is man! how farre from power,	127	Giddinesse		1
Go search this thing,	133	The Method		9
If ye have any thing to send or write,	152	The Bag		31
Any thing to me. Heark despair, away.	152	The Bag		42
O let not that of any thing;	163	The Search		33
Verses, ye are too fine a thing, too wise	164	Grief		13
What is this strange and uncouth thing?	164	The Crosse		1
I am in all a weak disabled thing,	165	The Crosse		17
As if there were no such cold thing.	165	The Flower		7
And what I do in any thing,	184	The Elixer		3
Death, thou wast once an uncouth hideous thing,	185	Death		1
If I lack'd any thing.	188	Love 3		6
Ah, what a thing is man devoid of grace,	193	Ch.-Milit.		111
O what a poore thing 'tis to bee a Queene	212	Bohemia	D	23
If I have done this thing, O Lord,	221	Psalm VII	D	9
the Fathers, or Schoolmen, a Minister is made, and the thing done.	226	Priest 2		12
For the Law required one thing, and the Gospel another:	229	Priest 4		15
and a thing required under Canonicall obedience, the expounding	230	Priest 5		13
Neither let any think this a slight thing.	230	Priest 5		23
Let him communicate the thing often by prayer unto God,	237	Priest 9		5

THING (cont'd)

	PAGE	TITLE	LINE
Originall concupisence is such an active thing, by reason	238	Priest 9	12
if God give any thing above those, and not spent in them,	240	Priest 10	11
and veal, if he addes any thing for a great day, or a stranger,	241	Priest 10	17
For it is as unnatural to do any thing, that leads me to a sicknesse,	242	Priest 10	36
One thing is evident, that an English body, and a Students body,	242	Priest 10	38
When-ever hee gives any thing, and sees them labour in thanking	245	Priest 12	31
for it is a good and just thing for every one to do their own	247	Priest 14	22
or else if the thing will admit interpretation;	252	Priest 18	10
an illustrating the thing by something else, which he knows,	256	Priest 21	37
that it is no complementall or light thing to sustain that place,	258	Priest 22	11
and so the thing passeth with more authority, and lesse envy.	260	Priest 23	12
God is wonderfully to be seen, one thing would be carefully observed;	261	Priest 23	28
or doing any thing of aversenesse, save in the very act	263	Priest 25	28
if I do not give every thing its end, I abuse the Creature,	265	Priest 26	9
contempt shall proceed so far as to do any thing punishable by law,	268	Priest 28	31
If himselfe reforme any thing, it is out of the overflowing of his	269	Priest 29	30
and exerciseth a threefold power in every thing which concernes man.	271	Priest 30	1
sustaining power he preserves and actuates every thing in his being;	271	Priest 30	4
and that the chiefe thing, which God in Scriptures requires,	279	Priest 33	16
then in their Countrey under so many miracles were a stranger thing,	282	Priest 34	9
that this very thing was intended by God, that the Jewes should be	282	Priest 34	11
it not onely a grave, and reverend thing, but a beneficial also.	285	Priest 36	3
and saw that it was no hard thing to do so, but the proper duty	292	Cornaro	32
with a deep Melancholie (a thing usuall to disorderly lives)	294	Cornaro	18
But my experience taught me another thing also, to wit,	295	Cornaro	16
comforts and condoles, doth perform an acceptable thing to thee;	298	Cornaro	7
that an orderly life is so hard a thing that it cannot be kept.	298	Cornaro	37
and later yeares, it is no such thing which may not be performed;	299	Cornaro	6
That a long life is no such desirable thing, because that after one	300	Cornaro	28
neither omit I any thing that may either teach, or delight me.	302	Cornaro	5
For death to all young men is a terrible thing, as also to those that	303	Cornaro	18
not onely a shamefull thing to fear that which cannot be avoided;	303	Cornaro	22
Since therefore a temperate life is so happie and pleasant a thing;	303	Cornaro	31
but lest in any thing I forsake that Temperance which I have found so	303	Cornaro	34
he sheweth through all his Considerations) a thing strangely buried,	305	Valdesso	1
Hee that trusts in the Kings word for any thing trusts in the King.	307	Valdesso	4
in regard it presents us not with the same thing only when it is read	310	Valdesso	33
and that no other sin or vertue hath any thing to doe with us;	311	Valdesso	24
But it is one thing not to judge, another to defend them.	316	Valdesso	14
that I may speak with him or doe some thing else when I doe come.	318	Valdesso	17
Every thing is of use to a houskeeper.	323	Proverbs	70
Every thing new is fine.	323	Proverbs	76
He that riseth betimes hath some thing in his head.	329	Proverbs	235
if you will know the truth of the thing.	332	Proverbs	331
The horse thinkes one thing, and he that sadles him another.	334	Proverbs	387
Hee that makes a thing too fine, breakes it.	336	Proverbs	440
A scepter is one thing, and a ladle another.	339	Proverbs	545
Of a little thing a little displeaseth.	348	Proverbs	814
It's a wicked thing to make a dearth ones garner.	351	Proverbs	898
but every thing else in this world.	358	Proverbs	D 1077
There is a remedy for every thing, could men find it.	360	Proverbs	D 1142
for it sets a dearer price on every thing.	361	Proverbs	D 1178
and now the only thing I long for, is to hear of my dear sick Sister;	371	Letters	7
What an admirable thing is this, that God puts his shoulder to our	374	Letters	17
if at length they may find out some thing not unworthy of those hands	376	Letters	29
And as I am glad for the thing, so no less glad for the Heart,	379	Letters	14
It is a different thing to advize you now, & before you took Sir	380	Woodnoth	7
The case of ministers and magistrates is another thing,	381	Woodnoth	28
any body els that owe me any thing else of old debt I forgive them.	383	G.H.'s Will	26
glorious shew is there, either of garments, or of any thing else?	442	Oration	32

THINGES

	PAGE	TITLE	LINE
Meane while, if hee (which all thinges weares)	208	H. Danvers D	5
I forgett all thinges, so I may doe them good who want it.	376	Letters	5

THINGS

	PAGE	TITLE	LINE
Wine above all things doth Gods stamp deface.	8	Ch.-Porch	48
Doe all things like a man, not sneakingly:	11	Ch.-Porch	121
To all things els. Wealth is the conjurers devil;	13	Ch.-Porch	165
Lesse at thine own things laugh; lest in the jest	15	Ch.-Porch	231
All things are bigge with jest: nothing that's plain,	16	Ch.-Porch	239
Who follows all things, forfeiteth his will.	21	Ch.-Porch	364
Affect in things about thee cleanlinesse,	21	Ch.-Porch	367
To worldly things are sharp, but to me blinde;	26	Sacrifice	2
I him obey, who all things else command:	29	Sacrifice	83
See how spite cankers things. These words aright	30	Sacrifice	109
But there are two vast, spacious things,	37	The Agonie	4
And bring by Faith all things to him?	49	Faith	4
A kinde of tune, which all things heare and fear;	51	Prayer 1	8
All things are busie; onely I	57	Employm. 1	17
Of all these things, or all of them in one?	62	Mattens	8
For above all things he abhorres deceit:	72	Constancie	18
Did th' earth and all things with it move.	76	Sunday	46
He sayes, in things which use hath justly got,	86	Lent	10
All things are in decay.	90	Man	6
All things unto our flesh are kinde	91	Man	34
Then how are all things neat?	92	Man	42
The world thinks all things bigg and tall	97	Charms & K W	17
And calling Justice, all things burn.	99	Decay	20
And those things most, which are most pure and fine:	101	Miserie	38
The spring, whence all things flow:	101	Miserie	60
By it do all things live their measur'd houre:	103	Prayer 2	10

THINGS (cont'd)

	PAGE	TITLE		LINE
By it do all things live their silly houre:	103	Prayer 2	W	10
Where most things were of purest gold;	106	Sion		3
And truly brasse and stones are heavie things, ...	107	Sion		19
We talk of harvests; there are no such things, ...	108	Home		55
To answer these fine things shall come;	111	The Quip		22
While all things have their will, yet none but thine.	117	Providence		32
Thou art in small things great, not small in any:	118	Providence		41
Thou art in all things one, in each thing many:	118	Providence		43
Hard things are glorious; easie things good cheap.	119	Providence		97
If they seek fine things, thou dost make them run	120	Providence		106
Most things move th' under-jaw; the Crocodile not.	121	Providence		139
Most things move th' underchaw; the Crocodile not.	121	Providence	V	139
Most things sleep lying; th' Elephant leans or stands.	121	Providence		140
Most things sleep lying; th' Elephant leane or stand.	121	Providence	V	140
All things that are, though they have sev'rall wayes, ...	121	Providence		145
Who above all things lov'd this life;	122	Time		8
To this life things of sense	131	Mans medly		7
He hath two winters, other things but one:	131	Mans medly		27
And he of all things fears two deaths alone.	131	Mans medly		30
More bowels have, then such hard things.	136	Ephes.		24
And giving all things their set forms and houres, ...	137	Familie		11
In hope of great things. Call to minde thy dream, ...	138	The Size		44
The starres and all things are; If I refuse, ...	139	Artillerie		12
That all things were more ours by being his.	143	Holdfast		12
What present things requir'd of thee.	144	Discharge		25
Things present shrink and die: but they that spend	145	Discharge		41
And single things grow fruitfull by deserts.	147	Offering		10
Hast thou left all things to their course, ...	149	Longing		44
Where all things have their leafe assign'd:	149	Longing		50
Yea, when both rocks and all things shall disband, ...	156	Assurance		34
All things concurre to give it a perfection.	158	Praise 3		9
Thousands of things do thee employ	158	Praise 3		19
Who changeth all things, as him pleaseth best.	159	Jos.coat		4
And force of fire, what curious things are made	161	Priesthood		14
O what pure things, most pure must those things be, ...	161	Priesthood		29
Are things of nought.	163	The Search		40
My grief hath need of all the watry things, ...	164	Grief		3
Besides, things sort not to my will, ...	165	The Crosse		19
Thou turnest th' edge of all things on me still, ...	165	The Crosse		21
Where all things burn, ...	166	The Flower		33
(As sweet things traffick when they meet)	175	The Odour		27
There are no such things to me, ...	177	The Rose		11
In all things thee to see, ...	184	The Elixer		2
All things I doe to thee	184	The Elixer	W	2
Seest and rulest all things ev'n as one:	190	Ch.-Milit.		2
For things misshapen, things of highest use.	191	Ch.-Milit.		46
(As dying things are wont) untill it flew	192	Ch.-Milit.		80
And judge of things but Mediocritie.	210	Paradox	D	12
When all things full & hale, that they may bring	212	Bohemia	D	27
he labours most in those things which are most apt to scandalize	227	Priest 3		11
In the Scriptures hee findes four things;	228	Priest 4		24
which if it be necessary even in temporall things, how much more in	228	Priest 4		34
how much more in things of another world, where the well is deep,	228	Priest 4		34
open mine eyes, that I may see the wondrous things of thy Law.	229	Priest 4		3
and that as one Countrey doth not bear all things, that there may be	229	Priest 4		24
that Sermons are dangerous things, that none goes out of Church as he	233	Priest 7		19
he takes occasion to discourse of such things as are both profitable,	236	Priest 8		22
and that the Ministry requires the best and highest things, . . .	236	Priest 9		33
As hee is just in all things, so is he to his wife also, . . .	238	Priest 9		34
but that he sometimes looks how things go, demanding an account,	239	Priest 9		2
he teacheth them, that three things make a compleate servant, Truth,	240	Priest 10		17
to preserve a directnesse, and open plainnesse in all things;	240	Priest 10		34
for he hath no mony for such things, charity being his only perfume,	241	Priest 10		13
and arising from the improvement of things, which otherwise would be	241	Priest 10		23
for there being two things, which as they are, are unuseful to man,	241	Priest 10		26
for the foulnesse, as wash, and durt, and things thereinto fallen;	241	Priest 10		29
or over-nourishing things, as the Israelites did eate sowre herbs:	242	Priest 10		4
then if it had taken before either fish, or rootes, or such things;	242	Priest 10		24
because countrey people are very observant of such things, . .	243	Priest 11		21
For many and wonderfull things are spoken of thee, thou great Vertue.	244	Priest 12		7
that all things there be decent, and befitting his Name by which it	246	Priest 13		2
Therefore first he takes order, that all things be in good repair;	246	Priest 13		4
or as putting a holiness in the things, but as desiring to keep	246	Priest 13		24
the Apostles two great and admirable Rules in things of this nature:	246	Priest 13		26
The first whereof is, Let all things be done decently, and in order:	246	Priest 13		27
The second, Let all things be done to edification, 1 Cor. 14.	246	Priest 13		28
even in externall and indifferent things, what course is to be taken;	246	Priest 13		33
But then he admonisheth them of two things;	247	Priest 14		23
If the Parson were ashamed of particularizing in these things,	249	Priest 14		1
and then he suits things faithfully according to that end. . .	253	Priest 19		4
that we should do whatsoever things are honest, or just, . .	253	Priest 19		23
where things are otherwise equall, therefore he satisfies this duty	253	Priest 19		27
Then are there some things to be beleeved that are not seen?	256	Priest 21		9
Is not Christianity full of such things, as are not to be seen,	256	Priest 21		10
not hold in Christianity, because it contains things above nature:	256	Priest 21		24
shewing that things of ordinary use are not only to serve in the way	257	Priest 21		13
but there being two things in Sermons, the one Informing, . .	257	Priest 21		21
with himself, how or what behaviour to assume for so holy things.	257	Priest 22		28
their understandings being ripe enough for ill things, and why	259	Priest 22		1
himself some insight in things ordinarily incident and controverted,	259	Priest 23		34

THINGS (cont'd)

	PAGE	TITLE	LINE
householder, who bringeth out of his treasure things new and old;	261	Priest 23	15
the old things of Philosophy, and the new of Grace; . . .	261	Priest 23	16
that by familiar things hee might make his Doctrine slip the more	261	Priest 23	18
but sometimes lift up their minds to better things, even in the midst	261	Priest 23	25
he doth not onely prefer home-bred things before them, but condemns	261	Priest 23	37
at least in fundamentall things, the obscurity in some points being	263	Priest 24	4
whether things once indifferent, being made by the precept . .	263	Priest 24	11
and to do such things of legall opposition either in the presenting,	263	Priest 25	23
in perverting that order which he hath set both to things, . .	265	Priest 26	12
that servants for their mony are as other things that they buy,	265	Priest 26	25
since there is a Justice in the least things, and for the least there	265	Priest 26	32
One act in these things is bad, but it is the custome and habit that	266	Priest 26	17
Yet of hurtfull things, I am more bound to abstain from those,	266	Priest 26	23
this is foretold, that it shall be so still, until things be no more.	268	Priest 28	16
people have to think that all things come by a kind of naturall	270	Priest 30	25
labours to reduce them to see Gods hand in all things, ...	270	Priest 30	29
that things are not set in such an inevitable order, but that God	270	Priest 30	30
he preserves and orders the references of things one to the other,	271	Priest 30	14
yet if he suite not other things to the growth, as seasons, . .	271	Priest 30	16
and therefore he often overturnes things, when they are thought past	271	Priest 30	20
and above all things, they are to frequent Sessions and Sizes;	277	Priest 32	1
And the Parson is a lover of and exciter to justice in all things,	277	Priest 32	22
all other things shall be added, even it selfe is a Sermon. . .	278	Priest 33	14
of all diseases, and were recovered of all by things that he knew;	278	Priest 33	31
sometimes to weepe more for the losse of some temporall things,	279	Priest 33	13
Particularly, he counselleth them to two things:	280	Priest 34	17
that there is none that can or will look after things, but all goes	281	Priest 34	8
though there be a great Governour of all things, yet to them he is	281	Priest 34	10
sea rage so much as it can, and all things do what they can, and all,	281	Priest 34	22
if he had been at the Creation of all things, should lesse beleeve	281	Priest 34	29
should lesse beleeve it, seeing the Preservation of all things;	281	Priest 34	30
He that is ashamed in small things, will extend his pusillanimity	284	Priest 35	34
Thou hast exalted thy mercy above all things;	288	Priest	23
who onely doth wondrous things.	289	Priest	9
and thy right hand shall teach thee terrible things. . . .	289	Priest	24
Yet with this diet I avoided other hurtfull things also, . .	293	Cornaro	30
yet these forenamed things have also their force.	293	Cornaro	34
That they who in these two things that enter in at the mouth,	294	Cornaro	4
But all these things could not defend me against their importunities.	296	Cornaro	5
so that all things were troublesome to me:	296	Cornaro	16
if he will give his minde to those things which he should, . .	297	Cornaro	22
which things in others cannot be known without such observation,	297	Cornaro	28
And that I may say nothing of other things, are not almost all	298	Cornaro	32
there needs not many and curious things, but onely that a man should	299	Cornaro	8
in all things wherein they deal, may be more lively and vigorous.	299	Cornaro	20
making it my aim in all things, how I may help others to the furthest	301	Cornaro	8
All these things I do at my ease, and at fit seasons, and in mine own	301	Cornaro	9
Many things more might be said in commendation hereof: . . .	303	Cornaro	33
there are some things which I like not in him, as my fragments will	304	Valdesso	16
to publish it, for these three eminent things observable therein:	304	Valdesso	19
These three things are very eminent in the Author, and overweigh	305	Valdesso	12
to open his eyes that he might see the wondrous things of his Lawes,	309	Valdesso	26
In indifferent things there is roome for motions [notions] . .	313	Valdesso	12
but in things good, as to relieve my Neighbour, God hath already	313	Valdesso	13
meanes a mans fre-will is only in outward, not in spirituall things.	313	Valdesso	34
Things hard to bee understood.	317	Valdesso	24
Things needing great Consideration. Mat. 24. 15.	317	Valdesso	25
He lives unsafely, that lookes too neere on things. . . .	322	Proverbs	43
Men speake of the faire, as things went with them there. . .	326	Proverbs	151
All things require skill, but an appetite.	334	Proverbs	378
All things have their place, knew wee how to place them. . .	334	Proverbs	379
Things well fitted abide.	337	Proverbs	483
Patience, time and money accommodate all things.	338	Proverbs	498
All things in their beeing are good for something. . . .	339	Proverbs	520
Of faire things, the Autumne is faire.	340	Proverbs	572
The soule needs few things, the body many.	342	Proverbs	640
The soule needs some things, the body many.	342	Proverbs	V 640
If things were to be done twice, all would be wise. . . .	344	Proverbs	700
If all things might be done twice, all would be wise. . . .	343	Proverbs	V 700
Manie things are lost for want of asking.	353	Proverbs	968
When one is on horsebacke hee knowes all things.	353	Proverbs	982
New things are fair.	359	Proverbs	D 1117
A man is known to be mortal by two things, Sleep and Lust. . .	361	Proverbs	D 1159
To seek these things is lost labour; Geese in an oyle pot, . .	361	Proverbs	D 1163
as that if all things proved not well, I had rather the fault should	364	Letters	29
pardon my boldness, and consider but these three things. . .	365	Letters	16
These are the things I am to acquaint you with, of whose rude	369	Letters	1
I have received the things you sent me, safe;	371	Letters	6
And above all, If any care of future things molest you? . .	374	Letters	13
Yf I should regard such things, it were in another's power to defeat	376	Letters	9
You write very lovingly that all your things are mine. . . .	378	Letters	21
by the Apostles rule (Philip 4, 8.) not only to pursue pure things,	380	Woodnoth	13
but things that are lovely, & of good report if there be any vertue	380	Woodnoth	13
As in things inwardly good to have an eye to the world may be	380	Woodnoth	16
so in things naturally visible & apparent, as the course of our life	380	Woodnoth	17
4. When two things dislike you:	380	Woodnoth	21
of God (whose the success of things is) & not into the hands of men	380	Woodnoth	24
things may grow worse by your withdrawing which grow not better	381	Woodnoth	10
but a Trade having two things, the one imployment, the other profitt,	381	Woodnoth	30

	PAGE	TITLE		LINE
THINK				
If this seeme Monkish; think which brings most paine	7	Ch.-Porch	W	15
If thou art nothing, think what thou wouldst bee	10	Ch.-Porch	W	90
Think the king sees thee still; for his King does. . . .	11	Ch.-Porch		122
Look on meat, think it dirt, then eat a bit;	11	Ch.-Porch		131
Think not thy fame at ev'ry twitch will break:	15	Ch.-Porch		219
Think heav'n a better bargain, then to give	21	Ch.-Porch		374
Sundaies observe: think when the bells do chime, ...	22	Ch.-Porch		387
In all, I think my foot doth ever tread	71	Frailtie		7
In friendship, first I think, if that agree, ...	93	Unkindness		2
Let me not think an action mine own way, ...	104	Obedience		18
The windes, who think they rule the mariner, ...	119	Providence		91
So must he sip and think	131	Mans medly		22
So he must sip and think	131	Mans medly	V	22
Who think me eager, hot, and undertaking, ...	169	The Answer		6
We think we rob them, but we think amisse:	197	Ch.-Milit.		253
And shrodely, as I think, Lord wash my soule	202	love	W	8
Not that I think, if a man do not all which is here expressed,	224	Priest		10
and not to think, that when they have read the Fathers, . .	226	Priest 2		10
Let not Chaplains think themselves so free, as many of them do,	226	Priest 2		19
and because they have different Names, think their Office different.	226	Priest 2		21
Neither let any think this a slight thing.	230	Priest 5		23
it being naturall to men to think, that where is much earnestness,	232	Priest 7		32
and think it behoves them to be so, when God is so neer them,	233	Priest 7		10
binding them prentices (in case he think fit to do so) he takes care	239	Priest 10		34
because men usually think, that servants for their mony are as other	265	Priest 26		24
Many think they are at more liberty then they are, as if they were	266	Priest 26		18
the Parson think it in his discretion either unfit, or bootelesse	269	Priest 28		4
aptnesse Countrey people have to think that all things come by a kind	270	Priest 30		25
hand to sickle, shall then secure himself, and think all cock-sure;	271	Priest 30		30
God further, even till he imbarn his corn, and then think all sure;	271	Priest 30		32
or at midnight, or as they think fit, & see cause, or rather as Gods	272	Priest 31		27
But if the young Gallant think these Courses dull, and phlegmatick,	278	Priest 32		4
either they think, that there is none that can or will look after	281	Priest 34		7
Or else, because they think it empty and superfluous.	285	Priest 36		8
and that even some good men think, so they speak truth, . .	286	Priest 37		31
to consider the force of Temperance, and to think thus with my self:	293	Cornaro		2
be silent, least while I think I am modest, I wrong both my self,	364	Letters		7
my case unto you, which I think deserves the reading at the least;	364	Letters		10
brothers house of his own name (as I think) at the sign of the Pedler	370	Letters		27
who cannot think me lazy, since I rode 200 mile to see a Sister,	371	Letters		2
Think not my silence forgetfulness;	371	Letters		25
If you could think of taking her, as once you did, surely it were	375	Letters		30
I doe my part to them, lett them think of me what they will or can.	376	Letters		7
Truly it grieves me to think of the child, how destitute she is,	376	Letters		12
and not as many who think they have done fairly, if they leave them	376	Letters		15
THINKE				
And thinke it contrary to Natures Lawes	209	Paradox	D	3
That makes you thinke us poore:	210	Paradox	D	8
and those that thinke this superstitious, neither know superstition,	284	Priest 35		28
Where you thinke there is bacon, there is no Chimney.	324	Proverbs		99
Thinke of ease, but worke on.	327	Proverbs		178
The first degree of folly is to thinke ourselves wise, ...	337	Proverbs	V	460
On a good bargaine thinke twice.	339	Proverbs		529
God is at the end, when we thinke he is furthest off it. . .	341	Proverbs		598
THINKES				
Mee thinkes, in that Dutch optick I doe see	211	Bohemia	D	13
He therefore thinkes it not enough for him to observe the fasting	237	Priest 9		21
The Wolfe knowes, what the ill beast thinkes.	321	Proverbs		16
He that is warme, thinkes all so.	323	Proverbs		80
The horse thinkes one thing, and he that sadles him another.	334	Proverbs		387
He that commits a fault, thinkes every one speakes of it. . .	340	Proverbs		554
Every one thinkes his sacke heaviest.	346	Proverbs		748
He thinkes not well, that thinkes not againe.	349	Proverbs		836
Hee that is in a Taverne thinkes he is in a vine-garden. . .	353	Proverbs		989
THINKETH				
and thinketh the Ceremony not onely innocent, but reverend. . .	258	Priest 22		8
The fatt man knoweth not, what the leane thinketh. . . .	341	Proverbs		605
THINKING				
I took, without more thinking, in good part	94	Life		8
Thinking with that, which I did thus present, ...	129	Love unkn.		31
of their answer, but gently and pausably, thinking what they say;	231	Priest 6		32
thinking that their own labour is the cause of their thriving,	247	Priest 14		29
you take her not, I am thinking to do it, even beyond my strengthe;	375	Letters		35
had done that (which you are thinking to doe) to blessed Mary Magd.	381	Woodnoth		4
THINKS				
Whom when he thinks he hath, the devil hath him.	13	Ch.-Porch		166
But while he thinks to spoil the room, he sweeps.	67	Ch.-floore		18
The world thinks all things bigg and tall	97	Charms & K	W	17
Thinks on it, and thinks again:	114	Businesse		35
And now, me thinks, I am where I began	128	Bunch Gr.		3
Me thinks delight should have	154	Glimpse		6
This he thinks naturall, and sweet, and grave.	235	Priest 7		5
the afternoone, he thinks he hath in some measure, according to poor,	236	Priest 8		8
At night he thinks it a very fit time, both sutable to the joy	236	Priest 8		18
he thinks it the most usefull way that a Pastor can take, . .	256	Priest 21		1
for example sake, and because they are most common, he thus thinks:	265	Priest 26		4
(for one thinks in eating, that he can eat more, then afterwards he	267	Priest 26		3
whereas he thinks it not onely a grave, and reverend thing, . .	285	Priest 36		2
Hee is a foole that thinks not that another thinks. . . .	330	Proverbs		287
He that thinks amiss, concludes worse.	357	Proverbs	D	1046

THINKS (cont'd)	PAGE	TITLE	LINE
much from Divinity, at which, not without cause, he thinks, I aim;	370	Letters	21
THINNE			
'Tis a thinne webbe, which poysonous fancies make:	15	Ch.-Porch	224
Most thinne.	43	East.wings	15
Thus thinne and lean without a fence or friend,	47	Afflict.1	35
Is not a corpulent, but a thinne and spare,	138	The Size	32
THIRD			
Drink not the third glasse, which thou canst not tame,	7	Ch.-Porch	25
Stay at the third glasse: if thou lose thy hold,	8	Ch.-Porch	41
Stay at the third cup, or forgo the place.	8	Ch.-Porch	47
Unto a third, that ten leaves off doth lie:	58	H.Script.2	6
The third means is a diligent Collation of Scripture with Scripture.	229	Priest 4	4
are much more essentiall to a true fast, then the third and last;	242	Priest 10	8
the third, to inflame this knowledge, to presse, and drive it	255	Priest 21	5
The third means is the observation what is the main foundation,	262	Priest 24	28
The third is the observation with what appetite they sit down.	267	Priest 26	4
the third a spirituall power.	271	Priest 30	2
The third power is spirituall, by which God turnes all outward	271	Priest 30	36
taken from Nature, the second from the Law, the third from Grace.	281	Priest 34	17
and in our age, Paul the third, and Cardinal Bembo, who therefore	299	Cornaro	1
the second to professe it, the third to despise counsell.	337	Proverbs	460
Two ill meales make the third a glutton.	340	Proverbs	575
It is true there is a third sister, whom to receive were the greatest	375	Letters	23
THIRDLY			
Thirdly, Christ being not to continue on earth, but after hee had	225	Priest 1	6
Thirdly, because Countrey people (as indeed all honest men) do much	228	Priest 3	1
Thirdly, by turning often, and making many Apostrophes to God,	233	Priest 7	32
Thirdly, a providing for her family in such sort, as that neither	239	Priest 10	17
Thirdly, of eating no flesh, which is but the determination	242	Priest 10	5
Thirdly, That there be fit, and proper texts of Scripture every where	246	Priest 13	10
Thirdly, he keeps good Correspondence with all the neighbouring	253	Priest 19	15
Thirdly, that those of the elder sort, who are not well grounded,	255	Priest 21	29
Thirdly, when the answerer sticks, an illustrating the thing	256	Priest 21	36
Thirdly, For the manner of receiving, as the Parson useth all	259	Priest 22	10
Thirdly, that he might set a Copy for Parsons.	261	Priest 23	26
Thirdly, by a bold and impartial reproof, even of the best in	268	Priest 28	27
Thirdly, for Grace. Besides the continuall succession (since	282	Priest 34	18
Thirdly, Charity in loving walking, and neighbourly accompanying one	284	Priest 35	5
Thirdly for the Churches sake, to whom by Printing it I would have	304	Valdesso	8
Thirdly, the many pious rules of ordering our life, about	305	Valdesso	9
Thirdly, what I desire, and to what end, not vain pleasures,	365	Letters	18
THIRDS			
To gain thy thirds and little part.	99	Decay	15
THIRST			
that so the hunger and thirst after it may come rather from	250	Priest 15	5
the beginning of the Gout, with almost a continuall fever and thirst.	291	Cornaro	23
nor for every thirst to the pot.	331	Proverbs	290
The wine in the bottell doth not quench thirst.	342	Proverbs	616
THIRSTED			
As when the people hungred and thirsted after our Saviours Doctrine,	267	Priest 26	22
THIRSTETH			
to the person, hungreth and thirsteth after righteous punishment	254	Priest 20	28
THIRSTY			
Hee that goes to bed thirsty riseth healthy.	354	Proverbs	1003
THIRTEENE			
To Sara thirteene shillings foure pence, Alsoe my will and pleasure	382	G.H.'s Will	26
THIRTIE			
For thirtie pence he did my death devise,	27	Sacrifice	17
was thus affected [afflicted] from the thirtie fifth yeare of my age	292	Cornaro	1
came a terrible fever, which continued thirtie five dayes and nights;	296	Cornaro	20
THIRTY			
Reckon right, and February hath one and thirty daies.	328	Proverbs	229
besides that which is due to her, to Ann I leave thirty shillings:	382	G.H.'s Will	24
To Amy Danvers thirty shillings, To Mrs Anne Danvers twenty	383	G.H.'s Will	9
shillings To Elizabeth Burthen thirty shillings To Mary Gifford tenn	383	G.H.'s Will	15
THIS			
If this seeme Monkish; think which brings most paine	7	Ch.-Porch W	15
This is Earth's language, for if Heaven come in,	10	Ch.-Porch W	90
This losse springs chiefly from our education.	10	Ch.-Porch	97
Studie this art, make it thy great designe;	10	Ch.-Porch	101
All that they leave: this is flat povertie.	10	Ch.-Porch	106
All that is left: this is flat povertie.	10	Ch.-Porch W	106
Old courtiers know this; therefore set out so,	14	Ch.-Porch	185
Say not then, This with that lace will do well;	14	Ch.-Porch	189
But, This with my discretion will be brave.	14	Ch.-Porch	190
Learn this, that hath old gamesters deerely cost:	14	Ch.-Porch	200
Learn this, it hath old gamesters deerely cost:	14	Ch.-Porch W	200
To compasse this. Finde out mens wants and will,	19	Ch.-Porch	328
All forrain wisdome doth amount to this,	20	Ch.-Porch	355
For this French sluttery which so currant goes:	21	Ch.-Porch W	368
Meets in this frame,	26	The Altar	11
And sanctifie this ALTAR to be thine.	26	The Altar	16
Had to this day been an Egyptian slave.	27	Sacrifice	10
O let this cup passe, if it be thy pleasure:	27	Sacrifice	23
And readie Paschal Lambe of this great week:	28	Sacrifice	59
Sends me to Pilate. This makes them agree;	29	Sacrifice	74
Bywords, but this by sorrow I must win:	33	Sacrifice	207
Sharp nails pierce this, but sharper that confound;	33	Sacrifice	218
What ever sinne did this pure rock commit,	41	Sepulchre	10
And missing this, most falsly did arraigne thee;	41	Sepulchre	14

THIS (cont'd)

	PAGE	TITLE		LINE
Is best to celebrate this most high day.	41	Easter		12
Can there be any day but this,	42	Easter		27
Teach it to sing thy praise, this day,	42	Easter	W	29
And then this day, my life shall date.	42	Easter	W	30
And sing this day thy victories:	43	East.wings		9
And sing this day thy sacrifice,	43	East.wings	W	9
And feel this day thy victorie:	43	East.wings		18
If thou shalt let this venome lurk,	45	Nature		7
Looking on this side, & beyond us all:	48	Repentance	W	9
Sweeten at length this bitter bowl,	49	Repentance		19
I and this day,	49	Repentance		23
And in this shew, what Christ hath done.	51	Faith		36
This shadowes out what Christ hath done.	51	Faith	W	36
Another lift like this will make	52	H.Commun.		27
Thou hast restor'd us to this ease	53	H.Commun.		37
By this thy heav'nly bloud;	53	H.Commun.		38
Immortall Love, authour of this great frame,	54	Love 1		1
This is but tuning of my breast,	55	Temper 1		23
The measure of our joyes is in this place,	57	Employm. 1		11
Ladies, look here; this is the thankfull glasse,	58	H.Script.1		8
That mends the lookers eyes: this is the well	58	H.Script.1		9
This verse marks that, and both do make a motion	58	H.Script.2		5
This book of starres lights to eternall blisse.	58	H.Script.2		14
This book of starres can spell eternall blisse.	58	H.Script.2	W	14
Restore this day, for thy great name,	60	Whitsunday		27
That this new light, which now I see,	63	Mattens		18
Who gave me eyes, and light, and power this day,	63	Even-song		2
For this thy love? have I discharg'd the debt,	64	Even-song		10
Which this dayes favour did beget?	64	Even-song		11
The day or night: that is the gale, this th' harbour;	64	Even-song		26
That is the walk, and this the arbour;	64	Even-song		27
Or that the garden, this the grove.	64	Even-song		28
And in this love, more then in bed, I rest.	64	Even-song		32
May take acquaintance of this heap of dust;	64	Ch.-monum.		3
My bodie to this school, that it may learn	65	Ch.-monum.		7
O what a state is this, which never knew	65	Ch.-mus.	W	8
This glorious and transcendent place,	67	Windows		4
This soul doth span the world, and hang content	69	Content		17
Humilitie, who held the plume, at this	71	Humilitie		25
O brook not this, lest if what even now	71	Frailtie		17
O brook not this, lest if that, which just now	71	Frailtie	W	17
This is the Mark-man, safe and sure,	73	Constancie		34
The fruit of this, the next worlds bud,	75	Sunday		2
This day my Saviour rose,	76	Sunday		36
And did inclose this light for his:	76	Sunday		37
Christ hath took in this piece of ground,	76	Sunday		40
To this great kingdome, which thou now hast got,	77	Avarice		6
This fully to us, till death blow	82	Ungratef.		16
This to us fully, till death blow	82	Ungratef.	W	16
For by this powder thou wilt make us see.	82	Ungratef.	W	18
This may allure us with delights;	82	Ungratef.		22
Because this box we know;	82	Ungratef.		23
My words & thoughts do both expresse this notion,	84	Coloss.		1
So that we need not say, Where's this command?	86	Vanitie 1		26
Betwixt this world and that of grace.	90	Afflict.4		6
My God, I heard this day,	90	Man		1
My life within this band.	94	Life		3
My God, I read this day,	97	Afflict.5		1
Is my God this way? no, they would reply:	99	Decay		8
Yet either this,	101	Miserie		41
He doth not like this vertue, no;	101	Miserie		45
For this he wondrous well doth know	101	Miserie	W	45
Who made the arbour: this exceeds her wit.	101	Miserie		58
This was not quick enough, and that was dead.	102	Jordan 2		10
Whisper, How wide is all this long pretence!	103	Jordan 2		16
Whisper, How wide is all this preparation	103	Jordan 2	W	16
If this poore paper do as much as they.	104	Obedience		5
As if this passed with a reservation,	104	Obedience		13
And heart unto this deed, when he hath read;	105	Obedience		38
And heart unto this deed, when he doth read	105	Obedience	W	38
Yet all this glorie, all this pomp and state	106	Sion		7
After all this canst thou be strange?	108	Home		26
My God, what is this world to me?	108	Home		32
This world of wo? hence all ye clouds, away,	108	Home		33
What is this weary world; this meat and drink,	108	Home		37
What is this woman-kinde, which I can wink	108	Home		39
Oh loose this frame, this knot of man untie!	109	Home		61
Come dearest Lord, passe not this holy season,	109	Home		73
What tune is this, poore man? said he:	110	The Quip		10
Leading to this favour:	115	Dialogue		18
In all my other hymnes, but in this twice.	121	Providence		148
Extolleth many wayes, yet this one more.	121	Providence		152
Who above all things lov'd this life;	122	Time		8
And this is that makes life so long,	123	Time		19
Then chafing said, This man deludes:	123	Time		28
And sayes, If he in this be crost,	123	Gratefulnes		6
This not withstanding, thou wentst on,	124	Gratefulnes		17
This is the lace of Peaces coat:	124	Peace		9
Take of this grain, which in my garden grows,	125	Peace		37
Is this same grief! within my heart I made	126	Confession		2

THIS (cont'd)

	PAGE	TITLE		LINE
To this life things of sense	131	Mans medly		7
Go search this thing,	133	The Method		9
What doth this noise of thoughts within my heart	136	Familie		1
This is thy house, with these it doth abound:	137	Familie		21
This, this hath done it, this did bite the root	140	Ch.-rents		5
Lifting to heaven from this well of tears.	141	Justice 2		18
That we have nought. I stood amaz'd at this,	143	Holdfast		10
And well it was for thee, when this befell,	144	Discharge		16
This houre is mine: if for the next I care,	145	Discharge		33
Small it is, in this poore sort	146	Praise 2		25
Seek out this All-heal, and seek no repose,	147	Offering		22
Then bring thy gift; and let thy hymne be this;	147	Offering		24
(For this heart is none)	148	Offering		33
To this poore oblation;	148	Offering		39
Will use me in this kinde, the doore	152	The Bag		38
When as my fears foretold this, did replie,	154	Glimpse		19
And what to this? what more	155	Assurance		13
And in this league, which now my foes invade,	156	Assurance		26
Since this being mine, brings with it thine,	157	Clasping		7
This spacious globe: Angels must have their joy,	158	Praise 3		21
Bestow this jewell also on my creature,	160	The Pulley		12
What is this strange and uncouth thing?	164	The Crosse		1
Much wrastling, many a combate, this deare end,	164	The Crosse		8
This or that is:	166	The Flower		20
With onely this, My joy, my life, my crown.	168	a true Hymn		5
Since the condition of this world is frail,	170	Water-crs.		2
This worlds delights before true Christian joy,	170	Self-cond.		8
And all this not for my desert,	172	23 Psalme		11
What cordials make this curious broth,	175	The Odour		9
This broth of smells, that feeds and fats my minde.	175	The Odour		10
This breathing would with gains by sweetning me	175	The Odour		26
And so this new commerce and sweet	175	The Odour		29
This were the better skie, the brighter place.	175	The Foil		4
Yet in this wretched world we toil,	176	The Foil		7
In this world of sugred lies,	177	The Rose		2
Onely take this gentle rose,	177	The Rose		15
So this flower doth judge and sentence	178	The Rose		25
And drink this,	180	Invitation		11
In this cheer,	180	Invitation		17
Let the wonder of this pitie	182	Banquet	V	49
Strive in this, and love the strife.	182	Banquet		54
This on my ring,	183	The Posie		5
This by my picture, in my book I write:	183	The Posie		6
Or say, or dictate, this is my delight.	183	The Posie		8
Thou saist, this fruit is mine.	184	The Elixer	W	12
Which with this tincture (for thy sake)	184	The Elixer	V	15
A servant with this clause	185	The Elixer		17
This is the famous stone	185	The Elixer		21
For this poore wreath, give thee a crown of praise.	185	A Wreath		12
We lookt on this side of thee, shooting short;	186	Death		9
While this member jogs the other,	186	Dooms-day		5
Make this the day.	186	Dooms-day		8
Early didst thou arise to plant this vine,	190	Ch.-Milit.		11
Thou didst rise early for to plant this vine,	190	Ch.-Milit.	W	11
Moses pursu'd this: but King Solomon	190	Ch.-Milit.		21
Constantines British line meant this of old,	192	Ch.-Milit.		93
And did this mysterie wrap up and fold	192	Ch.-Milit.		94
None will beleeve this now, though money be	193	Ch.-Milit.		119
To this great lotterie, and all would pull.	193	Ch.-Milit.		134
From this contagious infidelitie.	194	Ch.-Milit.		158
And this is all the Rock, whereof they boast,	194	Ch.-Milit.		159
Being in this their old crackt looking-glasse.	196	Ch.-Milit.		208
We are more poore, and they more rich by this.	197	Ch.-Milit.		254
Then of this also I am sure	200	H. Commun.	W	19
Into my soule this cannot pass	201	H. Commun.	W	37
This gift of all gifts is the best,	201	H. Commun.	W	43
If thou deferr this light, then shadow mee:	203	Even-song	W	9
Yet Thou art not so dark, since I know this,	203	Even-song	W	17
But onely while thou speak'st; This Anchor will.	439	Walton 5		4
This certain Anchor adde a Seal, and so	439	Walton 5		6
This holy Cable's of all storms secure.	439	Walton 5		10
This holy Cable's from all storms secure.	439	Walton 5	V	10
He gave this Seal, and, so gave ore.	439	walton 6		2
This Anchor keeps my faith, that, me secure.	439	walton 6		4
Against this meane & humble Blackamore.	209	L. Bacon	D	10
But that my Inke was factious for this side.	209	L. Bacon	D	12
This is thy empire yet: till better season	213	Bohemia	D	60
This oure great Sublunary Ball,	213	L' Envoy	D	12
this day have I begotten thee:	216	Psalm II	D	18
If I have done this thing, O Lord,	221	Psalm VII	D	9
This definition is evident, and containes the direct steps	225	Priest 1		2
therefore St. Paul in the beginning of his Epistles, professeth this:	225	Priest 1		10
Out of this Chartre of the Priesthood may be plainly gathered both	225	Priest 1		14
to whom this discourse ariseth not) some live in the Universities,	225	Priest 2		22
To this may be added the consideration of any text with the coherence	229	Priest 4		9
book of Scripture, and ploughing with this, and his own meditations,	229	Priest 4		29
this being to be done in his younger and preparatory times,	230	Priest 5		5
This Body he made by way of expounding the Church Catechisme,	230	Priest 5		7
besides this laborious work, a slighter forme of Catechizing,	230	Priest 5		15
Neither let any think this a slight thing.	230	Priest 5		23

THIS (cont'd)

	PAGE	TITLE	LINE
This Liberty he compasseth by one distinction, and that is, . .	272	Priest 31	19
This is so necessary, and essentiall to a Christian, that he cannot	272	Priest 31	23
that he cannot without this maintain himself in a Christian state.	272	Priest 31	24
Besides this, the Godly have ever added some houres of prayer,	272	Priest 31	25
Upon this his mind begins to be perplexed, and troubled, . .	272	Priest 31	32
Christian, that this prayer being additionary, not necessary;	273	Priest 31	4
And of this he is so to assure himself, as to admit no scruple,	273	Priest 31	10
By this it is evident, that the distinction is of singular use	273	Priest 31	12
that this interruption proceed not out of slacknes, or coldness,	273	Priest 31	15
Secondly, that this interruption proceede not out of shame. . .	273	Priest 31	21
and this briefly. But it happens, that neer the place where he is	273	Priest 31	27
as that by this he may take into his Prayer humiliation also.	273	Priest 31	32
in my heart) because this kinde of Prayer is additionary, . .	273	Priest 31	36
This distinction may runne through all Christian duties, . .	274	Priest 31	1
The great and nationall sin of this Land he esteems to be Idlenesse;	274	Priest 32	9
Wherefore the Parson strongly opposeth this sin, whersoever he goes.	274	Priest 32	14
The reason of this assertion is taken from the nature of man,	274	Priest 32	18
Now this reason crosseth not our Saviours precept of selling what we	274	Priest 32	31
Now because the onely opposer to this Doctrine is the Gallant,	275	Priest 32	6
But it will not be amisse in this exceeding usefull point to descend	275	Priest 32	17
Could men finde out this delight, they would seldome be from home;	275	Priest 32	34
But if after all this care well dispatched, the house-keepers Family	275	Priest 32	36
they are not in this Consideration, because we are about a Calling,	276	Priest 32	36
This is the duty of each to other, which they ought to fulfill:	277	Priest 32	20
whose neglect in this point is intolerable, and a shamefull wrong	277	Priest 32	26
at table about his appetite, if he tell this to another, preacheth;	278	Priest 33	19
And it fares in this as it doth in Physick:	278	Priest 33	25
Neither is this true onely in the military state of a Christian life,	279	Priest 33	2
he came at length to this resolution, that repentance is an act	279	Priest 33	14
since we are not Masters of our bodies, this sufficeth. . .	279	Priest 33	19
This Instruction and comfort the Parson getting for himself,	279	Priest 33	31
that there is a double state of a Christian even in this Life,	280	Priest 34	2
their peace and mirth have carryed them further then this moderation,	280	Priest 34	34
they are Circumcised to this day, and expect the promises . .	282	Priest 34	1
that this very thing was intended by God, that the Jews should be	282	Priest 34	11
And therefore this kind of Punishment was chosen rather then any	282	Priest 34	17
and this as the more faulty in him, so the more glorious in God.	283	Priest 34	21
There is much preaching in this friendliness.	284	Priest 35	22
And the Parson likes this very well;	284	Priest 35	24
and those that thinke this superstitious, neither know superstition,	284	Priest 35	28
As for those that are ashamed to use this forme, as being old,	284	Priest 35	30
But this was not proper to Christ, or the Apostles only, . .	285	Priest 36	12
The fruit of this blessing good Hannah found, and received with great	285	Priest 36	20
The neglect of this duty in Ministers themselves, hath made . .	286	Priest 36	11
they are so far from craving this benefit from their ghostly Father,	286	Priest 36	13
this unusuall form begets a reverence, and makes him esteemed	286	Priest 36	24
finds it somwhat difficult how to proceed in this point. . .	286	Priest 37	33
Now the Parson taking this point to task, which is so exceeding	287	Priest 37	8
But some may say, though the Law allow this, the Gospel doth not,	287	Priest 37	22
But this is easily answered:	287	Priest 37	24
for, this word of thy rich peace, and reconciliation, thou hast	289	Priest	3
wher-ever spoken this day throughout the universall Church. . .	289	Priest	14
blesse it in this thy own Kingdom, which thou hast made a Land	289	Priest	17
and unworthy hearts rob us of the continuance of this thy sweet love:	289	Priest	20
blesse this portion here assembled together, with thy unworthy	289	Priest	24
Thou hast given us the blessings of this life, and of a better.	290	Priest	5
Grant this dear Father, for thy Son's sake, our only Saviour:	290	Priest	13
who will take this into consideration, I will declare the causes	291	Cornaro	14
From this ill temper there remained little else to be expected of me,	291	Cornaro	24
for this had every way great force for the recovering and preserving	292	Cornaro	5
Upon this, weighing their reasons with my self, and abhorring from so	292	Cornaro	17
This they had told me before:	292	Cornaro	26
I so addicted my self to this course of life, that I never went	292	Cornaro	33
Upon this, I found within a few dayes, that I was exceedingly helped,	292	Cornaro	34
This upon triall I found most false:	293	Cornaro	10
By this means, within lesse then a yeare I was not onely freed from	293	Cornaro	19
Yet with this diet I avoided other hurtfull things also, . .	293	Cornaro	30
which gained me this experience, that I perceived, that they had no	294	Cornaro	1
This Galen confirms, when he sayes, that immoderate heats and colds,	294	Cornaro	6
But mine own experience confirmeth this more;	294	Cornaro	11
that this suit and contention was raised by the Divine Providence,	294	Cornaro	23
This I found by experience, when I was seventie yeares old: . .	294	Cornaro	35
To this agreed two Italian Proverbs, the one whereof was, . .	295	Cornaro	33
This addition after ten dayes wrought so much upon me, that . .	296	Cornaro	14
Besides all this, I could not sleep, no not a quarter of an houre:	296	Cornaro	21
By this it may cleerely be perceived, how great is the power of order	297	Cornaro	3
Neither can any man denie this, who will narrowly consider it.	297	Cornaro	14
prescribes this Physick first, That he use a moderate diet: . .	297	Cornaro	16
hath cured him, commends this also to him, if he will live in health.	297	Cornaro	18
because this will cut off all causes of diseases, so that he shall	297	Cornaro	20
The reason whereof is this, Every one by long experience may know	297	Cornaro	26
Many have thought that this could be done by Aurum potabile,	298	Cornaro	19
To this I answer, that Galen kept it, and held it for the best	298	Cornaro	37
Because since this is at the best but uncertain, dangerous, . .	300	Cornaro	19
recounting the delights and pleasures in this age of eighty three,	300	Cornaro	31
that they are in the fairest place of this learned Citie of Padua,	301	Cornaro	11
are verie beautifull and convenient above most in this age, . .	301	Cornaro	12
This place is washed with the river Brenta;	301	Cornaro	23
By this means the place is come to that perfection we now see it is:	301	Cornaro	30
and husbandrie, whereof in this age there is great plentie. . .	301	Cornaro	37

	PAGE	TITLE		LINE
THIS (cont'd)				
Neither is this my pleasure made lesse by the decaying dulnesse of my	302	Cornaro		7
But this chiefly delights me, that my advice hath taken effect in	302	Cornaro		14
Moreover, by this also, in what estate I am, may be discovered,	302	Cornaro		27
it is evident, That the life which I live at this age, is not a dead,	303	Cornaro		9
by MR. GEORGE HERBERT to his friend the Translator of this Book.	304	Valdesso		T
and God hath put this into your hands (as he sent the fish with mony	304	Valdesso		10
happily also with this (as his thoughts are fruitfull) intending	304	Valdesso		12
in his own country he would have to flourish in this land of light,	304	Valdesso		14
This place together with many other, as namely Consid. 71. upon Our	307	Valdesso		16
He often useth this manner of speech Beleeving by Revelation,	308	Valdesso		29
this I call beleeving by Revelation, and not by Relation. . .	309	Valdesso		6
but the meaning is this, That God in the dayes of the Gospell will	310	Valdesso		4
The Doctrine of this Consideration cleareth that of the precedent	310	Valdesso		26
wee to doe with the Scriptures and this is the use of the promises	310	Valdesso		31
but this sufficeth, he himselfe allowes it for a holy conversation	311	Valdesso		1
All the discourse from this line [place] till the end of this Chapter	311	Valdesso		20
this line [place] till the end of this Chapter may seeme strange,	311	Valdesso		20
And with this exposition the Chapter is cleare enough, but the truth	311	Valdesso		30
The Authors good meaning in this, will better appear by his 98	312	Valdesso	V	4
This doctrine however true in substance, yet needeth [requireth]	314	Valdesso		1
This Chapter is considerable. The intent of it, that the world	315	Valdesso		29
this cannot stand, and it is ill Doctrine in a common-wealth.	316	Valdesso		16
so a Scholar judgeth in his study, and censureth this or that;	317	Valdesso		3
perhaps he meant all of this later not of the former. . . .	317	Valdesso		4
and surely this the Author meant by the word Jurisdiction, . .	317	Valdesso	V	7
I wonder how this opinion could befall so good a man as it seems	317	Valdesso		31
There is no more to be said of this Chapter but that his opinion	318	Valdesso		5
2 Ep. 1. 19. which he makes the ground of his [this] Consideration,	318	Valdesso		7
this being given only to the godly, and the other sometimes . .	319	Valdesso		8
Though this were the Authors opinion, yet the truth of it would be	319	Valdesso	V	15
This is true onley of the Popish Cases of Conscience, which depend	319	Valdesso	V	28
This being well weighed, will make the Consideration easy, . .	320	Valdesso		4
Mend your cloathes, and you may hold out this yeare. . . .	324	Proverbs		100
This world is nothing except it tend to another.	334	Proverbs		382
The chiefe disease that raignes this yeare is folly. . . .	346	Proverbs		765
but every thing else in this world.	358	Proverbs	D	1077
and it is this, I want Books extremely;	364	Letters		10
This also is aggravated, in that I apprehend what my Friends would	364	Letters		19
Now this Lent I am forbid utterly to eat any Fish, so that I am fain	365	Letters		1
the time when I desire this (which is now, when I must lay . .	365	Letters		17
I have wrote to my dear sick Sister this week already, and therefore	367	Letters		21
This letter runs to you with much eagernes, for I am enjoined	367	Letters		27
to those busnesses which justly excuse him from writing at this time,	367	Letters		31
because my recompenses of your favours consist in this only.	367	Letters		32
to acquaint you with those passages of newes which this time affords;	368	Letters		1
now to the answering of this demand of the Kings these Agents pretend	368	Letters		14
this passeth in Spaine freely with consent of King & counsell.	368	Letters		28
upon this he was forbid Court & kingdome, yet was seene lately neere	368	Letters		34
only my comfort is that this is but an occasion for you to amplify	369	Letters		3
This Week hath loaded me with your Favours;	369	Letters		10
yet have I sent it thither by a faithful Messenger this day:	369	Letters		16
I hope I shall get this place without all your London helps,	370	Letters		7
since this place being civil may divert me too much from Divinity,	370	Letters		19
wrote him back, that this dignity, hath no such earthiness in it,	370	Letters		22
cause this inclosed to be carried to his brothers house of his own	370	Letters		26
God who knows and sees this Writing, knows also that my solliciting	372	Letters		2
also deliver me out of the hands of this uncircumcised Philistin.	374	Letters		8
What an admirable thing is this, that God puts his shoulder to our	374	Letters		17
and that upon this ground, because they were to come into an unknown	375	Letters		13
especially at this time, being more beggarly now than I have been	375	Letters		36
But though I both consider this, and your observation, also,	376	Letters		3
how destitute she is, and that in this necessary time of education.	376	Letters		13
But take this rule, and it is an outlandish one, which I commend	376	Letters		16
let this of Leighton Church the care, be amongst the chiefest also,	378	Letters		22
and also what becomes of you this sommer.	379	Letters		25
It is the whole amount of this letter, and therefore entertaine it	379	Letters		25
Doe this & be a man as David, after Gods hart.	381	Woodnoth		20
this whole sum of five hundred pounds I bequeath unto my Neeces	382	G.H.'s Will		12
payd out of it unto some whose names shal be annexed unto this bill.	382	G.H.'s Will		16
twenty pounds unto the poore of this parish to be devided according	382	G.H.'s Will		17
John Danvers that he would be pleased to be Overseer of this Will.	382	G.H.'s Will		32
same order and habit, of which wee all in this Kingdome glorie to be.	442	Oration		21
Fame is sowne in this age, that it may be reaped in the following;	443	Oration		3
THISTLES				
If the braine sowes not corne, it plants thistles.	355	Proverbs		1024
THITHER				
Bring not thy plough, thy plots, thy pleasures thither. . .	23	Ch.-Porch		422
My bodie also thither.	52	H.Commun.		26
His praise may thither flie:	53	Antiphon 1		4
Will thither flie;	61	Praise 1		6
Thy mercies thither flock and flow:	82	Ungratef.		20
Offring at heav'n, growing and groning thither:	166	The Flower		25
But borrow'd thence to light us thither.	177	Forerunners		29
Yet as the Church shall thither westward flie, ...	197	Ch.-Milit.		259
and thither lift mine eye.	218	Psalm V	D	8
may go the right way, and thither onely, where they are onely due.	245	Priest 12		34
that if any be willing to partake, they may resort thither. . .	251	Priest 17		13
because many wayes thither are so ordered, that they all meet and end	301	Cornaro		21
Whereupon men flockt thither, and built houses with happy successe.	301	Cornaro		29
yet have I sent it thither by a faithful Messenger this day:	369	Letters		16

THOSE (cont'd)

	PAGE	TITLE		LINE
And those wayes which the wicked go	215	Psalm I	D	23
Thou hat'st those that unjustly do:	218	Psalm V	D	13
But let all those that trust in thee	219	Psalm V	D	35
those that in heart are right:	222	Psalm VII	D	38
He judgeth both the good, and those	222	Psalm VII	D	39
my poor labours, but add to those points, which I have observed,	224	Priest		15
Of those that live in the Universities, some live there in office,	226	Priest 2		2
Those that live in Noble Houses are called Chaplains, whose duty	226	Priest 2		15
in these points he labours most in those things which are most apt	227	Priest 3		11
at least all those which he observeth are most incident to his	230	Priest 5		34
as of those of antient times, so especially of the late ones;	233	Priest 7		7
and those most, which are nearest to his Parish;	233	Priest 7		8
and that the good God would pardon all those, who come with lesse	235	Priest 8		31
but only by those means, by which at first it was obtained.	237	Priest 9		20
because those trades, for the most part, serve but the vices	240	Priest 10		3
if God give any thing above those, and not spent in them,	240	Priest 10		11
Those that can read, are allowed times for it, and those that cannot,	240	Priest 10		19
are allowed times for it, and those that cannot, are taught;	240	Priest 10		20
so that as in the house of those that are skill'd in Musick,	240	Priest 10		30
But those which his home produceth, he refuseth not, as coming cheap,	241	Priest 10		21
his money for the poor, and his table for those that are above Alms.	243	Priest 11		9
Yet doth hee oftenest invite those, whom hee sees take best courses,	243	Priest 11		25
working those that are able to the same charity, still pressing it in	245	Priest 12		12
so doth he also to those at his door, whom God puts in his way,	245	Priest 12		20
be as they ought, for those great duties that are performed in them.	246	Priest 13		7
appointed by Authority be there, and those not torne, or fouled,	246	Priest 13		14
Those that he findes religiously imployed, hee both commends them	247	Priest 14		12
Those that he finds busie in the works of their calling,	247	Priest 14		20
Those that the Parson findes idle, or ill imployed, he chides	248	Priest 14		13
For both God is there also, and those for whom God dyed:	249	Priest 14		6
and even in those wrongs which either in tithing, or otherwise are	250	Priest 16		12
Therefore those he meets on the way he blesseth audibly,	251	Priest 17		2
and with those he overtakes or that overtake him, hee begins good	251	Priest 17		3
rather then to those that are further, where things are otherwise	253	Priest 19		27
Those he Catechizeth publickly, these privately, giving age honour,	255	Priest 21		23
that those of the elder sort, who are not well grounded,	255	Priest 21		29
that those who are well grown in the knowledg of Religion,	255	Priest 21		32
or Sundayes before the Communion, or on the Eves of all those dayes.	258	Priest 22		28
the people so order their affairs as to receive just at those times,	259	Priest 22		27
especially canvasing those, whose natures are most stealing,	264	Priest 26		33
in all these, and those more which concerne me, I either do nothing,	265	Priest 26		16
I am more bound to abstain from those, which by mine own experience I	266	Priest 26		24
then from those which by a Common tradition, and vulgar knowledge are	266	Priest 26		25
and those that are weakly,) but that they must rise so,	266	Priest 26		34
Yet Phisicians bid those that would live in health, not keep	267	Priest 26		10
he gives him those freer rules:	267	Priest 26		18
minde being defixed on it with those nailes wherewith his Master was:	267	Priest 27		29
and much more for those rules, which out of his choysest judgment hee	268	Priest 28		11
at least of those, who are apt to despise:	268	Priest 28		24
for this may produce hatred in those that are reproved,	268	Priest 28		29
to the examination, and punishment of those which are in Authority;	269	Priest 28		1
and dishonour him with those mouths, which he continually fils,	269	Priest 28		11
ingenuous and fit imployment is never wanting to those that seek it.	275	Priest 32		10
and to restrain all those, who else might both trouble him	276	Priest 32		15
those whom the Parson finds loose, and not ingaged into some	277	Priest 32		24
busie himself better, then in those new Plantations, and discoveryes,	278	Priest 32		5
Those that he findes in the peaceable state, he adviseth to be very	280	Priest 34		14
not to eate of all those dishes at table, which even their present	280	Priest 34		22
to store their house with all those furnitures which even their	280	Priest 34		24
Those that the Parson findes in the military state, he fortifyes,	281	Priest 34		4
Now in those that are tempted, whatsoever is unruly, falls upon two	281	Priest 34		6
perambulation, and those that withdraw, and sever themselves from it,	284	Priest 35		10
and those that thinke this superstitious, neither know superstition,	284	Priest 35		28
As for those that are ashamed to use this forme, as being old,	284	Priest 35		29
Those who use it not, do so either out of niceness, because they like	285	Priest 36		4
as appears Rom. 12. 14. how much more those, who are spiritual	286	Priest 36		28
known by common fame (and of these, those that know them, may talk,	287	Priest 37		13
and more, they may discover them to those that know them not:	287	Priest 37		17
Law intends, as is evident by those, which are branded for rogues,	287	Priest 37		19
even for those that derided him then, and still despise him.	288	Priest		29
to convert those who are not yet thine, and to confirme those that	289	Priest		16
convert those who are not yet thine, and to confirme those that are:	289	Priest		17
whether those that pleased my taste brought me commoditie	293	Cornaro		6
I was not onely freed from all those evils which had so long beset	293	Cornaro		20
that they had no great power to hurt those bodies, which were kept in	294	Cornaro		2
can bring little grief or hurt to those that are temperate.	294	Cornaro		34
if he will give his minde to those things which he should,	297	Cornaro		22
and those ten yeares, which they set at naught in regard of their	298	Cornaro		34
That those inconveniences are of no great moment (as I shewed before)	299	Cornaro		15
my gardens, and those divers, parted with rills of running water,	301	Cornaro		15
I view their pieces, I compare them with those of Antiquitie;	302	Cornaro		1
I was one of those that was deputed for the managing of that work,	302	Cornaro		17
and abode in those fenny places two whole moneths in the heat	302	Cornaro		18
the Grace of God I feel not those perturbations of bodie and minde,	302	Cornaro		24
as also to those that live in sinne, and follow their appetites:	303	Cornaro		19
and those that have inspirations must still use Peter, Gods Word:	310	Valdesso		10
and not those which are in themselves occasions of sinne;	314	Valdesso		18
but in those other occasions, Gods Spirit will mortify and try them	314	Valdesso		20
The ofspring of those that are very young, or very old, lasts not.	350	Proverbs		887
(applyed to those that have a blow).	356	Proverbs	D	1040

THOSE (cont'd)

	PAGE	TITLE		LINE
Those that God loves, do not live long.	358	Proverbs	D	1094
leaving the secrets of nature to those that have spare time.	361	Proverbs	D	1165
But I fear the heat of my late Ague hath dryed up those springs,	363	Letters		4
to reprove the vanity of those many Love-poems, that are daily writ	363	Letters		7
what is that to those infinite Volumes of Divinity, which yet every	365	Letters		14
to impart unto you some of those observations which I have framed	366	Letters		1
but upon the want of those Books which were not to be got in England;	367	Letters		4
am not over much beholding to those busnesses which justly excuse him	367	Letters		30
desire is to acquaint you with those passages of newes which this	368	Letters		1
judge me then by those waters, and not by my ink, and then you shall	372	Letters		4
therefore, if either Age or Sickness lead you to those Joyes?	372	Letters		32
have over Youth and Health, who are now so near those true Comforts.	372	Letters		33
hath made me unable to perform those Offices for which I came into	373	Letters		9
For those of Estate? of what poor regard ought they to be,	373	Letters		22
for those Afflictions of the Soul, consider that God intends that	374	Letters		8
remember those admirable words of the Psalmist:	374	Letters		13
He doubles it to take away the scruple of those that might say,	374	Letters		22
school-mistresse, and you know what those mercenary creatures are.	375	Letters		26
find out some thing not unworthy of those hands at which they aim.	377	Letters		1
the other side are the names of those to whome my deceased Neece left	383	G.H.'s Will		1
All those that are crost are discharged already the rest are to be	383	G.H.'s Will		3
entreating that you would a while lay aside those warlike lookes,	442	Oration		2
of his praise, no, not, as in past ages, those Pillars of Hercules.	442	Oration		13
the felicitie of so great Princes redound also to those servants,	442	Oration		26

THOU

	PAGE	TITLE		LINE
Thou, whose sweet youth and early hopes inhance	6	Ch.-Porch		1
Abstaine or wedd: if thou canst not abstaine	7	Ch.-Porch	W	13
If thou chuse bravely & rely on God	7	Ch.-Porch	W	17
Drink not the third glasse, which thou canst not tame,	7	Ch.-Porch		25
Mayst rule it, as thou list; and poure the shame,	7	Ch.-Porch		27
Stay at the third glasse: if thou lose thy hold,	8	Ch.-Porch		41
Then thou art modest, and the wine grows bold.	8	Ch.-Porch		42
Yet, if thou sinne in wine or wantonnesse,	8	Ch.-Porch		49
When thou dost tell anothers jest, therein	9	Ch.-Porch		61
If thou wilt die, the gates of hell are broad:	9	Ch.-Porch		71
Flie idlenesse, which yet thou canst not flie	9	Ch.-Porch		79
Art thou a Magistrate? then be severe:	10	Ch.-Porch		85
If thou art nothing, think what thou wouldst bee	10	Ch.-Porch	W	90
But if thou coole, then take some shame to thee	10	Ch.-Porch	W	90
Thou hast run all thy race, ere thou beginn.	10	Ch.-Porch	W	90
Then all thou addest may be call'd his treasure.	11	Ch.-Porch		114
When thou dost purpose ought within thy power,	11	Ch.-Porch		115
Thou hast two sconses, if thy stomack call;	11	Ch.-Porch		128
Thou liv'st by rule. What doth not so, but man?	12	Ch.-Porch		134
Thou liv'st by rule. What does not so, but man?	12	Ch.-Porch	W	134
Entice the trusty sunne, if that thou can,	12	Ch.-Porch	W	136
And tumble up and down what thou find'st there.	12	Ch.-Porch		148
That thou hast gotten. Surely use alone	12	Ch.-Porch		155
Will canker both, yett thou alone shallt smart:	13	Ch.-Porch	W	166
Gold thou mayst safely touch; but if it stick	13	Ch.-Porch		167
As all the day thou mayst hold out to go.	14	Ch.-Porch		186
That all the day thou mayst hold out to go.	14	Ch.-Porch	W	186
If yet thou love game at so deere a rate,	14	Ch.-Porch		199
By great deeds shew, that thou canst little do;	15	Ch.-Porch		220
Thy person share, and thou thy mirth inhanse.	15	Ch.-Porch	W	232
But may be wittie, if thou hast the vein.	16	Ch.-Porch		240
Hast thou the knack? pamper it not with liking:	16	Ch.-Porch		243
But if thou want it, buy it not too deere.	16	Ch.-Porch		244
Envie not greatnesse: for thou mak'st thereby	16	Ch.-Porch		259
The shrine is that which thou dost venerate;	17	Ch.-Porch		267
If cause require, thou art his sacrifice;	17	Ch.-Porch		273
Yet be not surety, if thou be a father.	17	Ch.-Porch		277
If thou be single, all thy goods and ground	17	Ch.-Porch		283
In thy discourse, if thou desire to please:	18	Ch.-Porch		289
For so thou dost thy self and him a pleasure:	18	Ch.-Porch		296
If thou be Master-gunner, spend not all	18	Ch.-Porch		301
That thou canst speak, at once; but husband it,	18	Ch.-Porch		302
As if thou mad'st thy will. A civil guest	18	Ch.-Porch		305
Be usefull where thou livest, that they may	19	Ch.-Porch		325
So shalt thou humble and magnanimous be:	19	Ch.-Porch		332
If thou observest strangers in each fit,	21	Ch.-Porch		365
Till thou change names, and be where he began.	21	Ch.-Porch		378
Write, So much giv'n to God; thou shalt be heard.	21	Ch.-Porch		382
Fast when thou wilt; but then 'tis gain, not losse.	22	Ch.-Porch		396
God is more there, then thou: for thou art there	22	Ch.-Porch		404
Stay not for th' other pin: why thou hast lost	23	Ch.-Porch		411
Christ purg'd his temple; so must thou thy heart.	23	Ch.-Porch		423
If thou mislike him, thou conceiv'st him not.	23	Ch.-Porch		428
How know'st thou, but thy sinnes made him miscarrie?	24	Ch.-Porch		440
Summe up at night, what thou hast done by day;	24	Ch.-Porch		451
Summe up at night, what thou hast done that day;	24	Ch.-Porch	W	451
And in the morning, what thou hast to do.	24	Ch.-Porch		452
If thou do ill; the joy fades, not the pains:	24	Ch.-Porch		461
Thou, whom the former precepts have	25	Superlim		1
Judas, dost thou betray me with a kisse?	28	Sacrifice		41
Canst thou finde hell about my lips? and misse	28	Sacrifice		42
But, O my God, my God! why leav'st thou me,	33	Sacrifice		213
The sonne, in whom thou dost delight to be?	33	Sacrifice		214
The sonne, in whom thou art well pleas'd to be?	33	Sacrifice	W	214
Shall I weep bloud? why, thou hast wept such store	35	Thanksgvng		5

THOU (cont'd)	PAGE	TITLE		LINE
My God, my God, why dost thou part from me?	35	Thanksgvng		9
If thou dost give me wealth, I will restore	35	Thanksgvng		19
If thou dost give me honour, men shall see,	35	Thanksgvng		21
If thou shalt give me wit, it shall appeare,	36	Thanksgvng		43
If thou hast giv'n it me, 'tis here.	36	Thanksgvng		44
Ah! was it not enough that thou	37	Reprisall		9
Couldst thou not griefs sad conquests me allow,	37	Reprisall		11
Remember that thou once didst write in stone.	38	The Sinner		14
Sinn being gone o doe thou fill	39	Good Fri.	W	29
Thou hast an ancient claime to mee.	39	Good Fri.	W	32
O blessed bodie! Whither art thou thrown?	40	Sepulchre		1
Was writ in stone; so thou, which also art	41	Sepulchre		18
Who takes thee by the hand, that thou likewise	41	Easter		3
But thou wast up by break of day,	42	Easter		21
But thou wast up before myne houre	42	Easter	W	21
Yet thou with sicknesses and shame	43	East.wings	W	12
Thou didst so punish sinne,	43	East.wings		13
Thou didst lay hold, and antedate	44	H. Bapt.2		4
That thou hast ought to do with me.	45	Nature		3
If thou shalt let this venome lurk,	45	Nature		7
Lord, with what care hast thou begirt us round!	45	Sinne 1		1
When first thou didst entice to thee my heart,	46	Afflict.1		1
At first thou gav'st me milk and sweetnesses;	47	Afflict.1		19
When I got health, thou took'st away my life,	47	Afflict.1		31
Thou didst betray me to a lingring book,	47	Afflict.1		39
Thou often didst with Academick praise	47	Afflict.1		45
Turning my purge to food, thou throwest me	48	Afflict.1		51
Now I am here, what thou wilt do with me	48	Afflict.1		55
Yet, though thou troublest me, I must be meek;	48	Afflict.1		61
Which thou hast pour'd into my soul;	49	Repentance		20
For if thou stay,	49	Repentance		22
When thou for sinne rebukest man,	49	Repentance		25
But thou wilt sinne and grief destroy;	49	Repentance		31
Lord, how couldst thou so much appease	49	Faith		1
Thus dost thou make proud knowledge bend & crouch	50	Faith		31
Thus dost thou make proud knowledge bow & crouch	50	Faith	W	31
Inherent in them, thou didst make the sunne	51	Faith		34
Thou, who from me wast sold,	52	H.Commun.		3
Thou, who for me wast sold,	52	H.Commun.	V	3
For so thou should'st without me still have been,	52	H.Commun.		5
Thou creep'st into my breast;	52	H.Commun.		8
Thou hast restor'd us to this ease	53	H.Commun.		37
Since thou hast taught us by thy word,	53	H.Commun.	W	39
And thrown it on that dust which thou hast made,	54	Love 1		4
And thrown it in that dust which thou hast made,	54	Love 1	W	4
Thou standing by: and though thy glorious name	54	Love 1		11
Thou shalt recover all thy goods in kinde,	54	Love 2		11
Wilt thou meet arms with man, that thou dost stretch	55	Temper 1		13
Then of a sinner thou art rid,	55	Temper 1		19
Lord, if thou must needs use thy dart,	56	Temper 2		3
Thou suddenly dost raise and race,	56	Temper 2		7
For when thou dost depart from hence,	56	Temper 2		11
Thou wouldst extend me to some good,	57	Employm. 1		2
For as thou dost impart thy grace,	57	Employm. 1		9
Thou art all health, health thriving, till it make	58	H.Script.1		5
A full eternitie: thou art a masse	58	H.Script.1		6
Thy praise too much? thou art heav'ns Lidger here,	58	H.Script.1		11
Thy praise enough? thou art heav'ns Lidger here,	58	H.Script.1	W	11
Thou art joyes handsell: heav'n lies flat in thee,	58	H.Script.1		13
On thy Apostles? thou didst then	59	Whitsunday		6
Such glorious gifts thou didst bestow,	59	Whitsunday		9
Thou shutt'st the doore, and keep'st within;	60	Whitsunday		21
Lord, though we change, thou art the same;	60	Whitsunday		25
What if I say thou seek'st delayes;	61	Grace	W	20
Wilt thou not then my fault reprove?	61	Grace	W	20
O come! for thou dost know the way.	61	Grace		21
Or if to me thou wilt not move,	61	Grace		22
Thou shalt have more.	61	Praise 1		4
Thou Lord of life; since thy one death for me	62	Afflict.2		2
Thou art my grief alone,	62	Afflict.2		11
Thou Lord conceal it not: and as thou art	62	Afflict.2		12
But thou art ready there to catch	62	Mattens		2
That thou shouldst it so eye, and wooe,	62	Mattens		10
As if that thou hadst nothing els to do?	62	Mattens		12
Yet still thou goest on,	64	Even-song		17
Thou dost inclose us, till the day	64	Even-song		22
My God, thou art all love.	64	Even-song		29
And true descent; that when thou shalt grow fat,	65	Ch.-monum.		18
And wanton in thy cravings, thou mayst know,	65	Ch.-monum.		19
That thou mayst fit thy self against thy fall.	65	Ch.-monum.		24
Yet in thy temple thou dost him afford	67	Windows		3
But when thou dost anneal in glasse thy storie,	67	Windows		6
When all thy deeds, whose brunt thou feel'st alone,	69	Content		29
Affront those joyes, wherewith thou didst endow,	71	Frailtie		19
By that I knew that thou wast in the grief,	73	Afflict.3		2
Hadst thou not had thy part,	73	Afflict.3		5
Thou knowst my tallies; and when there's assign'd	73	Afflict.3		8
Thy life on earth was grief, and thou art still	73	Afflict.3		13
Thou dying dayly, praise thee to thy losse.	73	Afflict.3		18
Canst thou be any where	74	The Starre		3

THOU (cont'd)

	PAGE	TITLE		LINE
Yet, if thou wilt from thence depart,	74	The Starre		5
For thou canst make a debter,	74	The Starre		7
Unto the place where thou	74	The Starre		19
Sure thou wilt joy, by gaining me	74	The Starre		29
The other dayes and thou	75	Sunday		8
Make up one man; whose face thcu art,	75	Sunday		9
To endlesse death: but thou dost pull	75	Sunday		16
Thou art a day of mirth:	76	Sunday		57
Money, thou bane of blisse, & sourse of wo,	77	Avarice		1
Whence com'st thou, that thou art so fresh and fine?	77	Avarice		2
Surely thou didst so little contribute	77	Avarice		5
To this great kingdome, which thou now hast got,	77	Avarice		6
That he was fain, when thou wert destitute,	77	Avarice		7
Nay, thou hast got the face of man; for we	77	Avarice		10
Thou art the man, and man but drosse to thee.	77	Avarice		12
Thou art the holy mine, whence came the gold,	78	Ang.&Sts.		11
Thou art the sacred mine, whence came the gold,	78	Ang.&Sts.	W	11
Thou art the cabinet where the jewell lay:	78	Ang.&Sts.		14
O that thou shouldst give dust a tongue	80	Deniall		16
O Thou, whose glorious, yet contracted light,	81	Christmas		9
To Man of all beasts be not thou a stranger:	81	Christmas		12
Furnish & deck my soul, that thou mayst have	81	Christmas		13
Of better lodging thou maist be possest.	80	Christmas	W	14
Hast thou redeem'd us from the grave!	82	Ungratef.		2
If thou hadst let us runne,	82	Ungratef.		3
Thou hast but two rare cabinets full of treasure,	82	Ungratef.		7
Thou hadst but two rich cabinets of treasure,	82	Ungratef.	W	7
Thou hast unlockt them both,	82	Ungratef.		9
Thou hast layd open both,	82	Ungratef.	W	9
Therefore thou dost not show	82	Ungratef.		15
For by that powder thou wilt make us see.	82	Ungratef.		18
For by this powder thou wilt make us see.	82	Ungratef.	W	18
When thou demandest but a heart,	82	Ungratef.		26
But on thy glorie! then thou wilt reform	83	Sighs & Gr.		3
And not refuse me: for thou onely art	83	Sighs & Gr.		4
For thou hast other vessels full of bloud,	83	Sighs & Gr.		21
For thou hast life and death at thy command;	83	Sighs & Gr.		26
Thou art both Judge and Saviour, feast and rod,	83	Sighs & Gr.		27
Poore man, thou searchest round	86	Vanitie 1		27
Give to thy Mother, what thou wouldst allow	86	Lent		5
For thou must die.	87	Vertue		4
And thou must die.	87	Vertue		8
Since then, my God, thou hast	92	Man		49
Lord thou dost deserve much more.	93	Antiphon 2	W	19
And thou within them starve at doore.	93	Unkindness		14
Yet can a friend what thou hast done fulfill?	94	Unkindness		21
But that thou art my wisdome, Lord,	95	Submission		1
How know I, if thou shouldst me raise,	95	Submission		13
Onely do thou lend me a hand,	95	Submission		19
Since thou hast both mine eyes.	95	Submission		20
Lord, thou didst make me, yet thou woundest me;	95	Justice 1		2
Lord, thou dost wound me, yet thou dost relieve me:	95	Justice 1		3
Lord, thou relievest, yet I die by thee:	95	Justice 1		4
Lord, thou dost kill me, yet thou dost reprieve me.	95	Justice 1		5
A poore mans rod, when thou dost ride,	96	Charms & K		3
A poore mans rod if thou wilt hire	96	Charms & K	W	3
And anchor thou art onely, to confirm	97	Afflict.5		4
Thine own delights thou didst to us impart:	97	Afflict.5		8
When we grew wanton, thou didst use displeasure	97	Afflict.5		9
Now thou wouldst taste our miserie.	97	Afflict.5		12
Sweet were the dayes, when thou didst lodge with Lot,	99	Decay		1
But now thou dost thy self immure and close	99	Decay		11
How canst thou brook his foolishnesse?	100	Miserie		7
That thou within his curtains drawn canst see:	100	Miserie		16
Thou art all brightnesse, perfect puritie;	101	Miserie		32
How hast thou lost them in a croud of cares?	101	Miserie		50
Thou pull'st the rug, and wilt not rise,	101	Miserie		51
Thou lyest warme, and wilt not rise,	101	Miserie	W	51
Thou must go sleep, or dine.	101	Miserie		54
My blessed Lord, art thou! how suddenly	103	Prayer 2		2
Art thou, my blessed King? how suddenly	103	Prayer 2	W	2
Thou canst no more not heare, then thou canst die.	103	Prayer 2		6
Art thou possest, who, when thou couldst not die,	103	Prayer 2		14
Thou mightst make way for liberalitie!	103	Prayer 2		18
That thou shouldst minde a rotten tree?	104	Obedience		22
Yet since thou canst not choose but see my actions;	104	Obedience		23
Thou mayst as well my actions guide, as see.	104	Obedience		25
Not a fair look, but thou dost call it foul:	105	Conscience		2
Not a sweet dish, but thou dost call it sowre:	105	Conscience		3
If thou persistest, I will tell thee,	105	Conscience		11
Yet if thou talkest still,	106	Conscience		19
Lord with what glorie wast thou serv'd of old,	106	Sion		1
Wherefore thou quitt'st thy ancient claim:	106	Sion		10
There thou art struggling with a peevish heart,	106	Sion		13
Which sometimes crosseth thee, thou sometimes it:	106	Sion		14
While thou dost ever, ever stay:	107	Home		2
How canst thou stay, considering the pace	107	Home		7
The bloud did make, which thou didst waste?	107	Home		8
After all this canst thou be strange?	108	Home		26
Yet if thou stayest still, why must I stay?	108	Home		31

THOU (cont'd)

	PAGE	TITLE		LINE
With one small sigh thou gav'st me th' other day	108	Home		43
But thou shalt answer, Lord, for me.	110	The Quip		8
But thou shalt answer, Lord, for me.	110	The Quip		12
But thou shalt answer, Lord, for me.	111	The Quip		16
But thou shalt answer, Lord, for me.	111	The Quip		20
But thou dost still lament, and pine, and crie;	112	Dawning		7
Arise sad heart; if thou dost not withstand,	112	Dawning		9
Arise sad heart; if thou doe not withstand,	112	Dawning	V	9
Canst be idle? canst thou play,	113	Businesse		1
Hast thou tears, or hast thou none?	113	Businesse		5
If, poore soul, thou hast no tears,	113	Businesse		6
Would thou hadst no faults or fears!	113	Businesse		7
Hast thou sighs, or hast thou not?	113	Businesse		11
If thou hast no sighs or grones,	113	Businesse		12
Would thou hadst no flesh and bones!	113	Businesse		13
But if yet thou idle be,	113	Businesse		15
Thou hadst di'd most wretchedly;	113	Businesse		21
Thou hadst liv'd in miserie.	113	Businesse		27
If I say, Thou shalt be mine;	114	Dialogue		11
Ah! no more: thou break'st my heart.	115	Dialogue		32
Thou art my lovelinesse, my life, my light,	115	Dulnesse		9
The very dust, where thou dost tread and go,	115	Dulnesse		15
Sure thou didst put a minde there, if I could	116	Dulnesse		23
Onely to Man thou hast made known thy wayes,	117	Providence		6
Thou art in small things great, not small in any:	118	Providence		41
Thou art in all things one, in each thing many:	118	Providence		43
For thou art infinite in one and all.	118	Providence		44
Which crie and follow. Thou hast made poore sand	118	Providence		47
How finely dost thou times and seasons spin,	118	Providence		57
Thou hast hid metals: man may take them thence;	119	Providence		81
If they seek fine things, thou dost make them run	120	Providence		106
When th' earth was dry, thou mad'st a sea of wet:	120	Providence		113
When that lay gather'd, thou didst broach the mountains:	120	Providence		114
Sometimes thou dost divide thy gifts to man,	120	Providence		125
To show thou art not bound, as if thy lot	121	Providence		137
Were worse then ours; sometimes thou shiftest hands.	121	Providence		138
And in his blessing thou art blest:	123	Time		13
For where thou onely wert before	123	Time		14
Thou art a gard'ner now, and more,	123	Time		16
Thou that hast giv'n so much to me,	123	Gratefulnes		1
All thou hast giv'n him heretofore	123	Gratefulnes		7
But thou didst reckon, when at first	123	Gratefulnes		9
This not withstanding, thou wentst on,	124	Gratefulnes		17
Nay thou hast made a sigh and grone	124	Gratefulnes		19
Not that thou hast not still above	124	Gratefulnes		21
And in no quiet canst thou be,	124	Gratefulnes		26
Sweet Peace, where dost thou dwell? I humbly crave,	124	Peace		1
Except thou make us dayly, we shall spurn	127	Giddinesse		27
When thou dost greater judgements SPARE,	133	Paradise		10
Quickly effect, what thou dost move;	133	The Method		6
If thou hadst lost a glove or ring,	133	The Method		11
Wouldst thou not look?	133	The Method		12
And art thou grieved, sweet and sacred Dove,	135	Ephes.		1
For where thou dwellest all is neat.	136	Familie		8
Perhaps thou com'st sometimes, and for a day;	137	Familie		23
Descend and fall, and thou dost flow.	137	The Size		6
If thou hast wherewithall to spice a draught,	137	The Size		9
Wouldst thou his laws of fasting disanull?	138	The Size		15
Wouldst thou both eat thy cake, and have it?	138	The Size		18
Grasp not at much, for fear thou losest all.	138	The Size		38
Which thou hast open'd: do not spread thy robe	138	The Size		43
Do as thou usest, disobey,	139	Artillerie		6
And work up to thee; yet thou dost refuse.	139	Artillerie		20
Then thou to grant mine: but because	139	Artillerie		23
Then we are shooters both, and thou dost deigne	139	Artillerie		25
Yet if thou shunnest, I am thine:	139	Artillerie		29
Brave rose, (alas!) where art thou? in the chair	140	Ch.-rents		1
Brave rose, (alas!) where art thou? in the place	140	Ch.-rents	V	1
Where thou didst lately so triumph and shine,	140	Ch.-rents		2
Are the more foul, the more thou wert divine.	140	Ch.-rents		4
Wast thou of old,	141	Justice 2		2
For where before thou still didst call on me,	141	Justice 2		19
Because thou art	143	Complaining		2
Thou art the Lord of glorie;	143	Complaining		6
Art thou all justice, Lord?	143	Complaining		11
Busie enquiring heart, what wouldst thou know?	144	Discharge		1
Why dost thou prie,	144	Discharge		2
Hast thou not made thy counts, and summ'd up all?	144	Discharge		6
For thou canst tell,	144	Discharge		19
And happy thou,	144	Discharge		22
If, though thou didst not beat thy future brow,	144	Discharge		23
Thou couldst well see	144	Discharge		24
They ask enough; why shouldst thou further go?	145	Discharge		26
Wilt thou forestall it, and now grieve to morrow,	145	Discharge		48
Thou hast granted my request,	146	Praise 2		5
Thou hast heard me:	146	Praise 2		6
Thou didst note my working breast,	146	Praise 2		7
Thou hast spar'd me.	146	Praise 2		8
Thou didst cleare me;	146	Praise 2		14
Thou didst heare me.	146	Praise 2		16

THOU (cont'd)

	PAGE	TITLE	LINE
Thou grew'st soft and moist with tears,	146	Praise 2	21
Thou relentedst:	146	Praise 2	22
Thou dissentedst.	146	Praise 2	24
What hast thou there? a heart? but is it pure?	147	Offering	3
And thou mayst offer many gifts in one.	147	Offering	18
Untill thou finde and use it to thy good:	147	Offering	23
Lord thou dost convert,	147	Offering	27
What thou hast kept,	147	Offering	29
Which thou dost curse.	147	Offering	29
Mothers are kinde, because thou art,	148	Longing	9
Lord Jesu, thou didst bow	148	Longing	14
Wilt thou deferre	149	Longing	31
Hast thou left all things to their course,	149	Longing	39
Thou tarriest, while I die,	149	Longing	44
And fall to nothing: thou dost reigne,	150	Longing	55
Lord, didst thou leave thy throne,	150	Longing	56
That thou art grown	150	Longing	61
Hast thou not heard, that my Lord JESUS di'd?	150	Longing	63
And thou hast hands.	151	The Bag	7
While thou didst wink and wouldst not see.	153	The Collar	18
Thou cam'st but now; wilt thou so soon depart,	153	The Collar	26
Wert thou a winde or wave,	154	Glimpse	2
Thou knowst how grief and sinne	154	Glimpse	8
Bitterly spitefull thought! Couldst thou invent	155	Glimpse	28
Thou said'st but even now,	155	Assurance	2
What is thy aim? wouldst thou unlock the doore	155	Assurance	7
Wouldst thou raise devils? I see, I know,	155	Assurance	15
But thou art my desert:	155	Assurance	17
Thou art not onely to perform thy part,	156	Assurance	25
Thou didst at once thy self indite,	156	Assurance	27
Wherefore if thou canst fail,	156	Assurance	29
And rivers stirre, thou canst not shrink or quail:	156	Assurance	31
Then shalt thou be my rock and tower,	156	Assurance	33
To hide thy shame: for thou hast cast a bone	156	Assurance	35
Lord, thou art mine, and I am thine,	156	Assurance	39
And thou with me dost thee restore.	157	Clasping	1
Lord, I am thine, and thou art mine:	157	Clasping	8
So mine thou art, that something more	157	Clasping	11
For thou didst suffer to restore	157	Clasping	12
Since thou in death wast none of thine,	157	Clasping	14
That thou mayst yet have more.	157	Clasping	17
When thou dost favour any action,	157	Praise 3	6
When thou dost blesse, hath twelve: one wheel doth rise	158	Praise 3	7
But when thou dost on businesse blow,	158	Praise 3	11
Thou heardst my call, and more.	158	Praise 3	13
But after thou hadst slipt a drop	158	Praise 3	24
And bloudie battell which thou once didst trie)	158	Praise 3	31
That with th' one hand thou liftest to the sky,	158	Praise 3	35
But thou art fire, sacred and hallow'd fire;	160	Priesthood	2
Whither, O, whither art thou fled,	160	Priesthood	7
That thou art there.	162	The Search	1
Lord, dost thou some new fabrick mold,	162	The Search	8
When thou dost turn, and wilt be neare;	162	The Search	25
Thou turnest th' edge of all things on me still,	163	The Search	53
When thou dost turn,	165	The Crosse	21
Thou hast a garden for us, where to bide.	166	The Flower	34
Let losers talk: yet thou shalt die;	167	The Flower	46
Thou so much worse, that thou shalt be no more.	169	Dial.-Anth	7
Thou who dost dwell and linger here below,	169	Dial.-Anth	10
That so in purenesse thou mayst him adore,	170	Water-crs.	1
Thou who condemnest Jewish hate,	170	Water-crs.	9
Since thou dost love, yet strike;	170	Self-cond.	1
When thou shalt look us out of pain,	171	Bittersweet	2
For thou art with me; and thy rod	172	The Glance	21
Nay, thou dost make me sit and dine,	173	23 Psalme	15
Yet have they left me, Thou art still my God.	173	23 Psalme	17
So Thou art still my God, be out of fear.	176	Forerunners	6
Hony of roses, whither wilt thou flie?	176	Forerunners	10
And wilt thou leave the Church, and love a stie?	176	Forerunners	20
Fie, thou wilt soil thy broider'd coat,	176	Forerunners	22
For, Thou art still my God, is all that ye	176	Forerunners	23
Thou art God:	177	Forerunners	32
Souls joy, when thou art gone,	179	Discipline	31
Because thou dost abide with me,	183	A Parodie	1
Yet when thou dost suppresse	183	A Parodie	4
And when thou dost but shine lesse cleare,	183	A Parodie	6
Say, that thcu art not here.	183	A Parodie	19
That I may seek, but thou art lost;	183	A Parodie	20
Thou and alone thou know'st.	183	A Parodie	24
Thou com'st and dost relieve.	183	A Parodie	25
Thou saist, this fruit is mine.	184	A Parodie	30
Death, thou wast once an uncouth hideous thing,	184	The Elixer W	12
Thy mouth was open, but thou couldst not sing.	185	Death	1
Thou art grown fair and full of grace,	185	Death	4
When thou shalt call	186	Death	15
But I resolve, when thou shalt call for mine,	187	Judgement	4
There thou shalt finde my faults are thine.	188	Judgement	11
Thou Echo, thou art mortall, all men know.	188	Judgement	15
Wert thou not born among the trees and leaves?	188	Heaven	3
Wert thou not born among the woods and leaves?	188	Heaven	5
	188	Heaven W	5

THOU (cont'd)

	PAGE	TITLE		LINE
Early didst thou arise to plant this vine,	190	Ch.-Milit.		11
Thou didst rise early for to plant this vine,	190	Ch.-Milit.	W	11
My God, thou dost prepare for them a way	197	Ch.-Milit.		249
Thou wilt revenge their quarrell, making grace	197	Ch.-Milit.		255
Whether in these gifts thou bee so	200	H. Commun.	W	2
As thou art evry-where;	200	H. Commun.	W	3
Or rather so, as thou alone	200	H. Commun.	W	4
But that both thou, and all thy traine	200	H. Commun.	W	10
Thou dost come first to them, that showes	200	H. Commun.	W	14
Or if that thou two stations makest	200	H. Commun.	W	16
In Bread & mee, the way thou takest	200	H. Commun.	W	17
That thou didst all those pains endure	200	H. Commun.	W	20
Thou drivest from his seat.	200	H. Commun.	W	24
If thou hadst dyde for Bread.	201	H. Commun.	W	27
Thou took'st that pledg from mee:	201	H. Commun.	W	45
Thou art too hard for me in Love:	201	love	W	1
Thou still, O Lord, outstrippest mee.	201	love	W	6
I took a time when thou didst sleep	202	love	W	13
Yet then I found, that thou didst creep	202	love	W	16
If thou subdue mortalitie	202	love	W	21
Thou do'st no more, then doth the grave:	202	love	W	22
If thou deferr this light, then shadow mee:	203	Even-song	W	9
But thou art Light & darknes both togeather:	203	Even-song	W	13
And thou more dark then either.	203	Even-song	W	16
Yet Thou art not so dark, since I know this,	203	Even-song	W	17
Or rather as thou movedst mee.	204	Persever.	W	4
For who can tell, though thou hast dyde to winn	205	Persever.	W	9
Thou art my rock, thou art my rest.	205	Persever.	W	16
If thou chance for to find	207	Walton 3		1
If thou dost find an house built to thy mind	207	Walton 4		1
Serve thou the more God and the poore;	207	Walton 4		3
But onely while thou speak'st; This Anchor will.	439	Walton 5		4
Nor canst thou be content, unlesse thou to	439	Walton 5		5
Thou art requited; for his Fame,	209	H. Danvers	D	8
Worthy had bin, thou hadst not lost thine owne:	211	Bohemia	D	2
And what is fortunes. Thou hast singled out	211	Bohemia	D	19
Thou shalt not bee a Queene and conquer there.	212	Bohemia	D	40
Yet hast thou more dominions: God doth give	212	Bohemia	D	41
But joyes are stord for thee: thou shalt returne	212	Bohemia	D	55
He said to me, Thou art my Son,	216	Psalm II	D	17
Thou shalt possess earth's farthest bounds	216	Psalm II	D	21
But thou, O Lord, art still the shield	216	Psalm III	D	5
Thou art my glory, Lord, and he	216	Psalm III	D	7
For thou upon the cheek-bone smit'st	217	Psalm III	D	19
And thou hast brok th' ungodly's teeth:	217	Psalm III	D	21
O thou that hast enlarged me	217	Psalm IV	D	3
do thou to us afford.	217	Psalm IV	D	24
Thou in the morn shalt have my mone,	218	Psalm V	D	5
Thou art a God whose puritie	218	Psalm V	D	9
Thou hat'st those that unjustly do:	218	Psalm V	D	13
thou slay'st the men that lye:	218	Psalm V	D	14
which Thou did'st preordain.	221	Psalm VII	D	24
Thou art that righteous God by whom	221	Psalm VII	D	35
Why dost thou preach my Laws, and takest my Covenant in thy mouth?	226	Priest 2		14
errand I come, let me hold my peace, and doe thou speak thy selfe;	233	Priest 7		36
for thou art Love, and when thou teachest, all are Scholers.	233	Priest 7		36
So Isa. 64. Oh that thou would'st rent the Heavens, that thou wouldst	234	Priest 7		2
that thou would'st rent the Heavens, that thou wouldst come down, &c.	234	Priest 7		3
every one is more awaked, when we come, and say, Thou art the man.	236	Priest 8		15
For many and wonderfull things are spoken of thee, thou great Vertue.	244	Priest 12		8
thou knowest what thou didst, when thou appointedst it to be done	257	Priest 22		32
knowest what thou didst, when thou appointedst it to be done thus;	257	Priest 22		33
therefore doe thou fulfill what thou didst appoint;	257	Priest 22		34
for thou art not only the feast, but the way to it.	257	Priest 22		34
yet art thou our Creatour, and we thy work:	288	Priest		12
then did'st thou place us in Paradise, and wert proceeding still	288	Priest		14
But thou Lord, art patience, and pity, and sweetnesse, and love;	288	Priest		20
Thou hast exalted thy mercy above all things;	288	Priest		22
had sinned beyond any help in heaven or earth, then thou saidest, Lo,	288	Priest		26
didst thou arise triumphant, and therein mad'st us victorious.	289	Priest		1
and reconciliation, thou hast committed, not to Thunder,	289	Priest		4
which thou hast made a Land of light, a store-house of thy treasures	289	Priest		18
but pardon our sins, and perfect what thou hast begun.	289	Priest		21
teach thou me, that I may teach them:	289	Priest		26
Thou hast elected us, thou hast called us, thou hast justified us,	290	Priest		2
Thou hast elected us, thou hast called us, thou hast justified us,	290	Priest		3
thou hast called us, thou hast justified us, sanctified,	290	Priest		3
Thou was born for us, and thou livedst and diedst for us:	290	Priest		4
Thou hast given us the blessings of this life, and of a better.	290	Priest		5
And now Lord, thou hast fed us with the bread of life:	290	Priest		8
Learne weeping, and thou shalt laugh gayning.	325	Proverbs		127
Welcome evill, if thou commest alone.	325	Proverbs		140
Call me not an olive, till thou see me gathered.	331	Proverbs		301
Thou hast death in thy house, and dost bewaile anothers.	334	Proverbs		376
My house, my house, though thou art small,	335	Proverbs		413
thou art to me the Escuriall.	335	Proverbs		413
Be what thou wouldst seeme to be.	345	Proverbs		724
If thou thy selfe canst doe it, attend no others helpe or hand.	348	Proverbs		813
Doe what thou oughtest, and come what come can.	348	Proverbs		818

THOUGH (cont'd)	PAGE	TITLE		LINE
2 Kings 2. 24. which though our Saviour reproved as unfitting for his	285	Priest 36		26
But some may say, though the Law allow this, the Gospel doth not,	287	Priest 37		22
But though the streams of thy bloud were currant through darknesse,	288	Priest		32
though it was but a little excesse, in a few dayes had so soon	297	Cornaro		5
better to please the Appetite (though they live ten yeares lesse then	298	Cornaro		27
quantitie of any meat or drink (though most agreeable to them) then	300	Cornaro		12
though they live disorderly, yet continue in health to their lives	300	Cornaro		18
and, though subject to death, yet continually afraid of it:	303	Cornaro		17
And David (though David) studied all the day long in it:	306	Valdesso		20
though it were the Authors opinion, yet the truth of it would be	307	Valdesso		21
or conditionally he prayed as man, though as God he knew the event.	315	Valdesso		11
the Scriptures, or to themselves being still men, though godly men.	316	Valdesso		4
though in the point of Resurrection he agreed with them,	316	Valdesso		9
Though this were the Authors opinion, yet the truth of it would be	319	Valdesso	V	15
Though the Mastiffe be gentle, yet bite him not by the lippe.	325	Proverbs		132
Though the Mastiffe be gentile, yet bite him not by the lippe.	325	Proverbs	V	132
Though a lie be well drest, it is ever overcome.	325	Proverbs		133
Though old and wise, yet still advise.	325	Proverbs		134
Though you rise early, yet the day comes	332	Proverbs		333
Serve a noble disposition, though poore,	333	Proverbs		368
My house, my house, though thou art small,	335	Proverbs		413
Though the Fox run, the chicken hath wings.	339	Proverbs		549
Though you see a Church-man ill, yet continue in the Church still.	344	Proverbs		698
Though God take the sunne out of the Heaven,	353	Proverbs		980
There is no man, though never so little,	359	Proverbs	D	1119
Though I had the best wit in the World, yet it would easily tyre me,	363	Letters		14
or five Shillings come in my way, I buy it, though I fast for it;	365	Letters		12
Now though they have hitherto travelled upon your charge,	366	Letters		31
though your noble disposition is infinitely free, yet I had rather	367	Letters		6
for though it is likely that the time after the Holydaye will bee	368	Letters		2
is the finest place in the University, though not the gainfullest;	369	Letters		31
though never so, but that I have both time and work to be Your	370	Letters		13
though for the reckoning of your favours, I shall never find time	370	Letters		30
though businesses may stop my hand, yet my heart, a much better	371	Letters		26
But though I both consider this, and your observation, also,	376	Letters		3
though it be none of the Court-stile, yet doubtless Madam,	377	Letters		2
so though you incline not, happily you restraine.	381	Woodnoth		9
7. Though you want all success either in inclining or restraining,	381	Woodnoth		14
THOUGHT				
Who never thought that any robberie:	28	Sacrifice		63
I thought the service brave:	46	Afflict.1		2
Which when I could not get, I thought it here:	50	Faith		10
And thought his god most brave;	82	Ungratef.		5
From the least spot or thought of blame.	93	Unkindness		9
Any thought of waving.	114	Dialogue		4
Surely, thought I,	124	Peace		8
But then a thought creeps in,	127	Giddinesse		6
But when I thought to sleep out all these faults	130	Love unkn.		49
To wash away my stubborn thought:	139	Artillerie		15
Thought to let out, the bleeding did you good,	140	Ch.-rents		14
O spitefull bitter thought!	155	Assurance		1
Bitterly spitefull thought! Couldst thou invent	155	Assurance		2
Now foolish thought go on,	156	Assurance		37
As passeth thought:	163	The Search		38
Who would have thought my shrivel'd heart	166	The Flower		8
Which doth not meet with an eternall thought.	190	Ch.-Milit.		8
Which does not meet with an eternall thought.	190	Ch.-Milit.	W	8
I thought it brave to praise thee then,	202	love	W	15
because all ages have thought that a competency, and he that profits	235	Priest 7		11
or painted there, which may excite the reader to a thought of piety;	240	Priest 10		25
being all his joy, and thought) leaveth not his Ministry behind him;	250	Priest 17		25
for if wise men have thought it the best way of preserving a state	258	Priest 22		15
he often overturnes things, when they are thought past danger;	271	Priest 30		21
I thought fit to discover in a short Treatise, that Intemperance was	291	Cornaro		5
Many have thought that this could be done by Aurum potabile,	298	Cornaro		19
A hundred loade of thought will not pay one of debts.	335	Proverbs		414
The thought hath good leggs, and the quill a good tongue.	342	Proverbs		612
injuries which they are thought to have offerd to our Merchants	368	Letters		6
THOUGHTS				
Let vain or busie thoughts have there no part:	23	Ch.-Porch		421
Let vain & busie thoughts have there no part:	23	Ch.-Porch	W	421
All worldly thoughts are but theeves met together	23	Ch.-Porch		424
Thus argu'd into hopes, my thoughts reserved	46	Afflict.1		15
Peace mutt'ring thoughts, and do not grudge to keep	68	Content		1
My bent thoughts, like a brittle bow,	80	Deniall		6
Of thoughts, and words, and deeds.	81	Christmas		18
My words & thoughts do both expresse this notion,	84	Coloss.		1
Quick thoughts and motions at a small expense,	86	Lent		20
My thoughts are all a case of knives,	90	Afflict.4		7
My thoughts began to burnish, sprout, and swell,	102	Jordan 2		4
My thoughts began to burnish, spredd, and swell,	102	Jordan 2	W	4
My thoughts must work, but like a noiselesse sphere;	105	Conscience		8
My thoughts and joyes are all packt up and gone,	109	Home		69
My thoughts are working like a busie flame,	122	Sinnes rd.		3
My words take fire from my inflamed thoughts.	122	Sinnes rd.		6
My words take fire from my inflamed thoughts.	122	Sinnes rd.		7
New thoughts of sinning: wherefore, to my shame,	122	Sinnes rd.		17
One aire of thoughts usurps my brain.	128	Bunch Gr.		5
I found that some had stuff'd the bed with thoughts,	130	Love unkn.		51
Both frosts and thoughts do nip,	131	Mans medly		28

THOUGHTS (cont'd)	PAGE	TITLE		LINE
What doth this noise of thoughts within my heart	136	Familie		1
Me thoughts a starre did shoot into my lap.	139	Artillerie		2
Their thoughts and sense	145	Discharge		42
My thoughts turn round,	148	Longing		10
Which pettie thoughts have made, and made to thee	153	The Collar		23
Me thoughts I heard one calling, childe:	154	The Collar		35
I shake my head, and all the thoughts and ends,	169	The Answer		2
Deeper then they, in words, and works, and thoughts.	173	Marie Magd		12
My Heart, that gave fond Thoughts their Food,	214	Convert	D	16
His thoughts are full of making the best of the day, and contriving	235	Priest 8		19
never raising their thoughts to God, nor sanctifying their labour	248	Priest 14		1
and find sparkes of such thoughts now and then to break forth,	281	Priest 34		13
and well-contented, free from all troubles and troublesome thoughts;	301	Cornaro		1
happily also with this (as his thoughts are fruitfull) intending	304	Valdesso		12
then a heart with thoughts.	341	Proverbs		582
Your thoughts close, and your countenance loose.	362	Proverbs	D	1183
that whether you turn your thoughts on the life past, or on the Joyes	373	Letters		18
I beseech you let such thoughts as these, moderate your present fear	374	Letters		3
you have layed out thoughts & prayers you have sowed.	380	Woodnoth		10
as God gives me higher thoughts, & to rise with his favours,	381	Woodnoth		25
THOUSAND				
For he, that needs five thousand pound to live,	10	Ch.-Porch		107
But robs a thousand who would praise thee fain,	117	Providence		19
More then a thousand sunnes disburse in light,	172	The Glance		23
Of thousand harts: that face doth figure thee	212	Bohemia	D	33
ten thousand enemies:	216	Psalm III	D	14
Because such are daily exposed to a thousand dangers and deaths,	303	Cornaro		14
men for one pleasure a thousand griefes prove.	328	Proverbs		228
THOUSANDS				
Thousands of toyes dwell there, yet out of doore	40	Sepulchre		7
I owed thousands and much more:	50	Faith		13
Thousands of notions in my brain did runne,	102	Jordan 2		7
Thousands of things do thee employ	158	Praise 3		19
Thousands of souls it hath and doth destroy	170	Self-cond.		11
how they have been burnt by thousands, and have endur'd such other	373	Letters		36
THRALDOME				
Thraldome from those, who would not at a feast	107	Home		21
THRALL				
When wanton pleasures becken us to thrall.	11	Ch.-Porch		118
To work for two, who brought himself to thrall.	17	Ch.-Porch		286
To work for two, that brought himself to thrall.	17	Ch.-Porch	W	286
From th' earth unto my brows, and bear the thrall:	32	Sacrifice		167
Is selfe-sufficient to bee the thrall	212	Bohemia	D	32
save me, my God, from thrall:	217	Psalm III	D	18
THREAD				
He wears a stuffe whose thread is course and round,	131	Mans medly		15
A slender thread a gentle guest will tie.	154	Glimpse		20
Spin out thy thread, and make thereof a coat	156	Assurance		38
By the needle you shall draw the thread,	332	Proverbs		329
The thread breakes, where it is weakest.	341	Proverbs		596
A gentle heart is tyed with an easie thread.	345	Proverbs		726
THREATEN				
& to threaten him that if he will not give her halfe her estate	368	Letters		23
THREATENS				
since hee shoots higher that threatens the Moon, then hee that aims	224	Priest		9
THREATNED				
Yet, for I threatned oft the siege to raise,	47	Afflict.1		43
And threatned man, that he should fill the space.	119	Providence		84
I threatned to observe the strict decree	143	Holdfast		1
I threatned to observe the sweet decree	143	Holdfast	V	1
There are more men threatned then stricken.	329	Proverbs		256
Threatned men eat bread, says the Spaniard.	358	Proverbs	D	1081
THREATNINGS				
And lay my threatnings bleeding on the ground.	164	The Crosse		12
THRED				
And thred the spheres with his quick-piercing minde:	85	Vanitie 1		2
I have alwaies observ'd the thred of Life to be like other threds	373	Letters		4
THREDDED				
Thredded together on times string,	76	Sunday		30
THREDS				
observ'd the thred of Life to be like other threds or skenes of silk,	373	Letters		5
THREE				
She loseth three for one; her soul, rest, fame.	13	Ch.-Porch		174
Who at three hundred did the ointment prize,	27	Sacrifice		18
In three dayes raz'd, and raised as before.	28	Sacrifice		66
That three yeares hence, if I survive,	36	Thanksgvng		32
Or since all musick is but three parts vied	42	Easter		15
We count three hundred, but we misse:	42	Easter		29
Mans age is two houres work, or three:	48	Repentance		7
These three make up some Christians destinie:	58	H.Script.2		8
Since then these three wait on thy throne,	103	Prayer 2		19
And so my sinnes ascend three stories high,	122	Sinnes rd.		14
To make a jest of Christs three offices:	195	Ch.-Milit.		174
Thrice blessed Three in One.	199	L'Envoy		18
that so in the mouth of two or three witnesses the truth may be more	232	Priest 7		29
stead of the qualities of the world, he requires onely three of her;	239	Priest 10		12
he teacheth them, that three things make a compleate servant, Truth,	240	Priest 10		17
if he be in full health, keeps the three obligations, eating fish,	242	Priest 10		26
for there being three points of his duty, the one, to infuse	255	Priest 21		2
Yet the skill consists but in these three points:	256	Priest 21		30

THREE (cont'd)	PAGE	TITLE	LINE
if there be but three Communions, neither can all the people so order	259	Priest 22	25
but sends for three or four of the ablest of the Parish to hear	260	Priest 23	9
And I conceive, our Saviour did this for three reasons:	261	Priest 23	18
These three rules generally comprehend the faults of eating,	266	Priest 26	12
To guide them in this, there are three rules:	266	Priest 26	37
as at nine, or at three, or at midnight, or as they think fit,	272	Priest 31	26
And whereas there are usually three Objections made against	276	Priest 32	19
for Atheisme) he scatters in his discourse three sorts of arguments;	281	Priest 34	15
that in the mouth of two or three witnesses every word may be	283	Priest 34	19
and the Holy Ghost, three Persons, but one most glorious,	290	Priest	14
what case I was, they concluded that I would die within three dayes.	295	Cornaro	3
recounting the delights and pleasures in this age of eighty three,	300	Cornaro	32
to publish it, for these three eminent things observable therein:	304	Valdesso	18
These three things are very eminent in the Author, and overweigh	305	Valdesso	12
Three helping one another, beare the burthen of sixe.	325	Proverbs	135
There are three waies, the Universities, the Sea, the Court.	334	Proverbs	383
Three women make a market.	345	Proverbs	713
Three can hold their peace, if two be away.	345	Proverbs	714
One houres sleepe before midnight is worth three after.	350	Proverbs	882
pardon my boldness, and consider but these three things.	365	Letters	16
three pound more besides that which is due to her, to Ann I leave	382	G.H.'s Will	23
THREEFOLD			
that God hath and exerciseth a threefold power in every thing which	270	Priest 30	33
THREW			
And threw it in a font, wherein did fall	129	Love unkn.	13
And threw my heart into the scalding pan;	130	Love unkn.	35
THRICE			
Thrice blessed Three in One.	199	L'Envoy	18
When once his anger burns, thrice blest	216	Psalm II D	31
who being to present all that receive not thrice a year;	259	Priest 22	25
nor the Church-Wardens so well take notice who receive thrice,	259	Priest 22	28
France is a meddow that cuts thrice a yeere.	350	Proverbs	892
Take heed of a person marked, and a Widdow thrice married.	360	Proverbs D	1152
THRIFT			
Least want of Graces seeme thy thrift:	59	Whitsunday W	18
the wonderfull providence and thrift of the great householder	241	Priest 10	25
I even study Thrift, and yet I am scarce able with much ado to make	365	Letters	9
THRIFTIE			
Be thriftie, but not covetous: therefore give	12	Ch.-Porch	151
THRIVE			
as if it were in their own hands to thrive, or not to thrive.	247	Priest 14	31
If a good man thrive, all thrive with him.	344	Proverbs	695
THRIVES			
Hee that labours and thrives spins gold.	332	Proverbs	341
THRIVING			
Yet in thy thriving still misdoubt some evil;	13	Ch.-Porch	163
Not thriving, I resolved to be bold,	40	Redemption	2
Thou art all health, health thriving, till it make	58	H.Script.1	5
thinking that their own labour is the cause of their thriving,	247	Priest 14	30
THROAT			
More attributes? Am I all throat or eye,	143	Complaining	13
My throat, my soul is hoarse;	148	Longing	7
Which bounds on thee, and will not down thy throat:	156	Assurance	40
Their throat an open Sepulcher,	219	Psalm V D	27
A flatterers throat is an open Sepulcher.	341	Proverbs	588
THROATE			
The singing man keepes his shop in his throate.	351	Proverbs	918
THROATS			
To thy renown: but all their hands and throats	117	Providence	11
THROBBING			
A throbbing conscience spurred by remorse	132	The Storm	9
THRONE			
In sev'rall ranks upon an azure throne,	70	Humilitie	2
They leapt upon the throne;	70	Humilitie	22
Since then these three wait on thy throne,	103	Prayer 2	19
Who did leave his Fathers throne,	113	Businesse	17
Lord, didst thou leave thy throne,	150	Longing	61
To the throne of grace.	179	Discipline	16
Almightie Lord, who from thy glorious throne	190	Ch.-Milit.	1
Or strength in th' other, did erect her throne.	192	Ch.-Milit.	78
Then in memoriall of his ancient throne	195	Ch.-Milit.	181
There is thy best Throne. For afflictions are	211	Bohemia D	15
Direct my prayers to thy Throne,	218	Psalm V D	7
Parson preacheth constantly, the pulpit is his joy and his throne:	232	Priest 7	21
but to throw himselfe down at the throne of grace, saying,	257	Priest 22	32
THRONES			
Of his two thrones he made the latter best,	196	Ch.-Milit.	213
THROUGH (see also thorow)			
But the cheap swearer through his open sluce	8	Ch.-Porch	58
To hunt his cruell food through ev'ry vein.	37	The Agonie	12
That thy distresse through all may runne,	39	Good Fri.	15
I was blown through with ev'ry storm and winde.	47	Afflict.1	36
Of those, who did themselves through their side wound,	59	Whitsunday	20
Scarce a good joy creeps through the chink:	60	Whitsunday	22
Did through my bodie wound my minde,	65	Ch.-mus.	2
To be a window, through thy grace.	67	Windows	5
And hast redeem'd me through thy bloud,	68	Trin.Sun.	2
Cuts through the working waves, that he may fetch	85	Vanitie 1	9
Yet through the labyrinths, not my groveling wit,	89	The Pearl	37
Yet through these labyrinths, not my groveling wit,	89	The Pearl W	37

THROUGH (cont'd)	PAGE	TITLE		LINE
When th' hair is sweet through pride or lust,	96	Charms & K		13
And not of thee, through whom my fingers bend	116	Providence		3
Through all the earth:	125	Peace		32
And through their glasse discolour thee!	141	Justice 2		5
So to cares cops I came, and there got through	142	Pilgrimage		11
But through a Church-yard which them bounds.	145	Discharge		40
Through th' old sinnes and new doctrines of our land.	161	Priesthood		33
Swelling through store,	167	The Flower		48
Or if he pleaseth, through it passe,	184	The Elixer		11
From Heaven, thrcugh Earth, to Hell.	202	Trin.Sun.	W	14
Through that black tiffany thy vertues shine	211	Bohemia	D	17
and my neerest way ly through the Church, I will not doubt to go	273	Priest 31		34
This distinction may runne through all Christian duties,	274	Priest 31		1
But though the streams of thy bloud were currant through darknesse,	288	Priest		32
righteousnesse (as he sheweth through all his Considerations) a thing	305	Valdesso		1
the Consideration of Gods Worke in his heart through the Word,	309	Valdesso		31
doubt not, through Gods blessing, but it shall be to the full;	379	Letters		18
neighboring Sea, wondrously sound through all our Coasts, and eares.	442	Oration		24
THROUGHLY				
therefore he hath throughly studied these, that he may be an absolute	227	Priest 3		8
Wherefore the Parson hath throughly canvassed al the particulars	230	Priest 5		33
To this end he hath throughly digested all the points of consolation,	249	Priest 15		18
but also professeth himselfe throughly of the opinion, carrying it	250	Priest 16		8
THROUGHOUT				
Throughout the world. Fool not: for all may have,	10	Ch.-Porch		89
hath so many dispersed Officers at his beck throughout the Kingdome,	276	Priest 32		11
wher-ever spoken this day throughout the universall Church.	289	Priest		15
THROW				
It is most just to throw that on the ground,	7	Ch.-Porch		29
Which would throw me there, if I keep the round.	7	Ch.-Porch		30
Who by aspersions throw a stone	96	Charms & K		9
I throw me at his feet.	161	Priesthood		36
Taking me up to throw me dcwn:	165	The Crosse		22
Throw away thy rod,	178	Discipline		1
Throw away thy wrath:	178	Discipline		2
Throw away thy rcd;	179	Discipline		29
Throw away thy wrath.	179	Discipline		32
who treads in his steps, and will not throw down what he hath built;	232	Priest 7		26
but to throw himself down at the throne of grace, saying,	257	Priest 22		31
or throw into the fire, and so they pay them their wages,	265	Priest 26		26
his Father bids him throw it away, and he will give him the gold	272	Priest 30		10
if any scruple arise, I will throw it away, and be most confident,	273	Priest 31		38
Whose house is of glasse, must not throw stones at another.	327	Proverbs		196
Although it raine, throw not away thy watering pot.	332	Proverbs		325
A foole may throw a stone into a well,	339	Proverbs		527
For any scruple of leaving your trade, throw it away.	381	Woodnoth		22
THROWES				
then a horse that throwes me.	329	Proverbs		258
THROWEST				
Turning my purge to food, thou throwest me	48	Afflict.1		51
And with the other throwest down to hell	160	Priesthood		3
THROWN				
O blessed bodie! Whither art thou thrown?	40	Sepulchre		1
And thrown it on that dust which thou hast made,	54	Love 1		4
And thrown it in that dust which thou hast made,	54	Love 1	W	4
Thrown down I fall into a bed, and rest:	159	Jos.coat		2
touch him no more, then a stone thrown against heaven, where he is,	269	Priest 28		8
THROWNE				
Hee that is throwne would ever wrestle.	347	Proverbs		797
THROWS				
he that throws a stone at another, hits himselfe;	269	Priest 28		13
THRUSHES				
Hee that hath patience hath fatt thrushes for a farthing.	336	Proverbs		430
THRUST				
That I did thrust into the Deitie,	28	Sacrifice		62
If some kinde man would thrust his heart	105	Obedience		42
My minde ev'n thrust into them both:	175	The Odour		7
And thrust a Testament into thy hand:	188	Judgement		13
THRUSTING				
The thrusting away of his arme makes us onely not embraced.	283	Priest 34		25
THUNDER				
The Jews refused thunder; and we, folly.	24	Ch.-Porch		449
To whose powre Thunder is but weake and slight:	29	Sacrifice	W	79
Reversed thunder, Christ-side-piercing spear,	51	Prayer 1		6
From private bodies, make as big a thunder,	69	Content		23
Some to the warres and thunder	80	Deniall		9
thou hast committed, not to Thunder, or Angels, but to silly	289	Priest		5
I escaped the Thunder, and fell into the Lightning.	358	Proverbs	D	1084
THUNDERS				
When it thunders, the theefe becomes honest.	344	Proverbs		690
THURSDAY				
Thursday come, and the week's gone.	341	Proverbs		587
THUS				
A joy for it worth worlds. Thus hell doth jest	23	Ch.-Porch		412
Thus Adam my first breathing rendereth:	28	Sacrifice		71
Thus trimmed forth they bring me to the rout,	32	Sacrifice		185
Whom devils flie, thus is he toss'd of men:	32	Sacrifice		191
Thus argu'd into hopes, my thoughts reserved	46	Afflict.1		15
Thus argu'd into hopes, I was preserved	46	Afflict.1	W	15
Thus thinne and lean without a fence or friend,	47	Afflict.1		35

THUS (cont'd)	PAGE	TITLE		LINE
Thus doth thy power crosse-bias me, not making	48	Afflict.1		53
Thus are we to delights: but we are all	48	Repentance		9
Thus dost thou make proud knowledge bend & crouch	50	Faith		31
Thus dost thou make proud knowledge bow & crouch	50	Faith	W	31
Thus in thy Ebony box	64	Even-song		21
Thus we creep on,	79	Employm.2	W	29
But when I thus dispute and grieve,	95	Submission		9
Why do I languish thus, drooping and dull,	115	Dulnesse		1
Thus farre Time heard me patiently:	123	Time		27
I did demand; he thus began:	125	Peace		21
Thinking with that, which I did thus present,	129	Love unkn.		31
Thus hard to me?	150	Longing		64
Thus we prevent the last great day,	171	Self-cond.		19
Thus are true Aarons drest.	174	Aaron		5
Poore priest thus am I drest.	174	Aaron		10
But will ye leave me thus? when ye before	176	Forerunners		14
Thus both the Church and Sunne together ran	192	Ch.-Milit.		97
Thus Sinne in Egypt sneaked for a while;	193	Ch.-Milit.		121
Thus Sinne triumphs in Western Babylon;	196	Ch.-Milit.		211
Thus do both lights, as well in Church as Sunne,	197	Ch.-Milit.		270
Thus also Sinne and Darknesse follow still	198	Ch.-Milit.		272
Thus also sinn and darknes constantly	198	Ch.-Milit.	W	272
They who do not thus, while they remember their earthly Lord,	226	Priest 2		32
that mony thus lent to God, is placed surer for his childrens	240	Priest 10		8
but generally he distributes it thus, To his Children he shewes more	241	Priest 10		9
poor and needy, whom he thus finds labouring, he gives them somewhat;	248	Priest 14		9
to do all the good he can, moves him to say thus and thus.	251	Priest 17		32
to do all the good he can, moves him to say thus and thus.	251	Priest 17		33
Your meaning is not thus, but thus;	252	Priest 18		11
Thus both in rewarding vertue, and in punishing vice, the Parson	254	Priest 20		29
as thus, in the Creed:	256	Priest 21		6
Socrates did thus in Philosophy, who held that the seeds of all	256	Priest 21		21
and doubtlesse the Holy Scripture intends thus much, when it	257	Priest 21		11
knowest what thou didst, when thou appointedst it to be done thus;	257	Priest 22		33
for example sake, and because they are most common, he thus thinks:	265	Priest 26		4
few bring covetousness thus low, or consider it so narrowly,	265	Priest 26		31
in a doctrinall way, saying to the contemner, Alas, why do you thus?	269	Priest 28		13
But if it should be, the Assertion stands thus:	275	Priest 32		11
Thus the Parson considering that repentance is the great vertue	279	Priest 33		6
of Conversation, hath proceeded thus far in the discussing of it.	287	Priest 37		10
When therefore I was thus affected [afflicted] from the thirtie fifth	292	Cornaro		1
to consider the force of Temperance, and to think thus with my self:	293	Cornaro		2
Almes never make poore. Or thus,	327	Proverbs		189
As I had written thus much, I received a Letter, from My Brother,	378	Letters		30
body to Almightie God that made them doe thus dispose of my goods.	382	G.H.'s Will		2
THWART				
Thwart not th' Almighty God: O be not crosse.	22	Ch.-Porch		395
Thwart not the mighty God: O be not crosse.	22	Ch.-Porch	W	395
THWARTED				
if it be not thwarted, the Parson having a due respect both	268	Priest 28		33
THY				
And make us strive, who shall sing best thy name.	5	Dedication		4
Thy rate and price, and mark thee for a treasure;	6	Ch.-Porch		2
It makes thy soule a blott: it is a rodd	6	Ch.-Porch	W	8
It blots thy lesson written in thy soul;	6	Ch.-Porch		9
It spoils an Angel: robs thee of thy God.	6	Ch.-Porch	W	10
Abstain wholly, or wed. Thy bounteous Lord	7	Ch.-Porch		13
Yet wedding marrs thy fortune, fast & pray:	7	Ch.-Porch	W	14
Not grudging, that thy lust hath bounds and staies.	7	Ch.-Porch		16
Hee'le make thy wife a blessing not a rodd.	7	Ch.-Porch	W	18
If it concurr with vertue: doe thy best	7	Ch.-Porch	W	21
And winne thy selfe: Compare the joyes & so	7	Ch.-Porch	W	23
Stay at the third glasse: if thou lose thy hold,	8	Ch.-Porch		41
Boast not thereof; nor make thy shame thy glorie.	8	Ch.-Porch		50
Take not his name, who made thy mouth, in vain:	8	Ch.-Porch		55
Which is thy best stake, when griefs make thee tame.	9	Ch.-Porch		66
O crumble not away thy souls fair heap.	9	Ch.-Porch		70
Lie not; but let thy heart be true to God,	9	Ch.-Porch		73
Thy mouth to it, thy actions to them both:	9	Ch.-Porch		74
If those take up thy day, the sunne will crie	9	Ch.-Porch		81
If those bee all thy day, the sunne will crie	9	Ch.-Porch	W	81
God gave thy soul brave wings; put not those feathers	9	Ch.-Porch		83
Desire and shame, will make thy labour, play:	10	Ch.-Porch	W	90
Thou hast run all thy race, ere thou beginn.	10	Ch.-Porch	W	90
Spit out thy flegme, and fill thy brest with glorie:	10	Ch.-Porch		92
Thy Gentrie bleats, as if thy native cloth	10	Ch.-Porch		93
Transfus'd a sheepishnesse into thy storie:	10	Ch.-Porch		94
Studie this art, make it thy great designe;	10	Ch.-Porch		101
The way to make thy sonne rich, is to fill	11	Ch.-Porch		109
But if thy sonne can make ten pound his measure,	11	Ch.-Porch		113
When thou dost purpose ought within thy power,	11	Ch.-Porch		115
Look to thy mouth; diseases enter there.	11	Ch.-Porch		127
Thou hast two sconses, if thy stomack call;	11	Ch.-Porch		128
Tast all, but feed not. if thy stomach call	11	Ch.-Porch	W	128
Lose not thy self, nor give thy humours way:	12	Ch.-Porch		143
Salute thy self: see what thy soul doth wear.	12	Ch.-Porch		146
Dare to look in thy chest; for 'tis thine own:	12	Ch.-Porch		147
Thy need, thine honour, and thy friend his due.	12	Ch.-Porch		152
Never exceed thy income. Youth may make	13	Ch.-Porch		157
Thy children, kindred, friends upon thee call;	13	Ch.-Porch		161

THY (cont'd)

	PAGE	TITLE		LINE
Before thy journey fairly part with all.	13	Ch.-Porch		162
Yet in thy thriving still misdoubt some evil;	13	Ch.-Porch		163
Yett in thy pursing still thy self distrust	13	Ch.-Porch	W	163
Least gaining gaine on thee, & fill thy hart	13	Ch.-Porch	W	164
Unto thy hands, it woundeth to the quick.	13	Ch.-Porch		168
As that thy self alone to hell shalt goe.	13	Ch.-Porch	W	168
About thy neck do drown thee? raise thy head;	13	Ch.-Porch		170
To stuffe thy minde with solid braverie;	15	Ch.-Porch		208
Be sweet to all. Is thy complexion sowre?	15	Ch.-Porch		211
Then keep such companie; make them thy allay:	15	Ch.-Porch		212
Command thy self in chief. He lifes warre knows,	15	Ch.-Porch		215
Think not thy fame at ev'ry twitch will break:	15	Ch.-Porch		219
And do them not: that shall thy wisdome be;	15	Ch.-Porch		221
And change thy temperance into braverie.	15	Ch.-Porch		222
If that thy fame with ev'ry toy be pos'd,	15	Ch.-Porch		223
Thy person share, and the conceit advance.	15	Ch.-Porch		232
Thy person share, and thou thy mirth inhanse.	15	Ch.-Porch	W	232
Make not thy sport, abuses: for the fly	15	Ch.-Porch		233
Pick out of mirth, like stones out of thy ground,	16	Ch.-Porch		235
Doth ratably thy fortunes marre or make.	16	Ch.-Porch		256
Thy self the worse, and so the distance greater.	16	Ch.-Porch		260
Is a good spurre. Correct thy passions spite;	16	Ch.-Porch		263
Thy friend put in thy bosome: wear his eies	17	Ch.-Porch		271
Still in thy heart, that he may see what's there.	17	Ch.-Porch		272
Thy drops of bloud must pay down all his fear:	17	Ch.-Porch		274
If thou be single, all thy goods and ground	17	Ch.-Porch		283
In thy discourse, if thou desire to please:	18	Ch.-Porch		289
That suites him best, of whom thy speech is heard.	18	Ch.-Porch		294
For so thou dost thy self and him a pleasure:	18	Ch.-Porch		296
The speaker to thee, and preserve thy stock.	18	Ch.-Porch		300
As if thou mad'st thy will. A civil guest	18	Ch.-Porch		305
If truth be with thy friend, be with them both:	19	Ch.-Porch		323
Both want, and wish thy pleasing presence still.	19	Ch.-Porch		326
Need & bee glad, & wish thy presence still:	19	Ch.-Porch	W	326
Pitch thy behaviour low, thy projects high;	19	Ch.-Porch		331
Let thy minde still be bent, still plotting where,	20	Ch.-Porch		337
Whether thy stock of credit swell, or fall.	20	Ch.-Porch		346
Much lesse make any one thy enemie.	20	Ch.-Porch	W	351
Keep all thy native good, and naturalize	21	Ch.-Porch		361
In time they'l runne thee out of all thy wit.	21	Ch.-Porch		366
Let thy mindes sweetnesse have his operation	21	Ch.-Porch		371
Upon thy body, clothes, and habitation.	21	Ch.-Porch		372
In Almes regard thy means, and others merit.	21	Ch.-Porch		373
Onely thy single market-money for it.	21	Ch.-Porch		375
Let thy almes go before, and keep heav'ns gate	21	Ch.-Porch		383
For all the week thy food so oft he gave thee.	22	Ch.-Porch		392
Thy cheere is mended; bate not of the food,	22	Ch.-Porch		393
Where it is warmest. Leave thy six and seven;	22	Ch.-Porch		401
When once thy foot enters the church, be bare.	22	Ch.-Porch		403
And make thy self all reverence and fear.	22	Ch.-Porch		406
Kneeling ne're spoil'd silk stocking: quit thy state.	22	Ch.-Porch		407
Away thy blessings, and extreamly flout thee,	23	Ch.-Porch		413
Thy clothes being fast, but thy soul loose about thee.	23	Ch.-Porch		414
And send them to thy heart; that spying sinne,	23	Ch.-Porch	W	416
Bring not thy plough, thy plots, thy pleasures thither.	23	Ch.-Porch		422
Christ purg'd his temple; so must thou thy heart.	23	Ch.-Porch		423
To couzin thee. Look to thy actions well:	23	Ch.-Porch		425
Judge not the preacher; for he is thy Judge:	23	Ch.-Porch		427
How know'st thou, but thy sinnes made him miscarrie?	24	Ch.-Porch		440
Then turn thy faults and his into confession:	24	Ch.-Porch		441
Then turn thy fault and his into confession:	24	Ch.-Porch	W	441
Dresse and undresse thy soul: mark the decay	24	Ch.-Porch		453
And growth of it: if with thy watch, that too	24	Ch.-Porch		454
Most surely judg'd, make thy accounts agree.	24	Ch.-Porch		456
Make not an ell, by trifling in thy wo.	24	Ch.-Porch		460
Thy self in church; approach, and taste	25	Superlim		3
A broken ALTAR, Lord, thy servant reares,	26	The Altar		1
Whose parts are as thy hand did frame;	26	The Altar		3
Thy pow'r doth cut.	26	The Altar		8
To praise thy Name:	26	The Altar		12
O let thy blessed SACRIFICE be mine,	26	The Altar		15
O let thy onely SACRIFICE be mine,	26	The Altar	W	15
O let this cup passe, if it be thy pleasure:	27	Sacrifice		23
Now heal thy self, Physician; now come down.	34	Sacrifice		221
That all thy body was one doore.	35	Thanksgvng		6
Shall I then sing, skipping, thy dolefull storie,	35	Thanksgvng		11
Shall I then sing, neglecting thy sad storie,	35	Thanksgvng	W	11
And side with thy triumphant glorie?	35	Thanksgvng		12
Shall thy strokes be my stroking? thorns, my flower?	35	Thanksgvng		13
Thy rod, my posie? crosse, my bower?	35	Thanksgvng		14
Copie thy fair, though bloudie hand?	35	Thanksgvng		16
Surely I will revenge me on thy love,	35	Thanksgvng		17
My bosome friend, if he blaspheme thy name,	35	Thanksgvng		25
As for thy passion - But of that anon,	35	Thanksgvng		29
For thy predestination I'le contrive,	36	Thanksgvng		31
Then I will use the works of thy creation,	36	Thanksgvng		35
Then will I use the works of thy creation,	36	Thanksgvng	W	35
Nay, I will reade thy book, and never move	36	Thanksgvng		45
Nay, I will reade thy book, and never linn	36	Thanksgvng	W	45
Till I have found therein thy love,	36	Thanksgvng		46

THY (cont'd)	PAGE	TITLE		LINE
Till I have found thy love therin,	36	Thanksgvng	W	46
Thy art of love, which I'le turn back on thee:	36	Thanksgvng		47
Then for thy passion - I will do for that -	36	Thanksgvng		49
There is no dealing with thy mighty passion:	36	Reprisall		2
There is no medling with thy mighty passion:	36	Reprisall	W	2
And yet thy wounds still my attempts defie,	36	Reprisall		7
For by thy death I die for thee.	36	Reprisall		8
By thy eternall glorie didst outgo me?	37	Reprisall		10
Into thy conquest, though I can do nought	37	Reprisall	W	14
To shew their face, since crosse to thy decrees:	38	The Sinner		7
How shall I measure out thy bloud?	38	Good Fri.		2
Shall I thy woes	38	Good Fri.		5
Number according to thy foes?	38	Good Fri.		6
Or, since one starre show'd thy first breath,	38	Good Fri.		7
Shall all thy death?	38	Good Fri.		8
That thy distresse through all may runne,	39	Good Fri.		15
Thy sorrows in, and bloudie fight;	39	Good Fri.		22
To write thy sorrows in, as blood	39	Good Fri.	W	22
Thy whips, thy nails, thy wounds, thy woes,	39	Good Fri.		26
And keep possession with thy grace;	39	Good Fri.		30
Rise heart; thy Lord is risen. Sing his praise	41	Easter		1
Awake, my lute, and struggle for thy part	41	Easter		7
With all thy art.	41	Easter		8
O let thy blessed Spirit bear a part,	42	Easter		17
I got me flowers to straw thy way;	42	Easter		19
To strow thy way and Victorie,	42	Easter	W	20
And brought'st thy sweets along with thee.	42	Easter		22
Bringinge thy sweets along with thee.	42	Easter	W	22
And brought thy sweets along with thee.	42	Easter	WC	22
With thy arising, they presume.	42	Easter		26
As thy discoverie presents.	42	Easter	W	26
Teach it to sing thy praise, this day,	42	Easter	W	29
And sing this day thy victories:	43	East.wings		9
And sing this day thy sacrifice,	43	East.wings	W	9
And feel this day thy victorie:	43	East.wings		18
Let me be soft and supple to thy will,	44	H. Bapt.2		8
It is thy highest art	45	Nature		5
Making thy workmanship deceit.	45	Nature		12
Engrave thy rev'rend law and fear;	45	Nature		14
Augmented with thy gracious benefits.	46	Afflict.1		6
Augmented with thy graces perquisites.	46	Afflict.1	W	6
I looked on thy furniture so fine,	46	Afflict.1		7
I looked on thy furniture so rich,	46	Afflict.1	W	7
Thy glorious houshold-stuffe did me entwine,	46	Afflict.1		9
Thy glorious houshold-stuffe did me bewitch	46	Afflict.1	W	9
Into thy familie.	46	Afflict.1	W	10
And made her youth and fiercenesse seek thy face.	46	Afflict.1		18
I took thy sweetned pill, till I came neare;	47	Afflict.1		47
I took thy sweetned pill, till I came where	47	Afflict.1	W	47
Thus doth thy power crosse-bias me, not making	48	Afflict.1		53
With thy quick flow'r, thy momentarie bloom;	48	Repentance		3
O let thy height of mercie then	49	Repentance		13
Thy wormwood turn to health, windes to fair weather:	49	Repentance		21
Thy wrath for sinne, as when mans sight was dimme,	49	Faith		2
To me dost now thy self convey;	52	H.Commun.		4
Making thy way my rest,	52	H.Commun.		9
And thy small quantities my length;	52	H.Commun.		10
My rebel-flesh, and carrying thy name,	52	H.Commun.		17
Onely thy grace, which with these elements comes,	52	H.Commun.		19
By this thy heav'nly bloud;	53	H.Commun.		38
Since thou hast taught us by thy word,	53	H.Commun.	W	39
How hath man parcel'd out thy glorious name,	54	Love 1		3
(Thy workmanship) and give thee share in neither.	54	Love 1		8
Thou standing by: and though thy glorious name	54	Love 1		11
Who sings thy praise? onely a skarf or glove	54	Love 1		13
Immortall Heat, O let thy greater flame	54	Love 2		1
And there in hymnes send back thy fire again:	54	Love 2		8
Thou shalt recover all thy goods in kinde,	54	Love 2		11
Gladly engrave thy love in steel,	55	Temper 1		2
The world's too little for thy tent,	55	Temper 1		11
Shall he thy stature spell?	55	Temper 1		16
O let me, when thy roof my soul hath hid,	55	Temper 1		17
Yet take thy way; for sure thy way is best:	55	Temper 1		21
Stretch or contract me thy poore debter:	55	Temper 1		22
Thy hands made both, and I am there:	55	Temper 1		26
Thy power and love, my love and trust	55	Temper 1		27
Lord, if thou must needs use thy dart,	56	Temper 2		3
The grosser world stands to thy word and art;	56	Temper 2		5
But thy diviner world of grace	56	Temper 2		6
O fix thy chair of grace, that all my powers	56	Temper 2		9
They grow unruly, and sit in thy bowers.	56	Temper 2		12
Let not thy higher Court remove,	56	Temper 2		15
Which in thy garland I should fill, were mine	57	Employm. 1		7
At thy great doom.	57	Employm. 1		8
For as thou dost impart thy grace,	57	Employm. 1		9
A life as barren to thy praise,	57	Employm. 1		14
I am no link of thy great chain,	57	Employm. 1		21
Lord place me in thy consort; give one strain	57	Employm. 1		23
Thy praise too much? thou art heav'ns Lidger here,	58	H.Script.1		11
Thy praise enough? thou art heav'ns Lidger here,	58	H.Script.1	W	11

THY (cont'd)	PAGE	TITLE		LINE
Oh that I knew how all thy lights combine,	58	H.Script.2		1
Such are thy secrets, which my life makes good,	58	H.Script.2		9
Thy words do finde me out, & parallels bring,	58	H.Script.2		11
And spread thy golden wings in me;	59	Whitsunday		2
Display thy golden wings in me;	59	Whitsunday	W	2
On thy Apostles? thou didst then	59	Whitsunday		6
With livery-graces furnishing thy men.	59	Whitsunday	W	8
Without thy help, leads us his way to Hell.	59	Whitsunday	W	16
Least want of Graces seeme thy thrift:	59	Whitsunday	W	18
And lay it on thy husbandry, for shift.	59	Whitsunday	W	20
Show that thy brests can not be dry,	59	Whitsunday	W	21
Restore this day, for thy great name,	60	Whitsunday		27
O let thy graces without cease	60	Grace		3
Thy house would but a dungeon prove,	60	Grace		6
Thy great house would a dungeon prove,	60	Grace	W	6
Thy works nights captives: O let grace	60	Grace		7
And shall the dew out-strip thy dove?	60	Grace		10
O lett thy grace, to crosse his art,	60	Grace	W	19
Thou Lord of life; since thy one death for me	62	Afflict.2		2
They would discolour thy most bloudy sweat.	62	Afflict.2		10
Thy crosse took up in one,	62	Afflict.2		14
Powring upon it all thy art,	62	Mattens		11
Teach me thy love to know;	63	Mattens		17
For this thy love? have I discharg'd the debt,	64	Even-song		10
Thy diet, care, and cost	64	Even-song		13
Thus in thy Ebony box	64	Even-song		21
Not one poore minute scapes thy breast,	64	Even-song		30
Deare flesh, while I do pray, learn here thy stemme	65	Ch.-monum.		17
And wanton in thy cravings, thou mayst know,	65	Ch.-monum.		19
That thou mayst fit thy self against thy fall.	65	Ch.-monum.		24
And bindes thy hands,	66	Ch.-lock		2
Not on my sinnes, or coldnesse, but thy will.	66	Ch.-lock		8
Lord, how can man preach thy eternall word?	67	Windows		1
Yet in thy temple thou dost him afford	67	Windows		3
To be a window, through thy grace.	67	Windows		5
But when thou dost anneal in glasse thy storie,	67	Windows		6
Making thy life to shine within	67	Windows		7
And hast redeem'd me through thy bloud,	68	Trin.Sun.		2
Onely thy Chronicle is lost; and yet	69	Content		25
Thy name in books, which may not rent:	69	Content		28
Thy name in books, which may not vent:	69	Content	W	28
When all thy deeds, whose brunt thou feel'st alone,	69	Content		29
Thy nourisht fame is weak or strong.	69	Content		32
Do not thy self or friends importune.	69	Content		34
Hadst thou not had thy part,	73	Afflict.3		5
But since thy breath gave me both life and shape,	73	Afflict.3		7
Thy life on earth was grief, and thou art still	73	Afflict.3		13
And in thy members suffer ill.	73	Afflict.3		16
Thou dying dayly, praise thee to thy losse.	73	Afflict.3		18
First with thy fire-work burn to dust	74	The Starre		9
Then with thy light refine,	74	The Starre		11
Touch it with thy celestiall quicknesse,	74	The Starre		14
After thy love.	74	The Starre		16
The week were dark, but for thy light:	75	Sunday		6
The week were dark, but that thy light	75	Sunday	W	6
Thy torch doth show the way.	75	Sunday		7
Knocking at heaven with thy brow:	75	Sunday		10
Till thy release appeare.	75	Sunday		14
Thy flight is higher, as thy birth.	76	Sunday		59
I know thy parentage is base and low:	77	Avarice		3
To digge thee out of thy dark cave and grot:	77	Avarice		8
Thy silent eares;	79	Deniall		2
That so thy favours granting my request,	80	Deniall		28
Since my dark soul and brutish is thy right,	81	Christmas		11
The pasture is thy word: the streams, thy grace	81	Christmas		19
The work of thy creation	82	Ungratef.		11
Unto thy self in everlasting pleasure.	82	Ungratef.		12
But all thy sweets are packt up in the other;	82	Ungratef.		19
Thy mercies thither flock and flow:	82	Ungratef.		20
But on thy glorie! then thou wilt reform	83	Sighs & Gr.		3
For what account can thy ill steward make?	83	Sighs & Gr.		8
I have abus'd thy stock, destroy'd thy woods,	83	Sighs & Gr.		9
Suckt all thy magazens: my head did ake,	83	Sighs & Gr.		10
Till it found out how to consume thy goods:	83	Sighs & Gr.		11
Hath still sow'd fig-leaves to exclude thy light:	83	Sighs & Gr.		16
With the turn'd viall of thy bitter wrath!	83	Sighs & Gr.		20
For thou hast life and death at thy command;	83	Sighs & Gr.		26
Cordiall and Corrosive: put not thy hand	83	Sighs & Gr.		28
Give to thy Mother, what thou wouldst allow	86	Lent		5
The dew shall weep thy fall to night;	87	Vertue		3
Thy root is ever in its grave,	87	Vertue		7
Thy root is ever in his grave,	87	Vertue	V	7
And at what rate and price I have thy love;	89	The Pearl		35
But thy silk twist let down from heav'n to me,	89	The Pearl		38
Enter thy pay,	90	Afflict.4		26
Labour thy praise, and my relief;	90	Afflict.4		28
And both thy servants be.	92	Man		54
Lord, thy praises should be more.	93	Antiphon 2		19
But when thy grace	94	Unkindness		18
Then should thy praises with me grow,	95	Submission		7

THY (cont'd)

	PAGE	TITLE	LINE
Disseize thee of thy right.	95	Submission	12
Perhaps great places and thy praise	95	Submission	15
I cannot skill of these thy wayes.	95	Justice 1	1
Thy justice me most fitly payes:	96	Justice 1	7
Thy horse shal never fall or tire.	96	Charms & K W	4
As was and is thy floting Ark; whose stay	97	Afflict.5	3
Take up the second, then thy double line	97	Afflict.5	16
Furnish thy table to thy minde.	97	Afflict.5	18
That thy bright beams may tame thy bow.	97	Afflict.5	24
Advise with Abraham, when thy power could not	99	Decay	3
Thy words were then, Let me alone.	99	Decay	5
But now thou dost thy self immure and close	99	Decay	11
Where yet both Sinne and Satan, thy old foes,	99	Decay	13
To gain thy thirds and little part.	99	Decay	15
Of thy great love once spread, as in an urn	99	Decay	17
Lord, let the Angels praise thy name.	100	Miserie	1
The best of men, turn but thy hand	100	Miserie	19
The bargain made to serve thee: but thy love	100	Miserie	26
Their follies with the wing of thy milde Dove,	100	Miserie	28
Their follies with the wings of thy milde Dove,	100	Miserie W	28
Who would, to be thy foes.	100	Miserie	30
My God, Man cannot praise thy name:	101	Miserie	31
Presume on thy perfection?	101	Miserie	36
To sing thy praises, make them lesse divine.	101	Miserie	40
Or none thy portion is.	101	Miserie	42
Can thy strange wayes rehearse?	102	Miserie	66
Who may thy follies span?	102	Miserie W	66
Is thy great arm which spans the east and west,	103	Prayer 2	8
That by destroying that which ty'd thy purse,	103	Prayer 2	17
Since then these three wait on thy throne,	103	Prayer 2	19
I here exclude the wrangler from thy treasure.	104	Obedience	15
I here shutt out the wrangler from thy treasure.	104	Obedience W	15
O let thy sacred will	104	Obedience	16
All thy delight in me fulfill!	104	Obedience	17
But as thy love shall sway,	104	Obedience	19
Resigning up the rudder to thy skill.	104	Obedience	20
So great are thy perfections,	104	Obedience	24
Besides, thy death and bloud	104	Obedience	26
Thy sorrows were in earnest; no faint proffer,	104	Obedience	28
By listning to thy chatting fears	105	Conscience	5
Did not affect thee much, was not thy aim;	106	Sion	8
Wherefore thou quitt'st thy ancient claim:	106	Sion	10
And now thy Architecture meets with sinne;	106	Sion	11
For all thy frame and fabrick is within.	106	Sion	12
Thy long deferrings wound me to the quick,	107	Home	3
O show thy self to me,	107	Home	5
When I behold it trickling down thy face,	107	Home	9
O show thy self to me,	107	Home	11
When man was lost, thy pitie lockt about	107	Home	13
The help did in thy bosome lie.	107	Home	16
O show thy self to me,	107	Home	17
There lay thy sonne: and must he leave that nest,	107	Home	19
Leave one poore apple for thy love?	107	Home	22
O show thy self to me,	107	Home	23
As if thy love could fail or change.	108	Home	28
O show thy self to me,	108	Home	29
O show thy self to me,	108	Home	35
O show thy self to me,	108	Home	41
O show thy self to me,	108	Home	47
O show thy self to me,	108	Home	53
O show thy self to me,	108	Home	59
O show thy self to me,	109	Home	65
O show thy self to me,	109	Home	71
O show thy self to me,	109	Home	77
Thy perfect lineaments, and hue	109	Brit. Ch.	2
And dates her letters from thy face,	109	Brit. Ch.	5
The mean, thy praise and glorie is,	110	Brit. Ch.	26
Yet when the houre of thy designe	111	The Quip	21
O heare betimes, lest thy relenting	111	Vanitie 2	7
Unfold thy forehead gather'd into frowns:	112	Dawning	3
Thy Saviour comes, and with him mirth:	112	Dawning	4
To assume thy flesh and bone;	113	Businesse	18
And two deaths had been thy fee.	113	Businesse	22
He so farre thy good did plot,	113	Businesse	23
Brings thy Saviours death no gain?	114	Businesse	36
To thy wretch so full of stains;	114	Dialogue	7
Thy bloudy death and undeserv'd, makes thee	115	Dulnesse	11
That those thy form doth show,	115	Dulnesse	14
Lord, cleare thy gift, that with a constant wit	116	Dulnesse	25
Onely to Man thou hast made known thy wayes,	117	Providence	6
And made him Secretarie of thy praise.	117	Providence	8
To thy renown: but all their hands and throats	117	Providence	11
We all acknowledge both thy power and love	117	Providence	29
For either thy command, or thy permission	117	Providence	33
Lay hands on all: they are thy right and left.	117	Providence	34
Thy skill and art, what musick would it be!	118	Providence	40
Thy even praise can neither rise, nor fall.	118	Providence	42
Tempests are calm to thee; they know thy hand,	118	Providence	45
Thy cupboard serves the world: the meat is set,	118	Providence	49
Is there an herb for that? O that thy care	119	Providence	75

THY (cont'd)

	PAGE	TITLE	LINE
And as thy house is full, so I adore	119	Providence	93
Thy curious art in marshalling thy goods.	119	Providence	94
Sometimes thou dost divide thy gifts to man,	120	Providence	125
Thy creatures leap not, but expresse a feast,	121	Providence	133
To show thou art not bound, as if thy lot	121	Providence	137
None can expresse thy works, but he that knows them:	121	Providence	142
And none can know thy works, which are so many,	121	Providence	143
To honour thee; and so each hymne thy fame	121	Providence	151
Thy sithe is dull; whet it for shame.	122	Time	2
To whom thy sithe a hatchet was,	122	Time	9
Christs coming hath made man thy debter,	122	Time	11
Since by thy cutting he grows better.	122	Time	12
See how thy beggar works on thee	123	Gratefulnes	3
He makes thy gifts occasion more,	123	Gratefulnes	5
Thy word our hearts and hands did crave,	123	Gratefulnes	10
Perpetuall knockings at thy doore,	124	Gratefulnes	13
Tears sullying thy transparent rooms,	124	Gratefulnes	14
Thy joyes.	124	Gratefulnes	20
But that these countrey-aires thy love	124	Gratefulnes	23
As if thy blessings had spare dayes:	124	Gratefulnes	30
Thy praise.	124	Gratefulnes	32
Lord, I acknowledge; take thy plagues away:	126	Confession	26
Dares to assault thee, and besiege thy doore.	132	The Storm	12
There it stands knocking, to thy musicks wrong,	132	The Storm	13
Among thy trees, which in a ROW	132	Paradise	2
Then let me want thy hand & ART.	133	Paradise	9
And with thy knife but prune and PARE,	133	Paradise	11
For since thy God refuseth still,	133	The Method	2
Thy Father could	133	The Method	5
Tumble thy breast, and turn thy book.	133	The Method	10
Down with thy knees, up with thy voice.	134	The Method	30
Then burn thy Epicycles, foolish man;	135	Divinitie	25
Break all thy spheres, and save thy head.	135	Divinitie	26
And crosse thy love?	135	Ephes.	3
Oh take thy lute, and tune it to a strain,	136	Ephes.	19
Lord, pardon, for thy sonne makes good	136	Ephes.	35
Turn out these wranglers, which defile thy seat:	136	Familie	7
This is thy house, with these it doth abound:	137	Familie	21
Lay out thy joy, yet hope to save it?	138	The Size	17
Wouldst thou both eat thy cake, and have it?	138	The Size	18
Thy Saviour sentenc'd joy,	138	The Size	25
Which thou hast open'd: do not spread thy robe	138	The Size	43
In hope of great things. Call to minde thy dream,	138	The Size	44
Expell good motions from thy breast,	139	Artillerie	7
Born where thy servants both artilleries use.	139	Artillerie	18
Much more oblig'd to do thy will,	139	Artillerie	22
Thy promise now hath ev'n set thee thy laws.	139	Artillerie	24
And those all bitten, in thy chair I see.	140	Ch.-rents	10
And those all sitten in thy chair I see.	140	Ch.-rents V	10
Did show and shape thy looks to me,	141	Justice 2	4
The dishes of thy ballance seem'd to gape,	141	Justice 2	7
Thy hand above did burn and glow,	141	Justice 2	11
Thy hand is white,	141	Justice 2	15
Thy scales like buckets, which attend	141	Justice 2	16
Thy clay that weeps, thy dust that calls.	143	Complaining	5
Are both thy due: but I a silly flie,	143	Complaining	8
Shows not thy word	143	Complaining	12
Let not thy wrathfull power	144	Complaining	16
My inch of life: or let thy gracious power	144	Complaining	18
And in thy lookings stretch and grow?	144	Discharge	5
Hast thou not made thy counts, and summ'd up all?	144	Discharge	6
Did not thy heart	144	Discharge	7
Thy life is Gods, thy time to come is gone,	144	Discharge	11
He is thy night at noon: he is at night	144	Discharge	13
Thy noon alone.	144	Discharge	14
Thy businesse his, and in thy life partake:	144	Discharge	18
Onely the present is thy part and fee.	144	Discharge	21
If, though thou didst not beat thy future brow,	144	Discharge	23
And wake thy sorrow?	145	Discharge	47
Grieve over freshly all thy pain?	145	Discharge	50
Come, bring thy gift. If blessings were as slow	147	Offering	1
In Christ two natures met to be thy cure.	147	Offering	6
But all I fear is lest thy heart displease,	147	Offering	13
Thy lusts have made, and not thy lusts alone;	147	Offering	15
Thy passions also have their set partitions.	147	Offering	16
These parcell out thy heart: recover these,	147	Offering	17
Untill thou finde and use it to thy good:	147	Offering	23
Then bring thy gift; and let thy hymne be this;	147	Offering	24
As thy due desert.	147	Offering	30
Yet thy favour	148	Offering	37
To be thy praise,	148	Offering	41
Thy name!	149	Longing	24
Thy dying head upon the tree:	149	Longing	32
Behold, thy dust doth stirre,	149	Longing	37
Thy pile of dust, wherein each crumme	149	Longing	41
Indeed the world's thy book,	149	Longing	49
Thy board is full, yet humble guests	149	Longing	53
Thy childe.	150	Longing	60
Lord, didst thou leave thy throne,	150	Longing	61
And all thy promises live and bide.	150	Longing	68

THY (cont'd)	PAGE	TITLE	LINE
And in thy bosome poure my tears,	150	Longing	71
Thy beggars grow; rid them away	150	Longing	77
By these thy feet, at which my heart	150	Longing	80
Pluck out thy dart,	150	Longing	82
Recover all thy sigh-blown age	153	The Collar	19
On double pleasures: leave thy cold dispute	153	The Collar	20
Of what is fit, and not. Forsake thy cage,	153	The Collar	21
Thy rope of sands,	153	The Collar	22
And be thy law,	153	The Collar	25
Call in thy deaths head there: tie up thy fears.	153	The Collar	29
Thy short abode and stay	154	Glimpse	11
Although thy heap be kept	154	Glimpse	23
The wheel shall go, so that thy stay be short.	155	Glimpse	27
Who by thy coming may be made a court!	155	Glimpse	30
What is thy aim? wouldst thou unlock the doore	155	Assurance	15
I writ thy purpose long ago.	155	Assurance	18
Thou art not onely to perform thy part,	156	Assurance	27
Thou didst at once thy self indite,	156	Assurance	29
Then can thy truth and I: but while rocks stand,	156	Assurance	32
And make their ruine praise thy power.	156	Assurance	36
Spin out thy thread, and make thereof a coat	156	Assurance	38
To hide thy shame: for thou hast cast a bone	156	Assurance	39
Which bounds on thee, and will not down thy throat:	156	Assurance	40
Lord, I will mean and speak thy praise,	157	Praise 3	1
Thy praise alone.	157	Praise 3	2
From thy right eye,	158	Praise 3	32
That to thy chests there might be coming in	159	Praise 3	41
That to thy chest there might be coming in	159	Praise 3 V	41
In thy just censures; fain would I draw nigh,	160	Priesthood	4
To wear thy habit, the severe attire	160	Priesthood	9
As having keyes unto thy love,	162	The Search	15
What covert dare eclipse thy face?	163	The Search	31
Is it thy will?	163	The Search	32
Or steel, or mountains be thy ring,	163	The Search	35
Thy will such an intrenching is,	163	The Search	37
Thy will such a strange distance is,	163	The Search	41
As is thy space,	163	The Search	46
Thy distance from me; see my charge,	163	The Search	47
For as thy absence doth excell	163	The Search	57
So doth thy nearenesse bear the bell,	163	The Search	59
To set thy honour up, as our designe.	164	The Crosse	6
Ev'n when my will doth studie thy renown:	165	The Crosse	20
And yet since these thy contradictions	165	The Crosse	34
Are properly a crosse felt by thy sonne,	165	The Crosse	35
With but foure words, my words, Thy will be done.	165	The Crosse	36
Are thy returns! ev'n as the flowers in spring;	165	The Flower	2
These are thy wonders, Lord of power,	166	The Flower	15
Thy word is all, if we could spell.	166	The Flower	21
Fast in thy Paradise, where no flower can wither!	166	The Flower	23
Thy anger comes, and I decline:	166	The Flower	31
On whom thy tempests fell all night.	166	The Flower	42
These are thy wonders, Lord of love,	167	The Flower	43
Alas, poore Death, where is thy glorie?	169	Dial.-Anth	1
Where is thy famous force, thy ancient sting?	169	Dial.-Anth	2
Go spell and reade how I have kill'd thy King.	169	Dial.-Anth	4
Thy curse being laid on him, makes thee accurst.	169	Dial.-Anth	6
These arms shall crush thee. Spare not, do thy worst.	169	Dial.-Anth	8
To serve thy sinnes, and furnish thee with store	170	Water-crs.	7
That choice may be thy storie.	170	Self-cond.	6
When first thy sweet and gracious eye	171	The Glance	1
But still thy sweet originall joy	172	The Glance	13
If thy first glance so powerfull be,	172	The Glance	17
Thy full-ey'd love!	172	The Glance	20
For thou art with me; and thy rod	173	23 Psalme	15
To guide, thy staffe to bear.	173	23 Psalme	16
Surely thy sweet and wondrous love	173	23 Psalme	21
So neither shall thy praise.	173	23 Psalme V	24
Hath some fond lover tic'd thee to thy bane?	176	Forerunners	21
Fie, thou wilt soil thy broider'd coat,	176	Forerunners	23
And hurt thy self, and him that sings the note.	176	Forerunners	24
Throw away thy rod,	178	Discipline	1
Throw away thy wrath:	178	Discipline	2
And thy book alone.	178	Discipline	12
Throw away thy rod;	179	Discipline	29
Throw away thy wrath.	179	Discipline	32
For thy neatnesse passeth sight,	181	Banquet	4
Thy delight	181	Banquet	5
Of all thy mercies, is my posie still.	182	The Posie	4
Comparisons go play, wit use thy will:	183	The Posie	10
Of thy abode,	183	A Parodie	8
As thy eclipsed light.	183	A Parodie	15
Which with his tincture (for thy sake)	184	The Elixer	15
Which with this tincture (for thy sake)	184	The Elixer V	15
Who sweeps a room, as for thy laws,	185	The Elixer	19
Who sweeps a chamber, for thy laws,	185	The Elixer W	19
So live and like, that I may know thy wayes,	185	A Wreath	10
Thy mouth was open, but thou couldst not sing.	185	Death	4
Into thy face;	186	Death	14
And all thy bones with beautie shall be clad.	186	Death	20
But thy trumpet: then it kneels,	186	Dooms-day	10

THY (cont'd)

	PAGE	TITLE		LINE
Thy flock doth stray.	187	Dooms-day		20
Lord, thy broken consort raise,	187	Dooms-day		29
Thy dreadfull lock,	187	Judgement		2
And thrust a Testament into thy hand:	188	Judgement		13
Almightie Lord, who from thy glorious throne	190	Ch.-Milit.		1
The smallest ant or atome knows thy power,	190	Ch.-Milit.		3
And wrap their policies in thy decree,	190	Ch.-Milit.		6
Complying with thy counsels, doing nought	190	Ch.-Milit.		7
But above all, thy Church and Spouse doth prove	190	Ch.-Milit.		9
Spices come from the East; so did thy Spouse,	190	Ch.-Milit.		13
Prepar'd and fitted to receive thy love.	190	Ch.-Milit.		16
All, Emblems, which thy Darling doth improve.	190	Ch.-Milit.	W	16
How deare to me, O God, thy counsels are!	191	Ch.-Milit.		47
How deare to me, O God, thy counsels are!	192	Ch.-Milit.		99
How deare to me, O God, thy counsels are!	194	Ch.-Milit.		155
How deare to me, O God, thy counsels are!	196	Ch.-Milit.		209
How deare to me, O God, thy counsels are!	198	Ch.-Milit.		278
With the other blesse thy sheep,	199	L'Envoy		3
Let not Sinne devoure thy fold,	199	L'Envoy		5
Bragging that thy bloud is cold,	199	L'Envoy		6
That thy death is also dead,	199	L'Envoy		7
That thy flesh hath lost his food,	199	L'Envoy		9
And thy Crosse is common wood.	199	L'Envoy		10
Till thy conquests and his fall	199	L'Envoy		13
Till thy conquest and his fall	199	L'Envoy	V	13
For thy poore creature there	200	H. Commun.	W	6
But that both thou, and all thy traine	200	H. Commun.	W	10
Bee there, to thy truth, & my gaine	200	H. Commun.	W	11
And if in comming to thy foes	200	H. Commun.	W	13
The hast of thy good will.	200	H. Commun.	W	15
Thy flesh the least that I request.	201	H. Commun.	W	44
That is thy Master-peece I see	201	love	W	3
Thy ancient baptism which when I was foule	202	love	W	11
Upon the matter 'twill thy conquest prove:	202	love	W	20
Whereas if I orecome thee & thy Love	202	love	W	23
With Glory may attaine thy Face.	202	Trin.Sun.	W	6
Since Light thy Darknes is.	203	Even-song	W	20
Which know nct thee, suck in thy beames	203	Even-song	W	23
Lord help thy servant whose perplexed Soule	204	The Knell	W	2
Lord make thy Blood	204	The Knell	W	13
Onely my soule hangs on thy promisses	205	Persever.	W	13
With face and hands clinging unto thy brest,	205	Persever.	W	14
Upon thine Altar burnt? Cannot thy love	206	Walton 1		6
Heighten a spirit to sound out thy praise	206	Walton 1		7
As well as any she? Cannot thy Dove	206	Walton 1		8
Or, since thy wayes are deep, and still the same,	206	Waltcn 1		10
Will not a verse run smooth that bears thy name?	206	Walton 1		11
Why doth that fire, which by thy power and might	206	Waltcn 1		12
Cover the Earth, so doth thy Majesty:	206	Walton 2		3
Each Cloud distills thy praise, and doth forbid	206	Walton 2		4
A pair of Cheeks of them, is thy abuse.	206	Walton 2		7
A new House to thy mind,	207	Walton 3		2
And built without thy Cost:	207	Walton 3		3
If thou dost find an house built to thy mind	207	Walton 4		1
Without thy cost,	207	Walton 4		2
Nor yet thy eloquence here keep him still,	439	Walton 5		3
Are shed for him, dissolve thy frame,	209	H. Danvers	D	7
No Earth can bee thy Jointure. For the sunne	211	Bohemia	D	3
And pace of thy swift vertues; onely they	211	Bohemia	D	5
Are thy dominion. Those that rule in clay	211	Bohemia	D	6
Stick fast therein, but thy transcendent soule	211	Bohemia	D	7
Yet thy brave beames excluded from their right	211	Bohemia	D	10
Thy curious vertues much more visibly:	211	Bohemia	D	14
There is thy bėst Throne. For afflictions are	211	Bohemia	D	15
Through that black tiffany thy vertues shine	211	Bohemia	D	17
And show thy undivided Majestye	212	Bohemia	D	34
About thy temples that the furious frowne	212	Bohemia	D	38
Those ravening Harpyes, which peck at thy face,	212	Bohemia	D	48
Is thy chief government, to manage woe,	212	Bohemia	D	57
Making a Head & spring against thy Reason.	213	Bohemia	D	59
This is thy empire yet: till better season	213	Bohemia	D	60
Thy teares not needing. For that hand Divine	213	Bohemia	D	63
Which mingles water with thy Rhenish wine	213	Bohemia	D	64
And meet theire tast, who are thy bitter foes.	213	Bohemia	D	66
Thy fruite shall with there drops contend;	213	L' Envoy	D	4
Then shall thy Glory, fresh as flowers	213	L' Envoy	D	7
And with that Ring thy fame shall wedd	213	L' Envoy	D	13
Make thy request, and I will grant	216	Psalm II	D	19
the Heathen shall thy portion be.	216	Psalm II	D	20
Belongs, O Lord, thy blessing shall	217	Psalm III	D	23
upon thy people be.	217	Psalm III	D	24
Thy countenances cheering light	217	Psalm IV	D	23
For thy protection, Lord, alone	218	Psalm IV	D	31
Direct my prayers to thy Throne,	218	Psalm V	D	7
nor fools stand in thy sight.	218	Psalm V	D	12
But in th' abundance of thy Grace	218	Psalm V	D	17
And toward thy most Holy place	218	Psalm V	D	19
Lord lead me in thy righteousness,	219	Psalm V	D	21
thy perfect way disclose.	219	Psalm V	D	24
Because against thy Majesty	219	Psalm V	D	33

	PAGE	TITLE		LINE
THY (cont'd)				
Let them that do thy name adore	219	Psalm V	D	39
shall I in vain thy Grace implore?	220	Psalm VI	D	8
my Soul for thy great mercy save;	220	Psalm VI	D	10
and high thy Glory raise.	221	Psalm VII	D	28
preach my Laws, and takest my Covenant in thy mouth? Psal. 50. 16.	226	Priest 2		14
open mine eyes, that I may see the wondrous things of thy Law.	229	Priest 4		3
errand I come, let me hold my peace, and doe thou speak thy selfe;	233	Priest 7		36
imprecation to Simon Magus, Act. 8. Thy mony perish with thee:	285	Priest 36		30
How shall we dare to appear before thy face, who are contrary	288	Priest		9
yet art thou our Creatour, and we thy work:	288	Priest		12
Thy hands both made us, and also made us Lords of all thy creatures;	288	Priest		12
Thy hands both made us, and also made us Lords of all thy creatures;	288	Priest		13
and wert proceeding still on in thy Favours, untill we interrupted	288	Priest		15
untill we interrupted thy Counsels, disappointed thy Purposes,	288	Priest		16
thy Counsels, disappointed thy Purposes, and sold our God,	288	Priest		16
Thou hast exalted thy mercy above all things;	288	Priest		22
and hast made our salvation, not our punishment, thy glory:	288	Priest		24
many waters could not quench thy love!	288	Priest		31
But though the streams of thy bloud were currant through darknesse,	288	Priest		32
yet by these thy conflicts, and seemingly hazards, didst thou arise	288	Priest		33
Neither doth thy love yet stay here!	289	Priest		3
for, this word of thy rich peace, and reconciliation, thou hast	289	Priest		3
pardoning my sins, and bidding me go feed the people of thy love.	289	Priest		6
in the power of thy Victories, and in the wayes of thy Ordinances,	289	Priest		12
and in the wayes of thy Ordinances, and in the truth of thy Love,	289	Priest		12
and in the wayes of thy Ordinances, and in the truth of thy Love, Lo,	289	Priest		13
beseeching thee to blesse thy word, wher-ever spoken this day	289	Priest		14
blesse it in this thy own Kingdom, which thou hast made a Land	289	Priest		18
made a Land of light, a store-house of thy treasures and mercies:	289	Priest		19
and unworthy hearts rob us of the continuance of this thy sweet love:	289	Priest		20
and thy right hand shall teach thee terrible things.	289	Priest		23
assembled together, with thy unworthy Servant speaking unto them:	289	Priest		25
that in their full strength they may deliver thy message reverently,	289	Priest		28
O make thy word a swift word, passing from the ear to the heart,	289	Priest		29
so neither may thy word, but accomplish that for which it is given.	289	Priest		32
and do so for thy blessed Son's sake, in whose sweet and pleasing	289	Priest		34
thy blessings hang in clusters, they come trooping upon us!	290	Priest		6
untill our obedience reach the measure of thy love, who hast done	290	Priest		12
Grant this dear Father, for thy Son's sake, our only Saviour:	290	Priest		13
For if a friend who visits thee in thy sicknesse, and onely comforts	298	Cornaro		6
Better thy foote slip then thy tongue.	322	Proverbs	V	53
Deceive not thy Physitian, Confessor, nor Lawyer.	324	Proverbs		105
Let an ill man lie in thy straw, and he lookes to be thy heire.	330	Proverbs		271
Neither bribe nor loose thy right.	330	Proverbs		284
Although it raine, throw not away thy watering pot.	332	Proverbs		325
Although the sun shine, leave not thy cloake at home.	332	Proverbs		326
Thou hast death in thy house, and dost bewaile anothers.	334	Proverbs		376
Helpe thy selfe, and God will helpe thee.	339	Proverbs		537
Pardon all but thy selfe.	344	Proverbs		677
Neither praise nor dispraise thy selfe,	347	Proverbs		771
thy actions serve the turne.	347	Proverbs		771
Prayse not thyself, thy actions serve the Turne.	347	Proverbs	V	771
If thou thy selfe canst doe it, attend no others helpe or hand.	348	Proverbs		813
Chuse none for thy servant who have served thy betters.	354	Proverbs		1014
Follow not truth too near the heels, lest it dash out thy teeth.	360	Proverbs	D	1138
Cast thy Care on the Lord and he shall nourish thee. (Psal. 55.)	374	Letters		14
THYSELF				
Prayse not thyself, thy actions serve the Turne.	347	Proverbs	V	771
TIBER				
When Sein shall swallow Tiber, and the Thames	197	Ch.-Milit.		241
TIBI				
Better is one Accipe, then twice to say, Dabo tibi.	358	Proverbs	D	1079
'TICE				
And 'tice me unto thee.	46	Afflict.1		10
TICE				
Doth tice us on to hopes of more,	138	The Size		29
TIC'D				
Hath some fond lover tic'd thee to thy bane?	176	Forerunners		21
TICING				
One of Joyes coats, ticing it with relief	159	Jos.coat		11
TICKLE				
not to exceed his bounds, but in tickle cases to call in help.	260	Priest 23		36
TIDE				
And clean and fair, as I one even-tide	129	Love unkn.		23
TIDES				
And both with moons and tides.	91	Man		18
TIE (see also ty)				
Which on the world a true-love-knot may tie,	88	The Pearl		16
Here will I smell my remnant out, and tie	94	Life		2
Call in thy deaths head there: tie up thy fears.	153	The Collar		29
A slender thread a gentle guest will tie.	154	Glimpse		20
TI'D				
Save one good Angell, which a friend had ti'd	142	Pilgrimage		17
TIES				
Ties the whole frame, is Love	67	Ch.-floore		11
Man ties them both alone,	131	Mans medly		10
TIFFANY				
Through that black tiffany thy vertues shine	211	Bohemia	D	17
TILL (noun)				
In those chests, boxes; in each box, a till:	126	Confession		5

	PAGE	TITLE		LINE
TILL (verb)				
Some till their ground, but let weeds choke their sonne:	10	Ch.-Porch		98
Then cease discoursing soul, till thine own ground,	69	Content		33
TILL				
Who cannot rest till hee good-fellows finde,	12	Ch.-Porch		149
Till labour come, and make my weaknesse score.	17	Ch.-Porch		288
Till thou change names, and be where he began.	21	Ch.-Porch		378
Till all were melted, though he were all steel:	33	Sacrifice		211
Till I have found therein thy love,	36	Thanksgvng		46
Till I have found thy love therin,	36	Thanksgvng	W	46
Till he became	43	East.wings		4
Till I became	43	East.wings	W	14
Till grief did tell me roundly, that I lived.	47	Afflict.1		30
I took thy sweetned pill, till I came neare;	47	Afflict.1		47
I took thy sweetned pill, till I came where	47	Afflict.1	W	47
Dust blown by wit, till that they both were blinde:	54	Love 2		10
Thou art all health, health thriving, till it make	58	H.Script.1		5
Till it get wing, and flie away with thee.	59	Whitsunday		4
Till I get wing to fly away with thee.	59	Whitsunday	W	4
Thou dost inclose us, till the day	64	Even-song		22
Till they fell out: which when the beasts espied,	70	Humilitie		21
Till he the thing and the example weigh:	72	Constancie		13
Till thy release appeare.	75	Sunday		14
Till that we both, being toss'd from earth,	77	Sunday		62
My dearest Lord, expecting till the grief	81	Christmas		6
I will go searching, till I finde a sunne	81	Christmas		27
Shall stay, till we have done;	81	Christmas		28
Till ev'n his beams sing, and my musick shine.	81	Christmas		34
This fully to us, till death blow	82	Ungratef.		16
This to us fully, till death blow	82	Ungratef.	W	16
Till it found out how to consume thy goods:	83	Sighs & Gr.		11
Till she had weakned all by alteration:	84	The World		8
And strip the creature naked, till he finde	85	Vanitie 1		16
Till I reach heav'n, and much more thee.	90	Afflict.4		30
Till then, afford us so much wit;	92	Man		52
Till all do melt, and drown his breath	98	Mortific.		27
Cold sinne still forcing it, till it return,	99	Decay		19
Into these lines; till in heav'ns court of rolls	105	Obedience		43
Till they regain their ancient nest.	111	Vanitie 2		16
Till I a thankfull heart obtain	124	Gratefulnes		27
And till they foot and clutch their prey,	126	Confession		15
Glorie and honour are set by till it	132	The Storm		15
Much troubled, till I heard a friend expresse,	143	Holdfast		11
God chains the dog till night: wilt loose the chain,	145	Discharge		46
Till it stirre, and rubbe the eyes;	186	Dooms-day		4
Till all depart: so went the Church her way,	191	Ch.-Milit.		33
Till all be gone. so went the Church her way,	191	Ch.-Milit.	W	33
Till both removed to the western clime.	191	Ch.-Milit.		36
Till such a darknesse do the world invade	196	Ch.-Milit.		230
Till thy conquests and his fall	199	L'Envoy		13
Till thy conquest and his fall	199	L'Envoy	V	13
Till your bright gift my darknesse did abate.	209	L. Bacon	D	8
This is thy empire yet: till better season	213	Bohemia	D	60
(Till now averse to all that's Good)	214	Convert	D	17
and till they have learned them, makes them kneel by him;	241	Priest 10		3
of the pulpit, and never leaving them, till he obtaine his desire.	245	Priest 12		14
God further, even till he imbarn his corn, and then think all sure;	271	Priest 30		32
generation should not passe, till all were fulfilled, Luke 21. 32.	282	Priest 34		29
till either they despise that Love, or despaire of his Mercy:	283	Priest 34		23
for all are honest, till the contrary be proved.	287	Priest 37		35
discourse from this line [place] till the end of this Chapter may	311	Valdesso		20
bidding the dispersed Hebrews attend to the word till the day dawn,	318	Valdesso		18
but however he would have them attend to it till that time,	318	Valdesso		20
Say no ill of the yeere, till it be past.	331	Proverbs		297
Call me not an olive, till thou see me gathered.	331	Proverbs		301
Stay till the lame messenger come,	332	Proverbs		331
at his time, and not till then.	332	Proverbs		333
The Cow knowes not what her taile is worth, till she have lost it.	350	Proverbs		870
Sinnes are not knowne till they bee acted.	352	Proverbs		942
All are presumed good, till they are found in a fault.	352	Proverbs		944
but you married men laugh till your hearts ake.	361	Proverbs	D	1175
till I take some opportunity to let them know your love,	375	Letters		21
TILLAGE				
He condescends even to the knowledge of tillage, and pastorage,	228	Priest 4		18
TIMBER				
Like season'd timber, never gives;	88	Vertue		14
Into a piece of timber work and winde,	126	Confession		8
TIME				
If studious, copie fair, what time hath blurr'd;	10	Ch.-Porch		86
In time they'l runne thee out of all thy wit.	21	Ch.-Porch		366
Restore to God his due in tithe and time:	22	Ch.-Porch		385
In time of service seal up both thine eies,	23	Ch.-Porch		415
Who marks in church-time others symmetrie,	23	Ch.-Porch		419
Who marks in church-time others comlines,	23	Ch.-Porch	W	419
In you Redemption measures all my time,	44	H. Bapt.1		10
Nor let them punish me with losse of time,	57	Jordan 1	V	14
That measures all our time; which also shall	65	Ch.-monum.		21
The Couch of Time, the balme of tears,	75	Sunday	W	2
The couch of time; cares balm and bay:	75	Sunday		5
Deferre no time;	80	Deniall		27
But time did becken to the flowers, and they	94	Life		4

TITLE (cont'd)	PAGE	TITLE		LINE
Yet one, if good, may title to a number;	147	Offering		9
to his earthly, having no title to either, except he do good to both.	239	Priest 10		22
upon condition that I should surcease from all title to it,	367	Letters		9
therfore God is styled with that glorious title, Long Suffering.	381	Woodnoth		6
The accession of which new title to your Excellencies, all the Muses	442	Oration		1
TITLES				
and other titles most pleasing, as well to us remembring,	441	Oration		25
T'				
As from one room t' another.	53	H.Commun.		36
Content and warm t' it self alone:	68	Content		10
Either t' his publick foot or private tricks.	195	Ch.-Milit.		196
TO				
Lord, my first fruits present themselves to thee;	5	Dedication		1
Ryme thee to good, and make a bait of pleasure.	6	Ch.-Porch		4
Let not each fansy make thee to detest	7	Ch.-Porch	W	19
Let not each motion make thee to detest	7	Ch.-Porch	WC	19
And God will show thee how to take the towne,	7	Ch.-Porch	W	22
Sure to be crosse he would shift feet and face.	7	Ch.-Porch		24
It is most just to throw that on the ground,	7	Ch.-Porch		29
Shall I, to please anothers wine-sprung minde,	8	Ch.-Porch		37
Because to shun them also is so cheap:	9	Ch.-Porch		68
For we have wit to mark them, and to spare.	9	Ch.-Porch		69
Lie not; but let thy heart be true to God,	9	Ch.-Porch		73
Thy mouth to it, thy actions to them both:	9	Ch.-Porch		74
Dare to be true. Nothing can need a ly:	9	Ch.-Porch		77
Into a bed, to sleep out all ill weathers.	9	Ch.-Porch		84
But if thou coole, then take some shame to thee	10	Ch.-Porch	W	90
Are gone to grasse, and in the pasture lost.	10	Ch.-Porch		96
For he, that needs five thousand pound to live,	10	Ch.-Porch		107
The way to make thy sonne rich, is to fill	11	Ch.-Porch		109
To feel those tempests, which fly over ditches.	11	Ch.-Porch		112
Be sure to doe it, though it be but small:	11	Ch.-Porch		116
When wanton pleasures becken us to thrall.	11	Ch.-Porch		118
Who fears to do ill, sets himself to task:	11	Ch.-Porch		125
Who fears to do well, sure should wear a mask.	11	Ch.-Porch		126
Look to thy mouth; diseases enter there.	11	Ch.-Porch		127
Who carves, is kind to two; who talks, to all.	11	Ch.-Porch		130
And say withall, Earth to earth I commit.	11	Ch.-Porch		132
But say withall, Earth to earth I commit.	11	Ch.-Porch	W	132
And rots to nothing at the next great thaw.	12	Ch.-Porch		140
God gave them to thee under lock and key.	12	Ch.-Porch		144
By all means use sometimes to be alone.	12	Ch.-Porch		145
Dare to look in thy chest; for 'tis thine own:	12	Ch.-Porch		147
Never was scraper brave man. Get to live;	12	Ch.-Porch		153
To all things els. Wealth is the conjurers devil;	13	Ch.-Porch		165
Which if it cleave to coine, one common rust	13	Ch.-Porch	W	165
Unto thy hands, it woundeth to the quick.	13	Ch.-Porch		168
As that thy self alone to hell shalt goe.	13	Ch.-Porch	W	168
Take starres for money; starres not to be told	13	Ch.-Porch		171
By any art, yet to be purchased.	13	Ch.-Porch		172
As all the day thou mayst hold out to go.	14	Ch.-Porch		186
That all the day thou mayst hold out to go.	14	Ch.-Porch	W	186
Who strive to sit out losing hands, are lost.	14	Ch.-Porch		202
To stuffe thy minde with solid braverie;	15	Ch.-Porch		208
Be sweet to all. Is thy complexion sowre?	15	Ch.-Porch		211
For wit is newes onely to ignorance.	15	Ch.-Porch		230
Have got to be a deare fool for an houre.	16	Ch.-Porch		246
Then may the beasts draw thee to happy light.	16	Ch.-Porch		264
Both friends should die, then hinder them to live.	17	Ch.-Porch		280
Fathers first enter bonds to natures ends;	17	Ch.-Porch		281
Submit to love; but yet not more then all.	17	Ch.-Porch		284
To work for two, who brought himself to thrall.	17	Ch.-Porch		286
To work for two, that brought himself to thrall.	17	Ch.-Porch	W	286
In thy discourse, if thou desire to please:	18	Ch.-Porch		289
Entice all neatly to what they know best;	18	Ch.-Porch		295
What to ask further. Doubts well rais'd do lock	18	Ch.-Porch		299
What to ask farther. Doubts well rais'd do lock	18	Ch.-Porch	W	299
The speaker to thee, and preserve thy stock.	18	Ch.-Porch		300
As cunning fencers suffer heat to tire.	19	Ch.-Porch		316
To compasse this. Finde out mens wants and will,	19	Ch.-Porch		328
To the one joy of doing kindnesses.	19	Ch.-Porch		330
To that one joy of doing kindnesses.	19	Ch.-Porch	W	330
And to instruct them, will not quit the cost.	20	Ch.-Porch		348
The meanest tool, that he may chance to use.	20	Ch.-Porch		354
All forrain wisdome doth amount to this,	20	Ch.-Porch		355
To take all that is given; whether wealth,	20	Ch.-Porch		356
A good digestion turneth all to health:	20	Ch.-Porch		358
First to bee Slovens, & forsake their nose.	21	Ch.-Porch	W	370
Think heav'n a better bargain, then to give	21	Ch.-Porch		374
Joyn hands with God to make a man to live.	21	Ch.-Porch		376
Give to all something; to a good poore man,	21	Ch.-Porch		377
Christs stamp to boot: both images regard.	21	Ch.-Porch		380
Write, So much giv'n to God; thou shalt be heard.	21	Ch.-Porch		382
Restore to God his due in tithe and time:	22	Ch.-Porch		385
Who would not haste, nay give, to see the show?	22	Ch.-Porch		390
And love's a weight to hearts, to eies a signe.	22	Ch.-Porch		399
Resort to sermons, but to prayers most:	23	Ch.-Porch		409
And send them to thine heart; that spying sinne,	23	Ch.-Porch		416
And send them to thy heart; that spying sinne,	23	Ch.-Porch	W	416
Turns all their beauty to his uglines.	23	Ch.-Porch	W	420

TO (cont'd)

	PAGE	TITLE		LINE
To couzin thee. Look to thy actions well:	23	Ch.-Porch		425
To pick out treasures from an earthen pot.	23	Ch.-Porch		430
He that loves Gods abode, and to combine	24	Ch.-Porch		437
And in the morning, what thou hast to do.	24	Ch.-Porch		452
Sprinkled and taught, how to behave	25	Superlim		2
Or that which groneth to be so,	25	Superlim		7
To praise thy Name:	26	The Altar		12
That if I chance to hold my peace,	26	The Altar		13
These stones to praise thee may not cease.	26	The Altar		14
And sanctifie this ALTAR to be thine.	26	The Altar		16
To worldly things are sharp, but to me blinde;	26	Sacrifice		2
To me, who took eyes that I might you finde:	26	Sacrifice		3
Had to this day been an Egyptian slave.	27	Sacrifice		10
To sell me also, and to put me there:	27	Sacrifice		15
Drops bloud (the onely beads) my words to measure:	27	Sacrifice		22
Alas! what haste they make to be undone!	27	Sacrifice		34
Most true to those, who are my greatest grief:	27	Sacrifice		39
Then from one ruler to another bound	28	Sacrifice		53
Some said, that I the Temple to the floore	28	Sacrifice		65
Sends me to Pilate. This makes them agree;	29	Sacrifice		74
Who teach all hands to warre, fingers to fight,	29	Sacrifice		78
To whose powre Thunder is but weake and slight:	29	Sacrifice	W	79
In him to do themselves a courtesie:	30	Sacrifice		114
Windes up my grief to a mysteriousnesse:	30	Sacrifice		127
Leaving his blindnesse to mine enemies:	31	Sacrifice		135
Leaving his blindnesse to my enemies:	31	Sacrifice	W	135
The souldiers lead me to the common hall;	31	Sacrifice		153
Which shews my bloud to be the onely way,	31	Sacrifice		158
And cordiall left to repair mans decay:	31	Sacrifice		159
Then with the reed they gave to me before,	32	Sacrifice		169
Of heav'nly blessings issue to the poore:	32	Sacrifice	W	171
They bow their knees to me, and cry, Hail king:	32	Sacrifice		173
Which Angels did desire to have the grace,	32	Sacrifice		182
Whom Angels did desire to have the grace,	32	Sacrifice	W	182
And Prophets once to see, but found no place:	32	Sacrifice		183
Thus trimmed forth they bring me to the rout,	32	Sacrifice		185
And now wearie of sport, glad to ingrosse	33	Sacrifice		193
They carrie me to my most bitter crosse:	33	Sacrifice		195
The tree of life to all, but onely me:	33	Sacrifice		203
Or feel his part, he would not cease to kneel,	33	Sacrifice		210
Or feel his share, he would not cease to kneel,	33	Sacrifice	W	210
The sonne, in whom thou dost delight to be?	33	Sacrifice		214
The sonne, in whom thou art well pleas'd to be?	33	Sacrifice	W	214
And fathers smile for you, to feel his frown:	34	Sacrifice		223
And fathers smile to feele for you his frown:	34	Sacrifice	W	223
Yet by my subjects am condemn'd to die	34	Sacrifice		234
To thee of all kings onely due)	35	Thanksgvng		2
'Tis but to tell the tale is told.	35	Thanksgvng		8
The honour doth belong to thee.	35	Thanksgvng		22
That honour doth belong to thee.	35	Thanksgvng	W	22
Shall have his attribute to sing;	36	Thanksgvng		40
Walk'd with a staffe to heav'n, and traced fountains:	37	The Agonie		3
The which to measure it doth more behove:	37	The Agonie		5
To hunt his cruell food through ev'ry vein.	37	The Agonie		12
Each seventh note by right is due to thee.	38	The Sinner		4
To shew their face, since crosse to thy decrees:	38	The Sinner		7
Comes to about the many hundredth part.	38	The Sinner		11
Comes to about the many hundred part.	38	The Sinner	W	11
And though my hard heart scarce to thee can grone,	38	The Sinner		13
Number according to thy foes?	38	Good Fri.		6
Since bloud is fittest, Lord, to write	39	Good Fri.		21
To write thy sorrows in, as blood	39	Good Fri.	W	22
All come to lodge there, sinne may say,	39	Good Fri.		27
All come to lodge there, he may say,	39	Good Fri.	W	27
Thou hast an ancient claime to mee.	39	Good Fri.	W	32
Having been tenant long to a rich Lord,	40	Redemption		1
Not thriving, I resolved to be bold,	40	Redemption		2
And make a suit unto him, to afford	40	Redemption		3
Long since on earth, to take possession.	40	Redemption		8
Where our hard hearts have took up stones to brain thee,	41	Sepulchre		13
To hold thee.	41	Sepulchre		20
That, as his death calcined thee to dust,	41	Easter		5
The crosse taught all wood to resound his name,	41	Easter		9
Is best to celebrate this most high day.	41	Easter		12
I got me flowers to straw thy way;	42	Easter		19
To strow thy way and Victorie,	42	Easter	W	20
If they should offer to contest	42	Easter		25
Though many sunnes to shine endeavour?	42	Easter		28
Teach it to sing thy praise, this day,	42	Easter	W	29
More backward still, and to that water flie,	43	H. Bapt.1		4
You give us teares to wash them: lett those beams	44	H. Bapt.1	W	7
Or else give tears to drown them, as they grow.	44	H. Bapt.1		9
And spreads the plaister equall to the crime:	44	H. Bapt.1		11
Spredding the plaister equall to the crime:	44	H. Bapt.1	W	11
Since, Lord, to thee	44	H. Bapt.2		1
Let me be soft and supple to thy will,	44	H. Bapt.2		8
Small to my self, to others milde,	44	H. Bapt.2		9
That thou hast ought to do with me.	45	Nature		3
To captivate strong holds to thee.	45	Nature		6
My soul will turn to bubbles straight,	45	Nature		9

TO (cont'd)

	PAGE	TITLE		LINE
To hide my dust, then thee to hold.	45	Nature		18
Deliver us to laws; they send us bound	45	Sinne 1		3
To rules of reason, holy messengers,	45	Sinne 1		4
Fine nets and stratagems to catch us in,	45	Sinne 1		7
Fine nets and casualties to catch us in,	45	Sinne 1	W	7
When first thou didst entice to thee my heart,	46	Afflict.1		1
And made it fine to me:	46	Afflict.1		8
And made it rich to me:	46	Afflict.1	W	8
And tune my breath to grones.	47	Afflict.1		28
Thou didst betray me to a lingring book,	47	Afflict.1		39
Before I had the power to change my life.	47	Afflict.1		42
Yet, for I threatned oft the siege to raise,	47	Afflict.1		43
Turning my purge to food, thou throwest me	48	Afflict.1		51
To fruit or shade: at least some bird would trust	48	Afflict.1		59
Her houshold to me, and I should be just.	48	Afflict.1		60
Thus are we to delights: but we are all	48	Repentance		9
To sorrows old,	48	Repentance		10
Thy wormwood turn to health, windes to fair weather:	49	Repentance		21
To smoke & fume	49	Repentance	W	29
To a salt rhume	49	Repentance	WC	29
Fretting to death our other parts.	49	Repentance	W	30
And could see little, to regard his ease,	49	Faith		3
And bring by Faith all things to him?	49	Faith		4
That I can walk to heav'n well neare.	50	Faith		12
What though my bodie runne to dust?	51	Faith		41
Gods breath in man returning to his birth,	51	Prayer 1		2
To me dost now thy self convey;	52	H.Commun.		4
Yet can these not get over to my soul,	52	H.Commun.		13
While those to spirits refin'd, at doore attend	52	H.Commun.		23
Them both to be together.	52	H.Commun.		28
Before that sinne turn'd flesh to stone,	53	H.Commun.		29
And all our lump to leaven;	53	H.Commun.		30
Our innocent earth to heaven.	53	H.Commun.		32
To sinne, or sinne to smother;	53	H.Commun.		34
He might to heav'n from Paradise go,	53	H.Commun.		35
Thou hast restor'd us to this ease	53	H.Commun.		37
Which I can go to, when I please,	53	H.Commun.		39
And leave th' earth to their food.	53	H.Commun.		40
Attract the lesser to it: let those fires,	54	Love 2		2
All knees shall bow to thee; all wits shall rise,	54	Love 2		13
Sometimes to hell I fall.	55	Temper 1		8
O rack me not to such a vast extent;	55	Temper 1		9
Those distances belong to thee:	55	Temper 1		10
A crumme of dust from heav'n to hell?	55	Temper 1		14
To make the musick better.	55	Temper 1		24
Whether I Angell it, or fall to dust.	55	Temper 1	W	25
The grosser world stands to thy word and art;	56	Temper 2		5
Scatter, or binde them all to bend to thee:	56	Temper 2		13
Not to a true, but painted chair?	56	Jordan 1		5
Thou wouldst extend me to some good,	57	Employm. 1		2
A life as barren to thy praise,	57	Employm. 1		14
As is the dust, to which that life doth tend,	57	Employm. 1		15
Nor flowres to make that, nor the husbandrie	57	Employm. 1		19
To water these.	57	Employm. 1		20
To my poore reed.	57	Employm. 1		24
To cleare the breast, to mollifie all pain.	58	H.Script.1		4
To cleare the breast, to suple outward pain.	58	H.Script.1	W	4
Subject to ev'ry mounters bended knee.	58	H.Script.1		14
This book of starres lights to eternall blisse.	58	H.Script.2		14
Till I get wing to fly away with thee.	59	Whitsunday	W	4
The starres were coming down to know	59	Whitsunday		11
But wee are falne from Heaven to Earth,	59	Whitsunday	W	13
Without thy help, leads us his way to Hell.	59	Whitsunday	W	16
That cordiall water to our ground,	59	Whitsunday		18
So wee may cease to suck: to praise thee, never.	59	Whitsunday	W	24
Let suppling grace, to crosse his art,	60	Grace		19
O lett thy grace, to crosse his art,	60	Grace	W	19
Prevent my Sinn to thine owne praise,	61	Grace	W	20
Or if to me thou wilt not move,	61	Grace		22
To write a verse or two is all the praise,	61	Praise 1		1
I go to Church; help me to wings, and I	61	Praise 1		5
I goe to Church; make me an Angel, I	61	Praise 1	W	5
Or, if I steale up to the skie,	61	Praise 1	W	7
To a brave soul: Exalt the poore,	61	Praise 1		15
To a brave soul: for to a poore,	61	Praise 1	W	15
What were they all, compar'd to thine?	62	Afflict.2		8
But thou art ready there to catch	62	Mattens		2
As if that thou hadst nothing els to do?	62	Mattens		12
Amounts (and richly) to serve thee:	63	Mattens		14
Teach me thy love to know;	63	Mattens		17
Then by a sunne-beam I will climbe to thee.	63	Mattens		20
Sinne is flat opposite to th' Almighty, seeing	63	Sinne 2		4
Both to be busie, and to play.	63	Even-song		3
Which to himself he did denie:	63	Even-song		6
Of winde to thee whom I have crost,	64	Even-song		15
But balls of wilde-fire to my troubled minde.	64	Even-song		16
Saying to man, It doth suffice:	64	Even-song		19
And give new wheels to our disorder'd clocks.	64	Even-song		24
While that my soul repairs to her devotion,	64	Ch.-monum.		1
To which the blast of deaths incessant motion,	64	Ch.-monum.		4

TO (cont'd)

	PAGE	TITLE		LINE
My bodie to this school, that it may learn	65	Ch.-monum.		7
To spell his elements, and finde his birth	65	Ch.-monum.		8
To sever the good fellowship of dust,	65	Ch.-monum.		13
To kisse those heaps, which now they have in trust?	65	Ch.-monum.		16
Which knoweth not, what means, to Morrow.	65	Ch.-mus.	W	8
You know the way to heavens doore.	66	Ch.-mus.		12
His blouds sweet current much more loud to be.	66	Ch.-lock		12
Leads to the Quire above,	67	Ch.-floore		8
But while he thinks to spoil the room, he sweeps.	67	Ch.-floore		18
To be a window, through thy grace.	67	Windows		5
Making thy life to shine within	67	Windows		7
And sanctif'd me to do good;	68	Trin.Sun.		3
And I will strive to sinne no more.	68	Trin.Sun.		6
Peace mutt'ring thoughts, and do not grudge to keep	68	Content		1
To court each place or fortune that doth fall,	68	Content		7
To court each place or fortune that does fall,	68	Content	W	7
But when it would appeare to others eye,	68	Content		11
Which can let loose to a crown, and yet with pleasure	69	Content		15
Then to have hellish moths still gnaw and fret	69	Content		27
To execute their call,	70	Humilitie		6
Gave them about to all.	70	Humilitie		8
Which by consent was giv'n to Mansuetude.	70	Humilitie		10
Humilitie did reach to Fortitude.	70	Humilitie		12
That went to Temperance.	70	Humilitie		14
Of that brave gift, each one began to fume,	70	Humilitie		19
And challenge it, as proper to his place,	70	Humilitie		20
And if the Fox had liv'd to rule their side,	70	Humilitie		23
And then amerc'd them, double gifts to bring	71	Humilitie		31
Commodious to conquer heav'n and thee	72	Frailtie		23
To God, his neighbour, and himself most true:	72	Constancie		3
To use in any thing a trick or sleight;	72	Constancie		17
The sunne to others writeth laws,	72	Constancie		24
Who, when he is to treat	73	Constancie		26
To writhe his limbes, and share, not mend the ill.	73	Constancie		33
To writhe his limbes, and thare, not mend the ill.	73	Constancie	V	33
Who still is right, and prayes to be so still.	73	Constancie		35
To guide and govern it to my relief,	73	Afflict.3		3
So much breath to a sigh, what's then behinde?	73	Afflict.3		9
A gale to bring me sooner to my blisse.	73	Afflict.3		12
Constant unto it, making it to be	73	Afflict.3		14
A point of honour, now to grieve in me,	73	Afflict.3		15
Thou dying dayly, praise thee to thy losse.	73	Afflict.3		18
First with thy fire-work burn to dust	74	The Starre		9
Of him, who dy'd to part	74	The Starre		23
To flie home like a laden bee	74	The Starre		30
Teaches it not to stumble.	75	Sunday	W	7
Making the whole to stoup and bow,	75	Sunday		13
To endlesse death: but thou dost pull	75	Sunday		16
And turn us round to look on one,	75	Sunday		17
Make bracelets to adorn the wife	76	Sunday		31
That was requir'd to make us gay,	76	Sunday		55
Leaping with thee from sev'n to sev'n,	77	Sunday		61
Flie hand in hand to heav'n!	77	Sunday		63
To this great kingdome, which thou now hast got,	77	Avarice		6
To digge thee out of thy dark cave and grot:	77	Avarice		8
Thou art the man, and man but drosse to thee.	77	Avarice		12
To all Angels and Saints.	77	Ang.&Sts.		T
Do I forbear to crave your speciall aid:	78	Ang.&Sts.		7
My vows to thee most gladly, blessed Maid,	78	Ang.&Sts.		9
Chiefly to thee would I my soul unfold:	78	Ang.&Sts.		15
To make a posie for inferiour power.	78	Ang.&Sts.		25
To make a garland for inferiour power.	78	Ang.&Sts.	W	25
Since we are ever ready to disburse,	78	Ang.&Sts.		29
Since we are ever ready to discourse,	78	Ang.&Sts.	V	29
To cold complexions needing it.	78	Employm.2		5
Ordain'd the highest to be best;	79	Employm.2		13
Watch an advantage to appeare.	79	Employm.2		20
Each took his way; some would to pleasures go,	80	Deniall		8
Some to the warres and thunder	80	Deniall		9
As to benumme	80	Deniall		12
To crie to thee,	80	Deniall		17
My feeble spirit, unable to look right,	80	Deniall		23
Of pleasures brought me to him, readie there	81	Christmas		7
To be all passengers most sweet relief?	81	Christmas		8
To Man of all beasts be not thou a stranger:	81	Christmas		12
my soule to thee, that being drest	80	Christmas	W	13
And made them jewels to betroth	82	Ungratef.		10
This fully to us, till death blow	82	Ungratef.		16
This to us fully, till death blow	82	Ungratef.	W	16
But man is close, reserv'd, and dark to thee:	82	Ungratef.		25
Till it found out how to consume thy goods:	83	Sighs & Gr.		11
Hath still sow'd fig-leaves to exclude thy light:	83	Sighs & Gr.		16
And spinning phansies, she was heard to say,	84	The World		2
Began to make Balcones, Terraces,	84	The World		7
To raze the building to the very floore:	84	The World		17
One life is wrapt In flesh, and tends to earth.	84	Coloss.		5
Taught me to live here so, That still one eye	85	Coloss.		7
To gain at harvest an eternall Treasure.	85	Coloss.		10
He views their stations, walks from doore to doore,	85	Vanitie 1		3
To make a purchase there: he sees their dances,	85	Vanitie 1		5

TO (cont'd)

	PAGE	TITLE		LINE
There he imparts to them his minde,	85	Vanitie 1		18
Admitted to their bed-chamber, before	85	Vanitie 1		19
To ordinarie suitours at the doore.	85	Vanitie 1		21
To finde out death, but missest life at hand.	86	Vanitie 1		28
Give to thy Mother, what thou wouldst allow	86	Lent		5
To ev'ry Corporation.	86	Lent		6
I am a scandall to the Church, and not	86	Lent		11
The Church is so to me.	86	Lent		12
To use their temperance, seeking no evasion,	86	Lent		14
Yet to go part of that religious way,	87	Lent		32
Is better then to rest:	87	Lent		33
Is much more sure to meet with him, then one	87	Lent		38
Yet Lord instruct us to improve our fast	87	Lent		43
The dew shall weep thy fall to night;	87	Vertue		3
But though the whole world turn to coal,	88	Vertue		15
To all expressions both of hand and eye,	88	The Pearl		15
To sell my life unto my friends or foes:	88	The Pearl		19
Then he that curbs them, being but one to five:	89	The Pearl		29
I flie to thee, and fully understand	89	The Pearl		33
But thy silk twist let down from heav'n to me,	89	The Pearl		38
To climbe to thee.	89	The Pearl		40
The elements are let loose to fight,	90	Afflict.4		17
But he that means to dwell therein.	90	Man		3
Or can be, then is Man? to whose creation	90	Man		5
Full of proportions, one limbe to another,	91	Man		14
And all to all the world besides:	91	Man		15
The starres have us to bed;	91	Man		31
In their descent and being; to our minde	91	Man		35
Another to attend him.	92	Man		48
That as the world to us is kind and free	92	Man	W	53
So we may bee to Thee.	92	Man	W	54
To his friend,	92	Antiphon 2		5
And to his foe;	92	Antiphon 2		6
Lord, make me coy and tender to offend:	93	Unkindness		1
It is my honour and my love to free	93	Unkindness		7
When that my friend pretendeth to a place,	94	Unkindness		16
Onely to purchase my good-will:	94	Unkindness		24
But time did becken to the flowers, and they	94	Life		4
My hand was next to them, and then my heart:	94	Life		7
Making my minde to smell my fatall day;	94	Life		11
Were it not better to bestow	95	Submission		5
Who goes to bed and doth not pray,	96	Charms & K		7
Who goes to bed and does not pray,	96	Charms & K	W	7
Maketh two nights to ev'ry day.	96	Charms & K		8
Findes himself there, and seeks to rise.	96	Charms & K		12
But who drinks on, to hell may go.	97	Charms & K		18
And anchor thou art onely, to confirm	97	Afflict.5		4
Thine own delights thou didst to us impart:	97	Afflict.5		8
To make us thine: yet that we might not part,	97	Afflict.5		10
Furnish thy table to thy minde.	97	Afflict.5		18
To swaddle infants, whose young breath	98	Mortific.		3
When boyes go first to bed,	98	Mortific.		7
That musick summons to the knell,	98	Mortific.		17
Which shall convey him to the house of death.	98	Mortific.		30
Which shall convey him to the place of death.	98	Mortific.	W	30
As yet to spare:	99	Mortific.		34
Yet Lord, instruct us so to die,	99	Mortific.		35
He is to Sinai gone, as we heard tell:	99	Decay		9
To gain thy thirds and little part.	99	Decay		15
Then to serve thee in fear.	100	Miserie		12
The bargain made to serve thee: but thy love	100	Miserie		26
Who would, to be thy foes.	100	Miserie		30
To sing thy praises, make them lesse divine.	101	Miserie		40
Give him his dirt to wallow in all night:	101	Miserie		46
His head to shoot and ake.	101	Miserie		48
His head to shoot and shake.	101	Miserie	V	48
No, not to purchase the whole pack of starres:	101	Miserie		52
Made in the tree, where she was wont to sit,	101	Miserie		56
And all the bloud of God to run in vain.	102	Miserie		64
To raise him to the glimpse of blisse:	102	Miserie		75
My thoughts began to burnish, sprout, and swell,	102	Jordan 2		4
My thoughts began to burnish, spredd, and swell,	102	Jordan 2	W	4
Decking the sense, as if it were to sell.	102	Jordan 2		6
Praising the sense, as if it were to sell.	102	Jordan 2	W	6
Nothing could seem too rich to clothe the sunne,	102	Jordan 2		11
To shew that state dislikes not easinesse.	103	Prayer 2		4
And tacks the centre to the sphere!	103	Prayer 2		9
Wert fain to take our flesh and curse,	103	Prayer 2		15
That were I to leave all but one,	103	Prayer 2		21
To passe it self and all it hath to thee.	104	Obedience		8
To passe it self and all it has to thee.	104	Obedience	W	8
To which I do agree,	104	Obedience		9
Resigning up the rudder to thy skill.	104	Obedience		20
Lord, what is man to thee,	104	Obedience		21
Show'd a strange love to all our good:	104	Obedience		27
To one word onely I say, No:	105	Obedience		32
To both our goods, if he to it will stand.	105	Obedience		40
Musick to thee doth howl.	105	Conscience		4
By listning to thy chatting fears	105	Conscience		5
That I have physick to expell thee.	105	Conscience		12

TO (cont'd)

	PAGE	TITLE	LINE
No, not a tooth or nail to scratch,	106	Conscience	17
Some wood and nails to make a staffe or bill	106	Conscience	21
Is not so deare to thee as one good grone.	106	Sion	18
Thy long deferrings wound me to the quick,	107	Home	3
O show thy self to me,	107	Home	5
Or take me up to thee!	107	Home	6
O show thy self to me,	107	Home	11
Or take me up to thee!	107	Home	12
To see what help in th' earth or skie:	107	Home	14
O show thy self to me,	107	Home	17
Or take me up to thee!	107	Home	18
That hive of sweetnesse, to remove	107	Home	20
O show thy self to me,	107	Home	23
Or take me up to thee!	107	Home	24
O show thy self to me,	108	Home	29
Or take me up to thee!	108	Home	30
My God, what is this world to me?	108	Home	32
O show thy self to me,	108	Home	35
Or take me up to thee!	108	Home	36
O show thy self to me,	108	Home	41
Or take me up to thee!	108	Home	42
O show thy self to me,	108	Home	47
Or take me up to thee!	108	Home	48
They dresse themselves and come to thee.	108	Home	52
O show thy self to me,	108	Home	53
Or take me up to thee!	108	Home	54
O show thy self to me,	108	Home	59
Or take me up to thee!	108	Home	60
O show thy self to me,	109	Home	65
Or take me up to thee!	109	Home	66
The most of me to heav'n is fled:	109	Home	68
O show thy self to me,	109	Home	71
Or take me up to thee!	109	Home	72
O show thy self to me,	109	Home	77
Or take me up to thee!	109	Home	78
Allureth all in hope to be	110	Brit. Ch.	14
To double-moat thee with his grace,	110	Brit. Ch.	29
To meet together, where I lay,	110	The Quip	3
And all in sport to geere at me.	110	The Quip	4
And, to be short, make an oration.	111	The Quip	19
To answer these fine things shall come;	111	The Quip	22
To whom the starres shine not so fair, as eyes;	111	Vanitie 2	3
To purchase heaven for repenting,	111	Vanitie 2	9
Ev'n all to pieces: which I went to seek:	112	JESU	4
I sat me down to spell them, and perceived	112	JESU	8
That to my broken heart he was I ease you,	112	JESU	9
And to my whole is JESU.	112	JESU	10
Foolish soul who sinn'd to day?	113	Businesse	2
To assume thy flesh and bone;	113	Businesse	18
Tells to all he meets, his crosse:	114	Businesse	32
To thy wretch so full of stains;	114	Dialogue	7
Do amount to, onely he,	114	Dialogue	14
That transferr'd th' accounts to me.	114	Dialogue	16
Leading to this favour:	115	Dialogue	18
So the way to fit me for it,	115	Dialogue	19
Left all joyes to feel all smart -	115	Dialogue	31
Beautie alone to me:	115	Dulnesse	10
Look onely; for to love thee, who can be,	116	Dulnesse	27
To spend my judgement), said, It seem'd to me	116	Love-joy	5
To be the bodie and the letters both	116	Love-joy	6
O sacred Providence, who from end to end	116	Providence	1
To hold my quill? shall they not do thee right?	116	Providence	4
Onely to Man thou hast made known thy wayes,	117	Providence	6
Beasts fain would sing; birds dittie to their notes;	117	Providence	9
To thy renown: but all their hands and throats	117	Providence	11
Are brought to Man, while they are lame and mute.	117	Providence	12
He that to praise and laud thee doth refrain,	117	Providence	17
The tongue is yours to eat, but mine to praise.	117	Providence	22
Is mine to write, as it is yours to raise.	117	Providence	24
For me and all my fellows praise to thee:	117	Providence	26
Because the benefit accrues to me.	117	Providence	28
To be exact, transcendent, and divine;	117	Providence	30
Tempests are calm to thee; they know thy hand,	118	Providence	45
Some creatures have in winter what to eat;	118	Providence	55
As fair as ever, and as fit to use;	118	Providence	67
Who hath the vertue to expresse the rare	119	Providence	73
The sea, which seems to stop the traveller,	119	Providence	89
Are rul'd by him, and taught to serve his trade.	119	Providence	92
Men therefore seek to have, and care to keep.	119	Providence	99
All countreys have enough to serve their need:	120	Providence	105
To be commerce and trade from sunne to sunne.	120	Providence	108
But he to wear them. Nothing useth fire,	120	Providence	110
But Man alone, to show his heav'nly breed:	120	Providence	111
Your hony drops: presse not to smell them here:	120	Providence	118
How harsh are thorns to pears! and yet they make	120	Providence	121
Sometimes thou dost divide thy gifts to man,	120	Providence	125
To show thou art not bound, as if thy lot	121	Providence	137
To honour thee: and so I give thee praise	121	Providence	147
To honour thee; and so each hymne thy fame	121	Providence	151
I gave to Hope a watch of mine: but he	121	Hope	1

TO (cont'd)

	PAGE	TITLE	LINE
An anchor gave to me.	121	Hope	2
My hands do joyn to finish the inventions.	122	Sinnes rd.	12
My hands do joyn to finish the inventions:	122	Sinnes rd.	13
New thoughts of sinning: wherefore, to my shame,	122	Sinnes rd.	17
To whom thy sithe a hatchet was,	122	Time	9
An usher to convey our souls	123	Time	17
Thou that hast giv'n so much to me,	123	Gratefulnes	1
What it would come to at the worst	123	Gratefulnes	11
To save.	123	Gratefulnes	12
A hollow winde did seem to answer, No:	124	Peace	5
Then went I to a garden, and did spy	125	Peace	13
To plant and set.	125	Peace	30
Closets are halls to them; and hearts, high-wayes.	126	Confession	18
Doth give a hold and handle to affliction.	126	Confession	24
They shall be thick and cloudie to my breast.	126	Confession	30
Now he will fight it out, and to the warres;	127	Giddinesse	9
Brought back to the Red Sea, the sea of shame.	128	Bunch Gr.	7
To him I brought a dish of fruit one day,	129	Love unkn.	6
(I sigh to say)	129	Love unkn.	8
(I sigh to tell)	129	Love unkn.	24
To fetch a sacrifice out of my fold,	129	Love unkn.	30
To warm his love, which I did fear grew cold.	129	Love unkn.	32
Who was to take it from me, slipt his hand,	130	Love unkn.	34
Began to spread and to expatiate there:	130	Love unkn.	39
To supple hardnesses. But at the length	130	Love unkn.	45
Unto my house, where to repair the strength	130	Love unkn.	47
Which I had lost, I hasted to my bed.	130	Love unkn.	48
But when I thought to sleep out all these faults	130	Love unkn.	49
(I sigh to speak)	130	Love unkn.	50
For I had giv'n the key to none, but one:	130	Love unkn.	55
For ought I heare, your Master shows to you	130	Love unkn.	62
All did but strive to mend, what you had marr'd.	130	Love unkn.	67
Wherefore be cheer'd, and praise him to the full	130	Love unkn.	68
To this life things of sense	131	Mans medly	7
He may attain to, after he is dead.	131	Mans medly	24
To turn his double pains to double praise.	132	Mans medly	36
Dares to assault thee, and besiege thy doore.	132	The Storm	12
There it stands knocking, to thy musicks wrong,	132	The Storm	13
To thee both fruit and order OW.	132	Paradise	3
Be to me rather sharp and TART,	133	Paradise	8
To such indifferents chained be,	134	The Method	18
I had a motion to forbear,	134	The Method	23
Which needs not man, be ty'd to those	134	The Method	26
To take and taste what he doth there designe,	135	Divinitie	23
To heav'n alone both go, and leade.	135	Divinitie	28
I sinne not to my grief alone,	136	Ephes.	17
But to my Gods too; he doth grone.	136	Ephes.	18
Oh take thy lute, and tune it to a strain,	136	Ephes.	19
Lord, I adjudge my self to tears and grief,	136	Ephes.	25
Yet if I wail not still, since still to wail	136	Ephes.	31
But not to make a constant stay.	137	Familie	24
Modest and moderate joyes to those, that have	137	The Size	2
Title to more hereafter when they part,	137	The Size	3
If thou hast wherewithall to spice a draught,	137	The Size	9
To th' Isle of spices, is't not fair?	137	The Size	12
To be in both worlds full	138	The Size	13
Lay out thy joy, yet hope to save it?	138	The Size	17
Doth tice us on to hopes of more,	138	The Size	29
Do seem to equally divide,	138	The Size	35
If comforts fell according to desert,	138	The Size	39
In hope of great things. Call to minde thy dream,	138	The Size	44
But not of speech in starres, began to muse:	139	Artillerie	10
But turning to my God, whose ministers	139	Artillerie	11
To wash away my stubborn thought:	139	Artillerie	15
And work up to thee; yet thou dost refuse.	139	Artillerie	20
Much more oblig'd to do thy will,	139	Artillerie	22
Then thou to grant mine: but because	139	Artillerie	23
To enter combate with us, and contest	139	Artillerie	26
Thought to let out, the bleeding did you good,	140	Ch.-rents	14
Your health and beautie both began to break.	140	Ch.-rents	20
Where shall I get me eyes enough to weep,	140	Ch.-rents	25
Did show and shape thy looks to me,	141	Justice 2	4
The dishes of thy ballance seem'd to gape,	141	Justice 2	7
Lifting to heaven from this well of tears.	141	Justice 2	18
And so I came to phansies medow strow'd	142	Pilgrimage	7
And so I came to Fancies medow strow'd	142	Pilgrimage V	7
So to cares cops I came, and there got through	142	Pilgrimage	11
That led me to the wilde of passion, which	142	Pilgrimage	13
Close to my side.	142	Pilgrimage	18
I threatned to observe the strict decree	143	Holdfast	1
I threatned to observe the sweet decree	143	Holdfast V	1
Yet I might trust in God to be my light.	143	Holdfast	4
Nay, ev'n to trust in him, was also his:	143	Holdfast	6
But to have nought is ours, not to confesse	143	Holdfast	9
My power and wisdome. Put me not to shame,	143	Complaining	3
To weep or crie?	143	Complaining	14
Thy life is Gods, thy time to come is gone,	144	Discharge	11
In times to come; for it will grow.	145	Discharge	30
Wilt thou forestall it, and now grieve to morrow,	145	Discharge	48
To enroll thee:	146	Praise 2	26

TO (cont'd)

	PAGE	TITLE		LINE
To extoll thee.	146	Praise 2		28
Yet one pure heart is nothing to bestow:	147	Offering		5
In Christ two natures met to be thy cure.	147	Offering		6
Yet one, if good, may title to a number;	147	Offering		9
Untill thou finde and use it to thy good:	147	Offering		23
To this poore oblation;	148	Offering		39
To be thy praise,	148	Offering		41
To thee my cries,	148	Longing		3
To thee my grones,	148	Longing		4
To thee my sighs, my tears ascend:	148	Longing		5
To them a part:	148	Longing		16
More dead to me!	149	Longing		34
To succour me,	149	Longing		40
To thee help appertains.	149	Longing		43
Hast thou left all things to their course,	149	Longing		44
And fall to nothing: thou dost reigne,	150	Longing		56
Not to relieve? how can it be,	150	Longing		62
Thus hard to me?	150	Longing		64
To bear.	150	Longing		66
To day.	150	Longing		78
Ev'n when the boat seems most to reel.	151	The Bag		4
Resolv'd to light; and so one day	151	The Bag		11
He did endure to cancell sinne:	151	The Bag		22
Here he gave up his life to pay our score.	151	The Bag		24
And straight he turn'd, and to his brethren cry'd,	151	The Bag		30
If ye have any thing to send or write,	152	The Bag		31
Not to his hurt. Sighs will convey	152	The Bag		41
Any thing to me. Heark despair, away.	152	The Bag		42
To let me bloud, and not restore	153	The Collar		8
Is the yeare onely lost to me?	153	The Collar		13
Have I no bayes to crown it?	153	The Collar		14
Which pettie thoughts have made, and made to thee	153	The Collar		23
Good cable, to enforce and draw,	153	The Collar		24
To suit and serve his need,	153	The Collar		31
And give me up to night?	154	Glimpse		3
But one half houre of comfort to my heart?	154	Glimpse	V	5
Feeds not, but addes to the desire of meat.	154	Glimpse		12
A neighbour spring to cool his inward heat;	154	Glimpse		14
But constant to his part	154	Glimpse		18
If I have more to spinne,	155	Glimpse		26
When wit contrives to meet with thee,	155	Assurance		5
And, that I had great cause to fear it.	155	Assurance		12
And what to this? what more	155	Assurance		13
To cold despairs, and gnawing pensivenesse?	155	Assurance		16
But I will to my Father,	155	Assurance		19
Not half a letter to oppose	155	Assurance		23
Thou art not onely to perform thy part,	156	Assurance		27
To hide thy shame: for thou hast cast a bone	156	Assurance		39
Yet to be thine, doth me restore;	157	Clasping		4
For thou didst suffer to restore	157	Clasping		14
Not thee, but me, and to be mine:	157	Clasping		15
All things concurre to give it a perfection.	158	Praise 3		9
To twentie then, or more.	158	Praise 3		12
Did weep to heav'n, they found a bottle there	158	Praise 3		27
Readie to take them in; yet of a size	158	Praise 3		29
Of some fair church to show the sore	158	Praise 3		34
That to thy chests there might be coming in	159	Praise 3		41
That to thy chest there might be coming in	159	Praise 3	V	41
To fetch the bodie; both being due to grief.	159	Jos.coat		9
But he hath spoil'd the race; and giv'n to anguish	159	Jos.coat		10
To linger in me, and together languish.	159	Jos.coat		12
I live to shew his power, who once did bring	159	Jos.coat		13
My joyes to weep, and now my griefs to sing.	159	Jos.coat		14
May tosse him to my breast.	160	The Pulley		20
That with th' one hand thou liftest to the sky,	160	Priesthood		2
And with the other throwest down to hell	160	Priesthood		3
To wear thy habit, the severe attire	160	Priesthood		9
To deal in holy Writ.	160	Priesthood		12
Of wretched earth. Where once I scorn'd to stand,	161	Priesthood		15
When God vouchsafeth to become our fare,	161	Priesthood		27
Who bring my God to me!	161	Priesthood		30
To hold the Ark, although it seem to shake	161	Priesthood		32
For some mean stuffe wherecn to show his skill:	161	Priesthood		38
And centre both to me denie	162	The Search		7
As if to meet thee they did know,	162	The Search		11
I sent a sigh to seek thee out,	162	The Search		17
To it all strength, all subtilties	163	The Search		39
As that to it	163	The Search		42
To come between?	163	The Search		56
Suck up a river to supply mine eyes,	164	Grief		5
To bear them out, and with my state agree.	164	Grief		8
Give up your feet and running to mine eyes,	164	Grief		15
To make me sigh, and seek, and faint, and die,	164	The Crosse		2
To set thy honour up, as our designe.	164	The Crosse		6
So much desir'd, is giv'n, to take away	164	The Crosse		9
My power to serve thee; to unbend	164	The Crosse		10
Besides, things sort not to my will,	165	The Crosse		19
Taking me up to throw me down:	165	The Crosse		22
So that, ev'n when my hopes seem to be sped,	165	The Crosse		23
I am to grief alive, to them as dead.	165	The Crosse		24

TO (cont'd)

	PAGE	TITLE	LINE
To have my aim, and yet to be	165	The Crosse	25
To make my hopes my torture, and the fee	165	The Crosse	27
Is in the midst of delicates to need,	165	The Crosse	29
And ev'n in Paradise to be a weed.	165	The Crosse	30
To which, besides their own demean,	165	The Flower	3
To see their mother-root, when they have blown;	166	The Flower	11
Dead to the world, keep house unknown.	166	The Flower	14
Killing and quickning, bringing down to hell	166	The Flower	16
And up to heaven in an houre;	166	The Flower	17
What frost to that? what pole is not the zone,	166	The Flower	32
To make us see we are but flowers that glide:	167	The Flower	44
Thou hast a garden for us, where to bide.	167	The Flower	46
To parents issue and the sunnes bright starre!	168	The Sonne	6
To parents issue and the sonnes bright starre!	168	The Sonne V	6
From the first man in th' East, to fresh and new	168	The Sonne	9
To make his verse, or write a hymne in kinde.	168	a true Hymn	15
As when th' heart sayes (sighing to be approved)	168	a true Hymn	19
Flyes of estates and sunne-shine. But to all,	169	The Answer	5
And setling to a cloud, doth live and die	169	The Answer	11
In that dark state of tears: to all, that so	169	The Answer	12
To serve thy sinnes, and furnish thee with store	170	Water-crs.	7
Who gives to man, as he sees fit Salvation. / Damnation.	170	Water-crs.	10
To look upon me, who before did lie	171	The Glance	3
My soul hath felt, ev'n able to destroy,	172	The Glance	10
He leads me to the tender grasse,	172	23 Psalme	5
Then to the streams that gently passe:	172	23 Psalme	7
To guide, thy staffe to bear.	173	23 Psalme	16
To make him clean, who could not be defil'd?	173	Marie Magd	8
To bear her filth; and that her sinnes did dash	173	Marie Magd	14
As she had brought wherewith to stain,	173	Marie Magd	16
So to bring in wherewith to wash:	173	Marie Magd	17
To leade them unto life and rest.	174	Aaron	4
That to the old man I may rest,	174	Aaron	19
My Master, shall I speak? O that to thee	175	The Odour	11
To some degree of spicinesse to thee!	175	The Odour	15
Return to thee.	175	The Odour	28
To set off vertues; griefs to set off sinning:	176	The Foil	6
Must dulnesse turn me to a clod?	176	Forerunners	5
Good men ye be, to leave me my best room,	176	Forerunners	7
Brought you to Church well drest and clad:	176	Forerunners	17
Hath some fond lover tic'd thee to thy bane?	176	Forerunners	21
But borrow'd thence to light us thither.	177	Forerunners	29
Presse me not to take more pleasure	177	The Rose	1
And to use a larger measure	177	The Rose	3
Such delights I meant to say;	177	The Rose	10
There are no such things to me,	177	The Rose	11
Be contracted to a rose;	178	The Rose	22
Worldly joyes to be a scourge:	178	The Rose	26
To a full consent.	178	Discipline	8
I affect to own,	178	Discipline	10
To the throne of grace.	179	Discipline	16
Naming you not to your good:	180	Invitation	9
Bringing all your sinnes to sight:	180	Invitation	15
And exalts you to the skie:	180	Invitation	27
Still invite, still call to thee:	180	Invitation	33
Passeth tongue to taste or tell.	181	Banquet	6
To subdue the smell of sinne;	181	Banquet	15
Such a sweetnesse to impart:	181	Banquet	21
God, to show how farre his love	181	Banquet	28
Having rais'd me to look up,	182	Banquet	37
To the skie:	182	Banquet	44
But leave me to my load:	183	A Parodie	10
Lord teach mee to referr	184	The Elixer W	1
In all things thee to see,	184	The Elixer	2
All things I doe to thee	184	The Elixer W	2
To do it as for thee:	184	The Elixer	4
To runne into an action;	184	The Elixer	6
But still to make thee prepossest,	184	The Elixer	7
Will not to Heaven grow.	184	The Elixer W	16
That turneth all to gold:	185	The Elixer	22
Lett in the Light to all their actions	185	The Elixer W	23
I give to thee, who knowest all my wayes,	185	A Wreath	3
Straight as a line, and ever tends to thee,	185	A Wreath	6
To thee, who art more farre above deceit,	185	A Wreath	7
Flesh being turn'd to dust, and bones to sticks.	186	Death	8
Summon all the dust to rise,	186	Dooms-day	3
Read that lesson to the grave.	187	Dooms-day	18
Some to windes their bodie lend,	187	Dooms-day	21
Some to windes their bodies lend,	187	Dooms-day W	21
To a plague and publick wo.	187	Dooms-day	24
Parcel'd out to all the world.	187	Dooms-day	28
Able a heart of iron to appall,	187	Judgement	3
What others mean to do, I know not well;	187	Judgement	6
That some will turn thee to some leaves therein	187	Judgement	8
That to decline,	188	Judgement	12
Light to the minde: what shall the will enjoy?	188	Heaven	15
Drew nearer to me, sweetly questioning,	188	Love 3	5
A guest, I answer'd, worthy to be here:	189	Love 3	7
Known also to each minute of an houre:	190	Ch.-Milit.	4
Early didst thou arise to plant this vine,	190	Ch.-Milit.	11

TO (cont'd)

	PAGE	TITLE		LINE
Thou didst rise early for to plant this vine,	190	Ch.-Milit.	W	11
Which might the more indeare it to be thine.	190	Ch.-Milit.		12
Prepar'd and fitted to receive thy love.	190	Ch.-Milit.		16
To bring the other Ark from Canaan.	190	Ch.-Milit.		20
To bring the other Ark to Canaan.	190	Ch.-Milit.	W	21
By nailing Christ to fasten it again.	190	Ch.-Milit.		24
But to the Gentiles he bore crosse and all,	190	Ch.-Milit.		25
Till both removed to the western clime.	191	Ch.-Milit.		36
To Egypt first she came, where they did prove	191	Ch.-Milit.		37
Such power hath mightie Baptisme to produce	191	Ch.-Milit.		45
How deare to me, O God, thy counsels are!	191	Ch.-Milit.		47
And wheel'd about again to spell Christ-Crosse.	191	Ch.-Milit.		54
Religion went to Rome, subduing those,	191	Ch.-Milit.		61
From Greece to Rome she went, subduing those	191	Ch.-Milit.	W	61
But seems to yeeld Christ hath the greater wounds,	191	Ch.-Milit.		64
But seems to yeeld Christ had the greater wounds,	191	Ch.-Milit.	W	64
Wounds willingly endur'd to work his blisse,	192	Ch.-Milit.		65
The Shepherds hook grew to a scepter here,	192	Ch.-Milit.		71
Giving new names and numbers to the yeare.	192	Ch.-Milit.		72
But th' Empire dwelt in Greece, to comfort them	192	Ch.-Milit.		73
At length to Germanie, still westward bending,	192	Ch.-Milit.		81
Then showres Religion, and makes all to bear.	192	Ch.-Milit.		88
Giving the Church a crown to keep her state,	192	Ch.-Milit.		91
How deare to me, O God, thy counsels are!	192	Ch.-Milit.		99
At first he got to Egypt, and did sow	193	Ch.-Milit.		107
And such poore game. Thence he to Greece doth passe,	193	Ch.-Milit.		123
And such small game. Thence he to Greece doth passe,	193	Ch.-Milit.	W	123
To make good that which ev'ry day he winnes.	193	Ch.-Milit.		126
To this great lotterie, and all would pull.	193	Ch.-Milit.		134
To credit him, and to discredit those	193	Ch.-Milit.		137
To credit him, and so discredit those	193	Ch.-Milit.	W	137
From Greece he went to Rome: and as before	194	Ch.-Milit.		139
Put him in trust to rule the Romane sphere.	194	Ch.-Milit.		142
Which soon was blown to such a mightie flame,	194	Ch.-Milit.		145
Setting affliction to encounter pleasure;	194	Ch.-Milit.		148
Setting afflictions to encounter pleasure;	194	Ch.-Milit.	W	148
To such Mahometan stupidities,	194	Ch.-Milit.		153
How deare to me, O God, thy counsels are!	194	Ch.-Milit.		155
Sinne being not able to extirpate quite	194	Ch.-Milit.		161
To be a Church-man too, and wear a Mitre:	194	Ch.-Milit.		163
To which he lent a corner of his eye.	195	Ch.-Milit.		170
To make a jest of Christs three offices:	195	Ch.-Milit.		174
He took fine vizards to conceal his crimes:	195	Ch.-Milit.		186
Whereby he grew apace and scorn'd to use	195	Ch.-Milit.		191
All poste to Rome: Princes submit their necks	195	Ch.-Milit.		195
It did not fit his gravitie to stirre,	195	Ch.-Milit.		197
How deare to me, O God, thy counsels are!	196	Ch.-Milit.		209
And to defray his journey from the east.	196	Ch.-Milit.		214
Old and new Babylon are to hell and night,	196	Ch.-Milit.		215
As is the moon and sunne to heav'n and light.	196	Ch.-Milit.		216
The latter Church is to the first a debter.	196	Ch.-Milit.		224
To these diminishings, as is between	196	Ch.-Milit.		233
The spacious world and Jurie to be seen.	196	Ch.-Milit.		234
Readie to passe to the American strand.	196	Ch.-Milit.		236
Then shall Religion to America flee:	197	Ch.-Milit.		247
To pay our debts, and leave our ancient place	197	Ch.-Milit.		256
To pay our debts, and leave her ancient place	197	Ch.-Milit.	W	256
To go to them, while that which now their nation	197	Ch.-Milit.		257
But lends to us, shall be our desolation.	197	Ch.-Milit.		258
Lendeth to us, shall be our desolation.	197	Ch.-Milit.	W	258
To time and place, where judgement shall appeare.	198	Ch.-Milit.		277
How deare to me, O God, thy counsels are!	198	Ch.-Milit.		278
With the one make warre to cease;	199	L'Envoy		2
With the one make warrs to cease;	199	L'Envoy	W	2
Thee to love, in thee to sleep.	199	L'Envoy		4
Make his sighs to use it all,	199	L'Envoy		14
To discharge what is behinde.	199	L'Envoy		16
Bee there, to thy truth, & my gaine	200	H. Commun.	W	11
And if in comming to thy foes	200	H. Commun.	W	13
Thou dost come first to them, that showes	200	H. Commun.	W	14
To' abolish Sinn, not Wheat.	200	H. Commun.	W	21
But that which made my soule to dye	201	H. Commun.	W	28
And cannot turn to soule.	201	H. Commun.	W	39
When I contrive & plott to prove	201	love	W	4
I thought it brave to praise thee then,	202	love	W	15
Never to thee aspire,	202	Trin.Sun.	W	9
From Heaven, through Earth, to Hell.	202	Trin.Sun.	W	14
To them that fall,	203	Trin.Sun.	W	16
And hope, that may teach it to shine,	203	Even-song	W	19
Which warme these lines, & serve them up to thee	204	Persever.	W	2
For who can tell, though thou hast dyde to winn	205	Persever.	W	9
Heighten a spirit to sound out thy praise	206	Walton 1		7
Sure, Lord, there is enough in thee to dry	206	Walton 2		1
Poets to turn it to another use.	206	Walton 2		5
Roses and Lillies speak thee; and to make	206	Walton 2		6
To praise, and on thee, Lord, some Ink bestow.	206	Walton 2		11
To my Successor.	207	Walton 3		T
If thou chance for to find	207	Walton 3		1
A new House to thy mind,	207	Walton 3		2
Be good to the Poor,	207	Walton 3		4

TO (cont'd)	PAGE	TITLE		LINE
To my Successor.	207	Walton 4		T
If thou dost find an house built to thy mind	207	Walton 4		1
Nor canst thou be content, unlesse thou to	439	Walton 5		5
Love neere his death desir'd to end	439	Walton 5	V	11
Of kinde Expressions to his friend,	439	Walton 5		12
With kinde Expressions to his friend,	439	Walton 5	V	12
(Where nothing should be broke) to adde a Seal.	439	Walton 5		18
Ther's no monument to a sonne,	208	J. Danvers	D	15
To the Right Hon. the L. Chancellor (Bacon).	209	L. Bacon	D	T
My Lord. A diamond to mee you sent,	209	L. Bacon	D	1
And I to you a Blackamore present.	209	L. Bacon	D	2
And thinke it contrary to Natures Lawes	209	Paradox	D	3
To want one ownce of sleepe,	209	Paradox	D	4
Your state, to ours, is contrary;	210	Paradox	D	7
Wheare health hath nought to doe;	210	Paradox	D	14
Cease then to judge calamityes	210	Paradox	D	25
You allwayes feare to feele those smarts	210	Paradox	D	31
Playntes to bad fortunes dew:	211	Paradox	D	38
Come to our bed	211	Paradox	D	41
To comforte us, or to bee comforted.	211	Paradox	D	42
To the Queene of Bohemia.	211	Bohemia	D	T
Turne watrish Holland to a chrystalline sphere.	211	Bohemia	D	12
A foile to sett of worth, & make it rare.	211	Bohemia	D	16
Sorrowes & griefs, to fight with them a bout	211	Bohemia	D	20
To second thee against there cunning hate.	211	Bohemia	D	22
O what a poore thing 'tis to bee a Queene	212	Bohemia	D	23
Lyes round about us to helpe out the story,	212	Bohemia	D	26
A slow behaviour to the style of king,	212	Bohemia	D	28
To serve it forth, & being stript of all	212	Bohemia	D	31
Is selfe-sufficient to bee the thrall	212	Bohemia	D	32
Addes to the union, as lights doe gather	212	Bohemia	D	36
Children for kingdomes to thee; they shall live	212	Bohemia	D	42
To conquere new ones, & shall share the frame	212	Bohemia	D	43
At once to Hell, without a baiting while	212	Bohemia	D	49
To deale with brimstone, that untamed stench	212	Bohemia	D	53
Laden with comforts thence, where now to morne	212	Bohemia	D	56
Is thy chief government, to manage woe,	212	Bohemia	D	57
To curbe some Rebell teares, which faine would flow,	213	Bohemia	D	58
Will pour full joyes to thee, but dregs to those,	213	Bohemia	D	65
Which now that moist land to thee beares.	213	L' Envoy	D	6
Strive each to play their Part.	213	Convert	D	5
Where treach'rous Syrens us'd to sing,	214	Convert	D	7
Frail Beauty's Charms to Heav'n did raise,	214	Convert	D	13
(Till now averse to all that's Good)	214	Convert	D	17
and makes that law alone to be	214	Psalm I	D	6
able to stand the Judges doom:	215	Psalm I	D	18
For God himself vouchsafes to know	215	Psalm I	D	21
and 'gainst his Christ, presume to say,	215	Psalm II	D	6
Then shall He speak to them in wrath,	215	Psalm II	D	11
He said to me, Thou art my Son,	216	Psalm II	D	17
the righteous man to love.	217	Psalm IV	D	12
O learn to stand in awe of him,	217	Psalm IV	D	15
offer to God on high	217	Psalm IV	D	18
do thou to us afford.	217	Psalm IV	D	24
Lord to my words encline thine ear,	218	Psalm V	D	1
My King, my God, vouchsafe to hear	218	Psalm V	D	3
my cry to thee, I pray.	218	Psalm V	D	4
Direct my prayers to thy Throne,	218	Psalm V	D	7
will I to thee draw near:	218	Psalm V	D	18
And to my dym and sinful eyes	219	Psalm V	D	23
all night I make my Couch to swim;	220	Psalm VI	D	14
the Lord vouchsafes to weigh my tears;	220	Psalm VI	D	22
And put them all to utter shame,	220	Psalm VI	D	27
and to confusion suddainly.	220	Psalm VI	D	28
his mallice to controul.	221	Psalm VII	D	8
yea, let him to the Clay	221	Psalm VII	D	18
resort to give Thee praise;	221	Psalm VII	D	26
According to my righteousness,	221	Psalm VII	D	31
To his own head his wickedness	222	Psalm VII	D	57
While Prince to Spaine, and King to Cambridge goes,	438	Lat.Trans.		1
TOE				
Religion stands on tip-toe in our land,	196	Ch.-Milit.		235
TOGEATHER				
But thou art Light & darknes both togeather:	203	Even-song	W	13
TOGETHER				
All worldly thoughts are but theeves met together	23	Ch.-Porch		424
That all together may accord in thee,	36	Thanksgvng		41
As we did rise, we die together.	49	Repentance		24
And tune together in a well-set song,	49	Repentance		33
Them both to be together.	52	H.Commun.		28
Which siding with invention, they together	54	Love 1		6
We both together sweetly live and love,	65	Ch.-mus.		7
Thredded together on times string,	76	Sunday		30
Hath put together a solemnitie,	99	Mortific.		32
I and deare prayer would together dwell,	103	Prayer 2		23
To meet together, where I lay,	110	The Quip		3
To linger in me, and together languish.	159	Jos.coat		12
Where they together	166	The Flower		12
My sinnes and I joining together:	166	The Flower		28
Beautie and beauteous words should go together.	177	Forerunners		30

TOGETHER (cont'd)

	PAGE	TITLE		LINE
Thus both the Church and Sunne together ran	192	Ch.-Milit.		97
So both together are one Antichrist,	196	Ch.-Milit.		206
Light one another, and together runne.	198	Ch.-Milit.		271
For sins make all equall, whom they finde together;	227	Priest 3		28
but taking his Parish together the next Sunday, or holy-day,	253	Priest 19		31
making together a summe either to be sent, or, which were more	253	Priest 19		36
all together choosing some fitt day to carry it themselves,	253	Priest 19		37
and goes with him to the other, and all dine or sup together.	284	Priest 35		21
blesse this portion here assembled together, with thy unworthy	289	Priest		25
considering what an orderly life I had led for many yeares together,	295	Cornaro		8
This place together with many other, as namely Consid. 71. upon Our	307	Valdesso		16
Fooles bite one another, but wise-men agree together.	336	Proverbs		452
working, still together, that I take a comfort therein;	375	Letters		19
TOIL				
Yet in this wretched world we toil,	176	The Foil		7
TOKENS				
Presented tokens of submission.	70	Humilitie		4
TOLD				
Take starres for money; starres not to be told	13	Ch.-Porch		171
'Tis but to tell the tale is told.	35	Thanksgvng		8
They told me there, that he was lately gone	40	Redemption		6
If life be told	48	Repentance		11
Who opens it, hath it twice told.	96	Charms & K		6
But I was told by one, it could not be;	143	Holdfast		3
Cannot for lesse be told.	185	The Elixer		24
overcome them, being told to another, whether in private conference,	278	Priest 33		16
on our Saviour, for which he told, that it should never be forgotten,	282	Priest 34		25
the Physicians told me that yet there was one help for me,	292	Cornaro		3
This they had told me before:	292	Cornaro		26
All truths are not to be told.	324	Proverbs		89
What your glasse telles you, will not be told by Councell.	329	Proverbs		255
Good newes may bee told at any time, but ill in the morning.	350	Proverbs		877
denounced to him, told the King & so he is committed to prison.	368	Letters		37
but he told her Grace, that he would by no meanes do so,	379	Letters		6
TOLL				
Talking payes no toll.	338	Proverbs		485
TOLLE				
The Bell doth tolle	204	The Knell	W	1
TOMBE				
A steadie aiming at a tombe.	48	Repentance		6
TOMBES				
Tombes for the dead, not temples fit for thee:	107	Sion		20
TONGUE				
Are chaw'd by others pens and tongue;	69	Content		30
Are chaw'd by others pen and tongue;	69	Content	W	30
O that thou shouldst give dust a tongue	80	Deniall		16
The tongue is yours to eat, but mine to praise.	117	Providence		22
Hath got a tongue!	150	Longing		76
Could poyson, if it had a tongue, expresse?	155	Assurance		14
What fine varietie each tongue affords:	167	The Sonne		2
Let follie speak in her own native tongue.	177	Forerunners		27
Passeth tongue to taste or tell.	181	Banquet		6
Then what was in their tongue, did overcome;	196	Ch.-Milit.		202
valerian, mercury, adders tongue, yerrow, melilot, and Saint Johns	262	Priest 23		6
Better the feet slip then the tongue.	322	Proverbs		53
Better thy foote slip then thy tongue.	322	Proverbs	V	53
The tongue walkes where the teeth speede not.	324	Proverbs		102
A long tongue is a signe of a short hand.	329	Proverbs		251
The tongue talkes at the heads cost.	331	Proverbs		312
Hee that strikes with his tongue, must ward with his head.	331	Proverbs		313
Hee that strikes with his tongue, must ward with his hand.	331	Proverbs	V	313
The thought hath good leggs, and the quill a good tongue.	342	Proverbs		612
The effect speakes, the tongue needes not.	345	Proverbs		709
Faire language grates not the tongue.	347	Proverbs		799
The tongue is not steele, yet it cuts.	349	Proverbs		838
An Oxe is taken by the horns, and a Man by the tongue.	353	Proverbs		967
Take an oxe by his hornes & a man by his tongue.	353	Proverbs	V	967
TONGUES				
their flattering tongues do fain.	219	Psalm V	D	28
One paire of eares drawes dry a hundred tongues.	339	Proverbs		526
Foolish tongues talke by the dozen.	343	Proverbs		645
TOO				
A kinde of thing that's for it self too deere.	13	Ch.-Porch		178
The curious unthrift makes his cloth too wide,	13	Ch.-Porch		179
Perhaps his wives too, and whom she hath bore:	14	Ch.-Porch		195
Laugh not too much: the wittie man laughs least:	15	Ch.-Porch		229
But if thou want it, buy it not too deere.	16	Ch.-Porch		244
Open for thee; or both may come too late.	21	Ch.-Porch		384
Open for thee; or they may come too late.	21	Ch.-Porch	W	384
And growth of it: if with thy watch, that too	24	Ch.-Porch		454
A hart can never come too late.	42	Easter	W	28
Yet lest perchance I should too happie be	48	Afflict.1		49
Beleeves so too, and lets me go.	50	Faith		16
My Creditour beleev'd so too.	50	Faith	W	16
The heav'ns are not too high,	53	Antiphon 1		3
The earth is not too low,	53	Antiphon 1		5
The world's too little for thy tent,	55	Temper 1		11
A grave too big for me.	55	Temper 1		12
Thy praise too much? thou art heav'ns Lidger here,	58	H.Script.1		11
Let grace work too, and on my soul	60	Grace		15

	PAGE	TITLE		LINE
TOO (cont'd)				
Which knoweth not, what means, too Morrow.	65	Ch.-mus.	W	9
For though sinnes plead too, yet like stones they make	66	Ch.-lock		11
His words and works and fashion too	72	Constancie		19
But we are still too young or old;	79	Employm.2		26
My soul's a shepherd too; a flock it feeds	81	Christmas		17
Nothing could seem too rich to clothe the sunne,	102	Jordan 2		11
Neither too mean, nor yet too gay,	109	Brit. Ch.		8
May come too late!	111	Vanitie 2		8
Twentie for one too sharp do finde it.	122	Time		6
They are too subtill for the subt'llest hearts;	126	Confession		11
Then have we too our guardian fires and clouds;	128	Bunch Gr.		15
The Caldron suppled, what was grown too hard:	130	Love unkn.		65
The Thorns did quicken, what was grown too dull:	130	Love unkn.		66
But to my Gods too; he doth grone.	136	Ephes.		18
But I have also starres and shooters too,	139	Artillerie		17
I grow too wide,	145	Discharge		34
Ev'n eternitie is too short	146	Praise 2		27
My weary weeping eyes too drie for me,	164	Grief		6
Verses, ye are too fine a thing, too wise	164	Grief		13
To be a Church-man too, and wear a Mitre:	194	Ch.-Milit.		163
Thou art too hard for me in Love:	201	love	W	1
The bloody man, the false one too,	218	Psalm V	D	15
that they dive not too deep into worldly affairs, plunging themselves	247	Priest 14		24
or Diet, or too open a Buttery, or reading vain books, or swearing,	251	Priest 17		19
of the Communion only (for then it is too late) but the Sunday,	258	Priest 22		27
Children and youths are usually deferred too long, under pretence	258	Priest 22		37
and I either provide too little for them, or that which is	265	Priest 26		20
baned meat, sometimes too salt, and so not competent nourishment,	265	Priest 26		22
or studying dainties too much, they cannot wel dispatch) nor of their	266	Priest 26		15
wisheth all to incline rather to too much, then to too little;	267	Priest 26		13
as I too wel by experience found.	292	Cornaro		7
other hurtfull things also, as too much heat and cold, wearinesse,	293	Cornaro		30
that the hurt of too much meat is greater, then the commoditie	296	Cornaro		3
But some, too much given to Appetite, object, That a long life is no	300	Cornaro		27
sheweth, and I also, when I was a young man, too well found.	303	Cornaro		16
But I like none of it, for it slights the Scripture too much:	306	Valdesso		17
But when he enlargeth he goes too farre.	315	Valdesso		35
they are equally exempt with God, that is dangerous and too farre.	316	Valdesso		33
The Authour doth still discover too slight a regard of the Scripture,	317	Valdesso		22
He lives unsafely, that lookes too neere on things.	322	Proverbs		43
Hee that makes a thing too fine, breakes it.	336	Proverbs		440
One enemy is too much.	339	Proverbs		523
To whirle the eyes too much shewes a Kites braine.	345	Proverbs		717
To be too busie gets contempt.	346	Proverbs		738
Praise none too much, for all are fickle.	347	Proverbs		774
He warmes too neere that burnes.	348	Proverbs		815
Hee payes too deare for honey that licks it from thorns.	350	Proverbs	V	880
Too much taking heede is losse.	350	Proverbs		889
The death of a young wolfe doth never come too soon.	360	Proverbs	D	1131
Follow not truth too near the heels, lest it dash out thy teeth.	360	Proverbs	D	1138
perhaps they will say, you are sickly, you must not study too hard;	364	Letters		26
since this place being civil may divert me too much from Divinity,	370	Letters		20
Is it not too much for me?	371	Letters		11
but, wou'd you divide and choose too?	373	Letters		2
TOOK				
To me, who took eyes that I might you finde:	26	Sacrifice		3
Where our hard hearts have took up stones to brain thee,	41	Sepulchre		13
Whereas my birth and spirit rather took	47	Afflict.1		37
I took thy sweetned pill, till I came neare;	47	Afflict.1		47
I took thy sweetned pill, till I came where	47	Afflict.1	W	47
Faith puts me there with him, who sweetly took	50	Faith		23
Which just now took up all my heart?	56	Temper 2		2
Thy crosse took up in one,	62	Afflict.2		14
You took me thence, and in your house of pleasure	65	Ch.-mus.		3
Christ hath took in this piece of ground,	76	Sunday		40
Each took his way; some would to pleasures go,	80	Deniall		8
I took up in the next inne I could finde.	80	Christmas		4
But Love took Grace & Glory by the hand,	84	Sighs & Gr.	W	19
But Love and Grace took Glorie by the hand,	84	The World		19
I took, without more thinking, in good part	94	Life		8
Who took the debt upon him. Truly, Friend,	130	Love unkn.		61
God took bloud, and needs would be	182	Banquet		34
Love took my hand, and smiling did reply,	189	Love 3		11
Though Greece took horse as soon as Egypt did,	191	Ch.-Milit.		57
Or strength in th' other, took possession.	192	Ch.-Milit.	W	78
Here Sinne took heart, and for a garden-bed	193	Ch.-Milit.		127
From Egypt he took pettie deities,	195	Ch.-Milit.		177
He took fine vizards to conceal his crimes:	195	Ch.-Milit.		186
I took a time when thou didst sleep	202	love	W	13
He took flesh, he wept, he died;	288	Priest		28
a pain of the side took me, which held me two and twentie houres.	296	Cornaro		18
thing to advize you now, & before you took Sir Johns affairs.	380	Woodnoth		8
TOOK'ST				
When I got health, thou took'st away my life,	47	Afflict.1		31
Thou took'st that pledg from mee:	201	H. Commun.	W	45
TOOKE				
I ever tooke that for a weaknesse in the great Patriark:	316	Valdesso		1
TOOL				
The meanest tool, that he may chance to use.	20	Ch.-Porch		354
No workmans tool hath touch'd the same.	26	The Altar		4

	PAGE	TITLE	LINE
TOWN			
The way that takes the town;	47	Afflict.1	38
Travell'd, and saw no town;	128	Bunch Gr.	9
TOWNE			
And God will show thee how to take the towne,	7	Ch.-Porch W	22
or hath generall Propositions to the whole Towne or Hamlet,	276	Priest 32	5
Hee that is in a towne in May loseth his spring.	353	Proverbs	988
TOWRE			
Engine against th' Almightie, sinners towre,	51	Prayer 1	5
TOY			
If that thy fame with ev'ry toy be pos'd,	15	Ch.-Porch	223
A toy shunn'd cleanly passeth with the best.	15	Ch.-Porch	228
A toy shunn'd cleanly is fames interest.	15	Ch.-Porch W	228
TOYES			
Thousands of toyes dwell there, yet out of doore	40	Sepulchre	7
TRACE			
So Sinne shall trace and dog her instantly:	197	Ch.-Milit.	260
TRACED			
Walk'd with a staffe to heav'n, and traced fountains:	37	The Agonie	3
TRACKER			
and tracker of Gods wayes, sets up as many encouragements	244	Priest 11	2
TRADE			
And trade in courtesies and wit,	78	Employm.2	3
Are rul'd by him, and taught to serve his trade.	119	Providence	92
To be commerce and trade from sunne to sunne.	120	Providence	108
And like a master in my trade,	126	Confession	4
That earth is fitted by the fire and trade	161	Priesthood	16
Vertue and a Trade are the best portion for Children.	324	Proverbs	107
He that hath no good trade, it is to his losse.	340	Proverbs	560
Hee that learnes a trade hath a purchase made.	353	Proverbs	978
A trade is better then service.	354	Proverbs	1005
for the nature thereof (as your trade) the other only for the success	380	Woodnoth	22
lying upon you either for the execution or benefitt of a trade,	380	Woodnoth	26
For any scruple of leaving your trade, throw it away.	381	Woodnoth	22
but a Trade having two things, the one imployment, the other profitt,	381	Woodnoth	30
TRADES			
think fit to do so) he takes care not to put them into vain trades,	240	Priest 10	1
because those trades, for the most part, serve but the vices	240	Priest 10	3
by questions well ordered he found Philosophy in silly Trades-men.	256	Priest 21	23
What Trades-man is there who will set up without his Tools?	364	Letters	14
the success of things is) & not into the hands of men or mens trades:	380	Woodnoth	25
TRADES-MAN			
What Trades-man is there who will set up without his Tools?	364	Letters	14
TRADES-MEN			
by questions well ordered he found Philosophy in silly Trades-men.	256	Priest 21	23
TRADITION			
then from those which by a Common tradition, and vulgar knowledge are	266	Priest 26	26
TRADITIONS			
Traditions are accounts without our host.	194	Ch.-Milit. W	160
TRAFFICK			
(As sweet things traffick when they meet)	175	The Odour	27
that there may be a traffick in knowledg between the servants of God,	229	Priest 4	26
TRAGEDIE			
as a Tragedie with old Age, by reason of the sad events which it	302	Cornaro	31
of old was praised, that at the age of 73 yeares he writ a Tragedie;	302	Cornaro	34
TRAIL			
And where the week-dayes trail on ground,	76	Sunday	58
TRAIN (see also trayning)			
Spoil'd all the train: then saying, Here it is	71	Humilitie	27
With his train-bands and mates agree	110	The Quip	2
TRAIN-BANDS			
With his train-bands and mates agree	110	The Quip	2
TRAINE			
But that both thou, and all thy traine	200	H. Commun. W	10
TRAMPLE			
Much lesse those joyes which trample on his head.	102	Jordan 2	12
TRAMPLED			
(Whose precepts she had trampled on before)	173	Marie Magd	2
TRANQUILITIE			
and silence here are reverenced, here is tranquilitie, repose,	442	Oration	36
TRANSCENDENT			
This glorious and transcendent place,	67	Windows	4
To be exact, transcendent, and divine;	117	Providence	30
Divinities transcendent skie:	134	Divinitie	6
Stick fast therein, but thy transcendent soule	211	Bohemia D	7
TRANSFERR'D			
Have with our stamp and seal transferr'd our right:	77	Avarice	11
That transferr'd th' accounts to me.	114	Dialogue	16
TRANSFIGURATION			
preferres the Word before the sight of the Transfiguration of Christ.	318	Valdesso	23
TRANSFORM'D			
And Ergo was transform'd into Amen.	191	Ch.-Milit.	56
TRANSFUS'D			
Transfus'd a sheepishnesse into thy storie:	10	Ch.-Porch	94
TRANSGRESSED			
sacrificed lest his Children should have transgressed in their mirth:	281	Priest 34	2
TRANSGRESSION			
Cut me not off for my most foul transgression:	49	Repentance	15
In hight of their transgression,	219	Psalm V D	31
TRANSGRESSIONS			
For they can lodge transgressions by the score:	40	Sepulchre	6

	PAGE	TITLE		LINE
TRANSLATED				
by Lud. Cornarus, Translated into English by Mr. George Herbert.	291	Cornaro		T
TRANSLATOR				
by MR. GEORGE HERBERT to his friend the Translator of this Book.	304	Valdesso		T
TRANSMIGRATION				
Into a voluntarie transmigration.	195	Ch.-Milit.		194
Unto a voluntarie transmigration.	195	Ch.-Milit.	W	194
TRANSMIGRATIONS				
And make that name good by their transmigrations;	195	Ch.-Milit.		184
TRANSPARENT				
Tears sullying thy transparent rooms, ...	124	Gratefulnes		14
TRANSPLANT				
and to transplant it in time to his own home, with the same care	276	Priest 32		30
there, transplant them hither, as divers have done lately, . .	278	Priest 32		9
TRANSPLANTED				
In us the same transplanted foolerie.	193	Ch.-Milit.		120
TRANSPORTING				
by transporting French commodities to your own country. . .	366	Letters		12
TRANSPORTS				
Hee that hath charge of soules transports them not in bundles.	353	Proverbs		986
TRANSPOSER				
Transposer of the world, wonders resort, ...	51	Prayer 1	W	7
TRANSPOSING				
The six-daies world transposing in an houre, ...	51	Prayer 1		7
The six-daies world-transposing in an houre, ...	51	Prayer 1	V	7
TRAVEL				
Or let him travel into Germany, and France, and observing . .	278	Priest 32		8
TRAVELL				
Or fight, or travell, or denie	45	Nature		2
But if I travell in your companie, ...	66	Ch.-mus.		11
who by hard usage increase their travell, the Countrey Parson is very	227	Priest 3		15
At other times he is to travell over the King's Dominions, . .	277	Priest 32		6
TRAVELL'D				
Travell'd, and saw no town;	128	Bunch Gr.		9
I travell'd on, seeing the hill, where lay	141	Pilgrimage		1
And travell'd westward also: journeying on	193	Ch.-Milit.		104
And travell'd Westward allso, coasting on, ...	193	Ch.-Milit.	W	104
TRAVELLED				
the places, and rivers travelled unto, and frequented by others,	282	Priest 34		3
Now though they have hitherto travelled upon your charge, . .	366	Letters		31
TRAVELLER				
Slacknesse breeds worms; but the sure traveller, ...	20	Ch.-Porch		339
The sea, which seems to stop the traveller, ...	119	Providence		89
Much spends the traveller, more then the abider.	330	Proverbs		276
TRAVELLERS				
When he was come, as travellers are wont, ...	151	The Bag		19
TRAVELLETH				
That travelleth by-wayes:	87	Lent		39
That travelleth crosswayes	87	Lent	W	39
Behold, the wicked travelleth	222	Psalm VII	D	49
TRAVELLOUR				
which may be unto him as the sunne to a Travellour in his journey,	312	Valdesso		18
TRAVELLS				
I am much pleased also in my travells, with the beauty of situation.	302	Cornaro		6
TRAYNING				
a trayning up of her children and mayds in the fear of God, . .	239	Priest 10		12
TREACH'ROUS				
Where treach'rous Syrens us'd to sing, ...	214	Convert	D	7
TREACHEROUS				
All beasts of prey are strong or treacherous.	355	Proverbs		1023
TREAD (see also tredd)				
In all, I think my foot doth ever tread	71	Frailtie		7
My foot did tread, ...	71	Frailtie		18
The very dust, where thou dost tread and go, ...	115	Dulnesse		15
Griev'd for a worm, which when I tread, ...	135	Ephes.		5
Where Pagans tread. O Mother deare and kinde, ...	140	Ch.-rents		24
With pensive humblenesse would live and tread:	173	Marie Magd		6
Tread down my life, and in the dust	221	Psalm VII	D	19
All feete tread not in one shoe.	338	Proverbs		497
TREADS				
He treads down that which doth befriend him, ...	92	Man		45
is ever very well supplyed by some able man who treads in his steps,	232	Priest 7		26
TREASURE				
Thy rate and price, and mark thee for a treasure;	6	Ch.-Porch		2
The price of thee, and mark thee for a treasure;	6	Ch.-Porch	W	2
Then all thou addest may be call'd his treasure.	11	Ch.-Porch		114
Rather then shew his cards.) Steal from his treasure	18	Ch.-Porch		298
Therefore my soul melts, and my hearts deare treasure	27	Sacrifice		21
Thou hast but two rare cabinets full of treasure, ...	82	Ungratef.		7
Thou hadst but two rich cabinets of treasure, ...	82	Ungratef.	W	7
To gain at harvest an eternall Treasure.	85	Coloss.		10
As our delight, or as our treasure:	91	Man		28
Indeed at first Man was a treasure, ...	102	Miserie		67
I here exclude the wrangler from thy treasure.	104	Obedience		15
I here shutt out the wrangler from thy treasure.	104	Obedience	W	15
Finger not my treasure.	114	Dialogue		12
One while he counts of heav'n, as of his treasure:	127	Giddinesse		5
Perceiving that alone of all his treasure	160	The Pulley		9
Disparking oracles, and all their treasure, ...	194	Ch.-Milit.		147
By free dispensings of the Churches treasure.	195	Ch.-Milit.		180
By dispensations of the Churches treasure.	195	Ch.-Milit.	W	180

	PAGE	TITLE		LINE
TROUBLES				
If troubles cvertake thee, do not wail:	170	Water-crs.		4
then that after many troubles and griefs I should quickly come	291	Cornaro		25
and troubles of the minde, all these did hurt me little,	294	Cornaro		13
and well-contented, free from all troubles and troublesome thoughts;	301	Cornaro		1
To change my bed, troubles me not;	302	Cornaro		12
of the heavens, so are earthly Troubles compar'd to heavenly Joyes;	372	Letters		30
TROUBLESCME				
so that all things were troublesome to me:	296	Cornaro		16
and well-contented, free from all troubles and troublesome thoughts;	301	Cornaro		1
TROUBLEST				
Yet, though thou troublest me, I must be meek;	48	Afflict.1		61
TROUBLING				
Troubling mine eyes.	71	Frailtie	W	16
TROUT				
You must loose a flie to catch a trout.	348	Proverbs		827
TRUE				
Omit the oathes, which true wit cannot need:	9	Ch.-Porch		62
Lie not; but let thy heart be true to God,	9	Ch.-Porch		73
Dare to be true. Nothing can need a ly:	9	Ch.-Porch		77
Then live, and use it: els, it is nct true	12	Ch.-Porch		154
Who am the way of truth, the true relief;	27	Sacrifice		38
Who am the way & Truth, the true relief;	27	Sacrifice	W	38
Most true to those, who are my greatest grief:	27	Sacrifice		39
Oh King of grief! (a title strange, yet true,	35	Thanksgvng		1
King of all Grief (a title strange, yet true,	35	Thanksgvng	W	1
Of the true vine?	38	Good Fri.		12
I pass the shades, & fixe upon the true	43	H. Bapt.1	W	4
And kindle in our hearts such true desires,	54	Love 2		4
Not to a true, but painted chair?	56	Jordan 1		5
And true descent; that when thou shalt grow fat,	65	Ch.-monum.		18
To God, his neighbour, and himself most true:	72	Constancie		3
True Christians should be glad of an occasion	86	Lent		13
It's true, we cannot reach Christs forti'th day;	87	Lent		31
Which on the world a true-love-knot may tie,	88	The Pearl		16
And crusht the building: and it's partly true,	127	Giddinesse		15
Indeed 'tis true. I did and do commit	129	Love unkn.		19
Indeed 'tis true. I found a callous matter	130	Love unkn.		38
Indeed it's true. I found a callous matter	130	Love unkn.	V	38
True earnest sorrows, rooted miseries,	167	Dotage		7
Where are no sorrows, but delights more true,	167	Dotage		17
We turn upon him in a sense most true:	168	The Sonne		12
A true Hymne.	168	a true Hymn		T
Of sov'raigne tears, springing frcm true remorse:	170	Water-crs.		8
This worlds delights before true Christian joy,	170	Self-cond.		8
False gain before the true,	171	Self-cond.		15
Thus are true Aarons drest.	174	Aaron		5
True beautie dwells on high: ours is a flame	177	Forerunners		28
That Sinne sayes true: but while I grieve,	184	A Parodie		29
I have resolved to set down the Form and Character of a true Pastour,	224	Priest		7
as this is the true reason of his inward feare, so he is content	231	Priest 6		11
The two former obligations are much more essentiall to a true fast,	242	Priest 10		8
yet considering that the Law allows these in case they be true,	245	Priest 12		25
or, So farr indeed what you say is true, and well said;	252	Priest 18		12
This is to be on Gods side, and be true to his party.	252	Priest 18		15
are every way fitting to do his Countrey true and laudable service,	252	Priest 19		28
and true in all his wayes, as being the servant of him,	253	Priest 19		1
for he was the true householder, who bringeth out of his treasure	261	Priest 23		14
It is true indeed, they are long a knowing it, being partiall	264	Priest 26		12
Wherefore the Parson being true to his businesse, hath exactly sifted	264	Priest 26		31
in eating, that he can eat more, then afterwards he finds true:)	267	Priest 26		4
kindle them rather to redeem the Dignity either from true faults,	276	Priest 32		24
Neither is this true onely in the military state of a Christian life,	279	Priest 33		2
whether his repentance were true, or at least in that degree it ought	279	Priest 33		11
temper then others) consisteth in a true detestation of the soul,	279	Priest 33		23
gives true strength to the bodie, all superfluities passing away	293	Cornaro		27
and long dayes, and the true and onely medicine of many diseases.	297	Cornaro		13
the Authors sake, whom I conceive to have been a true servant of God;	304	Valdesso		7
It is true, there are some things which I like not in him,	304	Valdesso		16
while applying himselfe to the [unquestioned] duties of true Piety,	312	Valdesso		20
This doctrine however true in substance, yet needeth [requireth]	314	Valdesso		1
is in some sort true because they are spiritually discerned,	315	Valdesso		31
This is true onley of the Popish Cases of Conscience, which depend	319	Valdesso	V	28
Love is the true price of love.	339	Proverbs		540
True praise rootes and spreedes.	342	Proverbs		638
Astrologie is true, but the Astrologers cannot finde it.	342	Proverbs		641
is still true to you, and hath nothing else to answer your infinite	363	Letters		18
it is true (God knows) I am weak, yet not so, but that every day,	364	Letters		26
have over Youth and Health, who are now so near those true Comforts.	372	Letters		33
It is true there is a third sister, whom to receive were the greatest	375	Letters		23
of kindred bredd up, (which generally is very true,) yet I care not;	376	Letters		5
TRUE-LOVE-KNOT				
Which on the world a true-love-knot may tie,	88	The Pearl		16
TRUELY				
parted with rills of running water, which truely is very delightfull.	301	Cornaro		16
TRULY				
I had it straight, and did as truly eat,	50	Faith		7
And truly brasse and stones are heavie things,	107	Sion		19
Who took the debt upon him. Truly, Friend,	130	Love unkn.		61
If truly said, they may take part	168	a true Hymn		7
as being truly touched and amazed with the Majesty of God,	231	Priest 6		5

TRULY (cont'd)	PAGE	TITLE		LINE
truly affecting, and cordially expressing all that we say; . . .	233	Priest 7		30
and with truly godly zeal, without hatred to the person, . .	254	Priest 20		27
have yet no imployment, if he truly, and seriously prepare for it,	275	Priest 32		13
so that he as truly repents, who performes the other acts . .	279	Priest 33		29
So that I can truly say, That they who in these two things that enter	294	Cornaro		3
So that I can truly say, That I have both given God a Temple,	301	Cornaro		31
To the truly Noble Sir J. D.	366	Letters		T
and then you shall justly value Your most truly, most heartily,	372	Letters		6
Yet truly it was none of my meaning, when I wrote, to putt one of our	375	Letters		4
Yet, truly if you take her not, I am thinking to do it, . .	375	Letters		34
Truly it grieves me to think of the child, how destitute she is,	376	Letters		11
TRUMP				
Should crie so loud, untill the trump were drown'd, ...	152	The Jews		10
TRUMPET				
Oh that some Angel might a trumpet sound;	152	The Jews		8
But thy trumpet: then it kneels, ...	186	Dooms-day		10
TRUNK				
His minde with rest, before his trunk with riches:	11	Ch.-Porch		110
TRUNKS				
His minde with rest, before his trunks with riches:	11	Ch.-Porch	W	110
TRUSS'D				
Man is a shop of rules, a well truss'd pack, ...	12	Ch.-Porch		141
TRUST				
To fruit or shade: at least some bird would trust	48	Afflict.1		59
With an exact and most particular trust, ...	51	Faith		43
Thy power and love, my love and trust	55	Temper 1		27
Drives all at last. Therefore I gladly trust	64	Ch.-monum.		6
To kisse those heaps, which now they have in trust?	65	Ch.-monum.		16
What upon trust	71	Frailtie		2
Yet I might trust in God to be my light.	143	Holdfast		4
Then will I trust, said I, in him alone.	143	Holdfast		5
Nay, ev'n to trust in him, was also his:	143	Holdfast		6
Therefore we can go die as sleep, and trust	186	Death		21
Put him in trust to rule the Romane sphere.	194	Ch.-Milit.		142
But let all those that trust in thee	219	Psalm V	D	35
I put my trust in Thee:	220	Psalm VII	D	2
him in the pulpit, whom they cannot trust in his Conversation.	228	Priest 3		8
And in so doing they doe not sever their trust from God. . . .	307	Valdesso		2
But by trusting in the word of God they trust in God.	307	Valdesso		3
The dog that licks ashes, trust not with meale.	334	Proverbs		389
Trust not one nights ice.	336	Proverbs		453
we ought not to trust another.	338	Proverbs		490
Trust no friend with that you need fear him if he were your enemy.	361	Proverbs	D	1169
TRUSTETH				
God provides for him that trusteth.	345	Proverbs		728
TRUSTING				
Therefore trusting on experience, I forsook all these kinde of meats	293	Cornaro		15
But by trusting in the word of God they trust in God.	307	Valdesso		2
TRUSTS				
Hee that trusts in the Kings word for any thing trusts in the King.	307	Valdesso		3
Hee that trusts in the Kings word for any thing trusts in the King.	307	Valdesso		4
He that sowes trusts in God.	332	Proverbs		342
He that trusts in a lie, shall perish in truth.	340	Proverbs		569
He that trusts in a lie, shall perish by the truth.	340	Proverbs	V	569
He that trusts much Obliges much, says the Spaniard.	357	Proverbs	D	1045
TRUSTY				
Entice the trusty sunne, if that you can, ...	12	Ch.-Porch		136
Entice the trusty sunne, if that thou can, ...	12	Ch.-Porch	W	136
TRUTH				
Redeem truth from his jawes: if souldier, ...	10	Ch.-Porch		87
Redeem truth from his chawes: if souldier, ...	10	Ch.-Porch	W	87
Errour a fault, and truth discourtesie.	18	Ch.-Porch		308
Truth dwels not in the clouds: the bow that's there	19	Ch.-Porch		317
Truth dwels not in the clouds: that Bow doth hit	19	Ch.-Porch	W	317
If truth be with thy friend, be with them both:	19	Ch.-Porch		323
Who am the way of truth, the true relief;	27	Sacrifice		38
Who am the way & Truth, the true relief;	27	Sacrifice	W	38
I, who am Truth, turn into truth their deeds:	32	Sacrifice		179
I, who am Truth, turn into truth their scorns:	32	Sacrifice	W	179
Become a verse? Is there in truth no beautie?	56	Jordan 1		2
At least those beams of truth, which onely save, ...	135	Divinitie		15
Then can thy truth and I: but while rocks stand, ...	156	Assurance		32
Now love and truth will end in man.	156	Assurance		42
Come, my Way, my Truth, my Life:	156	The Call		1
Such a Truth, as ends all strife:	156	The Call		3
Truth Lord, but I have marr'd them: let my shame	189	Love 3		13
While Truth sat by, counting his victories:	195	Ch.-Milit.		190
Bee there, to thy truth, & my gaine	200	H. Commun.	W	11
their mouths no truth retain.	219	Psalm V	D	26
For all Truth being consonant to it self, and all being penn'd by one.	229	Priest 4		5
his servants, to whom he hath revealed his Truth, as well as to him;	229	Priest 4		23
ability of a Parson to lead his people exactly in the wayes of Truth,	230	Priest 5		21
mouth of two or three witnesses the truth may be more established.	232	Priest 7		29
that three things make a compleate servant, Truth, and Diligence,	240	Priest 10		18
with comparisons, and making much even of a word of truth from him.	256	Priest 21		15
the other an humble, and ingenuous search of truth;	263	Priest 24		17
the faults of eating, and the truth of them needs no proofe:	266	Priest 26		13
and the spirit, and to worship him in truth, and spirit. . .	279	Priest 33		17
and turning unto God in truth of heart, and newnesse of life:	279	Priest 33		24
who have born witness to the truth, (there being no reason, . .	282	Priest 34		20

	PAGE	TITLE		LINE
TWENTIE (cont'd)				
To twentie then, or more.	158	Praise 3		12
a pain of the side took me, which held me two and twentie houres.	296	Cornaro		18
To John twentie shillings, all these are over and above their wages,	382	G.H.'s Will		25
TWENTY				
The worst of law is, that one suit breedes twenty.	329	Proverbs		253
Then I bequeath twenty pounds unto the poore of this parish to be	382	G.H.'s Will		16
to Margeret twenty shillings: To William Twenty Nobles, . .	382	G.H.'s Will		24
To William Twenty Nobles, To John twentie shillings, all these are	382	G.H.'s Will		25
Executor to whome I bequeath twenty pound whereof fifteene pound shal	382	G.H.'s Will		29
To Mrs Anne Danvers twenty shillings, To Mrs Mary Danvers twenty	383	G.H.'s Will		10
To Mrs Mary Danvers twenty shillings, To Mrs Michel twenty shillings,	383	G.H.'s Will		11
To Mrs Michel twenty shillings, To Mrs Elizabeth Danvers Mr Henry	383	G.H.'s Will		11
To Mrs Elizabeth Danvers Mr Henry Danvers wife twenty shillings,	383	G.H.'s Will		13
to the poore of the parish twenty pound To my Lord of Cherbury tenn	383	G.H.'s Will		13
shillings To William Scuce twenty shillings To Mrs Judith Spencer	383	G.H.'s Will		17
TWICE				
Twice on the day his due is understood;	22	Ch.-Porch		391
Twice on that day his due is understood;	22	Ch.-Porch	W	391
Who opens it, hath it twice told.	96	Charms & K		6
In all my other hymnes, but in this twice.	121	Providence		148
They who rely on them must reckon twice	194	Ch.-Milit.	W	160
Then having read divine Service twice fully, and preached in	236	Priest 8		7
that all Christians should pray twice a day, every day of the week,	272	Priest 31		22
Hee that dines and leaves, layes the cloth twice.	333	Proverbs		347
A penny spar'd is twice got.	338	Proverbs		506
On a good bargaine thinke twice.	339	Proverbs		529
If things were to be done twice, all would be wise. . . .	344	Proverbs		700
If all things might be done twice, all would be wise. . . .	343	Proverbs	V	700
that twice suffers shipwrack.	345	Proverbs		706
who twice suffers shipwrack.	345	Proverbs	V	706
To review ones store is to mow twice.	354	Proverbs		1007
Better is one Accipe, then twice to say, Dabo tibi. . . .	358	Proverbs	D	1079
Out of Lent also, twice a Week, on Fridayes and Saturdayes, . .	365	Letters		5
TWIGS				
Whose twigs are pleasures, & they whip thee bare, ...	6	Ch.-Porch	W	9
'TWILL				
Upon the matter 'twill thy conquest prove:	202	love	W	20
TWINE				
His beams shall cheer my breast, and both so twine, ...	81	Christmas		33
TWIST				
Consort both heart and lute, and twist a song	42	Easter		13
But with my yeares sorrow did twist and grow, ...	47	Afflict.1		23
But with my yeares sorrows did twist and grow, ...	47	Afflict.1	W	23
But thy silk twist let down from heav'n to me, ...	89	The Pearl		38
And make a twist checker'd with night and day!	118	Providence		58
As new and old Rome did one Empire twist;	196	Ch.-Milit.		205
TWITCH				
Think not thy fame at ev'ry twitch will break:	15	Ch.-Porch		219
TWO				
A fault, which needs it most, grows two thereby.	9	Ch.-Porch		78
Thou hast two sconses, if thy stomack call;	11	Ch.-Porch		128
Who carves, is kind to two; who talks, to all.	11	Ch.-Porch		130
Plainly and home, is coward of the two.	15	Ch.-Porch		218
To work for two, who brought himself to thrall.	17	Ch.-Porch		286
To work for two, that brought himself to thrall.	17	Ch.-Porch	W	286
The greater world o' th' two; for that came in	33	Sacrifice		206
The greater world o' th' two; for that comes in	33	Sacrifice	W	206
Betwixt two theeves I spend my utmost breath, ...	34	Sacrifice		229
But there are two vast, spacious things, ...	37	The Agonie		4
Mans age is two houres work, or three:	48	Repentance		7
The world is theirs; they two play out the game, ...	54	Love 1		10
Catching the sense at two removes?	56	Jordan 1		10
To write a verse or two is all the praise, ...	61	Praise 1		1
Thou hast but two rare cabinets full of treasure, ...	82	Ungratef.		7
Thou hadst but two rich cabinets of treasure, ...	82	Ungratef.	W	7
Defrauding thee, who gavest two for one.	82	Ungratef.		30
Who hath made of two folds one.	93	Antiphon 2		23
Which hath made of two folds one.	93	Antiphon 2	W	23
Maketh two nights to ev'ry day.	96	Charms & K		8
And two deaths had been thy fee.	113	Businesse		22
Two lives worse then ten deaths be.	113	Businesse		28
I hold for two lives, and both lives in me.	129	Love unkn.		5
He hath two winters, other things but one:	131	Mans medly		27
And he of all things fears two deaths alone.	131	Mans medly		30
With these two poore ones lick up all the dew, ...	140	Ch.-rents		29
Like two great pits;	141	Justice 2		8
In Christ two natures met to be thy cure.	147	Offering		6
That which had but two legs before, ...	158	Praise 3		10
Making two one.	163	The Search		60
What are two shallow foords, two little spouts	164	Grief		9
Embroider'd lyes, nothing between two dishes;	167	Dotage		5
That these two words might creep & grow	175	The Odour		14
Before the other two were in their prime.	191	Ch.-Milit.	W	60
Yet with two faces, as their Janus was;	196	Ch.-Milit.		207
Of his two thrones he made the latter best, ...	196	Ch.-Milit.		213
Or if that thou two stations makest	200	H. Commun.	W	16
Two reacheth thee	202	Trin.Sun.	W	3
Lett two of those alone	203	Trin.Sun.	W	15
Is of the two the far more desperate.	210	Paradox	D	30
Doth for two clods of earth ten spheres controule, ...	211	Bohemia	D	8

TWO (cont'd)	PAGE	TITLE		LINE
And because the two highest points of Life, wherein a Christian is	227	Priest 3		3
that so in the mouth of two or three witnesses the truth may be more	232	Priest 7		29
There are but two devouring elements, fire, and water, he hath both	234	Priest 7		33
The Parsons Methcd in handling of a text consists of two parts;	235	Priest 7		1
his state of Life, which are principally these two, Spirituall pride,	238	Priest 9		2
and good breeding, are his two great stocks for his children;	240	Priest 10		10
for there being two things, which as they are, are unuseful to man,	241	Priest 10		26
The two former obligations are much more essentiall to a true fast,	242	Priest 10		7
and fasting dayes were fully performed by keeping of the two former,	242	Priest 10		9
but only the two former, which also in diseases of exinanition	242	Priest 10		30
are two great obstructed vessels, and there is nothing that is food,	243	Priest 10		1
since of the two commands, we are more injoyned to be charitable,	245	Priest 12		28
and as following the Apostles two great and admirable Rules in things	246	Priest 13		26
For these twc rules comprize and include the double object of our	246	Priest 13		29
But then he admonisheth them of two things;	247	Priest 14		23
diligently the state thereof to Godward, and that in two points:	251	Priest 17		18
but there being two things in Sermons, the one Informing,	257	Priest 21		21
the Parson hath diligently examined these two with himselfe,	262	Priest 24		32
whether, there being two precepts, one of obeying Authority,	263	Priest 24		9
having ever besides two great helps and powerfull perswaders on his	263	Priest 24		15
which are two great lights able to dazle the eyes of the mis-led,	263	Priest 24		18
discovers two sorts of vices, and two sorts of vicious persons.	264	Priest 26		4
discovers two sorts of vices, and two sorts of vicious persons.	264	Priest 26		5
concerning these two vices, not because they are all that are of this	265	Priest 26		1
he meets continually with two most sad spectacles, Sin,	267	Priest 27		31
But here there are two Cautions to be added.	273	Priest 31		14
wherein God hath placed two great Instruments, Reason in the soul,	274	Priest 32		19
For there are two branches of his affaires;	275	Priest 32		21
to insist and dwell chiefly on the two noble branches therof,	278	Priest 32		1
These two states were in our Saviour, not only in the beginning	280	Priest 34		8
Particularly, he counselleth them to two things:	280	Priest 34		17
those that are tempted, whatsoever is unruly, falls upon two heads;	281	Priest 34		7
There are two Prophesies in the Gospel, which evidently argue Christs	282	Priest 34		22
hath two pledges of Gods Love, that in the mouth of two or three	283	Priest 34		18
that in the mouth of two or three witnesses every word may be	283	Priest 34		19
That they who in these two things that enter in at the mouth,	294	Cornaro		4
Neverthelesse at a venture two remedies might be used, letting	295	Cornaro		4
To this agreed two Italian Proverbs, the one whereof was,	295	Cornaro		33
the quantitie of meat to be increased, yet but two ounces onely.	296	Cornaro		8
I increased it to the quantitie of two ounces more;	296	Cornaro		11
a pain of the side took me, which held me two and twentie houres.	296	Cornaro		18
save now and then a little indisposition for a day or two.	296	Cornaro		31
abode in those fenny places two whole moneths in the heat of summer	302	Cornaro		18
There are two sorts of acts in religion;	312	Valdesso	V	23
and we meet with two sorts of these Saints of the world;	319	Valdesso	V	21
A Dwarfe on a Gyants shoulder sees further of the two.	322	Proverbs		50
A Dwarfe on a Gyants shoulder sees farther then they two.	322	Proverbs	V	50
Estate in two parishes is bread in two wallets.	328	Proverbs		231
Two ill meales make the third a glutton.	340	Proverbs		575
That which two will, takes effect.	345	Proverbs		705
Three can hold their peace, if two be away.	345	Proverbs		714
One foote is better then two crutches.	346	Proverbs		769
Amongst good men two men suffice.	350	Proverbs		885
'Tis easier to build two chimneys, then to maintaine one.	350	Proverbs		893
The first blow is as much as two.	351	Proverbs		913
Every mile is two in winter.	352	Proverbs		949
Two sparrows on one Ear of Corn make an ill agreement.	358	Proverbs	D	1074
A man is known to be mortal by two things, Sleep and Lust.	361	Proverbs	D	1159
also I ride to Newmarket, and there lie a day or two for fresh Air;	365	Letters		7
these many years, as having spent two hundred pounds in building;	376	Letters		1
4. When two things dislike you:	380	Woodnoth		21
but a Trade having two things, the one imployment, the other profitt,	381	Woodnoth		30
Mrs Dorothy Vaughan whereof two hundred pounds belongs to my two	382	G.H.'s Will		10
two hundred pounds belongs to my two Neeces that survive and the rest	382	G.H.'s Will		11
lately receaved an hundred and two pounds besides some Remainders	383	G.H.'s Will		24
since there is a two-fold brightnesse which dazeleth the eyes of men,	442	Oration		33
TWO-FOLD				
since there is a two-fold brightnesse which dazeleth the eyes of men,	442	Oration		33
TWOFOLD				
And because Idleness is twofold, the one in having no calling,	274	Priest 32		15
TY				
Ty it well, and let it goe.	342	Proverbs		642
TYE				
obligation tc God, and their own soul, is above any temporall tye.	270	Priest 29		23
No tye can oblige the perfidious.	357	Proverbs	D	1066
for my Cambridge necessities are stronger to tye me here,	369	Letters		19
TY'D				
That by destroying that which ty'd thy purse,	103	Prayer 2		17
Which needs not man, be ty'd to those	134	The Method		26
TYED				
The goate must browse where she is tyed.	323	Proverbs		56
A gentle heart is tyed with an easie thread.	345	Proverbs		726
TYES				
Blessings beforehand, tyes of gratefulnesse,	46	Sinne 1		9
TYING				
their Canon law and Decretals, knots of their own tying and untying:	319	Valdesso	V	30
It's good tying the sack before it be full.	349	Proverbs		842
who tying, as with a knot, both Indias to his Spaine, knowes no	442	Oration		11
TYPE				
My coat, the type of love, which once cur'd those	34	Sacrifice		242

	PAGE	TITLE	LINE
TYRANT			
A Tyrant is most tyrant to himselfe.	350	Proverbs	888
TYRE			
yet it would easily tyre me, to find out variety of thanks . .	363	Letters	15
U			
After, where ES, and next where U was graved.	112	JESU	6
UGLINES			
Turns all their beauty to his uglines.	23	Ch.-Porch W	420
UN			
that if after dinner they are not fit (or un-weeldy) either to pray,	266	Priest 26	31
UN-WEELDY			
that if after dinner they are not fit (or un-weeldy) either to pray,	266	Priest 26	31
UNABLE			
My feeble spirit, unable to look right, ...	80	Deniall	23
did the Lord of life, unable of himselfe to die, contrive to do it.	288	Priest	27
because sickness hath made me unable to perform those Offices	373	Letters	9
UNACCESSIBLE			
but to them an unpenetrable rock, an unaccessible desert. . .	282	Priest 34	4
UNANSWERABLE			
He hath one argument unanswerable.	283	Priest 34	9
UNAWARES			
And made a partie unawares for wo.	47	Afflict.1	24
UNBEFITTING			
and unbefitting the reverence of their Fathers calling, . .	240	Priest 10	1
and fashionableness is so exceeding unbefitting a Minister, . .	285	Priest 36	7
UNBELIEF			
or by good works, or condemned for unbelief, or evil works, . .	319	Valdesso V	17
UNBEND			
My power to serve thee; to unbend	164	The Crosse	10
UNBLAMEABLE			
This he procures, first by his holy and unblameable life; . .	268	Priest 28	21
UNBRIDLED			
I know the projects of unbridled store:	89	The Pearl	26
UNBROKEN			
as it lyes entire, and unbroken in the Scripture it self. . .	235	Priest 7	4
UNBUNDLED			
I know the projects of unbundled store:	89	The Pearl V	26
UNCERTAIN			
Because since this is at the best but uncertain, dangerous, . .	300	Cornaro	19
UNCERTAINE			
whose natures are most stealing, and beginnings uncertaine. . .	265	Priest 26	1
UNCERTAINTY			
and exposing to them the uncertainty of humane affairs, . .	253	Priest 19	32
UNCHARITABLE			
in his order, or length of eating, is scandalous and uncharitable.	266	Priest 26	11
he mislikes, and reproves as uncharitable, and unneighbourly;	284	Priest 35	12
As the executioner is not uncharitable, that takes away the life	287	Priest 37	25
UNCHARITABLENESSE			
oppose Theologicall vertues, as Uncharitablenesse opposes Charity;	308	Valdesso	7
UNCIRCUMCISED			
also deliver me out of the hands of this uncircumcised Philistin.	374	Letters	8
UNCONQUERED			
Skill and confidence are an unconquered army.	342	Proverbs	626
UNCOUTH			
What is this strange and uncouth thing?	164	The Crosse	1
Death, thou wast once an uncouth hideous thing, ...	185	Death	1
UNDECENTLY			
and squeeze blood undecently to the station wherein God hath placed	265	Priest 26	18
UNDER			
Whose every parcell under-writes a law.	12	Ch.-Porch	142
God gave them to thee under lock and key.	12	Ch.-Porch	144
And are like empty vessels under sail.	14	Ch.-Porch	184
Most things move th' under-jaw; the Crocodile not.	121	Providence	139
Did once perceive, it blew them under foot, ...	140	Ch.-rents	7
Did once perceive, it blew thee under foot, ...	140	Ch.-rents V	7
Quite under ground; as flowers depart	166	The Flower	10
Hearken under pain of death, ...	182	Banquet	52
His dust who under thee must sleepe	208	H. Danvers D	2
and a thing required under Cancnicall obedience, the expounding	230	Priest 5	13
and cheerfull dying under persecuting Emperours, (though that indeed	237	Priest 9	30
or place, under colour of accommodation, or necessary provision,	238	Priest 9	15
giving some corn outright, and selling other at under rates;	245	Priest 12	11
in the Company where he is, but comes under his Test and censure:	252	Priest 18	3
under pretence of devotion to the Sacrament, but it is for want	258	Priest 22	37
who hath in his hand an apple, and a piece of Gold under it;	272	Priest 30	8
living then in their Countrey under so many miracles were a stranger	282	Priest 34	9
that under God nothing holp me, but that exact rule which I had so	296	Cornaro	28
otherwise they should do) then alwayes to live under bit and bridle.	298	Cornaro	28
I doubt but if Abraham had lived in our Kingdome under government,	316	Valdesso	23
The filth under the white snow, the sunne discovers. . . .	338	Proverbs	495
Under water, famine; under snow, bread.	339	Proverbs	516
We cannot come tc honour under a Coverlet.	339	Proverbs	533
UNDER-JAW			
Most things move th' under-jaw; the Crocodile not.	121	Providence	139
UNDER-WRITES			
Whose every parcell under-writes a law.	12	Ch.-Porch	142
UNDERCHAW			
Most things move th' underchaw; the Crocodile not.	121	Providence V	139
UNDERMINES			
Time undermines us.	351	Proverbs	923

	PAGE	TITLE		LINE
UNDERSTAND				
I flie to thee, and fully understand	89	The Pearl		33
My heart, that brought it (do you understand?)	130	Love unkn.		36
because people by what they understand, are best led to what they	228	Priest 4		20
by what they understand, are best led to what they understand not.	228	Priest 4		20
labouring to make them understand the great good use of this antient	249	Priest 15		30
should open the eyes of one to understand and expresse so clearely	304	Valdesso		20
whereby I understand he meaneth only the effectuall operation	308	Valdesso		30
help of humane learning in the studying to understand holy Scripture,	314	Valdesso	V	4
That is not good language which all understand not.	331	Proverbs		302
I understand by a Letter from my Brother Henry, that he hath bought	366	Letters		29
Orators place (that you may understand what it is) is the finest	369	Letters		30
I understand by Sir Francis Nethersols Letter, that he fears I have	370	Letters		18
when I shall understand that a Letter will be seasonable,	371	Letters		15
UNDERSTANDING				
All understanding, more then heav'n doth glasse:	30	Sacrifice		119
As well our understanding as our sight.	190	Ch.-Milit.		18
But for the understanding of these;	228	Priest 4		27
be a singular help for the right understanding of the Scriptures.	229	Priest 4		9
ones first receiving is not so much by yeers, as by understanding:	258	Priest 22		33
When God will punish, hee will first take away the understanding.	344	Proverbs		688
UNDERSTANDINGS				
their understandings being ripe enough for ill things, and why	259	Priest 22		1
UNDERSTANDS				
of the world he every where understands the cunning hypocrite who	319	Valdesso	V	19
UNDERSTOOD				
The holy lines cannot be understood.	6	Ch.-Porch		10
Twice on the day his due is understood;	22	Ch.-Porch		391
Twice on that day his due is understood;	22	Ch.-Porch	W	391
The land of spices; something understood.	51	Prayer 1		14
And in another make me understood.	58	H.Script.2		12
Full well I understood, who had been there:	130	Love unkn.		54
and because they are not understood but with the same Spirit that	228	Priest 4		32
in the way I ought to hold, I understood, that the food I was to use,	292	Cornaro		24
The Doctrine of the last passage must be warily understood.	308	Valdesso		1
that it is not to be understood of actuall sinnes, but habituall,	308	Valdesso		2
so it be understood with the former distinction, for Fomes is	308	Valdesso		14
Things hard to bee understood.	317	Valdesso		25
UNDERTAKE				
which I undertake the more willingly, because divers worthy young men	291	Cornaro		7
UNDERTAKING				
Who think me eager, hot, and undertaking,	169	The Answer		6
and his Saints, and by way of undertaking for a Christian soul.	258	Priest 22		13
UNDERVALUE				
and it is the part of a poor spirit to undervalue himself and blush.	366	Letters		19
UNDESERV'D				
Thy bloudy death and undeserv'd, makes thee	115	Dulnesse		11
UNDIVIDED				
And show thy undivided Majestye	212	Bohemia	D	34
UNDO				
Who can these Gordian knots undo?	135	Divinitie		20
One sound blow will serve to undo all.	322	Proverbs		34
UNDOE				
With customes wee live well, but Lawes undoe us.	353	Proverbs		973
UNDOES				
Give it a corner, and the clue undoes.	11	Ch.-Porch		124
UNDONE				
Alas! what haste they make to be undone!	27	Sacrifice		34
wit and noble disposition, overthrown and undone by Intemperance;	291	Cornaro		3
UNDOUBTED				
in the world as he was, hath this undoubted pledge of his salvation.	269	Priest 28		18
UNDRESSE				
Dresse and undresse thy soul: mark the decay	24	Ch.-Porch		453
UNDRESSING				
Is one undressing,	48	Repentance		5
He did descend, undressing all the way.	151	The Bag		12
UNDREST				
Or else undrest.	109	Brit. Ch.		12
UNDUTIFULL				
or any undutifull behaviour in them, but causing them,	231	Priest 6		24
UNEVEN				
While grace fills up uneven nature.	50	Faith		32
UNEXPECTED				
and fresh bounties, unexpected to them, but resolved to himself,	245	Priest 12		1
UNFEYNED				
other gestures which may expresse a hearty, and unfeyned devotion.	231	Priest 6		4
UNFIT				
But that which shews them large, shews them unfit.	41	Sepulchre		9
And in the flesh condemn'd it as unfit,	138	The Size		26
I am both foul and brittle; much unfit	160	Priesthood		11
the Parson think it in his discretion either unfit, or bootelesse	269	Priest 28		4
UNFITTING				
which though our Saviour reproved as unfitting for his particular,	285	Priest 36		27
UNFOLD				
Chiefly to thee would I my soul unfold:	78	Ang.&Sts.		15
Before we do our wares unfold:	79	Employm.2		28
Unfold thy forehead gather'd into frowns:	112	Dawning		3
UNFRUITFULL				
with the unfruitfull works of darknesse, he disableth himself	227	Priest 3		26
UNGODLY				
in councels of th' ungodly share,	214	Psalm I	D	2

UNGODLY (cont'd)	PAGE	TITLE		LINE
For, Unto the ungodly, saith God, Why dost thou preach my Laws,	226	Priest 2		13
UNGODLY'S				
And thou hast brok th' ungodly's teeth:	217	Psalm III	D	21
UNGRATEFULL				
I the unkinde, ungratefull? Ah my deare, ...	189	Love 3		9
UNGRATEFULNESSE				
Ungratefulnesse.	82	Ungratef.		T
UNHALLOW'D				
Where rude unhallow'd steps do crush and grinde	140	Ch.-rents		8
UNHAPPINESSE				
In my unhappinesse, ...	48	Afflict.1		50
UNHEALTHY				
because the place was moorish and unhealthy, fitter for beasts then	301	Cornaro		27
UNHINGE				
And did unhinge that day.	76	Sunday		49
UNIFORM				
firm, and uniform, especially that the Pulpit, and Desk, . .	246	Priest 13		5
live in health, not keep an uniform diet, but to feed variously,	267	Priest 26		11
UNIFORMITY				
partly for uniformity sake, that the same common truths may be every	255	Priest 21		18
UNION				
Addes to the unicn, as lights doe gather	212	Bohemia	D	36
UNITE				
Sometimes unite. The Indian nut alone	120	Providence		126
UNITED				
Waters united are our navigation;	92	Man		38
United now in one both time and sphere.	195	Ch.-Milit.		176
to bee united with that bloud, which useth to infuse so great	442	Oration		14
UNIVERSALL				
wher-ever spoken this day throughout the universall Church. . .	289	Priest		15
UNIVERSE				
Of th' universe, like as the windes, & name	212	Bohemia	D	44
UNIVERSITIE				
of the Universitie of Cambridg.	356	Proverbs	D	T
Orator of the Universitie cf Cambridge, when the Ambassadours were	441	Oration		T
UNIVERSITIE'S				
will do well, for it expresseth the Universities inclination to me;	369	Letters		27
UNIVERSITIES				
to whom this discourse ariseth not) some live in the Universities,	226	Priest 2		1
Of those that live in the Universities, some live there in office,	226	Priest 2		2
There are three waies, the Universities, the Sea, the Court.	334	Proverbs		383
UNIVERSITY				
to make an Oraticn to the whole University of an hour long in Latin,	369	Letters		13
you may understand what it is) is the finest place in the University,	369	Letters		31
for the Orator writes all the University Letters, makes all . .	369	Letters		34
be it to King, Prince, or whatever comes to the University; . .	369	Letters		35
UNJUST				
counting nothing so much his owne, as that he may be unjust unto it.	238	Priest 9		35
to redeem the Dignity either from true faults, or unjust aspersions.	276	Priest 32		24
UNJUSTLY				
Thou hat'st those that unjustly do:	218	Psalm V	D	13
poorest man cf the Parish detain but a pin unjustly from the richest,	260	Priest 23		15
UNKIND				
whether my peace be yet made with her concerning my unkind departure.	371	Letters		9
UNKINDE				
I the unkinde, ungratefull? Ah my deare, ...	189	Love 3		9
UNKINDNESSE				
Unkindnesse.	93	Unkindness		T
UNKNOWN				
Love unknown.	129	Love unkn.		T
Dead to the world, keep house unknown.	166	The Flower		14
because they were to come into an unknown country, tender in	375	Letters		14
UNKNOWNE				
The charges of building and making of gardens are unknowne. . .	335	Proverbs		412
UNLAWFUL				
if it be unlawful to open faults, no benefit or advantage can make it	287	Priest 37		5
UNLAWFULL				
to that which is presently unlawfull, even in one continued action.	264	Priest 26		21
the bounds of the action, nor when his eating begins to be unlawfull.	264	Priest 26		25
his children, hardly perceives when his storing becomes unlawfull:	264	Priest 26		28
UNLAWFULLY				
but proceeding on, comes to do unlawfully, even before he is aware;	264	Priest 26		23
UNLAWFULNESS				
after he hath shew'd the unlawfulness of spending the day in	277	Priest 32		28
UNLESS				
Unless the wicked turn again, ...	222	Psalm VII	D	41
UNLESSE				
Unlesse Authoritie, which should increase	86	Lent		16
Unlesse they get new conduits, new supplies	164	Grief		7
Nor canst thou be content, unlesse thou to	439	Walton 5		5
exercise what he is, unlesse he forsake his plough, and look back.	226	Priest 2		26
that unlesse I speedily used that remedy, within a few moneths I	292	Cornaro		13
unlesse it be evident to others, as well as to themselves, . .	316	Valdesso		19
unlesse he could have made it appeare, that it was done by Gods	316	Valdesso		25
Hee that demands misseth not, unlesse his demands be foolish.	333	Proverbs		359
Old praise dies, unlesse you feede it.	344	Proverbs		699
The little cannot bee great, unlesse he devoure many. . . .	351	Proverbs		922
Speake not of my debts, unlesse you meane to pay them. . . .	354	Proverbs		998
Nothing secure unlesse suspected.	357	Proverbs	D	1065
you bee like great Alexander, unlesse Historie delivered his actions?	443	Oration		2

	PAGE	TITLE	LINE
UNLOCK			
What is thy aim? wouldst thou unlock the doore	155	Assurance	15
UNLOCKT			
Thou hast unlockt them both, ...	82	Ungratef.	9
UNLOOSE			
Then did your sev'rall parts unloose and start:	140	Ch.-rents	21
UNMARRIED			
like circumstances considered, he is rather married then unmarried.	237	Priest 9	5
If he be unmarried, and keepe house, he hath not a woman in his	237	Priest 9	7
UNMARRYED			
the best and highest things, is rather unmarryed, then marryed.	236	Priest 9	33
If he be unmarryed, and sojourne, he never talkes with any woman	237	Priest 9	10
If the Parson be unmarryed, and means to continue so, he doth	238	Priest 9	24
UNMEASURABLE			
Of what unmeasurable love	103	Prayer 2	13
UNMOVED			
being unmoved in arguing, and voyd of all contentiousnesse: . .	263	Priest 24	17
Therfore the Parson unmoved, sheweth, that ingenuous and fit	275	Priest 32	9
UNNATURAL			
For it is as unnatural to do any thing, that leads me to a sicknesse,	242	Priest 10	36
UNNATURALL			
an act against reason, because it is unnaturall to hurt ones self;	266	Priest 26	22
UNNECESSARY			
when on the Lords day they do unnecessary servile work, . .	248	Priest 14	3
UNNEIGHBOURLY			
he mislikes, and reproves as uncharitable, and unneighbourly;	284	Priest 35	12
UNPENETRABLE			
but to them an unpenetrable rock, an unaccessible desert. . .	282	Priest 34	4
UNPINNE			
Unpinne, or wrench from giving all their due.	72	Constancie	5
UNPLEASANT			
to eat little, and that unpleasant, is the naturall rule of fasting,	242	Priest 10	10
if a peece of dry flesh at my table be more unpleasant to me,	242	Priest 10	13
or roots, and that for quantity little, for quality unpleasant.	242	Priest 10	28
UNPREPAREDNESSE			
but man's unpreparednesse asks kneeling.	259	Priest 22	13
UNPROFITABLE			
Curiosity in prying into high speculative and unprofitable questions,	238	Priest 9	18
UNQUESTIONED			
while applying himselfe to the [unquestioned] duties of true Piety,	312	Valdesso	19
UNRIGHTEOUSNESSE			
and thirsteth after righteous punishment of unrighteousnesse.	254	Priest 20	29
UNRULY			
Wit's an unruly engine, wildly striking	16	Ch.-Porch	241
They grow unruly, and sit in thy bowers.	56	Temper 2	12
Sure the unruly sigh had broke my heart.	73	Afflict.3	6
not for emboldening the unruly, but for the comfort of the weak,	242	Priest 10	34
those that are tempted, whatsoever is unruly, falls upon two heads;	281	Priest 34	7
UNSAFELY			
He lives unsafely, that lookes too neere on things.	322	Proverbs	43
UNSOUND			
Unsound minds like unsound Bodies, if you feed, you poyson. . .	358	Proverbs	D 1076
UNSPEAKEABLE			
of Gods Love, and the unspeakeable riches of his loving kindnesse.	283	Priest 34	8
UNSTRUNG			
Untun'd, unstrung:	80	Deniall	22
UNSUFFERABLE			
may pretend motions, which is unsufferable in a Common-wealth.	316	Valdesso	22
this Chapter but that his opinion of the scripture is unsufferable.	318	Valdesso	6
UNTAMED			
To deale with brimstone, that untamed stench	212	Bohemia	D 53
UNTHANKFUL			
(applyed to rich men that are unthankful to God).	359	Proverbs	D 1100
UNTHANKFULNESS			
of the unthankfulness of kindred bredd up, (which generally is very	376	Letters	4
UNTHRIFT			
The curious unthrift makes his cloth too wide, ...	13	Ch.-Porch	179
UNTIE			
Oh loose this frame, this knot of man untie!	109	Home	61
UNTIL			
Shall flow nc more - until they bring	214	Convert	D 8
this is foretold, that it shall be so still, until things be no more.	268	Priest 28	16
UNTILL			
My crosse I bear my self, untill I faint:	33	Sacrifice	197
Untill the grave increase our cold.	79	Employm.2	30
Untill their cockatrice they hatch and bring:	122	Sinnes rd.	4
Untill thou finde and use it to thy good:	147	Offering	23
Should crie so loud, untill the trump were drown'd, ...	152	The Jews	10
And both would runne untill they found a biere	159	Jos.coat	8
There will I lie, untill my Maker seek	161	Priesthood	37
Untill I had some place, where I might sing, ...	164	The Crosse	3
(As dying things are wont) untill it flew	192	Ch.-Milit.	80
Untill the graves againe restore	208	H. Danvers	D 3
which I have observed, untill the Book grow to a compleat Pastorall.	224	Priest	15
perplexity, untill it spread, and taint his other duties of piety,	273	Priest 31	1
untill we interrupted thy Counsels, disappointed thy Purposes,	288	Priest	16
untill our obedience reach the measure of thy love, who hast done	290	Priest	11
building it all upon the word untill the day starre arise, . .	318	Valdesso	8
doe the Fathers bring about Untill against the Heretiques who	318	Valdesso	10
untill shee had brought forth her first borne Sonne, as if afterwards	318	Valdesso	12
if I bid a man stay in a place untill I come, I doe not then bid him	318	Valdesso	15

UNTILL (cont'd)	PAGE	TITLE		LINE
untill they have satisfied him also concerning the fishing which	368	Letters		9
& therfore deferr it untill they heare farther from the States.	368	Letters		15
UNTIMELY				
or untimely desire of promotion to an higher state, or place,	238	Priest 9		15
UNTO				
Hearken unto a Verser, who may chance	6	Ch.-Porch		3
Unto thy hands, it woundeth to the quick.	13	Ch.-Porch		168
Which I do give them daily, unto death.	28	Sacrifice		70
They binde, and leade me unto Herod: he	29	Sacrifice		73
And now I am deliver'd unto death,	31	Sacrifice		145
From th' earth unto my brows, and bear the thrall:	32	Sacrifice		167
All back unto thee by the poore.	35	Thanksgvng		20
All back unto thee in the poore.	35	Thanksgvng	W	20
Unto some Chappell, die or live.	35	Thanksgvng		28
Unto mount Olivet; there shall he see	37	The Agonie		8
And make a suit unto him, to afford	40	Redemption		3
And 'tice me unto thee.	46	Afflict.1		10
My flesh began unto my soul in pain,	47	Afflict.1		25
Faith cleaves unto it, counting evr'y grain	51	Faith		42
Unto a third, that ten leaves off doth lie:	58	H.Script.2		6
Listen sweet Dove unto my song,	59	Whitsunday		1
Unto his ancient and miraculous right.	60	Whitsunday		28
Unto a hardnesse, void of love:	60	Grace		18
Or, if I mount unto the skie,	61	Praise 1		7
From either pole unto the centre:	69	Content		18
From either pole unto the centure:	69	Content	W	18
Constant unto it, making it to be	73	Afflict.3		14
Unto the place where thou	74	The Starre		19
Unto that hive of beams	74	The Starre		31
Unto thy self in everlasting pleasure.	82	Ungratef.		12
Ev'n unto death: since he di'd for my good,	83	Sighs & Gr.		23
To sell my life unto my friends or foes:	88	The Pearl		19
Unto my face:	90	Afflict.4		15
All things unto our flesh are kinde	91	Man		34
Unto my friends intent and end.	93	Unkindness		4
Wherefore unto my gift I stand;	95	Submission		17
Which do consigne and send them unto death.	98	Mortific.		6
Unto the coffin, that attends his death.	98	Mortific.		24
Holds them unto it, and doth cover	100	Miserie		27
And heart unto this deed, when he hath read;	105	Obedience		38
And heart unto this deed, when he doth read	105	Obedience	W	38
Let them unto their kindred flie:	111	Vanitie 2		14
Unto the service mutter an assent,	117	Providence		15
Doth not refrain unto himself alone,	117	Providence		18
Unto my house, where to repair the strength	130	Love unkn.		47
Do as ye would be done unto.	135	Divinitie		18
At length I got unto the gladsome hill,	142	Pilgrimage		19
Unto those grounds,	145	Discharge		39
He did repair unto an inne.	151	The Bag		20
Unto my fathers hands and sight	152	The Bag		33
As having keyes unto thy love,	162	The Search		15
Unto their sinnes?	162	The Search		28
Is, when the soul unto the lines accords.	168	a true Hymn		10
Shines bright and cleare, ev'n unto condemnation,	171	Self-cond.		23
To leade them unto life and rest.	174	Aaron		4
Unto a place where is no rest.	174	Aaron		9
Unto the taster:	174	The Odour		3
Unto what you now advise:	177	The Rose		14
Unto thine is bent:	178	Discipline		6
Of praise deserved, unto thee I give,	185	A Wreath		2
Unto an honest faithfull grave;	186	Death		23
Unto the farthest old meridian.	192	Ch.-Milit.		98
As Rome will one day finde unto her cost.	194	Ch.-Milit.		160
Unto a voluntarie transmigration.	195	Ch.-Milit.	W	194
But when they were unto the Sorbon come,	196	Ch.-Milit.	W	202
Unto the brimme, and make our measure up;	197	Ch.-Milit.		240
With face and hands clinging unto thy brest,	205	Persever.	W	14
Though nail'd unto 't, but he ascends again,	439	Walton 5		2
When nail'd unto 't, but he ascends again	439	Walton 5	V	2
The Water, and the Earth both unto thee	439	Walton 5		7
And starres alone unto the pitch doe runne	211	Bohemia	D	4
I cry'd unto the Lord, he heard	216	Psalm III	D	9
Salvation unto thee	217	Psalm III	D	22
The Lord will harken unto me	217	Psalm IV	D	13
unto mine overthrow.	221	Psalm VII	D	16
For, Unto the ungodly, saith God, Why dost thou preach my Laws,	226	Priest 2		13
may be like hindes feet ever climbing up higher, and higher unto him.	236	Priest 8		30
Let him communicate the thing often by prayer unto God,	237	Priest 9		6
counting nothing so much his owne, as that he may be unjust unto it.	238	Priest 9		35
and resorting unto him in any difficulty, either in his studies or in	253	Priest 19		8
but invites and urges the best unto it, shewing that they do	270	Priest 29		9
when the evills which he is now subject unto, may be prevented,	274	Priest 32		23
which either he lives in, or is neer unto it, is his imployment.	276	Priest 32		2
and turning unto God in truth of heart, and newnesse of life:	279	Priest 33		24
the places, and rivers travelled unto, and frequented by others,	282	Priest 34		3
then he dives unto the boundlesse Ocean of Gods Love,	283	Priest 34		7
assembled together, with thy unworthy Servant speaking unto them:	289	Priest		26
O Lord, make it health and strength unto us;	290	Priest		10
because divers worthy young men have obliged me unto it.	291	Cornaro		8
to search out most diligently what meats were agreeable unto me,	293	Cornaro		5

UP (cont'd)	PAGE	TITLE		LINE
Or take me up to thee!	107	Home		24
Or take me up to thee!	108	Home		30
Away; I must get up and see.	108	Home		34
Or take me up to thee!	108	Home		36
Or take me up to thee!	108	Home		42
Or take me up to thee!	108	Home		48
Or take me up to thee!	108	Home		54
Or take me up to thee!	108	Home		60
Or take me up to thee!	109	Home		66
My thoughts and joyes are all packt up and gone,	109	Home		69
Or take me up to thee!	109	Home		72
Or take me up to thee!	109	Home		78
Beautie in thee takes up her place,	109	Brit. Ch.		4
Beautie in thee takes up the place,	109	Brit. Ch.	V	4
Take up thine eyes, which feed on earth;	112	Dawning		2
Joy, I did lock thee up: but some bad man	128	Bunch Gr.		1
Let me as well take up their joy, as sorrow.	128	Bunch Gr.		21
But as birds drink, and straight lift up their head,	131	Mans medly		21
Down with thy knees, up with thy voice.	134	The Method		30
And work up to thee; yet thou dost refuse.	139	Artillerie		20
With these two poore ones lick up all the dew,	140	Ch.-rents		29
He that did but look up, was proud and bold.	141	Justice 2		6
Hast thou not made thy counts, and summ'd up all?	144	Discharge		6
Give up the whole, and with the whole depart?	144	Discharge		8
Here he gave up his life to pay our score.	151	The Bag		24
Call in thy deaths head there: tie up thy fears.	153	The Collar		29
And give me up to night?	154	Glimpse		3
And so take up at use good store:	159	Praise 3		40
As serve him up, who all the world commands:	161	Priesthood		26
Suck up a river to supply mine eyes,	164	Grief		5
Give up your feet and running to mine eyes,	164	Grief		15
To set thy honour up, as our designe.	164	The Crosse		6
Taking me up to throw me down:	165	The Crosse		22
And up to heaven in an houre;	166	The Flower		17
Many a spring I shoot up fair,	166	The Flower		24
And still it runneth mutt'ring up and down	168	a true Hymn		4
A mirth but open'd and seal'd up again;	172	The Glance		18
Having rais'd me to look up,	182	Banquet		37
And take up my lines and life:	182	Banquet		51
And did this mysterie wrap up and fold	192	Ch.-Milit.		94
Unto the brimme, and make our measure up;	197	Ch.-Milit.		240
Lord make my Losses up, & sett mee free:	203	Even-song	W	5
Which warme these lines, & serve them up to thee	204	Persever.	W	2
His letters were broke rudely up, believ'd	439	Walton 5		16
And Spanish sents, wisely layd up, presume	212	Bohemia	D	52
to be received up into heaven, he constituted Deputies in his place,	225	Priest 1		8
that he fils up that which is behinde of the afflictions of Christ in	225	Priest 1		11
but to keep up with the Lord and Lady of the house, and to preserve	226	Priest 2		28
lifting up his heart and hands, and eyes, and using all other	231	Priest 6		2
or offer up such sacrifices as they did of old, which was of beasts	232	Priest 6		4
and to raise up their mindes to apprehend Gods good blessing to our	236	Priest 8		22
and that our feet may be like hindes feet ever climbing up higher,	236	Priest 8		29
against these ghostly enemies he girdeth up his loynes,	238	Priest 9		4
a trayning up of her children and mayds in the fear of God,	239	Priest 10		12
sets up as many encouragements to goodnesse as he can, both in	244	Priest 11		3
of well minded people, and to lay up treasure for the sick and needy.	246	Priest 13		22
or breeding up children to no Calling, but in idleness,	251	Priest 17		21
to multiply, and build up this knowledge to a spirituall Temple;	255	Priest 21		4
but hee that sits, or lies, puts up to an Apostle:	259	Priest 22		17
but sometimes lift up their minds to better things, even in the midst	261	Priest 23		25
So a man storing up mony for his necessary provisions, both in	264	Priest 26		26
without which supply the corne would instantly dry up, as a river	271	Priest 30		7
by bringing them up in the fear and nurture of the Lord;	275	Priest 32		23
For if he absolutely shut up mens mouths, and forbid all disclosing	286	Priest 37		34
and that at length they shut up their dayes like a Lamp,	298	Cornaro		17
of the ground, and sometimes I go up high stairs and hills on foot.	300	Cornaro		36
joy and peace have taken up their standing in my heart.	301	Cornaro		2
shall overthrow all means, save catechizing, and set up Enthusiasmes.	310	Valdesso		12
He that takes not up a pin, slights his wife.	333	Proverbs		361
That's the best gowne that goes up and downe the house.	346	Proverbs		742
He that hath not the craft, let him shut up shop.	349	Proverbs		860
But I fear the heat of my late Ague hath dryed up those springs,	363	Letters		4
by which Schclars say, the Muses use to take up their habitations.	363	Letters		5
What Trades-man is there who will set up without his Tools?	364	Letters		15
whose bottom is wound up and laid ready for work in the New	373	Letters		6
and so brought up your Children that they have attain'd to the years	373	Letters		13
of the unthankfulness of kindred bredd up, (which generally is very	376	Letters		4
UPBRAIDED				
An upbraided morsell never choaked any.	335	Proverbs		406
UPON				
How dare those eyes upon a Bible look,	6	Ch.-Porch		11
Which it would poure on thee, upon the floore.	7	Ch.-Porch		28
Who keeps no guard upon himself, is slack,	12	Ch.-Porch		139
Thy children, kindred, friends upon thee call;	13	Ch.-Porch		161
Upon thy body, clothes, and habitation.	21	Ch.-Porch		372
Upon my head: so I remove it all	32	Sacrifice		166
The souldiers also spit upon that face,	32	Sacrifice		181
The souldiers also spit upon my Face,	32	Sacrifice	W	181
I pass the shades, & fixe upon the true	43	H. Bapt.1	W	4
Powring upon it all thy art,	62	Mattens		11

UPON (cont'd)	PAGE	TITLE		LINE
In sev'rall ranks upon an azure throne, ...	70	Humilitie		2
They leapt upon the throne;	70	Humilitie		22
What upon trust	71	Fraltie		2
Upon their head.	71	Fraltie		8
If not upon his head, yet in his hands:	77	Ang.&Sts.		5
They go upon the score.	91	Man		12
My friend may spit upon my curious floore:	93	Unkindness		11
O write in brasse, My God upon a tree	94	Unkindness		22
Gift upon gift, much would have more, ...	124	Gratefulnes		15
And fall, like rheumes, upon the tendrest parts.	126	Confession		12
Who took the debt upon him. Truly, Friend, ...	130	Love unkn.		61
And do encroach upon deaths side.	145	Discharge		35
Thy dying head upon the tree:	149	Longing		32
Upon the horse?	149	Longing		46
That ran upon him with a spear.	151	The Bag		26
Receiv'd the blow upon his side, ...	151	The Bag		29
At which the Church falling upon her face	152	The Jews		9
We turn upon him in a sense most true:	168	The Sonne		12
Look back upon thine own estate, ...	170	Self-cond.		4
To look upon me, who before did lie	171	The Glance		3
Upon the matter 'twill thy conquest prove:	202	love	W	20
Upon thine Altar burnt? Cannot thy love	206	walton 1		6
For thou upon the cheek-bone smit'st	217	Psalm III	D	19
upon thy people be.	217	Psalm III	D	24
Wherfore he hath one Comment at least upon every book of Scripture,	229	Priest 4		28
it is an honest joy ever after to looke upon his well spent houres.	230	Priest 5		7
and of theirs also who gaze upon them when they come in, . . .	232	Priest 6		11
were with Saint Paul even sacrificed upon the service of their faith.	234	Priest 7		8
for then they will reckon upon it, as on a debt;	244	Priest 12		28
which otherwise they would reckon upon, and turn to idlenesse.	245	Priest 12		5
The Countrey Parson upon the afternoons in the weekdays, . . .	247	Priest 14		3
which exceedingly delights him as by way of exercise upon himself,	255	Priest 21		12
upon which and to which the questions are to be chained. . . .	256	Priest 21		33
step into their great and glorious calling) and upon what termes,	258	Priest 22		19
or not in some proportion to Gods blessing upon him, is covetous.	265	Priest 26		6
both for the generall ignominy which is cast upon the profession,	268	Priest 28		10
that so the sentence lighting upon one, the example may reach to all.	269	Priest 28		2
what a great Charge lyes upon them, and that indeed the whole order	269	Priest 29		28
which are grounded upon the Canons, that so they may know their duty,	270	Priest 29		15
So that if a farmer should depend upon God all the yeer, . . .	271	Priest 30		28
that the godly petitioner upon some emergent interruption in the day,	272	Priest 31		30
Upon this his mind begins to be perplexed, and troubled, . . .	272	Priest 31		32
the omission thereof upon just occasion ought by no means to trouble	273	Priest 31		6
for besides the blessing that that brings upon it, there being	278	Priest 33		12
those that are tempted, whatsoever is unruly, falls upon two heads;	281	Priest 34		7
if all men are to blesse upon occasion, as appears Rom. 12. 14. how	286	Priest 36		27
or put into the stocks, that they may be looked upon.	287	Priest 37		21
who continueth to pour his benefits upon us.	290	Priest		2
thy blessings hang in clusters, they come trooping upon us! . . .	290	Priest		7
Upon this, weighing their reasons with my self, and abhorring from so	292	Cornaro		17
Upon this, I found within a few dayes, that I was exceedingly helped,	292	Cornaro		34
This upon triall I found most false:	293	Cornaro		10
This addition after ten dayes wrought so much upon me, that . . .	296	Cornaro		14
Upon the neck of it came a terrible fever, which continued thirtie	296	Cornaro		19
without such observation, as is not easily to be made upon others;	297	Cornaro		30
the presuming upon it ought not to leade us to a disorderly life.	300	Cornaro		20
onely upon a hope of an happie issue, which yet befalls verie few.	300	Cornaro		23
together with many other, as namely Consid. 71. upon Our Father;	307	Valdesso		17
and Consid. 94. upon these words:	307	Valdesso		17
See the note upon Consid. 36.	307	Valdesso		23
Feare is given to Christ, but not doubt, and upon good ground.	315	Valdesso		12
is a judgment of authority (upon a fact) and there is a judgment	316	Valdesso		35
of his Considerations being grounded upon some text of scripture,	318	Valdesso		1
building it all upon the word untill the day starre arise, . . .	318	Valdesso		8
To go upon the Franciscans Hackney (i.e. on foot).	356	Proverbs	D	1035
Now though they have hitherto travelled upon your charge, . . .	366	Letters		31
she would make good her promise of taking five or six pound upon her,	367	Letters		3
but upon the want of those Books which were not to be got in England;	367	Letters		4
upon condition that I should surcease from all title to it, . . .	367	Letters		8
and yet still grew upon Your humblest Servant, GEORGE HERBERT.	367	Letters		16
upon this he was forbid Court & kingdome, yet was seene lately neere	368	Letters		34
wrote to our eldest brother, when he urged one upon me, and but one,	375	Letters		11
and that upon this ground, because they were to come into an unknown	375	Letters		13
Wherefore the Lord make good the blessing of your Mother upon you,	377	Letters		4
your care of Leighton, upon my accompt, & give you my self for it,	378	Letters		4
that creeps upon Gods earth, no not tho' the advice step so far,	378	Letters		12
especially no obligation lying upon you either for the execution	380	Woodnoth		26
& if upon your withdrawing it shold doe so, it would trouble your	381	Woodnoth		12
UPPER				
Let th' upper springs into the low	137	The Size		5
UPPON				
Comment of Lucas Brugensis uppon the Scripture and his halfe yeares	382	G.H.'s Will		19
pound whereof fifteene pound shal be bestowed uppon Leighton Church,	382	G.H.'s Will		30
UPRIGHT				
The Countrey Parson is sincere and upright in all his relations.	252	Priest 19		24
UPWARD				
And all their motions upward be;	107	Sion		22
Whose fire is wild, and doth not upward go	206	Walton 2		10
UPWARDS				
Still upwards bent, as if heav'n were mine own, ...	166	The Flower		30

	PAGE	TITLE		LINE
URGE				
O do not urge me!	83	Sighs & Gr.		7
URGED				
that he himself hath often urged with no great success,	232	Priest 7		28
wrote to our eldest brother, when he urged one upon me, and but one,	375	Letters		11
URGES				
but invites and urges the best unto it, shewing that they do	270	Priest 29		8
URGETH				
Enmitie forbearance urgeth.	178	The Rose		20
he also urgeth them to do some pious charitable works, as a necessary	249	Priest 15		32
times invite one another to their houses, and he urgeth them to it:	284	Priest 35		18
URGING				
They leade me; urging, that it was not sound	28	Sacrifice		54
by an often urging of the presence, and majesty of God,	234	Priest 7		25
that he would by no meanes do so, urging, that Charity must be free.	379	Letters		7
URN				
Of thy great love once spread, as in an urn	99	Decay		17
And be that Idol's URN.	214	Convert	D	20
US				
And make us strive, who shall sing best thy name.	5	Dedication		4
God hath impal'd us, on the contrarie	7	Ch.-Porch		21
Constancie knits the bones, and makes us stowre,	11	Ch.-Porch		117
Constancie knits the bones, and makes us sowre,	11	Ch.-Porch	W	117
When wanton pleasures becken us to thrall.	11	Ch.-Porch		118
We all are but cold suitours; let us move	22	Ch.-Porch		400
Our blessings from us, and extreamly flout thee,	23	Ch.-Porch	W	413
Though God do hedge us in, yet who is holy?	24	Ch.-Porch		450
You give us teares to wash them: lett those beams	44	H. Bapt.1	W	7
Lord, with what care hast thou begirt us round!	45	Sinne 1		1
Parents first season us: then schoolmasters	45	Sinne 1		2
Deliver us to laws; they send us bound	45	Sinne 1		3
Fine nets and stratagems to catch us in,	45	Sinne 1		7
Fine nets and casualties to catch us in,	45	Sinne 1	W	7
Each day doth round about us see.	48	Repentance		8
Looking on this side, & beyond us all:	48	Repentance	W	9
Fractures well cur'd make us more strong.	49	Repentance		36
Thou hast restor'd us to this ease	53	H.Commun.		37
Since thou hast taught us by thy word,	53	H.Commun.	W	39
Without thy help, leads us his way to Hell.	59	Whitsunday	W	16
But God more care of us hath had:	63	Sinne 2		6
If apparitions make us sad,	63	Sinne 2		7
Thou dost inclose us, till the day	64	Even-song		22
And turn us round to look on one,	75	Sunday		17
That was requir'd to make us gay,	76	Sunday		55
Hast thou redeem'd us from the grave!	82	Ungratef.		2
If thou hadst let us runne,	82	Ungratef.		3
This fully to us, till death blow	82	Ungratef.		16
This to us fully, till death blow	82	Ungratef.	W	16
For by that powder thou wilt make us see.	82	Ungratef.		18
For by this powder thou wilt make us see.	82	Ungratef.	W	18
This may allure us with delights;	82	Ungratef.		22
For we have all of us just such another.	82	Ungratef.		24
Embosomes in us, mellowing the ground	85	Vanitie 1		24
The Scriptures bid us fast; the Church sayes, now:	86	Lent		4
The obligation in us, make it lesse,	86	Lent		17
Yet Lord instruct us to improve our fast	87	Lent		43
Parrats may thank us, if they are not mute,	91	Man		11
For us the windes do blow,	91	Man		25
The starres have us to bed;	91	Man		31
Till then, afford us so much wit;	92	Man		52
That, as the world serves us, we may serve thee,	92	Man		53
That as the world to us is kind and free	92	Man	W	53
Us of old,	92	Antiphon 2		8
And us in th' end.	92	Antiphon 2		9
Us did make,	92	Antiphon 2		11
For us was sold.	92	Antiphon 2		12
Thine own delights thou didst to us impart:	97	Afflict.5		8
To make us thine: yet that we might not part,	97	Afflict.5		10
If either will convert us, we are thine:	97	Afflict.5		14
Yet Lord, instruct us so to die,	99	Mortific.		35
That chains us by the teeth so fast?	108	Home		38
Birds teach us hawking; fishes have their net:	118	Providence		51
Which as it lengthens windes, and windes us in,	118	Providence		59
While it detains us from our God.	123	Time		20
And didst allow us all our noise:	124	Gratefulnes		18
Like moles within us, heave, and cast about:	126	Confession		14
Lord, mend or rather make us: one creation	127	Giddinesse		25
Except thou make us dayly, we shall spurn	127	Giddinesse		27
Their storie pennes and sets us down.	128	Bunch Gr.		11
But he doth bid us take his bloud for wine.	135	Divinitie		21
Doth tice us on to hopes of more,	138	The Size		29
To enter combate with us, and contest	139	Artillerie		26
O that within us hearts had propagation,	147	Offering		7
Such a Way, as gives us breath:	156	The Call		2
Let us (said he) poure on him all we can:	159	The Pulley		3
To make us see we are but flowers that glide:	167	The Flower		44
Thou hast a garden for us, where to bide.	167	The Flower		46
When thou shalt look us out of pain,	172	The Glance		21
But borrow'd thence to light us thither.	177	Forerunners		29
So they might still, and point us out the place	192	Ch.-Milit.		85
In us the same transplanted foolerie.	193	Ch.-Milit.		120

US (cont'd)	PAGE	TITLE		LINE
But in the Jews and us deserveth tears.	196	Ch.-Milit.		228
When Italie of us shall have her will,	197	Ch.-Milit.		243
But lends to us, shall be our desolation.	197	Ch.-Milit.		258
Lendeth to us, shall be our desolation.	197	Ch.-Milit.	W	258
That makes you thinke us poore:	210	Paradox	D	8
So Blackamoores repute us fowle, and wee	210	Paradox	D	9
Then for yourselves not us embrace	211	Paradox	D	37
For though you vysit us, & wayle our case,	211	Paradox	D	39
To comforte us, or to bee comforted.	211	Paradox	D	42
Betwixt us & the people: when as glory	212	Bohemia	D	25
Lyes round about us to helpe out the story,	212	Bohemia	D	26
Let us in sunder break their bonds,	215	Psalm II	D	7
and from us cast their cords away.	215	Psalm II	D	8
will shew us good? But, Lord,	217	Psalm IV	D	22
do thou to us afford.	217	Psalm IV	D	24
as farre as wee can in pleasing of him, who hath done so much for us.	224	Priest		13
according to the grace that is given to us, whether prophecy,	226	Priest 2		5
prophecy, let us prophecy according to the proportion of faith;	226	Priest 2		5
or ministry, let us wait on our ministring;	226	Priest 2		6
which in the day of wrath hath not one dramme of comfort for us.	227	Priest 3		21
is careless before his Judg, and that the word of God shal judge us.	233	Priest 7		21
Oh let us all take heed what we do, God sees us, he sees whether I	234	Priest 7		26
heed what we do, God sees us, he sees whether I speak as I ought,	234	Priest 7		27
he is among us; for if we be here, hee must be here, since we are	234	Priest 7		29
where God is thanked for calling us to the knowledg of his grace,	258	Priest 22		6
God) stands fast in the Liberty wherewith Christ hath made us free.	272	Priest 31		19
when the Divell for a time leaves us, as he did our Saviour,	280	Priest 34		5
and the Angels minister to us their owne food, even joy,	280	Priest 34		6
The thrusting away of his arme makes us onely not embraced.	283	Priest 34		26
when light is brought in, God send us the light of heaven;	284	Priest 35		23
Thy hands both made us, and also made us Lords of all thy creatures;	288	Priest		13
giving us one world in our selves, and another to serve us:	288	Priest		13
giving us one world in our selves, and another to serve us:	288	Priest		14
then did'st thou place us in Paradise, and wert proceeding still	288	Priest		15
didst thou arise triumphant, and therein mad'st us victorious.	289	Priest		2
foolish and unworthy hearts rob us of the continuance of this thy	289	Priest		20
who continueth to pour his benefits upon us.	290	Priest		2
Thou hast elected us, thou hast called us, thou hast justified us,	290	Priest		3
thou hast called us, thou hast justified us, sanctified,	290	Priest		3
hast called us, thou hast justified us, sanctified, and glorified us:	290	Priest		4
Thou was born for us, and thou livedst and diedst for us:	290	Priest		4
Thou was born for us, and thou livedst and diedst for us:	290	Priest		5
Thou hast given us the blessings of this life, and of a better.	290	Priest		5
thy blessings hang in clusters, they come trooping upon us!	290	Priest		7
And now Lord, thou hast fed us with the bread of life:	290	Priest		8
O Lord, make it health and strength unto us;	290	Priest		10
still striving & prospering so long within us, untill our obedience	290	Priest		11
the measure of thy love, who hast done for us as much as may be.	290	Priest		12
is a naturall Physick most agreeable to us, and also doth preserve	298	Cornaro		14
much as she can, teacheth us how to govern our selves in sicknesse:	299	Cornaro		26
the presuming upon it ought not to leade us to a disorderly life.	300	Cornaro		21
and observation of Gods Kingdome within us, and the working thereof,	305	Valdesso		10
and Gods worke within us still observed, who workes by his Word,	309	Valdesso		32
in regard it presents us not with the same thing only when it is read	310	Valdesso		33
but enlightens us with new Considerations the more we read it.	310	Valdesso		34
it is Faith and Infidelity that shall judge us now since the Gospell,	311	Valdesso		23
and that no other sin or vertue hath any thing to doe with us;	311	Valdesso		24
if we believe, no sinne shall hurt us;	311	Valdesso		25
if we believe not, no vertue shall helpe us.	311	Valdesso		26
for it invites us to all good, according to that singular place,	313	Valdesso		19
because the anointing which we have received, and abideth in us,	314	Valdesso	V	6
I remember the Fathers forbid us to judge of the doubtfull actions	316	Valdesso		12
Yet doubtlesse the best faith in us is defective, and arrives	319	Valdesso		10
Our owne actions secure us not others judgements.	326	Proverbs	V	173
He that owes nothing, if he makes not mouthes at us, is courteous.	333	Proverbs		362
Time undermines us.	351	Proverbs		923
With customes wee live well, but Lawes undoe us.	353	Proverbs		973
What one day gives us, another takes away from us.	359	Proverbs	D	1111
Credit and estimation calls on us to live in a more splendid fashion?	373	Letters		26
entertains our Care for us that we may the more quietly intend his	374	Letters		18
so that it is not left to us to rejoyce or not rejoyce:	374	Letters		24
whatsoever befals us we must alwaies, at all times rejoyce in	374	Letters		25
at all times rejoyce in the Lord, who taketh care for us:	374	Letters		26
trouble not your selves, God is at hand to deliver us from all, or,	374	Letters		30
blessed Success, that God had given us, by moving the Duches's heart,	379	Letters		1
most pleasing, as well to us remembring, as to you deserving them,	441	Oration		26
what could have happened more pleasing to us, then the accesse	442	Oration		9
James is the protecting Saint unto us both;	442	Oration		19
your Excellencies to bee more deare unto us, in that you are	442	Oration		20
For amongst us what glorious shew is there, either of garments,	442	Oration		31
USAGE				
who by hard usage increase their travell, the Countrey Parson is very	227	Priest 3		15
means is a very loving, and sweet usage of them, both in going to,	262	Priest 24		25
USE				
By all means use sometimes to be alone.	12	Ch.-Porch		145
Then live, and use it: els, it is not true	12	Ch.-Porch		154
That thou hast gotten. Surely use alone	12	Ch.-Porch		155
Towards great persons use respective boldnesse:	16	Ch.-Porch		253
Towards great persons use respectfull boldnesse:	16	Ch.-Porch	W	253
The meanest tool, that he may chance to use.	20	Ch.-Porch		354

	PAGE	TITLE		LINE
USE (cont'd)				
They use that power against me, which I gave:	27	Sacrifice		11
Then I will use the works of thy creation,	36	Thanksgvng		35
Then will I use the works of thy creation,	36	Thanksgvng	W	35
Was of more use then I.	47	Afflict.1		34
Lord, if thou must needs use thy dart,	56	Temper 2		3
But it is that which while I use	70	Quidditie		11
To use in any thing a trick or sleight;	72	Constancie		17
O do not use me	83	Sighs & Gr.		1
He sayes, in things which use hath justly got,	86	Lent		10
To use their temperance, seeking no evasion,	86	Lent		14
Spoil the good use; lest by that argument	86	Lent		29
Spoil our good use; lest by that argument	86	Lent	W	29
I would not use a friend, as I use Thee.	93	Unkindness		5
I could not use a friend, as I use Thee.	93	Unkindness		10
I cannot use a friend, as I use Thee.	93	Unkindness		15
Nor would I use a friend, as I use Thee.	94	Unkindness		20
Yet use I not my foes, as I use thee.	94	Unkindness		25
When we grew wanton, thou didst use displeasure	97	Afflict.5		9
Do pinch and straiten thee, and use much art	99	Decay		14
That my free soul may use her wing,	109	Home		62
Such as springs use that fall, and windes that blow.	117	Providence		16
As fair as ever, and as fit to use;	118	Providence		67
Each thing that is, although in use and name	121	Providence		149
Born where thy servants both artilleries use.	139	Artillerie		18
Untill thou finde and use it to thy good:	147	Offering		23
Will use me in this kinde, the doore	152	The Bag		38
And use in baptisme, while ye pine and die:	152	The Jews		4
And so take up at use good store:	159	Praise 3		40
And to use a larger measure	177	The Rose		3
Comparisons go play, wit use thy will:	183	The Posie		10
For things misshapen, things of highest use.	191	Ch.-Milit.		46
Whereby he grew apace and scorn'd to use	195	Ch.-Milit.		191
Make his sighs to use it all,	199	L'Envoy		14
Whither my many crymes and use of sinn	205	Persever.	W	11
Poets to turn it to another use.	206	Walton 2		5
and makes great use of them in teaching, because people by what they	228	Priest 4		19
is best to be chosen, of which there is likelyest to be most use.	230	Priest 5		11
but when we use our reason, and apply our powers to the service	232	Priest 6		5
the Market day comes, or a shopkeeper, when customers use to come in.	235	Priest 8		19
making use of that excellent statute, which bindes all Parishes	244	Priest 12		22
as having continuall use of them, such as are from Gods generall	249	Priest 15		19
understand the great good use of this antient and pious ordinance,	249	Priest 15		30
And of this he makes great use.	250	Priest 16		10
Wherein a pleasantness of disposition is of great use, men being	252	Priest 18		19
and being there, makes due use of them, as of Clergy councels,	253	Priest 19		10
shewing that things of ordinary use are not only to serve in the way	257	Priest 21		13
he chooseth to permit his Parishioners rather to make use of the Law,	260	Priest 23		19
as may be of much use to him both for himself, and others.	261	Priest 23		3
be diligently perused, as being the practicall part, and of most use.	261	Priest 23		8
the Parson and his Family use to premise prayers, for this is to cure	262	Priest 23		9
he forbears not in any wise to use the delinquent as before,	263	Priest 25		26
and yet hee chuseth rather to use his neighbours, and wear out that,	265	Priest 26		29
being cunning to make use of another, and spare themselves:	265	Priest 26		34
the Law concerning such goods for the use and profit of their Parish:	270	Priest 29		3
yet if God give him not the Grace to use, and utter this well,	272	Priest 30		2
that the distinction is of singular use and comfort, especially	273	Priest 31		13
and disarmed with sedentary lives, are to know the use of their Arms:	277	Priest 32		18
having for his owne use examined the nature of it, is able	279	Priest 33		8
As for those that are ashamed to use this forme, as being old,	284	Priest 35		30
that Blessing the people is in so little use with his brethren:	285	Priest 36		2
Those who use it not, do so either out of niceness, because they like	285	Priest 36		4
that the food I was to use, was such as belonged to sickly	292	Cornaro		24
that Proverb, wherewith Gluttons use to defend themselves, to wit,	293	Cornaro		8
watching, ill aire, overmuch use of the benefit of marriage.	293	Cornaro		32
prescribes this Physick first, That he use a moderate diet:	297	Cornaro		17
what diet shall he use in diseases, which being in health he hath	299	Cornaro		24
they who finde benefit in these meats, may, yea ought to use them:	300	Cornaro		11
holy Scriptures have not only an Elementary use, but a use	306	Valdesso		18
but a use of perfection, and are able to make the man of God perfect,	306	Valdesso		18
H. Scriptures (as I wrote before) have not only an Elementary use,	309	Valdesso		21
but a use of perfection, neither can they ever be exhausted,	309	Valdesso		21
and those that have inspirations must still use Peter, Gods Word:	310	Valdesso		10
the Scriptures and this is the use of the promises of the Scriptures.	310	Valdesso		31
But the use of the Doctrinall part is more, in regard it presents us	310	Valdesso		32
to be in the dark, ought to use the first, and to forbear the second;	312	Valdesso	V	25
holy Scripture, he meaneth that we should not use it as the onely,	314	Valdesso	V	5
Every thing is of use to a houskeeper.	323	Proverbs		70
by which Scholars say, the Muses use to take up their habitations.	363	Letters		5
also concerning the fishing which the Hollanders use in our coasts,	368	Letters		10
so that the best use of them is, having, not to have them.	373	Letters		24
with which you use to conquer your enemies, and assume more mild	442	Oration		3
US'D				
As if I us'd them but for fashion.	36	Thanksgvng		36
Some Angels us'd the first; if our relief	97	Afflict.5		15
Where treach'rous Syrens us'd to sing,	214	Convert	D	7
USED				
Used, and wished, are the whole worlds light:	30	Sacrifice		110
what means of Piety, whether daily prayers be used, Grace,	251	Priest 17		23
This order being used to one, would be a little varyed to another.	256	Priest 21		16
to know what herbs may be used in stead of drugs of the same nature,	261	Priest 23		29

USED (cont'd)	PAGE	TITLE	LINE
and the ways which he used to overcome them, being told to another,	278	Priest 33	16
and largesse, which at that time is, or ought to be used.	284	Priest 35	9
But that which the Apostles used so diligently in their writings,	285	Priest 36	9
which our Saviour himselfe used, Marke 10. 16, cannot bee vain	285	Priest 36	11
And therfore St. Peter used that fearfull imprecation to Simon Magus,	285	Priest 36	29
a sober life, expressing also the means which I have used therein.	291	Cornaro	17
that unlesse I speedily used that remedy, within a few moneths I	292	Cornaro	13
Neverthelesse at a venture two remedies might be used, letting	295	Cornaro	4
the Scriptures still used, and Gods worke within us still observed,	309	Valdesso	32
and not used it for a time onely, and then cast it away,	318	Valdesso	3
I am glad I used you in it, and you have no cause to be sorry,	377	Letters	20
USEFUL			
which is so exceeding useful, and hath taken so deep roote,	287	Priest 37	8
and if there be any such which you have found useful to yourself,	366	Letters	4
USEFULL			
All such is courteous, usefull, new, or wittie.	18	Ch.-Porch	290
Be usefull where thou livest, that they may	19	Ch.-Porch	325
expounding of our Catechisme must needs be the most usefull forme.	230	Priest 5	15
This way he findes exceeding usefull, and winning;	236	Priest 8	15
he thinks it the most usefull way that a Pastor can take,	256	Priest 21	2
be amisse in this exceeding usefull point to descend to particulars:	275	Priest 32	18
The one being usefull to all Countreys, and the other especially	278	Priest 32	2
Not that weeping is not usefull, where it can be, that so the body	279	Priest 33	27
USEFULNESSE			
Usefulnesse comes by labour, wit by ease;	18	Ch.-Porch	291
USES			
Of lowly matter for high uses meet,	161	Priesthood	35
USEST			
Do as thou usest, disobey,	139	Artillerie	6
USETH			
But he to wear them. Nothing useth fire,	120	Providence	110
the means he useth are first, a holy Life, remembring what his Master	228	Priest 4	27
according as his audience is, so he useth one, or other;	230	Priest 5	17
He useth, and preferreth the ordinary Church-Catechism,	255	Priest 21	16
as the Parson useth all reverence himself, so he administers to none	259	Priest 22	11
So, where the Apothecary useth either for loosing, Rubarb,	261	Priest 23	33
the Parson useth damask or white Roses for the one, and plantaine,	261	Priest 23	34
useth all possible diligence to reduce them to the common Faith.	262	Priest 24	20
The first means he useth is Prayer, beseeching the Father of lights	262	Priest 24	21
which kinde of Poems useth to be the childe of Youth, which it most	302	Cornaro	30
He often useth this manner of speech Beleeving by Revelation,	308	Valdesso	29
when he useth the word Jurisdiction, allowing no Jurisdiction over	316	Valdesso	15
for so he useth the same word in Consideration 68 ad finem.	317	Valdesso V	8
Hee hath no leisure who useth it not.	351	Proverbs	897
yet useth his Restraining grace, even in the most wicked:	381	Woodnoth	8
with that bloud, which useth to infuse so great and worthie Spirits.	442	Oration	15
USHER			
An usher to convey our souls	123	Time	17
USHER'D			
Usher'd the Gospel ever in mens hearts,	197	Ch.-Milit.	264
USING			
Which using, and not fearing skill in th' one,	192	Ch.-Milit.	77
and using all other gestures which may expresse a hearty,	231	Priest 6	3
using pleasantly the outlandish proverb, that Prayers and Provender	251	Priest 17	13
USUALL			
admits no vaine or idle names, but such as are usuall and accustomed.	258	Priest 22	4
by taking away so much as the usuall seasons of summer and winter,	281	Priest 34	24
a deep Melancholie (a thing usuall to disorderly lives) which	294	Cornaro	18
of my friends, to adde something to my usuall stint and measure.	295	Cornaro	21
USUALLY			
Children and youths are usually deferred too long, under pretence	258	Priest 22	37
because men usually think, that servants for their mony are as other	265	Priest 26	24
For knowing what one usually can well disgest, and feeling when I go	267	Priest 26	6
And whereas there are usually three Objections made against	276	Priest 32	19
as usually happens in old mens bodies, which live without rule.	296	Cornaro	35
USURER			
To speake of an Usurer at the table marres the wine.	353	Proverbs	974
USURER'S			
an Usurers, a Taverne, a Spittle, and a Prison.	348	Proverbs	816
USURPING			
Who wert disseized by usurping lust:	54	Love 2	12
USURPS			
One aire of thoughts usurps my brain.	128	Bunch Gr.	5
UTMOST			
Which each one calls for so with utmost breath,	31	Sacrifice	146
Betwixt two theeves I spend my utmost breath,	34	Sacrifice	229
Beyond the utmost starres and poles.	123	Time	18
Wherefore with my utmost art	146	Praise 2	9
he is content to expresse this outwardly to the utmost of his power;	231	Priest 6	12
especially in his own Parish he suffers it not to his utmost power;	268	Priest 28	18
military state, he fortifyes, and strengthens with his utmost skill.	281	Priest 34	6
UTTER			
His utter foes?	134	The Method	28
And put them all to utter shame,	220	Psalm VI D	27
and utter this well, all his advantages are to his losse.	272	Priest 30	3
UTTERLY			
shall utterly be overthrown.	215	Psalm I D	24
give him the gold for it, which the Child utterly refusing, eats it,	272	Priest 30	11
Now this Lent I am forbid utterly to eat any Fish, so that I am fain	365	Letters	2

	PAGE	TITLE		LINE
VARIETY				
or for the variety of the hearers, that he may be heard at his	232	Priest 7		23
nor gravity, nor variety, since the words apart are not Scripture,	235	Priest 7		8
which it most suits withall for variety and pleasantnesse;	302	Cornaro		31
in the Church of God there is one fundamentall, but else variety.	312	Valdesso		3
to find out variety of thanks for the diversity of your favours,	363	Letters		15
VARIOUSLY				
not keep an uniform diet, but to feed variously, now more,	267	Priest 26		11
VARYED				
the order of the Catechisme would be kept, but the rest varyed:	256	Priest 21		6
This order being used to one, would be a little varyed to another.	256	Priest 21		16
VAST				
But there are two vast, spacious things,	37	The Agonie		4
O rack me not to such a vast extent;	55	Temper 1		9
VAUGHAN				
my deare Neece Mrs Dorothy Vaughan whereof two hundred pounds belongs	382	G.H.'s Will		10
To Mrss Magdalen Vaughan one hundred pound, To Mrs Catharine Vaughan	383	G.H.'s Will		5
To Mrs Catharine Vaughan One hundred pound, To Mr George Herbert one	383	G.H.'s Will		6
VAULT				
It cannot vault, or dance, or play;	70	Quidditie		5
VAUNT (see also vanting)				
VEAL				
beefe, and veal, if he addes any thing for a great day,	241	Priest 10		17
VEIL (see also vail)				
VEIN				
But may be wittie, if thou hast the vein.	16	Ch.-Porch		240
To hunt his cruell food through ev'ry vein.	37	The Agonie		12
Consuming agues dwell in ev'ry vein,	47	Afflict.1		27
He that findes a silver vein,	114	Businesse		34
Sev'n yeares ago: one vogue and vein,	128	Bunch Gr.		4
That nature hath produc'd. Let ev'ry vein	164	Grief		4
VEINS				
Did with his liquour slide into his veins.	7	Ch.-Porch		34
The marbles neat and curious veins:	67	Ch.-floore		14
And calls for musick, while his veins do swell,	98	Mortific.		14
VENERATE				
The shrine is that which thou dost venerate;	17	Ch.-Porch		267
VENGEANCE				
with shafts of vengeance stor'd.	222	Psalm VII	D	44
VENISON				
All flesh is not venison.	358	Proverbs	D	1096
Princes are venison in Heaven.	360	Proverbs	D	1156
VENOME				
If thou shalt let this venome lurk,	45	Nature		7
VENT				
Which is above the heav'ns, whose spring and vent	44	H. Bapt.1	V	5
Thy name in books, which may not vent:	69	Content	W	28
Springs vent their streams, and by expense get store:	119	Providence		71
They vent the wares, and passe them with their faults,	122	Sinnes rd.		9
They vent the wares, and passe them with their fauts	122	Sinnes rd.	V	9
VENTILATE				
And by their breathing ventilate the ill.	122	Sinnes rd.		10
VENTROUS				
On purpose from the ventrous wretch;	85	Vanitie 1		11
VENTURE				
But shreds of holinesse, that dare not venture	38	The Sinner		6
Neverthelesse at a venture two remedies might be used, letting	295	Cornaro		3
VENUS				
those many Love-poems, that are daily writ and consecrated to Venus;	363	Letters		8
VENUS'				
Wear Venus Livery? only serve her turn?	206	Walton 1		4
VERDICT				
confirmeth, and the continuance of which verdict is yet evident.	282	Priest 34		30
VERGE				
A boyling caldron, round about whose verge	129	Love unkn.		27
VERIE				
onely upon a hope of an happie issue, which yet befalls verie few.	300	Cornaro		24
are verie beautifull and convenient above most in this age,	301	Cornaro		11
VERSE				
A verse may finde him, who a sermon flies,	6	Ch.-Porch		5
Become a verse? Is there in truth no beautie?	56	Jordan 1		2
Is it no verse, except enchanted groves	56	Jordan 1		6
Seeing not onely how each verse doth shine,	58	H.Script.2		3
This verse marks that, and both do make a motion	58	H.Script.2		5
To write a verse or two is all the praise,	61	Praise 1		1
My God, a verse is not a crown,	69	Quidditie		1
Then was my heart broken, as was my verse:	79	Deniall		3
Ah wretch! what verse	102	Miserie		65
When first my verse of heav'nly joyes made mention,	102	Jordan 2	W	1
And ev'n my verse, when by the ryme and reason	109	Home		75
To make his verse, or write a hymne in kinde.	168	a true Hymn		15
Although the verse be somewhat scant,	168	a true Hymn		17
Will not a verse run smooth that bears thy name?	206	Walton 1		11
or Christ, verse 23. which, setting aside his care of his Flock,	234	Priest 7		16
and, it follows in the next verse:	374	Letters		27
VERSED				
esteemes also of cases of conscience, wherein he is much versed.	230	Priest 5		20
VERSER				
Hearken unto a Verser, who may chance	6	Ch.-Porch		3
VERSES				
Verses, ye are too fine a thing, too wise	164	Grief		13

	PAGE	TITLE		LINE
VICES (cont'd)				
discovers two sorts of vices, and two sorts of vicious persons.	264	Priest 26		5
There are some vices, whose natures are alwayes cleer, and evident,	264	Priest 26		6
There are other vices, whose natures, at least in the beginning,	264	Priest 26		8
because the natures of these vices being not evidently discussed,	264	Priest 26		17
hath exactly sifted the definitions of all vertues, and vices;	264	Priest 26		32
concerning these two vices, not because they are all that are of this	265	Priest 26		1
VICIOUS				
discovers two sorts of vices, and two sorts of vicious persons.	264	Priest 26		5
VICTORIE				
O my deare Saviour, Victorie!	36	Thanksgvng		48
To strow thy way and Victorie,	42	Easter	W	20
And feel this day thy victorie:	43	East.wings		18
And feel his death, but not his victorie.	112	Dawning		8
But England in the higher victorie:	192	Ch.-Milit.		90
For in the end I got the victorie, to my great honour, and no lesse	294	Cornaro		28
VICT'RIES				
But in all vict'ries overthrow me?	37	Reprisall		12
VICTORIES				
And sing this day thy victories:	43	East.wings		9
While Truth sat by, counting his victories:	195	Ch.-Milit.		190
But it shall spy some of there victories.	212	Bohemia	D	46
hath ever so many sermons ready penn'd, as he hath victories.	278	Priest 33		24
in the power of thy Victories, and in the wayes of thy Ordinances,	289	Priest		12
VICTORIOUS				
And trie who shall victorious prove.	35	Thanksgvng		18
didst thou arise triumphant, and therein mad'st us victorious.	289	Priest		2
and armies victorious, and retains and confirms kingdomes,	297	Cornaro		10
VICTORY				
yet the victory is alike in all, being by the self-same Spirit.	279	Priest 33		1
and with an exceeding great victory, which in the Creation needed	283	Priest 34		15
It is a great victory that comes without blood.	328	Proverbs		227
VIED (see also vye)				
Or since all musick is but three parts vied	42	Easter		15
VIES				
In vies of favours whether partie gains,	88	The Pearl		13
VIEW (see also veywe)				
And then beyond them all my Baptisme view	43	H. Bapt.1	W	2
So when I view my sinnes, mine eyes remove	43	H. Bapt.1		3
But when I view abroad both Regiments;	71	Frailtie		9
I joy, deare Mother, when I view	109	Brit. Ch.		1
The help stands close, and keeps the fear in view.	119	Providence		88
Him I view,	182	Banquet		47
I view their pieces, I compare them with those of Antiquitie;	302	Cornaro		1
VIEWS				
He views their stations, walks from doore to doore,	85	Vanitie 1		3
Where are my lines then? my approaches? views?	116	Dulnesse		17
VIGILANT				
he adviseth to be very vigilant, and not to let go the raines as soon	280	Priest 34		15
VIGOROUS				
wherein wisdome and all kinde of vertues is most vigorous;	298	Cornaro		30
in all things wherein they deal, may be more lively and vigorous.	299	Cornaro		21
VIGOUR				
which are all in their perfect vigour, but especially my Taste;	302	Cornaro		8
VILIFIED				
Wherefore the Parson suffers not the place to be vilified or debased,	270	Priest 29		7
VILLAGE				
if any neighbouring village be overburdened with poore,	254	Priest 19		1
the Village or Parish which either he lives in, or is neer unto it,	276	Priest 32		1
At other times, I repair to a village of mine, seated in the valley;	301	Cornaro		19
VILLAGES				
not onely in the citie, but also in villages and hamlets.	299	Cornaro		4
VILLANY				
My flesh, & fleshly villany,	201	H. Commun.	W	29
VINE				
Though I my vine planted and watred there:	31	Sacrifice		163
Of the true vine?	38	Good Fri.		12
I saw a vine drop grapes with J and C	116	Love-joy		2
But can he want the grape, who hath the vine?	128	Bunch Gr.	V	22
Blessed be God, who prosper'd Noahs vine,	128	Bunch Gr.		24
Early didst thou arise to plant this vine,	190	Ch.-Milit.		11
Thou didst rise early for to plant this vine,	190	Ch.-Milit.	W	11
Of Noahs shadie vine, chaste as the dove;	190	Ch.-Milit.		15
Hee that is in a Taverne thinkes he is in a vine-garden.	353	Proverbs		989
VINE-GARDEN				
Hee that is in a Taverne thinkes he is in a vine-garden.	353	Proverbs		989
VINEGER				
They gave me vineger mingled with gall,	34	Sacrifice		237
They give me vineger mingled with gall,	34	Sacrifice	W	237
VINEYARD				
Fear keepes and looks to the vineyard, and not the owner.	358	Proverbs	D	1072
VINIGER				
Take heede of the viniger of sweet wine.	336	Proverbs		451
VINTAGE				
Short boughs, long vintage.	338	Proverbs		508
VIOL				
Awake therefore, my Lute, and my Viol!	289	Priest		9
VIOLENT				
by reason of their fierce, strong, and violent natures:	271	Priest 30		11
VIRGILL				
or Tertullian, or Chrysostome, more then Tully, Virgill, or Livy;)	282	Priest 34		22

	PAGE	TITLE		LINE
VIRGIN				
A Virgin-bed, which hath a speciall Crowne	7	Ch.-Porch	W	20
that he will keep himself a virgin, he spends his dayes in fasting	237	Priest 9		18
the Virginity of the blessed Virgin out of that text Mat. 1. 25.	318	Valdesso		11
VIRGIN-BED				
A Virgin-bed, which hath a speciall Crowne	7	Ch.-Porch	W	20
VIRGINITY				
Parson considering that virginity is a higher state then Matrimony,	236	Priest 9		31
who disputed against the Virginity of the blessed Virgin out	318	Valdesso		11
VIRGINS				
and virgins, and wondreth not so much at their patient suffering,	237	Priest 9		29
VIRTUE (see alsc vertue)				
VISIBLE				
Secondly because Luxury is a very visible sinne, the Parson is very	227	Priest 3		22
so in things naturally visible & apparent, as the course of our life	380	Woodnoth		17
VISIBLY				
Thy curious vertues much more visibly:	211	Bohemia	D	14
VISICNS				
So that the Word hath the precedence even of Revelations and Visions.	318	Valdesso		25
VISIT				
if I am to visit the sick in haste, and my neerest way ly through	273	Priest 31		33
when he cometh to visit his patient, prescribes this Physick first,	297	Cornaro		16
who not onely as a friend doth visit thee, but help thee! . .	298	Cornaro		9
VISITATION				
as also the visitation Articles, which are grounded upon the Canons,	270	Priest 29		14
VISITATIONS				
He observes Visitations, and being there, makes due use of them,	253	Priest 19		9
VISITE				
takes occasion sometimes to visite in person, now one quarter of his	247	Priest 14		4
VISITING				
or in visiting the sick, or in exhortations to some of his flock	236	Priest 8		12
in visiting other sick children, and tending their wounds, . .	239	Priest 10		25
Besides this, in his visiting the sick, or otherwise afflicted,	249	Priest 15		28
Complementing, visiting, and sporting, he first commends the study	277	Priest 32		29
VISITS				
For if a friend who visits thee in thy sicknesse, and onely comforts	298	Cornaro		6
VIZ				
For whereas before the measure of my whole dayes meat, viz. . .	296	Cornaro		9
because at these yeares (viz. 83) I have made a most pleasant	302	Cornaro		28
Chuse not an house neere an Inne (viz. for noise)	330	Proverbs		286
VIZARDS				
He took fine vizards to conceal his crimes:	195	Ch.-Milit.		186
VIZARS				
both of them having forms or vizars of godlinesse, but denying	319	Valdesso	V	26
VOCATION				
and to take more paines in their vocation, as not knowing when they	245	Priest 12		3
that so they go cn more cheerfully in their vocation, and himself be	248	Priest 14		12
and so not be drowned altogether in the works of their vocation,	261	Priest 23		24
he first represents to every body the necessity of a vocation.	274	Priest 32		18
When we exhort people to continue in their vocation, it is in	381	Woodnoth		23
VOGUE				
Sev'n yeares ago: one vogue and vein, ...	128	Bunch Gr.		4
VOICE (see also voyce)				
Down with thy knees, up with thy voice.	134	The Method		30
With her enchanting voice.	170	Self-cond.		12
If ever Voice was hoarse with Cries, ...	213	Convert	D	2
Let now my Eyes, my Voice, my Heart, ...	213	Convert	D	4
My Voice, that oft with foolish Lays, ...	214	Convert	D	11
because I have now a clearer voice, then ever I had in my life.	303	Cornaro		7
VOID (see also voyd)				
Unto a hardnesse, void of love:	60	Grace		18
Alas poore mcrtall, vcid of storie, ...	169	Dial.-Anth		3
So void of sinne, ...	187	Judgement		9
either void of knowledge, or of the fear of God.	361	Proverbs	D	1176
VOLUMES				
what is that to those infinite Volumes of Divinity, which yet every	365	Letters		14
VOLUNTARIE				
They step into their voluntarie graves, ...	98	Mortific.		8
Into a voluntarie transmigration.	195	Ch.-Milit.		194
Unto a voluntarie transmigration.	195	Ch.-Milit.	W	194
VOLUNTARY				
esteeming that this private praying is a more voluntary act in them,	241	Priest 10		5
VOUCHSAFE				
Deare soul, she knew who did vouchsafe and deigne	173	Marie Magd		13
My King, my God, vouchsafe to hear	218	Psalm V	D	3
VOUCHSAF'D				
Vouchsaf'd ev'n in the midst of youth and night	171	The Glance		2
VOUCHSAFES				
For God himself vouchsafes to know	215	Psalm I	D	21
the Lord vouchsafes to weigh my tears;	220	Psalm VI	D	22
VOUCHSAFETH				
When God vouchsafeth to become our fare, ...	161	Priesthood		27
VOW				
I protest and vow, I even study Thrift, and yet I am scarce able	365	Letters		9
poore duties wish, and vow unto you of the last a plenteous Harvest.	443	Oration		6
VOWES				
examine their grounds, renew their vowes, and by occasion of both,	255	Priest 21		33
and upon what termes, and with what vowes they were Baptized.	258	Priest 22		20
VOWS				
My vows to thee most gladly, blessed Maid, ...	78	Ang.&Sts.		9
With Vows and Rants, and sensless Praise, ...	214	Convert	D	12

	PAGE	TITLE		LINE
VOYCE				
Accordingly his voyce is humble, his words treatable, and slow;	231	Priest 6		16
His voyce is as the sound of many waters, Revelations 1. . .	234	Priest 7		34
VOYD				
being unmoved in arguing, and voyd of all contentiousnesse: . .	263	Priest 24		18
VULGAR				
punishing of any, as the vulgar ever consters for signes of ill will;	263	Priest 25		25
by a Common tradition, and vulgar knowledge are reputed to be so.	266	Priest 26		26
VYE				
Armies of blessings would contend & vye	66	Ch.-lock	W	4
VYING				
And vying malice with my gentlenesse, ...	29	Sacrifice		86
VYSIT				
For though you vysit us, & wayle our case, ...	211	Paradox	D	39
WAGES				
Payd me my wages in a world of mirth.	46	Afflict.1		12
If they might mend their wages, and serve here.	59	Whitsunday		12
throw into the fire, and so they pay them their wages, all is well.	265	Priest 26		27
He that serves well needes not ask his wages.	347	Proverbs		798
Brugensis uppon the Scripture and his halfe yeares wages aforehand,	382	G.H.'s Will		20
Bostocke St. Augustines workes and his halfe yeares wages aforehand,	382	G.H.'s Will		21
then I leave to my servant Elizabeth her dubble wages given her,	382	G.H.'s Will		22
all these are over and above their wages, To Sara thirteene shillings	382	G.H.'s Will		26
WAGGONERS				
Parsons are soules waggoners.	352	Proverbs		938
WAIES				
For when he sees my waies, I dy:	63	Even-song		7
Convey a Lordship any waies.	104	Obedience	V	2
There are three waies, the Universities, the Sea, the Court.	334	Proverbs		383
There are many waies to fame.	339	Proverbs		539
To him that will, waies are not wanting.	345	Proverbs		730
WAIGHES				
He carries well, to whom it waighes not.	334	Proverbs		391
WAIGHS				
In a long journey straw waighs.	348	Proverbs		820
WAIGHT				
One common waight will press downe both, yet so	13	Ch.-Porch	W	167
The waight was such they left the doctrins there	196	Ch.-Milit.	W	203
Waight and measure take away strife.	328	Proverbs		213
WAIL (see also wayle)				
Yet if I wail not still, since still to wail	136	Ephes.		31
If troubles overtake thee, do not wail:	170	Water-crs.		4
WAIT				
More servants wait on Man, ...	92	Man		43
Since then these three wait on thy throne, ...	103	Prayer 2		19
or ministry, let us wait on our ministring;	226	Priest 2		6
WAITING				
Then whom in waiting nothing seems more slow, ...	137	Familie		15
WAITS				
and waits, least hee should determine Gods houre of coming; . .	250	Priest 16		20
Hee puls with a long rope, that waits for anothers death. . .	322	Proverbs		25
WAK'D				
I laid me down and slept, I wak'd;	216	Psalm III	D	11
WAKE				
Some may dream merrily, but when they wake, ...	108	Home		51
And wake thy sorrow?	145	Discharge		47
And wake with thee for ever.	203	Even-song	W	24
Wake and confirm that judgment now, ...	221	Psalm VII	D	23
Sleepe without supping, and wake without owing.	324	Proverbs		93
WAKING				
As a young exhalation, newly waking, ...	169	The Answer		8
WALK				
That I can walk to heav'n well neare.	50	Faith		12
That is the walk, and this the arbour;	64	Even-song		27
And ever as I walk my foot doth tredd	71	Frailtie	W	7
Well may I walk, not fear:	173	23 Psalme		14
WALKE				
He that hath a head of waxe must not walke in the sunne. . .	335	Proverbs		425
WALK'D				
Walk'd with a staffe to heav'n, and traced fountains:	37	The Agonie		3
WALKES				
The tongue walkes where the teeth speede not.	324	Proverbs		102
WALKETH				
he is not afraid of the pestilence that walketh in darkenesse,	238	Priest 9		6
WALKING				
the other in walking carelesly in our calling, he first represents	274	Priest 32		16
Charity in loving walking, and neighbourly accompanying one another,	284	Priest 35		5
It's good walking with a horse in ones hand.	348	Proverbs		804
lying, eating, walking, praying, working, still together, . .	375	Letters		19
WALKS				
He views their stations, walks from doore to doore, ...	85	Vanitie 1		3
Makes of wilde woods sweet walks and bowres.	137	Familie		12
WALKT				
Walkt by my self abroad, I saw a large	129	Love unkn.		25
WALL				
Leaping the wall that parts	52	H.Commun.		14
Rending with earthquakes the partition-wall:	190	Ch.-Milit.		26
A white wall is the paper of a foole.	349	Proverbs		839
WALLET				
In the kingdome of a cheater the wallet is carried before. . .	337	Proverbs		465

	PAGE	TITLE	LINE
WALLETS			
Estate in two parishes is bread in two wallets.	328	Proverbs	231
WALLETT			
Count not fowre except you have them in a wallett.	352	Proverbs	962
WALLOW			
Give him his dirt to wallow in all night:	101	Miserie	46
WALLOWING			
most naturally as they are, wallowing in the midst of their affairs:	247	Priest 14	6
WALLS			
Within the walls of your own breast:	68	Content	2
The inward walls and Sommers cleft and tore:	84	The World	14
as walls plaistered, windows glazed, floore paved, seats whole,	246	Priest 13	4
WALS			
Even the wals are not idle, but something is written, or painted	240	Priest 10	23
WAN			
Forthwith he waxeth wo and wan:	49	Repentance	26
When sicknesse makes him pale and wan.	92	Man	46
WANDER			
in this, that at Sermons, and Prayers, men may sleep or wander;	257	Priest 21	19
WANDERER			
Call home thine eye (that busie wanderer)	170	Self-cond.	5
WANDRINGS			
Mark all his wandrings, and enjoy his frets;	19	Ch.-Porch	315
WANT			
But if thou want it, buy it not too deere.	16	Ch.-Porch	244
Both want, and wish thy pleasing presence still.	19	Ch.-Porch	326
The worst speak something good: if all want sense,	23	Ch.-Porch	431
What pleasures could I want, whose King I served,	46	Afflict.1	13
Least want of Graces seeme thy thrift:	59	Whitsunday W	18
So I do lay the want of my desire,	66	Ch.-lock	7
Who want herbs for their wound.	76	Sunday	42
And never want	79	Employm.2	24
Draws tears, or bloud, not want an handkerchief.	112	Dawning	16
Should creatures want for want of heed their due?	119	Providence	86
But can he want the grape, who hath the wine?	128	Bunch Gr.	22
But can he want the grape, who hath the vine?	128	Bunch Gr. V	22
Then let me want thy hand & ART.	133	Paradise	9
My want of tears with store of bloud.	136	Ephes.	36
And when it stops for want of store,	157	Praise 3	4
Which want provision in the midst of all.	164	Grief	12
Want a spring-showre,	166	The Flower	27
Who cannot dresse it well, want wit, not words.	167	The Sonne	4
God doth supplie the want.	168	a true Hymn	18
What can I want or need?	172	23 Psalme	4
Lest want of aw	183	A Parodie	17
To want one ownce of sleepe,	209	Paradox D	4
it is either for want of health, or against some great Festivall,	232	Priest 7	22
as that neither they want a competent sustentation, nor her husband	239	Priest 10	18
hee receives, to want a good meal suting to the joy of the occasion.	245	Priest 12	8
of devotion to the Sacrament, but it is for want of Instruction;	258	Priest 22	38
a wonder sent to Posterity, least they complaine of want of wonders.	282	Priest 34	36
Brabling Curres never want torne eares.	322	Proverbs	52
Brawling Curres never want sore eares.	322	Proverbs V	52
If all fooles had bables, wee should want fuell.	323	Proverbs	63
All griefes with bread are lesse, or Nor woe to want.	334	Proverbs V	377
Mills and wives ever want.	334	Proverbs	388
For want of a naile the shoe is lost,	338	Proverbs	499
for want of a shoe the horse is lost,	338	Proverbs	499
for want of a horse the rider is lost.	338	Proverbs	499
To have money is a feare, to want it is a griefe.	341	Proverbs V	591
Manie things are lost for want of asking.	353	Proverbs	968
and it is this, I want Books extremely;	364	Letters	11
had taken ill courses, Follow your Book, and you shall want nothing:	364	Letters	22
but upon the want of those Books which were not to be got in England;	367	Letters	4
I forgett all thinges, so I may doe them good who want it.	376	Letters	6
5. Whereas you complaine of want of success consider how long God	381	Woodnoth	1
6. you doe not want all success.	381	Woodnoth	7
7. Though you want all success either in inclining or restraining,	381	Woodnoth	14
Complaine not of the want of success, when you have the fruit of it.	381	Woodnoth	16
WANTE			
From wante of breath proceede,	210	Paradox D	20
WANTED			
to doe) to blessed Mary Magd. & Paul, heaven had wanted chief saints:	381	Woodnoth	5
WANTING			
the one, in wanting many excitings of grace;	259	Priest 22	5
that God cannot be wanting to them in Doctrine, to whom he is so	263	Priest 24	20
ingenuous and fit imployment is never wanting to those that seek it.	275	Priest 32	10
But surely there is no such matter, if Temperance be wanting.	298	Cornaro	22
Now lest there should be any delight wanting to my old age,	302	Cornaro	37
To him that will, waies are not wanting.	345	Proverbs	730
WANTON			
When wanton pleasures becken us to thrall.	11	Ch.-Porch	118
And wanton in thy cravings, thou mayst know,	65	Ch.-monum.	19
When we grew wanton, thou didst use displeasure	97	Afflict.5	9
While blustring windes destroy the wanton bowres,	97	Afflict.5	21
The wanton lover in a curious strain	115	Dulnesse	5
WANTONLY			
She on the hills, which wantonly	110	Brit. Ch.	13
WANTONNESSE			
Yet, if thou sinne in wine or wantonnesse,	8	Ch.-Porch	49
Is wantonnesse in contemplation.	68	Content	8

	PAGE	TITLE		LINE
WARRES (cont'd)				
Some to the warres and thunder	80	Deniall		9
Doubtlesse our plaques and plentie, peace and warres	119	Providence		79
Now he will fight it out, and to the warres;	127	Giddinesse		9
He that is not in the warres is not out of danger.	354	Proverbs		999
WARRIER				
The Warrier his deere skarres no more resounds,	191	Ch.-Milit.		63
WARRS				
With the one make warrs to cease;	199	L'Envoy	W	2
WARS				
Civill Wars of France made	361	Proverbs	D	1174
WARY				
in substance, yet needeth [requireth] discreet, and wary explaining.	314	Valdesso		2
WAS (see also 'twas)				
Against thee: for his light was onely lent.	9	Ch.-Porch		82
Never was scraper brave man. Get to live;	12	Ch.-Porch		153
But the great souldiers honour was compos'd	15	Ch.-Porch		225
Was ever grief like mine?	26	Sacrifice		4
Was ever grief like mine?	26	Sacrifice		8
Was ever grief like mine?	27	Sacrifice		12
Was ever grief like mine?	27	Sacrifice		16
Was ever grief like mine?	27	Sacrifice		20
Was ever grief like mine?	27	Sacrifice		24
Was ever grief like mine?	27	Sacrifice		28
Was ever grief like mine?	27	Sacrifice		32
Was ever grief like mine?	27	Sacrifice		36
Was ever grief like mine?	27	Sacrifice		40
Was ever grief like mine?	28	Sacrifice		44
Was ever grief like mine?	28	Sacrifice		48
Was ever grief like mine?	28	Sacrifice		52
They leade me; urging, that it was not sound	28	Sacrifice		54
Was ever grief like mine?	28	Sacrifice		56
Was ever grief like mine?	28	Sacrifice		60
Was ever grief like mine?	28	Sacrifice		64
Was ever grief like mine?	28	Sacrifice		68
Was ever grief like mine?	28	Sacrifice		72
Was ever grief like mine?	29	Sacrifice		76
Was ever grief like mine?	29	Sacrifice		80
Was ever grief like mine?	29	Sacrifice		84
Was ever grief like mine?	29	Sacrifice		88
Was ever grief like mine?	29	Sacrifice		92
Was ever grief like mine?	29	Sacrifice		96
Was ever grief like mine?	29	Sacrifice		100
Was ever grief like mine?	29	Sacrifice		104
Was ever grief like mine?	30	Sacrifice		108
Was ever grief like mine?	30	Sacrifice		112
For it was their own cause who killed me:	30	Sacrifice		115
For it was their own case who killed me:	30	Sacrifice	W	115
Was ever grief like mine?	30	Sacrifice		116
And a seditious murderer he was:	30	Sacrifice		117
Was ever grief like mine?	30	Sacrifice		120
Was ever grief like mine?	30	Sacrifice		124
Was ever grief like mine?	30	Sacrifice		128
Was ever grief like mine?	30	Sacrifice		132
Was ever grief like mine?	31	Sacrifice		136
As Moses face was vailed, so is mine,	31	Sacrifice		138
As Moses face was vailed, so was mine,	31	Sacrifice	W	138
Was ever grief like mine?	31	Sacrifice		140
Was ever grief like mine?	31	Sacrifice		144
Was ever grief like mine?	31	Sacrifice		148
Was ever grief like mine?	31	Sacrifice		152
Was ever grief like mine?	31	Sacrifice		156
Was ever grief like mine?	31	Sacrifice		160
Was ever grief like mine?	31	Sacrifice		164
Was ever grief like mine?	32	Sacrifice		168
Was ever grief like mine?	32	Sacrifice		172
Was ever grief like mine?	32	Sacrifice		176
Was ever grief like mine?	32	Sacrifice		180
Was ever grief like mine?	32	Sacrifice		184
Was ever grief like mine?	32	Sacrifice		188
Was ever grief like mine?	32	Sacrifice		192
Was ever grief like mine?	33	Sacrifice		196
Was ever grief like mine?	33	Sacrifice		200
Was ever grief like mine?	33	Sacrifice		204
Was ever grief like mine?	33	Sacrifice		208
Was ever grief like mine?	33	Sacrifice		212
Never was grief like mine.	33	Sacrifice		216
Was ever grief like mine?	33	Sacrifice		220
Was ever grief like mine?	34	Sacrifice		224
Was ever grief like mine?	34	Sacrifice		228
Was ever grief like mine?	34	Sacrifice		232
Was ever grief like mine?	34	Sacrifice		236
Was ever grief like mine?	34	Sacrifice		240
Was ever grief like mine?	34	Sacrifice		244
Was ever grief like mine?	34	Sacrifice		248
Never was grief like mine.	34	Sacrifice		252
That all thy body was one doore.	35	Thanksgvng		6
Was such a grief as cannot be.	35	Thanksgvng		10
Ah! was it not enough that thou	37	Reprisall		9
They told me there, that he was lately gone	40	Redemption		6
Was writ in stone; so thou, which also art	41	Sepulchre		18

WAS (cont'd)

	PAGE	TITLE	LINE
Thus argu'd into hopes, I was preserved	46	Afflict.1 W	15
There was no moneth but May.	47	Afflict.1	22
Sorrow was all my soul; I scarce beleeved,	47	Afflict.1	29
Sorrow was all my soul; I did not know	47	Afflict.1 W	29
My mirth and edge was lost; a blunted knife	47	Afflict.1	33
Was of more use then I.	47	Afflict.1	34
I was blown through with ev'ry storm and winde.	47	Afflict.1	36
I was entangled in the world of strife,	47	Afflict.1	41
Thy wrath for sinne, as when mans sight was dimme,	49	Faith	2
Hungrie I was, and had no meat:	50	Faith	5
That which before was darkned clean	51	Faith	37
I ranne; but all I brought, was fome.	64	Even-song	12
It never was in France or Spain;	70	Quidditie	6
Which by consent was giv'n to Mansuetude.	70	Humilitie	10
On Justice was bestow'd the Foxes brain,	70	Humilitie	15
That which was dust before, doth quickly rise,	71	Frailtie	15
Thy life on earth was grief, and thou art still	73	Afflict.3	13
That was requir'd to make us gay,	76	Sunday	55
That he was fain, when thou wert destitute,	77	Avarice	7
Then was my heart broken, as was my verse:	79	Deniall	3
My breast was full of fears	79	Deniall	4
My heart was in my knee,	80	Deniall	19
And spinning phansies, she was heard to say,	84	The World	2
For us was sold.	92	Antiphon 2	12
My hand was next to them, and then my heart:	94	Life	7
That planted Paradise was not so firm,	97	Afflict.5	2
As was and is thy floting Ark; whose stay	97	Afflict.5	3
Made in the tree, where she was wont to sit,	101	Miserie	56
Indeed at first Man was a treasure,	102	Miserie	67
A ring, whose posie was, My pleasure:	102	Miserie	69
He was a garden in a Paradise:	102	Miserie	70
Such was their lustre, they did so excell,	102	Jordan 2	2
This was not quick enough, and that was dead.	102	Jordan 2	10
Where in the deed there was an intimation	105	Obedience	33
The wood was all embellished	106	Sion	4
Did not affect thee much, was not thy aim;	106	Sion	8
Something there was, that sow'd debate:	106	Sion	9
When man was lost, thy pitie lookt about	107	Home	13
But there was none; at least no help without:	107	Home	15
Blessed be God, whose love it was	110	Brit. Ch.	28
And first I found the corner, where was J,	112	JESU	5
After, where ES, and next where U was graved.	112	JESU	6
That to my broken heart he was I ease you,	112	JESU	9
Who for man was sold, can see;	114	Dialogue	15
When th' earth was dry, thou mad'st a sea of wet:	120	Providence	113
To whom thy sithe a hatchet was,	122	Time	9
There was a Prince of old	125	Peace	22
And have good cause: there it was dipt and di'd,	129	Love unkn.	16
Enforceth tears. Your heart was foul, I fear.	129	Love unkn.	18
Yet still askt pardon, and was not deni'd.	129	Love unkn.	21
But you shall heare. After my heart was well,	129	Love unkn.	22
Was in great letters set AFFLICTION.	129	Love unkn.	28
Who was to take it from me, slipt his hand,	130	Love unkn.	34
The offerers heart. Your heart was hard, I fear.	130	Love unkn.	37
When with my pleasures ev'n my rest was gone?	130	Love unkn.	53
It must be he. Your heart was dull, I fear.	130	Love unkn.	56
The Font did onely, what was old, renew:	130	Love unkn.	64
The Caldron suppled, what was grown too hard:	130	Love unkn.	65
The Thorns did quicken, what was grown too dull:	130	Love unkn.	66
Was cleare as heav'n, from whence it came.	135	Divinitie	14
Is more then God was, who was hungrie here.	138	The Size	14
On whose meridian was engraven,	138	The Size	46
He that did but look up, was proud and bold.	141	Justice 2	6
A long it was and weary way.	141	Pilgrimage	3
But I was quicken'd by my houre.	142	Pilgrimage	10
Here I was robb'd of all my gold,	142	Pilgrimage	16
Was all I found.	142	Pilgrimage	24
I was deceiv'd:	142	Pilgrimage	30
My hill was further: so I flung away,	142	Pilgrimage	31
But I was told by one, it could not be;	143	Holdfast	3
Nay, ev'n to trust in him, was also his:	143	Holdfast	6
And well it was for thee, when this befell,	144	Discharge	16
When he was come, as travellers are wont,	151	The Bag	19
But as he was returning, there came one	151	The Bag	25
Sure there was wine	153	The Collar	10
Before my sighs did drie it: there was corn	153	The Collar	11
That all was not so fair, as I conceiv'd,	155	Assurance	8
And coin large hopes; but, that I was deceiv'd:	155	Assurance	10
Either the league was broke, or neare it;	155	Assurance	11
But also mine; as when the league was made	156	Assurance	28
The glasse was full and more.	158	Praise 3	36
When almost all was out, God made a stay,	160	The Pulley	8
Because the search was dumbe before:	162	The Search	23
But all was one.	162	The Search	24
Could have recover'd greennesse? It was gone	166	The Flower	9
My heart was meaning all the day,	168	a true Hymn	2
Poore death! and who was hurt thereby?	169	Dial.-Anth	5
Ev'n God himself: wherefore she was not loth,	173	Marie Magd	15
Then should the Pomander, which was before	175	The Odour	16
In delights of earth was drown'd;	182	Banquet	33

WAS (cont'd)

	PAGE	TITLE		LINE
Thy mouth was open, but thou couldst not sing.	185	Death		4
The course was westward, that the sunne might light	190	Ch.-Milit.		17
Goshen was darknesse, Egypt full of lights,	191	Ch.-Milit.		43
Learning was pos'd, Philosophie was set,	191	Ch.-Milit.		51
And Ergo was transform'd into Amen.	191	Ch.-Milit.		56
Him in his members, who for him was slain.	192	Ch.-Milit.		70
Within a sheet of paper, which was rent	192	Ch.-Milit.		95
His highest was an ox or crocodile,	193	Ch.-Milit.		122
And being craftier much then Goodnesse was,	193	Ch.-Milit.		124
But all was glorious cheating, brave deceit,	193	Ch.-Milit.		135
He was a God, now he's an Emperour.	194	Ch.-Milit.		140
Glorie was his chief instrument of old:	194	Ch.-Milit.		143
Which soon was blown to such a mightie flame,	194	Ch.-Milit.		145
His grave aspect was liker heav'n then hell:	194	Ch.-Milit.	W	168
Onely there was a handsome picture by,	194	Ch.-Milit.		169
As Sinne in Greece a Prophet was before,	195	Ch.-Milit.		171
Then what was in their tongue, did overcome;	196	Ch.-Milit.		202
The waight was such they left the doctrins there	196	Ch.-Milit.	W	203
Yet with two faces, as their Janus was;	196	Ch.-Milit.		207
Thy ancient baptism which when I was foule	202	love	W	11
How sweet a friend was he, who being griev'd	439	Walton 5		15
But that my Inke was factious for this side.	209	L. Bacon	D	12
If ever Voice was hoarse with Cries,	213	Convert	D	2
If ever Heart was sore with Sighs;	213	Convert	D	3
when I was in distress.	217	Psalm IV	D	4
that was at peace with me:	221	Psalm VII	D	12
that was my causeless foe:	221	Psalm VII	D	14
so that while they answer, As it was in the beginning, &c.	231	Priest 6		33
sacrifices as they did of old, which was of beasts devoyd of reason;	232	Priest 6		5
never was there such care of a flock expressed, save in the great	234	Priest 7		20
but only by those means, by which at first it was obtained.	237	Priest 9		21
the choyce of his wife was made rather by his eare, then by his eye;	238	Priest 9		26
or was not fit for him to do, by taking both sorts of food into them,	241	Priest 10		32
For meat was made for man, not man for meat.	242	Priest 10		32
This was not so well said, as it might have been forborn;	252	Priest 18		8
as being the servant of him, in whom there was no guile.	253	Priest 19		2
Was it made, or came it by chance?	256	Priest 21		7
made the answer so plaine, that he was even ashamed of his ignorance;	257	Priest 21		6
or whether he needed a helper, and who was that helper.	257	Priest 21		9
for he was the true householder, who bringeth out of his treasure	261	Priest 23		14
because of the suddain passing from that which was just now lawfull,	264	Priest 26		21
when his storing, which was even now good, passeth from good to bad.	264	Priest 26		30
minde being defixed on it with those nailes wherewith his Master was:	267	Priest 27		30
and being in the world as he was, hath this undoubted pledge of his	269	Priest 28		18
do it, then he that is generally learned, and was never sick.	278	Priest 33		29
his preaching, but afterwards also, as Mat. 22. 35. He was tempted:	280	Priest 34		9
that this very thing was intended by God, that the Jewes should be	282	Priest 34		11
in all Lands, was intended not only for a punishment to them;	282	Priest 34		14
therefore this kind of Punishment was chosen rather then any other.	282	Priest 34		17
But this was not proper to Christ, or the Apostles only,	285	Priest 36		12
no more then to be a spirituall Father was appropriated to them.	285	Priest 36		13
for it was not the person, but Priesthood, that blessed;	285	Priest 36		22
who was to shew all humility before his Passion, yet he allows in his	285	Priest 36		27
Thou was born for us, and thou livedst and diedst for us:	290	Priest		4
that Intemperance was not such an evil, but it might easily be	291	Cornaro		6
first caused me to leave Intemperance, to which I was much addicted:	291	Cornaro		19
as farre from it by Nature, as it was neare it by Intemperance.	291	Cornaro		27
When therefore I was thus affected [afflicted] from the thirtie fifth	292	Cornaro		1
the Physicians told me that yet there was one help for me,	292	Cornaro		3
that the food I was to use, was such as belonged to sickly	292	Cornaro		24
was such as belonged to sickly constitutions, and that in a small	292	Cornaro		24
and saw that it was no hard thing to do so, but the proper duty	292	Cornaro		32
that I was exceedingly helped, and by continuance thereof,	292	Cornaro		35
seem to some incredible) I was perfectly cured of all my infirmities.	292	Cornaro		37
within lesse then a yeare I was not onely freed from all those evils	293	Cornaro		20
whereinto I was wont, when I pleased my Sense & Appetite.	293	Cornaro		23
because from the time that I was made whole, I never since departed	293	Cornaro		25
and therefore never was sick by any of these inconveniences,	294	Cornaro		9
that this suit and contention was raised by the Divine Providence,	294	Cornaro		24
This I found by experience, when I was seventie yeares old:	294	Cornaro		35
it happened that the coach was overturned, and then was dragged	294	Cornaro		37
and then was dragged for a good space by the furie of the horses,	294	Cornaro		37
whereby my head and whole bodie was sore hurt, and also one of my	294	Cornaro		39
when the Physicians saw in what case I was, they concluded that I	295	Cornaro		2
and fever (which was certainly expected) might be hindred.	295	Cornaro		6
I was led by the advice of Physicians, and the dayly importunitie	295	Cornaro		19
that Nature was contented with a little, and that I had for many	295	Cornaro		26
that Custome was turned into Nature, and therefore it was agreeable	295	Cornaro		28
and therefore it was agreeable to reason, that my yeares increasing,	295	Cornaro		28
two Italian Proverbs, the one whereof was, He that will eat much,	295	Cornaro		34
The other Proverb was, The meat which remaineth, profits more then	296	Cornaro		1
and flesh, and broth, was twelve ounces exactly weighed;	296	Cornaro		10
of my drink, which before was foureteen ounces, I made now sixteen.	296	Cornaro		12
although I was now seventie eight yeares old, and my bodie spent	296	Cornaro		25
and the season of the yeare was winter and most cold aire.	296	Cornaro		27
although it was a sore evil, yet had no power to kill me.	297	Cornaro		2
though it was but a little excesse, in a few dayes had so soon	297	Cornaro		5
and that in much smaller quantitie then when he was well.	299	Cornaro		32
In former time it was not so, because the place was moorish	301	Cornaro		26
because the place was moorish and unhealthy, fitter for beasts then	301	Cornaro		26

WAS (cont'd)	PAGE	TITLE		LINE
when I was given to disorder and all the delights that could be.	302	Cornaro		10
I was one of those that was deputed for the managing of that work,	302	Cornaro		16
I was one of those that was deputed for the managing of that work,	302	Cornaro		17
And if a Greek Poet of old was praised, that at the age of 73 yeares	302	Cornaro		33
sheweth, and I also, when I was a young man, too well found.	303	Cornaro		15
and the working thereof, of which he was a very diligent observer.	305	Valdesso		11
And Joshua was to meditate therein Day and Night.	306	Valdesso		21
same Psalme it is evident, that he was not meanly conversant in them.	309	Valdesso		28
yet Peter was to be sent for, and those that have inspirations must	310	Valdesso		9
which strictly he was not, though in the point of Resurrecticn he	316	Valdesso		8
have made it appeare, that it was done by Gods immediate precept.	316	Valdesso		26
on both sides, and was just in the Canaanites and Israelites both.	316	Valdesso		29
how this opinion could befall so good a man as it seems Valdesso was,	317	Valdesso		32
shewes that he was continually conversant in it, and not used it	318	Valdesso		2
I wept when I was borne, and every day shewes why.	327	Proverbs		199
Never was strumpet faire.	336	Proverbs		431
I was taken by a morsell, saies the fish.	342	Proverbs		627
Mention not a halter in the house of him that was hanged. . .	343	Proverbs		671
Long jesting was never good.	344	Proverbs		694
Divine grace was never slow.	345	Proverbs		710
There comes nought out of the sacke but what was there. . .	348	Proverbs		833
There come nought out of the sacke but what was there. . . .	348	Proverbs	V	833
Saint Luke was a Saint and a Physitian, yet is dead. . . .	354	Proverbs		1008
Amiens was taken by the Fox, and retaken by the Lion. . . .	356	Proverbs	D	1036
Whatsoever was the father of a disease, ...	357	Proverbs	D	1048
an ill dyet was the mother.	357	Proverbs	D	1048
You know I was sick last Vacation, neither am I yet recovered,	364	Letters		32
Letter in yours, for it was because I know your Lodging, but not his.	367	Letters		24
My Lord of Buckingham was cbserved on Christmas day to bee so devout	368	Letters		16
upon this he was forbid Court & kingdome, yet was seene lately neere	368	Letters		34
yet was seene lately neere the king, which scme observing who heard	368	Letters		35
I was the better content because I was in hope I should my self carry	372	Letters		14
was the better content because I was in hope I should my self carry	372	Letters		15
but advance them, was lovingly done, and like a good brother.	375	Letters		3
Yet truly it was none of my meaning, when I wrote, to putt one of our	375	Letters		4
I was desirous to putt a good mind into the way of charity, . . .	375	Letters		7
a good mind into the way of charity, and that was all I intended.	375	Letters		8
I was glad of your Cambridge newes, but you joyed me exceedingly	377	Letters		18
therfore your choice at first was good	380	Woodnoth		6
WASH				
You give us teares to wash them: lett those beams	44	H. Bapt.1	W	7
To wash away my stubborn thought:	139	Artillerie		15
So to bring in wherewith to wash:	173	Marie Magd		17
Then did I wash you with my tears, and more, ...	176	Forerunners		16
Sometimes, when as I wash, I say	202	love	W	7
And shrodely, as I think, Lord wash my soule	202	love	W	8
And wash away my Shame.	214	Convert	D	10
the other for the foulnesse, as wash, and durt, and things thereinto	241	Priest 10		29
WASHED				
And yet in washing one, she washed both.	173	Marie Magd		18
altar to be bathed, and washed in the sacred Laver of Christs blood.	231	Priest 6		9
services done by men-servants at home, and his linnen washed abroad.	237	Priest 9		10
only to serve in the way of drudgery, but to be washed, and cleansed,	257	Priest 21		15
This place is washed with the river Brenta;	301	Cornaro		23
WASHES				
That washes what it shows. Who can indeare	58	H.Script.1		10
WASHETH				
One hand washeth another, and both the face.	329	Proverbs		239
WASHING				
And yet in washing one, she washed both.	173	Marie Magd		18
For washing his hands, none sels his lands.	323	Proverbs		54
WASHT				
Whom God in Baptisme washt with his own blood.	6	Ch.-Porch		8
And washt, and wrung: the very wringing yet	129	Love unkn.		17
WAST				
But thou wast up by break of day, ...	42	Easter		21
But thou wast up before myne houre	42	Easter	W	21
Thou, who from me wast sold, ...	52	H.Commun.		3
Thou, who for me wast sold, ...	52	H.Commun.	V	3
By that I knew that thou wast in the grief, ...	73	Afflict.3		2
Lord with what glorie wast thou serv'd of old, ...	106	Sion		1
Wast thou of old, ...	141	Justice 2		2
Since thou in death wast none of thine, ...	157	Clasping		17
Death, thou wast once an uncouth hideous thing, ...	185	Death		1
WASTE				
The bloud did make, which thou didst waste?	107	Home		8
Is your waste;	179	Invitation		2
WASTED				
A wasted place, but sometimes rich.	142	Pilgrimage		15
All wasted?	153	The Collar		16
WASTEFULL				
None is so wastefull as the scraping dame.	13	Ch.-Porch		173
WASTERS				
Building and marrying of Children are great wasters.	321	Proverbs		11
WATCH				
And growth of it: if with thy watch, that too	24	Ch.-Porch		454
Then as dispersed herbs do watch a potion, ...	58	H.Script.2		7
Watch an advantage to appeare.	79	Employm.2		20
I gave to Hope a watch of mine: but he	121	Hope		1
Love God, and love your neighbour. Watch and pray.	135	Divinitie		17

WATCH (cont'd)	PAGE	TITLE		LINE
He keepeth his watch and ward, night and day against the proper	238	Priest 9		1
The Countrey Parson, where ever he is, keeps Gods watch;	252	Priest 18		2
This is called keeping Gods watch, when the baits which the enemy	252	Priest 18		13
WATCHING				
One houre of watching; but their drowsie brain	27	Sacrifice		30
wearinesse, watching, ill aire, overmuch use of the benefit	293	Cornaro		31
WATCHINGS				
abstinence, watchings, and constant prayers, and mortifications in	237	Priest 9		32
WATER				
More backward still, and to that water flie,	43	H. Bapt.1		4
To water these.	57	Employm. 1		20
That cordiall water to our ground,	59	Whitsunday		18
But with a richer drug, then scalding water,	130	Love unkn.		40
The Water-course.	170	Water-crs.		T
The Water, and the Earth both unto thee	439	Walton 5		7
Which mingles water with thy Rhenish wine	213	Bohemia	D	64
In water kept, maugre the powers	213	L' Envoy	D	8
And water with salt tears my Bed,	220	Psalm VI	D	15
are but two devouring elements, fire, and water, he hath both in him;	234	Priest 7		33
the Priests Benedicite, and his holy water were over highly valued;	286	Priest 36		16
parted with rills of running water, which truely is very delightfull.	301	Cornaro		16
The scalded dog feares cold water.	321	Proverbs		13
The scalded head feares cold water.	321	Proverbs	V	13
Water trotted is as good as oates.	325	Proverbs		131
The mill cannot grind with the water that's past.	326	Proverbs		153
you can have but water of it.	327	Proverbs		180
Good words quench more then a bucket of water.	329	Proverbs		263
Soft words quench more then cold water.	329	Proverbs	V	263
Let none say, I will not drinke water.	331	Proverbs		310
Water a farre off quencheth not fire.	334	Proverbs		398
and his horse drinke at every water,	336	Proverbs		434
Water, fire, and souldiers, quickly make roome.	338	Proverbs		514
Under water, famine; under snow, bread.	339	Proverbs		516
Ships feare fire more then water.	351	Proverbs		909
WATER-COURSE				
The Water-course.	170	Water-crs.		T
WATER'S				
But rather turn the pipe, and waters course	170	Water-crs.		6
WATERING				
Although it raine, throw not away thy watering pot.	332	Proverbs		325
Folly growes without watering.	341	Proverbs		581
WATERS				
Because the raging waters still are high:	29	Sacrifice		95
Waters above the Heavens. O sweet streams	44	H. Bapt.1	W	5
Waters united are our navigation;	92	Man		38
In shallow waters heav'n doth show;	97	Charms & K		17
If as the windes and waters here below	132	The Storm		1
A lake of brackish waters on the ground	142	Pilgrimage		23
Hir waters alsoe and desired Bathe.	210	Paradox	D	18
Which, planted by the waters, shall	214	Psalm I	D	9
His voyce is as the sound of many waters, Revelations 1.	234	Priest 7		34
many waters could not quench thy love!	288	Priest		31
they break forth like mighty waters on every side.	290	Priest		7
Take heede of still waters, the quick passe away.	326	Proverbs		171
A great ship askes deepe waters.	336	Proverbs		449
judge me then by those waters, and not by my ink, and then you shall	372	Letters		4
WATRED				
Though I my vine planted and watred there:	31	Sacrifice		163
WATRING				
As watring pots give flowers their lives.	90	Afflict.4		10
WATRISH				
Which else shows watrish, bleak, & thin.	67	Windows		10
Turne watrish Holland to a chrystalline sphere.	211	Bohemia	D	12
WATRY				
My grief hath need of all the watry things,	164	Grief		3
WAVE				
Wert thou a winde or wave,	154	Glimpse		8
WAVERING				
at severall times and occasions, the Parson setleth wavering minds.	283	Priest 34		5
WAVES				
Cuts through the working waves, that he may fetch	85	Vanitie 1		9
When waves do rise, and tempests rage.	97	Afflict.5		6
Successive nights, like rolling waves,	98	Mortific.		11
Though windes and waves assault my keel,	151	The Bag		2
Great waves of trouble combating my brest:	202	love	W	14
When winds and waves rise highest, I am sure,	439	walton 6		3
WAVING				
Any thought of waving.	114	Dialogue		4
WAXE				
He that hath a head of waxe must not walke in the sunne.	335	Proverbs		425
WAXETH				
Forthwith he waxeth wo and wan:	49	Repentance		26
my sight with sorrow waxeth dim.	220	Psalm VI	D	16
WAY				
Need or Incontinency: the first way	7	Ch.-Porch	W	16
(All in a shipwrack shift their severall way)	8	Ch.-Porch		44
Pride and full sinnes have made the way a road.	9	Ch.-Porch		72
Hee that desires is more then halfe the way.	10	Ch.-Porch	W	90
The way to make thy sonne rich, is to fill	11	Ch.-Porch		109
Lose not thy self, nor give thy humours way:	12	Ch.-Porch		143

WAY (cont'd)

	PAGE	TITLE		LINE
Onely a herauld, who that way doth passe,	14	Ch.-Porch		197
A stumbler stumbles least in rugged way.	15	Ch.-Porch		214
But love is lost, the way of friendship's gone,	17	Ch.-Porch		275
Kindnesse, good parts, great places are the way	19	Ch.-Porch		327
As those, who mock at Gods way of salvation.	24	Ch.-Porch		446
Who am the way of truth, the true relief;	27	Sacrifice		38
Who am the way & Truth, the true relief;	27	Sacrifice	W	38
Which shews my bloud to be the onely way,	31	Sacrifice		158
I got me flowers to straw thy way;	42	Easter		19
To strow thy way and Victorie,	42	Easter	W	20
A narrow way and little gate	44	H. Bapt.2		2
I had my wish and way:	47	Afflict.1		20
The way that takes the town;	47	Afflict.1		38
The milkie way, the bird of Paradise,	51	Prayer 1		12
But by the way of nourishment and strength	52	H.Commun.		7
Making thy way my rest,	52	H.Commun.		9
Knoweth the ready way,	52	H.Commun.		20
As may consume our lusts, and make thee way.	54	Love 2		5
Yet take thy way; for sure thy way is best:	55	Temper 1		21
Without thy help, leads us his way to Hell.	59	Whitsunday	W	16
O come! for thou dost know the way.	61	Grace		21
By way of imprest, all my future mone.	62	Afflict.2		15
Put our amendment in our way,	64	Even-song		23
You know the way to heavens doore.	66	Ch.-mus.		12
Kill'd in the way by chance.	70	Humilitie		16
Allows for that, and keeps his constant way:	73	Constancie		28
Thy torch doth show the way.	75	Sunday		7
Each took his way; some would to pleasures go,	80	Deniall		8
Yet to go part of that religious way,	87	Lent		32
Who goeth in the way which Christ hath gone,	87	Lent		37
Who goeth in that way which Christ hath gone,	87	Lent	V	37
Who goeth in the way that Christ hath gone,	87	Lent	W	37
Scarce knows the way;	98	Mortific.		4
Is my God this way? no, they would reply:	99	Decay		8
Thou mightst make way for liberalitie!	103	Prayer 2		18
Convey a Lordship any way	104	Obedience		2
Let me not think an action mine own way,	104	Obedience		18
Lord, let it now by way of purchase go.	105	Obedience		35
Which way so-e're I look, I see.	108	Home		50
So the way to fit me for it,	115	Dialogue		19
So the way is none of mine:	115	Dialogue		22
As bouls go on, but turning all the way.	118	Providence		60
Which knows his way without a guide:	134	Divinitie		4
A long it was and weary way.	141	Pilgrimage		3
Can both the way and end be tears?	142	Pilgrimage		28
Just as I went, None goes that way	142	Pilgrimage		33
He did descend, undressing all the way.	151	The Bag		12
Doubtlesse, but in the way of punishment,	155	Assurance		4
Come, my Way, my Truth, my Life:	156	The Call		1
Such a Way, as gives us breath:	156	The Call		2
So strength first made a way;	160	The Pulley		6
But cooling by the way, grows pursie and slow,	169	The Answer		10
Yet if you go, I passe not; take your way:	177	Forerunners		31
Till all depart: so went the Church her way,	191	Ch.-Milit.		33
Till all be gone. so went the Church her way,	191	Ch.-Milit.	W	33
That as before Empire and Arts made way,	192	Ch.-Milit.		83
My God, thou dost prepare for them a way	197	Ch.-Milit.		249
Like Comick Lovers ever one way runn:	198	Ch.-Milit.	W	271
In Bread & mee, the way thou takest	200	H. Commun.	W	17
But then there comes into my way	202	love	W	10
Nor hath in way of sinners stood,	214	Psalm I	D	3
the way that right'ous men have gone:	215	Psalm I	D	22
and straight ye perish from the way:	216	Psalm II	D	30
thy perfect way disclose.	219	Psalm V	D	24
That the way to please him, is to feed my Flocke diligently	224	Priest		4
Some in a preparatory way, whose aim and labour must be not only	226	Priest 2		8
This Body he made by way of expounding the Church Catechisme,	230	Priest 5		8
Oh Lord, I know that the way of man is not in himself, &c.	234	Priest 7		5
Whereas the other way of crumbling a text into small parts,	235	Priest 7		6
This way he findes exceeding usefull, and winning;	236	Priest 8		15
knowing that it can no way be preserved, but only by those means,	237	Priest 9		20
for then commonly the stream of temptations is turned another way,	238	Priest 9		23
demanding an account, but not by the way of an account.	239	Priest 9		3
that he may, if not the best way, yet any way, make his Parish good.	244	Priest 11		5
if not the best way, yet any way, make his Parish good.	244	Priest 11		5
but that all bee in a competent way of getting their living.	244	Priest 12		21
at his door, whom God puts in his way, and makes his neighbours.	245	Priest 12		20
that so the thanks may go the right way, and thither onely,	245	Priest 12		33
but as desiring to keep the middle way between superstition,	246	Priest 13		24
So that they excellently score out the way, and fully, and exactly	246	Priest 13		32
However, one way or other, he ever reproves them, that he may keep	248	Priest 14		23
perfecting our Redemption no other way, then by sorrow;	249	Priest 15		23
Therefore those he meets on the way he blesseth audibly,	251	Priest 17		2
but such as are every way fitting to do his Countrey true	252	Priest 19		28
hee findes some way of releeving it, and reducing the Manna,	254	Priest 19		3
which exceedingly delights him as by way of exercise upon himself,	255	Priest 21		11
and by way of preaching to himself, for the advancing of his own	255	Priest 21		12
may then by an honourable way take occasion to be better instructed.	255	Priest 21		31
he thinks it the most usefull way that a Pastor can take,	256	Priest 21		2
And this is an admirable way of teaching, wherein the Catechized will	256	Priest 21		17

WAY (cont'd)	PAGE	TITLE		LINE
things of ordinary use are not only to serve in the way of drudgery,	257	Priest 21		14
for thou art not only the feast, but the way to it. . . .	258	Priest 22		1
and his Saints, and by way of undertaking for a Christian soul.	258	Priest 22		13
wise men have thought it the best way of preserving a state to reduce	258	Priest 22		15
they are most eminent, is the most gainfull way of Conversation.	260	Priest 23		7
as also by way of illustration, even as our Saviour made plants	261	Priest 23		13
he takes it either in an humble way, saying nothing at all; . .	269	Priest 28		6
or else in a slighting way, shewing that reproaches touch him no	269	Priest 28		7
or in a sad way, greived at his own, and others sins, which	269	Priest 28		9
or else in a doctrinall way, saying to the contemner, Alas, . .	269	Priest 28		12
or lastly, in a Triumphant way, being glad, and joyfull, . .	269	Priest 28		16
and my neerest way ly through the Church, I will not doubt to go	273	Priest 31		34
which way soever he turnes, hath two pledges of Gods Love, .	283	Priest 34		17
because it is not performed by way of request, but of confidence,	286	Priest 36		7
they had a great desire to know the way of my life, and how I came	291	Cornaro		12
for this had every way great force for the recovering and preserving	292	Cornaro		5
being directed by them in the way I ought to hold, I understood,	292	Cornaro		23
self to this course of life, that I never went a foot out of the way.	292	Cornaro		34
orderly life is the most sure way & ground of health and long dayes,	297	Cornaro		12
the experience of so many yeares have learned to give way to Reason:	303	Cornaro		21
a fair and desirable death, which Nature brings by way of resolution.	303	Cornaro		29
should have weaknesses is no way repugnant to the way of Gods Spirit	316	Valdesso		3
weaknesses is no way repugnant to the way of Gods Spirit in them,	316	Valdesso		3
Make hast to an ill way that you may get out of it.	325	Proverbs		124
Good land, evill way.	347	Proverbs		802
Hee goes not out of his way, that goes to a good Inne.	348	Proverbs		831
The life of man is a winter way.	351	Proverbs		914
The way is an ill neighbour.	351	Proverbs		915
Princes have no way.	352	Proverbs		956
puts not himselfe into a good way.	354	Proverbs		995
and that the Horse is every way fit for me, and I will strive	364	Letters		1
And yet if a Book of four or five Shillings come in my way, . .	365	Letters		12
either by engaging my future Annuity, or any other way, I desire you,	365	Letters		21
to see a Sister, in a way I knew not, in the midst of much business,	371	Letters		3
I was desirous to putt a good mind into the way of charity, . .	375	Letters		8
by the way of supporting either it (in regard of the citty) or your	380	Woodnoth		27
WAYES				
Allows thee choise of paths: take no by-wayes;	7	Ch.-Porch		14
I'le build a spittle, or mend common wayes, ...	36	Thanksgvng		33
Thine own gift good, yet me from my wayes taking.	48	Afflict.1		54
Mend my estate in any wayes, ...	61	Praise 1		3
That travelleth by-wayes:	87	Lent		39
I know the wayes of Learning; both the head	88	The Pearl		1
I know the wayes of Honour, what maintains	88	The Pearl		11
I know the wayes of Pleasure, the sweet strains, ...	89	The Pearl		21
I cannot skill of these thy wayes.	95	Justice 1		1
I cannot skill of these my wayes.	96	Justice 1		12
Can thy strange wayes rehearse?	102	Miserie		66
Onely to Man thou hast made known thy wayes, ...	117	Providence		6
All things that are, though they have sev'rall wayes, ...	121	Providence		145
It go for one, hath many wayes in store	121	Providence		150
Extolleth many wayes, yet this one more.	121	Providence		152
Closets are halls to them; and hearts, high-wayes.	126	Confession		18
Could he but take them right, and in their wayes.	132	Mans medly		33
I give to thee, who knowest all my wayes, ...	185	A Wreath		3
My crooked winding wayes, wherein I live, ...	185	A Wreath		4
So live and like, that I may know thy wayes, ...	185	A Wreath		10
Or, since thy wayes are deep, and still the same, ...	206	Walton 1		10
And those wayes which the wicked go	215	Psalm I	D	23
just, prudent, temperate, bold, grave in all his wayes. . . .	227	Priest 3		3
ability of a Parson to lead his people exactly in the wayes of Truth,	230	Priest 5		21
and tracker of Gods wayes, sets up as many encouragements . .	244	Priest 11		2
and true in all his wayes, as being the servant of him, . .	253	Priest 19		2
and in the wayes of thy Ordinances, and in the truth of thy Love,	289	Priest		12
because many wayes thither are so ordered, that they all meet and end	301	Cornaro		21
by the regularitie of my life I have shut out death all other wayes.	303	Cornaro		28
Take heed of foul dirty wayes, and long sicknesse.	360	Proverbs	D	1153
& have endeavoured many wayes, to find out a man for it. . .	378	Letters		7
not considering you any other wayes, as neyther I my self desire	378	Letters		15
& so turn you all, in your severall wayes, one to the other,	378	Letters		26
WAYLE				
For though you vysit us, & wayle our case, ...	211	Paradox	D	39
WAYS (see also waies)				
or any ways distressed, fails not to afford his best comforts,	249	Priest 15		14
and the ways which he used to overcome them, being told to another,	278	Priest 33		16
WE (see also wee)				
For we have wit to mark them, and to spare.	9	Ch.-Porch		69
We all are but cold suitours; let us move	22	Ch.-Porch		400
The Jews refused thunder; and we, folly.	24	Ch.-Porch		449
Be down, then winde up both; since we shall be	24	Ch.-Porch		455
Yet do we still persist as we began, ...	41	Sepulchre		21
We count three hundred, but we misse:	42	Easter		29
Thus are we to delights: but we are all	48	Repentance		9
As we did rise, we die together.	49	Repentance		24
Of strange delights, where we may wish & take.	58	H.Script.1		7
Did not excite thee, we should wholly sink.	60	Whitsunday		24
Lord, though we change, thou art the same;	60	Whitsunday		25
Then we must needs for that day make a match.	62	Mattens		4
We paint the devil foul, yet he	63	Sinne 2		2
By sight of sinne we should grow mad.	63	Sinne 2		8

WE (cont'd)

	PAGE	TITLE		LINE
Yet as in sleep we see foul death, and live:	63	Sinne 2		9
We both together sweetly live and love,	65	Ch.-mus.		7
Whom, if we were not very dull,	75	Sunday		18
We could not choose but look on still;	75	Sunday		19
We sullied by our foul offence:	76	Sunday		51
Wherefore that rcbe we cast away,	76	Sunday		52
Till that we both, being toss'd from earth,	77	Sunday		62
Nay, thou hast got the face of man; for we	77	Avarice		10
Whom we do all jcyntly adore and praise,	78	Ang.&Sts.		17
Therefore we dare not from his garland steal,	78	Ang.&Sts.		24
What's done on earth, we shall not fare the worse,	78	Ang.&Sts.		27
What's done on earth, we shall not feare the worse,	78	Ang.&Sts.	V	27
Since we are ever ready to disburse,	78	Ang.&Sts.		29
Since we are ever ready to discourse,	78	Ang.&Sts.	V	29
But we are still too young or old;	79	Employm.2		26
But we are ever young or old;	79	Employm.2	W	26
Before we do our wares unfcld:	79	Employm.2		28
So we freeze cn,	79	Employm.2		29
Thus we creep on,	79	Employm.2	W	29
Then we will chide the sunne for letting night	81	Christmas		23
We sing one common Lord; wherefore he should	81	Christmas		25
Shall stay, till we have done;	81	Christmas		28
Then we will sing, and shine all our own day,	81	Christmas		31
Where now we shall be better Gods then he.	82	Ungratef.		6
Because this box we know;	82	Ungratef.		23
For we have all of us just such another.	82	Ungratef.		24
So that we need not say, Where's this command?	86	Vanitie 1		26
We forfeit all our Creed.	86	Lent		30
It's true, we cannot reach Christs forti'th day;	87	Lent		31
We cannot reach our Saviours puritie;	87	Lent		34
Yet are we bid, Be holy ev'n as he.	87	Lent		35
Reason and speech we onely bring.	91	Man		10
Nothing we see, but means cur good,	91	Man		27
That, as the world serves us, we may serve thee,	92	Man		53
So we may bee to Thee.	92	Man	W	54
Him we touch;	93	Antiphon 2		14
And him we take.	93	Antiphon 2		15
We adore,	93	Antiphon 2		17
And we do crouch.	93	Antiphon 2		18
We have none,	93	Antiphon 2		20
And we no store.	93	Antiphon 2		21
At first we liv'd in pleasure;	97	Afflict.5		7
When we grew wanton, thou didst use displeasure	97	Afflict.5		9
To make us thine: yet that we might not part,	97	Afflict.5		10
As we at first did board with thee,	97	Afflict.5		11
If either will convert us, we are thine:	97	Afflict.5		14
We are the trees, whom shaking fastens more,	97	Afflict.5		20
He is to Sinai gone, as we heard tell:	99	Decay		9
Dead with eclipses, when we speak of thee:	101	Miserie		34
So our clay hearts, ev'n when we crouch	101	Miserie		39
We cannot ask the thing, which is not there,	103	Prayer 2		11
Of what we might not take, or be withstood.	104	Obedience		30
We talk of harvests; there are no such things,	108	Home		55
But when we leave our corn and hay:	108	Home		56
Christ left his grave-clothes, that we might, when grief	112	Dawning		15
Christ left his grave-cloths, that we might, when grief	112	Dawning	V	15
We all acknowledge both thy power and love	117	Providence		29
Who sweetly temper'st all. If we could heare	118	Providence		39
We are the earth; and they,	126	Confession		13
Except thou make us dayly, we shall spurn	127	Giddinesse		27
Then have we too our guardian fires and clouds;	128	Bunch Gr.		15
We have our sands and serpents, tents and shrowds;	128	Bunch Gr.		17
Yet if we rightly measure,	131	Mans medly		4
As well as we.	132	The Storm		8
For we should count, Since the last joy.	138	The Size		41
Then we are shooters both, and thou dost deigne	139	Artillerie		25
We must confesse that nothing is our own.	143	Holdfast		7
That we have nought. I stood amaz'd at this,	143	Holdfast		10
Whose streams we got by the Apostles sluce,	152	The Jews		3
(As we have boxes for the poore)	158	Praise 3		28
Let us (said he) poure on him all we can:	159	The Pulley		3
We say amisse,	166	The Flower		19
Thy word is all, if we could spell.	166	The Flower		21
To make us see we are but flowers that glide:	167	The Flower		44
Which when we once can finde and prove,	167	The Flower		45
How neatly doe we give one onely name	168	The Sonne		5
We turn upon him in a sense most true:	168	The Sonne		12
We him in glorie call, The Sonne of Man.	168	The Sonne		14
Thus we prevent the last great day,	171	Self-cond.		19
What wonders shall we feel, when we shall see	172	The Glance		19
And not his feet? Though we could dive	173	Marie Magd		10
If we could see below	175	The Foil		1
Yet in this wretched world we toil,	176	The Foil		7
As we sugar melt in wine?	181	Banquet		12
For we consider'd thee as at some six	186	Death		5
We lookt on this side of thee, shooting short;	186	Death		9
Where we did finde	186	Death		10
For we do now behold thee gay and glad,	186	Death		17
Therefore we can go die as sleep, and trust	186	Death		21
Half that we have	186	Death		22

WE (cont'd)

	PAGE	TITLE		LINE
They have their times of Gospel, ev'n as we.	197	Ch.-Milit.		248
They have their time of Gospel, ev'n as we.	197	Ch.-Milit.	W	248
We think we rob them, but we think amisse:	197	Ch.-Milit.		253
We are more poore, and they more rich by this.	197	Ch.-Milit.		254
If that bee dark we can not see:	203	Even-song	W	14
Let the world reel, we and all ours stand sure,	439	Walton 5		9
How know you that the sighes we send	210	Paradox	D	19
Not from excesse, and therefore doe we spende	210	Paradox	D	21
the well is deep, and we have nothing of our selves to draw with?	228	Priest 4		35
service, Rom. 12. when we speak not as Parrats, without reason,	232	Priest 6		3
but when we use our reason, and apply our powers to the service	232	Priest 6		5
truly affecting, and cordially expressing all that we say;	233	Priest 7		31
Oh let us all take heed what we do, God sees us, he sees whether I	234	Priest 7		27
or you hear as you ought, he sees hearts, as we see faces:	234	Priest 7		28
for if we be here, hee must be here, since we are here by him,	234	Priest 7		29
since we are here by him, and without him could not be here.	234	Priest 7		29
And every one is more awaked, when we come, and say, Thou art	236	Priest 8		14
that we may grow therein, and that our feet may be like hindes feet	236	Priest 8		28
although we should love him onely for his own sake, yet out of his	243	Priest 11		30
the two commands, we are more injoyned to be charitable, then wise.	245	Priest 12		28
from the certainty both of deliverance, and reward, if we faint not;	249	Priest 15		26
We cannot allow this: or else if the thing will admit interpretation;	252	Priest 18		9
that we should do whatsoever things are honest, or just,	253	Priest 19		23
say they, we have nothing to do, lets go to the Tavern,	274	Priest 32		12
reason crosseth not our Saviours precept of selling what we have,	274	Priest 32		32
because when we have sold all, and given it to the poor,	274	Priest 32		33
given it to the poor, we must not be idle, but labour to get more,	274	Priest 32		33
to get more, that we may give more, according to St. Pauls rule,	275	Priest 32		1
because we are about a Calling, and a preparation thereunto.	276	Priest 32		36
since we are not Masters of our bodies, this sufficeth.	279	Priest 33		19
when we are assaulted with temptations either from within or from	280	Priest 34		3
If we would judg ourselves, we should not be judged;	280	Priest 34		30
If we would judg ourselves, we should not be judged;	280	Priest 34		31
and if we would bound our selves, we should not be bounded.	280	Priest 34		31
and if we would bound our selves, we should not be bounded.	280	Priest 34		32
weather be what it will, still we have bread, though sometimes more,	281	Priest 34		25
Matthew 24. 14. which we see even miraculously effected in these new	282	Priest 34		32
is a great Blessing, and as great as food, for which we give thanks:	284	Priest 35		27
and now we are fallen to the clean contrary, even from superstition	286	Priest 36		16
for we must not do evill, that good may come of it.	287	Priest 37		6
How shall we dare to appear before thy face, who are contrary	288	Priest		8
before thy face, who are contrary to thee, in all we call thee?	288	Priest		10
for we are darknesse, and weaknesse, and filthinesse, and shame.	288	Priest		10
yet art thou our Creatour, and we thy work:	288	Priest		12
untill we interrupted thy Counsels, disappointed thy Purposes,	288	Priest		16
for an apple once we lost our God, and still lose him for no more;	288	Priest		19
therefore we sons of men are not consumed.	288	Priest		22
when we had sinned beyond any help in heaven or earth, then thou	288	Priest		25
We praise thee! we blesse thee!	289	Priest		10
we blesse thee! we magnifie thee for ever!	289	Priest		10
we magnifie thee for ever!	289	Priest		11
Lo, we stand here, beseeching thee to blesse thy word, wher-ever	289	Priest		13
in whose sweet and pleasing words, we say, Our Father, &c.	289	Priest		35
are not almost all the learned books that we have, written by their	298	Cornaro		33
so that we can eat but a very little, wherewith she is very well	299	Cornaro		28
yeares old, all the time we live after, is rather death then life.	300	Cornaro		29
By this means the place is come to that perfection we now see it is:	301	Cornaro		30
if we make another sence of that Text, wee shall overthrow all means,	310	Valdesso		11
but enlightens us with new Considerations the more we read it.	310	Valdesso		35
if we believe, no sinne shall hurt us;	311	Valdesso		24
if we believe not, no vertue shall helpe us.	311	Valdesso		25
we shall not be punished (which word I like here better then	311	Valdesso		26
holy Scripture, he meaneth that we should not use it as the onely,	314	Valdesso	V	4
because the anointing which we have received, and abideth in us,	314	Valdesso	V	6
and we meet with two sorts of these Saints of the world;	319	Valdesso	V	21
Ever since we weare cloathes, we know not one another.	326	Proverbs		168
We are fooles one to another.	334	Proverbs		381
we ought not to trust another.	338	Proverbs		490
We cannot come to honour under a Coverlet.	339	Proverbs		533
At the games end we shall see who gaines.	339	Proverbs		538
God is at the end, when we thinke he is furthest off it.	341	Proverbs		598
By doing nothing we learne to do ill.	346	Proverbs		757
In doing we learne.	347	Proverbs		803
Life is halfe spent before we know what it is.	351	Proverbs		917
yet we must have patience.	353	Proverbs		980
Without danger we cannot get beyond danger.	354	Proverbs		1010
We do it soon enough, if that we do be well.	359	Proverbs	D	1109
Cruelty is more cruell, if we defer the pain.	359	Proverbs	D	1110
We must recoile a little, to the end we may leap the better.	359	Proverbs	D	1121
We must love, as looking one day to hate.	359	Proverbs	D	1126
Stay a while, that we may make an end the sooner.	361	Proverbs	D	1161
We Batchelors laugh and shew our teeth,	361	Proverbs	D	1175
since if we had Riches we are commanded to give them away:	373	Letters		23
when we consider that the Blessings in the holy Scripture,	373	Letters		28
entertains our Care for us that we may the more quietly intend his	374	Letters		19
of those that might say, What shall we rejoyce in afflictions?	374	Letters		23
whatsoever befals us we must alwaies, at all times rejoyce in	374	Letters		25
a much better Paymaster then my self, even him, whome we both serve:	378	Letters		3
thereof, we are to regard others, & neither to scandalize them,	380	Woodnoth		18
To desire good & endeavour it when we can doe no more, is to doe it.	381	Woodnoth		15

WE (cont'd)	PAGE	TITLE		LINE
When we exhort people to continue in their vocation, it is in	381	Woodnoth		23
by which we well know how to convince the sterne, and more austere	442	Oration		5
all we and our whole Kingdome exult with joy, to bee united with that	442	Oration		13
we have as much failed, as your Excellencies doe excel,	442	Oration		34
we for your gracious acceptance of these poore duties wish,	443	Oration		5
WEAK				
Could build so strong in a weak heart.	67	Ch.-floore		20
Thy nourisht fame is weak or strong.	69	Content		32
When age grows low and weak,	98	Mortific.		25
I am in all a weak disabled thing,	165	The Crosse		17
that a weak stomack being prepossessed with flesh, shall much better	242	Priest 10		21
If his body be weak and obstructed, as most Students are,	242	Priest 10		28
but for the comfort of the weak, that not onely sicknesse breaks	242	Priest 10		34
For I eat little, because a little sufficeth my weak stomack:	300	Cornaro		9
Willowes are weak, yet they bind other wood.	341	Proverbs		594
it is true (God knows) I am weak, yet not so, but that every day,	364	Letters		26
WEAKE				
To whose powre Thunder is but weake and slight:	29	Sacrifice	W	79
A disarmed peace is weake.	342	Proverbs		628
WEAKEST				
Wealth is like rheume, it falles on the weakest parts.	337	Proverbs		475
The thread breakes, where it is weakest.	341	Proverbs		596
WEAKLY				
and those that are weakly,) but that they must rise so,	266	Priest 26		34
WEAKNED				
Till she had weakned all by alteration:	84	The World		8
that are now weakned, and disarmed with sedentary lives,	277	Priest 32		17
WEAKNESSE				
Till labour come, and make my weaknesse score.	17	Ch.-Porch		288
In weaknesse must be stout.	48	Afflict.1		62
Man is all weaknesse; there is no such thing	61	Praise 1		9
for we are darknesse, and weaknesse, and filthinesse, and shame.	288	Priest		10
I ever tooke that for a weaknesse in the great Patriark:	316	Valdesso		1
WEAKNESSES				
the best of Gods Servants should have weaknesses is no way repugnant	316	Valdesso		2
WEAL				
My wo, mans weal: and now I bow my head.	34	Sacrifice		250
'Twas more secure in great Loves Common-weal	439	Walton 5		17
WEALS				
Much more do Common-weals acknowledge thee,	190	Ch.-Milit.		5
which is both easie for common-weals-men, and very convenient,	299	Cornaro		17
WEALTH				
For wealth without contentment, climbes a hill	11	Ch.-Porch		111
To all things els. Wealth is the conjurers devil;	13	Ch.-Porch		165
To take all that is given; whether wealth,	20	Ch.-Porch		356
If thou dost give me wealth, I will restore	35	Thanksgvng		19
Lord, who createdst man in wealth and store,	43	East.wings		1
My soul bid nothing, but preserve her wealth:	44	H. Bapt.2		13
My soul bid nothing, but keep hir first wealth:	44	H. Bapt.2	W	13
Man calleth thee his wealth, who made thee rich;	77	Avarice		13
Wealth, fame, endowments, vertues, all should go;	103	Prayer 2		22
But all my wealth, and familie might combine	164	The Crosse		5
nor nigardly to keep, nor troubled to lose any worldly wealth;	227	Priest 3		18
that the world should so much value wealth, which in the day of wrath	227	Priest 3		20
he adviseth them so to labour for wealth and maintenance,	248	Priest 14		6
Now it is a justice and debt to the Common-wealth he lives in,	262	Priest 23		16
because wealth is given to that end to supply our occasions.	265	Priest 26		8
and it concernes the Common-wealth, that none should be idle,	274	Priest 32		27
No Common-wealth in the world hath a braver [better] Institution then	276	Priest 32		8
and a shamefull wrong both to the Common-wealth, and their own House:	277	Priest 32		27
which even their present plenty of wealth otherwise admits;	280	Priest 34		25
it concerns the Common-Wealth, that Rogues should be known,	287	Priest 37		36
That they who are employed in the common wealth, cannot live	299	Cornaro		12
this cannot stand, and it is ill Doctrine in a common-wealth.	316	Valdesso		17
may pretend motions, which is unsufferable in a Common-wealth.	316	Valdesso		22
Wealth is like rheume, it falles on the weakest parts.	337	Proverbs		475
Little wealth, little care.	338	Proverbs		501
Hee that marries for wealth sells his liberty.	347	Proverbs		784
Knowledge makes one laugh, but wealth makes one dance.	352	Proverbs		957
Either wealth is much increased, or moderation is much decayed.	360	Proverbs	D	1139
WEALTHS				
Houses are built by rule, and common-wealths.	12	Ch.-Porch		135
WEAPON				
Is both a weapon and a guide.	96	Charms & K		4
There's no such conquering weapon as the necessity of conquering.	357	Proverbs	D	1064
WEAPONS				
At there owne weapons, without pomp or state	211	Bohemia	D	21
WEAR				
Who fears to do well, sure should wear a mask.	11	Ch.-Porch		126
Salute thy self: see what thy soul doth wear.	12	Ch.-Porch		146
Thy friend put in thy bosome: wear his eies	17	Ch.-Porch		271
Then on my head a crown of thorns I wear:	31	Sacrifice		161
But he to wear them. Nothing useth fire,	120	Providence		110
And when they ask'd, what he would wear;	151	The Bag		16
To wear thy habit, the severe attire	160	Priesthood		9
When souls shall wear their new aray,	186	Death		19
To be a Church-man too, and wear a Mitre:	194	Ch.-Milit.		163
Wear Venus Livery? only serve her turn?	206	Walton 1		4
rather to use his neighbours, and wear out that, he is covetous.	265	Priest 26		29

	PAGE	TITLE		LINE
WEARE				
Ever since we weare cloathes, we know not one another.	326	Proverbs		168
WEARER				
The wearer knowes, where the shoe wrings.	338	Proverbs		491
WEARES				
Meane while, if hee (which all thinges weares)	208	H. Danvers	D	5
The gowne is his that weares it,	337	Proverbs		476
WEARIE				
And now wearie of sport, glad to ingrosse	33	Sacrifice		193
And now with darknesse closest wearie eyes,	64	Even-song		18
Let him be rich and wearie, that at least,	160	The Pulley		18
I am not wearie of life, which I passe with great delight.	301	Cornaro		3
WEARIED				
With groaning I am wearied,	220	Psalm VI	D	13
WEARINESSE				
If goodnesse leade him not, yet wearinesse	160	The Pulley		19
as too much heat and cold, wearinesse, watching, ill aire,	293	Cornaro		31
WEARS				
Her own destruction and his danger wears.	85	Vanitie 1		14
His own destruction and his danger wears.	85	Vanitie 1	V	14
And nothing wears.	110	Brit. Ch.		24
Nothing wears clothes, but Man; nothing doth need	120	Providence		109
He wears a stuffe whose thread is course and round,	131	Mans medly		15
My beauty wears and doth decay	220	Psalm VI	D	17
WEARY (see also wearie)				
He that is weary, let him sit.	78	Employm.2		1
What is this weary world; this meat and drink,	108	Home		37
A long it was and weary way.	141	Pilgrimage		3
With doubling knees and weary bones,	148	Longing		2
My weary weeping eyes too drie for me,	164	Grief		6
When Love being weary made an end	439	Walton 5		11
making him then weary, and so he grows from not relishing,	235	Priest 7		14
Every one is weary, the poore in seeking,	344	Proverbs		678
WEATHER				
Thy wormwood turn to health, windes to fair weather:	49	Repentance		21
According as the weather falls.	143	Complaining		10
All the hard weather,	166	The Flower		13
and weather, and other accidents by his governing power,	271	Priest 30		17
then God sends such weather, as lays the corn, and destroys it:	271	Priest 30		31
Let the weather be what it will, still we have bread, though	281	Priest 34		25
To a child all weather is cold.	345	Proverbs		732
WEATHERS				
Into a bed, to sleep out all ill weathers.	9	Ch.-Porch		84
WEAVE				
So did I weave my self into the sense.	103	Jordan 2		14
WEBBE				
'Tis a thinne webbe, which poysonous fancies make:	15	Ch.-Porch		224
WED				
Abstain wholly, or wed. Thy bounteous Lord	7	Ch.-Porch		13
And long since wed	71	Frailtie		20
What strange pollutions doth he wed,	100	Miserie		13
WEDD				
Abstaine or wedd: if thou canst not abstaine	7	Ch.-Porch	W	13
And wedd my soule in glorious paradise;	205	Persever.	W	10
And with that Ring thy fame shall wedd	213	L' Envoy	D	13
WEDDING				
Yet wedding marrs thy fortune, fast & pray:	7	Ch.-Porch	W	14
He that hath made a sorrie wedding	171	Self-cond.		13
WEDGE				
Nor in a wedge of gold,	52	H.Commun.		2
He is a foole that makes a wedge of his fist.	341	Proverbs		585
WEE				
Wee are born old.	48	Repentance	W	10
But wee strangers grown, o Lord,	53	H.Commun.	W	37
That wee may gaine by crosses.	53	H.Commun.	W	40
But wee are falne from Heaven to Earth,	59	Whitsunday	W	13
And if wee can stay there, it's well.	59	Whitsunday	W	14
So wee may cease to suck: to praise thee, never.	59	Whitsunday	W	24
Wee have no store.	93	Antiphon 2	W	21
Julips & Cordials when wee call on thee	204	The Knell	W	17
So Blackamoores repute us fowle, and wee	210	Paradox	D	9
That which wee doe not neede:	210	Paradox	D	22
Which wee but somtymes prove:	210	Paradox	D	32
Wee doubt much whether you	211	Paradox	D	40
Fairer & richer. Now wee know, what's thine,	211	Bohemia	D	18
it is a good strife to go as farre as wee can in pleasing of him,	224	Priest		12
sence of that Text, wee shall overthrow all means, save catechizing,	310	Valdesso		11
so are wee to doe with the Scriptures and this is the use	310	Valdesso		30
Therefore wee ought to proceed, except there be a restraining motion	313	Valdesso		15
If all fooles had bables, wee should want fuell.	323	Proverbs		63
All things have their place, knew wee how to place them.	334	Proverbs		379
If all fooles wore white Caps, wee should seeme a flock of geese.	338	Proverbs		513
It's an ill aire where wee gaine nothing.	350	Proverbs		872
Wee know not who lives or dies.	353	Proverbs		966
Wee leave more to do when wee dye, then wee have done.	353	Proverbs		972
With customes wee live well, but Lawes undoe us.	353	Proverbs		973
as to you deserving them, Wee at last salute you Masters of Arts;	441	Oration		26
and wee also putting off that countenance and gravitie,	442	Oration		4
wee might the more by love grow on, both the Spanish and Brittish	442	Oration		17
same order and habit, of which wee all in this Kingdome glorie to be.	442	Oration		21
your selves, wee justly feare that there is nothing here answerable	442	Oration		29

	PAGE	TITLE		LINE
WEE (cont'd)				
slight glories, which wee raise from bookes, and painefull industrie.	443	Oration		1
WEED				
But all my companie is a weed.	57	Employm. 1		22
The great prey on the lesse, they on some weed.	118	Providence		52
And ev'n in Paradise to be a weed.	165	The Crosse		30
WEEDS				
Some till their ground, but let weeds choke their sonne:	10	Ch.-Porch		98
And thorny all their crowns, bloudie their weeds;	32	Sacrifice		178
Full of glorie and gay weeds,	71	Frailtie		13
WEEK				
For all the week thy food so oft he gave thee.	22	Ch.-Porch		392
And readie Paschal Lambe of this great week:	28	Sacrifice		59
Since, if my soul make even with the week,	38	The Sinner		3
The week were dark, but for thy light:	75	Sunday		6
The week were dark, but that thy light	75	Sunday	W	6
The burden of the week lies there,	75	Sunday		12
And where the week-dayes trail on ground,	76	Sunday		58
Is deeply carved there: but th' other week	112	JESU		2
Each day, each houre, each moment of the week,	131	Love unkn.		69
pray twice a day, every day of the week, and four times on Sunday,	272	Priest 31		22
Thursday come, and the week's gone.	341	Proverbs		587
Out of Lent also, twice a Week, on Fridayes and Saturdayes,	365	Letters		5
I have wrote to my dear sick Sister this week already, and therefore	367	Letters		21
This Week hath loaded me with your Favours;	369	Letters		10
WEEK-DAYES				
And where the week-dayes trail on ground,	76	Sunday		58
WEEKDAYS				
The Countrey Parson upon the afternoons in the weekdays,	247	Priest 14		3
WEEKS				
For many weeks of lingring pain and smart	154	Glimpse		4
WEELDY				
that if after dinner they are not fit (or un-weeldy) either to pray,	266	Priest 26		31
WEENING				
Weening is not measure.	348	Proverbs		811
WEEP				
They may weep out the stains by them did rise:	23	Ch.-Porch		417
Weep not, deare friends, since I for both have wept	31	Sacrifice		149
Shall I weep bloud? why, thou hast wept such store	35	Thanksgvng		5
Did weep so fast, that the tears trickling down	71	Humilitie		26
The dew shall weep thy fall to night;	87	Vertue		3
Then weep mine eyes, the God of love doth grieve:	135	Ephes.		7
Weep foolish heart,	135	Ephes.		8
Marbles can weep; and surely strings	136	Ephes.		23
Where shall I get me eyes enough to weep,	140	Ch.-rents		25
To weep or crie?	143	Complaining		14
Did weep to heav'n, they found a bottle there	158	Praise 3		27
My joyes to weep, and now my griefs to sing.	159	Jos.coat		14
Though I fail, I weep:	179	Discipline		13
Weep what ye have drunk amisse,	180	Invitation		10
Wherefore in case a Christian endeavour to weep, and cannot,	279	Priest 33		18
WEEPE				
You neither groane nor weepe	209	Paradox	D	2
found himselfe sometimes to weepe more for the losse of some	279	Priest 33		12
Who hath none to still him, may weepe out his eyes.	321	Proverbs		17
If folly were griefe every house would weepe.	334	Proverbs		370
He that sings on friday, will weepe on Sunday.	335	Proverbs		411
To weepe for joy is a kinde of Manna.	337	Proverbs		462
Women laugh when they can, and weepe when they will.	348	Proverbs		821
WEEPING				
And weeping live:	135	Ephes.		9
My weary weeping eyes too drie for me,	164	Grief		6
alike in all Gods children (which as concerning weeping it cannot be,	279	Priest 33		22
Not that weeping is not usefull, where it can be, that so the body	279	Priest 33		26
Learne weeping, and thou shalt laugh gayning.	325	Proverbs		127
WEEPS				
But all is cleansed when the marble weeps.	67	Ch.-floore		15
Thy clay that weeps, thy dust that calls.	143	Complaining		5
when he cannot more, as he that weeps a floud of tears.	279	Priest 33		31
WEIGH (see also waighs)				
Continence hath his joy: weigh both; and so	7	Ch.-Porch		17
Till he the thing and the example weigh:	72	Constancie		13
my meditation weigh:	218	Psalm V	D	2
the Lord vouchsafes to weigh my tears;	220	Psalm VI	D	22
Weigh justly and sell dearely.	338	Proverbs		500
The reasons of the poore weigh not.	342	Proverbs		633
WEIGHED				
therefore the spirit of both is to be considered, and weighed.	229	Priest 4		17
and flesh, and broth, was twelve ounces exactly weighed;	296	Cornaro		11
This being well weighed, will make the Consideration easy,	320	Valdesso		4
WEIGHETH				
he diligently, and strictly weigheth, his Parish being all his joy,	250	Priest 17		25
WEIGHING				
weighing their reasons with my self, and abhorring from so sudden	292	Cornaro		17
WEIGHS				
with God, who weighs even childrens actions, 1 Kings 14. 12, 13.	239	Priest 10		29
WEIGHT				
And love's a weight to hearts, to eies a signe.	22	Ch.-Porch		399
Light without winde is glasse: warm without weight	120	Providence		101
of the moment of griefs here with the weight of joyes hereafter.	249	Priest 15		27
Weight justly and sell dearely.	338	Proverbs	V	500

	PAGE	TITLE		LINE
WEIGHT (cont'd)				
None knowes the weight of anothers burthen.	350	Proverbs		880
God gives his wrath by weight, and without weight his mercy.	359	Proverbs	D	1115
WEL				
that have glorified him as wel as now, and that he shall have so	231	Priest 6		35
Wherefore there is nothing done either wel or ill, whereof he is	254	Priest 20		10
they cannot wel dispatch) nor of their estate, nor of their brethren.	266	Priest 26		16
which none can perform so wel in trouble, as in calmness.	273	Priest 31		2
God knows the occasion as wel as he, and He is as a gracious Father,	273	Priest 31		7
as I too wel by experience found.	292	Cornaro		7
WELCOME				
But gladly welcome what he doth afford;	7	Ch.-Porch		15
As ever did a welcome guest.	50	Faith		8
Welcome deare feast of Lent: who loves not thee,	86	Lent		1
Then my strict, yet welcome size.	177	The Rose		4
Welcome sweet and scared cheer,	181	Banquet		1
Welcome deare;	181	Banquet		2
Love bade me welcome: yet my soul drew back,	188	Love 3		1
Not but that the poor are welcome also to his table, whom he	243	Priest 11		10
in their vocation, and himself be ever the more welcome to them.	248	Priest 14		13
which may make his other discourses more welcome, and lesse tedious.	251	Priest 17		6
Welcome evill, if thou commest alone.	325	Proverbs		140
Milke saies to wine, welcome friend.	327	Proverbs		184
move my Lords of Manchester and Boollingbrook is very welcome to mee.	377	Letters		24
WELCOMES				
Likewise he welcomes to his house any Minister, how poor or mean	253	Priest 19		18
WELDOING				
not punished) for evill doing nor rewarded for weldoing or living,	311	Valdesso		29
WELL (noun)				
That mends the lookers eyes: this is the well	58	H.Script.1		9
At some fair oak, or bush, or cave, or well:	99	Decay		7
Lifting to heaven from this well of tears.	141	Justice 2		18
where the well is deep, and we have nothing of our selves to draw	228	Priest 4		35
A foole may throw a stone into a well,	339	Proverbs		527
A stone in a well is not lost.	349	Proverbs		845
WELL (see also wel)				
Who fears to do well, sure should wear a mask.	11	Ch.-Porch		126
Man is a shop of rules, a well truss'd pack,	12	Ch.-Porch		141
Say not then, This with that lace will do well;	14	Ch.-Porch		189
The fine may spare these well, yet not go lesse.	16	Ch.-Porch		238
What to ask further. Doubts well rais'd do lock	18	Ch.-Porch		299
What to ask farther. Doubts well rais'd do lock	18	Ch.-Porch	W	299
To couzin thee. Look to thy actions well:	23	Ch.-Porch		425
If well; the pain doth fade, the joy remains.	24	Ch.-Porch		462
But surely not their hearts, as I well trie:	30	Sacrifice		123
That he before me well nigh suffereth:	31	Sacrifice		147
The sonne, in whom thou art well pleas'd to be?	33	Sacrifice	W	214
For they will pierce my side, I full well know;	34	Sacrifice		246
Well, I will change the service, and go seek	48	Afflict.1		63
And tune together in a well-set song,	49	Repentance		33
Fractures well cur'd make us more strong.	49	Repentance		36
That apprehension cur'd so well my foot,	50	Faith		11
That I can walk to heav'n well neare.	50	Faith		12
Heaven in ordinarie, man well drest,	51	Prayer 1		11
A fervent sigh might well have blown	53	H.Commun.		31
And if wee can stay there, it's well.	59	Whitsunday	W	14
Who have a work, as well as they,	61	Praise 1		19
Where in each room of the well-furnisht tent	69	Content		19
Where in each room of that well-furnisht tent	69	Content	W	19
So well as there?	74	The Starre		4
How well her name an Army doth present,	77	Anagram		1
Do not so well agree.	95	Submission		16
I would do well, yet sinne the hand hath got:	96	Justice 1		10
For this he wondrous well doth know	101	Miserie	W	45
Thou mayst as well my actions guide, as see.	104	Obedience		25
What show'd so well.	125	Peace		18
Let me as well take up their joy, as sorrow.	128	Bunch Gr.		21
Of a great rock: I well remember all,	129	Love unkn.		15
But you shall heare. After my heart was well,	129	Love unkn.		22
Full well I understood, who had been there:	130	Love unkn.		54
As well as we.	132	The Storm		8
I rose, and shook my clothes, as knowing well,	139	Artillerie		3
And well it was for thee, when this befell,	144	Discharge		16
If it be his once, all is well.	144	Discharge		20
Thou couldst well see	144	Discharge		24
Search well and see; for hearts have many holes.	147	Offering		4
Mark well my furnace! O what flames,	149	Longing		26
Well may he close his eyes, but not his heart.	151	The Bag		6
For well he knows, if but one grief and smart	159	Jos.coat		5
Shadows well mounted, dreams in a career,	167	Dotage		4
Who cannot dresse it well, want wit, not words.	167	The Sonne		4
Well may I walk, not fear:	173	23 Psalme		14
In him I am well drest.	174	Aaron		15
Brought you to Church well drest and clad:	176	Forerunners		17
What others mean to do, I know not well;	187	Judgement		6
As well our understanding as our sight.	190	Ch.-Milit.		18
As well what should befall, as what befell.	193	Ch.-Milit.		130
A gown and pen became him wondrous well:	194	Ch.-Milit.		167
Thus do both lights, as well in Church as Sunne,	197	Ch.-Milit.		270
As well as any she? Cannot thy Dove	206	Walton 1		8
As well show inward warblinge as decay.	210	Paradox	D	24

WELL (cont'd)

	PAGE	TITLE		LINE
his servants, to whom he hath revealed his Truth, as well as to him;	229	Priest 4		23
it is an honest joy ever after to looke upon his well spent houres.	230	Priest 5		7
he is ever very well supplyed by some able man who treads in his	232	Priest 7		25
but stories and sayings they will well remember.	233	Priest 7		18
his profit, for none are so well served, as by religious servants,	240	Priest 10		14
and others spurred to do well, that they may enjoy the like	243	Priest 11		27
For though he desire, that all should live well, and vertuously,	243	Priest 11		28
and those not torne, or fouled, but whole and clean, and well bound;	246	Priest 13		15
to receive the charity of well minded people, and to lay up treasure	246	Priest 13		21
If it be well spoken, or done, he takes occasion to commend,	252	Priest 18		4
This was not so well said, as it might have been forborn;	252	Priest 18		9
or, So farr indeed what you say is true, and well said;	252	Priest 18		12
who are not well grounded, may then by an honourable way take	255	Priest 21		30
that those who are well grown in the knowledg of Religion,	255	Priest 21		32
and accordingly by questions well ordered he found Philosophy in	256	Priest 21		22
nor the Church-Wardens so well take notice who receive thrice,	259	Priest 22		28
throw into the fire, and so they pay them their wages, all is well.	265	Priest 26		27
of their health, and so they will stand to the pain, all is well.	266	Priest 26		20
and knowledg of their own body, and what it can well digest:	267	Priest 26		1
For knowing what one usually can well disgest, and feeling when I go	267	Priest 26		6
The Countrey Parson knows well, that both for the generall ignominy	268	Priest 28		9
Do well, and right, and let the world sinke.	270	Priest 29		23
if they keep and fodder well their cattel, they must have milk,	270	Priest 30		27
hath both a faire harvest, and that also well inned, and imbarned,	272	Priest 30		1
and utter this well, all his advantages are to his losse.	272	Priest 30		3
every day of the week, and four times on Sunday, if they be well.	272	Priest 31		23
But if after all this care well dispatched, the house-keepers Family	275	Priest 32		36
for with such sacrifices God is well pleased.	281	Priest 34		4
wherefore he likes well, that his Parish at good times invite one	284	Priest 35		17
And the Parson likes this very well;	284	Priest 35		24
Being now sound and well, I began to consider the force	293	Cornaro		1
with a full stomack, but so as I might well both eat and drink more.	293	Cornaro		19
neither did I know well, what I did or said.	296	Cornaro		17
whereof the one kept me well for many yeares;	297	Cornaro		4
we can eat but a very little, wherewith she is very well contented:	299	Cornaro		28
and that in much smaller quantitie then when he was well.	299	Cornaro		32
and well-contented, free from all troubles and troublesome thoughts;	300	Cornaro		37
and fruitfull fields, well manured and adorned with many habitations.	301	Cornaro		25
I sleep well and quietly any where, and my dreams are fair	302	Cornaro		12
very apt and well given both for learning and behaviour.	303	Cornaro		5
sheweth, and I also, when I was a young man, too well found.	303	Cornaro		16
be evident to others, as well as to themselves, that God moved them.	316	Valdesso		20
This being well weighed, will make the Consideration easy,	320	Valdesso		4
All is well with him, who is beloved of his neighbours.	321	Proverbs		10
All is well to him, that is loved of his neighbours.	321	Proverbs	V	10
Hee that lives well is learned enough.	323	Proverbs		86
Hee who lives well is learned enough.	323	Proverbs	V	86
A full belly neither fights nor flies well.	324	Proverbs		88
Though a lie be well drest, it is ever overcome.	325	Proverbs		133
Well may hee smell fire, whose gowne burnes.	325	Proverbs		138
Shee spins well that breedes her children.	325	Proverbs		144
Shee spins well that breedes her child.	325	Proverbs	V	144
It costs more to doe ill then to doe well.	329	Proverbs		262
A well-bred youth neither speakes of himselfe,	330	Proverbs		278
He that lives well sees a farre off.	333	Proverbs		352
Hee that would bee well old, must bee old betimes.	334	Proverbs		371
He carries well, to whom it waighes not.	334	Proverbs		391
He that would be well, needs not goe from his owne house.	336	Proverbs		442
Things well fitted abide.	337	Proverbs		483
He that looseth is Marchant as well as he that gaines.	339	Proverbs		518
Living well is the best revenge.	339	Proverbs		524
He plaies well that winnes.	339	Proverbs		550
He that can make a fire well, can end a quarrell.	340	Proverbs		557
He that lives not well one yeare, sorrowes seven after.	340	Proverbs		562
Ty it well, and let it goe.	342	Proverbs		642
He that serves well needes not ask his wages.	347	Proverbs		798
Hee lookes not well to himselfe that lookes not ever.	349	Proverbs		835
He thinkes not well, that thinkes not againe.	349	Proverbs		836
He that gaines well and spends well, needes no count booke.	349	Proverbs		853
He that gaines well and spends well, needes no count books.	349	Proverbs	V	853
and a latin-bred woman, seldome end well.	349	Proverbs		866
He quits his place well, that leaves his friend there.	350	Proverbs		875
With customes wee live well, but Lawes undoe us.	353	Proverbs		973
If you must flie, flie well.	355	Proverbs		1021
A man well mounted is ever Cholerick.	355	Proverbs		1025
We do it soon enough, if that we do be well.	359	Proverbs	D	1109
as well as naturall bodies.	361	Proverbs	D	1166
and I love my friends so well, as that if all things proved not well,	364	Letters		28
as that if all things proved not well, I had rather the fault should	364	Letters		29
it will do well, for it expresseth the Universities inclination	369	Letters		26
and such like Gaynesses, which will please a young man well.	370	Letters		4
no such earthiness in it, but it may very well be joined with Heaven;	370	Letters		23
Can I be so happy, as to hear of both these that they succeed well?	371	Letters		10
Concerning the Orators place all goes well yet, the next Friday it is	371	Letters		16
So that now if they do not well the falt cannot be charg'd on you;	373	Letters		15
Well: the good GOD bless you more and more;	376	Letters		18
She liked our Book well, & has given order to the Tenants,	379	Letters		8
3. To Change shewes not well & you are by the Apostles rule (Philip	380	Woodnoth		12
most pleasing, as well to us remembring, as to you deserving them,	441	Oration		26
by which we well know how to convince the sterne, and more austere	442	Oration		5

WELL (cont'd)	PAGE	TITLE		LINE
that you may well conceive, your Excellencies to bee more deare unto	442	Oration		19
WELL-BRED				
A well-bred youth neither speakes of himselfe,	330	Proverbs		278
WELL-CONTENTED				
and well-contented, free from all troubles and troublesome thoughts;	300	Cornaro		37
WELL-FURNISHT				
Where in each room of the well-furnisht tent	69	Content		19
Where in each rocm of that well-furnisht tent	69	Content	W	19
WELL-SET				
And tune together in a well-set song,	49	Repentance		33
WELTRING				
Weltring in sinne;	171	The Glance		4
WENCH				
Take heed of a ycung wench,	360	Proverbs	D	1151
WENT				
That went to Temperance.	70	Humilitie		14
Ev'n all to pieces: which I went to seek:	112	JESU		4
Then went I to a garden, and did spy	125	Peace		13
The greatnesse shew'd the owner. So I went	129	Love unkn.		29
Though my lips went, my heart did stay behinde.	130	Love unkn.		59
Yet I went on.	134	The Method		24
Just as I went, None goes that way	142	Pilgrimage		33
Knocking at all doores, ever as she went.	190	Ch.-Milit.		30
Till all depart: so went the Church her way,	191	Ch.-Milit.		33
Till all be gone. so went the Church her way,	191	Ch.-Milit.	W	33
Religion went to Rome, subduing those,	191	Ch.-Milit.		61
From Greece to Rome she went, subduing those	191	Ch.-Milit.	W	61
From Greece he went to Rome: and as before	194	Ch.-Milit.		139
I went the slower, yet more paces,	203	Even-song	W	3
self to this course of life, that I never went a foot out of the way.	292	Cornaro		34
Men speake of the faire, as things went with them there.	326	Proverbs		151
WENTST				
This not withstanding, thou wentst on,	124	Gratefulnes		17
WEPT				
Weep not, deare friends, since I for both have wept	31	Sacrifice		149
Shall I weep bloud? why, thou hast wept such store	35	Thanksgvng		5
Yet if the heart that wept	154	Glimpse		21
He took flesh, he wept, he died;	288	Priest		28
I wept when I was borne, and every day shewes why.	327	Proverbs		199
WERE				
O what were man, might he himself misplace!	7	Ch.-Porch		23
Were I an Epicure, I could bate swearing.	8	Ch.-Porch		60
He clave the stonie rock, when they were drie;	30	Sacrifice		122
When all my tears were bloud, the while you slept:	31	Sacrifice		150
Till all were melted, though he were all steel:	33	Sacrifice		211
Where joyes my fellows were?	46	Afflict.1		14
My dayes were straw'd with flow'rs and happinesse;	47	Afflict.1		21
My dayes were strowd with flow'rs and happinesse;	47	Afflict.1	W	21
I reade, and sigh, and wish I were a tree;	48	Afflict.1		57
Dust blown by wit, till that they both were blinde:	54	Love 2		10
Although there were some fourtie heav'ns, or more,	55	Temper 1		5
Although there were a hundred heav'ns, or more,	55	Temper 1	W	5
Before I were by frosts extremitie	57	Employm. 1		3
The sweetnesse and the praise were thine;	57	Employm. 1		5
Which in thy garland I should fill, were mine	57	Employm. 1		7
The starres were coming down to know	59	Whitsunday		11
Were cut and martyr'd by the fault	59	Whitsunday		19
If all mens tears were let	62	Afflict.2		6
What were they all, compar'd to thine?	62	Afflict.2		8
Wherein if they were set,	62	Afflict.2		9
When by the beasts the presents tendred were,	70	Humilitie		7
The week were dark, but for thy light:	75	Sunday		6
The week were dark, but that thy light	75	Sunday	W	6
Whom, if we were not very dull,	75	Sunday		18
Oh that I were an Orenge-tree,	79	Employm.2		21
Whereas they were supported by the same:	84	The World		4
Were it not better to bestow	95	Submission		5
Sweet were the dayes, when thou didst lodge with Lot,	99	Decay		1
Thy words were then, Let me alone.	99	Decay		5
Decking the sense, as if it were to sell.	102	Jordan 2		6
Praising the sense, as if it were to sell.	102	Jordan 2	W	6
Off'ring their service, if I were nct sped:	102	Jordan 2		8
That were I to leave all but one,	103	Prayer 2		21
Thy sorrows were in earnest; no faint proffer,	104	Obedience		28
How happie were my part,	105	Obedience		41
They were by winged souls	105	Obedience		44
Where most things were of purest gold;	106	Sion		3
Were but worth the having,	114	Dialogue		2
As if I were all earth?	115	Dulnesse		2
Were worse then ours; sometimes thou shiftest hands.	121	Providence		138
As Babel grew, before there were dissensions.	122	Sinnes rd.		15
And ask'd, if Peace were there.	124	Peace		4
O what a sight were Man, if his attires	127	Giddinesse		17
But all my scores were by another paid,	130	Love unkn.		60
My sighs and tears as busie were above;	132	The Storm		3
As if a starre were duller then a clod,	134	Divinitie		3
If my deserts were masters of mine eyes:	136	Ephes.		34
As if there were no rule or eares?	136	Familie		4
That all things were more ours by being his.	143	Holdfast		12
Come, bring thy gift. If blessings were as slow	147	Offering		1

WERE (cont'd)	PAGE	TITLE		LINE
All were thine	148	Offering		34
Were sinne alive, good cause there were	150	Longing		65
Should crie so loud, untill the trump were drown'd,	152	The Jews		10
Were from my self, I had not half a word,	155	Assurance		22
As if there were no such cold thing.	165	The Flower		7
O that I once past changing were,	166	The Flower		22
Still upwards bent, as if heav'n were mine own,	166	The Flower		30
My servant were a little so,	175	The Odour		12
This were the better skie, the brighter place.	175	The Foil		4
As if grief were not foul, nor vertue winning.	176	The Foil		8
Those sparkling notions, which therein were bred?	176	Forerunners		4
Plato and Aristotle were at a losse,	191	Ch.-Milit.		53
Before the other two were in their prime.	191	Ch.-Milit.	W	60
Who were cut short in Alexanders stemme.	192	Ch.-Milit.		74
Fresh and fine deities. They were at great cost,	193	Ch.-Milit.		109
Where some poore truths were shuffled for a bait	193	Ch.-Milit.		136
The rather since his scatter'd jugglings were	195	Ch.-Milit.		175
But when they were unto the Sorbon come,	196	Ch.-Milit.	W	202
His letters were broke rudely up, believ'd	439	Walton 5		16
they were reproved, as ignorant of what spirit they were.	229	Priest 4		13
they were reproved, as ignorant of what spirit they were.	229	Priest 4		14
though he himself were with Saint Paul even sacrificed upon	234	Priest 7		8
setting aside his care of his Flock, were a madnesse to doubt of.	234	Priest 7		17
and that much more being single, then if he were marryed;	238	Priest 9		22
childrens advantage, then if it were given to the Chamber of London.	240	Priest 10		9
and were it not his duty to have them so, it were his profit,	240	Priest 10		13
to have them so, it were his profit, for none are so well served,	240	Priest 10		14
do as it were dresse and prepare both for man in themselves,	241	Priest 10		33
and fasting dayes were fully performed by keeping of the two former,	242	Priest 10		8
as if it were in their own hands to thrive, or not to thrive.	247	Priest 14		31
he chides not at first, for that were neither civill, nor profitable;	248	Priest 14		14
If the Parson were ashamed of particularizing in these things,	248	Priest 14		38
of particularizing in these things, hee were not fit to be a Parson:	249	Priest 14		1
from his promises, from the examples of all Saints, that ever were;	249	Priest 15		22
propounds among his Brethren what were fitting to be done.	253	Priest 19		14
as joyfull a countenance, as if he were to entertain some great Lord.	253	Priest 19		20
which were more comfortable, all together choosing some fitt day	253	Priest 19		37
This I do, because at such, and such a time you were charitable.	254	Priest 20		17
some dialogues in Plato were worth the reading, where the singular	256	Priest 21		28
He asked him again, what he would do, if he were in a ditch?	257	Priest 21		5
and upon what termes, and with what vowes they were Baptized.	258	Priest 22		20
as if they were Masters of their health, and so they will stand	266	Priest 26		19
instantly dry up, as a river would if the fountain were stopped.	271	Priest 30		7
Better were his corne burnt, then not spiritually improved.	272	Priest 30		4
the Professours whereof were much imployed by Queen Elizabeth,	277	Priest 32		31
of all diseases, and were recovered of all by things that he knew;	278	Priest 33		30
there were no such Physician as he, both for skill and tendernesse.	278	Priest 33		31
whether his repentance were true, or at least in that degree it ought	279	Priest 33		10
These two states were in our Saviour, not only in the beginning	280	Priest 34		8
as they remember themselves were, when affliction did blow the Coals.	280	Priest 34		20
then in their Countrey under so many miracles were a stranger thing,	282	Priest 34		9
generation should not passe, till all were fulfilled, Luke 21. 32.	282	Priest 34		29
the Priests of the Old Testament were commanded to Blesse the people,	285	Priest 36		16
the Priests Benedicite, and his holy water were over highly valued;	286	Priest 36		16
But though the streams of thy bloud were currant through darknesse,	288	Priest		32
to search out most diligently what meats were agreeable unto me,	293	Cornaro		5
evils which had so long beset me, and were almost become incurable;	293	Cornaro		21
hurt those bodies, which were kept in good order by a moderate Diet:	294	Cornaro		2
by any of these inconveniences, except it were for one onely day.	294	Cornaro		10
they were possessed with a deep Melancholie (a thing usuall	294	Cornaro		17
so that all things were troublesome to me:	296	Cornaro		16
I doe so love him, that were there nothing else, I would Print it,	305	Valdesso		7
though it were the Authors opinion, yet the truth of it would be	307	Valdesso		21
as if they were both but Alphabets and after a time to be left.	309	Valdesso		19
These in diverse cases ought, and were of old forborn for a time.	312	Valdesso	V	27
as if it were but childrens meat, whereas there is not onely milke	317	Valdesso		23
Though this were the Authors opinion, yet the truth of it would be	319	Valdesso	V	15
are come now, to what the Pharisees were come in our Saviours time.	320	Valdesso		7
Were there no fooles, badd ware would not passe.	323	Proverbs		66
Were there no hearers, there would be no backbiters.	323	Proverbs		69
There would bee no great ones if there were no little ones.	331	Proverbs		292
There would bee no great ones if there were no mean ones.	331	Proverbs	V	292
There were no ill language, if it were not ill taken.	331	Proverbs		294
If folly were griefe every house would weepe.	334	Proverbs		370
If things were to be done twice, all would be wise.	344	Proverbs		700
Were it not for the bone in the legge,	355	Proverbs		1020
if it were not begun on particular ends, it would last).	361	Proverbs	D	1160
Trust no friend with that you need fear him if he were your enemy.	361	Proverbs	D	1169
yet if my Sister were acquainted that they are ready, I dare say she	367	Letters		1
but upon the want of those Books which were not to be got in England;	367	Letters		5
to which mine owne obligations were occasion inough, & therfore I am	367	Letters		29
or rather increaseth, I wish earnestly that I were again with you:	372	Letters		18
because they were to come into an unknown country, tender in	375	Letters		13
whom to receive were the greatest charitie of all, for she is	375	Letters		23
surely it were a great good deed, and I would have her conveyed	375	Letters		31
it were in another's power to defeat my charity, and evill shold be	376	Letters		9
of Cambridge, when the Ambassadours were made Masters of Arts.	441	Oration		T
WERT				
Who wert disseized by usurping lust:	54	Love 2		12
That he was fain, when thou wert destitute,	77	Avarice		7

WERT (cont'd)	PAGE	TITLE		LINE
Wert fain to take our flesh and curse,	103	Prayer 2		15
For where thou onely wert before	123	Time		14
Are the more foul, the more thou wert divine.	140	Ch.-rents		4
Wert thou a winde or wave,	154	Glimpse		8
Wert thou not born among the trees and leaves?	188	Heaven		5
Wert thou not born among the woods and leaves?	188	Heaven	W	5
and wert proceeding still on in thy Favours, untill we interrupted	288	Priest		15
WEST				
Is thy great arm which spans the east and west,	103	Prayer 2		8
East and West touch, the poles do kisse,	163	The Search		43
Onely the West and Rome do keep them free	194	Ch.-Milit.		157
They are Sinnes nipples, feeding th' east and west.	196	Ch.-Milit.		220
But as the Sunne still goes both west and east;	198	Ch.-Milit.		274
So also did the Church by going west	198	Ch.-Milit.		275
WESTERN				
Western discov'ries of posteritie.	168	The Sonne		10
Till both removed to the western clime.	191	Ch.-Milit.		36
Thus Sinne triumphs in Western Babylon;	196	Ch.-Milit.		211
WESTWARD				
The course was westward, that the sunne might light	190	Ch.-Milit.		17
Religion, like a pilgrime, westward bent,	190	Ch.-Milit.		29
At length to Germanie, still westward bending,	192	Ch.-Milit.		81
And travell'd westward also: journeying on	193	Ch.-Milit.		104
And travell'd Westward also, coasting on,	193	Ch.-Milit.	W	104
Yet as the Church shall thither westward flie,	197	Ch.-Milit.		259
WET				
When th' earth was dry, thou mad'st a sea of wet:	120	Providence		113
WHAT				
But gladly welcome what he doth afford;	7	Ch.-Porch		15
O what were man, might he himself misplace!	7	Ch.-Porch		23
All worldly right, save what he hath by beast.	7	Ch.-Porch		36
If studious, copie fair, what time hath blurr'd;	10	Ch.-Porch		86
If thou art nothing, think what thou wouldst bee	10	Ch.-Porch	W	90
What nature made a ship, he makes a shelf.	11	Ch.-Porch		120
Thou liv'st by rule. What doth not so, but man?	12	Ch.-Porch		134
Thou liv'st by rule. What does not so, but man?	12	Ch.-Porch	W	134
Salute thy self: see what thy soul doth wear.	12	Ch.-Porch		146
And tumble up and down what thou find'st there.	12	Ch.-Porch		148
What skills it, if a bag of stones or gold	13	Ch.-Porch		169
Still in thy heart, that he may see what's there.	17	Ch.-Porch		272
Entice all neatly to what they know best;	18	Ch.-Porch		295
What to ask further. Doubts well rais'd do lock	18	Ch.-Porch		299
What to ask farther. Doubts well rais'd do lock	18	Ch.-Porch	W	299
Mark what another sayes: for many are	19	Ch.-Porch		319
Whom oil and balsames kill, what salve can cure?	24	Ch.-Porch		447
Whom oil and mercies kill, what salve can cure?	24	Ch.-Porch	W	447
Summe up at night, what thou hast done by day;	24	Ch.-Porch		451
Summe up at night, what thou hast done that day;	24	Ch.-Porch	W	451
And in the morning, what thou hast to do.	24	Ch.-Porch		452
Alas! what haste they make to be undone!	27	Sacrifice		34
What I taught: Comments would the text confound.	28	Sacrifice		55
What ever scoffes or scornfulnesse can bring,	32	Sacrifice		174
What ever scoffes & scornfulnesse can bring,	32	Sacrifice	W	174
Alas! what have I stollen from you? Death.	34	Sacrifice		231
Alas, my God, I know not what.	36	Thanksgvng		50
What I have treasur'd in my memorie!	38	The Sinner		2
How shall I count what thee befell,	38	Good Fri.		3
What ever sinne did this pure rock commit,	41	Sepulchre		10
His stretched sinews taught all strings, what key	41	Easter		11
What ever future sinnes should me miscall,	44	H. Bapt.1		13
Lord, with what care hast thou begirt us round!	45	Sinne 1		1
Besides what I might have	46	Afflict.1		4
What pleasures could I want, whose King I served,	46	Afflict.1		13
Now I am here, what thou wilt do with me	48	Afflict.1		55
From what life feeleth, Adams fall.	48	Repentance		12
What can be lower then the common manger?	50	Faith		22
And in this shew, what Christ hath done.	51	Faith		36
This shadowes out what Christ hath done.	51	Faith	W	36
What though my bodie runne to dust?	51	Faith		41
If what my soul doth feel sometimes,	55	Temper 1		3
That washes what it shows. Who can indeare	58	H.Script.1		10
What if I say thou seek'st delayes;	61	Grace	W	20
What were they all, compar'd to thine?	62	Afflict.2		8
My God, what is a heart?	62	Mattens		5
My God, what is a heart,	62	Mattens		9
What have I brought thee home	64	Even-song		9
And spoil the meeting. What shall point out them,	65	Ch.-monum.		14
O what a state is this, which never knew	65	Ch.-mus.	W	8
Which knoweth not, what means, to Morrow.	65	Ch.-mus.	W	8
Which knoweth not, what means, too Morrow.	65	Ch.-mus.	W	9
What upon trust	71	Frailtie		2
O brook not this, lest if what even now	71	Frailtie		17
What place or person calls for, he doth pay.	72	Constancie		15
So much breath to a sigh, what's then behinde?	73	Afflict.3		9
Setting in order what they tumble:	75	Sunday	W	5
What's done on earth, we shall not fare the worse,	78	Ang.&Sts.		27
What's done on earth, we shall not feare the worse,	78	Ang.&Sts.	V	27
Lord, with what bountie and rare clemencie	82	Ungratef.		1
For what account can thy ill steward make?	83	Sighs & Gr.		8
What hath not man sought out and found,	85	Vanitie 1		22

WHAT (cont'd)

	PAGE	TITLE		LINE
What hath not man wrought out and found,	85	Vanitie 1	V	22
Give to thy Mother, what thou wouldst allow	86	Lent		5
What reason hath from nature borrowed,	88	The Pearl		3
What reason hath from nature purchased,	88	The Pearl	W	3
In laws and policie; what the starres conspire,	88	The Pearl		5
What willing nature speaks, what forc'd by fire;	88	The Pearl		6
I know the wayes of Honour, what maintains	88	The Pearl		11
What mirth and musick mean; what love and wit	89	The Pearl		24
What both the steps and pegs of pleasure bee:	89	The Pearl	W	28
And at what rate and price I have thy love;	89	The Pearl		35
What house more stately hath there been,	90	Man		4
Yet can a friend what thou hast done fulfill?	94	Unkindness		21
And pilfring what I once did give,	95	Submission		11
Take one from ten, and what remains?	96	Charms & K		15
What strange pollutions doth he wed,	100	Miserie		13
Ah wretch! what verse	102	Miserie		65
I often blotted what I had begunne;	102	Jordan 2		9
Of what an easie quick accesse,	103	Prayer 2		1
Of what supreme almightie power	103	Prayer 2		7
Of what unmeasurable love	103	Prayer 2		13
Lord, what is man to thee,	104	Obedience		21
Of what we might not take, or be withstood.	104	Obedience		30
Lord with what glorie wast thou serv'd of old,	106	Sion		1
To see what help in th' earth or skie:	107	Home		14
My God, what is this world to me?	108	Home		32
What is this weary world; this meat and drink,	108	Home		37
What is this woman-kinde, which I can wink	108	Home		39
What have I left, that I should stay and grone?	109	Home		67
But dearest Mother, (what those misse),	110	Brit. Ch.		25
What tune is this, poore man? said he:	110	The Quip		10
Heark and beware, lest what you now do measure	111	Vanitie 2		5
What delight or hope remains?	114	Dialogue		8
What, (childe), is the ballance thine,	114	Dialogue		9
What the gains in having thee	114	Dialogue		13
What angel fit?	116	Dulnesse		28
Ask'd what it meant. I, (who am never loth	116	Love-joy		4
Thy skill and art, what musick would it be!	118	Providence		40
Some creatures have in winter what to eat;	118	Providence		55
And if an herb hath power, what have the starres?	119	Providence		77
Of what strange length must that needs be,	123	Time		25
What do I here before his doore?	123	Time		29
What it would come to at the worst	123	Gratefulnes		11
What show'd so well.	125	Peace		18
O what a cunning guest	126	Confession		1
Oh, what a thing is man! how farre from power,	127	Giddinesse		1
O what a sight were Man, if his attires	127	Giddinesse		17
The Font did onely, what was old, renew:	130	Love unkn.		64
The Caldron suppled, what was grown too hard:	130	Love unkn.		65
The Thorns did quicken, what was grown too dull:	130	Love unkn.		66
All did but strive to mend, what you had marr'd.	130	Love unkn.		67
What open force, or hidden CHARM	133	Paradise		4
Quickly effect, what thou dost move;	133	The Method		6
What do I see	133	The Method		13
But stay! what's there?	134	The Method		21
Bid what he please; yet I am sure,	135	Divinitie		22
To take and taste what he doth there designe,	135	Divinitie		23
I am no Crystall, what shall I?	136	Ephes.		30
What doth this noise of thoughts within my heart	136	Familie		1
What do these loud complaints and pulling fears,	136	Familie		3
What do these loud complaints and puling fears,	136	Familie	V	3
What is so shrill as silent tears?	137	Familie		20
What though some have a fraught	137	The Size		7
Those have their hopes; these what they have renounce,	138	The Size		21
For I will do, or suffer what I ought.	139	Artillerie		16
O dreadfull Justice, what a fright and terrour	141	Justice 2		1
What Adam had, and forfeited for all,	143	Holdfast		13
Busie enquiring heart, what wouldst thou know?	144	Discharge		1
Let what will fall:	144	Discharge		9
What present things requir'd of thee.	144	Discharge		25
As mens returns, what would become of fools?	147	Offering		2
What hast thou there? a heart? but is it pure?	147	Offering		3
What thou hast kept,	147	Offering		29
Mark well my furnace! O what flames,	149	Longing		26
What heats abound!	149	Longing		27
What griefs, what shames!	149	Longing		28
And when they ask'd, what he would wear;	151	The Bag		16
That I shall minde, what you impart;	152	The Bag		35
Shall still be open; what he sends	152	The Bag		39
What? shall I ever sigh and pine?	153	The Collar		3
What I have lost with cordiall fruit?	153	The Collar		9
Of what is fit, and not. Forsake thy cage,	153	The Collar		21
And what to this? what more	155	Assurance		13
What is thy aim? wouldst thou unlock the doore	155	Assurance		15
What is objected by my foes.	155	Assurance		24
What for it self love once began,	156	Assurance		41
And force of fire, what curious things are made	161	Priesthood		14
O what pure things, most pure must those things be,	161	Priesthood		29
What pride by opposition.	161	Priesthood		42
Where is my God? what hidden place	163	The Search		29
What covert dare eclipse thy face?	163	The Search		31

WHAT (cont'd)

	PAGE	TITLE	LINE
What edge so keen,	163	The Search	54
What point so piercing can appeare	163	The Search	55
What are two shallow foords, two little spouts	164	Grief	9
What is this strange and uncouth thing?	164	The Crosse	1
What I would do for thee, if once my grones	165	The Crosse	15
What frost to that? what pole is not the zone,	166	The Flower	32
What fine varietie each tongue affords:	167	The Sonne	2
For what Christ once in humblenesse began,	168	The Sonne	13
Hath done what he condemnes in reading:	171	Self-cond.	16
What wonders shall we feel, when we shall see	172	The Glance	19
What can I want or need?	172	23 Psalme	4
What cordials make this curious broth,	175	The Odour	9
Ev'n all my heart, and what is lodged there:	176	Forerunners	8
I passe not, I, what of the rest become,	176	Forerunners	9
Unto what you now advise:	177	The Rose	14
What is fairer then a rose?	178	The Rose	17
What is sweeter? yet it purgeth.	178	The Rose	18
Weep what ye have drunk amisse,	180	Invitation	10
O what sweetnesse from the bowl	181	Banquet	7
What I seek, for what I sue;	182	Banquet	46
O what a damp and shade	183	A Parodie	11
And then what life I have,	183	A Parodie	21
O what a deadly cold	184	A Parodie	26
And what I do in any thing,	184	The Elixer	3
What others mean to do, I know not well;	187	Judgement	6
What leaves are they? impart the matter wholly.	188	Heaven	9
Then tell me, what is that supreme delight?	188	Heaven	13
Light to the minde: what shall the will enjoy?	188	Heaven	15
Ah, what a thing is man devoid of grace,	193	Ch.-Milit.	111
What wretchednesse can give him any room,	193	Ch.-Milit.	117
As well what should befall, as what befell.	193	Ch.-Milit.	130
Then what was in their tongue, did overcome;	196	Ch.-Milit.	202
Whereby one may foretell, what sinnes next yeare	197	Ch.-Milit.	245
To discharge what is behinde.	199	L'Envoy	16
And what shold flesh but flesh discry,	201	H. Commun. W	32
But what shall issue, whither these my words	204	Persever. W	5
What makes a Danvers	208	J. Danvers D	5
Fairer & richer. Now wee know, what's thine,	211	Bohemia D	18
And what is fortunes. Thou hast singled out	211	Bohemia D	19
O what a poore thing 'tis to bee a Queene	212	Bohemia D	23
where he shall not exercise what he is, unlesse he forsake his	226	Priest 2	26
because people by what they understand, are best led to what they	228	Priest 4	20
by what they understand, are best led to what they understand not.	228	Priest 4	20
remembring what his Master saith, that if any do Gods will,	228	Priest 4	28
coherence thereof, touching what goes before, and what follows after,	229	Priest 4	11
and what follows after, as also the scope of the Holy Ghost.	229	Priest 4	11
they were reproved, as ignorant of what spirit they were.	229	Priest 4	14
the grace of God in himself, and what the Holy Spirit teacheth him;	229	Priest 4	20
as attending to what is done in the Church, and every one,	231	Priest 6	27
of their answer, but gently and pausably, thinking what they say;	231	Priest 6	33
who treads in his steps, and will not throw down what he hath built;	232	Priest 7	27
What an admirable Epistle is the second to the Corinthians?	234	Priest 7	17
Oh let us all take heed what we do, God sees us, he sees whether I	234	Priest 7	26
he contrives how and in what manner to induce it to the best	236	Priest 8	1
both because they do best, and because what they do, is blessed,	240	Priest 10	16
and knows what prayers they say, and till they have learned them,	241	Priest 10	3
and common, but wholsome, what hee hath, is little, but very good;	241	Priest 10	16
he bethinketh himselfe what good deeds he can do that day,	244	Priest 12	16
even in externall and indifferent things, what course is to be taken;	247	Priest 13	1
the Parson questions what order is kept in the house, as about	248	Priest 14	31
what strength, and joy, and peace it administers against all	250	Priest 15	2
First, what disorders there are either in Apparell, or Diet,	251	Priest 17	19
Secondly, what means of Piety, whether daily prayers be used,	251	Priest 17	22
what kind of remedy fits the temper of the house best, and then hee	251	Priest 17	26
or, So farr indeed what you say is true, and well said;	252	Priest 18	11
he considers what is the end of any Command, and then he suits things	253	Priest 19	4
propounds among his Brethren what were fitting to be done.	253	Priest 19	14
stead to his Parish, and dischargeth God what he can of his promises.	254	Priest 20	9
making what hee knows to serve him in that which he knows not:	256	Priest 21	38
since man is so miserable, what is to be done?	257	Priest 21	3
He asked him again, what he would do, if he were in a ditch?	257	Priest 21	4
but when one is asked a question, he must discover what he is.	257	Priest 21	20
with himself, how or what behaviour to assume for so holy things.	257	Priest 22	27
thou knowest what thou didst, when thou appointedst it to be done	257	Priest 22	32
therefore doe thou fulfill what thou didst appoint;	257	Priest 22	34
step into their great and glorious calling) and upon what termes,	258	Priest 22	19
and upon what termes, and with what vowes they were Baptized.	258	Priest 22	20
and the difference, hee ought to receive, of what age soever.	258	Priest 22	36
loosely and wildely, and then the Answerer will discover what hee is.	259	Priest 22	10
of which he gathers, in case he be ignorant himself, what to hold;	260	Priest 23	12
to know what herbs may be used in stead of drugs of the same nature,	261	Priest 23	29
The third means is the observation what is the main foundation,	262	Priest 24	28
these two with himselfe, as what the Church is, how it began,	262	Priest 24	32
what scandall is, when given or taken;	263	Priest 24	8
and knowledg of their own body, and what it can well disgest:	267	Priest 26	1
The third is the observation with what appetite they sit down.	267	Priest 26	5
For knowing what one usually can well disgest, and feeling when I go	267	Priest 26	6
and feeling when I go to meat in what disposition I am,	267	Priest 26	7
what a great Charge lyes upon them, and that indeed the whole order	269	Priest 29	27
and that is, of what is Necessary, and what is Additionary.	272	Priest 31	20

WHAT (cont'd)	PAGE	TITLE		LINE
and prevent such interruptions, what he may, before they come,	273	Priest 31		17
nothing to do, lets go to the Tavern, or to the stews, or what not.	274	Priest 32		13
reason crosseth not our Saviours precept of selling what we have,	274	Priest 32		32
and who is ready to ask, if he shall mend shoos, or what he shall do?	275	Priest 32		8
what they are fittest for, and to prepare for that with all	275	Priest 32		16
and house-keeper hath his hands full, if he do what he ought to do.	275	Priest 32		21
the Baptist squared out to every one (even to Souldiers) what to do.	277	Priest 32		24
and knows what recovered him, is a Physitian so far as he meetes	278	Priest 33		26
sea rage so much as it can, and all things do what they can, and all,	281	Priest 34		22
Let the weather be what it will, still we have bread, though	281	Priest 34		25
but pardon our sins, and perfect what thou hast begun.	289	Priest		21
to search out most diligently what meats were agreeable unto me,	293	Cornaro		5
diligently what meats were agreeable unto me, and what disagreeable:	293	Cornaro		5
that I might know what great power a sober and temperate life hath	294	Cornaro		25
when the Physicians saw in what case I was, they concluded that I	295	Cornaro		2
considering what an orderly life I had led for many yeares together,	295	Cornaro		7
neither did I know well, what I did or said.	296	Cornaro		17
and what hidden properties it hath, what meat and drink agrees best	297	Cornaro		27
hidden properties it hath, what meat and drink agrees best with it:	297	Cornaro		28
What Physician could have discovered these hidden qualities to me,	297	Cornaro		34
what diet shall he use in diseases, which being in health he hath	299	Cornaro		23
by this also, in what estate I am, may be discovered, because	302	Cornaro		27
what remains, but that I should wish all who have the care	303	Cornaro		31
words about the H. Scripture suite with what he writes elsewhere,	306	Valdesso		15
but it is sutable to what the Author holds elsewhere, for he	311	Valdesso		21
and that by restraining him from what he would not have him doe.	313	Valdesso		23
the scripture, yet what the scripture teacheth, the spirit teacheth,	317	Valdesso		29
are come now, to what the Pharisees were come in our Saviours time.	320	Valdesso		6
The Wolfe knowes, what the ill beast thinkes.	321	Proverbs		16
God complaines not, but doth what is fitting.	327	Proverbs		182
What your glasse telles you, will not be told by Councell.	329	Proverbs		255
The groundsell speakes not save what it heard at the hinges.	331	Proverbs		295
The child saies nothing, but what it heard by the fire.	331	Proverbs		300
tell me what I dreamed last night.	332	Proverbs		336
Hee that doth what hee will, doth not what he ought.	333	Proverbs		350
Would you know what mony is, Go borrow some.	334	Proverbs		374
Hee that knowes what may bee gained in a day never steales.	336	Proverbs		445
Hee that should have what hee hath not,	340	Proverbs		559
should doe what he doth not.	340	Proverbs		559
Hee that would have what hee hath not,	340	Proverbs	V	559
must doe what he doth not.	340	Proverbs	V	559
The fatt man knoweth not, what the leane thinketh.	341	Proverbs		605
but he will drinke when and what he pleaseth.	342	Proverbs		623
A wise man cares not for what he cannot have.	343	Proverbs		662
Be what thou wouldst seeme to be.	345	Proverbs		724
He that doth what he should not, shall feele what he would not.	347	Proverbs		783
Doe what thou oughtest, and come what come can.	348	Proverbs		818
There comes nought out of the sacke but what was there.	348	Proverbs		833
There come nought out of the sacke but what was there.	348	Proverbs	V	833
The Cow knowes not what her taile is worth, till she have lost it.	350	Proverbs		870
Life is halfe spent before we know what it is.	351	Proverbs		917
Conversation makes one what he is.	351	Proverbs		926
Conversation makes one what they are.	351	Proverbs	V	926
When all men have what belongs to them, it cannot bee much.	353	Proverbs		979
knowes nothing sure but what hee hath laid out.	354	Proverbs		1001
If gold knew what gold is, gold would get gold I wis.	354	Proverbs		1012
A woman conceales what shee knowes not.	355	Proverbs		1031
What one day gives us, another takes away from us.	359	Proverbs	D	1111
What Trades-man is there who will set up without his Tools?	364	Letters		14
in that I apprehend what my Friends would have been forward to say,	364	Letters		20
but they will object again, What becomes of your Annuity?	364	Letters		30
what is that to those infinite Volumes of Divinity, which yet every	365	Letters		13
Thirdly, what I desire, and to what end, not vain pleasures,	365	Letters		18
what I desire, and to what end, not vain pleasures, nor to a vain	365	Letters		19
of your wit, mark what I say, have a good conceit of your wit;	366	Letters		15
burden to you, since I can never answer what I have already received;	367	Letters		14
place (that you may understand what it is) is the finest place in	369	Letters		30
What hath Affliction grievous in it more then for a moment?	372	Letters		26
consider what advantage you have over Youth and Health,	372	Letters		32
of what poor regard ought they to be, since if we had Riches we are	373	Letters		22
What an admirable thing is this, that God puts his shoulder to our	374	Letters		17
of those that might say, What shall we rejoyce in afflictions?	374	Letters		23
What can be said more comfortably?	374	Letters		28
one of our neeces into your hands but barely what I wrote I meant,	375	Letters		5
I will tell you what I wrote to our eldest brother, when he urged one	375	Letters		10
school-mistresse, and you know what those mercenary creatures are.	375	Letters		26
I doe my part to them, lett them think of me what they will or can.	376	Letters		7
What a trouble hath your Goodness brought on you, by admitting our	376	Letters		26
to name at first, what the summe should be, but he told her Grace,	379	Letters		6
and also what becomes of you this sommer.	379	Letters		24
what could have happened more pleasing to us, then the accesse	442	Oration		8
For amongst us what glorious shew is there, either of garments,	442	Oration		31
what splendor? surely, since there is a two-fold brightnesse which	442	Oration		32
WHATEVER				
Whatever is made by the hand of man,	362	Proverbs	D	1184
be it to King, Prince, or whatever comes to the University;	369	Letters		35
WHATSOE'RE				
God sent him, whatsoe're he be: O tarry,	24	Ch.-Porch		442
WHATSOEVER				
that we should do whatsoever things are honest, or just,	253	Priest 19		23

WHEN (cont'd)

	PAGE	TITLE		LINE
When waves do rise, and tempests rage.	97	Afflict.5		6
When we grew wanton, thou didst use displeasure	97	Afflict.5		9
When clothes are taken from a chest of sweets	98	Mortific.		2
When cloths are taken from a chest of sweets	98	Mortific.	V	2
When boyes go first to bed,	98	Mortific.		7
When youth is frank and free,	98	Mortific.		13
When man grows staid and wise,	98	Mortific.		19
When age grows low and weak,	98	Mortific.		25
When he would speak;	98	Mortific.		28
Sweet were the dayes, when thou didst lodge with Lot,	99	Decay		1
Advise with Abraham, when thy power could not	99	Decay		3
I see the world grows old, when as the heat	99	Decay		16
Dead with eclipses, when we speak of thee:	101	Miserie		34
So our clay hearts, ev'n when we crouch	101	Miserie		39
When first my lines of heav'nly joyes made mention,	102	Jordan 2		1
When first my verse of heav'nly joyes made mention,	102	Jordan 2	W	1
As flames do work and winde, when they ascend,	103	Jordan 2		13
Art thou possest, who, when thou couldst not die,	103	Prayer 2		14
And heart unto this deed, when he hath read;	105	Obedience		38
And heart unto this deed, when he doth read	105	Obedience	W	38
My Saviours bloud: when ever at his board	106	Conscience		14
When Solomons temple stood and flourished!	106	Sion		2
When I behold it trickling down thy face,	107	Home		9
When man was lost, thy pitie lookt about	107	Home		13
Some may dream merrily, but when they wake,	108	Home		51
But when we leave our corn and hay:	108	Home		56
And ev'n my verse, when by the ryme and reason	109	Home		75
I joy, deare Mother, when I view	109	Brit. Ch.		1
When she doth write.	109	Brit. Ch.		6
Which when I pluckt not, Sir, said she,	110	The Quip		6
Yet when the houre of thy designe	111	The Quip		21
Christ left his grave-clothes, that we might, when grief	112	Dawning		15
Christ left his grave-cloths, that we might, when grief	112	Dawning	V	15
When I had got these parcels, instantly	112	JESU		7
But when all my care and pains	114	Dialogue		5
When all perfections as but one appeare,	115	Dulnesse		13
Check the proud sea, ev'n when it swells and gathers.	118	Providence		48
When they are callow; but withdraw their food	118	Providence		63
When they are fledge, that need may teach them flying.	118	Providence		64
But at his perill: when he digs the place,	119	Providence		82
When th' earth was dry, thou mad'st a sea of wet:	120	Providence		113
When that lay gather'd, thou didst broach the mountains:	120	Providence		114
When yet some places could no moisture get,	120	Providence		115
When they are ripe, their odour will ascend,	120	Providence		119
And when they once have perfected their draughts,	122	Sinnes rd.		5
But thou didst reckon, when at first	123	Gratefulnes		9
Not thankfull, when it pleaseth me;	124	Gratefulnes		29
But when I digg'd, I saw a worm devoure	125	Peace		17
Whom when for Peace	125	Peace		20
Yet grief knows all, and enters when he will.	126	Confession		6
When he a torture hath design'd.	126	Confession		10
But when I thought to sleep out all these faults	130	Love unkn.		49
When with my pleasures ev'n my rest was gone?	130	Love unkn.		53
Did oft possesse me, so that when I pray'd,	130	Love unkn.		58
When thou dost greater judgements SPARE,	133	Paradise		10
When I did pray.	133	The Method		16
Late when I would have something done,	134	The Method		22
When I am sowre,	135	Ephes.		2
Griev'd for a worm, which when I tread,	135	Ephes.		5
When sawcie mirth shall knock or call at doore,	136	Ephes.		13
Nothing more quick when she doth go.	137	Familie		16
Title to more hereafter when they part,	137	The Size		3
When griefs prevail;	137	The Size		10
When suddenly I heard one say,	139	Artillerie		5
And bottome of the leaves: which when the winde	140	Ch.-rents		6
Gave you a colour once; which when your foes	140	Ch.-rents		13
But when debates and fretting jealousies	140	Ch.-rents		16
Which when your neighbours saw, like a north-winde,	140	Ch.-rents		22
When sinne and errour	141	Justice 2		3
When I had gain'd the brow and top,	142	Pilgrimage		22
And well it was for thee, when this befell,	144	Discharge		16
And alone, when they replied,	146	Praise 2		15
And when Justice call'd for fears,	146	Praise 2		23
Ev'n when the boat seems most to reel.	151	The Bag		4
And when they ask'd, what he would wear;	151	The Bag		16
When he was come, as travellers are wont,	151	The Bag		19
When as my fears foretold this, did replie,	154	Glimpse		19
Must let thee go, return when it doth knock.	154	Glimpse		22
When wit contrives to meet with thee,	155	Assurance		5
But also mine; as when the league was made	156	Assurance		28
Yea, when both rocks and all things shall disband,	156	Assurance		34
And when it stops for want of store,	157	Praise 3		4
When thou dost favour any action,	158	Praise 3		7
When thou dost blesse, hath twelve: one wheel doth rise	158	Praise 3		11
But when thou dost on businesse blow,	158	Praise 3		13
The windes their stint: and yet when I did call,	158	Praise 3		23
But when mine eyes	158	Praise 3		26
When God at first made man,	159	The Pulley		1
When almost all was out, God made a stay,	160	The Pulley		8
When God vouchsafeth to become our fare,	161	Priesthood		27

WHEN (cont'd)

	PAGE	TITLE		LINE
When thou dost turn, and wilt be neare;	163	The Search		53
And then when after much delay,	164	The Crosse		7
Ev'n when my will doth studie thy renown:	165	The Crosse		20
So that, ev'n when my hopes seem to be sped,	165	The Crosse		23
Farther from it then when I bent my bow;	165	The Crosse		26
Further from it then when I bent my bow;	165	The Crosse	V	26
To see their mother-root, when they have blown;	166	The Flower		11
When thou dost turn,	166	The Flower		34
Which when we once can finde and prove,	167	The Flower		45
Is, when the soul unto the lines accords.	168	a true Hymn		10
As when th' heart sayes (sighing to be approved)	168	a true Hymn		19
When once those snuffes are ta'ne away,	171	Self-cond.		22
When first thy sweet and gracious eye	171	The Glance		1
And surging griefs, when they grew bold, controll,	172	The Glance		15
What wonders shall we feel, when we shall see	172	The Glance		19
When thou shalt look us out of pain,	172	The Glance		21
When blessed Marie wip'd her Saviours feet,	173	Marie Magd		1
For when My Master, which alone is sweet,	175	The Odour		21
(As sweet things traffick when they meet)	175	The Odour		27
But will ye leave me thus? when ye before	176	Forerunners		14
When I had forgot my birth,	182	Banquet		31
Souls joy, when thou art gone,	183	A Parodie		1
Yet when thou dost suppresse	183	A Parodie		6
And when thou dost but shine lesse cleare,	183	A Parodie		19
And when the Divel shakes the tree,	184	The Elixer	W	12
When souls shall wear their new aray,	186	Death		19
When thou shalt call	187	Judgement		4
But I resolve, when thou shalt call for mine,	188	Judgement		11
When it grew loose, the Jews did hope in vain	190	Ch.-Milit.		23
Both where and when the Church began her race,	192	Ch.-Milit.		102
Pleasure succeeded straight, when that grew cold.	194	Ch.-Milit.		144
When written Truths shall censure mans devise.	194	Ch.-Milit.	W	160
But when they were unto the Sorbon come,	196	Ch.-Milit.	W	202
When th' one did set, the other did take place,	196	Ch.-Milit.		217
When height of malice, and prodigious lusts,	197	Ch.-Milit.		237
When Sein shall swallow Tiber, and the Thames	197	Ch.-Milit.		241
When Italie of us shall have her will,	197	Ch.-Milit.		243
Spain hath done one; when Arts perform the other,	197	Ch.-Milit.		265
That when they have accomplished the round,	197	Ch.-Milit.		267
That when they have accomplished their round,	197	Ch.-Milit.	W	267
When I contrive & plott to prove	201	love	W	4
Sometimes, when as I wash, I say	202	love	W	7
Thy ancient baptism which when I was foule	202	love	W	11
I took a time when thou didst sleep	202	love	W	13
Julips & Cordials when wee call on thee	204	The Knell	W	17
In the best face but filth, when, Lord, in thee	206	Walton 2		13
When nail'd unto 't, but he ascends again	439	Walton 5	V	2
When Love being weary made an end	439	Walton 5		11
He writ; when 's hand could write no more,	439	Walton 5		13
When my dear Friend, could write no more,	439	walton 6		1
When winds and waves rise highest, I am sure,	439	walton 6		3
When scepters, state, Attendants are the screen	212	Bohemia	D	24
Betwixt us & the people: when as glory	212	Bohemia	D	25
When all things pull & hale, that they may bring	212	Bohemia	D	27
When sense is made by Comments. But that face	212	Bohemia	D	29
When once his anger burns, thrice blest	216	Psalm II	D	31
Lord hear me when I call on Thee,	217	Psalm IV	D	1
when I was in distress.	217	Psalm IV	D	4
when I his grace implore:	217	Psalm IV	D	14
and not to think, that when they have read the Fathers, or Schoolmen,	226	Priest 2		10
their very face, when occasion cals, but seasonably and discreetly.	226	Priest 2		30
that when death takes him, as the Jewes and Judas did Christ,	227	Priest 3		32
When the Apostles would have called down fire from Heaven,	229	Priest 4		12
when it is a sin to take something for mony lent, or when not;	230	Priest 5		24
when it is a sin to take something for mony lent, or when not;	230	Priest 5		25
when it is a fault to discover anothers fault, or when not;	230	Priest 5		25
when it is a fault to discover anothers fault, or when not;	230	Priest 5		26
when the affections of the soul in desiring and procuring increase	230	Priest 5		26
or honour, be a sin of covetousnes or ambition, and when not;	230	Priest 5		28
when the appetites of the body in eating, drinking, sleep,	230	Priest 5		28
lust, and when not, and so in many circumstances of actions.	230	Priest 5		30
when he is to read divine services, composeth himselfe to all	231	Priest 6		1
when they come to pray, as a devout behaviour in the very act	231	Priest 6		15
in them, but causing them, when they sit, or stand, or kneel,	231	Priest 6		25
service, Rom. 12. when we speak not as Parrats, without reason,	232	Priest 6		3
but when we use our reason, and apply our powers to the service	232	Priest 6		5
and of theirs also who gaze upon them when they come in,	232	Priest 6		11
When he intermits, he is ever very well supplyed by some able man who	232	Priest 7		25
When he preacheth, he procures attention by all possible art,	232	Priest 7		30
them to be so, when God is so neer them, and even over their heads.	233	Priest 7		10
for thou art Love, and when thou teachest, all are Scholers.	233	Priest 7		36
so as a Market-man is, when the Market day comes, or a shopkeeper,	235	Priest 8		18
the Market day comes, or a shopkeeper, when customers use to come in.	235	Priest 8		19
Afterwards when the hour calls, with his family attending him,	236	Priest 8		2
And every one is more awaked, when we come, and say, Thou art	236	Priest 8		14
And when they go abroad, his wife among her neighbours is	240	Priest 10		27
act in them, then when they are called to others prayers, and that,	241	Priest 10		5
which when they leave the family, they carry with them.	241	Priest 10		6
being his only perfume, which deserves cost when he can spare it.	241	Priest 10		14
as not to get out of that sicknesse, when I am in it, by any diet.	242	Priest 10		38

WHEN (cont'd)

	PAGE	TITLE	LINE
When he riseth in the morning, he bethinketh himselfe what good deeds	244	Priest 12	15
paines in their vocation, as not knowing when they shal be relieved;	245	Priest 12	4
and when his own stock serves not, working those that are able	245	Priest 12	11
When-ever hee gives any thing, and sees them labour in thanking	245	Priest 12	30
When he comes to any house, first he blesseth it, and then as hee	247	Priest 14	10
and furthers them when hee is gone, in their imployment;	247	Priest 14	14
labour anxiously, when they overdo it, to the loss of their quiet,	247	Priest 14	28
when they doubt Gods providence, thinking that their own labour is	247	Priest 14	29
when they set themselves to work like brute beasts, never raising	247	Priest 14	32
when on the Lords day they do unnecessary servile work,	248	Priest 14	2
for as when the offence is particular, and against mee,	248	Priest 14	26
so when the offence is publicke, and against God, I am then to follow	248	Priest 14	28
when any of his cure is sick, or afflicted with losse of friend,	249	Priest 15	13
For by this means, when any sinns, he hateth him not as an officer,	250	Priest 16	11
so also when after many admonitions, any continue to be refractory,	250	Priest 16	15
when a just occasion calleth him out of his Parish (which he	250	Priest 17	23
And when he comes to his Inn, he refuseth not to joyne,	251	Priest 17	6
When he comes to any other house, where his kindred, or other	251	Priest 17	15
when the baits which the enemy lays in company, are discovered	252	Priest 18	13
as when he is set at an armour, or horse, he borrowes them	252	Priest 19	25
to do his Countrey true and laudable service, when occasion requires.	252	Priest 19	29
and then when he hath affrighted them with this, exposing	253	Priest 19	33
him in his Tithes, telling him when he hath forgotten it, This I do,	254	Priest 20	16
answers prove, may when they come home, either commend or reprove,	255	Priest 21	28
When once all have learned the words of the Catechisme,	255	Priest 21	34
when the answerer sticks, an illustrating the thing by something	256	Priest 21	36
when the Parson once demanded after other questions about mans	257	Priest 21	1
when it condescends to the naming of a plough, a hatchet,	257	Priest 21	11
but when one is asked a question, he must discover what he is.	257	Priest 21	19
knowest what thou didst, when thou appointedst it to be done thus;	257	Priest 22	33
When any one can distinguish the Sacramentall from common bread,	258	Priest 22	34
whom he hath ever some cases to ask, when he meets with them;	260	Priest 23	5
Yet when ever any controversie is brought to him, he never decides it	260	Priest 23	7
but when he hath so done, then he assumes the Parson, and exhorts	260	Priest 23	16
when the persons in difference are of a contentious disposition,	260	Priest 23	22
of diversion, and the benefit of application when need requires;	261	Priest 23	12
what scandall is, when given or taken;	263	Priest 24	8
who when they know a sin evidently, they commit it not.	264	Priest 26	11
the bounds of the action, nor when his eating begins to be unlawfull.	264	Priest 26	25
his children, hardly perceives when his storing becomes unlawfull:	264	Priest 26	28
or center, when his storing, which was even now good, passeth from	264	Priest 26	29
Whosoever when a just occasion cals, either spends not at all,	265	Priest 26	5
and feeling when I go to meat in what disposition I am,	267	Priest 26	7
When he deals with any that is heavy, and carnall;	267	Priest 26	17
but when he meets with a refined, and heavenly disposition,	267	Priest 26	18
knowing that there is one, who when they forget, remembers for them;	267	Priest 26	21
As when the people hungred and thirsted after our Saviours Doctrine,	267	Priest 26	22
but also for that when they are in company, instructions seasoned	268	Priest 27	3
even of the best in the Parish, when occasion requires:	268	Priest 28	28
then when any despises him, he takes it either in an humble way,	269	Priest 28	5
yet when God pleased, the sun stood stil, the fire burned not.	271	Priest 30	12
he often overturnes things, when they are thought past danger;	271	Priest 30	20
As when a Merchant hath a ship come home after many a storme,	271	Priest 30	22
and when for all that they do come, he be a little affected	273	Priest 31	18
when his occasions carry him abroad, or bring strangers to him,	274	Priest 32	6
For when men have nothing to do, then they fall to drink,	274	Priest 32	10
when the evills which he is now subject unto, may be prevented,	274	Priest 32	22
them honestly, and seasonably, when they are not better imployed.	274	Priest 32	31
because when we have sold all, and given it to the poor,	274	Priest 32	33
when they see any remarkable point of Education or good husbandry,	276	Priest 32	29
when they meet with good fruit, get a graffe of the tree,	276	Priest 32	31
When there is a Parliament, he is to endeavour by all means to be	277	Priest 32	8
And when he is there, he must not only be a morning man,	277	Priest 32	11
When none of these occasions call him abroad, every morning that hee	277	Priest 32	14
so must they fight for, and defend them, when occasion calls.	277	Priest 32	20
when the servant of God, freed for a while from temptation,	279	Priest 33	4
when he cannot more, as he that weeps a floud of tears.	279	Priest 33	30
getting for himself, when he tels it to others, becomes a Sermon.	279	Priest 33	32
when we are assaulted with temptations either from within or from	280	Priest 34	3
when the Divell for a time leaves us, as he did our Saviour,	280	Priest 34	5
as they remember themselves were, when affliction did blow the Coals.	280	Priest 34	20
nor when they are among them that are merry, to extend themselves	280	Priest 34	26
will they last the longer, and when they depart, returne the sooner.	280	Priest 34	29
when light is brought in, God send us the light of heaven;	284	Priest 35	23
when the other gives him just opportunity, by speaking any good,	286	Priest 36	23
when they are at leasure, make others faults their entertainment	286	Priest 37	29
when we had sinned beyond any help in heaven or earth, then thou	288	Priest	25
For when they saw their parents and kindred snatcht away in the midst	291	Cornaro	9
When therefore I was thus affected [afflicted] from the thirtie fifth	292	Cornaro	1
and, when I felt inward heats, drank delightfull wines,	292	Cornaro	28
whereinto I was wont, when I pleased my Sense & Appetite.	293	Cornaro	23
This Galen confirms, when he sayes, that immoderate heats and colds,	294	Cornaro	6
For when my brother and others of my kindred saw some great powerfull	294	Cornaro	15
This I found by experience, when I was seventie yeares old:	294	Cornaro	35
when the Physicians saw in what case I was, they concluded that I	295	Cornaro	1
when he cometh to visit his patient, prescribes this Physick first,	297	Cornaro	15
and when he hath cured him, commends this also to him, if he will	297	Cornaro	17
heretofore orderly or disorderly, when he is sick, ought not to eat,	299	Cornaro	30
and that in much smaller quantitie then when he was well.	299	Cornaro	32
When I cannot have their companie, I give my self to the reading	301	Cornaro	5

WHEN (cont'd)	PAGE	TITLE		LINE
when I was given to disorder and all the delights that could be.	302	Cornaro		10
For when I come home, I finde eleven grand-children of mine,	303	Cornaro		2
sheweth, and I also, when I was a young man, too well found.	303	Cornaro		15
when I shall come to that point, I shall finde no little comfort in	303	Cornaro		23
I like not in him, as my fragments will expresse, when you read them;	304	Valdesso		17
ever outrunning the Teacher, as it did when Peter taught Cornelius:	310	Valdesso		8
For as the servant leaves not the letter when he hath read it,	310	Valdesso		27
us not with the same thing only when it is read as the promises doe,	310	Valdesso		33
restraining motion (as S. Paul had when hee would have preached in	313	Valdesso		16
But when he enlargeth he goes too farre.	315	Valdesso		34
when he professed himselfe a Pharisee, which strictly he was not,	316	Valdesso		7
when he useth the word Jurisdiction, allowing no Jurisdiction over	316	Valdesso		15
when they doe amisse, and they are to be judged according	316	Valdesso		18
but when he sayes they are equally exempt with God, that is dangerous	316	Valdesso		32
that I may speak with him or doe some thing else when I doe come.	318	Valdesso		17
When all sinnes grow old, coveteousnesse is young.	321	Proverbs		18
When all sinnes grow old, coveteousnesse grows young.	321	Proverbs	V	18
When a friend askes, there is no to morrow.	322	Proverbs		32
When prayers are done, my Lady is ready.	323	Proverbs		71
When a dog is a drowning, every one offers him drink.	323	Proverbs		77
To a gratefull man give mony when he askes.	324	Proverbs		115
The Fox, when hee cannot reach the grapes,	325	Proverbs		130
Marry your sonne when you will; your daughter when you can.	326	Proverbs		149
I wept when I was borne, and every day shewes why.	327	Proverbs		199
When God will, no winde but brings raine.	332	Proverbs		332
When the Foxe preacheth, beware your geese.	332	Proverbs		337
When you are an Anvill, hold you still;	332	Proverbs		338
when you are a hammer, strike your fill.	332	Proverbs		338
When your will is ready, the feete are swift.	336	Proverbs	V	448
When children stand quiet, they have done some ill.	338	Proverbs		504
When a knave is in a plumtree he hath neither friend nor kin.	338	Proverbs		507
When there are many to strike on one Anvile.	340	Proverbs		551
When the tree is fallen, all goe with their hatchet.	340	Proverbs		566
Old men, when they scorne young, make much of death.	341	Proverbs		597
God is at the end, when we thinke he is furthest off it.	341	Proverbs		598
but he will drinke when and what he pleaseth.	342	Proverbs		623
When age is jocond it makes sport for death.	342	Proverbs		637
When my house burnes, it's not good playing at Chesse.	343	Proverbs		666
When God will punish, hee will first take away the understanding.	344	Proverbs		688
When it thunders, the theefe becomes honest.	344	Proverbs		690
Women laugh when they can, and weepe when they will.	348	Proverbs		821
When you enter into a house, leave the anger ever at the doore.	350	Proverbs		896
Children when they are little make parents fooles,	352	Proverbs		939
when they are great they make them mad.	352	Proverbs		939
Children when they are little make their parents fooles,	352	Proverbs	V	939
The house is a fine house, when good folke are within.	352	Proverbs		952
The house is a fine house, when good folks are within.	352	Proverbs	V	952
Wee leave more to do when wee dye, then wee have done.	353	Proverbs		972
When all men have what belongs to them, it cannot bee much.	353	Proverbs		979
When a man sleepes, his head is in his stomach.	353	Proverbs		981
When one is on horsebacke hee knowes all things.	353	Proverbs		982
When God is made master of a family, he orders the disorderly.	353	Proverbs		983
When a Lackey comes to hells doore, the devills locke the gates.	353	Proverbs		984
To seek in a Sheep five feet when there is but four.	359	Proverbs	D	1112
To play at Chesse when the house is on fire.	360	Proverbs	D	1136
When war begins, then hell openeth.	360	Proverbs	D	1141
the time when I desire this (which is now, when I must lay	365	Letters		17
this (which is now, when I must lay the foundation of my whole life).	365	Letters		17
as when you meet with a witty French speech, try to speak the like in	366	Letters		10
not with a foolish vanting of yourself when there is no caus,	366	Letters		17
when I have more time, you shall hear more;	366	Letters		20
when I shall understand that a Letter will be seasonable,	371	Letters		14
when we consider that the Blessings in the holy Scripture,	373	Letters		28
when I wrote, to putt one of our neeces into your hands but barely	375	Letters		4
wrote to our eldest brother, when he urged one upon me, and but one,	375	Letters		10
4. When two things dislike you:	380	Woodnoth		21
To desire good & endeavour it when we can doe no more, is to doe it.	381	Woodnoth		15
Complaine not of the want of success, when you have the fruit of it.	381	Woodnoth		17
When we exhort people to continue in their vocation, it is in	381	Woodnoth		22
of Cambridge, when the Ambassadours were made Masters of Arts.	441	Oration		T
perpetuall povertie, but when your Excellencies appeare.	442	Oration		37
WHEN-EVER				
When-ever hee gives any thing, and sees them labour in thanking	245	Priest 12		30
WHENCE				
They strike my head, the rock from whence all store	32	Sacrifice		170
Whence com'st thou, that thou art so fresh and fine?	77	Avarice		2
Thou art the holy mine, whence came the gold,	78	Ang.&Sts.		11
Thou art the sacred mine, whence came the gold,	78	Ang.&Sts.	W	11
The spring, whence all things flow:	101	Miserie		60
Was cleare as heav'n, from whence it came.	135	Divinitie		14
Come from the earth, from whence those vessels come;	161	Priesthood		20
My Eyes, from whence these Tears did spring,	214	Convert	D	6
Whence I conclude, That they that live a temperate life,	295	Cornaro		14
Whence I conclude, That an orderly life is the most sure way & ground	297	Cornaro		11
whence it seems to me, not onely a shamefull thing to fear that which	303	Cornaro		21
whence come so many Books of severall mens opinions:	317	Valdesso		3
WHENEVER				
that how or whenever he punish him, it be not in his Ministry:	235	Priest 8		26
resolves whenever he enters into a Church, to kneel down,	273	Priest 31		23
that whenever he repaires to his house, he may behave himself so	273	Priest 31		26

	PAGE	TITLE		LINE
WHENSOEVER				
Whensoever the Countrey Parson proceeds so farre as to call in	263	Priest 25		22
WHER				
wher-ever spoken this day throughout the universall Church. . . .	289	Priest		14
WHER-EVER				
wher-ever spoken this day throughout the universall Church. . . .	289	Priest		14
WHERE (see also wheare)				
Be usefull where thou livest, that they may	19	Ch.-Porch		325
Let thy minde still be bent, still plotting where, . . .	20	Ch.-Porch		337
They dye in holes where glory never shone.	20	Ch.-Porch	W	348
Till thou change names, and be where he began.	21	Ch.-Porch		378
Where it is warmest. Leave thy six and seven;	22	Ch.-Porch		401
Pray with the most: for where most pray, is heaven. . . .	22	Ch.-Porch		402
I am the floore, the sink, where they it fling:	32	Sacrifice		175
My heart hath store, write there, where in	39	Good Fri.		23
Where our hard hearts have took up stones to brain thee, .	41	Sepulchre		13
Where joyes my fellows were?	46	Afflict.1		14
I took thy sweetned pill, till I came where	47	Afflict.1	W	47
And where sinne placeth me in Adams fall, ...	50	Faith		19
And where sinne places me in Adams fall, ...	50	Faith	W	19
Where now by Faith all arms are of a length;	50	Faith		27
Make one place ev'ry where.	55	Temper 1		28
It cannot be. Where is that mightie joy, ...	56	Temper 2		1
Of strange delights, where we may wish & take.	58	H.Script.1		7
Where is that fire which once descended	59	Whitsunday		5
Remove me, where I need not say, ...	61	Grace		23
Where all my debts are payd, none can accrue	65	Ch.-mus.	W	8
Where in each room of the well-furnisht tent	69	Content		19
Where in each room of that well-furnisht tent	69	Content	W	19
Where all the beasts and fowls by their command	70	Humilitie		3
Where all the beasts and Foule by their command	70	Humilitie	W	3
Where beams surround my Saviours face, ...	74	The Starre		2
Canst thou be any where	74	The Starre		3
Unto the place where thou	74	The Starre		19
And where the week-dayes trail on ground, ...	76	Sunday		58
Where ev'ry one is king, and hath his crown, ...	77	Ang.&Sts.		4
Thou art the cabinet where the jewell lay:	78	Ang.&Sts.		14
And where his pleasure no injunction layes, ...	78	Ang.&Sts.		19
As good go any where, they say, ...	80	Deniall		11
Where now we shall be better Gods then he.	82	Ungratef.		6
Love built a stately house; where Fortune came, ...	84	The World		1
So that we need not say, Where's this command?	86	Vanitie 1		26
A box where sweets compacted lie;	88	Vertue		10
Where both their baskets are with all their store, ...	89	The Pearl	W	26
Getting a house and home, where he may move	98	Mortific.		20
Where yet both Sinne and Satan, thy old foes, ...	99	Decay		13
Not he: he knows, where he can better be, ...	100	Miserie		10
Where never yet came moth.	100	Miserie		18
Oh foolish man! where are thine eyes?	101	Miserie		49
Made in the tree, where she was wont to sit, ...	101	Miserie		56
Where in the deed there was an intimation	105	Obedience		33
Where most things were of purest gold;	106	Sion		3
To meet together, where I lay, ...	110	The Quip		3
And first I found the corner, where was J, ...	112	JESU		5
After, where ES, and next where U was graved.	112	JESU		6
The very dust, where thou dost tread and go, ...	115	Dulnesse		15
Where are my lines then? my approaches? views?	116	Dulnesse		17
Where are my window-songs?	116	Dulnesse		18
Finde where it lies.	116	Dulnesse		24
Where all may reach: no beast but knows his feed.	118	Providence		50
Since where are poysons, antidotes are most:	119	Providence		87
Where all the guests sit close, and nothing wants.	121	Providence		134
But words suffice not, where are lewd intentions:	122	Sinnes rd.		11
But where one man would have me grinde it, ...	122	Time		5
For where thou onely wert before	123	Time		14
Who wants the place, where God doth dwell, ...	123	Time		23
Sweet Peace, where dost thou dwell? I humbly crave, ...	124	Peace		1
And peace, which ev'ry where	125	Peace		40
And now, me thinks, I am where I began	128	Bunch Gr.		3
But where's the cluster? where's the taste	128	Bunch Gr.		19
Unto my house, where to repair the strength	130	Love unkn.		47
For where thou dwellest all is neat.	136	Familie		8
And where these are not found, ...	137	Familie		22
Born where thy servants both artilleries use.	139	Artillerie		18
Brave rose, (alas!) where art thou? in the chair	140	Ch.-rents		1
Brave rose, (alas!) where art thou? in the place	140	Ch.-rents	V	1
Where thou didst lately so triumph and shine, ...	140	Ch.-rents		2
Where rude unhallow'd steps do crush and grinde	140	Ch.-rents		8
Where Pagans tread. O Mother deare and kinde, ...	140	Ch.-rents		24
Where shall I get me eyes enough to weep, ...	140	Ch.-rents		25
For where before thou still didst call on me, ...	141	Justice 2		19
I travell'd on, seeing the hill, where lay	141	Pilgrimage		1
Where lay my hope, ...	142	Pilgrimage		20
Where lay my heart; and climbing still, ...	142	Pilgrimage		21
Where all things have their leafe assign'd:	149	Longing		50
Of wretched earth. Where once I scorn'd to stand, ...	161	Priesthood		15
Where is my God? what hidden place	163	The Search		29
Untill I had some place, where I might sing, ...	164	The Crosse		3
Save in the sight thereof, where strength doth sting. . . .	165	The Crosse		18
Where they together	166	The Flower		12
Fast in thy Paradise, where no flower can wither!	166	The Flower		23

WHERE (cont'd)

	PAGE	TITLE		LINE
Where all things burn,	166	The Flower		33
Thou hast a garden for us, where to bide.	167	The Flower		46
Where are no sorrows, but delights more true,	167	Dotage		17
Alas, poore Death, where is thy glorie?	169	Dial.-Anth		1
Where is thy famous force, thy ancient sting?	169	Dial.-Anth		2
Where of all plants afflictions soonest grow;	170	Water-crs.		3
Where I both feed and rest;	172	23 Psalme		6
Unto a place where is no rest.	174	Aaron		9
Where is all, there all should be.	180	Invitation		36
Where I wipe mine eyes, and see	182	Banquet		45
Where we did finde	186	Death		10
Go where it doth deserve.	189	Love 3		14
Go where it does deserve.	189	Love 3	W	14
Where th' Ark did rest, there Abraham began	190	Ch.-Milit.		19
To Egypt first she came, where they did prove	191	Ch.-Milit.		37
Religion thence fled into Greece, where arts	191	Ch.-Milit.		49
Thence into Greece she fled, where curious Arts	191	Ch.-Milit.	W	49
Where first the Church should raise her down-cast face.	192	Ch.-Milit.		86
Both where and when the Church began her race,	192	Ch.-Milit.		102
He chid the Church away, where e're he came,	193	Ch.-Milit.		105
Where some poore truths were shuffled for a bait	193	Ch.-Milit.		136
I saw him in his studie, where he sate	194	Ch.-Milit.		165
And where of old the Empire and the Arts	197	Ch.-Milit.		263
Follow the Church & sunn where ere they fly.	198	Ch.-Milit.	W	273
To time and place, where judgement shall appeare.	198	Ch.-Milit.		277
As thou art evry-where;	200	H. Commun.	W	3
Even there, where they deceive?	201	H. Commun.	W	36
My God, where is that ancient heat towards thee,	206	Walton 1		1
(Where nothing should be broke) to adde a Seal.	439	Walton 5		18
Of opposition cannot place thee, where	212	Bohemia	D	39
Laden with comforts thence, where now to morne	212	Bohemia	D	56
Where treach'rous Syrens us'd to sing,	214	Convert	D	7
The Temple where an Idol stood,	214	Convert	D	18
where he shall not exercise what he is, unlesse he forsake his	226	Priest 2		26
where the well is deep, and we have nothing of our selves to draw	228	Priest 4		35
that where is much earnestness, there is somewhat worth hearing;	232	Priest 7		32
where he takes occasion to discourse of such things as are both	236	Priest 8		21
where he may have occasion to converse with women, and that among	237	Priest 9		2
from hot Countreys, where both flesh alone, and much more with wine,	242	Priest 10		16
and where flesh may be much better spared, and with more safety then	242	Priest 10		18
where both the people and the drink being cold and flegmatick,	242	Priest 10		19
knowing that where there are such conceits, there is no room for his	243	Priest 11		23
may go the right way, and thither onely, where they are onely due.	245	Priest 12		34
and proper texts of Scripture every where painted, and that all	246	Priest 13		11
but is himselfe where ever he is.	251	Priest 17		1
where his kindred, or other relations give him any authority over	251	Priest 17		16
The Countrey Parson, where ever he is, keeps Gods watch;	252	Priest 18		1
or done in the Company where he is, but comes under his Test	252	Priest 18		3
where things are otherwise equall, therefore he satisfies this duty	253	Priest 19		27
that the same common truths may be every where professed,	255	Priest 21		19
where the singular dexterity of Socrates in this kind may be	256	Priest 21		28
where God is thanked for calling us to the knowledg of his grace,	258	Priest 22		5
chiefly considered) might have every where monuments of his Doctrine,	261	Priest 23		21
So, where the Apothecary useth either for loosing, Rubarb,	261	Priest 23		32
for that, where contempt is, there is no room for instruction.	268	Priest 28		19
then a stone thrown against heaven, where he is, and lives;	269	Priest 28		8
that neer the place where he is to pray, he spyes some scoffing	273	Priest 31		28
where can he busie himself better, then in those new Plantations,	278	Priest 32		5
where it can be, that so the body may joyn in the grief,	279	Priest 33		27
where he knowes there hath been or is a little difference,	284	Priest 35		19
so that then where sin abounded, not death, but grace superabounded;	288	Priest		24
where also I have fountains and gardens, and a very convenient house.	301	Cornaro		18
I sleep well and quietly any where, and my dreams are fair	302	Cornaro		13
which he every where beares towards our deare [great] Master	305	Valdesso		4
Where he sayes the Inflammation of the naturall, he sayes aptly,	308	Valdesso		13
especially considering the time and place where he lived.	311	Valdesso	V	8
of the blessed Virgin out of that text Mat. 1. 25. where it is said,	318	Valdesso		12
Saints of the world he every where understands the cunning hypocrite	319	Valdesso	V	19
The goate must browse where she is tyed.	323	Proverbs		56
Whether goest, griefe? where I am wont.	324	Proverbs		96
Whether shall the Oxe goe, where he shall not labour?	324	Proverbs		98
Where you thinke there is bacon, there is no Chimney.	324	Proverbs		99
The tongue walkes where the teeth speede not.	324	Proverbs		102
Where there is no honour, there is no griefe.	327	Proverbs		186
Where the drink goes in, there the wit goes out.	327	Proverbs		187
A discontented man knowes not where to sit easie.	333	Proverbs		345
Where your will is ready, your feete are light.	336	Proverbs		448
Woe to the house where there is no chiding.	336	Proverbs		450
The wearer knowes, where the shoe wrings.	338	Proverbs		491
Every one fastens where there is gaine.	338	Proverbs		496
The thread breakes, where it is weakest.	341	Proverbs		596
Where there is peace, God is.	345	Proverbs		733
It's an ill aire where wee gaine nothing.	350	Proverbs		872
Gifts enter every where without a wimble.	352	Proverbs		955
The eyes have one language every where.	352	Proverbs		959
To go where the King goes afoot (i.e. to the stool).	356	Proverbs	D	1034
but he would chuse to dy in Spain (where they say	357	Proverbs	D	1047
You live in a brave nation, where, except you wink, you cannot	366	Letters		6
before lower, even where to continue in the lower is no sinn.	380	Woodnoth		4
As God where he finds no roome for his Inclining grace,	381	Woodnoth		7

WHEREIN (cont'd)	PAGE	TITLE	LINE
in all things wherein they deal, may be more lively and vigorous.	299	Cornaro	20
There is an hour wherein a man might be happy	360	Proverbs D	1143
wherein consisteth the making good of my former education,	364	Letters	16
at the Indies, wherein they have satisfied the King reasonably.	368	Letters	7
wherein, my absence by how much it naturally augmenteth suspicion,	372	Letters	20
WHEREINTO			
whereinto I was wont, when I pleased my Sense & Appetite.	293	Cornaro	23
WHEREOF (see also wherof)			
A pain in that, whereof he findes a pleasure?	8	Ch.-Porch W	40
A part whereof my Saviour empti'd hath,	83	Sighs & Gr.	22
And this is all the Rock, whereof they boast,	194	Ch.-Milit.	159
moving and ravishing texts, whereof the Scriptures are full.	233	Priest 7	28
The first whereof is, Let all things be done decently, and in order:	246	Priest 13	27
done either wel or ill, whereof he is not the rewarder, or punisher.	254	Priest 20	10
the Professours whereof were much imployed by Queen Elizabeth,	277	Priest 32	31
two Italian Proverbs, the one whereof was, He that will eat much,	295	Cornaro	34
whereof the one kept me well for many yeares;	297	Cornaro	4
The reason whereof is this, Every one by long experience may know	297	Cornaro	26
in the midst whereof is a Church suitable to the condition	301	Cornaro	22
on both sides whereof are great and fruitfull fields, well manured	301	Cornaro	24
The memorie whereof is exceeding delightfull to me.	301	Cornaro	33
and husbandrie, whereof in this age there is great plentie.	301	Cornaro	37
and whereof I would not have you ignorant.	366	Letters	2
my deare Neece Mrs Dorothy Vaughan whereof two hundred pounds belongs	382	G.H.'s Will	10
whome I bequeath twenty pound whereof fifteene pound shal be bestowed	382	G.H.'s Will	29
WHEREON			
For some mean stuffe whereon to show his skill:	161	Priesthood	38
is the main foundation, and pillar of their cause, whereon they rely;	262	Priest 24	29
WHERESOE'RE			
And bear the bundle, wheresoe're it goes:	88	The Pearl	17
WHEREUPON			
Whereupon, being directed by them in the way I ought to hold,	292	Cornaro	23
whereupon also I joyed exceedingly;	294	Cornaro	29
whereupon all gave me for dead.	296	Cornaro	22
Whereupon I conclude, since none can have a better Physician then	297	Cornaro	37
Whereupon men flockt thither, and built houses with happy successe.	301	Cornaro	28
WHEREWITH			
And th' other black and grave, wherewith each one	67	Ch.-floore	4
Affront those joyes, wherewith thou didst endow,	71	Frailtie	19
As she had brought wherewith to stain,	173	Marie Magd	16
So to bring in wherewith to wash:	173	Marie Magd	17
Wherewith whole showls of Martyrs once did burn,	206	Walton 1	2
minde being defixed on it with those nailes wherewith his Master was:	267	Priest 27	29
five shields, wherewith the Godly receive the darts of the wicked;	269	Priest 28	19
God) stands fast in the Liberty wherewith Christ hath made us free.	272	Priest 31	18
wherewith also a carefull Joseph might meet.	281	Priest 34	26
interesting of that dignity wherewith God hath invested the Priest,	286	Priest 36	9
that Proverb, wherewith Gluttons use to defend themselves, to wit,	293	Cornaro	8
we can eat but a very little, wherewith she is very well contented:	299	Cornaro	28
bodie and minde, wherewith infinite both young and old are afflicted.	302	Cornaro	25
WHEREWITHALL			
If thou hast wherewithall to spice a draught,	137	The Size	9
but that they may have wherewithall to serve God the better,	248	Priest 14	8
if a man hath wherewithall to buy a spade, and yet hee chuseth rather	265	Priest 26	28
of his affairs, that hee may have wherewithall to do good.	275	Priest 32	30
WHERFORE			
Wherfore they are not to be over-submissive, and base, but to keep up	226	Priest 2	27
Wherfore he hath one Comment at least upon every book of Scripture,	229	Priest 4	27
Wherfore neither disdaineth he to enter into the poorest Cottage,	249	Priest 14	4
WHERIN			
of that, wherin they are most eminent, is the most gainfull way	260	Priest 23	6
WHEROF			
besides some Remainders of monyes wherof he is to give as I know he	383	G.H.'s Will	25
WHERSOEVER			
Wherefore the Parson strongly opposeth this sin, whersoever he goes.	274	Priest 32	15
WHET (see also whett)			
Thy sithe is dull; whet it for shame.	122	Time	2
the Lord will whet his Sword:	222	Psalm VII D	42
WHETHER			
Slight not the smallest losse, whether it be	20	Ch.-Porch	343
Whether thy stock of credit swell, or fall.	20	Ch.-Porch	346
To take all that is given; whether wealth,	20	Ch.-Porch	356
Whether I fliє with angels, fall with dust,	55	Temper 1	25
Whether I Angell it, or fall to dust.	55	Temper 1 W	25
In vies of favours whether partie gains,	88	The Pearl	13
Whether I sing,	183	The Posie	7
Whether in these gifts thou bee so	200	H. Commun. W	2
First I am sure, whether bread stay	200	H. Commun. W	7
Or whether Bread doe fly away	200	H. Commun. W	8
Wee doubt much whether you	211	Paradox D	40
whether prophecy, let us prophecy according to the proportion	226	Priest 2	5
he sees whether I speak as I ought, or you hear as you ought,	234	Priest 7	27
what means of Piety, whether daily prayers be used, Grace,	251	Priest 17	22
whether he could get out of the ditch alone, or whether he needed	257	Priest 21	8
or whether he needed a helper, and who was that helper.	257	Priest 21	9
whether it be a rule to it selfe, whether it hath a rule,	263	Priest 24	1
be a rule to it selfe, whether it hath a rule, whether having a rule,	263	Priest 24	2
whether having a rule, it ought not to be guided by it;	263	Priest 24	2
whether any rule in the world be obscure, and how then should	263	Priest 24	3
whether, there being two precepts, one of obeying Authority,	263	Priest 24	8

WHETHER (cont'd)	PAGE	TITLE		LINE
whether things once indifferent, being made by the precept . .	263	Priest 24		11
told to another, whether in private conference, or in the Church,	278	Priest 33		17
whether his repentance were true, or at least in that degree it ought	279	Priest 33		10
a just doubt, whether, considering the stubbornnesse of the Nation,	282	Priest 34		7
whether those that pleased my taste brought me commoditie . .	293	Cornaro		6
and whether that Proverb, wherewith Gluttons use to defend . .	293	Cornaro		8
whether he hath lived heretofore orderly or disorderly, . .	299	Cornaro		29
Whether goest, griefe? where I am wont.	324	Proverbs		96
Whether shall the Oxe goe, where he shall not labour? . . .	324	Proverbs		98
Whether you boyle snow or pound it, ...	327	Proverbs		180
you see in Frenchmen, whether it be in knowledge, or in fashion,	366	Letters		8
of which is doubted whether it have some further meaning. . .	368	Letters		18
whether my peace be yet made with her concerning my unkind departure.	371	Letters		8
that whether you turn your thoughts on the life past, or on the Joyes	373	Letters		17
and bookes and howshould stuffe whether in my possession or out of my	382	G.H.'s Will		5
WHETT				
are so farr from cooling christians, that they whett them. . .	376	Letters		11
WHEY				
The whey of milk doth loose, the milk doth binde.	120	Providence		132
WHICH				
If this seeme Monkish; think which brings most paine	7	Ch.-Porch	W	15
A Virgin-bed, which hath a speciall Crowne	7	Ch.-Porch	W	20
Drink not the third glasse, which thou canst not tame, ...	7	Ch.-Porch		25
Which it would poure on thee, upon the floore.	7	Ch.-Porch		28
Which would throw me there, if I keep the round.	7	Ch.-Porch		30
Omit the oathes, which true wit cannot need:	9	Ch.-Porch		62
Which is thy best stake, when griefs make thee tame.	9	Ch.-Porch		66
A fault, which needs it most, grows two thereby.	9	Ch.-Porch		78
Flie idlenesse, which yet thou canst not flie	9	Ch.-Porch		79
To feel those tempests, which fly over ditches.	11	Ch.-Porch		112
Which if it cleave to coine, one common rust	13	Ch.-Porch	W	165
'Tis a thinne webbe, which poysonous fancies make:	15	Ch.-Porch		224
Of thicker stuffe, which would endure a shake.	15	Ch.-Porch		226
These are the scumme, with which course wits abound:	16	Ch.-Porch		237
The shrine is that which thou dost venerate;	17	Ch.-Porch		267
For this French sluttery which so currant goes:	21	Ch.-Porch	W	368
He that gets patience, and the blessing which	24	Ch.-Porch		433
Which he might fall in by companions, gains.	24	Ch.-Porch		436
Or that which groneth to be so, ...	25	Superlim		7
They use that power against me, which I gave:	27	Sacrifice		11
Which I do give them daily, unto death.	28	Sacrifice		70
Which each one calls for so with utmost breath, ...	31	Sacrifice		146
Which shews my bloud to be the onely way, ...	31	Sacrifice		158
Which Angels did desire to have the grace, ...	32	Sacrifice		182
Reproches, which are free, while I am bound.	33	Sacrifice		219
All that salvation, which ye now resist;	34	Sacrifice		226
My coat, the type of love, which once cur'd those	34	Sacrifice		242
Thy art of love, which I'le turn back on thee:	36	Thanksgvng		47
The which to measure it doth more behove:	37	The Agonie		5
Sinne is that presse and vice, which forceth pain	37	The Agonie		11
And taste that juice, which on the crosse a pike	37	The Agonie		14
Which my God feels as bloud; but I, as wine.	37	The Agonie		18
Which falls in Autumne, score a grief?	38	Good Fri.		10
About some land, which he had dearly bought	40	Redemption		7
But that which shews them large, shews them unfit.	41	Sepulchre		9
Which holds thee now? Who hath indited it	41	Sepulchre		11
Was writ in stone; so thou, which also art	41	Sepulchre		18
Which is above the heav'ns, whose spring and rent	44	H. Bapt.1		5
Which is above the heav'ns, whose spring and vent	44	H. Bapt.1	V	5
Which then join'd with you still meet in my brest	44	H. Bapt.1	W	8
Which thou hast pour'd into my soul;	49	Repentance		20
Which when I could not get, I thought it here:	50	Faith		10
That which before was darkned clean	51	Faith		37
A kinde of tune, which all things heare and fear;	51	Prayer 1		8
Which spread their forces into every part, ...	52	H.Commun.		11
Onely thy grace, which with these elements comes, ...	52	H.Commun.		19
Which I can go to, when I please, ...	53	H.Commun.		39
Sprung from that beautie which can never fade;	54	Love 1		2
Sprung from the beautie which can never fade;	54	Love 1	W	2
And thrown it on that dust which thou hast made, ...	54	Love 1		4
And thrown it in that dust which thou hast made, ...	54	Love 1	W	4
Which siding with invention, they together	54	Love 1		6
Which shall consume the world, first make it tame;	54	Love 2		3
Our eies shall see thee, which before saw dust;	54	Love 2		9
Which just now took up all my heart?	56	Temper 2		2
Which in thy garland I should fill, were mine	57	Employm. 1		7
As is the dust, to which that life doth tend, ...	57	Employm. 1		15
Such are thy secrets, which my life makes good, ...	58	H.Script.2		9
Where is that fire which once descended	59	Whitsunday		5
The sunne, which once did shine alone, ...	59	Whitsunday		13
But since those pipes of gold, which brought	59	Whitsunday		17
The dew, for which grasse cannot call, ...	60	Grace		11
That this new light, which now I see, ...	63	Mattens		18
Which to himself he did denie:	63	Even-song		6
Which this dayes favour did beget?	64	Even-song		11
I muse, which shows more love, ...	64	Even-song		25
To which the blast of deaths incessant motion, ...	64	Ch.-monum.		4
Which dissolution sure doth best discern, ...	65	Ch.-monum.		10
To kisse those heaps, which now they have in trust?	65	Ch.-monum.		16
That flesh is but the glasse, which holds the dust	65	Ch.-monum.		20

WHICH (cont'd)

	PAGE	TITLE		LINE
That measures all our time; which also shall	65	Ch.-monum.		21
O what a state is this, which never knew	65	Ch.-mus.	W	8
Which knoweth not, what means, to Morrow.	65	Ch.-mus.	W	8
Which knoweth not, what means, too Morrow.	65	Ch.-mus.	W	9
I know it is my sinne, which locks thine eares,	66	Ch.-lock		1
I know it is my sinne, which stops thine eares,	66	Ch.-lock	W	1
Which of them soonest should attaine my hart.	66	Ch.-lock	W	4
Which pleads for me:	66	Ch.-lock		10
Which looks so firm and strong,	66	Ch.-floore		2
The gentle rising, which on either hand	67	Ch.-floore		7
But the sweet cement, which in one sure band	67	Ch.-floore		10
Which else shows watrish, bleak, & thin.	67	Windows		10
Which can let loose to a crown, and yet with pleasure	69	Content		15
As those which rise from a huge King.	69	Content		24
Thy name in books, which may not rent:	69	Content		28
Thy name in books, which may not vent:	69	Content	W	28
But it is that which while I use	70	Quidditie		11
Which by consent was giv'n to Mansuetude.	70	Humilitie		10
The fearfull Hare her eares, which by their law	70	Humilitie		11
The fearfull Hare her eares, which by the law	70	Humilitie	W	11
Till they fell out: which when the beasts espied,	70	Humilitie		21
For which ye wrangle, made them turn their frown	71	Humilitie		28
That which was dust before, doth quickly rise,	71	Frailtie		15
O brook not this, lest if that, which just now	71	Frailtie	W	17
Among the beams, which crown the face	74	The Starre		22
The which he doth not fill.	75	Sunday		21
On which heav'ns palace arched lies:	75	Sunday		23
On which heav'ens kingdome arch'd doth stand:	75	Sunday	W	23
Which parts their ranks and orders.	75	Sunday		28
With the same shake, which at his passion	76	Sunday		45
To this great kingdome, which thou now hast got,	77	Avarice		6
Which they effected, none could them withstand.	84	The World		18
Should aim and shoot at that which Is on high:	85	Coloss.		8
His dearely-earned pearl, which God did hide	85	Vanitie 1		10
He sayes, in things which use hath justly got,	86	Lent		10
Unlesse Authoritie, which should increase	86	Lent		16
Then those same pendant profits, which the spring	86	Lent		25
Who goeth in the way which Christ hath gone,	87	Lent		37
Who goeth in that way which Christ hath gone,	87	Lent	V	37
Which on the world a true-love-knot may tie,	88	The Pearl		16
Then shall those powers, which work for grief,	90	Afflict.4		25
Night draws the curtain, which the sunne withdraws;	91	Man		32
He treads down that which doth befriend him,	92	Man		45
Which hath made of two folds one.	93	Antiphon 2	W	23
Which I intend,	93	Unkindness		3
Which do consigne and send them unto death.	98	Mortific.		6
Which shall befriend him at the house of death.	98	Mortific.		18
Which shall befriend him at the houre of death.	98	Mortific.	W	18
Which shall convey him to the house of death.	98	Mortific.		30
Which shall convey him to the place of death.	98	Mortific.	W	30
And those things most, which are most pure and fine:	101	Miserie		38
Much lesse those joyes which trample on his head.	102	Jordan 2		12
Is thy great arm which spans the east and west,	103	Prayer 2		8
We cannot ask the thing, which is not there,	103	Prayer 2		11
That by destroying that which ty'd thy purse,	103	Prayer 2		17
To which I do agree,	104	Obedience		9
Which sometimes crosseth thee, thou sometimes it:	106	Sion		14
The bloud did make, which thou didst waste?	107	Home		8
What is this woman-kinde, which I can wink	108	Home		39
Which way so-e're I look, I see.	108	Home		50
There is no fruitfull yeare, but that which brings	108	Home		57
Which now is pinion'd with mortalitie,	109	Home		63
She on the hills, which wantonly	110	Brit. Ch.		13
Which when I pluckt not, Sir, said she,	110	The Quip		6
Take up thine eyes, which feed on earth;	112	Dawning		2
Which as it riseth, raiseth thee:	112	Dawning		12
Ev'n all to pieces: which I went to seek:	112	JESU		4
Which crie and follow. Thou hast made poore sand	118	Providence		47
Which as it lengthens windes, and windes us in,	118	Providence		59
The sea, which seems to stop the traveller,	119	Providence		89
The common all men have; that which is rare,	119	Providence		98
And none can know thy works, which are so many,	121	Providence		143
Which spit it forth like the Sicilian hill.	122	Sinnes rd.		8
Which now is but a pruning-knife.	122	Time		10
Which ev'n eternitie excludes!	123	Time		26
Which many wondring at, got some of those	125	Peace		29
Take of this grain, which in my garden grows,	125	Peace		37
And peace, which ev'ry where	125	Peace		40
He builds a house, which quickly down must go,	127	Giddinesse		13
And have, of whom some grounds which may improve,	129	Love unkn.		4
Better then you know me, or (which is one)	129	Love unkn.		10
Better then you knew me, or (which is one)	129	Love unkn.	V	10
A stream of bloud, which issu'd from the side	129	Love unkn.		14
Thinking with that, which I did thus present,	129	Love unkn.		31
To warm his love, which I did fear grew cold.	129	Love unkn.		32
Which at a board, while many drunk bare wine,	130	Love unkn.		42
Which I had lost, I hasted to my bed.	130	Love unkn.		48
Among thy trees, which in a ROW	132	Paradise		2
Which cools his will.	133	The Method		4
Which needs not man, be ty'd to those	134	The Method		26

WHICH (cont'd)

	PAGE	TITLE		LINE
Which knows his way without a guide:	134	Divinitie		4
Which with the edge of wit they cut and carve.	134	Divinitie		7
Could not that wisdome, which first broacht the wine,	134	Divinitie		9
But all the doctrine, which he taught and gave,	135	Divinitie		13
At least those beams of truth, which onely save,	135	Divinitie		15
Griev'd for a worm, which when I tread,	135	Ephes.		5
Which may with thee	136	Ephes.		20
Turn out these wranglers, which defile thy seat:	136	Familie		7
Which thou hast open'd: do not spread thy robe	138	The Size		43
Which have the face of fire, but end in rest.	139	Artillerie		8
And bottome of the leaves: which when the winde	140	Ch.-rents		6
Gave you a colour once; which when your foes	140	Ch.-rents		13
Which when your neighbours saw, like a north-winde,	140	Ch.-rents		22
Which falls by night, and poure it out for you!	140	Ch.-rents		30
Thy scales like buckets, which attend	141	Justice 2		16
That led me to the wilde of passion, which	142	Pilgrimage		13
Save one good Angell, which a friend had ti'd	142	Pilgrimage		17
That which is past who can recall?	144	Discharge		10
But through a Church-yard which them bounds.	145	Discharge		40
Dropping from heav'n, which doth both cleanse and close	147	Offering		20
Which thou dost curse.	148	Longing		9
Which hath been broken now so long,	150	Longing		74
By these thy feet, at which my heart	150	Longing		80
And heal my troubled breast which cryes,	150	Longing		83
Which dyes.	150	Longing		84
At which the Church falling upon her face	152	The Jews		9
Which pettie thoughts have made, and made to thee	153	The Collar		23
Which by the springs accesse grew much more great.	154	Glimpse		15
And in this league, which now my foes invade,	156	Assurance		26
Which bounds on thee, and will not down thy throat:	156	Assurance		40
That which had but two legs before,	158	Praise 3		10
(Which there did hang like streamers neare the top	158	Praise 3		33
And bloudie battell which thou once didst trie)	158	Praise 3		35
Let the worlds riches, which dispersed lie,	159	The Pulley		4
Blest Order, which in power dost so excell,	160	Priesthood		1
Blest Order, which in power doth so excell,	160	Priesthood	V	1
Which favour winnes,	162	The Search		26
Which want provision in the midst of all.	164	Grief		12
To which, besides their own demean,	165	The Flower		3
Which when we once can finde and prove,	167	The Flower		45
The finenesse which a hymne or psalme affords,	168	a true Hymn		9
Which my fierce youth did bandie, fall and flow	169	The Answer		3
Which they that know the rest, know more then I.	169	The Answer		14
And judge our selves. That light, which sin & passion	171	Self-cond.		20
Then should the Pomander, which was before	175	The Odour		16
For when My Master, which alone is sweet,	175	The Odour		21
Those sparkling notions, which therein were bred?	176	Forerunners		4
That which wrought on thee,	179	Discipline		26
Which before ye drink is bloud.	180	Invitation		12
Here is love, which having breath	180	Invitation		28
Which cannot be,	183	A Parodie		3
Which with his tincture (for thy sake)	184	The Elixer		15
Which with this tincture (for thy sake)	184	The Elixer	V	15
For that which God doth touch and own	185	The Elixer		23
Dry dust, which sheds no tears, but may extort.	186	Death		12
And are there any leaves, which still abide?	188	Heaven	W	7
Which doth not meet with an eternall thought.	190	Ch.-Milit.		8
Which does not meet with an eternall thought.	190	Ch.-Milit.	W	8
Which might the more indeare it to be thine.	190	Ch.-Milit.		12
All, Emblems, which thy Darling doth improve.	190	Ch.-Milit.	W	16
Which using, and not fearing skill in th' one,	192	Ch.-Milit.		77
Within a sheet of paper, which was rent	192	Ch.-Milit.		95
Gardens of Gods, which ev'ry yeare did grow,	193	Ch.-Milit.		108
Begging his food of that which he may eat,	193	Ch.-Milit.		113
To make good that which ev'ry day he winnes.	193	Ch.-Milit.		126
Which soon was blown to such a mightie flame,	194	Ch.-Milit.		145
To which he lent a corner of his eye.	195	Ch.-Milit.		170
To go to them, while that which now their nation	197	Ch.-Milit.		257
Sinn onely, which did all deface	200	H. Commun.	W	23
But that which made my soule to dye	201	H. Commun.	W	28
Thy ancient baptism which when I was foule	202	love	W	11
That which beleefe	202	Trin.Sun.	W	11
Which know not thee, suck in thy beames	203	Even-song	W	23
Which warme these lines, & serve them up to thee	204	Persever.	W	2
Why doth that fire, which by thy power and might	206	walton 1		12
Than that, which one day Worms may chance refuse?	206	walton 1		14
Meane while, if hee (which all thinges weares)	208	H. Danvers	D	5
That which wee doe not neede:	210	Paradox	D	22
Which wee but somtymes prove:	210	Paradox	D	32
Which misery cannot untwist but rather	212	Bohemia	D	35
Those ravening Harpyes, which peck at thy face,	212	Bohemia	D	48
To curbe some Rebell teares, which faine would flow,	213	Bohemia	D	58
Which mingles water with thy Rhenish wine	213	Bohemia	D	64
Which now that moist land to thee beares.	213	L' Envoy	D	6
Which, planted by the waters, shall	214	Psalm I	D	9
are like the chaff, which from the face	215	Psalm I	D	14
And those wayes which the wicked go	215	Psalm I	D	23
which Thou did'st preordain.	221	Psalm VII	D	24
But in the pit which he hath made	222	Psalm VII	D	55
which also I will set as high as I can, since hee shoots higher that	224	Priest		8

WHICH (cont'd)	PAGE	TITLE	LINE
when his storing, which was even now good, passeth from good to bad.	264	Priest 26	29
I am false to my reason which should guide me, I offend the supreme	265	Priest 26	10
in perverting that order which he hath set both to things,	265	Priest 26	11
in all these, and those more which concerne me, I either do nothing,	265	Priest 26	16
or that which is unwholsome, being sometimes baned meat,	265	Priest 26	21
even as a piece of wood, which they may cut, or hack, or throw into	265	Priest 26	25
which yet ought to be done, since there is a Justice in the least	265	Priest 26	31
which while they dwell in their bookes, they will never finde;	266	Priest 26	1
(which being overburdened, or studying dainties too much,	266	Priest 26	15
which by mine own experience I have found hurtfull, then from those	266	Priest 26	24
then from those which by a Common tradition, and vulgar knowledge are	266	Priest 26	25
That which is said of hurtfull meats, extends to hurtfull drinks	266	Priest 26	27
of themselves in time of eating, which because it is deceitfull;	267	Priest 26	2
both for the generall ignominy which is cast upon the profession,	268	Priest 28	10
which out of his choysest judgment hee hath resolved to observe,	268	Priest 28	11
and which are described in this Book, he must be despised;	268	Priest 28	12
which carries a reverence with it, even above contempt.	268	Priest 28	21
which is not easily despised, except it degenerate to pride.	268	Priest 28	26
to the examination, and punishment of those which are in Authority;	269	Priest 28	1
which continually breake Gods Laws, and dishonour him with those	269	Priest 28	9
him with those mouths, which he continually fils, and feeds:	269	Priest 28	11
they resist not the evill which takes hold of them, and is farr	269	Priest 28	24
which are grounded upon the Canons, that so they may know their duty,	270	Priest 29	14
in which regard, considering the great Consequence of their place,	270	Priest 29	16
and exerciseth a threefold power in every thing which concernes man.	271	Priest 30	1
then by that which he continually supplyes, as the corn needs it;	271	Priest 30	5
without which supply the corne would instantly dry up, as a river	271	Priest 30	6
which it hath escaped, he destroyes it sometimes in the very Haven;	271	Priest 30	23
by which God turnes all outward blessings to inward advantages.	271	Priest 30	37
give him the gold for it, which the Child utterly refusing, eats it,	272	Priest 30	11
which none can perform so wel in trouble, as in calmness.	273	Priest 31	2
especially to pious minds, which are ever tender, and delicate.	273	Priest 31	14
which will appear if the Pious soul foresee and prevent such	273	Priest 31	16
when the evills which he is now subject unto, may be prevented,	274	Priest 32	23
the Village or Parish which either he lives in, or is neer unto it,	276	Priest 32	2
for it is both an honor which they owe to the Reverend Judges	277	Priest 32	2
the Kingdome into Portions, which every yeer he surveys peece-meal.	277	Priest 32	8
which are brought from thence to the House but in generall.	277	Priest 32	13
This is the duty of each to other, which they ought to fulfill:	277	Priest 32	21
which are not only a noble, but also as they may be handled,	278	Priest 32	6
For the temptations with which a good man is beset, and the ways	278	Priest 33	15
and the ways which he used to overcome them, being told to another,	278	Priest 33	16
the chiefe thing, which God in Scriptures requires, is the heart,	279	Priest 33	16
be alike in all Gods children (which as concerning weeping it cannot	279	Priest 33	21
Which acts of repentance are and must be found in all Gods servants:	279	Priest 33	25
dishes at table, which even their present health otherwise admits;	280	Priest 34	23
their house with all those furnitures which even their present plenty	280	Priest 34	25
which the present occasion of wit and company otherwise admits;	280	Priest 34	27
which evidently argue Christs Divinity by their success:	282	Priest 34	23
on our Saviour, for which he told, that it should never be forgotten,	282	Priest 34	25
of which our Saviour said, that that generation should not passe,	282	Priest 34	28
Which Josephus's History confirmeth, and the continuance of which	282	Priest 34	29
confirmeth, and the continuance of which verdict is yet evident.	282	Priest 34	30
Matthew 24. 14. which we see even miraculously effected in these new	282	Priest 34	32
and sent, which to the bearer is but paper, but to the receiver,	282	Priest 34	37
which in the Creation needed not, gave them love for love,	283	Priest 34	15
which way soever he turnes, hath two pledges of Gods Love,	283	Priest 34	17
and largesse, which at that time is, or ought to be used.	284	Priest 35	9
is a great Blessing, and as great as food, for which we give thanks:	284	Priest 35	27
of Christs Cross, or for any shame to leave that which is good.	284	Priest 35	33
which conformity and fashionableness is so exceeding unbefitting	285	Priest 36	6
But that which the Apostles used so diligently in their writings,	285	Priest 36	9
which our Saviour himselfe used, Marke 10. 16, cannot bee vain	285	Priest 36	10
2 Kings 2. 24. which though our Saviour reproved as unfitting for his	285	Priest 36	26
without any remedy (which cannot be applyed without notice)	287	Priest 37	2
which is so exceeding useful, and hath taken so deep roote,	287	Priest 37	8
against malefactours, which the Law intends, as is evident by those,	287	Priest 37	19
by those, which are branded for rogues, that they may be known;	287	Priest 37	19
which hath so much advanced Charity, and ranked backbiters among	287	Priest 37	22
which before their offence and Judgment they had in all mens brests:	287	Priest 37	33
it is a duty rather, which may do much good, and save much harme.	288	Priest 37	1
and forbear to speak of that, which even God himself hath forgotten.	288	Priest 37	5
which thou hast made a Land of light, a store-house of thy treasures	289	Priest	18
so neither may thy word, but accomplish that for which it is given.	289	Priest	32
which I undertake the more willingly, because divers worthy young men	291	Cornaro	7
I will declare the causes which moved me to forsake Intemperance,	291	Cornaro	15
a sober life, expressing also the means which I have used therein.	291	Cornaro	16
which did not onely begin, but had already gone farre in me,	291	Cornaro	17
first caused me to leave Intemperance, to which I was much addicted:	291	Cornaro	19
to wit, That which savours, is good and nourisheth, be consonant	293	Cornaro	9
was not onely freed from all those evils which had so long beset me,	293	Cornaro	21
Which benefits also still continue, because from the time that I was	293	Cornaro	24
of the minde, which have a great power over our constitutions.	293	Cornaro	36
which gained me this experience, that I perceived, that they had no	293	Cornaro	38
hurt those bodies, which were kept in good order by a moderate Diet:	294	Cornaro	2
(a thing usuall to disorderly lives) which increased so much in them,	294	Cornaro	19
which excesse of joy neither could do me any hurt.	294	Cornaro	29
By which it is manifest, That neither melancholie, nor any other	294	Cornaro	30
which often kill others, can bring little grief or hurt to those that	294	Cornaro	34
and fever (which was certainly expected) might be hindred.	295	Cornaro	6

WHICH (cont'd)

	PAGE	TITLE		LINE
which must needs so temper the humours of the bodie, that they could	295	Cornaro		8
which seemed as a miracle to the Physicians.	295	Cornaro		13
which yet needs not onely to be sustained, but also to gather	295	Cornaro		23
but also to gather strength, which could not be but by meat & drink.	295	Cornaro		24
The meat which remaineth, profits more then that which is eaten.	296	Cornaro		1
The meat which remaineth, profits more then that which is eaten.	296	Cornaro		2
By which is intimated, that the hurt of too much meat is greater,	296	Cornaro		2
of my drink, which before was foureteen ounces, I made now sixteen.	296	Cornaro		12
a pain of the side took me, which held me two and twentie houres.	296	Cornaro		18
came a terrible fever, which continued thirtie five dayes and nights;	296	Cornaro		19
nothing holp me, but that exact rule which I had so long continued.	296	Cornaro		29
In all which time I felt no grief, save now and then a little	296	Cornaro		30
as usually happens in old mens bodies, which live without rule.	296	Cornaro		35
of old age in the humours of my bodie, which commonly kills men.	296	Cornaro		37
which I contracted by breaking my diet, although it was a sore evil,	297	Cornaro		1
if he will give his minde to those things which he should, . .	297	Cornaro		23
which things in others cannot be known without such observation,	297	Cornaro		28
curing of diseases, into which they often fall, who live disorderly:	298	Cornaro		5
regular life is to be embraced, which, as is manifest by experience,	298	Cornaro		13
which, but in that age, can hardly be perfected.	298	Cornaro		31
those ten yeares, which they set at naught in regard of their belly?	298	Cornaro		34
and later yeares, it is no such thing which may not be performed;	299	Cornaro		6
and divers labours, which suit not with an orderly life: . .	299	Cornaro		14
which is both easie for common-weals-men, and very convenient,	299	Cornaro		17
preserve themselves from diseases, which hinder publick employment;	299	Cornaro		19
He which lives a regular life, eating alwayes light meats, . .	299	Cornaro		22
shall he use in diseases, which being in health he hath anticipated?	299	Cornaro		24
which endeavours to preserve a man as much as she can, teacheth us	299	Cornaro		25
which is alreadie burdened with a disease, would be wholly oppressed.	299	Cornaro		33
That he which lives a temperate life, cannot fall into diseases,	299	Cornaro		35
No man is forbidden to eat fruit or fish, which I eat not: . .	300	Cornaro		8
So that he which is offended with no kinde of meat and drink,	300	Cornaro		14
not the qualitie for his rule, which is very easie to be observed.	300	Cornaro		16
onely upon a hope of an happie issue, which yet befalls verie few.	300	Cornaro		24
in this age of eighty three, which now I take, and which are such,	300	Cornaro		32
and which are such, as that men generally account me happie.	300	Cornaro		32
I am not wearie of life, which I passe with great delight. . .	301	Cornaro		3
which, besides that they are in the fairest place of this learned	301	Cornaro		10
parted with rills of running water, which truely is very delightfull.	301	Cornaro		16
which is therefore very pleasant, because many wayes thither are so	301	Cornaro		20
and ever I learn somewhat which is worthy of my knowledge: . .	302	Cornaro		2
which are all in their perfect vigour, but especially my Taste;	302	Cornaro		8
moneths in the heat of summer (which in Italie is very great)	302	Cornaro		19
the power and efficacie of that Temperance which ever accompanied me.	302	Cornaro		21
which is altogether to be preferred before others youth: . .	302	Cornaro		22
which kinde of Poems useth to be the childe of Youth, which it most	302	Cornaro		29
which it most suits withall for variety and pleasantnesse; . .	302	Cornaro		30
Tragedie with old Age, by reason of the sad events which it contains.	302	Cornaro		32
By which it is evident, That the life which I live at this age,	303	Cornaro		9
it is evident, That the life which I live at this age, is not a dead,	303	Cornaro		9
not onely a shamefull thing to fear that which cannot be avoided;	303	Cornaro		22
a fair and desirable death, which Nature brings by way of resolution.	303	Cornaro		29
in any thing I forsake that Temperance which I have found so good,	303	Cornaro		34
in which perhaps you will discover some care, which I forbare not in	304	Valdesso		2
discover some care, which I forbare not in the midst of my griefes;	304	Valdesso		3
there are some things which I like not in him, as my fragments will	304	Valdesso		16
which he every where beares towards our deare [great] Master	305	Valdesso		4
for which I doe so love him, that were there nothing else, . .	305	Valdesso		6
and the working thereof, of which he was a very diligent observer.	305	Valdesso		11
is not that which filleth the heart with joy and peace in believing;	309	Valdesso		2
we shall not be punished (which word I like here better then	311	Valdesso		27
which may be unto him as the sunne to a Travellour in his journey,	312	Valdesso		18
God often chuseth which he shall doe, and that by restraining him	313	Valdesso		22
because the anointing which we have received, and abideth in us,	314	Valdesso	V	6
and not those which are in themselves occasions of sinne; . .	314	Valdesso		18
which strictly he was not, though in the point of Resurrection he	316	Valdesso		8
which is a modest admonition.	316	Valdesso		13
may pretend motions, which is unsufferable in a Common-wealth.	316	Valdesso		21
spirit to the teaching of the scripture, which the holy spirit wrot.	317	Valdesso		27
text of S. Pet. 2 Ep. 1. 19. which he makes the ground of his [this]	318	Valdesso		7
not to the point it should, which if it did, it would doe more,	319	Valdesso		11
which depend almost wholly on their Canon law and Decretals,	319	Valdesso	V	28
generall rules to particular actions, which are a most noble study.	319	Valdesso	V	32
the very Ceremonies of the Jewes, which no Christian observes now;	320	Valdesso		1
like to that of the Jewes, which they added to their divine law.	320	Valdesso		3
It takes much from the account, to which his sin doth amount.	327	Proverbs		192
That is not good language which all understand not. . . .	331	Proverbs		302
and by that which is past, see	332	Proverbs		329
how that which is to come will be drawne on.	332	Proverbs		329
Faire is not faire, but that which pleaseth.	338	Proverbs		492
which a hundred wise men cannot pull out.	339	Proverbs		527
That which will not be spun, ...	343	Proverbs		665
That which two will, takes effect.	345	Proverbs		705
That is gold which is worth gold.	349	Proverbs		841
That which sufficeth is not little.	350	Proverbs		876
by which Scholars say, the Muses use to take up their habitations.	363	Letters		5
the same heart, which you have won long since, is still true to you,	363	Letters		17
my case unto you, which I think deserves the reading at the least;	364	Letters		9
education, of obeying that Spirit which hath guided me hitherto,	364	Letters		18
on Fridayes and Saturdayes, I must do so, which yet sometimes I fast.	365	Letters		6

WHICH (cont'd)	PAGE	TITLE		LINE
all which tend to avoiding of costlier matters, if I should fall	365	Letters		7
Volumes of Divinity, which yet every day swell, and grow bigger.	365	Letters		14
the time when I desire this (which is now, when I must lay	365	Letters		17
The disease which I am troubled with now is the shortness of time,	365	Letters		30
some of those observations which I have framed to myself in	366	Letters		1
and if there be any such which you have found useful to yourself,	366	Letters		4
of all good which you see in Frenchmen, whether it be in knowledge,	366	Letters		7
there be no kind of excellency which it is possible for you to attain	366	Letters		13
which it is possible for you to attain to, which you seek not;	366	Letters		14
which she hath hitherto deferred to do, not of her self,	367	Letters		3
but upon the want of those Books which were not to be got in England;	367	Letters		4
for that which surmounts, though your noble disposition is infinitely	367	Letters		5
to which mine owne obligations were occasion inough, & therfore I am	367	Letters		28
beholding to those busnesses which justly excuse him from writing	367	Letters		30
to acquaint you with those passages of newes which this time affords;	368	Letters		1
as of certaine injuries which they are thought to have offerd to our	368	Letters		6
also concerning the fishing which the Hollanders use in our coasts,	368	Letters		10
which the King would so appropriate to himselfe, as that either his	368	Letters		10
of which is doubted whether it have some further meaning.	368	Letters		18
which he refusing to doe hath given her occasion to protest shee will	368	Letters		21
which some observing who heard the interdiction denounced to him,	368	Letters		36
which if you can sent to Sir Francis before his departure,	369	Letters		25
and such like Gaynesses, which will please a young man well.	370	Letters		4
of which I am very proud, not but that I joy in your favours,	370	Letters		8
yet you will pardon my haste, which is very great, though never so,	370	Letters		13
may divert me too much from Divinity, at which, not without cause,	370	Letters		20
and which is more, with our good and gracious God, incessantly	371	Letters		28
me unable to perform those Offices for which I came into the world,	373	Letters		9
and yours (which praised be God are less) are not like to continue	374	Letters		2
To which joyn that of St. peter, Casting all your Care on the Lord,	374	Letters		15
to let them know your love, for which both they shall, and I doe,	375	Letters		22
which, you know, is the encouragement of learning all the year after,	375	Letters		28
take pitty of her, which yet at that distance is some difficulty.	375	Letters		29
doe that which GOD shall put into your hart, and the LORD bless all	375	Letters		33
which to me that have nothing yett, is very much.	376	Letters		2
of kindred bredd up, (which generally is very true,) yet I care not;	376	Letters		4
which I commend to you as being now a father, "the best-bredd child	376	Letters		17
find out some thing not unworthy of those hands at which they aim.	377	Letters		1
for which I humbly thank him, & am so far from giving you cause,	378	Letters		9
if God had done that (which you are thinking to doe) to blessed Mary	381	Woodnoth		4
worse by your withdrawing which grow not better by your presence.	381	Woodnoth		11
hands a Merchant of London which fell to me by the death of my	382	G.H.'s Will		9
legacies of my deceased Neece which are to be payd out of it unto	382	G.H.'s Will		14
three pound more besides that which is due to her, to Ann I leave	382	G.H.'s Will		23
The accession of which new title to your Excellencies, all the Muses	441	Oration		28
with which you use to conquer your enemies, and assume more mild	442	Oration		3
by which we well know how to convince the sterne, and more austere	442	Oration		5
with that bloud, which useth to infuse so great and worthie Spirits.	442	Oration		15
And that which first deserveth our observation, to the end,	442	Oration		16
same order and habit, of which wee all in this Kingdome glorie to be.	442	Oration		21
since there is a two-fold brightnesse which dazeleth the eyes of men,	442	Oration		33
slight glories, which wee raise from bookes, and painefull industrie.	443	Oration		1
WHILE				
Herod in judgement sits, while I do stand;	29	Sacrifice		81
When all my tears were bloud, the while you slept:	31	Sacrifice		150
Reproches, which are free, while I am bound.	33	Sacrifice		219
While grace fills up uneven nature.	50	Faith		32
While those to spirits refin'd, at doore attend	52	H.Commun.		23
While mortall love doth all the title gain!	54	Love 1		5
While mortall love does all the title gain!	54	Love 1	W	5
Must all be vail'd, while he that reades, divines,	56	Jordan 1		9
While that my soul repairs to her devotion,	64	Ch.-monum.		1
Deare flesh, while I do pray, learn here thy stemme	65	Ch.-monum.		17
But while he thinks to spoil the room, he sweeps.	67	Ch.-floore		18
But it is that which while I use	70	Quidditie		11
While the world now rides by, now lags behinde.	72	Constancie		10
And while he digs out thee, falls in the ditch.	77	Avarice		14
While they do wound and prick my soul.	90	Afflict.4		12
While they do wound and pinke my soul.	90	Afflict.4	W	12
And while I live, trie out their right.	90	Afflict.4		18
I made a posie, while the day ran by:	94	Life		1
Fit, while ye liv'd, for smell or ornament,	94	Life		14
While blustring windes destroy the wanton bowres,	97	Afflict.5		21
And calls for musick, while his veins do swell,	98	Mortific.		14
And drest his herse, while he has breath	99	Mortific.		33
But while I bustled, I might heare a friend	103	Jordan 2		15
While thou dost ever, ever stay:	107	Home		2
While she avoids her neighbours pride,	110	Brit. Ch.		22
Are brought to Man, while they are lame and mute.	117	Providence		12
The sacrifice for all; while they below	117	Providence		14
While all things have their will, yet none but thine.	117	Providence		32
While it detains us from our God.	123	Time		20
But while I lookt, the clouds immediately	124	Peace		11
One while he counts of heav'n, as of his treasure:	127	Giddinesse		5
Which at a board, while many drunk bare wine,	130	Love unkn.		42
While the inclosure is thine ARM?	133	Paradise		6
And while it cometh, it is almost past.	145	Discharge		53
And fence a plague, while others sleep and slumber.	147	Offering		12
Thou tarriest, while I die,	150	Longing		55
While I remain	150	Longing		58

WHILE (cont'd)	PAGE	TITLE		LINE
And use in baptisme, while ye pine and die:	152	The Jews		4
While thou didst wink and wouldst not see.	153	The Collar		26
And hold my hand, while I did write.	156	Assurance		30
Then can thy truth and I: but while rocks stand,	156	Assurance		32
While I decay.	162	The Search		12
While poore I pine.	162	The Search		16
But while I grow in a straight line,	166	The Flower		29
While he is mine, and I am his,	172	23 Psalme		3
But lives in me while I do rest)	174	Aaron		24
While ye graze without your bounds:	180	Invitation		21
While Sinne doth rave,	183	A Parodie		22
That Sinne sayes true: but while I grieve,	184	A Parodie		29
While this member jogs the other,	186	Dooms-day		5
Letting, while one foot stept, the other stay	191	Ch.-Milit.		34
Starving the while he worshippeth his meat!	193	Ch.-Milit.		114
Whose house is foul, while he adores his broom?	193	Ch.-Milit.		118
Thus Sinne in Egypt sneaked for a while;	193	Ch.-Milit.		121
While Truth sat by, counting his victories:	195	Ch.-Milit.		190
To go to them, while that which now their nation	197	Ch.-Milit.		257
While his conquests dayly spread;	199	L'Envoy		8
But onely while thou speak'st; This Anchor will.	439	Walton 5		4
Meane while, if hee (which all thinges weares)	208	H. Danvers	D	5
At once to Hell, without a baiting while	212	Bohemia	D	49
And peace-meal rent it, while there's none	221	Psalm VII	D	7
While Prince to Spaine, and King to Cambridge goes,	438	Lat.Trans.		1
while they remember their earthly Lord, do much forget their	226	Priest 2		32
so that while they answer, As it was in the beginning, &c.	231	Priest 6		33
which while they deferr, both sides suffer;	259	Priest 22		4
while they consider, that God cannot be wanting to them in Doctrine,	263	Priest 24		19
which while they dwell in their bookes, they will never finde;	266	Priest 26		1
For while they resist the person that reviles, they resist	269	Priest 28		23
freed for a while from temptation, in a quiet sweetnesse seeks how	279	Priest 33		4
hee in the meane while applying himselfe to the [unquestioned] duties	312	Valdesso		19
While the discreet advise, the foole doth his busines.	330	Proverbs		273
Gaming, women, and wine, while they laugh they make men pine.	341	Proverbs		604
Benefits please like flowers while they are fresh.	356	Proverbs	D	40
Stay a while, that we may make an end the sooner.	361	Proverbs	D	1161
be silent, least while I think I am modest, I wrong both my self,	364	Letters		7
entreating that you would a while lay aside those warlike lookes,	442	Oration		2
WHILES				
And fence a plague, whiles others sleep and slumber.	147	Offering	V	12
Leave jesting whiles it pleaseth, lest it turne to earnest.	324	Proverbs		104
WHIP				
Whose twigs are pleasures, & they whip thee bare,	6	Ch.-Porch	W	9
WHIPPING				
passed judgment, & been corrected either by whipping, or imprisoning,	287	Priest 37		15
WHIPS				
Thy whips, thy nails, thy wounds, thy woes,	39	Good Fri.		26
WHIRLE				
To whirle the eyes too much shewes a Kites braine.	345	Proverbs		717
WHIRLWINDE				
As if a whirlwinde blew	127	Giddinesse		14
WHISPER				
Whisper, How wide is all this long pretence!	103	Jordan 2		16
Whisper, How wide is all this preparation	103	Jordan 2	W	16
WHISPRING				
Each one whispring, Live ye brother?	186	Dooms-day		6
WHISTLED				
In silks that whistled, who but he?	111	The Quip		14
WHIT				
in our publick Halls, you know, is nothing but Fish and Whit-meats:	365	Letters		4
WHIT-MEATS				
in our publick Halls, you know, is nothing but Fish and Whit-meats:	365	Letters		4
WHITE				
Pure red and white.	115	Dulnesse		12
Thy hand is white,	141	Justice 2		15
White is their colour, and behold my head.	176	Forerunners		2
being himselfe in white, he requires the presence of all,	258	Priest 22		2
the Parson useth damask or white Roses for the one, and plantaine,	261	Priest 23		34
then borrow of my neighbour white.	330	Proverbs		269
The filth under the white snow, the sunne discovers.	338	Proverbs		495
If all fooles wore white Caps, wee should seeme a flock of geese.	338	Proverbs		513
A white wall is the paper of a foole.	349	Proverbs		839
WHITEN				
Thornes whiten yet doe nothing.	352	Proverbs		943
The Bathe of the Blackamoor hath sworne not to whiten.	359	Proverbs	D	1105
WHITHER				
O blessed bodie! Whither art thou thrown?	40	Sepulchre		1
Whither the buyer and the seller please;	104	Obedience		3
Whither away delight?	154	Glimpse		1
Whither, O, whither art thou fled,	162	The Search		1
Hony of roses, whither wilt thou flie?	176	Forerunners		20
But what shall issue, whither these my words	204	Persever.	W	5
Whither my many crymes and use of sinn	205	Persever.	W	11
And is in contention for them whither to live, or dy;	234	Priest 7		15
whither the nature of man, loving refreshment, gladly betakes it	252	Priest 18		21
whither to drive the Answerer, which the Questionist must have in his	256	Priest 21		31
WHITSUNDAY				
Whitsunday.	59	Whitsunday		T

	PAGE	TITLE		LINE
WHITSUNTIDE				
Christmasse, Whitsuntide, afore and after Harvest, and the beginning	259	Priest 22		22
WHO				
And make us strive, who shall sing best thy name.	5	Dedication		4
Turn their eyes hither, who shall make a gain:	5	Dedication		5
Theirs, who shall hurt themselves or me, refrain.	5	Dedication		6
Hearken unto a Verser, who may chance	6	Ch.-Porch		3
A verse may finde him, who a sermon flies,	6	Ch.-Porch		5
Take not his name, who made thy mouth, in vain:	8	Ch.-Porch		55
Who breaks his own bond, forfeiteth himself:	11	Ch.-Porch		119
Who fears to do ill, sets himself to task:	11	Ch.-Porch		125
Who fears to do well, sure should wear a mask.	11	Ch.-Porch		126
Who carves, is kind to two; who talks, to all.	11	Ch.-Porch		130
Slight those who say amidst their sickly healths,	12	Ch.-Porch		133
Who lives by rule then, keeps good companie.	12	Ch.-Porch		138
Who keeps no guard upon himself, is slack,	12	Ch.-Porch		139
Who cannot rest till hee good-fellows finde,	12	Ch.-Porch		149
Who cannot live on twentie pound a yeare,	13	Ch.-Porch		176
Play not for gain, but sport. Who playes for more	14	Ch.-Porch		193
Onely a herauld, who that way doth passe,	14	Ch.-Porch		197
Who strive to sit out losing hands, are lost.	14	Ch.-Porch		202
To work for two, who brought himself to thrall.	17	Ch.-Porch		286
Sink not in spirit: who aimeth at the sky,	19	Ch.-Porch		333
Who say, I care not, those I give for lost;	20	Ch.-Porch		347
Who say, I care not, I give those for gone;	20	Ch.-Porch	W	347
Who follows all things, forfeiteth his will.	21	Ch.-Porch		364
As if none could bee brave, but who profess	21	Ch.-Porch	W	369
Who would not haste, nay give, to see the show?	22	Ch.-Porch		390
Who marks in church-time others symmetrie,	23	Ch.-Porch		419
Who marks in church-time others comlines,	23	Ch.-Porch	W	419
As those, who mock at Gods way of salvation.	24	Ch.-Porch		446
Though God do hedge us in, yet who is holy?	24	Ch.-Porch		450
Oh all ye, who passe by, whose eyes and minde	26	Sacrifice		1
To me, who took eyes that I might you finde:	26	Sacrifice		3
Who cannot wish, except I give them bread:	26	Sacrifice		7
Without me each one, who doth now me brave,	27	Sacrifice		9
Mine own Apostle, who the bag did beare,	27	Sacrifice		13
Who at three hundred did the ointment prize,	27	Sacrifice		18
Who am the way of truth, the true relief;	27	Sacrifice		38
Who am the way & Truth, the true relief;	27	Sacrifice	W	38
Most true to those, who are my greatest grief:	27	Sacrifice		39
I suffer binding, who have loos'd their bands:	28	Sacrifice		47
'Gainst him, who seeks not life, but is the meek	28	Sacrifice		58
Who never thought that any robberie:	28	Sacrifice		63
Who teach all hands to warre, fingers to fight,	29	Sacrifice		78
I him obey, who all things else command:	29	Sacrifice		83
But who does hawk at eagles with a dove?	29	Sacrifice		91
Who cannot live lesse then eternally:	29	Sacrifice		99
For it was their own cause who killed me:	30	Sacrifice		115
For it was their own case who killed me:	30	Sacrifice	W	115
Who grasp the earth and heaven with my fist,	30	Sacrifice		130
Who graspes the earth and heaven in his fist,	30	Sacrifice	W	130
Who by my spittle gave the blinde man eies,	31	Sacrifice		134
Who by my spittle gave that blinde man eies,	31	Sacrifice	W	134
Now prophesie who strikes thee, is their dittie.	31	Sacrifice		142
I, who am Truth, turn into truth their deeds:	32	Sacrifice		179
I, who am Truth, turn into truth their scorns:	32	Sacrifice	W	179
Who Crucifie him, crie with one strong shout.	32	Sacrifice		186
O all ye who passe by, behold and see;	33	Sacrifice		201
Who sought for help, never malicious foes:	34	Sacrifice		243
Who in all grief preventest me?	35	Thanksgvng		4
And trie who shall victorious prove.	35	Thanksgvng		18
The man, who once against thee fought.	37	Reprisall		16
Who would know Sinne, let him repair	37	The Agonie		7
Who knows not Love, let him assay	37	The Agonie		13
Who straight, Your suit is granted, said, & died.	40	Redemption		14
Which holds thee now? Who hath indited it	41	Sepulchre		11
Who takes thee by the hand, that thou likewise	41	Easter		3
Who bore the same.	41	Easter		10
Lord, who createdst man in wealth and store,	43	East.wings		1
Who dead men raises.	49	Repentance		35
Faith puts me there with him, who sweetly took	50	Faith		23
Thou, who from me wast sold,	52	H.Commun.		3
Thou, who for me wast sold,	52	H.Commun.	V	3
Who sings thy praise? onely a skarf or glove	54	Love 1		13
Who wert disseized by usurping lust:	54	Love 2		12
And praise him who did make and mend our eies.	54	Love 2		14
Who sayes that fictions onely and false hair	56	Jordan 1		1
Riddle who list, for me, and pull for Prime:	57	Jordan 1		12
Who plainly say, My God, My King.	57	Jordan 1		15
That washes what it shows. Who can indeare	58	H.Script.1		10
Of those, who did themselves through their side wound,	59	Whitsunday		20
Who have a work, as well as they,	61	Praise 1		19
Who doe no more.	61	Praise 1	W	20
Who gave me eyes, and light, and power this day,	63	Even-song		2
Who gave me sight alone,	63	Even-song		5
Lord, who hast form'd me out of mud,	68	Trin.Sun.		1
Lord, who hast made me living mudd,	68	Trin.Sun.	W	1
Lord, who hast rais'd me from the mudd	68	Trin.Sun.	WC	1
Who cannot on his own bed sweetly sleep,	68	Content		3
Humilitie, who sat the lowest there	70	Humilitie		5

WHO (cont'd)

	PAGE	TITLE		LINE
Humilitie, who held the plume, at this	71	Humilitie		25
Who is the honest man?	72	Constancie		1
Who rides his sure and even trot,	72	Constancie		9
Who, when great trials come,	72	Constancie		11
Who never melts or thaws	72	Constancie		21
Who, when he is to treat	73	Constancie		26
Who still is right, and prayes to be so still.	73	Constancie		35
They who lament one crosse,	73	Afflict.3		17
Of him, who dy'd to part	74	The Starre		23
Who want herbs for their wound.	76	Sunday		42
Man calleth thee his wealth, who made thee rich;	77	Avarice		13
Oh glorious spirits, who after all your bands	77	Ang.&Sts.		1
Who do not so;	78	Ang.&Sts.		28
Who blows it not, nor doth controll	79	Employm.2		8
Defrauding thee, who gavest two for one.	82	Ungratef.		30
Then Pleasure came, who liking not the fashion,	84	The World		6
Who with excessive pride	85	Vanitie 1		13
But his deare God? who yet his glorious law	85	Vanitie 1		23
Welcome deare feast of Lent: who loves not thee,	86	Lent		1
Who goeth in the way which Christ hath gone,	87	Lent		37
Who goeth in that way which Christ hath gone,	87	Lent	V	37
Who goeth in the way that Christ hath gone,	87	Lent	W	37
Who art my life: dissolve the knot,	90	Afflict.4		22
Who hath dealt his mercies so,	92	Antiphon 2		4
Who hath made of two folds one.	93	Antiphon 2		23
Who did so sweetly deaths sad taste convey,	94	Life		10
Who reade a chapter when they rise,	96	Charms & K		1
Who shuts his hand, hath lost his gold:	96	Charms & K		5
Who opens it, hath it twice told.	96	Charms & K		6
Who goes to bed and doth not pray,	96	Charms & K		7
Who goes to bed and does not pray,	96	Charms & K	W	7
Who by aspersions throw a stone	96	Charms & K		9
Who looks on ground with humble eyes,	96	Charms & K		11
Who turnes a trencher, setteth free	96	Charms & K	W	14
But who drinks on, to hell may go.	97	Charms & K		18
Who dives on further may find Hell.	97	Charms & K	W	22
Convey them quickly, who are bound for death.	98	Mortific.		12
Who would, to be thy foes.	100	Miserie		30
Who made the arbour: this exceeds her wit.	101	Miserie		58
Who may thy follies span?	102	Miserie	W	66
Art thou possest, who, when thou couldst not die,	103	Prayer 2		14
Thraldome from those, who would not at a feast	107	Home		21
Shows who is best.	109	Brit. Ch.		9
In silks that whistled, who but he?	111	The Quip		14
Foolish soul who sinn'd to day?	113	Businesse		2
Who hath these, those ill forbears.	113	Businesse		8
Foolish soul, Who di'd for thee?	113	Businesse		16
Who did leave his Fathers throne,	113	Businesse		17
Who in heart not ever kneels,	114	Businesse		37
Who for man was sold, can see;	114	Dialogue		15
Look onely; for to love thee, who can be,	116	Dulnesse		27
Ask'd what it meant. I, (who am never loth	116	Love-joy		4
O sacred Providence, who from end to end	116	Providence		1
But robs a thousand who would praise thee fain,	117	Providence		19
Who dost so strongly and so sweetly move,	117	Providence		31
Who sweetly temper'st all. If we could heare	118	Providence		39
Who hath the vertue to expresse the rare	119	Providence		73
The windes, who think they rule the mariner,	119	Providence		91
But who hath praise enough? nay who hath any?	121	Providence		141
Who above all things lov'd this life;	122	Time		8
Who wants the place, where God doth dwell,	123	Time		23
At Salem dwelt, who liv'd with good increase	125	Peace		23
And calls him coward, who for fear of sinne	127	Giddinesse		7
But can he want the grape, who hath the wine?	128	Bunch Gr.		22
But can he want the grape, who hath the vine?	128	Bunch Gr.	V	22
Blessed be God, who prosper'd Noahs vine,	128	Bunch Gr.		24
Who of the laws sowre juice sweet wine did make,	128	Bunch Gr.		27
Lookt on a servant, who did know his eye	129	Love unkn.		9
Who was to take it from me, slipt his hand,	130	Love unkn.		34
Full well I understood, who had been there:	130	Love unkn.		54
Who took the debt upon him. Truly, Friend,	130	Love unkn.		61
Who fain would have you be new, tender, quick.	131	Love unkn.		70
Who do not their own motions heare?	134	The Method		19
Who heare not him, but quickly heare	134	The Method		27
Who can these Gordian knots undo?	135	Divinitie		20
Is more then God was, who was hungrie here.	138	The Size		14
I, who had heard of musick in the spheres,	139	Artillerie		9
Christ keepeth now, who cannot fail or fall.	143	Holdfast		14
That which is past who can recall?	144	Discharge		10
He, who came hither all alone,	151	The Bag		27
Who by not keeping once, became a debter;	152	The Jews		5
Who by thy coming may be made a court!	155	Glimpse		30
Who heard thee say it. O most gracious Lord,	155	Assurance		20
Who changeth all things, as him pleaseth best.	159	Jos.coat		4
I live to shew his power, who once did bring	159	Jos.coat		13
Who make the bravest shows.	161	Priesthood		18
As serve him up, who all the world commands:	161	Priesthood		26
Their hands convey him, who conveys their hands.	161	Priesthood		28
Who bring my God to me!	161	Priesthood		30
O who will give me tears? Come all ye springs,	164	Grief		1

WHO (cont'd)

	PAGE	TITLE	LINE
Who would have thought my shrivel'd heart	166	The Flower	8
Who would be more,	167	The Flower	47
Who griefs in earnest, joyes in jest pursue;	167	Dotage	14
Who cannot dresse it well, want wit, not words.	167	The Sonne	4
He who craves all the minde,	168	a true Hymn	11
Who think me eager, hot, and undertaking,	169	The Answer	6
Poore death! and who was hurt thereby?	169	Dial.-Anth	5
Thou who dost dwell and linger here below,	170	Water-crs.	1
For who can look for lesse, that loveth Life. / Strife.	170	Water-crs.	5
Who gives to man, as he sees fit Salvation. / Damnation.	170	Water-crs.	10
Thou who condemnest Jewish hate,	170	Self-cond.	1
To look upon me, who before did lie	171	The Glance	3
To make him clean, who could not be defil'd?	173	Marie Magd	8
Deare soul, she knew who did vouchsafe and deigne	173	Marie Magd	13
My doctrine tun'd by Christ, (who is not dead,	174	Aaron	23
Who have pass'd my right away.	177	The Rose	12
Who can scape his bow?	179	Discipline	25
Onely God, who gives perfumes,	181	Banquet	22
Who hath done so much for me.	182	Banquet	48
Who sweeps a room, as for thy laws,	185	The Elixer	19
Who sweeps a chamber, for thy laws,	185	The Elixer W	19
I give to thee, who knowest all my wayes,	185	A Wreath	3
To thee, who art more farre above deceit,	185	A Wreath	7
O who will show me those delights on high?	188	Heaven	1
Who made the eyes but I?	189	Love 3	12
And know you not, sayes Love, who bore the blame?	189	Love 3	15
Almightie Lord, who from thy glorious throne	190	Ch.-Milit.	1
Who may with thee compare?	191	Ch.-Milit.	48
Who, that they might subdue, made all their foes.	191	Ch.-Milit.	62
Who had subdued all the world for foes.	191	Ch.-Milit. W	62
Who by an ambush lost his Paradise.	192	Ch.-Milit.	66
Him in his members, who for him was slain.	192	Ch.-Milit.	70
Who were cut short in Alexanders stemme.	192	Ch.-Milit.	74
Who may with thee compare?	192	Ch.-Milit.	100
Who for a God clearely a sallet lost.	193	Ch.-Milit.	110
Who makes a root his God, how low is he,	193	Ch.-Milit.	115
Who after him should braver truths disclose.	194	Ch.-Milit.	138
Cheat the most subtill nations. Who so coy,	194	Ch.-Milit.	150
Who may with thee compare?	194	Ch.-Milit.	156
They who rely on them must reckon twice	194	Ch.-Milit. W	160
Who without spear, or sword, or other drumme	195	Ch.-Milit.	201
Who brought his doctrins & his deeds from Rome	195	Ch.-Milit. W	201
Who may with thee compare?	196	Ch.-Milit.	210
Who may with thee compare?	198	Ch.-Milit.	279
Who God & Saints and Angels loose at last.	203	Trin.Sun. W	17
That I who cannot now by day	203	Even-song W	6
For who can tell, though thou hast dyde to winn	205	Persever. W	9
How sweet a friend was he, who being griev'd	439	Walton 5	15
His dust who under thee must sleepe	208	H. Danvers D	2
And meet theire tast, who are thy bitter foes.	213	Bohemia D	66
Many there are that say, O who	217	Psalm IV D	21
For who in death remember Thee?	220	Psalm VI D	11
or who shall praise Thee in the grave?	220	Psalm VI D	12
God is my shield, who doth preserve	222	Psalm VII D	37
and live, and who giveth mee my Desires and Performances;	224	Priest	2
as farre as wee can in pleasing of him, who hath done so much for us.	224	Priest	12
who may not despise my poor labours, but add to those points,	224	Priest	14
They who do not thus, while they remember their earthly Lord,	226	Priest 2	31
They who for the hope of promotion neglect any necessary admonition,	226	Priest 2	36
who by hard usage increase their travell, the Countrey Parson is very	227	Priest 3	14
and then they are worst, who ought to be best.	227	Priest 3	28
who have handled the places controverted, which the Parson by no	229	Priest 4	18
who somtimes make it a piece of state not to come at the beginning	232	Priest 6	7
and of theirs also who gaze upon them when they come in,	232	Priest 6	10
is ever very well supplyed by some able man who treads in his steps,	232	Priest 7	26
with letting them know, that he observes who marks, and who not;	233	Priest 7	2
who first shed teares over Jerusalem, and afterwards blood.	234	Priest 7	21
all those, who come with lesse prepared hearts then they ought.	235	Priest 8	31
with God, who weighs even childrens actions, 1 Kings 14. 12, 13.	239	Priest 10	28
it absurd, that he should exceed, who teacheth others temperance.	241	Priest 10	21
and their comfort, who are much cheered with such friendliness.	243	Priest 11	12
Parson, who is a diligent observer, and tracker of Gods wayes,	244	Priest 11	2
giving them most, who live best, and take most paines, and are most	245	Priest 12	15
and put them to great shame, who deny the Scripture to be perfect.	247	Priest 13	1
who can read, who not;	248	Priest 14	34
who wish them best, and that not a desire to meddle with others	251	Priest 17	30
and therefore not for him, who is hearty, and true in all his wayes,	253	Priest 19	1
this life, who hath promised, that Godlinesse shall be gainfull:	254	Priest 20	19
who like Christian Souldiers are to give the word, and to satisfie	255	Priest 21	20
who are not well grounded, may then by an honourable way take	255	Priest 21	30
that those who are well grown in the knowledg of Religion,	255	Priest 21	32
Who made it? Did you see God make it?	256	Priest 21	8
Who is God? And so forward, requiring answers to all these,	256	Priest 21	12
who held that the seeds of all truths lay in every body,	256	Priest 21	21
or whether he needed a helper, and who was that helper.	257	Priest 21	9
who having not received yet, are to enter into this great work,	258	Priest 22	29
who being to present all that receive not thrice a year;	259	Priest 22	24
nor the Church-Wardens so well take notice who receive thrice,	259	Priest 22	28
Church-Wardens so well take notice who receive thrice, and who not.	259	Priest 22	28
householder, who bringeth out of his treasure things new and old;	261	Priest 23	15

WHO (cont'd)

	PAGE	TITLE		LINE
there are some persons, who abstain not even from known sins;	264	Priest 26		10
who when they know a sin evidently, they commit it not. . .	264	Priest 26		11
to themselves, and witty to others who shall reprove them from it.	264	Priest 26		13
knowing that there is one, who when they forget, remembers for them;	267	Priest 26		21
at least of those, who are apt to despise:	268	Priest 28		24
who hath in his hand an apple, and a piece of Gold under it;	272	Priest 30		8
the manifold wiles of Satan (who playes his part sometimes in	272	Priest 31		16
and Satan, who knows the exigent, blows the fire, endeavouring	272	Priest 31		33
who more accepts a common course of devotion, then dislikes . .	273	Priest 31		8
some scoffing ruffian, who is likely to deride him for his paines:	273	Priest 31		29
the Gallant, who is witty enough to abuse both others, and himself,	275	Priest 32		6
and himself, and who is ready to ask, if he shall mend shoos,	275	Priest 32		7
who hath so many dispersed Officers at his beck throughout . .	276	Priest 32		10
all those, who else might both trouble him and the whole State.	276	Priest 32		15
who are come to the gravitie, and ripenesse of judgement for so	276	Priest 32		16
who performes the other acts of repentance, when he cannot more,	279	Priest 33		29
who sacrificed lest his Children should have transgressed in their	281	Priest 34		1
and then who can deny the stretched out arme of a mighty God?	282	Priest 34		6
who have born witness to the truth, (there being no reason, . .	282	Priest 34		19
Those who use it not, do so either out of niceness, because they like	285	Priest 36		4
who was to shew all humility before his Passion, yet he allows in his	285	Priest 36		27
who had withstood his preaching, The Lord (saith he) reward him	285	Priest 36		33
appears Rom. 12. 14. how much more those, who are spiritual Fathers?	286	Priest 36		28
before thy face, who are contrary to thee, in all we call thee?	288	Priest		9
who onely doth wondrous things.	289	Priest		8
to convert those who are not yet thine, and to confirme those that	289	Priest		16
who continueth to pour his benefits upon us.	290	Priest		1
the measure of thy love, who hast done for us as much as may be.	290	Priest		12
who, if they had lived, would have been an ornament to the world,	291	Cornaro		3
who will take this into consideration, I will declare the causes	291	Cornaro		14
That they who in these two things that enter in at the mouth,	294	Cornaro		3
whereas they hurt them very much who live intemperately. . .	294	Cornaro		15
Neither can any man denie this, who will narrowly consider it.	297	Cornaro		14
Who would beleeve that old wine should hurt my stomack, . .	297	Cornaro		31
curing of diseases, into which they often fall, who live disorderly:	298	Cornaro		5
For if a friend who visits thee in thy sicknesse, and onely comforts	298	Cornaro		6
who not onely as a friend doth visit thee, but help thee! . .	298	Cornaro		9
Paul the third, and Cardinal Bembo, who therefore lived so long;	299	Cornaro		2
That they who are employed in the common wealth, cannot live	299	Cornaro		11
But they who finde benefit in these meats, may, yea ought to use	300	Cornaro		10
That there are many, who, though they live disorderly, yet continue	300	Cornaro		18
sure of life, then the most strong young man who lives disorderly.	300	Cornaro		26
or lesse my self, who being ten yeares older have made a Comedie?	302	Cornaro		35
age and constitution with them who follow their youthfull appetites,	303	Cornaro		12
but that I should wish all who have the care of themselves, . .	303	Cornaro		31
who being obscured in his own country he would have to flourish in	304	Valdesso		13
observed, who workes by his Word, and ever in the reading of it.	310	Valdesso		1
Untill against the Heretiques who disputed against the Virginity	318	Valdesso		10
understands the cunning hypocrite who by the world is counted a very	319	Valdesso	V	20
All is well with him, who is beloved of his neighbours. . .	321	Proverbs		10
Who hath none to still him, may weepe out his eyes. . . .	321	Proverbs		17
Hee puls with a long rope, who looks for anothers death. . .	322	Proverbs	V	25
Who gives to all, denies all.	322	Proverbs		38
Who remove stones, bruise their fingers.	322	Proverbs		40
Who hath a Wolfe for his mate, needes a Dog for his man. . .	323	Proverbs		57
Who is so deafe, as he that will not heare?	323	Proverbs		79
Who is so deafe, as he who will not heare?	323	Proverbs	V	79
He who will learne to pray, let him goe to Sea.	323	Proverbs	V	84
Hee who lives well is learned enough.	323	Proverbs	V	86
Assaile who will, the valiant attends.	324	Proverbs		95
Who would doe ill ne're wants occasion.	324	Proverbs		116
Who hath no more bread then neede, must not keepe a dog. . .	325	Proverbs		128
Who must account for himselfe and others, must know both. . .	328	Proverbs		209
In the world who knowes not to swimme, goes to the bottome. . .	330	Proverbs		285
In the world who can not swimme, goe to the bottome. . . .	330	Proverbs	V	285
Who spits against heaven, it falls in his face.	333	Proverbs		346
Who eates his cock alone must saddle his horse alone. . . .	333	Proverbs		348
Who eates his cake alone must saddle his horse alone. . . .	333	Proverbs	V	348
Who likes not the drinke, God deprives him of bread. . . .	334	Proverbs		394
Who so once deceives is ever suspected.	335	Proverbs	V	417
Who doth his owne businesse, foules not his hands. . . .	335	Proverbs		419
Who hath bitter in his mouth, spits not all sweet. . . .	335	Proverbs		422
He who hath children, all his morsels are not his owne. . .	335	Proverbs	V	423
He who hath the spice, may season as he pleaseth.	335	Proverbs	V	424
Hee who hath but one sonne makes him fat, ...	336	Proverbs	V	433
Who letts his wife goe to every feast, ...	336	Proverbs		434
Who is fed by anothers hand stays long ere he be full. . . .	336	Proverbs	V	439
At the games end we shall see who gaines.	339	Proverbs		538
who twice suffers shipwrack.	345	Proverbs	V	706
Who will sell the Cow, must say the word.	347	Proverbs		791
He who talkes much of his happinesse summons griefe. . . .	349	Proverbs	V	856
Who hastens a glutton choakes him.	349	Proverbs		858
Who praiseth Saint Peter, doth not blame Saint Paul. . . .	349	Proverbs		859
The Rich knowes not who is his friend.	349	Proverbs		865
Who paies the Physitian, does the cure.	350	Proverbs		879
Hee hath no leisure who useth it not.	351	Proverbs		897
Wee know not who lives or dies.	353	Proverbs		966
Who hath no head, needes no hatt.	354	Proverbs		996
Who hath no head, needes no heart.	354	Proverbs	V	996
Who hath no hast in his businesse, ...	354	Proverbs		997

WHO (cont'd)	PAGE	TITLE		LINE
Who will make a doore of gold must knock a naile every day. . . .	354	Proverbs		1004
Chuse none for thy servant who have served thy betters. . . .	354	Proverbs		1014
What Trades-man is there who will set up without his Tools? . . .	364	Letters		14
There is a Frenchman who writt a poem heere in England & presented it	368	Letters		30
who because of his importunities gave him a reward, but not so great	368	Letters		31
which some observing who heard the interdiction denounced to him,	368	Letters		36
who cannot think me lazy, since I rode 200 mile to see a Sister,	371	Letters		1
God who knows and sees this Writing, knows also that my solliciting	372	Letters		1
of all Comfort, who is not willing to behold any sorrow but for sin.	372	Letters		25
have over Youth and Health, who are now so near those true Comforts.	372	Letters		33
who have already abundantly discharg'd that part, having both ordered	373	Letters		11
That God who hath delivered me out of the paws of the Lyon and Bear,	374	Letters		6
at all times rejoyce in the Lord, who taketh care for us: . .	374	Letters		26
and age, and knew none but one who could be no company to them.	375	Letters		15
I forgett all thinges, so I may doe them good who want it. . .	376	Letters		6
and not as many who think they have done fairly, if they leave them	376	Letters		15
who tying, as with a knot, both Indias to his Spaine, knowes no	442	Oration		11
WHOE				
You whoe admire yourselves because	209	Paradox	D	1
WHOLE				
Blowing up houses with their whole increase.	14	Ch.-Porch		204
A tithe purloin'd cankers the whole estate.	22	Ch.-Porch		386
Used, and wished, are the whole worlds light:	30	Sacrifice		110
Of my whole life one grief devoure;	39	Good Fri.		14
Yet all these fences and their whole aray	46	Sinne 1		13
Indeed mans whole estate	63	Mattens		13
Ties the whole frame, is Love	67	Ch.-floore		11
Making the whole to stoup and bow, ...	75	Sunday		13
But though the whole world turn to coal, ...	88	Vertue		15
The whole is, either our cupboard of food, ...	91	Man		29
No, not to purchase the whole pack of starres:	101	Miserie		52
And to my whole is JESU.	112	JESU		10
I disclaim the whole designe:	115	Dialogue		23
Give up the whole, and with the whole depart?	144	Discharge		8
Sev'n whole dayes, not one in seven, ...	146	Praise 2		17
That the whole world did seem but the Popes mule.	196	Ch.-Milit.		204
Wherewith whole showls of Martyrs once did burn, ...	206	Walton 1		2
A Paradox. That the Sicke are in better State then the Whole.	209	Paradox	D	T
but as presenting with himself the whole Congregation, whose sins he	231	Priest 6		8
some choyce Observations drawn out of the whole text, as it lyes	235	Priest 7		3
puts on the whole Armour of God, and by the vertue of the shield	238	Priest 9		5
but clean, whole, and sweet, as sweet as his garden can make;	241	Priest 10		12
windows glazed, floore paved, seats whole, firm, and uniform,	246	Priest 13		5
and those not torne, or fouled, but whole and clean, and well bound;	246	Priest 13		15
it about with him as fully, as if he had begot his whole Parish.	250	Priest 16		10
an aim and mark of the whole discourse, whither to drive . .	256	Priest 21		31
referreth the whole matter to the examination, and punishment	268	Priest 28		34
and that indeed the whole order and discipline of the Parish is put	269	Priest 29		28
or hath generall Propositions to the whole Towne or Hamlet, . .	276	Priest 32		5
all those, who else might both trouble him and the whole State.	276	Priest 32		15
and the whole Army of Temptations without, hath ever so many sermons	278	Priest 33		23
not only without dissolution of the whole, but also of any part,	281	Priest 34		23
because from the time that I was made whole, I never since departed	293	Cornaro		25
whereby my head and whole bodie was sore hurt, and also one of my	294	Cornaro		39
my arm and legge should be set, and my whole bodie anointed with oyl:	295	Cornaro		11
For whereas before the measure of my whole dayes meat, viz. . .	296	Cornaro		9
abode in those fenny places two whole moneths in the heat of summer	302	Cornaro		18
The best salve for the whole Chapter, is to distinguish Judgment:	316	Valdesso		34
And so his whole discourse and sevenfold observation falls . .	318	Valdesso		25
A naughty child is better sick then whole.	328	Proverbs		233
Your pot broken seemes better then my whole one.	330	Proverbs		270
Hee will spend a whole yeares rent at one meales meate. . .	331	Proverbs		305
A faire death honours the whole life.	339	Proverbs		522
He that mockes a cripple, ought to be whole.	340	Proverbs		565
this (which is now, when I must lay the foundation of my whole life).	365	Letters		18
am to make an Oration to the whole University of an hour long in	369	Letters		13
It is the whole amount of this letter, and therefore entertaine it	379	Letters		25
7, 21. & in the whole chapter	380	Woodnoth		5
this whole sum of five hundred pounds I bequeath unto my Neeces	382	G.H.'s Will		12
all we and our whole Kingdome exult with joy, to bee united with that	442	Oration		14
WHOLLY				
Abstain wholly, or wed. Thy bounteous Lord	7	Ch.-Porch		13
Did not excite thee, we should wholly sink.	60	Whitsunday		24
She wholly goes on th' other side, ...	110	Brit. Ch.		23
What leaves are they? impart the matter wholly.	188	Heaven		9
which is alreadie burdened with a disease, would be wholly oppressed.	299	Cornaro		34
which depend almost wholly on their Canon law and Decretals,	319	Valdesso	V	29
WHOLSOME				
fare is plain, and common, but wholsome, what hee hath, is little,	241	Priest 10		15
WHOLY				
O make mee wholy guiltles, or at least	66	Ch.-lock	W	9
WHOM				
Whom God in Baptisme washt with his own blood.	6	Ch.-Porch		8
Whom when he thinks he hath, the devil hath him.	13	Ch.-Porch		166
Perhaps his wives too, and whom she hath bore:	14	Ch.-Porch		195
Whom all his passions follow, as he goes.	15	Ch.-Porch		216
The gigler is a milk-maid, whom infection, ...	16	Ch.-Porch		249
That suites him best, of whom thy speech is heard.	18	Ch.-Porch		294
Whom oil and balsames kill, what salve can cure?	24	Ch.-Porch		447
Whom oil and mercies kill, what salve can cure?	24	Ch.-Porch	W	447

WHOM (cont'd)	PAGE	TITLE		LINE
Thou, whom the former precepts have	25	Superlim		1
And never yet, whom I would punish, miss'd:	30	Sacrifice		131
And never yet, whom he would punish, miss'd:	30	Sacrifice	W	131
Whom Angels did desire to have the grace,	32	Sacrifice	W	182
Whom devils flie, thus is he toss'd of men:	32	Sacrifice		191
The sonne, in whom thou dost delight to be?	33	Sacrifice		214
The sonne, in whom thou art well pleas'd to be?	33	Sacrifice	W	214
Yet studies them, not him by whom they be.	63	Mattens		16
Of winde to thee whom I have crost,	64	Even-song		15
Whom neither force nor fawning can	72	Constancie		4
Whom none can work or wooe	72	Constancie		16
With sick folks, women, those whom passions sway,	73	Constancie		27
Whom others faults do not defeat;	73	Constancie		29
Whom nothing can procure,	73	Constancie		31
Whom, if we were not very dull,	75	Sunday		18
In whom the Lord of hosts did pitch his tent!	77	Anagram		2
Whom we do all joyntly adore and praise,	78	Ang.&Sts.		17
Of his rich crown, from whom lyes no appeal	78	Ang.&Sts.		22
Of his great crown, from whom lyes no appeal	78	Ang.&Sts.	W	22
There when I came, whom found I but my deare,	81	Christmas		5
We are the trees, whom shaking fastens more,	97	Afflict.5		20
To whom the starres shine not so fair, as eyes;	111	Vanitie 2		3
Awake sad heart, whom sorrow ever drowns;	112	Dawning		1
And not of thee, through whom my fingers bend	116	Providence		3
To whom thy sithe a hatchet was,	122	Time		9
Whom when for Peace	125	Peace		20
And have, of whom some grounds which may improve,	129	Love unkn.		4
Then whom in waiting nothing seems more slow,	137	Familie		15
On whom thy tempests fell all night.	166	The Flower		42
Without whom I could have no rest:	174	Aaron		14
God, in whom all dainties are.	179	Invitation		6
Come ye hither all, whom wine	180	Invitation		7
Come ye hither all, whom pain	180	Invitation		13
Come ye hither all, whom joy	180	Invitation		19
(Whom Schollers Habitt & Obscurity	209	L. Bacon	D	6
Thou art that righteous God by whom	221	Psalm VII	D	35
(thorow the Mercy of GOD) to please Him, for whom I am, and live,	224	Priest		2
to whom this discourse ariseth not) some live in the Universities,	225	Priest 2		22
For sins make all equall, whom they finde together;	227	Priest 3		28
him in the pulpit, whom they cannot trust in his Conversation.	228	Priest 3		7
his servants, to whom he hath revealed his Truth, as well as to him;	229	Priest 4		22
amazed with the Majesty of God, before whom he then presents himself;	231	Priest 6		6
whom also he intreats to press some point, that he himself hath often	232	Priest 7		27
his flock by themselves, whom his Sermons cannot, or doe not reach.	236	Priest 8		13
whom he sometimes purposely takes home with him, setting them close	243	Priest 11		10
whom hee sees take best courses, that so both they may be encouraged	243	Priest 11		25
at his door, whom God puts in his way, and makes his neighbours.	245	Priest 12		20
poor and needy, whom he thus finds labouring, he gives them somewhat;	248	Priest 14		9
For both God is there also, and those for whom God dyed:	249	Priest 14		7
as being the servant of him, in whom there was no guile.	253	Priest 19		2
whom he hath ever some cases to ask, when he meets with them;	260	Priest 23		4
the cause with him, whom he makes to deliver their opinion first;	260	Priest 23		10
of whom in stead of the qualities of the world, he asks no other,	260	Priest 23		30
whom yet he ever exhorts not to exceed his bounds, but in tickle	260	Priest 23		35
that labouring people (whom he chiefly considered) might have every	261	Priest 23		20
be wanting to them in Doctrine, to whom he is so gracious in Life.	263	Priest 24		21
whom anothers ill mastereth, and leadeth captive without any	269	Priest 28		21
those whom the Parson finds loose, and not ingaged into some	277	Priest 32		24
whom the Law would have defamed, except he also do it out of rancour.	287	Priest 37		28
To whom with thee, and the Holy Ghost, three Persons, but one most	290	Priest		14
whom that matter ought to have affected most, received no	294	Cornaro		20
the Authors sake, whom I conceive to have been a true servant of God;	304	Valdesso		6
Churches sake, to whom by Printing it I would have you consecrate it.	304	Valdesso		8
He carries well, to whom it waighes not.	334	Proverbs		391
In time comes he whom God sends.	334	Proverbs		397
A kinsman, a friend, or whcm you intreate,	347	Proverbs		794
whom to receive were the greatest charitie of all, for she is	375	Letters		23
I have another judge, to whom I stand or fall.	376	Letters		8
Gods accepting you have done the good you intended, & whom serve you?	381	Woodnoth		18
or whom would you please?	381	Woodnoth		18
in the choice of whom their judgement doth even now appeare.	442	Oration		26
WHOME				
Bright soule, of whome if any countrey knowne	211	Bohemia	D	1
a much better Paymaster then my self, even him, whome we both serve:	378	Letters		3
whome I esteem to be God's faithfull & diligent Servant,	378	Letters		14
should be mine Executor to whome I bequeath twenty pound whereof	382	G.H.'s Will		28
side are the names of those to whome my deceased Neece left legacyes.	383	G.H.'s Will		1
WHORE				
then they fall to drink, to steal, to whore, to scoffe, to revile,	274	Priest 32		11
WHOSE				
Thou, whose sweet youth and early hopes inhance	6	Ch.-Porch		1
Whose twigs are pleasures, & they whip thee bare,	6	Ch.-Porch	W	9
Much lesse towards God, whose lust is all their book?	6	Ch.-Porch		12
Whose every parcell under-writes a law.	12	Ch.-Porch		142
Whose parts are as thy hand did frame;	26	The Altar		3
Oh all ye, who passe by, whose eyes and minde	26	Sacrifice		1
To whose powre Thunder is but weake and slight:	29	Sacrifice	W	79
Which is above the heav'ns, whose spring and rent	44	H. Bapt.1		5
Which is above the heav'ns, whose spring and vent	44	H. Bapt.1	V	5
What pleasures could I want, whose King I served,	46	Afflict.1		13

	PAGE	TITLE	LINE
WHOSE (cont'd)			
Whose life still pressing	48	Repentance	4
Blest be the Architect, whose art	67	Ch.-floore	19
Give me the pliant minde, whose gentle measure	69	Content	13
When all thy deeds, whose brunt thou feel'st alone,	69	Content	29
Whose honestie is not	72	Constancie	6
Make up one man; whose face thou art,	75	Sunday	9
Whose drops of bloud paid the full price,	76	Sunday	54
With him, whose will	79	Employm.2	12
O Thou, whose glorious, yet contracted light,	81	Christmas	9
Whose sparkling light accesse denies:	82	Ungratef.	14
Whose leaves first sheltred man from drought & dew,	84	The World	12
The other winds towards Him, whose happie birth	84	Coloss.	6
Sweet rose, whose hue angrie and brave	87	Vertue	5
Or can be, then is Man? to whose creation	90	Man	5
As was and is thy floting Ark; whose stay	97	Afflict.5	3
To swaddle infants, whose young breath	98	Mortific.	3
A ring, whose posie was, My pleasure:	102	Miserie	69
Blessed be God, whose love it was	110	Brit. Ch.	28
Tell me, I pray, Whose hands are those?	110	The Quip	7
Poore silly soul, whose hope and head lies low;	111	Vanitie 2	1
Whose flat delights on earth do creep and grow;	111	Vanitie 2	2
But I am lost in flesh, whose sugred lyes	116	Dulnesse	21
But such a heart, whose pulse may be	124	Gratefulnes	31
A boyling caldron, round about whose verge	129	Love unkn.	27
He wears a stuffe whose thread is course and round,	131	Mans medly	15
Happie is he, whose heart	132	Mans medly	34
End as the night, whose sable hue	135	Ephes.	11
Yet active strength: whose long and bonie face	138	The Size	33
On whose meridian was engraven,	138	The Size	46
But turning to my God, whose ministers	139	Artillerie	11
A worm doth sit, whose many feet and hair	140	Ch.-rents	3
Poore nation, whose sweet sap, and juice	152	The Jews	1
Whose streams we got by the Apostles sluce,	152	The Jews	3
Whose grief allows him musick and a ryme:	164	Grief	17
(Whose precepts she had trampled on before)	173	Marie Magd	2
Come ye hither all, whose taste	179	Invitation	1
Come ye hither all, whose love	180	Invitation	25
Whose house is foul, while he adores his broom?	193	Ch.-Milit.	118
O lett my Soule, whose keyes I must deliver	203	Even-song W	21
Lord help thy servant whose perplexed Soule	204	The Knell W	2
Whose fire is wild, and doth not upward go	206	Walton 2	10
Whose native beauty needs not dresse or lace	212	Bohemia D	30
Whose fier, like there malice, nought can quench.	212	Bohemia D	54
Whose pow'r shall dash and break them all	216	Psalm II D	23
Thou art a God whose puritie	218	Psalm V D	9
The question is, whose love the greater showes:	438	Lat.Trans.	2
some live there in office, whose rule is that of the Apostle;	226	Priest 2	3
whose aim and labour must be not only to get knowledg, but to subdue	226	Priest 2	8
whose duty and obligation being the same to the Houses they live in,	226	Priest 2	16
whose sins he then beares, and brings with his own to the heavenly	231	Priest 6	8
Oh my Master, on whose errand I come, let me hold my peace,	233	Priest 7	35
whose humble, and liberall disposition he preferred before beauty,	238	Priest 9	28
none knowing whose turne may be next, and then when he hath	253	Priest 19	33
the secret of whose good consists in this, that at Sermons,	257	Priest 21	17
There are some vices, whose natures are alwayes cleer, and evident,	264	Priest 26	6
There are other vices, whose natures, at least in the beginning,	264	Priest 26	8
whose natures are most stealing, and beginnings uncertaine.	264	Priest 26	33
whose neglect in this point is intolerable, and a shamefull wrong	277	Priest 32	26
thy blessed Son's sake, in whose sweet and pleasing words, we say,	289	Priest	34
whose admirable power causeth that the meat and drink that is taken	293	Cornaro	26
in whose place, joy and peace have taken up their standing in my	301	Cornaro	1
whose holinesse consists in a few ceremonious and superstitious	319	Valdesso V	22
Well may hee smell fire, whose gowne burnes.	325	Proverbs	138
Whose house is of glasse, must not throw stones at another.	327	Proverbs	196
They favour learning whose actions are worthy of a learned pen.	357	Proverbs D	1061
of whose rude delivery my hast makes mee ashamed, only my comfort is	369	Letters	2
whose bottom is wound up and laid ready for work in the New	373	Letters	6
whose Example and Care of them will justifie you both to the world	373	Letters	15
your self into the hands of God (whose the success of things is) &	380	Woodnoth	24
to be payd out of it unto some whose names shal be annexed unto this	382	G.H.'s Will	15
whose exceeding glory is equally round with the world it selfe:	442	Oration	10
WHOSOEVER			
Whosoever when a just occasion cals, either spends not at all,	265	Priest 26	5
WHY			
Why should I feel another mans mistakes	18	Ch.-Porch	309
Stay not for th' other pin: why thou hast lost	23	Ch.-Porch	411
Why, he that built the world can do much more:	28	Sacrifice	67
Why, Caesar is their onely King, not I:	30	Sacrifice	121
But, O my God, my God! why leav'st thou me,	33	Sacrifice	213
Shall I weep bloud? why, thou hast wept such store	35	Thanksgvng	5
My God, my God, why dost thou part from me?	35	Thanksgvng	9
Why he'l not lose a cup of drink for thee:	100	Miserie	8
Yet if thou stayest still, why must I stay?	108	Home	31
Why do I languish thus, drooping and dull,	115	Dulnesse	1
Why doth my Mother blush? is she the rose,	140	Ch.-rents	11
Why should I justice now decline?	141	Justice 2	23
Why dost thou prie,	144	Discharge	2
They ask enough; why shouldst thou further go?	145	Discharge	26
She being stain'd her self, why did she strive	173	Marie Magd	7
Why kept she not her tears for her own faults,	173	Marie Magd	9

WHY (cont'd)	PAGE	TITLE		LINE
Why kept she not her tears for her own fauts, ...	173	Marie Magd	V	9
Why are not Sonnets made of thee? and layes	206	Walton 1		5
Why doth that fire, which by thy power and might	206	Walton 1		12
Why should I Womens eyes for Chrystal take?	206	Walton 2		8
Why then confesse	210	Paradox	D	35
Why are the Heathen swell'd with rage, ...	215	Psalm II	D	1
Why dost thou preach my Laws, and takest my Covenant in thy mouth?	226	Priest 2		13
being ripe enough for ill things, and why not then for better?	259	Priest 22		2
in a doctrinall way, saying to the contemner, Alas, why do you thus?	269	Priest 28		12
being no reason, why any should distrust Saint Luke, or Tertullian,	282	Priest 34		20
why should I be accounted lesse happie, or lesse my self, . . .	302	Cornaro		34
I wept when I was borne, and every day shewes why.	327	Proverbs		199
or why should our afflictions here, have so much power or boldness	372	Letters		27
WICKED				
The wicked are not so, but they	215	Psalm I	D	13
Therefore shall not the wicked be	215	Psalm I	D	17
of good men shall the wicked come.	215	Psalm I	D	20
And those wayes which the wicked go	215	Psalm I	D	23
Unless the wicked turn again, ...	222	Psalm VII	D	41
Behold, the wicked travelleth	222	Psalm VII	D	49
The wicked digged, and a pit	222	Psalm VII	D	53
John 7. and assuring himself, that wicked men, however learned,	228	Priest 4		30
five shields, wherewith the Godly receive the darts of the wicked;	269	Priest 28		20
and ranked backbiters among the generation of the wicked, . . .	287	Priest 37		24
being given only to the godly, and the other sometimes to the wicked.	319	Valdesso		10
A wicked mans gift hath a touch of his master.	326	Proverbs		162
It's a wicked thing to make a dearth ones garner.	351	Proverbs		898
yet useth his Restraining grace, even in the most wicked: . . .	381	Woodnoth		9
WICKED'S				
The wicked's malice, Lord, confound, ...	221	Psalm VII	D	33
WICKEDNESS				
For wickedness their insides are, ...	219	Psalm V	D	25
To his own head his wickedness	222	Psalm VII	D	57
either by the wickedness or quarrelsomnesse thereof, he either	252	Priest 18		17
WICKEDNESSES				
and many other spirituall wickednesses in high places doth the Parson	238	Priest 9		20
WIDDOW				
Marry a widdow before she leave mourning.	329	Proverbs		252
Take heed of a person marked, and a Widdow thrice married. . . .	360	Proverbs	D	1152
WIDE				
The curious unthrift makes his cloth too wide, ...	13	Ch.-Porch		179
And stop our sinnes from growing thick and wide, ...	44	H. Bapt.1		8
When the wide world runnes bias, from his will	73	Constancie		32
Whisper, How wide is all this long pretence!	103	Jordan 2		16
Whisper, How wide is all this preparation	103	Jordan 2	W	16
Gods works are wide, and let in future times;	128	Bunch Gr.		13
I grow too wide, ...	145	Discharge		34
Little pitchers have wide eares.	334	Proverbs		380
WIFE				
Hee'le make thy wife a blessing not a rodd.	7	Ch.-Porch	W	18
Get a sharp wife, a servant that will lowre.	15	Ch.-Porch		213
Make bracelets to adorn the wife	76	Sunday		31
Make bracelets for the spouse & wife	76	Sunday	W	31
the choyce of his wife was made rather by his eare, then by his eye;	238	Priest 9		26
not his affection found out a fit wife for him, whose humble,	238	Priest 9		28
so is he to his wife also, counting nothing so much his owne,	238	Priest 9		34
His wife is either religious, or night and day he is winning her	239	Priest 10		10
his wife among her neighbours is the beginner of good discourses,	240	Priest 10		27
He himselfe, or his Wife, takes account of Sermons, and how every one	240	Priest 10		36
or at least his Wife, of whom in stead of the qualities of the world,	260	Priest 23		30
if neither himselfe, nor his wife have the skil, and his means serve,	260	Priest 23		33
his wife seeks not the city, but preferrs her garden and fields	262	Priest 23		3
A faire wife and a frontire Castle breede quarrels.	324	Proverbs		103
He that takes not up a pin, slights his wife.	333	Proverbs		361
Who letts his wife goe to every feast, ...	336	Proverbs		434
shall neither have good wife nor good horse.	336	Proverbs		434
In chusing a wife, and buying a sword, ...	338	Proverbs		490
In the husband wisedome, in the wife gentlenesse.	343	Proverbs		658
Hee that hath a wife and children wants not businesse. . . .	347	Proverbs		778
Chuse a horse made, and a wife to make.	350	Proverbs		871
The wife is the key of the house.	351	Proverbs		904
Hee that tells his wife newes is but newly married.	353	Proverbs		987
belonge to me unto my deare wife excepting onely these legacies	382	G.H.'s Will		6
To Mrs Elizabeth Danvers Mr Henry Danvers wife twenty shillings,	383	G.H.'s Will		13
WIFE'S (see also wive's)				
the seldomer, according as hee is satisfied of his Wifes discretion.	239	Priest 9		4
My wife's and neeces' service.	376	Letters		23
My wife's and neeces' service to you.	379	Letters		30
WIL				
that if he be not so, he wil quickly be discovered, and disregarded:	228	Priest 3		6
he that wil be respected, must respect;	268	Priest 28		23
WILD				
Whose fire is wild, and doth not upward go	206	Walton 2		10
Let not him that feares feathers come among wild-foule. . . .	322	Proverbs		48
The rage of a wild boar is able to spoil more then one wood.	360	Proverbs	D	1132
WILD-FOULE				
Let not him that feares feathers come among wild-foule. . . .	322	Proverbs		48
WILDE				
But balls of wilde-fire to my troubled minde.	64	Even-song		16
Makes of wilde woods sweet walks and bowres.	137	Familie		12

	PAGE	TITLE		LINE
WILDE (cont'd)				
That led me to the wilde of passion, which	142	Pilgrimage		13
But as I rav'd and grew more fierce and wilde	153	The Collar		33
WILDE-FIRE				
But balls of wilde-fire to my troubled minde.	64	Even-song		16
WILDELY				
but the Questions must be propounded loosely and wildely,	259	Priest 22		9
WILDLY				
Wit's an unruly engine, wildly striking	16	Ch.-Porch		241
WILES				
Parson observing the manifold wiles of Satan (who playes his part	272	Priest 31		15
WILFULL				
So is the carnall and wilfull man with the worm of the grave in this	272	Priest 30		13
'LE				
Hee'le make thy wife a blessing not a rodd.	7	Ch.-Porch	W	18
In time they'l runne thee out of all thy wit.	21	Ch.-Porch		366
One half of me being gone, the rest I'le give	35	Thanksgvng	W	27
For thy predestination I'le contrive,	36	Thanksgvng		31
I'le build a spittle, or mend common wayes,	36	Thanksgvng		33
Thy art of love, which I'le turn back on thee:	36	Thanksgvng		47
Comfort, I'le die; for if you poste from me,	66	Ch.-mus.		9
Comfort, I'le die; for if you part from me,	66	Ch.-mus.	W	9
Then he'l take notice of: in ev'ry path	92	Man		44
Why he'l not lose a cup of drink for thee:	100	Miserie		8
Ah Loyterer! I'le no more, no more I'le bring:	121	Hope		7
Shew me a lyer, and I'le shew thee a theefe.	343	Proverbs		652
WILL (volition)				
He pares his apple, that will cleanly feed.	9	Ch.-Porch		64
As if thou mad'st thy will. A civil guest	18	Ch.-Porch		305
To compasse this. Finde out mens wants and will,	19	Ch.-Porch		328
Who follows all things, forfeiteth his will.	21	Ch.-Porch		364
Surely I will revenge me on thy love,	35	Thanksgvng		17
If thou dost give me wealth, I will restore	35	Thanksgvng		19
I will not marry; or, if she be mine,	35	Thanksgvng		23
Then for thy passion - I will do for that -	36	Thanksgvng		49
Let me be soft and supple to thy will,	44	H. Bapt.2		8
I will do more.	61	Praise 1		8
Not on my sinnes, or coldnesse, but thy will.	66	Ch.-lock		8
When the wide world runnes bias, from his will	73	Constancie		32
With him, whose will	79	Employm.2		12
Onely to purchase my good-will:	94	Unkindness		24
O let thy sacred will	104	Obedience		16
He that will passe his land,	105	Obedience		36
While all things have their will, yet none but thine.	117	Providence		32
Yet grief knows all, and enters when he will.	126	Confession		6
Which cools his will.	133	The Method		4
Much more oblig'd to do thy will,	139	Artillerie		22
Then will I trust, said I, in him alone.	143	Holdfast		5
Let what will fall:	144	Discharge		9
I will love thee:	146	Praise 2		2
I will move thee.	146	Praise 2		4
I will sing thee,	146	Praise 2		10
I will bring thee.	146	Praise 2		12
I will praise thee.	146	Praise 2		18
I will abroad.	153	The Collar		2
I will abroad.	153	The Collar		28
But I will to my Father,	155	Assurance		19
Sorrow hath chang'd its note: such is his will,	159	Jos.coat		3
There will I lie, untill my Maker seek	161	Priesthood		37
Is it thy will?	163	The Search		32
Thy will such an intrenching is,	163	The Search		37
Thy will such a strange distance is,	163	The Search		41
Besides, things sort not to my will,	165	The Crosse		19
Ev'n when my will doth studie thy renown:	165	The Crosse		20
With but foure words, my words, Thy will be done.	165	The Crosse		36
Let foolish lovers, if they will love dung,	177	Forerunners		25
Comparisons go play, wit use thy will:	183	The Posie		10
Light to the minde: what shall the will enjoy?	188	Heaven		15
When Italie of us shall have her will,	197	Ch.-Milit.		243
The hast of thy good will.	200	H. Commun.	W	15
The Day is spent, & hath his will on mee:	203	Even-song	W	1
nor can I hide his sacred will.	215	Psalm II	D	16
that if any do Gods will, he shall know of the Doctrine,	228	Priest 4		29
that not any ill will draws him to it, but the debt and obligation	232	Priest 6		18
that he will keep himself a virgin, he spends his dayes in fasting	237	Priest 9		18
of such things, and will not be perswaded, but being not invited,	243	Priest 11		21
punishing of any, as the vulgar ever consters for signes of ill will;	263	Priest 25		25
either blessing God, that he will be pleased to dwell among men;	273	Priest 31		24
that there is none that can or will look after things, but all goes	281	Priest 34		8
Let the weather be what it will, still we have bread, though	281	Priest 34		25
and if they will not reforme, presents them.	284	Priest 35		13
the one whereof was, He that will eat much, let him eat little;	295	Cornaro		34
hath cured him, commends this also to him, if he will live in health.	297	Cornaro		18
to relieve my Neighbour, God hath already reveled his Will about it.	313	Valdesso		14
He meanes a mans fre-will is only in outward, not in spirituall	313	Valdesso		33
He that will take the bird, must not skare it.	322	Proverbs		42
Who is so deafe, as he that will not heare?	323	Proverbs		79
Who is so deafe, as he who will not heare?	323	Proverbs	V	79
He that will learne to pray, let him goe to Sea.	323	Proverbs		84
He who will learne to pray, let him goe to Sea.	323	Proverbs	V	84
Assaile who will, the valiant attends.	324	Proverbs		95

WILL (cont'd)

	PAGE	TITLE		LINE
Marry your sonne when you will; your daughter when you can.	326	Proverbs		149
He will burne his house, to warme his hands.	331	Proverbs		304
Let none say, I will not drinke water.	331	Proverbs		310
if you will know the truth of the thing.	332	Proverbs		331
When God will, no winde but brings raine.	332	Proverbs		332
Hee that doth what hee will, doth not what he ought.	333	Proverbs		350
Hee that will deceive the fox, must rise betimes.	333	Proverbs		351
He that will be served must bee patient.	333	Proverbs		354
Where your will is ready, your feete are light.	336	Proverbs		448
When your will is ready, the feete are swift.	336	Proverbs	V	448
The eye will have his part.	337	Proverbs		466
The good mother sayes not, Will you? but gives.	337	Proverbs		467
When God will punish, hee will first take away the understanding.	344	Proverbs		688
That which two will, takes effect.	345	Proverbs		705
He that will not have peace, God gives him warre.	345	Proverbs		729
To him that will, waies are not wanting.	345	Proverbs		730
Who will sell the Cow, must say the word.	347	Proverbs		791
take not to serve you, if you will be served neately.	347	Proverbs		794
Women laugh when they can, and weepe when they will.	348	Proverbs		821
He that will enter into Paradise, must have a good key.	350	Proverbs		895
Who will make a doore of gold must knock a naile every day.	354	Proverbs		1004
He that will do thee a good turne, either he will be gon or dye.	358	Proverbs	D	1083
He that will be surety, shall pay.	358	Proverbs	D	1091
There is no body will go to hell for company.	361	Proverbs	D	1177
I doe my part to them, lett them think of me what they will or can.	376	Letters		7
The Will of George Herbert	382	G.H.'s Will		T
Alsoe my will and pleasure is that Mr Woodnoth should be mine	382	G.H.'s Will		27
John Danvers that he would be pleased to be Overseer of this Will.	382	G.H.'s Will		32

WILL (see also 'twill,wil)

	PAGE	TITLE		LINE
Man breaks the fence, and every ground will plough.	7	Ch.-Porch		22
And God will show thee how to take the towne,	7	Ch.-Porch	W	22
If those take up thy day, the sunne will crie	9	Ch.-Porch		81
If those bee all thy day, the sunne will crie	9	Ch.-Porch	W	81
Desire and shame, will make thy labour, play:	10	Ch.-Porch	W	90
Ev'n with the yeare: but age, if it will hit,	13	Ch.-Porch		158
Will canker both, yett thou alone shallt smart:	13	Ch.-Porch	W	166
One common waight will press downe both, yet so	13	Ch.-Porch	W	167
Say not then, This with that lace will do well;	14	Ch.-Porch		189
But, This with my discretion will be brave.	14	Ch.-Porch		190
Boldnesse guilds finely, and will set it forth.	15	Ch.-Porch		210
Get a sharp wife, a servant that will lowre.	15	Ch.-Porch		213
Think not thy fame at ev'ry twitch will break:	15	Ch.-Porch		219
(But a proud ignorance will lose his rest,	18	Ch.-Porch		297
Will no more talk all, then eat all the feast.	18	Ch.-Porch		306
And to instruct them, will not quit the cost.	20	Ch.-Porch		348
If stonie hearts will melt with gentle love.	29	Sacrifice		90
But surely not their hearts, as I will trie:	30	Sacrifice	V	123
For they will pierce my side, I full well know;	34	Sacrifice		246
I will tear thence his love and fame.	35	Thanksgvng		26
I will ripp out his love and fame.	35	Thanksgvng	W	26
I will teare out his love and fame.	35	Thanksgvng	WC	26
Then I will use the works of thy creation,	36	Thanksgvng		35
Then will I use the works of thy creation,	36	Thanksgvng	W	35
The world and I will quarrell; and the yeare	36	Thanksgvng		37
Nay, I will reade thy book, and never move	36	Thanksgvng		45
Nay, I will reade thy book, and never linn	36	Thanksgvng	W	45
Yet by confession will I come	37	Reprisall		13
Against thee, in thee I will overcome	37	Reprisall		15
My soul will turn to bubbles straight,	45	Nature		9
My soul will bee all bubble straight,	45	Nature	W	9
None of my books will show:	48	Afflict.1		56
Well, I will change the service, and go seek	48	Afflict.1		63
Another lift like this will make	52	H.Commun.		27
Will great God measure with a wretch?	55	Temper 1		15
Will thither flie;	61	Praise 1		6
Then by a sunne-beam I will climbe to thee.	63	Mattens		20
And I will strive to sinne no more.	68	Trin.Sun.		6
Then we will chide the sunne for letting night	81	Christmas		23
I will go searching, till I finde a sunne	81	Christmas		27
Then we will sing, and shine all our own day,	81	Christmas		31
Here will I smell my remnant out, and tie	94	Life		2
I will no more advise:	95	Submission		18
If either will convert us, we are thine:	97	Afflict.5		14
As he will swear,	100	Miserie		11
They will be kind, and all his pains requite,	101	Miserie	W	46
To both our goods, if he to it will stand.	105	Obedience		40
If thou persistest, I will tell thee,	105	Conscience		11
When they are ripe, their odour will ascend,	120	Providence		119
I will search out the matter.	124	Peace		10
Will lose a pleasure.	127	Giddinesse		8
Now he will fight it out, and to the warres;	127	Giddinesse		9
Will not suffice our turn:	127	Giddinesse		26
Will more complie, then help. A Lord I had,	129	Love unkn.		3
Many a fault more then my lease will bear;	129	Love unkn.		20
Seek pardon first, and God will say,	134	The Method		31
For I will do, or suffer what I ought.	139	Artillerie		16
In times to come; for it will grow.	145	Discharge		30
Either grief will not come: or if it must,	145	Discharge		51
Will use me in this kinde, the doore	152	The Bag		38
I will present, and somewhat more,	152	The Bag		40

WILL (cont'd)

	PAGE	TITLE	LINE
Not to his hurt. Sighs will convey	152	The Bag	41
A slender thread a gentle guest will tie.	154	Glimpse	20
Which bounds on thee, and will not down thy throat:	156	Assurance	40
Now love and truth will end in man.	156	Assurance	42
Lord, I will mean and speak thy praise,	157	Praise 3	1
Then will I wring it with a sigh or grone,	157	Praise 3	5
And I will passe.	163	The Search	36
O who will give me tears? Come all ye springs,	164	Grief	1
Sure I will do the like.	171	Bittersweet	4
I will complain, yet praise;	171	Bittersweet	5
I will bewail, approve:	171	Bittersweet	6
I will lament, and love.	171	Bittersweet	8
He will be pleased with that dittie;	176	Forerunners	11
But will ye leave me thus? when ye before	176	Forerunners	14
But I will not much oppose	177	The Rose	13
Love will do the deed:	179	Discipline	18
Stonie hearts will bleed.	179	Discipline	20
Will not grow bright and clean.	184	The Elixer	16
Will not to Heaven grow.	184	The Elixer W	16
That some will turn thee to some leaves therein	187	Judgement	8
O who will show me those delights on high?	188	Heaven	1
My deare, then I will serve.	189	Love 3	16
None will beleeve this now, though money be	193	Ch.-Milit.	119
As Rome will one day finde unto her cost.	194	Ch.-Milit.	160
Will not a verse run smooth that bears thy name?	206	Walton 1	11
But onely while thou speak'st; This Anchor will.	439	Walton 5	4
Will pour full joyes to thee, but dregs to those,	213	Bohemia D	65
Great God will surely dry those teares,	213	L' Envoy D	5
I will declare the Lords decree,	215	Psalm II D	15
Make thy request, and I will grant	216	Psalm II D	19
Aided by him, I will not fear	216	Psalm III D	13
How long will ye, vain men, convert	217	Psalm IV D	7
How long will ye seek after lies,	217	Psalm IV D	9
The Lord will harken unto me	217	Psalm IV D	13
will shew us good? But, Lord,	217	Psalm IV D	22
Therefore will I lie down in peace,	218	Psalm IV D	29
for in the morn will I	218	Psalm V D	6
will I to thee draw near:	218	Psalm V D	18
will worship thee in fear.	218	Psalm V D	20
And now my foes the Lord will blame	220	Psalm VI D	25
the Lord will whet his Sword:	222	Psalm VII D	42
the Lord will magnifie:	222	Psalm VII D	62
which also I will set as high as I can, since hee shoots higher that	224	Priest	8
is indeed the bent of my Discourse) the other will be manifest.	226	Priest 2	19
neither will they beleeve him in the pulpit, whom they cannot trust	228	Priest 3	7
or will open all to one, that there may be a traffick in knowledg	229	Priest 4	25
Now if a shepherd know not which grass will bane, or which not,	230	Priest 5	32
who treads in his steps, and will not throw down what he hath built;	232	Priest 7	26
but stories and sayings they will well remember.	233	Priest 7	18
which will make them appear exceeding reverend, and holy.	234	Priest 7	23
will lesse afterwards, the same affection which made him not profit	235	Priest 7	12
but hath power over his own will, and hath so decreed in his heart,	237	Priest 9	17
sensitive faculty, will runne out more or lesse in her intellectuall.	238	Priest 9	11
which will discover it selfe by spitting, and rheume, or flegme.	242	Priest 10	24
yet that will not be so:	243	Priest 11	29
men to Piety, and is content, if at least so, they will become good:	244	Priest 11	1
for this in time will lose the name and effect of Charity	244	Priest 12	26
for then they will reckon upon it, as on a debt;	244	Priest 12	28
though justly, they will murmur, and repine as much, as he that is	244	Priest 12	29
that he will have prayers in the hall, wishing him to informe his	251	Priest 17	11
or else if the thing will admit interpretation;	252	Priest 18	10
but this will not stand.	252	Priest 18	12
wherein the Catechized will at length finde delight, and by which	256	Priest 21	18
will draw out of ignorant and silly souls, even the dark and deep	256	Priest 21	19
That position will not hold in Christianity, because it contains	256	Priest 21	23
loosely and wildely, and then the Answerer will discover what hee is.	259	Priest 22	9
which while they dwell in their bookes, they will never finde;	266	Priest 26	2
and doing their duty faithfully, they will soon discover:	266	Priest 26	3
for quantity eats more then his health or imployments will bear,	266	Priest 26	7
as he that eats more then his estate will bear, is a Prodigall;	266	Priest 26	9
of their health, and so they will stand to the pain, all is well.	266	Priest 26	20
as knowing that nature will not bear everlasting droopings,	267	Priest 27	34
and he will give him the gold for it, which the Child utterly	272	Priest 30	10
which will appear if the Pious soul foresee and prevent such	273	Priest 31	16
I will not doubt to go without staying to pray there (but onely,	273	Priest 31	34
if any scruple arise, I will throw it away, and be most confident,	273	Priest 31	38
But it will not be amisse in this exceeding usefull point to descend	275	Priest 32	17
so will they last the longer, and when they depart, returne	280	Priest 34	29
is ashamed in small things, will extend his pusillanimity to greater.	284	Priest 35	34
who will take this into consideration, I will declare the causes	291	Cornaro	14
I will declare the causes which moved me to forsake Intemperance,	291	Cornaro	14
Neither can any man denie this, who will narrowly consider it.	297	Cornaro	14
after live free from diseases, if he will keep such a course of life;	297	Cornaro	20
because this will cut off all causes of diseases, so that he shall	297	Cornaro	20
if he will give his minde to those things which he should,	297	Cornaro	22
he will prove himself a Physician, and that a very compleat one:	297	Cornaro	23
as I will shew by my self, recounting the delights and pleasures in	300	Cornaro	30
in which perhaps you will discover some care, which I forbare not in	304	Valdesso	3
I like not in him, as my fragments will expresse, when you read them;	304	Valdesso	17
That God in the dayes of the Gospell will not give an outward Law	310	Valdesso	5

WILL (cont'd)	PAGE	TITLE		LINE
will better appear by his 98 Consideration of faith and good works.	312	Valdesso	V	4
Gods Spirit will mortify and try them as gold in the fire. . .	314	Valdesso		21
and then afterward they will attend it of themselves without his	318	Valdesso		21
will make the Consideration easy, and very observeable: . .	320	Valdesso		5
One sound blow will serve to undo all.	322	Proverbs		34
All came from, and will goe to others.	322	Proverbs		41
Harken to reason or shee will bee heard.	323	Proverbs		74
Give a clowne your finger, and he will take your hand. . . .	324	Proverbs		111
and he will play with you in the market.	325	Proverbs		146
Without favour none will know you, ...	326	Proverbs		159
and with it you will not know your selfe.	326	Proverbs		159
with it you will hardly know your selfe.	326	Proverbs	V	159
What your glasse telles you, will not be told by Councell. . .	329	Proverbs		255
Hee will spend a whole yeares rent at one meales meate. . .	331	Proverbs		305
No lock will hold against the power of gold.	332	Proverbs		317
how that which is to come will be drawne on.	332	Proverbs		329
Stay a little and news will find you.	332	Proverbs		330
nor wise at 50, will never bee handsome, strong, rich, or wise.	333	Proverbs		349
the time comes that hee will repay thee.	333	Proverbs		368
He that sings on friday, will weepe on Sunday.	335	Proverbs		411
A hundred loade of thought will not pay one of debts. . . .	335	Proverbs		414
Helpe thy selfe, and God will helpe thee.	339	Proverbs		537
but he will drinke when and what he pleaseth.	342	Proverbs		623
That which will not be spun, ...	343	Proverbs		665
When God will punish, hee will first take away the understanding.	344	Proverbs		688
It's a proud horse that will not carry his owne provender. . .	345	Proverbs		712
All the Armes of England will not arme feare.	345	Proverbs		722
You cannot make the fire so low but it will get out. . . .	353	Proverbs		965
Favour will as surely perish as life.	357	Proverbs	D	1055
He that will do thee a good turne, either he will be gon or dye.	358	Proverbs	D	1083
He that steals an egge, will steal an oxe.	358	Proverbs	D	1090
A wolfe will never make war against another wolfe. . . .	359	Proverbs	D	1125
Say to pleasure, Gentle Eve, I will none of your apple. . .	360	Proverbs	D	1140
only hereafter I will take heed how I propose my desires unto you,	363	Letters		20
and I will strive to imitate the compleatness of your love, . .	364	Letters		2
wherefore I will open my case unto you, which I think deserves	364	Letters		9
What Trades-man is there who will set up without his Tools? . .	364	Letters		14
But perhaps they will say, you are sickly, you must not study too	364	Letters		25
but they will object again, What becomes of your Annuity? . .	364	Letters		30
and perhaps a little more mild, but you will hardly perceive it.	366	Letters		25
that the time after the Holydaye will bee fruitfuller of novelties,	368	Letters		3
but yet he will heare of no other affaires, untill they have	368	Letters		8
given her occasion to protest shee will never speake with him againe,	368	Letters		22
& to threaten him that if he will not give her halfe her estate	368	Letters		23
(for shee desires no more) shee will find friends to compell him	368	Letters		25
opinion of him, that if he can do me a courtesie, he will of himself;	369	Letters		23
it will do well, for it expresseth the Universities inclination	369	Letters		26
yet that will be about 30 l. per an. but the commodiousness is beyond	369	Letters		32
and such like Gaynesses, which will please a young man well.	370	Letters		4
circumstance, yet you will pardon my haste, which is very great,	370	Letters		12
when I shall understand that a Letter will be seasonable, . .	371	Letters		15
your Courtesie will pardon the haste of Your humblest Servant,	371	Letters		18
whose Example and Care of them will justifie you both to the world	373	Letters		16
will also deliver me out of the hands of this uncircumcised . .	374	Letters		7
and will not allow any room there for such an in-mate as Grief;	374	Letters		10
am glad that although you offer more, yet you will doe, as you write,	375	Letters		7
I will tell you what I wrote to our eldest brother, when he urged one	375	Letters		10
and still they will be presenting or wishing to see, if at length	376	Letters		28
of monyes wherof he is to give as I know he will a Just account:	383	G.H.'s Will		25
WILLIAM				
To William Twenty Nobles, To John twentie shillings, all these are	382	G.H.'s Will		25
Anne Hibbert tenn shillings To William Scuce twenty shillings To Mrs	383	G.H.'s Will		17
WILLING				
A willing shiner, that shall shine as gladly, ...	81	Christmas		29
What willing nature speaks, what forc'd by fire;	88	The Pearl		6
that if any be willing to partake, they may resort thither. . .	251	Priest 17		12
men being willing to sell the interest, and ingagement of their	252	Priest 18		20
unto you, since I find you so willing to yield to my requests;	363	Letters		21
of all Comfort, who is not willing to behold any sorrow but for sin.	372	Letters		25
WILLINGLY				
Wounds willingly endur'd to work his blisse, ...	192	Ch.-Milit.		65
the presence of all, and Baptizeth not willingly, but on Sundayes,	258	Priest 22		3
He willingly and cheerfully crosseth the child, and thinketh	258	Priest 22		8
which I undertake the more willingly, because divers worthy young men	291	Cornaro		7
WILLOWES				
Willowes are weak, yet they bind other wood.	341	Proverbs		594
WILT				
If thou wilt die, the gates of hell are broad:	9	Ch.-Porch		71
Fast when thou wilt; but then 'tis gain, not losse.	22	Ch.-Porch		396
Now I am here, what thou wilt do with me	48	Afflict.1		55
But thou wilt sinne and grief destroy;	49	Repentance		31
Wilt thou meet arms with man, that thou dost stretch . . .	55	Temper 1		13
Wilt thou not then my fault reprove?	61	Grace	W	20
Or if to me thou wilt not move, ...	61	Grace		22
Yet, if thou wilt from thence depart, ...	74	The Starre		5
Sure thou wilt joy, by gaining me	74	The Starre		29
For by that powder thou wilt make us see.	82	Ungratef.		18
For by this powder thou wilt make us see.	82	Ungratef.	W	18
But on thy glorie! then thou wilt reform	83	Sighs & Gr.		3
A poore mans rod if thou wilt hire	96	Charms & K	W	3

	PAGE	TITLE		LINE
WILT (cont'd)				
Thou pull'st the rug, and wilt not rise,	101	Miserie		51
Thou lyest warme, and wilt not rise,	101	Miserie	W	51
God chains the dog till night: wilt loose the chain,	145	Discharge		46
Wilt thou forestall it, and now grieve to morrow,	145	Discharge		48
Wilt thou deferre	149	Longing		39
Thou cam'st but now; wilt thou so soon depart,	154	Glimpse		2
When thou dost turn, and wilt be neare;	163	The Search		53
Hony of roses, whither wilt thou flie?	176	Forerunners		20
And wilt thou leave the Church, and love a stie?	176	Forerunners		22
Fie, thou wilt soil thy broider'd coat,	176	Forerunners		23
Thou wilt revenge their quarrell, making grace	197	Ch.-Milit.		255
WIMBLE				
Gifts enter every where without a wimble.	352	Proverbs		955
WIN (see also winn)				
Bywords, but this by sorrow I must win:	33	Sacrifice		207
More rev'rend grows, & more doth win:	67	Windows		9
so that to favour them therein is to win their hearts, and to oppose	283	Priest 35		30
WIND				
You cannot make a wind-mill goe with a paire of bellowes.	344	Proverbs		676
A litle wind kindles; much puts out the fire.	344	Proverbs		680
The wind in ones face makes one wise.	345	Proverbs		721
To a close shorne sheepe, God gives wind by measure.	349	Proverbs		867
Words and feathers the wind carries away.	359	Proverbs	D	1103
WIND-MILL				
You cannot make a wind-mill goe with a paire of bellowes.	344	Proverbs		676
WIND'S				
Pull downe your hatt on the winds side.	332	Proverbs		334
WINDE (verb)				
Be down, then winde up both; since we shall be	24	Ch.-Porch		455
Glitter, and curle, and winde as they:	74	The Starre		26
As flames do work and winde, when they ascend,	103	Jordan 2		13
Into a piece of timber work and winde,	126	Confession		8
Doe winde a rope about, and cut my heart:	165	The Crosse		33
WINDE				
Vanish into a winde,	45	Nature		11
I was blown through with ev'ry storm and winde.	47	Afflict.1		36
Do end in bubbles, balls of winde;	64	Even-song		14
Of winde to thee whom I have crost,	64	Even-song		15
So loose or easie, that a ruffling winde	72	Constancie		7
Light without winde is glasse: warm without weight	120	Providence		101
Cold fruits warm kernells help against the winde.	120	Providence		130
A hollow winde did seem to answer, No:	124	Peace		5
And bottome of the leaves: which when the winde	140	Ch.-rents		6
Which when your neighbours saw, like a north-winde,	140	Ch.-rents		22
Let not the winde	149	Longing		22
Loose as the winde, as large as store.	153	The Collar		5
Wert thou a winde or wave,	154	Glimpse		8
And then bargain with the winde	199	L'Envoy		15
Corne is cleaned with winde, and the soule with chastnings.	326	Proverbs		154
When God will, no winde but brings raine.	332	Proverbs		332
An idle head is a boxe for the winde.	343	Proverbs		651
The tree that God plants, no winde hurts it.	344	Proverbs		691
Take heed of winde that comes in at a hole,	360	Proverbs	D	1154
WINDES (verb)				
Windes up my grief to a mysteriousnesse:	30	Sacrifice		127
Which as it lengthens windes, and windes us in,	118	Providence		59
WINDES				
Thy wormwood turn to health, windes to fair weather:	49	Repentance		21
For us the windes do blow,	91	Man		25
While blustring windes destroy the wanton bowres,	97	Afflict.5		21
Windes still work: it is their plot,	113	Businesse		9
Such as springs use that fall, and windes that blow.	117	Providence		16
The windes, who think they rule the mariner,	119	Providence		91
The windes grew gard'ners, and the clouds good fountains.	120	Providence		116
If as the windes and waters here below	132	The Storm		1
Though windes and waves assault my keel,	151	The Bag		2
The windes their stint: and yet when I did call,	158	Praise 3		23
Some to windes their bodie lend,	187	Dooms-day		21
Some to windes their bodies lend,	187	Dooms-day	W	21
Of th' universe, like as the windes, & name	212	Bohemia	D	44
how the windes should blow so much as they can, and the sea rage so	281	Priest 34		20
and windes and labours did little hurt him, because in his meats	294	Cornaro		7
and colds, and windes, and showers, and divers labours,	299	Cornaro		13
WINDING				
Is all good structure in a winding stair?	56	Jordan 1		3
That winding is their fashion	74	The Starre		27
Working and winding slily evermore,	84	The World		13
Those clouts are little winding sheets,	98	Mortific.		5
My crooked winding wayes, wherein I live,	185	A Wreath		4
WINDOW				
To be a window, through thy grace.	67	Windows		5
Where are my window-songs?	116	Dulnesse		18
As on a window late I cast mine eye,	116	Love-joy		1
To a fair day open the window, but make you ready as to a foule.	325	Proverbs		119
WINDOW-SONGS				
Where are my window-songs?	116	Dulnesse		18
WINDOWS				
The Windows.	67	Windows		T
And with their words and posies windows fill:	182	The Posie		2
as walls plaistered, windows glazed, floore paved, seats whole,	246	Priest 13		4

WINDS (verb)	PAGE	TITLE		LINE
The other winds towards Him, whose happie birth	84	Coloss.		6
WINDS				
When winds and waves rise highest, I am sure,	439	Walton 6		3
Of earth is driven by winds away,	215	Psalm I	D	15
To a crazy ship all winds are contrary.	334	Proverbs		395
WINE				
Shall I, to please anothers wine-sprung minde,	8	Ch.-Porch		37
Then thou art modest, and the wine grows bold.	8	Ch.-Porch		42
Wine above all things doth Gods stamp deface.	8	Ch.-Porch		48
Yet, if thou sinne in wine or wantonnesse,	8	Ch.-Porch		49
Lust and wine plead a pleasure, avarice gain:	8	Ch.-Porch		57
Lust and wine plead a pleasure, cheating gain:	8	Ch.-Porch	W	57
Which my God feels as bloud; but I, as wine.	37	The Agonie		18
But can he want the grape, who hath the wine?	128	Bunch Gr.		22
Who of the laws sowre juice sweet wine did make,	128	Bunch Gr.		27
Which at a board, while many drunk bare wine,	130	Love unkn.		42
Could not that wisdome, which first broacht the wine,	134	Divinitie		9
But he doth bid us take his bloud for wine.	135	Divinitie		21
Sure there was wine	153	The Collar		10
My head with oyl, my cup with wine	173	23 Psalme		19
Come ye hither all, whom wine	180	Invitation		7
As we sugar melt in wine?	181	Banquet		12
Wine becomes a wing at last.	182	Banquet		42
Which mingles water with thy Rhenish wine	213	Bohemia	D	64
of corn and wine can be.	218	Psalm IV	D	28
and much more with wine, is apt to nourish more then in cold regions,	242	Priest 10		17
and chose that wine that fitted my stomack, and in such measure,	293	Cornaro		16
Who would beleeve that old wine should hurt my stomack,	297	Cornaro		32
You cannot know wine by the barrell.	321	Proverbs		20
Old wine, and an old friend, are good provisions.	325	Proverbs		136
Milke saies to wine, welcome friend.	327	Proverbs		184
Take heede of the viniger of sweet wine.	336	Proverbs		451
Gaming, women, and wine, while they laugh they make men pine.	341	Proverbs		604
The wine in the bottell doth not quench thirst.	342	Proverbs		616
Wine-Counsels seldome prosper.	348	Proverbs		810
A morning sunne, and a wine-bred child,	349	Proverbs		866
Wine is a turne-coate (first a friend, then an enemy).	351	Proverbs		929
Wine ever paies for his lodging.	352	Proverbs		930
Wine makes all sorts of creatures at table.	352	Proverbs		931
Wine that cost nothing is digested before it be drunke.	352	Proverbs		932
To speake of an Usurer at the table marres the wine.	353	Proverbs		974
fat Hogs among Jews, and Wine in a fishing net.	361	Proverbs	D	1163
WINE-BRED				
A morning sunne, and a wine-bred child,	349	Proverbs		866
WINE-COUNSELS				
Wine-Counsels seldome prosper.	348	Proverbs		810
WINE-SPRUNG				
Shall I, to please anothers wine-sprung minde,	8	Ch.-Porch		37
WINES				
inward heats, drank delightfull wines, and that in great quantitie,	292	Cornaro		29
for strong and very cool wines pleased my taste best, as also melons,	293	Cornaro		11
WING				
For, if I imp my wing on thine,	43	East.wings		19
Till it get wing, and flie away with thee.	59	Whitsunday		4
Till I get wing to fly away with thee.	59	Whitsunday	W	4
('Tis your own case) ye never move a wing.	78	Ang.&Sts.		20
'tis your own case, ye never move your wing.	78	Ang.&Sts.	W	20
O that I had the wing and thigh	79	Employm.2	W	21
Their follies with the wing of thy milde Dove,	100	Miserie		28
A lump of flesh, without a foot or wing	102	Miserie		74
That my free soul may use her wing,	109	Home		62
Wine becomes a wing at last.	182	Banquet		42
He that gives thee a Capon, give him the leg and the wing.	324	Proverbs		109
WING'D				
Wing'd like an arrow: but my scout	162	The Search		19
WINGED				
They were by winged souls	105	Obedience		44
WINGES				
There hands shall clipp the Eagles winges, & chase	212	Bohemia	D	47
WINGS				
God gave thy soul brave wings; put not those feathers	9	Ch.-Porch		83
Easter-wings.	43	East.wings		T
And spread thy golden wings in me;	59	Whitsunday		2
Display thy golden wings in me;	59	Whitsunday	W	2
I go to Church; help me to wings, and I	61	Praise 1		5
Rising and falling with your wings:	65	Ch.-mus.		6
Their follies with the wings of thy milde Dove,	100	Miserie	W	28
But grones are quick, and full of wings,	107	Sion		21
Though the Fox run, the chicken hath wings.	339	Proverbs		549
The ignorant hath an Eagles wings, and an Owles eyes.	351	Proverbs		902
It is better to have wings then hornes.	352	Proverbs		960
WINK				
What is this woman-kinde, which I can wink	108	Home		39
While thou didst wink and wouldst not see.	153	The Collar		26
except you wink, you cannot but see many brave examples.	366	Letters		6
WINKS				
His knowledge winks, and lets his humours reigne;	102	Miserie		62
WINN				
For who can tell, though thou hast dyde to winn	205	Persever.	W	9

WINNE	PAGE	TITLE		LINE
And winne thy selfe: Compare the joyes & so	7	Ch.-Porch	W	23
Dost lose? rise up: dost winne? rise in that state.	14	Ch.-Porch		201
Lest the enemie should winne?	181	Banquet		18
WINNES				
For since confession pardon winnes,	126	Confession		27
Which favour winnes,	162	The Search		26
To make good that which ev'ry day he winnes.	193	Ch.-Milit.		126
He plaies well that winnes.	339	Proverbs		550
WINNING				
As if grief were not foul, nor vertue winning.	176	The Foil		8
This way he findes exceeding usefull, and winning;	236	Priest 8		16
wife is either religious, or night and day he is winning her to it.	239	Priest 10		11
Secondly, by a courteous carriage, & winning behaviour:	268	Priest 28		22
WINS				
hee wins them to praise God more, to live more religiously,	245	Priest 12		2
WINTER				
Some creatures have in winter what to eat;	118	Providence		55
Go birds of spring: let winter have his fee,	177	Forerunners		34
by taking away so much as the usuall seasons of summer and winter,	281	Priest 34		24
and the season of the yeare was winter and most cold aire.	296	Cornaro		27
of Architecture, that they are cool in summer, and warm in winter.	301	Cornaro		14
The life of man is a winter way.	351	Proverbs		914
Every mile is two in winter.	352	Proverbs		949
One faire day in winter makes not birds merrie.	353	Proverbs		977
feeles it all the winter after.	354	Proverbs		992
A fair day in winter is the mother of a storme.	360	Proverbs	D	1145
WINTER'S				
He that passeth a winters day escapes an enemy.	349	Proverbs		864
WINTERS				
He hath two winters, other things but one:	131	Mans medly		27
WIPE				
Bids the rash gazer wipe his eye:	87	Vertue		6
Where I wipe mine eyes, and see	182	Banquet		45
WIP'D				
When blessed Marie wip'd her Saviours feet,	173	Marie Magd		1
Better a snotty child, then his nose wip'd off.	348	Proverbs		828
WIPES				
Hee that wipes the childs nose, kisseth the mothers cheeke.	355	Proverbs		1032
WIS				
If gold knew what gold is, gold would get gold I wis.	354	Proverbs		1012
WISDOME				
And do them not: that shall thy wisdome be;	15	Ch.-Porch		221
Wisdome picks friends; civilitie playes the rest.	15	Ch.-Porch		227
Nor wisdome neither: therefore gently move.	18	Ch.-Porch		312
All forrain wisdome doth amount to this,	20	Ch.-Porch		355
But Wisdome quickly swept them all away.	84	The World		5
But that thou art my wisdome, Lord,	95	Submission		1
Each creature hath a wisdome for his good.	118	Providence		61
Could not that wisdome, which first broacht the wine,	134	Divinitie		9
My power and wisdome. Put me not to shame,	143	Complaining		3
Then beautie flow'd, then wisdome, honour, pleasure:	160	The Pulley		7
wherein wisdome and all kinde of vertues is most vigorous;	298	Cornaro		30
WISE				
A sad wise valour is the brave complexion,	16	Ch.-Porch		247
That brought the wise men of the East from farre.	28	Sacrifice		51
Behold, they spit on me in scornfull wise,	31	Sacrifice		133
None but the wise or strong had gained it:	50	Faith		26
When man grows staid and wise,	98	Mortific.		19
Verses, ye are too fine a thing, too wise	164	Grief		13
Now therefore, O ye Kings, be wise,	216	Psalm II	D	25
of God to bring women to heaven) a wise and loving husband could out	238	Priest 9		31
the two commands, we are more injoyned to be charitable, then wise.	245	Priest 12		29
for if wise men have thought it the best way of preserving a state	258	Priest 22		15
he forbears not in any wise to use the delinquent as before,	263	Priest 25		26
and wise knowledg, the Professours whereof were much imployed	277	Priest 32		31
It is not the part of a wise man, to expose himself to so many	300	Cornaro		22
An old wise mans shaddow is better then a young buzzards sword.	324	Proverbs		90
Though old and wise, yet still advise.	325	Proverbs		134
Send a wise man on an errand, and say nothing unto him.	328	Proverbs		217
The wise hand doth not all that the foolish mouth speakes.	329	Proverbs		246
A foole knowes more in his house, then a wise man in anothers.	329	Proverbs		257
nor wise at 50, will never bee handsome, strong, rich, or wise.	333	Proverbs		349
Fooles bite one another, but wise-men agree together.	336	Proverbs		452
The first degree of folly is to hold ones selfe wise,	337	Proverbs		460
The first degree of folly is to thinke ourselves wise,	337	Proverbs	V	460
If the wise erred not, it would goe hard with fooles.	338	Proverbs		510
If wise men erred not, it would goe hard with fooles.	338	Proverbs	V	510
which a hundred wise men cannot pull out.	339	Proverbs		527
Hee commands enough that obeyes a wise man.	339	Proverbs		547
let him be wise in the punishment.	340	Proverbs		555
A wise man needes not blush for changing his purpose.	342	Proverbs		613
A wise man cares not for what he cannot have.	343	Proverbs		662
If things were to be done twice, all would be wise.	344	Proverbs		700
If all things might be done twice, all would be wise.	343	Proverbs	V	700
The wind in ones face makes one wise.	345	Proverbs		721
None is so wise, but the foole overtakes him.	345	Proverbs		734
None is so wise, but that the foole overtakes him.	345	Proverbs	V	734
The least foolish is wise.	351	Proverbs		910
The Italians are wise before the deede,	352	Proverbs		947

	PAGE	TITLE		LINE
WISE-MEN				
Fooles bite one another, but wise-men agree together.	336	Proverbs		452
WISEDOME				
Wisedome's a trimmer thing, then shop e're gave.	14	Ch.-Porch		188
wherein the manifold wisedome of God is wonderfully to be seen,	261	Priest 23		27
Wisedome hath one foot on Land, and another on Sea. . . .	341	Proverbs		611
In the husband wisedome, in the wife gentlenesse.	343	Proverbs		658
WISELY				
And Spanish sents, wisely layd up, presume	212	Bohemia	D	52
Speake fitly, or be silent wisely.	342	Proverbs		625
WISH				
Both want, and wish thy pleasing presence still.	19	Ch.-Porch		326
Need & bee glad, & wish thy presence still:	19	Ch.-Porch	W	326
Against their Maker: they do wish me dead, ...	26	Sacrifice		6
Who cannot wish, except I give them bread:	26	Sacrifice		7
And therefore wish my bloud on them and theirs:	30	Sacrifice		107
I had my wish and way:	47	Afflict.1		20
I reade, and sigh, and wish I were a tree;	48	Afflict.1		57
Of strange delights, where we may wish & take.	58	H.Script.1		7
who wish them best, and that not a desire to meddle with others	251	Priest 17		30
if I had my wish, would I change age and constitution with them who	303	Cornaro		11
but that I should wish all who have the care of themselves, . .	303	Cornaro		31
neverthelesse I wish you by all meanes to publish it, for these three	304	Valdesso		18
Many kisse the hand they wish cut off.	330	Proverbs		283
I wish I could have come in person to thank you, but it is . .	369	Letters		10
or rather increaseth, I wish earnestly that I were again with you:	372	Letters		17
would quickly make good my wish but that my employment does fix me	372	Letters		19
we for your gracious acceptance of these poore duties wish, . .	443	Oration		6
WISHED				
Used, and wished, are the whole worlds light:	30	Sacrifice		110
WISHES				
Foolish night-fires, womens and childrens wishes, ...	167	Dotage		2
by frequent wishes of the peoples good, and joying therein, . .	234	Priest 7		6
of your Mother upon you, and cause all her wishes, diligence,	377	Letters		5
WISHETH				
wisheth all to incline rather to too much, then to too little;	267	Priest 26		12
he wisheth them by no means to spare any, though never so great;	270	Priest 29		18
WISHING				
and wishing them ever to do the Cures with their own hands, . .	247	Priest 14		19
wishing him to informe his guests thereof, that if any be willing	251	Priest 17		11
and still they will be presenting or wishing to see, if at length	376	Letters		28
WISHINGS				
Hell is full of good meanings and wishings.	326	Proverbs		170
WISHLY				
Doth wishly look	204	The Knell	W	3
WISHT				
Hung down his head, and wisht for night, ...	59	Whitsunday		14
WIT				
Omit the oathes, which true wit cannot need:	9	Ch.-Porch		62
For we have wit to mark them, and to spare.	9	Ch.-Porch		69
For wit is newes onely to ignorance.	15	Ch.-Porch		230
Wit's an unruly engine, wildly striking	16	Ch.-Porch		241
Many affecting wit beyond their power, ...	16	Ch.-Porch		245
Usefulnesse comes by labour, wit by ease;	18	Ch.-Porch		291
By lavishnesse thine own, and others wit, ...	18	Ch.-Porch		304
In time they'l runne thee out of all thy wit.	21	Ch.-Porch		366
If thou shalt give me wit, it shall appeare, ...	36	Thanksgvng		43
Wit fancies beautie, beautie raiseth wit:	54	Love 1		9
Dust blown by wit, till that they both were blinde:	54	Love 2		10
And as their wit is, their digestion, ...	69	Content		31
And trade in courtesies and wit, ...	78	Employm.2		3
The quick returns of courtesie and wit:	88	The Pearl		12
What mirth and musick mean; what love and wit	89	The Pearl		24
Yet through the labyrinths, not my groveling wit, ...	89	The Pearl		37
Yet through these labyrinths, not my groveling wit, ...	89	The Pearl	W	37
Till then, afford us so much wit;	92	Man		52
Who made the arbour: this exceeds her wit.	101	Miserie		58
Then came quick Wit and Conversation, ...	111	The Quip		17
Lord, cleare thy gift, that with a constant wit	116	Dulnesse		25
Which with the edge of wit they cut and carve.	134	Divinitie		7
When wit contrives to meet with thee, ...	155	Assurance		5
Who cannot dresse it well, want wit, not words.	167	The Sonne		4
Comparisons go play, wit use thy will:	183	The Posie		10
Ours (like himselfe) o'recomes; for his wit's more	438	Lat.Trans.		3
which the present occasion of wit and company otherwise admits;	280	Priest 34		28
that can or will look after things, but all goes by chance, or wit:	281	Priest 34		9
of excellent wit and noble disposition, overthrown and undone	291	Cornaro		2
I fell into divers diseases, to wit, into the pain of the stomack,	291	Cornaro		21
if I could constantly pursue it, to wit, A sober and orderly life:	292	Cornaro		4
Gluttons use to defend themselves, to wit, That which savours,	293	Cornaro		9
to wit, That an orderly and regular life can hardly be altered	295	Cornaro		16
I conferre often with worthie men, excelling in wit, learning,	301	Cornaro		4
have made a most pleasant comedie, full of honest wit and merriment:	302	Cornaro		29
The Germans wit is in his fingers.	322	Proverbs		36
The Germans wit lies in his fingers.	322	Proverbs	V	36
Where the drink goes in, there the wit goes out.	327	Proverbs		187
(to wit - with a moderate and contented heart).	328	Proverbs		208
Though I had the best wit in the World, yet it would easily tyre me,	363	Letters		14
and have a good conceit of your wit, mark what I say, have a good	366	Letters		15
of your wit, mark what I say, have a good conceit of your wit;	366	Letters		16

	PAGE	TITLE		LINE
WITCHCRAFTS				
Impudent sinning, witchcrafts, and distrusts	197	Ch.-Milit.		238
WITCHES				
a million of Atheists, and 30000 Witches.	361	Proverbs	D	1174
WITH				
Whom God in Baptisme washt with his own blood.	6	Ch.-Porch		8
If it concurr with vertue: doe thy best	7	Ch.-Porch	W	21
Bigge with his sister: he hath lost the reins,	7	Ch.-Porch		32
Bigge with his sister: he hath lost his reins,	7	Ch.-Porch	W	32
Did with his liquour slide into his veins.	7	Ch.-Porch		34
He makes flat warre with God, and doth defie	8	Ch.-Porch		53
With his poore clod of earth the spacious sky.	8	Ch.-Porch		54
Chase brave employments with a naked sword	10	Ch.-Porch		88
Chase brave employment with a naked sword	10	Ch.-Porch	W	88
Spit out thy fleqme, and fill thy brest with glorie:	10	Ch.-Porch		92
His minde with rest, before his trunk with riches:	11	Ch.-Porch		110
His minde with rest, before his trunks with riches:	11	Ch.-Porch	W	110
Ev'n with the yeare: but age, if it will hit,	13	Ch.-Porch		158
As the day lessens, and his life with it.	13	Ch.-Porch		160
Before thy journey fairly part with all.	13	Ch.-Porch		162
Say not then, This with that lace will do well;	14	Ch.-Porch		189
But, This with my discretion will be brave.	14	Ch.-Porch		190
Nothing with labour, folly long a-doing.	14	Ch.-Porch		192
Then he can lose with pleasure, stakes his heart;	14	Ch.-Porch		194
Blowing up houses with their whole increase.	14	Ch.-Porch		204
To stuffe thy minde with solid braverie;	15	Ch.-Porch		208
If that thy fame with ev'ry toy be pos'd,	15	Ch.-Porch		223
A toy shunn'd cleanly passeth with the best.	15	Ch.-Porch		228
These are the scumme, with which course wits abound:	16	Ch.-Porch		237
All things are bigge with jest: nothing that's plain,	16	Ch.-Porch		239
Hast thou the knack? pamper it not with liking:	16	Ch.-Porch		243
Take all into thee; then with equall care	19	Ch.-Porch		321
If truth be with thy friend, be with them both:	19	Ch.-Porch		323
A grain of glorie mixt with humblenesse	19	Ch.-Porch		335
Joyn hands with God to make a man to live.	21	Ch.-Porch		376
Pray with the most: for where most pray, is heaven.	22	Ch.-Porch		402
Preachers conclude with, hath not lost his pains.	24	Ch.-Porch		434
With saints on earth, shall one day with them shine.	24	Ch.-Porch		438
They drink with greedinesse a full damnation.	24	Ch.-Porch		448
And growth of it: if with thy watch, that too	24	Ch.-Porch		454
Made of a heart, and cemented with teares:	26	The Altar		2
These drops being temper'd with a sinners tears,	27	Sacrifice		25
How with their lanterns do they seek the sunne!	27	Sacrifice		35
With clubs and staves they seek me, as a thief,	27	Sacrifice		37
Judas, dost thou betray me with a kisse?	28	Sacrifice		41
See, they lay hold on me, not with the hands	28	Sacrifice		45
Then they condemne me all with that same breath,	28	Sacrifice		69
Examines me with a censorious hand:	29	Sacrifice		82
The Jews accuse me with despitefulnesse;	29	Sacrifice		85
And vying malice with my gentlenesse,	29	Sacrifice		86
Pick quarrels with their onely happinesse:	29	Sacrifice		87
I answer nothing, but with patience prove	29	Sacrifice		89
If stonie hearts will melt with gentle love.	29	Sacrifice		90
But who does hawk at eagles with a dove?	29	Sacrifice		91
With noises confused frighting the day:	29	Sacrifice		103
Who grasp the earth and heaven with my fist,	30	Sacrifice		130
Which each one calls for so with utmost breath,	31	Sacrifice		146
Then with a scarlet robe they me aray;	31	Sacrifice		157
Then with the reed they gave to me before,	32	Sacrifice		169
Then with the reed they gave mee heertofore,	32	Sacrifice	W	169
Who Crucifie him, crie with one strong shout.	32	Sacrifice		186
With stronger blows strike mee as I come out:	32	Sacrifice	W	187
Lo, here I hang, charg'd with a world of sinne,	33	Sacrifice		205
They gave me vineger mingled with gall,	34	Sacrifice		237
They give me vineger mingled with gall,	34	Sacrifice	W	237
But more with malice: yet, when they did call,	34	Sacrifice		238
With Manna, Angels food, I fed them all:	34	Sacrifice		239
And side with thy triumphant glorie?	35	Thanksgvng		12
When with the other I have done.	35	Thanksgvng		30
There is no dealing with thy mighty passion:	36	Reprisall		2
There is no medling with thy mighty passion:	36	Reprisall	W	2
Walk'd with a staffe to heav'n, and traced fountains:	37	The Agonie		3
A man so wrung with pains, that all his hair,	37	The Agonie		9
Since, if my soul make even with the week,	38	The Sinner		3
And keep possession with thy grace;	39	Good Fri.		30
With him mayst rise:	41	Easter		4
With all thy art.	41	Easter		8
And make up our defects with his sweet art.	42	Easter		18
And brought'st thy sweets along with thee.	42	Easter		22
Bringinge thy sweets along with thee.	42	Easter	W	22
And brought thy sweets along with thee.	42	Easter	WC	22
With thy arising, they presume.	42	Easter		26
With thee	43	East.wings		6
And still with sicknesses and shame	43	East.wings		12
Yet thou with sicknesses and shame	43	East.wings	W	12
With thee	43	East.wings		16
Which then join'd with you still meet in my brest	44	H. Bapt.1	W	8
That thou hast ought to do with me.	45	Nature		3
Lord, with what care hast thou begirt us round!	45	Sinne 1		1
Yet all these fences with one bosome sinn	46	Sinne 1	W	13
Augmented with thy gracious benefits.	46	Afflict.1		6

WITH (cont'd)

	PAGE	TITLE		LINE
Augmented with thy graces perquisites.	46	Afflict.1	W	6
My dayes were straw'd with flow'rs and happinesse;	47	Afflict.1		21
My dayes were strowd with flow'rs and happinesse;	47	Afflict.1	W	21
But with my yeares sorrow did twist and grow,	47	Afflict.1		23
But with my yeares sorrows did twist and grow,	47	Afflict.1	W	23
I was blown through with ev'ry storm and winde.	47	Afflict.1		36
Thou often didst with Academick praise	47	Afflict.1		45
Now I am here, what thou wilt do with me	48	Afflict.1		55
With thy quick flow'r, thy momentarie bloom;	48	Repentance		3
And carrie with them th' other parts.	49	Repentance		30
And livd accordingly with no new score,	50	Faith	W	15
Faith puts me there with him, who sweetly took	50	Faith		23
My nature on him, with the danger	50	Faith	W	24
With bushie groves, pricking the lookers eie,	51	Faith		38
With an exact and most particular trust,	51	Faith		43
Onely thy grace, which with these elements comes,	52	H.Commun.		19
The church with psalms must shout,	53	Antiphon 1		9
Which siding with invention, they together	54	Love 1		6
Wilt thou meet arms with man, that thou dost stretch	55	Temper 1		13
Will great God measure with a wretch?	55	Temper 1		15
Whether I flie with angels, fall with dust,	55	Temper 1		25
Nor let them punish me with losse of ryme,	57	Jordan 1		14
Nor let them punish me with losse of time,	57	Jordan 1	V	14
The stuffe with thee.	57	Employm. 1		12
But with delaies.	57	Employm. 1		16
Neither bring hony with the bees,	57	Employm. 1		18
Come blessed Dove charm'd with my song,	59	Whitsunday	W	1
Till it get wing, and flie away with thee.	59	Whitsunday		4
Till I get wing to fly away with thee.	59	Whitsunday	W	4
With livery-graces furnishing thy men.	59	Whitsunday	W	8
His arm is short; yet with a sling	61	Praise 1		11
And now with darknesse closest wearie eyes,	64	Even-song		18
Fed with the exhalation of our crimes,	64	Ch.-monum.		5
Comparing dust with dust, and earth with earth.	65	Ch.-monum.		11
Rising and falling with your wings:	65	Ch.-mus.		6
But as cold hands are angrie with the fire,	66	Ch.-lock		5
Yet as cold hands are angrie with the fire,	66	Ch.-lock	W	5
With faith, with hope, with charitie;	68	Trin.Sun.		8
That I may runne, rise, rest with thee.	68	Trin.Sun.		9
Complies and suits with all estates;	69	Content		14
Which can let loose to a crown, and yet with pleasure	69	Content		15
With a great stable or demain:	70	Quidditie		8
With my great stable or demain:	70	Quidditie	W	8
I am with thee, and Most take all.	70	Quidditie		12
Thine clad with simplenesse, and sad events;	71	Frailtie		11
With sick folks, women, those whom passions sway,	73	Constancie		27
Or if some yeares with it escape,	73	Afflict.3		10
First with thy fire-work burn to dust	74	The Starre		9
Then with thy light refine,	74	The Starre		11
Touch it with thy celestiall quicknesse,	74	The Starre		14
Then with our trinitie of light,	74	The Starre		17
Writ by a friend, and with his bloud;	75	Sunday		4
Knocking at heaven with thy brow:	75	Sunday		10
And hollow room with vanities.	75	Sunday		25
Parted with alleys or with grass	75	Sunday	W	27
With the same shake, which at his passion	76	Sunday		45
Did th' earth and all things with it move.	76	Sunday		46
Leaping with thee from sev'n to sev'n,	77	Sunday		61
Have with our stamp and seal transferr'd our right:	77	Avarice		11
With him, whose will	79	Employm.2		12
With full crie of affections, quite astray;	80	Christmas		3
Lord, with what bountie and rare clemencie	82	Ungratef.		1
This may allure us with delights;	82	Ungratef.		22
Quickly reformed all with menaces.	84	Sighs & Gr.	W	10
With the turn'd viall of thy bitter wrath!	83	Sighs & Gr.		20
Reformed all at length with menaces.	84	The World		10
Then enter'd Sinne, and with that Sycomore,	84	The World		11
Then Sinne combin'd with Death in a firm band	84	The World		16
Coloss. 3. 3. Our life is hid with Christ in God.	84	Coloss.		T
That Life hath with the sun a double motion.	84	Coloss.		2
Quitting with daily labour all My pleasure,	85	Coloss.		9
And thred the spheres with his quick-piercing minde:	85	Vanitie 1		2
The nimble Diver with his side	85	Vanitie 1		8
Who with excessive pride	85	Vanitie 1		13
With showres and frosts, with love & aw,	85	Vanitie 1		25
Is much more sure to meet with him, then one	87	Lent		38
Where both their baskets are with all their store,	89	The Pearl	W	26
Therefore not sealed, but with open eyes	89	The Pearl		32
Therefore not seeled, but with open eyes	89	The Pearl	W	32
With all the circumstances that may move:	89	The Pearl		36
With scatter'd smart,	90	Afflict.4		9
With care and courage building me,	90	Afflict.4		29
For head with foot hath private amitie,	91	Man		17
And both with moons and tides.	91	Man		18
That it may dwell with thee at last!	92	Man		51
Then should thy praises with me grow,	95	Submission		7
Shall ne're be troubled with ill eyes.	96	Charms & K		2
Shall ne're be troubled with sore eyes.	96	Charms & K	W	2
Who looks on ground with humble eyes,	96	Charms & K		11
A prisoner crusht with gluttonie.	96	Charms & K	W	14

WITH (cont'd)

	PAGE	TITLE	LINE
As we at first did board with thee,	97	Afflict.5	11
Sweet were the dayes, when thou didst lodge with Lot,	99	Decay	1
Struggle with Jacob, sit with Gideon,	99	Decay	2
Advise with Abraham, when thy power could not	99	Decay	3
Their follies with the wing of thy milde Dove,	100	Miserie	28
Their follies with the wings of thy milde Dove,	100	Miserie W	28
Dead with eclipses, when we speak of thee:	101	Miserie	34
And feed the swine, with all his mind & might:	101	Miserie W	44
Curling with metaphors a plain intention,	102	Jordan 2	5
As if this passed with a reservation,	104	Obedience	13
Lord with what glorie wast thou serv'd of old,	106	Sion	1
With flowers and carvings, mysticall and rare:	106	Sion	5
And now thy Architecture meets with sinne;	106	Sion	11
There thou art struggling with a peevish heart,	106	Sion	13
With one small sigh thou gav'st me th' other day	108	Home	43
Which now is pinion'd with mortalitie,	109	Home	63
To double-moat thee with his grace,	110	Brit. Ch.	29
With his train-bands and mates agree	110	The Quip	2
Thy Saviour comes, and with him mirth:	112	Dawning	4
And with a thankfull heart his comforts take.	112	Dawning	6
And with his buriall-linen drie thine eyes:	112	Dawning	14
With my glorie and desert,	115	Dialogue	30
O give me quicknesse, that I may with mirth	115	Dulnesse	3
And with quaint metaphors her curled hair	115	Dulnesse	7
Lord, cleare thy gift, that with a constant wit	116	Dulnesse	25
I saw a vine drop grapes with J and C	116	Love-joy	2
The first puts on with speed and expedition;	117	Providence	35
And make a twist checker'd with night and day!	118	Providence	58
The hills with health abound; the vales with store;	119	Providence	95
The South with marble; North with furres & woods.	119	Providence	96
The healthy frosts with summer-fruits compare.	119	Providence	100
And at your lodging with their thanks appeare.	120	Providence	120
How smooth are silks compared with a stake,	120	Providence	123
Or with a stone! yet make no good foundation.	120	Providence	124
Yet in their being joyn with one advise	121	Providence	146
With that I gave a viall full of tears:	121	Hope	5
They vent the wares, and passe them with their faults,	122	Sinnes rd.	9
They vent the wares, and passe them with their fauts	122	Sinnes rd. V	9
Meeting with Time, Slack thing, said I,	122	Time	1
At Salem dwelt, who liv'd with good increase	125	Peace	23
With so much earnestnesse you do pursue,	125	Peace	41
Did alter with his minde;	127	Giddinesse	18
With his desires!	127	Giddinesse	20
Thinking with that, which I did thus present,	129	Love unkn.	31
But with a richer drug, then scalding water,	130	Love unkn.	40
I bath'd it often, ev'n with holy bloud,	130	Love unkn.	41
I found that some had stuff'd the bed with thoughts,	130	Love unkn.	51
When with my pleasures ev'n my rest was gone?	130	Love unkn.	53
With th'one hand touching heav'n, with th' other earth.	131	Mans medly	12
But trimm'd with curious lace,	131	Mans medly	16
And with thy knife but prune and PARE,	133	Paradise	11
Down with thy knees, up with thy voice.	134	The Method	30
Which with the edge of wit they cut and carve.	134	Divinitie	7
Have thicken'd it with definitions?	134	Divinitie	10
With curious questions and divisions?	134	Divinitie	12
Which may with thee	136	Ephes.	20
My want of tears with store of bloud.	136	Ephes.	36
This is thy house, with these it doth abound:	137	Familie	21
Then I refuse not ev'n with bloud	139	Artillerie	14
To enter combate with us, and contest	139	Artillerie	26
With thine own clay. But I would parley fain:	139	Artillerie	27
There is no articling with thee:	139	Artillerie	31
With these two poore ones lick up all the dew,	140	Ch.-rents	29
With many a flower:	142	Pilgrimage	8
With much ado.	142	Pilgrimage	12
With that abash'd and struck with many a sting	142	Pilgrimage	25
Of my deare God with all my power & might.	143	Holdfast	2
And turn, and leer, and with a licorous eye	144	Discharge	3
Give up the whole, and with the whole depart?	144	Discharge	8
Wherefore with my utmost art	146	Praise 2	9
Thou grew'st soft and moist with tears,	146	Praise 2	21
With sick and famisht eyes,	148	Longing	1
With doubling knees and weary bones,	148	Longing	2
That ran upon him with a spear.	151	The Bag	26
What I have lost with cordiall fruit?	153	The Collar	9
They quickly go and come with lesser crime:	154	Glimpse	9
When wit contrives to meet with thee,	155	Assurance	5
And with advantage mine the more.	157	Clasping	6
Since this being mine, brings with it thine,	157	Clasping	7
And thou with me dost thee restore.	157	Clasping	8
And with advantage mine the more,	157	Clasping	16
Then will I wring it with a sigh or grone,	157	Praise 3	5
Sure it would carrie with it ev'n my heart,	159	Jos.coat	7
One of Joyes coats, ticing it with relief	159	Jos.coat	11
But keep them with repining restlesnesse:	160	The Pulley	17
That with th' one hand thou liftest to the sky,	160	Priesthood	2
And with the other throwest down to hell	160	Priesthood	3
To bear them out, and with my state agree.	164	Grief	8
With but foure words, my words, Thy will be done.	165	The Crosse	36
With onely this, My joy, my life, my crown.	168	a true Hymn	5

WITH (cont'd)

	PAGE	TITLE		LINE
To serve thy sinnes, and furnish thee with store	170	Water-crs.		7
With her enchanting voice.	170	Self-cond.		12
For thou art with me; and thy rod	173	23 Psalme		15
My head with oyl, my cup with wine	173	23 Psalme		19
With pensive humblenesse would live and tread:	173	Marie Magd		6
With these all day I do perfume my minde,	175	The Odour		6
This breathing would with gains by sweetning me	175	The Odour		26
He will be pleased with that dittie;	176	Forerunners		11
Then did I wash you with my tears, and more,	176	Forerunners		16
With canvas, not with arras clothe their shame:	177	Forerunners		26
Perhaps with more embellishment can say,	177	Forerunners		33
For with love	179	Discipline		19
With me, in me, live and dwell:	181	Banquet		3
And with it perfumes my heart.	181	Banquet		24
Spilt with me,	182	Banquet		35
For with it alone I flie	182	Banquet		43
And with their words and posies windows fill:	182	The Posie		2
Because thou dost abide with me,	183	A Parodie		4
Which with his tincture (for thy sake)	184	The Elixer		15
Which with this tincture (for thy sake)	184	The Elixer	V	15
A servant with this clause	185	The Elixer		17
And all thy bones with beautie shall be clad.	186	Death		20
But are their cares and businesse with the pleasure?	188	Judgement	V	17
But are there cares and businesse with the pleasure?	188	Heaven		17
Complying with thy counsels, doing nought	190	Ch.-Milit.		7
Which doth not meet with an eternall thought.	190	Ch.-Milit.		8
Which does not meet with an eternall thought.	190	Ch.-Milit.	W	8
Rending with earthquakes the partition-wall:	190	Ch.-Milit.		26
Now with the crosse, as with a staffe, alone,	190	Ch.-Milit.		28
Who may with thee compare?	191	Ch.-Milit.		48
Spain in the Empire shar'd with Germanie,	192	Ch.-Milit.		89
Who may with thee compare?	192	Ch.-Milit.		100
Adoring garlick with an humble face,	193	Ch.-Milit.		112
The world came both with hands and purses full	193	Ch.-Milit.		133
The world came in with hands and purses full	193	Ch.-Milit.	W	133
Yet did a rogue with hope of carnall joy	194	Ch.-Milit.		149
Who may with thee compare?	194	Ch.-Milit.		156
Yet with two faces, as their Janus was;	196	Ch.-Milit.		207
Who may with thee compare?	196	Ch.-Milit.		210
Compare with ancient times and purer yeares;	196	Ch.-Milit.		227
Religion alwaies sides with povertie.	197	Ch.-Milit.		252
Religion alway sides with povertie.	197	Ch.-Milit.	W	252
The Church and Sunne with all their power and skill.	198	Ch.-Milit.		273
Who may with thee compare?	198	Ch.-Milit.		279
With the one make warre to cease;	199	L'Envoy		2
With the one make warrs to cease;	199	L'Envoy	W	2
With the other blesse thy sheep,	199	L'Envoy		3
And then bargain with the winde	199	L'Envoy		15
There is no dealing with thee in that Art:	201	love	W	2
Into my hart with joye, giving more rest	202	love	W	17
With Glory may attaine thy Face.	202	Trin.Sun.	W	6
And wake with thee for ever.	203	Even-song	W	24
Each with his rodd.	204	The Knell	W	12
But kill the man, is seald with thee.	204	Persever.	W	8
With face and hands clinging unto thy brest,	205	Persever.	W	14
With kinde Expressions to his friend,	439	Walton 5	V	12
Hath soild with Black) the colour of my state,	209	L. Bacon	D	7
Are quit with them and more.	210	Paradox	D	10
Sorrowes & griefs, to fight with them a bout	211	Bohemia	D	20
To deale with brimstone, that untamed stench	212	Bohemia	D	53
Laden with comforts thence, where now to morne	212	Bohemia	D	56
Which mingles water with thy Rhenish wine	213	Bohemia	D	64
Thy fruite shall with there drops contend;	213	L' Envoy	D	4
And with that Ring thy fame shall wedd	213	L' Envoy	D	13
If ever Voice was hoarse with Cries,	213	Convert	D	2
If ever Heart was sore with Sighs;	213	Convert	D	3
My Voice, that oft with foolish Lays,	214	Convert	D	11
With Vows and Rants, and sensless Praise,	214	Convert	D	12
with timely fruit still laden stand:	214	Psalm I	D	10
Why are the Heathen swell'd with rage,	215	Psalm II	D	1
For that, O Lord, with perfect joy	218	Psalm IV	D	25
Then worldlings joy'd with all their store	218	Psalm IV	D	27
No evil, Lord, shall dwell with thee,	218	Psalm V	D	11
with perfect joy be fill'd.	219	Psalm V	D	36
With groaning I am wearied,	220	Psalm VI	D	13
And water with salt tears my Bed,	220	Psalm VI	D	15
my sight with sorrow waxeth dim.	220	Psalm VI	D	16
Lest like a Lion swollen with rage	221	Psalm VII	D	5
that was at peace with me:	221	Psalm VII	D	12
with shafts of vengeance stor'd.	222	Psalm VII	D	44
with his iniquitie:	222	Psalm VII	D	50
and considering with my self, That the way to please him,	224	Priest		3
he that ruleth, let him do it with diligence, &c.	226	Priest 2		7
but to keep up with the Lord and Lady of the house, and to preserve	226	Priest 2		28
and to preserve a boldness with them and all, even so farre	226	Priest 2		29
so farre from that which they seek with their over-submissivenesse,	226	Priest 2		35
admonition, or reproofe, sell (with Judas) their Lord and Master.	226	Priest 2		37
are offended much with any, who by hard usage increase their travell,	227	Priest 3		14
with the unfruitfull works of darknesse, he disableth himself	227	Priest 3		26
he may say as He did, I sate daily with you teaching in the Temple.	228	Priest 3		1

WITH (cont'd)

	PAGE	TITLE	LINE
they are not understood but with the same Spirit that writ them.	228	Priest 4	32
the well is deep, and we have nothing of our selves to draw with?	229	Priest 4	1
the reading of the Scripture with some short inward ejaculation,	229	Priest 4	2
The third means is a diligent Collation of Scripture with Scripture.	229	Priest 4	5
and judicious comparing of place with place must be a singular help	229	Priest 4	8
be added the consideration of any text with the coherence thereof,	229	Priest 4	10
book of Scripture, and ploughing with this, and his own meditations,	229	Priest 4	29
and the pleasure that comes with sleep, be sins of gluttony,	230	Priest 5	29
as being truly touched and amazed with the Majesty of God,	231	Priest 6	5
but as presenting with himself the whole Congregation, whose sins he	231	Priest 6	7
and brings with his own to the heavenly altar to be bathed,	231	Priest 6	9
speaking, but with a grave livelinesse, between fear and zeal,	231	Priest 6	19
not to come at the beginning of service with their poor neighbours,	232	Priest 6	9
or if the poor Church-wardens be affrighted with their greatness,	232	Priest 6	14
that he himself hath often urged with no great success,	232	Priest 7	28
on his auditors, with letting them know, that he observes who marks,	233	Priest 7	1
and with particularizing of his speech now to the younger sort,	233	Priest 7	2
yet often dy with the Sermon, especially with Countrey people;	233	Priest 7	14
yet often dy with the Sermon, especially with Countrey people;	233	Priest 7	15
though he himself were with Saint Paul even sacrificed upon	234	Priest 7	8
And for the Philippians made request with joy, ch. 1. 4.	234	Priest 7	14
be with them, or Christ, verse 23. which, setting aside his care	234	Priest 7	16
himself, but that all may be done with reverence to his glory,	235	Priest 8	24
and with edification to his flock, humbly beseeching his Master,	235	Priest 8	25
that they may come with holy hearts, and awfull mindes into	235	Priest 8	29
all those, who come with lesse prepared hearts then they ought.	235	Priest 8	31
the hour calls, with his family attending him, he goes to Church,	236	Priest 8	3
As he opened the day with prayer, so he closeth it, humbly beseeching	236	Priest 8	26
where he may have occasion to converse with women, and that among	237	Priest 9	3
he never talkes with any woman alone, but in the audience of others,	237	Priest 9	11
with other exemplary vertues of that sort, and to keep them on in	237	Priest 9	34
as to be cloathed with perfect patience, and Christian fortitude in	237	Priest 9	37
and accordingly either meets with their vices, or advanceth their	239	Priest 10	9
children and mayds in the fear of God, with prayers, and catechizing,	239	Priest 10	13
and healing of all wounds and sores with her owne hands;	239	Priest 10	15
which skill either she brought with her, or he takes care she shall	239	Priest 10	16
Therefore having seasoned them with all Piety, not only of words in	239	Priest 10	23
and enter favour with God, who weighs even childrens actions,	239	Priest 10	28
turnes his care to fit all their dispositions with some calling,	239	Priest 10	30
he resolves with himself never to omit any present good deed	240	Priest 10	5
and how every one profits, comparing this yeer with the last:	240	Priest 10	38
which when they leave the family, they carry with them.	241	Priest 10	7
which he celebrates not only with abstinence of diet, but also	241	Priest 10	38
with confession of sins, and all acts of Mortification.	241	Priest 10	39
and much more with wine, is apt to nourish more then in cold regions,	242	Priest 10	17
and with more safety then elsewhere, where both the people	242	Priest 10	19
that a weak stomack being prepossessed with flesh, shall much better	242	Priest 10	22
whom he sometimes purposely takes home with him, setting them close	243	Priest 11	11
and their comfort, who are much cheered with such friendliness.	243	Priest 11	13
hee hath them all with him, because countrey people are very	243	Priest 11	20
time will lose the name and effect of Charity with the poor people,	244	Priest 12	27
name and effect of Charity with the poor people, though not with God:	244	Priest 12	27
except the evidence of the misery bring testimony with it.	245	Priest 12	23
festivalls strawed, and stuck with boughs, and perfumed with incense.	246	Priest 13	10
and reverend, not with light colours, or foolish anticks.	246	Priest 13	13
with an handsome, and seemly Carpet of good and costly Stuffe,	246	Priest 13	17
in a strong and decent chest, with a Chalice, and Cover,	246	Priest 13	19
as if hee findes them reading, hee furnisheth them with good books;	247	Priest 14	16
hee supplies them with Receipts, and instructs them further in that	247	Priest 14	17
and wishing them ever to do the Cures with their own hands,	247	Priest 14	19
thoughts to God, nor sanctifying their labour with daily prayer;	248	Priest 14	2
but with these he mingles other discourses for conversation sake,	249	Priest 14	10
of his cure is sick, or afflicted with losse of friend, or estate,	249	Priest 15	14
of the moment of griefs here with the weight of joyes hereafter.	249	Priest 15	27
carrying it about with him as fully, as if he had begot his whole	250	Priest 16	9
and with those he overtakes or that overtake him, hee begins good	251	Priest 17	3
hee first considers with himselfe, what kind of remedy fits	251	Priest 17	26
wish them best, and that not a desire to meddle with others affairs,	251	Priest 17	31
But this he doth discretely, with mollifying, and suppling words;	252	Priest 18	8
he keeps good Correspondence with all the neighbouring Pastours round	253	Priest 19	15
with as joyfull a countenance, as if he were to entertain some great	253	Priest 19	19
and then when he hath affrighted them with this, exposing	253	Priest 19	34
if any neighbouring village be overburdened with poore,	254	Priest 19	2
and with truly godly zeal, without hatred to the person,	254	Priest 20	27
growing with the growth of his Parish.	255	Priest 21	15
by making the Question very plaine with comparisons, and making much	256	Priest 21	14
is at a stand with himself, how or what behaviour to assume for so	257	Priest 22	27
Hee says that prayer with great devotion, where God is thanked	258	Priest 22	5
and upon what termes, and with what vowes they were Baptized.	258	Priest 22	20
he first takes order with the Church-Wardens, that the elements be	258	Priest 22	21
and accordingly applies himselfe with Catechizings, and lively	258	Priest 22	25
he takes the more pains with them, that hee may lay the foundation	258	Priest 22	30
with Daltons Justice of Peace, and the Abridgements of the Statutes,	260	Priest 23	2
as also by discourse with men of that profession, whom he hath ever	260	Priest 23	3
whom he hath ever some cases to ask, when he meets with them;	260	Priest 23	5
three or four of the ablest of the Parish to hear the cause with him,	260	Priest 23	10
and so the thing passeth with more authority, and lesse envy.	260	Priest 23	12
then he keeps good correspondence with some neighbour Phisician,	260	Priest 23	37
knot-grasse for the other, and that with better successe.	261	Priest 23	36
the Parson hath diligently examined these two with himselfe,	262	Priest 24	32

WITH (cont'd)

	PAGE	TITLE	LINE
The third is the observation with what appetite they sit down.	267	Priest 26	5
This last rule joyned with the first, never fails.	267	Priest 26	5
When he deals with any that is heavy, and carnall;	267	Priest 26	17
but when he meets with a refined, and heavenly disposition,	267	Priest 26	18
his minde being defixed on it with those nailes wherewith his Master	267	Priest 27	29
he meets continually with two most sad spectacles, Sin,	267	Priest 27	31
instructions seasoned with pleasantnesse, both enter sooner,	268	Priest 27	4
which carries a reverence with it, even above contempt.	268	Priest 28	21
and dishonour him with those mouths, which he continually fils,	269	Priest 28	10
The Parson with his Church-Wardens.	269	Priest 29	T
in this, how Gods goodnesse strives with mans refractorinesse;	272	Priest 30	5
and with pulling, gets the apple out of his Fathers hand:	272	Priest 30	9
the Child utterly refusing, eats it, and is troubled with wormes:	272	Priest 30	12
is the carnall and wilfull man with the worm of the grave in this	272	Priest 30	13
Here the Parson interposeth with his distinction, and shews	273	Priest 31	3
or else to examine with care, and advice, what they are fittest for,	275	Priest 32	16
they are fittest for, and to prepare for that with all diligence.	275	Priest 32	17
inabling him with power to do good, and to restrain all those,	276	Priest 32	14
with the same care as others, when they meet with good fruit,	276	Priest 32	31
when they meet with good fruit, get a graffe of the tree,	276	Priest 32	32
and disarmed with sedentary lives, are to know the use of their Arms:	277	Priest 32	18
For the temptations with which a good man is beset, and the ways	278	Priest 33	15
is a Physitian so far as he meetes with the same disease,	278	Priest 33	27
when we are assaulted with temptations either from within or from	280	Priest 34	4
nor to store their house with all those furnitures which even their	280	Priest 34	24
for with such sacrifices God is well pleased.	281	Priest 34	4
military state, he fortifyes, and strengthens with his utmost skill.	281	Priest 34	6
but with the Gospel it selfe be preached to all ages, Matth. 26. 13.	282	Priest 34	26
With some of these heads enlarged, and woven into his discourse,	283	Priest 34	3
and with an exceeding great victory, which in the Creation needed	283	Priest 34	15
with reconciling of differences at that time, if there be any:	284	Priest 35	6
and goes with him to the other, and all dine or sup together.	284	Priest 35	20
that Blessing the people is in so little use with his brethren:	285	Priest 36	2
and received with great joy, 1 Sam. 1. 18. though it came from a man	285	Priest 36	21
imprecation to Simon Magus, Act. 8. Thy mony perish with thee:	285	Priest 36	30
that if a Minister talke with a great man in the ordinary course	286	Priest 36	20
may talk, so they do it not with sport, but commiseration;)	287	Priest 37	14
assembled together, with thy unworthy Servant speaking unto them:	289	Priest	25
And now Lord, thou hast fed us with the bread of life:	290	Priest	8
To whom with thee, and the Holy Ghost, three Persons, but one most	290	Priest	14
the beginning of the Gout, with almost a continuall fever and thirst.	291	Cornaro	23
weighing their reasons with my self, and abhorring from so sudden	292	Cornaro	17
and finding my self continually oppressed with pain and sicknesse,	292	Cornaro	19
to consider the force of Temperance, and to think thus with my self:	293	Cornaro	2
taking care never to rise with a full stomack, but so as I might well	293	Cornaro	18
Yet with this diet I avoided other hurtfull things also,	293	Cornaro	30
they were possessed with a deep Melancholie (a thing usuall	294	Cornaro	18
my arm and legge should be set, and my whole bodie anointed with oyl:	295	Cornaro	12
that old age could not be sustained with so little meat and drink;	295	Cornaro	22
that Nature was contented with a little, and that I had for many	295	Cornaro	26
for many yeares continued in good health, with that little measure;	295	Cornaro	27
onely with returning to my former course of Diet, although I was now	296	Cornaro	25
and my bodie spent with extream leannesse, and the season	296	Cornaro	26
hidden properties it hath, what meat and drink agrees best with it:	297	Cornaro	28
and divers labours, which suit not with an orderly life:	299	Cornaro	14
which is alreadie burdened with a disease, would be wholly oppressed.	299	Cornaro	34
So that he which is offended with no kinde of meat and drink,	300	Cornaro	14
I am not wearie of life, which I passe with great delight.	301	Cornaro	3
I conferre often with worthie men, excelling in wit, learning,	301	Cornaro	4
parted with rills of running water, which truely is very delightfull.	301	Cornaro	15
This place is washed with the river Brenta;	301	Cornaro	24
and fruitfull fields, well manured and adorned with many habitations.	301	Cornaro	25
Whereupon men flockt thither, and built houses with happy successe.	301	Cornaro	29
I view their pieces, I compare them with those of Antiquitie;	302	Cornaro	1
I am much pleased also in my travells, with the beauty of situation.	302	Cornaro	6
as a Tragedie with old Age, by reason of the sad events which it	302	Cornaro	32
I am delighted with their musick and fashion, and I my self also sing	303	Cornaro	6
I change age and constitution with them who follow their youthfull	303	Cornaro	12
all who have the care of themselves, to embrace it with open arms?	303	Cornaro	32
your Valdesso I now returne with many thanks, and some notes,	304	Valdesso	2
put this into your hands (as he sent the fish with mony to S. Peter,)	304	Valdesso	11
happily also with this (as his thoughts are fruitfull) intending	304	Valdesso	12
concluding every Consideration almost with his holy Name,	305	Valdesso	5
Print it, that with it the honour of my Lord might be published.	305	Valdesso	8
words about the H. Scripture suite with what he writes elsewhere,	306	Valdesso	15
This place together with many other, as namely Consid. 71. upon Our	307	Valdesso	16
so it be understood with the former distinction, for Fomes is	308	Valdesso	15
is not that which filleth the heart with joy and peace in believing;	309	Valdesso	2
but the spirits bearing witnesse with our spirit, revealing	309	Valdesso	3
promises to every one in particular with such syncerity and efficacy,	309	Valdesso	5
is delayed, the more he reads it, and fortifies himselfe with it;	310	Valdesso	30
so are wee to doe with the Scriptures and this is the use	310	Valdesso	31
in regard it presents us not with the same thing only when it is read	310	Valdesso	33
but enlightens us with new Considerations the more we read it.	310	Valdesso	34
and that no other sin or vertue hath any thing to doe with us;	311	Valdesso	24
And with this exposition the Chapter is cleare enough, but the truth	311	Valdesso	30
To say our Saviour prayed with doubtfulnesse, is more then I can	315	Valdesso	9
But with condition, or conditionally he prayed as man, though as God	315	Valdesso	10
though in the point of Resurrection he agreed with them,	316	Valdesso	9
in the point of Resurrection he agreed with them, and they with him.	316	Valdesso	10

WITH (cont'd)

	PAGE	TITLE		LINE
but when he sayes they are equally exempt with God, that is dangerous	316	Valdesso		32
that I may speak with him or doe some thing else when I doe come.	318	Valdesso		16
and we meet with two sorts of these Saints of the world;	319	Valdesso	V	21
a few cheap and easie duties of religion, with no less superstition;	319	Valdesso	V	25
Every day brings his bread with it.	321	Proverbs		5
All is well with him, who is beloved of his neighbours.	321	Proverbs		10
Hee puls with a long rope, that waits for anothers death.	322	Proverbs		25
Hee puls with a long rope, who looks for anothers death.	322	Proverbs	V	25
Play with a foole at home,	325	Proverbs		146
and he will play with you in the market.	325	Proverbs		146
Dally not with mony or women.	326	Proverbs		150
Men speake of the faire, as things went with them there.	326	Proverbs		151
The mill cannot grind with the water that's past.	326	Proverbs		153
Corne is cleaned with winde, and the soule with chastnings.	326	Proverbs		154
Jest not with the eye or with Religion.	326	Proverbs		157
and with it you will not know your selfe.	326	Proverbs		159
with it you will hardly know your selfe.	326	Proverbs	V	159
Cover your selfe with your shield, and care not for cryes.	326	Proverbs		161
Diseases of the eye are to bee cured with the elbow.	327	Proverbs		203
Diseases of the eyes are to bee cured with the elbow.	326	Proverbs	V	203
(to wit - with a moderate and contented heart).	328	Proverbs		208
The thorne comes forth with his point forwards.	329	Proverbs		238
It's no sure rule to fish with a cros-bow.	331	Proverbs		293
Hee that strikes with his tongue, must ward with his head.	331	Proverbs		313
Hee that strikes with his tongue, must ward with his hand.	331	Proverbs	V	313
God strikes not with both hands,	331	Proverbs		315
Peace, and Patience, and death with repentance.	332	Proverbs		319
A little with quiet is the onely dyet.	332	Proverbs		327
Hee that lies with the dogs, riseth with fleas.	332	Proverbs		343
He that hath no ill fortune is troubled with good.	333	Proverbs		358
All griefes with bread are lesse.	334	Proverbs		377
All griefes with bread are lesse, or Nor woe to want.	334	Proverbs	V	377
The dog that licks ashes, trust not with meale.	334	Proverbs		389
An ill labourer quarrells with his tooles.	335	Proverbs		408
If the wise erred not, it would goe hard with fooles.	338	Proverbs		510
If wise men erred not, it would goe hard with fooles.	338	Proverbs	V	510
Beare with evill, and expect good.	338	Proverbs		511
The tooth-ach is more ease then to deale with ill people.	340	Proverbs		558
When the tree is fallen, all goe with their hatchet.	340	Proverbs		566
Hee that blowes in the dust fills his eyes with it.	340	Proverbs		570
Happier are the hands compast with yron,	341	Proverbs		582
then a heart with thoughts.	341	Proverbs		582
To take the nuts from the fire with the dogges foot.	341	Proverbs		584
A noble plant suites not with a stubborne ground.	342	Proverbs		622
Before you make a friend, eate a bushell of salt with him.	342	Proverbs		624
You cannot make a wind-mill goe with a paire of bellowes.	344	Proverbs		676
If a good man thrive, all thrive with him.	344	Proverbs		695
A gentle heart is tyed with an easie thread.	345	Proverbs		726
Every sin brings its punishment with it.	346	Proverbs		760
It's good walking with a horse in ones hand.	348	Proverbs		804
To live peaceably with all breedes good blood.	353	Proverbs		963
With customes wee live well, but Lawes undoe us.	353	Proverbs		973
He that is surprized with the first frost	354	Proverbs		992
An old cat sports not with her prey.	355	Proverbs		1030
the Catholick Religion is professed with greatest strictness).	357	Proverbs	D	1047
with some idlenesse of brain, says the Spaniard.	357	Proverbs	D	1050
God strikes with his finger, and not with all his arme.	359	Proverbs	D	1114
Great Fortune brings with it Great misfortune.	360	Proverbs	D	1144
Trust no friend with that you need fear him if he were your enemy.	361	Proverbs	D	1169
of your love, with being in some proportion, and after my manner,	364	Letters		3
and yet I am scarce able with much ado to make one half years	365	Letters		10
ado to make one half years allowance, shake hands with the other:	365	Letters		11
The disease which I am troubled with now is the shortness of time,	365	Letters		30
as when you meet with a witty French speech, try to speak the like in	366	Letters		10
not with a foolish vanting of yourself when there is no caus,	366	Letters		16
This letter runs to you with much eagernes, for I am enjoined	367	Letters		27
Now his desire is to acquaint you with those passages of newes which	368	Letters		1
being at London sent for him (as shee sayes) to make peace with him,	368	Letters		21
given her occasion to protest shee will never speake with him againe,	368	Letters		23
this passeth in Spaine freely with consent of King & counsell.	368	Letters		29
These are the things I am to acquaint you with, of whose rude	369	Letters		1
This Week hath loaded me with your Favours;	369	Letters		10
yet if you cannot send it with much convenience, it is no matter,	369	Letters		28
no such earthiness in it, but it may very well be joined with Heaven;	370	Letters		23
whether my peace be yet made with her concerning my unkind departure.	371	Letters		9
yet my heart, a much better member, is alwayes with you:	371	Letters		27
with our good and gracious God, incessantly begging some ease of your	371	Letters		28
ease of your pains, with that earnestness, that becomes your griefs,	371	Letters		29
or rather increaseth, I wish earnestly that I were again with you:	372	Letters		18
and I shou'd account my self most happy if I might change with you;	373	Letters		3
yet you may say with David, That God who hath delivered me out	374	Letters		6
but you joyed me exceedingly with your relation of my Lady Duchess's	377	Letters		19
in signing 100 lib. with her own hands (& promising to get her Son	379	Letters		2
to get her Son to doe as much) with some little Apology that she had	379	Letters		3
Herberts reasons for Arth. Woodenoths Living with Sir John Danvers.	380	Woodnoth		T
now Constancy is such & of great esteem with all.	380	Woodnoth		15
to be without dores with him, is no ill company.	381	Woodnoth		3
therfore God is styled with that glorious title, Long Suffering.	381	Woodnoth		6
& to rise with his favours, can not but be not only allowable	381	Woodnoth		26
with which you use to conquer your enemies, and assume more mild	442	Oration		3

WITH (cont'd)	PAGE	TITLE	LINE
whose exceeding glory is equally round with the world it selfe:	442	Oration	10
who tying, as with a knot, both Indias to his Spaine, knowes no	442	Oration	11
all we and our whole Kingdome exult with joy, to bee united with that	442	Oration	14
to bee united with that bloud, which useth to infuse so great	442	Oration	14
repose, peace with all but Booke-wormes, perpetuall povertie,	442	Oration	36
WITHALL			
And say withall, Earth to earth I commit.	11	Ch.-Porch	132
But say withall, Earth to earth I commit.	11	Ch.-Porch W	132
and withall help many others, who will take this into consideration,	291	Cornaro	13
They added withall, that unlesse I speedily used that remedy,	292	Cornaro	13
which it most suits withall for variety and pleasantnesse; . .	302	Cornaro	31
WITHDRAW			
When they are callow; but withdraw their food	118	Providence	63
Ah Lord! do not withdraw, ...	183	A Parodie	16
perambulation, and those that withdraw, and sever themselves from it,	284	Priest 35	11
From a chollerick man withdraw a little;	326	Proverbs	164
WITHDRAWING			
is rather by withdrawing his bounty and courtesie from the parties	254	Priest 20	22
things may grow worse by your withdrawing which grow not better	381	Woodnoth	11
& if upon your withdrawing it shold doe so, it would trouble your	381	Woodnoth	12
WITHDRAWS			
Night draws the curtain, which the sunne withdraws;	91	Man	32
WITHER			
Fast in thy Paradise, where no flower can wither!	166	The Flower	23
WITHER'D			
And wither'd in my hand.	94	Life	6
My heart is wither'd like a ground	148	Longing	8
WITHHOLD			
Withhold thee.	41	Sepulchre	24
WITHIN			
When once it is within thee; but before	7	Ch.-Porch	26
When thou dost purpose ought within thy power, ...	11	Ch.-Porch	115
All equall are within the churches gate.	22	Ch.-Porch	408
Sure there is room within our hearts good store;	40	Sepulchre	5
Without, our shame; within, our consciences;	46	Sinne 1	11
Leaving within me sinne:	52	H.Commun.	6
Thou shutt'st the doore, and keep'st within;	60	Whitsunday	21
Making thy life to shine within	67	Windows	7
Within the walls of your own breast:	68	Content	2
Take up within a cloisters gates.	69	Content	16
The callow principles within their nest:	85	Vanitie 1	17
And thou within them starve at doore.	93	Unkindness	14
My life within this band.	94	Life	3
Within the circle of his breath, ...	98	Mortific.	21
That thou within his curtains drawn canst see:	100	Miserie	16
For all thy frame and fabrick is within.	106	Sion	12
Is this same grief! within my heart I made	126	Confession	2
Like moles within us, heave, and cast about:	126	Confession	14
They purge the aire without, within the breast.	132	The Storm	18
What doth this noise of thoughts within my heart	136	Familie	1
Did worm and work within you more and more, ...	140	Ch.-rents	17
O that within us hearts had propagation, ...	147	Offering	7
Sprung from thine eye, did work within my soul, ...	172	The Glance	14
So all within be livelier then before.	177	Forerunners	36
Within a sheet of paper, which was rent	192	Ch.-Milit.	95
Statesmen within, without doores cloisterers:	195	Ch.-Milit.	200
Within your chamber try your hearts, ...	217	Psalm IV D	17
The greatest and hardest preparation is within:	226	Priest 2	13
and seriously prepare for it, he is safe and within bounds. . .	275	Priest 32	13
and mastered all his lusts and affections within, and the whole Army	278	Priest 33	23
we are assaulted with temptations either from within or from without.	280	Priest 34	4
not any sin else, but is within his Love;	283	Priest 34	24
still striving & prospering so long within us, untill our obedience	290	Priest	11
within a few moneths I should be driven to that exigent, . .	292	Cornaro	14
I found within a few dayes, that I was exceedingly helped, . .	292	Cornaro	34
within lesse then one yeare (although it may seem to some incredible)	292	Cornaro	36
within lesse then a yeare I was not onely freed from all those evils	293	Cornaro	20
what case I was, they concluded that I would die within three dayes.	295	Cornaro	3
and observation of Gods Kingdome within us, and the working thereof,	305	Valdesso	10
and Gods worke within us still observed, who workes by his Word,	309	Valdesso	32
The house is a fine house, when good folke are within. . . .	352	Proverbs	952
The house is a fine house, when good folks are within. . . .	352	Proverbs V	952
I give all my goods both within doores and without doores both	382	G.H.'s Will	3
WITHOUT			
For wealth without contentment, climbes a hill	11	Ch.-Porch	111
Without me each one, who doth now me brave, ...	27	Sacrifice	9
But mend mine own without delayes.	36	Thanksgvng	34
But mend my own without delayes.	36	Thanksgvng W	34
Without delayes, ...	41	Easter	2
Without, our shame; within, our consciences;	46	Sinne 1	11
Thus thinne and lean without a fence or friend, ...	47	Afflict.1	35
For so thou should'st without me still have been, ...	52	H.Commun.	5
Without thy help, leads us his way to Hell.	59	Whitsunday W	16
O let thy graces without cease	60	Grace	3
Now I in you without a bodie move, ...	65	Ch.-mus.	5
Without a knock it never shone.	68	Content	12
He lies warm, and without adventure.	69	Content	20
See the smooth face of God, without a frown	77	Ang.&Sts.	2
I took, without more thinking, in good part	94	Life	8
I follow straight without complaints or grief, ...	94	Life	16

WITHOUT (cont'd)	PAGE	TITLE	LINE
A lump of flesh, without a foot or wing	102	Miserie	74
But there was none; at least no help without:	107	Home	15
Get without repining;	115	Dialogue	26
Light without winde is glasse: warm without weight	120	Providence	101
Is wooll and furres: cool without closenesse, shade:	120	Providence	102
Is wooll and furre: cool without closenesse, shade:	120	Providence V	102
Speed without pains, a horse: tall without height,	120	Providence	103
A servile hawk: low without losse, a spade.	120	Providence	104
They purge the aire without, within the breast.	132	The Storm	18
Which knows his way without a guide:	134	Divinitie	4
Without relief.	136	Ephes.	27
But griefs without a noise:	137	Familie	18
If I without thee would be mine,	157	Clasping	9
Without excuse or cloke.	171	Self-cond.	24
Without whom I could have no rest:	174	Aaron	14
While ye graze without your bounds:	180	Invitation	21
Traditions are accounts without our host.	194	Ch.-Milit. W	160
Statesmen within, without doores cloisterers:	195	Ch.-Milit.	200
Who without spear, or sword, or other drumme	195	Ch.-Milit.	201
Clinging and crying, crying without cease,	205	Persever. W	15
And built without thy Cost:	207	Walton 3	3
Without thy cost,	207	Walton 4	2
At there owne weapons, without pomp or state	211	Bohemia D	21
At once to Hell, without a baiting while	212	Bohemia D	49
but reverend, and clean, without spots, or dust, or smell;	228	Priest 3	11
without reason, or offer up such sacrifices as they did of old,	232	Priest 6	3
since we are here by him, and without him could not be here.	234	Priest 7	30
and without hinderance to publick duties, either to entertaine some	236	Priest 8	19
without disturbance, or interruption of publick divine offices.	236	Priest 8	24
But these he helps not without some testimony, except the evidence	245	Priest 12	21
but allows by no means to give without testimony, as he obeys	245	Priest 12	25
that the Church be swept, and kept cleane without dust, or Cobwebs,	246	Priest 13	9
without hatred to the person, hungreth and thirsteth after righteous	254	Priest 20	27
as parrats, without ever piercing into the sense of it.	256	Priest 21	4
and leadeth captive without any resistance, even in resistance,	269	Priest 28	22
without which supply the corne would instantly dry up, as a river	271	Priest 30	6
that he cannot without this maintain himself in a Christian state.	272	Priest 31	24
I will not doubt to go without staying to pray there (but onely,	273	Priest 31	35
and the whole Army of Temptations without, hath ever so many sermons	278	Priest 33	23
Just so it is in Divinity, and that not without manifest reason:	278	Priest 33	33
we are assaulted with temptations either from within or from without.	280	Priest 34	4
then without opposing directly (for disputation is no Cure	281	Priest 34	14
he sees not how a house could be either built without a builder,	281	Priest 34	19
built without a builder, or kept in repaire without a house-keeper.	281	Priest 34	19
not only without dissolution of the whole, but also of any part,	281	Priest 34	22
but the despising of Love must needs be without it.	283	Priest 34	25
without any remedy (which cannot be applyed without notice)	287	Priest 37	2
any remedy (which cannot be applyed without notice) to the dishonor	287	Priest 37	2
all superfluities passing away without difficultie, and no ill	293	Cornaro	28
and so without other remedie or inconvenience I recovered;	295	Cornaro	12
regular life can hardly be altered without exceeding great danger.	295	Cornaro	17
as usually happens in old mens bodies, which live without rule.	296	Cornaro	36
which things in others cannot be known without such observation,	297	Cornaro	29
of the radicall moisture, without grief or perturbation of humours.	298	Cornaro	18
I can easily get on horseback without the advantage of the ground,	300	Cornaro	35
then I could of Originall before, and without Baptisme.	308	Valdesso	5
afterward they will attend it of themselves without his exhortation.	318	Valdesso	21
Sleepe without supping, and wake without owing.	324	Proverbs	93
Without favour none will know you,	326	Proverbs	159
It is a great victory that comes without blood.	328	Proverbs	227
Honour without profit is a ring on the finger.	328	Proverbs	230
God comes to see without a bell.	334	Proverbs	384
Life without a friend is death without a witnesse.	334	Proverbs	385
Health without money is halfe an ague.	338	Proverbs	509
Love rules his kingdome without a sword.	339	Proverbs	541
Folly growes without watering.	341	Proverbs	581
He that contemplates hath a day without night.	341	Proverbs	601
Gifts enter every where without a wimble.	352	Proverbs	955
He that dies without the company of good men	354	Proverbs	995
Hee that lives in hope danceth without musick.	354	Proverbs	1006
Without businesse debauchery.	354	Proverbs	1009
Without danger we cannot get beyond danger.	354	Proverbs	1010
Service without reward is punishment.	354	Proverbs	1015
One month doth nothing without another.	355	Proverbs	1028
One mouth doth nothing without another.	355	Proverbs V	1028
A man of a great memory without learning	358	Proverbs D	1085
God gives his wrath by weight, and without weight his mercy.	359	Proverbs D	1115
Love without end, hath no end, says the Spaniard: (meaning,	361	Proverbs D	1160
What Trades-man is there who will set up without his Tools?	364	Letters	15
I hope I shall get this place without all your London helps,	370	Letters	8
much from Divinity, at which, not without cause, he thinks, I aim;	370	Letters	21
to be without dores with him, is no ill company.	381	Woodnoth	3
& therfore not relinquishable without their masters consent.	381	Woodnoth	29
goods both within doores and without doores both monneys and bookes	382	G.H.'s Will	4
WITHSTAND			
Which they effected, none could them withstand.	84	The World	18
Arise sad heart; if thou dost not withstand,	112	Dawning	9
Arise sad heart; if thou doe not withstand,	112	Dawning V	9
WITHSTANDING			
This not withstanding, thou wentst on,	124	Gratefulnes	17

	PAGE	TITLE		LINE
WITHSTOOD				
Of what we might not take, or be withstood.	104	Obedience		30
who had withstood his preaching, The Lord (saith he) reward him	285	Priest 36		33
WITNESS				
who have born witness to the truth, (there being no reason, . . .	282	Priest 34		19
WITNESSE				
The Priest and rulers all false witnesse seek	28	Sacrifice		57
The Priests and rulers all false witnesse seek	28	Sacrifice	W	57
they have their Law and Language bearing witnesse to them, . .	281	Priest 34		36
but the spirits bearing witnesse with our spirit, revealing . .	309	Valdesso		3
Life without a friend is death without a witnesse. . . .	334	Proverbs		385
WITNESSES				
mouth of two or three witnesses the truth may be more established.	232	Priest 7		29
that the Jewes should be his proof, and witnesses, as he calls them,	282	Priest 34		12
in the mouth of two or three witnesses every word may be established;	283	Priest 34		19
WITS				
These are the scumme, with which course wits abound:	16	Ch.-Porch		237
All knees shall bow to thee; all wits shall rise, ...	54	Love 2		13
Danting the stoutest hearts, the proudest wits.	141	Justice 2		12
Let wits contest, ...	182	The Posie		1
WITT				
Witt & desire	202	Trin.Sun.	W	8
WITTIE				
Laugh not too much: the wittie man laughs least:	15	Ch.-Porch		229
But may be wittie, if thou hast the vein.	16	Ch.-Porch		240
All such is courteous, usefull, new, or wittie.	18	Ch.-Porch		290
Servants and abjects flout me; they are wittie:	31	Sacrifice		141
And if I please him, I write fine and wittie.	176	Forerunners		12
WITTY				
he is not witty, or learned, or eloquent, but Holy.	233	Priest 7		23
to themselves, and witty to others who shall reprove them from it.	264	Priest 26		13
the Gallant, who is witty enough to abuse both others, and himself,	275	Priest 32		6
Every one is witty for his owne purpose.	346	Proverbs		754
as when you meet with a witty French speech, try to speak the like in	366	Letters		10
WIVE'S				
Perhaps his wives too, and whom she hath bore:	14	Ch.-Porch		195
of this parish to be devided according to my deare wives discretion.	382	G.H.'s Will		17
WIVES				
Mills and wives ever want.	334	Proverbs		388
WO				
Make not an ell, by trifling in thy wo.	24	Ch.-Porch		460
My wo, mans weal: and now I bow my head.	34	Sacrifice		250
And made a partie unawares for wo.	47	Afflict.1		24
Forthwith he waxeth wo and wan:	49	Repentance		26
Money, thou bane of blisse, & sourse of wo, ...	77	Avarice		1
My God, so temper joy and wo, ...	97	Afflict.5		23
This world of wo? hence all ye clouds, away, ...	108	Home		33
Dig not for wo	145	Discharge		29
Of all my woes another wo, ...	165	The Crosse		28
To a plague and publick wo.	187	Dooms-day		24
Wo be to him that reads but one book.	360	Proverbs	D	1146
WOE				
That I did live, but by a pang of woe.	47	Afflict.1	W	30
How know you that our teares proceed from woe	210	Paradox	D	15
Is thy chief government, to manage woe, ...	212	Bohemia	D	57
All griefes with bread are lesse, or Nor woe to want.	334	Proverbs	V	377
Woe to the house where there is no chiding.	336	Proverbs		450
The cholerick man never wants woe.	339	Proverbs		536
WOES				
Shall I thy woes	38	Good Fri.		5
Thy whips, thy nails, thy wounds, thy woes, ...	39	Good Fri.		26
Of all my woes another wo, ...	165	The Crosse		28
Blushing woes, that look as cleare	177	The Rose		7
WOLD				
Some call the wold;	142	Pilgrimage		14
WOLFE				
The Wolfe knowes, what the ill beast thinkes.	321	Proverbs		16
Who hath a Wolfe for his mate, needes a Dog for his man. . .	323	Proverbs		57
A bad dog never sees the Wolfe.	323	Proverbs		59
The Wolfe must dye in his owne skinne.	349	Proverbs		849
Hee that makes himself a sheep, shall be eat by the wolfe. . .	358	Proverbs	D	1089
A wolfe will never make war against another wolfe. . . .	359	Proverbs	D	1125
The death of a young wolfe doth never come too soon. . . .	360	Proverbs	D	1131
The wolfe eats oft of the sheep that have been warn'd. . . .	360	Proverbs	D	1134
WOLVES				
The death of wolves is the safety of the sheep.	358	Proverbs	D	1086
WOMAN				
What is this woman-kinde, which I can wink	108	Home		39
he hath not a woman in his house, but findes opportunities of having	237	Priest 9		8
he never talkes with any woman alone, but in the audience of others,	237	Priest 9		11
the one concerning the woman that spent the oyntment on our Saviour,	282	Priest 34		24
A woman and a glasse are ever in danger.	329	Proverbs		244
A journying woman speakes much of all, and all of her.	330	Proverbs		279
A house and a woman sute excellently.	337	Proverbs		468
A shippe and a woman are ever repairing.	347	Proverbs		780
and a latin-bred woman, seldome end well.	349	Proverbs		866
A woman conceales what shee knowes not.	355	Proverbs		1031
a prophetesse, and a Lattin bred woman.	360	Proverbs	D	1151
WOMAN-KINDE				
What is this woman-kinde, which I can wink	108	Home		39

WOMAN'S	PAGE	TITLE		LINE
then he that reads the womans oyntment in the Gospell, or sees	283	Priest 34		2
WOMEN				
With sick folks, women, those whom passions sway,	73	Constancie		27
where he may have occasion to converse with women, and that among	237	Priest 9		3
good instrument of God to bring women to heaven) a wise and loving	238	Priest 9		30
such as are tavernes for men, and lace-making for women;	240	Priest 10		3
Dally not with mony or women.	326	Proverbs		150
The more women looke in their glasse,	329	Proverbs		250
Discreet women have neither eyes nor eares.	337	Proverbs		482
Gaming, women, and wine, while they laugh they make men pine.	341	Proverbs		604
Three women make a market.	345	Proverbs		713
Women laugh when they can, and weepe when they will.	348	Proverbs		821
Words are women, deedes are men.	349	Proverbs		843
WOMEN'S				
Foolish night-fires, womens and childrens wishes,	167	Dotage		2
Why should I Womens eyes for Chrystal take?	206	Walton 2		8
WON				
the same heart, which you have won long since, is still true to you,	363	Letters		18
WONDER				
The brags of life are but a nine dayes wonder;	69	Content		21
Once a poore creature, now a wonder,	89	Afflict.4		4
A wonder tortur'd in the space	90	Afflict.4		5
I do not greatly wonder at the sight,	161	Priesthood		23
Let the wonder of his pitie	182	Banquet		49
Let the wonder of this pitie	182	Banquet	V	49
as the only wonder-working knowledg, and therefore requiring the best	277	Priest 32		35
Now a prophesie is a wonder sent to Posterity, least they complaine	282	Priest 34		35
it is no wonder that order should preserve, and disorder destroy.	297	Cornaro		8
I wonder how this opinion could befall so good a man as it seems	317	Valdesso		31
WONDER-WORKING				
as the only wonder-working knowledg, and therefore requiring the best	277	Priest 32		35
WONDER'S				
Transposer of the world, wcnders resort,	51	Prayer 1	W	7
WONDERFULL				
Wherein he admires and imitates the wonderfull providence and thrift	241	Priest 10		25
For many and wonderfull things are spoken of thee, thou great Vertue.	244	Priest 12		7
WONDERFULLY				
wherein the manifold wisedome of God is wonderfully to be seen,	261	Priest 23		28
WONDERS				
Wonders and sings, but not his power	101	Miserie		57
These are thy wonders, Lord of power,	166	The Flower		15
These are thy wcnders, Lord of love,	167	The Flower		43
What wonders shall we feel, when we shall see	172	The Glance		19
Wonders of anger once, but now of love.	191	Ch.-Milit.		38
all the great wonders of old live in them, and then who can deny	282	Priest 34		5
a wonder sent to Posterity, least they complaine of want of wonders.	282	Priest 34		36
The Countrey Parson wonders, that Blessing the people is in so little	285	Priest 36		1
WONDRETH				
and wondreth not so much at their patient suffering, and cheerfull	237	Priest 9		29
WONDRING				
Which many wondring at, got some of those	125	Peace		29
even to a wondring, that the world should so much value wealth,	227	Priest 3		19
WONDROUS				
For this he wondrous well doth know	101	Miserie	W	45
Surely thy sweet and wondrous love	173	23 Psalme		21
A gown and pen became him wondrous well:	194	Ch.-Milit.		167
open mine eyes, that I may see the wondrous things of thy Law.	229	Priest 4		3
who onely doth wondrous things.	289	Priest		9
to open his eyes that he might see the wondrous things of his Lawes,	309	Valdesso		26
WONDROUSLY				
neighboring Sea, wondrously sound through all our Coasts, and eares.	442	Oration		24
WONT				
Made in the tree, where she was wont to sit,	101	Miserie		56
When he was come, as travellers are wont,	151	The Bag		19
(As dying things are wont) untill it flew	192	Ch.-Milit.		80
whereinto I was wont, when I pleased my Sense & Appetite.	293	Cornaro		23
Whether goest, griefe? where I am wont.	324	Proverbs		96
WONTED				
feele my self, either I take my wonted proportion, or diminish of it.	267	Priest 26		9
WOOD				
The crosse taught all wood to resound his name,	41	Easter		9
Some wood and nails to make a staffe or bill	106	Conscience		21
The wood was all embellished	106	Sion		4
But as Pomanders and wood	181	Banquet		25
And thy Crosse is common wood.	199	L'Envoy		10
things that they buy, even as a piece of wood, which they may cut,	265	Priest 26		25
Willowes are weak, yet they bind other wood.	341	Proverbs		594
Wood halfe burnt is easily kindled.	341	Proverbs		606
He that feares leaves, let him not goe into the wood.	346	Proverbs		768
Greene wood makes a hott fire.	349	Proverbs		862
He that is afraid of leaves, goes not to the wood.	358	Proverbs	D	1092
The rage of a wild boar is able to spoil more then one wood.	360	Proverbs	D	1132
WOODDEN				
To the counsell of fooles a woodden bell.	339	Proverbs		535
WOODENOTH'S				
Herberts reasons for Arth. Woodenoths Living with Sir John Danvers.	380	Woodnoth		T
WOODNOTH				
the chiefest also, so also have I required Mr W. for his part.	378	Letters		23
my will and pleasure is that Mr Woodnoth should be mine Executor	382	G.H.'s Will		28

WOODS	PAGE	TITLE	LINE
I have abus'd thy stock, destroy'd thy woods,	83	Sighs & Gr.	9
The South with marble; North with furres & woods.	119	Providence	96
And woods do ring.	131	Mans medly	2
Makes of wilde woods sweet walks and bowres.	137	Familie	12
Wert thou not born among the woods and leaves?	188	Heaven W	5
and managing Commons, or Woods, according as the place suggests.	276	Priest 32	6
WOOE			
That thou shouldst it so eye, and wooe,	62	Mattens	10
Whom none can work or wooe	72	Constancie	16
My tears and prayers night and day do wooe,	139	Artillerie	19
WOOING			
Much curiousnesse is a perpetuall wooing	14	Ch.-Porch	191
WOOLL			
Is wooll and furres: cool without closenesse, shade:	120	Providence	102
Is wooll and furre: cool without closenesse, shade:	120	Providence V	102
WORD			
The letter of the word, find'st no fit heart	41	Sepulchre	19
Since thou hast taught us by thy word,	53	H.Commun. W	39
The grosser world stands to thy word and art;	56	Temper 2	5
Lord, how can man preach thy eternall word?	67	Windows	1
The pasture is thy word: the streams, thy grace	81	Christmas	19
To one word onely I say, No:	105	Obedience	32
And leaves thee not a word;	106	Conscience	16
The word is, Stay, sayes ever, Come.	109	Home	76
Thy word our hearts and hands did crave,	123	Gratefulnes	10
Shows not thy word	143	Complaining	12
At every word,	153	The Collar	34
Were from my self, I had not half a word,	155	Assurance	22
For that of th' holy word.	160	Priesthood	6
Thy word is all, if we could spell.	166	The Flower	21
So in one word our Lords humilitie	168	The Sonne	11
Not a word or look	178	Discipline	9
Countrey people (as indeed all honest men) do much esteem their word,	228	Priest 3	3
therfore the Parson is very strict in keeping his word,	228	Priest 3	5
is careless before his Judg, and that the word of God shal judge us.	233	Priest 7	21
that the auditors may plainly perceive that every word is hart-deep.	233	Priest 7	32
to his Diocesan, honouring him both in word, and behaviour,	253	Priest 19	7
who like Christian Souldiers are to give the word, and to satisfie	255	Priest 21	20
with comparisons, and making much even of a word of truth from him.	256	Priest 21	15
Baptisme being a blessing, that the word hath not the like.	258	Priest 22	7
mens Covetousnesse, and Ambitions to the effecting of his word.	282	Priest 34	35
in the mouth of two or three witnesses every word may be established;	283	Priest 34	19
for, this word of thy rich peace, and reconciliation, thou hast	289	Priest	3
beseeching thee to blesse thy word, wher-ever spoken this day	289	Priest	14
O make it a word of power and peace, to convert those who are not yet	289	Priest	15
Ride on Lord, because of the word of truth, and meeknesse,	289	Priest	22
O make thy word a swift word, passing from the ear to the heart,	289	Priest	29
so neither may thy word, but accomplish that for which it is given.	289	Priest	32
but not as a naked Word severed from God, but as the Word of God:	306	Valdesso	29
but not as a naked Word severed from God, but as the Word of God:	307	Valdesso	1
But by trusting in the word of God they trust in God.	307	Valdesso	3
Hee that trusts in the Kings word for any thing trusts in the King.	307	Valdesso	4
the Consideration of Gods Worke in his heart through the Word,	309	Valdesso	31
observed, who workes by his Word, and ever in the reading of it.	310	Valdesso	1
and those that have inspirations must still use Peter, Gods Word:	310	Valdesso	11
shall not be punished (which word I like here better then	311	Valdesso	27
when he useth the word Jurisdiction, allowing no Jurisdiction over	316	Valdesso	15
and surely this the Author meant by the word Jurisdiction,	317	Valdesso V	7
for so he useth the same word in Consideration 68 ad finem.	317	Valdesso V	8
God in all ages have ever held in so pretious esteem the word of God,	317	Valdesso	33
building it all upon the word untill the day starre arise,	318	Valdesso	8
bidding the dispersed Hebrews attend to the word till the day dawn,	318	Valdesso	18
doth not bid them then cast away the word, or leave it off:	318	Valdesso	19
that in that very place he preferres the Word before the sight	318	Valdesso	23
So that the Word hath the precedence even of Revelations and Visions.	318	Valdesso	24
Of him that speakes ill, consider the life more then the word.	346	Proverbs V	761
Who will sell the Cow, must say the word.	347	Proverbs	791
WORDLY			
And meet them there. All wordly joyes go lesse	19	Ch.-Porch W	329
WORDS			
Drops bloud (the onely beads) my words to measure:	27	Sacrifice	22
See how spite cankers things. These words aright	30	Sacrifice	109
Thy words do finde me out, & parallels bring,	58	H.Script.2	11
His words and works and fashion too	72	Constancie	19
Of thoughts, and words, and deeds.	81	Christmas	18
My words & thoughts do both expresse this notion,	84	Coloss.	1
Thy words were then, Let me alone.	99	Decay	5
That I sought out quaint words, and trim invention;	102	Jordan 2	3
Or some such words in fashion;	104	Obedience	14
My words take fire from my inflamed thoughts.	122	Sinnes rd.	6
My words take fire from my inflamed thoughts.	122	Sinnes rd.	7
But words suffice not, where are lewd intentions:	122	Sinnes rd.	11
Scatter my words, and in the same	149	Longing	23
With but foure words, my words, Thy will be done.	165	The Crosse	36
Who cannot dresse it well, want wit, not words.	167	The Sonne	4
Yet slight not these few words:	168	a true Hymn	6
If the words onely ryme,	168	a true Hymn	13
Deeper then they, in words, and works, and thoughts.	173	Marie Magd	12
So do these words a sweet content,	174	The Odour	4
That these two words might creep & grow	175	The Odour	14

WORDS (cont'd)	PAGE	TITLE		LINE
Beautie and beauteous words should go together.	177	Forerunners		30
And with their words and posies windows fill:	182	The Posie		2
But what shall issue, whither these my words	204	Persever.	W	5
Lord to my words encline thine ear,	218	Psalm V	D	1
but in all his words and actions slighting, and disesteeming it,	227	Priest 3		18
Accordingly his voyce is humble, his words treatable, and slow;	231	Priest 6		17
and seasoning all our words and sentences in our hearts,	233	Priest 7		29
since the words apart are not Scripture, but a dictionary,	235	Priest 7		9
them with all Piety, not only of words in praying, and reading;	239	Priest 10		24
But this he doth discretely, with mollifying, and suppling words;	252	Priest 18		8
of the younger sort, the very words;	255	Priest 21		23
When once all have learned the words of the Catechisme,	256	Priest 21		1
way that a Pastor can take, to go over the same, but in other words:	256	Priest 21		3
doubtlesse then also mens affections and words must turne,	288	Priest 37		4
thy blessed Son's sake, in whose sweet and pleasing words, we say,	289	Priest		35
These words about the H. Scripture suite with what he writes	306	Valdesso		15
and Consid. 94. upon these words:	307	Valdesso		17
Although by other words of the same Psalme it is evident,	309	Valdesso		27
Evening words are not like to morning.	323	Proverbs		65
Good words are worth much, and cost little.	326	Proverbs		155
Good words quench more then a bucket of water.	329	Proverbs		263
Soft words quench more then cold water.	329	Proverbs	V	263
Vertue now is in herbs and stones and words onely.	337	Proverbs		478
Vertue now is in stones, herbs & words only.	337	Proverbs	V	478
Fine words dresse ill deedes.	337	Proverbs		479
Faire words make mee looke to my purse.	339	Proverbs		548
Of him that speakes ill, consider the life more then the words.	346	Proverbs		761
Words are women, deedes are men.	349	Proverbs		843
The words ending in Ique do mocke the Physician	357	Proverbs	D	1044
Words and feathers the wind carries away.	359	Proverbs	D	1103
whether it be in knowledge, or in fashion, or in words;	366	Letters		9
remember those admirable words of the Psalmist:	374	Letters		14
WORE				
And wore them for a jewell on her head,	173	Marie Magd		3
If all fooles wore white Caps, wee should seeme a flock of geese.	338	Proverbs		513
WORK				
To work for two, who brought himself to thrall.	17	Ch.-Porch		286
To work for two, that brought himself to thrall.	17	Ch.-Porch	W	286
And in suggestions fume and work,	45	Nature		8
Mans age is two houres work, or three:	48	Repentance		7
Let grace work too, and on my soul	60	Grace		15
O raise me then! poore bees, that work all day,	61	Praise 1		17
Who have a work, as well as they,	61	Praise 1		19
May both the work and workman show:	63	Mattens		19
Henceforth repose; your work is done.	64	Even-song		20
Whom none can work or wooe	72	Constancie		16
First with thy fire-work burn to dust	74	The Starre		9
The work of thy creation	82	Ungratef.		11
Then shall those powers, which work for grief,	90	Afflict.4		25
As flames do work and winde, when they ascend,	103	Jordan 2		13
My thoughts must work, but like a noiselesse sphere;	105	Conscience		8
Nor solid work, as false embroyderies;	111	Vanitie 2		4
Windes still work: it is their plot,	113	Businesse		9
Bees work for man; and yet they never bruise	118	Providence		65
Into a piece of timber work and winde,	126	Confession		8
And work up to thee; yet thou dost refuse.	139	Artillerie		20
Did worm and work within you more and more,	140	Ch.-rents		17
Disturb the work. O make me not their sport,	155	Glimpse		29
Sprung from thine eye, did work within my soul,	172	The Glance		14
Would warm and work it sweeter then before.	175	The Odour		20
Needs must work on me.	179	Discipline		28
Wounds willingly endur'd to work his blisse,	192	Ch.-Milit.		65
But did bewitch, and finely work each nation	195	Ch.-Milit.		193
all ye that work Iniquities.	220	Psalm VI	D	20
but after hee had fulfilled the work of Reconciliation,	225	Priest 1		7
Now Catechizing being a work of singular, and admirable benefit	230	Priest 5		12
besides this laborious work, a slighter forme of Catechizing,	230	Priest 5		15
presently falls to work, and seems to himselfe so as a Market-man is,	235	Priest 8		17
when they set themselves to work like brute beasts, never raising	247	Priest 14		32
when on the Lords day they do unnecessary servile work,	248	Priest 14		3
catechizing, singing of Psalms at their work, and on holy days;	248	Priest 14		34
First, for the authority of the work;	255	Priest 21		27
are to enter into this great work, he takes the more pains with them,	258	Priest 22		30
not onely for the benefit of the work, but also for the discharge	259	Priest 22		23
not fit (or un-weeldy) either to pray, or work, they are gluttons.	266	Priest 26		32
Not that all must presently work after dinner;	266	Priest 26		33
(For they rather must not work, especially Students, and those that	266	Priest 26		33
establisheth it, since they that have nothing, are fittest to work.	275	Priest 32		5
yet art thou our Creatour, and we thy work:	288	Priest		12
I was one of those that was deputed for the managing of that work,	302	Cornaro		17
Love makes one fitt for any work.	343	Proverbs		646
to me as soon as you can, that I may work the heads to my purpose.	370	Letters		7
but that I have both time and work to be Your extreme Servant,	370	Letters		14
bottom is wound up and laid ready for work in the New Jerusalem.	373	Letters		7
God Almighty prosper the Work.	379	Letters		10
work rather then doe nothing.	381	Woodnoth		24
but to chuse a higher work, as God gives me higher thoughts,	381	Woodnoth		25
the other profitt, the work I may change, the profitt, I am master	381	Woodnoth		31
WORKE				
for no perfect Artist ever yet hated his owne worke.	283	Priest 34		12

WORLD (cont'd)	PAGE	TITLE		LINE
While the world now rides by, now lags behinde.	72	Constancie		10
When the wide world runnes bias, from his will	73	Constancie		32
The World.	84	The World		T
But though the whole world turn to coal,	88	Vertue		15
Which on the world a true-love-knot may tie,	88	The Pearl		16
Betwixt this world and that of grace.	90	Afflict.4		6
And all to all the world besides:	91	Man		15
Oh mightie love! Man is one world, and hath	92	Man		47
That, as the world serves us, we may serve thee,	92	Man		53
That as the world to us is kind and free	92	Man	W	53
The world thinks all things bigg and tall	97	Charms & K	W	17
I see the world grows old, when as the heat	99	Decay		16
All Solomons sea of brasse and world of stone	106	Sion		17
My God, what is this world to me?	108	Home		32
This world of wo? hence all ye clouds, away,	108	Home		33
What is this weary world; this meat and drink,	108	Home		37
The merrie world did on a day	110	The Quip		1
And doth commit a world of sinne in one.	117	Providence		20
Thy cupboard serves the world: the meat is set,	118	Providence		49
Some call the world;	142	Pilgrimage	V	14
Indeed the world's thy book,	149	Longing		49
As serve him up, who all the world commands:	161	Priesthood		26
Of a lesse world? the greater is but small,	164	Grief		10
Dead to the world, keep house unknown.	166	The Flower		14
Since the condition of this world is frail,	170	Water-crs.		2
The world an ancient murderer is;	170	Self-cond.		10
Yet in this wretched world we toil,	176	The Foil		7
In this world of sugred lies,	177	The Rose		2
Parcel'd out to all the world.	187	Dooms-day		28
Who had subdued all the world for foes.	191	Ch.-Milit.	W	62
The world came both with hands and purses full	193	Ch.-Milit.		133
The world came in with hands and purses full	193	Ch.-Milit.	W	133
That the whole world did seem but the Popes mule.	196	Ch.-Milit.		204
Till such a darknesse do the world invade	196	Ch.-Milit.		230
The spacious world and Jurie to be seen.	196	Ch.-Milit.		234
Let the world reel, we and all ours stand sure,	439	Walton 5		9
The world anew: the sunne shall never rise	212	Bohemia	D	45
that the world should so much value wealth, which in the day of wrath	227	Priest 3		19
it being the Life of buying, and selling, and dealing in the world;	228	Priest 3		4
how much more in things of another world, where the well is deep,	228	Priest 4		35
For though the world is full of such composures, yet every mans own	230	Priest 5		3
but even to let the world sinke, so they do their duty;	232	Priest 6		16
In stead of the qualities of the world, he requires onely three	239	Priest 10		11
serve but the vices and vanities of the world, which he is to deny,	240	Priest 10		4
any entertainment, lest he goe into the world, esteeming it absurd,	241	Priest 10		20
providence and thrift of the great householder of the world:	241	Priest 10		26
How came this world to be as it is?	256	Priest 21		7
You said, God made the world;	256	Priest 21		12
of whom in stead of the qualities of the world, he asks no other,	260	Priest 23		31
whether any rule in the world be obscure, and how then should	263	Priest 24		3
and being in the world as he was, hath this undoubted pledge of his	269	Priest 28		17
and revenge to the children of the world, whom anothers ill	269	Priest 28		21
it being the greatest honor of this world, to do God and his chosen	270	Priest 29		10
Do well, and right, and let the world sinke.	270	Priest 29		23
Man would sit down at this world, God bids him sell it,	272	Priest 30		6
the carnall and wilfull man with the worm of the grave in this world,	272	Priest 30		13
No Common-wealth in the world hath a braver [better] Institution then	276	Priest 32		8
giving us one world in our selves, and another to serve us:	288	Priest		14
would have been an ornament to the world, and a comfort to their	291	Cornaro		4
If the world consist of order, if our corporall life depend	297	Cornaro		6
that the world pierceth not godly mens actions no more then Gods,	315	Valdesso		30
By the Saints of the world he every where understands the cunning	319	Valdesso	V	19
the cunning hypocrite who by the world is counted a very Saint,	319	Valdesso	V	20
and we meet with two sorts of these Saints of the world;	319	Valdesso	V	22
In the world who knowes not to swimme, goes to the bottome.	330	Proverbs		285
In the world who can not swimme, goe to the bottome.	330	Proverbs	V	285
He that hath lost his credit is dead to the world.	333	Proverbs		357
This world is nothing except it tend to another.	334	Proverbs		382
and the world his that enjoyes it.	337	Proverbs		476
Had you the world on your Chesse-bord,	344	Proverbs		701
He that deales in the world needes foure seeves.	351	Proverbs		899
Halfe the world knowes not how the other halfe lives.	351	Proverbs		907
Halfe the world knowes not how the other halfe lies.	351	Proverbs	V	907
If you would bee at ease, all the world is not.	355	Proverbs		1019
all the world would turne Carpenters (to make them crutches).	355	Proverbs		1020
The world is now adayes, God save the Conquerour.	358	Proverbs	D	1075
but every thing else in this world.	358	Proverbs	D	1077
The Divell divides the world between Atheisme and Superstition	359	Proverbs	D	1107
Though I had the best wit in the World, yet it would easily tyre me,	363	Letters		14
me unable to perform those Offices for which I came into the world,	373	Letters		10
of them will justifie you both to the world and your own Conscience:	373	Letters		16
things inwardly good to have an eye to the world may be pharisaicall:	380	Woodnoth		16
whose exceeding glory is equally round with the world it selfe:	442	Oration		11
WORLD-TRANSPOSING				
The six-daies world-transposing in an houre,	51	Prayer 1	V	7
WORLD'S				
Used, and wished, are the whole worlds light:	30	Sacrifice		110
The worlds, and thine:	71	Frailtie		10
The fruit of this, the next worlds bud,	75	Sunday		2
Man is the worlds high Priest: he doth present	117	Providence		13

	PAGE	TITLE	LINE
WORTHY			
A quest, I answer'd, worthy to be here:	189	Love 3	7
Worthy had bin, thou hadst not lost thine owne:	211	Bohemia D	2
because divers worthy young men have obliged me unto it.	291	Cornaro	8
so decent, and so holy, it is worthy by all means to be embraced;	300	Cornaro	4
and ever I learn somewhat which is worthy of my knowledge:	302	Cornaro	2
They favour learning whose actions are worthy of a learned pen.	357	Proverbs D	1061
WOT			
More favour then you wot of. Mark the end.	130	Love unkn.	63
WOU'D			
but, wou'd you divide and choose too?	373	Letters	1
WOULD			
Man would have been th' incloser: but since now	7	Ch.-Porch	20
Sure to be crosse he would shift feet and face.	7	Ch.-Porch	24
Which it would poure on thee, upon the floore.	7	Ch.-Porch	28
Which would throw me there, if I keep the round.	7	Ch.-Porch	30
And spares himself, but would his taylor chide.	13	Ch.-Porch	180
Would have their tale beleeved for their oathes,	14	Ch.-Porch	183
Of thicker stuffe, which would endure a shake.	15	Ch.-Porch	226
Who would not haste, nay give, to see the show?	22	Ch.-Porch	390
What I taught: Comments would the text confound.	28	Sacrifice	55
And never yet, whom I would punish, miss'd:	30	Sacrifice	131
And never yet, whom he would punish, miss'd:	30	Sacrifice W	131
Or feel his part, he would not cease to kneel,	33	Sacrifice	210
Or feel his share, he would not cease to kneel,	33	Sacrifice W	210
Who would know Sinne, let him repair	37	The Agonie	7
Full of rebellion, I would die,	45	Nature	1
To fruit or shade: at least some bird would trust	48	Afflict.1	59
For sinn would faine remove the dearth	59	Whitsunday W	19
Thy house would but a dungeon prove,	60	Grace	6
Thy great house would a dungeon prove,	60	Grace W	6
They would discolour thy most bloudy sweat.	62	Afflict.2	10
Armies of blessings would contend & vye	66	Ch.-lock W	4
But when it would appeare to others eye,	68	Content	11
(For he would not) as they beheld the grace	70	Humilitie	18
I would addresse	78	Ang.&Sts.	8
Chiefly to thee would I my soul unfold:	78	Ang.&Sts.	15
My soul would stirre	78	Employm.2	2
Then would I mount up instantly	79	Employm.2 W	23
Each took his way; some would to pleasures go,	80	Deniall	8
I would not use a friend, as I use Thee.	93	Unkindness	5
Would he have gold? I lend it instantly;	93	Unkindness	12
Nor would I use a friend, as I use Thee.	94	Unkindness	20
My minde would be extreamly stirr'd	95	Submission	3
I would do well, yet sinne the hand hath got:	96	Justice 1	10
When he would speak;	98	Mortific.	28
Is my God this way? no, they would reply:	99	Decay	8
They would not have their actions scann'd,	100	Miserie	21
They quarrell thee, and would give over	100	Miserie	25
Who would, to be thy foes.	100	Miserie	30
I and deare prayer would together dwell,	103	Prayer 2	23
If some kinde man would thrust his heart	105	Obedience	42
Thraldome from those, who would not at a feast	107	Home	21
And he would needs a comfort be,	111	The Quip	18
Would thou hadst no faults or fears!	113	Businesse	7
Would thou hadst no flesh and bones!	113	Businesse	13
And my clay my creature would	115	Dialogue	27
Beasts fain would sing; birds dittie to their notes;	117	Providence	9
Trees would be tuning on their native lute	117	Providence	10
But robs a thousand who would praise thee fain,	117	Providence	19
Thy skill and art, what musick would it be!	118	Providence	40
Would show a root, that gives expressions!	119	Providence	76
But where one man would have me grinde it,	122	Time	5
What it would come to at the worst	123	Gratefulnes	11
Gift upon gift, much would have more,	124	Gratefulnes	15
There would be no commerce,	127	Giddinesse	22
No sale or bargain passe: all would disperse,	127	Giddinesse	23
I would say thorns. Deare, could my heart not break,	130	Love unkn.	52
Who fain would have you be new, tender, quick.	131	Love unkn.	70
Sure they would move	132	The Storm	4
For he is Power: and sure he would;	133	The Method	7
Late when I would have something done,	134	The Method	22
Do as ye would be done unto.	135	Divinitie	18
And flesh would fail,	136	Ephes.	33
They would great frosts and snows destroy:	138	The Size	40
With thine own clay. But I would parley fain:	139	Artillerie	27
And ev'n all Africk; would at least I might	140	Ch.-rents	28
Fain would I here have made abode,	142	Pilgrimage	9
Some call the would;	142	Pilgrimage V	14
He that would know	145	Discharge	37
As mens returns, what would become of fools?	147	Offering	2
And when they ask'd, what he would wear;	151	The Bag	16
Pickt here and there a crumme, and would not die;	154	Glimpse	17
If I without thee would be mine,	157	Clasping	9
That would contain much more.	158	Praise 3	30
Sure it would carrie with it ev'n my heart,	159	Jos.coat	7
And both would runne untill they found a biere	159	Jos.coat	8
He would adore my gifts in stead of me,	160	The Pulley	13
In thy just censures; fain would I draw nigh,	160	Priesthood	4
What I would do for thee, if once my grones	165	The Crosse	15
Who would have thought my shrivel'd heart	166	The Flower	8

WOULD (cont'd)

	PAGE	TITLE		LINE
Who would be more,	167	The Flower		47
Somewhat it fain would say:	168	a true Hymn		3
With pensive humblenesse would live and tread:	173	Marie Magd		6
Would warm and work it sweeter then before.	175	The Odour		20
This breathing would with gains by sweetning me	175	The Odour		26
God took bloud, and needs would be	182	Banquet		34
(For no lesse Harbingers would serve then they)	192	Ch.-Milit.		84
He grew a gallant, and would needs foretell	193	Ch.-Milit.		129
Nay, he became a poet, and would serve	193	Ch.-Milit.		131
To this great lotterie, and all would pull.	193	Ch.-Milit.		134
As the old heathen would deem prodigies.	194	Ch.-Milit.		154
The old debauched ruffian would turn writer.	194	Ch.-Milit.		164
Would you find?	208	J. Danvers	D	6
To curbe some Rebell teares, which faine would flow,	213	Bohemia	D	58
Blest is the man that never would	214	Psalm I	D	1
When the Apostles would have called down fire from Heaven,	229	Priest 4		12
that the Lord would be pleased to sanctifie them all, that they may	235	Priest 8		28
and that the good God would pardon all those, who come with lesse	235	Priest 8		30
from the improvement of things, which otherwise would be lost.	241	Priest 10		24
which otherwise they would reckon upon, and turn to idlenesse.	245	Priest 12		5
In this course the order of the Catechisme would be kept,	256	Priest 21		5
This order being used to one, would be a little varyed to another.	256	Priest 21		16
He asked him again, what he would do, if he were in a ditch?	257	Priest 21		4
he could not but say, he would hast out of it as fast as he could.	257	Priest 21		7
God is wonderfully to be seen, one thing would be carefully observed;	261	Priest 23		28
The application of the ground would be infinite;	265	Priest 26		13
Yet Phisicians bid those that would live in health, not keep	267	Priest 26		10
so long at it, that they would have fainted, had they returned empty,	267	Priest 26		23
without which supply the corne would instantly dry up, as a river	271	Priest 30		6
instantly dry up, as a river would if the fountain were stopped.	271	Priest 30		7
Man would sit down at this world, God bids him sell it,	272	Priest 30		6
Could men finde out this delight, they would seldome be from home;	275	Priest 32		35
If we would judg ourselves, we should not be judged;	280	Priest 34		30
and if we would bound our selves, we should not be bounded.	280	Priest 34		31
how he that would beleeve a Divinity, if he had been at the Creation	281	Priest 34		28
whom the Law would have defamed, except he also do it out of rancour.	287	Priest 37		29
would have been an ornament to the world, and a comfort to their	291	Cornaro		3
to that exigent, that there would be no help for me, but Death,	292	Cornaro		15
what case I was, they concluded that I would die within three dayes.	295	Cornaro		3
Who would beleeve that old wine should hurt my stomack,	297	Cornaro		31
which is alreadie burdened with a disease, would be wholly oppressed.	299	Cornaro		34
would I change age and constitution with them who follow their	303	Cornaro		11
because I would doe nothing negligently that you commit unto mee;	304	Valdesso		5
Churches sake, to whom by Printing it I would have you consecrate it.	304	Valdesso		9
obscured in his own country he would have to flourish in this land	304	Valdesso		14
I would Print it, that with it the honour of my Lord might be	305	Valdesso		7
it were the Authors opinion, yet the truth of it would be examined.	307	Valdesso		22
wondrous things of his Lawes, and that he would make them his study.	309	Valdesso		27
but the truth of the Doctrine would be examined, however it may passe	312	Valdesso		1
motion (as S. Paul had when hee would have preached in Asia),	313	Valdesso		16
and that by restraining him from what he would not have him doe.	313	Valdesso		23
but however he would have them attend to it till that time,	318	Valdesso		20
point it should, which if it did, it would doe more, then it does.	319	Valdesso		11
this were the Authors opinion, yet the truth of it would be examined.	319	Valdesso	V	16
If yee would know a knave, give him a staffe.	321	Proverbs		19
Were there no fooles, badd ware would not passe.	323	Proverbs		66
Were there no hearers, there would be no backbiters.	323	Proverbs		69
Who would doe ill ne're wants occasion.	324	Proverbs		116
There would bee no great ones if there were no little ones.	331	Proverbs		292
There would bee no great ones if there were no mean ones.	331	Proverbs	V	292
Hee that would deceive the fox, must rise betimes.	333	Proverbs	V	351
Hee that gives thee a bone, would not have thee die.	333	Proverbs		355
If you would know secrets, looke them in griefe or pleasure.	333	Proverbs		367
If folly were griefe every house would weepe.	334	Proverbs		370
Hee that would bee well old, must bee old betimes.	334	Proverbs		371
Would you know what mony is, Go borrow some.	334	Proverbs		374
He that blames would buy.	335	Proverbs		410
He that would be well, needs not goe from his owne house.	336	Proverbs		442
If the wise erred not, it would goe hard with fooles.	338	Proverbs		510
If wise men erred not, it would goe hard with fooles.	338	Proverbs	V	510
Hee that would have what hee hath not,	340	Proverbs	V	559
If great men would have care of little ones,	344	Proverbs		697
both would last long.	344	Proverbs		697
If things were to be done twice, all would be wise.	344	Proverbs		700
If all things might be done twice, all would be wise.	343	Proverbs	V	700
Let all live as they would die.	345	Proverbs		725
He that doth what he should not, shall feele what he would not.	347	Proverbs		783
Hee that is throwne would ever wrestle.	347	Proverbs		797
Hee that would be a Gentleman, let him goe to an assault.	350	Proverbs		878
The great would have none great and the little all little.	352	Proverbs		946
that a man would desire straight to bee buried there.	353	Proverbs		969
He that gives me small gifts would have me live.	354	Proverbs		1000
If gold knew what gold is, gold would get gold I wis.	354	Proverbs		1012
If you would bee at ease, all the world is not.	355	Proverbs		1019
all the world would turne Carpenters (to make them crutches).	355	Proverbs		1020
A man would live in Italy (a place of pleasure)	357	Proverbs	D	1047
but he would chuse to dy in Spain (where they say	357	Proverbs	D	1047
if it were not begun on particular ends, it would last).	361	Proverbs	D	1160
yet it would easily tyre me, to find out variety of thanks	363	Letters		14
in that I apprehend what my Friends would have been forward to say,	364	Letters		20

WOULD (cont'd)	PAGE	TITLE		LINE
and whereof I would not have you ignorant.	366	Letters		2
for I would have you, even in speeches, to observe so much,	366	Letters		9
I dare say she would make good her promise of taking five or six	367	Letters		2
which the King would so appropriate to himselfe, as that either his	368	Letters		10
would quickly make good my wish but that my employment does fix me	372	Letters		18
I wrote to him that I would have both or neither;	375	Letters		12
that if one only came, the comfort intended would prove a discomfort.	375	Letters		17
and would not have to part them yet, till I take some opportunity	375	Letters		20
it were a great good deed, and I would have her conveyed to you.	375	Letters		32
but he told her Grace, that he would by no meanes do so, urging,	379	Letters		7
your withdrawing it shold doe so, it would trouble your conscience.	381	Woodnoth		12
or whom would you please?	381	Woodnoth		19
I besech Sir John Danvers that he would be pleased to be Overseer	382	G.H.'s Will		31
entreating that you would a while lay aside those warlike lookes,	442	Oration		2
WOULD'ST				
So Isa. 64. Oh that thou would'st rent the Heavens, that thou wouldst	234	Priest 7		2
WOULDST				
If thou art nothing, think what thou wouldst bee	10	Ch.-Porch	W	90
Thou wouldst extend me to some good,	57	Employm. 1		2
Give to thy Mother, what thou wouldst allow	86	Lent		5
Now thou wouldst taste our miserie.	97	Afflict.5		12
Wouldst thou not look?	133	The Method		12
Wouldst thou his laws of fasting disanull?	138	The Size		15
Wouldst thou both eat thy cake, and have it?	138	The Size		18
Busie enquiring heart, what wouldst thou know?	144	Discharge		1
While thou didst wink and wouldst not see.	153	The Collar		26
What is thy aim? wouldst thou unlock the doore	155	Assurance		15
Wouldst thou raise devils? I see, I know,	155	Assurance		17
that thou would'st rent the Heavens, that thou wouldst come down, &c.	234	Priest 7		3
Be what thou wouldst seeme to be.	345	Proverbs		724
WOUND				
Shame tears my soul, my bodie many a wound;	33	Sacrifice		217
My soule is full of shame, my flesh of wound:	33	Sacrifice	W	217
Of those, who did themselves through their side wound,	59	Whitsunday		20
Did through my bodie wound my minde,	65	Ch.-mus.		2
Who want herbs for their wound.	76	Sunday		42
While they do wound and prick my soul.	90	Afflict.4		12
While they do wound and pinke my soul.	90	Afflict.4	W	12
Lord, thou dost wound me, yet thou dost relieve me:	95	Justice 1		3
Thy long deferrings wound me to the quick,	107	Home		3
but to have the skill of healing a wound, or helping the sick.	260	Priest 23		32
An ill wound is cured, not an ill name.	329	Proverbs		245
whose bottom is wound up and laid ready for work in the New	373	Letters		6
& neither to scandalize them, nor wound our owne reputation.	380	Woodnoth		19
WOUNDED				
Wounded I sing, tormented I indite,	159	Jos.coat		1
WOUNDEST				
Lord, thou didst make me, yet thou woundest me;	95	Justice 1		2
WOUNDETH				
Unto thy hands, it woundeth to the quick.	13	Ch.-Porch		168
WOUNDING				
Wounding my heart	90	Afflict.4		8
WOUNDS				
Curing all wounds, but mine; all, but my fears:	27	Sacrifice		27
Oh King of wounds! how shall I grieve for thee,	35	Thanksgvng		3
King of all wounds, how shall I grieve for thee,	35	Thanksgvng	W	3
And yet thy wounds still my attempts defie,	36	Reprisall		7
Thy whips, thy nails, thy wounds, thy woes,	39	Good Fri.		26
All sorts of wounds; of such strange force it is.	147	Offering		21
But seems to yeeld Christ hath the greater wounds,	191	Ch.-Milit.		64
But seems to yeeld Christ had the greater wounds,	191	Ch.-Milit.	W	64
Wounds willingly endur'd to work his blisse,	192	Ch.-Milit.		65
and healing of all wounds and sores with her owne hands;	239	Priest 10		15
and tending their wounds, and sending his charity by them	239	Priest 10		26
WOVEN				
and then woven into Sermons, which will make them appear exceeding	234	Priest 7		23
and woven into his discourse, at severall times and occasions,	283	Priest 34		3
WRANGLE				
For which ye wrangle, made them turn their frown	71	Humilitie		28
WRANGLER				
I here exclude the wrangler from thy treasure.	104	Obedience		15
I here shutt out the wrangler from thy treasure.	104	Obedience	W	15
WRANGLERS				
Turn out these wranglers, which defile thy seat:	136	Familie		7
WRANGLING				
The parter of my wrangling feares,	75	Sunday	W	4
The partner of my wrangling feares,	75	Sunday	WC	4
WRAP				
And wrap me in a gown.	47	Afflict.1		40
And wrap their policies in thy decree,	190	Ch.-Milit.		6
And did this mysterie wrap up and fold	192	Ch.-Milit.		94
WRAPT				
Wrapt in nights mantle, stole into a manger;	81	Christmas		10
One life is wrapt In flesh, and tends to earth.	84	Coloss.		5
To fine folkes a little ill finely wrapt.	324	Proverbs		117
WRASTLING				
Much wrastling, many a combate, this deare end,	164	The Crosse		8
WRATH				
Thy wrath for sinne, as when mans sight was dimme,	49	Faith		2
With the turn'd viall of thy bitter wrath!	83	Sighs & Gr.		20

	PAGE	TITLE		LINE
WRATH (cont'd)				
Throw away thy wrath:	178	Discipline		2
Then let wrath remove;	179	Discipline		17
Throw away thy wrath.	179	Discipline		32
Then shall He speak to them in wrath,	215	Psalm II	D	11
O kiss the Son, lest he be wrath,	216	Psalm II	D	29
Rebuke me not in wrath, O Lord,	219	Psalm VI	D	1
Arise in wrath, O Lord, advance	221	Psalm VII	D	21
which in the day of wrath hath not one dramme of comfort for us.	227	Priest 3		20
God gives his wrath by weight, and without weight his mercy.	359	Proverbs	D	1115
Take heed of the wrath of a mighty man,	360	Proverbs	D	1148
WRATHFULL				
Let not thy wrathfull power	144	Complaining		16
WREATH				
A Wreath.	185	A Wreath		T
For this poore wreath, give thee a crown of praise.	185	A Wreath		12
WREATHED				
A wreathed garland of deserved praise,	185	A Wreath		1
WRENCH				
Unpinne, or wrench from giving all their due.	72	Constancie		5
WRESTLE (see also wrastling)				
Hee that is throwne would ever wrestle.	347	Proverbs		797
WRETCH				
Will great God measure with a wretch?	55	Temper 1		15
On purpose from the ventrous wretch;	85	Vanitie 1		11
Ah wretch! what verse	102	Miserie		65
To thy wretch so full of stains;	114	Dialogue		7
WRETCHED				
Ah wretched man	102	Miserie	W	65
Of wretched earth. Where once I scorn'd to stand,	161	Priesthood		15
Yet in this wretched world we toil,	176	The Foil		7
'Tis hard to be wretched, but worse to be knowne so.	340	Proverbs		577
WRETCHEDLY				
Thou hadst di'd most wretchedly;	113	Businesse		21
WRETCHEDNESSE				
What wretchednesse can give him any room,	193	Ch.-Milit.		117
WRETCHES				
Almightie Judge, how shall poore wretches brook	187	Judgement		1
WRING				
Then will I wring it with a sigh or grone,	157	Praise 3		5
WRINGING				
And washt, and wrung: the very wringing yet	129	Love unkn.		17
WRINGS				
The wearer knowes, where the shoe wrings.	338	Proverbs		491
WRIT				
Was writ in stone; so thou, which also art	41	Sepulchre		18
So many joyes I writ down for my part,	46	Afflict.1		3
Writ by a friend, and with his bloud;	75	Sunday		4
I writ thy purpose long ago.	155	Assurance		18
To deal in holy Writ.	160	Priesthood		12
He writ; when 's hand could write no more,	439	Walton 5		13
they are not understood but with the same Spirit that writ them.	228	Priest 4		32
of old was praised, that at the age of 73 yeares he writ a Tragedie;	302	Cornaro		34
Nay they are purposely recorded in holy Writ.	316	Valdesso		5
those many Love-poems, that are daily writ and consecrated to Venus;	363	Letters		7
nor to bewail that so few are writ, that look towards God and Heaven.	363	Letters		9
WRITE				
Write on the others, Here lies such a one.	20	Ch.-Porch		342
Write, So much giv'n to God; thou shalt be heard.	21	Ch.-Porch		382
Remember that thou once didst write in stone.	38	The Sinner		14
Since bloud is fittest, Lord, to write	39	Good Fri.		21
To write thy sorrows in, as blood	39	Good Fri.	W	22
My heart hath store, write there, where in	39	Good Fri.		23
Write thee great God, and me a childe:	44	H. Bapt.2		7
Doth warm our hands, and make them write of love.	54	Love 1		14
To write a verse or two is all the praise,	61	Praise 1		1
O write in brasse, My God upon a tree	94	Unkindness		22
When she doth write.	109	Brit. Ch.		6
And write for sweet, prove a most sowre displeasure.	111	Vanitie 2		6
Strongly and sweetly movest, shall I write,	116	Providence		2
Is mine to write, as it is yours to raise.	117	Providence		24
If ye have any thing to send or write,	152	The Bag		31
And hold my hand, while I did write.	156	Assurance		30
After so many deaths I live and write;	166	The Flower		37
To make his verse, or write a hymne in kinde.	168	a true Hymn		15
And if I please him, I write fine and wittie.	176	Forerunners		12
This by my picture, in my book I write:	183	The Posie		6
He writ; when 's hand could write no more,	439	Walton 5		13
When my dear Friend, could write no more,	439	Walton 6		1
O write it! O brand it in our foreheads for ever:	288	Priest		18
nor can I write coldly in that, wherein consisteth the making good	364	Letters		16
Now I write to you, Sir, because to you I have ever opened my heart;	365	Letters		23
and write you freely to mee in your letters, for I am your ever	366	Letters		20
for I am enjoined to write to you by Sir John Danvers, to which mine	367	Letters		28
I cannot yet find leisure to write to my Lord, or Sir Benjamin	370	Letters		29
although you offer more, yet you will doe, as you write, that alsoe.	375	Letters		7
You write very lovingly that all your things are mine.	378	Letters		21
WRITER				
The old debauched ruffian would turn writer.	194	Ch.-Milit.		164
WRITERS				
the Schoolmen, and the later Writers, or a good proportion of all,	229	Priest 5		32

YE (cont'd)	PAGE	TITLE		LINE
Do as ye would be done unto.	135	Divinitie		18
For death is drie as dust. Yet if ye part,	135	Ephes.		10
If ye have any thing to send or write,	152	The Bag		31
And use in baptisme, while ye pine and die:	152	The Jews		4
O who will give me tears? Come all ye springs,	164	Grief		1
Verses, ye are too fine a thing, too wise	164	Grief		13
Good men ye be, to leave me my best room,	176	Forerunners		7
But will ye leave me thus? when ye before	176	Forerunners		14
For, Thou art still my God, is all that ye	177	Forerunners		32
Come ye hither all, whose taste	179	Invitation		1
Come ye hither all, whom wine	180	Invitation		7
Weep what ye have drunk amisse,	180	Invitation		10
Which before ye drink is bloud.	180	Invitation		12
Come ye hither all, whom pain	180	Invitation		13
Come ye hither all, whom joy	180	Invitation		19
While ye graze without your bounds:	180	Invitation		21
Come ye hither all, whose love	180	Invitation		25
Each one whispring, Live ye brother?	186	Dooms-day		6
Now therefore, O ye Kings, be wise,	216	Psalm II	D	25
be learned, ye that judge the earth:	216	Psalm II	D	26
and straight ye perish from the way:	216	Psalm II	D	30
How long will ye, vain men, convert	217	Psalm IV	D	7
How long will ye seek after lies,	217	Psalm IV	D	9
all ye that work Iniquities.	220	Psalm VI	D	20
one to the other, that ye may be a heavenly comfort, to his prayse,	378	Letters		26
YEA				
Yea, when both rocks and all things shall disband,	156	Assurance		34
Yea, in deaths shadie black abode	173	23 Psalme		13
Yea, shout for joy for evermore,	219	Psalm V	D	37
Yea, he my prayer from on high	220	Psalm VI	D	23
Yea, have not oft deliver'd him	221	Psalm VII	D	13
yea, let him to the Clay	221	Psalm VII	D	18
The Parsons yea is yea, and nay nay;	228	Priest 3		10
yea though they be tenants, or otherwise ingaged to the delinquent:	270	Priest 29		20
yea, if he will give his minde to those things which he should,	297	Cornaro		22
they who finde benefit in these meats, may, yea ought to use them:	300	Cornaro		11
yea, sometimes of Ten Shillings:	365	Letters		12
yea, indeed of all, both Courtly, Militarie, Academicall.	441	Oration		27
YEAR (see also yeer)				
exercises, either from the time of the year, or from the State,	235	Priest 8		35
so that in the compasse of the year, hee hath them all with him,	243	Priest 11		19
if not duly once a month, yet at least five or six times in the year;	259	Priest 22		21
who being to present all that receive not thrice a year;	259	Priest 22		25
is the encouragement of learning all the year after, except my cousin	375	Letters		29
YEAR'S				
yet I am scarce able with much ado to make one half years allowance,	365	Letters		10
YEARE				
Ev'n with the yeare: but age, if it will hit,	13	Ch.-Porch		158
Who cannot live on twentie pound a yeare,	13	Ch.-Porch		176
The world and I will quarrell; and the yeare	36	Thanksgvng		37
Marking his grave, and thawing ev'ry yeare,	98	Mortific.		26
There is no fruitfull yeare, but that which brings	108	Home		57
Lies all the yeare,	150	Longing		81
Is the yeare onely lost to me?	153	The Collar		13
Giving new names and numbers to the yeare.	192	Ch.-Milit.		72
Gardens of Gods, which ev'ry yeare did grow,	193	Ch.-Milit.		108
Nay, it shall ev'ry yeare decrease and fade;	196	Ch.-Milit.		229
Whereby one may foretell, what sinnes next yeare	197	Ch.-Milit.		245
[afflicted] from the thirtie fifth yeare of my age to the fortieth,	292	Cornaro		2
within lesse then one yeare (although it may seem to some incredible)	292	Cornaro		36
within lesse then a yeare I was not onely freed from all those evils	293	Cornaro		20
and the season of the yeare was winter and most cold aire.	296	Cornaro		27
Some times of the yeare I enjoy the pleasure of the Euganean hills,	301	Cornaro		17
Mend your cloathes, and you may hold out this yeare.	324	Proverbs		100
A snow yeare, a rich yeare.	325	Proverbs		125
It's a poore stake that cannot stand one yeare in the ground.	340	Proverbs		553
He that lives not well one yeare, sorrowes seven after.	340	Proverbs		562
The chiefe disease that raignes this yeare is folly.	346	Proverbs		765
The yeare doth nothing else but open and shut.	351	Proverbs		901
Once a yeare a man may say: On his conscience.	353	Proverbs		971
YEARE'S				
Hee will spend a whole yeares rent at one meales meate.	331	Proverbs		305
Brugensis uppon the Scripture and his halfe yeares wages aforehand,	382	G.H.'s Will		19
Bostocke St. Augustines workes and his halfe yeares wages aforehand,	382	G.H.'s Will		21
YEARELY				
but also afterwards I fell not into that yearely disease,	293	Cornaro		22
YEARES				
That three yeares hence, if I survive,	36	Thanksgvng		32
But with my yeares sorrow did twist and grow,	47	Afflict.1		23
But with my yeares sorrows did twist and grow,	47	Afflict.1	W	23
Or if some yeares with it escape,	73	Afflict.3		10
Have done these twentie hundred yeares, and more:	89	The Pearl		25
Have done these many hundred yeares, and more:	89	The Pearl	W	25
So many yeares baptiz'd, and not appeare?	108	Home		27
Sev'n yeares ago: one vogue and vein,	128	Bunch Gr.		4
Or ten yeares hence,	186	Death		6
Compare with ancient times and purer yeares;	196	Ch.-Milit.		227
This I found by experience, when I was seventie yeares old:	294	Cornaro		36
considering what an orderly life I had led for many yeares together,	295	Cornaro		8
About foure yeares since, I was led by the advice of Physicians,	295	Cornaro		19

	PAGE	TITLE		LINE
YEARES (cont'd)				
and that I had fcr many yeares continued in good health,	295	Cornaro		26
to reason, that my yeares increasing, and strength decreasing,	295	Cornaro		29
although I was now seventie eight yeares old, and my bodie spent	296	Cornaro		26
For the Temperance of so many yeares spent all ill humours,	296	Cornaro		32
whereof the one kept me well for many yeares;	297	Cornaro		5
that they prolong their life even to a hundred yeares and more,	298	Cornaro		16
Appetite (though they live ten yeares lesse then otherwise they	298	Cornaro		27
of how great moment ten yeares are in mature age, wherein wisdome	298	Cornaro		29
and those ten yeares, which they set at naught in regard of their	298	Cornaro		34
both of old times and later yeares, it is no such thing which may	299	Cornaro		6
because that after one is once sixtie five yeares old, all the time	300	Cornaro		29
because at these yeares (viz. 83) I have made a most pleasant	302	Cornaro		28
of old was praised, that at the age of 73 yeares he writ a Tragedie;	302	Cornaro		34
or lesse my self, who being ten yeares older have made a Comedie?	302	Cornaro		35
I by the experience of so many yeares have learned to give way	303	Cornaro		20
In good yeares corne is hay, in ill yeares straw is corne.	328	Proverbs		216
YEARS				
up your Children that they have attain'd to the years of Discretion,	373	Letters		13
being more beggarly now than I have been these many years,	376	Letters		1
YEE				
If yee would know a knave, give him a staffe.	321	Proverbs		19
Yet doe not yee contemne these our slight glories, which wee raise	442	Oration		38
YEELD				
But seems to yeeld Christ hath the greater wounds,	191	Ch.-Milit.		64
But seems to yeeld Christ had the greater wounds,	191	Ch.-Milit.	W	64
YEELDED				
at length I yeelded, and permitted the quantitie of meat to be	296	Cornaro		7
YEELDING				
Valour that parlies is neare yeelding.	341	Proverbs		586
YEER				
and how every one profits, comparing this yeer with the last:	240	Priest 10		38
So that if a farmer should depend upon God all the yeer,	271	Priest 30		29
the Kingdome into Portions, which every yeer he surveys peece-meal.	277	Priest 32		8
YEERE				
Say no ill of the yeere, till it be past.	331	Proverbs		297
As the yeere is, your pot must seeth.	332	Proverbs		335
The constancy of the benefits of the yeere	347	Proverbs		773
France is a meddow that cuts thrice a yeere.	350	Proverbs		892
YEERES				
Yeeres know more then bookes.	351	Proverbs		928
YEERS				
The time of every ones first receiving is not so much by yeers,	258	Priest 22		33
YERROW				
adders tongue, yerrow, melilot, and Saint Johns wort made into	262	Priest 23		6
YES				
Echo. Yes.	188	Heaven		12
yes, I say again rejoyce;	374	Letters		23
YESTERDAY				
Written above there? Yesterday	133	The Method		14
YET				
Yet not mine neither: for from thee they came,	5	Dedication		2
Yet wedding marrs thy fortune, fast & pray:	7	Ch.-Porch	W	14
Yet, if thou sinne in wine or wantonnesse,	8	Ch.-Porch		49
Flie idlenesse, which yet thou canst not flie	9	Ch.-Porch		79
Yet in thy thriving still misdoubt some evil;	13	Ch.-Porch		163
One common waight will press downe both, yet so	13	Ch.-Porch	W	167
By any art, yet to be purchased.	13	Ch.-Porch		172
If yet thou love game at so deere a rate,	14	Ch.-Porch		199
The fine may spare these well, yet not go lesse.	16	Ch.-Porch		238
That temper gives them theirs, and yet doth take	16	Ch.-Porch		254
Be not thine own worm: yet such jealousie,	16	Ch.-Porch		261
Yet be not surety, if thou be a father.	17	Ch.-Porch		277
Submit to love; but yet not more then all.	17	Ch.-Porch		284
Yet publick hath more promises, more love:	22	Ch.-Porch		398
Yet publick has more promises, more love:	22	Ch.-Porch	W	398
Though God do hedge us in, yet who is holy?	24	Ch.-Porch		450
Yet my Disciples sleep: I cannot gain	27	Sacrifice		29
Of faith, but furie: yet at their commands	28	Sacrifice		46
But yet their friendship is my enmitie:	29	Sacrifice		75
Yet still they shout, and crie, and stop their eares,	30	Sacrifice		105
Ah! how they scourge me! yet my tendernesse	30	Sacrifice		125
Doubles each lash: and yet their bitternesse	30	Sacrifice		126
And never yet, whom I would punish, miss'd:	30	Sacrifice		131
And never yet, whom he would punish, miss'd:	30	Sacrifice	W	131
Yet for twelve heav'nly legions I could call:	31	Sacrifice		155
Yet since mans scepters are as frail as reeds,	32	Sacrifice		177
Yet since in frailty, cruelty, shrowd turns,	32	Sacrifice	W	177
Yet by my subjects am condemn'd to die	34	Sacrifice		234
But more with malice: yet, when they did call,	34	Sacrifice		238
Oh King of grief! (a title strange, yet true,	35	Thanksgvng		1
King of all Grief (a title strange, yet true,	35	Thanksgvng	W	1
And yet thy wounds still my attempts defie,	36	Reprisall		7
Yet by confession will I come	37	Reprisall		13
Yet few there are that sound them; Sinne and Love.	37	The Agonie		6
Yet Lord restore thine image, heare my call:	38	The Sinner		12
So many hearts on earth, and yet not one	40	Sepulchre		3
Thousands of toyes dwell there, yet out of doore	40	Sepulchre		7
Yet do we still persist as we began,	41	Sepulchre		21
Yet though my flours be lost, they say	42	Easter	W	27
Yet thou with sicknesses and shame	43	East.wings	W	12

YET (cont'd)

	PAGE	TITLE		LINE
My flesh get on; yet let her sister	44	H. Bapt.2		12
Yet all these fences and their whole aray	46	Sinne 1		13
Yet all these fences with one bosome sinn	46	Sinne 1	W	13
Yet, for I threatned oft the siege to raise,	47	Afflict.1		43
Yet lest perchance I should too happie be	48	Afflict.1		49
Thine own gift good, yet me from my wayes taking.	48	Afflict.1		54
Yet, though thou troublest me, I must be meek;	48	Afflict.1		61
Yet can these not get over to my soul,	52	H.Commun.		13
Yet take thy way; for sure thy way is best:	55	Temper 1		21
His arm is short; yet with a sling	61	Praise 1		11
Yet studies them, not him by whom they be.	63	Mattens		16
We paint the devil foul, yet he	63	Sinne 2		2
Yet as in sleep we see foul death, and live:	63	Sinne 2		9
Yet still thou goest on,	64	Even-song		17
Yet say sometimes, God help poore Kings.	65	Ch.-mus.		8
Yet as cold hands are angrie with the fire,	66	Ch.-lock	W	5
Yet heare, O God, onely for his blouds sake	66	Ch.-lock		9
For though sinnes plead too, yet like stones they make	66	Ch.-lock		11
Yet in thy temple thou dost him afford	67	Windows		3
Which can let loose to a crown, and yet with pleasure	69	Content		15
Onely thy Chronicle is lost; and yet	69	Content		25
Nor a good sword, nor yet a lute:	69	Quidditie		4
Nor a good sword, not yet a lute:	69	Quidditie	W	4
But though men fail him, yet his part doth play.	73	Constancie		30
Yet, if thou wilt from thence depart,	74	The Starre		5
If not upon his head, yet in his hands:	77	Ang.&Sts.		5
Yet no hearing.	80	Deniall	W	20
O Thou, whose glorious, yet contracted light,	81	Christmas		9
But his deare God? who yet his glorious law	85	Vanitie 1		23
Yet to go part of that religious way,	87	Lent		32
Yet are we bid, Be holy ev'n as he.	87	Lent		35
Yet Lord instruct us to improve our fast	87	Lent		43
Yet I love thee.	88	The Pearl		10
Yet I love thee.	88	The Pearl		20
Yet I love thee.	89	The Pearl		30
Yet through the labyrinths, not my groveling wit,	89	The Pearl		37
Yet through these labyrinths, not my groveling wit,	89	The Pearl	W	37
And more: He is a tree, yet bears no fruit;	91	Man		8
And more: He is a tree, yet bears more fruit;	91	Man	W	8
A beast, yet is, or should be more:	91	Man		9
Yet can a friend what thou hast done fulfill?	94	Unkindness		21
Yet use I not my foes, as I use thee.	94	Unkindness		25
Yet sugring the suspicion.	94	Life		12
Lord, thou didst make me, yet thou woundest me;	95	Justice 1		2
Lord, thou dost wound me, yet thou dost relieve me:	95	Justice 1		3
Lord, thou relievest, yet I die by thee:	95	Justice 1		4
Lord, thou dost kill me, yet thou dost reprieve me.	95	Justice 1		5
For, I do praise thee, yet I praise thee not:	96	Justice 1		8
My prayers mean thee, yet my prayers stray:	96	Justice 1		9
I would do well, yet sinne the hand hath got:	96	Justice 1		10
My soul doth love thee, yet it loves delay.	96	Justice 1		11
To make us thine: yet that we might not part,	97	Afflict.5		10
As yet to spare:	99	Mortific.		34
Yet Lord, instruct us so to die,	99	Mortific.		35
Where yet both Sinne and Satan, thy old foes,	99	Decay		13
His house still burns, and yet he still doth sing,	100	Miserie		4
Where never yet came moth.	100	Miserie		18
Yet either this,	101	Miserie		41
And yet as though he knew it not,	102	Miserie		61
Yet since thou canst not choose but see my actions;	104	Obedience		23
Yet if thou talkest still,	106	Conscience		19
Yet all this glorie, all this pomp and state	106	Sion		7
The note is sad, yet musick for a king.	107	Sion		24
Yet if thou stayest still, why must I stay?	108	Home		31
Neither too mean, nor yet too gay,	109	Brit. Ch.		8
Yet when the houre of thy designe	111	The Quip		21
But if yet thou idle be,	113	Businesse		15
While all things have their will, yet none but thine.	117	Providence		32
Bees work for man; and yet they never bruise	118	Providence		65
When yet some places could no moisture get,	120	Providence		115
How harsh are thorns to pears! and yet they make	120	Providence		121
Or with a stone! yet make no good foundation.	120	Providence		124
Yet in their being joyn with one advise	121	Providence		146
Extolleth many wayes, yet this one more.	121	Providence		152
Yet ill deeds loyter not: for they supplie	122	Sinnes rd.		16
He sweetly liv'd; yet sweetnesse did not save	125	Peace		25
Yet grief knows all, and enters when he will.	126	Confession		6
And washt, and wrung: the very wringing yet	129	Love unkn.		17
Yet still askt pardon, and was not deni'd.	129	Love unkn.		21
Yet if we rightly measure,	131	Mans medly		4
Yet ev'n the greatest griefs	132	Mans medly		31
Yet I went on.	134	The Method		24
Bid what he please; yet I am sure,	135	Divinitie		22
For death is drie as dust. Yet if ye part,	135	Ephes.		10
Yet if I wail not still, since still to wail	136	Ephes.		31
Yet speak they louder then distemper'd fears.	137	Familie		19
Lay out thy joy, yet hope to save it?	138	The Size		17
Yet active strength: whose long and bonie face	138	The Size		33
And work up to thee; yet thou dost refuse.	139	Artillerie		20
Yet if thou shunnest, I am thine:	139	Artillerie		29

YET (cont'd)

	PAGE	TITLE		LINE
I am but finite, yet thine infinitely.	139	Artillerie		32
Yet taking heart I rose, and then perceiv'd	142	Pilgrimage		29
Yet heard a crie	142	Pilgrimage		32
Yet I might trust in God to be my light.	143	Holdfast		4
Yet one pure heart is nothing to bestow:	147	Offering		5
Yet one, if good, may title to a number;	147	Offering		9
Yet thy favour	148	Offering		37
Yet call.	148	Longing		12
Yet a meek look	149	Longing		51
Thy board is full, yet humble guests	149	Longing		53
In bitter grief: yet am I stil'd	150	Longing		59
Yet if the heart that wept	154	Glimpse		21
Yet to be thine, doth me restore;	157	Clasping		4
Yet then as mine didst me restore.	157	Clasping		18
That thou mayst yet have more.	157	Praise 3		6
The windes their stint: and yet when I did call,	158	Praise 3		23
Readie to take them in; yet of a size	158	Praise 3		29
Wherefore I sing. Yet since my heart,	159	Praise 3		37
Yet let him keep the rest,	160	The Pulley		16
If goodnesse leade him not, yet wearinesse	160	The Pulley		19
Yet have I often seen, by cunning hand	161	Priesthood		13
Yet never prove.	162	The Search		4
And yet the sphere	162	The Search		6
Yet can I mark how herbs below	162	The Search		9
Yet can I mark how starres above	162	The Search		13
To have my aim, and yet to be	165	The Crosse		25
And yet since these thy contradictions	165	The Crosse		34
Yet slight not these few words:	168	a true Hymn		6
Let losers talk: yet thou shalt die;	169	Dial.-Anth		7
Since thou dost love, yet strike;	171	Bittersweet		2
Cast down, yet help afford;	171	Bittersweet		3
I will complain, yet praise;	171	Bittersweet		5
And yet in washing one, she washed both.	173	Marie Magd		18
Yet in this wretched world we toil,	176	The Foil		7
Yet have they left me, Thou art still my God.	176	Forerunners		6
Yet if you go, I passe not; take your way:	177	Forerunners		31
Then my strict, yet welcome size.	177	The Rose		4
What is sweeter? yet it purgeth.	178	The Rose		18
Yet I creep	179	Discipline		15
Yet being bruis'd are better sented:	181	Banquet		27
Yet when thou dost suppresse	183	A Parodie		6
Yet I heare tell,	187	Judgement		7
Love bade me welcome: yet my soul drew back,	188	Love 3		1
Yet as the sunne, though forward be his flight,	190	Ch.-Milit.		31
And Rome as both; yet Egypt faster rid,	191	Ch.-Milit.		58
Yet did a rogue with hope of carnall joy	194	Ch.-Milit.		149
So trimme, as Greece and Egypt? yet their hearts	194	Ch.-Milit.		151
So spruse, as Greece and Egypt? yet their hearts	194	Ch.-Milit.	W	151
Yet that he might the better gain all nations,	195	Ch.-Milit.		183
Yet with two faces, as their Janus was;	196	Ch.-Milit.		207
Yet not as Sinne, but as Religion.	196	Ch.-Milit.		212
Yet must there such proportions be assign'd	196	Ch.-Milit.		232
Yet must there such proportion be assign'd	196	Ch.-Milit.	W	232
For gold and grace did never yet agree:	197	Ch.-Milit.		251
Yet as the Church shall thither westward flie,	197	Ch.-Milit.		259
And knew it not, yet cleansed mee.	202	love	W	12
Yet then I found, that thou didst creep	202	love	W	16
I went the slower, yet more paces,	203	Even-song	W	3
Yet Thou art not so dark, since I know this,	203	Even-song	W	17
May yet forbid the banes and bliss.	205	Persever.	W	12
Nor yet thy eloquence here keep him still,	439	Walton 5		3
Yet thy brave beames excluded from their right	211	Bohemia	D	10
Yet hast thou more dominions: God doth give	212	Bohemia	D	41
This is thy empire yet: till better season	213	Bohemia	D	60
Yet in these points he labours most in those things which are most	227	Priest 3		10
yet as diverse, not as repugnant:	229	Priest 4		15
is full of such composures, yet every mans own is fittest, readyest,	230	Priest 5		4
Yet hath the Parson, besides this laborious work, a slighter forme	230	Priest 5		15
yet not as himself alone, but as presenting with himself the whole	231	Priest 6		6
yet not so slow neither, as to let the fervency of the supplicant	231	Priest 6		17
between fear and zeal, pausing yet pressing, he performes his duty.	231	Priest 6		20
yet often dy with the Sermon, especially with Countrey people;	233	Priest 7		14
But yet as the temper of his body may be, or as the temper of his	237	Priest 9		1
yet never so giving over the raines, but that he sometimes looks how	239	Priest 9		1
Yet in binding them prentices (in case he think fit to do so) he	239	Priest 10		33
Yet doth hee oftenest invite those, whom hee sees take best courses,	243	Priest 11		24
yet that will not be so:	243	Priest 11		29
yet out of his infinite pity hath set forth heaven for a reward	243	Priest 11		31
if not the best way, yet any way, make his Parish good.	244	Priest 11		5
Yet in all his Charity, he distinguisheth, giving them most,	245	Priest 12		14
yet considering that the Law allows these in case they be true,	245	Priest 12		24
yet in this he distinguisheth;	248	Priest 14		16
yet hee gives him not over, but is long before hee proceede	250	Priest 16		16
yet seasonably, and discreetly, by taking aside the Lord,	251	Priest 17		28
And yet as the malice of the person, or hainousness of the crime may	254	Priest 20		25
Yet the skill consists but in these three points:	256	Priest 21		29
who having not received yet, are to enter into this great work,	258	Priest 22		29
if not duly once a month, yet at least five or six times in the year;	259	Priest 22		20
Yet when ever any controversie is brought to him, he never decides it	260	Priest 23		7
whom yet he ever exhorts not to exceed his bounds, but in tickle	260	Priest 23		35

YET (cont'd)

	PAGE	TITLE		LINE
Yet is it easie for any Scholer to attaine to such a measure	261	Priest 23		1
yet he looks not in this point of Curing beyond his own Parish,	262	Priest 23		12
and yet hear Sermons against both, and himselfe condemn both in good	264	Priest 26		15
yet is there a period for his storing, and a point, or center,	264	Priest 26		28
to descend yet more particularly, if a man hath wherewithall to buy	265	Priest 26		27
and yet hee chuseth rather to use his neighbours, and wear out that,	265	Priest 26		29
which yet ought to be done, since there is a Justice in the least	265	Priest 26		31
Yet of hurtfull things, I am more bound to abstain from those,	266	Priest 26		23
Yet Phisicians bid those that would live in health, not keep	267	Priest 26		9
yet when God pleased, the sun stood stil, the fire burned not.	271	Priest 30		11
yet if he suite not other things to the growth, as seasons,	271	Priest 30		16
yet if God give him not the Grace to use, and utter this well,	272	Priest 30		2
Yet is it also a debt to our Countrey to have a Calling,	274	Priest 32		26
He that hath or can have yet no imployment, if he truly,	275	Priest 32		12
yet the victory is alike in all, being by the self-same Spirit.	279	Priest 33		1
Governour of all things, yet to them he is lost, as if they said,	281	Priest 34		10
The Jewes yet live, and are known:	281	Priest 34		35
confirmeth, and the continuance of which verdict is yet evident.	282	Priest 34		31
for no perfect Artist ever yet hated his owne worke.	283	Priest 34		12
shew all humility before his Passion, yet he allows in his Apostles.	285	Priest 36		28
yet art thou our Creatour, and we thy work:	288	Priest		11
yet by these thy conflicts, and seemingly hazards, didst thou arise	288	Priest		33
Neither doth thy love yet stay here!	289	Priest		3
to convert those who are not yet thine, and to confirme those that	289	Priest		16
the Physicians told me that yet there was one help for me,	292	Cornaro		3
and yet all these I found hurtfull.	293	Cornaro		14
Yet with this diet I avoided other hurtfull things also,	293	Cornaro		30
yet these forenamed things have also their force.	293	Cornaro		34
Yet could I not so avoid all these, but that now and then I fell into	293	Cornaro		37
which yet needs not onely to be sustained, but also to gather	295	Cornaro		23
the quantitie of meat to be increased, yet but two ounces onely.	296	Cornaro		8
although it was a sore evil, yet had no power to kill me.	297	Cornaro		2
ill handled by their intemperance, yet shunne a sober life:	298	Cornaro		25
yet all must [needs] take heed, lest they take a greater quantitie	300	Cornaro		11
they live disorderly, yet continue in health to their lives end:	300	Cornaro		18
onely upon a hope of an happie issue, which yet befalls verie few.	300	Cornaro		24
and, though subject to death, yet continually afraid of it:	303	Cornaro		17
Yet I am sure, that my end is farre from me:	303	Cornaro		24
it were the Authors opinion, yet the truth of it would be examined.	307	Valdesso		22
yet Peter was to be sent for, and those that have inspirations must	310	Valdesso		9
in substance, yet needeth [requireth] discreet, and wary explaining.	314	Valdesso		1
yet I remember the Fathers forbid us to judge of the doubtfull	316	Valdesso		11
and yet he had been punished justly, that is in humano foro &	316	Valdesso		27
the scripture, yet what the scripture teacheth, the spirit teacheth,	317	Valdesso		28
Yet his owne practice seemes to confute his opinion, for the most	317	Valdesso		34
Yet doubtlesse the best faith in us is defective, and arrives	319	Valdesso		10
this were the Authors opinion, yet the truth of it would be examined.	319	Valdesso	V	15
Though the Mastiffe be gentle, yet bite him not by the lippe.	325	Proverbs		132
Though the Mastiffe be gentile, yet bite him not by the lippe.	325	Proverbs	V	132
Though old and wise, yet still advise.	325	Proverbs		134
Love your neighbour, yet pull not downe your hedge.	325	Proverbs		141
yet hee is no little foole that despiseth it.	327	Proverbs		206
Though you rise early, yet the day comes	332	Proverbs		333
Willowes are weak, yet they bind other wood.	341	Proverbs		594
yet robbe the Altar.	343	Proverbs		650
Though you see a Church-man ill, yet continue in the Church still.	344	Proverbs		698
The tongue is not steele, yet it cuts.	349	Proverbs		838
Thornes whiten yet doe nothing.	352	Proverbs		943
You may be on land, yet not in a garden.	353	Proverbs		964
yet we must have patience.	353	Proverbs		980
Saint Luke was a Saint and a Physitian, yet is dead.	354	Proverbs		1008
yet it would easily tyre me, to find out variety of thanks	363	Letters		14
it is true (God knows) I am weak, yet not so, but that every day,	364	Letters		26
neither am I yet recovered, so that I am fain ever and anon,	364	Letters		33
on Fridayes and Saturdayes, I must do so, which yet sometimes I fast.	365	Letters		6
and yet I am scarce able with much ado to make one half years	365	Letters		9
And yet if a Book of four or five Shillings come in my way,	365	Letters		11
Volumes of Divinity, which yet every day swell, and grow bigger.	365	Letters		14
yet if my Sister were acquainted that they are ready, I dare say she	367	Letters		1
yet I had rather flie to my old ward, that if any course could be	367	Letters		6
and yet still grow upon Your humblest Servant, GEORGE HERBERT.	367	Letters		15
yet his love expects them not but first certifies you that there are	368	Letters		3
but yet he will heare of no other affaires, untill they have	368	Letters		8
yet was seene lately neere the king, which some observing who heard	368	Letters		35
yet have I sent it thither by a faithful Messenger this day:	369	Letters		16
yet your appearing in it, affects me strangely.	369	Letters		23
yet if you cannot send it with much convenience, it is no matter,	369	Letters		27
yet that will be about 30 l. per an. but the commodiousness is beyond	369	Letters		32
that if all fail, yet I am able to stand on mine own legs.	370	Letters		10
circumstance, yet you will pardon my haste, which is very great,	370	Letters		12
if it had to others, yet to me it should not, for ought I yet knew;	370	Letters		23
if it had to others, yet to me it should not, for ought I yet knew;	370	Letters		24
I cannot yet find leisure to write to my Lord, or Sir Benjamin	370	Letters		29
and paper enough, yet am I Your readiest Servant, GEORGE HERBERT.	370	Letters		32
whether my peace be yet made with her concerning my unkind departure.	371	Letters		8
Concerning the Orators place all goes well yet, the next Friday it is	371	Letters		16
businesses may stop my hand, yet my heart, a much better member,	371	Letters		27
Offices for which I came into the world, and must yet be kept in it;	373	Letters		10
And yet, Oh God! most carry themselves so, as if they not only	373	Letters		32
yet you may say with David, That God who hath delivered me out	374	Letters		5

	PAGE	TITLE		LINE
YET (cont'd)				
Yet truly it was none of my meaning, when I wrote, to putt one of our	375	Letters		4
am glad that although you offer more, yet you will doe, as you write,	375	Letters		7
and would not have to part them yet, till I take some opportunity	375	Letters		21
take pitty of her, which yet at that distance is some difficulty.	375	Letters		29
Yet, truly if you take her not, I am thinking to do it,	375	Letters		34
of kindred bredd up, (which generally is very true,) yet I care not;	376	Letters		5
be none of the Court-stile, yet doubtless Madam, can do you no hurt:	377	Letters		2
If there fall out yet any rubb, you shall heare of me;	377	Letters		22
yet I shall ever put your care of Leighton, upon my accompt,	378	Letters		3
2. yet are you now ingaged.	380	Woodnoth		7
long God knocks at our harts, before he be heard, & yet desists not.	381	Woodnoth		2
yet useth his Restraining grace, even in the most wicked:	381	Woodnoth		8
But yet the Arts in quietnes and silence here are reverenced,	442	Oration		35
Yet doe not yee contemne these our slight glories, which wee raise	442	Oration		38
YETT				
Yett in thy pursing still thy self distrust	13	Ch.-Porch	W	163
Will canker both, yett thou alone shallt smart:	13	Ch.-Porch	W	166
which to me that have nothing yett, is very much.	376	Letters		2
YF				
Yf I should regard such things, it were in another's power to defeat	376	Letters		8
YIELD				
unto you, since I find you so willing to yield to my requests;	363	Letters		21
YOU				
Entice the trusty sunne, if that you can,	12	Ch.-Porch		136
To me, who took eyes that I might you finde:	26	Sacrifice		3
When all my tears were bloud, the while you slept:	31	Sacrifice		150
And fathers smile for you, to feel his frown:	34	Sacrifice		223
And fathers smile to feele for you his frown:	34	Sacrifice	W	223
Alas! what have I stollen from you? Death.	34	Sacrifice		231
You doe prevent most sins & for the rest	44	H. Bapt.1	W	6
You give us teares to wash them: lett those beams	44	H. Bapt.1	W	7
Which then join'd with you still meet in my brest	44	H. Bapt.1	W	8
In you Redemption measures all my time,	44	H. Bapt.1		10
You taught the book of life my name, that so	44	H. Bapt.1		12
Sweetest of sweets, I thank you: when displeasure	65	Ch.-mus.		1
You took me thence, and in your house of pleasure	65	Ch.-mus.		3
Now I in you without a bodie move,	65	Ch.-mus.		5
Comfort, I'le die; for if you poste from me,	66	Ch.-mus.		9
Comfort, I'le die; for if you part from me,	66	Ch.-mus.	W	9
You know the way to heavens doore.	66	Ch.-mus.		12
Mark you the floore? that square & speckled stone,	66	Ch.-floore		1
Although then others court you, if ye know	78	Ang.&Sts.		26
I heard in Musick you had skill.	110	The Quip		11
Heark and beware, lest what you now do measure	111	Vanitie 2		5
That to my broken heart he was I ease you,	112	JESU		9
Of Joy and Charitie. Sir, you have not miss'd,	116	Love-joy		7
The trees say, Pull me: but the hand you stretch,	117	Providence		23
And grows for you;	125	Peace		38
With so much earnestnesse you do pursue,	125	Peace		41
Better then you know me, or (which is one)	129	Love unkn.		10
Better then you knew me, or (which is one)	129	Love unkn.	V	10
But you shall heare. After my heart was well,	129	Love unkn.		22
My heart, that brought it (do you understand?)	130	Love unkn.		36
For ought I heare, your Master shows to you	130	Love unkn.		62
More favour then you wot of. Mark the end.	130	Love unkn.		63
All did but strive to mend, what you had marr'd.	130	Love unkn.		67
Who fain would have you be new, tender, quick.	131	Love unkn.		70
Gave you a colour once; which when your foes	140	Ch.-rents		13
Thought to let out, the bleeding did you good,	140	Ch.-rents		14
And made you look much fresher then before.	140	Ch.-rents		15
Did worm and work within you more and more,	140	Ch.-rents		17
Which falls by night, and poure it out for you!	140	Ch.-rents		30
That I shall minde, what you impart;	152	The Bag		35
Look, you may put it very neare my heart.	152	The Bag		36
Our cyens have purloin'd, and left you drie:	152	The Jews		2
Our sinnes have purloin'd, and left you drie:	152	The Jews	V	2
Then did I wash you with my tears, and more,	176	Forerunners		16
Brought you to Church well drest and clad:	176	Forerunners		17
Yet if you go, I passe not; take your way:	177	Forerunners		31
Unto what you now advise:	177	The Rose		14
Onely though I you oppose,	178	The Rose		30
Naming you not to your good:	180	Invitation		9
And exalts you to the skie:	180	Invitation		27
Love said, you shall be he.	189	Love 3		8
And know you not, sayes Love, who bore the blame?	189	Love 3		15
You must sit down, sayes Love, and taste my meat:	189	Love 3		17
Open the bones, and you shall nothing find	206	Walton 2		12
Search and you may	208	J. Danvers	D	2
Would you find?	208	J. Danvers	D	6
My Lord. A diamond to mee you sent,	209	L. Bacon	D	1
And I to you a Blackamore present.	209	L. Bacon	D	2
So by the Other, you may read in mee	209	L. Bacon	D	5
You whoe admire yourselves because	209	Paradox	D	1
You neither groane nor weepe	209	Paradox	D	2
That makes you thinke us poore:	210	Paradox	D	8
How know you that our teares proceed from woe	210	Paradox	D	15
How know you that the sighes we send	210	Paradox	D	19
Then you shall fully knowe	210	Paradox	D	28
You allwayes feare to feele those smarts	210	Paradox	D	31
None but gross joyes you move:	210	Paradox	D	34

YOU (cont'd)

	PAGE	TITLE		LINE
For though you vysit us, & wayle our case,	211	Paradox	D	39
Wee doubt much whether you	211	Paradox	D	40
he may say as He did, I sate daily with you teaching in the Temple.	228	Priest 3		1
This is for you, and This is fcr you;	233	Priest 7		5
whether I speak as I ought, or you hear as you ought, he sees hearts,	234	Priest 7		28
or, So farr indeed what you say is true, and well said;	252	Priest 18		12
This I do, because at such, and such a time you were charitable.	254	Priest 20		17
Did you see God make it?	256	Priest 21		8
You said, God made the world;	256	Priest 21		11
in a doctrinall way, saying to the contemner, Alas, why do you thus?	269	Priest 28		13
you hurt your selfe, not me;	269	Priest 28		13
in which perhaps you will discover some care, which I forbare not in	304	Valdesso		3
because I would doe nothing negligently that you commit unto mee;	304	Valdesso		5
Churches sake, to whom by Printing it I would have you consecrate it.	304	Valdesso		9
You owe the Church a debt, and God hath put this into your hands	304	Valdesso		9
I like not in him, as my fragments will expresse, when you read them;	304	Valdesso		17
neverthelesse I wish you by all meanes to publish it, for these three	304	Valdesso		18
You cannot know wine by the barrell.	321	Proverbs		20
Where you thinke there is bacon, there is no Chimney.	324	Proverbs		99
Mend your cloathes, and you may hold out this yeare.	324	Proverbs		100
Ill natures, the more you aske them, the more they stick.	324	Proverbs		106
To a fair day open the window, but make you ready as to a foule.	325	Proverbs		119
Keepe good men company, and you shall be of the number.	325	Proverbs		120
Make hast to an ill way that you may get out of it.	325	Proverbs		124
and he will play with you in the market.	325	Proverbs		146
Marry your sonne when you will; your daughter when you can.	326	Proverbs		149
Without favour none will know you,	326	Proverbs		159
and with it you will not know your selfe.	326	Proverbs		159
with it you will hardly know your selfe.	326	Proverbs	V	159
but take heede, lest you bee drowned.	326	Proverbs		167
Whether you boyle snow or pound it,	327	Proverbs		180
you can have but water of it.	327	Proverbs		180
In life you lov'd me not, in death you bewaile me.	328	Proverbs		218
What your glasse telles you, will not be told by Councell.	329	Proverbs		255
Bee not idle and you shall not bee longing.	331	Proverbs		308
Keep not ill men company, lest you increase the number.	331	Proverbs		314
If you loose your time, you cannot get mony nor gaine.	332	Proverbs		320
By the needle you shall draw the thread,	332	Proverbs		329
Stay a little and news will find you.	332	Proverbs		330
if you will know the truth of the thing.	332	Proverbs		331
Though you rise early, yet the day comes	332	Proverbs		333
Since you know all, and I nothing,	332	Proverbs		336
When you are an Anvill, hold you still;	332	Proverbs		338
when you are a hammer, strike your fill.	332	Proverbs		338
If you would know secrets, looke them in griefe or pleasure.	333	Proverbs		367
Sit in your place and none can make you rise.	334	Proverbs		372
If you could runne, as you drinke, you might catch a hare.	334	Proverbs		373
Would you know what mony is, Go borrow some.	334	Proverbs		374
The good mother sayes not, Will you? but gives.	337	Proverbs		467
You must strike in measure,	340	Proverbs		551
You may bring a horse to the river,	342	Proverbs		623
Before you make a friend, eate a bushell of salt with him.	342	Proverbs		624
You cannot make a wind-mill goe with a paire of bellowes.	344	Proverbs		676
Though you see a Church-man ill, yet continue in the Church still.	344	Proverbs		698
Old praise dies, unlesse you feede it.	344	Proverbs		699
you could not fill all tc your mind.	343	Proverbs	V	700
Had you the world on your Chesse-bord,	344	Proverbs		701
you could not fit all to your mind.	344	Proverbs		701
You cannot hide an eele in a sacke.	346	Proverbs		762
You cannot hide a needle in a sacke.	346	Proverbs	V	762
You cannot flea a stone.	346	Proverbs		764
A kinsman, a friend, or whom you intreate,	347	Proverbs		794
take not to serve you, if you will be served neately.	347	Proverbs		794
You must loose a flie to catch a trout.	348	Proverbs		827
When you enter into a house, leave the anger ever at the doore.	350	Proverbs		896
Count not fowre except you have them in a wallett.	352	Proverbs		962
You may be on land, yet not in a garden.	353	Proverbs		964
You cannot make the fire so low but it will get out.	353	Proverbs		965
Speake not of my debts, unlesse you meane to pay them.	354	Proverbs		998
If you would bee at ease, all the world is not.	355	Proverbs		1019
If you must flie, flie well.	355	Proverbs		1021
Unsound minds like unsound Bodies, if you feed, you poyson.	358	Proverbs	D	1076
Of a pigs taile you can never make a good shaft.	359	Proverbs	D	1104
Trust no friend with that you need fear him if he were your enemy.	361	Proverbs	D	1169
but you married men laugh till your hearts ake.	361	Proverbs	D	1175
the same heart, which you have won long since, is still true to you,	363	Letters		17
is still true to you, and hath nothing else to answer your infinite	363	Letters		18
only hereafter I will take heed how I propose my desires unto you,	363	Letters		21
unto you, since I find you so willing to yield to my requests;	363	Letters		21
but that you have performed your kindness to the full, and that	363	Letters		24
wherefore I will open my case unto you, which I think deserves	364	Letters		9
You know Sir, how I am now setting foot into Divinity, to lay	364	Letters		11
had taken ill courses, Follow your Book, and you shall want nothing:	364	Letters		22
You know Sir, it is their ordinary speech, and now let them make it	364	Letters		22
perhaps they will say, you are sickly, you must not study too hard;	364	Letters		25
You know I was sick last Vacation, neither am I yet recovered,	364	Letters		32
in our publick Halls, you know, is nothing but Fish and Whit-meats:	365	Letters		3
or any other way, I desire you, Sir, to be my Mediator to them in my	365	Letters		21
Now I write to you, Sir, because to you I have ever opened my heart;	365	Letters		23
for I am sure you love Your faithfullest Servant, GEORGE HERBERT.	365	Letters		25

YOU (cont'd)

	PAGE	TITLE	LINE
have not leazure to impart unto you some of those observations which	365	Letters	32
and whereof I would not have you ignorant.	366	Letters	2
As I shal find occasion, you shal receive them by peeces; . .	366	Letters	3
and if there be any such which you have found useful to yourself,	366	Letters	4
You live in a brave nation, where, except you wink, you cannot	366	Letters	5
except you wink, you cannot but see many brave examples. . .	366	Letters	6
of all good which you see in Frenchmen, whether it be in knowledge,	366	Letters	7
for I would have you, even in speeches, to observe so much, . .	366	Letters	9
as when you meet with a witty French speech, try to speak the like in	366	Letters	10
so shall you play a good marchant, by transporting French commodities	366	Letters	11
be no kind of excellency which it is possible for you to attain to,	366	Letters	14
which it is possible for you to attain to, which you seek not;	366	Letters	14
when I have more time, you shall hear more;	366	Letters	20
and write you freely to mee in your letters, for I am your ever	366	Letters	20
and perhaps a little more mild, but you will hardly perceive it.	366	Letters	25
It is high time now that I should be no more a burden to you,	367	Letters	13
This letter runs to you with much eagernes, for I am enjoined	367	Letters	27
for I am enjoined to write to you by Sir John Danvers, to which mine	367	Letters	28
Now his desire is to acquaint you with those passages of newes which	368	Letters	1
them not but first certifies you that there are come agents hither	368	Letters	4
These are the things I am to acquaint you with, of whose rude	369	Letters	1
that this is but an occasion for you to amplify your favour to mee in	369	Letters	3
I wish I could have come in person to thank you, but it is . .	369	Letters	11
I beseech you all, you and my dear Mother and Sister to pardon me,	369	Letters	17
you and my dear Mother and Sister to pardon me, for my Cambridge	369	Letters	17
I have sent you here inclosed a Letter from our Master in my behalf,	369	Letters	24
which if you can sent to Sir Francis before his departure, . .	369	Letters	25
yet if you cannot send it with much convenience, it is no matter,	369	Letters	27
The Orators place (that you may understand what it is) is the finest	369	Letters	30
I pray Sir send the Letter you receive from him to me as soon as you	370	Letters	6
Sir send the Letter you receive from him to me as soon as you can,	370	Letters	6
that I joy in your favours, but that you may see, that if all fail,	370	Letters	9
I thank you for your infinite favours, I fear only that I have	370	Letters	11
circumstance, yet you will pardon my haste, which is very great,	370	Letters	12
I have received the things you sent me, safe;	371	Letters	6
the next Friday it is tryed, and accordingly you shall hear.	371	Letters	17
yet my heart, a much better member, is alwayes with you: . .	371	Letters	27
that my solliciting him has been much, and my tears many for you;	372	Letters	3
and then you shall justly value Your most truly, most heartily,	372	Letters	4
At my last parting from you, I was the better content because I was	372	Letters	14
or rather increaseth, I wish earnestly that I were again with you:	372	Letters	18
constant and the more earnest for you to the God of all Consolation.	372	Letters	23
I beseech you to be chearful, and comfort your self in the God of all	372	Letters	24
therefore, if either Age or Sickness lead you to those Joyes?	372	Letters	31
consider what advantage you have over Youth and Health, . .	372	Letters	32
but, wou'd you divide and choose too?	373	Letters	1
and I shou'd account my self most happy if I might change with you;	373	Letters	3
but you are freed from that fear, who have already abundantly	373	Letters	10
So that now if they do not well the falt cannot be charg'd on you;	373	Letters	15
and Care of them will justifie you both to the world and your own	373	Letters	16
that whether you turn your thoughts on the life past, or on the Joyes	373	Letters	17
that are to come, you have strong preservatives against all disquiet.	373	Letters	19
I beseech you consider all that can happen to you are either	373	Letters	20
consider all that can happen to you are either afflictions of Estate,	373	Letters	21
I beseech you let such thoughts as these, moderate your present fear	374	Letters	3
yet you may say with David, That God who hath delivered me out	374	Letters	5
And above all, If any care of future things molest you? . .	374	Letters	13
all your Care on the Lord, for he careth for you. (1 Pet. 5.7.)	374	Letters	16
commend only one place more to you (Philip. 4. 4.) St. Paul saith	374	Letters	20
That you did not only entertain my proposals, but advance them,	375	Letters	2
and am glad that although you offer more, yet you will doe, . .	375	Letters	6
am glad that although you offer more, yet you will doe, as you write,	375	Letters	7
although you offer more, yet you will doe, as you write, that alsoe.	375	Letters	7
I will tell you what I wrote to our eldest brother, when he urged one	375	Letters	10
them know your love, for which both they shall, and I doe, thank you.	375	Letters	22
school-mistresse, and you know what those mercenary creatures are.	375	Letters	26
you know, is the encouragement of learning all the year after,	375	Letters	28
If you could think of taking her, as once you did, surely it were	375	Letters	30
of taking her, as once you did, surely it were a great good deed,	375	Letters	31
it were a great good deed, and I would have her conveyed to you.	375	Letters	32
But I judge you not:	375	Letters	32
Yet, truly if you take her not, I am thinking to do it, . .	375	Letters	34
which I commend to you as being now a father, "the best-bredd child	376	Letters	17
the good GOD bless you more and more;	376	Letters	19
What a trouble hath your Goodness brought on you, by admitting our	376	Letters	26
be none of the Court-stile, yet doubtless Madam, can do you no hurt:	377	Letters	3
Wherefore the Lord make good the blessing of your Mother upon you,	377	Letters	4
but you joyed me exceedingly with your relation of my Lady Duchess's	377	Letters	18
I am glad I used you in it, and you have no cause to be sorry,	377	Letters	20
and you have no cause to be sorry, since it is GOD's business.	377	Letters	21
If there fall out yet any rubb, you shall heare of me; . . .	377	Letters	22
The LORD bless you, and make you abound in every good worke,	377	Letters	26
and make you abound in every good worke, to the joy of your ever	377	Letters	26
Although you have a much better Paymaster then my self, . .	378	Letters	2
upon my accompt, & give you my self for it, to be yours for ever. .	378	Letters	4
gratious Lord God, is pleased to give me you for the Man, I desired,	378	Letters	8
I humbly thank him, & am so far from giving you cause, to apology,	378	Letters	9
that I take it exceeding kindly of you.	378	Letters	11
much less can I disesteem it from you, whome I esteem to be God's	378	Letters	14
not considering you any other wayes, as neyther I my self desire	378	Letters	15

YOU (cont'd)	PAGE	TITLE		LINE
You write very lovingly that all your things are mine.	378	Letters		21
Now God the Father of our Lord Jesus Christ bless you more & more,	378	Letters		25
bless you more & more, & so turn you all, in your severall wayes,	378	Letters		25
I thanke you heartily for Leighton, your care, your Counsell,	379	Letters		13
glad for the Heart, that God has given you & yours, to pious works.	379	Letters		15
It is so long since I heard from you, that I long to heare both how	379	Letters		23
I heard from you, that I long to heare both how you and your's doe:	379	Letters		24
and also what becomes of you this sommer.	379	Letters		24
My wife's and neeces' service to you.	379	Letters		30
2. yet are you now ingaged.	380	Woodnoth		7
It is a different thing to advize you now, & before you took Sir	380	Woodnoth		8
thing to advize you now, & before you took Sir Johns affairs.	380	Woodnoth		8
you have bin at charges:	380	Woodnoth		8
you have stockd the grounds:	380	Woodnoth		9
you have layed out thoughts & prayers you have sowed. . . .	380	Woodnoth		9
you have layed out thoughts & prayers you have sowed. . . .	380	Woodnoth		10
3. To Change shewes not well & you are by the Apostles rule (Philip	380	Woodnoth		12
4. When two things dislike you:	380	Woodnoth		21
especially no obligation lying upon you either for the execution	380	Woodnoth		26
5. Whereas you complaine of want of success consider how long God	381	Woodnoth		1
if God had done that (which you are thinking to doe) to blessed Mary	381	Woodnoth		4
6. you doe not want all success.	381	Woodnoth		7
so though you incline not, happily you restraine.	381	Woodnoth		9
so though you incline not, happily you restraine.	381	Woodnoth		10
7. Though you want all success either in inclining or restraining,	381	Woodnoth		14
Complaine not of the want of success, when you have the fruit of it.	381	Woodnoth		17
In Gods accepting you have done the good you intended, & whom serve	381	Woodnoth		17
In Gods accepting you have done the good you intended, & whom serve	381	Woodnoth		18
Gods accepting you have done the good you intended, & whom serve you?	381	Woodnoth		18
or whom would you please?	381	Woodnoth		19
as to you deserving them, Wee at last salute you Masters of Arts;	441	Oration		26
as to you deserving them, Wee at last salute you Masters of Arts;	441	Oration		27
entreating that you would a while lay aside those warlike lookes,	442	Oration		2
with which you use to conquer your enemies, and assume more mild	442	Oration		3
of Philosophie, for respect to you, embrace all that is cheerefull,	442	Oration		7
that you may well conceive, your Excellencies to bee more deare unto	442	Oration		19
in that you are of the same order and habit, of which wee all in this	442	Oration		20
since you are so great both in your Princes, and your selves,	442	Oration		28
How could you bee like great Alexander, unlesse Historie delivered	443	Oration		2
poore duties wish, and vow unto you of the last a plenteous Harvest.	443	Oration		6
YOUNG				
In young and old;	78	Ang.&Sts.		13
But we are still too young or old;	79	Employm.2		26
But we are ever young or old;	79	Employm.2	W	26
To swaddle infants, whose young breath	98	Mortific.		3
As a young exhalation, newly waking, ...	169	The Answer		8
and his soul fervent, active, young, and lusty as an eagle. . .	237	Priest 9		27
least the poyson steal into some young and unwary spirits, . .	252	Priest 18		6
hee keepes some young practicioner in his house for the benefit	260	Priest 23		34
But if the young Gallant think these Courses dull, and phlegmatick,	278	Priest 32		4
because divers worthy young men have obliged me unto it. . .	291	Cornaro		8
sure of life, then the most strong young man who lives disorderly.	300	Cornaro		26
bodie and minde, wherewith infinite both young and old are afflicted.	302	Cornaro		26
sheweth, and I also, when I was a young man, too well found.	303	Cornaro		16
For death to all young men is a terrible thing, as also to those that	303	Cornaro		18
When all sinnes grow old, coveteousnesse is young. . . .	321	Proverbs		18
When all sinnes grow old, coveteousnesse grows young. . . .	321	Proverbs	V	18
An old wise mans shaddow is better then a young buzzards sword.	324	Proverbs		90
Pension never inriched young man.	339	Proverbs		515
Old men, when they scorne young, make much of death. . . .	341	Proverbs		597
An old Physitian, and a young Lawyer.	343	Proverbs		648
The ofspring of those that are very young, or very old, lasts not.	350	Proverbs		887
Old men go to Death, Death comes to Young men.	356	Proverbs	D	1
Old Camels carry young Camels skins to the Market. . . .	359	Proverbs	D	1101
The death of a young wolfe doth never come too soon. . . .	360	Proverbs	D	1131
Take heed of a young wench, ...	360	Proverbs	D	1151
and such like Gaynesses, which will please a young man well.	370	Letters		4
YOUNGER				
this being to be done in his younger and preparatory times, . .	230	Priest 5		6
and with particularizing of his speech now to the younger sort,	233	Priest 7		3
of the younger sort, the very words;	255	Priest 21		22
for single men, they are either Heirs, or younger Brothers: . .	276	Priest 32		25
As for younger Brothers, those whom the Parson finds loose, . .	277	Priest 32		24
YOUNGEST				
greatest charitie of all, for she is youngest, and least looked unto;	375	Letters		24
YOUR				
Your tears for your own fortunes should be kept:	31	Sacrifice		151
Your safetie in my sicknesse doth subsist:	34	Sacrifice		227
Who straight, Your suit is granted, said, & died.	40	Redemption		14
Your first acquaintance might discredit all.	44	H. Bapt.1		14
Henceforth repose; your work is done.	64	Even-song		20
You took me thence, and in your house of pleasure	65	Ch.-mus.		3
Rising and falling with your wings:	65	Ch.-mus.		6
But if I travell in your companie, ...	66	Ch.-mus.		11
Within the walls of your own breast:	68	Content		2
Oh glorious spirits, who after all your bands	77	Ang.&Sts.		1
Do I forbear to crave your speciall aid:	78	Ang.&Sts.		7
('Tis your own case) ye never move a wing.	78	Ang.&Sts.		20
'tis your own case, ye never move your wing.	78	Ang.&Sts.	W	20
My musick shows ye have your closes, ...	88	Vertue		11

YOUR (cont'd)

	PAGE	TITLE		LINE
Farewell deare flowers, sweetly your time ye spent,	94	Life		13
Your hony drops: presse not to smell them here:	120	Providence		118
And at your lodging with their thanks appeare.	120	Providence		120
And in my faintings I presume your love	129	Love unkn.		2
Enforceth tears. Your heart was foul, I fear.	129	Love unkn.		18
The offerers heart. Your heart was hard, I fear.	130	Love unkn.		37
It must be he. Your heart was dull, I fear.	130	Love unkn.		56
For ought I heare, your Master shows to you	130	Love unkn.		62
Love God, and love your neighbour. Watch and pray.	135	Divinitie		17
Your sinnes expresse; melt into dew.	135	Ephes.		12
Gave you a colour once; which when your foes	140	Ch.-rents		13
Your colour faded, and calamities	140	Ch.-rents		18
Your colour vaded, and calamities	140	Ch.-rents	V	18
Turned your ruddie into pale and bleak:	140	Ch.-rents		19
Your health and beautie both began to break.	140	Ch.-rents		20
Then did your sev'rall parts unloose and start:	140	Ch.-rents		21
Which when your neighbours saw, like a north-winde,	140	Ch.-rents		22
That your sweet sap might come again!	152	The Jews		12
Give up your feet and running to mine eyes,	164	Grief		15
And keep your measures for some lovers lute,	164	Grief		16
Yet if you go, I passe not; take your way:	177	Forerunners		31
Is your waste;	179	Invitation		2
Save your cost, and mend your fare.	179	Invitation		3
Naming you not to your good:	180	Invitation		9
Bringing all your sinnes to sight:	180	Invitation		15
While ye graze without your bounds:	180	Invitation		21
Your delight,	180	Invitation		23
Is your dove,	180	Invitation		26
Worth your stay.	208	J. Danvers	D	4
Shining and sharp, point out your rare Perfections;	209	L. Bacon	D	4
Till your bright gift my darknesse did abate.	209	L. Bacon	D	8
Your stronge beliefe	209	Paradox	D	5
Your state, to ours, is contrary;	210	Paradox	D	7
But veywe yourselves, & inward turn your eyes;	210	Paradox	D	27
That your estate	210	Paradox	D	29
Your feares in number more, your joyes are lesse.	210	Paradox	D	36
but tremble in your highest mirth.	216	Psalm II	D	28
Within your chamber try your hearts,	217	Psalm IV	D	17
Your meaning is not thus, but thus;	252	Priest 18		11
you hurt your selfe, not me;	269	Priest 28		13
your Valdesso I now returne with many thanks, and some notes,	304	Valdesso		1
First for your sake, because I would doe nothing negligently that you	304	Valdesso		4
and God hath put this into your hands (as he sent the fish with mony	304	Valdesso		10
Mend your cloathes, and you may hold out this yeare.	324	Proverbs		100
Give a clowne your finger, and he will take your hand.	324	Proverbs		111
Love your neighbour, yet pull not downe your hedge.	325	Proverbs		141
Love your neighbour, but pull not downe your hedge.	325	Proverbs	V	141
Marry your sonne when you will; your daughter when you can.	326	Proverbs		149
and with it you will not know your selfe.	326	Proverbs		159
with it you will hardly know your selfe.	326	Proverbs	V	159
Cover your selfe with your shield, and care not for cryes.	326	Proverbs		161
What your glasse telles you, will not be told by Councell.	329	Proverbs		255
Your pot broken seemes better then my whole one.	330	Proverbs		270
If you loose your time, you cannot get mony nor gaine.	332	Proverbs		320
Bee not a Baker, if your head be of butter.	332	Proverbs		321
Pull downe your hatt on the winds side.	332	Proverbs		334
As the yeere is, your pot must seeth.	332	Proverbs		335
When the Foxe preacheth, beware your geese.	332	Proverbs		337
when you are a hammer, strike your fill.	332	Proverbs		338
Sit in your place and none can make you rise.	334	Proverbs		372
Where your will is ready, your feete are light.	336	Proverbs		448
When your will is ready, the feete are swift.	336	Proverbs	V	448
The Lame goes as farre as your staggerer.	339	Proverbs		517
you could not fill all to your mind.	343	Proverbs	V	700
Had you the world on your Chesse-bord,	344	Proverbs		701
you could not fit all to your mind.	344	Proverbs		701
For a morning raine leave not your journey.	353	Proverbs		976
Say to pleasure, Gentle Eve, I will none of your apple.	360	Proverbs	D	1140
Trust no friend with that you need fear him if he were your enemy.	361	Proverbs	D	1169
Marry your daughters betimes, lest they marry themselves.	361	Proverbs	D	1171
but you married men laugh till your hearts ake.	361	Proverbs	D	1175
Your thoughts close, and your countenance loose.	362	Proverbs	D	1183
to find out variety of thanks for the diversity of your favours,	363	Letters		15
and hath nothing else to answer your infinite kindnesses,	363	Letters		19
for, since your favours come a Horse-back, there is reason,	363	Letters		22
but that you have performed your kindness to the full, and that	363	Letters		24
and I will strive to imitate the compleatness of your love,	364	Letters		2
and after my manner, Your most obedient Servant, GEORGE HERBERT.	364	Letters		4
had taken ill courses, Follow your Book, and you shall want nothing:	364	Letters		21
but they will object again, What becomes of your Annuity?	364	Letters		31
by the Patents of your perpetual favour to do so still,	365	Letters		24
for I am sure you love Your faithfullest Servant, GEORGE HERBERT.	365	Letters		26
by transporting French commodities to your own country.	366	Letters		12
and have a good conceit of your wit, mark what I say, have a good	366	Letters		15
of your wit, mark what I say, have a good conceit of your wit;	366	Letters		16
when there is no caus, but by setting a just price of your qualities:	366	Letters		18
and write you freely to mee in your letters, for I am your ever	366	Letters		21
mee in your letters, for I am your ever loving brother, G. HERBERT.	366	Letters		22
Now though they have hitherto travelled upon your charge,	367	Letters		1
though your noble disposition is infinitely free, yet I had rather	367	Letters		6

YOUR (cont'd)	PAGE	TITLE	LINE
for your favours are so ancient, that they prevent my memory,	367	Letters	14
and yet still grow upon Your humblest Servant, GEORGE HERBERT.	367	Letters	16
Letter in yours, for it was because I know your Lodging, but not his.	367	Letters	24
because my recompenses of your favours consist in this only.	367	Letters	32
an occasion for you to amplify your favour to mee in pardoning Your	369	Letters	4
your favour to mee in pardoning Your most indebted kinsman GEORGE	369	Letters	5
This Week hath loaded me with your Favours;	369	Letters	10
and deliver your Letter, yet have I sent it thither by a faithful	369	Letters	15
yet your appearing in it, affects me strangely.	369	Letters	23
I hope I shall get this place without all your London helps,	370	Letters	8
not but that I joy in your favours, but that you may see,	370	Letters	9
I thank you for your infinite favours, I fear only that I have	370	Letters	11
but that I have both time and work to be Your extreme Servant,	370	Letters	15
though for the reckoning of your favours, I shall never find time	370	Letters	31
and paper enough, yet am I Your readiest Servant, GEORGE HERBERT.	370	Letters	33
your Courtesie will pardon the haste of Your humblest Servant,	371	Letters	18
your Courtesie will pardon the haste of Your humblest Servant,	371	Letters	20
incessantly begging some ease of your pains, with that earnestness,	371	Letters	29
with that earnestness, that becomes your griefs, and my love.	372	Letters	1
and then you shall justly value Your most truly, most heartily,	372	Letters	6
I was in hope I should my self carry all sickness out of your family:	372	Letters	16
know I did not, and that your share continues, or rather increaseth,	372	Letters	16
and comfort your self in the God of all Comfort, who is not willing	372	Letters	24
Your last Letter gave me Earthly preferment, and kept Heavenly	372	Letters	34
Letter gave me Earthly preferment, and kept Heavenly for your self:	373	Letters	1
having both ordered your Family, and so brought up your Children that	373	Letters	12
and so brought up your Children that they have attain'd to the years	373	Letters	13
of them will justifie you both to the world and your own Conscience:	373	Letters	17
that whether you turn your thoughts on the life past, or on the Joyes	373	Letters	18
let such thoughts as these, moderate your present fear and sorrow;	374	Letters	4
Casting all your Care on the Lord, for he careth for you. (1 Pet.	374	Letters	16
Let your moderation appear to all men, the Lord is at hand:	374	Letters	27
trouble not your selves, God is at hand to deliver us from all,	374	Letters	29
accept the good meaning of, Your most obedient Son, GEORGE HERBERT.	374	Letters	32
to putt one of our neeces into your hands but barely what I wrote I	375	Letters	5
For concerning your offer of receiving one, I will tell you what I	375	Letters	9
till I take some opportunity to let them know your love,	375	Letters	22
doe that which GOD shall put into your hart, and the LORD bless all	375	Letters	33
into your hart, and the LORD bless all your purposes to his glory.	375	Letters	34
But though I both consider this, and your observation, also,	376	Letters	3
and make your family, a housefull of GOD's servants.	376	Letters	20
So prayes Your ever loving brother, G. HERBERT.	376	Letters	21
What a trouble hath your Goodness brought on you, by admitting our	376	Letters	26
Wherefore the Lord make good the blessing of your Mother upon you,	377	Letters	4
to bud, blow and bear fruit in your Soul, to his glory,	377	Letters	6
to his glory, your own good, and the great joy of Madam,	377	Letters	6
Your most faithful Servant in Christ Jesu, GEORGE HERBERT.	377	Letters	9
Your poor Colony of Servants present their humble duties.	377	Letters	13
I was glad of your Cambridge newes, but you joyed me exceedingly	377	Letters	18
but you joyed me exceedingly with your relation of my Lady Duchess's	377	Letters	19
and your offering of yourself to move my Lords of Manchester	377	Letters	23
every good worke, to the joy of your ever loving brother, G. HERBERT.	377	Letters	28
yet I shall ever put your care of Leighton, upon my accompt,	378	Letters	4
from giving you cause, to apology, about your counselling me herein:	378	Letters	10
Particularly, I like all your Addresses, & for ought I see,	378	Letters	17
You write very lovingly that all your things are mine.	378	Letters	21
& so turn you all, in your severall wayes, one to the other,	378	Letters	25
& the great Joy of Your Brother & Servant in Christ Jesus GEORGE	378	Letters	28
I thanke you heartily for Leighton, your care, your Counsell,	379	Letters	13
you heartily for Leighton, your care, your Counsell, your Cost.	379	Letters	13
you heartily for Leighton, your care, your Counsell, your Cost.	379	Letters	14
I have sent my Letters, to your Brother, investing him,	379	Letters	19
therefore entertaine it accordingly from Your very affectionate bro;	379	Letters	27
therfore your choice at first was good	380	Woodnoth	6
the one for the nature thereof (as your trade) the other only	380	Woodnoth	22
putt your self into the hands of God (whose the success of things is)	380	Woodnoth	23
either it (in regard of the citty) or your self or your kindred.	380	Woodnoth	28
things may grow worse by your withdrawing which grow not better	381	Woodnoth	10
worse by your withdrawing which grow not better by your presence.	381	Woodnoth	11
& if upon your withdrawing it shold doe so, it would trouble your	381	Woodnoth	12
your withdrawing it shold doe so, it would trouble your conscience.	381	Woodnoth	12
For any scruple of leaving your trade, throw it away.	381	Woodnoth	22
The accession of which new title to your Excellencies, all the Muses	442	Oration	1
with which you use to conquer your enemies, and assume more mild	442	Oration	3
your Excellencies to bee more deare unto us, in that you are	442	Oration	19
since you are so great both in your Princes, and your selves,	442	Oration	28
and your selves, wee justly feare that there is nothing here	442	Oration	29
there is nothing here answerable to the greatnesse of your presence.	442	Oration	30
we have as much failed, as your Excellencies doe excel, in both.	442	Oration	34
perpetuall povertie, but when your Excellencies appeare.	442	Oration	37
let the first be the care of your Excellencies;	443	Oration	4
we for your gracious acceptance of these poore duties wish,	443	Oration	5
YOUR'S			
I heard from you, that I long to heare both how you and your's doe:	379	Letters	24
YOURS			
It be as short as yours.	94	Life	18
The tongue is yours to eat, but mine to praise.	117	Providence	22
Is mine to write, as it is yours to raise.	117	Providence	24
pardon my boldness of inclosing my Brothers Letter in yours,	367	Letters	24
necessities are stronger to tye me here, than yours to London:	369	Letters	19

	PAGE	TITLE		LINE
YOURS (cont'd)				
and yours (which praised be God are less) are not like to continue	374	Letters		2
that if any of ycurs shou'd prove a Goliah-like trouble, . .	374	Letters		5
and all yours; and make your family, à housefull of GOD's servants.	376	Letters		19
upon my accompt, & give you my self for it, to be yours for ever.	378	Letters		5
glad for the Heart, that God has given you & yours, to pious works.	379	Letters		15
YOURSELF				
and if there be any such which you have found useful to yourself,	366	Letters		5
not with a foolish vanting of yourself when there is no caus,	366	Letters		17
and your offering of yourself to move my Lords of Manchester	377	Letters		23
YOURSELVES				
You whoe admire yourselves because	209	Paradox	D	1
Acquitts yourselves and gives the sicke all greife.	209	Paradox	D	6
But veywe yourselves, & inward turn your eyes;	210	Paradox	D	27
Then for yourselves not us embrace	211	Paradox	D	37
YOUTH				
Thou, whose sweet youth and early hopes inhance	6	Ch.-Porch		1
Never exceed thy income. Youth may make	13	Ch.-Porch		157
And made her youth and fiercenesse seek thy face.	46	Afflict.1		18
When youth is frank and free, ...	98	Mortific.		13
Which my fierce youth did bandie, fall and flow	169	The Answer		3
Vouchsaf'd ev'n in the midst of youth and night	171	The Glance		2
which is altogether to be preferred before others youth: . .	302	Cornaro		23
which kinde of Poems useth to be the childe of Youth, which it most	302	Cornaro		30
Dresse a stick, and it seemes a youth.	324	Proverbs		101
Presse a stick, and it seemes a youth.	324	Proverbs	V	101
A well-bred youth neither speakes of himselfe, ...	330	Proverbs		278
Time is the Rider that breakes youth.	342	Proverbs		615
An Idle youth, a needy Age.	356	Proverbs	D	1042
consider what advantage you have over Youth and Health, . .	372	Letters		33
YOUTHFULL				
age and constitution with them who follow their youthfull appetites,	303	Cornaro		13
YOUTHS				
Children and youths are usually deferred too long, under pretence	258	Priest 22		37
YRON				
Happier are the hands compast with yron, ...	341	Proverbs		582
ZEAL				
a grave livelinesse, between fear and zeal, pausing yet pressing,	231	Priest 6		20
and heavy, and hard to raise to a poynt of Zeal, and fervency,	233	Priest 7		16
and with truly godly zeal, without hatred to the person, . .	254	Priest 20		27
in a zeal against these, and in a strict performance of a few cheap	319	Valdesso	V	24
ZELE				
That zele and purenes circling my request	66	Ch.-lock	W	11
ZONE				
What frost to that? what pole is not the zone, ...	166	The Flower		32

Concordance to Writings in Latin

	PAGE	TITLE		LINE
A				
Illa quidem a nostro non multum abludit imago,	396	Musae 26		5
A Te Turture defluos,	403	Musae 40		13
Nos autem, a cunis, omnes sententia Mortis	415	Lucus 23		3
A nobis etenim procul remoti	415	Lucus 24		7
A veteri trunco & nobilitate cadit.	416	Lucus 25		6
Non a nobis vapulant Iesuitae, sed a scriptis vestris, quae ingenti	443	Orationes		19
sed a scriptis vestris, quae ingenti cum lucro quotidie legimus.	443	Orationes		19
cum non solum tuearis nos a maleuolorum insidijs, sed etiam doceas	443	Orationes		22
omnes ad Aulam, atque ab eo consilium peteremus a quo et fortunas?	443	Orationes		28
a re instructus nos doceat, tuosque fauores populo tuo communicans	444	Orationes		6
qui symbola sunt spei, quoniam a floribus fructus sperantur.	446	Orationes		33
& contracte King, a Con verbo deduci, quod tria complectitur,	447	Orationes		7
ac si Fatis a fuso essent atque consilijs, sine quibus ne vnum quidem	449	Orationes		29
Politicos audiamus, salus regnorum pendet a vicinis, quorum consilia,	450	Orationes		26
at IACOBVS a nobis est:	451	Orationes		25
indicantes, se non amare patriam terram, a qua adeo remouentur.	452	Orationes		12
Imperatorum incredibilem luxum a Tiberio Caesare ad Constantinum	452	Orationes		22
hic enim securi sumus a pluuia, imo a fulmine:	455	Orationes		15
hic enim securi sumus a pluuia, imo a fulmine:	455	Orationes		16
proin vt Fluuij quas aquas a Fonte accipiunt non retinent ipsi,	456	Epistolae		9
sic disparatae foelicitates hinc a populo, illinc a Principe,	456	Epistolae		24
foelicitates hinc a populo, illinc a Principe, in Te conueniunt,	456	Epistolae		24
ad legendum, quantum a nobis ad scribendum, cum humanitatis Tuae,	457	Epistolae		9
vestra solum dextra (quamuis a scriptione terrestribusque istis	458	Epistolae		6
quia dederunt, non a se compositos, scriptos, editosque:	458	Epistolae		24
Quod si Artaxerxes olim paululum aquae a Sinaeta, subiecto suo,	460	Epistolae		11
subiectos, integro Fluuio a Rege nostro donatos, triumphare?	460	Epistolae		13
Quod quidem non minus expectamus a Te, quem singularis doctrina	461	Epistolae		25
quem singularis doctrina exemit a populo, & quasi mixtam personam	461	Epistolae		26
conseruantes sibi Illos Fontes, a quibus ipsi olim hauserunt?	461	Epistolae		31
instructior ad omnem causam, paratiorue siue a doctrina, siue ab vsu;	462	Epistolae		22
Sic a Natura comparatum est, Ignis et Virtus semper ascendunt,	466	Epistolae		10
ratione habita Chartae nostrae a Serenissimo Principe Henrico 8	467	Epistolae		22
orantes vt immunitates nostrae a Serenissimis Regibus concessae ab	468	Epistolae		21
Statim a solatio aspectus Tui, Ego auctior iam gaudio atque	471	Epistolae		17
AB				
Mersis reuertens laetus ab hostibus	394	Musae 23		30
Aut potius Christi sanguis demissus ab alto,	399	Musae 35		9
Ante diem vestro mundus ab igne ruat.	399	Musae 35		12
Ipse etiam Christus coelo speculatus ab alto,	402	Musae 39		11
Cuius ab oppositis fluxit origo locis.	417	Lucus 31		4
Mag. Sigilli Custodis post editam ab eo Instaurationem Magnam.	436	Poem.Lat.		T
Non tot abest, quot nos Regis ab ingenio.	437	Poem.Lat.		4
Oratio in Discessum Regis ab Academia Cantabrigiae habita 12o die	443	Orationes		T
omnes ad Aulam, atque ab eo consilium peteremus a quo et fortunas?	443	Orationes		27
quod quidem vbi gentium si non ab Hispano sperandum?	447	Orationes		30
sic Tu etiam dignitates ab optimo Rege desumptas in vniuersam	456	Epistolae		11
quanquam quem alium fructum potuimus expectare ab Eo, in quem fauor	456	Epistolae		18
rotunditas Clementiae vestrae, quae ab omni parte nobis succurrit!	460	Epistolae		10
instructior ad omnem causam, paratiorue siue a doctrina, siue ab vsu;	462	Epistolae		22
cum olim ab Archiepiscopo Eboracensi Summo Angliae Cancellario	463	Epistolae		30
nunc denuo ex aedibus Eboracensibus ab altero Cancellario INSTAVRARI,	464	Epistolae		1
Serenissimis Regibus concessae ab Augustissimo Iacobo auctae tua	468	Epistolae		22
non solum rectum de Bene-merentibus iudicium hausisse ab Antiquis,	469	Epistolae		13
quidem multum, neque nostrae matronae conuenit, cui tu es ab ornatu.	471	Epistolae		3
non adeo sanatae ab optimo Rege nostro quin turgescat indies,	473	Epistolae		21
ABDOMINE				
Progenies, mundique aetas abdomine nostro	418	Tr.Mortis		4
Progenies, mundique aetas abdomine tanto	418	Tr.Mortis	V	4
ABEAM				
quam non longe abeam Oratorum more, qui nullum non angulum verrunt	445	Orationes		35
ABELEM				
Sanguinis, innocuum tandem luet orbis Abelem.	272	Tr.Mortis	VS	101
ABERAS				
Atque hoc quidem statu res erant, Suauissime CAROLE, cum tu aberas;	451	Orationes		28
ABEST				
Non tot abest, quot nos Regis ab ingenio.	437	Poem.Lat.		4
ABEUNT				
Pro lapsu stillarum abeunt peccata; nec acres	406	Passio 13		3
In laudes abeunt secula quaeque tuas;	435	Poem.Lat.		2
In laudes abeunt iam loca quaeque tuas:	435	Poem.Lat.		4
ABIECTIS				
illecebris melitaiais agxonais abiectis, iter aggreditur & labores,	452	Orationes		32
ABIECTUS				
si tam abiectus sim, vt laboribus meis plurimis atque assidua	472	Epistolae		12
ABIGAT				
tuus amor et authoritas istos sorices nobis abigat.	469	Epistolae		1
ABIJCIEBANT				
quos in arca repositos abijciebant in fluuium, his verbis:	452	Orationes		28
ABIJCITE				
Quamobrem abijcite quisque libros, non est locus grauitati,	454	Orationes		34
ABIJSTI				
siccine abijsti solus? cur non nos omnes tecum?	451	Orationes		7
ABIJT				
Heus, abijtne Noster? miseros nos;	450	Orationes		37
ABIOI				
Hinc Thraces dicti sunt abioi, & Licurgus magnus Legislator atimian	446	Orationes		20
ABIRENT				
ac si corpora sua non abirent olim in elementa, sed in bellaria aut	452	Orationes		14

ABITO	PAGE	TITLE	LINE
Abito, trunce, cum tuis pudoribus.	423	Mem.Matr.2	54
Abito, barde. Quam pie istic sum impudens!	424	Mem.Matr.2	60
ABLATUS			
sed si ablatus fuisset Fluuius noster, per quem vicini agri opulentia	460	Epistolae	22
ABLUDIT			
Illa quidem a nostro non multum abludit imago,	396	Musae 26	5
ABRUPERE			
Non tibi nunc soli filum abrupere sorores,	428	Mem.Matr.11	11
ABRUPTUM			
vlciscimur mortem, ligantes abruptum vitae filum, vnde consequimur,	446	Orationes	23
ABSCINDERE			
abscindere non possim, absque molesta aliorum ac frigida	472	Epistolae	14
ABSCONDUNTUR			
consilia nostra, absconduntur Diuina & Regia, praecipue pharetrata,	449	Orationes	26
ABSENTEM			
Dum torus absentem quisque reponit heram.	425	Mem.Matr.5	10
certe nos te absentem omnes acerrime concitatissimeque desiderauimus.	451	Orationes	33
ABSENTIA			
absentia magis quam praesentia. Nunc enim exploratos habet nostros	450	Orationes	33
ABSENTIAM			
ditat patriam, suamque absentiam cum foenore compensat.	454	Orationes	33
ABSIMILIS			
Cui non absimilis sensus inesse solet.	396	Musae 26	8
ABSIT			
Absit vt ingenuum pungant mea verba pudorem;	400	Musae 36	3
Interim curiositas absit, neque eorum satagamus, quae ad nos	449	Orationes	19
ABSOLUAS			
vtque mature absoluas quae complexus es animo, ad eius gloriam,	464	Epistolae	4
ABSORBENDAS			
Libandas nobis absorbendasque propinat!	401	Musae 39	3
ABSQUE			
Suauiter efficient, absque rigore Scholae.	417	Lucus 28	4
Absque nuptijs foret populus virorum, essemus vnius seculi;	446	Orationes	21
victoriaeque gloriam absque crudelitate effusi sanguinis delibas.	458	Epistolae	15
absque molesta aliorum ac frigida commendatione, si huc reciderit	472	Epistolae	14
ABSTULISTI			
Ipse scribendo irrupisti in compensationes nostras, et abstulisti:	459	Epistolae	2
ABUNDANT			
nos tam defecimus in vtroque quam Excellentiae Vestrae abundant.	441	Orationes	13
ABUNDANTEM			
Principem omnibus delicijs abundantem, obseptum illecebris,	452	Orationes	4
ABUNDANTIA			
etenim abundantia morosa est & sternax, vnde diuites syluas ac saltus	450	Orationes	20
ABUNDE			
O nimium Latro! reliquis furatus abunde,	406	Passio 11	1
Nec hoc abunde est tibi, nisi certae Anchorae	438	Poem.Lat.	5
collisis ignis elicitur) qui nunc mansueti sunt, abunde rugient.	449	Orationes	19
Tu vicissim abunde compensas nos, gratissimoque Almam Matrem	456	Epistolae	8
vt iam compensemur abunde, neque amplius quaerendum sit Tibi,	462	Epistolae	15
abunde succurres Magnificentiae tuae addicitissimis Procancellario	469	Epistolae	25
ABUTAR			
limatae auris atque tersae, quorum grauitate ac purpura non abutar.	445	Orationes	27
ABYSSUS			
et precium, quae abyssus crumenae tantos sumptus aequabit?	468	Epistolae	3
AC			
Reuerendissimo in Christo Patri ac Domino,	385	Musae	T
certa, ac perfacilis mihi!	395	Musae 25	7
sentire ac sapere addecet,	395	Musae 25	17
Ac zephyris, carnis flos remeare nequit.	415	Lucus 23	14
Tristis, vbi ac ferrum tellure reciditur ima,	419	Tr.Mortis	36
ac merentibus vobis gratissimos, Saluete tandem Magistri Artium,	440	Orationes	4
hilare est, laetum, ac lubens, vestram in gratiam amplectimur.	440	Orationes	13
ad Theologiam expeditissimos, tanto ac tam stupendo iudicio, vt,	443	Orationes	25
populo tuo communicans coelum ac terram minori quam cernimus	444	Orationes	7
vita nostra atque calor, longo animi deliquio fugitiuus ac desertor.	444	Orationes	23
limatae auris atque tersae, quorum grauitate ac purpura non abutar.	445	Orationes	27
nullum non angulum verrunt (ac si perdiderint ingenium) vt Spartam	445	Orationes	36
aliae contra semper pertinaces ac tribunitiae, vti Appij.	447	Orationes	21
bello, tubae ac tympana: pax nouum orbem aperuit;	448	Orationes	12
quam subito dispereunt, simul ac concrepuit incendium militare:	448	Orationes	19
ac si Fatis a fuso essent atque consilijs, sine quibus ne vnum quidem	449	Orationes	29
quid enim vtilius quam ex obseruatione exterarum Legum ac morum,	450	Orationes	15
vnde diuites syluas ac saltus quaerunt vbi aedificent, ac	450	Orationes	21
ac si non gregaria essent animalia, sed tigres aut vrsi.	450	Orationes	21
tanquam catenam, qua dissitas nationes ac superbas constringeret.	450	Orationes	24
apparatus, foedera, munitiones, aeque ac nostra spectari debent:	450	Orationes	27
hinc Reges Legatos habent statarios ac resides, quem locum Noster	450	Orationes	30
inspexi facies hominum ac vultus curiosius tanquam emptor;	451	Orationes	13
ac si corpora sua non abirent olim in elementa, sed in bellaria aut	452	Orationes	13
vapores seruiles ad nubes educti aeque magnum tonitru edent ac regij.	452	Orationes	18
quantum quidem ego homuncio ac nanus coniectando assequor.	453	Orationes	21
ac si iuuenili potius impetu correptus, quam adductus maturo	471	Epistolae	25
absque molesta aliorum ac frigida commendatione, si huc reciderit	472	Epistolae	15
ACADEMIA			
De gemina Academia.	388	Musae 8	T
Quare adsis Princeps, aliis Academia mons sit,	210	Cam.1613-a BR	7
Oratio in Discessum Regis ab Academia Cantabrigiae habita 12o die	443	Orationes	T
tantisper supplere donec Academia orationem tuam imbibat probetque,	470	Epistolae	6
Academia vniuersim sumpta vna est e proceribus, inter patritios	470	Epistolae	23

	PAGE	TITLE	LINE
ACADEMIAE			
Oratoris Academiae Cantabrigiensis, habita coram Dominis Legatis	440	Orationes	T
sed etiam doceas tanquam communis defensor fidei et Academiae,	443	Orationes	23
celebrauit Georgius Herbert Academiae Cantabrigiensis Orator.	444	Orationes	T
3. Ad Iacobum Regem Gratiae de Scriptis suis Academiae donatis	458	Epistolae	T
sericatam hanc stultitiam contere, Academiaeque iura, dignitatem,	461	Epistolae	23
sub specie publici commodi, Academiae incommodum videntur allaturi;	462	Epistolae	31
Cancel. Gratiae de Instaurationis Libro Academiae donato	463	Epistolae	T
tum Academiae nostrae, quae per Tuum Partum, ex Matre nunc Auia facta	463	Epistolae	25
neque quotidianae virtutis prouincia gerere personam Academiae,	465	Epistolae	10
Antiquitas praeripuit Tibi gloriam extruendae Academiae,	465	Epistolae	17
quae est vestra felicitas qui puro Academiae farre vtimini.	470	Epistolae	3
tibi conueniat scribenti, quam quod Academiae tuo calamo scribenti:	470	Epistolae	14
ACADEMIAM			
Quid fauores erga hanc Academiam inenarrabiles, cum non solum tuearis	443	Orationes	21
nostram Rempublicam, Academiam, pax adeo Musis summe necessaria est,	448	Orationes	16
Peregrinis Academiam nostram inuisentibus	459	Epistolae	29
dignissime praeficiaris Fisco, etiam Academiam in Thesauris habe:	469	Epistolae	21
Quare et Procancellarius Academiam simulans vel maximos magnatum	470	Epistolae	25
ACADEMIAS			
multi Academias integras subuersas volunt, neque illi e faece vulgi	461	Epistolae	16
ACADEMICARUM			
Magistri Artium, & quidem omnium Aulicarum, Militarium, Academicarum.	440	Orationes	6
ACADEMICI			
Non rhetoricor, Academici, non tinnio:	445	Orationes	22
Recte facitis, Academici, attollentes oculos cum stupore;	450	Orationes	1
Dicam vobis, Academici; ego tunc temporis liberior eram,	451	Orationes	11
ACADEMICIS			
Nunc obrutus Academicis negotijs, aegre hoc tempus illis succido:	471	Epistolae	20
Vna cum promotionibus Academicis maternisque, assumsi mecum	473	Epistolae	8
ACCEDANT			
accidere potest, quam vt ministri Regis Catholici ad nos accedant?	440	Orationes	15
ACCEDIS			
Accedis bene doctus, et poeta.	401	Musae 37	47
ACCEDIT			
Accedit Pyrius puluis, laquearibus Orci	419	Tr.Mortis	57
Hocine accedit ad incredibiles laudes vestras quod quae nos audiamus	443	Orationes	30
ACCEDUNT			
Iuris-consultos, partus sequitur ventrem: quibus accedunt Poetae,	447	Orationes	13
ACCENDENS			
illustrans nos omnes, lumenque accendens de suo lumine,	461	Epistolae	4
ACCENDERIT			
Vt nihilo-minus Tibi luceat, cum nobis accenderit.	461	Epistolae	5
ACCENDIT			
Mulcetur vento, accendit cum fomite partem	420	Tr.Mortis	68
Miscetur vento, accendit cum fomite partem	271	Tr.Mortis VS	68
ACCEPIMUS			
& ipsum accepimus saluum & annulum, annulum Coniugalem,	444	Orationes	18
Accepimus enim Londinenses Librarios omnia transmarina scripta	467	Epistolae	19
ACCEPISTIS			
Accepistis, Viri attentissimi, causas itineris huius, quantum quidem	453	Orationes	20
ACCEPTAM			
contra grassantes flammas aedificijs Honori Tuo acceptam ferimus:	457	Epistolae	19
ACCEPTI			
quae nos soluendo non sumus, in suas tabulas accepti transferat.	467	Epistolae	15
ACCERSERE			
Sic quasi Dijs certem, magnos accersere montes:	432	Poem.Lat.	6
ACCESSIONEM			
Cuius noui tituli accessionem summe gratulantur Excellentijs Vestris	440	Orationes	6
ACCIDERE			
Quid enim iucundius accidere potest, quam vt ministri Regis Catholici	440	Orationes	14
Hoc quidem illis accidere amat, qui celeritatem affectuum raptim	472	Epistolae	1
ACCIPE			
Accipe; ni talem des, tibi qualis erat.	434	Poem.Lat.	6
ACCIPERENT			
Mites acciperent Lampada Praesules,	391	Musae 17	5
ACCIPIUNT			
proin vt Fluuij quas aquas a Fonte accipiunt non retinent ipsi,	456	Epistolae	10
ACCLAMATIONE			
Iustitiam prius tanto cum honore atque acclamatione administrans,	464	Epistolae	15
ACCOLAE			
et quasi accolae Maiestatis, literaturae suae et vicinitati	463	Epistolae	22
ACCREUERIT			
Olim accreuerit Herculi furenti:	401	Musae 37	27
ACCURRENS			
tanquam partubus Virtutum Tuarum, Alma Mater accurrens gratuletur:	469	Epistolae	9
ACER			
Cur non lugentes Elegi? non acer Iambus?	387	Musae 5	5
ACERRIME			
certe nos te absentem omnes acerrime concitatissimeque desiderauimus.	451	Orationes	34
ACETO			
si Reges ipsi quandoque suauitates suas populari aceto condiant.	453	Orationes	19
ACIES			
Instructaeque acies, hyemesque in pellibus actae,	418	Tr.Mortis	28
eadem acies & stipulam secat & lignum:	453	Orationes	28
ACQUIESCAT			
circumspiciens reperisset Te, quasi in tuis palpebris acquiescat.	465	Epistolae	15
ACQUIRENDAM			
nihil ad cognitionem acquirendam peregrinatione conducibilius esse	450	Orationes	6
ACQUIRITE			
Lumina, nutantes paulatim acquirite vires,	432	Poem.Lat.	14

	PAGE	TITLE	LINE
ACRE			
Non potui non ire acre stimulante flagello:	431	Mem.Matr.19	5
Granum Sinapis, acre Alijs, crescens sibi:	437	Poem.Lat.	26
ACRES			
Nascentes radij fugant, vel acres	385	Musae	8
Pro lapsu stillarum abeunt peccata; nec acres	406	Passio 13	3
ACRI			
Adorta numen acri & ignea prece.	422	Mem.Matr.2	17
Pensilis, atque acri dirimens Examine lites.	426	Mem.Matr.7	13
ACRIBUS			
Quo dictis minus acribus notetur.	391	Musae 15	6
ACRIUS			
solebant signa in hostes inijcere, vt milites acrius ea repeterent:	451	Orationes	33
ACTA			
Diuina Christi scriberet acta manu?	412	Lucus 9	2
ACTAE			
Instructaeque acies, hyemesque in pellibus actae,	418	Tr.Mortis	28
ACTIBUS			
Ambitio Cathari quinque constat Actibus.	398	Musae 32	1
ACTIONE			
istis sublimitate solij asserta) vita et actione orbem vegetat.	458	Epistolae	7
ACTIONEM			
vnam actionem e multis seligam, quam vobis amplectendam	445	Orationes	32
ACTIONES			
Tuasque librans actiones, gloriam	414	Lucus 20	13
ACTIONUM			
recte diuinaret, non respiciat materiam actionum, sed quo spiritu,	454	Orationes	10
ACTOS			
Haec vestra spolia actosque ex orbe triumphos communicas cum Alma	458	Epistolae	16
ACTUM			
Imperij hic culmen figo: mortalibus actum est	421	Tr.Mortis	100
ACU			
Illi magnetica acu freti sunt.	463	Epistolae	16
ACUISSEM			
conuertissem, & ex altera parte acuissem me aspectu virtutum Tuarum;	472	Epistolae	6
ACUMINE			
Nec transire licet quo mentis acumine findis	402	Musae 39	27
Tu penetrantiori intellectus acumine; cuius nisi incredibilis fuisset	463	Epistolae	17
ACUTA			
Ecce decus vestrum spinis horrescit, acuta	425	Mem.Matr.5	3
ACUTI			
Sunt tamen acuti quidam & emuncti, qui omnia praeuident:	449	Orationes	28
ACUTO			
Quam nihil illudis! cum quo magis angar acuto	405	Passio 7	3
ACUUNT			
Sic acuunt zelum frigora tanta tuum?	399	Musae 35	6
AD			
Ad Andreae Melvini Scoti Anti-Tami-Cami-Categoriam.	384	Musae	T
Ad Regem Instituti Epigrammatici ratio.	385	Musae 1	T
Ad Melvinum	386	Musae 2	T
Ad eundem In Monstrum vocabuli Anti-Tami-Cami-Categoria.	386	Musae 3	T
Cum tener ad sacros infans sistatur aquales,	388	Musae 9	1
Forsitan & prohibes infans portetur ad vndas,	388	Musae 9	7
Nunc redit ad mitem, ceu benedicta, Deum.	390	Musae 12	16
Haec facit ad nasum sola loquela tuum.	391	Musae 16	6
Hos ad se trahere et mergere gestiens.	391	Musae 17	10
Ad Melvinum De ijsdem.	392	Musae 18	T
Age, prouocemus vsque ad Angelos ipsos,	392	Musae 20	3
Ad fratres.	393	Musae 21	T
Et nos reducas ad lapides auos:	393	Musae 23	6
Percussa dum currunt ad vrbem	394	Musae 23	15
Ad Dominum properare cantus.	394	Musae 23	32
Sionis excelsas ad arces	394	Musae 23	39
nostram Caesar ad insulam	395	Musae 25	2
atque ad barbariem patrum	395	Musae 25	11
Dum gladium stringens Paulus ad arma vocat.	398	Musae 33	12
Haec etiam ad pugnam praesens, qua viuimus, aetas	399	Musae 33	21
Interea ad sacrum stimulat sacra Musica bellum,	399	Musae 33	25
Vna dies Catharos ad bellum miserat omnes:	399	Musae 33	31
Ad bellum missos perdidit vna dies.	399	Musae 33	32
Ad Scotiam. Protrepticon ad Pacem.	399	Musae 35	T
Ad seductos innocentes.	400	Musae 36	T
Ad Melvinum.	400	Musae 37	T
Caesar sobrius ad rei Latinae	401	Musae 37	42
Et tu solus ad Angliae procellas	401	Musae 37	44
Ad Eundem.	401	Musae 38	T
Ad Seren. Regem.	401	Musae 39	T
Ad Deum.	402	Musae 40	T
Ad Dominum morientem.	404	Passio 1	T
Sic omnibus videris ad modum visus.	406	Passio 12	4
Ad Solem deficientem.	407	Passio 16	T
Nec tu pro socio doleas, qui fugit ad illud	415	Lucus 23	15
Non tantum est iter Angelis ad vndas,	415	Lucus 24	11
Vnde MARO laudes duxit ad astra tuas.	416	Lucus 25	4
Respons. ad Vrb. VIII.	416	Lucus 27	T
Ad Vrbanum VIII Pont.	417	Lucus 28	T
Res redit ad vates, Pieriosque duces:	417	Lucus 28	2
Confluere interea passim ad Floralia pubes	418	Tr.Mortis	9
Nempe & millenos ad palum interficit hostes	418	Tr.Mortis	31
Ad Dominum.	421	Lucus 35	T
Ad nos cum radio tam rutilante potes?	424	Mem.Matr.3	2

AD (cont'd)	PAGE	TITLE	LINE
Cuncta ad radices redeant, tumulosque paternos;	425	Mem.Matr.5	13
Nec sic parentem ducar ad optimam:	425	Mem.Matr.6	10
Non exigatur crasis ad alterum.	426	Mem.Matr.6	22
Ad saxa speciem retrahentis humanam,	429	Mem.Matr.12	7
Somnis (nescio queis) nocturna ad vota vocabo:	432	Poem.Lat.	3
Ad Autorem Instaurationis Magnae.	435	Poem.Lat.	T
Ad famae properes vera Tropaea tuae,	435	Poem.Lat.	2
Ad se suaeque matris Arcam regredi:	436	Poem.Lat.	21
Ad se suamque mentis Arcam regredi:	436	Poem.Lat. V	21
Ah! metuo ne me ad luctus mea fata crearint	437	Poem.Lat. V	11
Nec qua consuleres, populumve ad bella vocares,	211	Cam.1613-b BR	9
accidere potest, quam vt ministri Regis Catholici ad nos accedant?	440	Orationes	15
etiam libros indicans ad Theologiam expeditissimos, tanto ac tam	443	Orationes	25
conflueremus omnes ad Aulam, atque ab eo consilium peteremus a quo	443	Orationes	27
Hocine accedit ad incredibiles laudes vestras quod quae nos audiamus	443	Orationes	30
nondum ad spicam barbamque adultum.	445	Orationes	21
Quod ad nostram Rempublicam, Academiam, pax adeo Musis summe	448	Orationes	16
cum anima vinculum impedimento esse ad contemplandum causaris,	448	Orationes	27
perrumpit primipilus, & te cum coelis tuis ad inferos deturbat.	448	Orationes	30
pauxillum vitae, quantum satis ad dolendum, vrbium incendia,	449	Orationes	5
vbi velut ex continentibus tectis ad nos traiecturum est incendium:	449	Orationes	14
curiositas absit, neque eorum satagamus, quae ad nos non spectant;	449	Orationes	20
praecipue pharetrata, quae ad poenam gentium & Bellum spectant.	449	Orationes	27
nihil ad cognitionem acquirendam peregrinatione conducibilius esse	450	Orationes	6
vapores seruiles ad nubes educti aeque magnum tonitru edent ac regij.	452	Orationes	17
incredibilem luxum a Tiberio Caesare ad Constantinum magnum aperirem,	452	Orationes	22
satietas quaedam honoris, quem ad tempus deponere famem excitat:	453	Orationes	10
signo meritus est, ad vera castra traductus, hostem interficiet:	453	Orationes	30
vbi tamen ad vsum tralatae fuerint, machinas conficiunt	454	Orationes	5
machinas conficiunt ad defensionem Reipublicae mirabiles:	454	Orationes	6
qui furtim ascendit ad nubes, vbi iam ingrauescit humore,	454	Orationes	28
vsque ad Pyrenaeas nubes conscendens, reuersus per mare,	454	Orationes	31
commode peruenimus ad laurum hanc, vbi sub vmbra eius paulisper	455	Orationes	13
1. Ad Buckingh. C. Gratulatio de Marchionatu	456	Epistolae	T
manu prehendis Regem, alteram nobis ad radices haerentibus porrigis.	456	Epistolae	15
vt lineae, quamuis diuersa via, omnes tamen ad centrum properant;	456	Epistolae	23
2. Ad R. Naunton Gratiae de Fluuio et de tegendis Tectis stramineis	457	Epistolae	T
si tantum Honori Tuo superesset otij ad legendum, quantum a nobis	457	Epistolae	8
ad legendum, quantum a nobis ad scribendum, cum humanitatis Tuae,	457	Epistolae	9
3. Ad Iacobum Regem Gratiae de Scriptis suis Academiae donatis	458	Epistolae	T
4. Ad Iacobum Regem Gratiae de Fluuio contra Redemptores	460	Epistolae	T
5. Ad F. Bacon, Cancell. Gratiae de Fluuio	460	Epistolae	T
6. Ad R. Naunton, Secret. Gratiae de Fluuio	461	Epistolae	T
certe adeo festinasti ad gratitudines tuas cum emolumento nostro	462	Epistolae	14
Ad Ful. Grevil Gratiae de Fluuio	462	Epistolae	T
Neque sane quispiam incedit Te instructior ad omnem causam,	462	Epistolae	21
8. Ad F. bacon, Cancel. Gratiae de Instaurationis Libro Academiae	463	Epistolae	T
quae complexus es animo, ad eius gloriam, Reipublicae emolumentum,	464	Epistolae	5
9. Ad Mounteg., Thesaurar. Gratulatio	464	Epistolae	T
merita tua ita ascensura, vt eorum vis et virtus ad nos descendat.	464	Epistolae	19
10. Ad R. Naunt. Burgen. Elect.	465	Epistolae	T
Quare nos omnes ad prudentiae eloquentiaeque tuae praesidium	465	Epistolae	15
paratos nos habebis ad gratulationem, vt sic vna opera vtriusque	465	Epistolae	26
12. Ad Heath, Sollicitorem Procuratorem Gratulatio	466	Epistolae	T
13. Ad Archiep. Cantuar. De Bibliopolis Lond.	466	Epistolae	T
vti sanguis solet in re dubia ad cor festinare, ita ad Te confugimus	467	Epistolae	9
ita ad Te confugimus primariam partem ecclesiastici corporis,	467	Epistolae	9
14. Ad Fr. Bacon, Cancell. De Bibliop. Lond.	467	Epistolae	T
Librarios omnia transmarina scripta ad monopolium reuocare moliri,	467	Epistolae	20
vt qui tot subsidia attuleris ad progressum doctrinae, hac etiam	467	Epistolae	28
feracem gloriae, et coeleste ingenium quasi ad metalla damnari.	468	Epistolae	6
15. Ad J. Leigh, Capitalem Iustitiarium Angl. (Camden) Gratulatio	468	Epistolae	T
promotionis tuae gratissime appulit ad nos omnes haud ita certe	468	Epistolae	12
virtutibus, tuo exemplo compensatis, ad vnum omnes incumbamus.	468	Epistolae	17
16. Ad Cranfield, Thesaurar. Gratulatio	469	Epistolae	T
hausisse ab Antiquis, sed et ad Posteros transmissuri videantur.	469	Epistolae	13
17. Ad R. Creighton	470	Epistolae	T
Quin nec demisso, quando ad magnates cogitas, stylo vtare,	470	Epistolae	21
18. Ad Lanc. Andrewes, Episc.	471	Epistolae	T
affectuum raptim sequentes, ad omnem eorum auram vacillant.	472	Epistolae	2
Ego, non nisi meditato, obrepsi ad fauorem Tuum;	472	Epistolae	3
donec lacteam aliquam viam ad candorem Mentis Tuae ducentem aut	472	Epistolae	9
ad mea in Honorem Tuum officia erectior solutiorque redibo,	473	Epistolae	2
ADAM			
Haud secus ingenitis dotibus orbus Adam.	410	Lucus 1	4
ADAME			
Crudum olim pomum, tristis Adame, tibi.	412	Lucus 9	4
ADDAS			
Addas sigillum: nempe Symbolum suae	438	Poem.Lat.	6
ADDE			
Adde pijs animis quaeuis occasio lucro est,	390	Musae 12	11
Adde etiam currus, & cum temone Britanno	419	Tr.Mortis	45
Adde his trientem Musices, quae molliens	423	Mem.Matr.2	42
adde quod angusti est animi aut superbi sua tantum nosse,	450	Orationes	17
ADDECET			
sentire ac sapere addecet,	395	Musae 25	17
ADDI			
praemium consequare, cui neque addi quicquam potest, neque detrahi.	457	Epistolae	5
ADDICITISSIMIS			
succurres Magnificentiae tuae addicitissimis Procancellario Rel.	469	Epistolae	26

	PAGE	TITLE	LINE
ADDISCERE			
Mentibus attonitis cupiunt addiscere ritus:	402	Musae 39	9
ADDIT			
Innumeram nostris partibus addit opem.	399	Musae 33	22
Vltra loquendi tempus; addit Anchora:	438	Poem.Lat.	4
ADDITI			
Quod Crux nequibat fixa, Clavique additi, ...	438	Poem.Lat.	1
ADDUCTUS			
quam adductus maturo consilio, primas dedissem literas, . .	471	Epistolae	26
ADDUNT			
Angelicae turmae nostris se coetibus addunt:	402	Musae 39	10
ADEAS			
prouecta atque adulta, ipsam possessionem adeas, agathei ge tuxei.	470	Epistolae	8
ADEO			
Nunc adeo per te viuunt, vt repere possint, ...	384	Musae	5
Cur adeo immodica relligione cales?	399	Musae 35	2
Quantum caedi? adeon' vnam vos pascere vitam, ...	419	Tr.Mortis	34
Quantum caedi? adeon' vnam nos vivere vitam, ...	271	Tr.Mortis VS	34
Tam demissa, ipsamque adeo subeuntia terram?	420	Tr.Mortis	94
Iisque siccis adeo vt os Molossorum	429	Mem.Matr.12	3
Adeo inficetae, plumbeae, Meduseae, ...	429	Mem.Matr.12	6
quam Nuptiae, quas adeo laudant Poetae, vt in coelum transtulerint:	446	Orationes	17
pax adeo Musis summe necessaria est, vt sine ea nihil simus.	448	Orationes	16
at cur adeo dolent? cur ringuntur?	451	Orationes	22
adeon' nihili videtur res, Principem omnibus delicijs abundantem,	452	Orationes	3
indicantes, se non amare patriam terram, a qua adeo remouentur.	452	Orationes	13
quod sane adeo nobile fuit & honorificum, vt nihil habeat Inuidia	453	Orationes	23
praesertim donec transeat nubes illa, quae vicinos adeo infestat:	455	Orationes	15
adeo vt qui non subijciuntur ditioni, eruditioni vestrae obtemperent:	458	Epistolae	13
adeon' es praedo omnis gloriae, vt ne gratitudinis laudem nobis	459	Epistolae	2
certe adeo festinasti ad gratitudines tuas cum emolumento nostro	462	Epistolae	14
eccum nunc altera occasio, adeo festinat virtus tua:	465	Epistolae	24
caute incipe, cohibens adeo stylum ingeniumque;	470	Epistolae	11
magis id adeo factum esse mansuetudine Tua incomparabili, . .	472	Epistolae	21
illustrissime) quod pronomina mea adeo audacter incedant in hac	473	Epistolae	15
non adeo sanatae ab optimo Rege nostro quin turgescat indies,	473	Epistolae	21
ADEST			
Primus adest nobis, Pharisaeis omnibus hostis, ...	398	Musae 33	9
Hipponensis adest properans, & torquet in hostes	398	Musae 33	17
Christus adest: crebris aedes percurrite scopis, ...	413	Lucus 15	1
(Nam post Babelem linguae adest confusio)	422	Mem.Matr.2	13
Adest tamen anus illa querula, & philegklemon, quam audire videor	453	Orationes	25
ADHIBEAS			
Iam si inter commendandum adhibeas ei calamistros vti iuuenculae,	470	Epistolae	18
Cui sententiae si fidem adhibeas, assensumque Tuum veritati omni	473	Epistolae	10
ADHIBENDA			
quo eorum conditio sublimior, eo maior cura adhibenda sit. . .	446	Orationes	35
ADHIBENDAM			
viam aperiens & methodum in studijs adhibendam, etiam libros indicans	443	Orationes	24
ADHUC			
Deerat adhuc vitijs hominum dignissima mundo	419	Tr.Mortis	49
Deerat adhuc vitijs nostris dignissima mundo	271	Tr.Mortis VS	49
ADIJCITUR			
Huic Glans adijcitur (non quam ructare vetustas	419	Tr.Mortis	60
Hinc Glans adijcitur (non quam ructare vetustas	419	Tr.Mortis V	60
ADIMI			
vestem non adimi suam, ...	396	Musae 25	21
ADIPISCARIS			
vtriusque Reipublicae calculum et ciuilis et literariae adipiscaris.	466	Epistolae	1
ADIRE			
Sintque ausae thalamum solis adire tui.	384	Musae	6
Et per se Templi limen adire velis:	388	Musae 9	8
ADIUNGAT			
vestrae coronae ciuili & literariae tertiam Coelestem sero adiungat.	459	Epistolae	21
ADIUNGIMUS			
Quare nos tertium praedictis adiungimus Gratiarum Fluuium, . . .	462	Epistolae	23
ADMINISTRANS			
Iustitiam prius tanto cum honore atque acclamatione administrans,	464	Epistolae	15
ADMIRANS			
occurrit ei Democritus, & ingenium admirans, domum secum duxit,	453	Orationes	36
ADMODUM			
Protagoras cum eleganter admodum caudices ligni fasciculo vinxisset,	453	Orationes	33
Philosophus de Tactu & Visu, id apposite admodum huc transferatur.	472	Epistolae	36
ADMONUIT			
Euentum Naso vidit et admonuit;	399	Musae 33	30
ADMOUEAS			
Suauiter admoueas notum tibi carne flagellum, ...	406	Passio 9	3
ADNECTAM			
Ipse tuae solum adnectam, sine murmure, thensae.	426	Mem.Matr.7	16
ADOLERI			
post ingentes Hecatombas, exiguam thuris micam adoleri legimus.	469	Epistolae	17
ADOLESCAT			
Ne, si flamma nouis adolescat mota flabellis, ...	399	Musae 35	11
ADORIANTUR			
cum leunculum & dominum suum contra naturam adoriantur: . .	454	Orationes	18
ADORTA			
Adorta numen acri & ignea prece.	422	Mem.Matr.2	17
ADSIS			
Quare adsis Princeps, aliis Academia mons sit, ...	210	Cam.1613-a BR	7
ADSIT			
vt nullus sit angulus corporis, nulla venula, vbi non adsit CAROLVS.	445	Orationes	3

AEQUOR (cont'd)	PAGE	TITLE	LINE
Et tibi vicinas porrigit aequor aquas:	399	Musae 35	8
AEQUORE			
Scilicet has olim diuisas aequore terras	402	Musae 39	14
AEQUOS			
Vicini populi passim mirantur, & aequos	401	Musae 39	8
AEQUUM			
Magnatumque inopumque aequum certamen & ardor:	429	Mem.Matr.13	3
aequumne est vt tot labores & sollicitudines Principum sine . .	446	Orationes	11
AER			
Tranquillus aer nascitur:	396	Musae 27	2
Aura volans, vitamque aer, quam pauerat, aufert.	420	Tr.Mortis	84
Tuque aer inflato tubam, dum plurimus ignis	211	Cam.1613-b BR	5
AERARIUM			
Aerarium; sequester experientiae, ...	436	Poem.Lat.	8
AERE			
Quod si tam integrum tibi esset gratificari nobis in terra & aere,	457	Epistolae	22
AEREA			
Vberaque aerea hiscentem fallentia natum?	426	Mem.Matr.7	4
AEREM			
Recte, quem trahit, aerem repellit	428	Mem.Matr.10	6
AESTATE			
lucos aestate, pinguem togam hyeme:	448	Orationes	23
superiori aestate sponte suauiterque patefacta, nunc etiam . .	467	Epistolae	2
AESTATEM			
nunquam frigidiorem aestatem sensimus; at quo tandem?	450	Orationes	37
AESTIMATUR			
Et vnus impar aestimatur viribus, ...	388	Musae 8	5
AESTIMEMUS			
incubat artibus, & obstetricatur, minus quam par est, aestimemus.	448	Orationes	34
AESTUANS			
Tentando sanum: si calet, aestuans, ...	426	Mem.Matr.6	14
AESTUANTI			
Plumbo ducta fuisset aestuanti, ...	400	Musae 37	22
AETAS			
Non mea fert aetas, vt te, veterane, lacessam;	386	Musae 2	1
Aspice, dum perstas, vt te tua deserat aetas, ...	386	Musae 2	5
Scilicet emptorem si res aut parcior aetas	388	Musae 9	5
Haec etiam ad pugnam praesens, qua viuimus, aetas	399	Musae 33	21
Progenies, mundique aetas abdomine nostro	418	Tr.Mortis	4
Progenies, mundique aetas abdomine tanto	418	Tr.Mortis V	4
Debuit ista pati prima & non nobilis aetas:	432	Poem.Lat.	29
vos, vos, inquam, excutite, quorum aetas teritur in libris: . .	445	Orationes	15
AETATE			
tripudiet Alma Mater licet aetate prouectior, etiam anus subsultans	454	Orationes	35
AETATEM			
etiam senectus, quam aetatem in hac palaestra consecutus mihi videor.	471	Epistolae	8
AETATI			
sed et ambabus vlnis osculisque ei aetati debitis excipientes,	463	Epistolae	7
denique huic aetati quae talem virum protulit, cum quinque millibus	463	Epistolae	26
AETATIS			
Aetatis numerum supplebit causa minorem:	386	Musae 2	3
AETERNA			
Aeterna summae gloria regiae, ...	433	Poem.Lat.	2
AETERNI			
Comparat aeterni regna beata Dei.	388	Musae 9	4
AETERNITATE			
nos chartis et aeternitate occupatos, temporarijs hisce negotiolis	466	Epistolae	6
AETERNITATEM			
vnde consequimur, vel inuitis Fatis, quasi nodosam aeternitatem.	446	Orationes	24
aeternitatem nominis Tui subsidiumque Magnificentiae Tuae . .	464	Epistolae	5
AETERNITATI			
Maiestatem vestram aeternitati in scriptis nostris certissime	458	Epistolae	31
AETERNO			
Longius aeterno, latius orbe decus?	435	Poem.Lat.	6
AETERNOS			
Humana aeternos agerent praecordia questus:	433	Poem.Lat.	39
AETERNUM			
Responde aeternum titulo; quoque ordine felix	402	Musae 39	18
aeternum illud praemium consequare, cui neque addi quicquam potest,	457	Epistolae	4
AETHER			
Compita feruescunt pedibus, clamoribus aether.	418	Tr.Mortis	11
AETHIOPISSA			
Aethiopissa ambit Cestum Diuersi Coloris Virum.	437	Poem.Lat.	T
AETNA			
Aetna Cacum igniuomum dedit, hic Ixiona multis	420	Tr.Mortis	87
Aetna Cacum igniuomum dedit, hic Ixiona Graecis	272	Tr.Mortis VS	87
AETNAM			
Nox Aetnam, noctemque Chaos genuere priores.	420	Tr.Mortis	86
AEUI			
Deducens lacrymas prioris aeui	428	Mem.Matr.10	11
AEUUM			
Quae sapiunt aeuum, ceu cariosa iacent.	386	Musae 3	4
Quid memorem tormenta, quibus prius horruit aeuum;	419	Tr.Mortis	39
Machina, quam nullum satis execrabitur aeuum;	419	Tr.Mortis	50
Sic aeuum exigitur tardum, dum praepetis anni	428	Mem.Matr.9	13
AFFECTI			
Nos igitur hoc metu affecti, vti sanguis solet in re dubia ad cor	467	Epistolae	8
AFFECTUS			
Affectus socijs tuis remittens.	401	Musae 37	32
Affectusque mei similem; nec languida misce	427	Mem.Matr.7	30

	PAGE	TITLE	LINE
AFFECTUS (cont'd)			
Nunc enim exploratos habet nostros in se affectus, timores, . .	450	Orationes	34
hoc enim fastum amputat, affectus explorat, adulationem ventilat,	453	Orationes	1
AFFECTUUM			
qui celeritatem affectuum raptim sequentes, ad omnem eorum auram	472	Epistolae	1
AFFLAT			
Corda furor, spissaque afflat caligine sensus?	401	Musae 39	5
Contiguas stirpes afflat, eaeque rosas.	425	Mem.Matr.5	6
AFFLATA			
Non quia Pontificum sunt olim afflata veneno, ...	390	Musae 13	1
AFFLATU			
Afflatu perimunt: en, Cymba Cocytia turbis	420	Tr.Mortis	81
Fluuium placidissimo fauorum tuorum afflatu nobis tuere. . .	461	Epistolae	25
AFFLES			
Obtutu placido benignus affles, ...	384	Musae	3
AFFLICTIO			
Afflictio.	414	Lucus 19	T
AFFRICTU			
vt ex affrictu Libri vestri hominem illico contundamus. . .	459	Epistolae	8
AGAM			
Ah! Cheiragra vetat, quo minus, inquit, agam.	389	Musae 11	2
Quare vt parcius agam vobiscum, simulque & laboribus meis, . .	445	Orationes	28
quam simpliciter vobiscum agam, quam non longe abeam Oratorum more,	445	Orationes	35
AGAMOIS			
& Licurgus magnus Legislator atimian prosetheke tois agamois.	446	Orationes	21
AGAMUS			
neque de priuato agamus bono, sed publico;	448	Orationes	6
AGANT			
Nosse sui quid agant, quaedam est quoque musica sanctis, . .	427	Mem.Matr.9	3
AGAS			
Mitis agas: tenerae duplicant sibi verbera mentes, ...	406	Passio 9	5
AGATHEI			
prouecta atque adulta, ipsam possessionem adeas, agathei ge tuxei.	470	Epistolae	9
AGATHON			
Ou pheggos, koinon t' agathon, mian eis thuran eirgein . . .	430	Mem.Matr.17	5
Otan nomeus agathon kuna exei, kai oi alloi nomeis boulontai plesion	447	Orationes	31
AGE			
Age, prouocemus vsque ad Angelos ipsos, ...	392	Musae 20	3
Quare age, Mens, effare, precor, quo numine laeso? . . .	432	Poem.Lat.	17
AGEDUM			
Eia, agedum scribo: vicisti, Musa; sed audi, ...	431	Mem.Matr.19	7
AGELAS			
kai oi alloi nomeis boulontai plesion autou tas agelas istanai.	447	Orationes	32
AGER			
Nam te nunc Ager, Vrbs, & Aula plorant:	428	Mem.Matr.10	8
AGERENT			
Humana aeternos agerent praecordia questus:	433	Poem.Lat.	39
AGGERUM			
Qualis nescius aggerum	403	Musae 40	9
AGGOS			
Psuxes asthenes erkos, amauron pneumatos aggos, ...	429	Mem.Matr.14	1
AGGREDERIS			
Nunc etiam Christum callidus aggrederis.	406	Passio 11	2
AGGREDIATUR			
quo spiritu, qua arte, quanto impetu atque vigore res aggrediatur:	454	Orationes	11
AGGREDIENDUS			
Tunc Dominus clauis aggrediendus erit.	408	Passio 18	4
AGGREDITUR			
Aggreditur Matrem (conductis carmine Parcis)	431	Mem.Matr.19	3
agxonais abiectis, iter aggreditur & labores, haud ignarus, . .	452	Orationes	32
AGIMUS			
Quid agimus? hoc saltem solutio est;	459	Epistolae	4
AGIS			
Pastor agis proprios, medio tutissimus, agnos.	402	Musae 39	32
AGITET			
Si-quas mens agitet moles (dum pectora saeuo	432	Poem.Lat.	9
AGITUR			
idque pro Libris, de quibus nusquam rectius quam apud Te agitur.	467	Epistolae	19
AGMEN			
Si ducat agmen, reprime; sin claudat, sinas.	414	Lucus 20	14
AGMINA			
Quod non Lanigerae pecudes, non Agmina lustrent?	432	Poem.Lat.	19
AGNOS			
Pastor agis proprios, medio tutissimus, agnos.	402	Musae 39	32
AGNOSCAM			
quam meis meritis vllis, semper lubentissimeque agnoscam: . .	472	Epistolae	23
AGNOSCAS			
extra mortalitatis aleam, et quo magis Tuum agnoscas, in ipso partu,	459	Epistolae	11
AGNOSCERE			
tam communi hac luce, quam Tua, cum id agnoscere vnquam desinam.	472	Epistolae	24
AGNOSCIT			
Agnoscitque tuam Machina tota Crucem.	409	Passio 21	2
nullas Herculeas columnas, quas iam olim possidet, agnoscit.	440	Orationes	18
AGNUM			
Alapas nec Arietes? Quid ergo? Agnum & Crucem.	421	Lucus 33	6
AGNUS			
Vbique est Deus, Agnus, Ara, Flamen.	408	Passio 19	14
Venditus est Agnus, non tamen emptus erit.	410	Lucus 4	2
AGO			
Cur sine te, votis immoriturus, ago?	421	Lucus 35	6

	PAGE	TITLE	LINE
ALIAE (cont'd)			
Quod aliae gentes manibus in coelum sublatis, lachrymis in terram	448	Orationes	34
ALIAS			
vt semper post nouas dignitates, alias tibi quaerant et moliantur.	464	Epistolae	23
ALIENA			
Cur sic displiceat vox aliena tibi?	388	Musae 9	10
cum quanto plus possint in sua terra, tanto minus in aliena.	450	Orationes	12
ALIENAS			
Neque alienas tantum ex hoc itinere cognouit Respublicas sed quod	450	Orationes	32
ALIENIS			
re vna omnium grauissima, alienis oculis iudicioque inniti;	447	Orationes	23
ALIENOS			
Sin, Melvine, pedes alienos postulet infans,	388	Musae 9	9
ALIENUM			
Omne regnum suo Principi carcer est, aut si excedat, alienum:	450	Orationes	13
ALIIS			
Quare adsis Princeps, aliis Academia mons sit,	210	Cam.1613-a BR	7
ALIJ			
In patinas alij: furit inconstantia vini	418	Tr.Mortis	21
ipso Parnasso siti sumus, liberiorem, quam alij, prospectum habeamus.	449	Orationes	34
Quare quomodo alij molem hanc laetitiae suae exprimant,	456	Epistolae	25
praedia, alij immunitates carpunt, nonnulli Fluuium inuident,	461	Epistolae	15
si qui alij exurgant promissores magnifici et hiantes, qui,	462	Epistolae	30
cuius Libri si alij alijs (tanquam montes olim) imponerentur,	467	Epistolae	30
ALIJS			
Naufragij causa est alijs mare, roboris Anglo,	411	Lucus 6	5
Suamque in alijs possidet prudentiam.	412	Lucus 13	4
Granum Sinapis, acre Alijs, crescens sibi:	437	Poem.Lat.	26
cuius Libri si alij alijs (tanquam montes olim) imponerentur,	467	Epistolae	30
ALIO			
Non alio Cathari modo	395	Musae 25	8
Vt morbi perimant, alioque in puluere prostet?	433	Poem.Lat.	35
ALIOQUI			
Et amor alioqui loquax est;	471	Epistolae	7
ALIORUM			
Sed aliorum iniuriae tuarum virtutum pabula sunt, qui lemas istas	462	Epistolae	11
absque molesta aliorum ac frigida commendatione, si huc reciderit	472	Epistolae	15
ALIOS			
aliosque titulos aeque nobis memorantibus, ac merentibus vobis	440	Orationes	3
ALIQUAM			
donec lacteam aliquam viam ad candorem Mentis Tuae ducentem aut	472	Epistolae	9
ALIQUANDO			
Non nego bellum aliquando necessarium esse, belliqué miserias gratas,	449	Orationes	12
vt aliquando existimen id egisse prudentissimum Patrem tuum,	451	Orationes	30
Nihil vtilius Regi quam aliquando non regnare:	452	Orationes	38
ALIQUANTISPER			
vt cedam aliquantisper expectationi hominum, rariusque paulo fodiam	472	Epistolae	27
ALIQUANTULUM			
ipse egit oratorem, vt & ego aliquantulum hoc nomine glorier.	450	Orationes	31
ALIQUAS			
Quin liceat nobis aliquas procudere voces:	386	Musae 3	5
dignitatem diu expectantem magnas aliquas virtutes tandem meritis	464	Epistolae	12
ALIQUEM			
Iam dari nobis vellemus Iesuitam aliquem, vt ex affrictu Libri vestri	459	Epistolae	7
receptusque sim in aliquem apud Honorem Tuum locum, magis id adeo	472	Epistolae	20
ALIQUID			
Quin populo, clemens, aliquid largire caloris:	397	Musae 29	3
ALIQUIS			
Si per haec ludicra nostra pars aliquis eius laetitiae,	443	Orationes	9
ALIQUO			
si quis de Principe aliquo, quis sit futurus aut qualis,	454	Orationes	9
ALIQUOS			
vt nullus fere elabatur dies, qui non hostes aliquos nobis apériat:	461	Epistolae	14
ALIT			
Liber alit rixas: potantibus omnia bina	418	Tr.Mortis	18
ALITER			
Haud aliter cum Christus obit, prae funere tanto	409	Passio 20	5
tanquam ligna obliqua, aliter magna haec mundi domus corrueret:	450	Orationes	28
& metalla ei inserendo, aliter mundus iam diu fuisset deuoratus.	452	Orationes	25
ALIUD			
Aliud oratio, aliud epistola. Parce doctrinae in epistolis;	470	Epistolae	32
ALIUM			
quanquam quem alium fructum potuimus expectare ab Eo, in quem fauor	456	Epistolae	17
ALLA			
Ou sathron, oude melon epleto, alla voos:	429	Mem.Matr.14	6
Alla meneit', ou gar taraxos poti metera bainei,	431	Mem.Matr.18	5
on me themiton en, ou di' emauton emarton, alla dia tauta.	452	Orationes	31
ALLATURI			
sub specie publici commodi, Academiae incommodum videntur allaturi;	463	Epistolae	1
ALLO			
Ainon omou Zoein kai pneumatos allo genesthai	431	Mem.Matr.17	22
ALLOI			
Aiazo geneteiran, epaiazousi kai alloi,	430	Mem.Matr.17	1
kai oi alloi nomeis boulontai plesion autou tas agelas istanai.	447	Orationes	31
ALLOS			
Thanein suneidos kreitton, e allos bioun.	430	Mem.Matr.15	16
ALMA			
Praetulit Astraea, aut solio Themis alma vetusto	426	Mem.Matr.7	12
tripudiet Alma Mater licet aetate prouectior, etiam anus subsultans	454	Orationes	35
aut tantum de nullo vnquam Filio Alma Mater, quantum de Te sibi	457	Epistolae	26
vestra spolia actosque ex orbe triumphos communicas cum Alma Matre,	458	Epistolae	17

ALMA (cont'd)	PAGE	TITLE	LINE
Quanta hilaritate aspicit Alma Mater filios suos iam emancipatos,	461	Epistolae	30
vt Alma Mater libentissime caput reclinet in tuo sinu, oculusque	465	Epistolae	12
tanquam partubus Virtutum Tuarum, Alma Mater accurrens gratuletur:	469	Epistolae	9
ALMAE			
Arbor & ipse inuersa vocer: dumque insitus almae	428	Mem.Matr.11	5
neque amplius quaerendum sit Tibi, Almae Nutrici quid reponas.	462	Epistolae	16
expectamus indies futurum, Almae Matris amorem tecum simul euehas.	462	Epistolae	29
meo quadrabunt, quae almae matri inconcinna erunt atque enormia.	470	Epistolae	15
ALMAM			
abunde compensas nos, gratissimoque Almam Matrem prosequeris animo:	456	Epistolae	8
Quis enim tunc inuiseret Almam Matrem destitutam omni commeatu?	461	Epistolae	2
vt Almam Matrem spe noua grauidam semper atque praegnantem	464	Epistolae	25
ALMI			
Nec dextra te fugit, almi Amoris emblema?	397	Musae 31	1
Almi choragus luminis?	407	Passio 16	2
ALMOS			
Nos misere flemus, solesque obducimus almos	427	Mem.Matr.9	5
ALPHA			
Ei en en o anthropos, inquit Medicorum Alpha, ouk an elgeen.	446	Orationes	19
ALTA			
Tu Synodosque, Patresque, & quod dedit alta vetustas	402	Musae 39	25
Vt, fluuio currente, vadum sonat, alta quiescunt.	433	Poem.Lat.	48
ALTER			
Quid vetat vt pueri vagitus suppleat alter,	388	Musae 9	13
Primo, vnus aut alter parum ritus placet:	398	Musae 32	2
Sunt, praeter vitam: saxis hic sternitur, alter	418	Tr.Mortis	19
Vnde vagans passim recte vocer alter Vlysses,	428	Mem.Matr.11	13
ALTERA			
Ritibus vna Sacris opponitur; altera Sanctos	386	Musae 4	3
Quo fugies, sudor? quamuis pars altera Christi	404	Passio 2	1
Alteraque haec tua mors, Ilias esto mihi.	428	Mem.Matr.11	14
& cum ipse sis in summa arbore altera manu prehendis Regem,	456	Epistolae	14
eccum nunc altera occasio, adeo festinat virtus tua:	465	Epistolae	24
conuertissem, & ex altera parte acuissem me aspectu virtutum Tuarum;	472	Epistolae	6
ALTERAM			
manu prehendis Regem, alteram nobis ad radices haerentibus porrigis.	456	Epistolae	14
ALTERNIS			
Teque Deum alternis cantans Ambrosius iram,	398	Musae 33	19
ALTERO			
fecisti Fluuium nostrum conseruans altero eloquentiae Fluuio,	462	Epistolae	19
nunc denuo ex aedibus Eboracensibus ab altero Cancellario INSTAVRARI,	464	Epistolae	1
cum excusso altero iugo, dimidiaque operis parte leuatus,	473	Epistolae	1
ALTEROS			
alterosque maris quasi Flagellatores expugnatos fusosque nobis	462	Epistolae	8
ALTERUM			
Exemploque tuo nascor in alterum:	425	Mem.Matr.4	14
Non exigatur crasis ad alterum.	426	Mem.Matr.6	22
date mihi CAROLVM alterum, quamlibet Magnum, modo detis eum in flore,	445	Orationes	19
foetum vestrum, hunc alterum Carolum, hunc fasciculum Prudentiae,	459	Epistolae	10
communes Reipublicae lachrymae alterum nobis Fluuium effunderent.	462	Epistolae	6
ALTERUTRI			
non quod nunc indulgeas alterutri, sed quod deinceps indultum nollem.	470	Epistolae	12
ALTIS			
An quod semotum populo laquearibus altis	387	Musae 7	3
ALTITUDO			
velut Romani lacum, cuius altitudo ignota erat, dedicabant victoriae;	449	Orationes	21
ALTIUS			
quanto altius crescunt, tanto etiam altius agunt radices:	464	Epistolae	18
ALTO			
Aut potius Christi sanguis demissus ab alto,	399	Musae 35	9
Ipse etiam Christus coelo speculatus ab alto,	402	Musae 39	11
ALTUS			
Ille tamen, quamuis altus, tua crimina ridens	387	Musae 7	7
ALUEOS			
Contaminatis alueosque caelestes	404	Passio 5	4
ALUEUS			
Ex Veritate matre; Mellis alueus;	436	Poem.Lat.	23
ALUMNI			
Artificesque necis clueant, & mortis alumni.	418	Tr.Mortis	30
Arma tui metuunt alumni.	434	Poem.Lat.	24
ALUMNIS			
alumnis suis orbarentur, quin communes Reipublicae lachrymae alterum	462	Epistolae	5
AMA			
Tu vero vale, mi proorator, amaque Tuum G. H.	471	Epistolae	12
AMABILI			
Exundat fluuio Nilus amabili.	403	Musae 40	10
AMABILIS			
Nudetur illic lucus amabilis,	434	Poem.Lat.	30
AMANTE			
quam audire videor dicentem, Pulchrum quidem iter & Amante dignum;	453	Orationes	26
AMARE			
indicantes, se non amare patriam terram, a qua adeo remouentur.	452	Orationes	12
AMARTEKUIA			
Ergou amartekuia, neon peplon aimati stikton	431	Mem.Matr.17	13
AMAT			
Nempe Nouatores quis Veteranus amat?	398	Musae 33	14
Amat varietatem Natura omnis, flores, animalia, tum maxime homo,	453	Orationes	15
Hoc quidem illis accidere amat, qui celeritatem affectuum raptim	472	Epistolae	1
AMATO			
Quondam fessus Amor loquens Amato,	439	Poem.Lat.	10

	PAGE	TITLE	LINE
AMAUIT			
Ergon' amauit Princeps? Quippini; homo est, non statua;	446	Orationes	9
AMAURON			
Psuxes asthenes erkos, amauron pneumatos aggos,	429	Mem.Matr.14	1
AMBABUS			
Postremis ambabus idem sentimus vterque;	386	Musae 4	5
solum (quod innuis) sed et ambabus vlnis osculisque ei aetati debitis	463	Epistolae	7
AMBIENTEM			
summouet Oceanum ambientem, adeo vt qui non subijciuntur ditioni,	458	Epistolae	12
AMBIS			
Ante tuum tempus coelum gratissimus ambis.	402	Musae 39	29
AMBIT			
Aethiopissa ambit Cestum Diuersi Coloris Virum.	437	Poem.Lat.	T
Ah longum, quae te deperit, ambit iter.	437	Poem.Lat. V	4
AMBITIO			
Ambitio Cathari quinque constat Actibus.	398	Musae 32	1
AMBITIONIBUS			
Indulgens proprijs ambitionibus,	391	Musae 17	8
AMBITIONIS			
ambitionisque strumae, non adeo sanatae ab optimo Rege nostro quin	473	Epistolae	21
AMBITIOSA			
Cum per te sit res ambitiosa mori.	435	Poem.Lat.	8
AMBITIOSAE			
an inter lauros principis hederae nostrae ambitiosae locus est?	456	Epistolae	4
AMBITUM			
intra ambitum amplexusque foelicitatis Tuae receptae, communi calore	469	Epistolae	18
AMBITUS			
Labes, somniaque, ambitusque diros,	401	Musae 37	38
AMBIUIT			
at ille ambiuit nobilissimam Austriacam familiam, Aquilamque illam,	446	Orationes	14
AMBROSIUS			
Teque Deum alternis cantans Ambrosius iram,	398	Musae 33	19
AMBULAT			
Quis iste tandem? non enim vultu ambulat	436	Poem.Lat.	1
AMBUSTIS			
Ambustis sudibus: pars vitam in pocula fundunt,	418	Tr.Mortis	20
AMENTATA			
Non fert Vcalegon, atque amentata retorquet	418	Tr.Mortis	14
AMETIS			
ita me ametis omnes, vt ego nihil vspiam laetum, nihil candidum	451	Orationes	14
AMICA			
Aut saeuum reputes. Amica nostra est	400	Musae 37	11
Principibus, sed amica fiunt.	434	Poem.Lat.	28
Tot & tanta loquens amica, scripsit:	439	Poem.Lat.	11
AMICO			
praesertim cum amico fidere periculosius sit, quam hostem superare.	453	Orationes	32
AMICORUM			
Sunt hostium legata, non amicorum,	406	Passio 10	2
AMICTU			
Non ego vos posthac hederae velatus amictu	432	Poem.Lat.	2
AMICUM			
Quis sic amicum excipiet, vt Cathari Deum,	397	Musae 28	13
AMICUS			
Impediant, apices legis amicus obit.	388	Musae 9	6
Candor amicus.	390	Musae 14	16
AMNES			
Tu flectis amnes, tu mare caerulum	433	Poem.Lat.	13
AMO			
Et quid tu tandem desidiosus? AMO.	413	Lucus 16	6
AMOR			
Nec vel tantillum pignus habebit amor?	396	Musae 26	2
Amor.	413	Lucus 16	T
Roma. Anagr. Oram. Maro. / Ramo. Armo. / Mora. Amor.	416	Lucus 25	T
Et cum sublata laude recedit AMOR.	416	Lucus 25	12
Inuertis nomen. Quid tibi dicit? AMOR.	416	Lucus 26	6
Nempe es totus amor, medulla amoris,	417	Lucus 30	3
Sunt etiam tenebrae, quas tamen optat amor.	437	Poem.Lat.	2
Quisnam horum maior sit, dubitatur, amor.	437	Poem.Lat.	2
Cuiusnam maior sit, dubitatur, amor.	437	Poem.Lat. V	2
Quondam fessus Amor loquens Amato,	439	Poem.Lat.	10
Notissimus est Codri amor, cuius manifestationem in gentem suam	453	Orationes	7
si amor virginis eo pertraxit Principem, quo tandem ducet amor	453	Orationes	27
amor virginis eo pertraxit Principem, quo tandem ducet amor Patriae?	453	Orationes	28
Daphnen suam, cuius amor deinceps in triumphos & laurus mutabitur.	455	Orationes	11
sed perspectissimus tuus in nos amor, praestantissimaeque animi dotes	465	Epistolae	11
curesque vt tuus in nos amor, antehac satis perspectus,	466	Epistolae	3
tuus amor et authoritas istos sorices nobis abigat.	468	Epistolae	26
Et amor alioqui loquax est;	471	Epistolae	7
etiam teneor, sed laxioribus vinculis, quaeque amor saepe remittit:	472	Epistolae	34
AMORE			
Sic nunc plena boni sunt omnia Fratris, amore	393	Musae 21	3
Christus Apostolici cinctus amore gregis.	398	Musae 33	10
Hoc saltem officio fungar amore tui.	437	Poem.Lat.	8
dignum est, quo magis amore coalescamus, vtraque gens Hispanica,	440	Orationes	22
gaudeo quidem de ingenti amore in Principem, cui nulla dilectio par	451	Orationes	21
AMOREM			
nimirum infinitum Principis in suam gentem amorem, cui pacem	449	Orationes	37
timores, suspiria, expostulationes, iras, amorem rursus.	450	Orationes	35
expectamus indies futurum, Almae Matris amorem tecum simul euehas.	462	Epistolae	29
sume tecum amorem illum quo soles beare Amplitudini tuae deuotissimos	464	Epistolae	27

AMORES	PAGE	TITLE	LINE
Maturusque suos coquens amores	408	Passio 19	12
Crescent illae, crescetis amores. Cui sententiae si fidem adhibeas,	473	Epistolae	9
AMORIS			
audent amoris Symbolum?	397	Musae 28	15
Nec dextra te fugit, almi Amoris emblema?	397	Musae 31	1
Nempe es totus amor, medulla amoris,	417	Lucus 30	3
Sanctius in Regno Magni credebat Amoris	439	Poem.Lat.	14
idem feruor qui impar sub amoris signo meritus est, ad vera castra	453	Orationes	29
quis scit an & amoris onus scite vinctum ligatumque, & per tot	453	Orationes	38
hunc quidem gradum pignus habes amoris nostri, haec est ansa qua	456	Epistolae	5
plurimumque suspicimus cumulum amoris Tui, qui vtrumque curasti,	457	Epistolae	20
Tu vero promptitudinem amoris nostri, non passim expositam,	466	Epistolae	2
non est quod nostram quoque, cum amoris symbolo festinantem, recuses.	469	Epistolae	15
AMOUES			
et festucas, Reipublicae oculo haerentes, tam diligenter amoues;	462	Epistolae	13
AMPAUESTHAI			
Dakruontas ampauesthai.	430	Mem.Matr.16	4
AMPHIONIS			
Amphionis testudine nobili	394	Musae 23	14
AMPLECTENDAM			
e multis seligam, quam vobis amplectendam dissuauiandamque praebebo:	445	Orationes	32
AMPLECTIMUR			
hilare est, laetum, ac lubens, vestram in gratiam amplectimur.	440	Orationes	13
Quare amplectimur, fouemus, exosculamur, hunc foetum vestrum,	459	Epistolae	9
AMPLEXIBUS			
contineat se patria, cuius arctis amplexibus nunquam se expediet.	455	Orationes	2
AMPLEXUS			
intra ambitum amplexusque foelicitatis Tuae receptae, communi calore	469	Epistolae	18
AMPLIANTUR			
Res ampliantur, sin per aduersam videt,	388	Musae 8	13
AMPLISSIMIS			
Reges Collegia, eaque fundarunt amplissimis praedijs, immunitatibus:	458	Epistolae	22
AMPLITUDINE			
etiam imperium tenuius est quam pro amplitudine virtutum vestrarum:	458	Epistolae	11
AMPLITUDINI			
illum quo soles beare Amplitudini tuae deuotissimos Procancellarium	464	Epistolae	28
AMPLIUS			
neque amplius quaerendum sit Tibi, Almae Nutrici quid reponas.	462	Epistolae	15
AMPUTAT			
hoc enim fastum amputat, affectus explorat, adulationem ventilat,	453	Orationes	1
AMSTELLODAMUM			
Amstellodamum corripit se. Plaudite.	398	Musae 32	10
AN			
An quod semotum populo laquearibus altis	387	Musae 7	3
Quis hic superbit, oro? tune, an Praesules,	388	Musae 8	1
An rectius nos, si vices vertas, probi,	388	Musae 8	9
An quia Textores Artificesque probas?	392	Musae 18	2
Anne tuas flammas ipsa Antiperistasis auget,	399	Musae 35	3
Dic mihi, mons sterilis, vallis an vber eris?	413	Lucus 18	2
vnde pluuia futura, an sudum, facile conijcitur ex coelo,	445	Orationes	5
Ei en en o anthropos, inquit Medicorum Alpha, ouk an elgeen.	446	Orationes	19
vbi in dubio est, qui facit, an qui patitur, miserior.	449	Orationes	11
quis scit an & amoris onus scite vinctum ligatumque, & per tot	453	Orationes	38
quae materia sit, coelestis an sublunaris, sed quae signa,	454	Orationes	13
an inter lauros principis hederae nostrae ambitiosae locus est?	456	Epistolae	3
ANAGKE			
Orthos, anagke dustuxein tous ekgonous.	447	Orationes	15
ANAGR			
Roma. Anagr. Oram. Maro. / Ramo. Armo. / Mora. Amor.	416	Lucus 25	T
ANAGRAMMATE			
Dicti fidem firmabimus Anagrammate.	397	Musae 30	7
ANALECTA			
Grata mihi mensae sunt analecta tuae.	385	Musae 1	6
ANAPODEMETOUS			
tuphlous einai pros oksu blepontas, anapodemetous pros ekdedemekotas.	450	Orationes	9
ANCHORA			
Vltra loquendi tempus; addit Anchora:	438	Poem.Lat.	4
ANCHORAE			
Nec hoc abunde est tibi, nisi certae Anchorae	438	Poem.Lat.	5
ANCHORAM			
In Sacram Anchoram Piscatoris G. Herbert.	438	Poem.Lat.	T
AND			
To the right honourable and reverend Father in God, my L. Bishop of	473	Epistolae	23
ANDREAE			
Ad Andreae Melvini Scoti Anti-Tami-Cami-Categoriam.	384	Musae	T
ANDREWES			
18. Ad Lanc. Andrewes, Episc.	471	Epistolae	T
ANDRON			
Geneteiran ou tis andron	430	Mem.Matr.16	5
ANGAR			
Quam nihil illudis! cum quo magis angar acuto	405	Passio 7	3
ANGELI			
Angeli vultu radiante candent;	390	Musae 14	10
ANGELICAE			
Angelicae turmae nostris se coetibus addunt:	402	Musae 39	10
ANGELIS			
Non tantum est iter Angelis ad vndas,	415	Lucus 24	11
ANGELORUM			
Intellectus adultus Angelorum	415	Lucus 24	1

ANGELOS	PAGE	TITLE	LINE
Age, prouocemus vsque ad Angelos ipsos,	392	Musae 20	3
In Angelos.	415	Lucus 24	T
ANGIPORTUS			
Atque omnes peragrata es angiportus	411	Lucus 5	13
Per angiportus & maeandros labitur,	423	Mem.Matr.2	33
plena erant fora, nundinae, conciliabula, angiportus, Maeandri.	451	Orationes	10
ANGL			
15. Ad J. Leigh, Capitalem Iustitiarium Angl. (Camden) Gratulatio	468	Epistolae	T
ANGLI			
Georgii Herbertii Angli Musae Responsoriae	384	Musae	T
ANGLIA			
Sola mihi plenos, ait, exhibet Anglia cultus.	402	Musae 39	13
Anglia cur solum fuso sine sanguine sicca est,	411	Lucus 6	1
Te nunc Anglia, Scotiaeque binae,	428	Mem.Matr.10	9
ANGLIAE			
Et tu solus ad Angliae procellas	401	Musae 37	44
Archiepiscopo Eboracensi Summo Angliae Cancellario extructa fuerit,	463	Epistolae	31
ANGLIAM			
rogamusque vt quando beneficia tua peruagantur Angliam,	466	Epistolae	17
ANGLICE			
more maiorum, multos iam annos Anglice viuens garriensque.	470	Epistolae	5
ANGLIGENUM			
Angligenumque arces gaudentes sanguine Galli,	419	Tr.Mortis V	42
ANGLO			
Naufragij causa est alijs mare, roboris Anglo,	411	Lucus 6	5
ANGLORUM			
Anglorumque arcus gaudentes sanguine Galli,	419	Tr.Mortis	42
ANGLUS			
Te Germana tamen pubes, te Graecus & Anglus	416	Lucus 26	3
ANGUIBUS			
Nexas, capillos anguibus oblitos,	434	Poem.Lat.	18
ANGUILLAE			
vno semper saginantur in loco, vti anguillae, aut si mutant locum,	452	Orationes	10
ANGULIS			
Paulo, secretis mussitans in angulis	398	Musae 32	5
ANGULUM			
qui nullum non angulum verrunt (ac si perdiderint ingenium)	445	Orationes	36
ANGULUS			
Non sic effugit angulus vel vnus	391	Musae 15	5
Non est angulus vspiam serenus,	428	Mem.Matr.10	13
vbique deferentibus, vt nullus sit angulus corporis, nulla venula,	445	Orationes	3
ANGUSTI			
adde quod angusti est animi aut superbi sua tantum nosse,	450	Orationes	17
ANGUSTIOR			
Angustior erat Scotia, quam vt pennas nido plene explicare posses:	458	Epistolae	8
ANIMA			
Sic Hominis moles animaque & corpore constat,	417	Lucus 31	3
cum corporis cum anima vinculum impedimento esse ad contemplandum	448	Orationes	27
ANIMAE			
Non remanent nobis corpora, non animae.	390	Musae 13	4
Quas spargit animae corporis propius lutum?	393	Musae 22	4
Cordis apex, animae pugnaque paxque meae,	421	Lucus 35	2
ANIMALIA			
ac si non gregaria essent animalia, sed tigres aut vrsi.	450	Orationes	22
flores, animalia, tum maxime homo, cui soli ideo insunt oculi	453	Orationes	16
ANIMALIUM			
vt Rex animalium fiat Rex hominum, apponimus nos manibus Sceptrum,	447	Orationes	2
ANIMAM			
Hunc ponas animam mundi, Plato: vel tua mundum	409	Passio 21	3
Animam recentem rite curauit sacris	422	Mem.Matr.2	16
Siccam animam sapientissimam esse dixit obscurus ille philosophus;	460	Epistolae	20
ANIMANTIA			
insunt oculi variegati, cum caetera animantia vnicolores habeant.	453	Orationes	17
ANIMARUM			
Mundique & Animarum sacerdos vnicus;	436	Poem.Lat.	24
ANIMAS			
Non animas, raroque ornantur sanguine regum	420	Tr.Mortis	98
ANIMATA			
Asserit & vitam Mors animata tuam.	407	Passio 17	4
ANIMI			
O caecos animi fratres! quis vestra fatigat	401	Musae 39	4
vita nostra atque calor, longo animi deliquio fugitiuus ac desertor.	444	Orationes	23
minimeque omnium coelestiores animi, quorum pietatis interest	445	Orationes	11
Non vnum quid spectant aut singulare Magni animi, sed varia solent	446	Orationes	4
adde quod angusti est animi aut superbi sua tantum nosse,	450	Orationes	17
Quis enim impetus animi celeritatem tantae munificentiae assequi	460	Epistolae	4
praestantissimaeque animi dotes effecerunt, vt Alma Mater	465	Epistolae	12
ANIMIS			
Adde pijs animis quaeuis occasio lucro est,	390	Musae 12	11
Si numero starent praelia, non animis.	398	Musae 33	8
ANIMO			
Corporeque atque animo. Totus mihi seruiat Orbis.	421	Tr.Mortis	101
Animo renidentes prius. Sin rarior	423	Mem.Matr.2	25
Ne membra culpes, causa animo latet	426	Mem.Matr.6	18
Atque animo medicatur vnum.	426	Mem.Matr.6	24
abunde compensas nos, gratissimoque Almam Matrem prosequeris animo:	456	Epistolae	9
ne literae nostrae animo Tuo tot negotijs meritissime distincto,	457	Epistolae	11
et mammas arentes tam nobilis parentis aequo animo ferre posset?	462	Epistolae	1
vtque mature absoluas quae complexus es animo, ad eius gloriam,	464	Epistolae	4
illuc commeando, eo deueni animo, vt nunquam cessandum mihi ducerem,	472	Epistolae	7

	PAGE	TITLE	LINE
ANIMOS			
Commotos animos rectius ista decent.	387	Musae 5	6
si vestros animos regant	395	Musae 25	18
Sic lactare animos & sic ostendere gemmam	432	Poem.Lat.	31
in promptu erat, rudesque animos vi verborum percellere:	445	Orationes	17
spiritus, generososque animos frangere et retundere clamitant.	461	Epistolae	20
erectior solutiorque redibo, ex ipsa intermissione animos ducens.	473	Epistolae	4
ANIMOSA			
Votaque scintillae sunt animosa meae.	410	Lucus 2	4
ANIMUM			
cor Regium vigore, animum clementia, vt frequenter nos inuisat,	444	Orationes	5
Vicini quo pacto niteant, id animum aduertito;	450	Orationes	16
ANIMUS			
Vltra animus spatiatur exlex.	425	Mem.Matr.6	8
Ecce meus torpens animus succumbit vtrique,	435	Poem.Lat.	3
dum animus grandis, suique impos, triumphos & victorias quasi fraena	447	Orationes	33
sic idem animus, qui nuper versatus est in forma & figuris vultus,	454	Orationes	6
ANISTAMENOIS			
Oulumponde biban ummin anistamenois.	431	Mem.Matr.18	4
ANNA			
Quo Te, foelix Anna, modo deflere licebit?	435	Poem.Lat.	1
ANNAE			
In Obitum Serenissimae Reginae Annae.	435	Poem.Lat.	T
Namque Annae laudes coelo scribuntur aperto,	435	Poem.Lat.	9
ANNALES			
percurrite Annales regnorum, excutite scrinia politiarum omnium;	445	Orationes	13
ANNI			
Sint tibi vel stellis laudes, & laudibus anni:	402	Musae 39	34
Sic aeuum exigitur tardum, dum praepetis anni	428	Mem.Matr.9	13
Sed siccitas anni huius derisit incoeptum et plus effecit quam mille	461	Epistolae	11
o quot iam anni sunt ex quo vel apicem Latinum pertuli!	471	Epistolae	6
ANNIS			
qua tot iam annis impune fruimur, hoc pacto fundatam cupit	447	Orationes	29
ANNON			
Annon sic mercamur agros? quibus ecce Redemptor	388	Musae 9	3
Annon longa fames miseraeque iniuria pestis	432	Poem.Lat.	20
annon eius consilio res gesta est?	451	Orationes	24
ANNORUM			
virum protulit, cum quinque millibus annorum de palma certantem.	463	Epistolae	27
ANNOS			
Trecentos obijt Nestor, non transijt annos,	415	Lucus 23	7
more maiorum, multos iam annos Anglice viuens garriensque.	470	Epistolae	4
ANNOSA			
Cui caecas tribuit vires annosa vetustas.	433	Poem.Lat.	42
ANNULO			
De annulo coniugali.	396	Musae 26	T
ANNULUM			
Polycrates cum annulum sibi dilectum in mare dimisisset,	444	Orationes	14
& ipsum accepimus saluum & annulum, annulum Coniugalem,	444	Orationes	18
accepimus saluum & annulum, annulum Coniugalem, nunc denuo nostrum,	444	Orationes	19
ANNULUS			
Annulus & plenus tempore forsan erit.	396	Musae 26	6
Annulus hos reuocet, sistatque libidinis vndas	396	Musae 26	11
ANNUM			
fungar apud Meos, Rhetoris in hunc annum, & in plures Oratoris,	472	Epistolae	26
ANNUUNT			
gaudia praestolantur, quae iamdudum annuunt mihi vt perorem.	454	Orationes	23
ANSA			
haec est ansa qua prehendimus Te, et tanquam Aquilam inter nouas	456	Epistolae	5
ANSATUS			
Rotundus in te: namque si ansatus sies,	414	Lucus 20	7
ANTE			
Ante tui, CAESAR, quam fulserat aura fauoris,	384	Musae	3
Scilicet, vt quos ante suas cum coniuge tedas	396	Musae 26	9
Ante diem vestro mundus ab igne ruat.	399	Musae 35	12
Ante tuum tempus coelum gratissimus ambis.	402	Musae 39	29
Circumferre potes; Sampson vt ante fores.	408	Passio 18	2
Te petet, ante diem quisquis obire cupit.	414	Lucus 21	6
Creditur, ante satas prono cum numine fruges)	419	Tr.Mortis	61
Creditur, ante satas prono cum vertice fruges)	419	Tr.Mortis V	61
Ego vero non dicam vobis quod factum est ante seculum vestrum,	445	Orationes	38
ANTEA			
Sane, gestabaris antea in cordibus nostris;	458	Epistolae	18
ANTEAMBULONES			
Vt natura omnis suos habet anteambulones, vnde pluuia futura,	445	Orationes	5
ANTECELLERE			
significantes oportere Reges ijs partibus antecellere homines,	447	Orationes	4
ANTEFERENDAM			
anteferendam bello pacem, sine qua omnis vita procella,	448	Orationes	7
ANTEHAC			
in nos amòr, antehac satis perspectus, nunc cum honore geminetur.	466	Epistolae	3
ANTEIT			
Longe pileus anteit galerum,	391	Musae 15	8
ANTELUCANA			
Atheniensis doluit se victum opificum antelucana industria,	469	Epistolae	2
ANTEQUAM			
qui antequam condiebant corpora Nobilium, solebant ventres eximere,	452	Orationes	26
ANTHINEN			
Kepou sunothon anthinen euodian,	430	Mem.Matr.15	12
ANTHROPON			
Meter, gunaikon aigle, anthropon eris,	429	Mem.Matr.15	1

	PAGE	TITLE		LINE
ANTHROPOS				
Ei en en o anthropos, inquit Medicorum Alpha, ouk an elgeen.	446	Orationes		18
ANTI				
Ad Andreae Melvini Scoti Anti-Tami-Cami-Categoriam.	384	Musae		T
Ad eundem In Monstrum vocabuli Anti-Tami-Cami-Categoria.	386	Musae 3		T
Istas Anti-Tami-Cami-Categorias!	386	Musae 3		2
Hoc erit, Anti-furi-Puri-Categoria.	386	Musae 3		8
Est Anti-pelvi-Melvi-Categoria.	386	Musae 3		10
Partitio Anti-Tami-Cami-Categoriae.	386	Musae 4		T
ANTI-FURI-PURI-CATEGORIA				
Hoc erit, Anti-furi-Puri-Categoria.	386	Musae 3		8
ANTI-PELVI-MELVI-CATEGORIA				
Est Anti-pelvi-Melvi-Categoria.	386	Musae 3		10
ANTI-TAMI-CAMI-CATEGORIA				
Ad eundem In Monstrum vocabuli Anti-Tami-Cami-Categoria.	386	Musae 3		T
ANTI-TAMI-CAMI-CATEGORIAE				
Partitio Anti-Tami-Cami-Categoriae.	386	Musae 4		T
ANTI-TAMI-CAMI-CATEGORIAM				
Ad Andreae Melvini Scoti Anti-Tami-Cami-Categoriam.	384	Musae		T
ANTI-TAMI-CAMI-CATEGORIAS				
Istas Anti-Tami-Cami-Categorias!	386	Musae 3		2
ANTICATEGORIAE				
Anticategoriae, Scoto-Britanne, tuae:	386	Musae 4		2
ANTICHRISTI				
De Antichristi decore Pontificali.	390	Musae 13		T
ANTICHRISTUS				
Quisnam Antichristus cessemus quaerere; Papa	412	Lucus 10		1
ANTIDOTIS				
sua sibi sufficere, neque externis indigere auxilijs atque antidotis:	444	Orationes		26
ANTIPERISTASIS				
Anne tuas flammas ipsa Antiperistasis auget,	399	Musae 35		3
ANTIQUA				
Cur, vbi tot ludat numeris antiqua poesis,	387	Musae 5		1
Laus antiqua & honor perijt: quasi scilicet ARMO	416	Lucus 25		7
Laus antiqua & honor perierunt, te velut ARMO	416	Lucus 25	V	7
ANTIQUI				
Immemor antiqui mellis, eundo coquit.	398	Musae 33		20
vnde cuncti antiqui Philosophi peregrinati sunt, existimantes	450	Orationes		8
ANTIQUIS				
non solum rectum de Bene-merentibus iudicium hausisse ab Antiquis,	469	Epistolae		13
ANTIQUITAS				
Antiquitas praeripuit Tibi gloriam extruendae Academiae,	465	Epistolae		16
ANTIQUITATIS				
creberrima Antiquitatis lectione tersis atque expolitis,	473	Epistolae		19
ANTRA				
Vulpibus antra feris, nidique volucribus adsunt,	407	Passio 15		1
ANTRO				
Materiam vexat: nec iam se continet antro	420	Tr.Mortis		70
ANUS				
Adest tamen anus illa querula, & philegklemon, quam audire videor	453	Orationes		25
aetate prouectior, etiam anus subsultans multum excitet pulueris:	454	Orationes		36
ANXIETATE				
Cultricem reuocans anxietate manum:	425	Mem.Matr.5		4
ANXIOS				
Morsus increpat anxios;	403	Musae 40		5
APARKTIAS				
Pheron to pan, kagon: e os Aparktias	430	Mem.Matr.15		11
APAUGOUS				
Nun oraas, oti kallos apeiriton opos apaugous	429	Mem.Matr.14		5
APAURAMENES				
Photos apauramenes ogkou epheisthe pleon,	431	Mem.Matr.18		2
APEIRITON				
Nun oraas, oti kallos apeiriton opos apaugous	429	Mem.Matr.14		5
APELLAXTHAI				
Menouge sophien, ei s' apellaxthai xreon,	430	Mem.Matr.15		5
APEM				
Nunquid mel comedens, apem comedi	411	Lucus 5		8
APERI				
Aut aperi, & cernes corpus quas proijcit vmbras;	437	Poem.Lat.		7
Aut aperi, & cernis corpus quas proijcit vmbras;	437	Poem.Lat.	V	7
APERIAT				
vt nullus fere elabatur dies, qui non hostes aliquos nobis aperiat:	461	Epistolae		14
APERIENS				
viam aperiens & methodum in studijs adhibendam, etiam libros indicans	443	Orationes		24
APERIREM				
incredibilem luxum a Tiberio Caesare ad Constantinum magnum aperirem,	452	Orationes		23
APERIS				
Tu aperis illum populo, & cum ipse sis in summa arbore altera manu	456	Epistolae		13
APERTA				
Monumenta aperta.	407	Passio 17		T
APERTO				
Namque Annae laudes coelo scribuntur aperto,	435	Poem.Lat.		9
APERUIT				
pax nouum orbem aperuit; bellum destruit veterem.	448	Orationes		12
APES				
Imo, me nec apes, nec astra pungunt:	411	Lucus 5		10
APEX				
Humanae decus atque apex iuuentae,	384	Musae		2
Cordis apex, animae pugnaque paxque meae,	421	Lucus 35		2
APHIPTASAI				
Pos nun aphiptasai, qoou kai kindunou	429	Mem.Matr.15		3

	PAGE	TITLE	LINE
APICEM			
o quot iam anni sunt ex quo vel apicem Latinum pertuli!	471	Epistolae	7
APICES			
Impediant, apices legis amicus obit.	388	Musae 9	6
omnia fauorum tucrum momenta apicesque perpensuris et compensaturis.	466	Epistolae	8
APOLLO			
Apollo olim depositis radijs Daphnen deperijt, at illa mutata est	455	Orationes	8
APOLOGETICA			
Pro Disciplina Ecclesiae Nostrae Epigrammata Apologetica	385	Musae 1	T
APOSTOLICI			
Christus Apostolici cinctus amore gregis.	398	Musae 33	10
APOSTOLORUM			
Apostolorum culpa non leuis fuit	389	Musae 10	4
In Lotionem pedum Apostolorum.	412	Lucus 8	T
APOSTOLOS			
Quos charos habuit Christus Apostolos,	391	Musae 17	1
APOTHECA			
Ira facit, mundusque ipse est apotheca furoris.	418	Tr.Mortis	17
APPARATUS			
pendet a vicinis, quorum consilia, apparatus, foedera, munitiones,	450	Orationes	26
APPARET			
redundet, quorum in eligendis illis iudicium iampridem apparet.	441	Orationes	7
APPELLERET			
olim appelleret, intuens	395	Musae 25	3
APPETIT			
Appetit tempus, cum excusso altero iugo, dimidiaque operis parte	473	Epistolae	1
APPETITUS			
Et flexus fugientis appetitus.	411	Lucus 5	14
APPIJ			
aliae contra semper pertinaces ac tribunitiae, vti Appij.	447	Orationes	21
APPONIMUS			
apponimus nos manibus Sceptrum, capiti & faciei coronam,	447	Orationes	3
APPONIS			
Et lucro apponis gaudia sancta tuo.	424	Mem.Matr.3	6
APPONIT			
Scilicet apponit pretium tua dextera fato,	435	Poem.Lat.	5
APPOSITE			
Apposite quem commotum subfugerat olim,	390	Musae 12	15
Scite et apposite fecisti Fluuium nostrum conseruans altero	462	Epistolae	18
Philosophus de Tactu & Visu, id apposite admodum huc transferatur.	472	Epistolae	36
APPOSITISSIMUM			
Vos ergo puri! o nomen appositissimum	393	Musae 22	5
APPRIME			
Scio Hispanum versutum, callidum, artis & aucupij apprime gnarum:	451	Orationes	25
APPULIT			
promotionis tuae gratissime appulit ad nos omnes haud ita certe	468	Epistolae	12
APPULSU			
Magnatis appulsu extulit se occasio,	423	Mem.Matr.2	26
APRILE			
Constat, Aprile vno te potuisse mori:	438	Poem.Lat.	4
APTIOR			
Sepia concurrat, peccatis aptior humor,	404	Passio 1	3
me deficeret (& quidem nox aptior esset tali historiae) si Romanorum	452	Orationes	21
APUD			
Quis enim apud nos splendor, aut rerum, aut vestium?	441	Orationes	10
tam grauem) & apud quos dico, viros limatae auris atque tersae,	445	Orationes	26
non dicam vobis quod factum est ante seculum vestrum, aut apud Indos;	446	Orationes	1
Non ignoro apud quos haec dico, eos scilicet, qui innuptam Palladem	446	Orationes	25
Apud Iuris-consultos, partus sequitur ventrem:	447	Orationes	12
hinc contigisse arbitror apud Romanos, quod nonnullae familiae semper	447	Orationes	19
apud poetas deorum pharetrae operculum habuere, humanae non item:	449	Orationes	25
apud nos agri tantum sunt fertiles, illic etiam arenae.	451	Orationes	4
Florent apud nos artes omnes, inter quas & Mathematicae,	454	Orationes	2
abijcite quisque libros, non est locus grauitati, neque apud vos:	454	Orationes	34
idque pro Libris, de quibus nusquam rectius quam apud Te agitur.	467	Epistolae	19
Sic apud veterum aras, post ingentes Hecatombas, exiguam thuris micam	469	Epistolae	16
tanta Humanitatis massa, quae apud Te visitur, abscindere non possim,	472	Epistolae	14
receptusque sim in aliquem apud Honorem Tuum locum, magis id adeo	472	Epistolae	20
cum grauibus duobus muneribus fungar apud Meos, Rhetoris in hunc	472	Epistolae	25
AQUA			
Et quae corrumpit moenia, murus aqua est.	411	Lucus 6	6
Fusaque decurrit notis aqua ferrea sulcis:	419	Tr.Mortis	52
quam in aqua & igne fecisti, non dubitamus quin benignitas tua omnia	457	Epistolae	22
AQUAE			
Eripe coelesti qui moderatur aquae.	396	Musae 26	4
Graues lagenas, Vester est Aquae-ductus.	405	Passio 5	9
Quod si Artaxerxes olim paululum aquae a Sinaeta, subiecto suo,	460	Epistolae	11
sane dubitamus vlli, si prae defectu aquae, commeatusque inopia,	462	Epistolae	2
AQUAE-DUCTUS			
Graues lagenas, Vester est Aquae-ductus.	405	Passio 5	9
AQUALES			
Cum tener ad sacros infans sistatur aquales,	388	Musae 9	1
AQUAS			
Et ipse Iordan sistit aquas stupens;	394	Musae 23	42
Et tibi vicinas porrigit aequor aquas:	399	Musae 35	8
Sputando, praedicando? sic Aquas vitae	404	Passio 5	3
Tuque super nostras, Christe, moueris aquas.	411	Lucus 6	8
Sin pluuiam, fletus suppeditasset aquas.	427	Mem.Matr.9	10
Diluit oppositas candidus humor aquas.	428	Mem.Matr.9	18
proin vt Fluuij quas aquas a Fonte accipiunt non retinent ipsi,	456	Epistolae	9
cum olim gauderent Fluuijs, nunc etiam aquas, in quibus habitant,	460	Epistolae	9

AQUAS (cont'd)	PAGE	TITLE	LINE
Quid enim inuident aquas, quas non nobis habemus sed irrigati ipsi	462	Epistolae	10
AQUILAM			
Austriacam familiam, Aquilamque illam, quae non capit muscas.	446	Orationes	15
et tanquam Aquilam inter nouas honorum nubes e conspectu nostro	456	Epistolae	6
AQUIS			
Postquam se gelidis nocte refecit aquis:	412	Lucus 8	2
Vespere ros maestis funus honestet aquis.	425	Mem.Matr.5	16
Mille rotae nimijs impediuntur aquis.	428	Mem.Matr.9	14
ARA			
Pollubra vel cum olim damnaris Regia in ara,	386	Musae 3	9
Vbique est Deus, Agnus, Ara, Flamen.	408	Passio 19	14
Cespes viuus, Homo; mortuus, Ara fuit:	417	Lucus 29	2
Conueniunt; & Homo viua fit Ara Dei.	417	Lucus 29	4
ARARUM			
Ararumque Hominumque ortum si mente pererres,	417	Lucus 29	1
ARAS			
Et pro pectoribus recenset aras,	408	Passio 19	6
Sic apud veterum aras, post ingentes Hecatombas, exiguam thuris micam	469	Epistolae	16
ARATRA			
Coeperat, agricolis mentemque & aratra solutis:	418	Tr.Mortis	10
ARBITER			
Rationis & sensus stupendus Arbiter;	436	Poem.Lat.	16
Rationis & sensus peritus Arbiter;	436	Poem.Lat. V	16
ARBITRI			
Auresque superas: arbitri ipsi sint litis,	392	Musae 20	4
ARBITROR			
hinc contigisse arbitror apud Romanos, quod nonnullae familiae semper	447	Orationes	19
ARBOR			
Arbor & ipse inuersa vocer: dumque insitus almae	428	Mem.Matr.11	5
ARBORE			
Nec tamen excludor: namque vna ex arbore vitam	418	Tr.Mortis	7
Pulchre renatam ex arbore mortua,	434	Poem.Lat.	34
& cum ipse sis in summa arbore altera manu prehendis Regem,	456	Epistolae	14
ARBOREAS			
Quid ipse faciam? qui nec arboreas sudes	421	Lucus 33	3
ARBOREM			
Zacchaeus, vt Te cernat, arborem scandit:	406	Passio 12	1
deperijt, at illa mutata est in arborem triumphantium propriam:	455	Orationes	9
ARBORES			
e qua liberi quaerantur, quam qualis terra, e qua arbores.	447	Orationes	12
Arionem Delphino reuectum excepere arbores tripudiantes,	454	Orationes	37
nobis remotior, confidimus tamen vt arbores, quanto altius crescunt,	464	Epistolae	17
ARBORIBUS			
Vt si recisis arboribus meis	434	Poem.Lat.	29
ARCA			
quos in arca repositos abijciebant in fluuium, his verbis:	452	Orationes	28
ARCAM			
Ad se suaeque matris Arcam regredi:	436	Poem.Lat.	21
Ad se suamque mentis Arcam regredi:	436	Poem.Lat. V	21
ARCANA			
Nunc Arcana patent, nec inuolutam	408	Passio 19	9
Cancellario INSTAVRARI, inter Arcana Prouidentiae plane reponimus.	464	Epistolae	2
ARCE			
Ceu fida statione & arce certa,	417	Lucus 30	7
ARCES			
Sionis excelsas ad arces	394	Musae 23	39
Angligenumque arces gaudentes sanguine Galli,	419	Tr.Mortis V	42
ARCHIEP			
13. Ad Archiep. Cantuar. De Bibliopolis Lond.	466	Epistolae	T
ARCHIEPISCOPO			
cum olim ab Archiepiscopo Eboracensi Summo Angliae Cancellario	463	Epistolae	30
ARCHIMEDES			
Sensit hoc Archimedes, figuras iam nunc pulueri inscriptas corpore	448	Orationes	31
ARCTIS			
contineat se patria, cuius arctis amplexibus nunquam se expediet.	455	Orationes	2
ARCTO			
Scotia quae frigente iaces porrecta sub Arcto,	399	Musae 35	1
ARCUM			
Nulla tibi si signa placent, e nubibus arcum	396	Musae 26	3
ARCUS			
Anglorumque arcus gaudentes sanguine Galli,	419	Tr.Mortis	42
In te, nec arcus, scorpionesue, aut rotas,	421	Lucus 33	4
ARDEN			
Tes peri sullaleousin, eou poikilmatos arden	431	Mem.Matr.17	11
ARDENS			
In flumen moerore nigrum si funderer ardens,	422	Mem.Matr.1	5
ARDENTI			
Liquitur ardenti candens fornace metallum,	419	Tr.Mortis	51
liquitur ardenti cadens fornace metallum;	271	Tr.Mortis VS	51
ARDOR			
Magnatumque inopumque aequum certamen & ardor:	429	Mem.Matr.13	3
ARDORE			
Ardore Moses concitus entheo,	394	Musae 23	29
Ardore scribendi calescit,	426	Mem.Matr.6	15
ARENA			
Pactoli arena tibi tumulus est vnicus.	423	Mem.Matr.2	41
Dij te perdant, cum malis tuis & arena sine calce;	451	Orationes	6
ARENAE			
apud nos agri tantum sunt fertiles, illic etiam arenae.	451	Orationes	5

ARENTES	PAGE	TITLE		LINE
enim sicca vbera et mammas arentes tam nobilis parentis aequo animo	462	Epistolae		1
ARESCENS				
In posterum, maledicta Ficus arescens	405	Passio 5		6
ARETAS				
Aretas diakritheisas	430	Mem.Matr.16		11
ARETES				
Prounomioi d' aretes koinen geneteiran elontes.	430	Mem.Matr.17		3
ARGOS				
Talas, eithe y' Argos eien	430	Mem.Matr.16		8
ARGUIT				
Arguit, exceptos quos pia Roma fouet:	416	Lucus 26		4
Iniuste satis arguit viator.	428	Mem.Matr.10		4
ARGUS				
Quis, nisi qui manibus Briareus, oculisque sit Argus,	435	Poem.Lat.		5
ARIDITATE				
floribus suis sternentes Rempublicam, prae ariditate flaccescerent.	461	Epistolae		10
ARIDUS				
Herbae exoletae, ros-marinus aridus?	424	Mem.Matr.2		58
ARIES				
Quin Aries ruit, & multa Demetrius arte:	419	Tr.Mortis		47
Tamque aries ruit et multa Demetrius arte,	271	Tr.Mortis	VS	47
ARIETES				
Alapas nec Arietes? Quid ergo? Agnum & Crucem.	421	Lucus 33		6
ARIONEM				
Arionem Delphino reuectum excepere arbores tripudiantes,	454	Orationes		36
ARISTES				
Ei pou tuxoimi tesd' aristes atrapou,	430	Mem.Matr.15		15
ARMA				
Dum gladium stringens Paulus ad arma vocat.	398	Musae 33		12
Arma tui metuunt alumni.	434	Poem.Lat.		24
ARMIS				
O vos inualidos! Audi quem talibus armis	399	Musae 33		29
ARMO				
Roma. Anagr. Oram. Maro. / Ramo. Armo. / Mora. Amor.	416	Lucus 25		T
Laus antiqua & honor perijt: quasi scilicet ARMO	416	Lucus 25		7
Laus antiqua & honor perierunt, te velut ARMO	416	Lucus 25	V	7
ARMORUM				
Iam fulgor armorum fugaces	448	Orationes		3
AROGON				
Ouk et' emen idias phules grapsantes arogon,	430	Mem.Matr.17		2
AROMATA				
Quid iactas mihi aromata Orientis?	444	Orationes		24
ARRIDENT				
Cui dulcis arrident Camoenae	433	Poem.Lat.		3
ARRISERE				
Cur tibi tam facile non arrisere poetae	387	Musae 5		3
ARRODANT				
si oppidani nostri (more suo) Musarum iura et diplomata arrodant;	468	Epistolae		26
ARTAXERXES				
Quod si Artaxerxes olim paululum aquae a Sinaeta, subiecto suo,	460	Epistolae		11
ARTE				
Femineum blanda fallitis arte genus:	387	Musae 5		10
Quin Aries ruit, & multa Demetrius arte:	419	Tr.Mortis		47
Tamque aries ruit et multa Demetrius arte,	271	Tr.Mortis	VS	47
quo spiritu, qua arte, quanto impetu atque vigore res aggrediatur:	454	Orationes		10
ARTEM				
Ille quoque inuadit Diuinam Flaminis artem,	392	Musae 19		3
ARTERIAS				
Arterias tractans micantes	425	Mem.Matr.6		3
ARTERIJS				
arterijs micantibus, spiritibusque tabellarijs laetum hunc nuncium	445	Orationes		1
ARTES				
Quinimo Artes hic sunt quiete & silentio cultae, tranquillitas,	441	Orationes		14
Otium poscunt artes, mentem tranquillam, serenam, sudam:	448	Orationes		23
Florent apud nos artes omnes, inter quas & Mathematicae,	454	Orationes		2
nostrae etiam Athenae artesque obscuris opificum artibus superari	469	Epistolae		3
ARTIB				
Dominis Legatis cum Magistro. in Artib. titulis insignirentur. 27.	440	Orationes		T
ARTIBUS				
Columba Noae, quae in vetustis artibus	436	Poem.Lat.		19
Columba Noae, quae in vetustatis artibus	436	Poem.Lat.	V	19
ne pacem, quae sola incubat artibus, & obstetricatur, minus quam par	448	Orationes		33
& ingenium admirans, domum secum duxit, & erudiuit artibus;	453	Orationes		36
in quo paucorum auaritia liberalibus artibus dominatura est,	467	Epistolae		1
etiam Athenae artesque obscuris opificum artibus superari dolebunt.	469	Epistolae		3
ARTICULARE				
Ordinis osores articulare malum.	389	Musae 11		4
ARTICULIS				
Articulis sacris quidam subscribere iussus,	389	Musae 11		1
ARTIFEX				
Sarcasmos quibus artifex triumphas;	400	Musae 37		4
Tum quanta tabulis artifex? quae scriptio?	423	Mem.Matr.2		35
ARTIFICES				
An quia Textores Artificesque probas?	392	Musae 18		2
Artificesque necis clueant, & mortis alumni.	418	Tr.Mortis		30
quemadmodum artifices non omnes licitantibus producunt merces,	445	Orationes		29
ARTIS				
Scio Hispanum versutum, callidum, artis & aucupij apprime gnarum:	451	Orationes		25
ARTIUM				
Rerum magister vnicus, at non Artium;	436	Poem.Lat.		5

ARTIUM (cont'd)	PAGE	TITLE	LINE
Saluete tandem Magistri Artium, & quidem omnium Aulicarum,	440	Orationes	5
titulos caput vndique munientes meministi Magistrum Te esse Artium?	456	Epistolae	3
tanquam Nobilem Filium (more nostro) Magistrum Artium renunciauimus.	463	Epistolae	9
crassissimum elementum, Tu subtilitates Artium infinitas.	463	Epistolae	14
omniumque Artium molem et pondus sustinere, sed perspectissimus tuus	465	Epistolae	10
ARTUBUS			
Vis, & vena sacris regnat in artubus;	403	Musae 40	8
ARTUS			
nusquam benignius, soluens obstupefactos artus, atque exhilarans,	444	Orationes	28
ARUA			
Sed nec Cyrrhaei saltus Libethriaue arua	432	Poem.Lat.	4
ARUI			
Vnusquisque hominum, Terra est; & filius arui.	413	Lucus 18	1
ARUIRAGUM			
Aruiragum, falcesque obstantia quaeque metentes.	419	Tr.Mortis	46
ARUND			
In Arund. Spin. Genuflex. Purpur.	405	Passio 7	T
ARUNDO			
Scommata! Pastorem semper Arundo decet.	405	Passio 7	2
ARUSPEX			
Naturae Aruspex intimus; Philosophiae	436	Poem.Lat.	7
ARUUM			
Si nigro sit terra solo, quis despicit aruum?	437	Poem.Lat.	5
ASCENDANT			
Nec facile ascendant, sed tibi vallis erit.	210	Cam.1613-a BR	8
ASCENDAS			
ascendas, sume tecum amorem illum quo soles beare Amplitudini tuae	464	Epistolae	27
ASCENDERET			
(Tenere Christum scilicet, ne ascenderet)	438	Poem.Lat.	2
ASCENDIT			
qui furtim ascendit ad nubes, vbi iam ingrauescit humore,	454	Orationes	28
ASCENDUNT			
Ignis et Virtus semper ascendunt, vtriusque enim splendor et claritas	466	Epistolae	11
ASCENSURA			
sic merita tua ita ascensura, vt eorum vis et virtus ad nos	464	Epistolae	19
ASCENSUROS			
verisimile est, eos illuc, quo cognitio ipsa pertingit, ascensuros.	468	Epistolae	2
ASCENSURUM			
In Christum crucem ascensurum.	406	Passio 12	T
ASPECTIBUS			
Namque aspectibus e tuis vel vnus	384	Musae	4
ASPECTU			
conuertissem, & ex altera parte acuissem me aspectu virtutum Tuarum;	472	Epistolae	6
ASPECTUS			
in potestatem redigere, lenioresque aspectus, & dulciores assumatis;	440	Orationes	10
Statim a solatio aspectus Tui, Ego auctior iam gaudio atque	471	Epistolae	17
ASPERGIMUS			
quas non nobis habemus sed irrigati ipsi vniuersum regnum aspergimus?	462	Epistolae	11
ASPERGIS			
Saepius aspergis. Siste, pudore vacas.	387	Musae 7	2
ASPICE			
Aspice, dum perstas, vt te tua deserat aetas,	386	Musae 2	5
Aspice quam pleno descendat Iuppiter imbre,	210	Cam.1613-a BR	5
ASPICIS			
Aspicis multitudinem Librorum indies gliscentem, praesertim	467	Epistolae	29
ASPICIT			
Quanta hilaritate aspicit Alma Mater filios suos iam emancipatos,	461	Epistolae	30
ASSECUTA			
Nimirum id assecuta sunt merita Tua maxima, vt Almam Matrem spe noua	464	Epistolae	24
ASSECUTUS			
ex quo illustrius assecutus es nomen, quam Repertores Noui Orbis	463	Epistolae	12
ASSENSUM			
assensumque Tuum veritati omni familiarem largiaris, sun tei eulogiai	473	Epistolae	10
ASSEQUANTUR			
& polymiti, vt si minus id assequantur, quod primum intendunt,	446	Orationes	6
ASSEQUATUR			
enim sic effugies cum honoribus, quin laetitia nostra te assequatur.	465	Epistolae	23
ASSEQUENDA			
incerta sint, & nullis perspicillis, ne Belgicis quidem, assequenda:	449	Orationes	25
ASSEQUI			
Quid ipsi sumus, assequi putando.	415	Lucus 24	10
enim impetus animi celeritatem tantae munificentiae assequi potest?	460	Epistolae	4
ASSEQUOR			
quantum quidem ego homuncio ac nanus coniectando assequor.	453	Orationes	21
ASSERIT			
Asserit & vitam Mors animata tuam.	407	Passio 17	4
ASSERTA			
istis sublimitate solij asserta) vita et actione orbem vegetat.	458	Epistolae	7
ASSERUNT			
asserunt Medici vnamquamque regionem sua sibi sufficere,	444	Orationes	25
ASSIDEO			
Assideo Matri, robore vinco cedros.	428	Mem.Matr.11	6
ASSIDUA			
vt laboribus meis plurimis atque assidua obseruantia, ramenta	472	Epistolae	12
ASSIDUO			
Assiduo vilem lumine cingit humum.	387	Musae 7	8
Assiduo stimulo carnem Mens vlta lacessit,	410	Lucus 2	5
ASSIDUUS			
Assiduus nostri papilionis erat.	398	Musae 33	6
Assiduus tyro, si sit spectanda voluntas.	419	Tr.Mortis	32

	PAGE	TITLE	LINE
ASSUAS			
Vt, quae Papicolis propria, assuas nobis,	392	Musae 20	8
ASSUETA			
Hinc tyrocinium, paruoque assueta iuuentus,	418	Tr.Mortis	26
ASSUMATIS			
in potestatem redigere, lenioresque aspectus, & dulciores assumatis;	440	Orationes	10
ASSUMSI			
Academicis maternisque, assumsi mecum propensionem in Patrem.	473	Epistolae	8
ASTER			
Nou d' autou taphos est' aster: pheggos gar ekeinou	429	Mem.Matr.14	3
ASTHENES			
Psuxes asthenes erkos, amauron pneumatos aggos,	429	Mem.Matr.14	1
ASTRA			
Terra nihil, nec quo sanctius astra vident;	385	Musae	2
Astra rogant, Nouus hic quis hospes?	394	Musae 23	28
Imo, me nec apes, nec astra pungunt:	411	Lucus 5	10
Vnde MARO laudes duxit ad astra tuas.	416	Lucus 25	4
Ipse suos tanquam digno pallentiaque astra.	426	Mem.Matr.7	21
Quicquid habet tellus, quicquid & astra, fruens.	429	Mem.Matr.13	6
Harmoniam dabit inter astra.	434	Poem.Lat.	36
Quod calamum excusent Pontus & Astra meum:	435	Poem.Lat.	8
qui astra scrutaris, dum globos tractas & coelos fictitios,	448	Orationes	29
ASTRAEA			
Praetulit Astraea, aut solio Themis alma vetusto	426	Mem.Matr.7	12
ASTRAPTON			
Astrapton, Thuridon os dia, neime selas.	429	Mem.Matr.14	8
ASTRIS			
Viscera naturae, commistusque omnibus astris	402	Musae 39	28
ASTROLOGIA			
sic bonorum Principum facilis Astrologia:	445	Orationes	7
ASTRONOMUS			
Astronomus olim (vt fama) dum maculas diu,	393	Musae 22	7
AT			
Quo vulgus ornat vos! At audias parum;	393	Musae 22	6
At cui videri prodigium potest	395	Musae 23	49
At non lusus erit, si quem tu laeta necasti	405	Passio 7	9
At nunc fatiscis. Nempe Dominus aedium	407	Passio 16	5
At sibi collisit fictile Daemon opus.	408	Passio 20	2
At Caelum e saxis elicuit Stephanus.	410	Lucus 3	2
At nunc exucco similis tua gloria RAMO	416	Lucus 25	5
At tu qui inepte haec dicta censes filio,	423	Mem.Matr.2	52
At superat caput illa tuum, quantum ipsa cadauer	424	Mem.Matr.3	3
At te commoriente, Magna Mater,	428	Mem.Matr.10	5
At forte matrem perdere haud soles demens:	429	Mem.Matr.12	9
Rerum magister vnicus, at non Artium;	436	Poem.Lat.	5
at ille ambiuit nobilissimam Austriacam familiam, Aquilamque illam,	446	Orationes	14
at Noster difficultatem superans, fructum consecutus est:	450	Orationes	13
at quo tandem? Madritum? hui!	451	Orationes	1
at ego Principem vellem, CAROLVM, CAROLVM;	451	Orationes	6
at cur adeo dolent? cur ringuntur?	451	Orationes	22
at IACOBVS a nobis est:	451	Orationes	25
At Noster, spretis voluptatibus, illecebris melitaiais agxonais	452	Orationes	31
at fuerit; si amor virginis eo pertraxit Principem, quo tandem ducet	453	Orationes	27
deperijt, at illa mutata est in arborem triumphantium propriam:	455	Orationes	9
ATARPON			
Mian t' atarpon sumporeuesthai drasas.	430	Mem.Matr.15	13
ATHENAE			
Aut laesae mihi suggerunt Athenae,	400	Musae 37	17
nostrae etiam Athenae artesque obscuris opificum artibus superari	469	Epistolae	3
ATHENIENSIS			
Demosthenes Atheniensis doluit se victum opificum antelucana	469	Epistolae	2
ATIMIAN			
& Licurgus magnus Legislator atimian prosetheke tois agamois.	446	Orationes	20
ATLAS			
Repumicator mentis; Atlas Physicus,	436	Poem.Lat.	17
ATQUE			
Humanae decus atque apex iuuentae,	384	Musae	2
Te perspicaci atque integro.	388	Musae 8	8
Cur teretem Graecam damnas, atque Hellada totam,	391	Musae 16	3
atque ad barbariem patrum	395	Musae 25	11
Atque edentula Musa, nec veneno	400	Musae 37	12
Quas Latij Catharique mouent, atque inter vtrasque	402	Musae 39	31
Gens tota fiet, atque vtrinque plectetur.	405	Passio 5	7
Atque omnes peragrata es angiportus	411	Lucus 5	13
Atque euehens, bonum facit faecundius,	412	Lucus 13	2
Atque ipsi sibi sunt mola & farina.	415	Lucus 24	15
Non fert Vcalegon, atque amentata retorquet	418	Tr.Mortis	14
Non placuit rudis atque ignara occisio: Morti	418	Tr.Mortis	24
Non placuit rudis atque ignara occasio; morti	271	Tr.Mortis VS	24
Exoritur tubus, atque instar Cyclopis Homeri	419	Tr.Mortis	53
Inde rotae atque axes subeunt, quasi sella curulis	419	Tr.Mortis	55
Versatos neget, atque humiles, queis talis cordi	420	Tr.Mortis	93
Corporeque atque animo. Totus mihi seruiat Orbis.	421	Tr.Mortis	101
Struices superbas atque turritum caput	422	Mem.Matr.2	11
Ergo ipse solum mutus atque excors ero	423	Mem.Matr.2	55
Atque animo medicatur vnum.	426	Mem.Matr.6	24
Pallida materni Genij atque exanguis imago,	426	Mem.Matr.7	1
Pensilis, atque acri dirimens Examine lites.	426	Mem.Matr.7	13
Atque inter reliquos horti crescentia foetus	427	Mem.Matr.7	33
Atque vbi per te sanctificer natalibus ipsis,	434	Poem.Lat.	9
Profunditatis pinus, atque Elegantiae;	436	Poem.Lat.	6

	PAGE	TITLE	LINE
ATQUE (cont'd)			
Profunditatis cinnus, atque Elegantiae;	436	Poem.Lat. V	6
Promus; Fugator Idolum, atque nubium;	436	Poem.Lat.	12
Atque haeret dubio tabida vita pede,	438	Poem.Lat.	2
cuius ingens gloria aeque rotunda est atque ipse orbis:	440	Orationes	16
cum eo sitis ordine atque habitu, quo nos in hoc regno omnes esse	441	Orationes	1
quotidie transnatantes, litora nostra atque aures mire circumsonant.	441	Orationes	4
omnes ad Aulam, atque ab eo consilium peteremus a quo et fortunas?	443	Orationes	27
occurrant, oratio nostra est silentium, atque eloquentia, stupor.	444	Orationes	3
atque vbiuis terrarum pro iudicio prudentissimi Regis, & in rebus	444	Orationes	19
& cum eo vita nostra atque calor, longo animi deliquio fugitiuus ac	444	Orationes	22
sua sibi sufficere, neque externis indigere auxilijs atque antidotis:	444	Orationes	26
soluens obstupefactos artus, atque exhilarans, tumentibus iam venis,	444	Orationes	28
viros limatae auris atque tersae, quorum grauitate ac purpura	445	Orationes	26
& sollicitudines Principum sine condimento sint atque embammate?	446	Orationes	12
in virginum, flores atque herbas depinxere:	446	Orationes	31
ingenium ipsum atque indoles (veluti Conclusio sequitur infirmiorem	447	Orationes	17
illic tuta cognitio est, atque extra teli iactum.	449	Orationes	3
ac si Fatis a fuso essent atque consilijs, sine quibus ne vnum quidem	449	Orationes	30
Atque hoc quidem statu res erant, Suauissime CAROLE, cum tu aberas;	451	Orationes	27
Natura montibus vallibusque sublimitate atque humilitate distinxit:	453	Orationes	12
vt laeuitatem illam aequabilem atque politiem perturbent.	453	Orationes	14
cum grandi atque impedito onere facillime incedens, occurrit ei	453	Orationes	34
quo spiritu, qua arte, quanto impetu atque vigore res aggrediatur:	454	Orationes	11
interim vestra hac scribendi laude intacta manente atque illibata.	458	Epistolae	27
corrumpuntur statuae, haec imago atque character, tempore melior,	459	Epistolae	13
Iustitiam prius tanto cum honore atque acclamatione administrans,	464	Epistolae	15
nostrorum, atque immortalitas, vt semper post nouas dignitates,	464	Epistolae	22
Almam Matrem spe noua grauidam semper atque praegnantem effecerint.	464	Epistolae	26
singularem iam olim Regi notam atque signatam dignissime praeficiaris	469	Epistolae	21
hoc Principe, in quo doctrinae fructus atque vsus mirifice relucet.	469	Epistolae	23
Comiter scribis atque eleganter; quae est vestra felicitas qui puro	470	Epistolae	2
quo minus, spe prouecta atque adulta, ipsam possessionem adeas,	470	Epistolae	8
meo quadrabunt, quae almae matri inconcinna erunt atque enormia.	470	Epistolae	15
finge tibi matronam sanctam, venerandam, oris prisci atque augusti;	470	Epistolae	17
huius tu es commotria atque ornatrix.	470	Epistolae	17
Tandem, ne et ipse peccem, breuis sit sermo, atque pressus.	470	Epistolae	32
Ego auctior iam gaudio atque distentior, Cantabrigiam redij.	471	Epistolae	17
atque effusissimum in omnia officia, quae praestet mea paruitas;	471	Epistolae	21
qui primo caloris suasu excitati atque expergefacti, vbi sursum	471	Epistolae	29
vt laboribus meis plurimis atque assidua obseruantia, ramenta	472	Epistolae	12
creberrima Antiquitatis lectione tersis atque expolitis,	473	Epistolae	20
Rege nostro quin turgescat indies, atque efferat se, indulgere.	473	Epistolae	22
ATQUI			
Atqui vos secus, o boni,	395	Musae 25	16
Atqui manus imponere integras praestat,	397	Musae 31	2
Atqui te precor vnice per ipsam,	400	Musae 37	1
ATRA			
Nunc primum socij mors foret atra tui?	415	Lucus 23	2
ATRAMENTO			
Nos nunc conspersi atramento regio, nihil non sublime et excelsum	459	Epistolae	5
ATRAPOU			
Ei pou tuxoimi tesd' aristes atrapou,	430	Mem.Matr.15	15
ATRIS			
Dentibus atris?	390	Musae 14	4
Cantatum; deinde Ixion cum nubibus atris	420	Tr.Mortis	88
Sol sine sole tuo! quam te tum nubibus atris	433	Poem.Lat.	37
ATROPI			
Perrumpens, Atropi vetulae marcentibus vlnis.	419	Tr.Mortis	65
ATTAMEN			
Attamen VRBANI delecto nomine, constat	416	Lucus 27	5
ATTENTISSIMI			
Accepistis, Viri attentissimi, causas itineris huius, quantum quidem	453	Orationes	20
ATTOLLENTES			
Recte facitis, Academici, attollentes oculos cum stupore;	450	Orationes	1
ATTONITIS			
Mentibus attonitis cupiunt addiscere ritus:	402	Musae 39	9
ATTORN			
11.Ad T. Coventry, Attorn. Cognitorem Gratulatio	465	Epistolae	T
ATTULERIS			
vt qui tot subsidia attuleris ad progressum doctrinae, hac etiam	467	Epistolae	27
AU			
Autar od' au thanatos kuries, os elios auos	431	Mem.Matr.17	19
AUARITIA			
Claudis auaritia Satyram; statuisque sacrorum	399	Musae 34	1
Auaritia.	411	Lucus 7	T
in quo paucorum auaritia liberalibus artibus dominatura est,	467	Epistolae	1
orantes vt quicquid consilij auaritia ceperit aduersus aut	467	Epistolae	11
AUARUS			
Plusque habet hic laetus, quam vel Auarus habet.	411	Lucus 7	4
AUCTAE			
concessae ab Augustissimo Iacobo auctae tua opera conseruentur;	468	Epistolae	22
AUCTIOR			
gloria, prudentia auctior, ditat patriam, suamque absentiam	454	Orationes	32
Ego auctior iam gaudio atque distentior, Cantabrigiam redij.	471	Epistolae	17
AUCTUM			
ex quo timemus Librorum precia auctum iri, et priuilegia nostra	467	Epistolae	7
AUCTUS			
dein Hon. Tuo gratulamur, qui filio auctus es tali ingenio praedito:	463	Epistolae	24
AUCUPATUR			
Et flatulentas aucupatur glorias,	414	Lucus 20	2

	PAGE	TITLE	LINE
AUCUPIJ			
Scio Hispanum versutum, callidum, artis & aucupij apprime gnarum:	451	Orationes	25
AUDACTER			
quod pronomina mea adeo audacter incedant in hac epistola: . .	473	Epistolae	16
AUDENT			
audent amoris Symbolum?	397	Musae 28	15
AUDEO			
a Con verbo deduci, quod tria complectitur, Possum, Scio, Audeo:	447	Orationes	8
AUDI			
O vos inualidos! Audi quem talibus armis	399	Musae 33	29
Eia, agedum scribo: vicisti, Musa; sed audi, ...	431	Mem.Matr.19	7
Proinde audi Platonem: Dokei moi xrenai para ton presbuton . .	471	Epistolae	9
AUDIAMUS			
laudes vestras quod quae nos audiamus summo cum gaudio ea Maiestas	443	Orationes	31
Porro si Politicos audiamus, salus regnorum pendet a vicinis,	450	Orationes	25
AUDIAS			
Quo vulgus ornat vos! At audias parum;	393	Musae 22	6
AUDIES			
Quotidiano! Nescis, ignare? Audies!	436	Poem.Lat.	2
AUDIJT			
Isthaec pileus audijt propinquus, ...	391	Musae 15	3
AUDIMUS			
Omnesque stulti audimus, aut hypocritae, ...	388	Musae 8	7
AUDIO			
In ritibus nostris? Ego audio nullum.	392	Musae 20	2
Quid hocce? Psalmos audion'? o dapes!	394	Musae 23	33
AUDIRE			
quam audire videor dicentem, Pulchrum quidem iter & Amante dignum;	453	Orationes	25
AUDIS			
Et nullus audis? cantibus obstrepens, ...	395	Musae 23	46
O qui Defensor Fidei meritissimus audis, ...	402	Musae 39	17
AUDITIONES			
quae auditiones? qui susurri? Heus, abijtne Noster? . . .	450	Orationes	36
AUDITORES			
Nos vero, Auditores, diu iam peregrinati cum Principe, commode	455	Orationes	12
AUES			
Cum Romam nequeas, quod aues, euertere, nomen	416	Lucus 26	1
AUFERENS			
Nato parentis auferens Encomium, ...	423	Mem.Matr.2	53
AUFERT			
Aura volans, vitamque aer, quam pauerat, aufert.	420	Tr.Mortis	84
AUGENDO			
eorum gloriam conseruando nobis quae illi dederunt, etiam augendo;	458	Epistolae	26
AUGENT			
Qui augent precia Librorum, prosunt vendentibus Libros non ementibus,	468	Epistolae	6
AUGERI			
haud ignarus, ignem vitae augeri ventilatione, desidia corrumpi,	452	Orationes	33
AUGET			
Anne tuas flammas ipsa Antiperistasis auget, ...	399	Musae 35	3
AUGMENTUM			
etiam & scientiae augmentum ex hoc itinere captauit solertissimus	450	Orationes	5
AUGUSTA			
Verum augusta parens, sanctum os caeloque locandum, ...	426	Mem.Matr.7	10
AUGUSTI			
finge tibi matronam sanctam, venerandam, oris prisci atque augusti;	470	Epistolae	17
AUGUSTISSIME			
Perge, decus Regum; sic, Augustissime, plures	402	Musae 39	33
Augustissime Monarcha, Si per haec ludicra nostra pars aliquis eius	443	Orationes	8
AUGUSTISSIMO			
Augustissimo Potentissimoque Monarchae	384	Musae	T
Regibus concessae ab Augustissimo Iacobo auctae tua opera . .	468	Epistolae	22
AUIA			
nostrae, quae per Tuum Partum, ex Matre nunc Auia facta est:	463	Epistolae	26
AUIDE			
tibique non tam auide veterum beneficiorum memoriam recolenti,	457	Epistolae	12
AUIDO			
Qui sugit auido spiritu rumusculos	414	Lucus 20	1
AUIDOS			
Excitat optatus auidos, & ventilat ignem.	432	Poem.Lat.	32
AUIUM			
facile conijcitur ex coelo, ex garritu auium, ex lapidum exhalatione:	445	Orationes	6
pace, auium cantus expergefacit; bello, tubae ac tympana: . .	448	Orationes	11
AULA			
Nam te nunc Ager, Vrbs, & Aula plorant:	428	Mem.Matr.10	8
En Aurora vocat, lectus genialis in aula est, ...	210	Cam.1613-b BR	1
AULAEA			
Excutite aulaea, & luceat igne focus.	413	Lucus 15	2
AULAM			
confluereemus omnes ad Aulam, atque ab eo consilium peteremus a quo	443	Orationes	27
AULICARUM			
tandem Magistri Artium, & quidem omnium Aulicarum, Militarium,	440	Orationes	5
AUOS			
Et nos reducas ad lapides auos:	393	Musae 23	6
Autar od' au thanatos kuries, os elios auos	431	Mem.Matr.17	19
AURA			
Ante tui, CAESAR, quam fulserat aura fauoris, ...	384	Musae	3
Aura volans, vitamque aer, quam pauerat, aufert.	420	Tr.Mortis	84
AURAM			
affectuum raptim sequentes, ad omnem eorum auram vacillant. . .	472	Epistolae	2
AURE			
Sydera, pendenti sedulus aure bibis:	413	Lucus 16	2

AURE (cont'd)	PAGE	TITLE	LINE
Susurrat aure quispiam,	427	Mem.Matr.8	8
AUREA			
Aurea pro naulo lingua Charontis erit.	414	Lucus 22	4
Falleris, nusquam plura bona, cum etiam mala illic sint aurea:	451	Orationes	3
AUREAE			
Doctrinae fluuios clauderet aureae,	391	Musae 17	4
AURES			
Nunc etiam teneras quo versus gratior aures	387	Musae 5	11
Auresque superas: arbitri ipsi sint litis,	392	Musae 20	4
Tun' obdis aures, grex noue, barbaras,	395	Musae 23	45
quotidie transnatantes, litora nostra atque aures mire circumsonant.	441	Orationes	4
Stringuntur aures: iam litui strepunt,	448	Orationes	2
qui semper titillant aures Principum, Osper tois pterois knomenoi ta	453	Orationes	2
certe studijs chartisque obuolutos, quin aures nostrae tibi pateant.	468	Epistolae	13
AURI			
De auri sacra fame.	399	Musae 34	T
AURIBUS			
Quare malui seruire auribus Tuis, creberrima Antiquitatis lectione	473	Epistolae	19
AURIS			
viros limatae auris atque tersae, quorum grauitate ac purpura	445	Orationes	26
AURORA			
En Aurora vocat, lectus genialis in aula est,	210	Cam.1613-b BR	1
AURORAE			
Tam segnis facies aurorae nescia vernae,	426	Mem.Matr.7	8
AURUM			
Aurum nocte videns, vidisse insomnia dicit:	411	Lucus 7	1
Aurum luce videns, nulla videre putat.	411	Lucus 7	2
O falsos homines! Vigilat, qui somniat aurum,	411	Lucus 7	3
AUSAE			
Sintque ausae thalamum solis adire tui.	384	Musae	6
AUSCULTAS			
Quos tu rotatus, quale murmur auscultas	392	Musae 20	1
AUSINT			
Sic pulsare tuas, exclusis luctibus, ausint	402	Musae 39	35
AUSIS			
Interea classem magnis Rex instruit ausis:	427	Mem.Matr.9	7
AUSPICATISSIMUM			
Oratio Qua auspicatissimum Serenissimi Principis Caroli Reditum ex	444	Orationes	T
AUSTRIACAM			
at ille ambiuit nobilissimam Austriacam familiam, Aquilamque illam,	446	Orationes	15
AUT			
Omnesque stulti audimus, aut hypocritae,	388	Musae 8	7
Scilicet emptorem si res aut parcior aetas	388	Musae 9	5
(cum dignius nil posset aut melius dare)	397	Musae 28	10
Primo, vnus aut alter parum ritus placet:	398	Musae 32	2
Aut vt pruna gelu summo mordacius vrit,	399	Musae 35	5
Aut potius Christi sanguis demissus ab alto,	399	Musae 35	9
O vtinam aut illorum oculi (quod comprecor vnum)	400	Musae 36	5
Vobis, aut illis pectora vestra forent.	400	Musae 36	6
Aut saeuum reputes. Amica nostra est	400	Musae 37	11
Quam aut Ecclesia despicata vobis,	400	Musae 37	16
Aut laesae mihi suggerunt Athenae,	400	Musae 37	17
Quasque habet aut patulas, aut caeco tramite, moles	402	Musae 39	21
In te, nec arcus, scorpionesue, aut rotas,	421	Lucus 33	4
Non video, certum est iurare; aut si hoc vetuisti,	421	Lucus 35	9
Aut si negotio hora sumenda est, rei	423	Mem.Matr.2	32
Occidite; aut sane tantisper viuite, donec	425	Mem.Matr.5	15
Praetulit Astraea, aut solio Themis alma vetusto	426	Mem.Matr.7	12
Aut spes productas, barbataque somnia vertam	426	Mem.Matr.7	19
Dolere prohibes? aut dolere me gentis	429	Mem.Matr.12	5
Aut cita mors est danda bonis aut longa senectus:	432	Poem.Lat.	30
Aut aperi, & cernes corpus quas proijcit vmbras;	437	Poem.Lat.	7
Aut aperi, & cernis corpus quas proijcit vmbras;	437	Poem.Lat. V	7
Quis enim apud nos splendor, aut rerum, aut vestium?	441	Orationes	11
vestrae gaudia responderint aut nostris votis aut virtutibus	443	Orationes	13
vestrae gaudia responderint aut nostris votis aut virtutibus vestris,	443	Orationes	13
non rusticis loquor aut barbaris, quos magnificentia promissi	445	Orationes	15
aut eorum certe, qui cymbala sunt fanaticae iuuentutis:	445	Orationes	24
non dicam vobis quod factum est ante seculum vestrum, aut apud Indos;	445	Orationes	38
Non vnum quid spectant aut singulare Magni animi, sed varia solent	446	Orationes	4
quod primum intendunt, saltem in secundis aut tertijs consistant.	446	Orationes	7
Nihil habet humana vita maioris momenti aut ponderis, quam Nuptiae,	446	Orationes	17
aut tanquam oues taedulae & fastidiosae, cibum respuamus.	449	Orationes	1
Omne regnum suo Principi carcer est, aut si excedat, alienum:	450	Orationes	12
adde quod angusti est animi aut superbi sua tantum nosse,	450	Orationes	17
ac si non gregaria essent animalia, sed tigres aut vrsi.	450	Orationes	22
immersi, aut vno semper saginantur in loco, vti anguillae,	452	Orationes	9
vti anguillae, aut si mutant locum, gestantur, tanquam onera,	452	Orationes	10
sua non abirent olim in elementa, sed in bellaria aut tragemata:	452	Orationes	14
resolutione illa vltima, nulla sit distinctio populi aut principis:	452	Orationes	16
nulla sunt sceptra in elementis, nulli fasces aut secures:	452	Orationes	17
Quid ego vobis Neronum aut Heliogabalorum ingluuiem memorem?	452	Orationes	19
vt quid priuata habeat in se vita commodi aut voluptatis,	452	Orationes	37
vt nihil habeat Inuidia ipsa, quod contra hiscat aut mussitet.	453	Orationes	24
de Principe aliquo, quis sit futurus aut qualis, recte diuinaret,	454	Orationes	9
aut nostra vota gratiam Principis, aut Tuae virtutes et vota nostra	456	Epistolae	21
aut Tuae virtutes et vota nostra et Principis gratiam superarent.	456	Epistolae	21
aut enim misere fallimur, aut tantum de nullo vnquam Filio Alma	457	Epistolae	25
aut tantum de nullo vnquam Filio Alma Mater, quantum de Te sibi	457	Epistolae	25
aut si suos, quia dederunt, non a se compositos, scriptos,	458	Epistolae	24

AUT (cont'd)	PAGE	TITLE	LINE
viduae effoetae, aut ligna exucca & marcida, alumnis suis orbarentur,	462	Epistolae	4
auaritia ceperit aduersus aut immunitates nostras aut commune	467	Epistolae	11
aduersus aut immunitates nostras aut commune literarum et literatorum	467	Epistolae	11
viam ad candorem Mentis Tuae ducentem aut reperissem aut fecissem.	472	Epistolae	9
viam ad candorem Mentis Tuae ducentem aut reperissem aut fecissem.	472	Epistolae	10
AUTAI			
Autar axei megaloi kentoumenai: eute gar autai	431	Mem.Matr.17	10
AUTAR			
Autar axei megaloi kentoumenai: eute gar autai	431	Mem.Matr.17	10
Autar od' au thanatos kuries, os elios auos	431	Mem.Matr.17	19
AUTEM			
Quo tinqimur parui. Ecquis autem brachijs	389	Musae 10	8
Haec autem hospitio latere turpi	411	Lucus 5	6
Nos autem, a cunis, omnes sententia Mortis	415	Lucus 23	3
Nos autem flemus: res ea sola tuis.	427	Mem.Matr.9	8
Necesse est autem vt foelicitas tantorum Principum etiam in ministros	441	Orationes	5
esto autem hoc ipsum iter, quod nuper emensus est, vt sciatis omnes	445	Orationes	33
Quid autem? Ergon' amauit Princeps?	446	Orationes	9
Illud autem, quod cuiuis clarissime patet, etiam lusco, . . .	449	Orationes	34
Quid autem illic? sterilem aiunt regionem:	451	Orationes	2
AUTES			
Zo d' autos, braxu ti pneion, ost' empalin autes	431	Mem.Matr.17	21
AUTHOREM			
perfundis nos omnes quotidianis beneficijs, redundarit in authorem;	443	Orationes	11
AUTHORITAS			
tuus amor et authoritas istos sorices nobis abigat.	469	Epistolae	1
AUTHORITATE			
os importunorum hominum Authoritate tua plurima & Eloquentia	463	Epistolae	2
AUTHORITATIS			
Authoritatis exuens tyrannidem;	436	Poem.Lat.	15
AUTOREM			
Ad Autorem Instaurationis Magnae.	435	Poem.Lat.	T
AUTORES			
Praedicat autores; tertia plena Deo est.	386	Musae 4	4
AUTORUM			
De Autorum enumeratione.	398	Musae 33	T
Per strages licet autorum veterumque ruinam	435	Poem.Lat.	1
AUTOS			
Zo d' autos, braxu ti pneion, ost' empalin autes	431	Mem.Matr.17	21
AUTOU			
Nou d' autou taphos est' aster: pheggos gar ekeinou	429	Mem.Matr.14	3
kai oi alloi nomeis boulontai plesion autou tas agelas istanai.	447	Orationes	32
AUXILIJ			
Christus, vt auxilij	396	Musae 28	8
AUXILIJS			
sua sibi sufficere, neque externis indigere auxilijs atque antidotis:	444	Orationes	26
AXEI			
Autar axei megaloi kentoumenai: eute gar autai	431	Mem.Matr.17	10
AXES			
Inde rotae atque axes subeunt, quasi sella curulis	419	Tr.Mortis	55
BABELEM			
(Nam post Babelem linquae adest confusio)	422	Mem.Matr.2	13
BACCHANTUR			
Bacchantur Lapithae, furit inconstantia vini	271	Tr.Mortis VS	21
BACCHATA			
Euolat, horrendumque ciet bacchata fragorem.	420	Tr.Mortis	72
BACON			
5. Ad F. Bacon, Cancell. Gratiae de Fluuio	460	Epistolae	T
8. Ad F. bacon, Cancel. Gratiae de Instaurationis Libro Academiae	463	Epistolae	T
14. Ad Fr. Bacon, Cancell. De Bibliop. Lond.	467	Epistolae	T
BACULUS			
Lanquentium baculus, teges iacentium, ...	423	Mem.Matr.2	46
BAINEI			
Alla meneit', ou gar taraxos poti metera bainei, ...	431	Mem.Matr.18	5
BAIULO			
qui inde e baiulo euasit Philosophus, eodem ingenio vsus in lignis	453	Orationes	37
BALISTAS			
Balistasque Onagrosque & quicquid Scorpio saeuus	419	Tr.Mortis	40
BALLOMENES			
Ouk eti ballomenes xarisin bebolemenai etor, ...	431	Mem.Matr.17	9
BALSAMA			
O succulenti balsama spiritus!	394	Musae 23	34
BALSAMUM			
Commune cordis palpitantis balsamum:	423	Mem.Matr.2	47
certe nostrate Principe nusquam praesentius Balsamum, nusquam	444	Orationes	27
BAPTISMI			
De S. Baptismi Ritu.	388	Musae 9	T
BARBAM			
nondum ad spicam barbamque adultum.	445	Orationes	21
ego vero sentio, & quis sum ipse (barbam, hui, tam grauem) & apud	445	Orationes	25
BARBARA			
Illi barbara omnia, Tu non nisi cultissima, elegantiasque ipsas	463	Epistolae	14
BARBARAS			
Tun' obdis aures, grex noue, barbaras, ...	395	Musae 23	45
BARBARIEM			
atque ad barbariem patrum	395	Musae 25	11
quod pereleganter & supra barbariem seculi innuebant Maiores nostri,	446	Orationes	29
BARBARIES			
Hos nunc barbaries impia vellicat	391	Musae 17	7
Cedito Barbaries: Helicon iam litibus instat, ...	417	Lucus 28	5

	PAGE	TITLE	LINE
BENEDICTA			
Nunc redit ad mitem, ceu benedicta, Deum.	390	Musae 12	16
BENEDICTIONES			
Benedictiones publicae cingunt caput,	423	Mem.Matr.2	48
BENEFICIA			
Infinita vestra in nos Beneficia non solum verba omnia,	460	Epistolae	2
roqamusque vt quando beneficia tua peruagantur Angliam,	466	Epistolae	17
Deus Opti: Max. tua beneficia, quae nos soluendo non sumus,	467	Epistolae	14
BENEFICIJS			
qua perfundis nos omnes quotidianis beneficijs, redundarit	443	Orationes	10
infinitis vestris in nos beneficijs Maiestatem vestram aeternitati	458	Epistolae	30
alacrius illud impenderemus Doctrinae) beneficijs etiam obligasti.	460	Epistolae	6
quam nunc pleno gradu ingrediens beneficijs tuis percurres.	468	Epistolae	19
BENEFICIO			
cum Alma Matre, vtrumque splendorem cum beneficio nostro coniungis.	458	Epistolae	17
BENEFICIORUM			
tibique non tam auide veterum beneficiorum memoriam recolenti,	457	Epistolae	13
vt si officia nostra minus respondeant magnitudini beneficiorum,	460	Epistolae	16
BENIGNITAS			
non dubitamus quin benignitas tua omnia elementa percurreret.	457	Epistolae	23
BENIGNITATE			
concede vt nos etiam benignitate alarum tuarum et virtute fruamur.	466	Epistolae	22
BENIGNIUS			
praesentius Balsamum, nusquam benignius, soluens obstupefactos artus,	444	Orationes	28
ita excipiemus illa, vt benignius hospitium, et erga te propensius,	466	Epistolae	18
BENIGNUS			
Obtutu placido benignus affles,	384	Musae	3
BERECYNTHIOS			
Tinnitus Berecynthios omittens	401	Musae 37	39
BEZAM			
Martyra, Calvinum, Bezam, doctumque Bucerum,	398	Musae 33	3
BIBAN			
Oulumponde biban ummin anistamenois.	431	Mem.Matr.18	4
BIBERUNT			
Sistimus hic, inquit fatum, sat prata biberunt	272	Tr.Mortis	VS 100
BIBIS			
Sydera, pendenti sedulus aure bibis:	413	Lucus 16	2
BIBLIOP			
14. Ad Fr. Bacon, Cancell. De Bibliop. Lond.	467	Epistolae	T
BIBLIOPOLAS			
Ferunt enim Londinenses Bibliopclas suum potius emolumentum quam	467	Epistolae	4
BIBLIOPOLIS			
13. Ad Archiep. Cantuar. De Bibliopolis Lond.	466	Epistolae	T
BIBLIOTHECA			
Vnicus est nobis Bibliotheca Liber.	459	Epistolae	31
BIBLIOTHECAM			
Bibliothecam nostram rudiorem esse impexioremque, quam vt tantum	463	Epistolae	28
BINA			
Liber alit rixas: potantibus omnia bina	418	Tr.Mortis	18
BINAE			
Te nunc Anglia, Scotiaeque binae,	428	Mem.Matr.10	9
BINAS			
Conditis binas homini sequendas	390	Musae 14	14
BION			
theoi pantes, ei ti kata ton emautou Bion emarton, e phagon e pion,.	452	Orationes	30
BIOS			
Es bios eelioio diken, aktinas ientos	431	Mem.Matr.17	17
BIOU			
Exren phugousa, ten t' epistemen biou.	430	Mem.Matr.15	7
Pneuma, biou parodon mounois epeessi metresan.	431	Mem.Matr.17	23
BIOUN			
Thanein suneidos kreitton, e allos bioun.	430	Mem.Matr.15	16
BIS			
Daunia, non satiat bis ter millesima caedis	418	Tr.Mortis	3
Bis tu mater eras mihi,	425	Mem.Matr.4	15
Est mihi bis quinis laqueata domuncula tignis	426	Mem.Matr.7	22
praegnantes bis intersectas, infantulos plus lactis quam cruoris	449	Orationes	7
BISHOP			
my L. Bishop of Winchester, one of the Kings most honorable	473	Epistolae	24
BLANDA			
Femineum blanda fallitis arte genus:	387	Musae 5	10
Christe, dolor tibi supplicio, mihi blanda voluptas;	405	Passio 6	1
O blanda dextra, neutiquam istoc pulueris,	423	Mem.Matr.2	39
BLASPHEMANDO			
Sputando, blasphemando? nempe ne hoc fiat	405	Passio 5	5
BLATTAS			
Mordaces tineas, nigrasque blattas,	385	Musae	5
BLATTIS			
literatos, eosque cum tineis et blattis rixantes, exuens puluere,	462	Epistolae	26
BLEPONTAS			
existimantes tuphlous einai pros oksu blepontas, anapodemetous pros	450	Orationes	9
BODLEIUM			
Quid Vaticanam Bodleiumque obijcis, Hospes?	459	Epistolae	30
BOMBARDAS			
Ridens Bombardas miseras, quae corpora perdunt	420	Tr.Mortis	97
BONA			
O caecum populum! si bona res siet	392	Musae 17	11
Falleris, nusquam plura bona, cum etiam mala illic sint aurea:	451	Orationes	3
BONAS			
Profanos fremitus bonasque sannas:	400	Musae 37	24

	PAGE	TITLE	LINE
BONE			
Quin redde formas, o bone, pristinas, ...	393	Musae 23	5
Deus bone! qui tum rumores?	450	Orationes	35
BONI			
Sic nunc plena boni sunt omnia Fratris, amore	393	Musae 21	3
Atqui vos secus, o boni, ...	395	Musae 25	16
posterioris largam messem Vobis haec tenuia boni consulentibus,	441	Orationes	22
Quam facile sentiuntur boni Principes!	445	Orationes	4
non passim expositam, boni consulas, curesque vt tuus in nos amor,	466	Epistolae	2
BONIS			
Aut cita mors est danda bonis aut longa senectus:	432	Poem.Lat.	30
BONO			
neque de priuato agamus bono, sed publico;	448	Orationes	6
censemus nostram, et in honoribus Tuis nostro bono gratulamur;	456	Epistolae	17
BONORUM			
sic bonorum Principum facilis Astrologia:	445	Orationes	7
vt bonorum praemia citissime promulgentur, quo suauius virtutibus,	468	Epistolae	15
BONOS			
Sagax Humilitas, eligens viros bonos	412	Lucus 13	1
BONUM			
Atque euehens, bonum facit faecundius, ...	412	Lucus 13	2
BONUS			
Christianus extundi bonus.	396	Musae 27	4
Bonus Ciuis.	412	Lucus 13	T
BOREAE			
Edenem Boreae flatibus inuium.	424	Mem.Matr.4	4
BOULEMASI			
Seiriou ettetheis boulemasi, panta marainei.	431	Mem.Matr.17	20
BOULONTAI			
kai oi alloi nomeis boulontai plesion autou tas agelas istanai.	447	Orationes	32
BRACHIA			
Ni facias, vt opes linguae per brachia serpant, ...	414	Lucus 22	3
BRACHIJS			
Quo tingimur parui. Ecquis autem brachijs	389	Musae 10	8
BRACHIUM			
Quin cerne vt erres, inscie, brachium	426	Mem.Matr.6	13
BRAXU			
Zo d' autos, braxu ti pneion, ost' empalin autes	431	Mem.Matr.17	21
BREUE			
Caelestis harmoniae breue praeludium.	423	Mem.Matr.2	44
BREUEM			
Substructionem capitis & nimbum breuem, ...	422	Mem.Matr.2	15
BREUI			
Qui spissae fidei breuique menti	417	Lucus 30	4
BREUIORE			
Breuiore nodc stringe vitae sarcinas, ...	414	Lucus 20	6
BREUIS			
Rure; breuisque hortus, cuius cum vellere florum	426	Mem.Matr.7	23
Tandem, ne et ipse peccem, breuis sit sermo, atque pressus. . .	470	Epistolae	32
BRIAREUS			
Quis, nisi qui manibus Briareus, oculisque sit Argus, ...	435	Poem.Lat.	5
BRITANNE			
Anticategoriae, Scoto-Britanne, tuae:	386	Musae 4	2
Interea procede Comes Germano-britanne	211	Cam.1613-b BR	7
BRITANNI			
Mors semper iuuenem, senem Britanni.	385	Musae	11
BRITANNIAE			
IACOBO, D. G. Magnae Britanniae, Franciae, & Hiberniae	384	Musae	T
BRITANNIAM			
nulla pulchritudo per vniuersam Britanniam, disparuit forma,	451	Orationes	17
BRITANNICA			
coalescamus, vtraque gens Hispanica, Britannica, colimus Iacobum.	440	Orationes	22
BRITANNICAE			
Tellurisque Britannicae saliuam	428	Mem.Matr.10	3
BRITANNICAM			
Britannicam in Vulpem, inque Romanam Lupam.	397	Musae 30	6
In pacem Britannicam.	411	Lucus 6	T
BRITANNICAS			
Britannicas insulas omnes occupasti. Hoc etiam imperium tenuius est	458	Epistolae	9
BRITANNICI			
Leones Britannici (e quorum ossibus collisis ignis elicitur) qui nunc	449	Orationes	17
licet celebres sint canes Britannici, & plus iusto celebres,	454	Orationes	17
BRITANNO			
Adde etiam currus, & cum temone Britanno	419	Tr.Mortis	45
BRITANNOS			
Minima contentos nocte Britannos.	451	Orationes	20
BRITANNUS			
Quae dicteria fuderat Britannus	391	Musae 15	1
BRITONUM			
Et tu gemma etiam Britonum, Septentrionum	211	Cam.1613-b BR	11
BRUTA			
homines, quibus homo bruta, iustitia scilicet & prudentia. . . .	447	Orationes	5
BRUTUS			
Sophismatomastix; Brutus Literarius, ...	436	Poem.Lat.	14
BUCERUM			
Martyra, Calvinum, Bezam, doctumque Bucerum, ...	398	Musae 33	3
BUCKINGH			
1. Ad Buckingh. C. Gratulatio de Marchionatu	456	Epistolae	T
BULLA			
Magnas es; esto. Bulla si vocaberis, ...	413	Lucus 17	1

	PAGE	TITLE	LINE
BULLAE			
bullae & crepitacula puerorum sunt, aut eorum certe, qui cymbala sunt	445	Orationes	23
BURGEN			
10. Ad R. Naunt. Burgen. Elect.	465	Epistolae	T
C			
1. Ad Buckingh. C. Gratulatio de Marchionatu	456	Epistolae	T
CACUM			
Aetna Cacum igniuomum dedit, hic Ixiona multis	420	Tr.Mortis	87
Aetna Cacum igniuomum dedit, hic Ixiona Graecis	272	Tr.Mortis VS	87
CADAUER			
At superat caput illa tuum, quantum ipsa cadauer	424	Mem.Matr.3	3
Terram & funus olent flores: Dominaeque cadauer	425	Mem.Matr.5	5
CADAUERA			
Strata iacent toto millena cadauera campo	420	Tr.Mortis	79
Strata, iacent toto prostrata cadauera campo	272	Tr.Mortis VS	79
CADENS			
liquitur ardenti cadens fornace metallum;	271	Tr.Mortis VS	51
CADIS			
Cum tu, Christe, cadis, nascor; mentemque ligauit	434	Poem.Lat.	1
CADIT			
Quas Luna habet, tuetur, in foueam cadit,	393	Musae 22	8
A veteri trunco & nobilitate cadit.	416	Lucus 25	6
CADUNT			
Praecipitata; cadunt vrbes, formidine muri	420	Tr.Mortis	77
CAECAS			
Cui caecas tribuit vires annosa vetustas.	433	Poem.Lat.	42
CAECI			
Pennata caeci dextra Cupidinis,	434	Poem.Lat.	22
CAECO			
Quasque habet aut patulas, aut caeco tramite, moles	402	Musae 39	21
CAECOS			
O caecos animi fratres! quis vestra fatigat	401	Musae 39	4
Quae cordis latebras sinusque caecos	411	Lucus 5	12
Ah, cernam; Tu, qui caecos sanare solebas,	421	Lucus 35	7
CAECUM			
O caecum populum! si bona res siet	392	Musae 17	11
CAEDERIS			
Ah! quam caederis hinc & inde palmis!	405	Passio 8	1
CAEDI			
Quantum caedi? adeon' vnam vos pascere vitam,	419	Tr.Mortis	34
Quantum caedi? adeon' vnam nos vivere vitam,	271	Tr.Mortis VS	34
CAEDIS			
Daunia, non satiat bis ter millesima caedis	418	Tr.Mortis	3
CAELESTEM			
Flumina caelestem ducite lenta chorum:	210	Cam.1613-b BR	4
CAELESTES			
Contaminatis alueosque caelestes	404	Passio 5	4
CAELESTIS			
Caelestis harmoniae breue praeludium.	423	Mem.Matr.2	44
CAELI			
Quid hoc? & ipse deficis, Caeli gigas,	407	Passio 16	1
Coniugium Caeli Terraeque haec machina praestat;	417	Lucus 31	1
Non iam exaudiri quicquam vel Musica caeli	420	Tr.Mortis	74
Caelique referunt & praeoccupant modum.	423	Mem.Matr.2	49
Quin caeli mihi sunt mei,	424	Mem.Matr.4	5
CAELO			
Vnicus est nummus, caelo Christoque petitus,	410	Lucus 4	9
Debetur Caelo lumen, & vmbra solo:	417	Lucus 31	2
Verum heus, si nequeas caelo demittere matrem,	424	Mem.Matr.3	7
Verum augusta parens, sanctum os caeloque locandum,	426	Mem.Matr.7	10
CAELOS			
It stridor, caelosque omnes & Tartara findit.	420	Tr.Mortis	73
It stridor, caelosque omnes et sydera findit.	271	Tr.Mortis VS	73
CAELUM			
Vt tenuis flammae species caelum vsque minatur,	410	Lucus 2	1
At Caelum e saxis elicuit Stephanus.	410	Lucus 3	2
Ecquid emes Caelum? quin stellam rectius vnam	410	Lucus 4	5
Et maestum nimio madore Caelum	428	Mem.Matr.10	2
CAENO			
Caeno profani corporis exuens	394	Musae 23	26
CAENUM			
Totusque caenum Cynthiae ignoscit notis.	393	Musae 22	9
CAERULUM			
Tu flectis amnes, tu mare caerulum	433	Poem.Lat.	13
CAESAR			
Ante tui, CAESAR, quam fulserat aura fauoris,	384	Musae	3
Pro solido, CAESAR, carmine frusta dabo.	385	Musae 1	4
nostram Caesar ad insulam	395	Musae 25	2
Caesar sobrius ad rei Latinae	401	Musae 37	42
CAESARE			
incredibilem luxum a Tiberio Caesare ad Constantinum magnum aperirem,	452	Orationes	22
CAESARI			
Piscis tributum soluit; & tu Caesari:	412	Lucus 11	1
CAESARUM			
Quam pudet me delicatorum Caesarum, qui cupiditatibus immersi,	452	Orationes	9
CAESIA			
Pallas retortis caesia vocibus	434	Poem.Lat.	25
CAETERA			
Nunc sudas solus; caetera turba riget.	397	Musae 29	4
Caetera condonabo tibi, scombrisque remittam:	399	Musae 34	3
Caetera displiceat turba, necesse, tibi:	404	Passio 2	4

	PAGE	TITLE	LINE
CAETERA (cont'd)			
Quae contrita tamen caetera damna leuant.	409	Passio 20	8
Cum natet in tantis caetera terra malis?	411	Lucus 6	2
Corde tuo forsan, caetera munda, SOROR.	413	Lucus 15	6
insunt oculi variegati, cum caetera animantia vnicolores habeant.	453	Orationes	17
CAETERAE			
Cum caeterae ecclesiae tam perspicaci diligentia incubes, . . .	466	Epistolae	21
CAETERAS			
Mulcensque dotes caeteras visa est quasi	423	Mem.Matr.2	43
CAETERIS			
in qua dextra et fide coniuncti, in caeteris haud diuellamur.	468	Epistolae	25
CAETEROS			
Tu qui superbos caeteros existimas	388	Musae 8	15
CALAMI			
Pieria supellex, charta, calami, codices, quam subito dispereunt,	448	Orationes	18
CALAMISTROS			
Iam si inter commendandum adhibeas ei calamistros vti iuuenculae,	470	Epistolae	18
CALAMO			
Quid nugor calamo fauens?	424	Mem.Matr.4	1
tibi conueniat scribenti, quam quod Academiae tuo calamo scribenti:	470	Epistolae	14
sed vt facilius ignoscas occupato calamo, qui etiam ferians nihil Tua	471	Epistolae	23
CALAMOS			
Excussos manibus calamos, falcemque resumptam	431	Mem.Matr.19	1
CALAMUM			
Quod calamum excusent Pontus & Astra meum:	435	Poem.Lat.	8
Eximia tua in nos merita frequentiorem calamum postulant, . .	457	Epistolae	7
CALAMUS			
Non maeret calamus; non queritur caput:	403	Musae 40	6
CALCASTI			
Quos tu calcasti fluctus, me, Christe, lacessunt, ...	414	Lucus 19	1
CALCE			
Dij te perdant, cum malis tuis & arena sine calce;	451	Orationes	6
CALCEAT			
Illum volo, qui calceat lixam tuum.	413	Lucus 17	7
CALCITRO			
Vtrumque sternis calcitro:	388	Musae 8	6
CALCULO			
Prudenter inito quot-diebus calculo.	423	Mem.Matr.2	23
CALCULUM			
opera vtriusque Reipublicae calculum et ciuilis et literariae	466	Epistolae	1
CALES			
Cur adeo immodica relligione cales?	399	Musae 35	2
CALESCIT			
Ardore scribendi calescit, ...	426	Mem.Matr.6	15
CALET			
Tentando sanum: si calet, aestuans, ...	426	Mem.Matr.6	14
CALICES			
Musarum calices, per & beatos	400	Musae 37	3
CALIGINE			
Corda furor, spissaque afflat caligine sensus?	401	Musae 39	5
CALIGULA			
Quid si cochleas colligeret cum Caligula, praesertim cum possit	446	Orationes	13
CALLENT			
Saxa lyras citharasque callent.	393	Musae 23	8
CALLES			
Ah, quam docta perambulare calles	411	Lucus 5	15
CALLET			
administrans, distribuendi modum omnem rationemque callet? . .	464	Epistolae	16
CALLIDUM			
Scio Hispanum versutum, callidum, artis & aucupij apprime gnarum:	451	Orationes	25
CALLIDUS			
Nunc etiam Christum callidus aggrederis.	406	Passio 11	2
CALOR			
& cum eo vita nostra atque calor, longo animi deliquio fugitiuus ac	444	Orationes	23
CALORE			
amplexusque foelicitatis Tuae receptae, communi calore foueantur.	469	Epistolae	19
CALORIS			
Quin populo, clemens, aliquid largire caloris:	397	Musae 29	3
qui primo caloris suasu excitati atque expergefacti, vbi sursum	471	Epistolae	29
CALUMNIAE			
quanto citius fugient calumniae, si speculum Inuidiae ostendas,	454	Orationes	20
CALUMNIANDI			
Calumniandi concitauit vrtica, ...	392	Musae 20	7
CALUMNIARUM			
Calumniarum nec pudor quis nec modus?	397	Musae 30	1
CALVINUM			
Martyra, Calvinum, Bezam, doctumque Bucerum, ...	398	Musae 33	3
CAMBRIA			
Quin te Cambria peruetusta deflet, ...	428	Mem.Matr.10	10
CAMDEN			
15. Ad J. Leigh, Capitalem Iustitiarium Angl. (Camden) Gratulatio	468	Epistolae	T
CAMI			
Ad Andreae Melvini Scoti Anti-Tami-Cami-Categoriam.	384	Musae	T
Ad eundem In Monstrum vocabuli Anti-Tami-Cami-Categoria. . .	386	Musae 3	T
Istas Anti-Tami-Cami-Categorias!	386	Musae 3	2
Partitio Anti-Tami-Cami-Categoriae.	386	Musae 4	T
CAMOENAE			
Cui dulcis arrident Camoenae	433	Poem.Lat.	3
CAMOENARUM			
Tu duplicem solus Camoenarum thronum	388	Musae 8	3

	PAGE	TITLE	LINE
CAPITIS			
Et partem capitis petit supremam;	391	Musae 15	4
Substructionem capitis & nimbum breuem,	422	Mem.Matr.2	15
CAPTARET			
Quid si muscas captaret cum Domitiano?	446	Orationes	14
CAPTAUIT			
& scientiae augmentum ex hoc itinere captauit solertissimus Princeps?	450	Orationes	5
CAPTUS			
eundemque retulisset captus piscis, foelicissimus mortalium habitus	444	Orationes	15
CAPULUM			
Ornastis capulum, nec superesse licet.	425	Mem.Matr.5	2
CAPUT			
Ne tandem caput eius impetatis.	391	Musae 15	13
Non maeret calamus; non queritur caput:	403	Musae 40	6
Qui Caput es, spinas & tua Membra tuas.	405	Passio 6	4
Si sursum iacias, in caput ipsa ruit.	410	Lucus 4	8
Transiliuntque caput, qui subiere pedes.	414	Lucus 19	2
Nempe Caput Romae es, cuius mysteria velles	416	Lucus 27	3
Struices superbas atque turritum caput	422	Mem.Matr.2	11
Benedictiones publicae cingunt caput,	423	Mem.Matr.2	48
At superat caput illa tuum, quantum ipsa cadauer	424	Mem.Matr.3	3
Exere terra caput, servatos projice flores,	210	Cam.1613-b BR	3
soli caput rotundum & coeleste, soli facies tanquam vestibulum magni	446	Orationes	38
Ecquid inter tot gloriae titulos caput vndique munientes meministi	456	Epistolae	2
vt Alma Mater libentissime caput reclinet in tuo sinu, oculusque	465	Epistolae	13
neque vlla negotia (quippe quae caput petant, non cor) Tui in me	473	Epistolae	6
CARCER			
Omne regnum suo Principi carcer est, aut si excedat, alienum:	450	Orationes	12
CARERE			
Carere discat verna, quo summus caret	407	Passio 16	9
CARET			
Qui tamen excipiat, Christus caret hospite: tantum	407	Passio 15	3
Carere discat verna, quo summus caret	407	Passio 16	9
CARIOSA			
Quae sapiunt aeuum, ceu cariosa iacent.	386	Musae 3	4
CARMEN			
Tu perstrepis tamen; vtque turgeat carmen	392	Musae 20	10
Sacrilegum carmen, censeo, flamma voret.	399	Musae 34	4
CARMINA			
Heroum grandi carmina fulta pede?	387	Musae 5	4
Perstringunt vestros carmina sola duces.	400	Musae 36	4
Sola Iacobaeum decantent carmina nomen.	402	Musae 39	40
Non deerat vel fama tibi, vel carmina famae,	416	Lucus 25	3
Non deerint vel fama tibi, vel carmina famae,	416	Lucus 25 V	3
Quin Matris superans carmina poscit honos.	431	Mem.Matr.19	6
Musa, vale, & tu Phoebe; dolor mea carmina dictet;	432	Poem.Lat.	12
CARMINE			
Pro solido, CAESAR, carmine frusta dabo.	385	Musae 1	4
Potentiori carmine percitas	393	Musae 23	10
Whitaker, erranti quem praefers carmine, miles	398	Musae 33	5
Quin hoc carmine Lexicon probrorum	401	Musae 37	28
Non te carmine turbidum vocaui,	401	Musae 37	33
Incipis irridens; stomachans in carmine pergis;	401	Musae 38	1
Aggreditur Matrem (conductis carmine Parcis)	431	Mem.Matr.19	3
Hic habitant Musae, facilisque in carmine Pallas,	210	Cam.1613-a BR	3
CARMINIBUS			
Ne me carminibus nimis dicacem,	400	Musae 37	10
CARNE			
Suauiter admoueas notum tibi carne flagellum,	406	Passio 9	3
CARNEM			
Assiduo stimulo carnem Mens vlta lacessit,	410	Lucus 2	5
Quin, mitte nugas; teque carnem & sanguinem	413	Lucus 17	5
CARNIS			
Ac zephyris, carnis flos remeare nequit.	415	Lucus 23	14
Exuta strato carnis, ossibus constans,	429	Mem.Matr.12	2
CARO			
Nostra caro sanctae nescia laudis erit?	389	Musae 12	10
Vel sine luce solum, vel sine mente caro.	417	Lucus 31	6
CAROLE			
Atque hoc quidem statu res erant, Suauissime CAROLE, cum tu aberas;	451	Orationes	28
CAROLI			
Serenissimi Principis Caroli Reditum ex Hispanijs celebrauit	444	Orationes	T
CAROLO			
Illustriss. Celsissimoque CAROLO, Walliae, & Iuventutis Principi.	384	Musae	T
CAROLUM			
foetum vestrum, hunc alterum Carolum, hunc fasciculum Prudentiae,	459	Epistolae	10
CAROLVM			
date mihi CAROLVM alterum, quamlibet Magnum, modo detis eum in flore,	445	Orationes	19
at ego Principem vellem, CAROLVM, CAROLVM;	451	Orationes	6
at ego Principem vellem, CAROLVM, CAROLVM;	451	Orationes	7
CAROLVS			
redijt CAROLVS, & cum eo vita nostra atque calor, longo animi	444	Orationes	22
vt nullus sit angulus corporis, nulla venula, vbi non adsit CAROLVS.	445	Orationes	4
Redijt Princeps, CAROLVS redijt, honore grauidus, grauidus scientia,	454	Orationes	27
CARPIS			
Inuertis, mores carpis & obloqueris:	416	Lucus 26	2
CARPSIT			
Carpsit malignum sydus hanc modestiam	427	Mem.Matr.8	3
CARPUNT			
praedia, alij immunitates carpunt, nonnulli Fluuium inuident,	461	Epistolae	15

	PAGE	TITLE		LINE
CEDAM				
vt cedam aliquantisper expectationi hominum, rariusque paulo fodiam	472	Epistolae		27
CEDAT				
Nobis facilitas cedat & tibi sudor.	406	Passio 12		3
CEDERE				
Nescia vulturnis cedere, firma manet.	428	Mem.Matr.11		2
CEDET				
sed tamen comparatio & in honorem tuum cedet, nostrumque emolumentum.	467	Epistolae		26
CEDITO				
Cedito Barbaries: Helicon iam litibus instat,	417	Lucus 28		5
CEDO				
In vicium mundo sterili, cui cedo cometas	426	Mem.Matr.7		20
CEDROS				
Assideo Matri, robore vinco cedros.	428	Mem.Matr.11		6
CEDUNT				
Quam nihil illudis, Gens improba! quam male cedunt	405	Passio 7		1
CELARE				
ipsa durissima ingenia, meum praesertim, celare non possunt:	445	Orationes		9
CELEBRANS				
Te, Mater, celebrans diu,	424	Mem.Matr.4		11
Noctu te celebrans luminis aemulo.	424	Mem.Matr.4		12
CELEBRARE				
Quod nectar, nisi cum te celebrare diem?)	428	Mem.Matr.9		16
CELEBRAUIT				
Caroli Reditum ex Hispanijs celebrauit Georgius Herbert Academiae	444	Orationes		T
CELEBREM				
Vt celebrem decus insusurras?	394	Musae 23		24
omnia Danorum expiscatus consilia, victoriam celebrem consecutus est.	453	Orationes		7
CELEBRES				
licet celebres sint canes Britannici, & plus iusto celebres,	454	Orationes		16
& plus iusto celebres, cum leunculum & dominum suum contra naturam	454	Orationes		17
CELEBRIS				
qua in re celebris est Gracchorum mater, ingenium ipsum atque indoles	447	Orationes		16
CELERITATEM				
Quis enim impetus animi celeritatem tantae munificentiae assequi	460	Epistolae		4
qui celeritatem affectuum raptim sequentes, ad omnem eorum auram	472	Epistolae		1
CELLA				
Nescia sit metae; venula, cella tua est.	404	Passio 2		2
CELLAE				
Triste colens cellae, noctuque & Daemone plenum,	420	Tr.Mortis		90
CELSISSIMO				
Illustriss. Celsissimoque CAROLO, Walliae, & Iuventutis Principi.	384	Musae		T
CELSITUD				
Honoribus, Magnif., Celsitud., sed non patitur, vt mihi videtur,	473	Epistolae		17
CENSEMUS				
Tuam gloriam censemus nostram, et in honoribus Tuis nostro bono	456	Epistolae		16
Imo prorsus censemus permultum interesse alacritatis publicae,	468	Epistolae		14
CENSEO				
Sacrilegum carmen, censeo, flamma voret.	399	Musae 34		4
CENSES				
At tu qui inepte haec dicta censes filio,	423	Mem.Matr.2		52
Quod tu febrem censes, salubre est	426	Mem.Matr.6		23
CENTRUM				
vt lineae, quamuis diuersa via, omnes tamen ad centrum properant;	456	Epistolae		23
CENTUM				
O plena centum Musica Gratijs,	394	Musae 23		21
Centum stigmatibus tuos inurens	400	Musae 37		23
Christe, decus, dulcedo, & centum circiter Hyblae,	421	Lucus 35		1
CENTURIONIS				
tanquam flos molliculus rudiore Centurionis manu tactus flaccescit.	448	Orationes		25
CEPERIT				
quicquid consilij auaritia ceperit aduersus aut immunitates nostras	467	Epistolae		11
CERDONIBUS				
Communem habere crede cum Cerdonibus:	413	Lucus 17		6
CEREBRI				
Vt feruor cerebri refrigeretur,	391	Musae 15		9
CERNAM				
Quin, sine, te cernam; quoties iam dixero, cernam;	421	Lucus 35		3
Ah, cernam; Tu, qui caecos sanare solebas,	421	Lucus 35		7
CERNAT				
Zacchaeus, vt Te cernat, arborem scandit:	406	Passio 12		1
CERNE				
Quin cerne vt erres, inscie, brachium	426	Mem.Matr.6		13
CERNENS				
Nullum locum requiemue cernens perstitit	436	Poem.Lat.		20
Nullum locum requiemue cernens praestitit	436	Poem.Lat.	V	20
CERNES				
Aut aperi, & cernes corpus quas proijcit vmbras;	437	Poem.Lat.		7
CERNIMUS				
coelum ac terram minori quam cernimus interuallo connectat.	444	Orationes		8
CERNIS				
Cernis vt exusta semper sit fronte viator;	437	Poem.Lat.		3
Aut aperi, & cernis corpus quas proijcit vmbras;	437	Poem.Lat.	V	7
CERNITE				
Cernite, quam formosa suas Ecclesia pennas	401	Musae 39		6
CERNITIS				
cernitis Regem & nomine & re magnum quid polliceri, ideoque ex	447	Orationes		8
CERTA				
certa, ac perfacilis mihi!	395	Musae 25		7
Ceu fida statione & arce certa,	417	Lucus 30		7
Ratione certa vita constat & domus,	423	Mem.Matr.2		22

	PAGE	TITLE	LINE
CERTAE			
Nec hoc abunde est tibi, nisi certae Anchorae	438	Poem.Lat.	5
CERTAMEN			
Magnatumque inopumque aequum certamen & ardor:	429	Mem.Matr.13	3
inter quae etiam certamen oritur et pia contentio, vtrum gratia	456	Epistolae	19
CERTANTEM			
virum protulit, cum quinque millibus annorum de palma certantem.	463	Epistolae	27
CERTAT			
Occasione certat, imo & obtinet.	423	Mem.Matr.2	28
CERTE			
Sum, quis nescit, Imago Dei, sed saxea certe:	410	Lucus 1	1
certe cum duplex fulgor sit, qui mundi oculos perstringat,	441	Orationes	11
certe nostrate Principe nusquam praesentius Balsamum, nusquam	444	Orationes	26
aut eorum certe, qui cymbala sunt fanaticae iuuentutis:	445	Orationes	24
certe fatendum est, anteferendam bello pacem, sine qua omnis vita	448	Orationes	7
certe nos te absentem omnes acerrime concitatissimeque desiderauimus.	451	Orationes	33
nos certe precamur, vt neque virtutibus tuis desint honores neque	457	Epistolae	1
certe adeo festinasti ad gratitudines tuas cum emolumento nostro	462	Epistolae	13
Certe non diu est ex quo gratulati sumus tibi:	465	Epistolae	23
appulit ad nos omnes haud ita certe studijs chartisque obuolutos,	468	Epistolae	13
Certe, si quantum eruditio Regis profuerit Reipublicae,	469	Epistolae	23
certe non tam ornas illam, qui infers manum grauitati.	470	Epistolae	20
CERTEM			
Sic quasi Dijs certem, magnos accersere montes:	432	Poem.Lat.	6
CERTENT			
Tibi & concedat vt terrestres tui honores cum coelestibus certent,	465	Epistolae	19
CERTISSIME			
vestram aeternitati in scriptis nostris certissime traderemus?	458	Epistolae	31
CERTITUDINIS			
Collega Solis; Quadra Certitudinis;	436	Poem.Lat.	13
Tibi debet Vnda & Terra certitudinis.	438	Poem.Lat.	7
CERTUM			
Intus agunt, habeat certum meditatio finem:	402	Musae 39	37
Non video, certum est iurare; aut si hoc vetuisti,	421	Lucus 35	9
CERUICIBUS			
Quam cruenta gloria est, quae super ceruicibus hominum erigitur?	449	Orationes	10
CESPES			
Cespes viuus, Homo; mortuus, Ara fuit:	417	Lucus 29	2
CESSANDUM			
vt nunquam cessandum mihi ducerem, nunquam fatiscendum,	472	Epistolae	8
CESSATORIBUS			
vendentibus Libros non ementibus, hoc est cessatoribus non studiosis.	468	Epistolae	8
CESSATRICES			
O cessatrices! eccum puluisculus illic!	413	Lucus 15	5
CESSEMUS			
Quisnam Antichristus cessemus quaerere; Papa	412	Lucus 10	1
CESSENT			
Christe, fluas semper; ne, si tua flumina cessent,	406	Passio 13	5
CESTE			
Quid mihi si facies nigra est? hoc, Ceste, colore	437	Poem.Lat.	1
CESTUM			
Aethiopissa ambit Cestum Diuersi Coloris Virum.	437	Poem.Lat.	T
CEU			
Ceu, quas culta timet seges, pruinas	385	Musae	7
Quae sapiunt aeuum, ceu cariosa iacent.	386	Musae 3	4
Ingemat ob partus, ceu maledicta, suos,	390	Musae 12	14
Nunc redit ad mitem, ceu benedicta, Deum.	390	Musae 12	16
Ceu fida statione & arce certa,	417	Lucus 30	7
Scinditur in partes vulgus ceu compita: telum	418	Tr.Mortis	16
Ceu Polypus, chelis saxa prehendo tenax:	428	Mem.Matr.11	10
Ceu victa, Musis porrigit herbulas	434	Poem.Lat.	21
CHALIBS			
Faecundusque chalibs sceleris, iam sanguine tectus	271	Tr.Mortis VS	37
CHALYBS			
Faecundusque chalybs sceleris, iam sanguine tinctus,	419	Tr.Mortis	37
CHAOS			
Nox Aetnam, noctemque Chaos genuere priores.	420	Tr.Mortis	86
CHARA			
pignora chara sui	397	Musae 28	11
CHARACTER			
corrumpuntur statuae, haec imago atque character, tempore melior,	459	Epistolae	13
CHARAS			
Per charas tibi nobilesque dextras,	400	Musae 37	7
CHARIORES			
Excellentias vestras tanto chariores esse, cum eo sitis ordine atque	441	Orationes	1
CHARONTIS			
Aurea pro naulo lingua Charontis erit.	414	Lucus 22	4
CHAROS			
Quos charos habuit Christus Apostolos,	391	Musae 17	1
CHARTA			
Plus charta haec mea delibuta dictis	400	Musae 37	25
Sacratissima Charta, tu fuisti	411	Lucus 5	11
Nam primum tota haec Pieria supellex, charta, calami, codices,	448	Orationes	18
charta conspiciendum Te praebes, quo familiarius inter nos verseris.	458	Epistolae	19
CHARTACEI			
vestra disquisitio, qui tineae estis & helluones chartacei;	445	Orationes	19
CHARTAE			
neque ratione habita Chartae nostrae a Serenissimo Principe Henrico 8	467	Epistolae	21
CHARTAM			
Quam chartam tibi porrigo recentem,	384	Musae	1

	PAGE	TITLE	LINE
CHARTAS			
Queis me educasti; sponte chartas illinunt	424	Mem.Matr.2	63
CHARTIS			
contemnere has gloriolas nostras quas e chartis & puluere eruimus.	441	Orationes	17
nos chartis et aeternitate occupatos, temporarijs hisce negotiolis	466	Epistolae	5
appulit ad nos omnes haud ita certe studijs chartisque obuolutos,	468	Epistolae	13
CHARYBDIM			
Illam Charybdim cautionè nouimus	397	Musae 30	4
CHEIRAGRA			
Ah! Cheiragra vetat, quo minus, inquit, agam.	389	Musae 11	2
CHELIS			
Ceu Polypus, chelis saxa prehendo tenax:	428	Mem.Matr.11	10
CHLAMYDIS			
Polluens castum chlamydis colorem	390	Musae 14	3
CHORAGUS			
Almi choragus luminis?	407	Passio 16	2
CHORIS			
Qui templa sacris expoliant choris, ...	394	Musae 23	18
CHORO			
Virtutumque choro siccior ipse tuo.	422	Mem.Matr.1	4
CHORUM			
Flumina caelestem ducite lenta chorum:	210	Cam.1613-b BR	4
CHRISTE			
Christe, vbi tam duro patet in te semita ferro, ...	404	Passio 4	1
Christe, dolor tibi supplicio, mihi blanda voluptas; . . .	405	Passio 6	1
Christe, flagellati spes & victoria mundi, ...	406	Passio 9	1
Si, Christe, dum suffigeris, tuae vestes	406	Passio 10	1
Christe, fluas semper; ne, si tua flumina cessent, . . .	406	Passio 13	5
Tuque super nostras, Christe, moueris aquas.	411	Lucus 6	8
Verius hoc olim factum est, vbi, Christe, lauares	412	Lucus 8	3
Cum dormis, surgit pelagus: cum, Christe, resurgis, . . .	412	Lucus 12	1
Quos tu calcasti fluctus, me, Christe, lacessunt, ...	414	Lucus 19	1
Christe, super fluctus si non discurrere detur:	414	Lucus 19	3
Christe, decus, dulcedo, & centum circiter Hyblae, . . .	421	Lucus 35	1
Cum tu, Christe, cadis, nascor; mentemque ligauit	434	Poem.Lat.	1
Cur mihi das vitam, quam tibi, Christe, negas?	434	Poem.Lat.	4
Christe, duplex fiet mors tua vita mihi:	434	Poem.Lat.	8
CHRISTI			
Non plus maligni daemones Christi cruce	389	Musae 10	2
Vitasse Christi spiritum efflantis crucem.	389	Musae 10	5
Quo sanguis est Christi, nisi vt maculas lauet, ...	393	Musae 22	3
Aut potius Christi sanguis demissus ab alto, ...	399	Musae 35	9
Quo fugies, sudor? quamuis pars altera Christi	404	Passio 2	1
Diuina Christi scriberet acta manu?	412	Lucus 9	2
Quae diuisa nocent, Christi per foedus, in vnum	417	Lucus 29	3
CHRISTIANAE			
tantum qui eruditionem simplicitati Christianae putant aduersam,	461	Epistolae	18
CHRISTIANI			
Triumphus Christiani. In Mortem.	421	Lucus 33	T
CHRISTIANUS			
Et Christianus quisque piscis dicitur	389	Musae 10	6
Christianus extundi bonus.	396	Musae 27	4
CHRISTO			
Reuerendissimo in Christo Patri ac Domino, ...	385	Musae	T
In Mundi sympathiam cum Christo.	409	Passio 21	T
Vnicus est nummus, caelo Christoque petitus, ...	410	Lucus 4	9
Tempestas Christo dormiente.	412	Lucus 12	T
CHRISTUM			
Nunc etiam Christum callidus aggrederis.	406	Passio 11	2
In Christum crucem ascensurum.	406	Passio 12	T
Ecquid emes Christum? pro nobis scilicet olim	410	Lucus 4	1
(Tenere Christum scilicet, ne ascenderet)	438	Poem.Lat.	2
Tuiue Christum deuocans facundia	438	Poem.Lat.	3
CHRISTUS			
Quos charos habuit Christus Apostolos, ...	391	Musae 17	1
Quam Christus immortalis innocuo gregi	396	Musae 28	1
Christus, vt auxilij	396	Musae 28	8
Christus Apostolici cinctus amore gregis.	398	Musae 33	10
Ipse etiam Christus coelo speculatus ab alto, ...	402	Musae 39	11
Christus in cruce.	406	Passio 13	T
Qui tamen excipiat, Christus caret hospite: tantum . . .	407	Passio 15	3
Haud aliter cum Christus obit, prae funere tanto	409	Passio 20	5
Nec Deus est nec Homo: Christus vterque fuit.	412	Lucus 10	2
Christus adest: crebris aedes percurrite scopis, ...	413	Lucus 15	1
CIBOS			
Dum prono rapis ore cibos, & fercula verris, ...	414	Lucus 21	1
CIBUM			
aut tanquam oues taedulae & fastidiosae, cibum respuamus. . .	449	Orationes	2
CIBUS			
Praeclariorum spirituum cibus, ...	394	Musae 23	22
CIET			
Euolat, horrendumque ciet bacchata fragorem.	420	Tr.Mortis	72
CINCTA			
Tisiphone; flamma & fallaci fulmine cincta	420	Tr.Mortis	71
CINCTUS			
Christus Apostolici cinctus amore gregis.	398	Musae 33	10
CINE			
siccine abijsti solus? cur non nos omnes tecum?	451	Orationes	7
CINERI			
Tam languens genitrix cineri supposta fugaci:	426	Mem.Matr.7	9

	PAGE	TITLE	LINE
CINGIT			
Assiduo vilem lumine cingit humum.	387	Musae 7	8
Nec cingit mare, nunc inundat omnes.	428	Mem.Matr.10	14
CINGUNT			
Benedictiones publicae cingunt caput,	423	Mem.Matr.2	48
CINNUS			
Profunditatis cinnus, atque Elegantiae;	436	Poem.Lat. V	6
CIRCITER			
Christe, decus, dulcedo, & centum circiter Hyblae,	421	Lucus 35	1
CIRCUITU			
Nullo circuitu scienda pungunt,	415	Lucus 24	12
CIRCUMCURSITANS			
tunc temporis liberior eram, huc illuc pro libitu circumcursitans:	451	Orationes	12
CIRCUMDATUM			
voluptatibus quasi fascijs circumdatum, enatare e delicijs,	452	Orationes	5
CIRCUMFERRE			
Circumferre potes; Sampson vt ante fores.	408	Passio 18	2
CIRCUMFERUNTUR			
tanquam onera, circumferuntur mollissimis lecticis, indicantes,	452	Orationes	11
CIRCUMIERE			
Illos, qui mundum circumiere, pedes.	412	Lucus 8	4
CIRCUMSCRIBERE			
quos magnificentia promissi circumscribere in promptu erat,	445	Orationes	16
CIRCUMSCRIBERERIS			
sphaera quam pro latitudine meritorum tuorum circumscribereris.	466	Epistolae	15
CIRCUMSONANT			
quotidie transnatantes, litora nostra atque aures mire circumsonant.	441	Orationes	4
CIRCUMSPICE			
Circumspice, si placet, Terrarum Reges, mutus est mundus vniuersus,	458	Epistolae	5
CIRCUMSPICIENS			
postquam circumspiciens reperisset Te, quasi in tuis palpebris	465	Epistolae	14
CIRCUMSTANT			
O sec'lum lepidum! circumstant vndique Fratres,	393	Musae 21	1
CITA			
Aut cita mors est danda bonis aut longa senectus:	432	Poem.Lat.	30
CITHARAS			
Saxa lyras citharasque callent.	393	Musae 23	8
CITHARIS			
Cum citharis lituisque miscet.	394	Musae 23	40
CITISSIME			
vt bonorum praemia citissime promulgentur, quo suauius virtutibus,	468	Epistolae	15
CITIUS			
quanto citius fugient calumniae, si speculum Inuidiae ostendas,	454	Orationes	20
CIUILI			
nisi Rex esses in ciuili Republica, eligereris in Literaria?	443	Orationes	18
vt vestrae coronae ciuili & literariae tertiam Coelestem sero	459	Epistolae	21
CIUILIS			
vtriusque Reipublicae calculum et ciuilis et literariae adipiscaris.	466	Epistolae	1
CIUIS			
Bonus Ciuis.	412	Lucus 13	T
CLADEM			
Vnus dicitur aduenire cladem:	401	Musae 37	43
CLAMAS			
Dicterijs mordacibus notans, clamas	392	Musae 20	13
CLAMITANT			
spiritus, generososque animos frangere et retundere clamitant.	461	Epistolae	20
CLAMITAT			
O victoria, clamitat,	395	Musae 25	6
CLAMORIBUS			
Compita ferueścunt pedibus, clamoribus aether.	418	Tr.Mortis	11
CLANCULUM			
sic & Noster qui clanculum exijt, vsque ad Pyrenaeas nubes	454	Orationes	31
CLARA			
Dein, oratio clara sit, perspicua, pellucens.	470	Epistolae	28
CLARAS			
Cum nequeat claras ipse litare preces?	388	Musae 9	14
CLARE			
Nempe in quo clare lucet Imago Dei.	410	Lucus 4	10
CLARISSIMA			
Natare sine clarissima potest cruce?	389	Musae 10	9
CLARISSIME			
Illud autem, quod cuiuis clarissime patet, etiam lusco,	449	Orationes	35
Clarissime Vir. Permitte vt nos etiam in praedam partemque tecum	465	Epistolae	20
CLARITAS			
vtriusque enim splendor et claritas humilia loca deprecantur.	466	Epistolae	11
CLARITATEM			
splendida plerumque vitrea sint, claritatem fragilitate corrumpentia;	448	Orationes	5
CLASSEM			
Interea classem magnis Rex instruit ausis:	427	Mem.Matr.9	7
CLAUDAT			
Si ducat agmen, reprime; sin claudat, sinas.	414	Lucus 20	14
CLAUDE			
Claude oculos, & erunt omnia nigra tibi:	437	Poem.Lat.	6
CLAUDERET			
Doctrinae fluuios clauderet aureae,	391	Musae 17	4
CLAUDI			
Claudi, pene tuas praeteriere fores.	385	Musae	4
CLAUDIS			
Claudis auaritia Satyram; statuisque sacrorum	399	Musae 34	1
CLAUIBUS			
Seruarentque sacrum clauibus ordinem;	391	Musae 17	6

	PAGE	TITLE		LINE
COENUM				
in terram hanc, incidit in coenum, quod innuebat eum hic mansurum:	455	Orationes		4
COEPERAT				
Coeperat, agricolis mentemque & aratra solutis:	418	Tr.Mortis		10
COEPISTI				
Coepisti, pergas simili res texere filo.	402	Musae 39		19
COETIBUS				
Angelicae turmae nostris se coetibus addunt:	402	Musae 39		10
COGITABIMUS				
nihil non sublime et excelsum cogitabimus, perrumpemus controuersias	459	Epistolae		5
COGITANTI				
memoriam recolenti, quam cogitanti noua, improbe molestiam creent.	457	Epistolae		13
COGITAS				
Quin nec demisso, quando ad magnates cogitas, stylo vtare,	470	Epistolae		21
COGITAT				
Prorsus nescia, cogitat recessum?	411	Lucus 5		7
COGITATIONES				
Imo pectore cogitationes?	411	Lucus 5		3
non solum verba omnia, sed etiam cogitationes nostras exhauriunt.	460	Epistolae		3
COGITATIONUM				
Cum enim vim cogitationum in vitam meam omnem conuertissem,	472	Epistolae		5
COGNITIO				
illic tuta cognitio est, atque extra teli iactum.	449	Orationes		3
verisimile est, eos illuc, quo cognitio ipsa pertingit, ascensuros.	468	Epistolae		1
COGNITIONEM				
nihil ad cognitionem acquirendam peregrinatione conducibilius esse	450	Orationes		6
COGNITIS				
Tuis, meis desiderijs probe cognitis, excussis perpensisque.	472	Epistolae		4
COGNITOREM				
11.Ad T. Coventry, Attorn. Cognitorem Gratulatio	465	Epistolae		T
COGNOUIT				
alienas tantum ex hoc itinere cognouit Respublicas sed quod plus est,	450	Orationes		32
COHIBENS				
caute incipe, cohibens adeo stylum ingeniumque;	470	Epistolae		11
COHIBERE				
Vt nequeat paulo se cohibere domi.	404	Passio 3		2
COIERE				
Illa cauerna, in qua tot coiere ferae.	414	Lucus 21		4
COLENS				
Triste colens cellae, noctuque & Daemone plenum,	420	Tr.Mortis		90
Triste colens sellae, noctuque & Daemone plenum,	420	Tr.Mortis	V	90
COLI				
Horti, colique distributim pensitat.	423	Mem.Matr.2		19
COLIMUS				
coalescamus, vtraque gens Hispanica, Britannica, colimus Iacobum.	440	Orationes		23
COLIT				
Horto pro tenui colit	424	Mem.Matr.4		3
COLLECTU				
ex quo facile collectu erat, quantum deperimus te;	451	Orationes		28
COLLEGA				
Collega Solis; Quadra Certitudinis;	436	Poem.Lat.		13
COLLEGIA				
Aedificarunt olim nobis Serenissimi Reges Collegia, eaque fundarunt	458	Epistolae		22
desererentur collegia, pulcherrimaeque Musarum domus tanquam viduae	462	Epistolae		3
COLLIGE				
Tu vero collige te, tibique insistito,	414	Lucus 20		5
COLLIGEBAM				
quippe, qui sic colligebam; si tam abiectus sim, vt laboribus meis	472	Epistolae		11
COLLIGERET				
Quid si cochleas colligeret cum Caligula, praesertim cum possit	446	Orationes		12
COLLISIS				
Britannici (e quorum ossibus collisis ignis elicitur) qui nunc	449	Orationes		18
COLLISIT				
At sibi collisit fictile Daemon opus.	408	Passio 20		2
COLLUM				
humile os, collum pensile, manus decussatae, ipsae mulieres	451	Orationes		15
COLO				
Ipse pios laudo; Numen & ipse colo.	386	Musae 4		6
COLORE				
Et mea iam lacrymet culpa colore suo.	404	Passio 1		4
Quid mihi si facies nigra est? hoc, Ceste, colore	437	Poem.Lat.		1
COLOREM				
Polluens castum chlamydis colorem	390	Musae 14		3
COLORIS				
Mens sub insigni specie coloris	390	Musae 14		7
Aethiopissa ambit Cestum Diuersi Coloris Virum.	437	Poem.Lat.		T
COLOS				
Plumbis obsignata, colosque & stamina vitae	419	Tr.Mortis		64
COLUMBA				
Columba Noae, quae in vetustis artibus	436	Poem.Lat.		19
Columba Noae, quae in vetustatis artibus	436	Poem.Lat.	V	19
COLUMNAS				
metas laudum, nullas Herculeas columnas, quas iam olim possidet,	440	Orationes		18
COLUNT				
Qualia parturiente colunt sub rupe sorores:	432	Poem.Lat.		8
eos scilicet, qui innuptam Palladem colunt, Musasque coelibes,	446	Orationes		26
COMEDANT				
Non comedant famam, sic nulla obliuia potent.	432	Poem.Lat.		16
COMEDENS				
Nunquid mel comedens, apem comedi	411	Lucus 5		8

	PAGE	TITLE	LINE
COMEDI			
Nunquid mel comedens, apem comedi	411	Lucus 5	8
COMES			
Interea procede Comes Germano-britanne	211	Cam.1613-b BR	7
COMETAE			
Vtque ouis in dumis, haeres in crine Cometae,	413	Lucus 16	3
quemadmodum in Cometae praesagio, non respicitur, quae materia sit,	454	Orationes	12
COMETAS			
In vicium mundo sterili, cui cedo cometas	426	Mem.Matr.7	20
COMITAS			
Proh! quantus imber, quanta labri comitas,	423	Mem.Matr.2	29
COMITER			
Tandem prehensa comiter lacernula	427	Mem.Matr.8	7
Comiter scribis atque eleganter; quae est vestra felicitas qui puro	470	Epistolae	2
COMMEANDO			
huc, illuc commeando, eo deueni animo, vt nunquam cessandum mihi	472	Epistolae	7
COMMEATU			
Quis enim tunc inuiseret Almam Matrem destitutam omni commeatu?	461	Epistolae	2
COMMEATUS			
si prae defectu aquae, commeatusque inopia, desererentur collegia,	462	Epistolae	2
COMMENDAMUS			
nosque ipsos Tibi, Teque Deo Opti: Max: intimis precibus commendamus.	468	Epistolae	10
COMMENDANDUM			
Iam si inter commendandum adhibeas ei calamistros vti iuuenculae,	470	Epistolae	18
COMMENDANTES			
quam de futuro supplicem, integerrimae tuae fidei commendantes.	465	Epistolae	8
COMMENDATIONE			
absque molesta aliorum ac frigida commendatione, si huc reciderit	472	Epistolae	15
COMMISTUS			
Viscera naturae, commistusque omnibus astris	402	Musae 39	28
COMMITTERE			
Quae suberant causae? quid nos committere tantum,	432	Poem.Lat.	18
COMMODE			
commode peruenimus ad laurum hanc, vbi sub vmbra eius paulisper	455	Orationes	13
COMMODI			
vt quid priuata habeat in se vita commodi aut voluptatis,	452	Orationes	37
sub specie publici commodi, Academiae incommodum videntur allaturi;	462	Epistolae	31
COMMODUM			
immunitates nostras aut commune literarum et literatorum commodum,	467	Epistolae	12
COMMORIENTE			
At te commoriente, Magna Mater,	428	Mem.Matr.10	5
COMMOTOS			
Commotos animos rectius ista decent.	387	Musae 5	6
COMMOTRIA			
huius tu es commotria atque ornatrix.	470	Epistolae	17
COMMOTUM			
Apposite quem commotum subfugerat olim,	390	Musae 12	15
COMMUNE			
Commune cordis palpitantis balsamum:	423	Mem.Matr.2	47
aut immunitates nostras aut commune literarum et literatorum	467	Epistolae	12
COMMUNEM			
Communem habere crede cum Cerdonibus:	413	Lucus 17	6
COMMUNES			
quin communes Reipublicae lachrymae alterum nobis Fluuium	462	Epistolae	5
COMMUNI			
amplexusque foelicitatis Tuae receptae, communi calore foueantur.	469	Epistolae	19
imo precabor enixe, me tum priuari tam communi hac luce, quam Tua,	472	Epistolae	23
COMMUNICANS			
tuosque fauores populo tuo communicans coelum ac terram minori quam	444	Orationes	7
COMMUNICAS			
vestra spolia actosque ex orbe triumphos communicas cum Alma Matre,	458	Epistolae	16
COMMUNIS			
sed etiam doceas tanquam communis defensor fidei et Academiae,	443	Orationes	23
COMMUTANS			
virgam cum sceptro commutans, vt quid priuata habeat in se vita	452	Orationes	36
COMPARARUNT			
assecutus es nomen, quam Repertores Noui Orbis compararunt.	463	Epistolae	13
COMPARAT			
Comparat aeterni regna beata Dei.	388	Musae 9	4
COMPARATIO			
Comparatio inter Munus Summi Cancellariatus et Librum.	435	Poem.Lat.	T
sed tamen comparatio & in honorem tuum cedet, nostrumque emolumentum.	467	Epistolae	25
COMPARATUM			
Sic a Natura comparatum est, Ignis et Virtus semper ascendunt,	466	Epistolae	10
COMPEDES			
Loquitur numellas, compedes & retia:	423	Mem.Matr.2	31
COMPENSAS			
Tu vicissim abunde compensas nos, gratissimoque Almam Matrem	456	Epistolae	8
COMPENSAT			
ditat patriam, suamque absentiam cum foenore compensat.	454	Orationes	33
COMPENSATIONES			
Nunc vero Ipse scribendo irrupisti in compensationes nostras,	459	Epistolae	2
COMPENSATIS			
virtutibus, tuo exemplo compensatis, ad vnum omnes incumbamus.	468	Epistolae	17
COMPENSATURIS			
omnia fauorum tuorum momenta apicesque perpensuris et compensaturis.	466	Epistolae	8
COMPENSEMUR			
vt iam compensemur abunde, neque amplius quaerendum sit Tibi,	462	Epistolae	15
COMPITA			
Compita feruescunt pedibus, clamoribus aether.	418	Tr.Mortis	11
Scinditur in partes vulgus ceu compita: telum	418	Tr.Mortis	16

	PAGE	TITLE	LINE
COMPLACUERE			
Mulceat, imbelles complacuere modi.	387	Musae 5	12
COMPLECTITUR			
a Con verbo deduci, quod tria complectitur, Possum, Scio, . . .	447	Orationes	7
COMPLEXUS			
vtque mature absoluas quae complexus es animo, ad eius gloriam,	464	Epistolae	4
COMPLICANT			
Phylacteria complicant latriam.	408	Passio 19	10
COMPOSITOS			
quia dederunt, non a se compositos, scriptos, editosque: . .	458	Epistolae	24
COMPRECOR			
O vtinam aut illorum oculi (quod comprecor vnum)	400	Musae 36	5
COMPROBAT			
Quos Ecclesia comprobat, verendum	391	Musae 15	12
COMPTU			
Non illa soles terere comptu lubricos, ...	422	Mem.Matr.2	10
CON			
& contracte King, a Con verbo deduci, quod tria complectitur,	447	Orationes	7
CONATIBUS			
Obrue feruentes, ruptis conatibus, hostes:	402	Musae 39	20
CONCEDAT			
Deus faueat Tibi & concedat vt terrestres tui honores cum coelestibus	465	Epistolae	18
CONCEDE			
concede vt nos etiam benignitate alarum tuarum et virtute fruamur.	466	Epistolae	22
Concede vt Honoribus nuperis, tanquam partubus Virtutum Tuarum,	469	Epistolae	8
CONCESSAE			
a Serenissimis Regibus concessae ab Augustissimo Iacobo auctae	468	Epistolae	22
CONCILIABULA			
plena erant fora, nundinae, conciliabula, angiportus, Maeandri.	451	Orationes	10
CONCIPIT			
Concipit albi.	390	Musae 14	8
CONCITATISSIME			
certe nos te absentem omnes acerrime concitatissimeque desiderauimus.	451	Orationes	34
CONCITAUIT			
Calumniandi concitauit vrtica, ...	392	Musae 20	7
CONCITUS			
Ardore Moses concitus entheo, ...	394	Musae 23	29
CONCLUSIO			
ipsum atque indoles (veluti Conclusio sequitur infirmiorem partem)	447	Orationes	18
CONCOLOR			
Ridenti lacrymas quibus vnis concolor vnda est.	426	Mem.Matr.7	6
CONCREPUIT			
quam subito dispereunt, simul ac concrepuit incendium militare:	448	Orationes	19
CONCURRAT			
Sepia concurrat, peccatis aptior humor, ...	404	Passio 1	3
CONCURRENTES			
In Natales et Pascha Concurrentes.	434	Poem.Lat.	T
CONDAT			
Quo se condat & implicet volutans	417	Lucus 30	6
CONDERET			
Seposuit Diuina sibi, cum conderet orbem, ...	402	Musae 39	15
CONDIANT			
si Reges ipsi quandoque suauitates suas populari aceto condiant.	453	Orationes	19
CONDIDIT			
Quae vis condidit, ipsa nouit aedes.	411	Lucus 5	17
CONDIEBANT			
qui antequam condiebant corpora Nobilium, solebant ventres eximere,	452	Orationes	27
CONDIMENTO			
& sollicitudines Principum sine condimento sint atque embammate?	446	Orationes	12
CONDIS			
Tu promis Orbem mane, condis vesperi, ...	407	Passio 16	3
CONDITIO			
quo eorum conditio sublimior, eo maior cura adhibenda sit. . .	446	Orationes	35
CONDITIS			
Conditis binas homini sequendas	390	Musae 14	14
CONDONABO			
Caetera condonabo tibi, scombrisque remittam:	399	Musae 34	3
CONDUCIBILIUS			
acquirendam peregrinatione conducibilius esse nouistis omnes,	450	Orationes	7
CONDUCTIS			
Aggreditur Matrem (conductis carmine Parcis)	431	Mem.Matr.19	3
CONFABULANTUR			
hinc a populo, illinc a Principe, in Te conueniunt, et confabulantur.	456	Epistolae	25
CONFERTE			
Conferte lacrymas: Illa, quae vos miscuit	422	Mem.Matr.2	3
CONFICIUNT			
machinas conficiunt ad defensionem Reipublicae mirabiles: . .	454	Orationes	5
CONFIDIMUS			
nobis remotior, confidimus tamen vt arbores, quanto altius crescunt,	464	Epistolae	17
CONFIRMAUIT			
et tuum tibi largita est honorem, et priuilegia nostra confirmauit;	468	Epistolae	24
CONFLES			
Quo magis inuidiam nobis & crimina confles, ...	398	Musae 33	1
CONFLUERE			
Confluere interea passim ad Floralia pubes	418	Tr.Mortis	9
CONFLUEREMUS			
confluleremus omnes ad Aulam, atque ab eo consilium peteremus a quo	443	Orationes	27
CONFLUXERUNT			
in quem fauor Regius, nostra vota, virtutes tantae confluxerunt?	456	Epistolae	19
CONFOSSO			
figuras iam nunc pulueri inscriptas corpore confosso obliterans.	448	Orationes	32

	PAGE	TITLE	LINE
CONFREGIT			
Omnia, praeter corda, scelus confregit & error,	409	Passio 20	7
CONFUGIMUS			
ita ad Te confugimus primariam partem ecclesiastici corporis,	467	Epistolae	9
CONFUSIO			
(Nam post Babelem linguae adest confusio)	422	Mem.Matr.2	13
CONGREDIENS			
Congrediens genuit Monachum, qui limen opacae	420	Tr.Mortis	89
CONGRESSUS			
telam explices, perit negotium quasi ex nubibus Ixionis congressus.	470	Epistolae	31
CONIECTANDO			
quantum quidem ego homuncio ac nanus coniectando assequor.	453	Orationes	21
CONIJCITUR			
an sudum, facile conijcitur ex coelo, ex garritu auium,	445	Orationes	6
CONIUGALEM			
accepimus saluum & annulum, annulum Coniugalem, nunc denuo nostrum,	444	Orationes	19
CONIUGALI			
De annulo coniugali.	396	Musae 26	T
CONIUGE			
Scilicet, vt quos ante suas cum coniuge tedas	396	Musae 26	9
CONIUGIJ			
Sed nec coniugij signum, Melvine, probabis?	396	Musae 26	1
CONIUGIUM			
Coniugium Caeli Terraeque haec machina praestat;	417	Lucus 31	1
CONIUNCTAS			
festinasti ad gratitudines tuas cum emolumento nostro coniunctas,	462	Epistolae	15
vt res nostras omnes cum Honore Tuo coniunctas esse velimus.	465	Epistolae	3
CONIUNCTI			
in qua dextra et fide coniuncti, in caeteris haud diuellamur.	468	Epistolae	25
CONIUNGIS			
cum Alma Matre, vtrumque splendorem cum beneficio nostro coniungis.	458	Epistolae	18
CONIUNXIMUS			
Quare coniunximus nunc officia nostra, tuosque fauores temporibus	457	Epistolae	14
CONNECTAT			
coelum ac terram minori quam cernimus interuallo connectat.	444	Orationes	8
Natura suas dotes, vt indigentia singularum regionum omnes connectat:	450	Orationes	20
CONNECTENS			
qui vtrasque Indias Hispania sua quasi nodo connectens,	440	Orationes	17
CONNIXUS			
Connixus, digitis impiger vrgeo:	424	Mem.Matr.4	10
CONNUBIALE			
Legitimi signum connubiale tori.	396	Musae 26	12
CONSCENDENS			
vsque ad Pyrenaeas nubes conscendens, reuersus per mare,	454	Orationes	31
CONSCIA			
Sic vbi iam mulier decerpti conscia pomi	390	Musae 12	13
Plumbea glans, liuensque suae quasi conscia noxae,	419	Tr.Mortis	62
Iam foelix Philomela, & menti conscia Dido!	432	Poem.Lat.	22
CONSCIUS			
tantae eruditionis nobis conscius est, palustri opere & vliginoso	461	Epistolae	7
CONSCRIBERE			
Nos quoque possemus longas conscribere turmas,	398	Musae 33	7
CONSECUTAE			
Fructum laborum consecutae maximum	424	Mem.Matr.2	64
CONSECUTUS			
Et ius pectoris inde consecutus	421	Lucus 34	5
at Noster difficultatem superans, fructum consecutus est:	450	Orationes	14
omnia Danorum expiscatus consilia, victoriam celebrem consecutus est.	453	Orationes	7
etiam senectus, quam aetatem in hac palaestra consecutus mihi videor.	471	Epistolae	8
CONSEQUARE			
aeternum illud praemium consequare, cui neque addi quicquam potest,	457	Epistolae	4
CONSEQUI			
Nec tarda possunt pharmaca consequi,	425	Mem.Matr.6	6
CONSEQUIMUR			
ligantes abruptum vitae filum, vnde consequimur, vel inuitis Fatis,	446	Orationes	23
CONSERUANDAE			
praeripuit Tibi gloriam extruendae Academiae, reliquit conseruandae.	465	Epistolae	17
CONSERUANDO			
tam de conseruando Fluuio nostro, quam de muniendis contra grassantes	457	Epistolae	17
Tu inuaseris eorum gloriam conseruando nobis quae illi dederunt,	458	Epistolae	26
CONSERUANS			
fecisti Fluuium nostrum conseruans altero eloquentiae Fluuio,	462	Epistolae	18
CONSERUANTES			
conseruantes sibi Illos Fontes, a quibus ipsi olim hauserunt?	461	Epistolae	31
CONSERUENTUR			
concessae ab Augustissimo Iacobo auctae tua opera conseruentur;	468	Epistolae	23
CONSERUES			
omnipotens, conserues nobis haec gaudia, imbuas cor Regium vigore,	444	Orationes	4
CONSILIA			
sed varia solent esse eorum consilia, finesque multiplices	446	Orationes	5
pariter & nos consilia regia, tanquam gurgitem imperuestigabilem,	449	Orationes	22
patent enim consilia nostra, absconduntur Diuina & Regia,	449	Orationes	26
salus regnorum pendet a vicinis, quorum consilia, apparatus,	450	Orationes	26
omnia Danorum expiscatus consilia, victoriam celebrem consecutus est.	453	Orationes	6
CONSILIJ			
orantes vt quicquid consilij auaritia ceperit aduersus aut	467	Epistolae	10
CONSILIJS			
ac si Fatis a fuso essent atque consilijs, sine quibus ne vnum quidem	449	Orationes	30
CONSILIO			
Deus ipse cum crearet hominem, mundi regem, consilio vsus est.	446	Orationes	37
annon eius consilio res gesta est?	451	Orationes	24

CONSILIO (cont'd)	PAGE	TITLE	LINE
quam adductus maturo consilio, primas dedissem literas,	471	Epistolae	27
CONSILIUM			
omnes ad Aulam, atque ab eo consilium peteremus a quo et fortunas?	443	Orationes	27
CONSISTANT			
quod primum intendunt, saltem in secundis aut tertijs consistant.	446	Orationes	7
CONSOLATIO			
Consolatio.	415	Lucus 23	T
CONSONUM			
quamuis rationi consonum videtur, vt qui hic in Musarum monte	449	Orationes	32
CONSPECTU			
inter nouas honorum nubes e conspectu nostro fugientem reuocamus.	456	Epistolae	7
CONSPERSI			
Nos nunc conspersi atramento regio, nihil non sublime et excelsum	459	Epistolae	4
CONSPICIARE			
Hac facie dominae conspiciare tuae:	211	Cam.1613-b BR	10
CONSPICIENDUM			
charta conspiciendum Te praebes, quo familiarius inter nos verseris.	458	Epistolae	20
CONSPICIT			
Qui tam sublimi conspicit orbe viam:	387	Musae 7	6
CONSPIRANTIBUS			
tandem meritis tuis votisque nostris conspirantibus obtinuisti.	464	Epistolae	13
CONSTANS			
Exuta strato carnis, ossibus constans,	429	Mem.Matr.12	2
CONSTANTIAE			
Quare plurimum debemus constantiae fauoris tui, qui restinxisti sitim	462	Epistolae	7
CONSTANTINUM			
incredibilem luxum a Tiberio Caesare ad Constantinum magnum aperirem,	452	Orationes	22
CONSTANTINUS			
Iam Constantinus multo se milite miscet;	398	Musae 33	15
CONSTAT			
Ambitio Cathari quinque constat Actibus.	398	Musae 32	1
Constat inaccessas dissiluisse petras.	409	Passio 20	6
Attamen VRBANI delecto nomine, constat	416	Lucus 27	5
Sic Hominis moles animaque & corpore constat,	417	Lucus 31	3
Ratione certa vita constat & domus,	423	Mem.Matr.2	22
Constat, Aprile vno te potuisse mori:	438	Poem.Lat.	4
CONSTET			
Constet, & ex illa pendeat orbis ope;	385	Musae 1	2
Pudorque constet vel solutis crinibus;	422	Mem.Matr.2	6
CONSTRINGERET			
tanquam catenam, qua dissitas nationes ac superbas constringeret.	450	Orationes	25
CONSTRINGOR			
illic constringor debito; hic etiam teneor, sed laxioribus vinculis,	472	Epistolae	33
CONSUIAM			
& vestrae fidei consulam, quemadmodum artifices non omnes	445	Orationes	29
CONSULAS			
non passim expositam, boni consulas, curesque vt tuus in nos amor,	466	Epistolae	2
CONSULENTIBUS			
posterioris largam messem Vobis haec tenuia boni consulentibus,	441	Orationes	22
CONSULERES			
Nec qua consuleres, populumve ad bella vocares,	211	Cam.1613-b BR	9
CONSULERET			
vt ingenti labore suo & periculo consuleret & praesenti Reipublicae	447	Orationes	24
CONSULITE			
consulite historias; illic tuta cognitio est, atque extra teli	449	Orationes	2
CONSULTOS			
Apud Iuris-consultos, partus sequitur ventrem:	447	Orationes	12
CONSULUISSE			
optime consuluisse Deum orbi terrarum lapides & metalla ei inserendo,	452	Orationes	24
CONSULUIT			
Quamobrem optime consuluit gentibus natura, cum paupertatem daret	450	Orationes	23
CONTAMINATIS			
Contaminatis alueosque caelestes	404	Passio 5	4
CONTEMNERE			
Nolite tamen contemnere has gloriolas nostras quas e chartis	441	Orationes	17
CONTEMNITIS			
Militat & nobis, quem vos contemnitis, Ordo;	399	Musae 33	27
CONTEMPLANDUM			
cum anima vinculum impedimento esse ad contemplandum causaris,	448	Orationes	27
CONTEMPLARE			
Contemplare, miser, quantum terroris haberet	417	Lucus 31	5
CONTENTIO			
inter quae etiam certamen oritur et pia contentio, vtrum gratia	456	Epistolae	20
CONTENTOS			
Minima contentos nocte Britannos.	451	Orationes	20
CONTERE			
praesertim sericatam hanc stultitiam contere, Academiaeque iura,	461	Epistolae	23
CONTIGISSE			
hinc contigisse arbitror apud Romanos, quod nonnullae familiae semper	447	Orationes	19
CONTIGIT			
Hae tibi sunt alae laudum. Cui contigit vnquam	435	Poem.Lat.	5
Hae tibi sunt alae laudis. Cui contigit vnquam	435	Poem.Lat. V	5
CONTIGUAS			
Contiguas stirpes afflat, eaeque rosas.	425	Mem.Matr.5	6
CONTINEAT			
posthac contineat se patria, cuius arctis amplexibus nunquam se	455	Orationes	1
CONTINENTIBUS			
praecipue vbi velut ex continentibus tectis ad nos traiecturum est	449	Orationes	13
CONTINERI			
Erumpit inde, & contineri nescius	398	Musae 32	7

	PAGE	TITLE	LINE
CONTINET			
Materiam vexat: nec iam se continet antro	420	Tr.Mortis	70
CONTRA			
aliae contra semper pertinaces ac tribunitiae, vti Appij.	447	Orationes	21
vt nihil habeat Inuidia ipsa, quod contra hiscat aut mussitet.	453	Orationes	24
cum leunculum & dominum suum contra naturam adoriantur:	454	Orationes	18
quam de muniendis contra grassantes flammas aedificijs Honori Tuo	457	Epistolae	18
Hibernico lignum nascitur permanens, contra omnia venena validum:	459	Epistolae	16
4. Ad Iacobum Regem Gratiae de Fluuio contra Redemptores	460	Epistolae	T
CONTRACTE			
Koning, & contracte King, a Con verbo deduci, quod tria complectitur,	447	Orationes	6
CONTRAHAS			
Quare, peritus nauta, vela contrahas,	414	Lucus 20	11
CONTRARIA			
naturae legibus et hominum summe contraria est) monopolijs quibusdam	467	Epistolae	6
CONTRIBUERE			
Moenia contribuere Thebis.	394	Musae 23	16
Quae mihi lugubres contribuere genas!	437	Poem.Lat.	12
CONTRITA			
Quae contrita tamen caetera damna leuant.	409	Passio 20	8
CONTROUERSIAS			
perrumpemus controuersias omnes, superabimus quoscunque.	459	Epistolae	6
CONTULIT			
Hanc mihi duritiem contulit improbitas.	410	Lucus 1	2
CONTUMACI			
Te contumaci & liuido?	388	Musae 8	10
CONTUMELIOSI			
Splenis perlita contumeliosi.	400	Musae 37	13
CONTUNDAMUS			
vt ex affrictu Libri vestri hominem illico contundamus.	459	Epistolae	8
CONTUNDIS			
Cum tu contundis Catharos, vultuque librisque,	385	Musae 1	5
CONTUSAS			
hominum fame, frigore, illuuie, enectas, contusas, debilitatas.	449	Orationes	9
CONUENIAT			
non tam quod tibi conueniat scribenti, quam quod Academiae tuo calamo	470	Epistolae	13
CONUENIRE			
Non conuenire precibus ista Diuinis.	392	Musae 20	14
CONUENIT			
Sententiae cum voce mire conuenit,	423	Mem.Matr.2	37
Optime enim hoc conuenit Partui tuo, qui nouas scientiarum regiones	463	Epistolae	10
quidem multum, neque nostrae matronae conuenit, cui tu es ab ornatu.	471	Epistolae	3
CONUENIUNT			
Conueniunt; & Homo viua fit Ara Dei.	417	Lucus 29	4
hinc a populo, illinc a Principe, in Te conueniunt, et confabulantur.	456	Epistolae	25
CONUERTISSEM			
Cum enim vim cogitationum in vitam meam omnem conuertissem,	472	Epistolae	6
CONUICIA			
In Sputum & Conuicia.	404	Passio 5	T
CONUINCUNT			
Conuincunt vnam multa sepulcra Crucem.	408	Passio 17	6
CONUITIA			
Dicta ferox: haerent lateri conuitia fixo.	418	Tr.Mortis	15
Dicta ferox, haerent lateri conuitia fixa:	271	Tr.Mortis VS	15
COPULAUIMUS			
temporibus et diligentia diuisos in gratijs nostris copulauimus.	457	Epistolae	16
COPULETUR			
Si gratia tanta copuletur	421	Lucus 34	7
COQUENS			
Maturusque suos coquens amores	408	Passio 19	12
COQUIT			
Immemor antiqui mellis, eundo coquit.	398	Musae 33	20
COR			
Posteritas flectet corque genuque mihi.	405	Passio 7	6
Dum cor omne suum sibi requirat	408	Passio 19	7
Haud mihi cor saxo durius esse sinas.	410	Lucus 1	6
nobis haec gaudia, imbuas cor Regium vigore, animum clementia,	444	Orationes	5
cor sacrum, sentiatque Rex ipse nos haec intime precari.	444	Orationes	8
vti sanguis solet in re dubia ad cor festinare, ita ad Te confugimus	467	Epistolae	9
non cor) Tui in me dominij ius imminuere posse, nedum rescindere.	473	Epistolae	6
CORALLIA			
Durescunt proprijs euulsa corallia fundis,	410	Lucus 1	3
CORAM			
habita coram Dominis Legatis cum Magistro. in Artib. titulis	440	Orationes	T
CORDA			
Corda furor, spissaque afflat caligine sensus?	401	Musae 39	5
Ipsaque sunt ferulae mollia corda suae.	406	Passio 9	6
Omnia, praeter corda, scelus confregit & error,	409	Passio 20	7
CORDE			
Qua possint humili fundere corde preces.	390	Musae 12	12
Corde tuo forsan, caetera munda, SOROR.	413	Lucus 15	6
CORDI			
Spero meo cordi posse patere viam.	404	Passio 4	2
Versatos neget, atque humiles, queis talis cordi	420	Tr.Mortis	93
CORDIBUS			
Sane, gestabaris antea in cordibus nostris;	458	Epistolae	18
CORDIS			
Quae cordis latebras sinusque caecos	411	Lucus 5	12
Cordis apex, animae pugnaque paxque meae,	421	Lucus 35	2
Commune cordis palpitantis balsamum:	423	Mem.Matr.2	47

CORNELIAE	PAGE	TITLE	LINE
Corneliae sanctae, graues Semproniae,	422	Mem.Matr.2	1
CORNUUM			
Iam nunc minaci murmure cornuum	448	Orationes	1
CORONA			
Dignamque coelesti corona	434	Poem.Lat.	35
Corona Musica, qui optimum Principem spe nuptiarum mari nuper	444	Orationes	17
CORONAE			
si spinula vlla Coronae Regiae emollita sit vel retusa;	443	Orationes	11
vt vestrae coronae ciuili & literariae tertiam Coelestem sero	459	Epistolae	20
CORONAM			
In Coronam spineam.	405	Passio 6	T
capiti & faciei coronam, significantes oportere Reges ijs partibus	447	Orationes	3
CORPORA			
Non remanent nobis corpora, non animae.	390	Musae 13	4
Ridens Bombardas miseras, quae corpora perdunt	420	Tr.Mortis	97
Ecce lanienas omnimodas, truncata corpora, mutilatam imaginem Dei,	449	Orationes	4
ac si corpora sua non abirent olim in elementa, sed in bellaria aut	452	Orationes	13
qui antequam condiebant corpora Nobilium, solebant ventres eximere,	452	Orationes	27
CORPORE			
Sic Hominis moles animaque & corpore constat,	417	Lucus 31	3
Corporeque atque animo. Totus mihi seruiat Orbis.	421	Tr.Mortis	101
figuras iam nunc pulueri inscriptas corpore confosso obliterans.	448	Orationes	32
CORPOREAE			
Corporeae fluidaeque molis?	425	Mem.Matr.6	4
CORPORI			
Produxit Vmbram corpus, Vmbra corpori	413	Lucus 14	1
CORPORIBUS			
qui olim glasto se inficientes, in vxorum corporibus, Solem,	446	Orationes	30
CORPORIS			
Quas spargit animae corporis propius lutum?	393	Musae 22	4
Caeno profani corporis exuens	394	Musae 23	26
vbique deferentibus, vt nullus sit angulus corporis, nulla venula,	445	Orationes	3
cum corporis cum anima vinculum impedimento esse ad contemplandum	448	Orationes	26
ita ad Te confugimus primariam partem ecclesiastici corporis,	467	Epistolae	10
CORPUS			
Si tibi non illud placeat mirabile corpus,	404	Passio 2	3
Produxit Vmbram corpus, Vmbra corpori	413	Lucus 14	1
Mens superat; corpus solum Elementa tenent.	424	Mem.Matr.3	4
Aut aperi, & cernes corpus quas proijcit vmbras;	437	Poem.Lat.	7
Aut aperi, & cernis corpus quas proijcit vmbras;	437	Poem.Lat. V	7
CORREPTUS			
ac si iuuenili potius impetu correptus, quam adductus maturo	471	Epistolae	26
CORRIPIS			
Quos dente nigro corripis?	388	Musae 8	2
CORRIPIT			
Amstellodamum corripit se. Plaudite.	398	Musae 32	10
CORRUERET			
tanquam ligna obliqua, aliter magna haec mundi domus corrueret:	450	Orationes	29
CORRUMPENTIA			
splendida plerumque vitrea sint, claritatem fragilitate corrumpentia;	448	Orationes	6
CORRUMPI			
ventilatione, desidia corrumpi, neminemque esse sui negligentiorem,	452	Orationes	34
CORRUMPIT			
Et quae corrumpit moenia, murus aqua est.	411	Lucus 6	6
CORRUMPUNTUR			
aedificia, corrumpuntur statuae, haec imago atque character,	459	Epistolae	13
COSMICO			
Sic ex profano Cosmico & Catharo potest	396	Musae 27	3
COSTAS			
Omniaque haec vt transadigant sine crimine costas,	418	Tr.Mortis	29
COUNSAILE			
of Winchester, one of the Kings most honorable privy-Counsaile.	473	Epistolae	25
COVENTRY			
11.Ad T. Coventry, Attorn. Cognitorem Gratulatio	465	Epistolae	T
CRANFIELD			
16. Ad Cranfield, Thesaurar. Gratulatio	469	Epistolae	T
CRAPULAE			
quid ructus crapulae solium possidentis?	452	Orationes	20
CRASIS			
Non exigatur crasis ad alterum.	426	Mem.Matr.6	22
CRASSISSIMUM			
crassissimum elementum, Tu subtilitates Artium infinitas.	463	Epistolae	13
CRASSIUS			
Nil sit crassius, impolitiusue)	401	Musae 37	46
CREANS			
Tu, qui cuncta creans docuisti marmora flere,	410	Lucus 1	5
CREARET			
Deus ipse cum crearet hominem, mundi regem, consilio vsus est.	446	Orationes	36
CREARINT			
Ah! metuo ne me ad luctus mea fata crearint	437	Poem.Lat. V	11
CREATUM			
et quo magis Tuum agnoscas, in ipso partu, Librorum regem creatum.	459	Epistolae	12
CREATURIS			
E creaturis sine mentis vsu	390	Musae 14	13
CREBERRIMA			
creberrima Antiquitatis lectione tersis atque expolitis,	473	Epistolae	19
CREBRIS			
Christus adest: crebris aedes percurrite scopis,	413	Lucus 15	1
CREDAT			
Sic o te (iuuenem, senemue) credat	385	Musae	10

	PAGE	TITLE	LINE
CREDE			
Communem habere crede cum Cerdonibus:	413	Lucus 17	6
CREDEBAT			
Sanctius in Regno Magni credebat Amoris	439	Poem.Lat.	14
CREDERET			
quis crederet mortalibus	396	Musae 28	3
CREDIMUS			
Non laudare Deum, credimus esse nefas.	389	Musae 12	8
CREDITIS			
Et populi spurcas creditis esse vias:	387	Musae 5	8
CREDITUR			
Creditur, ante satas prono cum numine fruges)	419	Tr.Mortis	61
Creditur, ante satas prono cum vertice fruges)	419	Tr.Mortis V	61
CREENT			
memoriam recolenti, quam cogitanti noua, improbe molestiam creent.	457	Epistolae	14
CREIGHTON			
17. Ad R. Creighton	470	Epistolae	T
Erudite Creighton. Comiter scribis atque eleganter;	470	Epistolae	1
CREPANT			
Diffugiunt, fragilisque crepant coenacula mundi.	420	Tr.Mortis	78
CREPAX			
Si totus infler, si tumeam crepax,	426	Mem.Matr.6	17
CREPES			
Falsumque potius quam crepes versu?	392	Musae 20	9
CREPITACULA			
bullae & crepitacula puerorum sunt, aut eorum certe, qui cymbala sunt	445	Orationes	23
CREPITANTE			
Et Musa crepitante subruissem:	400	Musae 37	20
CRESCENS			
Sit quasi fasciculus crescens, & nidus odorum.	427	Mem.Matr.7	27
Granum Sinapis, acre Alijs, crescens sibi:	437	Poem.Lat.	26
CRESCENT			
Crescent illae, crescetis amores. Cui sententiae si fidem adhibeas,	473	Epistolae	9
CRESCENTES			
Prisci, crescentesque vna cum prole cauernas:	418	Tr.Mortis	6
CRESCENTIA			
Atque inter reliquos horti crescentia foetus	427	Mem.Matr.7	33
CRESCET			
Perdere sexcentas? crescet tamen hydra nocendi	419	Tr.Mortis V	35
CRESCETIS			
Crescent illae, crescetis amores. Cui sententiae si fidem adhibeas,	473	Epistolae	9
CRESCIT			
Perdere sexcentas? crescit tamen hydra nocendi	419	Tr.Mortis	35
CRESCUNT			
quanto altius crescunt, tanto etiam altius agunt radices:	464	Epistolae	18
CRIMEN			
Obstreperae stulto sonitu, crimenque fatentes.	420	Tr.Mortis	99
CRIMINA			
Ille tamen, quamuis altus, tua crimina ridens	387	Musae 7	7
Quo magis inuidiam nobis & crimina confles,	398	Musae 33	1
Crimina cum turgent, & mea poena prope est,	406	Passio 9	2
CRIMINE			
Sic tuus effundi gestit pro crimine sanguis,	404	Passio 3	1
Omniaque haec vt transadigant sine crimine costas,	418	Tr.Mortis	29
CRINE			
Vtque ouis in dumis, haeres in crine Cometae,	413	Lucus 16	3
CRINIBUS			
Pudorque constet vel solutis crinibus;	422	Mem.Matr.2	6
CRITT			
multa Critt meo quadrabunt, quae almae matri inconcinna erunt atque	470	Epistolae	14
CRUCE			
Non plus maligni daemones Christi cruce	389	Musae 10	2
Natare sine clarissima potest cruce?	389	Musae 10	9
Christus in cruce.	406	Passio 13	T
Eriperet nobis, in Cruce fixus eras;	407	Passio 14	2
In cruce suspendens, vnde reclinet, habet.	407	Passio 15	4
Te fixo vel Terra mouet: nam, cum Cruce, totam	408	Passio 18	1
CRUCEM			
Cur tanta sufflas probra in innocuam Crucem?	389	Musae 10	1
Vitasse Christi spiritum efflantis crucem.	389	Musae 10	5
Inuisamque tuis erigit hasta Crucem.	398	Musae 33	16
In Christum crucem ascensurum.	406	Passio 12	T
Conuincunt vnam multa sepulcra Crucem.	408	Passio 17	6
Agnoscitque tuam Machina tota Crucem.	409	Passio 21	2
Alapas nec Arietes? Quid ergo? Agnum & Crucem.	421	Lucus 33	6
CRUCI			
Aduoluor madidae laetus hiansque Cruci:	406	Passio 13	2
Vna meam membris horula, teque cruci.	434	Poem.Lat.	2
CRUCIFIXUM			
Scilicet in tumulis Crucifixum quaerite, viuit:	408	Passio 17	5
CRUCIS			
De Signaculo Crucis.	389	Musae 10	T
CRUDELEM			
Post vbi crudelem sentit diuisa securem,	428	Mem.Matr.11	3
CRUDELITATE			
victoriaeque gloriam absque crudelitate effusi sanguinis delibas.	458	Epistolae	15
CRUDO			
Inde exiguntur pensa crudo vespere.	423	Mem.Matr.2	21
CRUDUM			
Crudum olim pomum, tristis Adame, tibi.	412	Lucus 9	4

	PAGE	TITLE	LINE
CRUENTA			
Quam cruenta gloria est, quae super ceruicibus hominum erigitur?	449	Orationes	9
CRUMENAE			
et precium, quae abyssus crumenae tantos sumptus aequabit?	468	Epistolae	3
CRUORIS			
bis intersectas, infantulos plus lactis quam cruoris emittentes;	449	Orationes	7
CRURIBUS			
honore grauidus, grauidus scientia, cruribus thymo plenis:	454	Orationes	27
CRUX			
Sed non moramur: namque vestra crux erit,	389	Musae 10	10
Quod Crux nequibat fixa, Clavique additi,	438	Poem.Lat.	1
CUBILE			
Quodque suum nouit stroma, cubile suum.	407	Passio 15	2
CUDIT			
Saepe ex se nihil otiosa cudit.	415	Lucus 24	6
CUI			
At cui videri prodigium potest	395	Musae 23	49
Cui non absimilis sensus inesse solet.	396	Musae 26	8
Haud nostro similis, cui necesse,	415	Lucus 24	2
In vicium mundo sterili, cui cedo cometas	426	Mem.Matr.7	20
Quin nec potes; cui praebuit Tigris partum.	429	Mem.Matr.12	10
Cui caecas tribuit vires annosa vetustas.	433	Poem.Lat.	42
Cui dulcis arrident Camoenae	433	Poem.Lat.	3
Cui magnum imperium, gloria maior erat:	435	Poem.Lat.	2
Cui tenuis fama est, ingeniumque minus.	435	Poem.Lat.	4
Hae tibi sunt alae laudum. Cui contigit vnquam	435	Poem.Lat.	5
Hae tibi sunt alae laudis. Cui contigit vnquam	435	Poem.Lat. V	5
suam gentem amorem, cui pacem quaesiuit suo capite, periculis suis.	449	Orationes	37
de ingenti amore in Principem, cui nulla dilectio par esse potest;	451	Orationes	22
in Principibus virtus, & cui cum sceptro lites saepius intercedunt?	452	Orationes	2
cui soli ideo insunt oculi variegati, cum caetera animantia	453	Orationes	16
praemium consequare, cui neque addi quicquam potest, neque detrahi.	457	Epistolae	4
cui natura spiritum dederit feracem gloriae, et coeleste ingenium	468	Epistolae	5
quidem multum, neque nostrae matronae conuenit, cui tu es ab ornatu.	471	Epistolae	3
Cui sententiae si fidem adhibeas, assensumque Tuum veritati omni	473	Epistolae	10
CUIPIAM			
Namque haec, iure, cuipiam	395	Musae 25	20
CUIQUE			
Suum cuique tempus & locus datur.	423	Mem.Matr.2	20
CUIUIS			
Illud autem, quod cuiuis clarissime patet, etiam lusco,	449	Orationes	34
CUIUS			
Nempe Caput Romae es, cuius mysteria velles	416	Lucus 27	3
Cuius ab oppositis fluxit origo locis.	417	Lucus 31	4
Rure; breuisque hortus, cuius cum vellere florum	426	Mem.Matr.7	23
Cuius noui tituli accessionem summe gratulantur Excellentijs Vestris	440	Orationes	6
cuius ingens gloria aeque rotunda est atque ipse orbis:	440	Orationes	15
velut Romani lacum, cuius altitudo ignota erat, dedicabant victoriae;	449	Orationes	21
mirabilius, cuius tamen fructum omnem nondum habetis enucleatum.	450	Orationes	3
cuius manifestationem in gentem suam priuatae personae & habitui	453	Orationes	7
contineat se patria, cuius arctis amplexibus nunquam se expediet.	455	Orationes	2
Daphnen suam, cuius amor deinceps in triumphos & laurus mutabitur.	455	Orationes	11
Cuius fauoris magnitudo ita inuoluit nos, vt etiam rependendi vias	458	Epistolae	28
cuius nisi incredibilis fuisset vis, nunquam in tantis negotijs,	463	Epistolae	17
cuius Libri si alij alijs (tanquam montes olim) imponerentur,	467	Epistolae	30
CUIUSNAM			
Cuiusnam maior sit, dubitatur, amor.	437	Poem.Lat. V	2
CULMEN			
Foelicitatis culmen extra se locat,	414	Lucus 20	3
Culmen, vbi pro te nemo dolere potest.	415	Lucus 23	16
Imperij hic culmen figo: mortalibus actum est	421	Tr.Mortis	100
CULPA			
Apostolorum culpa non leuis fuit	389	Musae 10	4
Et mea iam lacrymet culpa colore suo.	404	Passio 1	4
Culpa redux iugem te neget esse Deum.	406	Passio 13	6
CULPES			
Ne membra culpes, causa animo latet	426	Mem.Matr.6	18
CULTA			
Ceu, quas culta timet seges, pruinas	385	Musae	7
CULTAE			
Quinimo Artes hic sunt quiete & silentio cultae, tranquillitas,	441	Orationes	14
CULTISSIMA			
barbara omnia, Tu non nisi cultissima, elegantiasque ipsas exhibes.	463	Epistolae	15
CULTRICEM			
Cultricem reuocans anxietate manum:	425	Mem.Matr.5	4
CULTU			
Ora meae memori menti: ne dispare cultu	427	Mem.Matr.7	31
CULTUM			
Funereque hoc cultum vindicat aegra suum.	431	Mem.Matr.19	4
CULTUS			
Sola mihi plenos, ait, exhibet Anglia cultus.	402	Musae 39	13
Frustra, Verpe, tumes, propola cultus,	408	Passio 19	1
CUM			
Cum mea futilibus numeris se verba viderent	385	Musae	3
Cum millena tuam pulsare negotia mentem	385	Musae 1	1
Cum tu contundis Catharos, vultuque librisque,	385	Musae 1	5
Ecce tamen quam suauis ero! cum, fine duelli,	386	Musae 2	7
Cum sacra perturbet vester furor omnia, scriptum	386	Musae 3	7
Pollubra vel cum olim damnaris Regia in ara,	386	Musae 3	9
Cum prope sit nobis Musa, Medusa procul?	387	Musae 6	2
(Superbius cum te nihil)	388	Musae 8	16

CUM (cont'd)

	PAGE	TITLE		LINE
Cum tener ad sacros infans sistatur aquales,	388	Musae 9		1
Cum nequeat claras ipse litare preces?	388	Musae 9		14
O vere dictum, & belle! cum torqueat omnes	389	Musae 11		3
Forte quidem, cum per vestras Ecclesia turbas	389	Musae 12		3
Sed nos, cum nequeat paruorum lingua, parentem	389	Musae 12		7
Vt, cum mors rabidis vnguibus imminens	391	Musae 17		3
Cum piscatores Textor legit esse vocatos,	392	Musae 19		1
Cum nil fraterno rarius esse queat.	393	Musae 21		4
Cum citharis lituisque miscet.	394	Musae 23		40
Cum primum ratibus suis	395	Musae 25		1
Scilicet, vt quos ante suas cum coniuge tedas	396	Musae 26		9
(cum dignius nil posset aut melius dare)	397	Musae 28		10
Cum templis effare, madent sudaria, mappae,	397	Musae 29		1
Extruxissem, vbi, cum moneret vsus,	401	Musae 37		29
(Cum plerumque tua sodalitate	401	Musae 37		45
Seposuit Diuina sibi, cum conderet orbem,	402	Musae 39		15
Cum lacrymas oculosque duos tot vulnera vincant,	404	Passio 1		1
Quam nihil illudis! cum quo magis angar acuto	405	Passio 7		3
Crimina cum turgent, & mea poena prope est,	406	Passio 9		2
Te fixo vel Terra mouet: nam, cum Cruce, totam	408	Passio 18		1
Haud aliter cum Christus obit, prae funere tanto	409	Passio 20		5
In Mundi sympathiam cum Christo.	409	Passio 21		T
Ipsa cum domina domum vorando?	411	Lucus 5		9
Cum natet in tantis caetera terra malis?	411	Lucus 6		2
Cum qui plus terrae, plus habuere maris.	411	Lucus 6		4
Cum dormis, surgit pelagus: cum, Christe, resurgis,	412	Lucus 12		1
Communem habere crede cum Cerdonibus:	413	Lucus 17		6
Cum Latium ferrent secula prisca iugum?	416	Lucus 25		2
Et cum sublata laude recedit AMOR.	416	Lucus 25		12
Cum Romam nequeas, quod aues, euertere, nomen	416	Lucus 26		1
Prisci, crescentesque vna cum prole cauernas:	418	Tr.Mortis		6
Fustibalos fundasque, quibus, cum Numine, fretus	419	Tr.Mortis		43
fustibulos fundusque quibus cum numine fretus	271	Tr.Mortis	VS	43
Adde etiam currus, & cum temone Britanno	419	Tr.Mortis		45
Creditur, ante satas prono cum numine fruges)	419	Tr.Mortis		61
Creditur, ante satas prono cum vertice fruges)	419	Tr.Mortis	V	61
Haec vbi iuncta, subit viuo cum fune minister,	420	Tr.Mortis		66
Haec vbi vincta, subit viuo cum fune minister,	271	Tr.Mortis	VS	66
Mulcetur vento, accendit cum fomite partem	420	Tr.Mortis		68
Miscetur vento, accendit cum fomite partem	271	Tr.Mortis	VS	68
Cantatum; deinde Ixion cum nubibus atris	420	Tr.Mortis		88
Protulit horrendum hoc primus cum puluere monstrum.	420	Tr.Mortis		91
Protulit horrendum hoc primum cum puluere monstrum.	420	Tr.Mortis	V	91
Lac cum sanguine posco deuolutum;	421	Lucus 34		6
Cum te non videam, mene videre putas?	421	Lucus 35		8
Sententiae cum voce mire conuenit,	423	Mem.Matr.2		37
Abito, trunce, cum tuis pudoribus.	423	Mem.Matr.2		54
Laudando Matrem, cum repugnant inscij.	424	Mem.Matr.2		65
Ad nos cum radio tam rutilante potes?	424	Mem.Matr.3		2
Hunc vultum ostendas, & tecum, nobile spectrum,	426	Mem.Matr.7		14
Rure; breuisque hortus, cuius cum vellere florum	426	Mem.Matr.7		23
Quod nectar, nisi cum te celebrare diem?)	428	Mem.Matr.9		16
Cum probro madidum, reumque difflat.	428	Mem.Matr.10		7
Cum tu, Christe, cadis, nascor; mentemque ligauit	434	Poem.Lat.		1
O me disparibus natum cum numine fatis!	434	Poem.Lat.		3
Quin moriar tecum: vitam, quam negligis ipse,	434	Poem.Lat.		5
Cum per te sit res ambitiosa mori.	435	Poem.Lat.		8
Cum mihi sit facies fumus, quas pectore flammas	437	Poem.Lat.		9
Cum petit Hispanam Princeps, Grantamque Iacobus,	437	Poem.Lat.	V	1
habita coram Dominis Legatis cum Magistro. in Artib. titulis	440	Orationes		T
Et quod obseruatione cum primis dignum est, quo magis amore	440	Orationes		21
cum eo sitis ordine atque habitu, quo nos in hoc regno omnes esse	441	Orationes		1
cum tanti sitis & in Principibus Vestris, & in vobismetipsis,	441	Orationes		8
certe cum duplex fulgor sit, qui mundi oculos perstringat,	441	Orationes		11
sed a scriptis vestris, quae ingenti cum lucro quotidie legimus.	443	Orationes		20
cum non solum tuearis nos a maleuolorum insidijs, sed etiam doceas	443	Orationes		21
quod quae nos audiamus summo cum gaudio ea Maiestas vestra summa	443	Orationes		31
nos audiamus summo cum gaudio ea Maiestas vestra summa cum molestia?	444	Orationes		1
Polycrates cum annulum sibi dilectum in mare dimisisset,	444	Orationes		14
& cum eo vita nostra atque calor, longo animi deliquio fugitiuus ac	444	Orationes		22
quam simpliciter vobiscum agam, quam non longe abeam Oratorum more,	445	Orationes		35
Quid si cochleas colligeret cum Caligula, praesertim cum possit	446	Orationes		13
colligeret cum Caligula, praesertim cum possit in eodem litore?	446	Orationes		13
Quid si muscas captaret cum Domitiano?	446	Orationes		14
tamen nimium efferre vos, cum Virginitas ipsa fructus sit Nuptiarum:	446	Orationes		27
quanto magis Principum, cum, quo eorum conditio sublimior,	446	Orationes		35
Deus ipse cum crearet hominem, mundi regem, consilio vsus est.	446	Orationes		36
Cum tamen splendida plerumque vitrea sint, claritatem fragilitate	448	Orationes		5
Dein quid Musis cum tumultu?	448	Orationes		22
cum corporis cum anima vinculum impedimento esse ad contemplandum	448	Orationes		26
cum corporis cum anima vinculum impedimento esse ad contemplandum	448	Orationes		27
perrumpit primipilus, & te cum coelis tuis ad inferos deturbat.	448	Orationes		30
praesertim cum futura incerta sint, & nullis perspicillis,	449	Orationes		23
Recte facitis, Academici, attollentes oculos cum stupore;	450	Orationes		1
cum quanto plus possint in sua terra, tanto minus in aliena.	450	Orationes		11
superbi sua tantum nosse, praesertim cum in vno regno non sint omnia:	450	Orationes		18
cum paupertatem daret tanquam catenam, qua dissitas nationes ac	450	Orationes		23
Falleris, nusquam plura bona, cum etiam mala illic sint aurea:	451	Orationes		3
Dij te perdant, cum malis tuis & arena sine calce;	451	Orationes		5
cur non vt elephanti turres, ita tu patriam tecum portasti?	451	Orationes		8

	PAGE	TITLE	LINE
DAMNARI			
feracem gloriae, et coeleste ingenium quasi ad metalla damnari.	468	Epistolae	6
DAMNARIS			
Pollubra vel cum olim damnaris Regia in ara,	386	Musae 3	9
DAMNAS			
Cur teretem Graecam damnas, atque Hellada totam,	391	Musae 16	3
DANDA			
Aut cita mors est danda bonis aut longa senectus:	432	Poem.Lat.	30
DANO			
Tillius incumbit Dano, Gallusque marinis,	427	Mem.Matr.9	11
DANORUM			
omnia Danorum expiscatus consilia, victoriam celebrem consecutus est.	453	Orationes	6
DANTUR			
Soli homini dantur manus, soli caput rotundum & coeleste,	446	Orationes	38
DAPES			
Quid hocce? Psalmos audion'? o dapes!	394	Musae 23	33
Tuque etiam Dapifer, quas fero, sume dapes:	210	Cam.1613-a BR	2
DAPHNEN			
Apollo olim depositis radijs Daphnen deperijt, at illa mutata est	455	Orationes	9
Noster etiam Princeps habuit Daphnen suam, cuius amor deinceps	455	Orationes	10
DAPIFER			
Tuque etiam Dapifer, quas fero, sume dapes:	210	Cam.1613-a BR	2
DARE			
(cum dignius nil posset aut melius dare)	397	Musae 28	10
DARET			
cum paupertatem daret tanquam catenam, qua dissitas nationes ac	450	Orationes	23
DARI			
Iam dari nobis vellemus Iesuitam aliquem, vt ex affrictu Libri vestri	459	Epistolae	7
DAS			
Cur mihi das vitam, quam tibi, Christe, negas?	434	Poem.Lat.	4
DATE			
date mihi CAROLVM alterum, quamlibet Magnum, modo detis eum in flore,	445	Orationes	19
DATUM			
satis virtuti datum est, satis Reipublicae.	455	Orationes	6
DATUR			
Pulueris inferni properat, datur ignis, & omnem	420	Tr.Mortis V	69
Suum cuique tempus & locus datur.	423	Mem.Matr.2	20
DATUS			
Pulueris inferni; properat datus ignis, & omnem	420	Tr.Mortis	69
Sulphuris inferni, properat datus ignis et omnem	271	Tr.Mortis VS	69
DAUNIA			
Daunia, non satiat bis ter millesima caedis	418	Tr.Mortis	3
DAVID			
Quos David, ipsae deliciae Dei,	394	Musae 23	37
DE			
De Laruata Gorgone.	387	Musae 6	T
De Praesulum fastu.	387	Musae 7	T
De gemina Academia.	388	Musae 8	T
De S. Baptismi Ritu.	388	Musae 9	T
De Signaculo Crucis.	389	Musae 10	T
De iuramento Ecclesiae.	389	Musae 11	T
De Purificatione post puerperium.	389	Musae 12	T
De Antichristi decore Pontificali.	390	Musae 13	T
De Superpelliceo.	390	Musae 14	T
De Pileo quadrato.	391	Musae 15	T
De Episcopis.	391	Musae 17	T
Ad Melvinum De ijsdem.	392	Musae 18	T
De Textore Catharo.	392	Musae 19	T
De Magicis rotatibus.	392	Musae 20	T
De labe maculisque.	393	Musae 22	T
De Musica Sacra.	393	Musae 23	T
De eadem.	395	Musae 24	T
De rituum vsu.	395	Musae 25	T
De annulo coniugali.	396	Musae 26	T
De Mundis & mundanis.	396	Musae 27	T
De oratione Dominica.	396	Musae 28	T
De lupa lustri Vaticani.	397	Musae 30	T
De impositione manuum.	397	Musae 31	T
De Autorum enumeratione.	398	Musae 33	T
De auri sacra fame.	399	Musae 34	T
Non placet vrbanus noster de nomine lusus	416	Lucus 27	1
Qua Mors ipsa sedens hominum de gente triumphat.	419	Tr.Mortis	56
Ego de rini ksumbalon ixnelato	430	Mem.Matr.15	14
Xalepoteron de panton	430	Mem.Matr.16	3
Nec vaga de summo deducam flumina monte,	432	Poem.Lat.	7
Quare etiam nuper Pyrij de pulueris ictu	433	Poem.Lat.	33
Sume Palatini versus de numine Phoebi,	210	Cam.1613-a BR	1
in rebus humanis diuinisque exercitatissimi, de integro disponendum.	444	Orationes	21
Otan de krepis me katablethei genous	447	Orationes	14
neque de priuato agamus bono, sed publico;	448	Orationes	6
Polemos de kan pedioi kakos ephu.	448	Orationes	15
nihil inaudisti de Tago, Pactolo?	451	Orationes	4
gaudeo quidem de ingenti amore in Principem, cui nulla dilectio par	451	Orationes	21
hic ego me erexi & de dolore remisi plurimum, de desiderio nihil.	451	Orationes	26
hic ego me erexi & de dolore remisi plurimum, de desiderio nihil.	451	Orationes	27
quam stulte de te rixamur:	451	Orationes	29
si quis de Principe aliquo, quis sit futurus aut qualis,	454	Orationes	8
1. Ad Buckingh. C. Gratulatio de Marchionatu	456	Epistolae	T
2. Ad R. Naunton Gratiae de Fluuio et de tegendis Tectis stramineis	457	Epistolae	T
tam de conseruando Fluuio nostro, quam de muniendis contra grassantes	457	Epistolae	17
quam de muniendis contra grassantes flammas aedificijs Honori Tuo	457	Epistolae	17

DE (cont'd)	PAGE	TITLE	LINE
aut tantum de nullo vnquam Filio Alma Mater, quantum de Te sibi	457	Epistolae	25
de nullo vnquam Filio Alma Mater, quantum de Te sibi polliceatur.	457	Epistolae	26
3. Ad Iacobum Regem Gratiae de Scriptis suis Academiae donatis	458	Epistolae	T
4. Ad Iacobum Regem Gratiae de Fluuio contra Redemptores . .	460	Epistolae	T
5. Ad F. Bacon, Cancell. Gratiae de Fluuio	460	Epistolae	T
illustrans nos omnes, lumenque accendens de suo lumine, . .	461	Epistolae	4
6. Ad R. Naunton, Secret. Gratiae de Fluuio	461	Epistolae	T
Ad Ful. Grevil Gratiae de Fluuio	462	Epistolae	T
de humanitate tua singulari, studioque in nos iam olim . .	462	Epistolae	24
Cancel. Gratiae de Instaurationis Libro Academiae donato . .	463	Epistolae	T
virum protulit, cum quinque millibus annorum de palma certantem.	463	Epistolae	27
Quare summe gratulamur tibi de nouo hoc cumulo honorum, . .	464	Epistolae	20
Tam eximie de nobis meritus es, vt res nostras omnes cum Honore Tuo	465	Epistolae	2
etiam Fluuium non minus de praeterito gratum, quam de futuro	465	Epistolae	7
quam de futuro supplicem, integerrimae tuae fidei commendantes.	465	Epistolae	7
Nos vero de hoc tuo progressu non minus Reipublicae gratulamur quam	466	Epistolae	15
13. Ad Archiep. Cantuar. De Bibliopolis Lond.	466	Epistolae	T
14. Ad Fr. Bacon, Cancell. De Bibliop. Lond.	467	Epistolae	T
idque pro Libris, de quibus nusquam rectius quam apud Te agitur.	467	Epistolae	19
quum ipsi non solum rectum de Bene-merentibus iudicium hausisse	469	Epistolae	12
vt quod Philosophus de Tactu & Visu, id apposite admodum huc	472	Epistolae	36
DEBEMUS			
Quare plurimum debemus constantiae fauoris tui, qui restinxisti sitim	462	Epistolae	7
DEBENT			
Nato dolenti: literae hoc debent tibi	424	Mem.Matr.2	62
apparatus, foedera, munitiones, aeque ac nostra spectari debent:	450	Orationes	27
DEBET			
Tibi debet Vnda & Terra certitudinis.	438	Poem.Lat.	7
DEBETUR			
Debetur Caelo lumen, & vmbra solo:	417	Lucus 31	2
DEBILITATAS			
hominum fame, frigore, illuuie, enectas, contusas, debilitatas.	449	Orationes	9
DEBITA			
Materni decus, & debita nominis, ...	424	Mem.Matr.4	6
DEBITIS			
sed et ambabus vlnis osculisque ei aetati debitis excipientes,	463	Epistolae	8
DEBITO			
illic constringor debito; hic etiam teneor, sed laxioribus vinculis,	472	Epistolae	33
DEBUIT			
Debuit ista pati prima & non nobilis aetas:	432	Poem.Lat.	29
manifestationem in gentem suam priuatae personae & habitui debuit.	453	Orationes	9
DECANTENT			
Sola Iacobaeum decantent carmina nomen.	402	Musae 39	40
DECENT			
Commotos animos rectius ista decent.	387	Musae 5	6
DECERPTI			
Sic vbi iam mulier decerpti conscia pomi	390	Musae 12	13
DECET			
Scommata! Pastorem semper Arundo decet.	405	Passio 7	2
Quam tribuit, verum multiplicare decet.	408	Passio 17	8
Quin post modestam, qualis integras decet, ...	422	Mem.Matr.2	14
DECIDUAE			
Deciduae melioris orbis!	394	Musae 23	36
DECORE			
De Antichristi decore Pontificali.	390	Musae 13	T
DECURRIT			
Fusaque decurrit notis aqua ferrea sulcis:	419	Tr.Mortis	52
DECUS			
Humanae decus atque apex iuuentae, ...	384	Musae	2
Vt celebrem decus insusurras?	394	Musae 23	24
Perge, decus Regum; sic, Augustissime, plures	402	Musae 39	33
Christe, decus, dulcedo, & centum circiter Hyblae, . . .	421	Lucus 35	1
Decus mulierum perijt: & metuunt viri	422	Mem.Matr.2	8
Tota renident aede decus & suauitas	423	Mem.Matr.2	24
Materni decus, & debita nominis, ...	424	Mem.Matr.4	6
Ecce decus vestrum spinis horrescit, acuta	425	Mem.Matr.5	3
Longius aeterno, latius orbe decus?	435	Poem.Lat.	6
India, non solitum profer Eliza decus:	211	Cam.1613-b BR	12
DECUSSATAE			
collum pensile, manus decussatae, ipsae mulieres inelegantes,	451	Orationes	16
DEDERAT			
voce sua dederat, ...	396	Musae 28	2
Sanguine, quem dederat, spolians. Primordia Mortis . . .	418	Tr.Mortis	22
Sanguine, quem dederat, spolians. Primordia belli	271	Tr.Mortis VS	22
DEDERIT			
cui natura spiritum dederit feracem gloriae, et coeleste ingenium	468	Epistolae	5
DEDERUNT			
etiam libros dederunt, sed non suos:	458	Epistolae	23
aut si suos, quia dederunt, non a se compositos, scriptos, . .	458	Epistolae	24
Tu inuaseris eorum gloriam conseruando nobis quae illi dederunt,	458	Epistolae	26
DEDICABANT			
velut Romani lacum, cuius altitudo ignota erat, dedicabant victoriae;	449	Orationes	21
DEDISSEM			
primas dedissem literas, ideoque praeferuida illa desideria silentio	471	Epistolae	27
DEDISTI			
Nuper enim dedisti nobis Librum, plenissimum Musarum, quae cum olim	460	Epistolae	7
maris quasi Flagellatores expugnatos fusosque nobis dedisti.	462	Epistolae	9
DEDIT			
Tu Synodosque, Patresque, & quod dedit alta vetustas . . .	402	Musae 39	25
Glans dedit, & truncus tectum, & ramalia mortem.	418	Tr.Mortis	8

DEDIT (cont'd)	PAGE	TITLE		LINE
Aetna Cacum igniuomum dedit, hic Ixiona multis	420	Tr.Mortis		87
Aetna Cacum igniuomum dedit, hic Ixiona Graecis	272	Tr.Mortis	VS	87
(Nempe sepulcra Satis numen inempta dedit.)	425	Mem.Matr.5		14
Tandem & fessa manus, dedit sigillum.	439	Poem.Lat.		12
DEDUCAM				
Nec vaga de summo deducam flumina monte,	432	Poem.Lat.		7
DEDUCANT				
Deducant linguae funera sola tuae.	438	Poem.Lat.		6
DEDUCENS				
Deducens lacrymas prioris aeui	428	Mem.Matr.10		11
DEDUCI				
& contracte King, a Con verbo deduci, quod tria complectitur,	447	Orationes		7
DEERAT				
Non deerat vel fama tibi, vel carmina famae,	416	Lucus 25		3
Deerat adhuc vitijs hominum dignissima mundo	419	Tr.Mortis		49
Deerat adhuc vitijs nostris dignissima mundo	271	Tr.Mortis	VS	49
DEERINT				
Non deerint vel fama tibi, vel carmina famae,	416	Lucus 25	V	3
DEESEI				
proeleluthoton, en kai emas isos deesei poreuesthai, poia tis esti.	471	Epistolae		11
DEESSE				
maius tamen piaculum reor, deesse publico muneri, quam priuato,	472	Epistolae		31
DEFECIMUS				
nos tam defecimus in vtroque quam Excellentiae Vestrae abundant.	441	Orationes		13
DEFECTU				
sane dubitamus vlli, si prae defectu aquae, commeatusque inopia,	462	Epistolae		2
DEFENDIT				
Defendit veram mente manuque fidem.	399	Musae 33		24
DEFENSIONEM				
machinas conficiunt ad defensionem Reipublicae mirabiles:	454	Orationes		6
DEFENSOR				
O qui Defensor Fidei meritissimus audis,	402	Musae 39		17
sed etiam doceas tanquam communis defensor fidei et Academiae,	443	Orationes		23
DEFENSORI				
Regi, Fidei Defensori &c. Geo. Herbertus.	384	Musae		T
DEFERENTIBUS				
spiritibusque tabellarijs laetum hunc nuncium vbique deferentibus,	445	Orationes		2
DEFESSUS				
Ingemit, & defessus opem iam Portitor orat.	420	Tr.Mortis		82
DEFICERET				
Dies me deficeret (& quidem nox aptior esset tali historiae)	452	Orationes		20
DEFICIENTEM				
Ad Solem deficientem.	407	Passio 16		T
DEFICIS				
Quid hoc? & ipse deficis, Caeli gigas,	407	Passio 16		1
DEFLEAT				
Namque hanc ruinam salua Grauitas defleat,	422	Mem.Matr.2		5
DEFLERE				
Quo Te, foelix Anna, modo deflere licebit?	435	Poem.Lat.		1
DEFLET				
Quin te Cambria peruetusta deflet,	428	Mem.Matr.10		10
DEFLUOS				
A Te Turture defluos,	403	Musae 40		13
DEFORMITATEM				
si speculum Inuidiae ostendas, quo deformitatem suam intueatur!	454	Orationes		21
DEGENTIUM				
Degentium olim, Emancipator; Luminis	436	Poem.Lat.		11
DEI				
Comparat aeterni regna beata Dei.	388	Musae 9		4
Qua tamen occisi foedera scripta Dei?	391	Musae 16		4
Quos David, ipsae deliciae Dei,	394	Musae 23		37
improbe, verba Dei,	397	Musae 28		17
Sum, quis nescit, Imago Dei, sed saxea certe:	410	Lucus 1		1
Nempe in quo clare lucet Imago Dei.	410	Lucus 4		10
Conueniunt; & Homo viua fit Ara Dei.	417	Lucus 29		4
truncata corpora, mutilatam imaginem Dei, pauxillum vitae,	449	Orationes		5
DEIECISSENT				
Te deiecissent tempora longa suo.	416	Lucus 25		8
DEIECTI				
oculi omnium deiecti, humile os, collum pensile, manus decussatae,	451	Orationes		15
DEIN				
Syluas pererrat. Fibulis dein omnibus	398	Musae 32		8
Dein familiam lustrat, & res prandij,	422	Mem.Matr.2		18
Dein quid Musis cum tumultu?	448	Orationes		22
dein Hon. Tuo gratulamur, qui filio auctus es tali ingenio praedito:	463	Epistolae		23
Dein, oratio clara sit, perspicua, pellucens.	470	Epistolae		27
DEINCEPS				
Daphnen suam, cuius amor deinceps in triumphos & laurus mutabitur.	455	Orationes		11
non quod nunc indulgeas alterutri, sed quod deinceps indultum nollem.	470	Epistolae		12
DEINDE				
Cantatum; deinde Ixion cum nubibus atris	420	Tr.Mortis		88
Molita, reliquum deinde garriens diem	422	Mem.Matr.2		12
DELECTAT				
non minus vitae inaequalitas delectat, quam terrae, quam Natura	453	Orationes		11
DELECTO				
Attamen VRBANI delecto nomine, constat	416	Lucus 27		5
DELECTU				
noluit Princeps optimus, in delectu vxoris, re vna omnium grauissima,	447	Orationes		22
DELENTUR				
& beatae fabricae, vnico ictu sulphurei tubi, vnica litura delentur?	448	Orationes		22

	PAGE	TITLE	LINE
DELIBAS			
victoriaeque gloriam absque crudelitate effusi sanguinis delibas.	458	Epistolae	15
DELIBUTA			
Plus charta haec mea delibuta dictis	400	Musae 37	25
DELICATA			
delicata res est eruditio & tenera, tanquam flos molliculus rudiore	448	Orationes	24
DELICATORUM			
Quam pudet me delicatorum Caesarum, qui cupiditatibus immersi,	452	Orationes	9
DELICIAE			
Quos David, ipsae deliciae Dei,	394	Musae 23	37
Horti, deliciae Dominae, marcescite tandem;	425	Mem.Matr.5	1
tractus (Oceani praeda et deliciae) vt irrigui Musarum horti,	461	Epistolae	9
DELICIJS			
Principem omnibus delicijs abundantem, obseptum illecebris,	452	Orationes	4
quasi fascijs circumdatum, enatare e delicijs, transilire sepes,	452	Orationes	6
DELIQUIO			
vita nostra atque calor, longo animi deliquio fugitiuus ac desertor.	444	Orationes	23
DELITUISSE			
Iamdudum tacite delituisse putes?	437	Poem.Lat.	10
Iamdudum tacite delituisse putas?	437	Poem.Lat. V	10
DELPHINO			
Arionem Delphino reuectum excepere arbores tripudiantes,	454	Orationes	36
DEMENS			
At forte matrem perdere haud soles demens:	429	Mem.Matr.12	9
DEMETENDAM			
segetem perspicio, nulla verborum, nulla temporis falce demetendam.	446	Orationes	3
DEMETRIUS			
Quin Aries ruit, & multa Demetrius arte:	419	Tr.Mortis	47
Tamque aries ruit et multa Demetrius arte,	271	Tr.Mortis VS	47
DEMISSA			
Tam demissa, ipsamque adeo subeuntia terram?	420	Tr.Mortis	94
DEMISSO			
Quin nec demisso, quando ad magnates cogitas, stylo vtare,	470	Epistolae	21
DEMISSUS			
Aut potius Christi sanguis demissus ab alto,	399	Musae 35	9
DEMITTERE			
Cur splendes, O Phoebe? ecquid demittere matrem	424	Mem.Matr.3	1
Verum heus, si nequeas caelo demittere matrem,	424	Mem.Matr.3	7
DEMOCRITUS			
facillime incedens, occurrit ei Democritus, & ingenium admirans,	453	Orationes	35
DEMONSTRAT			
regiones terrasque veteribus incognitas primus demonstrat:	463	Epistolae	11
DEMOSION			
Demosion t' indalma kalou, theion te katoptron.	430	Mem.Matr.17	7
DEMOSTHENES			
Demosthenes Atheniensis doluit se victum opificum antelucana	469	Epistolae	1
DEMUM			
vbi sursum processerint paulo, frigefacti demum relabuntur.	471	Epistolae	30
DENEGET			
te deneget VERBVM Deus.	397	Musae 28	18
DENIQUE			
denique huic aetati quae talem virum protulit, cum quinque millibus	463	Epistolae	26
DENTE			
Quos dente nigro corripis?	388	Musae 8	2
sunt, vt sic scripta vestra omni dente, tum edacis temporis,	459	Epistolae	18
DENTIBUS			
Dentibus atris?	390	Musae 14	4
DENTUR			
Vt dentur species, rogare sensum:	415	Lucus 24	3
DENUO			
nunc denuo nostrum, atque vbiuis terrarum pro iudicio prudentissimi	444	Orationes	19
illam nunc denuo ex aedibus Eboracensibus ab altero Cancellario	463	Epistolae	31
DEO			
Praedicat autores; tertia plena Deo est.	386	Musae 4	4
Displicet, & laudis tura litare Deo.	389	Musae 12	2
Quos inter plenusque Deo genioque Iacobus	399	Musae 33	23
nosque ipsos Tibi, Teque Deo Opti: Max: intimis precibus commendamus.	468	Epistolae	9
DEORUM			
apud poetas deorum pharetrae operculum habuere, humanae non item:	449	Orationes	25
DEPASCITUR			
Expleri nequit, & totum depascitur Orbem.	419	Tr.Mortis	38
DEPERIJT			
Apollo olim depositis radijs Daphnen deperijt, at illa mutata est	455	Orationes	9
DEPERIMUS			
ex quo facile collectu erat, quantum deperimus te;	451	Orationes	29
DEPERIT			
Ah longum, quae te deperit, errat iter.	437	Poem.Lat.	4
Ah longum, quae te deperit, ambit iter.	437	Poem.Lat. V	4
DEPINXERE			
in virginum, flores atque herbas depinxere:	446	Orationes	31
DEPLOREM			
Ah Mater, quo te deplorem fonte? Dolores	422	Mem.Matr.1	1
DEPONATIS			
vt deponatis paulisper vultus illos bellicos, quibus hostes soletis	440	Orationes	8
DEPONERE			
satietas quaedam honoris, quem ad tempus deponere famem excitat:	453	Orationes	10
DEPONIT			
personam Principis, deponit Maiestatem, virgam cum sceptro commutans,	452	Orationes	36
DEPOSITIS			
Apollo olim depositis radijs Daphnen deperijt, at illa mutata est	455	Orationes	8

	PAGE	TITLE		LINE
DEPOSUI				
ulomanian illam & inanem verborum strepitum iamdudum deposui:	445	Orationes		23
DEPRECANTUR				
vtriusque enim splendor et claritas humilia loca deprecantur.	466	Epistolae		12
DERIDET				
Deridet motus sancta catena tuos.	438	Poem.Lat.		9
DERIDICULUM				
Non deridiculumue, siue ineptum, ...	401	Musae 37		34
DERISIT				
Sed siccitas anni huius derisit incoeptum et plus effecit quam mille	461	Epistolae		11
DES				
Accipe; ni talem des, tibi qualis erat.	434	Poem.Lat.		6
DESCENDAT				
Aspice quam pleno descendat Iuppiter imbre, ...	210	Cam.1613-a	BR	5
merita tua ita ascensura, vt eorum vis et virtus ad nos descendat.	464	Epistolae		20
DESCENSURUS				
Gulielmus Victor descensurus primum e nauibus in terram hanc,	455	Orationes		3
DESCRIBENDIS				
quae licet versentur in figuris describendis, quibus nihil imperito	454	Orationes		4
DESERAT				
Aspice, dum perstas, vt te tua deserat aetas, ...	386	Musae 2		5
DESERERENTUR				
desererentur collegia, pulcherrimaeque Musarum domus tanquam viduae	462	Epistolae		3
DESERTOR				
vita nostra atque calor, longo animi deliquio fugitiuus ac desertor.	444	Orationes		23
DESIDERAUIMUS				
certe nos te absentem omnes acerrime concitatissimeque desiderauimus.	451	Orationes		34
DESIDERIA				
ideoque praeferuida illa desideria silentio suo sepulta nunc	471	Epistolae		28
DESIDERIJS				
Tuis, meis desiderijs probe cognitis, excussis perpensisque.	472	Epistolae		4
DESIDERIO				
hic ego me erexi & de dolore remisi plurimum, de desiderio nihil.	451	Orationes		27
sic existimes nihil Mortalium firmiori flagrare in Te desiderio,	473	Epistolae		5
DESIDERIORUM				
Ea est enim pertinacia desideriorum nostrorum, atque immortalitas,	464	Epistolae		22
DESIDIA				
ventilatione, desidia corrumpi, neminemque esse sui negligentiorem,	452	Orationes		34
DESIDIOSUS				
Et quid tu tandem desidiosus? AMO.	413	Lucus 16		6
DESINAM				
tam communi hac luce, quam Tua, cum id agnoscere vnquam desinam.	472	Epistolae		24
DESINES				
Nec Vaticanae desines vnquam Lupae	397	Musae 30		2
DESINIS				
Desinis exclamans: tota figura, vale.	401	Musae 38		2
DESINT				
vt neque virtutibus tuis desint honores neque vtrisque vita,	457	Epistolae		2
DESPERATAE				
Quin tibi tam desperatae MORA nulla medetur, ...	416	Lucus 25		9
Quin tibi jam desperatae MORA nulla medetur, ...	416	Lucus 25	V	9
DESPICATA				
Quam aut Ecclesia despicata vobis, ...	400	Musae 37		16
DESPICIT				
Si nigro sit terra solo, quis despicit aruum?	437	Poem.Lat.		5
DESPOINES				
Ouk eti despoines glukerai meledoni trapheisai:	431	Mem.Matr.17		16
DESPONDEAS				
Tu vero mentem neutiquam despondeas, ...	407	Passio 16		11
DESPOTA				
O despota elie kai theoi pantes, ei ti kata ton emautou Bion emarton,	452	Orationes		29
DESTITUTAM				
Quis enim tunc inuiseret Almam Matrem destitutam omni commeatu?	461	Epistolae		2
DESTRUIT				
pax nouum orbem aperuit; bellum destruit veterem.	448	Orationes		13
DESUMPTAS				
dignitates ab optimo Rege desumptas in vniuersam Rempublicam	456	Epistolae		11
DETIS				
quamlibet Magnum, modo detis eum in flore, in vagina, in herbescenti	445	Orationes		20
DETRAHI				
praemium consequare, cui neque addi quicquam potest, neque detrahi.	457	Epistolae		5
DETUR				
Christe, super fluctus si non discurrere detur:	414	Lucus 19		3
quod si tertia detur et quarta, paratos nos habebis ad gratulationem,	465	Epistolae		25
DETURBARUNT				
Jam deturbarunt tempora longa suo.	416	Lucus 25	V	8
DETURBAT				
perrumpit primipilus, & te cum coelis tuis ad inferos deturbat.	448	Orationes		31
DEUCALION				
Cur efficaci, Deucalion, manu, ...	393	Musae 23		1
DEUENI				
illuc commeando, eo deueni animo, vt nunquam cessandum mihi ducerem,	472	Epistolae		7
DEUM				
Non laudare Deum, credimus esse nefas.	389	Musae 12		8
Nunc redit ad mitem, ceu benedicta, Deum.	390	Musae 12		16
Quis sic amicum excipiet, vt Cathari Deum, ...	397	Musae 28		13
Teque Deum alternis cantans Ambrosius iram, ...	398	Musae 33		19
Ad Deum.	402	Musae 40		T
Culpa redux iugem te neget esse Deum.	406	Passio 13		6
Sic, pro Maiestate, Deum, non perdere vitam	408	Passio 17		7
Diffissum reserat Deum latentem, ...	408	Passio 19		3

DEUM (cont'd)	PAGE	TITLE	LINE
optime consuluisse Deum orbi terrarum lapides & metalla ei inserendo,	452	Orationes	24
Tantum precemur Deum immortalem, vt Princeps optimus nulla secunda	454	Orationes	38
DEUOCANS			
Tuiue Christum deuocans facundia	438	Poem.Lat.	3
DEUOLUTUM			
Lac cum sanguine posco deuolutum;	421	Lucus 34	6
DEUORAT			
& inuidiam, quae semper se deuorat primum, vti vermis nucleum,	454	Orationes	15
DEUORATUS			
& metalla ei inserendo, aliter mundus iam diu fuisset deuoratus.	452	Orationes	26
DEUOTISSIMORUM			
subsidiumque Magnificentiae Tuae deuotissimorum Procancellarij Reliq.	464	Epistolae	7
DEUOTISSIMOS			
quo soles beare Amplitudini tuae deuotissimos Procancellarium Rel.	464	Epistolae	28
DEUS			
te deneget VERBVM Deus.	397	Musae 28	18
Quem tu, summe Deus, semel	402	Musae 40	1
Vbique est Deus, Agnus, Ara, Flamen.	408	Passio 19	14
Cur Deus elegit Medicum, qui numine plenus	412	Lucus 9	1
Papae titulus Nec Deus Nec Homo.	412	Lucus 10	T
Nec Deus est nec Homo: Christus vterque fuit.	412	Lucus 10	2
Tu vero, Deus omnipotens, conserues nobis haec gaudia, imbuas cor	444	Orationes	4
Deus ipse cum crearet hominem, mundi regem, consilio vsus est.	446	Orationes	36
Deus bone! qui tum rumores?	450	Orationes	35
Faxit Deus vt quos profectus feceris in Sphaera Naturae,	464	Epistolae	2
Deus faueat Tibi & concedat vt terrestres tui honores cum coelestibus	465	Epistolae	18
Deus Opti: Max. tua beneficia, quae nos soluendo non sumus,	467	Epistolae	14
Deus fortunet tibi hunc honorem, et faxit, vt tibi gloriae sit,	469	Epistolae	5
DEXTERA			
Fac radios saltem ingemines, vt dextera tortos	424	Mem.Matr.3	9
Scilicet apponit pretium tua dextera fato,	435	Poem.Lat.	5
DEXTERRIMA			
id omne dexterrima tua in obeundis rebus prudentia dissipetur.	467	Epistolae	13
DEXTRA			
Nec dextra te fugit, almi Amoris emblema?	397	Musae 31	1
O blanda dextra, neutiquam istoc pulueris,	423	Mem.Matr.2	39
Pennata caeci dextra Cupidinis,	434	Poem.Lat.	22
vestra solum dextra (quamuis a scriptione terrestribusque istis	458	Epistolae	6
in qua dextra et fide coniuncti, in caeteris haud diuellamur.	468	Epistolae	24
DEXTRAM			
Fatalemque leuans dextram, qua stupeus ignis	420	Tr.Mortis	67
DEXTRAS			
Per charas tibi nobilesque dextras,	400	Musae 37	7
DEXTRE			
Sed propere dextreque reduxit euntia sensus,	385	Musae	5
DI'			
Os dia somatiou proteron kai nun di' Olumpou	429	Mem.Matr.14	7
on me themiton en, ou di' emauton emarton, alla dia tauta.	452	Orationes	30
DIA			
Os dia somatiou proteron kai nun di' Olumpou	429	Mem.Matr.14	7
Astrapton, Thuridon os dia, neime selas.	429	Mem.Matr.14	8
on me themiton en, ou di' emauton emarton, alla dia tauta.	452	Orationes	31
DIAKRITHEISAS			
Aretas diakritheisas	430	Mem.Matr.16	11
DIATHEINAI			
Zoes ksunergon tende diatheinai teknois	430	Mem.Matr.15	6
DIC			
Dic mihi, mons sterilis, vallis an vber eris?	413	Lucus 18	2
DICACEM			
Ne me carminibus nimis dicacem,	400	Musae 37	10
DICAM			
Ego vero non dicam vobis quod factum est ante seculum vestrum,	445	Orationes	38
Dicam vobis, Academici; ego tunc temporis liberior eram,	451	Orationes	11
Vt semel dicam; Oratio perfecta, vti vir, tetragonos est,	471	Epistolae	3
DICAS			
Ergo etiam Solem dicas, ignaue, superbum,	387	Musae 7	5
DICENTEM			
quam audire videor dicentem, Pulchrum quidem iter & Amante dignum;	453	Orationes	26
DICERIS			
Vssisse prono fulmine diceris,	433	Poem.Lat.	14
DICIT			
Aurum nocte videns, vidisse insomnia dicit:	411	Lucus 7	1
Inuertis nomen. Quid tibi dicit? AMOR.	416	Lucus 26	6
DICITE			
Dicite, vos Furiae, qua gaudet origine Monstrum.	420	Tr.Mortis	85
Dicite vos Stutiae, qua gaudet origine monstrum	272	Tr.Mortis VS	85
DICITUR			
Et Christianus quisque piscis dicitur	389	Musae 10	6
Vnus dicitur aduenire cladem:	401	Musae 37	43
in Geoponicis dicitur, Katoptron ean epideikseis toi epikeimenoi	454	Orationes	19
DICO			
Quin te laudibus orno: quippe dico,	401	Musae 37	41
Quare haud vos hortos, sed coemeteria dico,	425	Mem.Matr.5	9
tam grauem) & apud quos dico, viros limatae auris atque tersae,	445	Orationes	26
Non ignoro apud quos haec dico, eos scilicet, qui innuptam Palladem	446	Orationes	25
neque eo dico: sed lubet garrire paulo.	471	Epistolae	5
DICTA			
Dicta ferox: haerent lateri conuitia fixo.	418	Tr.Mortis	15
Dicta ferox, haerent lateri conuitia fixa:	271	Tr.Mortis VS	15
At tu qui inepte haec dicta censes filio,	423	Mem.Matr.2	52

	PAGE	TITLE	LINE
DICTA (cont'd)			
In mea dicta ruant; non tam mihi pendula mens est,	432	Poem.Lat.	5
DICTERIA			
Quae dicteria fuderat Britannus	391	Musae 15	1
DICTERIJS			
Dicterijs mordacibus notans, clamas	392	Musae 20	13
DICTET			
Musa, vale, & tu Phoebe; dolor mea carmina dictet;	432	Poem.Lat.	12
DICTI			
Dicti fidem firmabimus Anagrammate.	397	Musae 30	7
Hinc Thraces dicti sunt abioi, & Licurgus magnus Legislator atimian	446	Orationes	19
DICTIS			
Quo dictis minus acribus notetur.	391	Musae 15	6
Plus charta haec mea delibuta dictis	400	Musae 37	25
Sericus es dictis, factis pannusia Baucis:	414	Lucus 22	1
DICTUM			
O vere dictum, & belle! cum torqueat omnes	389	Musae 11	3
DIDO			
Iam foelix Philomela, & menti conscia Dido!	432	Poem.Lat.	22
DIDUMAIS			
Didumais korais toiauten	430	Mem.Matr.16	6
DIDYMUM			
In Thomam Didymum.	417	Lucus 30	T
DIE			
Discessum Regis ab Academia Cantabrigiae habita 12o die Martij 1622	443	Orationes	T
vbi trecenta foliorum iugera vno die sedentes percurritis;	454	Orationes	25
DIEBUS			
Prudenter inito quot-diebus calculo.	423	Mem.Matr.2	23
DIEM			
Ante diem vestro mundus ab igne ruat.	399	Musae 35	12
Te petet, ante diem quisquis obire cupit.	414	Lucus 21	6
Molita, reliquum deinde garriens diem	422	Mem.Matr.2	12
Quod nectar, nisi cum te celebrare diem?)	428	Mem.Matr.9	16
Hos oculos laetos, hunc sine nube diem:	211	Cam.1613-b BR	14
DIES			
Vna dies Catharos ad bellum miserat omnes:	399	Musae 33	31
Ad bellum missos perdidit vna dies.	399	Musae 33	32
Effluxisse dies, suffocatamue Mineruam,	426	Mem.Matr.7	18
Dies me deficeret (& quidem nox aptior esset tali historiae)	452	Orationes	20
Hilaris haec sumenda est dies.	454	Orationes	23
vnde fit vt nullus fere elabatur dies, qui non hostes aliquos nobis	461	Epistolae	13
DIESPITRE			
Innupta Pallas, nata Diespitre,	433	Poem.Lat.	1
DIFFICILIS			
Difficilis esse haud soleo: nam, pol, si forem,	413	Lucus 17	3
DIFFICILLIMA			
Principibus vt vtilissima ita difficillima factu, cum quanto plus	450	Orationes	11
DIFFICULTATEM			
at Noster difficultatem superans, fructum consecutus est:	450	Orationes	13
DIFFIDUNT			
num diffidunt prudentiae Regis? annon eius consilio res gesta est?	451	Orationes	23
DIFFISSUM			
Diffissum reserat Deum latentem,	408	Passio 19	3
DIFFLAT			
Cum probro madidum, reumque difflat.	428	Mem.Matr.10	7
DIFFLAUERIS			
Famamque nec difflaueris, nec suxeris:	414	Lucus 20	12
DIFFLUENTES			
quae fugerunt tot philosophos vmbra et otio diffluentes,	463	Epistolae	19
DIFFUGIUNT			
Diffugiunt, fragilisque crepant coenacula mundi.	420	Tr.Mortis	78
DIFFUNDIS			
ab optimo Rege desumptas in vniuersam Rempublicam diffundis:	456	Epistolae	12
DIGITIS			
Dum te vel digitis minister vrget,	417	Lucus 30	1
Connixus, digitis impiger vrgeo:	424	Mem.Matr.4	10
DIGNAM			
Dignamque coelesti corona	434	Poem.Lat.	35
DIGNIOR			
Tu mihi subueniens dignior esse potes.	404	Passio 2	6
DIGNISSIMA			
Deerat adhuc vitijs hominum dignissima mundo	419	Tr.Mortis	49
Deerat adhuc vitijs nostris dignissima mundo	271	Tr.Mortis VS	49
DIGNISSIME			
Vir Dignissime. Sic a Natura comparatum est, Ignis et Virtus semper	466	Epistolae	9
iam olim Regi notam atque signatam dignissime praeficiaris Fisco,	469	Epistolae	21
DIGNITATEM			
dignitatem, Fluuium placidissimo fauorum tuorum afflatu nobis tuere.	461	Epistolae	24
Pendulam hanc dignitatem diu expectantem magnas aliquas virtutes	464	Epistolae	11
DIGNITATES			
sic Tu etiam dignitates ab optimo Rege desumptas in vniuersam	456	Epistolae	11
vt semper post nouas dignitates, alias tibi quaerant et moliantur.	464	Epistolae	23
DIGNIUS			
Subtegmen reti dignius esse putans,	392	Musae 19	4
(cum dignius nil posset aut melius dare)	397	Musae 28	10
DIGNO			
Ipse suos tanquam digno pallentiaque astra.	426	Mem.Matr.7	21
DIGNUM			
Scribere, Te dignum, vel lachrymare queat!	435	Poem.Lat.	6
Et quod obseruatione cum primis dignum est, quo magis amore	440	Orationes	21
quam audire videor dicentem, Pulchrum quidem iter & Amante dignum;	453	Orationes	26

	PAGE	TITLE	LINE
DIGNUM (cont'd)			
qui etiam ferians nihil Tua perfectione dignum procudere possit.	471	Epistolae	24
DIJ			
Dij te perdant, cum malis tuis & arena sine calce;	451	Orationes	5
DIJS			
Sic quasi Dijs certem, magnos accersere montes:	432	Poem.Lat.	6
DIKEN			
Es bios eelioio diken, aktinas ientos	431	Mem.Matr.17	17
DILATAT			
nunc itaque Liber hic vester dilatat pomoeria, summouet Oceanum	458	Epistolae	12
DILECTIO			
de ingenti amore in Principem, cui nulla dilectio par esse potest;	451	Orationes	22
DILECTUM			
Polycrates cum annulum sibi dilectum in mare dimisisset,	444	Orationes	14
DILIGENTER			
et festucas, Reipublicae oculo haerentes, tam diligenter amoues;	462	Epistolae	13
DILIGENTIA			
tuosque fauores temporibus et diligentia diuisos in gratijs nostris	457	Epistolae	15
Cum caeterae ecclesiae tam perspicaci diligentia incubes,	466	Epistolae	21
DILUE			
dilue, fuga hos omnes, praesertim sericatam hanc stultitiam contere,	461	Epistolae	22
DILUIT			
Diluit oppositas candidus humor aquas.	428	Mem.Matr.9	18
DIMIDIA			
dimidiaque operis parte leuatus, ad mea in Honorem Tuum officia	473	Epistolae	2
DIMISISSET			
Polycrates cum annulum sibi dilectum in mare dimisisset,	444	Orationes	15
DIMITTERET			
cum dimitteret te in Hispaniam, quod Romani Imperatores in bello,	451	Orationes	31
DIMITTUNT			
aquas a Fonte accipiunt non retinent ipsi, sed in mare dimittunt;	456	Epistolae	10
DIPLOMATA			
si oppidani nostri (more suo) Musarum iura et diplomata arrodant;	468	Epistolae	26
DIRAM			
Gorgona cur diram laruasque obtrudis inanes,	387	Musae 6	1
DIREPTIONES			
fragores, direptiones, stupratas virgines, praegnantes bis	449	Orationes	6
DIRIMENS			
Pensilis, atque acri dirimens Examine lites.	426	Mem.Matr.7	13
DIRIS			
Et saxa diris hispida montibus	394	Musae 23	13
DIROS			
Labes, somniaque, ambitusque diros,	401	Musae 37	38
DIRUM			
Praesulibus dirum te Musa coarguit hostem,	392	Musae 18	1
DIRUUNTUR			
Diruuntur aedificia, corrumpuntur statuae, haec imago atque	459	Epistolae	12
DISCAT			
Carere discat verna, quo summus caret	407	Passio 16	9
Vt discat sibi quisque, quid vtile: nempe nocebat	412	Lucus 9	3
DISCERNI			
Ordine discerni maxima bella solent.	399	Musae 33	28
DISCERPTA			
Passio Discerpta	404	Passio	T
DISCESSUM			
Oratio in Discessum Regis ab Academia Cantabrigiae habita 12o die	443	Orationes	T
DISCIDISTI			
Tu discidisti Gorgoneas manus	434	Poem.Lat.	17
DISCIPLINA			
Pro Disciplina Ecclesiae Nostrae Epigrammata Apologetica	385	Musae 1	T
DISCORDIJS			
Discordijs plenas sonoris	395	Musae 23	51
DISCUMBUNT			
Hic vbi discumbunt per gramina, salsior vnus	418	Tr.Mortis	12
DISCURRERE			
Christe, super fluctus si non discurrere detur:	414	Lucus 19	3
DISERTAE			
quanto minus tacebunt lusciniae nostrae disertae, minimeque omnium	445	Orationes	10
DISERTUM			
In Improbum disertum.	414	Lucus 22	T
DISPARATAE			
sic disparatae foelicitates hinc a populo, illinc a Principe,	456	Epistolae	24
DISPARE			
Ora meae memori menti: ne dispare cultu	427	Mem.Matr.7	31
DISPARIBUS			
O me disparibus natum cum numine fatis!	434	Poem.Lat.	3
DISPARUIT			
per vniuersam Britanniam, disparuit forma, Albion nomine excidit:	451	Orationes	17
DISPEREUNT			
quam subito dispereunt, simul ac concrepuit incendium militare:	448	Orationes	19
DISPLICEAT			
Cur sic displiceat vox aliena tibi?	388	Musae 9	10
Caetera displiceat turba, necesse, tibi:	404	Passio 2	4
DISPLICENT			
Mox displicent omnes. Vbi hoc permanserit	398	Musae 32	4
DISPLICET			
Displicet, & laudis tura litare Deo.	389	Musae 12	2
DISPONENDUM			
in rebus humanis diuinisque exercitatissimi, de integro disponendum.	444	Orationes	21
DISPONIT			
qua optime ostendis te eius vicarium qui omnia disponit suauiter?	443	Orationes	17

	PAGE	TITLE	LINE
DISQUISITIO			
vestra disquisitio, qui tineae estis & helluones chartacei; . . .	445	Orationes	18
DISSENTIMUS			
Hoc vno Rex et populus dissentimus.	444	Orationes	1
DISSILUISSE			
Constat inaccessas dissiluisse petras.	409	Passio 20	6
DISSIPETUR			
id omne dexterrima tua in obeundis rebus prudentia dissipetur.	467	Epistolae	13
DISSITA			
Sic excelsa humilisque simul loca dissita iunxit, ...	429	Mem.Matr.13	5
DISSITAS			
tanquam catenam, qua dissitas nationes ac superbas constringeret.	450	Orationes	24
DISSUAUIANDAM			
e multis seligam, quam vobis amplectendam dissuauiandamque praebebo:	445	Orationes	33
DISSUTUS			
Dissutus videor funere & ipse tuo.	428	Mem.Matr.11	12
DISTENTIOR			
Ego auctior iam gaudio atque distentior, Cantabrigiam redij.	471	Epistolae	18
DISTINCTIO			
resolutione illa vltima, nulla sit distinctio populi aut principis:	452	Orationes	15
DISTINCTIUS			
Tres video partes, quo re distinctius vtar, ...	386	Musae 4	1
DISTINCTO			
ne literae nostrae animo Tuo tot negotijs meritissime distincto,	457	Epistolae	11
DISTINGUERE			
Vel potius liceat distinguere. Tuque tuique	387	Musae 6	5
DISTINXIT			
Natura montibus vallibusque sublimitate atque humilitate distinxit:	453	Orationes	12
DISTRACTUS			
nisi tot negotijs distractus esses, conflueremus omnes ad Aulam,	443	Orationes	26
DISTRIBUENDI			
administrans, distribuendi modum omnem rationemque callet? . .	464	Epistolae	15
DISTRIBUTIM			
Horti, colique distributim pensitat.	423	Mem.Matr.2	19
DISTRICTUS			
nunquam in tantis negotijs, quibus meritissime districtus es, ea,	463	Epistolae	18
DITARE			
quam ex obseruatione exterarum Legum ac morum, patriam ditare?	450	Orationes	15
DITAT			
ditat patriam, suamque absentiam cum foenore compensat. . .	454	Orationes	32
DITIONI			
adeo vt qui non subijciuntur ditioni, eruditioni vestrae obtemperent:	458	Epistolae	13
DIU			
Astronomus olim (vt fama) dum maculas diu, ...	393	Musae 22	7
Te, Mater, celebrans diu, ...	424	Mem.Matr.4	11
& metalla ei inserendo, aliter mundus iam diu fuisset deuoratus.	452	Orationes	25
diu iam peregrinati cum Principe, commode peruenimus ad laurum hanc,	455	Orationes	12
Pendulam hanc dignitatem diu expectantem magnas aliquas virtutes	464	Epistolae	11
Certe non diu est ex quo gratulati sumus tibi:	465	Epistolae	23
DIUA			
Tu Diua miro pollice spiritum	394	Musae 23	25
DIUELLAMUR			
in qua dextra et fide coniuncti, in caeteris haud diuellamur.	468	Epistolae	25
DIUERSA			
vt lineae, quamuis diuersa via, omnes tamen ad centrum properant;	456	Epistolae	23
DIUERSI			
Aethiopissa ambit Cestum Diuersi Coloris Virum.	437	Poem.Lat.	T
DIUES			
Os & lingua tibi diues, egena manus:	414	Lucus 22	2
DIUINA			
Seposuit Diuina sibi, cum conderet orbem, ...	402	Musae 39	15
Diuina Christi scriberet acta manu?	412	Lucus 9	2
consilia nostra, absconduntur Diuina & Regia, praecipue pharetrata,	449	Orationes	27
DIUINAM			
Ille quoque inuadit Diuinam Flaminis artem, ...	392	Musae 19	3
DIUINARET			
futurus aut qualis, recte diuinaret, non respiciat materiam actionum,	454	Orationes	9
DIUINIS			
Non conuenire precibus ista Diuinis.	392	Musae 20	14
& in rebus humanis diuinisque exercitatissimi, de integro . .	444	Orationes	21
DIUINUS			
Strauit Idumaeum diuinus Tityrus hostem?	419	Tr.Mortis	44
DIUISA			
Quae diuisa nocent, Christi per foedus, in vnum	417	Lucus 29	3
Post vbi crudelem sentit diuisa securem, ...	428	Mem.Matr.11	3
DIUISAS			
Scilicet has olim diuisas aequore terras	402	Musae 39	14
In vestes diuisas.	406	Passio 10	T
DIUISIT			
diuisit Natura suas dotes, vt indigentia singularum regionum omnes	450	Orationes	18
DIUISOS			
temporibus et diligentia diuisos in gratijs nostris copulauimus.	457	Epistolae	15
DIUITES			
vnde diuites syluas ac saltus quaerunt vbi aedificent, ac . .	450	Orationes	21
DIUUS			
Iacobus tutelaris Diuus est vtrique nostrum;	440	Orationes	23
DIXERAT			
ipsum coelum nubilum semper, & poeta stultus qui dixerat, . .	451	Orationes	19
DIXERE			
Si, quia felices olim dixere poetae	387	Musae 6	3

	PAGE	TITLE	LINE
DIXERO			
Quin, sine, te cernam; quoties iam dixero, cernam;	421	Lucus 35	3
DIXI			
cor sacrum, sentiatque Rex ipse nos haec intime precari. DIXI.	444	Orationes	10
nostram hanc Inter victrices hederam sibi serpere Lauros. DIXI.	455	Orationes	19
DIXIT			
Rure, sibi dixit Musa fuisse probro.	431	Mem.Matr.19	2
esti me perimenein, ote polemein umin omologesei, dixit Mithridates.	449	Orationes	15
Siccam animam sapientissimam esse dixit obscurus ille philosophus;	460	Epistolae	20
DIZEO			
Toide para tumboi dizeo, phile, monon.	429	Mem.Matr.14	2
DOCEAS			
sed etiam doceas tanquam communis defensor fidei et Academiae,	443	Orationes	22
sed etiam doceas, viam aperiens & methodum in studijs adhibendam,	443	Orationes	23
DOCEAT			
a re instructus nos doceat, tuosque fauores populo tuo communicans	444	Orationes	6
DOCENS			
Ista docens soli scripta quadrare tibi.	385	Musae	6
DOCENT			
Quaeque domus Dominae sit, grauitate docent.	425	Mem.Matr.5	8
DOCTA			
Ah, quam docta perambulare calles	411	Lucus 5	15
DOCTISSIME			
Ecce pererratas, Regum doctissime, nugas, ...	401	Musae 39	1
DOCTIUS			
Sancte Pater, coeli custos, quo doctius vno	385	Musae	1
DOCTOR			
Torquet, & in Textu Doctor vtroque cluet.	392	Musae 19	6
DOCTORIBUS			
Vos ducibus missis, missis doctoribus, omnes	387	Musae 5	9
DOCTRINA			
quem singularis doctrina exemit a populo, & quasi mixtam personam	461	Epistolae	26
instructior ad omnem causam, paratiorue siue a doctrina, siue ab vsu;	462	Epistolae	22
DOCTRINAE			
Doctrinae fluuios clauderet aureae, ...	391	Musae 17	4
alacrius illud impenderemus Doctrinae) beneficijs etiam obligasti.	460	Epistolae	6
qui elegantias doctrinae nitoremque spirans purpuram et eruditionem	461	Epistolae	21
vt qui tot subsidia attuleris ad progressum doctrinae, hac etiam	467	Epistolae	28
hoc Principe, in quo doctrinae fructus atque vsus mirifice relucet.	469	Epistolae	23
Parce doctrinae in epistolis; perorans, paululum indulge: . . .	471	Epistolae	1
DOCTUM			
Martyra, Calvinum, Bezam, doctumque Bucerum, ...	398	Musae 33	3
DOCTUS			
Accedis bene doctus, et poeta.	401	Musae 37	47
Quaeritur ingenium, doctusque homicida probatur.	418	Tr.Mortis	25
DOCUISTI			
Tu, qui cuncta creans docuisti marmora flere, ...	410	Lucus 1	5
DOKEI			
Xalepon dokei dakrusai, ...	430	Mem.Matr.16	1
Dokei moi xrenai para ton presbuton punthanesthai, osper tina odon	471	Epistolae	9
DOLEAS			
Nec tu pro socio doleas, qui fugit ad illud	415	Lucus 23	15
DOLEBUNT			
etiam Athenae artesque obscuris opificum artibus superari dolebunt.	469	Epistolae	4
DOLEMUS			
Id vnum dolemus, Bibliothecam nostram rudiorem esse impexioremque,	463	Epistolae	28
DOLENDUM			
pauxillum vitae, quantum satis ad dolendum, vrbium incendia,	449	Orationes	5
DOLENS			
Suauis erat, qui scripta dolens lacerando recludi, ...	439	Poem.Lat.	13
DOLENT			
at cur adeo dolent? cur ringuntur?	451	Orationes	23
DOLENTI			
Nato dolenti: literae hoc debent tibi	424	Mem.Matr.2	62
DOLERE			
Culmen, vbi pro te nemo dolere potest.	415	Lucus 23	16
Dolere prohibes? aut dolere me gentis	429	Mem.Matr.12	5
DOLI			
Te mille rixae, mille prensabunt doli, ...	414	Lucus 20	8
DOLIUM			
Gusto proboque Dolium.	427	Mem.Matr.8	10
DOLOR			
Exercet miserum; non dolor vnguium	403	Musae 40	4
Christe, dolor tibi supplicio, mihi blanda voluptas;	405	Passio 6	1
Mater: & ista Dolor nunc tibi Metra parit.	422	Mem.Matr.1	8
Quandoque voltus sola maiestas, Dolor.	422	Mem.Matr.2	7
Musa, vale, & tu Phoebe; dolor mea carmina dictet;	432	Poem.Lat.	12
DOLORE			
hic ego me erexi & de dolore remisi plurimum, de desiderio nihil.	451	Orationes	26
DOLORES			
Ah Mater, quo te deplorem fonte? Dolores	422	Mem.Matr.1	1
Solum dolores, & dolores, stellulae.	423	Mem.Matr.2	51
DOLORIS			
Expeto, tanquam haec sit nostri medicina doloris?	433	Poem.Lat.	46
Dure, negas? O fata mihi praesaga doloris, ...	437	Poem.Lat.	11
DOLOSUM			
Mutata? & pro matre mihi phantasma dolosum	426	Mem.Matr.7	3
DOLUIT			
Demosthenes Atheniensis doluit se victum opificum antelucana	469	Epistolae	2
DOMI			
Vt nequeat paulo se cohibere domi.	404	Passio 3	2

	PAGE	TITLE	LINE
DOMINA			
Ipsa cum domina domum vorando?	411	Lucus 5	9
DOMINAE			
Horti, deliciae Dominae, marcescite tandem;	425	Mem.Matr.5	1
Terram & funus olent flores: Dominaeque cadauer	425	Mem.Matr.5	5
Quaeque domus Dominae sit, grauitate docent.	425	Mem.Matr.5	8
Hac facie dominae conspiciare tuae:	211	Cam.1613-b BR	10
DOMINAM			
Quaesitum Dominam gemma vel herba suam.	425	Mem.Matr.5	12
DOMINATURA			
in quo paucorum auaritia liberalibus artibus dominatura est,	467	Epistolae	1
DOMINE			
Tangas, Domine, cor sacrum, sentiatque Rex ipse nos haec intime	444	Orationes	8
Illustrissime Domine. Ecquid inter tot gloriae titulos caput vndique	456	Epistolae	1
Serenissime Domine noster, Iacobe Inuictissime.	458	Epistolae	1
Serenissime Domine noster, Iacobe Potentissime.	460	Epistolae	1
Illustrissime Domine. Siccam animam sapientissimam esse dixit	460	Epistolae	19
Illustrissime Domine. Prolem Tuam suauissimam, nuper in lucem	463	Epistolae	4
Illustrissime Domine. Pendulam hanc dignitatem diu expectantem magnas	464	Epistolae	10
Tantum quocunque, Domine, ascendas, sume tecum amorem illum quo soles	464	Epistolae	26
Honoratissime Domine. Tam eximie de nobis meritus es, vt res nostras	465	Epistolae	1
Illustrissime Domine. Tu quidem semper Patronus noster es,	467	Epistolae	16
Ecquid permittis, Domine? Curasti tu quidem Instauratione tua,	467	Epistolae	24
Honoratissime Domine. Fama promotionis tuae gratissime appulit ad nos	468	Epistolae	11
Illustrissime Domine. Concede vt Honoribus nuperis, tanquam partubus	469	Epistolae	7
Tu, Domine, vicisti; tuere nos ita vt fortunae nostrae,	469	Epistolae	17
DOMINI			
Vt sanctum Domini persequerentur opus;	392	Musae 19	2
dum sponsam Domini pijs	395	Musae 25	9
Haec fuerat olim potio Domini tui.	427	Mem.Matr.8	9
Oratio Domini Georgij Herbert, Oratoris Academiae Cantabrigiensis,	440	Orationes	T
Excellentissimi Magnificentissimi Domini, Post honores eximios,	440	Orationes	1
Splendidissimi Domini, cum tanti sitis & in Principibus Vestris,	441	Orationes	8
DOMINICA			
De oratione Dominica.	396	Musae 28	T
DOMINIJ			
non cor) Tui in me dominij ius imminuere posse, nedum rescindere.	473	Epistolae	7
DOMINIS			
habita coram Dominis Legatis cum Magistro. in Artib. titulis	440	Orationes	T
DOMINO			
Reuerendissimo in Christo Patri ac Domino,	385	Musae	T
DOMINUM			
Ad Dominum properare cantus.	394	Musae 23	32
Ad Dominum morientem.	404	Passio 1	T
Ad Dominum.	421	Lucus 35	T
cum leunculum & dominum suum contra naturam adoriantur:	454	Orationes	18
quanto magis virtutes istae in Dominum agri transferendae sunt,	459	Epistolae	17
DOMINUS			
At nunc fatiscis. Nempe Dominus aedium	407	Passio 16	5
Tunc Dominus clauis aggrediendus erit.	408	Passio 18	4
Iudicij dominus, flores vt iunctius halent	427	Mem.Matr.7	25
Inductionis Dominus, & Verulamij;	436	Poem.Lat.	4
DOMITIANO			
Quid si muscas captaret cum Domitiano?	446	Orationes	14
DOMUM			
Ipsa cum domina domum vorando?	411	Lucus 5	9
& ingenium admirans, domum secum duxit, & erudiuit artibus;	453	Orationes	36
DOMUNCULA			
Est mihi bis quinis laqueata domuncula tignis	426	Mem.Matr.7	22
DOMUS			
Parcite luminibus, sitque lucerna domus:	413	Lucus 15	4
Ratione certa vita constat & domus,	423	Mem.Matr.2	22
Quaeque domus Dominae sit, grauitate docent.	425	Mem.Matr.5	8
tanquam ligna obliqua, aliter magna haec mundi domus corrueret:	450	Orationes	29
pulcherrimaeque Musarum domus tanquam viduae effoetae, aut ligna	462	Epistolae	4
DONARE			
(In quo fas nihil est rumpi) donare sigillum.	439	Poem.Lat.	15
DONATIS			
3. Ad Iacobum Regem Gratiae de Scriptis suis Academiae donatis	458	Epistolae	T
DONATO			
Cancel. Gratiae de Instaurationis Libro Academiae donato	463	Epistolae	T
DONATOS			
subiectos, integro Fluuio a Rege nostro donatos, triumphare?	460	Epistolae	14
DONATUM			
Se quasi donatum funere quisque putat.	435	Poem.Lat.	4
DONEC			
Ducentque, donec incidentem in cassidem	414	Lucus 20	9
Occidite; aut sane tantisper viuite, donec	425	Mem.Matr.5	15
praesertim donec transeat nubes illa, quae vicinos adeo infestat:	455	Orationes	14
vices meas tantisper supplere donec Academia orationem tuam imbibat	470	Epistolae	6
donec lacteam aliquam viam ad candorem Mentis Tuae ducentem aut	472	Epistolae	8
DORMIENTE			
Tempestas Christo dormiente.	412	Lucus 12	T
DORMIS			
Cum dormis, surgit pelagus: cum, Christe, resurgis,	412	Lucus 12	1
DORMITAT			
Dormitat pelagus: Quam bene fraena tenes!	412	Lucus 12	2
DOTE			
Vtrumque sexum dote ne mulctauerit.	422	Mem.Matr.2	9
DOTES			
Mulcensque dotes caeteras visa est quasi	423	Mem.Matr.2	43

	PAGE	TITLE		LINE
DOTES (cont'd)				
diuisit Natura suas dotes, vt indigentia singularum regionum omnes	450	Orationes		19
praestantissimaeque animi dotes effecerunt, vt Alma Mater	465	Epistolae		12
DOTIBUS				
Haud secus ingenitis dotibus orbus Adam.	410	Lucus 1		4
DRASAS				
Mian t' atarpon sumporeuesthai drasas.	430	Mem.Matr.15		13
DUBIA				
vti sanquis solet in re dubia ad cor festinare, ita ad Te confugimus	467	Epistolae		9
DUBIO				
Atque haeret dubio tabida vita pede,	438	Poem.Lat.		2
vbi in dubio est, qui facit, an qui patitur, miserior.	449	Orationes		10
DUBITAMUS				
non dubitamus quin benignitas tua omnia elementa percurreret.	457	Epistolae		23
neque sane dubitamus vlli, si prae defectu aquae, commeatusque	462	Epistolae		2
DUBITATUR				
Quisnam horum maior sit, dubitatur, amor.	437	Poem.Lat.		2
Cuiusnam maior sit, dubitatur, amor.	437	Poem.Lat.	V	2
DUBIUM				
O bene quod dubium possideamus agrum!	386	Musae 4		8
DUCAR				
Nec sic parentem ducar ad optimam:	425	Mem.Matr.6		10
DUCAT				
Si ducat agmen, reprime; sin claudat, sinas.	414	Lucus 20		14
DUCE				
Qua Fabio quondam sub duce nata salus.	416	Lucus 25		10
Quae Fabio quondam sub duce tuta salus.	416	Lucus 25	V	10
DUCENS				
erectior solutiorque redibo, ex ipsa intermissione animos ducens.	473	Epistolae		4
DUCENT				
Ducentque, donec incidentem in cassidem	414	Lucus 20		9
DUCENTEM				
viam ad candorem Mentis Tuae ducentem aut reperissem aut fecissem.	472	Epistolae		9
DUCEREM				
vt nunquam cessandum mihi ducerem, nunquam fatiscendum,	472	Epistolae		8
DUCES				
Perstringunt vestros carmina sola duces.	400	Musae 36		4
Res redit ad vates, Pieriosque duces:	417	Lucus 28		2
DUCET				
amor virginis eo pertraxit Principem, quo tandem ducet amor Patriae?	453	Orationes		28
DUCIBUS				
Vos ducibus missis, missis doctoribus, omnes	387	Musae 5		9
DUCITE				
Flumina caelestem ducite lenta chorum:	210	Cam.1613-b BR		4
DUCITUR				
Ducitur illimi candida vita fide,	400	Musae 36		2
DUCTA				
Plumbo ducta fuisset aestuanti,	400	Musae 37		22
DUCTUM				
Quicquid ex vrna meliore ductum	390	Musae 14		5
DUCTUS				
Graues lagenas, Vester est Aquae-ductus.	405	Passio 5		9
DUCUM				
Nos flendo: haec nostrum tessera sola ducum.	427	Mem.Matr.9		12
DUELLI				
Ecce tamen quam suauis ero! cum, fine duelli,	386	Musae 2		7
DULCEDO				
Christe, decus, dulcedo, & centum circiter Hyblae,	421	Lucus 35		1
DULCEM				
Paras hospitium torumque dulcem,	417	Lucus 30		5
Dulcem rependent tum mihi tibiam	434	Poem.Lat.		33
DULCI				
Qui dulci miseros irradiabit ope.	387	Musae 7		10
DULCIA				
Tantum dulcia leniunt catarrhos.	385	Musae		9
DULCIORES				
in potestatem redigere, lenioresque aspectus, & dulciores assumatis;	440	Orationes		10
DULCIS				
Cui dulcis arrident Camoenae	433	Poem.Lat.		3
DULCISSIME				
O dulcissime Spiritus,	403	Musae 40		11
DUM				
Aspice, dum perstas, vt te tua deserat aetas,	386	Musae 2		5
Dum suum nomen tenet, & triumphat	390	Musae 14		19
Astronomus olim (vt fama) dum maculas diu,	393	Musae 22		7
Percussa dum currunt ad vrbem	394	Musae 23		15
dum sponsam Domini pijs	395	Musae 25		9
Tu vero quisquis es, caue ne, dum neges,	397	Musae 28		16
Dum gladium stringens Paulus ad arma vocat.	398	Musae 33		12
Si, Christe, dum suffigeris, tuae vestes	406	Passio 10		1
Dum moreris, Mea Vita, ipsi vixere sepulti,	407	Passio 17		1
Dum cor omne suum sibi requirat	408	Passio 19		7
Dum prono rapis ore cibos, & fercula verris,	414	Lucus 21		1
Dum lacrymas, it vita: tuus tibi clepsydra fletus,	415	Lucus 23		9
Dum te vel digitis minister vrget,	417	Lucus 30		1
Dumque his inuigilo frequens	424	Mem.Matr.4		7
Dum torus absentem quisque reponit heram.	425	Mem.Matr.5		10
Nec querar ingratos, studijs dum tabidus insto,	426	Mem.Matr.7		17
Paruam piamque dum lubenter semitam	427	Mem.Matr.8		1
Siste parum cantus, dum legis ista, tuos.	427	Mem.Matr.9		2
Sic aeuum exigitur tardum, dum praepetis anni	428	Mem.Matr.9		13

DUM (cont'd)	PAGE	TITLE	LINE
Sed partem in scriptis etiam dum lacryma poscit,	428	Mem.Matr.9	17
Dum librata suis haeret radicibus ilex	428	Mem.Matr.11	1
Arbor & ipse inuersa vocer: dumque insitus almae	428	Mem.Matr.11	5
Si-quas mens agitet moles (dum pectora saeuo	432	Poem.Lat.	9
Viuite, dum mortem ostendam: sic tempora vestram	432	Poem.Lat.	15
Munere dum nobis prodes, Libroque futuris,	435	Poem.Lat.	1
Munere dum nobis prodes, Libroque remotis,	435	Poem.Lat.	3
Dum petit Infantem.	437	Poem.Lat.	T
Dum petit Infantem Princeps, Grantamque Iacobus,	437	Poem.Lat.	1
Dum longi lentique gemis sub pondere morbi	438	Poem.Lat.	1
Tuque aer inflato tubam, dum plurimus ignis	211	Cam.1613-b BR	5
etiam praesenti seculo, dum pacem, qua tot iam annis impune fruimur,	447	Orationes	28
dum animus grandis, suique impos, triumphos & victorias quasi fraena	447	Orationes	33
dum globos tractas & coelos fictitios, perrumpit primipilus,	448	Orationes	29
Quod si forense quippiam nos spectans, dum incumbis muneri, occurrat,	466	Epistolae	5
rariusque paulo fodiam in Vintoniensi agro, dum Rhetorici satagam:	472	Epistolae	29
DUMIS			
Vtque ouis in dumis, haeres in crine Cometae,	413	Lucus 16	3
DUNATON			
E themis, e dunaton. semnomatos epleto stathme,	430	Mem.Matr.17	6
DUOBUS			
cum grauibus duobus muneribus fungar apud Meos, Rhetoris in hunc	472	Epistolae	25
DUOS			
Cum lacrymas oculosque duos tot vulnera vincant,	404	Passio 1	1
DUPLEX			
Christe, duplex fiet mors tua vita mihi:	434	Poem.Lat.	8
certe cum duplex fulgor sit, qui mundi oculos perstringat,	441	Orationes	12
DUPLICANT			
Mitis agas: tenerae duplicant sibi verbera mentes,	406	Passio 9	5
DUPLICE			
Occiduis, tanquam duplice nube, genis.	427	Mem.Matr.9	6
DUPLICEM			
Tu duplicem solus Camoenarum thronum	388	Musae 8	3
DURE			
Dure, negas? O fata mihi praesaga doloris,	437	Poem.Lat.	11
DURESCUNT			
Durescunt proprijs euulsa corallia fundis,	410	Lucus 1	3
DURISSIMA			
aduentum ipsi lapides, ipsa durissima ingenia, meum praesertim,	445	Orationes	8
DURITIA			
Duritia superare cautes.	394	Musae 23	20
DURITIEM			
Hanc mihi duritiem contulit improbitas.	410	Lucus 1	2
DURIUS			
Haud mihi cor saxo durius esse sinas.	410	Lucus 1	6
DURO			
Christe, vbi tam duro patet in te semita ferro,	404	Passio 4	1
DUSTUXEIN			
Orthos, anagke dustuxein tous ekgonous.	447	Orationes	15
DUX			
Dux Notionum; veritatis Pontifex;	436	Poem.Lat.	3
Dux Nationum; veritatis Pontifex;	436	Poem.Lat. V	3
DUXIT			
Vnde MARO laudes duxit ad astra tuas.	416	Lucus 25	4
& ingenium admirans, domum secum duxit, & erudiuit artibus;	453	Orationes	36
E			
Namque aspectibus e tuis vel vnus	384	Musae	4
E creaturis sine mentis vsu	390	Musae 14	13
Nulla tibi si signa placent, e nubibus arcum	396	Musae 26	3
At Caelum e saxis elicuit Stephanus.	410	Lucus 3	2
Pheron to pan, kagon: e os Aparktias	430	Mem.Matr.15	11
Thanein suneidos kreitton, e allos bioun.	430	Mem.Matr.15	16
E themis, e dunaton. semnomatos epleto stathme,	430	Mem.Matr.17	6
Lesmones, e belone sphaleroi kep traumati vuttei	431	Mem.Matr.17	12
Fluminaque e ripis obvia facta tibi:	210	Cam.1613-a BR	6
contemnere has gloriolas nostras quas e chartis & puluere eruimus.	441	Orationes	17
sic & ipse excerpam e Principis rebus gestis pugillum, vnam actionem	445	Orationes	31
vnam actionem e multis seligam, quam vobis amplectendam	445	Orationes	32
qualis quaeque sit mater, e qua liberi quaerantur, quam qualis terra,	447	Orationes	11
e qua liberi quaerantur, quam qualis terra, e qua arbores.	447	Orationes	11
Leones Britannici (e quorum ossibus collisis ignis elicitur) qui nunc	449	Orationes	17
quasi fascijs circumdatum, enatare e delicijs, transilire sepes,	452	Orationes	5
ti kata ton emautou Bion emarton, e phagon e pion, on me themiton en,	452	Orationes	30
qui inde e baiulo euasit Philosophus, eodem ingenio vsus in lignis	453	Orationes	37
quae semper se deuorat primum, vti vermis nucleum, e quo nascitur;	454	Orationes	15
ean epideikseis toi epikeimenoi nephei, pareleusetai e xalaza:	454	Orationes	20
e gurgustijs vestris, vbi trecenta foliorum iugera vno die sedentes	454	Orationes	24
Gulielmus Victor descensurus primum e nauibus in terram hanc,	455	Orationes	3
Aquilam inter nouas honorum nubes e conspectu nostro fugientem	456	Epistolae	7
neque illi e faece vulgi tantum qui eruditionem simplicitati	461	Epistolae	17
Academia vniuersim sumpta vna est e proceribus, inter patritios	470	Epistolae	24
EA			
Nos autem flemus: res ea sola tuis.	427	Mem.Matr.9	8
nos audiamus summo cum gaudio ea Maiestas vestra summa cum molestia?	443	Orationes	31
pax adeo Musis summe necessaria est, vt sine ea nihil simus.	448	Orationes	17
solebant signa in hostes inijcere, vt milites acrius ea repeterent:	451	Orationes	33
Reges Collegia, eaque fundarunt amplissimis praedijs, immunitatibus:	458	Epistolae	22
ea, quae fugerunt tot philosophos vmbra et otio diffluentes,	463	Epistolae	18
Ea est enim pertinacia desideriorum nostrorum, atque immortalitas,	464	Epistolae	22

	PAGE	TITLE	LINE
EADEM			
De eadem.	395	Musae 24	T
eadem acies & stipulam secat & lignum:	453	Orationes	28
eadem manus et tuum tibi largita est honorem, et priuilegia nostra	468	Epistolae	23
EAE			
Contiguas stirpes afflat, eaeque rosas.	425	Mem.Matr.5	6
EAN			
Katoptron ean epideikseis toi epikeimenoi nephei, pareleusetai e	454	Orationes	19
EAS			
Prae spiritu ruptis, quo eas resarciat	398	Musae 32	9
EBORACENSI			
cum olim ab Archiepiscopo Eboracensi Summo Angliae Cancellario	463	Epistolae	30
EBORACENSIBUS			
nunc denuo ex aedibus Eboracensibus ab altero Cancellario INSTAVRARI,	464	Epistolae	1
ECCE			
Ecce recedentis foecundo in littore Nili	384	Musae	1
Ecce tamen quam suauis ero! cum, fine duelli,	386	Musae 2	7
Annon sic mercamur agros? quibus ecce Redemptor	388	Musae 9	3
Ecce pererratas, Regum doctissime, nugas,	401	Musae 39	1
Vitam reduxit: ecce gratitudinem.	413	Lucus 14	2
Ecce decus vestrum spinis horrescit, acuta	425	Mem.Matr.5	3
Ecce solutura est, ventos causata morantes:	427	Mem.Matr.9	9
Ecce meus torpens animus succumbit vtrique,	435	Poem.Lat.	3
Ecce lanienas omnimodas, truncata corpora, mutilatam imaginem Dei,	449	Orationes	3
ECCLESIA			
Forte quidem, cum per vestras Ecclesia turbas	389	Musae 12	3
Quos Ecclesia comprobat, verendum	391	Musae 15	12
Ecclesia est mihi Luna; perge in Fabula.	393	Musae 22	10
Quam aut Ecclesia despicata vobis,	400	Musae 37	16
Cernite, quam formosa suas Ecclesia pennas	401	Musae 39	6
ECCLESIAE			
Pro Disciplina Ecclesiae Nostrae Epigrammata Apologetica	385	Musae 1	T
De iuramento Ecclesiae.	389	Musae 11	T
Cum caeterae ecclesiae tam perspicaci diligentia incubes,	466	Epistolae	21
ECCLESIASTICI			
ita ad Te confugimus primariam partem ecclesiastici corporis,	467	Epistolae	10
ECCUM			
O cessatrices! eccum puluisculus illic!	413	Lucus 15	5
eccum nunc altera occasio, adeo festinat virtus tua:	465	Epistolae	24
ECQUID			
Aequabili facta. Ecquid ergo te tanta	392	Musae 20	6
Ecquid emes Christum? pro nobis scilicet olim	410	Lucus 4	1
Ecquid emes Caelum? quin stellam rectius vnam	410	Lucus 4	5
Cur splendes, O Phoebe? ecquid demittere matrem	424	Mem.Matr.3	1
Ecquid nescitis miserias Belli? consulite historias;	449	Orationes	2
Ecquid videtis tandem quam vtile hoc iter, per quod optimus Princeps	451	Orationes	35
Ecquid inter tot gloriae titulos caput vndique murientes meministi	456	Epistolae	2
Ecquid inter tantas mundi trepidationes nobis & Musis vacas?	458	Epistolae	2
Ecquid permittis, Domine? Curasti tu quidem Instauratione tua,	467	Epistolae	24
ECQUIS			
Quo tingimur parui. Ecquis autem brachijs	389	Musae 10	8
EDACIS			
vestra omni dente, tum edacis temporis, tum venenatorum haereticorum,	459	Epistolae	18
EDAX			
Tempus edax rerum, tuque o mors improba sola es,	433	Poem.Lat.	41
EDENEM			
Edenem Boreae flatibus inuium.	424	Mem.Matr.4	4
EDENT			
vapores seruiles ad nubes educti aeque magnum tonitru edent ac regij.	452	Orationes	18
EDENTULA			
Atque edentula Musa, nec veneno	400	Musae 37	12
EDIT			
Qui vestras edit intime medullas.	391	Musae 15	10
EDITAM			
Mag. Sigilli Custodis post editam ab eo Instaurationem Magnam.	436	Poem.Lat.	T
editam, non gremio solum (quod innuis) sed et ambabus vlnis	463	Epistolae	6
EDITISSIMO			
vt qui hic in Musarum monte editissimo, in ipso Parnasso siti sumus,	449	Orationes	33
EDITOS			
quia dederunt, non a se compositos, scriptos, editosque:	458	Epistolae	25
EDUCASTI			
Queis me educasti; sponte chartas illinunt	424	Mem.Matr.2	63
EDUCATIONEM			
Nam vt educationem liberorum mittam, qua in re celebris est	447	Orationes	16
EDUCTI			
vapores seruiles ad nubes educti aeque magnum tonitru edent ac regij.	452	Orationes	17
EELIOIO			
Es bios eelioio diken, aktinas ientos	431	Mem.Matr.17	17
EFFARE			
Cum templis effare, madent sudaria, mappae,	397	Musae 29	1
Quare age, Mens, effare, precor, quo numine laeso?	432	Poem.Lat.	17
EFFARI			
si per tempus liceret effari, non licet per multitudinem,	443	Orationes	29
EFFECERINT			
Almam Matrem spe noua grauidam semper atque praegnantem effecerint.	464	Epistolae	26
EFFECERUNT			
praestantissimaeque animi dotes effecerunt, vt Alma Mater	465	Epistolae	12
EFFECIT			
huius derisit incoeptum et plus effecit quam mille Redemptores exequi	461	Epistolae	12
EFFERAT			
Rege nostro quin turgescat indies, atque efferat se, indulgere.	473	Epistolae	22

	PAGE	TITLE	LINE
EFFERRE			
Nolite tamen nimium efferre vos, cum Virginitas ipsa fructus sit	446	Orationes	27
EFFICACI			
Cur efficaci, Deucalion, manu,	393	Musae 23	1
EFFICIENT			
Suauiter efficient, absque rigore Scholae.	417	Lucus 28	4
EFFIGIES			
effigies, imo vmbras hominum fame, frigore, illuuie, enectas,	449	Orationes	8
EFFLANTIS			
Vitasse Christi spiritum efflantis crucem.	389	Musae 10	5
EFFLUXISSE			
Effluxisse dies, suffocatamue Mineruam,	426	Mem.Matr.7	18
EFFOETAE			
pulcherrimaeque Musarum domus tanquam viduae effoetae, aut ligna	462	Epistolae	4
EFFUGIES			
neque enim sic effugies cum honoribus, quin laetitia nostra te	465	Epistolae	22
EFFUGIT			
Non sic effugit angulus vel vnus	391	Musae 15	5
EFFUNDERE			
Cur ideo verbis tristes effundere curas	433	Poem.Lat.	45
EFFUNDERENT			
communes Reipublicae lachrymae alterum nobis Fluuium effunderent.	462	Epistolae	6
EFFUNDI			
Sic tuus effundi gestit pro crimine sanguis,	404	Passio 3	1
EFFUSI			
victoriaeque gloriam absque crudelitate effusi sanguinis delibas.	458	Epistolae	15
EFFUSISSIMUM			
atque effusissimum in omnia officia, quae praestet mea paruitas;	471	Epistolae	21
EGENA			
Os & lingua tibi diues, egena manus:	414	Lucus 22	2
EGENTIBUS			
sed nudis & egentibus	396	Musae 25	22
EGISSE			
vt aliquando existimen id egisse prudentissimum Patrem tuum,	451	Orationes	30
EGIT			
ipse egit oratorem, vt & ego aliquantulum hoc nomine glorier.	450	Orationes	31
EGO			
Sic tu nunc iuuenis factus, egoque senex.	386	Musae 2	4
In ritibus nostris? Ego audio nullum.	392	Musae 20	2
Hic ego tuque erimus, variae suffitibus herbae	427	Mem.Matr.7	28
Ego de rini ksumbalon ixnelato	430	Mem.Matr.15	14
Non ego vos posthac hederae velatus amictu	432	Poem.Lat.	2
ego vero sentio, & quis sum ipse (barbam, hui, tam grauem) & apud	445	Orationes	25
Ego vero non dicam vobis quod factum est ante seculum vestrum,	445	Orationes	37
ipse egit oratorem, vt & ego aliquantulum hoc nomine glorier.	450	Orationes	31
at ego Principem vellem, CAROLVM, CAROLVM;	451	Orationes	6
ego tunc temporis liberior eram, huc illuc pro libitu	451	Orationes	11
vt ego nihil vspiam laetum, nihil candidum expiscari possem;	451	Orationes	14
Inde ego sic mecum: gaudeo quidem de ingenti amore in Principem,	451	Orationes	21
hic ego me erexi & de dolore remisi plurimum, de desiderio nihil.	451	Orationes	26
Quid ego vobis Neronum aut Heliogabalorum ingluuiem memorem?	452	Orationes	18
quantum quidem ego homuncio ac nanus coniectando assequor.	453	Orationes	21
Ego hic pultibus vescor et glande, more maiorum, multos iam annos	470	Epistolae	3
Ego auctior iam gaudio atque distentior, Cantabrigiam redij.	471	Epistolae	17
Ego, non nisi meditato, obrepsi ad fauorem Tuum;	472	Epistolae	2
Cur ego laborem notus esse tam praue,	472	Epistolae	17
EGOMET			
Quare Sphaeram egomet meam	424	Mem.Matr.4	9
EI			
Menouge sophien, ei s' apellaxthai xreon,	430	Mem.Matr.15	5
Ei pou tuxoimi tesd' aristes atrapou,	430	Mem.Matr.15	15
Ei en en o anthropos, inquit Medicorum Alpha, ouk an elgeen.	446	Orationes	18
optime consuluisse Deum orbi terrarum lapides & metalla ei inserendo,	452	Orationes	25
theoi pantes, ei ti kata ton emautou Bion emarton, e phagon e pion,	452	Orationes	29
facillime incedens, occurrit ei Democritus, & ingenium admirans,	453	Orationes	35
relabitur in terram, qua ortus est, eique cum foecundia remuneratur:	454	Orationes	30
sed et ambabus vlnis osculisque ei aetati debitis excipientes,	463	Epistolae	7
Iam si inter commendandum adhibeas ei calamistros vti iuuenculae,	470	Epistolae	18
EIA			
Eia, agedum scribo: vicisti, Musa; sed audi,	431	Mem.Matr.19	7
Respondit: Eia, ne metuas, precor,	434	Poem.Lat.	26
EIARINOUS			
Praeis eiarinous te xarais epikidnato kepon:	431	Mem.Matr.17	18
EIEN			
Talas, eithe y' Argos eien	430	Mem.Matr.16	8
EIKOS			
Pheggode monon, os eikos, epaulin exei.	429	Mem.Matr.14	4
EINAI			
existimantes tuphlous einai pros oksu blepontas, anapodemetous pros	450	Orationes	9
EIRENE			
Eirene georgon kan petrais trephei kalos,	448	Orationes	14
EIRGEIN			
Ou pheggos, koinon t' agathon, mian eis thuran eirgein	430	Mem.Matr.17	5
EIS			
Ou pheggos, koinon t' agathon, mian eis thuran eirgein	430	Mem.Matr.17	5
EITHE			
Talas, eithe y' Argos eien	430	Mem.Matr.16	8
EIUS			
Ne tandem caput eius impetatis.	391	Musae 15	13
nostrumque regnum gestimus fieri participes eius sanguinis,	440	Orationes	20
esse Alexandro Magno nisi eius res gestas tradidisset historia?	441	Orationes	19

EIUS (cont'd)	PAGE	TITLE	LINE
Si per haec ludicra nostra pars aliquis eius laetitiae,	443	Orationes	9
qua optime ostendis te eius vicarium qui omnia disponit suauiter?	443	Orationes	16
annon eius consilio res gesta est?	451	Orationes	24
peruenimus ad laurum hanc, vbi sub vmbra eius paulisper requiescamus:	455	Orationes	13
quae complexus es animo, ad eius gloriam, Reipublicae emolumentum,	464	Epistolae	5
EKDEDEMEKOTAS			
tuphlous einai pros oksu blepontas, anapodemetous pros ekdedemekotas.	450	Orationes	9
EKEINOU			
Nou d' autou taphos est' aster: pheggos gar ekeinou	429	Mem.Matr.14	3
EKGONOUS			
Orthos, anaqke dustuxein tous ekgonous.	447	Orationes	15
ELABATUR			
vnde fit vt nullus fere elabatur dies, qui non hostes aliquos nobis	461	Epistolae	13
ELECT			
10. Ad R. Naunt. Burgen. Elect.	465	Epistolae	T
ELEGANTER			
Protagoras cum eleganter admodum caudices ligni fasciculo vinxisset,	453	Orationes	33
Comiter scribis atque eleganter; quae est vestra felicitas qui puro	470	Epistolae	2
ELEGANTIA			
vt mihi videtur, Romana elegantia, periodique vetus rotunditas.	473	Epistolae	18
ELEGANTIAE			
Profunditatis pinus, atque Elegantiae;	436	Poem.Lat.	6
Profunditatis cinnus, atque Elegantiae;	436	Poem.Lat. V	6
ELEGANTIAS			
qui elegantias doctrinae nitoremque spirans purpuram et eruditionem	461	Epistolae	21
barbara omnia, Tu non nisi cultissima, elegantiasque ipsas exhibes.	463	Epistolae	15
ELEGI			
Cur non lugentes Elegi? non acer Iambus?	387	Musae 5	5
ELEGIMUS			
plenissimis suffragijs elegimus Te tribunum Parlamentarium,	465	Epistolae	4
ELEGIT			
Cur Deus elegit Medicum, qui numine plenus	412	Lucus 9	1
ELEMENTA			
Mens superat; corpus solum Elementa tenent.	424	Mem.Matr.3	4
ac si corpora sua non abirent olim in elementa, sed in bellaria aut	452	Orationes	14
non dubitamus quin benignitas tua omnia elementa percurreret.	457	Epistolae	23
ELEMENTIS			
nulla sunt sceptra in elementis, nulli fasces aut secures:	452	Orationes	16
ELEMENTUM			
crassissimum elementum, Tu subtilitates Artium infinitas.	463	Epistolae	14
ELEPHANTI			
cur non vt elephanti turres, ita tu patriam tecum portasti?	451	Orationes	8
ELFREDUS			
Elfredus, nobilissimus Saxonum nostrorum Princeps, sub ementito	453	Orationes	3
ELGEEN			
Ei en en o anthropos, inquit Medicorum Alpha, ouk an elgeen.	446	Orationes	19
ELICIT			
Qui silicem tundit, (mirum tamen) elicit ignem:	410	Lucus 3	1
ELICITUR			
(e quorum ossibus collisis ignis elicitur) qui nunc mansueti sunt,	449	Orationes	18
ELICUIT			
At Caelum e saxis elicuit Stephanus.	410	Lucus 3	2
ELIE			
O despota elie kai theoi pantes, ei ti kata ton emautou Bion emarton,	452	Orationes	29
ELIGENDIS			
redundet, quorum in eligendis illis iudicium iampridem apparet.	441	Orationes	6
ELIGENS			
Sagax Humilitas, eligens viros bonos	412	Lucus 13	1
ELIGERERIS			
nisi Rex esses in ciuili Republica, eligereris in Literaria?	443	Orationes	18
ELIGIT			
Luctatur spacium, qualem tamen eligit aequi	426	Mem.Matr.7	24
ELIOS			
Autar od' au thanatos kuries, os elios auos	431	Mem.Matr.17	19
ELIZA			
India, non solitum profer Eliza decus:	211	Cam.1613-b BR	12
Nec plus te rubeat vesper, Eliza, precor.	211	Cam.1613-b BR	16
ELONTES			
Prounomioi d' aretes koinen geneteiran elontes.	430	Mem.Matr.17	3
ELOQUENTIA			
occurrant, oratio nostra est silentium, atque eloquentia, stupor.	444	Orationes	3
Authoritate tua plurima & Eloquentia non minori nobis obstrue.	463	Epistolae	2
ELOQUENTIAE			
fecisti Fluuium nostrum conseruans altero eloquentiae Fluuio,	462	Epistolae	19
nos omnes ad prudentiae eloquentiaeque tuae praesidium festinantes	465	Epistolae	15
EMANAT			
Vulnereque emanat sanguis, vt intret honos.	435	Poem.Lat.	6
EMANCIPATOR			
Degentium olim, Emancipator; Luminis	436	Poem.Lat.	11
EMANCIPATOS			
Quanta hilaritate aspicit Alma Mater filios suos iam emancipatos,	461	Epistolae	31
EMARTON			
theoi pantes, ei ti kata ton emautou Bion emarton, e phagon e pion,	452	Orationes	30
on me themitcn en, ou di' emauton emarton, alla dia tauta.	452	Orationes	31
EMAS			
Emas lipousa kuklothen metaixmious?	429	Mem.Matr.15	4
proeleluthoton, en kai emas isos deesei poreuesthai, poia tis esti.	471	Epistolae	11
EMATHIUS			
Quem non Emathius torrens, non sanguine pinguis	418	Tr.Mortis	2

	PAGE	TITLE	LINE
EMAUTON			
on me themiton en, ou di' emauton emarton, alla dia tauta.	452	Orationes	31
EMAUTOU			
theoi pantes, ei ti kata ton emautou Bion emarton, e phagon e pion,	452	Orationes	30
EMBAMMATE			
& sollicitudines Principum sine condimento sint atque embammate?	446	Orationes	12
EMBLEMA			
Nec dextra te fugit, almi Amoris emblema?	397	Musae 31	1
EMEN			
Ouk et' emen idias phules grapsantes arogon,	430	Mem.Matr.17	2
EMENSUS			
hoc ipsum iter, quod nuper emensus est, vt sciatis omnes quam nude,	445	Orationes	34
EMENTIBUS			
prosunt vendentibus Libros non ementibus, hoc est cessatoribus	468	Epistolae	7
EMENTITO			
sub ementito habitu fidicinis castra hostium ingressus,	453	Orationes	4
EMES			
Ecquid emes Christum? pro nobis scilicet olim	410	Lucus 4	1
Ecquid emes Caelum? quin stellam rectius vnam	410	Lucus 4	5
EMICANT			
Quare operosior in eo structura, & praerogatiuae regiae emicant.	446	Orationes	38
EMINET			
Eminet, id tumidum protinus esse feres?	387	Musae 7	4
EMIT			
Quin nos Ipse emit, precioso faenora soluens	410	Lucus 4	3
Sanquine: nec precium merx emit vlla suum.	410	Lucus 4	4
EMITTENTES			
bis intersectas, infantulos plus lactis quam cruoris emittentes;	449	Orationes	8
EMOLLITA			
si spinula vlla Coronae Regiae emollita sit vel retusa;	443	Orationes	11
EMOLUMENTO			
festinasti ad gratitudines tuas cum emolumento nostro coniunctas,	462	Epistolae	14
EMOLUMENTUM			
Reipublicae emolumentum, aeternitatem nominis Tui subsidiumque	464	Epistolae	5
Bibliopolas suum potius emolumentum quam publicum spectantes (quae	467	Epistolae	4
sed tamen comparatio & in honorem tuum cedet, nostrumque emolumentum.	467	Epistolae	26
EMPALIN			
Zo d' autos, braxu ti pneion, ost' empalin autes	431	Mem.Matr.17	21
EMPTOR			
inspexi facies hominum ac vultus curiosius tanquam emptor;	451	Orationes	13
EMPTOREM			
Scilicet emptorem si res aut parcior aetas	388	Musae 9	5
EMPTUS			
Venditus est Agnus, non tamen emptus erit.	410	Lucus 4	2
EMUNCTI			
Sunt tamen acuti quidam & emuncti, qui omnia praeuident:	449	Orationes	29
EN			
Afflatu perimunt: en, Cymba Cocytia turbis	420	Tr.Mortis	81
En Aurora vocat, lectus genialis in aula est,	210	Cam.1613-b BR	1
Ei en en o anthropos, inquit Medicorum Alpha, ouk an elgeen.	446	Orationes	18
e phagon e pion, on me themiton en, ou di' emauton emarton,	452	Orationes	30
proeleluthoton, en kai emas isos deesei poreuesthai, poia tis esti.	471	Epistolae	10
ENATARE			
quasi fascijs circumdatum, enatare e delicijs, transilire sepes,	452	Orationes	5
ENCELADUM			
Enceladum pharetramque Rhoeci.	434	Poem.Lat.	20
ENCOMIUM			
Nato parentis auferens Encomium,	423	Mem.Matr.2	53
ENECTAS			
hominum fame, frigore, illuuie, enectas, contusas, debilitatas.	449	Orationes	9
ENI			
Ouk eni thauma toson spheterizein: oude gar udor,	430	Mem.Matr.17	4
ENIM			
Haeresis, euertas. Quid enim te fallere possit?	402	Musae 39	22
Quis iste tandem? non enim vultu ambulat	436	Poem.Lat.	1
Quid enim iucundius accidere potest, quam vt ministri Regis Catholici	440	Orationes	14
Quis enim apud ncs splendor, aut rerum, aut vestium?	441	Orationes	10
Quae enim vspiam gens, quod vnquam seculum meliorem habuit Principem?	445	Orationes	12
vt enim Vxores, Virgines; ita Sol & Coelum producunt flores,	446	Orationes	32
neque enim minus refert, qualis quaeque sit mater, e qua liberi	447	Orationes	10
patent enim consilia nostra, absconduntur Diuina & Regia,	449	Orationes	26
neque enim quicquam hoc itinere mirabilius, cuius tamen fructum omnem	450	Orationes	2
Quid enim si praeter Nuptias, prolem, tranquillitatem, etiam	450	Orationes	4
quid enim vtilius quam ex obseruatione exterarum Legum ac morum,	450	Orationes	14
Nunc enim exploratos habet nostros in se affectus, timores,	450	Orationes	34
Quid enim? adeon' nihili videtur res, Principem omnibus delicijs	452	Orationes	3
hoc enim fastum amputat, affectus explorat, adulationem ventilat,	453	Orationes	1
vt enim vapor, qui furtim ascendit ad nubes, vbi iam ingrauescit	454	Orationes	28
hic enim securi sumus a pluuia, imo a fulmine:	455	Orationes	15
gloria, id enim nostra interest, vt hoc precemur, aut enim misere	457	Epistolae	24
aut enim misere fallimur, aut tantum de nullo vnquam Filio Alma	457	Epistolae	25
Quae enim alia spes reliqua erat, quam vt pro infinitis vestris	458	Epistolae	29
Si enim in regno vestro Hibernico lignum nascitur permanens,	459	Epistolae	15
Quis enim impetus animi celeritatem tantae munificentiae assequi	460	Epistolae	3
Nuper enim dedisti nobis Librum, plenissimum Musarum, quae cum olim	460	Epistolae	7
Quis enim tunc inuiseret Almam Matrem destitutam omni commeatu?	461	Epistolae	1
Neque enim passus es illum Fluuium, qui tantae poeticae,	461	Epistolae	6
Quis enim sicca vbera et mammas arentes tam nobilis parentis aequo	461	Epistolae	32
Quid enim inuident aquas, quas non nobis habemus sed irrigati ipsi	462	Epistolae	10
Optime enim hoc conuenit Partui tuo, qui nouas scientiarum regiones	463	Epistolae	9
Quis enim rectius Thesauris Regijs praefici possit quam qui,	464	Epistolae	13

ENIM (cont'd)	PAGE	TITLE	LINE
Ea est enim pertinacia desideriorum nostrorum, atque immortalitas,	464	Epistolae	22
neque enim sic effugies cum honoribus, quin laetitia nostra te	465	Epistolae	22
vtriusque enim splendor et claritas humilia loca deprecantur.	466	Epistolae	11
Ferunt enim Londinenses Bibliopolas suum potius emolumentum quam	467	Epistolae	3
Accepimus enim Londinenses Librarios omnia transmarina scripta	467	Epistolae	20
solent enim Studiosorum suffragia enixus gloriae, sollicitudine	469	Epistolae	10
Quid enim manerem? Habui viaticum fauoris Tui, quod longiori multo	471	Epistolae	18
Cum enim vim cogitationum in vitam meam omnem conuertissem, . .	472	Epistolae	5
quamuis enim sexcenta huiusmodi praediola Tua gratia permutare nolim,	472	Epistolae	29
ENIXAS			
Enixas pueros matres se sistere templis	389	Musae 12	1
ENIXE			
imo precabor enixe, me tum priuari tam communi hac luce, . .	472	Epistolae	23
ENIXUS			
solent enim Studiosorum suffragia enixus gloriae, sollicitudine	469	Epistolae	10
ENORMIA			
meo quadrabunt, quae almae matri inconcinna erunt atque enormia.	470	Epistolae	15
ENSIS			
Foelices, quos bella premunt, & plurimus ensis!	432	Poem.Lat.	23
ENTHEND'			
Nun d' oxou enthend' os stratos nikephoros	430	Mem.Matr.15	10
ENTHEO			
Ardore Moses concitus entheo, ...	394	Musae 23	29
ENUCLEATUM			
mirabilius, cuius tamen fructum omnem nondum habetis enucleatum.	450	Orationes	3
ENUMERARE			
Quae guttae poterunt enumerare meos?	422	Mem.Matr.1	2
ENUMERATIONE			
De Autorum enumeratione.	398	Musae 33	T
ENUMERATIONI			
quarum enumerationi nulla vnquam vis, nulla latera sufficere possunt.	443	Orationes	14
EO			
Mag. Sigilli Custodis post editam ab eo Instaurationem Magnam.	436	Poem.Lat.	T
cum eo sitis ordine atque habitu, quo nos in hoc regno omnes esse	441	Orationes	1
omnes ad Aulam, atque ab eo consilium peteremus a quo et fortunas?	443	Orationes	27
& cum eo vita nostra atque calor, longo animi deliquio fugitiuus ac	444	Orationes	22
quo eorum conditio sublimior, eo maior cura adhibenda sit. . . .	446	Orationes	35
Quare operosior in eo structura, & praerogatiuae regiae emicant.	446	Orationes	37
si amor virginis eo pertraxit Principem, quo tandem ducet amor	453	Orationes	27
quanquam quem alium fructum potuimus expectare ab Eo, in quem fauor	456	Epistolae	18
eo videaris nobis remotior, confidimus tamen vt arbores, . .	464	Epistolae	17
neque eo dico: sed lubet garrire paulo.	471	Epistolae	5
illuc commeando, eo deueni animo, vt nunquam cessandum mihi ducerem,	472	Epistolae	7
EODEM			
colligeret cum Caligula, praesertim cum possit in eodem litore?	446	Orationes	13
e baiulo euasit Philosophus, eodem ingenio vsus in lignis & literis:	453	Orationes	37
incomparabilem, quae eodem vultu et moderatur mundum et nos respicit.	458	Epistolae	4
EORUM			
aut eorum certe, qui cymbala sunt fanaticae iuuentutis: . . .	445	Orationes	24
sed varia solent esse eorum consilia, finesque multiplices . .	446	Orationes	5
quo eorum conditio sublimior, eo maior cura adhibenda sit. . .	446	Orationes	35
curiositas absit, neque eorum satagamus, quae ad nos non spectant;	449	Orationes	19
quum tamen Tu inuaseris eorum gloriam conseruando nobis quae illi	458	Epistolae	25
merita tua ita ascensura, vt eorum vis et virtus ad nos descendat.	464	Epistolae	19
affectuum raptim sequentes, ad omnem eorum auram vacillant. . .	472	Epistolae	2
EOS			
apud quos haec dico, eos scilicet, qui innuptam Palladem colunt,	446	Orationes	25
nihil eos latet, ac si Fatis a fuso essent atque consilijs, . .	449	Orationes	29
literatos, eosque cum tineis et blattis rixantes, exuens puluere,	462	Epistolae	26
verisimile est, eos illuc, quo cognitio ipsa pertingit, . .	468	Epistolae	1
EOU			
Tes peri sullaleousin, eou poikilmatos arden	431	Mem.Matr.17	11
EPAIAZOUSI			
Aiazo geneteiran, epaiazousi kai alloi, ...	430	Mem.Matr.17	1
Aiazo geneteiran, epaiazousi gunaikes, ...	431	Mem.Matr.17	8
EPAIAZOUSIN			
Aiazo geneteiran, epaiazousin oporai, ...	431	Mem.Matr.17	15
EPAPHRIOONTA			
Kumat' epaphrioonta Thameseos, aike selenes	431	Mem.Matr.18	1
EPAULIN			
Pheggode monon, os eikos, epaulin exei.	429	Mem.Matr.14	4
EPEESSI			
Pneuma, biou parodon mounois epeessi metresan.	431	Mem.Matr.17	23
EPHEBIS			
Excessit tener Orbis ex Ephebis, ...	408	Passio 19	11
EPHEISTHE			
Photos apauramenes ogkou epheisthe pleon, ...	431	Mem.Matr.18	2
EPHU			
Polemos de kan pedioi kakos ephu.	448	Orationes	15
EPI			
Nun themis orphnaiei megales epi geitonos aisei	431	Mem.Matr.18	3
EPIDEIKSEIS			
Katoptron ean epideikseis toi epikeimenoi nephei, pareleusetai e	454	Orationes	19
EPIGRAMMATA			
Pro Disciplina Ecclesiae Nostrae Epigrammata Apologetica . .	385	Musae 1	T
EPIGRAMMATICI			
Ad Regem Instituti Epigrammatici ratio.	385	Musae 1	T
EPIKEIMENOI			
Katoptron ean epideikseis toi epikeimenoi nephei, pareleusetai e	454	Orationes	19

	PAGE	TITLE	LINE
ERIS			
Dic mihi, mons sterilis, vallis an vber eris?	413	Lucus 18	2
Meter, gunaikon aigle, anthropon eris,	429	Mem.Matr.15	1
ERIT			
Hoc erit, Anti-furi-Puri-Categoria.	386	Musae 3	8
Sumite gorgoneam, nostraque Pallas erit.	387	Musae 6	6
Sic laudandus erit nactus sublimia Praesul,	387	Musae 7	9
Sed non moramur: namque vestra crux erit,	389	Musae 10	10
Nostra caro sanctae nescia laudis erit?	389	Musae 12	10
Annulus & plenus tempore forsan erit.	396	Musae 26	6
At non lusus erit, si quem tu laeta necasti	405	Passio 7	9
Tunc Dominus clauis aggrediendus erit.	408	Passio 18	4
Venditus est Agnus, non tamen emptus erit.	410	Lucus 4	2
Aurea pro naulo lingua Charontis erit.	414	Lucus 22	4
Sera nimis lacryma haec, si lacrymabis, erit.	415	Lucus 23	12
Nec facile ascendant, sed tibi vallis erit.	210	Cam.1613-a BR	8
prius Excellentijs Vestris curae erit;	441	Orationes	21
ERKOS			
Psuxes asthenes erkos, amauron pneumatos aggos,	429	Mem.Matr.14	1
ERO			
Ecce tamen quam suauis ero! cum, fine duelli,	386	Musae 2	7
Impar, & in fletum vel resolutus, ero;	404	Passio 1	2
Ergo ipse solum mutus atque excors ero	423	Mem.Matr.2	55
ERRANTI			
Whitaker, erranti quem praefers carmine, miles	398	Musae 33	5
ERRAT			
Ah longum, quae te deperit, errat iter.	437	Poem.Lat.	4
ERRES			
Quin cerne vt erres, inscie, brachium	426	Mem.Matr.6	13
ERROR			
Omnia, praeter corda, scelus confregit & error,	409	Passio 20	7
ERRORES			
Errores, maculas, superbiamque,	401	Musae 37	37
ERRORUM			
Securis errorum; inque Naturalibus	437	Poem.Lat.	25
Securique errorum; inque Natalibus	437	Poem.Lat. V	25
ERUBESCENTES			
Non erubescentes vel ipsas	394	Musae 23	19
ERUCTANS			
Totamque eructans nubem, Glans proruit imo	420	Tr.Mortis	76
ERUDITE			
Erudite Creighton. Comiter scribis atque eleganter;	470	Epistolae	1
ERUDITIO			
delicata res est eruditio & tenera, tanquam flos molliculus rudiore	448	Orationes	24
si quantum eruditio Regis profuerit Reipublicae, tantum fauoris nobis	469	Epistolae	24
ERUDITIONEM			
Quid eruditionem, quae tanta est vt, nisi Rex esses in ciuili	443	Orationes	17
e faece vulgi tantum qui eruditionem simplicitati Christianae putant	461	Epistolae	17
doctrinae nitoremque spirans purpuram et eruditionem miscuisti;	461	Epistolae	22
ERUDITIONI			
adeo vt qui non subijciuntur ditioni, eruditioni vestrae obtemperent:	458	Epistolae	13
ERUDITIONIS			
tantae eruditionis nobis conscius est, palustri opere & vliginoso	461	Epistolae	7
vt cum ipse eruditionis Princeps sit, illi etiam honores qui finitimi	463	Epistolae	21
ERUDIUIT			
& ingenium admirans, domum secum duxit, & erudiuit artibus;	453	Orationes	36
ERUIMUS			
contemnere has gloriolas nostras quas e chartis & puluere eruimus.	441	Orationes	18
ERUISSES			
quae fugerunt tot philosophos vmbra et otio diffluentes, eruisses.	463	Epistolae	19
ERUMPIT			
Erumpit inde, & contineri nescius	398	Musae 32	7
ERUNT			
Claude oculos, & erunt omnia nigra tibi:	437	Poem.Lat.	6
meo quadrabunt, quae almae matri inconcinna erunt atque enormia.	470	Epistolae	15
ERUTUS			
Erutus, infernae pretiosa tragemata mensae,	419	Tr.Mortis	58
ES			
O quam bellus homo es! lepido quam nomine fingis	386	Musae 3	1
Saeuus es eripiens paruis vadimonia coeli:	389	Musae 9	15
Tu vero quisquis es, caue ne, dum neges,	397	Musae 28	16
Qui Caput es, spinas & tua Membra tuas.	405	Passio 6	4
Iam meus es: nunc Te teneo: Pastorque prehensus	407	Passio 14	3
Atque omnes peragrata es angiportus	411	Lucus 5	13
Maeandrosque plicasque, quam perita es!	411	Lucus 5	16
Magnas es; esto. Bulla si vocaberis,	413	Lucus 17	1
Intra extraque graui plenus es illuuie.	414	Lucus 21	2
Sericus es dictis, factis pannusia Baucis:	414	Lucus 22	1
Nempe Caput Romae es, cuius mysteria velles	416	Lucus 27	3
Nempe es totus amor, medulla amoris,	417	Lucus 30	3
Magnificus es screator, homicida inclytus.	421	Lucus 33	2
Galene, frustra es, cur miserum premens	425	Mem.Matr.6	1
Es bios eelioio diken, aktinas ientos	431	Mem.Matr.17	17
Tempus edax rerum, tuque o mors improba sola es,	433	Poem.Lat.	41
adeon' es praedo omnis gloriae, vt ne gratitudinis laudem nobis	459	Epistolae	2
Neque enim passus es illum Fluuium, qui tantae poeticae,	461	Epistolae	6
vtrinque mirus es et exercitatissimus.	462	Epistolae	22
ex quo illustrius assecutus es nomen, quam Repertores Noui Orbis	463	Epistolae	12
nunquam in tantis negotijs, quibus meritissime districtus es, ea,	463	Epistolae	18
dein Hon. Tuo gratulamur, qui filio auctus es tali ingenio praedito:	463	Epistolae	24
vtque mature absoluas quae complexus es animo, ad eius gloriam,	464	Epistolae	4

ES (cont'd)	PAGE	TITLE	LINE
Tam eximie de nobis meritus es, vt res nostras omnes cum Honore Tuo	465	Epistolae	2
Tu quidem semper Patronus noster es, etiam tacentibus nobis,	467	Epistolae	17
huius tu es commotria atque ornatrix.	470	Epistolae	17
quidem multum, neque nostrae matronae conuenit, cui tu es ab ornatu.	471	Epistolae	3
ESCAE			
Haud glubat inde tres teruncios escae.	429	Mem.Matr.12	4
ESSE			
Et populi spurcas creditis esse vias:	387	Musae 5	8
Eminet, id tumidum protinus esse feres?	387	Musae 7	4
Non laudare Deum, credimus esse nefas.	389	Musae 12	8
Scilicet talem liquet esse solem;	390	Musae 14	9
Cur Latiam linguam reris nimis esse profanam,	391	Musae 16	1
Cum piscatores Textor legit esse vocatos,	392	Musae 19	1
Subtegmen reti dignius esse putans,	392	Musae 19	4
Cum nil fraterno rarius esse queat.	393	Musae 21	4
Esse recidendas, Aeace noster, opes.	399	Musae 34	2
Tu mihi subueniens dignior esse potes.	404	Passio 2	6
Culpa redux iugem te neget esse Deum.	406	Passio 13	6
Haud mihi cor saxo durius esse sinas.	410	Lucus 1	6
Difficilis esse haud soleo: nam, pol, si forem,	413	Lucus 17	3
Esse iocum soli, plebe stupente, tibi:	416	Lucus 27	4
Excellentias vestras tanto chariores esse, cum eo sitis ordine atque	441	Orationes	1
sitis ordine atque habitu, quo nos in hoc regno omnes esse gloriamur.	441	Orationes	2
Quomodo possetis similes esse Alexandro Magno nisi eius res gestas	441	Orationes	18
sed varia solent esse eorum consilia, finesque multiplices	446	Orationes	5
ideoque ex quolibet ligno, qualibet vxore non esse fingendum:	447	Orationes	9
Scio Belli nomen splendidum esse & gloriosum:	447	Orationes	33
cum anima vinculum impedimento esse ad contemplandum causaris,	448	Orationes	27
Non nego bellum aliquando necessarium esse, bellique miserias gratas,	449	Orationes	12
nobis non licet esse tam perspicacibus, quamuis rationi consonum	449	Orationes	31
acquirendam peregrinatione conducibilius esse nouistis omnes,	450	Orationes	7
de ingenti amore in Principem, cui nulla dilectio par esse potest;	451	Orationes	22
neminemque esse sui negligentiorem, quam qui sibi parcat.	452	Orationes	34
titulos caput vndique munientes meministi Magistrum Te esse Artium?	456	Epistolae	3
Siccam animam sapientissimam esse dixit obscurus ille philosophus;	460	Epistolae	20
Bibliothecam nostram rudiorem esse impexioremque, quam vt tantum	463	Epistolae	28
vt res nostras omnes cum Honore Tuo coniunctas esse velimus.	465	Epistolae	3
Cur ego laborem notus esse tam praue,	472	Epistolae	17
magis id adeo factum esse mansuetudine Tua incomparabili,	472	Epistolae	21
ESSEMUS			
Absque nuptijs foret populus virorum, essemus vnius seculi;	446	Orationes	21
ESSENT			
quod nonnullae familiae semper mites essent, vti Valerij,	447	Orationes	20
ac si Fatis a fuso essent atque consilijs, sine quibus ne vnum quidem	449	Orationes	30
ac si non gregaria essent animalia, sed tigres aut vrsi.	450	Orationes	22
ESSES			
nisi Rex esses in ciuili Republica, eligereris in Literaria?	443	Orationes	18
nisi tot negotijs distractus esses, conflueremus omnes ad Aulam,	443	Orationes	26
ESSET			
deficeret (& quidem nox aptior esset tali historiae) si Romanorum	452	Orationes	21
Quod si tam integrum tibi esset gratificari nobis in terra & aere,	457	Epistolae	21
EST			
Est Anti-pelvi-Melvi-Categoria.	386	Musae 3	10
Praedicat autores; tertia plena Deo est.	386	Musae 4	4
Vitaque neglectas est satis vlta preces.	389	Musae 12	6
Adde pijs animis quaeuis occasio lucro est,	390	Musae 12	11
Spiritus proponit, & est vtrique	390	Musae 14	15
Quid? hoccine est mirum? Viatores sumus.	393	Musae 22	2
Quo sanguis est Christi, nisi vt maculas lauet,	393	Musae 22	3
Ecclesia est mihi Luna; perge in Fabula.	393	Musae 22	10
Tantum repertum est trux hominum genus,	394	Musae 23	17
Aiacis est praestantior?	396	Musae 28	6
Quanto Impositio melior est Impostura!	397	Musae 31	4
Quin nocuas extingue faces, precor: vnda propinqua est,	399	Musae 35	7
Aut saeuum reputes. Amica nostra est	400	Musae 37	11
Quod scribo, & placeo, si placeo, tuum est.	403	Musae 40	14
Nescia sit metae; venula, cella tua est.	404	Passio 2	2
Graues lagenas, Vester est Aquae-ductus.	405	Passio 5	9
Crimina cum turgent, & mea poena prope est,	406	Passio 9	2
Hoc ligno, his clauis est, quasi Falce sua.	407	Passio 14	4
Vbique est Deus, Agnus, Ara, Flamen.	408	Passio 19	14
Venditus est Agnus, non tamen emptus erit.	410	Lucus 4	2
Vnicus est nummus, caelo Christoque petitus,	410	Lucus 4	9
Anglia cur solum fuso sine sanguine sicca est,	411	Lucus 6	1
Sit licet in pelago semper, sine fluctibus illa est,	411	Lucus 6	3
Naufragij causa est alijs mare, roboris Anglo,	411	Lucus 6	5
Et quae corrumpit moenia, murus aqua est.	411	Lucus 6	6
Verius hoc olim factum est, vbi, Christe, lauares	412	Lucus 8	3
Nec Deus est nec Homo: Christus vterque fuit.	412	Lucus 10	2
Vtrumque mirum est: hoc tamen mirum magis,	412	Lucus 11	2
Vnusquisque hominum, Terra est; & filius arui.	413	Lucus 18	1
Morosus, oxygala est: leuis, coagulum.	414	Lucus 20	15
Non tantum est iter Angelis ad vndas,	415	Lucus 24	11
Romano, sed res seria Roma tibi est:	416	Lucus 27	2
Pontificem tandem nacta est sibi Roma poetam:	417	Lucus 28	1
Ira facit, mundusque ipse est apotheca furoris.	418	Tr.Mortis	17
Imperij hic culmen figo: mortalibus actum est	421	Tr.Mortis	100
Si licet, immoriar: vel si tua visio vita est,	421	Lucus 35	5
Non video, certum est iurare; aut si hoc vetuisti,	421	Lucus 35	9
Et quicquid vspiam est seuerae foeminae,	422	Mem.Matr.2	2

EST (cont'd)	PAGE	TITLE	LINE
Aut si negotio hora sumenda est, rei	423	Mem.Matr.2	32
Quo nunc recumbis, scriptio merita est tua,	423	Mem.Matr.2	40
Pactoli arena tibi tumulus est vnicus.	423	Mem.Matr.2	41
Mulcensque dotes caeteras visa est quasi	423	Mem.Matr.2	43
Mihine matris vrna clausa est vnico,	424	Mem.Matr.2	57
Scilicet id splendes: haec est tibi causa micandi,	424	Mem.Matr.3	5
Nec grauidis medicina tuta est.	426	Mem.Matr.6	20
Irregularis nunc habitus mihi est:	426	Mem.Matr.6	21
Quod tu febrem censes, salubre est	426	Mem.Matr.6	23
Ridenti lacrymas quibus vnis concolor vnda est.	426	Mem.Matr.7	6
Est mihi bis quinis laqueata domuncula tignis	426	Mem.Matr.7	22
Nosse sui quid agant, quaedam est quoque musica sanctis,	427	Mem.Matr.9	3
Ecce solutura est, ventos causata morantes:	427	Mem.Matr.9	9
Non est angulus vspiam serenus,	428	Mem.Matr.10	13
In mea dicta ruant; non tam mihi pendula mens est,	432	Poem.Lat.	5
Aut cita mors est danda bonis aut longa senectus:	432	Poem.Lat.	30
Quid non mutatum est? requierunt flumina cursus;	433	Poem.Lat.	43
Numne Hydra talis, tantane bellua est	433	Poem.Lat.	9
Cui tenuis fama est, ingeniumque minus.	435	Poem.Lat.	4
Quid mihi si facies nigra est? hoc, Ceste, colore	437	Poem.Lat.	1
Nec hoc abunde est tibi, nisi certae Anchorae	438	Poem.Lat.	5
(In quo fas nihil est rumpi) donare sigillum.	439	Poem.Lat.	15
En Aurora vocat, lectus genialis in aula est,	210	Cam.1613-b BR	1
Philosophiam expugnare nouimus, quicquid hilare est, laetum,	440	Orationes	12
cuius ingens gloria aeque rotunda est atque ipse orbis:	440	Orationes	16
Et quod obseruatione cum primis dignum est, quo magis amore	440	Orationes	21
Iacobus tutelaris Diuus est vtrique nostrum;	440	Orationes	23
Necesse est autem vt foelicitas tantorum Principum etiam in ministros	441	Orationes	5
eruditionem, quae tanta est vt, nisi Rex esses in ciuili Republica,	443	Orationes	18
nostra occurrant, oratio nostra est silentium, atque eloquentia,	444	Orationes	2
retulisset captus piscis, foelicissimus mortalium habitus est.	444	Orationes	16
vestra est optio, vestra disquisitio, qui tineae estis & helluones	445	Orationes	18
hoc ipsum iter, quod nuper emensus est, vt sciatis omnes quam nude,	445	Orationes	34
Ego vero non dicam vobis quod factum est ante seculum vestrum,	445	Orationes	38
homo est, non statua; Sceptriger, non sceptrum:	446	Orationes	10
aequumne est vt tot labores & sollicitudines Principum sine	446	Orationes	11
Deus ipse cum crearet hominem, mundi regem, consilio vsus est.	446	Orationes	37
qua in re celebris est Gracchorum mater, ingenium ipsum atque indoles	447	Orationes	17
ipse profectus est, vt ingenti labore suo & periculo consuleret	447	Orationes	24
certe fatendum est, anteferendam bello pacem, sine qua omnis vita	448	Orationes	7
pace, securitas in agris est;	448	Orationes	10
pax adeo Musis summe necessaria est, vt sine ea nihil simus.	448	Orationes	17
delicata res est eruditio & tenera, tanquam flos molliculus rudiore	448	Orationes	24
incubat artibus, & obstetricatur, minus quam par est, aestimemus.	448	Orationes	34
illic tuta cognitio est, atque extra teli iactum.	449	Orationes	3
Quam cruenta gloria est, quae super ceruicibus hominum erigitur?	449	Orationes	10
vbi in dubio est, qui facit, an qui patitur, miserior.	449	Orationes	11
vbi velut ex continentibus tectis ad nos traiecturum est incendium:	449	Orationes	14
Sed non est nostri bellum indicere:	449	Orationes	16
Omne regnum suo Principi carcer est, aut si excedat, alienum:	450	Orationes	12
at Noster difficultatem superans, fructum consecutus est:	450	Orationes	14
Catonianum praeceptum est: Vicini quo pacto niteant, id animum	450	Orationes	16
adde quod angusti est animi aut superbi sua tantum nosse,	450	Orationes	17
etenim abundantia morosa est & sternax, vnde diuites syluas ac saltus	450	Orationes	20
alienas tantum ex hoc itinere cognouit Respublicas sed quod plus est,	450	Orationes	33
annon eius consilio res gesta est?	451	Orationes	24
at IACOBVS a nobis est:	451	Orationes	26
omnia Danorum expiscatus consilia, victoriam celebrem consecutus est.	453	Orationes	7
Notissimus est Codri amor, cuius manifestationem in gentem suam	453	Orationes	7
est etiam interdum satietas quaedam honoris, quem ad tempus deponere	453	Orationes	9
In picturis locus est vmbris & recessibus, etiam si quis Principem	453	Orationes	14
Quamobrem non est mirandum, si Reges ipsi quandoque suauitates suas	453	Orationes	18
idem feruor qui impar sub amoris signo meritus est, ad vera castra	453	Orationes	30
qui nuper versatus est in forma & figuris vultus, vbi res postulat,	454	Orationes	7
non est tanti respondere latratibus maleuolorum;	454	Orationes	16
Hilaris haec sumenda est dies.	454	Orationes	23
relabitur in terram, qua ortus est, eique cum foecundia remuneratur:	454	Orationes	30
abijcite quisque libros, non est locus grauitati, neque apud vos:	454	Orationes	34
satis virtuti datum est, satis Reipublicae.	455	Orationes	6
deperijt, at illa mutata est in arborem triumphantium propriam:	455	Orationes	9
an inter lauros principis hederae nostrae ambitiosae locus est?	456	Epistolae	4
haec est ansa qua prehendimus Te, et tanquam Aquilam inter nouas	456	Epistolae	5
mutus est mundus vniuersus, vestra solum dextra (quamuis a scriptione	458	Epistolae	5
Hoc etiam imperium tenuius est quam pro amplitudine virtutum	458	Epistolae	10
hoc saltem solutio est; Nos nunc conspersi atramento regio,	459	Epistolae	4
Vnicus est nobis Bibliotheca Liber.	459	Epistolae	31
laetissime sumeret, quanto magis par est, nos humillimos subiectos,	460	Epistolae	12
tantae eruditionis nobis conscius est, palustri opere & vliginoso	461	Epistolae	7
cum non est tanti totus ille maritimus tractus (Oceani praeda	461	Epistolae	8
Quare multiplex est laetitia nostra:	463	Epistolae	20
nostrae, quae per Tuum Partum, ex Matre nunc Auia facta est:	463	Epistolae	26
Ea est enim pertinacia desideriorum nostrorum, atque immortalitas,	464	Epistolae	22
Magna est haec, neque quotidianae virtutis prouincia gerere personam	465	Epistolae	9
Certe non diu est ex quo gratulati sumus tibi:	465	Epistolae	23
Sic a Natura comparatum est, Ignis et Virtus semper ascendunt,	466	Epistolae	10
in quo paucorum auaritia liberalibus artibus dominatura est,	467	Epistolae	1
legibus et hominum summe contraria est) monopolijs quibusdam inhiare,	467	Epistolae	6
alijs (tanquam montes olim) imponerentur, verisimile est, eos illuc,	468	Epistolae	1
Iam vero miserum est, pecuniam retardare illam, cui natura spiritum	468	Epistolae	4
vendentibus Libros non ementibus, hoc est cessatoribus non studiosis.	468	Epistolae	8

EST (cont'd)	PAGE	TITLE	LINE
eadem manus et tuum tibi largita est honorem, et priuilegia nostra	468	Epistolae	23
non est quod nostram quoque, cum amoris symbolo festinantem,	469	Epistolae	15
quae est vestra felicitas qui puro Academiae farre vtimini.	470	Epistolae	2
ni graue est, librum tibi Oratorium lampademque tradat.	470	Epistolae	9
Academia vniuersim sumpta vna est e proceribus, inter patritios	470	Epistolae	24
Oratio perfecta, vti vir, tetragonos est, grauis, nobilis,	471	Epistolae	4
Et amor aliogui loquax est;	471	Epistolae	7
EST'			
Nou d' autou taphos est' aster: pheggos gar ekeinou	429	Mem.Matr.14	3
ESTI			
Sophronon esti me perimenein, ote polemein umin omologesei,	449	Orationes	14
proeleluthoton, en kai emas isos deesei poreuesthai, poia tis esti.	471	Epistolae	11
ESTIS			
vestra disquisitio, qui tineae estis & helluones chartacei;	445	Orationes	18
ESTO			
Magnas es; esto. Bulla si vocaberis,	413	Lucus 17	1
Alteraque haec tua mors, Ilias esto mihi.	428	Mem.Matr.11	14
esto autem hoc ipsum iter, quod nuper emensus est, vt sciatis omnes	445	Orationes	33
tu hanc personam indue scripturus, tuumque iudicium tibi Lictor esto.	470	Epistolae	27
&			
IACOBO, D. G. Magnae Britanniae, Franciae, & Hiberniae	384	Musae	T
Illustriss. Celsissimoque CAROLO, Walliae, & Iuventutis Principi.	384	Musae	T
Constet, & ex illa pendeat orbis ope;	385	Musae 1	2
Ipse pios laudo; Numen & ipse colo.	386	Musae 4	6
Te contumaci & liuido?	388	Musae 8	10
Forsitan & prohibes infans portetur ad vndas,	388	Musae 9	7
O vere dictum, & belle! cum torqueat omnes	389	Musae 11	3
Displicet, & laudis tura litare Deo.	389	Musae 12	2
Spiritus proponit, & est vtrique	390	Musae 14	15
Dum suum nomen tenet, & triumphat	390	Musae 14	19
Scilicet Hebraeam cantas, & perstrepis vnam:	391	Musae 16	5
Torquet, & in Textu Doctor vtroque cluet.	392	Musae 19	6
Magicos rotatus, & perhorridas Striges,	392	Musae 20	12
Rupes tenaces & silices ferunt	393	Musae 23	9
prorsus Daemoni & hostibus	395	Musae 25	14
sed nudis & egentibus	396	Musae 25	22
Annulus & plenus tempore forsan erit.	396	Musae 26	6
Sin nebulis parcas, & nostro parcito signo,	396	Musae 26	7
De Mundis & mundanis.	396	Musae 27	T
Sic ex profano Cosmico & Catharo potest	396	Musae 27	3
Erumpit inde, & contineri nescius	398	Musae 32	7
Quo magis inuidiam nobis & crimina confles,	398	Musae 33	1
Inde Patres pergunt quadrati, & tota Vetustas.	398	Musae 33	13
Hipponensis adest properans, & torquet in hostes	398	Musae 33	17
Militat & nobis, quem vos contemnitis, Ordo;	399	Musae 33	27
Musarum calices, per & beatos	400	Musae 37	3
Explicat, & radijs ipsum pertingit Olympum!	401	Musae 39	7
Vicini populi passim mirantur, & aequos	401	Musae 39	8
Tu Synodosque, Patresque, & quod dedit alta vetustas	402	Musae 39	25
Sint tibi vel stellis laudes, & laudibus anni:	402	Musae 39	34
Vis, & vena sacris regnat in artubus;	403	Musae 40	8
Quod scribo, & placeo, si placeo, tuum est.	403	Musae 40	14
Impar, & in fletum vel resolutus, ero;	404	Passio 1	2
In Sputum & Conuicia.	404	Passio 5	T
Qui Caput es, spinas & tua Membra tuas.	405	Passio 6	4
Viuat, & in mortem vita sit illa tuam.	405	Passio 7	10
Ah! quam caederis hinc & inde palmis!	405	Passio 8	1
Christe, flagellati spes & victoria mundi,	406	Passio 9	1
Crimina cum turgent, & mea poena prope est,	406	Passio 9	2
Nobis facilitas cedat & tibi sudor.	406	Passio 12	3
Quid hoc? & ipse deficis, Caeli gigas,	407	Passio 16	1
Tibi supererunt & mihi.	407	Passio 16	14
Asserit & vitam Mors animata tuam.	407	Passio 17	4
Structorem, & Solomon vbique regnet.	408	Passio 19	8
Omnia, praeter corda, scelus confregit & error,	409	Passio 20	7
Piscis tributum soluit; & tu Caesari:	412	Lucus 11	1
Excutite aulaea, & luceat igne focus.	413	Lucus 15	2
Largiar & istud: scilicet Magnatibus	413	Lucus 17	2
Quin, mitte nugas; teque carnem & sanguinem	413	Lucus 17	5
Vnusquisque hominum, Terra est; & filius arui.	413	Lucus 18	1
Dum prono rapis ore cibos, & fercula verris,	414	Lucus 21	1
Os & lingua tibi diues, egena manus:	414	Lucus 22	2
Cur lacrymas & tarda trahis suspiria, tanquam	415	Lucus 23	1
Siste tuum fletum & gemitus: namque imbribus istis	415	Lucus 23	13
Atque ipsi sibi sunt mola & farina.	415	Lucus 24	15
A veteri trunco & nobilitate cadit.	416	Lucus 25	6
Laus antiqua & honor perijt: quasi scilicet ARMO	416	Lucus 25	7
Laus antiqua & honor perierunt, te velut ARMO	416	Lucus 25 V	7
Inuertis, mores carpis & obloqueris:	416	Lucus 26	2
Te Germana tamen pubes, te Graecus & Anglus	416	Lucus 26	3
Quam satur & suauis sit tibi Roma iocus.	416	Lucus 27	6
Conueniunt; & Homo viua fit Ara Dei.	417	Lucus 29	4
Quo se condat & implicet volutans	417	Lucus 30	6
Ceu fida statione & arce certa,	417	Lucus 30	7
Debetur Caelo lumen, & vmbra solo:	417	Lucus 31	2
Sic Hominis moles animaque & corpore constat,	417	Lucus 31	3
Glans dedit, & truncus tectum, & ramalia mortem.	418	Tr.Mortis	8
Coeperat, agricolis mentemque & aratra solutis:	418	Tr.Mortis	10
Fictaque Bellona & verae ludibria pugnae,	418	Tr.Mortis	27
Artificesque necis clueant, & mortis alumni.	418	Tr.Mortis	30

& (cont'd)

	PAGE	TITLE		LINE
Nempe & millenos ad palum interficit hostes	418	Tr.Mortis		31
Expleri nequit, & totum depascitur Orbem.	419	Tr.Mortis		38
Balistasque Onagrosque & quicquid Scorpio saeuus	419	Tr.Mortis		40
Adde etiam currus, & cum temone Britanno	419	Tr.Mortis		45
Quin Aries ruit, & multa Demetrius arte:	419	Tr.Mortis		47
Plumbis obsignata, colosque & stamina vitae	419	Tr.Mortis		64
Pulueris inferni; properat datus ignis, & omnem	420	Tr.Mortis		69
Pulueris inferni properat, datur ignis, & omnem	420	Tr.Mortis	V	69
Tisiphone; flamma & fallaci fulmine cincta	420	Tr.Mortis		71
It stridor, caelosque omnes & Tartara findit.	420	Tr.Mortis		73
Ingemit, & defessus opem iam Portitor orat.	420	Tr.Mortis		82
Triste colens cellae, noctuque & Daemone plenum,	420	Tr.Mortis		90
Triste colens sellae, noctuque & Daemone plenum,	420	Tr.Mortis	V	90
Quis Monachos mortem meditari, & puluere tristi	420	Tr.Mortis		92
Tormento peior Iesuita, & fulminat Orbem,	420	Tr.Mortis		96
Alapas nec Arietes? Quid ergo? Agnum & Crucem.	421	Lucus 33		6
Christe, decus, dulcedo, & centum circiter Hyblae,	421	Lucus 35		1
Mater: & ista Dolor nunc tibi Metra parit.	422	Mem.Matr.1		8
Vestrasque laudes, poscit & mixtas genas.	422	Mem.Matr.2		4
Decus mulierum perijt: & metuunt viri	422	Mem.Matr.2		8
Substructionem capitis & nimbum breuem,	422	Mem.Matr.2		15
Adorta numen acri & ignea prece.	422	Mem.Matr.2		17
Dein familiam lustrat, & res prandij,	422	Mem.Matr.2		18
Suum cuique tempus & locus datur.	423	Mem.Matr.2		20
Ratione certa vita constat & domus,	423	Mem.Matr.2		22
Tota renident aede decus & suauitas	423	Mem.Matr.2		24
Surrexit vna & illa, seseque extulit:	423	Mem.Matr.2		27
Occasione certat, imo & obtinet.	423	Mem.Matr.2		28
Loquitur numellas, compedes & retia:	423	Mem.Matr.2		31
Per angiportus & maeandros labitur,	423	Mem.Matr.2		33
Caelique referunt & praeoccupant modum.	423	Mem.Matr.2		49
Solum dolores, & dolores, stellulae.	423	Mem.Matr.2		51
Implicet, & matrem, matre manente, petam.	424	Mem.Matr.3		10
Materni decus, & debita nominis,	424	Mem.Matr.4		6
Terram & funus olent flores: Dominaeque cadauer	425	Mem.Matr.5		5
Mutata? & pro matre mihi phantasma dolosum	426	Mem.Matr.7		3
Hunc vultum ostendas, & tecum, nobile spectrum,	426	Mem.Matr.7		14
Sit quasi fasciculus crescens, & nidus odorum.	427	Mem.Matr.7		27
Hinc fremere totus & minari gestio	427	Mem.Matr.8		5
Nam te nunc Ager, Vrbs, & Aula plorant:	428	Mem.Matr.10		8
Arbor & ipse inuersa vocer: dumque insitus almae	428	Mem.Matr.11		5
Lubricus, & superans mobilitate salum.	428	Mem.Matr.11		8
Dissutus videor funere & ipse tuo.	428	Mem.Matr.11		12
Hic sita foeminei laus & victoria sexus:	429	Mem.Matr.13		1
Magnatumque inopumque aequum certamen & ardor:	429	Mem.Matr.13		3
Quicquid habet tellus, quicquid & astra, fruens.	429	Mem.Matr.13		6
Musa, vale, & tu Phoebe; dolor mea carmina dictet;	432	Poem.Lat.		12
Iam foelix Philomela, & menti conscia Dido!	432	Poem.Lat.		22
Foelices, quos bella premunt, & plurimus ensis!	432	Poem.Lat.		23
Fataque Fortunasque & spem laesere futuram.	432	Poem.Lat.		25
Debuit ista pati prima & non nobilis aetas:	432	Poem.Lat.		29
Sic lactare animos & sic ostendere gemmam	432	Poem.Lat.		31
Excitat optatus auidos, & ventilat ignem.	432	Poem.Lat.		32
In vitam & neruos Pascha coaeua fluet.	434	Poem.Lat.		10
Quod calamum excusent Pontus & Astra meum:	435	Poem.Lat.		8
Inductionis Dominus, & Verulamij;	436	Poem.Lat.		4
Promus; Fugator Idolorum & nubium;	436	Poem.Lat.	V	12
Rationis & sensus stupendus Arbiter;	436	Poem.Lat.		16
Rationis & sensus peritus Arbiter;	436	Poem.Lat.	V	16
Mundique & Animarum sacerdos vnicus;	436	Poem.Lat.		24
Claude oculos, & erunt omnia nigra tibi:	437	Poem.Lat.		6
Aut aperi, & cernes corpus quas proijcit vmbras;	437	Poem.Lat.		7
Aut aperi, & cernis corpus quas proijcit vmbras;	437	Poem.Lat.	V	7
Tibi debet Vnda & Terra certitudinis.	438	Poem.Lat.		7
Tot & tanta loquens amica, scripsit:	439	Poem.Lat.		11
Tandem & fessa manus, dedit sigillum.	439	Poem.Lat.		12
tandem Magistri Artium, & quidem omnium Aulicarum, Militarium,	440	Orationes		5
in potestatem redigere, lenioresque aspectus, & dulciores assumatis;	440	Orationes		10
& supercilium quibus caperatam seuerioremque Philosophiam expugnare	440	Orationes		11
Quin & Serenissimae Principis Isabellae laudes, virtutesque,	441	Orationes		2
cum tanti sitis & in Principibus Vestris, & in vobismetipsis,	441	Orationes		8
in Principibus Vestris, & in vobismetipsis, veremur ne nihil hic sit,	441	Orationes		9
Quinimo Artes hic sunt quiete & silentio cultae, tranquillitas,	441	Orationes		14
contemnere has gloriolas nostras quas e chartis & puluere eruimus.	441	Orationes		17
viam aperiens & methodum in studijs adhibendam, etiam libros indicans	443	Orationes		24
& ipsum accepimus saluum & annulum, annulum Coniugalem,	444	Orationes		18
& in rebus humanis diuinisque exercitatissimi, de integro	444	Orationes		20
& cum eo vita nostra atque calor, longo animi deliquio fugitiuus ac	444	Orationes		22
vestra disquisitio, qui tineae estis & helluones chartacei;	445	Orationes		18
ulomanian illam & inanem verborum strepitum iamdudum deposui:	445	Orationes		22
bullae & crepitacula puerorum sunt, aut eorum certe, qui cymbala sunt	445	Orationes		23
ego vero sentio, & quis sum ipse (barbam, hui, tam grauem) & apud	445	Orationes		25
tam grauem) & apud quos dico, viros limatae auris atque tersae,	445	Orationes		26
agam vobiscum, simulque & laboribus meis, & vestrae fidei consulam,	445	Orationes		28
& vestrae fidei consulam, quemadmodum artifices non omnes	445	Orationes		29
sic & ipse excerpam e Principis rebus gestis pugillum, vnam actionem	445	Orationes		31
finesque multiplices & polymiti, vt si minus id assequantur,	446	Orationes		5
Quare & Principis iter multiplicem nobis exhibet prudentiam;	446	Orationes		7
aequumne est vt tot labores & sollicitudines Principum sine	446	Orationes		11
& Licurgus magnus Legislator atimian prosetheke tois agamois.	446	Orationes		20

& (cont'd)

	PAGE	TITLE	LINE
quod pereleganter & supra barbariem seculi innuebant Maiores nostri,	446	Orationes	28
glasto se inficientes, in vxorum corporibus, Solem, Lunam, & Stellas;	446	Orationes	31
ita Sol & Coelum producunt flores, qui symbola sunt spei, . .	446	Orationes	32
Quare operosior in eo structura, & praerogatiuae regiae emicant.	446	Orationes	37
soli caput rotundum & coeleste, soli facies tanquam vestibulum magni	447	Orationes	1
capiti & faciei coronam, significantes oportere Reges ijs partibus	447	Orationes	3
homines, quibus homo bruta, iustitia scilicet & prudentia. . .	447	Orationes	5
Koning, & contracte King, a Con verbo deduci, quod tria complectitur,	447	Orationes	6
cernitis Regem & nomine & re magnum quid polliceri, ideoque ex	447	Orationes	8
vt ingenti labore suo & periculo consuleret & praesenti Reipublicae	447	Orationes	24
labore suo & periculo consuleret & praesenti Reipublicae & futurae;	447	Orationes	24
labore suo & periculo consuleret & praesenti Reipublicae & futurae;	447	Orationes	25
neque vnius seculi Princeps, sed & omnium, quae ventura sunt,	447	Orationes	26
tot iam annis impune fruimur, hoc pacto fundatam cupit & perpetuam;	447	Orationes	29
Scio Belli nomen splendidum esse & gloriosum:	447	Orationes	33
triumphos & victorias quasi fraena ferox spumantia mandit, . .	447	Orationes	34
ferox spumantia mandit, iuuat micare gladio & mucronem intueri.	447	Orationes	35
bello pacem, sine qua omnis vita procella, & mundus solitudo.	448	Orationes	8
quando ipsae hae turres & beatae fabricae, vnico ictu sulphurei tubi,	448	Orationes	20
delicata res est eruditio & tenera, tanquam flos molliculus rudiore	448	Orationes	24
causaris, irruit Miles in Musaeum tuum, & gladio te liberat.	448	Orationes	28
dum globos tractas & coelos fictitios, perrumpit primipilus,	448	Orationes	29
perrumpit primipilus, & te cum coelis tuis ad inferos deturbat.	448	Orationes	30
quae sola incubat artibus, & obstetricatur, minus quam par est,	448	Orationes	33
aut tanquam oues taedulae & fastidiosae, cibum respuamus. . .	449	Orationes	1
pariter & nos consilia regia, tanquam gurgitem imperuestigabilem,	449	Orationes	22
cum futura incerta sint, & nullis perspicillis, ne Belgicis quidem,	449	Orationes	24
consilia nostra, absconduntur Diuina & Regia, praecipue pharetrata,	449	Orationes	27
praecipue pharetrata, quae ad poenam gentium & Bellum spectant.	449	Orationes	28
Sunt tamen acuti quidam & emuncti, qui omnia praeuident: . .	449	Orationes	28
etiam & scientiae augmentum ex hoc itinere captauit solertissimus	450	Orationes	5
etenim abundantia morosa est & sternax, vnde diuites syluas ac saltus	450	Orationes	20
ipse egit oratorem, vt & ego aliquantulum hoc nomine glorier.	450	Orationes	31
Dij te perdant, cum malis tuis & arena sine calce; . . .	451	Orationes	5
huiusmodi lamentis & quiritationibus plena erant fora, nundinae,	451	Orationes	9
ipsum coelum nubilum semper, & poeta stultus qui dixerat, . .	451	Orationes	18
Scio Hispanum versutum, callidum, artis & aucupij apprime gnarum:	451	Orationes	25
hic ego me erexi & de dolore remisi plurimum, de desiderio nihil.	451	Orationes	26
in Principibus virtus, & cui cum sceptro lites saepius intercedunt?	452	Orationes	2
Dies me deficeret (& quidem nox aptior esset tali historiae)	452	Orationes	20
optime consuluisse Deum orbi terrarum lapides & metalla ei inserendo,	452	Orationes	25
agxonais abiectis, iter aggreditur & labores, haud ignarus, . .	452	Orationes	32
ventilat, & adulatores, qui semper titillant aures Principum,	453	Orationes	2
manifestationem in gentem suam priuatae personae & habitui debuit.	453	Orationes	8
quin & venti imperant pelago, vt laeuitatem illam aequabilem atque	453	Orationes	13
In picturis locus est vmbris & recessibus, etiam si quis Principem	453	Orationes	14
quod sane adeo nobile fuit & honorificum, vt nihil habeat Inuidia	453	Orationes	23
tamen anus illa querula, & philegklemon, quam audire videor dicentem,	453	Orationes	25
quam audire videor dicentem, Pulchrum quidem iter & Amante dignum;	453	Orationes	26
eadem acies & stipulam secat & lignum:	453	Orationes	28
eadem acies & stipulam secat & lignum:	453	Orationes	29
occurrit ei Democritus, & ingenium admirans, domum secum duxit,	453	Orationes	35
& ingenium admirans, domum secum duxit, & erudiuit artibus; . .	453	Orationes	36
e baiulo euasit Philosophus, eodem ingenio vsus in lignis & literis:	453	Orationes	38
quis scit an & amoris onus scite vinctum ligatumque, & per tot	453	Orationes	38
& per tot milliaria facile transmissum, mentem maiorum capacem	454	Orationes	1
inter quas & Mathematicae, quae licet versentur in figuris . .	454	Orationes	3
qui nuper versatus est in forma & figuris vultus, vbi res postulat,	454	Orationes	7
Verum mittamus inuidos & inuidiam, quae semper se deuorat primum,	454	Orationes	14
& plus iusto celebres, cum leunculum & dominum suum contra naturam	454	Orationes	17
cum leunculum & dominum suum contra naturam adoriantur: . .	454	Orationes	18
sic & Noster qui clanculum exijt, vsque ad Pyrenaeas nubes . .	454	Orationes	30
Delphino reuectum excepere arbores tripudiantes, & Vos statis?	454	Orationes	37
vtinam & nunc sit tanta patriae tenacitas, vt nunquam Princeps se	455	Orationes	5
Daphnen suam, cuius amor deinceps in triumphos & laurus mutabitur.	455	Orationes	11
& cum ipse sis in summa arbore altera manu prehendis Regem, . .	456	Epistolae	13
Quod si tam integrum tibi esset gratificari nobis in terra & aere,	457	Epistolae	22
quam in aqua & igne fecisti, non dubitamus quin benignitas tua omnia	457	Epistolae	22
Ecquid inter tantas mundi trepidationes nobis & Musis vacas?	458	Epistolae	2
vt vestrae coronae ciuili & literariae tertiam Coelestem sero	459	Epistolae	21
eruditionis nobis conscius est, palustri opere & vliginoso intercipi:	461	Epistolae	7
& quasi mixtam personam reddidit quam si Episcopi more pristino	461	Epistolae	26
viduae effoetae, aut ligna exucca & marcida, alumnis suis orbarentur,	462	Epistolae	4
& inter nouos honorum cumulos, quod expectamus indies futurum,	462	Epistolae	28
hominum Authoritate tua plurima & Eloquentia non minori nobis	463	Epistolae	2
Deus faueat Tibi & concedat vt terrestres tui honores cum coelestibus	465	Epistolae	18
sed tamen comparatio & in honorem tuum cedet, nostrumque emolumentum.	467	Epistolae	26
conuertissem, & ex altera parte acuissem me aspectu virtutum Tuarum;	472	Epistolae	6
Rhetoris in hunc annum, & in plures Oratoris, permitte, . .	472	Epistolae	26
vt quod Philosophus de Tactu & Visu, id apposite admodum huc	472	Epistolae	36
ET			
Et mea sint canis scripta referta tuis.	386	Musae 2	6
Et populi spurcas creditis esse vias:	387	Musae 5	8
Et vnus impar aestimatur viribus, ...	388	Musae 8	5
Et per se Templi limen adire velis:	388	Musae 9	8
Et tibi sit nemo praes, vbi poscis opem.	389	Musae 9	16
Et Christianus quisque piscis dicitur	389	Musae 10	6
Et partem capitis petit supremam;	391	Musae 15	4
Et, quos ipsa nequit scandere vertices, ...	391	Musae 17	9
Hos ad se trahere et mergere gestiens.	391	Musae 17	10

ET (cont'd)

	PAGE	TITLE	LINE
Et nunc perlongas Scripturae stamine telas	392	Musae 19	5
Et nos reducas ad lapides auos:	393	Musae 23	6
Et saxa diris hispida montibus	394	Musae 23	13
Et ipse Iordan sistit aquas stupens;	394	Musae 23	42
Et nullus audis? cantibus obstrepens,	395	Musae 23	46
Euentum Naso vidit et admonuit;	399	Musae 33	30
Et tibi vicinas porrigit aequor aquas:	399	Musae 35	8
(Et quem non stimularet haec simultas?)	400	Musae 37	18
Et Musa crepitante subruissem:	400	Musae 37	20
Et tu solus ad Angliae procellas	401	Musae 37	44
Accedis bene doctus, et poeta.	401	Musae 37	47
Et mea iam lacrymet culpa colore suo.	404	Passio 1	4
Et Templi parasite; namque velum	408	Passio 19	2
Et pomoeria terminosque sanctos	408	Passio 19	4
Et pro pectoribus recenset aras,	408	Passio 19	6
Et flexus fugientis appetitus.	411	Lucus 5	14
Et quae corrumpit moenia, murus aqua est.	411	Lucus 6	6
Et quid tu tandem desidiosus? AMO.	413	Lucus 16	6
Et flatulentas aucupatur glorias,	414	Lucus 20	2
Et numerat mortes singula gutta pares;	415	Lucus 23	10
Et ni lumina ianuam resignent,	415	Lucus 24	4
Et nostrae tribuant molae farinam,	415	Lucus 24	5
Et cum sublata laude recedit AMOR.	416	Lucus 25	12
Et hoc indicium subis, Redemptor?	417	Lucus 30	2
Tamque aries ruit et multa Demetrius arte,	271	Tr.Mortis VS	47
Sulphuris inferni, properat datus ignis et omnem	271	Tr.Mortis VS	69
It stridor, caelosque omnes et sydera findit.	271	Tr.Mortis VS	73
Quis mortem Monachos meditari, et puluere tristi	272	Tr.Mortis VS	92
Et ius pectoris inde consecutus	421	Lucus 34	5
Et quicquid vspiam est seuerae foeminae,	422	Mem.Matr.2	2
Et lucro appcnis gaudia sancta tuo.	424	Mem.Matr.3	6
Et maestum nimio madore Caelum	428	Mem.Matr.10	2
Et patrio regno (sub quo iam Principe nobis	432	Poem.Lat.	27
In Natales et Pascha Concurrentes.	434	Poem.Lat.	T
Comparatio inter Munus Summi Cancellariatus et Librum.	435	Poem.Lat.	T
Et melius coelum, te veniente, subest:	210	Cam.1613-a BR	4
Et coelum vultus exhilarato tui,	211	Cam.1613-b BR	8
Et tu gemma etiam Britonum, Septentrionum	211	Cam.1613-b BR	11
Et quod obseruatione cum primis dignum est, quo magis amore	440	Orationes	21
sed etiam doceas tanquam communis defensor fidei et Academiae,	443	Orationes	23
omnes ad Aulam, atque ab eo consilium peteremus a quo et fortunas?	443	Orationes	28
Hoc vno Rex et populus dissentimus.	444	Orationes	1
et tanquam Aquilam inter nouas honorum nubes e conspectu nostro	456	Epistolae	6
censemus nostram, et in honoribus Tuis nostro bono gratulamur;	456	Epistolae	16
inter quae etiam certamen oritur et pia contentio, vtrum gratia	456	Epistolae	20
aut Tuae virtutes et vota nostra et Principis gratiam superarent.	456	Epistolae	21
aut Tuae virtutes et vota nostra et Principis gratiam superarent.	456	Epistolae	22
hinc a populo, illinc a Principe, in Te conueniunt, et confabulantur.	456	Epistolae	25
2. Ad R. Naunton Gratiae de Fluuio et de tegendis Tectis stramineis	457	Epistolae	T
tuosque fauores temporibus et diligentia diuisos in gratijs nostris	457	Epistolae	15
incomparabilem, quae eodem vultu et moderatur mundum et nos respicit.	458	Epistolae	4
istis sublimitate solij asserta) vita et actione orbem vegetat.	458	Epistolae	7
Ipse scribendo irrupisti in compensationes nostras, et abstulisti:	459	Epistolae	2
nihil non sublime et excelsum cogitabimus, perrumpemus controuersias	459	Epistolae	5
extra mortalitatis aleam, et quo magis Tuum agnoscas, in ipso partu,	459	Epistolae	11
maritimus tractus (Oceani praeda et deliciae) vt irrigui Musarum	461	Epistolae	9
anni huius derisit incoeptum et plus effecit quam mille Redemptores	461	Epistolae	11
spiritus, generososque animos frangere et retundere clamitant.	461	Epistolae	20
doctrinae nitoremque spirans purpuram et eruditionem miscuisti;	461	Epistolae	22
Quis enim sicca vbera et mammas arentes tam nobilis parentis aequo	461	Epistolae	32
et Xerxes istos, alterosque maris quasi Flagellatores expugnatos	462	Epistolae	8
qui lemas istas et festucas, Reipublicae oculo haerentes,	462	Epistolae	12
Scite et apposite fecisti Fluuium nostrum conseruans altero	462	Epistolae	18
vtrinque mirus es et exercitatissimus.	462	Epistolae	22
literatos, eosque cum tineis et blattis rixantes, exuens puluere,	462	Epistolae	26
et blattis rixantes, exuens puluere, in theatrum et lucem produxisti.	462	Epistolae	27
si qui alij exurgant promissores magnifici et hiantes, qui,	462	Epistolae	31
gremio solum (quod innuis) sed et ambabus vlnis osculisque ei aetati	463	Epistolae	7
quae fugerunt tot philosophos vmbra et otio diffluentes,	463	Epistolae	19
et quasi accolae Maiestatis, literaturae suae et vicinitati	463	Epistolae	22
quasi accolae Maiestatis, literaturae suae et vicinitati respondeant:	463	Epistolae	23
Et licet, quo proprior sis Regi, eo videaris nobis remotior,	464	Epistolae	16
merita tua ita ascensura, vt eorum vis et virtus ad nos descendat.	464	Epistolae	19
vt semper post nouas dignitates, alias tibi quaerant et moliantur.	464	Epistolae	24
omniumque Artium molem et pondus sustinere, sed perspectissimus tuus	465	Epistolae	10
vt terrestres tui honores cum coelestibus certent, et superentur.	465	Epistolae	19
quod si tertia detur et quarta, paratos nos habebis ad gratulationem,	465	Epistolae	25
vtriusque Reipublicae calculum et ciuilis et literariae adipiscaris.	466	Epistolae	1
nos chartis et aeternitate occupatos, temporarijs hisce negotiolis	466	Epistolae	5
omnia fauorum tuorum momenta apicesque perpensuris et compensaturis.	466	Epistolae	8
Ignis et Virtus semper ascendunt, vtriusque enim splendor et claritas	466	Epistolae	10
vtriusque enim splendor et claritas humilia loca deprecantur.	466	Epistolae	11
hospitium, et erga te propensius, haud vsquam forsitan reperias.	466	Epistolae	18
concede vt nos etiam benignitate alarum tuarum et virtute fruamur.	466	Epistolae	22
publicum spectantes (quae res et naturae legibus et hominum summe	467	Epistolae	5
(quae res et naturae legibus et hominum summe contraria est)	467	Epistolae	5
timemus Librorum precia auctum iri, et priuilegia nostra imminutum.	467	Epistolae	7
immunitates nostras aut commune literarum et literatorum commodum,	467	Epistolae	12
neque Studiosorum Sacculi, qui etiam nunc maeret et ingemiscit.	467	Epistolae	23
Quod si et numerus Scriptorum intumescat, et precium, quae abyssus	468	Epistolae	2

ET (cont'd)	PAGE	TITLE	LINE
et precium, quae abyssus crumenae tantos sumptus aequabit?	468	Epistolae	3
feracem gloriae, et coeleste ingenium quasi ad metalla damnari.	468	Epistolae	5
eadem manus et tuum tibi largita est honorem, et priuilegia nostra	468	Epistolae	23
et tuum tibi largita est honorem, et priuilegia nostra confirmauit;	468	Epistolae	24
in qua dextra et fide coniuncti, in caeteris haud diuellamur.	468	Epistolae	24
si oppidani nostri (more suo) Musarum iura et diplomata arrodant;	468	Epistolae	26
tuus amor et authoritas istos sorices nobis abigat.	469	Epistolae	1
Deus fortunet tibi hunc honorem, et faxit, vt tibi gloriae sit,	469	Epistolae	5
hausisse ab Antiquis, sed et ad Posteros transmissuri videantur.	469	Epistolae	13
Et cum ob perspicacitatem singularem iam olim Regi notam atque	469	Epistolae	19
Ego hic pultibus vescor et glande, more maiorum, multos iam annos	470	Epistolae	4
sumpta vna est e proceribus, inter patritios sedens et praetextatos.	470	Epistolae	24
Quare et Procancellarius Academiam simulans vel maximos magnatum	470	Epistolae	25
Tandem, ne et ipse peccem, breuis sit sermo, atque pressus.	470	Epistolae	31
Et amor alioqui loquax est;	471	Epistolae	7
ET'			
Ouk et' emen idias phules grapsantes arogon,	430	Mem.Matr.17	2
&C			
Regi, Fidei Defensori &c. Geo. Herbertus.	384	Musae	T
EPISCOPO VINTONIENSI, &c.	385	Musae	T
ETENIM			
A nobis etenim procul remoti	415	Lucus 24	7
Tantum etenim vestras (Parcae) non flectit habenas	433	Poem.Lat.	40
etenim abundantia morosa est & sternax, vnde diuites syluas ac saltus	450	Orationes	20
ETHNICI			
Parate situlas, Ethnici, lagenasque,	405	Passio 5	8
ETI			
Ouk eti ballomenes xarisin bebolemenai etor,	431	Mem.Matr.17	9
Ouk eti despoines glukerai meledoni trapheisai:	431	Mem.Matr.17	16
ETIAM			
Nostrae etiam Musae vile fuere lutum:	384	Musae	4
Nunc etiam teneras quo versus gratior aures	387	Musae 5	11
Ergo etiam Solem dicas, ignaue, superbum,	387	Musae 7	5
Haec etiam ad pugnam praesens, qua viuimus, aetas	399	Musae 33	21
Ipse etiam Christus coelo speculatus ab alto,	402	Musae 39	11
Nunc etiam Christum callidus aggrederis.	406	Passio 11	2
Hostibus haec etiam parcens imitatur Iesum.	416	Lucus 26	5
Adde etiam currus, & cum temone Britanno	419	Tr.Mortis	45
Nostra etiam paribus marcescant gaudia fatis.	427	Mem.Matr.7	34
Sed partem in scriptis etiam dum lacryma poscit,	428	Mem.Matr.9	17
Quare etiam nuper Pyrij de pulueris ictu	433	Poem.Lat.	33
Plus etiam veteres coelum videre remotum:	433	Poem.Lat.	44
Sunt etiam tenebrae, quas tamen optat amor.	437	Poem.Lat.	2
Tuque etiam Dapifer, quas fero, sume dapes:	210	Cam.1613-a BR	2
Et tu gemma etiam Britonum, Septentrionum	211	Cam.1613-b BR	11
nos etiam exuentes os illud, & supercilium quibus caperatam	440	Orationes	10
autem vt foelicitas tantorum Principum etiam in ministros redundet,	441	Orationes	6
sed etiam doceas tanquam communis defensor fidei et Academiae,	443	Orationes	22
sed etiam doceas, viam aperiens & methodum in studijs adhibendam,	443	Orationes	23
etiam libros indicans ad Theologiam expeditissimos, tanto ac tam	443	Orationes	24
suauissimus Princeps, verum etiam praesenti seculo, dum pacem,	447	Orationes	28
bello, etiam sani intereunt: pace, securitas in agris est;	448	Orationes	10
etiam lusco, nunquam intueri satis vel mirari possumus,	449	Orationes	35
etiam & scientiae augmentum ex hoc itinere captauit solertissimus	450	Orationes	5
Falleris, nusquam plura bona, cum etiam mala illic sint aurea:	451	Orationes	3
apud nos agri tantum sunt fertiles, illic etiam arenae.	451	Orationes	5
non tantum exteras regiones habuit perspectas, verum etiam suam?	452	Orationes	1
Quid si hic lateat etiam Temperantia, rara in Principibus virtus,	452	Orationes	1
est etiam interdum satietas quaedam honoris, quem ad tempus deponere	453	Orationes	9
locus est vmbris & recessibus, etiam si quis Principem pingat.	453	Orationes	15
aetate prouectior, etiam anus subsultans multum excitet pulueris:	454	Orationes	35
Noster etiam Princeps habuit Daphnen suam, cuius amor deinceps	455	Orationes	10
sic Tu etiam dignitates ab optimo Rege desumptas in vniuersam	456	Epistolae	11
inter quae etiam certamen oritur et pia contentio, vtrum gratia	456	Epistolae	19
Hoc etiam imperium tenuius est quam pro amplitudine virtutum	458	Epistolae	10
sed Tu vis etiam manibus teri, semotaque Maiestate, charta	458	Epistolae	19
etiam libros dederunt, sed non suos:	458	Epistolae	23
eorum gloriam conseruando nobis quae illi dederunt, etiam augendo;	458	Epistolae	26
ita inuoluit nos, vt etiam rependendi vias omnes praecludat.	458	Epistolae	28
non solum verba omnia, sed etiam cogitationes nostras exhauriunt.	460	Epistolae	3
alacrius illud impenderemus Doctrinae) beneficijs etiam obligasti.	460	Epistolae	6
cum olim gauderent Fluuijs, nunc etiam aquas, in quibus habitant,	460	Epistolae	8
illi etiam honores qui finitimi sunt, et quasi accolae Maiestatis,	463	Epistolae	22
quos profectus feceris in Sphaera Naturae, facias etiam in Gratiae:	464	Epistolae	3
quanto altius crescunt, tanto etiam altius agunt radices:	464	Epistolae	18
etiam Fluuium non minus de praeterito gratum, quam de futuro	465	Epistolae	6
Permitte vt nos etiam in praedam partemque tecum veniamus:	465	Epistolae	21
vt quando beneficia tua peruagantur Angliam, nos etiam inuisant:	466	Epistolae	17
concede vt nos etiam benignitate alarum tuarum et virtute fruamur.	466	Epistolae	22
suauiterque patefacta, nunc etiam laborantibus Musis succurrat.	467	Epistolae	3
Patronus noster es, etiam tacentibus nobis, quanto magis cum rogamus,	467	Epistolae	17
neque Studiosorum Sacculi, qui etiam nunc maeret et ingemiscit.	467	Epistolae	23
ad progressum doctrinae, hac etiam in parte nobis opituleris.	467	Epistolae	28
nec minus etiam Reipublicae, quam nunc pleno gradu ingrediens	468	Epistolae	18
Nos etiam haud minimam fauoris tui partem speramus, orantes	468	Epistolae	20
nostrae etiam Athenae artesque obscuris opificum artibus superari	469	Epistolae	3
dignissime praeficiaris Fisco, etiam Academiam in Thesauris habe:	469	Epistolae	21
vti etiam senectus, quam aetatem in hac palaestra consecutus mihi	471	Epistolae	8
qui etiam ferians nihil Tua perfectione dignum procudere possit.	471	Epistolae	23
hic etiam teneor, sed laxioribus vinculis, quaeque amor saepe	472	Epistolae	33

ETOR	PAGE	TITLE	LINE
Ouk eti ballomenes xarisin bebolemenai etor,	431	Mem.Matr.17	9
ETSI			
etsi tu qui scribis (vti quiuis priuatus) inferioris sis subsellij,	470	Epistolae	22
ETTETHEIS			
Seiriou ettetheis boulemasi, panta marainei.	431	Mem.Matr.17	20
EUASIT			
qui inde e baiulo euasit Philosophus, eodem ingenio vsus in lignis	453	Orationes	37
EUEHAS			
expectamus indies futurum, Almae Matris amorem tecum simul euehas.	462	Epistolae	30
EUEHENS			
Atque euehens, bonum facit faecundius,	412	Lucus 13	2
EUENTUM			
Euentum Naso vidit et admonuit;	399	Musae 33	30
EUERTAS			
Haeresis, euertas. Quid enim te fallere possit?	402	Musae 39	22
EUERTERE			
Cum Romam nequeas, quod aues, euertere, nomen	416	Lucus 26	1
EUGE			
Euge, perite omnes; nec posthac exeat vlla	425	Mem.Matr.5	11
EULOGIAI			
sun tei eulogiai scu prosepimetroumenei beabis Filium tuum	473	Epistolae	11
EUM			
quamlibet Magnum, modo detis eum in flore, in vagina, in herbescenti	445	Orationes	20
in terram hanc, incidit in coenum, quod innuebat eum hic mansurum:	455	Orationes	4
Obsecremus eum tantum vt permittat nostram hanc Inter victrices	455	Orationes	16
EUNDEM			
Ad eundem In Monstrum vocabuli Anti-Tami-Cami-Categoria.	386	Musae 3	T
Ad Eundem.	401	Musae 38	T
In eundem.	404	Passio 3	T
In eundem.	413	Lucus 18	T
eundemque retulisset captus piscis, foelicissimus mortalium habitus	444	Orationes	15
EUNDO			
Immemor antiqui mellis, eundo coquit.	398	Musae 33	20
EUNDUM			
Academiam simulans vel maximos magnatum inter eundum summouet:	470	Epistolae	26
EUNTIA			
Sed propere dextreque reduxit euntia sensus,	385	Musae	5
EUODIAN			
Kepou sunothon anthinen euodian,	430	Mem.Matr.15	12
EUOLAT			
Euolat, horrendumque ciet bacchata fragorem.	420	Tr.Mortis	72
EUOMEREM			
Totamque euomerem potenter iram	400	Musae 37	15
EUTE			
Autar axei megaloi kentoumenai: eute gar autai	431	Mem.Matr.17	10
EUTHENOUSES			
Ina metros euthenouses	430	Mem.Matr.16	10
EUULSA			
Durescunt proprijs euulsa corallia fundis,	410	Lucus 1	3
EX			
Constet, & ex illa pendeat orbis ope;	385	Musae 1	2
Quicquid ex vrna meliore ductum	390	Musae 14	5
Ex praelio vndae ignisque (si Physicis fides)	396	Musae 27	1
Sic ex profano Cosmico & Catharo potest	396	Musae 27	3
Excessit tener Orbis ex Ephebis,	408	Passio 19	11
Solem ex Oceano Veteres exurgere fingunt	412	Lucus 8	1
Saepe ex se nihil otiosa cudit.	415	Lucus 24	6
Nec tamen excludor: namque vna ex arbore vitam	418	Tr.Mortis	7
Pulchre renatam ex arbore mortua,	434	Poem.Lat.	34
Ex Veritate matre; Mellis alueus;	436	Poem.Lat.	23
Serenissimi Principis Caroli Reditum ex Hispanijs celebrauit Georgius	444	Orationes	T
an sudum, facile conijcitur ex coelo, ex garritu auium,	445	Orationes	6
facile conijcitur ex coelo, ex garritu auium, ex lapidum exhalatione:	445	Orationes	6
ideoque ex quolibet ligno, qualibet vxore non esse fingendum:	447	Orationes	9
praecipue vbi velut ex continentibus tectis ad nos traiecturum est	449	Orationes	13
etiam & scientiae augmentum ex hoc itinere captauit solertissimus	450	Orationes	5
quid enim vtilius quam ex obseruatione exterarum Legum ac morum,	450	Orationes	14
Neque alienas tantum ex hoc itinere cognouit Respublicas sed quod	450	Orationes	32
ex quo facile collectu erat, quantum deperimus te;	451	Orationes	28
Quare nunc vobis ex pede Herculem, ex itinere Principem metiri licet,	453	Orationes	22
ex itinere Principem metiri licet, quod sane adeo nobile fuit	453	Orationes	22
Haec vestra spolia actosque ex orbe triumphos communicas cum Alma	458	Epistolae	16
vt ex affrictu Libri vestri hominem illico contundamus.	459	Epistolae	8
ex quo illustrius assecutus es nomen, quam Repertores Noui Orbis	463	Epistolae	11
nostrae, quae per Tuum Partum, ex Matre nunc Auia facta est:	463	Epistolae	25
illam nunc denuo ex aedibus Eboracensibus ab altero Cancellario	463	Epistolae	31
Certe non diu est ex quo gratulati sumus tibi:	465	Epistolae	23
ex quo timemus Librorum precia auctum iri, et priuilegia nostra	467	Epistolae	6
telam explices, perit negotium quasi ex nubibus Ixionis congressus.	470	Epistolae	30
o quot iam anni sunt ex quo vel apicem Latinum pertuli!	471	Epistolae	6
conuertissem, & ex altera parte acuissem me aspectu virtutum Tuarum;	472	Epistolae	6
ramenta quaepiam ex tanta Humanitatis massa, quae apud Te visitur,	472	Epistolae	13
Quod tamen haec omnia succedant ex voto, quod reclusae sint fores,	472	Epistolae	19
erectior solutiorque redibo, ex ipsa intermissione animos ducens.	473	Epistolae	3
EXAESTUET			
Tota stupent luctu) lachrymisque exaestuet aequis	432	Poem.Lat.	10
EXAGITATA			
Fluctibus internis exagitata natet,	389	Musae 12	4
EXAMINE			
Pensilis, atque acri dirimens Examine lites.	426	Mem.Matr.7	13

	PAGE	TITLE	LINE
EXANGUIS			
Pallida materni Genij atque exanguis imago,	426	Mem.Matr.7	1
EXANIMATA			
Sanguinis insultus exanimata ferunt.	406	Passio 13	4
EXARESCENTIUM			
qui restinxisti sitim exarescentium Musarum, et Xerxes istos,	462	Epistolae	8
EXAUDIRI			
Non iam exaudiri quicquam vel Musica caeli	420	Tr.Mortis	74
Non iam exaudiri quicquam, vel musica sphaerae	271	Tr.Mortis VS	74
EXCEDAT			
Omne regnum suo Principi carcer est, aut si excedat, alienum:	450	Orationes	13
EXCELLENTIAE			
nos tam defecimus in vtroque quam Excellentiae Vestrae abundant.	441	Orationes	13
paupertas perpetua, nisi vbi vestrae adsunt Excellentiae.	441	Orationes	16
EXCELLENTIAS			
Excellentias vestras tanto chariores esse, cum eo sitis ordine atque	440	Orationes	24
EXCELLENTIJS			
accessionem summe gratulantur Excellentijs Vestris Musae omnes,	440	Orationes	7
prius Excellentijs Vestris curae erit;	441	Orationes	20
EXCELLENTISSIMI			
Excellentissimi Magnificentissimi Domini, Post honores eximios,	440	Orationes	1
Quare Excellentissimi, Splendididissimi Domini, cum tanti sitis	441	Orationes	7
EXCELSA			
Sic excelsa humilisque simul loca dissita iunxit,	429	Mem.Matr.13	5
EXCELSAS			
Sionis excelsas ad arces	394	Musae 23	39
EXCELSUM			
nihil non sublime et excelsum cogitabimus, perrumpemus controuersias	459	Epistolae	5
EXCEPERE			
Arionem Delphino reuectum excepere arbores tripudiantes,	454	Orationes	37
EXCEPTOS			
Arguit, exceptos quos pia Roma fouet:	416	Lucus 26	4
EXCERPAM			
sic & ipse excerpam e Principis rebus gestis pugillum, vnam actionem	445	Orationes	31
EXCESSIT			
Excessit tener Orbis ex Ephebis,	408	Passio 19	11
EXCIDIT			
per vniuersam Britanniam, disparuit forma, Albion nomine excidit:	451	Orationes	18
EXCIPE			
ad prudentiae eloquentiaeque tuae praesidium festinantes excipe:	465	Epistolae	16
EXCIPIAT			
Qui tamen excipiat, Christus caret hospite: tantum	407	Passio 15	3
rudiorem esse impexioremque, quam vt tantum Hospitem excipiat:	463	Epistolae	29
EXCIPIEMUS			
ita excipiemus illa, vt benignius hospitium, et erga te propensius,	466	Epistolae	18
EXCIPIENTES			
sed et ambabus vlnis osculisque ei aetati debitis excipientes,	463	Epistolae	8
EXCIPIET			
Quis sic amicum excipiet, vt Cathari Deum,	397	Musae 28	13
EXCIPIS			
Hac ope munitus securior excipis vndas,	402	Musae 39	30
EXCITAT			
Excitat optatus auidos, & ventilat ignem.	432	Poem.Lat.	32
satietas quaedam honoris, quem ad tempus deponere famem excitat:	453	Orationes	10
EXCITATI			
qui primo caloris suasu excitati atque expergefacti, vbi sursum	471	Epistolae	29
EXCITET			
aetate prouectior, etiam anus subsultans multum excitet pulueris:	454	Orationes	36
EXCLAMANS			
Desinis exclamans: tota figura, vale.	401	Musae 38	2
EXCLUDI			
Hinc tamen excludi mors noluit, ipsaque vitam	271	Tr.Mortis VS	7
EXCLUDOR			
Nec tamen excludor: namque vna ex arbore vitam	418	Tr.Mortis	7
EXCLUSIS			
Sic pulsare tuas, exclusis luctibus, ausint	402	Musae 39	35
EXCORS			
Ergo ipse solum mutus atque excors ero	423	Mem.Matr.2	55
EXCUSENT			
Quod calamum excusent Pontus & Astra meum:	435	Poem.Lat.	8
EXCUSSIS			
Tuis, meis desiderijs probe cognitis, excussis perpensisque.	472	Epistolae	4
EXCUSSO			
cum excusso altero iugo, dimidiaque operis parte leuatus,	473	Epistolae	1
EXCUSSOS			
Excussos manibus calamos, falcemque resumptam	431	Mem.Matr.19	1
EXCUTITE			
Excutite aulaea, & luceat igne focus.	413	Lucus 15	2
percurrite Annales regnorum, excutite scrinia politiarum omnium;	445	Orationes	13
vos, vos, inquam, excutite, quorum aetas teritur in libris:	445	Orationes	14
EXEAT			
Euge, perite omnes; nec posthac exeat vlla	425	Mem.Matr.5	11
EXECRABITUR			
Machina, quam nullum satis execrabitur aeuum;	419	Tr.Mortis	50
EXEI			
Pheggode monon, os eikos, epaulin exei.	429	Mem.Matr.14	4
Otan nomeus agathon kuna exei, kai oi alloi nomeis boulontai plesion	447	Orationes	31
EXEMIT			
quem singularis doctrina exemit a populo, & quasi mixtam personam	461	Epistolae	26
EXEMPLO			
Exemploque tuo nascor in alterum:	425	Mem.Matr.4	14

EXEMPLO (cont'd)	PAGE	TITLE	LINE
virtutibus, tuo exemplo compensatis, ad vnum cmnes incumbamus.	468	Epistolae	16
EXEQUI			
incoeptum et plus effecit quam mille Redemptores exequi possent.	461	Epistolae	12
EXERCET			
Exercet miserum; non dolor vnguium	403	Musae 40	4
EXERCITATISSIMI			
& in rebus humanis diuinisque exercitatissimi, de integro	444	Orationes	21
EXERCITATISSIMUS			
vtrinque mirus es et exercitatissimus.	462	Epistolae	23
EXERE			
Exere terra caput, servatos projice flores,	210	Cam.1613-b BR	3
EXESAS			
Aiacis exesas triremes	433	Poem.Lat.	15
EXHALATIONE			
facile conijcitur ex coelo, ex garritu auium, ex lapidum exhalatione:	445	Orationes	7
EXHAURIUNT			
non solum verba omnia, sed etiam cogitationes nostras exhauriunt.	460	Epistolae	3
EXHIBES			
barbara omnia, Tu non nisi cultissima, elegantiasque ipsas exhibes.	463	Epistolae	15
EXHIBET			
Sola mihi plenos, ait, exhibet Anglia cultus.	402	Musae 39	13
Quare & Principis iter multiplicem nobis exhibet prudentiam;	446	Orationes	8
EXHILARANS			
soluens obstupefactos artus, atque exhilarans, tumentibus iam venis,	444	Orationes	28
EXHILARATO			
Et coelum vultus exhilarato tui,	211	Cam.1613-b BR	8
EXIGATUR			
Non exigatur crasis ad alterum.	426	Mem.Matr.6	22
EXIGITUR			
Sic aeuum exigitur tardum, dum praepetis anni	428	Mem.Matr.9	13
EXIGUAM			
post ingentes Hecatombas, exiguam thuris micam adoleri legimus.	469	Epistolae	17
EXIGUNTUR			
Inde exiguntur pensa crudo vespere.	423	Mem.Matr.2	21
EXIJT			
sic & Noster qui clanculum exijt, vsque ad Pyrenaeas nubes	454	Orationes	31
EXILIT			
Nec tamen hic noster stetit impetus: exilit omni	420	Tr.Mortis	95
Nec tamen hic mortis rabies stetit; exilit omni	272	Tr.Mortis VS	95
EXIMERE			
solebant ventres eximere, quos in arca repositos abijciebant	452	Orationes	27
EXIMIA			
Eximia tua in nos merita frequentiorem calamum postulant,	457	Epistolae	7
EXIMIE			
quippe qui eximie semper fouisti literatos, eosque cum tineis	462	Epistolae	25
Tam eximie de nobis meritus es, vt res nostras omnes cum Honore Tuo	465	Epistolae	2
EXIMIOS			
Domini, Post honores eximios, praefecturas insignes,	440	Orationes	2
EXIRE			
Quod si necesse sit iterum exire patria, qui nunc inuenit viam,	455	Orationes	7
EXISTIMANTES			
existimantes tuphlous einai pros oksu blepontas, anapodemetous pros	450	Orationes	8
EXISTIMAS			
Tu qui superbos caeteros existimas	388	Musae 8	15
EXISTIMEN			
vt aliquando existimen id egisse prudentissimum Patrem tuum,	451	Orationes	30
EXISTIMES			
notionum aequare nunquam potest, non voluntati tribuendum existimes.	460	Epistolae	18
sic existimes nihil Mortalium firmiori flagrare in Te desiderio,	473	Epistolae	4
EXLEX			
Vltra animus spatiatur exlex.	425	Mem.Matr.6	8
EXOLETAE			
Herbae exoletae, ros-marinus aridus?	424	Mem.Matr.2	58
EXORITUR			
Exoritur tubus, atque instar Cyclopis Homeri	419	Tr.Mortis	53
EXORNENT			
verrunt (ac si perdiderint ingenium) vt Spartam exornent suam:	445	Orationes	37
EXORTI			
sane exorti sunt nuperi quidam homines, qui libenter sapientiores nos	460	Epistolae	21
EXOSCULAMUR			
fouemus, exosculamur, hunc foetum vestrum, hunc alterum Carolum,	459	Epistolae	9
EXPECTAMUS			
Quod quidem non minus expectamus a Te, quem singularis doctrina	461	Epistolae	25
quod expectamus indies futurum, Almae Matris amorem tecum simul	462	Epistolae	28
EXPECTANTEM			
Pendulam hanc dignitatem diu expectantem magnas aliquas virtutes	464	Epistolae	11
EXPECTARE			
quanquam quem alium fructum potuimus expectare ab Eo, in quem fauor	456	Epistolae	18
EXPECTATIONI			
vt cedam aliquantisper expectationi hominum, rariusque paulo fodiam	472	Epistolae	28
EXPEDIET			
contineat se patria, cuius arctis amplexibus nunquam se expediet.	455	Orationes	2
Sed tua humanitas haec nobis expediet.	469	Epistolae	4
EXPEDITISSIMOS			
etiam libros indicans ad Theologiam expeditissimos, tanto ac tam	443	Orationes	25
EXPERGEFACIT			
pace, auium cantus expergefacit; bello, tubae ac tympana:	448	Orationes	11
EXPERGEFACTI			
qui primo caloris suasu excitati atque expergefacti, vbi sursum	471	Epistolae	29

	PAGE	TITLE	LINE
EXPERIENTIAE			
Aerarium; sequester experientiae,	436	Poem.Lat.	8
EXPERIRETUR			
quid priuata habeat in se vita commodi aut voluptatis, experiretur.	452	Orationes	38
EXPETO			
Expeto, tanquam haec sit nostri medicina doloris?	433	Poem.Lat.	46
EXPETUNT			
orbam ritibus expetunt,	395	Musae 25	10
EXPISCARI			
vt ego nihil vspiam laetum, nihil candidum expiscari possem;	451	Orationes	15
EXPISCATUS			
omnia Danorum expiscatus consilia, victoriam celebrem consecutus est.	453	Orationes	6
EXPLERI			
Expleri nequit, & totum depascitur Orbem.	419	Tr.Mortis	38
EXPLICABO			
vnicum hoc iter nuperum explicabo, in quo longe vberrimam gloriae	446	Orationes	1
EXPLICARE			
Angustior erat Scotia, quam vt pennas nido plene explicare posses:	458	Epistolae	9
EXPLICAT			
Explicat, & radijs ipsum pertingit Olympum!	401	Musae 39	7
EXPLICES			
nisi candida phrasi telam explices, perit negotium quasi ex nubibus	470	Epistolae	30
EXPLORAT			
hoc enim fastum amputat, affectus explorat, adulationem ventilat,	453	Orationes	1
EXPLORATOS			
Nunc enim exploratos habet nostros in se affectus, timores,	450	Orationes	34
EXPOLIANT			
Qui templa sacris expoliant choris,	394	Musae 23	18
EXPOLITIS			
creberrima Antiquitatis lectione tersis atque expolitis,	473	Epistolae	20
EXPONUNT			
exponunt superabilem.	395	Musae 25	15
EXPOSITAM			
promptitudinem amoris nostri, non passim expositam, boni consulas,	466	Epistolae	2
EXPOSITUS			
Nunc sorti pateo, expositus sine matre procellis,	428	Mem.Matr.11	7
EXPOSTULATIONES			
timores, suspiria, expostulationes, iras, amorem rursus.	450	Orationes	35
EXPRIMANT			
Quare quomodo alij molem hanc laetitiae suae exprimant,	457	Epistolae	1
EXPUGNARE			
quibus caperatam seuerioremque Philosophiam expugnare nouimus,	440	Orationes	12
EXPUGNATOS			
maris quasi Flagellatores expugnatos fusosque nobis dedisti.	462	Epistolae	9
EXREN			
Exren phugousa, ten t' epistemen biou.	430	Mem.Matr.15	7
EXTERARUM			
quid enim vtilius quam ex obseruatione exterarum Legum ac morum,	450	Orationes	15
EXTERAS			
quod optimus Princeps non tantum exteras regiones habuit perspectas,	451	Orationes	36
EXTERIS			
quo minus exteris Libris indigeremus, sed tamen comparatio	467	Epistolae	25
EXTERNIS			
sua sibi sufficere, neque externis indigere auxilijs atque antidotis:	444	Orationes	26
EXTINGUE			
Quin nocuas extingue faces, precor: vnda propinqua est,	399	Musae 35	7
EXTRA			
Foelicitatis culmen extra se locat,	414	Lucus 20	3
Intra extraque graui plenus es illuuie.	414	Lucus 21	2
illic tuta cognitio est, atque extra teli iactum.	449	Orationes	3
positum extra mortalitatis aleam, et quo magis Tuum agnoscas,	459	Epistolae	11
EXTREMAS			
Clauserit extremas pugna peracta vices,	386	Musae 2	8
EXTRICET			
& nunc sit tanta patriae tenacitas, vt nunquam Princeps se extricet:	455	Orationes	6
EXTRUCTA			
Archiepiscopo Eboracensi Summo Angliae Cancellario extructa fuerit,	463	Epistolae	31
EXTRUENDAE			
Antiquitas praeripuit Tibi gloriam extruendae Academiae,	465	Epistolae	17
EXTRUXISSEM			
Extruxissem, vbi, cum moneret vsus,	401	Musae 37	29
EXTULIT			
Magnatis appulsu extulit se occasio,	423	Mem.Matr.2	26
Surrexit vna & illa, seseque extulit:	423	Mem.Matr.2	27
EXTUNDI			
Christianus extundi bonus.	396	Musae 27	4
EXUCCA			
viduae effoetae, aut ligna exucca & marcida, alumnis suis orbarentur,	462	Epistolae	4
EXUCCO			
At nunc exucco similis tua gloria RAMO	416	Lucus 25	5
EXUENS			
Caeno profani corporis exuens	394	Musae 23	26
Authoritatis exuens tyrannidem;	436	Poem.Lat.	15
et blattis rixantes, exuens puluere, in theatrum et lucem produxisti.	462	Epistolae	26
EXUENTES			
nos etiam exuentes os illud, & supercilium quibus caperatam	440	Orationes	10
EXUIT			
Quin exuit personam Principis, deponit Maiestatem, virgam cum sceptro	452	Orationes	35
EXULIS			
Exulis, infernae pretiosa tragemata mensae,	419	Tr.Mortis V	58

	PAGE	TITLE	LINE
EXUNDAT			
Exundat fluuio Nilus amabili.	403	Musae 40	10
EXUOR			
Stellarum socius, pellibus exuor.	424	Mem.Matr.4	8
EXURGANT			
si qui alij exurgant promissores magnifici et hiantes, qui,	462	Epistolae	30
EXURGERE			
Solem ex Oceano Veteres exurgere fingunt	412	Lucus 8	1
EXUSCITAT			
Exuscitat plebem sacratos	394	Musae 23	31
EXUSTA			
Cernis vt exusta semper sit fronte viator;	437	Poem.Lat.	3
EXUTA			
Exuta strato carnis, ossibus constans,	429	Mem.Matr.12	2
F			
5. Ad F. Bacon, Cancell. Gratiae de Fluuio	460	Epistolae	T
8. Ad F. bacon, Cancel. Gratiae de Instaurationis Libro Academiae	463	Epistolae	T
FABIO			
Qua Fabio quondam sub duce nata salus.	416	Lucus 25	10
Quae Fabio quondam sub duce tuta salus.	416	Lucus 25 V	10
FABRICAE			
quando ipsae hae turres & beatae fabricae, vnico ictu sulphurei tubi,	448	Orationes	21
FABULA			
Ecclesia est mihi Luna; perge in Fabula.	393	Musae 22	10
Quaerit recessus. Incalescit fabula:	398	Musae 32	6
FAC			
Quo precio venit, fac, liceare prius.	410	Lucus 4	6
Per fluctus saltem, fac, precor, ipse vadem.	414	Lucus 19	4
Ah nunc, helluo, fac, vt ipse sugam:	421	Lucus 34	1
Fac radios saltem ingemines, vt dextera tortos	424	Mem.Matr.3	9
FACES			
Quin nocuas extingue faces, precor: vnda propinqua est,	399	Musae 35	7
Incendat tacitas, sole morante, faces:	211	Cam.1613-b BR	6
FACESSE			
Facesse, Stoica plebs, obambulans cautes,	429	Mem.Matr.12	1
FACIAM			
Quid ipse faciam? qui nec arboreas sudes	421	Lucus 33	3
FACIAS			
Ni facias, vt opes linguae per brachia serpant,	414	Lucus 22	3
quos profectus feceris in Sphaera Naturae, facias etiam in Gratiae:	464	Epistolae	3
FACIAT			
iterum exire patria, qui nunc inuenit viam, proximo itinere faciat.	455	Orationes	8
FACIE			
Hac facie dominae conspiciare tuae:	211	Cam.1613-b BR	10
FACIEI			
capiti & faciei coronam, significantes oportere Reges ijs partibus	447	Orationes	3
FACIENDA			
Praeuenias vultu non facienda tuo.	421	Lucus 35	10
FACIES			
Tam segnis facies aurorae nescia vernae,	426	Mem.Matr.7	8
Quid mihi si facies nigra est? hoc, Ceste, colore	437	Poem.Lat.	1
Cum mihi sit facies fumus, quas pectore flammas	437	Poem.Lat.	9
rotundum & coeleste, soli facies tanquam vestibulum magni palatij.	447	Orationes	1
inspexi facies hominum ac vultus curiosius tanquam emptor;	451	Orationes	13
FACILE			
Cur tibi tam facile non arrisere poetae	387	Musae 5	3
Nec facile ascendant, sed tibi vallis erit.	210	Cam.1613-a BR	8
Quam facile sentiuntur boni Principes!	445	Orationes	4
an sudum, facile conijcitur ex coelo, ex garritu auium,	445	Orationes	6
ex quo facile collectu erat, quantum deperimus te;	451	Orationes	28
& per tot milliaria facile transmissum, mentem maiorum capacem	454	Orationes	1
FACILI			
Se per se facili modo scientes,	415	Lucus 24	14
FACILIS			
Hic habitant Musae, facilisque in carmine Pallas,	210	Cam.1613-a BR	3
sic bonorum Principum facilis Astrologia:	445	Orationes	7
FACILITAS			
Nobis facilitas cedat & tibi sudor.	406	Passio 12	3
FACILIUS			
sed vt facilius ignoscas occupato calamo, qui etiam ferians nihil Tua	471	Epistolae	22
FACILLIME			
cum grandi atque impedito onere facillime incedens, occurrit ei	453	Orationes	35
FACILLIMI			
Ipsi sibi sunt nequiter facillimi.	413	Lucus 17	4
FACIT			
Quae ratio per se, si sit adulta, facit.	388	Musae 9	12
Haec facit ad nasum sola loquela tuum.	391	Musae 16	6
Fides gigantem sola, vel facit nanum.	406	Passio 12	5
Non vrbem facit vnicam, sed Orbem.	408	Passio 19	5
Atque euehens, bonum facit faecundius,	412	Lucus 13	2
Ira facit, mundusque ipse est apotheca furoris.	418	Tr.Mortis	17
vbi in dubio est, qui facit, an qui patitur, miserior.	449	Orationes	11
FACITIS			
Recte facitis, Academici, attollentes oculos cum stupore;	450	Orationes	1
FACTA			
Aequabili facta. Ecquid ergo te tanta	392	Musae 20	6
Infectas tabulas facta iuuenca scidit.	408	Passio 20	4
Fluminaque e ripis obvia facta tibi:	210	Cam.1613-a BR	6
nostrae, quae per Tuum Partum, ex Matre nunc Auia facta est:	463	Epistolae	26
FACTIS			
Sericus es dictis, factis pannusia Baucis:	414	Lucus 22	1

	PAGE	TITLE		LINE
FACTU				
Principibus vt vtilissima ita difficillima factu, cum quanto plus	450	Orationes		11
illud necessarium magis factu, hoc vero longe iucundius,	472	Epistolae		35
FACTUM				
Verius hoc olim factum est, vbi, Christe, lauares	412	Lucus 8		3
Ego vero non dicam vobis quod factum est ante seculum vestrum,	445	Orationes		38
magis id adeo factum esse mansuetudine Tua incomparabili,	472	Epistolae		21
FACTUS				
Sic tu nunc iuuenis factus, egoque senex.	386	Musae 2		4
Sanus Homo factus, vitiorum purus vterque;	408	Passio 20		1
FACUNDIA				
Tuiue Christum deuocans facundia	438	Poem.Lat.		3
FAECE				
neque illi e faece vulgi tantum qui eruditionem simplicitati	461	Epistolae		17
FAECUNDA				
Sed faecunda poeseos	403	Musae 40		7
FAECUNDIUS				
Atque euehens, bonum facit faecundius,	412	Lucus 13		2
FAECUNDUS				
Faecundusque chalybs sceleris, iam sanguine tinctus,	419	Tr.Mortis		37
Faecundusque chalibs sceleris, iam sanguine tectus	271	Tr.Mortis	VS	37
FAENORA				
Quin nos Ipse emit, precioso faenora soluens	410	Lucus 4		3
FALCE				
Hoc ligno, his clauis est, quasi Falce sua.	407	Passio 14		4
segetem perspicio, nulla verborum, nulla temporis falce demetendam.	446	Orationes		3
FALCEM				
Excussos manibus calamos, falcemque resumptam	431	Mem.Matr.19		1
FALCES				
Aruiragum, falcesque obstantia quaeque metentes.	419	Tr.Mortis		46
FALLACI				
Tisiphone; flamma & fallaci fulmine cincta	420	Tr.Mortis		71
FALLENTIA				
Vberaque aerea hiscentem fallentia natum?	426	Mem.Matr.7		4
FALLERE				
Haeresis, euertas. Quid enim te fallere possit?	402	Musae 39		22
FALLERIS				
Falleris, nusquam plura bona, cum etiam mala illic sint aurea:	451	Orationes		2
FALLIMUR				
aut enim misere fallimur, aut tantum de nullo vnquam Filio Alma	457	Epistolae		25
FALLITIS				
Femineum blanda fallitis arte genus:	387	Musae 5		10
FALSOS				
O falsos homines! Vigilat, qui somniat aurum,	411	Lucus 7		3
FALSUM				
Falsumque potius quam crepes versu?	392	Musae 20		9
FAMA				
Astronomus olim (vt fama) dum maculas diu,	393	Musae 22		7
Non deerat vel fama tibi, vel carmina famae,	416	Lucus 25		3
Non deerint vel fama tibi, vel carmina famae,	416	Lucus 25	V	3
Cui tenuis fama est, ingeniumque minus.	435	Poem.Lat.		4
Seritur fama in hoc saeculo, vt in sequenti metatur:	441	Orationes		19
Fama promotionis tuae gratissime appulit ad nos omnes haud ita certe	468	Epistolae		12
FAMAE				
Non deerat vel fama tibi, vel carmina famae,	416	Lucus 25		3
Non deerint vel fama tibi, vel carmina famae,	416	Lucus 25	V	3
Ad famae properes vera Tropaea tuae,	435	Poem.Lat.		2
FAMAM				
Famamque nec difflaueris, nec suxeris:	414	Lucus 20		12
Non comedant famam, sic nulla obliuia potent.	432	Poem.Lat.		16
FAME				
De auri sacra fame.	399	Musae 34		T
effigies, imo vmbras hominum fame, frigore, illuuie, enectas,	449	Orationes		8
FAMEM				
satietas quaedam honoris, quem ad tempus deponere famem excitat:	453	Orationes		10
FAMES				
O mortis longaeua fames, venterque perennis	271	Tr.Mortis	VS	1
Annon longa fames miseraeque iniuria pestis	432	Poem.Lat.		20
FAMILIAE				
Negat familiae suae.	407	Passio 16		8
quod nonnullae familiae semper mites essent, vti Valerij,	447	Orationes		20
FAMILIAM				
Dein familiam lustrat, & res prandij,	422	Mem.Matr.2		18
at ille ambiuit nobilissimam Austriacam familiam, Aquilamque illam,	446	Orationes		15
FAMILIAREM				
assensumque Tuum veritati omni familiarem largiaris, sun tei eulogiai	473	Epistolae		11
FAMILIARIUS				
charta conspiciendum Te praebes, quo familiarius inter nos verseris.	458	Epistolae		20
FANATICAE				
aut eorum certe, qui cymbala sunt fanaticae iuuentutis:	445	Orationes		24
FARINA				
Atque ipsi sibi sunt mola & farina.	415	Lucus 24		15
FARINAM				
Et nostrae tribuant molae farinam,	415	Lucus 24		5
FARRE				
quae est vestra felicitas qui puro Academiae farre vtimini.	470	Epistolae		3
FAS				
(In quo fas nihil est rumpi) donare sigillum.	439	Poem.Lat.		15
FASCES				
nulla sunt sceptra in elementis, nulli fasces aut secures:	452	Orationes		17

	PAGE	TITLE	LINE
FEBREM			
Quod tu febrem censes, salubre est	426	Mem.Matr.6	23
FECERIS			
Faxit Deus vt quos profectus feceris in Sphaera Naturae,	464	Epistolae	3
FECISSEM			
viam ad candorem Mentis Tuae ducentem aut reperissem aut fecissem.	472	Epistolae	10
FECISTI			
quam in aqua & igne fecisti, non dubitamus quin benignitas tua omnia	457	Epistolae	22
Scite et apposite fecisti Fluuium nostrum conseruans altero	462	Epistolae	18
FECIT			
Quare optime fecit Rex Serenissimus, qui virtutes tuas magnis	466	Epistolae	12
FELICES			
Si, quia felices olim dixere poetae	387	Musae 6	3
O quam felices sunt, qui tua castra sequuntur,	435	Poem.Lat.	7
FELICITAS			
quae est vestra felicitas qui puro Academiae farre vtimini.	470	Epistolae	2
FELIX			
Responde aeternum titulo; quoque ordine felix	402	Musae 39	18
FELLE			
Vinumque felle miscuit.	427	Mem.Matr.8	4
FEMINA			
Sola tibi Sappho, feminaque vna placet?	387	Musae 5	2
FEMINEUM			
Femineum blanda fallitis arte genus:	387	Musae 5	10
FENESTRAE			
Illis perpetuae patent fenestrae,	415	Lucus 24	13
FERACEM			
cui natura spiritum dederit feracem gloriae, et coeleste ingenium	468	Epistolae	5
FERAE			
Illa cauerna, in qua tot coiere ferae.	414	Lucus 21	4
FERCULA			
Quotidiana suas poscant si fercula grates,	389	Musae 12	9
Dum prono rapis ore cibos, & fercula verris,	414	Lucus 21	1
FERE			
vnde fit vt nullus fere elabatur dies, qui non hostes aliquos nobis	461	Epistolae	13
FERES			
Eminet, id tumidum protinus esse feres?	387	Musae 7	4
FERET			
Non vt te superem: res tamen ipsa feret.	386	Musae 2	2
FERIANS			
qui etiam ferians nihil Tua perfectione dignum procudere possit.	471	Epistolae	23
FERIMUS			
contra grassantes flammas aedificijs Honori Tuo acceptam ferimus:	457	Epistolae	19
FERIS			
Vulpibus antra feris, nidique volucribus adsunt,	407	Passio 15	1
FERO			
Tuque etiam Dapifer, quas fero, sume dapes:	210	Cam.1613-a BR	2
FEROCITER			
O saeuus hostis! quam ferociter pugnas!	392	Musae 20	15
FEROX			
Dicta ferox: haerent lateri conuitia fixo.	418	Tr.Mortis	15
Dicta ferox, haerent lateri conuitia fixa:	271	Tr.Mortis VS	15
triumphos & victorias quasi fraena ferox spumantia mandit,	447	Orationes	34
FERRE			
Perpetuos mihi ferre rami,	434	Poem.Lat.	32
et mammas arentes tam nobilis parentis aequo animo ferre posset?	462	Epistolae	1
FERREA			
Fusaque decurrit notis aqua ferrea sulcis:	419	Tr.Mortis	52
FERRENT			
Cum Latium ferrent secula prisca iugum?	416	Lucus 25	2
FERRO			
Christe, vbi tam duro patet in te semita ferro,	404	Passio 4	1
FERRUM			
Tristis, vbi ac ferrum tellure reciditur ima,	419	Tr.Mortis	36
FERT			
Non mea fert aetas, vt te, veterane, lacessam;	386	Musae 2	1
Non fert Vcalegon, atque amentata retorquet	418	Tr.Mortis	14
FERTILES			
apud nos agri tantum sunt fertiles, illic etiam arenae.	451	Orationes	5
FERTUR			
Nempe graui fertur scelerata pecunia motu,	410	Lucus 4	7
Quo placet oblato, mortua fertur, hero:	428	Mem.Matr.11	4
FERUENTES			
Obrue feruentes, ruptis conatibus, hostes:	402	Musae 39	20
FERUESCUNT			
Compita feruescunt pedibus, clamoribus aether.	418	Tr.Mortis	11
FERULAE			
Ipsaque sunt ferulae mollia corda suae.	406	Passio 9	6
FERUNT			
Rupes tenaces & silices ferunt	393	Musae 23	9
Sanguinis insultus exanimata ferunt.	406	Passio 13	4
Ferunt enim Londinenses Bibliopolas suum potius emolumentum quam	467	Epistolae	3
FERUNTUR			
Ingluuieque minor. Quercus habitare feruntur	418	Tr.Mortis	5
FERUOR			
Vt feruor cerebri refrigeretur,	391	Musae 15	9
idem feruor qui impar sub amoris signo meritus est, ad vera castra	453	Orationes	29
FESSA			
Tandem & fessa manus, dedit sigillum.	439	Poem.Lat.	12
FESSUS			
Quondam fessus Amor loquens Amato,	439	Poem.Lat.	10

	PAGE	TITLE	LINE
FESTINANTEM			
non est quod nostram quoque, cum amoris symbolo festinantem, recuses.	469	Epistolae	15
FESTINANTES			
ad prudentiae eloquentiaeque tuae praesidium festinantes excipe:	465	Epistolae	16
FESTINARE			
vti sanguis solet in re dubia ad cor festinare, ita ad Te confugimus	467	Epistolae	9
FESTINASTI			
certe adeo festinasti ad gratitudines tuas cum emolumento nostro	462	Epistolae	14
FESTINAT			
eccum nunc altera occasio, adeo festinat virtus tua:	465	Epistolae	24
FESTUCAS			
qui lemas istas et festucas, Reipublicae oculo haerentes, . .	462	Epistolae	12
FIAT			
Sputando, blasphemando? nempe ne hoc fiat	405	Passio 5	5
vt Rex animalium fiat Rex hominum, apponimus nos manibus Sceptrum,	447	Orationes	2
FIBULIS			
Syluas pererrat. Fibulis dein omnibus	398	Musae 32	8
FICTA			
Fictaque Bellona & verae ludibria pugnae, ...	418	Tr.Mortis	27
FICTILE			
At sibi collisit fictile Daemon opus.	408	Passio 20	2
FICTITIOS			
dum globos tractas & coelos fictitios, perrumpit primipilus,	448	Orationes	29
FICUS			
In posterum, maledicta Ficus arescens	405	Passio 5	6
FIDA			
Ceu fida statione & arce certa, ...	417	Lucus 30	7
Virgo pudens, vxor fida, seuera parens:	429	Mem.Matr.13	2
FIDE			
Ducitur illimi candida vita fide, ...	400	Musae 36	2
in qua dextra et fide coniuncti, in caeteris haud diuellamur.	468	Epistolae	24
FIDEI			
Regi, Fidei Defensori &c. Geo. Herbertus.	384	Musae	T
O qui Defensor Fidei meritissimus audis, ...	402	Musae 39	17
Qui spissae fidei breuique menti	417	Lucus 30	4
sed etiam doceas tanquam communis defensor fidei et Academiae,	443	Orationes	23
& vestrae fidei consulam, quemadmodum artifices non omnes . .	445	Orationes	29
quam de futuro supplicem, integerrimae tuae fidei commendantes.	465	Epistolae	8
FIDELIS			
Mundi fidelis clauiger:	407	Passio 16	4
FIDEM			
Dicti fidem firmabimus Anagrammate.	397	Musae 30	7
Defendit veram mente manuque fidem.	399	Musae 33	24
Cui sententiae si fidem adhibeas, assensumque Tuum veritati omni	473	Epistolae	10
FIDERE			
praesertim cum amico fidere periculosius sit, quam hostem superare.	453	Orationes	32
FIDES			
Ex praelio vndae ignisque (si Physicis fides)	396	Musae 27	1
Fides gigantem sola, vel facit nanum.	406	Passio 12	5
FIDIBUS			
Praetorium, fidibus canendo, omnia Danorum expiscatus consilia,	453	Orationes	5
FIDICINIS			
sub ementito habitu fidicinis castra hostium ingressus, . .	453	Orationes	4
FIEREM			
Laudibus haud fierem sepia iusta tuis.	422	Mem.Matr.1	6
FIERI			
Quam cunctos fieri praestat Episcopos.	392	Musae 17	13
nostrumque regnum gestimus fieri participes eius sanguinis, . .	440	Orationes	19
FIET			
Gens tota fiet, atque vtrinque plectetur.	405	Passio 5	7
Christe, duplex fiet mors tua vita mihi:	434	Poem.Lat.	8
FIGITE			
Heu stolidi, primum fugientem figite Terram, ...	408	Passio 18	3
FIGO			
Imperij hic culmen figo: mortalibus actum est	421	Tr.Mortis	100
FIGURA			
Desinis exclamans: tota figura, vale.	401	Musae 38	2
FIGURAM			
Mutas in humanam figuram	393	Musae 23	3
FIGURAS			
figuras iam nunc pulueri inscriptas corpore confosso obliterans.	448	Orationes	31
FIGURIS			
quae licet versentur in figuris describendis, quibus nihil imperito	454	Orationes	3
qui nuper versatus est in forma & figuris vultus, vbi res postulat,	454	Orationes	7
FILIJ			
Filij noctis, populus malignus, ...	390	Musae 14	18
Pace, filij sepeliunt patres; bello, patres filios:	448	Orationes	9
FILIO			
At tu qui inepte haec dicta censes filio, ...	423	Mem.Matr.2	52
aut tantum de nullo vnquam Filio Alma Mater, quantum de Te sibi	457	Epistolae	26
dein Hon. Tuo gratulamur, qui filio auctus es tali ingenio praedito:	463	Epistolae	24
FILIOS			
bello, patres filios: pace, aegri sanantur;	448	Orationes	9
Quanta hilaritate aspicit Alma Mater filios suos iam emancipatos,	461	Epistolae	30
FILIUM			
protinus tanquam Nobilem Filium (more nostro) Magistrum Artium	463	Epistolae	8
sou prosepimetroumenei beabis Filium tuum obsequentissimum GEORGIUM	473	Epistolae	13
FILIUS			
Vnusquisque hominum, Terra est; & filius arui.	413	Lucus 18	1
FILO			
Coepisti, pergas simili res texere filo.	402	Musae 39	19

	PAGE	TITLE		LINE
FILUM				
Non tibi nunc soli filum abrupere sorores, ...	428	Mem.Matr.11		11
vlciscimur mortem, ligantes abruptum vitae filum, vnde consequimur,	446	Orationes		23
essent atque consilijs, sine quibus ne vnum quidem filum torquerent:	449	Orationes		31
FINDIS				
Nec transire licet quo mentis acumine findis	402	Musae 39		27
FINDIT				
It stridor, caelosque omnes & Tartara findit.	420	Tr.Mortis		73
It stridor, caelosque omnes et sydera findit.	271	Tr.Mortis	VS	73
FINE				
Ecce tamen quam suauis ero! cum, fine duelli, ...	386	Musae 2		7
FINEM				
Intus agunt, habeat certum meditatio finem:	402	Musae 39		37
FINES				
finesque multiplices & polymiti, vt si minus id assequantur,	446	Orationes		5
FINGE				
Quare scripturus, finge tibi matronam sanctam, venerandam, . .	470	Epistolae		16
FINGENDI				
Non tibi fingendi sola taberna patet.	386	Musae 3		6
FINGENDUM				
ideoque ex quolibet ligno, qualibet vxore non esse fingendum:	447	Orationes		10
FINGIS				
O quam bellus homo es! lepido quam nomine fingis	386	Musae 3		1
FINGIT				
Quam nihil illudis! si, quae tua purpura fingit, ...	405	Passio 7		7
FINGUNT				
Solem ex Oceano Veteres exurgere fingunt	412	Lucus 8		1
FINITIMI				
illi etiam honores qui finitimi sunt, et quasi accolae Maiestatis,	463	Epistolae		22
FINITIMUM				
Miratur aequor finitimum sonos, ...	394	Musae 23		41
FIRMA				
Nescia vulturnis cedere, firma manet.	428	Mem.Matr.11		2
FIRMABIMUS				
Dicti fidem firmabimus Anagrammate.	397	Musae 30		7
FIRMIORI				
sic existimes nihil Mortalium firmiori flagrare in Te desiderio,	473	Epistolae		5
FIRMISSIMA				
Tu radix, tu petra mihi firmissima, Mater, ...	428	Mem.Matr.11		9
FISCO				
iam olim Regi notam atque signatam dignissime praeficiaris Fisco,	469	Epistolae		21
FIT				
Conueniunt; & Homo viua fit Ara Dei.	417	Lucus 29		4
vnde fit vt nullus fere elabatur dies, qui non hostes aliquos nobis	461	Epistolae		13
FIUNT				
Minora fiunt omnia:	388	Musae 8		14
Principibus, sed amica fiunt.	434	Poem.Lat.		28
FIXA				
Dicta ferox, haerent lateri conuitia fixa:	271	Tr.Mortis	VS	15
Quod Crux nequibat fixa, Clavique additi, ...	438	Poem.Lat.		1
FIXI				
Munde, fluas fugiasque licet, nos nostraque fixi:	438	Poem.Lat.		8
FIXO				
Te fixo vel Terra mouet: nam, cum Cruce, totam	408	Passio 18		1
Dicta ferox: haerent lateri conuitia fixo.	418	Tr.Mortis		15
FIXUS				
Eriperet nobis, in Cruce fixus eras;	407	Passio 14		2
FLABELLIS				
Ne, si flamma nouis adolescat mota flabellis, ...	399	Musae 35		11
FLACCESCERENT				
floribus suis sternentes Rempublicam, prae ariditate flaccescerent.	461	Epistolae		11
FLACCESCIT				
tanquam flos molliculus rudiore Centurionis manu tactus flaccescit.	448	Orationes		26
FLAGELLATI				
Christe, flagellati spes & victoria mundi, ...	406	Passio 9		1
FLAGELLATORES				
alterosque maris quasi Flagellatores expugnatos fusosque nobis	462	Epistolae		9
FLAGELLO				
Non potui non ire acre stimulante flagello:	431	Mem.Matr.19		5
FLAGELLUM				
In Flagellum.	406	Passio 9		T
Suauiter admoueas notum tibi carne flagellum, ...	406	Passio 9		3
FLAGITANT				
pernoctes flagitant, cauendum ne id nobis nauseam moueat, . .	448	Orationes		36
FLAGRARE				
sic existimes nihil Mortalium firmiori flagrare in Te desiderio,	473	Epistolae		5
FLAGRARENT				
qui vtrumque curasti, vt neque sitirent Musae, neque flagrarent.	457	Epistolae		21
FLAMEN				
Vbique est Deus, Agnus, Ara, Flamen.	408	Passio 19		14
FLAMINIS				
Ille quoque inuadit Diuinam Flaminis artem, ...	392	Musae 19		3
FLAMMA				
Sacrilegum carmen, censeo, flamma voret.	399	Musae 34		4
Ne, si flamma nouis adolescat mota flabellis, ...	399	Musae 35		11
Tisiphone; flamma & fallaci fulmine cincta	420	Tr.Mortis		71
FLAMMAE				
Vt tenuis flammae species caelum vsque minatur, ...	410	Lucus 2		1
FLAMMAS				
Anne tuas flammas ipsa Antiperistasis auget, ...	399	Musae 35		3
Cum mihi sit facies fumus, quas pectore flammas	437	Poem.Lat.		9

FLUUIO (cont'd)	PAGE	TITLE	LINE
2. Ad R. Naunton Gratiae de Fluuio et de tegendis Tectis stramineis	457	Epistolae	T
tam de conseruando Fluuio nostro, quam de muniendis contra grassantes	457	Epistolae	17
4. Ad Iacobum Regem Gratiae de Fluuio contra Redemptores	460	Epistolae	T
subiectos, integro Fluuio a Rege nostro donatos, triumphare?	460	Epistolae	13
5. Ad F. Bacon, Cancell. Gratiae de Fluuio	460	Epistolae	T
6. Ad R. Naunton, Secret. Gratiae de Fluuio	461	Epistolae	T
Ad Ful. Grevil Gratiae de Fluuio	462	Epistolae	T
fecisti Fluuium nostrum conseruans altero eloquentiae Fluuio,	462	Epistolae	19
FLUUIOS			
Doctrinae fluuios clauderet aureae,	391	Musae 17	4
FLUUIUM			
quos in arca repositos abijciebant in fluuium, his verbis:	452	Orationes	28
Neque enim passus es illum Fluuium, qui tantae poeticae,	461	Epistolae	6
nonnulli Fluuium inuident, multi Academias integras subuersas volunt,	461	Epistolae	15
Fluuium placidissimo fauorum tuorum afflatu nobis tuere.	461	Epistolae	24
communes Reipublicae lachrymae alterum nobis Fluuium effunderent.	462	Epistolae	6
Scite et appcsite fecisti Fluuium nostrum conseruans altero	462	Epistolae	18
Quare nos tertium praedictis adiungimus Gratiarum Fluuium,	462	Epistolae	24
etiam Fluuium non minus de praeterito gratum, quam de futuro	465	Epistolae	7
FLUUIUS			
sed si ablatus fuisset Fluuius noster, per quem vicini agri opulentia	460	Epistolae	23
FLUXIT			
Cuius ab oppositis fluxit origo locis.	417	Lucus 31	4
FOCUS			
Excutite aulaea, & luceat igne focus.	413	Lucus 15	2
FODIAM			
rariusque paulo fodiam in Vintoniensi agro, dum Rhetorici satagam:	472	Epistolae	28
FOECUNDIA			
relabitur in terram, qua ortus est, eique cum foecundia remuneratur:	454	Orationes	30
FOECUNDO			
Ecce recedentis foecundo in littore Nili	384	Musae	1
FOEDERA			
Qua tamen occisi foedera scripta Dei?	391	Musae 16	4
apparatus, foedera, munitiones, aeque ac nostra spectari debent:	450	Orationes	26
FOEDUS			
Quae diuisa nocent, Christi per foedus, in vnum	417	Lucus 29	3
FOELICES			
Foelices, quos bella premunt, & plurimus ensis!	432	Poem.Lat.	23
o foelices! Optamus quidem vt Maiestatis vestrae gaudia responderint	443	Orationes	12
FOELICIORES			
Quanto foeliciores nos omnes, Corona Musica, qui optimum Principem	444	Orationes	16
FOELICISSIMUS			
retulisset captus piscis, foelicissimus mortalium habitus est.	444	Orationes	15
FOELICITAS			
Necesse est autem vt foelicitas tantorum Principum etiam in ministros	441	Orationes	5
FOELICITATES			
sic disparatae foelicitates hinc a populo, illinc a Principe,	456	Epistolae	24
FOELICITATIS			
Foelicitatis culmen extra se locat,	414	Lucus 20	3
intra ambitum amplexusque foelicitatis Tuae receptae, communi calore	469	Epistolae	19
FOELIX			
Iam foelix Philomela, & menti conscia Dido!	432	Poem.Lat.	22
Quo Te, foelix Anna, modo deflere licebit?	435	Poem.Lat.	1
FOEMINAE			
Et quicquid vspiam est seuerae foeminae,	422	Mem.Matr.2	2
FOEMINEI			
Hic sita foeminei laus & victoria sexus:	429	Mem.Matr.13	1
FOENORE			
ditat patriam, suamque absentiam cum foenore compensat.	454	Orationes	33
FOETUM			
exosculamur, hunc foetum vestrum, hunc alterum Carolum,	459	Epistolae	9
FOETUS			
Atque inter reliquos horti crescentia foetus	427	Mem.Matr.7	33
FOLIORUM			
vbi trecenta foliorum iugera vno die sedentes percurritis;	454	Orationes	25
FOMITE			
Mulcetur vento, accendit cum fomite partem	420	Tr.Mortis	68
Miscetur vento, accendit cum fomite partem	271	Tr.Mortis VS	68
FONTE			
Ah Mater, quo te deplorem fonte? Dolores	422	Mem.Matr.1	1
proin vt Fluuij quas aquas a Fonte accipiunt non retinent ipsi,	456	Epistolae	10
FONTEM			
Fontem intercipis omnibus patentem?	421	Lucus 34	3
FONTES			
conseruantes sibi Illos Fontes, a quibus ipsi olim hauserunt?	461	Epistolae	31
FORA			
huiusmodi lamentis & quiritationibus plena erant fora, nundinae,	451	Orationes	10
FORAMINE			
Luscum prodigium, medioque foramine gaudens.	419	Tr.Mortis	54
FORAS			
Omnia sunt temere proijcienda foras.	390	Musae 13	2
FOREM			
Difficilis esse haud soleo: nam, pol, si forem,	413	Lucus 17	3
FORENSE			
Quod si forense quippiam nos spectans, dum incumbis muneri,	466	Epistolae	4
FORENT			
Vobis, aut illis pectora vestra forent.	400	Musae 36	6
FORES			
Claudi, pene tuas praeteriere fores.	385	Musae	4
Gaudia sola fores: sic quicquid somnia mentis	402	Musae 39	36

FORES (cont'd)	PAGE	TITLE	LINE
Circumferre potes; Sampson vt ante fores.	408	Passio 18	2
quod reclusae sint fores, receptusque sim in aliquem apud Honorem	472	Epistolae	20
FORET			
Nunc primum socij mors foret atra tui?	415	Lucus 23	2
Absque nuptijs foret populus virorum, essemus vnius seculi;	446	Orationes	21
FORIBUS			
Nunquid pro foribus sedendo nuper	411	Lucus 5	4
FORMA			
per vniuersam Britanniam, disparuit forma, Albion nomine excidit:	451	Orationes	17
qui nuper versatus est in forma & figuris vultus, vbi res postulat,	454	Orationes	7
FORMAS			
Quin redde formas, o bone, pristinas,	393	Musae 23	5
FORMIDINE			
Praecipitata; cadunt vrbes, formidine muri	420	Tr.Mortis	77
FORMOSA			
Cernite, quam formosa suas Ecclesia pennas	401	Musae 39	6
FORNACE			
Liquitur ardenti candens fornace metallum,	419	Tr.Mortis	51
liquitur ardenti cadens fornace metallum;	271	Tr.Mortis VS	51
FORSAN			
Annulus & plenus tempore forsan erit.	396	Musae 26	6
Corde tuo forsan, caetera munda, SOROR.	413	Lucus 15	6
FORSITAN			
Forsitan & prohibes infans portetur ad vndas,	388	Musae 9	7
vniuersum tempus nostrum (forsitan quo alacrius illud impenderemus	460	Epistolae	5
hospitium, et erga te propensius, haud vsquam forsitan reperias.	466	Epistolae	19
FORTASSE			
Quod Bellarminus nequijt, fortasse poetae	417	Lucus 28	3
FORTE			
Forte quidem, cum per vestras Ecclesia turbas	389	Musae 12	3
Ni me forte petas; nam quanto indignior ipse,	404	Passio 2	5
At forte matrem perdere haud soles demens:	429	Mem.Matr.12	9
FORTITER			
Qui tamen in nostros fortiter ire negant.	398	Musae 33	4
FORTUNAE			
tuere nos ita vt fortunae nostrae, intra ambitum amplexusque	469	Epistolae	18
FORTUNAS			
Fataque Fortunasque & spem laesere futuram.	432	Poem.Lat.	25
omnes ad Aulam, atque ab eo consilium peteremus a quo et fortunas?	443	Orationes	28
FORTUNET			
Deus fortunet tibi hunc honorem, et faxit, vt tibi gloriae sit,	469	Epistolae	5
FOUEAM			
Quas Luna habet, tuetur, in foueam cadit,	393	Musae 22	8
FOUEANTUR			
amplexusque foelicitatis Tuae receptae, communi calore foueantur.	469	Epistolae	19
FOUEMUS			
Quare amplectimur, fouemus, exosculamur, hunc foetum vestrum,	459	Epistolae	9
FOUENTE			
Sol generat populum luce fouente nouum.	384	Musae	2
FOUET			
Arguit, exceptos quos pia Roma fouet:	416	Lucus 26	4
FOUISTI			
quippe qui eximie semper fouisti literatos, eosque cum tineis	462	Epistolae	26
FR			
14. Ad Fr. Bacon, Cancell. De Bibliop. Lond.	467	Epistolae	T
FRAENA			
Dormitat pelagus: Quam bene fraena tenes!	412	Lucus 12	2
triumphos & victorias quasi fraena ferox spumantia mandit,	447	Orationes	34
FRAGILIS			
Diffugiunt, fragilisque crepant coenacula mundi.	420	Tr.Mortis	78
FRAGILITATE			
splendida plerumque vitrea sint, claritatem fragilitate corrumpentia;	448	Orationes	6
FRAGMINA			
Post vbi Mosaicae repararent fragmina Leges,	408	Passio 20	3
FRAGOREM			
Euolat, horrendumque ciet bacchata fragorem.	420	Tr.Mortis	72
FRAGORES			
vrbium incendia, fragores, direptiones, stupratas virgines,	449	Orationes	6
FRANCIAE			
IACOBO, D. G. Magnae Britanniae, Franciae, & Hiberniae	384	Musae	T
FRANCISCI			
In obitum incomparabilis Francisci Vicecomitis	438	Poem.Lat.	T
FRANGERE			
spiritus, generososque animos frangere et retundere clamitant.	461	Epistolae	20
FRATERNO			
Cum nil fraterno rarius esse queat.	393	Musae 21	4
FRATRES			
Ad fratres.	393	Musae 21	T
O sec'lum lepidum! circumstant vndique Fratres,	393	Musae 21	1
O caecos animi fratres! quis vestra fatigat	401	Musae 39	4
FRATRIS			
Sic nunc plena boni sunt omnia Fratris, amore	393	Musae 21	3
FREMERE			
Hinc fremere totus & minari gestio	427	Mem.Matr.8	5
FREMITUS			
Profanos fremitus bonasque sannas:	400	Musae 37	24
FREQUENS			
Dumque his inuigilo frequens	424	Mem.Matr.4	7
FREQUENTER			
clementia, vt frequenter nos inuisat, a re instructus nos doceat,	444	Orationes	5

	PAGE	TITLE		LINE
FREQUENTIOREM				
Eximia tua in nos merita frequentiorem calamum postulant,	457	Epistolae		7
FREQUENTISSIMO				
Quare frequentissimo Senatu, plenissimis suffragijs elegimus Te	465	Epistolae		4
FRETI				
Illi magnetica acu freti sunt.	463	Epistolae		16
FRETUM				
vicinum fretum quotidie transnatantes, litora nostra atque aures mire	441	Orationes		3
FRETUS				
Fustibalos fundasque, quibus, cum Numine, fretus	419	Tr.Mortis		43
fustibulos fundusque quibus cum numine fretus	271	Tr.Mortis	VS	43
FRICARI				
Sic vnguenta solent manu fricari:	405	Passio 8		2
FRIGEFACTI				
vbi sursum processerint paulo, frigefacti demum relabuntur.	471	Epistolae		30
FRIGENTE				
Scotia quae frigente iaces porrecta sub Arcto,	399	Musae 35		1
FRIGIDA				
absque molesta aliorum ac frigida commendatione, si huc reciderit	472	Epistolae		15
FRIGIDIOREM				
nunquam frigidiorem aestatem sensimus; at quo tandem?	450	Orationes		37
FRIGORA				
Sic acuunt zelum frigora tanta tuum?	399	Musae 35		6
FRIGORE				
effigies, imo vmbras hominum fame, frigore, illuuie, enectas,	449	Orationes		8
FRONTE				
Cernis vt exusta semper sit fronte viator;	437	Poem.Lat.		3
FRUAMUR				
concede vt nos etiam benignitate alarum tuarum et virtute fruamur.	466	Epistolae		23
FRUARE				
Ipse fruare, licet, solus graueolente sepulcro;	414	Lucus 21		5
FRUCTUM				
Fructum laborum consecutae maximum	424	Mem.Matr.2		64
mirabilius, cuius tamen fructum omnem nondum habetis enucleatum.	450	Orationes		3
at Noster difficultatem superans, fructum consecutus est:	450	Orationes		13
quanquam quem alium fructum potuimus expectare ab Eo, in quem fauor	456	Epistolae		17
FRUCTUS				
Fructusque post mortem recusent	434	Poem.Lat.		31
tamen nimium efferre vos, cum Virginitas ipsa fructus sit Nuptiarum:	446	Orationes		28
qui symbola sunt spei, quoniam a floribus fructus sperantur.	446	Orationes		33
hoc Principe, in quo doctrinae fructus atque vsus mirifice relucet.	469	Epistolae		23
commendatione, si huc reciderit omnis studiorum spes fructusque:	472	Epistolae		16
FRUENDA				
fruenda nobis tradidit.	397	Musae 28		12
FRUENS				
Quicquid habet tellus, quicquid & astra, fruens.	429	Mem.Matr.13		6
FRUGES				
Creditur, ante satas prono cum numine fruges)	419	Tr.Mortis		61
Creditur, ante satas prono cum vertice fruges)	419	Tr.Mortis	V	61
FRUIMUR				
qua tot iam annis impune fruimur, hoc pacto fundatam cupit	447	Orationes		29
per quem vicini agri opulentia fruimur, veremur ne non tam sapientes	460	Epistolae		23
FRUSTA				
Pro solido, CAESAR, carmine frusta dabo.	385	Musae 1		4
FRUSTRA				
Frustra, Verpe, tumes, propola cultus,	408	Passio 19		1
Frustra itaque in tot funeribus miraberis vnum,	415	Lucus 23		11
Galene, frustra es, cur miserum premens	425	Mem.Matr.6		1
Frustra igitur sudo: superest mihi sola voluptas,	435	Poem.Lat.		7
Haud frustra impendes operam nobis omnia fauorum tuorum momenta	466	Epistolae		7
FUDERAT				
Quae dicteria fuderat Britannus	391	Musae 15		1
FUERANT				
Haec fuerant: sic Tisiphone virguncula lusit.	418	Tr.Mortis		23
FUERAT				
Quin fugias? mea non fuerat tam nubila Iuno,	426	Mem.Matr.7		7
Haec fuerat olim potio Domini tui.	427	Mem.Matr.8		9
Quaeque olim fuerat cura, manere potest.	427	Mem.Matr.9		4
Poena minor fuerat, quam fatum Principis aegrum?	432	Poem.Lat.		21
FUERE				
Nostrae etiam Musae vile fuere lutum:	384	Musae		4
FUERINT				
vbi tamen ad vsum tralatae fuerint, machinas conficiunt	454	Orationes		5
FUERIT				
Sedula si fuerit, perterebrare potest.	410	Lucus 2		6
at fuerit; si amor virginis eo pertraxit Principem, quo tandem ducet	453	Orationes		27
Archiepiscopo Eboracensi Summo Angliae Cancellario extructa fuerit,	463	Epistolae		31
FUGA				
fuga hos omnes, praesertim sericatam hanc stultitiam contere,	461	Epistolae		22
FUGACES				
Iam fulgor armorum fugaces	448	Orationes		3
FUGACI				
Tam languens genitrix cineri supposta fugaci:	426	Mem.Matr.7		9
FUGANT				
Nascentes radij fugant, vel acres	385	Musae		8
FUGARI				
Vnquam fugari, quam tui socij solent.	389	Musae 10		3
FUGAT				
Squaloremque togae candida Musa fugat.	417	Lucus 28		6
FUGATOR				
Promus; Fugator Idolum, atque nubium;	436	Poem.Lat.		12

	PAGE	TITLE	LINE
FUGATOR (cont'd)			
Promus; Fugator Idolorum & nubium;	436	Poem.Lat. V	12
FUGERUNT			
quae fugerunt tot philosophos vmbra et otio diffluentes,	463	Epistolae	19
FUGIAS			
Quin fugias? mea non fuerat tam nubila Iuno,	426	Mem.Matr.7	7
Munde, fluas fugiasque licet, nos nostraque fixi:	438	Poem.Lat.	8
FUGIENT			
quanto citius fugient calumniae, si speculum Inuidiae ostendas,	454	Orationes	20
FUGIENTEM			
Heu stolidi, primum fugientem figite Terram,	408	Passio 18	3
inter nouas honorum nubes e conspectu nostro fugientem reuocamus.	456	Epistolae	7
FUGIENTIA			
Tum tibi, si placeat, fugientia tempora reddam;	386	Musae 2	9
FUGIENTIS			
Et flexus fugientis appetitus.	411	Lucus 5	14
FUGIES			
Quo fugies, sudor? quamuis pars altera Christi	404	Passio 2	1
FUGIT			
Nec dextra te fugit, almi Amoris emblema?	397	Musae 31	1
Nec tu pro socio doleas, qui fugit ad illud	415	Lucus 23	15
Invitoque fugit singula stella pede:	210	Cam.1613-b BR	2
FUGITIUUS			
vita nostra atque calor, longo animi deliquio fugitiuus ac desertor.	444	Orationes	23
FUISSE			
Rure, sibi dixit Musa fuisse probro.	431	Mem.Matr.19	2
FUISSET			
Plumbo ducta fuisset aestuanti,	400	Musae 37	22
& metalla ei inserendo, aliter mundus iam diu fuisset deuoratus.	452	Orationes	25
sed si ablatus fuisset Fluuius noster, per quem vicini agri opulentia	460	Epistolae	22
cuius nisi incredibilis fuisset vis, nunquam in tantis negotijs,	463	Epistolae	17
FUISTI			
Sacratissima Charta, tu fuisti	411	Lucus 5	11
FUIT			
Apostolorum culpa non leuis fuit	389	Musae 10	4
Proque vno vincto turba soluta fuit.	407	Passio 17	2
Nec Deus est nec Homo: Christus vterque fuit.	412	Lucus 10	2
Cespes viuus, Homo; mortuus, Ara fuit:	417	Lucus 29	2
quod sane adeo nobile fuit & honorificum, vt nihil habeat Inuidia	453	Orationes	23
FUL			
Ad Ful. Grevil Gratiae de Fluuio	462	Epistolae	T
FULGOR			
certe cum duplex fulgor sit, qui mundi oculos perstringat,	441	Orationes	12
Iam fulgor armorum fugaces	448	Orationes	3
FULMINAT			
Tormento peior Iesuita, & fulminat Orbem,	420	Tr.Mortis	96
FULMINE			
Tisiphone; flamma & fallaci fulmine cincta	420	Tr.Mortis	71
Vssisse prono fulmine diceris,	433	Poem.Lat.	14
hic enim securi sumus a pluuia, imo a fulmine:	455	Orationes	16
FULSERAT			
Ante tui, CAESAR, quam fulserat aura fauoris,	384	Musae	3
FULTA			
Heroum grandi carmina fulta pede?	387	Musae 5	4
FUMUS			
Cum mihi sit facies fumus, quas pectore flammas	437	Poem.Lat.	9
FUNDARUNT			
Reges Collegia, eaque fundarunt amplissimis praedijs, immunitatibus:	458	Epistolae	22
FUNDAS			
Fustibalos fundasque, quibus, cum Numine, fretus	419	Tr.Mortis	43
FUNDATAM			
tot iam annis impune fruimur, hoc pacto fundatam cupit & perpetuam;	447	Orationes	29
FUNDERE			
Qua possint humili fundere corde preces.	390	Musae 12	12
FUNDERER			
In flumen moerore nigrum si funderer ardens,	422	Mem.Matr.1	5
FUNDIS			
Durescunt proprijs euulsa corallia fundis,	410	Lucus 1	3
FUNDITUS			
Iam te funditus igneis Camoenis,	400	Musae 37	19
FUNDOS			
nos nostraque omnia priuilegia, fundos, aedificia, vniuersam Musarum	465	Epistolae	6
FUNDUNT			
Ambustis sudibus: pars vitam in pocula fundunt,	418	Tr.Mortis	20
FUNDUS			
fustibulos fundusque quibus cum numine fretus	271	Tr.Mortis VS	43
FUNE			
Haec vbi iuncta, subit viuo cum fune minister,	420	Tr.Mortis	66
Haec vbi vincta, subit viuo cum fune minister,	271	Tr.Mortis VS	66
FUNERA			
Deducant linguae funera sola tuae.	438	Poem.Lat.	6
FUNERE			
Haud aliter cum Christus obit, prae funere tanto	409	Passio 20	5
Dissutus videor funere & ipse tuo.	428	Mem.Matr.11	12
Funereque hoc cultum vindicat aegra suum.	431	Mem.Matr.19	4
Hoc mihi legatum tristi si funere praestes,	434	Poem.Lat.	7
Se quasi donatum funere quisque putat.	435	Poem.Lat.	4
FUNERIBUS			
Frustra itaque in tot funeribus miraberis vnum,	415	Lucus 23	11
FUNGAR			
Hoc saltem officio fungar amore tui.	437	Poem.Lat.	8

FUNGAR (cont'd)	PAGE	TITLE		LINE
cum grauibus duobus muneribus fungar apud Meos, Rhetoris in hunc	472	Epistolae		25
FUNUS				
Terram & funus olent flores: Dominaeque cadauer	425	Mem.Matr.5		5
Vespere ros maestis funus honestet aquis.	425	Mem.Matr.5		16
FURATUS				
O nimium Latro! reliquis furatus abunde, ...	406	Passio 11		1
FURENTI				
Olim accreuerit Herculi furenti:	401	Musae 37		27
FURENTIS				
Non vlla Bellonae furentis	434	Poem.Lat.		23
FURI				
Hoc erit, Anti-furi-Puri-Categoria.	386	Musae 3		8
FURIAE				
Dicite, vos Furiae, qua gaudet origine Monstrum.	420	Tr.Mortis		85
FURIT				
In patinas alij: furit inconstantia vini	418	Tr.Mortis		21
Bacchantur Lapithae, furit inconstantia vini	271	Tr.Mortis	VS	21
FUROR				
Cum sacra perturbet vester furor omnia, scriptum	386	Musae 3		7
Corda furor, spissaque afflat caligine sensus?	401	Musae 39		5
FURORIS				
Ira facit, mundusque ipse est apotheca furoris.	418	Tr.Mortis		17
FURTIM				
qui furtim ascendit ad nubes, vbi iam ingrauescit humore, . .	454	Orationes		28
FURUOS				
Furuosque vicisti Gigantes, ...	434	Poem.Lat.		19
FUSA				
Fusaque decurrit notis aqua ferrea sulcis:	419	Tr.Mortis		52
FUSO				
Anglia cur solum fuso sine sanguine sicca est, ...	411	Lucus 6		1
ac si Fatis a fuso essent atque consilijs, sine quibus ne vnum quidem	449	Orationes		30
FUSOS				
maris quasi Flagellatores expugnatos fusosque nobis dedisti.	462	Epistolae		9
FUSTIBALOS				
Fustibalos fundasque, quibus, cum Numine, fretus	419	Tr.Mortis		43
FUSTIBULOS				
fustibulos fundusque quibus cum numine fretus	271	Tr.Mortis	VS	43
FUSUS				
Eridanusque pudore fusus.	394	Musae 23		44
FUTILIBUS				
Cum mea futilibus numeris se verba viderent	385	Musae		3
FUTURA				
natura omnis suos habet anteambulones, vnde pluuia futura, an sudum,	445	Orationes		5
praesertim cum futura incerta sint, & nullis perspicillis, . .	449	Orationes		23
FUTURAE				
labore suo & periculo consuleret & praesenti Reipublicae & futurae;	447	Orationes		25
FUTURAM				
Fataque Fortunasque & spem laesere futuram.	432	Poem.Lat.		25
FUTURAS				
Praeflorat sibi nuptias futuras.	408	Passio 19		13
FUTURIS				
Munere dum nobis prodes, Libroque futuris, ...	435	Poem.Lat.		1
FUTURO				
quam de futuro supplicem, integerrimae tuae fidei commendantes.	465	Epistolae		7
FUTURUM				
quod expectamus indies futurum, Almae Matris amorem tecum simul	462	Epistolae		29
enixus gloriae, sollicitudine in futurum plenos, haud parum leuare;	469	Epistolae		11
FUTURUS				
de Principe aliquo, quis sit futurus aut qualis, recte diuinaret,	454	Orationes		9
G				
IACOBO, D. G. Magnae Britanniae, Franciae, & Hiberniae	384	Musae		T
In Sacram Anchoram Piscatoris G. Herbert.	438	Poem.Lat.		T
Tu vero vale, mi proorator, amaque Tuum G. H.	471	Epistolae		12
GALENE				
Galene, frustra es, cur miserum premens	425	Mem.Matr.6		1
GALERUM				
Longe pileus anteit galerum, ...	391	Musae 15		8
GALLI				
Anglorumque arcus gaudentes sanguine Galli, ...	419	Tr.Mortis		42
Angligenumque arces gaudentes sanguine Galli, ...	419	Tr.Mortis	V	42
GALLUS				
Tillius incumbit Dano, Gallusque marinis, ...	427	Mem.Matr.9		11
GAR				
Nou d' autou taphos est' aster: pheggos gar ekeinou	429	Mem.Matr.14		3
Ouk eni thauma toson spheterizein: oude gar udor, ...	430	Mem.Matr.17		4
Autar axei megaloi kentoumenai: eute gar autai	431	Mem.Matr.17		10
Alla meneit', ou gar taraxos poti metera bainei, ...	431	Mem.Matr.18		5
GARRIENS				
Molita, reliquum deinde garriens diem	422	Mem.Matr.2		12
more maiorum, multos iam annos Anglice viuens garriensque. . .	470	Epistolae		5
GARRIRE				
sed lubet garrire paulo. Iupiter!	471	Epistolae		6
GARRITU				
facile conijcitur ex coelo, ex garritu auium, ex lapidum exhalatione:	445	Orationes		6
GAUDENS				
Luscum prodigium, medioque foramine gaudens.	419	Tr.Mortis		54
GAUDENTES				
Anglorumque arcus gaudentes sanguine Galli, ...	419	Tr.Mortis		42
Angligenumque arces gaudentes sanguine Galli, ...	419	Tr.Mortis	V	42

	PAGE	TITLE	LINE
GAUDEO			
gaudeo quidem de ingenti amore in Principem, cui nulla dilectio par	451	Orationes	21
GAUDERENT			
Musarum, quae cum olim gauderent Fluuijs, nunc etiam aquas,	460	Epistolae	8
GAUDES			
Pagina, gustasti, multoque interprete gaudes:	402	Musae 39	24
GAUDET			
Dicite, vos Furiae, qua gaudet origine Monstrum.	420	Tr.Mortis	85
Dicite vos Stutiae, qua gaudet origine monstrum	272	Tr.Mortis VS	85
GAUDIA			
Gaudia sola fores: sic quicquid somnia mentis	402	Musae 39	36
Et lucro apponis gaudia sancta tuo.	424	Mem.Matr.3	6
In nebulas similesque tui res gaudia nunquid	426	Mem.Matr.7	2
Nostra etiam paribus marcescant gaudia fatis.	427	Mem.Matr.7	34
quidem vt Maiestatis vestrae gaudia responderint aut nostris votis	443	Orationes	13
omnipotens, conserues nobis haec gaudia, imbuas cor Regium vigore,	444	Orationes	4
gaudia praestolantur, quae iamdudum annuunt mihi vt perorem.	454	Orationes	22
GAUDIJS			
Mater perpetuis vuida gaudijs,	424	Mem.Matr.4	2
GAUDIO			
quod quae nos audiamus summo cum gaudio ea Maiestas vestra summa	443	Orationes	31
Ego auctior iam gaudio atque distentior, Cantabrigiam redij.	471	Epistolae	17
GE			
prouecta atque adulta, ipsam possessionem adeas, agathei ge tuxei.	470	Epistolae	9
GEITONOS			
Nun themis orphnaiei megales epi geitonos aisei	431	Mem.Matr.18	3
GELIDIS			
Postquam se gelidis nocte refecit aquis:	412	Lucus 8	2
GELU			
Aut vt pruna gelu summo mordacius vrit,	399	Musae 35	5
GEMINA			
De gemina Academia.	388	Musae 8	T
GEMINAS			
Tu geminas belli portas, o Petre, repandis,	398	Musae 33	11
GEMINETUR			
in nos amor, antehac satis perspectus, nunc cum honore geminetur.	466	Epistolae	4
GEMIS			
Dum longi lentique gemis sub pondere morbi	438	Poem.Lat.	1
GEMITUS			
Sanctos qui gemitus mentibus inseris	403	Musae 40	12
Siste tuum fletum & gemitus: namque imbribus istis	415	Lucus 23	13
Vel gemitus Erebi: piceo se turbine voluens	420	Tr.Mortis	75
GEMMA			
Quaesitum Dominam gemma vel herba suam.	425	Mem.Matr.5	12
Et tu gemma etiam Britonum, Septentrionum	211	Cam.1613-b BR	11
GEMMAM			
Progenies, gemmamque sua quasi pyxide clausit.	402	Musae 39	16
Sic lactare animos & sic ostendere gemmam	432	Poem.Lat.	31
GENAS			
Vestrasque laudes, poscit & mixtas genas.	422	Mem.Matr.2	4
Quae mihi lugubres contribuere genas!	437	Poem.Lat.	12
GENERAT			
Sol generat populum luce fouente nouum.	384	Musae	2
GENEROSOS			
spiritus, generososque animos frangere et retundere clamitant.	461	Epistolae	19
GENESTHAI			
Ainon omou Zoein kai pneumatos allo genesthai	431	Mem.Matr.17	22
GENETEIRAN			
Geneteiran ou tis andron	430	Mem.Matr.16	5
Aiazo geneteiran, epaiazousi kai alloi,	430	Mem.Matr.17	1
Prounomioi d' aretes koinen geneteiran elontes.	430	Mem.Matr.17	3
Aiazo geneteiran, epaiazousi gunaikes,	431	Mem.Matr.17	8
Aiazo geneteiran, epaiazousin oporai,	431	Mem.Matr.17	15
GENIALIS			
En Aurora vocat, lectus genialis in aula est,	210	Cam.1613-b BR	1
GENIJ			
Pallida materni Genij atque exanguis imago,	426	Mem.Matr.7	1
GENIO			
Quos inter plenusque Deo genioque Iacobus	399	Musae 33	23
GENIS			
Occiduis, tanquam duplice nube, genis.	427	Mem.Matr.9	6
GENITRIX			
Tam languens genitrix cineri supposta fugaci:	426	Mem.Matr.7	9
Hoc, Genitrix, scriptum proles tibi sedula mittit.	427	Mem.Matr.9	1
GENOUS			
Otan de krepis me katablethei genous	447	Orationes	14
GENS			
Quas gens inconsulta, suis vexata procellis,	401	Musae 39	2
Gens tota fiet, atque vtrinque plectetur.	405	Passio 5	7
Quam nihil illudis, Gens improba! quam male cedunt	405	Passio 7	1
quo magis amore coalescamus, vtraque gens Hispanica, Britannica,	440	Orationes	22
Quae enim vspiam gens, quod vnquam seculum meliorem habuit Principem?	445	Orationes	12
GENTE			
Qua Mors ipsa sedens hominum de gente triumphat.	419	Tr.Mortis	56
GENTEM			
nimirum infinitum Principis in suam gentem amorem, cui pacem	449	Orationes	36
cuius manifestationem in gentem suam priuatae personae & habitui	453	Orationes	8
GENTES			
Hinc te olim gentes miratae odere vicissim;	416	Lucus 25	11
Quod aliae gentes manibus in coelum sublatis, lachrymis in terram	448	Orationes	34

	PAGE	TITLE	LINE
GENTIBUS			
Quamobrem optime consuluit gentibus natura, cum paupertatem daret	450	Orationes	23
GENTIS			
Dolere prohibes? aut dolere me gentis	429	Mem.Matr.12	5
GENTIUM			
quod quidem vbi gentium si non ab Hispano sperandum? . . .	447	Orationes	30
praecipue pharetrata, quae ad poenam gentium & Bellum spectant.	449	Orationes	28
GENU			
Posteritas flectet corque genuque mihi.	405	Passio 7	6
GENUERE			
Nox Aetnam, noctemque Chaos genuere priores.	420	Tr.Mortis	86
GENUFLEX			
In Arund. Spin. Genuflex. Purpur.	405	Passio 7	T
GENUIT			
Congrediens genuit Monachum, qui limen opacae	420	Tr.Mortis	89
GENUS			
In metri genus.	387	Musae 5	T
Femineum blanda fallitis arte genus:	387	Musae 5	10
Tantum repertum est trux hominum genus, ...	394	Musae 23	17
GEO			
Regi, Fidei Defensori &c. Geo. Herbertus.	384	Musae	T
GEOPONICIS			
in Geoponicis dicitur, Katoptron ean epideikseis toi epikeimenoi	454	Orationes	18
GEORGII			
Georgii Herbertii Angli Musae Responsoriae	384	Musae	T
GEORGIJ			
Oratio Domini Georgij Herbert, Oratoris Academiae Cantabrigiensis,	440	Orationes	T
GEORGION			
Odurma Daimonon, Theou georgion, ...	429	Mem.Matr.15	2
GEORGIUM			
beabis Filium tuum obsequentissimum GEORGIUM HERBERT. . . .	473	Epistolae	13
GEORGIUS			
ex Hispanijs celebrauit Georgius Herbert Academiae Cantabrigiensis	444	Orationes	T
GEORGON			
Eirene georgon kan petrais trephei kalos, ...	448	Orationes	14
GERERE			
neque quotidianae virtutis prouincia gerere personam Academiae,	465	Epistolae	9
GERIT			
Spargitque per tot capita, quot vulgus gerit.	414	Lucus 20	4
GERMANA			
Te Germana tamen pubes, te Graecus & Anglus	416	Lucus 26	3
GERMANO			
Interea procede Comes Germano-britanne	211	Cam.1613-b BR	7
GERMANO-BRITANNE			
Interea procede Comes Germano-britanne	211	Cam.1613-b BR	7
GESTA			
annon eius consilio res gesta est?	451	Orationes	24
GESTABARIS			
Sane, gestabaris antea in cordibus nostris;	458	Epistolae	18
GESTANTUR			
aut si mutant locum, gestantur, tanquam onera, circumferuntur	452	Orationes	11
GESTAS			
esse Alexandro Magno nisi eius res gestas tradidisset historia?	441	Orationes	19
GESTIENS			
Hos ad se trahere et mergere gestiens.	391	Musae 17	10
GESTIMUS			
nostrumque regnum gestimus fieri participes eius sanguinis, . . .	440	Orationes	19
GESTIO			
Hinc fremere totus & minari gestio	427	Mem.Matr.8	5
GESTIS			
sic & ipse excerpam e Principis rebus gestis pugillum, vnam actionem	445	Orationes	31
GESTIT			
Sic tuus effundi gestit pro crimine sanguis, ...	404	Passio 3	1
GIGANTEM			
Fides gigantem sola, vel facit nanum.	406	Passio 12	5
GIGANTES			
Furuosque vicisti Gigantes, ...	434	Poem.Lat.	19
GIGAS			
Quid hoc? & ipse deficis, Caeli gigas, ...	407	Passio 16	1
GLADIO			
ferox spumantia mandit, iuuat micare gladio & mucronem intueri.	447	Orationes	35
causaris, irruit Miles in Musaeum tuum, & gladio te liberat.	448	Orationes	28
GLADIOS			
Gladiosue, Catapultasue teneam, quin neque	421	Lucus 33	5
GLADIUM			
Dum gladium stringens Paulus ad arma vocat.	398	Musae 33	12
GLANDE			
Ego hic pultibus vescor et glande, more maiorum, multos iam annos	470	Epistolae	4
GLANS			
Glans dedit, & truncus tectum, & ramalia mortem.	418	Tr.Mortis	8
Huic Glans adijcitur (non quam ructare vetustas	419	Tr.Mortis	60
Hinc Glans adijcitur (non quam ructare vetustas	419	Tr.Mortis V	60
Plumbea glans, liuensque suae quasi conscia noxae, ...	419	Tr.Mortis	62
Totamque eructans nubem, Glans proruit imo	420	Tr.Mortis	76
Nec Glans sola nocet; mortem quandoque susurrat	420	Tr.Mortis	83
GLAPHURON			
Menoun to glaphuron, kai melirroon tropon, ...	430	Mem.Matr.15	8
GLASTO			
Maiores nostri, qui olim glasto se inficientes, in vxorum corporibus,	446	Orationes	30
GLISCENTEM			
Aspicis multitudinem Librorum indies gliscentem, praesertim . .	467	Epistolae	29

	PAGE	TITLE		LINE
GLOBOS				
dum globos tractas & coelos fictitios, perrumpit primipilus,	448	Orationes		29
GLOBUM				
Per te nascor in hunc globum	425	Mem.Matr.4		13
GLORIA				
Ingens piorum gloria Principum,	394	Musae 23		38
At nunc exucco similis tua gloria RAMO	416	Lucus 25		5
Vt currat paribus gloria tibijs.	425	Mem.Matr.4		16
Aeterna summae gloria regiae,	433	Poem.Lat.		2
Cui magnum imperium, gloria maior erat:	435	Poem.Lat.		2
cuius ingens gloria aeque rotunda est atque ipse orbis:	440	Orationes		15
Quam cruenta gloria est, quae super ceruicibus hominum erigitur?	449	Orationes		9
reuersus per mare, gloria, prudentia auctior, ditat patriam,	454	Orationes		32
Tu vero macte honoribus, gloria, id enim nostra interest,	457	Epistolae		24
GLORIAE				
in quo longe vberrimam gloriae segetem perspicio, nulla verborum,	446	Orationes		2
Ecquid inter tot gloriae titulos caput vndique munientes meministi	456	Epistolae		2
adeon' es praedo omnis gloriae, vt ne gratitudinis laudem nobis	459	Epistolae		3
cui natura spiritum dederit feracem gloriae, et coeleste ingenium	468	Epistolae		5
tibi hunc honorem, et faxit, vt tibi gloriae sit, omnibus saluti.	469	Epistolae		5
solent enim Studiosorum suffragia enixus gloriae, sollicitudine	469	Epistolae		10
GLORIAM				
Tuasque librans actiones, gloriam	414	Lucus 20		13
Tuam gloriam censemus nostram, et in honoribus Tuis nostro bono	456	Epistolae		16
victoriaeque gloriam absque crudelitate effusi sanguinis delibas.	458	Epistolae		15
quum tamen Tu inuaseris eorum gloriam conseruando nobis quae illi	458	Epistolae		26
quae complexus es animo, ad eius gloriam, Reipublicae emolumentum,	464	Epistolae		5
Antiquitas praeripuit Tibi gloriam extruendae Academiae,	465	Epistolae		17
GLORIAMUR				
sitis ordine atque habitu, quo nos in hoc regno omnes esse gloriamur.	441	Orationes		2
GLORIAS				
Et flatulentas aucupatur glorias,	414	Lucus 20		2
GLORIER				
ipse egit oratorem, vt & ego aliquantulum hoc nomine glorier.	450	Orationes		31
GLORIOLAS				
Nolite tamen contemnere has gloriolas nostras quas e chartis	441	Orationes		17
GLORIOSUM				
Scio Belli nomen splendidum esse & gloriosum:	447	Orationes		33
GLUBAT				
Haud glubat inde tres teruncios escae.	429	Mem.Matr.12		4
GLUKERAI				
Ouk eti despoines glukerai meledoni trapheisai:	431	Mem.Matr.17		16
GNARUM				
Scio Hispanum versutum, callidum, artis & aucupij apprime gnarum:	451	Orationes		25
GOD				
To the right honourable and reverend Father in God, my L. Bishop of	473	Epistolae		23
GOOI				
Meteri tektainousa, gooi kai penthesi sugxroun.	431	Mem.Matr.17		14
GOOU				
Pos nun aphiptasai, goou kai kindunou	429	Mem.Matr.15		3
GORGONA				
Gorgona cur diram laruasque obtrudis inanes,	387	Musae 6		1
GORGONE				
De Laruata Gorgone.	387	Musae 6		T
GORGONEAM				
Pallada gorgoneam, sic tua verba placent.	387	Musae 6		4
Sumite gorgoneam, nostraque Pallas erit.	387	Musae 6		6
GORGONEAS				
Tu discidisti Gorgoneas manus	434	Poem.Lat.		17
GOROPIUS				
Goropius Becanus ait vetus vocabulum nostrum, Koning, & contracte	447	Orationes		5
GRACCHORUM				
qua in re celebris est Gracchorum mater, ingenium ipsum atque indoles	447	Orationes		17
GRADU				
quam nunc pleno gradu ingrediens beneficijs tuis percurres.	468	Epistolae		19
GRADUM				
hunc quidem gradum pignus habes amoris nostri, haec est ansa qua	456	Epistolae		5
GRADUS				
postquam omnes honorum gradus hic percurreris, aeternum illud	457	Epistolae		3
GRAECAM				
Cur teretem Graecam damnas, atque Hellada totam,	391	Musae 16		3
GRAECIS				
Aetna Cacum igniuomum dedit, hic Ixiona Graecis	272	Tr.Mortis	VS	87
GRAECUS				
Te Germana tamen pubes, te Graecus & Anglus	416	Lucus 26		3
GRAMINA				
Hic vbi discumbunt per gramina, salsior vnus	418	Tr.Mortis		12
GRANDI				
Heroum grandi carmina fulta pede?	387	Musae 5		4
Grandi reaeque praefero,	427	Mem.Matr.8		2
cum grandi atque impedito onere facillime incedens, occurrit ei	453	Orationes		34
quando ad magnates cogitas, stylo vtare, sed modeste grandi;	470	Epistolae		22
GRANDIS				
dum animus grandis, suique impos, triumphos & victorias quasi fraena	447	Orationes		33
GRANTAM				
Dum petit Infantem Princeps, Grantamque Iacobus,	437	Poem.Lat.		1
Cum petit Hispanam Princeps, Grantamque Iacobus,	437	Poem.Lat.	V	1
GRANUM				
Granum Sinapis, acre Alijs, crescens sibi:	437	Poem.Lat.		26
GRAPSANTES				
Ouk et' emen idias phules grapsantes arogon,	430	Mem.Matr.17		2

	PAGE	TITLE	LINE
GRASSANTES			
quam de muniendis contra grassantes flammas aedificijs Honori Tuo	457	Epistolae	18
GRATA			
Grata mihi mensae sunt analecta tuae.	385	Musae 1	6
GRATAS			
bellique miserias gratas, praecipue vbi velut ex continentibus tectis	449	Orationes	13
GRATES			
Quotidiana suas poscant si fercula grates, ...	389	Musae 12	9
GRATIA			
Vt, si gratia tanta copuletur	421	Lucus 34	7
vtrum gratia Principis virtutes tuas, aut nostra vota gratiam	456	Epistolae	20
quamuis enim sexcenta huiusmodi praediola Tua gratia permutare nolim,	472	Epistolae	30
GRATIAE			
Excellentijs Vestris Musae omnes, Gratiaeque, obsecrantes, . .	440	Orationes	7
2. Ad R. Naunton Gratiae de Fluuio et de tegendis Tectis stramineis	457	Epistolae	T
3. Ad Iacobum Regem Gratiae de Scriptis suis Academiae donatis	458	Epistolae	T
4. Ad Iacobum Regem Gratiae de Fluuio contra Redemptores . .	460	Epistolae	T
5. Ad F. Bacon, Cancell. Gratiae de Fluuio	460	Epistolae	T
6. Ad R. Naunton, Secret. Gratiae de Fluuio	461	Epistolae	T
Ad Ful. Grevil Gratiae de Fluuio	462	Epistolae	T
Cancel. Gratiae de Instaurationis Libro Academiae donato . .	463	Epistolae	T
quos profectus feceris in Sphaera Naturae, facias etiam in Gratiae:	464	Epistolae	4
GRATIAM			
hilare est, laetum, ac lubens, vestram in gratiam amplectimur.	440	Orationes	13
aut nostra vota gratiam Principis, aut Tuae virtutes et vota nostra	456	Epistolae	21
aut Tuae virtutes et vota nostra et Principis gratiam superarent.	456	Epistolae	22
GRATIARUM			
Quare nos tertium praedictis adiungimus Gratiarum Fluuium, . .	462	Epistolae	24
GRATIFICARI			
Quod si tam integrum tibi esset gratificari nobis in terra & aere,	457	Epistolae	21
GRATIJS			
O plena centum Musica Gratijs, ...	394	Musae 23	21
Lepos seuerus, Pallas mixta Gratijs;	423	Mem.Matr.2	30
temporibus et diligentia diuisos in gratijs nostris copulauimus.	457	Epistolae	16
GRATIOR			
Nunc etiam teneras quo versus gratior aures	387	Musae 5	11
GRATIS			
Cum stare gratis cum silentio possim?	472	Epistolae	18
GRATISSIME			
Fama promotionis tuae gratissime appulit ad nos omnes haud ita certe	468	Epistolae	12
GRATISSIMO			
abunde compensas nos, gratissimoque Almam Matrem prosequeris animo:	456	Epistolae	8
GRATISSIMOS			
ac merentibus vobis gratissimos, Saluete tandem Magistri Artium,	440	Orationes	4
GRATISSIMUS			
Ante tuum tempus coelum gratissimus ambis.	402	Musae 39	29
GRATITUDINEM			
Vitam reduxit: ecce gratitudinem.	413	Lucus 14	2
GRATITUDINES			
certe adeo festinasti ad gratitudines tuas cum emolumento nostro	462	Epistolae	14
GRATITUDINIS			
cum humanitatis Tuae, tum gratitudinis nostrae ratio postulat.	457	Epistolae	10
es praedo omnis gloriae, vt ne gratitudinis laudem nobis reliqueris?	459	Epistolae	3
GRATULAMUR			
censemus nostram, et in honoribus Tuis nostro bono gratulamur;	456	Epistolae	17
primo gratulamur optimo Regi nostro, qui prospicit, vt cum ipse	463	Epistolae	20
dein Hon. Tuo gratulamur, qui filio auctus es tali ingenio praedito:	463	Epistolae	24
Quare summe gratulamur tibi de nouo hoc cumulo honorum, . .	464	Epistolae	20
vero de hoc tuo progressu non minus Reipublicae gratulamur quam tibi,	466	Epistolae	16
Quare tam vere quam libenter gratulamur tibi, nec minus etiam	468	Epistolae	18
GRATULANTUR			
noui tituli accessionem summe gratulantur Excellentijs Vestris Musae	440	Orationes	7
GRATULATI			
Certe non diu est ex quo gratulati sumus tibi:	465	Epistolae	23
GRATULATIO			
1. Ad Buckingh. C. Gratulatio de Marchionatu	456	Epistolae	T
9. Ad Mounteg., Thesaurar. Gratulatio	464	Epistolae	T
11.Ad T. Coventry, Attorn. Cognitorem Gratulatio	465	Epistolae	T
12. Ad Heath, Sollicitorem Procuratorem Gratulatio	466	Epistolae	T
15. Ad J. Leigh, Capitalem Iustitiarium Angl. (Camden) Gratulatio	468	Epistolae	T
16. Ad Cranfield, Thesaurar. Gratulatio	469	Epistolae	T
GRATULATIONEM			
paratos nos habebis ad gratulationem, vt sic vna opera vtriusque	465	Epistolae	26
GRATULETUR			
tanquam partubus Virtutum Tuarum, Alma Mater accurrens gratuletur:	469	Epistolae	9
GRATUM			
etiam Fluuium non minus de praeterito gratum, quam de futuro	465	Epistolae	7
GRATUS			
Tantum istaec scribo gratus, ne tu mihi tantum	422	Mem.Matr.1	7
GRAUE			
ni graue est, librum tibi Oratorium lampademque tradat. . .	470	Epistolae	9
GRAUEM			
tam grauem) & apud quos dico, viros limatae auris atque tersae,	445	Orationes	26
GRAUEOLENTE			
Ipse fruare, licet, solus graueolente sepulcro;	414	Lucus 21	5
GRAUES			
Graues lagenas, Vester est Aquae-ductus.	405	Passio 5	9
Corneliae sanctae, graues Semproniae, ...	422	Mem.Matr.2	1
Quod si Nuptiae in se graues sunt, quanto magis Principum, . .	446	Orationes	34
GRAUI			
Nempe graui fertur scelerata pecunia motu, ...	410	Lucus 4	7

	PAGE	TITLE	LINE
GRAUI (cont'd)			
Intra extraque graui plenus es illuuie.	414	Lucus 21	2
GRAUIBUS			
cum grauibus duobus muneribus fungar apud Meos, Rhetoris in hunc	472	Epistolae	25
GRAUIDAE			
Vae nubi pluuia grauidae, non lacte, measque	426	Mem.Matr.7	5
GRAUIDAM			
vt Almam Matrem spe noua grauidam semper atque praegnantem	464	Epistolae	25
GRAUIDIS			
Nec grauidis medicina tuta est.	426	Mem.Matr.6	20
GRAUIDUS			
CAROLVS redijt, honore grauidus, grauidus scientia, cruribus thymo	454	Orationes	27
honore grauidus, grauidus scientia, cruribus thymo plenis:	454	Orationes	27
GRAUIORE			
Praecipitans grauiore casu.	433	Poem.Lat.	16
GRAUIS			
vti vir, tetragonos est, grauis, nobilis, perspicua, succincta.	471	Epistolae	4
GRAUISSIMA			
re vna omnium grauissima, alienis oculis iudicioque inniti;	447	Orationes	23
GRAUISSIMI			
Veneranda Capita, Viri grauissimi, Pubes lectissima.	444	Orationes	11
GRAUITAS			
Namque hanc ruinam salua Grauitas defleat,	422	Mem.Matr.2	5
GRAUITATE			
Quaeque domus Dominae sit, grauitate docent.	425	Mem.Matr.5	8
limatae auris atque tersae, quorum grauitate ac purpura non abutar.	445	Orationes	27
GRAUITATI			
abijcite quisque libros, non est locus grauitati, neque apud vos:	454	Orationes	34
certe non tam ornas illam, qui infers manum grauitati.	470	Epistolae	21
GREGARIA			
ac si non gregaria essent animalia, sed tigres aut vrsi.	450	Orationes	22
GREGI			
Testatosque suo tradiderat gregi;	391	Musae 17	2
Quam Christus immortalis innocuo gregi	396	Musae 28	1
GREGIS			
Christus Apostolici cinctus amore gregis.	398	Musae 33	10
GREMIO			
non gremio solum (quod innuis) sed et ambabus vlnis osculisque ei	463	Epistolae	6
GREVIL			
Ad Ful. Grevil Gratiae de Fluuio	462	Epistolae	T
GREX			
Tun' obdis aures, grex noue, barbaras,	395	Musae 23	45
GULAE			
magnum aperirem, quorum imperium gulae impar erat, vt interdum putem,	452	Orationes	23
GULIELMUS			
Gulielmus Victor descensurus primum e nauibus in terram hanc,	455	Orationes	3
GULOSUM			
In Gulosum.	414	Lucus 21	T
GUNAIKES			
Aiazo geneteiran, epaiazousi gunaikes,	431	Mem.Matr.17	8
GUNAIKON			
Meter, gunaikon aigle, anthropon eris,	429	Mem.Matr.15	1
GURGITEM			
tanquam gurgitem imperuestigabilem, victoriae nuncupemus:	449	Orationes	22
GURGUSTIJS			
e gurgustijs vestris, vbi trecenta foliorum iugera vno die sedentes	454	Orationes	24
GUSTASTI			
Pagina, gustasti, multoque interprete gaudes:	402	Musae 39	24
GUSTO			
Gusto proboque Dolium.	427	Mem.Matr.8	10
GUTTA			
Et numerat mortes singula gutta pares;	415	Lucus 23	10
Quacunque gutta temporis imminent?	433	Poem.Lat.	6
GUTTAE			
Quae guttae poterunt enumerare meos?	422	Mem.Matr.1	2
GUTTULAE			
Ramenta coeli; guttulaeque	394	Musae 23	35
HABE			
dignissime praeficiaris Fisco, etiam Academiam in Thesauris habe:	469	Epistolae	22
HABEAMUS			
ipso Parnasso siti sumus, liberiorem, quam alij, prospectum habeamus.	449	Orationes	34
HABEANT			
insunt oculi variegati, cum caetera animantia vnicolores habeant.	453	Orationes	18
HABEAT			
Intus agunt, habeat certum meditatio finem:	402	Musae 39	37
vt quid priuata habeat in se vita commodi aut voluptatis,	452	Orationes	37
vt nihil habeat Inuidia ipsa, quod contra hiscat aut mussitet.	453	Orationes	24
HABEBIS			
paratos nos habebis ad gratulationem, vt sic vna opera vtriusque	465	Epistolae	25
HABEBIT			
Nec vel tantillum pignus habebit amor?	396	Musae 26	2
HABEMUS			
quas non nobis habemus sed irrigati ipsi vniuersum regnum aspergimus?	462	Epistolae	10
HABENAS			
Tantum etenim vestras (Parcae) non flectit habenas	433	Poem.Lat.	40
HABENT			
Vertas specillum: nam, prout se res habent,	388	Musae 8	17
hinc Reges Legatos habent statarios ac resides, quem locum Noster	450	Orationes	29
HABERE			
Communem habere crede cum Cerdonibus:	413	Lucus 17	6

	PAGE	TITLE	LINE
HABERET			
Contemplare, miser, quantum terroris haberet	417	Lucus 31	5
HABERETUR			
vnius seculi Princeps, sed & omnium, quae ventura sunt, haberetur.	447	Orationes	26
HABES			
hunc quidem gradum pignus habes amoris nostri, haec est ansa qua	456	Epistolae	5
HABET			
Quas Luna habet, tuetur, in foueam cadit,	393	Musae 22	8
Quasque habet aut patulas, aut caeco tramite, moles	402	Musae 39	21
In cruce suspendens, vnde reclinet, habet.	407	Passio 15	4
Plusque habet hic laetus, quam vel Auarus habet.	411	Lucus 7	4
Quicquid habet tellus, quicquid & astra, fruens.	429	Mem.Matr.13	6
Vt natura omnis suos habet anteambulones, vnde pluuia futura,	445	Orationes	5
Nihil habet humana vita maioris momenti aut ponderis, quam Nuptiae,	446	Orationes	16
Nunc enim exploratos habet nostros in se affectus, timores,	450	Orationes	34
HABETIS			
Sed qui tam male pileos habetis,	391	Musae 15	11
mirabilius, cuius tamen fructum omnem nondum habetis enucleatum.	450	Orationes	3
HABITA			
habita coram Dominis Legatis cum Magistro. in Artib. titulis	440	Orationes	T
Discessum Regis ab Academia Cantabrigiae habita 12o die Martij 1622	443	Orationes	T
neque ratione habita Chartae nostrae a Serenissimo Principe Henrico 8	467	Epistolae	21
HABITACULA			
Intuituque vno stringens habitacula mundi,	402	Musae 39	12
HABITANT			
Hic habitant Musae, facilisque in carmine Pallas,	210	Cam.1613-a BR	3
gauderent Fluuijs, nunc etiam aquas, in quibus habitant, impertis!	460	Epistolae	9
HABITARE			
Ingluuieque minor. Quercus habitare feruntur	418	Tr.Mortis	5
HABITU			
cum eo sitis ordine atque habitu, quo nos in hoc regno omnes esse	441	Orationes	1
sub ementito habitu fidicinis castra hostium ingressus,	453	Orationes	4
HABITUI			
manifestationem in gentem suam priuatae personae & habitui debuit.	453	Orationes	9
HABITUS			
Irregularis nunc habitus mihi est:	426	Mem.Matr.6	21
retulisset captus piscis, foelicissimus mortalium habitus est.	444	Orationes	16
HABUERE			
Cum qui plus terrae, plus habuere maris.	411	Lucus 6	4
apud poetas deorum pharetrae operculum habuere, humanae non item:	449	Orationes	25
HABUI			
Habui viaticum fauoris Tui, quod longiori multo itineri sufficeret.	471	Epistolae	18
HABUIT			
Quos charos habuit Christus Apostolos,	391	Musae 17	1
Quae enim vspiam gens, quod vnquam seculum meliorem habuit Principem?	445	Orationes	13
quod optimus Princeps non tantum exteras regiones habuit perspectas,	451	Orationes	36
Noster etiam Princeps habuit Daphnen suam, cuius amor deinceps	455	Orationes	10
HAC			
Hac ope munitus securior excipis vndas,	402	Musae 39	30
Hac facie dominae conspiciare tuae:	211	Cam.1613-b BR	10
hac re solum vlciscimur mortem, ligantes abruptum vitae filum,	446	Orationes	22
interim vestra hac scribendi laude intacta manente atque illibata.	458	Epistolae	27
iniurias seculi scriptaque hac illac pereuntia securius praeterit.	459	Epistolae	14
ad progressum doctrinae, hac etiam in parte nobis opituleris.	467	Epistolae	28
etiam senectus, quam aetatem in hac palaestra consecutus mihi videor.	471	Epistolae	8
imo precabor enixe, me tum priuari tam communi hac luce, quam Tua,	472	Epistolae	24
quod pronomina mea adeo audacter incedant in hac epistola:	473	Epistolae	16
HAE			
Hae tibi sunt alae laudum. Cui contigit vnquam	435	Poem.Lat.	5
Hae tibi sunt alae laudis. Cui contigit vnquam	435	Poem.Lat. V	5
quando ipsae hae turres & beatae fabricae, vnico ictu sulphurei tubi,	448	Orationes	20
HAEC			
Haec facit ad nasum sola loquela tuum.	391	Musae 16	6
Namque haec, iure, cuipiam	395	Musae 25	20
Haec verba superos aduolaturus thronos	396	Musae 28	7
Haec etiam ad pugnam praesens, qua viuimus, aetas	399	Musae 33	21
(Et quem non stimularet haec simultas?)	400	Musae 37	18
Plus charta haec mea delibuta dictis	400	Musae 37	25
Nunc haec omnia sustuli, tonantes	401	Musae 37	31
Haec autem hospitio latere turpi	411	Lucus 5	6
Sera nimis lacryma haec, si lacrymabis, erit.	415	Lucus 23	12
Hostibus haec etiam parcens imitatur Iesum.	416	Lucus 26	5
Coniugium Caeli Terraeque haec machina praestat;	417	Lucus 31	1
Haec fuerant: sic Tisiphone virguncula lusit.	418	Tr.Mortis	23
Omniaque haec vt transadigant sine crimine costas,	418	Tr.Mortis	29
Haec vbi iuncta, subit viuo cum fune minister,	420	Tr.Mortis	66
Haec vbi vincta, subit viuo cum fune minister,	271	Tr.Mortis VS	66
At tu qui inepte haec dicta censes filio,	423	Mem.Matr.2	52
Scilicet id splendes: haec est tibi causa micandi,	424	Mem.Matr.3	5
Haec fuerat olim potio Domini tui.	427	Mem.Matr.8	9
Nos flendo: haec nostrum tessera sola ducum.	427	Mem.Matr.9	12
Alteraque haec tua mors, Ilias esto mihi.	428	Mem.Matr.11	14
Spiritus, hi mihi iam montes, haec flumina sunto.	432	Poem.Lat.	11
Expeto, tanquam haec sit nostri medicina doloris?	433	Poem.Lat.	46
posterioris largam messem Vobis haec tenuia boni consulentibus,	441	Orationes	21
Si per haec ludicra nostra pars aliquis eius laetitiae,	443	Orationes	9
omnipotens, conserues nobis haec gaudia, imbuas cor Regium vigore,	444	Orationes	4
cor sacrum, sentiatque Rex ipse nos haec intime precari.	444	Orationes	9
Non ignoro apud quos haec dico, eos scilicet, qui innuptam Palladem	446	Orationes	25
Nam primum tota haec Pieria supellex, charta, calami, codices,	448	Orationes	18
Quamuis res haec. Principibus vt vtilissima ita difficillima factu,	450	Orationes	10

HAEC (cont'd)	PAGE	TITLE	LINE
tanquam ligna obliqua, aliter magna haec mundi domus corrueret:	450	Orationes	28
Hilaris haec sumenda est dies.	454	Orationes	23
haec est ansa qua prehendimus Te, et tanquam Aquilam inter nouas	456	Epistolae	5
Haec vestra spolia actosque ex orbe triumphos communicas cum Alma	458	Epistolae	15
corrumpuntur statuae, haec imago atque character, tempore melior,	459	Epistolae	13
Magna est haec, neque quotidianae virtutis prouincia gerere personam	465	Epistolae	9
Haec tu omnium optime vides, quare causam nostram nosque ipsos Tibi,	468	Epistolae	8
Sed tua humanitas haec nobis expediet.	469	Epistolae	4
Haec tu optime nosti; neque eo dico:	471	Epistolae	5
Tua lenitas non ita interpretabitur mea haec scribendi interualla,	471	Epistolae	25
Quod tamen haec omnia succedant ex voto, quod reclusae sint fores,	472	Epistolae	19
HAERENT			
Dicta ferox: haerent lateri conuitia fixo.	418	Tr.Mortis	15
Dicta ferox, haerent lateri conuitia fixa:	271	Tr.Mortis VS	15
HAERENTES			
et festucas, Reipublicae oculo haerentes, tam diligenter amoues;	462	Epistolae	13
HAERENTIBUS			
manu prehendis Regem, alteram nobis ad radices haerentibus porrigis.	456	Epistolae	15
HAERES			
Vtque ouis in dumis, haeres in crine Cometae,	413	Lucus 16	3
HAERESIS			
Haeresis, euertas. Quid enim te fallere possit?	402	Musae 39	22
HAERET			
Dum librata suis haeret radicibus ilex	428	Mem.Matr.11	1
Atque haeret dubio tabida vita pede,	438	Poem.Lat.	2
HAERETICORUM			
tum venenatorum haereticorum, insita vi sua liberentur.	459	Epistolae	19
HAESISSET			
Haesisset tibi, quam suprema vestis	400	Musae 37	26
HALENT			
Iudicij dominus, flores vt iunctius halent	427	Mem.Matr.7	25
HALITUS			
vt halitus tenuiores solent, qui primo caloris suasu excitati atque	471	Epistolae	28
HANC			
Hanc mihi duritiem contulit improbitas.	410	Lucus 1	2
Namque hanc ruinam salua Grauitas defleat,	422	Mem.Matr.2	5
Carpsit malignum sydus hanc modestiam	427	Mem.Matr.8	3
Quid fauores erga hanc Academiam inenarrabiles, cum non solum tuearis	443	Orationes	21
Gulielmus Victor descensurus primum e nauibus in terram hanc,	455	Orationes	4
commode peruenimus ad laurum hanc, vbi sub vmbra eius paulisper	455	Orationes	13
eum tantum vt permittat nostram hanc Inter victrices hederam sibi	455	Orationes	17
Quare quomodo alij molem hanc laetitiae suae exprimant,	457	Epistolae	1
praesertim sericatam hanc stultitiam contere, Academiaeque iura,	461	Epistolae	23
Pendulam hanc dignitatem diu expectantem magnas aliquas virtutes	464	Epistolae	11
tu hanc personam indue scripturus, tuumque iudicium tibi Lictor esto.	470	Epistolae	26
HARMONIAE			
Caelestis harmoniae breue praeludium.	423	Mem.Matr.2	44
HARMONIAM			
Harmoniam tolerare nullam?	395	Musae 23	52
Harmoniam dabit inter astra.	434	Poem.Lat.	36
HAS			
Scilicet has olim diuisas aequore terras	402	Musae 39	14
Nolite tamen contemnere has gloriolas nostras quas e chartis	441	Orationes	17
HASTA			
Inuisamque tuis erigit hasta Crucem.	398	Musae 33	16
HAUD			
nos haud inanes linqueret,	396	Musae 28	9
Haud per te moritura, Scholamque introspicis omnem.	402	Musae 39	26
Tu tamen, haud tibi tam moreris, quam viuis in illis,	407	Passio 17	3
Haud aliter cum Christus obit, prae funere tanto	409	Passio 20	5
Haud secus ingenitis dotibus orbus Adam.	410	Lucus 1	4
Haud mihi cor saxo durius esse sinas.	410	Lucus 1	6
Difficilis esse haud soleo: nam, pol, si forem,	413	Lucus 17	3
Haud nostro similis, cui necesse,	415	Lucus 24	2
Laudibus haud fierem sepia iusta tuis.	422	Mem.Matr.1	6
Quare haud vos hortos, sed coemeteria dico,	425	Mem.Matr.5	9
Haud glubat inde tres teruncios escae.	429	Mem.Matr.12	4
At forte matrem perdere haud soles demens:	429	Mem.Matr.12	9
aggreditur & labores, haud ignarus, ignem vitae augeri ventilatione,	452	Orationes	33
Haud frustra impendes operam nobis omnia fauorum tuorum momenta	466	Epistolae	7
hospitium, et erga te propensius, haud vsquam forsitan reperias.	466	Epistolae	19
gratissime appulit ad nos omnes haud ita certe studijs chartisque	468	Epistolae	13
Nos etiam haud minimam fauoris tui partem speramus, orantes	468	Epistolae	20
in qua dextra et fide coniuncti, in caeteris haud diuellamur.	468	Epistolae	25
enixus gloriae, sollicitudine in futurum plenos, haud parum leuare;	469	Epistolae	11
HAURIRENT			
Haurirent tibi tota plaustra Musae.	401	Musae 37	30
HAUSERUNT			
conseruantes sibi Illos Fontes, a quibus ipsi olim hauserunt?	461	Epistolae	32
HAUSISSE			
non solum rectum de Bene-merentibus iudicium hausisse ab Antiquis,	469	Epistolae	13
HEATH			
12. Ad Heath, Sollicitorem Procuratorem Gratulatio	466	Epistolae	T
HEBRAEAM			
Scilicet Hebraeam cantas, & perstrepis vnam:	391	Musae 16	5
HECATOMBAS			
post ingentes Hecatombas, exiguam thuris micam adoleri legimus.	469	Epistolae	16
HEDERAE			
Non ego vos posthac hederae velatus amictu	432	Poem.Lat.	2
an inter lauros principis hederae nostrae ambitiosae locus est?	456	Epistolae	4

	PAGE	TITLE	LINE
HEDERAM			
permittat nostram hanc Inter victrices hederam sibi serpere Lauros.	455	Orationes	18
HELICON			
Cedito Barbaries: Helicon iam litibus instat,	417	Lucus 28	5
HELIOGABALORUM			
Quid ego vobis Neronum aut Heliogabalorum ingluuiem memorem?	452	Orationes	19
HELLADA			
Cur teretem Graecam damnas, atque Hellada totam,	391	Musae 16	3
HELLUO			
Ah nunc, helluo, fac, vt ipse sugam:	421	Lucus 34	1
HELLUONES			
vestra disquisitio, qui tineae estis & helluones chartacei;	445	Orationes	18
HENRICI			
In Obitum Henrici Principis Walliae.	432	Poem.Lat.	T
HENRICO			
habita Chartae nostrae a Serenissimo Principe Henrico 8 indultae,	467	Epistolae	22
HERAM			
Dum torus absentem quisque reponit heram.	425	Mem.Matr.5	10
HERBA			
Quaesitum Dominam gemma vel herba suam.	425	Mem.Matr.5	12
HERBAE			
Herbae exoletae, ros-marinus aridus?	424	Mem.Matr.2	58
Hic ego tuque erimus, variae suffitibus herbae	427	Mem.Matr.7	28
HERBAS			
in virginum, flores atque herbas depinxere:	446	Orationes	31
HERBERT			
In Sacram Anchoram Piscatoris G. Herbert.	438	Poem.Lat.	T
Oratio Domini Georgij Herbert, Oratoris Academiae Cantabrigiensis,	440	Orationes	T
Hispanijs celebrauit Georgius Herbert Academiae Cantabrigiensis	444	Orationes	T
Tu vero vale, mi proorator, amaque Tuum G. H.	471	Epistolae	12
beabis Filium tuum obsequentissimum GEORGIUM HERBERT.	473	Epistolae	13
HERBERTII			
Georgii Herbertii Angli Musae Responsoriae	384	Musae	T
HERBERTUS			
Regi, Fidei Defensori &c. Geo. Herbertus.	384	Musae	T
HERBESCENTI			
modo detis eum in flore, in vagina, in herbescenti viriditate;	445	Orationes	20
HERBULAS			
Ceu victa, Musis porrigit herbulas	434	Poem.Lat.	21
HERCLE			
Ain' vero? quanta praedicas? hercle aedepol,	421	Lucus 33	1
HERCULE			
rumpere fascias cum Hercule, serpentesque interficere voluptatis,	452	Orationes	6
HERCULEAS			
metas laudum, nullas Herculeas columnas, quas iam olim possidet,	440	Orationes	18
HERCULEM			
Quare nunc vobis ex pede Herculem, ex itinere Principem metiri licet,	453	Orationes	22
HERCULI			
Olim accreuerit Herculi furenti:	401	Musae 37	27
HERO			
Quo placet oblato, mortua fertur, hero:	428	Mem.Matr.11	4
HEROS			
Ignosce (Heros illustrissime) quod pronomina mea adeo audacter	473	Epistolae	15
HEROUM			
Heroum grandi carmina fulta pede?	387	Musae 5	4
HERUS			
Resurget occumbens Herus:	407	Passio 16	12
HESTERNAM			
Viuimus in praesens: hesternam viuere vitam	415	Lucus 23	5
HEU			
Heu stolidi, primum fugientem figite Terram,	408	Passio 18	3
Heu, quis spiritus, igneusque turbo	411	Lucus 5	1
Heu miseri! Quis tantum ipsis virtutibus instat	419	Tr.Mortis	33
HEUS			
Verum heus! si reputes, tibi tuisque	391	Musae 15	7
Verum heus, si nequeas caelo demittere matrem,	424	Mem.Matr.3	7
Heus, abijtne Noster? miseros nos;	450	Orationes	36
Verum heus! caute incipe, cohibens adeo stylum ingeniumque;	470	Epistolae	10
HI			
Spiritus, hi mihi iam montes, haec flumina sunto.	432	Poem.Lat.	11
HIANS			
Aduoluor madidae laetus hiansque Cruci:	406	Passio 13	2
HIANTES			
si qui alij exurgant promissores magnifici et hiantes, qui,	462	Epistolae	31
HIBERNIAE			
IACOBO, D. G. Magnae Britanniae, Franciae, & Hiberniae	384	Musae	T
HIBERNICO			
Si enim in regno vestro Hibernico lignum nascitur permanens,	459	Epistolae	15
HIC			
Quis hic superbit, oro? tune, an Praesules,	388	Musae 8	1
Astra rogant, Nouus hic quis hospes?	394	Musae 23	28
Hic, vbi sanati stillant opobalsama mundi,	406	Passio 13	1
Nempe hic Religio floret, regina quietis,	411	Lucus 6	7
Plusque habet hic laetus, quam vel Auarus habet.	411	Lucus 7	4
Hic vbi discumbunt per gramina, salsior vnus	418	Tr.Mortis	12
Sunt, praeter vitam: saxis hic sternitur, alter	418	Tr.Mortis	19
Aetna Cacum igniuomum dedit, hic Ixiona multis	420	Tr.Mortis	87
Aetna Cacum igniuomum dedit, hic Ixiona Graecis	272	Tr.Mortis VS	87
Nec tamen hic noster stetit impetus: exilit omni	420	Tr.Mortis	95
Nec tamen hic mortis rabies stetit; exilit omni	272	Tr.Mortis VS	95
Imperij hic culmen figo: mortalibus actum est	421	Tr.Mortis	100

	PAGE	TITLE	LINE
HIC (cont'd)			
Sistimus hic, inquit fatum, sat prata biberunt	272	Tr.Mortis VS	100
Hic ego tuque erimus, variae suffitibus herbae	427	Mem.Matr.7	28
Hic sita foeminei laus & victoria sexus:	429	Mem.Matr.13	1
Hic habitant Musae, facilisque in carmine Pallas,	210	Cam.1613-a BR	3
veremur ne nihil hic sit, quod magnitudini praesentiae vestrae	441	Orationes	9
Quinimo Artes hic sunt quiete & silentio cultae, tranquillitas,	441	Orationes	14
vt qui hic in Musarum monte editissimo, in ipso Parnasso siti sumus,	449	Orationes	32
hic ego me erexi & de dolore remisi plurimum, de desiderio nihil.	451	Orationes	26
Quid si hic lateat etiam Temperantia, rara in Principibus virtus,	452	Orationes	1
in terram hanc, incidit in coenum, quod innuebat eum hic mansurum:	455	Orationes	4
hic enim securi sumus a pluuia, imo a fulmine:	455	Orationes	15
postquam omnes honorum gradus hic percurreris, aeternum illud	457	Epistolae	4
nunc itaque Liber hic vester dilatat pomoeria, summouet Oceanum	458	Epistolae	11
Ego hic pultibus vescor et glande, more maiorum, multos iam annos	470	Epistolae	3
hic etiam teneor, sed laxioribus vinculis, quaeque amor saepe	472	Epistolae	33
HILARE			
Philosophiam expugnare nouimus, quicquid hilare est, laetum,	440	Orationes	12
HILARIS			
Hilaris haec sumenda est dies.	454	Orationes	23
HILARITATE			
Quanta hilaritate aspicit Alma Mater filios suos iam emancipatos,	461	Epistolae	30
HINC			
Ah! quam caederis hinc & inde palmis!	405	Passio 8	1
Hinc te olim gentes miratae odere vicissim;	416	Lucus 25	11
Hinc tamen excludi mors noluit, ipsaque vitam	271	Tr.Mortis VS	7
Hinc tyrocinium, paruoque assueta iuuentus,	418	Tr.Mortis	26
Hinc Glans adijcitur (non quam ructare vetustas	419	Tr.Mortis V	60
Hinc fremere totus & minari gestio	427	Mem.Matr.8	5
Hinc mihi principium: vos o labentia mentis	432	Poem.Lat.	13
Vt Flos hinc lacrymis, illinc Philomela querelis,	438	Poem.Lat.	5
Hinc Thraces dicti sunt abioi, & Licurgus magnus Legislator atimian	446	Orationes	19
hinc contigisse arbitror apud Romanos, quod nonnullae familiae semper	447	Orationes	19
hinc Reges Legatos habent statarios ac resides, quem locum Noster	450	Orationes	29
sic disparatae foelicitates hinc a populo, illinc a Principe,	456	Epistolae	24
HIPPONENSIS			
Hipponensis adest properans, & torquet in hostes	398	Musae 33	17
HIS			
Hoc ligno, his clauis est, quasi Falce sua.	407	Passio 14	4
Adde his trientem Musices, quae molliens	423	Mem.Matr.2	42
Dumque his inuigilo frequens	424	Mem.Matr.4	7
quos in arca repositos abijciebant in fluuium, his verbis:	452	Orationes	28
opportune his tenebris Fauor Tuus occurrit, illustrans nos omnes,	461	Epistolae	2
HISCAT			
vt nihil habeat Inuidia ipsa, quod contra hiscat aut mussitet.	453	Orationes	24
HISCE			
Neque in hisce Nuptijs posteritati tantum prospexit suauissimus	447	Orationes	27
et aeternitate occupatos, temporarijs hisce negotiolis libera.	466	Epistolae	6
HISCENTEM			
Vberaque aerea hiscentem fallentia natum?	426	Mem.Matr.7	4
HISPANAM			
Cum petit Hispanam Princeps, Grantamque Iacobus,	437	Poem.Lat. V	1
HISPANIA			
qui vtrasque Indias Hispania sua quasi nodo connectens,	440	Orationes	16
HISPANIAM			
cum dimitteret te in Hispaniam, quod Romani Imperatores in bello,	451	Orationes	31
idem impetus, qui peragrauit Hispaniam, si opus sit, superabit;	453	Orationes	31
HISPANICA			
quo magis amore coalescamus, vtraque gens Hispanica, Britannica,	440	Orationes	22
HISPANIJS			
Principis Caroli Reditum ex Hispanijs celebrauit Georgius Herbert	444	Orationes	T
HISPANO			
quod quidem vbi gentium si non ab Hispano sperandum?	447	Orationes	30
HISPANUM			
Scio Hispanum versutum, callidum, artis & aucupij apprime gnarum:	451	Orationes	24
HISPIDA			
Et saxa diris hispida montibus	394	Musae 23	13
HISTORIA			
esse Alexandro Magno nisi eius res gestas tradidisset historia?	441	Orationes	19
HISTORIAE			
quidem nox aptior esset tali historiae) si Romanorum Imperatorum	452	Orationes	21
HISTORIAS			
consulite historias; illic tuta cognitio est, atque extra teli	449	Orationes	3
HOC			
Hoc erit, Anti-furi-Puri-Categoria.	386	Musae 3	8
Scilicet hoc vobis proprium, qui purius itis,	387	Musae 5	7
Mox displicent omnes. Vbi hoc permanserit	398	Musae 32	4
Quin hoc carmine Lexicon probrorum	401	Musae 37	28
Sputando, blasphemando? nempe ne hoc fiat	405	Passio 5	5
Hoc ligno, his clauis est, quasi Falce sua.	407	Passio 14	4
Quid hoc? & ipse deficis, Caeli gigas,	407	Passio 16	1
Verius hoc olim factum est, vbi, Christe, lauares	412	Lucus 8	3
Vtrumque mirum est: hoc tamen mirum magis,	412	Lucus 11	2
Et hoc indicium subis, Redemptor?	417	Lucus 30	2
Protulit horrendum hoc primus cum puluere monstrum.	420	Tr.Mortis	91
Protulit horrendum hoc primum cum puluere monstrum.	420	Tr.Mortis V	91
Non video, certum est iurare; aut si hoc vetuisti,	421	Lucus 35	9
Nato dolenti: literae hoc debent tibi	424	Mem.Matr.2	62
Hoc, Genitrix, scriptum proles tibi sedula mittit.	427	Mem.Matr.9	1
Funereque hoc cultum vindicat aegra suum.	431	Mem.Matr.19	4
Hoc mihi legatum tristi si funere praestes,	434	Poem.Lat.	7

HOC (cont'd)	PAGE	TITLE	LINE
Quid mihi si facies nigra est? hoc, Ceste, colore	437	Poem.Lat.	1
Hoc saltem officio fungar amore tui.	437	Poem.Lat.	8
Nec hoc abunde est tibi, nisi certae Anchorae	438	Poem.Lat.	5
sitis ordine atque habitu, quo nos in hoc regno omnes esse gloriamur.	441	Orationes	2
Seritur fama in hoc saeculo, vt in sequenti metatur:	441	Orationes	19
Hoc vno Rex et populus dissentimus.	444	Orationes	1
esto autem hoc ipsum iter, quod nuper emensus est, vt sciatis omnes	445	Orationes	33
vnicum hoc iter nuperum explicabo, in quo longe vberrimam gloriae	446	Orationes	1
tot iam annis impune fruimur, hoc pacto fundatam cupit & perpetuam;	447	Orationes	29
Sensit hoc Archimedes, figuras iam nunc pulueri inscriptas corpore	448	Orationes	31
neque enim quicquam hoc itinere mirabilius, cuius tamen fructum omnem	450	Orationes	2
etiam & scientiae augmentum ex hoc itinere captauit solertissimus	450	Orationes	5
ipse egit oratorem, vt & ego aliquantulum hoc nomine glorier.	450	Orationes	31
Neque alienas tantum ex hoc itinere cognouit Respublicas sed quod	450	Orationes	32
Atque hoc quidem statu res erant, Suauissime CAROLE, cum tu aberas;	451	Orationes	27
Ecquid videtis tandem quam vtile hoc iter, per quod optimus Princeps	451	Orationes	35
hoc enim fastum amputat, affectus explorat, adulationem ventilat,	453	Orationes	1
id enim nostra interest, vt hoc precemur, aut enim misere fallimur,	457	Epistolae	25
Hoc etiam imperium tenuius est quam pro amplitudine virtutum	458	Epistolae	10
hoc saltem solutio est; Nos nunc conspersi atramento regio,	459	Epistolae	4
Optime enim hoc conuenit Partui tuo, qui nouas scientiarum regiones	463	Epistolae	10
Quare summe gratulamur tibi de nouo hoc cumulo honorum,	464	Epistolae	20
Nos vero de hoc tuo progressu non minus Reipublicae gratulamur quam	466	Epistolae	15
Praesertim hoc tempore, in quo paucorum auaritia liberalibus artibus	466	Epistolae	23
Nos igitur hoc metu affecti, vti sanguis solet in re dubia ad cor	467	Epistolae	8
vendentibus Libros non ementibus, hoc est cessatoribus non studiosis.	468	Epistolae	8
iustissime potes sub hoc Principe, in quo doctrinae fructus atque	469	Epistolae	22
Nunc obrutus Academicis negotijs, aegre hoc tempus illis succido:	471	Epistolae	20
Hoc quidem illis accidere amat, qui celeritatem affectuum raptim	471	Epistolae	30
hoc impetrem, vt cedam aliquantisper expectationi hominum,	472	Epistolae	27
illud necessarium magis factu, hoc vero longe iucundius, nobiliusque:	472	Epistolae	35
HOCCE			
Quid hocce? Þsalmos audion'? o dapes!	394	Musae 23	33
HOCCINE			
Quid? hoccine est mirum? Viatores sumus.	393	Musae 22	2
HOCINE			
Hocine accedit ad incredibiles laudes vestras quod quae nos audiamus	443	Orationes	30
HODIE			
Nemo potest: hodie vita sepulta prior.	415	Lucus 23	6
HOMERI			
Exoritur tubus, atque instar Cyclopis Homeri	419	Tr.Mortis	53
HOMICIDA			
Quaeritur ingenium, doctusque homicida probatur.	418	Tr.Mortis	25
Magnificus es screator, homicida inclytus.	421	Lucus 33	2
HOMINEM			
Deus ipse cum crearet hominem, mundi regem, consilio vsus est.	446	Orationes	36
vt ex affrictu Libri vestri hominem illico contundamus.	459	Epistolae	8
HOMINES			
O falsos homines! Vigilat, qui somniat aurum,	411	Lucus 7	3
Quid metuant homines infra, supraue minentur	413	Lucus 16	1
Perstringas homines vultu, miretur vt orbis	211	Cam.1613-b BR	13
significantes oportere Reges ijs partibus antecellere homines,	447	Orationes	4
sane exorti sunt nuperi quidam homines, qui libenter sapientiores nos	460	Epistolae	21
sed homines nobilioris ignorantiae, qui literas imminuere spiritus,	461	Epistolae	18
HOMINI			
Conditis binas homini sequendas	390	Musae 14	14
Soli homini dantur manus, soli caput rotundum & coeleste,	446	Orationes	38
HOMINIS			
Sic Hominis moles animaque & corpore constat,	417	Lucus 31	3
HOMINUM			
Tantum repertum est trux hominum genus,	394	Musae 23	17
Vnusquisque hominum, Terra est; & filius arui.	413	Lucus 18	1
Ararumque Hominumque ortum si mente pererres,	417	Lucus 29	1
Deerat adhuc vitijs hominum dignissima mundo	419	Tr.Mortis	49
Qua Mors ipsa sedens hominum de gente triumphat.	419	Tr.Mortis	56
vt Rex animalium fiat Rex hominum, apponimus nos manibus Sceptrum,	447	Orationes	2
effigies, imo vmbras hominum fame, frigore, illuuie, enectas,	449	Orationes	8
Quam cruenta gloria est, quae super ceruicibus hominum erigitur?	449	Orationes	10
inspexi facies hominum ac vultus curiosius tanquam emptor;	451	Orationes	13
os importunorum hominum Authoritate tua plurima & Eloquentia	463	Epistolae	1
res et naturae legibus et hominum summe contraria est) monopolijs	467	Epistolae	5
vt cedam aliquantisper expectationi hominum, rariusque paulo fodiam	472	Epistolae	28
HOMO			
O quam bellus homo es! lepido quam nomine fingis	386	Musae 3	1
Sanus Homo factus, vitiorum purus vterque;	408	Passio 20	1
Homo, Statua.	410	Lucus 1	T
Papae titulus Nec Deus Nec Homo.	412	Lucus 10	T
Nec Deus est nec Homo: Christus vterque fuit.	412	Lucus 10	2
Cespes viuus, Homo; mortuus, Ara fuit:	417	Lucus 29	2
Conueniunt; & Homo viua fit Ara Dei.	417	Lucus 29	4
homo est, non statua; Sceptriger, non sceptrum:	446	Orationes	10
homines, quibus homo bruta, iustitia scilicet & prudentia.	447	Orationes	5
animalia, tum maxime homo, cui soli ideo insunt oculi variegati,	453	Orationes	16
HOMUNCIO			
quantum quidem ego homuncio ac nanus coniectando assequor.	453	Orationes	21
HON			
dein Hon. Tuo gratulamur, qui filio auctus es tali ingenio praedito:	463	Epistolae	24
HONESTET			
Vespere ros maestis funus honestet aquis.	425	Mem.Matr.5	16

	PAGE	TITLE		LINE
HONOR				
Laus antiqua & honor perijt: quasi scilicet ARMO	416	Lucus 25		7
Laus antiqua & honor perierunt, te velut ARMO	416	Lucus 25	V	7
HONORABLE				
of Winchester, one of the Kings most honorable privy-Counsaile.	473	Epistolae		24
HONORATISSIME				
Vir Honoratissime. Eximia tua in nos merita frequentiorem calamum	457	Epistolae		6
Vir Honoratissime. Quanta hilaritate aspicit Alma Mater filios suos	461	Epistolae		29
Vir Honoratissime. Scite et apposite fecisti Fluuium nostrum	462	Epistolae		17
Honoratissime Domine. Tam eximie de nobis meritus es, vt res nostras	465	Epistolae		1
Honoratissime Domine. Fama promotionis tuae gratissime appulit ad nos	468	Epistolae		11
HONORE				
Luce praelustri, vel honore pollet,	390	Musae 14		6
CAROLVS redijt, honore grauidus, grauidus scientia, cruribus thymo	454	Orationes		27
Iustitiam prius tanto cum honore atque acclamatione administrans,	464	Epistolae		15
vt res nostras omnes cum Honore Tuo coniunctas esse velimus.	465	Epistolae		3
in nos amor, antehac satis perspectus, nunc cum honore geminetur.	466	Epistolae		4
HONOREM				
In Honorem Illustr. D. D. Verulamij, Sti Albani,	436	Poem.Lat.		T
sed tamen comparatio & in honorem tuum cedet, nostrumque emolumentum.	467	Epistolae		26
eadem manus et tuum tibi largita est honorem, et priuilegia nostra	468	Epistolae		23
Deus fortunet tibi hunc honorem, et faxit, vt tibi gloriae sit,	469	Epistolae		5
receptusque sim in aliquem apud Honorem Tuum locum, magis id adeo	472	Epistolae		20
ad mea in Honorem Tuum officia erectior solutiorque redibo,	473	Epistolae		2
HONORES				
Domini, Post honores eximios, praefecturas insignes,	440	Orationes		2
vt neque virtutibus tuis desint honores neque vtrisque vita,	457	Epistolae		2
illi etiam honores qui finitimi sunt, et quasi accolae Maiestatis,	463	Epistolae		22
Tibi & concedat vt terrestres tui honores cum coelestibus certent,	465	Epistolae		18
HONORI				
si tantum Honori Tuo superesset otij ad legendum, quantum a nobis	457	Epistolae		8
contra grassantes flammas aedificijs Honori Tuo acceptam ferimus:	457	Epistolae		18
HONORIBUS				
censemus nostram, et in honoribus Tuis nostro bono gratulamur;	456	Epistolae		16
Tu vero macte honoribus, gloria, id enim nostra interest,	457	Epistolae		24
neque enim sic effugies cum honoribus, quin laetitia nostra te	465	Epistolae		22
Concede vt Honoribus nuperis, tanquam partubus Virtutum Tuarum,	469	Epistolae		8
Quare post Principis manum honoribus refertam, non est quod nostram	469	Epistolae		14
potui refercire lineas Honoribus, Magnif., Celsitud., sed	473	Epistolae		17
HONORIFICUM				
quod sane adeo nobile fuit & honorificum, vt nihil habeat Inuidia	453	Orationes		23
HONORIS				
est etiam interdum satietas quaedam honoris, quem ad tempus deponere	453	Orationes		10
HONORUM				
tanquam Aquilam inter nouas honorum nubes e conspectu nostro	456	Epistolae		7
postquam omnes honorum gradus hic percurreris, aeternum illud	457	Epistolae		3
& inter nouos honorum cumulos, quod expectamus indies futurum,	462	Epistolae		28
Quare summe gratulamur tibi de nouo hoc cumulo honorum,	464	Epistolae		21
HONOS				
Quin Matris superans carmina poscit honos.	431	Mem.Matr.19		6
Vulnereque emanat sanguis, vt intret honos.	435	Poem.Lat.		6
HONOURABLE				
To the right honourable and reverend Father in God, my L. Bishop of	473	Epistolae		23
HORA				
Aut si negotio hora sumenda est, rei	423	Mem.Matr.2		32
HORRENDUM				
Euolat, horrendumque ciet bacchata fragorem.	420	Tr.Mortis		72
Protulit horrendum hoc primus cum puluere monstrum.	420	Tr.Mortis		91
Protulit horrendum hoc primum cum puluere monstrum.	420	Tr.Mortis	V	91
HORRESCIT				
Ecce decus vestrum spinis horrescit, acuta	425	Mem.Matr.5		3
HORRUIT				
Quid memorem tormenta, quibus prius horruit aeuum;	419	Tr.Mortis		39
HORTI				
Horti, colique distributim pensitat.	423	Mem.Matr.2		19
Horti, deliciae Dominae, marcescite tandem;	425	Mem.Matr.5		1
Atque inter reliquos horti crescentia foetus	427	Mem.Matr.7		33
tractus (Oceani praeda et deliciae) vt irrigui Musarum horti,	461	Epistolae		9
HORTO				
Horto pro tenui colit	424	Mem.Matr.4		3
HORTOS				
Quare haud vos hortos, sed coemeteria dico,	425	Mem.Matr.5		9
HORTUS				
Rure; breuisque hortus, cuius cum vellere florum	426	Mem.Matr.7		23
Stipati, rudibusque volis imperuius hortus	427	Mem.Matr.7		26
HORULA				
Vna meam membris horula, teque cruci.	434	Poem.Lat.		2
HORUM				
Nil horum regero tibi merenti.	401	Musae 37		40
Quisnam horum maior sit, dubitatur, amor.	437	Poem.Lat.		2
HOS				
Hos nunc barbaries impia vellicat	391	Musae 17		7
Hos ad se trahere et mergere gestiens.	391	Musae 17		10
Annulus hos reuocet, sistatque libidinis vndas	396	Musae 26		11
Nobilitate illos, hos pietate rapit.	429	Mem.Matr.13		4
Hos oculos laetos, hunc sine nube diem:	211	Cam.1613-b BR		14
fuga hos omnes, praesertim sericatam hanc stultitiam contere,	461	Epistolae		22
HOSPES				
Astra rogant, Nouus hic quis hospes?	394	Musae 23		28
Quid Vaticanam Bodleiumque obijcis, Hospes?	459	Epistolae		30

	PAGE	TITLE	LINE
HOSPITE			
Qui tamen excipiat, Christus caret hospite: tantum	407	Passio 15	3
HOSPITEM			
rudiorem esse impexioremque, quam vt tantum Hospitem excipiat:	463	Epistolae	29
HOSPITIO			
Haec autem hospitio latere turpi	411	Lucus 5	6
HOSPITIUM			
Paras hospitium torumque dulcem,	417	Lucus 30	5
ita excipiemus illa, vt benignius hospitium, et erga te propensius,	466	Epistolae	18
HOSTEM			
Praesulibus dirum te Musa coarguit hostem,	392	Musae 18	1
Strauit Idumaeum diuinus Tityrus hostem?	419	Tr.Mortis	44
signo meritus est, ad vera castra traductus, hostem interficiet:	453	Orationes	30
praesertim cum amico fidere periculosius sit, quam hostem superare.	453	Orationes	33
HOSTES			
Ergo ringantur pietatis hostes,	390	Musae 14	17
Hipponensis adest properans, & torquet in hostes	398	Musae 33	17
Obrue feruentes, ruptis conatibus, hostes:	402	Musae 39	20
Nempe & millenos ad palum interficit hostes	418	Tr.Mortis	31
Tam nitide tamen occidis, tam suauiter, hostes,	435	Poem.Lat.	3
quibus hostes soletis in potestatem redigere, lenioresque aspectus,	440	Orationes	9
qui solebant signa in hostes inijcere, vt milites acrius ea	451	Orationes	32
vt nullus fere elabatur dies, qui non hostes aliquos nobis aperiat:	461	Epistolae	14
HOSTIBUS			
Mersis reuertens laetus ab hostibus	394	Musae 23	30
prorsus Daemoni & hostibus	395	Musae 25	14
Hostibus haec etiam parcens imitatur Iesum.	416	Lucus 26	5
HOSTIS			
Superpellicei tremendus hostis,	391	Musae 15	2
O saeuus hostis! quam ferociter pugnas!	392	Musae 20	15
Primus adest nobis, Pharisaeis omnibus hostis,	398	Musae 33	9
HOSTIUM			
Sunt hostium legata, non amicorum,	406	Passio 10	2
sub ementito habitu fidicinis castra hostium ingressus,	453	Orationes	5
HUC			
Nempe huc vsque notos tenebricosos	428	Mem.Matr.10	1
tunc temporis liberior eram, huc illuc pro libitu circumcursitans:	451	Orationes	12
huc, illuc commeando, eo deueni animo, vt nunquam cessandum mihi	472	Epistolae	7
commendatione, si huc reciderit omnis studiorum spes fructusque:	472	Epistolae	15
Philosophus de Tactu & Visu, id apposite admodum huc transferatur.	472	Epistolae	36
HUI			
& quis sum ipse (barbam, hui, tam grauem) & apud quos dico,	445	Orationes	25
hui! iter bene longum! Quid autem illic?	451	Orationes	1
HUIC			
Huic Glans adijcitur (non quam ructare vetustas	419	Tr.Mortis	60
denique huic aetati quae talem virum protulit, cum quinque millibus	463	Epistolae	26
HUIUS			
causas itineris huius, quantum quidem ego homuncio ac nanus	453	Orationes	20
Sed siccitas anni huius derisit incoeptum et plus effecit quam mille	461	Epistolae	11
huius tu es commotria atque ornatrix.	470	Epistolae	17
HUIUSMODI			
huiusmodi lamentis & quiritationibus plena erant fora, nundinae,	451	Orationes	9
quamuis enim sexcenta huiusmodi praediola Tua gratia permutare nolim,	472	Epistolae	30
HUMANA			
Humana aeternos agerent praecordia questus:	433	Poem.Lat.	39
Nihil habet humana vita maioris momenti aut ponderis, quam Nuptiae,	446	Orationes	16
HUMANAE			
Humanae decus atque apex iuuentae,	384	Musae	2
apud poetas deorum pharetrae operculum habuere, humanae non item:	449	Orationes	26
HUMANAM			
Mutas in humanam figuram	393	Musae 23	3
Ad saxa speciem retrahentis humanam,	429	Mem.Matr.12	7
HUMANIS			
& in rebus humanis diuinisque exercitatissimi, de integro	444	Orationes	21
HUMANITAS			
nisi humanitas tua, superiori aestate sponte suauiterque patefacta,	467	Epistolae	1
Sed tua humanitas haec nobis expediet.	469	Epistolae	4
HUMANITATE			
de humanitate tua singulari, studioque in nos iam olim	462	Epistolae	24
HUMANITATIS			
cum humanitatis Tuae, tum gratitudinis nostrae ratio postulat.	457	Epistolae	9
ramenta quaepiam ex tanta Humanitatis massa, quae apud Te visitur,	472	Epistolae	13
HUMERO			
Occumbens humero Thronos lacessam.	421	Lucus 34	9
HUMILE			
oculi omnium deiecti, humile os, collum pensile, manus decussatae,	451	Orationes	15
HUMILES			
Versatos neget, atque humiles, queis talis cordi	420	Tr.Mortis	93
HUMILI			
Qua possint humili fundere corde preces.	390	Musae 12	12
HUMILIA			
vtriusque enim splendor et claritas humilia loca deprecantur.	466	Epistolae	11
HUMILIS			
Sic excelsa humilisque simul loca dissita iunxit,	429	Mem.Matr.13	5
HUMILITAS			
Sagax Humilitas, eligens viros bonos	412	Lucus 13	1
HUMILITATE			
Natura montibus vallibusque sublimitate atque humilitate distinxit:	453	Orationes	12
HUMILLIMI			
Humillimi serui subditique vestri Procancellarius Reliquusque Senatus	459	Epistolae	22

	PAGE	TITLE		LINE
HUMILLIMOS				
nos humillimos subiectos, integro Fluuio a Rege nostro donatos,	460	Epistolae		13
HUMOR				
Sepia concurrat, peccatis aptior humor,	404	Passio 1		3
Diluit oppositas candidus humor aquas.	428	Mem.Matr.9		18
HUMORE				
ascendit ad nubes, vbi iam ingrauescit humore, relabitur in terram,	454	Orationes		29
HUMUM				
Assiduo vilem lumine cingit humum.	387	Musae 7		8
HUNC				
Hunc ponas animam mundi, Plato: vel tua mundum	409	Passio 21		3
Per te nascor in hunc globum	425	Mem.Matr.4		13
Hunc vultum ostendas, & tecum, nobile spectrum,	426	Mem.Matr.7		14
Hos oculos laetos, hunc sine nube diem:	211	Cam.1613-b	BR	14
spiritibusque tabellarijs laetum hunc nuncium vbique deferentibus,	445	Orationes		2
hunc quidem gradum pignus habes amoris nostri, haec est ansa qua	456	Epistolae		4
per hunc imperas orbi vniuerso, victoriaeque gloriam absque	458	Epistolae		14
exosculamur, hunc foetum vestrum, hunc alterum Carolum,	459	Epistolae		9
foetum vestrum, hunc alterum Carolum, hunc fasciculum Prudentiae,	459	Epistolae		10
hunc fasciculum Prudentiae, positum extra mortalitatis aleam,	459	Epistolae		10
Deus fortunet tibi hunc honorem, et faxit, vt tibi gloriae sit,	469	Epistolae		5
fungar apud Meos, Rhetoris in hunc annum, & in plures Oratoris,	472	Epistolae		26
HYBLAE				
Christe, decus, dulcedo, & centum circiter Hyblae,	421	Lucus 35		1
HYDRA				
Perdere sexcentas? crescit tamen hydra nocendi	419	Tr.Mortis		35
Perdere sexcentas? crescet tamen hydra nocendi	419	Tr.Mortis	V	35
Numne Hydra talis, tantane bellua est	433	Poem.Lat.		9
HYEME				
lucos aestate, pinguem togam hyeme:	448	Orationes		24
HYEMES				
Instructaeque acies, hyemesque in pellibus actae,	418	Tr.Mortis		28
HYMNIS				
Vos sine maternis hymnis infantia vidit,	389	Musae 12		5
HYPOCRITAE				
Omnesque stulti audimus, aut hypocritae,	388	Musae 8		7
IACENT				
Quae sapiunt aeuum, ceu cariosa iacent.	386	Musae 3		4
Strata iacent toto millena cadauera campo	420	Tr.Mortis		79
Strata, iacent toto prostrata cadauera campo	272	Tr.Mortis	VS	79
IACENTIUM				
Languentium baculus, teges iacentium,	423	Mem.Matr.2		46
IACES				
Scotia quae frigente iaces porrecta sub Arcto,	399	Musae 35		1
IACIAS				
Si sursum iacias, in caput ipsa ruit.	410	Lucus 4		8
IACOBAEUM				
Sola Iacobaeum decantent carmina nomen.	402	Musae 39		40
IACOBE				
Serenissime Domine noster, Iacobe Inuictissime.	458	Epistolae		1
Serenissime Domine noster, Iacobe Potentissime.	460	Epistolae		1
IACOBO				
IACOBO, D. G. Magnae Britanniae, Franciae, & Hiberniae	384	Musae		T
concessae ab Augustissimo Iacobo auctae tua opera conseruentur;	468	Epistolae		22
IACOBUM				
coalescamus, vtraque gens Hispanica, Britannica, colimus Iacobum.	440	Orationes		23
3. Ad Iacobum Regem Gratiae de Scriptis suis Academiae donatis	458	Epistolae		T
4. Ad Iacobum Regem Gratiae de Fluuio contra Redemptores	460	Epistolae		T
IACOBUS				
Quos inter plenusque Deo genioque Iacobus	399	Musae 33		23
Dum petit Infantem Princeps, Grantamque Iacobus,	437	Poem.Lat.		1
Cum petit Hispanam Princeps, Grantamque Iacobus,	437	Poem.Lat.	V	1
Iacobus tutelaris Diuus est vtrique nostrum;	440	Orationes		23
per Te illucet nobis Iacobus noster.	456	Epistolae		13
IACOBVS				
at IACOBVS a nobis est:	451	Orationes		25
IACTAS				
Quid iactas mihi aromata Orientis?	444	Orationes		24
IACTUM				
illic tutà cognitio est, atque extra teli iactum.	449	Orationes		3
IACULIS				
Quas malus liuor iaculis lacessit	390	Musae 14		2
IAM				
Sic vbi iam mulier decerpti conscia pomi	390	Musae 12		13
Iam repit impietas volatura illico.	398	Musae 32		3
Iam Constantinus multo se milite miscet;	398	Musae 33		15
Iam te funditus igneis Camoenis,	400	Musae 37		19
Et mea iam lacrymet culpa colore suo.	404	Passio 1		4
Iam meus es: nunc Te teneo: Pastorque prehensus	407	Passio 14		3
Non iam ventriculus, verum spelunca vocetur	414	Lucus 21		3
Cedito Barbaries: Helicon iam litibus instat,	417	Lucus 28		5
Faecundusque chalybs sceleris, iam sanguine tinctus,	419	Tr.Mortis		37
Faecundusque chalibs sceleris, iam sanguine tectus	271	Tr.Mortis	VS	37
Materiam vexat: nec iam se continet antro	420	Tr.Mortis		70
Non iam exaudiri quicquam vel Musica caeli	420	Tr.Mortis		74
Non iam exaudiri quicquam, vel musica sphaerae	271	Tr.Mortis	VS	74
Ingemit, & defessus opem iam Portitor orat.	420	Tr.Mortis		82
Quin, sine, te cernam; quoties iam dixero, cernam;	421	Lucus 35		3
Spiritus, hi mihi iam montes, haec flumina sunto.	432	Poem.Lat.		11
Iam foelix Philomela, & menti conscia Dido!	432	Poem.Lat.		22
Et patrio regno (sub quo iam Principe nobis	432	Poem.Lat.		27

IAM (cont'd)	PAGE	TITLE	LINE
In laudes abeunt iam loca quaeque tuas:	435	Poem.Lat.	4
In laudes properant iam loca quaeque tuas:	435	Poem.Lat. V	4
Quid voluit prudens Fatum, iam sentio tandem:	438	Poem.Lat.	3
Sic non Phoebeus iam plus te splendeat ortus	211	Cam.1613-b BR	15
nullas Herculeas columnas, quas iam olim possidet, agnoscit.	440	Orationes	18
atque exhilarans, tumentibus iam venis, arterijs micantibus,	445	Orationes	1
Iam vero, vt Rex animalium fiat Rex hominum, apponimus nos manibus	447	Orationes	2
qua tot iam annis impune fruimur, hoc pacto fundatam cupit	447	Orationes	29
Iam nunc minaci murmure cornuum	448	Orationes	1
Stringuntur aures: iam litui strepunt,	448	Orationes	2
Iam fulgor armorum fugaces	448	Orationes	3
figuras iam nunc pulueri inscriptas corpore confosso obliterans.	448	Orationes	31
& metalla ei inserendo, aliter mundus iam diu fuisset deuoratus.	452	Orationes	25
ascendit ad nubes, vbi iam ingrauescit humore, relabitur in terram,	454	Orationes	29
diu iam peregrinati cum Principe, commode peruenimus ad laurum hanc,	455	Orationes	12
Iam dari nobis vellemus Iesuitam aliquem, vt ex affrictu Libri vestri	459	Epistolae	7
Quanta hilaritate aspicit Alma Mater filios suos iam emancipatos,	461	Epistolae	30
vt iam compensemur abunde, neque amplius quaerendum sit Tibi,	462	Epistolae	15
studioque in nos iam olim perspectissimo, quippe qui eximie semper	462	Epistolae	25
Iam vero miserum est, pecuniam retardare illam, cui natura spiritum	468	Epistolae	4
cum ob perspicacitatem singularem iam olim Regi notam atque signatam	469	Epistolae	20
more maiorum, multos iam annos Anglice viuens garriensque.	470	Epistolae	4
Iam si inter commendandum adhibeas ei calamistros vti iuuenculae,	470	Epistolae	18
o quot iam anni sunt ex quo vel apicem Latinum pertuli!	471	Epistolae	6
Ego auctior iam gaudio atque distentior, Cantabrigiam redij.	471	Epistolae	17
IAMBUS			
Cur non lugentes Elegi? non acer Iambus?	387	Musae 5	5
IAMDUDUM			
Iamdudum tacite delituisse putes?	437	Poem.Lat.	10
Iamdudum tacite delituisse putas?	437	Poem.Lat. V	10
Iamdudum nos omnes, nostrumque regnum gestimus fieri participes eius	440	Orationes	19
ulomanian illam & inanem verborum strepitum iamdudum deposui:	445	Orationes	23
gaudia praestolantur, quae iamdudum annuunt mihi vt perorem.	454	Orationes	22
IAMIAM			
Quale paludosos iamiam lictura recessus	426	Mem.Matr.7	11
IAMPRIDEM			
redundet, quorum in eligendis illis iudicium iampridem apparet.	441	Orationes	7
IANUAM			
Et ni lumina ianuam resignent,	415	Lucus 24	4
ICTU			
Vno ictu: non sic pestis, non stella maligno	420	Tr.Mortis	80
Quare etiam nuper Pyrij de pulueris ictu	433	Poem.Lat.	33
& beatae fabricae, vnico ictu sulphurei tubi, vnica litura delentur?	448	Orationes	21
ID			
Eminet, id tumidum protinus esse feres?	387	Musae 7	4
Scilicet id splendes: haec est tibi causa micandi,	424	Mem.Matr.3	5
& polymiti, vt si minus id assequantur, quod primum intendunt,	446	Orationes	6
cauendum ne id nobis nauseam moueat, aut tanquam oues taedulae	448	Orationes	36
Vicini quo pacto niteant, id animum aduertito;	450	Orationes	16
vt aliquando existimen id egisse prudentissimum Patrem tuum,	451	Orationes	30
gloria, id enim nostra interest, vt hoc precemur, aut enim misere	457	Epistolae	24
imbecillitati id nostrae, quae fastigium regiarum notionum aequare	460	Epistolae	16
Id vnum dolemus, Bibliothecam nostram rudiorem esse impexioremque,	463	Epistolae	28
Nimirum id assecuta sunt merita Tua maxima, vt Almam Matrem spe noua	464	Epistolae	24
id omne dexterrima tua in obeundis rebus prudentia dissipetur.	467	Epistolae	12
idque pro Libris, de quibus nusquam rectius quam apud Te agitur.	467	Epistolae	.18
magis id adeo factum esse mansuetudine Tua incomparabili,	472	Epistolae	21
tam communi hac luce, quam Tua, cum id agnoscere vnquam desinam.	472	Epistolae	24
Philosophus de Tactu & Visu, id apposite admodum huc transferatur.	472	Epistolae	36
IDEM			
Postremis ambabus idem sentimus vterque;	386	Musae 4	5
idem feruor qui impar sub amoris signo meritus est, ad vera castra	453	Orationes	29
idem impetus, qui peragrauit Hispaniam, si opus sit, superabit;	453	Orationes	31
sic idem animus, qui nuper versatus est in forma & figuris vultus,	454	Orationes	6
IDEO			
Cur ideo verbis tristes effundere curas	433	Poem.Lat.	45
ideoque ex quolibet ligno, qualibet vxore non esse fingendum:	447	Orationes	9
cui soli ideo insunt oculi variegati, cum caetera animantia	453	Orationes	17
ideoque praeferuida illa desideria silentio suo sepulta nunc	471	Epistolae	27
IDIAIS			
Idiais koraisi klauso.	430	Mem.Matr.16	12
IDIAS			
Ouk et' emen idias phules grapsantes arogon,	430	Mem.Matr.17	2
IDOLORUM			
Promus; Fugator Idolorum & nubium;	436	Poem.Lat. V	12
IDOLUM			
Promus; Fugator Idolum, atque nubium;	436	Poem.Lat.	12
IDUMAEUM			
Strauit Idumaeum diuinus Tityrus hostem?	419	Tr.Mortis	44
IEIUNAE			
lachrymis in terram manantibus, ieiunae, squalidae, perdiae,	448	Orationes	35
IENTOS			
Es bios eelioio diken, aktinas ientos	431	Mem.Matr.17	17
IESUITA			
Tormento peior Iesuita, & fulminat Orbem,	420	Tr.Mortis	96
IESUITAE			
Non a nobis vapulant Iesuitae, sed a scriptis vestris, quae ingenti	443	Orationes	19
IESUITAM			
Iam dari nobis vellemus Iesuitam aliquem, vt ex affrictu Libri vestri	459	Epistolae	7

	PAGE	TITLE	LINE
IESUM			
Hostibus haec etiam parcens imitatur Iesum.	416	Lucus 26	5
IGITUR			
Frustra igitur sudo: superest mihi sola voluptas,	435	Poem.Lat.	7
Nos igitur hoc metu affecti, vti sanguis solet in re dubia ad cor	467	Epistolae	8
IGNARA			
Non placuit rudis atque ignara occisio: Morti	418	Tr.Mortis	24
Non placuit rudis atque ignara occasio; morti	271	Tr.Mortis VS	24
IGNARE			
Quotidiano! Nescis, ignare? Audies!	436	Poem.Lat.	2
IGNARUS			
aggreditur & labores, haud ignarus, ignem vitae augeri ventilatione,	452	Orationes	33
IGNAUE			
Ergo etiam Solem dicas, ignaue, superbum,	387	Musae 7	5
IGNE			
Ante diem vestro mundus ab igne ruat.	399	Musae 35	12
Excutite aulaea, & luceat igne focus.	413	Lucus 15	2
Immodicus luctus tacito vorat igne medullas,	433	Poem.Lat.	47
quam in aqua & igne fecisti, non dubitamus quin benignitas tua omnia	457	Epistolae	22
IGNEA			
Adorta numen acri & ignea prece.	422	Mem.Matr.2	17
IGNEIS			
Iam te funditus igneis Camoenis,	400	Musae 37	19
IGNEM			
Qui silicem tundit, (mirum tamen) elicit ignem:	410	Lucus 3	1
Excitat optatus auidos, & ventilat ignem.	432	Poem.Lat.	32
haud ignarus, ignem vitae augeri ventilatione, desidia corrumpi,	452	Orationes	33
IGNEUS			
Heu, quis spiritus, igneusque turbo	411	Lucus 5	1
IGNICULOS			
Igniculos legans, manserit ipsa licet;	410	Lucus 2	2
IGNIS			
Ex praelio vndae ignisque (si Physicis fides)	396	Musae 27	1
Fatalemque leuans dextram, qua stupeus ignis	420	Tr.Mortis	67
Pulueris inferni; properat datus ignis, & omnem	420	Tr.Mortis	69
Pulueris inferni properat, datur ignis, & omnem	420	Tr.Mortis V	69
Sulphuris inferni, properat datus ignis et omnem	271	Tr.Mortis VS	69
Tuque aer inflato tubam, dum plurimus ignis	211	Cam.1613-b BR	5
(e quorum ossibus collisis ignis elicitur) qui nunc mansueti	449	Orationes	18
Ignis et Virtus semper ascendunt, vtriusque enim splendor et claritas	466	Epistolae	10
IGNIUOMUM			
Aetna Cacum igniuomum dedit, hic Ixiona multis	420	Tr.Mortis	87
Aetna Cacum igniuomum dedit, hic Ixiona Graecis	272	Tr.Mortis VS	87
IGNORANTIAE			
sed homines nobilioris ignorantiae, qui literas imminuere spiritus,	461	Epistolae	19
IGNORAT			
Quod puer ignorat, verba profana putas?	388	Musae 9	2
IGNORO			
Non ignoro apud quos haec dico, eos scilicet, qui innuptam Palladem	446	Orationes	25
IGNOSCAS			
sed vt facilius ignoscas occupato calamo, qui etiam ferians nihil Tua	471	Epistolae	23
IGNOSCE			
Ignosce (Heros illustrissime) quod pronomina mea adeo audacter	473	Epistolae	15
IGNOSCIT			
Totusque caenum Cynthiae ignoscit notis.	393	Musae 22	9
IGNOTA			
velut Romani lacum, cuius altitudo ignota erat, dedicabant victoriae;	449	Orationes	21
IGNOTIOR			
Neque quod ignotior eram, retundebatur vnquam impetus:	472	Epistolae	10
IIS			
Iisque siccis adeo vt os Molossorum	429	Mem.Matr.12	3
IJS			
significantes oportere Reges ijs partibus antecellere homines,	447	Orationes	4
IJSDEM			
Ad Melvinum De ijsdem.	392	Musae 18	T
ILEX			
Dum librata suis haeret radicibus ilex	428	Mem.Matr.11	1
ILIAS			
Alteraque haec tua mors, Ilias esto mihi.	428	Mem.Matr.11	14
ILLA			
Constet, & ex illa pendeat orbis ope;	385	Musae 1	2
Illa quidem a nostro non multum abludit imago,	396	Musae 26	5
Viuat, & in mortem vita sit illa tuam.	405	Passio 7	10
Sit licet in pelago semper, sine fluctibus illa est,	411	Lucus 6	3
Illa cauerna, in qua tot coiere ferae.	414	Lucus 21	4
Conferte lacrymas: Illa, quae vos miscuit	422	Mem.Matr.2	3
Non illa soles terere comptu lubricos,	422	Mem.Matr.2	10
Surrexit vna & illa, seseque extulit:	423	Mem.Matr.2	27
At superat caput illa tuum, quantum ipsa cadauer	424	Mem.Matr.3	3
Morte magis viduabor illa.	425	Mem.Matr.6	12
cum tamen in resolutione illa vltima, nulla sit distinctio populi aut	452	Orationes	15
Adest tamen anus illa querula, & philegklemon, quam audire videor	453	Orationes	25
deperijt, at illa mutata est in arborem triumphantium propriam:	455	Orationes	9
praesertim donec transeat nubes illa, quae vicinos adeo infestat:	455	Orationes	15
ita excipiemus illa, vt benignius hospitium, et erga te propensius,	466	Epistolae	18
ideoque praeferuida illa desideria silentio suo sepulta nunc	471	Epistolae	27
ILLAC			
iniurias seculi scriptaque hac illac pereuntia securius praeterit.	459	Epistolae	14
ILLAE			
Crescent illae, crescetis amores. Cui sententiae si fidem adhibeas,	473	Epistolae	9

	PAGE	TITLE	LINE
ILLAM			
illam teqminis insciam	395	Musae 25	13
Illam Charybdim cautione nouimus	397	Musae 30	4
ulomanian illam & inanem verborum strepitum iamdudum deposui:	445	Orationes	22
Austriacam familiam, Aquilamque illam, quae non capit muscas.	446	Orationes	15
vt laeuitatem illam aequabilem atque politiem perturbent.	453	Orationes	13
Nam vtramque illam curam insignem, tam de conseruando Fluuio nostro,	457	Epistolae	16
illam nunc denuo ex aedibus Eboracensibus ab altero Cancellario	463	Epistolae	31
pecuniam retardare illam, cui natura spiritum dederit feracem	468	Epistolae	5
certe non tam ornas illam, qui infers manum grauitati.	470	Epistolae	20
ILLE			
Ille tamen, quamuis altus, tua crimina ridens	387	Musae 7	7
Ille quoque inuadit Diuinam Flaminis artem,	392	Musae 19	3
at ille ambiuit nobilissimam Austriacam familiam, Aquilamque illam,	446	Orationes	14
vbi ille signum sustulerit, Leones Britannici (e quorum ossibus	449	Orationes	17
Siccam animam sapientissimam esse dixit obscurus ille philosophus;	460	Epistolae	20
cum non est tanti totus ille maritimus tractus (Oceani praeda	461	Epistolae	8
ILLECEBRIS			
obseptum illecebris, voluptatibus quasi fascijs circumdatum,	452	Orationes	4
illecebris melitaiais agxonais abiectis, iter aggreditur & labores,	452	Orationes	32
ILLI			
Quod si fata illi longam invidere salutem	432	Poem.Lat.	26
Tu inuaseris eorum gloriam conseruando nobis quae illi dederunt,	458	Epistolae	26
neque illi e faece vulgi tantum qui eruditionem simplicitati	461	Epistolae	17
Illi terram inuenerunt, crassissimum elementum, Tu subtilitates	463	Epistolae	13
Illi barbara omnia, Tu non nisi cultissima, elegantiasque ipsas	463	Epistolae	14
Illi magnetica acu freti sunt.	463	Epistolae	16
illi etiam honores qui finitimi sunt, et quasi accolae Maiestatis,	463	Epistolae	22
ILLIBATA			
interim vestra hac scribendi laude intacta manente atque illibata.	458	Epistolae	28
ILLIC			
O cessatrices! eccum puluisculus illic!	413	Lucus 15	5
Nudetur illic lucus amabilis,	434	Poem.Lat.	30
illic tuta cognitio est, atque extra teli iactum.	449	Orationes	3
Quid autem illic? sterilem aiunt regionem:	451	Orationes	2
Falleris, nusquam plura bona, cum etiam mala illic sint aurea:	451	Orationes	3
apud nos agri tantum sunt fertiles, illic etiam arenae.	451	Orationes	5
illic constringor debito; hic etiam teneor, sed laxioribus vinculis,	472	Epistolae	33
ILLICO			
Iam repit impietas volatura illico.	398	Musae 32	3
vt ex affrictu Libri vestri hominem illico contundamus.	459	Epistolae	8
ILLIMI			
Ducitur illimi candida vita fide,	400	Musae 36	2
ILLINC			
Vt Flos hinc lacrymis, illinc Philomela querelis,	438	Poem.Lat.	5
foelicitates hinc a populo, illinc a Principe, in Te conueniunt,	456	Epistolae	24
ILLINUNT			
Queis me educasti; sponte chartas illinunt	424	Mem.Matr.2	63
ILLIS			
Vobis, aut illis pectora vestra forent.	400	Musae 36	6
Tu tamen, haud tibi tam moreris, quam viuis in illis,	407	Passio 17	3
Illis perpetuae patent fenestrae,	415	Lucus 24	13
redundet, quorum in eligendis illis iudicium iampridem apparet.	441	Orationes	6
Nunc obrutus Academicis negotijs, aegre hoc tempus illis succido:	471	Epistolae	20
Hoc quidem illis accidere amat, qui celeritatem affectuum raptim	472	Epistolae	1
ILLORUM			
O vtinam aut illorum oculi (quod comprecor vnum)	400	Musae 36	5
ILLOS			
Illos, qui mundum circumiere, pedes.	412	Lucus 8	4
Nobilitate illos, hos pietate rapit.	429	Mem.Matr.13	4
vt deponatis paulisper vultus illos bellicos, quibus hostes soletis	440	Orationes	8
conseruantes sibi Illos Fontes, a quibus ipsi olim hauserunt?	461	Epistolae	31
ILLUC			
tunc temporis liberior eram, huc illuc pro libitu circumcursitans:	451	Orationes	12
verisimile est, eos illuc, quo cognitio ipsa pertingit,	468	Epistolae	1
huc, illuc commeando, eo deueni animo, vt nunquam cessandum mihi	472	Epistolae	7
ILLUCET			
per Te illucet nobis Iacobus noster.	456	Epistolae	12
ILLUD			
Si tibi non illud placeat mirabile corpus,	404	Passio 2	3
Nec tu pro socio doleas, qui fugit ad illud	415	Lucus 23	15
nos etiam exuentes os illud, & supercilium quibus caperatam	440	Orationes	11
Illud autem, quod cuiuis clarissime patet, etiam lusco,	449	Orationes	34
aeternum illud praemium consequare, cui neque addi quicquam potest,	457	Epistolae	4
nostrum (forsitan quo alacrius illud impenderemus Doctrinae)	460	Epistolae	6
illud necessarium magis factu, hoc vero longe iucundius,	472	Epistolae	34
ILLUDIS			
Quam nihil illudis, Gens improba! quam male cedunt	405	Passio 7	1
Quam nihil illudis! cum quo magis angar acuto	405	Passio 7	3
Quam nihil illudis flectens! namque integra posthac	405	Passio 7	5
Quam nihil illudis! si, quae tua purpura fingit,	405	Passio 7	7
ILLUM			
Illum non labor irritus	402	Musae 40	3
Illum volo, qui calceat lixam tuum.	413	Lucus 17	7
Tu aperis illum populo, & cum ipse sis in summa arbore altera manu	456	Epistolae	13
Neque enim passus es illum Fluuium, qui tantae poeticae,	461	Epistolae	6
sume tecum amorem illum quo soles beare Amplitudini tuae deuotissimos	464	Epistolae	27
ILLUSTR			
In Honorem Illustr. D. D. Verulamij, Sti Albani,	436	Poem.Lat.	T
ILLUSTRANS			
illustrans nos omnes, lumenque accendens de suo lumine,	461	Epistolae	3

	PAGE	TITLE	LINE
ILLUSTRISS			
Illustriss. Celsissimoque CAROLO, Walliae, & Iuventutis Principi.	384	Musae	T
ILLUSTRISSIME			
Illustrissime Domine. Ecquid inter tot gloriae titulos caput vndique	456	Epistolae	1
Illustrissime Domine. Siccam animam sapientissimam esse dixit	460	Epistolae	19
Illustrissime Domine. Prolem Tuam suauissimam, nuper in lucem	463	Epistolae	4
Illustrissime Domine. Pendulam hanc dignitatem diu expectantem magnas	464	Epistolae	10
Illustrissime Domine. Tu quidem semper Patronus noster es,	467	Epistolae	16
Illustrissime Domine. Concede vt Honoribus nuperis, tanquam partubus	469	Epistolae	7
Ignosce (Heros illustrissime) quod pronomina mea adeo audacter	473	Epistolae	15
ILLUSTRIUS			
ex quo illustrius assecutus es nomen, quam Repertores Noui Orbis	463	Epistolae	12
ILLUUIE			
Intra extraque graui plenus es illuuie.	414	Lucus 21	2
imo vmbras hominum fame, frigore, illuuie, enectas, contusas,	449	Orationes	9
IMA			
Tristis, vbi ac ferrum tellure reciditur ima,	419	Tr.Mortis	36
IMAGINEM			
truncata corpora, mutilatam imaginem Dei, pauxillum vitae,	449	Orationes	4
IMAGO			
Illa quidem a nostro non multum abludit imago,	396	Musae 26	5
Sum, quis nescit, Imago Dei, sed saxea certe:	410	Lucus 1	1
Nempe in quo clare lucet Imago Dei.	410	Lucus 4	10
Pallida materni Genij atque exanguis imago,	426	Mem.Matr.7	1
corrumpuntur statuae, haec imago atque character, tempore melior,	459	Epistolae	13
IMBECILLITATI			
imbecillitati id nostrae, quae fastigium regiarum notionum aequare	460	Epistolae	16
IMBELLES			
Mulceat, imbelles complacuere modi.	387	Musae 5	12
IMBER			
Proh! quantus imber, quanta labri comitas,	423	Mem.Matr.2	29
IMBIBAT			
tantisper supplere donec Academia orationem tuam imbibat probetque,	470	Epistolae	7
IMBRE			
Aspice quam pleno descendat Iuppiter imbre,	210	Cam.1613-a BR	5
IMBRIBUS			
Siste tuum fletum & gemitus: namque imbribus istis	415	Lucus 23	13
IMBUAS			
nobis haec gaudia, imbuas cor Regium vigore, animum clementia,	444	Orationes	5
IMBUTA			
Sulphureoque lacu, totaque imbuta Mephiti.	419	Tr.Mortis	59
IMITATUR			
Hostibus haec etiam parcens imitatur Iesum.	416	Lucus 26	5
IMMEMOR			
Immemor antiqui mellis, eundo coquit.	398	Musae 33	20
IMMERSI			
qui cupiditatibus immersi, aut vno semper saginantur in loco,	452	Orationes	9
IMMINENS			
Vt, cum mors rabidis vnguibus imminens	391	Musae 17	3
IMMINENT			
Quacunque gutta temporis imminent?	433	Poem.Lat.	6
IMMINUERE			
qui literas imminuere spiritus, generososque animos frangere	461	Epistolae	19
non cor) Tui in me dominij ius imminuere posse, nedum rescindere.	473	Epistolae	7
IMMINUTUM			
timemus Librorum precia auctum iri, et priuilegia nostra imminutum.	467	Epistolae	8
IMMODICA			
Cur adeo immodica relligione cales?	399	Musae 35	2
IMMODICUS			
Immodicus luctus tacito vorat igne medullas,	433	Poem.Lat.	47
IMMORIAR			
Immoriarque oculis, o mea vita, tuis.	421	Lucus 35	4
Si licet, immoriar: vel si tua visio vita est,	421	Lucus 35	5
IMMORITURUS			
Cur sine te, votis immoriturus, ago?	421	Lucus 35	6
IMMORTALEM			
Tantum precemur Deum immortalem, vt Princeps optimus nulla secunda	454	Orationes	38
IMMORTALIS			
Quam Christus immortalis innocuo gregi	396	Musae 28	1
IMMORTALITAS			
nostrorum, atque immortalitas, vt semper post nouas dignitates,	464	Epistolae	23
IMMUNITATES			
praedia, alij immunitates carpunt, nonnulli Fluuium inuident,	461	Epistolae	15
ceperit aduersus aut immunitates nostras aut commune literarum	467	Epistolae	11
orantes vt immunitates nostrae a Serenissimis Regibus concessae ab	468	Epistolae	21
IMMUNITATIBUS			
Reges Collegia, eaque fundarunt amplissimis praedijs, immunitatibus:	458	Epistolae	23
IMO			
Imo pectore cogitationes?	411	Lucus 5	3
Imo, me nec apes, nec astra pungunt:	411	Lucus 5	10
Totamque eructans nubem, Glans proruit imo	420	Tr.Mortis	76
Occasione certat, imo & obtinet.	423	Mem.Matr.2	28
Quid sperare, imo quid non sperare licebat?)	432	Poem.Lat.	28
effari, non licet per multitudinem, imo per modestiam vestram?	443	Orationes	29
effigies, imc vmbras hominum fame, frigore, illuuie, enectas,	449	Orationes	8
imo in vniuersum, si quis de Principe aliquo, quis sit futurus aut	454	Orationes	8
hic enim securi sumus a pluuia, imo a fulmine:	455	Orationes	16
Imo prorsus censemus permultum interesse alacritatis publicae,	468	Epistolae	14
imo precabor enixe, me tum priuari tam communi hac luce,	472	Epistolae	23
IMPAR			
Et vnus impar aestimatur viribus,	388	Musae 8	5

	PAGE	TITLE	LINE
IMPROBA (cont'd)			
Tempus edax rerum, tuque o mors improba sola es,	433	Poem.Lat.	41
IMPROBE			
improbe, verba Dei,	397	Musae 28	17
memoriam recolenti, quam cogitanti noua, improbe molestiam creent.	457	Epistolae	14
IMPROBITAS			
Hanc mihi duritiem contulit improbitas.	410	Lucus 1	2
IMPROBUM			
In Improbum disertum.	414	Lucus 22	T
IMPUDENS			
Abito, barde. Quam pie istic sum impudens!	424	Mem.Matr.2	60
IMPUNE			
qua tot iam annis impune fruimur, hoc pacto fundatam cupit	447	Orationes	29
IMPUTABIS			
Num totum tibi pectus imputabis?	421	Lucus 34	2
IN			
Ecce recedentis foecundo in littore Nili	384	Musae	1
Reuerendissimo in Christo Patri ac Domino,	385	Musae	T
Ad eundem In Monstrum vocabuli Anti-Tami-Cami-Categoria.	386	Musae 3	T
Pollubra vel cum olim damnaris Regia in ara,	386	Musae 3	9
In metri genus.	387	Musae 5	T
Cur tanta sufflas probra in innocuam Crucem?	389	Musae 10	1
In Catharum.	391	Musae 16	T
Torquet, & in Textu Doctor vtroque cluet.	392	Musae 19	6
In ritibus nostris? Ego audio nullum.	392	Musae 20	2
Quas Luna habet, tuetur, in foueam cadit,	393	Musae 22	8
Ecclesia est mihi Luna; perge in Fabula.	393	Musae 22	10
Mutas in humanam figuram	393	Musae 23	3
Merserat in lustris perniciosa venus,	396	Musae 26	10
In Catharum quendam.	397	Musae 29	T
Britannicam in Vulpem, inque Romanam Lupam.	397	Musae 30	6
Paulo, secretis mussitans in angulis	398	Musae 32	5
Pertrahis in partes nomina magna tuas;	398	Musae 33	2
Qui tamen in nostros fortiter ire negant.	398	Musae 33	4
Hipponensis adest properans, & torquet in hostes	398	Musae 33	17
Incipis irridens; stomachans in carmine pergis;	401	Musae 38	1
Vis, & vena sacris regnat in artubus;	403	Musae 40	8
Impar, & in fletum vel resolutus, ero;	404	Passio 1	2
In sudorem sanguineum.	404	Passio 2	T
In eundem.	404	Passio 3	T
In latus perfossum.	404	Passio 4	T
Christe, vbi tam duro patet in te semita ferro,	404	Passio 4	1
In Sputum & Conuicia.	404	Passio 5	T
In posterum, maledicta Ficus arescens	405	Passio 5	6
In Coronam spineam.	405	Passio 6	T
In Arund. Spin. Genuflex. Purpur.	405	Passio 7	T
Viuat, & in mortem vita sit illa tuam.	405	Passio 7	10
In Alapas.	405	Passio 8	T
In Flagellum.	406	Passio 9	T
In vestes diuisas.	406	Passio 10	T
In pium Latronem.	406	Passio 11	T
In Christum crucem ascensurum.	406	Passio 12	T
Christus in cruce.	406	Passio 13	T
In Clauos.	407	Passio 14	T
Eriperet nobis, in Cruce fixus eras;	407	Passio 14	2
In cruce suspendens, vnde reclinet, habet.	407	Passio 15	4
Tu tamen, haud tibi tam moreris, quam viuis in illis,	407	Passio 17	3
Scilicet in tumulis Crucifixum quaerite, viuit:	408	Passio 17	5
In Mundi sympathiam cum Christo.	409	Passio 21	T
Non moreris solus: Mundus simul interit in te,	409	Passio 21	1
In Stephanum lapidatum.	410	Lucus 3	T
In Simonem Magum.	410	Lucus 4	T
Si sursum iacias, in caput ipsa ruit.	410	Lucus 4	8
Nempe in quo clare lucet Imago Dei.	410	Lucus 4	10
In S. Scripturas.	411	Lucus 5	T
In pacem Britannicam.	411	Lucus 6	T
Cum natet in tantis caetera terra malis?	411	Lucus 6	2
Sit licet in pelago semper, sine fluctibus illa est,	411	Lucus 6	3
In Lotionem pedum Apostolorum.	412	Lucus 8	T
In D. Lucam.	412	Lucus 9	T
Suamque in alijs possidet prudentiam.	412	Lucus 13	4
In Vmbram Petri.	413	Lucus 14	T
Vtque ouis in dumis, haeres in crine Cometae,	413	Lucus 16	3
In Superbum.	413	Lucus 17	T
In eundem.	413	Lucus 18	T
In kenodoksian.	414	Lucus 20	T
Rotundus in te: namque si ansatus sies,	414	Lucus 20	7
Ducentque, donec incidentem in cassidem	414	Lucus 20	9
In Gulosum.	414	Lucus 21	T
Illa cauerna, in qua tot coiere ferae.	414	Lucus 21	4
In Improbum disertum.	414	Lucus 22	T
Viuimus in praesens: hesternam viuere vitam	415	Lucus 23	5
Frustra itaque in tot funeribus miraberis vnum,	415	Lucus 23	11
In Angelos.	415	Lucus 24	T
Quae diuisa nocent, Christi per foedus, in vnum	417	Lucus 29	3
In Thomam Didymum.	417	Lucus 30	T
In Solarium.	417	Lucus 31	T
Scinditur in partes vulgus ceu compita: telum	418	Tr.Mortis	16
Ambustis sudibus: pars vitam in pocula fundunt,	418	Tr.Mortis	20
In patinas alij: furit inconstantia vini	418	Tr.Mortis	21
Instructaeque acies, hyemesque in pellibus actae,	418	Tr.Mortis	28

IN (cont'd)

	PAGE	TITLE		LINE
Triumphus Christiani. In Mortem.	421	Lucus 33		T
In te, nec arcus, scorpionesue, aut rotas,	421	Lucus 33		4
In Johannem epistethion.	421	Lucus 34		T
In flumen moerore nigrum si funderer ardens,	422	Mem.Matr.1		5
Per te nascor in hunc globum	425	Mem.Matr.4		13
Exemploque tuo nascor in alterum:	425	Mem.Matr.4		14
In terram violae capite inclinantur opaco,	425	Mem.Matr.5		7
In nebulas similesque tui res gaudia nunquid	426	Mem.Matr.7		2
In vicium mundo sterili, cui cedo cometas	426	Mem.Matr.7		20
Sed partem in scriptis etiam dum lacryma poscit,	428	Mem.Matr.9		17
In Obitum Henrici Principis Walliae.	432	Poem.Lat.		T
In mea dicta ruant; non tam mihi pendula mens est,	432	Poem.Lat.		5
Vt morbi perimant, alioque in puluere prostet?	433	Poem.Lat.		35
In Natales et Pascha Concurrentes.	434	Poem.Lat.		T
In vitam & neruos Pascha coaeua fluet.	434	Poem.Lat.		10
In Obitum Serenissimae Reginae Annae.	435	Poem.Lat.		T
In laudes abeunt secula quaeque tuas;	435	Poem.Lat.		2
In laudes properant secula quaeque tuas;	435	Poem.Lat.	V	2
In laudes abeunt iam loca quaeque tuas:	435	Poem.Lat.		4
In laudes properant iam loca quaeque tuas:	435	Poem.Lat.	V	4
In Honorem Illustr. D. D. Verulamij, Sti Albani,	436	Poem.Lat.		T
Columba Noae, quae in vetustis artibus	436	Poem.Lat.		19
Columba Noae, quae in vetustatis artibus	436	Poem.Lat.	V	19
Securis errorum; inque Naturalibus	437	Poem.Lat.		25
Securique errorum; inque Natalibus	437	Poem.Lat.	V	25
In obitum incomparabilis Francisci Vicecomitis	438	Poem.Lat.		T
In Sacram Anchoram Piscatoris G. Herbert.	438	Poem.Lat.		T
Sanctius in Regno Magni credebat Amoris	439	Poem.Lat.		14
(In quo fas nihil est rumpi) donare sigillum.	439	Poem.Lat.		15
Hic habitant Musae, facilisque in carmine Pallas,	210	Cam.1613-a	BR	3
En Aurora vocat, lectus genialis in aula est,	210	Cam.1613-b	BR	1
coram Dominis Legatis cum Magistro. in Artib. titulis insignirentur.	440	Orationes		T
quibus hostes soletis in potestatem redigere, lenioresque aspectus,	440	Orationes		9
hilare est, laetum, ac lubens, vestram in gratiam amplectimur.	440	Orationes		13
sitis ordine atque habitu, quo nos in hoc regno omnes esse gloriamur.	441	Orationes		1
autem vt foelicitas tantorum Principum etiam in ministros redundet,	441	Orationes		6
redundet, quorum in eligendis illis iudicium iampridem apparet.	441	Orationes		6
cum tanti sitis & in Principibus Vestris, & in vobismetipsis,	441	Orationes		8
in Principibus Vestris, & in vobismetipsis, veremur ne nihil hic sit,	441	Orationes		9
nos tam defecimus in vtroque quam Excellentiae Vestrae abundant.	441	Orationes		13
Seritur fama in hoc saeculo, vt in sequenti metatur:	441	Orationes		19
Seritur fama in hoc saeculo, vt in sequenti metatur:	441	Orationes		20
Oratio in Discessum Regis ab Academia Cantabrigiae habita 12o die	443	Orationes		T
perfundis nos omnes quotidianis beneficijs, redundarit in authorem;	443	Orationes		11
nisi Rex esses in ciuili Republica, eligereris in Literaria?	443	Orationes		18
nisi Rex esses in ciuili Republica, eligereris in Literaria?	443	Orationes		19
viam aperiens & methodum in studijs adhibendam, etiam libros indicans	443	Orationes		24
Polycrates cum annulum sibi dilectum in mare dimisisset,	444	Orationes		14
& in rebus humanis diuinisque exercitatissimi, de integro	444	Orationes		20
vos, vos, inquam, excutite, quorum aetas teritur in libris:	445	Orationes		15
quos magnificentia promissi circumscribere in promptu erat,	445	Orationes		16
quamlibet Magnum, modo detis eum in flore, in vagina, in herbescenti	445	Orationes		20
modo detis eum in flore, in vagina, in herbescenti viriditate;	445	Orationes		20
in quo longe vberrimam gloriae segetem perspicio, nulla verborum,	446	Orationes		1
quod primum intendunt, saltem in secundis aut tertijs consistant.	446	Orationes		7
colligeret cum Caligula, praesertim cum possit in eodem litore?	446	Orationes		13
quam Nuptiae, quas adeo laudant Poetae, vt in coelum transtulerint:	446	Orationes		18
qui olim glasto se inficientes, in vxorum corporibus, Solem,	446	Orationes		30
in virginum, flores atque herbas depinxere:	446	Orationes		31
Quod si Nuptiae in se graues sunt, quanto magis Principum,	446	Orationes		34
Quare operosior in eo structura, & praerogatiuae regiae emicant.	446	Orationes		37
qua in re celebris est Gracchorum mater, ingenium ipsum atque indoles	447	Orationes		16
noluit Princeps optimus, in delectu vxoris, re vna omnium grauissima,	447	Orationes		22
Neque in hisce Nuptijs posteritati tantum prospexit suauissimus	447	Orationes		27
pace, securitas in agris est;	448	Orationes		10
causaris, irruit Miles in Musaeum tuum, & gladio te liberat.	448	Orationes		28
Quod aliae gentes manibus in coelum sublatis, lachrymis in terram	448	Orationes		34
manibus in coelum sublatis, lachrymis in terram manantibus, ieiunae,	448	Orationes		35
vbi in dubio est, qui facit, an qui patitur, miserior.	449	Orationes		10
vt qui hic in Musarum monte editissimo, in ipso Parnasso siti sumus,	449	Orationes		32
in Musarum monte editissimo, in ipso Parnasso siti sumus, liberiorem,	449	Orationes		33
nimirum infinitum Principis in suam gentem amorem, cui pacem	449	Orationes		36
cum quanto plus possint in sua terra, tanto minus in aliena.	450	Orationes		11
cum quanto plus possint in sua terra, tanto minus in aliena.	450	Orationes		12
superbi sua tantum nosse, praesertim cum in vno regno non sint omnia:	450	Orationes		18
Nunc enim exploratos habet nostros in se affectus, timores,	450	Orationes		34
gaudeo quidem de ingenti amore in Principem, cui nulla dilectio par	451	Orationes		22
cum dimitteret te in Hispaniam, quod Romani Imperatores in bello,	451	Orationes		31
quod Romani Imperatores in bello, qui solebant signa in hostes	451	Orationes		32
qui solebant signa in hostes inijcere, vt milites acrius ea	451	Orationes		32
rara in Principibus virtus, & cui cum sceptro lites saepius	452	Orationes		2
immersi, aut vno semper saginantur in loco, vti anguillae,	452	Orationes		10
ac si corpora sua non abirent olim in elementa, sed in bellaria aut	452	Orationes		14
sua non abirent olim in elementa, sed in bellaria aut tragemata:	452	Orationes		14
cum tamen in resolutione illa vltima, nulla sit distinctio populi aut	452	Orationes		15
nulla sunt sceptra in elementis, nulli fasces aut secures:	452	Orationes		16
quos in arca repositos abijciebant in fluuium, his verbis:	452	Orationes		28
vt quid priuata habeat in se vita commodi aut voluptatis,	452	Orationes		37
cuius manifestationem in gentem suam priuatae personae & habitui	453	Orationes		8
In picturis locus est vmbris & recessibus, etiam si quis Principem	453	Orationes		14

IN (cont'd)	PAGE	TITLE	LINE
e baiulo euasit Philosophus, eodem ingenio vsus in lignis & literis:	453	Orationes	37
quae licet versentur in figuris describendis, quibus nihil imperito	454	Orationes	3
qui nuper versatus est in forma & figuris vultus, vbi res postulat,	454	Orationes	7
imo in vniuersum, si quis de Principe aliquo, quis sit futurus aut	454	Orationes	8
quemadmodum in Cometae praesagio, non respicitur, quae materia sit,	454	Orationes	12
in Geoponicis dicitur, Katoptron ean epideikseis toi epikeimenoi	454	Orationes	18
vbi iam ingrauescit humore, relabitur in terram, qua ortus est,	454	Orationes	29
Gulielmus Victor descensurus primum e nauibus in terram hanc,	455	Orationes	3
in terram hanc, incidit in coenum, quod innuebat eum hic mansurum:	455	Orationes	4
deperijt, at illa mutata est in arborem triumphantium propriam:	455	Orationes	9
Daphnen suam, cuius amor deinceps in triumphos & laurus mutabitur.	455	Orationes	11
aquas a Fonte accipiunt non retinent ipsi, sed in mare dimittunt;	456	Epistolae	10
ab optimo Rege desumptas in vniuersam Rempublicam diffundis:	456	Epistolae	11
& cum ipse sis in summa arbore altera manu prehendis Regem, . .	456	Epistolae	13
censemus nostram, et in honoribus Tuis nostro bono gratulamur;	456	Epistolae	16
fructum potuimus expectare ab Eo, in quem fauor Regius, nostra vota,	456	Epistolae	18
hinc a populo, illinc a Principe, in Te conueniunt, et confabulantur.	456	Epistolae	25
Eximia tua in nos merita frequentiorem calamum postulant, . .	457	Epistolae	7
temporibus et diligentia diuisos in gratijs nostris copulauimus.	457	Epistolae	15
Quod si tam integrum tibi esset gratificari nobis in terra & aere,	457	Epistolae	22
quam in aqua & igne fecisti, non dubitamus quin benignitas tua omnia	457	Epistolae	22
Sane, gestabaris antea in cordibus nostris;	458	Epistolae	18
quam vt pro infinitis vestris in nos beneficijs Maiestatem vestram	458	Epistolae	30
Maiestatem vestram aeternitati in scriptis nostris certissime	458	Epistolae	31
Nunc vero Ipse scribendo irrupisti in compensationes nostras,	459	Epistolae	1
et quo magis Tuum agnoscas, in ipso partu, Librorum regem creatum.	459	Epistolae	12
Si enim in regno vestro Hibernico lignum nascitur permanens,	459	Epistolae	15
quanto magis virtutes istae in Dominum agri transferendae sunt,	459	Epistolae	17
Infinita vestra in nos Beneficia non solum verba omnia, . .	460	Epistolae	2
gauderent Fluuijs, nunc etiam aquas, in quibus habitant, impertis!	460	Epistolae	9
studioque in nos iam olim perspectissimo, quippe qui eximie semper	462	Epistolae	25
et blattis rixantes, exuens puluere, in theatrum et lucem produxisti.	462	Epistolae	27
Tuam suauissimam, nuper in lucem publicam, nostramque praesertim,	463	Epistolae	5
nunquam in tantis negotijs, quibus meritissime districtus es,	463	Epistolae	17
Faxit Deus vt quos profectus feceris in Sphaera Naturae, . .	464	Epistolae	3
quos profectus feceris in Sphaera Naturae, facias etiam in Gratiae:	464	Epistolae	3
sed perspectissimus tuus in nos amor, praestantissimaeque animi dotes	465	Epistolae	11
vt Alma Mater libentissime caput reclinet in tuo sinu, oculusque	465	Epistolae	13
circumspiciens reperisset Te, quasi in tuis palpebris acquiescat.	465	Epistolae	14
Permitte vt nos etiam in praedam partemque tecum veniamus: . .	465	Epistolae	21
curesque vt tuus in nos amor, antehac satis perspectus, . .	466	Epistolae	3
in quo paucorum auaritia liberalibus artibus dominatura est,	466	Epistolae	23
vti sanguis solet in re dubia ad cor festinare, ita ad Te confugimus	467	Epistolae	9
id omne dexterrima tua in obeundis rebus prudentia dissipetur.	467	Epistolae	13
quae nos soluendo non sumus, in suas tabulas accepti transferat.	467	Epistolae	15
sed tamen comparatio & in honorem tuum cedet, nostrumque emolumentum.	467	Epistolae	26
ad progressum doctrinae, hac etiam in parte nobis opituleris.	467	Epistolae	28
praesertim in Theologia, cuius Libri si alij alijs (tanquam montes	467	Epistolae	30
in qua dextra et fide coniuncti, in caeteris haud diuellamur.	468	Epistolae	24
in qua dextra et fide coniuncti, in caeteris haud diuellamur.	468	Epistolae	25
enixus gloriae, sollicitudine in futurum plenos, haud parum leuare;	469	Epistolae	11
dignissime praeficiaris Fisco, etiam Academiam in Thesauris habe:	469	Epistolae	22
hoc Principe, in quo doctrinae fructus atque vsus mirifice relucet.	469	Epistolae	23
Parce doctrinae in epistolis; perorans, paululum indulge: . .	471	Epistolae	1
etiam senectus, quam aetatem in hac palaestra consecutus mihi videor.	471	Epistolae	8
atque effusissimum in omnia officia, quae praestet mea paruitas;	471	Epistolae	22
Cum enim vim cogitationum in vitam meam omnem conuertissem, . .	472	Epistolae	5
receptusque sim in aliquem apud Honorem Tuum locum, magis id adeo	472	Epistolae	20
fungar apud Meos, Rhetoris in hunc annum, & in plures Oratoris,	472	Epistolae	26
Rhetoris in hunc annum, & in plures Oratoris, permitte, . .	472	Epistolae	26
rariusque paulo fodiam in Vintoniensi agro, dum Rhetorici satagam:	472	Epistolae	28
ad mea in Honorem Tuum officia erectior solutiorque redibo, . .	473	Epistolae	2
sic existimes nihil Mortalium firmiori flagrare in Te desiderio,	473	Epistolae	5
non cor) Tui in me dominij ius imminuere posse, nedum rescindere.	473	Epistolae	6
Academicis maternisque, assumsi mecum propensionem in Patrem.	473	Epistolae	9
quod pronomina mea adeo audacter incedant in hac epistola: . .	473	Epistolae	16
To the right honourable and reverend Father in God, my L. Bishop of	473	Epistolae	23
INA			
Ina metros euthenouses	430	Mem.Matr.16	10
INACCESSAS			
Constat inaccessas dissiluisse petras.	409	Passio 20	6
INAEQUALITAS			
non minus vitae inaequalitas delectat, quam terrae, quam Natura	453	Orationes	11
INANEM			
ulomanian illam & inanem verborum strepitum iamdudum deposui:	445	Orationes	22
INANES			
Gorgona cur diram laruasque obtrudis inanes, ...	387	Musae 6	1
nos haud inanes linqueret, ...	396	Musae 28	9
Metus inanes? Nos pari praeteruehi	397	Musae 30	3
INAUDISTI			
nihil inaudisti de Tago, Pactolo?	451	Orationes	4
INCALESCIT			
Quaerit recessus. Incalescit fabula:	398	Musae 32	6
INCALUERE			
Vt niue torpentes incaluere manus?	399	Musae 35	4
INCEDANT			
quod pronomina mea adeo audacter incedant in hac epistola: . .	473	Epistolae	16
INCEDENS			
cum grandi atque impedito onere facillime incedens, occurrit ei	453	Orationes	35

INCEDIT	PAGE	TITLE	LINE
Neque sane quispiam incedit Te instructior ad omnem causam,	462	Epistolae	21
INCENDAT			
Incendat tacitas, sole morante, faces:	211	Cam.1613-b BR	6
INCENDIA			
quantum satis ad dolendum, vrbium incendia, fragores, direptiones,	449	Orationes	6
INCENDIUM			
quam subito dispereunt, simul ac concrepuit incendium militare:	448	Orationes	19
vbi velut ex continentibus tectis ad nos traiecturum est incendium:	449	Orationes	14
INCERTA			
praesertim cum futura incerta sint, & nullis perspicillis,	449	Orationes	24
INCIDENTEM			
Ducentque, donec incidentem in cassidem	414	Lucus 20	9
INCIDIT			
in terram hanc, incidit in coenum, quod innuebat eum hic mansurum:	455	Orationes	4
INCIPE			
caute incipe, cohibens adeo stylum ingeniumque;	470	Epistolae	11
INCIPIS			
Incipis irridens; stomachans in carmine pergis;	401	Musae 38	1
INCLINANTUR			
In terram violae capite inclinantur opaco,	425	Mem.Matr.5	7
INCLINATO			
Inclinato capite. Joh. 19.	407	Passio 15	T
INCLYTUS			
Magnificus es screator, homicida inclytus.	421	Lucus 33	2
INCOEPTUM			
siccitas anni huius derisit incoeptum et plus effecit quam mille	461	Epistolae	11
INCOGNITAS			
regiones terrasque veteribus incognitas primus demonstrat:	463	Epistolae	11
INCOLAE			
Incolae coeli melioris alba	390	Musae 14	11
INCOMMODUM			
sub specie publici commodi, Academiae incommodum videntur allaturi;	463	Epistolae	1
INCOMPARABILEM			
Quid memorem prudentiam vestram incomparabilem, qua optime ostendis	443	Orationes	16
O prudentiam incomparabilem, quae eodem vultu et moderatur mundum	458	Epistolae	3
INCOMPARABILI			
magis id adeo factum esse mansuetudine Tua incomparabili,	472	Epistolae	22
INCOMPARABILIS			
In obitum incomparabilis Francisci Vicecomitis	438	Poem.Lat.	T
INCONCINNA			
meo quadrabunt, quae almae matri inconcinna erunt atque enormia.	470	Epistolae	15
INCONSTANTIA			
In patinas alij: furit inconstantia vini	418	Tr.Mortis	21
Bacchantur Lapithae, furit inconstantia vini	271	Tr.Mortis VS	21
INCONSULTA			
Quas gens inconsulta, suis vexata procellis,	401	Musae 39	2
INCREDIBILEM			
si Romanorum Imperatorum incredibilem luxum a Tiberio Caesare	452	Orationes	22
INCREDIBILES			
Hocine accedit ad incredibiles laudes vestras quod quae nos audiamus	443	Orationes	30
INCREDIBILIS			
cuius nisi incredibilis fuisset vis, nunquam in tantis negotijs,	463	Epistolae	17
INCREPAT			
Morsus increpat anxios;	403	Musae 40	5
INCUBAT			
ne pacem, quae sola incubat artibus, & obstetricatur, minus quam par	448	Orationes	33
INCUBES			
Cum caeterae ecclesiae tam perspicaci diligentia incubes,	466	Epistolae	21
INCULTOS			
Saltus per incultos lacusque	393	Musae 23	11
INCUMBAMUS			
virtutibus, tuo exemplo compensatis, ad vnum omnes incumbamus.	468	Epistolae	17
INCUMBANT			
incumbant sibi inuicem imperia, tanquam ligna obliqua, aliter magna	450	Orationes	27
INCUMBIS			
qui Philosophiae incumbis, cum corporis cum anima vinculum	448	Orationes	26
Quod si forense quippiam nos spectans, dum incumbis muneri, occurrat,	466	Epistolae	5
INCUMBIT			
Tillius incumbit Dano, Gallusque marinis,	427	Mem.Matr.9	11
INDALMA			
Demosion t' indalma kalou, theion te katoptron.	430	Mem.Matr.17	7
INDE			
Erumpit inde, & contineri nescius	398	Musae 32	7
Inde Patres pergunt quadrati, & tota Vetustas.	398	Musae 33	13
Munere, Rex tanto verior inde prober.	405	Passio 7	4
Ah! quam caederis hinc & inde palmis!	405	Passio 8	1
Inde rotae atque axes subeunt, quasi sella curulis	419	Tr.Mortis	55
Et ius pectoris inde consecutus	421	Lucus 34	5
Inde exiguntur pensa crudo vespere.	423	Mem.Matr.2	21
Haud glubat inde tres teruncios escae.	429	Mem.Matr.12	4
Inde ego sic mecum: gaudeo quidem de ingenti amore in Principem,	451	Orationes	21
qui inde e baiulo euasit Philosophus, eodem ingenio vsus in lignis	453	Orationes	37
quid Tu inde? Britannicas insulas omnes occupasti.	458	Epistolae	9
INDIA			
India, non solitum profer Eliza decus:	211	Cam.1613-b BR	12
INDIAS			
qui vtrasque Indias Hispania sua quasi nodo connectens,	440	Orationes	16
INDICANS			
etiam libros indicans ad Theologiam expeditissimos, tanto ac tam	443	Orationes	25

	PAGE	TITLE		LINE
INDICANTES				
mollissimis lecticis, indicantes, se non amare patriam terram,	452	Orationes		12
INDICERE				
Sed non est nostri bellum indicere:	449	Orationes		16
INDICET				
per tot milliaria facile transmissum, mentem maiorum capacem indicet?	454	Orationes		2
INDICIUM				
Et hoc indicium subis, Redemptor?	417	Lucus 30		2
INDIES				
Sic pascunt se indies, ac si corpora sua non abirent olim	452	Orationes		13
quod expectamus indies futurum, Almae Matris amorem tecum simul	462	Epistolae		29
Aspicis multitudinem Librorum indies gliscentem, praesertim	467	Epistolae		29
non adeo sanatae ab optimo Rege nostro quin turgescat indies,	473	Epistolae		22
INDIGENAS				
omnes indigenas loci	395	Musae 25		4
INDIGENTIA				
Natura suas dotes, vt indigentia singularum regionum omnes connectat:	450	Orationes		19
INDIGERE				
sua sibi sufficere, neque externis indigere auxilijs atque antidotis:	444	Orationes		26
INDIGEREMUS				
quc minus exteris Libris indigeremus, sed tamen comparatio	467	Epistolae		25
INDIGNIOR				
Ni me forte petas; nam quanto indignior ipse,	404	Passio 2		5
INDOLES				
ingenium ipsum atque indoles (veluti Conclusio sequitur infirmiorem	447	Orationes		17
INDOS				
non dicam vobis quod factum est ante seculum vestrum, aut apud Indos;	446	Orationes		1
INDUCENS				
ophthalmon upographas kai epitrimmata pareion inducens;	470	Epistolae		20
INDUCTIONIS				
Inductionis Dominus, & Verulamij;	436	Poem.Lat.		4
INDUE				
Quotidie pasti: tantum verum indue vultum	427	Mem.Matr.7		29
tu hanc personam indue scripturus, tuumque iudicium tibi Lictor esto.	470	Epistolae		27
INDULGE				
perorans, paululum indulge: ne tum quidem multum, neque nostrae	471	Epistolae		2
INDULGEAS				
non quod nunc indulgeas alterutri, sed quod deinceps indultum nollem.	470	Epistolae		12
INDULGENS				
Indulgens proprijs ambitionibus,	391	Musae 17		8
INDULGERE				
Rege nostro quin turgescat indies, atque efferat se, indulgere.	473	Epistolae		22
INDULTAE				
habita Chartae nostrae a Serenissimo Principe Henrico 8 indultae,	467	Epistolae		22
INDULTUM				
non quod nunc indulgeas alterutri, sed quod deinceps indultum nollem.	470	Epistolae		12
INDUM				
Vtrumque si praederis Indum,	425	Mem.Matr.6		7
INDUSTRIA				
Atheniensis doluit se victum opificum antelucana industria,	469	Epistolae		2
INELEGANTES				
ipsae mulieres inelegantes, nulla pulchritudo per vniuersam	451	Orationes		16
INEMPTA				
(Nempe sepulcra Satis numen inempta dedit.)	425	Mem.Matr.5		14
INENARRABILES				
Quid fauores erga hanc Academiam inenarrabiles, cum non solum tuearis	443	Orationes		21
INEPTE				
At tu qui inepte haec dicta censes filio,	423	Mem.Matr.2		52
INEPTUM				
Non deridiculumue, siue ineptum,	401	Musae 37		34
INEPTUS				
Obscurus sermo negotijs ineptus; quae cum plerumque implicata sint,	470	Epistolae		29
INESSE				
Cui non absimilis sensus inesse solet.	396	Musae 26		8
INEST				
Mater inest saliente vena.	426	Mem.Matr.6		16
INFANS				
Cum tener ad sacros infans sistatur aquales,	388	Musae 9		1
Forsitan & prohibes infans portetur ad vndas,	388	Musae 9		7
Sin, Melvine, pedes alienos postulet infans,	388	Musae 9		9
Vincit more suo Noster: nam millibus Infans	437	Poem.Lat.		3
Vicit more suo Noster: nam millibus Infans	437	Poem.Lat.	V	3
INFANTEM				
Dum petit Infantem.	437	Poem.Lat.		T
Dum petit Infantem Princeps, Grantamque Iacobus,	437	Poem.Lat.		1
INFANTIA				
Vos sine maternis hymnis infantia vidit,	389	Musae 12		5
INFANTULOS				
bis intersectas, infantulos plus lactis quam cruoris emittentes;	449	Orationes		7
INFECTAS				
Infectas tabulas facta iuuenca scidit.	408	Passio 20		4
INFERIORIS				
etsi tu qui scribis (vti quiuis priuatus) inferioris sis subsellij,	470	Epistolae		23
INFERNAE				
Erutus, infernae pretiosa tragemata mensae,	419	Tr.Mortis		58
Exulis, infernae pretiosa tragemata mensae,	419	Tr.Mortis	V	58
INFERNI				
Pulueris inferni; properat datus ignis, & omnem	420	Tr.Mortis		69
Pulueris inferni properat, datur ignis, & omnem	420	Tr.Mortis	V	69
Sulphuris inferni, properat datus ignis et omnem	271	Tr.Mortis	VS	69

	PAGE	TITLE	LINE
INFEROS			
perrumpit primipilus, & te cum coelis tuis ad inferos deturbat.	448	Orationes	30
INFERS			
certe non tam ornas illam, qui infers manum grauitati.	470	Epistolae	20
INFESTAT			
praesertim donec transeat nubes illa, quae vicinos adeo infestat:	455	Orationes	15
INFICETAE			
Adeo inficetae, plumbeae, Meduseae, ...	429	Mem.Matr.12	6
INFICIENTES			
Maiores nostri, qui olim glasto se inficientes, in vxorum corporibus,	446	Orationes	30
INFINITA			
Infinita vestra in nos Beneficia non solum verba omnia, . . .	460	Epistolae	2
INFINITAS			
crassissimum elementum, Tu subtilitates Artium infinitas. . .	463	Epistolae	14
INFINITIS			
quam vt pro infinitis vestris in nos beneficijs Maiestatem vestram	458	Epistolae	30
INFINITUM			
nimirum infinitum Principis in suam gentem amorem, cui pacem	449	Orationes	36
INFIRMIOREM			
(veluti Conclusio sequitur infirmiorem partem) plerumque matrissat:	447	Orationes	18
INFLATO			
Tuque aer inflato tubam, dum plurimus ignis	211	Cam.1613-b BR	5
INFLER			
Si totus infler, si tumeam crepax, ...	426	Mem.Matr.6	17
INFORTUNIA			
Non metuunt vltra; nostra infortunia tantum	432	Poem.Lat.	24
INFRA			
Quid metuant homines infra, supraue minentur	413	Lucus 16	1
INFUNDERE			
fieri participes eius sanguinis, qui tantos spiritus solet infundere.	440	Orationes	20
INGEMAT			
Ingemat ob partus, ceu maledicta, suos, ...	390	Musae 12	14
INGEMINES			
Fac radios saltem ingemines, vt dextera tortos	424	Mem.Matr.3	9
INGEMISCIT			
neque Studiosorum Sacculi, qui etiam nunc maeret et ingemiscit.	467	Epistolae	23
INGEMIT			
Ingemit, & defessus opem iam Portitor orat.	420	Tr.Mortis	82
INGENIA			
aduentum ipsi lapides, ipsa durissima ingenia, meum praesertim,	445	Orationes	8
INGENIO			
Non tot abest, quot nos Regis ab ingenio.	437	Poem.Lat.	4
e baiulo euasit Philosophus, eodem ingenio vsus in lignis & literis:	453	Orationes	37
dein Hon. Tuo gratulamur, qui filio auctus es tali ingenio praedito:	463	Epistolae	24
INGENITIS			
Haud secus ingenitis dotibus orbus Adam.	410	Lucus 1	4
INGENIUM			
Quaeritur ingenium, doctusque homicida probatur.	418	Tr.Mortis	25
Cui tenuis fama est, ingeniumque minus.	435	Poem.Lat.	4
verrunt (ac si perdiderint ingenium) vt Spartam exornent suam:	445	Orationes	37
ingenium ipsum atque indoles (veluti Conclusio sequitur infirmiorem	447	Orationes	17
occurrit ei Democritus, & ingenium admirans, domum secum duxit,	453	Orationes	35
feracem gloriae, et coeleste ingenium quasi ad metalla damnari.	468	Epistolae	6
caute incipe, cohibens adeo stylum ingeniumque;	470	Epistolae	11
INGENS			
Ingens piorum gloria Principum, ...	394	Musae 23	38
cuius ingens gloria aeque rotunda est atque ipse orbis: . .	440	Orationes	15
INGENTES			
post ingentes Hecatombas, exiguam thuris micam adoleri legimus.	469	Epistolae	16
INGENTI			
sed a scriptis vestris, quae ingenti cum lucro quotidie legimus.	443	Orationes	20
vt ingenti labore suo & periculo consuleret & praesenti Reipublicae	447	Orationes	24
gaudeo quidem de ingenti amore in Principem, cui nulla dilectio par	451	Orationes	21
INGENUUM			
Absit vt ingenuum pungant mea verba pudorem;	400	Musae 36	3
INGLUUIE			
Ingluuieque minor. Quercus habitare feruntur	418	Tr.Mortis	5
INGLUUIEM			
Quid ego vobis Neronum aut Heliogabalorum ingluuiem memorem?	452	Orationes	19
INGRATOS			
Nec querar ingratos, studijs dum tabidus insto, ...	426	Mem.Matr.7	17
INGRAUESCIT			
ascendit ad nubes, vbi iam ingrauescit humore, relabitur in terram,	454	Orationes	29
INGREDIENS			
quam nunc pleno gradu ingrediens beneficijs tuis percurres. . .	468	Epistolae	19
INGRESSUS			
sub ementito habitu fidicinis castra hostium ingressus, . .	453	Orationes	5
INHIARE			
legibus et hominum summe contraria est) monopolijs quibusdam inhiare,	467	Epistolae	6
INIJCERE			
qui solebant signa in hostes inijcere, vt milites acrius ea . .	451	Orationes	32
INITO			
Prudenter inito quot-diebus calculo.	423	Mem.Matr.2	23
INIURIA			
Annon longa fames miseraeque iniuria pestis	432	Poem.Lat.	20
INIURIAE			
Sed aliorum iniuriae tuarum virtutum pabula sunt, qui lemas istas	462	Epistolae	11
INIURIAS			
iniurias seculi scriptaque hac illac pereuntia securius praeterit.	459	Epistolae	14
INIUSTE			
Iniuste satis arguit viator.	428	Mem.Matr.10	4

	PAGE	TITLE	LINE
INIUSTITIAE			
latiusque manare iniustitiae peccatum, quam negligentiae.	472	Epistolae	32
INNITI			
re vna omnium grauissima, alienis oculis iudicioque inniti;	447	Orationes	23
INNOCENTES			
Ad seductos innocentes.	400	Musae 36	T
INNOCUAE			
Innocuae mentes, quibus inter flumina mundi	400	Musae 36	1
INNOCUAM			
Cur tanta sufflas probra in innocuam Crucem?	389	Musae 10	1
Principis innocuam seruastis numina Vitam,	433	Poem.Lat.	34
INNOCUIS			
Rectius innocuis lactentibus omnia praestes,	388	Musae 9	11
INNOCUO			
Quam Christus immortalis innocuo gregi	396	Musae 28	1
INNOCUUM			
Sanguinis, innocuum tandem luet orbis Abelem.	272	Tr.Mortis VS	101
INNUEBANT			
quod pereleganter & supra barbariem seculi innuebant Maiores nostri,	446	Orationes	29
INNUEBAT			
in terram hanc, incidit in coenum, quod innuebat eum hic mansurum:	455	Orationes	4
INNUIS			
non gremio solum (quod innuis) sed et ambabus vlnis osculisque ei	463	Epistolae	7
INNUMERA			
Quid innumera alia, quae, si per tempus liceret effari,	443	Orationes	28
INNUMERAM			
Innumeram nostris partibus addit opem.	399	Musae 33	22
INNUMEROS			
Innumeros mergit vitiata mente poetas,	402	Musae 39	39
INNUPTA			
Innupta Pallas, nata Diespitre,	433	Poem.Lat.	1
INNUPTAM			
eos scilicet, qui innuptam Palladem colunt, Musasque coelibes,	446	Orationes	25
INOPIA			
si prae defectu aquae, commeatusque inopia, desererentur collegia,	462	Epistolae	3
INOPUM			
Magnatumque inopumque aequum certamen & ardor:	429	Mem.Matr.13	3
INQUAM			
Ite leues (inquam), Parnassia numina, Musae,	432	Poem.Lat.	1
vos, vos, inquam, excutite, quorum aetas teritur in libris:	445	Orationes	14
INQUINAUIT			
Quas subscriptio neutiquam inquinauit;	400	Musae 37	8
INQUIT			
Ah! Cheiragra vetat, quo minus, inquit, agam.	389	Musae 11	2
Sistimus hic, inquit fatum, sat prata biberunt	272	Tr.Mortis VS	100
Ei en en o anthropos, inquit Medicorum Alpha, ouk an elgeen.	446	Orationes	18
INSCIAM			
illam tegminis insciam	395	Musae 25	13
INSCIE			
Quin cerne vt erres, inscie, brachium	426	Mem.Matr.6	13
INSCIJ			
Laudando Matrem, cum repugnant inscij.	424	Mem.Matr.2	65
INSCIO			
Quam (more vestro) imponere inscio vulgo.	397	Musae 31	3
INSCRIPTAS			
figuras iam nunc pulueri inscriptas corpore confosso obliterans.	448	Orationes	32
INSERENDO			
optime consuluisse Deum orbi terrarum lapides & metalla ei inserendo,	452	Orationes	25
INSERIS			
Sanctos qui gemitus mentibus inseris	403	Musae 40	12
INSIDIJS			
cum non solum tuearis nos a maleuolorum insidijs, sed etiam doceas	443	Orationes	22
INSIGNEM			
Nam vtramque illam curam insignem, tam de conseruando Fluuio nostro,	457	Epistolae	17
INSIGNES			
Post honores eximios, praefecturas insignes, Legationes Nobilissimas,	440	Orationes	2
INSIGNI			
Mens sub insigni specie coloris	390	Musae 14	7
INSIGNIRENTUR			
cum Magistro. in Artib. titulis insignirentur. 27. Febr. 1622.	440	Orationes	T
INSISTITO			
Tu vero collige te, tibique insistito,	414	Lucus 20	5
INSITA			
tum venenatorum haereticorum, insita vi sua liberentur.	459	Epistolae	19
INSITUS			
Arbor & ipse inuersa vocer: dumque insitus almae	428	Mem.Matr.11	5
INSOMNIA			
Aurum nocte videns, vidisse insomnia dicit:	411	Lucus 7	1
INSPEXI			
inspexi facies hominum ac vultus curiosius tanquam emptor;	451	Orationes	12
INSTAR			
Exoritur tubus, atque instar Cyclopis Homeri	419	Tr.Mortis	53
INSTAT			
Cedito Barbaries: Helicon iam litibus instat,	417	Lucus 28	5
Heu miseri! Quis tantum ipsis virtutibus instat	419	Tr.Mortis	33
O superi: Quis tantum ipsis virtutibus instat	271	Tr.Mortis VS	33
INSTAURARI			
nunc denuo ex aedibus Eboracensibus ab altero Cancellario INSTAVRARI,	464	Epistolae	1
INSTAURATIONE			
Curasti tu quidem Instauratione tua, quo minus exteris Libris	467	Epistolae	24

	PAGE	TITLE	LINE
INSTAURATIONEM			
Mag. Sigilli Custodis post editam ab eo Instaurationem Magnam.	436	Poem.Lat.	T
INSTAURATIONIS			
Ad Autorem Instaurationis Magnae.	435	Poem.Lat.	T
Cancel. Gratiae de Instaurationis Libro Academiae donato	463	Epistolae	T
INSTITUTI			
Ad Regem Instituti Epigrammatici ratio.	385	Musae 1	T
INSTO			
Nec querar ingratos, studijs dum tabidus insto,	426	Mem.Matr.7	17
INSTRUCTAE			
Instructaeque acies, hyemesque in pellibus actae,	418	Tr.Mortis	28
INSTRUCTIOR			
Neque sane quispiam incedit Te instructior ad omnem causam,	462	Epistolae	21
INSTRUCTUS			
a re instructus nos doceat, tuosque fauores populo tuo communicans	444	Orationes	6
INSTRUETUR			
Tunc instruetur lautius radijs penu,	407	Passio 16	13
INSTRUIT			
Interea classem magnis Rex instruit ausis:	427	Mem.Matr.9	7
INSULAM			
nostram Caesar ad insulam	395	Musae 25	2
INSULAS			
Britannicas insulas omnes occupasti. Hoc etiam imperium tenuius est	458	Epistolae	9
INSULTUS			
Sanguinis insultus exanimata ferunt.	406	Passio 13	4
INSUMAM			
Quod superest vitae, insumam: Solisque iugales	426	Mem.Matr.7	15
INSUNT			
cui soli ideo insunt oculi variegati, cum caetera animantia	453	Orationes	17
INSUSURRAS			
Vt celebrem decus insusurras?	394	Musae 23	24
INTACTA			
interim vestra hac scribendi laude intacta manente atque illibata.	458	Epistolae	27
INTEGERRIMAE			
quam de futuro supplicem, integerrimae tuae fidei commendantes.	465	Epistolae	8
INTEGRA			
Quam nihil illudis flectens! namque integra posthac	405	Passio 7	5
INTEGRAS			
Atqui manus imponere integras praestat,	397	Musae 31	2
Quin post modestam, qualis integras decet,	422	Mem.Matr.2	14
multi Academias integras subuersas volunt, neque illi e faece vulgi	461	Epistolae	16
INTEGRO			
Te perspicaci atque integro.	388	Musae 8	8
in rebus humanis diuinisque exercitatissimi, de integro disponendum.	444	Orationes	21
subiectos, integro Fluuio a Rege nostro donatos, triumphare?	460	Epistolae	13
INTEGRUM			
Prodegit integrum penu,	407	Passio 16	6
Quod si tam integrum tibi esset gratificari nobis in terra & aere,	457	Epistolae	21
INTELLECTUS			
Intellectus adultus Angelorum	415	Lucus 24	1
Tu penetrantiori intellectus acumine; cuius nisi incredibilis fuisset	463	Epistolae	16
INTELLIGATIS			
vt satis intelligatis, Excellentias vestras tanto chariores esse,	440	Orationes	24
INTENDUNT			
quod primum intendunt, saltem in secundis aut tertijs consistant.	446	Orationes	6
INTER			
Quos inter plenusque Deo genioque Iacobus	399	Musae 33	23
Innocuae mentes, quibus inter flumina mundi	400	Musae 36	1
Quas Latij Catharique mouent, atque inter vtrasque	402	Musae 39	31
Atque inter reliquos horti crescentia foetus	427	Mem.Matr.7	33
Harmoniam dabit inter astra.	434	Poem.Lat.	36
Comparatio inter Munus Summi Cancellariatus et Librum.	435	Poem.Lat.	T
inter quas & Mathematicae, quae licet versentur in figuris	454	Orationes	3
tantum vt permittat nostram hanc Inter victrices hederam sibi serpere	455	Orationes	18
Ecquid inter tot gloriae titulos caput vndique munientes meministi	456	Epistolae	2
an inter lauros principis hederae nostrae ambitiosae locus est?	456	Epistolae	3
et tanquam Aquilam inter nouas honorum nubes e conspectu nostro	456	Epistolae	6
inter quae etiam certamen oritur et pia contentio, vtrum gratia	456	Epistolae	19
Ecquid inter tantas mundi trepidationes nobis & Musis vacas?	458	Epistolae	2
charta conspiciendum Te praebes, quo familiarius inter nos verseris.	458	Epistolae	20
& inter nouos honorum cumulos, quod expectamus indies futurum,	462	Epistolae	28
Cancellario INSTAVRARI, inter Arcana Prouidentiae plane reponimus.	464	Epistolae	2
Iam si inter commendandum adhibeas ei calamistros vti iuuenculae,	470	Epistolae	18
sumpta vna est e proceribus, inter patritios sedens et praetextatos.	470	Epistolae	24
Academiam simulans vel maximos magnatum inter eundum summouet:	470	Epistolae	26
INTERCEDUNT			
in Principibus virtus, & cui cum sceptro lites saepius intercedunt?	452	Orationes	3
INTERCIPI			
eruditionis nobis conscius est, palustri opere & vliginoso intercipi:	461	Epistolae	8
INTERCIPIS			
Fontem intercipis omnibus patentem?	421	Lucus 34	3
INTERDUM			
vt interdum putem, optime consuluisse Deum orbi terrarum lapides	452	Orationes	24
est etiam interdum satietas quaedam honoris, quem ad tempus deponere	453	Orationes	9
INTEREA			
Interea ad sacrum stimulat sacra Musica bellum,	399	Musae 33	25
Confluere interea passim ad Floralia pubes	418	Tr.Mortis	9
Interea classem magnis Rex instruit ausis:	427	Mem.Matr.9	7
Interea procede Comes Germano-britanne	211	Cam.1613-b BR	7
INTERESSE			
Imo prorsus censemus permultum interesse alacritatis publicae,	468	Epistolae	15

INUIDIAM	PAGE	TITLE	LINE
Quo magis inuidiam nobis & crimina confles,	398	Musae 33	1
Verum mittamus inuidos & inuidiam, quae semper se deuorat primum,	454	Orationes	14
INUIDOS			
Verum mittamus inuidos & inuidiam, quae semper se deuorat primum,	454	Orationes	14
INUIGILARE			
Lampada, qua studijs inuigilare solet.	398	Musae 33	18
INUIGILO			
Dumque his inuigilo frequens	424	Mem.Matr.4	7
INUISAM			
Inuisamque tuis erigit hasta Crucem.	398	Musae 33	16
INUISANT			
vt quando beneficia tua peruagantur Angliam, nos etiam inuisant:	466	Epistolae	17
INUISAT			
clementia, vt frequenter nos inuisat, a re instructus nos doceat,	444	Orationes	6
INUISENTIBUS			
Peregrinis Academiam nostram inuisentibus	459	Epistolae	29
INUISERET			
Quis enim tunc inuiseret Almam Matrem destitutam omni commeatu?	461	Epistolae	1
INUITIS			
vnde consequimur, vel inuitis Fatis, quasi nodosam aeternitatem.	446	Orationes	23
INUIUM			
Edenem Boreae flatibus inuium.	424	Mem.Matr.4	4
INUNDAT			
Nec cingit mare, nunc inundat omnes.	428	Mem.Matr.10	14
INUOLUIT			
Cuius fauoris magnitudo ita inuoluit nos, vt etiam rependendi vias	458	Epistolae	28
INUOLUTAM			
Nunc Arcana patent, nec inuolutam	408	Passio 19	9
INURENS			
Centum stigmatibus tuos inurens	400	Musae 37	23
INUTILIUS			
quibus nihil imperito vanius inutiliusue videatur, vbi tamen ad vsum	454	Orationes	4
INVENTA			
Inventa bellica.	271	Tr.Mortis VS	T
INVIDERE			
Quod si fata illi longam invidere salutem	432	Poem.Lat.	26
INVITO			
Invitoque fugit singula stella pede:	210	Cam.1613-b BR	2
IOCUM			
Esse iocum scli, plebe stupente, tibi:	416	Lucus 27	4
IOCUS			
Quam satur & suauis sit tibi Roma iocus.	416	Lucus 27	6
IORDAN			
Et ipse Iordan sistit aquas stupens;	394	Musae 23	42
IPSA			
Non vt te superem: res tamen ipsa feret.	386	Musae 2	2
Et, quos ipsa nequit scandere vertices,	391	Musae 17	9
Anne tuas flammas ipsa Antiperistasis auget,	399	Musae 35	3
Ipsaque sunt ferulae mollia corda suae.	406	Passio 9	6
Igniculos legans, manserit ipsa licet;	410	Lucus 2	2
Si sursum iacias, in caput ipsa ruit.	410	Lucus 4	8
Ipsa cum domina domum vorando?	411	Lucus 5	9
Quae vis condidit, ipsa nouit aedes.	411	Lucus 5	17
Hinc tamen excludi mors noluit, ipsaque vitam	271	Tr.Mortis VS	7
Qua Mors ipsa sedens hominum de gente triumphat.	419	Tr.Mortis	56
At superat caput illa tuum, quantum ipsa cadauer	424	Mem.Matr.3	3
aduentum ipsi lapides, ipsa durissima ingenia, meum praesertim,	445	Orationes	8
tamen nimium efferre vos, cum Virginitas ipsa fructus sit Nuptiarum:	446	Orationes	28
vt nihil habeat Inuidia ipsa, quod contra hiscat aut mussitet.	453	Orationes	24
verisimile est, eos illuc, quo cognitio ipsa pertingit, ascensuros.	468	Epistolae	2
erectior solutiorque redibo, ex ipsa intermissione animos ducens.	473	Epistolae	3
IPSAE			
Quos David, ipsae deliciae Dei,	394	Musae 23	37
quando ipsae hae turres & beatae fabricae, vnico ictu sulphurei tubi,	448	Orationes	20
ipsae mulieres inelegantes, nulla pulchritudc per vniuersam	451	Orationes	16
IPSAM			
Atqui te precor vnice per ipsam,	400	Musae 37	1
Tam demissa, ipsamque adeo subeuntia terram?	420	Tr.Mortis	94
prouecta atque adulta, ipsam possessionem adeas, agathei ge tuxei.	470	Epistolae	8
IPSAS			
Non erubescentes vel ipsas	394	Musae 23	19
primo nuptias ipsas spectate. Quid autem?	446	Orationes	9
barbara omnia, Tu non nisi cultissima, elegantiasque ipsas exhibes.	463	Epistolae	15
IPSE			
Ipse pios laudo; Numen & ipse colo.	386	Musae 4	6
Cum nequeat claras ipse litare preces?	388	Musae 9	14
Et ipse Iordan sistit aquas stupens;	394	Musae 23	42
Ipse etiam Christus coelo speculatus ab alto,	402	Musae 39	11
Ni me forte petas; nam quanto indignior ipse,	404	Passio 2	5
Tu spina misere pungeris, ipse Rosa.	405	Passio 6	2
Sic toti medicaris ipse mundo.	405	Passio 8	3
Nunc ipse scandis, vt labore mutato	406	Passio 12	2
Quid hoc? & ipse deficis, Caeli gigas,	407	Passio 16	1
Quamque ipse lucis tesseram sibi negat,	407	Passio 16	7
Quin nos Ipse emit, precioso faenora soluens	410	Lucus 4	3
Quam si ipse solus omnia interuerteret,	412	Lucus 13	3
Per fluctus saltem, fac, precor, ipse vadem.	414	Lucus 19	4
Ipse fruare, licet, solus graueolente sepulcro;	414	Lucus 21	5
Ira facit, mundusque ipse est apotheca furoris.	418	Tr.Mortis	17
Quid ipse faciam? qui nec arboreas sudes	421	Lucus 33	3

IPSE (cont'd)	PAGE	TITLE	LINE
Ah nunc, helluo, fac, vt ipse sugam:	421	Lucus 34	1
Virtutumque choro siccior ipse tuo.	422	Mem.Matr.1	4
Ergo ipse solum mutus atque excors ero	423	Mem.Matr.2	55
Ipse tuae solum adnectam, sine murmure, thensae.	426	Mem.Matr.7	16
Ipse suos tanquam digno pallentiaque astra.	426	Mem.Matr.7	21
Arbor & ipse inuersa vocer: dumque insitus almae	428	Mem.Matr.11	5
Dissutus videor funere & ipse tuo.	428	Mem.Matr.11	12
Quin moriar tecum: vitam, quam negligis ipse,	434	Poem.Lat.	5
cuius ingens gloria aeque rotunda est atque ipse orbis:	440	Orationes	16
cor sacrum, sentiatque Rex ipse nos haec intime precari.	444	Orationes	9
ego vero sentio, & quis sum ipse (barbam, hui, tam grauem) & apud	445	Orationes	25
sic & ipse excerpam e Principis rebus gestis pugillum, vnam actionem	445	Orationes	31
Deus ipse cum crearet hominem, mundi regem, consilio vsus est.	446	Orationes	36
Ipse, ipse profectus est, vt ingenti labore suo & periculo consuleret	447	Orationes	23
ipse profectus est, vt ingenti labore suo & periculo consuleret	447	Orationes	23
ipse egit oratorem, vt & ego aliquantulum hoc nomine glorier.	450	Orationes	30
& cum ipse sis in summa arbore altera manu prehendis Regem,	456	Epistolae	13
Nunc vero Ipse scribendo irrupisti in compensationes nostras,	459	Epistolae	1
vt cum ipse eruditionis Princeps sit, illi etiam honores qui finitimi	463	Epistolae	21
Tandem, ne et ipse peccem, breuis sit sermo, atque pressus.	470	Epistolae	31
IPSI			
Auresque superas: arbitri ipsi sint litis,	392	Musae 20	4
Dum moreris, Mea Vita, ipsi vixere sepulti,	407	Passio 17	1
Ipsi sibi sunt nequiter facillimi.	413	Lucus 17	4
Si non per species, nequimus ipsi,	415	Lucus 24	9
Quid ipsi sumus, assequi putando.	415	Lucus 24	10
Atque ipsi sibi sunt mola & farina.	415	Lucus 24	15
quorum aduentum ipsi lapides, ipsa durissima ingenia, meum	445	Orationes	8
si Reges ipsi quandoque suauitates suas populari aceto condiant.	453	Orationes	18
proin vt Fluuij quas aquas a Fonte accipiunt non retinent ipsi,	456	Epistolae	10
quomodo alij molem hanc laetitiae suae exprimant, ipsi viderint:	457	Epistolae	1
conseruantes sibi Illos Fontes, a quibus ipsi olim hauserunt?	461	Epistolae	32
quas non nobis habemus sed irrigati ipsi vniuersum regnum aspergimus?	462	Epistolae	11
praesertim quum ipsi non solum rectum de Bene-merentibus iudicium	469	Epistolae	12
IPSIS			
Heu miseri! Quis tantum ipsis virtutibus instat	419	Tr.Mortis	33
O superi: Quis tantum ipsis virtutibus instat	271	Tr.Mortis VS	33
Ipsis seuerus orbibus;	427	Mem.Matr.8	6
Atque vbi per te sanctificer natalibus ipsis,	434	Poem.Lat.	9
IPSO			
in Musarum monte editissimo, in ipso Parnasso siti sumus, liberiorem,	449	Orationes	33
et quo magis Tuum agnoscas, in ipso partu, Librorum regem creatum.	459	Epistolae	12
IPSOS			
Age, prouocemus vsque ad Angelos ipsos,	392	Musae 20	3
Peccati veniae mei, vel ipsos	421	Lucus 34	8
Ipsos Catones prouocans oraculis.	423	Mem.Matr.2	34
quare causam nostram nosque ipsos Tibi, Teque Deo Opti: Max: intimis	468	Epistolae	9
IPSUM			
Explicat, & radijs ipsum pertingit Olympum!	401	Musae 39	7
& ipsum accepimus saluum & annulum, annulum Coniugalem,	444	Orationes	18
esto autem hoc ipsum iter, quod nuper emensus est, vt sciatis omnes	445	Orationes	33
ingenium ipsum atque indoles (veluti Conclusio sequitur infirmiorem	447	Orationes	17
ipsum coelum nubilum semper, & poeta stultus qui dixerat,	451	Orationes	18
castra hostium ingressus, ipsumque Praetorium, fidibus canendo,	453	Orationes	5
IRA			
Ira facit, mundusque ipse est apotheca furoris.	418	Tr.Mortis	17
IRAM			
Teque Deum alternis cantans Ambrosius iram,	398	Musae 33	19
Totamque euomerem potenter iram	400	Musae 37	15
IRAS			
timores, suspiria, expostulationes, iras, amorem rursus.	450	Orationes	35
IRASCOR			
Proinde parco belluis, nec irascor.	429	Mem.Matr.12	11
IRE			
Qui tamen in nostros fortiter ire negant.	398	Musae 33	4
Non potui non ire acre stimulante flagello:	431	Mem.Matr.19	5
IRI			
ex quo timemus Librorum precia auctum iri, et priuilegia nostra	467	Epistolae	7
IRRADIABIT			
Qui dulci miseros irradiabit ope.	387	Musae 7	10
IRREGULARIS			
Irregularis nunc habitus mihi est:	426	Mem.Matr.6	21
IRRETITA			
Sic positis nugis, quibus irretita libido	402	Musae 39	38
IRRIDENS			
Incipis irridens; stomachans in carmine pergis;	401	Musae 38	1
IRRIGATI			
quas non nobis habemus sed irrigati ipsi vniuersum regnum aspergimus?	462	Epistolae	10
IRRIGUI			
tractus (Oceani praeda et deliciae) vt irrigui Musarum horti,	461	Epistolae	9
IRRITUS			
Illum non labor irritus	402	Musae 40	3
IRRUIT			
causaris, irruit Miles in Musaeum tuum, & gladio te liberat.	448	Orationes	28
IRRUPISTI			
Nunc vero Ipse scribendo irrupisti in compensationes nostras,	459	Epistolae	1
ISABELLAE			
Quin & Serenissimae Principis Isabellae laudes, virtutesque,	441	Orationes	3
ISOS			
proeleluthoton, en kai emas isos deesei poreuesthai, poia tis esti.	471	Epistolae	11

ISTA	PAGE	TITLE		LINE
Ista docens soli scripta quadrare tibi.	385	Musae		6
Sufficiet votis ista iuuenta meis.	386	Musae 2		10
Commotos animos rectius ista decent.	387	Musae 5		6
Non conuenire precibus ista Diuinis.	392	Musae 20		14
Mater: & ista Dolor nunc tibi Metra parit.	422	Mem.Matr.1		8
Siste parum cantus, dum legis ista, tuos.	427	Mem.Matr.9		2
Debuit ista pati prima & non nobilis aetas:	432	Poem.Lat.		29
ISTAE				
quanto magis virtutes istae in Dominum agri transferendae sunt,	459	Epistolae		17
ISTAEC				
Tantum istaec scribo gratus, ne tu mihi tantum	422	Mem.Matr.1		7
ISTANAI				
kai oi alloi nomeis boulontai plesion autou tas agelas istanai.	447	Orationes		32
ISTAS				
Istas Anti-Tami-Cami-Categorias!	386	Musae 3		2
qui lemas istas et festucas, Reipublicae oculo haerentes,	462	Epistolae		12
ISTE				
Quis iste tandem? non enim vultu ambulat	436	Poem.Lat.		1
ISTHAEC				
Isthaec pileus audijt propinquus,	391	Musae 15		3
ISTIC				
Abito, barde. Quam pie istic sum impudens!	424	Mem.Matr.2		60
ISTIS				
Siste tuum fletum & gemitus: namque imbribus istis	415	Lucus 23		13
a scriptione terrestribusque istis sublimitate solij asserta) vita	458	Epistolae		7
ISTOC				
O blanda dextra, neutiquam istoc pulueris,	423	Mem.Matr.2		39
ISTOS				
et Xerxes istos, alterosque maris quasi Flagellatores expugnatos	462	Epistolae		8
paludumque istos siccatores (solem officio suo priuantes) vi verborum	462	Epistolae		19
tuus amor et authoritas istos sorices nobis abigat.	469	Epistolae		1
ISTUD				
Largiar & istud: scilicet Magnatibus	413	Lucus 17		2
IT				
Dum lacrymas, it vita: tuus tibi clepsydra fletus,	415	Lucus 23		9
It stridor, caelosque omnes & Tartara findit.	420	Tr.Mortis		73
It stridor, caelosque omnes et sydera findit.	271	Tr.Mortis	VS	73
ITA				
ita Sol & Coelum producunt flores, qui symbola sunt spei,	446	Orationes		32
Principibus vt vtilissima ita difficillima factu, cum quanto plus	450	Orationes		10
cur non vt elephanti turres, ita tu patriam tecum portasti?	451	Orationes		8
ita me ametis omnes, vt ego nihil vspiam laetum, nihil candidum	451	Orationes		13
Cuius fauoris magnitudo ita inuoluit nos, vt etiam rependendi vias	458	Epistolae		28
sic merita tua ita ascensura, vt eorum vis et virtus ad nos	464	Epistolae		19
ita excipiemus illa, vt benignius hospitium, et erga te propensius,	466	Epistolae		17
ita ad Te confugimus primariam partem ecclesiastici corporis,	467	Epistolae		9
appulit ad nos omnes haud ita certe studijs chartisque obuolutos,	468	Epistolae		13
tuere nos ita vt fortunae nostrae, intra ambitum amplexusque	469	Epistolae		18
Vtcunque Tua lenitas non ita interpretabitur mea haec scribendi	471	Epistolae		25
ITAQUE				
Frustra itaque in tot funeribus miraberis vnum,	415	Lucus 23		11
nunc itaque Liber hic vester dilatat pomoeria, summouet Oceanum	458	Epistolae		11
ITE				
Ite leues (inquam), Parnassia numina, Musae,	432	Poem.Lat.		1
ITEM				
apud poetas deorum pharetrae operculum habuere, humanae non item:	449	Orationes		26
ITER				
Non tantum est iter Angelis ad vndas,	415	Lucus 24		11
Ah longum, quae te deperit, errat iter.	437	Poem.Lat.		4
Ah longum, quae te deperit, ambit iter.	437	Poem.Lat.	V	4
esto autem hoc ipsum iter, quod nuper emensus est, vt sciatis omnes	445	Orationes		34
vnicum hoc iter nuperum explicabo, in quo longe vberrimam gloriae	446	Orationes		1
Quare & Principis iter multiplicem nobis exhibet prudentiam;	446	Orationes		8
iter bene longum! Quid autem illic?	451	Orationes		1
Ecquid videtis tandem quam vtile hoc iter, per quod optimus Princeps	451	Orationes		35
interficere voluptatis, vt iter tantum, tantis laboribus,	452	Orationes		7
agxonais abiectis, iter aggreditur & labores, haud ignarus,	452	Orationes		32
quam audire videor dicentem, Pulchrum quidem iter & Amante dignum;	453	Orationes		26
ITERUM				
Quod si necesse sit iterum exire patria, qui nunc inuenit viam,	455	Orationes		7
ITINERA				
Deum immortalem, vt Princeps optimus nulla secunda itinera meditetur;	455	Orationes		1
ITINERE				
neque enim quicquam hoc itinere mirabilius, cuius tamen fructum omnem	450	Orationes		2
& scientiae augmentum ex hoc itinere captauit solertissimus Princeps?	450	Orationes		5
Neque alienas tantum ex hoc itinere cognouit Respublicas sed quod	450	Orationes		32
ex itinere Principem metiri licet, quod sane adeo nobile fuit	453	Orationes		22
iterum exire patria, qui nunc inuenit viam, proximo itinere faciat.	455	Orationes		8
ITINERI				
Habui viaticum fauoris Tui, quod longiori multo itineri sufficeret.	471	Epistolae		19
ITINERIS				
causas itineris huius, quantum quidem ego homuncio ac nanus	453	Orationes		20
ITIS				
Scilicet hoc vobis proprium, qui purius itis,	387	Musae 5		7
Qua sine vos miseri lentius itis ope.	399	Musae 33		26
IUBE				
Proin iube Thorndick nostrum, ni graue est, librum tibi Oratorium	470	Epistolae		9
IUBET				
non suam tribui iubet.	396	Musae 25		23

	PAGE	TITLE	LINE
IUCUNDIUS			
Quid enim iucundius accidere potest, quam vt ministri Regis Catholici	440	Orationes	14
illud necessarium magis factu, hoc vero longe iucundius, nobiliusque:	472	Epistolae	35
IUDICIJ			
Iudicij dominus, flores vt iunctius halent	427	Mem.Matr.7	25
IUDICIO			
ad Theologiam expeditissimos, tanto ac tam stupendo iudicio, vt,	443	Orationes	26
atque vbiuis terrarum pro iudicio prudentissimi Regis, & in rebus	444	Orationes	20
re vna omnium grauissima, alienis oculis iudicioque inniti;	447	Orationes	23
IUDICIUM			
redundet, quorum in eligendis illis iudicium iampridem apparet.	441	Orationes	7
non solum rectum de Bene-merentibus iudicium hausisse ab Antiquis,	469	Epistolae	12
tu hanc personam indue scripturus, tuumque iudicium tibi Lictor esto.	470	Epistolae	27
IUGALES			
Quod superest vitae, insumam: Solisque iugales	426	Mem.Matr.7	15
IUGEM			
Culpa redux iugem te neget esse Deum.	406	Passio 13	6
IUGERA			
vbi trecenta foliorum iugera vno die sedentes percurritis;	454	Orationes	25
IUGO			
cum excusso altero iugo, dimidiaque operis parte leuatus,	473	Epistolae	1
IUGULAT			
Quotidie iugulat, nec semel vllus obit.	415	Lucus 23	4
IUGUM			
Cum Latium ferrent secula prisca iugum?	416	Lucus 25	2
IUNCTA			
Haec vbi iuncta, subit viuo cum fune minister,	420	Tr.Mortis	66
IUNCTIUS			
Iudicij dominus, flores vt iunctius halent	427	Mem.Matr.7	25
IUNO			
Quin fugias? mea non fuerat tam nubila Iuno,	426	Mem.Matr.7	7
IUNXIT			
Sic excelsa humilisque simul loca dissita iunxit,	429	Mem.Matr.13	5
IUPITER			
Iupiter! o quot iam anni sunt ex quo vel apicem Latinum pertuli!	471	Epistolae	6
IUPPITER			
Aspice quam pleno descendat Iuppiter imbre,	210	Cam.1613-a BR	5
IURA			
sericatam hanc stultitiam contere, Academiaeque iura, dignitatem,	461	Epistolae	24
si oppidani nostri (more suo) Musarum iura et diplomata arrodant;	468	Epistolae	26
IURAMENTO			
De iuramento Ecclesiae.	389	Musae 11	T
IURARE			
Non video, certum est iurare; aut si hoc vetuisti,	421	Lucus 35	9
IURE			
Namque haec, iure, cuipiam	395	Musae 25	20
IURIS			
Apud Iuris-consultos, partus sequitur ventrem:	447	Orationes	12
IURIS-CONSULTOS			
Apud Iuris-consultos, partus sequitur ventrem:	447	Orationes	12
IUS			
Et ius pectoris inde consecutus	421	Lucus 34	5
non cor) Tui in me dominij ius imminuere posse, nedum rescindere.	473	Epistolae	7
IUSSUS			
Articulis sacris quidam subscribere iussus,	389	Musae 11	1
IUSTA			
Laudibus haud fierem sepia iusta tuis.	422	Mem.Matr.1	6
IUSTIS			
Nam fata non iustis repugnant	434	Poem.Lat.	27
IUSTISSIME			
iustissime potes sub hoc Principe, in quo doctrinae fructus atque	469	Epistolae	22
IUSTITIA			
homines, quibus homo bruta, iustitia scilicet & prudentia.	447	Orationes	5
IUSTITIAM			
Iustitiam prius tanto cum honore atque acclamatione administrans,	464	Epistolae	14
IUSTITIARIUM			
15. Ad J. Leigh, Capitalem Iustitiarium Angl. (Camden) Gratulatio	468	Epistolae	T
IUSTO			
& plus iusto celebres, cum leunculum & dominum suum contra naturam	454	Orationes	17
IUUAT			
ferox spumantia mandit, iuuat micare gladio & mucronem intueri.	447	Orationes	35
IUUATE			
O me probe lassum! Iuuate, Posteri!	437	Poem.Lat.	27
O me prope lassum! Iuuate, Posteri!	437	Poem.Lat. V	27
IUUENCA			
Infectas tabulas facta iuuenca scidit.	408	Passio 20	4
IUUENCULAE			
Iam si inter commendandum adhibeas ei calamistros vti iuuenculae,	470	Epistolae	19
IUUENEM			
Sic o te (iuuenem, senemue) credat	385	Musae	10
Mors semper iuuenem, senem Britanni.	385	Musae	11
IUUENILI			
ac si iuuenili potius impetu correptus, quam adductus maturo	471	Epistolae	26
IUUENIS			
Sic tu nunc iuuenis factus, egoque senex.	386	Musae 2	4
IUUENTA			
Sufficiet votis ista iuuenta meis.	386	Musae 2	10
IUUENTAE			
Humanae decus atque apex iuuentae,	384	Musae	2
IUUENTUS			
Hinc tyrocinium, paruoque assueta iuuentus,	418	Tr.Mortis	26

	PAGE	TITLE		LINE
IUUENTUTIS				
aut eorum certe, qui cymbala sunt fanaticae iuuentutis:	445	Orationes		25
IUVENTUTIS				
Illustriss. Celsissimoque CAROLO, Walliae, & Iuventutis Principi.	384	Musae		T
IXION				
Cantatum; deinde Ixion cum nubibus atris	420	Tr.Mortis		88
IXIONA				
Aetna Cacum igniuomum dedit, hic Ixiona multis	420	Tr.Mortis		87
Aetna Cacum igniuomum dedit, hic Ixiona Graecis	272	Tr.Mortis	VS	87
IXIONIS				
telam explices, perit negotium quasi ex nubibus Ixionis congressus.	470	Epistolae		31
IXNELATO				
Ego de rini ksumbalon ixnelato	430	Mem.Matr.15		14
J				
15. Ad J. Leigh, Capitalem Iustitiarium Angl. (Camden) Gratulatio	468	Epistolae		T
JAM				
Jam deturbarunt tempora longa suo.	416	Lucus 25	V	8
Quin tibi jam desperatae MORA nulla medetur,	416	Lucus 25	V	9
JOH				
Inclinato capite. Joh. 19.	407	Passio 15		T
JOHANNEM				
In Johannem epistethion.	421	Lucus 34		T
KAGON				
Pheron to pan, kagon: e os Aparktias	430	Mem.Matr.15		11
KAI				
Os dia somatiou proteron kai nun di' Olumpou	429	Mem.Matr.14		7
Pos nun aphiptasai, goou kai kindunou	429	Mem.Matr.15		3
Menoun to glaphuron, kai melirroon tropon,	430	Mem.Matr.15		8
Aiazo geneteiran, epaiazousi kai alloi,	430	Mem.Matr.17		1
Meteri tektainousa, gooi kai penthesi sugxroun.	431	Mem.Matr.17		14
Ainon omou Zoein kai pneumatos allo genesthai	431	Mem.Matr.17		22
Kai prepon ode para dakruoessi reein.	431	Mem.Matr.18		6
kai oi alloi nomeis boulontai plesion autou tas agelas istanai.	447	Orationes		31
O despota elie kai theoi pantes, ei ti kata ton emautou Bion emarton,	452	Orationes		29
ophthalmon upographas kai epitrimmata pareion inducens;	470	Epistolae		19
proeleluthoton, en kai emas isos deesei poreuesthai, poia tis esti.	471	Epistolae		11
KAKOS				
Polemos de kan pedioi kakos ephu.	448	Orationes		15
KALLOS				
Nun oraas, oti kallos apeiriton opos apaugous	429	Mem.Matr.14		5
KALOS				
Eirene georgon kan petrais trephei kalos,	448	Orationes		14
KALOU				
Demosion t' indalma kalou, theion te katoptron.	430	Mem.Matr.17		7
KAN				
Eirene georgon kan petrais trephei kalos,	448	Orationes		14
Polemos de kan pedioi kakos ephu.	448	Orationes		15
KATA				
theoi pantes, ei ti kata ton emautou Bion emarton, e phagon e pion,	452	Orationes		29
KATABLETHEI				
Otan de krepis me katablethei genous	447	Orationes		14
KATOPTRON				
Demosion t' indalma kalou, theion te katoptron.	430	Mem.Matr.17		7
Katoptron ean epideikseis toi epikeimenoi nephei, pareleusetai e	454	Orationes		19
KENODOKSIAN				
In kenodoksian.	414	Lucus 20		T
KENTOUMENAI				
Autar axei megaloi kentoumenai: eute gar autai	431	Mem.Matr.17		10
KEP				
Lesmones, e belone sphaleroi kep traumati vuttei	431	Mem.Matr.17		12
KEPON				
Praeis eiarinous te xarais epikidnato kepon:	431	Mem.Matr.17		18
KEPOU				
Kepou sunothon anthinen euodian,	430	Mem.Matr.15		12
KINDUNOU				
Pos nun aphiptasai, goou kai kindunou	429	Mem.Matr.15		3
KING				
Koning, & contracte King, a Con verbo deduci, quod tria complectitur,	447	Orationes		7
KING'S				
of Winchester, one of the Kings most honorable privy-Counsaile.	473	Epistolae		24
KLAUSO				
Idiais koraisi klauso.	430	Mem.Matr.16		12
KNOMENOI				
semper titillant aures Principum, Osper tois pterois knomenoi ta ota.	453	Orationes		3
KOINEN				
Prounomioi d' aretes koinen geneteiran elontes.	430	Mem.Matr.17		3
KOINON				
Ou pheggos, koinon t' agathon, mian eis thuran eirgein	430	Mem.Matr.17		5
KOMOIDOUMENOS				
Supplicum Ministrorum raptus komoidoumenos.	398	Musae 32		T
KONING				
Becanus ait vetus vocabulum nostrum, Koning, & contracte King,	447	Orationes		6
KORAIS				
Didumais korais toiauten	430	Mem.Matr.16		6
KORAISI				
Idiais koraisi klauso.	430	Mem.Matr.16		12
KREITTON				
Thanein suneidos kreitton, e allos bioun.	430	Mem.Matr.15		16
KREPIS				
Otan de krepis me katablethei genous	447	Orationes		14

	PAGE	TITLE	LINE
KSUMBALON			
Ego de rini ksumbalon ixnelato	430	Mem.Matr.15	14
KSUNERGON			
Zoes ksunergon tende diatheinai teknois	430	Mem.Matr.15	6
KUKLOTHEN			
Emas lipousa kuklothen metaixmious?	429	Mem.Matr.15	4
KUMAT'			
Kumat' epaphrioonta Thameseos, aike selenes	431	Mem.Matr.18	1
KUNA			
Otan nomeus agathon kuna exei, kai oi alloi nomeis boulontai plesion	447	Orationes	31
KURIES			
Autar od' au thanatos kuries, os elios auos	431	Mem.Matr.17	19
L			
my L. Bishop of Winchester, one of the Kings most honorable	473	Epistolae	24
LABE			
De labe maculisque.	393	Musae 22	T
LABECULAS			
Labeculas maculasque nobis obijcis:	393	Musae 22	1
LABENTIA			
Hinc mihi principium: vos o labentia mentis	432	Poem.Lat.	13
LABES			
Labes, somniaque, ambitusque diros,	401	Musae 37	38
LABITUR			
Per angiportus & maeandros labitur,	423	Mem.Matr.2	33
LABOR			
Illum non labor irritus	402	Musae 40	3
LABORANTIBUS			
suauiterque patefacta, nunc etiam laborantibus Musis succurrat.	467	Epistolae	3
LABORE			
Nunc ipse scandis, vt labore mutato	406	Passio 12	2
vt ingenti labore suo & periculo consuleret & praesenti Reipublicae	447	Orationes	24
LABOREM			
Cur ego laborem notus esse tam praue,	472	Epistolae	17
LABORES			
aequumne est vt tot labores & sollicitudines Principum sine	446	Orationes	11
agxonais abiectis, iter aggreditur & labores, haud ignarus,	452	Orationes	33
LABORIBUS			
agam vobiscum, simulque & laboribus meis, & vestrae fidei consulam,	445	Orationes	28
vt iter tantum, tantis laboribus, periculis obnoxium, susciperet?	452	Orationes	8
vt laboribus meis plurimis atque assidua obseruantia, ramenta	472	Epistolae	12
LABORUM			
Fructum laborum consecutae maximum	424	Mem.Matr.2	64
LABRI			
Proh! quantus imber, quanta labri comitas,	423	Mem.Matr.2	29
LABUNTUR			
Labuntur fluuij scientiarum:	415	Lucus 24	8
LAC			
Lac cum sanguine posco deuolutum;	421	Lucus 34	6
LACERANDO			
Suauis erat, qui scripta dolens lacerando recludi,	439	Poem.Lat.	13
LACERNULA			
Tandem prehensa comiter lacernula	427	Mem.Matr.8	7
LACESSAM			
Non mea fert aetas, vt te, veterane, lacessam;	386	Musae 2	1
Occumbens humero Thronos lacessam.	421	Lucus 34	9
LACESSIT			
Quas malus liuor iaculis lacessit	390	Musae 14	2
Assiduo stimulo carnem Mens vlta lacessit,	410	Lucus 2	5
Omnia suspendit naso, sociosque lacessit:	418	Tr.Mortis	13
LACESSUNT			
Quos tu calcasti fluctus, me, Christe, lacessunt,	414	Lucus 19	1
LACHRYMAE			
communes Reipublicae lachrymae alterum nobis Fluuium effunderent.	462	Epistolae	6
LACHRYMARE			
Scribere, Te dignum, vel lachrymare queat!	435	Poem.Lat.	6
LACHRYMIS			
Tota stupent luctu) lachrymisque exaestuet aequis	432	Poem.Lat.	10
manibus in coelum sublatis, lachrymis in terram manantibus, ieiunae,	448	Orationes	35
LACRYMA			
Sera nimis lacryma haec, si lacrymabis, erit.	415	Lucus 23	12
Sed partem in scriptis etiam dum lacryma poscit,	428	Mem.Matr.9	17
LACRYMABIS			
Sera nimis lacryma haec, si lacrymabis, erit.	415	Lucus 23	12
LACRYMAS			
Cum lacrymas oculosque duos tot vulnera vincant,	404	Passio 1	1
Cur lacrymas & tarda trahis suspiria, tanquam	415	Lucus 23	1
Dum lacrymas, it vita: tuus tibi clepsydra fletus,	415	Lucus 23	9
Conferte lacrymas: Illa, quae vos miscuit	422	Mem.Matr.2	3
Ridenti lacrymas quibus vnis concolor vnda est.	426	Mem.Matr.7	6
Deducens lacrymas prioris aeui	428	Mem.Matr.10	11
LACRYMET			
Et mea iam lacrymet culpa colore suo.	404	Passio 1	4
LACRYMIS			
Sicca meis lacrymis Thamesis vicina videtur,	422	Mem.Matr.1	3
Vt Flos hinc lacrymis, illinc Philomela querelis,	438	Poem.Lat.	5
LACTARE			
Sic lactare animos & sic ostendere gemmam	432	Poem.Lat.	31
LACTE			
Vae nubi pluuia grauidae, non lacte, measque	426	Mem.Matr.7	5
LACTEAM			
donec lacteam aliquam viam ad candorem Mentis Tuae ducentem aut	472	Epistolae	9

LACTENTIBUS	PAGE	TITLE	LINE
Rectius innocuis lactentibus omnia praestes, ...	388	Musae 9	11
LACTIS			
bis intersectas, infantulos plus lactis quam cruoris emittentes;	449	Orationes	7
LACU			
Sulphureoque lacu, totaque imbuta Mephiti.	419	Tr.Mortis	59
LACUM			
sed velut Romani lacum, cuius altitudo ignota erat, dedicabant	449	Orationes	21
LACUS			
Saltus per incultos lacusque	393	Musae 23	11
LAENA			
Trux caper alarum, suppara, laena, sagum.	397	Musae 29	2
LAESAE			
Aut laesae mihi suggerunt Athenae, ...	400	Musae 37	17
LAESERE			
Fataque Fortunasque & spem laesere futuram.	432	Poem.Lat.	25
LAESO			
Quare age, Mens, effare, precor, quo numine laeso? . . .	432	Poem.Lat.	17
LAETA			
At non lusus erit, si quem tu laeta necasti	405	Passio 7	9
LAETISSIME			
subiecto suo, laetissime sumeret, quanto magis par est, . .	460	Epistolae	12
LAETITIA			
Quare multiplex est laetitia nostra:	463	Epistolae	20
enim sic effugies cum honoribus, quin laetitia nostra te assequatur.	465	Epistolae	23
LAETITIAE			
Si per haec ludicra nostra pars aliquis eius laetitiae, . .	443	Orationes	9
Quare quomodo alij molem hanc laetitiae suae exprimant, . .	457	Epistolae	1
LAETOS			
Hos oculos laetos, hunc sine nube diem:	211	Cam.1613-b BR	14
LAETUM			
quicquid hilare est, laetum, ac lubens, vestram in gratiam . .	440	Orationes	13
spiritibusque tabellarijs laetum hunc nuncium vbique deferentibus,	445	Orationes	2
vt ego nihil vspiam laetum, nihil candidum expiscari possem;	451	Orationes	14
LAETUS			
Mersis reuertens laetus ab hostibus	394	Musae 23	30
Aduoluor madidae laetus hiansque Cruci:	406	Passio 13	2
Plusque habet hic laetus, quam vel Auarus habet.	411	Lucus 7	4
LAEUITATEM			
vt laeuitatem illam aequabilem atque politiem perturbent. . .	453	Orationes	13
LAGENAS			
Parate situlas, Ethnici, lagenasque, ...	405	Passio 5	8
Graues lagenas, Vester est Aquae-ductus.	405	Passio 5	9
LAMENTIS			
huiusmodi lamentis & quiritationibus plena erant fora, nundinae,	451	Orationes	9
LAMPADA			
Mites acciperent Lampada Praesules, ...	391	Musae 17	5
Lampada, qua studijs inuigilare solet.	398	Musae 33	18
LAMPADEM			
ni graue est, librum tibi Oratorium lampademque tradat. . .	470	Epistolae	10
LANC			
18. Ad Lanc. Andrewes, Episc.	471	Epistolae	T
LANGUENS			
Tam languens genitrix cineri supposta fugaci:	426	Mem.Matr.7	9
LANGUENTIUM			
Languentium baculus, teges iacentium, ...	423	Mem.Matr.2	46
LANGUESCERE			
praeferuida illa desideria silentio suo sepulta nunc languescere,	471	Epistolae	28
LANGUIDA			
Affectusque mei similem; nec languida misce	427	Mem.Matr.7	30
LANIENAS			
Ecce lanienas omnimodas, truncata corpora, mutilatam imaginem Dei,	449	Orationes	4
LANIGERAE			
Quod non Lanigerae pecudes, non Agmina lustrent?	432	Poem.Lat.	19
LAPIDATUM			
In Stephanum lapidatum.	410	Lucus 3	T
LAPIDES			
Et nos reducas ad lapides auos:	393	Musae 23	6
quorum aduentum ipsi lapides, ipsa durissima ingenia, meum . .	445	Orationes	8
optime consuluisse Deum orbi terrarum lapides & metalla ei inserendo,	452	Orationes	25
LAPIDUM			
facile conijcitur ex coelo, ex garritu auium, ex lapidum exhalatione:	445	Orationes	7
LAPITHAE			
Bacchantur Lapithae, furit inconstantia vini	271	Tr.Mortis VS	21
LAPSU			
Pro lapsu stillarum abeunt peccata; nec acres	406	Passio 13	3
LAQUEARIBUS			
An quod semotum populo laquearibus altis	387	Musae 7	3
Accedit Pyrius puluis, laquearibus Orci	419	Tr.Mortis	57
LAQUEATA			
Est mihi bis quinis laqueata domuncula tignis	426	Mem.Matr.7	22
LARGAM			
posterioris largam messem Vobis haec tenuia boni consulentibus,	441	Orationes	21
LARGIAR			
Largiar & istud: scilicet Magnatibus	413	Lucus 17	2
LARGIARIS			
assensumque Tuum veritati omni familiarem largiaris, sun tei eulogiai	473	Epistolae	11
LARGIRE			
Quin populo, clemens, aliquid largire caloris:	397	Musae 29	3
LARGITA			
eadem manus et tuum tibi largita est honorem, et priuilegia nostra	468	Epistolae	23

	PAGE	TITLE	LINE
LAUDO			
Ipse pios laudo; Numen & ipse colo.	386	Musae 4	6
laudo vos, neque enim quicquam hoc itinere mirabilius, cuius tamen	450	Orationes	2
LAUDUM			
Hae tibi sunt alae laudum. Cui contigit vnquam	435	Poem.Lat.	5
nodo connectens, nullas metas laudum, nullas Herculeas columnas,	440	Orationes	17
LAUET			
Quo sanguis est Christi, nisi vt maculas lauet,	393	Musae 22	3
LAUROS			
permittat nostram hanc Inter victrices hederam sibi serpere Lauros.	455	Orationes	18
an inter lauros principis hederae nostrae ambitiosae locus est?	456	Epistolae	4
LAURUM			
commode peruenimus ad laurum hanc, vbi sub vmbra eius paulisper	455	Orationes	13
LAURUS			
Plura tibi missurus eram (nam quae mihi laurus,	428	Mem.Matr.9	15
Daphnen suam, cuius amor deinceps in triumphos & laurus mutabitur.	455	Orationes	11
LAUS			
Laus antiqua & honor perijt: quasi scilicet ARMO	416	Lucus 25	7
Laus antiqua & honor perierunt, te velut ARMO	416	Lucus 25 V	7
Hic sita foeminei laus & victoria sexus:	429	Mem.Matr.13	1
LAUTIUS			
Tunc instruetur lautius radijs penu,	407	Passio 16	13
LAXIORIBUS			
etiam teneor, sed laxioribus vinculis, quaeque amor saepe remittit:	472	Epistolae	33
LECTICIS			
tanquam onera, circumferuntur mollissimis lecticis, indicantes,	452	Orationes	12
LECTIONE			
creberrima Antiquitatis lectione tersis atque expolitis,	473	Epistolae	20
LECTISSIMA			
Veneranda Capita, Viri grauissimi, Pubes lectissima.	444	Orationes	11
LECTUS			
En Aurora vocat, lectus genialis in aula est,	210	Cam.1613-b BR	1
LEGANS			
Igniculos legans, manserit ipsa licet;	410	Lucus 2	2
LEGATA			
Sunt hostium legata, non amicorum,	406	Passio 10	2
LEGATIONES			
Legationes Nobilissimas, aliosque titulos aeque nobis memorantibus,	440	Orationes	2
LEGATIS			
habita coram Dominis Legatis cum Magistro. in Artib. titulis	440	Orationes	T
LEGATOS			
hinc Reges Legatos habent statarios ac resides, quem locum Noster	450	Orationes	29
LEGATUM			
Hoc mihi legatum tristi si funere praestes,	434	Poem.Lat.	7
LEGENDUM			
si tantum Honori Tuo superesset otij ad legendum, quantum a nobis	457	Epistolae	9
LEGES			
Post vbi Mosaicae repararent fragmina Leges,	408	Passio 20	3
LEGIBUS			
spectantes (quae res et naturae legibus et hominum summe contraria	467	Epistolae	5
LEGIMUS			
sed a scriptis vestris, quae ingenti cum lucro quotidie legimus.	443	Orationes	20
post ingentes Hecatombas, exiguam thuris micam adoleri legimus.	469	Epistolae	17
LEGIS			
Impediant, apices legis amicus obit.	388	Musae 9	6
Siste parum cantus, dum legis ista, tuos.	427	Mem.Matr.9	2
LEGISLATOR			
& Licurgus magnus Legislator atimian prosetheke tois agamois.	446	Orationes	20
LEGIT			
Cum piscatores Textor legit esse vocatos,	392	Musae 19	1
LEGITIMI			
Legitimi signum connubiale tori.	396	Musae 26	12
LEGUM			
quid enim vtilius quam ex obseruatione exterarum Legum ac morum,	450	Orationes	15
LEIGH			
15. Ad J. Leigh, Capitalem Iustitiarium Angl. (Camden) Gratulatio	468	Epistolae	T
LEMAS			
qui lemas istas et festucas, Reipublicae oculo haerentes,	462	Epistolae	12
LENIORES			
in potestatem redigere, lenioresque aspectus, & dulciores assumatis;	440	Orationes	9
LENITAS			
Vtcunque Tua lenitas non ita interpretabitur mea haec scribendi	471	Epistolae	24
LENIUNT			
Tantum dulcia leniunt catarrhos.	385	Musae	9
LENTA			
Flumina caelestem ducite lenta chorum:	210	Cam.1613-b BR	4
LENTI			
Dum longi lentique gemis sub pondere morbi	438	Poem.Lat.	1
LENTIUS			
Qua sine vos miseri lentius itis ope.	399	Musae 33	26
LEO			
Ne perdat Leo rugiens vagantem.	417	Lucus 30	8
LEON			
Logon te philtron, osth' upekselthein leon.	430	Mem.Matr.15	9
LEONES			
Leones Britannici (e quorum ossibus collisis ignis elicitur) qui nunc	449	Orationes	17
LEPIDO			
O quam bellus homo es! lepido quam nomine fingis	386	Musae 3	1
LEPIDUM			
O sec'lum lepidum! circumstant vndique Fratres,	393	Musae 21	1

	PAGE	TITLE	LINE
LEPOS			
Lepos seuerus, Pallas mixta Gratijs;	423	Mem.Matr.2	30
LESMONES			
Lesmones, e belone sphaleroi kep traumati vuttei	431	Mem.Matr.17	12
LEUANS			
Fatalemque leuans dextram, qua stupeus ignis	420	Tr.Mortis	67
LEUANT			
Quae contrita tamen caetera damna leuant.	409	Passio 20	8
LEUARE			
enixus gloriae, sollicitudine in futurum plenos, haud parum leuare;	469	Epistolae	11
LEUATUS			
dimidiaque operis parte leuatus, ad mea in Honorem Tuum officia	473	Epistolae	2
LEUES			
Ite leues (inquam), Parnassia numina, Musae,	432	Poem.Lat.	1
LEUIS			
Apostolorum culpa non leuis fuit	389	Musae 10	4
Morosus, oxygala est: leuis, coagulum.	414	Lucus 20	15
LEUNCULUM			
cum leunculum & dominum suum contra naturam adoriantur:	454	Orationes	17
LEXICON			
Quin hoc carmine Lexicon probrorum	401	Musae 37	28
LIBANDAS			
Libandas nobis absorbendasque propinat!	401	Musae 39	3
LIBENTER			
sunt nuperi quidam homines, qui libenter sapientiores nos redderent:	460	Epistolae	22
Quare tam vere quam libenter gratulamur tibi, nec minus etiam	468	Epistolae	18
LIBENTISSIME			
vt Alma Mater libentissime caput reclinet in tuo sinu, oculusque	465	Epistolae	13
LIBER			
Liber alit rixas: potantibus omnia bina	418	Tr.Mortis	18
nunc itaque liber hic vester dilatat pomoeria, summouet Oceanum	458	Epistolae	11
Vnicus est nobis Bibliotheca Liber.	459	Epistolae	31
LIBERA			
et aeternitate occupatos, temporarijs hisce negotiolis libera.	466	Epistolae	6
LIBERALIBUS			
in quo paucorum auaritia liberalibus artibus dominatura est,	467	Epistolae	1
LIBERAT			
causaris, irruit Miles in Musaeum tuum, & gladio te liberat.	448	Orationes	28
LIBERENTUR			
tum venenatorum haereticorum, insita vi sua liberentur.	459	Epistolae	19
LIBERI			
qualis quaeque sit mater, e qua liberi quaerantur, quam qualis terra,	447	Orationes	11
LIBERIOR			
ego tunc temporis liberior eram, huc illuc pro libitu	451	Orationes	12
LIBERIOREM			
in ipso Parnasso siti sumus, liberiorem, quam alij, prospectum	449	Orationes	33
LIBERIS			
Musasque coelibes, qui posteros libris non liberis quaeritis.	446	Orationes	27
LIBERORUM			
Nam vt educationem liberorum mittam, qua in re celebris est	447	Orationes	16
LIBETHRIA			
Sed nec Cyrrhaei saltus Libethriaue arua	432	Poem.Lat.	4
LIBIDINIS			
Annulus hos reuocet, sistatque libidinis vndas	396	Musae 26	11
LIBIDO			
Sic positis nugis, quibus irretita libido	402	Musae 39	38
LIBITU			
tunc temporis liberior eram, huc illuc pro libitu circumcursitans:	451	Orationes	12
LIBRANS			
Tuasque librans actiones, gloriam	414	Lucus 20	13
LIBRARIOS			
Accepimus enim Londinenses Librarios omnia transmarina scripta	467	Epistolae	20
LIBRATA			
Dum librata suis haeret radicibus ilex	428	Mem.Matr.11	1
LIBRI			
vt ex affrictu Libri vestri hominem illico contundamus.	459	Epistolae	8
cuius Libri si alij alijs (tanquam montes olim) imponerentur,	467	Epistolae	30
LIBRIS			
Cum tu contundis Catharos, vultuque librisque,	385	Musae 1	5
vos, vos, inquam, excutite, quorum aetas teritur in libris:	445	Orationes	15
Musasque coelibes, qui posteros libris non liberis quaeritis.	446	Orationes	26
idque pro Libris, de quibus nusquam rectius quam apud Te agitur.	467	Epistolae	18
quo minus exteris Libris indigeremus, sed tamen comparatio	467	Epistolae	25
LIBRO			
Munere dum nobis prodes, Libroque futuris,	435	Poem.Lat.	1
Munere dum nobis prodes, Libroque remotis,	435	Poem.Lat.	3
Cancel. Gratiae de Instaurationis Libro Academiae donato	463	Epistolae	T
LIBRORUM			
et quo magis Tuum agnoscas, in ipso partu, Librorum regem creatum.	459	Epistolae	12
ex quo timemus Librorum precia auctum iri, et priuilegia nostra	467	Epistolae	7
Aspicis multitudinem Librorum indies gliscentem, praesertim	467	Epistolae	29
Qui augent precia Librorum, prosunt vendentibus Libros non ementibus,	468	Epistolae	7
LIBROS			
etiam libros indicans ad Theologiam expeditissimos, tanto ac tam	443	Orationes	25
Quamobrem abijcite quisque libros, non est locus grauitati,	454	Orationes	34
etiam libros dederunt, sed non suos:	458	Epistolae	23
prosunt vendentibus Libros non ementibus, hoc est cessatoribus	468	Epistolae	7
LIBRUM			
Comparatio inter Munus Summi Cancellariatus et Librum.	435	Poem.Lat.	T
Nuper enim dedisti nobis Librum, plenissimum Musarum, quae cum olim	460	Epistolae	7
ni graue est, librum tibi Oratorium lampademque tradat.	470	Epistolae	10

	PAGE	TITLE	LINE
LICEARE			
Quo precio venit, fac, liceare prius.	410	Lucus 4	6
LICEAT			
Quin liceat nobis aliquas procudere voces:	386	Musae 3	5
Vel potius liceat distinguere. Tuque tuique	387	Musae 6	5
LICEBAT			
Quid sperare, imo quid non sperare licebat?)	432	Poem.Lat.	28
LICEBIT			
Quo Te, foelix Anna, modo deflere licebit?	435	Poem.Lat.	1
LICERET			
si per tempus liceret effari, non licet per multitudinem, . .	443	Orationes	29
LICET			
Nec transire licet quo mentis acumine findis	402	Musae 39	27
Igniculos legans, manserit ipsa licet;	410	Lucus 2	2
Sit licet in pelago semper, sine fluctibus illa est, ...	411	Lucus 6	3
Ipse fruare, licet, solus graueolente sepulcro;	414	Lucus 21	5
Si licet, immoriar: vel si tua visio vita est, ...	421	Lucus 35	5
Ornastis capulum, nec superesse licet.	425	Mem.Matr.5	2
Per strages licet autorum veterumque ruinam	435	Poem.Lat.	1
Munde, fluas fugiasque licet, nos nostraque fixi:	438	Poem.Lat.	8
effari, non licet per multitudinem, imo per modestiam vestram?	443	Orationes	29
nobis non licet esse tam perspicacibus, quamuis rationi consonum	449	Orationes	31
ex itinere Principem metiri licet, quod sane adeo nobile fuit	453	Orationes	23
quae licet versentur in figuris describendis, quibus nihil imperito	454	Orationes	3
licet celebres sint canes Britannici, & plus iusto celebres,	454	Orationes	16
tripudiet Alma Mater licet aetate prouectior, etiam anus subsultans	454	Orationes	35
Et licet, quo proprior sis Regi, eo videaris nobis remotior,	464	Epistolae	16
LICITANTIBUS			
quemadmodum artifices non omnes licitantibus producunt merces,	445	Orationes	30
LICTOR			
Purpureus lictor Plutonis, epistola Fati	419	Tr.Mortis	63
tu hanc personam indue scripturus, tuumque iudicium tibi Lictor esto.	470	Epistolae	27
LICTURA			
Quale paludosos iamiam lictura recessus	426	Mem.Matr.7	11
LICURGUS			
& Licurgus magnus Legislator atimian prosetheke tois agamois.	446	Orationes	20
LIGANTES			
vlciscimur mortem, ligantes abruptum vitae filum, vnde consequimur,	446	Orationes	22
LIGATUM			
quis scit an & amoris onus scite vinctum ligatumque, & per tot	454	Orationes	1
LIGAUIT			
Cum tu, Christe, cadis, nascor; mentemque ligauit	434	Poem.Lat.	1
LIGNA			
tanquam ligna obliqua, aliter magna haec mundi domus corrueret:	450	Orationes	28
viduae effoetae, aut ligna exucca & marcida, alumnis suis orbarentur,	462	Epistolae	4
LIGNI			
Protagoras cum eleganter admodum caudices ligni fasciculo vinxisset,	453	Orationes	34
LIGNIS			
e baiulo euasit Philosophus, eodem ingenio vsus in lignis & literis:	453	Orationes	38
LIGNO			
Hoc ligno, his clauis est, quasi Falce sua.	407	Passio 14	4
ideoque ex quolibet ligno, qualibet vxore non esse fingendum:	447	Orationes	9
LIGNUM			
eadem acies & stipulam secat & lignum:	453	Orationes	29
Si enim in regno vestro Hibernico lignum nascitur permanens,	459	Epistolae	16
LIMATAE			
viros limatae auris atque tersae, quorum grauitate ac purpura	445	Orationes	26
LIMEN			
Et per se Templi limen adire velis:	388	Musae 9	8
Congrediens genuit Monachum, qui limen opacae	420	Tr.Mortis	89
LINEA			
Omnis linea sepiam recusans	400	Musae 37	21
LINEAE			
Nimirum vt lineae, quamuis diuersa via, omnes tamen ad centrum	456	Epistolae	22
LINEAS			
potui refercire lineas Honoribus, Magnif., Celsitud., sed . .	473	Epistolae	16
LINGUA			
Sed nos, cum nequeat paruorum lingua, parentem	389	Musae 12	7
Os & lingua tibi diues, egena manus:	414	Lucus 22	2
Aurea pro naulo lingua Charontis erit.	414	Lucus 22	4
LINGUAE			
Ni facias, vt opes linguae per brachia serpant, ...	414	Lucus 22	3
(Nam post Babelem linguae adest confusio)	422	Mem.Matr.2	13
Deducant linguae funera sola tuae.	438	Poem.Lat.	6
LINGUAM			
Cur Latiam linguam reris nimis esse profanam, ...	391	Musae 16	1
Matrine linguam refero, solum vt mordeam?	424	Mem.Matr.2	59
LINQUERET			
nos haud inanes linqueret, ...	396	Musae 28	9
LIPOUSA			
Emas lipousa kuklothen metaixmious?	429	Mem.Matr.15	4
LIQUET			
Scilicet talem liquet esse solem;	390	Musae 14	9
LIQUITUR			
Liquitur ardenti candens fornace metallum, ...	419	Tr.Mortis	51
liquitur ardenti cadens fornace metallum;	271	Tr.Mortis VS	51
LITARE			
Cum nequeat claras ipse litare preces?	388	Musae 9	14
Displicet, & laudis tura litare Deo.	389	Musae 12	2
LITERAE			
Volant per orbem literae notissimae:	423	Mem.Matr.2	38

LITERAE (cont'd)	PAGE	TITLE	LINE
Nato dolenti: literae hoc debent tibi	424	Mem.Matr.2	62
ne literae nostrae animo Tuo tot negotijs meritissime distincto,	457	Epistolae	11
LITERARIA			
nisi Rex esses in ciuili Republica, eligereris in Literaria?	443	Orationes	19
LITERARIAE			
vestrae coronae ciuili & literariae tertiam Coelestem sero adiungat.	459	Epistolae	21
vtriusque Reipublicae calculum et ciuilis et literariae adipiscaris.	466	Epistolae	1
LITERARIJ			
Quare prodite, tenebriones literarij, e gurgustijs vestris, . .	454	Orationes	24
LITERARIUS			
Sophismatomastix; Brutus Literarius, ...	436	Poem.Lat.	14
LITERARUM			
immunitates nostras aut commune literarum et literatorum commodum,	467	Epistolae	12
LITERAS			
qui literas imminuere spiritus, generososque animos frangere	461	Epistolae	19
primas dedissem literas, ideoque praeferuida illa desideria silentio	471	Epistolae	27
LITERATORUM			
immunitates nostras aut commune literarum et literatorum commodum,	467	Epistolae	12
LITERATOS			
quippe qui eximie semper fouisti literatos, eosque cum tineis	462	Epistolae	26
LITERATURAE			
quasi accolae Maiestatis, literaturae suae et vicinitati respondeant:	463	Epistolae	23
LITERIS			
e baiulo euasit Philosophus, eodem ingenio vsus in lignis & literis:	453	Orationes	38
LITES			
Non nisi prima suas patiuntur praelia lites.	386	Musae 4	7
Pensilis, atque acri dirimens Examine lites.	426	Mem.Matr.7	13
in Principibus virtus, & cui cum sceptro lites saepius intercedunt?	452	Orationes	2
LITIBUS			
Cedito Barbaries: Helicon iam litibus instat, ...	417	Lucus 28	5
LITIS			
Auresque superas: arbitri ipsi sint litis, ...	392	Musae 20	4
LITORA			
quotidie transnatantes, litora nostra atque aures mire circumsonant.	441	Orationes	4
LITORE			
colligeret cum Caligula, praesertim cum possit in eodem litore?	446	Orationes	13
LITTORE			
Ecce recedentis foecundo in littore Nili	384	Musae	1
LITUI			
Stringuntur aures: iam litui strepunt, ...	448	Orationes	2
LITUIS			
Cum citharis lituisque miscet.	394	Musae 23	40
LITURA			
& beatae fabricae, vnico ictu sulphurei tubi, vnica litura delentur?	448	Orationes	21
LIUENS			
Plumbea glans, liuensque suae quasi conscia noxae, ...	419	Tr.Mortis	62
LIUIDO			
Te contumaci & liuido?	388	Musae 8	10
LIUOR			
Quas liuor mihi parturit, retundet, ...	385	Musae	6
Quas malus liuor iaculis lacessit	390	Musae 14	2
LIXAM			
Illum volo, qui calceat lixam tuum.	413	Lucus 17	7
LOCA			
Sic excelsa humilisque simul loca dissita iunxit, ...	429	Mem.Matr.13	5
In laudes abeunt iam loca quaeque tuas:	435	Poem.Lat.	4
In laudes properant iam loca quaeque tuas:	435	Poem.Lat. V	4
vtriusque enim splendor et claritas humilia loca deprecantur.	466	Epistolae	12
LOCANDUM			
Verum augusta parens, sanctum os caeloque locandum, ...	426	Mem.Matr.7	10
LOCAT			
Foelicitatis culmen extra se locat, ...	414	Lucus 20	3
LOCI			
omnes indigenas loci	395	Musae 25	4
LOCIS			
Cuius ab oppositis fluxit origo locis.	417	Lucus 31	4
LOCO			
immersi, aut vno semper saginantur in loco, vti anguillae, . . .	452	Orationes	10
LOCUM			
Nullum locum requiemue cernens perstitit	436	Poem.Lat.	20
Nullum locum requiemue cernens praestitit	436	Poem.Lat. V	20
quem locum Noster suauissimus impleuit, ipse egit oratorem, . .	450	Orationes	30
vti anguillae, aut si mutant locum, gestantur, tanquam onera,	452	Orationes	11
receptusque sim in aliquem apud Honorem Tuum locum, magis id adeo	472	Epistolae	21
LOCUS			
Suum cuique tempus & locus datur.	423	Mem.Matr.2	20
In picturis locus est vmbris & recessibus, etiam si quis Principem	453	Orationes	14
abijcite quisque libros, non est locus grauitati, neque apud vos:	454	Orationes	34
an inter lauros principis hederae nostrae ambitiosae locus est?	456	Epistolae	4
LOGIKE			
Logike Thusia.	417	Lucus 29	T
LOGON			
Logon te philtron, osth' upekselthein leon.	430	Mem.Matr.15	9
LOND			
13. Ad Archiep. Cantuar. De Bibliopolis Lond.	466	Epistolae	T
14. Ad Fr. Bacon, Cancell. De Bibliop. Lond.	467	Epistolae	T
LONDINENSES			
Ferunt enim Londinenses Bibliopolas suum potius emolumentum quam	467	Epistolae	3
Accepimus enim Londinenses Librarios omnia transmarina scripta	467	Epistolae	20

LONGA	PAGE	TITLE		LINE
Te deiecissent tempora longa suo.	416	Lucus 25		8
Jam deturbarunt tempora longa suo.	416	Lucus 25	V	8
Annon longa fames miseraeque iniuria pestis	432	Poem.Lat.		20
Aut cita mors est danda bonis aut longa senectus:	432	Poem.Lat.		30
LONGAEUA				
O mortis longaeua fames, venterque perennis	271	Tr.Mortis	VS	1
LONGAM				
Quod si fata illi longam invidere salutem	432	Poem.Lat.		26
LONGAS				
Nos quoque possemus longas conscribere turmas,	398	Musae 33		7
LONGE				
Longe pileus anteit galerum,	391	Musae 15		8
quam non longe abeam Oratorum more, qui nullum non angulum verrunt	445	Orationes		35
in quo longe vberrimam gloriae segetem perspicio, nulla verborum,	446	Orationes		2
illud necessarium magis factu, hoc vero longe iucundius, nobiliusque:	472	Epistolae		35
LONGI				
Dum longi lentique gemis sub pondere morbi	438	Poem.Lat.		1
LONGIORI				
Habui viaticum fauoris Tui, quod longiori multo itineri sufficeret.	471	Epistolae		19
LONGIUS				
Longius aeterno, latius orbe decus?	435	Poem.Lat.		6
LONGO				
vita nostra atque calor, longo animi deliquio fugitiuus ac desertor.	444	Orationes		23
LONGUM				
Ah longum, quae te deperit, errat iter.	437	Poem.Lat.		4
Ah longum, quae te deperit, ambit iter.	437	Poem.Lat.	V	4
iter bene longum! Quid autem illic?	451	Orationes		2
LOQUAX				
Et amor alioqui loquax est;	471	Epistolae		7
LOQUELA				
Haec facit ad nasum sola loquela tuum.	391	Musae 16		6
LOQUENDI				
Vltra loquendi tempus; addit Anchora:	438	Poem.Lat.		4
LOQUENS				
Quondam fessus Amor loquens Amato,	439	Poem.Lat.		10
Tot & tanta loquens amica, scripsit:	439	Poem.Lat.		11
LOQUITUR				
Loquitur numellas, compedes & retia:	423	Mem.Matr.2		31
LOQUOR				
non rusticis loquor aut barbaris, quos magnificentia promissi	445	Orationes		15
LOTIONEM				
In Lotionem pedum Apostolorum.	412	Lucus 8		T
LUBENS				
hilare est, laetum, ac lubens, vestram in gratiam amplectimur.	440	Orationes		13
LUBENTER				
Paruam piamque dum lubenter semitam	427	Mem.Matr.8		1
LUBENTISSIME				
quam meis meritis vllis, semper lubentissimeque agnoscam:	472	Epistolae		22
LUBET				
sed lubet garrire paulo. Iupiter!	471	Epistolae		5
LUBRICOS				
Non illa soles terere comptu lubricos,	422	Mem.Matr.2		10
LUBRICUS				
Lubricus, & superans mobilitate salum.	428	Mem.Matr.11		8
LUCAM				
In D. Lucam.	412	Lucus 9		T
LUCE				
Sol generat populum luce fouente nouum.	384	Musae		2
Luce praelustri, vel honore pollet,	390	Musae 14		6
Aurum luce videns, nulla videre putat.	411	Lucus 7		2
Vel sine luce solum, vel sine mente caro.	417	Lucus 31		6
imo precabor enixe, me tum priuari tam communi hac luce, quam Tua,	472	Epistolae		24
LUCEAT				
Excutite aulaea, & luceat igne focus.	413	Lucus 15		2
Vt nihilo-minus Tibi luceat, cum nobis accenderit.	461	Epistolae		5
LUCEM				
et blattis rixantes, exuens puluere, in theatrum et lucem produxisti.	462	Epistolae		27
Tuam suauissimam, nuper in lucem publicam, nostramque praesertim,	463	Epistolae		5
LUCERNA				
Parcite luminibus, sitque lucerna domus:	413	Lucus 15		4
LUCET				
Nempe in quo clare lucet Imago Dei.	410	Lucus 4		10
LUCIS				
Quamque ipse lucis tesseram sibi negat,	407	Passio 16		7
LUCOS				
lucos aestate, pinguem togam hyeme:	448	Orationes		23
LUCRERIS				
Pulpita, plus spatij lucreris?	395	Musae 23		48
LUCRO				
Adde pijs animis quaeuis occasio lucro est,	390	Musae 12		11
Et lucro apponis gaudia sancta tuo.	424	Mem.Matr.3		6
sed a scriptis vestris, quae ingenti cum lucro quotidie legimus.	443	Orationes		20
LUCTATUR				
Luctatur spacium, qualem tamen eligit aequi	426	Mem.Matr.7		24
LUCTIBUS				
Sic pulsare tuas, exclusis luctibus, ausint	402	Musae 39		35
LUCTU				
Tota stupent luctu) lachrymisque exaestuet aequis	432	Poem.Lat.		10
LUCTUS				
Immodicus luctus tacito vorat igne medullas,	433	Poem.Lat.		47

LUCTUS (cont'd)	PAGE	TITLE	LINE
Sed luctus ncster scribitur Oceano.	435	Poem.Lat.	10
Ah! metuo ne me ad luctus mea fata crearint	437	Poem.Lat. V	11
LUCUS			
Lucus	410	Lucus	T
Nudetur illic lucus amabilis,	434	Poem.Lat.	30
LUDAT			
Cur, vbi tot ludat numeris antiqua poesis,	387	Musae 5	1
LUDIBRIA			
Fictaque Bellona & verae ludibria pugnae,	418	Tr.Mortis	27
LUDICRA			
Si per haec ludicra nostra pars aliquis eius laetitiae,	443	Orationes	9
LUET			
Sanguinis, innocuum tandem luet orbis Abelem.	272	Tr.Mortis VS	101
LUGENTES			
Cur non lugentes Elegi? non acer Iambus?	387	Musae 5	5
LUGUBRES			
Quae mihi lugubres contribuere genas!	437	Poem.Lat.	12
LUMEN			
Debetur Caelo lumen, & vmbra solo:	417	Lucus 31	2
illustrans nos omnes, lumenque accendens de suo lumine,	461	Epistolae	3
LUMINA			
Et ni lumina ianuam resignent,	415	Lucus 24	4
Lumina, nutantes paulatim acquirite vires,	432	Poem.Lat.	14
LUMINE			
Assiduo vilem lumine cingit humum.	387	Musae 7	8
illustrans nos omnes, lumenque accendens de suo lumine,	461	Epistolae	4
LUMINIBUS			
Parcite luminibus, sitque lucerna domus:	413	Lucus 15	4
LUMINIS			
Almi choragus luminis?	407	Passio 16	2
Paterfamilias luminis.	407	Passio 16	10
Noctu te celebrans luminis aemulo.	424	Mem.Matr.4	12
Degentium olim, Emancipator; Luminis	436	Poem.Lat.	11
LUNA			
Quas Luna habet, tuetur, in foueam cadit,	393	Musae 22	8
Ecclesia est mihi Luna; perge in Fabula.	393	Musae 22	10
LUNAM			
glasto se inficientes, in vxorum corporibus, Solem, Lunam, & Stellas;	446	Orationes	30
LUPA			
De lupa lustri Vaticani.	397	Musae 30	T
LUPAE			
Nec Vaticanae desines vnquam Lupae	397	Musae 30	2
LUPAM			
Britannicam in Vulpem, inque Romanam Lupam.	397	Musae 30	6
LUSCINIAE			
quanto minus tacebunt lusciniae nostrae disertae, minimeque omnium	445	Orationes	10
LUSCO			
etiam lusco, nunquam intueri satis vel mirari possumus,	449	Orationes	35
LUSCUM			
Luscum prodigium, medioque foramine gaudens.	419	Tr.Mortis	54
LUSIT			
Haec fuerant: sic Tisiphone virguncula lusit.	418	Tr.Mortis	23
LUSTRAT			
Dein familiam lustrat, & res prandij,	422	Mem.Matr.2	18
LUSTRENT			
Quod non Lanigerae pecudes, non Agmina lustrent?	432	Poem.Lat.	19
LUSTRI			
De lupa lustri Vaticani.	397	Musae 30	T
LUSTRIS			
Merserat in lustris perniciosa venus,	396	Musae 26	10
LUSUS			
At non lusus erit, si quem tu laeta necasti	405	Passio 7	9
Non placet vrbanus noster de nomine lusus	416	Lucus 27	1
LUTUM			
Nostrae etiam Musae vile fuere lutum:	384	Musae	4
Quas spargit animae corporis propius lutum?	393	Musae 22	4
LUXUM			
Imperatorum incredibilem luxum a Tiberio Caesare ad Constantinum	452	Orationes	22
LUXURIAE			
tersis atque expolitis, quam luxuriae saeculi, ambitionisque strumae,	473	Epistolae	20
LYRAS			
Saxa lyras citharasque callent.	393	Musae 23	8
M			
m. Ad Ful. Grevil Gratiae de Fluuio	462	Epistolae	T
MACHINA			
Agnoscitque tuam Machina tota Crucem.	409	Passio 21	2
Coniugium Caeli Terraeque haec machina praestat;	417	Lucus 31	1
Machina, quam nullum satis execrabitur aeuum;	419	Tr.Mortis	50
MACHINAS			
machinas conficiunt ad defensionem Reipublicae mirabiles:	454	Orationes	5
MACTE			
Tu vero macte honoribus, gloria, id enim nostra interest,	457	Epistolae	24
MACULAS			
Labeculas maculasque nobis obijcis:	393	Musae 22	1
Quo sanguis est Christi, nisi vt maculas lauet,	393	Musae 22	3
Astronomus olim (vt fama) dum maculas diu,	393	Musae 22	7
Errores, maculas, superbiamque,	401	Musae 37	37
MACULIS			
De labe maculisque.	393	Musae 22	T

	PAGE	TITLE	LINE
MADENT			
Cum templis effare, madent sudaria, mappae,	397	Musae 29	1
MADIDAE			
Aduoluor madidae laetus hiansque Cruci:	406	Passio 13	2
MADIDUM			
Cum probro madidum, reumque difflat.	428	Mem.Matr.10	7
MADORE			
Et maestum nimio madore Caelum	428	Mem.Matr.10	2
MADRITUM			
Madritum? hui! iter bene longum!	451	Orationes	1
MAEANDRI			
plena erant fora, nundinae, conciliabula, angiportus, Maeandri.	451	Orationes	11
MAEANDROS			
Maeandrosque plicasque, quam perita es!	411	Lucus 5	16
Per angiportus & maeandros labitur,	423	Mem.Matr.2	33
MAERET			
Non maeret calamus; non queritur caput:	403	Musae 40	6
neque Studiosorum Sacculi, qui etiam nunc maeret et ingemiscit.	467	Epistolae	23
MAESTIS			
Vespere ros maestis funus honestet aquis.	425	Mem.Matr.5	16
MAESTUM			
Et maestum nimio madore Caelum	428	Mem.Matr.10	2
MAG			
Mag. Sigilli Custodis post editam ab eo Instaurationem Magnam.	436	Poem.Lat.	T
MAGIAM			
Non striges, magiamue, vel rotatus,	401	Musae 37	35
MAGICIS			
De Magicis rotatibus.	392	Musae 20	T
MAGICOS			
Magicos rotatus, & perhorridas Striges,	392	Musae 20	12
MAGIS			
Quo magis inuidiam nobis & crimina confles,	398	Musae 33	1
Vicinusque magis nobiliorque fluit:	399	Musae 35	10
Quam nihil illudis! cum quo magis angar acuto	405	Passio 7	3
Vtrumque mirum est: hoc tamen mirum magis,	412	Lucus 11	2
Morte magis viduabor illa.	425	Mem.Matr.6	12
dignum est, quo magis amore coalescamus, vtraque gens Hispanica,	440	Orationes	21
Quod si Nuptiae in se graues sunt, quanto magis Principum, cum,	446	Orationes	34
absentia magis quam praesentia. Nunc enim exploratos habet nostros	450	Orationes	33
extra mortalitatis aleam, et quo magis Tuum agnoscas, in ipso partu,	459	Epistolae	11
quanto magis virtutes istae in Dominum agri transferendae sunt,	459	Epistolae	17
laetissime sumeret, quanto magis par est, nos humillimos subiectos,	460	Epistolae	12
etiam tacentibus nobis, quanto magis cum rogamus, idque pro Libris,	467	Epistolae	18
magis id adeo factum esse mansuetudine Tua incomparabili,	472	Epistolae	21
illud necessarium magis factu, hoc vero longe iucundius,	472	Epistolae	35
MAGISTER			
Rerum magister vnicus, at non Artium;	436	Poem.Lat.	5
MAGISTRI			
Vel Catapulta potest, Siculique inuenta magistri,	419	Tr.Mortis	41
Saluete tandem Magistri Artium, & quidem omnium Aulicarum,	440	Orationes	5
MAGISTRO			
coram Dominis Legatis cum Magistro. in Artib. titulis insignirentur.	440	Orationes	T
MAGISTRUM			
titulos caput vndique munientes meministi Magistrum Te esse Artium?	456	Epistolae	3
tanquam Nobilem Filium (more nostro) Magistrum Artium renunciauimus.	463	Epistolae	9
MAGNA			
Pertrahis in partes nomina magna tuas;	398	Musae 33	2
At te commoriente, Magna Mater,	428	Mem.Matr.10	5
tanquam ligna obliqua, aliter magna haec mundi domus corrueret:	450	Orationes	28
Magna est haec, neque quotidianae virtutis prouincia gerere personam	465	Epistolae	8
MAGNAE			
IACOBO, D. G. Magnae Britanniae, Franciae, & Hiberniae	384	Musae	T
Ad Autorem Instaurationis Magnae.	435	Poem.Lat.	T
MAGNAM			
Mag. Sigilli Custodis post editam ab eo Instaurationem Magnam.	436	Poem.Lat.	T
MAGNAS			
Magnas es; esto. Bulla si vocaberis,	413	Lucus 17	1
dignitatem diu expectantem magnas aliquas virtutes tandem meritis	464	Epistolae	11
MAGNATES			
Quin nec demisso, quando ad magnates cogitas, stylo vtare,	470	Epistolae	21
MAGNATIBUS			
Largiar & istud: scilicet Magnatibus	413	Lucus 17	2
MAGNATIS			
Magnatis appulsu extulit se occasio,	423	Mem.Matr.2	26
MAGNATUM			
Magnatumque inopumque aequum certamen & ardor:	429	Mem.Matr.13	3
Academiam simulans vel maximos magnatum inter eundum summouet:	470	Epistolae	26
MAGNETICA			
Illi magnetica acu freti sunt.	463	Epistolae	16
MAGNI			
Sanctius in Regno Magni credebat Amoris	439	Poem.Lat.	14
Non vnum quid spectant aut singulare Magni animi, sed varia solent	446	Orationes	4
rotundum & coeleste, soli facies tanquam vestibulum magni palatij.	447	Orationes	1
MAGNIF			
potui refercire lineas Honoribus, Magnif., Celsitud., sed	473	Epistolae	17
MAGNIFICENTIA			
quos magnificentia promissi circumscribere in promptu erat,	445	Orationes	16
MAGNIFICENTIAE			
nominis Tui subsidiumque Magnificentiae Tuae deuotissimorum	464	Epistolae	7
abunde succurres Magnificentiae tuae addicitissimis Procancellario	469	Epistolae	26

	PAGE	TITLE	LINE
MAGNIFICENTISSIMI			
Excellentissimi Magnificentissimi Domini, Post honores eximios,	440	Orationes	1
MAGNIFICI			
si qui alij exurgant promissores magnifici et hiantes, qui,	462	Epistolae	30
MAGNIFICUS			
Magnificus es screator, homicida inclytus.	421	Lucus 33	2
MAGNIS			
Interea classem magnis Rex instruit ausis:	427	Mem.Matr.9	7
qui virtutes tuas magnis negotijs pares prouexit, noluitque vt minori	466	Epistolae	13
MAGNITUDINI			
ne nihil hic sit, quod magnitudini praesentiae vestrae respondeat.	441	Orationes	9
vt si officia nostra minus respondeant magnitudini beneficiorum,	460	Epistolae	16
MAGNITUDO			
Cuius fauoris magnitudo ita inuoluit nos, vt etiam rependendi vias	458	Epistolae	28
MAGNO			
similes esse Alexandro Magno nisi eius res gestas tradidisset	441	Orationes	18
MAGNOS			
Sic quasi Dijs certem, magnos accersere montes:	432	Poem.Lat.	6
MAGNUM			
Cui magnum imperium, gloria maior erat:	435	Poem.Lat.	2
date mihi CAROLVM alterum, quamlibet Magnum, modo detis eum in flore,	445	Orationes	19
cernitis Regem & nomine & re magnum quid polliceri, ideoque ex	447	Orationes	8
vapores seruiles ad nubes educti aeque magnum tonitru edent ac regij.	452	Orationes	18
incredibilem luxum a Tiberio Caesare ad Constantinum magnum aperirem,	452	Orationes	23
MAGNUS			
& Licurgus magnus Legislator atimian prosetheke tois agamois.	446	Orationes	20
MAGUM			
In Simonem Magum.	410	Lucus 4	T
MAIESTAS			
Quandoque voltus sola maiestas, Dolor.	422	Mem.Matr.2	7
nos audiamus summo cum gaudio ea Maiestas vestra summa cum molestia?	443	Orationes	31
MAIESTATE			
Sic, pro Maiestate, Deum, non perdere vitam	408	Passio 17	7
manibus teri, semotaque Maiestate, charta conspiciendum Te praebes,	458	Epistolae	19
MAIESTATEM			
personam Principis, deponit Maiestatem, virgam cum sceptro commutans,	452	Orationes	36
vestris in nos beneficijs Maiestatem vestram aeternitati in scriptis	458	Epistolae	31
Tantum Maiestatem vestram subiectissime oramus, vt si officia nostra	460	Epistolae	14
MAIESTATIS			
Optamus quidem vt Maiestatis vestrae gaudia responderint aut nostris	443	Orationes	13
et quasi accolae Maiestatis, literaturae suae et vicinitati	463	Epistolae	23
MAIOR			
Cui magnum imperium, gloria maior erat:	435	Poem.Lat.	2
Quisnam horum maior sit, dubitatur, amor.	437	Poem.Lat.	2
Cuiusnam maior sit, dubitatur, amor.	437	Poem.Lat. V	2
quo eorum conditio sublimior, eo maior cura adhibenda sit.	446	Orationes	35
MAIORES			
quod pereleganter & supra barbariem seculi innuebant Maiores nostri,	446	Orationes	29
MAIORIS			
Nihil habet humana vita maioris momenti aut ponderis, quam Nuptiae,	446	Orationes	16
MAIORUM			
per tot milliaria facile transmissum, mentem maiorum capacem indicet?	454	Orationes	2
more maiorum, multos iam annos Anglice viuens garriensque.	470	Epistolae	4
MAIUS			
permutare nolim, maius tamen piaculum reor, deesse publico muneri,	472	Epistolae	30
MALA			
Praesul, cur renuis? sin mala, pauculos	392	Musae 17	12
Falleris, nusquam plura bona, cum etiam mala illic sint aurea:	451	Orationes	3
MALE			
Sed qui tam male pileos habetis,	391	Musae 15	11
Quam nihil illudis, Gens improba! quam male cedunt	405	Passio 7	1
MALEDICTA			
Ingemat ob partus, ceu maledicta, suos,	390	Musae 12	14
In posterum, maledicta Ficus arescens	405	Passio 5	6
MALEUOLORUM			
cum non solum tuearis nos a maleuolorum insidijs, sed etiam doceas	443	Orationes	22
non est tanti respondere latratibus maleuolorum;	454	Orationes	16
MALIGNI			
Non plus maligni daemones Christi cruce	389	Musae 10	2
MALIGNO			
Vno ictu: non sic pestis, non stella maligno	420	Tr.Mortis	80
MALIGNUM			
Carpsit malignum sydus hanc modestiam	427	Mem.Matr.8	3
MALIGNUS			
Filij noctis, populus malignus,	390	Musae 14	18
MALIS			
Cum natet in tantis caetera terra malis?	411	Lucus 6	2
Dij te perdant, cum malis tuis & arena sine calce;	451	Orationes	5
MALUI			
Quare malui seruire auribus Tuis, creberrima Antiquitatis lectione	473	Epistolae	19
MALUM			
Ordinis osores articulare malum.	389	Musae 11	4
MALUS			
Tollantur si cuncta malus quae polluit vsus,	390	Musae 13	3
Quas malus liuor iaculis lacessit	390	Musae 14	2
MAMMAS			
Quis enim sicca vbera et mammas arentes tam nobilis parentis aequo	461	Epistolae	32
MANANTIBUS			
manibus in coelum sublatis, lachrymis in terram manantibus, ieiunae,	448	Orationes	35
MANARE			
latiusque manare iniustitiae peccatum, quam negligentiae.	472	Epistolae	32

	PAGE	TITLE	LINE
MANDIT			
triumphos & victorias quasi fraena ferox spumantia mandit, . . .	447	Orationes	35
MANE			
Tu promis Orbem mane, condis vesperi, ...	407	Passio 16	3
Phoebe, tui puduit quum summo mane redires	433	Poem.Lat.	36
MANENTE			
Implicet, & matrem, matre manente, petam.	424	Mem.Matr.3	10
interim vestra hac scribendi laude intacta manente atque illibata.	458	Epistolae	27
MANERE			
Quaeque olim fuerat cura, manere potest.	427	Mem.Matr.9	4
MANEREM			
Quid enim manerem? Habui viaticum fauoris Tui, quod longiori multo	471	Epistolae	18
MANET			
Nescia vulturnis cedere, firma manet.	428	Mem.Matr.11	2
MANIBUS			
Excussos manibus calamos, falcemque resumptam	431	Mem.Matr.19	1
Quis, nisi qui manibus Briareus, oculisque sit Argus, . . .	435	Poem.Lat.	5
apponimus nos manibus Sceptrum, capiti & faciei coronam, . .	447	Orationes	3
Quod aliae gentes manibus in coelum sublatis, lachrymis in terram	448	Orationes	34
sed Tu vis etiam manibus teri, semotaque Maiestate, charta . .	458	Epistolae	19
MANIFESTATIONEM			
cuius manifestationem in gentem suam priuatae personae & habitui	453	Orationes	8
MANSERIT			
Igniculos legans, manserit ipsa licet;	410	Lucus 2	2
MANSUETI			
(e quorum ossibus collisis ignis elicitur) qui nunc mansueti sunt,	449	Orationes	18
MANSUETUDINE			
magis id adeo factum esse mansuetudine Tua incomparabili, . .	472	Epistolae	21
MANSURUM			
in terram hanc, incidit in coenum, quod innuebat eum hic mansurum:	455	Orationes	4
MANU			
Cur efficaci, Deucalion, manu, ...	393	Musae 23	1
Defendit veram mente manuque fidem.	399	Musae 33	24
Sic vnguenta solent manu fricari:	405	Passio 8	2
Diuina Christi scriberet acta manu?	412	Lucus 9	2
tanquam flos molliculus rudiore Centurionis manu tactus flaccescit.	448	Orationes	25
& cum ipse sis in summa arbore altera manu prehendis Regem, . .	456	Epistolae	14
MANUM			
Quae scripsit numeros, manum; per omnes	400	Musae 37	2
Cultricem reuocans anxietate manum:	425	Mem.Matr.5	4
Quare post Principis manum honoribus refertam, non est quod nostram	469	Epistolae	14
certe non tam ornas illam, qui infers manum grauitati. . . .	470	Epistolae	20
MANUS			
Atqui manus imponere integras praestat, ...	397	Musae 31	2
Vt niue torpentes incaluere manus?	399	Musae 35	4
Os & lingua tibi diues, egena manus:	414	Lucus 22	2
O mea suspicienda manus, venterque perennis!	418	Tr.Mortis	1
Tu discidisti Gorgoneas manus	434	Poem.Lat.	17
Tandem & fessa manus, dedit sigillum.	439	Poem.Lat.	12
Soli homini dantur manus, soli caput rotundum & coeleste, . .	446	Orationes	38
collum pensile, manus decussatae, ipsae mulieres inelegantes,	451	Orationes	16
eadem manus et tuum tibi largita est honorem, et priuilegia nostra	468	Epistolae	23
MANUUM			
De impositione manuum.	397	Musae 31	T
MAPPAE			
Cum templis effare, madent sudaria, mappae, ...	397	Musae 29	1
MARAINEI			
Seiriou ettetheis boulemasi, panta marainei.	431	Mem.Matr.17	20
MARCENTIBUS			
Perrumpens, Atropi vetulae marcentibus vlnis.	419	Tr.Mortis	65
MARCESCANT			
Nostra etiam paribus marcescant gaudia fatis.	427	Mem.Matr.7	34
MARCESCITE			
Horti, deliciae Dominae, marcescite tandem;	425	Mem.Matr.5	1
MARCHIO			
Quare, meritissime Marchio, Tuam gloriam censemus nostram, . . .	456	Epistolae	15
MARCHIONATU			
1. Ad Buckingh. C. Gratulatio de Marchionatu	456	Epistolae	T
MARCIDA			
viduae effoetae, aut ligna exucca & marcida, alumnis suis orbarentur,	462	Epistolae	4
MARE			
Naufragij causa est alijs mare, roboris Anglo, ...	411	Lucus 6	5
Nec cingit mare, nunc inundat omnes.	428	Mem.Matr.10	14
Tu flectis amnes, tu mare caerulum	433	Poem.Lat.	13
Polycrates cum annulum sibi dilectum in mare dimisisset, . .	444	Orationes	14
vsque ad Pyrenaeas nubes conscendens, reuersus per mare, gloria,	454	Orationes	32
aquas a Fonte accipiunt non retinent ipsi, sed in mare dimittunt;	456	Epistolae	10
MARI			
qui optimum Principem spe nuptiarum mari nuper tradentes, . .	444	Orationes	18
MARIA			
Martha: Maria.	413	Lucus 15	T
MARINIS			
Tillius incumbit Dano, Gallusque marinis, ...	427	Mem.Matr.9	11
MARINUS			
Herbae exoletae, ros-marinus aridus?	424	Mem.Matr.2	58
MARIS			
Cum qui plus terrae, plus habuere maris.	411	Lucus 6	4
alterosque maris quasi Flagellatores expugnatos fusosque nobis	462	Epistolae	8
MARITIMUS			
cum non est tanti totus ille maritimus tractus (Oceani praeda	461	Epistolae	8

	PAGE	TITLE	LINE
MARMORA			
Tu, qui cuncta creans docuisti marmora flere,	410	Lucus 1	5
MARO			
Roma. Anagr. Oram. Maro. / Ramo. Armo. / Mora. Amor.	416	Lucus 25	T
Vnde MARO laudes duxit ad astra tuas.	416	Lucus 25	4
MARTHA			
Martha: Maria.	413	Lucus 15	T
MARTIJ			
Discessum Regis ab Academia Cantabrigiae habita 12o die Martij 1622	443	Orationes	T
MARTYRA			
Martyra, Calvinum, Bezam, doctumque Bucerum,	398	Musae 33	3
MASSA			
ramenta quaepiam ex tanta Humanitatis massa, quae apud Te visitur,	472	Epistolae	13
MATER			
Ah Mater, quo te deplorem fonte? Dolores	422	Mem.Matr.1	1
Mater: & ista Dolor nunc tibi Metra parit.	422	Mem.Matr.1	8
Tu vero mater perpetim laudabere	424	Mem.Matr.2	61
Mater perpetuis vuida gaudijs,	424	Mem.Matr.4	2
Te, Mater, celebrans diu,	424	Mem.Matr.4	11
Bis tu mater eras mihi,	425	Mem.Matr.4	15
Ni sancte, vti mater, recedam,	425	Mem.Matr.6	11
Mater inest saliente vena.	426	Mem.Matr.6	16
At te commoriente, Magna Mater,	428	Mem.Matr.10	5
Tu radix, tu petra mihi firmissima, Mater,	428	Mem.Matr.11	9
enim minus refert, qualis quaeque sit mater, e qua liberi quaerantur,	447	Orationes	11
qua in re celebris est Gracchorum mater, ingenium ipsum atque indoles	447	Orationes	17
tripudiet Alma Mater licet aetate prouectior, etiam anus subsultans	454	Orationes	35
aut tantum de nullo vnquam Filio Alma Mater, quantum de Te sibi	457	Epistolae	26
Quanta hilaritate aspicit Alma Mater filios suos iam emancipatos,	461	Epistolae	30
vt Alma Mater libentissime caput reclinet in tuo sinu, oculusque	465	Epistolae	12
tanquam partubus Virtutum Tuarum, Alma Mater accurrens gratuletur:	469	Epistolae	9
MATERIA			
non respicitur, quae materia sit, coelestis an sublunaris,	454	Orationes	12
MATERIAM			
Materiam vexat: nec iam se continet antro	420	Tr.Mortis	70
recte diuinaret, non respiciat materiam actionum, sed quo spiritu,	454	Orationes	10
MATERNI			
Materni decus, & debita nominis,	424	Mem.Matr.4	6
Pallida materni Genij atque exanguis imago,	426	Mem.Matr.7	1
MATERNIS			
Vos sine maternis hymnis infantia vidit,	389	Musae 12	5
Vna cum promotionibus Academicis maternisque, assumsi mecum	473	Epistolae	8
MATHEMATICAE			
inter quas & Mathematicae, quae licet versentur in figuris	454	Orationes	3
MATRE			
Implicet, & matrem, matre manente, petam.	424	Mem.Matr.3	10
Mutata? & pro matre mihi phantasma dolosum	426	Mem.Matr.7	3
Nunc sorti pateo, expositus sine matre procellis,	428	Mem.Matr.11	7
Ex Veritate matre; Mellis alueus;	436	Poem.Lat.	23
vestra spolia actosque ex orbe triumphos communicas cum Alma Matre,	458	Epistolae	17
nostrae, quae per Tuum Partum, ex Matre nunc Auia facta est:	463	Epistolae	25
MATREM			
Laudando Matrem, cum repugnant inscij.	424	Mem.Matr.2	65
Cur splendes, O Phoebe? ecquid demittere matrem	424	Mem.Matr.3	1
Verum heus, si nequeas caelo demittere matrem,	424	Mem.Matr.3	7
Implicet, & matrem, matre manente, petam.	424	Mem.Matr.3	10
At forte matrem perdere haud soles demens:	429	Mem.Matr.12	9
Aggreditur Matrem (conductis carmine Parcis)	431	Mem.Matr.19	3
abunde compensas nos, gratissimoque Almam Matrem prosequeris animo:	456	Epistolae	9
Quis enim tunc inuiseret Almam Matrem destitutam omni commeatu?	461	Epistolae	2
vt Almam Matrem spe noua grauidam semper atque praegnantem	464	Epistolae	25
MATRES			
Enixas pueros matres se sistere templis	389	Musae 12	1
MATRI			
Matrine linguam refero, solum vt mordeam?	424	Mem.Matr.2	59
Assideo Matri, robore vinco cedros.	428	Mem.Matr.11	6
meo quadrabunt, quae almae matri inconcinna erunt atque enormia.	470	Epistolae	15
MATRIS			
Memoriae Matris Sacrum	422	Mem.Matris	T
Mihine matris vrna clausa est vnico,	424	Mem.Matr.2	57
Quin Matris superans carmina poscit honos.	431	Mem.Matr.19	6
Ad se suaeque matris Arcam regredi:	436	Poem.Lat.	21
expectamus indies futurum, Almae Matris amorem tecum simul euehas.	462	Epistolae	29
MATRISSAT			
(veluti Conclusio sequitur infirmiorem partem) plerumque matrissat:	447	Orationes	19
MATRONAE			
quidem multum, neque nostrae matronae conuenit, cui tu es ab ornatu.	471	Epistolae	2
MATRONAM			
Quare scripturus, finge tibi matronam sanctam, venerandam,	470	Epistolae	16
MATURE			
prudentissimus Rex mature prospiciet: vbi ille signum sustulerit,	449	Orationes	16
vtque mature absoluas quae complexus es animo, ad eius gloriam,	464	Epistolae	4
MATURO			
quam adductus maturo consilio, primas dedissem literas,	471	Epistolae	26
MATURUS			
Maturusque suos coquens amores	408	Passio 19	12
MAUELIM			
Mugire multo mauelim quam rudere.	395	Musae 24	2
MAX			
Deus Opti: Max. tua beneficia, quae nos soluendo non sumus,	467	Epistolae	14
nosque ipsos Tibi, Teque Deo Opti: Max: intimis precibus commendamus.	468	Epistolae	10

MAXIMA	PAGE	TITLE		LINE
Ordine discerni maxima bella solent.	399	Musae 33		28
Nimirum id assecuta sunt merita Tua maxima, vt Almam Matrem spe noua	464	Epistolae		25
MAXIME				
animalia, tum maxime homo, cui soli ideo insunt oculi variegati,	453	Orationes		16
MAXIMOS				
Academiam simulans vel maximos magnatum inter eundum summouet:	470	Epistolae		25
MAXIMUM				
Fructum laborum consecutae maximum	424	Mem.Matr.2		64
ME				
Quo me vocas tandem, tuumque	394	Musae 23		23
Ne me carminibus nimis dicacem,	400	Musae 37		10
Ni me forte petas; nam quanto indignior ipse,	404	Passio 2		5
Imo, me nec apes, nec astra pungunt:	411	Lucus 5		10
Quos tu calcasti fluctus, me, Christe, lacessunt,	414	Lucus 19		1
Quin pro me quoque sanguinem profudit,	421	Lucus 34		4
Cum te non videam, mene videre putas?	421	Lucus 35		8
Queis me educasti; sponte chartas illinunt	424	Mem.Matr.2		63
Dolere prohibes? aut dolere me gentis	429	Mem.Matr.12		5
O me disparibus natum cum numine fatis!	434	Poem.Lat.		3
O me probe lassum! Iuuate, Posteri!	437	Poem.Lat.		27
O me prope lassum! Iuuate, Posteri!	437	Poem.Lat.	V	27
Ah! metuo ne me ad luctus mea fata crearint	437	Poem.Lat.	V	11
Otan de krepis me katablethei genous	447	Orationes		14
Sophronon esti me perimenein, ote polemein umin omologesei,	449	Orationes		14
ita me ametis omnes, vt ego nihil vspiam laetum, nihil candidum	451	Orationes		13
Inde ego sic mecum: gaudeo quidem de ingenti amore in Principem,	451	Orationes		21
hic ego me erexi & de dolore remisi plurimum, de desiderio nihil.	451	Orationes		26
Quam pudet me delicatorum Caesarum, qui cupiditatibus immersi,	452	Orationes		8
Dies me deficeret (& quidem nox aptior esset tali historiae)	452	Orationes		20
e phagon e pion, on me themiton en, ou di' emauton emarton,	452	Orationes		30
per me non stabit quo minus, spe prouecta atque adulta,	470	Epistolae		7
conuertissem, & ex altera parte acuissem me aspectu virtutum Tuarum;	472	Epistolae		6
imo precabor enixe, me tum priuari tam communi hac luce, quam Tua,	472	Epistolae		23
non cor) Tui in me dominij ius imminuere posse, nedum rescindere.	473	Epistolae		6
Academicis maternisque, assumsi mecum propensionem in Patrem.	473	Epistolae		8
MEA				
Cum mea futilibus numeris se verba viderent	385	Musae		3
Non mea fert aetas, vt te, veterane, lacessam;	386	Musae 2		1
Et mea sint canis scripta referta tuis.	386	Musae 2		6
Absit vt ingenuum pungant mea verba pudorem;	400	Musae 36		3
Plus charta haec mea delibuta dictis	400	Musae 37		25
Et mea iam lacrymet culpa colore suo.	404	Passio 1		4
Crimina cum turgent, & mea poena prope est,	406	Passio 9		2
Dum moreris, Mea Vita, ipsi vixere sepulti,	407	Passio 17		1
O mea suspicienda manus, venterque perennis!	418	Tr.Mortis		1
Immoriarque oculis, o mea vita, tuis.	421	Lucus 35		4
Quin fugias? mea non fuerat tam nubila Iuno,	426	Mem.Matr.7		7
In mea dicta ruant; non tam mihi pendula mens est,	432	Poem.Lat.		5
Musa, vale, & tu Phoebe; dolor mea carmina dictet;	432	Poem.Lat.		12
Ah! metuo ne me ad luctus mea fata crearint	437	Poem.Lat.	V	11
atque effusissimum in omnia officia, quae praestet mea paruitas;	471	Epistolae		22
Tua lenitas non ita interpretabitur mea haec scribendi interualla,	471	Epistolae		25
ad mea in Honorem Tuum officia erectior solutiorque redibo,	473	Epistolae		2
illustrissime) quod pronomina mea adeo audacter incedant in hac	473	Epistolae		15
MEAE				
Votaque scintillae sunt animosa meae.	410	Lucus 2		4
Cordis apex, animae pugnaque paxque meae,	421	Lucus 35		2
Ora meae memori menti: ne dispare cultu	427	Mem.Matr.7		31
MEAM				
Ne nimium vexet quaestio, pone meam.	409	Passio 21		4
Quare Sphaeram egomet meam	424	Mem.Matr.4		9
Vna meam membris horula, teque cruci.	434	Poem.Lat.		2
Cum enim vim cogitationum in vitam meam omnem conuertissem,	472	Epistolae		5
MEAS				
Regnat visceribus, measque versat	411	Lucus 5		2
Vae nubi pluuia grauidae, non lacte, measque	426	Mem.Matr.7		5
si placeat vices meas tantisper supplere donec Academia orationem	470	Epistolae		6
MEDENDI				
Impos medendi, occidere si potes,	425	Mem.Matr.6		9
MEDETUR				
Quin tibi tam desperatae MORA nulla medetur,	416	Lucus 25		9
Quin tibi jam desperatae MORA nulla medetur,	416	Lucus 25	V	9
MEDICARIS				
Sic toti medicaris ipse mundo.	405	Passio 8		3
MEDICATUR				
Atque animo medicatur vnum.	426	Mem.Matr.6		24
MEDICI				
asserunt Medici vnamquamque regionem sua sibi sufficere,	444	Orationes		25
MEDICINA				
Nec grauidis medicina tuta est.	426	Mem.Matr.6		20
Expeto, tanquam haec sit nostri medicina doloris?	433	Poem.Lat.		46
MEDICORUM				
Ei en en o anthropos, inquit Medicorum Alpha, ouk an elgeen.	446	Orationes		19
MEDICUM				
Cur Deus elegit Medicum, qui numine plenus	412	Lucus 9		1
MEDIO				
Pastor agis proprios, medio tutissimus, agnos.	402	Musae 39		32
Luscum prodigium, medioque foramine gaudens.	419	Tr.Mortis		54
MEDITARI				
Quis Monachos mortem meditari, & puluere tristi	420	Tr.Mortis		92

MEDITARI (cont'd)	PAGE	TITLE	LINE
Quis mortem Monachos meditari, et puluere tristi	272	Tr.Mortis VS	92
MEDITATIO			
Intus agunt, habeat certum meditatio finem:	402	Musae 39	37
MEDITATO			
Ego, non nisi meditato, obrepsi ad fauorem Tuum;	472	Epistolae	3
MEDITETUR			
Deum immortalem, vt Princeps optimus nulla secunda itinera meditetur;	455	Orationes	1
MEDULLA			
Nempe es totus amor, medulla amoris,	417	Lucus 30	3
MEDULLAS			
Qui vestras edit intime medullas.	391	Musae 15	10
Immodicus luctus tacito vorat igne medullas,	433	Poem.Lat.	47
MEDUSA			
Cum prope sit nobis Musa, Medusa procul?	387	Musae 6	2
MEDUSEAE			
Adeo inficetae, plumbeae, Meduseae,	429	Mem.Matr.12	6
MEGALES			
Nun themis orphnaiei megales epi geitonos aisei	431	Mem.Matr.18	3
MEGALOI			
Autar axei megaloi kentoumenai: eute gar autai	431	Mem.Matr.17	10
MEI			
Peccati veniae mei, vel ipsos	421	Lucus 34	8
Fatisco referens tanta quae numerant mei	423	Mem.Matr.2	50
Quin caeli mihi sunt mei,	424	Mem.Matr.4	5
Affectusque mei similem; nec languida misce	427	Mem.Matr.7	30
MEIS			
Sufficiet votis ista iuuenta meis.	386	Musae 2	10
Sicca meis lacrymis Thamesis vicina videtur,	422	Mem.Matr.1	3
Vt si recisis arboribus meis	434	Poem.Lat.	29
agam vobiscum, simulque & laboribus meis, & vestrae fidei consulam,	445	Orationes	29
Tuis, meis desiderijs probe cognitis, excussis perpensisque.	472	Epistolae	4
vt laboribus meis plurimis atque assidua obseruantia, ramenta	472	Epistolae	12
quam meis meritis vllis, semper lubentissimeque agnoscam:	472	Epistolae	22
MEL			
Nunquid mel comedens, apem comedi	411	Lucus 5	8
MELEDONI			
Ouk eti despoines glukerai meledoni trapheisai:	431	Mem.Matr.17	16
MELIOR			
Quanto Impositio melior est Impostura!	397	Musae 31	4
Qualis eras, qui, ne melior natura minorem	407	Passio 14	1
tempore melior, iniurias seculi scriptaque hac illac pereuntia	459	Epistolae	14
MELIORE			
Quicquid ex vrna meliore ductum	390	Musae 14	5
MELIOREM			
Quae enim vspiam gens, quod vnquam seculum meliorem habuit Principem?	445	Orationes	12
MELIORIS			
Incolae coeli melioris alba	390	Musae 14	11
Deciduae melioris orbis!	394	Musae 23	36
MELIRROON			
Menoun to glaphuron, kai melirroon tropon,	430	Mem.Matr.15	8
MELITAIAIS			
illecebris melitaiais agxonais abiectis, iter aggreditur & labores,	452	Orationes	32
MELIUS			
(cum dignius nil posset aut melius dare)	397	Musae 28	10
Purpureo melius sanguine Regna probem.	405	Passio 7	8
Et melius coelum, te veniente, subest:	210	Cam.1613-a BR	4
MELLIFLUUM			
Orphea mellifluum secutas.	393	Musae 23	12
MELLIS			
Immemor antiqui mellis, eundo coquit.	398	Musae 33	20
Ex Veritate matre; Mellis alueus;	436	Poem.Lat.	23
MELON			
Ou sathron, oude melon epleto, alla voos:	429	Mem.Matr.14	6
MELVI			
Est Anti-pelvi-Melvi-Categoria.	386	Musae 3	10
MELVINE			
Praesulibus nostris fastus, Melvine, tumentes	387	Musae 7	1
Sin, Melvine, pedes alienos postulet infans,	388	Musae 9	9
Sed nec coniugij signum, Melvine, probabis?	396	Musae 26	1
MELVINI			
Ad Andreae Melvini Scoti Anti-Tami-Cami-Categoriam.	384	Musae	T
MELVINUM			
Ad Melvinum	386	Musae 2	T
Ad Melvinum De ijsdem.	392	Musae 18	T
Ad Melvinum.	400	Musae 37	T
MEMBRA			
Qui Caput es, spinas & tua Membra tuas.	405	Passio 6	4
Ne membra culpes, causa animo latet	426	Mem.Matr.6	18
MEMBRIS			
Vna meam membris horula, teque cruci.	434	Poem.Lat.	2
MEMINISTI			
titulos caput vndique munientes meministi Magistrum Te esse Artium?	456	Epistolae	3
MEMORANTIBUS			
aliosque titulos aeque nobis memorantibus, ac merentibus vobis	440	Orationes	3
MEMOREM			
Quid memorem tormenta, quibus prius horruit aeuum;	419	Tr.Mortis	39
Quid memorem prudentiam vestram incomparabilem, qua optime ostendis	443	Orationes	15
Quid ego vobis Neronum aut Heliogabalorum ingluuiem memorem?	452	Orationes	19
MEMORI			
Ora meae memori menti: ne dispare cultu	427	Mem.Matr.7	31

MEMORIAE	PAGE	TITLE	LINE
Memoriae Matris Sacrum	422	Mem.Matris	T
MEMORIAM			
tibique non tam auide veterum beneficiorum memoriam recolenti,	457	Epistolae	13
MEN			
Xalepon men ou dakrusai:	430	Mem.Matr.16	2
MENEIT'			
Alla meneit', ou qar taraxos poti metera bainei,	431	Mem.Matr.18	5
MENOUGE			
Menouge sophien, ei s' apellaxthai xreon,	430	Mem.Matr.15	5
MENOUN			
Menoun to glaphuron, kai melirroon tropon,	430	Mem.Matr.15	8
MENS			
Mens sub insigni specie coloris	390	Musae 14	7
Assiduo stimulo carnem Mens vlta lacessit,	410	Lucus 2	5
Mens superat; corpus solum Elementa tenent.	424	Mem.Matr.3	4
In mea dicta ruant; non tam mihi pendula mens est,	432	Poem.Lat.	5
Si-quas mens agitet moles (dum pectora saeuo	432	Poem.Lat.	9
Quare age, Mens, effare, precor, quo numine laeso?	432	Poem.Lat.	17
MENSAE			
Grata mihi mensae sunt analecta tuae.	385	Musae 1	6
Erutus, infernae pretiosa tragemata mensae,	419	Tr.Mortis	58
Exulis, infernae pretiosa tragemata mensae,	419	Tr.Mortis V	58
MENTE			
Defendit veram mente manuque fidem.	399	Musae 33	24
Innumeros mergit vitiata mente poetas,	402	Musae 39	39
Ararumque Hominumque ortum si mente pererres,	417	Lucus 29	1
Vel sine luce solum, vel sine mente caro.	417	Lucus 31	6
MENTEM			
Cum millena tuam pulsare negotia mentem	385	Musae 1	1
Tu vero mentem neutiquam despondeas,	407	Passio 16	11
Sic mucronatam reddunt suspiria mentem,	410	Lucus 2	3
Coeperat, agricolis mentemque & aratra solutis:	418	Tr.Mortis	10
Cum tu, Christe, cadis, nascor; mentemque ligauit	434	Poem.Lat.	1
Otium poscunt artes, mentem tranquillam, serenam, sudam:	448	Orationes	23
per tot milliaria facile transmissum, mentem maiorum capacem indicet?	454	Orationes	1
MENTES			
Mentes, quietis tympana publicae,	395	Musae 23	50
Innocuae mentes, quibus inter flumina mundi	400	Musae 36	1
Mitis agas: tenerae duplicant sibi verbera mentes,	406	Passio 9	5
MENTI			
Qui spissae fidei breuique menti	417	Lucus 30	4
Ora meae memori menti: ne dispare cultu	427	Mem.Matr.7	31
Iam foelix Philomela, & menti conscia Dido!	432	Poem.Lat.	22
MENTIBUS			
Mentibus attonitis cupiunt addiscere ritus:	402	Musae 39	9
Sanctos qui gemitus mentibus inseris	403	Musae 40	12
MENTIS			
E creaturis sine mentis vsu	390	Musae 14	13
Nec transire licet quo mentis acumine findis	402	Musae 39	27
Gaudia sola fores: sic quicquid somnia mentis	402	Musae 39	36
Aegroto mentis: quam neque pixides	425	Mem.Matr.6	5
Hinc mihi principium: vos o labentia mentis	432	Poem.Lat.	13
Repumicator mentis; Atlas Physicus,	436	Poem.Lat.	17
Ad se suamque mentis Arcam regredi:	436	Poem.Lat. V	21
lacteam aliquam viam ad candorem Mentis Tuae ducentem aut reperissem	472	Epistolae	9
MEO			
Spero meo cordi posse patere viam.	404	Passio 4	2
multa Critt meo quadrabunt, quae almae matri inconcinna erunt atque	470	Epistolae	14
MEOS			
Quae guttae poterunt enumerare meos?	422	Mem.Matr.1	2
cum grauibus duobus muneribus fungar apud Meos, Rhetoris in hunc	472	Epistolae	26
MEPHITI			
Sulphureoque lacu, totaque imbuta Mephiti.	419	Tr.Mortis	59
MERCAMUR			
Annon sic mercamur agros? quibus ecce Redemptor	388	Musae 9	3
MERCES			
quemadmodum artifices non omnes licitantibus producunt merces,	445	Orationes	30
MERENTI			
Nil horum regero tibi merenti.	401	Musae 37	40
MERENTIBUS			
ac merentibus vobis gratissimos, Saluete tandem Magistri Artium,	440	Orationes	4
non solum rectum de Bene-merentibus iudicium hausisse ab Antiquis,	469	Epistolae	12
MERGERE			
Hos ad se trahere et mergere gestiens.	391	Musae 17	10
MERGIT			
Innumeros mergit vitiata mente poetas,	402	Musae 39	39
MERITA			
Quo nunc recumbis, scriptio merita est tua,	423	Mem.Matr.2	40
Eximia tua in nos merita frequentiorem calamum postulant,	457	Epistolae	7
sic merita tua ita ascensura, vt eorum vis et virtus ad nos	464	Epistolae	19
Nimirum id assecuta sunt merita Tua maxima, vt Almam Matrem spe noua	464	Epistolae	24
MERITIS			
Ne serae meritis tuis venirent.	428	Mem.Matr.10	12
aliquas virtutes tandem meritis tuis votisque nostris conspirantibus	464	Epistolae	12
quam meis meritis vllis, semper lubentissimeque agnoscam:	472	Epistolae	22
MERITISSIME			
Quare, meritissime Marchio, Tuam gloriam censemus nostram,	456	Epistolae	15
ne literae nostrae animo Tuo tot negotijs meritissime distincto,	457	Epistolae	11
nunquam in tantis negotijs, quibus meritissime districtus es, ea,	463	Epistolae	18

	PAGE	TITLE	LINE
MERITISSIMUS			
O qui Defensor Fidei meritissimus audis, ...	402	Musae 39	17
MERITORUM			
sphaera quam pro latitudine meritorum tuorum circumscribereris.	466	Epistolae	14
MERITUS			
idem feruor qui impar sub amoris signo meritus est, ad vera castra	453	Orationes	30
Tam eximie de nobis meritus es, vt res nostras omnes cum Honore Tuo	465	Epistolae	2
MERSERAT			
Merserat in lustris perniciosa venus, ...	396	Musae 26	10
MERSIS			
Mersis reuertens laetus ab hostibus	394	Musae 23	30
MERUERE			
Quid sacrae tandem meruere vestes, ...	390	Musae 14	1
MERX			
Sanguine: nec precium merx emit vlla suum.	410	Lucus 4	4
MESSEM			
posterioris largam messem Vobis haec tenuia boni consulentibus,	441	Orationes	21
METAE			
Nescia sit metae; venula, cella tua est.	404	Passio 2	2
METAIXMIOUS			
Emas lipousa kuklothen metaixmious?	429	Mem.Matr.15	4
METALLA			
optime consuluisse Deum orbi terrarum lapides & metalla ei inserendo,	452	Orationes	25
feracem gloriae, et coeleste ingenium quasi ad metalla damnari.	468	Epistolae	6
METALLUM			
Liquitur ardenti candens fornace metallum, ...	419	Tr.Mortis	51
liquitur ardenti cadens fornace metallum;	271	Tr.Mortis VS	51
METAS			
nodo connectens, nullas metas laudum, nullas Herculeas columnas,	440	Orationes	17
METATUR			
Seritur fama in hoc saeculo, vt in sequenti metatur:	441	Orationes	20
METENTES			
Aruiragum, falcesque obstantia quaeque metentes.	419	Tr.Mortis	46
METER			
Meter, gunaikon aigle, anthropon eris, ...	429	Mem.Matr.15	1
METERA			
Alla meneit', ou gar taraxos poti metera bainei, ...	431	Mem.Matr.18	5
METERI			
Meteri tektainousa, gooi kai penthesi sugxroun.	431	Mem.Matr.17	14
METHODUM			
viam aperiens & methodum in studijs adhibendam, etiam libros indicans	443	Orationes	24
METIRI			
ex itinere Principem metiri licet, quod sane adeo nobile fuit	453	Orationes	23
METRA			
Mater: & ista Dolor nunc tibi Metra parit.	422	Mem.Matr.1	8
METRESAN			
Pneuma, biou parodon mounois epeessi metresan.	431	Mem.Matr.17	23
METRI			
In metri genus.	387	Musae 5	T
METROS			
Ina metros euthenouses	430	Mem.Matr.16	10
METU			
Nos igitur hoc metu affecti, vti sanguis solet in re dubia ad cor	467	Epistolae	8
METUANT			
Quid metuant homines infra, supraue minentur	413	Lucus 16	1
METUAS			
Respondit: Eia, ne metuas, precor, ...	434	Poem.Lat.	26
METUO			
Ah! metuo ne me ad luctus mea fata crearint	437	Poem.Lat. V	11
METUS			
Metus inanes? Nos pari praeteruehi	397	Musae 30	3
METUUNT			
Decus mulierum perijt: & metuunt viri	422	Mem.Matr.2	8
Non metuunt vltra; nostra infortunia tantum	432	Poem.Lat.	24
Arma tui metuunt alumni.	434	Poem.Lat.	24
MEUM			
Quod calamum excusent Pontus & Astra meum:	435	Poem.Lat.	8
ipsa durissima ingenia, meum praesertim, celare non possunt:	445	Orationes	9
non quin pectus meum plenum Tui sit, atque effusissimum in omnia	471	Epistolae	21
nihil Mortalium firmiori flagrare in Te desiderio, quam meum pectus;	473	Epistolae	5
MEUS			
Iam meus es: nunc Te teneo: Pastorque prehensus	407	Passio 14	3
Ecce meus torpens animus succumbit vtrique, ...	435	Poem.Lat.	3
MI			
Tu vero vale, mi proorator, amaque Tuum G. H.	471	Epistolae	12
MIAN			
Mian t' atarpon sumporeuesthai drasas.	430	Mem.Matr.15	13
Ou pheggos, koinon t' agathon, mian eis thuran eirgein . . .	430	Mem.Matr.17	5
MICAM			
post ingentes Hecatombas, exiguam thuris micam adoleri legimus.	469	Epistolae	17
MICANDI			
Scilicet id splendes: haec est tibi causa micandi, ...	424	Mem.Matr.3	5
MICANTES			
Arterias tractans micantes	425	Mem.Matr.6	3
MICANTIBUS			
arterijs micantibus, spiritibusque tabellarijs laetum hunc nuncium .	445	Orationes	1
MICARE			
ferox spumantia mandit, iuuat micare gladio & mucronem intueri.	447	Orationes	35
MIHI			
Quas liuor mihi parturit, retundet, ...	385	Musae	6
Grata mihi mensae sunt analecta tuae.	385	Musae 1	6

MIHI (cont'd)	PAGE	TITLE	LINE
Ecclesia est mihi Luna; perge in Fabula.	393	Musae 22	10
certa, ac perfacilis mihi!	395	Musae 25	7
Aut laesae mihi suggerunt Athenae,	400	Musae 37	17
Sola mihi plenos, ait, exhibet Anglia cultus.	402	Musae 39	13
Tu mihi subueniens dignior esse potes.	404	Passio 2	6
Christe, dolor tibi supplicio, mihi blanda voluptas;	405	Passio 6	1
Posteritas flectet corque genuque mihi.	405	Passio 7	6
Tibi supererunt & mihi.	407	Passio 16	14
Hanc mihi duritiem contulit improbitas.	410	Lucus 1	2
Haud mihi cor saxo durius esse sinas.	410	Lucus 1	6
Omnia purgentur, niteat mihi tota supellex,	413	Lucus 15	3
Dic mihi, mors sterilis, vallis an vber eris?	413	Lucus 16	2
Corporeque atque animo. Totus mihi seruiat Orbis.	421	Tr.Mortis	101
Tantum istaec scribo gratus, ne tu mihi tantum	422	Mem.Matr.1	7
Mihine matris vrna clausa est vnico,	424	Mem.Matr.2	57
Quin caeli mihi sunt mei,	424	Mem.Matr.4	5
Bis tu mater eras mihi,	425	Mem.Matr.4	15
Irregularis nunc habitus mihi est:	426	Mem.Matr.6	21
Mutata? & pro matre mihi phantasma dolosum	426	Mem.Matr.7	3
Est mihi bis quinis laqueata domuncula tignis	426	Mem.Matr.7	22
Plura tibi missurus eram (nam quae mihi laurus,	428	Mem.Matr.9	15
Tu radix, tu petra mihi firmissima, Mater,	428	Mem.Matr.11	9
Alteraque haec tua mors, Ilias esto mihi.	428	Mem.Matr.11	14
In mea dicta ruant; non tam mihi pendula mens est,	432	Poem.Lat.	5
Spiritus, hi mihi iam montes, haec flumina sunto.	432	Poem.Lat.	11
Hinc mihi principium: vos o labentia mentis	432	Poem.Lat.	13
Perpetuos mihi ferre rami,	434	Poem.Lat.	32
Dulcem rependent tum mihi tibiam	434	Poem.Lat.	33
Cur mihi das vitam, quam tibi, Christe, negas?	434	Poem.Lat.	4
Hoc mihi legatum tristi si funere praestes,	434	Poem.Lat.	7
Christe, duplex fiet mors tua vita mihi:	434	Poem.Lat.	8
Frustra igitur sudo: superest mihi sola voluptas,	435	Poem.Lat.	7
Quid mihi si facies nigra est? hoc, Ceste, colore	437	Poem.Lat.	1
Cum mihi sit facies fumus, quas pectore flammas	437	Poem.Lat.	9
Dure, negas? O fata mihi praesaga doloris,	437	Poem.Lat.	11
Quae mihi lugubres contribuere genas!	437	Poem.Lat.	12
Quid iactas mihi aromata Orientis?	444	Orationes	24
date mihi CAROLVM alterum, quamlibet Magnum, modo detis eum in flore,	445	Orationes	19
gaudia praestolantur, quae iamdudum annuunt mihi vt perorem.	454	Orationes	23
etiam senectus, quam aetatem in hac palaestra consecutus mihi videor.	471	Epistolae	9
vt nunquam cessandum mihi ducerem, nunquam fatiscendum,	472	Epistolae	8
sed non patitur, vt mihi videtur, Romana elegantia, periodique vetus	473	Epistolae	17
MILES			
Whitaker, erranti quem praefers carmine, miles	398	Musae 33	5
causaris, irruit Miles in Musaeum tuum, & gladio te liberat.	448	Orationes	28
MILITARE			
quam subito dispereunt, simul ac concrepuit incendium militare:	448	Orationes	19
MILITARIUM			
Magistri Artium, & quidem omnium Aulicarum, Militarium, Academicarum.	440	Orationes	5
MILITAT			
Militat & nobis, quem vos contemnitis, Ordo;	399	Musae 33	27
MILITE			
Iam Constantinus multo se milite miscet;	398	Musae 33	15
MILITES			
solebant signa in hostes inijcere, vt milites acrius ea repeterent:	451	Orationes	33
MILLE			
Te mille rixae, mille prensabunt doli,	414	Lucus 20	8
Te mille nasi, mille rideant sinus.	414	Lucus 20	10
Mille rotae nimijs impediuntur aquis.	428	Mem.Matr.9	14
incoeptum et plus effecit quam mille Redemptores exequi possent.	461	Epistolae	12
MILLENA			
Cum millena tuam pulsare negotia mentem	385	Musae 1	1
Strata iacent toto millena cadauera campo	420	Tr.Mortis	79
MILLENOS			
Nempe & millenos ad palum interficit hostes	418	Tr.Mortis	31
MILLESIMA			
Daunia, non satiat bis ter millesima caedis	418	Tr.Mortis	3
MILLIARIA			
& per tot milliaria facile transmissum, mentem maiorum capacem	454	Orationes	1
MILLIBUS			
Vincit more suo Noster: nam millibus Infans	437	Poem.Lat.	3
Vicit more suo Noster: nam millibus Infans	437	Poem.Lat. V	3
virum protulit, cum quinque millibus annorum de palma certantem.	463	Epistolae	27
MILLIES			
Ter millies coelo regnis:	394	Musae 23	27
MINACI			
Iam nunc minaci murmure cornuum	448	Orationes	1
MINARI			
Hinc fremere totus & minari gestio	427	Mem.Matr.8	5
MINATUR			
Vt tenuis flammae species caelum vsque minatur,	410	Lucus 2	1
MINAX			
Vtque minax superetur Aegis?	433	Poem.Lat.	12
MINENTUR			
Quid metuant homines infra, supraue minentur	413	Lucus 16	1
MINERUAE			
Vt mucro rumpatur Mineruae,	433	Poem.Lat.	11
MINERUAM			
Effluxisse dies, suffocatamue Mineruam,	426	Mem.Matr.7	18

	PAGE	TITLE	LINE
MINIMA			
Minima contentos nocte Britannos.	451	Orationes	20
MINIMAM			
Nos etiam haud minimam fauoris tui partem speramus, orantes	468	Epistolae	20
MINIME			
minimeque omnium coelestiores animi, quorum pietatis interest	445	Orationes	10
MINISTER			
Dum te vel digitis minister vrget,	417	Lucus 30	1
Haec vbi iuncta, subit viuo cum fune minister,	420	Tr.Mortis	66
Haec vbi vincta, subit viuo cum fune minister,	271	Tr.Mortis VS	66
MINISTRI			
accidere potest, quam vt ministri Regis Catholici ad nos accedant?	440	Orationes	14
MINISTRORUM			
Supplicum Ministrorum raptus komoidoumenos.	398	Musae 32	T
MINISTROS			
autem vt foelicitas tantorum Principum etiam in ministros redundet,	441	Orationes	6
MINOR			
Ingluuieque minor. Quercus habitare feruntur	418	Tr.Mortis	5
Poena minor fuerat, quam fatum Principis aegrum?	432	Poem.Lat.	21
MINORA			
Minora fiunt omnia:	388	Musae 8	14
MINOREM			
Aetatis numerum supplebit causa minorem:	386	Musae 2	3
Qualis eras, qui, ne melior natura minorem	407	Passio 14	1
MINORI			
communicans coelum ac terram minori quam cernimus interuallo	444	Orationes	7
Authoritate tua plurima & Eloquentia non minori nobis obstrue.	463	Epistolae	2
noluitque vt minori sphaera quam pro latitudine meritorum tuorum	466	Epistolae	14
MINUS			
Vitro minus recte vteris.	388	Musae 8	18
Ah! Cheiragra vetat, quo minus, inquit, agam.	389	Musae 11	2
Quo dictis minus acribus notetur.	391	Musae 15	6
Cui tenuis fama est, ingeniumque minus.	435	Poem.Lat.	4
quanto minus tacebunt lusciniae nostrae disertae, minimeque omnium	445	Orationes	9
& polymiti, vt si minus id assequantur, quod primum intendunt,	446	Orationes	6
neque enim minus refert, qualis quaeque sit mater, e qua liberi	447	Orationes	10
incubat artibus, & obstetricatur, minus quam par est, aestimemus.	448	Orationes	33
cum quanto plus possint in sua terra, tanto minus in aliena.	450	Orationes	12
non minus vitae inaequalitas delectat, quam terrae, quam Natura	453	Orationes	11
vt si officia nostra minus respondeant magnitudini beneficiorum,	460	Epistolae	15
Vt nihilo-minus Tibi luceat, cum nobis accenderit.	461	Epistolae	5
Quod quidem non minus expectamus a Te, quem singularis doctrina	461	Epistolae	25
etiam Fluuium non minus de praeterito gratum, quam de futuro	465	Epistolae	7
vero de hoc tuo progressu non minus Reipublicae gratulamur quam tibi,	466	Epistolae	15
quo minus exteris Libris indigeremus, sed tamen comparatio	467	Epistolae	25
nec minus etiam Reipublicae, quam nunc pleno gradu ingrediens	468	Epistolae	18
per me non stabit quo minus, spe prouecta atque adulta,	470	Epistolae	8
MIRA			
Quam mira tandem Subleuatrix pauperum!	423	Mem.Matr.2	45
MIRABERIS			
Frustra itaque in tot funeribus miraberis vnum,	415	Lucus 23	11
MIRABILE			
Si tibi non illud placeat mirabile corpus,	404	Passio 2	3
MIRABILES			
machinas conficiunt ad defensionem Reipublicae mirabiles:	454	Orationes	6
MIRABILIUS			
neque enim quicquam hoc itinere mirabilius, cuius tamen fructum omnem	450	Orationes	2
MIRACULIS			
vt miraculis vestris nostra occurrant, oratio nostra est silentium,	444	Orationes	2
MIRANDUM			
Quamobrem non est mirandum, si Reges ipsi quandoque suauitates suas	453	Orationes	18
MIRANTUR			
Nam saxa mirantur canentes,	393	Musae 23	7
Vicini populi passim mirantur, & aequos	401	Musae 39	8
MIRARI			
nunquam intueri satis vel mirari possumus, nimirum infinitum	449	Orationes	35
Quanquam non mirari non possumus, vnde fit vt nullus fere elabatur	461	Epistolae	13
MIRATAE			
Hinc te olim gentes miratae odere vicissim;	416	Lucus 25	11
MIRATUR			
Miratur aequor finitimum sonos,	394	Musae 23	41
MIRE			
Sententiae cum voce mire conuenit,	423	Mem.Matr.2	37
quotidie transnatantes, litora nostra atque aures mire circumsonant.	441	Orationes	4
MIRETUR			
Perstringas homines vultu, miretur vt orbis	211	Cam.1613-b BR	13
MIRIFICAM			
O, mirificam Clementiam! Aedificarunt olim nobis Serenissimi Reges	458	Epistolae	21
MIRIFICE			
hoc Principe, in quo doctrinae fructus atque vsus mirifice relucet.	469	Epistolae	23
MIRO			
Tu Diua miro pollice spiritum	394	Musae 23	25
MIRUM			
Quid? hoccine est mirum? Viatores sumus.	393	Musae 22	2
Qui silicem tundit, (mirum tamen) elicit ignem:	410	Lucus 3	1
Vtrumque mirum est: hoc tamen mirum magis,	412	Lucus 11	2
MIRUS			
vtrinque mirus es et exercitatissimus.	462	Epistolae	22
MISCE			
Affectusque mei similem; nec languida misce	427	Mem.Matr.7	30

	PAGE	TITLE	LINE
MISCET			
Cum citharis lituisque miscet.	394	Musae 23	40
Iam Ccnstartinus multo se milite miscet;	398	Musae 33	15
MISCETUR			
Miscetur vento, accendit cum fcmite partem	271	Tr.Mortis VS	68
MISCUISTI			
doctrinae nitoremque spirans purpuram et eruditionem miscuisti;	461	Epistclae	22
MISCUIT			
Conferte lacrymas: Illa, quae vcs miscuit	422	Mem.Matr.2	3
Vinumque felle miscuit.	427	Mem.Matr.8	4
MISER			
Contemplare, miser, quantum terrcris haberet	417	Lucus 31	5
MISERAE			
Annon longa fames miseraeque iniuria pestis	432	Poem.Lat.	20
MISERAS			
Ridens Bcmbardas miseras, quae ccrpora perdunt	420	Tr.Mcrtis	97
MISERAT			
Vna dies Catharos ad bellum miserat cmnes:	399	Musae 33	31
MISERE			
Tu spina misere pungeris, ipse Rcsa.	405	Passio 6	2
Nos misere flemus, sclesque obducimus almos	427	Mem.Matr.9	5
aut enim misere fallimur, aut tantum de nullo vnquam Filio Alma	457	Epistolae	25
MISERI			
Qua sine vos miseri lentius itis ope.	399	Musae 33	26
Heu miseri! Quis tantum ipsis virtutibus instat	419	Tr.Mcrtis	33
MISERIAS			
Ecquid nescitis miserias Belli? consulite historias;	449	Orationes	2
bellique miserias gratas, praecipue vbi velut ex continentibus tectis	449	Oraticnes	13
MISERIOR			
vbi in dubio est, qui facit, an qui patitur, miserior.	449	Oraticnes	11
MISERIS			
quae miseris clypec	396	Musae 28	5
MISEROS			
Qui dulci miseros irradiabit ope.	387	Musae 7	10
miseros nos; nunquam frigidiorem aestatem sensimus;	450	Orationes	37
MISERUM			
Exercet miserum; non dolor vnguium	403	Musae 40	4
Galene, frustra es, cur miserum premens	425	Mem.Matr.6	1
Iam vero miserum est, pecuniam retardare illam, cui natura spiritum	468	Epistclae	4
MISSIS			
Vos ducibus missis, missis doctoribus, cmnes	387	Musae 5	9
MISSOS			
Ad bellum missos perdidit vna dies.	399	Musae 33	32
MISSURUS			
Plura tibi missurus eram (nam quae mihi laurus,	428	Mem.Matr.9	15
MITEM			
Nunc redit ad mitem, ceu benedicta, Deum.	390	Musae 12	16
MITES			
Mites acciperent Lampada Praesules,	391	Musae 17	5
quod nonnullae familiae semper mites essent, vti Valerij,	447	Oraticnes	20
MITHRIDATES			
esti me perimenein, ote polemein umin omologesei, dixit Mithridates.	449	Orationes	15
MITIS			
Mitis agas: tenerae duplicant sibi verbera mentes,	406	Passio 9	5
MITTAM			
Nam vt educationem liberorum mittam, qua in re celebris est	447	Orationes	16
MITTAMUS			
Verum mittamus inuidos & inuidiam, quae semper se deuorat primum,	454	Orationes	14
MITTE			
Quin, mitte nugas; teque carnem & sanguinem	413	Lucus 17	5
MITTIT			
Hoc, Genitrix, scriptum proles tibi sedula mittit.	427	Mem.Matr.9	1
MIXTA			
Lepos seuerus, Pallas mixta Gratijs;	423	Mem.Matr.2	30
MIXTAM			
& quasi mixtam personam reddidit quam si Episcopi more pristino	461	Epistolae	27
MIXTAS			
Vestrasque laudes, poscit & mixtas genas.	422	Mem.Matr.2	4
MOBILITATE			
Lubricus, & superans mobilitate salum.	428	Mem.Matr.11	8
MODERATUR			
Eripe coelesti qui moderatur aquae.	396	Musae 26	4
incomparabilem, quae eodem vultu et moderatur mundum et nos respicit.	458	Epistclae	4
MODESTAM			
Quin post modestam, qualis integras decet,	422	Mem.Matr.2	14
MODESTE			
quando ad magnates cogitas, stylo vtare, sed modeste grandi;	470	Epistclae	22
MODESTIAM			
Carpsit malignum sydus hanc modestiam	427	Mem.Matr.8	3
effari, non licet per multitudinem, imo per modestiam vestram?	443	Orationes	29
MODI			
Mulceat, imbelles complacuere modi.	387	Musae 5	12
MODO			
Non alio Cathari modo	395	Musae 25	8
Se per se facili modo scientes,	415	Lucus 24	14
Quo Te, foelix Anna, modo deflere licebit?	435	Poem.Lat.	1
quamlibet Magnum, modo detis eum in flore, in vagina, in herbescenti	445	Orationes	20
MODUM			
Sic omnibus videris ad modum visus.	406	Passio 12	4
Caelique referunt & praeoccupant modum.	423	Mem.Matr.2	49
administrans, distribuendi modum omnem rationemque callet?	464	Epistolae	15

	PAGE	TITLE		LINE
MODUS				
Calumniarum nec pudor quis nec modus?	397	Musae 30		1
MOENIA				
Moenia contribuere Thebis.	394	Musae 23		16
Et quae corrumpit moenia, murus aqua est.	411	Lucus 6		6
MOERORE				
In flumen moerore nigrum si funderer ardens,	422	Mem.Matr.1		5
MOI				
Dokei moi xrenai para ton presbuton punthanesthai, osper tina odon	471	Epistolae		9
MOLA				
Atque ipsi sibi sunt mola & farina.	415	Lucus 24		15
MOLAE				
Et nostrae tribuant molae farinam,	415	Lucus 24		5
MOLEM				
Quare quomodo alij molem hanc laetitiae suae exprimant,	457	Epistolae		1
omniumque Artium molem et pondus sustinere, sed perspectissimus tuus	465	Epistolae		10
MOLES				
Quasque habet aut patulas, aut caeco tramite, moles	402	Musae 39		21
Sic Hominis moles animaque & corpore constat,	417	Lucus 31		3
Si-quas mens agitet moles (dum pectora saeuo	432	Poem.Lat.		9
MOLESTA				
absque molesta aliorum ac frigida commendatione, si huc reciderit	472	Epistolae		14
MOLESTIA				
nos audiamus summo cum gaudio ea Maiestas vestra summa cum molestia?	444	Orationes		1
MOLESTIAM				
memoriam recolenti, quam cogitanti noua, improbe molestiam creent.	457	Epistolae		14
MOLIANTUR				
vt semper post nouas dignitates, alias tibi quaerant et moliantur.	464	Epistolae		24
MOLIRI				
Librarios omnia transmarina scripta ad monopolium reuocare moliri,	467	Epistolae		21
MOLIS				
Corporeae fluidaeque molis?	425	Mem.Matr.6		4
MOLITA				
Molita, reliquum deinde garriens diem	422	Mem.Matr.2		12
MOLLIA				
Ipsaque sunt ferulae mollia corda suae.	406	Passio 9		6
MOLLICULUS				
tanquam flos molliculus rudiore Centurionis manu tactus flaccescit.	448	Orationes		25
MOLLIENS				
Adde his trientem Musices, quae molliens	423	Mem.Matr.2		42
MOLLISSIMIS				
tanquam onera, circumferuntur mollissimis lecticis, indicantes,	452	Orationes		11
MOLOSSORUM				
Iisque siccis adeo vt os Molossorum	429	Mem.Matr.12		3
MOMENTA				
operam nobis omnia fautorum tuorum momenta apicesque perpensuris	466	Epistolae		8
MOMENTI				
Nihil habet humana vita maioris momenti aut ponderis, quam Nuptiae,	446	Orationes		17
MONACHOS				
Quis Monachos mortem meditari, & puluere tristi	420	Tr.Mortis		92
Quis mortem Monachos meditari, et puluere tristi	272	Tr.Mortis	VS	92
MONACHUM				
Congrediens genuit Monachum, qui limen opacae	420	Tr.Mortis		89
MONARCHA				
Augustissime Monarcha, Si per haec ludicra nostra pars aliquis eius	443	Orationes		8
MONARCHAE				
Augustissimo Potentissimoque Monarchae	384	Musae		T
MONERET				
Extruxissem, vbi, cum moneret vsus,	401	Musae 37		29
MONON				
Toide para tumboi dizeo, phile, monon.	429	Mem.Matr.14		2
Rheggode monon, os eikos, epaulin exei.	429	Mem.Matr.14		4
MONOPOLIJS				
legibus et hominum summe contraria est) monopolijs quibusdam inhiare,	467	Epistolae		6
MONOPOLIUM				
Librarios omnia transmarina scripta ad monopolium reuocare moliri,	467	Epistolae		21
MONS				
Dic mihi, mons sterilis, vallis an vber eris?	413	Lucus 18		2
Quare adsis Princeps, aliis Academia mons sit,	210	Cam.1613-a	BR	7
MONSTRUM				
Ad eundem In Monstrum vocabuli Anti-Tami-Cami-Categoria.	386	Musae 3		T
Dicite, vos Furiae, qua gaudet origine Monstrum.	420	Tr.Mortis		85
Dicite vos Stutiae, qua gaudet origine monstrum	272	Tr.Mortis	VS	85
Protulit horrendum hoc primus cum puluere monstrum.	420	Tr.Mortis		91
Protulit horrendum hoc primum cum puluere monstrum.	420	Tr.Mortis	V	91
MONTE				
Nec vaga de summo deducam flumina monte,	432	Poem.Lat.		7
vt qui hic in Musarum monte editissimo, in ipso Parnasso siti sumus,	449	Orationes		33
MONTES				
Sic quasi Dijs certem, magnos accersere montes:	432	Poem.Lat.		6
Spiritus, hi mihi iam montes, haec flumina sunto.	432	Poem.Lat.		11
cuius libri si alij alijs (tanquam montes olim) imponerentur,	467	Epistolae		30
MONTIBUS				
Et saxa diris hispida montibus	394	Musae 23		13
quam Natura montibus vallibusque sublimitate atque humilitate	453	Orationes		12
MONUMENTA				
Monumenta aperta.	407	Passio 17		T
MORA				
Roma. Anagr. Oram. Maro. / Ramo. Armo. / Mora. Amor.	416	Lucus 25		T
Quin tibi tam desperatae MORA nulla medetur,	416	Lucus 25		9
Quin tibi jam desperatae MORA nulla medetur,	416	Lucus 25	V	9

	PAGE	TITLE	LINE
MORAMUR			
Sed non moramur: namque vestra crux erit,	389	Musae 10	10
MORANTE			
Incendat tacitas, sole morante, faces:	211	Cam.1613-b BR	6
MORANTES			
Ecce solutura est, ventos causata morantes:	427	Mem.Matr.9	9
MORBI			
Vt morbi perimant, alicque in puluere prostet?	433	Poem.Lat.	35
Dum longi lentique gemis sub pondere morbi	438	Poem.Lat.	1
MORDACES			
Mordaces tineas, nigrasque blattas,	385	Musae	5
MORDACIBUS			
Dicterijs mordacibus notans, clamas	392	Musae 20	13
MORDACIUS			
Aut vt pruna gelu summo mordacius vrit,	399	Musae 35	5
MORDEAM			
Matrine linguam refero, solum vt mordeam?	424	Mem.Matr.2	59
MORE			
Quam (more vestro) imponere inscio vulgo.	397	Musae 31	3
Vincit more suo Noster: nam millibus Infans	437	Poem.Lat.	3
Vicit more suo Noster: nam millibus Infans	437	Poem.Lat. V	3
quam non longe abeam Oratorum more, qui nullum non angulum verrunt	445	Orationes	36
reddidit quam si Episcopi more pristino Cancellis praeficerentur.	461	Epistolae	27
protinus tanquam Nobilem Filium (more nostro) Magistrum Artium	463	Epistolae	8
Quod si oppidani nostri (more suo) Musarum iura et diplomata	468	Epistolae	26
more maiorum, multos iam annos Anglice viuens garriensque.	470	Epistolae	4
MORERIS			
Dum moreris, Mea Vita, ipsi vixere sepulti,	407	Passio 17	1
Tu tamen, haud tibi tam moreris, quam viuis in illis,	407	Passio 17	3
Non moreris solus: Mundus simul interit in te,	409	Passio 21	1
MORES			
Inuertis, mores carpis & obloqueris:	416	Lucus 26	2
MORI			
Cum per te sit res ambitiosa mori.	435	Poem.Lat.	8
Constat, Aprile vno te potuisse mori:	438	Poem.Lat.	4
MORIAR			
Quin moriar tecum: vitam, quam negligis ipse,	434	Poem.Lat.	5
MORIENTEM			
Ad Dominum morientem.	404	Passio 1	T
MORITUR			
Vel quia tot moritur, tot viguisse probes.	415	Lucus 23	8
MORITURA			
Haud per te moritura, Scholamque introspicis omnem.	402	Musae 39	26
MOROSA			
etenim abundantia morosa est & sternax, vnde diuites syluas ac saltus	450	Orationes	20
MOROSUS			
Morosus, oxygala est: leuis, coagulum.	414	Lucus 20	15
MORS			
Mors semper iuuenem, senem Britanni.	385	Musae	11
Vt, cum mors rabidis vnguibus imminens	391	Musae 17	3
Asserit & vitam Mors animata tuam.	407	Passio 17	4
Nunc primum socij mors foret atra tui?	415	Lucus 23	2
Hinc tamen excludi mors noluit, ipsaque vitam	271	Tr.Mortis VS	7
Qua Mors ipsa sedens hominum de gente triumphat.	419	Tr.Mortis	56
Alteraque haec tua mors, Ilias esto mihi.	428	Mem.Matr.11	14
Aut cita mors est danda bonis aut longa senectus:	432	Poem.Lat.	30
Tempus edax rerum, tuque o mors improba sola es,	433	Poem.Lat.	41
Mors tot virorum sordida sanguine,	433	Poem.Lat.	10
Christe, duplex fiet mors tua vita mihi:	434	Poem.Lat.	8
MORSUS			
Morsus increpat anxios;	403	Musae 40	5
MORTALIBUS			
quis crederet mortalibus	396	Musae 28	3
Imperij hic culmen figo: mortalibus actum est	421	Tr.Mortis	100
MORTALITATIS			
positum extra mortalitatis aleam, et quo magis Tuum agnoscas,	459	Epistolae	11
MORTALIUM			
retulisset captus piscis, foelicissimus mortalium habitus est.	444	Orationes	16
sic existimes nihil Mortalium firmiori flagrare in Te desiderio,	473	Epistolae	4
MORTE			
Morte magis viduabor illa.	425	Mem.Matr.6	12
MORTEM			
Viuat, & in mortem vita sit illa tuam.	405	Passio 7	10
Glans dedit, & truncus tectum, & ramalia mortem.	418	Tr.Mortis	8
Nec Glans sola nocet; mortem quandoque susurrat	420	Tr.Mortis	83
Quis Monachos mortem meditari, & puluere tristi	420	Tr.Mortis	92
Quis mortem Monachos meditari, et puluere tristi	272	Tr.Mortis VS	92
Triumphus Christiani. In Mortem.	421	Lucus 33	T
Viuite, dum mortem ostendam: sic tempora vestram	432	Poem.Lat.	15
Fructusque post mortem recusent	434	Poem.Lat.	31
hac re solum vlciscimur mortem, ligantes abruptum vitae filum,	446	Orationes	22
MORTES			
Et numerat mortes singula gutta pares;	415	Lucus 23	10
MORTI			
Non placuit rudis atque ignara occisio: Morti	418	Tr.Mortis	24
Non placuit rudis atque ignara occasio; morti	271	Tr.Mortis VS	24
MORTIS			
Nos autem, a cunis, omnes sententia Mortis	415	Lucus 23	3
Triumphus Mortis.	418	Tr.Mortis	T
O mortis longaeua fames, venterque perennis	271	Tr.Mortis VS	1
Sanguine, quem dederat, spolians. Primordia Mortis	418	Tr.Mortis	22

MORTIS (cont'd)	PAGE	TITLE	LINE
Artificesque necis clueant, & mortis alumni.	418	Tr.Mortis	30
Nec tamen hic mortis rabies stetit; exilit omni	272	Tr.Mortis VS	95
Cur tela Mortis vel tibi vel tuis	433	Poem.Lat.	5
MORTUA			
Quo placet oblato, mortua fertur, hero:	428	Mem.Matr.11	4
Pulchre renatam ex arbore mortua,	434	Poem.Lat.	34
MORTUUS			
Cespes viuus, Homo; mortuus, Ara fuit:	417	Lucus 29	2
MORUM			
quid enim vtilius quam ex obseruatione exterarum Legum ac morum,	450	Orationes	15
MOS			
Vt postulat mos; quid tuis dabis? Teipsum.	406	Passio 10	3
MOSAICAE			
Post vbi Mosaicae repararent fragmina Leges,	408	Passio 20	3
MOSES			
Ardore Moses concitus enthec,	394	Musae 23	29
MOST			
of Winchester, one of the Kings most honorable privy-Counsaile.	473	Epistolae	24
MOTA			
Ne, si flamma nouis adolescat mota flabellis,	399	Musae 35	11
MOTU			
Nempe graui fertur scelerata pecunia motu,	410	Lucus 4	7
coelestis an sublunaris, sed quae signa, quo motu transeat.	454	Orationes	13
MOTUS			
Terrae-motus.	408	Passio 18	T
Sitque omnis motus nescia tanta quies,	424	Mem.Matr.3	8
Deridet motus sancta catena tuos.	438	Poem.Lat.	9
MOUEAT			
cauendum ne id nobis nauseam moueat, aut tanquam oues taedulae	449	Orationes	1
MOUENT			
Quas Latij Catharique mouent, atque inter vtrasque	402	Musae 39	31
MOUERIS			
Tuque super nostras, Christe, moueris aquas.	411	Lucus 6	8
MOUET			
Te fixo vel Terra mouet: nam, cum Cruce, totam	408	Passio 18	1
MOUNOIS			
Pneuma, biou parodon mounois epeessi metresan.	431	Mem.Matr.17	23
MOUNTEG			
9. Ad Mounteg., Thesaurar. Gratulatio	464	Epistolae	T
MOX			
Mox displicent omnes. Vbi hoc permanserit	398	Musae 32	4
MUCRO			
Vt mucro rumpatur Mineruae,	433	Poem.Lat.	11
MUCRONATAM			
Sic mucronatam reddunt suspiria mentem,	410	Lucus 2	3
MUCRONEM			
ferox spumantia mandit, iuuat micare gladio & mucronem intueri.	447	Orationes	35
MUGIRE			
Mugire multo mauelim quam rudere.	395	Musae 24	2
MUGITUS			
Cantus sacros, profane, mugitus vocas?	395	Musae 24	1
MULCEAT			
Mulceat, imbelles complacuere modi.	387	Musae 5	12
MULCENS			
Mulcensque dotes caeteras visa est quasi	423	Mem.Matr.2	43
MULCETUR			
Mulcetur vento, accendit cum fomite partem	420	Tr.Mortis	68
MULCTAUERIT			
Vtrumque sexum dote ne mulctauerit.	422	Mem.Matr.2	9
MULIER			
Sic vbi iam mulier decerpti conscia pomi	390	Musae 12	13
MULIERES			
ipsae mulieres inelegantes, nulla pulchritudo per vniuersam	451	Orationes	16
MULIERUM			
Decus mulierum perijt: & metuunt viri	422	Mem.Matr.2	8
MULTA			
Conuincunt vnam multa sepulcra Crucem.	408	Passio 17	6
Quin Aries ruit, & multa Demetrius arte:	419	Tr.Mortis	47
Tamque aries ruit et multa Demetrius arte,	271	Tr.Mortis VS	47
multa Critt mec quadrabunt, quae almae matri inconcinna erunt atque	470	Epistolae	14
MULTI			
multi Academias integras subuersas volunt, neque illi e faece vulgi	461	Epistolae	16
MULTIPLEX			
Quare multiplex est laetitia nostra:	463	Epistolae	20
MULTIPLICARE			
Quam tribuit, verum multiplicare decet.	408	Passio 17	8
MULTIPLICEM			
Quare & Principis iter multiplicem nobis exhibet prudentiam;	446	Orationes	8
MULTIPLICES			
finesque multiplices & polymiti, vt si minus id assequantur,	446	Orationes	5
MULTIS			
Aetna Cacum igniuomum dedit, hic Ixiona multis	420	Tr.Mortis	87
vnam actionem e multis seligam, quam vobis amplectendam	445	Orationes	32
MULTITUDINEM			
effari, non licet per multitudinem, imo per modestiam vestram?	443	Orationes	29
Aspicis multitudinem Librorum indies gliscentem, praesertim	467	Epistolae	29
MULTO			
Mugire multo mauelim quam rudere.	395	Musae 24	2
Iam Constantinus multo se milite miscet;	398	Musae 33	15
Pagina, gustasti, multoque interprete gaudes:	402	Musae 39	24

MULTO (cont'd)	PAGE	TITLE	LINE
Habui viaticum fauoris Tui, quod longiori multo itineri sufficeret.	471	Epistolae	19
MULTOS			
more maiorum, multos iam annos Anglice viuens garriensque.	470	Epistolae	4
MULTUM			
Illa quidem a nostro non multum abludit imago,	396	Musae 26	5
aetate prouectior, etiam anus subsultans multum excitet pulueris:	454	Orationes	36
ne tum quidem multum, neque nostrae matronae conuenit, cui tu es ab	471	Epistolae	2
MUNDA			
Corde tuo forsan, caetera munda, SOFOR.	413	Lucus 15	6
MUNDANIS			
De Mundis & mundanis.	396	Musae 27	T
MUNDE			
Munde, fluas fugiasque licet, nos nostraque fixi:	438	Poem.Lat.	8
MUNDI			
Innocuae mentes, quibus inter flumina mundi	400	Musae 36	1
Intuituque vno stringens habitacula mundi,	402	Musae 39	12
Christe, flagellati spes & victoria mundi,	406	Passio 9	1
Hic, vbi sanati stillant opobalsama mundi,	406	Passio 13	1
Mundi fidelis clauiger:	407	Passio 16	4
In Mundi sympathiam cum Christo.	409	Passio 21	T
Hunc ponas animam mundi, Plato: vel tua mundum	409	Passio 21	3
Progenies, mundique aetas abdomine nostro	418	Tr.Mortis	4
Progenies, mundique aetas abdomine tanto	418	Tr.Mortis V	4
Diffugiunt, fragilisque crepant coenacula mundi.	420	Tr.Mortis	78
Mundique & Animarum sacerdos vnicus;	436	Poem.Lat.	24
qui mundi oculos perstringat, nos tam defecimus in vtroque quam	441	Orationes	12
Deus ipse cum crearet hominem, mundi regem, consilio vsus est.	446	Orationes	36
tanquam ligna obliqua, aliter magna haec mundi domus corrueret:	450	Orationes	29
Ecquid inter tantas mundi trepidationes nobis & Musis vacas?	458	Epistolae	2
MUNDIS			
De Mundis & mundanis.	396	Musae 27	T
MUNDO			
Sic toti medicaris ipse mundo.	405	Passio 8	3
Deerat adhuc vitijs hominum dignissima mundo	419	Tr.Mortis	49
Deerat adhuc vitijs nostris dignissima mundo	271	Tr.Mortis VS	49
Strepente mundo tinnulis praeconijs?	423	Mem.Matr.2	56
In vicium mundo sterili, cui cedo cometas	426	Mem.Matr.7	20
MUNDUM			
Hunc ponas animam mundi, Plato: vel tua mundum	409	Passio 21	3
Illos, qui mundum circumiere, pedes.	412	Lucus 8	4
incomparabilem, quae eodem vultu et moderatur mundum et nos respicit.	458	Epistolae	4
MUNDUS			
Ante diem vestro mundus ab igne ruat.	399	Musae 35	12
Non moreris solus: Mundus simul interit in te,	409	Passio 21	1
Ira facit, mundusque ipse est apotheca furoris.	418	Tr.Mortis	17
bello pacem, sine qua omnis vita procella, & mundus solitudo.	448	Orationes	8
& metalla ei inserendo, aliter mundus iam diu fuisset deuoratus.	452	Orationes	25
mutus est mundus vniuersus, vestra solum dextra (quamuis a scriptione	458	Epistolae	5
MUNERE			
Munere, Rex tanto verior inde prober.	405	Passio 7	4
Munere dum nobis prodes, Libroque futuris,	435	Poem.Lat.	1
Munere dum nobis prodes, Libroque remotis,	435	Poem.Lat.	3
MUNERI			
Quod si forense quippiam nos spectans, dum incumbis muneri, occurrat,	466	Epistolae	5
maius tamen piaculum reor, deesse publico muneri, quam priuato,	472	Epistolae	31
MUNERIBUS			
cum grauibus duobus muneribus fungar apud Meos, Rhetoris in hunc	472	Epistolae	25
MUNIENDIS			
quam de muniendis contra grassantes flammas aedificijs Honori Tuo	457	Epistolae	18
MUNIENTES			
gloriae titulos caput vndique munientes meministi Magistrum Te esse	456	Epistolae	2
MUNIFICENTIAE			
enim impetus animi celeritatem tantae munificentiae assequi potest?	460	Epistolae	4
MUNITIONES			
apparatus, foedera, munitiones, aeque ac nostra spectari debent:	450	Orationes	27
MUNITUS			
Hac ope munitus securior excipis vndas,	402	Musae 39	30
MUNUS			
Comparatio inter Munus Summi Cancellariatus et Librum.	435	Poem.Lat.	T
MURI			
Praecipitata; cadunt vrbes, formidine muri	420	Tr.Mortis	77
MURMUR			
Quos tu rotatus, quale murmur auscultas	392	Musae 20	1
MURMURE			
Ipse tuae solum adnectam, sine murmure, thensae.	426	Mem.Matr.7	16
Iam nunc minaci murmure cornuum	448	Orationes	1
MUROS			
bello, neque intra muros: pace, auium cantus expergefacit;	448	Orationes	11
MURUS			
Et quae corrumpit moenia, murus aqua est.	411	Lucus 6	6
MUSA			
Cum prope sit nobis Musa, Medusa procul?	387	Musae 6	2
Praesulibus dirum te Musa coarguit hostem,	392	Musae 18	1
Atque edentula Musa, nec veneno	400	Musae 37	12
Et Musa crepitante subruissem:	400	Musae 37	20
Squaloremque togae candida Musa fugat.	417	Lucus 28	6
Rure, sibi dixit Musa fuisse probro.	431	Mem.Matr.19	2
Eia, agedum scribo: vicisti, Musa; sed audi,	431	Mem.Matr.19	7
Musa, vale, & tu Phoebe; dolor mea carmina dictet;	432	Poem.Lat.	12

MUSAE	PAGE	TITLE	LINE
Georgii Herbertii Angli Musae Responsoriae	384	Musae	T
Nostrae etiam Musae vile fuere lutum:	384	Musae	4
Haurirent tibi tota plaustra Musae.	401	Musae 37	30
Ite leues (irquam), Parnassia numina, Musae,	432	Poem.Lat.	1
Pieridis Latiaeque Musae,	433	Poem.Lat.	4
Hic habitant Musae, facilisque in carmine Pallas,	210	Cam.1613-a BR	3
accessionem summe gratulantur Excellentijs Vestris Musae omnes,	440	Orationes	7
qui vtrumque curasti, vt neque sitirent Musae, neque flagrarent.	457	Epistolae	20
MUSAEUM			
causaris, irruit Miles in Musaeum tuum, & gladio te liberat.	448	Orationes	28
MUSARUM			
Musarum calices, per & beatos	400	Musae 37	3
vt qui hic in Musarum monte editissimo, in ipso Parnasso siti sumus,	449	Orationes	32
nobis librum, plenissimum Musarum, quae cum olim gauderent Fluuijs,	460	Epistolae	8
tractus (Oceani praeda et deliciae) vt irrigui Musarum horti,	461	Epistolae	9
pulcherrimaeque Musarum domus tanquam viduae effoetae, aut ligna	462	Epistolae	3
qui restinxisti sitim exarescentium Musarum, et Xerxes istos,	462	Epistolae	8
vniuersam Musarum supellectilem, etiam Fluuium non minus de	465	Epistolae	6
si oppidani nostri (more suo) Musarum iura et diplomata arrodant;	468	Epistolae	26
MUSAS			
Musasque coelites, qui posteros libris non liberis quaeritis.	446	Orationes	26
MUSCAS			
Quid si muscas captaret cum Domitiano?	446	Orationes	14
Austriacam familiam, Aquilamque illam, quae non capit muscas.	446	Orationes	16
MUSICA			
De Musica Sacra.	393	Musae 23	T
O plena centum Musica Gratijs,	394	Musae 23	21
Interea ad sacrum stimulat sacra Musica bellum,	399	Musae 33	25
Non iam exaudiri quicquam vel Musica caeli	420	Tr.Mortis	74
Non iam exaudiri quicquam, vel musica sphaerae	271	Tr.Mortis VS	74
Nosse sui quid agant, quaedam est quoque musica sanctis,	427	Mem.Matr.9	3
Corona Musica, qui optimum Principem spe nuptiarum mari nuper	444	Orationes	17
MUSICES			
Adde his trientem Musices, quae molliens	423	Mem.Matr.2	42
MUSIS			
Ceu victa, Musis porrigit herbulas	434	Poem.Lat.	21
pax adeo Musis summe necessaria est, vt sine ea nihil simus.	448	Orationes	16
Dein quid Musis cum tumultu?	448	Orationes	22
Ecquid inter tantas mundi trepidationes nobis & Musis vacas?	458	Epistolae	3
suauiterque patefacta, nunc etiam laborantibus Musis succurrat.	467	Epistolae	3
MUSSITANS			
Paulo, secretis mussitans in angulis	398	Musae 32	5
MUSSITET			
vt nihil habeat Inuidia ipsa, quod contra hiscat aut mussitet.	453	Orationes	24
MUTABITUR			
Daphnen suam, cuius amor deinceps in triumphos & laurus mutabitur.	455	Orationes	11
MUTANT			
vti anguillae, aut si mutant locum, gestantur, tanquam onera,	452	Orationes	10
MUTAS			
Mutas in humanam figuram	393	Musae 23	3
MUTATA			
Mutata? & pro matre mihi phantasma dolosum	426	Mem.Matr.7	3
deperijt, at illa mutata est in arborem triumphantium propriam:	455	Orationes	9
MUTATO			
Nunc ipse scandis, vt labore mutato	406	Passio 12	2
MUTATUM			
Quid non mutatum est? requierunt flumina cursus;	433	Poem.Lat.	43
MUTEMUS			
Spicula mutemus: capias Tu serta Rosarum,	405	Passio 6	3
MUTILATAM			
truncata corpora, mutilatam imaginem Dei, pauxillum vitae,	449	Orationes	4
MUTUS			
Ergo ipse solum mutus atque excors ero	423	Mem.Matr.2	55
mutus est murdus vniuersus, vestra solum dextra (quamuis a scriptione	458	Epistolae	5
MY			
my L. Bishop of Winchester, one of the Kings most honorable	473	Epistolae	23
MYSTERIA			
Nempe Caput Romae es, cuius mysteria velles	416	Lucus 27	3
MYSTES			
Tuum tibi, poeta belle, non mystes,	392	Musae 20	11
N'			
Quid hocce? Psalmos audion'? o dapes!	394	Musae 23	33
Tun' obdis aures, grex noue, barbaras,	395	Musae 23	45
Quantum caedi? adeon' vnam vos pascere vitam,	419	Tr.Mortis	34
Quantum caedi? adeon' vnam nos viuere vitam,	271	Tr.Mortis VS	34
Ain' vero? quanta praedicas? hercle aedepol,	421	Lucus 33	1
Ergon' amauit Princeps? Quippini; homo est, non statua;	446	Orationes	9
adeon' nihili videtur res, Principem omnibus delicijs abundantem,	452	Orationes	3
adeon' es praedo omnis gloriae, vt ne gratitudinis laudem nobis	459	Epistolae	2
NACTA			
Pontificem tandem nacta est sibi Roma poetam:	417	Lucus 28	1
NACTUS			
Sic laudandus erit nactus sublimia Praesul,	387	Musae 7	9
NAM			
Vertas specillum: nam, prout se res habent,	388	Musae 8	17
Nam saxa mirantur canentes,	393	Musae 23	7
Nam si te cuperem secare versu,	400	Musae 37	14
Ni me forte petas; nam quanto indignior ipse,	404	Passio 2	5
Te fixo vel Terra mouet: nam, cum Cruce, totam	408	Passio 18	1
Difficilis esse haud soleo: nam, pol, si forem,	413	Lucus 17	3

NAM (cont'd)	PAGE	TITLE		LINE
(Nam post Babelem linguae adest confusio)	422	Mem.Matr.2		13
Plura tibi missurus eram (nam quae mihi laurus, ...	428	Mem.Matr.9		15
Nam te nunc Ager, Vrbs, & Aula plorant:	428	Mem.Matr.10		8
Nam fata non iustis repugnant	434	Poem.Lat.		27
Vincit more suo Noster: nam millibus Infans	437	Poem.Lat.		3
Vicit more suo Noster: nam millibus Infans	437	Poem.Lat.	V	3
Nam vt educationem liberorum mittam, qua in re celebris est . .	447	Orationes		16
Nam primum tota haec Pieria supellex, charta, calami, codices,	448	Orationes		17
Nam vtramque illam curam insignem, tam de conseruando Fluuio nostro,	457	Epistolae		16
NAMQUE				
Namque aspectibus e tuis vel vnus	384	Musae		4
Sed non moramur: namque vestra crux erit, ...	389	Musae 10		10
Namque haec, iure, cuipiam	395	Musae 25		20
Quam nihil illudis flectens! namque integra posthac . . .	405	Passio 7		5
Et Templi parasite; namque velum	408	Passio 19		2
Rotundus in te: namque si ansatus sies, ...	414	Lucus 20		7
Siste tuum fletum & gemitus: namque imbribus istis	415	Lucus 23		13
Nec tamen excludor: namque vna ex arbore vitam	418	Tr.Mortis		7
Namque hanc ruinam salua Grauitas defleat, ...	422	Mem.Matr.2		5
Namque Annae laudes coelo scribuntur aperto, ...	435	Poem.Lat.		9
NANUM				
Fides gigantem sola, vel facit nanum.	406	Passio 12		5
NANUS				
quantum quidem ego homuncio ac nanus coniectando assequor. . .	453	Orationes		21
NASCENTES				
Nascentes radij fugant, vel acres	385	Musae		8
NASCITUR				
Tranquillus aer nascitur:	396	Musae 27		2
quae semper se deuorat primum, vti vermis nucleum, e quo nascitur;	454	Orationes		15
Si enim in regno vestro Hibernico lignum nascitur permanens,	459	Epistolae		16
NASCOR				
Per te nascor in hunc globum	425	Mem.Matr.4		13
Exemploque tuo nascor in alterum:	425	Mem.Matr.4		14
Cum tu, Christe, cadis, nascor; mentemque ligauit	434	Poem.Lat.		1
NASI				
Te mille nasi, mille rideant sinus.	414	Lucus 20		10
NASO				
Euentum Naso vidit et admonuit;	399	Musae 33		30
Omnia suspendit naso, sociosque lacessit:	418	Tr.Mortis		13
NASUM				
Haec facit ad nasum sola loquela tuum.	391	Musae 16		6
NATA				
Qua Fabio quondam sub duce nata salus.	416	Lucus 25		10
Innupta Pallas, nata Diespitre, ...	433	Poem.Lat.		1
NATALES				
In Natales et Pascha Concurrentes.	434	Poem.Lat.		T
NATALIBUS				
Atque vbi per te sanctificer natalibus ipsis, ...	434	Poem.Lat.		9
Securique errorum; inque Natalibus	437	Poem.Lat.	V	25
NATARE				
Natare sine clarissima potest cruce?	389	Musae 10		9
NATET				
Fluctibus internis exagitata natet, ...	389	Musae 12		4
Cum natet in tantis caetera terra malis?	411	Lucus 6		2
NATIONES				
tanquam catenam, qua dissitas nationes ac superbas constringeret.	450	Orationes		24
NATIONUM				
Dux Nationum; veritatis Pontifex;	436	Poem.Lat.	V	3
NATO				
Nato parentis auferens Encomium, ...	423	Mem.Matr.2		53
Nato dolenti: literae hoc debent tibi	424	Mem.Matr.2		62
NATUM				
Vberaque aerea hiscentem fallentia natum?	426	Mem.Matr.7		4
O me disparibus natum cum numine fatis!	434	Poem.Lat.		3
NATURA				
Qualis eras, qui, ne melior natura minorem	407	Passio 14		1
Vt natura omnis suos habet anteambulones, vnde pluuia futura,	445	Orationes		4
diuisit Natura suas dotes, vt indigentia singularum regionum omnes	450	Orationes		19
Quamobrem optime consuluit gentibus natura, cum paupertatem daret	450	Orationes		23
quam Natura montibus vallibusque sublimitate atque humilitate	453	Orationes		11
Amat varietatem Natura omnis, flores, animalia, tum maxime homo,	453	Orationes		16
Sic a Natura comparatum est, Ignis et Virtus semper ascendunt,	466	Epistolae		10
cui natura spiritum dederit feracem gloriae, et coeleste ingenium	468	Epistolae		5
NATURAE				
Viscera naturae, commistusque omnibus astris	402	Musae 39		28
Naturae Aruspex intimus; Philosophiae	436	Poem.Lat.		7
Faxit Deus vt quos profectus feceris in Sphaera Naturae, . .	464	Epistolae		3
spectantes (quae res et naturae legibus et hominum summe contraria	467	Epistolae		5
NATURALIBUS				
Securis errorum; inque Naturalibus	437	Poem.Lat.		25
NATURAM				
cum leunculum & dominum suum contra naturam adoriantur: . . .	454	Orationes		18
NAUFRAGIJ				
Naufragij causa est alijs mare, roboris Anglo, ...	411	Lucus 6		5
NAUIBUS				
Gulielmus Victor descensurus primum e nauibus in terram hanc,	455	Orationes		3
NAULO				
Aurea pro naulo lingua Charontis erit.	414	Lucus 22		4
NAUNT				
10. Ad R. Naunt. Burgen. Elect.	465	Epistolae		T

	PAGE	TITLE	LINE
NAUNTON			
2. Ad R. Naunton Gratiae de Fluuio et de tegendis Tectis stramineis	457	Epistolae	T
6. Ad R. Naunton, Secret. Gratiae de Fluuio	461	Epistolae	T
NAUSEAM			
cauendum ne id nobis nauseam moueat, aut tanquam oues taedulae	449	Orationes	1
NAUTA			
Quare, peritus nauta, vela contrahas,	414	Lucus 20	11
NE			
Ne te productis videar lassare Camoenis,	385	Musae 1	3
Quis hic superbit, oro? tune, an Praesules,	388	Musae 8	1
Ne tandem caput eius impetatis.	391	Musae 15	13
Nihilne respondebimus tibi? Fatemur.	392	Musae 20	16
Tu vero quisquis es, caue ne, dum neges,	397	Musae 28	16
Anne tuas flammas ipsa Antiperistasis auget,	399	Musae 35	3
Ne, si flamma nouis adolescat mota flabellis,	399	Musae 35	11
Ne me carminibus nimis dicacem,	400	Musae 37	10
Sputando, blasphemando? nempe ne hoc fiat	405	Passio 5	5
Christe, fluas semper; ne, si tua flumina cessent,	406	Passio 13	5
Qualis eras, qui, ne melior natura minorem	407	Passio 14	1
Ne nimium vexet quaestio, pone meam.	409	Passio 21	4
Sollicitus, ne te stella perita notet:	413	Lucus 16	4
Ne perdat Leo rugiens vagantem.	417	Lucus 30	8
Cum te non videam, mene videre putas?	421	Lucus 35	8
Tantum istaec scribo gratus, ne tu mihi tantum	422	Mem.Matr.1	7
Vtrumque sexum dote ne mulctauerit.	422	Mem.Matr.2	9
Mihine matris vrna clausa est vnico,	424	Mem.Matr.2	57
Matrine linguam refero, solum vt mordeam?	424	Mem.Matr.2	59
Ne membra culpes, causa animo latet	426	Mem.Matr.6	18
Ora meae memori menti: ne dispare cultu	427	Mem.Matr.7	31
Ne serae meritis tuis venirent.	428	Mem.Matr.10	12
Numne Hydra talis, tantane bellua est	433	Poem.Lat.	9
Respondit: Eia, ne metuas, precor,	434	Poem.Lat.	26
Ah! metuo ne me ad luctus mea fata crearint	437	Poem.Lat. V	11
(Tenere Christum scilicet, ne ascenderet)	438	Poem.Lat.	2
veremur ne nihil hic sit, quod magnitudini praesentiae vestrae	441	Orationes	9
aequumne est vt tot labores & sollicitudines Principum sine	446	Orationes	11
Quare cauendum, ne pacem, quae sola incubat artibus, & obstetricatur,	448	Orationes	32
cauendum ne id nobis nauseam moueat, aut tanquam oues taedulae	448	Orationes	36
incerta sint, & nullis perspicillis, ne Belgicis quidem, assequenda:	449	Orationes	24
essent atque consilijs, sine quibus ne vnum quidem filum torquerent:	449	Orationes	30
Heus, abijtne Noster? miseros nos;	450	Orationes	37
ne literae nostrae animo Tuo tot negotijs meritissime distincto,	457	Epistolae	11
es praedo omnis gloriae, vt ne gratitudinis laudem nobis reliqueris?	459	Epistolae	3
veremur ne non tam sapientes nos, quam obscuros philosophos	460	Epistolae	24
Tandem, ne et ipse peccem, breuis sit sermo, atque pressus.	470	Epistolae	31
ne tum quidem multum, neque nostrae matronae conuenit, cui tu es ab	471	Epistolae	2
NEBULAS			
In nebulas similesque tui res gaudia nunquid	426	Mem.Matr.7	2
NEBULIS			
Sin nebulis parcas, & nostro parcito signo,	396	Musae 26	7
NEC			
Terra nihil, nec quo sanctius astra vident;	385	Musae	2
Sed nec coniugij signum, Melvine, probabis?	396	Musae 26	1
Nec vel tantillum pignus habebit amor?	396	Musae 26	2
Calumniarum nec pudor quis nec modus?	397	Musae 30	1
Nec Vaticanae desines vnquam Lupae	397	Musae 30	2
Nec dextra te fugit, almi Amoris emblema?	397	Musae 31	1
Atque edentula Musa, nec veneno	400	Musae 37	12
Nec transire licet quo mentis acumine findis	402	Musae 39	27
Pro lapsu stillarum abeunt peccata; nec acres	406	Passio 13	3
Nunc Arcana patent, nec inuclutam	408	Passio 19	9
Sanguine: nec precium merx emit vlla suum.	410	Lucus 4	4
Imo, me nec apes, nec astra pungunt:	411	Lucus 5	10
Papae titulus Nec Deus Nec Homo.	412	Lucus 10	T
Nec Deus est nec Homo: Christus vterque fuit.	412	Lucus 10	2
Famamque nec difflaueris, nec suxeris:	414	Lucus 20	12
Quotidie iugulat, nec semel vllus obit.	415	Lucus 23	4
Nec tu pro socio doleas, qui fugit ad illud	415	Lucus 23	15
Nec tamen excludor: namque vna ex arbore vitam	418	Tr.Mortis	7
Materiam vexat: nec iam se continet antro	420	Tr.Mortis	70
Nec Glans sola nocet; mortem quandoque susurrat	420	Tr.Mortis	83
Nec tamen hic noster stetit impetus: exilit omni	420	Tr.Mortis	95
Nec tamen hic mortis rabies stetit; exilit omni	272	Tr.Mortis VS	95
Quid ipse faciam? qui nec arboreas sudes	421	Lucus 33	3
In te, nec arcus, scorpionesue, aut rotas,	421	Lucus 33	4
Alapas nec Arietes? Quid ergo? Agnum & Crucem.	421	Lucus 33	6
Ornastis capulum, nec superesse licet.	425	Mem.Matr.5	2
Euge, perite omnes; nec posthac exeat vlla	425	Mem.Matr.5	11
Nec tarda possunt pharmaca consequi,	425	Mem.Matr.6	6
Nec sic parentem ducar ad optimam:	425	Mem.Matr.6	10
Nec grauidis medicina tuta est.	426	Mem.Matr.6	20
Nec querar ingratos, studijs dum tabidus insto,	426	Mem.Matr.7	17
Affectusque mei similem; nec languida misce	427	Mem.Matr.7	30
Nec cingit mare, nunc inundat omnes.	428	Mem.Matr.10	14
Quin nec potes; cui praebuit Tigris partum.	429	Mem.Matr.12	10
Proinde parco belluis, nec irascor.	429	Mem.Matr.12	11
Sed nec Cyrrhaei saltus Libethriaue arua	432	Poem.Lat.	4
Nec vaga de summo deducam flumina monte,	432	Poem.Lat.	7
Nec hoc aburde est tibi, nisi certae Anchorae	438	Poem.Lat.	5
Nec facile ascendant, sed tibi vallis erit.	210	Cam.1613-a BR	8
Nec qua consuleres, populumve ad bella vocares,	211	Cam.1613-b BR	9

NEC (cont'd)	PAGE	TITLE	LINE
Nec plus te rubeat vesper, Eliza, precor.	211	Cam.1613-b BB	16
nec minus etiam Reipublicae, quam nunc pleno gradu ingrediens	468	Epistolae	18
Quin nec demissc, quando ad magnates cogitas, stylo vtare,	470	Epistolae	21
NECASTI			
At non lusus erit, si quem tu laeta necasti	405	Passio 7	9
NECESSARIA			
pax adeo Musis summe necessaria est, vt sine ea nihil simus.	448	Orationes	17
NECESSARIUM			
Non nego bellum aliquando necessarium esse, bellique miserias gratas,	449	Orationes	12
illud necessarium magis factu, hoc vero longe iucundius,	472	Epistolae	34
NECESSE			
Caetera displiceat turba, necesse, tibi:	404	Passio 2	4
Haud nostro similis, cui necesse,	415	Lucus 24	2
Necesse est autem vt foelicitas tantorum Principum etiam in ministros	441	Orationes	5
Quod si necesse sit iterum exire patria, qui nunc inuenit viam,	455	Orationes	7
NECIS			
Artificesque necis clueant, & mortis alumni.	418	Tr.Mortis	30
NECNE			
Vtrum tenore sacra nostra sint necne	392	Musae 20	5
NECTAR			
Quod nectar, nisi cum te celebrare diem?)	428	Mem.Matr.9	16
NEDUM			
non cor) Tui in me dominij ius imminuere posse, nedum rescindere.	473	Epistolae	7
NEFAS			
Non laudare Deum, credimus esse nefas.	389	Musae 12	8
NEGANT			
Qui tamen in nostros fortiter ire negant.	398	Musae 33	4
NEGANTIBUS			
Vobis fauentibusue, vel negantibus.	389	Musae 10	11
NEGAS			
Cur mihi das vitam, quam tibi, Christe, negas?	434	Poem.Lat.	4
Dure, negas? O fata mihi praesaga doloris,	437	Poem.Lat.	11
NEGAT			
Quamque ipse lucis tesseram sibi negat,	407	Passio 16	7
Negat familiae suae.	407	Passio 16	8
NEGES			
Tu vero quisquis es, caue ne, dum neges,	397	Musae 28	16
NEGET			
Culpa redux iugem te neget esse Deum.	406	Passio 13	6
Versatos neget, atque humiles, queis talis cordi	420	Tr.Mortis	93
NEGLECTAS			
Vitaque neglectas est satis vlta preces.	389	Musae 12	6
NEGLIGENTIAE			
latiusque manare iniustitiae peccatum, quam negligentiae.	472	Epistolae	32
NEGLIGENTIOREM			
neminemque esse sui negligentiorem, quam qui sibi parcat.	452	Orationes	34
NEGLIGIS			
Quin moriar tecum: vitam, quam negligis ipse,	434	Poem.Lat.	5
NEGO			
Non nego bellum aliquando necessarium esse, bellique miserias gratas,	449	Orationes	12
NEGOTIA			
Cum millena tuam pulsare negotia mentem	385	Musae 1	1
neque vlla negotia (quippe quae caput petant, non cor) Tui in me	473	Epistolae	6
NEGOTIJS			
nisi tot negotijs distractus esses, confluueremus omnes ad Aulam,	443	Orationes	26
ne literae nostrae animo Tuo tot negotijs meritissime distincto,	457	Epistolae	11
nunquam in tantis negotijs, quibus meritissime districtus es,	463	Epistolae	18
qui virtutes tuas magnis negotijs pares prouexit, noluitque vt minori	466	Epistolae	13
Obscurus sermo negotijs ineptus; quae cum plerumque implicata sint,	470	Epistolae	29
Nunc obrutus Academicis negotijs, aegre hoc tempus illis succido:	471	Epistolae	20
NEGOTIO			
Aut si negotio hora sumenda est, rei	423	Mem.Matr.2	32
NEGOTIOLIS			
et aeternitate occupatos, temporarijs hisce negotiolis libera.	466	Epistolae	6
NEGOTIUM			
telam explices, perit negotium quasi ex nubibus Ixionis congressus.	470	Epistolae	30
NEIME			
Astrapton, Thuridon os dia, neime selas.	429	Mem.Matr.14	8
NEMINEM			
neminemque esse sui negligentiorem, quam qui sibi parcat.	452	Orationes	34
NEMO			
Et tibi sit nemo praes, vbi poscis opem.	389	Musae 9	16
Quod omnibus tute imperes, nemo tibi.	412	Lucus 11	3
Nemo potest: hodie vita sepulta prior.	415	Lucus 23	6
Culmen, vbi pro te nemo dolere potest.	415	Lucus 23	16
NEMPE			
Nempe Nouatores quis Veteranus amat?	398	Musae 33	14
Sputando, blasphemando? nempe ne hoc fiat	405	Passio 9	9
At nunc fatiscis. Nempe Dominus aedium	407	Passio 16	5
Nempe graui fertur scelerata pecunia motu,	410	Lucus 4	7
Nempe in quo clare lucet Imago Dei.	410	Lucus 4	10
Nempe hic Religio floret, regina quietis,	411	Lucus 6	7
Vt discat sibi quisque, quid vtile: nempe nocebat	412	Lucus 9	3
Nempe Caput Romae es, cuius mysteria velles	416	Lucus 27	3
Nempe es totus amor, medulla amoris,	417	Lucus 30	3
Nempe & millenos ad palum interficit hostes	418	Tr.Mortis	31
(Nempe sepulcra Satis numen inempta dedit.)	425	Mem.Matr.5	14
Nempe huc vsque notos tenebricosos	428	Mem.Matr.10	1
Addas sigillum: nempe Symbolum suae	438	Poem.Lat.	6

NEON	PAGE	TITLE	LINE
Ergou amartekuia, neon peplon aimati stikton	431	Mem.Matr.17	13
NEPHEI			
Katoptron ean epideikseis toi epikeimenoi nephei, pareleusetai e	454	Orationes	19
NEPOS			
Subtilitatis Terebra; Temporis Nepos	436	Poem.Lat.	22
NEQUE			
Gladiosue, Catapultasue teneam, quin neque	421	Lucus 33	5
Aegroto mentis: quam neque pixides	425	Mem.Matr.6	5
sua sibi sufficere, neque externis indigere auxilijs atque antidotis:	444	Orationes	26
neque enim minus refert, qualis quaeque sit mater, e qua liberi	447	Orationes	10
neque vnius seculi Princeps, sed & omnium, quae ventura sunt,	447	Orationes	25
Neque in hisce Nuptijs posteritati tantum prospexit suauissimus	447	Orationes	26
neque de priuato agamus bono, sed publico;	448	Orationes	6
bello, neque intra muros: pace, auium cantus expergefacit; . .	448	Orationes	11
curiositas absit, neque eorum satagamus, quae ad nos non spectant;	449	Orationes	19
neque enim quicquam hoc itinere mirabilius, cuius tamen fructum omnem	450	Orationes	2
Neque alienas tantum ex hoc itinere cognouit Respublicas sed quod	450	Orationes	32
abijcite quisque libros, non est locus grauitati, neque apud vos:	454	Orationes	34
vt neque virtutibus tuis desint honores neque vtrisque vita,	457	Epistolae	2
praemium consequare, cui neque addi quicquam potest, neque detrahi.	457	Epistolae	5
qui vtrumque curasti, vt neque sitirent Musae, neque flagrarent.	457	Epistolae	20
qui vtrumque curasti, vt neque sitirent Musae, neque flagrarent.	457	Epistolae	21
Neque enim passus es illum Fluuium, qui tantae poeticae, . .	461	Epistolae	6
neque illi e faece vulgi tantum qui eruditiorem simplicitati	461	Epistolae	16
neque sane dubitamus vlli, si prae defectu aquae, commeatusque	462	Epistolae	1
neque amplius quaerendum sit Tibi, Almae Nutrici quid repones.	462	Epistolae	15
Neque sane quispiam incedit Te instructior ad omnem causam, . .	462	Epistolae	20
neque quotidianae virtutis prouincia gerere personam Academiae,	465	Epistolae	9
neque enim sic effugies cum honoribus, quin laetitia nostra te	465	Epistolae	22
neque ratione habita Chartae nostrae a Serenissimo Principe Henrico 8	467	Epistolae	21
neque Studiosorum Sacculi, qui etiam nunc maeret et ingemiscit.	467	Epistolae	22
quidem multum, neque nostrae matronae conuenit, cui tu es ab ornatu.	471	Epistolae	2
neque eo dico: sed lubet garrire paulo.	471	Epistolae	5
Neque quod ignotior eram, retundebatur vnguam impetus: . . .	472	Epistolae	10
neque vlla negotia (quippe quae caput petant, non cor) Tui in me	473	Epistolae	5
NEQUEAS			
Cum Romam nequeas, quod aues, euertere, nomen	416	Lucus 26	1
Verum heus, si nequeas caelo demittere matrem, ...	424	Mem.Matr.3	7
NEQUEAT			
Cum nequeat claras ipse litare preces?	388	Musae 9	14
Sed nos, cum nequeat paruorum lingua, parentem	389	Musae 12	7
Vt nequeat paulo se cohibere domi.	404	Passio 3	2
NEQUEO			
Quam curto nequeo referre versu;	400	Musae 37	6
NEQUIBAT			
Quod Crux nequibat fixa, Clavique additi, ...	438	Poem.Lat.	1
NEQUIJT			
Quod Bellarminus nequijt, fortasse poetae	417	Lucus 28	3
NEQUIMUS			
Si non per species, nequimus ipsi, ...	415	Lucus 24	9
NEQUIORIS			
Tantoque nequioris optima Pirrha?	429	Mem.Matr.12	8
NEQUIT			
Et, quos ipsa nequit scandere vertices, ...	391	Musae 17	9
Ac zephyris, carnis flos remeare nequit.	415	Lucus 23	14
Expleri nequit, & totum depascitur Orbem.	419	Tr.Mortis	38
NEQUITER			
Ipsi sibi sunt nequiter facillimi.	413	Lucus 17	4
NERONUM			
Quid ego vobis Neronum aut Heliogabalorum ingluuiem memorem?	452	Orationes	18
NERUOS			
In vitam & neruos Pascha coaeua fluet.	434	Poem.Lat.	10
NESCIA			
Nostra caro sanctae nescia laudis erit?	389	Musae 12	10
Nescia sit metae; venula, cella tua est.	404	Passio 2	2
Prorsus nescia, cogitat recessum?	411	Lucus 5	7
Sitque omnis motus nescia tanta quies, ...	424	Mem.Matr.3	8
Tam segnis facies aurorae nescia vernae, ...	426	Mem.Matr.7	8
Nescia vulturnis cedere, firma manet.	428	Mem.Matr.11	2
NESCIO			
Somnis (nescio queis) nocturna ad vota vocabo:	432	Poem.Lat.	3
NESCIS			
Quotidiano! Nescis, ignare? Audies!	436	Poem.Lat.	2
NESCIT			
Sum, quis nescit, Imago Dei, sed saxea certe:	410	Lucus 1	1
NESCITIS			
Ecquid nescitis miserias Belli? consulite historias;	449	Orationes	2
NESCIUS			
Erumpit inde, & contineri nescius	398	Musae 32	7
Qualis nescius aggerum	403	Musae 40	9
NESTOR			
Trecentos obijt Nestor, non transijt annos, ...	415	Lucus 23	7
NEUTIQUAM			
Quas subscriptio neutiquam inquinauit;	400	Musae 37	8
Tu vero mentem neutiquam despondeas, ...	407	Passio 16	11
O blanda dextra, neutiquam istoc pulueris, ...	423	Mem.Matr.2	39
NEXAS			
Nexas, capillos anguibus oblitos, ...	434	Poem.Lat.	18
NI			
Ni me forte petas; nam quanto indignior ipse, ...	404	Passio 2	5

NI (cont'd)	PAGE	TITLE	LINE
Ni facias, vt opes linguae per brachia serpant, ...	414	Lucus 22	3
Et ni lumina ianuam resignent, ...	415	Lucus 24	4
Ni sancte, vti mater, recedam, ...	425	Mem.Matr.6	11
Accipe; ni talem des, tibi qualis erat.	434	Poem.Lat.	6
ni graue est, librum tibi Oratorium lampademque tradat. . .	470	Epistolae	9
NIDI			
Vulpibus antra feris, nidique volucribus adsunt, ...	407	Passio 15	1
NIDO			
Angustior erat Scotia, quam vt pennas nido plene explicare posses:	458	Epistolae	8
NIDUS			
Sit quasi fasciculus crescens, & nidus odorum.	427	Mem.Matr.7	27
NIGRA			
Quid mihi si facies nigra est? hoc, Ceste, colore	437	Poem.Lat.	1
Claude oculos, & erunt omnia nigra tibi:	437	Poem.Lat.	6
NIGRAS			
Mordaces tineas, nigrasque blattas, ...	385	Musae	5
NIGRO			
Quos dente nigro corripis?	388	Musae 8	2
Si nigro sit terra solo, quis despicit aruum?	437	Poem.Lat.	5
NIGRUM			
In flumen moerore nigrum si funderer ardens, ...	422	Mem.Matr.1	5
NIHIL			
Terra nihil, nec quo sanctius astra vident;	385	Musae	2
(Superbius cum te nihil)	388	Musae 8	16
Nihilne respondebimus tibi? Fatemur.	392	Musae 20	16
Quam nihil illudis, Gens improba! quam male cedunt	405	Passio 7	1
Quam nihil illudis! cum quo magis angar acuto	405	Passio 7	3
Quam nihil illudis flectens! namque integra posthac	405	Passio 7	5
Quam nihil illudis! si, quae tua purpura fingit, ...	405	Passio 7	7
Saepe ex se nihil otiosa cudit.	415	Lucus 24	6
(In quo fas nihil est rumpi) donare sigillum.	439	Poem.Lat.	15
veremur ne nihil hic sit, quod magnitudini praesentiae vestrae	441	Orationes	9
Nihil habet humana vita maioris momenti aut ponderis, quam Nuptiae,	446	Orationes	16
pax adeo Musis summe necessaria est, vt sine ea nihil simus.	448	Orationes	17
nihil eos latet, ac si Fatis a fuso essent atque consilijs, . .	449	Orationes	29
nihil ad cognitionem acquirendam peregrinatione conducibilius esse	450	Orationes	6
nihil inaudisti de Tago, Pactolo?	451	Orationes	3
vt ego nihil vspiam laetum, nihil candidum expiscari possem;	451	Orationes	14
hic ego me erexi & de dolore remisi plurimum, de desiderio nihil.	451	Orationes	27
Nihil vtilius Regi quam aliquando non regnare:	452	Orationes	38
vt nihil habeat Inuidia ipsa, quod contra hiscat aut mussitet.	453	Orationes	24
quibus nihil imperito vanius inutiliusue videatur, vbi tamen ad vsum	454	Orationes	4
nihil non sublime et excelsum cogitabimus, perrumpemus controuersias	459	Epistolae	5
qui etiam ferians nihil Tua perfectione dignum procudere possit.	471	Epistolae	23
sic existimes nihil Mortalium firmiori flagrare in Te desiderio,	473	Epistolae	4
NIHILI			
adeon' nihili videtur res, Principem omnibus delicijs abundantem,	452	Orationes	3
NIHILO			
Vt nihilo-minus Tibi luceat, cum nobis accenderit.	461	Epistolae	5
NIHILO-MINUS			
Vt nihilo-minus Tibi luceat, cum nobis accenderit.	461	Epistolae	5
NIKEPHOROS			
Nun d' oxou enthend' os stratos nikephoros	430	Mem.Matr.15	10
NIL			
Cum nil fraterno rarius esse queat.	393	Musae 21	4
(cum dignius nil posset aut melius dare)	397	Musae 28	10
Nil horum regero tibi merenti.	401	Musae 37	40
Nil sit crassius, impolitiusue)	401	Musae 37	46
NILI			
Ecce recedentis foecundo in littore Nili	384	Musae	1
NILUS			
Exundat fluuio Nilus amabili.	403	Musae 40	10
NIMBUM			
Substructionem capitis & nimbum breuem, ...	422	Mem.Matr.2	15
NIMIJS			
Mille rotae nimijs impediuntur aquis.	428	Mem.Matr.9	14
NIMIO			
Et maestum nimio madore Caelum	428	Mem.Matr.10	2
NIMIRUM			
nimirum infinitum Principis in suam gentem amorem, cui pacem	449	Orationes	36
Nimirum vt lineae, quamuis diuersa via, omnes tamen ad centrum	456	Epistolae	22
Nimirum id assecuta sunt merita Tua maxima, vt Almam Matrem spe noua	464	Epistolae	24
NIMIS			
Cur Latiam linguam reris nimis esse profanam, ...	391	Musae 16	1
Ne me carminibus nimis dicacem, ...	400	Musae 37	10
Sera nimis lacryma haec, si lacrymabis, erit.	415	Lucus 23	12
NIMIUM			
O nimium Latro! reliquis furatus abunde, ...	406	Passio 11	1
Ne nimium vexet quaestio, pone meam.	409	Passio 21	4
Nolite tamen nimium efferre vos, cum Virginitas ipsa fructus sit	446	Orationes	27
NISI			
Non nisi prima suas patiuntur praelia lites.	386	Musae 4	7
Quo sanguis est Christi, nisi vt maculas lauet, ...	393	Musae 22	3
Quod nectar, nisi cum te celebrare diem?)	428	Mem.Matr.9	16
Quis, nisi qui manibus Briareus, oculisque sit Argus, . . .	435	Poem.Lat.	5
Nec hoc abunde est tibi, nisi certae Anchorae	438	Poem.Lat.	5
paupertas perpetua, nisi vbi vestrae adsunt Excellentiae. . .	441	Orationes	16
similes esse Alexandro Magno nisi eius res gestas tradidisset	441	Orationes	19
nisi Rex esses in ciuili Republica, eligereris in Literaria?	443	Orationes	18
nisi tot negotijs distractus esses, confluereremus omnes ad Aulam,	443	Orationes	26

	PAGE	TITLE	LINE
NISI (cont'd)			
barbara omnia, Tu non nisi cultissima, elegantiasque ipsas exhibes.	463	Epistolae	15
cuius nisi incredibilis fuisset vis, nunquam in tantis negotijs,	463	Epistolae	17
nisi humanitas tua, superiori aestate sponte suauiterque patefacta,	467	Epistolae	1
nisi candida phrasi telam explices, perit negotium quasi ex nubibus	470	Epistolae	29
Ego, non nisi meditato, obrepsi ad fauorem Tuum;	472	Epistolae	3
NITEANT			
Vicini quo pacto niteant, id animum aduertito;	450	Orationes	16
NITEAT			
Omnia purgentur, niteat mihi tota supellex, ...	413	Lucus 15	3
NITIDE			
Tam nitide tamen occidis, tam suauiter, hostes, ...	435	Poem.Lat.	3
NITOREM			
qui elegantias doctrinae nitoremque spirans purpuram et eruditionem	461	Epistolae	21
NIUE			
Vt niue torpentes incaluere manus?	399	Musae 35	4
NOAE			
Columba Noae, quae in vetustis artibus	436	Poem.Lat.	19
Columba Noae, quae in vetustatis artibus	436	Poem.Lat. V	19
NOBILE			
Hunc vultum ostendas, & tecum, nobile spectrum, ...	426	Mem.Matr.7	14
quod sane adeo nobile fuit & honorificum, vt nihil habeat Inuidia	453	Orationes	23
NOBILEM			
protinus tanquam Nobilem Filium (more nostro) Magistrum Artium	463	Epistolae	8
NOBILES			
Per charas tibi nobilesque dextras, ...	400	Musae 37	7
NOBILI			
Amphionis testudine nobili	394	Musae 23	14
NOBILIOR			
Vicinusque magis nobiliorque fluit:	399	Musae 35	10
NOBILIORIS			
sed homines nobilioris ignorantiae, qui literas imminuere spiritus,	461	Epistolae	18
NOBILIS			
Debuit ista pati prima & non nobilis aetas:	432	Poem.Lat.	29
vbera et mammas arentes tam nobilis parentis aequo animo ferre	462	Epistolae	1
vti vir, tetragonos est, grauis, nobilis, perspicua, succincta.	471	Epistolae	4
NOBILISSIMAM			
at ille ambiuit nobilissimam Austriacam familiam, Aquilamque illam,	446	Orationes	15
NOBILISSIMAS			
Legationes Nobilissimas, aliosque titulos aeque nobis memorantibus,	440	Orationes	3
NOBILISSIMUS			
nobilissimus Saxonum nostrorum Princeps, sub ementito habitu	453	Orationes	3
NOBILITATE			
A veteri trunco & nobilitate cadit.	416	Lucus 25	6
Nobilitate illos, hos pietate rapit.	429	Mem.Matr.13	4
NOBILIUM			
qui antequam condiebant corpora Nobilium, solebant ventres eximere,	452	Orationes	27
NOBILIUS			
illud necessarium magis factu, hoc vero longe iucundius, nobiliusque:	472	Epistolae	35
NOBIS			
Quin liceat nobis aliquas procudere voces:	386	Musae 3	5
Cum prope sit nobis Musa, Medusa procul?	387	Musae 6	2
Non remanent nobis corpora, non animae.	390	Musae 13	4
Vt, quae Papicolis propria, assuas nobis, ...	392	Musae 20	8
Labeculas maculasque nobis obijcis:	393	Musae 22	1
fruenda nobis tradidit.	397	Musae 28	12
Quo magis inuidiam nobis & crimina confles, ...	398	Musae 33	1
Primus adest nobis, Pharisaeis omnibus hostis, ...	398	Musae 33	9
Militat & nobis, quem vos contemnitis, Ordo;	399	Musae 33	27
Libandas nobis absorbendasque propinat!	401	Musae 39	3
Nobis facilitas cedat & tibi sudor.	406	Passio 12	3
Eriperet nobis, in Cruce fixus eras;	407	Passio 14	2
Ecquid emes Christum? pro nobis scilicet olim	410	Lucus 4	1
A nobis eterim procul remoti	415	Lucus 24	7
Et patrio regno (sub quo iam Principe nobis	432	Poem.Lat.	27
Munere dum nobis prodes, Libroque futuris, ...	435	Poem.Lat.	1
Munere dum nobis prodes, Libroque remotis, ...	435	Poem.Lat.	3
aliosque titulos aeque nobis memorantibus, ac merentibus vobis	440	Orationes	3
Non a nobis vapulant Iesuitae, sed a scriptis vestris, quae ingenti	443	Orationes	19
omnipotens, conserues nobis haec gaudia, imbuas cor Regium vigore,	444	Orationes	4
Quare & Principis iter multiplicem nobis exhibet prudentiam;	446	Orationes	8
cauendum ne id nobis nauseam moueat, aut tanquam oues taedulae	448	Orationes	36
nobis non licet esse tam perspicacibus, quamuis rationi consonum	449	Orationes	31
at IACOBVS a nobis est:	451	Orationes	26
per Te illucet nobis Iacobus noster.	456	Epistolae	12
manu prehendis Regem, alteram nobis ad radices haerentibus porrigis.	456	Epistolae	14
ad legendum, quantum a nobis ad scribendum, cum humanitatis Tuae,	457	Epistolae	9
Quod si tam integrum tibi esset gratificari nobis in terra & aere,	457	Epistolae	22
Ecquid inter tantas mundi trepidationes nobis & Musis vacas?	458	Epistolae	2
Aedificarunt olim nobis Serenissimi Reges Collegia, eaque fundarunt	458	Epistolae	21
Tu inuaseris eorum gloriam conseruando nobis quae illi dederunt,	458	Epistolae	26
es praedo omnis gloriae, vt ne gratitudinis laudem nobis reliqueris?	459	Epistolae	3
Iam dari nobis vellemus Iesuitam aliquem, vt ex affrictu Libri vestri	459	Epistolae	7
Vnicus est nobis Bibliotheca Liber.	459	Epistolae	31
Nuper enim dedisti nobis Librum, plenissimum Musarum, quae cum olim	460	Epistolae	7
rotunditas Clementiae vestrae, quae ab omni parte nobis succurrit!	460	Epistolae	10
Vt nihilo-minus Tibi luceat, cum nobis accenderit. . . .	461	Epistolae	5
tantae eruditionis nobis conscius est, palustri opere & vliginoso	461	Epistolae	7
vt nullus fere elabatur dies, qui non hostes aliquos nobis aperiat:	461	Epistolae	14
Fluuium placidissimo fauorum tuorum afflatu nobis tuere. . .	461	Epistolae	25
communes Reipublicae lachrymae alterum nobis Fluuium effunderent.	462	Epistolae	6

NOBIS (cont'd)	PAGE	TITLE		LINE
maris quasi Flagellatores expugnatos fuscosque nobis dedisti.	462	Epistolae		9
quas non nobis habemus sed irrigati ipsi vniuersum regnum aspergimus?	462	Epistolae		10
Authoritate tua plurima & Eloquentia non minori nobis obstrue.	463	Epistolae		2
eo videaris nobis remotior, confidimus tamen vt arbores, . . .	464	Epistolae		17
Tam eximie de nobis meritus es, vt res nostras omnes cum Honore Tuo	465	Epistolae		2
Haud frustra impendes operam nobis omnia faucrum tuorum momenta	466	Epistolae		7
Patronus noster es, etiam tacentibus nobis, quanto magis cum rogamus,	467	Epistolae		18
ad progressum doctrinae, hac etiam in parte nobis opituleris.	467	Epistolae		28
tuus amor et authoritas istos sorices nobis abigat.	469	Epistolae		1
Sed tua humanitas haec nobis expediet.	469	Epistolae		4
tantum faucris nobis impertias, abunde succurres Magnificentiae tuae	469	Epistolae		25
NOCEBAT				
Vt discat sibi quisque, quid vtile: nempe nocebat	412	Lucus 9		3
NOCENDI				
Perdere sexcentas? crescit tamen hydra nocendi	419	Tr.Mortis		35
Perdere sexcentas? crescet tamen hydra nocendi	419	Tr.Mortis	V	35
NOCENT				
Quae diuisa nocent, Christi per foedus, in vnum	417	Lucus 29		3
NOCET				
Nec Glans sola nocet; mortem quandoque susurrat	420	Tr.Mortis		83
NOCTE				
Aurum nocte videns, vidisse insomnia dicit:	411	Lucus 7		1
Postquam se gelidis nocte refecit aquis:	412	Lucus 8		2
Totum offuscari peteres, vt nocte silenti	433	Poem.Lat.		38
Minima contentos nocte Britannos.	451	Orationes		20
NOCTEM				
Nox Aetnam, noctemque Chaos genuere priores.	420	Tr.Mortis		86
NOCTIS				
Filij noctis, populus malignus, ...	390	Musae 14		18
NOCTU				
Triste colens cellae, noctuque & Daemone plenum, ...	420	Tr.Mortis		90
Triste colens sellae, noctuque & Daemone plenum, ...	420	Tr.Mortis	V	90
Noctu te celebrans luminis aemulo.	424	Mem.Matr.4		12
NOCTURNA				
Somnis (nescio queis) nocturna ad vota vocabo:	432	Poem.Lat.		3
NOCUAS				
Quin nocuas extingue faces, precor: vnda propinqua est, . . .	399	Musae 35		7
NODO				
Breuiore nodo stringe vitae sarcinas, ...	414	Lucus 20		6
qui vtrasque Indias Hispania sua quasi nodo connectens, . .	440	Orationes		17
NODOSAM				
vnde consequimur, vel inuitis Fatis, quasi nodosam aeternitatem.	446	Orationes		24
NOLIM				
quamuis enim sexcenta huiusmodi praediola Tua gratia permutare nolim,	472	Epistolae		30
NOLITE				
Nolite tamen contemnere has gloriolas nostras quas e chartis	441	Orationes		16
Nolite tamen nimium efferre vos, cum Virginitas ipsa fructus sit	446	Orationes		27
NOLLEM				
non quod nunc indulgeas alterutri, sed quod deinceps indultum nollem.	470	Epistolae		12
NOLUIT				
Hinc tamen excludi mors noluit, ipsaque vitam	271	Tr.Mortis	VS	7
Quare noluit Princeps optimus, in delectu vxoris, re vna omnium	447	Orationes		22
noluitque vt minori sphaera quam pro latitudine meritorum tuorum	466	Epistolae		13
NOMEIS				
kai oi alloi nomeis boulontai plesion autou tas agelas istanai.	447	Orationes		31
NOMEN				
Dum suum nomen tenet, & triumphat	390	Musae 14		19
Vos ergo puri! o nomen appositissimum	393	Musae 22		5
Sola Iacchaeum decantent carmina nomen.	402	Musae 39		40
ROMA, tuum nomen quam non pertransijt ORAM, ...	416	Lucus 25		1
Cum Romam nequeas, quod aues, euertere, nomen	416	Lucus 26		1
Inuertis nomen. Quid tibi dicit? AMOR.	416	Lucus 26		6
Scio Belli nomen splendidum esse & gloriosum:	447	Orationes		32
ex quo illustrius assecutus es nomen, quam Repertores Noui Orbis	463	Epistolae		12
NOMEUS				
Otan nomeus agathon kuna exei, kai oi alloi nomeis boulontai plesion	447	Orationes		31
NOMINA				
Pertrahis in partes nomina magna tuas;	398	Musae 33		2
NOMINE				
O quam bellus homo es! lepido quam nomine fingis	386	Musae 3		1
Non placet vrbanus noster de nomine lusus	416	Lucus 27		1
Attamen VRBANI delecto nomine, constat	416	Lucus 27		5
cernitis Regem & nomine & re magnum quid polliceri, ideoque ex	447	Orationes		8
ipse egit oratorem, vt & ego aliquantulum hoc nomine glorier.	450	Orationes		31
per vniuersam Britanniam, disparuit forma, Albion nomine excidit:	451	Orationes		18
NOMINIS				
Materni decus, & debita nominis, ...	424	Mem.Matr.4		6
aeternitatem nominis Tui subsidiumque Magnificentiae Tuae . .	464	Epistolae		6
NON				
Non mea fert aetas, vt te, veterane, lacessam;	386	Musae 2		1
Non vt te superem: res tamen ipsa feret.	386	Musae 2		2
Non tibi fingendi sola taberna patet.	386	Musae 3		6
Non nisi prima suas patiuntur praelia lites.	386	Musae 4		7
Cur tibi tam facile non arrisere poetae	387	Musae 5		3
Cur non lugentes Elegi? nor acer Iambus?	387	Musae 5		5
Non plus maligni daemones Christi cruce	389	Musae 10		2
Apostolorum culpa non leuis fuit	389	Musae 10		4
Sed non moramur: namque vestra crux erit, ...	389	Musae 10		10
Non laudare Deum, credimus esse nefas.	389	Musae 12		8
Non quia Pontificum sunt olim afflata veneno, ...	390	Musae 13		1

NON (cont'd)

	PAGE	TITLE		LINE
Non remanent nobis corpora, non animae.	390	Musae 13		4
Non sic effugit angulus vel vnus	391	Musae 15		5
Tuum tibi, poeta belle, non mystes,	392	Musae 20		11
Non conuenire precibus ista Diuinis.	392	Musae 20		14
Non erubescentes vel ipsas	394	Musae 23		19
Non alio Cathari modo	395	Musae 25		8
vestem non adimi suam,	396	Musae 25		21
non suam tritui iubet.	396	Musae 25		23
Illa quidem a nostro non multum abludit imago,	396	Musae 26		5
Cui non absimilis sensus inesse solet.	396	Musae 26		8
Si numero starent praelia, non animis.	398	Musae 33		8
(Et quem non stimularet haec simultas?)	400	Musae 37		18
Non te carmine turbidum vocaui,	401	Musae 37		33
Non deridiculumue, siue ineptum,	401	Musae 37		34
Non striges, magiamue, vel rotatus,	401	Musae 37		35
Non fastus tibi turgidos repono;	401	Musae 37		36
Illum non labor irritus	402	Musae 40		3
Exercet miserum; non dolor vnguium	403	Musae 40		4
Non maeret calamus; non queritur caput:	403	Musae 40		6
Si tibi non illud placeat mirabile corpus,	404	Passio 2		3
At non lusus erit, si quem tu laeta necasti	405	Passio 7		9
Sunt hostium legata, non amicorum,	406	Passio 10		2
Sic, pro Maiestate, Deum, non perdere vitam	408	Passio 17		7
Non vrbem facit vnicam, sed Orbem.	408	Passio 19		5
Non moreris solus: Mundus simul interit in te,	409	Passio 21		1
Venditus est Agnus, non tamen emptus erit.	410	Lucus 4		2
Christe, super fluctus si non discurrere detur:	414	Lucus 19		3
Non iam ventriculus, verum spelunca vocetur	414	Lucus 21		3
Trecentos obijt Nestor, non transijt annos,	415	Lucus 23		7
Si non per species, nequimus ipsi,	415	Lucus 24		9
Non tantum est iter Angelis ad vndas,	415	Lucus 24		11
ROMA, tuum nomen quam non pertransijt ORAM,	416	Lucus 25		1
Non deerat vel fama tibi, vel carmina famae,	416	Lucus 25		3
Non deerint vel fama tibi, vel carmina famae,	416	Lucus 25	V	3
Non placet vrbanus noster de nomine lusus	416	Lucus 27		1
Quem non Emathius torrens, non sanguine pinguis	418	Tr.Mortis		2
Daunia, non satiat bis ter millesima caedis	418	Tr.Mortis		3
Non fert Vcalegon, atque amentata retorquet	418	Tr.Mortis		14
Non placuit rudis atque ignara occisio: Morti	418	Tr.Mortis		24
Non placuit rudis atque ignara occasio; morti	271	Tr.Mortis	VS	24
Huic Glans adijcitur (non quam ructare vetustas	419	Tr.Mortis		60
Hinc Glans adijcitur (non quam ructare vetustas	419	Tr.Mortis	V	60
Non iam exaudiri quicquam vel Musica caeli	420	Tr.Mortis		74
Non iam exaudiri quicquam, vel musica sphaerae	271	Tr.Mortis	VS	74
Vno ictu: non sic pestis, non stella maligno	420	Tr.Mortis		80
Non animas, raroque ornantur sanguine regum	420	Tr.Mortis		98
Cum te non videam, mene videre putas?	421	Lucus 35		8
Non video, certum est iurare; aut si hoc vetuisti,	421	Lucus 35		9
Praeuenias vultu non facienda tuo.	421	Lucus 35		10
Non illa soles terere compta lubricos,	422	Mem.Matr.2		10
Non exigatur crasis ad alterum.	426	Mem.Matr.6		22
Vae nubi pluuia grauidae, non lacte, measque	426	Mem.Matr.7		5
Quin fugias? mea non fuerat tam nubila Iuno,	426	Mem.Matr.7		7
Non est angulus vspiam serenus,	428	Mem.Matr.10		13
Non tibi nunc soli filum abrupere sorores,	428	Mem.Matr.11		11
Non potui non ire acre stimulante flagello:	431	Mem.Matr.19		5
Non ego vos posthac hederae velatus amictu	432	Poem.Lat.		2
In mea dicta ruant; non tam mihi pendula mens est,	432	Poem.Lat.		5
Non comedant famam, sic nulla obliuia potent.	432	Poem.Lat.		16
Quod non lanigerae pecudes, non Agmina lustrent?	432	Poem.Lat.		19
Non metuunt vltra; nostra infortunia tantum	432	Poem.Lat.		24
Quid sperare, imo quid non sperare licebat?)	432	Poem.Lat.		28
Debuit ista pati prima & non nobilis aetas:	432	Poem.Lat.		29
Tantum etenim vestras (Parcae) non flectit habenas	433	Poem.Lat.		40
Quid non mutatum est? requierunt flumina cursus;	433	Poem.Lat.		43
Non vlla Bellonae furentis	434	Poem.Lat.		23
Nam fata non iustis repugnant	434	Poem.Lat.		27
Quis iste tandem? non enim vultu ambulat	436	Poem.Lat.		1
Rerum magister vnicus, at non Artium;	436	Poem.Lat.		5
Non tot abest, quot nos Regis ab ingenio.	437	Poem.Lat.		4
India, non solitum prefer Eliza decus:	211	Cam.1613-b	BR	12
Sic non Phoebeus iam plus te splendeat ortus	211	Cam.1613-b	BR	15
Non a nobis vapulant Iesuitae, sed a scriptis vestris, quae ingenti	443	Orationes		19
cum non solum tuearis nos a maleuolorum insidijs, sed etiam doceas	443	Orationes		21
effari, non licet per multitudinem, imo per modestiam vestram?	443	Orationes		29
vt nullus sit angulus corporis, nulla venula, vbi non adsit CAROLVS.	445	Orationes		3
ipsa durissima ingenia, meum praesertim, celare non possunt:	445	Orationes		9
omnium coelestiores animi, quorum pietatis interest non silere.	445	Orationes		11
non rusticis loquor aut barbaris, quos magnificentia promissi	445	Orationes		15
Non rhetoricor, Academici, non tinnio:	445	Orationes		21
Non rhetoricor, Academici, non tinnio:	445	Orationes		22
limatae auris atque tersae, quorum grauitate ac purpura non abutar.	445	Orationes		27
quemadmodum artifices non omnes licitantibus producunt merces,	445	Orationes		30
quam non longe abeam Oratorum more, qui nullum non angulum verrunt	445	Orationes		35
qui nullum non angulum verrunt (ac si perdiderint ingenium)	445	Orationes		36
Ego vero non dicam vobis quod factum est ante seculum vestrum,	445	Orationes		38
Non vnum quid spectant aut singulare Magni animi, sed varia solent	446	Orationes		4
homo est, non statua; Sceptriger, non sceptrum:	446	Orationes		10
Sceptriger, non sceptrum: aequumne est vt tot labores	446	Orationes		10
Austriacam familiam, Aquilamque illam, quae non capit muscas.	446	Orationes		16

NON (cont'd)

	PAGE	TITLE	LINE
Non ignoro apud quos haec dico, eos scilicet, qui innuptam Palladem	446	Orationes	25
Musasque coelibes, qui posteros libris non liberis quaeritis.	446	Orationes	26
ideoque ex quolibet ligno, qualibet vxore non esse fingendum:	447	Orationes	9
quod quidem vbi gentium si non ab Hispano sperandum? . . .	447	Orationes	30
Non nego bellum aliquando necessarium esse, belliique miserias gratas,	449	Orationes	12
Sed non est nostri bellum indicere:	449	Orationes	15
curiositas absit, neque eorum satagamus, quae ad nos non spectant;	449	Orationes	20
apud poetas deorum pharetrae operculum habuere, humanae non item:	449	Orationes	26
nobis non licet esse tam perspicacibus, quamuis rationi consonum	449	Orationes	31
superbi sua tantum nosse, praesertim cum in vno regno non sint omnia:	450	Orationes	18
ac si non gregaria essent animalia, sed tigres aut vrsi. . .	450	Orationes	21
cur non nos omnes tecum?	451	Orationes	7
cur non vt elephanti turres, ita tu patriam tecum portasti? . .	451	Orationes	8
per quod optimus Princeps non tantum exteras regiones habuit	451	Orationes	36
indicantes, se non amare patriam terram, a qua adeo remouentur.	452	Orationes	12
ac si corpora sua non abirent olim in elementa, sed in bellaria aut	452	Orationes	14
Nihil vtilius Regi quam aliquando non regnare:	452	Orationes	38
non minus vitae inaequalitas delectat, quam terrae, quam Natura	453	Orationes	10
Quamobrem non est mirandum, si Reges ipsi quandoque suauitates suas	453	Orationes	18
recte diuinaret, non respiciat materiam actionum, sed quo spiritu,	454	Orationes	9
quemadmodum in Cometae praesagio, non respicitur, quae materia sit,	454	Orationes	12
non est tanti respondere latratibus maleuolorum;	454	Orationes	15
abijcite quisque libros, non est locus grauitati, neque apud vos:	454	Orationes	34
proin vt Fluuij quas aquas a Fonte accipiunt non retinent ipsi,	456	Epistolae	10
Tuo tot negotijs meritissime distincto, tempore non suo obrepant:	457	Epistolae	12
tibique non tam auide veterum beneficiorum memoriam recolenti,	457	Epistolae	12
non dubitamus quin benignitas tua omnia elementa percurreret.	457	Epistolae	22
adeo vt qui non subijciuntur ditioni, eruditioni vestrae obtemperent:	458	Epistolae	13
etiam libros dederunt, sed non suos:	458	Epistolae	23
quia dederunt, non a se compositos, scriptos, editosque: . . .	458	Epistolae	24
nihil non sublime et excelsum cogitabimus, perrumpemus controuersias	459	Epistolae	5
Infinita vestra in nos Beneficia non solum verba omnia, . .	460	Epistolae	2
notionum aequare nunquam potest, non voluntati tribuendum existimes.	460	Epistolae	17
veremur ne non tam sapientes nos, quam obscuros philosophos . .	460	Epistolae	24
cum non est tanti totus ille maritimus tractus (Oceani praeda	461	Epistolae	8
Quanquam non mirari non possumus, vnde fit vt nullus fere elabatur	461	Epistolae	13
vt nullus fere elabatur dies, qui non hostes aliquos nobis aperiat:	461	Epistolae	14
Quod quidem non minus expectamus a Te, quem singularis doctrina	461	Epistolae	25
quas non nobis habemus sed irrigati ipsi vniuersum regnum aspergimus?	462	Epistolae	10
Authoritate tua plurima & Eloquentia non minori nobis obstrue.	463	Epistolae	2
non gremio solum (quod innuis) sed et ambabus vlnis osculisque ei	463	Epistolae	6
barbara omnia, Tu non nisi cultissima, elegantiasque ipsas exhibes.	463	Epistolae	15
etiam Fluuium non minus de praeterito gratum, quam de futuro	465	Epistolae	7
Certe non diu est ex quo gratulati sumus tibi:	465	Epistolae	23
promptitudinem amoris nostri, non passim expositam, boni consulas,	466	Epistolae	2
Nos vero de hoc tuo progressu non minus Reipublicae gratulamur quam	466	Epistolae	15
quae nos soluendo non sumus, in suas tabulas accepti transferat.	467	Epistolae	14
prosunt vendentibus Libros non ementibus, hoc est cessatoribus	468	Epistolae	7
vendentibus Libros non ementibus, hoc est cessatoribus non studiosis.	468	Epistolae	8
praesertim quum ipsi non solum rectum de Bene-merentibus iudicium	469	Epistolae	12
non est quod nostram quoque, cum amoris symbolo festinantem,	469	Epistolae	14
per me non stabit quo minus, spe prouecta atque adulta, . .	470	Epistolae	7
non quod nunc indulgeas alterutri, sed quod deinceps indultum nollem.	470	Epistolae	11
non tam quod tibi conueniat scribenti, quam quod Academiae tuo calamo	470	Epistolae	13
certe non tam ornas illam, qui infers manum grauitati. . . .	470	Epistolae	20
non quin pectus meum plenum Tui sit, atque effusissimum in omnia	471	Epistolae	21
Vtcunque Tua lenitas non ita interpretabitur mea haec scribendi	471	Epistolae	25
Ego, non nisi meditato, obrepsi ad fauorem Tuum;	472	Epistolae	2
abscindere non possim, absque molesta aliorum ac frigida . .	472	Epistolae	14
non cor) Tui in me dominij ius imminuere posse, nedum rescindere.	473	Epistolae	6
Celsitud., sed non patitur, vt mihi videtur, Romana elegantia,	473	Epistolae	17
non adeo sanatae ab optimo Rege nostro quin turgescat indies,	473	Epistolae	21
NONDUM			
nondum ad spicam barbamque adultum.	445	Orationes	21
mirabilius, cuius tamen fructum omnem nondum habetis enucleatum.	450	Orationes	3
nouo hoc cumulo honorum, qui tamen votis nostris nondum respondent.	464	Epistolae	21
NONNULLAE			
quod nonnullae familiae semper mites essent, vti Valerij, . .	447	Orationes	20
NONNULLI			
nonnulli Fluuium inuident, multi Academias integras subuersas volunt,	461	Epistolae	15
NOS			
An rectius nos, si vices vertas, probi, ...	388	Musae 8	9
Sed nos, cum nequeat paruorum lingua, parentem	389	Musae 12	7
Et nos reducas ad lapides auos:	393	Musae 23	6
nos haud inares linqueret, ...	396	Musae 28	9
Metus inanes? Nos pari praeteruehi	397	Musae 30	3
Nos quoque possemus longas conscribere turmas, ...	398	Musae 33	7
Quin nos Ipse emit, precioso faenora soluens	410	Lucus 4	3
Nos autem, a cunis, omnes sententia Mortis	415	Lucus 23	3
Quantum caedi? adeon' vnam nos viuere vitam, ...	271	Tr.Mortis VS	34
Ad nos cum radio tam rutilante potes?	424	Mem.Matr.3	2
Nos misere flemus, solesque obducimus almos	427	Mem.Matr.9	5
Nos autem flemus: res ea sola tuis.	427	Mem.Matr.9	8
Nos flendo: haec nostrum tessera sola ducum.	427	Mem.Matr.9	12
Quae suberant causae? quid nos committere tantum, ...	432	Poem.Lat.	18
Non tot abest, quot nos Regis ab ingenio.	437	Poem.Lat.	4
Munde, fluas fugiasque licet, nos nostraque fixi:	438	Poem.Lat.	8
nos etiam exuentes os illud, & supercilium quibus caperatam . .	440	Orationes	10
accidere potest, quam vt ministri Regis Catholici ad nos accedant?	440	Orationes	15
Iamdudum nos omnes, nostrumque regnum gestimus fieri participes eius	440	Orationes	19

	PAGE	TITLE	LINE
NOS (cont'd)			
sitis ordine atque habitu, quo nos in hoc regno omnes esse gloriamur.	441	Orationes	1
Quis enim apud nos splendor, aut rerum, aut vestium?	441	Orationes	10
nos tam defecimus in vtroque quam Excellentiae Vestrae abundant.	441	Orationes	12
qua perfundis nos omnes quotidianis beneficijs, redundarit	443	Orationes	10
O beatos nos! o foelices!	443	Orationes	12
cum non solum tuearis nos a maleuolorum insidijs, sed etiam doceas	443	Orationes	22
incredibiles laudes vestras quod quae nos audiamus summo cum gaudio	443	Orationes	31
clementia, vt frequenter nos inuisat, a re instructus nos doceat,	444	Orationes	6
a re instructus nos doceat, tuosque fauores populo tuo communicans	444	Orationes	6
cor sacrum, sentiatque Rex ipse nos haec intime precari.	444	Orationes	9
Quanto foeliciores nos omnes, Corona Musica, qui optimum Principem	444	Orationes	16
apponimus nos manibus Sceptrum, capiti & faciei coronam,	447	Orationes	3
vbi velut ex continentibus tectis ad nos traiecturum est incendium:	449	Orationes	14
curiositas absit, neque eorum satagamus, quae ad nos non spectant;	449	Orationes	20
pariter & nos consilia regia, tanquam gurgitem imperuestigabilem,	449	Orationes	22
miseros nos; nunquam frigidiorem aestatem sensimus;	450	Orationes	37
apud nos agri tantum sunt fertiles, illic etiam arenae.	451	Orationes	4
cur non nos omnes tecum?	451	Orationes	7
certe nos te absentem omnes acerrime concitatissimeque desiderauimus.	451	Orationes	33
Florent apud nos artes omnes, inter quas & Mathematicae,	454	Orationes	2
Nos vero, flores Parnassi, gaudia praestolantur, quae iamdudum	454	Orationes	21
Nos vero, Auditores, diu iam peregrinati cum Principe, commode	455	Orationes	12
Tu vicissim abunde compensas nos, gratissimoque Almam Matrem	456	Epistolae	8
nos certe precamur, vt neque virtutibus tuis desint honores neque	457	Epistolae	1
Eximia tua in nos merita frequentiorem calamum postulant,	457	Epistolae	7
incomparabilem, quae eodem vultu et moderatur mundum et nos respicit.	458	Epistolae	4
charta conspiciendum Te praebes, quo familiarius inter nos verseris.	458	Epistolae	20
Cuius fauoris magnitudo ita inualuit nos, vt etiam rependendi vias	458	Epistolae	28
quam vt pro infinitis vestris in nos beneficijs Maiestatem vestram	458	Epistolae	30
Nos nunc conspersi atramento regio, nihil non sublime et excelsum	459	Epistolae	4
Infinita vestra in nos Beneficia non solum verba omnia,	460	Epistolae	2
nos humillimos subiectos, integro Fluuio a Rege nostro donatos,	460	Epistolae	12
sunt nuperi quidam homines, qui libenter sapientiores nos redderent:	460	Epistolae	22
veremur ne non tam sapientes nos, quam obscuros philosophos	460	Epistolae	24
illustrans nos omnes, lumenque accendens de suo lumine,	461	Epistolae	3
Quare nos tertium praedictis adiungimus Gratiarum Fluuium,	462	Epistolae	23
studioque in nos iam olim perspectissimo, quippe qui eximie semper	462	Epistolae	25
merita tua ita ascensura, vt eorum vis et virtus ad nos descendat.	464	Epistolae	19
Te tribunum Parlamentarium, nos nostraque omnia priuilegia, fundos,	465	Epistolae	5
sed perspectissimus tuus in nos amor, praestantissimaeque animi dotes	465	Epistolae	11
Quare nos omnes ad prudentiae eloquentiaeque tuae praesidium	465	Epistolae	15
Permitte vt nos etiam in praedam partemque tecum veniamus:	465	Epistolae	21
paratos nos habebis ad gratulationem, vt sic vna opera vtriusque	465	Epistolae	25
curesque vt tuus in nos amor, antehac satis perspectus,	466	Epistolae	3
Quod si forense quippiam nos spectans, dum incumbis muneri,	466	Epistolae	4
nos chartis et aeternitate occupatos, temporarijs hisce negotiolis	466	Epistolae	5
Nos vero de hoc tuo progressu non minus Reipublicae gratulamur quam	466	Epistolae	15
vt quando beneficia tua peruagantur Angliam, nos etiam inuisant:	466	Epistolae	17
concede vt nos etiam benignitate alarum tuarum et virtute fruamur.	466	Epistolae	22
Nos igitur hoc metu affecti, vti sanguis solet in re dubia ad cor	467	Epistolae	8
quae nos soluendo non sumus, in suas tabulas accepti transferat.	467	Epistolae	14
quare causam nostram nosque ipsos Tibi, Teque Deo Opti: Max: intimis	468	Epistolae	9
tuae gratissime appulit ad nos omnes haud ita certe studijs	468	Epistolae	12
Nos etiam haud minimam fauoris tui partem speramus, orantes	468	Epistolae	20
tuere nos ita vt fortunae nostrae, intra ambitum amplexusque	469	Epistolae	18
NOSSE			
Nosse sui quid agant, quaedam est quoque musica sanctis,	427	Mem.Matr.9	3
adde quod angusti est animi aut superbi sua tantum nosse,	450	Orationes	18
NOSTER			
Esse recidendas, Aeace noster, opes.	399	Musae 34	2
Non placet vrbanus noster de nomine lusus	416	Lucus 27	1
Nec tamen hic noster stetit impetus: exilit omni	420	Tr.Mortis	95
Sed luctus noster scribitur Oceano.	435	Poem.Lat.	10
Vincit more suo Noster: nam millibus Infans	437	Poem.Lat.	3
Vicit more suo Noster: nam millibus Infans	437	Poem.Lat. V	3
at Noster difficultatem superans, fructum consecutus est:	450	Orationes	13
quem locum Noster suauissimus impleuit, ipse egit oratorem,	450	Orationes	30
Heus, abijtne Noster? miseros nos;	450	Orationes	37
At Noster, spretis voluptatibus, illecebris melitaiais agxonais	452	Orationes	31
sic & Noster qui clanculum exijt, vsque ad Pyrenaeas nubes	454	Orationes	30
Noster etiam Princeps habuit Daphnen suam, cuius amor deinceps	455	Orationes	10
per Te illucet nobis Iacobus noster.	456	Epistolae	13
Serenissime Domine noster, Iacobe Inuictissime.	458	Epistolae	1
Serenissime Domine noster, Iacobe Potentissime.	460	Epistolae	1
sed si ablatus fuisset Fluuius noster, per quem vicini agri opulentia	460	Epistolae	23
Patrone noster, qui elegantias doctrinae nitoremque spirans purpuram	461	Epistolae	21
Tu quidem semper Patronus noster es, etiam tacentibus nobis,	467	Epistolae	17
NOSTI			
Haec tu optime nosti; neque eo dico:	471	Epistolae	5
NOSTRA			
Sumite gorgoneam, nostraque Pallas erit.	387	Musae 6	6
Nostra caro sanctae nescia laudis erit?	389	Musae 12	10
Quam praemissa probant secula, nostra probant?	391	Musae 16	2
Vtrum tenore sacra nostra sint necne	392	Musae 20	5
Aut saeuum reputes. Amica nostra est	400	Musae 37	11
Nostra etiam paribus marcescant gaudia fatis.	427	Mem.Matr.7	34
Non metuunt vltra; nostra infortunia tantum	432	Poem.Lat.	24
Munde, fluas fugiasque licet, nos nostraque fixi:	438	Poem.Lat.	8
quotidie transnatantes, litora nostra atque aures mire circumsonant.	441	Orationes	4
Si per haec ludicra nostra pars aliquis eius laetitiae,	443	Orationes	9

NOSTRA (cont'd)	PAGE	TITLE	LINE
vt miraculis vestris nostra occurrant, oratio nostra est silentium,	444	Orationes	2
nostra occurrant, oratio nostra est silentium, atque eloquentia,	444	Orationes	2
& cum eo vita nostra atque calor, longo animi deliquio fugitiuus ac	444	Orationes	22
patent enim consilia nostra, absconduntur Diuina & Regia, . .	449	Orationes	26
apparatus, foedera, munitiones, aeque ac nostra spectari debent:	450	Orationes	27
in quem fauor Regius, nostra vota, virtutes tantae confluxerunt?	456	Epistolae	18
aut nostra vota gratiam Principis, aut Tuae virtutes et vota nostra	456	Epistolae	21
aut Tuae virtutes et vota nostra et Principis gratiam superarent.	456	Epistolae	22
Quare coniunximus nunc officia nostra, tuosque fauores temporibus	457	Epistolae	15
gloria, id enim nostra interest, vt hoc precemur, aut enim misere	457	Epistolae	24
vt si officia nostra minus respondeant magnitudini beneficiorum,	460	Epistolae	15
Quare multiplex est laetitia nostra:	463	Epistolae	20
Te tribunum Parlamentarium, nos nostraque omnia priuilegia, fundos,	465	Epistolae	5
enim sic effugies cum honoribus, quin laetitia nostra te assequatur.	465	Epistolae	23
timemus Librorum precia auctum iri, et priuilegia nostra imminutum.	467	Epistolae	7
et tuum tibi largita est honorem, et priuilegia nostra confirmauit;	468	Epistolae	24
NOSTRAE			
Nostrae etiam Musae vile fuere lutum:	384	Musae	4
Pro Disciplina Ecclesiae Nostrae Epigrammata Apologetica . . .	385	Musae 1	T
Et nostrae tribuant molae farinam, ...	415	Lucus 24	5
quanto minus tacebunt lusciniae nostrae disertae, minimeque omnium	445	Orationes	10
an inter lauros principis hederae nostrae ambitiosae locus est?	456	Epistolae	4
cum humanitatis Tuae, tum gratitudinis nostrae ratio postulat.	457	Epistolae	10
ne literae nostrae animo Tuo tot negotijs meritissime distincto,	457	Epistolae	11
imbecillitati id nostrae, quae fastigium regiarum notionum aequare	460	Epistolae	16
tum Academiae nostrae, quae per Tuum Partum, ex Matre nunc Auia facta	463	Epistolae	25
neque ratione habita Chartae nostrae a Serenissimo Principe Henrico 8	467	Epistolae	22
certe studijs chartisque obuolutos, quin aures nostrae tibi pateant.	468	Epistolae	14
orantes vt immunitates nostrae a Serenissimis Regibus concessae ab	468	Epistolae	21
nostrae etiam Athenae artesque obscuris opificum artibus superari	469	Epistolae	3
tuere nos ita vt fortunae nostrae, intra ambitum amplexusque	469	Epistolae	18
quidem multum, neque nostrae matronae conuenit, cui tu es ab ornatu.	471	Epistolae	2
NOSTRAM			
nostram Caesar ad insulam	395	Musae 25	2
Quod ad nostram Rempublicam, Academiam, pax adeo Musis summe	448	Orationes	16
eum tantum vt permittat nostram hanc Inter victrices hederam	455	Orationes	17
Tuam gloriam censemus nostram, et in honoribus Tuis nostro bono	456	Epistolae	16
Peregrinis Academiam nostram inuisentibus	459	Epistolae	29
nuper in lucem publicam, nostramque praesertim, editam, . .	463	Epistolae	6
Bibliothecam nostram rudiorem esse impexioremque, quam vt tantum	463	Epistolae	28
quare causam nostram nosque ipsos Tibi, Teque Deo Opti: Max: intimis	468	Epistolae	9
non est quod nostram quoque, cum amoris symbolo festinantem,	469	Epistolae	15
NOSTRAS			
Tuque super nostras, Christe, moueris aquas.	411	Lucus 6	8
contemnere has gloriolas nostras quas e chartis & puluere eruimus.	441	Orationes	17
Nunc vero Ipse scribendo irrupisti in compensationes nostras,	459	Epistolae	2
non solum verba omnia, sed etiam cogitationes nostras exhauriunt.	460	Epistolae	3
vt res nostras omnes cum Honore Tuo coniunctas esse velimus.	465	Epistolae	2
aduersus aut immunitates nostras aut commune literarum et literatorum	467	Epistolae	11
NOSTRATE			
certe nostrate Principe nusquam praesentius Balsamum, nusquam	444	Orationes	27
NOSTRI			
Assiduus nostri papilionis erat.	398	Musae 33	6
Expeto, tanquam haec sit nostri medicina doloris?	433	Poem.Lat.	46
quod pereleganter & supra barbariem seculi innuebant Maiores nostri,	446	Orationes	29
Sed non est nostri bellum indicere:	449	Orationes	16
hunc quidem gradum pignus habes amoris nostri, haec est ansa qua	456	Epistolae	5
Tu vero promptitudinem amoris nostri, non passim expositam, . .	466	Epistolae	2
Quod si oppidani nostri (more suo) Musarum iura et diplomata	468	Epistolae	25
NOSTRIS			
Praesulibus nostris fastus, Melvine, tumentes	387	Musae 7	1
In ritibus nostris? Ego audio nullum.	392	Musae 20	2
Innumeram nostris partibus addit opem.	399	Musae 33	22
Angelicae turmae nostris se coetibus addunt:	402	Musae 39	10
Deerat adhuc vitijs nostris dignissima mundo	271	Tr.Mortis VS	49
vestrae gaudia responderint aut nostris votis aut virtutibus vestris,	443	Orationes	13
temporibus et diligentia diuisos in gratijs nostris copulauimus.	457	Epistolae	16
Sane, gestabaris antea in cordibus nostris;	458	Epistolae	18
vestram aeternitati in scriptis nostris certissime traderemus?	458	Epistolae	31
tandem meritis tuis votisque nostris conspirantibus obtinuisti.	464	Epistolae	12
nouo hoc cumulo honorum, qui tamen votis nostris nondum respondent.	464	Epistolae	21
NOSTRO			
Illa quidem a nostro non multum abludit imago, ...	396	Musae 26	5
Sin nebulis parcas, & nostro parcito signo, ...	396	Musae 26	7
Haud nostro similis, cui necesse, ...	415	Lucus 24	2
Progenies, mundique aetas abdomine nostro	418	Tr.Mortis	4
inter nouas honorum nubes e conspectu nostro fugientem reuocamus.	456	Epistolae	7
censemus nostram, et in honoribus Tuis nostro bono gratulamur;	456	Epistolae	17
tam de conseruando Fluuio nostro, quam de muniendis contra grassantes	457	Epistolae	17
cum Alma Matre, vtrumque splendorem cum beneficio nostro coniungis.	458	Epistolae	17
subiectos, integro Fluuio a Rege nostro donatos, triumphare?	460	Epistolae	13
festinasti ad gratitudines tuas cum emolumento nostro coniunctas,	462	Epistolae	14
tanquam Nobilem Filium (more nostro) Magistrum Artium renunciauimus.	463	Epistolae	9
primo gratulamur optimo Regi nostro, qui prospicit, vt cum ipse	463	Epistolae	21
non adeo sanatae ab optimo Rege nostro quin turgescat indies,	473	Epistolae	22
NOSTRORUM			
nobilissimus Saxonum nostrorum Princeps, sub ementito habitu	453	Orationes	4
Ea est enim pertinacia desideriorum nostrorum, atque immortalitas,	464	Epistolae	22
NOSTROS			
Qui tamen in nostros fortiter ire negant.	398	Musae 33	4

NOSTROS (cont'd)	PAGE	TITLE	LINE
Nunc enim explcratos habet nostros in se affectus, timores,	450	Orationes	34
NOSTRUM			
Nos flendo: haec nostrum tessera sola ducum.	427	Mem.Matr.9	12
nostrumque regnum gestimus fieri participes eius sanguinis,	440	Orationes	19
Iacobus tutelaris Diuus est vtrique nostrum;	440	Orationes	24
nunc denuo nostrum, atque vbiuis terrarum pro iudicio prudentissimi	444	Orationes	19
Goropius Becanus ait vetus vocabulum nostrum, Koning, & contracte	447	Orationes	6
quippe qui vniuersum tempus nostrum (forsitan quo alacrius illud	460	Epistolae	5
et apposite fecisti Fluuium nostrum conseruans altero eloquentiae	462	Epistolae	18
sed tamen comparatio & in honorem tuum cedet, nostrumque emolumentum.	467	Epistolae	26
Proin iube Thorndick nostrum, ni graue est, librum tibi Oratorium	470	Epistolae	9
NOTA			
Nota sunt tarixeumata Aegyptiorum, qui antequam condiebant corpora	452	Orationes	26
NOTAM			
singularem iam olim Regi notam atque signatam dignissime praeficiaris	469	Epistolae	20
NOTANS			
Dicterijs mordacibus notans, clamas	392	Musae 20	13
NOTET			
Sollicitus, ne te stella perita notet:	413	Lucus 16	4
NOTETUR			
Quo dictis minus acribus notetur.	391	Musae 15	6
NOTICNUM			
Dux Noticnum; veritatis Pontifex;	436	Poem.Lat.	3
quae fastigium regiarum notionum aequare nunquam potest,	460	Epistolae	17
NOTIS			
Totusque caenum Cynthiae ignoscit notis.	393	Musae 22	9
Fusaque decurrit notis aqua ferrea sulcis:	419	Tr.Mortis	52
NOTISSIMAE			
Volant per orbem literae notissimae:	423	Mem.Matr.2	38
NOTISSIMUS			
Notissimus est Codri amor, cuius manifestationem in gentem suam	453	Orationes	7
NOTOS			
Nempe huc vsque notos tenebricosos	428	Mem.Matr.10	1
NOTUM			
Suauiter admoueas notum tibi carne flagellum,	406	Passio 9	3
NOTUS			
Cur ego laborem notus esse tam praue,	472	Epistolae	17
NOU			
Nou d' autou taphos est' aster: pheggos gar ekeinou	429	Mem.Matr.14	3
NOUA			
Sic Catharis noua sola placent; res, verba nouantur:	386	Musae 3	3
memoriam recolenti, quam cogitanti noua, improbe molestiam creent.	457	Epistolae	13
vt Almam Matrem spe noua grauidam semper atque praegnantem	464	Epistolae	25
NOUANTUR			
Sic Catharis noua sola placent; res, verba nouantur:	386	Musae 3	3
NOUAS			
et tanquam Aquilam inter nouas honorum nubes e conspectu nostro	456	Epistolae	6
qui nouas scientiarum regiones terrasque veteribus incognitas primus	463	Epistolae	10
vt semper post nouas dignitates, alias tibi quaerant et moliantur.	464	Epistolae	23
NOUATORES			
Nempe Nouatores quis Veteranus amat?	398	Musae 33	14
NOUE			
Tun' obdis aures, grex noue, barbaras,	395	Musae 23	45
NOUI			
Cuius noui tituli accessionem summe gratulantur Excellentijs Vestris	440	Orationes	6
Quid noui? Quid noui, stupide?	454	Orationes	26
Quid noui, stupide? Redijt Princeps, CAROLVS redijt, honore grauidus,	454	Orationes	26
assecutus es nomen, quam Repertores Noui Orbis compararunt.	463	Epistolae	12
NOUIMUS			
Illam Charybdim cautione nouimus	397	Musae 30	4
quibus caperatam seuericremque Philosophiam expugnare nouimus,	440	Orationes	12
NOUIS			
Ne, si flamma nouis adolescat mota flabellis,	399	Musae 35	11
NOUISTIS			
acquirendam peregrinatione conducibilius esse nouistis omnes,	450	Orationes	7
NOUIT			
Quodque suum nouit stroma, cubile suum.	407	Passio 15	2
Quae vis condidit, ipsa nouit aedes.	411	Lucus 5	17
NOUO			
Quare summe gratulamur tibi de nouo hoc cumulo honorum,	464	Epistolae	20
NOUOS			
& inter nouos honorum cumulos, quod expectamus indies futurum,	462	Epistolae	28
NOUUM			
Sol generat populum luce fouente nouum.	384	Musae	2
pax nouum orbem aperuit; bellum destruit veterem.	448	Orationes	12
NOUUS			
Astra rogant, Nouus hic quis hospes?	394	Musae 23	28
NOX			
Nox Aetnam, noctemque Chaos genuere priores.	420	Tr.Mortis	86
Dies me deficeret (& quidem nox aptior esset tali historiae)	452	Orationes	21
NOXAE			
Plumbea glans, liuensque suae quasi conscia noxae,	419	Tr.Mortis	62
NUBE			
Occiduis, tanquam duplice nube, genis.	427	Mem.Matr.9	6
Hos oculos laetos, hunc sine nube diem:	·211	Cam.1613-b BR	14
NUBEM			
Totamque eructans nubem, Glans proruit imo	420	Tr.Mortis	76
NUBES			
vapores seruiles ad nubes educti aeque magnum tonitru edent ac regij.	452	Orationes	17
qui furtim ascendit ad nubes, vbi iam ingrauescit humore,	454	Orationes	28

NUBES (cont'd)	PAGE	TITLE		LINE
vsque ad Pyrenaeas nubes conscendens, reuersus per mare, . .	454	Orationes		31
praesertim donec transeat nubes illa, quae vicinos adeo infestat:	455	Orationes		14
Aquilam inter nouas honorum nubes e conspectu nostro fugientem	456	Epistolae		7
NUBI				
Vae nubi pluuia grauidae, non lacte, measque	426	Mem.Matr.7		5
NUBIBUS				
Nulla tibi si signa placent, e nubibus arcum	396	Musae 26		3
Cantatum; deinde Ixion cum nubibus atris	420	Tr.Mortis		88
Sol sine sole tuo! quam te tum nubibus atris	433	Poem.Lat.		37
telam explices, perit negotium quasi ex nubibus Ixionis congressus.	470	Epistolae		31
NUBILA				
Quin fugias? mea non fuerat tam nubila Iuno, ...	426	Mem.Matr.7		7
NUBILUM				
ipsum coelum nubilum semper, & poeta stultus qui dixerat, . .	451	Orationes		18
NUBIUM				
Promus; Fugator Idolum, atque nubium;	436	Poem.Lat.		12
Promus; Fugator Idolorum & nubium;	436	Poem.Lat.	V	12
NUCLEUM				
quae semper se deuorat primum, vti vermis nucleum, e quo nascitur;	454	Orationes		15
NUCLEUS				
Bellum putamen, nucleus bellissimus, ...	423	Mem.Matr.2		36
NUDE				
vt sciatis omnes quam nude, quam simpliciter vobiscum agam, . .	445	Orationes		34
NUDETUR				
Nudetur illic lucus amabilis, ...	434	Poem.Lat.		30
NUDIS				
sed nudis & egentibus	396	Musae 25		22
NUGAS				
Ecce pererratas, Regum doctissime, nugas, ...	401	Musae 39		1
Quin, mitte nugas; teque carnem & sanguinem	413	Lucus 17		5
NUGIS				
Sic positis nugis, quibus irretita libido	402	Musae 39		38
NUGOR				
Quid nugor calamo fauens?	424	Mem.Matr.4		1
NULLA				
Nulla tibi si signa placent, e nubibus arcum	396	Musae 26		3
Aurum luce videns, nulla videre putat.	411	Lucus 7		2
Quin tibi tam desperatae MORA nulla medetur, ...	416	Lucus 25		9
Quin tibi iam desperatae MORA nulla medetur, ...	416	Lucus 25	V	9
Non comedant famam, sic nulla obliuia potent.	432	Poem.Lat.		16
quarum enumerationi nulla vnquam vis, nulla latera sufficere possunt.	443	Orationes		14
quarum enumerationi nulla vnquam vis, nulla latera sufficere possunt.	443	Orationes		15
vt nullus sit angulus corporis, nulla venula, vbi non adsit CARCIVS.	445	Orationes		3
segetem perspicic, nulla verborum, nulla temporis falce demetendam.	446	Orationes		2
segetem perspicio, nulla verborum, nulla temporis falce demetendam.	446	Orationes		3
nulla pulchritudo per vniuersam Britanniam, disparuit forma,	451	Orationes		16
de ingenti amore in Principem, cui nulla dilectio par esse potest;	451	Orationes		22
resolutione illa vltima, nulla sit distinctio populi aut principis:	452	Orationes		15
nulla sunt sceptra in elementis, nulli fasces aut secures: . .	452	Orationes		16
Deum immortalem, vt Princeps optimus nulla secunda itinera meditetur;	455	Orationes		1
NULLAM				
Harmoniam tolerare nullam?	395	Musae 23		52
NULLAS				
nodo connectens, nullas metas laudum, nullas Herculeas columnas,	440	Orationes		17
metas laudum, nullas Herculeas columnas, quas iam olim possidet,	440	Orationes		17
NULLI				
nulla sunt sceptra in elementis, nulli fasces aut secures: . .	452	Orationes		16
NULLIS				
cum futura incerta sint, & nullis perspicillis, ne Belgicis quidem,	449	Orationes		24
NULLO				
Nullo circuitu scienda pungunt, ...	415	Lucus 24		12
aut tantum de nullo vnquam Filio Alma Mater, quantum de Te sibi	457	Epistolae		26
NULLUM				
In ritibus nostris? Ego audio nullum.	392	Musae 20		2
Machina, quam nullum satis execrabitur aeuum;	419	Tr.Mortis		50
Nullum locum requiemue cernens perstitit	436	Poem.Lat.		20
Nullum locum requiemue cernens praestitit	436	Poem.Lat.	V	20
qui nullum non angulum verrunt (ac si perdiderint ingenium) . .	445	Orationes		36
NULLUS				
Et nullus audis? cantibus obstrepens, ...	395	Musae 23		46
vbique deferentibus, vt nullus sit angulus corporis, nulla venula,	445	Orationes		3
vnde fit vt nullus fere elabatur dies, qui non hostes aliquos nobis	461	Epistolae		13
NUM				
Num totum tibi pectus imputabis?	421	Lucus 34		2
Numne Hydra talis, tantane bellua est	433	Poem.Lat.		9
num diffidunt prudentiae Regis? annon eius consilio res gesta est?	451	Orationes		23
NUMELLAS				
Loquitur numellas, compedes & retia:	423	Mem.Matr.2		31
NUMEN				
Ipse pios laudo; Numen & ipse colo.	386	Musae 4		6
Adorta numen acri & ignea prece.	422	Mem.Matr.2		17
(Nempe sepulcra Satis numen inempta dedit.)	425	Mem.Matr.5		14
NUMERANT				
Fatisco referens tanta quae numerant mei	423	Mem.Matr.2		50
NUMERAT				
Et numerat mortes singula gutta pares;	415	Lucus 23		10
NUMERIS				
Cum mea futilibus numeris se verba viderent	385	Musae		3
Cur, vbi tot ludat numeris antiqua poesis, ...	387	Musae 5		1

	PAGE	TITLE	LINE
NUMERO			
Si numero starent praelia, non animis.	398	Musae 33	8
NUMEROS			
Quae scripsit numeros, manum; per omnes	400	Musae 37	2
NUMERUM			
Aetatis numerum supplebit causa minorem:	386	Musae 2	3
NUMERUS			
Quod si et numerus Scriptorum intumescat, et precium, quae abyssus	468	Epistolae	2
NUMINA			
Ite leues (inquam), Parnassia numina, Musae,	432	Poem.Lat.	1
Principis inuocuam seruastis numina Vitam,	433	Poem.Lat.	34
NUMINE			
Cur Deus elegit Medicum, qui numine plenus	412	Lucus 9	1
Fustibalos fundasque, quibus, cum Numine, fretus	419	Tr.Mortis	43
fustibulos fundusque quibus cum numine fretus	271	Tr.Mortis VS	43
Creditur, ante satas prono cum numine fruges)	419	Tr.Mortis	61
Quare age, Mens, effare, precor, quo numine laeso?	432	Poem.Lat.	17
O me disparibus natum cum numine fatis!	434	Poem.Lat.	3
Sume Palatini versus de numine Phoebi,	210	Cam.1613-a BR	1
NUMMUS			
Vnicus est nummus, caelo Christoque petitus,	410	Lucus 4	9
NUN			
Nun oraas, oti kallos apeiriton opos apaugous	429	Mem.Matr.14	5
Os dia somatiou proteron kai nun di' Olumpou	429	Mem.Matr.14	7
Pos nun aphiptasai, gocu kai kirduncu	429	Mem.Matr.15	3
Nun d' oxou enthend' os stratos nikephoros	430	Mem.Matr.15	10
Nun themis orphnaiei megales epi geitonos aisei	431	Mem.Matr.18	3
NUNC			
Nunc adeo per te viuunt, vt repere possint,	384	Musae	5
Sic tu nunc iuueris factus, egoque senex.	386	Musae 2	4
Nunc etiam teneras quo versus gratior aures	387	Musae 5	11
Nunc redit ad mitem, ceu benedicta, Deum.	390	Musae 12	16
Hos nunc barbaries impia vellicat	391	Musae 17	7
Et nunc perlongas Scripturae stamine telas	392	Musae 19	5
Sic nunc plena boni sunt omnia Fratris, amore	393	Musae 21	3
Nunc sudas solus; caetera turba riget.	397	Musae 29	4
Nunc haec omnia sustuli, tonantes	401	Musae 37	31
Nunc etiam Christum callidus aggrederis.	406	Passio 11	2
Nunc ipse scandis, vt labore mutato	406	Passio 12	2
Iam meus es: nunc Te teneo: Pastorque prehensus	407	Passio 14	3
At nunc fatiscis. Nempe Dominus aedium	407	Passio 16	5
Nunc Arcana patent, nec inuolutam	408	Passio 19	9
Nunc primum socij mors foret atra tui?	415	Lucus 23	2
At nunc exucco similis tua gloria RAMO	416	Lucus 25	5
Ah nunc, helluc, fac, vt ipse sugam:	421	Lucus 34	1
Mater: & ista Dolor nunc tibi Metra parit.	422	Mem.Matr.1	8
Quo nunc recumbis, scriptio merita est tua,	423	Mem.Matr.2	40
Irregularis nunc habitus mihi est:	426	Mem.Matr.6	21
Nam te nunc Ager, Vrbs, & Aula plorant:	428	Mem.Matr.10	8
Te nunc Anglia, Scotiaeque binae,	428	Mem.Matr.10	9
Nec cingit mare, nunc inundat omnes.	428	Mem.Matr.10	14
Nunc sorti pateo, expositus sine matre procellis,	428	Mem.Matr.11	7
Non tibi nunc soli filum abrupere sorores,	428	Mem.Matr.11	11
nunc denuo nostrum, atque vbiuis terrarum pro iudicio prudentissimi	444	Orationes	19
Iam nunc minaci murmure cornuum	448	Orationes	1
figuras iam nunc pulueri inscriptas corpore confosso obliterans.	448	Orationes	31
(e quorum ossibus collisis ignis elicitur) qui nunc mansueti sunt,	449	Orationes	18
Nunc enim exploratos habet nostros in se affectus, timores,	450	Orationes	34
Quare nunc vobis ex pede Herculem, ex itinere Principem metiri licet,	453	Orationes	22
vtinam & nunc sit tanta patriae tenacitas, vt nunquam Princeps se	455	Orationes	5
iterum exire patria, qui nunc inuenit viam, proximo itinere faciat.	455	Orationes	7
Quare coniunximus nunc officia nostra, tuosque fauores temporibus	457	Epistolae	14
nunc itaque liber hic vester dilatat pomoeria, summouet Oceanum	458	Epistolae	11
Nunc vero Ipse scribendo irrupisti in compensationes nostras,	459	Epistolae	1
Nos nunc conspersi atramento regio, nihil non sublime et excelsum	459	Epistolae	4
cum olim gauderent Fluuijs, nunc etiam aquas, in quibus habitant,	460	Epistolae	8
nostrae, quae per Tuum Partum, ex Matre nunc Auia facta est:	463	Epistolae	26
illam nunc denuo ex aedibus Eboracensibus ab altero Cancellario	463	Epistolae	31
eccum nunc altera occasio, adeo festinat virtus tua:	465	Epistolae	24
in nos amor, antehac satis perspectus, nunc cum honore geminetur.	466	Epistolae	3
suauiterque patefacta, nunc etiam laborantibus Musis succurrat.	467	Epistolae	2
neque Studiosorum Sacculi, qui etiam nunc maeret et ingemiscit.	467	Epistolae	23
quam nunc pleno gradu ingrediens beneficijs tuis percurres.	468	Epistolae	19
non quod nunc indulgeas alterutri, sed quod deinceps indultum nollem.	470	Epistolae	12
Nunc obrutus Academicis negotijs, aegre hoc tempus illis succido:	471	Epistolae	19
praeferuida illa desideria silentio suo sepulta nunc languescere,	471	Epistolae	28
NUNCIUM			
spiritibusque tabellarijs laetum hunc nuncium vbique deferentibus,	445	Orationes	2
NUNCUPEMUS			
tanquam gurgitem imperuestigabilem, victoriae nuncupemus:	449	Orationes	23
NUNDINAE			
lamentis & quiritationibus plena erant fora, nundinae, conciliabula,	451	Orationes	10
NUNQUAM			
nunquam intueri satis vel mirari possumus, nimirum infinitum	449	Orationes	35
nunquam frigidiorem aestatem sensimus; at quo tandem?	450	Orationes	37
contineat se patria, cuius arctis amplexibus nunquam se expediet.	455	Orationes	2
& nunc sit tanta patriae tenacitas, vt nunquam Princeps se extricet:	455	Orationes	5
quae fastigium regiarum notionum aequare nunquam potest,	460	Epistolae	17
nunquam in tantis negotijs, quibus meritissime districtus es,	463	Epistolae	17
vt nunquam cessandum mihi ducerem, nunquam fatiscendum,	472	Epistolae	8
nunquam fatiscendum, donec lacteam aliquam viam ad candorem Mentis	472	Epistolae	8

	PAGE	TITLE	LINE
NUNQUID			
Nunquid pro foribus sedendo nuper	411	Lucus 5	4
Nunquid mel comedens, apem comedi	411	Lucus 5	8
In nebulas similesque tui res gaudia nunquid	426	Mem.Matr.7	2
NUPER			
Nunquid pro foribus sedendo nuper	411	Lucus 5	4
Quare etiam nuper Pyrij de pulueris ictu	433	Poem.Lat.	33
qui optimum Principem spe nuptiarum mari nuper tradentes,	444	Orationes	18
hoc ipsum iter, quod nuper emensus est, vt sciatis omnes quam nude,	445	Orationes	34
qui nuper versatus est in forma & figuris vultus, vbi res postulat,	454	Orationes	7
Nuper enim dedisti nobis Librum, plenissimum Musarum, quae cum olim	460	Epistolae	7
Tuam suauissimam, nuper in lucem publicam, nostramque praesertim,	463	Epistolae	5
NUPERI			
sane exorti sunt nuperi quidam homines, qui libenter sapienticres nos	460	Epistolae	21
NUPERIS			
Concede vt Honoribus nuperis, tanquam partubus Virtutum Tuarum,	469	Epistolae	8
NUPERUM			
vnicum hoc iter nuperum explicabo, in quo longe vberrimam gloriae	446	Orationes	1
NUPTIAE			
maioris momenti aut ponderis, quam Nuptiae, quas adeo laudant Poetae,	446	Orationes	17
Quod si Nuptiae in se graues sunt, quanto magis Principum,	446	Orationes	34
NUPTIARUM			
qui optimum Principem spe nuptiarum mari nuper tradentes,	444	Orationes	17
tamen nimium efferre vos, cum Virginitas ipsa fructus sit Nuptiarum:	446	Orationes	28
NUPTIAS			
Praeflorat sibi nuptias futuras.	408	Passio 19	13
primo nuptias ipsas spectate. Quid autem?	446	Orationes	8
Quid enim si praeter Nuptias, prolem, tranquillitatem, etiam	450	Orationes	4
NUPTIJS			
Absque nuptijs foret populus virorum, essemus vnius seculi;	446	Orationes	21
Neque in hisce Nuptijs posteritati tantum prospexit suauissimus	447	Orationes	27
NUSQUAM			
certe nostrate Principe nusquam praesentius Balsamum, nusquam	444	Orationes	27
praesentius Balsamum, nusquam benignius, soluens obstupefactos artus,	444	Orationes	27
Falleris, nusquam plura bona, cum etiam mala illic sint aurea:	451	Orationes	3
idque pro Libris, de quibus nusquam rectius quam apud Te agitur.	467	Epistolae	19
NUTANTES			
Lumina, nutantes paulatim acquirite vires,	432	Poem.Lat.	14
NUTRICI			
neque amplius quaerendum sit Tibi, Almae Nutrici quid repnas.	462	Epistolae	16
O			
Sic o te (iuuenem, senemue) credat	385	Musae	10
O quam bellus homo es! lepido quam nomine fingis	386	Musae 3	1
O bene quod dubium possideamus agrum!	386	Musae 4	8
O vere dictum, & belle! cum torqueat omnes	389	Musae 11	3
O caecum populum! si bona res siet	392	Musae 17	11
O saeuus hostis! quam ferociter pugnas!	392	Musae 20	15
O sec'lum lepidum! circumstant vndique Fratres,	393	Musae 21	1
Vos ergo puri! o nomen appositissimum	393	Musae 22	5
Quin redde formas, o bone, pristinas,	393	Musae 23	5
O plena centum Musica Gratijs,	394	Musae 23	21
Quid hocce? Psalmos audion'? o dapes!	394	Musae 23	33
O succulenti balsama spiritus!	394	Musae 23	34
O victoria, clamitat,	395	Musae 25	6
Atqui vos secus, o boni,	395	Musae 25	16
Tu geminas belli portas, o Petre, repandis,	398	Musae 33	11
O vos inualidos! Audi quem talibus armis	399	Musae 33	29
O vtinam aut illorum oculi (quod comprecor vnum)	400	Musae 36	5
O caecos animi fratres! quis vestra fatigat	401	Musae 39	4
O qui Defensor Fidei meritissimus audis,	402	Musae 39	17
O dulcissime Spiritus,	403	Musae 40	11
O barbaros! sic os rependitis sanctum,	404	Passio 5	1
O nimium Latro! reliquis furatus abunde,	406	Passio 11	1
O falsos homines! Vigilat, qui somniat aurum,	411	Lucus 7	3
O cessatrices! eccum puluisculus illic!	413	Lucus 15	5
O mea suspicienda manus, venterque perennis!	418	Tr.Mortis	1
O mortis longaeua fames, venterque perennis	271	Tr.Mortis VS	1
O superi: Quis tantum ipsis virtutibus instat	271	Tr.Mortis VS	33
Immoriarque oculis, o mea vita, tuis.	421	Lucus 35	4
O blanda dextra, neutiquam istoc pulueris,	423	Mem.Matr.2	39
Cur splendes, O Phoebe? ecquid demittere matrem	424	Mem.Matr.3	1
Hinc mihi principium: vos o labentia mentis	432	Poem.Lat.	13
Tempus edax rerum, tuque o mors improba sola es,	433	Poem.Lat.	41
O me disparibus natum cum numine fatis!	434	Poem.Lat.	3
O quam felices sunt, qui tua castra sequuntur,	435	Poem.Lat.	7
O me probe lassum! Iuuate, Posteri!	437	Poem.Lat.	27
O me prope lassum! Iuuate, Posteri!	437	Poem.Lat. V	27
Dure, negas? O fata mihi praesaga doloris,	437	Poem.Lat.	11
O beatos nos! o foelices!	443	Orationes	12
o foelices! Optamus quidem vt Maiestatis vestrae gaudia respondérint	443	Orationes	12
Ei en en o anthropos, inquit Medicorum Alpha, ouk an elgeen.	446	Orationes	18
O despota elie kai theoi pantes, ei ti kata ton emautou Bion emarton,	452	Orationes	29
O prudentiam incomparabilem, quae eodem vultu et moderatur mundum	458	Epistolae	3
O, mirificam Clementiam! Aedificarunt olim nobis Serenissimi Reges	458	Epistolae	21
o quot iam anni sunt ex quo vel apicem Latinum pertuli!	471	Epistolae	6
OB			
Ingemat ob partus, ceu maledicta, suos,	390	Musae 12	14
Et cum ob perspicacitatem singularem iam olim Regi notam atque	469	Epistolae	20
OBAMBULANS			
Facesse, Stoica plebs, obambulans cautes,	429	Mem.Matr.12	1

	PAGE	TITLE	LINE
OBDIS			
Tun' obdis aures, grex noue, barbaras,	395	Musae 23	45
OBDUCIMUS			
Nos misere flemus, sclesque obducimus almos	427	Mem.Matr.9	5
OBEUNDIS			
id omne dexterrima tua in obeundis rebus prudentia dissipetur.	467	Epistolae	13
OBICES			
Post restitutos fluctibus obices,	393	Musae 23	2
OBIJCIS			
Labeculas maculasque nobis obijcis:	393	Musae 22	1
Quid Vaticanam Bodleiumque obijcis, Hospes?	459	Epistolae	30
OBIJT			
Trecentos obijt Nestor, non transijt annos,	415	Lucus 23	7
OBIRE			
Te petet, ante diem quisquis obire cupit.	414	Lucus 21	6
OBIT			
Impediant, apices legis amicus obit.	388	Musae 9	6
Haud aliter cum Christus obit, prae funere tanto	409	Passio 20	5
Quotidie iugulat, nec semel vllus obit.	415	Lucus 23	4
OBITUM			
In Obitum Henrici Principis Walliae.	432	Poem.Lat.	T
In Obitum Serenissimae Reginae Annae.	435	Poem.Lat.	T
In obitum incomparabilis Francisci Vicecomitis	438	Poem.Lat.	T
OBLATO			
Quo placet oblato, mortua fertur, hero:	428	Mem.Matr.11	4
OBLIGASTI			
alacrius illud impenderemus Doctrinae) beneficijs etiam obligasti.	460	Epistolae	7
OBLIQUA			
tanquam ligna obliqua, aliter magna haec mundi domus corrueret:	450	Orationes	28
OBLITERANS			
figuras iam nunc pulueri inscriptas corpore confosso obliterans.	448	Orationes	32
OBLITOS			
Nexas, capillos anguibus oblitos,	434	Poem.Lat.	18
OBLIUIA			
Non comedant famam, sic nulla obliuia potent.	432	Poem.Lat.	16
OBLOQUERIS			
Inuertis, mores carpis & obloqueris:	416	Lucus 26	2
OBNOXIUM			
vt iter tantum, tantis laboribus, periculis obnoxium, susciperet?	452	Orationes	8
OBREPANT			
Tuo tot negotijs meritissime distincto, tempore non suo obrepant:	457	Epistolae	12
OBREPSI			
Ego, non nisi meditato, obrepsi ad fauorem Tuum;	472	Epistolae	3
OBRUE			
Obrue feruentes, ruptis conatibus, hostes:	402	Musae 39	20
OBRUENS			
siccatores (solem officio suo priuantes) vi verborum lucrum obruens.	462	Epistolae	20
OBRUIS			
Tot quaestionum fluctibus obruis,	425	Mem.Matr.6	2
OBRUTUS			
Nunc obrutus Academicis negotijs, aegre hoc tempus illis succido:	471	Epistolae	20
OBSCURIS			
nostrae etiam Athenae artesque obscuris opificum artibus superari	469	Epistolae	3
OBSCUROS			
ne non tam sapientes nos, quam obscuros philosophos reddidissent.	460	Epistolae	24
OBSCURUS			
Siccam animam sapientissimam esse dixit obscurus ille philosophus;	460	Epistolae	20
Obscurus sermo negotijs ineptus; quae cum plerumque implicata sint,	470	Epistolae	28
OBSECRAMUS			
Quare vnice obsecramus, vt qui tot subsidia attuleris ad progressum	467	Epistolae	27
OBSECRANTES			
obsecrantes, vt dequatis paulisper vultus illos bellicos,	440	Orationes	8
OBSECREMUS			
Obsecremus eum tantum vt permittat nostram hanc Inter victrices	455	Orationes	16
OBSEPTUM			
obseptum illecebris, voluptatibus quasi fascijs circumdatum,	452	Orationes	4
OBSEQUENTISSIMUM			
beabis Filium tuum obsequentissimum GEORGIUM HERBERT.	473	Epistolae	13
OBSERUANTIA			
vt laboribus meis plurimis atque assidua obseruantia, ramenta	472	Epistolae	13
OBSERUATIONE			
Et quod obseruatione cum primis dignum est, quo magis amore	440	Orationes	21
quid enim vtilius quam ex obseruatione exterarum Legum ac morum,	450	Orationes	14
OBSIGNATA			
Plumbis obsignata, colosque & stamina vitae	419	Tr.Mortis	64
OBSTANTIA			
Aruiragum, falcesque obstantia quaeque metentes.	419	Tr.Mortis	46
OBSTETRICATUR			
quae sola incubat artibus, & obstetricatur, minus quam par est,	448	Orationes	33
OBSTREPENS			
Et nullus audis? cantibus obstrepens,	395	Musae 23	46
OBSTREPERAE			
Obstreperae stulto sonitu, crimenque fatentes.	420	Tr.Mortis	99
OBSTRUE			
Authoritate tua plurima & Eloquentia non minori nobis obstrue.	463	Epistolae	3
OBSTUPEFACTOS			
nusquam benignius, soluens obstupefactos artus, atque exhilarans,	444	Orationes	28
OBTEMPERENT			
adeo vt qui non subijciuntur ditioni, eruditioni vestrae obtemperent:	458	Epistolae	14
OBTINET			
Occasione certat, imo & obtinet.	423	Mem.Matr.2	28

	PAGE	TITLE	LINE
OBTINUISTI			
tandem meritis tuis votisque nostris conspirantibus obtinuisti.	464	Epistolae	13
OBTRUDIS			
Gorgona cur diram laruasque obtrudis inanes, ...	387	Musae 6	1
OBTUTU			
Obtutu placido benignus affles, ...	384	Musae	3
OBUOLUTOS			
appulit ad nos omnes haud ita certe studijs chartisque obuolutos,	468	Epistolae	13
OBVIA			
Fluminaque e ripis obvia facta tibi:	210	Cam.1613-a BR	6
OCCASIO			
Adde pijs animis quaeuis occasio lucro est, ...	390	Musae 12	11
Non placuit rudis atque ignara occasio; morti	271	Tr.Mortis VS	24
Magnatis appulsu extulit se occasio, ...	423	Mem.Matr.2	26
eccum nunc altera occasio, adeo festinat virtus tua:	465	Epistolae	24
OCCASIONE			
Occasione certat, imo & obtinet.	423	Mem.Matr.2	28
OCCIDERE			
Impos medendi, occidere si potes, ...	425	Mem.Matr.6	9
OCCIDIS			
Tam nitide tamen occidis, tam suauiter, hostes, ...	435	Poem.Lat.	3
OCCIDITE			
Occidite; aut sare tantisper viuite, donec	425	Mem.Matr.5	15
OCCIDUIS			
Occiduis, tanquam duplice nube, genis.	427	Mem.Matr.9	6
OCCISI			
Qua tamen occisi foedera scripta Dei?	391	Musae 16	4
OCCISIO			
Non placuit rudis atque ignara occisio: Morti	418	Tr.Mortis	24
OCCUMBENS			
Resurget occumbens Herus:	407	Passio 16	12
Occumbens humero Thronos lacessam.	421	Lucus 34	9
OCCUPASTI			
Britannicas insulas omnes occupasti. Hoc etiam imperium tenuius est	458	Epistolae	10
OCCUPATO			
sed vt facilius ignoscas occupato calamo, qui etiam ferians nihil Tua	471	Epistolae	23
OCCUPATOS			
nos chartis et aeternitate occupatos, temporarijs hisce negotiolis	466	Epistolae	6
OCCURRANT			
vt miraculis vestris nostra occurrant, oratio nostra est silentium,	444	Orationes	2
OCCURRAT			
dum incumbis muneri, occurrat, nos chartis et aeternitate occupatos,	466	Epistolae	5
OCCURRIT			
facillime incedens, occurrit ei Democritus, & ingenium admirans,	453	Orationes	35
opportune his tenebris Fauor Tuus occurrit, illustrans nos omnes,	461	Epistolae	3
OCEANI			
totus ille maritimus tractus (Oceani praeda et deliciae) vt irrigui	461	Epistolae	9
OCEANO			
Solem ex Oceano Veteres exurgere fingunt	412	Lucus 8	1
Sed luctus noster scribitur Oceano.	435	Poem.Lat.	10
OCEANUM			
summouet Oceanum ambientem, adeo vt qui non subijciuntur ditioni,	458	Epistolae	12
OCULI			
O vtinam aut illorum oculi (quod comprecor vnum)	400	Musae 36	5
oculi omnium deiecti, humile os, collum pensile, manus decussatae,	451	Orationes	15
cui soli ideo insunt oculi variegati, cum caetera animantia . .	453	Orationes	17
OCULIS			
Immoriarque oculis, o mea vita, tuis.	421	Lucus 35	4
Quis, nisi qui manibus Briareus, oculisque sit Argus, . . .	435	Poem.Lat.	5
re vna omnium grauissima, alienis oculis iudicioque inniti; . .	447	Orationes	23
OCULO			
et festucas, Reipublicae oculo haerentes, tam diligenter amoues;	462	Epistolae	13
OCULOS			
Cum lacrymas oculosque duos tot vulnera vincant, ...	404	Passio 1	1
Claude oculos, & erunt omnia nigra tibi:	437	Poem.Lat.	6
Hos oculos laetos, hunc sine nube diem:	211	Cam.1613-b BR	14
qui mundi oculos perstringat, nos tam defecimus in vtroque quam	441	Orationes	12
Recte facitis, Academici, attollentes oculos cum stupore; . .	450	Orationes	1
OCULUS			
Alma Mater libentissime caput reclinet in tuo sinu, oculusque Reipub:	465	Epistolae	13
OD'			
Autar od' au thanatos kuries, os elios auos	431	Mem.Matr.17	19
ODE			
Kai prepon ode para dakruoessi reein.	431	Mem.Matr.18	6
ODERE			
Hinc te olim gentes miratae odere vicissim;	416	Lucus 25	11
ODON			
osper tina odon proeleluthoton, en kai emas isos deesei poreuesthai,	471	Epistolae	10
ODORES			
Pugnaces, teneros florum turbemus odores, ...	427	Mem.Matr.7	32
ODORUM			
Sit quasi fasciculus crescens, & nidus odorum.	427	Mem.Matr.7	27
ODURMA			
Odurma Daimonon, Theou georgion, ...	429	Mem.Matr.15	2
OF			
my L. Bishop of Winchester, one of the Kings most honorable . .	473	Epistolae	24
of Winchester, one of the Kings most honorable privy-Counsaile.	473	Epistolae	24
OFFICIA			
Quare coniunximus nunc officia nostra, tuosque fauores temporibus	457	Epistolae	14
vt si officia nostra minus respondeant magnitudini beneficiorum,	460	Epistolae	15
atque effusissimum in omnia officia, quae praestet mea paruitas;	471	Epistolae	22

OFFICIA (cont'd)	PAGE	TITLE	LINE
ad mea in Honorem Tuum officia erectior solutiorque redibo,	473	Epistolae	3
OFFICIO			
Hoc saltem officio fungar amore tui.	437	Poem.Lat.	8
paludumque istos siccatores (solem officio suo priuantes) vi verborum	462	Epistolae	20
OFFUSCARI			
Totum offuscari peteres, vt nocte silenti	433	Poem.Lat.	38
OGKOU			
Photos apauramenes ogkou epheisthe pleon,	431	Mem.Matr.18	2
OI			
kai oi alloi nomeis boulontai plesion autou tas agelas istanai.	447	Orationes	31
OKSU			
existimantes tuphlous einai pros oksu blepontas, anapodemetous pros	450	Orationes	9
OLENT			
Terram & funus olent flores: Dominaeque cadauer	425	Mem.Matr.5	5
OLIM			
Pollubra vel cum olim damnaris Regia in ara,	386	Musae 3	9
Si, quia felices olim dixere poetae	387	Musae 6	3
Apposite quem commotum subfugerat olim,	390	Musae 12	15
Non quia Pontificum sunt olim afflata veneno,	390	Musae 13	1
Astronomus olim (vt fama) dum maculas diu,	393	Musae 22	7
olim appelleret, intuens	395	Musae 25	3
Olim accreuerit Herculi furenti:	401	Musae 37	27
Scilicet has olim diuisas aequore terras	402	Musae 39	14
Ecquid emes Christum? pro nobis scilicet olim	410	Lucus 4	1
Verius hoc olim factum est, vbi, Christe, lauares	412	Lucus 8	3
Crudum olim pomum, tristis Adame, tibi.	412	Lucus 9	4
Hinc te olim gentes miratae odere vicissim;	416	Lucus 25	11
Sic olim cecidere.	419	Tr.Mortis	48
Haec fuerat olim potio Domini tui.	427	Mem.Matr.8	9
Quaeque olim fuerat cura, manere potest.	427	Mem.Matr.9	4
Degentium olim, Emancipator; luminis	436	Poem.Lat.	11
nullas Herculeas columnas, quas iam olim possidet, agnoscit.	440	Orationes	18
Maiores nostri, qui olim glasto se inficientes, in vxorum corporibus,	446	Orationes	29
ac si corpora sua non abirent olim in elementa, sed in bellaria aut	452	Orationes	14
Apollo olim depositis radijs Daphnen deperijt, at illa mutata est	455	Orationes	8
Aedificarunt olim nobis Serenissimi Reges Collegia, eaque fundarunt	458	Epistolae	21
Musarum, quae cum olim gauderent Fluuijs, nunc etiam aquas,	460	Epistolae	8
Quod si Artaxerxes olim paulum aquae a Sinaeta, subiecto suo,	460	Epistolae	11
conseruantes sibi Illos Fontes, a quibus ipsi olim hauserunt?	461	Epistolae	32
studioque in nos iam olim perspectissimo, quippe qui eximie semper	462	Epistolae	25
cum olim ab Archiepiscopo Eboracensi Summo Angliae Cancellario	463	Epistolae	30
cuius libri si alij alijs (tanquam montes olim) imponerentur,	468	Epistolae	1
perspicacitatem singularem iam olim Regi notam atque signatam	469	Epistolae	20
OLUMPOU			
Os dia somaticu proteron kai nun di' Olumpou	429	Mem.Matr.14	7
OLYMPUM			
Explicat, & radijs ipsum pertingit Olympum!	401	Musae 39	7
OMITTENS			
Tinnitus Berecynthios omittens	401	Musae 37	39
OMNE			
Dum cor omne suum sibi requirat	408	Passio 19	7
Omne regnum suo Principi carcer est, aut si excedat, alienum:	450	Orationes	12
id omne dexterrima tua in obeundis rebus prudentia dissipetur.	467	Epistolae	12
OMNEM			
Haud per te moritura, Scholamque introspicis omnem.	402	Musae 39	26
Pulueris inferni; properat datus ignis, & omnem	420	Tr.Mortis	69
Pulueris inferni properat, datur ignis, & omnem	420	Tr.Mortis V	69
Sulphuris inferni, properat datus ignis et omnem	271	Tr.Mortis VS	69
mirabilius, cuius tamen fructum omnem nondum habetis enucleatum.	450	Orationes	3
Neque sane quispiam incedit Te instructior ad omnem causam,	462	Epistolae	21
administrans, distribuendi modum omnem rationemque callet?	464	Epistolae	16
affectuum raptim sequentes, ad omnem eorum auram vacillant.	472	Epistolae	2
Cum enim vim cogitationum in vitam meam omnem conuertissem,	472	Epistolae	5
OMNES			
Vos ducibus missis, missis doctoribus, omnes	387	Musae 5	9
Omnesque stulti audimus, aut hypocritae,	388	Musae 8	7
O vere dictum, & belle! cum torqueat omnes	389	Musae 11	3
omnes indigenas loci	395	Musae 25	4
Mox displicent omnes. Vbi hoc permanserit	398	Musae 32	4
Vna dies Catharos ad bellum miserat omnes:	399	Musae 33	31
Quae scripsit numeros, manum; per omnes	400	Musae 37	2
Tu venas laticesque omnes, quos sacra recludit	402	Musae 39	23
Atque omnes peragrata es angiportus	411	Lucus 5	13
Nos autem, a cunis, omnes sententia Mortis	415	Lucus 23	3
It stridor, caelosque omnes & Tartara findit.	420	Tr.Mortis	73
It stridor, caelosque omnes et sydera findit.	271	Tr.Mortis VS	73
Euge, perite omnes; nec posthac exeat vlla	425	Mem.Matr.5	11
Nec cingit mare, nunc inundat omnes.	428	Mem.Matr.10	14
accessionem summe gratulantur Excellentijs Vestris Musae omnes,	440	Orationes	7
Iamdudum nos omnes, nostrumque regnum gestimus fieri participes eius	440	Orationes	19
sitis ordine atque habitu, quo nos in hoc regno omnes esse gloriamur.	441	Orationes	2
qua perfundis nos omnes quotidianis beneficijs, redundarit	443	Orationes	10
conflueremus omnes ad Aulam, atque ab eo consilium peteremus a quo	443	Orationes	27
Quanto foeliciores nos omnes, Corona Musica, qui optimum Principem	444	Orationes	16
quemadmodum artifices non omnes licitantibus producunt merces,	445	Orationes	30
vt sciatis omnes quam nude, quam simpliciter vobiscum agam,	445	Orationes	34
acquirendam peregrinatione conducibilius esse nouistis omnes,	450	Orationes	7
Natura suas dotes, vt indigentia singularum regionum omnes connectat:	450	Orationes	19
cur non nos omnes tecum?	451	Orationes	7
Sic tunc omnes strepebant: huiusmodi lamentis & quiritationibus plena	451	Orationes	9

CMNES (cont'd)	PAGE	TITIE	LINE
ita me ametis cmnes, vt egc nihil vspiam laetum, nihil candidum	451	Oraticnes	14
certe nos te absentem cmnes acerrime concitatissimeque desiderauimus.	451	Orationes	33
Flcrent apud ncs artes omnes, inter quas & Mathematicae,	454	Orationes	2
prodite cmnes. Quid noui? Quid noui, stupide?	454	Oraticnes	26
vt lineae, quamuis diuersa via, omnes tamen ad centrum prcperant;	456	Epistolae	23
postquam omnes hcncrum gradus hic percurreris, aeternum illud	457	Epistolae	3
Britannicas insulas cmnes occupasti. Hoc etiam imperium tenuius est	458	Epistolae	9
ita inuoluit ncs, vt etiam rependendi vias cmnes praecludat.	458	Epistclae	29
perrumpemus controuersias omnes, superabimus qucscunque.	459	Epistolae	6
illustrans nos omnes, lumenque accendens de suo lumine,	461	Epistolae	3
fuga hcs cmnes, praesertim sericatam hanc stultitiam contere,	461	Epistclae	22
vt res nostras cmnes cum Honore Tuo coniunctas esse velimus.	465	Epistolae	2
Quare nos cmnes ad prudentiae elcquentiaeque tuae praesidium	465	Epistolae	15
gratissime appulit ad nos omnes haud ita certe studijs chartisque	468	Epistclae	12
virtutibus, tuo exemplo compensatis, ad vnum cmnes incumbamus.	468	Epistolae	17
CMNI			
Nec tamen hic noster stetit impetus: exilit cmni	420	Tr.Mortis	95
Nec tamen hic mcrtis rabies stetit; exilit cmni	272	Tr.Mcrtis VS	95
sunt, vt sic scripta vestra omni dente, tum edacis temporis,	459	Epistolae	18
rotunditas Clementiae vestrae, quae ab omni parte nobis succurrit!	460	Epistolae	10
Quis enim turc inuiseret Almam Matrem destitutam cmni commeatu?	461	Epistclae	2
assensumque Tuum veritati omni familiarem largiaris, sun tei eulcgiai	473	Epistolae	11
CMNIA			
Cum sacra perturbet vester furor omnia, scriptum	386	Musae 3	7
Minora fiunt cmnia:	388	Musae 8	14
Rectius innocuis lactentibus cmnia praestes,	388	Musae 9	11
Cmnia sunt temere proijcienda foras.	390	Musae 13	2
Sic nunc plena bcni sunt cmnia Fratris, amore	393	Musae 21	3
vellent cmnia regredi,	395	Musae 25	12
Nunc haec cmnia sustuli, tcnantes	401	Musae 37	31
Omnia, praeter corda, scelus confregit & errcr,	409	Passic 20	7
Quam si ipse sclus cmnia interuerteret,	412	Lucus 13	3
Cmnia purgentur, niteat mihi tcta supellex,	413	Lucus 15	3
Cmnia quaerendo, sed te, super cmnia, vexas:	413	Lucus 16	5
Omnia suspendit naso, sccicsque lacessit:	418	Tr.Mortis	13
Liber alit rixas: pctantibus cmnia bina	418	Tr.Mortis	18
Cmniaque haec vt transadigant sine crimine ccstas,	418	Tr.Mortis	29
Claude oculcs, & erunt cmnia nigra tibi:	437	Poem.Lat.	6
qua optime ostendis te eius vicarium qui omnia disponit suauiter?	443	Oraticnes	17
Sunt tamen acuti quidam & emuncti, qui cmnia praeuident:	449	Orationes	29
superbi sua tantum ncsse, praesertim cum in vno regno non sint cmnia:	450	Craticnes	18
cmnia Danorum expiscatus consilia, victoriam celebrem consecutus est.	453	Orationes	6
non dubitamus quin benignitas tua omnia elementa percurreret.	457	Epistolae	23
Hibernico lignum nascitur permanens, contra cmnia venena validum:	459	Epistclae	16
Infinita vestra in nos Beneficia non solum verba cmnia,	460	Epistolae	2
Illi barbara omnia, Tu ncn nisi cultissima, elegantiasque ipsas	463	Epistolae	15
Te tribunum Parlamentarium, nos nostraque cmnia priuilegia, fundos,	465	Epistclae	5
frustra impendes operam nobis omnia fauorum tuorum mcmenta apicesque	466	Epistclae	7
enim Lcndinenses Librarics cmnia transmarina scripta ad moncpolium	467	Epistclae	20
atque effusissimum in omnia officia, quae praestet mea paruitas;	471	Epistolae	22
Quod tamen haec cmnia succedant ex voto, quod reclusae sint fores,	472	Epistclae	19
CMNIBUS			
Syluas pererrat. Fibulis dein cmnibus	398	Musae 32	8
Primus adest nobis, Pharisaeis cmnibus hcstis,	398	Musae 33	9
Viscera naturae, ccmmistusque cmnibus astris	402	Musae 39	28
Visum quod vni praebet, cmnibus vitam,	404	Passio 5	2
Sic cmnibus videris ad modum visus.	406	Passio 12	4
Quod cmnibus tute imperes, nemc tibi.	412	Lucus 11	3
Fontem intercipis cmnibus patentem?	421	Lucus 34	3
otium, pax cmnibus praeterquam tineis, paupertas perpetua,	441	Orationes	15
Principem cmnibus delicijs abundantem, obseptum illecebris,	452	Oraticnes	4
tibi hunc hcnorem, et faxit, vt tibi gloriae sit, omnibus saluti.	469	Epistolae	6
OMNIMODAS			
Ecce lanienas omnimodas, truncata ccrpora, mutilatam imaginem Dei,	449	Orationes	4
CMNIPOTENS			
Tu vero, Deus cmnipotens, conserues nobis haec gaudia, imbuas cor	444	Crationes	4
CMNIS			
Cmnis linea sepiam recusans	400	Musae 37	21
Sitque omnis mctus nescia tanta quies,	424	Mem.Matr.3	8
Vt natura cmnis suos habet anteambulones, vnde pluuia futura,	445	Orationes	5
bello pacem, sine qua cmnis vita prccella, & mundus solitudo.	448	Orationes	8
Amat varietatem Natura omnis, flores, animalia, tum maxime hcmo,	453	Orationes	16
adeon' es praedo omnis gloriae, vt ne gratitudinis laudem ncbis	459	Epistolae	2
commendaticne, si huc reciderit cmnis studiorum spes fructusque:	472	Epistclae	15
CMNIUM			
tandem Magistri Artium, & quidem cmnium Aulicarum, Militarium,	440	Craticnes	5
minimeque cmnium coelestiores animi, qucrum pietatis interest	445	Orationes	10
percurrite Annales regncrum, excutite scrinia politiarum omnium;	445	Craticnes	14
re vna omnium grauissima, alienis oculis iudicioque inniti;	447	Oraticnes	22
neque vnius seculi Princeps, sed & cmnium, quae ventura sunt,	447	Orationes	26
oculi cmnium deiecti, humile os, cellum pensile, manus decussatae,	451	Oraticnes	15
cmniumque Artium molem et pondus sustinere, sed perspectissimus tuus	465	Epistolae	10
Haec tu cmnium optime vides, quare causam nostram nosque ipsos Tibi,	468	Epistolae	8
CMCLCGESEI			
esti me perimenein, cte polemein umin cmclogesei, dixit Mithridates.	449	Oraticnes	15
CMCU			
Ainon cmcu Zcein kai pneumatcs allo genesthai	431	Mem.Matr.17	22
CN			
e phagcn e picn, on me themitcn en, ou di' emauton emarton,	452	Oraticnes	30

	PAGE	TITLE	LINE
ONAGROS			
Balistasque Onagrosque & quicquid Scorpio saeuus	419	Tr.Mortis	40
ONE			
of Winchester, one of the Kings most honorable privy-Counsaile.	473	Epistolae	24
ONERA			
gestantur, tanquam onera, circumferuntur mollissimis lecticis,	452	Orationes	11
ONERE			
cum grandi atque impedito onere facillime incedens, occurrit ei	453	Orationes	35
ONUS			
quis scit an & amoris onus scite vinctum ligatumque, & per tot	453	Orationes	38
OPACAE			
Congrediens genuit Monachum, qui limen opacae	420	Tr.Mortis	89
OPACO			
In terram violae capite inclinantur opaco,	425	Mem.Matr.5	7
OPE			
Constet, & ex illa pendeat orbis ope;	385	Musae 1	2
Qui dulci miseros irradiabit ope.	387	Musae 7	10
Qua sine vos miseri lentius itis ope.	399	Musae 33	26
Hac ope munitus securior excipis vndas,	402	Musae 39	30
OPEM			
Et tibi sit nemo praes, vbi poscis opem.	389	Musae 9	16
Innumeram nostris partibus addit opem.	399	Musae 33	22
Ingemit, & defessus opem iam Portitor orat.	420	Tr.Mortis	82
OPERA			
vt sic vna opera vtriusque Reipublicae calculum et ciuilis	465	Epistolae	26
concessae ab Augustissimo Iacobo auctae tua opera conseruentur;	468	Epistolae	22
OPERAM			
Haud frustra impendes operam nobis omnia faucrum tuorum momenta	466	Epistolae	7
OPERCULUM			
apud poetas deorum pharetrae operculum habuere, humanae non item:	449	Orationes	25
OPERE			
eruditionis nobis conscius est, palustri opere & vliginoso intercipi:	461	Epistolae	7
OPERIS			
dimidiaque operis parte leuatus, ad mea in Honorem Tuum officia	473	Epistolae	2
OPEROSIOR			
Quare operosior in eo structura, & praerogatiuae regiae emicant.	446	Orationes	37
OPES			
Esse recidendas, Aeace noster, opes.	399	Musae 34	2
Ni facias, vt opes linguae per brachia serpant,	414	Lucus 22	3
OPHTHALMON			
ophthalmon upographas kai epitrimmata pareion inducens;	470	Epistolae	19
OPIFICUM			
Atheniensis doluit se victum opificum antelucana industria,	469	Epistolae	2
etiam Athenae artesque obscuris opificum artibus superari dolebunt.	469	Epistolae	3
OPITULERIS			
ad progressum doctrinae, hac etiam in parte nobis opituleris.	467	Epistolae	28
OPOBALSAMA			
Hic, vbi sanati stillant opobalsama mundi,	406	Passio 13	1
OPORAI			
Aiazo geneteiran, epaiazousin oporai,	431	Mem.Matr.17	15
OPORTERE			
significantes oportere Reges ijs partibus antecellere homines,	447	Orationes	4
OPOS			
Nun oraas, oti kallos apeiriton opos apaugous	429	Mem.Matr.14	5
OPPIDANI			
Quod si oppidani nostri (more suo) Musarum iura et diplomata	468	Epistolae	25
OPPONITUR			
Ritibus vna Sacris opponitur; altera Sanctos	386	Musae 4	3
OPPORTUNE			
opportune his tenebris Fauor Tuus occurrit, illustrans nos omnes,	461	Epistolae	2
OPPOSITAS			
Diluit oppositas candidus humor aquas.	428	Mem.Matr.9	18
OPPOSITIS			
Cuius ab oppositis fluxit origo locis.	417	Lucus 31	4
OPTAMUS			
Optamus quidem vt Maiestatis vestrae gaudia responderint aut nostris	443	Orationes	12
OPTAT			
Sunt etiam tenebrae, quas tamen optat amor.	437	Poem.Lat.	2
OPTATUS			
Excitat optatus auidos, & ventilat ignem.	432	Poem.Lat.	32
OPTI			
Deus Opti: Max. tua beneficia, quae nos soluendo non sumus,	467	Epistolae	14
nosque ipsos Tibi, Teque Deo Opti: Max: intimis precibus commendamus.	468	Epistolae	10
OPTIMA			
Tantoque nequioris optima Pirrha?	429	Mem.Matr.12	8
OPTIMAM			
Nec sic parentem ducar ad optimam:	425	Mem.Matr.6	10
OPTIME			
qua optime ostendis te eius vicarium qui omnia disponit suauiter?	443	Orationes	16
Quamobrem optime consuluit gentibus natura, cum paupertatem daret	450	Orationes	23
optime consuluisse Deum orbi terrarum lapides & metalla ei inserendo,	452	Orationes	24
Optime enim hoc conuenit Partui tuo, qui nouas scientiarum regiones	463	Epistolae	9
Quare optime fecit Rex Serenissimus, qui virtutes tuas magnis	466	Epistolae	12
Haec tu omnium optime vides, quare causam nostram nosque ipsos Tibi,	468	Epistolae	8
Haec tu optime nosti; neque eo dico:	471	Epistolae	5
OPTIMO			
sic Tu etiam dignitates ab optimo Rege desumptas in vniuersam	456	Epistolae	11
primo gratulamur optimo Regi nostro, qui prospicit, vt cum ipse	463	Epistolae	20
non adeo sanatae ab optimo Rege nostro quin turgescat indies,	473	Epistolae	21
OPTIMUM			
qui optimum Principem spe nuptiarum mari nuper tradentes,	444	Orationes	17

OPTIMUS	PAGE	TITLE	LINE
Quare noluit Princeps optimus, in delectu vxoris, re vna omnium	447	Orationes	22
per quod optimus Princeps non tantum exteras regiones habuit	451	Orationes	36
Deum immortalem, vt Princeps optimus nulla secunda itinera meditetur;	454	Orationes	38
OPTIO			
vestra est optio, vestra disquisitio, qui tineae estis & helluones	445	Orationes	18
OPULENTIA			
per quem vicini agri opulentia fruimur, veremur ne non tam sapientes	460	Epistolae	23
OPUS			
Vt sanctum Domini persequerentur opus;	392	Musae 19	2
At sibi collisit fictile Daemon opus.	408	Passio 20	2
idem impetus, qui peragrauit Hispaniam, si opus sit, superabit;	453	Orationes	31
ORA			
Ora meae memori menti: ne dispare cultu	427	Mem.Matr.7	31
ORAAS			
Nun oraas, oti kallos apeiriton opos apaugous	429	Mem.Matr.14	5
ORACULIS			
Ipsos Catones prouocans oraculis.	423	Mem.Matr.2	34
ORAM			
Roma. Anagr. Oram. Marc. / Ramo. Armo. / Mora. Amor.	416	Lucus 25	T
ROMA, tuum nomen quam non pertransijt ORAM, ...	416	Lucus 25	1
ORAMUS			
Tantum Maiestatem vestram subiectissime oramus, vt si officia nostra	460	Epistolae	15
ORANTES			
orantes vt quicquid consilij auaritia ceperit aduersus aut . . .	467	Epistolae	10
orantes vt immunitates nostrae a Serenissimis Regibus concessae ab	468	Epistolae	21
ORAT			
Ingemit, & defessus opem iam Portitor orat.	420	Tr.Mortis	82
ORATIO			
Oratio Domini Georgij Herbert, Oratoris Academiae Cantabrigiensis,	440	Orationes	T
Oratio in Discessum Regis ab Academia Cantabrigiae habita 12o die	443	Orationes	T
nostra occurrant, oratio nostra est silentium, atque eloquentia,	444	Orationes	2
Oratio Qua auspicatissimum Serenissimi Principis Caroli Reditum ex	444	Orationes	T
Dein, oratio clara sit, perspicua, pellucens.	470	Epistolae	28
Aliud oratio, aliud epistola. Parce doctrinae in epistolis; . .	470	Epistolae	32
Oratio perfecta, vti vir, tetragonos est, grauis, nobilis, . .	471	Epistolae	3
ORATIONE			
De oratione Dominica.	396	Musae 28	T
ORATIONEM			
orationem reijci septemplicem, ...	396	Musae 28	4
tantisper supplere donec Academia orationem tuam imbibat probetque,	470	Epistolae	7
ORATOR			
celebrauit Georgius Herbert Academiae Cantabrigiensis Orator.	444	Orationes	T
ORATOREM			
ipse egit oratorem, vt & ego aliquantulum hoc nomine glorier.	450	Orationes	31
ORATORIS			
Oratoris Academiae Cantabrigiensis, habita coram Dominis Legatis	440	Orationes	T
Rhetoris in hunc annum, & in plures Oratoris, permitte, . .	472	Epistolae	26
ORATORIUM			
ni graue est, librum tibi Oratorium lampademque tradat. . .	470	Epistolae	10
ORATORUM			
quam non longe abeam Oratorum more, qui nullum non angulum verrunt	445	Orationes	36
ORBAM			
orbam ritibus expetunt, ...	395	Musae 25	10
ORBARENTUR			
alumnis suis orbarentur, quin communes Reipublicae lachrymae alterum	462	Epistolae	5
ORBE			
Qui tam sublimi conspicit orbe viam:	387	Musae 7	6
Longius aeterno, latius orbe decus?	435	Poem.Lat.	6
Haec vestra spolia actosque ex orbe triumphos communicas cum Alma	458	Epistolae	16
ORBEM			
Seposuit Diuina sibi, cum conderet orbem, ...	402	Musae 39	15
Tu promis Orbem mane, condis vesperi, ...	407	Passio 16	3
Non vrbem facit vnicam, sed Orbem.	408	Passio 19	5
Expleri nequit, & totum depascitur Orbem.	419	Tr.Mortis	38
Tormento peior Iesuita, & fulminat Orbem, ...	420	Tr.Mortis	96
Volant per orbem literae notissimae:	423	Mem.Matr.2	38
pax nouum orbem aperuit; bellum destruit veterem.	448	Orationes	12
istis sublimitate solij asserta) vita et actione orbem vegetat.	458	Epistolae	7
ORBI			
optime consuluisse Deum orbi terrarum lapides & metalla ei inserendo,	452	Orationes	24
per hunc imperas orbi vniuerso, victoriaeque gloriam absque . .	458	Epistolae	14
ORBIBUS			
Ipsis seuerus orbibus;	427	Mem.Matr.8	6
ORBIS			
Constet, & ex illa pendeat orbis ope;	385	Musae 1	2
Deciduae melioris orbis!	394	Musae 23	36
Excessit tener Orbis ex Ephebis, ...	408	Passio 19	11
Corporeque atque animo. Ictus mihi seruiat Orbis.	421	Tr.Mortis	101
Sanguinis, innocuum tandem luet orbis Abelem.	272	Tr.Mortis VS	101
Perstringas homines vultu, miretur vt orbis	211	Cam.1613-b EF	13
cuius ingens gloria aeque rotunda est atque ipse orbis: . .	440	Orationes	16
assecutus es nomen, quam Repertores Noui Orbis compararunt. . .	463	Epistolae	12
ORBUS			
Haud secus ingenitis dotibus orbus Adam.	410	Lucus 1	4
ORCI			
Accedit Pyrius puluis, laquearibus Orci	419	Tr.Mortis	57
ORDINE			
Ordine discerni maxima bella solent.	399	Musae 33	28
Responde aeternum titulo; quoque ordine felix	402	Musae 39	18
cum eo sitis ordine atque habitu, quo nos in hoc regno omnes esse	441	Orationes	1

	PAGE	TITLE	LINE
ORDINEM			
Seruarentque sacrum clauibus ordinem;	391	Musae 17	6
ORDINIS			
Ordinis osores articulare malum.	389	Musae 11	4
ORDO			
Militat & nobis, quem vos contemnitis, Ordo;	399	Musae 33	27
ORE			
Dum prono rapis ore cibos, & fercula verris, ...	414	Lucus 21	1
ORIENTIS			
Quid iactas mihi aromata Orientis?	444	Orationes	24
ORIGINE			
Dicite, vos Furiae, qua gaudet origine Monstrum.	420	Tr.Mortis	85
Dicite vos Stutiae, qua gaudet origine monstrum	272	Tr.Mortis VS	85
ORIGO			
Cuius ab oppositis fluxit origo locis.	417	Lucus 31	4
ORIS			
finge tibi matronam sanctam, venerandam, oris prisci atque augusti;	470	Epistolae	17
ORITUR			
inter quae etiam certamen oritur et pia contentio, vtrum gratia	456	Epistolae	20
ORNANTUR			
Non animas, raroque ornantur sanguine regum	420	Tr.Mortis	98
ORNAS			
certe non tam ornas illam, qui infers manum grauitati.	470	Epistolae	20
ORNASTIS			
Ornastis capulum, nec superesse licet.	425	Mem.Matr.5	2
ORNAT			
Quo vulgus ornat vos! At audias parum;	393	Musae 22	6
ORNATRIX			
huius tu es commotria atque ornatrix.	470	Epistolae	17
ORNATU			
quidem multum, neque nostrae matronae conuenit, cui tu es ab ornatu.	471	Epistolae	3
ORNO			
Quin te laudibus orno: quippe dico, ...	401	Musae 37	41
ORO			
Quis hic superbit, oro? tune, an Praesules, ...	388	Musae 8	1
ORPHEA			
Orphea mellifluum secutas.	393	Musae 23	12
ORPHNAIEI			
Nun themis orphnaiei megales epi geitonos aisei	431	Mem.Matr.18	3
ORTHOS			
Orthos, anagke dustuxein tous ekgonous.	447	Orationes	15
ORTUM			
Ararumque Hominumque ortum si mente pererres, ...	417	Lucus 29	1
ORTUS			
Sic non Phoebeus iam plus te splendeat ortus	211	Cam.1613-b BB	15
relabitur in terram, qua ortus est, eique cum foecundia remuneratur:	454	Orationes	29
OS			
O barbaros! sic os rependitis sanctum, ...	404	Passio 5	1
Os & lingua tibi diues, egena manus:	414	Lucus 22	2
Verum augusta parens, sanctum os caeloque locandum, ...	426	Mem.Matr.7	10
Iisque siccis adeo vt os Molossorum	429	Mem.Matr.12	3
Pheggode monon, os eikos, epaulin exei.	429	Mem.Matr.14	4
Os dia somatiou proteron kai nun di' Olumpou	429	Mem.Matr.14	7
Astrapton, Thuridon os dia, neime selas.	429	Mem.Matr.14	8
Nun d' oxou enthend' os stratos nikephoros	430	Mem.Matr.15	10
Pheron to pan, kagon: e os Aparktias	430	Mem.Matr.15	11
Autar od' au thanatos kuries, os elios auos	431	Mem.Matr.17	19
nos etiam exuentes os illud, & supercilium quibus caperatam . .	440	Orationes	10
oculi omnium deiecti, humile os, collum pensile, manus decussatae,	451	Orationes	15
os importunorum hominum Authoritate tua plurima & Eloquentia	463	Epistolae	1
OSCULIS			
sed et ambabus vlnis osculisque ei aetati debitis excipientes,	463	Epistolae	7
OSORES			
Ordinis osores articulare malum.	389	Musae 11	4
OSPER			
semper titillant aures Principum, Osper tois pterois knomenoi ta ota.	453	Orationes	3
osper tina odon proeleluthoton, en kai emas isos deesei poreuesthai,	471	Epistolae	10
OSSIBUS			
Exuta strato carris, ossibus constans, ...	429	Mem.Matr.12	2
Leones Britannici (e quorum ossibus collisis ignis elicitur) qui nunc	449	Orationes	18
OST'			
Zo d' autos, braxu ti pneion, ost' empalin autes	431	Mem.Matr.17	21
OSTENDAM			
Viuite, dum mortem ostendam: sic tempora vestram	432	Poem.Lat.	15
OSTENDAS			
Hunc vultum ostendas, & tecum, nobile spectrum, ...	426	Mem.Matr.7	14
si speculum Inuidiae ostendas, quo deformitatem suam intueatur!	454	Orationes	21
OSTENDERE			
Sic lactare animos & sic ostendere gemmam	432	Poem.Lat.	31
OSTENDIS			
qua optime ostendis te eius vicarium qui omnia disponit suauiter?	443	Orationes	16
OSTH'			
Logon te philtron, osth' upekselthein loon.	430	Mem.Matr.15	9
OTA			
semper titillant aures Principum, Osper tois pterois knomenoi ta ota.	453	Orationes	3
OTAN			
Otan de krepis me katablethei genous	447	Orationes	14
Otan nomeus agathon kuna exei, kai oi alloi nomeis boulontai plesion	447	Orationes	31
OTE			
esti me perimenein, ote polemein umin omologesei, dixit Mithridates.	449	Orationes	15

	PAGE	TITLE	LINE
OTI			
Nun oraas, oti kallos apeiriton opos apaugous	429	Mem.Matr.14	5
OTIJ			
si tantum Honori Tuo superesset otij ad legendum, quantum a nobis	457	Epistolae	8
OTIO			
quae fugerunt tot philosophos vmbra et otio diffluentes, . .	463	Epistolae	19
OTIOSA			
Saepe ex se nihil otiosa cudit.	415	Lucus 24	6
OTIUM			
tranquillitas, otium, pax omnibus praeterquam tineis, paupertas	441	Orationes	15
Otium poscunt artes, mentem tranquillam, serenam, sudam: . .	448	Orationes	22
OU			
Ou sathron, oude melon epleto, alla voos:	429	Mem.Matr.14	6
Xalepon men ou dakrusai:	430	Mem.Matr.16	2
Geneteiran ou tis andron	430	Mem.Matr.16	5
Ou pheggos, koinon t' agathon, mian eis thuran eirgein . . .	430	Mem.Matr.17	5
Alla meneit', ou gar taraxos poti metera bainei, ...	431	Mem.Matr.18	5
on me themiton en, ou di' emauton emarton, alla dia tauta. . .	452	Orationes	30
OUDE			
Ou sathron, oude melon epleto, alla voos:	429	Mem.Matr.14	6
Ouk eni thauma toson spheterizein: oude gar udor, ...	430	Mem.Matr.17	4
OUES			
aut tanquam oues taedulae & fastidiosae, cibum respuamus. . .	449	Orationes	1
OUIS			
Vtque ouis in dumis, haeres in crine Cometae, ...	413	Lucus 16	3
OUK			
Ouk et' emen idias phules grapsantes arogon, ...	430	Mem.Matr.17	2
Ouk eni thauma toson spheterizein: oude gar udor, ...	430	Mem.Matr.17	4
Ouk eti ballomenes xarisin bebolemenai etor, ...	431	Mem.Matr.17	9
Ouk eti despoines glukerai meledoni trapheisai:	431	Mem.Matr.17	16
Ei en en o anthropos, inquit Medicorum Alpha, ouk an elgeen.	446	Orationes	19
OULUMPONDE			
Oulumponde biban ummin anistamenois.	431	Mem.Matr.18	4
OXOU			
Nun d' oxou enthend' os stratos nikephoros	430	Mem.Matr.15	10
OXYGALA			
Morosus, oxygala est: leuis, coagulum.	414	Lucus 20	15
PABULA			
Sed aliorum iniuriae tuarum virtutum pabula sunt, qui lemas istas	462	Epistolae	12
PACE			
Pace, filij sepeliunt patres; bello, patres filios:	448	Orationes	8
pace, aegri sanantur; bello, etiam sani intereunt:	448	Orationes	9
pace, securitas in agris est;	448	Orationes	10
pace, auium cantus expergefacit; bello, tubae ac tympana: . .	448	Orationes	11
PACEM			
Ad Scotiam. Protrepticon ad Pacem.	399	Musae 35	T
In pacem Britannicam.	411	Lucus 6	T
etiam praesenti seculo, dum pacem, qua tot iam annis impune fruimur,	447	Orationes	28
anteferendam bello pacem, sine qua omnis vita procella, . .	448	Orationes	7
Quare cauendum, ne pacem, quae sola incubat artibus, & obstetricatur,	448	Orationes	33
suam gentem amorem, cui pacem quaesiuit suo capite, periculis suis.	449	Orationes	37
PACTO			
tot iam annis impune fruimur, hoc pacto fundatam cupit & perpetuam;	447	Orationes	29
Vicini quo pacto niteant, id animum aduertito;	450	Orationes	16
PACTOLI			
Pactoli arena tibi tumulus est vnicus.	423	Mem.Matr.2	41
PACTOLO			
nihil inaudisti de Tago, Pactolo?	451	Orationes	4
PAGINA			
Pagina, gustasti, multoque interprete gaudes:	402	Musae 39	24
PALAESTRA			
etiam senectus, quam aetatem in hac palaestra consecutus mihi videor.	471	Epistolae	8
PALATIJ			
rotundum & coeleste, soli facies tanquam vestibulum magni palatij.	447	Orationes	2
PALATINI			
Sume Palatini versus de numine Phoebi, ...	210	Cam.1613-a BR	1
PALLADA			
Pallada gorgoneam, sic tua verba placent.	387	Musae 6	4
PALLADEM			
eos scilicet, qui innuptam Palladem colunt, Musasque coelibes,	446	Orationes	26
PALLAS			
Sumite gorgoneam, nostraque Pallas erit.	387	Musae 6	6
Lepos seuerus, Pallas mixta Gratijs;	423	Mem.Matr.2	30
Innupta Pallas, nata Diespitre, ...	433	Poem.Lat.	1
Pallas retortis caesia vocibus	434	Poem.Lat.	25
Hic habitant Musae, facilisque in carmine Pallas, ...	210	Cam.1613-a BR	3
PALLENTIA			
Ipse suos tanquam digno pallentiaque astra.	426	Mem.Matr.7	21
PALLIDA			
Pallida materni Genij atque exanguis imago, ...	426	Mem.Matr.7	1
PALMA			
virum protulit, cum quinque millibus annorum de palma certantem.	463	Epistolae	27
PALMIS			
Ah! quam caederis hinc & inde palmis!	405	Passio 8	1
PALPEBRIS			
circumspiciens reperisset Te, quasi in tuis palpebris acquiescat.	465	Epistolae	14
PALPITANTIS			
Commune cordis palpitantis balsamum:	423	Mem.Matr.2	47
PALUDOSOS			
Quale paludosos iamiam lictura recessus	426	Mem.Matr.7	11

	PAGE	TITLE	LINE
PALUDUM			
paludumque istos siccatores (solem officio suo priuantes) vi verborum	462	Epistolae	19
PALUM			
Nempe & millenos ad palum interficit hostes	418	Tr.Mortis	31
PALUSTRI			
eruditionis nobis conscius est, palustri opere & vliginoso intercipi:	461	Epistolae	7
PAN			
Pheron to pan, kagon: e os Aparktias	430	Mem.Matr.15	11
PANNUSIA			
Sericus es dictis, factis pannusia Baucis:	414	Lucus 22	1
PANTA			
Seiriou ettetheis boulemasi, panta marainei.	431	Mem.Matr.17	20
PANTES			
O despota elie kai theoi pantes, ei ti kata ton emautou Bion emarton,	452	Orationes	29
PANTON			
Xalepoteron de panton	430	Mem.Matr.16	3
PAPA			
Quisnam Antichristus cessemus quaerere; Papa	412	Lucus 10	1
PAPAE			
Papae titulus Nec Deus Nec Homo.	412	Lucus 10	1
PAPICOLIS			
Vt, quae Papicolis propria, assuas nobis,	392	Musae 20	8
Papicolisque sui sunt, Catharisque sui.	393	Musae 21	2
PAPILIONIS			
Assiduus nostri papilionis erat.	398	Musae 33	6
PAR			
incubat artibus, & obstetricatur, minus quam par est, aestimemus.	448	Orationes	34
de ingenti amore in Principem, cui nulla dilectio par esse potest;	451	Orationes	22
laetissime sumeret, quanto magis par est, nos humillimos subiectos,	460	Epistolae	12
PARA			
Toide para tumboi dizeo, phile, monon.	429	Mem.Matr.14	2
Kai prepon ode para dakruoessi reein.	431	Mem.Matr.18	6
Dokei moi xrenai para ton presbuton punthanesthai, osper tina odon	471	Epistolae	9
PARAS			
Paras hospitium torumque dulcem,	417	Lucus 30	5
PARASITE			
Et Templi parasite; namque velum	408	Passio 19	2
PARATE			
Parate situlas, Ethnici, lagenasque,	405	Passio 5	8
PARATI			
Vestramque Scyllam, aequis parati spiculis	397	Musae 30	5
PARATIOR			
instructior ad omnem causam, paratiorue siue a doctrina, siue ab vsu;	462	Epistolae	22
PARATOS			
paratos nos habebis ad gratulationem, vt sic vna opera vtriusque	465	Epistolae	25
PARCAE			
Tantum etenim vestras (Parcae) non flectit habenas	433	Poem.Lat.	40
PARCAS			
Sin nebulis parcas, & nostro parcito signo,	396	Musae 26	7
PARCAT			
neminemque esse sui negligentiorem, quam qui sibi parcat.	452	Orationes	35
PARCE			
Parce doctrinae in epistolis; perorans, paululum indulge:	471	Epistolae	1
PARCENS			
Hostibus haec etiam parcens imitatur Iesum.	416	Lucus 26	5
PARCIOR			
Scilicet emptorem si res aut parcior aetas	388	Musae 9	5
PARCIS			
Aggreditur Matrem (conductis carmine Parcis)	431	Mem.Matr.19	3
PARCITE			
Parcite luminibus, sitque lucerna domus:	413	Lucus 15	4
PARCITO			
Sin nebulis parcas, & nostro parcito signo,	396	Musae 26	7
PARCIUS			
Quare vt parcius agam vobiscum, simulque & laboribus meis,	445	Orationes	28
PARCO			
Proinde parco belluis, nec irascor.	429	Mem.Matr.12	11
PAREION			
ophthalmon upographas kai epitrimmata pareion inducens;	470	Epistolae	19
PARELEUSETAI			
ean epideikseis toi epikeimenoi nephei, pareleusetai e xalaza:	454	Orationes	19
PARENS			
Verum augusta parens, sanctum os caeloque locandum,	426	Mem.Matr.7	10
Virgo pudens, vxor fida, seuera parens:	429	Mem.Matr.13	2
PARENTEM			
Sed nos, cum nequeat paruorum lingua, parentem	389	Musae 12	7
Nec sic parentem ducar ad optimam:	425	Mem.Matr.6	10
PARENTIS			
Nato parentis auferens Encomium,	423	Mem.Matr.2	53
Qui parturit laudes parentis:	426	Mem.Matr.6	19
et mammas arentes tam nobilis parentis aequo animo ferre posset?	462	Epistolae	1
PARES			
Et numerat mortes singula gutta pares;	415	Lucus 23	10
qui virtutes tuas magnis negotijs pares prouexit, noluitque vt minori,	466	Epistolae	13
PARI			
Metus inanes? Nos pari praeteruehi	397	Musae 30	3
PARIBUS			
Vt currat paribus gloria tibijs.	425	Mem.Matr.4	16
Nostra etiam paribus marcescant gaudia fatis.	427	Mem.Matr.7	34
PARIT			
Mater: & ista Dolor nunc tibi Metra parit.	422	Mem.Matr.1	8

	PAGE	TITLE	LINE
PASSUS			
Neque enim passus es illum Fluuium, qui tantae poeticae, . . .	461	Epistolae	6
PASTI			
Quotidie pasti: tantum verum indue vultum	427	Mem.Matr.7	29
PASTOR			
Pastor agis proprios, medic tutissimus, agnos.	402	Musae 39	32
Iam meus es: nunc Te teneo: Pastorque prehensus	407	Passio 14	3
PASTOREM			
Scommata! Pastorem semper Arundo decet.	405	Passio 7	2
PATEANT			
certe studijs chartisque obuolutos, quin aures nostrae tibi pateant.	468	Epistolae	14
PATEFACTA			
superiori aestate sponte suauiterque patefacta, nunc etiam . . .	467	Epistolae	2
PATENT			
Nunc Arcana patent, nec inuolutam	408	Passio 19	9
Illis perpetuae patent fenestrae, ...	415	Lucus 24	13
patent enim consilia nostra, absconduntur Diuina & Regia, . .	449	Orationes	26
PATENTEM			
Fontem intercipis omnibus patentem?	421	Lucus 34	3
PATEO			
Nunc sorti pateo, expositus sine matre procellis, ...	428	Mem.Matr.11	7
PATER			
Sancte Pater, coeli custos, quo doctius vno	385	Musae	1
Sanctissime Pater. Cum caeterae ecclesiae tam perspicaci diligentia	466	Epistolae	20
Sanctissime Pater, Statim a solatio aspectus Tui, Ego auctior iam	471	Epistolae	16
permitte, Pater, hoc impetrem, vt cedam aliquantisper expectationi	472	Epistolae	27
PATERE			
Spero meo cordi posse patere viam.	404	Passio 4	2
PATERFAMILIAS			
Paterfamilias luminis.	407	Passio 16	10
PATERNOS			
Cuncta ad radices redeant, tumulosque paternos;	425	Mem.Matr.5	13
PATET			
Non tibi fingendi sola taberna patet.	386	Musae 3	6
Christe, vbi tam duro patet in te semita ferro, ...	404	Passio 4	1
Illud autem, quod cuiuis clarissime patet, etiam lusco, . .	449	Orationes	39
PATI			
Debuit ista pati prima & non nobilis aetas:	432	Poem.Lat.	29
PATINAS			
In patinas alij: furit inconstantia vini	418	Tr.Mortis	21
PATITUR			
vbi in dubio est, qui facit, an qui patitur, miserior.	449	Orationes	11
Celsitud., sed non patitur, vt mihi videtur, Romana elegantia,	473	Epistolae	17
PATIUNTUR			
Non nisi prima suas patiuntur praelia lites.	386	Musae 4	7
PATREM			
vt aliquando existimen id egisse prudentissimum Patrem tuum,	451	Orationes	30
Academicis maternisque, assumsi mecum propensionem in Patrem.	473	Epistolae	9
PATRES			
Inde Patres pergunt quadrati, & tota Vetustas.	398	Musae 33	13
Tu Synodosque, Patresque, & quod dedit alta vetustas	402	Musae 39	25
Pace, filij sepeliunt patres; bello, patres filios:	448	Orationes	9
bello, patres filios: pace, aegri sanantur;	448	Orationes	9
PATRI			
Reuerendissimo in Christo Patri ac Domino, ...	385	Musae	T
PATRIA			
Patria.	410	Lucus 2	T
posthac contineat se patria, cuius arctis amplexibus nunquam se	455	Orationes	2
Quod si necesse sit iterum exire patria, qui nunc inuenit viam,	455	Orationes	7
PATRIAE			
amor virginis eo pertraxit Principem, quo tandem ducet amor Patriae?	453	Orationes	28
vtinam & nunc sit tanta patriae tenacitas, vt nunquam Princeps se	455	Orationes	5
PATRIAM			
quam ex obseruatione exterarum legum ac morum, patriam ditare?	450	Orationes	15
cur non vt elephanti turres, ita tu patriam tecum portasti? . .	451	Orationes	8
indicantes, se non amare patriam terram, a qua adeo remouentur.	452	Orationes	12
ditat patriam, suamque absentiam cum foenore compensat. . .	454	Orationes	32
PATRIO			
Et patrio regno (sub quo iam Principe nobis	432	Poem.Lat.	27
PATRITIOS			
sumpta vna est e proceribus, inter patritios sedens et praetextatos.	470	Epistolae	24
PATRONE			
Patrone noster, qui elegantias doctrinae nitoremque spirans purpuram	461	Epistolae	21
PATRONUS			
Tu quidem semper Patronus noster es, etiam tacentibus nobis,	467	Epistolae	17
PATRUM			
atque ad barbariem patrum	395	Musae 25	11
PATULAS			
Quasque habet aut patulas, aut caeco tramite, moles . . .	402	Musae 39	21
PAUCORUM			
in quo paucorum auaritia liberalibus artibus dominatura est,	466	Epistolae	23
PAUCULOS			
Praesul, cur renuis? sin mala, pauculos	392	Musae 17	12
PAUERAT			
Aura volans, vitamque aer, quam pauerat, aufert.	420	Tr.Mortis	84
PAULATIM			
Lumina, nutantes paulatim acquirite vires, ...	432	Poem.Lat.	14
PAULISPER			
vt deponatis paulisper vultus illos bellicos, quibus hostes scletis	440	Orationes	8
peruenimus ad laurum hanc, vbi sub vmbra eius paulisper requiescamus:	455	Orationes	14

PAULO	PAGE	TITLE	LINE
Paulo, secretis mussitans in angulis	398	Musae 32	5
Vt nequeat paulo se cohibere domi.	404	Passio 3	2
sed lubet garrire paulo. Iupiter!	471	Epistolae	6
vbi sursum processerint paulo, frigefacti demum relabuntur. . .	471	Epistolae	30
rariusque paulo fodiam in Vintoniensi agro, dum Rhetorici satagam:	472	Epistolae	28
PAULULUM			
Quod si Artaxerxes olim paululum aquae a Sinaeta, subiecto suo,	460	Epistolae	11
perorans, paululum indulge: ne tum quidem multum, neque nostrae	471	Epistolae	1
PAULUS			
Dum gladium stringens Paulus ad arma vocat.	398	Musae 33	12
PAUPERTAS			
paupertas perpetua, nisi vbi vestrae adsunt Excellentiae. . .	441	Orationes	15
PAUPERTATEM			
cum paupertatem daret tanquam catenam, qua dissitas nationes ac	450	Orationes	23
PAUPERUM			
Quam mira tandem Subleuatrix pauperum!	423	Mem.Matr.2	45
PAUXILLUM			
mutilatam imaginem Dei, pauxillum vitae, quantum satis ad dolendum,	449	Orationes	5
PAX			
Cordis apex, animae pugnaque paxque meae, ...	421	Lucus 35	2
otium, pax omnibus praeterquam tineis, paupertas perpetua, . .	441	Orationes	15
pax nouum orbem aperuit; bellum destruit veterem.	448	Orationes	12
pax adeo Musis summe necessaria est, vt sine ea nihil simus.	448	Orationes	16
PECCATA			
Pro lapsu stillarum abeunt peccata; nec acres	406	Passio 13	3
PECCATI			
Peccati veniae mei, vel ipsos	421	Lucus 34	8
PECCATIS			
Sepia concurrat, peccatis aptior humor, ...	404	Passio 1	3
PECCATUM			
latiusque manare iniustitiae peccatum, quam negligentiae. . .	472	Epistolae	32
PECCEM			
Tandem, ne et ipse peccem, breuis sit sermo, atque pressus. . .	470	Epistolae	31
PECTORA			
Vobis, aut illis pectora vestra forent.	400	Musae 36	6
Si-quas mens agitet moles (dum pectora saeuo	432	Poem.Lat.	9
PECTORE			
Imo pectore cogitationes?	411	Lucus 5	3
Cum mihi sit facies fumus, quas pectore flammas	437	Poem.Lat.	9
PECTORIBUS			
Et pro pectoribus recenset aras, ...	408	Passio 19	6
PECTORIS			
Et ius pectoris inde consecutus	421	Lucus 34	5
PECTUS			
Num totum tibi pectus imputabis?	421	Lucus 34	2
non quin pectus meum plenum Tui sit, atque effusissimum in omnia	471	Epistolae	21
nihil Mortalium firmiori flagrare in Te desiderio, quam meum pectus;	473	Epistolae	5
PECUDES			
Quod non Lanigerae pecudes, non Agmina lustrent?	432	Poem.Lat.	19
PECUNIA			
Nempe graui fertur scelerata pecunia motu, ...	410	Lucus 4	7
PECUNIAM			
pecuniam retardare illam, cui natura spiritum dederit feracem	468	Epistolae	4
PEDE			
Heroum grandi carmina fulta pede?	387	Musae 5	4
Atque haeret dubio tabida vita pede, ...	438	Poem.Lat.	2
Invitoque fugit singula stella pede:	210	Cam.1613-b ER	2
Quare nunc vobis ex pede Herculem, ex itinere Principem metiri licet,	453	Orationes	22
PEDES			
Sin, Melvine, pedes alienos postulet infans, ...	388	Musae 9	9
Illos, qui mundum circumiere, pedes.	412	Lucus 8	4
Transiliuntque caput, qui subiere pedes.	414	Lucus 19	2
PEDIBUS			
Compita feruescunt pedibus, clamoribus aether.	418	Tr.Mortis	11
PEDIOI			
Polemos de kan pedioi kakos ephu.	448	Orationes	15
PEDUM			
In lotionem pedum Apostolorum.	412	Lucus 8	T
PEIOR			
Tormento peior Iesuita, & fulminat Orbem, ...	420	Tr.Mortis	96
PELAGO			
Sit licet in pelago semper, sine fluctibus illa est, ...	411	Lucus 6	3
quin & venti imperant pelago, vt laeuitatem illam aequabilem atque	453	Orationes	13
PELAGUS			
Cum dormis, surgit pelagus: cum, Christe, resurgis, ...	412	Lucus 12	1
Dormitat pelagus: Quam bene fraena tenes!	412	Lucus 12	2
PELLIBUS			
Instructaeque acies, hyemesque in pellibus actae, ...	418	Tr.Mortis	28
Stellarum socius, pellibus exuor.	424	Mem.Matr.4	8
PELLUCENS			
Dein, oratio clara sit, perspicua, pellucens.	470	Epistolae	28
PELVI			
Est Anti-pelvi-Melvi-Categoria.	386	Musae 3	10
PENDEAT			
Constet, & ex illa pendeat orbis ope;	385	Musae 1	2
PENDENTI			
Sydera, pendenti sedulus aure bibis:	413	Lucus 16	2
PENDET			
Politicos audiamus, salus regnorum pendet a vicinis, quorum consilia,	450	Orationes	26

	PAGE	TITLE	LINE
PENDULA			
In mea dicta ruant; non tam mihi pendula mens est,	432	Poem.Lat.	5
PENDULAM			
Pendulam hanc dignitatem diu expectantem magnas aliquas virtutes	464	Epistolae	11
PENE			
Claudi, pene tuas praeteriere fores.	385	Musae	4
PENETRANTIORI			
Tu penetrantiori intellectus acumine; cuius nisi incredibilis fuisset	463	Epistolae	16
PENNAS			
Cernite, quam formosa suas Ecclesia pennas	401	Musae 39	6
Angustior erat Scotia, quam vt pennas nido plene explicare posses:	458	Epistolae	8
PENNATA			
Pennata caeci dextra Cupidinis,	434	Poem.Lat.	22
PENSA			
Inde exiguntur pensa crudo vespere.	423	Mem.Matr.2	21
PENSILE			
humile os, collum pensile, manus decussatae, ipsae mulieres	451	Orationes	16
PENSILIS			
Pensilis, atque acri dirimens Examine lites.	426	Mem.Matr.7	13
PENSITAT			
Horti, colique distributim pensitat.	423	Mem.Matr.2	19
PENTHESI			
Meteri tektaincusa, gooi kai penthesi sugxroun.	431	Mem.Matr.17	14
PENU			
Prodegit integrum penu,	407	Passio 16	6
Tunc instruetur lautius radijs penu,	407	Passio 16	13
PEPLON			
Ergou amartekuia, neon peplon aimati stikton	431	Mem.Matr.17	13
PER			
Nunc adeo per te viuunt, vt repere possint,	384	Musae	5
Res ampliantur, sin per aduersam videt,	388	Musae 8	13
Et per se Templi limen adire velis:	388	Musae 9	8
Quae ratio per se, si sit adulta, facit.	388	Musae 9	12
Forte quidem, cum per vestras Ecclesia turbas	389	Musae 12	3
Saltus per incultos lacusque	393	Musae 23	11
Atqui te precor vnice per ipsam,	400	Musae 37	1
Quae scripsit numeros, manum; per omnes	400	Musae 37	2
Musarum calices, per & beatos	400	Musae 37	3
Quin per Presbyteros tuos; per vrbem	400	Musae 37	5
Per charas tibi nobilesque dextras,	400	Musae 37	7
Per quicquid tibi suauiter probatur;	400	Musae 37	9
Haud per te moritura, Scholamque introspicis omnem.	402	Musae 39	26
Per fluctus saltem, fac, precor, ipse vadem.	414	Lucus 19	4
Spargitque per tot capita, quot vulgus gerit.	414	Lucus 20	4
Ni facias, vt opes linguae per brachia serpant,	414	Lucus 22	3
Si non per species, nequimus ipsi,	415	Lucus 24	9
Se per se facili modo scientes,	415	Lucus 24	14
Quae diuisa nocent, Christi per foedus, in vnum	417	Lucus 29	3
Hic vbi discumbunt per gramina, salsior vnus	418	Tr.Mortis	12
Per angiportus & maeandros labitur,	423	Mem.Matr.2	33
Volant per orbem literae notissimae:	423	Mem.Matr.2	38
Per te nascor in hunc globum	425	Mem.Matr.4	13
Atque vbi per te sanctificer natalibus ipsis,	434	Poem.Lat.	9
Per strages licet autorum veterumque ruinam	435	Poem.Lat.	1
Cum per te sit res ambitiosa mori.	435	Poem.Lat.	8
Si per haec ludicra nostra pars aliquis eius laetitiae,	443	Orationes	9
si per tempus liceret effari, non licet per multitudinem,	443	Orationes	28
effari, non licet per multitudinem, imo per modestiam vestram?	443	Orationes	29
nulla pulchritudo per vniuersam Britanniam, disparuit forma,	451	Orationes	17
per quod optimus Princeps non tantum exteras regiones habuit	451	Orationes	35
& per tot milliaria facile transmissum, mentem maiorum capacem	454	Orationes	1
vsque ad Pyrenaeas nubes conscendens, reuersus per mare, gloria,	454	Orationes	32
per Te illucet nobis Iacobus noster.	456	Epistolae	12
per hunc imperas orbi vniuerso, victoriaeque gloriam absque	458	Epistolae	14
per quem vicini agri opulentia fruimur, veremur ne non tam sapientes	460	Epistolae	23
nostrae, quae per Tuum Partum, ex Matre nunc Auia facta est:	463	Epistolae	25
per me non stabit quo minus, spe prouecta atque adulta,	470	Epistolae	7
PERACTA			
Clauserit extremas pugna peracta vices,	386	Musae 2	8
PERAGRATA			
Atque omnes peragrata es angiportus	411	Lucus 5	13
PERAGRAUIT			
idem impetus, qui peragrauit Hispaniam, si opus sit, superabit;	453	Orationes	31
PERAMBULARE			
Ah, quam docta perambulare calles	411	Lucus 5	15
PERCELLERE			
in promptu erat, rudesque animos vi verborum percellere:	445	Orationes	17
PERCELLIS			
Virtute percellis tua;	388	Musae 8	4
PERCITAS			
Potentiori carmine percitas	393	Musae 23	10
PERCURRERET			
non dubitamus quin benignitas tua omnia elementa percurreret.	457	Epistolae	23
PERCURRERIS			
postquam omnes honorum gradus hic percurreris, aeternum illud	457	Epistolae	4
PERCURRES			
quam nunc pleno gradu ingrediens beneficijs tuis percurres.	468	Epistolae	19
PERCURRITE			
Christus adest: crebris aedes percurrite scopis,	413	Lucus 15	1
percurrite Annales regnorum, excutite scrinia politiarum omnium;	445	Orationes	13

	PAGE	TITLE	LINE
PERCURRITIS			
vbi trecenta foliorum iugera vno die sedentes percurritis;	454	Orationes	25
PERCUSSA			
Percussa dum currunt ad vrbem	394	Musae 23	15
PERDANT			
Dij te perdant, cum malis tuis & arena sine calce;	451	Orationes	5
PERDAT			
Ne perdat Leo rugiens vagantem.	417	Lucus 30	8
PERDERE			
Sic, pro Maiestate, Deum, non perdere vitam	408	Passio 17	7
Perdere sexcentas? crescit tamen hydra nocendi	419	Tr.Mortis	35
Perdere sexcentas? crescet tamen hydra nocendi	419	Tr.Mortis V	35
At forte matrem perdere haud scies demens:	429	Mem.Matr.12	9
PERDIAE			
squalidae, perdiae, pernoctes flagitant, cauendum ne id nobis nauseam	448	Orationes	36
PERDIDERINT			
non angulum verrunt (ac si perdiderint ingenium) vt Spartam exornent	445	Orationes	37
PERDIDIT			
Ad bellum missos perdidit vna dies.	399	Musae 33	32
PERDUNT			
Ridens Bombardas miseras, quae corpora perdunt	420	Tr.Mortis	97
PEREGRINAS			
Quid Theriacas peregrinas? asserunt Medici vnamquamque regionem sua	444	Orationes	24
PEREGRINATI			
vnde cuncti antiqui Philosophi peregrinati sunt, existimantes	450	Orationes	8
diu iam peregrinati cum Principe, commode peruenimus ad laurum hanc,	455	Orationes	12
PEREGRINATIONE			
ad cognitionem acquirendam peregrinatione conducibilius esse nouistis	450	Orationes	7
PEREGRINIS			
Peregrinis Academiam nostram inuisentibus	459	Epistolae	29
PERELEGANTER			
quod pereleganter & supra barbariem seculi innuebant Maiores nostri,	446	Orationes	28
PERENNIS			
O mea suspicienda manus, venterque perennis!	418	Tr.Mortis	1
O mortis longaeua fames, venterque perennis	271	Tr.Mortis VS	1
PERERRAT			
Syluas pererrat. Fibulis dein omnibus	398	Musae 32	8
PERERRATAS			
Ecce pererratas, Regum doctissime, nugas,	401	Musae 39	1
PERERRES			
Ararumque Hominumque ortum si mente pererres,	417	Lucus 29	1
PEREUNTIA			
iniurias seculi scriptaque hac illac pereuntia securius praeterit.	459	Epistolae	14
PERFACILIS			
certa, ac perfacilis mihi!	395	Musae 25	7
PERFECTA			
Oratio perfecta, vti vir, tetragonos est, grauis, nobilis,	471	Epistolae	4
PERFECTIONE			
qui etiam ferians nihil Tua perfectione dignum procudere possit.	471	Epistolae	24
PERFECTIONIBUS			
perfectionibus Tuis, meis desiderijs probe cognitis, excussis	472	Epistolae	3
PERFOSSUM			
In latus perfossum.	404	Passio 4	1
PERFUNDIS			
qua perfundis nos omnes quotidianis beneficijs, redundarit	443	Orationes	10
PERGAS			
Coepisti, pergas simili res texere filo.	402	Musae 39	19
Tantum rogamus, vt pergas, & inter nouos honorum cumulos,	462	Epistolae	28
PERGE			
Ecclesia est mihi Luna; perge in Fabula.	393	Musae 22	10
Perge, decus Regum; sic, Augustissime, plures	402	Musae 39	33
PERGIS			
Incipis irridens; stomachans in carmine pergis;	401	Musae 38	1
PERGUNT			
Inde Patres pergunt quadrati, & tota Vetustas.	398	Musae 33	13
PERHORRIDAS			
Magicos rotatus, & perhorridas Striges,	392	Musae 20	12
PERI			
Tes peri sullalecusin, eou poikilmatos arden	431	Mem.Matr.17	11
PERICULIS			
suam gentem amorem, cui pacem quaesiuit suo capite, periculis suis.	449	Orationes	37
vt iter tantum, tantis laboribus, periculis obnoxium, susciperet?	452	Orationes	8
PERICULO			
vt ingenti labore suo & periculo consuleret & praesenti Reipublicae	447	Orationes	24
PERICULOSIUS			
praesertim cum amico fidere periculosius sit, quam hostem superare.	453	Orationes	32
PERIERUNT			
Laus antiqua & honor perierunt, te velut ARMO	416	Lucus 25 V	7
PERIJT			
Laus antiqua & honor perijt: quasi scilicet ARMO	416	Lucus 25	7
Decus mulierum perijt: & metuunt viri	422	Mem.Matr.2	8
PERIMANT			
Vt morbi perimant, alioque in puluere prostet?	433	Poem.Lat.	35
PERIMENEIN			
Sophronon esti me perimenein, ote polemein umin omologesei,	449	Orationes	14
PERIMUNT			
Afflatu perimunt: en, Cymba Cocytia turbis	420	Tr.Mortis	81
PERIODI			
vt mihi videtur, Romana elegantia, periodique vetus rotunditas.	473	Epistolae	18
PERIT			
telam explices, perit negotium quasi ex nubibus Ixionis congressus.	470	Epistolae	30

	PAGE	TITLE	LINE
PERITA			
Maeandrosque plicasque, quam perita es!	411	Lucus 5	16
Sollicitus, ne te stella perita notet:	413	Lucus 16	4
PERITE			
Euge, perite omnes; nec posthac exeat vlla	425	Mem.Matr.5	11
PERITUS			
Quare, peritus nauta, vela contrahas, ...	414	Lucus 20	11
Rationis & sensus peritus Arbiter;	436	Poem.Lat. V	16
PERLITA			
Splenis perlita contumeliosi.	400	Musae 37	13
PERLONGAS			
Et nunc perlongas Scripturae stamine telas	392	Musae 19	5
PERMANENS			
Si enim in regno vestro Hibernico lignum nascitur permanens,	459	Epistolae	16
PERMANSERIT			
Mox displicent omnes. Vbi hoc permanserit	398	Musae 32	4
PERMITTAT			
Obsecremus eum tantum vt permittat nostram hanc Inter victrices	455	Orationes	16
PERMITTE			
Permitte vt nos etiam in praedam partemque tecum veniamus: . .	465	Epistolae	21
in hunc annum, & in plures Oratoris, permitte, Pater, hoc impetrem,	472	Epistolae	27
PERMITTIS			
Ecquid permittis, Domine? Curasti tu quidem Instauratione tua,	467	Epistolae	24
PERMULTUM			
Imo prorsus censemus permultum interesse alacritatis publicae,	468	Epistolae	14
PERMUTARE			
quamuis enim sexcenta huiusmodi praediola Tua gratia permutare nolim,	472	Epistolae	30
PERNICIOSA			
Merserat in lustris perniciosa venus, ...	396	Musae 26	10
PERNOCTES			
pernoctes flagitant, cauendum ne id nobis nauseam moueat, . .	448	Orationes	36
PERORANS			
perorans, paululum indulge: ne tum quidem multum, neque nostrae	471	Epistolae	1
PERORER			
gaudia praestolantur, quae iamdudum annuunt mihi vt perorem.	454	Orationes	23
PERPENDE			
Perpende, non tam quod tibi conueniat scribenti, quam quod Academiae	470	Epistolae	13
PERPENSIS			
Tuis, meis desiderijs probe cognitis, excussis perpensisque.	472	Epistolae	4
PERPENSURIS			
omnia fauorum tuorum momenta apicesque perpensuris et compensaturis.	466	Epistolae	8
PERPETIM			
Tu vero mater perpetim laudabere	424	Mem.Matr.2	61
PERPETUA			
paupertas perpetua, nisi vbi vestrae adsunt Excellentiae. . .	441	Orationes	16
PERPETUAE			
Illis perpetuae patent fenestrae, ...	415	Lucus 24	13
PERPETUAM			
tot iam annis impune fruimur, hoc pacto fundatam cupit & perpetuam;	447	Orationes	30
PERPETUIS			
Mater perpetuis vuida gaudijs, ...	424	Mem.Matr.4	2
PERPETUO			
Stulta: semel scribo, perpetuo vt sileam.	431	Mem.Matr.19	8
PERPETUOS			
Perpetuos mihi ferre rami, ...	434	Poem.Lat.	32
PERRUMPEMUS			
perrumpemus controuersias omnes, superabimus quoscunque. . .	459	Epistolae	6
PERRUMPENS			
Perrumpens, Atropi vetulae marcentibus vlnis.	419	Tr.Mortis	65
PERRUMPIT			
perrumpit primipilus, & te cum coelis tuis ad inferos deturbat.	448	Orationes	30
PERSEQUERENTUR			
Vt sanctum Domini persequerentur opus;	392	Musae 19	2
PERSONAE			
manifestationem in gentem suam priuatae personae & habitui debuit.	453	Orationes	8
PERSONAM			
Quin exuit personam Principis, deponit Maiestatem, virgam cum sceptro	452	Orationes	35
& quasi mixtam personam reddidit quam si Episcopi more pristino	461	Epistolae	27
neque quotidianae virtutis prouincia gerere personam Academiae,	465	Epistolae	10
tu hanc personam indue scripturus, tuumque iudicium tibi Lictor esto.	470	Epistolae	26
PERSPECTAS			
quod optimus Princeps non tantum exteras regiones habuit perspectas,	452	Orationes	1
PERSPECTISSIMO			
studioque in nos iam olim perspectissimo, quippe qui eximie semper	462	Epistolae	25
PERSPECTISSIMUS			
sed perspectissimus tuus in nos amor, praestantissimaeque animi dotes	465	Epistolae	11
PERSPECTUS			
in nos amor, antehac satis perspectus, nunc cum honore geminetur.	466	Epistolae	3
PERSPICACI			
Te perspicaci atque integro.	388	Musae 8	8
Cum caeterae ecclesiae tam perspicaci diligentia incubes, . .	466	Epistolae	21
PERSPICACIBUS			
nobis non licet esse tam perspicacibus, quamuis rationi consonum	449	Orationes	31
PERSPICACITATEM			
Et cum ob perspicacitatem singularem iam olim Regi notam atque	469	Epistolae	20
PERSPICILLIS			
Quisquis tuetur perspicillis Belgicis	388	Musae 8	11
cum futura incerta sint, & nullis perspicillis, ne Belgicis quidem,	449	Orationes	24
PERSPICIO			
in quo longe vberrimam gloriae segetem perspicio, nulla verborum,	446	Orationes	2

	PAGE	TITLE	LINE
PERSPICUA			
Dein, oratio clara sit, perspicua, pellucens.	470	Epistolae	28
vti vir, tetragonos est, grauis, nobilis, perspicua, succincta.	471	Epistolae	4
PERSTAS			
Aspice, dum perstas, vt te tua deserat aetas,	386	Musae 2	5
PERSTITIT			
Nullum locum requiemue cernens perstitit	436	Poem.Lat.	20
PERSTREPIS			
Scilicet Hebraeam cantas, & perstrepis vnam:	391	Musae 16	5
Tu perstrepis tamen; vtque turgeat carmen	392	Musae 20	10
PERSTRINGAS			
Perstringas homines vultu, miretur vt orbis	211	Cam.1613-b BR	13
PERSTRINGAT			
qui mundi oculos perstringat, nos tam defecimus in vtroque quam	441	Orationes	12
PERSTRINGUNT			
Perstringunt vestros carmina sola duces.	400	Musae 36	4
PERTEREBRARE			
Sedula si fuerit, pereterebrare potest.	410	Lucus 2	6
PERTINACES			
aliae contra semper pertinaces ac tribunitiae, vti Appij.	447	Orationes	21
PERTINACIA			
Ea est enim pertinacia desideriorum nostrorum, atque immortalitas,	464	Epistolae	22
PERTINGIT			
Explicat, & radijs ipsum pertingit Olympum!	401	Musae 39	7
verisimile est, eos illuc, quo cognitio ipsa pertingit, ascensuros.	468	Epistolae	2
PERTRAHIS			
Pertrahis in partes nomina magna tuas;	398	Musae 33	2
PERTRANSIJT			
ROMA, tuum nomen quam non pertransijt ORAM,	416	Lucus 25	1
PERTRAXIT			
si amor virginis eo pertraxit Principem, quo tandem ducet amor	453	Orationes	27
PERTULI			
o quot iam anni sunt ex quo vel apicem Latinum pertuli!	471	Epistolae	7
PERTURBENT			
vt laeuitatem illam aequabilem atque politiem perturbent.	453	Orationes	14
PERTURBET			
Cum sacra perturbet vester furor omnia, scriptum	386	Musae 3	7
PERUAGANTUR			
rogamusque vt quando beneficia tua peruagantur Angliam,	466	Epistolae	17
PERUENIMUS			
commode peruenimus ad laurum hanc, vbi sub vmbra eius paulisper	455	Orationes	13
PERUETUSTA			
Quin te Cambria peruetusta deflet,	428	Mem.Matr.10	10
PESSIMA			
siccine pessima? at fuerit; si amor virginis eo pertraxit Principem,	453	Orationes	27
PESTIS			
Vno ictu: non sic pestis, non stella maligno	420	Tr.Mortis	80
Annon longa fames miseraeque iniuria pestis	432	Poem.Lat.	20
PETAM			
Implicet, & matrem, matre manente, petam.	424	Mem.Matr.3	10
PETANT			
neque vlla negotia (quippe quae caput petant, non cor) Tui in me	473	Epistolae	6
PETAS			
Ni me forte petas; nam quanto indignior ipse,	404	Passio 2	5
PETEREMUS			
omnes ad Aulam, atque ab eo consilium peteremus a quo et fortunas?	443	Orationes	27
PETERES			
Totum offuscari peteres, vt nocte silenti	433	Poem.Lat.	38
PETET			
Te petet, ante diem quisquis obire cupit.	414	Lucus 21	6
PETIT			
Et partem capitis petit supremam;	391	Musae 15	4
Dum petit Infantem.	437	Poem.Lat.	T
Dum petit Infantem Princeps, Grantamque Iacobus,	437	Poem.Lat.	1
Cum petit Hispanam Princeps, Grantamque Iacobus,	437	Poem.Lat. V	1
PETITUS			
Vnicus est nummus, caelo Christoque petitus,	410	Lucus 4	9
PETRA			
Tu radix, tu petra mihi firmissima, Mater,	428	Mem.Matr.11	9
PETRAE			
Petrae scissae.	408	Passio 20	T
PETRAIS			
Eirene georgon kan petrais trephei kalos,	448	Orationes	14
PETRAS			
Constat inaccessas dissiluisse petras.	409	Passio 20	6
PETRE			
Tu geminas belli portas, o Petrè, repandis,	398	Musae 33	11
PETRI			
In Vmbram Petri.	413	Lucus 14	T
PHAGON			
ti kata ton emautou Bion emarton, e phagon e pion, on me themiton en,	452	Orationes	30
PHANTASMA			
Mutata? & pro matre mihi phantasma dolosum	426	Mem.Matr.7	3
PHARETRAE			
apud poetas deorum pharetrae operculum habuere, humanae non item:	449	Orationes	25
PHARETRAM			
Enceladum pharetramque Rhoeci.	434	Poem.Lat.	20
PHARETRATA			
praecipue pharetrata, quae ad poenam gentium & Bellum spectant.	449	Orationes	27
PHARISAEIS			
Primus adest nobis, Pharisaeis omnibus hostis,	398	Musae 33	9

	PAGE	TITLE	LINE
PHARMACA			
Nec tarda possunt pharmaca consequi,	425	Mem.Matr.6	6
PHEGGODE			
Pheggode monon, os eikos, epaulin exei.	429	Mem.Matr.14	4
PHEGGOS			
Nou d' autou taphos est' aster: pheggos gar ekeinou	429	Mem.Matr.14	3
Ou pheggos, keinon t' agathon, mian eis thuran eirgein	430	Mem.Matr.17	5
PHERON			
Pheron to pan, kagon: e os Aparktias	430	Mem.Matr.15	11
PHILE			
Toide para tumboi dizeo, phile, monon.	429	Mem.Matr.14	2
PHILEGKLEMON			
tamen anus illa querula, & philegklemon, quam audire videor dicentem,	453	Orationes	29
PHILOMELA			
Iam foelix Philomela, & menti conscia Dido!	432	Poem.Lat.	22
Vt Flos hinc lacrymis, illinc Philomela querelis,	438	Poem.Lat.	5
PHILOSOPHI			
vnde cuncti antiqui Philosophi peregrinati sunt, existimantes	450	Orationes	8
PHILOSOPHIAE			
Naturae Aruspex intimus; Philosophiae	436	Poem.Lat.	7
qui Philosophiae incumbis, cum corporis cum anima vinculum	448	Orationes	26
PHILOSOPHIAM			
quibus caperatam seuerioremque Philosophiam expugnare nouimus,	440	Orationes	12
PHILOSOPHOS			
ne non tam sapientes nos, quam obscuros philosophos reddidissent.	461	Epistolae	1
quae fugerunt tot philosophos vmbra et otio diffluentes,	463	Epistolae	19
PHILOSOPHUS			
qui inde e baiulo euasit Philosophus, eodem ingenio vsus in lignis	453	Orationes	37
Siccam animam sapientissimam esse dixit obscurus ille philosophus;	460	Epistolae	21
vt quod Philosophus de Tactu & Visu, id apposite admodum huc	472	Epistolae	36
PHILTRON			
Logon te philtron, osth' upekselthein leon.	430	Mem.Matr.15	9
PHOEBE			
Cur splendes, O Phoebe? ecquid demittere matrem	424	Mem.Matr.3	1
Musa, vale, & tu Phoebe; dolor mea carmina dictet;	432	Poem.Lat.	12
Phoebe, tui puduit quum summo mane redires	433	Poem.Lat.	36
PHOEBEUS			
Sic non Phoebeus iam plus te splendeat ortus	211	Cam.1613-b BF	15
PHOEBI			
Sume Palatini versus de numine Phoebi,	210	Cam.1613-a BF	1
PHOTOS			
Photos apauramenes ogkou epheisthe pleon,	431	Mem.Matr.18	2
PHRASI			
nisi candida phrasi telam explices, perit negotium quasi ex nubibus	470	Epistolae	30
PHUGOUSA			
Exren phugousa, ten t' epistemen biou.	430	Mem.Matr.15	7
PHULES			
Ouk et' emen idias phules grapsantes arogon,	430	Mem.Matr.17	2
PHYLACTERIA			
Phylacteria complicant latriam.	408	Passio 19	10
PHYSICIS			
Ex praelio vndae ignisque (si Physicis fides)	396	Musae 27	1
PHYSICUS			
Repumicator mentis; Atlas Physicus,	436	Poem.Lat.	17
PIA			
Arguit, exceptos quos pia Roma fouet:	416	Lucus 26	4
inter quae etiam certamen oritur et pia contentio, vtrum gratia	456	Epistolae	20
PIACULUM			
permutare nolim, maius tamen piaculum reor, deesse publico muneri,	472	Epistolae	31
PIAM			
Paruam piamque dum lubenter semitam	427	Mem.Matr.8	1
PICEO			
Vel gemitus Erebi: piceo se turbine voluens	420	Tr.Mortis	75
PICTURIS			
In picturis locus est vmbris & recessibus, etiam si quis Principem	453	Orationes	14
PIE			
Abito, barde. Quam pie istic sum impudens!	424	Mem.Matr.2	60
PIERIA			
Nam primum tota haec Pieria supellex, charta, calami, codices,	448	Orationes	18
PIERIDIS			
Pieridis Latiaeque Musae,	433	Poem.Lat.	4
PIERIOS			
Res redit ad vates, Pieriosque duces:	417	Lucus 28	2
PIETATE			
Nobilitate illos, hos pietate rapit.	429	Mem.Matr.13	4
PIETATIS			
Ergo ringantur pietatis hostes,	390	Musae 14	17
omnium coelestiores animi, quorum pietatis interest non silere.	445	Orationes	11
PIGNORA			
pignora chara sui	397	Musae 28	11
PIGNUS			
Nec vel tantillum pignus habebit amor?	396	Musae 26	2
hunc quidem gradum pignus habes amoris nostri, haec est ansa qua	456	Epistolae	5
PIJS			
Adde pijs animis quaeuis occasio lucro est,	390	Musae 12	11
dum sponsam Domini pijs	395	Musae 25	9
PILEO			
De Pileo quadrato.	391	Musae 15	T
PILEOS			
Sed qui tam male pileos habetis,	391	Musae 15	11

	PAGE	TITLE	LINE
PILEUS			
Isthaec pileus audijt propinquus, ...	391	Musae 15	3
Longe pileus anteit galerum, ...	391	Musae 15	8
PINGAT			
locus est vtris & recessibus, etiam si quis Principem pingat.	453	Orationes	15
PINGUEM			
lucos aestate, pinguem togam hyeme:	448	Orationes	24
PINGUIS			
Quem non Emathius torrens, non sanguine pinguis	418	Tr.Mortis	2
PINUS			
Profunditatis pinus, atque Elegantiae;	436	Poem.Lat.	6
PION			
ti kata ton emautou Bion emarton, e phagon e pion, on me themiton en,	452	Orationes	30
PIORUM			
Ingens piorum gloria Principum, ...	394	Musae 23	38
PIOS			
Ipse pios laudo; Numen & ipse colo.	386	Musae 4	6
PIRRHA			
Tantoque nequioris optima Pirrha?	429	Mem.Matr.12	8
PISCATORES			
Cum piscatores Textor legit esse vocatos, ...	392	Musae 19	1
PISCATORIS			
In Sacram Anchoram Piscatoris G. Herbert.	438	Poem.Lat.	T
PISCIS			
Et Christianus quisque piscis dicitur	389	Musae 10	6
Piscis tributum soluit; & tu Caesari:	412	Lucus 11	1
eundemque retulisset captus piscis, foelicissimus mortalium habitus	444	Orationes	15
PIUM			
In pium Latronem.	406	Passio 11	T
PIXIDES			
Aegroto mentis: quam neque pixides	425	Mem.Matr.6	5
PLACEAT			
Tum tibi, si placeat, fugientia tempora reddam;	386	Musae 2	9
Si tibi non illud placeat mirabile corpus, ...	404	Passio 2	3
si placeat vices meas tantisper supplere donec Academia orationem	470	Epistolae	6
PLACENT			
Sic Catharis noua scla placent; res, verba nouantur:	386	Musae 3	3
Pallada gorgoneam, sic tua verba placent.	387	Musae 6	4
Nulla tibi si signa placent, e nubibus arcum	396	Musae 26	3
PLACEO			
Quod scribo, & placeo, si placeo, tuum est.	403	Musae 40	14
PLACET			
Sola tibi Sappho, feminaque vna placet?	387	Musae 5	2
Primo, vnus aut alter parum ritus placet:	398	Musae 32	2
Non placet vrbanus noster de nomine lusus	416	Lucus 27	1
Quo placet oblato, mortua fertur, hero:	428	Mem.Matr.11	4
Circumspice, si placet, Terrarum Reges, mutus est mundus vniuersus,	458	Epistolae	5
PLACIDISSIMO			
Fluuium placidissimo faucium tuorum afflatu nobis tuere. . .	461	Epistolae	24
PLACIDO			
Obtutu placido benignus affles, ...	384	Musae	3
Scribentem placido rore beaueris, ...	402	Musae 40	2
PLACUIT			
Non placuit rudis atque ignara occisio: Morti	418	Tr.Mortis	24
Non placuit rudis atque ignara occasio; morti	271	Tr.Mortis VS	24
PLANE			
Cancellario INSTAVRARI, inter Arcana Prouidentiae plane reponimus.	464	Epistolae	2
PLATO			
Hunc poenas animam mundi, Plato: vel tua mundum	409	Passio 21	3
PLATONEM			
Proinde audi Platonem: Dokei moi xrenai para ton presbuton . .	471	Epistolae	9
PLAUDITE			
Amstellodamum corripit se. Plaudite.	398	Musae 32	10
PLAUSTRA			
Haurirent tibi tota plaustra Musae.	401	Musae 37	30
PLEBE			
Esse iocum soli, plebe stupente, tibi:	416	Lucus 27	4
PLEBEM			
Exuscitat plebem sacratos	394	Musae 23	31
PLEBS			
Facesse, Stoica plebs, obambulans cautes, ...	429	Mem.Matr.12	1
PLECTETUR			
Gens tota fiet, atque vtringue plectetur.	405	Passio 5	7
PLENA			
Praedicat autores; tertia plena Deo est.	386	Musae 4	4
Sic nunc plena boni sunt omnia Fratris, amore	393	Musae 21	3
O plena centum Musica Gratijs, ...	394	Musae 23	21
huiusmodi lamentis & quiritationibus plena erant fora, nundinae,	451	Orationes	10
PLENAS			
Discordijs plenas sonoris	395	Musae 23	51
PLENE			
Angustior erat Scotia, quam vt pennas nido plene explicare posses:	458	Epistolae	8
PLENIS			
honore grauidus, grauidus scientia, cruribus thymo plenis: . . .	454	Orationes	28
PLENISSIMIS			
plenissimis suffragijs elegimus Te tribunum Parlamentarium, . . .	465	Epistolae	4
PLENISSIMUM			
nobis Librum, plenissimum Musarum, quae cum olim gauderent Fluuijs,	460	Epistolae	7
PLENO			
Aspice quam pleno descendat Iuppiter imbre, ...	210	Cam.1613-a BR	5
quam nunc pleno gradu ingrediens beneficijs tuis percurres. . .	468	Epistolae	19

	PAGE	TITLE	LINE
PLENOS			
Sola mihi plenos, ait, exhibet Anglia cultus.	402	Musae 39	13
enixus gloriae, sollicitudine in futurum plenos, haud parum leuare;	469	Epistolae	11
PLENUM			
Triste colens cellae, noctuque & Daemone plenum, ...	420	Tr.Mortis	90
Triste colens sellae, noctuque & Daemone plenum, ...	420	Tr.Mortis V	90
non quin pectus meum plenum Tui sit, atque effusissimum in omnia	471	Epistolae	21
PLENUS			
Annulus & plenus tempore forsan erit.	396	Musae 26	6
Quos inter plerusque Deo genioque Iacobus	399	Musae 33	23
Cur Deus elegit Medicum, qui numine plenus	412	Lucus 9	1
Intra extraque graui plenus es illuuie.	414	Lucus 21	2
PLEON			
Photos apauramenes ogkou epheisthe pleon, ...	431	Mem.Matr.18	2
PLERUMQUE			
(Cum plerumque tua sodalitate	401	Musae 37	45
(veluti Conclusio sequitur infirmiorem partem) plerumque matrissat:	447	Orationes	18
Cum tamen splendida plerumque vitrea sint, claritatem fragilitate	448	Orationes	5
quae cum plerumque implicata sint, nisi candida phrasi telam	470	Epistolae	29
PLESION			
kai oi alloi nomeis boulontai plesion autou tas agelas istanai.	447	Orationes	32
PLICAS			
Maeandrosque plicasque, quam perita es!	411	Lucus 5	16
PLORANT			
Nam te nunc Ager, Vrbs, & Aula plorant:	428	Mem.Matr.10	8
PLUMBEA			
Plumbea glans, liuensque suae quasi conscia noxae, ...	419	Tr.Mortis	62
PLUMBEAE			
Adeo inficetae, plumbeae, Meduseae, ...	429	Mem.Matr.12	6
PLUMBIS			
Plumbis obsignata, colosque & stamina vitae	419	Tr.Mortis	64
PLUMBO			
Plumbo ducta fuisset aestuanti, ...	400	Musae 37	22
PLURA			
Plura tibi missurus eram (nam quae mihi laurus, ...	428	Mem.Matr.9	15
Falleris, nusquam plura bona, cum etiam mala illic sint aurea:	451	Orationes	3
PLURES			
Perge, decus Regum; sic, Augustissime, plures	402	Musae 39	33
Rhetoris in hunc annum, & in plures Oratoris, permitte, . .	472	Epistolae	26
PLURIMA			
hominum Authoritate tua plurima & Eloquentia non minori nobis	463	Epistolae	2
PLURIMIS			
vt laboribus meis plurimis atque assidua obseruantia, ramenta	472	Epistolae	12
PLURIMUM			
hic ego me erexi & de dolore remisi plurimum, de desiderio nihil.	451	Orationes	26
plurimumque suspicimus cumulum amoris Tui, qui vtrumque curasti,	457	Epistolae	19
Quare plurimum debemus constantiae fauoris tui, qui restinxisti sitim	462	Epistolae	7
PLURIMUS			
Foelices, quos bella premunt, & plurimus ensis!	432	Poem.Lat.	23
Tuque aer inflato tubam, dum plurimus ignis	211	Cam.1613-b BR	5
PLUS			
Non plus maligni daemones Christi cruce	389	Musae 10	2
Pulpita, plus spatij lucreris?	395	Musae 23	48
Plus charta haec mea delibuta dictis	400	Musae 37	25
Cum qui plus terrae, plus habuere maris.	411	Lucus 6	4
Plusque habet hic laetus, quam vel Auarus habet.	411	Lucus 7	4
Plus etiam veteres coelum videre remotum:	433	Poem.Lat.	44
Sic non Phoebeus iam plus te splendeat ortus	211	Cam.1613-b BR	15
Nec plus te rubeat vesper, Eliza, precor.	211	Cam.1613-b BR	16
bis intersectas, infantulos plus lactis quam crucris emittentes;	449	Orationes	7
cum quanto plus possint in sua terra, tanto minus in aliena.	450	Orationes	11
alienas tantum ex hoc itinere cognouit Respublicas sed quod plus est,	450	Orationes	33
& plus iusto celebres, cum leunculum & dominum suum contra naturam	454	Orationes	17
anni huius derisit incoeptum et plus effecit quam mille Redemptores	461	Epistolae	12
PLUTONIS			
Purpureus lictor Plutonis, epistola Fati	419	Tr.Mortis	63
PLUUIA			
Vae nubi pluuia grauidae, non lacte, measque	426	Mem.Matr.7	5
natura omnis suos habet anteambulones, vnde pluuia futura, an sudum,	445	Orationes	5
hic enim securi sumus a pluuia, imo a fulmine:	455	Orationes	16
PLUUIAM			
Sin pluuiam, fletus suppeditasset aquas.	427	Mem.Matr.9	10
PNEION			
Zo d' autos, braxu ti pneion, ost' empalin autes	431	Mem.Matr.17	21
PNEUMA			
Pneuma, biou parodon mounois epeessi metresan.	431	Mem.Matr.17	23
PNEUMATOS			
Psuxes asthenes erkos, amauron pneumatos aggos, ...	429	Mem.Matr.14	1
Aiona omou Zoein kai pneumatos allo genesthai	431	Mem.Matr.17	22
POCULA			
Ambustis sudibus: pars vitam in pocula fundunt, ...	418	Tr.Mortis	20
POENA			
Crimina cum turgent, & mea poena prope est, ...	406	Passio 9	2
Poena minor fuerat, quam fatum Principis aegrum?	432	Poem.Lat.	21
POENAM			
praecipue pharetrata, quae ad poenam gentium & Bellum spectant.	449	Orationes	27
POESEOS			
Sed faecunda poeseos	403	Musae 40	7
POESIS			
Cur, vbi tot ludat numeris antiqua poesis, ...	387	Musae 5	1

POETA	PAGE	TITLE	LINE
Tuum tibi, poeta belle, non mystes, ...	392	Musae 20	11
Accedis bene doctus, et poeta.	401	Musae 37	47
ipsum coelum nubilum semper, & poeta stultus qui dixerat, . .	451	Orationes	19
POETAE			
Cur tibi tam facile non arrisere poetae	387	Musae 5	3
Si, quia felices olim dixere poetae	387	Musae 6	3
Quod Bellarminus nequijt, fortasse poetae	417	Lucus 28	3
quam Nuptiae, quas adeo laudant Poetae, vt in coelum transtulerint:	446	Orationes	18
Iuris-consultos, partus sequitur ventrem: quibus accedunt Poetae,	447	Orationes	13
POETAM			
Pontificem tandem nacta est sibi Roma poetam:	417	Lucus 28	1
POETAS			
Innumeros mergit vitiata mente poetas, ...	402	Musae 39	39
apud poetas deorum pharetrae operculum habuere, humanae non item:	449	Orationes	25
POETICAE			
qui tantae poeticae, tantae eruditionis nobis conscius est, . . .	461	Epistolae	6
POIA			
proeleluthoton, en kai emas isos deesei poreuesthai, poia tis esti.	471	Epistolae	11
POIKILMATOS			
Tes peri sullalecusin, ecu poikilmatos arden	431	Mem.Matr.17	11
POL			
Difficilis esse haud solec: nam, pol, si forem, ...	413	Lucus 17	3
POLEMEIN			
esti me perimenein, ote polemein umin omologesei, dixit Mithridates.	449	Orationes	15
POLEMOS			
Polemos de kan pedioi kakos ephu.	448	Orationes	15
POLITIARUM			
percurrite Annales regnorum, excutite scrinia politiarum omnium;	445	Orationes	14
POLITICOS			
Porro si Politicos audiamus, salus regnorum pendet a vicinis,	450	Orationes	25
POLITIEM			
vt laeuitatem illam aequabilem atque politiem perturbent. . .	453	Orationes	14
POLLET			
Luce praelustri, vel honore pollet, ...	390	Musae 14	6
POLLICE			
Tu Diua miro pollice spiritum	394	Musae 23	25
POLLICEATUR			
de nullo vnquam Filio Alma Mater, quantum de Te sibi polliceatur.	457	Epistolae	27
POLLICERI			
cernitis Regem & nomine & re magnum quid polliceri, ideoque ex	447	Orationes	9
POLLUBRA			
Pollubra vel cum olim damnaris Regia in ara, ...	386	Musae 3	9
POLLUBRUM			
Tertulliano, propter vndae pollubrum, ...	389	Musae 10	7
POLLUENS			
Polluens castum chlamydis colorem	390	Musae 14	3
POLLUIT			
Tollantur si cuncta malus quae polluit vsus, ...	390	Musae 13	3
POLUOMMATOS			
Poluommatos, polutlas, ...	430	Mem.Matr.16	9
POLUTLAS			
Poluommatos, polutlas, ...	430	Mem.Matr.16	9
POLYCRATES			
Polycrates cum annulum sibi dilectum in mare dimisisset, . . .	444	Orationes	14
POLYMITI			
finesque multiplices & polymiti, vt si minus id assequantur,	446	Orationes	6
POLYPUS			
Ceu Polypus, chelis saxa prehendo tenax:	428	Mem.Matr.11	10
POMI			
Sic vbi iam mulier decerpti conscia pomi	390	Musae 12	13
POMOERIA			
Et pomoeria terminosque sanctos	408	Passio 19	4
nunc itaque liber hic vester dilatat pomoeria, summouet Oceanum	458	Epistolae	12
POMUM			
Crudum olim pomum, tristis Adame, tibi.	412	Lucus 9	4
PONAS			
Hunc ponas animam mundi, Plato: vel tua mundum	409	Passio 21	3
PONDERE			
Dum longi lentique gemis sub pondere morbi	438	Poem.Lat.	1
PONDERIS			
Nihil habet humana vita maioris momenti aut ponderis, quam Nuptiae,	446	Orationes	17
PONDUS			
omniumque Artium molem et pondus sustinere, sed perspectissimus tuus	465	Epistolae	10
PONE			
Ne nimium vexet quaestio, pone meam.	409	Passio 21	4
PONT			
Vrbani VIII Pont. Respons.	416	Lucus 26	T
Ad Vrbanum VIII Pont.	417	Lucus 28	T
PONTIFEX			
Dux Notionum; veritatis Pontifex;	436	Poem.Lat.	3
Dux Nationum; veritatis Pontifex;	436	Poem.Lat. V	3
PONTIFICALI			
De Antichristi decore Pontificali.	390	Musae 13	T
PONTIFICEM			
Pontificem tandem nacta est sibi Roma poetam:	417	Lucus 28	1
PONTIFICUM			
Non quia Pontificum sunt olim afflata veneno, ...	390	Musae 13	1
PONTUS			
Quod calamum excusent Pontus & Astra meum:	435	Poem.Lat.	8

	PAGE	TITLE	LINE
POPULARI			
si Reges ipsi quandoque suauitates suas populari acetc condiant.	453	Orationes	19
POPULI			
Et populi spurcas creditis esse vias:	387	Musae 5	8
Vicini populi passim mirantur, & aequos	401	Musae 39	8
resolutione illa vltima, nulla sit distinctio populi aut principis:	452	Orationes	16
POPULO			
An quod semotum populo laquearibus altis	387	Musae 7	3
Quin populo, clemens, aliquid largire caloris:	397	Musae 29	3
tuosque fauores populo tuo communicans coelum ac terram minori quam	444	Orationes	7
Tu aperis illum populo, & cum ipse sis in summa arbore altera manu	456	Epistolae	13
sic disparatae foelicitates hinc a populo, illinc a Principe,	456	Epistolae	24
quem singularis doctrina exemit a populo, & quasi mixtam personam	461	Epistolae	26
POPULUM			
Sol generat populum luce fouente nouum.	384	Musae	2
O caecum populum! si bona res siet	392	Musae 17	11
Nec qua consuleres, populumve ad bella vocares,	211	Cam.1613-b BR	9
POPULUS			
Filij noctis, populus malignus,	390	Musae 14	18
Hoc vno Rex et populus dissentimus.	444	Orationes	1
Absque nuptijs foret populus virorum, essemus vnius seculi;	446	Orationes	21
POREUESTHAI			
proeleluthoton, en kai emas isos deesei poreuesthai, poia tis esti.	471	Epistolae	11
PORRECTA			
Scotia quae frigente iaces porrecta sub Arcto,	399	Musae 35	1
PORRIGIS			
manu prehendis Regem, alteram nobis ad radices haerentibus porrigis.	456	Epistolae	15
PORRIGIT			
Et tibi vicinas porrigit aequor aquas:	399	Musae 35	8
Ceu victa, Musis porrigit herbulas	434	Poem.Lat.	21
PORRIGO			
Quam chartam tibi porrigo recentem,	384	Musae	1
PORRO			
Porro si Politicos audiamus, salus regnorum pendet a vicinis,	450	Orationes	25
Porro, est etiam interdum satietas quaedam honoris, quem ad tempus	453	Orationes	9
PORTAS			
Tu geminas belli portas, o Petre, repandis,	398	Musae 33	11
PORTASTI			
cur non vt elephanti turres, ita tu patriam tecum portasti?	451	Orationes	8
PORTETUR			
Forsitan & prohibes infans portetur ad vndas,	388	Musae 9	7
PORTITOR			
Ingemit, & defessus opem iam Portitor orat.	420	Tr.Mortis	82
POS			
Pos nun aphiptasai, goou kai kindunou	429	Mem.Matr.15	3
POSCANT			
Quotidiana suas poscant si fercula grates,	389	Musae 12	9
POSCIS			
Et tibi sit nemo praes, vbi poscis opem.	389	Musae 9	16
POSCIT			
Vestrasque laudes, poscit & mixtas genas.	422	Mem.Matr.2	4
Sed partem in scriptis etiam dum lacryma poscit,	428	Mem.Matr.9	17
Quin Matris superans carmina poscit honos.	431	Mem.Matr.19	6
POSCO			
Lac cum sanguine posco deuolutum;	421	Lucus 34	6
POSCUNT			
Otium poscunt artes, mentem tranquillam, serenam, sudam:	448	Orationes	22
POSITIS			
Sic positis rugis, quibus irretita libido	402	Musae 39	38
POSITUM			
positum extra mortalitatis aleam, et quo magis Tuum agnoscas,	459	Epistolae	11
POSSE			
Spero meo cordi posse patere viam.	404	Passio 4	2
non cor) Tui in me dominij ius imminuere posse, nedum rescindere.	473	Epistolae	7
POSSEM			
vt ego nihil vspiam laetum, nihil candidum expiscari possem;	451	Orationes	15
POSSEMUS			
Nos quoque possemus longas conscribere turmas,	398	Musae 33	7
POSSENT			
incoeptum et plus effecit quam mille Redemptores exequi possent.	461	Epistolae	12
POSSES			
Angustior erat Scotia, quam vt pennas nido plene explicare posses:	458	Epistolae	9
POSSESSIONEM			
prouecta atque adulta, ipsam possessionem adeas, agathei ge tuxei.	470	Epistolae	8
POSSET			
(cum dignius nil posset aut melius dare)	397	Musae 28	10
et mammas arentes tam nobilis parentis aequo animo ferre posset?	462	Epistolae	1
POSSETIS			
Quomodo possetis similes esse Alexandro Magno nisi eius res gestas	441	Orationes	18
POSSIDEAMUS			
O bene quod dubium possideamus agrum!	386	Musae 4	8
POSSIDENTIS			
quid ructus crapulae solium possidentis?	452	Orationes	20
POSSIDET			
Suamque in alijs possidet prudentiam.	412	Lucus 13	4
nullas Herculeas columnas, quas iam olim possidet, agnoscit.	440	Orationes	18
POSSIM			
abscindere non possim, absque molesta aliorum ac frigida	472	Epistolae	14
Cum stare gratis cum silentio possim?	472	Epistolae	18
POSSINT			
Nunc adeo per te viuunt, vt repere possint,	384	Musae	5

POSSINT (cont'd)	PAGE	TITLE	LINE
Qua possint humili fundere corde preces.	390	Musae 12	12
cum quanto plus possint in sua terra, tanto minus in aliena.	450	Orationes	11
POSSIT			
Haeresis, euertas. Quid enim te fallere possit?	402	Musae 39	22
colligeret cum Caligula, praesertim cum possit in eodem litore?	446	Orationes	13
Quis enim rectius Thesauris Regijs praefici possit quam qui,	464	Epistolae	14
qui etiam ferians nihil Tua perfectione dignum procudere possit.	471	Epistolae	24
POSSUM			
a Con verbo deduci, quod tria complectitur, Possum, Scio, Audeo:	447	Orationes	7
POSSUMUS			
nunquam intueri satis vel mirari possumus, nimirum infinitum	449	Orationes	36
Quanquam non mirari non possumus, vnde fit vt nullus fere elabatur	461	Epistolae	13
POSSUNT			
Nec tarda possunt pharmaca consequi, ...	425	Mem.Matr.6	6
quarum enumerationi nulla vnquam vis, nulla latera sufficere possunt.	443	Orationes	15
ipsa durissima ingenia, meum praesertim, celare non possunt:	445	Orationes	9
POST			
De Purificatione post puerperium.	389	Musae 12	T
Post restitutos fluctibus obices, ...	393	Musae 23	2
Post vbi Mosaicae repararent fragmina Leges, ...	408	Passio 20	3
(Nam post Babelem linguae adest confusio)	422	Mem.Matr.2	13
Quin post modestam, qualis integras decet, ...	422	Mem.Matr.2	14
Post vbi crudelem sentit diuisa securem, ...	428	Mem.Matr.11	3
Fructusque post mortem recusent	434	Poem.Lat.	31
Mag. Sigilli Custodis post editam ab eo Instaurationem Magnam.	436	Poem.Lat.	T
Domini, Post honores eximios, praefecturas insignes, . . .	440	Orationes	2
vt semper post nouas dignitates, alias tibi quaerant et moliantur.	464	Epistolae	23
Quare post Principis manum honoribus refertam, non est quod nostram	469	Epistolae	14
post ingentes Hecatombas, exiguam thuris micam adoleri legimus.	469	Epistolae	16
POSTERI			
O me probe lassum! Iuuate, Posteri!	437	Poem.Lat.	27
O me prope lassum! Iuuate, Posteri!	437	Poem.Lat. V	27
POSTERIORIS			
posterioris largam messem Vobis haec tenuia boni consulentibus,	441	Orationes	21
POSTERITAS			
Posteritas flectet corque genuque mihi.	405	Passio 7	6
POSTERITATI			
Neque in hisce Nuptijs posteritati tantum prospexit suauissimus	447	Orationes	27
POSTEROS			
Musasque coelibes, qui posteros libris non liberis quaeritis.	446	Orationes	26
hausisse ab Antiquis, sed et ad Posteros transmissuri videantur.	469	Epistolae	13
POSTERUM			
In posterum, maledicta Ficus arescens	405	Passio 5	6
POSTHAC			
Quam nihil illudis flectens! namque integra posthac	405	Passio 7	5
Euge, perite omnes; nec posthac exeat vlla	425	Mem.Matr.5	11
Non ego vos posthac hederae velatus amictu	432	Poem.Lat.	2
posthac contineat se patria, cuius arctis amplexibus nunquam se	455	Orationes	1
POSTQUAM			
Postquam se gelidis nocte refecit aquis:	412	Lucus 8	2
postquam omnes honorum gradus hic percurreris, aeternum illud	457	Epistolae	3
postquam circumspiciens reperisset Te, quasi in tuis palpebris	465	Epistolae	13
POSTREMIS			
Postremis ambabus idem sentimus vterque;	386	Musae 4	5
POSTULANT			
Eximia tua in nos merita frequentiorem calamum postulant, . .	457	Epistolae	8
POSTULAT			
Vt postulat mos; quid tuis dabis? Teipsum.	406	Passio 10	3
est in forma & figuris vultus, vbi res postulat, regnum tuebitur:	454	Orationes	7
cum humanitatis Tuae, tum gratitudinis nostrae ratio postulat.	457	Epistolae	10
POSTULET			
Sin, Melvine, pedes alienos postulet infans, ...	388	Musae 9	9
POTANTIBUS			
Liber alit rixas: potantibus omnia bina	418	Tr.Mortis	18
POTENT			
Non comedant famam, sic nulla obliuia potent.	432	Poem.Lat.	16
POTENTER			
Totamque eucmerem potenter iram	400	Musae 37	15
POTENTIORI			
Potentiori carmine percitas	393	Musae 23	10
POTENTISSIME			
Serenissime Domine noster, Iacobe Potentissime.	460	Epistolae	1
POTENTISSIMO			
Augustissimo Potentissimoque Monarchae	384	Musae	T
POTERUNT			
Quae guttae poterunt enumerare meos?	422	Mem.Matr.1	2
POTES			
Tu mihi subueniens dignior esse potes.	404	Passio 2	6
Circumferre potes; Sampson vt ante fores.	408	Passio 18	2
Ad nos cum radio tam rutilante potes?	424	Mem.Matr.3	2
Impos medendi, occidere si potes, ...	425	Mem.Matr.6	9
Quin nec potes; cui praebuit Tigris partum.	429	Mem.Matr.12	10
iustissime potes sub hoc Principe, in quo doctrinae fructus atque	469	Epistolae	22
POTEST			
Natare sine clarissima potest cruce?	389	Musae 10	9
At cui videri prodigium potest	395	Musae 23	49
Sic ex profano Cosmico & Catharo potest	396	Musae 27	3
Sedula si fuerit, perterebrare potest.	410	Lucus 2	6
Nemo potest: hodie vita sepulta prior.	415	Lucus 23	6
Culmen, vbi pro te nemo dolere potest.	415	Lucus 23	16

POTEST (cont'd)	PAGE	TITLE	LINE
Vel Catapulta potest, Siculique inuenta magistri, ...	419	Tr.Mortis	41
Quaeque olim fuerat cura, manere potest.	427	Mem.Matr.9	4
Quid enim iucundius accidere potest, quam vt ministri Regis Catholici	440	Orationes	14
de ingenti amore in Principem, cui nulla dilectio par esse potest;	451	Orationes	22
praemium consequare, cui neque addi quicquam potest, neque detrahi.	457	Epistolae	5
enim impetus animi celeritatem tantae munificentiae assequi potest?	460	Epistolae	5
quae fastigium regiarum actionum aequare nunquam potest, . .	460	Epistolae	17
POTESTATEM			
quibus hostes scletis in potestatem redigere, lenioresque aspectus,	440	Orationes	9
POTI			
Alla meneit', ou gar taraxos poti metera bainei, ...	431	Mem.Matr.18	5
POTIO			
Haec fuerat olim potio Domini tui.	427	Mem.Matr.8	9
POTIUS			
Vel potius liceat distinguere. Tuque tuique	387	Musae 6	5
Falsumque potius quam crepes versu?	392	Musae 20	9
Aut potius Christi sanguis demissus ab alto, ...	399	Musae 35	9
Londinenses Bibliopolas suum potius emolumentum quam publicum	467	Epistolae	4
ac si iuuenili potius impetu correptus, quam adductus maturo	471	Epistolae	26
POTUI			
Non potui non ire acre stimulante flagello:	431	Mem.Matr.19	5
potui refercire lineas Honoribus, Magnif., Celsitud., sed . .	473	Epistolae	16
POTUIMUS			
quanquam quem alium fructum potuimus expectare ab Eo, in quem fauor	456	Epistolae	18
POTUISSE			
Constat, Aprile vno te potuisse mori:	438	Poem.Lat.	4
POU			
Ei pou tuxoimi tesd' aristes atrapou, ...	430	Mem.Matr.15	15
PRAE			
Prae quo Tibris vultum recondit, ...	394	Musae 23	43
Prae spiritu ruptis, quo eas resarciat	398	Musae 32	9
Haud aliter cum Christus obit, prae funere tanto	409	Passio 20	5
floribus suis sternentes Rempublicam, prae ariditate flaccescerent.	461	Epistolae	10
sane dubitamus vlli, si prae defectu aquae, commeatusque inopia,	462	Epistolae	2
PRAEBEBO			
e multis seligam, quam vobis amplectendam dissuauiandamque praebebo:	445	Orationes	33
PRAEBES			
charta conspiciendum Te praebes, quo familiarius inter nos verseris.	458	Epistolae	20
PRAEBET			
Visum quod vni praebet, omnibus vitam, ...	404	Passio 5	2
PRAEBUIT			
Quin nec potes; cui praebuit Tigris partum.	429	Mem.Matr.12	10
PRAECEPTUM			
Catonianum praeceptum est: Vicini quo pacto niteant, id animum	450	Orationes	16
PRAECIPITANS			
Praecipitans grauiore casu.	433	Poem.Lat.	16
PRAECIPITATA			
Praecipitata; cadunt vrbes, formidine muri	420	Tr.Mortis	77
PRAECIPUE			
praecipue vbi velut ex continentibus tectis ad nos traiecturum est	449	Orationes	13
praecipue pharetrata, quae ad poenam gentium & Bellum spectant.	449	Orationes	27
PRAECLARIORUM			
Praeclariorum spirituum cibus, ...	394	Musae 23	22
PRAECLUDAT			
ita inuoluit nos, vt etiam rependendi vias omnes praecludat.	458	Epistolae	29
PRAECONIJS			
Strepente mundo tinnulis praeconijs?	423	Mem.Matr.2	56
PRAECORDIA			
Humana aeternos agerent praecordia questus:	433	Poem.Lat.	39
PRAEDA			
ille maritimus tractus (Oceani praeda et deliciae) vt irrigui Musarum	461	Epistolae	9
PRAEDAM			
Permitte vt nos etiam in praedam partemque tecum veniamus: . .	465	Epistolae	21
PRAEDERIS			
Vtrumque si praederis Indum, ...	425	Mem.Matr.6	7
PRAEDIA			
quidam stomachantur praedia, alij immunitates carpunt, nonnulli	461	Epistolae	19
PRAEDICANDO			
Sputando, praedicando? sic Aquas vitae	404	Passio 5	3
PRAEDICAS			
Ain' vero? quanta praedicas? hercle aedepol, ...	421	Lucus 33	1
PRAEDICAT			
Praedicat autores; tertia plena Deo est.	386	Musae 4	4
PRAEDICTIS			
Quare nos tertium praedictis adiungimus Gratiarum Fluuium, . .	462	Epistolae	23
PRAEDIJS			
Reges Collegia, eaque fundarunt amplissimis praedijs, immunitatibus:	458	Epistolae	23
PRAEDIOLA			
quamuis enim sexcenta huiusmodi praediola Tua gratia permutare nolim,	472	Epistolae	30
PRAEDITO			
dein Hon. Tuo gratulamur, qui filio auctus es tali ingenio praedito:	463	Epistolae	24
PRAEDO			
adeon' es praedo omnis gloriae, vt ne gratitudinis laudem nobis	459	Epistolae	2
PRAEFECTURAS			
Post honores eximios, praefecturas insignes, Legationes Nobilissimas,	440	Orationes	2
PRAEFERO			
Grandi reaeque praefero, ...	427	Mem.Matr.8	2
PRAEFERS			
Whitaker, erranti quem praefers carmine, miles	398	Musae 33	5

	PAGE	TITLE	LINE
PRAEFERUIDA			
ideoque praeferuida illa desideria silentio suo sepulta nunc	471	Epistolae	27
PRAEFICERENTUR			
reddidit quam si Episcopi more pristino Cancellis praeficerentur.	461	Epistolae	28
PRAEFICI			
Quis enim rectius Thesauris Regijs praefici possit quam qui,	464	Epistolae	14
PRAEFICIARIS			
iam olim Regi notam atque signatam dignissime praeficiaris Fisco,	469	Epistolae	21
PRAEFLORAT			
Praeflorat sibi nuptias futuras.	408	Passio 19	13
PRAEGNANTEM			
Almam Matrem spe noua grauidam semper atque praegnantem effecerint.	464	Epistolae	26
PRAEGNANTES			
praegnantes bis intersectas, infantulos plus lactis quam crucis	449	Orationes	7
PRAEIS			
Praeis eiarinous te xarais epikidnato kepon:	431	Mem.Matr.17	18
PRAELIA			
Non nisi prima suas patiuntur praelia lites.	386	Musae 4	7
Si numero starent praelia, non animis.	398	Musae 33	8
PRAELIO			
Ex praelio vndae ignisque (si Physicis fides)	396	Musae 27	1
PRAELUDIUM			
Caelestis harmoniae breue praeludium.	423	Mem.Matr.2	44
PRAELUSTRI			
Luce praelustri, vel honore pollet, ...	390	Musae 14	6
PRAEMIA			
vt bonorum praemia citissime promulgentur, quo suauius virtutibus,	468	Epistolae	15
PRAEMISSA			
Quam praemissa probant secula, nostra probant?	391	Musae 16	2
PRAEMIUM			
aeternum illud praemium consequare, cui neque addi quicquam potest,	457	Epistolae	4
PRAEOCCUPANT			
Caelique referunt & praeoccupant modum.	423	Mem.Matr.2	49
PRAEPETIS			
Sic aeuum exigitur tardum, dum praepetis anni	428	Mem.Matr.9	13
PRAERIPUIT			
Antiquitas praeripuit Tibi gloriam extruendae Academiae, . .	465	Epistolae	16
PRAEROGATIUAE			
Quare operosior in eo structura, & praerogatiuae ragiae emicant.	446	Orationes	38
PRAES			
Et tibi sit nemo praes, vbi poscis opem.	389	Musae 9	16
PRAESAGA			
Dure, negas? O fata mihi praesaga doloris, ...	437	Poem.Lat.	11
PRAESAGIO			
quemadmodum in Cometae praesagio, non respicitur, quae materia sit,	454	Orationes	12
PRAESENS			
Haec etiam ad pugnam praesens, qua viuimus, aetas	399	Musae 33	21
Viuimus in praesens: hesternam viuere vitam	415	Lucus 23	5
PRAESENTI			
labore suo & periculo consuleret & praesenti Reipublicae & futurae;	447	Orationes	25
suauissimus Princeps, verum etiam praesenti seculo, dum pacem,	447	Orationes	28
PRAESENTIA			
absentia magis quam praesentia. Nunc enim exploratos habet nostros	450	Orationes	33
PRAESENTIAE			
ne nihil hic sit, quod magnitudini praesentiae vestrae respondeat.	441	Orationes	10
PRAESENTIUS			
certe nostrate Principe nusquam praesentius Balsamum, nusquam	444	Orationes	27
PRAESERTIM			
ipsa durissima ingenia, meum praesertim, celare non possunt:	445	Orationes	9
colligeret cum Caligula, praesertim cum possit in eodem litore?	446	Orationes	13
praesertim cum futura incerta sint, & nullis perspicillis, . .	449	Orationes	23
superbi sua tantum nosse, praesertim cum in vno regno non sint omnia:	450	Orationes	18
praesertim cum amico fidere periculosius sit, quam hostem superare.	453	Orationes	32
praesertim donec transeat nubes illa, quae vicinos adeo infestat:	455	Orationes	14
praesertim sericatam hanc stultitiam contere, Academiaeque iura,	461	Epistolae	23
nuper in lucem publicam, nostramque praesertim, editam, . .	463	Epistolae	6
Praesertim hoc tempore, in quo paucorum auaritia liberalibus artibus	466	Epistolae	23
praesertim in Theologia, cuius Libri si alij alijs (tanquam montes	467	Epistolae	30
praesertim quum ipsi non solum rectum de Bene-merentibus iudicium	469	Epistolae	11
PRAESIDIUM			
ad prudentiae eloquentiaeque tuae praesidium festinantes excipe:	465	Epistolae	16
PRAESTANTIOR			
Aiacis est praestantior?	396	Musae 28	6
PRAESTANTISSIMAE			
praestantissimaeque animi dotes effecerunt, vt Alma Mater . .	465	Epistolae	12
PRAESTAT			
Quam cunctos fieri praestat Episcopos.	392	Musae 17	13
Atqui manus imponere integras praestat, ...	397	Musae 31	2
Coniugium Caeli Terraeque haec machina praestat;	417	Lucus 31	1
PRAESTES			
Rectius innocuis lactentibus omnia praestes, ...	388	Musae 9	11
Hoc mihi legatum tristi si funere praestes, ...	434	Poem.Lat.	7
PRAESTET			
atque effusissimum in omnia officia, quae praestet mea paruitas;	471	Epistolae	22
PRAESTITIT			
Nullum locum requiemue cernens praestitit	436	Poem.Lat. V	20
PRAESTOLANTUR			
gaudia praestolantur, quae iamdudum annuunt mihi vt perorem.	454	Orationes	22
PRAESUL			
Sic laudandus erit nactus sublimia Praesul, ...	387	Musae 7	9
Praesul, cur renuis? sin mala, pauculos	392	Musae 17	12

	PAGE	TITLE		LINE
PREPON				
Kai prepon ode para dakruoessi reein.	431	Mem.Matr.18		6
PREPONTOS				
Epoduretai prepontos.	430	Mem.Matr.16		7
PRESBUTON				
Dokei moi xrenai para ton presbuton punthanesthai, osper tina odon	471	Epistolae		10
PRESBYTEROS				
Quin per Presbyteros tuos; per vrbem	400	Musae 37		5
PRESSUS				
Tandem, ne et ipse peccem, breuis sit sermo, atque pressus. . . .	470	Epistolae		32
PRETICSA				
Erutus, infernae preticsa tragemata mensae, ...	419	Tr.Mortis		58
Exulis, infernae pretiosa tragemata mensae, ...	419	Tr.Mortis	V	58
PRETIUM				
Scilicet apponit pretium tua dextera fato, ...	435	Poem.Lat.		5
PRIMA				
Non nisi prima suas patiuntur praelia lites.	386	Musae 4		7
Debuit ista pati prima & non nobilis aetas:	432	Poem.Lat.		29
PRIMARIAM				
ita ad Te confugimus primariam partem ecclesiastici corporis,	467	Epistolae		9
PRIMAS				
primas dedissem literas, ideoque praeferuida illa desideria silentio	471	Epistolae		27
PRIMIPILUS				
perrumpit primipilus, & te cum coelis tuis ad inferos deturbat.	448	Orationes		30
PRIMIS				
Et quod obseruatione cum primis dignum est, quo magis amore . . .	440	Orationes		21
PRIMO				
Primo, vnus aut alter parum ritus placet:	398	Musae 32		2
primo nuptias ipsas spectate. Quid autem?	446	Orationes		8
primo gratulamur optimo Regi nostro, qui prospicit, vt cum ipse	463	Epistolae		20
qui primo caloris suasu excitati atque expergefacti, vbi sursum	471	Epistolae		29
PRIMORDIA				
Sanguine, quem dederat, spolians. Primordia Mortis	418	Tr.Mortis		22
Sanguine, quem dederat, spolians. Primordia belli	271	Tr.Mortis	VS	22
PRIMUM				
Cum primum ratibus suis	395	Musae 25		1
Heu stolidi, primum fugientem figite Terram, ...	408	Passio 18		3
Nunc primum socij mors foret atra tui?	415	Lucus 23		2
Protulit horrendum hoc primum cum puluere monstrum. . . .	420	Tr.Mortis	V	91
quod primum intendunt, saltem in secundis aut tertijs consistant.	446	Orationes		6
Nam primum tota haec Pieria supellex, charta, calami, codices,	448	Orationes		17
& inuidiam, quae semper se deuorat primum, vti vermis nucleum,	454	Orationes		15
Gulielmus Victor descensurus primum e nauibus in terram hanc,	455	Orationes		3
PRIMUS				
Primus adest nobis, Pharisaeis omnibus hostis, ...	398	Musae 33		9
Protulit horrendum hoc primus cum puluere monstrum. . . .	420	Tr.Mortis		91
regiones terrasque veteribus incognitas primus demonstrat: . .	463	Epistolae		11
PRINCEPS				
Dum petit Infantem Princeps, Grantamque Iacobus, ...	437	Poem.Lat.		1
Cum petit Hispanam Princeps, Grantamque Iacobus, ...	437	Poem.Lat.	V	1
Quare adsis Princeps, aliis Academia mons sit, ...	210	Cam.1613-a	BR	7
Ergon' amauit Princeps? Quippini; homo est, non statua; . .	446	Orationes		9
Quare noluit Princeps optimus, in delectu vxoris, re vna omnium	447	Orationes		22
neque vnius seculi Princeps, sed & omnium, quae ventura sunt,	447	Orationes		25
in hisce Nuptijs posteritati tantum prospexit suauissimus Princeps,	447	Orationes		28
& scientiae augmentum ex hoc itinere captauit solertissimus Princeps?	450	Orationes		6
per quod optimus Princeps non tantum exteras regiones habuit	451	Orationes		36
nobilissimus Saxonum nostrorum Princeps, sub ementito habitu	453	Orationes		4
Redijt Princeps, CAROLVS redijt, honore grauidus, grauidus scientia,	454	Orationes		26
Deum immortalem, vt Princeps optimus nulla secunda itinera meditetur;	454	Orationes		38
& nunc sit tanta patriae tenacitas, vt nunquam Princeps se extricet:	455	Orationes		6
Noster etiam Princeps habuit Daphnen suam, cuius amor deinceps	455	Orationes		10
vt cum ipse eruditionis Princeps sit, illi etiam honores qui finitimi	463	Epistolae		21
PRINCIPE				
Et patrio regno (sub quo iam Principe nobis	432	Poem.Lat.		27
certe nostrate Principe nusquam praesentius Balsamum, nusquam	444	Orationes		27
si quis de Principe aliquo, quis sit futurus aut qualis, . . .	454	Orationes		8
diu iam peregrinati cum Principe, commode peruenimus ad laurum hanc,	455	Orationes		12
foelicitates hinc a populo, illinc a Principe, in Te conueniunt,	456	Epistolae		24
habita Chartae nostrae a Serenissimo Principe Henrico 8 indultae,	467	Epistolae		22
iustissime potes sub hoc Principe, in quo doctrinae fructus atque	469	Epistolae		22
PRINCIPEM				
qui optimum Principem spe nuptiarum mari nuper tradentes, . . .	444	Orationes		17
Quae enim vspiam gens, quod vnquam seculum melicrem habuit Principem?	445	Orationes		13
at ego Principem vellem, CAROLVM, CAROLVM;	451	Orationes		6
gaudeo quidem de ingenti amore in Principem, cui nulla dilectio par	451	Orationes		22
Principem cirribus delicijs abundantem, obseptum illecebris, . .	452	Orationes		4
locus est vmbris & recessibus, etiam si quis Principem pingat.	453	Orationes		15
ex itinere Principem metiri licet, quod sane adeo nobile fuit	453	Orationes		22
si amor virginis eo pertraxit Principem, quo tandem ducet amor	453	Orationes		28
PRINCIPES				
Quam facile sentiuntur boni Principes!	445	Orationes		4
PRINCIPI				
Illustriss. Celsissimoque CAROLO, Walliae, & Iuventutis Principi.	384	Musae		T
Omne regnum suo Principi carcer est, aut si excedat, alienum:	450	Orationes		12
PRINCIPIBUS				
Principibus, sed amica fiunt.	434	Poem.Lat.		28
cum tanti sitis & in Principibus Vestris, & in vobismetipsis,	441	Orationes		8
Principibus vt vtilissima ita difficillima factu, cum quanto plus	450	Orationes		10
rara in Principibus virtus, & cui cum sceptro lites saepius . .	452	Orationes		2

	PAGE	TITLE	LINE
PRINCIPIS			
In Obitum Henrici Principis Walliae.	432	Poem.Lat.	T
Poena minor fuerat, quam fatum Principis aegrum?	432	Poem.Lat.	21
Principis incocuam seruastis numina Vitam,	433	Poem.Lat.	34
Quin & Serenissimae Principis Isabellae laudes, virtutesque,	441	Orationes	3
auspicatissimum Serenissimi Principis Caroli Reditum ex Hispanijs	444	Orationes	T
sic & ipse excerpam e Principis rebus gestis pugillum, vnam actionem	445	Orationes	31
Quare & Principis iter multiplicem nobis exhibet prudentiam;	446	Orationes	7
nimirum infinitum Principis in suam gentem amorem, cui pacem	449	Orationes	36
resolutione illa vltima, nulla sit distinctio populi aut principis:	452	Orationes	16
Quin exuit personam Principis, deponit Maiestatem, virgam cum sceptro	452	Orationes	35
an inter lauros principis hederae nostrae ambitiosae locus est?	456	Epistolae	4
vtrum gratia Principis virtutes tuas, aut nostra vota gratiam	456	Epistolae	20
aut nostra vota gratiam Principis, aut Tuae virtutes et vota nostra	456	Epistolae	21
aut Tuae virtutes et vota nostra et Principis gratiam superarent.	456	Epistolae	22
Quare post Principis manum honoribus refertam, non est quod nostram	469	Epistolae	14
PRINCIPIUM			
Hinc mihi principium: vos o labentia mentis	432	Poem.Lat.	13
PRINCIPUM			
Ingens piorum gloria Principum,	394	Musae 23	38
autem vt foelicitas tantorum Principum etiam in ministros redundet,	441	Orationes	5
sic bonorum Principum facilis Astrologia:	445	Orationes	7
tot labores & sollicitudines Principum sine condimento sint atque	446	Orationes	11
Quod si Nuptiae in se graues sunt, quanto magis Principum, cum,	446	Orationes	34
qui semper titillant aures Principum, Osper tois ptercis knomenci ta	453	Orationes	2
PRIOR			
Nemo potest: hodie vita sepulta prior.	415	Lucus 23	6
PRIORES			
Nox Aetnam, noctemque Chaos genuere priores.	420	Tr.Mortis	86
PRIORIS			
Deducens lacrymas prioris aeui	428	Mem.Matr.10	11
PRISCA			
Cum Latium ferrent secula prisca iugum?	416	Lucus 25	2
PRISCI			
Prisci, crescentesque vna cum prole cauernas:	418	Tr.Mortis	6
finge tibi matronam sanctam, venerandam, oris prisci atque augusti;	470	Epistolae	17
PRISTINAS			
Quin redde formas, o bone, pristinas,	393	Musae 23	5
PRISTINO			
reddidit quam si Episcopi more pristino Cancellis praeficerentur.	461	Epistolae	27
PRIUANTES			
siccatores (solem officio suo priuantes) vi verborum Tuorum obruens.	462	Epistolae	20
PRIUARI			
imo precabor enixe, me tum priuari tam communi hac luce, quam Tua,	472	Epistolae	23
PRIUATA			
vt quid priuata habeat in se vita commodi aut voluptatis,	452	Orationes	37
PRIUATAE			
manifestationem in gentem suam priuatae personae & habitui debuit.	453	Orationes	8
PRIUATO			
neque de priuato agamus bono, sed publico;	448	Orationes	6
publico muneri, quam priuato, latiusque manare iniustitiae peccatum,	472	Epistolae	31
PRIUATUS			
etsi tu qui scribis (vti quiuis priuatus) inferioris sis subsellij,	470	Epistolae	23
PRIUILEGIA			
Te tribunum Parlamentarium, nos nostraque omnia priuilegia, fundos,	465	Epistolae	5
timemus Librorum precia auctum iri, et priuilegia nostra imminutum.	467	Epistolae	7
et tuum tibi largita est honorem, et priuilegia nostra confirmauit;	468	Epistolae	24
PRIUS			
Quo precio venit, fac, liceare prius.	410	Lucus 4	6
Quid memorem tormenta, quibus prius horruit aeuum;	419	Tr.Mortis	39
Animo renidentes prius. Sir rarior	423	Mem.Matr.2	25
prius Excellentijs Vestris curae erit;	441	Orationes	20
Iustitiam prius tanto cum honore atque acclamatione administrans,	464	Epistolae	14
PRIVY			
of Winchester, one of the Kings most honorable privy-Counsaile.	473	Epistolae	25
PRIVY-COUNSAILE			
of Winchester, one of the Kings most honorable privy-Counsaile.	473	Epistolae	25
PRO			
Pro Disciplina Ecclesiae Nostrae Epigrammata Apologetica	385	Musae 1	T
Pro solido, CAESAR, carmine frusta dabo.	385	Musae 1	4
Sic tuus effundi gestit pro crimine sanguis,	404	Passio 3	1
Pro lapsu stillarum abeunt peccata; nec acres	406	Passio 13	3
Proque vno vincto turba soluta fuit.	407	Passio 17	2
Sic, pro Maiestate, Deum, non perdere vitam	408	Passio 17	7
Et pro pectoribus recenset aras,	408	Passio 19	6
Ecquid emes Christum? pro nobis scilicet olim	410	Lucus 4	1
Nunquid pro foribus sedendo nuper	411	Lucus 5	4
Aurea pro naulo lingua Charontis erit.	414	Lucus 22	4
Nec tu pro socio doleas, qui fugit ad illud	415	Lucus 23	15
Culmen, vbi pro te nemo dolere potest.	415	Lucus 23	16
Quin pro me quoque sanguinem profudit,	421	Lucus 34	4
Horto pro tenui colit	424	Mem.Matr.4	3
Mutata? & pro matre mihi phantasma dolosum	426	Mem.Matr.7	3
atque vbiuis terrarum pro iudicio prudentissimi Regis, & in rebus	444	Orationes	20
tunc temporis liberior eram, huc illuc pro libitu circumcursitans:	451	Orationes	12
etiam imperium tenuius est quam pro amplitudine virtutum vestrarum:	458	Epistolae	10
quam vt pro infinitis vestris in nos beneficijs Maiestatem vestram	458	Epistolae	30
noluitque vt minori sphaera quam pro latitudine meritorum tuorum	466	Epistolae	14
idque pro Libris, de quibus nusquam rectius quam apud Te agitur.	467	Epistolae	18
PROBABIS			
Sed nec coniugij signum, Melvine, probabis?	396	Musae 26	1

	PAGE	TITLE	LINE
PROBANT			
Quam praemissa probant secula, nostra probant?	391	Musae 16	2
PROBAS			
An quia Textores Artificesque probas?	392	Musae 18	2
PROBATUR			
Per quicquid tibi suauiter probatur;	400	Musae 37	9
Quaeritur ingenium, doctusque homicida probatur.	418	Tr.Mortis	25
PROBE			
O me probe lassum! Iuuate, Posteri!	437	Poem.Lat.	27
Tuis, meis desiderijs probe cognitis, excussis perpensisque.	472	Epistolae	4
PROBEM			
Purpureo melius sanguine Regna probem.	405	Passio 7	8
PROBER			
Munere, Rex tanto verior inde prober.	405	Passio 7	4
PROBES			
Vel quia tot moritur, tot viquisse probes.	415	Lucus 23	8
PROBET			
tantisper supplere donec Academia orationem tuam imbibat probetque,	470	Epistolae	7
PROBI			
An rectius nos, si vices vertas, probi, ...	388	Musae 8	9
PROBO			
Gusto proboque Dolium.	427	Mem.Matr.8	10
PROBRA			
Cur tanta sufflas probra in innocuam Crucem?	389	Musae 10	1
PROBRO			
Cum probro madidum, reumque difflat.	428	Mem.Matr.10	7
Bure, sibi dixit Musa fuisse probro.	431	Mem.Matr.19	2
PROBRORUM			
Quin hoc carmine Lexicon probrorum	401	Musae 37	28
PROCANCELLARIJ			
subsidiumque Magnificentiae Tuae deuotissimorum Procancellarij Relig.	464	Epistolae	7
PROCANCELLARIO			
succurres Magnificentiae tuae addicitissimis Procancellario Rel.	469	Epistolae	26
PROCANCELLARIUM			
quo soles beare Amplitudini tuae deuotissimos Procancellarium Rel.	464	Epistolae	28
PROCANCELLARIUS			
serui subditique vestri Procancellarius Reliquusque Senatus . .	459	Epistolae	22
Quare et Procancellarius Academiam simulans vel maximos magnatum	470	Epistolae	25
PROCEDE			
Interea procede Comes Germano-britanne	211	Cam.1613-b BR	7
PROCELLA			
bello pacem, sine qua omnis vita procella, & mundus solitudo.	448	Orationes	8
PROCELLAS			
Et tu solus ad Angliae procellas	401	Musae 37	44
PROCELLIS			
Quas gens inconsulta, suis vexata procellis, ...	401	Musae 39	2
Nunc sorti pateo, expositus sine matre procellis, ...	428	Mem.Matr.11	7
PROCERIBUS			
Academia vniuersim sumpta vna est e proceribus, inter patritios	470	Epistolae	24
PROCESSERINT			
vbi sursum processerint paulo, frigefacti demum relabuntur. . .	471	Epistolae	30
PROCUDERE			
Quin liceat nobis aliquas procudere voces:	386	Musae 3	5
qui etiam ferians nihil Tua perfectione dignum procudere possit.	471	Epistolae	24
PROCUL			
Cum prope sit nobis Musa, Medusa procul?	387	Musae 6	2
A nobis etenim procul remoti	415	Lucus 24	7
PROCURATOREM			
12. Ad Heath, Sollicitorem Procuratorem Gratulatio . . .	466	Epistolae	T
PRODEGIT			
Prodegit integrum penu, ...	407	Passio 16	6
PRODERUNT			
quid proderunt scalpella vestra, quando ipsae hae turres & beatae	448	Orationes	20
PRODES			
Munere dum nobis prodes, Libroque futuris, ...	435	Poem.Lat.	1
Munere dum nobis prodes, Libroque remotis, ...	435	Poem.Lat.	3
PRODIGIUM			
At cui videri prodigium potest	395	Musae 23	49
Luscum prodigium, medioque foramine gaudens.	419	Tr.Mortis	54
PRODITE			
Quare prodite, tenebriones literarij, e gurgustijs vestris, . .	454	Orationes	24
prodite omnes. Quid noui? Quid noui, stupide?	454	Orationes	25
PRODUCTAS			
Aut spes productas, barbataque somnia vertam	426	Mem.Matr.7	19
PRODUCTIS			
Ne te productis videar lassare Camoenis, ...	385	Musae 1	3
PRODUCUNT			
quemadmodum artifices non omnes licitantibus producunt merces,	445	Orationes	30
ita Sol & Coelum producunt flores, qui symbola sunt spei, . .	446	Orationes	32
PRODUXISTI			
et blattis rixantes, exuens puluere, in theatrum et lucem produxisti.	462	Epistolae	27
PRODUXIT			
Produxit Vmbram corpus, Vmbra corpori	413	Lucus 14	1
PROELELUTHOTON			
osper tina odon proeleluthoton, en kai emas isos deesei poreuesthai,	471	Epistolae	10
PROFANA			
Quod puer ignorat, verba profana putas?	388	Musae 9	2
PROFANAM			
Cur Latiam linguam reris nimis esse profanam, ...	391	Musae 16	1
PROFANE			
Cantus sacros, profane, mugitus vocas?	395	Musae 24	1

	PAGE	TITLE		LINE
PROFANI				
Caeno profani corporis exuens	394	Musae 23		26
PROFANO				
Sic ex profano Cosmico & Catharo potest	396	Musae 27		3
PROFANOS				
Profanos fremitus bonasque sannas:	400	Musae 37		24
PROFECTUS				
ipse profectus est, vt ingenti labore suo & periculo consuleret	447	Orationes		24
Faxit Deus vt quos profectus feceris in Sphaera Naturae, . .	464	Epistolae		3
PROFER				
India, non solitum profer Eliza decus:	211	Cam.1613-b BB		12
PROFUDIT				
Quin pro me quoque sanguinem profudit, ...	421	Lucus 34		4
PROFUERIT				
si quantum eruditio Regis profuerit Reipublicae, tantum fauoris nobis	469	Epistolae		24
PROFUNDITATIS				
Profunditatis pinus, atque Elegantiae;	436	Poem.Lat.		6
Profunditatis cirnus, atque Elegantiae;	436	Poem.Lat.	V	6
PROGENIES				
Progenies, gemmamque sua quasi pyxide clausit.	402	Musae 39		16
Progenies, mundique aetas abdomine nostro	418	Tr.Mortis		4
Progenies, mundique aetas abdomine tanto	418	Tr.Mortis	V	4
PROGRESSU				
Nos vero de hoc tuo progressu non minus Reipublicae gratulamur quam	466	Epistolae		15
PROGRESSUM				
vt qui tot subsidia attuleris ad progressum doctrinae, hac etiam	467	Epistolae		28
PROH				
Proh! quantus imber, quanta latri comitas, ...	423	Mem.Matr.2		29
PROHIBES				
Forsitan & prohibes infans portetur ad vndas, ...	388	Musae 9		7
Dolere prohibes? aut dolere me gentis	429	Mem.Matr.12		5
PROIJCIENDA				
Omnia sunt temere proijcienda foras.	390	Musae 13		2
PROIJCIT				
Aut aperi, & cernes corpus quas proijcit vmbras;	437	Poem.Lat.		7
Aut aperi, & cernis corpus quas proijcit vmbras;	437	Poem.Lat.	V	7
PROIN				
proin vt Fluuij quas aquas a Fonte accipiunt non retinent ipsi,	456	Epistolae		9
Proin iube Thorndick nostrum, ni graue est, librum tibi Oratorium	470	Epistolae		9
PROINDE				
Proinde parco belluis, nec irascor.	429	Mem.Matr.12		11
Proinde audi Platonem: Dokei moi xrenai para ton presbuton . .	471	Epistolae		9
PROJICE				
Exere terra caput, servatos projice flores, ...	210	Cam.1613-b BB		3
PROLE				
Prisci, crescentesque vna cum prole cauernas:	418	Tr.Mortis		6
PROLEM				
Quid enim si praeter Nuptias, prolem, tranquillitatem, etiam	450	Orationes		4
Prolem Tuam suauissimam, nuper in lucem publicam, nostramque	463	Epistolae		5
PROLES				
Hoc, Genitrix, scriptum proles tibi sedula mittit.	427	Mem.Matr.9		1
PROMIS				
Tu promis Orbem mane, condis vesperi, ...	407	Passio 16		3
PROMISSI				
quos magnificentia promissi circumscribere in promptu erat, . . .	445	Orationes		16
PROMISSORES				
si qui alij exurgant promissores magnifici et hiantes, qui, . .	462	Epistolae		30
PROMOTIONIBUS				
Vna cum promotionibus Academicis maternisque, assumsi mecum . .	473	Epistolae		8
PROMOTIONIS				
Fama promotionis tuae gratissime appulit ad nos omnes haud ita certe	468	Epistolae		12
PROMPTITUDINEM				
Tu vero promptitudinem amoris nostri, non passim expositam, . .	466	Epistolae		1
PROMPTU				
quos magnificentia promissi circumscribere in promptu erat, . . .	445	Orationes		17
PROMULGENTUR				
vt bonorum praemia citissime promulgentur, quo suauius virtutibus,	468	Epistolae		16
PROMUS				
Promus; Fugator Idolum, atque nubium;	436	Poem.Lat.		12
Promus; Fugator Idolorum & nubium;	436	Poem.Lat.	V	12
PRONO				
Dum prono rapis ore cibos, & fercula verris, ...	414	Lucus 21		1
Creditur, ante satas prono cum numine fruges)	419	Tr.Mortis		61
Creditur, ante satas prono cum vertice fruges)	419	Tr.Mortis	V	61
Vssisse prono fulmine diceris, ...	433	Poem.Lat.		14
PRONOMINA				
(Heros illustrissime) quod pronomina mea adeo audacter incedant	473	Epistolae		15
PROORATOR				
Tu vero vale, mi proorator, amaque Tuum G. H.	471	Epistolae		12
PROPE				
Cum prope sit nobis Musa, Medusa procul?	387	Musae 6		2
Crimina cum turgent, & mea poena prope est, ...	406	Passio 9		2
O me prope lassum! Iuuate, Posteri!	437	Poem.Lat.	V	27
PROPENDET				
Tantaque propendet statera	433	Poem.Lat.		7
PROPENSIONEM				
Academicis maternisque, assumsi mecum propensionem in Patrem.	473	Epistolae		9
PROPENSIUS				
hospitium, et erga te propensius, haud vsquam forsitan reperias.	466	Epistolae		18
PROPERANS				
Hipponensis adest properans, & torquet in hostes	398	Musae 33		17

	PAGE	TITLE	LINE
PROUINCIA			
neque quotidianae virtutis prouincia gerere personam Academiae,	465	Epistolae	9
PROUNOMIOI			
Prounomioi d' aretes koinen geneteiran elontes.	430	Mem.Matr.17	3
PROUOCANS			
Ipsos Catones prouocans oraculis.	423	Mem.Matr.2	34
PROUOCEMUS			
Age, prouocemus vsque ad Angelos ipsos, ...	392	Musae 20	3
PROUT			
Vertas specillum: nam, prout se res habent, ...	388	Musae 8	17
PROXIMO			
iterum exire patria, qui nunc inuenit viam, proximo itinere faciat.	455	Orationes	8
PRUDENS			
Quid voluit prudens Fatum, iam sentio tandem:	438	Poem.Lat.	3
PRUDENTER			
Prudenter inito quot-diebus calculo.	423	Mem.Matr.2	23
PRUDENTIA			
homines, quibus homo bruta, iustitia scilicet & prudentia. . .	447	Orationes	5
gloria, prudentia auctior, ditat patriam, suamque absentiam . .	454	Orationes	32
id omne dexterrima tua in obeundis rebus prudentia dissipetur.	467	Epistolae	13
PRUDENTIAE			
num diffidunt prudentiae Regis? annon eius consilio res gesta est?	451	Orationes	23
hunc fasciculum Prudentiae, positum extra mortalitatis aleam,	459	Epistolae	10
Quare nos omnes ad prudentiae eloquentiaeque tuae praesidium	465	Epistolae	15
PRUDENTIAM			
Suamque in alijs possidet prudentiam.	412	Lucus 13	4
Quid memorem prudentiam vestram incomparabilem, qua optime ostendis	443	Orationes	15
Quare & Principis iter multiplicem nobis exhibet prudentiam;	446	Orationes	8
O prudentiam incomparabilem, quae eodem vultu et moderatur mundum	458	Epistolae	3
PRUDENTISSIMI			
atque vbiuis terrarum pro iudicio prudentissimi Regis, & in rebus	444	Orationes	20
PRUDENTISSIMUM			
vt aliquando existimen id egisse prudentissimum Patrem tuum,	451	Orationes	30
PRUDENTISSIMUS			
prudentissimus Rex mature prospiciet: vbi ille signum sustulerit,	449	Orationes	16
PRUINAS			
Ceu, quas culta timet seges, pruinas	385	Musae	7
PRUNA			
Aut vt pruna gelu summo mordacius vrit, ...	399	Musae 35	5
PSALMOS			
Quid hocce? Psalmos audion'? o dapes!	394	Musae 23	33
PSUXES			
Psuxes asthenes erkos, amauron pneumatos aggos, ...	429	Mem.Matr.14	1
PTEROIS			
semper titillant aures Principum, Osper tois pterois knomenoi ta ota.	453	Orationes	3
PUBES			
Te Germana tamen pubes, te Graecus & Anglus	416	Lucus 26	3
Confluere interea passim ad Floralia pubes	418	Tr.Mortis	9
Veneranda Capita, Viri grauissimi, Pubes lectissima.	444	Orationes	11
PUBLICAE			
Mentes, quietis tympana publicae, ...	395	Musae 23	50
Benedictiones publicae cingunt caput, ...	423	Mem.Matr.2	48
Imo prorsus censemus permultum interesse alacritatis publicae,	468	Epistolae	15
PUBLICAM			
Tuam suauissimam, nuper in lucem publicam, nostramque praesertim,	463	Epistolae	5
PUBLICI			
sub specie publici commodi, Academiae incommodum videntur allaturi;	462	Epistolae	31
PUBLICO			
neque de priuato agamus bono, sed publico;	448	Orationes	7
maius tamen piaculum reor, deesse publico muneri, quam priuato,	472	Epistolae	31
PUBLICUM			
suum potius emolumentum quam publicum spectantes (quae res et naturae	467	Epistolae	4
PUDENS			
Virgo pudens, vxor fida, seuera parens:	429	Mem.Matr.13	2
PUDET			
Quam pudet me delicatorum Caesarum, qui cupiditatibus immersi,	452	Orationes	8
PUDOR			
Calumniarum nec pudor quis nec modus?	397	Musae 30	1
Pudorque constet vel solutis crinibus;	422	Mem.Matr.2	6
PUDORE			
Saepius aspergis. Siste, pudore vacas.	387	Musae 7	2
Eridanusque pudore fusus.	394	Musae 23	44
PUDOREM			
Absit vt ingenuum pungant mea verba pudorem;	400	Musae 36	3
PUDORIBUS			
Abito, trunce, cum tuis pudoribus.	423	Mem.Matr.2	54
PUDUIT			
Phoebe, tui puduit quum summo mane redires	433	Poem.Lat.	36
PUER			
Quod puer ignorat, verba profana putas?	388	Musae 9	2
PUERI			
Quid vetat vt pueri vagitus suppleat alter, ...	388	Musae 9	13
PUERORUM			
bullae & crepitacula puerorum sunt, aut eorum certe, qui cymbala sunt	445	Orationes	23
PUEROS			
Enixas pueros matres se sistere templis	389	Musae 12	1
PUERPERIUM			
De Purificatione post puerperium.	389	Musae 12	T
PUGILLUM			
sic & ipse excerpam e Principis rebus gestis pugillum, vnam actionem	445	Orationes	31

PUGNA	PAGE	TITLE		LINE
Clauserit extremas pugna peracta vices, ...	386	Musae 2		8
Cordis apex, animae pugnaque paxque meae, ...	421	Lucus 35		2
PUGNACES				
Pugnaces, teneros florum turbemus odores, ...	427	Mem.Matr.7		32
PUGNAE				
Fictaque Bellona & verae ludibria pugnae, ...	418	Tr.Mortis		27
PUGNAM				
Haec etiam ad pugnam praesens, qua viuimus, aetas	399	Musae 33		21
PUGNAS				
O saeuus hostis! quam ferociter pugnas!	392	Musae 20		15
PULCHERRIMAE				
pulcherrimaeque Musarum domus tanquam viduae effoetae, aut ligna	462	Epistolae		3
PULCHRE				
Pulchre renatam ex arbore mortua, ...	434	Poem.Lat.		34
PULCHRITUDO				
nulla pulchritudo per vniuersam Britanniam, disparuit forma,	451	Orationes		17
PULCHRUM				
quam audire videor dicentem, Pulchrum quidem iter & Amante dignum;	453	Orationes		26
PULPITA				
Pulpita, plus spatij lucreris?	395	Musae 23		48
PULSARE				
Cum millena tuam pulsare negotia mentem	385	Musae 1		1
Sic pulsare tuas, exclusis luctibus, ausint	402	Musae 39		35
PULTIBUS				
Ego hic pultibus vescor et glande, more maiorum, multos iam annos	470	Epistolae		4
PULUERE				
Protulit horrendum hoc primus cum puluere monstrum.	420	Tr.Mortis		91
Protulit horrendum hoc primum cum puluere monstrum.	420	Tr.Mortis	V	91
Quis Monachos mortem meditari, & puluere tristi	420	Tr.Mortis		92
Quis mortem Monachos meditari, et puluere tristi	272	Tr.Mortis	VS	92
Vt morti perimant, alioque in puluere prostet?	433	Poem.Lat.		35
contemnere has gloriolas nostras quas e chartis & puluere eruimus.	441	Orationes		17
et blattis rixantes, exuens puluere, in theatrum et lucem produxisti.	462	Epistolae		27
PULUERI				
figuras iam nunc pulueri inscriptas corpore confosso obliterans.	448	Orationes		31
PULUERIS				
Pulueris inferni; properat datus ignis, & omnem	420	Tr.Mortis		69
Pulueris inferni properat, datur ignis, & omnem	420	Tr.Mortis	V	69
O blanda dextra, neutiquam istoc pulueris, ...	423	Mem.Matr.2		39
Quare etiam nuper Pyrij de pulueris ictu	433	Poem.Lat.		33
aetate prouectior, etiam anus subsultans multum excitet pulueris:	454	Orationes		36
PULUIS				
Accedit Pyrius puluis, laquearibus Orci	419	Tr.Mortis		57
PULUISCULUS				
O cessatrices! eccum puluisculus illic!	413	Lucus 15		5
PUNGANT				
Absit vt ingenuum pungant mea verba pudorem;	400	Musae 36		3
PUNGERIS				
Tu spina misere pungeris, ipse Rosa.	405	Passio 6		2
PUNGUNT				
Imo, me nec apes, nec astra pungunt:	411	Lucus 5		10
Nullo circuitu scienda pungunt, ...	415	Lucus 24		12
PUNTHANESTHAI				
Dokei moi xrenai para ton presbuton punthanesthai, osper tina odon	471	Epistolae		10
PUPILLARI				
Scientiarum, sub pupillari statu	436	Poem.Lat.		10
PURGENTUR				
Omnia purgentur, niteat mihi tota supellex, ...	413	Lucus 15		3
PURI				
Hoc erit, Anti-furi-Puri-Categoria.	386	Musae 3		8
Vos ergo puri! o nomen appositissimum	393	Musae 22		5
PURIFICATIONE				
De Purificatione post puerperium.	389	Musae 12		T
PURIUS				
Scilicet hoc vobis proprium, qui purius itis, ...	387	Musae 5		7
PURO				
quae est vestra felicitas qui puro Academiae farre vtimini. . . .	470	Epistolae		3
PURPUR				
In Arund. Spin. Genuflex. Purpur.	405	Passio 7		T
PURPURA				
Quam nihil illudis! si, quae tua purpura fingit, ...	405	Passio 7		7
limatae auris atque tersae, quorum grauitate ac purpura non abutar.	445	Orationes		27
PURPURAM				
doctrinae nitoremque spirans purpuram et eruditionem miscuisti;	461	Epistolae		22
PURPUREO				
Purpureo melius sanguine Regna probem.	405	Passio 7		8
PURPUREUS				
Purpureus lictor Plutonis, epistola Fati	419	Tr.Mortis		63
PURUS				
Sanus Homo factus, vitiorum purus vterque;	408	Passio 20		1
PUTAMEN				
Bellum putamen, nucleus bellissimus, ...	423	Mem.Matr.2		36
PUTANDO				
Quid ipsi sumus, assequi putando.	415	Lucus 24		10
PUTANS				
Subtegmen reti dignius esse putans, ...	392	Musae 19		4
PUTANT				
tantum qui eruditionem simplicitati Christianae putant aduersam,	461	Epistolae		18
PUTAS				
Quod puer ignorat, verba profana putas?	388	Musae 9		2

PUTAS (cont'd)	PAGE	TITLE		LINE
Cum te non videam, mene videre putas?	421	Lucus 35		8
Iamdudum tacite delituisse putas?	437	Poem.Lat.	V	10
PUTAT				
Aurum luce videns, nulla videre putat.	411	Lucus 7		2
Se quasi donatum funere quisque putat.	435	Poem.Lat.		4
PUTEM				
vt interdum putem, optime consuluisse Deum orbi terrarum lapides	452	Orationes		24
PUTES				
Iamdudum tacite delituisse putes?	437	Poem.Lat.		10
PYRENAEAS				
vsque ad Pyrenaeas nubes conscendens, reuersus per mare,	454	Orationes		31
PYRIJ				
Quare etiam nuper Pyrij de pulueris ictu	433	Poem.Lat.		33
PYRIUS				
Accedit Pyrius puluis, laquearibus Orci	419	Tr.Mortis		57
PYXIDE				
Progenies, gemmamque sua quasi pyxide clausit.	402	Musae 39		16
QUA				
Qua parte tractari solent,	388	Musae 8		12
Qua possint humili fundere corde preces.	390	Musae 12		12
Qua tamen occisi foedera scripta Dei?	391	Musae 16		4
Lampada, qua studijs inuigilare solet.	398	Musae 33		18
Haec etiam ad pugnam praesens, qua viuimus, aetas	399	Musae 33		21
Qua sine vos miseri lentius itis ope.	399	Musae 33		26
Illa cauerna, in qua tot ociere ferae.	414	Lucus 21		4
Qua Fabio quondam sub duce nata salus.	416	Lucus 25		10
Qua Mors ipsa sedens hominum de gente triumphat.	419	Tr.Mortis		56
Fatalemque leuans dextram, qua stupeus ignis	420	Tr.Mortis		67
Dicite, vos Furiae, qua gaudet origine Monstrum.	420	Tr.Mortis		85
Dicite vos Stutiae, qua gaudet origine monstrum	272	Tr.Mortis	VS	85
Nec qua consuleres, populumve ad bella vocares,	211	Cam.1613-b	BR	9
qua perfundis nos omnes quotidianis beneficijs, redundarit	443	Orationes		9
qua optime ostendis te eius vicarium qui omnia disponit suauiter?	443	Orationes		16
Oratio Qua auspicatissimum Serenissimi Principis Caroli Reditum ex	444	Orationes		T
qualis quaeque sit mater, e qua liberi quaerantur, quam qualis terra,	447	Orationes		11
e qua liberi quaerantur, quam qualis terra, e qua arbores.	447	Orationes		11
qua in re celebris est Gracchorum mater, ingenium ipsum atque indoles	447	Orationes		16
qua tot iam annis impune fruimur, hoc pacto fundatam cupit	447	Orationes		28
bello pacem, sine qua omnis vita procella, & mundus solitudo.	448	Orationes		8
tanquam catenam, qua dissitas nationes ac superbas constringeret.	450	Orationes		24
indicantes, se non amare patriam terram, a qua adeo remouentur.	452	Orationes		12
quo spiritu, qua arte, quanto impetu atque vigore res aggrediatur:	454	Orationes		10
relabitur in terram, qua ortus est, eique cum foecundia remuneratur:	454	Orationes		29
haec est ansa qua prehendimus Te, et tanquam Aquilam inter nouas	456	Epistolae		6
in qua dextra et fide coniuncti, in caeteris haud diuellamur.	468	Epistolae		24
QUACUNQUE				
Quacunque gutta temporis imminent?	433	Poem.Lat.		6
QUADRA				
Collega Solis; Quadra Certitudinis;	436	Poem.Lat.		13
QUADRABUNT				
multa Critt meo quadrabunt, quae almae matri inconcinna erunt atque	470	Epistolae		14
QUADRARE				
Ista docens soli scripta quadrare tibi.	385	Musae		6
QUADRATI				
Inde Patres pergunt quadrati, & tota Vetustas.	398	Musae 33		13
QUADRATO				
De Pileo quadrato.	391	Musae 15		T
QUAE				
Quae sapiunt aeuum, ceu cariosa iacent.	386	Musae 3		4
Quae ratio per se, si sit adulta, facit.	388	Musae 9		12
Tollantur si cuncta malus quae polluit vsus,	390	Musae 13		3
Quae dicteria fuderat Britannus	391	Musae 15		1
Vt, quae Papicolis propria, assuas nobis,	392	Musae 20		8
quae miseris clypeo	396	Musae 28		5
Scotia quae frigente iaces porrecta sub Arcto,	399	Musae 35		1
Quae scripsit numeros, manum; per omnes	400	Musae 37		2
Quam nihil illudis! si, quae tua purpura fingit,	405	Passio 7		7
Quae contrita tamen caetera damna leuant.	409	Passio 20		8
Quae cordis latebras sinusque caecos	411	Lucus 5		12
Quae vis condidit, ipsa nouit aedes.	411	Lucus 5		17
Et quae corrumpit moenia, murus aqua est.	411	Lucus 6		6
Quae Fabio quondam sub duce tuta salus.	416	Lucus 25	V	10
Quae diuisa nocent, Christi per foedus, in vnum	417	Lucus 29		3
Bidens Bombardas miseras, quae corpora perdunt	420	Tr.Mortis		97
Quae guttae poterunt enumerare meos?	422	Mem.Matr.1		2
Conferte lacrymas: Illa, quae vos miscuit	422	Mem.Matr.2		3
Tum quanta tabulis artifex? quae scriptio?	423	Mem.Matr.2		35
Adde his trientem Musices, quae molliens	423	Mem.Matr.2		42
Fatisco referens tanta quae numerant mei	423	Mem.Matr.2		50
Plura tibi missurus eram (nam quae mihi laurus,	428	Mem.Matr.9		15
Quae suberant causae? quid nos committere tantum,	432	Poem.Lat.		18
Columba Noae, quae in vetustis artibus	436	Poem.Lat.		19
Columba Noae, quae in vetustatis artibus	436	Poem.Lat.	V	19
Ah longum, quae te deperit, errat iter.	437	Poem.Lat.		4
Ah longum, quae te deperit, ambit iter.	437	Poem.Lat.	V	4
Quae mihi lugubres contribuere genas!	437	Poem.Lat.		12
quae rutilatio? certe cum duplex fulgor sit, qui mundi oculos	441	Orationes		11
eruditionem, quae tanta est vt, nisi Rex esses in ciuili Republica,	443	Orationes		18
sed a scriptis vestris, quae ingenti cum lucro quotidie legimus.	443	Orationes		20
Quid innumera alia, quae, si per tempus liceret effari,	443	Orationes		28

QUAE (cont'd)	PAGE	TITLE		LINE
incredibiles laudes vestras quod quae nos audiamus summo cum gaudio	443	Orationes		31
Quae enim vspiam gens, quod vnquam seculum meliorem habuit Principem?	445	Orationes		12
Austriacam familiam, Aquilamque illam, quae non capit muscas.	446	Orationes		16
vnius seculi Princeps, sed & omnium, quae ventura sunt, haberetur.	447	Orationes		26
ne pacem, quae sola incubat artibus, & obstetricatur, minus quam par	448	Orationes		33
Quam cruenta gloria est, quae super ceruicibus hominum erigitur?	449	Orationes		10
curiositas absit, neque eorum satagamus, quae ad nos non spectant;	449	Orationes		20
praecipue pharetrata, quae ad poenam gentium & Bellum spectant.	449	Orationes		27
quae auditiones? qui susurri? Heus, abijtne Noster?	450	Orationes		36
quae licet versentur in figuris describendis, quibus nihil imperito	454	Orationes		3
non respicitur, quae materia sit, coelestis an sublunaris,	454	Orationes		12
coelestis an sublunaris, sed quae signa, quo motu transeat.	454	Orationes		13
& inuidiam, quae semper se deuorat primum, vti vermis nucleum,	454	Orationes		14
gaudia praestolantur, quae iamdudum annuunt mihi vt perorem.	454	Orationes		22
praesertim donec transeat nubes illa, quae vicinos adeo infestat:	455	Orationes		15
inter quae etiam certamen oritur et pia contentio, vtrum gratia	456	Epistolae		19
incomparabilem, quae eodem vultu et moderatur mundum et nos respicit.	458	Epistolae		3
Tu inuaseris eorum gloriam conseruando nobis quae illi dederunt,	458	Epistolae		26
Quae enim alia spes reliqua erat, quam vt pro infinitis vestris	458	Epistolae		29
Musarum, quae cum olim gauderent Fluuijs, nunc etiam aquas,	460	Epistolae		8
rotunditas Clementiae vestrae, quae ab omni parte nobis succurrit!	460	Epistolae		10
quae fastigium regiarum noticnum aequare nunquam potest,	460	Epistolae		16
quae fugerunt tot philosophos vmbra et otio diffluentes,	463	Epistolae		18
nostrae, quae per Tuum Partum, ex Matre nunc Auia facta est:	463	Epistolae		25
denique huic aetati quae talem virum protulit, cum quinque millibus	463	Epistolae		26
vtque mature absoluas quae complexus es animo, ad eius gloriam,	464	Epistolae		4
quam publicum spectantes (quae res et naturae legibus et hominum	467	Epistolae		5
quae nos soluendo non sumus, in suas tabulas accepti transferat.	467	Epistolae		14
et precium, quae abyssus crumenae tantos sumptus aequabit?	468	Epistolae		3
quae est vestra felicitas qui puro Academiae farre vtimini.	470	Epistolae		2
meo quadrabunt, quae almae matri inconcinna erunt atque enormia.	470	Epistolae		15
quae cum plerumque implicata sint, nisi candida phrasi telam	470	Epistolae		29
atque effusissimum in omnia officia, quae praestet mea paruitas;	471	Epistolae		22
tanta Humanitatis massa, quae apud Te visitur, abscindere non possim,	472	Epistolae		14
neque vlla negotia (quippe quae caput petant, non cor) Tui in me	473	Epistolae		6
QUAEDAM				
Nosse sui quid agant, quaedam est quoque musica sanctis,	427	Mem.Matr.9		3
est etiam interdum satietas quaedam honoris, quem ad tempus deponere	453	Orationes		9
QUAEPIAM				
ramenta quaepiam ex tanta Humanitatis massa, quae apud Te visitur,	472	Epistolae		13
QUAEQUE				
Aruiraqum, falcesque obstantia quaeque metentes.	419	Tr.Mortis		46
Quaeque domus Dominae sit, grauitate docent.	425	Mem.Matr.5		8
Quaeque olim fuerat cura, manere potest.	427	Mem.Matr.9		4
In laudes abeunt secula quaeque tuas;	435	Poem.Lat.		2
In laudes properant secula quaeque tuas;	435	Poem.Lat.	V	2
In laudes abeunt iam loca quaeque tuas:	435	Poem.Lat.		4
In laudes properant iam loca quaeque tuas:	435	Poem.Lat.	V	4
enim minus refert, qualis quaeque sit mater, e qua liberi quaerantur,	447	Orationes		10
etiam tenero, sed laxioribus vinculis, quaeque amor saepe remittit:	472	Epistolae		34
QUAERANT				
vt semper post nouas dignitates, alias tibi quaerant et moliantur.	464	Epistolae		24
QUAERANTUR				
qualis quaeque sit mater, e qua liberi quaerantur, quam qualis terra,	447	Orationes		11
QUAERENDO				
Omnia quaerendo, sed te, super omnia, vexas:	413	Lucus 16		5
QUAERENDUM				
neque amplius quaerendum sit Tibi, Almae Nutrici quid reponas.	462	Epistolae		16
QUAERERE				
Quisnam Antichristus cessemus quaerere; Papa	412	Lucus 10		1
QUAERIT				
Quaerit recessus. Incalescit fabula:	398	Musae 32		6
QUAERITE				
Scilicet in tumulis Crucifixum quaerite, viuit:	408	Passio 17		5
QUAERITIS				
Musasque coelibes, qui posteros libris non liberis quaeritis.	446	Orationes		27
QUAERITUR				
Quaeritur ingenium, doctusque homicida probatur.	418	Tr.Mortis		25
QUAERUNT				
vnde diuites syluas ac saltus quaerunt vbi aedificent, ac	450	Orationes		21
QUAESITUM				
Quaesitum Dominam gemma vel herba suam.	425	Mem.Matr.5		12
QUAESIUIT				
suam gentem amorem, cui pacem quaesiuit suo capite, periculis suis.	449	Orationes		37
QUAESTIO				
Ne nimium vexet quaestio, pone meam.	409	Passio 21		4
QUAESTIONUM				
Tot quaestionum fluctibus obruis,	425	Mem.Matr.6		2
QUAEUIS				
Adde pijs animis quaeuis occasio lucro est,	390	Musae 12		11
QUALE				
Quos tu rotatus, quale murmur auscultas	392	Musae 20		1
Quale paludosos iamiam lictura recessus	426	Mem.Matr.7		11
QUALEM				
Luctatur spacium, qualem tamen eligit aequi	426	Mem.Matr.7		24
QUALIA				
Qualia parturiente colunt sub rupe sorores:	432	Poem.Lat.		8
QUALIBET				
ideoque ex quolibet ligno, qualibet vxore non esse fingendum:	447	Orationes		9

QUALIS	PAGE	TITLE	LINE
Qualis nescius aggerum	403	Musae 40	9
Qualis eras, qui, ne melior natura minorem	407	Passio 14	1
Quin post modestam, qualis integras decet,	422	Mem.Matr.2	14
Accipe; ni talem des, tibi qualis erat.	434	Poem.Lat.	6
enim minus refert, qualis quaeque sit mater, e qua liberi quaerantur,	447	Orationes	10
e qua liberi quaerantur, quam qualis terra, e qua arbores.	447	Orationes	11
de Principe aliquo, quis sit futurus aut qualis, recte diuinaret,	454	Orationes	9
QUAM			
Ante tui, CAESAR, quam fulserat aura fauoris,	384	Musae	3
Quam chartam tibi porrigo recentem,	384	Musae	1
Ecce tamen quam suauis ero! cum, fine duelli,	386	Musae 2	7
O quam bellus homo es! lepido quam nomine fingis	386	Musae 3	1
Vnquam fugari, quam tui socij solent.	389	Musae 10	3
Quam praemissa probant secula, nostra probant?	391	Musae 16	2
Quam cunctos fieri praestat Episcopos.	392	Musae 17	13
Falsumque potius quam crepes versu?	392	Musae 20	9
O saeuus hostis! quam ferociter pugnas!	392	Musae 20	15
Mugire multo mauelim quam rudere.	395	Musae 24	2
Quam Christus immortalis innocuo gregi	396	Musae 28	1
Quam (more vestro) imponere inscio vulgo.	397	Musae 31	3
Quam curto nequeo referre versu;	400	Musae 37	6
Quam aut Ecclesia despicata vobis,	400	Musae 37	16
Haesisset tibi, quam suprema vestis	400	Musae 37	26
Cernite, quam formosa suas Ecclesia pennas	401	Musae 39	6
Quam nihil illudis, Gens improba! quam male cedunt	405	Passio 7	1
Quam nihil illudis! cum quo magis angar acuto	405	Passio 7	3
Quam nihil illudis flectens! namque integra posthac	405	Passio 7	5
Quam nihil illudis! si, quae tua purpura fingit,	405	Passio 7	7
Ah! quam caederis hinc & inde palmis!	405	Passio 8	1
Quamque ipse lucis tesseram sibi negat,	407	Passio 16	7
Tu tamen, haud tibi tam moreris, quam viuis in illis,	407	Passio 17	3
Quam tribuit, verum multiplicare decet.	408	Passio 17	8
Ah, quam docta perambulare calles	411	Lucus 5	15
Maeandrosque plicasque, quam perita es!	411	Lucus 5	16
Plusque habet hic laetus, quam vel Auarus habet.	411	Lucus 7	4
Dormitat pelagus: Quam bene fraena tenes!	412	Lucus 12	2
Quam si ipse solus omnia interuerteret,	412	Lucus 13	3
ROMA, tuum nomen quam non pertransijt ORAM,	416	Lucus 25	1
Quam satur & suauis sit tibi Roma iocus.	416	Lucus 27	6
Machina, quam nullum satis execrabitur aeuum;	419	Tr.Mortis	50
Huic Glans adijcitur (non quam ructare vetustas	419	Tr.Mortis	60
Hinc Glans adijcitur (non quam ructare vetustas	419	Tr.Mortis V	60
Aura volans, vitamque aer, quam pauerat, aufert.	420	Tr.Mortis	84
Quam mira tandem Subleuatrix pauperum!	423	Mem.Matr.2	45
Abito, tarde. Quam pie istic sum impudens!	424	Mem.Matr.2	60
Aegroto mentis: quam neque pixides	425	Mem.Matr.6	5
Poena minor fuerat, quam fatum Principis aegrum?	432	Poem.Lat.	21
Sol sine sole tuo! quam te tum nubibus atris	433	Poem.Lat.	37
Cur mihi das vitam, quam tibi, Christe, negas?	434	Poem.Lat.	4
Quin moriar tecum: vitam, quam negligis ipse,	434	Poem.Lat.	5
O quam felices sunt, qui tua castra sequuntur,	435	Poem.Lat.	7
Aspice quam pleno descendat Iuppiter imbre,	210	Cam.1613-a BR	5
accidere potest, quam vt ministri Regis Catholici ad nos accedant?	440	Orationes	14
nos tam defecimus in vtroque quam Excellentiae Vestrae abundant.	441	Orationes	13
coelum ac terram minori quam cernimus interuallo connectat.	444	Orationes	7
Quam facile sentiuntur boni Principes!	445	Orationes	4
e multis seligam, quam vobis amplectendam dissuauiandamque praebebo:	445	Orationes	32
vt sciatis omnes quam nude, quam simpliciter vobiscum agam,	445	Orationes	34
quam simpliciter vobiscum agam, quam non longe abeam Oratorum more,	445	Orationes	35
quam non longe abeam Oratorum more, qui nullum non angulum verrunt	445	Orationes	35
maioris momenti aut ponderis, quam Nuptiae, quas adeo laudant Poetae,	446	Orationes	17
e qua liberi quaerantur, quam qualis terra, e qua arbores.	447	Orationes	11
quam subito dispereunt, simul ac concrepuit incendium militare:	448	Orationes	18
incubat artibus, & obstetricatur, minus quam par est, aestimemus.	448	Orationes	34
bis intersectas, infantulos plus lactis quam cruoris emittentes;	449	Orationes	7
Quam cruenta gloria est, quae super ceruicibus hominum erigitur?	449	Orationes	9
ipso Parnasso siti sumus, liberiorem, quam alij, prospectum habeamus.	449	Orationes	34
quid enim vtilius quam ex obseruatione exterarum Legum ac morum,	450	Orationes	14
absentia magis quam praesentia. Nunc enim exploratos habet nostros	450	Orationes	33
quam stulte de te rixamur:	451	Orationes	29
Ecquid videtis tandem quam vtile hoc iter, per quod optimus Princeps	451	Orationes	35
Quam pudet me delicatorum Caesarum, qui cupiditatibus immersi,	452	Orationes	8
neminemque esse sui negligentiorem, quam qui sibi parcat.	452	Orationes	35
Nihil vtilius Regi quam aliquando non regnare:	452	Orationes	38
quam terrae, quam Natura montibus vallibusque sublimitate atque	453	Orationes	11
quam Natura montibus vallibusque sublimitate atque humilitate	453	Orationes	11
quam audire videor dicentem, Pulchrum quidem iter & Amante dignum;	453	Orationes	25
praesertim cum amico fidere periculosius sit, quam hostem superare.	453	Orationes	33
memoriam recolenti, quam cogitanti noua, improbe molestiam creent.	457	Epistolae	13
quam de muniendis contra grassantes flammas aedificijs Honori Tuo	457	Epistolae	17
quam in aqua & igne fecisti, non dubitamus quin benignitas tua omnia	457	Epistolae	22
Angustior erat Scotia, quam vt pennas nido plene explicare posses:	458	Epistolae	8
etiam imperium tenuius est quam pro amplitudine virtutum vestrarum:	458	Epistolae	10
quam vt pro infinitis vestris in nos beneficijs Maiestatem vestram	458	Epistolae	30
ne non tam sapientes nos, quam obscuros philosophos reddidissent.	460	Epistolae	24
incoeptum et plus effecit quam mille Redemptores exequi possent.	461	Epistolae	12
quasi mixtam personam reddidit quam si Episcopi more pristino	461	Epistolae	27
assecutus es nomen, quam Repertores Noui Orbis compararunt.	463	Epistolae	12
rudiorem esse impexioremque, quam vt tantum Hospitem excipiat:	463	Epistolae	29
Quis enim rectius Thesauris Regijs praefici possit quam qui,	464	Epistolae	14

QUAM (cont'd)	PAGE	TITLE	LINE
quam de futuro supplicem, integerrimae tuae fidei commendantes.	465	Epistolae	7
noluitque vt minori sphaera quam pro latitudine meritorum tuorum	466	Epistolae	14
vero de hoc tuo progressu non minus Reipublicae gratulamur quam tibi,	466	Epistolae	16
Bibliopolas suum potius emolumentum quam publicum spectantes (quae	467	Epistolae	4
idque pro libris, de quibus nusquam rectius quam apud Te agitur.	467	Epistolae	19
Quare tam vere quam libenter gratulamur tibi, nec minus etiam	468	Epistolae	18
quam nunc pleno gradu ingrediens beneficijs tuis percurres.	468	Epistolae	19
tibi conueniat scribenti, quam quod Academiae tuo calamo scribenti:	470	Epistolae	13
etiam senectus, quam aetatem in hac palaestra consecutus mihi videor.	471	Epistolae	8
quam adductus maturo consilio, primas dedissem literas,	471	Epistolae	26
quam meis meritis vllis, semper lubentissimeque agnoscam:	472	Epistolae	22
tam communi hac luce, quam Tua, cum id agnoscere vnquam desinam.	472	Epistolae	24
publico muneri, quam priuato, latiusque manare iniustitiae peccatum,	472	Epistolae	31
latiusque manare iniustitiae peccatum, quam negligentiae.	472	Epistolae	32
nihil Mortalium firmiori flagrare in Te desiderio, quam meum pectus;	473	Epistolae	5
tersis atque expolitis, quam luxuriae saeculi, ambitionisque strumae,	473	Epistolae	20
QUAMLIBET			
date mihi CAROLVM alterum, quamlibet Magnum, modo detis eum in flore,	445	Orationes	19
QUAMOBREM			
Quamobrem optime consuluit gentibus natura, cum paupertatem daret	450	Orationes	22
Quamobrem non est mirandum, si Reges ipsi quandoque suauitates suas	453	Orationes	18
Quamobrem abijcite quisque libros, non est locus grauitati,	454	Orationes	33
QUAMUIS			
Ille tamen, quamuis altus, tua crimina ridens	387	Musae 7	7
Quo fugies, sudor? quamuis pars altera Christi	404	Passio 2	1
quamuis rationi consonum videtur, vt qui hic in Musarum monte	449	Orationes	32
Quamuis res haec. Principibus vt vtilissima ita difficillima factu,	450	Orationes	10
vt lineae, quamuis diuersa via, omnes tamen ad centrum properant;	456	Epistolae	23
vestra solum dextra (quamuis a scriptione terrestribusque istis	458	Epistolae	6
quamuis enim sexcenta huiusmodi praediola Tua gratia permutare nolim,	472	Epistolae	29
QUANDO			
quando ipsae hae turres & beatae fabricae, vnico ictu sulphurei tubi,	448	Orationes	20
rogamusque vt quando beneficia tua peruagantur Angliam,	466	Epistolae	16
Quin nec demisso, quando ad magnates cogitas, stylo vtare,	470	Epistolae	21
QUANDOQUE			
Nec Glans sola nocet; mortem quandoque susurrat	420	Tr.Mortis	83
Quandoque voltus sola maiestas, Dolor.	422	Mem.Matr.2	7
si Reges ipsi quandoque suauitates suas populari aceto condiant.	453	Orationes	19
QUANQUAM			
quanquam quem alium fructum potuimus expectare ab Eo, in quem fauor	456	Epistolae	17
Quanquam non mirari non possumus, vnde fit vt nullus fere elabatur	461	Epistolae	12
Quanquam, cum grauibus duobus muneribus fungar apud Meos,	472	Epistolae	25
QUANTA			
Ain' vero? quanta praedicas? hercle aedepol,	421	Lucus 33	1
Proh! quantus imber, quanta labri comitas,	423	Mem.Matr.2	29
Tum quanta tabulis artifex? quae scriptio?	423	Mem.Matr.2	35
Quanta rotunditas Clementiae vestrae, quae ab omni parte nobis	460	Epistolae	9
Quanta hilaritate aspicit Alma Mater filios suos iam emancipatos,	461	Epistolae	30
QUANTO			
Quanto Impositio melior est Impostura!	397	Musae 31	4
Ni me forte petas; nam quanto indignior ipse,	404	Passio 2	5
Quanto foeliciores nos omnes, Corona Musica, qui optimum Principem	444	Orationes	16
quanto minus tacebunt lusciniae nostrae disertae, minimeque omnium	445	Orationes	9
Quod si Nuptiae in se graues sunt, quanto magis Principum, cum,	446	Orationes	34
cum quanto plus possint in sua terra, tanto minus in aliena.	450	Orationes	11
quo spiritu, qua arte, quanto impetu atque vigore res aggrediatur:	454	Orationes	11
quanto citius fugient calumniae, si speculum Inuidiae ostendas,	454	Orationes	20
quanto magis virtutes istae in Dominum agri transferendae sunt,	459	Epistolae	17
laetissime sumeret, quanto magis par est, nos humillimos subiectos,	460	Epistolae	12
quanto altius crescunt, tanto etiam altius agunt radices:	464	Epistolae	18
etiam tacentibus nobis, quanto magis cum rogamus, idque pro Libris,	467	Epistolae	18
QUANTUM			
Contemplare, miser, quantum terroris haberet	417	Lucus 31	5
Quantum caedi? adeon' vnam vos pascere vitam,	419	Tr.Mortis	34
Quantum caedi? adeon' vnam nos viuere vitam,	271	Tr.Mortis VS	34
At superat caput illa tuum, quantum ipsa cadauer	424	Mem.Matr.3	3
pauxillum vitae, quantum satis ad dolendum, vrbium incendia,	449	Orationes	5
ex quo facile collectu erat, quantum deperimus te;	451	Orationes	29
quantum quidem ego homuncio ac nanus coniectando assequor.	453	Orationes	20
ad legendum, quantum a nobis ad scribendum, cum humanitatis Tuae,	457	Epistolae	9
de nullo vnquam Filio Alma Mater, quantum de Te sibi polliceatur.	457	Epistolae	26
si quantum eruditio Regis profuerit Reipublicae, tantum fauoris nobis	469	Epistolae	24
QUANTUS			
Proh! quantus imber, quanta labri comitas,	423	Mem.Matr.2	29
QUARE			
Quare, peritus nauta, vela contrahas,	414	Lucus 20	11
Quare Sphaeram egomet meam	424	Mem.Matr.4	9
Quare haud vos hortos, sed coemeteria dico,	425	Mem.Matr.5	9
Quare age, Mens, effare, precor, quo numine laeso?	432	Poem.Lat.	17
Quare etiam nuper Pyrij de pulueris ictu	433	Poem.Lat.	33
Quare adsis Princeps, aliis Academia mons sit,	210	Cam.1613-a BR	7
Quare Excellentissimi, Splendidissimi Domini, cum tanti sitis	441	Orationes	7
Quare, vt miraculis vestris nostra occurrant, oratio nostra est	444	Orationes	2
Quare vt parcius agam vobiscum, simulque & laboribus meis,	445	Orationes	28
Quare & Principis iter multiplicem nobis exhibet prudentiam;	446	Orationes	7
Quare operosior in eo structura, & praerogatiuae regiae emicant.	446	Orationes	37
Quare noluit Princeps optimus, in delectu vxoris, re vna omnium	447	Orationes	21
Quare cauendum, ne pacem, quae sola incubat artibus, & obstetricatur,	448	Orationes	32
Quare nunc vobis ex pede Herculem, ex itinere Principem metiri licet,	453	Orationes	22
Quare prodite, tenebriones literarij, e gurgustijs vestris,	454	Orationes	24

QUARE (cont'd)	PAGE	TITLE	LINE
Quare, meritissime Marchio, Tuam gloriam censemus nostram,	456	Epistolae	15
Quare quomodo alij molem hanc laetitiae suae exprimant,	456	Epistolae	25
Quare coniunximus nunc officia nostra, tuosque fauores temporibus	457	Epistolae	14
Quare amplectimur, fouemus, exosculamur, hunc foetum vestrum,	459	Epistolae	8
Quare plurimum debemus constantiae fauoris tui, qui restinxisti sitim	462	Epistolae	6
Quare nos tertium praedictis adiungimus Gratiarum Fluuium,	462	Epistolae	23
Quare multiplex est laetitia nostra:	463	Epistolae	20
Quare summe gratulamur tibi de nouo hoc cumulo honorum,	464	Epistolae	20
Quare frequentissimo Senatu, plenissimis suffragijs elegimus Te	465	Epistolae	3
Quare nos omnes ad prudentiae eloquentiaeque tuae praesidium	465	Epistolae	15
Quare optime fecit Rex Serenissimus, qui virtutes tuas magnis	466	Epistolae	12
Quare vnice obsecramus, vt qui tot subsidia attuleris ad progressum	467	Epistolae	27
quare causam nostram nosque ipsos Tibi, Teque Deo Opti: Max: intimis	468	Epistolae	9
Quare tam vere quam libenter gratulamur tibi, nec minus etiam	468	Epistolae	17
Quare post Principis manum honoribus refertam, non est quod nostram	469	Epistolae	14
Quare scripturus, finge tibi matronam sanctam, venerandam,	470	Epistolae	16
Quare et Procancellarius Academiam simulans vel maximos magnatum	470	Epistolae	25
Quare malui seruire auribus Tuis, creberrima Antiquitatis lectione	473	Epistolae	19
QUARTA			
quod si tertia detur et quarta, paratos nos habebis ad gratulationem,	465	Epistolae	25
QUARUM			
quarum enumerationi nulla vnquam vis, nulla latera sufficere possunt.	443	Orationes	14
QUAS			
Quas liuor mihi parturit, retundet,	385	Musae	6
Ceu, quas culta timet seges, pruinas	385	Musae	7
Quas malus liuor iaculis lacessit	390	Musae 14	2
Quas spargit animae corporis propius lutum?	393	Musae 22	4
Quas Luna habet, tuetur, in foueam cadit,	393	Musae 22	8
Quas subscriptio neutiquam inquinauit;	400	Musae 37	8
Quas gens inconsulta, suis vexata procellis,	401	Musae 39	2
Quas Latij Catharique mouent, atque inter vtrasque	402	Musae 39	31
Si-quas mens agitet moles (dum pectora saeuo	432	Poem.Lat.	9
Sunt etiam tenebrae, quas tamen optat amor.	437	Poem.Lat.	2
Aut aperi, & cernes corpus quas proijcit vmbras;	437	Poem.Lat.	7
Aut aperi, & cernis corpus quas proijcit vmbras;	437	Poem.Lat. V	7
Cum mihi sit facies fumus, quas pectore flammas	437	Poem.Lat.	9
Tuque etiam Dapifer, quas fero, sume dapes:	210	Cam.1613-a BR	2
nullas Herculeas columnas, quas iam olim possidet, agnoscit.	440	Orationes	18
contemnere has gloriolas nostras quas e chartis & puluere eruimus.	441	Orationes	17
quam Nuptiae, quas adeo laudant Poetae, vt in coelum transtulerint:	446	Orationes	17
inter quas & Mathematicae, quae licet versentur in figuris	454	Orationes	3
proin vt Fluuij quas aquas a Fonte accipiunt non retinent ipsi,	456	Epistolae	9
quas non nobis habemus sed irrigati ipsi vniuersum regnum aspergimus?	462	Epistolae	10
QUASI			
Progenies, gemmamque sua quasi pyxide clausit.	402	Musae 39	16
Hoc ligno, his clauis est, quasi Falce sua.	407	Passio 14	4
Laus antiqua & honor perijt: quasi scilicet ARMO	416	Lucus 25	7
Inde rotae atque axes subeunt, quasi sella curulis	419	Tr.Mortis	55
Plumbea glans, liuensque suae quasi conscia noxae,	419	Tr.Mortis	62
Mulcensque dotes caeteras visa est quasi	423	Mem.Matr.2	43
Sit quasi fasciculus crescens, & nidus odorum.	427	Mem.Matr.7	27
Sic quasi Dijs certem, magnos accersere montes:	432	Poem.Lat.	6
Se quasi donatum funere quisque putat.	435	Poem.Lat.	4
qui vtrasque Indias Hispania sua quasi nodo connectens,	440	Orationes	17
vnde consequimur, vel inuitis Fatis, quasi nodosam aeternitatem.	446	Orationes	24
triumphos & victorias quasi fraena ferox spumantia mandit,	447	Orationes	34
voluptatibus quasi fascijs circumdatum, enatare e delicijs,	452	Orationes	5
& quasi mixtam personam reddidit quam si Episcopi more pristino	461	Epistolae	26
alterosque maris quasi Flagellatores expugnatos fusosque nobis	462	Epistolae	9
et quasi accolae Maiestatis, literaturae suae et vicinitati	463	Epistolae	22
circumspiciens reperisset Te, quasi in tuis palpebris acquiescat.	465	Epistolae	14
feracem gloriae, et coeleste ingenium quasi ad metalla damnari.	468	Epistolae	6
telam explices, perit negotium quasi ex nubibus Ixionis congressus.	470	Epistolae	30
QUASQUE			
Quasque habet aut patulas, aut caeco tramite, moles	402	Musae 39	21
QUE			
Augustissimo Potentissimoque Monarchae	384	Musae	T
Sintque ausae thalamum solis adire tui.	384	Musae	6
Illustriss. Celsissimoque CAROLO, Walliae, & Iuuentutis Principi.	384	Musae	T
Mordaces tineas, nigrasque blattas,	385	Musae	5
Sed propere dextreque reduxit euntia sensus,	385	Musae	5
Cum tu conturdis Catharos, vultuque librisque,	385	Musae 1	5
Sic tu nunc iuuenis factus, egoque senex.	386	Musae 2	4
Sola tibi Sappho, feminaque vna placet?	387	Musae 5	2
Gorgona cur diram laruasque obtrudis inanes,	387	Musae 6	1
Vel potius liceat distinguere. Tuque tuique	387	Musae 6	5
Sumite gorgoneam, nostraque Pallas erit.	387	Musae 6	6
Omnesque stulti audimus, aut hypocritae,	388	Musae 8	7
Vitaque neglectas est satis vlta preces.	389	Musae 12	6
Verum heus! si reputes, tibi tuisque	391	Musae 15	7
Testatosque suo tradiderat gregi;	391	Musae 17	2
Seruarentque sacrum clauibus ordinem;	391	Musae 17	6
An quia Textores Artificesque probas?	392	Musae 18	2
Auresque superas: arbitri ipsi sint litis,	392	Musae 20	4
Falsumque potius quam crepes versu?	392	Musae 20	9
Tu perstrepis tamen; vtque turgeat carmen	392	Musae 20	10
Papicolisque sui sunt, Catharisque sui.	393	Musae 21	2
De labe maculisque.	393	Musae 22	T
Labeculas maculasque nobis obijcis:	393	Musae 22	1
Totusque caenum Cynthiae ignoscit noctis.	393	Musae 22	9

QUE (cont'd)

QUE (cont'd)

	PAGE	TITLE		LINE
Artificesque necis clueant, & mortis alumni.	418	Tr.Mortis		30
Faecundusque chalybs sceleris, iam sanguine tinctus,	419	Tr.Mortis		37
Faecundusque chalibs sceleris, iam sanguine tectus	271	Tr.Mortis	VS	37
Balistasque Cnagrosque & quicquid Scorpio saeuus	419	Tr.Mortis		40
Vel Catapulta potest, Siculique inuenta magistri,	419	Tr.Mortis		41
Anglorumque arcus gaudentes sanguine Galli,	419	Tr.Mortis		42
Angligenumque arces gaudentes sanguine Galli,	419	Tr.Mortis	V	42
Fustibalos fundasque, quibus, cum Numine, fretus	419	Tr.Mortis		43
fustibulos fundusque quibus cum numine fretus	271	Tr.Mortis	VS	43
Aruiragum, falcesque obstantia quaeque metentes.	419	Tr.Mortis		46
Tamque aries ruit et multa Demetrius arte,	271	Tr.Mortis	VS	47
Fusaque decurrit noctis aqua ferrea sulcis:	419	Tr.Mortis		52
Luscum prodigium, medicque foramine gaudens.	419	Tr.Mortis		54
Sulphureoque lacu, totaque imbuta Mephiti.	419	Tr.Mortis		59
Plumbea glans, liuensque suae quasi conscia noxae,	419	Tr.Mortis		62
Plumbis obsignata, colosque & stamina vitae	419	Tr.Mortis		64
Fatalemque leuans dextram, qua stupeus ignis	420	Tr.Mortis		67
Euclat, horrendumque ciet bacchata fragorem.	420	Tr.Mortis		72
It stridor, caelosque omnes & Tartara findit.	420	Tr.Mortis		73
It stridor, caelosque omnes et sydera findit.	271	Tr.Mortis	VS	73
Totamque eructans nubem, Glans proruit imo	420	Tr.Mortis		76
Diffugiunt, fragilisque crepant coenacula mundi.	420	Tr.Mortis		78
Aura volans, vitamque aer, quam pauerat, aufert.	420	Tr.Mortis		84
Nox Aetnam, noctemque Chaos genuere priores.	420	Tr.Mortis		86
Triste colens cellae, noctuque & Daemone plenum,	420	Tr.Mortis		90
Triste colens sellae, noctuque & Daemone plenum,	420	Tr.Mortis	V	90
Tam demissa, ipsamque adeo subeuntia terram?	420	Tr.Mortis		94
Non animas, raroque ornantur sanguine regum	420	Tr.Mortis		98
Obstreperae stulto sonitu, crimenque fatentes.	420	Tr.Mortis		99
Corporeque atque animo. Totus mihi seruiat Orbis.	421	Tr.Mortis		101
Cordis apex, animae pugnaque paxque meae,	421	Lucus 35		2
Immoriarque oculis, o mea vita, tuis.	421	Lucus 35		4
Virtutumque choro siccior ipse tuo.	422	Mem.Matr.1		4
Vestrasque laudes, poscit & mixtas genas.	422	Mem.Matr.2		4
Pudorque constet vel solutis crinibus;	422	Mem.Matr.2		6
Horti, colique distributim pensitat.	423	Mem.Matr.2		19
Surrexit vna & illa, seseque extulit:	423	Mem.Matr.2		27
Mulcensque dotes caeteras visa est quasi	423	Mem.Matr.2		43
Caelique referunt & praeoccupant modum.	423	Mem.Matr.2		49
Sitque omnis motus nescia tanta quies,	424	Mem.Matr.3		8
Dumque his inuigilo frequens	424	Mem.Matr.4		7
Exemploque tuo nascor in alterum:	425	Mem.Matr.4		14
Terram & funus olent flores: Dominaeque cadauer	425	Mem.Matr.5		5
Contiguas stirpes afflat, eaeque rosas.	425	Mem.Matr.5		6
Cuncta ad radices redeant, tumulosque paternos;	425	Mem.Matr.5		13
Corporeae fluidaeque molis?	425	Mem.Matr.6		4
In nebulas similesque tui res gaudia nunquid	426	Mem.Matr.7		2
Vberaque aerea hiscentem fallentia natum?	426	Mem.Matr.7		4
Vae nubi pluuia grauidae, non lacte, measque	426	Mem.Matr.7		5
Verum augusta parens, sanctum os caeloque locandum,	426	Mem.Matr.7		10
Quod superest vitae, insumam: Solisque iugales	426	Mem.Matr.7		15
Aut spes productas, barbataque somnia vertam	426	Mem.Matr.7		19
Ipse suos tanquam digno pallentiaque astra.	426	Mem.Matr.7		21
Rure; breuisque hortus, cuius cum vellere florum	426	Mem.Matr.7		23
Stipati, rudibusque volis imperuius hortus	427	Mem.Matr.7		26
Hic ego tuque erimus, variae suffitibus herbae	427	Mem.Matr.7		28
Affectusque mei similem; nec languida misce	427	Mem.Matr.7		30
Paruam piamque dum lubenter semitam	427	Mem.Matr.8		1
Grandi reaeque praefero,	427	Mem.Matr.8		2
Vinumque felle miscuit.	427	Mem.Matr.8		4
Gusto proboque Dolium.	427	Mem.Matr.8		10
Nos misere flemus, solesque obducimus almos	427	Mem.Matr.9		5
Tillius incumbit Dano, Gallusque marinis,	427	Mem.Matr.9		11
Tellurisque Britannicae saliuam	428	Mem.Matr.10		3
Cum probro madidum, reumque difflat.	428	Mem.Matr.10		7
Te nunc Anglia, Scotiaeque binae,	428	Mem.Matr.10		9
Arbor & ipse inuersa vocer: dumque insitus almae	428	Mem.Matr.11		5
Alteraque haec tua mors, Ilias esto mihi.	428	Mem.Matr.11		14
Iisque siccis adeo vt os Molossorum	429	Mem.Matr.12		3
Tantoque nequioris optima Pirrha?	429	Mem.Matr.12		8
Magnatumque inopumque aequum certamen & ardor:	429	Mem.Matr.13		3
Sic excelsa humilisque simul loca dissita iunxit,	429	Mem.Matr.13		5
Excussos manibus calamos, falcemque resumptam	431	Mem.Matr.19		1
Funereque hoc cultum vindicat aegra suum.	431	Mem.Matr.19		4
Tota stupent luctu) lachrymisque exaestuet aequis	432	Poem.Lat.		10
Annon longa fames miseraeque iniuria pestis	432	Poem.Lat.		20
Fataque Fortunasque & spem laesere futuram.	432	Poem.Lat.		25
Vt morbi perimant, alicque in puluere prostet?	433	Poem.Lat.		35
Tempus edax rerum, tuque o mors improba sola es,	433	Poem.Lat.		41
Pieridis Latiaeque Musae,	433	Poem.Lat.		4
Tantaque propendet statera	433	Poem.Lat.		7
Vtque minax superetur Aegis?	433	Poem.Lat.		12
Furuosque vicisti Gigantes,	434	Poem.Lat.		19
Enceladum pharetramque Rhoeci.	434	Poem.Lat.		20
Fructusque post mortem recusent	434	Poem.Lat.		31
Dignamque caelesti corona	434	Poem.Lat.		35
Cum tu, Christe, cadis, nascor; mentemque liquauit	434	Poem.Lat.		1
Vna meam membris horula, teque cruci.	434	Poem.Lat.		2
Cui tenuis fama est, ingeniumque minus.	435	Poem.Lat.		4
Quis, nisi qui manibus Briareus, oculisque sit Argus,	435	Poem.Lat.		5

QUE (cont'd)

	PAGE	TITLE		LINE
Per strages licet autorum veterumque ruinam	435	Poem.Lat.		1
Vulnereque emanat sanguis, vt intret honos.	435	Poem.Lat.		6
Munere dum nobis prodes, Libroque futuris,	435	Poem.Lat.		1
Munere dum nobis prodes, Libroque remotis,	435	Poem.Lat.		3
Speculationisque; Aequitatis signifer;	436	Poem.Lat.		9
Ad se suaeque matris Arcam regredi:	436	Poem.Lat.		21
Ad se suamque mentis Arcam regredi:	436	Poem.Lat.	V	21
Mundique & Animarum sacerdos vnicus;	436	Poem.Lat.		24
Securis errorum; inque Naturalibus	437	Poem.Lat.		25
Securique errorum; inque Natalibus	437	Poem.Lat.	V	25
Dum petit Infantem Princeps, Grantamque Iacobus,	437	Poem.Lat.		1
Cum petit Hispanam Princeps, Grantamque Iacobus,	437	Poem.Lat.	V	1
Dum longi lentique gemis sub pondere morbi	438	Poem.Lat.		1
Quod Crux nequibat fixa, Clavique additi,	438	Poem.Lat.		1
Munde, fluas fugiasque licet, nos nostraque fixi:	438	Poem.Lat.		8
Tuque etiam Dapifer, quas fero, sume dapes:	210	Cam.1613-a	BR	2
Hic habitant Musae, facilisque in carmine Pallas,	210	Cam.1613-a	BR	3
Fluminaque e ripis obvia facta tibi:	210	Cam.1613-a	BR	6
Invitoque fugit singula stella pede:	210	Cam.1613-b	BR	2
Tuque aer inflato tubam, dum plurimus ignis	211	Cam.1613-b	BR	5
aliosque titulos aeque nobis memorantibus, ac merentibus vobis	440	Orationes		3
Excellentijs Vestris Musae omnes, Gratiaeque, obsecrantes,	440	Orationes		7
in potestatem redigere, lenioresque aspectus, & dulciores assumatis;	440	Orationes		9
supercilium quibus caperatam seuerioremque Philosophiam expugnare	440	Orationes		11
nostrumque regnum gestimus fieri participes eius sanguinis,	440	Orationes		19
Isabellae laudes, virtutesque, vicinum fretum quotidie transnatantes,	441	Orationes		3
tuosque fauces populo tuo communicans coelum ac terram minori quam	444	Orationes		6
cor sacrum, sentiatque Rex ipse nos haec intime precari.	444	Orationes		9
eundemque retulisset captus piscis, foelicissimus mortalium habitus	444	Orationes		15
& in rebus humanis diuinisque exercitatissimi, de integro	444	Orationes		21
spiritibusque tabellarijs laetum hunc nuncium vbique deferentibus,	445	Orationes		1
minimeque omnium coelestiores animi, quorum pietatis interest	445	Orationes		10
in promptu erat, rudesque animos vi verborum percellere:	445	Orationes		17
nondum ad spicam barbamque adultum.	445	Orationes		21
agam vobiscum, simulque & laboribus meis, & vestrae fidei consulam,	445	Orationes		28
e multis seligam, quam vobis amplectendam dissuauiandamque praebebo:	445	Orationes		33
finesque multiplices & polymiti, vt si minus id assequantur,	446	Orationes		5
Austriacam familiam, Aquilamque illam, quae non capit muscas.	446	Orationes		15
Musasque coelibes, qui posteros libris non liberis quaeritis.	446	Orationes		26
ideoque ex quolibet ligno, qualibet vxore non esse fingendum:	447	Orationes		9
re vna omnium grauissima, alienis oculis iudicioque inniti;	447	Orationes		23
suique impos, triumphos & victorias quasi fraena ferox spumantia	447	Orationes		33
Terret equos equitumque vultus.	448	Orationes		4
bellique miserias gratas, praecipue vbi velut ex continentibus tectis	449	Orationes		12
certe nos te absentem omnes acerrime concitatissimeque desiderauimus.	451	Orationes		34
cum Hercule, serpentesque interficere voluptatis, vt iter tantum,	452	Orationes		7
neminemque esse sui negligentiorem, quam qui sibi parcat.	452	Orationes		34
castra hostium ingressus, ipsumque Praetorium, fidibus canendo,	453	Orationes		5
quis scit an & amoris onus scite vinctum ligatumque, & per tot	454	Orationes		1
relabitur in terram, qua ortus est, eique cum foecundia remuneratur:	454	Orationes		30
ditat patriam, suamque absentiam cum foenore compensat.	454	Orationes		33
abunde compensas nos, gratissimoque Almam Matrem prosequeris animo:	456	Epistolae		8
tibique non tam auide veterum beneficiorum memoriam recolenti,	457	Epistolae		12
tuosque fauores temporibus et diligentia diuisos in gratijs nostris	457	Epistolae		15
plurimumque suspicimus cumulum amoris Tui, qui vtrumque curasti,	457	Epistolae		19
dextra (quamuis a scriptione terrestribusque istis sublimitate solij	458	Epistolae		6
victoriaeque gloriam absque crudelitate effusi sanguinis delibas.	458	Epistolae		14
Haec vestra spolia actosque ex orbe triumphos communicas cum Alma	458	Epistolae		16
manibus teri, sanctaque Maiestate, charta conspiciendum Te praebes,	458	Epistolae		19
Reges Collegia, eaque fundarunt amplissimis praedijs, immunitatibus:	458	Epistolae		22
quia dederunt, non a se compositos, scriptos, editosque:	458	Epistolae		25
Humillimi serui subditique vestri Procancellarius Reliquusque Senatus	459	Epistolae		22
vestri Procancellarius Reliquusque Senatus Cantabrigiensis.	459	Epistolae		23
Quid Vaticanam Bodleiumque obijcis, Hospes?	459	Epistolae		30
illustrans nos omnes, lumenque accendens de suo lumine,	461	Epistolae		3
spiritus, generososque animos frangere et retundere clamitant.	461	Epistolae		19
qui elegantias doctrinae nitoremque spirans purpuram et eruditionem	461	Epistolae		21
sericatam hanc stultitiam contere, Academiaeque iura, dignitatem,	461	Epistolae		23
si prae defectu aquae, commeatusque inopia, desererentur collegia,	462	Epistolae		2
pulcherrimaeque Musarum domus tanquam viduae effoetae, aut ligna	462	Epistolae		3
alterosque maris quasi Flagellatores expugnatos fusosque nobis	462	Epistolae		8
maris quasi Flagellatores expugnatos fusosque nobis dedisti.	462	Epistolae		9
paludumque istos siccatores (solem officio suo priuantes) vi verborum	462	Epistolae		19
studioque in nos iam olim perspectissimo, quippe qui eximie semper	462	Epistolae		24
literatos, eosque cum tineis et blattis rixantes, exuens puluere,	462	Epistolae		26
nuper in lucem publicam, nostramque praesertim, editam,	463	Epistolae		6
sed et ambabus vlnis osculisque ei aetati debitis excipientes,	463	Epistolae		7
qui nouas scientiarum regiones terrasque veteribus incognitas primus	463	Epistolae		11
barbara omnia, Tu non nisi cultissima, elegantiasque ipsas exhibes.	463	Epistolae		15
Bibliothecam nostram rudiorem esse impexioremque, quam vt tantum	463	Epistolae		29
vtque mature absoluas quae complexus es animo, ad eius gloriam,	464	Epistolae		4
aeternitatem nominis Tui subsidiumque Magnificentiae Tuae	464	Epistolae		6
virtutes tandem meritis tuis votisque nostris conspirantibus	464	Epistolae		12
administrans, distribuendi modum omnem rationemque callet?	464	Epistolae		16
Te tribunum Parlamentarium, nos nostraque omnia priuilegia, fundos,	465	Epistolae		5
omniumque Artium molem et pondus sustinere, sed perspectissimus tuus	465	Epistolae		10
praestantissimaeque animi dotes effecerunt, vt Alma Mater	465	Epistolae		12
Alma Mater libentissime caput reclinet in tuo sinu, oculusque Reipub:	465	Epistolae		13
nos omnes ad prudentiae eloquentiaeque tuae praesidium festinantes	465	Epistolae		15
Permitte vt nos etiam in praedam partemque tecum veniamus:	465	Epistolae		21

QUE (cont'd)	PAGE	TITLE	LINE
curesque vt tuus in nos amor, antehac satis perspectus,	466	Epistolae	3
omnia fauorum tuorum momenta apicesque perpensuris et compensaturis.	466	Epistolae	8
noluitque vt minori sphaera quam pro latitudine meritorum tuorum	466	Epistolae	13
rogamusque vt quando beneficia tua peruagantur Angliam,	466	Epistolae	16
superiori aestate sponte suauiterque patefacta, nunc etiam	467	Epistolae	2
idque pro libris, de quibus nusquam rectius quam apud Te agitur.	467	Epistolae	18
sed tamen comparatio & in honorem tuum cedet, nostrumque emolumentum.	467	Epistolae	26
quare causam nostram nosque ipsos Tibi, Teque Deo Opti: Max: intimis	468	Epistolae	9
nosque ipsos Tibi, Teque Deo Opti: Max: intimis precibus commendamus.	468	Epistolae	9
appulit ad nos omnes haud ita certe studijs chartisque obuclutos,	468	Epistolae	13
nostrae etiam Athenae artesque obscuris opificum artibus superari	469	Epistolae	3
intra ambitum amplexusque foelicitatis Tuae receptae, communi calore	469	Epistolae	18
more maiorum, multos iam annos Anglice viuens garriensque.	470	Epistolae	5
tantisper supplere donec Academia orationem tuam imbibat probetque,	470	Epistolae	7
ni graue est, librum tibi Oratorium lampademque tradat.	470	Epistolae	10
caute incipe, cohibens adeo stylum ingeniumque;	470	Epistolae	11
tu hanc personam indue scripturus, tuumque iudicium tibi Lictor esto.	470	Epistolae	27
Tu vero vale, mi procrator, amaque Tuum G. H.	471	Epistolae	12
ideoque praeferuida illa desideria silentio suo sepulta nunc	471	Epistolae	27
Tuis, meis desiderijs probe cognitis, excussis perpensisque.	472	Epistolae	4
commendatione, si huc reciderit omnis studiorum spes fructusque:	472	Epistolae	16
receptusque sim in aliquem apud Honorem Tuum locum, magis id adeo	472	Epistolae	20
quam meis meritis vllis, semper lubentissimeque agnoscam:	472	Epistolae	22
rariusque paulo fodiam in Vintoniensi agro, dum Rhetorici satagam:	472	Epistolae	28
latiusque manare iniustitiae peccatum, quam negligentiae.	472	Epistolae	32
illud necessarium magis factu, hoc vero longe iucundius, nobiliusque:	472	Epistolae	35
dimidiaque operis parte leuatus, ad mea in Honorem Tuum officia	473	Epistolae	2
ad mea in Honorem Tuum officia erectior solutiorque redibo,	473	Epistolae	3
Vna cum promotioribus Academicis maternisque, assumsi mecum	473	Epistolae	8
assensumque Tuum veritati omni familiarem largiaris, sun tei eulogiai	473	Epistolae	10
vt mihi videtur, Romana elegantia, periodique vetus rotunditas.	473	Epistolae	18
ambitionisque strumae, non adeo sanatae ab optimo Rege nostro quin	473	Epistolae	21
QUEAT			
Cum nil fraterno rarius esse queat.	393	Musae 21	4
Scribere, Te dignum, vel lachrymare queat!	435	Poem.Lat.	6
QUEIS			
Versatos neget, atque humiles, queis talis cordi	420	Tr.Mortis	93
Queis me educasti; sponte chartas illinunt	424	Mem.Matr.2	63
Somnis (nescio queis) nocturna ad vota vocabo:	432	Poem.Lat.	3
QUEM			
Apposite quem commotum subfugerat olim,	390	Musae 12	15
Whitaker, erranti quem praefers carmine, miles	398	Musae 33	5
Militat & nobis, quem vos contemnitis, Ordo;	399	Musae 33	27
O vos inualidos! Audi quem talibus armis	399	Musae 33	29
(Et quem non stimularet haec simultas?)	400	Musae 37	18
Quem tu, summe Deus, semel	402	Musae 40	1
At non lusus erit, si quem tu laeta necasti	405	Passio 7	9
Quem non Emathius torrens, non sanguine pinguis	418	Tr.Mortis	2
Sanguine, quem dederat, spolians. Primordia Mortis	418	Tr.Mortis	22
Sanguine, quem dederat, spolians. Primordia belli	271	Tr.Mortis VS	22
Recte, quem trahit, aerem repellit	428	Mem.Matr.10	6
quem locum Noster suauissimus impleuit, ipse egit oratorem,	450	Orationes	30
satietas quaedam honoris, quem ad tempus deponere famem excitat:	453	Orationes	10
quanquam quem alium fructum potuimus expectare ab Eo, in quem fauor	456	Epistolae	17
fructum potuimus expectare ab Eo, in quem fauor Regius, nostra vota,	456	Epistolae	18
per quem vicini agri opulentia fruimur, veremur ne non tam sapientes	460	Epistolae	23
quem singularis doctrina exemit a populo, & quasi mixtam personam	461	Epistolae	26
QUEMADMODUM			
quemadmodum artifices non omnes licitantibus producunt merces,	445	Orationes	29
quemadmodum in Cometae praesagio, non respicitur, quae materia sit,	454	Orationes	11
QUENDAM			
In Catharum quendam.	397	Musae 29	T
QUERAR			
Nec querar ingratos, studijs dum tabidus insto,	426	Mem.Matr.7	17
QUERCUS			
Ingluuieque minor. Quercus habitare feruntur	418	Tr.Mortis	5
QUERELIS			
Vt Flos hinc lacrymis, illinc Philomela querelis,	438	Poem.Lat.	5
QUERITUR			
Non maeret calamus; non queritur caput:	403	Musae 40	6
QUERULA			
Adest tamen anus illa querula, & philegklemon, quam audire videor	453	Orationes	25
QUESTUS			
Humana aeternos agerent praecordia questus:	433	Poem.Lat.	39
QUI			
Scilicet hoc vobis proprium, qui purius itis,	387	Musae 5	7
Qui tam sublimi conspicit orbe viam:	387	Musae 7	6
Qui dulci miseros irradiabit ope.	387	Musae 7	10
Tu qui superbos caeteros existimas	388	Musae 8	15
Qui vestras edit intime medullas.	391	Musae 15	10
Sed qui tam male pileos habetis,	391	Musae 15	11
Qui templa sacris expoliant choris,	394	Musae 23	18
Eripe coelesti qui moderatur aquae.	396	Musae 26	4
qui renouare sacre	397	Musae 28	14
Qui tamen in nostros fortiter ire negant.	398	Musae 33	4
O qui Defensor Fidei meritissimus audis,	402	Musae 39	17
Sanctos qui gemitus mentibus inseris	403	Musae 40	12
Qui Caput es, spinas & tua Membra tuas.	405	Passio 6	4
Qualis eras, qui, ne melior natura minorem	407	Passio 14	1
Qui tamen excipiat, Christus caret hospite: tantum	407	Passio 15	3

QUI (cont'd)	PAGE	TITLE	LINE
Tu, qui cuncta creans docuisti marmora flere,	410	Lucus 1	5
Qui silicem tundit, (mirum tamen) elicit ignem:	410	Lucus 3	1
Cum qui plus terrae, plus habuere maris.	411	Lucus 6	4
O falsos homines! Vigilat, qui somniat aurum,	411	Lucus 7	3
Illos, qui mundum circumiere, pedes.	412	Lucus 8	4
Cur Deus elegit Medicum, qui numine plenus	412	Lucus 9	1
Illum volo, qui calceat lixam tuum.	413	Lucus 17	7
Transiliuntque caput, qui subiere pedes.	414	Lucus 19	2
Qui sugit auido spiritu rumusculos	414	Lucus 20	1
Nec tu pro socio doleas, qui fugit ad illud	415	Lucus 23	15
Qui spissae fidei breuique menti	417	Lucus 30	4
Congrediens genuit Monachum, qui limen opacae	420	Tr.Mortis	89
Quid ipse faciam? qui nec arboreas sudes	421	Lucus 33	3
Ah, cernam; Tu, qui caecos sanare solebas,	421	Lucus 35	7
At tu qui inepte haec dicta censes filio,	423	Mem.Matr.2	52
Qui parturit laudes parentis:	426	Mem.Matr.6	19
Quis, nisi qui manibus Briareus, oculisque sit Argus,	435	Poem.Lat.	5
O quam felices sunt, qui tua castra sequuntur,	435	Poem.Lat.	7
Suauis erat, qui scripta dolens lacerando recludi,	439	Poem.Lat.	13
qui vtrasque Indias Hispania sua quasi nodo connectens,	440	Orationes	16
fieri participes eius sanguinis, qui tantos spiritus solet infundere.	440	Orationes	20
qui mundi oculos perstringat, nos tam defecimus in vtroque quam	441	Orationes	12
qua optime ostendis te eius vicarium qui omnia disponit suauiter?	443	Orationes	17
qui optimum Principem spe nuptiarum mari nuper tradentes,	444	Orationes	17
vestra disquisitio, qui tineae estis & helluones chartacei;	445	Orationes	18
aut eorum certe, qui cymbala sunt fanaticae iuuentutis:	445	Orationes	24
qui nullum non angulum verrunt (ac si perdiderint ingenium)	445	Orationes	36
eos scilicet, qui innuptam Palladem colunt, Musasque coelibes,	446	Orationes	25
Musasque coelibes, qui posteros libris non liberis quaeritis.	446	Orationes	26
Maiores nostri, qui olim glasto se inficientes, in vxorum corporibus,	446	Orationes	29
qui symbola sunt spei, quoriam a floribus fructus sperantur.	446	Orationes	33
qui Philosophiae incumbis, cum corporis cum anima vinculum	448	Orationes	26
qui astra scrutaris, dum globos tractas & coelos fictitios,	448	Orationes	29
vbi in dubio est, qui facit, an qui patitur, miserior.	449	Orationes	11
(e quorum ossibus collisis ignis elicitur) qui nunc mansueti sunt,	449	Orationes	18
Sunt tamen acuti quidam & emuncti, qui omnia praeuident:	449	Orationes	29
vt qui hic in Musarum monte editissimo, in ipso Parnasso siti sumus,	449	Orationes	32
qui tum rumores? quae auditiones?	450	Orationes	36
qui susurri? Heus, abijtne Noster?	450	Orationes	36
ipsum coelum nubilum semper, & poeta stultus qui dixerat,	451	Orationes	19
qui solebant signa in hostes inijcere, vt milites acrius ea	451	Orationes	32
qui cupiditatibus immersi, aut vno semper saginantur in loco,	452	Orationes	9
qui antequam condiebant corpora Nobilium, solebant ventres eximere,	452	Orationes	26
neminemque esse sui negligentiorem, quam qui sibi parcat.	452	Orationes	35
qui semper titillant aures Principum, Osper tois pterois knomenci ta	453	Orationes	2
idem feruor qui impar sub amoris signo meritus est, ad vera castra	453	Orationes	29
idem impetus, qui peragrauit Hispaniam, si opus sit, superabit;	453	Orationes	31
qui inde e baiulo euasit Philosophus, eodem ingenio vsus in lignis	453	Orationes	36
qui nuper versatus est in forma & figuris vultus, vbi res postulat,	454	Orationes	6
qui furtim ascendit ad nubes, vbi iam ingrauescit humore,	454	Orationes	28
sic & Noster qui clanculum exijt, vsque ad Pyrenaeas nubes	454	Orationes	30
iterum exire patria, qui nunc inuenit viam, proximo itinere faciat.	455	Orationes	7
cumulum amoris Tui, qui vtrumque curasti, vt neque sitirent Musae,	457	Epistolae	20
adeo vt qui non subijciuntur ditioni, eruditioni vestrae obtemperent:	458	Epistolae	13
quippe qui vniuersum tempus nostrum (forsitan quo alacrius illud	460	Epistolae	5
sunt nuperi quidam homines, qui libenter sapientiores nos redderent:	460	Epistolae	22
qui tantae poeticae, tantae eruditionis nobis conscius est,	461	Epistolae	6
vt nullus fere elabatur dies, qui non hostes aliquos nobis aperiat:	461	Epistolae	14
illi e faece vulgi tantum qui eruditionem simplicitati Christianae	461	Epistolae	17
qui literas imminuere spiritus, generososque animos frangere	461	Epistolae	19
qui elegantias doctrinae nitoremque spirans purpuram et eruditionem	461	Epistolae	21
qui restinxisti sitim exarescentium Musarum, et Xerxes istos,	462	Epistolae	7
qui lemas istas et festucas, Reipublicae oculo haerentes,	462	Epistolae	12
quippe qui eximie semper fouisti literatos, eosque cum tineis	462	Epistolae	25
si qui alij exurgant promissores magnifici et hiantes, qui,	462	Epistolae	30
promissores magnifici et hiantes, qui, sub specie publici commodi,	462	Epistolae	31
qui nouas scientiarum regiones terrasque veteribus incognitas primus	463	Epistolae	10
Regi nostro, qui prospicit, vt cum ipse eruditionis Princeps sit,	463	Epistolae	21
illi etiam honores qui finitimi sunt, et quasi accolae Maiestatis,	463	Epistolae	22
dein Hon. Tuo gratulamur, qui filio auctus es tali ingenio praedito:	463	Epistolae	24
Quis enim rectius Thesauris Regijs praefici possit quam qui,	464	Epistolae	14
nouc hoc cumulo honorum, qui tamen votis nostris nondum respondent.	464	Epistolae	21
qui virtutes tuas magnis negotijs pares prouexit, noluitque vt minori	466	Epistolae	13
neque Studiosorum Sacculi, qui etiam nunc maeret et ingemiscit.	467	Epistolae	23
vt qui tot subsidia attuleris ad progressum doctrinae, hac etiam	467	Epistolae	27
Qui augent precia Librorum, prosunt vendentibus Libros non ementibus,	468	Epistolae	6
quae est vestra felicitas qui puro Academiae farre vtimini.	470	Epistolae	3
certe non tam ornas illam, qui infers manum grauitati.	470	Epistolae	20
etsi tu qui scribis (vti quiuis priuatus) inferioris sis subsellij,	470	Epistolae	22
qui etiam ferians nihil Tua perfectione dignum procudere possit.	471	Epistolae	23
qui primo caloris suasu excitati atque expergefacti, vbi sursum	471	Epistolae	29
qui celeritatem affectuum raptim sequentes, ad omnem eorum auram	472	Epistolae	1
quippe, qui sic colligebam; si tam abiectus sim, vt laboribus meis	472	Epistolae	11
QUIA			
Si, quia felices olim dixere poetae	387	Musae 6	3
Non quia Pontificum sunt olim afflata veneno,	390	Musae 13	1
An quia Textores Artificesque probas?	392	Musae 18	2
Vel quia tot moritur, tot viguisse probes.	415	Lucus 23	8
aut si suos, quia dederunt, non a se compositos, scriptos,	458	Epistolae	24

	PAGE	TITLE		LINE
QUIBUS				
Annon sic mercamur agros? quibus ecce Redemptor	388	Musae 9		3
Innocuae mentes, quibus inter flumina mundi	400	Musae 36		1
Sarcasmos quibus artifex triumphas;	400	Musae 37		4
Sic positis nugis, quibus irretita libido	402	Musae 39		38
Quid memorem tormenta, quibus prius horruit aeuum;	419	Tr.Mortis		39
Fustibalos fundasque, quibus, cum Numine, fretus	419	Tr.Mortis		43
fustibulos fundusque quibus cum numine fretus	271	Tr.Mortis	VS	43
Ridenti lacrymas quibus vnis concolor vnda est.	426	Mem.Matr.7		6
quibus hostes soletis in potestatem redigere, lenioresque aspectus,	440	Orationes		9
& supercilium quibus caperatam seuerioremque Philosophiam expugnare	440	Orationes		11
homines, quibus homo bruta, iustitia scilicet & prudentia. . .	447	Orationes		5
Iuris-consultos, partus sequitur ventrem: quibus accedunt Poetae,	447	Orationes		13
essent atque consilijs, sine quibus ne vnum quidem filum torquerent:	449	Orationes		30
quibus nihil imperito vanius inutiliusue videatur, vbi tamen ad vsum	454	Orationes		4
gauderent Fluuijs, nunc etiam aquas, in quibus habitant, impertis!	460	Epistolae		9
conseruantes sibi Illos Fontes, a quibus ipsi olim hauserunt?	461	Epistolae		31
nunquam in tantis negotijs, quibus meritissime districtus es, ea,	463	Epistolae		18
idque pro Libris, de quibus nusquam rectius quam apud Te agitur.	467	Epistolae		19
QUIBUSDAM				
legibus et hominum summe contraria est) monopolijs quibusdam inhiare,	467	Epistolae		6
QUICQUAM				
Non iam exaudiri quicquam vel Musica caeli	420	Tr.Mortis		74
Non iam exaudiri quicquam, vel musica sphaerae	271	Tr.Mortis	VS	74
neque enim quicquam hoc itinere mirabilius, cuius tamen fructum omnem	450	Orationes		2
praemium consequare, cui neque addi quicquam potest, neque detrahi.	457	Epistolae		5
QUICQUID				
Quicquid ex vrna meliore ductum	390	Musae 14		5
Per quicquid tibi suauiter probatur;	400	Musae 37		9
Gaudia sola fores: sic quicquid somnia mentis	402	Musae 39		36
Balistasque Onagrosque & quicquid Scorpio saeuus	419	Tr.Mortis		40
Et quicquid vspiam est seuerae foeminae, ...	422	Mem.Matr.2		2
Quicquid habet tellus, quicquid & astra, fruens.	429	Mem.Matr.13		6
Philosophiam expugnare nouimus, quicquid hilare est, laetum,	440	Orationes		12
orantes vt quicquid consilij auaritia ceperit aduersus aut . .	467	Epistolae		10
QUID				
Quid vetat vt pueri vagitus suppleat alter, ...	388	Musae 9		13
Quid sacrae tandem meruere vestes, ...	390	Musae 14		1
Quid? hoccine est mirum? Viatores sumus.	393	Musae 22		2
Quid hocce? Psalmos audion'? o dapes!	394	Musae 23		33
Haeresis, euertas. Quid enim te fallere possit?	402	Musae 39		22
Vt postulat mos; quid tuis dabis? Teipsum.	406	Passio 10		3
Quid hoc? & ipse deficis, Caeli gigas, ...	407	Passio 16		1
Vt discat sibi quisque, quid vtile: nempe nocebat	412	Lucus 9		3
Quid metuant homines infra, supraue minentur	413	Lucus 16		1
Et quid tu tandem desidiosus? AMO.	413	Lucus 16		6
Quid ipsi sumus, assequi putando.	415	Lucus 24		10
Inuertis nomen. Quid tibi dicit? AMOR.	416	Lucus 26		6
Quid memorem tormenta, quibus prius horruit aeuum;	419	Tr.Mortis		39
Quid ipse faciam? qui nec arboreas sudes	421	Lucus 33		3
Alapas nec Arietes? Quid ergo? Agnum & Crucem.	421	Lucus 33		6
Quid nugor calamo fauens?	424	Mem.Matr.4		1
Nosse sui quid agant, quaedam est quoque musica sanctis, . .	427	Mem.Matr.9		3
Quae suberant causae? quid nos committere tantum, ...	432	Poem.Lat.		18
Quid sperare, imo quid non sperare licebat?)	432	Poem.Lat.		28
Quid non mutatum est? requierunt flumina cursus;	433	Poem.Lat.		43
Quid mihi si facies nigra est? hoc, Ceste, colore	437	Poem.Lat.		1
Quid voluit prudens Fatum, iam sentio tandem:	438	Poem.Lat.		3
Quid enim iucundius accidere potest, quam vt ministri Regis Catholici	440	Orationes		13
Quid memorem prudentiam vestram incomparabilem, qua optime ostendis	443	Orationes		15
Quid eruditionem, quae tanta est vt, nisi Rex esses in ciuili	443	Orationes		17
Quid fauores erga hanc Academiam inenarrabiles, cum non solum tuearis	443	Orationes		20
Quid innumera alia, quae, si per tempus liceret effari, . .	443	Orationes		28
Quid iactas mihi aromata Orientis?	444	Orationes		23
Quid Theriacas peregrinas? asserunt Medici vnamquamque regionem sua	444	Orationes		24
Non vnum quid spectant aut singulare Magni animi, sed varia solent	446	Orationes		4
Quid autem? Ergon' amauit Princeps?	446	Orationes		9
Quid si cochleas colligeret cum Caligula, praesertim cum possit	446	Orationes		12
Quid si muscas captaret cum Domitiano?	446	Orationes		14
cernitis Regem & nomine & re magnum quid polliceri, ideoque ex	447	Orationes		8
quid proderunt scalpella vestra, quando ipsae hae turres & beatae	448	Orationes		20
Dein quid Musis cum tumultu?	448	Orationes		22
Quid enim si praeter Nuptias, prolem, tranquillitatem, etiam	450	Orationes		4
quid enim vtilius quam ex obseruatione exterarum Legum ac morum,	450	Orationes		14
Quid autem illic? sterilem aiunt regionem:	451	Orationes		2
Quid si hic lateat etiam Temperantia, rara in Principibus virtus,	452	Orationes		1
Quid enim? adeon' nihili videtur res, Principem omnibus delicijs	452	Orationes		3
Quid ego vobis Neronum aut Heliogabalorum ingluuiem memorem?	452	Orationes		18
quid ructus crapulae solium possidentis?	452	Orationes		19
vt quid priuata habeat in se vita commodi aut voluptatis, . .	452	Orationes		37
Quid noui? Quid noui, stupide?	454	Orationes		26
Quid noui, stupide? Redijt Princeps, CAROLVS redijt, honore grauidus,	454	Orationes		26
quid Tu inde? Britannicas insulas omnes occupasti.	458	Epistolae		9
Quid agimus? hoc saltem solutio est;	459	Epistolae		3
Quid Vaticanam Bodleiumque obijcis, Hospes?	459	Epistolae		30
Quid enim inuiderent aquas, quas non nobis habemus sed irrigati ipsi	462	Epistolae		9
neque amplius quaerendum sit Tibi, Almae Nutrici quid reponas.	462	Epistolae		16
Quid enim manerem? Habui viaticum fauoris Tui, quod longiori multo	471	Epistolae		18
QUIDAM				
Articulis sacris quidam subscribere iussus, ...	389	Musae 11		1
Sunt tamen acuti quidam & emuncti, qui omnia praeuident: . .	449	Orationes		28

QUIDAM (cont'd)	PAGE	TITLE	LINE
sane exorti sunt nuperi quidam homines, qui libenter sapientiores nos	460	Epistolae	21
quidam stomachantur praedia, alij immunitates carpunt, nonnulli	461	Epistolae	14
QUIDEM			
Forte quidem, cum per vestras Ecclesia turbas	389	Musae 12	3
Illa quidem a nostro non multum abludit imago,	396	Musae 26	5
tandem Magistri Artium, & quidem omnium Aulicarum, Militarium,	440	Orationes	5
Optamus quidem vt Maiestatis vestrae gaudia responderint aut nostris	443	Orationes	12
quod quidem vbi gentium si non ab Hispano sperandum?	447	Orationes	30
incerta sint, & nullis perspicillis, ne Belgicis quidem, assequenda:	449	Orationes	24
essent atque consilijs, sine quibus ne vnum quidem filum torquerent:	449	Orationes	30
gaudeo quidem de ingenti amore in Principem, cui nulla dilectio par	451	Orationes	21
Atque hoc quidem statu res erant, Suauissime CAROLE, cum tu aberas;	451	Orationes	27
Dies me deficeret (& quidem nox aptior esset tali historiae)	452	Orationes	20
quantum quidem ego homuncio ac nanus coniectando assequor.	453	Orationes	21
quam audire videor dicentem, Pulchrum quidem iter & Amante dignum;	453	Orationes	26
hunc quidem gradum pignus habes amoris nostri, haec est ansa qua	456	Epistolae	5
Quod quidem non minus expectamus a Te, quem singularis doctrina	461	Epistolae	25
Tu quidem semper Patronus noster es, etiam tacentibus nobis,	467	Epistolae	17
Curasti tu quidem Instauratione tua, quo minus exteris Libris	467	Epistolae	24
ne tum quidem multum, neque nostrae matronae conuenit, cui tu es ab	471	Epistolae	2
Hoc quidem illis accidere amat, qui celeritatem affectuum raptim	472	Epistolae	1
QUIES			
Sitque omnis motus nescia tanta quies,	424	Mem.Matr.3	8
QUIESCUNT			
Vt, fluuio currente, vadum sonat, alta quiescunt.	433	Poem.Lat.	48
QUIETE			
Quinimo Artes hic sunt quiete & silentio cultae, tranquillitas,	441	Orationes	14
QUIETIS			
Mentes, quietis tympana publicae,	395	Musae 23	50
Nempe hic Religio floret, regina quietis,	411	Lucus 6	7
QUIN			
Quin liceat nobis aliquas procudere voces:	386	Musae 3	5
Quin redde formas, o bone, pristinas,	393	Musae 23	5
Quin populo, clemens, aliquid largire caloris:	397	Musae 29	3
Quin nocuas extingue faces, precor: vnda propinqua est,	399	Musae 35	7
Quin per Presbyteros tuos; per vrbem	400	Musae 37	5
Quin hoc carmine Lexicon probrorum	401	Musae 37	28
Quin te laudibus orno: quippe dico,	401	Musae 37	41
Quin nos Ipse emit, pretioso faenora soluens	410	Lucus 4	3
Ecquid emes Caelum? quin stellam rectius vnam	410	Lucus 4	5
Quin, mitte nugas; teque carnem & sanguinem	413	Lucus 17	5
Quin tibi tam desperatae MORA nulla medetur,	416	Lucus 25	9
Quin tibi jam desperatae MORA nulla medetur,	416	Lucus 25 V	9
Quin Aries ruit, & multa Demetrius arte:	419	Tr.Mortis	47
Gladiosue, Catapultasue teneam, quin neque	421	Lucus 33	5
Quin pro me quoque sanguinem profudit,	421	Lucus 34	4
Quin, sine, te cernam; quoties iam dixero, cernam;	421	Lucus 35	3
Quin post modestam, qualis integras decet,	422	Mem.Matr.2	14
Quin caeli mihi sunt mei,	424	Mem.Matr.4	5
Quin cerne vt erres, inscie, brachium	426	Mem.Matr.6	13
Quin fugias? mea non fuerat tam nubila Iuno,	426	Mem.Matr.7	7
Quin te Cambria peruetusta deflet,	428	Mem.Matr.10	10
Quin nec potes; cui praebuit Tigris partum.	429	Mem.Matr.12	10
Quin Matris superans carmina poscit honos.	431	Mem.Matr.19	6
Quin moriar tecum: vitam, quam negligis ipse,	434	Poem.Lat.	5
Quin & Serenissimae Principis Isabellae laudes, virtutesque,	441	Orationes	2
Quin exuit personam Principis, deponit Maiestatem, virgam cum sceptro	452	Orationes	35
quin & venti imperant pelago, vt laeuitatem illam aequabilem atque	453	Orationes	13
non dubitamus quin benignitas tua omnia elementa percurreret.	457	Epistolae	23
quin communes Reipublicae lachrymae alterum nobis Fluuium	462	Epistolae	5
enim sic effugies cum honoribus, quin laetitia nostra te assequatur.	465	Epistolae	22
certe studijs chartisque obuolutos, quin aures nostrae tibi pateant.	468	Epistolae	13
Quin nec demisso, quando ad magnates cogitas, stylo vtare,	470	Epistolae	21
non quin pectus meum plenum Tui sit, atque effusissimum in omnia	471	Epistolae	21
non adeo sanatae ab optimo Rege nostro quin turgescat indies,	473	Epistolae	22
QUINIMO			
Quinimo Artes hic sunt quiete & silentio cultae, tranquillitas,	441	Orationes	14
QUINIS			
Est mihi bis quinis laqueata domuncula tignis	426	Mem.Matr.7	22
QUINQUE			
Ambitio Cathari quinque constat Actibus.	398	Musae 32	1
virum protulit, cum quinque millibus annorum de palma certantem.	463	Epistolae	27
QUIPPE			
Quin te laudibus orno: quippe dico,	401	Musae 37	41
quippe qui vniuersum tempus nostrum (forsitan quo alacrius illud	460	Epistolae	5
quippe qui eximie semper fouisti literatos, eosque cum tineis	462	Epistolae	25
quippe, qui sic colligebam; si tam abiectus sim, vt laboribus meis	472	Epistolae	11
neque vlla negotia (quippe quae caput petant, non cor) Tui in me	473	Epistolae	6
QUIPPIAM			
Quod si forerse quippiam nos spectans, dum incumbis muneri,	466	Epistolae	4
QUIPPINI			
Quippini; homo est, non statua;	446	Orationes	10
QUIRITATIONIBUS			
huiusmodi lamentis & quiritationibus plena erant fora, nundinae,	451	Orationes	9
QUIS			
Quis hic superbit, oro? tune, an Praesules,	388	Musae 8	1
Astra rogant, Nouus hic quis hospes?	394	Musae 23	28
quis crederet mortalibus	396	Musae 28	3
Quis sic amicum excipiet, vt Cathari Deum,	397	Musae 28	13
Calumniarum nec pudor quis nec modus?	397	Musae 30	1

QUO (cont'd)	PAGE	TITLE	LINE
ex quo timemus Librorum precia auctum iri, et priuilegia nostra	467	Epistolae	6
quo minus exteris Libris indigeremus, sed tamen comparatic . .	467	Epistolae	25
verisimile est, eos illuc, quo cognitio ipsa pertingit, ascensuros.	468	Epistolae	1
promulgentur, quo suauius virtutibus, tuo exemplo compensatis,	468	Epistolae	16
hoc Principe, in quo doctrinae fructus atque vsus mirifice relucet.	469	Epistolae	23
per me non stabit quo minus, spe prouecta atque adulta, . . .	470	Epistolae	7
o quot iam anni sunt ex quo vel apicem Latinum pertuli! . . .	471	Epistolae	6
QUOCUNQUE			
Tantum quocunque, Domine, ascendas, sume tecum amorem illum quo soles	464	Epistolae	26
QUOD			
O bene quod dubium possideamus agrum!	386	Musae 4	8
An quod semotum populo laquearibus altis	387	Musae 7	3
Quod puer ignorat, verba profana putas?	388	Musae 9	2
O vtinam aut illorum oculi (quod comprecor vnum)	400	Musae 36	5
Tu Synodosque, Patresque, & quod dedit alta vetustas	402	Musae 39	25
Quod scribo, & placeo, si placeo, tuum est.	403	Musae 40	14
Visum quod vni praebet, omnibus vitam, ...	404	Passio 5	2
Quod omnibus tute imperes, nemo tibi.	412	Lucus 11	3
Cum Romam nequeas, quod aues, euertere, nomen	416	Lucus 26	1
Quod Bellarminus nequijt, fortasse poetae	417	Lucus 28	3
Quod tu febrem censes, salubre est	426	Mem.Matr.6	23
Quod superest vitae, insumam: Solisque iugales	426	Mem.Matr.7	15
Quod nectar, nisi cum te celebrare diem?)	428	Mem.Matr.9	16
Quod non Lanigerae pecudes, non Agmina lustrent?	432	Poem.Lat.	19
Quod si fata illi longam invidere salutem	432	Poem.Lat.	26
Quod calamum excusent Pontus & Astra meum:	435	Poem.Lat.	8
Quod Crux nequibat fixa, Clavique additi, ...	438	Poem.Lat.	1
Et quod obseruatione cum primis dignum est, quo magis amore . .	440	Orationes	21
ne nihil hic sit, quod magnitudini praesentiae vestrae respondeat.	441	Orationes	9
incredibiles laudes vestras quod quae nos audiamus summo cum gaudio	443	Orationes	30
Quae enim vspiam gens, quod vnquam seculum meliorem habuit Principem?	445	Orationes	12
hoc ipsum iter, quod nuper emensus est, vt sciatis omnes quam nude,	445	Orationes	34
Ego vero non dicam vobis quod factum est ante seculum vestrum,	445	Orationes	38
quod primum intendunt, saltem in secundis aut tertijs consistant.	446	Orationes	6
quod pereleganter & supra barbariem seculi innuebant Maiores nostri,	446	Orationes	28
Quod si Nuptiae in se graues sunt, quanto magis Principum, . .	446	Orationes	34
a Con verbo deduci, quod tria complectitur, Possum, Scio, . .	447	Orationes	7
quod nonnullae familiae semper mites essent, vti Valerij, . .	447	Orationes	19
quod quidem vbi gentium si non ab Hispano sperandum? . . .	447	Orationes	30
Quod ad nostram Rempublicam, Academiam, pax adeo Musis summe	448	Orationes	16
Quod aliae gentes manibus in coelum sublatis, lachrymis in terram	448	Orationes	34
Illud autem, quod cuiuis clarissime patet, etiam lusco, . .	449	Orationes	34
adde quod angusti est animi aut superbi sua tantum nosse, . .	450	Orationes	17
alienas tantum ex hoc itinere cognouit Respublicas sed quod plus est,	450	Orationes	33
quod Romani Imperatores in bello, qui solebant signa in hostes	451	Orationes	31
per quod optimus Princeps non tantum exteras regiones habuit	451	Orationes	35
quod sane adeo nobile fuit & honorificum, vt nihil habeat Inuidia	453	Orationes	23
vt nihil habeat Inuidia ipsa, quod contra hiscat aut mussitet.	453	Orationes	24
in terram hanc, incidit in coenum, quod innuebat eum hic mansurum:	455	Orationes	4
Quod si necesse sit iterum exire patria, qui nunc inuenit viam,	455	Orationes	7
Quod si tam integrum tibi esset gratificari nobis in terra & aere,	457	Epistolae	21
Quod superest, precamur S. S. Trinitatem, vt vestrae coronae ciuili	459	Epistolae	20
Quod si Artaxerxes olim paululum aquae a Sinaeta, subiecto suo,	460	Epistolae	11
Quod quidem non minus expectamus a Te, quem singularis doctrina	461	Epistolae	25
quod expectamus indies futurum, Almae Matris amorem tecum simul	462	Epistolae	28
non gremio solum (quod innuis) sed et ambabus vlnis osculisque ei	463	Epistolae	7
quod si tertia detur et quarta, paratos nos habebis ad gratulationem,	465	Epistolae	25
Quod si forense quippiam nos spectans, dum incumbis muneri, . .	466	Epistolae	4
Quod si et numerus Scriptorum intumescat, et precium, quae abyssus	468	Epistolae	2
Quod si oppidani nostri (more suo) Musarum iura et diplomata	468	Epistolae	25
non est quod nostram quoque, cum amoris symbolo festinantem,	469	Epistolae	15
quod rem spectat, si placeat vices meas tantisper supplere donec	470	Epistolae	5
non quod nunc indulgeas alterutri, sed quod deinceps indultum nollem.	470	Epistolae	11
non quod nunc indulgeas alterutri, sed quod deinceps indultum nollem.	470	Epistolae	12
non tam quod tibi conueniat scribenti, quam quod Academiae tuo calamo	470	Epistolae	13
tibi conueniat scribenti, quam quod Academiae tuo calamo scribenti:	470	Epistolae	13
Habui viaticum fauoris Tui, quod longiori multo itineri sufficeret.	471	Epistolae	19
Neque quod ignotior eram, retundebatur vnquam impetus: . . .	472	Epistolae	10
Quod tamen haec omnia succedant ex voto, quod reclusae sint fores,	472	Epistolae	19
quod reclusae sint fores, receptusque sim in aliquem apud Honorem	472	Epistolae	19
vt quod Philosophus de Tactu & Visu, id apposite admodum huc	472	Epistolae	35
Ignosce (Heros illustrissime) quod pronomina mea adeo audacter	473	Epistolae	15
QUODQUE			
Quodque suum nouit stroma, cubile suum.	407	Passio 15	2
QUOLIBET			
ideoque ex quolibet ligno, qualibet vxore non esse fingendum:	447	Orationes	9
QUOMODO			
Quomodo possetis similes esse Alexandro Magno nisi eius res gestas	441	Orationes	18
Quare quomodo alij molem hanc laetitiae suae exprimant, . .	456	Epistolae	25
QUONDAM			
Qua Fabio quondam sub duce nata salus.	416	Lucus 29	10
Quae Fabio quondam sub duce tuta salus.	416	Lucus 29 V	10
Quondam fessus Amor loquens Amato, ...	439	Poem.Lat.	10
QUONIAM			
qui symbola sunt spei, quoniam a floribus fructus sperantur.	446	Orationes	33
QUOQUE			
Ille quoque inuadit Diuinam Flaminis artem, ...	392	Musae 19	3
Nos quoque possemus longas conscribere turmas, ...	398	Musae 33	7
Cuin pro me quoque sanguinem profudit, ...	421	Lucus 34	4
Nosse sui quid agant, quaedam est quoque musica sanctis, . . .	427	Mem.Matr.9	3

	PAGE	TITLE	LINE
QUOQUE (cont'd)			
non est quod nostram quoque, cum amoris symbolo festinantem,	469	Epistolae	15
QUORUM			
redundet, quorum in eligendis illis iudicium iampridem apparet.	441	Orationes	6
quorum aduentum ipsi lapides, ipsa durissima ingenia, meum	445	Orationes	8
omnium coelestiores animi, quorum pietatis interest non silere.	445	Orationes	11
vos, vos, inquam, excutite, quorum aetas teritur in libris:	445	Orationes	15
limatae auris atque tersae, quorum grauitate ac purpura non abutar.	445	Orationes	27
Leones Britannici (e quorum ossibus collisis ignis elicitur) qui nunc	449	Orationes	18
salus regnorum pendet a vicinis, quorum consilia, apparatus,	450	Orationes	26
magnum aperirem, quorum imperium gulae impar erat, vt interdum putem,	452	Orationes	23
QUOS			
Quos dente nigro corripis?	388	Musae 8	2
Quos Ecclesia comprobat, verendum	391	Musae 15	12
Quos charos habuit Christus Apostolos,	391	Musae 17	1
Et, quos ipsa nequit scandere vertices,	391	Musae 17	9
Quos tu rotatus, quale murmur auscultas	392	Musae 20	1
Quos David, ipsae deliciae Dei,	394	Musae 23	37
Scilicet, vt quos ante suas cum coniuge tedas	396	Musae 26	9
Quos inter plenusque Deo genioque Iacobus	399	Musae 33	23
Tu venas laticesque omnes, quos sacra recludit	402	Musae 39	23
Quos tu calcasti fluctus, me, Christe, lacessunt,	414	Lucus 19	1
Arguit, exceptos quos pia Roma fouet:	416	Lucus 26	4
Foelices, quos bella premunt, & plurimus ensis!	432	Poem.Lat.	23
quos magnificentia promissi circumscribere in promptu erat,	445	Orationes	16
tam grauem) & apud quos dico, viros limatae auris atque tersae,	445	Orationes	26
Non ignoro apud quos haec dico, eos scilicet, qui innuptam Palladem	446	Orationes	25
quos in arca repositos abijciebant in fluuium, his verbis:	452	Orationes	28
Faxit Deus vt quos profectus feceris in Sphaera Naturae,	464	Epistolae	3
QUOSCUNQUE			
perrumpemus controuersias omnes, superabimus quoscunque.	459	Epistolae	7
QUOT			
Spargitque per tot capita, quot vulgus gerit.	414	Lucus 20	4
Prudenter inito quot-diebus calculo.	423	Mem.Matr.2	23
Non tot abest, quot nos Regis ab ingenio.	437	Poem.Lat.	4
o quot iam anni sunt ex quo vel apicem Latinum pertuli!	471	Epistolae	6
QUOT-DIEBUS			
Prudenter inito quot-diebus calculo.	423	Mem.Matr.2	23
QUOTIDIANA			
Quotidiana suas poscant si fercula grates,	389	Musae 12	9
QUOTIDIANAE			
neque quotidianae virtutis prouincia gerere personam Academiae,	465	Epistolae	9
QUOTIDIANIS			
qua perfundis nos omnes quotidianis beneficijs, redundarit	443	Orationes	10
QUOTIDIANO			
Quotidiano! Nescis, ignare? Audies!	436	Poem.Lat.	2
QUOTIDIE			
Quotidie iugulat, nec semel vllus obit.	415	Lucus 23	4
Quotidie pasti: tantum verum indue vultum	427	Mem.Matr.7	29
vicinum fretum quotidie transnatantes, litora nostra atque aures mire	441	Orationes	4
sed a scriptis vestris, quae ingenti cum lucro quotidie legimus.	443	Orationes	20
QUOTIES			
Quin, sine, te cernam; quoties iam dixero, cernam;	421	Lucus 35	3
QUUM			
Phoebe, tui puduit quum summo mane redires	433	Poem.Lat.	36
quum tamen Tu inuaseris eorum gloriam conseruando nobis quae illi	458	Epistolae	25
praesertim quum ipsi non solum rectum de Bene-merentibus iudicium	469	Epistolae	12
R			
2. Ad R. Naunton Gratiae de Fluuio et de tegendis Tectis stramineis	457	Epistolae	T
6. Ad R. Naunton, Secret. Gratiae de Fluuio	461	Epistolae	T
10. Ad R. Naunt. Burgen. Elect.	465	Epistolae	T
17. Ad R. Creighton	470	Epistolae	T
RABIDIS			
Vt, cum mors rabidis vnguibus imminens	391	Musae 17	3
RABIES			
Nec tamen hic mortis rabies stetit; exilit omni	272	Tr.Mortis VS	95
RADIANTE			
Angeli vultu radiante candent;	390	Musae 14	10
RADICES			
Cuncta ad radices redeant, tumulosque paternos;	425	Mem.Matr.5	13
manu prehendis Regem, alteram nobis ad radices haerentibus porrigis.	456	Epistolae	15
quanto altius crescunt, tanto etiam altius agunt radices:	464	Epistolae	18
RADICIBUS			
Dum librata suis haeret radicibus ilex	428	Mem.Matr.11	1
RADIJ			
Nascentes radij fugant, vel acres	385	Musae	8
RADIJS			
Explicat, & radijs ipsum pertingit Olympum!	401	Musae 39	7
Tunc instruetur lautius radijs penu,	407	Passio 16	13
Apollo olim depositis radijs Daphnen deperijt, at illa mutata est	455	Orationes	8
RADIO			
Ad nos cum radio tam rutilante potes?	424	Mem.Matr.3	2
RADIOS			
Fac radios saltem ingemines, vt dextera tortos	424	Mem.Matr.3	9
RADIX			
Tu radix, tu petra mihi firmissima, Mater,	428	Mem.Matr.11	9
RAMALIA			
Glans dedit, & truncus tectum, & ramalia mortem.	418	Tr.Mortis	8
RAMENTA			
Ramenta coeli, guttulaeque	394	Musae 23	35
ramenta quaepiam ex tanta Humanitatis massa, quae apud Te visitur,	472	Epistolae	13

RAMI	PAGE	TITLE	LINE
Perpetuos mihi ferre rami, ...	434	Poem.Lat.	32
RAMO			
Roma. Anagr. Oram. Maro. / Ramo. Armo. / Mora. Amor. . . .	416	Lucus 25	T
At nunc exucco similis tua gloria RAMO	416	Lucus 25	5
RAPIS			
Dum prono rapis ore cibos, & fercula verris, ...	414	Lucus 21	1
RAPIT			
Nobilitate illos, hos pietate rapit.	429	Mem.Matr.13	4
RAPTIM			
qui celeritatem affectuum raptim sequentes, ad omnem eorum auram	472	Epistolae	1
RAPTUS			
Supplicum Ministrorum raptus komoidoumenos.	398	Musae 32	T
RARA			
rara in Principibus virtus, & cui cum sceptro lites saepius . .	452	Orationes	2
RARIOR			
Animo renidentes prius. Sin rarior	423	Mem.Matr.2	25
RARIUS			
Cum nil fraterno rarius esse queat.	393	Musae 21	4
rariusque paulo fodiam in Vintoniensi agro, dum Rhetorici satagam:	472	Epistolae	28
RARO			
Non animas, raroque ornantur sanguine regum	420	Tr.Mortis	98
RATIBUS			
Cum primum ratibus suis	395	Musae 25	1
RATIO			
Ad Regem Instituti Epigrammatici ratio.	385	Musae 1	T
Quae ratio per se, si sit adulta, facit.	388	Musae 9	12
cum humanitatis Tuae, tum gratitudinis nostrae ratio postulat.	457	Epistolae	10
RATIONE			
Ratione certa vita constat & domus, ...	423	Mem.Matr.2	22
neque ratione habita Chartae nostrae a Serenissimo Principe Henrico 8	467	Epistolae	21
RATIONEM			
administrans, distribuendi modum omnem rationemque callet? . .	464	Epistolae	16
RATIONI			
quamuis rationi consonum videtur, vt qui hic in Musarum monte	449	Orationes	32
RATIONIS			
Rationis & sensus stupendus Arbiter;	436	Poem.Lat.	16
Rationis & sensus peritus Arbiter;	436	Poem.Lat. V	16
RE			
Tres video partes, quo re distinctius vtar, ...	386	Musae 4	1
a re instructus nos doceat, tuosque fauores populo tuo communicans	444	Orationes	6
hac re solum vlciscimur mortem, ligantes abruptum vitae filum,	446	Orationes	22
cernitis Regem & nomine & re magnum quid polliceri, ideoque ex	447	Orationes	8
qua in re celebris est Gracchorum mater, ingenium ipsum atque indoles	447	Orationes	16
re vna omnium grauissima, alienis oculis iudicioque inniti; . .	447	Orationes	22
vti sanguis solet in re dubia ad cor festinare, ita ad Te confugimus	467	Epistolae	9
REAE			
Grandi reaeque praefero, ...	427	Mem.Matr.8	2
REBUS			
& in rebus humanis diuinisque exercitatissimi, de integro . . .	444	Orationes	20
sic & ipse excerpam e Principis rebus gestis pugillum, vnam actionem	445	Orationes	31
id omne dexterrima tua in obeundis rebus prudentia dissipetur.	467	Epistolae	13
RECEDAM			
Ni sancte, vti mater, recedam, ...	425	Mem.Matr.6	11
RECEDENTIS			
Ecce recedentis foecundo in littore Nili	384	Musae	1
RECEDIT			
Et cum sublata laude recedit AMOR.	416	Lucus 25	12
RECENSET			
Et pro pectoribus recenset aras, ...	408	Passio 19	6
RECENTEM			
Quam chartam tibi porrigo recentem, ...	384	Musae	1
Animam recentem rite curauit sacris	422	Mem.Matr.2	16
RECEPTAE			
intra ambitum amplexusque foelicitatis Tuae receptae, communi calore	469	Epistolae	19
RECEPTUS			
receptusque sim in aliquem apud Honorem Tuum locum, magis id adeo	472	Epistolae	20
RECESSIBUS			
In picturis locus est vmbris & recessibus, etiam si quis Principem	453	Orationes	15
RECESSUM			
Prorsus nescia, cogitat recessum?	411	Lucus 5	7
RECESSUS			
Quaerit recessus. Incalescit fabula:	398	Musae 32	6
Quale paludosos iamiam lictura recessus	426	Mem.Matr.7	11
RECIDENDAS			
Esse recidendas, Aeace noster, opes.	399	Musae 34	2
RECIDERIT			
commendatione, si huc reciderit omnis studiorum spes fructusque:	472	Epistolae	15
RECIDITUR			
Tristis, vbi ac ferrum tellure reciditur ima, ...	419	Tr.Mortis	36
RECISIS			
Vt si recisis arboribus meis	434	Poem.Lat.	29
RECLINET			
In cruce suspendens, vnde reclinet, habet.	407	Passio 15	4
vt Alma Mater libentissime caput reclinet in tuo sinu, oculusque	465	Epistolae	13
RECLUDI			
Suauis erat, qui scripta dolens lacerando recludi, ...	439	Poem.Lat.	13
RECLUDIT			
Tu venas laticesque omnes, quos sacra recludit	402	Musae 39	23
RECLUSAE			
quod reclusae sint fores, receptusque sim in aliquem apud Honorem	472	Epistolae	19

	PAGE	TITLE	LINE
RECOLENTI			
tibique non tam auide veterum beneficiorum memoriam recolenti,	457	Epistolae	13
RECONDIT			
Prae quo Tibris vultum recondit,	394	Musae 23	43
RECTE			
Vitro minus recte vteris.	388	Musae 8	18
Recte, quem trahit, aerem repellit	428	Mem.Matr.10	6
Vnde vagans passim recte vocer alter Vlysses,	428	Mem.Matr.11	13
Recte facitis, Academici, attollentes oculos cum stupore;	450	Orationes	1
futurus aut qualis, recte diuinaret, non respiciat materiam actionum,	454	Orationes	9
RECTIUS			
Commotos animos rectius ista decent.	387	Musae 5	6
An rectius nos, si vices vertas, probi,	388	Musae 8	9
Rectius innocuis lactentibus omnia praestes,	388	Musae 9	11
Ecquid emes Caelum? quin stellam rectius vnam	410	Lucus 4	5
Quis enim rectius Thesauris Regijs praefici possit quam qui,	464	Epistolae	13
idque pro libris, de quibus nusquam rectius quam apud Te agitur.	467	Epistolae	19
RECTUM			
praesertim quum ipsi non solum rectum de Bene-merentibus iudicium	469	Epistolae	12
RECUMBIS			
Quo nunc recumbis, scriptio merita est tua,	423	Mem.Matr.2	40
RECUSANS			
Omnis linea sepiam recusans	400	Musae 37	21
RECUSENT			
Fructusque post mortem recusent	434	Poem.Lat.	31
RECUSES			
non est quod nostram quoque, cum amoris symbolo festinantem, recuses.	469	Epistolae	16
REDDAM			
Tum tibi, si placeat, fugientia tempora reddam;	386	Musae 2	9
REDDE			
Quin redde formas, o bone, pristinas,	393	Musae 23	5
REDDERENT			
sunt nuperi quidam homines, qui libenter sapientiores nos redderent:	460	Epistolae	22
REDDIDISSENT			
ne non tam sapientes nos, quam obscuros philosophos reddidissent.	461	Epistolae	1
REDDIDIT			
& quasi mixtam personam reddidit quam si Episcopi more pristino	461	Epistolae	27
REDDUNT			
Sic mucronatam reddunt suspiria mentem,	410	Lucus 2	3
REDEANT			
Cuncta ad radices redeant, tumulosque paternos;	425	Mem.Matr.5	13
REDEMPTOR			
Annon sic mercamur agros? quibus ecce Redemptor	388	Musae 9	3
Et hoc indicium subis, Redemptor?	417	Lucus 30	2
REDEMPTORES			
4. Ad Iacobum Regem Gratiae de Fluuio contra Redemptores	460	Epistolae	T
incoeptum et plus effecit quam mille Redemptores exequi possent.	461	Epistolae	12
REDIBO			
ad mea in Honorem Tuum officia erectior solutiorque redibo,	473	Epistolae	3
REDIGERE			
quibus hostes soletis in potestatem redigere, lenioresque aspectus,	440	Orationes	9
REDIJ			
Ego auctior iam gaudio atque distentior, Cantabrigiam redij.	471	Epistolae	18
REDIJT			
Redijt! redijt CAROLVS, & cum eo vita nostra atque calor,	444	Orationes	22
redijt CAROLVS, & cum eo vita nostra atque calor, longo animi	444	Orationes	22
Redijt Princeps, CAROLVS redijt, honore grauidus, grauidus scientia,	454	Orationes	26
Redijt Princeps, CAROLVS redijt, honore grauidus, grauidus scientia,	454	Orationes	27
REDIRES			
Phoebe, tui puduit quum summo mane redires	433	Poem.Lat.	36
REDIT			
Nunc redit ad mitem, ceu benedicta, Deum.	390	Musae 12	16
Res redit ad vates, Pieriosque duces:	417	Lucus 28	2
REDITUM			
Serenissimi Principis Caroli Reditum ex Hispanijs celebrauit Georgius	444	Orationes	T
REDUCAS			
Et nos reducas ad lapides aucs:	393	Musae 23	6
REDUNDARIT			
perfundis nos omnes quotidianis beneficijs, redundarit in authorem;	443	Orationes	10
REDUNDET			
autem vt foelicitas tantorum Principum etiam in ministros redundet,	441	Orationes	6
REDUX			
Culpa redux iugem te neget esse Deum.	406	Passio 13	6
REDUXIT			
Sed propere dextreque reduxit euntia sensus,	385	Musae	5
Vitam reduxit: ecce gratitudinem.	413	Lucus 14	2
REEIN			
Kai prepon ode para dakrucessi reein.	431	Mem.Matr.18	6
REFECIT			
Postquam se gelidis nocte refecit aquis:	412	Lucus 8	2
REFERCIRE			
potui refercire lineas Honoribus, Magnif., Celsitud., sed	473	Epistolae	16
REFERENS			
Fatisco referens tanta quae numerant mei	423	Mem.Matr.2	50
REFERO			
Matrine linguam refero, solum vt mordeam?	424	Mem.Matr.2	59
REFERRE			
Quam curto nequeo referre versu;	400	Musae 37	6
REFERT			
neque enim minus refert, qualis quaeque sit mater, e qua liberi	447	Orationes	10

REFERTA	PAGE	TITLE	LINE
Et mea sint canis scripta referta tuis.	386	Musae 2	6
REFERTAM			
Quare post Principis manum honoribus refertam, non est quod nostram	469	Epistolae	14
REFERUNT			
Caelique referunt & praeoccupant modum.	423	Mem.Matr.2	49
REFRIGERETUR			
Vt feruor cerebri refrigeretur,	391	Musae 15	9
REGANT			
si vestros animos regant	395	Musae 25	18
REGE			
Tu etiam dignitates ab optimo Rege desumptas in vniuersam Rempublicam	456	Epistolae	11
subiectos, integro Fluuio a Rege nostro donatos, triumphare?	460	Epistolae	13
non adeo sanatae ab optimo Rege nostro quin turgescat indies,	473	Epistolae	21
REGEM			
Ad Regem Instituti Epigrammatici ratio.	385	Musae 1	T
Ad Seren. Regem.	401	Musae 39	T
Deus ipse cum crearet hominem, mundi regem, consilio vsus est.	446	Orationes	36
cernitis Regem & nomine & re magnum quid polliceri, ideoque ex	447	Orationes	8
& cum ipse sis in summa arbore altera manu prehendis Regem,	456	Epistolae	14
3. Ad Iacobum Regem Gratiae de Scriptis suis Academiae donatis	458	Epistolae	T
et quo magis Tuum agnoscas, in ipso partu, Librorum regem creatum.	459	Epistolae	12
4. Ad Iacobum Regem Gratiae de Fluuio contra Redemptores	460	Epistolae	T
REGERO			
Nil horum regero tibi merenti.	401	Musae 37	40
REGES			
significantes oportere Reges ijs partibus antecellere homines,	447	Orationes	4
hinc Reges Legatos habent statarios ac resides, quem locum Noster	450	Orationes	29
si Reges ipsi quandoque suauitates suas populari aceto condiant.	453	Orationes	18
si placet, Terrarum Reges, mutus est mundus vniuersus, vestra solum	458	Epistolae	5
Aedificarunt olim nobis Serenissimi Reges Collegia, eaque fundarunt	458	Epistolae	22
REGI			
Regi, Fidei Defensori &c. Geo. Herbertus.	384	Musae	T
Nihil vtilius Regi quam aliquando non regnare:	452	Orationes	38
primo gratulamur optimo Regi nostro, qui prospicit, vt cum ipse	463	Epistolae	21
Et licet, quo propior sis Regi, eo videaris nobis remotior,	464	Epistolae	16
perspicacitatem singularem iam olim Regi notam atque signatam	469	Epistolae	20
REGIA			
Pollubra vel cum olim damnaris Regia in ara,	386	Musae 3	9
pariter & nos consilia regia, tanquam gurgitem imperuestigabilem,	449	Orationes	22
consilia nostra, absconduntur Diuina & Regia, praecipue pharetrata,	449	Orationes	27
REGIAE			
Aeterna summae gloria regiae,	433	Poem.Lat.	2
si spinula vlla Coronae Regiae emollita sit vel retusa;	443	Orationes	11
Quare operosior in eo structura, & praerogatiuae regiae emicant.	446	Orationes	38
REGIARUM			
quae fastigium regiarum noticnum aequare nunquam potest,	460	Epistolae	17
REGIBUS			
immunitates nostrae a Serenissimis Regibus concessae ab Augustissimo	468	Epistolae	21
REGIJ			
vapores seruiles ad nubes educti aeque magnum tonitru edent ac regij.	452	Orationes	18
REGIJS			
Quis enim rectius Thesauris Regijs praefici possit quam qui,	464	Epistolae	14
REGINA			
Nempe hic Religio floret, regina quietis,	411	Lucus 6	7
REGINAE			
In Obitum Serenissimae Reginae Annae.	435	Poem.Lat.	T
REGIO			
Nos nunc conspersi atramento regio, nihil non sublime et excelsum	459	Epistolae	5
REGIONEM			
asserunt Medici vnamquamque regionem sua sibi sufficere,	444	Orationes	25
sterilem aiunt regionem: Falleris, nusquam plura bona, cum etiam mala	451	Orationes	2
REGIONES			
quod optimus Princeps non tantum exteras regiones habuit perspectas,	451	Orationes	36
qui nouas scientiarum regiones terrasque veteribus incognitas primus	463	Epistolae	10
REGIONUM			
Natura suas dotes, vt indigentia singularum regionum omnes connectat:	450	Orationes	19
REGIS			
Non tot abest, quot nos Regis ab ingenio.	437	Poem.Lat.	4
accidere potest, quam vt ministri Regis Catholici ad nos accedant?	440	Orationes	14
Oratio in Discessum Regis ab Academia Cantabrigiae habita 12o die	443	Orationes	T
atque vbiuis terrarum pro iudicio prudentissimi Regis, & in rebus	444	Orationes	20
num diffidunt prudentiae Regis? annon eius consilio res gesta est?	451	Orationes	23
si quantum eruditio Regis profuerit Reipublicae, tantum fauoris nobis	469	Epistolae	24
REGIUM			
nobis haec gaudia, imbuas cor Regium vigore, animum clementia,	444	Orationes	5
REGIUS			
fructum potuimus expectare ab Eo, in quem fauor Regius, nostra vota,	456	Epistolae	18
REGNA			
Comparat aeterni regna beata Dei.	388	Musae 9	4
Purpureo melius sanguine Regna probem.	405	Passio 7	8
REGNARE			
Nihil vtilius Regi quam aliquando non regnare:	452	Orationes	38
REGNAT			
Vis, & vena sacris regnat in artubus;	403	Musae 40	8
Regnat visceribus, measque versat	411	Lucus 5	2
REGNET			
Structorem, & Solomon vbique regnet.	408	Passio 19	8
REGNO			
Et patrio regno (sub quo iam Principe nobis	432	Poem.Lat.	27
Sanctius in Regno Magni credebat Amoris	439	Poem.Lat.	14

REGNO (cont'd)	PAGE	TITLE	LINE
sitis ordine atque habitu, quo nos in hoc regno omnes esse gloriamur.	441	Orationes	2
superbi sua tantum nosse, praesertim cum in vno regno non sint omnia:	450	Orationes	18
Si enim in regno vestro Hibernico lignum nascitur permanens,	459	Epistolae	15
REGNORUM			
percurrite Annales regnorum, excutite scrinia politiarum omnium;	445	Orationes	13
Politicos audiamus, salus regnorum pendet a vicinis, quorum consilia,	450	Orationes	25
REGNUM			
nostrumque regnum gestimus fieri participes eius sanguinis, . . .	440	Orationes	19
Omne regnum suo Principi carcer est, aut si excedat, alienum:	450	Orationes	12
est in forma & figuris vultus, vbi res postulat, regnum tuebitur:	454	Orationes	8
quas non nobis habemus sed irrigati ipsi vniuersum regnum aspergimus?	462	Epistolae	11
REGREDI			
vellent omnia regredi, ...	395	Musae 25	12
Ad se suaeque matris Arcam regredi:	436	Poem.Lat.	21
Ad se suamque mentis Arcam regredi:	436	Poem.Lat. V	21
REGULA			
Regula sanguinolenta fati?	433	Poem.Lat.	8
REGUM			
Ecce pererratas, Regum doctissime, nugas, ...	401	Musae 39	1
Perge, decus Regum; sic, Augustissime, plures	402	Musae 39	33
Non animas, raroque ornantur sanguine regum	420	Tr.Mortis	98
REI			
Caesar sobrius ad rei Latinae	401	Musae 37	42
Aut si negotio hora sumenda est, rei	423	Mem.Matr.2	32
REIJCI			
orationem reijci septemplicem, ...	396	Musae 28	4
REIPUB			
Alma Mater libentissime caput reclinet in tuo sinu, oculusque Reipub:	465	Epistolae	13
REIPUBLICAE			
labore suo & periculo consuleret & praesenti Reipublicae & futurae;	447	Orationes	25
machinas conficiunt ad defensionem Reipublicae mirabiles: . .	454	Orationes	6
satis virtuti datum est, satis Reipublicae.	455	Orationes	6
quin communes Reipublicae lachrymae alterum nobis Fluuium . .	462	Epistolae	5
et festucas, Reipublicae oculo haerentes, tam diligenter amoues;	462	Epistolae	13
Reipublicae emolumentum, aeternitatem nominis Tui subsidiumque	464	Epistolae	5
sic vna opera vtriusque Reipublicae calculum et ciuilis et literariae	465	Epistolae	26
vero de hoc tuo progressu non minus Reipublicae gratulamur quam tibi,	466	Epistolae	16
nec minus etiam Reipublicae, quam nunc pleno gradu ingrediens	468	Epistolae	18
si quantum eruditio Regis profuerit Reipublicae, tantum fauoris nobis	469	Epistolae	24
REL			
quo soles beare Amplitudini tuae deuotissimos Procancellarium Rel.	464	Epistolae	28
succurres Magnificentiae tuae addicitissimis Procancellario Rel.	469	Epistolae	26
RELABITUR			
vbi iam ingrauescit humore, relabitur in terram, qua ortus est,	454	Orationes	29
RELABUNTUR			
vbi sursum processerint paulo, frigefacti demum relabuntur. . .	471	Epistolae	30
RELIGIO			
Nempe hic Religio floret, regina quietis, ...	411	Lucus 6	7
RELIQ			
subsidiumque Magnificentiae Tuae deuotissimorum Procancellarij Reliq.	464	Epistolae	7
RELIQUA			
Quae enim alia spes reliqua erat, quam vt pro infinitis vestris	458	Epistolae	30
RELIQUERIS			
es praedo omnis gloriae, vt ne gratitudinis laudem nobis reliqueris?	459	Epistolae	3
RELIQUIS			
O nimium Latro! reliquis furatus abunde, ...	406	Passio 11	1
RELIQUIT			
praeripuit Tibi gloriam extruendae Academiae, reliquit conseruandae.	465	Epistolae	17
RELIQUOS			
Atque inter reliquos horti crescentia foetus	427	Mem.Matr.7	33
RELIQUUM			
Molita, reliquum deinde garriens diem	422	Mem.Matr.2	12
RELIQUUS			
vestri Procancellarius Reliquusque Senatus Cantabrigiensis. . .	459	Epistolae	23
RELLIGIONE			
Cur adeo immodica relligione cales?	399	Musae 35	2
RELUCET			
hoc Principe, in quo doctrinae fructus atque vsus mirifice relucet.	469	Epistolae	23
REM			
quod rem spectat, si placeat vices meas tantisper supplere donec	470	Epistolae	5
REMANENT			
Non remanent nobis corpora, non animae.	390	Musae 13	4
REMEARE			
Ac zephyris, carnis flos remeare nequit.	415	Lucus 23	14
REMISI			
hic ego me erexi & de dolore remisi plurimum, de desiderio nihil.	451	Orationes	26
REMITTAM			
Caetera condonabo tibi, scombrisque remittam:	399	Musae 34	3
REMITTENS			
Affectus socijs tuis remittens.	401	Musae 37	32
REMITTIT			
etiam teneor, sed laxioribus vinculis, quaeque amor saepe remittit:	472	Epistolae	34
REMOTI			
A nobis etenim procul remoti	415	Lucus 24	7
REMOTIOR			
eo videaris nobis remotior, confidimus tamen vt arbores, . .	464	Epistolae	17
REMOTIS			
Munere dum nobis prodes, Libroque remotis, ...	435	Poem.Lat.	3
REMOTUM			
Plus etiam veteres coelum videre remotum:	433	Poem.Lat.	44

	PAGE	TITLE	LINE
REMOUENTUR			
indicantes, se non amare patriam terram, a qua adeo remouentur.	452	Orationes	13
REMPUBLICAM			
Quod ad nostram Rempublicam, Academiam, pax adeo Musis summe	448	Orationes	16
ab optimo Rege desumptas in vniuersam Rempublicam diffundis:	456	Epistolae	12
floribus suis sternentes Rempublicam, prae ariditate flaccescerent.	461	Epistolae	10
REMUNERATUR			
relabitur in terram, qua ortus est, eique cum foecundia remuneratur:	454	Orationes	30
RENATAM			
Pulchre renatam ex arbore mortua,	434	Poem.Lat.	34
RENIDENT			
Tota renident aede decus & suauitas	423	Mem.Matr.2	24
RENIDENTES			
Animo renidentes prius. Sin rarior	423	Mem.Matr.2	25
RENOUARE			
qui renouare sacre	397	Musae 28	14
RENUIS			
Praesul, cur renuis? sin mala, pauculos	392	Musae 17	12
RENUNCIAUIMUS			
tanquam Nobilem Filium (more nostro) Magistrum Artium renunciauimus.	463	Epistolae	9
REOR			
permutare nolim, maius tamen piaculum reor, deesse publico muneri,	472	Epistolae	31
REPANDIS			
Tu geminas belli portas, o Petre, repandis,	398	Musae 33	11
REPARARENT			
Post vbi Mosaicae repararent fragmina Leges,	408	Passio 20	3
REPELLIT			
Recte, quem trahit, aerem repellit	428	Mem.Matr.10	6
REPENDENDI			
ita inuoluit nos, vt etiam rependendi vias omnes praecludat.	458	Epistolae	29
REPENDENT			
Dulcem rependent tum mihi tibiam	434	Poem.Lat.	33
REPENDITIS			
O barbaros! sic os rependitis sanctum,	404	Passio 5	1
REPERE			
Nunc adeo per te viuunt, vt repere possint,	384	Musae	5
REPERIAS			
hospitium, et erga te propensius, haud vsquam forsitan reperias.	466	Epistolae	19
REPERISSEM			
viam ad candorem Mentis Tuae ducentem aut reperissem aut fecissem.	472	Epistolae	10
REPERISSET			
postquam circumspiciens reperisset Te, quasi in tuis palpebris	465	Epistolae	14
REPERTORES			
assecutus es nomen, quam Repertores Noui Orbis compararunt.	463	Epistolae	12
REPERTUM			
Tantum repertum est trux hominum genus,	394	Musae 23	17
REPETERENT			
solebant signa in hostes inijcere, vt milites acrius ea repeterent:	451	Orationes	33
REPIT			
Iam repit impietas velatura illico.	398	Musae 32	3
REPONAS			
neque amplius quaerendum sit Tibi, Almae Nutrici quid reponas.	462	Epistolae	16
REPONIMUS			
Cancellario INSTAVRARI, inter Arcana Prouidentiae plane reponimus.	464	Epistolae	2
REPONIS			
Ter millies coelo reponis:	394	Musae 23	27
REPONIT			
Dum torus absentem quisque reponit heram.	425	Mem.Matr.5	10
REPONO			
Non fastus tibi turgidos repono;	401	Musae 37	36
REPOSITOS			
quos in arca repositos abijciebant in fluuium, his verbis:	452	Orationes	28
REPRIME			
Si ducat agmen, reprime; sin claudat, sinas.	414	Lucus 20	14
REPUBLICA			
nisi Rex esses in ciuili Republica, eligereris in Literaria?	443	Orationes	18
REPUGNANT			
Laudando Matrem, cum repugnant inscij.	424	Mem.Matr.2	65
Nam fata non iustis repugnant	434	Poem.Lat.	27
REPUMICATOR			
Repumicator mentis; Atlas Physicus,	436	Poem.Lat.	17
REPUTES			
Verum heus! si reputes, tibi tuisque	391	Musae 15	7
Aut saeuum reputes. Amica nostra est	400	Musae 37	11
REQUIEM			
Nullum locum requiemue cernens perstitit	436	Poem.Lat.	20
Nullum locum requiemue cernens praestitit	436	Poem.Lat. V	20
REQUIERUNT			
Quid non mutatum est? requierunt flumina cursus;	433	Poem.Lat.	43
REQUIESCAMUS			
peruenimus ad laurum hanc, vbi sub vmbra eius paulisper requiescamus:	455	Orationes	14
REQUIRAT			
Dum cor omne suum sibi requirat	408	Passio 19	7
RERIS			
Cur Latiam linguam reris nimis esse profanam,	391	Musae 16	1
RERUM			
Tempus edax rerum, tuque o mors improba sola es,	433	Poem.Lat.	41
Rerum magister vnicus, at non Artium;	436	Poem.Lat.	5
Quis enim apud nos splendor, aut rerum, aut vestium?	441	Orationes	11
RES			
Non vt te superem: res tamen ipsa feret.	386	Musae 2	2

RES (cont'd)	PAGE	TITLE	LINE
Sic Catharis noua sola placent; res, verba nouantur:	386	Musae 3	3
Res ampliantur, sin per aduersam videt, ...	388	Musae 8	13
Vertas specillum: nam, prout se res habent, ...	388	Musae 8	17
Scilicet emptorem si res aut parcior aetas	388	Musae 9	5
O caecum populum! si bona res siet	392	Musae 17	11
Coepisti, pergas simili res texere filo.	402	Musae 39	19
Romano, sed res seria Roma tibi est:	416	Lucus 27	2
Res redit ad vates, Pieriosque duces:	417	Lucus 28	2
Dein familiam lustrat, & res prandij, ...	422	Mem.Matr.2	18
In nebulas similesque tui res gaudia nunquid	426	Mem.Matr.7	2
Nos autem flemus: res ea sola tuis.	427	Mem.Matr.9	8
Cum per te sit res ambitiosa mori.	435	Poem.Lat.	8
esse Alexandro Magno nisi eius res gestas tradidisset historia?	441	Orationes	19
delicata res est eruditio & tenera, tanquam flos molliculus rudiore	448	Orationes	24
Quamuis res haec. Principibus vt vtilissima ita difficillima factu,	450	Orationes	10
annon eius consilio res gesta est?	451	Orationes	24
Atque hoc quidem statu res erant, Suauissime CAROLE, cum tu aberas;	451	Orationes	27
adeon' nihili videtur res, Principem omnibus delicijs abundantem,	452	Orationes	3
est in forma & figuris vultus, vbi res postulat, regnum tuebitur:	454	Orationes	7
quo spiritu, qua arte, quarto impetu atque vigore res aggrediatur:	454	Orationes	11
vt res nostras omnes cum Honore Tuo coniunctas esse velimus.	465	Epistolae	2
quam publicum spectantes (quae res et naturae legibus et hominum	467	Epistolae	5
RESARCIAT			
Prae spiritu ruptis, quo eas resarciat	398	Musae 32	9
RESCINDERE			
non cor) Tui in me dominij ius imminuere posse, nedum rescindere.	473	Epistolae	7
RESERAT			
Diffissum reserat Deum latentem, ...	408	Passio 19	3
RESIDES			
hinc Reges legatos habent statarios ac resides, quem locum Noster	450	Orationes	30
RESIGNENT			
Et ni lumina ianuam resignent, ...	415	Lucus 24	4
RESOLUTIONE			
cum tamen in resolutione illa vltima, nulla sit distinctio populi aut	452	Orationes	15
RESOLUTUS			
Impar, & in fletum vel resolutus, ero;	404	Passio 1	2
RESPICIAT			
recte diuinaret, non respiciat materiam actionum, sed quo spiritu,	454	Orationes	10
RESPICIT			
incomparabilem, quae eodem vultu et moderatur mundum et nos respicit.	458	Epistolae	4
RESPICITUR			
quemadmodum in Cometae praesagio, non respicitur, quae materia sit,	454	Orationes	12
RESPONDE			
Responde aeternum titulo; quoque ordine felix	402	Musae 39	18
RESPONDEANT			
vt si officia nostra minus respondeant magnitudini beneficiorum,	460	Epistolae	15
quasi accolae Maiestatis, literaturae suae et vicinitati respondeant:	463	Epistolae	23
RESPONDEAT			
ne nihil hic sit, quod magnitudini praesentiae vestrae respondeat.	441	Orationes	10
RESPONDEBIMUS			
Nihilne respondebimus tibi? Fatemur.	392	Musae 20	16
RESPONDENT			
nouo hoc cumulo honorum, qui tamen votis nostris nondum respondent.	464	Epistolae	21
RESPONDERE			
non est tanti respondere latratibus maleuolorum;	454	Orationes	16
RESPONDERINT			
Maiestatis vestrae gaudia responderint aut nostris votis aut	443	Orationes	13
RESPONDIT			
Respondit: Eia, ne metuas, precor, ...	434	Poem.Lat.	26
RESPONS			
Vrbani VIII Pont. Respons.	416	Lucus 26	T
Respons. ad Vrb. VIII.	416	Lucus 27	T
RESPONSORIAE			
Georgii Herbertii Angli Musae Responsoriae	384	Musae	T
RESPUAMUS			
aut tanquam oues taedulae & fastidiosae, cibum respuamus. . . .	449	Orationes	2
RESPUBLICAS			
alienas tantum ex hoc itinere cognouit Respublicas sed quod plus est,	450	Orationes	32
RESTINXISTI			
qui restinxisti sitim exarescentium Musarum, et Xerxes istos,	462	Epistolae	7
RESTITUTOS			
Post restitutos fluctibus obices, ...	393	Musae 23	2
RESUMPTAM			
Excussos manibus calamos, falcemque resumptam	431	Mem.Matr.19	1
RESURGET			
Resurget occumbens Herus:	407	Passio 16	12
RESURGIS			
Cum dormis, surgit pelagus: cum, Christe, resurgis, ...	412	Lucus 12	1
RETARDARE			
pecuniam retardare illam, cui natura spiritum dederit feracem	468	Epistolae	4
RETI			
Subtegmen reti dignius esse putans, ...	392	Musae 19	4
RETIA			
loquitur numellas, compedes & retia:	423	Mem.Matr.2	31
RETINENT			
proin vt Fluuij quas aquas a Fonte accipiunt non retinent ipsi,	456	Epistolae	10
RETORQUET			
Non fert Vcalegon, atque amentata retorquet	418	Tr.Mortis	14
RETORTIS			
Pallas retortis caesia vocibus	434	Poem.Lat.	25

RETRAHENTIS	PAGE	TITLE	LINE
Ad saxa speciem retrahentis humanam,	429	Mem.Matr.12	7
RETULISSET			
eundemque retulisset captus piscis, foelicissimus mortalium habitus	444	Orationes	15
RETUNDEBATUR			
Neque quod ignotior eram, retundebatur vnquam impetus:	472	Epistolae	11
RETUNDERE			
spiritus, generososque animos frangere et retundere clamitant.	461	Epistolae	20
RETUNDET			
Quas liuor mihi parturit, retundet,	385	Musae	6
RETUSA			
si spinula vlla Coronae Regiae emollita sit vel retusa;	443	Orationes	12
REUECTUM			
Arionem Delphino reuectum excepere arbores tripudiantes,	454	Orationes	37
REUERENDISSIMO			
Reuerendissimo in Christo Patri ac Domino,	385	Musae	T
REUERSUS			
vsque ad Pyrenaeas nubes conscendens, reuersus per mare, gloria,	454	Orationes	32
REUERTENS			
Mersis reuertens laetus ab hostibus	394	Musae 23	30
REUM			
Cum probro madidum, reumque difflat.	428	Mem.Matr.10	7
REUOCAMUS			
inter nouas honorum nubes e conspectu nostro fugientem reuocamus.	456	Epistolae	7
REUOCANS			
Cultricem reuocans anxietate manum:	425	Mem.Matr.5	4
REUOCARE			
Librarios omnia transmarina scripta ad monopolium reuocare moliri,	467	Epistolae	21
REUOCET			
Annulus hos reuocet, sistatque libidinis vndas	396	Musae 26	11
REVEREND			
To the right honourable and reverend Father in God, my L. Bishop of	473	Epistolae	23
REX			
Munere, Rex tanto verior inde prober.	405	Passio 7	4
Interea classem magnis Rex instruit ausis:	427	Mem.Matr.9	7
nisi Rex esses in ciuili Republica, eligereris in Literaria?	443	Orationes	18
Hoc vno Rex et populus dissentimus.	444	Orationes	1
cor sacrum, sentiatque Rex ipse nos haec intime precari.	444	Orationes	9
vt Rex animalium fiat Rex hominum, apponimus nos manibus Sceptrum,	447	Orationes	2
prudentissimus Rex mature prospiciet: vbi ille signum sustulerit,	449	Orationes	16
Quare optime fecit Rex Serenissimus, qui virtutes tuas magnis	466	Epistolae	12
RHETORICI			
rariusque paulo fodiam in Vintoniensi agro, dum Rhetorici satagam:	472	Epistolae	29
RHETORICOR			
Non rhetoricor, Academici, non tinnio:	445	Orationes	21
RHETORIS			
fungar apud Meos, Rhetoris in hunc annum, & in plures Oratoris,	472	Epistolae	26
RHOECI			
Enceladum pharetramque Rhoeci.	434	Poem.Lat.	20
RIDEANT			
Te mille nasi, mille rideant sinus.	414	Lucus 20	10
RIDENS			
Ille tamen, quamuis altus, tua crimina ridens	387	Musae 7	7
Ridens Bombardas miseras, quae corpora perdunt	420	Tr.Mortis	97
RIDENTI			
Ridenti lacrymas quibus vnis concolor vnda est.	426	Mem.Matr.7	6
RIGET			
Nunc sudas solus; caetera turba riget.	397	Musae 29	4
RIGHT			
To the right honourable and reverend Father in God, my L. Bishop of	473	Epistolae	23
RIGORE			
Suauiter efficient, absque rigore Scholae.	417	Lucus 28	4
RINGANTUR			
Ergo ringantur pietatis hostes,	390	Musae 14	17
RINGUNTUR			
cur ringuntur? num diffidunt prudentiae Regis?	451	Orationes	23
RINI			
Ego de rini ksumbalon ixnelato	430	Mem.Matr.15	14
RIPIS			
Fluminaque e ripis obvia facta tibi:	210	Cam.1613-a BR	6
RITE			
Animam recentem rite curauit sacris	422	Mem.Matr.2	16
RITIBUS			
Ritibus vna Sacris opponitur; altera Sanctos	386	Musae 4	3
In ritibus nostris? Ego audio nullum.	392	Musae 20	2
orbam ritibus expetunt,	395	Musae 25	10
RITU			
De S. Baptismi Ritu.	388	Musae 9	T
RITUS			
Primo, vnus aut alter parum ritus placet:	398	Musae 32	2
Mentibus attonitis cupiunt addiscere ritus:	402	Musae 39	9
RITUUM			
De rituum vsu.	395	Musae 25	T
RIXAE			
Te mille rixae, mille prensabunt doli,	414	Lucus 20	8
RIXAMUR			
quam stulte de te rixamur:	451	Orationes	29
RIXANTES			
literatos, eosque cum tineis et blattis rixantes, exuens puluere,	462	Epistolae	26
RIXAS			
Liber alit rixas: potantibus omnia bina	418	Tr.Mortis	18

	PAGE	TITLE	LINE
ROBORE			
Assideo Matri, robore vinco cedros.	428	Mem.Matr.11	6
ROBORIS			
Naufragij causa est alijs mare, roboris Anglo,	411	Lucus 6	5
ROGAMUS			
Tantum rogamus, vt pergas, & inter nouos honorum cumulos,	462	Epistolae	27
rogamusque vt quando beneficia tua peruagantur Angliam,	466	Epistolae	16
etiam tacentibus nobis, quanto magis cum rogamus, idque pro Libris,	467	Epistolae	18
ROGANT			
Astra rogant, Nouus hic quis hospes?	394	Musae 23	28
ROGARE			
Vt dentur species, rogare sensum:	415	Lucus 24	3
ROMA			
Roma. Anagr. Oram. Maro. / Ramo. Armo. / Mora. Amor.	416	Lucus 25	T
ROMA, tuum nomen quam non pertransijt ORAM,	416	Lucus 25	1
Arguit, exceptos quos pia Roma fouet:	416	Lucus 26	4
Romano, sed res seria Roma tibi est:	416	Lucus 27	2
Quam satur & suauis sit tibi Roma iocus.	416	Lucus 27	6
Pontificem tandem nacta est sibi Roma poetam:	417	Lucus 28	1
ROMAE			
Nempe Caput Romae es, cuius mysteria velles	416	Lucus 27	3
ROMAM			
Cum Romam nequeas, quod aues, euertere, nomen	416	Lucus 26	1
ROMANA			
vt mihi videtur, Romana elegantia, periodique vetus rotunditas.	473	Epistolae	18
ROMANAM			
Britannicam in Vulpem, inque Romanam Lupam.	397	Musae 30	6
ROMANI			
sed velut Romani lacum, cuius altitudo ignota erat, dedicabant	449	Orationes	20
quod Romani Imperatores in bello, qui solebant signa in hostes	451	Orationes	31
ROMANO			
Romano, sed res seria Roma tibi est:	416	Lucus 27	2
ROMANORUM			
esset tali historiae) si Romanorum Imperatorum incredibilem luxum	452	Orationes	21
ROMANOS			
hinc contigisse arbitror apud Romanos, quod nonnullae familiae semper	447	Orationes	19
RORE			
Scribentem placido rore beaueris,	402	Musae 40	2
ROS			
Herbae exoletae, ros-marinus aridus?	424	Mem.Matr.2	58
Vespere ros maestis funus honestet aquis.	425	Mem.Matr.5	16
ROS-MARINUS			
Herbae exoletae, ros-marinus aridus?	424	Mem.Matr.2	58
ROSA			
Tu spina misere pungeris, ipse Rosa.	405	Passio 6	2
ROSARUM			
Spicula mutemus: capias Tu serta Rosarum,	405	Passio 6	3
ROSAS			
Contiguas stirpes afflat, eaeque rosas.	425	Mem.Matr.5	6
ROTAE			
Inde rotae atque axes subeunt, quasi sella curulis	419	Tr.Mortis	55
Mille rotae nimijs impediuntur aquis.	428	Mem.Matr.9	14
ROTAS			
In te, nec arcus, scorpionesue, aut rotas,	421	Lucus 33	4
ROTATIBUS			
De Magicis rotatibus.	392	Musae 20	T
ROTATUS			
Quos tu rotatus, quale murmur auscultas	392	Musae 20	1
Magicos rotatus, & perhorridas Striges,	392	Musae 20	12
Non striges, magiamue, vel rotatus,	401	Musae 37	35
ROTUNDA			
cuius ingens gloria aeque rotunda est atque ipse orbis:	440	Orationes	16
ROTUNDITAS			
Quanta rotunditas Clementiae vestrae, quae ab omni parte nobis	460	Epistolae	9
vt mihi videtur, Romana elegantia, periodique vetus rotunditas.	473	Epistolae	18
ROTUNDUM			
soli caput rotundum & coeleste, soli facies tanquam vestibulum magni	447	Orationes	1
ROTUNDUS			
Rotundus in te: namque si ansatus sies,	414	Lucus 20	7
RUANT			
In mea dicta ruant; non tam mihi pendula mens est,	432	Poem.Lat.	5
RUAT			
Ante diem vestro mundus ab igne ruat.	399	Musae 35	12
RUBEAT			
Nec plus te rubeat vesper, Eliza, precor.	211	Cam.1613-b BF	16
RUCTARE			
Huic Glans adijcitur (non quam ructare vetustas	419	Tr.Mortis	60
Hinc Glans adijcitur (non quam ructare vetustas	419	Tr.Mortis V	60
RUCTUS			
quid ructus crapulae solium possidentis?	452	Orationes	19
RUDERE			
Mugire multo mauelim quam rudere.	395	Musae 24	2
RUDES			
in promptu erat, rudesque animos vi verborum percellere:	445	Orationes	17
RUDIBUS			
Stipati, rudibusque volis imperuius hortus	427	Mem.Matr.7	26
RUDIORE			
tanquam flos molliculus rudiore Centurionis manu tactus flaccescit.	448	Orationes	25
RUDIOREM			
Bibliothecam nostram rudiorem esse impexioremque, quam vt tantum	463	Epistolae	28

	PAGE	TITLE		LINE
RUDIS				
Non placuit rudis atque ignara occisio: Morti	418	Tr.Mortis		24
Non placuit rudis atque ignara occasio; morti	271	Tr.Mortis	VS	24
RUGIENS				
Ne perdat Lec rugiens vagantem.	417	Lucus 30		8
RUGIENT				
collisis ignis elicitur) qui nunc mansueti sunt, abunde rugient.	449	Orationes		19
RUINAM				
Namque hanc ruinam salua Grauitas defleat, ...	422	Mem.Matr.2		5
Per strages licet autorum veterumque ruinam	435	Poem.Lat.		1
RUIT				
Si sursum iacias, in caput ipsa ruit.	410	Lucus 4		8
Quin Aries ruit, & multa Demetrius arte:	419	Tr.Mortis		47
Tamque aries ruit et multa Demetrius arte, ...	271	Tr.Mortis	VS	47
RUMORES				
qui tum rumores? quae auditiones?	450	Orationes		36
RUMPATUR				
Vt mucro rumpatur Mineruae, ...	433	Poem.Lat.		11
RUMPERE				
rumpere fascias cum Hercule, serpentesque interficere voluptatis,	452	Orationes		6
RUMPI				
(In quo fas nihil est rumpi) donare sigillum.	439	Poem.Lat.		15
RUMUSCULOS				
Qui sugit auido spiritu rumusculos	414	Lucus 20		1
RUPE				
Qualia parturiente colunt sub rupe sorores:	432	Poem.Lat.		8
RUPES				
Rupes tenaces & silices ferunt	393	Musae 23		9
RUPTIS				
Prae spiritu ruptis, quo eas resarciat	398	Musae 32		9
Obrue feruentes, ruptis conatibus, hostes:	402	Musae 39		20
RURE				
Rure; breuisque hortus, cuius cum vellere florum	426	Mem.Matr.7		23
Rure, sibi dixit Musa fuisse probro.	431	Mem.Matr.19		2
RURSUS				
timores, suspiria, expostulationes, iras, amorem rursus. . .	450	Orationes		35
RUSTICIS				
non rusticis loquor aut barbaris, quos magnificentia promissi	445	Orationes		15
RUTILANTE				
Ad nos cum radio tam rutilante potes?	424	Mem.Matr.3		2
RUTILATIO				
quae rutilatio? certe cum duplex fulgor sit, qui mundi oculos	441	Orationes		11
S				
De S. Baptismi Ritu.	388	Musae 9		T
In S. Scripturas.	411	Lucus 5		T
precamur S. S. Trinitatem, vt vestrae coronae ciuili & literariae	459	Epistolae		20
S'				
Menouge sophien, ei s' apellaxthai xreon, ...	430	Mem.Matr.15		5
SACCULI				
neque Studiosorum Sacculi, qui etiam nunc maeret et ingemiscit.	467	Epistolae		23
SACERDOS				
Mundique & Animarum sacerdos vnicus;	436	Poem.Lat.		24
SACRA				
Cum sacra perturbet vester furor omnia, scriptum	386	Musae 3		7
Vtrum tenore sacra nostra sint necne	392	Musae 20		5
De Musica Sacra.	393	Musae 23		T
Interea ad sacrum stimulat sacra Musica bellum, ...	399	Musae 33		25
De auri sacra fame.	399	Musae 34		T
Tu venas laticesque omnes, quos sacra recludit	402	Musae 39		23
SACRAE				
Quid sacrae tandem meruere vestes, ...	390	Musae 14		1
Scripturae canones sacrae:	395	Musae 25		19
SACRAM				
In Sacram Anchoram Piscatoris G. Herbert.	438	Poem.Lat.		T
SACRATISSIMA				
Sacratissima Charta, tu fuisti	411	Lucus 5		11
SACRATOS				
Exuscitat plebem sacratos	394	Musae 23		31
SACRE				
qui renouare sacre	397	Musae 28		14
SACRILEGUM				
Sacrilegum carmen, censeo, flamma voret.	399	Musae 34		4
SACRIS				
Ritibus vna Sacris opponitur; altera Sanctos	386	Musae 4		3
Articulis sacris quidam subscribere iussus, ...	389	Musae 11		1
Qui templa sacris expoliant choris, ...	394	Musae 23		18
Vis, & vena sacris regnat in artubus;	403	Musae 40		8
Animam recentem rite curauit sacris	422	Mem.Matr.2		16
SACRORUM				
Claudis auaritia Satyram; statuisque sacrorum	399	Musae 34		1
SACROS				
Cum tener ad sacros infans sistatur aquales, ...	388	Musae 9		1
Cantus sacros, profane, mugitus vocas?	395	Musae 24		1
SACRUM				
Seruarentque sacrum clauibus ordinem;	391	Musae 17		6
Interea ad sacrum stimulat sacra Musica bellum, ...	399	Musae 33		25
Memoriae Matris Sacrum	422	Mem.Matris		T
cor sacrum, sentiatque Rex ipse nos haec intime precari. . .	444	Orationes		9
SAECULI				
tersis atque expolitis, quam luxuriae saeculi, ambitionisque strumae,	473	Epistolae		20

	PAGE	TITLE	LINE
SAECULO			
Seritur fama in hoc saeculo, vt in sequenti metatur:	441	Orationes	20
SAEPE			
Saepe ex se nihil otiosa cudit.	415	Lucus 24	6
etiam tenecr, sed laxicribus vinculis, quaeque amor saepe remittit:	472	Epistolae	34
SAEPIUS			
Saepius aspergis. Siste, pudore vacas.	387	Musae 7	2
Sufficiat virgae saepius vmbra tuae.	406	Passio 9	4
in Principibus virtus, & cui cum sceptro lites saepius intercedunt?	452	Orationes	3
SAEUO			
Si-quas mens agitet moles (dum pectora saeuo	432	Poem.Lat.	9
SAEUUM			
Aut saeuum reputes. Amica nostra est	400	Musae 37	11
SAEUUS			
Saeuus es eripiens paruis vadimonia coeli:	389	Musae 9	15
O saeuus hostis! quam ferociter pugnas!	392	Musae 20	15
Balistasque Onagrosque & quicquid Scorpio saeuus	419	Tr.Mortis	40
SAGAX			
Sagax Humilitas, eligens viros bonos	412	Lucus 13	1
SAGINANTUR			
immersi, aut vno semper saginantur in loco, vti anguillae, . . .	452	Orationes	10
SAGUM			
Trux caper alarum, suppara, laena, sagum.	397	Musae 29	2
SALIENTE			
Mater inest saliente vena.	426	Mem.Matr.6	16
SALIUAM			
Tellurisque Britannicae saliuam	428	Mem.Matr.10	3
SALSIOR			
Hic vbi discumbunt per gramina, salsior vnus	418	Tr.Mortis	12
SALTEM			
Per fluctus saltem, fac, precor, ipse vadem.	414	Lucus 19	4
Fac radios saltem ingemines, vt dextera tortos	424	Mem.Matr.3	9
Hoc saltem officio fungar amore tui.	437	Poem.Lat.	8
quod primum intendunt, saltem in secundis aut tertijs consistant.	446	Orationes	7
hoc saltem solutio est; Nos nunc conspersi atramento regio, . .	459	Epistolae	4
SALTUS			
Saltus per incultos lacusque	393	Musae 23	11
Sed nec Cyrrhaei saltus Libethriaue arua	432	Poem.Lat.	4
vnde diuites syluas ac saltus quaerunt vbi aedificent, ac . .	450	Orationes	21
SALUA			
Namque hanc ruinam salua Grauitas defleat, ...	422	Mem.Matr.2	5
SALUBRE			
Quod tu febrem censes, salubre est	426	Mem.Matr.6	23
SALUETE			
Saluete tandem Magistri Artium, & quidem omnium Aulicarum, . .	440	Orationes	4
SALUM			
Lubricus, & superans mobilitate salum.	428	Mem.Matr.11	8
SALUS			
Qua Fabio quondam sub duce nata salus.	416	Lucus 25	10
Quae Fabio quondam sub duce tuta salus.	416	Lucus 25 V	10
Politicos audiamus, salus regnorum pendet a vicinis, quorum consilia,	450	Orationes	25
SALUTEM			
Quod si fata illi longam inuidere salutem	432	Poem.Lat.	26
SALUTI			
tibi hunc honorem, et faxit, vt tibi gloriae sit, omnibus saluti.	469	Epistolae	6
SALUUM			
& ipsum accepimus saluum & annulum, annulum Coniugalem, . .	444	Orationes	18
SAMPSON			
Circumferre potes; Sampson vt ante fores.	408	Passio 18	2
SANANTUR			
pace, aegri sanantur; bello, etiam sani intereunt:	448	Orationes	9
SANARE			
Ah, cernam; Tu, qui caecos sanare solebas, ...	421	Lucus 35	7
SANATAE			
non adeo sanatae ab optimo Rege nostro quin turgescat indies,	473	Epistolae	21
SANATI			
Hic, vbi sanati stillant opobalsama mundi, ...	406	Passio 13	1
SANCTA			
Et lucro apponis gaudia sancta tuo.	424	Mem.Matr.3	6
Deridet motus sancta catena tuos.	438	Poem.Lat.	9
SANCTAE			
Nostra caro sanctae nescia laudis erit?	389	Musae 12	10
Corneliae sanctae, graues Semproniae, ...	422	Mem.Matr.2	1
SANCTAM			
Quare scripturus, finge tibi matronam sanctam, venerandam, . .	470	Epistolae	16
SANCTE			
Sancte Pater, coeli custos, quo doctius vno	385	Musae	1
Ni sancte, vti mater, recedam, ...	425	Mem.Matr.6	11
SANCTI			
Sancti Albani, Baronis Verulamij.	438	Poem.Lat.	T
SANCTIFICER			
Atque vbi per te sanctificer natalibus ipsis, ...	434	Poem.Lat.	9
SANCTIS			
Nosse sui quid agant, quaedam est quoque musica sanctis, . .	427	Mem.Matr.9	3
SANCTISSIME			
Sanctissime Pater. Cum caeterae ecclesiae tam perspicaci diligentia	466	Epistolae	20
Sanctissime Pater, Statim a solatio aspectus Tui, Ego auctior iam	471	Epistolae	16
SANCTIUS			
Terra nihil, nec quo sanctius astra vident;	385	Musae	2
Sanctius in Regno Magni credebat Amoris	439	Poem.Lat.	14

	PAGE	TITLE		LINE
SANCTOS				
Ritibus vna Sacris opponitur; altera Sanctos	386	Musae 4		3
Sanctos qui gemitus mentibus inseris	403	Musae 40		12
Et pomoeria terminosque sanctos	408	Passio 19		4
SANCTUM				
Vt sanctum Domini persequerentur opus;	392	Musae 19		2
O barbaros! sic os rependitis sanctum,	404	Passio 5		1
Verum augusta parens, sanctum os caeloque locandum,	426	Mem.Matr.7		10
SANE				
Occidite; aut sane tantisper viuite, donec	425	Mem.Matr.5		15
quod sane adeo nobile fuit & honorificum, vt nihil habeat Inuidia	453	Orationes		23
Sane, gestabaris antea in corditus nostris;	458	Epistolae		18
sane exorti sunt nuperi quidam homines, qui libenter sapientiores nos	460	Epistolae		21
neque sane dubitamus vlli, si prae defectu aquae, commeatusque	462	Epistolae		2
Neque sane quispiam incedit Te instructior ad omnem causam,	462	Epistolae		21
SANGUINE				
Purpureo melius sanguine Regna probem.	405	Passio 7		8
Sanguine: nec precium merx emit vlla suum.	410	Lucus 4		4
Anglia cur solum fuso sine sanguine sicca est,	411	Lucus 6		1
Quem non Emathius torrens, non sanguine pinguis	418	Tr.Mortis		2
Sanguine, quem dederat, spolians. Primordia Mortis	418	Tr.Mortis		22
Sanguine, quem dederat, spolians. Primordia belli	271	Tr.Mortis	VS	22
Faecundusque chalybs sceleris, iam sanguine tinctus,	419	Tr.Mortis		37
Faecundusque chalibs sceleris, iam sanguine tectus	271	Tr.Mortis	VS	37
Anglorumque arcus gaudentes sanguine Galli,	419	Tr.Mortis		42
Angligenumque arces gaudentes sanguine Galli,	419	Tr.Mortis	V	42
Non animas, rarcque cruantur sanguine regum	420	Tr.Mortis		98
Lac cum sanguine posco deuolutum;	421	Lucus 34		6
Mors tot virorum sordida sanguine,	433	Poem.Lat.		10
SANGUINEM				
Quin, mitte nugas; teque carnem & sanguinem	413	Lucus 17		5
Quin pro me quoque sanguinem profudit,	421	Lucus 34		4
SANGUINEUM				
In sudorem sanguineum.	404	Passio 2		7
SANGUINIS				
Sanguinis insultus exanimata ferunt.	406	Passio 13		4
Sanguinis, innocuum tandem luet orbis Abelem.	272	Tr.Mortis	VS	101
nostrumque regnum gestimus fieri participes eius sanguinis,	440	Orationes		20
victoriaeque gloriam absque crudelitate effusi sanguinis delibas.	458	Epistolae		15
SANGUINOLENTA				
Regula sanguinolenta fati?	433	Poem.Lat.		8
SANGUIS				
Quo sanguis est Christi, nisi vt maculas lauet,	393	Musae 22		3
Aut potius Christi sanguis demissus ab alto,	399	Musae 35		9
Sic tuus effundi gestit pro crimine sanguis,	404	Passio 3		1
Vulnereque emanat sanguis, vt intret honos.	435	Poem.Lat.		6
vti sanguis solet in re dubia ad cor festinare, ita ad Te confugimus	467	Epistolae		8
SANI				
bello, etiam sani intereunt: pace, securitas in agris est;	448	Orationes		10
SANNAS				
Profanos fremitus bonasque sannas:	400	Musae 37		24
SANUM				
Tentando sanum: si calet, aestuans,	426	Mem.Matr.6		14
SANUS				
Sanus Homo factus, vitiorum purus vterque;	408	Passio 20		1
SAPERE				
sentire ac sapere addecet,	395	Musae 25		17
SAPIENTES				
veremur ne non tam sapientes nos, quam obscuros philosophos	460	Epistolae		24
SAPIENTIORES				
sunt nuperi quidam homines, qui libenter sapientiores nos redderent:	460	Epistolae		22
SAPIENTISSIMAM				
Siccam animam sapientissimam esse dixit obscurus ille philosophus;	460	Epistolae		20
SAPIUNT				
Quae sapiunt aeuum, ceu cariosa iacent.	386	Musae 3		4
SAPPHO				
Sola tibi Sappho, feminaque vna placet?	387	Musae 5		2
SARCASMOS				
Sarcasmos quibus artifex triumphas;	400	Musae 37		4
SARCINAS				
Breuiore nodo stringe vitae sarcinas,	414	Lucus 20		6
SAT				
Sistimus hic, inquit fatum, sat prata biberunt	272	Tr.Mortis	VS	100
SATAGAM				
rariusque paulo fodiam in Vintoniensi agro, dum Rhetorici satagam:	472	Epistolae		29
SATAGAMUS				
curiositas absit, neque eorum satagamus, quae ad nos non spectant;	449	Orationes		20
SATAS				
Creditur, ante satas prono cum numine fruges)	419	Tr.Mortis		61
Creditur, ante satas prono cum vertice fruges)	419	Tr.Mortis	V	61
SATHRON				
Ou sathron, oude melon epleto, alla voos:	429	Mem.Matr.14		6
SATIAT				
Daunia, non satiat bis ter millesima caedis	418	Tr.Mortis		3
SATIETAS				
est etiam interdum satietas quaedam honoris, quem ad tempus deponere	453	Orationes		9
SATIS				
Vitaque neglectas est satis vlta preces.	389	Musae 12		6
Machina, quam nullum satis execrabitur aeuum;	419	Tr.Mortis		50
(Nempe sepulcra Satis nuper inempta dedit.)	425	Mem.Matr.5		14
Iniuste satis arguit viator.	428	Mem.Matr.10		4

	PAGE	TITLE	LINE
SATIS (cont'd)			
vt satis intelligatis, Excellentias vestras tanto chariores esse,	440	Orationes	24
pauxillum vitae, quantum satis ad dolendum, vrbium incendia,	449	Orationes	5
nunquam intueri satis vel mirari possumus, nimirum infinitum	449	Orationes	35
satis virtuti datum est, satis Reipublicae.	455	Orationes	6
in nos amor, antehac satis perspectus, nunc cum honore geminetur.	466	Epistolae	3
SATUR			
Quam satur & suauis sit tibi Roma iocus.	416	Lucus 27	6
SATYRAM			
Claudis auaritia Satyram; statuisque sacrorum	399	Musae 34	1
SAXA			
Saxa superuacuasque cautes?	393	Musae 23	4
Nam saxa mirantur canentes,	393	Musae 23	7
Saxa lyras citharasque callent.	393	Musae 23	8
Et saxa diris hispida montibus	394	Musae 23	13
Ceu Polypus, chelis saxa prehendo tenax:	428	Mem.Matr.11	10
Ad saxa speciem retrahentis humanam,	429	Mem.Matr.12	7
SAXEA			
Sum, quis nescit, Imago Dei, sed saxea certe:	410	Lucus 1	1
SAXIS			
At Caelum e saxis elicuit Stephanus.	410	Lucus 3	2
Sunt, praeter vitam: saxis hic sternitur, alter	418	Tr.Mortis	19
SAXO			
Haud mihi cor saxo durius esse sinas.	410	Lucus 1	6
SAXONUM			
nobilissimus Saxonum nostrorum Princeps, sub ementito habitu	453	Orationes	4
SCALPELLA			
quid proderunt scalpella vestra, quando ipsae hae turres & beatae	448	Orationes	20
SCANDERE			
Et, quos ipsa nequit scandere vertices,	391	Musae 17	9
SCANDIS			
Nunc ipse scandis, vt labore mutato	406	Passio 12	2
SCANDIT			
Zacchaeus, vt Te cernat, arborem scandit:	406	Passio 12	1
SCELERATA			
Nempe graui fertur scelerata pecunia motu,	410	Lucus 4	7
SCELERIS			
Faecundusque chalybs sceleris, iam sanguine tinctus,	419	Tr.Mortis	37
Faecundusque chalibs sceleris, iam sanguine tectus	271	Tr.Mortis VS	37
SCELUS			
Omnia, praeter corda, scelus confregit & error,	409	Passio 20	7
SCEPTRA			
nulla sunt sceptra in elementis, nulli fasces aut secures:	452	Orationes	16
SCEPTRIGER			
Sceptriger, non sceptrum: aequumne est vt tot labores	446	Orationes	10
SCEPTRO			
in Principibus virtus, & cui cum sceptro lites saepius intercedunt?	452	Orationes	2
virgam cum sceptro commutare, vt quid priuata habeat in se vita	452	Orationes	36
SCEPTRUM			
Sceptriger, non sceptrum: aequumne est vt tot labores	446	Orationes	10
apponimus nos manibus Sceptrum, capiti & faciei coronam,	447	Orationes	3
SCHOLAE			
Suauiter efficient, absque rigore Scholae.	417	Lucus 28	4
SCHOLAM			
Haud per te moritura, Scholamque introspicis omnem.	402	Musae 39	26
SCIATIS			
vt sciatis omnes quam nude, quam simpliciter vobiscum agam,	445	Orationes	34
SCIDIT			
Infectas tabulas facta iuuenca scidit.	408	Passio 20	4
SCIENDA			
Nullo circuitu scienda pungunt,	415	Lucus 24	12
SCIENTES			
Se per se facili modo scientes,	415	Lucus 24	14
SCIENTIA			
honore grauidus, grauidus scientia, cruribus thymo plenis:	454	Orationes	27
SCIENTIAE			
etiam & scientiae augmentum ex hoc itinere captauit solertissimus	450	Orationes	5
SCIENTIARUM			
Labuntur fluuij scientiarum:	415	Lucus 24	8
Scientiarum, sub pupillari statu	436	Poem.Lat.	10
qui nouas scientiarum regiones terrasque veteribus incognitas primus	463	Epistolae	10
SCILICET			
Scilicet hoc vobis proprium, qui purius itis,	387	Musae 5	7
Scilicet emptorem si res aut parcior aetas	388	Musae 9	5
Scilicet talem liquet esse solem;	390	Musae 14	9
Scilicet Hebraeam cantas, & perstrepis vnam:	391	Musae 16	5
Scilicet, vt quos ante suas cum coniuge tedas	396	Musae 26	9
Scilicet has olim diuisas aequore terras	402	Musae 39	14
Scilicet in tumulis Crucifixum quaerite, viuit:	408	Passio 17	5
Ecquid emes Christum? pro nobis scilicet olim	410	Lucus 4	1
Largiar & istud: scilicet Magnatibus	413	Lucus 17	2
Laus antiqua & honor perijt: quasi scilicet ARMO	416	Lucus 25	7
Scilicet id splendes: haec est tibi causa micandi,	424	Mem.Matr.3	5
Scilicet apponit pretium tua dextera fato,	435	Poem.Lat.	5
(Tenere Christum scilicet, ne ascenderet)	438	Poem.Lat.	2
apud quos haec dico, eos scilicet, qui innuptam Palladem colunt,	446	Orationes	25
homines, quibus homo bruta, iustitia scilicet & prudentia.	447	Orationes	5
SCINDITUR			
Scinditur in partes vulgus ceu compita: telum	418	Tr.Mortis	16
SCINTILLAE			
Votaque scintillae sunt animosa meae.	410	Lucus 2	4

	PAGE	TITLE	LINE
SCIO			
a Con verbo deduci, quod tria complectitur, Possum, Scio, Audeo:	447	Orationes	8
Scio Belli nomen splendidum esse & gloriosum:	447	Orationes	32
Scio Hispanum versutum, callidum, artis & aucupij apprime gnarum:	451	Orationes	24
SCISSAE			
Petrae scissae.	408	Passio 20	T
SCISSUM			
Velum scissum.	408	Passio 19	T
SCIT			
quis scit an & amoris onus scite vinctum ligatumque, & per tot	453	Orationes	38
SCITE			
quis scit an & amoris onus scite vinctum ligatumque, & per tot	453	Orationes	38
Scite et apposite fecisti Fluuium nostrum conseruans altero	462	Epistolae	18
SCOMBRIS			
Caetera condonabo tibi, scombrisque remittam:	399	Musae 34	3
SCOMMATA			
Scommata! Pastorem semper Arundo decet.	405	Passio 7	2
SCOPIS			
Christus adest: crebris aedes percurrite scopis,	413	Lucus 15	1
SCORPIO			
Balistasque Onagrosque & quicquid Scorpio saeuus	419	Tr.Mortis	40
SCORPIONES			
In te, nec arcus, scorpionesue, aut rotas,	421	Lucus 33	4
SCOTI			
Ad Andreae Melvini Scoti Anti-Tami-Cami-Categoriam.	384	Musae	T
SCOTIA			
Scotia quae frigente iaces porrecta sub Arcto,	399	Musae 35	1
Angustior erat Scotia, quam vt pennas nido plene explicare posses:	458	Epistolae	8
SCOTIAE			
Te nunc Anglia, Scotiaeque binae,	428	Mem.Matr.10	9
SCOTIAM			
Ad Scotiam. Protrepticon ad Pacem.	399	Musae 35	T
SCOTO			
Anticategoriae, Scoto-Britanne, tuae:	386	Musae 4	2
SCOTO-BRITANNE			
Anticategoriae, Scoto-Britanne, tuae:	386	Musae 4	2
SCREATOR			
Magnificus es screator, homicida inclytus.	421	Lucus 33	2
SCRIBENDI			
Ardore scribendi calescit,	426	Mem.Matr.6	15
interim vestra hac scribendi laude intacta manente atque illibata.	458	Epistolae	27
Tua lenitas non ita interpretabitur mea haec scribendi interualla,	471	Epistolae	25
SCRIBENDO			
Nunc vero Ipse scribendo irrupisti in compensationes nostras,	459	Epistolae	1
SCRIBENDUM			
ad legendum, quantum a nobis ad scribendum, cum humanitatis Tuae,	457	Epistolae	9
SCRIBENTEM			
Scribentem placido rore beaueris,	402	Musae 40	2
SCRIBENTI			
non tam quod tibi conueniat scribenti, quam quod Academiae tuo calamo	470	Epistolae	13
tibi conueniat scribenti, quam quod Academiae tuo calamo scribenti:	470	Epistolae	14
SCRIBERE			
Scribere, Te dignum, vel lachrymare queat!	435	Poem.Lat.	6
SCRIBERET			
Diuina Christi scriberet acta manu?	412	Lucus 9	2
SCRIBIS			
Comiter scribis atque eleganter; quae est vestra felicitas qui puro	470	Epistolae	2
etsi tu qui scribis (vti quiuis priuatus) inferioris sis subsellij,	470	Epistolae	22
SCRIBITUR			
Sed luctus noster scribitur Oceano.	435	Poem.Lat.	10
SCRIBO			
Quod scribo, & placeo, si placeo, tuum est.	403	Musae 40	14
Tantum istaec scribo gratus, ne tu mihi tantum	422	Mem.Matr.1	7
Eia, agedum scribo: vicisti, Musa; sed audi,	431	Mem.Matr.19	7
Stulta: semel scribo, perpetuo vt sileam.	431	Mem.Matr.19	8
SCRIBUNTUR			
Namque Annae laudes coelo scribuntur aperto,	435	Poem.Lat.	9
SCRINIA			
percurrite Annales regnorum, excutite scrinia politiarum omnium;	445	Orationes	14
SCRIPSIT			
Quae scripsit numeros, manum; per omnes	400	Musae 37	2
Tot & tanta loquens amica, scripsit:	439	Poem.Lat.	11
SCRIPTA			
Ista docens soli scripta quadrare tibi.	385	Musae	6
Et mea sint canis scripta referta tuis.	386	Musae 2	6
Qua tamen occisi foedera scripta Dei?	391	Musae 16	4
Suauis erat, qui scripta dolens lacerando recludi,	439	Poem.Lat.	13
sunt, vt sic scripta vestra omni dente, tum edacis temporis,	459	Epistolae	18
Librarios omnia transmarina scripta ad monopolium reuocare moliri,	467	Epistolae	20
SCRIPTAQUE			
iniurias seculi scriptaque hac illac pereuntia securius praeterit.	459	Epistolae	14
SCRIPTIO			
Tum quanta tabulis artifex? quae scriptio?	423	Mem.Matr.2	35
Quo nunc recumbis, scriptio merita est tua,	423	Mem.Matr.2	40
SCRIPTIONE			
solum dextra (quamuis a scriptione terrestribusque istis sublimitate	458	Epistolae	6
SCRIPTIS			
Sed partem in scriptis etiam dum lacryma poscit,	428	Mem.Matr.9	17
sed a scriptis vestris, quae ingenti cum lucro quotidie legimus.	443	Orationes	19
3. Ad Iacobum Regem Gratiae de Scriptis suis Academiae donatis	458	Epistolae	T
vestram aeternitati in scriptis nostris certissime traderemus?	458	Epistolae	31

	PAGE	TITLE		LINE
SCRIPTORUM				
Quod si et numerus Scriptorum intumescat, et precium, quae abyssus	468	Epistolae		2
SCRIPTOS				
quia dederunt, non a se compositos, scriptos, editosque:	458	Epistolae		25
SCRIPTUM				
Cum sacra perturbet vester furor omnia, scriptum	386	Musae 3		7
Hoc, Genitrix, scriptum proles tibi sedula mittit.	427	Mem.Matr.9		1
SCRIPTURAE				
Et nunc perlongas Scripturae stamine telas	392	Musae 19		5
Scripturae canones sacrae:	395	Musae 25		19
SCRIPTURAS				
In S. Scripturas.	411	Lucus 5		T
SCRIPTURUS				
Quare scripturus, finge tibi matronam sanctam, venerandam,	470	Epistolae		16
tu hanc personam indue scripturus, tuumque iudicium tibi Lictor esto.	470	Epistolae		27
SCRUTARIS				
qui astra scrutaris, dum globos tractas & coelos fictitios,	448	Orationes		29
SCYLLAM				
Vestramque Scyllam, aequis parati spiculis	397	Musae 30		5
SE				
Cum mea futilibus numeris se verba viderent	385	Musae		3
Vertas specillum: nam, prout se res habent,	388	Musae 8		17
Et per se Templi limen adire velis:	388	Musae 9		8
Quae ratio per se, si sit adulta, facit.	388	Musae 9		12
Enixas pueros matres se sistere templis	389	Musae 12		1
Hos ad se trahere et mergere gestiens.	391	Musae 17		10
Amstellodamum corripit se. Plaudite.	398	Musae 32		10
Iam Constantinus multo se milite miscet;	398	Musae 33		15
Angelicae turmae nostris se coetibus addunt:	402	Musae 39		10
Vt nequeat paulo se cohibere domi.	404	Passio 3		2
Postquam se gelidis nocte refecit aquis:	412	Lucus 8		2
Foelicitatis culmen extra se locat,	414	Lucus 20		3
Saepe ex se nihil otiosa cudit.	415	Lucus 24		6
Se per se facili modo scientes,	415	Lucus 24		14
Quo se condat & implicet volutans	417	Lucus 30		6
Materiam vexat: nec iam se continet antro	420	Tr.Mortis		70
Vel gemitus Erebi: piceo se turbine voluens	420	Tr.Mortis		75
Magnatis appulsu extulit se occasio,	423	Mem.Matr.2		26
Se quasi donatum funere quisque putat.	435	Poem.Lat.		4
Ad se suaeque matris Arcam regredi:	436	Poem.Lat.		21
Ad se suamque mentis Arcam regredi:	436	Poem.Lat.	V	21
Maiores nostri, qui olim glasto se inficientes, in vxorum corporibus,	446	Orationes		30
Quod si Nuptiae in se graues sunt, quanto magis Principum,	446	Orationes		34
Nunc enim exploratos habet nostros in se affectus, timores,	450	Orationes		34
indicantes, se non amare patriam terram, a qua adeo remouentur.	452	Orationes		12
Sic pascunt se indies, ac si corpora sua non abirent olim	452	Orationes		13
vt quid priuata habeat in se vita commodi aut voluptatis,	452	Orationes		37
& inuidiam, quae semper se deuorat primum, vti vermis nucleum,	454	Orationes		14
posthac contineat se patria, cuius arctis amplexibus nunquam se	455	Orationes		1
contineat se patria, cuius arctis amplexibus nunquam se expediet.	455	Orationes		2
& nunc sit tanta patriae tenacitas, vt nunquam Princeps se extricet:	455	Orationes		6
quia dederunt, non a se compositos, scriptos, editosque:	458	Epistolae		24
Demosthenes Atheniensis doluit se victum opificum antelucana	469	Epistolae		2
Rege nostro quin turgescat indies, atque efferat se, indulgere.	473	Epistolae		22
SEC'LUM				
O sec'lum lepidum! circumstant vndique Fratres,	393	Musae 21		1
SECARE				
Nam si te cuperem secare versu,	400	Musae 37		14
SECAT				
eadem acies & stipulam secat & lignum:	453	Orationes		29
SECRET				
6. Ad R. Naunton, Secret. Gratiae de Fluuio	461	Epistolae		T
SECRETIS				
Paulo, secretis mussitans in angulis	398	Musae 32		5
SECULA				
Quam praemissa probant secula, nostra probant?	391	Musae 16		2
Cum Latium ferrent secula prisca iugum?	416	Lucus 25		2
In laudes abeunt secula quaeque tuas;	435	Poem.Lat.		2
In laudes properant secula quaeque tuas;	435	Poem.Lat.	V	2
SECULI				
Absque nuptijs foret populus virorum, essemus vnius seculi;	446	Orationes		22
quod pereleganter & supra barbariem seculi innuebant Maiores nostri,	446	Orationes		29
neque vnius seculi Princeps, sed & omnium, quae ventura sunt,	447	Orationes		25
iniurias seculi scriptaque hac illac pereuntia securius praeterit.	459	Epistolae		14
SECULO				
suauissimus Princeps, verum etiam praesenti seculo, dum pacem,	447	Orationes		28
SECULUM				
Quae enim vspiam gens, quod vnquam seculum meliorem habuit Principem?	445	Orationes		12
Ego vero non dicam vobis quod factum est ante seculum vestrum,	445	Orationes		38
SECUM				
& ingenium admirans, domum secum duxit, & erudiuit artibus;	453	Orationes		36
SECUNDA				
Deum immortalem, vt Princeps optimus nulla secunda itinera meditetur;	455	Orationes		1
SECUNDIS				
quod primum intendunt, saltem in secundis aut tertijs consistant.	446	Orationes		7
SECUREM				
Post vbi crudelem sentit diuisa securem,	428	Mem.Matr.11		3
SECURES				
nulla sunt sceptra in elementis, nulli fasces aut secures:	452	Orationes		17
SECURI				
Securique errorum; inque Natalibus	437	Poem.Lat.	V	25

SECURI (cont'd)

	PAGE	TITLE	LINE
hic enim securi sumus a pluuia, imo a fulmine:	455	Orationes	15
SECURIOR			
Hac ope munitus securior excipis vndas,	402	Musae 39	30
SECURIS			
Securis errorum; inque Naturalibus	437	Poem.Lat.	25
SECURITAS			
pace, securitas in agris est;	448	Orationes	10
SECURIUS			
iniurias seculi scriptaque hac illac pereuntia securius praeterit.	459	Epistolae	15
SECUS			
Atqui vos secus, o boni,	395	Musae 25	16
Haud secus ingenitis dotibus orbus Adam.	410	Lucus 1	4
SECUTAS			
Orphea mellifluum secutas.	393	Musae 23	12
SED			
Sed propere dextreque reduxit euntia sensus,	385	Musae	5
Sed non moramur: namque vestra crux erit,	389	Musae 10	10
Sed nos, cum nequeat paruorum lingua, parentem	389	Musae 12	7
Sed qui tam male pileos habetis,	391	Musae 15	11
sed nudis & egentibus	396	Musae 25	22
Sed nec coniugij signum, Melvine, probatis?	396	Musae 26	1
Sed faecunda poeseos	403	Musae 40	7
Non vrbem facit vnicam, sed Orbem.	408	Passio 19	5
Sum, quis nescit, Imago Dei, sed saxea certe:	410	Lucus 1	1
Omnia quaerendo, sed te, super omnia, vexas:	413	Lucus 16	5
Romano, sed res seria Roma tibi est:	416	Lucus 27	2
Quare haud vos hortos, sed coemeteria dico,	425	Mem.Matr.5	9
Sed partem in scriptis etiam dum lacryma poscit,	428	Mem.Matr.9	17
Eia, agedum scribo: vicisti, Musa; sed audi,	431	Mem.Matr.19	7
Sed nec Cyrrhaei saltus Libethriaue arua	432	Poem.Lat.	4
Principibus, sed amica fiunt.	434	Poem.Lat.	28
Sed luctus noster scribitur Oceano.	435	Poem.Lat.	10
Nec facile ascendant, sed tibi vallis erit.	210	Cam.1613-a BR	8
sed a scriptis vestris, quae ingenti cum lucro quotidie legimus.	443	Orationes	19
sed etiam doceas tanquam communis defensor fidei et Academiae,	443	Orationes	22
sed etiam doceas, viam aperiens & methodum in studijs adhibendam,	443	Orationes	23
non omnes licitantibus producunt merces, sed specimen tantum:	445	Orationes	30
sed varia solent esse eorum consilia, finesque multiplices	446	Orationes	4
neque vnius seculi Princeps, sed & omnium, quae ventura sunt,	447	Orationes	26
neque de priuato agamus bono, sed publico;	448	Orationes	7
Sed non est nostri bellum indicere:	449	Orationes	15
sed velut Romani lacum, cuius altitudo ignota erat, dedicabant	449	Orationes	20
ac si non gregaria essent animalia, sed tigres aut vrsi.	450	Orationes	22
alienas tantum ex hoc itinere cognouit Respublicas sed quod plus est,	450	Orationes	33
sua non abirent olim in elementa, sed in bellaria aut tragemata:	452	Orationes	14
non respiciat materiam actionum, sed quo spiritu, qua arte,	454	Orationes	10
coelestis an sublunaris, sed quae signa, quo motu transeat.	454	Orationes	13
aquas a Fonte accipiunt non retinent ipsi, sed in mare dimittunt;	456	Epistolae	10
Sed veremur, ne literae nostrae animo Tuo tot negotijs meritissime	457	Epistolae	10
sed Tu vis etiam manibus teri, semotaque Maiestate, charta	458	Epistolae	18
etiam libros dederunt, sed non suos:	458	Epistolae	23
non solum verba omnia, sed etiam cogitationes nostras exhauriunt.	460	Epistolae	3
sed si ablatus fuisset Fluuius noster, per quem vicini agri opulentia	460	Epistolae	22
Sed siccitas anni huius derisit incoeptum et plus effecit quam mille	461	Epistolae	11
sed homines nobilioris ignorantiae, qui literas imminuere spiritus,	461	Epistolae	18
quas non nobis habemus sed irrigati ipsi vniuersum regnum aspergimus?	462	Epistolae	10
Sed aliorum iniuriae tuarum virtutum pabula sunt, qui lemas istas	462	Epistolae	11
non gremio solum (quod innuis) sed et ambabus vlnis osculisque ei	463	Epistolae	7
sed perspectissimus tuus in nos amor, praestantissimaeque animi dotes	465	Epistolae	11
sed tamen comparatio & in honorem tuum cedet, nostrumque emolumentum.	467	Epistolae	25
Sed tua humanitas haec nobis expediet.	469	Epistolae	4
hausisse ab Antiquis, sed et ad Posteros transmissuri videantur.	469	Epistolae	13
non quod nunc indulgeas alterutri, sed quod deinceps indultum nollem.	470	Epistolae	12
quando ad magnates cogitas, stylo vtare, sed modeste grandi;	470	Epistolae	22
sed lubet garrire paulo. Iupiter!	471	Epistolae	5
sed vt facilius ignoscas occupato calamo, qui etiam ferians nihil Tua	471	Epistolae	22
etiam teneor, sed laxioribus vinculis, quaeque amor saepe remittit:	472	Epistolae	33
Celsitud., sed non patitur, vt mihi videtur, Romana elegantia,	473	Epistolae	17
SEDENDO			
Nunquid pro foribus sedendo nuper	411	Lucus 5	4
SEDENS			
Qua Mors ipsa sedens hominum de gente triumphat.	419	Tr.Mortis	56
sumpta vna est e proceribus, inter patritios sedens et praetextatos.	470	Epistolae	24
SEDENTES			
vbi trecenta foliorum iugera vno die sedentes percurritis;	454	Orationes	25
SEDUCTOS			
Ad seductos innocentes.	400	Musae 36	T
SEDULA			
Sedula si fuerit, perterebrare potest.	410	Lucus 2	6
Hoc, Genitrix, scriptum proles tibi sedula mittit.	427	Mem.Matr.9	1
SEDULUS			
Sydera, pendenti sedulus aure bibis:	413	Lucus 16	2
SEGES			
Ceu, quas culta timet seges, pruinas	385	Musae	7
SEGETEM			
in quo longe vberrimam gloriae segetem perspicio, nulla verborum,	446	Orationes	2
SEGNIS			
Tam segnis facies aurorae nescia vernae,	426	Mem.Matr.7	8
SEIRIOU			
Seiriou ettetheis boulemasi, panta marainei.	431	Mem.Matr.17	20

	PAGE	TITLE		LINE
SELAS				
Astrapton, Ibaridon cs dia, neime selas.	429	Mem.Matr.14		8
SELENES				
Kumat' epaphriccnta Thameseos, aike selenes	431	Mem.Matr.18		1
SELIGAM				
vnam actionem e multis seligam, quam vobis amplectendam	445	Orationes		32
SELLA				
Inde rotae atque axes subeunt, quasi sella curulis	419	Tr.Mortis		55
SELLAE				
Triste colens sellae, noctuque & Daemone plenum,	420	Tr.Mortis	V	90
SEMEL				
Quem tu, summe Deus, semel	402	Musae 40		1
Quotidie iugulat, nec semel vllus obit.	415	Lucus 23		4
Stulta: semel scribo, perpetuo vt sileam.	431	Mem.Matr.19		8
Vt semel dicam; Oratio perfecta, vti vir, tetragonos est,	471	Epistolae		3
SEMITA				
Christe, vbi tam duro patet in te semita ferro,	404	Passio 4		1
SEMITAM				
Paruam piamque dum lubenter semitam	427	Mem.Matr.8		1
SEMNOMATOS				
E themis, e dunaton. semnomatos epleto stathme,	430	Mem.Matr.17		6
SEMOTA				
manibus teri, semotaque Maiestate, charta conspiciendum Te praebes,	458	Epistolae		19
SEMOTUM				
An quod semotum populo laquearibus altis	387	Musae 7		3
SEMPER				
Mors semper iuuenem, senem Britanni.	385	Musae		11
Scommata! Pastorem semper Arundo decet.	405	Passio 7		2
Christe, fluas semper; ne, si tua flumina cessent,	406	Passio 13		5
Sit licet in pelago semper, sine fluctibus illa est,	411	Lucus 6		3
Cernis vt exusta semper sit fronte viator;	437	Poem.Lat.		3
quod nonnullae familiae semper mites essent, vti Valerij,	447	Orationes		20
aliae contra semper pertinaces ac tribunitiae, vti Appij.	447	Orationes		21
ipsum coelum nubilum semper, & poeta stultus qui dixerat,	451	Orationes		18
immersi, aut vno semper saginantur in loco, vti anguillae,	452	Orationes		10
qui semper titillant aures Principum, Osper tois pterois knomenci ta	453	Orationes		2
& inuidiam, quae semper se deuorat primum, vti vermis nucleum,	454	Orationes		14
quippe qui eximie semper fouisti literatos, eosque cum tineis	462	Epistolae		25
vt semper post nouas dignitates, alias tibi quaerant et moliantur.	464	Epistolae		23
Almam Matrem spe noua grauidam semper atque praegnantem effecerint.	464	Epistolae		25
Ignis et Virtus semper ascendunt, vtriusque enim splendor et claritas	466	Epistolae		10
Tu quidem semper Patronus noster es, etiam tacentibus nobis,	467	Epistolae		17
quam meis meritis vllis, semper lubentissimeque agnoscam:	472	Epistolae		22
SEMPRONIAE				
Corneliae sanctae, graues Semproniae,	422	Mem.Matr.2		1
SENATU				
Quare frequentissimo Senatu, plenissimis suffragijs elegimus Te	465	Epistolae		4
SENATUS				
vestri Procancellarius Reliquusque Senatus Cantabrigiensis.	459	Epistolae		23
SENECTUS				
Aut cita mors est danda bonis aut longa senectus:	432	Poem.Lat.		30
vti etiam senectus, quam aetatem in hac palaestra consecutus mihi	471	Epistolae		8
SENEM				
Sic o te (iuuenem, senemue) credat	385	Musae		10
Mors semper iuuenem, senem Britanni.	385	Musae		11
SENEX				
Sic tu nunc iuuenis factus, egoque senex.	386	Musae 2		4
SENSIMUS				
nunquam frigidiorem aestatem sensimus; at quo tandem?	451	Orationes		1
SENSIT				
Sensit hoc Archimedes, figuras iam nunc pulueri inscriptas corpore	448	Orationes		31
SENSUM				
Vt dentur species, rogare sensum:	419	Lucus 24		3
SENSUS				
Sed propere dextreque reduxit euntia sensus,	385	Musae		5
Cui non absimilis sensus inesse solet.	396	Musae 26		8
Corda furor, spissaque afflat caligine sensus?	401	Musae 39		5
Rationis & sensus stupendus Arbiter;	436	Poem.Lat.		16
Rationis & sensus peritus Arbiter;	436	Poem.Lat.	V	16
SENTENTIA				
Nos autem, a cunis, omnes sententia Mortis	415	Lucus 23		3
SENTENTIAE				
Sententiae cum voce mire conuenit,	423	Mem.Matr.2		37
Cui sententiae si fidem adhibeas, assensumque Tuum veritati omni	473	Epistolae		10
SENTIAT				
cor sacrum, sentiatque Rex ipse nos haec intime precari.	444	Orationes		9
SENTIMUS				
Postremis ambabus idem sentimus vterque;	386	Musae 4		5
SENTIO				
Quid voluit prudens Fatum, iam sentio tandem:	438	Poem.Lat.		3
ego vero sentio, & quis sum ipse (barbam, hui, tam grauem) & apud	445	Orationes		25
SENTIRE				
sentire ac sapere addecet,	395	Musae 25		17
SENTIT				
Post vbi crudelem sentit diuisa securem,	428	Mem.Matr.11		3
SENTIUNTUR				
Quam facile sentiuntur boni Principes!	445	Orationes		4
SEPELIUNT				
Pace, filij sepeliunt patres; bello, patres filios:	448	Orationes		9
SEPES				
enatare e delicijs, transilire sepes, rumpere fascias cum Hercule,	452	Orationes		6

SEPIA	PAGE	TITLE	LINE
Sepia concurrat, peccatis aptior humor, ...	404	Passio 1	3
Laudibus haud fierem sepia iusta tuis.	422	Mem.Matr.1	6
SEPIAM			
Omnis linea sepiam recusans	400	Musae 37	21
SEPOSUIT			
Seposuit Diuina sibi, cum conderet orbem, ...	402	Musae 39	15
SEPTEMPLICEM			
orationem reijci septemplicem, ...	396	Musae 28	4
SEPTENTRIONUM			
Et tu gemma etiam Britonum, Septentrionum	211	Cam.1613-b BR	11
SEPULCRA			
Conuincunt vram multa sepulcra Crucem.	408	Passio 17	6
(Nempe sepulcra Satis numen inempta dedit.)	425	Mem.Matr.5	14
SEPULCRO			
Ipse fruare, licet, solus graueolente sepulcro;	414	Lucus 21	5
SEPULTA			
Nemo potest: hodie vita sepulta prior.	415	Lucus 23	6
praeferuida illa desideria silentio suo sepulta nunc languescere,	471	Epistolae	28
SEPULTI			
Dum moreris, Mea Vita, ipsi vixere sepulti, ...	407	Passio 17	1
SEQUENDAS			
Conditis binas homini sequendas	390	Musae 14	14
SEQUENTES			
qui celeritatem affectuum raptim sequentes, ad omnem eorum auram	472	Epistolae	2
SEQUENTI			
Seritur fama in hoc saeculo, vt in sequenti metatur:	441	Orationes	20
SEQUESTER			
Aerarium; sequester experientiae, ...	436	Poem.Lat.	8
SEQUITUR			
Apud Iuris-consultos, partus sequitur ventrem:	447	Orationes	12
indoles (veluti Conclusio sequitur infirmiorem partem) plerumque	447	Orationes	18
SEQUUNTUR			
O quam felices sunt, qui tua castra sequuntur, ...	435	Poem.Lat.	7
SERA			
Sera nimis lacryma haec, si lacrymabis, erit.	415	Lucus 23	12
SERAE			
Ne serae meritis tuis venirent.	428	Mem.Matr.10	12
SEREN			
Ad Seren. Regem.	401	Musae 39	T
SERENAM			
Otium poscunt artes, mentem tranquillam, serenam, sudam: . .	448	Orationes	23
SERENISSIMAE			
In Obitum Serenissimae Reginae Annae.	435	Poem.Lat.	T
Quin & Serenissimae Principis Isabellae laudes, virtutesque,	441	Orationes	2
SERENISSIME			
Serenissime Domine noster, Iacobe Inuictissime.	458	Epistolae	1
Serenissime Domine noster, Iacobe Potentissime.	460	Epistolae	1
SERENISSIMI			
Oratio Qua auspicatissimum Serenissimi Principis Caroli Reditum ex	444	Orationes	T
Aedificarunt olim nobis Serenissimi Reges Collegia, eaque fundarunt	458	Epistolae	22
SERENISSIMIS			
immunitates nostrae a Serenissimis Regibus concessae ab Augustissimo	468	Epistolae	21
SERENISSIMO			
habita Chartae nostrae a Serenissimo Principe Henrico 8 indultae,	467	Epistolae	22
SERENISSIMUS			
Quare optime fecit Rex Serenissimus, qui virtutes tuas magnis	466	Epistolae	12
SERENUS			
Non est angulus vspiam serenus, ...	428	Mem.Matr.10	13
SERIA			
Romano, sed res seria Roma tibi est:	416	Lucus 27	2
SERICATAM			
praesertim sericatam hanc stultitiam contere, Academiaeque iura,	461	Epistolae	23
SERICUS			
Sericus es dictis, factis pannusia Baucis:	414	Lucus 22	1
SERITUR			
Seritur fama in hoc saeculo, vt in sequenti metatur:	441	Orationes	19
SERMO			
Obscurus sermo negotijs ineptus; quae cum plerumque implicata sint,	470	Epistolae	28
Tandem, ne et ipse peccem, breuis sit sermo, atque pressus. . .	470	Epistolae	32
SERO			
vestrae coronae ciuili & literariae tertiam Coelestem sero adiungat.	459	Epistolae	21
SERPANT			
Ni facias, vt opes linguae per brachia serpant, ...	414	Lucus 22	3
SERPENTES			
cum Hercule, serpentesque interficere voluptatis, vt iter tantum,	452	Orationes	7
SERPERE			
permittat nostram hanc Inter victrices hederam sibi serpere Lauros.	455	Orationes	18
SERTA			
Spicula mutemus: capias Tu serta Rosarum, ...	405	Passio 6	3
SERUARENT			
Seruarentque sacrum clauibus ordinem;	391	Musae 17	6
SERUASTIS			
Principis innocuam seruastis numina Vitam, ...	433	Poem.Lat.	34
SERUI			
Humillimi serui subditique vestri Procancellarius Reliquusque Senatus	459	Epistolae	22
SERUIAT			
Corporeque atque animo. Totus mihi seruiat Orbis.	421	Tr.Mortis	101
SERUILES			
vapores seruiles ad nubes educti aeque magnum tonitru edent ac regij.	452	Orationes	17

	PAGE	TITLE	LINE
SERUIRE			
Quare malui seruire auritus Tuis, creberrima Antiquitatis lectione	473	Epistolae	19
SERVATOS			
Exere terra caput, servatos proijce flores,	210	Cam.1613-b BR	3
SESE			
Surrexit vna & illa, seseque extulit:	423	Mem.Matr.2	27
SEUERA			
Virgo pudens, vxor fida, seuera parens:	429	Mem.Matr.13	2
SEUERAE			
Et quicquid vspiam est seuerae foeminae,	422	Mem.Matr.2	2
SEUERIOREM			
supercilium quibus caperatam seucrioremque Philosophiam expugnare	440	Orationes	11
SEUERUS			
Lepos seuerus, Pallas mixta Gratijs;	423	Mem.Matr.2	30
Ipsis seuerus orbibus;	427	Mem.Matr.8	6
SEXCENTA			
quamuis enim sexcenta huiusmodi praediola Tua gratia permutare nolim,	472	Epistolae	29
SEXCENTAS			
Perdere sexcentas? crescit tamen hydra nocendi	419	Tr.Mortis	35
Perdere sexcentas? crescet tamen hydra nocendi	419	Tr.Mortis V	35
SEXUM			
Vtrumque sexum dote ne mulctauerit.	422	Mem.Matr.2	9
SEXUS			
Hic sita foeminei laus & victoria sexus:	429	Mem.Matr.13	1
SI			
Tum tibi, si placeat, fugientia tempora reddam;	386	Musae 2	9
Si, quia felices olim dixere poetae	387	Musae 6	3
An rectius nos, si vices vertas, probi,	388	Musae 8	9
Scilicet emptorem si res aut parcior aetas	388	Musae 9	5
Quae ratio per se, si sit adulta, facit.	388	Musae 9	12
Quotidiana suas poscant si fercula grates,	389	Musae 12	9
Tollantur si cuncta malus quae polluit vsus,	390	Musae 13	3
Verum heus! si reputes, tibi tuisque	391	Musae 15	7
O caecum populum! si bona res siet	392	Musae 17	11
si vestros animos regant	395	Musae 25	18
Nulla tibi si signa placent, e nubibus arcum	396	Musae 26	3
Ex praelio vndae ignisque (si Physicis fides)	396	Musae 27	1
Si numero starent praelia, non animis.	398	Musae 33	8
Ne, si flamma nouis adolescat mota flabellis,	399	Musae 35	11
Nam si te cuperem secare versu,	400	Musae 37	14
Quod scribo, & placeo, si placeo, tuum est.	403	Musae 40	14
Si tibi non illud placeat mirabile corpus,	404	Passio 2	3
Quam nihil illudis! si, quae tua purpura fingit,	405	Passio 7	7
At non lusus erit, si quem tu laeta necasti	405	Passio 7	9
Si, Christe, dum suffigeris, tuae vestes	406	Passio 10	1
Christe, fluas semper; ne, si tua flumina cessent,	406	Passio 13	5
Sedula si fuerit, perterebrare potest.	410	Lucus 2	6
Si sursum iacias, in caput ipsa ruit.	410	Lucus 4	8
Quam si ipse solus omnia interuerteret,	412	Lucus 13	3
Magnas es; esto. Bulla si vocaberis,	413	Lucus 17	1
Difficilis esse haud soleo: nam, pol, si forem,	413	Lucus 17	3
Christe, super fluctus si non discurrere detur:	414	Lucus 19	3
Rotundus in te: ramque si ansatus sies,	414	Lucus 20	7
Si ducat agmen, reprime; sin claudat, sinas.	414	Lucus 20	14
Sera nimis lacryma haec, si lacrymabis, erit.	415	Lucus 23	12
Si non per species, nequimus ipsi,	415	Lucus 24	9
Ararumque Hominumque ortum si mente pererres,	417	Lucus 29	1
Assiduus tyro, si sit spectanda voluntas.	419	Tr.Mortis	32
Vt, si gratia tanta copuletur	421	Lucus 34	7
Si licet, immoriar: vel si tua visio vita est,	421	Lucus 35	5
Non video, certum est iurare; aut si hoc vetuisti,	421	Lucus 35	9
In flumen moerore nigrum si funderer ardens,	422	Mem.Matr.1	5
Aut si negotio hora sumenda est, rei	423	Mem.Matr.2	32
Verum heus, si nequeas caelo demittere matrem,	424	Mem.Matr.3	7
Vtrumque si praederis Indum,	425	Mem.Matr.6	7
Impos medendi, occidere si potes,	425	Mem.Matr.6	9
Tentando sanum: si calet, aestuans,	426	Mem.Matr.6	14
Si totus infler, si tumeam crepax,	426	Mem.Matr.6	17
Si-quas mens agitet moles (dum pectora saeuo	432	Poem.Lat.	9
Quod si fata illi longam invidere salutem	432	Poem.Lat.	26
Vt si recisis arboribus meis	434	Poem.Lat.	29
Hoc mihi legatum tristi si funere praestes,	434	Poem.Lat.	7
Quid mihi si facies nigra est? hoc, Ceste, colore	437	Poem.Lat.	1
Si nigro sit terra solo, quis despicit aruum?	437	Poem.Lat.	5
Si per haec ludicra nostra pars aliquis eius laetitiae,	443	Orationes	9
si spinula vlla Coronae Regiae emollita sit vel retusa;	443	Orationes	11
si per tempus liceret effari, non licet per multitudinem,	443	Orationes	28
nullum non angulum verrunt (ac si perdiderint ingenium) vt Spartam	445	Orationes	36
& polymiti, vt si minus id assequantur, quod primum intendunt,	446	Orationes	6
Quid si cochleas colligeret cum Caligula, praesertim cum possit	446	Orationes	12
Quid si muscas captaret cum Domitiano?	446	Orationes	14
Quod si Nuptiae in se graues sunt, quanto magis Principum,	446	Orationes	34
quod quidem vbi gentium si non ab Hispano sperandum?	447	Orationes	30
ac si Fatis a fuso essent atque consilijs, sine quibus ne vnum quidem	449	Orationes	29
Quid enim si praeter Nuptias, prolem, tranquillitatem, etiam	450	Orationes	4
Omne regnum suo Principi carcer est, aut si excedat, alienum:	450	Orationes	13
ac si non gregaria essent animalia, sed tigres aut vrsi.	450	Orationes	21
Porro si Politicos audiamus, salus regnorum pendet a vicinis,	450	Orationes	25
Quid si hic lateat etiam Temperantia, rara in Principibus virtus,	452	Orationes	1
vti anguillae, aut si mutant locum, gestantur, tanquam onera,	452	Orationes	10
ac si corpora sua non abirent olim in elementa, sed in bellaria aut	452	Orationes	13

SI (cont'd)	PAGE	TITLE	LINE
aptior esset tali historiae) si Romanorum Imperatorum incredibilem	452	Orationes	21
locus est vmbris & recessibus, etiam si quis Principem pingat.	453	Orationes	15
si Reges ipsi quandoque suauitates suas populari aceto condiant.	453	Orationes	18
si amor virginis eo pertraxit Principem, quo tandem ducet amor	453	Orationes	27
idem impetus, qui peragrauit Hispaniam, si opus sit, superabit;	453	Orationes	31
si quis de Principe aliquo, quis sit futurus aut qualis,	454	Orationes	8
si speculum Inuidiae ostendas, quo deformitatem suam intueatur!	454	Orationes	20
Quod si necesse sit iterum exire patria, qui nunc inuenit viam,	455	Orationes	7
si tantum Honori Tuo superesset otij ad legendum, quantum a nobis	457	Epistolae	8
Quod si tam integrum tibi esset gratificari nobis in terra & aere,	457	Epistolae	21
Circumspice, si placet, Terrarum Reges, mutus est mundus vniuersus,	458	Epistolae	5
aut si suos, quia dederunt, non a se compositos, scriptos,	458	Epistolae	24
Si enim in regno vestro Hibernico lignum nascitur permanens,	459	Epistolae	15
Quod si Artaxerxes olim paululum aquae a Sinaeta, subiecto suo,	460	Epistolae	11
vt si officia nostra minus respondeant magnitudini beneficiorum,	460	Epistolae	15
sed si ablatus fuisset Fluuius noster, per quem vicini agri opulentia	460	Epistolae	22
mixtam personam reddidit quam si Episcopi more pristino Cancellis	461	Epistolae	27
sane dubitamus vlli, si prae defectu aquae, commeatusque inopia,	462	Epistolae	2
si qui alij exurgant promissores magnifici et hiantes, qui,	462	Epistolae	30
quod si tertia detur et quarta, paratos nos habebis ad gratulationem,	465	Epistolae	25
Quod si forense quippiam nos spectans, dum incumbis muneri,	466	Epistolae	4
cuius Libri si alij alijs (tanquam montes olim) imponerentur,	467	Epistolae	30
Quod si et numerus Scriptorum intumescat, et precium, quae abyssus	468	Epistolae	2
Quod si oppidani nostri (more suo) Musarum iura et diplomata	468	Epistolae	25
si quantum eruditio Regis profuerit Reipublicae, tantum fauoris nobis	469	Epistolae	24
si placeat vices meas tantisper supplere donec Academia orationem	470	Epistolae	5
Iam si inter commendandum adhibeas ei calamistros vti iuuenculae,	470	Epistolae	18
ac si iuuenili potius impetu correptus, quam adductus maturo	471	Epistolae	25
si tam abiectus sim, vt laboribus meis plurimis atque assidua	472	Epistolae	12
commendatione, si huc reciderit omnis studiorum spes fructusque:	472	Epistolae	15
Cui sententiae si fidem adhibeas, assensumque Tuum veritati omni	473	Epistolae	10
SI-QUAS			
Si-quas mens agitet moles (dum pectora saeuo	432	Poem.Lat.	9
SIBI			
Seposuit Diuina sibi, cum conderet orbem,	402	Musae 39	15
Mitis agas: tenerae duplicant sibi verbera mentes,	406	Passio 9	5
Quamque ipse lucis tesseram sibi negat,	407	Passio 16	7
Dum cor omne suum sibi requirat	408	Passio 19	7
Praeflorat sibi nuptias futuras.	408	Passio 19	13
At sibi collisit fictile Daemon opus.	408	Passio 20	2
Vt discat sibi quisque, quid vtile: nempe nocebat	412	Lucus 9	3
Ipsi sibi sunt nequiter facillimi.	413	Lucus 17	4
Atque ipsi sibi sunt mola & farina.	415	Lucus 24	15
Pontificem tandem nacta est sibi Roma poetam:	417	Lucus 28	1
Rure, sibi dixit Musa fuisse probro.	431	Mem.Matr.19	2
Granum Sinapis, acre Alijs, crescens sibi:	437	Poem.Lat.	26
Polycrates cum annulum sibi dilectum in mare dimisisset,	444	Orationes	14
asserunt Medici vnamquamque regionem sua sibi sufficere,	444	Orationes	25
incumbant sibi inuicem imperia, tanquam ligna obliqua, aliter magna	450	Orationes	27
neminemque esse sui negligentiorem, quam qui sibi parcat.	452	Orationes	35
permittat nostram hanc Inter victrices hederam sibi serpere Lauros.	455	Orationes	18
de nullo vnquam Filio Alma Mater, quantum de Te sibi polliceatur.	457	Epistolae	26
conseruantes sibi Illos Fontes, a quibus ipsi olim hauserunt?	461	Epistolae	31
SIC			
Sic o te (iuuenem, senemue) credat	385	Musae	10
Sic tu nunc iuuenis factus, egoque senex.	386	Musae 2	4
Sic Catharis noua sola placent; res, verba nouantur:	386	Musae 3	3
Pallada gorgoneam, sic tua verba placent.	387	Musae 6	4
Sic laudandus erit nactus sublimia Praesul,	387	Musae 7	9
Annon sic mercamur agros? quibus ecce Redemptor	388	Musae 9	3
Cur sic displiceat vox aliena tibi?	388	Musae 9	10
Sic vbi iam mulier decerpti conscia pomi	390	Musae 12	13
Non sic effugit angulus vel vnus	391	Musae 15	5
Sic nunc plena boni sunt omnia Fratris, amore	393	Musae 21	3
Sic ex profano Cosmico & Catharo potest	396	Musae 27	3
Quis sic amicum excipiet, vt Cathari Deum,	397	Musae 28	13
Sic acuunt zelum frigora tanta tuum?	399	Musae 35	6
Perge, decus Regum; sic, Augustissime, plures	402	Musae 39	33
Sic pulsare tuas, exclusis luctibus, ausint	402	Musae 39	35
Gaudia sola fores: sic quicquid somnia mentis	402	Musae 39	36
Sic positis rugis, quibus irretita libido	402	Musae 39	38
Sic tuus effundi gestit pro crimine sanguis,	404	Passio 3	1
O barbaros! sic os rependitis sanctum,	404	Passio 5	1
Sputando, praedicando? sic Aquas vitae	404	Passio 5	3
Sic vnguenta solent manu fricari:	405	Passio 8	2
Sic toti medicaris ipse mundo.	405	Passio 8	3
Sic omnibus videris ad modum visus.	406	Passio 12	4
Sic, pro Maiestate, Deum, non perdere vitam	408	Passio 17	7
Sic mucronatam reddunt suspiria mentem,	410	Lucus 2	3
Sic Hominis moles animaque & corpore constat,	417	Lucus 31	3
Haec fuerant: sic Tisiphone virguncula lusit.	418	Tr.Mortis	23
Sic olim cecidere.	419	Tr.Mortis	48
Vno ictu: non sic pestis, non stella maligno	420	Tr.Mortis	80
Nec sic parentem ducar ad optimam:	425	Mem.Matr.6	10
Sic aeuum exigitur tardum, dum praepetis anni	428	Mem.Matr.9	13
Sic excelsa humilisque simul loca dissita iunxit,	429	Mem.Matr.13	5
Sic quasi Dijs certem, magnos accersere montes:	432	Poem.Lat.	6
Viuite, dum mortem ostendam: sic tempora vestram	432	Poem.Lat.	15
Non comedant famam, sic nulla obliuia potent.	432	Poem.Lat.	16
Sic lactare animos & sic ostendere gemmam	432	Poem.Lat.	31

SIC (cont'd)	PAGE	TITLE	LINE
Sic non Phoebus iam plus te splendeat ortus	211	Cam.1613-b BR	15
sic bonorum Principum facilis Astrologia:	445	Orationes	7
sic & ipse excerpam e Principis rebus gestis pugillum, vnam actionem	445	Orationes	31
siccine abijsti solus? cur non nos omnes tecum?	451	Orationes	7
Sic tunc omnes strepebant: huiusmodi lamentis & quiritationibus plena	451	Orationes	9
Inde ego sic mecum: gaudeo quidem de ingenti amore in Principem,	451	Orationes	21
Sic pascunt se indies, ac si corpora sua non abirent olim . .	452	Orationes	13
sic idem animus, qui nuper versatus est in forma & figuris vultus,	454	Orationes	6
sic & Noster qui clanculum exijt, vsque ad Pyrenaeas nubes . .	454	Orationes	30
sic Tu etiam dignitates ab optimo Rege desumptas in vniuersam	456	Epistolae	11
sic disparatae foelicitates hinc a populo, illinc a Principe,	456	Epistolae	24
sunt, vt sic scripta vestra omni dente, tum edacis temporis,	459	Epistolae	18
sic merita tua ita ascensura, vt eorum vis et virtus ad nos . .	464	Epistolae	18
neque enim sic effugies cum honoribus, quin laetitia nostra te	465	Epistolae	22
vt sic vna opera vtriusque Reipublicae calculum et ciuilis . .	465	Epistolae	26
Sic a Natura comparatum est, Ignis et Virtus semper ascendunt,	466	Epistolae	10
Sic apud veterum aras, post ingentes Hecatombas, exiguam thuris micam	469	Epistolae	16
quippe, qui sic colligebam; si tam abiectus sim, vt laboribus meis	472	Epistolae	11
sic existimes nihil Mortalium firmiori flagrare in Te desiderio,	473	Epistolae	4
SICCA			
Anglia cur solum fuso sine sanguine sicca est, ...	411	Lucus 6	1
Sicca meis lacrymis Thamesis vicina videtur, ...	422	Mem.Matr.1	3
Quis enim sicca vbera et mammas arentes tam nobilis parentis aequo	461	Epistolae	32
SICCAM			
Siccam animam sapientissimam esse dixit obscurus ille philosophus;	460	Epistolae	20
SICCATORES			
paludumque istos siccatores (solem officio suo priuantes) vi verborum	462	Epistolae	19
SICCINE			
siccine pessima? at fuerit; si amor virginis eo pertraxit Principem,	453	Orationes	27
SICCIOR			
Virtutumque choro siccior ipse tuo.	422	Mem.Matr.1	4
SICCIS			
Iisque siccis adeo vt os Molossorum	429	Mem.Matr.12	3
SICCITAS			
Sed siccitas anni huius derisit inceptum et plus effecit quam mille	461	Epistolae	11
SICULI			
Vel Catapulta potest, Siculique inuenta magistri, ...	419	Tr.Mortis	41
SIES			
Rotundus in te: namque si ansatus sies, ...	414	Lucus 20	7
SIET			
O caecum populum! si bona res siet	392	Musae 17	11
SIGILLI			
Mag. Sigilli Custodis post editam ab eo Instaurationem Magnam.	436	Poem.Lat.	T
SIGILLUM			
Addas sigillum: nempe Symbolum suae	438	Poem.Lat.	6
Tandem & fessa manus, dedit sigillum.	439	Poem.Lat.	12
(In quo fas nihil est rumpi) donare sigillum.	439	Poem.Lat.	15
SIGNA			
Nulla tibi si signa placent, e nubibus arcum	396	Musae 26	3
qui solebant signa in hostes inijcere, vt milites acrius ea . .	451	Orationes	32
coelestis an sublunaris, sed quae signa, quo motu transeat. . .	454	Orationes	13
SIGNACULO			
De Signaculo Crucis.	389	Musae 10	T
SIGNATAM			
iam olim Regi notam atque signatam dignissime praeficiaris Fisco,	469	Epistolae	21
SIGNIFER			
Speculationisque; Aequitatis signifer;	436	Poem.Lat.	9
SIGNIFICANTES			
significantes oportere Reges ijs partibus antecellere homines,	447	Orationes	4
SIGNO			
Sin nebulis parcas, & nostro parcito signo, ...	396	Musae 26	7
idem feruor qui impar sub amoris signo meritus est, ad vera castra	453	Orationes	30
SIGNUM			
Sed nec coniugij signum, Melvine, probabis?	396	Musae 26	1
Legitimi signum connubiale tori.	396	Musae 26	12
vbi ille signum sustulerit, Leones Britannici (e quorum ossibus	449	Orationes	17
SILEAM			
Stulta: semel scribo, perpetuo vt sileam.	431	Mem.Matr.19	8
SILENTI			
Totum offuscari peteres, vt nocte silenti	433	Poem.Lat.	38
SILENTIO			
Quinimo Artes hic sunt quiete & silentio cultae, tranquillitas,	441	Orationes	14
praeferuida illa desideria silentio suo sepulta nunc languescere,	471	Epistolae	28
Cum stare gratis cum silentio possim?	472	Epistolae	18
SILENTIUM			
nostra occurrant, oratio nostra est silentium, atque eloquentia,	444	Orationes	3
SILERE			
omnium coelestiores animi, quorum pietatis interest non silere.	445	Orationes	11
SILICEM			
Qui silicem tundit, (mirum tamen) elicit ignem:	410	Lucus 3	1
SILICES			
Rupes tenaces & silices ferunt	393	Musae 23	9
SIM			
si tam abiectus sim, vt laboribus meis plurimis atque assidua	472	Epistolae	12
receptusque sim in aliquem apud Honorem Tuum locum, magis id adeo	472	Epistolae	20
SIMILEM			
Affectusque mei similem; nec languida misce	427	Mem.Matr.7	30
SIMILES			
In nebulas similesque tui res gaudia nunquid	426	Mem.Matr.7	2
Quomodo possetis similes esse Alexandro Magno nisi eius res gestas	441	Orationes	18

SIMILI	PAGE	TITLE	LINE
Coepisti, pergas simili res texere filo.	402	Musae 39	19
SIMILIS			
Haud nostro similis, cui necesse,	415	Lucus 24	2
At nunc exucco similis tua gloria RAMO	416	Lucus 25	5
SIMONEM			
In Simonem Magum.	410	Lucus 4	T
SIMPLICITATI			
tantum qui eruditionem simplicitati Christianae putant aduersam,	461	Epistolae	17
SIMPLICITER			
quam simpliciter vobiscum agam, quam non longe abeam Oratorum more,	445	Orationes	35
SIMUL			
Non moreris solus: Mundus simul interit in te,	409	Passio 21	1
Sic excelsa humilisque simul loca dissita iunxit,	429	Mem.Matr.13	5
agam vobiscum, simulque & laboribus meis, & vestrae fidei consulam,	445	Orationes	28
quam subito dispereunt, simul ac concrepuit incendium militare:	448	Orationes	19
expectamus indies futurum, Almae Matris amorem tecum simul euehas.	462	Epistolae	29
SIMULANS			
et Procancellarius Academiam simulans vel maximos magnatum inter	470	Epistolae	25
SIMULTAS			
(Et quem non stimularet haec simultas?)	400	Musae 37	18
SIMUS			
pax adeo Musis summe necessaria est, vt sine ea nihil simus.	448	Orationes	17
SIN			
Res ampliantur, sin per aduersam videt,	388	Musae 8	13
Sin, Melvine, pedes alienos postulet infans,	388	Musae 9	9
Praesul, cur renuis? sin mala, pauculos	392	Musae 17	12
Sin nebulis parcas, & nostro parcito signo,	396	Musae 26	7
Si ducat agmen, reprime; sin claudat, sinas.	414	Lucus 20	14
Animo renidentes prius. Sin rarior	423	Mem.Matr.2	25
Sin pluuiam, fletus suppeditasset aquas.	427	Mem.Matr.9	10
SINAETA			
Quod si Artaxerxes olim paululum aquae a Sinaeta, subiecto suo,	460	Epistolae	11
SINAPIS			
Granum Sinapis, acre Alijs, crescens sibi:	437	Poem.Lat.	26
SINAS			
Haud mihi cor saxo durius esse sinas.	410	Lucus 1	6
Si ducat agmen, reprime; sin claudat, sinas.	414	Lucus 20	14
SINE			
Natare sine clarissima potest cruce?	389	Musae 10	9
Vos sine maternis hymnis infantia vidit,	389	Musae 12	5
E creaturis sine mentis vsu	390	Musae 14	13
viuentes sine vestibus,	395	Musae 25	5
Qua sine vos miseri lentius itis ope.	399	Musae 33	26
Anglia cur solum fuso sine sanguine sicca est,	411	Lucus 6	1
Sit licet in pelago semper, sine fluctibus illa est,	411	Lucus 6	3
Vel sine luce solum, vel sine mente caro.	417	Lucus 31	6
Omniaque haec vt transadigant sine crimine costas,	418	Tr.Mortis	29
Quin, sine, te cernam; quoties iam dixero, cernam;	421	Lucus 35	3
Cur sine te, votis immoriturus, ago?	421	Lucus 35	6
Ipse tuae solum adnectam, sine murmure, thensae.	426	Mem.Matr.7	16
Nunc sorti patec, expositus sine matre procellis,	428	Mem.Matr.11	7
Sol sine sole tuo! quam te tum nubibus atris	433	Poem.Lat.	37
Hos oculos laetos, hunc sine nube diem:	211	Cam.1613-b BR	14
& sollicitudines Principum sine condimento sint atque embammate?	446	Orationes	11
bello pacem, sine qua omnis vita procella, & mundus solitudo.	448	Orationes	8
pax adeo Musis summe necessaria est, vt sine ea nihil simus.	448	Orationes	17
essent atque consilijs, sine quibus ne vnum quidem filum torquerent:	449	Orationes	30
Dij te perdant, cum malis tuis & arena sine calce;	451	Orationes	6
SINGULA			
Et numerat mortes singula gutta pares;	415	Lucus 23	10
Invitoque fugit singula stella pede:	210	Cam.1613-b BR	2
SINGULARE			
Non vnum quid spectant aut singulare Magni animi, sed varia solent	446	Orationes	4
SINGULAREM			
Et cum ob perspicacitatem singularem iam olim Regi notam atque	469	Epistolae	20
SINGULARI			
de humanitate tua singulari, studioque in nos iam olim	462	Epistolae	24
SINGULARIS			
quem singularis doctrina exemit a populo, & quasi mixtam personam	461	Epistolae	26
SINGULARUM			
Natura suas dotes, vt indigentia singularum regionum omnes connectat:	450	Orationes	19
SINT			
Sintque ausae thalamum solis adire tui.	384	Musae	6
Et mea sint canis scripta referta tuis.	386	Musae 2	6
Auresque superas: arbitri ipsi sint litis,	392	Musae 20	4
Vtrum tenore sacra nostra sint necne	392	Musae 20	5
Sint tibi vel stellis laudes, & laudibus anni:	402	Musae 39	34
& sollicitudines Principum sine condimento sint atque embammate?	446	Orationes	12
Cum tamen splendida plerumque vitrea sint, claritatem fragilitate	448	Orationes	5
praesertim cum futura incerta sint, & nullis perspicillis,	449	Orationes	24
superbi sua tantum nosse, praesertim cum in vno regno non sint omnia:	450	Orationes	18
Falleris, nusquam plura bona, cum etiam mala illic sint aurea:	451	Orationes	3
licet celebres sint canes Britannici, & plus iusto celebres,	454	Orationes	17
quae cum plerumque implicata sint, nisi candida phrasi telam	470	Epistolae	29
quod reclusae sint fores, receptusque sim in aliquem apud Honorem	472	Epistolae	20
SINU			
vt Alma Mater libentissime caput reclinet in tuo sinu, oculusque	465	Epistolae	13
SINUS			
Quae cordis latebras sinusque caecos	411	Lucus 5	12
Te mille nasi, mille rideant sinus.	414	Lucus 20	10

	PAGE	TITLE	LINE
SICNIS			
Sicnis excelsas ad arces	394	Musae 23	39
SIS			
& cum ipse sis in summa arbore altera manu prehendis Regem,	456	Epistolae	13
Et licet, quo proprior sis Regi, eo videaris nobis remotior,	464	Epistolae	16
etsi tu qui scribis (vti quiuis priuatus) inferioris sis subsellij,	470	Epistolae	23
SISTAT			
Annulus hos reuocet, sistatque libidinis vndas	396	Musae 26	11
SISTATUR			
Cum tener ad sacros infans sistatur aquales,	388	Musae 9	1
SISTE			
Saepius aspergis. Siste, pudore vacas.	387	Musae 7	2
Siste tuum fletum & gemitus: namque imbribus istis	415	Lucus 23	13
Siste parum cantus, dum legis ista, tuos.	427	Mem.Matr.9	2
SISTERE			
Enixas pueros matres se sistere templis	389	Musae 12	1
SISTIMUS			
Sistimus hic, inquit fatum, sat prata biberunt	272	Tr.Mortis VS	100
SISTIT			
Et ipse Iordan sistit aquas stupens;	394	Musae 23	42
SIT			
Cum prope sit nobis Musa, Medusa procul?	387	Musae 6	2
Quae ratio per se, si sit adulta, facit.	388	Musae 9	12
Et tibi sit nemo praes, vbi poscis opem.	389	Musae 9	16
Nil sit crassius, impolitiusue)	401	Musae 37	46
Nescia sit metae; venula, cella tua est.	404	Passio 2	2
Viuat, & in mortem vita sit illa tuam.	405	Passio 7	10
Sit licet in pelago semper, sine fluctibus illa est,	411	Lucus 6	3
Parcite luminibus, sitque lucerna domus:	413	Lucus 15	4
Quam satur & suauis sit tibi Roma iocus.	416	Lucus 27	6
Assiduus tyro, si sit spectanda voluntas.	419	Tr.Mortis	32
Sitque omnis motus nescia tanta quies,	424	Mem.Matr.3	8
Quaeque domus Dominae sit, grauitate docent.	425	Mem.Matr.5	8
Sit quasi fasciculus crescens, & nidus odorum.	427	Mem.Matr.7	27
Expeto, tanquam haec sit nostri medicina doloris?	433	Poem.Lat.	46
Quis, nisi qui manibus Briareus, oculisque sit Argus,	435	Poem.Lat.	5
Cum per te sit res ambitiosa mori.	435	Poem.Lat.	8
Cernis vt exusta semper sit fronte viator;	437	Poem.Lat.	3
Si nigro sit terra solo, quis despicit aruum?	437	Poem.Lat.	5
Cum mihi sit facies fumus, quas pectore flammas	437	Poem.Lat.	9
Quisnam horum maior sit, dubitatur, amor.	437	Poem.Lat.	2
Cuiusnam maior sit, dubitatur, amor.	437	Poem.Lat. V	2
Quare adsis Princeps, aliis Academia mons sit,	210	Cam.1613-a BR	7
veremur ne nihil hic sit, quod magnitudini praesentiae vestrae	441	Orationes	9
certe cum duplex fulgor sit, qui mundi oculos perstringat,	441	Orationes	12
si spinula vlla Coronae Regiae emollita sit vel retusa;	443	Orationes	11
vbique deferentibus, vt nullus sit angulus corporis, nulla venula,	445	Orationes	3
tamen nimium efferre vos, cum Virginitas ipsa fructus sit Nuptiarum:	446	Orationes	28
quo eorum conditio sublimior, eo maior cura adhibenda sit.	446	Orationes	36
enim minus refert, qualis quaeque sit mater, e qua liberi quaerantur,	447	Orationes	10
resolutione illa vltima, nulla sit distinctio populi aut principis:	452	Orationes	15
idem impetus, qui peragrauit Hispaniam, si opus sit, superabit;	453	Orationes	32
praesertim cum amico fidere periculosius sit, quam hostem superare.	453	Orationes	32
de Principe aliquo, quis sit futurus aut qualis, recte diuinaret,	454	Orationes	9
non respicitur, quae materia sit, coelestis an sublunaris,	454	Orationes	12
vtinam & nunc sit tanta patriae tenacitas, vt nunquam Princeps se	455	Orationes	5
Quod si necesse sit iterum exire patria, qui nunc inuenit viam,	455	Orationes	7
neque amplius quaerendum sit Tibi, Almae Nutrici quid repones.	462	Epistolae	16
vt cum ipse eruditionis Princeps sit, illi etiam honores qui finitimi	463	Epistolae	22
tibi hunc honorem, et faxit, vt tibi gloriae sit, omnibus saluti.	469	Epistolae	5
Dein, oratio clara sit, perspicua, pellucens.	470	Epistolae	28
Tandem, ne et ipse peccem, breuis sit sermo, atque pressus.	470	Epistolae	32
non quin pectus meum plenum Tui sit, atque effusissimum in omnia	471	Epistolae	21
SITA			
Hic sita foeminei laus & victoria sexus:	429	Mem.Matr.13	1
SITI			
in Musarum monte editissimo, in ipso Parnasso siti sumus, liberiorem,	449	Orationes	33
SITIM			
qui restinxisti sitim exarescentium Musarum, et Xerxes istos,	462	Epistolae	7
SITIRENT			
qui vtrumque curasti, vt neque sitirent Musae, neque flagrarent.	457	Epistolae	20
SITIS			
cum eo sitis ordine atque habitu, quo nos in hoc regno omnes esse	441	Orationes	1
cum tanti sitis & in Principibus Vestris, & in vobismetipsis,	441	Orationes	8
SITULAS			
Parate situlas, Ethnici, lagenasque,	405	Passio 5	8
SIUE			
Non derididiculumue, siue ineptum,	401	Musae 37	34
instructior ad omnem causam, paratiorue siue a doctrina, siue ab vsu;	462	Epistolae	22
SOBRIUS			
Caesar sobrius ad rei Latinae	401	Musae 37	42
SOCIJ			
Vnquam fugari, quam tui socij solent.	389	Musae 10	3
Nunc primum socij mors foret atra tui?	415	Lucus 23	2
SOCIJS			
Affectus socijs tuis remittens.	401	Musae 37	32
SOCIO			
Nec tu pro socio doleas, qui fugit ad illud	415	Lucus 23	15
SOCIOS			
Omnia suspendit naso, sociosque lacessit:	418	Tr.Mortis	13

SOCIUS	PAGE	TITLE	LINE
Stellarum socius, pellitus exuor.	424	Mem.Matr.4	8
SOLALITATE			
(Cum plerumque tua sodalitate	401	Musae 37	45
SOL			
Sol generat populum luce fouente nouum.	384	Musae	2
Sol sine sole tuo! quam te tum nubibus atris	433	Poem.Lat.	37
ita Sol & Coelum producunt flores, qui symbola sunt spei, . .	446	Orationes	32
SOLA			
Sic Catharis noua sola placent; res, verba nouantur:	386	Musae 3	3
Non tibi fingendi sola taberna patet.	386	Musae 3	6
Sola tibi Sappho, feminaque vna placet?	387	Musae 5	2
Haec facit ad nasum sola loquela tuum.	391	Musae 16	6
Perstringunt vestros carmina sola duces.	400	Musae 36	4
Sola mihi plenos, ait, exhibet Anglia cultus.	402	Musae 39	13
Gaudia sola fores: sic quicquid somnia mentis	402	Musae 39	36
Sola Iacobaeum decantent carmina nomen.	402	Musae 39	40
Fides gigantem sola, vel facit nanum.	406	Passio 12	5
Nec Glans sola nocet; mortem quandoque susurrat	420	Tr.Mortis	83
Quandoque voltus sola maiestas, Dolor.	422	Mem.Matr.2	7
Nos autem flemus: res ea sola tuis.	427	Mem.Matr.9	8
Nos flendo: haec nostrum tessera sola ducum.	427	Mem.Matr.9	12
Tempus edax rerum, tuque o mors improba sola es, ...	433	Poem.Lat.	41
Frustra igitur sudo: superest mihi sola voluptas, ...	435	Poem.Lat.	7
Deducant linguae funera sola tuae.	438	Poem.Lat.	6
ne pacem, quae sola incubat artibus, & obstetricatur, minus quam par	448	Orationes	33
SOLARIUM			
In Solarium.	417	Lucus 31	T
SOLATIO			
Statim a solatio aspectus Tui, Ego auctior iam gaudio atque . . .	471	Epistolae	17
SOLE			
Sol sine sole tuo! quam te tum nubibus atris	433	Poem.Lat.	37
Incendat tacitas, sole morante, faces:	211	Cam.1613-b BR	6
SOLEBANT			
qui solebant signa in hostes inijcere, vt milites acrius ea . . .	451	Orationes	32
solebant ventres eximere, quos in arca repositos abijciebant	452	Orationes	27
SOLEBAS			
Ah, cernam; Tu, qui caecos sanare solebas, ...	421	Lucus 35	7
SOLEM			
Ergo etiam Solem dicas, ignaue, superbum, ...	387	Musae 7	5
Scilicet talem liquet esse solem;	390	Musae 14	9
Ad Solem deficientem.	407	Passio 16	T
Solem ex Oceano Veteres exurgere fingunt	412	Lucus 8	1
glasto se inficientes, in vxorum corporibus, Solem, Lunam, & Stellas;	446	Orationes	30
paludumque istos siccatores (solem officio suo priuantes) vi verborum	462	Epistolae	19
SOLENT			
Qua parte tractari solent, ...	388	Musae 8	12
Vnquam fugari, quam tui socij solent.	389	Musae 10	3
Ordine discerni maxima bella solent.	399	Musae 33	28
Sic vnguenta solent manu fricari:	405	Passio 8	2
sed varia solent esse eorum consilia, finesque multiplices . . .	446	Orationes	5
solent enim Studiosorum suffragia enixus gloriae, sollicitudine	469	Epistolae	9
vt halitus tenuiores solent, qui primo caloris suasu excitati atque	471	Epistolae	29
SOLEO			
Difficilis esse haud soleo: nam, pol, si forem, ...	413	Lucus 17	3
SOLERTISSIMUS			
& scientiae augmentum ex hoc itinere captauit solertissimus Princeps?	450	Orationes	6
SOLES			
Non illa soles terere comptu lubricos, ...	422	Mem.Matr.2	10
Nos misere flemus, solesque obducimus almos	427	Mem.Matr.9	5
At forte matrem perdere haud soles demens:	429	Mem.Matr.12	9
sume tecum amorem illum quo soles beare Amplitudini tuae deuotissimos	464	Epistolae	27
SOLET			
Cui non absimilis sensus inesse solet.	396	Musae 26	8
Lampada, qua studijs inuigilare solet.	398	Musae 33	18
fieri participes eius sanguinis, qui tantos spiritus solet infundere.	440	Orationes	20
vti sanguis solet in re dubia ad cor festinare, ita ad Te confugimus	467	Epistolae	8
SOLETIS			
quibus hostes soletis in potestatem redigere, leniores que aspectus,	440	Orationes	9
SOLI			
Ista docens soli scripta quadrare tibi.	385	Musae	6
Esse iocum soli, plebe stupente, tibi:	416	Lucus 27	4
Non tibi nunc soli filum abrupere sorores, ...	428	Mem.Matr.11	11
Soli homini dantur manus, soli caput rotundum & coeleste, . . .	446	Orationes	38
soli caput rotundum & coeleste, soli facies tanquam vestibulum magni	446	Orationes	38
rotundum & coeleste, soli facies tanquam vestibulum magni palatij.	447	Orationes	1
cui soli ideo insunt oculi variegati, cum caetera animantia . . .	453	Orationes	16
SOLIDO			
Pro solido, CAESAR, carmine frusta dabo.	385	Musae 1	4
SOLIJ			
terrestribusque istis sublimitate solij asserta) vita et actione	458	Epistolae	7
SOLIO			
Praetulit Astraea, aut solio Themis alma vetusto	426	Mem.Matr.7	12
SOLIS			
Sintque ausae thalamum solis adire tui.	384	Musae	6
Quod superest vitae, insumam: Solisque iugales	426	Mem.Matr.7	15
Collega Solis; Quadra Certitudinis;	436	Poem.Lat.	13
SOLITUDO			
bello pacem, sine qua omnis vita procella, & mundus solitudo.	448	Orationes	8
SOLITUM			
India, non solitum profer Eliza decus:	211	Cam.1613-b BR	12

SOLIUM	PAGE	TITLE	LINE
quid ructus crapulae solium possidentis?	452	Orationes	20
SOLLICITOREM			
12. Ad Heath, Sollicitorem Procuratorem Gratulatio . . .	466	Epistolae	T
SOLLICITUDINE			
enixus gloriae, sollicitudine in futurum plenos, haud parum leuare;	469	Epistolae	10
SOLLICITUDINES			
est vt tot labores & sollicitudines Principum sine condimento	446	Orationes	11
SOLLICITUS			
Sollicitus, ne te stella perita notet:	413	Lucus 16	4
SOLO			
Debetur Caelo lumen, & vmbra solo:	417	Lucus 31	2
Si nigro sit terra solo, quis despicit aruum?	437	Poem.Lat.	5
SOLOMON			
Structorem, & Solomon vbique regnet.	408	Passio 19	8
SOLUENDO			
quae nos soluendo non sumus, in suas tabulas accepti transferat.	467	Epistolae	14
SOLUENS			
Quin nos Ipse emit, precioso faenora soluens	410	Lucus 4	3
nusquam benignius, soluens obstupefactos artus, atque exhilarans,	444	Orationes	28
SOLUIT			
Piscis tributum soluit; & tu Caesari:	412	Lucus 11	1
SOLUM			
Anglia cur solum fuso sine sanguine sicca est, ...	411	Lucus 6	1
Vel sine luce solum, vel sine mente caro.	417	Lucus 31	6
Solum dolores, & dolores, stellulae.	423	Mem.Matr.2	51
Ergo ipse solum mutus atque excors ero	423	Mem.Matr.2	55
Matrine linguam refero, solum vt mordeam?	424	Mem.Matr.2	59
Mens superat; corpus solum Elementa tenent.	424	Mem.Matr.3	4
Ipse tuae solum adnectam, sine murmure, thensae.	426	Mem.Matr.7	16
cum non solum tuearis nos a maleuolorum insidijs, sed etiam doceas	443	Orationes	21
hac re solum vlciscimur mortem, ligantes abruptum vitae filum,	446	Orationes	22
vestra solum dextra (quamuis a scriptione terrestribusque istis	458	Epistolae	6
Infinita vestra in nos Beneficia non solum verba omnia, . .	460	Epistolae	2
non gremio solum (quod innuis) sed et ambabus vlnis osculisque ei	463	Epistolae	6
praesertim quum ipsi non solum rectum de Bene-merentibus iudicium	469	Epistolae	12
SOLUS			
Tu duplicem solus Camoenarum thronum	388	Musae 8	3
Nunc sudas solus; caetera turba riget.	397	Musae 29	4
Et tu solus ad Angliae procellas	401	Musae 37	44
Non moreris solus: Mundus simul interit in te, ...	409	Passio 21	1
Quam si ipse solus omnia interuerteret, ...	412	Lucus 13	3
Ipse fruare, licet, solus graueolente sepulcro;	414	Lucus 21	5
siccine abijsti solus? cur non nos omnes tecum?	451	Orationes	7
SOLUTA			
Proque vno vincto turba soluta fuit.	407	Passio 17	2
SOLUTIO			
Tributi solutio.	412	Lucus 11	T
hoc saltem solutio est; Nos nunc conspersi atramento regio, . .	459	Epistolae	4
SOLUTIOR			
ad mea in Honorem Tuum officia erectior solutiorque redibo, . .	473	Epistolae	3
SOLUTIS			
Coeperat, agricolis mentemque & aratra solutis:	418	Tr.Mortis	10
Pudorque constet vel solutis crinibus;	422	Mem.Matr.2	6
SOLUTURA			
Ecce solutura est, ventos causata morantes:	427	Mem.Matr.9	9
SOMATIOU			
Os dia somatiou proteron kai nun di' Olumpou	429	Mem.Matr.14	7
SOMNIA			
Labes, somniaque, ambitusque diros, ...	401	Musae 37	38
Gaudia sola fores: sic quicquid somnia mentis	402	Musae 39	36
Aut spes productas, barbataque somnia vertam	426	Mem.Matr.7	19
SOMNIAT			
O falsos homines! Vigilat, qui somniat aurum, ...	411	Lucus 7	3
SOMNIS			
Somnis (nescio queis) nocturna ad vota vocabo:	432	Poem.Lat.	3
SONAT			
Vt, fluuio currente, vadum sonat, alta quiescunt.	433	Poem.Lat.	48
SONITU			
Obstreperae stulto sonitu, crimenque fatentes.	420	Tr.Mortis	99
SONORIS			
Discordijs plenas sonoris	395	Musae 23	51
SONOS			
Miratur aequor finitimum sonos, ...	394	Musae 23	41
SOPHIEN			
Menouge sophien, ei s' apellaxthai xreon, ...	430	Mem.Matr.15	5
SOPHISMATOMASTIX			
Sophismatomastix; Brutus Literarius, ...	436	Poem.Lat.	14
SOPHRONON			
Sophronon esti me perimenein, ote polemein umin omologesei, . .	449	Orationes	14
SORDIDA			
Mors tot virorum sordida sanguine, ...	433	Poem.Lat.	10
SORICES			
tuus amor et authoritas istos sorices nobis abigat.	469	Epistolae	1
SOROR			
Corde tuo forsan, caetera munda, SOROR.	413	Lucus 15	6
SORORES			
Non tibi nunc soli filum abrupere sorores, ...	428	Mem.Matr.11	11
Qualia parturiente colunt sub rupe sorores:	432	Poem.Lat.	8
SORTI			
Nunc sorti pateo, expositus sine matre procellis, ...	428	Mem.Matr.11	7

	PAGE	TITLE	LINE
SPICULIS			
Vestramque Scyllam, aequis parati spiculis	397	Musae 30	5
SPIN			
In Arund. Spin. Genuflex. Purpur.	405	Passio 7	T
SPINA			
Tu spina misere pungeris, ipse Rosa.	405	Passio 6	2
SPINAS			
Qui Caput es, spinas & tua Membra tuas.	405	Passio 6	4
SPINEAM			
In Coronam spineam.	405	Passio 6	T
SPINIS			
Ecce decus vestrum spinis horrescit, acuta	425	Mem.Matr.5	3
SPINULA			
si spinula vlla Coronae Regiae emollita sit vel retusa;	443	Orationes	11
SPIRANS			
elegantias doctrinae nitoremque spirans purpuram et eruditionem	461	Epistolae	21
SPIRITIBUS			
spiritibusque tabellarijs laetum hunc nuncium vbique deferentibus,	445	Orationes	1
SPIRITU			
Prae spiritu ruptis, quo eas resarciat	398	Musae 32	9
Qui sugit auido spiritu rumusculos	414	Lucus 20	1
non respiciat materiam actionum, sed quo spiritu, qua arte,	454	Orationes	10
SPIRITUM			
Vitasse Christi spiritum efflantis crucem.	389	Musae 10	5
Tu Diua miro pollice spiritum	394	Musae 23	25
cui natura spiritum dederit feracem gloriae, et coeleste ingenium	468	Epistolae	5
SPIRITUS			
Spiritus proponit, & est vtrique	390	Musae 14	15
O succulenti balsama spiritus!	394	Musae 23	34
O dulcissime Spiritus,	403	Musae 40	11
Heu, quis spiritus, igneusque turbo	411	Lucus 5	1
Spiritus, hi mihi iam montes, haec flumina sunto.	432	Poem.Lat.	11
fieri participes eius sanguinis, qui tantos spiritus solet infundere.	440	Orationes	20
qui literas imminuere spiritus, generososque animos frangere	461	Epistolae	19
SPIRITUUM			
Praeclariorum spirituum cibus,	394	Musae 23	22
SPISSA			
Corda furor, spissaque afflat caligine sensus?	401	Musae 39	5
SPISSAE			
Qui spissae fidei breuique menti	417	Lucus 30	4
SPLENDEAT			
Sic non Phoebeus iam plus te splendeat ortus	211	Cam.1613-b BR	15
SPLENDES			
Cur splendes, O Phoebe? ecquid demittere matrem	424	Mem.Matr.3	1
Scilicet id splendes: haec est tibi causa micandi,	424	Mem.Matr.3	5
SPLENDIDA			
Cum tamen splendida plerumque vitrea sint, claritatem fragilitate	448	Orationes	5
SPLENDIDISSIMI			
Splendidissimi Domini, cum tanti sitis & in Principibus Vestris,	441	Orationes	8
SPLENDIDUM			
Scio Belli nomen splendidum esse & gloriosum:	447	Orationes	33
SPLENDOR			
Quis enim apud nos splendor, aut rerum, aut vestium?	441	Orationes	11
vtriusque enim splendor et claritas humilia loca deprecantur.	466	Epistolae	11
SPLENDOREM			
cum Alma Matre, vtrumque splendorem cum beneficio nostro coniungis.	458	Epistolae	17
SPLENIS			
Splenis perlita contumeliosi.	400	Musae 37	13
SPOLIA			
Haec vestra spolia actosque ex orbe triumphos communicas cum Alma	458	Epistolae	16
SPOLIANS			
Sanguine, quem dederat, spolians. Primordia Mortis	418	Tr.Mortis	22
Sanguine, quem dederat, spolians. Primordia belli	271	Tr.Mortis VS	22
SPONSAM			
dum sponsam Domini pijs	395	Musae 25	9
SPONTE			
Queis me educasti; sponte chartas illinunt	424	Mem.Matr.2	63
superiori aestate sponte suauiterque patefacta, nunc etiam	467	Epistolae	2
SPRETIS			
spretis voluptatibus, illecebris melitaiais agxonais abiectis,	452	Orationes	31
SPUMANTIA			
triumphos & victorias quasi fraena ferox spumantia mandit,	447	Orationes	34
SPURCAS			
Et populi spurcas creditis esse vias:	387	Musae 5	8
SPUTANDO			
Sputando, praedicando? sic Aquas vitae	404	Passio 5	3
Sputando, blasphemando? nempe ne hoc fiat	405	Passio 5	5
SPUTUM			
In Sputum & Conuicia.	404	Passio 5	T
SQUALIDAE			
terram manantibus, ieiunae, squalidae, perdiae, pernoctes flagitant,	448	Orationes	36
SQUALOREM			
Squaloremque togae candida Musa fugat.	417	Lucus 28	6
STABIT			
per me non stabit quo minus, spe prouecta atque adulta,	470	Epistolae	7
STAGIRITICO			
Alcide succumbente Stagiritico;	436	Poem.Lat.	18
STAMINA			
Plumbis obsignata, colosque & stamina vitae	419	Tr.Mortis	64
STAMINE			
Et nunc perlongas Scripturae stamine telas	392	Musae 19	5

	PAGE	TITLE	LINE
STARE			
Cum stare gratis cum silentio possim?	472	Epistolae	18
STARENT			
Si numero starent praelia, non animis.	398	Musae 33	8
STATARIOS			
hinc Reges Legatos habent statarios ac resides, quem locum Noster	450	Orationes	29
STATERA			
Tantaque propendet statera	433	Poem.Lat.	7
STATHME			
E themis, e duraton. semnomatos epleto stathme,	430	Mem.Matr.17	6
STATIM			
Statim a solatio aspectus Tui, Ego auctior iam gaudio atque	471	Epistolae	17
STATIONE			
Ceu fida statione & arce certa,	417	Lucus 30	7
STATIS			
Delphino reuectum excepere arbores tripudiantes, & Vos statis?	454	Orationes	37
STATU			
Scientiarum, sub pupillari statu	436	Poem.Lat.	10
Atque hoc quidem statu res erant, Suauissime CAROLE, cum tu aberas;	451	Orationes	27
STATUA			
Homo, Statua.	410	Lucus 1	T
homo est, non statua; Sceptriger, non sceptrum:	446	Orationes	10
STATUAE			
aedificia, corrumpuntur statuae, haec imago atque character,	459	Epistolae	13
STATUIS			
Claudis auaritia Satyram; statuisque sacrorum	399	Musae 34	1
STELLA			
Sollicitus, ne te stella perita notet:	413	Lucus 16	4
Vno ictu: non sic pestis, non stella maligno	420	Tr.Mortis	80
Invitoque fugit singula stella pede:	210	Cam.1613-b BR	2
STELLAM			
Ecquid emes Caelum? quin stellam rectius vnam	410	Lucus 4	5
Stellam vespere suxerim volantem,	411	Lucus 5	5
STELLARUM			
Stellarum socius, pellitus exuor.	424	Mem.Matr.4	8
STELLAS			
glasto se inficientes, in vxorum corporibus, Solem, Lunam, & Stellas;	446	Orationes	31
STELLIS			
Sint tibi vel stellis laudes, & laudibus anni:	402	Musae 39	34
STELLULAE			
Solum dolores, & dolores, stellulae.	423	Mem.Matr.2	51
STEPHANUM			
In Stephanum lapidatum.	410	Lucus 3	T
STEPHANUS			
At Caelum e saxis elicuit Stephanus.	410	Lucus 3	2
STERILEM			
sterilem aiunt regionem: Falleris, nusquam plura bona, cum etiam mala	451	Orationes	2
STERILI			
In vicium mundo sterili, cui cedo cometas	426	Mem.Matr.7	20
STERILIS			
Dic mihi, mons sterilis, vallis an vber eris?	413	Lucus 18	2
STERNAX			
etenim abundantia morosa est & sternax, vnde diuites syluas ac saltus	450	Orationes	20
STERNENTES			
floribus suis sternentes Rempublicam, prae ariditate flaccescerent.	461	Epistolae	10
STERNIS			
Vtrumque sternis calcitro:	388	Musae 8	6
STERNITUR			
Sunt, praeter vitam: saxis hic sternitur, alter	418	Tr.Mortis	19
STETIT			
Nec tamen hic noster stetit impetus: exilit omni	420	Tr.Mortis	95
Nec tamen hic mortis rabies stetit; exilit omni	272	Tr.Mortis VS	95
STI			
In Honorem Illustr. D. D. Verulamij, Sti Albani,	436	Poem.Lat.	T
STIGMATIBUS			
Centum stigmatibus tuos inurens	400	Musae 37	23
STIKTON			
Ergou amartekuia, necn peplon aimati stikton	431	Mem.Matr.17	13
STILLANT			
Hic, vbi sanati stillant opobalsama mundi,	406	Passio 13	1
STILLARUM			
Pro lapsu stillarum abeunt peccata; nec acres	406	Passio 13	3
STIMULANTE			
Non potui non ire acre stimulante flagello:	431	Mem.Matr.19	5
STIMULARET			
(Et quem non stimularet haec simultas?)	400	Musae 37	18
STIMULAT			
Interea ad sacrum stimulat sacra Musica bellum,	399	Musae 33	25
STIMULO			
Assiduo stimulo carnem Mens vlta lacessit,	410	Lucus 2	5
STIPATI			
Stipati, rudibusque volis imperuius hortus	427	Mem.Matr.7	26
STIPULAM			
eadem acies & stipulam secat & lignum:	453	Orationes	29
STIRPES			
Contiguas stirpes afflat, eaeque rosas.	425	Mem.Matr.5	6
STOICA			
Facesse, Stoica plebs, obambulans cautes,	429	Mem.Matr.12	1
STOLIDI			
Heu stolidi, primum fugientem figite Terram,	408	Passio 18	3

STOMACHANS	PAGE	TITLE	LINE
Incipis irridens; stomachans in carmine pergis;	401	Musae 38	1
STOMACHANTUR			
quidam stomachantur praedia, alij immunitates carpunt, nonnulli	461	Epistolae	14
STRAGES			
Per strages licet autorum veterumque ruinam	435	Poem.Lat.	1
STRAMINEIS			
2. Ad R. Naunton Gratiae de Fluuio et de tegendis Tectis stramineis	457	Epistolae	1
STRATA			
Strata iacent toto millena cadauera campo	420	Tr.Mortis	79
Strata, iacent toto prostrata cadauera campo	272	Tr.Mortis VS	79
STRATO			
Exuta strato carnis, ossibus constans,	429	Mem.Matr.12	2
STRATOS			
Nun d' oxou enthend' os stratos nikephoros	430	Mem.Matr.15	10
STRAUIT			
Strauit Idumaeum diuinus Tityrus hostem?	419	Tr.Mortis	44
STREPEBANT			
Sic tunc omnes strepebant: huiusmodi lamentis & quiritationibus plena	451	Orationes	9
STREPENTE			
Strepente mundo tinnulis praeconijs?	423	Mem.Matr.2	56
STREPITUM			
ulemanian illam & inanem verborum strepitum iamdudum deposui:	445	Orationes	23
STREPUNT			
Stringuntur aures: iam litui strepunt,	448	Orationes	2
STRIDOR			
It stridor, caelosque omnes & Tartara findit.	420	Tr.Mortis	73
It stridor, caelosque omnes et sydera findit.	271	Tr.Mortis VS	73
STRIGES			
Magicos rotatus, & perhorridas Striges,	392	Musae 20	12
Non striges, magiamue, vel rotatus,	401	Musae 37	35
STRINGE			
Breuiore nodo stringe vitae sarcinas,	414	Lucus 20	6
STRINGENS			
Dum gladium stringens Paulus ad arma vocat.	398	Musae 33	12
Intuituque vno stringens habitacula mundi,	402	Musae 39	12
STRINGUNTUR			
Stringuntur aures: iam litui strepunt,	448	Orationes	2
STROMA			
Quodque suum nouit stroma, cubile suum.	407	Passio 15	2
STRUCTOREM			
Structorem, & Solomon vbique regnet.	408	Passio 19	8
STRUCTURA			
Quare operosior in eo structura, & praerogatiuae regiae emicant.	446	Orationes	37
STRUICES			
Struices superbas atque turritum caput	422	Mem.Matr.2	11
STRUMAE			
ambitionisque strumae, non adeo sanatae ab optimo Rege nostro quin	473	Epistolae	21
STUDIJS			
Lampada, qua studijs inuigilare solet.	398	Musae 33	18
Nec querar ingratos, studijs dum tabidus insto,	426	Mem.Matr.7	17
viam aperiens & methodum in studijs adhibendam, etiam libros indicans	443	Orationes	24
appulit ad nos omnes haud ita certe studijs chartisque obuclutos,	468	Epistolae	13
STUDIO			
studioque in nos iam olim perspectissimo, quippe qui eximie semper	462	Epistolae	24
STUDIORUM			
commendatione, si huc reciderit omnis studiorum spes fructusque:	472	Epistolae	16
STUDIOSIS			
vendentibus libros non ementibus, hoc est cessatoribus non studiosis.	468	Epistolae	8
STUDIOSORUM			
neque Studiosorum Sacculi, qui etiam nunc maeret et ingemiscit.	467	Epistolae	23
solent enim Studiosorum suffragia enixus gloriae, sollicitudine	469	Epistolae	10
STULTA			
Stulta: semel scribo, perpetuo vt sileam.	431	Mem.Matr.19	8
STULTE			
quam stulte de te rixamur:	451	Orationes	29
STULTI			
Omnesque stulti audimus, aut hypocritae,	388	Musae 8	7
STULTITIAM			
praesertim sericatam hanc stultitiam contere, Academiaeque iura,	461	Epistolae	23
STULTO			
Obstreperae stulto sonitu, crimenque fatentes.	420	Tr.Mortis	99
STULTUS			
ipsum coelum nubilum semper, & poeta stultus qui dixerat,	451	Orationes	19
STUPENDO			
ad Theologiam expeditissimos, tanto ac tam stupendo iudicio, vt,	443	Orationes	26
STUPENDUS			
Rationis & sensus stupendus Arbiter;	436	Poem.Lat.	16
STUPENS			
Et ipse Iordan sistit aquas stupens;	394	Musae 23	42
STUPENT			
Tota stupent luctu) lachrymisque exaestuet aequis	432	Poem.Lat.	10
STUPENTE			
Esse iocum soli, plebe stupente, tibi:	416	Lucus 27	4
STUPEUS			
Fatalemque leuans dextram, qua stupeus ignis	420	Tr.Mortis	67
STUPIDE			
Quid noui, stupide? Redijt Princeps, CAROLVS redijt, honore grauidus,	454	Orationes	26
STUPOR			
occurrant, oratio nostra est silentium, atque eloquentia, stupor.	444	Orationes	3

STUPORE	PAGE	TITLE		LINE
Recte facitis, Academici, attollentes oculos cum stupore;	450	Orationes		1
STUPRATAS				
direptiones, stupratas virgines, praegnantes bis intersectas,	449	Orationes		6
STUTIAE				
Dicite vos Stutiae, qua gaudet origine monstrum	272	Tr.Mortis	VS	85
STYLO				
quando ad magnates cogitas, stylo vtare, sed modeste grandi;	470	Epistolae		22
STYLUM				
caute incipe, cohibens adeo stylum ingeniumque;	470	Epistolae		11
SUA				
voce sua dederat,	396	Musae 28		2
Progenies, gemmamque sua quasi pyxide clausit.	402	Musae 39		16
Hoc ligno, his clauis est, quasi Falce sua.	407	Passio 14		4
qui vtrasque Indias Hispania sua quasi nodo connectens,	440	Orationes		17
asserunt Medici vnamquamque regionem sua sibi sufficere,	444	Orationes		25
cum quanto plus possint in sua terra, tanto minus in aliena.	450	Orationes		11
adde quod angusti est animi aut superbi sua tantum nosse,	450	Orationes		17
ac si corpora sua non abirent olim in elementa, sed in bellaria aut	452	Orationes		13
tum venenatorum haereticorum, insita vi sua liberentur.	459	Epistolae		19
SUAE				
Ipsaque sunt ferulae mollia corda suae.	406	Passio 9		6
Negat familiae suae.	407	Passio 16		8
Plumbea glans, liuensque suae quasi conscia noxae,	419	Tr.Mortis		62
Ad se suaeque matris Arcam regredi:	436	Poem.Lat.		21
Addas sigillum: nempe Symbolum suae	438	Poem.Lat.		6
Quare quomodo alij molem hanc laetitiae suae exprimant,	457	Epistolae		1
quasi accolae Maiestatis, literaturae suae et vicinitati respondeant:	463	Epistolae		23
SUAM				
vestem non adimi suam,	396	Musae 25		21
non suam tribui iubet.	396	Musae 25		23
Suamque in alijs possidet prudentiam.	412	Lucus 13		4
Quaesitum Dominam gemma vel herba suam.	425	Mem.Matr.5		12
Ad se suamque mentis Arcam regredi:	436	Poem.Lat.	V	21
verrunt (ac si perdiderint ingenium) vt Spartam exornent suam:	445	Orationes		37
nimirum infinitum Principis in suam gentem amorem, cui pacem	449	Orationes		36
tantum ex hoc itinere cognouit Respublicas sed quod plus est, suam;	450	Orationes		33
non tantum exteras regiones habuit perspectas, verum etiam suam?	452	Orationes		1
cuius manifestationem in gentem suam priuatae personae & habitui	453	Orationes		8
si speculum Inuidiae ostendas, quo deformitatem suam intueatur!	454	Orationes		21
ditat patriam, suamque absentiam cum foenore compensat.	454	Orationes		33
Noster etiam Princeps habuit Daphnen suam, cuius amor deinceps	455	Orationes		10
SUAS				
Non nisi prima suas patiuntur praelia lites.	386	Musae 4		7
Quotidiana suas poscant si fercula grates,	389	Musae 12		9
Scilicet, vt quos ante suas cum coniuge tedas	396	Musae 26		9
Cernite, quam formosa suas Ecclesia pennas	401	Musae 39		6
diuisit Natura suas dotes, vt indigentia singularum regionum omnes	450	Orationes		19
si Reges ipsi quandoque suauitates suas populari aceto condiant.	453	Orationes		19
quae nos soluendo non sumus, in suas tabulas accepti transferat.	467	Epistolae		15
SUASU				
qui primo caloris suasu excitati atque expergefacti, vbi sursum	471	Epistolae		29
SUAUIS				
Ecce tamen quam suauis ero! cum, fine duelli,	386	Musae 2		7
Quam satur & suauis sit tibi Roma iocus.	416	Lucus 27		6
Suauis erat, qui scripta dolens lacerando recludi,	439	Poem.Lat.		13
SUAUISSIMAM				
Prolem Tuam suauissimam, nuper in lucem publicam, nostramque	463	Epistolae		5
SUAUISSIME				
Atque hoc quidem statu res erant, Suauissime CAROLE, cum tu aberas;	451	Orationes		28
SUAUISSIMUS				
in hisce Nuptijs posteritati tantum prospexit suauissimus Princeps,	447	Orationes		27
quem locum Noster suauissimus impleuit, ipse egit oratorem,	450	Orationes		30
SUAUITAS				
Tota renident aede decus & suauitas	423	Mem.Matr.2		24
SUAUITATES				
si Reges ipsi quandoque suauitates suas populari aceto condiant.	453	Orationes		19
SUAUITER				
Per quicquid tibi suauiter probatur;	400	Musae 37		9
Suauiter admoueas notum tibi carne flagellum,	406	Passio 9		3
Suauiter efficient, absque rigore Scholae.	417	Lucus 28		4
Tam nitide tamen occidis, tam suauiter, hostes,	435	Poem.Lat.		3
qua optime ostendis te eius vicarium qui omnia disponit suauiter?	443	Orationes		17
superiori aestate sponte suauiterque patefacta, nunc etiam	467	Epistolae		2
SUAUIUS				
promulgentur, quo suauius virtutibus, tuo exemplo compensatis,	468	Epistolae		16
SUB				
Mens sub insigni specie coloris	390	Musae 14		7
Scotia quae frigente iaces porrecta sub Arcto,	399	Musae 35		1
Qua Fabio quondam sub duce nata salus.	416	Lucus 25		10
Quae Fabio quondam sub duce tuta salus.	416	Lucus 25	V	10
Qualia parturiente colunt sub rupe sorores:	432	Poem.Lat.		8
Et patrio regno (sub quo iam Principe nobis	432	Poem.Lat.		27
Scientiarum, sub pupillari statu	436	Poem.Lat.		10
Dum longi lentique gemis sub pondere morbi	438	Poem.Lat.		1
sub ementito habitu fidicinis castra hostium ingressus,	453	Orationes		4
idem feruor qui impar sub amoris signo meritus est, ad vera castra	453	Orationes		29
peruenimus ad laurum hanc, vbi sub vmbra eius paulisper requiescamus:	455	Orationes		13
sub specie publici commodi, Academiae incommodum videntur allaturi;	462	Epistolae		31
iustissime potes sub hoc Principe, in quo doctrinae fructus atque	469	Epistolae		22

	PAGE	TITLE	LINE
SUBDITI			
Humillimi serui subditique vestri Procancellarius Reliquusque Senatus	459	Epistolae	22
SUBERANT			
Quae suberant causae? quid nos committere tantum, ...	432	Poem.Lat.	18
SUBEST			
Et melius coelum, te veniente, subest:	210	Cam.1613-a BR	4
SUBEUNT			
Inde rotae atque axes subeunt, quasi sella curulis . . .	419	Tr.Mortis	55
SUBEUNTIA			
Iam demissa, ipsamque adeo subeuntia terram?	420	Tr.Mortis	94
SUBFUGERAT			
Apposite quem commotum subfugerat olim, ...	390	Musae 12	15
SUBIECTISSIME			
Tantum Maiestatem vestram subiectissime oramus, vt si officia nostra	460	Epistolae	15
SUBIECTO			
olim paululum aquae a Sinaeta, subiecto suo, laetissime sumeret,	460	Epistolae	12
SUBIECTOS			
nos humillimos subiectos, integro Fluuio a Rege nostro donatos,	460	Epistolae	13
SUBIERE			
Transiliuntque caput, qui subiere pedes.	414	Lucus 19	2
SUBIJCIUNTUR			
adeo vt qui non subijciuntur ditioni, eruditioni vestrae obtemperent:	458	Epistolae	13
SUBIS			
Et hoc indicium subis, Redemptor?	417	Lucus 30	2
SUBIT			
Haec vbi iuncta, subit viuo cum fune minister, ...	420	Tr.Mortis	66
Haec vbi vincta, subit viuo cum fune minister, ...	271	Tr.Mortis VS	66
SUBITO			
quam subito dispereunt, simul ac concrepuit incendium militare:	448	Orationes	19
SUBLATA			
Et cum sublata laude recedit AMOR.	416	Lucus 25	12
SUBLATIS			
Quod aliae gentes manibus in coelum sublatis, lachrymis in terram	448	Orationes	35
SUBLEUATRIX			
Quam mira tardem Subleuatrix pauperum!	423	Mem.Matr.2	45
SUBLIME			
nihil non sublime et excelsum cogitabimus, perrumpemus controuersias	459	Epistolae	5
SUBLIMI			
Qui tam sublimi conspicit orbe viam:	387	Musae 7	6
SUBLIMIA			
Sic laudandus erit nactus sublimia Praesul, ...	387	Musae 7	9
SUBLIMIOR			
quo eorum conditio sublimior, eo maior cura adhibenda sit. . .	446	Orationes	35
SUBLIMITATE			
Natura montibus vallibusque sublimitate atque humilitate distinxit:	453	Orationes	12
terrestribusque istis sublimitate solij asserta) vita et actione	458	Epistolae	7
SUBLUNARIS			
quae materia sit, coelestis an sublunaris, sed quae signa, . .	454	Orationes	13
SUBRUISSEM			
Et Musa crepitante subruissem:	400	Musae 37	20
SUBSCRIBERE			
Articulis sacris quidam subscribere iussus, ...	389	Musae 11	1
SUBSCRIPTIO			
Quas subscriptio neutiquam inquinauit;	400	Musae 37	8
SUBSELLIJ			
etsi tu qui scribis (vti quiuis priuatus) inferioris sis subsellij,	470	Epistolae	23
SUBSIDIA			
vt qui tot subsidia attuleris ad progressum doctrinae, hac etiam	467	Epistolae	27
SUBSIDIUM			
aeternitatem nominis Tui subsidiumque Magnificentiae Tuae . .	464	Epistolae	6
SUBSTRUCTIONEM			
Substructionem capitis & nimbum breuem, ...	422	Mem.Matr.2	15
SUBSULTANS			
aetate prouectior, etiam anus subsultans multum excitet pulueris:	454	Orationes	36
SUBTEGMEN			
Subtegmen reti dignius esse putans, ...	392	Musae 19	4
SUBTILITATES			
crassissimum elementum, Tu subtilitates Artium infinitas. . .	463	Epistolae	14
SUBTILITATIS			
Subtilitatis Terebra; Temporis Nepos	436	Poem.Lat.	22
SUBUENIENS			
Tu mihi subueniens dignior esse potes.	404	Passio 2	6
SUBUERSAS			
multi Academias integras subuersas volunt, neque illi e faece vulgi	461	Epistolae	16
SUCCEDANT			
Quod tamen haec omnia succedant ex voto, quod reclusae sint fores,	472	Epistolae	19
SUCCIDO			
Nunc obrutus Academicis negotijs, aegre hoc tempus illis succido:	471	Epistolae	20
SUCCINCTA			
vti vir, tetragonos est, grauis, nobilis, perspicua, succincta.	471	Epistolae	5
SUCCULENTI			
O succulenti balsama spiritus!	394	Musae 23	34
SUCCUMBENTE			
Alcide succumbente Stagiritico;	436	Poem.Lat.	18
SUCCUMBIT			
Ecce meus torpens animus succumbit vtrique, ...	435	Poem.Lat.	3
SUCCURRAT			
suauiterque patefacta, nunc etiam laborantibus Musis succurrat.	467	Epistolae	3
SUCCURRES			
abunde succurres Magnificentiae tuae addicitissimis Procancellario	469	Epistolae	25

	PAGE	TITLE	LINE
SUCCURRIT			
rotunditas Clementiae vestrae, quae ab omni parte nobis succurrit!	460	Epistolae	10
SUDAM			
Otium poscunt artes, mentem tranquillam, serenam, sudam:	448	Orationes	23
SUDARIA			
Cum templis effare, madent sudaria, mappae,	397	Musae 29	1
SUDAS			
Nunc sudas solus; caetera turba riget.	397	Musae 29	4
SUDES			
Quid ipse faciam? qui nec arboreas sudes	421	Lucus 33	3
SUDIBUS			
Ambustis sudibus: pars vitam in pocula fundunt,	418	Tr.Mortis	20
SUDO			
Frustra igitur sudo: superest mihi sola voluptas,	435	Poem.Lat.	7
SUDOR			
Quo fugies, sudor? quamuis pars altera Christi	404	Passio 2	1
Nobis facilitas cedat & tibi sudor.	406	Passio 12	3
SUDOREM			
In sudorem sanguineum.	404	Passio 2	T
SUDUM			
vnde pluuia futura, an sudum, facile conijcitur ex coelo,	445	Orationes	6
SUFFICERE			
quarum enumerationi nulla vnquam vis, nulla latera sufficere possunt.	443	Orationes	15
asserunt Medici vnamquamque regionem sua sibi sufficere,	444	Orationes	26
SUFFICERET			
Habui viaticum fauoris Tui, quod longiori multo itineri sufficeret.	471	Epistolae	19
SUFFICIAT			
Sufficiat virgae saepius vmbra tuae.	406	Passio 9	4
SUFFICIET			
Sufficiet votis ista iuuenta meis.	386	Musae 2	10
SUFFIGERIS			
Si, Christe, dum suffigeris, tuae vestes	406	Passio 10	1
SUFFITIBUS			
Hic ego tuque erimus, variae suffitibus herbae	427	Mem.Matr.7	28
SUFFLAS			
Cur tanta sufflas probra in innocuam Crucem?	389	Musae 10	1
SUFFOCATAM			
Effluxisse dies, suffocatamue Mineruam,	426	Mem.Matr.7	18
SUFFRAGIA			
solent enim Studiosorum suffragia erixus gloriae, sollicitudine	469	Epistolae	10
SUFFRAGIJS			
plenissimis suffragijs elegimus Te tribunum Parlamentarium,	465	Epistolae	4
SUGAM			
Ah nunc, helluo, fac, vt ipse sugam:	421	Lucus 34	1
SUGGERUNT			
Aut laesae mihi suggerunt Athenae,	400	Musae 37	17
SUGIT			
Qui sugit auido spiritu rumusculos	414	Lucus 20	1
SUGXROUN			
Meteri tektaincusa, qoci kai penthesi sugxroun.	431	Mem.Matr.17	14
SUI			
Papicolisque sui sunt, Catharisque sui.	393	Musae 21	2
pignora chara sui	397	Musae 28	11
Nosse sui quid agant, quaedam est quoque musica sanctis,	427	Mem.Matr.9	3
suique impos, triumphos & victorias quasi fraena ferox spumantia	447	Orationes	33
neminemque esse sui negligentiorem, quam qui sibi parcat.	452	Orationes	34
SUIS			
Cum primum ratibus suis	395	Musae 25	1
Quas gens inconsulta, suis vexata procellis,	401	Musae 39	2
Dum librata suis haeret radicibus ilex	428	Mem.Matr.11	1
suam gentem amorem, cui pacem quaesiuit suo capite, periculis suis.	449	Orationes	37
3. Ad Iacobum Regem Gratiae de Scriptis suis Academiae donatis	458	Epistolae	T
floribus suis sternentes Rempublicam, prae ariditate flaccescerent.	461	Epistolae	10
alumnis suis orbarentur, quin communes Reipublicae lachrymae alterum	462	Epistolae	5
SULCIS			
Fusaque decurrit notis aqua ferrea sulcis:	419	Tr.Mortis	52
SULLALEOUSIN			
Tes peri sullaleousin, eou poikilmatos arden	431	Mem.Matr.17	11
SULPHUREI			
& beatae fabricae, vnico ictu sulphurei tubi, vnica litura delentur?	448	Orationes	21
SULPHUREO			
Sulphureoque lacu, totaque imbuta Mephiti.	419	Tr.Mortis	59
SULPHURIS			
Sulphuris inferni, properat datus ignis et omnem	271	Tr.Mortis VS	69
SUM			
Sum, quis nescit, Imago Dei, sed saxea certe:	410	Lucus 1	1
Abito, barde. Quam pie istic sum impudens!	424	Mem.Matr.2	60
ego vero sentio, & quis sum ipse (barbam, hui, tam grauem) & apud	445	Orationes	25
SUME			
Sume Palatini versus de numine Phoebi,	210	Cam.1613-a BR	1
Tuque etiam Dapifer, quas fero, sume dapes:	210	Cam.1613-a BR	2
sume tecum amorem illum quo soles beare Amplitudini tuae deuotissimos	464	Epistolae	27
SUMENDA			
Aut si negotio hora sumenda est, rei	423	Mem.Matr.2	32
Hilaris haec sumenda est dies.	454	Orationes	23
SUMERET			
subiecto suo, laetissime sumeret, quanto magis par est,	460	Epistolae	12
SUMITE			
Sumite gorgoneam, nostraque Pallas erit.	387	Musae 6	6
SUMMA			
nos audiamus summo cum gaudio ea Maiestas vestra summa cum molestia?	444	Orationes	1

SUO (cont'd)	PAGE	TITLE	LINE
Tuo tot negotijs meritissime distincto, tempore non suo obrepant:	457	Epistolae	12
olim paululum aquae a Sinaeta, subiecto suo, laetissime sumeret,	460	Epistolae	12
illustrans nos omnes, lumenque accendens de suo lumine,	461	Epistolae	4
istos siccatores (solem officio suo priuantes) vi verborum Tuorum	462	Epistolae	20
Quod si oppidani nostri (more suo) Musarum iura et diplomata	468	Epistolae	26
praeferuida illa desideria silentio suo sepulta nunc languescere,	471	Epistolae	28
SUOS			
Ingemat ob partus, ceu maledicta, suos,	390	Musae 12	14
Maturusque suos coquens amores	408	Passio 19	12
Ipse suos tanquam digno pallentiaque astra.	426	Mem.Matr.7	21
Vt natura omnis sucs habet anteambulones, vnde pluuia futura,	445	Orationes	5
etiam libros dederunt, sed non suos:	458	Epistolae	24
aut si suos, quia dederunt, non a se compositos, scriptos,	458	Epistolae	24
Quanta hilaritate aspicit Alma Mater filios suos iam emancipatos,	461	Epistolae	30
SUPELLECTILEM			
vniuersam Musarum supellectilem, etiam Fluuium non minus de	465	Epistolae	6
SUPELLEX			
Omnia purgentur, niteat mihi tota supellex,	413	Lucus 15	3
Nam primum tota haec Pieria supellex, charta, calami, codices,	448	Orationes	18
SUPER			
Tuque super nostras, Christe, moueris aquas.	411	Lucus 6	8
Omnia quaerendo, sed te, super omnia, vexas:	413	Lucus 16	5
Christe, super fluctus si non discurrere detur:	414	Lucus 19	3
Quam cruenta gloria est, quae super ceruicibus hominum erigitur?	449	Orationes	10
SUPERABILEM			
exponunt superabilem.	395	Musae 25	15
SUPERABIMUS			
perrumpemus controuersias omnes, superabimus quoscunque.	459	Epistolae	6
SUPERABIT			
idem impetus, qui peragrauit Hispaniam, si opus sit, superabit;	453	Orationes	32
SUPERANS			
Lubricus, & superans mobilitate salum.	428	Mem.Matr.11	8
Quin Matris superans carmina posscit honos.	431	Mem.Matr.19	6
at Noster difficultatem superans, fructum consecutus est:	450	Orationes	13
SUPERARE			
Duritia superare cautes.	394	Musae 23	20
praesertim cum amico fidere periculosius sit, quam hostem superare.	453	Orationes	33
SUPERARENT			
aut Tuae virtutes et vota nostra et Principis gratiam superarent.	456	Epistolae	22
SUPERARI			
etiam Athenae artesque obscuris opificum artibus superari dolebunt.	469	Epistolae	4
SUPERAS			
Auresque superas: arbitri ipsi sint litis,	392	Musae 20	4
SUPERAT			
At superat caput illa tuum, quantum ipsa cadauer	424	Mem.Matr.3	3
Mens superat; corpus solum Elementa tenent.	424	Mem.Matr.3	4
SUPERBAS			
Struices superbas atque turritum caput	422	Mem.Matr.2	11
tanquam catenam, qua dissitas nationes ac superbas constringeret.	450	Orationes	24
SUPERBI			
adde quod angusti est animi aut superbi sua tantum nosse,	450	Orationes	17
SUPERBIAM			
Errores, maculas, superbiamque,	401	Musae 37	37
SUPERBIT			
Quis hic superbit, oro? tune, an Praesules,	388	Musae 8	1
SUPERBIUS			
(Superbius cum te nihil)	388	Musae 8	16
SUPERBOS			
Tu qui superbos caeteros existimas	388	Musae 8	15
SUPERBUM			
Ergo etiam Solem dicas, ignaue, superbum,	387	Musae 7	5
In Superbum.	413	Lucus 17	T
SUPERCILIUM			
& supercilium quibus caperatam seuerioremque Philosophiam expugnare	440	Orationes	11
SUPEREM			
Non vt te superem: res tamen ipsa feret.	386	Musae 2	2
SUPERENTUR			
vt terrestres tui honores cum coelestibus certent, et superentur.	465	Epistolae	19
SUPERERUNT			
Tibi supererunt & mihi.	407	Passio 16	14
SUPERESSE			
Ornastis capulum, nec superesse licet.	425	Mem.Matr.5	2
SUPERESSET			
si tantum Honori Tuo superesset otij ad legendum, quantum a nobis	457	Epistolae	8
SUPEREST			
Quod superest vitae, insumam: Solisque iugales	426	Mem.Matr.7	15
Frustra igitur sudo: superest mihi sola voluptas,	435	Poem.Lat.	7
Quod superest, precamur S. S. Trinitatem, vt vestrae coronae ciuili	459	Epistolae	20
SUPERETUR			
Vtque minax superetur Aegis?	433	Poem.Lat.	12
SUPERI			
O superi: Quis tantum ipsis virtutibus instat	271	Tr.Mortis VS	33
SUPERIORI			
superiori aestate sponte suauiterque patefacta, nunc etiam	467	Epistolae	2
SUPEROS			
Haec verba superos aduolaturus thronos	396	Musae 28	7
SUPERPELLICEI			
Superpellicei tremendus hostis,	391	Musae 15	2
SUPERPELLICEO			
De Superpelliceo.	390	Musae 14	T

	PAGE	TITLE	LINE
T			
11.Ad T. Coventry, Attorn. Cognitorem Gratulatio	465	Epistolae	T
T'			
Exren phugousa, ten t' epistemen biou.	430	Mem.Matr.15	7
Mian t' atarpon sumporeuesthai drasas.	430	Mem.Matr.15	13
Ou pheggos, koinon t' agathon, mian eis thuran eirgein . . .	430	Mem.Matr.17	5
Demosion t' indalma kalou, theion te katoptron.	430	Mem.Matr.17	7
TA			
semper titillant aures Principum, Osper tois pterois knomenoi ta ota.	453	Orationes	3
TABELLARIJS			
spiritibusque tabellarijs laetum hunc nuncium vbique deferentibus,	445	Orationes	2
TABERNA			
Non tibi fingendi sola taberna patet.	386	Musae 3	6
TABIDA			
Atque haeret dubio tabida vita pede, ...	438	Poem.Lat.	2
TABIDUS			
Nec querar ingratos, studijs dum tabidus insto, ...	426	Mem.Matr.7	17
TABULAS			
Infectas tabulas facta iuuenca scidit.	408	Passio 20	4
quae nos soluendo non sumus, in suas tabulas accepti transferat.	467	Epistolae	15
TABULIS			
Tum quanta tabulis artifex? quae scriptio?	423	Mem.Matr.2	35
TACEBUNT			
quanto minus tacebunt lusciniae nostrae disertae, minimeque omnium	445	Orationes	9
TACENTIBUS			
Patronus noster es, etiam tacentibus nobis, quanto magis cum rogamus,	467	Epistolae	17
TACITAS			
Incendat tacitas, sole morante, faces:	211	Cam.1613-b BR	6
TACITE			
Iamdudum tacite delituisse putes?	437	Poem.Lat.	10
Iamdudum tacite delituisse putas?	437	Poem.Lat. V	10
TACITO			
Immodicus luctus tacito vorat igne medullas, ...	433	Poem.Lat.	47
TACTU			
vt quod Philosophus de Tactu & Visu, id apposite admodum huc	472	Epistolae	36
TACTUS			
tanquam flos molliculus rudiore Centurionis manu tactus flaccescit.	448	Orationes	25
TAEDULAE			
aut tanquam oues taedulae & fastidiosae, cibum respuamus. . .	449	Orationes	1
TAGO			
nihil inaudisti de Tago, Pactolo?	451	Orationes	4
TALAS			
Talas, eithe y' Argos eien	430	Mem.Matr.16	8
TALEM			
Scilicet talem liquet esse solem;	390	Musae 14	9
Accipe; ni talem des, tibi qualis erat.	434	Poem.Lat.	6
denique huic aetati quae talem virum protulit, cum quinque millibus	463	Epistolae	26
TALI			
(& quidem nox aptior esset tali historiae) si Romanorum Imperatorum	452	Orationes	21
dein Hon. Tuo gratulamur, qui filio auctus es tali ingenio praedito:	463	Epistolae	24
TALIBUS			
O vos inualidos! Audi quem talibus armis	399	Musae 33	29
TALIS			
Versatos neget, atque humiles, queis talis cordi	420	Tr.Mortis	93
Numne Hydra talis, tantane bellua est	433	Poem.Lat.	9
TAM			
Cur tibi tam facile non arrisere poetae	387	Musae 5	3
Qui tam sublimi conspicit orbe viam:	387	Musae 7	6
Sed qui tam male pileos habetis, ...	391	Musae 15	11
Christe, vbi tam duro patet in te semita ferro, ...	404	Passio 4	1
Tu tamen, haud tibi tam moreris, quam viuis in illis, ...	407	Passio 17	3
Quin tibi tam desperatae MORA nulla medetur, ...	416	Lucus 25	9
Tamque aries ruit et multa Demetrius arte, ...	271	Tr.Mortis VS	47
Tam demissa, ipsamque adeo subeuntia terram?	420	Tr.Mortis	94
Ad nos cum radio tam rutilante potes?	424	Mem.Matr.3	2
Quin fugias? mea non fuerat tam nubila Iuno, ...	426	Mem.Matr.7	7
Tam segnis facies aurorae nescia vernae, ...	426	Mem.Matr.7	8
Tam languens genitrix cineri supposta fugaci:	426	Mem.Matr.7	9
In mea dicta ruant; non tam mihi pendula mens est, ...	432	Poem.Lat.	5
Tam nitide tamen occidis, tam suauiter, hostes, ...	435	Poem.Lat.	3
nos tam defecimus in vtroque quam Excellentiae Vestrae abundant.	441	Orationes	12
ad Theologiam expeditissimos, tanto ac tam stupendo iudicio, vt,	443	Orationes	25
tam grauem) & apud quos dico, viros limatae auris atque tersae,	445	Orationes	26
nobis non licet esse tam perspicacibus, quamuis rationi consonum	449	Orationes	31
tibique non tam auide veterum beneficiorum memoriam recolenti,	457	Epistolae	12
tam de conseruando Fluuio nostro, quam de muniendis contra grassantes	457	Epistolae	17
Quod si tam integrum tibi esset gratificari nobis in terra & aere,	457	Epistolae	21
veremur ne non tam sapientes nos, quam obscuros philosophos . .	460	Epistolae	24
sicca vbera et mammas arentes tam nobilis parentis aequo animo ferre	462	Epistolae	1
et festucas, Reipublicae oculo haerentes, tam diligenter amoues;	462	Epistolae	13
Tam eximie de nobis meritus es, vt res nostras omnes cum Honore Tuo	465	Epistolae	2
Cum caeterae ecclesiae tam perspicaci diligentia incubes, . .	466	Epistolae	21
Quare tam vere quam libenter gratulamur tibi, nec minus etiam	468	Epistolae	17
non tam quod tibi conueniat scribenti, quam quod Academiae tuo calamo	470	Epistolae	13
certe non tam ornas illam, qui infers manum grauitati. . . .	470	Epistolae	20
si tam abiectus sim, vt laboribus meis plurimis atque assidua	472	Epistolae	12
Cur ego laborem notus esse tam praue, ...	472	Epistolae	17
imo precabor enixe, me tum priuari tam communi hac luce, quam Tua,	472	Epistolae	23
TAMEN			
Non vt te superem: res tamen ipsa feret.	386	Musae 2	2
Ecce tamen quam suauis ero! cum, fine duelli, ...	386	Musae 2	7

TAMEN (cont'd)	PAGE	TITLE	LINE
Ille tamen, quamuis altus, tua crimina ridens	387	Musae 7	7
Qua tamen occisi fcedera scripta Dei?	391	Musae 16	4
Tu perstrepis tamen; vtque turgeat carmen	392	Musae 20	10
Qui tamen in nostros fortiter ire negant.	398	Musae 33	4
Qui tamen excipiat, Christus caret hospite: tantum	407	Passio 15	3
Tu tamen, haud tibi tam moreris, quam viuis in illis,	407	Passio 17	3
Quae contrita tamen caetera damna leuant.	409	Passio 20	8
Qui silicem tundit, (mirum tamen) elicit ignem:	410	Lucus 3	1
Venditus est Agnus, non tamen emptus erit.	410	Lucus 4	2
Vtrumque mirum est: hoc tamen mirum magis,	412	Lucus 11	2
Te Germana tamen pubes, te Graecus & Anglus	416	Lucus 26	3
Nec tamen excluder: namque vna ex arbore vitam	418	Tr.Mortis	7
Hinc tamen excludi mors noluit, ipsaque vitam	271	Tr.Mortis VS	7
Perdere sexcentas? crescit tamen hydra nocendi	419	Tr.Mortis	35
Perdere sexcentas? crescet tamen hydra nocendi	419	Tr.Mortis V	35
Nec tamen hic noster stetit impetus: exilit omni	420	Tr.Mortis	95
Nec tamen hic mortis rabies stetit; exilit omni	272	Tr.Mortis VS	95
Luctatur spacium, qualem tamen eligit aequi	426	Mem.Matr.7	24
Tam nitide tamen occidis, tam suauiter, hostes,	435	Poem.Lat.	3
Sunt etiam tenebrae, quas tamen optat amor.	437	Poem.Lat.	2
Nolite tamen contemnere has gloriolas nostras quas e chartis	441	Orationes	16
Nolite tamen nimium efferre vos, cum Virginitas ipsa fructus sit	446	Orationes	27
Cum tamen splendida plerumque vitrea sint, claritatem fragilitate	448	Orationes	5
Sunt tamen acuti quidam & emuncti, qui omnia praeuident:	449	Orationes	28
mirabilius, cuius tamen fructum omnem nondum habetis enucleatum.	450	Orationes	3
cum tamen in resolutione illa vltima, nulla sit distinctio populi aut	452	Orationes	15
Adest tamen anus illa querula, & philegklemor, quam audire videor	453	Orationes	25
vbi tamen ad vsum tralatae fuerint, machinas conficiunt	454	Orationes	5
vt lineae, quamuis diuersa via, omnes tamen ad centrum properant;	456	Epistolae	23
quum tamen Tu inuaseris eorum gloriam conseruando nobis quae illi	458	Epistolae	25
nobis remotior, confidimus tamen vt arbores, quanto altius crescunt,	464	Epistolae	17
nouo hoc cumulo honorum, qui tamen votis nostris nondum respondent.	464	Epistolae	21
sed tamen comparatio & in honorem tuum cedet, nostrumque emolumentum.	467	Epistolae	25
Quod tamen haec omnia succedant ex voto, quod reclusae sint fores,	472	Epistolae	19
permutare nolim, maius tamen piaculum reor, deesse publico muneri,	472	Epistolae	31
TAMI			
Ad Andreae Melvini Scoti Anti-Tami-Cami-Categoriam.	384	Musae	T
Ad eundem In Monstrum vocabuli Anti-Tami-Cami-Categoria.	386	Musae 3	T
Istas Anti-Tami-Cami-Categorias!	386	Musae 3	2
Partitio Anti-Tami-Cami-Categoriae.	386	Musae 4	T
TANDEM			
Quid sacrae tandem meruere vestes,	390	Musae 14	1
Ne tandem caput eius impetatis.	391	Musae 15	13
Quo me vocas tandem, tuumque	394	Musae 23	23
Et quid tu tandem desidiosus? AMO.	413	Lucus 16	6
Pontificem tandem nacta est sibi Roma poetam:	417	Lucus 28	1
Sanguinis, innocuum tandem luet orbis Abelem.	272	Tr.Mortis VS	101
Quam mira tandem Subleuatrix pauperum!	423	Mem.Matr.2	45
Horti, deliciae Dominae, marcescite tandem;	425	Mem.Matr.5	1
Tandem prehensa comiter lacernula	427	Mem.Matr.8	7
Quis iste tandem? non enim vultu ambulat	436	Poem.Lat.	1
Quid voluit prudens Fatum, iam sentio tandem:	438	Poem.Lat.	3
Tandem & fessa manus, dedit sigillum.	439	Poem.Lat.	12
Saluete tandem Magistri Artium, & quidem omnium Aulicarum,	440	Orationes	4
at quo tandem? Madritum? hui!	451	Orationes	1
Ecquid videtis tandem quam vtile hoc iter, per quod optimus Princeps	451	Orationes	35
amor virginis eo pertraxit Principem, quo tandem ducet amor Patriae?	453	Orationes	28
magnas aliquas virtutes tandem meritis tuis votisque nostris	464	Epistolae	12
Tandem, ne et ipse peccem, breuis sit sermo, atque pressus.	470	Epistolae	31
TANGAS			
Tangas, Domine, cor sacrum, sentiatque Rex ipse nos haec intime	444	Orationes	8
TANQUAM			
Cur lacrymas & tarda trahis suspiria, tanquam	415	Lucus 23	1
Ipse suos tanquam digno pallentiaque astra.	426	Mem.Matr.7	21
Occiduis, tanquam duplice nube, genis.	427	Mem.Matr.9	6
Expeto, tanquam haec sit nostri medicina doloris?	433	Poem.Lat.	46
sed etiam doceas tanquam communis defensor fidei et Academiae,	443	Orationes	22
rotundum & coeleste, soli facies tanquam vestibulum magni palatij.	447	Orationes	1
tanquam flos molliculus rudiore Centurionis manu tactus flaccescit.	448	Orationes	25
aut tanquam oues taedulae & fastidiosae, cibum respuamus.	449	Orationes	1
tanquam gurgitem imperuestigabilem, victoriae nuncupemus:	449	Orationes	22
cum paupertatem daret tanquam catenam, qua dissitas nationes ac	450	Orationes	24
tanquam ligna obliqua, aliter magna haec mundi domus corrueret:	450	Orationes	28
inspexi facies hominum ac vultus curiosius tanquam emptor;	451	Orationes	13
gestantur, tanquam onera, circumferuntur mollissimis lecticis,	452	Orationes	11
et tanquam Aquilam inter nouas honorum nubes e conspectu nostro	456	Epistolae	6
pulcherrimaeque Musarum domus tanquam viduae effoetae, aut ligna	462	Epistolae	4
protinus tanquam Nobilem Filium (more nostro) Magistrum Artium	463	Epistolae	8
cuius libri si alij alijs (tanquam montes olim) imponerentur,	467	Epistolae	30
tanquam partubus Virtutum Tuarum, Alma Mater accurrens gratuletur:	469	Epistolae	8
TANTA			
Cur tanta sufflas probra in innocuam Crucem?	389	Musae 10	1
Aequabili facta. Ecquid ergo te tanta	392	Musae 20	6
Sic acuunt zelum frigora tanta tuum?	399	Musae 35	6
Vt, si gratia tanta copuletur	421	Lucus 34	7
Fatisco referens tanta quae numerant mei	423	Mem.Matr.2	50
Sitque omnis motus nescia tanta quies,	424	Mem.Matr.3	8
Tantaque propendet statera	433	Poem.Lat.	7
Numne Hydra talis, tantane bellua est	433	Poem.Lat.	9
Tot & tanta loquens amica, scripsit:	439	Poem.Lat.	11

TANTA (cont'd)	PAGE	TITLE	LINE
eruditionem, quae tanta est vt, nisi Rex esses in ciuili Republica,	443	Orationes	18
vtinam & nunc sit tanta patriae tenacitas, vt nunquam Princeps se	455	Orationes	5
ramenta quaepiam ex tanta Humanitatis massa, quae apud Te visitur,	472	Epistolae	13
TANTAE			
in quem fauor Regius, nostra vota, virtutes tantae confluxerunt?	456	Epistolae	19
enim impetus animi celeritatem tantae munificentiae assequi potest?	460	Epistolae	4
qui tantae poeticae, tantae eruditionis nobis conscius est,	461	Epistolae	6
tantae eruditionis nobis conscius est, palustri opere & vliginoso	461	Epistolae	7
TANTAS			
Ecquid inter tantas mundi trepidationes nobis & Musis vacas?	458	Epistolae	2
TANTI			
cum tanti sitis & in Principibus Vestris, & in vobismetipsis,	441	Orationes	8
non est tanti respondere latratibus maleuolorum;	454	Orationes	16
cum non est tanti totus ille maritimus tractus (Oceani praeda	461	Epistolae	8
TANTILLUM			
Nec vel tantillum pignus habebit amor?	396	Musae 26	2
TANTIS			
Cum natet in tantis caetera terra malis?	411	Lucus 6	2
vt iter tantum, tantis laboribus, periculis obnoxium, susciperet?	452	Orationes	7
nunquam in tantis negotijs, quibus meritissime districtus es,	463	Epistolae	18
TANTISPER			
Occidite; aut sane tantisper viuite, donec	425	Mem.Matr.5	15
si placeat vices meas tantisper supplere donec Academia orationem	470	Epistolae	6
TANTO			
Munere, Rex tanto verior inde prober.	405	Passio 7	4
Haud aliter cum Christus obit, prae funere tanto	409	Passio 20	5
Progenies, mundique aetas abdomine tanto	418	Tr.Mortis V	4
Tantoque nequioris optima Pirrha?	429	Mem.Matr.12	8
Excellentias vestras tanto chariores esse, cum eo sitis ordine atque	440	Orationes	24
ad Theologiam expeditissimos, tanto ac tam stupendo iudicio, vt,	443	Orationes	25
cum quanto plus possint in sua terra, tanto minus in aliena.	450	Orationes	11
Iustitiam prius tanto cum honore atque acclamatione administrans,	464	Epistolae	14
quanto altius crescunt, tanto etiam altius agunt radices:	464	Epistolae	18
TANTORUM			
Necesse est autem vt foelicitas tantorum Principum etiam in ministros	441	Orationes	5
TANTOS			
fieri participes eius sanguinis, qui tantos spiritus solet infundere.	440	Orationes	20
et precium, quae abyssus crumenae tantos sumptus aequabit?	468	Epistolae	3
TANTUM			
Tantum dulcia leniunt catarrhos.	385	Musae	9
Tantum repertum est trux hominum genus,	394	Musae 23	17
Qui tamen excipiat, Christus caret hospite: tantum	407	Passio 15	3
Non tantum est iter Angelis ad vndas,	415	Lucus 24	11
Heu miseri! Quis tantum ipsis virtutibus instat	419	Tr.Mortis	33
O superi: Quis tantum ipsis virtutibus instat	271	Tr.Mortis VS	33
Tantum istaec scribo gratus, ne tu mihi tantum	422	Mem.Matr.1	7
Quotidie pasti: tantum verum indue vultum	427	Mem.Matr.7	29
Quae suberant causae? quid nos committere tantum,	432	Poem.Lat.	18
Non metuunt vltra; nostra infortunia tantum	432	Poem.Lat.	24
Tantum etenim vestras (Parcae) non flectit habenas	433	Poem.Lat.	40
non omnes licitantibus producunt merces, sed specimen tantum:	445	Orationes	31
in hisce Nuptijs posteritati tantum prospexit suauissimus Princeps,	447	Orationes	27
adde quod angusti est animi aut superbi sua tantum nosse,	450	Orationes	17
Neque alienas tantum ex hoc itinere cognouit Respublicas sed quod	450	Orationes	32
apud nos agri tantum sunt fertiles, illic etiam arenae.	451	Orationes	4
quod optimus Princeps non tantum exteras regiones habuit perspectas,	451	Orationes	36
interficere voluptatis, vt iter tantum, tantis laboribus,	452	Orationes	7
Tantum precemur Deum immortalem, vt Princeps optimus nulla secunda	454	Orationes	38
Obsecremus eum tantum vt permittat nostram hanc Inter victrices	455	Orationes	16
si tantum Honori Tuo superesset otij ad legendum, quantum a nobis	457	Epistolae	8
aut tantum de nullo vnquam Filio Alma Mater, quantum de Te sibi	457	Epistolae	25
Tantum Maiestatem vestram subiectissime oramus, vt si officia nostra	460	Epistolae	14
neque illi e faece vulgi tantum qui eruditionem simplicitati	461	Epistolae	17
Tantum rogamus, vt pergas, & inter nouos honorum cumulos,	462	Epistolae	27
rudiorem esse impexioremque, quam vt tantum Hospitem excipiat:	463	Epistolae	29
Tantum quocunque, Domine, ascendas, sume tecum amorem illum quo soles	464	Epistolae	26
tantum fauoris nobis impertias, abunde succurres Magnificentiae tuae	469	Epistolae	24
TAPHOS			
Nou d' autou taphos est' aster: pheggos gar ekeinou	429	Mem.Matr.14	3
TARAXOS			
Alla meneit', ou gar taraxos poti metera bainei,	431	Mem.Matr.18	5
TARDA			
Cur lacrymas & tarda trahis suspiria, tanquam	415	Lucus 23	1
Nec tarda possunt pharmaca consequi,	425	Mem.Matr.6	6
TARDUM			
Sic aeuum exigitur tardum, dum praepetis anni	428	Mem.Matr.9	13
TARIXEUMATA			
Nota sunt tarixeumata Aegyptiorum, qui antequam condiebant corpora	452	Orationes	26
TARTARA			
It stridor, caelosque omnes & Tartara findit.	420	Tr.Mortis	73
TAS			
kai oi alloi nomeis boulontai plesion autou tas agelas istanai.	447	Orationes	32
TAUTA			
on me themiton en, ou di' emauton emarton, alla dia tauta.	452	Orationes	31
TE			
Nunc adeo per te viuunt, vt repere possint,	384	Musae	5
Sic o te (iuuerem, senemue) credat	385	Musae	10
Ne te productis videar lassare Camoenis,	385	Musae 1	3
Non mea fert aetas, vt te, veterane, lacessam;	386	Musae 2	1
Non vt te superem: res tamen ipsa feret.	386	Musae 2	2

TE (cont'd)	PAGE	TITLE		LINE
Aspice, dum perstas, vt te tua deserat aetas,	386	Musae 2		5
Te perspicaci atque integro.	388	Musae 8		8
Te contumaci & liuido?	388	Musae 8		10
(Superbius cum te nihil)	388	Musae 8		16
Praesulibus dirum te Musa coarguit hostem,	392	Musae 18		1
Aequabili facta. Ecquid ergo te tanta	392	Musae 20		6
te deneget VERBVM Deus.	397	Musae 28		18
Nec dextra te fugit, almi Amoris emblema?	397	Musae 31		1
Teque Deum alternis cantans Ambrosius iram,	398	Musae 33		19
Atqui te precor vnice per ipsam,	400	Musae 37		1
Nam si te cuperem secare versu,	400	Musae 37		14
Iam te funditus igneis Camoenis,	400	Musae 37		19
Non te carmine turbidum vocaui,	401	Musae 37		33
Quin te laudibus orno: quippe dico,	401	Musae 37		41
Haeresis, euertas. Quid enim te fallere possit?	402	Musae 39		22
Haud per te moritura, Scholamque introspicis omnem.	402	Musae 39		26
A Te Turture defluos,	403	Musae 40		13
Christe, vbi tam duro patet in te semita ferro,	404	Passio 4		1
Zacchaeus, vt Te cernat, arborem scandit:	406	Passio 12		1
Culpa redux iugem te neget esse Deum.	406	Passio 13		6
Iam meus es: nunc Te teneo: Pastorque prehensus	407	Passio 14		3
Te fixo vel Terra mouet: nam, cum Cruce, totam	408	Passio 18		1
Non moreris solus: Mundus simul interit in te,	409	Passio 21		1
Sollicitus, ne te stella perita notet:	413	Lucus 16		4
Omnia quaerendo, sed te, super omnia, vexas:	413	Lucus 16		5
Quin, mitte rugas; teque carnem & sanguinem	413	Lucus 17		5
Tu vero collige te, tibique insistito,	414	Lucus 20		5
Rotundus in te: namque si ansatus sies,	414	Lucus 20		7
Te mille rixae, mille prensabunt doli,	414	Lucus 20		8
Te mille nasi, mille rideant sinus.	414	Lucus 20		10
Te petet, ante diem quisquis obire cupit.	414	Lucus 21		6
Culmen, vbi pro te nemo dolere potest.	415	Lucus 23		16
Laus antiqua & honor perierunt, te velut ARMO	416	Lucus 25	V	7
Te deiecissent tempora longa suo.	416	Lucus 25		8
Hinc te olim gentes miratae odere vicissim;	416	Lucus 25		11
Te Germana tamen pubes, te Graecus & Anglus	416	Lucus 26		3
Dum te vel digitis minister vrget,	417	Lucus 30		1
In te, nec arcus, scorpionesue, aut rotas,	421	Lucus 33		4
Quin, sine, te cernam; quoties iam dixero, cernam;	421	Lucus 35		3
Cur sine te, votis immoriturus, ago?	421	Lucus 35		6
Cum te non videam, mene videre putas?	421	Lucus 35		8
Ah Mater, quo te deplorem fonte? Dolores	422	Mem.Matr.1		1
Te, Mater, celebrans diu,	424	Mem.Matr.4		11
Noctu te celebrans luminis aemulo.	424	Mem.Matr.4		12
Per te nascor in hunc globum	425	Mem.Matr.4		13
Hunc vultum ostendas, & tecum, nobile spectrum,	426	Mem.Matr.7		14
Quod nectar, nisi cum te celebrare diem?)	428	Mem.Matr.9		16
At te commoriente, Magna Mater,	428	Mem.Matr.10		5
Nam te nunc Ager, Vrbs, & Aula plorant:	428	Mem.Matr.10		8
Te nunc Anglia, Scotiaeque binae,	428	Mem.Matr.10		9
Quin te Cambria peruetusta deflet,	428	Mem.Matr.10		10
Logon te philtron, osth' upekselthein leon.	430	Mem.Matr.15		9
Demosion t' indalma kalou, theion te katoptron.	430	Mem.Matr.17		7
Praeis eiarinous te xarais epikidnato kepon:	431	Mem.Matr.17		18
Sol sine sole tuo! quam te tum nubibus atris	433	Poem.Lat.		37
Vna meam membris horula, teque cruci.	434	Poem.Lat.		2
Quin moriar tecum: vitam, quam negligis ipse,	434	Poem.Lat.		5
Atque vbi per te sanctificer natalibus ipsis,	434	Poem.Lat.		9
Quo Te, foelix Anna, modo deflere licebit?	435	Poem.Lat.		1
Scribere, Te dignum, vel lachrymare queat!	435	Poem.Lat.		6
Cum per te sit res ambitiosa mori.	435	Poem.Lat.		8
Ah longum, quae te deperit, errat iter.	437	Poem.Lat.		4
Ah longum, quae te deperit, ambit iter.	437	Poem.Lat.	V	4
Constat, Aprile vno te potuisse mori:	438	Poem.Lat.		4
Et melius coelum, te veniente, subest:	210	Cam.1613-a	BR	4
Sic non Phoebeus iam plus te splendeat ortus	211	Cam.1613-b	BR	15
Nec plus te rubeat vesper, Eliza, precor.	211	Cam.1613-b	BR	16
qua optime ostendis te eius vicarium qui omnia disponit suauiter?	443	Orationes		16
causaris, irruit Miles in Musaeum tuum, & gladio te liberat.	448	Orationes		28
perrumpit primipilus, & te cum coelis tuis ad inferos deturbat.	448	Orationes		30
Dij te perdant, cum malis tuis & arena sine calce;	451	Orationes		5
cur non vt elephanti turres, ita tu patriam tecum portasti?	451	Orationes		8
ex quo facile collectu erat, quantum deperimus te;	451	Orationes		29
quam stulte de te rixamur:	451	Orationes		29
cum dimitteret te in Hispaniam, quod Romani Imperatores in bello,	451	Orationes		31
certe nos te absentem omnes acerrime concitatissimeque desiderauimus.	451	Orationes		33
titulos caput vndique munientes meministi Magistrum Te esse Artium?	456	Epistolae		3
haec est ansa qua prehendimus Te, et tanquam Aquilam inter nouas	456	Epistolae		6
per Te illucet nobis Iacobus noster.	456	Epistolae		12
hinc a populo, illinc a Principe, in Te conueniunt, et confabulantur.	456	Epistolae		25
de nullo vnquam Filio Alma Mater, quantum de Te sibi polliceatur.	457	Epistolae		26
charta conspiciendum Te praebes, quo familiarius inter nos verseris.	458	Epistolae		20
Quod quidem non minus expectamus a Te, quem singularis doctrina	461	Epistolae		26
Neque sane quispiam incedit Te instructior ad omnem causam,	462	Epistolae		21
plenissimis suffragijs elegimus Te tribunum Parlamentarium,	465	Epistolae		4
postquam circumspiciens reperisset Te, quasi in tuis palpebris	465	Epistolae		14
enim sic effugies cum honoribus, quin laetitia nostra te assequatur.	465	Epistolae		23
hospitium, et erga te propensius, haud vsquam forsitan reperias.	466	Epistolae		18
ita ad Te confugimus primariam partem ecclesiastici corporis,	467	Epistolae		9
idque pro libris, de quibus nusquam rectius quam apud Te agitur.	467	Epistolae		19

TE (cont'd)	PAGE	TITLE		LINE
nosque ipsos Tibi, Teque Deo Opti: Max: intimis precibus commendamus.	468	Epistolae		9
tanta Humanitatis massa, quae apud Te visitur, abscindere non possim,	472	Epistolae		14
sic existimes nihil Mortalium firmiori flagrare in Te desiderio,	473	Epistolae		5
TECTIS				
vbi velut ex continentibus tectis ad nos traiecturum est incendium:	449	Orationes		13
2. Ad R. Naunton Gratiae de Fluuio et de tegendis Tectis stramineis	457	Epistolae		T
TECTUM				
Glans dedit, & truncus tectum, & ramalia mortem.	418	Tr.Mortis		8
TECTUS				
Faecundusque chalibs sceleris, iam sanguine tectus	271	Tr.Mortis	VS	37
TECUM				
cur non nos omnes tecum?	451	Orationes		7
expectamus indies futurum, Almae Matris amorem tecum simul euehas.	462	Epistolae		29
sume tecum amorem illum quo scles beare Amplitudini tuae deuotissimos	464	Epistolae		27
Permitte vt nos etiam in praedam partemque tecum veniamus: . .	465	Epistolae		21
TEDAS				
Scilicet, vt quos ante suas cum coniuge tedas	396	Musae 26		9
TEGENDIS				
2. Ad R. Naunton Gratiae de Fluuio et de tegendis Tectis stramineis	457	Epistolae		T
TEGES				
Languentium baculus, teges iacentium, ...	423	Mem.Matr.2		46
TEGMINIS				
illam tegminis insciam	395	Musae 25		13
TEI				
sun tei eulogiai sou prosepimetroumenei beabis Filium tuum . .	473	Epistolae		11
TEIPSUM				
Vt postulat nos; quid tuis dabis? Teipsum.	406	Passio 10		3
TEKNOIS				
Zoes ksunergon tende diatheinai teknois	430	Mem.Matr.15		6
TEKTAINOUSA				
Meteri tektainousa, gooi kai penthesi sugxroun.	431	Mem.Matr.17		14
TELA				
Cur tela Mortis vel tibi vel tuis	433	Poem.Lat.		5
TELAM				
nisi candida phrasi telam explices, perit negotium quasi ex nubibus	470	Epistolae		30
TELAS				
Et nunc perlongas Scripturae stamine telas	392	Musae 19		5
TELI				
illic tuta cognitio est, atque extra teli iactum.	449	Orationes		3
TELLURE				
Tristis, vbi ac ferrum tellure reciditur ima, ...	419	Tr.Mortis		36
TELLURIS				
Tellurisque Britannicae saliuam	428	Mem.Matr.10		3
TELLUS				
Quicquid habet tellus, quicquid & astra, fruens.	429	Mem.Matr.13		6
TELUM				
Scinditur in partes vulgus ceu compita: telum	418	Tr.Mortis		16
TEMERE				
Omnia sunt temere proijcienda foras.	390	Musae 13		2
TEMONE				
Adde etiam currus, & cum temone Britanno	419	Tr.Mortis		45
TEMPERANTIA				
Quid si hic lateat etiam Temperantia, rara in Principibus virtus,	452	Orationes		2
TEMPESTAS				
Tempestas Christo dormiente.	412	Lucus 12		T
TEMPLA				
Qui templa sacris expoliant choris, ...	394	Musae 23		18
TEMPLI				
Et per se Templi limen adire velis:	388	Musae 9		8
Et Templi parasite; namque velum	408	Passio 19		2
TEMPLIS				
Enixas pueros matres se sistere templis	389	Musae 12		1
Cum templis effare, madent sudaria, mappae, ...	397	Musae 29		1
TEMPORA				
Tum tibi, si placeat, fugientia tempora reddam;	386	Musae 2		9
Te deiecissent tempora longa suo.	416	Lucus 25		8
Jam deturbarunt tempora longa suo.	416	Lucus 25	V	8
Viuite, dum mortem ostendam: sic tempora vestram	432	Poem.Lat.		15
TEMPORARIJS				
et aeternitate occupatos, temporarijs hisce negotiolis libera.	466	Epistolae		6
TEMPORE				
Annulus & plenus tempore forsan erit.	396	Musae 26		6
Tuc tot negotijs meritissime distincto, tempore non suo obrepant:	457	Epistolae		12
tempore melior, iniurias seculi scriptaque hac illac pereuntia	459	Epistolae		14
Praesertim hoc tempore, in quo paucorum auaritia liberalibus artibus	466	Epistolae		23
TEMPORIBUS				
tuosque fauores temporibus et diligentia diuisos in gratijs nostris	457	Epistolae		15
TEMPORIS				
Quacunque gutta temporis imminent?	433	Poem.Lat.		6
Subtilitatis Terebra; Temporis Nepos	436	Poem.Lat.		22
segetem perspicio, nulla verborum, nulla temporis falce demetendam.	446	Orationes		3
ego tunc temporis liberior eram, huc illuc pro libitu	451	Orationes		11
vestra omni dente, tum edacis temporis, tum venenatorum haereticorum,	459	Epistolae		18
TEMPUS				
Ante tuum tempus coelum gratissimus ambis.	402	Musae 39		29
Suum cuique tempus & locus datur.	423	Mem.Matr.2		20
Tempus edax rerum, tuque o mors improba sola es, ...	433	Poem.Lat.		41
Vltra loquendi tempus; addit Anchora:	438	Poem.Lat.		4
si per tempus liceret effari, non licet per multitudinem, . .	443	Orationes		28
satietas quaedam honoris, quem ad tempus deponere famem excitat:	453	Orationes		10

	PAGE	TITLE	LINE
TEMPUS (cont'd)			
quippe qui vniuersum tempus nostrum (forsitan quo alacrius illud	460	Epistolae	5
Nunc obrutus Academicis negotijs, aegre hoc tempus illis succido:	471	Epistolae	20
Appetit tempus, cum excusso altero iugo, dimidiaque operis parte	473	Epistolae	1
TEN			
Exren phugousa, ten t' epistemen bicu.	430	Mem.Matr.15	7
TENACES			
Rupes tenaces & silices ferunt	393	Musae 23	9
TENACITAS			
vtinam & nunc sit tanta patriae tenacitas, vt nunquam Princeps se	455	Orationes	5
TENAX			
Ceu Polypus, chelis saxa prehendo tenax:	428	Mem.Matr.11	10
TENDE			
Zoes ksunergon tende diatheinai teknois	430	Mem.Matr.15	6
TENEAM			
Gladiosue, Catapultasue teneam, quin neque	421	Lucus 33	5
TENEBRAE			
Sunt etiam tenebrae, quas tamen optat amor.	437	Poem.Lat.	2
TENEBRICOSOS			
Nempe huc vsque notos tenebricosos	428	Mem.Matr.10	1
TENEBRIONES			
Quare prodite, tenebriones literarij, e gurgustijs vestris, . .	454	Orationes	24
TENEBRIS			
opportune his tenebris Fauor Tuus occurrit, illustrans nos omnes,	461	Epistolae	3
TENENT			
Mens superat; corpus solum Elementa tenent.	424	Mem.Matr.3	4
TENEO			
Iam meus es: nunc Te teneo: Pastorque prehensus	407	Passio 14	3
TENEOR			
hic etiam teneor, sed laxioribus vinculis, quaeque amor saepe	472	Epistolae	33
TENER			
Cum tener ad sacros infans sistatur aquales, ...	388	Musae 9	1
Excessit tener Orbis ex Ephebis, ...	408	Passio 19	11
TENERA			
delicata res est eruditio & tenera, tanquam flos molliculus rudiore	448	Orationes	24
TENERAE			
Mitis agas: tenerae duplicant sibi verbera mentes, ...	406	Passio 9	5
TENERAS			
Nunc etiam teneras quo versus gratior aures	387	Musae 5	11
TENERE			
(Tenere Christum scilicet, ne ascenderet)	438	Poem.Lat.	2
TENEROS			
Pugnaces, teneros florum turbemus odores, ...	427	Mem.Matr.7	32
TENES			
Dormitat pelagus: Quam bene fraena tenes!	412	Lucus 12	2
TENET			
Dum suum nomen tenet, & triumphat	390	Musae 14	19
TENORE			
Vtrum tenore sacra nostra sint necne	392	Musae 20	5
TENTANDO			
Tentando sanum: si calet, aestuans, ...	426	Mem.Matr.6	14
TENUI			
Horto pro tenui colit	424	Mem.Matr.4	3
TENUIA			
posterioris largam messem Vobis haec tenuia boni consulentibus,	441	Orationes	21
TENUIORES			
vt halitus tenuiores solent, qui primo caloris suasu excitati atque	471	Epistolae	28
TENUIS			
Vt tenuis flammae species caelum vsque minatur, ...	410	Lucus 2	1
Cui tenuis fama est, ingeniumque minus.	435	Poem.Lat.	4
TENUIUS			
Hoc etiam imperium tenuius est quam pro amplitudine virtutum	458	Epistolae	10
TER			
Ter millies coelo reponis:	394	Musae 23	27
Daunia, non satiat bis ter millesima caedis	418	Tr.Mortis	3
TEREBRA			
Subtilitatis Terebra; Temporis Nepos	436	Poem.Lat.	22
TERERE			
Non illa soles terere comptu lubricos, ...	422	Mem.Matr.2	10
TERETEM			
Cur teretem Graecam damnas, atque Hellada totam, ...	391	Musae 16	3
TERI			
sed Tu vis etiam manibus teri, semotaque Maiestate, charta . .	458	Epistolae	19
TERITUR			
vos, vos, inquam, excutite, quorum aetas teritur in libris: . .	445	Orationes	15
TERMINOS			
Et pomoeria terminosque sanctos	408	Passio 19	4
TERRA			
Terra nihil, nec quo sanctius astra vident;	385	Musae	2
Te fixo vel Terra mouet: nam, cum Cruce, totam	408	Passio 18	1
Cum natet in tantis caetera terra malis?	411	Lucus 6	2
Vnusquisque hominum, Terra est; & filius arui.	413	Lucus 18	1
Si nigro sit terra solo, quis despicit aruum?	437	Poem.Lat.	5
Tibi debet Vnda & Terra certitudinis.	438	Poem.Lat.	7
Exere terra caput, servatos projice flores, ...	210	Cam.1613-b BR	3
e qua liberi quaerantur, quam qualis terra, e qua arbores. . .	447	Orationes	11
cum quanto plus possint in sua terra, tanto minus in aliena.	450	Orationes	11
Quod si tam integrum tibi esset gratificari nobis in terra & aere,	457	Epistolae	22
TERRAE			
Terrae-motus.	408	Passio 18	1
Cum qui plus terrae, plus habuere maris.	411	Lucus 6	4

TERRAE (cont'd)	PAGE	TITLE	LINE
Coniugium Caeli Terraeque haec machina praestat;	417	Lucus 31	1
quam terrae, quam Natura montibus vallibusque sublimitate atque	453	Orationes	11
TERRAE-MOTUS			
Terrae-motus.	408	Passio 18	T
TERRAM			
Heu stolidi, primum fugientem figite Terram,	408	Passio 18	3
Tam demissa, ipsamque adeo subeuntia terram?	420	Tr.Mortis	94
Terram & funus olent flores: Dominaeque cadauer	425	Mem.Matr.5	5
In terram violae capite inclinantur opaco,	425	Mem.Matr.5	7
tuo communicans coelum ac terram minori quam cernimus interuallo	444	Orationes	7
manibus in coelum sublatis, lachrymis in terram manantibus, ieiunae,	448	Orationes	35
indicantes, se non amare patriam terram, a qua adeo remouentur.	452	Orationes	12
vbi iam ingrauescit humore, relabitur in terram, qua ortus est,	454	Orationes	29
Gulielmus Victor descensurus primum e nauibus in terram hanc,	455	Orationes	3
Illi terram inuenerunt, crassissimum elementum, Tu subtilitates	463	Epistolae	13
TERRARUM			
atque vbiuis terrarum pro iudicio prudentissimi Regis, & in rebus	444	Orationes	20
optime consuluisse Deum orbi terrarum lapides & metalla ei inserendo,	452	Orationes	24
si placet, Terrarum Reges, mutus est mundus vniuersus, vestra solum	458	Epistolae	5
TERRAS			
Scilicet has olim diuisas aequore terras	402	Musae 39	14
qui nouas scientiarum regiones terrasque veteribus incognitas primus	463	Epistolae	11
TERRESTRES			
Deus faueat Tibi & concedat vt terrestres tui honores cum coelestibus	465	Epistolae	18
TERRESTRIBUS			
dextra (quamuis a scriptione terrestribusque istis sublimitate solij	458	Epistolae	6
TERRET			
Terret equos equitumque vultus.	448	Orationes	4
TERRORIS			
Contemplare, miser, quantum terroris haberet	417	Lucus 31	5
TERSAE			
viros limatae auris atque tersae, quorum grauitate ac purpura	445	Orationes	27
TERSIS			
creberrima Antiquitatis lectione tersis atque expolitis,	473	Epistolae	20
TERTIA			
Praedicat autores; tertia plena Deo est.	386	Musae 4	4
quod si tertia detur et quarta, paratos nos habebis ad gratulationem,	465	Epistolae	25
TERTIAM			
vestrae coronae ciuili & literariae tertiam Coelestem sero adiungat.	459	Epistolae	21
TERTIJS			
quod primum intendunt, saltem in secundis aut tertijs consistant.	446	Orationes	7
TERTIUM			
Quare nos tertium praedictis adiungimus Gratiarum Fluuium,	462	Epistolae	23
TERTULLIANO			
Tertulliano, propter vndae pollubrum,	389	Musae 10	7
TERUNCIOS			
Haud glubat inde tres teruncios escae.	429	Mem.Matr.12	4
TES			
Tes peri sullalecusin, eou poikilmatos arden	431	Mem.Matr.17	11
TESD'			
Ei pou tuxcimi tesd' aristes atrapou,	430	Mem.Matr.15	15
TESSERA			
Nos flendo: haec nostrum tessera sola ducum.	427	Mem.Matr.9	12
TESSERAM			
Quamque ipse lucis tesseram sibi negat,	407	Passio 16	7
TESTATOS			
Testatosque suo tradiderat gregi;	391	Musae 17	2
TESTUDINE			
Amphionis testudine nobili	394	Musae 23	14
TETRAGONOS			
Oratio perfecta, vti vir, tetragonos est, grauis, nobilis,	471	Epistolae	4
TEXERE			
Coepisti, pergas simili res texere filo.	402	Musae 39	19
TEXTOR			
Cum piscatores Textor legit esse vocatos,	392	Musae 19	1
TEXTORE			
De Textore Catharo.	392	Musae 19	T
TEXTORES			
An quia Textores Artificesque probas?	392	Musae 18	2
TEXTU			
Torquet, & in Textu Doctor vtroque cluet.	392	Musae 19	6
THALAMUM			
Sintque ausae thalamum solis adire tui.	384	Musae	6
THAMESEOS			
Kumat' epaphriconta Thameseos, aike selenes	431	Mem.Matr.18	1
THAMESIS			
Sicca meis lacrymis Thamesis vicina videtur,	422	Mem.Matr.1	3
THANATOS			
Autar od' au thanatos kuries, os elios auos	431	Mem.Matr.17	19
THANEIN			
Thanein suneidos kreitton, e allos bioun.	430	Mem.Matr.15	16
THAUMA			
Ouk eni thauma toson spheterizein: oude gar udor,	430	Mem.Matr.17	4
THE			
To the right honourable and reverend Father in God, my L. Bishop of	473	Epistolae	23
of Winchester, one of the Kings most honorable privy-Counsaile.	473	Epistolae	24
THEATRUM			
et blattis rixantes, exuens puluere, in theatrum et lucem produxisti.	462	Epistolae	27
THEBIS			
Moenia contribuere Thebis.	394	Musae 23	16

	PAGE	TITLE		LINE
THEION				
Demosion t' indalma kalou, theion te katoptron.	430	Mem.Matr.17		7
THEMIS				
Praetulit Astraea, aut solic Themis alma vetusto	426	Mem.Matr.7		12
E themis, e dunaton. semnomatos epleto stathme, ...	430	Mem.Matr.17		6
Nun themis orphnaiei megales epi geitonos aisei	431	Mem.Matr.18		3
THEMITON				
e phagon e pion, on me themiton en, ou di' emauton emarton, . .	452	Orationes		30
THENSAE				
Ipse tuae solum adnectam, sine murmure, thensae.	426	Mem.Matr.7		16
THEOI				
O despota elie kai theoi pantes, ei ti kata ton emautou Bion emarton,	452	Orationes		29
THEOLOGIA				
praesertim in Theologia, cuius Libri si alij alijs (tanquam montes	467	Epistolae		30
THEOLOGIAM				
etiam libros indicans ad Theologiam expeditissimos, tanto ac tam	443	Orationes		25
THEOU				
Odurma Daimonon, Theou georgion, ...	429	Mem.Matr.15		2
THERIACAS				
Quid Theriacas peregrinas? asserunt Medici vramquamque regionem sua	444	Orationes		24
THESAURAR				
9. Ad Mounteg., Thesaurar. Gratulatio	464	Epistolae		T
16. Ad Cranfield, Thesaurar. Gratulatio	469	Epistolae		T
THESAURIS				
Quis enim rectius Thesauris Regijs praefici possit quam qui,	464	Epistolae		13
dignissime praeficiaris Fisco, etiam Academiam in Thesauris habe:	469	Epistolae		22
THOMAM				
In Thomam Didymum.	417	Lucus 30		T
THORNDICK				
Proin iube Thorndick nostrum, ni graue est, librum tibi Oratorium	470	Epistolae		9
THRACES				
Hinc Thraces dicti sunt abioi, & Licurgus magnus Legislator atimian	446	Orationes		19
THRONOS				
Haec verba superos aduclaturus thronos	396	Musae 28		7
Occumbens humero Thronos lacessam.	421	Lucus 34		9
THRONUM				
Tu duplicem solus Camoenarum thronum	388	Musae 8		3
THURAN				
Ou pheggos, koinon t' agathon, mian eis thuran eirgein . . .	430	Mem.Matr.17		5
THURIDON				
Astrapton, Thuridon os dia, neime selas.	429	Mem.Matr.14		8
THURIS				
post ingentes Hecatombas, exiguam thuris micam adoleri legimus.	469	Epistolae		17
THUSIA				
Logike Thusia.	417	Lucus 29		T
THYMO				
honore grauidus, grauidus scientia, cruribus thymo plenis: . .	454	Orationes		28
TI				
Zo d' autos, braxu ti pneion, ost' empalin autes	431	Mem.Matr.17		21
theoi pantes, ei ti kata ton emautou Bion emarton, e phagon e pion,	452	Orationes		29
TIBERIO				
Imperatorum incredibilem luxum a Tiberio Caesare ad Constantinum	452	Orationes		22
TIBI				
Quam chartam tibi porrigo recentem, ...	384	Musae		1
Ista decens soli scripta quadrare tibi.	385	Musae		6
Tum tibi, si placeat, fugientia tempora reddam;	386	Musae 2		9
Non tibi fingendi sola taberna patet.	386	Musae 3		6
Sola tibi Sappho, feminaque vna placet?	387	Musae 5		2
Cur tibi tam facile non arrisere poetae	387	Musae 5		3
Cur sic displiceat vox aliena tibi?	388	Musae 9		10
Et tibi sit nemo praes, vbi poscis opem.	389	Musae 9		16
Verum heus! si reputes, tibi tuisque	391	Musae 15		7
Tuum tibi, poeta belle, nor mystes, ...	392	Musae 20		11
Nihilne respondebimus tibi? Fatemur.	392	Musae 20		16
Nulla tibi si signa placent, e nubibus arcum	396	Musae 26		3
Caetera condonabo tibi, scombrisque remittam:	399	Musae 34		3
Et tibi vicinas porrigit aequor aquas:	399	Musae 35		8
Per charas tibi nobilesque dextras, ...	400	Musae 37		7
Per quicquid tibi suauiter probatur;	400	Musae 37		9
Haesisset tibi, quam suprema vestis	400	Musae 37		26
Haurirent tibi tota plaustra Musae.	401	Musae 37		30
Non fastus tibi turgidos repono;	401	Musae 37		36
Nil horum rogero tibi merenti.	401	Musae 37		40
Sint tibi vel stellis laudes, & laudibus anni:	402	Musae 39		34
Si tibi non illud placeat mirabile corpus, ...	404	Passio 2		3
Caetera displiceat turba, recesse, tibi:	404	Passio 2		4
Christe, dolor tibi supplicio, mihi blanda voluptas;	405	Passio 6		1
Suauiter admoueas notum tibi carne flagellum, ...	406	Passio 9		3
Nobis facilitas cedat & tibi sudor.	406	Passio 12		3
Tibi supererunt & mihi.	407	Passio 16		14
Tu tamen, haud tibi tam moreris, quam viuis in illis, ...	407	Passio 17		3
Crudum olim pomum, tristis Adame, tibi.	412	Lucus 9		4
Quod omnibus tute imperes, nemo tibi.	412	Lucus 11		3
Tu vero collige te, tibique insistito, ...	414	Lucus 20		5
Os & lingua tibi diues, egena manus:	414	Lucus 22		2
Dum lacrymas, it vita: tuus tibi clepsydra fletus, ...	415	Lucus 23		9
Non deerat vel fama tibi, vel carmina famae, ...	416	Lucus 25		3
Non deerint vel fama tibi, vel carmina famae, ...	416	Lucus 25	V	3
Quin tibi tam desperatae MORA nulla medetur, ...	416	Lucus 25		9
Quin tibi iam desperatae MORA nulla medetur, ...	416	Lucus 25	V	9
Inuertis nomen. Quid tibi dicit? AMOR.	416	Lucus 26		6

TIBI (cont'd)	PAGE	TITLE	LINE
Romano, sed res seria Roma tibi est:	416	Lucus 27	2
Esse iocum soli, plebe stupente, tibi:	416	Lucus 27	4
Quam satur & suauis sit tibi Roma iocus.	416	Lucus 27	6
Num totum tibi pectus imputabis?	421	Lucus 34	2
Mater: & ista Dolor nunc tibi Metra parit.	422	Mem.Matr.1	8
Pactoli arena tibi tumulus est vnicus.	423	Mem.Matr.2	41
Nato dolenti: literae hoc debent tibi	424	Mem.Matr.2	62
Scilicet id splendes: haec est tibi causa micandi,	424	Mem.Matr.3	5
Hoc, Genitrix, scriptum proles tibi sedula mittit.	427	Mem.Matr.9	1
Plura tibi missurus eram (nam quae mihi laurus,	428	Mem.Matr.9	15
Non tibi nunc soli filum abrupere sorores,	428	Mem.Matr.11	11
Cur tela Mortis vel tibi vel tuis	433	Poem.Lat.	5
Cur mihi das vitam, quam tibi, Christe, negas?	434	Poem.Lat.	4
Accipe; ni talem des, tibi qualis erat.	434	Poem.Lat.	6
Hae tibi sunt alae laudum. Cui contigit vnquam	435	Poem.Lat.	5
Hae tibi sunt alae laudis. Cui contigit vnquam	435	Poem.Lat. V	5
Claude oculos, & erunt omnia nigra tibi:	437	Poem.Lat.	6
Nec hoc abunde est tibi, nisi certae Anchorae	438	Poem.Lat.	5
Tibi debet Vnda & Terra certitudinis.	438	Poem.Lat.	7
Fluminaque e ripis obvia facta tibi:	210	Cam.1613-a BR	6
Nec facile ascendant, sed tibi vallis erit.	210	Cam.1613-a BR	8
tibique non tam auide veterum beneficiorum memoriam recolenti,	457	Epistolae	12
Quod si tam integrum tibi esset gratificari nobis in terra & aere,	457	Epistolae	21
Vt nihilo-minus Tibi luceat, cum nobis accenderit.	461	Epistolae	5
neque amplius quaerendum sit Tibi, Almae Nutrici quid reponas.	462	Epistolae	16
Quare summe gratulamur tibi de nouo hoc cumulo honorum,	464	Epistolae	20
vt semper post nouas dignitates, alias tibi quaerant et moliantur.	464	Epistolae	23
Antiquitas praeripuit Tibi gloriam extruendae Academiae,	465	Epistolae	17
Deus faueat Tibi & concedat vt terrestres tui honores cum coelestibus	465	Epistolae	18
Certe non diu est ex quo gratulati sumus tibi:	465	Epistolae	24
vero de hoc tuo progressu non minus Reipublicae gratulamur quam tibi,	466	Epistolae	16
quare causam nostram nosque ipsos Tibi, Teque Deo Opti: Max: intimis	468	Epistolae	9
certe studijs chartisque obuolutos, quin aures nostrae tibi pateant.	468	Epistolae	14
Quare tam vere quam libenter gratulamur tibi, nec minus etiam	468	Epistolae	18
eadem manus et tuum tibi largita est honorem, et priuilegia nostra	468	Epistolae	23
Deus fortunet tibi hunc honorem, et faxit, vt tibi gloriae sit,	469	Epistolae	5
tibi hunc honorem, et faxit, vt tibi gloriae sit, omnibus saluti.	469	Epistolae	5
ni graue est, librum tibi Oratorium lampademque tradat.	470	Epistolae	10
non tam quod tibi conueniat scribenti, quam quod Academiae tuo calamo	470	Epistolae	13
Quare scripturus, finge tibi matronam sanctam, venerandam,	470	Epistolae	16
tu hanc personam indue scripturus, tuumque iudicium tibi Lictor esto.	470	Epistolae	27
TIBIAM			
Dulcem rependent tum mihi tibiam	434	Poem.Lat.	33
TIBIJS			
Vt currat paribus gloria tibijs.	425	Mem.Matr.4	16
TIBRIS			
Prae quo Tibris vultum recondit,	394	Musae 23	43
TIGNIS			
Est mihi bis quinis laqueata domuncula tignis	426	Mem.Matr.7	22
TIGRES			
ac si non gregaria essent animalia, sed tigres aut vrsi.	450	Orationes	22
TIGRIS			
Quin nec potes; cui praebuit Tigris partum.	429	Mem.Matr.12	10
TILLIUS			
Tillius incumbit Dano, Gallusque marinis,	427	Mem.Matr.9	11
TIMEMUS			
ex quo timemus librorum precia auctum iri, et priuilegia nostra	467	Epistolae	7
TIMET			
Ceu, quas culta timet seges, pruinas	385	Musae	7
TIMORES			
Nunc enim exploratos habet nostros in se affectus, timores, suspiria,	450	Orationes	34
TINA			
osper tina odon proeleluthoton, en kai emas isos deesei poreuesthai,	471	Epistolae	10
TINCTUS			
Faecundusque chalybs sceleris, iam sanguine tinctus,	419	Tr.Mortis	37
TINEAE			
vestra disquisitio, qui tineae estis & helluones chartacei;	445	Orationes	18
TINEAS			
Mordaces tineas, nigrasque blattas,	385	Musae	5
TINEIS			
otium, pax omnibus praeterquam tineis, paupertas perpetua,	441	Orationes	15
literatos, eosque cum tineis et blattis rixantes, exuens puluere,	462	Epistolae	26
TINGIMUR			
Quo tingimur parui. Ecquis autem brachijs	389	Musae 10	8
TINNIO			
Non rhetoricor, Academici, non tinnio:	445	Orationes	22
TINNITUS			
Tinnitus Berecynthios omittens	401	Musae 37	39
TINNULIS			
Strepente mundo tinnulis praeconijs?	423	Mem.Matr.2	56
TIS			
Geneteiran ou tis andron	430	Mem.Matr.16	5
proeleluthoton, en kai emas isos deesei poreuesthai, poia tis esti.	471	Epistolae	11
TISIPHONE			
Haec fuerant: sic Tisiphone virguncula lusit.	418	Tr.Mortis	23
Tisiphone; flamma & fallaci fulmine cincta	420	Tr.Mortis	71
TITILLANT			
qui semper titillant aures Principum, Osper tois pterois knomenoi ta	453	Orationes	2
TITULI			
Cuius noui tituli accessionem summe gratulantur Excellentijs Vestris	440	Orationes	6

	PAGE	TITIE	LINE
TITUIIS			
Legatis cum Magistro. in Artib. titulis insignirentur. 27. Febr.	440	Oraticnes	T
TITUIC			
Responde aeternum titulc; quoque crdine felix	402	Musae 39	18
TITUICS			
aliosque titulcs aeque ncbis memorantibus, ac merentibus vobis	440	Oraticnes	3
Ecquid inter tot gloriae titulos caput vndique munientes meministi	456	Epistolae	2
TITULUS			
Papae titulus Nec Deus Nec Homo.	412	Lucus 10	T
TITYRUS			
Strauit Idumaeum diuinus Tityrus hostem?	419	Tr.Mortis	44
TO			
Mencun to glaphuron, kai melirrocn tropcn, ...	430	Mem.Matr.15	8
Phercn tc par, kagcn: e cs Aparktias	430	Mem.Matr.15	11
To the right hcnourable and reverend Father in Gcd, my L. Bishcp of	473	Epistolae	23
TCGAE			
Squaloremque tcgae candida Musa fugat.	417	Lucus 28	6
TCGAM			
lucos aestate, pinguem tcgam hyeme:	448	Orationes	24
TCI			
Katoptron ean epideikseis toi epikeimenoi nephei, pareleusetai e	454	Oraticnes	19
TCIAUTEN			
Didumais kcrais toiauten	430	Mem.Matr.16	6
TCIDE			
Toide para tumbci dizec, phile, mcncn.	429	Mem.Matr.14	2
TCIS			
& Licurgus magnus Legislatcr atimian prosetheke tois agamois.	446	Oraticnes	20
semper titillant aures Principum, Osper tcis ptercis kncmenci ta ota.	453	Orationes	3
TOLERARE			
Harmoniam tolerare nullam?	395	Musae 23	52
TOLLANTUR			
Tollantur si cuncta malus quae polluit vsus, ...	390	Musae 13	3
TCN			
theoi pantes, ei ti kata ton emautou Bicn emartcn, e phagcn e picn,	452	Crationes	29
Dokei moi xrenai para tcn presbutcn punthanesthai, osper tina odon	471	Epistolae	10
TCNANTES			
Nunc haec cmnia sustuli, tcnantes	401	Musae 37	31
TCNITRU			
vapores seruiles ad nubes educti aeque magnum tonitru edent ac regij.	452	Orationes	18
TCRI			
Legitimi signum ccnnubiale tcri.	396	Musae 26	12
TORMENTA			
Quid memorem tcrmenta, quibus prius horruit aeuum;	419	Tr.Mcrtis	39
TCRMENTC			
Tormento peicr Iesuita, & fulminat Crbem, ...	420	Tr.Mcrtis	96
TCRPENS			
Ecce meus tcrpens animus succumbit vtrique, ...	435	Poem.Lat.	3
TCRPENTES			
Vt niue torpentes incaluere manus?	399	Musae 35	4
TORQUEAT			
O vere dictum, & belle! cum tcrqueat cmnes	389	Musae 11	3
TORQUERENT			
essent atque ccnsilijs, sine quibus ne vnum quidem filum torquerent:	449	Oraticnes	31
TORQUET			
Torquet, & in Textu Dcctcr vtrcque cluet.	392	Musae 19	6
Hippcnensis adest properans, & tcrquet in hcstes	398	Musae 33	17
TORRENS			
Quem non Emathius torrens, ncn sanguine pinguis	418	Tr.Mcrtis	2
TCRTCS			
Fac radios saltem ingemines, vt dextera tortcs	424	Mem.Matr.3	9
TORUM			
Paras hospitium torumque dulcem, ...	417	Lucus 30	5
TCRUS			
Dum torus absentem quisque repcnit heram.	425	Mem.Matr.5	10
TOSCN			
Ouk eni thauma tcscn spheterizein: cude gar udor, ...	430	Mem.Matr.17	4
TCT			
Cur, vbi tct ludat numeris antiqua poesis, ...	387	Musae 5	1
Cum lacrymas oculosque duos tot vulnera vincant, ...	404	Passic 1	1
Spargitque per tct capita, quct vulgus gerit.	414	Lucus 20	4
Illa cauerna, in qua tot cciere ferae.	414	Lucus 21	4
Vel quia tot moritur, tot viguisse probes.	415	Lucus 23	8
Frustra itaque in tct funeribus miraberis vnum, ...	415	Lucus 23	11
Tot quaesticnum fluctibus ctruis, ...	425	Mem.Matr.6	2
Mors tct vircrum scrdida sanguine, ...	433	Poem.Lat.	10
Non tot abest, quot nos Regis ab ingenic.	437	Poem.Lat.	4
Tot & tanta loquens amica, scripsit:	439	Poem.Lat.	11
nisi tct negctijs distractus esses, confluerernus omnes ad Aulam,	443	Oraticnes	26
aequumne est vt tot labores & sollicitudines Principum sine . .	446	Orationes	11
qua tct iam annis impune fruimur, hoc pacto fundatam cupit . .	447	Crationes	28
& per tot milliaria facile transmissum, mentem maiorum capacem	454	Oraticnes	1
Ecquid inter tct gloriae titulos caput vndique munientes meministi	456	Epistolae	2
ne literae ncstrae animc Tuc tct negctijs meritissime distincto,	457	Epistclae	11
quae fugerunt tot philosophos vmbra et otio diffluentes, . .	463	Epistolae	19
vt qui tct subsidia attuleris ad prcgressum doctrinae, hac etiam	467	Epistclae	27
TOTA			
Inde Patres pergunt quadrati, & tota Vetustas.	398	Musae 33	13
Haurirent tibi tcta plaustra Musae.	401	Musae 37	30
Desinis exclamans: tota figura, vale.	401	Musae 38	2
Gens tcta fiet, atque vtrinque plectetur.	405	Passio 5	7
Agnoscitque tuam Machina tcta Crucem.	409	Passic 21	2

TOTA (cont'd)	PAGE	TITLE	LINE
Omnia purgentur, niteat mihi tota supellex,	413	Lucus 19	3
Sulphureoque lacu, totaque imbuta Mephiti.	419	Tr.Mortis	59
Tota renident aede decus & suauitas	423	Mem.Matr.2	24
Tota stupent luctu) lachrymisque exaestuet aequis	432	Poem.Lat.	10
Nam primum tota haec Pieria supellex, charta, calami, codices,	448	Orationes	18
TOTAM			
Cur teretem Graecam damnas, atque Hellada totam,	391	Musae 16	3
Totamque euomerem potenter iram	400	Musae 37	15
Te fixo vel Terra mouet: nam, cum Cruce, totam	408	Passio 18	1
Totamque eructans nubem, Glans proruit imo	420	Tr.Mortis	76
TOTI			
Sic toti medicaris ipse murdo.	405	Passio 8	3
TOTO			
Strata iacent toto millena cadauera campo	420	Tr.Mortis	79
Strata, iacent toto prostrata cadauera campo	272	Tr.Mortis VS	79
TOTUM			
Expleri nequit, & totum depascitur Orbem.	419	Tr.Mortis	38
Num totum tibi pectus imputabis?	421	Lucus 34	2
Totum offuscari peteres, vt nocte silenti	433	Poem.Lat.	38
TOTUS			
Totusque caerum Cynthiae ignoscit noctis.	393	Musae 22	9
Nempe es totus amor, medulla amoris,	417	Lucus 30	3
Corporeque atque animo. Totus mihi seruiat Orbis.	421	Tr.Mortis	101
Si totus infler, si tumeam crepax,	426	Mem.Matr.6	17
Hinc fremere totus & minari gestio	427	Mem.Matr.8	5
cum non est tanti totus ille maritimus tractus (Oceani praeda	461	Epistolae	8
TOUS			
Orthos, anagke dustuxein tous ekgonous.	447	Orationes	19
TRACTANS			
Arterias tractans micantes	425	Mem.Matr.6	3
TRACTARI			
Qua parte tractari solent,	388	Musae 8	12
TRACTAS			
dum globos tractas & coelos fictitios, perrumpit primipilus,	448	Orationes	29
TRACTUS			
est tanti totus ille maritimus tractus (Oceani praeda et deliciae)	461	Epistolae	9
TRADAT			
ni graue est, librum tibi Cratorium lampademque tradat.	470	Epistolae	10
TRADENTES			
qui optimum Principem spe nuptiarum mari nuper tradentes,	444	Orationes	18
TRADEREMUS			
vestram aeternitati in scriptis nostris certissime traderemus?	459	Epistolae	1
TRADIDERAT			
Testatosque suo tradiderat gregi;	391	Musae 17	2
TRADIDISSET			
esse Alexandro Magno nisi eius res gestas tradidisset historia?	441	Orationes	19
TRADIDIT			
fruenda nobis tradidit.	397	Musae 28	12
TRADUCTUS			
signo meritus est, ad vera castra traductus, hostem interficiet:	453	Orationes	30
TRAGEMATA			
Erutus, infernae pretiosa tragemata mensae,	419	Tr.Mortis	58
Exulis, infernae pretiosa tragemata mensae,	419	Tr.Mortis V	58
sua non abirent olim in elementa, sed in bellaria aut tragemata:	452	Orationes	14
TRAHERE			
Hos ad se trahere et mergere gestiens.	391	Musae 17	10
TRAHIS			
Cur lacrymas & tarda trahis suspiria, tanquam	415	Lucus 23	1
TRAHIT			
Recte, quem trahit, aerem repellit	428	Mem.Matr.10	6
TRAIECTURUM			
vbi velut ex continentibus tectis ad nos traiecturum est incendium:	449	Orationes	14
TRALATAE			
vbi tamen ad vsum tralatae fuerint, machinas conficiunt	454	Orationes	5
TRAMITE			
Quasque habet aut patulas, aut caeco tramite, moles	402	Musae 39	21
TRANQUILLAM			
Otium poscunt artes, mentem tranquillam, serenam, sudam:	448	Orationes	23
TRANQUILLITAS			
Artes hic sunt quiete & silentio cultae, tranquillitas, otium,	441	Orationes	14
TRANQUILLITATEM			
tranquillitatem, etiam & scientiae augmentum ex hoc itinere captauit	450	Orationes	4
TRANQUILLUS			
Tranquillus aer nascitur:	396	Musae 27	2
TRANSADIGANT			
Omniaque haec vt transadigant sine crimine costas,	418	Tr.Mortis	29
TRANSEAT			
coelestis an sublunaris, sed quae signa, quo motu transeat.	454	Orationes	13
praesertim donec transeat nubes illa, quae vicinos adeo infestat:	455	Orationes	14
TRANSFERAT			
quae nos soluendo non sumus, in suas tabulas accepti transferat.	467	Epistolae	19
TRANSFERATUR			
Philosophus de Tactu & Visu, id apposite admodum huc transferatur.	473	Epistolae	1
TRANSFERENDAE			
quanto magis virtutes istae in Dominum agri transferendae sunt,	459	Epistolae	17
TRANSIJT			
Trecentos obijt Nestor, non transijt annos,	415	Lucus 23	7
TRANSILIRE			
enatare e delicijs, transilire sepes, rumpere fascias cum Hercule,	452	Orationes	6

	PAGE	TITLE	LINE
TRANSILIUNT			
Transiliuntque caput, qui subiere pedes.	414	Lucus 19	2
TRANSIRE			
Nec transire licet quo mentis acumine findis	402	Musae 39	27
TRANSMARINA			
Londinenses librarios omnia transmarina scripta ad monopolium	467	Epistolae	20
TRANSMISSUM			
& per tot milliaria facile transmissum, mentem maiorum capacem	454	Orationes	1
TRANSMISSURI			
hausisse ab Antiquis, sed et ad Posteros transmissuri videantur.	469	Epistolae	13
TRANSNATANTES			
vicinum fretum quotidie transnatantes, litora nostra atque aures mire	441	Orationes	4
TRANSTULERINT			
quam Nuptiae, quas adeo laudant Poetae, vt in coelum transtulerint:	446	Orationes	18
TRAPHEISAI			
Ouk eti despoines glukerai meledoni trapheisai:	431	Mem.Matr.17	16
TRAUMATI			
Iesmones, e belone sphaleroi kep traumati vuttei	431	Mem.Matr.17	12
TRECENTA			
vbi trecenta foliorum iugera vno die sedentes percurritis; . . .	454	Orationes	25
TRECENTOS			
Trecentos obijt Nestor, non transijt annos, ...	415	Lucus 23	7
TREMENDUS			
Superpellicei tremendus hostis, ...	391	Musae 15	2
TREPHEI			
Eirene georgon kan petrais trephei kalos, ...	448	Orationes	14
TREPIDATIONES			
Ecquid inter tantas mundi trepidationes nobis & Musis vacas?	458	Epistolae	2
TRES			
Tres video partes, quo re distinctius vtar, ...	386	Musae 4	1
Haud glubat inde tres terunciosescae.	429	Mem.Matr.12	4
TRIA			
a Con verbo deduci, quod tria complectitur, Possum, Scio, . . .	447	Orationes	7
TRIBUANT			
Et nostrae tribuant molae farinam, ...	415	Lucus 24	5
TRIBUENDUM			
notionum aequare nunquam potest, non voluntati tribuendum existimes.	460	Epistolae	18
TRIBUI			
non suam tribui iubet.	396	Musae 25	23
TRIBUIT			
Quam tribuit, verum multiplicare decet.	408	Passio 17	8
Cui caecas tribuit vires annosa vetustas.	433	Poem.Lat.	42
TRIBUNITIAE			
aliae contra semper pertinaces ac tribunitiae, vti Appij. . .	447	Orationes	21
TRIBUNUM			
plenissimis suffragijs elegimus Te tribunum Parlamentarium, . .	465	Epistolae	5
TRIBUTI			
Tributi solutio.	412	Lucus 11	T
TRIBUTUM			
Piscis tributum soluit; & tu Caesari:	412	Lucus 11	1
TRIENTEM			
Adde his trientem Musices, quae molliens	423	Mem.Matr.2	42
TRINITATEM			
precamur S. S. Trinitatem, vt vestrae coronae ciuili & literariae	459	Epistolae	20
TRIPUDIANTES			
Arionem Delphino reuectum excepere arbores tripudiantes, . .	454	Orationes	37
TRIPUDIET			
tripudiet Alma Mater licet aetate prouectior, etiam anus subsultans	454	Orationes	35
TRIREMES			
Aiacis exesas triremes	433	Poem.Lat.	15
TRISTE			
Triste colens cellae, noctuque & Daemone plenum, ...	420	Tr.Mortis	90
Triste colens sellae, noctuque & Daemone plenum, ...	420	Tr.Mortis V	90
TRISTES			
Cur ideo verbis tristes effundere curas	433	Poem.Lat.	45
TRISTI			
Quis Monachos mortem meditari, & puluere tristi	420	Tr.Mortis	92
Quis mortem Monachos meditari, et puluere tristi	272	Tr.Mortis VS	92
Hoc mihi legatum tristi si funere praestes, ...	434	Poem.Lat.	7
TRISTIS			
Crudum olim pomum, tristis Adame, tibi.	412	Lucus 9	4
Tristis, vbi ac ferrum tellure reciditur ima, ...	419	Tr.Mortis	36
TRIUMPHANT			
Veste triumphant.	390	Musae 14	12
TRIUMPHANTIUM			
deperijt, at illa mutata est in arborem triumphantium propriam:	455	Orationes	9
TRIUMPHARE			
subiectos, integro Fluuio a Rege nostro donatos, triumphare?	460	Epistolae	14
TRIUMPHAS			
Sarcasmos quibus artifex triumphas;	400	Musae 37	4
TRIUMPHAT			
Dum suum nomen tenet, & triumphat	390	Musae 14	19
Qua Mors ipsa sedens hominum de gente triumphat.	419	Tr.Mortis	56
TRIUMPHOS			
triumphos & victorias quasi fraena ferox spumantia mandit, . .	447	Orationes	34
Daphnen suam, cuius amor deinceps in triumphos & laurus mutabitur.	455	Orationes	11
vestra spolia actosque ex orbe triumphos communicas cum Alma Matre,	458	Epistolae	16
TRIUMPHUS			
Triumphus Mortis.	418	Tr.Mortis	T
Triumphus Christiani. In Mortem.	421	Lucus 33	T

TUA	PAGE	TITLE	LINE
Aspice, dum perstas, vt te tua deserat aetas,	386	Musae 2	5
Pallada gorgoneam, sic tua verba placent.	387	Musae 6	4
Ille tamen, quamuis altus, tua crimina ridens	387	Musae 7	7
Virtute percellis tua;	388	Musae 8	4
(Cum plerumque tua sodalitate	401	Musae 37	45
Nescia sit metae; venula, cella tua est.	404	Passio 2	2
Qui Caput es, spinas & tua Membra tuas.	405	Passio 6	4
Quam nihil illudis! si, quae tua purpura fingit,	405	Passio 7	7
Christe, fluas semper; ne, si tua flumina cessent,	406	Passio 13	5
Hunc penas animam mundi, Plato: vel tua mundum	409	Passio 21	3
At nunc exucco similis tua gloria RAMO	416	Lucus 25	5
Si licet, immoriar: vel si tua visio vita est,	421	Lucus 35	5
Quo nunc recumbis, scriptio merita est tua,	423	Mem.Matr.2	40
Alteraque haec tua mors, Ilias esto mihi.	428	Mem.Matr.11	14
Christe, duplex fiet mors tua vita mihi:	434	Poem.Lat.	8
Scilicet appenit pretium tua dextera fato,	435	Poem.Lat.	5
O quam felices sunt, qui tua castra sequuntur,	435	Poem.Lat.	7
Eximia tua in nos merita frequentiorem calamum postulant,	457	Epistolae	7
non dubitamus quin benignitas tua omnia elementa percurreret.	457	Epistolae	23
de humanitate tua singulari, studioque in nos iam olim	462	Epistolae	24
importunorum hominum Authoritate tua plurima & Eloquentia non minori	463	Epistolae	2
sic merita tua ita ascensura, vt eorum vis et virtus ad nos	464	Epistolae	19
Nimirum id assecuta sunt merita Tua maxima, vt Almam Matrem spe noua	464	Epistolae	24
eccum nunc altera occasio, adeo festinat virtus tua:	465	Epistolae	25
rogamusque vt quando beneficia tua peruagantur Angliam,	466	Epistolae	17
nisi humanitas tua, superiori aestate sponte suauiterque patefacta,	467	Epistolae	2
id omne dexterrima tua in obeundis rebus prudentia dissipetur.	467	Epistolae	13
Deus Opti: Max. tua beneficia, quae nos soluendo non sumus,	467	Epistolae	14
Curasti tu quidem Instauratione tua, quo minus exteris Libris	467	Epistolae	24
concessae ab Augustissimo Iacobo auctae tua opera conseruentur;	468	Epistolae	22
Sed tua humanitas haec nobis expediet.	469	Epistolae	4
qui etiam ferians nihil Tua perfectione dignum procudere possit.	471	Epistolae	23
Vtcunque Tua lenitas non ita interpretabitur mea haec scribendi	471	Epistolae	24
magis id adeo factum esse mansuetudine Tua incomparabili,	472	Epistolae	21
tam communi hac luce, quam Tua, cum id agnoscere vnquam desinam.	472	Epistolae	24
quamuis enim sexcenta huiusmodi praedicla Tua gratia permutare nolim,	472	Epistolae	30
TUAE			
Grata mihi mensae sunt analecta tuae.	385	Musae 1	6
Anticategoriae, Scoto-Britanne, tuae:	386	Musae 4	2
Sufficiat virgae saepius vmbra tuae.	406	Passio 9	4
Si, Christe, dum suffigeris, tuae vestes	406	Passio 10	1
Ipse tuae solum adnectam, sine murmure, thensae.	426	Mem.Matr.7	16
Ad famae properes vera Tropaea tuae,	435	Poem.Lat.	2
Deducant linguae funera sola tuae.	438	Poem.Lat.	6
Hac facie dominae conspiciare tuae:	211	Cam.1613-b BB	10
aut Tuae virtutes et vota nostra et Principis gratiam superarent.	456	Epistolae	21
cum humanitatis Tuae, tum gratitudinis nostrae ratio postulat.	457	Epistolae	10
Tui subsidiumque Magnificentiae Tuae deuotissimorum Procancellarij	464	Epistolae	7
illum quo soles beare Amplitudini tuae deuotissimos Procancellarium	464	Epistolae	28
quam de futuro supplicem, integerrimae tuae fidei commendantes.	465	Epistolae	8
ad prudentiae eloquentiaeque tuae praesidium festinantes excipe:	465	Epistolae	16
Fama promotionis tuae gratissime appulit ad nos omnes haud ita certe	468	Epistolae	12
intra ambitum amplexusque foelicitatis Tuae receptae, communi calore	469	Epistolae	19
abunde succurres Magnificentiae tuae addicitissimis Procancellario	469	Epistolae	26
aliquam viam ad candorem Mentis Tuae ducentem aut reperissem aut	472	Epistolae	9
TUAM			
Cum millena tuam pulsare negotia mentem	385	Musae 1	1
Viuat, & in mortem vita sit illa tuam.	405	Passio 7	10
Asserit & vitam Mors animata tuam.	407	Passio 17	4
Agnoscitque tuam Machina tota Crucem.	409	Passio 21	2
Tuam gloriam censemus nostram, et in honoribus Tuis nostro bono	456	Epistolae	16
Prolem Tuam suauissimam, nuper in lucem publicam, nostramque	463	Epistolae	5
tantisper supplere donec Academia orationem tuam imbibat probetque,	470	Epistolae	7
TUARUM			
Sed aliorum iniuriae tuarum virtutum pabula sunt, qui lemas istas	462	Epistolae	12
concede vt nos etiam benignitate alarum tuarum et virtute fruamur.	466	Epistolae	22
tanquam partubus Virtutum Tuarum, Alma Mater accurrens gratuletur:	469	Epistolae	9
conuertissem, & ex altera parte acuissem me aspectu virtutum Tuarum;	472	Epistolae	7
TUAS			
Claudi, pene tuas praeteriere fores.	385	Musae	4
Pertrahis in partes nomina magna tuas;	398	Musae 33	2
Anne tuas flammas ipsa Antiperistasis auget,	399	Musae 35	3
Sic pulsare tuas, exclusis luctibus, ausint	402	Musae 39	35
Qui Caput es, spinas & tua Membra tuas.	405	Passio 6	4
Tuasque libans actiones, gloriam	414	Lucus 20	13
Vnde MARO laudes duxit ad astra tuas.	416	Lucus 25	4
In laudes abeunt secula quaeque tuas;	435	Poem.Lat.	2
In laudes properant secula quaeque tuas;	435	Poem.Lat. V	2
In laudes abeunt iam loca quaeque tuas:	435	Poem.Lat.	4
In laudes properant iam loca quaeque tuas:	435	Poem.Lat. V	4
vtrum gratia Principis virtutes tuas, aut nostra vota gratiam	456	Epistolae	20
festinasti ad gratitudines tuas cum emolumento nostro coniunctas,	462	Epistolae	14
qui virtutes tuas magnis negotijs pares prouexit, noluitque vt minori	466	Epistolae	13
TUBAE			
bello, tubae ac tympana: pax nouum orbem aperuit;	448	Orationes	12
TUBAM			
Tuque aer inflato tubam, dum plurimus ignis	211	Cam.1613-b BB	5
TUBI			
& beatae fabricae, vnico ictu sulphurei tubi, vnica litura delentur?	448	Orationes	21

TUBUS	PAGE	TITLE	LINE
Exoritur tubus, atque instar Cyclopis Homeri	419	Tr.Mortis	53
TUEARIS			
cum non solum tuearis nos a maleuolorum insidijs, sed etiam doceas	443	Orationes	22
TUEBITUR			
est in forma & figuris vultus, vbi res postulat, regnum tuebitur:	454	Orationes	8
TUERE			
Fluuium placidissimo faucrum tuorum afflatu nobis tuere. . .	461	Epistolae	25
tuere nos ita vt fortunae nostrae, intra ambitum amplexusque	469	Epistolae	18
TUETUR			
Quisquis tuetur perspicillis Belgicis	388	Musae 8	11
Quas Luna habet, tuetur, in foueam cadit, ...	393	Musae 22	8
TUI			
Ante tui, CAESAR, quam fulserat aura fauoris, ...	384	Musae	3
Sintque ausae thalamum solis adire tui.	384	Musae	6
Vel potius liceat distinguere. Tuque tuique	387	Musae 6	5
Vnquam fugari, quam tui socij solent.	389	Musae 10	3
Nunc primum socij mors foret atra tui?	415	Lucus 23	2
In nebulas similesque tui res gaudia nunquid	426	Mem.Matr.7	2
Haec fuerat olim potio Domini tui.	427	Mem.Matr.8	9
Phoebe, tui puduit quum summo mane redires	433	Poem.Lat.	36
Arma tui metuunt alumni.	434	Poem.Lat.	24
Hoc saltem officio fungar amore tui.	437	Poem.Lat.	8
Tuiue Christum deuocans facundia	438	Poem.Lat.	3
Et coelum vultus exhilarato tui, ...	211	Cam.1613-b BR	8
plurimumque suspicimus cumulum amoris Tui, qui vtrumque curasti,	457	Epistolae	20
Quare plurimum debemus constantiae fauoris tui, qui restinxisti sitim	462	Epistolae	7
aeternitatem nominis Tui subsidiumque Magnificentiae Tuae . .	464	Epistolae	6
Tibi & concedat vt terrestres tui honores cum coelestibus certent,	465	Epistolae	18
Nos etiam haud minimam fauoris tui partem speramus, orantes . .	468	Epistolae	20
Statim a solatio aspectus Tui, Ego auctior iam gaudio atque . .	471	Epistolae	17
Habui viaticum fauoris Tui, quod longiori multo itineri sufficeret.	471	Epistolae	19
non quin pectus meum plenum Tui sit, atque effusissimum in omnia	471	Epistolae	21
non cor) Tui in me dominij ius imminuere posse, nedum rescindere.	473	Epistolae	6
TUIS			
Namque aspectibus e tuis vel vnus	384	Musae	4
Et mea sint caris scripta referta tuis.	386	Musae 2	6
Verum heus! si reputes, tibi tuisque	391	Musae 15	7
Inuisamque tuis erigit hasta Crucem.	398	Musae 33	16
Affectus socijs tuis remittens.	401	Musae 37	32
Vt postulat mos; quid tuis dabis? Teipsum.	406	Passio 10	3
Immoriarque oculis, o mea vita, tuis.	421	Lucus 35	4
Laudibus haud fierem sepia iusta tuis.	422	Mem.Matr.1	6
Abito, trunce, cum tuis pudoribus.	423	Mem.Matr.2	54
Nos autem flemus: res ea sola tuis.	427	Mem.Matr.9	8
Ne serae meritis tuis venirent.	428	Mem.Matr.10	12
Cur tela Mortis vel tibi vel tuis	433	Poem.Lat.	5
perrumpit primipilus, & te cum ocelis tuis ad inferos deturbat.	448	Orationes	30
Dij te perdant, cum malis tuis & arena sine calce;	451	Orationes	5
censemus nostram, et in honoribus Tuis nostro bono gratulamur;	456	Epistolae	16
vt neque virtutibus tuis desint honores neque vtrisque vita,	457	Epistolae	2
aliquas virtutes tandem meritis tuis votisque nostris conspirantibus	464	Epistolae	12
circumspiciens reperisset Te, quasi in tuis palpebris acquiescat.	465	Epistolae	14
quam nunc pleno gradu ingrediens beneficijs tuis percurres. . .	468	Epistolae	19
perfectionibus Tuis, meis desiderijs probe cognitis, excussis	472	Epistolae	4
Quare malui seruire auribus Tuis, creberrima Antiquitatis lectione	473	Epistolae	19
TUM			
Tum tibi, si placeat, fugientia tempora reddam;	386	Musae 2	9
Tum quanta tabulis artifex? quae scriptio?	423	Mem.Matr.2	35
Sol sine sole tuo! quam te tum nubibus atris	433	Poem.Lat.	37
Dulcem rependent tum mihi tibiam	434	Poem.Lat.	33
qui tum rumores? quae auditiones?	450	Orationes	36
animalia, tum maxime homo, cui soli ideo insunt oculi variegati,	453	Orationes	16
cum humanitatis Tuae, tum gratitudinis nostrae ratio postulat.	457	Epistolae	10
vestra omni dente, tum edacis temporis, tum venenatorum haereticorum,	459	Epistolae	18
tum venenatorum haereticorum, insita vi sua liberentur. . .	459	Epistolae	19
tum Academiae nostrae, quae per Tuum Partum, ex Matre nunc Auia facta	463	Epistolae	25
ne tum quidem multum, neque nostrae matronae conuenit, cui tu es ab	471	Epistolae	2
imo precabor enixe, me tum priuari tam communi hac luce, quam Tua,	472	Epistolae	23
TUMBCI			
Toide para tumbci dizeo, phile, monon.	429	Mem.Matr.14	2
TUMEAM			
Si totus infler, si tumeam crepax, ...	426	Mem.Matr.6	17
TUMENTES			
Praesulibus nostris fastus, Melvine, tumentes	387	Musae 7	1
TUMENTIBUS			
atque exhilarans, tumentibus iam venis, arterijs micantibus,	445	Orationes	1
TUMES			
Frustra, Verpe, tumes, propola cultus, ...	408	Passio 19	1
TUMIDUM			
Eminet, id tumidum protinus esse feres?	387	Musae 7	4
TUMULIS			
Scilicet in tumulis Crucifixum quaerite, viuit:	408	Passio 17	5
TUMULOS			
Cuncta ad radices redeant, tumulosque paternos;	425	Mem.Matr.5	13
TUMULTU			
Dein quid Musis cum tumultu?	448	Orationes	22
TUMULUS			
Pactoli arena tibi tumulus est vnicus.	423	Mem.Matr.2	41
TUNC			
Tunc instruetur lautius radijs penu, ...	407	Passio 16	13

TUNC (cont'd)	PAGE	TITLE	LINE
Tunc Dominus clauis aggrediendus erit.	408	Passio 18	4
Sic tunc omnes strepebant: huiusmodi lamentis & quiritationibus plena	451	Orationes	9
ego tunc temporis liberior eram, huc illuc pro libitu . . .	451	Orationes	11
Quis enim tunc inuiseret Almam Matrem destitutam omni commeatu?	461	Epistolae	1
TUNDIT			
Qui silicem tundit, (mirum tamen) elicit ignem:	410	Lucus 3	1
TUO			
Corde tuo forsan, caetera munda, SOROR.	413	Lucus 15	6
Praeuenias vultu non facienda tuo.	421	Lucus 35	10
Virtutumque choro siccior ipse tuo.	422	Mem.Matr.1	4
Et lucro appcnis gaudia sancta tuo.	424	Mem.Matr.3	6
Exemploque tuo nascor in alterum:	425	Mem.Matr.4	14
Dissutus videor funere & ipse tuo.	428	Mem.Matr.11	12
Sol sine sole tuo! quam te tum nubibus atris	433	Poem.Lat.	37
tuosque fauores populo tuo communicans coelum ac terram minori quam	444	Orationes	7
si tantum Honori Tuo superesset otij ad legendum, quantum a nobis	457	Epistolae	8
ne literae nostrae animo Tuo tot negotijs meritissime distincto,	457	Epistolae	11
contra grassantes flammas aedificijs Honori Tuo acceptam ferimus:	457	Epistolae	18
Optime enim hoc conuenit Partui tuo, qui nouas scientiarum regiones	463	Epistolae	10
dein Hon. Tuo gratulamur, qui filio auctus es tali ingenio praedito:	463	Epistolae	24
vt res nostras omnes cum Honore Tuo coniunctas esse velimus.	465	Epistolae	3
vt Alma Mater libentissime caput reclinet in tuo sinu, oculusque	465	Epistolae	13
Nos vero de hoc tuo progressu non minus Reipublicae gratulamur quam	466	Epistolae	15
virtutibus, tuo exemplo compensatis, ad vnum omnes incumbamus.	468	Epistolae	16
tibi conueniat scribenti, quam quod Academiae tuo calamo scribenti:	470	Epistolae	14
TUORUM			
Fluuium placidissimo faucrum tuorum afflatu nobis tuere. . . .	461	Epistolae	24
siccatores (solem officio suo priuantes) vi verborum Tuorum obruens.	462	Epistolae	20
operam nobis omnia faucrum tuorum momenta apicesque perpensuris	466	Epistolae	7
sphaera quam pro latitudine meritorum tuorum circumscribereris.	466	Epistolae	14
TUOS			
Quin per Presbyteros tuos; per vrbem	400	Musae 37	5
Centum stigmatibus tuos inurens	400	Musae 37	23
Siste parum cantus, dum legis ista, tuos.	427	Mem.Matr.9	2
Deridet motus sancta catena tuos.	438	Poem.Lat.	9
tuosque faucres populo tuo communicans coelum ac terram minori quam	444	Orationes	6
tuosque faucres temporibus et diligentia diuisos in gratijs nostris	457	Epistolae	15
TUPHICUS			
existimantes tuphlous einai pros oksu blepontas, anapodemetous pros	450	Orationes	8
TURA			
Displicet, & laudis tura litare Deo.	389	Musae 12	2
TURBA			
Nunc sudas solus; caetera turba riget.	397	Musae 29	4
Caetera displiceat turba, necesse, tibi:	404	Passio 2	4
Proque vno vincto turba soluta fuit.	407	Passio 17	2
TURBAS			
Forte quidem, cum per vestras Ecclesia turbas	389	Musae 12	3
TURBEMUS			
Pugnaces, teneros florum turbemus odores, ...	427	Mem.Matr.7	32
TURBIDUM			
Non te carmine turbidum vocaui, ...	401	Musae 37	33
TURBINE			
Vel gemitus Erebi: piceo se turbine voluens	420	Tr.Mortis	75
TURBIS			
Afflatu perimunt: en, Cymba Cocytia turbis	420	Tr.Mortis	81
TURBO			
Heu, quis spiritus, igneusque turbo	411	Lucus 5	1
TURGEAT			
Tu perstrepis tamen; vtque turgeat carmen	392	Musae 20	10
TURGENT			
Crimina cum turgent, & mea poena prope est, ...	406	Passio 9	2
TURGESCAT			
non adeo sanatae ab optimo Rege nostro quin turgescat indies,	473	Epistolae	22
TURGIDOS			
Non fastus tibi turgidos repono;	401	Musae 37	36
TURMAE			
Angelicae turmae nostris se coetibus addunt:	402	Musae 39	10
TURMAS			
Nos quoque possemus longas conscribere turmas, ...	398	Musae 33	7
TURPI			
Haec autem hospitio latere turpi	411	Lucus 5	6
TURRES			
quando ipsae hae turres & beatae fabricae, vnico ictu sulphurei tubi,	448	Orationes	20
cur non vt elephanti turres, ita tu patriam tecum portasti? . .	451	Orationes	8
TURRITUM			
Struices superbas atque turritum caput	422	Mem.Matr.2	11
TURTURE			
A Te Turture defluos, ...	403	Musae 40	13
TUTA			
Quae Fabio quondam sub duce tuta salus.	416	Lucus 25 V	10
Nec grauidis medicina tuta est.	426	Mem.Matr.6	20
illic tuta cognitio est, atque extra teli iactum.	449	Orationes	3
TUTE			
Quod omnibus tute imperes, nemo tibi.	412	Lucus 11	3
TUTELARIS			
Iacchus tutelaris Diuus est vtrique nostrum;	440	Orationes	23
TUTISSIMUS			
Pastor agis proprios, medio tutissimus, agnos.	402	Musae 39	32
TUUM			
Haec facit ad nasum sola loquela tuum.	391	Musae 16	6

TUUM (cont'd)	PAGE	TITLE	LINE
Tuum tibi, poeta belle, non mystes,	392	Musae 20	11
Quo me vocas tandem, tuumque	394	Musae 23	23
Sic acuunt zelum frigora tanta tuum?	399	Musae 35	6
Ante tuum tempus coelum gratissimus ambis.	402	Musae 39	29
Quod scribo, & placeo, si placeo, tuum est.	403	Musae 40	14
Illum volo, qui calceat lixam tuum.	413	Lucus 17	7
Siste tuum fletum & gemitus: namque imbribus istis	415	Lucus 23	13
ROMA, tuum nomen quam non pertransijt ORAM,	416	Lucus 25	1
At superat caput illa tuum, quantum ipsa cadauer	424	Mem.Matr.3	3
causaris, irruit Miles in Musaeum tuum, & gladio te liberat.	448	Orationes	28
vt aliquando existimen id egisse prudentissimum Patrem tuum,	451	Orationes	31
extra mortalitatis aleam, et quo magis Tuum agnoscas, in ipso partu,	459	Epistolae	11
nostrae, quae per Tuum Partum, ex Matre nunc Auia facta est:	463	Epistolae	25
sed tamen comparatio & in honorem tuum cedet, nostrumque emolumentum.	467	Epistolae	26
eadem manus et tuum tibi largita est honorem, et priuilegia nostra	468	Epistolae	23
tu hanc personam indue scripturus, tuumque iudicium tibi Lictor estc.	470	Epistolae	27
Tu vero vale, mi procrator, amaque Tuum G. H.	471	Epistolae	12
Ego, non nisi meditato, obrepsi ad fauorem Tuum;	472	Epistolae	3
receptusque sim in aliquem apud Honorem Tuum locum, magis id adeo	472	Epistolae	20
ad mea in Honorem Tuum officia erectior solutiorque redibo,	473	Epistolae	2
assensumque Tuum veritati omni familiarem largiaris, sun tei eulogiai	473	Epistolae	10
prosepimetrcumenei beabis Filium tuum obsequentissimum GEORGIUM	473	Epistolae	13
TUUS			
Sic tuus effundi gestit pro crimine sanguis,	404	Passio 3	1
Dum lacrymas, it vita: tuus tibi clepsydra fletus,	415	Lucus 23	9
opportune his tenebris Fauor Tuus occurrit, illustrans nos omnes,	461	Epistolae	3
sed perspectissimus tuus in nos amor, praestantissimaeque animi dotes	465	Epistolae	11
curesque vt tuus in nos amor, antehac satis perspectus,	466	Epistolae	3
tuus amor et authoritas istos sorices nobis abigat.	468	Epistolae	26
TUXEI			
prouecta atque adulta, ipsam possessionem adeas, agathei ge tuxei.	470	Epistolae	9
TUXOIMI			
Ei pou tuxoimi tesd' aristes atrapou,	430	Mem.Matr.15	15
TYMPANA			
Mentes, quietis tympana publicae,	395	Musae 23	50
bello, tubae ac tympana: pax nouum orbem aperuit;	448	Orationes	12
TYRANNIDEM			
Authoritatis exuens tyrannidem;	436	Poem.Lat.	15
TYRO			
Assiduus tyro, si sit spectanda voluntas.	419	Tr.Mortis	32
TYROCINIUM			
Hinc tyrocinium, paruoque assueta iuuentus,	418	Tr.Mortis	26
UDOR			
Ouk eni thauma toson spheterizein: oude gar udor,	430	Mem.Matr.17	4
UE			
Sic o te (iuuerem, senemue) credat	385	Musae	10
Vobis fauentibusue, vel negantibus.	389	Musae 10	11
Non deridiculumue, siue ineptum,	401	Musae 37	34
Non striges, magiamue, vel rotatus,	401	Musae 37	35
Nil sit crassius, impolitiusue)	401	Musae 37	46
Quid metuant homines infra, supraue minentur	413	Lucus 16	1
In te, nec arcus, scorpionesue, aut rotas,	421	Lucus 33	4
Gladiosue, Catapultasue teneam, quin neque	421	Lucus 33	5
Effluxisse dies, suffocatamue Mineruam,	426	Mem.Matr.7	18
Sed nec Cyrrhaei saltus Libethriaue arua	432	Poem.Lat.	4
Nullum locum requiemue cernens perstitit	436	Poem.Lat.	20
Nullum locum requiemue cernens praestitit	436	Poem.Lat. V	20
Tuiue Christum deuocans facundia	438	Poem.Lat.	3
quibus nihil imperito vanius inutiliusue videatur, vbi tamen ad vsum	454	Orationes	4
instructior ad omnem causam, paratiorue siue a doctrina, siue ab vsu;	462	Epistolae	22
ULOMANIAN			
ulomanian illam & inanem verborum strepitum iamdudum deposui:	445	Orationes	22
UMIN			
esti me perimenein, ote polemein umin omologesei, dixit Mithridates.	449	Orationes	15
UMMIN			
Culumponde biban ummin anistamenois.	431	Mem.Matr.18	4
UPEKSELTHEIN			
Iogon te philtron, osth' upekselthein leon.	430	Mem.Matr.15	9
UPOGRAPHAS			
ophthalmon upographas kai epitrimmata pareion inducens;	470	Epistolae	19
VACAS			
Saepius aspergis. Siste, pudore vacas.	387	Musae 7	2
Ecquid inter tantas mundi trepidationes nobis & Musis vacas?	458	Epistolae	3
VACILLANT			
affectuum raptim sequentes, ad omnem eorum auram vacillant.	472	Epistolae	2
VADEM			
Per fluctus saltem, fac, precor, ipse vadem.	414	Lucus 19	4
VADIMONIA			
Saeuus es eripiens paruis vadimonia coeli:	389	Musae 9	15
VADUM			
Vt, fluuio currente, vadum sonat, alta quiescunt.	433	Poem.Lat.	48
VAE			
Vae nubi pluuia grauidae, non lacte, measque	426	Mem.Matr.7	5
VAGA			
Nec vaga de summo deducam flumina monte,	432	Poem.Lat.	7
VAGANS			
Vnde vagans passim recte vocer alter Vlysses,	428	Mem.Matr.11	13
VAGANTEM			
Ne perdat leo rugiens vagantem.	417	Lucus 30	8

VAGINA	PAGE	TITLE	LINE
modo detis eum in flore, in vagina, in herbescenti viriditate;	445	Orationes	20
VAGITUS			
Quid vetat vt pueri vagitus suppleat alter,	388	Musae 9	13
VALE			
Desinis exclamans: tota figura, vale.	401	Musae 38	2
Musa, vale, & tu Phoebe; dolor mea carmina dictet;	432	Poem.Lat.	12
Tu vero vale, mi procrator, amaque Tuum G. H.	471	Epistolae	12
VALERIJ			
vti Valerij, aliae contra semper pertinaces ac tribunitiae,	447	Orationes	20
VALIDUM			
Hibernico lignum nascitur permanens, contra omnia venena validum:	459	Epistolae	16
VALLIBUSQUE			
quam Natura montibus vallibusque sublimitate atque humilitate	453	Orationes	12
VALLIS			
Dic mihi, mons sterilis, vallis an vber eris?	413	Lucus 18	2
Nec facile ascendant, sed tibi vallis erit.	210	Cam.1613-a BR	8
VANIUS			
quibus nihil imperito vanius inutiliusue videatur, vbi tamen ad vsum	454	Orationes	4
VAPOR			
vt enim vapor, qui furtim ascendit ad nubes, vbi iam ingrauescit	454	Orationes	28
VAPORES			
vapores seruiles ad nubes educti aeque magnum tonitru edent ac regij.	452	Orationes	17
VAPULANT			
Non a nobis vapulant Iesuitae, sed a scriptis vestris, quae ingenti	443	Orationes	19
VARIA			
sed varia solent esse eorum consilia, finesque multiplices	446	Orationes	5
VARIAE			
Hic ego tuque erimus, variae suffitibus herbae	427	Mem.Matr.7	28
VARIEGATI			
cui soli ideo insunt oculi variegati, cum caetera animantia	453	Orationes	17
VARIETATEM			
Amat varietatem Natura omnis, flores, animalia, tum maxime homo,	453	Orationes	15
VATES			
Res redit ad vates, Pieriosque duces:	417	Lucus 28	2
VATICANAE			
Nec Vaticanae desines vnquam Lupae	397	Musae 30	2
VATICANAM			
Quid Vaticanam Bodleiumque obijcis, Hospes?	459	Epistolae	30
VATICANI			
De lupa lustri Vaticani.	397	Musae 30	T
VBER			
Dic mihi, mons sterilis, vallis an vber eris?	413	Lucus 18	2
VBERA			
Vberaque aerea hiscentem fallentia natum?	426	Mem.Matr.7	4
Quis enim sicca vbera et mammas arentes tam nobilis parentis aequo	461	Epistolae	32
VBERRIMAM			
in quo longe vberrimam gloriae segetem perspicio, nulla verborum,	446	Orationes	2
VBI			
Cur, vbi tot ludat numeris antiqua poesis,	387	Musae 5	1
Et tibi sit nemo praes, vbi poscis opem.	389	Musae 9	16
Sic vbi iam mulier decerpti conscia pomi	390	Musae 12	13
Mox displicent omnes. Vbi hoc permanserit	398	Musae 32	4
Extruxissem, vbi, cum moneret vsus,	401	Musae 37	29
Christe, vbi tam duro patet in te semita ferro,	404	Passio 4	1
Hic, vbi sanati stillant opobalsama mundi,	406	Passio 13	1
Post vbi Mosaicae repararent fragmina Leges,	408	Passio 20	3
Verius hoc olim factum est, vbi, Christe, lauares	412	Lucus 8	3
Culmen, vbi pro te nemo dolere potest.	415	Lucus 23	16
Hic vbi discumbunt per gramina, salsior vnus	418	Tr.Mortis	12
Tristis, vbi ac ferrum tellure reciditur ima,	419	Tr.Mortis	36
Haec vbi iuncta, subit viuo cum fune minister,	420	Tr.Mortis	66
Haec vbi vincta, subit viuo cum fune minister,	271	Tr.Mortis VS	66
Post vbi crudelem sentit diuisa securem,	428	Mem.Matr.11	3
Atque vbi per te sanctificer natalibus ipsis,	434	Poem.Lat.	9
paupertas perpetua, nisi vbi vestrae adsunt Excellentiae.	441	Orationes	16
vt nullus sit angulus corporis, nulla venula, vbi non adsit CAROLVS.	445	Orationes	3
quod quidem vbi gentium si non ab Hispano sperandum?	447	Orationes	30
vbi in dubio est, qui facit, an qui patitur, miserior.	449	Orationes	10
praecipue vbi velut ex continentibus tectis ad nos traiecturum est	449	Orationes	13
vbi ille signum sustulerit, Leones Britannici (e quorum ossibus	449	Orationes	17
vnde diuites syluas ac saltus quaerunt vbi aedificent, ac	450	Orationes	21
vbi tamen ad vsum tralatae fuerint, machinas conficiunt	454	Orationes	5
est in forma & figuris vultus, vbi res postulat, regnum tuebitur:	454	Orationes	7
vbi trecenta foliorum iugera vno die sedentes percurritis;	454	Orationes	24
ascendit ad nubes, vbi iam ingrauescit humore, relabitur in terram,	454	Orationes	29
peruenimus ad laurum hanc, vbi sub vmbra eius paulisper requiescamus:	455	Orationes	13
vbi sursum processerint paulo, frigefacti demum relabuntur.	471	Epistolae	29
VBIQUE			
Structorem, & Solomon vbique regnet.	408	Passio 19	8
Vbique est Deus, Agnus, Ara, Flamen.	408	Passio 19	14
spiritibusque tabellarijs laetum hunc nuncium vbique deferentibus,	445	Orationes	2
VBIUIS			
atque vbiuis terrarum pro iudicio prudentissimi Regis, & in rebus	444	Orationes	20
VCALEGON			
Non fert Vcalegon, atque amentata retorquet	418	Tr.Mortis	14
VE			
Nec qua consuleres, populumve ad bella vocares,	211	Cam.1613-b BR	9
VEGETAT			
istis sublimitate solij asserta) vita et actione orbem vegetat.	458	Epistolae	8

VEL	PAGE	TITLE		LINE
Namque aspectibus e tuis vel vnus	384	Musae		4
Nascentes radij fugant, vel acres	385	Musae		8
Pollubra vel cum olim damnaris Regia in ara,	386	Musae 3		9
Vel potius liceat distinquere. Tuque tuique	387	Musae 6		5
Vobis fauentibusue, vel negantibus.	389	Musae 10		11
Luce praelustri, vel honore pollet,	390	Musae 14		6
Non sic effugit angulus vel vnus	391	Musae 15		5
Non erubescentes vel ipsas	394	Musae 23		19
Nec vel tantillum pignus habebit amor?	396	Musae 26		2
Non striges, magiamue, vel rotatus,	401	Musae 37		35
Sint tibi vel stellis laudes, & laudibus anni:	402	Musae 39		34
Impar, & in fletum vel resolutus, ero;	404	Passio 1		2
Fides gigantem sola, vel facit nanum.	406	Passio 12		5
Te fixo vel Terra mouet: nam, cum Cruce, totam	408	Passio 18		1
Hunc poenas animam mundi, Plato: vel tua mundum	409	Passio 21		3
Plusque habet hic laetus, quam vel Auarus habet.	411	Lucus 7		4
Vel quia tot moritur, tot viguisse probes.	415	Lucus 23		8
Non deerat vel fama tibi, vel carmina famae,	416	Lucus 25		3
Non deerint vel fama tibi, vel carmina famae,	416	Lucus 25	V	3
Dum te vel digitis minister vrget,	417	Lucus 30		1
Vel sine luce solum, vel sine mente caro.	417	Lucus 31		6
Vel Catapulta potest, Siculique inuenta magistri,	419	Tr.Mortis		41
Non iam exaudiri quicquam vel Musica caeli	420	Tr.Mortis		74
Non iam exaudiri quicquam, vel musica sphaerae	271	Tr.Mortis	VS	74
Vel gemitus Erebi: piceo se turbine voluens	420	Tr.Mortis		75
Peccati veniae mei, vel ipsos	421	Lucus 34		8
Si licet, immoriar: vel si tua visio vita est,	421	Lucus 35		5
Pudorque constet vel solutis crinibus;	422	Mem.Matr.2		6
Quaesitum Domina gemma vel herba suam.	425	Mem.Matr.5		12
Cur tela Mortis vel tibi vel tuis	433	Poem.Lat.		5
Scribere, Te dignum, vel lachrymare queat!	435	Poem.Lat.		6
si spinula vlla Coronae Regiae emollita sit vel retusa;	443	Orationes		11
vnde consequimur, vel inuitis Fatis, quasi nodosam aeternitatem.	446	Orationes		23
nunquam intueri satis vel mirari possumus, nimirum infinitum	449	Orationes		35
Procancellarius Academiam simulans vel maximos magnatum inter eundum	470	Epistolae		25
o quot iam anni sunt ex quo vel apicem Latinum pertuli!	471	Epistolae		6
VELA				
Quare, peritus nauta, vela contrahas,	414	Lucus 20		11
VELATUS				
Non ego vos posthac hederae velatus amictu	432	Poem.Lat.		2
VELIMUS				
vt res nostras omnes cum Honore Tuo coniunctas esse velimus.	465	Epistolae		3
VELIS				
Et per se Templi limen adire velis:	388	Musae 9		8
VELLEM				
at ego Principem vellem, CAROLVM, CAROLVM;	451	Orationes		6
VELLEMUS				
Iam dari nobis vellemus Iesuitam aliquem, vt ex affrictu Libri vestri	459	Epistolae		7
VELLENT				
vellent omnia regredi,	395	Musae 25		12
VELLERE				
Rure; breuisque hortus, cuius cum vellere florum	426	Mem.Matr.7		23
VELLES				
Nempe Caput Romae es, cuius mysteria velles	416	Lucus 27		3
VELLICAT				
Hos nunc barbaries impia vellicat	391	Musae 17		7
VELUM				
Velum scissum.	408	Passio 19		T
Et Templi parasite; namque velum	408	Passio 19		2
VELUT				
Laus antiqua & honor perierunt, te velut ARMC	416	Lucus 25	V	7
praecipue vbi velut ex continentibus tectis ad nos traiecturum est	449	Orationes		13
sed velut Romani lacum, cuius altitudo ignota erat, dedicabant	449	Orationes		20
VELUTI				
ingenium ipsum atque indoles (veluti Conclusio sequitur infirmiorem	447	Orationes		18
VENA				
Vis, & vena sacris regnat in artubus;	403	Musae 40		8
Mater inest saliente vena.	426	Mem.Matr.6		16
VENAS				
Tu venas laticesque omnes, quos sacra recludit	402	Musae 39		23
VENDENTIBUS				
prosunt vendentibus Libros non ementibus, hoc est cessatoribus	468	Epistolae		7
VENDITUS				
Venditus est Agnus, non tamen emptus erit.	410	Lucus 4		2
VENENA				
Hibernico lignum nascitur permanens, contra omnia venena validum:	459	Epistolae		16
VENENATORUM				
tum venenatorum haereticorum, insita vi sua liberentur.	459	Epistolae		19
VENENO				
Non quia Pontificum sunt olim afflata veneno,	390	Musae 13		1
Atque edentula Musa, nec veneno	400	Musae 37		12
VENERANDA				
Veneranda Capita, Viri grauissimi, Pubes lectissima.	444	Orationes		11
VENERANDAM				
finge tibi matronam sanctam, venerandam, oris prisci atque augusti;	470	Epistolae		16
VENIAE				
Peccati veniae mei, vel ipsos	421	Lucus 34		8
VENIAMUS				
Permitte vt nos etiam in praedam partemque tecum veniamus:	465	Epistolae		22

	PAGE	TITLE	LINE
VENIENTE			
Et melius coelum, te veniente, subest:	210	Cam.1613-a BR	4
VENIRENT			
Ne serae meritis tuis venirent.	428	Mem.Matr.10	12
VENIS			
atque exhilarans, tumentibus iam venis, arterijs micantibus,	445	Orationes	1
VENIT			
Quo precio venit, fac, liceare prius.	410	Lucus 4	6
VENTER			
O mea suspicienda manus, venterque perennis!	418	Tr.Mortis	1
O mortis longaeua fames, venterque perennis	271	Tr.Mortis VS	1
VENTI			
quin & venti imperant pelago, vt laeuitatem illam aequabilem atque	453	Orationes	13
VENTILAT			
Excitat optatus auidos, & ventilat ignem.	432	Poem.Lat.	32
affectus explorat, adulationem ventilat, & adulatores, qui semper	453	Orationes	2
VENTILATIONE			
haud ignarus, ignem vitae augeri ventilatione, desidia corrumpi,	452	Orationes	33
VENTO			
Mulcetur vento, accendit cum fomite partem	420	Tr.Mortis	68
Miscetur vento, accendit cum fomite partem	271	Tr.Mortis VS	68
VENTOS			
Ecce solutura est, ventos causata morantes:	427	Mem.Matr.9	9
VENTREM			
Apud Iuris-consultos, partus sequitur ventrem:	447	Orationes	12
VENTRES			
solebant ventres eximere, quos in arca repositos abijciebant	452	Orationes	27
VENTRICULUS			
Non iam ventriculus, verum spelunca vocetur	414	Lucus 21	3
VENTURA			
vnius seculi Princeps, sed & omnium, quae ventura sunt, haberetur.	447	Orationes	26
VENULA			
Nescia sit metae; venula, cella tua est.	404	Passio 2	2
vt nullus sit angulus corporis, nulla venula, vbi non adsit CAROLVS.	445	Orationes	3
VENUS			
Merserat in lustris perniciosa venus, ...	396	Musae 26	10
VERA			
Ad famae properes vera Tropaea tuae, ...	435	Poem.Lat.	2
signo meritus est, ad vera castra traductus, hostem interficiet:	453	Orationes	30
VERAE			
Fictaque Bellona & verae ludibria pugnae, ...	418	Tr.Mortis	27
VERAM			
Defendit veram mente manuque fidem.	399	Musae 33	24
VERBA			
Cum mea futilibus numeris se verba viderent	385	Musae	3
Sic Catharis noua sola placent; res, verba nouantur:	386	Musae 3	3
Pallada gorgoneam, sic tua verba placent.	387	Musae 6	4
Quod puer ignorat, verba profana putas?	388	Musae 9	2
Haec verba superos aduolaturus thronos	396	Musae 28	7
improbe, verba Dei, ...	397	Musae 28	17
Absit vt ingenuum pungant mea verba pudorem;	400	Musae 36	3
Infinita vestra in nos Beneficia non solum verba omnia, . .	460	Epistolae	2
VERBERA			
Mitis agas: tenerae duplicant sibi verbera mentes, ...	406	Passio 9	5
VERBERES			
Vt, quo fatiges verberesque	395	Musae 23	47
VERBIS			
Cur ideo verbis tristes effundere curas	433	Poem.Lat.	45
quos in arca repositos abijciebant in fluuium, his verbis: . .	452	Orationes	29
VERBO			
& contracte King, a Con verbo deduci, quod tria complectitur,	447	Orationes	7
VERBORUM			
in promptu erat, rudesque animos vi verborum percellere: . . .	445	Orationes	17
ulcmanian illam & inanem verborum strepitum iamdudum deposui:	445	Orationes	22
segetem perspicio, nulla verborum, nulla temporis falce demetendam.	446	Orationes	2
siccatores (solem officio suo priuantes) vi verborum Tuorum obruens.	462	Epistolae	20
VERBVM			
te deneget VERBVM Deus.	397	Musae 28	18
VERE			
O vere dictum, & belle! cum torqueat omnes	389	Musae 11	3
Quare tam vere quam libenter gratulamur tibi, nec minus etiam	468	Epistolae	17
VEREMUR			
veremur ne nihil hic sit, quod magnitudini praesentiae vestrae	441	Orationes	9
Sed veremur, ne literae nostrae animo Tuo tot negotijs meritissime	457	Epistolae	10
veremur ne non tam sapientes nos, quam obscuros philosophos . .	460	Epistolae	24
VERENDUM			
Quos Ecclesia comprobat, verendum	391	Musae 15	12
VERIOR			
Munere, Rex, tanto verior inde probor.	405	Passio 7	4
VERISIMILE			
alijs (tanquam montes olim) imponerentur, verisimile est, eos illuc,	468	Epistolae	1
VERITATE			
Ex Veritate matre; Mellis alueus;	436	Poem.Lat.	23
VERITATI			
assensumque Tuum veritati omni familiarem largiaris, sun tei eulogiai	473	Epistolae	10
VERITATIS			
Dux Noticnum; veritatis Pontifex;	436	Poem.Lat.	3
Dux Nationum; veritatis Pontifex;	436	Poem.Lat. V	3
VERIUS			
Verius hoc olim factum est, vbi, Christe, lauares	412	Lucus 8	3

	PAGE	TITLE	LINE
VERMIS			
quae semper se deuorat primum, vti vermis nucleum, e quo nascitur;	454	Orationes	15
VERNA			
Carere discat verna, quo summus caret	407	Passio 16	9
VERNAE			
Tam segnis facies aurorae nescia vernae,	426	Mem.Matr.7	8
VERO			
Tu vero quisquis es, caue ne, dum neges,	397	Musae 28	16
Tu vero mentem neutiquam despondeas,	407	Passio 16	11
Tu vero collige te, tibique insistito,	414	Lucus 20	9
Ain' vero? quanta praedicas? hercle aedepol,	421	Lucus 33	1
Tu vero mater perpetim laudabere	424	Mem.Matr.2	61
Tu vero, Deus omnipotens, conserues nobis haec gaudia, imbuas cor	444	Orationes	4
ego vero sentio, & quis sum ipse (barbam, hui, tam grauem) & apud	445	Orationes	25
Ego vero non dicam vobis quod factum est ante seculum vestrum,	445	Orationes	37
Iam vero, vt Rex animalium fiat Rex hominum, apponimus nos manibus	447	Orationes	2
Nos vero, flores Parnassi, gaudia praestolantur, quae iamdudum	454	Orationes	22
Nos vero, Auditores, diu iam peregrinati cum Principe, commode	455	Orationes	12
Tu vero macte honoribus, gloria, id enim nostra interest,	457	Epistolae	24
Nunc vero Ipse scribendo irrupisti in compensationes nostras,	459	Epistolae	1
Tu vero, Patrone noster, qui elegantias doctrinae nitoremque spirans	461	Epistolae	20
Tu vero promptitudinem amoris nostri, non passim expositam,	466	Epistolae	1
Nos vero de hoc tuo progressu non minus Reipublicae gratulamur quam	466	Epistolae	15
Iam vero miserum est, pecuniam retardare illam, cui natura spiritum	468	Epistolae	4
Tu vero vale, mi procrator, amaque Tuum G. H.	471	Epistolae	12
illud necessarium magis factu, hoc vero longe iucundius, nobiliusque:	472	Epistolae	35
VERPE			
Frustra, Verpe, tumes, propola cultus,	408	Passio 19	1
VERRIS			
Dum prono rapis ore cibos, & fercula verris,	414	Lucus 21	1
VERRUNT			
qui nullum non angulum verrunt (ac si perdiderint ingenium)	445	Orationes	36
VERSAT			
Regnat visceribus, measque versat	411	Lucus 5	2
VERSATOS			
Versatos neget, atque humiles, queis talis cordi	420	Tr.Mortis	93
VERSATUS			
qui nuper versatus est in forma & figuris vultus, vbi res postulat,	454	Orationes	7
VERSENTUR			
quae licet versentur in figuris describendis, quibus nihil imperito	454	Orationes	3
VERSERIS			
charta conspiciendum Te praebes, quo familiarius inter nos verseris.	456	Epistolae	21
VERSU			
Falsumque potius quam crepes versu?	392	Musae 20	9
Quam curto nequeo referre versu;	400	Musae 37	6
Nam si te cuperem secare versu,	400	Musae 37	14
VERSUS			
Nunc etiam teneras quo versus gratior aures	387	Musae 5	11
Sume Palatini versus de numine Phoebi,	210	Cam.1613-a BR	1
VERSUTUM			
Scio Hispanum versutum, callidum, artis & aucupij apprime gnarum:	451	Orationes	24
VERTAM			
Aut spes productas, barbataque somnia vertam	426	Mem.Matr.7	19
VERTAS			
An rectius nos, si vices vertas, probi,	388	Musae 8	9
Vertas specillum: nam, prout se res habent,	388	Musae 8	17
VERTICE			
Creditur, ante satas prono cum vertice fruges)	419	Tr.Mortis V	61
VERTICES			
Et, quos ipsa nequit scandere vertices,	391	Musae 17	9
VERULAMIJ			
In Honorem Illustr. D. D. Verulamij, Sti Albani,	436	Poem.Lat.	T
Inductionis Dominus, & Verulamij;	436	Poem.Lat.	4
Sancti Albani, Baronis Verulamij.	438	Poem.Lat.	T
VERUM			
Verum heus! si reputes, tibi tuisque	391	Musae 19	7
Quam tribuit, verum multiplicare decet.	408	Passio 17	8
Non iam ventriculus, verum spelunca vocetur	414	Lucus 21	3
Verum heus, si nequeas caelo demittere matrem,	424	Mem.Matr.3	7
Verum augusta parens, sanctum os caeloque locandum,	426	Mem.Matr.7	10
Quotidie pasti: tantum verum indue vultum	427	Mem.Matr.7	29
suauissimus Princeps, verum etiam praesenti seculo, dum pacem,	447	Orationes	28
non tantum exteras regiones habuit perspectas, verum etiam suam?	452	Orationes	1
Verum mittamus inuidos & inuidiam, quae semper se deuorat primum,	454	Orationes	14
Verum, quod rem spectat, si placeat vices meas tantisper supplere	470	Epistolae	5
Verum heus! caute incipe, cohibens adeo stylum ingeniumque;	470	Epistolae	10
VESCOR			
Ego hic pultibus vescor et glande, more maiorum, multos iam annos	470	Epistolae	4
VESPER			
Nec plus te rubeat vesper, Eliza, precor.	211	Cam.1613-b BR	16
VESPERE			
Stellam vespere suxerim volantem,	411	Lucus 5	5
Inde exiguntur pensa crudo vespere.	423	Mem.Matr.2	21
Vespere ros maestis funus honestet aquis.	425	Mem.Matr.5	16
VESPERI			
Tu promis Orbem mane, condis vesperi,	407	Passio 16	3
VESTE			
Veste triumphant.	390	Musae 14	12
VESTEM			
vestem non adimi suam,	396	Musae 25	21

	PAGE	TITLE	LINE
VESTER			
Cum sacra perturbet vester furor omnia, scriptum	386	Musae 3	7
Graues lagenas, Vester est Aquae-ductus.	405	Passio 5	9
nunc itaque liber hic vester dilatat pomoeria, summouet Oceanum	458	Epistolae	12
VESTES			
Quid sacrae tandem meruere vestes, ...	390	Musae 14	1
In vestes diuisas.	406	Passio 10	T
Si, Christe, dum suffigeris, tuae vestes	406	Passio 10	1
VESTIBULUM			
rotundum & coeleste, soli facies tanquam vestibulum magni palatij.	447	Orationes	1
VESTIBUS			
viuentes sine vestibus, ...	395	Musae 25	5
VESTIS			
Haesisset tibi, quam suprema vestis	400	Musae 37	26
VESTIUM			
Quis enim apud nos splendor, aut rerum, aut vestium?	441	Orationes	11
VESTRA			
Sed non moramur: namque vestra crux erit, ...	389	Musae 10	10
Vobis, aut illis pectora vestra forent.	400	Musae 36	6
O caecos animi fratres! quis vestra fatigat	401	Musae 39	4
nos audiamus summo cum gaudio ea Maiestas vestra summa cum molestia?	443	Orationes	31
vestra est optio, vestra disquisitio, qui tineae estis & helluones	445	Orationes	18
vestra disquisitio, qui tineae estis & helluones chartacei; . .	445	Orationes	18
quid proderunt scalpella vestra, quando ipsae hae turres & beatae	448	Orationes	20
vestra solum dextra (quamuis a scriptione terrestribusque istis	458	Epistolae	6
Haec vestra spolia actosque ex orbe triumphos communicas cum Alma	458	Epistolae	16
interim vestra hac scribendi laude intacta manente atque illibata.	458	Epistolae	27
sunt, vt sic scripta vestra omni dente, tum edacis temporis,	459	Epistolae	18
Infinita vestra in nos Beneficia non solum verba omnia, . . .	460	Epistolae	2
quae est vestra felicitas qui puro Academiae farre vtimini. . .	470	Epistolae	2
VESTRAE			
ne nihil hic sit, quod magnitudini praesentiae vestrae respondeat.	441	Orationes	10
nos tam defecimus in vtroque quam Excellentiae Vestrae abundant.	441	Orationes	13
paupertas perpetua, nisi vbi vestrae adsunt Excellentiae. . .	441	Orationes	16
Optamus quidem vt Maiestatis vestrae gaudia responderint aut nostris	443	Orationes	13
& vestrae fidei consulam, quemadmodum artifices non omnes . .	445	Orationes	29
adeo vt qui non subijciuntur ditioni, eruditioni vestrae obtemperent:	458	Epistolae	13
vt vestrae coronae ciuili & literariae tertiam Coelestem sero	459	Epistolae	20
Quanta rotunditas Clementiae vestrae, quae ab omni parte nobis	460	Epistolae	10
VESTRAM			
Vestramque Scyllam, aequis parati spiculis	397	Musae 30	5
Viuite, dum mortem ostendam: sic tempora vestram	432	Poem.Lat.	15
hilare est, laetum, ac lubens, vestram in gratiam amplectimur.	440	Orationes	13
Quid memorem prudentiam vestram incomparabilem, qua optime ostendis	443	Orationes	16
effari, non licet per multitudinem, imo per modestiam vestram?	443	Orationes	30
in nos beneficijs Maiestatem vestram aeternitati in scriptis nostris	458	Epistolae	31
Tantum Maiestatem vestram subiectissime oramus, vt si officia nostra	460	Epistolae	14
VESTRARUM			
etiam imperium tenuius est quam pro amplitudine virtutum vestrarum:	458	Epistolae	11
VESTRAS			
Forte quidem, cum per vestras Ecclesia turbas	389	Musae 12	3
Qui vestras edit intime medullas.	391	Musae 15	10
Vestrasque laudes, poscit & mixtas genas.	422	Mem.Matr.2	4
Tantum etenim vestras (Parcae) non flectit habenas	433	Poem.Lat.	40
Excellentias vestras tanto chariores esse, cum eo sitis ordine atque	440	Orationes	24
accedit ad incredibiles laudes vestras quod quae nos audiamus summo	443	Orationes	30
VESTRI			
vt ex affrictu Libri vestri hominem illico contundamus. . . .	459	Epistolae	8
Humillimi serui subditique vestri Procancellarius Reliquusque Senatus	459	Epistolae	22
VESTRIS			
accessionem summe gratulantur Excellentijs Vestris Musae omnes,	440	Orationes	7
cum tanti sitis & in Principibus Vestris, & in vobismetipsis,	441	Orationes	8
prius Excellentijs Vestris curae erit;	441	Orationes	20
vestrae gaudia responderint aut nostris votis aut virtutibus vestris,	443	Orationes	14
sed a scriptis vestris, quae ingenti cum lucro quotidie legimus.	443	Orationes	20
vt miraculis vestris nostra occurrant, oratio nostra est silentium,	444	Orationes	2
e querquetis vestris, vbi trecenta foliorum iugera vno die sedentes	454	Orationes	24
quam vt pro infinitis vestris in nos beneficijs Maiestatem vestram	458	Epistolae	30
VESTRO			
Quam (more vestro) imponere inscio vulgo.	397	Musae 31	3
Ante diem vestro mundus ab igne ruat.	399	Musae 35	12
Si enim in regno vestro Hibernico lignum nascitur permanens,	459	Epistolae	19
VESTROS			
si vestros animos regant	395	Musae 25	18
Perstringunt vestros carmina sola duces.	400	Musae 36	4
VESTRUM			
Ecce decus vestrum spinis horrescit, acuta	425	Mem.Matr.5	3
Ego vero non dicam vobis quod factum est ante seculum vestrum,	445	Orationes	38
exosculamur, hunc foetum vestrum, hunc alterum Carolum, . .	459	Epistolae	9
VETAT			
Quid vetat vt pueri vagitus suppleat alter, ...	388	Musae 9	13
Ah! Cheiragra vetat, quo minus, inquit, agam.	389	Musae 11	2
VETERANE			
Non mea fert aetas, vt te, veterane, lacessam;	386	Musae 2	1
VETERANUS			
Nempe Nouatores quis Veteranus amat?	398	Musae 33	14
VETEREM			
pax nouum orbem aperuit; bellum destruit veterem.	448	Orationes	13
VETERES			
Solem ex Oceano Veteres exurgere fingunt	412	Lucus 8	1
Plus etiam veteres coelum videre remotum:	433	Poem.Lat.	44

VETERI	PAGE	TITLE		LINE
A veteri trunco & nobilitate cadit.	416	Lucus 25		6
VETERIBUS				
regiones terrasque veteribus incognitas primus demonstrat:	463	Epistolae		11
VETERUM				
Per strages licet autorum veterumque ruinam	435	Poem.Lat.		1
tibique non tam auide veterum beneficiorum memoriam recolenti,	457	Epistolae		12
Sic apud veterum aras, post ingentes Hecatombas, exiguam thuris micam	469	Epistolae		16
VETUISTI				
Non video, certum est iurare; aut si hoc vetuisti,	421	Lucus 35		9
VETULAE				
Perrumpens, Atropi vetulae marcentibus vlnis.	419	Tr.Mortis		65
VETUS				
Goropius Becanus ait vetus vocabulum nostrum, Koning, & contracte	447	Orationes		6
vt mihi videtur, Romana elegantia, periodique vetus rotunditas.	473	Epistolae		18
VETUSTAS				
Inde Patres pergunt quadrati, & tota Vetustas.	398	Musae 33		13
Tu Synodosque, Patresque, & quod dedit alta vetustas	402	Musae 39		25
Huic Glans adijcitur (non quam ructare vetustas	419	Tr.Mortis		60
Hinc Glans adijcitur (non quam ructare vetustas	419	Tr.Mortis	V	60
Cui caecas tribuit vires annosa vetustas.	433	Poem.Lat.		42
VETUSTATIS				
Columba Noae, quae in vetustatis artibus	436	Poem.Lat.	V	19
VETUSTIS				
Columba Noae, quae in vetustis artibus	436	Poem.Lat.		19
VETUSTO				
Praetulit Astraea, aut solio Themis alma vetusto	426	Mem.Matr.7		12
VEXAS				
Omnia quaerendo, sed te, super omnia, vexas:	413	Lucus 16		5
VEXAT				
Materiam vexat: nec iam se continet antro	420	Tr.Mortis		70
VEXATA				
Quas gens inconsulta, suis vexata procellis,	401	Musae 39		2
VEXET				
Ne nimium vexet quaestio, pone meam.	409	Passio 21		4
VI				
in promptu erat, rudesque animos vi verborum percellere:	445	Orationes		17
tum venenatorum haereticorum, insita vi sua liberentur.	459	Epistolae		19
siccatores (solem officio suo priuantes) vi verborum Tuorum obruens.	462	Epistolae		20
VIA				
vt lineae, quamuis diuersa via, omnes tamen ad centrum properant;	456	Epistolae		23
VIAM				
Qui tam sublimi conspicit orbe viam:	387	Musae 7		6
Spero meo cordi posse patere viam.	404	Passio 4		2
viam aperiens & methodum in studijs adhibendam, etiam libros indicans	443	Orationes		24
iterum exire patria, qui nunc inuenit viam, proximo itinere faciat.	455	Orationes		8
donec lacteam aliquam viam ad candorem Mentis Tuae ducentem aut	472	Epistolae		9
VIAS				
Et populi spurcas creditis esse vias:	387	Musae 5		8
ita inuoluit nos, vt etiam rependendi vias omnes praecludat.	458	Epistolae		29
VIATICUM				
Habui viaticum fauoris Tui, quod longiori multo itineri sufficeret.	471	Epistolae		19
VIATOR				
Iniuste satis arguit viator.	428	Mem.Matr.10		4
Cernis vt exusta semper sit fronte viator;	437	Poem.Lat.		3
VIATORES				
Quid? hoccine est mirum? Viatores sumus.	393	Musae 22		2
VICARIUM				
qua optime ostendis te eius vicarium qui omnia disponit suauiter?	443	Orationes		17
VICECOMITIS				
In obitum incomparabilis Francisci Vicecomitis	438	Poem.Lat.		T
VICES				
Clauserit extremas pugna peracta vices,	386	Musae 2		8
An rectius nos, si vices vertas, probi,	388	Musae 8		9
si placeat vices meas tantisper supplere donec Academia orationem	470	Epistólae		6
VICINA				
Sicca meis lacrymis Thamesis vicina videtur,	422	Mem.Matr.1		3
VICINAS				
Et tibi vicinas porrigit aequor aquas:	399	Musae 35		8
VICINI				
Vicini populi passim mirantur, & aequos	401	Musae 39		8
Vicini quo pacto niteant, id animum aduertito;	450	Orationes		16
per quem vicini agri opulentia fruimur, veremur ne non tam sapientes	460	Epistolae		23
VICINIS				
Politicos audiamus, salus regnorum pendet a vicinis, quorum consilia,	450	Orationes		26
VICINITATI				
quasi accolae Maiestatis, literaturae suae et vicinitati respondeant:	463	Epistolae		23
VICINOS				
praesertim donec transeat nubes illa, quae vicinos adeo infestat:	455	Orationes		15
VICINUM				
vicinum fretum quotidie transnatantes, litora nostra atque aures mire	441	Orationes		3
VICINUS				
Vicinusque magis nobiliorque fluit:	399	Musae 35		10
VICISSIM				
Hinc te olim gentes miratae odere vicissim;	416	Lucus 25		11
Tu vicissim abunde compensas nos, gratissimoque Almam Matrem	456	Epistolae		8
VICISTI				
Eia, agedum scribo: vicisti, Musa; sed audi,	431	Mem.Matr.19		7
Furuosque vicisti Gigantes,	434	Poem.Lat.		19
Tu, Domine, vicisti; tuere nos ita vt fortunae nostrae,	469	Epistolae		17

	PAGE	TITLE	LINE
VICIT			
Vicit more suo Noster: nam millibus Infans	437	Poem.Lat. V	3
VICIUM			
In vicium mundo sterili, cui cedo cometas	426	Mem.Matr.7	20
VICTA			
Ceu victa, Musis porrigit herbulas	434	Poem.Lat.	21
VICTOR			
Gulielmus Victor descensurus primum e nauibus in terram hanc,	455	Orationes	3
VICTORIA			
O victoria, clamitat,	395	Musae 25	6
Christe, flagellati spes & victoria mundi,	406	Passio 9	1
Hic sita foeminei laus & victoria sexus:	429	Mem.Matr.13	1
VICTORIAE			
velut Romani lacum, cuius altitudo ignota erat, dedicabant victoriae;	449	Orationes	21
tanquam gurgitem imperuestigabilem, victoriae nuncupemus:	449	Orationes	23
victoriaeque gloriam absque crudelitate effusi sanguinis delibas.	458	Epistolae	14
VICTORIAM			
omnia Danorum expiscatus consilia, victoriam celebrem consecutus est.	453	Orationes	6
VICTORIAS			
triumphos & victorias quasi fraena ferox spumantia mandit,	447	Orationes	34
VICTRICES			
permittat nostram hanc Inter victrices hederam sibi serpere Lauros.	455	Orationes	18
VICTUM			
Atheniensis doluit se victum opificum antelucana industria,	469	Epistolae	2
VIDEAM			
Cum te non videam, mene videre putas?	421	Lucus 35	8
VIDEANTUR			
hausisse ab Antiquis, sed et ad Posteros transmissuri videantur.	469	Epistolae	13
VIDEAR			
Ne te productis videar lassare Camoenis,	385	Musae 1	3
VIDEARIS			
eo videaris nobis remotior, confidimus tamen vt arbores,	464	Epistolae	17
VIDEATUR			
quibus nihil imperito vanius inutiliusue videatur, vbi tamen ad vsum	454	Orationes	4
VIDENS			
Aurum nocte videns, vidisse insomnia dicit:	411	Lucus 7	1
Aurum luce videns, nulla videre putat.	411	Lucus 7	2
VIDENT			
Terra nihil, nec quo sanctius astra vident;	385	Musae	2
VIDENTUR			
sub specie publici commodi, Academiae incommodum videntur allaturi;	463	Epistolae	1
VIDEO			
Tres video partes, quo re distinctius vtar,	386	Musae 4	1
Non video, certum est iurare; aut si hoc vetuisti,	421	Lucus 35	9
VIDEOR			
Dissutus videor funere & ipse tuo.	428	Mem.Matr.11	12
quam audire videor dicentem, Pulchrum quidem iter & Amante dignum;	453	Orationes	26
etiam senectus, quam aetatem in hac palaestra consecutus mihi videor.	471	Epistolae	9
VIDERE			
Aurum luce videns, nulla videre putat.	411	Lucus 7	2
Cum te non videam, mene videre putas?	421	Lucus 35	8
Plus etiam veteres coelum videre remotum:	433	Poem.Lat.	44
VIDERENT			
Cum mea futilibus numeris se verba viderent	385	Musae	3
VIDERI			
At cui videri prodigium potest	395	Musae 23	49
VIDERINT			
quomodo alij molem hanc laetitiae suae exprimant, ipsi viderint:	457	Epistolae	1
VIDERIS			
Sic omnibus videris ad modum visus.	406	Passio 12	4
VIDES			
Haec tu.omnium optime vides, quare causam nostram nosque ipsos Tibi,	468	Epistolae	9
VIDET			
Res ampliantur, sin per aduersam videt,	388	Musae 8	13
VIDETIS			
Ecquid videtis tandem quam vtile hoc iter, per quod optimus Princeps	451	Orationes	35
VIDETUR			
Sicca meis lacrymis Thamesis vicina videtur,	422	Mem.Matr.1	3
quamuis rationi consonum videtur, vt qui hic in Musarum monte	449	Orationes	32
adeon' nihili videtur res, Principem omnibus delicijs abundantem,	452	Orationes	3
sed non patitur, vt mihi videtur, Romana elegantia, periodique vetus	473	Epistolae	18
VIDISSE			
Aurum nocte videns, vidisse insomnia dicit:	411	Lucus 7	1
VIDIT			
Vos sine maternis hymnis infantia vidit,	389	Musae 12	5
Euentum Naso vidit et admonuit;	399	Musae 33	30
VIDUABOR			
Morte magis viduabor illa.	425	Mem.Matr.6	12
VIDUAE			
pulcherrimaeque Musarum domus tanquam viduae effoetae, aut ligna	462	Epistolae	4
VIGILAT			
O falsos homines! Vigilat, qui somniat aurum,	411	Lucus 7	3
VIGORE			
nobis haec gaudia, imbuas cor Regium vigore, animum clementia,	444	Orationes	5
quo spiritu, qua arte, quanto impetu atque vigore res aggrediatur:	454	Orationes	11
VIGUISSE			
Vel quia tot moritur, tot viguisse probes.	415	Lucus 23	8
VILE			
Nostrae etiam Musae vile fuere lutum:	384	Musae	4
VILEM			
Assiduo vilem lumine cingit humum.	387	Musae 7	8

	PAGE	TITLE	LINE
VIM			
Cum enim vim cogitationum in vitam meam omnem conuertissem,	472	Epistolae	5
VINCANT			
Cum lacrymas oculosque duos tot vulnera vincant,	404	Passio 1	1
VINCIT			
Vincit more suo Noster: nam millibus Infans	437	Poem.Lat.	3
VINCO			
Assideo Matri, robore vinco cedros.	428	Mem.Matr.11	6
VINCTA			
Haec vbi vincta, subit viuo cum fune minister,	271	Tr.Mortis VS	66
VINCTO			
Proque vno vincto turba soluta fuit.	407	Passio 17	2
VINCTUM			
quis scit an & amoris onus scite vinctum ligatumque, & per tot	453	Orationes	38
VINCULIS			
etiam teneor, sed laxioribus vinculis, quaeque amor saepe remittit:	472	Epistolae	34
VINCULUM			
cum corporis cum anima vinculum impedimento esse ad contemplandum	448	Orationes	27
VINDICAT			
Funereque hoc cultum vindicat aegra suum.	431	Mem.Matr.19	4
VINI			
In patinas alij: furit inconstantia vini	418	Tr.Mortis	21
Bacchantur Lapithae, furit inconstantia vini	271	Tr.Mortis VS	21
VINTONIENSI			
EPISCOPO VINTONIENSI, &c.	385	Musae	T
rariusque paulo fodiam in Vintoniensi agro, dum Rhetorici satagam:	472	Epistolae	28
VINUM			
Vinumque felle miscuit.	427	Mem.Matr.8	4
VINXISSET			
Protagoras cum eleganter admodum caudices ligni fasciculo vinxisset,	453	Orationes	34
VIOLAE			
In terram violae capite inclinantur opaco,	425	Mem.Matr.5	7
VIR			
Vir Honoratissime. Eximia tua in nos merita frequentiorem calamum	457	Epistolae	6
Vir Honoratissime. Quanta hilaritate aspicit Alma Mater filios suos	461	Epistolae	29
Vir Honoratissime. Scite et apposite fecisti Fluuium nostrum	462	Epistolae	17
Clarissime Vir. Permitte vt nos etiam in praedam partemque tecum	465	Epistolae	20
Vir Dignissime. Sic a Natura comparatum est, Ignis et Virtus semper	466	Epistolae	9
Oratio perfecta, vti vir, tetragonos est, grauis, nobilis,	471	Epistolae	4
VIRES			
Lumina, nutantes paulatim acquirite vires,	432	Poem.Lat.	14
Cui caecas tribuit vires annosa vetustas.	433	Poem.Lat.	42
VIRGAE			
Sufficiat virgae saepius vmbra tuae.	406	Passio 9	4
VIRGAM			
virgam cum sceptro commutans, vt quid priuata habeat in se vita	452	Orationes	36
VIRGINES			
vt enim Vxores, Virgines; ita Sol & Coelum producunt flores,	446	Orationes	32
direptiones, stupratas virgines, praegnantes bis intersectas,	449	Orationes	6
VIRGINIS			
si amor virginis eo pertraxit Principem, quo tandem ducet amor	453	Orationes	27
VIRGINITAS			
tamen nimium efferre vos, cum Virginitas ipsa fructus sit Nuptiarum:	446	Orationes	28
VIRGINUM			
in virginum, flores atque herbas depinxere:	446	Orationes	31
VIRGO			
Virgo pudens, vxor fida, seuera parens:	429	Mem.Matr.13	2
VIRGUNCULA			
Haec fuerant: sic Tisiphone virguncula lusit.	418	Tr.Mortis	23
VIRI			
Decus mulierum perijt: & metuunt viri	422	Mem.Matr.2	8
Veneranda Capita, Viri grauissimi, Pubes lectissima.	444	Orationes	11
Accepistis, Viri attentissimi, causas itineris huius, quantum quidem	453	Orationes	20
VIRIBUS			
Et vnus impar aestimatur viribus,	388	Musae 8	5
VIRIDITATE			
modo detis eum in flore, in vagina, in herbescenti viriditate;	445	Orationes	20
VIRORUM			
Mors tot virorum sordida sanguine,	433	Poem.Lat.	10
Absque nuptijs foret populus virorum, essemus vnius seculi;	446	Orationes	21
VIROS			
Sagax Humilitas, eligens viros bonos	412	Lucus 13	1
viros limatae auris atque tersae, quorum grauitate ac purpura	445	Orationes	26
VIRTUS			
rara in Principibus virtus, & cui cum sceptro lites saepius	452	Orationes	2
merita tua ita ascensura, vt eorum vis et virtus ad nos descendat.	464	Epistolae	19
eccum nunc altera occasio, adeo festinat virtus tua:	465	Epistolae	24
Ignis et Virtus semper ascendunt, vtriusque enim splendor et claritas	466	Epistolae	10
VIRTUTE			
Virtute percellis tua;	388	Musae 8	4
concede vt nos etiam benignitate alarum tuarum et virtute fruamur.	466	Epistolae	23
VIRTUTES			
Isabellae laudes, virtutesque, vicinum fretum quotidie transnatantes,	441	Orationes	3
in quem fauor Regius, nostra vota, virtutes tantae confluxerunt?	456	Epistolae	19
vtrum gratia Principis virtutes tuas, aut nostra vota gratiam	456	Epistolae	20
aut Tuae virtutes et vota nostra et Principis gratiam superarent.	456	Epistolae	21
quanto magis virtutes istae in Dominum agri transferendae sunt,	459	Epistolae	17
diu expectantem magnas aliquas virtutes tandem meritis tuis votisque	464	Epistolae	12
qui virtutes tuas magnis negotijs pares prouexit, noluitque vt minori	466	Epistolae	13
VIRTUTI			
satis virtuti datum est, satis Reipublicae.	455	Orationes	6

VIRTUTIBUS	PAGE	TITLE	LINE
Heu miseri! Quis tantum ipsis virtutibus instat	419	Tr.Mortis	33
O superi: Quis tantum ipsis virtutibus instat	271	Tr.Mortis VS	33
vestrae gaudia responderint aut nostris votis aut virtutibus vestris,	443	Orationes	14
vt neque virtutibus tuis desint honores neque vtrisque vita,	457	Epistolae	2
promulgentur, quo suauius virtutibus, tuo exemplo compensatis,	468	Epistolae	16
VIRTUTIS			
neque quotidianae virtutis prouincia gerere personam Academiae,	465	Epistolae	9
VIRTUTUM			
Virtutumque choro siccior ipse tuo.	422	Mem.Matr.1	4
etiam imperium tenuius est quam pro amplitudine virtutum vestrarum:	458	Epistolae	11
Sed aliorum iniuriae tuarum virtutum patula sunt, qui lemas istas	462	Epistolae	12
tanquam partubus Virtutum Tuarum, Alma Mater accurrens gratuletur:	469	Epistolae	9
conuertissem, & ex altera parte acuissem me aspectu virtutum Tuarum;	472	Epistolae	6
VIRUM			
Aethiopissa ambit Cestum Diuersi Coloris Virum.	437	Poem.Lat.	T
denique huic aetati quae talem virum protulit, cum quinque millibus	463	Epistolae	26
VIS			
Vis, & vena sacris regnat in artubus;	403	Musae 40	8
Quae vis condidit, ipsa nouit aedes.	411	Lucus 5	17
quarum enumerationi nulla vnquam vis, nulla latera sufficere possunt.	443	Orationes	14
sed Tu vis etiam manibus teri, semotaque Maiestate, charta	458	Epistolae	19
cuius nisi incredibilis fuisset vis, nunquam in tantis negotijs,	463	Epistolae	17
merita tua ita ascensura, vt eorum vis et virtus ad nos descendat.	464	Epistolae	19
VISA			
Mulcensque dotes caeteras visa est quasi	423	Mem.Matr.2	43
VISCERA			
Viscera naturae, commistusque omnibus astris	402	Musae 39	28
VISCERIBUS			
Regnat visceribus, measque versat	411	Lucus 5	2
VISIO			
Si licet, immoriar: vel si tua visio vita est,	421	Lucus 35	5
VISITUR			
tanta Humanitatis massa, quae apud Te visitur, abscindere non possim,	472	Epistolae	14
VISU			
vt quod Philosophus de Tactu & Visu, id apposite admodum huc	472	Epistolae	36
VISUM			
Visum quod vni praebet, omnibus vitam,	404	Passio 5	2
VISUS			
Sic omnibus videris ad modum visus.	406	Passio 12	4
VITA			
Vitaque neglectas est satis vlta preces.	389	Musae 12	6
Ducitur illimi candida vita fide,	400	Musae 36	2
Viuat, & in mortem vita sit illa tuam.	405	Passio 7	10
Dum moreris, Mea Vita, ipsi vixere sepulti,	407	Passio 17	1
Nemo potest: hodie vita sepulta prior.	415	Lucus 23	6
Dum lacrymas, it vita: tuus tibi clepsydra fletus,	415	Lucus 23	9
Immoriarque oculis, o mea vita, tuis.	421	Lucus 35	4
Si licet, immoriar: vel si tua visio vita est,	421	Lucus 35	5
Ratione certa vita constat & domus,	423	Mem.Matr.2	22
Christe, duplex fiet mors tua vita mihi:	434	Poem.Lat.	8
Atque haeret dubio tabida vita pede,	438	Poem.Lat.	2
& cum eo vita nostra atque calor, longo animi deliquio fugitiuus ac	444	Orationes	22
Nihil habet humana vita maioris momenti aut ponderis, quam Nuptiae,	446	Orationes	16
bello pacem, sine qua omnis vita procella, & mundus solitudo.	448	Orationes	8
vt quid priuata habeat in se vita commodi aut voluptatis,	452	Orationes	37
vt neque virtutibus tuis desint honores neque vtrisque vita,	457	Epistolae	3
istis sublimitate solij asserta) vita et actione orbem vegetat.	458	Epistolae	7
VITAE			
Sputando, praedicando? sic Aquas vitae	404	Passio 5	3
Breuiore nodo stringe vitae sarcinas,	414	Lucus 20	6
Plumbis obsignata, colosque & stamina vitae	419	Tr.Mortis	64
Quod superest vitae, insumam: Solisque iugales	426	Mem.Matr.7	15
vlciscimur mortem, ligantes abruptum vitae filum, vnde consequimur,	446	Orationes	23
mutilatam imaginem Dei, pauxillum vitae, quantum satis ad dolendum,	449	Orationes	5
haud ignarus, ignem vitae augeri ventilatione, desidia corrumpi,	452	Orationes	33
non minus vitae inaequalitas delectat, quam terrae, quam Natura	453	Orationes	11
VITAM			
Visum quod vni praebet, omnibus vitam,	404	Passio 5	2
Asserit & vitam Mors animata tuam.	407	Passio 17	4
Sic, pro Maiestate, Deum, non perdere vitam	408	Passio 17	7
Vitam reduxit: ecce gratitudinem.	413	Lucus 14	2
Viuimus in praesens: hesternam viuere vitam	415	Lucus 23	5
Nec tamen excludor: namque vna ex arbore vitam	418	Tr.Mortis	7
Hinc tamen excludi mors noluit, ipsaque vitam	271	Tr.Mortis VS	7
Sunt, praeter vitam: saxis hic sternitur, alter	418	Tr.Mortis	19
Ambustis sudibus: pars vitam in pocula fundunt,	418	Tr.Mortis	20
Quantum caedi? adeon' vnam vos pascere vitam,	419	Tr.Mortis	34
Quantum caedi? adeon' vnam nos viuere vitam,	271	Tr.Mortis VS	34
Aura volans, vitamque aer, quam pauerat, aufert.	420	Tr.Mortis	84
Principis innocuam seruastis numina Vitam,	433	Poem.Lat.	34
Cur mihi das vitam, quam tibi, Christe, negas?	434	Poem.Lat.	4
Quin moriar tecum: vitam, quam negligis ipse,	434	Poem.Lat.	5
In vitam & neruos Pascha coaeua fluet.	434	Poem.Lat.	10
Cum enim vim cogitationum in vitam meam omnem conuertissem,	472	Epistolae	5
VITASSE			
Vitasse Christi spiritum efflantis crucem.	389	Musae 10	5
VITIATA			
Innumeros mergit vitiata mente poetas,	402	Musae 39	39
VITIJS			
Deerat adhuc vitijs hominum dignissima mundo	419	Tr.Mortis	49

VITIJS (cont'd)	PAGE	TITLE		LINE
Deerat adhuc vitijs nostris dignissima mundo	271	Tr.Mortis	VS	49
VITIORUM				
Sanus Homo factus, vitiorum purus vterque;	408	Passio 20		1
VITREA				
Cum tamen splendida plerumque vitrea sint, claritatem fragilitate	448	Orationes		5
VITRO				
Vitro minus recte vteris.	388	Musae 8		18
VIUA				
Conueniunt; & Homo viua fit Ara Dei.	417	Lucus 29		4
VIUAT				
Viuat, & in mortem vita sit illa tuam.	405	Passio 7		10
VIUENS				
more maiorum, multos iam annos Anglice viuens garriensque.	470	Epistolae		5
VIUENTES				
viuentes sine vestibus,	395	Musae 25		5
VIUERE				
Viuimus in praesens: hesternam viuere vitam	415	Lucus 23		5
VIUIMUS				
Haec etiam ad pugnam praesens, qua viuimus, aetas	399	Musae 33		21
Viuimus in praesens: hesternam viuere vitam	415	Lucus 23		5
VIUIS				
Tu tamen, haud tibi tam moreris, quam viuis in illis,	407	Passio 17		3
VIUIT				
Scilicet in tumulis Crucifixum quaerite, viuit:	408	Passio 17		5
VIUITE				
Occidite; aut sane tantisper viuite, donec	425	Mem.Matr.5		15
Viuite, dum mortem ostendam: sic tempora vestram	432	Poem.Lat.		15
VIUO				
Haec vbi iuncta, subit viuo cum fune minister,	420	Tr.Mortis		66
Haec vbi vincta, subit viuo cum fune minister,	271	Tr.Mortis	VS	66
VIUUNT				
Nunc adeo per te viuunt, vt repere possint,	384	Musae		5
VIUUS				
Cespes viuus, Homo; mortuus, Ara fuit:	417	Lucus 29		2
VIVERE				
Quantum caedi? adeon' vnam nos vivere vitam,	271	Tr.Mortis	VS	34
VIXERE				
Dum moreris, Mea Vita, ipsi vixere sepulti,	407	Passio 17		1
VLCISCIMUR				
hac re solum vlciscimur mortem, ligantes abruptum vitae filum,	446	Orationes		22
VLIGINOSO				
eruditionis nobis conscius est, palustri opere & vliginoso intercipi:	461	Epistolae		8
VLLA				
Sanguine: nec precium merx emit vlla suum.	410	Lucus 4		4
Fuge, perite omnes; nec posthac exeat vlla	425	Mem.Matr.5		11
Non vlla Bellonae furentis	434	Poem.Lat.		23
si spinula vlla Coronae Regiae emollita sit vel retusa;	443	Orationes		11
neque vlla negotia (quippe quae caput petant, non cor) Tui in me	473	Epistolae		6
VLLI				
neque sane dubitamus vlli, si prae defectu aquae, commeatusque	462	Epistolae		2
VLLIS				
quam meis meritis vllis, semper lubentissimeque agnoscam:	472	Epistolae		22
VLLUS				
Quotidie iugulat, nec semel vllus obit.	415	Lucus 23		4
VLNIS				
Perrumpens, Atropi vetulae marcentibus vlnis.	419	Tr.Mortis		65
(quod innuis) sed et ambabus vlnis osculisque ei aetati debitis	463	Epistolae		7
VLTA				
Vitaque neglectas est satis vlta preces.	389	Musae 12		6
Assiduo stimulo carnem Mens vlta lacessit,	410	Lucus 2		5
VLTIMA				
cum tamen in resolutione illa vltima, nulla sit distinctio populi aut	452	Orationes		15
VLTRA				
Vltra animus spatiatur exlex.	425	Mem.Matr.6		8
Non metuunt vltra; nostra infortunia tantum	432	Poem.Lat.		24
Vltra loquendi tempus; addit Anchora:	438	Poem.Lat.		4
VLYSSES				
Vnde vagans passim recte vocer alter Vlysses,	428	Mem.Matr.11		13
VMBRA				
Sufficiat virgae saepius vmbra tuae.	406	Passio 9		4
Produxit Vmbram corpus, Vmbra corpori	413	Lucus 14		1
Debetur Caelo lumen, & vmbra solo:	417	Lucus 31		2
peruenimus ad laurum hanc, vbi sub vmbra eius paulisper requiescamus:	455	Orationes		13
quae fugerunt tot philosophos vmbra et otio diffluentes,	463	Epistolae		19
VMBRAM				
In Vmbram Petri.	413	Lucus 14		T
Produxit Vmbram corpus, Vmbra corpori	413	Lucus 14		1
VMBRAS				
Aut aperi, & cernes corpus quas proijcit vmbras;	437	Poem.Lat.		7
Aut aperi, & cernis corpus quas proijcit vmbras;	437	Poem.Lat.	V	7
effigies, imo vmbras hominum fame, frigore, illuuie, enectas,	449	Orationes		8
VMBRIS				
In picturis locus est vmbris & recessibus, etiam si quis Principem	453	Orationes		14
VNA				
Ritibus vna Sacris opponitur; altera Sanctos	386	Musae 4		3
Sola tibi Sappho, feminaque vna placet?	387	Musae 5		2
Vna dies Catharos ad bellum miserat omnes:	399	Musae 33		31
Ad bellum missos perdidit vna dies.	399	Musae 33		32
Prisci, crescentesque vna cum prole cauernas:	418	Tr.Mortis		6
Nec tamen excludor: namque vna ex arbore vitam	418	Tr.Mortis		7

VNA (cont'd)	PAGE	TITLE	LINE
Surrexit vna & illa, seseque extulit:	423	Mem.Matr.2	27
Vna meam membris horula, teque cruci.	434	Poem.Lat.	2
re vna omnium grauissima, alienis oculis iudicioque inniti;	447	Orationes	22
vt sic vna opera vtriusque Reipublicae calculum et ciuilis	465	Epistolae	26
Academia vniuersim sumpta vna est e proceritus, inter patritios	470	Epistolae	24
Vna cum promptioribus Academicis maternisque, assumsi mecum	473	Epistolae	7
VNAM			
Scilicet Hebraeam cantas, & perstrepis vnam:	391	Musae 16	5
Conuincunt vnam multa sepulcra Crucem.	408	Passio 17	6
Ecquid emes Caelum? quin stellam rectius vnam	410	Lucus 4	5
Quantum caedi? adeon' vnam vos pascere vitam,	419	Tr.Mortis	34
Quantum caedi? adeon' vnam nos vivere vitam,	271	Tr.Mortis VS	34
vnam actionem e multis seligam, quam vobis amplectendam	445	Orationes	32
VNAMQUAMQUE			
asserunt Medici vnamquamque regionem sua sibi sufficere,	444	Orationes	25
VNDA			
Quin nocuas extinque faces, precor: vnda propingua est,	399	Musae 35	7
Ridenti lacrymas quibus vnis concolor vnda est.	426	Mem.Matr.7	6
Tibi debet Vnda & Terra certitudinis.	438	Poem.Lat.	7
VNDAE			
Tertulliano, propter vndae pollutrum,	389	Musae 10	7
Ex praelio vndae ignisque (si Physicis fides)	396	Musae 27	1
VNDAS			
Forsitan & prohibes infans portetur ad vndas,	388	Musae 9	7
Annulus hos reuocet, sistatque libidinis vndas	396	Musae 26	11
Hac ope munitus securior excipis vndas,	402	Musae 39	30
Non tantum est iter Angelis ad vndas,	415	Lucus 24	11
VNDE			
In cruce suspendens, vnde reclinet, habet.	407	Passio 15	4
Vnde MARO laudes duxit ad astra tuas.	416	Lucus 25	4
Vnde vagans passim recte vocer alter Vlysses,	428	Mem.Matr.11	13
natura omnis suos habet anteambulones, vnde pluuia futura, an sudum,	445	Orationes	5
ligantes abruptum vitae filum, vnde consequimur, vel inuitis Fatis,	446	Orationes	23
vnde cuncti antiqui Philosophi peregrinati sunt, existimantes	450	Orationes	7
vnde diuites syluas ac saltus quaerunt vbi aedificent, ac	450	Orationes	20
vnde fit vt nullus fere elabatur dies, qui non hostes aliquos nobis	461	Epistolae	13
VNDIQUE			
O sec'lum lepidum! circumstant vndique Fratres,	393	Musae 21	1
inter tot gloriae titulos caput vndique munientes meministi Magistrum	456	Epistolae	2
VNGUENTA			
Sic vnguenta solent manu fricari:	405	Passio 8	2
VNGUIBUS			
Vt, cum mors rabidis vnguibus imminens	391	Musae 17	3
VNGUIUM			
Exercet miserum; non dolor vnguium	403	Musae 40	4
VNI			
Visum quod vni praebet, omnibus vitam,	404	Passio 5	2
VNICA			
& beatae fabricae, vnico ictu sulphurei tubi, vnica litura delentur?	448	Orationes	21
VNICAM			
Non vrbem facit vnicam, sed Orbem.	408	Passio 19	5
VNICE			
Atqui te precor vnice per ipsam,	400	Musae 37	1
Quare vnice obsecramus, vt qui tot subsidia attuleris ad progressum	467	Epistolae	27
VNICO			
Mihine matris vrna clausa est vnico,	424	Mem.Matr.2	57
& beatae fabricae, vnico ictu sulphurei tubi, vnica litura delentur?	448	Orationes	21
VNICOLORES			
insunt oculi variegati, cum caetera animantia vnicolores habeant.	453	Orationes	17
VNICUM			
vnicum hoc iter nuperum explicabo, in quo longe vberrimam gloriae	446	Orationes	1
VNICUS			
Vnicus est nummus, caelo Christoque petitus,	410	Lucus 4	9
Pactoli arena tibi tumulus est vnicus.	423	Mem.Matr.2	41
Rerum magister vnicus, at non Artium;	436	Poem.Lat.	5
Mundique & Animarum sacerdos vnicus;	436	Poem.Lat.	24
Vnicus est nobis Bibliotheca Liber.	459	Epistolae	31
VNIS			
Ridenti lacrymas quibus vnis concolor vnda est.	426	Mem.Matr.7	6
VNIUERSAM			
nulla pulchritudo per vniuersam Britanniam, disparuit forma,	451	Orationes	17
ab optimo Rege desumptas in vniuersam Rempublicam diffundis:	456	Epistolae	12
vniuersam Musarum supellectilem, etiam Fluuium non minus de	465	Epistolae	6
VNIUERSIM			
Academia vniuersim sumpta vna est e proceribus, inter patritios	470	Epistolae	23
VNIUERSO			
per hunc imperas orbi vniuerso, victoriaeque gloriam absque	458	Epistolae	14
VNIUERSUM			
imo in vniuersum, si quis de Principe aliquo, quis sit futurus aut	454	Orationes	8
quippe qui vniuersum tempus nostrum (forsitan quo alacrius illud	460	Epistolae	5
quas non nobis habemus sed irrigati ipsi vniuersum regnum aspergimus?	462	Epistolae	11
VNIUERSUS			
mutus est mundus vniuersus, vestra solum dextra (quamuis a scriptione	458	Epistolae	6
VNIUS			
Absque nuptijs foret populus virorum, essemus vnius seculi;	446	Orationes	22
neque vnius seculi Princeps, sed & omnium, quae ventura sunt,	447	Orationes	25
VNO			
Sancte Pater, coeli custos, quo doctius vno	385	Musae	1
Intuituque vno stringens habitacula mundi,	402	Musae 39	12
Proque vno vincto turba soluta fuit.	407	Passio 17	2

VNO (cont'd)	PAGE	TITLE	LINE
Vno ictu: non sic pestis, non stella maligno	420	Tr.Mortis	80
Constat, Aprile vno te potuisse mori:	438	Poem.Lat.	4
Hoc vno Rex et populus dissentimus.	444	Orationes	1
superbi sua tantum nosse, praesertim cum in vno regno non sint omnia:	450	Orationes	18
immersi, aut vno semper saginantur in loco, vti anguillae,	452	Orationes	9
vbi trecenta foliorum iugera vno die sedentes percurritis;	454	Orationes	25
VNQUAM			
Vnquam fugari, quam tui socij solent.	389	Musae 10	3
Nec Vaticanae desines vnquam Lupae	397	Musae 30	2
Hae tibi sunt alae laudum. Cui contigit vnquam	435	Poem.Lat.	5
Hae tibi sunt alae laudis. Cui contigit vnquam	435	Poem.Lat. V	5
quarum enumerationi nulla vnquam vis, nulla latera sufficere possunt.	443	Orationes	14
Quae enim vspiam gens, quod vnquam seculum felicrem habuit Principem?	445	Orationes	12
aut tantum de nullo vnquam Filio Alma Mater, quantum de Te sibi	457	Epistolae	26
Neque quod ignotior eram, retundebatur vnquam impetus:	472	Epistolae	11
tam communi hac luce, quam Tua, cum id agnoscere vnquam desinam.	472	Epistolae	24
VNUM			
O vtinam aut illorum oculi (quod comprecor vnum)	400	Musae 36	5
Frustra itaque in tot funeribus miraberis vnum,	415	Lucus 23	11
Quae diuisa nocent, Christi per foedus, in vnum	417	Lucus 29	3
Atque animo medicatur vnum.	426	Mem.Matr.6	24
Non vnum quid spectant aut singulare Magni animi, sed varia solent	446	Orationes	4
essent atque consilijs, sine quibus ne vnum quidem filum torquerent:	449	Orationes	30
Id vnum dolemus, Bibliothecam nostram rudiorem esse impexioremque,	463	Epistolae	28
virtutibus, tuo exemplo compensatis, ad vnum omnes incumbamus.	468	Epistolae	17
VNUS			
Namque aspectibus e tuis vel vnus	384	Musae	4
Et vnus impar aestimatur viribus,	388	Musae 8	5
Non sic effugit angulus vel vnus	391	Musae 15	5
Primo, vnus aut alter parum ritus placet:	398	Musae 32	2
Vnus dicitur aduenire cladem:	401	Musae 37	43
Hic vbi discumbunt per gramina, salsior vnus	418	Tr.Mortis	12
VNUSQUISQUE			
Vnusquisque hominum, Terra est; & filius arui.	413	Lucus 18	1
VOBIS			
Scilicet hoc vobis proprium, qui purius itis,	387	Musae 5	7
Vobis fauentibusue, vel negantibus.	389	Musae 10	11
Vobis, aut illis pectora vestra forent.	400	Musae 36	6
Quam aut Ecclesia despicata vobis,	400	Musae 37	16
ac merentibus vobis gratissimos, Saluete tandem Magistri Artium,	440	Orationes	4
posterioris largam messem Vobis haec tenuia boni consulentibus,	441	Orationes	21
e multis seligam, quam vobis amplectendam dissuauiandamque praebebo:	445	Orationes	32
quam simpliciter vobiscum agam, quam non longe abeam Oratorum more,	445	Orationes	35
Ego vero non dicam vobis quod factum est ante seculum vestrum,	445	Orationes	38
Dicam vobis, Academici; ego tunc temporis liberior eram,	451	Orationes	11
Quid ego vobis Neronum aut Heliogabalorum ingluuiem memorem?	452	Orationes	18
Quare nunc vobis ex pede Herculem, ex itinere Principem metiri licet,	453	Orationes	22
VOBISCUM			
Quare vt parcius agam vobiscum, simulque & laboribus meis,	445	Orationes	28
VOBISMETIPSIS			
in Principibus Vestris, & in vobismetipsis, veremur ne nihil hic sit,	441	Orationes	9
VOCABERIS			
Magnas es; esto. Bulla si vocaberis,	413	Lucus 17	1
VOCABO			
Somnis (nescio queis) nocturna ad vota vocabo:	432	Poem.Lat.	3
VOCABULI			
Ad eundem In Monstrum vocabuli Anti-Tami-Cami-Categoria.	386	Musae 3	T
VOCABULUM			
Goropius Becanus ait vetus vocabulum nostrum, Koning, & contracte	447	Orationes	6
VOCARES			
Nec qua consuleres, populumve ad bella vocares,	211	Cam.1613-b BR	9
VOCAS			
Quo me vocas tandem, tuumque	394	Musae 23	23
Cantus sacros, profane, mugitus vocas?	395	Musae 24	1
VOCAT			
Dum gladium stringens Paulus ad arma vocat.	398	Musae 33	12
En Aurora vocat, lectus genialis in aula est,	210	Cam.1613-b BR	1
VOCATOS			
Cum piscatores Textor legit esse vocatos,	392	Musae 19	1
VOCAUI			
Non te carmine turbidum vocaui,	401	Musae 37	33
VOCE			
voce sua dederat,	396	Musae 28	2
Sententiae cum voce mire conuenit,	423	Mem.Matr.2	37
VOCER			
Arbor & ipse inuersa vocer: dumque insitus almae	428	Mem.Matr.11	9
Vnde vagans passim recte vocer alter Vlysses,	428	Mem.Matr.11	13
VOCES			
Quin liceat nobis aliquas procudere voces:	386	Musae 3	5
VOCETUR			
Non iam ventriculus, verum spelunca vocetur	414	Lucus 21	3
VOCIBUS			
Pallas retortis caesia vocibus	434	Poem.Lat.	25
VOLANS			
Aura volans, vitamque aer, quam pauerat, aufert.	420	Tr.Mortis	84
VOLANT			
Volant per orbem literae notissimae:	423	Mem.Matr.2	38
VOLANTEM			
Stellam vespere suxerim volantem,	411	Lucus 5	5

	PAGE	TITLE	LINE
VOLATURA			
Iam repit impietas volatura illico.	398	Musae 32	3
VOLIS			
Stipati, rudibusque volis imperuius hortus	427	Mem.Matr.7	26
VOLO			
Illum volo, qui calceat lixam tuum.	413	Lucus 17	7
VOLTUS			
Quandoque voltus sola maiestas, Dolor.	422	Mem.Matr.2	7
VOLUCRIBUS			
Vulpibus antra feris, nidique volucribus adsunt,	407	Passio 15	1
VOLUENS			
Vel gemitus Erebi: piceo se turbine voluens	420	Tr.Mortis	75
VOLUIT			
Quid voluit prudens Fatum, iam sentio tandem:	438	Poem.Lat.	3
VOLUNT			
multi Academias integras subuersas volunt, neque illi e faece vulgi	461	Epistolae	16
VOLUNTAS			
Assiduus tyro, si sit spectanda voluntas.	419	Tr.Mortis	32
VOLUNTATI			
notionum aequare nunquam potest, non voluntati tribuendum existimes.	460	Epistolae	18
VOLUPTAS			
Christe, dolor tibi supplicio, mihi blanda voluptas;	405	Passio 6	1
Frustra igitur sudo: superest mihi sola voluptas,	435	Poem.Lat.	7
VOLUPTATIBUS			
voluptatibus quasi fascijs circumdatum, enatare e delicijs,	452	Orationes	5
spretis voluptatibus, illecebris melitaiais agxonais abiectis,	452	Orationes	31
VOLUPTATIS			
cum Hercule, serpentesque interficere voluptatis, vt iter tantum,	452	Orationes	7
vt quid priuata habeat in se vita commodi aut voluptatis,	452	Orationes	37
VOLUTANS			
Quo se condat & implicet volutans	417	Lucus 30	6
VOOS			
Cu sathron, cude melon epleto, alla voos:	429	Mem.Matr.14	6
VORANDO			
Ipsa cum domina domum vorando?	411	Lucus 5	9
VORAT			
Immodicus luctus tacito vorat igne medullas,	433	Poem.Lat.	47
VORET			
Sacrilegum carmen, censeo, flamma voret.	399	Musae 34	4
VOS			
Vos ducibus missis, missis doctoribus, omnes	387	Musae 5	9
Vos sine maternis hymnis infantia vidit,	389	Musae 12	5
Vos ergo puri! o nomen appositissimum	393	Musae 22	5
Quo vulgus ornat vos! At audias parum;	393	Musae 22	6
Atqui vos secus, o boni,	395	Musae 25	16
Qua sine vos miseri lentius itis ope.	399	Musae 33	26
Militat & nobis, quem vos contemnitis, Ordo;	399	Musae 33	27
O vos inualidos! Audi quem talibus armis	399	Musae 33	29
Quantum caedi? adeon' vram vos pascere vitam,	419	Tr.Mortis	34
Dicite, vos Furiae, qua gaudet origine Monstrum.	420	Tr.Mortis	85
Dicite vos Stutiae, qua gaudet origine monstrum	272	Tr.Mortis VS	85
Conferte lacrymas: Illa, quae vos miscuit	422	Mem.Matr.2	3
Quare haud vos hortos, sed coemeteria dico,	425	Mem.Matr.5	9
Non ego vos posthac hederae velatus amictu	432	Poem.Lat.	2
Hinc mihi principium: vos o labentia mentis	432	Poem.Lat.	13
vos, vos, inquam, excutite, quorum aetas teritur in libris:	445	Orationes	14
Nolite tamen nimium efferre vos, cum Virginitas ipsa fructus sit	446	Orationes	27
laudo vos, neque enim quicquam hoc itinere mirabilius, cuius tamen	450	Orationes	2
abijcite quisque libros, non est locus grauitati, neque apud vos:	454	Orationes	35
Delphino reuectum excepere arbores tripudiantes, & Vos statis?	454	Orationes	37
VOTA			
Votaque scintillae sunt animosa meae.	410	Lucus 2	4
Somnis (nescio queis) nocturna ad vota vocabo:	432	Poem.Lat.	3
in quem fauor Regius, nostra vota, virtutes tantae confluxerunt?	456	Epistolae	19
aut nostra vota gratiam Principis, aut Tuae virtutes et vota nostra	456	Epistolae	21
aut Tuae virtutes et vota nostra et Principis gratiam superarent.	456	Epistolae	21
VOTIS			
Sufficiet votis ista iuuenta meis.	386	Musae 2	10
Cur sine te, votis immoriturus, ago?	421	Lucus 35	6
vestrae gaudia responderint aut nostris votis aut virtutibus vestris,	443	Orationes	13
virtutes tandem meritis tuis votisque nostris conspirantibus	464	Epistolae	12
nouo hoc cumulo honorum, qui tamen votis nostris nondum respondent.	464	Epistolae	21
VOTO			
Quod tamen haec omnia succedant ex voto, quod reclusae sint fores,	472	Epistolae	19
VOUEMUS			
largam messem Vobis haec tenuia boni consulentibus, vouemus.	441	Orationes	22
VOX			
Cur sic displiceat vox aliena tibi?	388	Musae 9	10
VRBANI			
Vrbani VIII Pont. Respons.	416	Lucus 26	T
Attamen VRBANI delecto nomine, constat	416	Lucus 27	5
VRBANUM			
Respons. ad Vrb. VIII.	416	Lucus 27	T
Ad Vrbanum VIII Pont.	417	Lucus 28	T
VRBANUS			
Non placet vrbanus noster de nomine lusus	416	Lucus 27	1
VRBEM			
Percussa dum currunt ad vrbem	394	Musae 23	15
Quin per Presbyteros tuos; per vrbem	400	Musae 37	5
Non vrbem facit vnicam, sed Orbem.	408	Passio 19	5

	PAGE	TITLE	LINE
VRBES			
Praecipitata; cadunt vrbes, formidine muri	420	Tr.Mortis	77
VRBIUM			
quantum satis ad dolendum, vrbium incendia, fragores, direptiones,	449	Orationes	5
VRBS			
Nam te nunc Ager, Vrbs, & Aula plorant:	428	Mem.Matr.10	8
VRGEO			
Connixus, digitis impiger vrgeo:	424	Mem.Matr.4	10
VRGET			
Dum te vel digitis minister vrget,	417	Lucus 30	1
VRIT			
Aut vt pruna gelu summo mordacius vrit,	399	Musae 35	5
VRNA			
Quicquid ex vrna meliore ductum	390	Musae 14	5
Mihine matris vrna clausa est vnico,	424	Mem.Matr.2	57
VRSI			
ac si non gregaria essent animalia, sed tigres aut vrsi.	450	Orationes	22
VRTICA			
Calumniandi concitauit vrtica,	392	Musae 20	7
VSPIAM			
Et quicquid vspiam est seuerae foeminae,	422	Mem.Matr.2	2
Non est angulus vspiam serenus,	428	Mem.Matr.10	13
Quae enim vspiam gens, quod vnquam seculum meliorem habuit Principem?	445	Orationes	12
vt ego nihil vspiam laetum, nihil candidum expiscari possem;	451	Orationes	14
VSQUAM			
hospitium, et erga te propensius, haud vsquam forsitan reperias.	466	Epistolae	19
VSQUE			
Age, prouocemus vsque ad Angelos ipsos,	392	Musae 20	3
Vt tenuis flammae species caelum vsque minatur,	410	Lucus 2	1
Nempe huc vsque notos tenebricosos	428	Mem.Matr.10	1
vsque ad Pyrenaeas nubes conscendens, reuersus per mare,	454	Orationes	31
VSQUEDUM			
vsquedum, postquam omnes honorum gradus hic percurreris,	457	Epistolae	3
VSSISSE			
Vssisse prono fulmine diceris,	433	Poem.Lat.	14
VSU			
E creaturis sine mentis vsu	390	Musae 14	13
De rituum vsu.	395	Musae 25	T
instructior ad omnem causam, paratiorue siue a doctrina, siue ab vsu;	462	Epistolae	22
VSUM			
vbi tamen ad vsum tralatae fuerint, machinas conficiunt	454	Orationes	5
VSUS			
Tollantur si cuncta malus quae polluit vsus,	390	Musae 13	3
Extruxissem, vbi, cum moneret vsus,	401	Musae 37	29
Deus ipse cum crearet hominem, mundi regem, consilio vsus est.	446	Orationes	37
e baiulo euasit Philosophus, eodem ingenio vsus in lignis & literis:	453	Orationes	37
hoc Principe, in quo doctrinae fructus atque vsus mirifice relucet.	469	Epistolae	23
VT			
Nunc adeo per te viuunt, vt repere possint,	384	Musae	5
Non mea fert aetas, vt te, veterane, lacessam;	386	Musae 2	1
Non vt te superem: res tamen ipsa feret.	386	Musae 2	2
Aspice, dum perstas, vt te tua deserat aetas,	386	Musae 2	5
Quid vetat vt pueri vagitus suppleat alter,	388	Musae 9	13
Vt feruor cerebri refrigeretur,	391	Musae 15	9
Vt, cum mors rabidis vnguibus imminens	391	Musae 17	3
Vt sanctum Domini persequerentur opus;	392	Musae 19	2
Vt, quae Papicolis propria, assuas nobis,	392	Musae 20	8
Tu perstrepis tamen; vtque turgeat carmen	392	Musae 20	10
Quo sanguis est Christi, nisi vt maculas lauet,	393	Musae 22	3
Astronomus olim (vt fama) dum maculas diu,	393	Musae 22	7
Vt celebrem decus insusurras?	394	Musae 23	24
Vt, quo fatiges verberesque	395	Musae 23	47
Scilicet, vt quos ante suas cum coniuge tedas	396	Musae 26	9
Christus, vt auxilij	396	Musae 28	8
Quis sic amicum excipiet, vt Cathari Deum,	397	Musae 28	13
Vt niue torpentes incaluere manus?	399	Musae 35	4
Aut vt pruna gelu summo mordacius vrit,	399	Musae 35	5
Absit vt ingenuum pungant mea verba pudorem;	400	Musae 36	3
Vt nequeat paulo se cohibere domi.	404	Passio 3	2
Vt postulat mos; quid tuis dabis? Teipsum.	406	Passio 10	3
Zacchaeus, vt Te cernat, arborem scandit:	406	Passio 12	1
Nunc ipse scandis, vt labore mutato	406	Passio 12	2
Circumferre potes; Sampson vt ante fores.	408	Passio 18	2
Vt tenuis flammae species caelum vsque minatur,	410	Lucus 2	1
Vt discat sibi quisque, quid vtile: nempe nocebat	412	Lucus 9	3
Vtque ouis in dumis, haeres in crine Cometae,	413	Lucus 16	3
Ni facias, vt opes linguae per brachia serpant,	414	Lucus 22	3
Vt dentur species, rogare sensum:	415	Lucus 24	3
Omniaque haec vt transadigant sine crimine costas,	418	Tr.Mortis	29
Ah nunc, helluo, fac, vt ipse sugam:	421	Lucus 34	1
Vt, si gratia tanta copuletur	421	Lucus 34	7
Matrine linguam refero, solum vt mordeam?	424	Mem.Matr.2	59
Fac radios saltem ingemines, vt dextera tortos	424	Mem.Matr.3	9
Vt currat paribus gloria tibijs.	425	Mem.Matr.4	16
Quin cerne vt erres, inscie, brachium	426	Mem.Matr.6	13
Iudicij dominus, flores vt iunctius halent	427	Mem.Matr.7	25
Iisque siccis adeo vt os Molossorum	429	Mem.Matr.12	3
Stulta: semel scribo, perpetuo vt sileam.	431	Mem.Matr.19	8
Vt morbi perimant, alioque in puluere prostet?	433	Poem.Lat.	35
Totum offuscari peteres, vt nocte silenti	433	Poem.Lat.	38
Vt, fluuio currente, vadum sonat, alta quiescunt.	433	Poem.Lat.	48

VT (cont'd)

	PAGE	TITLE	LINE
Vt mucro rumpatur Mineruae, ...	433	Poem.Lat.	11
Vtque minax superetur Aegis?	433	Poem.Lat.	12
Vt si recisis arboribus meis	434	Poem.Lat.	29
Vulnereque emanat sanguis, vt intret honos.	435	Poem.Lat.	6
Cernis vt exusta semper sit fronte viator;	437	Poem.Lat.	3
Vt Flos hinc lacrymis, illinc Philomela querelis, ...	438	Poem.Lat.	5
Perstringas homines vultu, miretur vt orbis	211	Cam.1613-b BB	13
vt deponatis paulisper vultus illos bellicos, quibus hostes soletis	440	Orationes	8
accidere potest, quam vt ministri Regis Catholici ad nos accedant?	440	Orationes	14
vt satis intelligatis, Excellentias vestras tanto chariores esse,	440	Orationes	24
Necesse est autem vt foelicitas tantorum Principum etiam in ministros	441	Orationes	5
Seritur fama in hoc saeculo, vt in sequenti metatur:	441	Orationes	20
Optamus quidem vt Maiestatis vestrae gaudia responderint aut nostris	443	Orationes	12
eruditionem, quae tanta est vt, nisi Rex esses in ciuili Republica,	443	Orationes	18
ac tam stupendo iudicio, vt, nisi tot negotijs distractus esses,	443	Orationes	26
vt miraculis vestris nostra occurrant, oratio nostra est silentium,	444	Orationes	2
clementia, vt frequenter nos inuisat, a re instructus nos doceat,	444	Orationes	5
vbique deferentibus, vt nullus sit angulus corporis, nulla venula,	445	Orationes	2
Vt natura omnis suos habet anteambulones, vnde pluuia futura,	445	Orationes	4
Quare vt parcius agam vobiscum, simulque & laboribus meis, . .	445	Orationes	28
vt sciatis omnes quam nude, quam simpliciter vobiscum agam, . .	445	Orationes	34
verrunt (ac si perdiderint ingenium) vt Spartam excrnent suam:	445	Orationes	37
& polymiti, vt si minus id assequantur, quod primum intendunt,	446	Orationes	6
aequumne est vt tot labores & sollicitudines Principum sine . .	446	Orationes	11
quam Nuptiae, quas adeo laudant Poetae, vt in coelum transtulerint:	446	Orationes	18
vt enim Vxores, Virgines; ita Sol & Coelum producunt flores,	446	Orationes	31
vt Rex animalium fiat Rex hominum, apponimus nos manibus Sceptrum,	447	Orationes	2
Nam vt educationem liberorum mittam, qua in re celebris est . .	447	Orationes	16
vt ingenti labore suo & periculo consuleret & praesenti Reipublicae	447	Orationes	24
pax adeo Musis summe necessaria est, vt sine ea nihil simus.	448	Orationes	17
vt qui hic in Musarum monte editissimo, in ipso Parnasso siti sumus,	449	Orationes	32
Principibus vt vtilissima ita difficillima factu, cum quanto plus	450	Orationes	10
Natura suas dotes, vt indigentia singularum regionum omnes connectat:	450	Orationes	19
ipse egit oratorem, vt & ego aliquantulum hoc nomine glorier.	450	Orationes	31
cur non vt elephanti turres, ita tu patriam tecum portasti? . .	451	Orationes	8
vt ego nihil vspiam laetum, nihil candidum expiscari possem;	451	Orationes	14
vt aliquando existimen id egisse prudentissimum Patrem tuum,	451	Orationes	29
solebant signa in hostes inijcere, vt milites acrius ea repeterent:	451	Orationes	32
interficere voluptatis, vt iter tantum, tantis laboribus, . .	452	Orationes	7
vt interdum putem, optime consuluisse Deum orbi terrarum lapides	452	Orationes	23
vt quid priuata habeat in se vita commodi aut voluptatis, . .	452	Orationes	36
vt laeuitatem illam aequabilem atque politiem perturbent. . .	453	Orationes	13
vt nihil habeat Inuidia ipsa, quod contra hiscat aut mussitet.	453	Orationes	23
gaudia praestolantur, quae iamdudum annuunt mihi vt perorem.	454	Orationes	23
vt enim vapor, qui furtim ascendit ad nubes, vbi iam ingrauescit	454	Orationes	28
Deum immortalem, vt Princeps optimus nulla secunda itinera meditetur;	454	Orationes	38
& nunc sit tanta patriae tenacitas, vt nunquam Princeps se extricet:	455	Orationes	5
Obsecremus eum tantum vt permittat nostram hanc Inter victrices	455	Orationes	16
proin vt Fluuij quas aquas a Fonte accipiunt non retinent ipsi,	456	Epistolae	9
Nimirum vt lineae, quamuis diuersa via, omnes tamen ad centrum	456	Epistolae	22
vt neque virtutibus tuis desint honores neque vtrisque vita,	457	Epistolae	2
qui vtrumque curasti, vt neque sitirent Musae, neque flagrarent.	457	Epistolae	20
id enim nostra interest, vt hoc precemur, aut enim misere fallimur,	457	Epistolae	25
Angustior erat Scotia, quam vt pennas nido plene explicare posses:	458	Epistolae	8
adeo vt qui non subijciuntur ditioni, eruditioni vestrae obtemperent:	458	Epistolae	13
ita inuoluit nos, vt etiam rependendi vias omnes praecludat.	458	Epistolae	28
quam vt pro infinitis vestris in nos beneficijs Maiestatem vestram	458	Epistolae	30
es praedo omnis gloriae, vt ne gratitudinis laudem nobis reliqueris?	459	Epistolae	3
vt ex affrictu Libri vestri hominem illico contundamus. . .	459	Epistolae	7
sunt, vt sic scripta vestra omni dente, tum edacis temporis,	459	Epistolae	18
vt vestrae coronae ciuili & literariae tertiam Coelestem sero	459	Epistolae	20
vt si officia nostra minus respondeant magnitudini beneficiorum,	460	Epistolae	15
Vt nihilo-minus Tibi luceat, cum nobis accenderit. . . .	461	Epistolae	5
tractus (Oceani praeda et deliciae) vt irrigui Musarum horti,	461	Epistolae	9
vnde fit vt nullus fere elabatur dies, qui non hostes aliquos nobis	461	Epistolae	13
vt iam compensemur abunde, neque amplius quaerendum sit Tibi,	462	Epistolae	15
Tantum rogamus, vt pergas, & inter nouos honorum cumulos, . .	462	Epistolae	28
vt cum ipse eruditionis Princeps sit, illi etiam honores qui finitimi	463	Epistolae	21
rudiorem esse impexioremque, quam vt tantum Hospitem excipiat:	463	Epistolae	29
Faxit Deus vt quos profectus feceris in Sphaera Naturae, . .	464	Epistolae	2
vtque mature absoluas quae complexus es animo, ad eius gloriam,	464	Epistolae	4
nobis remotior, confidimus tamen vt arbores, quanto altius crescunt,	464	Epistolae	17
merita tua ita ascensura, vt eorum vis et virtus ad nos descendat.	464	Epistolae	19
vt semper post nouas dignitates, alias tibi quaerant et moliantur.	464	Epistolae	23
vt Almam Matrem spe noua grauidam semper atque praegnantem . .	464	Epistolae	25
vt res nostras omnes cum Honore Tuo coniunctas esse velimus.	465	Epistolae	2
vt Alma Mater libentissime caput reclinet in tuo sinu, oculusque	465	Epistolae	12
Deus faueat Tibi & concedat vt terrestres tui honores cum coelestibus	465	Epistolae	18
Permitte vt nos etiam in praedam partemque tecum veniamus: . .	465	Epistolae	21
vt sic vna opera vtriusque Reipublicae calculum et ciuilis . .	465	Epistolae	26
curesque vt tuus in nos amor, antehac satis perspectus, . .	466	Epistolae	3
noluitque vt minori sphaera quam pro latitudine meritorum tuorum	466	Epistolae	14
rogamusque vt quando beneficia tua peruagantur Angliam, . .	466	Epistolae	16
ita excipiemus illa, vt benignius hospitium, et erga te propensius,	466	Epistolae	18
concede vt nos etiam benignitate alarum tuarum et virtute fruamur.	466	Epistolae	22
orantes vt quicquid consilij auaritia ceperit aduersus aut . .	467	Epistolae	10
vt qui tot subsidia attuleris ad progressum doctrinae, hac etiam	467	Epistolae	27
vt bonorum praemia citissime promulgentur, quo suauius virtutibus,	468	Epistolae	15
orantes vt immunitates nostrae a Serenissimis Regibus concessae ab	468	Epistolae	21
tibi hunc honorem, et faxit, vt tibi gloriae sit, omnibus saluti.	469	Epistolae	5

VT (cont'd)	PAGE	TITLE	LINE
Concede vt Honoribus nuperis, tanquam partubus Virtutum Tuarum,	469	Epistolae	8
tuere nos ita vt fortunae nostrae, intra ambitum amplexusque	469	Epistolae	18
Vt semel dicam; Oratio perfecta, vti vir, tetragonos est,	471	Epistolae	3
sed vt facilius ignoscas occupato calamo, qui etiam ferians nihil Tua	471	Epistolae	22
vt halitus tenuiores solent, qui primo caloris suasu excitati atque	471	Epistolae	28
vt nunquam cessandum mihi ducerem, nunquam fatiscendum,	472	Epistolae	7
vt laboribus meis plurimis atque assidua obseruantia, ramenta	472	Epistolae	12
vt cedam aliquantisper expectationi hominum, rariusque paulo fodiam	472	Epistolae	27
vt quod Philosophus de Tactu & Visu, id apposite admodum huc	472	Epistolae	35
sed non patitur, vt mihi videtur, Romana elegantia, periodique vetus	473	Epistolae	17
VTAR			
Tres video partes, quo re distinctius vtar,	386	Musae 4	1
VTARE			
quando ad magnates cogitas, stylo vtare, sed modeste grandi;	470	Epistolae	22
VTCUMQUE			
vtcumque, cum olim ab Archiepiscopo Eboracensi Summo Angliae	463	Epistolae	30
VTCUNQUE			
Vtcunque Tua lenitas non ita interpretabitur mea haec scribendi	471	Epistolae	24
VTERIS			
Vitro minus recte vteris.	388	Musae 8	18
VTERQUE			
Postremis ambabus idem sentimus vterque;	386	Musae 4	5
Sanus Homo factus, vitiorum purus vterque;	408	Passio 20	1
Nec Deus est nec Homo: Christus vterque fuit.	412	Lucus 10	2
VTI			
Ni sancte, vti mater, recedam,	425	Mem.Matr.6	11
vti Valerij, aliae contra semper pertinaces ac tribunitiae,	447	Orationes	20
aliae contra semper pertinaces ac tribunitiae, vti Appij.	447	Orationes	21
vno semper saginantur in loco, vti anguillae, aut si mutant locum,	452	Orationes	10
quae semper se deuorat primum, vti vermis nucleum, e quo nascitur;	454	Orationes	15
vti sanguis solet in re dubia ad cor festinare, ita ad Te confugimus	467	Epistolae	8
Iam si inter commendandum adhibeas ei calamistros vti iuuenculae,	470	Epistolae	19
etsi tu qui scribis (vti quiuis priuatus) inferioris sis subsellij,	470	Epistolae	22
Oratio perfecta, vti vir, tetragonos est, grauis, nobilis,	471	Epistolae	4
vti etiam senectus, quam aetatem in hac palaestra consecutus mihi	471	Epistolae	7
VTILE			
Vt discat sibi quisque, quid vtile: nempe nocebat	412	Lucus 9	3
Ecquid videtis tandem quam vtile hoc iter, per quod optimus Princeps	451	Orationes	35
VTILISSIMA			
Principibus vt vtilissima ita difficillima factu, cum quanto plus	450	Orationes	10
VTILIUS			
quid enim vtilius quam ex obseruatione exterarum Legum ac morum,	450	Orationes	14
Nihil vtilius Regi quam aliquando non regnare:	452	Orationes	38
VTIMINI			
quae est vestra felicitas qui puro Academiae farre vtimini.	470	Epistolae	3
VTINAM			
O vtinam aut illorum oculi (quod comprecor vnum)	400	Musae 36	5
vtinam & nunc sit tanta patriae tenacitas, vt nunquam Princeps se	455	Orationes	5
VTRAMQUE			
Nam vtramque illam curam insignem, tam de conseruando Fluuio nostro,	457	Epistolae	16
VTRAQUE			
quo magis amore coalescamus, vtraque gens Hispanica, Britannica,	440	Orationes	22
VTRASQUE			
Quas Latij Catharique mouent, atque inter vtrasque	402	Musae 39	31
qui vtrasque Indias Hispania sua quasi nodo connectens,	440	Orationes	16
VTRINQUE			
Gens tota fiet, atque vtrinque plectetur.	405	Passio 5	7
vtrinque mirus es et exercitatissimus.	462	Epistolae	22
VTRIQUE			
Spiritus proponit, & est vtrique	390	Musae 14	15
Ecce meus torpens animus succumbit vtrique,	435	Poem.Lat.	3
Iacobus tutelaris Diuus est vtrique nostrum;	440	Orationes	23
VTRISQUE			
vt neque virtutibus tuis desint honores neque vtrisque vita,	457	Epistolae	3
VTRIUSQUE			
vt sic vna opera vtriusque Reipublicae calculum et ciuilis	465	Epistolae	26
vtriusque enim splendor et claritas humilia loca deprecantur.	466	Epistolae	11
VTROQUE			
Torquet, & in Textu Doctor vtroque cluet.	392	Musae 19	6
nos tam defecimus in vtroque quam Excellentiae Vestrae abundant.	441	Orationes	13
VTRUM			
Vtrum tenore sacra nostra sint necne	392	Musae 20	5
vtrum gratia Principis virtutes tuas, aut nostra vota gratiam	456	Epistolae	20
VTRUMQUE			
Vtrumque sternis calcitro:	388	Musae 8	6
Vtrumque mirum est: hoc tamen mirum magis,	412	Lucus 11	2
Vtrumque sexum dote ne mulctauerit.	422	Mem.Matr.2	9
Vtrumque si praederis Indum,	425	Mem.Matr.6	7
cumulum amoris Tui, qui vtrumque curasti, vt neque sitirent Musae,	457	Epistolae	20
cum Alma Matre, vtrumque splendorem cum beneficio nostro coniungis.	458	Epistolae	17
VUIDA			
Mater perpetuis vuida gaudijs,	424	Mem.Matr.4	2
VULGI			
neque illi e faece vulgi tantum qui eruditionem simplicitati	461	Epistolae	17
VULGO			
Quam (more vestro) imponere inscio vulgo.	397	Musae 31	3
VULGUS			
Quo vulgus ornat vos! At audias parum;	393	Musae 22	6
Spargitque per tot capita, quot vulgus gerit.	414	Lucus 20	4
Scinditur in partes vulgus ceu compita: telum	418	Tr.Mortis	16

	PAGE	TITLE	LINE
VULNERA			
Cum lacrymas oculosque duos tot vulnera vincant,	404	Passio 1	1
VULNERE			
Vulnereque emanat sanguis, vt intret honos.	435	Poem.Lat.	6
VULPEM			
Britannicam in Vulpem, inque Romanam Lupam.	397	Musae 30	6
VULPIBUS			
Vulpibus antra feris, nidique volucribus adsunt,	407	Passio 19	1
VULTU			
Cum tu contundis Catharos, vultuque librisque,	385	Musae 1	5
Angeli vultu radiante candent;	390	Musae 14	10
Praeuenias vultu non facienda tuo.	421	Lucus 35	10
Quis iste tandem? non enim vultu ambulat	436	Poem.Lat.	1
Perstringas homines vultu, miretur vt orbis	211	Cam.1613-b BR	13
incomparabilem, quae eodem vultu et moderatur mundum et nos respicit.	458	Epistolae	4
VULTUM			
Prae quo Tibris vultum recondit,	394	Musae 23	43
Hunc vultum ostendas, & tecum, nobile spectrum,	426	Mem.Matr.7	14
Quotidie pasti: tantum verum indue vultum	427	Mem.Matr.7	29
VULTURNIS			
Nescia vulturnis cedere, firma manet.	428	Mem.Matr.11	2
VULTUS			
Et coelum vultus exhilarato tui,	211	Cam.1613-b BR	8
vt deponatis paulisper vultus illos bellicos, quibus hostes soletis	440	Orationes	8
Terret equos equitumque vultus.	448	Orationes	4
inspexi facies hominum ac vultus curiosius tanquam emptor;	451	Orationes	13
qui nuper versatus est in forma & figuris vultus, vbi res postulat,	454	Orationes	7
VUTTEI			
Lesmones, e belone sphalerci kep traumati vuttei	431	Mem.Matr.17	12
VXOR			
Virgo pudens, vxor fida, seuera parens:	429	Mem.Matr.13	2
VXORE			
ideoque ex quolibet ligno, qualibet vxore non esse fingendum:	447	Orationes	9
VXORES			
vt enim Vxores, Virgines; ita Sol & Coelum producunt flores,	446	Orationes	32
VXORIS			
noluit Princeps optimus, in delectu vxoris, re vna omnium grauissima,	447	Orationes	22
VXORUM			
qui olim glasto se inficientes, in vxorum corporibus, Solem,	446	Orationes	30
WALLIAE			
Illustriss. Celsissimoque CAROLO, Walliae, & Iuventutis Principi.	384	Musae	T
In Obitum Henrici Principis Walliae.	432	Poem.Lat.	T
WHITAKER			
Whitaker, erranti quem praefers carmine, miles	398	Musae 33	5
WINCHESTER			
my L. Bishop of Winchester, one of the Kings most honorable	473	Epistolae	24
XALAZA			
ean epideikseis toi epikeimenoi nephei, pareleusetai e xalaza:	454	Orationes	20
XALEPON			
Xalepon dokei dakrusai,	430	Mem.Matr.16	1
Xalepon men ou dakrusai:	430	Mem.Matr.16	2
XALEPOTERON			
Xalepoteron de panton	430	Mem.Matr.16	3
XARAIS			
Praeis eiarinous te xarais epikidnato kepon:	431	Mem.Matr.17	18
XARISIN			
Ouk eti ballomenes xarisin bebolemenai etor,	431	Mem.Matr.17	9
XERXES			
et Xerxes istos, alterosque maris quasi Flagellatores expugnatos	462	Epistolae	8
XRENAI			
Dokei moi xrenai para ton presbuton punthanesthai, osper tina odon	471	Epistolae	9
XREON			
Menouge sophien, ei s' apellaxthai xreon,	430	Mem.Matr.15	5
Y'			
Talas, eithe y' Argos eien	430	Mem.Matr.16	8
ZACCHAEUS			
Zacchaeus, vt Te cernat, arborem scandit:	406	Passio 12	1
ZELUM			
Sic acuunt zelum frigora tanta tuum?	399	Musae 35	6
ZEPHYRIS			
Ac zephyris, carnis flos remeare nequit.	415	Lucus 23	14
ZO			
Zo d' autos, braxu ti pneion, ost' empalin autes	431	Mem.Matr.17	21
ZOEIN			
Ainon omou Zoein kai pneumatos allo genesthai	431	Mem.Matr.17	22
ZOES			
Zoes ksunergon tende diatheinai teknois	430	Mem.Matr.15	6

Frequencies

English, in Frequency Order
English, in Alphabetical Order
Latin, in Frequency Order
Latin, in Alphabetical Order

-3961-
THE

-3568-
AND

-2512-
TO

-2131-
OF

-1781-
A

-1575-
THAT

-1512-
IN

-1382-
IS

-1221-
I

-1104-
NOT

-1095-
HE

-1011-
MY

-990-
HIS

-937-
BUT

-924-
FOR

-923-
IT

-855-
ALL

-794-
AS

-768-
THY

-754-
BE

-657-
WITH

-625-
OR

-602-
ARE

-573-
WHICH

-553-
SO

-551-
THEY

-538-
THOU

-505-
ME

-494-
THEN

-488-
BY

-473-
IF

-462-
THIS

-444-
THEIR

-413-
WHEN

-408-
THEM

-391-
GOD

-384-
THEE

-380-
WHO

-378-
HAVE

-357-
ONE

-348-
THERE

-339-
MORE

-336-
WHAT

-329-
NO

-324-
YET

-323-
AT

-321-
MAY

-315-
HIM

-313-
HATH

-307-
ON

-302-
WILL

-301-
WAS

-300-
YOU

-274-
FROM
GOOD

-250-
MAN

-249-
DO

-242-
SHALL

-239-
OUR

-238-
DOTH

-236-
AN

-227-
BOTH

-224-
DID

-212-
MAKE

-210-
WE

-209-
LOVE

-208-
THINGS

-199-
GREAT
YOUR

-197-
CAN

-195-
MUCH

-190-
LORD

-183-
WOULD

-182-
THOSE

-180-
HEE

-179-
SOME

-178-
EVER

-176-
OUT
WHERE

-172-
ANY

-169-
NOW

-168-
LET

-166-
&

-164-
LIKE

-163-
DAY
OTHER

-161-
THESE

-158-
LIFE

-157-
MINE
O

-156-
US

-154-
WELL

-151-
HEART

-140-
WERE

-139-
FIRST
HAD
SUCH

-137-
BEING
HOW

-136-
SHOULD

-135-
MUST

-134-
ALSO
INTO
STILL

-133-
WAY

-132-
MOST

-128-
TAKE

-127-
THOUGH

-126-
ART

-125-
COME

-120-
MADE

-115-
BEFORE
HER

-112-
ONELY
UP

-110-
PARSON

-109-
GRIEF
MANY
MEN
TWO

-108-
NEVER
THING

-107-
NOTHING

-105-
UNTO

-104-
AM
KNOW
WITHOUT
WORLD

-103-
CANNOT
SINCE
TIME

-102-
NOR

-101-
BECAUSE
ILL

-100-
OWN

-99-
EITHER

-98-
GIVE

-97-
MAKES
SINNE

-96-
HOUSE

-95-
OLD

-93-
BETTER
PLACE

-92-
USE

-91-
CHURCH
DEATH

-90-
LITTLE
SAY

-88-
UPON

-87-
EVEN

-86-
AFTER
EVERY
HAST

-84-
SOUL

-83-
COULD
GO
HIMSELF

-81-
AWAY
HERE
SELF
WHOSE

-79-
POWER
WHOM

-78-
LIVE
NONE
SEE

-77-
PRAISE
THINE

-76-
ANOTHER
POORE
VERY
WHILE

-75-
BEST
DOE
LONG
TOO

-74-
DONE
HAND

-73-
DOST

-72-
EARTH

-71-
EYES
NEITHER

-71- (cont'd)

TILL

-70-

TH'

-69-

'S
LIGHT

-68-

HOLY
MIGHT

-67-

THEREFORE

-66-

BEE
FULL
PART

-65-

ONCE

-64-

GOD'S
GRACE
TRUE

-63-

JOY

-62-

HEAD

-61-

HANDS
SWEET

-59-

ALONE
COUNTREY

-58-

EACH

-57-

OTHERS

-55-

FIRE
HIMSELFE
PEACE

-53-

FLESH
LESSE
ONLY
RATHER
THUS
WORDS

-52-

WORD
WORK

-51-

END
EV'N
KING
WHOLE

-50-

AGAINST
FRIEND

-49-

DEARE
OUGHT

-48-

ABOVE
CARE
LOST
NIGHT
PEOPLE
SHE
SOMETIMES
THEMSELVES
TRUTH

-47-

REST

-46-

FEAR
HAVING
THINK
WANT

-45-

CHRIST
DUST
LEAST
PLEASURE

-44-

COMES
DIDST
TEARS

-43-

FALL
FOUND
HEALTH
HEARTS
LAW
PARISH
SERVE
WIT
WITHIN

-42-

BRING
CALL
DOWN
LOOK
MINDE
NAME
NEW
PUT
SURE
WHEREFORE

-41-

DIE
HEAVEN
KEEP
MEANS
SUNNE
THOUGHTS

-40-

ABOUT
CAME
FACE

-39-

FIT
GROW
HONOUR
LEAVE
NATURE
RULE
SINNES
THREE
YE

-38-

BESIDES
COMMON
GET
HEAV'N
MASTER
SAME
SET
SHOW
SIR
STAY

-37-

BLOUD
FINDE
GIVES
GOES
REASON
SERVANT
TURN
WISE

-36-

CHILDREN
JOYES
MEAT
PRESENT
WHETHER
WINE

-35-

AGE
GROUND
MAN'S
RICH
SPIRIT
STATE

-34-

DAYES
ESPECIALLY
JUST
RISE
SCRIPTURE
TIMES

-33-

BROUGHT
FAITH
FARRE
GOLD
HOPE
HORSE
MEE
OFTEN
OWNE
POOR
SAID
TAKEN
WAYES

-32-

DEAD
GAVE
GLORIE
HELP
HOLD
LEST
LIVES
MAKING
OPEN
PRAYERS
RIGHT
SING
STORE
WEE

-31-

BLESSED
BODY
EAT
EYE
FINE
MEASURE
PASSE
VERTUE

-30-

ACCORDING
BEEN
BOOK
HARD
HEARE
HERBERT
SELFE
THROUGH
WRITE
YEARES

-29-

BREAD
CHARITY
DOORE
HIGH
HOME
MUSICK
NEEDS
OCCASION
OVER
PRAYER
SECONDLY
SERVICE
SHAME
SICK
TAKES
THOUGHT
WHY

-28-

AMONG
BLESSING
BRAVE
COLD
DRINK
LAST
SEEK
SERVANTS
SIDE
SMALL
TOGETHER
WEALTH

-27-

AGAIN
ANSWER
EV'RY
FLIE
FREE
FRUIT
GIVEN
GOE
GRAVE
HELL
HOURE
LABOUR
LAY
LENGTH
LIES
ORDER
PRAY
STARRES
TOOK

-26-

COMFORT
CROSSE
DELIGHT
ELSE
FAIR
FATHER
GEORGE
GONE
HEARD
HURT
KINDE
KNOWS
MOTHER
RELIGION
STAND
YOUNG

-25-

ACTIONS
ALTHOUGH
ENOUGH
GIVING
GLORIOUS
INDEED
KEPT
MEET
MOVE
OFF
OH
SAVE
SHALT
WATER
WHEREIN
WIFE

-24-

BED
BREAST
BROTHER
CHRISTIAN
COURSE
DESIRE
DIVINE
FIND
HUNDRED
NEED
POINT
SHINE
SHORT
SLEEP
SOULE
TONGUE
UNDER
WILT
WINDE

-24- (cont'd)

YEARE

-23-

BEAR
CANST
FOOLE
FRIENDS
LEAVES
MARK
MIRTH
SEES
SIGHT
SPEAK
TREE
WORKS

-22-

ANOTHER'S
CAUSE
DUTY
FOOLISH
PERSON
RAISE
SEA
TELL
TREASURE

-21-

BEGAN
BODIE
BOW
BREATH
CHILD
CONSIDERATION
COURT
DARK
EARES
EXCEPT
FOOT
GOT
KNOWES
KNOWING
LEFT
LETTER
MORNING
NAY
READ
SAVIOUR
SIN
STONE
STRENGTH
STRONG
SURELY
THEREOF
WHEREAS

-20-

BOOKS
DISCOURSE
FAULT
FEAST
FLOCK
FOES
JUDGE
KNEW
LIE
MEN'S
NEXT
PARSON'S
POUND
QUICKLY
SENT
STRAIGHT
TASTE
TEMPERANCE
TEN
THEREIN
TRUST
UNTILL

-19-

BLESSINGS
COMPANY
DISEASES
DUE
DWELL
FAIRE
FAST
FOOD
GARDEN
GLASSE
JUSTICE
KNOWLEDGE
LAND
LOSE
MONY
MOUTH
MR
PAIN
PLAY
PROVE
RUNNE
SAYES
SCRIPTURES
SKILL
SPRING
TEACH
VERTUES
WINDES

-18-

ALAS
BEAUTIE
BREAK
CALLING
CASE
DOCTRINE
DOES
&C
FAULTS
FAVOUR
FEARS
FORTH
GLORY
GREATER
GRIEFS
HUMBLE
LATE
LOOSE
LOSSE
READY
ROOM
ROUND
SAD
SENSE
SHILLINGS
SONNE
THINKS
THROW

-17-

ABLE
ANCIENT
APPEARE
BRIGHT
BUSINESSE
CRIE
DELIGHTS
DREST
EASIE
ENTER
FAME
FAMILY
FURTHER
GENTLE
GIFT
HEED
HIGHER
LEARNED
MEND
MONEY
NECESSARY
NOBLE
PARDON
PASSION
PAY
PERFECT
PLEASURES
QUICK
SHEW
SIT
SORROW
TEMPER
THIRDLY
TWICE
WHEREOF
WISH

-16-

ADVANTAGE
BACK
BEASTS
BUSIE
CAST
CLEARE
CLOSE
CONSIDER
COST
CROWN
DARE
DOING
DUTIES
EASILY
FEEL
FILL
FINDES
FIVE
FOUL
FUTURE
GAIN
GREW
GROWS
HALFE
LOW
MEAN
OTHERS'
PUBLICK
READING
SAINT
SAKE
SAW
SECOND
STRANGE
TABLE
TAKING
THENCE
THIRD
TOLD
TRULY
USETH
VAIN
VERSE
WENT
WORKING

-15-

AUTHORITY
BROKEN
CHANGE
CURIOUS
DOUBLE
EATING
ESTATE
FEARE
FEED
FINDS
FISH
FOLLY
GODLY
LANGUAGE
NEIGHBOUR
OFT
OTHERWISE
PARADISE
RECEIVE
REGARD
RULES
SIGH
SOON
SOUGHT
SPARE
TOWARDS
USED
WEEP
WORTH

-14-

AFFLICTION
BEYOND
BLOW
BUILT
CURE
DANVERS
DEBT
EASE
EVILL
FAIN
FASTING
FEET
FEW
FLOWERS
FOLLOW
FOOLES
GENERALL
GIFTS
GREECE
HEAR
JOURNEY
KEEPS
KNOWN
LUST
MIND
PAINS
PARTS
PERHAPS
PHYSICIAN
PLEASE
PUNISHMENT
PURE
ROSE
SACRED
SEND
SERMON
SERMONS
SINS
STARRE
SWORD
TAUGHT
TEMPLE
THITHER
'TIS
TROUBLED
WARRE
WATERS
WEEK
WICKED
YOUTH

-13-

AFFLICTIONS
AH
ARISE
BLESSE
BONES
BRINGS
CEASE
CHRIST'S
CLEAN
COMMAND
CONCERNING
CONSCIENCE
CREATURES
DAILY
DEAR
DECAY
DEEDS
DIET
DIVINITY
DOG
DRAW
EVIDENT
EXCEEDING
EXPERIENCE
FORCE
FRAME
GLAD
HALF
HAS
HOPES
JOHN
KINGDOME
LINES
LOOKS
MRS
PAST
PATIENCE
PETER
PROMISES
REMOVE
REVERENCE
ROME
SICKNESSE
SOMETHING
SORT
SOULS
SOUND
SPEECH
SPIRITUALL
STONES
SWEETLY
SWEETNESSE
TEXT
THRONE
TOUCH
TRADE
TROUBLE
TURNE
UNDERSTAND
UNLESSE
WELCOME
WHEREWITH
WORSE
WOULDST
WOUND
YEA

-12-

ACCORDINGLY
ADMIRABLE
AGREE
ANGELS
BAPTISME
BEAST
BEHAVIOUR
BELEEVE
BELOW
BENEFIT
BETWEEN
BITTER
BOUNDS
BOX
CASES
CONSIDERING
CORN
DANGER
DESIRES
DESTROY
DIVERS
DROP
DRY
ECHO
FASHION
FATHERS
FAVOURS
FLOWER
GOODS
HADST
HEAT
HERBS
HIGHEST
HONEST
KNOWLEDG
LAWS
LEARNING
LIVING
MATTER
MAYST
MEANING
MIDST
OBSERVED
PLACES
PLEASING
PRESERVE
PRIDE
PRIVATE
PSALM
REACH
REMEMBER
REPENTANCE

-12- (cont'd)

RESTORE
REWARD
SAINTS
SAVIOUR'S
SHEE
SHOWS
SINN
SKIE
SORROWS
SPEND
STANDS
STOCK
STORIE
STREAMS
SUFFER
SUNDAY
THERFORE
UNDERSTOOD
WANTS
WHENCE
WOOD
WRATH
WEAR
WHITHER
WING
WINGS
WISDOME
WO
WOMAN
WOMEN
WOUNDS
WRIT

-11-

ABROAD
ACCOUNT
AIM
ALLOW
ARTS
BEHINDE
BID
BOUND
CARRY
CATECHIZING
CLOTHES
CONTENT
CONVERSATION
COURTESIE
CREATION
DEED
DOVE
EAST
EXPRESSE
FAR
FEARES
FELL
FLOW
FORMER
FRUITFULL
GOSPEL
GRACIOUS
GREATEST
H
HITHER
HOUSES
HUMOURS
IDLE
JUDGEMENT
JUSTLY
LIV'D
LOOKE
LOVES
NOUGHT
ONES
PARTICULAR
PARTICULARLY
PAUL
PLEASED
POINTS
PROPORTION
PUTS
RELIEF
REQUEST
REQUIRES
ROCK
ROD
SACRIFICE
SEEMS
SELL
SHARE
SPENT
SPHERE
SPREAD
STUFFE
TENDER
TITLE
TWENTY

-10-

ALWAIES
ATTEND
BEHOLD
BLISSE
CALLS
COMPARE
CONFESSION
CONTINUE
CONVEY
COUNTRY
CURED
CUSTOME
CUT
DEW
DISCOURSES
DISCOVER
DISPOSITION
DOORES
EARE
EGYPT
ENEMIES
EXAMPLE
FATHER'S
FLOORE
FORTUNE
FOX
FULLY
GAINE
GIV'N
GRIEFE
GRIEVE
GUIDE
HAPPIE
HART
HILL
INCREASE
KEEPES
KEY
KILL
LAUGH
LENT
MORTALL
NATURALL
NEARE
NEEDES
NEIGHBOURS
OBLIGATION
OBSERVATION
OPINION
PERSONS
PHYSICK
PLAIN
POWERS
PREACHING
PRESENCE
QUIET
RARE
REFUSE
RELIGIOUS
RENT
RING
SALVATION
SCORE
SEASON
SELDOME
SENDS
SETS
SETTING
SHAL
SISTER
SMELL
SOMEWHAT
SOWRE
SPEAKES
SPORT
STAFFE
STEP
STOMACK
TEMPERATE
THEIRS
THINKES
TREES
TURNES
WEAK
WINTER
WONDER
WRITTEN
YOURS

-9-

ACTS
ADVISE
AFFAIRS
AFFLICTED
AFTERWARDS
ALMES
APPETITE
BEAUTY
BENT
BIRD
BIRTH
BODIES
BONE
BOSOME
BRAIN
BRED
BUILDING
BURDEN
BURN
CHANCE
CHAPTER
CHEER
CLAY
CLOUDS
COMING
COMMUNION
CONSTANT
CONTEMPT
CONTINUALLY
CONVERT
CORNE
CORNER
DARKNESSE
DAVID
DEGREE
DELIVER
DIES
DISORDERLY
EARTHLY
EFFECT
ENEMY
ETERNALL
FAIL
FALLS
FALSE
FIGHT
FLIES
FOULE
GETS
GLADLY
GROUNDS
HAPPY
HEAVENLY
HOLDS
HONY
INFINITE
INWARD
ITS
JEST
JUDGMENT
KIND
KINGS
LARGE
LEARN
LEAVING
LETT
LETTERS
LODGING
LOVING
MEATS
MERCY
NATION
OBEDIENCE
OCCASIONS
ONE'S
ORDERLY
OURS
OUTWARD
PARENTS
PLAINLY
PLEASETH
PRESENTLY
PRESUME
PRICE
PRIEST
PRINCES
PROVIDENCE
PULL
PUNISH
PURCHASE
PURSE
QUESTIONS
RECEIVED
REJOYCE
RESOLVED
REVEREND
RICHES
ROMANS
SAFE
SAYING
SEARCH
SIGHS
SINGLE
SLIGHT
SOLD
SORTS
SUCCESS
SUIT
TAME
TEACHETH
TEARES
TEMPTATIONS
VICES
VINE
WARM
WAST
WERT
WHITE
WOLFE
WORLDLY

-8-

ACT
ACTION
ADDED
ALLOWS
ALMIGHTIE
ALREADY
AMISSE
ANGER
APPLE
APPLYING
ASK
BAD
BEAMS
BEGINNING
BEGINS
BIRDS
BLEST
BLOOD
BOLD
BORN
BUY
CATCH
CHAIR
COMFORTS
COMPANIE
CONCLUDE
CONDITION
CONFESSE
CONTROLL
COOL
COUNSELL
COUNSELS
CUNNING
DEATH'S
DEEP
DEPART
DESERT
DOUBT
DRESSE
DRIE
EATES
EIES
ELEMENTS
ERE
FLIGHT
FRESH
GAME
GARDENS
GOSPELL
GRONES
HARDLY
HARVEST
HEAV'NLY
HENRY
HEREAFTER
HIDE
IMPLOYMENT
INSTANTLY
INTEMPERANCE
JEWS
KNEES
LAYS
LEADE
LETS
LIGHTS
LUTE
LYES
MAJESTY
MANNER
MARKET
MARRY
MASTERS
MATTHEW
MEETS
MELT
MORTIFICATION
MOTIONS
NEGLECT
PASSETH
PASSING
PERFECTION
PHYSITIAN
PIECE
PIETY
PORTION
POSSESSION
POT
PRAISES
PREACHETH
PRESENTS
PROFIT
PROUD
QUANTITIE
REPROVE
RIVERS
ROOT
SEEM
SELVES
SHUT
SLOW
SON
SOONER
SORE
SPEAKE
ST
STEAD
STRIKE
STRIVE
SWEETS
TEACHING
THINKE
TREAD
TUNE
TURNING
USEFULL
VESSELS
WAGES
WASH
WATCH
WEARY
WIDE
WONDERS
WORM
WROTE

-7-

ADORE
AFFECTIONS
AFFORD
ALMOST
ALTAR
ALWAYES

-7- (cont'd)

ARMS
AWAKE
BECAME
BECOME
BECOMES
BELL
BETIMES
BLINDE
BLOWN
BREAKS
BRIGHTNESSE
BUILD
CALLED
CATECHISME
CHIEFLY
CHOOSE
CHRISTIANS
CHURCHE'S
CHUSE
CLOTH
COLOUR
COMMIT
COMMON-WEALTH
CONFIDENCE
CONQUEST
CONSIDERED
CONSIDERS
CORINTHIANS
COVETOUS
CREATURE
CREDIT
CREEP
CRYING
CUP
CURES
DEATHS
DEFEND
DESIGNE
DESPISE
DEVOTION
DILIGENT
DILIGENTLY
DISCRETION
DISEASE
DOUBTLESSE
DRINKE
DROPS
DULL
EARNEST
EATS
EMPIRE
EMPTY
ENGLAND
ENJOY
ESTEEM
EXACT
FLAME
FLAT
FLY
FOLD
FROSTS
GAINES
GAINS
GAY
GENERALLY
GRASSE
GRONE
GROWN
GUEST
HAIR
HANG
HASTE
HOWEVER
IGNORANT
IMPART
ISSUE
JESU
JESUS
JEWES
KEEPE
KINDRED
LABOURS
LAID
LASTLY
LIBERALL
LIBERTY
LIKEWISE
LIVED
LOCK
LONDON
LUSTS
MALICE
MANIFEST
MARY
MIGHTIE
MINISTER
MOTION
NAMES
NATURES
NEEDE
NEVERTHELESSE
NOISE
NOTE
OBJECT
OBSERVABLE
OFFER
OPPOSE
ORDINARY
OUTLANDISH
PIERCE
PIOUS
PLANT
PLEASANT
POSIE
PRACTICE
PRAYING
PREVENT
PREY
PROCEED
PURPOSE
QUITE
REPAIR
RETURN
RIDE
RIVER
RUN
RYME
SACKE
SAIES
SALT
SAYS
SCANDALL
SECURE
SEEN
SERVES
SHAKE
SHEEP
SHEPHERD
SHEWES
SHEWING
SHIP
SHOOT
SHOP
SIDES
SILLY
SMART
SNOW
SOMTIMES
SONG
SOULDIERS
SPELL
SPENDS
SPIRITS
SPOKEN
SPRINGS
STANDING
STEAL
STRAW
STRIFE
STUDY
SUDDENLY
TALKE
THANKS
THEREBY
THORNS
THOUSAND
THUNDER
TRUTHS
TWENTIE
UTMOST
VIEW
WARME
WEATHER
WEEPE
WEIGHT
WORKE
WORLD'S
WORST

-6-

ABIDE
ABODE
ABUSE
AGAINE
AGREEABLE
AIRE
ALMIGHTY
ANSWERS
APT
ARK
ASHAMED
ASIDE
ASKES
AUTHOUR
BEARS
BEHIND
BETWIXT
BEWARE
BITE
BLESS
BLOUDIE
BOARD
BOLDNESS
BORE
BORNE
BRETHREN
BRINGING
BURTHEN
CERTAINLY
CHARGE
CHARITABLE
CHEAP
CHEST
CHIEF
CHILDE
CHOICE
CHURCH-WARDENS
COAT
COLLEGE
COMMANDS
CONSISTS
CONSUME
CONTINUED
CONTRARY
COULDST
COUNT
CRIMES
CRY
CURING
DAINTIES
DAYS
DECEIT
DECEIVE
DEERE
DENIE
DI'D
DIGESTED
DIGNITY
DILIGENCE
DISH
DISTANCE
DOWNE
DRAWES
DY
DYING
EATE
EQUALL
EV'RY
EXCEED
EXCELLENT
EXPECT
EXPECTED
FAINT
FAT
FILLS
FLED
FORBID
FORSAKE
FOURE
FOURTHLY
GARLAND
GOING
GOODNESSE
HAPPINESSE
HATE
HELPE
HENCE
HINDER
HIT
HOLINESSE
HOURES
HUMILITIE
HURTFULL
HUSBAND
HYMNE
IMPROVE
INCREASED
INVADE
INVENTION
JOYN
KEEPING
KNEEL
LADEN
LADY
LEADS
LED
LEISURE
LETTING
LINE
LIST
LOOKES
LOOSETH
LOWER
LYON
MADAM
MARKS
MEANT
MERCIES
MIGHTY
MODERATE
MOMENT
MOUSE
NATIONS
NEWES
OBSERVE
OFFICE
OWE
PAPER
PATIENT
PERCEIVE
PERISH
PHILOSOPHY
PHYSICIANS
PICK
PINE
PITIE
POSSIBLE
POUNDS
POVERTIE
PREPARE
PRESSE
PRINCE
PRISON
PROVIDES
PURSUE
QUENCH
QUESTION
RAGE
READE
REMEDY
RESPECT
RIGHTEOUS
RISETH
SAITH
SCARCE
SEASONS
SECRET
SEEME
SERVED
SEVERALL
SEV'RALL
SHADE
SHARE
SILENCE
SILENT
SINGULAR
SITS
SIX
SKY
SMOOTH
SPACE
SPEAKING
SPECIALL
SPHERES
SPIT
STIRRE
STRICT
SUBJECT
SUFFERS
SUMME
SUMMER
SUPERSTITION
SWAY
TALK
THANK
THINKING
THOUSANDS
THRALL
THREAD
THREATNED
THRICE
TOUCHING
TRINITY
TROUBLES
TRUSTS
TRY
TWELVE
TWIST
UNDERSTANDING
VEIN
VERTUOUS
VICE
VICTORIE
VOICE
WANTING
WARDENS
WAVES
WEARS
WEIGH
WEL
WEST
WESTWARD
WHOLLY
'LE
WILLING
WOE
WONDROUS
WOODS
WORTHY
WRITES
WRONG
WROUGHT

-5-

ABOUND
ACCEPT
ACCESSE
ACQUAINTANCE
ADDITIONARY
ADVANCE
ADVICE
ADVISETH
AFFECT
AGES
AMEN
ANCHOR
ANGRIE
ANSWERER
APOSTLE
APOSTLE'S
APOSTLES
APPEAR
ARAY
ARME
ASHES
ASSIGN'D
AUTHOR'S
AVOID
BAG
BANDS
BANQUET
BARE
BELLY
BEND
BENEFITS
BEQUEATH
BESEECHING
BESTOW
BETWEENE
BLACK
BLAME
BLESSETH
BLOWS
BOLDNESSE
BOOKES
BOTTOME
BRASSE
BRAVER
BREAKES

-5- (cont'd)

BREEDES
BREST
BROKE
BURNES
CALM
CAMBRIDGE
CARES
CARRIES
CHAMBER
CHILDREN'S
CHOKE
CHOSEN
CHRISTMAS
CHURCHES
CITIE
CITIES
COMBINE
COMMENDS
COMMERCE
COMMONLY
COMPETENT
CONCEIVE
CONSIDERATIONS
CONTINUALL
COUNCELS
COUNTING
COVER
DANGEROUS
DARKNES
DAYLY
DEARELY
DEBTER
DEBTS
DEEDE
DESCEND
DESERVE
DIFFERENT
DISORDER
DISTINCTION
DISTINGUISHETH
DIVELL
DOUBLES
DROWN
DYE
EASTER
ELIZABETH
ELS
ELSEWHERE
EMBRACE
EMPLOYMENT
ENDS
ENDURE
ENEMIE
ENGINE
ENTERTAIN
EQUALLY
EVENING
EVIL
EXACTLY
EXACTS
EXALTED
EXAMINED
EXCELL
EXCELLENCIES
EXERCISE
EXERCISES
EXHORTATIONS
EXPRESSIONS
EY'D
FADE
FAITHFULLY
FALLES
FARE
FARTHER
FED
FEEDS
FELT
FEVER
FINGERS
FITTING
FORBEAR
FORGET
FORGOT
FORME
FORWARD
FOUNDATION
FOUNTAINS
FOUR
FRANCE
FROWN
FULFILL
GAINED
GALLANT
GENTLY
GOETH
GOVERNING
GRAPES
GROWES
GROWING
HABITATION
HEADS
HEAL
HEARING
HEATHEN
HEATS
HEAV'N'S
HEAV'NS
HEEDE
HEIGHT
HELD
HELPS
HID
HIDDEN
HOT
HUMANE
HUMBLY
HUMILITY
IGNORANCE
IMPLOYED
INDIFFERENT
INTENDED
INTERRUPTION
JUDGEMENTS
KEEPER
KEYES
KILLED
KNOT
KNOWETH
KNOWNE
LACE
LAME
LATELY
LAWES
LAWYER
LEAD
LEANE
LEARNE
LEIGHTON
LEND
LESS
LIFT
LOCKT
LUKE
LYING
MARRIED
MARRYED
MASTER'S
MEANETH
MEEK
MERIT
MILITARY
MILK
MILL
MINDS
MINISTERS
MINISTRY
MISERY
MISSE
MODERATION
MORROW
NAKED
NATIVE
NEERE
NEST
NET
NE'RE
NOTES
NUMBER
OBSERVING
OFFENCE
ORDERS
OVERCOME
OWES
OXE
PACE
PAINES
PAINTED
PARTICULARS
PASSIONS
PAYD
PERFECTIONS
PERFORM
PERFORMED
PHILIPPIANS
PHISICK
PLAINE
PLANTED
PLANTS
PLEAD
PLEASANTNESSE
POURE
POYSON
PRAISED
PRECEPTS
PRESENTED
PROFESSION
PROPER
PULPIT
PULSE
QUALITIES
QUARRELL
QUIT
QUITTING
RACE
RATE
READIE
REASONS
RECEIVING
RECKON
REFUSETH
RELIEVE
REPROOF
REQUESTS
RESORT
RESTRAINING
RETURNE
RETURNS
RIGHTEOUSNESS
RIPE
RUNNES
S
SAT
SEAL
SEASONABLY
SECRETS
SEEING
SEEKS
SEEMES
SHEWS
SHIELD
SHOULDST
SICKNESS
SICKNESSES
SINFULL
SLACK
SOBER
SORRIE
SPACIOUS
SPAIN
SPAINE
SPEAR
SPIN
SPITE
SPITTLE
SPOIL
SPRUNG
STAKE
STATES
STEPS
STICK
STING
STOOD
STORMS
STRANGELY
STRANGERS
STRIKES
SUCK
SUDDEN
SUFFICETH
SUN
SWELL
TALKES
TEETH
TENN
THROAT
THROWN
TIMOTHY
TRADES
TRIE
TURN'D
TURNS
UNRULY
UNWORTHY
USUALLY
VALUE
VANITIES
VARIETY
VENT
VICTORIES
VOCATION
WAIES
WAKE
WANTON
WAR
WARRES
WASHED
WEAKNESSE
WEEPING
WEPT
WHEREUPON
WHOME
WIND
WINDING
WITHALL
WITNESSE
WITTIE
WITTY
WONT
WORSHIP
YEAR
YOUNGER

-4-

ABRAHAM
ABSTAIN
ABSTINENCE
ACTIVE
ADAM'S
ADMITS
AFFECTED
AFRAID
'GAINST
AGUE
ALONG
ALTOGETHER
AMONGST
AMOUNT
ANGEL
ARGUMENT
ARM
ARMOUR
ARMY
ASCEND
ASKE
ASPECT
AUTHOR
BABYLON
BAIT
BALLANCE
BANE
BARGAIN
BATE
BEARE
BEES
BEGINNINGS
BELEEVED
BESEECH
BIDS
BIT
BOAST
BORROW
BOUGHS
BRAVELY
BREATHING
BRIDLE
BRITTLE
BROOK
BUD
BUILDS
BURNT
CABINET
CABLE
CAKE
CALS
CANAAN
CARNALL
CAUGHT
CAUSES
CAVE
CENTRE
CHARACTER
CHARITIE
CHEAPE
CHEERFULL
CHIME
CLIMBE
CLOATHES
COMMANDED
COMMEND
COMPLAINE
COMPLAINTS
CONCEIT
CONCEIVES
CONDEMNATION
CONFOUND
CONGREGATION
CONSENT
CONSTANCY
CONTENTED
CONTEST
CONTRACT
COPIE
CORDIALL
COUNTS
COVETOUSNESSE
COW
CRAVE
CREEPS
CRIME
CROUCH
CROWNE
CRY'D
CURSE
DEARTH
DECLINE
DECREE
DEFECTS
DEFEND
DELAY
DELAYES
DELINQUENT
DENY
DESERVES
DESIRED
DESTRUCTION
DEVIL
DEVILS
DEVOURE
DIFFERENCE
DINNER
DIRECT
DIRT
DISCHARGE
DISCLOSE
DISCOVERED
DISCOVERS
DISCREDIT
DISPERSED
DISTRUST
DITCH
DITTIE
DOCTRINES
DOUBTS
DRESSING
DRINKS
EARLY
EARTH'S
EDGE
EDUCATION
ELDER
EMBRACED
EMINENT
ENCOUNTER
ENDEAVOUR
ENTERS
ENTICE
ENVIE
EPHESIANS
ESCAPED
ESTEEMED
EVERMORE
EXCEEDINGLY
EXCEEDS
EXCESSE
EXCUSE
EXPECTS
EXTEND
FALLEN
FAMILIE
FARR
FARTHING

-4- (cont'd)

FEARING
FEE
FEELE
FENCE
FIERCE
FILTH
FINELY
FINGER
FIRES
FIRM
FISHING
FITTED
FITTEST
FIX
FLAMES
FLOUT
FOLLOWES
FOOTE
FORBEARS
FORGOTTEN
FORM
FORTUNES
FORTY
FRAILTIE
FRANCIS
FREED
FRENCH
FRIDAY
FRIENDSHIP
FROST
FRUITS
FURNITURE
FURRE
GALEN
GATE
GATES
GATHERS
GETTING
GLUTTON
GLUTTONY
GODS
GRACES
GRAIN
GREATLY
GRIEFES
GROUNDED
GROWTH
HABIT
HANDSOME
HAPPILY
HARE
HATRED
HEARR
HEAVENS
HEAVIE
HEDGE
HEREIN
HERETOFORE
HILLS
HITHERTO
HOLE
HORNES
HORSES
HOUR
HOUSE-KEEPER
HOUSHOLD
HUMBLENESSE
HUMILIATION
HUSBANDRIE
IDLENESSE
INK
INNE
INSTRUCT
INSTRUCTION
INSTRUMENT
INVITED
INVITES
J
JERUSALEM
JUDAS
JUDG
JUICE
KINDLE
KINDNESSES
KISSE
KNIFE
KNOCK
KNOTS
LAMENT
LASTS
LATER
LAYES
LIVELY
LODGE
LONGER
LOCKED
LOOKING
LORDS
LOUD
LOVELY
LOVER
LOVERS
LUSTRE
LYE
MAGISTRATE
MAKETH
MANNA
MARBLE
MEANE
MEASURES
MELANCHOLIE
MENTION
MERRIE
MET
METHOD
MODEST
MOUNT
MOUTHS
MURDERER
NATURALLY
NECESSITY
NEEDING
NEER
NEWS
NIGHTS
NOSE
NOTICE
OATH
OBLIGATIONS
OBSCURE
OBSERVES
OFFERING
OMIT
OPPORTUNITIES
OPPOSITION
ORIGINALL
OUNCES
OVERTHROWN
PAID
PALACE
PARISHES
PARSONS
PASTOR
PEACEABLE
PECULIAR
PEECE
PEN
PENCE
PERFUME
PERIOD
PERPETUALL
PERSWASION
PIECES
PIERCING
PIT
PLAIES
PLATO
PLOT
PLOUGH
POLE
POVERTY
POWDER
PREACHED
PREFERRED
PREPARED
PRESERVED
PRIESTHOOD
PRIESTS
PRIME
PROCURE
PROCURES
PRODUCE
PROFESSED
PROFITS
PROMISE
PROSPER
PROVENDER
PROVERBS
PSALME
PUNISHED
PUNISHING
PURGE
PURPOSES
PUTTING
QUARRELS
RAIN
RAIS'D
READS
RECOVERED
REGULAR
REINS
RELATION
RELY
REMAINS
REMEDIES
RENOWN
REPOSE
RESOLUTION
REVENGE
REV'REND
RID
ROPE
ROSES
RUDE
RUINE
SALVE
SATAN
SATISFIED
SCEPTER
SCHOOL
SCRUPLE
SEAS
SEAT
SEATED
SEEDS
SELLING
SENCE
SERVICES
SERVILE
SEV'N
SHADOW
SHINES
SHIPWRACK
SHOE
SHOUT
SHOW'D
SICKE
SICKLY
SIGNE
SINGS
SINNE'S
SIZE
SLEEPE
SLIP
SOEVER
SOFT
SONS
SOUL'S
SOWES
SPAN
SPANIARD
SPEED
SPICE
SPICES
STATELY
STOP
STOPS
STORING
STRANGER
STRETCH
STRONGLY
STUDIES
SUBDUE
SUFFICE
SUNDAYES
SUNN
SUNNES
SUPREME
SUSPECTED
SWIFT
TELLS
TEMPESTS
TEMPORALL
TEND
TENT
TERRIBLE
TESTIMONY
THAN
THANKFULL
THEEVES
THINNE
THIRST
THIRTY
THRIVE
THRIVING
THROUGHLY
THRUST
TIE
TOP
TRANSCENDENT
TRAVELL
TRAVELL'D
TRENCHER
TRINITIE
UNFIT
UNIVERSITY
USUALL
VISITING
VOID
WALK
WALKING
WARD
WEARIE
WHATSOEVER
WHEREBY
WHEREWITHALL
WILDE
WILLINGLY
WINDOW
WINDS
WINNES
WINNING
WISEDOME
WITHDRAW
WITS
WOES
WRETCH
WRETCHED
WRITING
WRITINGS
WRONGS
YEERE
YOURSELVES
ZEAL

-3-

ABSENCE
ABSOLUTELY
ACCOUNTS
ACE
ACKNOWLEDGE
ADAM
ADDE
ADDES
ADDICTED
ADMIT
ADMONITION
ADMONITIONS
ADVANTAGES
AFFAIRES
AFFECTION
AFFORDS
AIME
AIMS
AKE
ALEXANDER
ALIKE
ALLSO
ALSOE
ANGELS'
ANGUISH
ANNE
ANNUITY
APART
APOSTLES'
APPARELL
APPETITES
APPLYED
ARCHITECTURE
ARGUES
ARGUING
ARISING
ARRAS
ASK'D
ASKS
ASSAULT
ASSE
ASSISTANCE
ASSUME
ATHEISME
ATTAINE
ATTENDING
AUCTORITY
AUDIENCE
AVOIDING
AW
BAND
BASE
BEARES
BEARING
BECKEN
BEFALL
BEFELL
BEFRIEND
BEHAVE
BELIEVING
BELLS
BELONG
BELONGS
BEMERTON
BETRAY
BEWITCH
BIDE
BIGGE
BIN
BINDE
BINDES
BINDING
BLASTED
BLEAK
BLEW
BLIND
BLINDNESSE
BLUSH
BOSTOCKE
BOUGHT
BOUNTY
BOWELS
BREAKING
BREED
BREEDING
BRIEF
BRIEFE
BROTH
BROTHERS
BROW
BRUISE
BURNS
BUSHELL
BUSINESS
BUSINESSES
CALAMITIES
CALDRON
CALLETH
CAREFULL
CARRIAGE
CARRIE
CARRIED
CARRYING
CATECHISM
CENSURE
CHAIN
CHALLENGE
CHANGING
CHAPPELL
CHASE
CHASTENS
CHEERFULLY
CHESSE
CHIDE
CHIEFE
CHIMNEY
CHOLERICK
CHOOSING
CHOYCE
CIRCUMSTANCES
CIVIL
CIVILL
CLAD
CLEANLINESSE
CLEANLY
CLEANSED
CLEARELY
CLOD
CLOTHS
CLOUD
COCK
COLDNESSE
COLDS
COM'ST
COMBIN'D

-3- (cont'd)

COMFORTABLE
COMMENTS
COMPARING
COMPARISONS
COMPASSE
COMPLAINES
COMPOS'D
CONDESCENDS
CONQUER
CONQUESTS
CONSEQUENCE
CONSIST
CONSISTETH
CONSORT
CONSTANCIE
CONSTANTLY
CONSTITUTION
CONSTITUTIONS
CONTEND
CONTENTION
CONTINUANCE
CONTRACTED
CONTRARIE
CONTRIVE
CONTROVERSIE
CONVENIENT
COOLING
COPY
CORDIALS
CORNELIUS
CORRECT
COUCH
COUNCELL
COUNTENANCE
COUNTREYS
COURSES
COURTEOUS
COVETEOUSNESSE
COWARD
CRAFT
CREED
CRIES
CROCODILE
CROOKED
CROSSETH
CROST
CRUELTY
CRUMME
CRUSE
CRYES
CUPBOARD
CUR'D
CUTS
DAIES
DAMNATION
DANCE
DARKNED
DASH
DAUGHTER
DEAFE
DEALING
DEAREST
DECENT
DECLARE
DEEDES
DEFERR
DEFERRE
DELIGHTFULL
DELIVERANCE
DELIVERED
DEMANDS
DENIES
DEPARTURE
DERIDE
DESIR'D
DESIRING
DESOLATION
DESPISED
DEVISE
DEVOUT
DEXTERITY
DIED
DIFFICULTY
DIGS
DIMME
DINE
DISCREET
DISHES
DISPLEASURE
DISPOSE
DISSOLVE
DIVE
DIVERSE
DIVERSION
DIVIDE
DIVINES
DOCTRINS
DOGS
DOUBLING
DOUBTED
DRAWN
DRAWS
DREADFULL
DREW
DRIVE
DROUGHT
DROWNED
DROWNING
DRUNK
DULNESSE
DUMBE
DUNG
DYET
EAR
EARNESTNESSE
EMPLOY
ENDURES
ENGLISH
ENLARGE
ENMITIE
ERRE
ERROUR
ESCAPES
ESTATES
ESTEEMING
ETERNITIE
E'RE
EVIDENCE
EVIDENTLY
EVILS
EXAMPLES
EXCELLENTLY
EXEMPT
EXPECTING
EXPENSE
EXPRESSED
EXTREAMLY
FACES
FAIREST
FAIRLY
FALLING
FAMILIAR
FAMINE
FARES
FARTHEST
FAULTY
FAYRE
FEARFULL
FEATHERS
FEBRUARY
FEELES
FEELING
FEELS
FEETE
FELLOWS
FERVENT
FETCH
FIELD
FIST
FITTER
FLOWRE
FOLKS
FOLLIES
FOLLOWING
FOLLOWS
FONT
FOORDS
FORFEIT
FORMES
FORRAIN
FRAIL
FREELY
FREQUENT
FUME
FURIE
FURNISH
FURTHEST
GAINING
GALL
GARDINER
GARMENTS
GATHER
GEESE
GHOST
GHOSTLY
GLADSOME
GLORIFIED
GOTTEN
GOUT
GOVERN
GOVERNMENT
GOWNE
GRANT
GRASS
GRAVES
GRAVITIE
GREATNESSE
GREEDY
GRINDE
GUARD
GUESTS
HALL
HALTER
HANDLED
HANGS
HAPPENS
HARM
HARMONIE
HARTS
HATCHET
HATT
HAWK
HAY
HEALING
HEALTHY
HEAP
HEARKEN
HEARS
HEART'S
HEAVEN'S
HEBREWS
HELPING
HENCEFORTH
HERB
HERESIE
HEROD
HINDERANCE
HISTORIE
HOLINESS
HOLLOW
HONOURABLE
HOOK
HOST
HUE
HUSBANDRY
IE
ILLUSTRATION
IMAGE
IMPROVEMENT
INCH
INCLOSE
INCONVENIENCE
INCONVENIENCES
INFANTS
INFECTION
INFERIOUR
INFINITELY
INFIRMITIES
INGAGED
INHERITANCE
INNOCENT
INSTITUTION
INTENDS
INTENT
INTEREST
INVITE
ISRAELITES
'T
JAMES
JESTING
JEWELL
JOURNEYS
JOYNTLY
JUDGETH
JUDICIOUSLY
JURISDICTION
KING'S
KNAVE
KNEELING
KNEELS
KNOCKING
LABOURING
LANDS
LANGUISH
LARKS
LATTER
LEAGUE
LEGGES
LEGS
LESSENS
LESSER
LIKES
LIKING
LION
LO
LORD'S
LOSETH
LOSSES
LOT
LOVED
LOV'D
LOVINGLY
LUMP
LY
MAD
MAD'ST
MAINTAINE
MANGER
MARCH
MARCHANT
MARRIES
MATE
MEAL
MEANES
MEANEST
MEATE
MEDICINE
MEDITATE
MEDITATION
MEETING
MELTS
MEMORIE
MENDS
METAPHORS
MIDNIGHT
MILDE
MINDES
MINUTE
MISERABLE
MISERIE
MISERIES
MISLIKE
MISS'D
MOIST
MONE
MONTH
MOSES'
MOUNTAINS
MOVED
MOVES
MUDD
MUSE
MUTE
NAIL'D
NAILS
NARROW
NEAR
NEAT
NEATLY
NEECE
NEECES
NEEDLE
NEEDY
NEIGHBOURING
NEWLY
NIGHT'S
NIPT
NON
NOON
NOTIONS
OBSERVATIONS
OBSERVEABLE
OFFENDED
OFFICES
OFTENTIMES
OPE
OPENED
OPENLY
OPTICK
ORATION
ORATCH
ORDERED
ORDERING
O'RE
OVERTAKES
OVERTHROW
OWNER
PACK
PAINTING
PARCELL
PARDONS
PARRATS
PARTAKE
PARTIE
PARTLY
PASS
PASSAGE
PATH
PAUL'S
PAYES
PENN'D
PENNY
PERCEIVED
PERPLEXED
PERSEVERE
PHISICIAN
PIN
PITCH
PITY
PLACED
PLAGUE
PLAGUES
PLAYES
PLENTIFULL
POEMS
POETRY
POSSIBLY
POWERFULL
PRAISING
PREACH
PREACHERS
PRECEPT
PRECIOUS
PREPARATION
PRESENTING
PRESERVATION
PRESERVES
PRESSING
PRETENCE
PROCEEDE
PROCEEDED
PROFANENESSE
PROFITABLE
PROJECTS
PROSPERITY
PROVERB
PROVIDE
PROVISION
PUNISHABLE
PURCHASED
PURITIE
PURLOIN'D
PUTT
QUALITY
QUANTITY
QUEENE
QUITS
RAINE
RAISETH
RAN
RECOVER
REDEEM
REDEMPTION
REDUCE
REDUCING
REED
REFRAIN
REFUSED
REMEMBRING
REPAIRES
REPLY
REPROVED
REPROVES
REQUIRE
REQUIRED
RESERVE
RESIST
RETURNING
REVELATION
REVELATIONS
RISING
ROBE
ROBS

-3- (cont'd)

RODD
ROOME
RUDELY
RUGGED
SACRAMENT
SACRAMENTS
SADDLE
SAFELY
SAFETY
SAIL
SALUTE
SANCTIFIE
SATISFIE
SAVOUR
SCAPE
SCATTER
SCEPTERS
SCORNS
SCOURGE
SCRAPE
SEED
SEEKING
SENTENCE
SEVEN
SEVER
SEVERED
SHADIE
SHELF
SHEWETH
SHIFT
SHINING
SHOLD
SHONE
SHOOTING
SHOOTS
SHOULDER
SHUTS
SILK
SIMPRING
SINK
SINNING
SION
SIXE
SKINNE
SLUMBER
SMALLEST
SOCRATES
SOLID
SOULDIER
SPANISH
SPENDING
SPIES
SPINS
SPITS
SPITTING
SPOIL'D
SPOUSE
STAINS
STAMP
START
STEALING
STEEL
STEELE
STINT
STONIE
STORIES
STORM
STRAIN
STRAY
STRIP
STRONGER
STRUGGLING
STUDIE
STUDIED
STUMBLES
SUBDUING
SUBMISSION
SUBMIT
SUBSTANCE
SUFFERED
SUFFERING
SUGRED
SUITS
SUMMONS
SUNDAIES
SUPPERS
SUPPLY
SUPPOSE
SURVEYS
SUSTAINING
SUTABLE
SWEEPS
SWEETEST
SWEPT
SWINE
TAILE
TAKETH
TALE
TASK
TEMPLES
TENDING
TERROUR
TESTAMENT
TEXTS
THEEFE
THICK
THRIFTIE
THRIFT
THROUGHOUT
TINCTURE
TIRE
TITHE
T'
TONGUES
TOOTH
TORTURE
TOSS'D
TOWNE
TOY
TRAVELLER
TRAVELLETH
TREAT
TREATISE
TRIUMPHANT
TUMBLE
TUN'D
TURNED
TYE
TYING
UNABLE
UNCHARITABLE
UNFOLD
UNITED
UNIVERSITIES
UNKNOWN
UNLAWFULL
UNMARRYED
UNPLEASANT
UNTRAINED
URGETH
URGING
US'D
USING
UTTER
UTTERLY
VANISH
VAUGHAN
VEINS
VICTORIOUS
VICTORY
VILLAGE
VIRGIN
VISIT
VIZ
VOLUNTARIE
WAIGHT
WAIL
WAIT
WALL
WALLS
WARE
WARES
WED
WEDD
WEED
WEEDS
WEEPS
WEIGHED
WESTERN
WHEEL
WHENEVER
WHERFORE
WICKEDNESS
WIFE'S
WILD
'LE
WIN
WINDOWS
WINK
WINNE
WISHES
WISHING
WITHDRAWING
WITHSTAND
WITNESSES
WOOE
WORKES
WORMS
WRAP
WRAPT
YEARE'S
YEER
YETT
YOURSELF

-2-

AARON
ABHORRING
ABILITIES
ABILITY
ABOUNDED
ABSENT
ABSTAINE
ABSURD
ACCEPTABLE
ACCOMPLISHED
ACCOUNTED
ACCUSE
ACQUAINT
ACTUALL
ADD
ADDITION
ADDS
ADMINISTER
ADMINISTERS
ADO
ADORES
ADORING
ADULTERY
ADVANCING
ADVENTURE
ADVERSARIES
AFFECTING
AFFECTIONATE
AFFECTS
AFFLICT
AFFRIGHT
AFFRIGHTED
AFORE
AFOREHAND
AGEN
AGENTS
AGO
AGREED
AGREEMENT
AGUES
AKES
ALIVE
ALLOW'D
ALOUD
ALTERATION
AMAZE
AMBITION
AMENDMENT
ANGELL
ANON
ANSWERED
ANSWERING
ANTIENT
ANTIPHON
ANXIOUSLY
APOLOGY
APPEAL
APPLICATION
APPLIES
APPLY
APPREHEND
APPREHENSION
APPROVE
ARBOUR
ARGU'D
ARMIES
ARRAIGNE
ARROWS
ASCENDS
ASIA
ASKED
ASPECTS
ASPERSIONS
ASPIRE
ASSAY
ASSEMBLIES
ASSENT
ASSERTION
ASSUMES
ASSURANCE
ASSURE
ASUNDER
ATTAIN
ATTENDANTS
ATTENDED
ATTENDS
ATTENTION
AUDITORS
AUGMENT
AUGMENTED
AUTHORITIE
AUTUMNE
AVARICE
AVOIDED
AVOYDING
AWARE
AZURE
BABEL
BACKBITERS
BACKWARD
BACON
BAITS
BALLS
BALSOME
BAPTISM
BARGAINE
BARREN
BATHE
BEAM
BEAMES
BEAT
BEAUTEOUS
BEENE
BEFOREHAND
BEGET
BEGGING
BEGIN
BEGUN
BEHALF
BEHELD
BEHOVES
BELEEVETH
BELEEVING
BELIEFE
BELIEVE
BELOVED
BENDING
BESET
BEWAIL
BEWAILE
BEWAILES
BIAS
BIBLE
BIDDING
BIERE
BIG
BIGGER
BILL
BITTERNESSE
BLACKAMORE
BLASPHEME
BLAST
BLEED
BLEEDING
BLOCK
BLOT
BLOUD'S
BLOUDY
BLOWES
BOARDS
BOAT
BODYES
BOLDLY
BONDS
BOOKE
BOTTLE
BOUNDED
BOWL
BOWRES
BOXE
BOXES
BOYES
BOYLING
BRACELETS
BRAINE
BRAKE
BRANCHES
BRAVERIE
BREAKE
BREDD
BRESTS
BRIDGE
BRIEFLY
BRIGHTER
BRITISH
BROAD
BRUNT
BRUTE
BUBBLE
BUBBLES
BUFFET
BUNCH
BURIED
BURNISH
BUSH
BUSINES
BUYER
BUYING
BY-WAYES
CABINETS
CALENDER
CALL'D
CALLOUS
CALLOW
CANCELL
CANDLE
CANKERS
CANONICALL
CANONS
CAPTIVATE
CAPTIVE
CARE'S
CAREER
CARELESLY
CARRI'D
CARRYES
CARVE
CASTING
CASTLES
CASUALTIES
CATCHETH
CATCHING
CATECHIZED
CATHOLICK
CATT
CAUSETH
CAUSING
CELEBRATE
CELEBRATES
CENTURE
CEREMONIES
CERTAINE
CERTAINTY
CHAINED
CHAINS
CHANGETH
CHAPLAINS
CHARGED
CHARG'D
CHARGES
CHARMS
CHAW'D
CHEATING
CHECKER'D
CHEERE
CHEREFULL
CHESTS
CHICKEN
CHIEFEST
CHILD'S
CHIMNEYS
CHOLLERICK
CHOOSETH
CHRISTIAN'S
CHRISTIANITY
CHRONICLE
CHURCH-MAN
CHURCH-TIME
CHURCH-YARD
CHUSETH
CIRCUIT
CIRCUMFERENCE
CIRCUMSPECT
CITTIES
CITY

-2- (cont'd)

CLAIM
CLAMOROUS
CLEANLINES
CLEANSE
CLEAVE
CLIMBING
CLINGING
CLOATHS
CLOSENESSE
CLOSETS
CLOTHE
CLOTHING
COACH
COAL
COASTS
COBWEBS
COLOURS
COMBATE
COMEDIE
COMETH
COMFORTE
COMFORTED
COMMANDMENTS
COMMENT
COMMISSION
COMMITTED
COMMODITIE
COMMODITIES
COMMUNICATE
COMMUNIONS
COMPANIONS
COMPAR'D
COMPARISON
COMPLAIN
COMPLAINED
COMPLEAT
COMPLEMENTING
COMPLETE
COMPLEXION
CONCEAL
CONCERNES
CONCERNETH
CONDEMNED
CONDEMN'D
CONFIDENT
CONFIRM
CONFIRMETH
CONFIRMS
CONFORMITY
CONFUSION
CONQUERING
CONQUEROUR
CONSECRATED
CONSEQUENTLY
CONSIDER'D
CONSOLATION
CONSONANT
CONSUMED
CONSUMING
CONSUMPTION
CONTAIN
CONTAINED
CONTAINS
CONTEMPLATION
CONTENTIOUSNESSE
CONTRIVES
CONTROVERTED
CONVERSANT
COOLE
CORPORATION
CORRESPONDENCE
COSTLY
COSTS
COUNTED
COURAGE
COURTESIES
COURTS
COVENANT
COVERLET
COVETOUS
COVETOUSNES
COY
CRACKT
CRAFTY
CREATOUR
CROSS
CROW
CROWNS
CRUCIFIE
CRUELL
CRUSHT
CRUTCHES
CURES
CURRANT
CURRES
CURSING
CUSTOMES
CUTTING
DAIES'
DAINTIE
DANGERS
DANVERS'
DARES
DART
DAVID'S
DAYE'S
DEAL
DEALE
DEALS
DEARTHS
DECAYING
DECEASED
DECEIV'D
DECEIVES
DECREED
DECREES
DEEPER
DEEPLY
DEFACE
DEFAMED
DEFEAT
DEFERRED
DEFIE
DEFINITION
DEFINITIONS
DEIGNE
DEITIES
DELIVER'D
DELUGE
DEMAIN
DEMAND
DEN
DEPENDANCE
DEPTHS
DESCENT
DESCRIBED
DESERTS
DESERVED
DESERVETH
DESERVING
DESIGN'D
DESIRABLE
DESIRETH
DESIROUS
DESPAIR
DESPERATION
DESTITUTE
DESTROYES
DETAIN
DETEST
DEVEST
DEVIDED
DEVILL
DEVOTIONS
DIALOGUE
DIAMOND
DID'ST
DIFFERS
DIFFICULT
DIGESTION
DIRTIE
DISABLE
DISARMED
DISBURSE
DISCHARG'D
DISCHARGED
DISCHARGING
DISCIPLES
DISCIPLINE
DISCOLOUR
DISCOMFORT
DISCONTENT
DISCONTENTED
DISCOVERYES
DISCREETLY
DISCUSSED
DISGEST
DISHONOUR
DISLIKES
DISORDERS
DISPERSE
DISPLEASE
DISPOSETH
DISPUTE
DISQUIET
DISSEIZED
DISSOLUTION
DISTAFFE
DISTINGUISH
DISTRACTED
DISTRESS
DISTRESSE
DISTRUSTFULLY
DISTURBANCE
DIVEL
DIVES
DIVISIONS
DOCTRINALL
DOGGE'S
DOMINIONS
DONATION
DOOM
DOOMS
DOOMS-DAY
DOOR
DORES
DOUBTFULL
DRAMME
DRAUGHT
DRAUGHTS
DRAWNE
DREAM
DREAMS
DREGS
DRESS'D
DRINKING
DRIVEN
DROSSE
DROWN'D
DROWNS
DUNGEON
DURT
DUTIE
DWARFE
DWELS
DWELT
DYDE
EARNESTNESS
EASETH
EASIER
EASTERN
ECCLESIASTICALL
EDIFICATION
EFFECTED
EFFECTS
EFFECTUALLY
EGGE
EGYPTIAN
EIE
ELBOW
ELDEST
ELEMENTARY
ELEPHANT
ELL
ELOQUENCE
EMINENCY
EMPEROUR
ENCHANTING
ENDEAVOURS
ENDLESSE
ENDUR'D
ENEMIES'
ENGRAVE
ENLARGED
ENTER'D
ENTERTAINE
ENTERTAINED
ENTERTAINMENT
ENTHUSIASMES
ENTRANCE
ENVOY
EPISTLE
EPISTLES
EQUIVOCATION
ERRAND
ERRED
ESCAPE
ESPIED
ESSENTIALL
ESTABLISHED
EUROPE
EVE
EVEN-SONG
EVENT
EVENTS
EVERLASTING
EXALTATION
EXAMINE
EXCEPTING
EXCHANGING
EXCITE
EXCLUDE
EXCLUDES
EXCUSED
EXECUTIONER
EXECUTOR
EXEMPTION
EXHALATION
EXHORTS
EXIGENT
EXINANITION
EXPECTATION
EXPELL
EXPLOITS
EXPOSING
EXPOUNDING
EXPRESSING
EXTREME
FABRICK
FACT
FAILS
FAINE
FAIRER
FAITHFUL
FAITHFULL
FALSLY
FAMILIES
FAMOUS
FANCIES
FAREWELL
FARMER
FASTENS
FASTER
FATT
FAUTS
FEAR'D
FEEBLE
FELLOWSHIP
FENCES
FERVENCY
FESTIVALL
FIELDS
FIERCENESSE
FILS
FILTHINESSE
FIND'ST
FINDING
FINENESSE
FINISH
FITLY
FITT
FLAMING
FLEDGE
FLEGMATICK
FLEGME
FLESHLY
FLINT
FLOUD
FLOURISH
FLOW'RS
FLYES
FODDER
FOE
FOIL
FOLDS
FOND
FOOL
FOOLISHNESSE
FOOLS
FORBEARE
FORBORN
FORCING
FORESEENE
FORESTALL
FORETELL
FORETOLD
FORFEITETH
FORGIVE
FORGO
FORMS
FORTITUDE
FOULING
FOUNTAIN
FOURTIE
FRAILTIES
FRETTING
FRIEND'S
FRIENDLINESS
FRIGHT
FROGS
FUELL
FULFILLED
FULL-EY'D
FUMES
FUNDAMENTALL
FURNISHT
FURRES
GAIN'D
GAINFULL
GALE
GAMESTERS
GARNER
GATHERED
GATHER'D
GAV'ST
GENERATION
GENTLEMAN
GENTLENESSE
GERMAN'S
GERMANIE
GESTURES
GIRDLE
GIVETH
GLADNESSE
GLANCE
GLIMPSE
GLOBE
GLOOMY
GLORIES
GLOVE
GLUTTONS
GODLINESSE
GOEST
GOLDEN
GOODNESS
GOWN
GRANTED
GRAPE
GRASP
GRATEFULL
GRATEFULNESSE
GRATIA
GRATIOUS
GREEN
GRIEVED
GRIEV'D
GRIEVES
GROVE
GROVELING
GROVES
GRUDGE
GUIDED
GUILDED
GUILTLES
GYANT'S
HABITATIONS
HABITS
HAIE
HALLS
HAPPEN
HAPPENED
HAPPIER
HARBINGERS
HARKEN
HARMONIOUS
HARVESTS
HATED
HAVEN
HAWKE
HEALTHFULL
HEARERS
HEARTILY
HEARTY
HEAVE
HEAVY
HEIRE
HEIRS
HELL'S
HELPER
HEREOF
HIGHLY
HINDERS
HIR

-2- (cont'd)

HITTS
HIVE
HOARSE
HOLES
HOLLAND
HOLLANDERS
HOLY-DAY
HOME-BRED
HONEY
HONOR
HOOD
HOSTS
HOUSEHOLDER
HOUSHOLD-STUFFE
HUMBLEST
HUNG
HUNGER
HUNGRIE
HUNT
HURTS
HYMNES
IDLENESS
IMAGES
IMITATE
IMMEDIATE
IMMORTALL
IMPLORE
IMPLOYMENTS
IMPORTUNITIES
IMPROVED
IMPURITY
INCARNATION
INCIDENT
INCLINE
INCLINING
INCLOSED
INCLOSURE
INDEARE
INDITE
INEVITABLE
INFAMY
INFIDELITY
INFLAME
INFLAMED
INFLAMMATION
INFUSE
INGENDRED
INGENUOUS
INLARGE
INNED
INSTRUCTED
INSTRUCTIONS
INSTRUMENTS
INTANGLED
INTEND
INTENDING
INTENTION
INTERPOSED
INTERPOSING
INTERRUPTED
INTOLERABLE
INTOMBE
INVENTIONS
INWARDLY
ISAIAH
ITALIAN
ITALIE
JEWELS
JEWISH
JOHN'S
JORDAN
JOSEPH
JOSHUA
JOYE'S
JOYED
JOYFULL
JOYNED
JUDGED
JUDGES
JUDITH
JUSTIFIED
JUSTIFYING
KEEPETH
KILD
KILL'D
KILLS
KINDNESSE
KINDS
KINGDOMES
KINSMAN
KITCHIN
KNEE
KNELL
KNITS
KNOWEST
KNOW'ST
KNOWST
L
LABYRINTHS
LATE-PAST
LATIN
LAWFULL
LAWLY
LAYD
L'
LEAF
LEAP
LEAPING
LEARN'D
LEASE
LEAVEN
LEGACIES
LEGGE
LENDS
LESSON
LIBRARY
LICKS
LICOROUS
LIDGER
LIFE'S
LIFTING
LIKED
LIKELY
LILLYES
LIMBES
LINGER
LINGRING
LINNEN
LIPPE
LIPS
LIQUOUR
LISTENS
LITLE
LIVERY
LIV'ST
LOAD
LOCKS
LONGEST
LONGING
LOOKER'S
LORDSHIP
LOSERS
LOSS
LOTH
LOVER'S
LOWRE
MAGDALENE
MAGISTRATES
MAGNIFIE
MAID
MAIN
MAINTAINS
MAINTENANCE
MAJESTICK
MAKER
MALICIOUS
MANAGING
MANIFOLD
MANTLE
MARIE
MARKED
MARR'D
MARRES
MARTYRS
MASTIFFE
MATTERS
MEALE
MEASUR'D
MEDITATIONS
MEDOW
MEEKNESSE
MELTED
MEMBER
MEMBERS
MEMORY
MENACES
MERCENARY
MERCHANT
MERIDIAN
MERRY
MESSAGE
MESSENGER
MIDDLE
MILD
MILE
MILKE
MINGLED
MINGLES
MINISTRATION
MIRACLE
MIRACLES
MIRACULOUSLY
MISCARRY
MISCHIEF
MISSETH
MISSING
MOCK
MOISTURE
MOLD
MONETHS
MONKE
MONUMENT
MONUMENTS
MOON
MORALL
MOREOVER
MORN
MORSELL
MORSELS
MORTALITIE
MORTALS
MOSES
MOTHERS
MOULDED
MOUNTAINE
MOUNTAINES
MOUNTED
MOVING
MS
MURDER
MUSES
MUTT'RING
MYSTICALL
NAILE
NAMELY
NAMING
NARROWLY
NATURE'S
NAVIGATION
NEATNESSE
NECK
NEECES'
NEEDED
NEGLECTING
NEIGHBOUR-HOOD
NEIGHBOUR'S
NEIGHBOURHOOD
NEIGHBOURLY
NETS
NEVERTHELESS
NIGH
NIMBLE
NINE
NOAH'S
NOONE
NORTH
NOTION
NOTORIOUS
NOTWITHSTANDING
NOURISH
NOURISHMENT
NUMBERS
NUTS
OATHES
OBEDIENT
OBEY
OBEYING
OBLIGE
OBSCURITY
OBSERVER
OBSERVETH
OBSTRUCTED
OBTAIN
OCCASIONALL
ODE
ODOUR
O'
OFFEND
OFFENDER
OFFENDING
OFFERS
OFFICERS
OIL
OPEN'D
OPENS
OPERATION
OPPORTUNITY
OPPOSES
OPPOSETH
OPPRESSED
ORACLES
ORATOR'S
ORCHARD
ORDAIN'D
ORDINARIE
ORNAMENT
OURSELVES
OUT-STRIP
OUTLAWD
OVERBURDENED
OVERTAKE
OVERTURNED
OWING
OYL
OYLE
OYNTMENT
PACKT
PAIES
PAINE
PAINT
PAIRE
PALACES
PALE
PAMPER
PARALLELS
PARCEL'D
PARDONING
PARENTS'
PARES
PARIS
PARISHIONERS
PARLIAMENT
PARLIES
PARTED
PARTICULARIZING
PARTIES
PASSED
PASTORALL
PASTOUR
PASTURE
PAYMASTER
PEARL
PENSION
PERCEIVING
PERFECTED
PERFORMES
PERFUMES
PERILL
PERMISSION
PERSECUTE
PERSIST
PERSWADED
PERTURBATIONS
PETTIE
PETTY
PHILOSOPHIE
PICTURE
PILATE
PIL'D
PILGRIMAGE
PILL
PILLARS
PINCH
PINNE
PIPES
PITTIFULL
PLAISTER
PLENTIE
PLUME
POET
POETS
POLES
POLLUTE
POMP
POOREST
POPE
POPERY
PORTIONS
POS'D
POSSESSE
POSSEST
POSTE
POSTERITIE
POSTURE
POTION
POUR
POW'R
POYSONS
PRACTISE
PRAISETH
PRATLER
PRAYED
PRAYES
PRAYSE
PREACHER
PRECEDENCE
PREFERMENT
PREFERR'D
PREFIXED
PREPARATORY
PREPAR'D
PREROGATIVE
PRESERVING
PRESS
PRESUMED
PRETEND
PREVAIL
PRICK
PRIEST'S
PRINCIPALL
PRINCIPLES
PRIVATELY
PRIZE
PROCEEDING
PROCURING
PROFANELY
PROFESS
PROFESSE
PROFESSETH
PROFITT
PROMISING
PROMOTION
PROOF
PROOFE
PROPERLY
PROPHECY
PROPHESIE
PROPHETS
PROPORTIONS
PROPOSITIONS
PROPOUNDED
PROSPER'D
PROTEST
PROVED
PROVIDING
PROVISIONS
PRUNE
PSALMS
PUBLICKLY
PUFFING
PULLING
PULS
PURPOSELY
PURSES
PUSILLANIMITY
QUAINT
QUALITIE
QUARRELLS
QUARTER
QUICKNESSE
QUIETLY
QUILL
RACK
RAGING
RAINBOW
RAINES
RAISED
RAISES
RAISING
RANKS
READER
REASONABLE
REBUKE
RECONCILIATION
RECONCILING
RECREATION
RED
REDEEM'D
REDEEMER
REEDS
REEL
REFORMATION
REFORME

-2- (cont'd)

REFORMED
REFRESHMENT
REFUSING
REGENT
REHEARSE
REIGNE
RELATIONS
RELEEVING
RELIEVED
RELIGIOUSLY
RELISHES
REMARKABLE
REMEMBERS
REMORSE
RENEW
RENOUNCING
REPAST
REPENTS
REPINE
REPINING
REPLIE
REPLY'D
REPORT
REPRESENTS
REPRIEVE
REPROOFE
REPUGNANT
REPUTED
REQUIR'D
REQUIRING
REQUITE
REQUITED
RESCUE
RESERVING
RESIGNING
RESISTANCE
RESOLV'D
RESOLVES
RESORTING
RESORTS
RESPECTED
RESURRECTION
RETREAT
RETURNED
REVEALED
REWARDED
REWARDING
REWARDS
RHEUME
RHEUMES
RICHER
RICHLY
RIDER
RIDES
RIDING
RIGHTEOUSNESSE
RINGING
ROB
ROBBERIE
ROCKS
RODE
ROGUES
ROOMS
ROOTE
ROOTES
ROW
RUFFIAN
RULERS
RUNN
RUNNING
SACRIFICED
SACRIFICES
SAILE
SAKES
SALE
SANDS
SAP
SARA
SATE
SATINS
SAYINGS
SCALDED
SCALDING
SCANDALIZE
SCANN'D
SCARLET
SCATTER'D
SCATTERS
SCHOLARS
SCHOLERS
SCHOOLE
SCHOOLMEN
SCOFFES
SCORES
SCORN
SCORN'D
SCORNFULNESSE
SEALED
SEASONABLE
SEASONED
SECURITY
SEEKES
SEEMED
SEEM'D
SELECTED
SELF-SAME
SELLER
SENDING
SENSES
SENSIBLE
SENTENCES
SENTS
SEPULCHER
SERIOUS
SETLED
SETLING
SETT
SEVENTIE
SEVERE
SHADES
SHAKES
SHALLOW
SHAMEFULL
SHAPE
SHED
SHEEPE
SHEPHERD'S
SHEPHERDS
SHEW'D
SHOOTERS
SHORTLY
SHOU'D
SHOWES
SHOWRES
SHREDS
SHRINES
SHRINK
SHUN
SHUNNE
SHUNN'D
SHUTT
SIGN
SIGNES
SILKES
SILKS
SILVER
SIMON
SIMPLICITIE
SINGING
SINKE
SINNER
SINNER'S
SINNERS'
SINNS
SIP
SITHE
SITTEN
SITTING
SIX-DAIES'
SIZES
SKILFULL
SLANDERS
SLEEPES
SLEEVE
SLENDER
SLEPT
SLIGHTING
SLIGHTS
SLING
SLIPT
SLOTH
SLOTHFUL
SLOVENS
SLOWLY
SLUCE
SMELLS
SMILE
SMITH
SMOTHER
SOBRIETIE
SOIL
SOLOMON
SOLOMON'S
SON'S
SONNET
SONNETS
SOONEST
SOPHISTERS
SORROWES
SORRY
SOULES
SOW
SOW'D
SPADE
SPAR'D
SPARES
SPARKLING
SPECTACLES
SPED
SPEECHES
SPINDLE
SPIRITUALLY
SPITEFULL
SPOILS
SPORTS
SPUNNE
SPURRE
SPURRED
SPY
SPYES
SPYING
SQUARE
SQUINT
STABLE
STAIES
STAIN
STARR
STARVING
STATION
STATIONS
STATURE
STATUTE
STATUTES
STAYES
STEALE
STEALES
STEALS
STEALTH
STEMME
STEP-MOTHER
STEWS
STICKS
STOCKING
STOCKS
STOLE
STOMACH
STOREHOUSE
STORME
STORMIE
STRAINS
STRAIT
STRAND
STREAM
STRENGTHEN
STRETCHED
STRICTLY
STRIKING
STRING
STRINGS
STROKES
STROW'D
STRUCK
STRUGGLE
STUBBORN
STUBBORNNESSE
STUDENTS
STUDYING
STUMBLE
STUMBLING
STYLED
SUBJECTS
SUBMISSIVENESSE
SUBTILL
SUCCESSE
SUCCESSION
SUCCESSOR
SUCCOUR
SUE
SUFFERETH
SUFFICIENT
SUGAR
SUITE
SUITES
SUITOURS
SUNDAYS
SUPERFLUOUS
SUPERSTITIOUS
SUPPLE
SUPPLIE
SUPPLIES
SUPPLING
SUPPLYES
SUPPORT
SURER
SURETY
SURNAME
SURVEY
SURVIVE
SUSPICION
SUSTAINED
SUTES
SWALLOW
SWEARING
SWEAT
SWEETER
SWEETNED
SWELLS
SWIMME
SYMMETRIE
TAKEST
TALKING
TALL
TAST
TAVERNE
TAVERNES
TAYLE
TEACHES
TEAR
TEARE
TELLING
TELS
TEMPERS
TEMPTATION
TEMPTED
TENANTS
TENDERNESSE
TENDS
THANKES
THEIRE
THER
THERIN
THIEFE
THIN
THINGES
THINKETH
THORNES
THRED
THREW
THROWEST
THWART
TIES
TIMBER
TIME'S
TITHES
TOOK'ST
TOOL
TOOLES
TOOTH-ACH
TORNE
TOUCHED
TOWARD
TOWN
TRAFFICK
TRAGEDIE
TRAIN
TRANSFERR'D
TRANSGRESSION
TRANSMIGRATION
TRANSPLANT
TRANSPOSING
TRAVELLED
TREADS
TREASURES
TRIBUTES
TRICKLING
TRIM
TRIMME
TRIUMPH
TRIUMPHS
TROUBLESOME
TRUMPET
TRUSTING
TRUSTY
TRYED
TUNING
TURNETH
TYED
TY'D
TYRANT
UNBEFITTING
UNCOUTH
UNDERTAKING
UNDO
UNDONE
UNDRESSING
UNGODLY
UNIFORM
UNIVERSITIE
UNJUST
UNJUSTLY
UNMARRIED
UNMOVED
UNSOUND
UNSUFFERABLE
UNTIL
UNWHOLSOME
UPPON
UPWARD
URGED
URN
USAGE
USEFUL
VAILED
VAINE
VALDESSO
VALIANT
VALLEY
VALOUR
VALUES
VANITIE
VANITY
VARYED
VAST
VENISON
VENTURE
VERIE
VESSEL
VIALL
VIEWS
VIGOROUS
VINEGER
VIRGINITY
VISIBLE
VOUCHSAFE
VOUCHSAFES
VOW
VOWES
VOWS
VOYCE
VULGAR
WAITS
WALKS
WAN
WANTONNESSE
WARMES
WASHING
WASHT
WASTE
WASTED
WATCHING
WATERING
WATRISH
WAXETH
WAYS
WEAKE
WEAKEST
WEAKNED
WEAL
WEALS
WEAPON
WEARES
WEARINESSE
WEDDING
WEDGE
WELL-FURNISHT
WHATEVER
WHEAT
WHEELS
WHEREON
WHET
WHILES
WHISPER
WHITEN

-2- (ccnt'd)

WIDDCW
WIL
'L
WILLIAM
WINES
WIPE
WIE'D
WISELY
WISHETH
WITHEE'D
WITHSTOOL
WIVE'S
WCMEN'S
WCNDEEFUIL
WCNDEING
WOODNOTH
WCCLI
WORE
WOEKEMAN
WORKMAN
WORKMANSHIF
WORLDIINGS
WORLCS
WOEMES
WORTHIE
WOVEN
WEANGLER
WEANGIING
WREATH
WRITETH
WRITHE
WRONGFULLY
WRUNG
YARD
YEARS
YEE
YEELD
YES

-1-

A-DOING
A-FOCT
AARON'S
AAECNS
AEASH'D
ABATE
ABHORR'D
ABHORFES
ABIDEE
ABIDETH
ABIDING
ABJECTS
ABLEST
ABOLISH
ABRAHAM'S
ABRIEGEMENTS
ABEOACH
ABSOIUTE
ABSTINE
ABUNDANCE
ABUNDANTLY
ABUS'D
ABUSES
ABUSIVENESSE
ACADEMICALL
ACADEMICK
ACCENSIC
ACCEPTANCE
ACCEFTATICN
ACCEPTING
ACCEFTS
ACCESSARY
ACCESSICN
ACCIDENT
ACCIDENTS
ACCIPE
ACCCMMCDATE
ACCOMMCDATICN
ACCOMPANIED
ACCOMPANYING
ACCOMPLISH
ACCOMPT
ACCORD
ACCORDS
ACCOUNTABLE
ACCRUE
ACCRUES

ACCURATELY
ACCURSED
ACCUEST
ACCUSTOME
ACCUSTCMEL
ACKNOWLEDG
ACKNCWLEDGING
ACQUAINTED
ACQUIT
ACQUITTS
ACTED
ACTING
ACTIVENESSE
ACTUATES
AD
ADAYES
ADDER'S
ADDEST
ADDRESSE
ADDRESSES
ADJUDGE
ADMIRE
ADMIRES
ADMITTED
ADMITTING
ADMCNISHETH
ADORATION
ADOE'D
ADORN
ADCRNED
ADULATICN
ADVANCED
ADVANCEMENT
ADVANCETH
ADVEESITY
ADVIZE
AFAERE
AFFECTIONATELY
AFFLICTING
AFFEAID
AFFRIGHTS
AFFECNT
AFOOT
AFRICK
AFTERNOONE
AFTEENCCNS
AFTERWARD
AGENT
AGGRAVATED
AGCNIE
AGREES
AID
AIDED
AIMETH
AIMING
AIR
AIRES
AL
ALARMS
ALBION
ALCHYMY
ALE
ALE-HOUSES
ALEXANDER'S
ALIENATED
ALIGHT
ALL-HEAL
ALLAY
ALLEYS
ALLCWABLE
ALLCWANCE
ALLOWED
ALLCWES
ALLOWING
ALLUEE
ALLURETH
ALLWAYES
ALMANACK
ALMES-DEEDS
ALMES-GIVING
ALMS
ALOCFE
ALPHABETS
ALREADIE
ALTER
ALTERED
ALWAY
ALWAYS
AMAZED
AMAZ'D
AMAZEMENT

AMBASSADOURS
AMBASSAGES
AMBER
AMBER-GREESE
AMBITIONS
AMBUSH
AMENDED
AMERC'D
AMERICA
AMERICAN
AMIDST
AMIENS
AMISS
AMITIE
AMOUNTS
AMPLIFY
AMUSE
AMY
ANAGRAM
ANALCGAT
ANANIAS
ANATCMY
ANCHCRISME
ANCIENTS
ANEW
ANGEL'S
ANGRY
ANN
ANNEAL
ANNEAL'D
ANNEXED
ANCINTED
ANOINTING
ANSWEEABIE
ANSWER'D
ANT
ANTEDATE
ANTHEME
ANTHCNIE
ANTICHRIST
ANTICIPATE
ANTICIPATED
ANTICKS
ANTIDOTE
ANTIDCTES
ANTIQUITIE
ANTIQUITIES
ANVILE
ANVILL
ANYTHING
APACE
APE
APOPLECTIQUE
APCSTEOPHES
APOTHECARIE'S
APOTHECAEY
APPALL
APPARENT
APPARITICNS
APPARRELL
APPEAR'D
APPEARES
APPEARING
APPEARS
APPEASE
APPERTAINS
APPLYETH
APPCINT
APPOINTED
APPCINTEDST
APPROACH
APPROACHES
APPROPRIATE
APPRCPRIATED
APPROVED
APTLY
APTNESSE
ARBCURS
ARCH'D
ARCHED
ARCHITECT
ARGUE
ARGUED
ARGUMENTS
ARIGHT
ARISETH
ARISTIDES
ARISTOTLE
ARMED
ARMES
ARCSE

ARRIVAL
ARRIVES
ARROW
ARTHUR
ARTICLES
ARTICLING
ARTIFICERS
ARTIFICES
ARTILLERIE
ARTILLERIES
ARTIST
ARTISTS
ASCENDED
ASCENT
ASCRIBED
ASKING
ASKT
ASLEEP
ASMUCH
ASSAILE
ASSAILES
ASSAULTED
ASSEMBLED
ASSIGNS
ASSURANCES
ASSURES
ASSURING
ASSWAGED
ASTRAY
ASTRCLCGERS
ASTROLOGIE
ASTRCNCMER
ATCHIEVING
ATHEISM
ATHEIST
ATHEISTS
ATOME
ATTAIN'D
ATTAINED
ATTEMPTING
ATTEMPTS
ATTENTIVE
ATTENTIVELY
ATTIRE
ATTIRES
ATTRACT
ATTRIBUTE
ATTRIBUTES
AUDIBLY
AUGMENTETH
AUGUSTINE'S
AURUM
AUSTERE
AUTHORS
AUTHOUR'S
AUTUMNALL
AVERSE
AVERSENESSE
AVOIDS
AVCUCHETH
AVOYDED
AVOYDS
AWAKED
AWAKES
AWE
AWFUL
AWFULL
AYRE
BABLES
BACK-DOORE
BACK-PART
BACK-SIDE
BADD
BADE
BAITING
BAKER
BALCCNES
BALL
BALM
BALME
BALSAMES
BANDIE
BANDING
BANDYING
BANED
BANES
BANQUETTING
BAPTIST
BAPTIZED
BAPTIZ'D
BAPTIZETH

BARABBAS
BARBER
BAREFOCT
BARELY
BARGAINES
BARK
BARKE
BARKS
BARNE
BARRE
BARRELL
BARRES
BASENESSE
BASKETS
BASCN
BATCHELORS
BATHED
BATH'D
BATHS
BATS
BATTELL
BAY
BAYES
BEACCN
BEADES
BEADS
BEANE
BEARER
BEATE
BEATRICE
BEAUTIES
BEAUTIFULL
BEAUTY'S
BECK
BED-CHAMBER
BED-STRAW
BEDD
BEDEW
BEDLE
BEDS
BEE'S
BEEFE
BEEING
BEER
BEFALLS
BEFALS
BEFITS
BEFITTING
BEGETS
BEGGAR
BEGGARLY
BEGGARS
BEGG'D
BEGGER
BEGINN
BEGINNE
BEGINNER
BEGIRT
BEGOT
BEGCTTEN
BEGUILE
BEGUNNE
BEHITHER
BEHCLDING
BEHOVE
BELEEFE
BELEEV'D
BELEEVERS
BELEEVES
BELIEV'D
BELLCWES
BELLY-GODS
BELCNGE
BELONGED
BELCNGING
BELS
BEMBO
BEMMORTON
BENDED
BENEDICITE
BENEFICE
BENEFICIAL
BENEFITT
BENJAMIN
BENUMME
BERRY
BESECH
BESIDE
BESIEGE
BESPCKE
BEST-BREDD

-1- (cont'd)

BESTOWED
BESTOW'D
BETAKES
BETHINKETH
BETROTH
BETT
BETTERS
'TWIXT
BIBLES
BIGG
BIND
BITES
BITETH
BITTEN
BITTER-SWEET
BITTERLY
BLACKAMOOR
BLACKAMOORES
BLACKNESSE
BLAMES
BLAMING
BLASPHEMIE
BLEATS
BLENDING
BLISS
BLISTER
BLOODY
BLOOM
BLOSSOME
BLOTS
BLOTT
BLOTTED
BLOWING
BLOWNE
BLUNTED
BLURR'D
BLUSHING
BLUSTERING
BLUSTRING
BOAR
BOASTS
BODIE'S
BOHEMIA
BOIL
BOLEARMENA
BOND
BONDAGE
BONIE
BOOKE-WORMES
BOOKISH
BOOLLINGBROOK
BOOT
BOOTED
BOOTLESSE
BORD
BORDERS
BORROWED
BORROW'D
BORROWES
BOSOM
BOSOME-SINNE
BOTTELL
BOTTOM
BOULS
BOUNDLESSE
BOUNTEOUS
BOUNTIE
BOUNTIES
BOUNTIFULL
BOUT
BOWER
BOWERS
BOWRE
BOXED
BOY
BOYLE
BRABLES
BRABLING
BRACKISH
BRAGGING
BRAGS
BRAINS
BRAMPTON
BRANCH
BRAND
BRANDED
BRAVES
BRAVEST
BRAWLING
BREAK'ST
BREATHED
BREEDE
BREEDS
BRENTA
BRIBE
BRIBES
BRIDALL
BRIDE
BRIGHTEST
BRIGHTNES
BRIM
BRIM-FULL
BRIMME
BRIMSTONE
BRINE
BRINGETH
BRINGINGE
BRINISH
BRITAIN'S
BRITTISH
BROACH
BROACHT
BROIDER'D
BROK
BROOKE
BROOKS
BROOM
BROTHELS
BROTHER'S
BROUGHT'ST
BROWNE
BROWS
BROWSE
BRUGENSIS
BRUIS'D
BRUISES
BRUSHERS
BRUTISH
BUCKET
BUCKETS
BUCKINGHAM
BUGDEN
BUILDER
BUILDER'S
BULK
BUNDLE
BUNDLES
BURDENED
BURDENS
BURGESS
BURIALL
BURIALL-LINEN
BURNE
BURNED
BURST
BURTHENS
BUSHIE
BUSIED
BUSIEST
BUSNESSES
BUSTLED
BUSY
BUTTER
BUTTERY
BUZZARD'S
BYWORDS
C
CAESAR
CAGE
CALAMITY
CALAMITYES
CALCINED
CALMLY
CALMNESS
CALMNESSE
CALVES
CAM'ST
CAMELS
CAMELS'
CAMOMILL
CANAANITES
CANE
CANKER
CANNE
CANON
CANVAS
CANVASING
CANVASSED
CAPE
CAPON
CAPS
CAPTIVES
CAPUCH
CARD
CARDINAL
CARDS
CAREFUL
CAREFULLY
CARELESNESS
CARELESNESSE
CARELESS
CARETH
CARING
CARKING
CARP
CARPENTERS
CARPET
CARROWAY
CARRYED
CARVED
CARVES
CARVING
CARVINGS
CASKE
CASKS
CASTLE
CAT
CATECHIZER
CATECHIZETH
CATECHIZINGS
CATHARINE
CATHOLIKE
CATT'S
CATTEL
CAUS
CAUSED
CAUSELESS
CAUTIONS
CAVILL
CAVILS
CEASED
CEASING
CELESTIALL
CELL
CEMENT
CEMENTED
CENSORIOUS
CENSURES
CENSURETH
CENTER
CEREMONIOUS
CEREMONY
CERTAIN
CERTIFIES
CHAFE
CHAFF
CHAFING
CHAINE
CHALICE
CHALK
CHAMBERS
CHANCELLOR
CHANCES
CHANDLERS
CHANG'D
CHANGES
CHAP
CHARING
CHARLES
CHARM
CHARM'D
CHARTRE
CHAS'D
CHASES
CHASING
CHASTE
CHASTEN
CHASTIZED
CHASTIZEMENT
CHASTNINGS
CHATTELS
CHATTING
CHAWES
CHEAPEST
CHEARFUL
CHEAT
CHEATER
CHECK
CHEEK
CHEEK-BONE
CHEEKE
CHEEKS
CHEERED
CHEER'D
CHEERFULL
CHEERFULNESS
CHEERFULNESSE
CHEERING
CHELSEY
CHERBURY
CHERISHING
CHERRIES
CHESSE-BORD
CHID
CHIDES
CHIDING
CHILDE'S
CHILDHOOD
CHILNESSE
CHIMING
CHINK
CHINKING
CHOAKED
CHOAKES
CHOISE
CHOSE
CHOYSEST
CHRIST-CROSSE
CHRIST-SIDE-
 PIERCING
CHRISTMAS-DAY
CHRISTMASSE
CHRYSOSTOME
CHRYSTAL
CHRYSTALLINE
CHURCH-BELS
CHURCH-CATECHISM
CHURCH-FLOORE
CHURCH-GLASSE
CHURCH-LOCK
CHURCH-MONUMENTS
CHURCH-MUSICK
CHURCH-PORCH
CHURCH-RENTS
CHURCH-WARDENS'
CHURCHYARD
CHUSING
CHYMICK
CINAMON
CINNAMON
CIRCLE
CIRCLING
CIRCUMCISED
CIRCUMSPECTION
CIRCUMSTANCE
CITIZEN
CITTY
CIVILITIE
CLACKE
CLAIME
CLASPING
CLAUSE
CLAVE
CLEANE
CLEANED
CLEANNESSE
CLEANSETH
CLEAR
CLEARER
CLEAREST
CLEARETH
CLEAVES
CLEER
CLEERE
CLEERLY
CLEFT
CLEMENCIE
CLENSETH
CLERGY
CLERK
CLERK'S
CLIMBES
CLIME
CLIPP
CLOAK
CLOAKE
CLOATH
CLOATHED
CLOCKS
CLODS
CLOGS
CLOISTER'S
CLOISTERERS
CLOKE
CLOSES
CLOSEST
CLOSET
CLOSETH
CLOTHED
CLOUDIE
CLOUTS
CLOVES
CLOWNE
CLUBS
CLUE
CLUSTER
CLUSTERS
CLUTCH
COALS
COAST
COASTING
COATE
COATS
COCK-SURE
COCKATRICE
COCKERS
COFFERS
COFFIN
COHERENCE
COIN
COINE
COLDLY
COLDNES
COLDNESS
COLLAR
COLLATION
COLONY
COLOSS
COLOSSIANS
COLOUR'D
COLOURED
COMB
COMBAT
COMBATING
COMERS
COMFIT
COMFORTABLY
COMFORTER'S
COMFORTING
COMICK
COMLINES
COMMANDER
COMMENCEMENT
COMMENDABLE
COMMENDATION
COMMENDETH
COMMENDING
COMMENTERS
COMMEST
COMMINATION
COMMING
COMMISERATION
COMMITS
COMMITTEES
COMMODIOUS
COMMODIOUSNESS
COMMON-PRAYER-BOOK
COMMON-WEAL
COMMON-WEALS
COMMON-WEALS-MEN
COMMON-WEALTHS
COMMONS
COMMONWEALTH'S
COMMONWEALTHS
COMMONWEALTHS-MEN
COMMUNICATION
COMPACTED
COMPANYES
COMPARABLE
COMPARED
COMPASS
COMPASSETH
COMPASSIONATE
COMPAST
COMPELL
COMPETENCY
COMPETITOR
COMPHREY
COMPILED
COMPLAINING
COMPLAINS
COMPLEATE
COMPLEATNESS

-1- (cont'd)

COMPLEMENT
COMPLEMENTALL
COMPLEMENTERS
COMPLEMENTS
COMPLETENESSE
COMPLEXIONS
COMPLIE
COMPLIES
COMPLYING
COMPOSE
COMPOSETH
COMPOSITIONS
COMPOSURES
COMPREHEND
COMPREHENDS
COMPRIZE
COMPROMISES
CONCEALES
CONCEALS
CONCEITE
CONCEITS
CONCEIV'ST
CONCEIV'D
CONCERNE
CONCERNS
CONCLUDED
CONCLUDES
CONCLUDING
CONCOURSE
CONCUPISCENCE
CONCUPISENCE
CONCURR
CONCURRE
CONDEMN
CONDEMNE
CONDEMNES
CONDEMNEST
CONDEMNING
CONDEMNS
CONDESCENDING
CONDIGN
CONDITIONALLY
CONDITIONS
CONDOLES
CONDUCT
CONDUITS
CONFERENCE
CONFERRE
CONFESS
CONFESSETH
CONFESSOR
CONFIGURATIONS
CONFIRME
CONFIRMED
CONFLICTS
CONFORMABLE
CONFRONTING
CONFUSED
CONFUTE
CONGRATULATE
CONJECTURE
CONJURER'S
CONQUERE
CONQUER'D
CONQU'RING
CONSCIENCES
CONSECRATE
CONSERVE
CONSIDERABLE
CONSIGNE
CONSPIRE
CONSTANTINE'S
CONSTELLATIONS
CONSTERS
CONSTITUTED
CONSTRAINT
CONSUMES
CONSUMPTIONS
CONTAGIOUS
CONTAINE
CONTAINES
CONTAINING
CONTEMNE
CONTEMNER
CONTEMPLATES
CONTEMPTIBLE
CONTENTIOUS
CONTENTMENT
CONTENTMENTS
CONTINENCE
CONTINENCY
CONTINUES
CONTINUETH
CONTINUING
CONTRADICT
CONTRADICTIONS
CONTRARIETIES
CONTRARIWISE
CONTRIBUTE
CONTRIVING
CONTROUL
CONTROULE
CONTROVERSIES
CONVENIENCE
CONVENIENTLY
CONVERSATIONS
CONVERSE
CONVERSION
CONVERSIONS
CONVEYED
CONVEYS
CONVINCE
COOLS
COPIED
COPPERSMITH
COPPY
COPS
CORALL
CORALL-CHAIN
CORDIALLY
CORDS
CORNABUS
CORPORALL
CORPULENT
CORRECTED
CORROBORATE
CORROSIVE
CORRUPTED
COSTLIER
COTTAGE
COUGH
COUNSELLETH
COUNSELLING
COUNSELLOR
COUNTENANCE'S
COUNTERS
COUNTESS
COUNTREY-AIRES
COUNTREY-DUTY
COUNTREY'S
COUNTRIE'S
COUNTRYMAN
COURSE-SPUNNE
COURT-STILE
COURTIER
COURTIERS
COURTLY
COUSIN
COUZIN
COVERING
COVERS
COVERT
COVERTLY
COVET
COVETOUSNESS
COWARD'S
COWARDS
CRAFTIER
CRAV'D
CRAVES
CRAVING
CRAVINGS
CRAZIE
CRAZY
CREAM
CREATE
CREATEDST
CREDITOR
CREDITOUR
CREEP'ST
CREEPING
CREPT
CREST
CRIED
CRINGINGS
CRIPPLE
CRITICKS
CROP
CROS
CROS-BOW
CROSSE-BIAS
CROSSES
CROSSING
CROSSWAYES
CROUD
CRUMBLE
CRUMBLED
CRUMBLING
CRUMS
CRUST
CRYMES
CRYSTALL
CULTIVATION
CUNNINGLY
CUNTRIES
CUNTRY
CUPID
CURBE
CURIOSITY
CURIOUSNESSE
CURL
CURLE
CURLED
CURLING
CURRENT
CURSED
CURST
CURTAIN
CURTAINS
CURTESIE
CUSTOMARY
CUSTOMERS
CUSTOMS
CUTTINGS
CYENS
DABO
DALLY
DALTON'S
DAMASK
DAME
DAMP
DANBY
DANCES
DANCETH
DANCING
DANTING
DARING
DARKENESSE
DARKER
DARLING
DARTS
DASHING
DATA
DATE
DATES
DAUGHTERS
DAWN
DAWNING
DAY-LIGHT
DAYES'
DAZELETH
DAZLE
DEADING
DEADLY
DEALES
DEALT
DEARELY-EARNED
DEARER
DEARLY
DEBASED
DEBATE
DEBATES
DEBAUCHED
DEBAUCHERY
DEBTERS
DECAID
DECAYED
DECAYES
DECEASE
DECEITFULL
DECEITS
DECEIVED
DECENTLY
DECIDES
DECK
DECKING
DECLARATION
DECREASE
DECREASED
DECREASING
DECRETALS
DEDICATION
DEEM
DEEPE
DEEPLY
DEERE-CUNTRY-
CLEANLINES
DEFAMES
DEFAMING
DEFECT
DEFECTIVE
DEFER
DEFERRINGS
DEFILE
DEFIL'D
DEFINE
DEFIXED
DEFORMITIE
DEFRAUDING
DEFRAY
DEGENERATE
DEGREES
DEITIE
DEITY
DEJECT
DELAIES
DELAYED
DELICATE
DELICATES
DELICIOUS
DELIGHTED
DELINQUENT'S
DELIVERY
DELUDES
DEMANDED
DEMANDEST
DEMANDING
DEMEAN
DEMONSTRATIONS
DENIALL
DENI'D
DENOUNCED
DENYING
DEPARTED
DEPARTS
DEPOS'D
DEPRIVES
DEPUTED
DEPUTIES
DEPUTY
DERIDED
DESCENDED
DESCRIBING
DESERV'D
DESERVERS
DESIGNES
DESISTS
DESK
DESPAIRE
DESPAIRED
DESPAIRS
DESPERATE
DESPISES
DESPISETH
DESPISING
DESPITEFULNESSE
DESTILL'D
DESTINIE
DESTINY
DESTROYED
DESTROY'D
DESTROYETH
DESTROYING
DESTROYS
DETAINS
DETERMINABLE
DETERMINATION
DETERMINE
DETERRING
DETESTATION
DETRACTION
DEVILLS
DEVOID
DEVOUR
DEVOURING
DEVOYD
DIALOGUE-ANTHEME
DIALOGUES
DICTATE
DICTIONARY
DIEDST
DIFFERENCES
DIFFERING
DIFFICULTIE
DIFFICULTIES
DIG
DIGEST
DIGGE
DIGG'D
DIGGED
DILATING
DIM
DIMINISH
DIMINISHED
DIMINISHINGS
DIMNESSE
DINES
DINING
DINNERS
DIOCESAN
DIOCESE
DIPPING
DIPT
DIRECTED
DIRECTLY
DIRECTNESSE
DIRTY
DISABILITY
DISABLED
DISABLETH
DISAFFECTED
DISAGREE
DISAGREEABLE
DISALLOWED
DISANULL
DISAPPOINTED
DISBAND
DISBANDED
DISBURSMENTS
DISCERN
DISCERNED
DISCHARGETH
DISCLAIM
DISCLAIMS
DISCLOSING
DISCOMMODITIE
DISCOMMODITIES
DISCORD
DISCOURSERS
DISCOURSING
DISCOURTESIE
DISCOV'RIES
DISCOVERIE
DISCOVERIES
DISCOVERY
DISCREETLY
DISCRY
DISCUSSING
DISDAIN
DISDAINETH
DISENGAG'D
DISENTANGLED
DISESTEEM
DISESTEEMING
DISGRACES
DISHONEST
DISHONOR
DISHONOURED
DISINHERITING
DISLIKE
DISMOUNT
DISOBEDIENCE
DISOBEY
DISOBEYING
DISORDER'D
DISPARAGEMENT
DISPARK
DISPARKING
DISPATCH
DISPATCHED
DISPATCHES
DISPENSATIONS
DISPENSINGS
DISPERSION
DISPLACE
DISPLAY
DISPLEASED
DISPLEASES
DISPLEASETH
DISPLEASING
DISPOSED
DISPOS'D
DISPOSITIONS

-1- (cont'd)

DISPRAISE
DISPUTATION
DISPUTED
DISPUTES
DISPUTING
DISREGARDED
DISSEIZE
DISSENSIONS
DISSENTEDST
DISSOLVES
DISTANCES
DISTASTE
DISTEMPER'D
DISTILLS
DISTINGUISHED
DISTRESSED
DISTRIBUTES
DISTRIBUTION
DISTRUSTS
DISTURB
DITCHES
DITTIES
DIURNALL
DIVER
DIVERSITIE
DIVERSITIES
DIVERSITY
DIVERSLY
DIVERT
DIVERTED
DIVIDED
DIVIDES
DIVINER
DIVINITIE
DIVINITIE'S
DO'ST
DOCTOR
DOCTORS
DOEING
DOGGES
DOGGING
DOLEFULL
DOLPHIN'S
DOMINEER
DOMINION
DON
DONATUS
DOOR-KEEPER
DORE
DOROTHY
DOTAGE
DOUBLE-DARK
DOUBLE-MOAT
DOUBLY
DOUBTFULNESSE
DOUBTING
DOUBTLESS
DOWN-CAST
DOWRY
DOZEN
DRAGGED
DRAINED
DRAINING
DRAMMES
DRANK
DRAWING
DREAD
DREAM'D
DREAMED
DREAMES
DRESSED
DRIES
DRINKES
DRIVES
DRIVEST
DRIVING
DROOPING
DROOPINGS
DROPE
DROPP
DROPPING
DROPPINGS
DROWNETH
DROWSIE
DROWSINES
DRUDGERIE
DRUDGERY
DRUG
DRUGS
DRUMME
DRUNKARD
DRUNKARD'S
DRUNKARDS
DRUNKE
DRUNKEN
DRUNKENNESS
DRYED
DUBBLE
DUBIOUS
DUCHES'S
DUCHESS'S
DUKES
DULLER
DULY
DUMB
DUMPISH
DURST
DURTIE
DUSTIE
DUTCH
DWELLEST
DWELLETH
DWELLS
DYED
DY'D
DYES
DYINGS
DYM
EAGER
EAGERNES
EAGLE
EAGLE'S
EAGLES
EAGLES'
EARING
EARL
EARNED
EARNESTLY
EARS
EARTHEN
EARTHINESS
EARTHQUAKES
EASINESSE
EASTER-WINGS
EASTWARD
EASY
EATEN
EBONY
ECLIPSE
ECLIPSED
ECLIPSES
ECLIPTICK
EDIFY
EELE
EFFECTING
EFFECTUALL
EFFICACIE
EFFICACY
EGGES
EIGHT
EIGHTIE
EIGHTY
EJACULATION
EJACULATIONS
ELECTED
ELEMENT
ELEVEN
ELEVENTH
ELISHA
ELIXER
ELLES
ELLS
ELOQUENT
EMBALME
EMBELLISHED
EMBELLISHMENT
EMBLEMS
EMBOLDENING
EMBOSOMES
EMBRACETH
EMBROIDER'D
EMBROYDERIES
EMERGENT
EMPEROURS
EMPLOYED
EMPLOYMENTS
EMPTIE
EMPTI'D
EMPTINESSE
ENABLED
ENACT
ENCHANTED
ENCLINE
ENCOMPASS
ENCOUNTERS
ENCOURAGED
ENCOURAGEMENT
ENCOURAGEMENTS
ENCOURAGING
ENCROACH
ENDEAVOURED
ENDEAVOURETH
ENDEAVOURING
ENDING
ENDOW
ENDOWMENTS
ENDURED
ENDURING
ENFORCE
ENFORCETH
ENGAGING
ENGINEER
ENGRAVEN
ENJOINED
ENJOYES
ENJOYNED
ENLARGETH
ENLIGHTENS
ENQUIRING
ENRICH
ENRICHING
ENROLL
ENTANGLED
ENTERPRIZE
ENTERTAINES
ENTERTAINS
ENTIRE
ENTREATING
ENTRED
ENTWINE
ENVIRONS
ENVY
ENVYED
EPICURE
EPICURIAN
EPICYCLES
EPITAPH
EQUALITY
ERECT
ERGO
ERRADICATE
ER'ST
ES
ESCURIALL
ESPIE
ESSENCE
EST
ESTABLISHETH
ESTABLISHING
ESTEEMES
ESTEEMS
ESTIMATION
ESTRANGING
ETERNALLY
ETERNITY
EUGANEAN
EVASION
EVEN-TIDE
EV'NING
EVENINGE
EVER-LIVING
EVR'Y
EVES
EVILLS
EVRY
EVRY-WHERE
EXACTNESSE
EXALT
EXALTS
EXAMIN'D
EXAMINATION
EXAMINES
EXCEL
EXCELLED
EXCELLENCY
EXCELLING
EXCESSES
EXCESSIVE
EXCHANGE
EXCITER
EXCITING
EXCITINGS
EXCLUDED
EXCUSES
EXECUTE
EXECUTION
EXECUTIONERS
EXECUTORS
EXEMPLARY
EXERCISED
EXERCISETH
EXHALATIONS
EXHAUSTED
EXHORT
EXHORTATION
EXILE
EXPATIATE
EXPEDITION
EXPENCE
EXPERIMENT
EXPLAINE
EXPLAINING
EXPOSE
EXPOSED
EXPOSITION
EXPOUNDED
EXPRESSETH
EXPRESSION
EXTENDED
EXTENDS
EXTENSION
EXTENT
EXTERNALL
EXTINGUISHED
EXTIRPATE
EXTOLL
EXTOLLETH
EXTORT
EXTRACT
EXTRAORDINARY
EXTREAM
EXTREMELY
EXTREMITIE
EXULT
EYESIGHT
FABRICKS
FACIENS
FACTION
FACTIOUS
FACULTY
FADED
FADES
FAILED
FAINTED
FAINTINGS
FAITHFULLEST
FALNE
FALS
FALSIFYED
FALT
FAME'S
FAMISHT
FANCIE'S
FANCY
FANSY
FARMES
FASHIONABLENESS
FASTEN
FASTNING
FATAL
FATALL
FATE
FATHOM'D
FATS
FATTENS
FAULTIE
FAWNING
FEASTERS
FEASTING
FEATHER
FEEDE
FEEDER
FEEDING
FEEL'ST
FEELETH
FEELINGLY
FELICITIE
FELLOW
FELLOW-LABOURERS
FELLOWES
FELLS
FENCERS
FENCING
FENNELL
FENNY
FERNELIUS
FERRAR
FERVENCIE
FERVENTLY
FESTIVALLS
FESTIVALS
FETCHING
FETTER'D
FICKLE
FICTION
FICTIONS
FIDDLE
FIDLER
FIE
FIER
FIERY
FIERY-TRYALS
FIFTEENE
FIFTEENTH
FIFTH
FIFTY
FIG
FIG-LEAVES
FIGHTING
FIGHTS
FIGURE
FIGURES
FILL'D
FILLETH
FINALL
FINDETH
FINEM
FINEST
FINISH'D
FINISHED
FINISHT
FINITE
FIRE-WORK
FIR'D
FIRMENESSE
FISHER'S
FISHERNETT
FISHES
FISHETH
FITS
FITTS
FIXE
FIXT
FLAGON
FLARING
FLATTER
FLATTERER'S
FLATTERING
FLEA
FLEAS
FLEE
FLEET
FLEMMISH
FLESHE'S
FLESHY
FLEW
FLING
FLINTS
FLOCKE
FLOCKT
FLOOD
FLOTING
FLOURISHED
FLOURISHING
FLOURS
FLOUTED
FLOW'D
FLOW'R
FLOWRES
FLOWS
FLUNG
FLYING
FOES'
FOILE
FOLKE
FOLKES
FOLLIE
FOLLOWED
FOLLOWERS
FOLLOWETH
FOME
FOMES
FOMITIS

-1- (cont'd)

FOOL'D
FOOLERIE
FOOLISHLY
FOOTED
FORBARE
FORBEARANCE
FORBIDDEN
FORC'D
FORCES
FORCETH
FORE
FORE-MENTIONED
FORECAST
FOREHEAD
FOREHEADS
FORENAMED
FORERUNNERS
FORESEE
FORFEITED
FORFEITS
FORGETFULNESS
FORGETS
FORGETT
FORGETTING
FORGIVENESSE
FORGIVES
FORM'D
FORMOST
FORNACE
FORO
FORRAINE
FORRESTS
FORSOOK
FORT
FORTHWITH
FORTIETH
FORTI'TH
FORTIFICATION
FORTIFICATIONS
FORTIFIES
FORTIFYES
FORTNIGHT
FORTUNATE
FORTUNE'S
FORWARDNES
FORWARDNESS
FORWARDS
FOUGHT
FOULED
FOULES
FOULING-PEECE
FOULNESSE
FOULS
FOUNDATIONS
FOUNTAINES
FOURETEEN
FOURTH
FOWLE
FOWLER
FOWLS
FOWRE
FOXE
FOXE'S
FRACTURES
FRAGMENTS
FRAGRANCIE
FRAILE
FRAILTY
FRAMED
FRAMING
FRANCISCAN'S
FRANK
FRAUGHT
FRE
FRE-WILL
FREER
FREEZE
FRENCHMAN
FRENCHMEN
FREND
FRENZY
FREQUENCY
FREQUENTED
FRESHER
FRESHLY
FRET
FRETS
FRIDAYES
FRIER
FRIGHTETH
FRIGHTING
FRONTIRE
FROST-NIPT
FROST'S
FROTH
FROWNE
FROWNS
FRUITE
FRUITFULLER
FRUITFULLY
FRUITLESLY
FUEL
FULFILLING
FULFILLS
FULNESSE
FURIOUS
FURNACE
FURNISHETH
FURNISHING
FURNITURES
FURRIER
FURRS
FURTHERS
GAD
GAINFULLEST
GALLANTS
GAME'S
GAMING
GAMINGS
GAMSTERS
GAPE
GAPING
GARD'NER
GARD'NERS
GARDEN-BED
GARLAND-STREAMS
GARLANDS
GARLICK
GARRISONS
GASPETH
GAVEST
GAYNESSES
GAYNING
GAZE
GAZER
GAZING
GEERE
GENERALLS
GENTILE
GENTILES
GENTILITY
GENTLEMAN'S
GENTLEMEN
GENTRIE
GENTRY
GERMANES
GERMANY
GERSON
GETTS
GIDDIE
GIDDINESSE
GIDEON
GIFFORD
GIGLER
GIRDETH
GIVER
GIVERS
GIVINGS
GLANCES
GLAZED
GLIDE
GLISTERS
GLITTER
GLITTERING
GLORIFIE
GLORYES
GLOW
GLOZING
GLUTTONIE
GNAW
GNAWES
GNAWING
GOATE
GOD-FATHERS
GOD-MOTHERS
GODWARD
GOLIAH
GOLIAH-LIKE
GON
GOOD-FELLOWS
GOOD-WILL
GOOSE
GORDIAN
GOSHEN
GOSSIPS
GOVERNE
GOVERNED
GOVERNOUR
GOVERNOURS
GRACE'S
GRAFFE
GRAINE
GRAND
GRAND-CHILDREN
GRANTING
GRANTS
GRASPES
GRATES
GRATIFIE
GRATIS
GRATUM
GRAVE-CLOTHES
GRAVE-CLOTHS
GRAVED
GRAVITY
GRAYHOUND
GRAZE
GREATNESS
GREEDIE
GREEDINESSE
GREEK
GREENE
GREENNESSE
GREESE
GREIFE
GREIVED
GREW'ST
GRIEF'S
GRIEVOUS
GRIND
GRINDS
GROANE
GROANING
GRONETH
GRONING
GROSS
GROSSER
GROT
GROTTOS
GROUNDSELL
GROWE
GRUDGING
GRUMBLE
GRUMBLINGLY
GUARDIAN
GUIFTS
GUILDS
GUILE
GUILTIE
GUILTY
GUMMES
GUMS
GUNNER
GUNNES
GUNPOWDER
GUSTOS
HABITABLE
HABITT
HABITUALL
HACK
HACKNEY
HAIL
HAINOUSNESS
HALFE-KNEELING
HALLOW'D
HALT
HAMLET
HAMLETS
HAMMER
HAMMERING
HAMPER'D
HANDFULL
HANDKERCHIEF
HANDLE
HANDLING
HANDSELL
HANDSOM
HANDSOMNESSE
HANGED
HANGING
HANNAH
HARBOUR
HARDEN
HARDEST
HARDNESSE
HARDNESSES
HARLEY
HARME
HARMLESSE
HARMONIOUSLY
HARP
HARPYES
HARQUEBUZE
HARSH
HART-DEEP
HARTES
HASTED
HASTENS
HATCH
HATCHING
HAT'ST
HATETH
HAUNT
HAVENS
HAWKING
HAYS
HAZARDS
HEAD-ACH
HEAD'S
HEALES
HEALTHS
HEAPS
HEARDST
HEARE-SAY
HEARER
HEARTLESSE
HEATE
HEAV'EN
HEAV'EN'S
HEAVIEST
HEBREW
HECTIQUE
HEELS
HEERE
HEERTOFORE
HEIGHTEN
HEIR
HELLISH
HELPED
HELPES
HEMISPHERES
HEN
HERALDRIE
HERAULD
HERBALL
HERBERT'S
HERCULES
HERETICK
HERETIQUES
HERMITS
HERMOGENES
HERS
HERSE
HIBBERT
HIDEOUS
HIDES
HIGH-WAYES
HIGHT
HINDES'
HINDRED
HINGE
HINGES
HIRE
HISTORY
HITS
HOG
HOGGE
HOGS
HOLDETH
HOLDFAST
HOLDING
HOLP
HOLY-DAYES
HOLY-DAYS
HOLYDAYE
HONESTIE
HONESTLY
HONORABLE
HONORS
HONOURING
HONOURS
HOOKE
HOOPES
HORNS
HORSE-BACK
HORSEBACK
HORSEBACKE
HOTT
HOURE'S
HOURS
HOUSE-KEEPER'S
HOUSED
HOUSEFULL
HOUSKEEPER
HOUSKEEPERS
HOUSWIFE
HOWARD
HOWL
HOWRE
HOWSHOULD
HUDLING
HUGE
HUMANO
HUMBLING
HUMOUR
HUNDREDTH
HUNGRED
HUNGRETH
HUNGRY
HUNTING
HURL'D
HUSBANDMAN
HUSBANDS
HUSWIFE
HYMENEUS
HYPOCRISIE
HYPOCRITE
HYSSOPE
ICE
IDLENES
IDOL
IDOL'S
IGNOMINY
ILANDS
ILE
ILL-MEANING
ILL-TASTED
ILLUMINATION
ILLUSTRATE
ILLUSTRATED
ILLUSTRATING
ILLUSTRIOUS
IMAGINATION
IMBARN
IMBARNED
IMITATED
IMITATES
IMMEDIATELY
IMMODERATE
IMMODERATELY
IMMORTAL
IMMORTALITIE
IMMURE
IMP
IMPAL'D
IMPANATION
IMPARTIAL
IMPARTS
IMPERFECTION
IMPERIALL
IMPLICITE
IMPLOY
IMPLYES
IMPORTUNE
IMPORTUNITIE
IMPOVERISHING
IMPRECATION
IMPREST
IMPRISONING
IMPUDENT
IMPUTE
IN-MATE
INABLE
INABLING
INCENSE
INCESSANT
INCESSANTLY
INCHANTED
INCHANTMENT
INCHES
INCITATION
INCITES
INCLINATION

-1- (cont'd)

INCLINED
INCLOSER
INCLOSING
INCLUDE
INCOME
INCOMPOSSIBLE
INCOMPREHENSIBLE
INCONSIDERATE
INCONTINENCY
INCREASETH
INCREASING
INCREDIBLE
INCROACH
INCUMBRANCES
INCURABLE
INDEBTED
INDIAN
INDIAS
INDIES
INDIFFERENTS
INDISPOSITION
INDISPOSITIONS
INDITED
INDORSEMENT
INDUCE
INDUSTRIE
INDUSTRIOUS
INFALLIBILITIES
INFANCIE
INFANTS'
INFERNALL
INFIDELITIE
INFIRMITIE
INFLAMING
INFLICTED
INFOLD
INFORME
INFORMING
INGAGEMENT
INGAGEMENTS
INGAGING
INGROSSE
INHANCE
INHANSE
INHERENT
INHERITANCES
INIQUITIE
INIQUITIES
INITIATORY
INJOYNED
INJUNCTION
INJURIES
INJURY
INJUSTICES
INKE
INLARGED
INLARGETH
INN
INNES
INNOCENCE
INOUGH
INRICH
INRICHED
INRICHING
INSIDES
INSIGHT
INSINUATION
INSIST
INSOMUCH
INSPIRATIONS
INSTANCE
INSTRUCTETH
INSTRUCTS
INSUING
INTEGRITIE
INTELLECTUALL
INTEMPERATE
INTEMPERATELY
INTENTIONS
INTERCHANGEABLY
INTERDICTION
INTERESTING
INTERLIN'D
INTERMEDIATE
INTERMINGLES
INTERMIT
INTERMITS
INTERMIXED
INTERPOSE
INTERPOSETH
INTERPRETATION
INTERRUPTIONS
INTIMATE
INTIMATED
INTIMATETH
INTIMATION
INTREATE
INTREATS
INTRENCHING
INVENT
INVESTED
INVESTING
INVISIBLE
INVITATION
INVITING
IQUE
IRON
IRRADIATIONS
ISAAC
ISABEL
ISLE
ISOCRATES
ISRAEL
ISSU'D
ITALIANS
ITALY
ITCH
IUSTO
JACOB
JACULA
JADE
JAGG'D
JANE
JANUS
JAW
JAWES
JEALOUS
JEALOUSIE
JEALOUSIES
JEALOVSIE
JEAT
JEREMY
JESSUITT
JESTINGLY
JESTS
JEW
JOB'S
JOCOND
JOGS
JOIN'D
JOINED
JOINING
JOINTURE
JOLLITIE
JONATHAN
JOSEPH'S
JOSEPHUS'S
JOURNEYING
JOURNIE'S
JOURNYING
JOY'D
JOYE
JOYFUL
JOYING
JOYNE
JOYNT
JOYNTS
JOYOUS
JUDAS-JEW
JUDGE'S
JUDG'D
JUDGING
JUDICIOUS
JUGGLINGS
JULIPS
JURIE
JUSTICES
JUSTIFIE
JUSTIFY
KAN
KEEL
KEEN
KEEPER'S
KEEP'ST
KENNELL
KERNELLS
KILLETH
KILLING
KIN
KINDLED
KINDLES
KINDLY
KINDNESS
KINGDOM
KISS
KISS'D
KISSETH
KISSING
KITE'S
KNACK
KNIGHT
KNIVES
KNOCKES
KNOCKINGS
KNOCKS
KNOT-GRASSE
KNOWE
KNOWLEDGES
LABORIOUS
LABOURED
LABOURER
LABOURERS
LACE-MAKING
LACK
LACK'D
LACKEY
LADDER
LADIES
LADLE
LAGS
LAKE
LAMBE
LAMP
LAND-MARKS
LANDUS
LANTERNS
LANTHORNE
LAP
LARD
LARGER
LARGESSE
LASH
LASTLIE
LATIN-BRED
LATTIN
LAUD
LAUDABLE
LAUGHS
LAVER
LAVISHNESSE
LAW'S
LAWFULLY
LAWFULNES
LAWLEY'S
LAWYERS
LAWYERS'
LAY-HYPOCRISIE
LAY-SWORD
LAYED
LAZY
LEADETH
LEADING
LEAFE
LEAN
LEANING
LEANNESSE
LEANS
LEAPT
LEARNERS
LEARNES
LEASURE
LEASURELY
LEAV'ST
LEAVETH
LEAZURE
LEER
LEG
LEGACYES
LEGAL
LEGALEM
LEGALL
LEGGS
LEGIONS
LEMMON'S
LENDETH
LENGTHEN
LENGTHENS
LENGTHS
LEOPARD
LETHARGICKNESSE
LETHARGIQUE
LETTICE
LETTS
LEVELS
LEVY
LEWD
LEX
LIB
LIBERALITIE
LIBERALITY
LIBERALLY
LIBERTIE
LICK
LICKES
LIEN
LIFTEST
LIGHTING
LIGHTLY
LIGHTNING
LIKELYEST
LIKER
LILLIES
LIMBE
LIME
LIMITS
LINCOLN
LINEAMENTS
LINEN
LINK
LINN
LIP
LISTEN
LISTNING
LITTER
LIVD
LIVEDST
LIVELIER
LIVELINESSE
LIVERY-GRACES
LIVES'
LIVEST
LIVINGS
LIVY
LOADE
LOADED
LOATHING
LOCKE
LOCKES
LOCKT
LODGED
LODG'D
LOG
LOGS
LONDON-BRIDGE
LONG'D
LOOKING-GLASSE
LOOKINGS
LOOS'D
LOOSELY
LOOSERS
LOOSING
LOSEST
LOSING
LOTHSOME
LOTHSOMLY
LOTTERIE
LOUDER
LOVE-JOY
LOVE-POEMS
LOVE'S
LOVELINESSE
LOVETH
LOW-CUNTRIES
LOWEST
LOWLY
LOWT
LOYNES
LOYTER
LOYTERER
LUCAS
LUD
LULLINGS
LURK
LUSTIE
LUSTY
LUTER'S
LUXURY
LYER
LYERS
LYEST
LYON'S
LYZARD
MACARIUS
MADNESSE
MAGAZENE
MAGAZENS
MAGDALEN
MAGNANIMITY
MAGNANIMOUS
MAGNIFICENT
MAGUS
MAHOMETAN
MAIDES
MAINE
MAINTAIN
MAINTAINES
MAIST
MAJESTIE
MAJESTYE
MAKEST
MAK'ST
MALEFACTOR
MALEFACTORS
MALEFACTOUR
MALEFACTOURS
MALICIOUSNESSE
MALIGNITIE
MALLICE
MALLOWES
MANAGE
MANCHESTER
MANIE
MANNERS
MANOUR
MANS
MANSUETUDE
MANUFACTURES
MANURED
MARBLE'S
MARBLES
MARGERET
MARINER
MARK-MAN
MARKE
MARKET-MAN
MARKET-MONEY
MARKETH
MARKING
MARRE
MARRIAGE
MARRIAGES
MARRS
MARRYING
MARSHALLING
MARTYR'D
MARVELL
MASK
MASON
MASSE
MASTER-GUNNER
MASTER-PEECE
MASTERED
MASTERETH
MAST'RING
MASTERS'
MATCH
MATES
MATHEMATICKS
MATRIMONY
MATTENS
MATURE
MAUGRE
MAYDS
MEALE'S
MEALES
MEANER
MEANINGS
MEANLY
MEASURED
MEDDLE
MEDDOW
MEDIATOR
MEDICINES
MEDIOCRITIE
MEDLEY
MEDLING
MEETE
MEETES
MEETINGS
MELANCHOLICK
MELILOT
MELLOWING
MELONS

-1- (cont'd)

MELTING
MEMORIALL
MEN-SERVANTS
MENDED
MENDING
MENTIONED
MERCHANTS
MERCIE
MERCURY
MERES
MERRILY
MERRIMENT
MESSENGERS
METALS
METHEGLIN
METHUSALEM'S
MICHAELMAS
MICHEL
MIDPRAYERS
MIGHTST
MILES
MILITANT
MILITARIE
MILK-MAID
MILKIE
MILL-CLACKE
MILLER
MILLION
MILLIONS
MILLS
MINDE'S
MINDED
MINES
MINGLE
MINISTERIALL
MINISTRING
MINTS
MIRACLE-WORKING
MIRACULOUS
MIRROUR
MIS
MIS-LED
MISCALL
MISCARRIE
MISDOUBT
MISFORTUNE
MISHAP
MISLIKES
MISPLACE
MISSES
MISSEST
MISSHAPEN
MISTAKES
MISTRES
MISTRESSE
MISTRESSING
MISUSE
MITRE
MIXT
MOAT
MOCKE
MOCKES
MODELL
MODERATELY
MODESTY
MOLDETH
MOLE
MOLES
MOLEST
MOLLIFIE
MOLLIFYING
MOMENTARIE
MONETH
MONEYS
MONK
MONKISH
MONKS
MONNEYS
MONSTERS
MONTGOMERY
MONYES
MOONS
MOORISH
MORA
MORALITY
MORES
MORNE
MORNING-SOUL
MORTAL
MORTER
MORTIFICATIONS
MORTIFIE
MORTIFY
MOTH
MOTHER-ROOT
MOTHER'S
MOTHS
MOUNTER'S
MOUNTING
MOUNTS
MOURNERS
MOURNING
MOUTHES
MOVEABLE
MOVEDST
MOVEST
MOVETH
MOW
MRSS
MUD
MUDDE
MULE
MULTIPLIED
MULTIPLY
MURDERERS
MURMUR
MURMURINGS
MUSICIANS
MUSICK'S
MUSKE
MUSTARD
MUSTARD-SEED
MUTTER
MUTTON
MUTUALLY
MYNE
MYSELF
MYSTERIE
MYSTERIOUSNESSE
NAIL
NAILES
NAILING
NAMETH
NATHAN
NATHANIELL
NATIONALL
NATIVITIES
NATURALIZE
NAUGHT
NAUGHTY
NEARENESSE
NEARER
NEAREST
NEATELY
NECESSARIE
NECESSARILY
NECESSITIES
NECKS
NECROMANCER
NEEDETH
NEERER
NEEREST
NEGLIGENCE
NEGLIGENTLY
NEIGHBOR
NEIGHBORING
NEIGHBOUR-CITIES
NEIGHBOURS'
NERE
NERO
NESTLE
NESTLES
NESTS
NETHERSOL'S
NETHERSOLE
NEW-FOUND
NEWMARKET
NEWNESSE
NEYTHER
NICENESS
NICHOLAS
NIGARDLY
NIGHT-FIRES
NIGHTINGALE
NILUS
NIP
NIPPLES
NOBILITY
NOBLE-MAN
NOBLEMEN'S
NOBLES
NOBLEST
NOBODIE
NOD
NOISELESSE
NOISES
NOISOME
NOISOMNESSE
NON-REGENT
NON-SENSE
NORTH-WINDE
NOTHINGE
NOURISHETH
NOURISHING
NOURISHT
NOVELTIES
NURTURE
NUT
NUTMEGS
OAK
OATES
OATHS
OBEYED
OBEYES
OBEYS
OBJECTED
OBJECTIONS
OBLATION
OBLIG'D
OBLIGED
OBLIGES
OBLIQUELY
OBSCURED
OBSERV'D
OBSERVANT
OBSERVEST
OBSOLETE
OBSTINACIE
OBSTRUCT
OBSTRUCTIONS
OBSTRUCTIVE
OBTAINE
OBTAIN'D
OBTAINED
OBTAINES
OCCASIONALLY
OCEAN
OCEANS
ODIOUS
OFF-SPRING
OFFENCES
OFFENDERS
OFFENSIVE
OFFENSIVELY
OFFERD
OFFERER'S
OFF'RING
OFFERINGS
OFFICER
OFFRING
OFSPRING
OFTENEST
OFTNER
OINTMENT
OKE
OLDER
OLIVE
OLIVET
OMISSION
OMITS
OMITTED
ONLEY
OPENER
OPENETH
OPENING
OP'NING
OPERATIONS
OPINIONS
OPPOSER
OPPOSING
OPPOSITE
OPPREST
ORACULAR
ORATIONS
ORDAINED
ORDINANCE
ORDINANCES
ORDINARILY
ORE
ORECOME
ORENGE
ORENGE-TREE
ORIENTALL
OTHER'S
OUGHTEST
OURE
OUT-CRYING
OUT-SING
OUTGO
OUTRIGHT
OUTRUNNING
OUTSTRIPPEST
OUTWARDLY
OUTWORKS
OVEN
OVER-NOURISHING
OVER-SUBMISSIVE
OVER-
SUBMISSIVENESSE
OVERCAME
OVERCOMES
O'RECOMES
OVERDO
OVERFLOWING
OVERFLOWS
OVERMUCH
OVERRUNNE
OVERSEER
OVERSIGHT
OVERSLEEPING
OVERTHROWING
OVERTURNES
OVERWEIGH
OVERWEIGHS
OVERWHELME
OW
OWED
OWENS
OWLE'S
OWNCE
OX
OXEN
PACES
PADUA
PAGANS
PAINEFULL
PAINFUL
PAIR
PALENESSE
PAN
PANG
PANGS
PANT
PAPERS
PAPIST
PAPISTS
PARADICE
PARADOX
PARALITIQUE
PARAPHRASE
PARCEL
PARCELL-DEVILL
PARCELS
PARE
PARENTAGE
PARKS
PARLEY
PARLOUR
PARODIE
PARTAKES
PARTER
PARTIALL
PARTICIPATION
PARTING
PARTITION
PARTITION-WALL
PARTITIONS
PARTNER
PARTRIDGE
PARTY
PASCHAL
PASSAGES
PASS'D
PASSENGERS'
PASSING-BELL
PASTIME
PASTORAGE
PASTORS
PASTOUR'S
PASTOURS
PATE
PATENTS
PATHS
PATIENTLY
PATRIARK
PATTERN
PAUSABLY
PAUSING
PAVED
PAW
PAWS
PAY-MASTER
PAYER
PAYMENT
PEACE-MEAL
PEACE'S
PEACEABLY
PEACOCK'S
PEARS
PEASANT
PECK
PEDIGREES
PEDLER
PEECE-MEAL
PEECES
PEERE
PEEVISH
PEGS
PEMBROKE
PENALTIES
PENDANT
PENITENTIAL
PENNE
PENNES
PENNING
PENS
PENSIVE
PENSIVENESSE
PENY
PEOPLE'S
PEOPLES'
PEPPER
PER
PERAMBULATION
PERCEIV'D
PERCEIVES
PERCHANCE
PERFECTING
PERFECTLY
PERFIDIOUS
PERFORMANCE
PERFORMANCES
PERFORMING
PERFORMS
PERFUMED
PERIODS
PERIRRHANTERIUM
PERMIT
PERMITTED
PERPETUAL
PERPETUATE
PERPLEX'D
PERPLEXING
PERPLEXITY
PERQUISITES
PERSECUTETH
PERSECUTING
PERSECUTION
PERSEVER
PERSEVERANCE
PERSISTEST
PERSON'S
PERSONALL
PERSPECTIVE
PERSWADE
PERSWADERS
PERSWADING
PERTURBATION
PERUSED
PERVERSNES
PERVERTING
PESTILENCE
PETITIONER
PHANSIE'S
PHANSIES
PHARACH
PHARAOH'S
PHARISAICALL
PHARISEE
PHARISEES
PHILISTIN
PHILOSOPHER'S
PHILOSOPHERS

-1- (cont'd)

PHISICIANS
PHLEGMATICK
PHRASES
PHYSICKE
PHYSITIANS
PICK-PURSE
PICKS
PICKT
PICTURED
PICTURES
PIERCED
PIERCER
PIERCETH
PIG'S
PIGEONS
PIKE
PILE
PILFRING
PILGRIME
PILLAR
PILLOWS
PILLS
PIN'D
PINION'D
PINKE
PIOUSLY
PIPE
PIPING
PITCHERS
PITHY
PITS
PITTIES
PITTY
PITYES
PITYING
PLAC'D
PLACETH
PLAINNESSE
PLAISTERED
PLANTAINE
PLANTATIONS
PLANTING
PLATFORM
PLAYING
PLAYNTES
PLEA
PLEADING
PLEADS
PLEAS'D
PLEASANTLY
PLEASANTNESS
PLEDG
PLEDGE
PLEDGES
PLENARIE
PLENTEOUS
PLENTY
PLIANT
PLOTS
PLOTT
PLOTTING
PLOUGHING
PLUCK
PLUCKT
PLUMMET
PLUMTREE
PLUNGING
POEM
POISE
POLICIE
POLICIES
POLLUTES
POLLUTIONS
POMANDER
POMANDERS
POMPE
POOR-MAN'S
POPE'S
POPES
POPISH
POPULAR
PORCH
PORK
POSIES
POSITA
POSITION
POSITIVELY
POSSESS
POSSESSED
POSSESSING
POSTERITY
POSTURES
POTABILE
POTENTATES
POTS
POULTIS
POULTRY
POUR'D
POWDERS
POWRE
POWRING
POYNT
POYSONOUS
PRACTICALL
PRACTICIONER
PRAESUMPTIONEM
PRATLERS
PRAY'D
PRAYER-BOOK
PREACHER'S
PREACHERS'
PRECEDENT
PREDESTINATION
PREDOMINANT
PREFER
PREFERRES
PREFERRETH
PREFERRING
PREFERRS
PREFIXT
PREJUDICE
PRELATES
PREMISE
PRENTICES
PREORDAIN
PREPOSSESSED
PREPOSSEST
PRESCRIBED
PRESCRIBES
PRESERVATIVES
PRESS'D
PRESSED
PRESUMERS
PRESUMING
PRETENDER
PRETENDETH
PRETENDING
PRETIOUS
PRETTINESSE
PREVENTED
PREVENTEST
PREVENTS
PRICKING
PRIE
PRIMITIVE
PRINCESSE
PRINCIPALLY
PRINT
PRINTING
PRISONER
PRIVIE
PRIVILEDGE
PRIVY
PROCEEDINGS
PROCEEDS
PROCESSION
PROCLAMATION
PROCTORS
PRODIGALITY
PRODIGALL
PRODIGIES
PRODIGIOUS
PRODUC'D
PRODUCETH
PROFESSIONS
PROFESSOURS
PROFFER
PROFOUND
PROGENIE
PROHIBITING
PROLONG
PROLONGS
PROMISED
PROMIS'D
PROMISSES
PROOFS
PROPAGATION
PROPERTIES
PROPHESIES
PROPHET
PROPHETESSE
PROPORTIONABLE
PROPOSALS
PROPOSE
PROPOSETH
PROPOUNDS
PROSECUTIONS
PROSPERING
PROSPERS
PROSTITUTES
PROTECTED
PROTECTING
PROTECTION
PROTESTING
PROUDEST
PROVIDED
PROWESSE
PRUDENT
PRUDENTUM
PRUNING
PRUNING-KNIFE
PRYING
PS
PSALMES
PSALMIST
PUBLICAN
PUBLICKE
PUBLISH
PUBLISHED
PUBLISHING
PUDDLE
PULING
PULL'ST
PULLEY
PULPITS
PUNISHER
PUNISHMENTS
PUNISHT
PURENES
PURENESSE
PURER
PUREST
PURGATORY
PURG'D
PURGETH
PURGING
PURGINGS
PURITY
PURLE
PURLING
PURPOSED
PURPOSETHE
PURSIE
PURSING
PURSU'D
PY
PY-CRUST
QUAIL
QUANTITIES
QUARRELSOMNESSE
QUARRIES
QUEEN
QUENCHETH
QUEST
QUESTIONING
QUESTIONIST
QUICK-EY'D
QUICK-PIERCING
QUICKEN
QUICKEN'D
QUICKNING
QUIDDITIE
QUIETNES
QUINTESSENCE
QUIP
QUIRE
QUITT'ST
QUIVER
RACE-HORSES
RACES
RADICALL
RAGGED
RAIGNES
RANCOUR
RANK
RANKE
RANKED
RANNE
RANTS
RAPPER
RARELY
RARITIES
RASH
RATABLY
RATES
RAVE
RAV'D
RAVENING
RAVISH
RAVISHING
RAW
RAZE
RAZ'D
REACHETH
READES
READETH
READIEST
READILY
READYEST
REALL
REAPED
REARES
REASONABLY
REASONING
REBEL
REBEL-FLESH
REBELL
REBELL'D
REBELLION
REBELLIONS
REBUKEST
RECALL
RECALLING
RECEAVED
RECEIPTS
RECEIT
RECEIV'D
RECEIVER
RECEIVES
RECKONING
RECKONS
RECOILE
RECOMPENSES
RECONCILED
RECORDED
RECOUNTING
RECOVER'D
RECOVERING
REDEEMER'S
REDOUND
REDUCED
REFERENCE
REFERENCES
REFERR
REFERRED
REFERRETH
REFINE
REFINED
REFIN'D
REFLECTION
REFORM
REFORMES
REFRACTIONS
REFRACTORINESSE
REFRACTORY
REFRESH
REFRESHETH
REFRESHMENTS
REFUTATION
REGAIN
REGARDS
REGENERATION
REGIMENTS
REGION
REGIONS
REGULARITIE
REGULARLY
REJECT
REJOYCED
REJOYCING
RELATING
RELEASE
RELENTEDST
RELENTING
RELIEFS
RELIEVEST
RELINQUISHABLE
RELISH
RELISHING
RELLISH
REMAIN
REMAINDERS
REMAINED
REMAINETH
REMEDIE
REMEDIED
REMNANT
REMOTE
REMOVED
REMOVES
REND
RENDERETH
RENDING
RENOUNCE
RENOWNE
RENOWNED
RENTED
RENTS
REPAIRE
REPAIRING
REPAIRS
REPARATION
REPAY
REPENTED
REPENTING
REPLENISH
REPLETION
REPLIED
REPRESENTING
REPRISALL
REPROACHED
REPROACHES
REPROCHES
REPUTATION
REPUTE
REQUIRETH
RESENT
RESERVATION
RESERVED
RESERV'D
RESIDING
RESIGNE
RESOLVE
RESOUND
RESOUNDS
RESPECTFULL
RESPECTIVE
RESPECTIVELY
RESPECTS
RESTETH
RESTFUL
RESTLESNESSE
RESTORATIVE
RESTOR'D
RESTORES
RESTORING
RESTRAIN
RESTRAINE
RESTS
RESUME
RESUMING
RETAIN
RETAINS
RETAKEN
RETIREDNESSE
RETORTING
RETURN'D
REVEALING
REVELED
REVELL
REVENGERS
REVENGES
REVENGING
REVENUE
REVERENCED
REVERENT
REVERENTLY
REVERSED
REVIEW
REVILE
REVILES
REVILING
REVOKING
REWARDER
RHENISH
RHUME
RICHEST
RIDDLE
RIDS
RIFE
RIFLED
RIGHT'OUS
RIGHTLY

-1- (cont'd)

RIGOROUS
RILLS
RINDE
RINGS
RIPENESSE
RIPP
RISEN
RISES
ROAD
ROBBE
ROBB'D
ROBBES
ROBERT
ROBES
ROGUE
ROILING
ROLLS
ROMANE
ROOF
ROOST
ROOTED
ROOTS
ROSEMARY
ROST
ROTE
ROTS
ROTTEN
ROTTENNESS
ROTTENNESSE
ROUGH
ROUNDLY
ROUT
ROVING
ROWS
ROYALL
RUB
RUBARB
RUBB
RUBBE
RUDDER
RUDDIE
RUDDYARD
RUFFLE
RUFFLING
RUG
RUL'D
RULER
RULEST
RULETH
RULING
RUNNETH
RUNS
RUSHED
RUST
RYMES
SABLE
SACK
SACRAMENTALL
SADDER
SADLES
SADLY
SADNESS
SADNESSE
SAFEST
SAFETIE
SAID'ST
SAIDEST
SAIST
SALEM
SALLET
SALT-BOX
SALUTATIONS
SALVES
SAMPSON
SAMUEL
SANCTIF'D
SANCTIFIED
SANCTIFYING
SAND
SAPLESSE
SATAN'S
SATISFIES
SATURDAYES
SAUSAGES
SAVES
SAVING
SAVORY
SAVOURIE
SAVOURS
SAVOURY
SAWCIE
SCAB
SCAB'D
SCALD
SCALES
SCANDALOUS
SCANT
SCAPES
SCARED
SCATTERED
SCATTERINGLY
SCENE
SCHISMATICK
SCHISMES
SCHOLAR
SCHOLER
SCHOLLER
SCHOLLER'S
SCHOOL-MISTRESSE
SCHOOLEMASTERS
SCHOOLING
SCHOOLMASTERS
SCOFFE
SCOFFING
SCONSES
SCOPE
SCORNE
SCORNER'S
SCORNFULL
SCOULING
SCOURGED
SCOUT
SCRAPER
SCRAPING
SCRATCH
SCRATCHING
SCREEN
SCRIPTURE-DEW
SCRUE
SCUCE
SCUMME
SEALD
SEALE
SEAL'D
SEAM
SEAMLESSE
SEARCHES
SEARCHEST
SEARCHING
SEASON'D
SEASONING
SEATS
SEAVEN
SECRETARIE
SECULAR
SECUNDUM
SEDENTARY
SEDITIOUS
SEED-CORN
SEED-TIME
SEEK'ST
SEEKE
SEELED
SEEMINGLY
SEEMLY
SEENE
SEER'S
SEEST
SEETH
SEEVES
SEIN
SEIZ'D
SELDOM
SELDOMER
SELF-CONCEITE
SELF-CONDEMNATION
SELFE-SUFFICIENT
SELLS
SELS
SENCELES
SENDES
SENSITIVE
SENSLESS
SENSUAL
SENSUALL
SENTED
SENTENC'D
SENTINELL
SEPT
SEPULCHRE
SERIOUSLY
SERPENTS
SERVANT'S
SERV'D
SERVICEABLE
SERVING
SESSION
SESSION-DAY
SESSIONS
SETLETH
SETTETH
SETTLE
SEVENFOLD
SEVENTH
SEVERALLY
SEVER'D
SEVERITY
SEWER
SHADDOW
SHADOWES
SHADOWS
SHAFT
SHAFTS
SHAKING
SHALLOWNESSE
SHALT
SHAMES
SHAR'D
SHARPEN
SHARPER
SHARPNES
SHAVE
SHAVES
SHEATH
SHEDS
SHEEPISHNESSE
SHEET
SHEETS
SHELLS
SHELTRED
SHEWED
SHIE
SHIELDS
SHIFTEST
SHINER
SHINETH
SHIPPE
SHIPPING
SHIPS
SHIRE
SHIRES
SHOARE
SHOCK
SHOCKE
SHOOS
SHOPKEEPER
SHORE
SHOR'D
SHORNE
SHORT-BREATHED
SHORTEST
SHORTNESS
SHOT
SHOTT
SHOULDERS
SHOULD'ST
SHOWE
SHOWER
SHOWERS
SHOWIS
SHOWN
SHOWRE
SHRILL
SHRINE
SHRIVEL'D
SHRODELY
SHROWD
SHROWDS
SHUFFLED
SHUNNES
SHUNNEST
SHUTT'ST
SICILIAN
SICKLE
SICKLINESSE
SICKNES
SIDING
SIEGE
SIFTED
SIGH-BLOWN
SIGHES
SIGHING
SIGHTLY
SIGNIFIES
SIGNING
SILKE
SILLIE
SIMPER
SIMPLE
SIMPLENESSE
SIMPLES
SIN-SICK
SINAI
SINCERE
SINEWS
SINFUL
SINGLED
SINNED
SINN'D
SINNERS
SION'S
SIRE
SITUATION
SIXTEEN
SIXTIE
SKARE
SKARF
SKARRES
SKENES
SKIES
SKIL
SKILL'D
SKILLS
SKIN
SKINS
SKIPPING
SLACKNES
SLACKNESSE
SLAIN
SLANDER
SLAUGHTER'D
SLAVE
SLAY'ST
SLEEPIE
SLEEPING
SLEEPY
SLEIGHT
SLIDE
SLIGHTER
SLILY
SLIPS
SLIPTE
SLOATH
SLOVENLINESSE
SLOWER
SLUBBERING
SLUTTERY
SLUTTISH
SMACK
SMACKS
SMALL-RENTED
SMALLAGE
SMALLER
SMALNESSE
SMARTS
SMIL'D
SMILING
SMIT'ST
SMOKE
SNARLES
SNATCHT
SNEAKED
SNEAKINGLY
SNOTTY
SNOWS
SNUDGE
SNUFFES
SO-E'RE
SOCIETY
SOFTENS
SOFTNESSE
SOILD
SOJOURNE
SOLACES
SOLEMNITIE
SOLLICITING
SOMETIME
SOMMER
SOMMERS
SOMTYMES
SOMWHAT
SONGS
SONNE'S
SONNES
SORBON
SORELY
SORES
SORTED
SOULD
SOULDIER'S
SOULES'
SOUNDING
SOURSE
SOUTH
SOV'RAIGNE
SOVERAIGNE
SOWED
SOWING
SOWN
SOWNE
SOWRE-SWEET
SOYLE
SPANN'D
SPANS
SPANYARD
SPARED
SPARING
SPARK
SPARKES
SPARROWS
SPATTERETH
SPEAK'ST
SPEAKER
SPEAKS
SPECIALLY
SPECKLED
SPECULATIVE
SPEEDE
SPEEDIER
SPEEDILY
SPENCER
SPENDE
SPENDER
SPENSER
SPICINESSE
SPIDER
SPILL
SPILT
SPINNE
SPINNING
SPIRITUAL
SPLENDID
SPLENDOR
SPLENDOUR
SPOILES
SPONGES
SPORTFULLY
SPORTING
SPOT
SPOTS
SPOTTED
SPOTTS
SPOUTS
SPRANG
SPREADS
SPREDD
SPREDDING
SPREEDES
SPRING-SHOWRE
SPRING'S
SPRINGING
SPRINKLED
SPROUT
SPRUSE
SPUN
SPURN
SPURRES
SQUARED
SQUATS
SQUEEZE
STAGGERER
STAID
STAIN'D
STAIR
STAIRS
STAKES
STALKING
STALKS
STARS
STARTLE
STARTS
STARVE
STATELIER

-1- (cont'd)

STATELINESSE
STATESMEN
STATICNEE
STATUTE-LAW
STAVES
STAYEST
STAYING
STAYS
STEADFAST
STEADIE
STEADY
STEER
STENCH
STEPHENS'
STEPT
STERNE
STEWARD
STICKES
STIE
STIL
STILE
STIL'D
STINGS
STIR
STIRR'D
STIRRING
STOCKD
STOLLEN
STONECUTTING
STOOL
STOOP
STOOPS
STOPPED
STOR'D
STORE
STORE-HOUSE
STORMES
STORY
STOUP
STOUT
STOUTEST
STOUTLY
STOWRE
STRAIGHT-GROWING
STRAITEN
STRAITLY
STRANGENESS
STRATAGEMS
STRAW'D
STRAWED
STREAMERS
STREET
STRENGTHE
STRENGTHENS
STRETCHETH
STRICKEN
STRICTNESS
STRIPT
STRIVES
STRIVING
STROKE
STROKING
STRONGE
STROW
STROWD
STRUCTURE
STRUGLING
STRUMPET
STUBBORNE
STUCK
STUDENT'S
STUDIOUS
STUFF'D
STUMBLER
STUMBLING-BLOCK
STUMPS
STUPIDITIES
STUPIFYING
STYLE
SUBDUED
SUBLIMATE
SUBLUNARY
SUBMISSIVE
SUBSIST
SUBSTANTIALL
SUBT'LLEST
SUBTIL
SUBTILE
SUBTILTIES
SUCCEED
SUCCEEDED
SUCCESSIVE
SUCKS
SUCKT
SUDDAIN
SUDDAINLY
SUED
SUES
SUFF'RING
SUGAR-CANE
SUGGESTIONS
SUGGESTS
SUGRING
SUITABLE
SULLIED
SULLYING
SUM
SUMM'D
SUMMER-FRUITS
SUMMON
SUNDER
SUNN'S
SUNNE-BEAM
SUNNE-SHINE
SUNNE'S
SUNSHINE
SUP
SUPERABOUNDED
SUPERFICIALL
SUPERFLUITIES
SUPERINDUCED
SUPERLIMINARE
SUPLE
SUPPER
SUPPING
SUPPLED
SUPPLICANT
SUPPLICATION
SUPPLI'D
SUPPLYED
SUPPORTED
SUPPORTING
SUPPRESSE
SURCEASE
SURE-FOOTED
SURETIES
SURGING
SURMOUNTS
SURPASSE
SURPLUS
SURPLUSAGE
SURPRISES
SURPRIZED
SURROUND
SURROUNDED
SURROUNDS
SUSPECT
SUSPICIOUS
SUSPITION
SUSTAIN
SUSTAIN'D
SUSTENTATION
SUSTINE
SUTABLY
SUTE
SUTING
SWADDLE
SWAIES
SWALLOWS
SWARMING
SWEAR
SWEARER
SWEETE
SWEETEN
SWEETNESSES
SWEETNING
SWELL'T
SWELLING
SWIM
SWIMMERS
SWING
SWOLLEN
SWORDS
SWORNE
SYCOMORE
SYLLOGISMES
SYMBOLE
SYNCERE
SYNCERITY
SYRENS
TACKS
TAINT
TAINTING
TA'NE
TAK'ST
TALENT
TALES
TALKEST
TALKS
TALLIES
TAPESTRIE
TARANTULA'S
TARES
TARRIEST
TARRY
TARRYED
TART
TASTED
TASTER
TASTS
TATTERED
TAVERN
TAYLOR
TEACHER
TEACHERS
TEACHEST
TEAMS
TEDIOUS
TEEMES
TELLES
TEMPER'ST
TEMPER'D
TEMPEST
TEMPESTUOUS
TEMPORAL
TEMPORARY
TENANT
TENDRED
TENDREST
TENTATION
TENTATIONS
TENTS
TERMES
TERRACES
TERTULLIAN
TEST
TESTER
TESTES
TESTIFIE
TESTIFYING
TESTIMONIES
THAMES
THANKE
THANKED
THANKING
THANKS-GIVING
THANKSGIVING
THARE
THAW
THAWING
THAWS
THEATERS
THEATRES
THEFT
THENCEFORTH
THEOLOGICALL
THEREINTO
THEREON
THERETO
THEREUNTO
THEREWITH
THEROF
THESSALONIANS
THICKEN
THICKEN'D
THICKER
THICKET
THIEF
THIGH
THIRDS
THIRSTED
THIRSTETH
THIRSTY
THIRTEENE
THISTLES
THOMAS
THORN
THORNE
THORNY
THOROW
THO'
THRALDOME
THREATEN
THREATENS
THREATNINGS
THRELDED
THREDS
THREEFOLD
THRIFTIE
THRIVES
THROATE
THROATS
THROBBING
THRONES
THROWES
THROWNE
THROWS
THRUSHES
THRUSTING
THUNDERS
THURSDAY
THWARTED
THYSELF
TIBER
TIBI
'TICE
TICE
TIC'D
TICING
TICKLE
TIDE
TIDES
TI'D
TIFFANY
TILLAGE
TIMELY
TIP
TIP-TOE
TIR'D
TITHING
TITLES
TOE
TOGEATHER
TOIL
TOKENS
TOLL
TOLLE
TOMBE
TOMBES
TOCKE
TOOLS
TORCH
TORE
TORMENTED
TORTUR'D
TORTURES
TORTURING
TOSSE
TOTTERING
TOUCH'D
TOWER
TOWRE
TOYES
TRACE
TRACED
TRACKER
TRADES-MAN
TRADES-MEN
TRADITION
TRADITIONS
TRAIL
TRAIN-BANDS
TRAINE
TRAMPLE
TRAMPLED
TRANQUILITIE
TRANSFIGURATION
TRANSFORM'D
TRANSFUS'D
TRANSGRESSED
TRANSGRESSIONS
TRANSLATED
TRANSLATOR
TRANSMIGRATIONS
TRANSPARENT
TRANSPLANTED
TRANSPORTING
TRANSPORTS
TRANSPOSER
TRAVEL
TRAVELLERS
TRAVELLOUR
TRAVELLS
TRAYNING
TREACH'ROUS
TREACHEROUS
TREASUR'D
TREASURED
TREASURER
TREATABLE
TREATISES
TREBLE
TREDD
TREMBLE
TREMBLINGE
TRIALL
TRIALS
TRIBUNALL
TRIBUTE
TRICK
TRICKS
TRIED
TRIFLING
TRIMM'D
TRIMMED
TRIMMER
TRIMMING
TRIP
TRIPS
TROOPING
TROOPS
TROT
TROTH
TROTTED
TROUBLEST
TROUBLING
TROUT
TRUE-LOVE-KNOT
TRUELY
TRUMP
TRUNK
TRUNKS
TRUSS'D
TRUSTETH
TRY'D
TRYALS
TULLIE
TULLY
TUMULT
TUNES
TURK
TURKIE
TURNE-COATE
TURNEST
'TWAS
TWELFTH
TWIGS
'TWILL
TWINE
TWITCH
TWO-FOLD
TWOFOLD
TY
TYES
TYPE
TYRE
U
UGLINES
UN
UN-WEELDY
UNACCESSIBLE
UNANSWERABLE
UNAWARES
UNBELIEF
UNBEND
UNBLAMEABLE
UNBRIDLED
UNBROKEN
UNBUNDLED
UNCERTAIN
UNCERTAINE
UNCERTAINTY
UNCHARITABLENESSE
UNCIRCUMCISED
UNCONQUERED
UNDECENTLY
UNDER-JAW
UNDER-WRITES
UNDERCHAW
UNDERMINES
UNDERSTANDINGS
UNDERSTANDS
UNDERTAKE

-1- (ccnt'd)

UNDERVALUE
UNDESEBV'D
UNCIVIDEC
UNDOE
UNDOES
UNDOUBTEC
UNCRESSE
UNDREST
UNDUTIFULL
UNEVEN
UNEXPECTED
UNFEYNED
UNFITTING
UNFRUITFULL
UNGODLY'S
UNGRATEFULL
UNGRATEFULNESSE
UNHALLOW'D
UNHAPPINESSE
UNHEALTHY
UNHINGE
UNIFCRMITY
UNION
UNITE
UNIVERSALL
UNIVERSE
UNIVERSITIE'S
UNKIND
UNKINDE
UNKINDNESSE
UNKNCWNE
UNLAWFUL
UNLAWFULLY
UNLAWFULNESS
UNLESS
UNLOCK
UNLOCKT
UNLOOSE
UNMEASURABLE
UNNATURAL
UNNATURALL
UNNECESSARY
UNNEIGHBCURLY
UNPENETRABLE
UNPINNE
UNPREPAREDNESSE
UNPROFITABLE
UNQUESTICNED
UNRIGHTEOUSNESSE
UNSAFELY
UNSPEAKEABLE
UNSTRUNG
UNTAMEC
UNTHANKFUL
UNTHANKFULNESS
UNTHRIFT
UNTIE
UNTIMELY
UNTOILEC
UNTUN'D
UNTWIST
UNTYING
UNUSEC
UNUSEFUL
UNUSEFULL
UNUSUALL
UNWARY
UNWORTHINESSE
UPBRAICEC
UPPER
UPRIGHT
UPWARCS
URGE
URGES
USEFULNESSE
USES
USEST
USHER
USHER'D
USURER
USURER'S
USURPING
USURES
VACATION
VADEC
VAIL
VAIL'D
VAINLY
VALDESSC'S
VALERIAN
VALES
VALLEYS
VALUEC
VAN
VANISHT
VANTING
VAPCURS
VARIANCE
VARIETIE
VARIOUSLY
VAULT
VEAL
VENERATE
VENGEANCE
VENCME
VENTILATE
VENTROUS
VENUS
VENUS'
VERCICT
VERGE
VERSED
VERSER
VERSES
VERSING
VERTUE'S
VERTUOUSLY
VESSELLS
VEX
VEX'D
VEXATICNS
VEXEC
VEYWE
VICEGERENT
VICIOUS
VICT'RIES
VIED
VIES
VIGILANT
VIGOUR
VILIFIED
VILLAGES
VILLANY
VINE-GARCEN
VINEYARC
VINIGER
VINTAGE
VIOL
VICLENT
VIRGILL
VIRGIN-BEC
VIRGINS
VISIBLY
VISIONS
VISITATICN
VISITATIONS
VISITE
VISITS
VIZARCS
VIZARS
VOGUE
VOLUMES
VCLUNTARY
VCUCHSAF'C
VOUCHSAFETH
VCYC
VYE
VYING
VYSIT
WAGGCNERS
WAIGHES
WAIGHS
WAITING
WAK'D
WAKING
WALKE
WALK'C
WALKES
WALKETH
WALKT
WALLET
WALLETS
WALLETT
WALLCW
WALLOWING
WALS
WANDER
WANDERER
WANDRINGS
WANTE
WANTEC
WANTONLY
WARBLINGE
WARCENS'
WARILY
WARLIKE
WARMEST
WARN'D
WARNING
WARRIER
WARRS
WARS
WARY
WASHES
WASHETH
WASTEFULL
WASTERS
WATCHINGS
WATER-COURSE
WATER'S
WATRED
WATRING
WATRY
WAVE
WAVERING
WAVING
WAXE
WAYLE
WEAKLY
WEAKNESSES
WEALTHS
WEAPCNS
WEARE
WEARER
WEARIED
WEATHERS
WEAVE
WEBBE
WEEK-CAYES
WEEKCAYS
WEEKS
WEELDY
WEENING
WEIGHETH
WEIGHING
WEIGHS
WELCCMES
WELDOING
WELL-BREC
WELL-CONTENTED
WELL-SET
WELTRING
WENCH
WENTST
WET
WHATSOE'RE
WHEARE
WHEEL'D
WHEELING
WHEN-EVER
WHENSCEVER
WHER
WHER-EVER
WHEREINTO
WHERESOE'RE
WHERIN
WHEROF
WHERSCEVER
WHETT
WHEY
WHIP
WHIPPING
WHIPS
WHIRLE
WHIRLWINDE
WHISPRING
WHISTLED
WHIT
WHIT-MEATS
WHITSUNDAY
WHITSUNTIDE
WHOE
WHOLSOME
WHOLY
WHORE
WHOSCEVER
WICKED'S
WICKEDNESSES
WILD-FOULE
WILDE-FIRE
WILDELY
WILDLY
WILES
WILFULL
'LE
'L
WILLOWES
WIMBLE
WIND-MILL
WIND'S
WINDOW-SCNGS
WINE-BREC
WINE-CCUNSELS
WINE-SPRUNG
WINGED
WING'C
WINGES
WINKS
WINN
WINS
WINTER'S
WINTERS
WIPES
WIS
WISE-MEN
WISHEC
WISHINGS
WISHLY
WISHT
WITCHCRAFTS
WITCHES
WITHDRAWS
WITHER
WITHHCLD
WITHSTANCING
WITNESS
WITT
WIVES
WCLD
WCLVES
WOMAN-KINDE
WOMAN'S
WCN
WCNDER-WCRKING
WCNDER'S
WONDERFULLY
WCNDRETH
WCNDRCUSLY
WONTED
WCCDEN
WOODENOTH'S
WOOING
WORDLY
WORKEMEN
WORKMAN'S
WORKY
WORKY-DAIES
WORLC-TRANSPOSING
WORMWOOD
WORSHIPPETH
WORSHIPPING
WORT
WOT
WOU'C
WCULC'ST
WOUNDED
WCUNCEST
WOUNDETH
WCUNCING
WRANGLE
WRANGLERS
WRASTLING
WRATHFULL
WREATHED
WRENCH
WRESTLE
WRETCHEDLY
WRETCHEDNESSE
WRETCHES
WRING
WRINGING
WRINGS
WRITER
WRITERS
WRITT
WRCNG'D
WRCT
YEAR'S
YEARELY
YEELDED
YEELCING
YEERES
YEERS
YERRCW
YESTERDAY
YF
YIELD
YCUNGEST
YOUR'S
YOUTHFULL
YOUTHS
YRCN
ZELE
ZCNE

1781 A
6 ABIDE
17 AELE
6 ABODE
40 ABCUT
48 ABOVE
11 ABFOAD
6 ABUSE
30 ACCCFDING
12 ACCORDINGLY
11 ACCCUNT
8 ACT
8 ACTICN
25 ACTICNS
9 ACTS
8 ADDED
12 ADMIRABLE
7 ADCRE
16 ADVANTAGE
9 ADVISE
9 AFFAIRS
7 AFFECTICNS
9 AFFLICTED
14 AFFLICTICN
13 AFFLICTICNS
7 AFFORD
86 AFTER
9 AFTERWARDS
27 AGAIN
6 AGAINE
50 AGAINST
35 AGE
12 AGFEE
6 AGREEABLE
13 AH
11 AIM
6 AIRE
18 ALAS
855 AII
11 ALLOW
8 AIIOWS
9 ALMES
8 ALMIGHTIE
6 ALMIGHTY
7 ALMOST
59 ALCNE
8 ALREADY
134 AISO
7 ALTAR
25 AITHCUGH
10 ALWAIES
7 ALWAYES
104 AM
8 AMISSE
28 AMONG
236 AN
17 ANCIENT
166 &
3568 AND
12 ANGELS
8 ANGER
76 ANCTHER
22 ANCTHER'S
27 ANSWER
6 ANSWERS
172 ANY
17 APPEARE
9 APPETITE
8 APPLE
8 APPLYING
6 APT
602 ARE
13 ARISE
6 ARK
7 ARMS
126 ART
11 ARTS
794 AS
6 ASHAMED
6 ASIDE
8 ASK
6 ASKES
323 AT
10 ATTEND
15 AUTHCRITY
6 AUTHOUR
7 AWAKE
81 AWAY

16 BACK
8 BAD
12 BAPTISME
754 BE
8 BEAMS
23 BEAR
6 BEARS
12 BEAST
16 BEASTS
18 BEAUTIE
9 BEAUTY
7 BECAME
101 BECAUSE
7 BECCME
7 BECOMES
24 BED
66 BEE
30 BEEN
115 BEFORE
21 BEGAN
8 BEGINNING
8 BEGINS
12 BEHAVIOUR
6 BEHIND
11 BEHINDE
10 BEHCLD
137 BEING
12 BELEEVE
7 BELL
12 BELOW
12 BENEFIT
9 BENT
38 BESIDES
75 BEST
7 BETIMES
93 BETTER
12 BETWEEN
6 BETWIXT
6 BEWARE
14 BEYCND
11 BID
9 BIRD
8 BIRDS
9 BIRTH
6 BITE
12 BITTER
6 BLESS
13 BLESSE
31 BLESSED
28 BLESSING
19 BLESSINGS
8 BLEST
7 BLINDE
10 BLISSE
8 BLOOD
37 BLCUD
6 BLCUDIE
14 BLCW
7 BLCWN
6 BOARD
21 BODIE
9 BODIES
31 BODY
8 BOLD
6 BOLDNESS
9 BCNE
13 BCNES
30 BOCK
20 BOCKS
6 BORE
8 BORN
6 BORNE
9 BOSCME
227 BCTH
11 BOUND
12 BOUNDS
21 BOW
12 BOX
9 BRAIN
28 BRAVE
29 BREAD
18 BREAK
7 BREAKS
24 BREAST
21 BREATH
9 BRED
6 BRETHREN
17 BRIGHT
7 BRIGHTNESSE
42 BRING
6 BRINGING
13 BRINGS
15 BROKEN
24 BROTHER
33 BROUGHT
7 BUILD
9 BUILDING
14 BUILT
9 BURDEN
9 BURN
6 BURTHEN
16 BUSIE
17 BUSINESSE
937 BUT
8 BUY
488 BY

42 CALL
7 CALLED
18 CALLING
10 CALLS
40 CAME
197 CAN
103 CANNOT
23 CANST
48 CARE
11 CARRY
18 CASE
12 CASES
16 CAST
8 CATCH
7 CATECHISME
11 CATECHIZING
22 CAUSE
13 CEASE
6 CERTAINLY
8 CHAIR
9 CHANCE
15 CHANGE
9 CHAPTER
6 CHARGE
6 CHARITABLE
29 CHARITY
6 CHEAP
9 CHEER
6 CHEST
6 CHIEF
7 CHIEFLY
21 CHILD
6 CHILDE
36 CHILDREN
6 CHCICE
7 CHOOSE
45 CHRIST
13 CHRIST'S
24 CHRISTIAN
7 CHRISTIANS
91 CHURCH
6 CHURCH-WARDENS
7 CHURCHE'S
7 CHUSE
9 CLAY
13 CLEAN
16 CLEARE
16 CLOSE
7 CLCTH
11 CLOTHES
9 CLOUDS
6 COAT
28 COLD
6 COLLEGE
7 COLOUR
125 COME
44 CCMES
26 CCMFORT
8 CCMFORTS
9 CCMING
13 COMMAND
6 CCMMANDS
7 COMMIT
38 CCMMCN
7 COMMCN-WEALTH
9 CCMMUNICN
8 COMPANIE
19 CCMPANY
10 CCMPARE
13 CCNCERNING
8 CCNCLUDE
8 CONDITICN
8 CCNFESSE
10 CONFESSICN
7 CCNFIDENCE
7 CCNQUEST
13 CONSCIENCE
16 CCNSIDER
21 CONSIDERATION
7 CCNSIDERED
12 CONSIDERING
7 CCNSIDERS
6 CONSISTS
9 CCNSTANT
6 CONSUME
9 CCNTEMPT
11 CCNTENT
9 CCNTINUALLY
10 CCNTINUE
6 CONTINUED
6 CCNTRARY
8 CONTROLL
11 CCNVERSATICN
9 CONVERT
10 CCNVEY
8 COOL
7 CORINTHIANS
12 CORN
9 CCRNE
9 CORNER
16 COST
83 CCULD
6 COULDST
8 CCUNSELL
8 COUNSELS
6 CCUNT
59 COUNTREY
10 CCUNTRY
24 COURSE
21 CCURT
11 COURTESIE
7 COVETCUS
11 CREATICN
7 CREATURE
13 CREATURES
7 CREDIT
7 CREEP
17 CRIE
6 CRIMES
26 CROSSE
16 CRCWN
6 CRY
7 CRYING
8 CUNNING
7 CUP
14 CURE
10 CURED
7 CURES
6 CURING
15 CURICUS
10 CUSTCME
10 CUT

13 DAILY
6 DAINTIES
12 DANGER
14 DANVERS
16 DARE
21 DARK
9 DARKNESSE
9 DAVID
163 DAY
34 DAYES
6 DAYS
32 DEAD
13 DEAR
49 DEARE
91 DEATH
8 DEATH'S
7 DEATHS
14 DEBT
13 DECAY
6 DECEIT
6 DECEIVE
11 DEED
13 DEEDS
8 DEEP
6 DEERE
9 DEGREE
26 DELIGHT
17 DELIGHTS
9 DELIVER
6 DENIE
8 DEPART
7 DEPEND

8 DESERT
7 DESIGNE
24 DESIRE
12 DESIRES
7 DESPISE
12 DESTROY
7 DEVOTION
10 DEW
224 DID
44 DIDST
41 DIE
6 DI'D
9 DIES
13 DIET
6 DIGESTED
6 DIGNITY
6 DILIGENCE
7 DILIGENT
7 DILIGENTLY
20 DISCOURSE
10 DISCOURSES
10 DISCOVER
7 DISCRETION
7 DISEASE
19 DISEASES
6 DISH
9 DISORDERLY
10 DISPOSITION
6 DISTANCE
12 DIVERS
24 DIVINE
13 DIVINITY
249 DO
18 DOCTRINE
75 DOE
18 DOES
13 DOG
16 DOING
74 DONE
29 DOORE
10 DOORES
73 DOST
238 DOTH
15 DOUBLE
8 DOUBT
7 DOUBTLESSE
11 DOVE
42 DOWN
6 DOWNE
13 DRAW
6 DRAWES
8 DRESSE
17 DREST
8 DRIE
28 DRINK
7 DRINKE
12 DROP
7 DROPS
12 DRY
19 DUE
7 DULL
45 DUST
16 DUTIES
22 DUTY
19 DWELL
6 DY
6 DYING

58 EACH
10 EARE
21 EARES
7 EARNEST
72 EARTH
9 EARTHLY
14 EASE
17 EASIE
16 EASILY
11 EAST
31 EAT
6 EATE
8 EATES
15 EATING
7 EATS
12 ECHO
9 EFFECT
10 EGYPT
8 EIES
99 EITHER
8 ELEMENTS
26 ELSE
7 EMPIRE
7 EMPTY
51 END
10 ENEMIES
9 ENEMY
7 ENGLAND
7 ENJOY
25 ENOUGH
17 ENTER
6 EQUALL
8 ERE
34 ESPECIALLY
15 ESTATE
7 ESTEEM
18 &C
9 ETERNALL
51 EV'N
87 EVEN
178 EVER
6 EV'RY
27 EV'RY
86 EVERY
13 EVIDENT
14 EVILL
7 EXACT
10 EXAMPLE
6 EXCEED
13 EXCEEDING
6 EXCELLENT
21 EXCEPT
6 EXPECT
6 EXPECTED
13 EXPERIENCE
11 EXPRESSE
31 EYE
71 EYES

40 FACE
9 FAIL
14 FAIN
6 FAINT
26 FAIR
19 FAIRE
33 FAITH
43 FALL
9 FALLS
9 FALSE
17 FAME
17 FAMILY
11 FAR
33 FARRE
12 FASHION
19 FAST
14 FASTING
6 FAT
26 FATHER
10 FATHER'S
12 FATHERS
20 FAULT
18 FAULTS
18 FAVOUR
12 FAVOURS
46 FEAR
15 FEARE
11 FEARES
18 FEARS
20 FEAST
15 FEED
16 FEEL
14 FEET
11 FELL
14 FEW
9 FIGHT
16 FILL
6 FILLS
24 FIND
37 FINDE
16 FINDES
15 FINDS
31 FINE
55 FIRE
139 FIRST
15 FISH
39 FIT
16 FIVE
7 FLAME
7 FLAT
6 FLED
53 FLESH
27 FLIE
9 FLIES
8 FLIGHT
20 FLOCK
10 FLOCKE
11 FLOW
12 FLOWER
14 FLOWERS
7 FLY
20 FOES
7 FOLD
14 FOLLOW
15 FOLLY
19 FOOD
23 FOOLE
14 FOOLES
22 FOOLISH
21 FOOT
924 FOR
6 FORBID
13 FORCE
11 FORMER
6 FORSAKE
18 FORTH
10 FORTUNE
16 FOUL
9 FOULE
43 FOUND
6 FOURE
6 FOURTHLY
10 FOX
13 FRAME
27 FREE
8 FRESH
50 FRIEND
23 FRIENDS
274 FROM
7 FROSTS
27 FRUIT
11 FRUITFULL
66 FULL
10 FULLY
17 FURTHER
16 FUTURE

16 GAIN
10 GAINE
7 GAINES
7 GAINS
8 GAME
19 GARDEN
8 GARDENS
6 GARLAND
32 GAVE
7 GAY
14 GENERALL
7 GENERALLY
17 GENTLE
26 GEORGE
38 GET
9 GETS
17 GIFT
14 GIFTS
98 GIVE
10 GIV'N
27 GIVEN
37 GIVES
25 GIVING
13 GLAD
9 GLADLY
19 GLASSE
32 GLORIE
25 GLORIOUS
18 GLORY
83 GO
391 GOD
64 GOD'S
15 GODLY
27 GOE
37 GOES
6 GOING
33 GOLD
26 GONE
274 GOOD
6 GOODNESSE
12 GOODS
11 GOSPEL
8 GOSPELL
21 GOT
64 GRACE
11 GRACIOUS
7 GRASSE
27 GRAVE
199 GREAT
18 GREATER
11 GREATEST
14 GREECE
16 GREW
109 GRIEF
10 GRIEFE
18 GRIEFS
10 GRIEVE
7 GRONE
8 GRONES
35 GROUND
9 GROUNDS
39 GROW
7 GROWN
16 GROWS
7 GUEST
10 GUIDE

11 H
139 HAD
12 HADST
7 HAIR
13 HALF
16 HALFE
74 HAND
61 HANDS
7 HANG
10 HAPPIE
6 HAPPINESSE
9 HAPPY
30 HARD
8 HARDLY
10 HART
8 HARVEST
13 HAS
86 HAST
7 HASTE
6 HATE
313 HATH
378 HAVE
46 HAVING
1095 HE
62 HEAD
43 HEALTH
14 HEAR
26 HEARD
30 HEARE
151 HEART
43 HEARTS
12 HEAT
8 HEAV'NLY
38 HEAV'N
41 HEAVEN
9 HEAVENLY
180 HEE
17 HEED
27 HELL
32 HELP
6 HELPE
6 HENCE
8 HENRY
115 HER
30 HERBERT
12 HERBS
81 HERE
8 HEREAFTER
8 HIDE
29 HIGH
17 HIGHER
12 HIGHEST
10 HILL
315 HIM
83 HIMSELF
55 HIMSELFE
6 HINDER
990 HIS
6 HIT
11 HITHER
32 HOLD
9 HOLDS
6 HOLINESSE
68 HOLY
29 HOME
12 HONEST
39 HONOUR
9 HONY
33 HOPE

13 HOPES
33 HORSE
27 HOURE
6 HOURES
96 HOUSE
11 HOUSES
137 HOW
7 HOWEVER
18 HUMBLE
6 HUMILITIE
11 HUMOURS
24 HUNDRED
26 HURT
6 HURTFULL
6 HUSBAND
6 HYMNE

1221 I
11 IDLE
473 IF
7 IGNORANT
101 ILL
7 IMPART
8 IMPLOYMENT
6 IMPROVE
1512 IN
10 INCREASE
6 INCREASED
25 INDEED
9 INFINITE
8 INSTANTLY
8 INTEMPERANCE
134 INTO
6 INVADE
6 INVENTION
9 INWARD
69 'S
1382 IS
7 ISSUE
923 IT
9 ITS

9 JEST
7 JESU
7 JESUS
7 JEWES
8 JEWS
13 JOHN
14 JOURNEY
63 JOY
36 JOYES
6 JOYN
20 JUDGE
11 JUDGEMENT
9 JUDGMENT
34 JUST
19 JUSTICE
11 JUSTLY

41 KEEP
7 KEEPE
10 KEEPES
6 KEEPING
14 KEEPS
25 KEPT
10 KEY
10 KILL
9 KIND
26 KINDE
7 KINDRED
51 KING
13 KINGDOME
9 KINGS
6 KNEEL
8 KNEES
20 KNEW
104 KNOW
21 KNOWES
21 KNOWING
12 KNOWLEDG
19 KNOWLEDGE
14 KNOWN
26 KNOWS

27 LABOUR
7 LABOURS
6 LADEN
6 LADY
7 LAID
19 LAND
15 LANGUAGE
9 LARGE
28 LAST
7 LASTLY
18 LATE
10 LAUGH
43 LAW
12 LAWS
27 LAY
8 LAYS
8 LEADE
6 LEADS
9 LEARN
17 LEARNED
12 LEARNING
45 LEAST
39 LEAVE
23 LEAVES
9 LEAVING
6 LED
21 LEFT
6 LEISURE
27 LENGTH
10 LENT
53 LESSE
32 LEST
168 LET
8 LETS
9 LETT
21 LETTER
9 LETTERS
6 LETTING
7 LIBERALL
7 LIBERTY
20 LIE
27 LIES
158 LIFE
69 LIGHT
8 LIGHTS
164 LIKE
7 LIKEWISE
6 LINE
13 LINES
6 LIST
90 LITTLE
78 LIVE
11 LIV'D
7 LIVED
32 LIVES
12 LIVING
7 LOCK
9 LODGING
7 LONDON
75 LONG
42 LOOK
11 LOOKE
6 LOOKES
13 LOOKS
18 LOOSE
6 LOOSETH
190 LORD
19 LOSE
18 LOSSE
48 LOST
209 LOVE
11 LOVES
9 LOVING
16 LOW
6 LOWER
14 LUST
7 LUSTS
8 LUTE
8 LYES
6 LYON

6 MADAM
120 MADE
8 MAJESTY
212 MAKE
97 MAKES
32 MAKING
7 MALICE
250 MAN
35 MAN'S
7 MANIFEST
8 MANNER
109 MANY
23 MARK
8 MARKET
6 MARKS
8 MARRY
7 MARY
38 MASTER
8 MASTERS
12 MATTER
8 MATTHEW
321 MAY
12 MAYST
505 ME
16 MEAN
12 MEANING
41 MEANS
6 MEANT
31 MEASURE
36 MEAT
9 MEATS
33 MEE
25 MEET
8 MEETS
8 MELT
109 MEN
20 MEN'S
17 MEND
6 MERCIES
9 MERCY
12 MIDST
68 MIGHT
7 MIGHTIE
6 MIGHTY
14 MIND
42 MINDE
157 MINE
7 MINISTER
23 MIRTH
6 MODERATE
6 MOMENT
17 MONEY
19 MONY
339 MORE
21 MORNING
10 MORTALL
8 MORTIFICATION
132 MOST
26 MOTHER
7 MOTION
8 MOTIONS
6 MOUSE
19 MOUTH
25 MOVE
19 MR
13 MRS
195 MUCH
29 MUSICK
135 MUST
1011 MY

42 NAME
7 NAMES
9 NATION
6 NATIONS
10 NATURALL
39 NATURE
7 NATURES
21 NAY
10 NEARE
17 NECESSARY
24 NEED
7 NEEDE
10 NEEDES
29 NEEDS
8 NEGLECT
15 NEIGHBOUR
10 NEIGHBOURS
71 NEITHER
108 NEVER
7 NEVERTHELESSE
42 NEW
6 NEWES
20 NEXT
48 NIGHT
329 NO
17 NOBLE
7 NOISE
78 NONE
102 NOR
1104 NOT
7 NOTE
107 NOTHING
11 NOUGHT
169 NOW

9 OBEDIENCE
7 OBJECT
10 OBLIGATION
7 OBSERVABLE
10 OBSERVATION
6 OBSERVE
12 OBSERVED
29 OCCASION
9 OCCASIONS
2131 OF
25 OFF
7 OFFER
6 OFFICE
15 OFT
33 OFTEN
157 O
25 OH
95 OLD
307 ON
65 ONCE
357 ONE
9 ONE'S
112 ONELY
11 ONES
53 ONLY
32 OPEN
10 OPINION
7 OPPOSE
625 OR
27 ORDER
9 ORDERLY
7 ORDINARY
163 OTHER
57 OTHERS
16 OTHERS'
15 OTHERWISE
49 OUGHT
239 OUR
9 OURS
176 OUT
7 OUTLANDISH
9 OUTWARD
29 OVER
6 OWE
100 OWN
33 OWNE

19 PAIN
14 PAINS
6 PAPER
15 PARADISE
17 PARDON
9 PARENTS
43 PARISH
110 PARSON
20 PARSON'S
66 PART
11 PARTICULAR
11 PARTICULARLY
14 PARTS
31 PASSE
8 PASSETH
8 PASSING
17 PASSION
13 PAST
13 PATIENCE
6 PATIENT
11 PAUL
17 PAY
55 PEACE
48 PEOPLE
6 PERCEIVE
17 PERFECT
8 PERFECTION
14 PERHAPS
6 PERISH
22 PERSON
10 PERSONS
13 PETER
6 PHILOSOPHY
14 PHYSICIAN
6 PHYSICIANS
10 PHYSICK
8 PHYSITIAN
6 PICK

8 PIECE
7 PIERCE
8 PIETY
6 PINE
7 PIOUS
6 PITIE
93 PLACE
12 PLACES
10 PLAIN
9 PLAINLY
7 PLANT
19 PLAY
7 PLEASANT
14 PLEASE
11 PLEASED
9 PLEASETH
12 PLEASING
45 PLEASURE
17 PLEASURES
24 POINT
11 POINTS
33 POOR
76 POORE
8 PORTION
7 POSIE
8 POSSESSION
6 POSSIBLE
8 POT
20 POUND
6 POUNDS
6 POVERTIE
79 POWER
10 POWERS
7 PRACTICE
77 PRAISE
8 PRAISES
27 PRAY
29 PRAYER
32 PRAYERS
7 PRAYING
8 PREACHETH
10 PREACHING
6 PREPARE
10 PRESENCE
36 PRESENT
9 PRESENTLY
8 PRESENTS
12 PRESERVE
6 PRESSE
9 PRESUME
7 PREVENT
7 PREY
9 PRICE
12 PRIDE
9 PRIEST
6 PRINCE
9 PRINCES
6 PRISON
12 PRIVATE
7 PROCEED
8 PROFIT
13 PROMISES
11 PROPORTION
8 PROUD
19 PROVE
9 PROVIDENCE
6 PROVIDES
12 PSALM
16 PUBLICK
9 PULL
9 PUNISH
14 PUNISHMENT
9 PURCHASE
14 PURE
7 PURPOSE
9 PURSE
6 PURSUE
42 PUT
11 PUTS

8 QUANTITIE
6 QUENCH
6 QUESTION
9 QUESTIONS
17 QUICK
20 QUICKLY
10 QUIET
7 QUITE

6 RAGE
22 RAISE
10 RARE
53 RATHER
12 REACH
21 READ
6 READE
16 READING
18 READY
37 REASON
15 RECEIVE
9 RECEIVED
10 REFUSE
15 REGARD
9 REJOYCE
11 RELIEF
26 RELIGION
10 RELIGIOUS
6 REMEDY
12 REMEMBER
13 REMOVE
10 RENT
7 REPAIR
12 REPENTANCE
8 REPROVE
11 REQUEST
11 REQUIRES
9 RESOLVED
6 RESPECT
47 REST
12 RESTORE
7 RETURN
13 REVERENCE
9 REVEREND
12 REWARD
35 RICH
9 RICHES
7 RIDE
32 RIGHT
6 RIGHTEOUS
10 RING
34 RISE
6 RISETH
7 RIVER
8 RIVERS
11 ROCK
11 ROD
9 ROMANS
13 ROME
18 ROOM
8 ROOT
14 ROSE
18 ROUND
39 RULE
15 RULES
7 RUN
19 RUNNE
7 RYME

7 SACKE
14 SACRED
11 SACRIFICE
18 SAD
9 SAFE
33 SAID
7 SAIES
16 SAINT
12 SAINTS
6 SAITH
16 SAKE
7 SALT
10 SALVATION
38 SAME
25 SAVE
21 SAVIOUR
12 SAVIOUR'S
16 SAW
90 SAY
19 SAYES
9 SAYING
7 SAYS
7 SCANDALL
6 SCARCE
10 SCORE
34 SCRIPTURE
19 SCRIPTURES
22 SEA
9 SEARCH
10 SEASON
6 SEASONS
16 SECOND
29 SECONDLY
6 SECRET
7 SECURE
78 SEE
28 SEEK
8 SEEM
6 SEEME
11 SEEMS
7 SEEN
23 SEES
10 SELDOME
81 SELF
30 SELFE
11 SELL
8 SELVES
14 SEND
10 SENDS
18 SENSE
20 SENT
14 SERMON
14 SERMONS
37 SERVANT
28 SERVANTS
43 SERVE
6 SERVED
7 SERVES
29 SERVICE
38 SET
10 SETS
10 SETTING
6 SEV'RALL
6 SEVERALL
6 SHADE
7 SHAKE
10 SHAL
242 SHALL
25 SHALT
29 SHAME
11 SHARE
6 SHARP
48 SHE
12 SHEE
7 SHEEP
7 SHEPHERD
17 SHEW
7 SHEWES
7 SHEWING
18 SHILLINGS
24 SHINE
7 SHIP
7 SHOOT
7 SHOP
24 SHORT
136 SHOULD
38 SHOW
12 SHOWS
8 SHUT
29 SICK
13 SICKNESSE
28 SIDE
7 SIDES
15 SIGH
9 SIGHS
23 SIGHT
6 SILENCE
6 SILENT
7 SILLY
21 SIN
103 SINCE
32 SING
9 SINGLE
6 SINGULAR
12 SINN
97 SINNE
39 SINNES
14 SINS
38 SIR
10 SISTER
17 SIT
6 SITS
6 SIX
12 SKIE
19 SKILL
6 SKY
24 SLEEP
9 SLIGHT
8 SLOW
28 SMALL
7 SMART
10 SMELL
6 SMOOTH
7 SNOW
553 SO
9 SOLD
179 SOME
13 SOMETHING
48 SOMETIMES
10 SOMEWHAT
7 SOMTIMES
8 SON
7 SONG
18 SONNE
15 SOON
8 SOONER
8 SORE
17 SORROW
12 SORROWS
13 SORT
9 SORTS
15 SOUGHT
84 SOUL
7 SOULDIERS
24 SOULE
13 SOULS
13 SOUND
10 SOWRE
6 SPACE
15 SPARE
23 SPEAK
8 SPEAKE
10 SPEAKES
6 SPEAKING
6 SPECIALL
13 SPEECH
7 SPELL
12 SPEND
7 SPENDS
11 SPENT
11 SPHERE
6 SPHERES
35 SPIRIT
7 SPIRITS
13 SPIRITUALL
6 SPIT
7 SPOKEN
10 SPORT
11 SPREAD
19 SPRING
7 SPRINGS
8 ST
10 STAFFE
26 STAND
7 STANDING
12 STANDS
14 STARRE
27 STARRES
35 STATE
38 STAY
8 STEAD
7 STEAL
10 STEP
134 STILL
6 STIRRE
12 STOCK
10 STOMACK
21 STONE
13 STONES
32 STORE
12 STORIE
20 STRAIGHT
16 STRANGE
7 STRAW
12 STREAMS
21 STRENGTH
6 STRICT
7 STRIFE
8 STRIKE
8 STRIVE
21 STRONG
7 STUDY
11 STUFFE
6 SUBJECT
9 SUCCESS
139 SUCH
7 SUDDENLY
12 SUFFER
6 SUFFERS
9 SUIT
6 SUMME
6 SUMMER
12 SUNDAY

41 SUNNE
6 SUPEBSTITICN
42 SURE
21 SUBELY
6 SWAY
61 SWEET
13 SWEETLY
13 SWEETNESSE
8 SWEETS
14 SWCRD

16 TABLE
128 TAKE
33 TAKEN
29 TAKES
16 TAKING
6 TAIK
7 TALKE
9 TAME
20 TASTE
14 TAUGHT
19 TEACH
9 TEACHETH
8 TEACHING
9 TEARES
44 TEARS
22 TELL
17 TEMPER
20 TEMPERANCE
10 TEMPERATE
14 TEMPLE
9 TEMPTATICNS
20 TEN
11 TENDER
13 TEXT
6 THANK
7 THANKS
1575 THAT
70 TH'
3961 THE
384 THEE
444 THEIR
10 THEIRS
408 THEM
48 THEMSELVES
494 THEN
16 THENCE
348 THERE
7 THEREBY
67 THEBEFCBE
20 THEREIN
21 THEREOF
12 THERFOBE
161 THESE
551 THEY
77 THINE
108 THING
208 THINGS
46 THINK
8 THINKE
10 THINKES
6 THINKING
18 THINKS
16 THIRD
17 THIRDLY
462 THIS
14 THITHEB
7 THORNS
182 THCSE
538 THOU
127 THCUGH
29 THOUGHT
41 THCUGHTS
7 THOUSAND
6 THCUSANDS
6 THRALL
6 THREAD
6 THREATNED
39 THREE
6 THRICE
13 THBCNE
30 THROUGH
18 THBCW
7 THUNDER
53 THUS
768 THY
71 TILL
103 TIME
34 TIMES
14 'TIS
11 TITLE
2512 TO
28 TOGETHER
16 TOLD
24 TONGUE
75 TOO
27 TOCK
13 TOUCH
6 TOUCHING
15 TOWARDS
13 TRADE
8 TREAD
22 TREASURE
23 TREE
10 TREES
6 TRINITY
13 TRCUBLE
14 TRCUBLED
6 TRCUBLES
64 TRUE
16 TRULY
20 TRUST
6 TRUSTS
48 TRUTH
7 TRUTHS
6 TRY
8 TUNE
37 TURN
13 TURNE
10 TURNES
8 TURNING
6 TWELVE
7 TWENTIE
11 TWENTY
17 TWICE
6 TWIST
109 TWO

24 UNDER
13 UNDERSTAND
6 UNDERSTANDING
12 UNDERSTOOD
13 UNLESSE
20 UNTILL
105 UNTO
112 UP
88 UPCN
156 US
92 USE
15 USED
8 USEFULL
16 USETH
7 UTMOST

16 VAIN
6 VEIN
16 VERSE
31 VERTUE
19 VERTUES
6 VERTUOUS
76 VERY
8 VESSELS
6 VICE
9 VICES
6 VICTORIE
7 VIEW
9 VINE
6 VOICE

8 WAGES
46 WANT
6 WANTING
12 WANTS
6 WARDENS
9 WARM
7 WARME
14 WARRE
301 WAS
8 WASH
9 WAST
8 WATCH
25 WATER
14 WATERS
6 WAVES
133 WAY
33 WAYES
210 WE
10 WEAK
28 WEALTH
11 WEAR
6 WEARS
8 WEARY
7 WEATHER
32 WEE
14 WEEK
15 WEEP
7 WEEPE
6 WEIGH
7 WEIGHT
6 WEL
13 WELCOME
154 WELL
16 WENT
140 WERE
9 WERT
6 WEST
6 WESTWARD
336 WHAT
413 WHEN
12 WHENCE
176 WHERE
21 WHEREAS
42 WHEREFORE
25 WHEREIN
17 WHEREOF
13 WHEREWITH
36 WHETHER
573 WHICH
76 WHILE
9 WHITE
11 WHITHER
380 WHO
51 WHCLE
6 WHOLLY
79 WHCM
81 WHOSE
29 WHY
14 WICKED
8 WIDE
25 WIFE
6 'LE
302 WILL
6 WILLING
24 WILT
24 WINDE
19 WINDES
36 WINE
11 WING
11 WINGS
10 WINTER
11 WISDCME
37 WISE
17 WISH
43 WIT
657 WITH
43 WITHIN
104 WITHCUT
11 WO
6 WCE
9 WOLFE
11 WCMAN
11 WOMEN
10 WCNDER
8 WCNDERS
6 WCNDRCUS
12 WOOD
6 WCCDS
52 WORD
53 WORDS
52 WORK
7 WCRKE
16 WORKING
23 WCRKS
104 WORLD
7 WCRLD'S
9 WORLDLY
8 WCRM
13 WORSE
7 WCRST
15 WORTH
6 WCRTHY
183 WOULD
13 WCULDST
13 WOUND
11 WCUNDS
12 WRATH
11 WRIT
30 WRITE
6 WRITES
10 WRITTEN
6 WRCNG
8 WROTE
6 WRCUGHT

39 YE
13 YEA
24 YEARE
30 YEARES
324 YET
300 YOU
26 YOUNG
199 YOUR
10 YOURS
14 YOUTH

-344-
CUE

-243-
&

-236-
IN

-171-
NON

-144-
CUM

-143-
VT

-135-
EST

-118-
AD

-116-
ET

-100-
QUAM

-99-
QUI
SI
TE

-79-
TIBI

-76-
TU

-74-
NOS

-68-
DE

-67-
ATQUE
QUAE

-62-
QUOD

-60-
ETIAM

-57-
AUT
QUO

-56-
SIC

-53-
QUID
SED

-52-
NOBIS

-48-
HOC
NEC
NUNC

-44-
MIHI
O

-43-
IAM

-42-
SIT

-41-
OMNES

-40-
HAEC
PER
VEL

-39-
NE

-37-
ENIM
IPSE
TAMEN

-36-
SUNT
TUA

-35-
A
DUM
EX
SE

-34-
QUIN

-33-
QUARE
TAM

-32-
ESSE

-31-
NEQUE

-29-
OMNIA
TANTUM
VBI

-28-
AC
OLIM

-27-
E
ES
HIC
QUA

-26-
ME
NOSTRA
QUIS

-25-
CUR

-24-
NIHIL

-23-
RES
TUUM

-22-
ADEO

-21-
AT
PRO
SINE
TUI
TUIS
VOS

-20-
AB
QUAS

-19-
AMOR
CUI
EGO
HAUD
INTER
QUASI
SIBI
TOT
VERO

-18-
MEA
MINUS
NOSTER
QUIBUS
QUIDEM
TANDEM
TANQUAM
TUAE
TUO

-17-
MATER
QUEM
QUOS
SEMPER
SOLA
VITA
VITAM

-16-
ILLA
IPSA
UE

-15-
APUD
ID
LICET
MUNDI
NAM
NOSTRAE
NULLA
PRINCEPS
PRINCIPIS
SCILICET
SUO

-14-
CAPUT
CHRISTE
DOMINE
MAGIS
NISI
PLUS
TUAS

-13-
CUIUS
DEUS
ERIT
IPSI
NEMPE
NOSTRO
OS
POTEST
SANGUINE
SINT
SOLUM
SUAM
SUB
VESTRA

-12-
ACADEMIAE
AN
CERTE
HINC
HOMINUM
HUNC
POST
QUANTO
TANTA
TUM
VNA
VOBIS

-11-
EO
HANC
IMO
INDE
ITA
ITER
KAI
LAUDES
MORS
NOSTRIS
PRAESERTIM
VERUM

-10-
AMORIS
CHRISTUS
DECUS
DEUM
ERAT
FLUUIO
HOMO
NAMQUE
OMNIBUS
QUANTUM
REIPUBLICAE
SATIS
TERRA
TERRAM
TOTA
VTI

-9-
AH
ANIMO
ANTE
AQUAS
ASTRA
AUTEM
COELUM
ECCE
ECQUID
EI
GLORIA
GRATIAE
HABET
HAC
ILLAM
MANUS
MATREM
MORTEM
NOSTRAM
NOSTRUM
OMNEM
QUAEQUE
QUICQUID
REX
SUA
SUUM
TANTO
TEMPUS
VNO
VNQUAM

-8-
AETAS
BELLUM
CARMINE
DEU
DEI
EIUS
FLUUIUM
HOSTES
IGNIS
MENTIS
MORE
MUSA
MUSAE
MUSARUM
N'
NATURA
NOMEN
NUNQUAM
OMNIUM
ORBEM
ORBIS
PARTEM
PRIMUM
PRINCIPEM
QUORUM
REGEM
VERBA
VESTRAE
VESTRIS
VITAE
VNDE
VNUM

-7-
ALMA
ANIMI
AURES
CAETERA
CARMINA
CHRISTI
COR
CRUCEM
EA
EORUM
ERGO
FACIT
FLORES
FLUMINA
GAUDIA
IIII
ILLIC
ILLUD
ILLUSTRISSIME
INGENIUM
ISTA
MEIS
MENTEM
MORTIS
MUSICA
NOSTRI
NUMINE
NUPER
OMNIS
OPTIME
ORATIO
PRINCIPE
PULUERE
QUALIS
QUAMUIS
RE
SIN
SOLENT
SOLI
SOLUS
SPIRITUS
SUAE
SUAS
SUIS
SUOS
TUAM
VESTRAM
VIRTUTES

-6-
ABUNDE
ALIJ
ALTERA
ANIMOS
ANTI
ARTIBUS
ARTIUM
BELLO
CONSTAT
CONTRA
CRUCE
DEDIT
DIES
DIU
DOCTRINAE
DOMINI
EN
FACILE
FAMA
FAUCRIS
FIDEI
GIANS
GLORIAE
GLORIAM
GRATULAMUR
GRATULATIO
HOMINES
HONOREM
HONORIBUS
HOS
ILLE
ILLIS
IPSUM
LACRYMAS
MANU
MARE
MATRE
MENS
MILLE
MUNDUS
NEGOTIJS
NESCIA
NI
NOMINE
NOSTRAS
OMNI
OU

-6- (cont'd)

PACEM
POPULO
POTES
PRECOR
PRINCIPUM
RECTIUS
REGIS
ROMA
SACRA
SANE
SAXA
SCRIPTA
SCIEM
SUAUITER
SUI
SUMUS
TOTUS
TUOS
TUUS
VESTRAS
VIR
VIS
VNAM
VNUS
VTRUMQUE
VULTU

-5-

ACADEMIA
ACADEMIAM
ADEST
ALTERUM
AMORE
BELLI
BENE
BONI
CAELI
CHRISTUM
CONSILIA
CORPORA
CORPORIS
CORPUS
DEIN
DEXTRA
DICO
DIEM
DOLOR
DOMINUM
DOMUS
DONEC
ECCLESIA
EUNDEM
FACIES
FATA
FRUCTUS
FRUSTRA
FUIT
FUNERE
GENETEIRAN
GENS
HERBERT
HIS
HONORATISSIME
HONORE
HUC
IACOBUS
IAMDUDUM
ILIUM
IMAGO
INFANS
ITINERE
LIBRIS
LOCUM
LUCE
MAGNUM
MANIBUS
MATRIS
MONSTRUM
MUNDO
MUSIS
NUBES
NULLUM
NUN
OCULOS
OUK
PALLAS
PARTE
PAULO
PLACET
POETAE
POTIUS
PRAE
PRIUS
PULUERIS
QUANTA
QUIA
QUIPPE
QUISQUE
QUOQUE
RECTE
REGES
REGI
REGNO
SACRIS
SALTEM
SANGUIS
SENSUS
SIMUL
SUMME
SUMMO
TEMPORIS
TUNC
VETUSTAS
VIAM
VIRTUTIBUS
VIRTUTUM
VLLA
VMBRA
VNICUS
VOTA
VOTIS
VSUS
VULTUS

-4-

ABSQUE
ADDE
AEQUE
AEUUM
AFFECTUS
ALIJS
ALMAE
ALTER
AMOREM
ANIMUS
ANNI
AQUAE
ARA
ARTE
ARTES
AUARITIA
BENEFICIJS
BIS
CAELO
CAELUM
CAESAR
CAMI
CANTUS
CATHARI
CAUSA
CHARTA
CHRISTO
COELI
COELO
CONSECUTUS
D
D'
DEO
DICTA
DIGNUM
DOMINAE
DOMINUS
EOS
ESTO
EXTRA
FAC
FACTA
FATIS
FLUCTIBUS
FORES
FRUCTUM
FUERAT
FUISSET
GAR
GRANDI
HABUIT
HEUS
HONORES
HONORUM
HORTI
HOSTEM
IDEM
IDEO
IGNE
ILLOS
ILLUDIS
IMPAR
IMPETUS
INDIES
INTEREA
INTERIM
IPSIS
IPSOS
LIBRORUM
LIBROS
LOCA
LOCUS
LONGA
LONGE
LUMINIS
MACULAS
MAGNA
MAIOR
MANUM
MEAM
MEI
MENTE
MERITA
MEUM
MIRUM
MODO
MULTA
MULTO
NATURAE
NECESSE
NEMO
NIL
NOCTE
NOUI
NUBIBUS
NUSQUAM
OCCASIO
OFFICIA
OPE
PACE
PARUM
PASSIM
PATER
PATRES
PATRIAM
PAX
PEDE
PERDERE
PERSONAM
PETIT
PLENA
PLENUS
PLERUMQUE
POSSIT
POSTHAC
PRIMO
PRINCIPIBUS
PRONO
PRUDENTIAM
QUICQUAM
QUIDAM
QUOT
QUOTIDIE
R
REDIJT
REGNUM
S
SACRUM
SANGUINIS
SCRIBO
SCRIPTIS
SECULA
SECULI
SEMEL
SOLES
SOLET
SPES
STUDIJS
SUPER
T'
TAMI
TANTAE
TECUM
TEMPORA
TEMPORE
TERRAE
TOTAM
TUARUM
TUORUM
VERBORUM
VIDETUR
VIRTUS
VNDAS
VSPIAM
VSQUE

-3-

ABEUNT
ACADEMICI
AER
AGAM
AGRI
AIAZO
ALIQUANDO
ALITER
ALIA
ALMAM
ALTERO
AMAT
AMICA
ANGIPORTUS
ANGLIA
ANGULUS
ANIMAE
ANIMAM
ANNON
ANNULUM
ANTIQUA
APPOSITE
AQUA
AQUIS
ARBORE
ARBORES
ARMO
ARTIFICES
ATQUI
ATRIS
AUDI
AURUM
BACON
BELLA
BENEFICIA
BLANDA
CAECOS
CALAMO
CANDIDA
CANTABRIGIENSIS
CAPITE
CAROLVM
CAROLVS
CASTRA
CATEGORIA
CAUTES
CENTUM
CERNAM
CERTA
CHARTIS
CONSCIA
CONSILIO
CONUENIT
CORDA
CORDIS
CORPORE
CRIMINA
CULMEN
CULPA
CUNCTA
DECET
DEDERAT
DEDERUNT
DEERAT
DELICIAE
DIA
DICAM
DICITUR
DICTIS
DIUINA
DIXIT
DOLERE
DOLORES
DOTES
EADEM
ECCLESIAE
ELEMENTA
EMOLUMENTUM
EODEM
EPISTOLA
ERAM
ERAS
ERO
ERUDITIONEM
ESSENT
ETENIM
EUM
EXCUTITE
EXUENS
FACTUM
FAMAE
FATUM
FAUCRES
FEROX
FERUNT
FIDEM
FILIO
FILUM
FLAMMA
FLAMMAS
FLOS
FLUCTUS
FORSITAN
FORTE
FRATRES
FUERIT
FUGIT
FULMINE
G
GEMITUS
GENUS
GRATIA
GRATIAM
GRATIJS
GRAUES
HABEAT
HABITA
HAE
HEU
HORRENDUM
HOSTIBUS
HOSTIS
HUIUS
HYDRA
IACENT
IACOBUM
ICTU
IGNEM
ILLUC
IMMUNITATES
IMPERIUM
INANES
INFERNI
INGENIO
INGENTI
INQUIT
INSTAT
INTEGRAS
INTEGRO
INTRA
IPSAE
IPSAM
IPSAS
ISTOS
IT
IUDICIO
IUDICIUM
LABORIBUS
LACESSIT
LAETUM
LAETUS
LAPIDES
LAUDIBUS
LAUDIS
LAUS
LIBER
LIBRO
LIBRUM
LINGUA
LINGUAE
LITERAE
LITES
LONGUM
LUCRO
LUCTUS

-3- (cont'd)

MACHINA
MAGNI
MAIESTATEM
MATRI
MEAE
MEAS
MELIOR
MELIUS
MELVINE
MELVINUM
MEMOREM
MENSAE
MENTES
MENTI
MERITIS
MERITISSIME
METUUNT
MILLIBUS
MINISTER
MINORI
MISERE
MISERUM
MODUM
MOLES
MONTES
MORA
MORERIS
MOTUS
MULTUM
MUNDUM
MUNERE
NASCITUR
NASCOR
NEQUEAT
NEQUIT
NEUTIQUAM
NIMIRUM
NIMIS
NIMIUM
NOBILIS
NOCTU
NOLUIT
NONDUM
NOUA
NOUAS
NULLUS
NUM
NUMEN
NUNQUID
NUPTIAS
OBIT
OBITUM
OCULI
OCULIS
OMNE
OPEM
OPTIMO
OPTIMUS
OPUS
ORBE
ORDINE
PAR
PARA
PARENTIS
PARS
PARTES
PATENT
PATET
PATRIA
PECTUS
PEDES
PHILOSOPHUS
PHOEBE
PISCIS
PLACEAT
PLACENT
PLENUM
PLURIMUM
PLUUIA
POETA
POPULI
POPULUM
POPULUS
POSCIT
POSSINT
POSSUNT
POSTQUAM
POSTULAT
PRAESTAT
PRAETER
PRECES
PRIMUS
PRIUILEGIA
PROGENIES
PROLE
PROPERANT
PROPERAT
PRORSUS
PROTULIT
PRUDENTIA
PRUDENTIAE
PUBES
PUBLICAE
PUTAS
QUAMOBREM
QUANDO
QUANDOQUE
QUANQUAM
QUEIS
QUISQUIS
QUONDAM
QUUM
RADICES
RADIJS
RATIO
REBUS
REGE
REGIA
REGIAE
REGREDI
REGUM
REMPUBLICAM
RERUM
RITIBUS
ROGAMUS
ROTATUS
RUIT
SAEPIUS
SAEUUS
SALTUS
SALUS
SANCTOS
SANCTUM
SCIENTIARUM
SCIO
SCRIBENDI
SICCA
SIGILLUM
SIGNA
SIGNUM
SILENTIO
SIS
SISTE
SIUE
SOL
SOLIS
SOMNIA
SPE
SPECIES
SPECTANT
SPIRITU
SPIRITUM
STELLA
SUAUIS
SUM
SUME
SUPERANS
SUPEREST
SUSPIRIA
TALEM
TANTI
TANTIS
TERRARUM
THEMIS
TO
TOTUM
TRAGEMATA
TRISTI
TRIUMPHOS
TURBA
TUTA
VALE
VELQUE
VELUT
VEREMUR
VERSU
VERULAMIJ
VESPERE
VESTER
VESTES
VESTRO
VESTRUM
VETERUM
VI
VICES
VICINI
VICISTI
VICTORIA
VICTORIAE
VIDEOR
VIDERE
VIRI
VLTRA
VMBRAS
VNDA
VNIUERSAM
VNIUERSUM
VRBEM
VSU
VTERQUE
VTRIQUE
VULGUS
VULTUM

-2-

ABDOMINE
ABITO
ABSENTEM
ABSIT
ACADEMICIS
ACCEDIT
ACCENDIT
ACCEPIMUS
ACCIDERE
ACIES
ACRE
ACRES
ACRI
ACUMINE
ADDIT
ADHIBEAS
ADHUC
ADIJCITUR
ADIRE
ADMODUM
ADSUNT
ADUERSAM
ADULTA
AEDES
AEDIFICIA
AEQUIS
AEQUOR
AEQUUM
AESTATE
AETATI
AETERNITATEM
AETERNUM
AETNA
AFFLAT
AFFLATU
AGATHON
AGE
AGGREDITUR
AGNOSCIT
AGNUS
AGUNT
AIACIS
AIT
ALAE
ALAPAS
ALARUM
ALBANI
ALBION
ALIA
ALIAE
ALIENA
ALIO
ALIORUM
ALIQUAS
ALIQUEM
ALIUD
ALLOI
ALMI
ALTA
ALTIUS
ALTO
ALUMNI
AMBAEUS
AMBIT
AMICUS
AMORES
AMPLECTIMUR
ANGELOS
ANGLIAE
ANIMA
ANIMALIA
ANIMIS
ANIMUM
ANNAE
ANNOS
ANNULUS
ANTIQUI
ANUS
APERI
APEX
APICES
APOSTOLORUM
APTIOR
AQUILAM
ARAS
ARBITER
ARBOREM
ARCAM
ARCANA
ARCES
ARCUS
ARDENTI
ARDORE
ARENA
ARGUIT
ARIES
ARMA
ARTIFEX
ASPECTUS
ASPICE
ASSEQUI
ASSIDUO
ASSIDUUS
ATHENAE
AUCTIOR
AUDIAMUS
AUDIO
AUDIS
AUGUSTISSIME
AUGUSTISSIMO
AUIUM
AULA
AUOS
AURA
AURE
AUREA
AUTAR
AUTORUM
AUTOU
BALSAMUM
BARBAM
BARBARIEM
BARBARIES
BEATOS
BELGICIS
BELLE
BENEFICIORUM
BENIGNIUS
BIOU
BONA
BONE
BONO
BONORUM
BONUS
BREUIS
BRITANNE
BRITANNICAM
BRITANNICI
CACUM
CADAUER
CADAUERA
CADIT
CAEDI
CAELOS
CALAMUM
CALORIS
CAMOENIS
CAMPO
CANCELL
CANCELLARIO
CAPITA
CAPITIS
CARET
CARMEN
CARNEM
CARNIS
CARO
CATHARIS
CATHARO
CATHAROS
CATHARUM
CAUENDUM
CAUSAM
CELEBRANS
CELEBREM
CELEBRES
CELERITATEM
CENSEMUS
CENSES
CERNENS
CERNIS
CERTAMEN
CERTITUDINIS
CERTUM
CHRISTIANUS
CINGIT
CIUILI
CLARISSIME
CLAUIS
COELESTE
COELESTI
COGITATIONES
COGNITIO
COLENS
COLLEGIA
COLORE
COLORIS
COLUMBA
COLUNT
COMETAE
COMITER
COMMODI
COMMUNE
COMMUNI
COMPARATIO
COMPITA
CONCEDE
CONIUNCTAS
CONNECTAT
CONSERUANDO
CONSTET
CONTIGIT
CONTRIBUERE
CONUENIUNT
CONUITIA
CORDE
CORDI
CORONA
CORONAE
CORONAM
CREDITUR
CREIGHTON
CRESCENS
CRIMINE
CRUCI
CRUX
CULTUS
CUPIT
CURA
CURASTI
DAEMONE
DAKRUSAI
DAPES
DAPHNEN
DATUR
DATUS
DEBENT
DEBUIT
DEDISTI
DEFENSOR
DEINCEPS
DEINDE
DELICIJS
DELITUISSE
DEMETRIUS
DEMITTERE
DENTE
DENUO
DEPERIT
DESCENDAT
DESIDERIO
DESPERATAE
DETUR
DEXTERA
DI'
DICIT

-2- (cont'd)

DICITE
DICTI
DIE
DIGITIS
DIGNISSIMA
DIGNISSIME
DIGNITATEM
DIGNITATES
DIGNIUS
DILIGENTIA
DISCAT
DISPLICEAT
DIUINIS
DIUISA
DIUISAS
DIXI
DOCEAS
DOCTRINA
DOCTUS
DOKEI
DOLORIS
DOMUM
DUBIO
DUBITAMUS
DUBITATUR
DUCE
DUCES
DULCEM
DUPLEX
DUX
DUXIT
ECCUM
EDITAM
EFFARE
EIA
ELEGANTER
ELEGANTIAE
ELEGANTIAS
ELIZA
ELOQUENTIA
ELOQUENTIAE
EMARTON
EMAS
EMES
EMIT
EPAIAZOUSI
EPLETO
ERANT
ERGA
ERIS
ERRORUM
ERUDITIO
ERUDITIONIS
ERUNT
ESSES
ESSET
ESTI
&C
ETI
EXAUDIRI
EXCELLENTIAE
EXCELLENTIJS
EXCELLENTISSIMI
EXCIPIAT
EXCITAT
EXEI
EXEMPLO
EXHIBET
EXILIT
EXIMIE
EXISTIMES
EXPECTAMUS
EXPEDIET
EXTULIT
F
FABIO
FABULA
FACES
FACIAS
FACILIS
FACTU
FACTUS
FAECUNDUS
FALCE
FAMAM
FAME
FAMES
FAMILIAE
FAMILIAM
FASTUS
FATI
FAUOR
FAUORUM
FAXIT
FECISTI
FELICES
FERCULA
FERRE
FERT
FERTUR
FERUOR
FIAT
FIDA
FIDE
FIDES
FIERI
FIET
FIGURIS
FILIJ
FILIOS
FILIUM
FINDIT
FIT
FIUNT
FIXA
FIXO
FLAGELLUM
FLEMUS
FLETUM
FLETUS
FLORIBUS
FLORUM
FLUAS
FLUUIJ
FOEDERA
FOELICES
FOELICITATIS
FOELIX
FOMITE
FONTE
FORET
FORMA
FORNACE
FORSAN
FORTUNAS
FRAENA
FRETUS
FRUGES
FRUIMUR
FUGATOR
FUGIAS
FUGIENTEM
FULGOR
FUNE
FUNGAR
FUNUS
FURIT
FUROR
FUSC
FUTURA
FUTURUM
GALLI
GARRIENS
GAUDENTES
GAUDET
GAUDIO
GEMMA
GEMMAM
GENAS
GENITRIX
GENTEM
GENTES
GENTIUM
GLADIO
GORGONEAM
GRANTAM
GRATITUDINIS
GRAUI
GRAUIDUS
GRAUITATE
GRAUITATI
GREGI
GUTTA
HABENT
HABETIS
HABITANT
HABITU
HABITUS
HABUERE
HAERENT
HAERET
HARMONIAM
HAS
HEDERAE
HERBAE
HISCE
HISPANIAM
HOMICIDA
HOMINEM
HOMINI
HONOR
HONORI
HONOS
HORTUS
HORUM
HOSPES
HOSPITIUM
HOSTIUM
HUI
HUIC
HUIUSMODI
HUMANA
HUMANAE
HUMANAM
HUMANITAS
HUMANITATIS
HUMOR
IACOBE
IACOBO
IGITUR
IGNARA
IGNIUOMUM
ILLECEBRIS
ILLICO
ILLINC
ILLUUIE
IMMINUERE
IMMORIAR
IMPETU
IMPLICET
IMPONERE
IMPOS
IMPROBA
IMPROBE
INCENDIUM
INCOMPARABILEM
INCONSTANTIA
INCUMBIS
INDUE
INFANTEM
INFERNAE
INGENS
INNOCUAM
INQUAM
INSTAURATIONIS
INTEGRUM
INTELLECTUS
INTERDUM
INTEREST
INTIME
INTUERI
INUERTIS
INUIDENT
INUIDIAM
IPSO
IRAM
IRE
ISTAS
ISTIS
ITAQUE
ITIS
IUCUNDIUS
IURA
IUS
IUUATE
IUUENEM
IXIONA
JAM
KAN
KATOPTRON
LABORE
LABORES
LACESSAM
LACHRYMIS
LACRYMA
LACRYMIS
LAETITIA
LAETITIAE
LAGENAS
LAMPADA
LAQUEARIBUS
LASSUM
LATERI
LATET
LATIUS
LAUDE
LAUDO
LAUDUM
LAUROS
LAURUS
LEGIMUS
LEGIS
LEUIS
LIBENTER
LIBRI
LICEAT
LICTOR
LIGNA
LIGNO
LIGNUM
LIMEN
LINGUAM
LIQUITUR
LITARE
LITERARIAE
LITERAS
LIUOR
LOND
LONDINENSES
LOQUENS
LUCEAT
LUCEM
LUCUS
LUMEN
LUMINA
LUMINE
LUNA
LUSUS
LUTUM
MAEANDROS
MAERET
MAGISTRI
MAGISTRUM
MAGNAE
MAGNAS
MAGNATUM
MAGNIFICENTIAE
MAGNIS
MAGNITUDINI
MAIESTAS
MAIESTATE
MAIESTATIS
MAIORUM
MALA
MALE
MALEDICTA
MALEUOLORUM
MALIS
MALUS
MANE
MANENTE
MARIS
MARO
MATERIAM
MATERNI
MATERNIS
MATURE
MAX
MAXIMA
MEDETUR
MEDICINA
MEDIO
MEDITARI
MEDULLAS
MELIORIS
MELLIS
MEMBRA
MENTIBUS
MEO
MEOS
MERENTIBUS
MERITUS
METALLA
METALLUM
MEUS
MIAN
MILES
MILLENA
MINOR
MINOREM
MIRANTUR
MIRARI
MIRE
MISCET
MISCUIT
MISERI
MISERIAS
MISEROS
MISSIS
MITES
MODERATUR
MODESTIAM
MOENIA
MOLEM
MONACHOS
MONON
MONS
MONTE
MONTIBUS
MORBI
MORI
MORTALIBUS
MORTALIUM
MORTI
MORTUA
MOTU
MULTIS
MULTITUDINEM
MUNERI
MURMURE
MUSCAS
MUTATA
MUTUS
NASO
NATA
NATALIBUS
NATET
NATO
NATUM
NAUNTON
NECESSARIUM
NEGAS
NEGAT
NEGET
NEGOTIA
NEQUEAS
NESCIUS
NIGRA
NIGRO
NOAE
NOBILE
NOBILITATE
NOCENDI
NODO
NOLITE
NOMINIS
NOSSE
NOSTRORUM
NOSTROS
NOTIONUM
NOTIS
NOUIMUS
NOUIT
NOUUM
NOX
NUBE
NUBIUM
NUGAS
NULLAS
NULLO
NUMERIS
NUMINA
NUPTIAE
NUPTIARUM
NUPTIJS
OB
OBIJCIS
OBSCURUS
OBSERUATIONE
OCCUMBENS
OCCURRIT
OCEANO
OF
OFFICIO
OPERA
OPES
OPIFICUM
OPTI
ORAM
ORANTES
ORATIONEM
ORATORIS
ORBI

-2- (cont'd)

ORIGINE
ORTUS
OSPER
OSSIBUS
OSTENDAS
OTAN
OTIUM
OUDE
PACTO
PAPICOLIS
PARENS
PARENTEM
PARES
PARIBUS
PARTIBUS
PARTUM
PARTURIT
PARTUS
PASCHA
PASTOR
PATITUR
PATREM
PATRIAE
PAULISPER
PAULULUM
PECTORA
PECTORE
PELAGO
PELAGUS
PELLIBUS
PENNAS
PENU
PERCURRITE
PEREGRINATI
PERENNIS
PERGAS
PERGE
PERICULIS
PERIJT
PERITA
PERITUS
PERMITTE
PERSPICACI
PERSPICILLIS
PERSPICUA
PERSTREPIS
PERTINGIT
PESTIS
PHEGGOS
PHILOMELA
PHILOSOPHIAE
PHILOSOPHOS
PIA
PIETATIS
PIGNUS
PIJS
PILEUS
PLACEO
PLACIDO
PLACUIT
PLENO
PLENOS
PLURA
PLURES
PLURIMUS
PNEUMATOS
POENA
POETAS
POMOERIA
PONT
PONTIFEX
PORRIGIT
PORRO
POSSE
POSSET
POSSIDET
POSSIM
POSSUMUS
POSTERI
POSTEROS
POTUI
PRAECIPUE
PRAELIA
PRAESENS
PRAESENTI
PRAESTES
PRAESUL
PRAESULES
PRAESULIBUS
PRECAMUR
PRECEMUR
PRECIA
PRECIBUS
PRECIUM
PRETIOSA
PRIMA
PRIMORDIA
PRINCIPI
PRISCI
PRIUATO
PROBANT
PROBATUR
PROBE
PROBRO
PROCANCELLARIUS
PROCELLIS
PROCUDERE
PROCUL
PRODES
PRODIGIUM
PRODITE
PRODUCUNT
PROFECTUS
PROFUNDITATIS
PROHIBES
PROIJCIT
PROIN
PROINDE
PROLEM
PROMUS
PROPRIJS
PROS
PROTINUS
PUBLICO
PUDOR
PUDORE
PUGNA
PULSARE
PUNGUNT
PURI
PURPURA
PUTAT
QUAEDAM
QUALE
QUEAT
QUEMADMODUM
QUIETIS
QUINQUE
QUISNAM
QUISPIAM
QUOMODO
RAMENTA
RAMO
RARIUS
RATIONE
RATIONIS
RECENTEM
RECESSUS
RECLINET
REDEMPTOR
REDEMPTORES
REDIT
REDUXIT
REGIONEM
REGIONES
REGNA
REGNAT
REGNORUM
REI
REL
REPUGNANT
REPUTES
REQUIEM
RESPONDEANT
RESEONS
RIDENS
RITUS
ROMANI
ROS
ROTAE
ROTUNDITAS
RUCTARE
RUDIS
RUINAM
RUPTIS
RURE
SACRAE
SACROS
SAEPE
SANCTA
SANCTAE
SANCTE
SANCTISSIME
SANCTIUS
SANGUINEM
SATAS
SAXIS
SCELERIS
SCEPTRO
SCEPTRUM
SCITE
SCOTIA
SCRIBENTI
SCRIBIS
SCRIPSIT
SCRIPTIO
SCRIPTUM
SCRIPTURAE
SCRIPTURIS
SECULUM
SECURI
SECUS
SEDENS
SEDULA
SENECTUS
SENEM
SENTENTIAE
SENTIO
SEPIA
SEPULCRA
SEPULTA
SEQUITUR
SERENISSIMAE
SERENISSIME
SERENISSIMI
SERMO
SEUERUS
SEXCENTAS
SIGNO
SIM
SIMILES
SIMILIS
SINAS
SINGULA
SINUS
SITIS
SOCIJ
SOLE
SOLEBANT
SOLO
SOLUENS
SOLUTIO
SOLUTIS
SORORES
SPARGIT
SPECIE
SPERARE
SPHAERA
SPLENDES
SPLENDOR
SPOLIANS
SPONTE
SPUTANDO
STATU
STATUA
STELLAM
STETIT
STRATA
STRIDOR
STRIGES
STRINGENS
STUDIOSORUM
SUAUISSIMUS
SUBIT
SUBLIMITATE
SUDOR
SUFFICERE
SUMENDA
SUMMA
SUMMOUET
SUPELLEX
SUPERARE
SUPERAT
SUPERBAS
SUPERBUM
SUPRA
SURSUM
SUSURRAT
SYDERA
SYLUAS
SYMBOLUM
TABULAS
TACITE
TALI
TALIS
TANTISPER
TANTOS
TARDA
TECTIS
TEMPLI
TEMPLIS
TENER
TENUIS
TER
TERRAS
TERTIA
THE
THESAURAR
THESAURIS
THRONOS
TI
TINEIS
TIS
TISIPHONE
TITULOS
TOIS
TON
TORQUET
TOTO
TRANSEAT
TRES
TRIBUIT
TRISTE
TRISTIS
TRIUMPHAT
TRIUMPHUS
TRUX
TUERE
TUETUR
TURRES
TYMPANA
VACAS
VALLIS
VBERA
VELUM
VENA
VENENO
VENTER
VENTILAT
VENTO
VENULA
VERA
VERBIS
VERE
VERITATIS
VERSUS
VERTAS
VESTRI
VESTROS
VETAT
VETERES
VETUS
VIAS
VIATOR
VICISSIM
VIDENS
VIDEO
VIDIT
VIGORE
VINI
VINTONIENSI
VIRES
VIRGINES
VIRORUM
VIROS
VIRTUTE
VIRUM
VITIJS
VIUIMUS
VIUITE
VIUO
VLNIS
VLTA
VMBRAM
VNDAE
VNDIQUE
VNICE
VNICO
VNIUS
VOCAS
VOCAT
VOCE
VOCER
VOLUPTAS
VOLUPTATIBUS
VOLUPTATIS
VRBANI
VRBANUM
VRNA
VTILE
VTILIUS
VTINAM
VTRASQUE
VTRINQUE
VTRIUSQUE
VTROQUE
VTRUM
WALLIAE
XALEPON

35 A
20 AB
3 ABEUNT
4 ABSQUE
6 ABUNDE
28 AC
5 ACADEMIA
12 ACADEMIAE
5 ACADEMIAM
3 ACADEMICI
118 AD
4 ADDE
22 ADEO
5 ADEST
4 AEQUE
3 AER
8 AETAS
4 AEUUM
4 AFFECTUS
3 AGAM
3 AGRI
9 AH
3 AIAZO
6 ALIJ
4 ALIJS
3 ALIQUANDO
3 ALITER
3 ALLA
7 ALMA
4 ALMAE
3 ALMAM
4 ALTER
6 ALTERA
3 ALTERO
5 ALTERUM
3 AMAT
3 AMICA
19 AMOR
5 AMORE
4 AMOREM
10 AMORIS
12 AN
3 ANGIPORTUS
3 ANGLIA
3 ANGULUS
3 ANIMAE
3 ANIMAM
7 ANIMI
9 ANIMO
6 ANIMOS
4 ANIMUS
4 ANNI
3 ANNON
3 ANNULUM
9 ANTE
6 ANTI
3 ANTIQUA
3 APPOSITE
15 APUD
3 AQUA
4 AQUAE
9 AQUAS
3 AQUIS
4 ARA
3 ARBORE
3 ARBORES
3 ARMO
4 ARTE
4 ARTES
6 ARTIBUS
3 ARTIFICES
6 ARTIUM
9 ASTRA
21 AT
67 ATQUE
3 ATQUI
3 ATRIS
4 AUARITIA
3 AUDI
7 AURES
3 AURUM
57 AUT
9 AUTEM

3 BACON
3 BELLA
5 BELLI
6 BELLO
8 BELLUM
5 BENE
3 BENEFICIA
4 BENEFICIJS
4 BIS
3 BLANDA
5 BONI

3 CAECOS
5 CAELI
4 CAELO
4 CAELUM
4 CAESAR
7 CAETERA
3 CALAMO
4 CAMI
3 CANDIDA
3 CANTABRIGIENSIS
4 CANTUS
3 CAPITE
14 CAPUT
7 CARMINA
8 CARMINE
3 CAROLVM
3 CAROLVS
3 CASTRA
3 CATEGORIA
4 CATHARI
4 CAUSA
3 CAUTES
3 CENTUM
3 CERNAM
3 CERTA
12 CERTE
8 CEU
4 CHARTA
3 CHARTIS
14 CHRISTE
7 CHRISTI
4 CHRISTO
5 CHRISTUM
10 CHRISTUS
4 COELI
4 COELO
9 COELUM
3 CONSCIA
4 CONSECUTUS
5 CONSILIA
3 CONSILIO
6 CONSTAT
6 CONTRA
3 CONUENIT
7 COR
3 CORDA
3 CORDIS
5 CORPORA
3 CORPORE
5 CORPORIS
5 CORPUS
3 CRIMINA
6 CRUCE
7 CRUCEM
19 CUI
13 CUIUS
3 CULMEN
3 CULPA
144 CUM
3 CUNCTA
25 CUR

4 D
4 D'
68 DE
3 DECET
10 DECUS
3 DEDERAT
3 DEDERUNT
6 DEDIT
3 DEERAT
8 DEI
5 DEIN
3 DELICIAE
4 DEO
10 DEUM
13 DEUS
5 DEXTRA
3 DIA
3 DICAM
3 DICITUR
5 DICO
4 DICTA
3 DICTIS
5 DIEM
6 DIES
4 DIGNUM
6 DIU
3 DIUINA
3 DIXIT
6 DOCTRINAE
3 DOLERE
5 DOLOR
3 DOLORES
4 DOMINAE
14 DOMINE
6 DOMINI
5 DOMINUM
4 DOMINUS
5 DOMUS
5 DONEC
3 DOTES
35 DUM

27 E
7 EA
3 EADEM
9 ECCE
5 ECCLESIA
3 ECCLESIAE
9 ECQUID
19 EGO
9 EI
8 EIUS
3 ELEMENTA
3 EMOLUMENTUM
6 EN
37 ENIM
11 EO
3 EODEM
7 EORUM
4 EOS
3 EPISTOLA
3 ERAM
3 ERAS
10 ERAT
7 ERGO
13 ERIT
3 ERO
3 ERUDITIONEM
27 ES
32 ESSE
3 ESSENT
135 EST
4 ESTO
243 &
116 ET
3 ETENIM
60 ETIAM
3 EUM
5 EUNDEM
35 EX
3 EXCUTITE
4 EXTRA
3 EXUENS

4 FAC
5 FACIES
6 FACILE
7 FACIT
4 FACTA
3 FACTUM
6 FAMA
3 FAMAE
5 FATA
4 FATIS
3 FATUM
3 FAUORES
6 FAUORIS
3 FEROX
3 FERUNT
6 FIDEI
3 FIDEM
3 FILIO
3 FILIUM
3 FLAMMA
3 FLAMMAS
7 FLORES
3 FLOS
4 FLUCTIBUS
3 FLUCTUS
7 FLUMINA
10 FLUUIO
8 FLUUIUM
4 FORES
3 FORSITAN
3 FORTE
3 FRATRES
4 FRUCTUM
5 FRUCTUS
5 FRUSTRA
4 FUERAT
3 FUERIT
3 FUGIT
4 FUISSET
5 FUIT
3 FULMINE
5 FUNERE

3 G
4 GAR
7 GAUDIA
3 GEMITUS
5 GENETEIRAN
5 GENS
3 GENUS
6 GIANS
9 GLORIA
6 GLORIAE
6 GLORIAM
4 GRANDI
3 GRATIA
9 GRATIAE
3 GRATIAM
3 GRATIJS
6 GRATULAMUR
6 GRATULATIO
3 GRAUES

3 HABEAT
9 HABET
3 HABITA
4 HABUIT
9 HAC
3 HAE
40 HAEC
11 HANC
19 HAUD
5 HERBERT
3 HEU
4 HEUS
27 HIC
12 HINC
5 HIS
48 HOC
6 HOMINES
12 HOMINUM
10 HOMO
5 HONORATISSIME
5 HONORE
6 HONOREM
4 HONORES
6 HONORIBUS
4 HONORUM
3 HORRENDUM
4 HORTI
6 HOS
4 HOSTEM
8 HOSTES
3 HOSTIBUS
3 HOSTIS
5 HUC
3 HUIUS
12 HUNC
3 HYDRA

3 IACENT
3 IACOBUM
5 IACOBUS
43 IAM
5 IAMDUDUM
3 ICTU
15 ID
4 IDEM
4 IDEO
4 IGNE
3 IGNEM
8 IGNIS
16 ILLA
9 ILLAM

6 ILLE
7 ILLI
7 ILLIC
6 ILLIS
4 ILLOS
3 ILLUC
7 ILLUD
4 ILLUDIS
5 ILLUM
7 ILLUSTRISSIME
5 IMAGO
3 IMMUNITATES
11 IMO
4 IMPAR
3 IMPERIUM
4 IMPETUS
236 IN
3 INANES
11 INDE
4 INDIES
5 INFANS
3 INFERNI
3 INGENIO
7 INGENIUM
3 INGENTI
3 INQUIT
3 INSTAT
3 INTEGRAS
3 INTEGRO
19 INTER
4 INTEREA
4 INTERIM
3 INTRA
16 IPSA
3 IPSAE
3 IPSAM
3 IPSAS
37 IPSE
13 IPSI
4 IPSIS
4 IPSOS
6 IPSUM
7 ISTA
3 ISTOS
3 IT
11 ITA
11 ITER
5 ITINERE
3 IUDICIO
3 IUDICIUM

11 KAI

3 LABORIBUS
3 LACESSIT
6 LACRYMAS
3 LAETUM
3 LAETUS
3 LAPIDES
11 LAUDES
3 LAUDIBUS
3 LAUDIS
3 LAUS
3 LIBER
5 LIBRIS
3 LIBRO
4 LIBRORUM
4 LIBROS
3 LIBRUM
15 LICET
3 LINGUA
3 LINGUAE
3 LITERAE
3 LITES
4 LOCA
5 LOCUM
4 LOCUS
4 LONGA
4 LONGE
3 LONGUM
5 LUCE
3 LUCRO
3 LUCTUS
4 LUMINIS

3 MACHINA
4 MACULAS
14 MAGIS
4 MAGNA
3 MAGNI
5 MAGNUM
3 MAIESTATEM
4 MAIOR
5 MANIBUS
6 MANU
4 MANUM
9 MANUS
6 MARE
17 MATER
6 MATRE
9 MATREM
3 MATRI
5 MATRIS
26 ME
18 MEA
3 MEAE
4 MEAM
3 MEAS
4 MEI
7 MEIS
3 MELIOR
3 MELIUS
3 MELVINE
3 MELVINUM
3 MEMOREM
6 MENS
3 MENSAE
4 MENTE
7 MENTEM
3 MENTES
3 MENTI
8 MENTIS
4 MERITA
3 MERITIS
3 MERITISSIME
3 METUUNT
4 MEUM
44 MIHI
6 MILLE
3 MILLIBUS
3 MINISTER
3 MINORI
18 MINUS
4 MIRUM
3 MISERE
3 MISERUM
4 MODO
3 MODUM
3 MOLES
5 MONSTRUM
3 MONTES
3 MORA
8 MORE
3 MORERIS
11 MORS
9 MORTEM
7 MORTIS
3 MOTUS
4 MULTA
4 MULTO
3 MULTUM
15 MUNDI
5 MUNDO
3 MUNDUM
6 MUNDUS
3 MUNERE
8 MUSA
8 MUSAE
8 MUSARUM
7 MUSICA
5 MUSIS

8 N'
15 NAM
10 NAMQUE
3 NASCITUR
3 NASCOR
8 NATURA
4 NATURAE
39 NE
48 NEC
4 NECESSE
6 NEGOTIJS
4 NEMO
13 NEMPE
31 NEQUE
3 NEQUEAT
3 NEQUIT
6 NESCIA
3 NEUTIQUAM
6 NI
24 NIHIL
4 NIL
3 NIMIRUM
3 NIMIS
3 NIMIUM
14 NISI
3 NOBILIS
52 NOBIS
4 NOCTE
3 NOCTU
3 NOLUIT
8 NOMEN
6 NOMINE
171 NON
3 NONDUM
74 NOS
18 NOSTER
26 NOSTRA
15 NOSTRAE
9 NOSTRAM
6 NOSTRAS
7 NOSTRI
11 NOSTRIS
13 NOSTRO
9 NOSTRUM
3 NOUA
3 NOUAS
4 NOUI
5 NUBES
4 NUBIBUS
15 NULLA
5 NULLUM
3 NULLUS
3 NUM
3 NUMEN
7 NUMINE
5 NUN
48 NUNC
8 NUNQUAM
3 NUNQUID
7 NUPER
3 NUPTIAS
4 NUSQUAM

44 O
3 OBIT
3 OBITUM
4 OCCASIO
3 OCULI
3 OCULIS
5 OCULOS
4 OFFICIA
28 OLIM
3 OMNE
9 OMNEM
41 OMNES
6 OMNI
29 OMNIA
10 OMNIBUS
7 OMNIS
8 OMNIUM
4 OPE
3 OPEM
7 OPTIME
3 OPTIMO
3 OPTIMUS
3 OPUS
7 ORATIO
3 ORBE
8 ORBEM
8 ORBIS
3 ORDINE
13 OS
6 OU
5 OUK

4 PACE
6 PACEM
5 PALLAS
3 PAR
3 PARA
3 PARENTIS
3 PARS
5 PARTE
8 PARTEM
3 PARTES
4 PARUM
4 PASSIM
3 PATENT
4 PATER
3 PATET
4 PATRES
3 PATRIA
4 PATRIAM
5 PAULO
4 PAX
3 PECTUS
4 PEDE
3 PEDES
40 PER
4 PERDERE
4 PERSONAM
4 PETIT
3 PHILOSOPHUS
3 PHOEBE
3 PISCIS
3 PLACEAT
3 PLACENT
5 PLACET
4 PLENA
3 PLENUM
4 PLENUS
4 PLERUMQUE
3 PLURIMUM
14 PLUS
3 PLUUIA
3 POETA
5 POETAE
3 POPULI
6 POPULO
3 POPULUM
3 POPULUS
3 POSCIT
3 POSSINT
4 POSSIT
3 POSSUNT
12 POST
4 POSTHAC
3 POSTQUAM
3 POSTULAT
6 POTES
13 POTEST
5 POTIUS
5 PRAE
11 PRAESERTIM
3 PRAESTAT
3 PRAETER
3 PRECES
6 PRECOR
4 PRIMO
8 PRIMUM
3 PRIMUS
15 PRINCEPS
7 PRINCIPE
8 PRINCIPEM
4 PRINCIPIBUS
15 PRINCIPIS
6 PRINCIPUM
3 PRIUILEGIA
5 PRIUS
21 PRO
3 PROGENIES
4 PRONO
3 PROPE
3 PROPERANT
3 PROPERAT
3 PRORSUS
3 PROTULIT
3 PRUDENTIA
3 PRUDENTIAE
4 PRUDENTIAM
3 PUBES
3 PUBLICAE
7 PULUERE
5 PULUERIS
3 PUTAS

27 QUA
67 QUAE
9 QUAEQUE
7 QUALIS
100 QUAM
3 QUAMOBREM
7 QUAMUIS
3 QUANDO
3 QUANDOQUE

3 QUANQUAM
5 QUANTA
12 QUANTO
10 QUANTUM
33 QUARE
20 QUAS
19 QUASI
344 QUE
3 QUEIS
17 QUEM
99 QUI
5 QUIA
18 QUIBUS
4 QUICQUAM
9 QUICQUID
53 QUID
4 QUIDAM
18 QUIDEM
34 QUIN
5 QUIPPE
26 QUIS
5 QUISQUE
3 QUISQUIS
57 QUO
62 QUOD
3 QUONDAM
5 QUOQUE
8 QUORUM
17 QUOS
4 QUOT
4 QUOTIDIE
3 QUUM

4 R
3 RADICES
3 RADIJS
3 RATIO
7 RE
3 REBUS
5 RECTE
6 RECTIUS
4 REDIJT
3 REGE
8 REGEM
5 REGES
5 REGI
3 REGIA
3 REGIAE
6 REGIS
5 REGNO
4 REGNUM
3 REGREDI
3 REGUM
10 REIPUBLICAE
3 REMPUBLICAM
3 RERUM
23 RES
9 REX
3 RITIBUS
3 ROGAMUS
6 ROMA
3 ROTATUS
3 RUIT

4 S
6 SACRA
5 SACRIS
4 SACRUM
3 SAEPIUS
3 SAEUUS
5 SALTEM
3 SALTUS
3 SALUS
3 SANCTOS
3 SANCTUM
6 SANE
13 SANGUINE
4 SANGUINIS
5 SANGUIS
10 SATIS
6 SAXA
3 SCIENTIARUM
15 SCILICET
3 SCIO
3 SCRIBENDI
4 SCRIBO
6 SCRIPTA
4 SCRIPTIS
35 SE
4 SECULA
4 SECULI
53 SED
4 SEMEL
17 SEMPER
5 SENSUS
99 SI
19 SIBI
56 SIC
3 SICCA
3 SIGILLUM
3 SIGNA
3 SIGNUM
3 SILENTIO
5 SIMUL
7 SIN
21 SINE
13 SINT
3 SIS
3 SISTE
42 SIT
3 SIUE
3 SOL
17 SOLA
6 SOLEM
7 SOLENT
4 SOLES
4 SOLET
7 SOLI
3 SOLIS
13 SOLUM
7 SOLUS
3 SOMNIA
3 SPE
3 SPECIES
3 SPECTANT
4 SPES
3 SPIRITU
3 SPIRITUM
7 SPIRITUS
3 STELLA
4 STUDIJS
9 SUA
7 SUAE
13 SUAM
7 SUAS
3 SUAUIS
6 SUAUITER
13 SUB
6 SUI
7 SUIS
3 SUM
3 SUME
5 SUMME
5 SUMMO
6 SUMUS
36 SUNT
15 SUO
7 SUOS
4 SUPER
3 SUPERANS
3 SUPEREST
3 SUSPIRIA
9 SUUM

4 T'
3 TALEM
33 TAM
37 TAMEN
4 TAMI
18 TANDEM
18 TANQUAM
12 TANTA
4 TANTAE
3 TANTI
3 TANTIS
9 TANTO
29 TANTUM
99 TE
4 TECUM
4 TEMPORA
4 TEMPORE
5 TEMPORIS
9 TEMPUS
10 TERRA
4 TERRAE
10 TERRAM
3 TERRARUM
3 THEMIS
79 TIBI
3 TO
19 TOT
10 TOTA
4 TOTAM
3 TOTUM
6 TOTUS
3 TRAGEMATA
3 TRISTI
3 TRIUMPHOS
76 TU
36 TUA
18 TUAE
7 TUAM
4 TUARUM
14 TUAS
21 TUI
21 TUIS
12 TUM
5 TUNC
18 TUO
4 TUORUM
6 TUOS
3 TURBA
3 TUTA
23 TUUM
6 TUUS

16 UE

3 VALE
29 VBI
3 VBIQUE
40 VEL
3 VELUT
8 VERBA
4 VERBORUM
3 VEREMUR
19 VERO
3 VERSU
3 VERULAMIJ
11 VERUM
3 VESPERE
3 VESTER
3 VESTES
13 VESTRA
8 VESTRAE
7 VESTRAM
6 VESTRAS
8 VESTRIS
3 VESTRO
3 VESTRUM
3 VETERUM
5 VETUSTAS
3 VI
5 VIAM
3 VICES
3 VICINI
3 VICISTI
3 VICTORIA
3 VICTORIAE
3 VIDEOR
3 VIDERE
4 VIDETUR
6 VIR
3 VIRI
4 VIRTUS
7 VIRTUTES
5 VIRTUTIBUS
5 VIRTUTUM
6 VIS
17 VITA
8 VITAE
17 VITAM
5 VLLA
3 VLTRA
5 VMBRA
3 VMBRAS
12 VNA
6 VNAM
3 VNDA
4 VNDAS
8 VNDE
5 VNICUS
3 VNIUERSAM
3 VNIUERSUM
9 VNO
9 VNQUAM
8 VNUM
6 VNUS
12 VOBIS
21 VOS
5 VOTA
5 VOTIS
3 VRBEM
4 VSPIAM
4 VSQUE
3 VSU
5 VSUS
143 VT
3 VTERQUE
10 VTI
3 VTRIQUE
6 VTRUMQUE
3 VULGUS
6 VULTU
3 VULTUM
5 VULTUS

Library of Congress Cataloging in Publication Data
(For library cataloging purposes only)

Di Cesare, Mario A
A concordance to the complete writings of George Herbert.

(The Cornell concordances)
1. Herbert, George, 1593–1633—Concordances.
I. Mignani, Rigo, 1921– joint author. II. Title. III. Series.
PS3508.D5 821'.3 76-56642
ISBN 0-8014-1106-8